TESTS IN PRINT VIII

EARLIER PUBLICATIONS IN THIS SERIES

TESTS
IN PRINT VIII

AN INDEX TO TESTS, TEST REVIEWS, AND THE LITERATURE ON SPECIFIC TESTS

Edited by

LINDA L. MURPHY
KURT F. GEISINGER
JANET F. CARLSON
ROBERT A. SPIES

The Buros Institute of Mental Measurements
The University of Nebraska-Lincoln
Lincoln, Nebraska

2011
Distributed by The University of Nebraska Press

LC 83-18866
ISBN 978-0-910674-62-1

Manufactured in the United States of America.

The paper used in this publication meets the minimum requirements of American National Standard for Information Sciences—Permanence of Paper for Printed Library Materials, ANSI Z39.48-1984.

Note to Users

TABLE OF CONTENTS

124 192

INTRODUCTION

The *Tests in Print* (*TIP*) series consists of descriptive listings of commercially published tests. This volume also serves as a comprehensive index to all editions of the *Mental Measurements Yearbook* series (MMY) published to date.

There are key differences between the *Tests in Print* series and the *Mental Measurements Yearbook* series. In contrast to *TIP*, the *MMY* series contains both descriptive entries and critical reviews of commercially published tests available in the English language. Each *MMY*, of which there are now 18, includes reviews and descriptions of only those tests that are new or substantially revised since the previous *MMY*. The *MMY* series is, therefore, sequential and cumulative in nature.

Each *TIP*, of which there are now eight, is a comprehensive volume describing, to the best of our ability, every test that is currently commercially available. *TIP VII*, therefore, supersedes *TIP VI*. Although it is necessary to have the entire *MMY* series to be sure of finding a descriptive entry or a review of a particular test, only the latest addition to the TIP series is needed for comprehensive coverage of currently available testing products.

To complement these two publications, Tests Reviews Online (www.unl.edu/buros) has been developed to permit users instant access to test descriptions and reviews from the Buros Institute of Mental Measurements. Test information and reviews available from Tests Reviews Online appear exactly as in the *The Ninth* through *The Eighteenth Mental Measurements Yearbooks* with regular updates from our current database. A total of over 3,700 tests are briefly described and, for a small fee, users may download descriptive testing information and test critiques for over 2,700 tests. In addition, electronic versions of both the *Mental Measurements Yearbook* and *Tests in Print* series are now available to libraries through Ovid Technologies (Wolters Kluwer Health) and EBSCO Publishing with access to the contents of all previous editions of the *Yearbooks*.

TIP VIII may be best used as a means to locate and learn about commercially available testing products. Because *TIP VIII* indexes all 18 books in the MMY series (for tests still in print), it is an invaluable guide to both descriptive and analytical information. As a directory of commercially available tests, *TIP VIII* is not designed to include all known tests. Specifically, the TIP series does not include research or proprietary instruments. Research instruments are often published in journals and serve the limited uses of test authors. Proprietary instruments are frequently designed for specialized audiences (e.g., admissions, licensure, certification) or for highly secured markets (e.g., government, industry) and are not considered "commercially available" tests.

In the Preface of the first *Tests in Print* volume (1961), Oscar Buros noted that this work had been in preparation for over 20 years. The first two volumes of *The Mental Measurements Yearbook* were published in 1938 and 1940. It became increasingly apparent that a comprehensive bibliography of tests and an index to the contents of the MMY volumes was needed. The initial delay in *Tests in Print* was due to World War II, and then various other financial and production limitations postponed its publication. *Tests in Print II* was published in 1974. After the death of Oscar Buros in 1978, the Buros Institute was established at the University of Nebraska-Lincoln. The first publication from the new Institute was *Tests in Print III* in 1983. *Tests in Print IV* was published in 1994, *Tests in Print V* in 1999, *Tests in Print VI* in 2002, and *Tests in Print VII* in 2006.

The need for a comprehensive bibliography of tests has never been more essential. Because of the proliferation of commercially available tests, we have adopted a policy of reviewing in *The Mental*

Measurements Yearbook series only those tests with at least a minimum of technical and development information. This policy was implemented with tests reviewed in the *14th MMY*. Therefore, not all commercially available tests will be reviewed in the *MMY*. However, we continue to include descriptive information for all known in-print commercially available tests in the *Tests in Print* series. With the more rapid publication of *The Mental Measurements Yearbook* series (approximately every 24 months), it also became necessary to update our listing of commercially available tests on a more frequent basis. Beginning with *Tests in Print VI*, we embarked on a plan to publish *TIP* every 3 to 5 years.

Our efforts in this massive enterprise have been consistent with those initially proposed by Oscar K. Buros, that is, to improve the science and practice of testing by offering information and evaluative reviews of commercial products to informed consumers. *Tests in Print VIII* is a continuation of our efforts to provide a product for people who develop, evaluate, study, purchase, and/or use tests. We hope and expect that informed users will consider the reviews of tests, if available, prior to their purchasing tests for use with clients, especially in high stakes situations.

TESTS IN PRINT VIII

The contents of *Tests in Print VIII* include: (a) a comprehensive bibliography of commercially available tests published as separates for use with English-speaking individuals; (b) a list of contributing reviewers for the entire *MMY* series; (c) a test title index that includes all in-print tests, tests that have gone out of print since the publication of *TIP VII*, and alternative or superseded titles for some tests; (d) a separate listing of the tests that have gone out of print since the publication of *TIP III* (1983); (e) a list of test acronyms; (f) a classified subject index that also describes the population for which each test is intended; (g) a publishers directory and index, including contact information and test listings by publisher; (h) a name index, which includes the names of all authors of tests or of reviews; and (i) a score index listing all scores generated by tests listed in *TIP VIII*.

The organization of the volume is encyclopedic in nature, with tests being ordered alphabetically by title. Thus, if the title of a test is known, the reader can locate the test description immediately without having to consult the Index of Titles. Test classifications appear in the Classified Subject Index.

TABLE 1

Test Entries in *TIP VII* by Major Classification

Classification	Number of Test Entries
Achievement	81
Behavior Assessment	155
Developmental	145
Education	118
English and Language	164
Fine Arts	18
Foreign Language	47
Intelligence and General Aptitude	212
Mathematics	73
Miscellaneous	267
Neuropsychological	128
Personality	644
Reading	128
Science	46
Sensory-Motor	60
Social Studies	31
Speech and Hearing	92
Vocations	594

The page headings reflect the encyclopedic organization. The page heading of the left-hand page cites the number and title of the first test listed on that page, and the page heading of the right-hand page cites the number and title of the last test listed on that page. All numbers presented in the various indexes are test numbers, not page numbers. Page numbers, important only for the Table of Contents, are indicated at the bottom of each page.

TESTS

Tests in Print VIII contains 3,003 test entries. The in-print status of these tests was confirmed by direct correspondence with publishers. Table 1 presents the number of test entries included in each major classification of the Classified Subject Index. Any classification system is to some degree dependent on human judgment, but broad comparisons between categories are often useful. It is interesting to note, for example, that the Personality test category continues to include the greatest number of tests of any category in *TIP VIII*.

REVIEWS AND EXCERPTS

Tests in Print VIII serves as a master index of in-print tests that refers the reader to all the original test reviews and excerpted test reviews that appeared for these tests in all of the *Mental Measurements Yearbooks* to date. In addition, it provides references to entries and reviews in earlier Yearbooks for all tests that have gone out of print since *TIP III*. Authors of reviews and excerpts are named following the test entries in cross references to the appropriate *MMY*. Although *TIP VIII* will serve a very useful function by providing a comprehensive bibliography of tests in print, the cross references to the critical reviews are also of great importance if tests are to be used wisely. Thus *TIP* and the *MMY*s are inseparable partners in the cause of promoting effective selection and use of tests.

A total of 3,203 individuals have contributed reviews to one or more *MMY*s. Because of their important contributions to the *Mental Measurements Yearbooks*, a complete listing of *MMY* test reviewers is presented in the index section of *TIP VIII*.

REFERENCES

Earlier volumes have included specific test references selected by Buros staff who searched through hundreds of professional journals. Because of the current availability of online search features that allow users to do independent reference searches, it was our decision to discontinue providing these references in the *MMY* and *TIP* series. Cross references for a number of test descriptions will still indicate when references were provided in previous publications (e.g., "See T5:326 [10 references]").

INDEXES

As mentioned earlier, *TIP VIII* includes eight indexes invaluable as aids to effective use: (a) Index of *MMY* test reviewers, (b) Index of Titles, (c) Index of Recently-Out-of-Print Tests, (d) Index of Acronyms, (e) Classified Subject Index, (f) Publishers Directory and Index, (g) Index of Names, and (h) Score Index. Additional comment on these indexes is provided below.

Index of MMY Test Reviewers. This listing represents all test reviewers who have had their reviews published in *The Mental Measurements Yearbook* series and the volume number of their test reviews.

Index of Titles. Because the organization of *TIP* is comprehensive in nature, with the tests ordered alphabetically by title throughout the volume, the test title index does not have to be consulted to find a test for which the title is known. However, the title index has some features that make it useful beyond its function as a complete title listing. First, it includes cross-reference information useful for tests with superseded or alternative titles or tests

commonly (and sometimes inaccurately) known by multiple titles. Second, it lists the 43 tests that have gone out of print since being listed in *TIP VII* or the *17th* or *18th MMY*. To differentiate between in-print and out-of-print tests in the title index, it is important to read carefully the instructions on the use of the test title index that precede the title listing. One should keep in mind that the numbers in this index, like those for all *TIP* and *MMY* indexes, are test numbers and not page numbers.

Index of Recently Out-of-Print Tests. This index is a comprehensive listing of all tests that have gone out of print since the publication of *Tests in Print III* (1983). The number following the title indicates the last Buros publication in which the test was listed as an in-print test.

Index of Acronyms. Some tests seem to be better known by their acronyms than by their full titles. The Index of Acronyms can help in these instances; it refers the reader to the full title of the test and to the relevant descriptive information and reviews.

Classified Subject Index. The Classified Subject Index classifies all tests listed in *TIP VIII* into 18 major categories: Achievement, Behavior Assessment, Developmental, Education, English and Language, Fine Arts, Foreign Languages, Intelligence and General Aptitude, Mathematics, Miscellaneous, Neuropsychological, Personality, Reading, Science, Sensory-Motor, Social Studies, Speech and Hearing, and Vocations. Each test entry includes test title, population for which the test is intended, and test number. The Classified Subject Index is of great help to readers who seek a listing of tests in given subject areas. The Classified Subject Index represents a starting point for readers who know their area of interest but do not know how to further focus that interest in order to identify the best test(s) for their particular purposes. A descriptive listing of the categories precedes the Classified Subject Index.

Publishers Directory and Index. The Publishers Directory and Index includes the names and addresses of the publishers of all tests included in *TIP VIII* plus a listing of test numbers for each individual publisher. This index also includes telephone and FAX numbers and addresses for electronic access (email and web pages). Publishers were given an opportunity to provide this information as they wanted it listed. For those not providing contact information, only a mailing address is included. This index can be particularly useful in obtaining addresses for specimen sets or catalogs after the test descriptions have been read and evaluated. It can also be useful when a reader knows the publisher of a certain test but is uncertain about the test title, or when a reader is interested in the range of tests published by a given publisher. A few publishers are listed as "Status Unknown" because recent correspondence has been returned by the Post Office and we have been unable to obtain a current address.

Index of Names. The Index of Names provides a comprehensive list of names, indicating authorship of a test or a test review.

Score Index. The Score Index is an index to all scores generated by the tests in *TIP VIII.* Test titles are sometimes misleading or ambiguous, and test content may be difficult to define with precision. Test scores represent operational definitions of the variables the test author is trying to measure, and as such they often define test purpose and content more adequately than other descriptive information. A search for a particular test is most often a search for a test that measures some specific variables. Test scores and their associated labels can often be the best definitions of the variables of interest. It is, in fact, a detailed subject index based on the most critical operational features of any test–the scores and their associated labels.

HOW TO USE *TIP VIII*

A reference work like *TIP VIII* can be of far greater benefit to a reader if a little time is taken to become familiar with what it has to offer and how one might use it most effectively to obtain the information sought. The first step in this process is to read the Introduction to *TIP VIII.* The second step is to become familiar with the eight indexes and particularly with the instructions preceding each index listing. The third step is to make actual use of the book by looking up needed information. This third step is simple if one keeps in mind the following possibilities:

1. If you know the title of the test, use the alphabetical page headings to go directly to the test entry.

2. If you do not know, cannot find, or are unsure of the title of a test, consult the Index of Titles for possible variants of the title or consult the appropriate subject area of the Classified Subject Index for other possible leads or for similar or related tests in the same area. (Other uses for both of these indexes were described earlier.)

3. If you know the author of a test but not the title or publisher, consult the Index of Names and look up the author and corresponding test titles until you find the test you want.

4. If you know the test publisher but not the title or author, consult the Publishers Directory and Index and look up the publisher's titles until you find the test you want.

5. If you are looking for a test that yields a particular kind of score, but have no knowledge of which test that might be, look up the score in the Score Index and locate the test or tests that include the score variable of interest.

6. Once you have found the test or tests you are looking for, read the descriptive entries for these tests carefully so that you may take advantage of the information provided. A description of the information available in these test entries is presented later in this section.

7. After you have read the descriptive information, you may want to order a specimen set for a particular test so that you can examine it firsthand. The Publishers Directory and Index includes the address information needed to obtain specimen sets or catalogs.

Making Effective Use of the Test Entries. The test entries include extensive information. For each test, descriptive information is presented in the following order:

a) TITLE. Test titles are printed in boldface type. Secondary or series titles are set off from main titles by a colon.

b) PURPOSE. For each test a brief, clear statement is included describing the purpose of the test. Often these statements are quotations from the test manual.

c) POPULATION. This is a description of the groups for which the test is intended. The grade, chronological age, semester range, or employment category is usually given. "Grades 1.5–2.5, 2–3, 4–12, 13–17" means that there are four test booklets: a booklet for the middle of first grade through the middle of the second grade, a booklet for the beginning of the second grade through the end of third grade, a booklet for Grades 4 through 12 inclusive, and a booklet for undergraduate and graduate students in colleges and universities.

d) PUBLICATION DATE. The inclusive range of publication dates for the various forms, accessories, and editions of a test is reported.

e) ACRONYM. When a test is often referred to by an acronym by the test publisher, the acronym is provided in the test entry.

f) SCORES. The number of part scores (e.g., subscores or component scores) is presented along with their titles or descriptions of what they are intended to represent or measure.

g) ADMINISTRATION. Individual or group administration is indicated. A test is considered a group test unless it may be administered only individually.

h) FORMS, PARTS, AND LEVELS. All available forms, parts, and levels are listed.

i) MANUAL. Notation is made if no manual is available. All other manual information is included under Price Data.

j) RESTRICTED DISTRIBUTION. This is noted only for tests that are put on a special market by the publisher. Educational and psychological restrictions are not noted (unless a special training course is required for use).

k) PRICE DATA. Price information is reported for test packages (usually 20 to 35 tests), answer sheets, all other accessories, and specimen sets. The statement "$17.50 per 35 tests" means that all accessories are included unless otherwise indicated by the reporting of separate prices for accessories. The statement also means 35 tests of one level, one edition, or one part unless stated otherwise. Because test prices can change very quickly, the year that the listed test prices were obtained is also given. Foreign currency is assigned the appropriate symbol. When prices are given in foreign dollars, a qualifying symbol is added (e.g., A$16.50 refers to 16 dollars and 50 cents in Australian currency). Along with cost, the publication date and number of pages on which print occurs is reported for manuals and technical reports (e.g., 1995, 102 pages). All types of machine-scorable answer sheets available for use with a specific test are also reported in the descriptive entry. Scoring and reporting services provided by publishers are reported along with information on costs. In a few cases, special computerized scoring and interpretation services are given in separate entries immediately following the test.

l) FOREIGN LANGUAGE AND OTHER SPECIAL EDITIONS. This section concerns foreign language editions published by the same publisher who sells the English edition. It also indicates special editions (e.g., Braille, large type) available from the same or a different publisher.

m) TIME. The number of minutes of actual working time allowed examinees and the approximate length of time needed for administering a test are reported whenever obtainable. The latter figure is always enclosed in parentheses. Thus, "50(60) minutes" indicates that the examinees are allowed 50 minutes of working time and that a total of 60 minutes is needed to administer the test. A time of "40–50 minutes" indicates an untimed test that takes approximately 45 minutes to administer, or–in a few instances–a test so timed that working time and administration time are very difficult to disentangle. When the time necessary to administer a test is not reported or suggested in the test materials but has been obtained through correspondence with the test publisher or author, the time is enclosed in brackets.

n) COMMENTS. Some entries contain special notations, such as: "for research use only"; "revision of the ABC Test"; "tests administered monthly at centers throughout the United States"; "subtests available as separates"; and "verbal creativity." A statement such as "verbal creativity" is intended to further describe what the test claims to measure. Some of the test entries include additional factual statements that may influence one's perception of the test, such as "1990 test identical with test copyrighted 1970."

o) AUTHOR. For most tests, all authors are reported. In the case of tests that appear in a new form each year, typically only authors of the most recent forms are listed. Names are reported exactly as printed on test booklets. Names of editors generally are not reported.

p) PUBLISHER. The name of the publisher or distributor is reported for each test. Foreign publishers are identified by listing the country in brackets immediately following the name of the publisher. The Publishers Directory and Index must be consulted for a publisher's address and other contact information.

q) FOREIGN ADAPTATIONS. Revisions and adaptations of tests for foreign use are listed in a separate paragraph following the original edition.

r) SUBLISTINGS. Levels, editions, subtests, or parts of a test available in separate booklets are sometimes presented as sublistings with titles set in small capital letters. Sub-sublistings are indented and titles are set in italic type.

s) CROSS REFERENCES. For tests that have been listed previously in a Buros Institute publication, a test entry includes–if relevant–a final paragraph containing a cross reference to the reviews, excerpts, and references for that test in those volumes. For example, in the cross references, "T3:467" refers to test 467 in *Tests in Print III*,

"8:1023" refers to test 1023 in *The Eighth Mental Measurements Yearbook*, "T2:144" refers to test 144 in Tests in Print II, "7:637" refers to test 637 in *The Seventh Mental Measurements Yearbook*, "P:262" refers to test 262 in *Personality Tests and Reviews I*, "2:1427" refers to test 1427 in *The 1940 Yearbook*, and "1:1110" refers to test 1110 in *The 1938 Yearbook*. In the case of batteries and programs, the paragraph also includes cross references—from the battery to the separately listed subtests and vice versa—to entries in this volume and to entries and reviews in earlier editions of TIP and the MMY.

ACKNOWLEDGEMENTS

The publication of a volume of this kind is only accomplished with the effort and cooperation of many people. The editors are grateful to all who have given of their time and expertise in the publication process.

Staff members of the Buros Institute of Mental Measurements have been major contributors and vital to the success of gathering and compiling the information to be included in *TIP VIII*. It has truly been a team effort. Gary Anderson, Assistant Editor, and Jennifer Schlueter, Assistant Editor, have worked long and hard in helping to organize, proofread, and present the information included. Their careful and conscientious efforts are very important to our final product. The administrative support of Rasma Strautkalns, Institute Secretary, has also been very important and helpful, as has clerical assistance from student workers, Christa Hake and Kaley Smith. The Buros Institute for Assessment Consultation and Outreach professional staff of Elaine Rodeck, Katherine (Tzu-Yun) Chin, and Theresa Glanz have provided valuable assistance and insights into a range of testing products that have made this publication a better product. Jessica Jonson has provided needed assessment literacy information during the final stages of preparation of this volume.

The Buros Institute of Mental Measurements is part of the Buros Center for Testing within the Department of Educational Psychology of the University of Nebraska-Lincoln and many students from the department and the university have contributed to the publication of this volume. We thank the following graduate research assistants who helped with the preparation of *TIP VIII:* Nancy Anderson, Jeffrey Babl, Allison Champion-Wescott, Rebecca Norman Dvorak, Kristin Jones, Chelsi Klentz Davis, Natalie Koziol, Tabethah Mack, and Erin Rhoads.

Appreciation is also extended to our National Advisory Council for their willingness to assist in the operation of the Buros Center. The members of the National Advisory Council during the time of preparation of this volume were Angee Baker, Gregory Cizek, Terry Gutkin, John Fremer, Milton Hakel, Lawrence Rudner, Jonathan Sandoval, and Neal Schmitt.

Most of the publishers of the tests listed have been extremely cooperative in providing us with their materials and information to make these listings comprehensive and accurate. We appreciate their timely assistance. A small minority of publishers refuse to provide information and materials. We sincerely regret that we were not able to list their products. Some others did not respond to our requests for an accuracy check of information, so we have included the earlier information we have for their tests and addresses. We have made every effort to stay alert to new tests, publishers, and publisher addresses. We apologize for any oversights and hope that the test authors or publishers will make us aware of omissions and discrepancies so that their entries can be corrected in future editions, which may take the familiar tangible form or an electronic form.

And finally, we thank our friends and families for their patience and encouragement during the publication process.

Linda L. Murphy
Kurt F. Geisinger
Janet F. Carlson
Robert A. Spies

October 2011

Tests in Print

[1]

A-4 Police Officer Video Test.

Purpose: Designed as an entry-level test to "assess both cognitive and non-cognitive competencies that new police officers need to perform successfully on the job."
Population: Candidates for entry-level police officer positions.
Publication Date: 1999.
Scores: 3 abilities: Ability to Observe/Listen to/ and Remember Information, Ability to Use Situational Judgment and Interpersonal Skills, Ability to Learn and Apply Police Information.
Administration: Individual or group.
Price Data: Available from publisher.
Time: 155 minutes.
Comments: Administered via videotaped scenarios as an alternative to traditional multiple-choice tests; all instructions as well as count down timer are included on the video to facilitate test administration.
Author: International Public Management Association for Human Resources.
Publisher: International Public Management Association for Human Resources (IPMA-HR).
Cross References: For a review by Deniz S. Ones and Stephan Dilchert, see 18:1.

[2]

AAMR Adaptive Behavior Scale–Residential and Community, Second Edition.

Purpose: To determine "an individual's strengths and weaknesses among adaptive domains and factors."
Population: Persons with disabilities in residential and community settings.
Publication Dates: 1969–1993.
Acronym: ABS-RC:2.
Scores, 23: 18 domain scores (10 part one domain scores: Independent Functioning, Physical Develop-ment, Economic Activity, Language Development, Numbers and Time, Domestic Activity, Prevocational/ Vocational Activity, Self-Direction, Responsibil-ity, Socialization; 8 part two domain scores: Social Behavior, Conformity, Trustworthiness, Stereotyped and Hyperactive Behavior, Sexual Behavior, Self-Abusive Behavior, Social Engagement, Disturbing Interpersonal Behavior); 5 factor scores (Personal Self-Sufficiency, Community Self-Sufficiency, Personal-Social Responsibility, Social Adjustment, Personal Adjustment).
Administration: Individual.
Price Data, 2006: $150 per complete kit including examiner's manual (1993, 76 pages), 25 examination booklets, and 25 profile/summary forms; $225 per 100 examination booklets; $30 per 25 profile/summary forms; $63 per examiner's manual.
Time: Administration time varies but ranges between 25–30 minutes.
Authors: Kazuo Nihira, Henry Leland, and Nadine Lambert.
Publisher: PRO-ED.
Cross References: For reviews by Karen T. Carey and Patti L. Harrison, see 13:1.

[3]

AAMR Adaptive Behavior Scale–School, Second Edition.

Purpose: "Used to assess adaptive behavior."
Population: Ages 3–21.
Publication Dates: 1981–1993.
Acronym: ABS-S:2.
Scores, 21: 16 domain scores (9 part one domain scores: Independent Functioning, Physical Development, Economic Activity, Language Development, Numbers and Time, Prevocational/Vocational Activity, Self-Direction, Responsibility, Socialization; 7 part two domain scores:

Social Behavior, Conformity, Trustworthiness, Stereotyped and Hyperactive Behavior, Self-Abusive Behavior, Social Engagement, Disturbing Interpersonal Behavior), 5 factor scores (Personal Self-Sufficiency, Community Self-Sufficiency, Personal-Social Responsibility, Social Adjustment, Personal Adjustment).

Administration: Individual.

Price Data, 2006: $150 per complete kit including examiner's manual (1993, 118 pages), 25 examination booklets, and 25 profile/summary forms; $63 per 25 examination booklets; $30 per 25 profile/summary forms; $60 per examiner's manual.

Time: (15–30) minutes.

Comments: Previously called AAMD Adaptive Behavior Scale.

Authors: Nadine Lambert, Kazuo Nihira, and Henry Leland.

Publisher: PRO-ED.

Cross References: See T5:2 (2 references); for reviews by Robert G. Harrington and Terry A. Stinnett, see 13:2 (6 references); see also T4:2 (42 references); for a review of an earlier edition by Stephen N. Elliott, see 9:3 (9 references); see also T3:6 (55 references); for reviews of an earlier edition by Morton Bortner and by C. H. Ammons and R. B. Ammons, see 8:493 (25 references); see also T2:1092 (3 references); for reviews of an earlier edition by Lovick C. Miller and Melvyn I. Semmel, see 7:37 (9 references).

[4]

Abbreviated Torrance Test for Adults.

Purpose: To assess creative thinking ability.

Population: Adults.

Publication Date: 2002.

Acronym: ATTA.

Scores, 23: Norm-Referenced Measures (Fluency, Originality, Elaboration, Flexibility, Total Scaled Score), Criterion-Referenced Creativity Indicators (Richness and Colorfulness of Imagery, Emotions/Feelings, Future Orientation, Humor: Conceptual Incongruity, Provocative Questions, Verbal Responses Total, Openness: Resistance to Premature Closure, Unusual Visualization/Different Perspective, Movement and/or Sound, Richness and/or Colorfulness of Imagery, Abstractness of Titles, Articulateness in Telling Story, Combination/Synthesis of Two or More Figures, Internal Visual Perspective, Expressions of Feelings and Emotions, Fantasy, Figural Responses Total), Creativity Index.

Administration: Group.

Price Data: See www.ststesting.com for up-to-date prices.

Foreign Language Edition: Spanish edition available.

Time: 15 minutes.

Comments: Based on 1980 Demonstration Form of the Torrance Tests; may be self-administered; norm- and criterion-referenced.

Authors: Kathy Goff and E. Paul Torrance.

Publisher: Scholastic Testing Service, Inc.

Cross References: For reviews by James A. Athanasou and Alan C. Bugbee, Jr., see 17:1.

[5]

Aberrant Behavior Checklist.

Purpose: Constructed to rate "inappropriate and maladaptive behavior of mentally retarded individuals in residential and community settings, and developmental centers."

Population: Mentally retarded adolescents and adults.

Publication Date: 1986.

Acronym: ABC.

Scores, 5: Irritability, Lethargy, Stereotypy, Hyperactivity, Inappropriate Speech.

Administration: Individual.

Price Data, 2002: $63 per Residential complete kit including manual (32 pages) and Community supplemental manual; $70 per Community complete kit including manual, supplementary manual, and 50 Residential/Community forms/score sheets; $33 per 50 Residential/Community forms/score sheets; $33 per manual; $12 per Community supplemental manual.

Time: (5) minutes.

Comments: Ratings by direct care or professional staff member acquainted with individual.

Authors: Michael G. Aman and Nirbhay N. Singh.

Publisher: Slosson Educational Publications, Inc.

Cross References: See T5:4 (23 references); for reviews by Lena R. Gaddis and by J. Jeffrey Grill, see 12:1 (5 references); see T4:4 (2 references).

[6]

Abortion Scale.

Purpose: To measure attitudes toward abortion.

Population: Older adolescents and adults.

Publication Dates: 1972–1988.

Scores: Total score only.

Manual: No manual.

Price Data, 2002: $2 per scale.

Time: [10] minutes.

Comments: Supplementary article available.

Author: Panos D. Bardis.

Publisher: Donna Bardis.

Cross References: See T4:4 (2 references).

[7]

Abstract Reasoning Test.

Purpose: "Assesses student ability to use non-verbal reasoning skills."

Population: Middle primary through middle secondary school students.

Publication Date: 2008.

Acronym: ART.

Scores: Total score only.
Administration: Group.
Forms, 5: Level A Series 1, Level B Series 1, Level C Series 1, Level D Series 1, Level E Series 1.
Price Data, 2009: A\$7 per student; A\$60 batch charge for orders of less than 60 forms; contact publisher for cost of scoring and report service; manual (24 pages) is free to print from publisher's website: www.acer.edu.au/art.
Time: (30) minute time limit per Levels A and B; (40) minute time limit per Levels C, D, and E.
Comments: Online version available in 2010; publisher provides scoring and summary report; reports include individual and group level data; 1 total score per student represented in 4 different ways (Raw Score, Scaled Score, Percentile Rank, Stanine) and 1 total score per client school represented in 2 different ways (Raw Score, Scaled Score); stanines and percentile rankings "relative to students in the same year level at [client] school."
Author: Australian Council for Educational Research Ltd.
Publisher: Australian Council for Educational Research Ltd. [Australia].

[8]

Abuse Disability Questionnaire.

Purpose: "Designed to assess both the extent of exposure to partner abuse, as well as its associated consequences."
Population: Women ages 18 years and older.
Publication Date: 2005.
Acronym: ADQ.
Scores, 8: Relationship Disability, Psychological Dysfunction, Substance Abuse, Anxiety, Life Restriction, Health Status Issues, Inadequate Life Control, Concern with Physical Harm.
Administration: Individual or group.
Price Data, 2006: \$70 per complete kit including 50 questionnaires/profile forms and manual (27 pages); \$45 per 50 questionnaires/profile forms; \$30 per manual.
Time: (5-15) minutes.
Comments: Includes a self-report questionnaire/profile form and an information/diagnostics form to be completed via an interview.
Author: John R. McNamara.
Publisher: Stoelting Co.
Cross References: For reviews by Sheri Bauman and by Carl J. Sheperis and Tiffany D. Chandler, see 17:2.

[9]

Abuse Risk Inventory for Women.

Purpose: To identify women who are current victims of abuse or who are at risk for abuse by their male intimate partners or ex-partners.

Population: Women seeking medical or mental health services.
Publication Date: 1989.
Acronym: ARNW.
Scores: Total score only.
Administration: Group and individual.
Price Data: Available from publisher at www.mindgarden.com/products/arnws.htm.
Time: (10–15) minutes.
Comments: Test booklet title is Interpersonal Relationship Survey; self-administered; workbook available.
Author: Bonnie L. Yegidis.
Publisher: Mind Garden, Inc.
Cross References: For reviews by Cynthia A. Rohrbeck and Janice G. Williams, see 11:1.

[10]

Academic Advising Inventory.

Purpose: "Designed to measure three aspects of academic advising: (1) the nature of advising relationships, seen along a developmental-prescriptive continuum, (2) the frequency of activities taking place during advising sessions, and (3) satisfaction with advising."
Population: Undergraduate students.
Publication Dates: 1984–1986.
Acronym: AAI.
Scores, 3: Developmental-Prescriptive Advising, Advisor-Advisee Activity Scales, Student Satisfaction with Advising.
Administration: Group.
Price Data: Available from publisher.
Time: (20) minutes.
Comments: Manual entitled Evaluating Academic Advising; scoring service available from publisher.
Authors: Roger B. Winston, Jr. and Janet A. Sandor.
Publisher: Student Development Associates, Inc. [No reply from publisher; status unknown].
Cross References: See T5:8 (1 reference) and T4:7 (2 references); for a review by Robert D. Brown, see 10:3.

[11]

Academic Aptitude Test: Non-Verbal Intelligence: Acorn National Aptitude Tests.

Purpose: "Designed to evaluate that aspect of intelligence related to the aptitude for abstract academic work required in mathematical, engineering, designing and other physical sciences."
Population: Grades 7–16 and adults.
Publication Dates: 1943–1957.
Scores, 4: Spatial Relations, Physical Relations, Graphic Relations, Total.
Administration: Group.
Price Data: Available from publisher.

Time: 26 minutes.
Authors: Andrew Kobal, J. Wayne Wrightstone, and Karl R. Kunze.
Publisher: Psychometric Affiliates.
Cross References: For a review by William B. Schrader, see 4:274.

[12]

Academic Aptitude Test: Verbal Intelligence: Acorn National Aptitude Tests.

Purpose: "Designed to evaluate mental abilities and capacities that are important in academic work."
Population: Grades 7–16 and adults.
Publication Dates: 1943–1952.
Scores, 4: General Information, Mental Alertness, Comprehension of Relations, Total.
Administration: Group.
Price Data: Available from publisher.
Time: 40 minutes.
Authors: Andrew Kobal, J. Wayne Wrightstone, and Karl R. Kunze.
Publisher: Psychometric Affiliates.
Cross References: For a review by William B. Schrader, see 4:275; for a review by Marion A. Bills, see 3:215.

[13]

Academic Competence Evaluation Scales.

Purpose: "Measures academic skills (reading/language arts, mathematics, critical thinking) as well as academic enablers (motivation, study skills, engagement, interpersonal skills)."
Population: Grades K–12, Grades 6–12, 2- or 4-year college.
Publication Date: 2000.
Acronym: ACES.
Scores, 9: Academic Skills (Reading/Language Arts, Mathematics, Critical Thinking, Total), Academic Enablers (Interpersonal Skills, Motivation, Study Skills, Engagement, Total).
Administration: Group.
Forms, 3: Teacher (Grades K–12), Student (Grades 6–12), College (2- or 4-year college).
Price Data, 2001: $119 per K–12 basic kit including manual, 25 each of student and teacher record forms, boxed; $195 per K–12 complete kit including manual (154 pages), 25 each of student and teacher record forms, scoring assistant (disk or CD-ROM version); $165 per college complete kit including manual, 25 college record forms, scoring assistant (disk or CD-ROM version); $65 per K–12 manual or college manual; $34 per 25 record forms (specify Student, Teacher, or College), quantity discounts available; $91 per scoring assistant software (disk or CD-ROM version).
Time: (10–15) minutes.

Comments: Standardized; indicates confidence intervals for each subscale; allows ranking of scale and subscale scores into one of three competence levels (developing, competent, advanced); Assistant software (version 2.0) scores, monitors change in scores over time, graphs data, generates descriptive reports; system requirements: Windows 95/98/2000/NT 4.0/ME, 32 MB RAM, 100 MHz processor or higher, CD-ROM and 3.5-inch floppy diskette drive (CD-ROM version) or 3.5-diskette drive only (diskette version), 2 MB video card, 800 x 600 resolution, 256 colors, 25 MB free disk space.
Authors: James C. DiPerna and Stephen N. Elliott.
Publisher: Pearson.
Cross References: For reviews by Ronald K. Hambleton and by Darrell L. Sabers and Sarah Bonner, see 16:1.

[14]

Academic Freedom Survey.

Purpose: "Attempted to measure academic freedom" at college level.
Population: College students and faculty.
Publication Date: 1954.
Scores, 3: Student, Faculty, Total.
Administration: Group.
Price Data, 2001: $4 per specimen set.
Time: Administration time not reported.
Authors: Paul Slivnick and Academic Freedom Committee, Illinois Division, American Civil Liberties Union.
Publisher: Psychometric Affiliates.

[15]

Academic Intervention Monitoring System.

Purpose: Guidebook and intervention planning questionnaires "designed to provide teachers and other school-based professionals with the resources they need for developing, monitoring, and evaluating classroom-based, empirically supported interventions for academic difficulties."
Population: Grades K–12.
Publication Date: 2001.
Acronym: AIMS.
Scores: Not scored.
Administration: Individual.
Forms, 3: Student, Parent, Teacher.
Price Data, 2004: $133 per complete kit including manual (147 pages), 25 each of Student, Parent, and Teacher forms; $19 per 25 Student forms; $19 per 25 Parent forms; $36 per 25 Teacher forms; $95 per manual.
Time: (10–15) minutes.
Comments: Developed in conjunction with the Academic Competence Evaluation Scales (13); student and parent forms available in Spanish.
Authors: Stephen N. Elliott, James C. DiPerna, with Edward Shapiro.

Publisher: Pearson.
Cross References: For reviews by Kathleen M. Johnson and Jeffrey Smith, see 17:4.

[16]

Academic Perceptions Inventory [2000 Revision].

Purpose: "Developed to assess a profile of the academic self in various classrooms and in the learning environment … with perceptions of the self as a person, as a student, and at school."
Population: Grades K–16.
Publication Dates: 1979–2000.
Acronym: API.
Administration: Group.
Price Data, 2002: $20 per packet of 25 scales (specify level); $25 per test manual (specify Primary Level [2000, 83 pages], Intermediate Level [2000, 76 pages], Advanced Level [2000, 79 pages], or College Level [2000, 73 pages]); $40 per composite test manual (2000, 146 pages); $.40 per answer sheet; $.30 per scale for scoring.
Foreign Language Editions: Available in Spanish, Italian, and French.
Time: (5–20) minutes per test.
Comments: Ratings by self and others; previous edition entitled The Affective Perception Inventory.
Authors: Louise M. Soares and Anthony T. Soares.
Publisher: Castle Consultants.
a) PRIMARY LEVEL.
Population: Grades K–3.
Scores: 9 Scales: Self Concept, Student Self, School, Reading, Social Studies, Science, Arithmetic, Fine Arts, Sports and Games.
b) INTERMEDIATE LEVEL.
Population: Grades 4–8.
Scores: 11 Scales: Self Concept, Student Self, School, Language Arts, Reading, Foreign Languages, History and Geography, Science, Mathematics, Fine Arts, Physical Education.
c) ADVANCED LEVEL.
Population: Grades 9–12.
Scores: 13 Scales: Self Concept, Student Self, School, English, Foreign Languages, American History, Mathematics, Biology, Chemistry, Earth Sciences, Physics, Fine Arts, Sports.
d) COLLEGE LEVEL.
Population: Grades 13–16.
Scores: 15 Scales: Self Concept, Student Self, Campus, English, Foreign Languages, World History, Political Science, Business, Mathematics, Biology, Chemistry, Physics, Humanities, Fine Arts, Sports.
Cross References: For reviews by Carol E. Kessler and Aimin Wang, see 15:1; see T4:130 (3 references); for reviews by Rosa A. Hagin and Gerald R. Smith of The Affective Perception Inventory, see 9:59.

[17]

ACCESS–A Comprehensive Custody Evaluation Standard System.

Purpose: Constructed as a "total system for conducting child custody evaluations."
Population: Children, parents, and others involved in child custody evaluations.
Publication Dates: 1997–2002.
Administration: Individual.
Price Data, 2002: $1,495 per complete kit including Bricklin Perceptual Scales Comprehensive Starting Kit with 3.5-inch unlimited use computer scoring profile, Perception-of-Relationships Test Comprehensive Starting Kit with 3.5-inch unlimited use computer scoring profile, Parent Awareness Skills Survey Comprehensive Starting Kit; Parent Perception-of-Child Profile Comprehensive Starting Kit, Custody Evaluation Questionnaires Kit, Custody Evaluation Interview Kit, Custody Evaluation Observation Kit, Custody Evaluation Aggregation Kit, Discipline Index Kit with 3.5-inch unlimited use computer scoring profiles, Home-Visit Kit, and Assessment of Parenting Skills: Infant and Preschooler.
Time: Administration time not reported.
Comments: Ratings by parents, children, teachers, and health/mental health professionals.
Authors: Barry Bricklin and Gail Elliot.
Publisher: Village Publishing.
a) BRICKLIN PERCEPTUAL SCALES.
Comments: See T5:334.
b) PERCEPTION-OF-RELATIONSHIPS TEST.
Comments: See T5:1917.
c) PARENT AWARENESS SKILLS SURVEY.
Comments: See T5:1879.
d) PARENT PERCEPTION OF CHILD PROFILE.
Comments: See T5:1886.
e) CUSTODY EVALUATION QUESTIONNAIRES KIT.
Purpose: "Designed to gather self-report data … in every single area that are considered important in model custody statutes."
Population: Children, parents, grandparents, and collateral informants involved in a custody evaluation.
Scores: No scores, ratings only.
Forms, 6: Parent Self-Report Questionnaire, "Would" Questionnaire, Child Data Questionnaire, Child Self-Report Questionnaire, Child's Access to Parental Strengths Questionnaire, Child's Sexual Abuse Questionnaire.
f) CUSTODY EVALUATION INTERVIEW KIT.
Purpose: Designed for conducting custody evaluation interviews.
Population: Professionals conducting custody evaluation interviews.
Scores: No scores, structured interviews only.

Forms, 5: Parent Interview, Physician Interview, Teacher Interview, Mental Health Professional Interview, Corroborative Source Interview.

g) CUSTODY EVALUATION OBSERVATION KIT.

Purpose: Constructed to "discriminate among the different ways, positive and negative, a child responds to parental communications."

Population: Professionals conducting custody evaluations.

Scores: No scores, ratings by observers.

Forms, 2: Adult Observation Form, Child Observation Form.

h) CUSTODY EVALUATION AGGREGATION KIT.

Purpose: "Designed to aggregate the enormous amount of information gathered" in custody evaluations.

Population: Professionals conducting custody evaluations.

Scores: No scores.

Comments: Also includes phone logs, critical targets forms, and model contracts.

i) DISCIPLINE INDEX.

Comments: See 889.

j) HOME-VISIT KIT.

Comments: See 1262.

k) ASSESSMENT OF PARENTING SKILLS: INFANT AND PRESCHOOLER.

Comments: See 214.

Cross References: For a review by Mark W. Roberts, see 14:1.

[18]

Access Management Survey.

Purpose: Designed to measure the extent to which a manager provides opportunities and support for employee involvement, and the necessary resources for people to influence work-life issues.

Population: Adults.

Publication Dates: 1989–1995.

Acronym: AMS.

Scores, 5: Access to the Problem, Access to People, Access to Information and Resources, Access to Support, Access to the Solution.

Administration: Group.

Price Data, 2001: $8.95 per instrument.

Time: Untimed.

Comments: Self-assessment survey.

Author: Jay Hall.

Publisher: Teleometrics International, Inc.

Cross References: For reviews by Thomas M. Haladyna and Mary A. Lewis, see 12:2.

[19]

Accountant Staff Selector.

Purpose: Designed "to evaluate the administrative, intellectual and analytical skills necessary for successful performance as an accountant."

Population: Adult applicants for accounting positions.

Publication Dates: 1982–2002.

Scores, 7: Numerical Skills, Attention to Detail, Problem Solving Ability, Reading Comprehension, Spreadsheet Simulation, Verbal Fluency, Bookkeeping Skills.

Administration: Individual or group.

Price Data: Available from publisher.

Foreign Language Edition: French edition available.

Time: (66) minutes.

Comments: Scoring available by mail, courier service, fax, or telephone.

Author: Walden Personnel Testing and Consulting, Inc.

Publisher: Walden Personnel Performance, Inc. [Canada].

Cross References: For a review by JoEllen V. Carlson, see 16:2.

[20]

Accounting Aptitude Test.

Purpose: Designed to assess aptitude for an accounting career.

Population: First-year college students.

Publication Dates: 1982–1992.

Scores, 3: Communication Skills, Quantitative Skills, Problem-Solving Skills.

Administration: Group or individual.

Price Data, 2002: $53 per examination kit including Form Z test booklet, Ready-Score answer document, and administrator's handbook (1992, 22 pages); $30 per 10 test booklets; $64 per 20 answer documents; $37.50 per administrator's handbook.

Time: 50(55) minutes.

Author: The Psychological Corporation.

Publisher: Pearson.

Cross References: For reviews by JoEllen Carlson and Bikkar S. Randhawa, see 13:3.

[21]

Accounting Program Admission Test.

Purpose: Designed as "an objective measure of student achievement in elementary accounting."

Population: College level elementary accounting students.

Publication Date: 1988.

Acronym: APAT.

Scores, 3: Financial Accounting, Managerial Accounting, Total.

Administration: Group or individual.

Price Data: Available from publisher.

Time: 100(110) minutes.

Comments: Formerly called the AICPA Accounting Program Admission Test; no longer affiliated with the AICPA.

Author: American Institute of Certified Public Accountants.
Publisher: Pearson.
Cross References: For reviews by JoEllen Carlson and William R. Koch, see 12:3.

[22]

ACCUPLACER.

Purpose: Designed to assist with determining if students are prepared for a college-level course or if they would benefit from a developmental course; ACCUPLACER English-as-a-Second Language (ESL) tests are intended for use in placing nonnative speakers of English into ESL courses; the Diagnostic tests provide a detailed assessment of skills in English and mathematics in order to pinpoint academic strengths and weaknesses; can also serve to evaluate college readiness of high school students.
Population: Students in high schools, community colleges, four-year colleges, and technical schools.
Publication Dates: 1985–2010.
Acronym: ACCUPLACER.
Administration: Individual.
Price Data: Available from publisher.
Special Editions: All Companion tests are available in Braille and large print.
Time: Untimed.
Comments: All tests are delivered over the Internet and all but the Computer Skills Placement, WritePlacer, and WritePlacer ESL tests are computer adaptive; ACCUPLACER Companion tests provide a paper-and-pencil format for all the online tests except ESL Listening and the Computer Skills Placement tests; the Companion tests use the same score scale as the computer-adaptive tests.
Author: The College Board.
Publisher: The College Board.
 a) READING COMPREHENSION.
Scores: Total score only.
Comments: Each student is administered 20 items, which are adaptively delivered depending on student responses to prior items. The Reading Comprehension test measures students' ability to understand what they have read. There are four content areas on this test: identifying main ideas, direct statements/secondary ideas, inferences, and applications.
 b) SENTENCE SKILLS.
Scores: Total score only.
Comments: Each student is 20 items, which are adaptively delivered depending on student responses to prior items. The Sentence Skills test measures students' understanding of sentence structure. Three content areas are measure on this test: recognizing complete sentences, coordination/subordination, and clear sentence logic.
 c) ARITHMETIC.
Scores: Total score only.

Comments: Each student is administered 17 items, which are adaptively delivered depending on student responses to prior items. The Arithmetic test measures students' ability to perform basic arithmetic operations and to solve problems that involve fundamental arithmetic concepts. Three content areas are measured on this test: whole numbers and fractions, decimals and percents, and applications.
 d) ELEMENTARY ALGEBRA.
Scores: Total score only.
Comments: Each student is administered 12 items, which are adaptively delivered depending on student responses to prior items. The Elementary Algebra test measures a student's ability to perform basic algebraic operations and to solve problems that involve elementary algebraic concepts. Three content areas are measured with this test: integers and rationals; algebraic expressions; and equations, inequalities, and word problems.
 e) COLLEGE LEVEL MATH.
Scores: Total score only.
Comments: Each student is administered 20 items, which are adaptively delivered depending on student responses to prior items. The College Level Math test measures students' ability to solve problems that involve college-level mathematics concepts. Six content areas are measured on this test: algebraic operations, solutions of equations and inequalities, coordinate geometry, applications and other topics, functions, and trigonometry.
 f) COMPUTER SKILLS PLACEMENT–BASIC.
Scores: Percent correct with detailed category test results.
Comments: There are two forms of Computer Skills Placement–Basic: CSP Basic (XP/2003) reflects Microsoft's Windows XP operating system; and CSP Basic (Vista/2007) reflects Microsoft's Vista/Windows 7 operating system and the Office 2007 suite of applications. CSP Basic tests are linear tests consisting of 30 questions over three different categories: file management, word processing, information and communication.
 g) COMPUTER SKILLS PLACEMENT.
Scores: Percent correct with detailed category test results.
Comments: There are two forms of Computer Skills Placement: CSP (XP/2003 reflects Microsoft's Windows XP operating system; and CSP (Vista/2007) reflects Microsoft's Vista/Windows 7 operating system and the Office 2007 suite of applications. CSP tests are linear tests consisting of 70 questions over seven different categories: basic concepts of information technology; file management; word processing; spreadsheets; databases; presentations; and information and communication.

h) ESL LANGUAGE USE.

Scores: Total score only.

Comments: Each student is administered 20 items, which are adaptively delivered depending on student responses to prior items. The ESL Language Use test measures a student's proficiency in using correct grammar in English sentences. Six content areas are measured on this test: nouns, pronouns, pronoun case structure; sentence structure; subject-verb agreement; adverbs, adjective; verbs; and subordination/coordination.

i) ESL LISTENING.

Scores: Total score only.

Comments: Each student is administered 20 items, which are adaptively delivered depending on student responses to prior items. ESL Listening is a direct measure of the listening skills of non-native English-speaking students. The test measures the ability to listen to and understand one or more people speaking in English. Two content areas are measured on this test: literal comprehension and implied meaning.

j) ESL READING SKILLS.

Scores: Total score only.

Comments: Each student is administered 20 items, which are adaptively delivered depending on student responses to prior items. The ESL Reading Skills test measures a student's ability to read English. The test contains brief passages of 50 words or less and moderate length passages of 50 to 90 words. Two content areas are measured: literal comprehension and inference.

k) ESL SENTENCE MEANING.

Scores: Total score only.

Comments: Each student is administered 20 items, which are adaptively delivered depending on student responses to prior items. The ESL Sentence Meaning test measures how well students understand the meaning of sentences in English. Four content areas are measured: particles, phrasal verbs, and prepositions; adverbs, adjectives, connectives sequence; basic nouns and verbs; and basic and important idioms.

l) WRITERPLACER.

Scores: Holistic score and 6 dimension scores are reported.

Comments: Measures writing skill at the level expected of an entering level college student. Students are asked to type on a computer a writing sample of 300 to 600 words in response to one of 14 prompts available in the ACCUPLACER system. The essay is electronically scored by Intelligent Essay Assessor, a unique automated assessment technology that evaluates the meaning of text, not just grammatical correctness or spelling. In addition to the holistic score, six dimension scores are reported: purpose and focus; organization and structure; development

and support; sentence variety and style; mechanical conventions; and critical thinking.

m) WRITERPLACER COMPANION.

Scores: Holistic score and 6 dimension scores are reported.

Comments: Provides a paper-and-pencil format to WriterPlacer and like WriterPlacer measures writing skill at the level expected of an entering level college student. Students are asked to write an essay of 300 to 600 words in response to a prompt provided in a test booklet. The essay is sent for scoring by trainer readers and returned to the institution within 10 days. In addition to the holistic score, six dimension scores are reported: purpose and focus; organization and structure; development and support; sentence variety and style; mechanical conventions; and critical thinking.

n) WRITERPLACER ESL.

Scores: Holistic score and 4 dimension scores are reported.

Comments: WriterPlacer ESL provides a direct measure of the writing skills of students who are not native speakers of English. Examinees are asked to type an essay of 300 to 600 words in response to one of five prompts available in the system. Essays are electronically scored by Intelligent Essay Assessor. In addition to the holistic score, four dimension scores are reported: word use; sentence use; grammar; organization and development.

o) WRITERPLACER ESL COMPANION.

Scores: Holistic score and 4 dimension scores are reported.

Comments: WriterPlacer ESL COMPANION provides a paper-and-pencil format to WriterPlacer ESL and like WriterPlacer ESL provides a direct measure of the writing skills of students who are not native speakers of English. Students are asked to write an essay of 300 to 600 words in response to a prompt provided in a test booklet. The essay is sent for scoring by trainer readers and returned to the institution within 10 days. In addition to the holistic score, four dimension scores are reported: word use; sentence use; grammar; organization and development.

p) ARITHMETIC DIAGNOSTIC TESTS.

Scores: Both numerical and categorical scores for each of the 5 domains included in the diagnostic test are reported.

Comments: The five domains tested in the Arithmetic Diagnostic test are: computation with integers and fractions; computation with decimal numbers; problems involving percent; estimation, ordering, and number sense; and word problems and applications.

q) DIAGNOSTIC ELEMENTARY ALGEBRA TEST.

Scores: Both numerical and categorical scores for each of the 5 domains included in the diagnostic test are reported.

Comments: The five domains tested in the Diagnostic Elementary Algebra test are: real numbers; linear equations, inequalities, and systems; quadratic expressions and equations; algebraic expressions and equations; word problems and applications.

r) DIAGNOSTIC READING COMPREHENSION TEST.

Scores: Both numerical and categorical scores for each of the 5 domains included in the Reading Comprehension diagnostic test are reported.

Comments: The five domains tested in the Diagnostic Reading Comprehension test are: passage-based reading: main idea; passage-based reading: supporting detail; sentence relationships; passage-based reading: inference; passage-based reading: author's purpose/rhetorical strategies.

s) DIAGNOSTIC SENTENCE SKILLS TEST.

Scores: Both numerical and categorical scores for each of the 5 domains included in the Sentence Skills diagnostic test are reported.

Comments: The five domains tested in the Diagnostic Sentence Skills test are: agreement; modifiers; diction/logic; sentence structure; sentence boundaries.

Cross References: For reviews by Martin A. Fischer and Steven V. Owen, see 13:4.

[23]

ACDI-Corrections Version and Corrections Version II.

Purpose: "Designed for troubled youth screening and assessment."

Population: Troubled youth between the ages of 12 and 18 years in juvenile probation, parole, and corrections programs.

Publication Dates: 1988–1995.

Acronym: ACDI.

Administration: Group.

Price Data: Available from publisher.

Time: (15–25) minutes.

Comments: Both computer version and paper-pencil format are scored on IBM-PC compatibles.

Author: Risk & Needs Assessment, Inc.

Publisher: Behavior Data Systems, Ltd.

a) VERSION I.

Scores, 5: Truthfulness, Alcohol, Drug, Adjustment, Distress.

b) VERSION II.

Scores, 6: Truthfulness, Alcohol, Drug, Adjustment, Distress, Violence.

Cross References: For reviews by Carol Collins and Mark Pope, see 14:2.

[24]

ACER Advanced Test B40.

Purpose: Intended to assess general intellectual ability at the advanced adult level.

Population: Ages 15 and over.

Publication Dates: 1945–1983.

Acronym: B40.

Scores: Total score only.

Administration: Group.

Price Data, 2005: A$11.55 per 10 test booklets; $4.95 per scoring key; $19 per manual (1983, 7 pages); $24.20 per specimen set.

Time: 55(65) minutes.

Author: Australian Council for Educational Research Ltd.

Publisher: Australian Council for Educational Research Ltd. [Australia].

Cross References: For a review by Harriet C. Cobb, see 9:4; see also T2:323 (6 references) and 7:328 (4 references); for a review by C. Sanders, see 5:296 (3 references).

[25]

ACER Advanced Test B90: New Zealand Edition.

Purpose: "Designed to measure general intellectual ability."

Population: College students and adults.

Publication Date: 1991.

Scores: Total score only.

Administration: Group.

Price Data: Available from publisher for test materials including administrator's manual (5 pages).

Time: 50(55) minutes.

Comments: "Selected items from the ACER Advanced Test B40 and the ACER Test of Cognitive Ability."

Authors: Australian Council for Educational Research and manual by Neil Reid and Cedric Croft.

Publisher: New Zealand Council for Educational Research [New Zealand].

Cross References: For a review by John Rust, see 12:4; for a review of ACER Advanced Test B40 by Harriet C. Cobb, see 9:4; see also T2:323 (6 references) and 7:328 (4 references); for a review of ACER Advanced Test B40 by C. Sanders, see 5:296 (3 references).

[26]

ACER Advanced Tests AL and AQ (Second Edition) and BL-BQ.

Purpose: "To measure general intellectual ability at advanced secondary and college levels."

Population: College and senior high.

Publication Dates: 1953–1982.

Acronyms: AL-AQ (2nd Edition), BL-BQ.

Administration: Group.

Price Data, 2005: A$14.55 per 10 test booklets; A$4.95 per scoring key.

Author: Australian Council for Educational Research Ltd.

Publisher: Australian Council for Educational Research Ltd. [Australia].
   a) TEST AL-BL.
   Scores: Linguistic.
   Forms, 2: A, B.
   Time: 15(25) minutes.
   b) TEST AQ-BQ.
   Scores: Quantitative.
   Forms, 2: A, B.
   Time: 20(30) minutes.
Cross References: See T5:23 (1 reference); for reviews by Harriet C. Cobb and Leland K. Doebler, see 9:5; see also T3:21 (1 reference) and T2:324 (3 references); for a review by Duncan Howie, see 5:295.

[27]
ACER Applied Reading Test.

Purpose: Designed to measure ability to read and understand technical material.
Population: Apprentices, trainees, technical and trade personnel.
Publication Dates: 1989–1990.
Scores: Total score only.
Administration: Group.
Forms, 2: A, B.
Price Data, 2005: A$9.95 per test booklet; A$9.95 per 10 answer sheets; A$9.95 per score key; A$34.95 per manual (1990, 24 pages); A$54.95 per specimen set A–Personnel only or B–Personnel or Technical and Further Education Colleges.
Time: 40–45 minutes.
Authors: J. M. van den Berg and I. R. Woff.
Publisher: Australian Council for Educational Research Ltd. [Australia].
Cross References: For reviews by Mark H. Daniel and Michael S. Trevisan, see 12:5.

[28]
ACER Mechanical Reasoning Test [Revised 1997].

Purpose: "Designed to assess a person's aptitude for solving problems requiring the understanding of mechanical ideas."
Population: Ages 15 and over.
Publication Dates: 1951–1997.
Scores: Total score only.
Administration: Group.
Forms, 2: Parallel Forms A and B.
Price Data, 2005: A$10.95 per test booklet; A$9.95 per scoring key; A$19.95 per 10 answer sheets; A$55.95 per manual (1997, 58 pages); A$89.95 per specimen set.
Time: 20(25) minutes.
Comments: Revision of ACER Mechanical Comprehension Test (T7:27).

Author: Australian Council for Educational Research Ltd.
Publisher: Australian Council for Educational Research Ltd. [Australia].
Cross References: For a review by Gerald R. Schneck, see 15:2; see T2:2238 (3 references); for reviews by John R. Jennings and Hayden S. Williams of an earlier edition, see 5:875.

[29]
ACER Short Clerical Test.

Purpose: Designed to measure aptitudes for speed and accuracy in routine clerical work.
Population: Age 15 and over.
Publication Dates: 1953–2001.
Scores, 2: Checking, Arithmetic.
Administration: Group.
Price Data, 2005: A$15 per 10 test booklets; A$5.95 per score key; A$29.95 per manual; A$36 per specimen set.
Time: 5(10) minutes per test.
Author: Australian Council for Educational Research.
Publisher: Australian Council for Educational Research Ltd. [Australia].

[30]
ACER Test of Employment Entry Mathematics.

Purpose: "A group test of basic mathematical ability … used for the selection of apprentices, trainees, and any other technical and trades personnel."
Population: Apprentice, trainee, technical and trade applicants.
Publication Date: 1992.
Acronym: TEEM.
Scores: Total score only.
Administration: Group.
Price Data, 2006: A$9.95 per test booklet; A$9.95 per score key; A$9.95 per 10 answer sheets; A$69.95 per specimen set.
Time: 25 (40) minutes.
Comments: Can be hand scored or scored by testing service.
Authors: John Izard, Ian Woff, and Brian Doig.
Publisher: Australian Council for Educational Research Ltd. [Australia].
Cross References: For reviews by Jay R. Stewart and Patricia H. Wheeler, see 15:3.

[31]
ACER Word Knowledge Test.

Purpose: Designed to obtain a quick assessment of verbal or language ability.
Population: Australian years 9–12 and job applicants.

Publication Dates: 1984–1990.
Scores: Total score only.
Administration: Group.
Editions, 2: E, F.
Restricted Distribution: Distribution of Form E restricted to personnel use.
Price Data, 2005: A$9.95 per reusable test booklet; A$9.95 per 10 answer sheets; A$9.95 per score key; A$30 per manual (1990, 44 pages); A$49.95 per specimen set (specify Form E or F).
Time: 10(20) minutes.
Comments: Replacement for the ACER Adult Form B.
Author: Marion M. de Lemos.
Publisher: Australian Council for Educational Research Ltd. [Australia].
Cross References: See T5:34 (6 references); for reviews by Douglas Ayers and William R. Merz, Sr., see 11:2.

[32]

Achenbach System of Empirically Based Assessment.

Purpose: "An integrated ... [approach] designed to provide standardized descriptions of ... competencies, adaptive functioning, and problems."
Population: Ages 18 months to 90+ years.
Publication Dates: 1980–2004.
Acronym: ASEBA.
Administration: Individual or group.
Levels, 4: Preschool, School-Age, Adult, Older Adult.
Price Data, 2005: $150 per Preschool hand-scoring starter kit including 50 each of CBCL/1 1/2-5 & LDS forms, C-TRF forms, CBCL/1 1/2-5 hand-scoring profiles, C-TRF hand-scoring profiles, LDS hand-scoring forms, CBCL/1 1/2-5 and C-TRF templates, and Manual for the Preschool Forms & Profiles (2000, 189 pages); $230 per Preschool computer-scoring starter kit including 50 CBCL/1 1/2-5 & LDS forms, 50 C-TRF forms, Ages 1 1/2-5 entry scoring module, Manual for the Preschool Forms & Profiles; $325 per School-Age computer-scoring starter kit including 50 CBCL forms, 50 TRF forms, 50 YSR forms, Ages 6–18 entry scoring module, and Manual for the School-Age Forms & Profiles (2001, 238 pages); $35 per Manual for the Preschool Forms and Profiles, Manual for the School-Age Forms and profiles, or Manual for the SCICA (2001, 164 pages); $35 per Manual for the ASEBA Adult Forms and Profiles (2003, 216 pages); $35 per Manual for the ASEBA Older Adult Forms and Profiles (2004, 190 pages); $10 per Mental Health Practitioners' Guide for the ASEBA (2004, 42 pages), School-Based Practitioners' Guide for the ASEBA (2004, 48 pages), Child and Family Service Workers' Guide for the ASEBA (2003, 37 pages), Medical Practitioners' Guide for the ASEBA (2003, 33 pages), Guide for ASEBA Instruments for Adults/18-59 and Older Adults/60-90+ (2004, 39 pages); $695 per full set

of ADM Software Modules including Ages 1 1/2-5, 6–18, 18–59, 60-90+, SCICA, and Test Observation Form (TOF); $170 per ADM Software Modules for Ages 1 1/2-5, 18–59, 60-90+, SCICA, or TOF; $250 per ADM Software Module for Ages 6–18; $220 per Scanning Module or Client Entry Module for CBCL/6–18, TRF/6–18, and YSR/11–18; $220 per ASEBA Web-Link (following purchase of any ADM Module) including E-package of 100 E-units; $25 per 50 CBCL/1 1/2-5 & LDS, C-TRF, CBCL/6–18, TRF/6–18, YSR, DOF, SCICA, ASR, ABCL, OASR, OABCL, or TOF forms; $25 per 50 Profiles for hand scoring profiles for any of CBCL/1 1/2-5, C-TRF, CBCL/6–18 (specify gender), TRF (specify gender), YSR, DOF, SCICA, ASR, ABCL, OASR, OABCL, or TOF; $25 per 50 forms for hand-scoring LDS; $25 per 50 Combined SCICA Observation and Self-Report scoring forms; $25 per 50 CBCL, TRF, YSR, SCICA, ASR, ABCL, OASR, or OABCL DSM-Oriented Profiles; $7 per reusable templates for hand scoring CBCL/1 1/2-5, C-TRF, CBCL/6–18, TRF, YSR, ASR, ABCL, OASR, or OABCL Profiles.
Foreign Language Editions: One or more forms have been translated into 74 languages, check website (www.ASEBA.org) for availability.
Comments: Revised version of the Child Behavior Checklist; includes both empirically based syndrome scales and DSM-oriented scales for scoring consistent with DSM-IV categories; designed to be usable in diverse contexts, including schools, mental health, medical, child and family service, and other settings; all forms except DOF and SCICA are parallel, facilitating comparisons across informants; hand- or computer-scorable; reusable hand-scoring templates available; data processed by Assessment Data Manager (ADM); cross-informant bar graphs; minimum system requirements Windows 95/98/NT/2000, 64 MB RAM, 65 MB free hard disk space, Pentium recommended; can be completed using paper forms (hand- or machine-readable), by direct client-entry on computer, or via Web-Link; LDS, Preschool and School-Age manuals.
Authors: Thomas M. Achenbach (all forms and manuals), Leslie A. Rescorla (all forms and Mental Health Practitioners' Guide for the ASEBA), Stephanie H. McConaughy (SCICA, SCICA manual, and School-Based Practitioners' Guide for the ASEBA), Peter J. Pecora and Kathleen M. Wetherbee (Child and Family Service Workers' Guide for the ASEBA), Thomas M. Ruffle (Medical Practitioners' Guide for the ASEBA), Paul A. Newhouse (older adult forms, manual, and Guide for Adult and Older Adult Forms).
Publisher: ASEBA Research Center for Children, Youth, and Families
   a) PRESCHOOL FORMS AND PROFILES.
   Purpose: To provide "systematic assessment of maladaptive behavior among preschoolers."

Comments: DSM-Oriented Scales rated as very consistent with the following DSM-IV categories: Affective Problems consistent with Dysthymia, Major Depressive Disorder; Anxiety Problems consistent with Generalized Anxiety Disorder, Separation Anxiety Disorder, Specific Phobia; Pervasive Developmental Problems consistent with Asperger's Disorder and Autistic Disorder; Attention Deficit/Hyperactivity Problems consistent with Hyperactive-Impulsive and Inattentive types of ADHD.

1) *Child Behavior Checklist for Ages 1 1/2-5.*
Population: Ages 18 months to 5 years.
Publication Dates: 1988–2000.
Acronym: CBCL/1 1/2-5.
Scores: 7 Syndrome scales (Emotionally Reactive, Anxious/Depressed, Somatic Complaints, Withdrawn, Sleep Problems, Attention Problems, Aggressive Behavior), plus Internalizing, Externalizing, Total Problems; Language Development Survey (LDS) scored (for children age 18–35 months); 5 DSM-Oriented scales (Affective Problems, Anxiety Problems, Pervasive Developmental Problems, Attention Deficit/Hyperactivity Problems, Oppositional Defiant Problems).
Time: (10) minutes.
Comments: Designed to be completed by parents and others who see children in home-like settings; includes the Language Development Survey (LDS) for evaluating language delays in children under age 3 as well as those over age 3 suspected of having language delays.

2) *Caregiver-Teacher Report Form for Ages 1 1/2-5.*
Population: Ages 18 months to 5 years.
Publication Dates: 1997–2000.
Acronym: C-TRF.
Scores: 6 Syndrome scales (Emotionally Reactive, Anxious/Depressed, Somatic Complaints, Withdrawn, Attention Problems, Aggressive Behavior), plus Internalizing, Externalizing, Total Problems.
Time: (10) minutes.
Comments: Designed to be completed by daycare providers and preschool teachers who have known a child in daycare, preschool, or similar settings for at least 2 months.

b) SCHOOL-AGE FORMS AND PROFILES.
Comments: DSM-Oriented Scales rated as very consistent with the following DSM-IV categories: Affective Problems consistent with Dysthymia, Major Depressive Disorder; Anxiety Problems consistent with Generalized Anxiety Disorder, Separation Anxiety Disorder, Specific Phobia; Attention Deficit/Hyperactivity Problems consistent with Hyperactive-Impulsive and Inattentive types of ADHD; Somatic Problems consistent with Somatization Disorder and Somatoform Disorder.

1) *Child Behavior Checklist for Ages 6–18.*
Population: Ages 6–18.
Publication Dates: 1981–2001.
Acronym: CBCL/6–18.
Scores: 4 Competence scales (Activities, Social, School, Total Competence); 8 Syndrome scales (Anxious/Depressed, Withdrawn/Depressed, Somatic Complaints, Social Problems, Thought Problems, Attention Problems, Rule-Breaking Behavior, Aggressive Behavior), plus Internalizing, Externalizing, Total Problems; 6 DSM-Oriented scales (Affective Problems, Anxiety Problems, Somatic Problems, Attention Deficit/Hyperactivity Problems, Oppositional Defiant Problems, Conduct Problems).
Time: (15–20) minutes.

2) *Teacher's Report Form for Ages 6–18.*
Purpose: "Quickly obtain[s] a picture of children's functioning in school, as seen by teachers and other personnel."
Population: Teachers of children ages 6–18.
Publication Dates: 1981–2001.
Acronym: TRF.
Scores: 6 Adaptive Functioning scales (Academic Performance, Working Hard, Behaving Appropriately, Learning, Happy, Total); same Syndrome and DSM-Oriented scales as CBCL/6–18; yields separate scores for Inattention and Hyperactivity-Impulsivity.
Time: (15–20) minutes.

3) *Youth Self-Report for Ages 11–18.*
Purpose: To obtain youths' reports of their own problems and competencies in a standardized format.
Population: Ages 11–18.
Publication Dates: 1981–2001.
Acronym: YSR.
Scores: 2 Competence scales (Activities, Social) plus Total Competence; same Syndrome and DSM-Oriented scales as CBCL/6–18.

4) *Direct Observation Form for Ages 5–14.*
Purpose: "Used to record and rate behavior in group settings."
Publication Dates: 1983–1986.
Acronym: DOF.
Comments: Used to obtain 10-minute samples of children's behavior in classrooms and other group settings; enables users to compare an observed child with 2 control children for on-task, Internalizing, Externalizing, and Total Problems, averaged for up to 6 observation sessions; 6 syndrome scales available (computer-scored profiles only).

5) *Semistructured Clinical Interview for Children and Adolescents.*
Purpose: "Used to record and rate children's behavior and self-reports during an interview."
Population: Ages 6–18.
Publication Dates: 1989–2001.
Acronym: SCICA.
Scores: 8 Syndrome scales (Anxious, Anxious/Depressed, Withdrawn/Depressed, Language/Motor Problems, Aggressive/Rule-Breaking Behavior, Attention Problems, Self-Control Problems, Somatic Complaints (ages 12–18 only), plus Internalizing, Externalizing, Total Problems; same DSM-Oriented scales as CBCL/6–18.
Time: (60–90) minutes.
Comments: Designed for use by experienced clinical interviewers; protocol form includes topic questions and activities, such as kinetic family drawing and tasks for screening fine and gross motor functioning; observation and self-report form for rating what a child does and says during interview.
c) ADULT FORMS AND PROFILES.
Publication Dates: 1997–2003.
1) *Adult Self-Report for Ages 18–59.*
Population: Ages 18–59.
Acronym: ASR.
Scores: 5 Adaptive Functioning scales (Education, Friends, Job, Family, Spouse or Partner), 3 Substance Use scales (Tobacco, Alcohol, Drugs) plus Mean Substance Use score, 6 DSM-oriented scales (Depressive Problems, Anxiety Problems, Somatic Problems, Avoidant Personality Problems, Attention Deficit/Hyperactivity Problems, Antisocial Personality Problems), same Syndrome scales as CBCL/6–18, plus Intrusive, Internalizing, Externalizing, Total Problems.
Time: (15–20) minutes.
Comments: Upward extension of YASR.
2) *Adult Behavior Checklist for Ages 18–59.*
Population: Ages 18–59.
Acronym: ABCL.
Scores: 2 Adaptive Functioning scales (Friends, Spouse/Partner), other scales same as ASR.
Time: (10–15) minutes.
Comments: Upward extension of YABCL. Ratings by parents, surrogates, friends, and spouses of adults.
d) OLDER ADULT FORMS AND PROFILES.
Publication Date: 2004.
1) *Older Adult Self-Report for Ages 60-90+.*
Population: Ages 60-90+.
Acronym: OASR.
Scores: 3 Adaptive Functioning scales (Friends, Spouse/Partner, Personal Strengths), 7 Syndrome scales (Anxious/Depressed, Worries, Somatic Complaints, Functional Impairment, Memory/Cognition Problems, Thought Problems, Irritable/Disinhibited), 6 DSM-oriented scales (Depressive Problems, Anxiety Problems, Somatic Problems, Dementia Problems, Psychotic Problems, Antisocial Personality Problems), plus Total Problems.
Time: (15-20) minutes.
2) *Older Adult Behavior Checklist for Ages 60-90+.*
Population: Ages 60-90+.
Acronym: OABCL.
Scores: Same scales as OASR.
Time: (15-20) minutes.
Comment: Ratings by people who know the older adult well.
Cross References: For reviews by Rosemary Flanagan and T. Steuart Watson, see 16:3; see also T5:451 (292 references); for reviews by Beth Doll and by Michael J. Furlong and Michelle Wood of an earlier edition, see 13:55 (556 references); see also T4:433 (135 references); for reviews by Sandra L. Christenson and by Stephen N. Elliott and R. T. Busse of the Teacher's Report Form and the Youth Self-Report, see 11:64 (216 references); for additional information and reviews by B. J. Freeman and Mary Lou Kelley, see 9:213 (5 references).

[33]

Achievement Identification Measure.
Purpose: Developed to provide a measure of the characteristics that distinguish achieving students from underachievers.
Population: School age children.
Publication Date: 1985.
Acronym: AIM.
Scores, 6: Competition, Responsibility, Control, Achievement, Communication, Respect.
Administration: Individual.
Price Data, 2005: $120 per 30 tests, manual for administration (8 pages), manual for interpretation of scores (7 pages), and computer scoring of 30 tests; $15 per specimen set.
Foreign Language Edition: Spanish edition available.
Time: (20) minutes.
Comments: Parent report inventory.
Author: Sylvia B. Rimm.
Publisher: Educational Assessment Service, Inc.
Cross References: See T5:35 (1 reference); for reviews by Howard M. Knoff and Sharon B. Reynolds, see 10:5.

[34]

Achievement Identification Measure–Teacher Observation.
Purpose: Identify underachievers.
Population: School-age children.

Publication Date: 1988.
Acronym: AIM-TO.
Scores: 5 dimension scores: Competition, Responsibility, Achievement Communication, Independence/Dependence, Respect/Dominance.
Administration: Individual.
Price Data, 2005: $120 per set of 30 test booklets/answer sheets (scoring by publisher included); $15 per specimen set.
Foreign Language Edition: Spanish edition available.
Time: (20) minutes.
Comments: Ratings by teacher.
Author: Sylvia B. Rimm.
Publisher: Educational Assessment Service, Inc.
Cross References: For reviews by William P. Erchul and Geoffrey F. Schultz, see 11:3.

[35]

Achievement Motivation Inventory.

Purpose: Designed to evaluate "all major aspects of job-related achievement motivation."
Population: Adults.
Publication Date: 2004.
Acronym: AMI.
Scores, 17: Compensatory Effort, Competitiveness, Confidence in Success, Dominance, Eagerness to Learn, Engagement, Fearlessness, Flexibility, Flow, Goal Setting, Independence, Internality, Persistence, Preference for Difficult Tasks, Pride in Productivity, Self-Control, Status Orientation.
Administration: Individual or group.
Price Data, 2011: $235 per complete kit including manual (60 pages), question booklet, 20 response sheets, 20 score profiles, and case; $23 per question booklet; $85 per 20 response sheets; $15 per 20 score profiles; $123 per manual.
Time: Administration time not reported.
Authors: Heinz Schuler, George C. Thornton III, Andreas Frintrup, and Rose Mueller-Hanson.
Publisher: Hogrefe Publishing
Cross References: For reviews by Jeffrey A. Jenkins and Eleanor E. Sanford-Moore, see 17:4.

[36]

Achievement Motivation Profile.

Purpose: "Designed to be a measure of a student's motivation to achieve" and related personality characteristics.
Population: Ages 10 to 14 for AMP Juniors; 14 years and older in high school, junior college, and college.
Publication Dates: 1995–1996.
Acronym: AMP.
Scores, 18: Response style (Inconsistent Responding, Self-Enhancing, Self-Critical), Motivation for

Achievement (Achiever, Motivation, Competitiveness, Goal Orientation), Inner Resources (Relaxed Style, Happiness, Patience, Self-Confidence), Interpersonal Strengths (Assertiveness, Personal Diplomacy, Extroversion, Cooperativeness), Work Habits (Planning and Organization, Initiative, Team Player).
Administration: Group.
Price Data, 2006: $150 per complete kit including 25 AutoScore™ forms for High School; 25 College Student AutoScore forms, and manual (1996, 93 pages); $47 per 25 AutoScore™ forms; $58 per manual; $45 each for 1–9 AMP mail-in answer sheets; $231 per 25-use microcomputer disk (PC with Microsoft Windows); $16.50 per 100 microcomputer answer sheets; $9 per fax service scoring.
Time: (20–30) minutes.
Authors: Jotham G. Friedland, Harvey P. Mandel, and Sander I. Marcus.
Publisher: Western Psychological Services.

[37]

Achieving Behavioral Competencies.

Purpose: To develop a program of instruction in social/emotional skills.
Population: "Students who are seriously emotionally disturbed, closed head injured, juvenile offenders, learning disabled, or at-risk for school drop-out" and "adults served by voc rehab programs."
Publication Date: 1992.
Acronym: ABC.
Scores, 24: Relating to Others (Building Friendships, Maintaining Friendships, Apologizing, Compromising/Negotiating, Giving/Accepting Praise or Criticism, Total), Personal Responsibility (Goal Setting, Decision Making, Assuming Responsibility, Promptness, Asking for Assistance, Total), Coping with Stress (Handling Frustration, Coping with Anger, Dealing with Stress, Accepting Authority, Resisting Peer Pressure, Total), Personal/Affective Development (Building Self-Esteem, Coping with Depression, Coping with Anxiety, Controlling Impulsivity, Sensitivity to Others, Total).
Administration: Group.
Editions, 2: Individual Student Report, Class Report.
Price Data, 2011: $195 per set including curriculum, 25 rating forms, and computer program (Windows or Macintosh).
Time: Administration time not reported.
Comments: Computer reports generated from teacher ratings.
Authors: Lawrence T. McCarron, Kathleen McConnell Fad, and Melody B. McCarron.
Publisher: McCarron-Dial Systems, Inc.
Cross References: For reviews by Sally Kuhlenschmidt and Robert A. Leark, see 13:6.

[38]

Ackerman-Banks Neuropsychological Rehabilitation Battery.

Purpose: Designed as a comprehensive neuropsychological screening instrument.
Population: Adult clients referred for psychological or neuropsychological assessment and/or cognitive rehabilitation.
Publication Dates: 1991–2006.
Acronym: ABNRB.
Scores, 40: Alertness (Attention/Concentration), Prosody (Receptive Prosody, Expressive Prosody), Memory (Long-Term Memory, Short-Term Interference Memory, Short-Term Input Memory, Short-Term Retrieval Memory), Sensorimotor (Auditory Input, Auditory Discrimination, Tactile Input, Tactile Output, Visual Input, Visual Discrimination, Visual-Spatial Construction, Proprioception, Motor Quality, Motor Writing), Speech (Speech Production, Dysarthria, Dysnomia, Neologisms, Confabulation, Perseveration, Lisping), Academic Abilities (Mathematics, Reading, Writing), Cognitive Problem Solving (Concreteness, Integration, Judgment, Speed), Organic Emotions (Depression, Anxiety, Impulsivity), Asymmetry (Left-Right Confusion, Left-Brain Controlled Balance, Right-Brain Controlled Balance), Treatment Problems (Peripheral Control, Awareness of Deficits, Socially Appropriate Comments, Frustration Tolerance).
Administration: Individual.
Price Data, 2006: $800 per complete kit including professional manual (2006, 192 pages), stimulus card book, 10 administration protocols, 10 response booklets, 10 scoring forms, and processing fee for web-based, mail-in, or faxed computer score submission; $500 per administration package including 10 administration protocols, 10 response booklets, 10 scoring forms, and processing fee for web-based, mail-in, or faxed computer score submission; $300 per professional manual; student, volume, and research discounts available.
Time: (45–120) minutes.
Authors: Rosalie J. Ackerman and Martha E. Banks.
Publisher: ABackans DCP, Inc.
Cross References: For reviews by Surendra P. Singh and by Wilfred G. Van Gorp and Colleen A. Ewing, see 15:5.

[39]

Ackerman-Schoendorf Scales for Parent Evaluation of Custody.

Purpose: "A clinical tool designed to aid mental health professionals in making child custody recommendations."
Population: Parents engaged in a dispute over custody of their children.
Publication Date: 1992.
Acronym: ASPECT.

Scores, 3: Scales (Observational, Social, Cognitive-Emotional) yielding 1 score: Parental Custody Index (PCI).
Administration: Individual.
Price Data, 2006: $152 per kit including 20 parent questionnaires, 10 AutoScore™ answer forms, manual (77 pages), and 2 prepaid mail-in WPS test report answer sheets for computer scoring and interpretation; $40 per 20 answer forms; $32.50 per 20 parent questionnaires; $58 per manual; $19 or less per mail-in answer sheet; $13.75 each for test report fax service.
Time: Administration time varies.
Comments: For complete set of information to score, need results of each parent's MMPI or MMPI-2, Rorschach, WAIS-R, and WRAT-R or NEAT tests.
Authors: Marc J. Ackerman and Kathleen Schoendorf.
Publisher: Western Psychological Services.
Cross References: See T5:41 (1 reference); for reviews by Joyce A. Arditti and Gary R. Melton, see 12:9.

[40]

ACS Examination in Analytical Chemistry.

Purpose: Designed to measure a student's achievement in analytical chemistry.
Population: 1 year college.
Publication Dates: 1944–2001.
Scores: Total score only.
Administration: Group.
Manual: No specific manual; general directions (no date, 4 pages).
Price Data: Available from publisher.
Time: 90(100) minutes.
Comments: ACS test program is continually updated by retiring an older form of the test upon release of a new form; separate answer sheet must be used; exam carries secure copyright.
Author: ACS DivCHED Examinations Institute.
Publisher: ACS DivCHED Examinations Institute.
Cross References: See 7:836 (1 reference) and 6:907 (1 reference); for an excerpted review by H. E. Wilcox of an earlier form, see 5:735; for reviews by William B. Meldrum and William Rieman III, see 3:563.

[41]

ACS Examination in Biochemistry.

Purpose: Designed to measure a student's achievement in biochemistry.
Population: 1 year college.
Publication Dates: 1947–2003.
Scores: Total score only.
Administration: Group.
Manual: No specific manual; general directions (no date, 4 pages).
Price Data: Available from publisher.
Time: 120(130) minutes.

Comments: ACS test program is continually updated by retiring an older form of the test upon release of a new form; separate answer sheet must be used; exam carries secure copyright.
Author: ACS DivCHED Examinations Institute.
Publisher: ACS DivCHED Examinations Institute.
Cross References: See 7:823 (1 reference); for an excerpted review by Wilhelm R. Frisell of an earlier form, see 6:898 (2 references).

[42]

ACS Examination in General Chemistry.

Purpose: Designed to measure a student's achievement in general chemistry.
Population: 1 year college.
Publication Dates: 1934–2005.
Scores: Total score only.
Administration: Group.
Manual: No specific manual; general directions (no date, 4 pages).
Price Data: Available from publisher.
Time: 110(120) minutes.
Comments: ACS test program is continually updated by retiring an older form of the test upon release of a new form; separate answer sheet must be used; exam carries secure copyright.
Author: ACS DivCHED Examinations Institute.
Publisher: ACS DivCHED Examinations Institute.
Cross References: For a review by Frank J. Fornoff of an earlier edition, see 8:837 (3 references); see also T2:1819 (1 reference) and 7:826 (5 references); for reviews by J. A. Campbell and William Hered and an excerpted review by S. L. Burson, Jr., see 6:902 (3 references); for reviews by Frank P. Cassaretto and Palmer O. Johnson, see 5:732 (2 references); for a review by Kenneth E. Anderson, see 4:610 (1 reference); for reviews by Sidney J. French and Florence E. Hooper, see 3:557 (3 references); see also 2:1593 (5 references).

[43]

ACS Examination in General Chemistry (Brief Test).

Purpose: Designed to measure a student's achievement in general chemistry.
Population: 1 year college.
Publication Dates: 1981–2002.
Scores: Total score only.
Administration: Group.
Manual: No specific manual; general directions (no date, 4 pages).
Price Data: Available from publisher.
Time: 55(60) minutes.
Comments: ACS test program is continually updated by retiring an older form of the test upon release of a

new form; separate answer sheet must be used; exam carries secure copyright.
Author: ACS DivCHED Examinations Institute.
Publisher: ACS DivCHED Examinations Institute.

[44]

ACS Examination in General-Organic-Biological Chemistry.

Purpose: Designed to measure a student's achievement in general, organic, and biological chemistry.
Population: Nursing and other paramedical and home economics students.
Publication Dates: 1979–2000.
Scores, 10: General (Part A, Part B, Total), Organic (Part A, Part B, Total), Biological (Part A, Part B, Total), Part A Total.
Administration: Group.
Manual: No specific manual; general directions (no date, 4 pages).
Price Data: Available from publisher.
Time: 165(180) minutes.
Comments: ACS test program is continually updated by retiring an older form of the test upon release of a new form; separate answer sheet must be used; exam carries secure copyright.
Author: ACS DivCHED Examinations Institute.
Publisher: ACS DivCHED Examinations Institute.

[45]

ACS Examination in High School Chemistry [Advanced Level].

Purpose: To measure achievement in high school chemistry.
Population: Advanced high school chemistry students.
Publication Dates: 1963–2004.
Scores: Total score only.
Administration: Group.
Price Data: Available from publisher.
Time: 110(120) minutes.
Comments: ACS test program is continually updated by retiring an older form of the test upon release of a new form; exam carries secure copyright.
Author: ACS DivCHED Examinations Institute.
Publisher: ACS DivCHED Examinations Institute.
Cross References: See T5:48 (1 reference) and T4:57 (1 reference); for reviews by Peter A. Dahl and John P. Penna of an earlier form, see 8:844 (1 reference); for a review by Irvin J. Lehmann, see 7:838 (3 references); for reviews by Frank J. Fornoff and William Hered, see 6:909.

[46]

ACS Examination in High School Chemistry [Lower Level].

Purpose: To measure achievement in high school chemistry.

Population: High school first year chemistry students.
Publication Dates: 1957–2005.
Scores, 3: Part I, Part II, Total.
Administration: Group.
Price Data: Available from publisher.
Time: 80(90) minutes.
Comments: ACS test program is continually updated by retiring an older form of the test upon release of a new form; exam carries secure copyright.
Author: ACS DivCHED Examinations Institute.
Publisher: ACS DivCHED Examinations Institute.
Cross References: See T5:49 (1 reference), T4:59 (1 reference) and 9:41 (1 reference); for a review by Edward F. DeVillafranca of an earlier form, see 8:845 (11 references); see also T2:1830 (3 references); for reviews by William R. Crawford and Irvin J. Lehmann, see 7:837 (9 references); for reviews by Frank J. Fornoff and William Hered and excerpted reviews by Christine Jansing and Joseph Schmuckler, see 6:908 (5 references); for reviews by Edward G. Rietz and Willard G. Warrington, see 5:729.

[47]

ACS Examination in Inorganic Chemistry.
Purpose: Designed to measure a student's achievement in inorganic chemistry.
Population: 1 year college.
Publication Dates: 1961–2002.
Scores: Total score only.
Administration: Group.
Manual: No specific manual; general directions (no date, 4 pages).
Price Data: Available from publisher.
Time: 120(130) minutes.
Comments: ACS test program is continually updated by retiring an older form of the test upon release of a new form; separate answer sheet must be used; exam carries secure copyright.
Author: ACS DivCHED Examinations Institute.
Publisher: ACS DivCHED Examinations Institute.
Cross References: See T3:64 (1 reference), 8:838 (2 references), T2:1820 (1 reference), and 7:827 (2 references); for a review by Frank J. Fornoff and an excerpted review by George B. Kauffman of an earlier form, see 6:903 (1 reference).

[48]

ACS Examination in Instrumental Methods.
Purpose: Designed to measure a student's achievement in instrumental determinations.
Population: 1 year college.
Publication Dates: 1966–2001.
Scores: Total score only.
Administration: Group.
Manual: No specific manual; general directions (no date, 4 pages).

Price Data: Available from publisher.
Time: 110(120) minutes.
Comments: ACS test program is continually updated by retiring an older form of the test upon release of a new form; separate answer sheet must be used; exam carries secure copyright.
Author: ACS DivCHED Examinations Institute.
Publisher: ACS DivCHED Examinations Institute.
Cross References: See 7:830 (1 reference).

[49]

ACS Examination in Organic Chemistry.
Purpose: Designed to measure a student's achievement in organic chemistry.
Population: 1 year college.
Publication Dates: 1942–1986.
Scores: Total score only.
Administration: Group.
Manual: No specific manual; general directions (no date, 4 pages)
Price Data: Available from publisher.
Time: 115(125) minutes.
Comments: ACS test program is continually updated by retiring an older form of the test upon release of a new form; separate answer sheet must be used; Exam carries secure copyright.
Author: ACS DivCHED Examinations Institute.
Publisher: ACS DivCHED Examinations Institute.
Cross References: See 8:840 (3 references), 7:831 (3 references), and 6:905 (4 references); for a review by Shailer Peterson of an earlier form, see 3:558.

[50]

ACS Examination in Physical Chemistry.
Purpose: Designed to measure a student's mastery of physical chemistry.
Population: 1 year college.
Publication Dates: 1946–2001.
Administration: Group.
Manual: No specific manual.
Price Data: Available from publisher.
Comments: ACS test program is continually updated by retiring an older form of the test upon release of a new form; subtests may be administered separately or together; separate answer sheet must be used; includes a comprehensive exam and three subject matter exams.
Author: ACS DivCHED Examinations Institute.
Publisher: ACS DivCHED Examinations Institute.
  a) THERMODYNAMICS.
  Scores, 3: Part A, Part B, Total.
  Time: 90(100) minutes.
  b) CHEMICAL DYNAMICS.
  Scores, 3: Part A, Part B, Total.
  Time: 90(100) minutes.

c) QUANTUM CHEMISTRY.
Scores, 3: Part A, Part B, Total.
Time: 100(110) minutes.
Cross References: For a review by Gerald R. Van Hecke of an earlier form, see 8:842 (2 references); see also T2:1826 (2 references), 7:833 (2 references), and 6:904 (1 reference); for a review by Alfred S. Brown, see 3:559.

[51]

ACS Examination in Physical Chemistry for Life Sciences.

Purpose: Designed to measure a student's achievement in physical chemistry for life sciences.
Population: 1 year college.
Publication Date: 1982.
Scores: Total score only.
Administration: Group.
Manual: No specific manual; general directions (no date, 4 pages).
Price Data: Available from publisher.
Time: 100(110) minutes.
Comments: ACS test program is continually updated by retiring an older form of the test upon publication of a new form; separate answer sheet must be used.
Author: ACS DivCHED Examinations Institute.
Publisher: ACS DivCHED Examinations Institute.

[52]

ACS Examination in Polymer Chemistry.

Purpose: Designed to measure a student's achievement in polymer chemistry.
Population: 1 year college.
Publication Dates: 1978–1990.
Scores: Total score only.
Administration: Group.
Price Data: Available from publisher.
Time: 75(85) minutes.
Comments: ACS test program is continually updated by retiring an older form of the test upon release of a new form; separate answer sheet must be used; exam carries secure copyright.
Author: ACS DivCHED Examinations Institute.
Publisher: ACS DivCHED Examinations Institute.

[53]

ACS Toledo Chemistry Placement Examination.

Purpose: Designed to measure a student's achievement in general chemistry.
Population: 1 year college.
Publication Dates: 1959–1998.
Scores, 4: General Mathematics, General Chemical Knowledge, Specific Chemical Knowledge, Total.
Administration: Group.

Manual: No specific manual; general directions (no date, 4 pages).
Price Data: Available from publisher.
Time: 55(65) minutes.
Comments: ACS test program is continually updated by retiring an older form of the test upon release of a new form; separate answer sheet must be used; exam carries secure copyright.
Author: ACS DivCHED Examinations Institute.
Publisher: ACS DivCHED Examinations Institute.
Cross References: For a review by Frank J. Fornoff of an earlier form, see 8:853 (3 references); see also T2:1847 (2 references); for reviews by Kenneth E. Anderson and William R. Crawford, see 6:920 (1 reference).

[54]

ACT Survey Services.

Purpose: Designed to help educational institutions obtain reliable survey information that can be used to evaluate and enhance their programs.
Population: Secondary and postsecondary students and alumni.
Publication Dates: 1979–2006.
Acronym: ESS.
Administration: Group or individual.
Comments: For measurement of groups, not individuals.
Author: ACT, Inc.
Publisher: ACT, Inc.
 a) SECONDARY SCHOOL LEVEL.
 Population: High school.
 Publication Dates: 1979–2006.
 Price Data, 2005: $17.50 per 25 survey instruments; $9.20 per User's Guide; $46.00 per normative data reports; $8.70 per item catalog; $72 per institutional processing/handling fee; $1 per instrument scanning fee; $210-$350 per report fee.
 Time: (15–25) minutes.
  1) *High School Student Opinion Survey.*
  Publication Dates: 1980–2006.
  Acronym: HSSOS.
  Scores: Student's perceptions in 6 areas: High School Environment, Occupational Preparation, Educational Preparation, High School Characteristics, Additional Questions, Comments and Suggestions.
  2) *Student Needs Assessment Questionnaire.*
  Publication Dates: 1979–2006.
  Acronym: SNAQ.
  Scores: Student's personal and educational needs in 4 areas: Importance and Life Goals, Individual Growth/Development/Planning, Additional Questions, Comments and Suggestions.
  3) *High School Follow-Up Survey.*
  Publication Dates: 1990–2006.
  Acronym: HSFS.

Scores: Student's satisfaction with high school in 5 areas: Continuing Education, Employment History, High School Experiences, Additional Questions, Comments and Suggestions.

Comments: Administered to recent graduates.

b) POSTSECONDARY SCHOOL LEVEL.

Population: College.

Publication Dates: 1981–2006.

Price Data: $17.50 per 25 survey instruments; $9.20 per User's Guide; $46 per normative data reports; $8.70 per item catalog; $72 per institutional processing/handling fee; $1 per instrument scanning fee; $210-$350 per report fee.

Time: (15–25) minutes.

1) *Adult Learner Needs Assessment Survey.*

Publication Dates: 1981–2006.

Acronym: ALNAS.

Scores: Adult student's educational and persona needs in 4 areas: Personal and Educational Needs, Educational Plans and Preferences, Additional Questions, Comments and Suggestions.

2) *Alumni Survey.*

Publication Dates: 1981–2006.

Acronym: AS.

Scores: Impact of college on graduates in 5 areas: Continuing Education, College Experiences, Employment History, Additional Questions, Comments and Suggestions.

3) *Alumni Survey (2-Year College Form).*

Publication Dates: 1981–2006.

Scores: Same as 2 above but for 2-year colleges.

4) *Alumni Outcomes Survey.*

Publication Dates: 1993–2006.

Acronym: AOS.

Scores: Alumni outcomes in 7 areas: Employment History and Experiences, Educational Outcomes, Educational Experiences, Activities and Organizations, Additional Questions, Comments and Suggestions, Mailing Address.

5) *College Outcomes Survey.*

Publication Dates: 1992–2006.

Acronym: COS.

Scores: Student's perception of their college experience in 4 areas: College Outcomes, Satisfaction with Experiences at College, Additional Questions, Comments and Suggestions.

6) *College Student Needs Assessment Survey.*

Acronym: CSNAS.

Scores: Student's educational and personal needs in 4 areas: Career and Life Goals, Educational and Personal Needs, Additional Questions, Comments and Suggestions.

7) *Entering Student Survey.*

Publication Dates: 1982–2006.

Acronym: ESS.

Scores: Student's expectations for college in 4 areas: Educational Plans and Preferences, College Impressions, Additional Questions, Comments and Suggestions.

8) *Financial Aid Student Services Survey.*

Publication Dates: 1997-2006.

Acronym: FASSS.

Scores: Students' Perceptions of Financial Aid Services Received at Their College or University.

9) *Student Opinion Survey.*

Publication Dates: 1981–2006.

Acronym: SOS.

Scores: Student's perceptions of the institution in 4 areas: College Services, College Environment, Additional Questions, Comments and Suggestions.

Comments: Available via paper/pencil and online.

10) *Student Opinion Survey (2-Year College Form).*

Publication Dates: 1981–2006.

Scores: Student's perceptions of the 2-year college in 5 areas: College Impressions, College Services, College Environment, Additional Questions, Comments and Suggestions.

Comments: Available via paper/pencil and online.

11) *Survey of Academic Advising.*

Publication Dates: 1990-2006.

Acronym: SAA.

Scores: Student's perception of academic advising services in 6 areas: Advising Information, Academic Advising Needs, Impressions of Your Advisor, Additional Advising Information, Additional Questions, Comments and Suggestions.

12) *Survey of Current Activities and Plans.*

Publication Dates: 1988–2006.

Acronym: SCAP.

Scores: Student's current educational status in 5 areas: Impressions of This College, Educational Plans and Activities, Employment Plans, Additional Questions, Comments and Suggestions.

13) *Survey of Postsecondary Plans.*

Publication Dates: 1982–2006.

Acronym: SPP.

Scores: Student's educational plans in 4 areas: Educational Plans After High School, Impressions of This College, Additional Questions, Comments and Suggestions.

14) *Withdrawing/Nonreturning Student Survey.*

Publication Dates: 1979–2006.

Acronym: WNSS.

Scores: Student's reasons for leaving an institution in 4 areas: Reasons for Leaving This College, College Services and Characteristics, Additional Questions, Comments and Suggestions.

15) *Withdrawing/Nonreturning Student Survey (short form).*
Publication Dates: 1981–2006.
Acronym: WNSS-Short Form.
Scores: Student's reasons for leaving an institution in 2 areas: Reasons for Leaving This College, Additional Questions.
16) *Faces of the Future.*
Publication Dates: 1998–2006.
Acronym: FFS.
Scores: 6 areas: Employment Background, Education Background, Current College Experience, ID Number, Additional Questions, Comments and Suggestions.
Cross References: For reviews by Marcia J. Belcher and Claudia J. Morner of an earlier edition, see 12:10; see T4:61 (5 references); for a review by Rodney T. Hartnett of an earlier edition, see 9:44.

[55]

ACT Test.
Purpose: "Contains five curriculum-based tests (four multiple-choice tests and an optional Writing Test) that measure academic achievement in English/Writing, mathematics, reading, and science as well as noncognitive components (high school course/grade information, ACT interest inventory, and the student profile section). Results of the cognitive section are used by high schools and post-secondary institutions to understand what students are likely to know and ready to learn next in preparation for, and the transition to, post-secondary education. Results from the ACT Test are used in admissions, scholarship determination, academic advising, course placement, and career counseling."
Population: Grades 11–12.
Publication Dates: 1959–2005.
Administration: Group.
Price Data: Available from publisher.
Time: 175(190) minutes; 205(220) with the Optional Writing Test.
Comments: Tests administered nationally 6 times per year (February, April, June, September [in some states], October, December) at centers established by the publisher; also offered up to 5 times per year at international test centers outside the U.S.; special testing with extended time and alternate test formats are available for students who receive special accommodations in school due to professionally diagnosed and documented disabilities; a previous version was entitled Enhanced ACT Assessment.
Author: ACT, Inc.
Publisher: ACT, Inc.
a) ACT ENGLISH TEST.
Purpose: "Measures the student's understanding of the conventions of standard written English."
Scores, 3: Usage/Mechanics, Rhetorical Skills, Total.
Time: 45 minutes.
b) ACT MATHEMATICS TEST.
Purpose: "Measures reasoning and mathematical skills."
Scores, 4: Pre-Algebra/Elementary Algebra, Intermediate Algebra/Coordinate Geometry, Plane Geometry/Trigonometry, Total.
Time: 60 minutes.
c) ACT READING TEST.
Purpose: "Measures reading comprehension as a product of skill in referring and reasoning."
Scores, 3: Social Studies/Sciences, Arts/Literature, Total.
Time: 35 minutes.
d) ACT SCIENCE TEST.
Purpose: "Measures the interpretation, analysis, evaluation, reasoning, and problem-solving skills required in the natural sciences."
Scores: Total score only.
Time: 35 minutes.
e) ACT WRITING TEST (Optional).
Purpose: "Measures writing skills emphasized in high school English classes and in college-level composition courses."
Scores, 2: Writing Test subscore, Combined English/Writing Test score.
Time: 30 minutes.
Cross References: See T5:56 (19 references); for reviews by A. Harry Passow and James S. Terwilliger of the Enhanced ACT Assessment, see 12:139 (35 references); see also T4:913 (71 references); for reviews by Lewis R. Aiken and Edward Kifer of the ACT Assessment Program, see 9:43 (27 references); see also T3:76 (76 references); for a review by John R. Hills, see 8:469 (208 references); see also T2:1044 (97 references); for a review by Wimburn L. Wallace of an earlier program, see 7:330 (265 references); for reviews by Max D. Engelhart and Warren G. Findley and an excerpted review by David V. Tiedeman, see 6:1 (14 references).

[56]

Adaptability Test.
Purpose: "Designed to measure mental adaptability or mental alertness."
Population: Job applicants.
Publication Dates: 1942–1994.
Scores: Total score only.
Administration: Individual or group.
Forms, 2: A, B.
Price Data, 2002: $79 per start-up kit including 25 test booklets (specify Form A or Form B) and examiner's manual; $61 per 25 test booklets (specify Form A or Form B); $28 per examiner's manual.
Time: 15 minutes.

Authors: Joseph Tiffin and C. H. Lawshe.
Publisher: Pearson Performance Solutions [No reply from publisher; status unknown].
Cross References: See T4:80 (2 references), T3:111 (1 reference), T2:337 (3 references), and 7:333 (6 references); for a review by John M. Willits, see 5:305 (13 references); for reviews by Anne Anastasi and Marion A. Bills, see 3:216 (3 references).

[57]

Adaptive Behavior Assessment System®–Second Edition.

Purpose: Designed to provide a comprehensive norm-referenced assessment of adaptive skills.
Population: Birth to 89 years.
Publication Dates: 2002–2003.
Acronym: ABAS–Second Edition.
Scores, 14: 10 skill areas, 3 adaptive domains, 1 overall score: Conceptual (Communication, Functional Academics, Self-Direction, Composite), Social (Leisure, Social, Composite), Practical (Community Use, Home Living, Health and Safety, Self-Care, Work, Composite), Motor, General Adaptive Composite.
Administration: Individual.
Forms, 5: Parent/Primary Caregiver Form (Ages Birth–5), Parent Form (Ages 5–21), Teacher/Day Care Form (Ages 2–5), Teacher Form (Ages 5–21), Adult Form (Ages 16–89).
Price Data, 2006: $175 per examination kit including manual, 5 Parent/Primary Caregiver Forms (Ages 0–5), 5 Teacher/Daycare Provider Forms (Ages 2–5), 5 Parent Forms (Ages 5–21), 5 Teacher Forms (Ages 5–21), and 5 Adult Forms; $120 per manual; $59 per 25 Forms (specify respondent and age); $175 per Infant and Preschool kit including manual, 25 Parent/Primary Caregiver Forms, and 25 Teacher/Daycare Provider Forms; $175 per School kit including manual, 25 Parent Forms, and 25 Teacher Forms; $175 per Adult kit including manual and 25 Adult Forms; $199 per Scoring Assistant Windows CD-ROM.
Time: (15-20) minutes.
Comments: Personal computer scoring software available; incorporates current AAMR and DSM-IV diagnostic guidelines.
Authors: Patti Harrison and Thomas Oakland.
Publisher: Western Psychological Services.
Cross References: For reviews by Matthew K. Burns and by Joyce Meikamp and Carolyn H. Suppa, see 16:4; for a review by James K. Benish of the original edition, see 15:6.

[58]

Adaptive Behavior Evaluation Scale, Revised.

Purpose: Designed to assist in "making diagnostic, placement, and programming decisions for mentally re-tarded and emotionally disturbed/behaviorally disordered children and adolescents."
Population: Ages 5-0 to 18-0.
Publication Dates: 1983–1995.
Acronym: ABES-R.
Scores, 10: Communication, Self-Care, Home Living, Social, Community Use, Self-Direction, Health and Safety, Functional Academics, Leisure, Work.
Administration: Individual.
Forms, 2: Adaptive Behavior Evaluation Scale, School Version; Adaptive Behavior Evaluation Scale, Home Version.
Price Data: Available from publisher.
Time: (15–20) minutes.
Comments: Publisher advises that ABES-R2 replaces this test.
Author: Stephen B. McCarney.
Publisher: Hawthorne Educational Services, Inc.
Cross References: For reviews by John H. Kranzler and by Mark D. Shriver and Merilee McCurdy, see 14:4; for reviews by Mary Ross Moran and Harvey N. Switzky of an earlier edition, see 12:14.

[59]

Adaptive Behavior Inventory.

Purpose: Designed to evaluate functional daily living skills.
Population: Mentally retarded students ages 6-0 through 18-11 years and normal students ages 5-0 through 18-11 years
Publication Date: 1986.
Acronym: ABI.
Scores, 6: Self-Care Skills, Communication Skills, Social Skills, Academic Skills, Occupational Skills, Composite Quotient.
Administration: Individual.
Price Data, 2010: $103 per complete kit including 25 profile and response sheets, 25 short form response sheets, and examiner's manual (69 pages); $40 per 25 profile and response sheets; $18 per 25 short form response sheets; $51 per examiner's manual.
Time: (20–25) minutes.
Comments: Inventory is completed by classroom teacher or other professional having regular contact with the student; ABI-Short Form available for research and screening purposes.
Authors: Linda Brown and James E. Leigh.
Publisher: PRO-ED.
Cross References: For a review by Corinne Roth Smith, see 10:9 (2 references).

[60]

Adaptive Behavior Inventory for Children.

Purpose: Designed to "measure the child's social role performance in the family, the peer group, and the community."

Population: Ages 5–11.
Publication Dates: 1977–1982.
Acronym: ABIC.
Scores, 6: Family, Community, Peer Relations, Nonacademic School Roles, Earner/Consumer, Self-Maintenance.
Administration: Individual.
Price Data, 2002: $149 per basic kit including manual (1982, 121 pages), 6 keys, and 25 record forms; $44 per 6 scoring keys; $40 per 25 record forms.
Time: (45) minutes.
Comments: A component of the System of Multicultural Pluralistic Assessment; the manual includes the ABIC questions in Spanish as well as in English.
Authors: Jane R. Mercer and June F. Lewis.
Publisher: Pearson.
Cross References: See T5:61 (2 references) and T4:85 (10 references); for reviews by James E. Jirsa and Benson P. Low, see 9:48 (1 reference); see T3:2387 (9 references) for ABIC and related references.

[61]

Adaptive Behavior: Street Survival Skills Questionnaire.

Purpose: "To assess fundamental community living and prevocational skills of mentally disabled adolescents and adults."
Population: Ages 9.5 and over.
Publication Dates: 1979–1993.
Acronym: SSSQ.
Scores, 10: Basic Concepts, Functional Signs, Tools, Domestics, Health and Safety, Public Services, Time, Monetary, Measurements, Total.
Administration: Individual.
Price Data, 2011: $490 per complete kit including 9 picture volumes (1993, 50 pages each), 50 scoring forms, 50 planning charts, Curriculum Guide (1982, 272 pages), and manual (1993, 95 pages); $41 per 50 scoring forms; $26.75 per 50 planning charts; $75 per Curriculum Guide; $59.50 per manual; $250 per computer software (Windows or Macintosh) offered by publisher.
Time: [45] minutes.
Authors: Dan Linkenhoker and Lawrence McCarron.
Publisher: McCarron-Dial Systems, Inc.
Cross References: See T4:139 (1 reference); for a review by Thomas G. Haring, see 11:6.

[62]

Adaptive Functioning Index.

Purpose: "Training and assessment tool to be used by those working with the developmentally handicapped adolescent and adult."
Population: Ages 14 and over in rehabilitation or special education settings.
Publication Dates: 1971–1978.
Acronym: AFI.

Administration: Individual.
Price Data: Price information available from publisher for complete kit, administration manual (1976, 43 pages), standardization manual (1977, 42 pages), program manual (1978, 198 pages), Program Workbooks (1977, 19 pages), and Target Workbooks (1977, 12 pages).
Time: Administration time not reported.
Comments: Ratings by staff; 3 subtests: Social Education Test, Vocational Check List, Residential Check List, plus Adaptive Functioning of the Dependent Handicapped; Training Package available, includes Training Manual, Program Workbook, and Target Workbook; Program manual and workbooks not necessary for test administration; no norms.
Authors: Nancy J. Marlett and E. Anne Hughson (Program Workbook and Target Workbook).
Publisher: Vocational and Rehabilitation Research Institute [Canada].
   a) SOCIAL EDUCATION TEST.
   Scores, 9: Reading, Writing, Communication, Concept Attainment, Number Concepts, Time, Money Handling, Community Awareness, Motor Movements.
   b) VOCATIONAL CHECK LIST.
   Scores, 12: Basic Work Habits (Independence, Making Decisions, Use and Care of Equipment and Materials, Taking Direction), Work Skills (Speed of Movement, Ability to Follow Instructions, Competence, Skill Level), Acceptance Skills (Appearance, Attendance/Punctuality, Self-Expressions, Relation with Co-workers).
   c) RESIDENTIAL CHECK LIST.
   Scores, 15: Personal Routines (Cleanliness, Appearance and Eating, Room Management, Time Management, Health), Community Awareness (Transportation, Shopping, Leisure, Budgeting, Cooking and Home Management), Social Maturity (Communication, Consideration, Getting Friends, Keeping Friends, Handling Problems).
   d) ADAPTIVE FUNCTIONING OF THE DEPENDENT HANDICAPPED.
   Population: Profoundly handicapped of all ages.
   Scores, 20: Nursing Care (Medications, Body Tone, Medical Care, Observation for Injury, Feeding), Physical Development (Head, Legs, Body, Hands or Feet, Movement), Awareness (Eye Contact, Contact with His World, Contact with People, Communication, Contact with Things), Self Help (Feeding, Eating, Washing, Dressing, Toileting).
Cross References: See T5:63 (1 reference) and T4:87 (2 references); for reviews by Nadine M. Lambert and David J. Mealor, see 9:49 (1 reference).

[63]

Adaptive Style Inventory.

Purpose: "Designed to assess individuals' ability to adapt to different learning situations."

Population: Junior high through adult.
Publication Date: 1993.
Acronym: ASI.
Scores, 16: 4 scores: Concrete Experience, Reflective Observation, Abstract Conceptualization, Active Experimentation in each of 4 situations: Acting Situation, Deciding Situation, Thinking Situation, Valuing Situation.
Administration: Group or individual.
Price Data, 2006: $69 per complete kit including 10 questionnaires, 10 profiles and interpretive notes (14 pages), and 10 scoring booklets.
Time: [30–40] minutes.
Comments: Self-scored inventory.
Authors: Richard E. Boyatzis and David A. Kolb.
Publisher: Hay Group.
Cross References: For reviews by Thomas R. Knapp and Erich P. Prien, see 13:7.

[64]

Addiction Severity Index–Multimedia Version.

Purpose: "An interactive, multimedia administration of the Addiction Severity Index," "a measure of addiction severity."
Population: Adults seeking substance abuse treatment.
Publication Date: 1999.
Acronym: ASI-MV.
Scores, 7: Composite scores and severity ratings provided for 7 domains: Medical Status, Employment/Support Status, Alcohol Use, Drug Use, Legal Status, Family/Social Relationships, Psychiatric Status.
Administration: Individual or group.
Price Data: Available from publisher.
Time: (45) minutes.
Comments: Same clinical interview as Addiction Severity Index (5th edition) adapted for self-report, multimedia format; clients are guided through a series of on-screen offices and meet with virtual interviewers; produces narrative report, severity profile, utilization report; customized reports available; personal computer or mouse-driven computer kiosk versions available; PC system requirements: Windows 95/98/NT 4.0, 6 MB hard drive, 12 MB RAM, 100 MHz processor, SVGA monitor (256 colors), 4X CD-ROM, sound card, speakers with headphones, mouse, keyboard, printer; kiosk information available from publisher.
Author: Innovative Training Systems, Inc.
Publisher: Pearson.

[65]

AD/HD Comprehensive Teacher's Rating Scale, Second Edition [1998 Revision].

Purpose: "Designed to help identify attention disorder, with or without hyperactivity."
Population: Grades K–adult.

Publication Dates: 1986–2000.
Acronym: ACTeRS.
Administration: Individual.
Price Data, 2010: $67 per Teacher and Parent Form examiner's kit including manual (2000, 31 pages) and 50 rating/profile forms; $48 per 50 rating/profile forms; $72 per Self-Report examiner's kit including manual and 50 rating/profile forms; $53 per 50 rating/profile forms; $21 per introductory kit including manual, sample Parent rating/profile Form, sample Teacher rating/profile Form, sample Self-Report Form, and annotated bibliography of research; $21 per manual.
Time: [5–15] minutes.
Comments: Paper and pencil edition; parent forms available in Spanish.
Authors: Rina K. Ullmann, Esther K. Sleator, Robert L. Sprague, and MetriTech staff.
Publisher: MetriTech, Inc.
  a) ACTeRS TEACHER FORM.
  Population: Grades K–8.
  Scores, 4: Attention, Hyperactivity, Social Skills, Oppositional Behavior.
  Price Data: $67 including manual and 50 forms; $48 per 50 forms.
  Time: Untimed.
  b) ACTeRS PARENT FORM.
  Scores, 5: Attention, Hyperactivity, Social Skills, Oppositional Behavior, Early Childhood.
  Price Data: $67 including manual and 50 forms; $48 per 50 forms.
  Time: Untimed.
  c) ACTeRS SELF-REPORT.
  Population: Adolescence through adulthood.
  Scores, 3: Attention, Hyperactivity/Impulsivity, Social Adjustment.
  Price Data: $72 including manual and 50 forms; $53 per 50 forms.
  Time: Untimed [10–15 minutes].
Cross References: For reviews by Cederick O. Lindskog and Janet V. Smith and by Everett V. Smith, Jr., see 14:5; for reviews by Robert J. Miller and Judy Oehler-Stinnett of an earlier edition, see 12:15 (2 references); see also T4:89 (1 reference); for reviews by Ellen H. Bacon and Ayres G. D'Costa of an earlier edition, see 11:7 (2 references).

[66]

ADHD Rating Scale–IV.

Purpose: Designed to help identify the frequency of ADHD symptoms of a child as reported by a parent or educator.
Population: Ages 5–18 years
Publication Date: 1998.
Scores, 3: Inattention, Hyperactivity-Impulsivity, Total.
Administration: Individual.
Forms, 2: Home, School.

Price Data, 2010: $50 per scale including manual (79 pages) and photocopiable scales.
Foreign Language Edition: Spanish questionnaires available.
Time: Administration time not reported.
Comments: Symptom criteria based on the DSM-IV; 18-item rating scale.
Authors: George J. DuPaul, Thomas J. Power, Arthur D. Anastopolous, and Robert Reid.
Publisher: Guilford Publications, Inc.
Cross References: For reviews by Jill Ann Jenkins and Cederick O. Lindskog, see 15:7.

[67]
ADHD Symptom Checklist–4.
Purpose: Designed as "a screening instrument for the behavioral symptoms of attention-deficit/hyperactivity disorder (AD/HD) and oppositional defiant disorder (ODD)."
Population: Ages 3–18.
Publication Date: 1997.
Acronym: ADHD-SC4.
Scores, 3: Screening Cutoff, Symptom Count, Symptom Severity.
Administration: Individual.
Forms, 1: Same checklist completed by parent and teacher.
Price Data, 2006: $52 per kit including 50 checklists, 50 symptom count score sheets, 50 symptom severity profile score sheets, and manual (1997, 200 pages); $26 per 50 checklists.
Foreign Language Edition: Spanish edition available.
Time: (5) minutes.
Authors: Kenneth D. Gadow and Joyce Sprafkin.
Publisher: Checkmate Plus, Ltd.
Cross References: For reviews by James C. DiPerna and Robert J. Volpe and by Cynthia A. Rohrbeck, see 15:8.

[68]
ADHD Symptoms Rating Scale.
Purpose: Designed "to assess behaviors symptomatic of Attention Deficit Hyperactivity Disorder in children and adolescents."
Population: Ages 5–18 years.
Publication Date: 2001.
Acronym: ADHD-SRS.
Scores, 4: Hyperactive, Impulsive, Inattentive, Total.
Administration: Individual.
Price Data, 2006: $85 per starter set including manual (100 pages), 25 English forms, and 5 Spanish forms; $38 per 25 rating forms (specify English or Spanish); $50 per manual.
Foreign Language Edition: Spanish edition available.

Time: (10–15) minutes.
Authors: Melissa Lea Holland, Gretchen A. Gimpel, and Kenneth W. Merrell.
Publisher: Psychological Assessment Resources, Inc.
Cross References: For reviews by Kevin M. Jones and Ronald A. Madle, see 15:9.

[69]
The Adjective Check List.
Purpose: Designed to identify personal characteristics of individuals.
Population: High school and over.
Publication Dates: 1952–1983.
Acronym: ACL.
Scores, 37: Number of Adjectives Checked, Number of Favorable Adjectives, Number of Unfavorable Adjectives, Commonality, Achievement, Dominance, Endurance, Order, Intraception, Nurturance, Affiliation, Heterosexuality, Exhibition, Autonomy, Aggression, Change, Succorance, Abasement, Deference, Counseling Readiness, Self-Control, Self-Confidence, Personal Adjustment, Ideal Self, Creative Personality, Military Leadership, Masculine Attributes, Feminine Attributes, Critical Parent, Nurturing Parent, Adult, Free Child, Adapted Child, High Origence-Low Intellectence, High Origence-High Intellectence, Low Origence-Low Intellectence, Low Origence-High Intellectence.
Administration: Individual or group.
Price Data, 2011: $37.50 per combined item booklet/answer sheet, non-prepaid; $30.75 per 25 Profiles for hand scoring; $99.50 per manual (1980, 88 pages).
Foreign Language Edition: Spanish edition available.
Time: [15–20] minutes.
Authors: Harrison G. Gough and Alfred B. Heilbrun, Jr. (manual and bibliography).
Publisher: CPP, Inc.
Cross References: See T5:68 (62 references) and T4:93 (92 references); for reviews by Phyllis Anne Teeter and John A. Zarske, see 9:52 (39 references); see also T3:116 (117 references), 8:495 (202 references), and T2:1094 (85 references); for reviews by Leonard G. Rorer and Forrest L. Vance, see 7:38 (131 references); see also P:4 (102 references).

[70]
Adjustment Scales for Children and Adolescents.
Purpose: "Designed to assess through teacher observation behavior pathology in youths."
Population: Ages 5–17.
Publication Dates: 1993–1994.
Acronym: ASCA.
Scores, 10: Overactivity, Underactivity, Attention-Deficit Hyperactive, Solitary Aggressive-Provocative,

Solitary Aggressive-Impulsive, Oppositional Defiant, Diffident, Avoidant, Delinquent, Lethargic-Hypoactive.
Administration: Individual.
Price Data, 2006: $87 per complete kit including 25 male and 25 female self-scoring forms and profiles and manual (1994, 68 pages); $26.20 per 25 self-scoring forms and profiles (specify male or female); $34.95 per manual.
Time: (10–20) minutes.
Comments: Behavior checklist to be completed by a teacher about a student; scored by a psychologist or assessment specialist.
Authors: Paul A. McDermott, Neville C. Marston, and Denis H. Stott.
Publisher: Ed & Psych Associates.
Cross References: For reviews by Gary L. Canivez and Richard V. Schowengerdt, see 14:6; see also T5:69 (1 reference).

[71]
Administrative Series Modules.
Purpose: Designed to assess skills needed in various administrative positions.
Population: Candidates for administrative positions.
Publication Dates: 1975-1997.
Administration: Individual or group.
Price Data: Available from publisher.
Comments: "Designed in module format so test users can select the modules that best suit their testing needs"; "hand scoring is available for all individual and combined modules"; "machine scoring is available for all modules except I, K, and L"; previous version listed as SCC Clerical Skills Series.
Author: International Public Management Association for Human Resources.
Publisher: International Public Management Association for Human Resources (IPMA-HR).
a) INDIVIDUAL ADMINISTRATIVE MODULE TESTS.
  1) *Grammar (A).*
  Score: Total score only.
  Time: 15 minutes.
  2) *Punctuation (B).*
  Score: Total score only.
  Time: 11 minutes.
  3) *Vocabulary (C).*
  Score: Total score only.
  Time: 9 minutes.
  4) *Spelling (D).*
  Score: Total score only.
  Time: 6 minutes.
  5) *Basic Filing Skills (E).*
  Score: Total score only.
  Time: 18 minutes.
  6) *Reasoning (F).*
  Score: Total score only.
  Time: 9 minutes.

  7) *Following Oral Instructions (G).*
  Score: Total score only.
  Time: 33 minutes.
  8) *Following Written Instructions (H).*
  Score: Total score only.
  Time: 25 minutes.
  9) *Forms, Completion/Listening (I).*
  Score: Total score only.
  Time: 30 minutes.
  10) *Data Proofing (J).*
  Score: Total score only.
  Time: 13 minutes.
  11) *Document Proofing-Part A (K).*
  Score: Total score only.
  Time: 15 minutes.
  12) *Document Proofing-Part B (L).*
  Score: Total score only.
  Time: 20 minutes.
  13) *Mathematical Reasoning (M).*
  Score: Total score only.
  Time: 35 minutes.
  14) *Basic Math Calculations (N).*
  Score: Total score only.
  Time: 20 minutes.
b) COMBINED ADMINISTRATIVE MODULE TESTS.
  1) *Clerical Series 1-A.*
  Acronym: CS1-A.
  Scores: 5 modules: Grammar, Punctuation, Vocabulary, Spelling, Basic Filing.
  Time: 59 minutes.
  2) *Clerical Series 1-B.*
  Acronym: CS1-B.
  Scores: 3 modules: Reasoning, Following Written Instructions, Basic Math Calculations.
  Time: 54 minutes.
Cross References: For a review by Thomas R. O'Neill, see 18:2; for a review by Lorraine D. Eyde of a previous version, see 9:1074.

[72]
Adolescent/Adult Sensory Profile.
Purpose: Designed "to promote self-evaluation of behavioral responses to everyday sensory experiences."
Population: Ages 11–65+.
Publication Date: 2002.
Scores, 4: Low Registration, Sensation Seeking, Sensory Sensitivity, Sensation Avoiding.
Administration: Individual.
Price Data, 2003: $85 per complete kit including user's manual (144 pages) and 25 self-questionnaire/summary reports; $65 per user's manual; $27 per 25 self-questionnaire/summary reports.
Time: (10–15) minutes.
Comments: Self-report inventory based on the Sensory Profile (2429), a measure developed for children.

Authors: Catana E. Brown and Winnie Dunn.
Publisher: Pearson.
Cross References: For reviews by Corine Fitzpatrick and Janet V. Smith, see 16:5.

[73]

Adolescent American Drug and Alcohol Survey with Prevention Planning Survey.

Purpose: Designed to survey youth about their experiences with alcohol, tobacco and other drugs, and "about various risk and protective factors associated with the Prevention Planning Model."
Population: Grades 6–12.
Publication Dates: 1999-2005.
Acronym: ADAS/PPS.
Scores: Not scored.
Administration: Group.
Price Data: The publisher is dissolving in 2011 and releasing the copyright on this survey–it may be freely used hereafter.
Time: (20–30) minutes.
Comments: For information about the Children's ADAS, see T6:147; the publisher is dissolving in 2011 and releasing the copyright on this survey–it may be freely used hereafter.
Authors: Ruth Edwards, Fred Beauvais, and Eugene R. Oetting.
Publisher: Rocky Mountain Behavioral Science Institute, Inc.
Cross References: For reviews by Jody L. Kulstad and by Nathaniel J. Pallone and James J. Hennessy, see 16:6.

[74]

Adolescent and Child Urgent Threat Evaluation.

Purpose: Designed to "assess the risk of near-future violence (both homicidal and suicidal) among children and adolescents."
Population: Ages 8-18.
Publication Date: 2005.
Acronym: ACUTE.
Scores, 8: Threat Cluster, Precipitating Factors Cluster, Early Precipitating Factors Cluster, Late Precipitating Factors Cluster, Predisposing Factors Cluster, Impulsivity Cluster, Overall Threat Classification, Total Score.
Administration: Individual.
Price Data, 2009: $125 per professional manual (64 pages) and 50 rating forms.
Time: (20) minutes.
Comments: Some items may require the examiner to "obtain information from additional sources" to gather the most "accurate information regarding a client."
Authors: Russell Copelan and David Ashley.

Publisher: Psychological Assessment Resources, Inc.
Cross References: For reviews by Mary M. Clare and Thomas P. Hogan, see 18:3.

[75]

Adolescent Anger Rating Scale.

Purpose: Developed to "assess the intensity and frequency of anger expression in adolescents."
Population: Ages 11–19.
Publication Date: 2001.
Acronym: AARS.
Scores, 4: Instrumental Anger, Reactive Anger, Anger Control, Total Anger.
Administration: Individual or group.
Price Data, 2006: $142 per introductory kit including professional manual (69 pages) and 50 test booklets.
Time: (5–10) minutes for individuals; (10–20) minutes per group.
Comments: Self-rating scale.
Author: DeAnna McKinnie Burney.
Publisher: Psychological Assessment Resources, Inc.
Cross References: For reviews by Carlen Henington and Hugh Stephenson, see 15:10.

[76]

Adolescent Apperception Cards.

Purpose: "Intended to suggest themes and evoke narratives that include … family, sibling, and peer relationships; abuse and neglect."
Population: Ages 12–19.
Publication Date: 1993.
Acronym: AAC.
Scores: No scores.
Administration: Individual.
Forms, 2: Black, White.
Price Data, 2011: $115 per kit including Adolescent Apperception Cards (Black and White versions included); $67.50 per cards (specify version).
Time: [45–60] minutes.
Comments: Publisher recommends (a) training and experience in projective testing and in working with adolescents, and (b) that the test be used as one component of a comprehensive battery of measures.
Authors: Leigh Silverton; illustrated by Laurie Harden.
Publisher: Western Psychological Services
Cross References: For reviews by David M. Kaplan and Molly L. Vanduser and by Jody L. Swartz-Kulstad, see 14:7.

[77]

Adolescent Chemical Dependency Inventory.

Purpose: "Designed for assessing troubled youth in school settings, counseling or treatment programs."
Population: Ages 14-17.
Publication Dates: 1988-1998.

Acronym: ACDI.
Scores, 5: Truthfulness, Alcohol, Drugs, Adjustment, Distress.
Administration: Group.
Price Data, 2010: $8 per test; volume discounts available.
Foreign Language Edition: Spanish version available.
Time: (15-20) minutes.
Comments: May be administered via paper and pencil, computer, or human voice audio.
Author: Behavior Data Systems, Ltd.
Publisher: Behavior Data Systems, Ltd.

[78]

Adolescent Coping Scale.

Purpose: Assesses 18 possible coping strategies used by adolescents and young adults in dealing with stress.
Population: Ages 12–18.
Publication Dates: 1993–1997.
Acronym: ACS.
Scores, 18: Seek Social Support, Focus on Solving the Problem, Work Hard and Achieve, Worry, Invest in Close Friends, Seek to Belong, Wishful Thinking, Not Coping, Tension Reduction, Social Action, Ignore the Problem, Self-Blame, Keep to Self, Seek Spiritual Support, Focus on the Positive, Seek Professional Help, Seek Relaxing Diversions, Physical Recreation.
Administration: Group.
Price Data, 2005: A$121 per complete kit including manual (48 pages) and all required material in a notebook; A$24.95 per 10 questionnaires (short form); A$24.95 per 10 questionnaires (long form); A$11.55 per 10 scoring sheets; A$11.55 per 10 profile charts; A$51.80 per manual.
Time: 10 minutes for Long Form; 3 minutes for Short Form.
Authors: Erica Frydenberg and Ramon Lewis.
Publisher: Australian Council for Educational Research Ltd. [Australia].
Cross References: See T5:72 (3 references); for reviews by Frederick T. L. Leong and Judy J. Oehler-Stinnett, see 13:8.

[79]

Adolescent Diagnostic Interview.

Purpose: "Assesses psychoactive substance use disorders."
Population: Ages 12–18.
Publication Date: 1993.
Acronym: ADI.
Scores: 8 sections to indicate presence or absence of a DSM-III-R diagnosis of psychoactive substance use disorder: Sociodemographic Factors, Psychosocial Stressors, Substance Use/Consumption History, Alcohol Use Symptoms, Cannabis Use Symptoms, Additional Drug Use Symptoms, Level of Functioning Domains, Orientation and Memory Screen; plus 8 psychiatric status screens: Depression, Mania, Eating Disorder, Delusional Thinking, Hallucinations, Attention Deficit Disorder, Anxiety Disorder, Conduct Disorder.
Administration: Individual.
Price Data, 2002: $78 per complete kit including 5 administration booklets and manual (46 pages); $35 per 5 administration booklets; $45 per manual.
Time: (45–55) minutes.
Comments: Structured interview for use with adolescents; complements the Personal Experience Inventory (1997).
Authors: Ken C. Winters and George A. Henly.
Publisher: Western Psychological Services.
Cross References: See T5:73 (1 reference); for reviews by Tony Toneatto and by Logan Wright, Donna Ford, and Karyll Kiser, see 12:16.

[80]

Adolescent Dissociative Experiences Scale.

Purpose: Designed as a "screening measure for pathological dissociation during adolescence."
Population: Ages 11–17.
Publication Date: 1996.
Acronym: A-DES.
Scores, 5: Dissociative Amnesia, Absorption and Imaginative Involvement, Depersonalization and Derealization, Passive Influence, Total.
Administration: Individual or group.
Price Data: Available from publisher
Time: (10–15) minutes.
Comments: A 30-item self-report measure, derived from the Dissociative Experiences Scale (original adult version) (891).
Authors: Judith Armstrong, Frank Putnam, and Eve Carlson.
Publisher: The Sidran Institute.
Cross References: For reviews by Rosemary Flanagan and Ramasamy Manikam, see 14:8.

[81]

Adolescent Drinking Index.

Purpose: Constructed to "assess alcohol abuse in adolescents with psychological, emotional, or behavioral problems; identify referred adolescents who need further evaluation or treatment; and define the type of drinking problem the adolescent is experiencing."
Population: Ages 12–17.
Publication Dates: 1985–1989.
Acronym: ADI.
Scores, 3: Self-Medicated Drinking (MED), Aggressive/Rebellious Behavior (REB), Total.
Administration: Group or individual.

Price Data, 2005: $85 per Introductory Kit including manual (1989, 34 pages) and 25 test booklets.
Time: (5) minutes.
Comments: Test booklet title is Drinking & You.
Authors: Adele V. Harrell and Philip W. Wirtz.
Publisher: Psychological Assessment Resources, Inc.
Cross References: See T5:75 (1 reference); for reviews by Thomas F. Donlon and by Kevin J. McCarthy and Penelope W. Dralle, see 12:17.

[82]

Adolescent Language Screening Test.

Purpose: "Developed to screen for deficits in the dimensions of language use, content, and form" in adolescents.
Population: Ages 11–17.
Publication Date: 1984.
Acronym: ALST.
Scores: 7 subtests: Pragmatics, Receptive Vocabulary, Concepts, Expressive Vocabulary, Sentence Formulation, Morphology, Phonology.
Administration: Individual.
Price Data, 2010: $157 per complete kit including 50 test booklets, picture book, and examiner's manual (26 pages); $45 per 50 test booklets; $79 per picture book; $45 per examiner's manual.
Time: (10–15) minutes.
Authors: Denise L. Morgan and Arthur M. Guilford.
Publisher: PRO-ED.
Cross References: For reviews by Linda Crocker and by Robert T. Williams and Amy Finch-Williams, see 10:10.

[83]

Adolescent Psychopathology Scale.

Purpose: Designed to "evaluate symptoms of psychological disorders and distress in adolescents … measures psychopathology, personality, and social-emotional problems and competencies."
Population: Ages 12–19.
Publication Date: 1998.
Acronym: APS.
Scores: 40 scales in 4 domains: Clinical Disorders Domain (Attention-Deficit/Hyperactivity Disorder, Conduct Disorder, Oppositional-Defiant Disorder, Adjustment Disorder, Substance Abuse Disorder, Anorexia Nervosa, Bulimia Nervosa, Sleep Disorder, Somatization Disorder, Panic Disorder, Obsessive-Compulsive Disorder, Generalized Anxiety Disorder, Social Phobia, Separation Anxiety Disorder, Posttraumatic Stress Disorder, Major Depression, Dysthymic Disorder, Mania, Depersonalization Disorder, Schizophrenia); Personality Disorder Domain (Avoidant, Obsessive-Compulsive, Borderline, Schizotypal, Paranoid); Psychosocial Problem Content Domain (Self-Concept, Psycho-social Substance Use Difficulties, Introversion, Alienation-Boredom, Anger, Aggression, Interpersonal Problems, Emotional Lability, Disorientation, Suicide, Social Adaptation; Response Style Indicators (Lie, Consistency, Infrequency, Critical Item Endorsement); Factor Scales (Internalizing Disorder Factor, Externalizing Disorder Factor, Personality Disorder Factor).
Administration: Individual or group.
Price Data, 2006: $360 per introductory kit including CD ROM based scoring program, administration and interpretation manual, psychometric and technical manual, and 25 test booklets.
Time: (45–60) minutes.
Comments: A 346-item self-report scale; developed to be consistent with the DSM-IV disorders; test form is entitled Adolescent Mental Health Questionnaire; software for computerized (Windows) scoring program included.
Author: William M. Reynolds.
Publisher: Psychological Assessment Resources, Inc.
Cross References: For reviews by Timothy R. Konold and Wayne C. Piersel, see 14:9.

[84]

Adolescent Psychopathology Scale–Short Form.

Purpose: Constructed as a "multidimensional measure of psychopathology and personality characteristics derived from the APS to evaluate symptoms of psychological disorder and distress consistent with DSM-IV symptom specifications."
Population: Ages 12–19 years.
Publication Dates: 1998–2000.
Acronym: APS-SF.
Scores, 14: Defensiveness, Consistency Response, Conduct Disorder, Oppositional Defiant Disorder, Substance Abuse Disorder, Anger/Violence Proneness, Academic Problems, Generalized Anxiety Disorder, Posttraumatic Stress Disorder, Major Depression, Eating Disturbance, Suicide, Self-Concept, Interpersonal Problems.
Administration: Group or individual.
Price Data, 2006: $235 per Introductory kit including CD ROM based unlimited use scoring program with on-screen user's guide, professional manual, and 25 test booklets.
Time: (15–20) minutes.
Comments: Derived from the Adolescent Psychopathology Scale (APS; 83).
Author: William M. Reynolds.
Publisher: Psychological Assessment Resources, Inc.
Cross References: For reviews by Janet F. Carlson and Steven I. Pfeiffer, see 15:11.

[85]

Adolescent Separation Anxiety Test.

Purpose: "Provides a measure of emotional and personality patterns which adolescents show in reaction to separation experiences."

Population: Ages 11–18.
Publication Dates: 1972–1980.
Scores, 28: 18 association responses (Rejection, Impaired Concentration, Phobic Feeling, Anxiety, Loneliness, Withdrawal, Somatic, Adaptive Reaction, Anger, Projection, Empathy, Evasion, Fantasy, Well-Being, Sublimation, Intrapunitive, Identify Stress, Total), plus 10 derived response patterns (Attachment, Individuation, Hostility, Painful Tension, Reality Avoidance, Concentration Impairment and Sublimation, Self-Love, Identity Stress, Absurd Responses, Attachment-Individuation Balance).
Administration: Individual.
Forms: Separate forms for boys and girls.
Price Data: Not available.
Time: Administration time not reported.
Comments: Formerly titled Separation Anxiety Test.
Author: Henry G. Hansburg.
Publisher: Krieger Publishing Company [No reply from publisher; status unknown].
Cross References: See T5:78 (1 reference) and T4:100 (1 reference); for reviews by Brenda Bailey-Richardson and Carolyn S. Hartsough, see 9:53.

[86]
Adolescent Symptom Inventory-4.

Purpose: Designed as a "screening instrument for the behavioral, affective, and cognitive symptoms of a variety of adolescent psychiatric disorders."
Population: Ages 12–18.
Publication Dates: 1997–1998.
Acronym: ASI-4.
Scores, 15: 11 scores shared on both Parent and Teacher Forms: AD/HD Inattentive, Hyperactive-Impulsive, Combined, Conduct Disorder, Oppositional Defiant, Generalized Anxiety Disorder, Schizoid Personality, Schizophrenia, Major Depressive Disorder, Dysthymic Disorder, Bipolar Disorder; 4 additional scores on the Parent Form: Antisocial Personality Disorder, Separation Anxiety, Anorexia Nervosa, Bulimia Nervosa.
Administration: Individual.
Forms, 2: Teacher Checklist, Parent Checklist.
Price Data, 2006: $102 per deluxe kit including 25 parent checklists, 25 teacher checklists, 50 symptom count score sheets, 50 parent and teacher symptom severity profile score sheets, , screening manual (1997, 145 pages), and norms manual (1998, 168 pages); $52 per 50 parent checklists; $38 per 50 teacher checklists.
Foreign Language Edition: Spanish edition available.
Time: [10–15] minutes.
Comments: Checklists completed by teachers and caregivers about adolescents; scores are not intended for diagnostic purposes, only screening purposes.
Authors: Kenneth D. Gadow and Joyce Sprafkin.
Publisher: Checkmate Plus, Ltd.

Cross References: For reviews by Stephen N. Axford and Patti L. Harrison, see 15:12.

[87]
Adult Attention Deficit Disorders Evaluation Scale.

Purpose: Designed to provide a measure of inattention and hyperactivity-impulsivity in adults.
Population: Adults.
Publication Dates: 1996–1997.
Scores, 3: Inattentive, Hyperactive-Impulsive, Total Percentile Rank.
Administration: Individual.
Price Data, 2006: $175 per complete kit including 50 self-report rating forms, 50 Home Version rating forms, 50 Work Version rating forms, Self-Report technical manual (1996, 43 pages), Home Version technical manual (1996, 41 pages), Work Version technical manual (1996, 40 pages), and Adult Attention Deficit Disorders Intervention manual (1997, 183 pages); $35 per 50 rating forms (specify Self-Report, Home Version, or Work Version); $22 per 50 ADDES/DSM-IV forms; $15 per technical manual (specify Self-Report, Home Version, or Work Version); $25 per Adult Attention Deficit Disorders Intervention manual; $2 per Comparing the Technical Aspects of Adult Attention-Deficit/Hyperactivity Disorder Rating Scales review.
Time: Untimed.
Comments: Behavioral rating system with three forms: Home, Work, and Self-Report; may be completed in one sitting or over a period of days.
Authors: Stephen B. McCarney and Paul D. Anderson.
Publisher: Hawthorne Educational Services, Inc.
  a) HOME VERSION.
  Comments: To be completed by a spouse or other close relative/friend who observes daily behavior in the home; best when used in conjunction with Work and Self-Report versions.
  b) WORK VERSION.
  Comments: To be completed by an employer, supervisor, or fellow employee who can closely observe the subject's work behaviors; best when used in conjunction with Work and Self-Report versions.
Cross References: For reviews by Helen Kitchens and James C. Reed, see 14:10.

[88]
Adult Basic Learning Examination, Second Edition.

Purpose: "Designed to measure the educational achievement of adults who may or may not have completed twelve years of schooling . . . also useful in evaluating efforts to raise the educational level of these adults."
Population: Adults with less than 12 years of formal schooling.

Publication Dates: 1986–1990.
Acronym: ABLE.
Administration: Group.
Levels, 3: 1, 2, 3 and placement test (SelectABLE).
Forms, 2: E, F (equivalent forms).
Price Data, 2002: $67 per examination kit containing test booklets and directions for administering for 1 form of each of the 3 levels, hand-scorable answer sheet, Ready Score® Answer Sheet and group record for Level 2, and SelectABLE Ready Score® Answer Sheet; $43.50 per Handbook of Instructional Techniques and Materials (1986, 67 pages); $51.90 per norms booklet (specify level); $13.80 per Reading Supplement.
Foreign Language Edition: Spanish edition (1990) ABLE Screening Battery available for Level 2 Reading and Mathematics subtests only.
Authors: Bjorn Karlsen and Eric F. Gardner.
Publisher: Pearson.

a) SELECTABLE.
Purpose: A screening test to determine which level of ABLE is most suitable for use with a particular individual.
Price Data: $72.60 per 25 Ready Score® Answer Sheets; $44.50 per 50 hand-scorable test sheets; $37.60 per scoring key; $12.70 per SelectABLE Handbook (1986, 15 pages).
Time: (15) minutes.

b) LEVEL 1.
Population: Adults with 1–4 years of formal education.
Scores, 5: Vocabulary, Reading Comprehension, Spelling, Number Operations, Problem Solving.
Price Data: $89 per 25 hand-scorable test booklets and directions for administering including group record (specify Form E or F); $77.40 per scoring key (specify Form E or F); $10.60 per directions for administering (1986, 38 pages).
Time: (130–165) minutes.

c) LEVEL 2.
Population: Adults with 5–8 years of formal education.
Scores: Same as *b* plus Language.
Price Data: $89 per 25 hand-scorable or reusable test booklets (specify Form E or F); $77.40 per scoring key (specify Form E or F); $79.50 per 25 Ready Score® Answer Sheets (specify Form E or F); $66.80 per 50 hand-scorable answer sheets and 2 group records; $10.60 per directions for administering Levels 2 and 3.
Time: (175–215) minutes.

d) LEVEL 3.
Population: Adults with 9–12 years of formal schooling who may or may not have completed 12 years of schooling.

Scores: Same as *c* above.
Price Data: Same as *c* above.
Time: Same as *c* above.
Cross References: See T5:82 (1 reference); for reviews by Anne R. Fitzpatrick and Robert T. Williams, see 11:9 (1 reference); see also T3:121 (6 references), 8:2 (4 references), and T2:3 (3 references); for a review by A. N. Hieronymus of the earlier edition and excerpted reviews by Edward B. Fry and James W. Hall of Levels 1 and 2 of the earlier edition, see 7:3.

[89]

Adult Language Assessment Scales.

Purpose: "Designed to provide complete information about language proficiency of adults who speak English as a Second or Foreign Language."
Population: Adults.
Publication Date: 1991.
Acronym: A-LAS®.
Scores, 10: Listening (Conversations, Same/Different, Total), Speaking (Vocabulary, Making Sentences, Newscast, Sounds, Total), Pronunciation, Total.
Administration: Individual.
Forms, 2: A and B.
Price Data, 2002: $201.95 per complete kit (Form A) including oral administration manual (28 pages) (Forms A and B), oral scoring and interpretation manual (53 pages) (Forms A and B), cue picture book (Form A), audiocassette for the oral language component (Form A), audiocassette for the additional pronunciation section (Form A), audiocassette holder, and 50 answer booklets (Form A); $142.55 per augmentation kit (Form B including cue picture book (Form B), audiocassette for oral language component (Form B), audiocassette for pronunciation section (Form B), and 50 answer booklets (Form B); $110.15 per 25 reading and mathematics booklets (specify level and Form); $75.60 per 50 writing booklets (specify Form); $43.20 per 50 reading and mathematics answer sheets (specify level); $51.85 per 50 oral answer booklets (specify form); $45.35 per 50 oral profile sheets (specify form); $31.30 per oral administration manual; $32.40 per oral scoring and interpretation manual; $45.35 per cue picture book (specify form); $20.55 per audiocassette (specify form and story).
Time: (25–30) minutes.
Comments: Includes equivalent forms, A and B.
Authors: Sharon E. Duncan and Edward A. DeAvila.
Publisher: CTB/McGraw-Hill.
Cross References: For reviews by Roger A. Richards and Wayne H. Slater, see 14:11.

[90]

Adult Level of Care Index-2R.

Purpose: "To provide assessment summation and documentation for addictions treatment planning."

Population: Adults.
Publication Date: 2001.
Acronym: LOCI-2R.
Scores: 56 ratings: 5 Acute Intoxication/Withdrawal (Outpatient Detoxification, Ambulatory Detoxification with Extended On-Site Monitoring, Clinically Managed Residential Detoxification, Medically Monitored Inpatient Detoxification, Medically Managed Intensive Inpatient Detoxification); 8 Biomedical Conditions/Complications (Outpatient Treatment, Intensive Outpatient Treatment, Partial Hospitalization, Clinically Managed Low-/Medium-/High-Intensity Residential Treatment, Medically Monitored Intensive Inpatient, Medically Managed Inpatient Services); 9 Emotional, Behavioral, or Cognitive Conditions and Complications (Early Intervention, Outpatient Services, Intensive Outpatient, Partial Hospitalization, Clinically Managed Low-/Medium-/High-Intensity Residential Treatment, Medically Monitored Intensive Inpatient Services, Medically Managed Inpatient Services); 9 Readiness to Change (Early Intervention, Outpatient Services, Intensive Outpatient Treatment, Partial Hospitalization, Clinically Managed Low-/Medium-/High-Intensity Residential Treatment, Medically Monitored Inpatient Treatment, Medically Managed Inpatient Treatment); 9 Relapse, Continued Use, or Continued Problem Potential (Early Intervention, Outpatient Treatment, Intensive Outpatient Treatment, Partial Hospitalization, Clinically Managed Low-/Medium-/High-Intensity Residential Treatment, Medically Monitored Intensive Inpatient, Medically Managed Inpatient Treatment); 9 Recovery Environment (Early Intervention, Outpatient Treatment, Intensive Outpatient Treatment, Partial Hospitalization, Clinically Managed Low-/Medium-/High-Intensity Residential Treatment, Medically Monitored Inpatient Treatment, Medically Managed Inpatient Treatment); 6 Opioid Maintenance Therapy (Acute Intoxication/Withdrawal; Biomedical Conditions and Complications; Emotional, Behavioral, or Cognitive Conditions and Complications; Readiness to Change; Relapse, Continued Use, or Continued Problem Potential; Recovery Environment); Level of Care Indicated.
Administration: Individual.
Price Data: Available from publisher.
Time: Variable.
Comments: Not a psychometric instrument; summary checklist provides an estimate of the likelihood that an individual meets the criteria for substance abuse or dependency on six dimensions in accordance with the criteria of the American Society of Addiction Medicine; also indicates overall level of care needed.
Authors: Norman G. Hoffmann, David Mee-Lee, and Gerald D. Shulman.
Publisher: Change Companies.

[91]

The Adult Manifest Anxiety Scale.

Purpose: Used to evaluate the level of anxiety experienced by individuals across the age spectrum from early adulthood to elderly.
Population: Ages 19–59, college students, ages 60 and over.
Publication Date: 2003.
Administration: Group.
Levels, 3: AMAS-A, AMAS-C, AMAS-E.
Price Data, 2006: $102 per kit including 30 AutoScore™ answer forms (10 for each subtest) and manual (44 pages); $37.95 per 20 AutoScore™ answer forms; $49.50 per manual.
Time: 10 minutes.
Comments: All three scales together represent an upward extension of the Revised Children's Manifest Anxiety Scale (2270); the original CMAS was a downward extension of the Taylor Manifest Anxiety Scale.
Authors: Cecil R. Reynolds, Bert O. Richmond, and Patricia A. Lowe.
Publisher: Western Psychological Services.
 a) AMAS-A.
 Populat ion: Ages 19–59.
 Acronym: AMAS-A.
 Scores, 5: Worry/Oversensitivity, Physiological Anxiety, Social Concerns/Stress, Lie, Worry.
 b) AMAS-C.
 Population: College students.
 Acronym: AMAS-C.
 Scores, 6: Worry/Oversensitivity, Physiological Anxiety, Social Concerns/Stress, Test Anxiety, Lie, Total.
 c) AMAS-E.
 Population: Ages 60 and over.
 Acronym: AMAS-E.
 Scores, 5: Worry/Oversensitivity, Physiological Anxiety, Fear of Aging, Lie, Total.
Cross References: For a review by Ashraf Kagee, see 16:7.

[92]

Adult Presentence Evaluation.

Purpose: Designed to assess "defendants' attitudes and behavior … at presentence, before or after conviction."
Population: Presentenced defendants.
Publication Dates: 1998-2002.
Acronym: APE.
Scores, 7: Truthfulness, Resistance, Violence (Lethality), Stress Coping Abilities, Substance Abuse/Dependency, Alcohol, Drugs.
Administration: Group.
Price Data, 2011: $8 per test; volume discounts available.

Foreign Language Edition: Spanish version available.
Time: (30-35) minutes.
Comments: May be administered via paper and pencil, computer, or human voice audio.
Author: Risk & Needs Assessment, Inc.
Publisher: Behavior Data Systems, Ltd.

[93]

Adult Pretrial Test.

Purpose: Designed for "adult chemical dependency and substance (alcohol and other drugs) abuse assessment."
Population: Misdemeanor or felony charged defendants.
Publication Dates: 1997-2002.
Acronym: APT.
Scores, 7: Validity (Truthfulness), Alcohol Severity, Drugs Severity, Substance Abuse/Dependency, Lethality (Violence), Antisocial Reaction, Stress Quotient.
Administration: Group.
Price Data, 2011: $8 per test; volume discounts available.
Foreign Language Edition: Spanish version available.
Time: (35) minutes.
Comments: May be administered via paper and pencil, computer, or human voice audio.
Author: Risk & Needs Assessment, Inc.
Publisher: Behavior Data Systems, Ltd.

[94]

Adult Rating of Oral English.

Purpose: "Designed to assess the oral English language skills of secondary and adult students" who speak English as a second language.
Population: Adult and secondary students in vocational education and employment training programs.
Publication Date: 1995.
Acronym: AROE.
Scores, 15: Pronunciation, Grammar, General Vocabulary, Vocational Vocabulary, Building Blocks Subscore; Listener and Speaker scores for Conversation, Instructions, Explanations, Clarification/Verification; Discourse Subscore; Mean Proficiency Score; Total Score.
Administration: Individual.
Price Data, 2006: $75 per training kit including 5 user's handbooks (43 pages) and 25 matrix scoring sheets; $20 per set of 25 matrix scoring sheets; $15 per user's handbook; $10 per technical manual (16 pages); $15 per supplementary video explaining use and purpose.
Time: Untimed.
Comments: A rating scale completed by teachers about individual students' skills; supplementary video explaining use and purpose is available.
Authors: Annette M. Zehler and Patricia A. DiCerbo.

Publisher: Development Associates, Inc.
Cross References: For reviews by Roger A. Richards and Gerald Tindal, see 14:13.

[95]

The Adult Self Expression Scale.

Purpose: Assesses the assertiveness level of the respondent.
Population: Adults.
Publication Dates: 1974-1975.
Acronym: ASES.
Scores: Total score only.
Administration: Group or individual.
Price Data: Available from publisher.
Time: Administration time not reported.
Authors: Melvin L. Gay, James G. Hollandsworth, Jr., and John P. Galassi.
Publisher: Adult Self Expression Scale.
Cross References: See T5:88 (2 references) and T4:107 (1 reference); for reviews by Philip H. Dreyer and Goldine C. Gleser, see 9:55 (15 references).

[96]

Adult Self-Report Inventory-4.

Purpose: Designed to be "a guide for conducting clinical interviews" and be used "as a tool to assist the clinician in making a diagnosis" and to help identify possible psychiatric disorders.
Population: Ages 18-75.
Publication Dates: 2004-2008.
Acronyms: ASRI-4; AI-4.
Scores, 20: Symptom Severity Score (Normative Data Model): Anxiety Disorders, Mood Disorders, Eating Disorders, Somatoform Disorders, Psychotic Disorders, Sleep Disorders, Impulse Control Disorders, Personality Disorders, Child-Onset Disorders, Other Disorders; Symptom Count Cutoff Score (Diagnostic Model): Anxiety Disorders, Mood Disorders, Eating Disorders, Somatoform Disorders, Psychotic Disorders, Sleep Disorders, Impulse Control Disorders, Personality Disorders, Child-Onset Disorders, Other Disorders.
Administration: Individual.
Forms, 2: Adult Self Report Inventory-4, Adult Inventory-4.
Price Data, 2011: $112 per Deluxe Kit including manual (2004, 173 pages), 50 Adult Self-Report Inventories-4, 5 Adult Inventories-4, 50 Symptom Count score sheets, and 50 Symptom Severity Profile score sheets; $235 per Deluxe Kit plus Scoring Program CD; $57 per 50 copies of Adult Self-Report Inventory-4 Checklist in Spanish or 50 copies of Adult Inventory-4 Checklist in Spanish; $44 per manual.
Foreign Language Edition: Spanish edition available.
Time: (15-20) minutes.

Comments: The assessments are taken by the patient and by a person who knows the patient well "(e.g., parent, partner, roommate)."
Authors: Kenneth D. Gadow, Joyce Sprafkin, and Margaret D. Weiss.
Publisher: Checkmate Plus, Ltd.

[97]

Adult Suicidal Ideation Questionnaire.

Purpose: "Designed to evaluate the presence and frequency of suicidal thoughts."
Population: Ages 18 and over.
Publication Dates: 1987–1991.
Acronym: ASIQ.
Scores: Total score only.
Administration: Individual or group.
Price Data, 2006: $78 per introductory kit including manual (1991, 62 pages) and 25 respondent forms.
Time: (5–10) minutes.
Author: William M. Reynolds.
Publisher: Psychological Assessment Resources, Inc.
Cross References: See T5:89 (1 reference); for reviews by Debra E. Cole and Isadore Newman, see 12:21.

[98]

Advanced Measures of Music Audiation.

Purpose: Developed to measure music aptitude.
Population: Junior high school through college.
Publication Date: 1989.
Scores, 3: Tonal, Rhythm, Total.
Administration: Group.
Price Data, 2006: $70 per complete kit including compact disc, 100 answer sheets, and manual (54 pages); $20 per 100 answer sheets; $10 per manual; $20 per set of scoring stencils (scoring stencils not part of complete kit); $25 per compact disc; scoring service available from publisher at $1 per student.
Time: 16(20) minutes.
Comments: CD player necessary for administration; upward extension of the Intermediate Measures of Music Audiation (1260).
Author: Edwin E. Gordon.
Publisher: GIA Publications, Inc.
Cross References: For reviews by Rudolf E. Radocy and James W. Sherbon, see 12:22.

[99]

Advanced Placement Examination in Art History.

Purpose: Designed to measure college-level achievement of students in art history.
Population: High school students desiring credit for college-level courses and admission to advanced courses
Publication Dates: 1972–2011.

Scores: Total score only.
Administration: Group.
Price Data: Available from publisher.
Time: 180 minutes.
Comments: Available to secondary schools for annual administration on specific days in May; inactive form and previous free-response questions available; program sponsored by the College Board with exams administered by Educational Testing Service.
Author: Educational Testing Service.
Publisher: The College Board.
Cross References: For additional information concerning an earlier edition, see 8:83. For reviews of the AP® Program, see 8:471 (2 reviews) and 7:662 (2 reviews).

[100]

Advanced Placement Examination in Biology.

Purpose: Designed to measure college-level achievement of students in biology.
Population: High school students desiring credit for college-level courses and admission to advanced courses.
Publication Dates: 1956–2011.
Scores: Total score only.
Administration: Group.
Price Data: Available from publisher.
Time: 180 minutes.
Comments: Available to secondary schools for annual administration on specific days in May; inactive form and previous free-response questions available; program sponsored by the College Board with exams administered by Educational Testing Service.
Author: Educational Testing Service.
Publisher: The College Board.
Cross References: See T5:92 (1 reference), T4:110 (1 reference), 8:381 (1 reference), and 7:807 (1 reference); for a review by Clarence H. Nelson of earlier forms, see 6:893 (1 reference); for a review by Clark W. Horton, see 5:724. For reviews of the AP® Program, see 8:471 (2 reviews) and 7:662 (2 reviews).

[101]

Advanced Placement Examination in Calculus.

Purpose: Designed to measure college-level achievement of students in calculus.
Population: High school students desiring credit for college-level courses and admission to advanced courses.
Publication Dates: 1969–2011.
Score: Total score only.
Administration: Group.
Levels, 2: AB, BC (candidate elects only one).
Price Data: Available from publisher.
Time: 195 minutes.
Comments: Available to secondary schools for annual administration on specific days in May; inactive form

and previous free-response questions available; program sponsored by the College Board with exams administered by Educational Testing Service.
Author: Educational Testing Service.
Publisher: The College Board.
    a) CALCULUS AB.
    Scores: Total score only.
    Comments: Covers differential and integral calculus topics typically included in an introductory Calculus I college course.
    b) CALCULUS BC.
    Scores: Total score plus an AB subscore.
    Comments: Covers the Calculus AB topics, as well as additional topics in differential and integral calculus, and series.
Cross References: See T5:93 (1 reference), 8:309 (1 reference), T2:742 (1 reference), 7:451 (2 references), and 6:570 (4 references); for a review by Paul L. Dressel of an earlier form, see 5:419. For reviews of the AP® Program, see 8:471 (2 reviews) and 7:662 (2 reviews).

[102]

Advanced Placement Examination in Chemistry.

Purpose: Designed to measure college-level achievement of students in chemistry.
Population: High school students desiring credit for college-level courses and admission to advanced courses
Publication Dates: 1956–2011.
Scores: Total score only.
Administration: Group.
Price Data: Available from publisher.
Time: 180 minutes.
Comments: Available to secondary schools for annual administration on specific days in May; inactive form and previous free-response questions available; program sponsored by the College Board with exams administered by Educational Testing Service.
Author: Educational Testing Service.
Publisher: The College Board.
Cross References: See T5:94 (3 references) and T4:111 (1 reference); for a review by J. Arthur Campbell, see 8:846; see also T2:1832 (1 reference) and 6:915 (1 reference); for a review by Theo A. Ashford of an earlier form, see 5:743. For reviews of the AP® Program, see 8:471 (2 reviews) and 7:662 (2 reviews).

[103]

Advanced Placement Examination in Comparative Government and Politics.

Purpose: Designed to measure college-level achievement of students in comparative government and politics.
Population: High school students desiring credit for college-level courses and admission to advanced courses.
Publication Dates: 1987–2011.

Score: Total score only.
Administration: Group.
Price Data: Available from publisher.
Time: 145 minutes.
Comments: Available to secondary schools for annual administration on specific days in May; inactive forms and previous free-response questions available; program sponsored by the College Board with exams administered by Educational Testing Service.
Author: Educational Testing Service.
Publisher: The College Board.

[104]

Advanced Placement Examination in Computer Science A.

Purpose: Designed to measure college-level achievement of students in computer science.
Population: High school students desiring credit for college-level courses and admission to advanced courses.
Publication Dates: 1988–2011.
Scores: Total score only.
Administration: Group.
Price Data: Available from publisher.
Time: 180 minutes.
Comments: Covers topics in a first-semester introductory college course in computer science; emphasizes programming in C++, programming methodology (including recursion), and procedural abstraction; also includes algorithms, data structures, and data abstraction; available to secondary schools for annual administration on specific days in May; inactive forms and previous free-response questions available; program sponsored by the College Board with exams administered by Educational Testing Service.
Author: Educational Testing Service.
Publisher: The College Board.

[105]

Advanced Placement Examination in English–Language and Composition.

Purpose: Designed to measure college-level achievement of students in English language and composition.
Population: High school students desiring credit for college-level courses and admission to advanced courses
Publication Dates: 1980–2005.
Scores: Total score only.
Administration: Group.
Price Data: Available from publisher.
Time: 195 minutes.
Comments: Available to secondary schools for annual administration on specific days in May; inactive form and previous free-response questions available; program sponsored by the College Board with exams administered by Educational Testing Service.

Author: Educational Testing Service.
Publisher: The College Board.
Cross References: See T5:97 (1 reference); for additional information and a review by Ellis Batten Page of an earlier edition, see 8:39; see also T2:51 (2 references) and 7:184 (1 reference); for a review by Robert C. Pooley of an earlier form of the English composition test, see 5:205. For reviews of the AP® Program, see 8:471 (2 reviews) and 7:662 (2 reviews).

[106]

Advanced Placement Examination in English–Literature and Composition.

Purpose: Designed to measure college-level achievement of students in English literature and composition.
Population: High school students desiring credit for college-level courses and admission to advanced courses.
Publication Dates: 1980–2011.
Scores: Total score only.
Administration: Group.
Price Data: Available from publisher.
Time: 180 minutes.
Comments: Available to secondary schools for annual administration on specific days in May; inactive form and previous free-response questions available; program sponsored by the College Board with exams administered by Educational Testing Service.
Author: Educational Testing Service.
Publisher: The College Board.
Cross References: See T4:112 (2 references); for a review by Ellis Batten Page of an earlier edition, see 8:39; see also T2:51 (2 references) and 7:184 (1 reference); for a review by Robert C. Pooley of an earlier form of the English composition test, see 5:205; for a review by John S. Diekhoff of an earlier form of the literature test, see 5:211. For reviews of the AP® Program, see 8:471 (2 reviews) and 7:662 (2 reviews).

[107]

Advanced Placement Examination in Environmental Science.

Purpose: Designed to measure college-level achievement of students in environmental science.
Population: High school students desiring credit for college-level courses and admission to advanced courses.
Publication Dates: 1998–2011.
Score: Total score only.
Administration: Group.
Price Data: Available from publisher.
Time: 180 minutes.
Comments: Available to secondary schools for annual administration on specific days in May; inactive forms

and previous free-response questions available; program sponsored by the College Board with exams administered by Educational Testing Service.
Author: Educational Testing Service.
Publisher: The College Board.

[108]

Advanced Placement Examination in European History.

Purpose: Designed to measure college-level achievement of students in European history.
Population: High school students desiring credit for college-level courses and admission to advanced courses.
Publication Dates: 1956–2011.
Scores: Total score only.
Administration: Group.
Price Data: Available from publisher.
Time: 185 minutes.
Comments: Available to secondary schools for annual administration on specific days in May; inactive form and previous free-response questions available; program sponsored by the College Board with exams administered by Educational Testing Service.
Author: Educational Testing Service.
Publisher: The College Board.
Cross References: See T5:100 (1 reference), T4:114 (1 reference), 8:908 (1 reference), and 6:1001 (2 references). For reviews of the AP® Program, see 8:471 (2 reviews) and 7:662 (2 reviews).

[109]

Advanced Placement Examination in French Language.

Purpose: Designed to measure college-level achievement of students in the French language.
Population: High school students desiring credit for college-level courses and admission to advanced courses.
Publication Dates: 1971–2011.
Scores: Total score only.
Administration: Group.
Price Data: Available from publisher.
Time: 160 minutes.
Comments: Available to secondary schools for annual administration on specific days in May; inactive form and previous free-response questions available; program sponsored by the College Board with exams administered by Educational Testing Service.
Author: Educational Testing Service.
Publisher: The College Board.
Cross References: See T3:131 (1 reference); for additional information and a review by Michio Peter Hagiwara, see 8:112. For reviews of the AP® Program, see 8:471 (2 reviews).

[110]

Advanced Placement Examination in French Literature.

Purpose: Designed to measure college-level achievement of students in French literature.
Population: High school students desiring credit for college-level courses and admission to advanced courses.
Publication Dates: 1954–2005.
Scores: Total score only.
Administration: Group.
Price Data: Available from publisher.
Time: 180 minutes.
Comments: Available to secondary schools for annual administration on specific days in May; inactive form and previous free-response questions available; program sponsored by the College Board with exams administered by Educational Testing Service.
Author: Educational Testing Service.
Publisher: The College Board.
Cross References: For additional information and reviews by Michio Peter Hagiwara and Joseph A. Murphy, see 8:113 (3 references); see also 7:268 (1 reference) and 6:368 (3 references). For a review of the AP® Program, see 8:471 (2 reviews) and 7:662 (2 reviews).

[111]

Advanced Placement Examination in German Language.

Purpose: Designed to measure college-level achievement of students in German language.
Population: High school students desiring credit for college-level courses and admission to advanced courses
Publication Dates: 1956–2011.
Scores: Total score only.
Administration: Group.
Price Data: Available from publisher.
Time: 150 minutes.
Comments: Available to secondary schools for annual administration on specific days in May; inactive form and previous free-response questions available; program sponsored by the College Board with exams administered by Educational Testing Service.
Author: Educational Testing Service.
Publisher: The College Board.
Cross References: For reviews of the AP® Program, see 8:471 (2 reviews) and 7:662 (2 reviews).

[112]

Advanced Placement Examination in Human Geography.

Purpose: Designed to measure college-level achievement of students in human geography.
Population: High school students desiring credit for college-level courses and admission to advanced courses.

Publication Dates: 2001–2011.
Score: Total score only.
Administration: Group.
Price Data: Available from publisher.
Time: 135 minutes.
Comments: Available to secondary schools for annual administration on specific days in May; inactive form and previous free-response questions available; program sponsored by the College Board with exams administered by Educational Testing Service.
Author: Educational Testing Service.
Publisher: The College Board.

[113]

Advanced Placement Examination in Latin Literature.

Purpose: Designed to measure college-level achievement of students in Latin literature.
Population: High school students desiring credit for college-level courses and admission to advanced courses.
Publication Dates: 1980–2005.
Scores: Total score only.
Administration: Group.
Price Data: Available from publisher.
Time: 180 minutes.
Comments: Available to secondary schools for annual administration on specific days in May; inactive form and previous free-response questions available; program sponsored by the College Board with exams administered by Educational Testing Service.
Author: Educational Testing Service.
Publisher: The College Board.
Cross References: For additional information concerning an earlier edition of the Classics examination, see 8:144 (3 references). For reviews of the AP® Program, see 8:471 (2 reviews) and 7:662 (2 reviews).

[114]

Advanced Placement Examination in Latin–Vergil.

Purpose: Designed to measure college-level achievement of students in Latin (Vergil).
Population: High school students desiring credit for college-level courses and admission to advanced courses
Publication Dates: 1989–2011.
Scores: Total score only.
Administration: Group.
Price Data: Available from publisher.
Time: 180 minutes.
Comments: Available to secondary schools for annual administration on specific days in May; inactive form and previous free-response questions available; program sponsored by the College Board with exams administered by Educational Testing Service.
Author: Educational Testing Service.

Publisher: The College Board.
Cross References: For additional information concerning an earlier edition of the classics examination, see 8:144 (3 references). For reviews of the AP® Program, see 8:471 (2 reviews) and 7:662 (2 reviews).

[115]

Advanced Placement Examination in Macroeconomics.

Purpose: Designed to measure college-level achievement of students in macroeconomics.
Population: High school students desiring credit for college-level courses and admission to advanced courses
Publication Dates: 1989–2011.
Score: Total score only.
Administration: Group.
Price Data: Available from publisher.
Time: 130 minutes.
Comments: Available to secondary schools for annual administration on specific days in May; inactive forms and previous free-response questions available; program sponsored by the College Board with exams administered by Educational Testing Service.
Author: Educational Testing Service.
Publisher: The College Board.

[116]

Advanced Placement Examination in Microeconomics.

Purpose: Designed to measure college-level achievement of students in microeconomics.
Population: High school students desiring credit for college-level courses and admission to advanced courses
Publication Dates: 1989–2011.
Scores: Total score only.
Administration: Group.
Price Data: Available from publisher.
Time: 130 minutes.
Comments: Available to secondary schools for annual administration on specific days in May; inactive forms and previous free-response questions available; program sponsored by the College Board with exams administered by Educational Testing Service.
Author: Educational Testing Service.
Publisher: The College Board.

[117]

Advanced Placement Examination in Music Theory.

Purpose: Designed to measure college-level achievement of students in music theory.
Population: High school students desiring credit for college-level courses and admission to advanced courses

Publication Dates: 1978–2011.
Scores, 3: Aural, Nonaural, Total.
Administration: Group.
Price Data: Available from publisher.
Time: 180 minutes.
Comments: Available to secondary schools for annual administration on specific days in May; inactive form and previous free-response questions available; program sponsored by the College Board with exams administered by Educational Testing Service.
Author: Educational Testing Service.
Publisher: The College Board.
Cross References: For additional information regarding an earlier edition of the Music Examination, see 8:90. For reviews of the AP® Program, see 8:471 (2 reviews).

[118]

Advanced Placement Examination in Physics.

Purpose: Designed to measure college-level achievement of students in physics.
Population: High school students desiring credit for college-level courses and admission to advanced courses.
Publication Dates: 1954–2011.
Administration: Group.
Levels, 3: Physics B, Physics C: Electricity and Magnetism, Physics C: Mechanics (candidate chooses only one).
Price Data: Available from publisher.
Comments: Available to secondary schools for annual administration on specific days in May; inactive forms and previous free-response questions available; program sponsored by the College Board with exams administered by Educational Testing Service.
Author: Educational Testing Service.
Publisher: The College Board.
    a) PHYSICS B.
    Scores: Total score only.
    Comments: Equivalent of 1-year terminal course in noncalculus-based college physics.
    Time: 180 minutes.
    b) PHYSICS C: Electricity and Magnetism.
    Scores: Total scores only.
    Comments: Equivalent of 1-year nonterminal course in calculus-based college physics.
    Time: 90 minutes.
    c) PHYSICS C: Mechanics.
    Comments: Equivalent of 1-year nonterminal course in calculus-based college physics.
    Time: 90 minutes.
Cross References: See T3:143 (1 reference); for a review by Mario Iona, see 8:862 (3 references); see also 6:927 (2 references); for a review by Leo Nedelsky of an earlier form, see 5:750. For reviews of the AP® Program, see 8:471 (2 reviews) and 7:662 (2 reviews).

[119]

Advanced Placement Examination in Psychology.

Purpose: Designed to measure college-level achievement of students in psychology.
Population: High school students desiring credit for college-level courses and admission to advanced courses.
Publication Dates: 1992–2011.
Scores: Total score only.
Administration: Group.
Price Data: Available from publisher.
Time: 120 minutes.
Comments: Available to secondary schools for annual administration on specific days in May; inactive forms and previous free-response questions available; program sponsored by the College Board with exams administered by Educational Testing Service.
Author: Educational Testing Service.
Publisher: The College Board.

[120]

Advanced Placement Examination in Spanish Language.

Purpose: Designed to measure college-level achievement of students in Spanish language.
Population: High school students desiring credit for college-level courses and admission to advanced courses.
Publication Dates: 1977–2011.
Scores: Total score only.
Administration: Group.
Price Data: Available from publisher.
Time: 165 minutes.
Comments: Available to secondary schools for annual administration on specific days in May; inactive form and previous free-response questions available; program sponsored by the College Board with exams administered by Educational Testing Service.
Author: Educational Testing Service.
Publisher: The College Board.
Cross References: See T3:139 (1 reference); for a review by George W. Ayer of an earlier edition, see 8:153 (1 reference); see also 7:313 (2 references) and 6:421 (1 reference). For reviews of the AP® Program, see 8:471 (2 reviews) and 7:662 (2 reviews).

[121]

Advanced Placement Examination in Spanish Literature.

Purpose: Designed to measure college-level achievement of students in Spanish literature.
Population: High school students desiring credit for college-level courses and admission to advanced courses
Publication Dates: 1977–2011.
Score: Total score only.
Administration: Group.
Price Data: Available from publisher.
Time: 190 minutes.
Comments: Available to secondary schools for annual administration on specific days in May; inactive form and previous free-response questions available; program sponsored by the College Board with exams administered by Educational Testing Service.
Author: Educational Testing Service.
Publisher: The College Board.
Cross References: For a review by George W. Ayer of an earlier edition, see 8:153 (1 reference); see also 7:313 (2 references) and 6:421 (1 reference). For reviews of the AP® Program, see 8:471 (2 reviews) and 7:662 (2 reviews).

[122]

Advanced Placement Examination in Statistics.

Purpose: Designed to measure college-level achievement of students in statistics.
Population: High school students desiring credit for college-level courses and admission to advanced courses.
Publication Dates: 1997–2011.
Score: Total score only.
Administration: Group.
Price Data: Available from publisher.
Time: 180 minutes.
Comments: Available to secondary schools for annual administration on specific days in May; inactive forms and previous free-response questions available; program sponsored by the College Board with exams administered by Educational Testing Service.
Author: Educational Testing Service.
Publisher: The College Board.

[123]

Advanced Placement Examination in Studio Art.

Purpose: Designed to measure college-level achievement of students in studio art.
Population: High school students desiring credit for college-level courses and admission to advanced courses.
Publication Dates: 1972–2005.
Scores: Total score only.
Administration: Group.
Price Data: Available from publisher.
Comments: Candidate submits materials (original works, written commentary, slides) for evaluation of quality, concentration, and breadth; available to secondary schools for annual submission of materials on specific days in May; program sponsored by the College Board with exams administered by Educational Testing Service.

Author: Educational Testing Service.
Publisher: The College Board.
Cross References: For additional information concerning an earlier edition, see 8:83. For reviews of the AP® Program, see 8:471 (2 reviews).

[124]
Advanced Placement Examination in United States Government and Politics.

Purpose: Designed to measure college-level achievement of students in United States government and politics.
Population: High school students desiring credit for college-level courses and admission to advanced courses.
Publication Dates: 1987-2011.
Score: Total score only.
Administration: Group.
Price Data: Available from publisher.
Time: 145 minutes.
Comments: Available to secondary schools for annual administration on specific days in May; inactive forms and previous free-response questions available; program sponsored by the College Board with exams by Educational Testing Service.
Author: Educational Testing Service.
Publisher: The College Board.

[125]
Advanced Placement Examination in U.S. History.

Purpose: Designed to measure college-level achievement of students in U.S. history.
Population: High school students desiring credit for college-level courses and admission to advanced courses.
Publication Dates: 1956–2011.
Scores: Total score only.
Administration: Group.
Price Data: Available from publisher.
Time: 185 minutes.
Comments: Available to secondary schools for annual administration on specific days in May; inactive form and previous free-response questions available; program sponsored by the College Board with exams administered by Educational Testing Service.
Author: Educational Testing Service.
Publisher: The College Board.
Cross References: See T5:117 (4 references), T4:127 (1 reference) and T2:1980 (1 reference); for a review by Harry D. Berg of an earlier form, see 6:1000 (1 reference); for reviews by James A. Field, Jr. and Christine McGuire, see 5:812. For reviews of the AP® Program, see 8:471 (2 reviews) and 7:662 (2 reviews).

[126]
Advanced Placement Examination in World History.

Purpose: Designed to measure college-level achievement of students in world history.
Population: High school students desiring credit for college-level courses and admission to advanced courses.
Publication Dates: 2002–2011.
Score: Total score only.
Administration: Group.
Price Data: Available from publisher.
Time: 185 minutes.
Comments: Available to secondary schools for annual administration on specific days in May; inactive form and previous free-response questions available; program sponsored by the College Board with exams administered by Educational Testing Service.
Author: Educational Testing Service.
Publisher: The College Board.

[127]
Advanced Placement Examinations.

Purpose: Designed to measure college-level achievement of students in various subject areas.
Population: High school students desiring credit for college-level courses and admission to advanced courses.
Publication Dates: 1954–1999.
Acronym: AP®.
Scores: 32 tests in 18 subject areas: Art History, Studio Art (2 portfolios: Drawing and General), Biology, Calculus AB, Calculus BC, Chemistry, Computer Science A, Computer Science AB, English Language and Composition, English Literature and Composition, Environmental Science, European History, French Language, French Literature, German Language, Government & Politics–Comparative, Government & Politics–United States, International English Language, Latin Literature, Latin–Vergil, Macroeconomics, Microeconomics, Music Theory, Physics B., Physics C (2 tests: Electricity and Magnetism, Mechanics), Psychology, Spanish Language, Spanish Literature, Statistics, United States History.
Administration: Group.
Price Data: Available from publisher.
Time: 120–200 minutes.
Comments: Available to secondary schools for annual administration on specified days in May; inactive forms and previous essay/free-response sections available; program administered by the College Board and Educational Testing Service.
Author: Educational Testing Service.
Publisher: Educational Testing Service.
Cross References: See T5:118 (1 reference) and T3:124 (1 reference); for additional information and

reviews by Paul L. Dressel and David A. Frisbie, see 8:471 (5 references); see also T2:1045 (4 references); for reviews by Warren G. Findley and Alexander G. Wesman of an earlier program, see 7:662 (3 references); see also 6:761 (5 references). For reviews of individual tests, see 8:112 (1 review), 8:113 (2 reviews), 8:126 (1 review), 8:153 (1 review), 8:846 (1 review), 8:862 (1 review), 6:893 (1 review), 6:1000 (1 review), 5:205 (1 review), 5:211 (1 review), 5:273 (1 review), 5:419 (1 review), 5:724 (1 review), 5:743 (1 review), 5:750 (1 review), and 5:812 (2 reviews).

[128]

Advanced Test Battery.

Purpose: "Designed for use in the selection, development, or guidance of personnel at graduate level or in management positions."
Population: Personnel at graduate level or in management positions.
Publication Dates: 1979–1983.
Acronym: ATB.
Administration: Group.
Levels, 2: Higher order aptitudes, Higher order aptitudes in a work setting.
Restricted Distribution: Restricted to persons who have completed the publisher's training course or members of the Division of Occupational Psychology of the British Psychological Society.
Price Data: Available from publisher.
Comments: Subtests available as separates; separate answer sheets must be used.
Authors: Roger Holdsworth (VA3, NA4, manual); Peter Saville (VA1, NA2, manual), Gill Nyfield (manual), Dave Hawkey (DA5, ST7, DT8), Steve Blinkhorn (VA3), and Alan Iliffe (NA4).
Publisher: SHL Group plc [United Kingdom].
   a) LEVEL 1. 1979–1980; HIGHER ORDER APTITUDES, 3 TESTS.
      1) *Verbal Concepts.*
      Publication Date: 1980.
      Acronym: VA1.
      Time: 15(20) minutes.
      2) *Number Series.*
      Publication Date: 1980.
      Acronym: NA2.
      Time: 15(20) minutes.
      3) *Diagramming.*
      Publication Date: 1980.
      Acronym: DA5.
      Time: 20(25) minutes.
   b) LEVEL 2. 1979–1980; HIGHER ORDER APTITUDES IN A WORK CONTEST; 4 TESTS.
      1) *Verbal Critical Reasoning.*
      Publication Date: 1983.
      Acronym: VA3.
      Time: 30(35) minutes.
      2) *Numerical Critical Reasoning.*
      Publication Dates: 1979–1983.
      Acronym: NA4.
      Time: 35(40) minutes.
      3) *Spatial Reasoning.*
      Publication Dates: 1979–1981.
      Acronym: ST7.
      Time: 20(25) minutes.
      4) *Diagrammatic Reasoning.*
      Publication Dates: 1979–1981.
      Acronym: DT8.
      Time: 15(20) minutes.

[129]

Affair–Spouse's Comprehensive Worksheets.

Purpose: Designed to "analyze the spouse's reaction to [an] affair, the impact on the marriage and everyone involved, decisions that need to be made and what needs to be done to solve the problems caused by the affair."
Population: Spouses of persons who had an affair.
Publication Dates: 1996-2010.
Scores: 14 sections: Therapy, Marriage Before the Affair, Pre-Affair, Spouse's Relationship with the Lover, Cheating Opinions, Keeping It Secret, Reaction to the Affair, Others Finding Out, Spouse's Reaction, Effects on the Person, Sex After the Affair, Decisions and Planning, Repairing the Marriage, Other Problems.
Administration: Individual.
Manual: Instructions included with the worksheet.
Price Data, 2011: Now available only in the book, "Psychological Worksheets & Assignments," which includes all 68 tests available from the publisher; $98 per book version and $48 per CD version.
Time: [20-60] minutes.
Author: Allan Roe.
Publisher: Diagnostic Specialists, Inc.

[130]

Age Projection Test.

Purpose: Designed as "an imagery test aimed at revealing self-images at various age [and self] levels and their associated structures of imagery functioning useful toward the understanding of a presented problem or a symptom."
Population: Adults.
Publication Date: 1988.
Acronym: APT.
Scores: No scores.
Administration: Individual.
Price Data: Available from publisher.
Time: [60–120] minutes.
Author: Akhter Ahsen.
Publisher: Brandon House, Inc. [No reply from publisher; status unknown].
Cross References: For reviews by Edward Aronow and Michael D. Botwin, see 12:23.

[131]

Ages & Stages Questionnaires®: A Parent-Completed Child Monitoring System, Third Edition.

Purpose: Designed to "screen young children for developmental delays-that is, to identify those children who are in need of further evaluation and those who appear to be developing typically."
Population: Ages 1 to 66 months.
Publication Dates: 1995-2009.
Acronym: ASQ-3 ™.
Scores, 5: Communication, Gross Motor, Fine Motor, Problem Solving, Personal-Social.
Administration: Individual.
Levels, 21: 2, 4, 6, 8, 9, 10, 12, 14, 16, 18, 20, 22, 24, 27, 30, 33, 36, 42, 48, 54, and 60 months.
Price Data, 2009: $249.95 per starter kit including 21 copies of questionnaires and scoring sheets, CD-ROM, user's guide (2009, 256 pages), and quick start guide; $249.95 per starter kit with Spanish questionnaires; $199.95 per 21 questionnaires, scoring sheets, and CD-ROM in English or Spanish; $50 per user's guide.
Foreign Language Edition: Questionnaires available in Spanish.
Time: (10-15) minutes.
Comments: The questionnaire is to be completed by the child's primary caregiver in the home; the authors state, however, that "professionals will need to establish the screening and monitoring system, develop the necessary community interfaces, train individuals who will score the questionnaires, and provide feedback to parents of children who are completing the questionnaires."
Authors: Jane Squires and Diane Bricker (questionnaires and user's guide); Elizabeth Twombly and LaWanda Potter (user's guide only).
Publisher: Paul H. Brookes Publishing Co., Inc.
Cross References: For reviews by Kenneth M. Hanig and by Rachel J. Valleley and Brandy M. Roane, see 18:4; for reviews by B. Ann Boyce and G. Michael Poteat of the second edition, see 16:8; for reviews by Dorothy M. Singleton and Rhonda H. Solomon of the original edition, see 14:14.

[132]

Ages & Stages Questionnaires: Social-Emotional: A Parent-Completed, Child-Monitoring System for Social-Emotional Behaviors.

Purpose: Designed to assess "children's social-emotional development."
Population: Ages 3–66 months
Publication Dates: 2002–2003.
Acronym: ASQ-SE.
Scores, 7: Self-Regulation, Compliance, Communica-tion, Adaptive Functioning, Autonomy, Affect, Interaction with People.
Administration: Individual.
Levels, 8: 6, 12, 18, 24, 30, 36, 48, and 60 month questionnaires.
Price Data, 2011: $194.95 per complete kit including user's guide (2003, 192 pages), and a boxed set of 8 photocopiable master questionnaires and corresponding scoring sheets and printable questionnaires and scoring sheets on CD-ROM; $149.95 per boxed set of 8 photocopiable master questionnaires and corresponding scoring sheets and printable questionnaires and scoring sheets on CD-ROM; $45 per user's guide.
Foreign Language Edition: Questionnaires available in Spanish.
Time: (10–15) minutes.
Comments: Parent-completed questionnaires.
Authors: Jane Squires, Diane Bricker, Elizabeth Twombly, Suzanne Yockelson, Maura Schoen Davis, and Younghee Kim.
Publisher: Paul H. Brookes Publishing Co., Inc.
Cross References: For a review by John J. Vacca, see 16:9.

[133]

Aggression Questionnaire.

Purpose: Designed to aid in evaluating an individual's aggressive responses and ability to channel those responses in a safe and constructive manner.
Population: Ages 9–88.
Publication Date: 2000.
Scores, 7: Physical Aggression, Verbal Aggression, Anger, Hostility, Indirect Aggression, Inconsistent Re-sponding, Total Score.
Administration: Individual or group.
Price Data, 2006: $99 per complete kit; $43.50 per 25 AutoScore™ answer forms; $199 per computer disk; $16.50 per 100 answer sheets; $57.75 per manual (2000, 95 pages).
Time: (10) minutes.
Comments: Updated version of the Buss-Durkee Hostility Inventory; computer scoring is available from publisher.
Authors: Arnold H. Buss and W. L. Warren.
Publisher: Western Psychological Services.
Cross References: For reviews by Johnnie A. Brown and Mary Lou Kelley, see 15:13.

[134]

AH4: Group Test of General Intelligence.

Purpose: "Designed as a group test of general intel-ligence."
Population: Ages 10 and over.
Publication Dates: 1955–1984.
Scores: Total score only.

Administration: Group.
Price Data: Price information available from publisher for tests, answer sheets, marking key, data supplement, manual (1970, 17 pages), and specimen set.
Time: 20(30–45) minutes.
Authors: A. W. Heim, K. P. Watts (test), V. Simmonds (test), and Anne Walters (data supplement).
Publisher: GL Assessment [England].
Cross References: See T5:127 (5 references), T4:137 (5 references), and T2:331 (20 references); for a review by John Nisbet, see 7:331 (12 references); for a review by John Liggett of the original edition, see 6:506; for a review by George A. Ferguson, see 5:390 (11 references).

[135]
AH5 Group Test of High Grade Intelligence.
Purpose: Designed as a test of general intelligence "for use with selected, highly intelligent subjects."
Population: Ages 13 and over.
Publication Dates: 1968–1984.
Scores, 3: Verbal and Numeric, Diagrammatic, Total.
Administration: Group.
Price Data: Price information available from publisher for tests, answer sheets, manual (1983, 21 pages), and for specimen set including test, key, answer sheet, and manual.
Time: 40(60) minutes.
Author: A. W. Heim.
Publisher: GL Assessment [England].
Cross References: See T5:128 (3 references), T4:138 (2 references), and 9:66 (1 reference).

[136]
Air Conditioning Specialist (Form SWA-C).
Purpose: For selecting candidates with knowledge of air conditioning.
Population: Applicants and incumbents for jobs requiring air conditioning knowledge and skills.
Publication Dates: 1992–2008.
Scores, 7: Print Reading/Electrical/and Test Equipment, Controls, Welding/Piping and Plumbing, Mechanical Maintenance and Machines & Equipment, Heating & Ventilation and Combustion, Air Conditioning and Refrigeration, Total.
Administration: Group.
Price Data, 2011: $22 per consumable self-scoring test booklet (minimum order of 20); $24.95 per manual (2008, 16 pages).
Foreign Language Edition: Available in Spanish.
Time: (60-70) minutes.
Comments: Online test administration available.
Author: Roland T. Ramsay.
Publisher: Ramsay Corporation.
Cross References: For a review by James A. Penny, see 17:5.

[137]
The Alcadd Test, Revised Edition.
Purpose: "Designed to: a) provide an objective measurement of alcoholic addiction that could identify individuals whose behavior and personality structure indicated that they were alcoholic addicts or had serious alcoholic problems; b) identify specific areas of maladjustment in alcoholics to facilitate therapeutic and rehabilitation activities; and c) obtain better insight into the psychodynamics of alcoholic addiction."
Population: Adults.
Publication Dates: 1949–1988.
Scores, 6: Regularity of Drinking, Preference for Drinking over Other Activities, Lack of Controlled Drinking, Rationalization of Drinking, Excessive Emotionality, Total.
Administration: Individual or group.
Editions, 2: Paper-and-pencil, microcomputer.
Price Data, 2002: $60 per complete kit including 25 AutoScore™ test/profile forms (1988, 4 pages) and manual (1988, 24 pages); $32.50 per 25 AutoScore™ test booklets; $32.50 per manual; $139.50 per microcomputer edition (IBM) including diskette (tests up to 25) and user's guide; $9.50 or less per mail-in answer sheet.
Time: (5–15) minutes.
Comments: Self-administered.
Authors: Morse P. Manson, Lisa A. Melchior, and G. J. Huba.
Publisher: Western Psychological Services.
Cross References: For reviews by William L. Curlette and Paul Retzlaff, see 11:12 (1 reference); see also T3:152 (3 references), T2:1098 (1 reference), and P:7 (3 references); for a review by Dugal Campbell, see 6:60 (6 references); for reviews by Charles H. Honzik and Albert L. Hunsicker, see 4:30.

[138]
Alcohol Dependence Scale.
Purpose: "Provides a brief measure of the extent to which the use of alcohol has progressed from psychological involvement to impaired control."
Population: Problem drinkers.
Publication Date: 1984.
Acronym: ADS.
Scores: Total score only.
Administration: Group.
Price Data: Available from publisher.
Foreign Language Edition: Questionnaire available in French.
Time: (5–10) minutes.
Comments: Test booklet title is Alcohol Use Questionnaire.
Authors: Harvey A. Skinner and John L. Horn.
Publisher: Centre for Addiction and Mental Health [Canada].

Cross References: See T5:134 (41 references) and T4:145 (5 references); for reviews by Robert E. Deysach and Nick J. Piazza, see 10:12 (1 reference).

[139]

Alcohol Use Disorders Identification Test.

Purpose: A screening procedure "to identify persons whose alcohol consumption has become hazardous or harmful to their health."
Population: Adults.
Publication Dates: 1992–1993.
Acronym: AUDIT.
Scores: Total score only.
Administration: Individual or group.
Price Data, 2001: Test and manual (88 pages) are free; $75 per training module.
Foreign Language Editions: English, Japanese, Spanish, Norwegian, Romanian, Portuguese, German, Indian, French, Swedish, Russian, Catalan, and Italian.
Time: [2] minutes.
Comments: Developed by World Health Organization and validated on primary care patients in six countries.
Authors: Thomas F. Babor, Juan Ramon de la Fuente, John Saunders, O. G. Aasland, and Marcus Grant.
Publisher: World Health Organization [Switzerland].
Cross References: For reviews by Philip Ash and Herbert Bischoff, see 14:15; see T5:135 (6 references).

[140]

Alcohol Use Inventory.

Purpose: To assess patterns of behavior, attitudes, and symptoms associated with alcohol use and abuse.
Population: Individuals 16 years and older.
Publication Date: 1987.
Acronym: AUI.
Scores, 24: Social Improvement, Mental Improvement, Manage Moods, Marital Coping, Gregarious, Compulsive, Sustained, Loss of Control, Role Maladaptation, Delirium, Hangover, Marital Problems, Quantity, Guilt and Worry, Help Before, Receptivity, Awareness, Enhanced, Obsessed, Disruption 1, Disruption 2, Anxious Concern, Receptive Awareness, Alcohol Involvement.
Administration: Group.
Price Data, 2008: $120 per Q Local software starter kit; $125 per mail-in starter kit; $159 per hand-scoring starter kit; $45.50 per manual (1987, 95 pages); $37 per user's guide for computer-based reports; $41 per 10 reusable test booklets; $22 per 25 Q Local answer sheets; $57 per 50 hand-scoring answer sheets with 50 profile forms; $17.25 per Q Local interpretive report; $9.25 per Q Local profile report; $20.25 per mail-in interpretive report; $12.25 per mail-in profile report.
Time: (35–60) minutes.

Comments: Scoring options are: hand scoring, mail-in scoring, or Q Local software; report options are: Interpretive or Profile.
Authors: John L. Horn, Kenneth W. Wanberg, and F. Mark Foster.
Publisher: Pearson.
Cross References: See T5:136 (12 references); for reviews by Robert J. Drummond and Sharon McNeely, see 12:25 (3 references); see also T4:146 (6 references).

[141]

Algebra Test for Engineering and Science: National Achievement Tests.

Purpose: Designed to screen proficiency in trigonometry and geometry.
Population: College entrants.
Publication Dates: 1958–1961.
Scores, 2: Test 1, Total.
Administration: Group.
Price Data: Available from publisher.
Time: 50(55) minutes for Test 1; 80(85) minutes for total test.
Author: A. B. Lonski.
Publisher: Psychometric Affiliates.
Cross References: For a review by Peter A. Lappan, Jr., see 6:595.

[142]

Alleman Mentoring Activities Questionnaire.

Purpose: "Measures the amount, quality and impact of mentoring activity."
Population: Mentors, proteges, and bosses.
Publication Dates: 1987–2000.
Acronym: AMAQ.
Scores, 10: Teach the Job, Provide Challenge, Teach Politics, Career Help, Protect, Sponsor, Counsel, Friendship, Demonstrate Trust, Total.
Administration: Group or individual.
Price Data, 2011: $25 per pair for assessment and graph report; student, research, and large sample discounts available from publisher; sample test and manual are available through email for $25.
Time: (10–15) minutes.
Comments: Previously listed as Alleman Mentoring Scales Questionnaire; available in paper-and-pencil or electronic format.
Authors: Elizabeth Alleman and Diana Clarke.
Publisher: Silverwood Enterprises, LLC
Cross References: See T5:139 (1 reference).

[143]

Allied Health Professions Admission Test.

Purpose: Developed to measure general academic ability and scientific knowledge.

Population: Applicants to 4-year allied health programs.
Publication Dates: 1979–1999.
Acronym: AHPAT.
Scores, 5: Verbal Ability, Quantitative Ability, Biology, Chemistry, Reading Comprehension.
Administration: Group.
Restricted Distribution: Distribution restricted and test administered at licensed testing centers; details may be obtained from publisher.
Price Data: Available from publisher.
Time: 165 minutes.
Author: The Psychological Corporation.
Publisher: Pearson.
Cross References: For reviews by Alan C. Bugbee, Jr. and Richard C. Pugh, see 12:26.

[144]

Alternate Uses.

Purpose: "Designed to represent an expected factor of 'flexibility of thinking' in an investigation of creative thinking."
Population: Grades 6–16 and adults.
Publication Dates: 1960–1978.
Scores: Total score only.
Administration: Group.
Forms, 2: Form B, C.
Price Data: Available from publisher.
Time: 12(20) minutes.
Authors: Paul R. Christensen, J. P. Guilford, Philip R. Merrifield, and Robert C. Wilson.
Publisher: Charlotte Mackley [No reply from publisher; status unknown].
Cross References: See T5:142 (8 references) and T4:154 (4 references); for a review by Edys S. Quellmalz, see 9:71 (3 references); see also T3:157 (21 references), 8:235 (32 references), T2:542 (94 references), and 6:542 (7 references).

[145]

Alzheimer's Disease Caregiver's Questionnaire.

Purpose: Designed to "evaluate the likelihood that a specific individual has a dementia suggestive of Alzheimer's Disease."
Population: Ages 40 and over.
Publication Dates: 1998–2002.
Acronym: ADCQ.
Scores, 7: Likelihood of a Dementia Consistent with or Suggestive of Alzheimer's Disease (Memory, Confusion and Disorientation, Geographic Disorientation, Behavior, Reasoning and Judgment, Language Abilities, Total).
Administration: Individual.
Price Data, 2005: $299 per introductory kit on a 3.5-inch disk including 25 paper-and-pencil versions,

software program, on-screen user's manual, installation guide, and 25 caregiver's report generations; $350 per 50 record forms with 50-use key disk.
Time: (5–10) minutes.
Comments: Symptom checklist completed by caregiver; can be administered on-line, on desk-top computer, or in paper-and-pencil format; software requires Windows 95/98/ME/NT/2000/XP and standard 3.5-inch, 1.44 MB disk.
Authors: Paul R. Solomon and Cynthia A. Murphy (manual).
Publisher: Psychological Assessment Resources, Inc.
Cross References: For reviews by Mark A. Albanese and Matthew E. Lambert, see 16:10.

[146]

Am I Musical? Music Audiation Games.

Purpose: Designed to objectively reveal a general estimate of the extent of music potential a child or adult possess.
Population: Ages 7–12, 13–adult.
Publication Date: 2003.
Scores: Total score only.
Administration: Group.
Levels, 2: Youth Game, Adult Game.
Price Data: Available from publisher.
Time: (12) minutes.
Comments: Test administered via CD; CD player needed; self-administered, self-scored.
Author: Edwin E. Gordon.
Publisher: GIA Publications, Inc.
Cross References: For reviews by Christopher M. Johnson and James W. Sherbon, see 16:12.

[147]

The AMA DISC Survey.

Purpose: Personal styles survey that focuses on the ways in which people approach their work and relate to others within their organization.
Population: Adults.
Publication Date: 2000.
Scores: 4 styles of behavior: Directing, Influencing, Supportive, Contemplative.
Administration: Individual or group.
Price Data: Price data for test materials including Facilitator's Manual (84 pages) and Debriefing Guide (47 pages) available from Human Synergistics International.
Time: 20–25 minutes.
Author: Robert A. Cooke.
Publisher: American Management Association [distributed by Human Synergistics International].

[148]

The American Drug and Alcohol Survey.

Purpose: Designed to estimate levels of drug use in youth populations.
Population: Schools and school districts.

Publication Dates: 1989–2005.
Scores: Item scores, High/Moderate/Low Drug Involvement.
Administration: Group.
Levels, 2: Grades 4–6, Grades 6–12.
Price Data: The publisher is dissolving in 2011 after completing existing contracts. They are releasing copyright to this survey instrument, and give permission to freely use it hereafter.
Time: (20–30) minutes.
Authors: Eugene R. Oetting, Frederick Beauvais, and Ruth Edwards.
Publisher: Rocky Mountain Behavioral Science Institute, Inc.
Cross References: See T5:143 (1 reference); for reviews by Jeffrey Jenkins and Steven Schinke, see 12:27; see also T4:155 (1 reference).

[149]

The American Home Scale.

Purpose: "Designed to measure the socioeconomic status of individuals and groups."
Population: Grades 8–16.
Publication Date: 1942.
Scores, 5: Cultural, Aesthetic, Economic, Miscellaneous, Total.
Administration: Group.
Price Data: Available from publisher.
Time: (35–50) minutes.
Author: W. A. Kerr.
Publisher: Psychometric Affiliates.
Cross References: See T2:1039 (5 references) and 5:596 (2 references); for reviews by Henry S. Maas and Verner M. Sims, see 3:417 (7 references).

[150]

American Invitational Mathematics Examination.

Purpose: "Provides challenge and recognition to high school students in the United States and Canada who have exceptional mathematical ability."
Population: American and Canadian high school students.
Publication Dates: 1983–2002.
Acronym: AIME.
Score: Total score only.
Administration: Group.
Manual: No manual.
Price Data: Price information available from publisher for practice examination set including past exam (specify year desired 1983–present) and solution pamphlet; other price data available from publisher.
Time: 180 minutes.
Comments: Administered annually, three weeks after the American Mathematics Competitions 12 (AMC12;

153) to students attaining a predetermined cutoff score on the AMC12.
Authors: Sponsored jointly by the Mathematical Association of America, Society of Actuaries, Mu Alpha Theta, National Council on Teachers of Mathematics, Casualty Actuarial Society, American Statistical Association, and American Mathematical Association of Two Year Colleges, and others.
Publisher: Mathematical Association of America; American Mathematics Competitions.
Cross References: For reviews by Robert W. Lissitz and Claudia R. Wright, see 11:14.

[151]

American Literacy Test.

Purpose: Constructed to assess literacy based on vocabulary.
Population: Adults.
Publication Date: 1962.
Scores: Total score only.
Administration: Group.
Price Data: Available from publisher.
Time: 4 minutes.
Author: John J. McCarty.
Publisher: Psychometric Affiliates.
Cross References: For a review by Victor H. Noll, see 6:328.

[152]

American Mathematics Competitions, Contest 8 (AMC8).

Purpose: "To increase interest in mathematics and to develop problem solving ability through a friendly competition."
Population: American and Canadian students in grade 8 or below.
Publication Dates: 1985–2001.
Acronym: AMC8.
Scores: Total score only.
Administration: Group.
Price Data, 2001: $25 per school registration fee; $10 per 10 exam booklets.
Foreign Language and Special Editions: Spanish, Braille and large-print editions available.
Time: 40 minutes.
Comments: Test administered annually in December at participating schools; test previously called American Junior High School Mathematics Examination.
Authors: Sponsored jointly by Mathematical Association of America, Society of Actuaries, Mu Alpha Theta, National Council of Teachers of Mathematics, Casualty Actuarial Society, American Statistical Association, and American Mathematical Association of Two Year Colleges.
Publisher: Mathematical Association of America; American Mathematics Competitions.

Cross References: For reviews by John M. Enger and Darrell Sabers, see 11:15.

[153]

American Mathematics Competitions, Contest 12 (AMC12).

Purpose: "To identify, through friendly competition, students with an interest and a talent for mathematical problem solving."
Population: High school students competing for individual and school awards
Publication Dates: 1950–2011.
Acronym: AMC12.
Scores: Total score only.
Administration: Group.
Price Data, 2011: $30 per school registration fee; $1.60 per exam (specify English, French, or Spanish); $6 per 10 solutions pamphlets; $1.00 per practice set of prior year exams (specify year); price data available from publisher for additional study aids and supplementary materials.
Foreign Language and Special Editions: Spanish, French, Braille, and large-print editions available.
Time: (75) minutes.
Comments: Test administered annually in February at participating secondary schools; test previously called American High School Mathematics Examination (AHSME).
Authors: Sponsored jointly by the Mathematical Association of America, Society of Actuaries, Mu Alpha Theta, National Council of Teachers of Mathematics, Casualty Actuarial Society, American Statistical Association, and American Mathematical Association of Two-Year Colleges, and others.
Publisher: Mathematical Association of America; American Mathematics Competitions.
Cross References: For reviews by Camilla Persson Benbow and Randy W. Kamphaus of the American High School Mathematics Examination, see 11:13; for a review by Thomas P. Hogan, see 8:252 (1 reference); see also T2:598 (3 references).

[154]

American Mathematics Contest 10.

Purpose: Designed to "spur interest in mathematics and to develop talent through the excitement of solving challenging problems."
Population: Grades 10 and below.
Publication Dates: 1999-2011.
Acronym: AMC10.
Scores: Total score only.
Administration: Group.
Forms: Contest A, Contest B.

Price Data, 2011: $16 per bundle of 10 exams and answer forms; $62 per Registration and Shipping fee-Contest A; $62 per Registration and Shipping fee-Contest B.
Foreign Language and Other Special Editions: French, Spanish, Braille, and large-print editions available.
Time: (75) minutes.
Authors: Sponsored jointly by Mathematical Association of America, Society of Actuaries, Mu Alpha Theta, National Council of Teachers of Mathematics, Casualty Actuarial Society, American Statistical Association, and American Mathematical Association of Two Year Colleges.
Publisher: Mathematical Association of America.
Cross References: For reviews by Camilla Persson Benbow and Randy W. Kamphaus of the American High School Mathematics Examination, see 11:13; for a review by Thomas P. Hogan, see 8:252 (1 reference); see also T2:598 (3 references).

[155]

American Numerical Test.

Purpose: Designed to assess "numerical alertness and adaptation."
Population: Adults in "vocations which emphasize shop and white collar skills."
Publication Date: 1962.
Scores: Total score only.
Administration: Group.
Price Data: Available from publisher.
Time: 4 minutes.
Author: John J. McCarty.
Publisher: Psychometric Affiliates.
Cross References: For reviews by Marvin D. Glock and Richard T. Johnson, see 6:604.

[156]

The American Occupational Therapy Association, Inc. Fieldwork Evaluation for the Occupational Therapist.

Purpose: Constructed to evaluate "student competence at the completion of each Level II fieldwork experience."
Population: Occupational therapy students.
Publication Dates: 1973–1987.
Scores, 3: Performance, Judgment, Attitude.
Administration: Individual.
Price Data: Available from publisher.
Time: Administration time not reported.
Comments: Ratings by supervisor; revision of the Field Work Performance Report (T3:885).
Author: The American Occupational Therapy Association, Inc.

Publisher: The American Occupational Therapy Association, Inc.
Cross References: For reviews by James T. Austin and Brian Bolton, see 12:28; for information on the Field Work Performance Report, see T3:885 (2 references) and 8:1107 (1 reference).

[157]

Amsterdam Short-Term Memory Test.

Purpose: Designed to be used in "neuropsychological evaluation of persons who claim to have memory and/or concentration problems, but in whom these problems are not clinically obvious, while the possibility exists that they are exaggerating or simulating their problems."
Population: Individuals who claim to have memory and/or concentration problems, but do not have clinical symptoms.
Publication Dates: 1999-2005.
Acronym: ASTM.
Scores: Total score only.
Administration: Individual.
Price Data, 2006: €350 per complete kit including manual (2005, 75 pages), computer program for administration, and 100 record forms; €49.50 per manual; €29.95 per 100 record forms.
Foreign Language Editions: Manual and record forms are also available in German and Dutch.
Time: (10-30) minutes.
Comments: Test is administered via computer; computer program is available on a CD.
Authors: Ben Schmand and Jaap Lindeboom with collaboration of Thomas Merten and Scott R. Millis.
Publisher: PITS: Psychologische Instrumenten, Tests en Services [The Netherlands].
Cross References: For a review by Daniel C. Miller, see 17:6.

[158]

Analytic Learning Disability Assessment.

Purpose: Designed to match student learning style with instructional strategies.
Population: Ages 8-14.
Publication Date: 1982.
Acronym: ALDA.
Scores: Fail, Weak, or Solid in 77 unit skill subtests.
Administration: Individual.
Price Data, 2005: $174.25 per complete kit; $55.75 per 20 test forms including test score formulation sheet and student worksheets.
Time: (75) minutes.
Authors: Thomas D. Gnagey and Patricia A. Gnagey.
Publisher: Slosson Educational Publications, Inc.
Cross References: For a review by Marcia B. Shaffer, see 9:72.

[159]

Analytical Aptitude Skills Evaluation.

Purpose: To evaluate aptitude and potential for analyzing business problems.
Population: Entry-level and experienced candidates for positions requiring the ability to analyze business problems.
Publication Date: 1993.
Acronym: AASE.
Scores: Total Score, Narrative Evaluation, Rating, Recommendation.
Administration: Group.
Price Data, 2001: $235 per candidate; quantity discounts available.
Foreign Language Edition: French version available.
Time: (60) minutes.
Comments: Scored by publisher; must be proctored.
Author: Bruce A. Winrow.
Publisher: Walden Personnel Performance, Inc.
Cross References: For a review by John S. Geisler, see 15:14.

[160]

Analytical Reasoning Skills Battery.

Purpose: Measures high level analytical reasoning skills.
Population: Adults.
Publication Date: 1998.
Acronym: ANAL.
Scores: Total Score, Narrative Evaluation, Ranking, Recommendation.
Administration: Group.
Price Data, 2001: $150 per candidate; quantity discount available.
Time: (68) minutes.
Comments: Scored by publisher; must be proctored.
Author: Bruce A. Winrow.
Publisher: Walden Personnel Performance, Inc. [Canada].

[161]

Analytical Thinking Test.

Purpose: Designed as a self-assessment exercise in analytical thinking.
Population: Adults.
Publication Dates: 1992–1994.
Scores, 2: Situations, Proposals.
Administration: Group.
Manual: No manual.
Price Data: Available from publisher.
Time: [30–40] minutes.
Comments: Self-administered, self-scored.
Author: Training House, Inc.
Publisher: Training House, Inc.

[162]
Analyzing the Communication Environment.
Purpose: "An inventory of ways to encourage communication in functional activities."
Population: Preschool to adolescent children with severe disabilities.
Publication Date: 1993.
Acronym: ACE.
Scores: Total score only.
Administration: Individual.
Price Data: Price data available from publisher for complete kit including 90-minutes VHS videotape and softbound instructor's guide (85 pages).
Time: Administration time not reported.
Authors: Charity Rowland and Philip Schweigert.
Publisher: Pearson.
Cross References: For reviews by Pat Mirenda and Sheila Pratt, see 14:16.

[163]
Anger Disorders Scale.
Purpose: "Designed to help practitioners identify clinically dysfunctional anger by assessing anger as an independent problem, rather than as a secondary symptom to another issue."
Population: Ages 18 and over.
Publication Date: 2004.
Administration: Individual or group.
Forms, 2: Anger Disorders Scale; Anger Disorders Scale: Short.
Price Data, 2011: $171 per ADS complete kit including technical manual (2004, 172 pages), 10 reusable ADS item booklets, and 25 each ADS and ADS:S QuikScore forms; $78 per technical manual; $50 per 25 ADS QuikScore forms; $50 per 25 ADS:S QuikScore forms; $29 per 10 reusable ADS item booklets. $142 per ADS Online interpretive report kit including technical manual and 25 Interpretive Reports; $6 per ADS Online Interpretive Report; $5 per ADS Online Profile Report. $146 per ADS V.5 Software kit including technical manual and 25 interpretive Reports; $56 per ADS V.5 software preview version includes 3 Interpretive Reports; $6 per ADS Software Interpretive Report; $4 per ADS Software Profile Report; $34 per 50 ADS Data Entry Sheets; $34 per 50 ADS:S Data Entry Sheets.
Authors: Raymond DiGiuseppe and Raymond Chip Tafrate.
Publisher: Multi-Health Systems, Inc.
  a) ANGER DISORDERS SCALE.
  Acronym: ADS.
  Scores, 22: Reactivity/Expression (Scope of Anger Provocations, Physiological Arousal, Duration of Anger Problems, Rumination, Impulsivity, Coercion, Verbal Expression, Total), Anger-In (Hurt/Social Rejection, Episode Length, Suspiciousness, Resentment, Tension Reduction, Brooding, Total), Vengeance (Revenge, Physical Aggression, Relational Aggression, Passive Aggression, Indirect Aggression, Total), Total.
  Time: (20) minutes.
  b) ANGER DISORDERS SCALE; SHORT.
  Acronym: ADS:S.
  Scores, 4: Reactivity/Expression, Anger-In, Vengeance, Total.
  Time: (5-10) minutes.
Cross References: For reviews by Laura L. B. Barnes and Matthew E. Lambert, see 17:7.

[164]
Anger Regulation and Expression Scale.
Purpose: Designed as "a self-report assessment of the expression and regulation of anger in children and adolescents."
Population: Ages 10-17.
Publication Date: 2011.
Acronym: ARES; ARES(S).
Scores, 25: 3 clusters, 13 scales, 8 subscales, Total Score: Internalizing Anger [Arousal (Physiological Arousal, Cognitive Arousal), Rejection, Anger-In, Bitterness (Resentment, Suspiciousness)], Externalizing Anger [Overt Aggression/Expression (Physical Aggression, Verbal Expression), Covert Aggression, Revenge, Subversion (Relational Aggression, Passive Aggression), Bullying, Impulsivity], Extent of Anger [Scope of Triggers, Problem Duration, Episode Duration].
Administration: Group.
Forms, 2: Full-length, Short.
Price Data, 2011: $180 per online kit, including technical manual (114 pages), 15 online response forms, and 15 short online response forms; $250 per complete scoring software kit, including technical manual, unlimited use scoring software (USB key), 25 response forms, and 25 short response forms; $50 per 25 response forms (full-length or short); $120 per complete scoring software program (USB key); $1.80 per online response form (full-length or short); $80 per technical manual.
Time: (15) minutes for ARES; (5) minutes for ARES(S).
Comments: May be administered via paper-and-pencil or online; online scoring or software (USB key) is required for scoring paper-and-pencil assessments.
Authors: Raymond DiGiuseppe and Raymond Chip Tafrate.
Publisher: Multi-Health Systems, Inc.

[165]
The ANSER System-Aggregate Neurobehavioral Student Health and Educational Review [Revised 1997].
Purpose: Designed as a system of collecting and integrating information from several sources about children

suspected of having developmental and/or behavioral problems.
Population: Children ages 3+, suspected of having learning difficulties.
Publication Dates: 1980–1997.
Acronym: The ANSER System.
Scores: Not scored; questionnaires cover the following areas: Parent Questionnaires (Identifying Information, Initial Background Information, Possible Pregnancy Problems, Newborn Infant Problems, Health Problems or Conditions, Early Life Problems, Early Development, Family History), Attention Control Inventory (Skills and Interests, Attention Problems, Additional Behavior Traits, Behavioral Strengths, Open-Ended Comments), School Questionnaires (Identifying Information, Difficulties and Strengths, Specific Questions, School Facilities and Programs, Previous Reports and Assessments, Developmental Functions, Attention Control Inventory, Additional Behavior Traits, Open-Ended Comments), Self-Administered Student Profile (Attention, Language Function, Spatial Motor Function, Graphomotor Function, Gross Motor Function, Memory Function, Temporal-Sequential Ordering, Efficiency, Affect, Outlook, Academic Skills, Social Function, Weekend Activities, Strengths and Weaknesses, Open-Ended Comments), Self-Administered Follow-Up Profile ("How I Think I'm Doing").
Administration: Individual.
Forms, 6: Form 1 (Ages 3–5), Form 2 (Ages 6–11), Form 3 (Ages 12+), Form 4 (Ages 9+), Form 5 (All ages), Form 6 (Ages 9+).
Price Data, 2006: $18.60 per Interpreter's Guide (1997, 56 pages); $18.60 per specimen set; $36.00 each per Forms 1–3 (Parent Questionnaire); $30.40 each per Forms 1–3 (School Questionnaire); $29.25 each per Form 4; $29.60 per 24 each of Forms 5P and 5S or Form 6; quantity discounts available.
Time: Administration time not reported.
Comments: A series of questionnaires to be completed by parents, school personnel, and students.
Author: Melvin D. Levine.
Publisher: Educators Publishing Service, Inc.
Cross References: For reviews by Robert G. Harrington and Kenneth W. Howell of an earlier edition, see 9:74.

[166]

Antisocial Process Screening Device.

Purpose: Designed to assess personality processes related to antisocial behavior in young populations.
Population: Ages 6–13
Publication Date: 2001.
Acronym: APSD.
Scores, 4: Callous/Unemotional, Impulsivity, Narcissism, Total.
Administration: Individual.

Price Data, 2011: $177 per complete kit including technical manual (84 pages), and 25 Quikscore forms for each of APSD-T, APSD-P, and APSD-C; $73 per technical manual; $53 per 25 QuikScore forms.
Time: 10 minutes per rater for Parent and Teacher forms.
Comments: Individual Parent and Teacher ratings.
Authors: Paul J. Frick and Robert D. Hare.
Publisher: Multi-Health Systems, Inc.
Cross References: For reviews by Arthur S. Ellen and Mary Lou Kelley, see 16:13.

[167]

Aphasia Diagnostic Profiles.

Purpose: "Provides a systematic method of assessing language and communication impairment associated with aphasia."
Population: Adults with acquired brain damage.
Publication Date: 1992.
Acronym: ADP.
Scores: Behavioral Profile Score plus 9 subtests: Personal Information, Writing, Reading, Fluency, Naming, Auditory Comprehension, Repetition, Elicited Gestures, Singing.
Administration: Individual.
Price Data, 2010: $190 per complete kit including 25 record forms, manual (55 pages), stimulus cards/letterboard/pointer, and carrying case; $58 per 25 record forms; $74 per manual; $63 per stimulus cards/letterboard/pointer.
Time: (40–50) minutes.
Author: Nancy Helm-Estabrooks.
Publisher: PRO-ED.
Cross References: See T5:159 (2 references); for reviews by Wilfred G. Van Gorp and Richard G. Whitten, see 13:11.

[168]

Applicant Potential Inventory.

Purpose: Designed as a pre-employment screening assessment to help determine the employability of applicants.
Population: Job applicants.
Publication Date: 1996.
Acronym: API™.
Scores, 11: Candidness, Accuracy, Customer Service, Honesty, Drug Avoidance, Employee Relations, Safety Attitudes, Work Values, Supervision Attitudes, Tenure, Employability.
Administration: Group.
Price Data: Available from publisher.
Time: (15) minutes.
Author: National Computer Systems, Inc.
Publisher: Pearson Performance Solutions [No reply from publisher; status unknown].

[169]

Applicant Productivity Profile.

Purpose: Designed "to help screen applicants with limited reading abilities for low-skill positions."
Population: Age 18 and over.
Publication Dates: 1994–1997.
Acronym: APP.
Scores: 3 scores (Validity, Reading Ease, Employability Index), and 7 supplementary scores (Honesty II, Drug Avoidance II, Employee/Customer Relations II, Safety Attitude II, Work Values II, Supervision Attitudes II, Tenure II).
Administration: Individual or group.
Price Data, 2005: $22 for 1–999 Internet scoring with booklets $22 for 1–999 Internet scoring without booklets; $22 for 1–999 Scan scoring; $22 for 1–999 Quanta-TouchTest™ scoring; $22 for 1–999 Quanta® Fax scoring; $22 for 1–999 Quanta® software for Windows with booklets; $22 for 1–999 Quanta® software for Windows without booklets.
Foreign Language Editions: Spanish and Mexican Spanish versions available.
Time: (15) minutes.
Comments: Test can be scored online, by fax, optical screening; software is available.
Author: Reid London House.
Publisher: Pearson Performance Solutions [No reply from publisher; status unknown].

[170]

Applicant Risk Profiler.

Purpose: "Designed to assist companies in determining which applicants are a potential risk or threat to their supervisors, coworkers and/or themselves."
Population: Job applicants.
Publication Date: 2001.
Acronym: ARP.
Scores, 5: Deception, Integrity, Illegal Drug Use, Workplace Policy Compliance, Workplace Aggression.
Administration: Individual.
Price Data, 2005: $99.99 per starter kit including manual (44 pages), 5 tests, and 1 test log; $34.99 per manual; $13.29 per paper-and-pencil version test (sold in quantities of 10; quantity discounts available); $13.29 per on-line test.
Time: (30) minutes.
Comments: Online and paper-and-pencil administration available; online version includes interpretive reports and follow-up interview questions.
Author: J. M. Llobet.
Publisher: G. Neil.
Cross References: For reviews by Richard E. Harding and William I. Sauser, Jr., see 17:8.

[171]

Appraise Your World™.

Purpose: Constructed "to measure the complexity and richness of the way individuals develop their personal worlds and make life choices."

Population: Adults.
Publication Dates: 1983-2001.
Acronym: AYW.
Scores: 29 dimensions: Emphasis (Career, Economic, Community, Interpersonal, Recreation, Travel, Nature, Palate, Arts, Practical Arts, Home, Romance, Family, Intellectual, Ideological, Physical, Emotional, Spiritual), World Dynamics (Level of Security, Level of Insecurity, Level of Satisfaction, Level of Dissatisfaction, Internal Focus of World, External Focus of World, Flexibility of Boundaries, Level of Growth, Balance of World, Level of Public Success, Level of Present Support).
Administration: Group.
Price Data: Available from publisher.
Time: (45) minutes.
Comments: Purchase and use requires training by publisher.
Authors: James T. Mahoney, Joan W. Chadbourne (test), and Robert I. Kabacoff (manual).
Publisher: Management Research Group.

[172]

Apraxia Battery for Adults, Second Edition.

Purpose: Designed to "verify the presence of apraxia in the adult patient and to estimate the severity of the disorder."
Population: Adults.
Publication Dates: 1979–2000.
Acronym: ABA-2.
Scores: 6 subtests: Diadochokinetic Rate, Increasing Word Length, Limb Apraxia and Oral Apraxia, Latency Time and Utterance Time for Polysyllabic Words, Repeated Trials, Inventory of Articulation Characteristics of Apraxia.
Administration: Individual.
Price Data, 2010: $147 per complete kit including 25 profile/examiner record forms, picture book, and manual (2000, 46 pages); $51 per 25 profile/examiner record forms; $57 per manual; $45 per picture book.
Time: (20) minutes.
Comments: Publisher states that the "vocabulary and conceptual structure of the six subtests allows administration of the battery to adolescents and children down to about age 9"; however, the norming group included only adults.
Author: Barbara L. Dabul.
Publisher: PRO-ED.
Cross References: For reviews by Elaine Clark and by Raymond S. Dean and John J. Brinkman, Jr., see 15:15; see T5:163 (3 references) and T4:179 (4 references); for a review by Norma Cooke of an earlier edition, see 9:77 (1 reference).

[173]

Aprenda®: La prueba de logros en español– Segunda edición.

Purpose: Designed to measure the academic achievement of Spanish-speaking students.

Publication Dates: 1990–1998.
Acronym: Aprenda 2.
Administration: Group.
Price Data, 2002: $33.90 per multiple-choice assessment kit (Preprimer–Advanced) including test booklet and directions for administering (1997, 68 pages), practice test and directions, answer document, and reviewer's edition; $17.50 per 25 practice tests and directions (Preprimer–Intermediate 3); $5.30 per single copy directions for administering practice tests (Preprimer–Intermediate 3); $13.80 per directions for administering (Preprimer–Advanced); $102 per 25 reusable test booklets (Intermediate 1–Advanced); $42.90 each per overlay keys for scoring machine-scorable answer documents (Intermediate 1–Advanced); $28.60 each per response keys (Preprimer-Advanced); $125 per 25 machine-scorable test booklets (Preprimer-Primary 3); $79.50 per 100 type 1 machine-scorable answer documents (Intermediate 1–Advanced); $6.50 per package of 25 markers/rulers (Preprimer–Advanced); $64.60 per technical manual (1998, 331 pages); $71.55 per spring or fall multilevel norms book (all levels); $21.70 per 25 preview for parents (Preprimer–Advanced, in Spanish); $21.70 per 25 understanding test results (Preprimer–Advanced); $22.80 per compendium of instructional objectives (all levels); $33.40 per guide for classroom planning (all levels); $11 per open-ended assessment kit per level across Reading, Mathematics, and Writing (Primary 1–Advanced) including one open-ended directions for administering (1997, 68 pages), and reviewer's edition; $26 per 25 open-ended test booklets for Reading, Mathematics, or Writing (Primary 1–Advanced); $32.30 per single copy scoring guides for open-ended assessments for Reading, Mathematics (Primary 1–Advanced); $9 per single copy open-ended directions for administering Reading, Mathematics, Writing (Primary 1–Advanced); $23.30 per single copy manual for Interpreting Writing (Primary 1–Advanced); Information on optional score/reporting services, package services and electronic services can be obtained by contacting the publisher.
Foreign Language Edition: Test booklets written in Spanish; content mirrors Stanford Achievement Test Series (Stanford 9; 13:292).
Author: Harcourt Brace Educational Measurement.
Publisher: Pearson.
a) PREPRIMER (PREPRIMARIO).
Population: Grades K.5–1.5.
Scores, 6: Sounds and Letters, Word Reading, Sentence Reading, Total Reading, Mathematics, Listening to Words and Stories.
Time: (140) minutes.
b) PRIMARY 1 (PRIMARIO 1).
Population: Grades 1.5–2.5
Scores, 11: 8 multiple-choice scores (Word Reading, Reading Comprehension, Total Reading, Mathematics: Problem Solving, Mathematics: Procedures, Total Mathematics, Language, Listening), and 3 open-ended scores (Reading, Mathematics, Writing).
Time: (265) minutes.
c) PRIMARY 2 (PRIMARIO 2).
Population: Grades 2.5–3.5.
Scores, 11: 8 multiple-choice scores (Reading Vocabulary, Reading Comprehension, Total Reading, Mathematics: Problem Solving, Mathematics: Procedures, Total Mathematics, Language, Listening), and 3 open-ended scores (Reading, Mathematics, Writing).
Time: (260) minutes.
d) PRIMARY 3 (PRIMARIO 3).
Population: Grades 3.5–4.5.
Scores, 11: 8 multiple-choice scores (Reading Vocabulary, Reading Comprehension, Total Reading, Mathematics: Problem Solving, Mathematics: Procedures, Total Mathematics, Language, Listening), and 3 open-ended scores (Reading, Mathematics, Writing).
Time: (280) minutes.
e) INTERMEDIATE 1 (INTERMEDIO 1).
Population: Grades 4.5–5.5.
Scores, 12: 9 multiple-choice scores (Reading Vocabulary, Reading Comprehension, Total Reading, Mathematics: Problem Solving, Mathematics: Procedures, Total Mathematics, Language, Listening, English), and 3 open-ended scores (Reading, Mathematics, Writing).
Time: (320) minutes.
f) INTERMEDIATE 2 (INTERMEDIO 2).
Population: Grades 5.5–6.5.
Scores, 12: 9 multiple-choice scores (Reading Vocabulary, Reading Comprehension, Total Reading, Mathematics: Problem Solving, Mathematics: Procedures, Total Mathematics, Language, Listening, English), and 3 open-ended scores (Reading, Mathematics, Writing).
Time: (330) minutes.
g) INTERMEDIATE 3 (INTERMEDIO 3).
Population: Grades 6.5–8.9.
Scores, 12: 9 multiple-choice scores (Reading Vocabulary, Reading Comprehension, Total Reading, Mathematics: Problem Solving, Mathematics: Procedures, Total Mathematics, Language, Listening, English), and 3 open-ended scores (Reading, Mathematics, Writing).
Time: (330) minutes.
h) ADVANCED (AVANZADO).
Population: Grades 9.0–12.9.
Scores, 9: 6 multiple-choice scores (Reading Vocabulary, Reading Comprehension, Total Reading, Mathematics, Language, English), and 3 open-ended scores (Reading, Mathematics, Writing).
Time: (265) minutes.

Cross References: For reviews by Joseph O. Prewitt and by Maria Prendes Lintel and Francisca Esteban Peterson, see 14:18; for reviews by Maria Medina-Diaz and Salvador Hector Ochoa of an earlier edition, see 13:12.

[174]

The APT Inventory.

Purpose: Designed to measure an individual's relative strength on each of ten personal traits.
Population: Adults.
Publication Date: 1992.
Scores, 10: Communication, Analytical Thinking, Administrative, Relating to Others, Influencing, Achieving, Empowering, Developing, Leadership, Ethics.
Administration: Individual or group.
Manual: No manual.
Price Data: Price information per set available from publisher (each set includes assessment, response sheet, and interpretation booklet).
Time: (40) minutes.
Comments: Self-administered; self-scored.
Author: Training House, Inc.
Publisher: Training House, Inc.
Cross References: For reviews by E. Scott Huebner and Jayne E. Stake, see 13:13.

[175]

Aptitude Assessment Battery: Programming.

Purpose: Designed to measure programming aptitude.
Population: Programmers and trainees.
Publication Date: 1967.
Acronym: AABP.
Scores: Total score only.
Administration: Group.
Restricted Distribution: Restricted to employers of programmers, not available to school personnel.
Price Data, 2001: $290 per candidate.
Foreign Language and Special Editions: French, Spanish, Braille, and left-handed editions available.
Time: Untimed.
Comments: Percentile and qualitative information provided in detailed report.
Author: Jack M. Wolfe.
Publisher: Rose Wolfe Family Partnership LLP [Canada].
Cross References: See 7:1087 (1 reference).

[176]

Aptitude Profile Test Series.

Purpose: Designed to assess a range of core cognitive abilities relevant to and known to predict success in many occupations and areas of study.
Population: Years 9–11 in Australian school system to adults.

Publication Date: 2000.
Acronym: APTS and APTS-E.
Scores, 4: Abstract Reasoning, Quantitative Reasoning, Spatial-Visual Reasoning, Verbal Reasoning.
Administration: Individual or group.
Price Data, 2006: A$19.80 per Occupational Verbal Reasoning test book; $19.80 per Occupational Quantitative Reasoning test book; $19.80 per Occupational Abstract Reasoning test book; $19.80 per Occupational Spatial Reasoning test book; $13.20 per 10 Occupational answer sheets; $25.30 per score keys; $119.90 per Occupational manual; $225.50 per Occupational specimen set (incl. one each of the above); $7.70 per Educational Verbal Reasoning test book; $7.70 per Educational Quantitative Reasoning test book; $8.80 per Educational Abstract Reasoning test book; $9.90 per Educational Spatial Reasoning test book; $10.90 per 10 Educational answer sheets; $25.30 per score keys; $105 per Educational manual (incl. score keys); $137.50 per Educational specimen set (incl. one each of the above).
Time: 30(45) minutes per test.
Authors: George Morgan, Andrew Stephanou, and Brian Simpson.
Publisher: Australian Council for Educational Research Ltd. [Australia].
a) APTITUDE PROFILE TEST SERIES.
Purpose: "Developed for use … with assessing people's abilities in relation to employment and to occupational needs of organisations and industry."
Population: Adults.
Acronym: APTS.
b) APTITUDE PROFILE TEST SERIES–EDUCATIONAL.
Purpose: "Developed for … assessing students' abilities in an educational context."
Population: Years 9–11 in Australian school system.
Acronym: APTS-E.
Cross References: For a review by Robert M. Thorndike, see 15:16.

[177]

Aptitude Tests for School Beginners.

Purpose: "Obtain a differentiated picture of certain aptitudes of school beginners."
Population: Grade 1 entrants.
Publication Dates: 1974–1994.
Acronym: ASB.
Scores, 8: Perception, Spatial, Reasoning, Numerical, Gestalt, Co-ordination, Memory, Verbal Comprehension.
Administration: Group.
Price Data: Available from publisher.
Time: (390–450) minutes for full battery, (180–240) minutes for abbreviated battery.
Comments: An abbreviated battery (Reasoning, Numerical, and Gestalt subtests) may be administered to

obtain total score only; revised 1994 norms include norms for all South-Africans, norms for nonenvironmentally disadvantaged children, and norms for environmentally disadvantaged children.

Authors: D. J. Swart (manuals), T. M. Coetzee (manual), Margaretha Tredoux (manual), and N. M. Oliver (manual).

Publisher: Human Sciences Research Council [South Africa].

Cross References: See T5:169 (1 reference) and T4:186 (1 reference).

[178]

Aptitudes Associates Test of Sales Aptitude: A Test for Measuring Knowledge of Basic Principles of Selling, Revised.

Purpose: Designed to aid in the appraisal of one aspect of sales aptitude, understanding and appreciation of sales techniques.

Population: Applicants for sales positions and general population.

Publication Dates: 1947–1983.

Scores: Total score only.

Administration: Group.

Price Data, 2006: $94.20 per package; $52.20 per specimen set; $12.95 per manual; $3.75 per scoring key.

Time: (20–30) minutes.

Author: Martin M. Bruce.

Publisher: Martin M. Bruce, Ph.D.

Cross References: See 6:1169 (6 references); for reviews by Milton E. Hahn and Donald G. Paterson, see 4:824.

[179]

Arabic Proficiency Test.

Purpose: "Designed to assess the general proficiency in listening and reading attained by English-speaking learners of Arabic."

Population: Postsecondary to adult.

Publication Date: 1994.

Acronym: APT.

Scores, 2: Listening Comprehension, Reading Comprehension.

Administration: Group.

Price Data, 2005: $25 per test; quantity discounts available; $6 per official score report.

Time: 110(150) minutes.

Comments: Multiple-choice, machine-scorable test.

Authors: University of Michigan and Center for Applied Linguistics.

Publisher: Center for Applied Linguistics.

Cross References: For reviews by James D. Brown and Atiqa Hachimi and by Antony John Kunnan, see 16:14.

[180]

Arithmetic Skills Assessment Test.

Purpose: "Designed to quickly determine the approximate mathematical abilities of students with unknown math skills."

Population: High school and adults.

Publication Dates: 1993–1999.

Scores, 3: Whole Numbers, Fractions/Mixed Numbers, Decimals.

Administration: Group.

Price Data, 2006: $89 per computer application including 1 CD-ROM, management, and documentation; $445 per site license version.

Time: (15) minutes.

Comments: Computerized, self-administered; available in Macintosh Version and Windows Version.

Author: Howard Behrns.

Publisher: Educational Activities Software.

Cross References: For reviews by Michael B. Bunch and Kevin D. Crehan, see 14:19.

[181]

Arithmetic Test (Fundamentals and Reasoning): Municipal Tests: National Achievement Tests.

Purpose: Constructed to assess arithmetic skills.

Population: Grades 3–6, 6–8.

Publication Dates: 1938–1962.

Scores, 6: Computation, Number Comparisons, Comparisons, Problem Analysis, Problems, Total.

Administration: Group.

Forms, 2: A, B.

Price Data: Available from publisher.

Time: 60 minutes over 2 sessions.

Comments: Subtest of Municipal Battery.

Authors: Robert K. Speer and Samuel Smith.

Publisher: Psychometric Affiliates.

Cross References: For reviews by Foster E. Grossnickle and Charles S. Ross, see 4:406. For reviews of the complete battery, see 5:18 (1 review), 4:20 (1 review), and 2:1191 (2 reviews).

[182]

Arithmetic Test: National Achievement Tests.

Population: Grades 3–8.

Publication Dates: 1936–1961.

Administration: Group.

Forms, 2: A, B.

Manual: No manual.

Price Data: Available from publisher.

Authors: Robert K. Speer and Samuel Smith.

Publisher: Psychometric Affiliates.

a) FUNDAMENTALS.

Purpose: Constructed to assess "speed, knowledge, and accuracy in computation."

Scores, 4: Fundamentals-Speed, Number Comparisons, Fundamentals-Skills, Total.
Time: (55–85) minutes.
b) REASONING.
Purpose: Designed to measure ability to compare, comprehend, analyze, and solve problems.
Scores, 5: Comparisons, Problem Analysis, Finding the Key to a Problem, Problems, Total.
Time: (40) minutes.
Cross References: For reviews by R. L. Morton and Leroy H. Schnell, see 2:1449; for reviews by William A. Brownell and W. J. Osburn, see 1:889.

[183]

Arizona Articulation Proficiency Scale, Third Revision.

Purpose: An "assessment measure of articulatory proficiency in children, adolescents, and adults."
Population: Ages 1.5–18 years.
Publication Dates: 1963–2000.
Acronym: Arizona-3.
Scores: Total score only.
Administration: Individual.
Price Data, 2006: $147 per kit including 42 picture cards, 25 test booklets, and manual (2000, 60 pages); $70.50 per picture cards; $28.50 per 25 test booklets, quantity discounts available; $54.50 per manual.
Time: (3) minutes.
Comments: Replaces the Arizona Articulation Proficiency Scale, Second Edition (AAPS); has updated picture cards, new gender-specific norms.
Author: Janet Barker Fudala.
Publisher: Western Psychological Services.
Cross References: For reviews by Steven Long and Roger L. Towne, see 16:15; see also T5:175 (12 references) and T4:191 (4 references); for reviews by Penelope K. Hall and Charles Wm. Martin of a previous edition, see 11:17 (12 references); see also T3:200 (8 references); for reviews by Raphael M. Haller and Ronald K. Sommers, and an excerpted review by Barton B. Proger, see 8:954 (6 references); see also T2:2065 (2 references), 7:948 (2 references), and 6:307a (2 references).

[184]

The Arizona Battery for Communication Disorders of Dementia.

Purpose: To measure "the effects and severity of Alzheimer's Disease."
Population: Alzheimer's patients.
Publication Dates: 1991–1993.
Acronym: ABCD.
Scores: 6: Mental Status, Episodic Memory, Linguistic Expression, Linguistic Comprehension, Visuospatial Construction, Total.
Administration: Individual.

Price Data, 2010: $253 per complete kit including manual (77 pages), scoring and interpretation card, 25 response record forms, stimulus book A, stimulus book B, and nail and envelope; $40 per 25 response record forms; $62 per stimulus book A; $73 per stimulus book B; $23 per scoring and interpretation card; $67 per manual.
Time: (45–90) minutes.
Authors: Kathryn A. Bayles and Cheryl K. Tomoeda.
Publisher: PRO-ED.
Cross References: For reviews by Charles J. Long and Kenneth Sakauye, see 12:31.

[185]

Arlin Test of Formal Reasoning.

Purpose: Designed to assess "individual's ability to use the eight specific concepts associated with (Piaget's) stages of formal operations"; profiles individual as "concrete, high concrete, transitional, low formal, or high formal."
Population: Grades 6-12 and adults.
Publication Date: 1984.
Acronym: ATFR.
Scores, 9: Volume, Probability, Correlations, Combinations, Propositions, Momentum, Mechanical Equilibrium, Frames of Reference, Total.
Administration: Group.
Price Data, 2002: $69 per complete kit; $37 per 35 test question booklets; $12 per 35 answer sheets; $5 per hand-scoring template; $15 per manual (28 pages).
Time: (45–50) minutes.
Author: Patricia Kennedy Arlin.
Publisher: Slosson Educational Publications, Inc.
Cross References: See T5:178 (1 reference) and T4:194 (3 references); for a review by Toni E. Santmire, see 9:80 (5 references).

[186]

Armed Services-Civilian Vocational Interest Survey.

Purpose: Designed to assess interest in careers in the armed-services and related civilian jobs.
Population: Grades 11–12.
Publication Date: 1983.
Acronym: ASCVIS.
Scores: Ratings in 8 occupational groups: Administrative/Clerical/Personnel, Communications, Computer and Data-Processing, Construction/Engineering/Craft, Mechanical/Repairer/Machining, Service and Transportation, Health and Health Care, Scientific/Technical/Electronic.
Administration: Group.
Price Data: Available from publisher.
Time: (30) minutes.
Comments: Self-administering and self-scoring; may be used in conjunction with the ASVAB (187).
Author: Robert Kauk.

Publisher: CFKR Career Materials.
Cross References: For reviews by Bruce W. Hartman and Frederick A. Schrank, see 10:13.

[187]

Armed Services Vocational Aptitude Battery [Forms 18/19].

Purpose: Intended "for use in educational and vocational counseling and to stimulate interest in job and training opportunities in the Armed Forces."
Population: High school, junior college, and young adult applicants to the Armed Forces.
Publication Dates: 1967–1992.
Acronym: ASVAB.
Scores: 3 composite scores: Academic Ability, Verbal Ability, Math Ability.
Subtests, 10: General Science, Arithmetic Reasoning, Word Knowledge, Paragraph Comprehension, Numerical Operations, Coding Speed, Auto-Shop Information, Math Knowledge, Mechanical Comprehension, Electronics Information.
Administration: Group.
Price Data: Administered free of charge at participating high schools by Department of Defense personnel.
Time: 144(180) minutes.
Comments: Several supplemental publications provide support for counseling: Counselor Manual, an interpretive guide; Technical Manual; Exploring Careers: The ASVAB Workbook; Military Careers.
Author: United States Military Entrance Processing Command.
Publisher: United States Military Entrance Processing Command.
Cross References: See T5:180 (37 references) and T4:196 (27 references); for a review by R. A. Weitzman, see 9:81 (3 references); see also T3:202 (8 references); for a review by David J. Weiss, see 8:483 (4 references); see also T2:1067 (1 reference).

[188]

Arousal Seeking Tendency Scale.

Purpose: Designed to "assess individual differences in preference for change, novelty, and risk taking."
Population: Ages 15 and older.
Publication Dates: 1978–1994.
Acronym: MAST.
Scores: Total score only.
Administration: Group or individual.
Price Data: Available from publisher for test kit including scale, scoring directions, norms, and manual (1994, 6 pages).
Time: (10–15) minutes.
Comments: Previously listed as Measure of Arousal Seeking Tendency.
Author: Albert Mehrabian.

Publisher: Albert Mehrabian.
Cross References: For a review by Gregory J. Boyle, see 13:15; for reviews by Norman S. Endler and Jon D. Swartz of an earlier edition, see 9:677; see also T3:1438 (1 reference).

[189]

Ashland Interest Assessment.

Purpose: "A career interest inventory for individuals with restricted abilities developed in response to a need for a career measure to accommodate individuals with barriers to employment due to educational, physical, emotional, cognitive, or psychiatric conditions."
Population: Adults and adolescents.
Publication Date: 1997.
Acronym: AIA.
Scores, 12: Arts and Crafts, Sales, Clerical, Protective Service, Food Service, Personal Service, Health Care, General Service, Plant or Animal Care, Construction, Transportation, Mechanical.
Administration: Group or individual.
Price Data, 2010: $88 per examination kit including manual on CD (1997, 94 pages), 5 hand-scorable question and answer booklets, 5 profile sheets, 5 scoring sheets, one set of templates, and one machine-scorable question and answer booklet for a Mail-in Extended Report; $24 per test manual on CD; $60 per 25 hand-scorable question and answer booklets; $70 per 25 response sheets (includes 25 scoring sheets and 25 profile sheets); $36 per set of templates; $75–$85 (depending on volume) per 10 machine-scorable question and answer documents for Mail-in Extended Reports; $145 per software installation package, includes 10 scoring coupons; $8 per online report.
Foreign Language Edition: Hand-scorable and machine-scorable question and answer booklets and extended reports available in French.
Time: 35 minutes.
Comments: Scored by self, mail-in scoring, computer scoring, and online scoring at www.SigmaTesting.com.
Authors: Douglas N. Jackson and Connie W. Marshall.
Publisher: SIGMA Assessment Systems, Inc.
Cross References: For reviews by Richard J. McCowan and Sheila C. McCowan and by Mary Roznowski, see 14:20.

[190]

ASIST: A Structured Addictions Assessment Interview for Selecting Treatment.

Purpose: To assess alcohol and drug use for the purpose of selecting treatment.
Population: Adults.
Publication Dates: 1984–1990.
Acronym: ASIST.
Scores: 12 sections: Identifying Information, Basic Information, Alcohol Use, Psychoactive Drug Use, Health Screen-

ing, Other Life Areas, Previous Treatment, Client Preference for Treatment, Treatment Assessment Summary, Treatment Plan, Actual Referrals, Assessment Worker's Observation.
Administration: Individual.
Price Data, 2002: C$25 per 10 questionnaires; C$35 per Assessment Handbook (1990, 200 pages).
Time: Administration time not reported.
Author: Addiction Research Foundation.
Publisher: Centre for Addiction and Mental Health [Canada].
Cross References: For reviews by Wesley E. Sime and by Nicholas A. Vacc and Gerald A. Juhnke, see 13:16.

[191]

Asperger Syndrome Diagnostic Scale.

Purpose: "Designed to assess individuals who manifest the characteristics of Asperger syndrome."
Population: Ages 5–18.
Publication Date: 2001.
Acronym: ASDS.
Scores, 6: Language, Social, Maladaptive, Cognitive, Sensorimotor, Total.
Administration: Individual.
Price Data, 2010: $113 per complete kit including 50 summary/response forms, and examiner's manual (39 pages); $57 per 50 summary response forms; $62 per examiner's manual.
Time: (10–15) minutes.
Comments: Ratings by parents, teachers, and professionals at home and school.
Authors: Brenda Smith Myles, Stacey Jones-Bock, and Richard L. Simpson.
Publisher: PRO-ED.
Cross References: For reviews by Kimberly Ann Blair and Pat Mirenda, see 15:17.

[192]

The Assertiveness Skills Inventory.

Purpose: Developed to measure an individual's level of assertiveness.
Population: Adults.
Publication Date: 1997.
Acronym: ASI.
Scores: Total score only.
Administration: Group.
Manual: No manual; scoring/instruction sheet available.
Price Data: Available from publisher.
Time: Administration time not reported.
Author: Millard J. Bienvenu.
Publisher: Millard J. Bienvenu, Northwest Publications.

[193]

Assess Expert System.

Purpose: A web-based assessment system that provides assessment for selection and development of managers and professionals.

Population: Current employees, potential employees, and candidates for promotion in professional, managerial, and sales positions.
Publication Dates: 1997-2010.
Acronym: ASSESS.
Scores: Updated and shortened versions of the Guilford Zimmerman Temperament Survey (GZTS) and Dynamic Factors Opinion Survey (DFOS) provide normative results on 24 characteristics grouped in the areas of Thinking, Working, and Relating; Intellectual Ability Tests: 7 possible scores: Watson-Glaser Critical Thinking, Raven's Standard Progressive Matrices (Abstract Reasoning), Thurstone Test of Mental Alertness, Employee Aptitude Survey 7 (EAS-7)–Verbal Reasoning, RBH Arithmetic Reasoning Test, Employee Aptitude Survey 2 (EAS-2)–Numerical Ability, Employee Aptitude Survey 1 (EAS-1)–Verbal Comprehension.
Administration: Group or individual.
Parts, 8: Access v2 Personality Survey, Watson-Glaser Critical Thinking, Raven's Standard Progressive Matrices, Thurstone Test of Mental Alertness, Employee Aptitude Survey 7 (EAS-7)–Verbal Reasoning, RBH Arithmetic Reasoning Test, Employee Aptitude Survey 2 (EAS-2)–Numerical Ability, Employee Aptitude Survey 1 (EAS-1)–Verbal Comprehension.
Price Data, 2011: $295 per one-time fee for account set-up and user training; $170 to $220 per report (depending on quantity); annual licenses for larger volume usage are available.
Foreign Language Edition: German version available.
Time: Administration time varies for each assessment.
Comments: The personality survey is the main component of the assessment. Intellectual ability tests are optional and may be given in any combination.
Author: Bigby, Havis & Associates, Inc., d/b/a Assess Systems.
Publisher: Bigby, Havis & Associates, Inc., d/b/a Assess Systems.
Cross References: For reviews by Peter F. Merenda and Stephen Olejnik of an earlier version called Assess Expert Assessment System Internet Version 1.3, see 14:21.

[194]

Assessing and Teaching Phonological Knowledge.

Purpose: Designed to assess children's reading readiness and diagnose a child's reading difficulty.
Population: Young children.
Publication Date: 1998.
Scores, 5: Acquiring Implicit Awareness of Sound Patterns in Words, Segmenting Words into Sounds, Sound Blending, Manipulating Sounds Within Words, Phonemic Recoding: Bridging to Written Words.
Administration: Individual.

Forms, 3: Screening Checklist, Parental Referral Form, Profile Sheet.
Price Data, 2006: A$133.00 per starter set including manual (144 pages), record book, checklist, and task sheets; A$69.95 per manual; A$25.95 per record book; A$17.60 per checklist (10); A$19.80 per set of task sheets.
Time: Administration time not reported.
Author: John Munro.
Publisher: Australian Council for Educational Research Ltd. [Australia].
Cross References: For reviews by Rebecca McCauley and Steven A. Stahl, see 14:22.

[195]

Assessing Motivation to Communicate.

Purpose: Designed to assess communication apprehension and willingness to communicate.
Population: Postsecondary students.
Publication Date: 1994.
Acronym: AMTC.
Scores, 5: Group Discussions, Meetings, Interpersonal Conversations, Public Speaking, Total.
Administration: Group.
Price Data: Available from publisher.
Time: Administration time not reported.
Comments: Instrument consists of two assessment tools (The Personal Report of Communication Apprehension and The Willingness to Communicate) administered on a Macintosh computer, Operating System 7.0 or higher.
Author: Speech Communication Association.
Publisher: National Communication Association.
Cross References: For reviews by Ric Brown and Claudia R. Wright, see 14:23.

[196]

Assessing Reading: Multiple Measures-Second Edition.

Purpose: Designed to "identify why a student is having reading difficulty, determine what the next step in instruction should be to remediate that difficulty, and monitor progress throughout the course of instruction."
Publication Dates: 1999-2008.
Parts, 6: Phonological Awareness, Decoding and Word Attack, Vocabulary, Comprehension, Fluency, Assessments in Spanish.
Price Data, 2010: $39 per Assessing Reading: Multiple Measures, 2nd Edition.
Authors: Linda Diamond and B. J. Thorsnes (Editors).
Publisher: Consortium on Reading Excellence, Inc.
a) CORE PHONEME DELETION TEST.
   Population: Grades K-3.
   Scores, 4: Initial Sounds, Final Sounds, First Sound/Blend, Embedded Sound/Blend.
   Administration: Individual.
   Time: (10-15) minutes.
   Author: Orna Lenchner.
b) CORE PHONOLOGICAL SEGMENTATION TEST.
   Population: Grades K-1.
   Scores, 3: Sentences into Words, Words into Syllables, Words into Phonemes.
   Administration: Individual.
   Time: (5-10) minutes.
   Author: Orna Lenchner.
c) CORE PHONEME SEGMENTATION TEST.
   Population: Grades 2-12.
   Score: Performance Level.
   Administration: Individual.
   Time: (5-10) minutes.
   Author: Orna Lenchner.
d) CORE PHONICS SURVEY.
   Population: Grades K-12.
   Score: Mastery English.
   Administration: Individual.
   Time: (10-15) minutes.
   Author: Consortium On Reading Excellence.
e) SAN DIEGO QUICK ASSESSMENT OF READING ABILITY.
   Population: Grades K-11.
   Score: Reading Level.
   Administration: Individual.
   Time: 10 minutes.
   Author: Margaret La Pray et al.
f) CORE GRADED HIGH-FREQUENCY WORD SURVEY.
   Population: Grades K-4, older struggling readers.
   Score: Mastery.
   Administration: Individual.
   Time: (5-7) minutes.
   Author: Consortium on Reading Excellence.
g) CORE VOCABULARY SCREENING.
   Population: Grades 1-8.
   Score: Vocabulary Screening.
   Administration: Group.
   Time: (10-20) minutes.
   Author: Michael Milone.
h) CORE READING MAZE COMPREHENSION TEST.
   Population: Grades 2-10.
   Score: Correct Replacement.
   Administration: Group.
   Time: 3 minutes.
   Author: Michael Milone.
i) MASI-R ORAL READING FLUENCY MEASURE.
   Population: Grades 1-6.
   Score: Oral Reading Fluency.
   Administration: Individual.
   Time: (10-15) minutes.
   Authors: Kenneth W. Howell, Michelle K. Hosp, and Mada Kay Morehead.

j) CORE SPANISH PHONEMIC AWARENESS TEST.
Population: Grades K-2.
Scores, 2: Phoneme Oddity, Phoneme Deletion.
Administration: Individual.
Time: (5-10) minutes.
Author: Jacalyn Mahler.
k) CORE SPANISH PHONICS SURVEY.
Score: Mastery Spanish.
Administration: Individual.
Time: (10-15) minutes.
Author: Consortium On Reading Excellence.
l) CORE SPANISH SPELLING INVENTORY.
Population: Grades K-6.
Score: Performance Score.
Administration: Group.
Time: (10-15) minutes.
Author: Jacalyn Mahler.
m) CRITCHLOW SPANISH VERBAL LANGUAGE SCALES.
Population: Grades K-8.
Score: Grade Level.
Administration: Individual.
Time: 15 minutes.
Author: Donald E. Critchlow.

[197]

Assessing Your Team: Seven Measures of Team Success.

Purpose: Intended to give insight and understanding in assessing a team.
Population: Teams.
Publication Date: 1994.
Scores, 7: Purpose, Role, Strategy, Processes, People, Feedback, Interfaces.
Administration: Group.
Price Data: Available from publisher.
Time: [.5] day.
Authors: Dick Richards and Susan Smyth.
Publisher: Jossey-Bass, A Wiley Company.
Cross References: For a review by Peter F. Merenda, see 14:24.

[198]

Assessment, Evaluation, and Programming System for Infants and Children (AEPS®): Second Edition.

Purpose: Designed "to assist interventionists and caregivers in developing functional and coordinated assessment, goal development, intervention and evaluation activities for young children who have or who are at risk for disabilities."
Population: Birth to 3 years, 3 to 6 years.
Publication Dates: 1993-2002.
Acronym: AEPS®.

Scores, 7: 6 developmental areas: Fine Motor, Gross Motor, Adaptive, Cognitive, Social-Communication, Social; 1 Total raw score.
Administration: Individual or group.
Levels, 2: Birth to Three Years, Three to Six Years.
Price Data, 2009: $239 per 4-Volume Set, including Volume 1: Administration Guide (2002, 336 pages), Volume 2: Test: Birth to Three Years and Three to Six Years (2002, 304 pages), Volume 3: Curriculum for Birth to Three Years (2002, 512 pages), Volume 4: Curriculum for Three to Six Years (2002, 352 pages); $179 per Administration Guide, Test, and choice of Birth to Three Years Curriculum or Three to Six Years Curriculum; $65 per each Volume 1: Administration Guide, Volume 3: Curriculum for Birth to Three Years, Volume 4: Curriculum for Three to Six Years; $75 per Volume 2: Test: Birth to Three Years and Three to Six Years; $249.95 per Forms on CD-ROM; annual subscription to web-based management system AEPS-interactive (AEPSi) priced at $19.95-$16.95 per child record, depending on the number of children (1-500) for whom data are being managed (the user is directed to contact the publisher if data will be managed for more than 500 children).
Foreign Language Edition: CD-ROM Forms also available in Spanish; CODRF also available in AEPSi in Spanish.
Time: Administration time varies.
Comments: Administration time depends on several factors; recommended to be administered over a 2-week period to permit observation of the child in a variety of activities. AEPS can also be used for children up to age 9 with significant delays. AEPS is a curriculum-based assessment, not a norm-referenced assessment. As such, the Child Observation Data Recording Form (CODRF) is used by the professional to organize and display assessment information gathered in the six developmental areas that are assessed. Observations for up to four test sessions may be recorded on the CODRF. AEPS is a flexible assessment system designed so that professionals may choose the developmental areas and the number of children who are assessed at each testing session. Each developmental area in each level is composed of strands, or behaviors that are developmentally related. An appendix is included in the Administration Guide that links a child's performance on each developmental area with Individualized Family Service Plan or Individualized Education Program goals. The test elicits family participation through the use of the Family Report Form, which encourages family assessment of the child. AEPSinteractive (AEPSi) is a "web-based management system (www.aepsi.com) [that] streamlines AEPS administration, provides new reporting features, and includes sets of activities that allow users to assess multiple children at the same time."

Authors: Diane Bricker, Betty Capt, Kristie Pretti-Frontczak, JoAnn Johnson, Kristine Slentz, Elizabeth Straka, and Misti Waddell.
Publisher: Paul H. Brookes Publishing Co., Inc.
Cross References: For review by James Van Haneghan, see 18:5.

[199]

Assessment for Persons Profoundly or Severely Impaired.

Purpose: Designed to measure the responsiveness of a preverbal individual's communicative functioning.
Population: Infants through adults who are preverbal and functioning with a mental age between approximately 0 and 8 months.
Publication Dates: 1984–1998.
Acronym: APPSI.
Administration: Individual.
Price Data, 2010: $208 per complete kit including examiner's manual (1998, 31 pages), 25 record booklets, 25 profile/summary forms, set of cards, and other manipulatives; $57 per examiner's manual; $57 per 25 record booklets; $34 per 25 profile/summary forms; $67 per object kit.
Time: Untimed.
Comments: A revision of the Preverbal Assessment–Intervention Profile (T4:2093).
Authors: Patricia Connard and Sharon Bradley-Johnson.
Publisher: PRO-ED.
a) STAGE I.
Population: Mental age 0–1 month.
Scores: 4 domains: Visual Responsiveness, Auditory Responsiveness, Tactile Responsiveness, Interaction with Others.
b) STAGE II.
Population: Mental age 1–4 months.
Scores: Same as *a* above.
c) STAGE III.
Population: Mental age 4–8 months.
Scores: 2 domains: Responsiveness to Objects, Interaction with Others.
Cross References: For reviews by Carolyn Mitchell-Person and Lawrence J. Ryan, see 15:18; for reviews by Karen T. Carey and Joe Olmi of the earlier edition, see 11:301.

[200]

Assessment Inventory for Management.

Purpose: "For screening candidates for insurance field sales management positions."
Population: Managers.
Publication Dates: 1991–1993.
Acronym: AIM.
Scores, 19: 7 Job Task Areas [Basic Task Areas (Staffing/Recruiting and Selection, Training, Performance Management–Supervision, Total); Advanced Task Areas (Business Management, Field Office Development, Total)]; 12 Job Behaviors [Interpersonal Relations (Communicating, Counseling, Supporting), Leadership (Delegating, Motivating, Rewarding, Team Building, Networking), Organization (Coordinating, Monitoring, Planning, Problem-Solving and Decision-Making)].
Administration: Group.
Price Data: Available from publisher.
Foreign Language Edition: French Canadian edition (1992) available.
Time: (120–180) minutes.
Comments: Mail-in scoring.
Author: LIMRA International.
Publisher: LIMRA International.
Cross References: For reviews by Connie Kubo Della-Piana and Gabriel M. Della-Piana and by Cyril J. Sadowski, see 13:17.

[201]

Assessment of Adaptive Areas.

Purpose: Designed to identify deficits in 10 adaptive skill areas of mental retardation.
Population: Ages 3–60+ years.
Publication Date: 1996.
Acronym: AAA.
Scores, 10: Communication, Self-Care, Home-Living, Social, Community Use, Self-Direction, Health and Safety, Functional Academics, Leisure, Work.
Administration: Individual.
Price Data, 2006: $108 per complete kit including examiner's manual (143 pages) and 25 profile/examiner record booklets; $53 per examiner's manual; $59 per 25 profile/examiner record booklets.
Time: (30) minutes.
Comments: The AAA is a system of reassigning the items from the Adaptive Behavior Scale–Residential and Community: Second Edition (2) and the Adaptive Behavior Scale–School: Second Edition (3) into the 10 adaptive skill areas delineated by the American Association on Mental Retardation.
Authors: Brian R. Bryant, Ronald L. Taylor, and Diane Pedrotty Rivera.
Publisher: PRO-ED.
Cross References: For reviews by Jack A. Cummings and by Mark D. Shriver and Merilee McCurdy, see 14:25.

[202]

Assessment of Chemical Health Inventory.

Purpose: "Designed to evaluate the nature and extent of adolescent and adult chemical use and associated problems."
Population: Adolescents, adults.
Publication Dates: 1988–1992.

Acronym: ACHI.

Scores: 9 factors (Chemical Involvement, Alienation, Family Estrangement, Personal Consequence, Depression, Family Support, Social Impact, Self Regard, Family Chemical Use) yielding Total score.

Administration: Individual.

Price Data: Price available from publisher for starter set including microcomputer disk containing 25 administrations and user manual (1992, 119 pages), response forms, microcomputer disk (sold in multiples of 50) to administer and score ACHI, and manual.

Time: (15–25) minutes.

Comments: Requires 4th grade reading level; may be taken and scored on computer (or administered on paper); mail-in service available.

Authors: Daniel Krotz, Richard Kominowski, Barbara Berntson, and James W. Sipe.

Publisher: RENOVEX Corporation.

Cross References: For reviews by Philip Ash and Betsy Waterman, see 13:18.

[203]

Assessment of Classroom Communication and Study Skills.

Purpose: Designed to "provide classroom teachers and specialists with a tool that efficiently comments on the quality of a student's school language skills."

Population: Grades 5-12.

Publication Dates: 1998-2000.

Acronym: ACCSS.

Scores, 2: Total Score, Vocabulary Score.

Administration: Group or individual.

Forms, 3: ACCSS-Long Form, ACCSS-Short Form, ACCSS-esl.

Price Data, 2006: $40 per test and manual (1998, 211 pages).

Time: (40-60) minutes.

Comments: Criterion-referenced measure; includes an audio cassette containing the administration scenario; revised and expanded edition of the Classroom Communication Screening Procedure.

Author: Charlann S. Simon.

Publisher: Thinking Publications.

Cross References: For reviews by Thomas Emerson Hancock and S. Kathleen Krach, see 17:9.

[204]

Assessment of Classroom Environments.

Purpose: "Identifies [teachers'] preferences [and approaches] for establishing classroom environments [by comparing] the Leadership Model, the Guidance Model, and the Integrated Model."

Population: Teachers.

Publication Dates: 2000-2008.

Acronym: ACE.

Scores: 3 models (Leadership, Guidance, Integration) for each of 8 scales: Self-Attributions, Self-Reflections, Ideal Teacher, Peers, Students, Supervisors, General Form, Comparative Form.

Administration: Group.

Forms, 8: Self-Attributions (ratings by teacher), Self-Reflections (ratings by teacher [teacher's perception of how students, peers, and supervisors view teacher]), 4 Observation Checklists (General Form [ratings by "community members, parents, visitors, [or] college students in teacher preparation programs"], Peer Form [ratings by teacher's peers], Student Form [ratings by teacher's students], Supervisor Form [ratings by teacher's supervisors]), Ideal Checklist (ratings by teacher [teacher's perception of the ideal classroom environment]), Comparative Form (ratings by teacher [comparison of the teacher's classroom environment, other professional teachers' classroom environment, and the ideal classroom environment]).

Price Data, 2009: $50 per 25 Self-Attributions forms; $50 per 25 Self-Reflections forms; $50 per 25 Observation Checklist-General forms; $50 per 25 Observation Checklist-Peer forms; $50 per 25 Observation Checklist-Student forms; $50 per 25 Observation Checklist-Supervisor forms; $50 per 25 Ideal Checklist forms; $50 per 25 Comparative forms; $40 per test manual (2008, 34 pages); $.40 per scoring/profiling per scale; $40 per analysis report.

Time: Administration time not reported.

Authors: Louise M. Soares and Anthony T. Soares (test).

Publisher: Castle Consultants.

Cross References: For reviews by Amanda Nolen and Steven W. Schmidt, see 18:6.

[205]

Assessment of Competencies for Instructor Development.

Purpose: To measure six competencies important to being an effective instructor in an industrial setting.

Population: Instructors in industrial settings.

Publication Date: 1986.

Scores, 7: Analyzing the Needs and "Entering Behavior" of the Learner, Specifying Outcomes and "Terminal Behaviors" for a Course, Designing Instructional Sequences and Learning Materials, Instructing in Both the Inductive and Deductive Modes, Maintaining Adult-to-Adult (not "Parent-Child") Relationships in Class, Staying Learner-Centered not Information-Centered, Overall Instructional Competency.

Administration: Individual or group.

Manual: No manual.

Price Data: Price information available from publisher for 20 tests, 20 interpretation brochures, and 20 response sheets.

Time: (45) minutes.
Comments: Self-administered, self-scored.
Author: Training House, Inc.
Publisher: Training House, Inc.
Cross References: For a review by Stephen F. Davis, see 11:20.

[206]

Assessment of Comprehension and Expression 6–11.

Purpose: Designed to "assess language development."
Population: Ages 6-0 to 11-11.
Publication Date: 2002.
Acronym: ACE 6–11.
Administration: Individual.
Price Data: Available from publisher.
Comments: Subtests may be administered individually although it is recommended that a minimum of three subtests be employed.
Authors: Catherine Adams, Rosanne Cooke, Alison Crutchley, Anne Hesketh, and David Reeves.
Publisher: GL Assessment [England].
a) MAIN TEST.
    Scores, 6: Sentence Completion, Inferential Comprehension, Naming, Syntactic Formulation, Semantic Decisions, Total.
    Time: (26–32) minutes.
b) EXTENDED TEST.
    Scores, 10: Same as above with the addition of Non-Literal Comprehension, Narrative Propositions, Narrative Syntax/Discourse, Total.
    Time: (46–59) minutes.
Cross References: For reviews by Cleborne D. Maddux and Sheila Pratt, see 16:16.

[207]

Assessment of Conceptual Organization (ACO): Improving Writing, Thinking, and Reading Skills.

Purpose: Developed to assess "understanding of conceptual organization in written language."
Population: Grades 4-6, 7-12, 10-adult.
Publication Date: 1991.
Acronym: ACO.
Scores: 3 criteria: Correct Superordinate Word Chosen, Appropriateness of Topic Sentence, Relatedness of Topic Sentence and Three Other Sentences.
Administration: Group.
Price Data, 2001: $4.99 per set of 20 assessment and 20 scoring forms (select level); $9.99 per manual (57 pages).
Time: (15-20) minutes.
Comments: Optional administration and scoring procedures available for "reluctant" writers.

Author: Christian Gerhard.
Publisher: Research for Better Schools, Inc.
Cross References: For reviews by Deborah L. Bandalos and Dale P. Scannell, see 12:34.

[208]

Assessment of Core Goals.

Purpose: Constructed to define core goals and to identify activities that will lead to satisfaction of these goals.
Population: High school and over.
Publication Date: 1991.
Acronym: ACG.
Scores: No scores, workbook developmental format.
Administration: Group or individual.
Price Data: Available from publisher (www.mindgarden.com).
Time: (60-600) minutes.
Comments: Method and length of administration depends on desired depth of information.
Author: C. W. Nichols.
Publisher: Mind Garden, Inc.
Cross References: For reviews by Gary J. Dean and Carol Kehr Tittle, see 12:35.

[209]

Assessment of Individual Learning Style: The Perceptual Memory Task.

Purpose: "To provide measures of the individual's perception and memory for spatial relationships; visual and auditory sequential memory; intermediate term memory; and discrimination of detail."
Population: Ages 4 and over.
Publication Dates: 1984–1993.
Acronym: PMT.
Scores: 7 scores, 3 alternate scores: Spatial Relations, Visual Designs Recognition, Visual Designs-Sequencing, Auditory-Visual Colors Recognition, Auditory-Visual Colors Sequencing, Discrimination Recall, Total PMT, Visual-Visual (alternate), Auditory-Auditory (alternate), Visual-Auditory (alternate).
Administration: Individual.
Price Data, 2011: $550 per complete kit including carrying case containing various subtest components, 25 scoring forms, 25 alternate forms, and manual (129 pages); $49 per 25 scoring forms; $27.50 per 25 alternate forms; $82.50 per manual; $350 per PMT computer (Windows or Macintosh) report.
Time: (30–40) minutes.
Comments: PMT Computer Report (2003) is available for Windows or Macintosh and for use in profiling PMT scores for ages 14 through adult.
Author: Lawrence McCarron.
Publisher: McCarron-Dial Systems, Inc.
Cross References: For reviews by Steven Ferrara and Arlene Coopersmith Rosenthal, see 11:21 (1 reference).

[210]

Assessment of Intelligibility of Dysarthric Speech.

Purpose: Designed "to provide clinicians and researchers with a means of measuring intelligibility and speaking rate of dysarthric individuals."

Population: Adult and adolescent dysarthric speakers.

Publication Dates: 1981–1984.

Scores, 6: Single Word Intelligibility (Transcription, Multiple Choice), Sentence Intelligibility (Transcription, Speaking Rate, Rate of Intelligible Speech, Communication Efficiency Ratio).

Administration: Individual.

Price Data, 2010: $114 per complete kit including examiner's manual (60 pages) and picture book of stimulus words and sentences.

Time: Administration time not reported.

Authors: Kathryn M. Yorkston, David R. Beukelman, and Charles Traynor.

Publisher: PRO-ED.

Cross References: See T5:209 (5 references) and T4:217 (3 references); for reviews by Katharine G. Butler and C. Dale Carpenter, see 10:19.

[211]

Assessment of Language-Related Functional Activities.

Purpose: Designed to answer the question, "Despite this person's impairment, is he or she able to integrate skills adequately to perform selected functional daily activities?"

Population: People with suspected language or cognitive compromise, aged 16 to 95.

Publication Date: 1999.

Acronym: ALFA.

Scores: 10: Telling Time, Counting Money, Addressing an Envelope, Solving Daily Math Problems, Writing a Check and Balancing a Checkbook, Understanding Medicine Labels, Using a Calendar, Reading Instructions, Using the Telephone, Writing a Phone Message.

Administration: Individual.

Price Data, 2010: $179 per complete kit including 25 profile/examiner record forms, picture book, examiner's manual (39 pages), and an additional materials kit; $40 per materials kit including 10 tokens, clock, medicine chart, and 25 envelopes; $30 per 25 profile/examiner record forms; $63 per picture book; $51 per examiner's manual.

Time: (30–120) minutes.

Authors: Kathleen Anderson Baines, Heidi McMartin Heeringa, and Ann W. Martin.

Publisher: PRO-ED.

Cross References: For reviews by Steven R. Shaw and by T. Steuart Watson and R. Anthony Doggett, see 15:19.

[212]

Assessment of Literacy and Language.

Purpose: Designed to "diagnose children who exhibit language disorders and to identify children who are at risk for later reading disabilities."

Population: Grades PK-1.

Publication Date: 2005.

Acronym: ALL.

Administration: Individual.

Levels, 4: Pre-K (Fall and Spring), K-Fall, K-Spring, 1st Grade (Fall and Spring).

Price Data, 2007: $261 per complete kit including manual (2005, 200 pages), stimulus book, 25 parent questionnaires, 25 record forms, and story cards; $42 per 25 parent questionnaires; $52 per 25 record forms; $78 per stimulus book; $105 per manual.

Time: (60) minutes.

Authors: Linda J. Lombardino, R. Jane Lieberman, and Jaumeiko J. C. Brown.

Publisher: Pearson.

a) PRE-K.

Scores, 16: 6 subtest scores (Letter Knowledge, Rhyme Knowledge, Basic Concepts, Receptive Vocabulary, Parallel Sentence Production, Listening Comprehension); 4 index scores (Emergent Literacy, Language, Phonological, Phonological-Orthographic); 6 criterion-referenced scores (Book Handling, Concept of Word, Matching Symbols, Word Retrieval, Rapid Automatic Naming, Invented Spelling).

b) K-FALL.

Scores, 18: Same as for Pre-K plus Elision and Word Relationships subtest scores.

c) K-SPRING.

Scores, 21: Same as for K-Fall plus Phonics Knowledge, Sound Categorization, and Sight Word Recognition subtest scores.

d) 1st GRADE.

Scores, 21: Same as for K-Spring.

Cross References: For reviews by Abigail Baxter and Mildred Murray-Ward, see 18:7.

[213]

Assessment of Living Skills and Resources.

Purpose: Assesses "daily tasks that require a high level of cognitive function," or Instrumental Activities of Daily Living (IADLs), "in community-dwelling elders."

Population: Community-dwelling elders.

Publication Data: 1991.

Acronym: ALSAR.

Scores: 11 task scores: Telephoning, Reading, Leisure, Medication Management, Transportation, Shopping, Meal Preparation, Laundering, Housekeeping, Home Maintenance.

Administration: Individual.

Price Data: Price data available from publisher for master of the reproducible ALSAR, and each of two instructional videotapes ("An Overview of IADL Assessment" and "Administration of the ALSAR"); master of the ALSAR included in the latter videotape.

Time: (15–20) minutes.

Comments: Incorporates assessment of Instrumental Activities of Daily Living (IADL); administered by health professionals from any discipline.

Authors: Theresa J. K. Drinka, Jane H. Williams, Martha Schram, Jean Farrell-Holtan, and Reenie Euhardy.

Publisher: Madison Geriatric Research, Education, and Clinical Center, VA Medical Center.

Cross References: For reviews by Cameron J. Camp and Anita M. Hubley, see 13:20.

[214]

Assessment of Parenting Skills: Infant and Preschooler.

Purpose: Designed to "evaluate the parenting skills of parents of children between birth and five years of age."

Population: Parents of children between birth and 5 years of age.

Publication Dates: 1998–2002.

Acronym: APSIP.

Scores, 13: Discipline, Fears (Stranger Anxiety, Mobility Fears, Separation Fears, Nightmares and Night Terrors, Fears of Real Events, Abstract Fears, Doctors and Dentists), Tantrums, Crying, Individual Differences and Temperament, Daily Routine, Parental Strengths and Weaknesses.

Administration: Individual.

Price Data, 2002: $189 per complete kit including 8 booklets, 8 summary sheets, and instruction manual (21 pages); $99 per 8 booklets with summary sheets; $159 per 16 booklets with summary sheets; $199 per 24 booklets with summary sheets; $119 per instruction manual.

Time: [45] minutes.

Author: Gail Elliot.

Publisher: Village Publishing.

Cross References: For a review by T. Steuart Watson, see 14:26.

[215]

The Assessment of Personal Goals.

Purpose: Designed to assist the individual "to seriously consider life goals based on the APG Taxonomy of Human Goals, and organize them according to importance."

Population: Adults.

Publication Dates: 1988–2004

Scores, 24: Task Goals (Mastery, Task Creativity, Management, Material Gain, Safety), Self-Assertive Social Relationship Goals (Individuality, Self-Determination, Superiority, Resource Acquisition), Integrative Social Relationship Goals (Belongingness, Social Responsibility, Equity, Resource Provision), Cognitive Goals (Curiosity, Understanding, Intellectual Creativity, Positive Self-Evaluations), Affective Goals (Excitement, Tranquility, Happiness, Bodily Sensations, Physical Well-Being), Subjective Organization Goals (Unity, Transcendence).

Administration: Individual

Price Data: Available from publisher.

Time: Administration time not reported.

Comments: Self-administered and self-scored; web-based administration and reporting available (www.mindgarden.com).

Authors: Martin E. Ford and Charles W. Nichols.

Publisher: Mind Garden, Inc.

[216]

Assessment of Practices in Early Elementary Classrooms.

Purpose: "Designed to evaluate the use of developmentally appropriate practices in early elementary classrooms … that include children with disabilities."

Population: Kindergarten through Grade 3 classrooms.

Publication Date: 2001.

Acronym: APEEC.

Scores: Total score only.

Administration: Group or individual.

Manual: No manual.

Price Data, 2006: $13.95 per booklet (39 pages).

Time: Administration time not reported.

Comments: Assesses three domains of classroom practices: physical environment, curriculum and instruction, social context.

Authors: Mary Louise Hemmeter, Kelly L. Maxwell, Melinda Jones Ault, and John W. Schuster.

Publisher: Teachers College Press.

Cross References: For reviews by Edward J. Daly III and Michael Persampieri and by Kathleen A. Dolgos, see 15:20.

[217]

Assessment of Qualitative and Structural Dimensions of Object Representations, Revised Edition.

Purpose: Designed to measure aspects of an individual's conceptualization of others.

Population: Adolescents and adults (patients and normals).

Publication Dates: 1981–1992.

Acronym: AQSDOR.

Scores: Ratings in 4 areas: Personal Qualities, Degree of Ambivalence in Description, Length of Description, Conceptual Level.

Administration: Group.

Price Date: Available from publisher.

Time: (5) minutes per description.

Comments: Subjects' descriptions of significant figures (e.g., parent) rated by judges; no reading by examinees.
Authors: Sidney J. Blatt, Eve S. Chevron, Donald M. Quinlan, Carrie E. Schaffer, and Steven Wein.
Publisher: Sidney J. Blatt.
Cross References: For a review by C. H. Swensen, see 9:92.

[218]

Assessment of School Needs for Low-Achieving Students: Staff Survey.

Purpose: Designed to measure "staff perceptions as to whether certain behaviors are occurring in their school."
Population: Teachers and administrators.
Publication Dates: 1988–1989.
Acronym: ASNLAS.
Scores, 9: School Programs and Policies, Classroom Management, Instruction, Teacher Expectations, Principal Leadership, Staff Development, Student Involvement in Learning, School Climate, Parent Involvement.
Administration: Group.
Price Data, 2001: $2 per survey booklet; $.25 per scoring form; $18.95 per manual (1989, 44 pages).
Time: (45–50) minutes.
Authors: Francine S. Beyer and Ronald L. Houston.
Publisher: Research for Better Schools, Inc.
Cross References: For a review by Dean H. Nafziger and Ann M. Muench, see 11:22.

[219]

Assessment of Spirituality and Religious Sentiments.

Purpose: Designed to measure spirituality constructs "with individuals across a wide range of faith traditions."
Population: Ages 15 and over.
Publication Dates: 1999–2010.
Acronym: ASPIRES.
Scores, 7: Religiosity, Religious Crisis, Prayer Fulfillment, Universality, Connectedness, Total Religious Sentiments, Total Spiritual Transcendence.
Administration: Group or individual.
Forms, 4: Self-Report, Observer Rating, Self-Report Short Form, Observer Rating Short Form.
Price Data, 2010: $.50 per Self-Report Long Form; $.50 per Self-Report Short Form; $.50 per Observer Rating Long Form; $.50 per Observer Rating Short Form; $25 per Scoring and Interpretive Manual; $50 per Scoring Software 2007 Excel; $50 per Scoring Software 2003 Excel.
Foreign Language Editions: Also available in Spanish, Tagalog, Czech, Polish, Chinese, Malay, and Korean.
Time: Approximately 10 minutes.
Author: Ralph L. Piedmont.
Publisher: Ralph L. Piedmont [the author].

[220]

Assessor Employment Values Inventory.

Purpose: "A measure of personal values associated with work and the working environment."
Population: Adults.
Publication Dates: 1988–2001.
Scores, 14: Work Ethic, Social Outgoingness, Risk-Taking, Stability, Responsibility, Need For Achievement, Task Orientation, Leadership, Training and Development, Innovation, Intellectual Demands, Status, Structure, Inclusion.
Administration: Individual or group.
Price Data: Available from publisher.
Time: (30–40) minutes.
Comments: Computer administration and scoring available; test previously listed as Employment Values Inventory.
Author: Selby MillSmith Limited.
Publisher: Penna Assessment PLC [England] [No reply from publisher; status unknown].
Cross References: For reviews by Julie A. Allison and Nambury S. Raju, see 14:139.

[221]

Assessor Occupational Relationships Profile.

Purpose: Designed to assess a person's preferred styles of working with colleagues.
Population: Adults.
Publication Dates: 1991–2001.
Scores, 18: Core Scales (Contact at Work, Membership, Power, Responsiveness, Openness, Shyness); Composite Scales (Sociability, Proactivity); Special Scales (Team, Individual, Leadership Overall, Leadership-Coach, Leadership-Fighter, Leadership-Expert, Preferred Style of Leader Overall, Preferred Style of Leader-Coach, Preferred Style of Leader-Fighter, Preferred Style of Leader-Expert).
Administration: Individual or group.
Price Data: Available from publisher.
Time: (30) minutes.
Comments: Computer administration and scoring available; previously listed as Occupational Relationships Profile.
Author: Selby MillSmith, Ltd.
Publisher: Penna Assessment PLC [England] [No reply from publisher; status unknown].
Cross References: For a review by Robert W. Hiltonsmith, see 13:215.

[222]

Assessor Occupational Type Profile.

Purpose: Designed to measure individual's preferences related to the manner in which they acquire information and make decisions based on that information.
Population: Adults.

Publication Dates: 1991–2001.
Scores, 5: Extraversion/Introversion, Sensing/Intuition, Thinking/Feeling, Judgement/Perception, Uncertainty.
Administration: Individual or group.
Price Data: Available from publisher.
Time: (20) minutes.
Comments: Computer administration and scoring available; previously listed as Occupational Type Profile.
Author: Selby MillSmith Ltd.
Publisher: Penna Assessment PLC [England] [No reply from publisher; status unknown].
Cross References: For a review by Steven J. Lindner, see 14:261.

[223]

Association Adjustment Inventory.

Purpose: "Designed for use as a screening instrument for maladjustment and immaturity."
Population: Normal and institutionalized adults.
Publication Dates: 1959–1984.
Acronym: AAI.
Scores, 3: Juvenility, Psychotic Responses, Depressed-Optimistic, Hysteric-Non-Hysteric, Withdrawal-Sociable, Paranoid-Naive, Rigid-Flexible, Schizophrenic-Objective, Impulsive-Restrained, Sociopathic-Empathetic, Psychosomapathic-Physical Contentment, Anxious-Relaxed, Total.
Administration: Group.
Price Data, 2006: $98.75 per test package; $65.25 per IBM answer sheet/profile sheet package; $56.50 per set of IBM scoring stencils; $25 per set of fan type keys; $43.50 per manual (15 pages) and manuals supplement (1984, 17 pages); $76.50 per IBM format specimen set with keys; $26.50 per IBM format specimen set without keys; $49.50 per fan key specimen set.
Foreign Language Editions: Spanish and German editions available.
Time: (10) minutes.
Comments: Adaptation of the Kent-Rosanoff Word List.
Author: Martin M. Bruce.
Publisher: Martin M. Bruce, Ph.D.
Cross References: For reviews by W. Grant Dahlstrom and Bertram R. Forer and an excerpted review by Edward S. Bordin, see 6:201.

[224]

Athletic Motivation Inventory.

Purpose: Constructed to measure the personality and motivation of athletes participating in competitive sports.
Population: Male and female athletes ages 13 and older and coaches.
Publication Dates: 1969–1995.
Acronym: AMI.

Scores, 14: Drive, Aggressiveness, Determination, Responsibility, Leadership, Self-Confidence, Emotional Control, Mental Toughness, Coachability, Conscientiousness, Trust, Validity Scales (Accuracy, Desirability, Completion Rate).
Administration: Group or individual.
Price Data: Available from publisher.
Foreign Language Editions: French and Spanish editions available.
Time: (40–50) minutes.
Comments: May be used for individual self-assessment.
Authors: Thomas A. Tutko, Leland P. Lyon, and Bruce C. Ogilvie.
Publisher: Athletic Success Institute.
  a) ATHLETIC SUCCESS PROFILE.
  Publication Dates: 1968–1995.
  Acronym: ASP.
  Price Data: Available from publisher.
  Manual: No manual.
  Time: (20) minutes.
  Comments: Shortened version of the Athletic Motivation Inventory.
Cross References: For a review by John W. Shepard, see 12:37; for a review by Andrew L. Comrey of an earlier edition, see 8:409 (19 references).

[225]

Attention Deficit Disorder Checklist.

Purpose: Designed "to collect behavioral data" as a preliminary assessment for further in-depth evaluation.
Population: School-aged children.
Publication Dates: 1990–1995.
Scores: Not scored.
Administration: Individual or group.
Price Data, 2002: $10 per 25 checklists.
Time: Administration time not reported.
Comments: "This checklist is designed to collect behavioral data. It is not intended for diagnosis. It should be completed by adults familiar with the child's behavior in various settings—preferably the parent/guardian and the classroom teacher. It may be used for educational intervention or as a prereferral tool for further in-depth testing."
Author: Academic Consulting & Testing Service.
Publisher: Academic Consulting & Testing Service.

[226]

Attention Deficit Disorders Evaluation Scale Secondary-Age Student.

Purpose: "Designed to provide a measure of those characteristics of Attention-Deficit/Hyperactivity Disorder."
Population: Ages 11.5–19.
Publication Date: 1996.
Acronym: ADDES-S.
Scores, 3: Inattentive, Hyperactive/Impulsive, Total Percentile Rank.

Administration: Individual or group.

Forms, 3: Home, School, DSM-IV.

Price Data, 2006: $232 per complete kit including 50 Pre-Referral Attention Deficit Checklists, 50 Intervention Strategies documentation forms, 50 School Version rating forms, 50 Home Version rating forms, 50 ADDES/DSM-IV forms, School Version technical manual, Home Version technical manual, Attention Deficit Disorders Intervention Manual: Secondary-Age Student, and Parent's Guide; $30 per 50 Pre-Referral Attention Deficit Checklists; $30 per 50 intervention Strategies documentation forms; $35 per 50 rating forms (specify School Version or Home Version); $22 per 50 ADDES/DSM-IV forms; $15 per technical manual (specify School Version or Home Version); $30 per Attention Deficit Disorders Intervention Manual: Secondary-Age Student; $20 per Parent's Guide; $35 per computerized Quick Score (Windows).

Time: (15–20) minutes.

Comments: Ratings by parents/guardians and/or teachers.

Author: Stephen B. McCarney.

Publisher: Hawthorne Educational Services, Inc.

Cross References: For reviews by Helen Kitchens and Joseph G. Law, Jr., see 14:28.

[227]

Attention Deficit Disorders Evaluation Scale–Third Edition.

Purpose: Designed "to provide a measure of the ADHD characteristics of inattention and hyperactivity-impulsivity in the DSM-IV."

Population: Ages 4-18.

Publication Dates: 1989–2004.

Acronym: ADDES-3.

Scores: 3: Inattentive, Hyperactive-Impulsive, Total Score.

Administration: Individual.

Forms, 2: School Version, Home Version.

Price Data, 2006: $232 per complete kit including 50 Pre-Referral Attention Deficit checklists, 50 Intervention Strategies Documentation forms, School Version technical manual (2004, 48 pages), 50 School Version rating forms, Home Version technical manual (2004, 48 pages), 50 Home Version rating forms, 50 ADDES-3/DSM-IV forms, Attention Deficit Disorders Intervention manual, and the Parent's Guide to Attention Deficit Disorders; $15 per technical manual (specify School or Home Version); $30 per Attention Deficit Disorders Intervention manual; $35 per 50 rating forms (specify School or Home Version); $30 per 50 Intervention Strategies Documentation forms; $30 per 50 Pre-Referral Attention Deficit checklists; $22 per 50 ADDES-3/DSM-IV forms; $20 per Parent's Guide to Attention Deficit Disorders; $35 per Quick Score computerized Windows program (specify English or Spanish); $35 per 50 Spanish rating forms (specify School or Home Version).

Foreign Language Edition: Spanish edition available.

Time: (20) minutes.

Comments: Scale is rated by parent/caregiver or an educator.

Authors: Stephen B. McCarney and Tamara J. Arthaud.

Publisher: Hawthorne Educational Services, Inc.

Cross References: For reviews by Timothy J. Makatura and Jamie G. Wood, see 17:10; for reviews by Hugh W. Glenn and Beverly M. Klecker of the second edition, see 14:27; for reviews by Deborah Collins and Stephen Olejnik of the original edition, see 12:38 (1 reference).

[228]

Attention-Deficit/Hyperactivity Disorder Test.

Purpose: Designed to "contribute to the diagnosis of students with Attention-Deficit/Hyperactivity Disorder."

Population: Ages 3–23.

Publication Date: 1995.

Acronym: ADHDT.

Scores: 3 subtests (Hyperactivity, Impulsivity, Inattention), plus ADHD Quotient.

Administration: Individual.

Price Data, 2010: $124 per complete kit including manual (46 pages) and 50 summary/response forms in storage box; $57 per 50 summary/response forms; $73 per manual.

Time: (5–10) minutes.

Comments: Ratings by teacher, teacher's aide, or parent.

Author: James E. Gilliam.

Publisher: PRO-ED.

Cross References: For reviews by Robert S. Miller and Anthony W. Paolitto, see 14:30.

[229]

Attention-Deficit Scales for Adults.

Purpose: Designed as an objective measure of attention deficit in adults.

Population: Adults.

Publication Date: 1996.

Acronym: ADSA.

Scores, 11: Attention-Focus/Concentration, Interpersonal, Behavior-Disorganized Activity, Coordination, Academic Theme, Emotive, Consistency/Long Term, Childhood, Negative-Social, Internal Consistency, Total.

Administration: Individual.

Price Data: Available from publisher.

Time: Untimed.

Comments: A 54-item, Likert-scale questionnaire to be administered in a clinical setting; self-report.

Authors: Santo James Triolo and Kevin Richard Murphy.

Publisher: Routledge (Taylor and Francis Group) [England].
Cross References: For reviews by Joseph G. Law, Jr. and James C. Reed, see 14:29.

[230]

Attention Test Linking Assessment and Services.

Purpose: "To provide a comprehensive assessment system for diagnosing and remediating ADHD."
Population: Ages 8-18.
Publication Dates: 2001-2007.
Acronym: ATLAS.
Administration: Individual.
Forms, 5: Parent Attention Report, Teacher Attention Report, Attention Performance Assessment, Examiner's Observation Report, Mental Health Interview Screener.
Price Data, 2008: $250 per ATLAS kit including examiner's manual (2007, 129 pages) and 25 each of the Parent/Teacher Attention Report forms, Mental Health Interview Screener, Examiner's Observation Report forms, Attention Performance Summary Report forms, Youth Response booklets, and Client Profile Summary Report forms; $70 per 50 Parent/Teacher Attention Report forms; $40 per 25 Mental Health Interview Screener; $35 per 25 Examiner's Observation Report forms; $35 per 25 Attention Performance Summary Report forms; $40 per 25 Subject Response booklets; $35 per 25 Client Profile Summary Report forms; $65 per examiner's manual.
Time: (50) minutes.
Authors: Gregory R. Anderson and Patricia C. Post.
Publisher: Stoelting Co.

a) PARENT ATTENTION REPORT.
Scores, 6: Inattention, Concentration/Sustained Attention, Organization, Impulsivity, Hyperactivity, Divided Attention.
b) TEACHER ATTENTION REPORT.
Scores, 6: Inattention, Concentration/Sustained Attention, Organization, Impulsivity, Hyperactivity, Divided Attention.
c) ATTENTION PERFORMANCE ASSESSMENT.
Scores, 16: Sustained Attention/Vigilance, Random Letter Response-Vigilance, Trails A (Pathways 1), Complex Figure/Complex Figure for Organization, Memory (Verbal and Spatial), Digit Memory Span Forward, Verbal Memory-Superspan List, Complex Figure/Complex Figure by Memory, Working Memory, Trails B (Pathways 2) Shifting Sets/Attention, Serial Subtraction (7's), Digits Memory Span Reverse, Divided Attention, Divided/Alternating Attention: Cancellation of 4's/Trails A (Pathways 1), Verbal Fluency, Fluency for Names.
d) EXAMINER'S OBSERVATION.
Scores, 8: Inattention, Concentration, Impulse Control, Hyperactivity, Organization for Task Completion, Social Skills, Irritability, Motor Difficulties.

e) MENTAL HEALTH INTERVIEW SCREENER.
Scores, 8: Oppositional Defiant/Conduct Disorderd, Obsessive-Compulsive Disorder, Depression, Bipolar Disorder, Post-Traumatic Stress Disorder (PTSD), Generalized Anxiety Disorder (GAD), Autistic Spectrum Disorder.
Cross References: For reviews by Mary (Rina) M. Chittooran and by Tawnya J. Meadows and Eric Grady, see 18:8.

[231]

The Attentional and Interpersonal Style Inventory.

Purpose: "Developed to measure the critical concentration and interpersonal determinants of performance."
Population: Adults and adolescents.
Publication Dates: 1993–1996.
Acronym: TAIS.
Scores: 18 scales: Attentional (Broad External Awareness, External Distractibility, Conceptual/Analytical, Internal Distractibility, Narrow/Focused, Reduced Flexibility), Interpersonal (Information Processing, Orientation Toward Rules and Risk/Impulse Control, Need for Control, Self Esteem, Physical Competitiveness, Decision Making Speed, Extroversion, Introversion, Expression of Ideas, Expression of Criticism, Expression of Support, Self Critical).
Administration: Individual or group.
Price Data: Certification and test pricing available from publisher.
Time: [20–25] minutes.
Comments: Can be administered via pencil and paper, computer, or the internet.
Author: Robert M. Nideffer.
Publisher: Enhanced Performance Systems, Inc.
Cross References: For reviews by Phillip L. Ackerman and Eugene V. Aidman, see 14:31; see also T5:226 (2 references).

[232]

Attitudes and Values Questionnaire.

Purpose: Assesses "secondary school students' social, moral and spiritual development."
Population: Current and past (less than 10 years out) secondary school students.
Publication Date: 2008.
Acronym: AVQ.
Scores, 7: Conscience, Compassion, Emotional Growth, Social Growth, Service of Others, Commitment to God, Commitment to Jesus.
Administration: Group.
Forms, 3: Program A (focuses on social dimensions only), Program B (focuses on social dimensions and commitment to God), Program C (focuses on social dimensions, commitment to God, and commitment to Jesus).

Price Data, 2009: A$7.90 per Survey Form; contact publisher for cost of scoring and report service; manual (2008, 38 pages) is free to print from publisher's website: www.acer.edu.au/avq.

Time: (30) minutes.

Comments: Developed "with the support of John XXIII College in Perth"; available online or in paper-and-pencil format; publisher provides scoring and summary report; each form contains item level summaries (109 [Program A], 130 [Program B], 152 [Program C]) and averaged summaries for 5 social dimensions (Conscience, Compassion, Emotional growth, Social Growth, Service of Others) and 2 religious dimensions (Commitment to God [Programs B and C], Commitment to Jesus [Program C]; some items are "check statements [that] show whether respondents are answering the questionnaire thoughtfully" and are not included in report; data are aggregated across like subjects; client school's scores are separated by gender and year level, and are compared "against 'All Schools' results"; summary report does not provide data for individual students.

Author: Australian Council for Educational Research Ltd.

Publisher: Australian Council for Educational Research Ltd. [Australia].

[233]

Attitudes Toward Working Mothers Scale.

Purpose: "Designed to assess attitudes toward the … dual role of mother and worker."

Population: Adults.

Publication Date: No date on test materials.

Acronym: AWM.

Scores: Total score only.

Administration: Group.

Price Data: Free of charge for inventory, scoring instructions, and mimeographed paper on construction validation of scale (23 pages).

Time: Administration time not reported.

Authors: Toby J. Tetenbaum, Jessica Lighter, and Mary Travis.

Publisher: Toby J. Tetenbaum.

Cross References: See T4:229 (1 reference); for reviews by Mark W. Roberts and Charles Wenar, see 9:99 (1 reference).

[234]

Attitudes Towards Guns and Violence Questionnaire.

Purpose: Designed to measure "attitudes concerning guns, physical aggression, and interpersonal conflict."

Population: Ages 6–29.

Publication Date: 2000.

Acronym: AGVQ.

Scores, 6: Total (Favorable or Unfavorable to Violence and Guns), Inconsistent Responding, Aggressive Response to Shame, Comfort with Aggression, Excitement, Power/Safety.

Administration: Group.

Price Data, 2006: $99 per kit including 25 score forms, manual, and 50 Aggressive Behavior checklists (25 teacher forms and 25 student forms); $37.95 per 25 answer forms; $49.50 per manual; $27.50 per 100 Aggressive Behavior checklists (teacher or student form); $105 per Windows scoring computer disk (good for 50 uses); $16.50 per 100 PC answer sheets.

Time: (5–10) minutes.

Author: Jeremy P. Shapiro.

Publisher: Western Psychological Services.

Cross References: For reviews by Stephen E. Trotter and Delores D. Walcott, see 15:22.

[235]

Auditory Continuous Performance Test.

Purpose: "Designed to help … identify children who have auditory attention disorders … Also yields information that will help diagnose children as having Attention Deficit/Hyperactivity Disorder."

Population: Ages 6 to 11.

Publication Date: 1994.

Acronym: ACPT.

Scores, 4: Inattention Errors, Impulsivity Errors, Total Error Score, Vigilance Decrement.

Administration: Individual.

Price Data, 2002: $109 per complete kit including examiner's manual (52 pages), test audiocassette, and 12 record forms; $16 per 12 record forms; $48 per examiner's manual; $59 per 1 test audiocassette.

Time: (15) minutes.

Author: Robert W. Keith.

Publisher: Pearson.

Cross References: See T5:229 (1 reference); for reviews by Nadeen L. Kaufman and Alan S. Kaufman and by Joseph G. Law, Jr., see 13:22.

[236]

Auditory Processing Abilities Test.

Purpose: Designed to assess auditory processing.

Population: Ages 5-0 through 12-11.

Publication Date: 2004.

Acronym: APAT.

Scores, 20: Phonemic Awareness, Word Sequences, Semantic Relationships, Sentence Memory, Cued Recall, Content Memory, Complex Sentences, Sentence Absurdities, Following Directions, Passage Comprehension, Global Index, Auditory Memory Index, Linguistic Processing Index, Auditory Discrimination Index (optional), Auditory Sequencing Index (optional), Auditory Cohesion Index (optional), Immediate Recall Index (optional), Delayed Recall Index (optional), Sequential Recall Index (optional), Cued Recall Index (optional).

Administration: Individual.

Price Data, 2006: $112 per complete kit including examiner's manual (95 pages), 25 test booklets, 25 summary sheets in portfolio; $42 per manual; $45 per 25 test booklets; $25 per 25 summary sheets.
Time: (30–45) minutes.
Authors: Deborah Ross-Swain and Nancy Long.
Publisher: Academic Therapy Publications.
Cross References: For reviews by Jeffery P. Braden and Kelly M. Laugle and by Christopher A. Sink and Rick Eigenbrood, see 16:17.

[237]
Auditory Selective Attention Test.
Purpose: Designed as "a measure of auditory selective attention."
Population: Adults.
Publication Date: 1993.
Acronym: ASAT.
Scores: Total Errors.
Administration: Individual.
Price Data, 2002: $100 per test (cassette tape); $5 per manual (15 pages).
Time: 30(35) minutes.
Comments: Stereo tape player and a pair of stereo headphones must be supplied by the examiner.
Authors: Winfred Arthur, Jr., Gerald V. Barrett, and Dennis Doverspike.
Publisher: Barrett and Associates, Inc.
Cross References: See T5:231 (1 reference); for reviews by William W. Deardorff and Judy R. Dubno, see 13:23.

[238]
Auditory Skills Assessment.
Purpose: Designed for the "early identification of young children who might be at risk for auditory skill deficits and/or early literacy skill difficulties."
Publication Date: 2010.
Acronym: ASA.
Administration: Individual.
Price Data, 2010: $174 per complete test kit including examiner's manual (53 pages), 25 record forms, stimulus book, and stimulus CD-ROM; $72 per 25 record forms; $70 per examiner's manual; $57 per stimulus book; $30 per stimulus CD-ROM.
Authors: Donna Geffner and Ronald Goldman.
Publisher: Pearson.
a) ASA FOR AGES 3-6 TO 4-11.
Population: Ages 3-6 to 4-11.
Time: 5 minutes.
Scores, 4: Speech Discrimination (Speech Discrimination in Noise, Mimicry, Total), Total ASA.
b) ASA FOR AGES 5-0 TO 6-11.
Population: Ages 5-0 to 6-11.

Time: 15 minutes.
Scores, 10: Speech Discrimination (Speech Discrimination in Noise, Mimicry, Total), Phonological Awareness (Blending, Rhyming, Total), Nonspeech Processing (Tonal Discrimination, Tonal Patterning, Total), Total ASA.

[239]
Australian Developmental Screening Checklist.
Purpose: Designed to "provide a brief screening measure of early developmental delay."
Population: Ages 6 months–5 years.
Publication Dates: 1968–1994.
Acronym: ADSC.
Scores, 5: Personal/Social, Language, Cognition, Fine Motor, Gross Motor.
Administration: Individual.
Price Data, 2006: A$288.05 per complete kit; A$118.40 per 25 record forms.
Time: (10–15) minutes.
Author: Barry Burdon.
Publisher: Pearson Assesment and Information [Australia and New Zealand].
Cross References: For a review by James A. Athanasou, see 15:23.

[240]
Australian Developmental Screening Test.
Purpose: Designed to provide a brief screening measure of early developmental delay.
Population: Ages 6 months–5 years.
Publication Date: 1993.
Acronym: ADST.
Scores, 5: Personal-Social, Language, Cognitive, Fine Motor, Gross Motor.
Administration: Individual.
Price Data, 2006: A$675.15 per complete kit including manual (135 pages), stimulus cards, 25 record forms, and a set of toys; A$115 per 25 record forms.
Time: (15–20) minutes.
Author: Barry Burdon.
Publisher: Pearson Assessment and Information [Australia and New Zealand].
Cross References: For a review by Koressa Kutsick Malcolm, see 15:24.

[241]
Australian Second Language Proficiency Ratings.
Purpose: "Designed to measure general proficiency by matching observed language behavior against global descriptions."
Population: Adolescents and adults.

Publication Dates: 1982–1984.
Acronym: ASLPR.
Scores, 4: Speaking, Listening, Reading, Writing.
Administration: Individual.
Price Data: Available from publisher.
Foreign Language Editions: French, Italian, and Japanese versions available.
Time: Administration time not reported.
Authors: D. E. Ingram and Elaine Wylie.
Publisher: Australian Department of Immigration and Multicultural Affairs [Australia].
Cross References: See T5:233 (2 references).

[242]

Autism Detection in Early Childhood.

Purpose: "Developed to detect Autistic Disorder (AD) in pre-verbal infants ... and very young children."
Population: Ages 12-24 months.
Publication Date: 2007.
Acronym: ADEC.
Scores, 17: Response to Name, Imitation, Stereotypical Behaviour, Gaze Switching, Eye Contact in a Game of Peek-a-Boo, Functional Play, Pretend Play, Reciprocity of a Smile, Response to Everyday Sounds, Gaze Monitoring, Responds to a Verbal Command, Demonstrates Use of Words, Anticipatory Posture, Nestling into Caregiver, Use of Gestures, Ability to Switch from Task to Task, Total.
Administration: Individual.
Price Data, 2008: A$495 per kit including manual (56 pages), Introduction and Training DVD, 10 score sheets, and set of stimulus materials; A$29.95 per 10 score sheets; A$199.95 per manual and Introduction and Training DVD combination; A$269.95 per set of stimulus materials.
Time: (10) minutes or less.
Comments: Parent/guardian should be present during administration.
Author: Robyn Young.
Publisher: Australian Council for Educational Research Ltd. [Australia].
Cross References: For a review by John J. Vacca, see 18:9.

[243]

Autism Screening Instrument for Educational Planning, Second Edition.

Purpose: "Designed to help professionals identify individuals with autism and to provide information needed to develop appropriate educational plans."
Population: Autistic individuals ages 18 months to adult.
Publication Dates: 1978–1993.
Acronym: ASIEP-2.
Administration: Individual.
Price Data: Available from publisher.

Time: Administration time varies.
Comments: Subtests administered depends on results of Autism Behavior Checklist and purpose of assessment; publisher advises that a Third Edition is now available.
Authors: David A. Krug, Joel R. Arick, and Patricia J. Almond.
Publisher: PRO-ED.

a) AUTISM BEHAVIOR CHECKLIST.
Scores, 6: Sensory, Relating, Body and Object Use, Language, Social and Self Help, Total.
b) SAMPLE OF VOCAL BEHAVIOR.
Scores, 5: Repetitive, Noncommunicative, Babbling, Unintelligible, Total.
c) INTERACTION ASSESSMENT.
Scores, 4: Interaction, Independent Play, No Response, Negative.
d) EDUCATIONAL ASSESSMENT.
Scores, 6: In Seat, Receptive Language, Expressive Language, Body Concept, Speech Imitation, Total.
e) PROGNOSIS OF LEARNING RATE.
Scores, 5: Hand-Shaping, Random Position–A, Fixed Position–B, Fixed Position–C, Random Position–D.
Cross References: See T5:234 (3 references); for reviews by D. Joe Olmi and Donald P. Oswald, see 13:24 (3 references); see also T4:235 (1 reference); for reviews by Lawrence J. Turton and Richard L. Wikoff of an earlier edition, see 9:105 (1 reference).

[244]

Autism Spectrum Rating Scales.

Purpose: Measures behaviors associated with Autism Spectrum Disorders.
Population: Ages 2-18.
Publication Date: 2010.
Acronym: ASRS.
Scores, 13: 5 ASRS scale scores (Total Score, Social/Communication, Unusual Behaviors, Self-Regulation, Short Form Score) and 8 DSM-IV-TR Scale scores (Peer Socialization, Adult Socialization, Social/Emotional Reciprocity, Atypical Language, Stereotypy, Behavioral Rigidity, Sensory Sensitivity, Attention/Self-Regulation).
Administration: Group.
Levels, 2: 2-5 years, 6-18 years.
Price Data, 2009: $327 per complete kit including 25 each of the ASRS 2-5 Parent, Teacher, and Short QuikScore forms, 25 each of the ASRS 6-18 Parent, Teacher, and Short QuikScore forms, and technical manual (167 pages); $399 per complete software scoring kit including complete kit and scoring software; $195 per particular age range kit (2-5 years or 6-18 years) including 25 each of the Parent, Teacher, and Short QuikScore Forms for the appropriate age range; $280 per age range scoring software kit including the age range kit and scoring software; $45 per 25 forms; $40 per 25 short forms; $50 per 25 QuikScore forms; $45 per 25

QuikScore short forms; $119 for scoring software; $70 per technical manual.

Time: (5-15) minutes.

Comments: All scales include a parent and teacher score; Self-Regulation Scale only for the 6-18 years forms.

Authors: Sam Goldstein and Jack A. Naglieri.

Publisher: Multi-Health Systems, Inc.

[245]

The Autistic Continuum: An Assessment and Intervention Schedule.

Purpose: Designed to indicate the presence of autistic features and to aid in developing educational and therapeutic programs.

Population: Ages 2-8.

Publication Dates: 1987-1992.

Scores: Item scores only in 8 areas: General Observations, Attention Control, Sensory Function, Non-Verbal Symbolic Function, Concept Formation, Sequencing and Rhythmic Abilities, Speech and Language, Educational Attainments and Intelligence.

Administration: Individual.

Price Data, 1998: £60 per manual (1992, 78 pages) incorporating schedule; sample sheets are free.

Time: Untimed.

Comments: Revision of Is This Autism? A Checklist of Behaviours and Skills for Children Showing Autistic Features.

Authors: Maureen Aarons and Tessa Gittens.

Publisher: GL Assessment [England].

Cross References: For reviews by Doreen W. Fairbank and Pat Mirenda, see 15:25; for reviews by William M. Bart and Doreen Ward Fairbank of the earlier edition, see 12:197.

[246]

The Autobiographical Memory Interview.

Purpose: "Provides an assessment of a subject's personal remote (retrograde) memory."

Population: Ages 18-80.

Publication Date: 1990.

Acronym: AMI.

Scores, 8: Personal Semantic (Childhood, Young Adult, Recent, Total), Autobiographical Incidents (Childhood, Young Adult, Recent, Total).

Administration: Individual.

Price Data, 2006: £84 per complete kit including manual (24 pages) and 25 scoring sheets; £104 per 50 scoring sheets.

Time: Untimed.

Comments: Semistructured interview format.

Authors: Michael Kopelman, Barbara Wilson, and Alan Baddeley.

Publisher: Pearson Assessment [England].

Cross References: For reviews by Carolyn M. Callahan and by Michael Furlong and Diane Tanigawa, see 17:11.

[247]

Automated Office Battery.

Purpose: Aptitude tests designed for the selection of staff to work in offices with a high degree of automation.

Population: Student and employed clerical staff.

Publication Dates: 1985-1986.

Acronym: AOB.

Scores: 3 tests: Numerical Estimation, Computer Checking, Coded Instructions.

Administration: Group.

Price Data: Available from publisher.

Time: 40(60) minutes for entire battery.

Comments: "Tests may be used individually or as a complete battery as particular requirements dictate."

Authors: Bill Mabey and Hazel Stevenson.

Publisher: SHL Group plc [United Kingdom].

a) NUMERICAL ESTIMATION.

Purpose: A test to measure the ability to estimate the answer to a calculation.

Acronym: NE-1.

Time: 10(15) minutes.

b) COMPUTER CHECKING.

Purpose: A test to measure the ability to check machine input information with the corresponding output.

Acronym: CC-2.

Time: 12(17) minutes.

c) CODED INSTRUCTIONS.

Purpose: A test to measure the ability to comprehend and follow written instructions when a form of coded language is used.

Time: 18(23) minutes.

Cross References: For a review by Philip Ash, see 11:24.

[248]

The Awareness of Social Inference Test.

Purpose: To test "the ability of the viewer to recognize basic emotions shown by other people" and to test "the ability of the viewer to determine speaker intention, attitude, and meaning."

Population: Ages 14-60.

Publication Date: 2002.

Acronym: TASIT.

Scores: Emotion Evaluation Test (Happy, Surprised, Neutral, Sad, Angry, Anxious, Revolted, Total Positive Emotions, Total Negative Emotions, Total Positive and Negative Emotions), Social Inference [Minimal] Test (Sincere, Sarcasm, Total), Social Inference [Enriched] Test (Lies, Sarcasm, Total).

Administration: Individual.

Forms, 2: A, B.

Price Data, 2006: £215 per complete kit including manual (16 pages), 2 packs of 25 scoring sheets, 2 video tapes, and 2 stimulus books; £64.50 per 2 packs of 25 scoring sheets.
Time: (30–45) minutes.
Authors: Skye McDonald, Sharon Flanagan, and Jennifer Rollins.
Publisher: Pearson Assessment [England].

[249]

B-3R, B-4R, B-5, B-5a Firefighter Tests.
Purpose: Designed to assess critical abilities necessary for the successful job performance of entry-level firefighters.
Population: Candidates for entry-level firefighter positions.
Publication Dates: 1994-2001
Administration: Individual or group.
Price Data: Available from publisher.
Comments: Previous versions listed as Firefighter Exams (T6:1273) and IPMA Fire Service Tests (9:538); no prior taining or experience as a firefighter is assumed of candidates taking the tests.
Authors: International Public Management Association for Human Resources & Bruce Davey Associates.
Publisher: International Public Management Association for Human Resources (IPMA-HR).
  a) B-3R and B-R FIREFIGHTER TESTS.
  Scores: 10 knowledge areas: Reading Comprehension, Interpreting Tables, Situational Judgment, Logical Reasoning, Reading Gauges, Applying Basic Math Rules, Mechanical Aptitude, Spatial Sense, Map Reading, Vocabulary.
  Time: 120 minutes.
  Comments: B-3R and B-4R are parallel forms.
  b) B-5 and B-5a FIREFIGHTER TESTS.
  Scores: 5 knowledge areas: Ability to Learn/Remember and Apply Information, Reading Comprehension, Interests (B-5 only), Situational Judgment, Logical and Mathematical Reasoning Ability.
  Time: 140 minutes for B-5; 125 minutes for B-5a.
  Comments: The B-5 assesses a wider range of characteristics than typical entry-level firefighter tests and includes a noncognitive component that measures personal traits.
Cross References: For a review by Lawrence Allen of an earlier version, see 9:538.

[250]

Balanced Assessment in Mathematics.
Purpose: Designed to improve the teaching and learning of mathematics in schools by introducing goals and curricula based on national and international standards.
Population: Grades 3–10.
Publication Dates: 2001–2003.
Scores: Total score only.

Administration: Group.
Levels, 8: 3, 4, 5, 6, 7, 8, 9, 10.
Forms: 2 forms at all 8 levels for 2001-2002; one form for 2003.
Price Data: Available from publisher.
Foreign Language Edition: Spanish edition available.
Time: (40) minutes per form.
Comments: Two forms per grade each year (practice and secure tests) are published; scoring is done locally; performance is reported at four levels and cut scores are determined each year; no norms.
Author: Mathematics Assessment Resource Service.
Publisher: CTB/McGraw-Hill.
Cross References: For reviews by Matthew K. Burns and Joseph C. Ciechalski, see 16:18.

[251]

The Balanced Emotional Empathy Scale.
Purpose: To measure an individual's vicarious emotional response to perceived emotional experiences of others.
Population: Ages 15 and older.
Publication Dates: 1972–1996.
Acronym: BEES.
Scores: Total score only.
Administration: Group or individual.
Price Data: Available from publisher for test kit including scale, scoring directions, norms, manual (1996, 12 pages), and literature review.
Time: (10–15) minutes.
Comments: Replaces The Emotional Empathic Tendency Scale.
Author: Albert Mehrabian.
Publisher: Albert Mehrabian.
Cross References: For reviews by Richard W. Johnson and Susana Urbina, see 13:25.

[252]

The Balloons Test.
Purpose: "Designed to detect visual inattention following brain injury."
Population: Adults.
Publication Date: 1998.
Scores, 4: Total A, Total B, Generalized Inattention Index, Lateralized Inattention Index.
Administration: Individual.
Price Data, 2006: £130 per complete kit including manual (10 pages), test cards, and 20 scoring sheets; £39.50 per 50 scoring sheets.
Time: [5-10] minutes.
Authors: Jennifer A. Edgeworth, Ian H. Robertson, and Thomas M. McMillan.
Publisher: Pearson Assessment [England].
Cross References: For reviews by Mary (Rina) M. Chittooran and D. Ashley Cohen, see 17:12.

[253]

Bankson-Bernthal Test of Phonology.

Purpose: "Designed for use by speech-language clinicians to assess the phonology of preschool and school-age children."
Population: Ages 3-9.
Publication Dates: 1989–1990.
Acronym: BBTOP.
Scores, 3: Word Inventory, Consonants Composite, Phonological Processes Composite.
Administration: Individual.
Price Data, 2010: $191 per complete kit; $90 per picture book; $51 per 25 record forms; $57 per manual (1990, 111 pages).
Time: (10-15) minutes.
Authors: Nicholas W. Bankson and John E. Bernthal.
Publisher: PRO-ED.
Cross References: See T5:240 (4 references); for reviews by Lynn S. Bliss and Lawrence J. Turton, see 12:41.

[254]

Bankson Language Test—2.

Purpose: Constructed "to establish the presence of a language disorder and identify areas in need of further, in-depth testing."
Population: Ages 3-0 to 6-11.
Publication Dates: 1977–1990.
Acronym: BLT-2.
Scores, 4: Semantic Knowledge, Morphological and Syntactic Rules, Language Quotient, Pragmatic Knowledge (optional).
Administration: Individual.
Forms, 2: BLT-2; BLT-2 Screen.
Price Data, 2010: $129 per complete kit including 25 profile/examiner's record booklets, 25 screen record forms, picture book, and examiner's manual (1990, 32 pages); $57 per picture book; $40 per 25 profile/examiner's record booklets; $20 per 25 screen record forms; $51 per examiner's manual.
Time: (30) minutes.
Comments: Revision of Bankson Language Screening Test.
Author: Nicholas W. Bankson.
Publisher: PRO-ED.
Cross References: See T5:241 (4 references) and T4:241 (3 references); for reviews by Ronald B. Gillam and Roger L. Towne, see 11:26 (4 references); for a review of an earlier edition by Barry W. Jones, see 9:107 (1 reference).

[255]

Bar-Ilan Picture Test for Children.

Purpose: "A semi-projective device to pinpoint the child's perception of his place in society, in his formal educational setting, and in his home, as well as his perception of his weaker points and of his potential for coping with life."
Population: Ages 4–16.
Publication Dates: 1982–1989.
Scores: Guidelines for analysis in 8 areas: Emotional Makeup, Motivation, Interpersonal Behavior and Areas of Conflict, Attitudes of Teachers-Parents Toward Testee, Attitudes of Peers and Siblings Towards Testee, Degree of Mastery and Feeling of Competence, Quality of Thinking Process, Activity.
Administration: Individual.
Forms, 1: 9 drawings (6 of which have different versions for boys and girls).
Price Data, 2005: $50 per set of 15 drawings; $25 per manual (1982, 49 pages).
Time: Administration time not reported.
Comments: 1989 edition is identical to 1982 edition except Appendix II was added.
Authors: Rivkah Itskowitz and Helen Strauss.
Publisher: Hogrefe Psykologisk Forlag A/S [Denmark].
Cross References: See T5:242 (1 reference) and T4:242 (1 reference).

[256]

Barkley Adult ADHD Rating Scale-IV.

Purpose: Designed "for clinical purposes to evaluate the range of ADHD symptoms in clinic-referred or high-risk adults … includes a section of items for assessing … a subtype of ADHD known as sluggish cognitive tempo."
Population: Ages 18 to 89.
Publication Date: 2011.
Acronym: BAARS-IV.
Price Data, 2011: $149 for manual (160 pages) containing forms and score sheets (includes permission to photocopy).
Author: Russell A. Barkley.
Publisher: Guilford Publications, Inc.
  a) SELF-REPORT: CURRENT SYMPTOMS.
  Scores, 9: Inattention, Hyperactivity, Impulsivity, Sluggish Cognitive Tempo, Total ADHD Score, Symptom Counts (Inattention, Hyperactivity-Impulsivity, Total ADHD, Sluggish Cognitive Tempo).
  Time: (5-7) minutes.
  b) SELF-REPORT: CHILDHOOD SYMPTOMS.
  Scores, 6: Inattention, Hyperactivity-Impulsivity, Total, Symptom Count (Inattention, Hyperactivity-Impulsivity, Total).
  Time: (5-7) minutes.
  c) OTHER-REPORT: CURRENT SYMPTOMS.
  Scores, 10: Inattention, Hyperactivity, Impulsivity, Total, Sluggish Cognitive Tempo, Symptom Counts (Inattention, Hyperactivity, Impulsivity, Total, Sluggish Cognitive Tempo).
  Time: (5-7) minutes.

d) OTHER-REPORT: CHILDHOOD SYMPTOMS.
Scores, 6: Inattention, Hyperactivity-Impulsivity, Total, Symptom Counts (Inattention, Hyperactivity-Impulsivity, Total).
Time: (5-7) minutes.
e) SELF-REPORT: QUICK SCREEN.
Scores, 3: Current Symptoms, Childhood Symptoms, Total.
Time: (3-5) minutes.
f) OTHER-REPORT: QUICK SCREEN.
Scores, 2: Current Symptoms, Childhood Symptoms.
Time: (3-5) minutes.
g) SELF-REPORT: CURRENT SYMPTOMS INTERVIEW.
Scores, 5: Symptom Count (Inattention, Hyperactivity, Impulsivity, Total, Sluggish Cognitive Tempo).
Time: (5-7) minutes.
h) SELF-REPORT: CHILDHOOD SYMPTOMS INTERVIEW.
Scores, 3: Symptom Count (Inattention, Hyperactivity-Impulsivity, Total).
Time: (5-7) minutes.

[257]

Barkley Deficits in Executive Functioning Scale.

Purpose: Designed "for evaluating dimensions of adult executive functioning in daily life."
Population: Ages 18-81.
Publication Date: 2011.
Acronym: BDEFS.
Scores, 6: Self-Organize, Time Management, Self-Restraint, Emotion Regulation, Self-Motivation, EF Summary.
Administration: Individual.
Forms, 4: Self-Report, Other-Report, Short Form, Long Form.
Price Data, 2011: $149 per manual (184 pages) including all forms and score sheets (includes permission to photocopy).
Time: (15-20) minutes long form; (4-5) minutes short form.
Author: Russell A. Barkley.
Publisher: Guilford Publications, Inc.

[258]

Barkley Functional Impairment Scale.

Purpose: A self-report assessment "intended for clinical purposes–specifically, to be used to evaluate the range of functional impairment in clinic-referred or high-risk adults."
Population: Ages 18-89.
Publication Date: 2011.
Acronym: BFIS.

Scores, 2: Mean Impairment, Percent Domains Impaired; 15 domains: Home-Family, Home-Chores, Work, Social-Strangers, Social-Friends, Community Activities, Education, Marriage/Cohabitation/Dating, Money Management, Driving, Sexual Relations, Daily Responsibilities, Self-Care Routines, Health Maintenance, Childrearing.
Administration: Individual.
Forms, 4: Long Form: Self-Report, Quick Screen: Self-Report, Long Form: Other-Report, Quick Screen: Other-Report.
Price Data, 2011: $149 per manual, including all forms and scoresheets (including permission to photocopy).
Time: (5-7) minutes for Long Form; (3-5) minutes for Quick Screen.
Author: Russell A. Barkley.
Publisher: Guilford Publications, Inc.

[259]

Barrier to Employment Success Inventory, Second Edition.

Purpose: Designed to help identify personal barriers to getting or keeping a job.
Population: Adult and teenage job seekers and career planners.
Publication Date: 2002.
Acronym: BESI.
Scores, 5: Personal and Financial, Emotional and Physical, Career Decision-Making and Planning, Job Seeking Knowledge, Training and Education.
Administration: Group or individual.
Price Data, 2006: $39.95 per 25 inventories including copy of instructor's guide (12 pages).
Time: (10–15) minutes.
Comments: Self-administered and self-scored; revised version features simplified language, and color-coded response and scoring tables.
Author: John J. Liptak.
Publisher: JIST Publishing, Inc.
Cross References: For reviews by Wayne J. Camara and Kathy E. Green, see 16:22.

[260]

Barsch Learning Style Inventory-Revised.

Purpose: Designed to assess an individual's learning style.
Population: 14 through adult.
Publication Dates: 1980–1996.
Scores: 4: Visual Preference, Auditory Preference, Tactile Preference, Kinesthetic Preference.
Administration: Group.
Manual: No manual.
Price Data, 2006: $14 per kit (10 Inventories & 10 Effective Study Tips).

Time: Administration time not reported.

Comments: Intended as an "informal survey, such as would be used by teachers or education specialists to guide them in setting up an appropriate educational plan."

Author: Jeffrey R. Barsch.

Publisher: Academic Therapy Publications.

Cross References: For reviews by John Biggs and Jayne A. Parker, see 9:111.

[261]

BASC Monitor for ADHD.

Purpose: Designed to survey the primary symptoms of ADHD in a format suited to repeated assessments in order to see relationships between treatments and symptoms overtime.

Population: Ages 4–18.

Publication Date: 1998.

Acronym: BASC Monitor for ADHD.

Scores: 4 scales: Attention Problems, Hyperactivity, Internalizing Problems, Adaptive Skills; plus Student Observation System (13 adaptive and maladaptive behavior categories).

Administration: Group.

Forms, 2: Teacher Monitor Ratings, Parent Monitor Ratings.

Price Data, 2006: $135.99 per hand-scoring set including 25 Teacher Monitor rating forms, 25 Parent Monitor rating forms, scoring templates, and manual (112 pages); $33.99 per 25 Teacher Monitor rating forms or 25 Parent Monitor rating forms; $34.99 per 25 Student Observation System forms; $68.99 per manual; $277.99 per single-user complete software kit including 25 Teacher Monitor rating forms, 25 Parent Monitor rating forms, manual, and software disks (network version also available).

Time: (5–10) minutes.

Comments: Instrument is designed to supplement the BASC (297) or to be used independently; questionnaires are completed by parents and teachers; Parent Monitor Ratings form available in Spanish; BASC Monitor software available for Windows 95 or Windows NT, single-user or network versions.

Authors: Randy W. Kamphaus and Cecil R. Reynolds.

Publisher: Pearson.

Cross References: For reviews by Hugh W. Glenn and Kevin M. Jones, see 14:33.

[262]

BASC-2 Behavioral and Emotional Screening System.

Purpose: "Designed to determine behavioral and emotional strengths and weaknesses in children and adolescents in preschool through high school."

Population: Ages 3-18.

Publication Date: 2007.

Acronym: BASC-2 BESS.

Score: Total score only.

Administration: Individual.

Forms, 5: Teacher Form-Preschool, Teacher Form-Child/Adolescent, Parent Form-Preschool, Parent Form-Child/Adolescent, Student Form-Child/Adolescent.

Price Data, 2008: $60 per manual (100 pages); $22 per 25 Header Sheets (needed for group scanning); $34 per Test Items on Audio CD; $589 per ASSIST software.

Foreign Language Edition: Spanish edition available for the Parent Form-Preschool, Parent Form-Child/Adolescent, and Student Form-Child/Adolescent.

Time: (5-10) minutes.

Comments: Item development originated with items created for the Behavior Assessment System for Children [Second Edition] (BASC-2; 17:21).

Authors: Randy W. Kamphaus and Cecil R. Reynolds.

Publisher: Pearson.

　　a) TEACHER FORMS.

　　Price Data: $26.75 per 25 Teacher Forms-Preschool; $98 per 100 Teacher Forms-Preschool; $26.75 per 25 Teacher Forms-Child/Adolescent; $98 per 100 Teacher Forms-Child/Adolescent.

　　　　1) *Teacher Form-Preschool.*

　　　　Population: Ages 3-5.

　　　　2) *Teacher Form-Child/Adolescent.*

　　　　Population: Ages 5-18.

　　b) PARENT FORMS.

　　Price Data: $26.75 per 25 Parent Forms-Preschool; $26.75 per 25 Parent Forms-Child/Adolescent.

　　Time: (5-10) minutes.

　　　　1) *Parent Form-Preschool.*

　　　　Population: Ages 3-5.

　　　　2) *Parent Form-Child/Adolescent.*

　　　　Population: Ages 5-18 (Grades K-12).

　　c) STUDENT FORMS.

　　Price Data: $26.75 per 25 Student Forms; $98 per 100 Student Forms.

　　Time: (5-10) minutes.

　　　　1) *Student Form-Child/Adolescent.*

　　　　Population: Ages 8-18.

Cross References: For reviews by Michael J. Furlong and Lindsey O'Brennan and by Kathleen M. Johnson, see 18:10.

[263]

Basic Achievement Skills Individual Screener.

Purpose: "Designed to provide norm-referenced and criterion-referenced information for reading, mathematics, and spelling."

Population: Grades 1–12 and post high school.

Publication Date: 1983.

Acronym: BASIS.

Scores, 3 or 4: Mathematics, Reading, Spelling, Writing Exercise (optional).

Administration: Individual.
Price Data, 2002: $92.20 per content booklet; $81 per 25 record forms; $92.20 per manual (1983, 232 pages); $181 per examiner's kit.
Time: (50–60) minutes.
Author: The Psychological Corporation.
Publisher: Pearson.
Cross References: See T5:246 (7 references) and T4:244 (6 references); for reviews by Robert E. Floden and Richard E. Schutz, see 9:112.

[264]

Basic Achievement Skills Inventory.

Purpose: Designed "to measure reading, written language, and math skills among children and adults."
Population: Grades 3 & 4, 5 & 6, 7 & 8, 9–12, and ages 8 to 80.
Publication Date: 2004.
Acronym: BASI.
Administration: Individual or group.
Tests, 2: Comprehensive, Survey.
Price Data, 2007: $115 per Comprehensive starter kit including manual (382 pages), 1 test booklet for each level (Levels 1–4, Forms A and B), and 12 hand-scored answer sheets (3 for each level); $185 per Mail-in Scoring Service Comprehensive starter kit with Student Summary Report, includes same materials as hand-scored starter kit but with scannable answer sheets; $160 per Q Local Comprehensive starter kit with Student Summary Report, includes same materials as hand-scored starter kit but with scannable answer sheets and 12 Q Local administrations, which require separate purchase of Q Local Software of $89 (desktop version) or $250 (network version) annual license fee; $55 per Survey starter kit including manual (146 pages), 1 test booklet (Math and Verbal), and 3 hand-scored answer sheets; $65 per Q Local Survey starter kit with Summary Report, includes same materials as hand-scored starter kit but with scannable answer sheets, and 12 Q Local administrations, which require separate purchase of Q Local Software; quantity discounts available for the reports.
Comments: Form A is for August-December testing; Form B is for January-July testing.
Author: Achilles N. Bardos.
Publisher: Pearson.
a) BASI COMPREHENSIVE.
Population: Grades 3 & 4, 5 & 6, 7 & 8, 9–12.
Scores, 9: Reading (Vocabulary, Reading Comprehension, Total), Written Language (Spelling, Language Mechanics, Total), Math (Math Comprehension, Math Application, Total).
Subtests, 6: Vocabulary, Spelling, Language Mechanics, Reading Comprehension, Math Computation, Math Application.
Levels, 4: Grades 3 & 4, Grades 5 & 6, Grades 7 & 8, Grades 9–12.

Forms, 2: A, B at each level.
Time: 115 minutes.
b) BASI SURVEY.
Population: Ages 8 to 80.
Scores, 7: Verbal Skills (Vocabulary, Language Mechanics, Reading Comprehension, Total), Math Skills (Math Computation, Math Application, Total).
Subtests, 2: Verbal Skills, Math Skills.
Price Data: $36.05 per 10 test booklets (Math and Verbal).
Time: 50 minutes.
Comments: Brief version of the Comprehensive Test.
Cross References: For reviews by Elizabeth Kelley Rhoades and Michael S. Trevisan, see 17:13.

[265]

Basic Banking Skills Battery.

Purpose: Designed to "measure skills and abilities for financial services jobs."
Population: Age 18 and over.
Publication Dates: 1987–1995.
Acronym: BBSB.
Scores, 14: Number Comparison, Name Comparison, Arithmetic Computation, Error Recognition, Drive, School Achievement, Interpersonal Skills, Cognitive Skills, Motor Ability, Math Ability, Self Discipline, Leadership, Perceptual Skills, Error Perception.
Administration: Group.
Forms, 2: Timed, Untimed.
Price Data, 2005: $22 for 1–999 Internet scoring with booklets; $22 for 1–999 Internet scoring without booklets; $22 for 1–999 Scan scoring; $22 for 1–999 Quanta-TouchTest™ scoring (timed); $22 for 1–999 Quanta-TouchTest™ scoring (untimed); $22 for 1–999 Quanta® Fax scoring; $22 for 1–999 Quanta® software for Windows with booklets; $22 for 1–999 for Quanta® software for Windows without booklets.
Time: (45) minutes.
Comments: Test can be scored online, by fax, optical screening; software is available.
Author: Reid London House.
Publisher: Pearson Performance Solutions [No reply from publisher; status unknown].

[266]

Basic Early Assessment of Reading™.

Purpose: Designed "to assess young students' acquisition of the essential components of reading—phonemic awareness, phonics, vocabulary, comprehension, and oral reading fluency."
Population: Grades K–3.
Publication Date: 2002.
Acronym: BEAR®.

Levels, 4: K, 1, 2, 3.
Price Data, 2005: $280.75 per complete kit (specify Levels K and 1 or Levels 2 and 3) including 25 Initial-Skills Analysis student booklets for each level, 1 Initial-Skills Analysis administration and scoring guide for each level, 1 Specific-Skill Analysis–Reading Basics black-line master for each level, 1 Specific-Skill Analysis–Language Arts black-line master for each level, 1 Specific-Skill Analysis–Comprehension black-line master for each level, 1 Specific-Skill Analysis administration and scoring guide for each level, 13 Oral Reading Fluency Assessment Passage Sheets for Levels K–3, 1 Oral Reading Fluency Assessment administration and scoring guide for Levels K–3, 25 Summative Assessment–Reading Basics student booklets for each level, 25 Summative Assessment–Language Arts student booklets for each level, 25 Summative Assessment–Comprehension student booklets for each level, 1 Summative Assessment administration guide for each level, 1 Summative Assessment scoring guide for each level, and Scoring and Reporting Software; $23 per 25 Initial-Skills Analysis test booklets (specify level); $74.50 per set of 3 Specific-Skill Analysis black-line masters (specify Levels K and 1, or 2 and 3); $34.25 per 13 Oral Reading Fluency Assessment Passage sheets; $19.50 per 25 Summative Assessment test booklets (specify level and content area); $5.75 per administration and scoring guide–Initial-Skills Analysis (specify level); $5.75 per administration and scoring guide–Specific-Skill Analysis (specify Levels K and 1 or 2 and 3); $28.50 per administration and scoring guide–Oral Reading fluency Assessment; $5.75 per administration guide–Summative Assessment (specify level); $17.25 per scoring guide–Summative Assessment (specify level); $31.75 per technical manual; $86.25 per scoring and reporting software; $209 per computer-administered BEAR.
Comments: Criterion-referenced testing program with modules designed for use in conjunction with classroom activities; computer-scoring and reporting available for PC.
Author: Riverside Publishing.
Publisher: PRO-ED.
a) INITIAL-SKILLS ANALYSIS.
Purpose: Designed to provide a quick overview of students' skills in Reading Basics, Comprehension, and Language Arts.
Scores, 4: Reading Basics, Comprehension, Language Arts, Total.
Administration: Individual or group.
Time: (45–60) minutes.
b) SPECIFIC-SKILL ANALYSIS.
Purpose: Designed to provide diagnostic information about students' specific skills in Reading Basics, Comprehension, and Language Arts.
Scores, 4: Reading Basics, Comprehension, Language Arts, Total.

Administration: Individual or group.
Time: (30–40) minutes per content area.
c) ORAL READING FLUENCY ASSESSMENT.
Purpose: Designed to provide information about students' accuracy, ability to retell what was read, oral reading skills, and reading rate (for Levels 1–3).
Scores, 3: Letter Recognition, Informational, Narrative.
Administration: Individual.
Forms: 6 (8 at Level K).
Time: (15–30) minutes per passage or list.
d) SUMMATIVE ASSESSMENT.
Purpose: Designed to assess early reading and language arts skills for placement and instructional planning.
Scores, 4: Reading Basics, Comprehension, Language Arts, Total.
Administration: Individual or group.
Time: (30–40) minutes per content area.
Cross References: For reviews by Zandra S. Gratz and Annita Marie Ward, see 16:23.

[267]

Basic Economics Test, Second Edition.
Purpose: "An updated economics achievement test for curriculum development, for the assessment of student understanding, and for determining the effectiveness of educational materials and teaching strategies."
Population: Grades 5–6.
Publication Dates: 1980–1990.
Acronym: BET.
Scores: Total score only.
Administration: Group.
Forms, 2: A, B.
Price Data, 2001: $19.95 per 25 test booklets (specify Form A or B); $14.95 per examiner's manual (1990, 54 pages) which includes scoring keys and model answer sheet which may be duplicated locally.
Time: 30 minutes.
Authors: William B. Walstad and Denise Robson.
Publisher: Council for Economic Education.
Cross References: For reviews by Irvin J. Lehmann and A. Harry Passow of an earlier edition, see 11:27; for reviews by Mary Friend Adams and James O. Hodges of an earlier edition, see 8:901 (1 reference).

[268]

Basic English Literacy Skills Test.
Purpose: To measure the skills needed for a basic knowledge of the English language.
Population: Candidates for any position requiring a basic knowledge of the English language.
Publication Date: 1996.
Acronym: ENGLIT.

Scores: Total Score, Narrative Evaluation, Rating, Recommendation.
Administration: Group.
Price Data, 2001: $130 per candidate; quantity discounts available.
Time: (77) minutes.
Comments: Scored by publisher; must be proctored.
Author: Walden Personnel Performance, Inc.
Publisher: Walden Personnel Performance, Inc. [Canada].

[269]

Basic English Skills Test.
Purpose: Designed to test listening comprehension, speaking, reading, and writing skills at a basic level when information on the attainment of basic functional language skills is needed.
Population: Limited-English-speaking adults.
Publication Dates: 1982–1988.
Acronym: B.E.S.T.
Scores, 9: Oral Interview Section (Listening Comprehension, Communication, Fluency, Pronunciation, Reading/Writing, Total) and Literacy Skill Section (Reading Comprehension, Writing, Total).
Subtests, 2: Oral Interview Section, Literacy Skills Section.
Administration: Individual in part.
Parts: 4 forms (Forms B and C only in current circulation).
Price Data, 2002: $150 per complete test kit; $12 per picture cue book (1988, 15 pages); $13 per 5 interviewer's booklets (1988, 13 pages); $30 per 100 interview scoring sheets (1988, 2 pages); $45 per literacy skills testing package including 20 literacy skills test booklets (1988, 20 pages) and 20 literacy skills scoring sheets (1988, 2 pages); $25 per manual (1988, 79 pages); $50 per training video and guide.
Time: [75] minutes.
Comments: Orally administered in part; subtests available as separates; other test materials (e.g., 3 $1 bills, 2 dimes, etc.) must be supplied by examiner.
Authors: Center for Applied Linguistics (test), Dorry Kenyon (revised manual), and Charles W. Stansfield (revised manual) with assistance from Dora Johnson, Allene Grognet, and Dan Dreyfus.
Publisher: Center for Applied Linguistics.
Cross References: For reviews by Alan Garfinkel and Patsy Arnett Jaynes, see 11:28.

[270]

Basic Number Diagnostic Test [2001 Revision].
Purpose: Designed to "show what a child can do (and cannot do) so that teaching objectives for that child can be determined."

Population: Ages 5–7.
Publication Dates: 1980–2001.
Scores, 13: Reciting Numbers, Naming Numerals, Copying Over Numerals, Copying Underneath Numerals, Counting Bricks, Selecting Bricks, Writing Numerals in Sequence, Writing Numerals to Dictation, Addition with Objects, Addition with Numerals, Subtraction with Objects, Subtraction with Numerals, Total.
Administration: Individual.
Forms, 2: A, B.
Price Data, 2002: £8.99 per set of 10 copies; £13.99 per manual (2001, 30 pages); £14.99 per specimen set.
Time: (15–25) minutes.
Comments: "Criterion-referenced."
Author: Bill Gillham.
Publisher: Hodder & Stoughton Educational [England].
Cross References: For reviews by Cleborne D. Maddux and Jeffrey K. Smith, see 15:27; for a review by Mary Montgomery Lindquist of an earlier edition, see 9:117.

[271]

Basic Number Screening Test [2001 Edition].
Purpose: "Quick assessment of a child's understanding of … number concepts and number skills."
Population: Ages 7–12.
Publication Dates: 1976–2001.
Scores: No scores.
Administration: Group.
Forms, 2: A, B.
Price Data, 2002: £9.99 per 20 tests (Form A or B); £10.99 per manual; £11.99 per specimen set.
Time: (20–35) minutes.
Comments: May be orally administered.
Authors: Bill Gillham and Kenneth Heese.
Publisher: Hodder & Stoughton Educational [England].
Cross References: For reviews by Kevin D. Crehan and Thanos Patelis, see 16:24; for reviews by John O. Anderson and Suzanna Lance of the 1996 edition, see 15:28; for reviews by Mary Montgomery Lindquist and Marilyn N. Suydam of an earlier edition, see 9:118.

[272]

Basic Personality Inventory.
Purpose: Constructed to be a "measure of personality and psychopathology."
Population: Adult and adolescent.
Publication Dates: 1988-1997.
Acronym: BPI.
Scores: 12: Hypochondriasis, Depression, Denial, Interpersonal Problems, Alienation, Persecutory Ideas, Anxiety, Thinking Disorder, Impulse Expression, Social Introversion, Self Depreciation, Deviation.
Administration: Individual or group.

Price Data, 2010: $92 per examination kit including 5 reusable test booklets, scoring template, 5 hand-scorable answer sheets, 5 profile sheets, answer sheet and coupon for BPI Basic Report, and manual on CD (1996, 120 pages); $24 per test manual on CD; $65 per 25 test booklets; $50 per 25 hand-scorable answer sheets; $50 per 25 profile sheets (select adult or adolescent); $21 per scoring template; $75–$85 (depending on volume) per 10 machine-scorable answer sheets and coupons for Basic Reports; $145 per software package including installation package and 10 coupons for computer report; $12-$20 (depending on volume) per online password.
Foreign Language Editions: Test booklets available in French and Spanish.
Time: 35 minutes.
Author: Douglas N. Jackson.
Publisher: SIGMA Assessment Systems, Inc.
Cross References: See T5:256 (4 references); for reviews by Susana Urbina and Tamela Yelland, see 12:42 (1 reference); see also T4:254 (16 references).

[273]

Basic Reading Inventory, Eighth Edition.

Purpose: Designed as an informal measure of students' reading behavior.
Population: Pre-primer through Grade 12.
Publication Dates: 1978–2001.
Scores, 9–16: 3 reading scores (Independent, Instructional, Frustration, Word Recognition in Isolation, Word Recognition in Context, Comprehension—Oral, Comprehension—Silent, Listening Level); Rate of Reading (Optional); 9 informal Early Literacy Assessment ratings (Alphabet Knowledge, Writing, Literacy Knowledge, Wordless Picture Reading, Caption Reading, Auditory Discrimination, Phoneme Awareness, Phoneme Segmentation, Basic Word Knowledge).
Administration: Individual.
Levels, 2: Pre-primer through Grade 12; Grades 3–12.
Forms, 6: A, B, C, D, LN, LE.
Price Data: Price data available from publisher for manual with paper-and-pencil materials (2001, 472 pages), including CD-ROM (with videos, Performance Booklets, and Record Booklet, and demo disk for recording and tracking software); a training video is available to train administrators.
Time: [20] minutes.
Comments: Optional Basic Reading Inventory Tracking Software available to assist with advanced qualitative analysis available from publisher. System requirements: Windows or Macintosh, CD-ROM drive, 20 MB RAM, 20 MB hard drive, sound and video options.
Author: Jerry L. Johns.
Publisher: Kendall/Hunt Publishing Company.
Cross References: For reviews by Matthew K. Burns and Zandra S. Gratz of the eighth edition, see 15:29; for reviews by Michael Harwell and Steven A. Stahl of

the seventh edition, see 14:34 (6 references); see also T5:257 (4 references); for reviews by Jerrilyn V. Andrews and Robert T. Williams of the fifth edition, see 12:43 (3 references); see also T4:255 (4 references); for a review by Gus Plessas of the second edition, see 9:119.

[274]

Basic School Skills Inventory, Third Edition.

Purpose: Designed to locate children who are at-risk for school failure, who need more in-depth assessment, and who should be referred for additional study.
Population: Ages 4-0 to 8-11.
Publication Dates: 1975–1998.
Acronym: BSSI-3.
Scores, 7: Spoken Language, Reading, Writing, Mathematics, Classroom Behavior, Daily Living Skills, Overall Skill Level.
Administration: Individual.
Price Data, 2010: $118 per complete kit including examiner's manual (1998, 77 pages), and 25 profile/response forms; $67 per examiner's manual; $57 per 25 profile/response forms.
Time: (5–8) minutes.
Comments: Replaces the Basic School Skills Inventory–Diagnostic (T4:256).
Authors: Donald D. Hammill, James E. Leigh, Nils A. Pearson, and Taddy Maddox.
Publisher: PRO-ED.
Cross References: For reviews by R. W. Kamphaus and Leah M. Nellis, see 14:35; see also T5:258 and T4:256 (1 reference); for a review by William J. Webster of the Basic School Skills Inventory Diagnostic, see 9:120; for reviews by Byron R. Egeland and Lawrence M. Kasdon of an earlier edition, see 8:424 (2 references).

[275]

Basic Skills Locater Test.

Purpose: "Designed to assess a person's functional skill levels in math and language."
Population: Ages 15 to adult who are functioning below a 12th grade level.
Publication Date: 1998.
Scores, 2: Language, Math.
Administration: Group or individual.
Price Data, 2002: $195 per Basic Skills Locater Test (software version) including 1 guide, 1 reproducible test master, and software; $195 per Basic Skills Locater Test (print version) including 1 user's guide, 10 reusable test booklets, 100 answer sheets, 1 test key, and a Windows scoring disk; $995 per Network Version.
Time: (30–60) minutes.
Comments: Test results place test-takers into four levels corresponding to GED and grade levels: GED Level 1 (grades 1–3); GED Level 2 (grades 4–6); GED Level 3 (grades 7–8) and GED Level 4 (grades 9–12).

Bar graphs representing competency in each level in the two domains of Language and Math yield 8 levels of competency for each test-taker.
Author: Helena Hendrix-Frye.
Publisher: Piney Mountain Press, Inc.
Cross References: For a review by Hoi K. Suen, see 15:30.

[276]

Basic Tests Series.
Purpose: To assess basic skills and knowledge relevant to the world of work or postsecondary education.
Population: High school seniors and college entrants and job applicants.
Publication Dates: 1981–1993.
Scores: Total scores only.
Administration: Group.
Restricted Distribution: Distribution restricted and tests administered at licensed testing centers.
Price Data, 2001: £9 entry fee per candidate per test; £1 per Basic Tests booklet containing syllabus and specimen papers (specify test); price data for additional supplementary materials available from publisher.
Comments: Tests administered each May at centers established by the publisher; tests available as separates.
Author: The Assessment and Qualifications Alliance.
Publisher: The Assessment and Qualifications Alliance [England].
  a) BASIC TEST IN LIFE SKILLS.
  Time: 90(100) minutes.
  b) BASIC TEST IN GRAPHICACY.
  Time: 90(100) minutes.
  c) BASIC TEST IN HEALTH, HYGIENE AND SAFETY.
  Time: 75(85) minutes.
Cross References: For reviews by Steven Ferrara and Anne R. Fitzpatrick, see 11:29.

[277]

BASIS-A Inventory [Basic Adlerian Scales for Interpersonal Success–Adult].
Purpose: Designed "to help understand how an individual's life-style, based on beliefs developed in early childhood, contributes to one's effectiveness in social, work, and intimate relationships."
Population: Adults.
Publication Dates: 1993–1997.
Acronym: BASIS-A.
Scores, 10: BASIS scales (Belonging-Social Interest, Taking Charge, Going Along, Wanting Recognition, Being Cautious); HELPS scales (Harshness, Entitlement, Liked By All, Striving for Perfection, Softness).
Administration: Group or individual.
Price Data, 2001: $95 per introductory kit including 15 test booklets, technical manual (1997, 87 pages),

interpretive manual (1997, 61 pages), and 15 copies of interpretive guide; $85 per 25 test booklets; $34 per technical manual and interpretive manual; $7 per sampler kit including test booklet and BASIS-A interpretive guide; $35 per 25 BASIS-A interpretive guides.
Foreign Language Editions: Test items and instructions available in Spanish and German.
Time: (10–15) minutes.
Comments: Self-scored.
Authors: Mary S. Wheeler, Roy M. Kern, and William L. Curlette.
Publisher: TRT Associates, Inc.
Cross References: For reviews by James P. Choca and Peggy E. Gallaher, see 13:26.

[278]

Bass Orientation Inventory.
Purpose: Designed to measure kinds of satisfactions and rewards sought in jobs.
Population: College and industry.
Publication Dates: 1962–1977.
Acronym: RNVT.
Scores, 3: Self-Orientation, Interaction-Orientation, Task-Orientation.
Administration: Group.
Price Data: Available from publisher at www.mindgarden.com/products/rnvts.htm.
Time: (20–25) minutes.
Comments: Previously listed as The Orientation Inventory.
Author: Bernard M. Bass.
Publisher: Mind Garden, Inc.
Cross References: See T3:1748 (1 reference); for a review by Thomas J. Bouchard, Jr., see 8:636 (15 references); see also T2:1306 (26 references) and P:187 (13 references); for reviews by Richard S. Barrett and H. Bradley Sagen, see 6:153 (2 references).

[279]

Batería III Woodcock-Muñoz™.
Purpose: Designed to "measure intellectual abilities and academic achievement" in Spanish-speaking individuals.
Population: Ages 2–90+.
Publication Dates: 1982–2007.
Acronym: Batería III.
Price Data, 2007: $1,283.50 per complete Batería III with 2 carrying cases including Cognitive standard and extended test books, examiner's manual (158 pages), examiner's training workbook, audio recording, 25 test records with 25 subject response booklets, 5 BIA test records, scoring guides, Achievement standard and extended test books, examiner's manual (180 pages), examiner's training workbook, audio recording, 25 test records with 25 subject response booklets, WJ III NU Compuscore® and Profiles Program, and scoring guides;

$799 per Batería III Cognitive Battery with carrying case including Cognitive standard and extended test books, examiner's manual, examiner's training workbook, audio recording, 25 test records with 25 subject response booklets, 5 BIA test records, WJ III NU Compuscore and Profiles Program, and scoring guides; $374 per Diagnostic Supplement including test book, examiner's manual (2005, 151 pages), 25 test records, audio recording, WJII III NU Compuscore and Profile Program, and scoring guides; $597 per Batería III Achievement Battery with carrying case including Achievement standard and extended test books, examiner's manual, examiner's training workbook, audio recording, 25 test records with 25 subject response booklets, WJ III NU Compuscore and Profiles Program, and scoring guides.

Foreign Language Editions: All of the materials are in Spanish including the examiner's manuals and the technical manual.

Time: (5–10) minutes per test.

Comments: The Batería III Woodcock-Muñoz is the parallel Spanish adaption/translation of the Woodcock-Johnson III (2952).

Authors: Ana F. Muñoz-Sandoval, Richard W. Woodcock, Kevin S. McGrew, and Nancy Mather (test); Fredrick A. Schrank, Kevin S. McGrew, Mary L. Ruef, Criselda G. Alvarado, Ana F. Muñoz-Sandoval, and Richard W. Woodcock (manual).

Publisher: Riverside Publishing.

a) Pruebas de habilidades cognitivas (Tests of Cognitive Abilities).

Acronym: Batería III COG.

Scores: 20 tests: Standard Battery (Comprensión verbal, Aprendizaje visual-auditivo, Relaciones espaciales, Integración de sonidos, Formación de conceptos, Pareo visual, Inversión de números, Palabras incompletas, Memoria de trabajo auditiva, Memoria diferida–aprendizaje visual-auditivo), Extended Battery (Información general, Fluidez de recuperación, Reconocimiento de dibujos, Atención auditiva, Análisis-síntesis, Rapidez en la decisión, Memoria para palabras, Rapidez en la idenificación de dibujos, Planeamiento, Cancelación de pares).

1) *Suplemento Diagnóstico (Diagnostic Supplement).*

Acronym: Bateria III SD.

Scores: 11 tests: Memoria para nombres, Integración visual, Configuración de sonidos–vocalizada, Series numéricas, Números matrices, Tachar, Memoria para frases, Rotación de bloques, Configuración de sonidos–musical, Memoria diferida–Memoria para nombes, Comprensión verbal bilingüe–español/inglés.

b) Pruebas de aprovechamiento (Tests of Achievement).

Acronym: Batería III APROV.

Scores: 22 tests: Standard Battery (Identificación

de letras y palabras, Fluidez en la lectura, Rememoración de cuentos, Comprensión de indicaciones, Cálculo, Fluidez en matemáticas, Ortografiá, Fluidez en la escritura, Comprensión de textos, Problemas aplicados, Muestras de redacción, Memoria diferida–Rememoración de cuentos), Extended Battery (Análisis de palabras, Vocabulario sobre dibujos, Comprensión oral, Corrección de textos, Vocabulario de lectura, Conceptos cuantitativos, Conocimientos academicos, Análisis de sonidos, Discernimiento de sonidos, Puntuación y mayúsculas).

Cross References: For reviews by Beth Doll and Courtney LeClair and by Arturo Olivarz, Jr. and Allison Boroda, see 17:14; for reviews by Robert B. Frary and Maria Prendes Lintel of a previous edition, see 13:27; for reviews by Jack A. Cummings and by Steven W. Lee and Elaine Flory Stefany of the Woodcock-Johnson Psycho-Educational Battery–Revised, see 12:415 (36 references); see also T4:2973 (90 references) and T3:2639 (3 references); for reviews by Jack A. Cummings and Alan S. Kaufman of an earlier edition of the Woodcock-Johnson Psycho-Educational Battery, see 9:1387 (6 references).

[280]

Battelle Developmental Inventory™, 2nd Edition.

Purpose: "Screening, diagnosis, and evaluation of early development."

Population: Birth to 7 years, 11 months.

Publication Dates: 1984–2005.

Acronym: BDI-2™.

Administration: Individual.

Forms, 2: Full Assessment, Screening Test.

Foreign Language Editions: Test items available in Spanish translation/adaptation for use by bilingual examiner or with a Spanish monolingual examiner.

Comments: Screening Test available as separate; hand-scoring, web-based, or standalone computer scoring (current version is called Data Manager) and Palm-powered electronic data collection capability with Electronic Record Forms (ERF) available for full Assessment and Screening Test in English and Spanish.

Author: Jean Newborg.

Publisher: Riverside Publishing.

a) FULL ASSESSMENT.

Purpose: Assess and identify "strengths and opportunities for learning of typically developing infants, preschoolers, kindergarteners, and early primary school students, as well as those who are advanced," and "children who have a disability or delay in any area of development."

Scores, 19: Self-Care, Personal Responsibility, Adaptive Total, Adult Interaction, Peer Interaction, Self-Concept and Social Role, Personal-Social Total, Receptive Communication, Expressive Communication, Communication Total, Gross Motor, Fine Motor, Perceptual Motor, Motor Total, Attention and Memory, Reasoning and Academic Skills, Perception and Concepts, Cognitive Total, Total.

Domains, 5: Adaptive, Personal-Social, Communication, Motor, Cognitive.

Administration Methods, 3: Structured Procedure, Observation Procedure, Interview Procedure.

Price Data, 2007: $444.50 per complete kit including 5 test item books, examiner's manual (256 pages), stimulus book, set of presentation cards, 15 scoring booklets, 15 workbooks, the screening test item book with 30 screening test booklets, set of screening visuals, and carrying case; $489 per manipulatives kit; $902.25 per complete kit with manipulatives; $70.25 per examiner's manual; $43.75 per 15 scoring booklets; $43.75 per 15 workbooks; $238.25 per Data Manager (new program released 2007) software kit (PC); $238.25 per Data Manager software kit (Web) single; $59.25 per Palm Application Kit.

Time: (60–90) minutes.

b) SCREENING TEST.

Purpose: Provides "method for determining in which areas of development, if any, a comprehensive assessment is needed for a given child."

Scores, 6: Adaptive, Personal-Social, Communication, Motor, Cognitive, Total.

Price Data: $299 per Screener Kit including Screening Test Item Book with 30 Screening Test booklets, set of screening visuals, examiner's manual, Quick Reference Guide, manipulatives needed to administer the Screening Test, and a canvas carrying case; $178.25 per Screener Kit including the screening test item book with 30 screening test booklets, and set of screening visuals (must purchase BDI-2 examiner's manual separately); $70.25 per examiner's manual; $51.50 per 30 screening test booklets.

Time: (10-30) minutes.

Cross References: For reviews by Michelle Athanasiou and by Lauren R. Barton and Donna Spiker, see 17:15; see also T5:265 (15 references) and T4:263 (4 references); for reviews by Judy Oehler-Stinnett and Kathleen D. Paget of an earlier edition, see 10:25 (1 reference); for information about the Screening Test, see T5:266 (4 references) and T4:264 (1 reference); for reviews by David W. Barnett and by Joan Ershler and Stephen N. Elliott of an earlier edition of the Screening Test, see 11:30.

[281]

Battery for Health Improvement 2.

Purpose: A psychomedical assessment designed "to provide relevant information and treatment recommendations to professionals who treat injured patients in a variety of settings."

Population: Ages 18–65, individuals who are being treated for a physical injury.

Publication Dates: 1996–2003.

Acronym: BHI 2.

Scores: 18 scales: Validity (Self-Disclosure, Defensiveness), Physical Symptoms (Somatic Complaints, Pain Complaints, Functional Complaints, Muscular Bracing), Affective Scales (Depression, Anxiety, Hostility), Character Scales (Borderline, Symptom Dependency, Chronic Maladjustment, Substance Abuse, Perseverance), Psychosocial Scales (Family Dysfunction, Survivor of Violence, Doctor Dissatisfaction, Job Dissatisfaction).

Administration: Group or individual.

Price Data, 2007: $104 per Q Local scoring starter kit with enhanced interpretive reports including manual (2003, 291 pages), 1 soft-cover test booklet, and answer sheets; $91 per Q Local scoring starter kit with basic interpretive reports; $71 per Q Local scoring starter kit with profile reports; $114 per mail-in starter kit with enhanced interpretive reports including manual, 1 soft-cover test booklet, and answer sheets; $102 per mail-in starter kit with basic interpretive reports; $80 per mail-in starter kit with profile reports; $89 per Desktop Version Q Local Software (requires annual license fee); $250 per Network Version Q Local Software (requires annual license); $47 per manual; $10.25 per 5 test booklets; $21.50 per 25 answer sheets; $51.50 per compact disc; quantity discounts available for the reports.

Foreign Language Editions: Spanish forms available.

Time: (30–45) minutes.

Comments: Computer administration and audio CD; mail-in scoring, Q Local software, fax-scoring.

Authors: Daniel Bruns and John Mark Disorbio.

Publisher: Pearson.

Cross References: For reviews by Michael G. Kavan and Romeo Vitelli, see 17:16; for reviews by Gregory J. Boyle and Ephrem Fernandez of an earlier edition, see 14:36.

[282]

Bay Area Functional Performance Evaluation, Second Edition.

Purpose: Developed to assess "general components of functioning that are needed to perform activities of daily living."

Population: Psychiatric patients.

Publication Dates: 1978–1987.

Acronym: BaFPE.

Administration: Individual.

Price Data: Available from publisher.

Comments: Task-Oriented Assessment and Social Interaction Scale may be used separately.

Authors: Susan Lang Williams and Judith Bloomer.

Publisher: Maddak Inc.

a) TASK-ORIENTED ASSESSMENT.
Acronym: TOA.
Scores, 138: 16 Component scores: Cognitive (Memory for Written/Verbal Instruction, Organization of Time and Materials, Attention Span, Evidence of Thought Disorder, Ability to Abstract, Total), Performance (Task Completion, Errors, Efficiency, Total), Affective (Motivation/Compliance, Frustration Tolerance, Self-Confidence, General Affective Impression, Total), Total for the following 11 Parameters: Sorting Shells, Money/Marketing, Home Drawing, Block Design, Kinetic Person Drawing, Total; also 11 Qualitative Signs and Referral Indicators ratings: Language, Comprehension, Hemispatial Neglect, Memory, Abstraction, Task-Specific Observations, Total for the above parameters.
Time: (30–45) minutes.
b) SOCIAL INTERACTION SCALE.
Acronym: SIS.
Scores, 13: Parameter scores (Verbal Communication, Psychomotor Behavior, Socially Appropriate Behavior, Response to Authority Figures, Degree of Independence/Dependence, Ability to Work with Others, Participation in Group Activities), Social Situations (One-to-One, Mealtime, Unstructured Group, Structured Task or Activity Group, Structured Verbal Group), Total Interaction.
Time: [50–60] minutes.
Cross References: See T5:268 (1 reference); for reviews by Deborah D. Roman and Orest E. Wasyliw, see 12:44; see also T4:265 (1 reference).

[283]

Bayley Infant Neurodevelopmental Screener.

Purpose: "Designed to identify infants between the ages of 3 and 24 months who are developmentally delayed or have neurological impairments."
Population: Ages 3–24 months.
Publication Dates: 1992–1995.
Acronym: BINS.
Scores: 4 areas: Basic Neurological Functions/Intactness, Auditory and Visual Receptive Functions, Verbal and Motor Expressive Functions, Cognitive Processes; total score for each level.
Administration: Individual.
Levels, 6: 3–4 months, 5–6 months, 7–10 months, 11–15 months, 16–20 months, 21–24 months.
Price Data, 2002: $265 per complete kit including 25 record forms, manual (1995, 105 pages), stimulus cards, and necessary manipulables in soft-sided carrying case; $33 per 25 record forms; $80 per manual; $17 per stimulus card; $50 per training video.
Time: (10–15) minutes.
Comments: Includes a subset of items from the Bayley Scales of Infant Development–Second Edition

(BSID–II; T5:271), but is not an abbreviated form of the BSID-II.
Author: Glen P. Aylward.
Publisher: Pearson.
Cross References: For reviews by James K. Benish and by Damon Krug and Brandon Davis, see 13:28.

[284]

Bayley Scales of Infant and Toddler Development–Third Edition.

Purpose: Designed to "assess the developmental functioning of infants and young children."
Population: Ages 1-42 months.
Publication Dates: 1969-2006.
Acronym: Bayley-III.
Scores, 19: Cognitive, Language (Receptive Communication, Expressive Communication, Total), Motor (Fine Motor, Gross Motor, Total), Social-Emotional, Adaptive Behavior (Communication, Community Use, Functional Pre-Academics, Home Living, Health and Safety, Leisure, Self-Care, Self-Direction, Social, Motor, Total).
Administration: Individual.
Price Data, 2006: $895 per complete kit including administration manual (2006, 266 pages), technical manual (2006, 163 pages), 25 Cognitive, Language, and Motor record forms, stimulus booklet, picture book, manipulative set, 25 Social-Emotional/Adaptive Behavior Questionnaires, 25 Caregiver Report forms, rolling case, and PDA Administrative Assistant; $98 per 25 Cognitive, Language, and Motor record forms; $75 per 25 Social-Emotional/Adaptive Behavior Questionnaires; $225 per stimulus booklet; $15 per picture book; $150 per administration manual; $150 per technical manual.
Time: (30-60) minutes.
Comments: Hand scored or scored with use of a PDA.
Author: Nancy Bayley.
Publisher: Pearson.
Cross References: For reviews by Renee M. Tobin and Kathryn E. Hoff and by John J. Venn, see 17:17; see also T5:270 (48 references); for reviews by Carl J. Dunst and Mark H. Fugate of a previous edition, see 13:29 (130 references); see also T4:266 (58 references); for reviews by Michael J. Roszkowski and Jane A. Rysberg of an earlier edition, see 10:26 (80 references); see also 9:126 (42 references) and T3:270 (101 references); for a review by Fred Damarin, see 8:206 (28 references); see also T2:484 (11 references); for reviews by Roberta R. Collard and Raymond H. Holden, see 7:402 (20 references).

[285]

Bayley Scales of Infant and Toddler Development–Third Edition, Screening Test.

Purpose: Designed to "briefly assess the cognitive, language, and motor functioning of infants and young children."

Population: Ages 1-42 months.
Publication Date: 2006.
Acronym: Bayley-III Screening Test.
Scores, 5: Cognitive, Receptive Communication, Expressive Communication, Fine Motor, Gross Motor.
Administration: Individual.
Price Data, 2006: $225 per screening test kit including screening test manual (138 pages), 25 screening record forms, screening stimulus book, picture book, and screening manipulative set; $35 per 25 screening record forms; $100 per stimulus booklet; $15 per picture book; $50 per manual.
Time: (15-30) minutes.
Author: Nancy Bayley.
Publisher: Pearson.
Cross References: For reviews by R. Anthony Doggett and Kristin N. Johnson-Gros and by Theresa Graham, see 17:18.

[286]

BDI-FastScreen for Medical Patients.

Purpose: Designed to screen for depression in patients reporting somatic and behavioral symptoms that may be attributable to biological, medical, alcohol, and/or substance abuse problems.
Population: Ages 12–82.
Publication Date: 2000.
Acronym: BDI-FastScreen.
Scores: Total score only.
Administration: Group.
Price Data, 2003: $67 per complete kit including manual and 50 score forms; $39 per manual; $39 per 50 record forms; $43 per 50 scannable record forms; quantity discounts available.
Time: (5) minutes.
Comments: Formerly called Beck Depression Inventory for Primary Care; based upon Beck Depression Inventory–II (288).
Authors: Aaron T. Beck, Robert A. Steer, and Gregory K. Brown.
Publisher: Pearson.
Cross References: For reviews by James J. Hennessy and Nathaniel J. Pallone and by Susan C. Whiston and Kelly Eder, see 16:25.

[287]

Beck Anxiety Inventory [1993 Edition].

Purpose: "Measures the severity of anxiety in adults and adolescents."
Population: Adults and adolescents ages 17 and over.
Publication Dates: 1987–1993.
Acronym: BAI.
Scores: Total score only.
Administration: Group or individual.
Price Data, 2002: $66 per complete kit including

25 record forms and manual (1993, 23 pages); $34.50 per 25 record forms; $34 per manual.
Foreign Language Edition: Available in Spanish.
Time: (5–10) minutes.
Comments: Computer scoring and interpretation available.
Authors: Aaron T. Beck and Robert A. Steer.
Publisher: Pearson.
Cross References: See T5:271 (18 references); for reviews by E. Thomas Dowd and Niels G. Waller, see 13:30 (73 references); see also T4:267 (2 references).

[288]

Beck Depression Inventory—II.

Purpose: "Developed for the assessment of symptoms corresponding to criteria for diagnosing depressive disorders listed in the … DSM IV."
Population: Ages 13 and over.
Publication Dates: 1961–1996.
Acronym: BDI-II.
Scores: Total score only.
Administration: Group or individual.
Price Data, 2002: $66 per complete kit including manual (1996, 38 pages) and 25 recording forms; $34 per manual; $34.50 per 25 recording forms; $130 per 100 recording forms; $34.50 per 25 Spanish recording forms; $130 per 100 Spanish recording forms.
Foreign Language Edition: Available in Spanish.
Time: (5–10) minutes.
Comments: Hand-scored or computer-based administration, scoring, and interpretation available; "revision of BDI based upon new information about depression."
Authors: Aaron T. Beck, Robert A. Steer, and Gregory K. Brown.
Publisher: Pearson.
Cross References: For reviews by Paul A. Arbisi and Richard F. Farmer, see 14:37; see also T5:272 (384 references); for reviews by Janet F. Carlson and Niels G. Waller of an earlier edition, see 13:31 (1026 references); see also T4:268 (660 references); for reviews by Collie W. Conoley and Norman D. Sundberg of an earlier edition, see 11:31 (286 references).

[289]

Beck Hopelessness Scale [Revised].

Purpose: Measures "the extent of negative attitudes about the future (pessimism) as perceived by adolescents and adults."
Population: Adolescents and adults ages 17 and over.
Publication Dates: 1978–1993.
Acronym: BHS.
Scores: Total score only.
Administration: Group or individual.
Price Data, 2002: $66 per complete kit including 25 record forms and manual (1993, 29 pages);

$34.50 per 25 record forms; $34 per manual; $8.50 per scoring key.
Foreign Language Edition: Available in Spanish.
Time: (5–10) minutes.
Comments: Computer scoring and interpretation available.
Authors: Aaron T. Beck and Robert A. Steer.
Publisher: Pearson.
Cross References: See T5:273 (34 references); for a review by Ephrem Fernandez, see 13:32 (83 references); see also T4:269 (37 references); for reviews by E. Thomas Dowd and Steven V. Owen of an earlier edition, see 11:32 (13 references).

[290]

Beck Scale for Suicide Ideation.
Purpose: "To detect and measure the severity of suicidal ideation in adults and adolescents."
Population: Adults and adolescents ages 17 and over.
Publication Dates: 1991–1993.
Acronym: BSS.
Scores: Total score only; item score ranges.
Administration: Group or individual.
Price Data, 2002: $66 per complete kit including 25 record forms and manual (1993, 24 pages); $34.50 per 25 record forms; $34 per manual.
Foreign Language Edition: Spanish forms available.
Time: (5–10) minutes.
Comments: Computer scoring and interpretation available.
Authors: Aaron T. Beck and Robert A. Steer.
Publisher: Pearson.
Cross References: For reviews by Karl R. Hanes and Jay R. Stewart, see 13:33 (14 references).

[291]

BECK Youth Inventories for Children and Adolescents: Second Edition.
Purpose: Designed to "assess a child's experience of depression, anxiety, disruptive behavior, and self-concept."
Population: Ages 7-18.
Publication Dates: 2001-2005.
Acronyms: BYI-II, BDI-Y, BSCI-Y, BAI-Y, BANI-Y, BDBI-Y.
Scores, 5: Depression, Anxiety, Anger, Disruptive Behavior, Self-Concept.
Subtests, 5: Beck Depression Inventory for Youth, Beck Anxiety Inventory for Youth, Beck Anger Inventory for Youth, Beck Disruptive Inventory for Youth, Beck Self-Concept.
Administration: Individual or group.
Price Data, 2007: $165 per complete kit including manual (2005, 85 pages) and 25 combination inventory booklets; $95 per 25 combination inventory booklets; $46 per 25 depression inventory booklets; $46 per 25 anxiety inventory booklets; $46 per 25 anger inventory booklets; $46 per 25 disruptive behavior inventory booklets; $46 per self-concept inventory booklets; $85 per manual.
Time: (30-60) minutes for combination form.
Comments: Subtests may be administered separately or via combination form; previous edition was entitled Beck Youth Inventories of Emotional & Social Impairment.
Authors: Judith S. Beck, Aaron T. Beck, John B. Jolly, and Robert A. Steer.
Publisher: Pearson.
Cross References: For reviews by Rosemary Flanagan and Carlen Henington, see 18:11; for reviews by Mike Bonner and Hugh Stephenson of the earlier edition, see 15:31.

[292]

Becker Work Adjustment Profile: 2.
Purpose: Designed to "assess work habits, attitudes, and skills of people with special needs" and to assess level of supports needed.
Population: Individuals ages 13 and over, who are mentally retarded, physically disabled, emotionally disturbed, learning disabled, and/or economically disadvantaged.
Publication Dates: 1989-2005.
Acronym: BWAP:2.
Scores, 5: Work Habits/Attitudes, Interpersonal Relations, Cognitive Skills, Work Performance Skills, Broad Work Adjustment.
Administration: Individual.
Price Data, 2011: $79 per value kit including 25 test booklets and manual (2005, 76 pages); $38 per 25 test booklets; $44.50 per manual; $45 per starter set including 2 test booklets and manual; quantity discounts available.
Time: (15) minutes.
Comments: Ratings by teachers, counselors, or other vocational professionals; 5 levels of work supports are also assessed.
Author: Ralph L. Becker.
Publisher: Elbern Publications.
Cross References: For reviews by James T. Austin and Stephanie D. Tischendorf and by Pam Lindsey, see 17:19; see also T5:275 (1 reference); for reviews by Brian Bolton and Elliot L. Gory of an earlier form, see 11:33.

[293]

Bedside Evaluation of Dysphagia, Revised Edition.
Purpose: Designed to assess swallowing abilities and the factors that may influence those abilities.
Population: Adults neurologically impaired.
Publication Date: 1995.
Acronym: BED.
Scores, 13: Behavioral Characteristics, Cognition and Communication Screening (Cognition, Receptive

Language, Expressive Language/Speech Production), Oral Motor Examination (Lips, Tongue, Soft Palate, Cheeks, Mandible, Larynx), Oral-Pharyngeal Dysphagia Symptoms Assessment (Oral State, Pharyngeal State, Additional Observations).
Administration: Individual.
Price Data, 2010: $103 per complete kit including 25 evaluation forms, manual (54 pages), 25 evaluation forms, and 25 screening forms; $46 per 25 standard evaluation forms; $12 per 25 screening forms.
Time: (15–45) minutes.
Author: Edward Hardy.
Publisher: PRO-ED.
Cross References: For reviews by Carlos Inchaurralde and Steven B. Leder, see 14:38.

[294]

Bedside Evaluation Screening Test, Second Edition.

Purpose: "Designed to assess and quantify language disorders in adults resulting from aphasia."
Population: Patients with language deficits.
Publication Dates: 1987–1998.
Acronym: BEST-2.
Scores, 8: Conversational Expression, Naming Objects, Describing Objects, Repeating Sentences, Pointing to Objects, Pointing to Parts of a Picture, Reading, Total.
Administration: Individual.
Price Data, 2010: $186 per complete kit including examiner's manual (1998, 49 pages), picture book, 25 record forms, and 25 profile/summary sheets; $51 per examiner's manual; $67 per picture book; $51 per 25 record forms; $23 per 25 profile/summary sheets.
Time: (20–30) minutes.
Comments: Replaces the Bedside Evaluation and Screening Test of Aphasia (T4:272).
Authors: Joyce Fitch West, Elaine S. Sands, and Deborah Ross-Swain.
Publisher: PRO-ED.
Cross References: For reviews by Pamilla Morales and Carolyn Mitchell-Person, see 14:39; for a review by Malcolm R. McNeil of an earlier edition, see 11:34.

[295]

The Beery-Buktenica Developmental Test of Visual-Motor Integration, 5th Edition.

Purpose: "Designed to assess the extent to which individuals can integrate their visual and motor abilities (eye-hand coordination)."
Population: Ages 2–100.
Publication Dates: 1967-2004.
Acronym: BEERY VMI.
Scores: 3: Beery VMI, Visual Perception [optional], Motor Coordination [optional].
Administration: Group or individual.

Forms, 2: Full, Short.
Price Data, 2007: $110 per starter kit including manual (2004, 210 pages), 10 Full forms, 10 Short forms, 10 Visual Perception forms, and 10 Motor Coordination forms; $55 per manual; $90 per 25 Full forms; $67 per 25 Short forms; $14.95 per 25 Visual Perception forms; $14.95 per 25 Motor Coordination forms (bulk discounts available for forms); $140 per Teaching Materials starter kit including My Book of Shapes, My Book of Letters and Numbers, Developmental Teaching Activities, Developmental Wall Chart, and 25 Stepping Stones Parent Checklists; $36.25 per My Book of Shapes; $36.25 per My Book of Letters and Numbers; $47 per Developmental Teaching Activities; $26 per Stepping Stones Parent Checklist; $20.75 per Developmental Wall Chart for Visual-Motor Integration.
Comments: The subtests must be given in the appropriate sequence.
Authors: Keith E. Beery and Natasha A. Beery.
Publisher: Pearson.
  a) BEERY VMI.
    1) *Full form.*
    Population: Ages 2-100.
    Time: (10-15) minutes.
    2) *Short form.*
    Population: Ages 2-7.
    Time: (5-15) minutes.
  b) VISUAL PERCEPTION [OPTIONAL].
  Population: Ages 2-100.
  Time: (3-7) minutes.
  c) MOTOR COORDINATION [OPTIONAL].
  Population: Ages 2-100.
  Time: (3-7) minutes.
Cross References: For reviews by Theresa Graham and by Thomas McKnight and Tiffany Chandler, see 17:20; for a review by Jan Visser of an earlier version, see 14:119; see also T5:815 (52 references); for reviews by Darrell L. Sabers and James E. Ysseldyke of the Third Revision, see 12:111 (25 references); see also T4:768 (42 references), 9:329 (15 references), and T3:701 (57 references); for reviews by Donald A. Leton and James A. Rice of an earlier edition, see 8:870 (24 references); see also T2:1875 (6 references); for a review by Brad S. Chissom of an earlier edition, see 7:867 (5 references).

[296]

Behavior Analysis Forms for Clinical Intervention.

Purpose: To gather client interview data in a structured manner.
Population: Behavior therapy clients.
Publication Dates: 1977–1981.
Scores: Volume 1: 36 plans, questionnaires, scales, forms, schedules, and data forms in areas such as Client History, Motivation for Change, Reinforcement, Social Performance; Volume 2: 59 questionnaires, scales, forms,

schedules, and data forms in areas such as Reinforcers for Specific Populations, Survey of Phobic or Relationship Reactions, and Guidelines for Clients.
Administration: Group or individual.
Price Data, 2001: $79.95 for each volume.
Time: Administration times vary.
Author: Joseph R. Cautela.
Publisher: Cambridge Center for Behavioral Studies.
Cross References: For reviews by Mary Lou Kelley and Francis E. Lentz, Jr., see 9:127.

[297]

Behavior Assessment System for Children [Second Edition].

Purpose: Designed "to facilitate the differential diagnosis and educational classification of a variety of emotional and behavioral disorders of children and to aid in the design of treatment plans."
Population: Ages 2-25.
Publication Dates: 1992–2004.
Acronym: BASC-2.
Administration: Individual.
Forms, 11: Teacher Rating Scales-Preschool, Teacher Rating Scales-Child, Teacher Rating Scales-Adolescent, Parent Rating Scales-Preschool, Parent Rating Scales-Child, Parent Rating Scales-Adolescent, Self-Report of Personality-Child, Self-Report of Personality-Adolescent, Self-Report of Personality-College, Structured Developmental History, Student Observation System.
Price Data, 2007: $120 per examination set including manual (2004, 606 pages), and 1 sample each of the hand-scored forms for all levels of the Teacher Rating Scales, Parent Rating Scales, and Self-Report of Personality, Parent Feedback Report, the Structured Developmental History, and the Student Observation System; $249.99 per ASSIST software for Windows and Macintosh (nonscannable version); $589.99 per ASSIST software for Windows and Macintosh (scanning version); $85.75 per manual; $125 per BASC-2 Training Video (DVD or VHS); additional price data available on publisher's website (www.pearsonassessments.com).
Foreign Language Editions: Spanish edition available for the Parent Rating Scales, the Self-Report of Personality, and the Structured Developmental History.
Comments: Also available are Parent Feedback Reports for the Teacher Rating Scales, Parent Rating Scales, and Self-Report of Personality forms; computer programs (BASC-2 ASSIST and BASC-2 ASSIST Plus, which includes optional content scales) to score and report results are also available; computer version of the student Observation System (BASC-2 Portable Observation Program) is available for use with Windows (Win 98 SE, 4.0 NT, 2000, ME, XP), Macintosh (OS 9.2, 10.x), Palm (OS 3.x, 4.x, 5.x), and Pocket PC (2000, 2002); audiorecordings are available for administration of the Parent Rating Scales and Self-Report of Personality forms.

Authors: Cecil R. Reynolds and Randy W. Kamphaus.
Publisher: Pearson.
a) TEACHER RATING SCALES.
Price Data: $32.25 per 25 hand-scored forms; $26.75 per 25 computer-scored forms; $42.75 per 25 scannable forms; $26.75 per 25 Parent Feedback Reports.
Time: (10-15) minutes.
  1) *Teacher Rating Scales-Preschool.*
  Population: Ages 2-5.
  Scores, 19: Externalizing Problems (Aggression, Hyperactivity), Internalizing Problems (Anxiety, Depression, Somatization), Adaptive Skills (Adaptability, Social Skills, Functional Communication), Behavioral Symptoms Index, Attention Problems, Atypicality, Withdrawal, Content Scales (Anger Control, Bullying, Developmental Social Disorders, Emotional Self-Control, Executive Functioning, Negative Emotionality, Resiliency).
  2) *Teacher Rating Scales-Child.*
  Population: Ages 6-11.
  Scores, 23: Externalizing Problems (Aggression, Hyperactivity, Conduct Problems), Internalizing Problems (Anxiety, Depression, Somatization), School Problems (Attention Problems, Learning Problems), Adaptive Skills (Adaptability, Social Skills, Leadership, Study Skills, Functional Communication), Behavioral Symptoms Index, Atypicality, Withdrawal, Content Scales (Anger Control, Bullying, Developmental Social Disorders, Emotional Self-Control, Executive Functioning, Negative Emotionality, Resiliency).
  3) *Teacher Rating Scales-Adolescent.*
  Population: Ages 12-21.
  Scores, 23: Externalizing Problems (Aggression, Hyperactivity, Conduct Problems), Internalizing Problems (Anxiety, Depression, Somatization), School Problems (Attention Problems, Learning Problems), Adaptive Skills (Adaptability, Social Skills, Leadership, Study Skills, Functional Communication), Behavioral Symptoms Index, Atypicality, Withdrawal, Control Scales (Anger Control, Bullying, Developmental Social Disorders, Emotional Self-Control, Executive Functioning, Negative Emotionality, Resiliency).
b) PARENT RATING SCALES.
Price Data: $32.25 per 25 hand-scored forms; $26.75 per 25 computer-scored forms; $42.75 per 25 scannable forms; $26.75 per 25 Parent Feedback Reports.
Time: (10-20) minutes.
  1) *Parent Rating Scales-Preschool.*
  Population: Ages 2-5.

Scores, 20: Externalizing Problems (Aggression, Hyperactivity), Internalizing Problems (Anxiety, Depression, Somatization), Adaptive Skills (Adaptability, Social Skills, Activities of Daily Living, Functional Communication), Behavioral Symptoms Index, Attention Problems, Atypicality, Withdrawal, Control Scales (Anger Control, Bullying, Developmental Social Disorders, Emotional Self-Control, Executive Functioning, Negative Emotionality, Resiliency).
2) *Parent Rating Scales-Child.*
Population: Ages 6-11.
Scores, 22: Externalizing Problems (Aggression, Hyperactivity, Conduct Problems), Internalizing Problems (Anxiety, Depression, Somatization), Adaptive Skills (Adaptability, Social Skills, Leadership, Activities of Daily Living, Functional Communication), Behavioral Symptoms Index, Attention Problems, Atypicality, Withdrawal, Control Scales (Anger Control, Bullying, Developmental Social Disorders, Emotional Self-Control, Executive Functioning, Negative Emotionality, Resiliency).
3) *Parent Rating Scales–Adolescent.*
Population: Ages 12-21.
Scores, 22: Externalizing Problems (Aggression, Hyperactivity, Conduct Problems), Internalizing Problems (Anxiety, Depression, Somatization), Adaptive Skills (Adaptability, Social Skills, Leadership, Activities of Daily Living, Functional Communication), Behavioral Symptoms Index, Attention Problems, Atypicality, Withdrawal, Control Scales (Anger Control, Bullying, Developmental Social Disorders, Emotional Self-Control, Executive Functioning, Negative Emotionality, Resiliency).
c) SELF-REPORT OF PERSONALITY.
Price Data: $32.25 per 25 hand-scored forms; $26.75 per 25 computer-scored forms; $42.75 per 25 scannable forms; $26.75 per 25 Parent Feedback Reports.
Time: (20-30) minutes.
1) *Self-Report of Personality-Interview.*
Population: Ages 6-7.
Scores, 8: Anxiety, Attitude to School, Attitude to Teachers, Atypicality, Depression, Interpersonal Relations, Social Stress, Emotional Symptoms Index.
2) *Self-Report of Personality-Child.*
Population: Ages 8-11.
Scores, 20: School Problems (Attitude to School, Attitude to Teachers), Internalizing Problems (Atypicality, Locus of Control, Social Stress, Anxiety, Depression, Sense of Inadequacy), Inattention/Hyperactivity (Attention Problems, Hyperactivity), Emotional Symptoms

Index (Social Stress, Anxiety, Depression, Sense of Inadequacy, Self-Esteem, Self-Reliance), Personal Adjustment (Relations with Parents, Interpersonal Relations, Self-Esteem, Self-Reliance).
3) *Self-Report of Personality-Adolescent.*
Population: Ages 12-21.
Scores, 26: School Problems (Attitude to School, Attitude to Teachers, Sensation Seeking), Internalizing Problems (Atypicality, Locus of Control, Social Stress, Anxiety, Depression, Sense of Inadequacy, Somatization), Inattention/Hyperactivity (Attention Problems, Hyperactivity), Emotional Symptoms Index (Social Stress, Anxiety, Depression, Sense of Inadequacy, Self-Esteem, Self-Reliance), Personal Adjustment (Relations with Parents, Interpersonal Relations, Self-Esteem, Self-Reliance), Content Scales (Anger Control, Ego Strength, Mania, Test Anxiety).
4) *Self-Report of Personality-College.*
Population: Ages 18-25.
Scores, 23: Internalizing Problems (Atypicality, Locus of Control, Social Stress, Anxiety, Depression, Sense of Inadequacy, Somatization), Inattention/Hyperactivity (Attention Problems, Hyperactivity), Emotional Symptoms Index (Social Stress, Anxiety, Depression, Sense of Inadequacy, Self-Esteem, Self-Reliance), Personal Adjustment (Relations with Parents, Interpersonal Relations, Self-Esteem, Self-Reliance), Content Scales (Anger Control, Ego Strength, Mania, Test Anxiety).
d) STRUCTURED DEVELOPMENTAL HISTORY.
Price Data: $41.75 per 25 history forms.
e) STUDENT OBSERVATION SYSTEM.
Price Data: $35.25 per 25 observation forms.
Time: (15) minutes.
Cross References: For reviews by Stephanie Stein and by T. Steuart Watson and Katherine Wickstrom, see 17:21; for reviews by James Clyde DiPerna and by Robert Spies and Christina Finley Jones of an earlier version, see 14:40; see also T5:280 (6 references); for reviews by Jonathon Sandoval and by Joseph C. Witt and Kevin M. Jones of an earlier edition, see 13:34 (6 references).

[298]

Behavior Dimensions Rating Scale.
Purpose: Developed to screen for emotional/behavior disorders and for monitoring behavior change.
Population: Ages 5–adult.
Publication Date: 1989.
Acronym: BDRS.
Scores: 5: Aggressive/Acting Out, Irresponsible/Inattentive, Socially Withdrawn, Fearful/Anxious, Total.

Administration: Individual.
Price Data, 2006: $134 per complete kit including examiner's manual (77 pages) and 25 record forms; $93.50 per examiner's manaul; $50.50 per 25 test records
Time: [5–10] minutes.
Comments: Ratings by teachers, parents, and psychologists.
Authors: Lyndal M. Bullock and Michael J. Wilson.
Publisher: Riverside Publishing.
Cross References: For reviews by Martha W. Blackwell and Rosemery O. Nelson-Gray, see 11:37 (1 reference).

[299]

Behavior Dimensions Scale.

Purpose: Designed to categorize and document existing behavior patterns into recognized areas of behavior disorders to assist in making diagnostic, placement, and programming decisions.
Population: Ages 3–19.
Publication Date: 1995.
Acronym: BDS.
Scores, 7: Inattentive, Hyperactive-Impulsive, Oppositional Defiant, Conduct, Avoidant Personality, Anxiety, Depression.
Administration: Individual.
Price Data, 2006: $130 per complete kit including School Version (59 pages) and Home Version (55 pages) manuals, 50 rating forms (School and Home), intervention manual (323 pages); $15 per manual (School or Home); $35 per 50 rating forms (School or Home); $35 per 50 Home Version Spanish rating forms; $30 per intervention manual; $35 per computerized scoring disk (Windows).
Time: (20–25) minutes.
Author: Stephen B. McCarney.
Publisher: Hawthorne Educational Services, Inc.
Cross References: For reviews by Kevin M. Jones and Beverly M. Klecker, see 14:41.

[300]

Behavior Disorders Identification Scale–Second Edition.

Purpose: "To document the existence of behaviors which meet the criteria for identifying the student as behaviorally disordered."
Population: Ages 4.5-21.
Publication Dates: 1988–2000.
Acronym: BDIS-2 SV (School Version); BDIS-2 HV (Home Version).
Scores, 5: Learning Problems, Interpersonal Relations, Inappropriate Behavior, Unhappiness/Depression, Physical Symptoms/Fears.
Administration: Individual.
Forms, 2: School Version, Home Version.

Price Data, 2006: $190 per complete kit including 50 Pre-Referral Behavior Checklists, 50 Intervention Strategies Documentation forms, 50 School Version Rating forms, 50 Home Version Rating forms, School Version Technical Manual, Home Version Technical Manual, and Teacher's Guide to Behavioral Interventions; $30 per 50 Pre-Referral Behavior Checklists; $30 per 50 Intervention Strategies Documentation forms; $15 per Technical Manual (School Version or Home Version); $35 per 50 rating forms (School Version, Home Version, or Home Version Spanish); $30 per Teacher's Guide to Behavioral Interventions; $35 per BDIS-2 Quick Score; $225 per Teacher's Guide to Behavioral Interventions computer version (Windows®).
Time: [20] minutes for School Version; [15] minutes for Home Version.
Comments: Completed by adult observers; based on federal definitions of serious emotional disturbance (PL 94-142 and IDEA Amendments of 1997); available in paper or computer version; system requirements: IBM-compatible computer, 30 MB of drive space, 32–64 MB of free RAM, Windows 98 or newer, and a 2X CD-ROM drive, 580K memory; Quick Score computer scoring of school and Home Versions available, system requirements Windows 95 or newer, 8 MB RAM, 10 MB hard disk space, 2X CD-ROM drive; Quick Score provides individualized goals, objectives, interventions; Spanish language Home Version rating forms available.
Authors: Stephen B. McCarney and Tamara J. Arthaud (Technical Manuals, Home Version and School Version), and Kathy Cummins Wunderlich (Teacher's Guide to Behavioral Interventions).
Publisher: Hawthorne Educational Services, Inc.
Cross References: For reviews by Judy Oehler-Stinnett and by Stephanie Stein and Phil Diaz, see 16:26; for reviews by Doreen Ward Fairbank and Harlan J. Stientjes of an earlier edition, see 12:46.

[301]

Behavior Evaluation Scale–Third Edition.

Purpose: Designed "to contribute to the early identification and service delivery for students with serious emotional disturbance or behavior disorders."
Population: Ages 4-19.
Publication Dates: 1990-2005.
Acronym: BES-3:L, BES-3:S.
Scores: 6: Learning Problems, Interpersonal Difficulties, Inappropriate Behavior, Unhappiness/Depression, Physical Symptoms/Fears, Total Score.
Administration: Individual.
Forms, 4: Long-School Version, Long-Home Version, Short-School Version, Short-Home Version.
Price Data, 2006: LONG VERSION: $208.50 per complete kit including Long-School Version technical manual (2005, 77 pages), 50 Long-School Version rating forms, Long-Home Version technical manual (2005, 75

pages), 50 Long-Home Version rating forms, 50 Intervention Strategies Documentation forms, 50 Long-Pre-Referral checklists, Long-Intervention manual, and one Parent's Guide; $20 per Long-technical manual (specify School or Home Version); $30 per Long-Intervention manual; $35 per 50 Long-rating forms (specify School or Home Version); $35 per 50 Long-Home Version Spanish rating forms; $30 per 50 Intervention Strategies Documentation forms; $30 per 50 Long-Pre-Referral checklists; $8.50 per the Parent's Guide; $35 per Long-Quick Score computerized Windows program; SHORT VERSION: $206.50 per complete kit including Short-School Version technical manual (2005, 83 pages), 50 Short-School Version rating forms, Short-Home Version technical manual (2005, 77 pages), 50 Short-Home Version rating forms, 50 Intervention Strategies Documentation forms, 50 Long-Pre-Referral checklists, Short-Intervention manual, and one Parent's Guide; $20 per Short-technical manual (specify School or Home Version); $28 per Short-Intervention manual; $35 per 50 Short-rating forms (specify School or Home Version); $35 per 50 Short-Home Version Spanish rating forms; $30 per 50 Intervention Strategies Documentation forms; $30 per 50 Short-Pre-Referral checklists; $8.50 per the Parent's Guide; $35 per Short-Quick Score computerized Windows program.
Foreign Language Editions: Long-Home and Short-Home Version Spanish rating forms available.
Time: (20) minutes.
Comments: Includes Home Version and School Version; scale is completed by parent/caregiver or an educator.
Authors: Stephen B. McCarney and Tamara J. Arthaud.
Publisher: Hawthorne Educational Services, Inc.
Cross References: For reviews by Matthew K. Burns and by Mark E. Swerdlik and W. Joel Schneider, see 17:22; see also T5:284 (1 reference); for reviews by Bert A. Goldman and D. Joe Olmi of a previous edition, see 12:47; for reviews by J. Jeffrey Grill, Lester Mann, and Leonard Kenowitz of an earlier edition, see 9:128.

[302]

Behavior Rating Instrument for Autistic and Other Atypical Children, 2nd Edition.

Purpose: Designed to evaluate the status of autistic, atypical, and other developmentally delayed children by assessing their present levels of functioning and measuring changes in their behavior.
Population: Autistic children.
Publication Dates: 1977–1991.
Acronym: BRIAAC.
Scores: 9: Relationship to an Adult, Communication, Drive for Mastery, Vocalization and Expressive Speech, Sound and Speech Reception, Social Responsiveness, Psychobiological Development, Expressive Gesture and Sign Language, Receptive Gesture and Sign Language.
Administration: Individual.

Price Data, 2005: $130 per complete kit including manual (1991, 140 pages) and report form masters with permission to reproduce 50 copies; $50 per manual; $80 per reproducible masters and permission to make 50 copies.
Time: Untimed.
Authors: Bertram A. Ruttenberg, Enid G. Wolf-Schein, and Charles Wenar.
Publisher: Stoelting Co.
Cross References: For a review by Doreen Ward Fairbank, see 13:35; see also T4:280 (1 reference); for a review by Edward Workman of an earlier edition, see 9:129; see also T3:272 (1 reference).

[303]

Behavior Rating Inventory of Executive Function.

Purpose: Designed to assess impairment of executive function behaviors in the home and school environments using parent and teacher questionnaires.
Population: Ages 5–18.
Publication Dates: 1996–2000.
Acronym: BRIEF.
Scores, 11: Inhibit, Shift, Emotional Control, Behavioral Regulation Index, Initiate, Working Memory, Plan/Organize, Organization of Materials, Monitor, Metacognition Index, Global Executive Composite.
Administration: Individual or group.
Forms, 2: Parent Form, Teacher Form.
Price Data, 2006: $196 per introductory kit including professional manual (2000, 150 pages), 25 Parent Form Questionnaires, 25 Teacher Form Questionnaires, 50 Parent Form Scoring Summary/Profile Forms, and 50 Teacher Form Scoring Summary/Profile Forms; $525 per Scoring Program including unlimited scoring and reports for both BRIEF forms on CD-ROM.
Time: (10–15) minutes.
Comments: Ratings by teachers, parents, or guardians; CD-ROM-based Software Portfolio is also available for scoring and report generation.
Authors: Gerard A. Gioia, Peter K. Isquith, Steven C. Guy, and Lauren Kenworthy.
Publisher: Psychological Assessment Resources, Inc.
Cross References: For reviews by Corine Fitzpatrick and Gregory Schraw, see 15:32.

[304]

Behavior Rating Inventory of Executive Function–Adult Version.

Purpose: Designed to capture "views of an adult's own executive functions, or self-regulation, in his or her everyday environment."
Population: Ages 18–90.
Publication Dates: 1996-2005.

Acronym: BRIEF-A.

Scores, 12: 9 subscales: Inhibit, Shift, Emotional Control, Self-Monitor, Initiate, Working Memory, Plan/Organize, Task Monitor, Organization of Materials; 3 composite scores: Behavioral Regulation Index, Metacognition Index, Global Executive Composite.

Administration: Individual.

Price Data, 2007: $189 per introductory kit including professional manual (2005, 147 pages), 25 self-report forms, 25 informant report forms, 25 self-report scoring summary/profile forms, and 25 informant report scoring summary/profile forms; $55 per professional manual; $45 per 25 self-report forms; $45 per 25 informant report forms; $30 per 25 self-report scoring summary/profile forms; $30 per 25 informant report scoring summary/profile forms.

Time: (15) minutes.

Comments: It is preferable to administer the informant report form to a knowledgeable informant such as a spouse, adult child, caregiver, or other person who has frequent face-to-face interaction with the individual completing the self-report form.

Authors: Robert M. Roth, Peter K. Isquith, and Gerard A. Gioia.

Publisher: Psychological Assessment Resources, Inc.

Cross References: For reviews by Gary J. Dean and Sandra F. Dean and by Kathy E. Green, see 17:23.

[305]

Behavior Rating Inventory of Executive Function–Preschool Version.

Purpose: Designed to "assess executive function behaviors of preschool aged children in the home and preschool environments using the observations of parents, teachers, and daycare providers."

Population: Ages 2-0 to 5-11.

Publication Dates: 1996–2003.

Acronym: BRIEF-P™.

Scores, 9: Inhibit, Shift, Emotional Control, Working Memory, Plan/Organize, Inhibitory Self-Control Index, Flexibility Index, Emergent Metacognition Index, Global Executive Composite.

Administration: Individual.

Price Data, 2006: $125 per introductory kit including manual (2003, 111 pages), 25 rating forms, and 25 scoring summary/profile forms.

Time: (10–15) minutes.

Comments: Behavior rating scale is completed by parent or teacher/child care worker who is familiar with the child.

Authors: Gerard A. Gioia, Kimberly Andrews Espy, and Peter K. Isquith.

Publisher: Psychological Assessment Resources, Inc.

Cross References: For reviews by R. Anthony Doggett and Carl J. Sheperis and by Leah M. Nellis, see 16:27.

[306]

Behavior Rating Inventory of Executive Function–Self-Report Version.

Purpose: Designed to assess children's and adolescents' "views of their own executive functions, or self-regulation, in their everyday environment."

Population: Ages 11–18.

Publication Dates: 1996–2004.

Acronym: BRIEF-SR.

Scores, 15: Behavioral Regulation Index (Inhibit, Shift, Emotional Control, Monitor, Total), Metacognition Index (Working Memory, Plan/Organize, Organization of Materials, Task Completion, Total), Global Executive Composite, Behavioral Shift, Cognitive Shift, Inconsistency, Negativity.

Administration: Individual.

Price Data, 2006: $142 per introductory kit including professional manual (2004, 204 pages), 25 rating forms, and 50 scoring summary/profile forms.

Time: (10-15) minutes.

Authors: Steven C. Guy, Peter K. Isquith, and Gerard A. Gioia.

Publisher: Psychological Assessment Resources, Inc.

Cross References: For reviews by Stephen L. Benton and Sheryl Benton and by Manuel Martinez-Pons, see 16:28.

[307]

Behavior Rating Profile, Second Edition.

Purpose: "To evaluate students' behaviors at home, in school, and in interpersonal relationships."

Population: Ages 6-6 to 18-6.

Publication Dates: 1978–1990.

Acronym: BRP-2.

Scores: 5 checklists: Student Rating Scales (Home, School, Peers), Teacher Rating Scale, Parent Rating Scale, plus Sociogram score.

Administration: Individual.

Price Data, 2010: $229 per complete kit; $45 per 50 rating scale booklets (specify student, parent, or teacher form); $45 per 50 profile forms; $55 per examiner's manual (1990, 75 pages).

Time: (15–30) minutes per scale.

Authors: Linda Brown and Donald D. Hammill.

Publisher: PRO-ED.

Cross References: See T5:286 (3 references); for reviews by Sarah J. Allen and Lisa A. Bloom, see 12:48 (1 reference); see also T4:281 (1 reference); for reviews by Thomas R. Kratochwill and Joseph C. Witt of an earlier edition, see 9:130 (1 reference); see also T3:273 (1 reference).

[308]

Behavior Rating Scale.

Purpose: Designed to sample teachers' perceptions about their pupils' behavior in the classroom.

Population: Grades K–8.
Publication Dates: 1970–1975.
Score: Total score only.
Administration: Group.
Forms, 3: Forms differ only in number of rating categories.
Manual: No manual.
Price Data, 2001: Now free upon request from publisher.
Time: Administration time not reported.
Comments: Ratings by teachers; research instrument; may be used with or separately from Characteristics Scale (467).
Authors: Patricia B. Elmore and Donald L. Beggs.
Publisher: Patricia B. Elmore.
Cross References: See T5:287 (1 reference) and T4:282 (2 references); for a review by Jayne A. Parker, see 9:131 (2 references).

[309]

Behavioral and Emotional Rating Scale, Second Edition.

Purpose: Designed to "measure the personal strengths and competencies of children."
Population: Ages 5-0 to 18-11.
Publication Dates: 1998–2004.
Acronym: BERS-2.
Scores, 6: 5 subscales: Interpersonal Strength, Family Involvement, Intrapersonal Strength, School Functioning, Affective Strength, plus Strength Index.
Administration: Individual.
Price Data, 2010: $186 per complete kit including examiner's manual (2004, 112 pages), 25 teacher rating scales, 25 parent rating scales, 25 youth rating scales, and 50 summary forms; $64 per examiner's manual; $34 per 25 teacher rating scales; $34 per parent rating scales; $34 per youth rating scales; $34 per 50 summary forms.
Time: (10) minutes.
Comments: Revised edition adds Parent and Youth Rating Scales.
Author: Michael H. Epstein.
Publisher: PRO-ED.
Cross References: For reviews by John D. King and by Mark E. Swerdlik and W. Joel Schneider, see 16:29; for reviews by Beth Doll and D. Joe Olmi of an earlier edition, see 14:42.

[310]

Behavioral and Psychological Assessment of Dementia.

Purpose: Designed to "assess changes in behavior and mood associated with the onset of various dementia syndromes."
Population: Ages 30-90.
Publication Date: 2007.

Acronym: BPAD.
Scores, 24: Total Current, Total Past, Total Change, Perceptual/Delusional Current, Perceptual/Delusional Past, Perceptual/Delusional Change, Positive Mood/Anxiety Current, Positive Mood/Anxiety Past, Positive Mood/Anxiety Change, Negative Mood/Anxiety Current, Negative Mood/Anxiety Past, Negative Mood/Anxiety Change, Aggressive Current, Aggressive Past, Aggressive Change, Perseverative/Rigid Current, Perseverative/Rigid Past, Perseverative/Rigid Change, Disinhibited Current, Disinhibited Past, Disinhibited Change, Biological Rhythms Current, Biological Rhythms Past, Biological Rhythms Change.
Administration: Individual.
Price Data, 2010: $260 per software portfolio with on-screen help, quick start guide, professional manual (67 pages), and 25 response booklets; $63 per 25 response booklets; $67 per professional manual.
Time: (15) minutes.
Comments: "Should be completed by family members, paraprofessionals, or other professionals ages 18-90 who have regular contact with individuals who have suspected or diagnosed dementia."
Authors: Kara S. Schmidt and Jennifer L. Gallo.
Publisher: Psychological Assessment Resources, Inc.
Cross References: For reviews by Shawn K. Acheson and Anita M. Hubley, see 18:12.

[311]

Behavioral Assessment of Pain Questionnaire.

Purpose: "Used for gaining a better understanding of factors which may be maintaining the subacute and chronic noncancerous pain experience."
Population: Subacute and chronic pain patients.
Publication Dates: 1990-1992.
Administration: Individual.
Price Data, 2001: $30 per sample kit including manual (1992, 44 pages); answer sheet and Mercury scoring with interpretive clinical profile, general information, scale descriptions, sample BAP clinical profile, and reprint of journal article; $10 per manual.
Foreign Language Editions: Spanish and French editions available.
Time: (60) minutes.
Authors: Michael J. Lewandowski and Blake H. Tearnan.
Publisher: Pain Assessment Resources [No reply from publisher; status unknown].
 a) BEHAVIORAL ASSESSMENT OF PAIN.
 Acronym: BAP.
 Scores, 34: Demographic Information, Activity Interference Scale (Domestic/Household Activities, Heavy Activities, Social Activities, Personal Care Activities, Personal Hygiene Activities), Avoidance Scale, Spouse/Partner Influence Scale (Reinforce-

ment of Pain, Discouragement/Criticism of Pain, Reinforcement of Wellness, Discouragement/Criticism of Wellness), Physician Influence Scale (Discouragement/Criticism of Pain, Reinforcement of Wellness, Discouragement/Criticism of Wellness, Reinforcement of Pain), Physician Qualities Scale, Pain Beliefs Scale (Catastrophizing, Fear of Reinjury, Expectation for Cure, Blaming Self, Entitlement, Future Despair, Social Disbelief, Lack of Medical Comprehensiveness), Perceived Consequences Scale (Social Interference, Physical Harm, Psychological Harm, Pain Exacerbation, Productivity Interference), Coping Scale, Negative Mood Scale (Depression, Anxiety, Muscular Discomfort, Change in Weight).
Price Data: $21.50 per on-site scored interpretive report; $23.50 per Mercury scored interpretive report; $5 per BAP booklet.
b) POST BEHAVIORAL ASSESSMENT OF PAIN.
Acronym: P-BAP.
Scores, 23: Avoidance, Spouse/Partner Influence Scale (Reinforcement of Pain, Discouragement/Criticism of Pain, Reinforcement of Wellness, Discouragement/Criticism of Wellness), Pain Beliefs Scale (Catastrophizing, Fear of Reinjury, Expectation for Cure, Blaming Self, Entitlement, Future Despair, Social Disbelief, Lack of Medical Comprehensiveness), Perceived Consequences Scale (Social Interference, Physical Harm, Psychological Harm, Pain Exacerbation, Productivity Interference), Coping Scale, Negative Mood Scale (Depression, Anxiety, Muscular Discomfort, Change in Weight).
Price Data: $21.50 per on-site scored P-BAP report; $23.50 per Mercury scored P-BAP report; $5 per P-BAP booklet.
Cross References: For reviews by Gerald E. DeMauro and Ronald J. Ganellen, see 12:49.

[312]
Behavioral Characteristics Progression (BCP) Assessment Record.
Purpose: Assesses developmental skills/behaviors.
Population: Children and adults with mental and physical disabilities.
Publication Dates: 1973-1997.
Acronym: BCP.
Scores: Item scores only.
Administration: Individual.
Price Data, 2006: $5 per record booklet (1997, 64 pages); $59.95 per BCP Instructional Activities resource book (1997, 400 pages).
Time: Administration time not reported.
Comments: "Criterion-referenced" assessment for developmental ages 1-14 years.
Author: VORT Corporation.
Publisher: VORT Corporation.

Cross References: See T5:292 (1 reference); for reviews by Rosemery O. Nelson-Gray and Harvey N. Switzky of an earlier edition, see 11:38.

[313]
Behavioral Objective Sequence.
Purpose: Designed to "assist special educators and other professionals assess behavioral competencies of students with emotional and behavioral disorders."
Population: Students (grades 1-12) with emotional and behavioral disorders.
Publication Date: 1998.
Acronym: BOS.
Scores, 6: Adaptive Behaviors, Self-Management Behaviors, Communication Behaviors, Interpersonal Behaviors, Task Behaviors, Personal Behaviors.
Administration: Individual.
Price Data, 2006: $39.95 per manual (1998, 104 pages), recording forms, and test; $150 per report generating software (for Windows) Behavioral Objective Sequence Reports (BOSR) including BOS manual.
Time: Administration time not reported.
Comments: "Can be used as a bank of (behavioral) objectives, as a rating scale, or as a structured observational system"; completed by educational/psychological professionals about a student; software program available.
Authors: Sheldon Braaten (test and software program) and John B. Merbler (software program).
Publisher: Research Press.
Cross References: For reviews by M. David Miller and Stephanie Stein, see 15:33.

[314]
Behavioral Summary.
Purpose: Provides "screening of behavioral adjustment problems in children and adolescents."
Population: Grades K-12.
Publication Date: 2009.
Administration: Group.
Price Data, 2009: $60 per hand scoring kit including 10 Parent Report AutoScore forms, 10 Teacher Report AutoScore forms, 10 Student Report AutoScore forms, and manual (134 pages); $299 per computer scoring kit including 10 Parent Report AutoScore forms, 10 Teacher Report AutoScore forms, 10 Student Report AutoScore forms, manual, and Unlimited-Use CD for computer scoring; $18.75 per 25 AutoScore forms; $45 per manual; $275 per Unlimited-Use CD for computer scoring and interpretation.
Comments: Ratings by parents, teachers, and self-report; scoring on PC with Windows 98, ME, 2000, XP, or Vista.
Authors: David Lachar and Christian P. Gruber (all forms and manual), Sabine A. Wingenfeld and Rex B. Kline (teacher report form).
Publisher: Western Psychological Services.

a) PARENT REPORT.
Population: Grades K-12.
Scores, 14: 2 Validity scales (Inconsistent Responding, Exaggeration), 8 Adjustment scales (Impulsivity & Distractibility, Defiance, Family Problems, Atypical Behavior, Somatic Concern, Emotional Problems, Social Withdrawal, Social Skill Deficits), 3 Composite scales (Externalization, Internalization, Social Adjustment), Total score.
Time: (15) minutes.
b) STUDENT REPORT.
Population: Same as *a* above.
Scores: Same as *a* above.
Time: Same as *a* above.
c) TEACHER REPORT.
Population: Grades 4-12.
Scores, 15: 4 Academic Resources scales (Academic Performance, Academic Habits, Social Skills, Parent Participation), 7 Adjustment Problems scales (Health Concerns, Emotional Distress, Unusual Behavior, Social Problems, Verbal Aggression, Physical Aggression, Behavior Problems), 3 Disruptive Behavior scales (Attention-Deficit/Hyperactivity, Oppositional Defiant, Conduct Problems), Total score.
Time: (20) minutes.

[315]

Behaviors and Experiences Inventory.

Purpose: "An initial screen for Attention-Deficit/Hyperactivity Disorder (ADHD), Conduct Disorder (CD), and Antisocial Personality Disorder (ASPD)."
Population: Adults.
Publication Dates: 1998–1999.
Acronym: BEI.
Scores, 24: ADHD: Inattention (Difficulty Sustaining Attention, Fails to Finish Assignments, Inattention to Details/Careless, Difficulty Organizing Tasks/Activities, Tendency to Lose Things, Distractible), Hyperactivity, Impulsivity, Conduct Disorder as a Child/Adolescent (Aggression, Destruction of Property, Deceitfulness or Theft, Serious Violation of Rules, Cruelty to Animals and Fire-Setting), Antisocial Personality Disorder (Failure to Conform to Social Norms, Deceitfulness, Impulsivity, Irritability/Aggressiveness, Reckless Disregard for Safety, Irresponsibility, Lack of Remorse), History of Abuse as a Child/Adolescent (Physical, Sexual, Emotional).
Administration: Individual.
Price Data: Available from publisher.
Time: (15–20) minutes.
Comments: Can be administered as paper-and-pencil questionnaire or as a structured interview; screens for DSM-IV diagnostic criteria, providing an estimate of the likelihood that an individual meets the criteria for ADHD, CD, and ASPD; covers current problems only.

Authors: Norman G. Hoffmann, David Mee-Lee, and Gerald D. Shulman.
Publisher: Change Companies.
Cross References: For a review by Mark R. Cooper, see 15:34.

[316]

Behaviour Problems: A System of Management.

Purpose: "A systematic means of recording and analysing information on children's problem behaviour."
Population: Problem behavior children in a classroom situation.
Publication Date: 1984.
Scores: 8 areas of behavior: Classroom Conformity, Task Orientation, Emotional Control, Acceptance of Authority, Self-Worth, Peer Relationships, Self Responsibility/Problem Solving, Other.
Administration: Individual.
Price Data: Price information available from publisher for complete set including manual (15 pages), pad of 50 Daily Records, and pack of 10 Behaviour Checklist/Monthly Progress Charts.
Time: Administration time not reported.
Authors: Peter P. Galvin and Richard M. Singleton.
Publisher: GL Assessment [England].
Cross References: For reviews by Kathryn M. Benes and Terry Overton, see 11:39.

[317]

Behavioural Assessment of the Dysexecutive Syndrome.

Purpose: "A test battery aimed at predicting everyday problems arising from the Dysexecutive Syndrome."
Population: Ages 16–87.
Publication Date: 1996.
Acronym: BADS.
Scores, 7: Rule Shift Card, Action Program, Key Search, Temporal Judgement, Zoo Map, Modified Six Elements, Total.
Administration: Individual.
Price Data, 2006: £319.50 per complete kit including manual, 25 scoring sheets, 5 stimulus books, stimulus cards, three-dimensional plastic materials, timer, 25 self-rater dex questionnaires, and 25 independent rater questionnaires; £26 per 2 packs of 25 dex questionnaires (self-rater and independent rater).
Time: 40 minutes.
Comments: Subtest scores "may be used individually, although validation studies have indicated that the overall battery score is the most sensitive predictor of executive problems"; useful with brain-injured and schizophrenic patients for identifying general or specific deficits in executive functions; supplemental information about patients can be gathered using

the self-rating and caregiver rating forms included in the test kit.

Authors: Barbara A. Wilson, Nick Alderman, Paul W. Burgess, Hazel Emslie, and Jonathan J. Evans.

Publisher: Pearson Assessment [England].

Cross References: For reviews by Rik Carl D'Amato and Sandra D. Haynes, see 14:43.

[318]

Behavioural Assessment of the Dysexecutive Syndrome for Children.

Purpose: Tests the executive functioning of children and adolescents.

Population: Children and adolescents ages 7 to 16.

Publication Date: 2003.

Acronym: BADS-C.

Scores, 8: Playing Cards Test, Water Test, Key Search Test, Zoo Map Test 1, Zoo Map Test 2, Six Part Test, Dysexecutive Questionnaire for Children, Total Score.

Administration: Individual.

Price Data, 2007: £382 per complete kit including manual (41 pages), 25 scoring sheets, stimulus cards, three-dimensional plastic materials, timer, 25 Dysexecutive Questionnaire for Children (DEX-C), independent rater questionnaires, beads, nuts, bolts, and washers; £19.39 per 25 record sheets; £15.86 per 25 DEX-C questionnaires.

Time: (35–45) minutes.

Comments: Adaptation of Behavioural Assessment of the Dysexecutive Syndrome (317); examinee IQ-score must be available to determine scaled score and percentile rank.

Authors: Hazel Emslie, F. Colin Wilson, Vivian Burden, Ian Nimmo-Smith, and Barbara A. Wilson.

Publisher: Pearson Assessment [England].

Cross References: For reviews by Lorraine Cleeton and Rama K. Mishra, see 17:24.

[319]

Behavioural Inattention Test.

Purpose: Developed to measure unilateral visual neglect.

Population: Ages 19-83.

Publication Date: 1987.

Acronym: BIT.

Scores, 17: Conventional Subtest Scores (Line Crossing, Letter Cancellation, Star Cancellation, Figure and Shape Copying, Line Bisection, Representational Drawing, Total), Behavioural Subtests (Picture Scanning, Telephone Dialling, Menu Reading, Article Reading, Telling and Setting the Time, Coin Sorting, Address and Sentence Copying, Map Navigation, Card Sorting, Total).

Administration: Individual.

Price Data, 2006: £229.50 per complete kit including manual (19 pages), various stimuli, test, playing cards, and clock face; £60.50 per 50 scoring sheets.

Time: (40) minutes.

Authors: Barbara Wilson, Janet Cockburn, and Peter Halligan.

Publisher: Pearson Assessment [England].

Cross References: For reviews by William R. Horstman and Robert M. Thorndike, see 17:25.

[320]

Belbin Team-Roles Self-Perception Inventory.

Purpose: Designed to determine which contributions each team member can make best.

Population: Teams.

Publication Date: 1994.

Scores: 9 Profiles: Plant, Coordinator, Resource Investigator, Monitor Evaluator, Implementer, Team Worker, Completer-Finisher, Specialist, Shaper.

Administration: Group.

Price Data: Available from publisher.

Time: [1 day].

Author: Meredith Belbin.

Publisher: Jossey-Bass, A Wiley Company.

Cross References: For reviews by Keith Hattrup and by Kristin O. Prien and Erich P. Prien, see 14:44.

[321]

Bell Object Relations and Reality Testing Inventory.

Purpose: Designed to assess "dimensions of object relations and reality testing ego functioning."

Population: Ages 18 and older

Publication Date: 1995.

Acronym: BORRTI.

Scores, 8: Object Relations (Alienation, Insecure Attachment, Egocentricity, Social Incompetence); Reality Testing (Reality Distortion, Uncertainty of Perception, Hallucinations and Delusions); Inconsistent Responding; plus two validity indexes: FREQ, INFREQ.

Administration: Group.

Price Data, 2011: $130 for complete kit, including 20 Full Form AutoScore Forms, 2 WPS Test Report prepaid BORRTI (Full Form) mail-in answer sheets, and manual; $45 Full Form Autoscore Form (set of 20); $40 Form O Autoscore Form (set of 20); $55 manual; $19.25 BORRTI Full Form mail-in answer sheet; $18 BORRTI Form O mail-in answer sheet; $290 BORRTI CD for computer scoring and interpretation (BORRTI Full Form or Form O), includes interpretive report and free U.S. shipping; $125 BORRTI CD for computer scoring only (Full Form or Form O), includes free U.S. shipping; $17.50 BORRTI Full Form PC answer sheet for use with the BORRTI CDs (pads of 100); $17.50 BORRTI Form O PC answer sheet for use with the BORRTI CDs (pads of 100).

Time: (15–20) minutes.

Comments: Form O including only items measuring object relations also available; The BORRTI CD requires a PC with Windows 98, 2000, ME, XP, Vista, or Windows 7; each CD is good for 20 uses.
Author: Morris D. Bell.
Publisher: Western Psychological Services.
Cross References: For reviews by Glen Fox and Steven I. Pfeiffer, see 14:45; see also T5:297 (2 references).

[322]

Bell Relationship Inventory for Adolescents.

Purpose: Designed for use "in schools and clinical settings for quickly and accurately assessing object relations ego functioning in children and adolescents."
Population: Ages 11-17.
Publication Date: 2005.
Acronym: BRIA.
Scores, 6: Alienation, Insecure Attachment, Egocentricity, Social Incompetence, Positive Attachment, Response Bias.
Administration: Group.
Price Data, 2010: $99 per kit including Autoscore forms, 1 manual for the Bell Object Relations and Reality Testing Inventory (1995, 82 pages), and 1 manual supplement for the BRIA (2005, 27 pages); $37 per 25 Autoscore Forms; $55 per nanual for the Bell Object Relations and Reality Testing Inventory; $22 per manual supplement for the BRIA.
Time: (10-15) minutes.
Comments: The BRIA is a version of the Bell Object Relations and Reality Testing Inventory, Form O (321) adapted for use with adolescents aged 11-17.
Author: Morris D. Bell.
Publisher: Western Psychological Services.
Cross References: For reviews by Glen Fox and Steven I. Pfeiffer of the Bell Object Relations and Reality Testing Inventory, see 14:45; see also T5:297 (2 references).

[323]

Bem Sex-Role Inventory.

Purpose: Provides independent assessments of masculinity and femininity in terms of the respondent's self-reported possession of socially desirable, stereotypically masculine and feminine personality characteristics; can also be used as a measurement of the extent to which respondents spontaneously sort self-relevant information into distinct masculine and feminine categories; measures masculinity, femininity, androgyny, and undifferentiated, using the Masculinity and Femininity scales.
Population: High school and college and adults.
Publication Dates: 1978-1981.
Acronym: BSRI.
Scores, 4: Femininity, Masculinity, Androgeny, Undifferentiated.

Administration: Group.
Price Data: Available from publisher at www.mindgarden.com/products/bemss.htm
Time: (10-15) minutes.
Comments: Test is titled Bem Inventory; self-administered; short and long form available (short form consists of first 30 items only).
Author: Sandra Lipsitz Bem.
Publisher: Mind Garden, Inc.
Cross References: See T5:298 (167 references) and T4:288 (204 references); for reviews by Richard Lippa and Frank D. Rayne, see 9:137 (121 references).

[324]

Bench Mark Measures.

Purpose: Measures a student's general knowledge of phonics.
Population: Ungraded.
Publication Date: 1977.
Scores: 3 levels in 4 areas: Alphabet and Dictionary Skills, Reading, Handwriting, Spelling.
Administration: Individual in part.
Price Data, 2006: $77.60 per complete kit including administrator's guide (16 pages), test booklet (26 pages), 24 summary sheets (6 pages), graph of concepts and multisensory introductions (16 pages), sheet of block capitals, set of three-dimensional letters, skeleton dictionary (Anna Gillingham and Bessie Stillman, 1956, 79 pages), test cards (56), spirit duplicating master (1 page); $18 per 12 summary sheets; $8.20 per graph; $9.70 per skeleton dictionary; quantity discounts available.
Time: (30–60) minutes.
Comments: "Criterion-referenced"; follows the sequence of the Alphabetic Phonics curriculum developed in the Language Research and Training Laboratory of the Texas Scottish Rite Hospital for its remedial language training program.
Author: Aylett R. Cox.
Publisher: Educators Publishing Service, Inc.
Cross References: For a review by David J. Carroll, see 9:138.

[325]

Benchmark of Organizational Emotional Intelligence.

Purpose: "Designed to measure the level of emotional intelligence in an organization as a whole and across departments, teams, or divisions."
Population: Ages 18 and over.
Publication Date: 2005.
Acronym: BOEI.
Scores, 24: 7 scale scores (Job Happiness, Compensation, Work/Life Stress Management, Organizational Cohesiveness, Supervisory Leadership, Diversity and Anger Management, Organizational Responsiveness),

14 subscale scores (Pay, Benefits, Stability, Stress Management, Work/Life Balance, Coworker Relationships, Teamwork, Diversity Climate, Gender/Racial Acceptance, Anger Management, Training and Innovation, Optimism and Integrity, Courage and Adaptability, Top Management Leadership), 2 validity scale scores (Positive Impression, Negative Impression), Total Score.
Administration: Group or individual.
Price Data, 2011: $352 per Online Organizational Report kit including technical manual (176 pages) and 1 Organizational Report; $336 per Online Organizational Report; $56 per technical manual; $56 per Online Group Report comparing up to 5 groups; $15 per Online Individual Report.
Time: (30) minutes.
Comments: Test can be administered over the internet.
Authors: Steven J. Stein and Multi-Health Systems Staff.
Publisher: Multi-Health Systems, Inc.
Cross References: For reviews by Malinda Hendricks Green and Michael J. Zickar, see 17:26.

[326]

Benchmarks [Revised].

Purpose: "Assesses skills and perspectives that leaders can learn from experience; also, potential flaws that can derail a career."
Population: Middle- to upper-level managers and executives with at least 3–5 years of managerial experience.
Publication Dates: 1990–2001.
Scores, 21: 3 Skill Areas: Meeting Job Challenges (Resourcefulness, Doing Whatever It Takes, Being A Quick Study, Decisiveness), Leading People (Leading Employees, Confronting Problem Employees, Participative Management, Change Management), Respecting Self and Others (Building And Mending Relationships, Compassion And Sensitivity, Straightforwardness And Composure, Balance Between Personal Life And Work, Self-Awareness, Putting People At Ease, Differences Matter, Career Management), Potential for Derailment (Problems With Interpersonal Relationships, Difficulty Building And Leading A Team, Difficulty Changing Or Adapting, Failure To Meet Business Objectives, Too Narrow Functional Orientation).
Administration: Group.
Restricted Distribution: The publisher requires a 2-day certification program for those who wish to give feedback from Benchmarks in their own organization or as a consultant.
Price Data, 2006: $275 per set including 13 survey questionnaires (paper-and-pencil or internet), Feedback Reports, Developmental Learning Guide, and a Facilitators Guide; $40 handling fee charged per set; quantity discounts available; $300 per group profile (2005, 13 pages).
Foreign Language Editions: Translations available include British English, French, French-Canadian,

Dutch, German, Italian, and Spanish; normative comparisons are available for Belgium and the United Kingdom.
Time: (30–40) minutes.
Comments: Available in paper-and-pencil and online; hard copy Feedback Report is generated providing mean scores and normative comparisons for all items and the 21 scores as rated by all observers, self, boss, superior, peer, direct report, other; Developmental Learning Guide "suggests strategies for change" including exercises to help analyze feedback, presentation of "tactics and strategies."
Authors: Michael Lombardo, Cynthia McCauley, Dana McDonald-Mann, and Jean Brittain Leslie.
Publisher: Center for Creative Leadership.
  a) BENCHMARKS GROUP PROFILE.
  Purpose: "To assess the caliber and potential of management to fulfill … objectives, and to develop more appropriate and effective management and organizational development strategies."
  Price Data: $300 per group profile.
  Comments: Provides group-level mean scores and normative comparisons for the 21 scores as rated by all observers, self, boss/superior, peer, direct report, other.
Cross References: For reviews by Heidi M. Carty and Michael Spangler, see 15:35; for a review by Sheldon Zedeck of an earlier edition, see 12:50.

[327]

Bender® Visual-Motor Gestalt Test, Second Edition.

Purpose: Designed to measure visual-motor integration skills in children and adults.
Population: Ages 4–85+.
Publication Dates: 1938–2003.
Acronym: Bender®-Gestalt II.
Scores, 4: Copy Score, Recall Score, Motor Test Score, Perception Test Score.
Administration: Individual.
Price Data, 2006: $130.50 per complete kit including manual (2003, 181 pages), cards, 25 observation forms, 25 motor test booklets, and 25 perception test booklets; $68.50 per manual; $13 per 25 observation forms; $13 per 25 motor test booklets; $13 per 25 perception test booklets.
Time: Untimed; typically (10-15) minutes.
Comments: Revision of the Visual Motor Gestalt Test [Bender-Gestalt Test].
Authors: Gary G. Brannigan and Scott L. Decker.
Publisher: Riverside Publishing.
Cross References: For reviews by D. Joe Olmi and by Darrell L. Sabers and Sarah Bonner, see 16:30; see also T5:301 (61 references) and T4:291 (34 references); for reviews by Jack A. Naglieri and by John E. Obrzut and Carol A. Boliek of an earlier edition, see 11:40 (92 references) for reviews by Kenneth W. Howell and Jerome M. Sattler, see 9:139 (65 references); see also T3:280

(159 references), 8:506 (253 references), and T2:1447 (144 references); for a review by Phillip M. Kitay, see 7:161 (192 references); see also P:415 (170 references); for a review by C. B. Blakemore and an excerpted review by Fred Y. Billingslea, see 6:203 (99 references); see also 5:172 (118 references); for reviews by Arthur L. Benton and Howard R. White, see 4:144 (34 references); see also 3:108 (8 references).

[328]

Bennett Mechanical Comprehension Test, Second Edition.

Purpose: "Designed to measure the ability to perceive and understand the relationship of physical forces and mechanical elements in practical situations."

Population: Industrial employees and high school and adult applicants for mechanical positions or engineering schools.

Publication Dates: 1940–1994.

Acronym: BMCT.

Scores: Total score only.

Administration: Group.

Forms, 2: S, T (equivalent forms).

Price Data, 2006: $275 per complete starter kit including 10 forms test booklet, 50 answer booklets for both forms, and manual (1994, 89 pages); $195 per 25 test booklets; $100 per 10 test bookets; $115 per 50 answer documents; $35 per hand-scoring keys; $45 per manual; $135 per taped recordings of test questions.

Time: (30) minutes.

Comments: Tape recordings of test questions read aloud are available for use with examinees who have limited reading abilities; total assessment score and percentile score provided; available online and via pencil-and-paper; Spanish version available.

Author: George K. Bennett.

Publisher: Pearson.

Cross References: For reviews by Joseph C. Ciechalski and Michael Spangler, see 16:31; see also T5:302 (4 references) and T4:292 (2 references); for a review by Hilda Wing of an earlier edition, see 11:41 (3 references); see also T3:282 (7 references) and T2:2239 (9 references); for reviews by Harold P. Bechtoldt and A. Oscar H. Roberts, and an excerpted review by Ronald K. Hambleton of the first edition, see 7:1049 (22 references); see also 6:1094 (15 references) and 5:889 (46 references); for a review by N. W. Morton of earlier forms, see 4:766 (28 references); for reviews by Charles M. Harsh, Lloyd G. Humphreys, and George A. Satter, see 3:683 (19 references).

[329]

Benton Visual Retention Test, Fifth Edition.

Purpose: "To assess visual perception, visual memory, and visuoconstructive abilities."

Population: Age 8–adults.

Publication Dates: 1946–1991.

Acronym: BVRT.

Scores, 9: Omissions, Distortions, Perseverations, Rotations, Misplacements, Size Errors, Total Left, Total Right, Total.

Administration: Individual.

Forms, 3: C, D, E in a single booklet.

Price Data, 2002: $168 per complete set including stimulus booklet (all 30 designs), scoring template, 25 response booklets, record form, and manual (1992, 108 pages); $76 per stimulus booklet; $45 per 25 response booklets-record form; $10 per scoring template; $67 per manual.

Time: (15–20) minutes.

Author: Arthur L. Benton.

Publisher: Pearson.

Cross References: See T5:303 (32 references); for reviews by Anita M. Hubley and Cynthia A. Rohrbeck, see 13:36 (66 references); see also T4:293 (62 references), 9:140 (30 references), T3:283 (27 references), 8:236 (32 references), T2:543 (71 references), and 6:543 (22 references); for a review by Nelson G. Hanawalt, see 5:401 (5 references); for reviews by Ivan Norman Mensh, Joseph Newman, and William Schofield of the original edition, see 4:360 (3 references); for an excerpted review, see 3:297.

[330]

The Benziger Thinking Styles Assessment.

Purpose: Designed to "help individuals increase their general effectiveness, collaborative skills and overall well-being through enhanced self-awareness and understanding."

Population: Working adults, aged 18 or older.

Publication Dates: 1988–2004.

Acronym: BTSA, E-BTSA.

Scores, 5: Frontal Left, Basal Left, Basal Right, Frontal Right, Introversion/Extraversion.

Administration: Individual or group.

Restricted Distribution: Administrators must be persons (licensees) who have completed the publisher's training course.

Price Data, 2004: $100 per E-BTSA (electronic version); $25 per book Thriving in Mind (2003, 326 pages); North American and European licensee prices: $45 per BTSA and book Thriving in Mind; $15 per workbook, Thriving in Mind: The Workbook (specify English or Spanish); $75 per hour telephone feedback from author; price information for other countries available from publisher.

Time: (30–45) minutes.

Comments: Not intended as a psychometric measure; paper and electronic versions available.

Author: Katherine Benziger.

Publisher: KBA, LLC.

Cross References: For reviews by Richard E. Harding and Mark L. Pope, see 16:32.

[331]

The Ber-Sil Spanish Test.

Purpose: Screening and evaluation of Spanish-speaking children.
Population: Ages 5–12, 13–17.
Publication Dates: 1972–1987.
Administration: Individual.
Price Data: Available from publisher.
Author: Marjorie L. Beringer.
Publisher: Ber-Sil Co.

a) ELEMENTARY LEVEL.
Population: Ages 5–12.
Publication Date: 1987.
Scores, 7: Vocabulary, Response to Directions, Writing, Geometric Figures, Draw a Boy or Girl, Math Skills, English Vocabulary.
Foreign Language Editions: Cantonese, Mandarin, Ilokano, Tagalog, Korean, and Persian translations available.
Time: (45–55) minutes.
b) SECONDARY LEVEL.
Population: Ages 13–17.
Publication Date: 1984.
Scores, 4: Vocabulary, Dictation in Spanish, Draw a Person, Mathematics.
Foreign Language Editions: Philippine, Tagalog, and Ilokano translations available.
Time: (45) minutes.
Cross References: For reviews by J. Manuel Casas and David Strand and by Giuseppe Costantino, see 10:30; for reviews by Giuseppe Costantino and Jaclyn B. Spitzer of an earlier edition, see 9:141.

[332]

BEST Instruments.

Purpose: A series of learning instruments designed to help managers and employees understand their behavior.
Population: Adults.
Publication Dates: 1989–1994.
Acronym: BEST.
Administration: Group.
Price Data: Available from publisher.
Comments: Subtests available as separates.
Author: James H. Brewer.
Publisher: BEST Instruments, LLC.

a) MY BEST PROFILE.
Purpose: "To promote positive interpersonal relations."
Publication Date: 1989.
Scores: 4 personality types: Bold, Expressive, Sympathetic, Technical.
Time: (15–20) minutes.
b) MY BEST COMMUNICATION STYLE.
Purpose: "To improve communication skills."
Publication Dates: 1989–1990.
Scores: 4 styles: Bold, Expressive, Sympathetic, Technical.
Time: (15–20) minutes.
c) MY BEST LEADERSHIP STYLE.
Purpose: "To improve leadership skills."
Publication Dates: 1989–1994.
Scores: Same as *a* above.
Time: (15–20) minutes.
d) LEADERSHIP/PERSONALITY COMPATIBIL-ITY INVENTORY.
Purpose: "To promote more productive leadership in organizations."
Acronym: L/PCI.
Scores: Same as *a* above plus 4 Leadership Role Characteristics: Active/Competitive, Persuasive/Interactive, Precise/Systematic, Willing/Steady.
Publication Dates: 1990–1994.
Time: (15–20) minutes.
e) WORKING WITH MY BOSS.
Purpose: "To improve the productive relationship between employee and supervisor."
Publication Date: 1989.
Scores: Same as *a* above.
Time: (10–15) minutes.
f) PRE-EVALUATION PROFILE.
Purpose: "To prepare supervisors for performance evaluations of employees without personality type bias."
Acronym: PEP.
Publication Date: 1989.
Scores: Same as *a* above.
Time: (15–20) minutes.
Comments: Supervisor completes profile for self and employee.
g) OUR BEST TEAM.
Purpose: "To build a more productive team."
Publication Date: 1989.
Scores: Same as *a* above.
Time: (20–30) minutes.
Comments: Ratings of all team members are combined for a composite profile.
h) MY TIMESTYLE.
Purpose: "To develop more productive time usage."
Publication Date: 1990.
Scores: 4 timestyles: Road Runner, Race Horse, New Pup, Tom Cat.
Time: (10–15) minutes.
i) MY BEST PRESENTATION STYLE.
Purpose: "To assist individuals in making more effective presentations."
Publication Date: 1989.
Scores: Same as *a* above.
Time: (15–20) minutes.
j) SALES STYLE.
Purpose: "To sharpen sales skills."
Publication Date: 1990.

Scores: 4 sales styles: Quick-Sell, Persistent-Sell, Talkative-Sell, Precise-Sell.
Time: (10–15) minutes.
k) MY TEACHING STYLE.
Purpose: "To help teachers understand learning style."
Publication Date: 1989.
Scores: Bold, Expressive, Sympathetic, Technical.
Time: (15–20) minutes.
l) NEGOTIATING STYLE.
Purpose: "To build productive negotiating strategies."
Publication Date: 1991.
Scores: 4 negotiating styles: Pushy, Stand Pat, Buddy, Check All.
Time: (10–15) minutes.
m) CAREER/PERSONALITY COMPATIBILITY INVENTORY.
Purpose: "To improve career selection."
Publication Date: No date on materials.
Acronym: C/PCI.
Scores: Bold, Expressive, Sympathetic, Technical.
Time: (20–30) minutes.
Cross References: For reviews by Mary A. Lewis and Frank Schmidt, see 13:37.

[333]

BEST Literacy.

Purpose: Designed to "measure adult English language learners' ability to read and write in English in authentic situations in the United States."
Population: Ages 16 and over.
Publication Date: 2008.
Scores, 3: Reading, Writing, Final Scale Score.
Administration: Group.
Forms, 3: Form B, Form C, Form D.
Price Data, 2010: $45 per Form B (including 20 booklets with corresponding scoring sheets); $45 per Form C (including 20 booklets with corresponding scoring sheets); $45 per Form D (including 20 booklets with corresponding scoring sheets); $25 per test manual (64 pages); $25 per technical report (130 pages).
Time: (60) minutes.
Comments: May be used as a pretest and posttest using the different forms available.
Author: Center for Applied Linguistics.
Publisher: Center for Applied Linguistics.

[334]

BEST Plus: Oral English Proficiency Assessment.

Purpose: Designed "to assess the oral language proficiency of adult" English language learners enrolled in educational programs "who need to use English to function in day-to-day life in the United States."
Population: Adults.

Publication Dates: 2003–2005.
Acronym: BEST Plus.
Scores: 3 subscales: Listening Comprehension, Language Complexity, Communication; Total scale score.
Administration: Individual.
Levels: Aligned to Student Performance Level descriptors (SPL) for Listening Comprehension and Oral Communication 0-10; National Reporting System (NRS) Educational Functioning Levels (June 2006) – Beginning, ESL Literacy, Low Beginning ESL, High Beginning ESL, Low Intermediate ESL, High Intermediate ESL, Advanced ESL.
Versions, 2: Computer-adaptive version, semi-adaptive print-based version (3 parallel forms A, B, and C); the computer-adaptive version is available in two formats: CD-ROM or network version.
Price Data, 2011: $.95-$1.50 per computer-adaptive test administrations (quantity discounts available; must be ordered in multiples of 20 or 50; $30 per packet of 20 semi-adaptive print-based test administrations (consumable test booklets Forms A, B, and C (20 booklets per packet): $15 each per form for reusable Print-Based Picture Cue Booklets Forms A, B, and C; $150 per Scoring Refresher Toolkit (VHS or DVD); $6 per Scoring Refresher Workbook-Test Administrator's Edition; $30 per Administrator Guide; $10 per Replacement Test CD; $25 (bound copy) or $10 (PDF copy) per Technical Report; contact publisher (www.cal.org/store) for price information regarding Network Version.
Time: [5-20] minutes, depending on proficiency level of the examinee.
Comments: Training is required for all test administrators and must be conducted by a CAL certified BEST Plus trainer, who has authority to approve or not approve someone to administer the test; Scoring Refresher Toolkit is available for periodic recalibration of test administrators' scoring abilities after the initial training workshop; rubric scored; raw scores from the print-based version must be entered into the Score Management Software (received at training in the Test Administrator Guide) to receive a complete score report with scale score for reporting purposes; designed to be used in educational settings within the United States. (Publisher's test usage and accommodations policies are available online at www.cal.org/ae; complimentary user support is available by phone, email (best-plus@cal.org), or online at www.cal.org/aea/current/bestpluscurrentusersfaqs.html.
Author: Center for Applied Linguistics.
Publisher: Center for Applied Linguistics.
Cross References: For reviews by S. Kathleen Krach and Annita Ward, see 17:27.

[335]

Beta III.

Purpose: "Provides a quick ... measure of nonverbal intellectual ability."

Population: Ages 16–89.
Publication Dates: 1934–1999.
Scores, 6: Coding, Picture Completion, Clerical Checking, Picture Absurdities, Matrix Reasoning, IQ Score.
Administration: Group or individual.
Price Data, 2002: $145 per complete kit including manual (1999, 58 pages), 25 response booklets, and scoring key; $42 per manual; $104 per 25 response booklets; $299 per 100 response booklets; quantity discounts available; $16 per scoring key.
Time: 15(25–30) minutes including 10–15 minutes of instruction and practice.
Comments: Revision of the Revised Beta Examination, Second Edition.
Authors: C. E. Kellogg and N. W. Morton.
Publisher: Pearson.
Cross References: For reviews by C. G. Bellah and Louise M. Soares, see 16:33; for information regarding the previous edition, see T5:2212 (3 references) and T4:2255 (4 references); for reviews by Louis M. Hsu and Mark D. Reckase of the Revised Beta Examination, Second Edition, see 9:1044; see also T2:447 (29 references); for a review by Bert A. Goldman, see 6:494 (13 references); see also 5:375 (14 references); for reviews by Raleigh M. Drake and Walter C. Shipley, see 3:259 (5 references); for reviews by S. D. Porteus and David Wechsler, see 2:1419 (4 references).

[336]

Bilingual Syntax Measure [medida de Sintaxis Bilingüe].

Purpose: Designed to measure second-language oral proficiency with respect to syntactic structures in English and Spanish.
Population: Grades PK–2, 3–12.
Publication Dates: 1975–1980.
Acronym: BSM I, BSM II.
Scores: Scores consist of assigned levels of proficiency.
Administration: Individual.
Price Data, 2002: $476 per complete set including picture booklet, 35 English response booklets, 35 Spanish response booklets, class record, technical handbook, English manual, and Spanish manual (specify BSM I or BSM II); $133.50 per picture booklet (specify BSM I or BSM II); $118 per 35 BSM I response booklets (specify English or Spanish); $135 per 35 BSM II response booklets (specify English or Spanish); $10 per class record (specify BSM I or BSM II); $40.30 per BSM I technical handbook (1976, 53 pages); $40.30 per BSM II technical handbook (1980, 33 pages); $24.50 per BSM I manual (1975, 15 pages) (specify English or Spanish); $24.50 per BSM II manual (1978, 11 pages) (specify English or Spanish); $26 per English-Spanish reference handbook for educators.
Foreign Language Edition: English, Spanish (both of which may be administered as an indicator of language dominance).

Time: (10–15) minutes for each edition.
Comments: BSM II is an upward extension of the Bilingual Syntax Measure (BSM I).
Authors: Marina K. Burt, Heidi C. Dulay, and Eduardo Hernandez Ch.
Publisher: Pearson.
Cross References: See T5:307 (3 references) and T4:298 (2 references); for reviews of BSM II by Eugene E. Garcia and Sylvia Shellenberger, see 9:147 (1 reference); for reviews of BSM I by Isaac I. Bejar and C. Ray Graham, and an excerpted review by John W. Oller, Jr., see 8:156 (4 references); for information on BSM I, see T3:290 (5 references).

[337]

Bilingual Two-Language Assessment Battery of Tests.

Purpose: Designed to reveal "levels of language proficiency" and to determine language skills, acquisition, and loss.
Population: Students, adults, and potential employees with a language proficiency at second grade or higher level.
Publication Date: 1983-2008.
Scores, 13: First Letter Recognition, Second Letter Recognition, Spelling, Opposites, Similarities, Comparisons, Reading, Listening, Items, Actions, Relationships, Total, Oral Proficiency.
Administration: Individual or group.
Forms, 7: Spanish-English, Portuguese-English, Vietnamese-English, Italian-English, French-English, English-Russian, English-Chinese.
Price Data, 2005: $99 per battery including manual (2005, 104 pages), profile cards, one language test, student's test work pages, and test answers; $594 per complete battery including manual, profile cards, six language tests, student's test work pages, and test answers.
Foreign Language Editions: Spanish, Portuguese, Vietnamese, Italian, French, Russian, and Chinese.
Time: (20-30) minutes per language.
Comments: "Criterion-referenced"; each session consists of a Native language sitting followed by an English language sitting within 2 weeks; the battery is prerecorded and requires access to a CD player; optimal administration frequency is every 6 to 8 months.
Author: Adolph Caso.
Publisher: Branden Publishing Co.

[338]

Bilingual Verbal Ability Tests.

Purpose: "Provides a measure of overall verbal ability, and an unique combination of cognitive/academic language abilities for bilingual individuals."
Population: Ages 5 and older.
Publication Date: 1998.
Acronym: BVAT.

Scores, 5: Bilingual Verbal Ability, English Language Proficiency, Picture Vocabulary, Oral Vocabulary, Verbal Analogies.
Administration: Individual.
Price Data, 2006: $817.50 per complete kit including test book with English test pages, 16 sets of tests in languages (Arabic, Chinese Simplified, Chinese Traditional, French, German, Haitian-Creole, Hindi, Italian, Japanese, Korean, Polish, Portuguese, Russian, Spanish, Turkish, and Vietnamese), software (Windows and Mac), comprehensive manual (110 pages), and package of 25 assorted test records; $79.80 for Hmong or Navajo test pages; $199 per English test kit; $309 per Spanish test kit; $35 per 25 test records.
Time: (20–30) minutes.
Comments: Yields an aptitude measure that can be used in conjunction with the WJ-R® Tests of Achievement; an optional training video with administration procedures is available.
Authors: Ana F. Muñoz-Sandoval, Jim Cummins, Criselda G. Alvarado, and Mary L. Ruef.
Publisher: Riverside Publishing.
Cross References: For reviews by Alan Garfinkel and Charles W. Stansfield, see 14:46.

[339]

Biofeedback Certification Examination.

Purpose: A certification examination covering "the knowledge needed by providers of biofeedback services at the time they begin practice."
Population: Entry-level biofeedback service providers.
Publication Dates: 1980–1984.
Scores: 11 Blueprint Areas: Introduction to Biofeedback, Preparing for Clinical Intervention, Neuromuscular Intervention: General, Neuromuscular Intervention: Specific, Central Nervous System Interventions: General, Autonomic Nervous System Interventions: General, Autonomic Nervous System Interventions: Specific, Biofeedback and Distress, Instrumentation, Adjunctive Techniques and Cognitive Interventions, Professional Conduct.
Administration: Group.
Manual: No manual.
Price Data: Available from BCIA.
Time: (180) minutes.
Comments: Administration schedule available from BCIA.
Author: Biofeedback Certification Institute of America.
Publisher: Biofeedback Certification Institute of America.

[340]

Biographical Inventory Form U.

Purpose: "To obtain and analyze information about an individual's characteristics and background."

Population: Grades 7–12.
Publication Dates: 1976–1978.
Acronym: BI.
Scores, 6: Academic Performance, Creativity, Artistic Potential, Leadership, Career Maturity, Educational Orientation.
Administration: Group.
Price Data: Available from publisher.
Time: (60–65) minutes.
Comments: Replaces earlier Alpha Biographical Inventory (7:975).
Author: Institute for Behavioral Research in Creativity.
Publisher: Institute for Behavioral Research in Creativity.
Cross References: See T5:311 (1 reference); for reviews by Christopher Borman and Courtland C. Lee, see 9:150.

[341]

The Birkman Method.

Purpose: "Developed as a self-report questionnaire eliciting responses about perception of self, perception of social context and perception of occupational opportunities."
Population: Ages 25-65.
Publication Dates: 1992-2011.
Scores, 33: Esteem Usual, Esteem Need, Acceptance Usual, Acceptance Need, Structure Usual, Structure Need, Authority Usual, Authority Need, Advantage Usual, Advantage Need, Activity Usual, Activity Need, Challenge Usual, Challenge Need, Empathy Usual, Empathy Need, Change Usual, Change Need, Freedom Usual, Freedom Need, Thought Usual, Thought Need, Persuasive Interest, Social Service Interest, Scientific Interest, Mechanical Interest, Outoor Interest, Numerical Interest, Clerical Interest, Artistic Interest, Literacy Interest, Musical Interest, Stress Behaviors.
Administration: Group.
Price Data: Available from publisher.
Time: [30-45] minutes.
Comments: Publisher advises that 2011 edition is available for ages 15 and up. However, these new materials were not made available for review.
Author: Roger W. Birkman.
Publisher: Birkman International, Inc.
Cross References: For reviews by David F. Ciampi and Gypsy M. Denzine, see 17:28.

[342]

Birmingham Object Recognition Battery.

Purpose: Designed to assess neuropsychological disorders of visual object recognition.
Population: Available from publisher.
Publication Date: 1993.
Acronym: BORB.

Scores: Available from publisher.
Administration: Individual.
Price Data, 2001: $250 per book.
Time: Administration time not reported.
Authors: M. Jane Riddoch and Glyn W. Humphreys.
Publisher: Psychology Press.

[343]

Birth to Three Assessment and Intervention System, Second Edition.

Purpose: Designed to "identify children who are developmentally at risk in the areas of language and learning."
Population: Birth to 3 years.
Publication Dates: 1986–2000.
Acronym: BTAIS-2.
Scores, 5: Language Comprehension, Language Expression, Nonverbal Thinking, Social/Personal Behaviors, Motor Behaviors.
Administration: Individual.
Price Data, 2010: $277 per complete kit including screening test kit, comprehensive test kit, and teaching manual (2000, 163 pages); $76 per teaching manual.
Time: Untimed.
Authors: Jerome J. Ammer and Tina E. Bangs.
Publisher: PRO-ED.
a) SCREENING TEST OF DEVELOPMENTAL ABILITIES.
Purpose: Designed "to identify young children who may have developmental delays."
Price Data: $91 per complete screening test kit including manual (2000, 93 pages) and 25 record forms; $66 per manual; $28 per 25 record forms.
b) COMPREHENSIVE TEST OF DEVELOPMENTAL ABILITIES.
Purpose: Designed "to identify each child's specific strengths and weaknesses and to guide the preparation of instructional plans."
Price Data: $114 per complete comprehensive test kit including manual (2000, 107 pages) and 25 record forms; $66 per manual; $51 per 25 record forms.
Cross References: For reviews by Kimberly A. Blair and Leah M. Nellis, see 15:36; see T5:315; for a review by Donna Spiker of an earlier edition, see 11:45; for a review by Bonnie W. Camp of an earlier edition, see 9:152.

[344]

Bloomer Learning Test–Neurologically Enhanced.

Purpose: Designed as a "diagnostic, focused process assessment of cognitive processes and neurological substrates underlying academic learning."
Population: Grades 1–11 and adults.
Publication Dates: 1978–1998.

Acronym: BLT-NE.
Scores: 56 scores in 5 domains: Cognitive Processing Speed (Activity Persistence, Automaticity, Arousal Need, Association Index, Language/Abstract Processing Ratio), Processing in Short Term Memory (Visual Short Term Memory, Auditory Short Term Memory, Visual Apprehension Span, Short Term Memory Composite, Stimulus Complexity Ratio, Working Memory for Letters, Working Memory for Words, Impulsivity, Rehearsal Effects, Cross Modal Efficiency, Stimulus Mode, Response Mode, Memory Response Sequencing, Working Memory Sequencing Stimulus Number Effects, Stimulus Number Sequencing Effects), Learning and Retention Processes (Serial Learning, Learning Set Ratio, Acquisition, Seriation, Auditory Serial Learning, Auditory Acquisition, Auditory Seriation, Free Association, Verbal Response Association, Verbal Written Association Ratio, Free Spelling Error Ratio, Idiosyncratic Language Ratio, Language Complexity Ratio, Cortical Arousal, Paired Associate Index, Paired Associate Learning, Paired Associate Decrement, Recall, Relearning, Recall Ratio, Savings Ratio), Complex Conceptual Processes (Concept Recognition, Concept Production, Concept Synthesis, Problem Solving, Familiarity, Multiordinality), Emotional Mediating Processes (Emotional Passivity, Intensity, Lability, Valence, Emotional Ratio, Verbal Emotional Ratio, Suppression Index).
Administration: Individual or group.
Price Data: Available from publisher.
Time: (10–25) minutes per domain; (70–95) minutes total.
Author: Richard H. Bloomer.
Publisher: Brador Publications, Inc. [No reply from publisher; status unknown].
Cross References: For a review by Edward Earl Gotts of an earlier edition, see 9:154.

[345]

Blox Test.

Purpose: Designed to measure the individual's perceptual ability for spatial relations.
Population: Job applicants with at least 10 years of education.
Publication Dates: 1961–1963.
Scores: Total score only.
Administration: Group.
Manual: No manual.
Price Data: Available from publisher.
Time: 30(35) minutes.
Comments: Test previously known as Perceptual Battery (T3:1777).
Author: National Institute for Personnel Research of the Human Sciences Research Council.
Publisher: Human Sciences Research Council [South Africa].

[346]

The Boder Test of Reading-Spelling Patterns.

Purpose: Designed as a diagnostic screening test for developmental dyslexia.
Population: Grades K–12 and adult.
Publication Date: 1982.
Scores, 5: Reading (Level, Age, Quotient), Spelling (Known Words/Correct, Unknown Words/Phonetic Equivalence).
Administration: Individual.
Price Data, 2002: $175 per complete kit including 25 reading test record forms, 25 spelling test record forms, 25 alphabet tasks record forms, 25 diagnostic summary record forms, and manual (175 pages); $55 per 25 reading test record forms; $39 per 25 spelling test record forms; $39 per 25 alphabet tasks record forms; $39 per 25 diagnostic summary forms; $82 per manual.
Time: (10–30) minutes.
Authors: Elena Boder and Sylvia Jarrico.
Publisher: Pearson.
Cross References: See T5:322 (7 references) and T4:312 (5 references); for reviews by Frederick A. Schrank and Timothy Shanahan, see 9:155 (2 references).

[347]

Boehm Test of Basic Concepts–Third Edition.

Purpose: Designed to "assess ... [school] readiness or [to] identify students who may be at risk for learning difficulty."
Population: Grades K–2.
Publication Dates: 1967–2001.
Acronym: Boehm-3.
Scores: Total score only.
Administration: Group or individual.
Forms, 2: E, F.
Price Data, 2004: $62 per examination set including examiner's manual (2001, 145 pages), 1 Form E booklet, 1 Form F booklet, 1 Form E class key, 1 Form F class key, and 1 directions for administration (Forms E and F, English and Spanish); $83 per testing kit (Form E or F) including directions for administration (English and Spanish), 1 package of 25 booklets, and 1 class key; $57 per examiner's manual (Fall norms manual); $7 per class key (Form E or F); $18 per directions for administration (English and Spanish).
Foreign Language Edition: Directions for administering in Spanish are available for both forms.
Time: 30(45) minutes if administered in one session; 45(60) minutes if administered in two test sessions.
Comments: Revision of the Boehm Test of Basic Concepts–Revised; yields raw scores, percent correct, performance range, and percentiles by grade.
Author: Ann E. Boehm.
Publisher: Pearson.

Cross References: For reviews by Sherry K. Bain and James Hawkins and by Harold R. Keller, see 16:34; for information regarding previous editions, see T5:324 (12 references) and T4:314 (5 references); for reviews by Robert L. Linn and by Colleen Fitzmaurice and Joseph C. Witt, see 10:32 (16 references); see also T3:302 (18 references); for an excerpted review by Theodore A. Dahl, see 8:178 (22 references); se also T2:344 (1 reference); for reviews by Boyd R. McCandless and Charles D. Smock, and excerpted reviews by Frank S. Freeman, George Lawlor, Victor H. Noll, and Barton B. Proger, see 7:335 (1 reference).

[348]

Boehm Test of Basic Concepts–3 Preschool.

Purpose: "Designed to assess young children's understanding of the basic relational concepts" ("quality, spatial, temporal, quantity") "important for language and cognitive development."
Population: Ages 3-0 to 5-11.
Publication Dates: 1986–2001.
Scores: Total score only.
Administration: Individual.
Price Data, 2006: $159 per complete kit including examiner's manual (2001, 111 pages), picture manual, and 25 record forms; $52 per examiner's manual; $116 per picture manual; $34 per 25 record forms.
Foreign Language Edition: Spanish version available.
Time: (15–20) minutes.
Comments: Revision of Boehm Test of Basic Concepts–Preschool Version; norms extended upward; provides Parent Report Form, Ongoing Observation and Intervention Planning Form (Spanish versions included); includes directions for Spanish administration and scoring; separate English and Spanish norms available.
Author: Ann E. Boehm.
Publisher: Pearson.
Cross References: For reviews by Theresa Graham and Koressa Kutsick Malcolm, see 16:35; see also T5:323 (1 reference) and T4:313 (1 reference); for reviews by Judy Oehler-Stinnett and Stephanie Stein of an earlier edition, see 11:46 (1 reference).

[349]

The Booklet Category Test, Second Edition.

Purpose: Designed to "distinguish individuals with brain damage from normal individuals by measuring concept formation and abstract reasoning."
Population: Ages 15 and older.
Publication Dates: 1979–1997.
Acronym: BCT.
Scores: Total score only.
Administration: Individual.

Price Data, 2006: $460 per introductory kit including professional manual, 2-volume set of stimulus books, and 50 response forms.
Time: (30–60) minutes.
Authors: Nick A. DeFilippis and Elizabeth McCampbell.
Publisher: Psychological Assessment Resources, Inc.
Cross References: For reviews by Carolyn M. Callahan and David C. S. Richard, see 14:47; see also T5:326 (10 references) and T4:315 (4 references); for reviews by Raymond S. Dean and Thomas A. Hammeke of an earlier edition, see 9:156.

[350]
Borromean Family Index.

Purpose: Developed to measure "attitudes and feelings about one's family."
Population: Adolescents and adults.
Publication Dates: 1975–1988.
Scores: 2: Internal (forces that attract toward family), External (forces that pull away).
Subtests, 2: For Married Persons, For Single Persons.
Administration: Group.
Manual: No manual.
Price Data, 2005: $2 per test.
Time: [10] minutes.
Comments: Supplementary article available.
Author: Panos D. Bardis.
Publisher: Donna Bardis.
Cross References: For additional information, see 8:332 (1 reference).

[351]
Boston Assessment of Severe Aphasia.

Purpose: Developed to identify "preserved abilities that might form the beginning steps of rehabilitation programs for severely aphasic patients."
Population: Aphasic adults.
Publication Date: 1989.
Acronym: BASA.
Scores, 5: Auditory Comprehension, Praxis, Oral-Gestural Expression, Reading Comprehension, Other.
Administration: Individual.
Price Data, 2010: $311 per complete kit; $74 per package of manipulatives; $51 per set of stimulus cards; $46 per custom aluminum clipboard; $45 per 25 record forms; $63 per manual (96 pages).
Time: (30–40) minutes.
Comments: See T5:328 (1 reference); for reviews by Steven B. Leder and Roger L. Towne, see 12:52 (3 references).
Authors: Nancy Helm-Estabrooks, Gail Ramsberger, Alisa R. Morgan, and Marjorie Nicholas.
Publisher: PRO-ED.

Cross References: See T5:328 (1 reference); for reviews by Steven B. Leder and Roger L. Towne, see 12:52 (3 references).

[352]
Boston Diagnostic Aphasia Examination–Third Edition.

Purpose: Designed to help "identify and distinguish among disorders of language function and neurologically recognized aphasic syndromes."
Population: Individuals with aphasia
Publication Dates: 1972-2001.
Acronym: BDAE-3.
Scores, 59: Conversational and Expository Speech (Simple Social Responses, Free Conversation, Picture Description [Discourse Analysis-Segmentation into Utterances], Severity Rating and Profile of Speech Characteristics), Auditory Comprehension (Word Comprehension [Basic Word Discrimination, Supplemental Test], Commands and Complex Ideational Material Test), Oral Expression (Oral Agility [Nonverbal Agility and Verbal Agility], Automatized Sequences, Recitation, Melody, and Rhythm [Recitation, Melody and Rhythm], Repetition [Single Word Repetition and Repetition of Sentences], Naming [Responsive Naming, Boston Naming Test-Visual Confrontation Naming, Screening for Naming of Special Categories]), Reading (Basic Symbol Recognition [Matching Across Cases and Scripts and Number Matching], Word Identification [Picture-Word Match], Phonics [Homophone Matching], Derivational and Inflectional Morphology [Free Grammatical Morphemes], Oral Reading [Basic Oral Word Reading and Oral Reading of Special Word Lists (Mixed Morphological Types and Semantic Paralexia-Prone Words)], Oral Reading of Sentences with Comprehension, Reading Comprehension-Sentences and Paragraphs), Writing (Mechanics of Writing, Basic Encoding Skills [Primer Word Vocabulary, Regular Phonics and Common Irregular Forms], Written Picture Naming and Narrative Writing) and Apraxia Assessment (Natural Gestures, Conventional Gestures, Use of Pretend Objects without an Action Goal, Use of Pretend Objects with an Action Goal and Bucco-Facial Respiratory Movements).
Administration: Individual.
Forms, 3: Short, Standard (Long), Boston Naming Test (Short and Long combined).
Price Data, 2010: $449 per complete kit including manual (2001, 136 pages), 147 long form stimulus cards picture book, 25 long form record booklets, 27 short form stimulus cards picture book, 25 short form record booklets, Boston Naming Test stimulus cards picture book, 25 Boston Naming Test record booklets, and DVD; $101 per manual; $45 per DVD; $101 per Boston Naming Test kit including Boston Naming Test stimulus cards picture book and 25 Boston Naming Test record booklets; $39 per 25 Boston Naming Test

record booklets; $73 per Boston Naming Test stimulus cards picture book.

Time: (35-45) minutes.

Comments: Previously listed as The Assessment of Aphasia and Related Disorders and that is the title of the manual.

Authors: Harold Goodglass with the collaboration of Edith Kaplan and Barbara Barresi.

Publisher: PRO-ED.

a) SHORT FORM.

Purpose: Designed "to provide a comprehensive, but brief sampling of the performances necessary for an informed quantitative assessment" of individuals with aphasia.

Price Data: $90 per short form kit including 27 short form stimulus cards picture book and 25 short form record booklets; $40 per 25 short form record booklets; $67 per short form stimulus cards picture book.

Time: (30-45) minutes.

Comments: The short form consists of shortened or omitted sections that are included in the standard form.

b) STANDARD (Long) FORM.

Purpose: Designed to be a "more probing evaluation of particular language functions within each area of testing."

Scores, 18: Aesop's Fables, Word Comprehension in Categories, Syntactic Processing (Touching A with B, Reversible Possessives, Embedded Sentences), Repetition of Nonsense Words, Naming in Categories, Advanced Phonic Analysis–Pseudo-Homophone Matching, Bound Grammatical Morphemes, Derivational Morphemes, Uncommon Irregularities, Nonsense Words, Oral Spelling, and Cognitive/Grammatical Influences (Part of Speech Effects: Dictated Words, Subtest 2: "Dictated Functor Loaded Sentences").

Price Data: $214 per long form kit including manual, 147 long form stimulus cards picture book, and 25 long form record booklets; $45 per 25 long form record booklets; $85 per long form stimulus cards picture book.

Time: Administration time not reported.

Comments: All scores included in the standard form are also included in the extended form.

c) BOSTON NAMING TEST, SECOND EDITION.

Population: Ages 55-59.

Scores: Total score only.

Time: Administration time not reported.

Authors: Edith Kaplan, Harold Goodglass, and Sandra Weintraub.

Cross References: For reviews by Shawn K. Acheson and Anthony T. Dugbartey, see 17:29; see also T5:199 (18 references) and T4:207 (105 references); for reviews by Rita Sloan Berndt and Malcolm R. McNeil of an

earlier edition, see 10:15 (3 references); see also 9:86 (2 references) and T3:308 (28 references); for reviews by Daniel R. Boone and Manfred J. Meier of an earlier edition, see 8:955 (1 reference).

[353]

The Boston Qualitative Scoring System for the Rey-Osterrieth Complex Figure.

Purpose: Designed as a quantifiable approach to rating the qualitative features of the ROCF (which was designed to assess visuoconstructional ability and visual memory performance in brain-impaired patients).

Population: Ages 18–94.

Publication Dates: 1994–1999.

Acronym: BQSS.

Scores, 23: Qualitative (Configural Presence, Configural Accuracy, Cluster Presence, Cluster Accuracy, Cluster Placement, Detail Presence, Detail Placement, Fragmentation, Planning, Neatness, Vertical Expansion, Horizontal Expansion, Reduction, Rotation, Perseveration, Confabulation, Asymmetry), Summary (Copy Presence and Accuracy, Immediate Presence and Accuracy, Delayed Presence and Accuracy, Immediate Retention, Delayed Retention, Organization).

Administration: Individual.

Price Data, 2005: $202 per introductory kit including professional manual, 50 scoring booklets, 50 response sheets, stimulus card, reference guide, scoring templates, and metric ruler.

Time: (45) minutes, including a (20–30) minute delay interval.

Authors: Robert A. Stern, Debbie J. Javorsky, Elizabeth A. Singer, Naomi G. Singer Harris, Jessica A. Somerville, Lisa M. Duke, Jodi A. Thompson, and Edith Kaplan.

Publisher: Psychological Assessment Resources, Inc.

Cross References: For reviews by D. Ashley Cohen and Robert A. Leark, see 15:37.

[354]

Bracken Basic Concept Scale: Expressive.

Purpose: Used to measure "a child's ability to verbally label basic concepts."

Population: Ages 3-0 to 6-11.

Publication Date: 2006.

Acronym: BBCS:E.

Scores, 13: 10 subtest scores (Colors, Letters/Sounds, Numbers/Counting, Sizes/Comparisons, Shapes, Direction/Position, Self-/Social Awareness, Texture/Material, Quantity, Time/Sequence); 3 composite scores (School Readiness Composite, Expressive School Readiness Composite, Expressive Total Composite).

Administration: Individual.

Price Data, 2007: $235 per complete kit including manual (2006, 205 pages), stimulus book, and 25 English record forms; $219 per stimulus book; $47 per 25 English record forms; $47 per 25 Spanish record forms; $78 per manual; $149 per Bracken scoring assistant.

Foreign Language Edition: Criterion-referenced Spanish edition included.

Time: 25(30) minutes.

Comments: For use with the Bracken Basic Concept Scale-Third Edition: Receptive (355).

Author: Bruce A. Bracken.

Publisher: Pearson.

Cross References: For reviews by R. Anthony Doggett and Gregory Snyder, see 18:13.

[355]

Bracken Basic Concept Scale–Third Edition: Receptive.

Purpose: Designed to measure relevant educational concepts and receptive language skills.

Population: Ages 3-0 to 6-11.

Publication Dates: 1984-2006.

Acronym: BBCS-3:R.

Scores, 8: 5 subtest scores (Direction/Position, Self-/Social Awareness, Texture/Material, Quantity, Time/Sequence); 3 composite scores (School Readiness Composite, Receptive School Readiness Composite, Receptive Total Composite).

Administration: Individual.

Price Data, 2007: $312 per complete kit including manual (2006, 208 pages), stimulus book, and 25 English record forms; $219 per stimulus book; $47 per 25 English record forms; $47 per 25 Spanish record forms; $103 per manual, $149 per Bracken scoring assistant.

Foreign Language Edition: Criterion-referenced Spanish edition included.

Time: (30-40) minutes.

Comments: For use with the Bracken Basic Concept Scale: Expressive (354).

Author: Bruce A. Bracken.

Publisher: Pearson.

Cross References: For reviews by Gretchen Owens and Loraine J. Spenciner, see 18:14; for reviews of an earlier edition by Leah M. Nellis and Rhonda H. Solomon, see 14:48; see also T5:331 (6 references) and T4:319 (4 references); for reviews by Timothy L. Turco and James E. Ysseldyke of the original edition, see 10:33.

[356]

Bracken School Readiness Assessment.

Purpose: Designed to "assess academic readiness by evaluating a child's understanding of 88 important fundamental concepts in the categories of Colors, Letters, Numbers/Counting, Sizes, Comparisons and Shapes."

Population: Ages 2:6 to 7:11.

Publication Date: 2002.

Acronym: BSRA.

Scores, 7: Colors, Letters, Numbers/Counting, Sizes, Comparisons, Shapes, School Readiness Composite.

Administration: Individual.

Price Data, 2003: $119 per complete kit including administration manual (104 pages), stimulus manual, and 25 record forms (specify English or Spanish); $39 per administration manual; $89 per stimulus manual; $25 per 25 record forms (specify English or Spanish).

Foreign Language Edition: Spanish edition available.

Time: (10–15) minutes.

Comments: The subtests in this test are the first 6 of 11 subtests of the Bracken Basic Concept Scale–Revised (T7:339); national norms not available for Spanish edition.

Author: Bruce A. Bracken.

Publisher: Pearson.

Cross References: For reviews by Thomas McKnight and Gene Schwarting, see 16:36.

[357]

Brain Injury Rehabilitation Trust Memory and Information Processing Battery.

Purpose: Designed to "assess memory and information processing skills or to detect and/or assess impairments in these skills for either clinical, educational, occupational or research purposes."

Population: Adults.

Publication Date: 2007.

Acronym: BMIPB.

Administration: Individual.

Forms, 4: 1, 2, 3, 4.

Price Data, 2007: £445 per complete battery; £44 per 25 Memory and Learning forms and 25 Speed of Information Processing forms Form 1; £44 per 25 Memory and Learning forms and 25 Speed of Information Processing forms Form 2; £44 per 25 Memory and Learning Forms and 25 Speed of Information Processing forms Form 3; £44 per 25 Memory and Learning forms and 25 Speed of Information Processing forms Form 4.

Time: (45-60) minutes.

Comments: Test authors suggest the assessment be administered by "chartered psychologists with post qualification experience and knowledge of neuropsychology or the psychology of aging."

Authors: Anthony K. Coughlan, Michael Oddy, and John R. Crawford.

Publisher: The Brain Injury Rehabilitation Trust [England].

a) STORY RECALL.

Scores, 3: Immediate, Delayed, Retained%.

b) FIGURE RECALL.

Scores, 4: Copy%, Immediate%, Delayed%, Retained%.

c) LIST LEARNING.

Scores, 4: A1-A5 Total, A6, B, Intrusions.

d) WORD RECOGNITION.
Scores, 6: A Words, B Words, Total Word Recognition, List A, List B, Total List Recognition.
e) DESIGN LEARNING.
Scores, 4: A1-A5 Total, A6, B, Intrusions.
f) DESIGN RECOGNITION.
Scores, 6: Correct Positive, Correct Negative, Recognition Total, Design A Correct, Design B Correct, Identification Total.
g) SPEED OF INFORMATION PROCESSING.
Scores, 4: Total, Errors%, Speed, Adjusted Total.

[358]

The BrainMap™.

Purpose: "A tool for determining the world-building (or thinking/information-processing) style of individuals and of groups."
Population: Adults.
Publication Dates: 1981–1986.
Scores, 4: Posterior Brain Scale, Anterior Brain Scale, Left Brain Scale, Right Brain Scale.
Administration: Group.
Price Data: Available from publisher.
Time: [30–40] minutes.
Comments: Self-administered, self-scored.
Author: Dudley Lynch.
Publisher: Brain Technologies Corporation.
Cross References: For a review by Manfred J. Meier, see 11:47.

[359]

Bricklin Perceptual Scales.

Purpose: Yields information on a child's unconscious or nonverbal perception of his or her parents; for determining which of the parents would make the better primary caretaker for a particular child in child-custody decisions.
Population: Ages 6 and over.
Publication Dates: 1984–2002.
Acronym: BPS.
Scores, 10: 5 scores each for mother and father: Perception of Competency, Perception of Supportiveness, Perception of Follow-Up Consistency, Perception of Admirable Character Traits, Total.
Administration: Individual.
Price Data, 2002: $199 per complete kit including 8 sets of response cards, 8 scoring sheets, stylus-pen, placement dots, test box with foam insert, manual (1992, 141 pages), instructions, and Bricklin Updates; $99 per 8 additional sets of response cards; $159 per 16 sets of response cards with summaries; $199 per 24 sets of response cards with summaries; $198 per IBM computer scoring profile (3.5-inch disk).
Time: (40) minutes.
Comments: IBM or compatible computer required for computer scoring profile (unlimited uses).

Author: Barry Bricklin.
Publisher: Village Publishing.
Cross References: For reviews by Rosa A. Hagin and Marcia B. Shaffer, see 11:48.

[360]

Brief Battery for Health Improvement 2.

Purpose: Designed for "assessing medical patients who may be experiencing problems with pain, functioning, somatization, depression, anxiety, or other factors relevant to rehabilitation and recovery."
Population: 18–65 years.
Publication Date: 2002.
Acronym: BBHI 2.
Scores, 6: Validity Scale (Defensiveness), Physical Symptom Scales (Somatic Complaints, Pain Complaints, Functional Complaints), Affective Symptom Scales (Depression, Anxiety).
Administration: Individual.
Parts, 4: Part I (Pain Complaints scale), Part II (Somatic Complaints scale), Part III (Functional Complaints scale), Part IV (Depression, Anxiety, and Defensiveness scales).
Price Data, 2007: $140 per starter kit with Standard or Extended Reports including manual (151 pages) and 10 fax-in answer sheets and scoring; $110 per starter kit with Standard or Extended Reports including manual, 10 answer sheets, and 10 Q Local administrations; $36.50 per manual; $51.50 per compact disk administration; $26.50 per 25 fax-in answer sheets; $13.50 per fax-in service of 1 fax-in answer sheet; $9.50 per 5–9 Patient Assessment Device Reports; $89 per Q Local Software Desktop version (annual license fee); $26.50 per 25 Q Local answer sheets; $9.50 per 5–9 Q Local Standard or Extended Reports; no charge for Q Local Progress Reports; $12.50 per 5–9 mail-in answer sheets and Standard or Extended Reports; quantity discounts available for the reports.
Foreign Language Editions: Spanish materials available.
Time: (7–10) minutes.
Comments: Shorter version of the Battery for Health Improvement 2 (BHI 2; 281); mail-in and fax-in scoring available from publisher along with on-site computer (Q Local software) and hand-held electronic device (Patient Assessment Device) scoring; three automated reports available (Standard Report, Extended Report, Progress Report).
Authors: John Mark Disorbio and Daniel Bruns.
Publisher: Pearson.
Cross References: For reviews by Theodore L. Hayes and Wes Sime, see 17:30.

[361]

Brief Derogatis Psychiatric Rating Scale.

Purpose: To obtain clinical observers' ratings on nine personality dimensions.

Population: Psychiatric and medical patients.
Publication Dates: 1974–1978.
Acronym: B-DPRS™.
Scores: 9 dimensions: Somatization, Obsessive-Compulsive, Interpersonal Sensitivity, Depression, Anxiety, Hostility, Phobic Anxiety, Paranoid Ideation, Psychoticism.
Administration: Individual.
Manual: No manual.
Price Data, 2006: $50 per 100 tests.
Time: (5) minutes.
Comments: Formerly the Brief Hopkins Psychiatric Rating Scale; short form of the Derogatis Psychiatric Rating Scale; self-report; can also be used with Symptom Checklist-90-Revised or Brief Symptom Inventory.
Author: Leonard R. Derogatis.
Publisher: Pearson.
Cross References: See T5:335 (15 references) and T4:323 (5 references).

[362]

Brief Neuropsychological Cognitive Examination.

Purpose: Constructed as "an assessment of the severity and nature of cognitive impairment" for psychiatric and neurological patients.
Population: Ages 18 and older.
Publication Date: 1997.
Acronym: BNCE.
Scores, 4: Validity Index, Part I, Part II, Total.
Administration: Individual.
Price Data, 2006: $137.50 per complete kit including manual (58 pages), stimulus booklet, 20 response booklets, and 20 administration and scoring forms; $42.50 per 20 response booklets; $30 per 20 administration and scoring forms; $38.50 per stimulus booklet; $50.50 per manual.
Time: (30) minutes.
Author: Joseph Tonkonogy.
Publisher: Western Psychological Services.
Cross References: For reviews by Eugene V. Aidman and Sheila Mehta, see 14:50.

[363]

Brief Symptom Inventory.

Purpose: "Designed to reflect the psychological symptom patterns of psychiatric and medical patients as well as non-patients."
Population: Adults and adolescents age 13 or older.
Publication Date: 1975.
Acronym: BSI®.
Scores: 9 primary dimensions: Somatization, Obsessive-Compulsive, Interpersonal Sensitivity, Depression, Anxiety, Hostility, Phobic Anxiety, Paranoid Ideation, Psychoticism; plus 3 global indices: Global Severity Index, Positive Symptom Distress Index, Positive Symptom Total.

Administration: Group or individual.
Price Data, 2006: $100 per hand-scoring starter kit including manual, 50 answer sheets, 50 profile forms, 2 worksheets, and answer keys (specify Nonpatient Adult, Nonpatient Adolescent, Outpatient Psychiatric, or Inpatient Psychiatric); $52.50 per 50 hand-scoring answer sheets; $24.50 per answer keys; $24.50 per 50 profile forms and 2 worksheets (specify Nonpatient Adult, Nonpatient Adolescent, Outpatient Psychiatric, or Inpatient Psychiatric); $34 per manual; price information for Interpretive Report and Profile Report scoring and software available from publisher.; quantity discounts available for the reports; price information for Spanish materials available from publisher.
Foreign Language Editions: Spanish materials available.
Time: (8–10) minutes.
Comments: Essentially the brief form of the Symptom Checklist-90-Revised (2674); self-report; useful in initial evaluation and measurement of patient progress during treatment to monitor change and after treament for assessment of treatment outcome; companion clinician and observer rating forms are also available.
Author: Leonard R. Derogatis.
Publisher: Pearson.
Cross References: See T5:337 (198 references) and T4:324 (59 references); for reviews by Bert P. Cundick and Charles A. Peterson, see 10:35 (7 references); see also 9:160 (1 reference).

[364]

Brief Symptom Inventory 18.

Purpose: Designed to "screen for psychological distress and psychiatric disorders in medical and community populations."
Population: Age 18 and older.
Publication Dates: 2000–2001.
Acronym: BSI 18.
Scores, 4: Somatization, Depression, Anxiety, Total (Global Severity Index).
Administration: Individual or group.
Price Data, 2006: $44.50 per Q Local starter kit with profile reports including manual (2001, 54 pages), 3 answer sheets with test items to conduct and receive 3 Q local administrations; $26 per 25 answer sheets; $4.15 per profile report (quantity discounts available); $97.75 per hand-scoring starter kit including manual, 50 answer sheets with test items, and 50 profile forms (specify Community or Oncology norms); $52.50 per 50 answer sheets; $25.50 per 50 profile forms (specify Community or Oncology norms); $34 per manual; quantity discounts available for the reports; price information for Spanish materials available from publisher.
Foreign Language Editions: Spanish materials available.

Time: (4–5) minutes.
Comments: Abbreviated adaptation of Brief Symptom Inventory (363); self-report; may be administered in paper-and-pencil format or online.
Author: Leonard R. Derogatis.
Publisher: Pearson.
Cross References: For reviews by Roger A. Boothroyd and William E. Hanson, see 15:38; for information on the Brief Symptom Inventory, see T5:337 (198 references); for reviews by Bert P. Cundick and Charles A. Peterson of an earlier edition, see 10:35 (7 references); see also 9:160 (1 reference).

[365]

Brief Test of Attention.

Purpose: Designed "to assess the severity of attentional impairment among nonaphasic hearing adult patients."
Population: Ages 17–82.
Publication Date: 1997.
Acronym: BTA.
Scores: Total score only.
Administration: Individual.
Forms, 2: N (Numbers), L (Letters).
Price Data, 2006: $78 per introductory kit including professional manual (34 pages), stimulus audiotape, and 50 scoring forms.
Time: (10) minutes.
Author: David Schretlen.
Publisher: Psychological Assessment Resources, Inc.
Cross References: For reviews by Elizabeth Kelley Boyles and Steven R. Shaw, see 15:39.

[366]

Brief Test of Head Injury.

Purpose: Designed to provide information about cognitive, linguistic, and communicative abilities of patients with severe head trauma.
Population: Acute and long-term head-injured adults.
Publication Dates: 1989–1991.
Acronym: BTHI.
Scores, 8: Orientation/Attention, Following Commands, Linguistic Organization, Reading Comprehension, Naming, Memory, Visual-Spatial Skills, Total.
Administration: Individual.
Price Data, 2011: $201 per complete kit including 25 record forms, examiner's manual (1991, 85 pages), manipulatives package, stimulus cards and letter board, and carrying case; $58 per 25 record forms; $86 per stimulus cards; $86 per examiner's manual.
Time: (25–30) minutes.
Authors: Nancy Helm-Estabrooks and Gillian Hotz.
Publisher: PRO-ED.
Cross References: For reviews by Deborah D. Roman and Michael Lee Russell, see 13:39.

[367]

Brief Visuospatial Memory Test–Revised.

Purpose: Designed as an equivalent, multiple-test form assessment of visuospatial memory.
Population: Ages 18–79.
Publication Dates: 1988–1997.
Acronym: BVMT-R.
Scores, 12: Trial 1, Trial 2, Trial 3, Total Recall, Learning, Delayed Recall, Percent Retained, Recognition Hits, Recognition False Alarms, Recognition Discrimination Index, Recognition Response Bias, Copy (Optional).
Administration: Individual.
Forms, 6: 1, 2, 3, 4, 5, 6.
Price Data, 2006: $255 per introductory kit including professional manual (1997, 131 pages), recognition stimulus booklet, reusable recall stimulus booklet, and 25 response forms.
Time: (45) minutes including 25-minute delay.
Comments: Can be administered bed-side by appropriately trained personnel.
Author: Ralph H. B. Benedict.
Publisher: Psychological Assessment Resources, Inc.
Cross References: For review by Anita M. Hubley and Terry A. Stinnett, see 15:40.

[368]

BRIGANCE® Comprehensive Inventory of Basic Skills II.

Purpose: Designed to compare "a student's mastery of various skills to those of other students around the country" and can be completed "as part of a battery to determine eligibility for special education services."
Publication Dates: 1976-2010.
Acronym: CIBS-II.
Administration: Individual.
Price Data, 2010: $339 per classroom kit including Reading/ELA and Math Inventory, 20 record books, and 1 canvas tote; $249 per Standardized Inventory including assessments, Standardization and Validation manual (2010, 152 pages), and 20 record books; $49 per Standardization and Validation manual; $35 per 10 record books; $329 per 100 record books.
Authors: Brian F. French and Frances Page Glascoe.
Publisher: Curriculum Associates.
    a) READINESS ASSESSMENTS.
    Population: Ages 5-0 to 6-11.
    Scores, 40: 21 Task Scores (Personal Data Response, Identifies Body Parts, Understands Directional and Positional Concepts, Standing Gross-Motor Skills, Walking Gross-Motor Skills, Prints Uppercase Letters in Sequence, Prints Personal Data, Writes Numerals in Sequence, Readiness for Reading, Knows Common Signs, Oral Expression, Reads Lowercase Letters, Rote Counting, Understands Quantitative Concepts, Counts Objects, Reads

Numerals, Articulation-Initial Sounds of Words, Articulation-Final Sounds of Words, Auditory Discrimination, Identifies Initial Consonants in Spoken Words, Sounds of Letters), 13 Supplemental Task Scores (Recognizes Colors, Self-Help Skills, Running and Skipping Gross-Motor Skills, Draws a Person, Visual Motor Skills-Forms, Prints Lower-case Letters in Sequence, Prints Uppercase Letters Dictated, Prints Lowercase Letters Dictated, Reads Lowercase Letters, Visual Discrimination-Forms/ Letters/and Words, Recites Alphabet, Joins Sets, Numeral Comprehension), and 6 Composite Scores (General Knowledge and Language, Gross-Motor Skills, Graphomotor and Writing Skills, Reading, Math, Phonemic Awareness.
Time: (60) minutes.
b) FIRST-GRADE THROUGH SIXTH-GRADE ASSESSMENTS.
Forms, 2: Form A (Pretest), Form B (Post Test).
Population: Ages 7-0 to 12-0.
Scores, 16: 9 Task Scores (Word Recognition Grade-Placement Test, Word Analysis Survey, Reading Vocabulary Comprehension Grade-Placement Test, Comprehends Passages, Computational Skills Grade-Placement Test, Problem Solving Grade-Placement Test, Spelling Grade-Placement Test, Sentence- Writing Grade-Placement Test, Listening Vocabulary Comprehension Grade-Placement Test), 2 Supplemental Task Scores (Warning and Safety Signs, Warning Lables), and 5 Composite Scores (Basic Reading, Reading Comprehension, Math, Written Expression, Listening Comprehension).
Time: (45-60) minutes.
Cross References: For reviews by Gregory J. Cizek and Mary J. McLellan of an earlier edition, see 14:51; see also T5:340 (1 reference); for reviews by Craig N. Mills and Mark E. Swerdlik of the original edition, see 9:162.

[369]

BRIGANCE® Diagnostic Assessment of Basic Skills-Revised Spanish Edition.

Purpose: Designed to assess and progress monitor language dominance, oral and written English language proficiency, and basic math skills.
Population: Grades PreK-9.
Publication Dates: 1984-2007.
Acronym: ABS-R.
Scores, 163: Readiness, Speech, Listening, Word Recognition Grade Placement, Oral Reading, Reading Comprehension, Word Analysis, Functional Word Recognition, Spelling, Writing, Reference Skills, Graphs and Maps, Math Grade Placement, Numbers, Number Facts, Computation of Whole Numbers, Fractions and Mixed Numbers, Decimals, Percents, Time, Money, U.S. Customary Measurement and Geometry, Metrics.
Administration: Individual.

Price Data, 2007: $185 per administration binder (2007, 484 pages); $35 per 10 student record books; $14 per class record book; $39 per 10 profile test booklets; $59.95 per Goals & Objectives Writer CD-ROM.
Time: Administration time not reported.
Comments: Criterion-referenced testing system.
Author: Albert H. Brigance.
Publisher: Curriculum Associates, Inc.

[370]

BRIGANCE® Early Childhood Complete System.

Purpose: "Developed to help early childhood teachers screen, provide ongoing assessment, measure progress, and provide instruction … The screens assess a broad sampling of skills … helping identify learning delays, giftedness, and strengths and weaknesses in language, motor, self-help, social-emotional, and cognitive skills."
Population: Ages 0-5 years enrolled in early childhood programs; Grades K-1.
Publication Dates: 1982-2010.
Administration: Individual.
Price Data, 2011: $299 per Early Childhood Screening Kit (0-35 months, 3-5 years, or K & 1) including Screen Manual, 60 data sheets (assorted ages), Technical Report, accessories, tote bag, online training; $175 per Screen Manual (0-35 months, 3-5 years, or K & 1); $19 per 15 data sheets; $59 per 60 data sheets; $59 per Technical Report; $65 per set of accessories; $189 per Early Childhood Developmental Inventory.
Foreign Language Edition: Spanish directions available.
Time: (10-15) minutes.
Comments: The BRIGANCE Early Childhood Screen II 0-35 Months was compiled from the BRIGANCE Infant & Toddler Screen by Albert H. Brigance and Frances Page Glascoe and the BRIGANCE Early Preschool Screen-II by Albert H. Brigance." The BRIGANCE Early Childhood Screen II 3-5 Years was "compiled from the BRIGANCE Preschool Screen-II and the BRIGANCE K & 1 Screen-II by Albert H. Brigance."The BRIGANCE Early Childhood Screen II K & 1 was "compiled from the BRIGANCE K & 1 Screen-II by Albert H. Brigance." The BRIGANCE Early Childhood Developmental Inventory was "compiled from the BRIGANCE Inventory of Early Development II by Albert H. Brigance."
Authors: Curriculum Associates, Inc. (screens) and Frances Page Glascoe (Technical Report).
Publisher: Curriculum Associates, Inc.
   a) BRIGANCE EARLY CHILDHOOD SCREEN II 0-35 MONTHS.
      1) *Infant (birth–11 months).*
      Scores: 6 skills: Fine-Motor Skills, Receptive Language Skills, Expressive Language Skills, Gross-Motor Skills, Self-help Skills, Social-Emotional Skills.

2) *Toddler (12-23 months).*

Scores: 11 skills: Fine-Motor Skills, Receptive Language Skills–General, Receptive Language Skills–Body Parts, Receptive Language Skills–Picture Naming, Receptive Language Skills–Environmental Sounds, Receptive Language Skills–General, Receptive Language Skills–Object Naming, Receptive Language Skills–Phrases, Gross-Motor Skills, Self-help Skills, Social-Emotional Skills.

3) *Two-Year-Old Child.*

Scores: 8 skills: Identifies Body Parts, Gross-Motor Skills, Picture Vocabulary, Identifies People in Pictures by Naming, Knows Use of Objects, Visual Motor Skills, Verbal Fluency, Builds Tower with Blocks.

4) *Two-and-a-Half-Year-Old Child.*

Scores: 11 skills: Personal Data Response, Identifies Body Parts, Gross-Motor Skills, Knows Use of Objects, Repeats Sentences, Visual Motor Skills, Quantitative Concepts, Builds Tower With Blocks, Matches Colors, Picture Vocabulary, Plural s and –ing.

b) BRIGANCE EARLY CHILDHOOD SCREEN II 3-5 YEARS.

1) *Three-Year-Old Child.*

Scores: 11 skills: Personal Data Response, Color Recognition, Picture Vocabulary, Knows Use of Objects, Visual Motor Skills, Gross-Motor Skills, Number Concepts, Builds Tower with Blocks, Identifies Body Parts, Repeats Sentences, Prepositions and Irregular Plural Nouns.

2) *Four-Year-Old Child.*

Scores: 11 skills: Personal Data Response, Color Recognition, Picture Vocabulary, Visual Discrimination–Forms and Uppercase Letters, Visual Motor Skills, Gross-Motor Skills, Rote Counting, Identifies Body Parts, Follows Verbal Directions, Number Concepts, Syntax and Fluency.

3) *Five-Year-Old Child.*

Scores: 12 skills: Personal Data Response, Identifies Body Parts, Gross-Motor Skills, Color Recognition, Visual Motor Skills, Draws a Person (Body Image), Prints Personal Data, Rote Counting, Numerical Comprehension, Number Readiness, Reads Uppercase (or Lowercase) Letters, Syntax and Fluency.

c) BRIGANCE EARLY CHILDHOOD SCREEN II K & 1.

1) *Kindergarten.*

Scores: 12 skills: Personal Data Response, Identifies Body Parts, Gross-Motor Skills, Color Recognition, Visual Motor Skills, Draws a Person (Body Image), Prints Personal Data, Rote Counting, Numerical Comprehension, Number Readiness, Reads Uppercase (or Lowercase) Letters, Syntax and Fluency.

2) *First Grade.*

Scores: 12 skills: Personal Data Response, Recites Alphabet, Visual Discrimination—Lowercase Letters and Words, Reads Lowercase Letters, Auditory Discrimination, Phonemic Awareness and Decoding, Listening Vocabulary Comprehension, Word Recognition, Draws a Person (Body Image), Prints Personal Data, Computation, Numerals in Sequence.

d) BRIGANCE EARLY CHILDHOOD DEVELOPMENTAL INVENTORY.

Purpose: "Criterion-referenced assessment" designed to "identify children's specific strengths and needs … set individualized instructional goals, and measure and report progress over time."

Population: Ages birth to 7 years.

Scores: 39 assessments in 2 skill areas: Language Development [Prespeech Receptive Language, Prespeech Gestures, Prespeech Vocalization, Colors, General Speech and Language Development, Length of Sentences, Verbal Directions, Picture Vocabulary, Knows What to Do in Different Situations, Knows Use of Objects, Knows Function of Community Helpers, Recognizes Money, Repeats Numbers, Sentence Memory (With Picture Stimuli), Sentence Memory (Without Picture Stimuli), Plural s and –ing, Prepositions, and Irregular Plural Nouns]; Literacy [Response to and Experience with Books, Prehandwriting, Copies Forms, Identifies Common Signs, Identifies Rhymes, Visual Discrimination (Forms and Uppercase Words), Visual Discrimination (Lowercase Letters and Words), Identifies Uppercase Letters, Identifies Lowercase Letters, Prints Uppercase Letters, Prints Personal Data, Prints Lowercase Letters, Auditory Discrimination, Identifies Blended Words, Identifies Beginning Sounds, Matches Beginning Sounds and Letters with Pictures, Identifies Blended Phonemes, Substitutes Beginning Consonant Sounds, Reads Common Signs, Reads High-Frequency Words, Word Recognition Grade Placement Test, Reads Sentences (Preprimer), Reads Sentences (Primer).

Cross References: For reviews of the BRIGANCE Infant & Toddler Screen by Theresa Graham and Loraine J. Spenciner, see 15:41. For reviews of the BRIGANCE Early Preschool Screen-II by Michelle Athanasiou and Gene Schwarting, see 17:32; for reviews of an earlier edition by William M. Bart and Joseph M. Ryan, see 11:49. For reviews of the BRIGANCE Preschool Screen-II by Shawn Powell and John J. Vacca, see 17:14; for reviews of an earlier edition by Edith S. Heil and Timothy L. Turco, see 10:36. For reviews of the BRIGANCE K & 1 Screen-II by Koressa Kutsick Malcolm and Theresa Volpe-Johnstone, see 17:33; for reviews of the previous edition by Ronald A. Berk and T. Steuart Watson, see 12:53 (1 reference); see also T4:331 (3 references); for reviews of an earlier edition by Ann E. Boehm and Dan Wright, see 9:166.

[371]

BRIGANCE® Head Start and Early Head Start Complete System.

Purpose: "Developed to help Head Start teachers screen, provide ongoing assessment, measure progress, and provide instruction ... The screens assess a broad sampling of skills ... helping identify learning delays, giftedness, and strengths and weaknesses in language, motor, self-help, social-emotional, and cognitive skills."

Publication Dates: 1997-2010.

Administration: Individual.

Price Data, 2011: $259 per Head Start Screening Kit including Head Start Screen Manual, 60 data sheets (assorted ages), Technical Report (2010, 259 pages), accessories, tote bag, online training, and online scoring; $299 per Early Head Start Screening Kit including Early Head Start Screen Manual, 60 data sheets (assorted ages), Technical Report, accessories, tote bag, online training, and online scoring; $175 per Head Start Screen Manual or Early Head Start Screen Manual; $19 per 15 data sheets; $59 per 60 data sheets; $59 per Technical Report; $66 per set of accessories; $189 per Head Start Developmental Inventory.

Foreign Language Edition: Spanish directions available.

Time: (10-15) minutes.

Comments: The BRIGANCE Early Head Start Screen was "compiled from the BRIGANCE Infant & Toddler Screen by Albert H. Brigance and Frances Page Glascoe and the BRIGANCE Early Preschool Screen-II by Albert H. Brigance." The BRIGANCE Head Start Screen was "compiled from the BRIGANCE Preschool Screen-II and the BRIGANCE K & 1 Screen-II by Albert H. Brigance."

Authors: Curriculum Associates, Inc. (screens) and Frances Page Glascoe (Technical Report).

Publisher: Curriculum Associates, Inc.

a) BRIGANCE EARLY HEAD START SCREEN.

Population: Ages 0-3 years.

1) *Infant (birth-11 months).*

Scores: 6 skills: Fine-Motor Skills, Receptive Language Skills, Expressive Language Skills, Gross-Motor Skills, Self-help Skills, Social-Emotional Skills.

2) *Toddler (12-23 months).*

Scores: 11 skills: Fine-Motor Skills, Receptive Language Skills–General, Receptive Language Skills–Body Parts, Receptive Language Skills–Picture Naming, Receptive Language Skills–Environmental Sounds, Receptive Language Skills–General, Receptive Language Skills–Object Naming, Receptive Language Skills–Phrases, Gross-Motor Skills, Self-help Skills, Social-Emotional Skills.

3) *Two-Year-Old Child.*

Scores: 8 skills: Identifies Body Parts, Gross-Motor Skills, Picture Vocabulary, Identifies People in Pictures by Naming, Knows Use of Objects, Visual Motor Skills, Verbal Fluency, Builds Tower with Blocks.

4) *Two-and-a-Half-Year-Old Child.*

Scores: 11 skills: Personal Data Response, Identifies Body Parts, Gross-Motor Skills, Knows Use of Objects, Repeats Sentences, Visual Motor Skills, Quantitative Concepts, Builds Tower With Blocks, Matches Colors, Picture Vocabulary, Plural s and –ing.

b) BRIGANCE HEAD START SCREEN.

Population: Ages 3-5 years.

1) *Three-Year-Old Child.*

Scores: 11 skills: Personal Data Response, Color Recognition, Picture Vocabulary, Knows Use of Objects, Visual Motor Skills, Gross-Motor Skills, Number Concepts, Builds Tower with Blocks, Identifies Body Parts, Repeats Sentences, Prepositions and Irregular Plural Nouns.

2) *Four-Year-Old Child.*

Scores: 11 skills: Personal Data Response, Color Recognition, Picture Vocabulary, Visual Discrimination–Forms and Uppercase Letters, Visual Motor Skills, Gross-Motor Skills, Rote Counting, Identifies Body Parts, Follows Verbal Directions, Number Concepts, Syntax and Fluency.

3) *Five-Year-Old Child.*

Scores: 12 skills: Personal Data Response, Identifies Body Parts, Gross-Motor Skills, Color Recognition, Visual Motor Skills, Draws a Person (Body Image), Prints Personal Data, Rote Counting, Numerical Comprehension, Number Readiness, Reads Uppercase (or Lowercase) Letters, Syntax and Fluency.

c) BRIGANCE HEAD START DEVELOPMENTAL INVENTORY.

Population: Ages 0-6 years.

Purpose: "Criterion-referenced assessments" designed to "enable teachers to measure and report each child's progress over time by Head Start domain."

Comments: "Correlated to the BRIGANCE Head Start and Early Head Start Screens."

Cross References: For reviews of the BRIGANCE Infant & Toddler Screen by Theresa Graham and Loraine J. Spenciner, see 15:41. For reviews of the BRIGANCE Early Preschool Screen-II by Michelle Athanasiou and Gene Schwarting, see 17:32; for reviews of an earlier edition by William M. Bart and Joseph M. Ryan, see 11:49. For reviews of the BRIGANCE Preschool Screen-II by Shawn Powell and John J. Vacca, see 17:14; for reviews of an earlier edition by Edith S. Heil and Timothy L. Turco, see 10:36. For reviews of the BRIGANCE K & 1 Screen-II by Koressa Kutsick Malcolm and Theresa Volpe-Johnstone, see 17:33; for reviews of the previous edition by Ronald A. Berk and T. Steuart Watson, see 12:53 (1 reference); see also T4:331 (3 references); for reviews of an earlier edition by Ann E. Boehm and Dan Wright, see 9:166.

[372]

BRIGANCE® Inventory of Early Development II.

Purpose: Designed to "determine readiness for school; track developmental progress; provide a range of scores needed for documenting eligiblity for special education services; enable a comparison of children's skills within and across developmental domains/skill areas in order to view strengths and weaknesses; determine entry points for instruction;[and]assist with program evaluation."

Population: Developmental ages birth to age 7.

Publication Dates: 1978-2010.

Acronym: IED-II.

Scores, 22: Physical Development: Fine-Motor Subdomain (Drawing/Visual Motor, Writing, Total), Physical Development: Gross-Motor Subdomain (Nonlocomotor, Locomotor, Total), Total Physical Development Domain/ Skill Area, Language Development: Receptive Subdomain (Nouns and Early Listening, Actions, Total), Language Development: Expressive Subdomain (Isolated Skills, Contextual Skills, Total), Total Language Development Domain/Skill Area, Academic/Cognitive: Mathematical/ General Concepts Subdomain (Mathematical/General Concepts), Academic/ Cognitive: Literacy Subdomain (Literacy), Total Academic/Cognitive Domain/Skill Area, Daily Living Domain/Skill Area (Self-Help, Prevocational, Total), Total Social and Emotional Development Domain/Skill Area, Total Adaptive Behavior.

Administration: Individual.

Price Data, 2009: $299 per classroom kit including Inventory of Early Development II, 20 record books, testing accessories kit (blocks, scissors, and other manipulatives), canvas tote; $189 per standardized kit including standardized assessments, 20 standardized record books, testing accessories kit (blocks, scissors, and other manipulatives), canvas tote; $329 per 100 record books; $35 per per 10 record books.

Time: (20-25) minutes.

Comments: Previous edition was entitled BRIGANCE Diagnostic Inventory of Early Development-II.

Author: Frances Page Glascoe.

Publisher: Curriculum Associates, Inc.

Cross References: For reviews by Andrew S. Davis and W. Holmes Finch and by Lauren R. Barton and Donna Spiker of the previous edition, see 17:31; for reviews by C. Dale Carpenter and Douglas A. Penfield of an earlier edition, see 12:326; see also T4:2256 (3 references); for reviews by Stephen J. Bagnato and Elliot L. Gory of an earlier edition, see 9:164.

[373]

BRIGANCE Transition Skills Inventory.

Purpose: "Criterion-referenced" assessments designed to "help special educators and transition specialists identify a student's present level of performance, plan appropriate instruction, and monitor progress" in transition to adult life.

Population: Middle and high school students with special needs.

Publication Dates: 1994-2010.

Acronym: TSI.

Scores: 124 assessments in 17 skill areas: Academic [Reading Grade Placement (3 assessments), Listening and Speaking Skills (4 assessments), Functional Writing Skills (2 assessments), Math Skills (20 assessments)]; Post-Secondary [Interests & Choices (4 assessments), Job-Related Writing Skills (7 assessments), Job-Related Knowledge and Skills (14 assessments), Communication and Technology Skills (5 assessments)]; Independent Living [Food (11 assessments), Clothing (2 assessments), Housing (2 assessments), Money and Finance (10 assessments), Health (14 assessments), Travel and Transportation (7 assessments)]; Community Participation [Community Resources (9 assessments), Community Signs (8 assessments), Citizenship (2 assessments)].

Administration: Individual in part.

Price Data, 2011: $289 per kit including Transition Skills Inventory (2010, 537 pages), 20 record books, and canvas tote; $199 per Transition Skills Inventory; $35 per 10 record books; $329 per 100 record books.

Time: Administration time varies.

Comments: "Compiled from the BRIGANCE Employability Skills Inventory and the BRIGANCE Life Skills Inventory, both by Albert H. Brigance."

Author: Curriculum Associates, Inc.

Publisher: Curriculum Associates, Inc.

Cross References: For reviews of the BRIGANCE Diagnostic Employability Skills Inventory by JoEllen V. Carlson and William C. Tirre, see 14:52. For reviews of the BRIGANCE Diagnostic Life Skills Inventory by Cleborne D. Maddux and Rhoda Cummings and by James A. Wollack, see 14:53; see also T5:344 (1 reference).

[374]

British Ability Scales: Second Edition.

Purpose: Designed as a battery to assess "cognitive abilities and educational achievement."

Population: Ages 2.6 to 17.11.

Publication Dates: 1977–1997.

Acronym: BAS II.

Scores, 4: Early Years Core Scales (Block Building, Verbal Comprehension, Picture Similarities, Naming Vocabulary, Pattern Construction, Early Number Concepts, Copying), School Age Core Scales (Recall of Designs, Word Definitions, Pattern Construction, Matrices, Verbal Similarities, Quantitative Reasoning), Diagnostic Scales (Speed of Information Processing, Recall of Digits Forward, Recall of Objects–Immediate, Recall of Objects–Delayed, Matching Letter-Like Forms, Recognition of Pictures, Recall of Digits Backward), Achievement Scales (Number Skills, Spelling, Word Reading).

Administration: Individual.
Forms, 2: Early Years, School Age.
Price Data, 2005: £810 per full age range complete set including stimulus books, 10 relevant record forms and consumable booklets; £575 per early years complete set including stimulus books, 10 record forms and consumable booklets; £495 per school age complete set including stimulus books, 10 record forms and consumable booklets; £40.50 per 25 early years record booklets; £52.50 per 25 school age record booklets; £10.90 per 25 achievement scales record forms; £12 per 10 Speed of Information Processing booklets A, B, or C; £12 per 10 Quantitative Reasoning booklets set A; £6 per 100 sheets copying paper; £6 per 100 recall of designs sheets; £17.50 per 25 number skills/spelling worksheets; £8.75 per 25 number skills worksheets; $8.75 per 25 spelling worksheets; £87.25 per administration and scoring manual (1996, 544 pages); £70 per technical manual (1997, 341 pages); £168.80 per BAS II Scoring and Reporting Software.
Time: Administration time varies.
Comments: Considerations for testing special populations detailed in manual.
Authors: Colin D. Elliott with Pauline Smith and Kay McCulloch.
Publisher: GL Assessment [England].
Cross References: For reviews by Colin Cooper and Robert W. Hiltonsmith, see 16:37; see also T5:349 (39 references) and T4:336 (25 references); for reviews by Susan Embretson (Whitely), Benjamin D. Wright, and Mark H. Stone of an earlier edition, see 9:172 (5 references); for reviews by Steve Graham and William D. Schafer of an earlier edition of the British Ability Scales: Spelling Scale, see 12:55.

[375]

The British Picture Vocabulary Scale, Second Edition.

Purpose: Designed to serve as a "norm referenced wide-range test of hearing vocabulary for Standard English."
Population: Ages 3.0 to 15.8.
Publication Dates: 1982–1997.
Acronym: BPVS-II.
Scores: Total score only.
Administration: Individual.
Price Data: Available from publisher.
Time: (5–8) minutes.
Comments: Manual is incorporated in the easeled test book.
Authors: Lloyd M. Dunn, Leota M. Dunn, Chris Whetton, and Juliet Burley.
Publisher: GL Assessment [England].
Cross References: For reviews by Alfred P. Longo and Dolores Kluppel Vetter, see 16:38; for information regarding the original edition, see T5:350 (53 references) and T4:338 (16 references).

[376]

British Spelling Test Series.

Purpose: Developed to serve as a "comprehensive screening test that delivers detailed information about the spelling ability of groups or individuals."
Population: Ages 5–adult.
Publication Date: 1997.
Acronym: BSTS.
Administration: Individual or group.
Levels, 5: 1, 2, 3, 4, 5.
Forms, 2: X and Y, alternate forms.
Price Data: Available from publisher.
Time: (30–40) minutes.
Authors: Denis Vincent and Mary Crumpler.
Publisher: GL Assessment [England].
Cross References: For reviews by Timothy Z. Keith and S. Kathleen Krach, see 16:39.

[377]

Brown Attention-Deficit Disorder Scales.

Purpose: Designed to "elicit cognitive and affective indications of Attention-Deficit Disorder."
Publication Dates: 1996–2001.
Acronym: Brown ADD Scales.
Scores, 6: Organizing and Activating to Work, Sustaining Attention and Concentration, Sustaining Energy and Effort, Managing Affective Interference, Utilizing "Working Memory" and Assessing Recall, Total.
Administration: Individual or group.
Price Data, 2002: $270 per complete kit for Children and Adolescents including 25 Ready Score® Parent and Teacher forms for ages 3–7, 25 Ready Score® Parent, Teacher and self-report forms for ages 8–12, 25 Ready Score® answer documents for ages 12–18, diagnostic forms (10 each, Children and Adolescents), and manual for Children and Adolescents; $160 per complete kit for Adolescents and Adults including treatment monitoring worksheet, 50 Ready Score® answer documents (25 each for ages 12–18 and 18+), diagnostic forms (10 each for ages 12–18 and 18+), and manual for Adolescents and Adults; $40 per 25 Ready Score® parent forms (specify ages 3–7 or ages 8–12); $40 per 25 Ready Score® teacher forms (specify ages 3–7 or ages 8–12); $40 per 25 Ready Score® self-report forms/answer documents (specify ages 8–12, or ages 12–18, or ages 18+); $20 per 10 diagnostic forms (specify ages 3–12, ages 12–18, or ages 18+); $79 per manual for Children and Adolescents or manual for Adolescents and Adults; $150 per Scoring Assistant (3.5-inch diskette or CD-ROM Windows).
Time: (10–20) minutes.
Author: Thomas E. Brown.
Publisher: Pearson.
  a) PRIMARY/PRESCHOOL.
  Population: Ages 3–7.
  b) SCHOOL-AGE.
  Population: Ages 8–12.

c) ADOLESCENT SCALE.
Population: Ages 12 to 18.
d) ADULT SCALE.
Population: Ages 18 and over.
Cross References: For reviews by Nadeen L. Kaufman and Alan S. Kaufman, by E. Jean Newman, and by Judy Oehler-Stinnett, see 14:54.

[378]

Brown Attention-Deficit Disorder Scales for Children and Adolescents.

Purpose: "Designed to elicit ... [information] that may indicate impairment in executive functions related to Attention-Deficit/Hyperactivity Disorders (AD/HD)."
Population: Ages 3–18.
Publication Date: 2001.
Acronym: Brown ADD Scales for Children.
Scores, 7: 6 cluster scores (Organizing/Prioritizing/ and Activating to Work, Focusing/Sustaining/and Shifting Attention to Tasks, Regulating Alertness/Sustaining Effort/and Processing Speed, Managing Frustration and Modulating Emotions, Utilizing Working Memory and Accessing Recall, Monitoring and Self-Regulating Action), Total Score.
Administration: Group or individual.
Price Data, 2001: $270 per complete kit including manual (149 pages), 25 each Ready Score Parent Forms and Teacher Forms (ages 3–7), 25 each Ready Score Parent Forms, Teacher Forms, and Self-Report Forms (ages 8–12), 25 Ready Score Answer Documents (ages 12–18), and 10 each Child Diagnostic Forms (ages 3–12) and Adolescent Diagnostic Forms (ages 12–18); $79 per manual; $40 per 25 Ready Score Parent Forms (ages 3–7 or 8–12); $40 per 25 Ready Score Teacher Forms (ages 3–7 or 8–12); $40 per 25 Ready Score Self-Report Forms/Answer Documents (child, ages 8–12; or adolescent, ages 12–18); $20 per 10 Diagnostic Forms (child, ages 3–12; or adolescent, ages 12–18); $350 per Scoring Assistant kit including manual, 25 each Parent Forms (ages 3–7 and 8–12), 25 each Teacher Forms (ages 3–7 and 8–12), 25 each Self-Report Forms (ages 8–12 and 12–18), Brown ADD Scoring Assistant CD-ROM (3.5-inch diskette version available); $40 per 25 Parent or Teacher Forms (ages 3–7 or 8–12); $40 per 25 Self-Report Forms/Answer Documents (child, ages 8–12; or adolescent, ages 12–18).
Time: (10–20) minutes.
Comments: Downward extension of the Brown Attention Deficit Disorder Scales for Adolescents and Adults (377); describes cognitive, affective, behavioral symptoms beyond DSM-IV diagnostic criteria to assess executive function impairments; optional Brown ADD Scales Scoring Assistant software scores, analyzes results, maintains records, generates graphical and narrative reports; system requirements: Windows 95/98/2000/ME/NT 4.0, 100 MHz Pentium processor, 32 MB RAM, 2 MB video

card capable of 800 x 600 resolution (256 colors), 20 MB free hard disk space, 3.5-inch floppy drive, 50 MB temporary disk space.
Author: Thomas E. Brown.
Publisher: Pearson.
a) PRIMARY/PRESCHOOL LEVEL.
Population: Ages 3–7.
Forms, 2: Parent Form, Teacher Form.
Comments: Elicits parent and teacher reports of symptoms.
b) SCHOOL-AGE LEVEL.
Population: Ages 8–12.
Forms, 3: Self-Report Form, Parent Form, Teacher Form.
Comments: Elicits parent, teacher and self-reports of symptoms.
c) ADOLESCENT LEVEL.
Population: Ages 13–18.
Form, 1: Ready-Score Answer Document.
Comments: Elicits parent and self-reports of symptoms.
Cross References: For reviews by Karen E. Jennings and William K. Wilkinson, see 15:42.

[379]

Bruce Vocabulary Inventory.

Purpose: Constructed to measure vocabulary.
Population: Business and industry and general population.
Publication Dates: 1959–1984.
Scores: Total score only.
Administration: Group.
Price Data, 2006: $96 per test package; $36 per IBM answer sheet package; $12.50 per set of IBM scoring stencils; $5.50 per set of fan keys; $35 per manual (1959, 4 pages) and manual supplement (1984, 17 pages); $39 per IBM specimen set; $33.50 per fan key specimen set.
Time: (15–20) minutes.
Author: Martin M. Bruce.
Publisher: Martin M. Bruce, Ph.D.
Cross References: See T5:352 (1 reference); for reviews by Fred H. Borgen and Robert Fitzpatrick, see 7:231.

[380]

Bruininks-Oseretsky Test of Motor Proficiency, Second Edition.

Purpose: Designed to measure gross and fine motor skills of children.
Population: Ages 4–21.
Publication Dates: 1978–2005.
Acronym: BOT-2.
Scores: 3 scores: Gross Motor Composite, Fine Motor Composite, Battery Composite, for 8 subtests: Fine Motor Precision, Fine Motor Integration, Manual Dexterity,

Bilateral Coordination, Balance, Running Speed and Agility, Upper-Limb Coordination, Strength.
Administration: Individual.
Price Data, 2009: $795 per kit including manual (2005, 273 pages), administration easel, 25 record forms, 25 examinee booklets, scoring transparency, balance beam, blocks with string, penny box, penny pad, plastic pennies, knee pad, peg board and pegs, 2 red pencils, scissors, target, tennis ball, shape cards, and shuttle block; $44.50 per 25 record forms for complete battery/short form; $44.50 per 25 examinee booklets.
Time: (45–60) minutes for complete battery; (15–20) minutes for short form.
Comments: Second revised edition of the Oseretsky Tests of Motor Proficiency.
Authors: Robert H. Bruininks and Brett D. Bruininks.
Publisher: Pearson.
Cross References: For reviews by Katharine A. Snyder and Gabrielle Stutman, see 18:15; see T5:353 (22 references) and T4:340 (18 references); for a review by David A. Sabatino of an earlier edition, see 9:174 (7 references); see also T3:324 (3 references) and T2:1898 (15 references); for a review by Anna Espenschade, see 4:650 (10 references); for an excerpted review, see 3:472 (6 references).

[381]
Burks Behavior Rating Scales, Second Edition.

Purpose: Designed to measure child and adolescent behaviors that are relevant to school and community activities.
Population: Ages 4-18.
Publication Dates: 1968-2006.
Acronym: BBRS-2.
Scores, 7: Disruptive Behavior, Attention and Impulse Control Problems, Emotional Problems, Social Withdrawal, Ability Deficits, Physical Deficits, Weak Self-Confidence.
Administration: Individual.
Forms, 2: Teacher, Parent.
Price Data, 2007: $105 per complete kit including 25 parent autoscore forms, 25 teacher autoscore forms, and manual (2006, 74 pages); $40 per 25 autoscore forms (specify parent or teacher); $44 per manual.
Time: 15(20) minutes.
Comments: Ratings by teachers or parents; computer scoring options also available, contact publisher for details.
Authors: Harold F. Burks and Christian P. Gruber.
Publisher: Western Psychological Services.
Cross References: For reviews by Ronald A. Madle and Hoi K. Suen, see 18:16; see T5:355 (1 reference) and T4:342 (5 references); for reviews by Lisa G. Bischoff and by Leland C. Zlomke and Brenda R. Bush of an earlier edition, see 11:50 (7 references); see also T3:328 (1 reference), T2:1115 (1 reference), and 7:46 (2 references).

[382]
Burns Brief Inventory of Communication and Cognition.

Purpose: Designed to "assist in determining which of a client's cognitive or communication skills are impaired as a result of a neurological lesion or other disease process, and to assist in selecting appropriate treatment targets and functional treatment goals."
Population: Adults with neurological impairment.
Publication Date: 1997.
Acronym: Burns Inventory.
Scores: Left Hemisphere Inventory: 16 scores in 5 domains: Auditory Comprehension (Yes/No Questions, Comprehension of Words and Sentences, Comprehension of Paragraphs), Verbal Expression (Automatic Speech, Verbal Repetition, Responsive Naming-Nouns, Responsive Naming-Verbs, Confrontation Naming), Reading (Oral Reading of Words and Sentences, Reading Comprehension of Words and Sentences, Reading Comprehension of Functional Paragraphs), Writing (Writing to Dictation, Functional Writing), Numerical Reasoning (Time, Money, Calculation); Right Hemisphere Inventory: 12 scores in 3 domains: Scanning and Tracking (Functional Scanning and Tracking, Scanning and Tracking of Single Words), Visuo-Spatial Skills (Functional Spatial Distribution of Attention, Spatial Distribution of Attention, Recognition of Familiar Faces, Gestalt Perception, Visuo-Spatial Construction-Clock, Visuo-Spatial Organization for Writing), Prosody and Abstract Language (Spontaneous Expressive Prosody, Receptive Prosody, Inferences, Metaphorical Language); Complex Neuropathology Inventory: 15 scores in 4 domains: Orientation to Factual Memory (Orientation to Person/Place/Time, Factual Current and Remote Memory), Auditory Attention and Memory (Auditory Attention/Vigilance, Immediate Auditory Recall of Digits, Immediate Auditory Recall of Digits with Distractions, Immediate Auditory Recall of Functional Information); Visual Perception (Color Recognition, Picture Matching, Word Matching); Visual Attention and Memory (Functional Short-Term Recognition, Short-Term Recognition of Pictures, Short-Term Recognition of Words, Divided Visual Attention, Delayed Recognition of Pictures, Delayed Recognition of Words).
Administration: Individual.
Forms, 3: Inventories: Left Hemisphere Inventory, Right Hemisphere Inventory, Complex Neuropathology Inventory.
Price Data, 2002: $159 per complete kit; $23 per 15 Right Hemisphere record forms; $23 per 15 Complex Neuropathology record forms; $23 per 15 Left Hemisphere record forms; $52 per stimulus plates; $53 per examiner's manual (116 pages); $6 per 3-minute audiocassette.
Time: (30) minutes per inventory.

Comments: For use by speech pathologists; each inventory can be used separately or all three can be used as a battery.
Author: Martha S. Burns.
Publisher: Pearson.
Cross References: For reviews by Joan C. Ballard and Richard I. Frederick, see 14:55.

[383]

Burns/Roe Informal Reading Inventory: Preprimer to Twelfth Grade, Sixth Edition.

Purpose: Provides information about the reading skills, abilities, and needs of individual students in order to plan an appropriate program of reading intervention.
Population: Beginning readers–Grade 12.
Publication Dates: 1985–2002.
Acronym: IRI.
Scores, 2: Word Recognition, Comprehension.
Administration: Individual.
Levels, 14: Preprimer, Primer, First Reader, Second Grade, Third Grade, Fourth Grade, Fifth Grade, Sixth Grade, Seventh Grade, Eighth Grade, Ninth Grade, Tenth Grade, Eleventh Grade, Twelfth Grade.
Price Data, 2005: $55.56 per Informal Reading Inventory manual including reproducible teacher pages.
Time: (40–50 minutes).
Authors: Betty D. Roe and Paul C. Burns.
Publisher: Houghton Mifflin Company.
Cross References: For reviews by Joyce Meikamp and Carolyn H. Suppa and by Rayne A. Sperling and Crystal M. Ramsay, see 17:35; for reviews by Felice J. Green and Timothy Shanahan of the Fifth Edition, see 14:56; see also T5:357 (1 reference) and T4:343; for reviews by Steven V. Owen and Stephanie Stein of the Third Edition, see 12:56; for reviews by Carolyn Colvin Murphy and Roger H. Bruning and by Edward S. Shapiro of an earlier edition, see 10:37.

[384]

Burt Word Reading Test, New Zealand Revision.

Purpose: Designed to provide an estimate of word recognition skills for 110 words.
Population: Ages 6-0 to 12-11 years.
Publication Date: 1981.
Scores: 1 overall performance score.
Administration: Individual.
Price Data, 2001: NZ$3.60 per 20 record forms; $.99 per test card; $6.30 per manual (10 pages); $8.10 per specimen set.
Time: [5] minutes.
Comments: Revision and New Zealand standardization of the Burt Word Reading Test; identical to 1974 revision except for word order.
Authors: Alison Gilmore, Cedric Croft, and Neil Reid.

Publisher: New Zealand Council for Educational Research [New Zealand].
Cross References: See T5:358 (13 references) and T4:344 (4 references); for reviews by Mark W. Aulls and John Elkins, see 9:175 (2 references).

[385]

Bury Infant Check.
Purpose: To aid in identifying children with special needs.
Population: Children in second term of infant school.
Publication Date: 1986.
Acronym: BIC.
Administration: Individual.
Price Data: Price information available from publisher for Full Check record booklets, Quick Check record forms, and for teacher's set including Full Check record booklet, Quick Check record form, and manual (36 pages).
Authors: Lea Pearson and John Quinn.
Publisher: GL Assessment [England].
  a) QUICK CHECK.
  Scores, 3: Language Expression, Learning Style, Total.
  Time: (3–4) minutes.
  Comments: Teacher-rated.
  b) FULL CHECK.
  Scores, 12: Language Skills (Comprehension, Expression, Total), Learning Style, Memory Skills (Visual, Auditory, Total), Number Skills, Perceptual Motor Skills (Copying Shapes, Visual Discrimination, Total), Total.
  Time: (20) minutes.
Cross References: For a review by Stephan A. Henry, see 9:38.

[386]

Business Analyst Skills Evaluation [One-Hour].
Purpose: Measures practical and analytical skills for the position of Business Systems Analyst.
Population: Candidates for Business Analyst positions.
Publication Dates: 1984–1998.
Acronym: BUSAN.
Scores: Total Score, Narrative Evaluation, Ranking, Recommendation.
Administration: Group.
Price Data, 2001: $225 per candidate, quantity discounts available.
Foreign Language Edition: Available in French.
Time: (60) minutes.
Comments: Available in booklet and Internet formats; scored by publisher; must be proctored.
Author: Bruce A. Winrow.

Publisher: Walden Personnel Performance, Inc. [Canada].
Cross References: For reviews by Charles K. Parsons and Michael Spangler, see 16:40.

[387]

Business Analyst Skills Evaluation [Two-Hour].

Purpose: "Measures practical and analytical skills required for the position of Business Systems Analyst."
Population: Candidates for business analyst positions.
Publication Date: 1984.
Acronym: PRBUSAN.
Score: Total score, narrative evaluation, rating, recommendation.
Administration: Group.
Price Data, 2001: $350 per candidate; quantity discounts available.
Time: (120) minutes.
Comments: Also available with interpersonal skills; graded by publisher; must be proctored.
Author: Bruce A. Winrow.
Publisher: Walden Personnel Performance, Inc. [Canada].
Cross References: For a review by Lenore W. Harmon, see 10:39.

[388]

The Business Critical Thinking Skills Test.

Purpose: "Developed to assess the critical thinking skills of business professionals and business students."
Population: Adult business professionals and business students.
Publication Dates: 2007-2008.
Acronym: BCTST.
Scores, 6: Analysis, Inference, Evaluation, Deductive, Inductive, Total.
Administration: Group.
Price Data: Available from publisher.
Time: (50) minutes.
Comments: This test can be administered online or via paper and pencil.
Authors: Peter A. Facione, Stephen Blohm, and Noreen C. Facione.
Publisher: Insight Assessment-The California Academic Press LLC.
Cross References: For reviews by Patricia A. Bachelor and Jean P. Kirnan, see 18:17.

[389]

Business Judgment Test, Revised.

Purpose: "Designed to be a measure of empathy or 'feel' for the generally accepted ideas and opinions on desirable courses of action in interpersonal relationships."

Population: Adults.
Publication Dates: 1953–1984.
Acronym: BJT.
Scores: Total score only.
Administration: Group.
Price Data, 2006: $119.50 per test package; $3.25 per scoring key; $49.50 per manual (1965, 12 pages) and manual supplement (1984, 17 pages); $55.50 per specimen set.
Foreign Language Edition: French edition available.
Time: (10–20) minutes.
Author: Martin M. Bruce.
Publisher: Martin M. Bruce, Ph.D.
Cross References: See T2:2275 (1 reference); for a review by Jerome E. Doppelt, and an excerpted review by Kenneth D. Orton, see 7:1059 (1 reference); see also 6:1101 (4 references); for a review by Edward B. Greene, see 5:893.

[390]

Butcher Treatment Planning Inventory.

Purpose: Designed to provide psychotherapists with "relevant personality and symptomatic information early in the treatment process."
Population: Adults in therapy.
Publication Date: 1998.
Acronym: BTPI.
Administration: Individual or group.
Price Data, 2002: $147 per starter kit including manual (236 pages), 10 full form reusable question booklets, 25 full form answer/profile sheets, scoring templates, 1 free sample symptom monitoring form reusable question booklet, 1 free sample symptom monitoring ready score answer document; $74 per symptom monitoring supplement hand scoring kit including 10 reusable question booklets and 25 ready score answer booklets; $20 per 10 full form question booklets; $14 per 10 symptom monitoring form reusable question booklets; $32 per 25 full form answer sheets; $67 per 25 symptom monitoring ready score answer documents; $67 per manual; $39 per full form scoring templates.
Comments: Normed on ages 18 and over; hand- or computer-scored; paper-and-pencil or computerized administration; computer-generated interpretive reports available.
Author: James N. Butcher.
Publisher: Pearson.
   a) FULL FORM.
     Scores, 16: Validity Scales (Inconsistent Responding, Overly Virtuous Self-Views, Exaggerated Problem Presentation, Closed-Mindedness), Treatment Issues Scales (Problems in Relationship Formation, Somatization of Conflict, Low Expectation of Benefit, Self-Oriented/Narcissism, Perceived Lack of Environmental Support), Current Symptom

Scales (Depression, Anxiety, Anger-Out, Anger-In, Unusual Thinking), General Pathology Composite, Treatment Difficulty Composite.
Time: [30] minutes.
b) SYMPTOM MONITORING FORM.
Scores: Includes only Current Symptom Scales from *a* above.
Time: [12] minutes.
c) TREATMENT PROCESS/SYMPTOM FORM.
Scores: Includes only Treatment Issues Scales and Current Symptom Scales from *a* above.
Time: Administration time not reported.
d) TREATMENT ISSUES FORM.
Scores: Includes only Validity Scales and Treatment Issues Scales from *a* above.
Time: Administration time not reported.
Cross References: For reviews by Wiliam E. Hanson and Samuel Juni, see 14:57.

[391]

C-BDQ Correctional Officer Background Data Questionnaire.

Purpose: Developed to assess background and personal characteristics.
Population: Candidates for entry-level correctional officer positions.
Publication Date: 1995.
Acronym: C-BDQ.
Scores: 7 biodata subtypes: Unscored Demographic Information, Background, Lifestyle, Interest, Personality, Ability, Opinion-Based.
Administration: Individual or group.
Price Data: Available from publisher.
Time: 60 minutes.
Comments: "It is recommended that this test be given in conjunction with one of IPMA-HR's other entry-level correctional officer tests."
Authors: International Public Management Association for Human Resources & Bruce Davey Associates.
Publisher: International Public Management Association for Human Resources (IPMA-HR).
Cross References: For a review by Susan M. Brookhart, see 18:18.

[392]

C-1 and C-2 Correctional Officer Tests.

Purpose: Designed as entry-level tests for correctional officers.
Population: Candidates for entry-level correctional officer positions.
Publication Dates: 1991-1995.
Scores: 4 knowledge areas: Reading Comprehension, Counting Accuracy, Inductive Reasoning, Deductive Reasoning.
Administration: Individual or group.

Forms, 2: C-1, C-2.
Price Data: Available from publisher.
Time: 120 minutes per test.
Comments: No prior training or experience as a correctional officer is assumed of candidates taking these tests.
Author: International Public Management Association for Human Resources.
Publisher: International Public Management Association for Human Resources (IPMA-HR).
Cross References: For a review by Susan M. Brookhart, see 18:19.

[393]

California Achievement Tests, Fifth Edition.

Purpose: "Designed to measure achievement in the basic skills taught in schools throughout the nation."
Population: Grades K–12.
Publication Dates: 1957–1993.
Acronym: CAT/5.
Administration: Group.
Levels: 13.
Forms, 4: Complete Battery A, B; Survey A, B.
Price Data, 2006: $44 per 30 locator tests with directions and answer sheets (specify Grades 1–6 or Grades 6–12); $26 per 30 practice tests; $22 per Form A Complete Battery Examiner's Manual (1993, 45 pages); $209 per 30 Form A Complete Battery reflective machine-scorable booklets; $218 per 30 Form A Complete Battery (Trans-Optic) booklets; $61 per 50 CompuScan answer sheets, Levels 14–21/22 (specify Complete Battery or Survey tests); $1,488 per 1,250 continuous form (Trans-Optic) answer sheets (specify form and indicate Level 14–21/22); $2.30 per class record sheet for hand-recording; $63 per test coordinator's handbook; $59 per technical report; $45 per Class Management Guide; $20 per Multi-Level Norms book (specify Fall, Winter, or Spring); scoring service available from publisher.
Comments: California Achievement Tests, Sixth Edition is now the same as TerraNova, The Second Edition (T7:2563); additional information available from publisher.
Author: CTB Macmillan/McGraw-Hill.
Publisher: CTB/McGraw-Hill.
Cross References: See T5:364 (28 references); for reviews by Anthony J. Nitko and by Robert F. McMorris, Wei-Ping Liu, and Elizabeth L. Bringsjord, see 13:40 (113 references); see also T4:352 (52 references); for reviews by Peter W. Airasian and James L. Wardrop of the 1985 edition, see 10:41 (68 references); for reviews by Bruce G. Rogers and Victor L. Willson of the 1978 edition, see 9:180 (19 references); see also T3:344 (68 references); for reviews by Miriam M. Bryan and Frank Womer of the 1970 edition, see 8:10 (33 references); for reviews by Jack C. Merwin and Robert D. North of the 1957 edition, see 6:3 (19 references); for a review by Charles O. Neidt, see 5:2 (10 references); for reviews by

Warren G. Findley, Alvin W. Schindler, and J. Harlan Shores of the 1950 edition, see 4:2 (8 references); for a review by Paul A. Witty of the 1943 edition, see 2:1193 (1 reference); for a review by D. Welty Lefever and an excerpted review by E. L. Abell, see 7:876. For reviews of subtests, see 8:45 (2 reviews), 8:257 (1 review), 8:719 (2 reviews), see 6:251 (1 review), 5:177 (2 reviews), 5:468 (1 review), 4:151 (2 reviews), 4:411 (1 review), 4:530 (2 reviews, 1 excerpt), 2:1292 (2 reviews), 2:1459 (2 reviews), 2:1563 (1 review), 1:893 (1 review), and 1:1110 (2 reviews).

[394]
The California Child Q-Sort.

Purpose: "Designed to describe a child's behavior and personality."
Population: Children.
Publication Date: 1980.
Acronym: CAQC.
Scores: Q-sort rating of children by teachers and counselors in 9 categories ranging from extremely uncharacteristic to extremely characteristic.
Administration: Group.
Price Data: Available from publisher at www.mindgarden.com/products/caqrs.htm#children
Time: (35-60) minutes.
Comments: For an upward extension see The California Q-Sort (402).
Authors: Jeanne Block and Jack Block.
Publisher: Mind Garden, Inc.
Cross References: See T5:365 (11 references) and T4:354 (6 references); for a review by Alfred B. Heilbrun, Jr., see 9:181; see also T3:348 (2 references).

[395]
California Computerized Assessment Package.

Purpose: Designed as a "standardized assessment of reaction time and speed of information processing."
Population: Ages 10–90.
Publication Dates: 1986–1999.
Acronym: CalCAP.
Scores: 7: Simple Reaction Time, Choice Reaction Time for Single Digits, Serial Pattern Matching, Lexical Discrimination, Visual Selective Attention, Response Reversal and Rapid Visual Scanning, Form Discrimination.
Administration: Individual.
Forms, 2: Standard, Abbreviated.
Price Data, 2005: $495 per complete kit including manual (2001, 80 pages), standard battery and abbreviated battery; $10 per demonstration program; $15 per manual.
Foreign Language Editions: Danish, Flemish, French, Norwegian, and Spanish editions available.
Time: (20–25) minutes-Standard battery; (8-10) minutes-Abbreviated battery.

Comments: DOS or Windows PC running MS-DOS 3.1 or greater, Windows 95/98 required; see CalCAP web site (www.calcaprt.com) for workarounds if using Windows 2000/XP.
Author: Eric N. Miller.
Publisher: Norland Software.
Cross References: For reviews by Howard A. Lloyd and by Goran Westergren and Ingela Westergren, see 14:58.

[396]
The California Critical Thinking Disposition Inventory [2007 Edition].

Purpose: Designed to measure the dispositional dimension of critical thinking.
Population: Working professionals, high school, and college students.
Publication Dates: 1992-2007.
Acronym: CCTDI.
Scores, 8: Overall score, Truth-Seeking, Open-Mindedness, Analyticity, Systematicity, CT-Confidence, Inquisitiveness, Cognitive Maturity.
Administration: Group.
Price Data: Available from publisher.
Foreign Language Editions: French, Spanish, Chinese, Hebrew, Japanese, and Thai.
Time: Administration time not reported.
Comments: This test can be administered online or via paper and pencil.
Authors: Peter A. Facione and Noreen C. Facione.
Publisher: Insight Assessment.
Cross References: For reviews by Brad M. Merker and John F. Wakefield, see 18:20; for reviews by Carolyn M. Callahan and Salvador Hector Ochoa of an earlier edition, see 12:57.

[397]
The California Critical Thinking Skills Test [Revised].

Purpose: "Specifically designed to measure the skills dimension of critical thinking."
Population: College students and adults.
Publication Dates: 1990-2007.
Acronym: CCTST.
Administration: Group.
Price Data: Available from publisher.
Foreign Language Editions: All forms available in English; Form A is available in Chinese (Beijing and Taiwan), Hebrew, Korean, Spanish (Mexico), and Thai; Form B is available in Portuguese; Form 2000 is available in French (Canadian), Italian, Korean, and Spanish (Spain).
Time: (45) minutes or unlimited.
Comments: This test can be administered online or via paper and pencil.

Authors: Peter A. Facione, Noreen C. Facione, Stephen W. Blohm, and Carol Ann F. Giancarlo.
Publisher: Insight Assessment-The California Academic Press LLC.
  a) FORM A.
  Scores, 4: Analysis, Inference, Evaluation, Total.
  b) FORM B.
  Scores, 4: Analysis, Inference, Evaluation, Total.
  c) FORM C.
  Scores, 6: Analysis, Inference, Evaluation, Deductive Reasoning, Inductive Reasoning, Total.
Cross References: For reviews by Matthew E. Lambert and William E. Martin, Jr., see 18:21; for reviews by Robert F. McMorris and William B. Michael of an earlier edition, see 12:58.

[398]

California Diagnostic Mathematics Tests.

Purpose: Developed to assess mathematics achievement for use in instructional planning and program evaluation.
Publication Date: 1988.
Acronym: CDMT.
Administration: Group.
Price Data, 2002: $20.55 per 35 practice tests (select Levels A, B–C, D–F); $35.55 per 35 locator tests (select Levels A–C, D–F); $30.15 per 50 locator test answer sheets (Levels D–F); $140.65 per 35 scannable test bookes (specify Level A, B, or C); $64.90 per 35 reusable test books (specify Level D, E, or F); $23.15 per 50 CompuScore or Scantron answer sheets (for use with scanning); $29.25 per 25 SCOREZE answer sheets (for use with handscoring); $16.90 per set of hand scoring stencils (select Levels D, E, F); $49.55 per 100 student diagnostic profiles; $2.70 per class report form; $11.20 per locator test directions; $14.65 per examiner's manual and answer keys (select level); $20.40 per teacher's guide (select Levels A–B, C–D, or E–F); $64.85 per specimen set; price information for norms book and technical report available from publisher; scoring service available from publisher.
Time: Administration time not reported.
Author: CTB/McGraw-Hill.
Publisher: CTB/McGraw-Hill.
  a) LEVEL A.
  Population: Grades 1.1–2.9.
  Scores, 3: Number Concepts, Computation, Applications.
  b) LEVEL B.
  Population: Grades 2.6–3.9.
  Scores, 3: Same as *a* above.
  c) LEVEL C.
  Population: Grades 3.6–4.9.
  Scores, 3: Same as *a* above.
  d) LEVEL D.
  Population: Grades 4.6–6.9.
  Scores, 3: Same as *a* above.

  e) LEVEL E.
  Population: Grades 6.6–8.9.
  Scores, 3: Same as *a* above.
  f) LEVEL F.
  Population: Grades 8.6–12.
  Scores, 3: Same as *a* above plus Life Skills.
Cross References: For reviews by Michael B. Bunch and Jerry Johnson, see 11:52.

[399]

California Diagnostic Reading Tests.

Purpose: Developed to assess reading achievement for use in instructional planning and program evaluation.
Publication Date: 1989.
Acronym: CDRT.
Administration: Group.
Price Data, 2002: $20.55 per 35 practice books (select Levels A, B–C, D–F); $35.55 per 35 locator tests (select Levels A–C, D–F); $140.65 per 35 scannable test books (specify Level A, B, or C); $64.90 per 35 reusable test books (specify Level D, E, or F); $40.65 per 50 CompuScan answer sheets (use for scanning) (specify Level D, E, or F); $46.15 per 50 Scantron answer sheets (use for scanning) (specify Level D, E, or F); $58.50 per 25 SCOREZE answer sheets (use for handscoring) (specify Level D, E, or F); $30.15 per 50 locator test answer sheets (Levels D–F only); $50.95 per set of scoring stencils (Levels D–F only); $49.55 per 100 student diagnostic profiles; $2.70 per class record sheet for handscoring (select level); $11.20 per locator test directions; $14.55 per examiner's manual including answer keys (select level); $20.40 per teacher's guide (select Levels A–B, C–D, E–F); $14.55 per norms book (32 pages); $14.55 per technical report; $64.85 per review kit; scoring service available from publisher.
Time: Tests are untimed.
Author: CTB/McGraw-Hill.
Publisher: CTB/McGraw-Hill.
  a) LEVEL A.
  Population: Grades 1.1–2.9.
  Scores, 3: Word Analysis, Vocabulary, Comprehension.
  b) LEVEL B.
  Population: Grades 2.6–3.9.
  Scores, 3: Same as *a* above.
  c) LEVEL C.
  Population: Grades 3.6–4.9.
  Scores, 3: Same as *a* above.
  d) LEVEL D.
  Population: Grades 4.6–6.9.
  Scores, 4: Same as *a* above plus Applications.
  e) LEVEL E.
  Population: Grades 6.6–8.9.
  Scores, 4: Same as *d* above.
  f) LEVEL F.
  Population: Grades 8.6–12.

Scores, 3: Vocabulary, Comprehension, Applications.
Cross References: For a review by T. Steuart Watson, see 11:53.

[400]

California Measure of Mental Motivation.
Purpose: Designed to "measure the degree to which an individual is motivated toward thinking."
Population: Grade K through adult.
Publication Dates: 1997-2006.
Acronym: CM3.
Administration: Group.
Levels, 4: IA, IB, II, III.
Price Data: Available from publisher.
Time: (15-20) minutes.
Comments: This test can be administered online or via paper and pencil.
Authors: Carol A. F. Giancarlo and P. A. Facione.
Publisher: Insight Assessment-The California Academic Press LLC.
a) LEVEL IA.
Population: Grades K-2.
Scores, 4: Mental Focus/Self-Regulation, Learning Orientation, Creative Problem Solving, Cognitive Integrity.
b) LEVEL IB.
Population: Grades 3-5.
Scores, 4: Mental Focus/Self-Regulation, Learning Orientation, Creative Problem Solving, Cognitive Integrity.
c) LEVEL II.
Population: Grades 6-12.
Scores, 5: Mental Focus/Self-Regulation, Learning Orientation, Creative Problem Solving, Cognitive Integrity, Scholarly Rigor.
d) LEVEL III.
Population: Adults.
Scores, 4: Mental Focus/Self-Regulation, Learning Orientation, Creative Problem Solving, Cognitive Integrity.
Cross References: For reviews by John J. Brinkman and Amber Carter and by William D. Schafer, see 18:22.

[401]

California Psychological Inventory™ 434.
Purpose: Designed to assess personality characteristics and to predict what people will say and do in specified contexts.
Population: Ages 13 and over.
Publication Dates: 1956–1996.
Acronym: CPI 434.
Scores, 36: 20 Folk Scales: Dominance (Do), Capacity for Status (Cs), Sociability (Sy), Social Presence (Sp), Self-Acceptance (Sa), Independence (In), Empathy (Em), Responsibility (Re), Socialization (So), Self-Control (Sc), Good Impression (Gi), Communality (Cm), Well-Being (Wb), Tolerance (To), Achievement via Conformance (Ac), Achievement via Independence (Ai), Intellectual Efficiency (Ie), Psychological-Mindedness (Py), Flexibility (Fx), Femininity/Masculinity (F/M); 3 Vector Scales: v. 1 (Internality/Externality), v. 2 (Norm Questioning/Norm Favoring), v. 3 (Self-Realization), plus 13 Special Purpose scales: Managerial Potential, Work Orientation, Creative Temperament, Leadership, Amicability, Law Enforcement Orientation, Tough-mindedness, Baucom Scale for Masculinity, Baucom Scale for Femininity, Leventhal Scale for Anxiety, Wink-Gough Scale for Narcissism, Dicken Scale for Social Desirability, Dicken Scale for Aquiescence.
Administration: Individual or group.
Price Data, 2011: $19.95 each for the Profile (online); $39.95 each for the Narrative Report (online); $49.95 each for the Configural Analysis Report (online); $99.50 per manual; $89.50 per Practical Guide to CPI™ Interpretation.
Foreign Language Editions: French, German, Italian, and Spanish editions available in an earlier edition.
Time: (45–60) minutes.
Comments: Previous edition was entitled California Psychological Inventory, Third Edition and is still available; 1 form; reports available: Narrative, Configural Analysis, Profile; Scoring Options: Prepaid (mail-in), CPP Software System, skillsone.com.
Authors: Harrison G. Gough and Pamela Bradley (manual).
Publisher: CPP, Inc.
Cross References: For reviews by Mark J. Atkinson and Keith Hattrup, see 15:43; see also T5:372 (118 references) and T4:361 (57 references); for reviews by Brian Bolton and George Engelhard, Jr., see 11:54 (108 references); for reviews by Donald H. Baucom and H. J. Eysenck, see 9:182 (61 references); see also T3:354 (195 references); for a review by Malcolm D. Gynther, see 8:514 (452 references); see also T2:1121 (166 references); for reviews by Lewis R. Goldberg and James A. Walsh and an excerpted review by John O. Crites, see 7:49 (370 references); see also P:27 (249 references); for a review by E. Lowell Kelly, see 6:71 (116 references); for reviews by Lee J. Cronbach and Robert L. Thorndike and an excerpted review by Laurance F. Shaffer, see 5:37 (33 references).

[402]

California Q-Sort (Revised Adult Set).
Purpose: Designed as "a systematic way of comparing different [intra-individual] personalities with one another."
Population: Adults.
Publication Dates: 1961–1990.
Acronym: CAQR.

Scores: Ratings in 9 categories ranging from most uncharacteristic to most characteristic.
Administration: Individual.
Price Data: Available from publisher at www.mind-garden.com/products/caqrs.htm.
Time: (30–40) minutes.
Comments: For an adaptation for children, see The California Child Q-Sort (394).
Author: Jack Block.
Publisher: Mind Garden, Inc.
Cross References: For a review by George Domino, see 14:59; see also T5:373 (43 references); T4:362 (20 references), and T3:356 (1 reference); for reviews by Allen L. Edwards and David T. Lykken of an earlier edition and excerpted reviews by Samuel J. Beck and John E. Exner, Jr., see 6:72 (2 references); see also P:28 (1 reference).

[403]

California Verbal Learning Test, Children's Version.

Purpose: "Designed to assess multiple components of verbal learning/memory, interference effects on memory and recall strategy/control."
Population: Ages 5–16.
Publication Dates: 1989–1994.
Acronym: CVLT-C.
Scores, 13: List A Trials 1–5 Total, List B Free-Recall Trial, Short Delay Free Recall, Short-Delay Cued Recall, Long-Delay Free Recall, Long-Delay Cued Recall, Semantic Cluster Ratio, Perseverations, Free-Recall Intrusions, Cued-Recall Intrusions, Recognition Hits, Discriminability, False Positives.
Administration: Individual
Price Data, 2006: $168 per set including manual (1994, 147 pages) and 25 record forms; $58 per 25 record forms or $220 per 100 record forms; $349 per scoring assistant including CD-ROM, user's guide, and keyboard overlay (Macintosh or Windows).
Time: (55) minutes with 20 minute interval between short and long delay.
Authors: Dean C. Delis, Joel H. Kramer, Edith Kaplan, and Beth A. Ober; Alan J. Fridlund, and Dean C. Delis (Scoring Assistant User's Guide).
Publisher: Pearson.
Cross References: See T5:375 (8 references); for reviews by Billy T. Ogletree and LeAdelle Phelps, see 13:41 (2 references).

[404]

California Verbal Learning Test, Second Edition, Adult Version.

Purpose: To "assess multiple cognitive components of verbal learning and memory functioning including recall strategy/organization, interference effects, recall accuracy and effort."

Population: 16–89 years.
Publication Dates: 1983–2000.
Acronym: CVLT-II (Standard); CVLT-II SF (Short Form).
Scores, 29: Immediate Recall (Trial 1, Trials 2–5, Trials 1–5 Total), Learning Slope, Semantic Clustering, Serial Clustering, Subjective Clustering, Primacy/Recency Recall, Percentage of Recall Consistency, List B Trial, Proactive Interference, Short-Delay Free Recall, Retroactive Interference, Short-Delay Cued Recall, Long-Delay Free Recall, Long-Delay Free Recall Retention, Long-Delay Cued Recall, Repetition Errors, Synonym/Subordinate Intrusions, Across-List Intrusions, Categorical Intrusions, Non-Categorical Intrusions, Yes/No Recognition Testing, False-Positive Errors, Total Recognition Discriminability, Source Recognition Discriminability, Semantic Recognition Discriminability, Novel Recognition Discriminability, Response Bias, Critical Item Analysis, Forced-Choice Recognition [optional].
Administration: Individual.
Forms, 3: Standard Form, Alternate Form, Short Form.
Price Data, 2006: $525 per complete kit including software package (CD-ROM or diskette version), manual (2000, 287 pages), 25 Standard Record Forms, 1 Alternate Record Form, and 25 Short Record Forms; $58 per 25 Standard or Alternate Record Forms (quantity discounts available); $47 per 25 Short Record Forms (quantity discounts available).
Time: (30) minutes plus 30 minutes of delay for Standard and Alternate Forms; (15) minutes plus 15 minutes of delay for Short Form.
Comments: Comprehensive Scoring System software generates Core Report (generates 27 scores), Expanded Report (generates 66 scores), Research Report (generates over 260 scores); computer system requirements: Windows 95/98/NT 4.0, 100 MHz processor, 32 MB RAM, CD-ROM and 3.5-inch floppy diskette drive (CD-ROM version) or 3.5-inch diskette drive (diskette version), 2 MB video card with 800 x 600 resolution (256 colors), and 25 MB free disk space.
Authors: Dean C. Delis, Joel H. Kramer, Edith Kaplan, and Beth A. Ober.
Publisher: Pearson.
Cross References: For reviews by Anita M. Hubley and Cederick O. Lindskog, see 16:41; see also T5:376 (35 references); for a review by Ray Fenton of the previous edition, see 13:42 (57 references); see also T4:364 (12 references).

[405]

Caliper Profile.

Purpose: Designed for "consultants to provide clear, objective information on an individual's strengths, limitations and motivations, along with solid suggestions for improving performance."
Population: Potential and existing employees.

Publication Date: 2001.

Scores, 4: Persuasiveness, Interpersonal, Problem Solving/Decision Making, Personal Organization/Time Management.

Administration: Group.

Foreign Language Editions: Available in Chinese, Czech, Dutch, English, French, German, Italian, Japanese, Korean, Portuguese, Quebecois, Russian, Spanish, Swedish, and Taiwanese.

Manual: No manual.

Time: [120] minutes, untimed.

Comments: Can be administered online or in paper-pencil format.

Authors: Caliper.

Publisher: Caliper Corporation.

[406]
Call Center Skills Test.

Purpose: Measures practical and intellectual skills for call center positions.

Population: Candidates for call center positions.

Publication Date: 2001.

Acronym: CCTR.

Scores: Total Score, Narrative Evaluation, Ranking, Recommendation.

Administration: Group.

Price Data, 2001: $150 per candidate; quantity discounts available.

Foreign Language Edition: Available in French.

Time: (60) minutes.

Comments: Available in booklet and internet versions; scored by publisher; must be proctored.

Author: Bruce A. Winrow.

Publisher: Walden Personnel Performance, Inc. [Canada].

Cross References: For reviews by Theodore L. Hayes and Judith A. Rein, see 16:42.

[407]
The Callier-Azusa Scale: G Edition.

Purpose: A developmental scale "designed to aid in the assessment of deaf-blind and severely and profoundly handicapped children."

Population: Deaf-blind and severely/profoundly handicapped children.

Publication Date: 1978.

Scores: 18 subscales in 5 areas: Motor Development (Postural Control, Locomotion, Fine Motor, Visual Motor), Perceptual Development (Vision, Auditory, Tactile), Daily Living Skills (Dressing, Personal Hygiene, Feeding, Toileting), Cognition, Communication and Language (Cognition, Receptive, Expressive, Speech), Social Development (Adults, Peers, Environment).

Administration: Individual.

Price Data: Available from publisher.

Time: Administration time not reported.

Comments: Criterion-referenced.

Author: Robert Stillman (Editor).

Publisher: Callier Center for Communication Disorders.

Cross References: See T5:377 (1 reference).

[408]
Cambridge Prospective Memory Test.

Purpose: Designed to "assess prospective memory" (remembering to do previously planned actions).

Population: Ages 16 and over.

Publication Date: 2005.

Acronym: CAMPROMPT.

Score: Total score only.

Administration: Individual.

Forms, 2: Parallel Forms A and B.

Price Data, 2006: £171.50 per complete kit including manual (44 pages), 25 record forms, quiz question cards, puzzle cards, message card, clock, and two timers; £36.50 per 25 record forms.

Time: 20(25) minutes.

Authors: Barbara A. Wilson, Hazel Emslie, Jennifer Foley, Agnes Shiel, Peter Watson, Kari Hawkins, Yvonne Groot, and Jonathan J. Evans.

Publisher: Pearson Assessment [England].

Cross References: For reviews by Mark A. Albanese and Linda E. Brody, see 17:36.

[409]
The Camden Memory Tests.

Purpose: Designed "to fulfill a clinical need that was not met by existing memory tests."

Population: Available from publisher.

Publication Date: 1996.

Scores: 5 tests: Pictorial Recognition Memory Test, Topographical Recognition Memory Test, Paired Associate Learning Test, Short Recognition Memory Test for Words, Short Recognition Memory Test for Faces.

Administration: Available from publisher.

Price Data, 2001: $182 per Pictorial Recognition Memory Test; $182 per Topographical Recognition Memory Test; $59.95 per Paired Associate Learning Test; $59.95 per Short Recognition Memory Test for Words; $59.95 per Short Recognition Memory Test for Faces; $21.95 per test manual; $395 per set of all 5 tests including 1 manual and 5 packs of scoring sheets; and $16.95 plus postage per 25 scoring sheets.

Time: Administration time not reported.

Author: Elizabeth Warrington.

Publisher: Psychology Press.

[410]
Campbell-Hallam Team Development Survey.

Purpose: "Designed to give teams standardized feedback on their strengths and weaknesses."

Population: Members of intact working teams.
Publication Date: 1994.
Acronym: TDS.
Scores, 19: Resources (Time and Staffing, Information, Material Resources, Organizational Support, Skills, Commitment), Efficiency (Mission Clarity, Team Coordination, Team Unity, Individual Goals, Empowerment), Improvement (Team Assessment, Innovation, Feedback, Rewards, Leadership), Success (Satisfaction, Performance, Overall Index).
Administration: Group.
Price Data, 1999: $180 per preview package including 10 individual survey booklets, team report, individual report for each team member, manual (216 pages), administrator's guide (15 pages), and facilitator's guide (16 pages); $15 per individual survey and report; $10 per 10 observer survey forms; $60 per team report including scoring of one team report, narrative summary profile, miniature profile, and item response summary; $35 plus $10 per item per supplemental items summary reports; $30 per manual; $10 per administrator's guide; $20 per facilitator's guide; $50 per set of manual, administrator's guide, and facilitator's guide.
Time: (20–25) minutes.
Authors: Glenn Hallam and David Campbell.
Publisher: Pearson Performance Solutions [No reply from publisher; status unknown].
Cross References: For reviews by Frederick T. L. Leong and Mary A. Lewis, see 14:60; see also T5:379 (1 reference).

[411]

Campbell™ Interest and Skill Survey.

Purpose: "Measures self-reported interests and skills."
Population: Ages 15 years to adult.
Publication Dates: 1989–1992.
Acronym: CISS™.
Scores, 99: 7 Orientation Scales (Influencing, Organizing, Helping, Creating, Analyzing, Producing, Adventuring), 29 Basic Scales (Leadership, Law/Politics, Public Speaking, Sales, Advertising/Marketing, Supervision, Financial Services, Office Practices, Adult Development, Child Development, Counseling, Religious Activities, Medical Practice, Art/Design, Performing Arts, Writing, International Activities, Fashion, Culinary Arts, Mathematics, Science, Mechanical Crafts, Woodworking, Farming/Forestry, Plants/Gardens, Animal Care, Athletics/Physical Fitness, Military/Law Enforcement, Risks/Adventure), 58 Occupational Scales (Attorney, Financial Planner, Hotel Manager, Manufacturer's Representative, Marketing Director, Realtor, CEO/President, Human Resources Director, School Superintendent, Advertising Account Executive, Media Executive, Public Relations Director, Corporate Trainer, Secretary, Bank Manager, Insurance Agent, Retail Store Manager, Hospital Administrator, Accountant/CPA, Bookkeeper, Child Care Worker, Guidance Counselor, Religious Leader, Teacher K–12, Social Worker, Psychologist, Nursing Administrator, Commercial Artist, Fashion Designer, Liberal Arts Professor, Librarian, Musician, Translator/Interpreter, Writer/Editor, Restaurant Manager, Chef, Physician, Chemist, Medical Researcher, Math/Science Teacher, Computer Programmer, Statistician, Systems Analyst, Carpenter, Electrician, Veterinarian, Airline Mechanic, Agribusiness Manager, Landscape Architect, Architect, Police Officer, Military Officer, Ski Instructor, Test Pilot, Athletic Coach, Athletic Trainer, Emergency Medical Technician, Fitness Instructor), 2 Special Scales (Academic Focus, Extraversion), 3 Procedural Checks (Response Percentage Check, Inconsistency Check, Omitted Items Check).
Administration: Group.
Price Data, 2006: $2.30 per Career Planner; $51.50 per hardcover (ring-binder) manual; $33 per softcover manual; $12.50 per 50 interest/skill pattern worksheets; $21 per 25 Q Local answer sheets; $7.60 per Q Local report; $30.75 per 100 report cover sheets; $55 per Q Local starter kit including softcover manual, 3 career planners, interest/skill pattern worksheets, 3 answer sheets with test items, and 3 Q Local administrations; $60 per mail-in socring starter kit including softcover manual, 3 career planners, interest/skill pattern worksheets, 3 answer sheets with test items, and all materials necessary to generate 3 reports using mail-in scoring service; $10.95 per internet vouchers including profile report, career planner, and career web resources; quantity discounts available for the reports; price information for Spanish materials available from publisher.
Time: (35) minutes.
Comments: Each scale contains both an interest and a skill score; combined gender scales allow for broadest interpretation of survey results; workshops available.
Author: David Campbell.
Publisher: Pearson.
Cross References: See T5:380 (1 reference); for reviews by Richard C. Pugh and Michael J. Roszkowski, see 13:43; see also T4:368 (1 reference).

[412]

Campbell Leadership Index.

Purpose: "An adjective checklist designed to be used in the assessment of leadership characteristics."
Population: Leaders.
Publication Date: 1991.
Acronym: CLI.
Scores, 22: Ambitious, Daring, Dynamic, Enterprising, Experienced, Farsighted, Original, Persuasive, Energy, Affectionate, Considerate, Empowering, Entertaining, Friendly, Credible, Organized, Productive, Thrifty, Calm, Flexible, Optimistic, Trusting.
Administration: Group or individual.
Price Data: Available from publisher.

Time: (45–60) minutes.
Comments: Self-ratings plus 3–5 observer ratings.
Author: David Campbell.
Publisher: Pearson Performance Solutions [No reply from publisher; status unknown].
Cross References: See T5:381 (1 reference); for reviews by George Domino and Charles Houston, see 12:59; see also T4:369 (1 reference).

[413]

Campbell Organizational Survey.

Purpose: Designed to measure attitudes of employees regarding the organization.
Population: Working adults.
Publication Dates: 1988–1990.
Acronym: COS.
Scores, 14: The Work Itself, Working Conditions, Freedom from Stress, Co-Workers, Supervision, Top Leadership, Pay, Benefits, Job Security, Promotional Opportunities, Feedback/Communications, Organizational Planning, Support for Innovation, Overall Satisfaction Index.
Administration: Group.
Price Data: Available from publisher.
Time: (15–25) minutes.
Comments: A component of Campbell Development Surveys (CDS); scoring and reporting discounts for 50, 250, 1,000 or 2,500+ examinees.
Author: David Campbell.
Publisher: Pearson Performance Solutions [No reply from publisher; status unknown].
Cross References: For reviews by Ralph O. Mueller and Kevin R. Murphy, see 12:60; see T4:370 (1 reference).

[414]

Canadian Achievement Survey Tests for Adults.

Purpose: "Designed to measure achievement in reading, language, and mathematics … subject areas commonly found in adult basic education curricula."
Population: Adults.
Publication Date: 1994.
Acronym: CAST.
Scores, 6: Reading (Vocabulary, Comprehension), Language (Language Mechanics, Language Expression), Mathematics (Mathematics Computation, Mathematics Concepts and Applications).
Administration: Group.
Levels, 3: Completed up to Grade 6, completed Grades 7 to 9, completed Grades 10 and above.
Price Data, 2005: $67 per 25 test booklets (specify level); $34 per 25 hand-scorable answer sheets; $65 per 50 machine scorable answer sheets; $46 per manual (53 pages); $25 per review kit including brochure, 1 copy each of Levels 1, 2, and 3 test booklets, hand-scorable

answer sheet, machine-scorable answer sheet, and directions for administering.
Time: (90) minutes.
Author: Canadian Test Centre.
Publisher: Canadian Test Centre, Educational Assessment Services [Canada].
Cross References: For reviews by John O. Anderson and Mark H. Daniel, see 14:61.

[415]

Canadian Achievement Tests, Third Edition.

Purpose: Designed to measure achievement in reading, writing, and mathematics.
Population: Grades 1.6–postsecondary.
Publication Dates: 1981–2002.
Acronym: CAT-3.
Administration: Group.
Parts, 3: Basic Battery, Supplemental Tests, Constructed-Response Tests.
Levels, 10: 11 (Grades 1.6–2.5), 12 (Grades 2.6–3.5), 13 (Grades 3.6–4.5), 14 (Grades 4.6–5.5), 15 (Grades 5.6–6.5), 16 (Grades 6.6–7.5), 17 (Grades 7.6–8.5), 18 (Grades 8.6–9.5), 19 (Grades 9.6–11.5), 20 (Grades 11.6–postsecondary).
Price Data, 2002: C$205 per Teacher Resource Kit including 3 Student Books at each of Levels 11–13, 1 Student Book at each of Levels 14–19/20, 1 Test Directions for Teachers for each level, 3 Practice Tests for each level, 3 U-Score answer sheets each (Levels 14–19/20), 3 Student Diagnostic Profiles for each level, 9 each of Locator Tests 1 and 2, 1 Locator Test Directions, 18 Locator Test answer sheets, 1 scoring key at each of Levels 11–13, 1 scoring mask at each of Levels 14–18, 1 Norms Book (2001, 101 pages), 1 Teacher Resource Manual for CAT-3 (2002, 242 pages), 1 Parents' Guide to Understanding CAT Results, and 1 carrying bag; $105 per 30 Basic Battery Plus test books (Levels 11–13, specify level); $120 per 30 Basic Battery Plus test books (Levels 14–19/20, specify level); $90 per 30 Basic Battery test books (Levels 12, 13, specify level); $65 per 50 machine-scorable answer sheets (Levels 14–19/20, specify level); $42 per 30 hand-scorable answer sheets (Levels 14–19/20, specify level); $1 per machine-scoring Directions for Test Coordinators; $8 per Test Directions for Teachers (Levels 11–18) or Administering Directions (Levels 19/20), specify level; $40 per Norms Book; $48 per Technical Manual (2002, 156 pages); $35 per Teacher Resource Manual for CAT-3; $1.50 per Parents' Guide to CAT Results; $15 per 30 Student Diagnostic Profiles (Levels 11–19/20, specify level); $12 per 30 Practice Tests (Levels 11–19/20, specify level); $1.50 per scoring key (Levels 11–19/20, specify level); $21 per Locator Test 1 or 2 (specify Test 1 or 2) including directions and 35 answer sheets; $8 per additional directions for Locator Tests 1–2; $21 per 50 additional answer sheets for Locator Tests 1–2; $1.50 per Constructed Response

Dictation Worksheet Photocopy Master (Levels 14–16, specify level); $22.50 per Constructed Response Writing Directions including 30 Student Worksheets Narrative Prompts (Levels 12–16), Informational Prompts (Levels 14–16), Letter Prompts (Levels 17–19/20), or Persuasive Prompts (Levels 17–19/20), specify level and prompt; $22.50 per Constructed Response Mathematics directions including 30 Student Worksheets (Levels 11–18), specify level and task; $50 per scoring binder for Constructed-Response Writing or Mathematics including blackline masters for scoring manual, rubrics, and anchor papers (Levels 12–19/20, specify level); $.44 per Administrator's Summary/Graphic Frequency Distribution (per student); $2.90 per Class Record Sheet (per student, Level 11); $4 per Class Record Sheet (per student, Levels 12–13, specify level), $2.10 per Class Record Sheet (per student, Levels 14–19/20, specify level); $.61 per Objective Competency Report (per student); $.91 per Parent Report or Student Test Record (per student); additional price information available from publisher.

Time: Varies by level; (85–115) minutes for Basic Battery, (55–75) minutes for Supplemental Tests, (40–230) minutes for Constructed Response Test.

Comments: Hand- or machine-scored by the Canadian Test Centre; machine-scoring recommended when testing 30 or more students; Supplemental and Constructed Response Tests optional.

Author: Canadian Test Centre, Educational Assessment Services.

Publisher: Canadian Test Centre, Educational Assessment Services [Canada].

a) LOCATOR TESTS.
Population: Grades 2–12.
Scores, 2: Vocabulary, Mathematics.
Levels, 2: 1 (Grades 2–6), 2 (Grades 6–12).
Time: (10) minutes.

b) LEVEL 11.
Population: Grades 1.6–2.5.
Scores, 6: 2 Basic Battery Tests (Reading/Language, Mathematics), 3 Supplemental Tests (Word Analysis, Vocabulary, Computation), 1 Constructed Response Test (Mathematics).
Time: (85) minutes for Basic Battery, (55) minutes for Supplemental Tests, (40) minutes for Constructed Response Test.

c) LEVEL 12.
Population: Grades 2.6–3.5.
Scores, 9: 2 Basic Battery Tests (Reading/Language, Mathematics), 4 Supplemental Tests (Word Analysis, Vocabulary, Language/Writing, Computation), 3 Constructed Response Tests (Dictation, Mathematics, Writing-Narrative).
Time: (115) minutes for Basic Battery, (70) minutes for Supplemental Tests, (110) minutes for Constructed Response Test.

d) LEVEL 13.
Population: Grades 3.6–4.5.

Scores, 9: 2 Basic Battery Tests (Reading/Language, Mathematics), 4 Supplemental Tests (Word Analysis, Vocabulary, Language/Writing, Computation), 3 Constructed Response Tests (Dictation, Mathematics, Writing-Narrative).
Time: (110) minutes for Basic Battery, (70) minutes for Supplemental Tests, (110) minutes for Constructed Response Test.

e) LEVEL 14.
Population: Grades 4.6–5.5.
Scores, 10: 2 Basic Battery Tests (Reading/Language, Mathematics), 4 Supplemental Tests (Vocabulary, Spelling, Language/Writing, Computation), 4 Constructed Response Tests (Dictation, Mathematics, Writing-Narrative, Writing-Informational).
Time: (110) minutes for Basic Battery, (75) minutes for Supplemental Tests, (230) minutes for Constructed Response Test.

f) LEVEL 15.
Population: Grades 5.6–6.5.
Scores, 10: 2 Basic Battery Tests (Reading/Language, Mathematics), 4 Supplemental Tests (Vocabulary, Spelling, Language/Writing, Computation), 4 Constructed Response Tests (Dictation, Mathematics, Writing-Narrative, Writing-Informational).
Time: (110) minutes for Basic Battery, (75) minutes for Supplemental Tests, (220) minutes for Constructed Response Test.

g) LEVEL 16.
Population: Grades 6.6–7.5.
Scores, 10: 2 Basic Battery Tests (Reading/Language, Mathematics), 4 Supplemental Tests (Vocabulary, Spelling, Language/Writing, Computation), 4 Constructed Response Tests (Dictation, Mathematics, Writing-Narrative, Writing-Informational).
Time: (110) minutes for Basic Battery, (75) minutes for Supplemental Tests, (220) minutes for Constructed Response Test.

h) LEVEL 17.
Population: Grades 7.6–8.5.
Scores, 10: 2 Basic Battery Tests (Reading/Language, Mathematics), 4 Supplemental Tests (Vocabulary, Spelling, Language/Writing, Computation), 3 Constructed Response Tests (Mathematics, Writing-Letter, Writing-Persuasive).
Time: (110) minutes for Basic Battery, (75) minutes for Supplemental Tests, (220) minutes for Constructed Response Test.

i) LEVEL 18.
Population: Grades 8.6–9.5.
Scores, 10: 2 Basic Battery Tests (Reading/Language, Mathematics), 4 Supplemental Tests (Vocabulary, Spelling, Language/Writing, Computa-

tion), 3 Constructed Response Tests (Mathematics, Writing-Letter, Writing-Persuasive).
Time: (110) minutes for Basic Battery, (75) minutes for Supplemental Tests, (220) minutes for Constructed Response Test.
j) LEVEL 19.
Population: Grades 9.6–11.5.
Scores, 10: 2 Basic Battery Tests (Reading/ Language, Mathematics), 4 Supplemental Tests (Vocabulary, Spelling, Language/Writing, Computation), 2 Constructed Response Tests (Writing-Letter, Writing-Persuasive).
Time: (110) minutes for Basic Battery, (75) minutes for Supplemental Tests, (180) minutes for Constructed Response Test.
k) LEVEL 20.
Population: Grades 11.6-postsecondary.
Scores, 10: 2 Basic Battery Tests (Reading/ Language, Mathematics), 4 Supplemental Tests (Vocabulary, Spelling, Language/Writing, Computation), 2 Constructed Response Tests (Writing-Letter, Writing-Persuasive).
Time: (110) minutes for Basic Battery, (75) minutes for Supplemental Tests, (180) minutes for Constructed Response Test.
Cross References: For reviews by John O. Anderson and Louise M. Soares, see 16:43; see T5:384; for reviews by John Hattie and Leslie Eastman Lukin of the second edition, see 13:44 (2 references); see also T4:371 (3 references); for a review by L. A. Whyte of an earlier edition, see 9:187.

[416]

Canadian Cognitive Abilities Test, Form K.
Purpose: "Designed to assess the development of cognitive abilities related to verbal, quantitative, and nonverbal reasoning and problem solving."
Population: Grades K–2, 3–12.
Publication Dates: 1970–1997.
Acronym: CCAT.
Scores: 4: Verbal, Quantitative, Nonverbal, Composite.
Administration: Group.
Time: 90 minutes for Grades 3-12.
Comments: Canadian version of Cognitive Abilities Test, Form 5 (T4:537); statistical information for CCAT is available from publisher.
Authors: Original edition by Robert L. Thorndike and Elizabeth P. Hagen; Canadian version by Edgar N. Wright.
Publisher: Nelson Education Ltd. [Canada].
a) PRIMARY BATTERIES.
Population: Grades K–1, 2–3.
Levels, 2: 1, 2.
Price Data, 2005: $4.20 per test booklet; $8.70 per Directions for Administration; $9.20 per scoring key; $40.10 per norms booklet; $40.10 per Teacher's

Handbook; $12.10 per 10 class record folders; $181.10 per score conversion software; $13.80 per preview kit; scoring service available from publisher.
b) MULTILEVEL EDITION.
Population: Grades 3–12.
Levels, 8: A, B, C, D, E, F, G, and H.
Price Data: $5.20 per test booklet; $31.40 per 35 answer sheets; $76.50 per 100 answer sheets; $8.70 per Directions for Administration; $21.80 per scoring mask; $40.10 per norms booklet; $40.10 per Teacher's Handbook; $12.10 per 10 class record folders; $246 per score conversion software; $14.80 per preview kit; scoring service available from publisher.
Cross References: See T5:385 (3 references); for reviews by John O. Anderson and John Hattie of an earlier edition, see 12:61 (3 references); for reviews by Giuseppe Costantino and Jack A. Cummings of an earlier edition, see 10:42 (3 references); see also T3:361 (5 references) and 8:180 (2 references).

[417]

Canadian Dental Aptitude Test.
Purpose: "Designed to measure general academic achievement, comprehension of scientific information, perceptual ability, and manual dexterity."
Population: Canadian dental school applicants.
Publication Dates: 1946-2005.
Scores: 7: Reading Comprehension, Natural Sciences (Biology, General Chemistry, Total), Perceptual Ability Test, Chalk Carving Test, Academic Average.
Administration: Group.
Price Data: Available from publisher.
Time: 235(330) minutes in 2 sessions.
Comments: Based on the Dental Admission Testing program (807).
Authors: Department of Testing Services, American Dental Association.
Publisher: American Dental Association.

[418]

Canadian Test of Cognitive Skills.
Purpose: Designed to assess the academic aptitude important for scholastic success of students in grades 2 through 12.
Population: Grades 2–12.
Publication Dates: 1992–1996.
Acronym: CTCS.
Scores, 4: Sequences, Memory, Analogies, Verbal Reasoning.
Administration: Group.
Levels, 5: Level 1 (Grades 2–3); Level 2 (Grades 4–5); Level 3 (Grades 6–7); Level 4 (Grades 8–9); Level 5 (Grades 10–12+).
Price Data, 2005: C$85 per 35 consumable test booklets (Level 1); $105 per 35 reusable test booklets (specify Level 2–5); $12 per 35 practice tests including

directions; $65 per 50 machine-scorable answer sheets (specify level); $28 per 25 U-Score answer sheets; $1.50 per scoring keys (specify level); $17 per 50 individual record sheets; $1.50 per class record sheet; $8 per examiner's manual (1992, 26 pages; specify level); $32 per norms book (1992, 154 pages); $21 per handbook and technical bulletin (1996, 87 pages); $50 per Multi-Level specimen set; $25 per Primary, Junior, or Senior specimen set.

Time: (52) minutes for Level 1; (55) minutes for Level 2–5.

Comments: A Practice Test (15–20 minute administration time) is available and is recommended to be administered at least one day prior to the actual testing session; adapted from Test of Cognitive Skills, Second Edition (T5:2677).

Author: Canadian Test Centre, Educational Services.

Publisher: Canadian Test Centre, Educational Assessment Services [Canada]

Cross References: For reviews by Martine Hébert and Susan J. Maller, see 13:45.

[419]

Canadian Tests of Basic Skills, Forms K and L.

Purpose: Constructed to measure growth in the fundamental skills crucial to day-to-day learning.

Population: Grades K–2, 3–8, and 9–12.

Publication Dates: 1955–1997.

Acronym: CTBS.

Scores, 12: Vocabulary, Reading Comprehension, Spelling, Capitalization, Punctuation, Usage, Reference Materials, Math Concepts & Estimation, Math Problems & Data, Math Computation, Science, Maps & Diagrams.

Administration: Group.

Time: (280) minutes for Grades 3-8 Form K; (100) for Grades 3-8 Form L.

Comments: Scoring service available from publisher; statistical information available from publisher.

Authors: A. N. Hieronymus, H. D. Hoover, E. F. Lindquist, and others (original Level 5–14 tests); Dale P. Scannell and others (original Level 15–18 tests); Ethel King-Shaw and others (Canadian adaptation).

Publisher: Nelson Education Ltd. [Canada].

a) PRIMARY BATTERY FORM K.
Population: Grades K.1–1.5, K.8–1.9, 1.7–2.6, 2.5–3.5.
Levels, 4: 5, 6, 7, 8.
Price Data, 2005: $4 per test booklet; $11 per Directions for Administration; $13.40 per scoring key and skill guide; $40.10 per norms booklet; $40.10 per Teacher's Handbook; $12.10 per 10 class record folders; $12.10 per 10 profile charts; $17.50 per 35 student profile charts (K and L); $181.10 per score conversion software; $13.80 per preview kit.

b) LEVELS 9–14 FORM K.
Population: Grades 3–8.
Levels, 6: 9, 10, 11, 12, 13, 14.

Price Data: $4.20 per test booklet (Language Arts, or Math & Science); $31.10 per 35 answer sheets (select level); $8.70 per Directions for Administration; $21.80 per scoring mask (select level); $40.10 per norms booklet; $40.10 per Teacher's Handbook; $12.10 per 10 class record folders; $12.10 per 10 profile charts; $17.50 per 35 student profile charts; $246 per score conversion software; $21.20 per preview kit.

c) LEVELS 15–18 FORM K.
Population: Grades 9–12.
Levels, 3: 15, 16, 17/18.
Price Data: $4.20 per test booklet (English, or Math & Science); $31.10 per 35 answer sheets; $8.70 per Directions for Administration; $17.95 per scoring mask (select level); $40.10 per norms booklet; $40.10 per Teacher's Handbook; $12.10 per 10 class record folders; $12.10 per 10 profile charts; $17.50 per 35 student profile charts; $181.10 per score conversion software; $17.60 per preview kit.

d) LEVELS 9–14 FORM L.
Population: Grades 3–8.
Levels, 6: 9, 10, 11, 12, 13, 14.
Price Data: $5.20 per test booklet; $31.10 per 35 answer sheets; $8.70 per Directions for Administration; $21.80 per scoring mask (select level); $40.10 per norms booklet; $40.10 per Teacher's Handbook; $12.10 per 10 class record folders; $12.10 per 10 profile charts; $17.50 per 35 student profile charts; $246 per score conversion software; $14.80 per preview kit.

Cross References: See T5:389 (14 references) and T4:375 (5 references); for reviews by John O. Anderson and by Jean-Jacques Bernier and Martine Hébert of an earlier edition, see 11:55 (9 references); see also T3:363 (15 references) and 8:11 (1 reference); for a review by L. B. Birch of an earlier edition, see 7:6.

[420]

The Capute Scales.

Purpose: "Designed to help the clinician determine the presence of atypical development in the two streams of cognitive development: language and visual motor skills."

Population: Ages 1 month to 36 months.

Publication Date: 2005.

Acronyms: CAT; CLAMS.

Scores, 3: Cognitive Adaptive Test Developmental Quotient, Clinical Linguistic & Auditory Milestone Scale Quotient, Full Scale Developmental Quotient.

Administration: Individual.

Price Data, 2010: $375 per complete test system including manual (115 pages), scoring sheets, and test kit; $25 per 20 scoring sheets; $325 per test kit including laminated card of images, notepad, crayons, cloth, form board, plexiglass pane, pegboard, dowel, cup, plastic jar, 10 blocks, plastic ring, bell, and tote bag; $55 per manual.

Foreign Language Editions: Spanish and Russian editions available.
Time: (6-20) minutes per scale.
Comments: Developmental quotients are provided for the Cognitive Adaptive Test and Clinical Linguistic and Auditory Milestone Scale. These are summed to yield a Full Scale Developmental Quotient for the entire scale.
Authors: Pasquale J. Accardo and Arnold J. Capute.
Publisher: Paul H. Brookes, Co., Inc.

[421]

Cardall Test of Practical Judgement–Revised.

Purpose: To measure problem-solving ability in everyday life.
Population: Adults in business and industry.
Publication Dates: 1942–1999.
Scores, 3: Factual, Empathetic, Total.
Administration: Group.
Price Data, 2005: $22 per review set including manual (1961, 4 pages); $55 per 25 test booklets.
Foreign Language Edition: French edition available.
Time: (30) minutes.
Author: Alfred J. Cardall.
Publisher: Institute of Psychological Research, Inc. [Canada].
Cross References: See 6:1102 (4 references) and 4:784 (6 references); for reviews by Glen U. Cleeton and Howard R. Taylor of an earlier edition, see 3:694.

[422]

CARE-2 Assessment: Chronic Violent Behavior Risk and Needs Assessment.

Purpose: Designed to identify youth "at risk for violence and aggression and to determine the interventions needed to prevent any future risk of aggression."
Population: Ages 6-19.
Publication Dates: 2003-2007.
Acronym: CARE-2.
Scores, 3: Risk, Resiliency, Total.
Administration: Individual.
Price Data, 2007: $39.95 including manual (2007, 35 pages) and one assessment booklet; $45 per 25 assessment booklets.
Time: (15-30) minutes.
Comments: Clinician obtains information for assessment through interviews with the youth, family, and caregivers; earlier edition entitled Child and Adolescent Risk Evaluation: A Measure of the Risk for Violent Behavior.
Author: Kathryn Seifert.
Publisher: Acanthus Publishing.
Cross References: For reviews by Randy G. Floyd and by Michael J. Furlong and Amy-Jane Griffiths, see 18:23; for reviews by Christopher A. Sink and Beverly J. Wilson and by Jamie G. Wood of the original edition, see 17:40.

[423]

Career & Life Explorer.

Purpose: Designed to "engage youths in thinking about themselves and in planning their future."
Population: Grades 5-12.
Publication Date: 2002.
Acronym: CLE.
Scores: No formal scores; 6 interest groups: Realistic, Investigative, Artistic, Social, Enterprising, Conventional.
Administration: Individual or group.
Price Data, 2006: $29.95 per complete kit including 25 test booklets and 1 administrator's guide (12 pages).
Time: (55-65) minutes.
Comments: Self-guided, self-scored, and self-interpreted; includes a "My Ideal Job" poster.
Author: Michael Farr.
Publisher: JIST Publishing, Inc.

[424]

Career Ability Placement Survey.

Purpose: Designed to measure abilities as they relate to careers.
Population: Junior high, high school, college, and adults.
Publication Dates: 1976–1995.
Acronym: CAPS.
Scores: Scores in 14 COPSystem Career Clusters: Science-Professional, Science-Skilled, Technology-Professional, Technology-Skilled, Consumer Economics, Outdoor, Business-Professional, Business-Skilled, Clerical, Communication, Arts-Professional, Arts-Skilled, Service-Professional, Service-Skilled; and 8 ability scores: Mechanical Reasoning, Spatial Relations, Verbal Reasoning, Numerical Ability, Language Usage, Word Knowledge, Perceptual Speed and Accuracy, Manual Speed and Dexterity.
Administration: Group.
Price Data: Available from publisher.
Time: (5) minutes per test; (50) minutes for entire battery.
Authors: Lila F. Knapp and Robert R. Knapp.
Publisher: EdITS/Educational and Industrial Testing Service.
Cross References: See T5:395 (1 reference) and T4:382 (1 reference).

[425]

Career Anchors: Discovering Your Real Values, Revised Edition.

Purpose: Designed to help a person identify their career anchor, uncover their real values, and use them to make better career choices.
Population: Adults.
Publication Date: 1990.
Scores, 8: Technical/Functional Competence, General Managerial Competence, Autonomy/Independence,

Security/Stability, Entrepreneurial Creativity, Service/ Dedication to a Cause, Pure Challenge, Lifestyle.

Administration: Group.

Price Data: Price information available from publisher for complete kit including instrument (67 pages) and trainer's manual (20 pages).

Time: (180–240) minutes.

Comments: Self-rating plus interview with a partner.

Author: Edgar H. Schein.

Publisher: Jossey-Bass, A Wiley Company.

Cross References: See T5:396 (1 reference); for reviews by Michael B. Bunch and Gary J. Robertson, see 13:46.

[426]

Career Assessment Inventory™–The Enhanced Version.

Purpose: A vocational interest assessment tool focusing on careers requiring "various amounts of post-secondary education."

Population: Grade 9 through adult.

Publication Dates: 1975–1994.

Scores, 142: 6 themes (Realistic, Investigative, Artistic, Social, Enterprising, Conventional), 25 basic interest (Mechanical/Fixing, Electronics, Carpentry, Manual/ Skilled Trades, Protective Service, Athletics/Sports, Nature/ Outdoors, Animal Service, Mathematics, Scientific Research/ Development, Medical Science, Writing, Creative Arts, Performing/Entertaining, Educating, Community Service, Medical Service, Religious Activities, Public Speaking, Law/ Politics, Management/Supervision, Sales, Office Practices, Clerical/Clerking, Food Service), 111 occupational (Accountant, Advertising Artist/Writer, Advertising Executive, Aircraft Mechanic, Architect, Athletic Trainer, Author/ Writer, Auto Mechanic, Bank Manager, Bank Teller, Barber/Hairstylist, Biologist, Bookkeeper, Bus Driver, Buyer/ Merchandiser, Cafeteria Worker, Camera Repair Technician, Card/Gift Shop Manager, Carpenter, Caterer, Chef, Chemist, Child Care Assistant, Chiropractor, Computer Programmer, Computer Scientist, Conservation Officer, Cosmetologist, Counselor-Chemical Dependency, Court Reporter, Data Input Operator, Dental Assistant, Dental Hygienist, Dental Lab Technician, Dentist, Dietitian, Drafter, Economist, Elected Public Official, Electrician, Electronic Technician, Elementary School Teacher, Emergency Medical Technician, Engineer, Executive Housekeeper, Farmer/ Rancher, Firefighter, Florist, Food Service Manager, Forest Ranger, Guidance Counselor, Hardware Store Manager, Hospital Administrator, Hotel/Motel Manager, Insurance Agent, Interior Designer, Janitor/Janitress, Lawyer, Legal Assistant, Librarian, Machinist, Mail Carrier, Manufacturing Representative, Mathematician, Math-Science Teacher, Medical Assistant, Medical Lab Technician, Military Enlisted, Military Officer, Musical Instrument Repair, Musician, Newspaper Reporter, Nurse Aide, Nurse/LPN, Nurse/RN, Occupational Therapist, Operating Room Technician, Or-

thotist/Prosthetist, Painter, Park Ranger, Personnel Manager, Pharmacist, Pharmacy Technician, Photographer, Physical Therapist, Physician, Piano Technician, Pipefitter/Plumber, Police Officer, Printer, Private Investigator, Psychologist, Purchasing Agent, Radio/TV Repair, Radiologic Technician, Real Estate Agent, Religious Leader, Reservation Agent, Respiratory Therapy Technician, Restaurant Manager, Secretary, Security Guard, Sheet Metal Worker, Surveyor, Teacher Aide, Telephone Repair Technician, Tool and Die Maker, Travel Agent, Truck Driver, Veterinarian, Waiter/Waitress.

Administration: Group or individual.

Price Data, 2006: $33 per manual; $55 per mail-in starter kit including manual and 3 answer sheets with test items to conduct and receive 3 interpretive reports; $52 per Q Local starter kit including manual, 3 answer sheets with test items, and 3 Q Local administrations; $21 per 25 Q Local answer sheets with test items; $8.65 per Q Local interpretive reports; $5.30 per Q Local profile reports; $10.65 per mail-in interpretive answer sheets with test items; $7.30 per mail-in profile reports; quantity discounts available for the reports; price information available from publisher for Spanish/French Canadian materials.

Time: (35–40) minutes.

Author: Charles B. Johansson.

Publisher: Pearson.

Cross References: See T5:398 (4 references); for a review by James B. Rounds, see 10:43 (2 references); see also T3:367 (1 reference); for reviews by Jack L. Bodden and Paul R. Lohnes of an earlier edition, see 8:993.

[427]

Career Assessment Inventory™–Vocational Version.

Purpose: "A vocational interest assessment tool for individuals planning to enter occupations requiring 0-2 years of post-secondary training."

Population: Grade 9 through adult.

Publication Dates: 1973–1994.

Scores, 125: 2 Administrative Indices (Total Responses, Response Patterning), 4 Nonoccupational (Fine Arts-Mechanical, Occupational Extroversion-Introversion, Educational Orientation, Variability of Interests), 6 General Themes (Realistic, Investigative, Artistic, Social, Enterprising, Conventional), 22 Basic Interest Area Scales (Mechanical/ Fixing, Electronics, Carpentry, Manual/Skilled Trades, Agriculture, Nature/Outdoors, Animal Service, Science, Numbers, Writing, Performing/Entertaining, Arts/Crafts, Social Service, Teaching, Child Care, Medical Service, Religious Activities, Business, Sales, Office Practices, Clerical/Clerking, Food Service), 91 Occupational Scales (Aircraft Mechanic, Auto Mechanic, Bus Driver, Camera Repair Technician, Carpenter, Conservation Officer, Dental Laboratory Technician, Drafter, Electrician, Emergency Medical Technician, Farmer/Rancher, Firefighter, Forest Ranger, Hardware Store Manager, Janitor/Janitress, Machinist, Mail Carrier, Musical

Instrument Repair, Navy Enlisted, Orthodontist/Prosthetist, Painter, Park Ranger, Pipefitter/Plumber, Police Officer, Printer, Radio/TV Repair, Security Guard, Sheet Metal Worker, Telephone Repair, Tool/Die Maker, Truck Driver, Veterinary Technician, Chiropractor, Computer Programmer, Dental Hygienist, Electronic Technician, Math-Science Teacher, Medical Laboratory Technician, Radiological Technician, Respiratory Therapeutic Technician, Surveyor, Advertising Artist/Writer, Advertising Executive, Author/Writer, Counselor-Chemical Dependency, Interior Designer, Legal Assistant, Librarian, Musician, Newspaper Reporter, Photographer, Piano Technician, Athletic Trainer, Child Care Assistant, Cosmetologist, Elementary School Teacher, Licensed Practical Nurse, Nurse Aide, Occupational Therapist Assistant, Operating Room Technician, Physical Therapist Assistant, Registered Nurse, Barber/Hairstylist, Buyer/Merchandiser, Card/Gift Shop Manager, Caterer, Florist, Food Service Manager, Hotel/Motel Manager, Insurance Agent, Manufacturing Representative, Personnel Manager, Private Investigator, Purchasing Agent, Real Estate Agent, Reservation Agent, Restaurant Manager, Travel Agent, Accountant, Bank Teller, Bookkeeper, Cafeteria Worker, Court Reporter, Data Entry Operator, Dental Assistant, Executive Housekeeper, Medical Assistant, Pharmacy Technician, Secretary, Teacher Aide, Waiter/Waitress).

Administration: Group.

Price Data, 2006: $55 per manual (1984, 152 pages); $55 per mail-in starter kit including manual and 3 answer sheets with test items to conduct and receive 3 interpretive reports; $52 per Q Local starter kit including manual, 3 answer sheets with test items, and 3 Q Local administrations; $21 per 25 Q Local answer sheets with test items; $8.65 per Q Local interpretive reports; $5.30 per Q Local profile reports; $10.65 per mail-in interprtive answer sheets with tst items; $7.30 per mail-in profile reports; quantity discounts available for the reports; price information for Spanish/French Canadian materials available from publisher.

Foreign Language Editions: Spanish and French editions available.

Time: (30–45) minutes.

Author: Charles B. Johansson.

Publisher: Pearson.

Cross References: See T5:399 (5 references) and T4:385 (4 references); for reviews by Jerard F. Kehoe and Nicholas A. Vacc, see 11:59 (1 reference); see also T3:367 (1 reference); for reviews by Jack L. Bodden and Paul R. Lohnes of an earlier edition, see 8:993.

[428]

Career Attitudes and Strategies Inventory: An Inventory for Understanding Adult Careers.

Purpose: "Developed to assess some common attitudes, feelings, experiences, and obstacles that influence the careers of employed and unemployed adults."

Population: Adults seeking vocational counseling.

Publication Dates: 1992–1994.

Acronym: CASI.

Scores, 9: Job Satisfaction, Work Involvement, Skill Development, Dominant Style, Career Worries, Interpersonal Abuse, Family Commitment, Risk-Taking Style, Geographical Barriers.

Administration: Individual.

Price Data, 2005: $117 per introductory kit including professional manual (1994, 53 pages), 25 inventory booklets, 25 hand-scorable answer sheets, and 25 interpretive summary booklets.

Time: (35) minutes.

Comments: Also includes Career Obstacles Checklist designed to assess "personal problems that may influence an individual's job situation."

Authors: John L. Holland and Gary D. Gottfredson.

Publisher: Psychological Assessment Resources, Inc.

Cross References: For reviews by Michael B. Brown and Richard T. Kinnier, see 13:47.

[429]

Career Beliefs Inventory.

Purpose: Designed to assist people to identify career beliefs that may influence their career goals.

Population: 13 years and above.

Publication Dates: 1991–1998.

Acronym: CBI.

Scores, 25: Employment Status, Career Plans, Acceptance of Uncertainty, Openness, Achievement, College Education, Intrinsic Satisfaction, Peer Equality, Structured Work Environment, Control, Responsibility, Approval of Others, Self-Other Comparisons, Occupation/College Variation, Career Path Flexibility, Post-Training Transition, Job Experimentation, Relocation, Improving Self, Persisting While Uncertain, Taking Risks, Learning Job Skills, Negotiating/Searching, Overcoming Obstacles, Working Hard.

Administration: Individual or group.

Price Data, 2011: $69.50 per 25 test booklets; $59.50 per Applications and Technical Guide.

Time: (20–30) minutes.

Comments: Available in self-scorable booklets.

Authors: John D. Krumboltz.

Publisher: CPP, Inc.

Cross References: See T5:401 (3 references); for reviews by David L. Bolton and Robert M. Guion, see 12:64 (9 references).

[430]

Career Counseling Personal Data Form.

Purpose: "Designed to provide [background] information useful in career counseling."

Population: Vocational counselees.

Publication Date: 1962.

Scores: No scores.

Administration: Group.

Manual: No manual.
Price Data, 2006: $94.20 per package of forms; $43.50 per specimen set.
Time: (30-40) minutes.
Author: John B. Ahrens.
Publisher: Martin M. Bruce, Ph.D.

[431]

Career Decision Scale.

Purpose: Developed to provide "an estimate of career indecision and its antecedents."
Population: Grades 9–12 and college.
Publication Dates: 1976–1987.
Scores: 2: Certainty, Career Indecision.
Administration: Group or individual.
Price Data, 2006: $65 per introductory kit including 50 test booklets and manual (1987, 28 pages).
Time: (10-15) minutes.
Authors: Samuel H. Osipow, Clarke G. Carney (test), Jane Winer (test), Barbara Yanico (test), and Maryanne Koschier (test).
Publisher: Psychological Assessment Resources, Inc.
Cross References: See T5:404 (47 references) and T4:390 (49 references); for reviews by Lenore W. Harmon and David O. Herman, see 9:194 (4 references).

[432]

Career Decision Self-Efficacy Scale.

Purpose: "Measures an individual's degree of belief that he/she can successfully complete tasks necessary to making career decisions."
Population: College students.
Publication Dates: 1983–1994.
Acronym: CDMSE.
Scores, 6: Self-Appraisal, Occupational Information, Goal Selection, Planning, Problem Solving, Total.
Administration: Group.
Price Data: Available from publisher (now free of charge).
Time: Administration time not reported.
Comments: A 25-item short form is also available.
Authors: Nancy E. Betz and Karen M. Taylor.
Publisher: Nancy E. Betz (the author).
Cross References: For reviews by James K. Benish and Richard W. Johnson, see 14:62; see also T5:403 (1 reference).

[433]

Career Directions Inventory [Second Edition].

Purpose: "Designed to identify areas of greater or lesser interest from among a wide variety of occupations."
Population: Adolescents and adults ages 15 years or older.
Publication Dates: 1986–2003.

Acronym: CDI.
Scores, 49: 15 Basic Interest Scales (Administration, Art, Clerical, Food Service, Industrial Art, Health Service, Outdoors, Personal Service, Sales, Science, Teaching/Social Service, Writing, Assertive, Persuasive, Systematic); 7 General Occupational Themes (Realistic/Practical, Enterprising, Artistic/Communicative, Social/Helping, Investigative/Logical, Conventional, Serving); 27 Job Clusters (Computer and Mathematical Science, Science and Engineering, Electronic Technology, Medical and Health Care, Health Record Technology, Social Science, Banking and Accounting, Funeral Services, Architectural Technology/Drafting and Design, Word Processing and Administrative Assistant, Public and Protective Services, Art, Social Services, Sales, Administration, Performing Arts, Communication Arts, Food Services, Education, Hospitality and Travel Services, Law Enforcement, Agriculture and Animal Science, Personal Care, Renewable Resource Technology, Marketing and Merchandising, Skilled Trades, Library Science).
Administration: Group and individual.
Price Data, 2010: $30 per examination kit including manual on CD (2003, 116 pages) and question and answer document for the Mail-in Extended Report; $24 per test manual on CD; $95-$105 per 10 Mail-in Extended Reports; $145 per SigmaSoft CDI for Windows Software installation package and 10 coupons; $8 per online password.
Time: 30 minutes.
Comments: Test may be administered through Mail-in Scoring, SigmaSoft for Windows Software, or via the internet at www.sigmatesting.com.
Author: Douglas N. Jackson.
Publisher: SIGMA Assessment Systems, Inc.
Cross References: For reviews by Bert A. Goldman and Cleborne D. Maddux, see 17:37; for reviews by Darrell L. Sabers and Fredrick A. Schrank of an earlier edition, see 9:44.

[434]

Career Exploration Inventory: A Guide for Exploring Work, Leisure, and Learning, Third Edition.

Purpose: Designed to help participants explore and plan three major areas in their lives-work, leisure activities, and education or learning.
Population: Employed and unemployed youth and adults.
Publication Dates: 1992-2006.
Acronym: CEI.
Scores: 17 occupational categories: Agriculture and Natural Resources, Architecture and Construction, Arts and Communication, Business and Administration, Education and Training, Finance and Insurance, Government and Public Administration, Health Science, Hospitality, Tourism and Recreation, Human Service, Information

Technology, Law and Public Safety, Manufacturing, Retail and Wholesale Sales, Scientific Research/Engineering and Mathematics, Transportation/Distribution and Logistics.
Administration: Group or individual.
Price Data, 2006: $36.95 per 25 inventories including free administrator's guide (2006, 4 pages).
Time: (30) minutes.
Comments: Occupational categories correspond to the U.S. Department of Education Career Clusters; 12-panel foldout; self-scoring and self-interpreting; no other components needed.
Author: John J. Liptak.
Publisher: JIST Publishing, Inc.
Cross References: For reviews by Bert A. Goldman and Douglas J. McRae of an earlier edition, see 13:49.

[435]

Career Exploration Series, 1992 Revision.
Purpose: Designed for career guidance using "a series of six job interest inventories that focus on specific occupational fields."
Population: Grades 7–12 and college and adults.
Publication Dates: 1979–1992.
Acronym: CES.
Scores: 6 areas: Agriculture–Forestry–Conservation, Science–Mathematics–Health, Business, Industrial, Consumer Economics, Design–Art–Communications.
Administration: Group.
Price Data: Available from publisher.
Time: (50–60) minutes.
Comments: Self-administered and self-scored interest inventories.
Authors: Arthur Cutler, Francis Ferry, Robert Kauk, and Robert Robinett.
Publisher: CFKR Career Materials.
Cross References: For a review by Herbert C. Rudman, see 13:50; for reviews by Mark Pope and William I. Sauser, Jr. of an earlier edition, see 11:60; for reviews by Bruce R. Fretz and Robert B. Slaney of the original edition, see 9:196.

[436]

Career Factors Inventory.
Purpose: Designed to provide an understanding of career decision-making readiness.
Population: Ages 13 and over.
Publication Date: 1997.
Acronym: CFI.
Scores, 4: Need for Career Information, Need for Self-Knowledge, Career Choice Anxiety, Generalized Indecisiveness.
Administration: Individual or group.
Price Data, 2011: $9.95 each for Career Factors Inventory online administration; $52.50 per 10 Career Factors Inventory self-scorable booklets; $55.50 per Career Factors Inventory Application and Technical Guide.

Time: (5–10) minutes.
Comments: Self-scorable and online scoring available.
Authors: Judy M. Chartrand, Steven B. Robbins, and Weston H. Morrill.
Publisher: CPP, Inc.
Cross References: For a review by Ayres D'Costa, see 14:63.

[437]

Career Guidance Inventory.
Purpose: "Designed to provide measures of relative interest in postsecondary instructional programs."
Population: Students and prospective students at trade, vocational, or technical school, or at community college.
Publication Dates: 1972–1989.
Acronym: CGI.
Scores, 47: Agribusiness and Agricultural Production, Renewable Natural Resources, Business (Accounting and Finance, Data Processing, Clerical/Typing/Word Processing, Office Supervision and Management, Secretarial), Marketing and Distribution (General Marketing, Financial Services, Hospitality/Recreation/Tourism, Real Estate), Communications and Communications Technologies, Computer and Information Sciences, Cosmetology and Barbering, Engineering and Related Technologies (Architectural, Civil, Electrical and Electronic, Environmental Control, Industrial Production, Mechanical Engineering, Mining and Petroleum), Allied Health (Dental Services, Diagnostic and Treatment Services, Miscellaneous Services, Medical Laboratory Technologies, Mental Health/Human Services, Nursing and Related Services, Rehabilitation Services), Vocational Home Economics (Child Care and Guidance, Clothing/Apparel/Textiles, Food Production/Management/Services, Institutional/Home Management/Supporting Services), Protective Services, Construction Trades (Brickmason/Stonemason/Tile Setting, Carpentry, Electrical and Power Transmission Installation, Plumbing/Pipefitting/Steamfitting), Mechanics and Repairers (Electrical and Electronic Equipment Repair, Heating/Air Conditioning/Refrigeration Mechanics, Industrial Equipment Maintenance and Repair, Vehicle and Mobile Equipment), Precision Production (Drafting, Graphic and Printing Communications, Precision Metal Work, Woodworking), Transportation and Material Moving, Visual Arts (Fine Arts).
Administration: Group.
Price Data: Price information available from publisher for reusable test booklet, answer sheet/interpretation guides, administrator's manual (1989, 43 pages), and specimen set of all Career Guidance Inventory and Educational Interest Inventory (859) components.
Time: [45–60] minutes.
Comments: Self-administered, self-scored.
Author: James E. Oliver.
Publisher: Wintergreen/Orchard House, Inc.

Cross References: For reviews by E. Jack Asher, Jr., and Michael B. Bunch, see 11:61; for a review by James B. Rounds, Jr., of an earlier edition, see 9:197; for a review by Bert W. Westbrook, see 8:996.

[438]

Career Matchmaker.

Purpose: An online self-assessment for "people who want to find careers that suit their interests."
Population: Grade 6 to adults.
Publication Date: 2011.
Scores: Results include 40 suggested careers.
Administration: Individual.
Price Data, 2011: $595 per English site license for one year; $795 per Spanish and English site license for one year; $795 per French and English site license for one year; multi-year discounts available.
Foreign Language Editions: Spanish and French versions available.
Time: Administration time not reported.
Comments: "Interface helps users satisfy five...career guidance needs: self-assessment, career exploration, post-secondary education planning, work search, and portfolio development."
Author: Career Cruising.
Publisher: Career Cruising [Canada].

[439]

Career Occupational Preference System, Interest Inventory, Form R.

Purpose: Designed to measure interests as they relate to careers using simplified language.
Population: Grade 6 through high school.
Publication Dates: 1984–1992.
Acronym: COPS-R.
Scores: Scores in the 14 COPSystem Career Clusters: Science-Professional, Science-Skilled, Technology-Professional, Technology-Skilled, Consumer Economics, Outdoor, Business-Professional, Business-Skilled, Clerical, Communication, Arts-Professional, Arts-Skilled, Service-Professional, Service-Skilled.
Administration: Group.
Price Data: Available from publisher.
Time: (20) minutes.
Authors: Lila F. Knapp and Robert R. Knapp.
Publisher: EdITS/Educational and Industrial Testing Service.
Cross References: See T5:414 (2 references and T4:399 (12 references).

[440]

Career Occupational Preference System, Intermediate Inventory.

Purpose: To measure career interests and provide a rating of interests based on knowledge of school subjects and activities familiar to elementary and intermediate grade students.
Population: Elementary through high school with 4th grade reading level.
Publication Dates: 1981–1997.
Acronym: COPS-II.
Scores: Scores in 14 COPSystem Career Clusters: Science-Professional, Science-Skilled, Technology-Professional, Technology-Skilled, Consumer Economics, Outdoor, Business-Professional, Business-Skilled, Clerical, Communication, Arts-Professional, Arts-Skilled, Service-Professional, Service-Skilled.
Administration: Group.
Price Data: Available from publisher.
Time: (15–20) minutes.
Authors: Robert R. Knapp and Lila F. Knapp.
Publisher: EdITS/Educational and Industrial Testing Service.
Cross References: See T5:415 (1 reference).

[441]

Career Occupational Preference System–Professional Level Interest Inventory.

Purpose: Designed to measure career interest for those wanting to focus on the professional level careers.
Population: College and adult professionals, college-bound senior high school students.
Publication Dates: 1982–1989.
Acronym: COPS-P.
Scores: Scores in the 16 COPSystem Career Clusters: Service-Social, Service-Instructional, Science-Physical, Science-Medical/Life, Technology-Civil, Technology-Electrical, Technology-Mechanical, Outdoor-Agribusiness, Outdoor-Nature, Business-Management, Business-Finance, Computation, Communication-Written, Communication-Oral, Arts-Design, Arts-Performing.
Administration: Group.
Price Data: Available from publisher.
Time: (15–20) minutes.
Authors: Lisa Knapp-Lee, Lila F. Knapp, Robert R. Knapp.
Publisher: EdITS/Educational and Industrial Testing Service.
Cross References: For reviews by Mark A. Albanese and Jeffrey A. Jenkins, see 14:65; see also T5:416 (1 reference).

[442]

Career Orientation Placement and Evaluation Survey.

Purpose: Designed to measure values having a demonstrated effect on vocational motivation.
Population: Grade 7 through high school, college, and adult.
Publication Dates: 1981–1995.

Acronym: COPES.
Scores: Scores in 8 work values dimensions: Investigative v. Accepting, Practical v. Carefree, Independence v. Conformity, Leadership v. Supporting, Orderliness v. Flexibility, Recognition v. Privacy, Aesthetic v. Realistic, Social v. Reserved; and 14 COPSystem Career Clusters: Science-Professional, Science-Skilled, Technology-Professional, Technology-Skilled, Consumer Economics, Outdoor, Business-Professional, Business-Skilled, Clerical, Communication, Arts-Professional, Arts-Skilled, Service-Professional, Service-Skilled.
Administration: Group.
Price Data: Available from publisher.
Time: (15–20) minutes.
Authors: Robert R. Knapp and Lila F. Knapp.
Publisher: EdITS/Educational and Industrial Testing Service.

[443]

Career Planning Survey.

Purpose: Intended "to help students in grades 8–10 identify and explore personally relevant occupations and high school courses ... to provide students with a general sense of direction for career exploration ... show students how occupations relate to each other, thus giving students a context in which to explore their career options."
Population: Grades 8–10.
Publication Dates: 1997–2001.
Scores, 4: (UNIACT) Interest Inventory, Inventory of Work-Relevant Abilities, and 2 ability measures (Reading Skills, Numerical Skills).
Administration: Group.
Price Data, 2006: $4.10 per Assessment Set Option A (with ability measures); $3.50 per Assessment Set Option B (without ability measures) (each set includes an answer sheet [scored by ACT], a student guidebook, prepaid scoring, and two copies of the student report); $13.00 per examination kit (with detailed information and sample materials for the preview of Career Planning Survey, including test booklet, Directions for Administration, Counselor's Manual [2001, 48 pages], and student guidebook [2001, 24 pages]); $.75 per reusable test booklet; $8.60 per Counselor's Manual; $2.35 per Directions for Administration; volume discounts available.
Time: (90) minutes (Option A); (45) minutes (Option B).
Author: ACT, Inc.
Publisher: ACT, Inc.
Cross References: For a review by Sandra A. Loew, see 15:44.

[444]

Career Profile +.

Purpose: "Predicts an individual's probability of success in an insurance sales career."

Population: Candidates for financial services sales representative positions.
Publication Dates: 1983-2000.
Administration: Individual.
Price Data: Available from publisher.
Foreign Language Editions: English-speaking Canada and French-speaking Canada editions available; U.S. Spanish and Chinese editions of nonstudent version are available.
Time: Untimed.
Comments: Profiles processed by publisher.
Author: LIMRA International.
Publisher: LIMRA International.
  a) STUDENT CAREER PROFILE.
  Population: High school–college student.
  Scores: Career Profile rating.
  Comments: Career Profile rating indicates probability of success in financial services sales; versions available for Financial Services Sales, Life and Health Sales, and Multiple-Line & Property-Casualty Sales.
    1) *Personality Assessment.*
    Scores: 4 personality characteristics: Persuasiveness, Energy, Achievement Drive, Initiative & Persistence.
  b) NONSTUDENT CAREER PROFILE.
  Population: Inexperienced candidates.
  Scores: Same as *a* above.
  Comments: Versions available for Financial Services Sales, Life and Health Sales, and Multiple-Line & Property-Casualty Sales.
    1) *Personality Assessment.*
    Scores: Same as *a*-1 above.
Cross References: For reviews by Ayres G. D'Costa and Michael S. Trevisan, see 13:52.

[445]

Career Thoughts Inventory.

Purpose: Constructed to " identify an individual who is likely to need career counseling and identify the nature of the individual's career problems."
Population: Adults, college students, and high school students.
Publication Dates: 1994–1996.
Acronym: CTI.
Scores, 4: Decision Making Confusion, Commitment Anxiety, External Conflict, Total.
Administration: Group.
Price Data, 2006: $185 per introductory kit including manual (1996, 99 pages), 25 test booklets, and 10 workbooks (1996, 39 pages).
Time: (7–15) minutes.
Authors: James P. Samson, Jr., Gary W. Peterson, Janet G. Lenz, Robert C. Reardon, and Denise E. Saunders.
Publisher: Psychological Assessment Resources, Inc.
Cross References: For a review by Janet H. Fontaine, see 14:66.

[446]

Career Transitions Inventory.

Purpose: "Designed to assess the resources and barriers" experienced "in making a career transition."
Population: Adults.
Publication Date: 1991.
Acronym: CTI.
Scores, 5: Readiness, Confidence, Personal Control, Support, Independence.
Administration: Group.
Manual: No manual.
Price Data: Available from author.
Time: Administration time not reported.
Author: Mary J. Heppner.
Publisher: Mary J. Heppner (the author).
Cross References: For reviews by Robert J. Drummond and Jean Powell Kirnan, see 15:45.

[447]

Career Values Card Sort.

Purpose: Defines factors that affect career satisfaction, the intensity of feelings about these factors, determines areas of value conflict and congruence, helps make career decisions.
Population: Adults.
Publication Dates: 1977-2005.
Scores: No scores.
Administration: Group or individual.
Price Data, 2011: $9 per one card sort deck and one worksheet.
Time: (20–30) minutes.
Comments: Self-administered; worksheet includes career decision matrix; distributors are available in Canada, Australia, Egypt, and U.S.A. List of distributor information available online from www.CareerTrainer.Com.
Authors: Richard L. Knowdell.
Publisher: Career Research & Testing, Inc.
Cross References: For reviews by Esther E. Diamond and Richard T. Kinnier, see 13:53.

[448]

Careers for Me.

Purpose: Designed "to encourage students to think about their interests and the world of work around them."
Population: Grades K-9.
Publication Dates: 2000-2009.
Scores: Not scored.
Administration: Group.
Manual: No manual.
Author: Career Kids.
Publisher: Career Kids.

a) CAREERS FOR ME JUNIOR.
Purpose: Designed to "start the process of career awareness with young children."
Population: Grades K-3.
Publication Date: 2000.
Price Data, 2010: $33.75 per 25 consumable folders; volume discounts available.
Foreign Language Edition: Spanish translation available.

b) CAREERS FOR ME II.
Purpose: Designed to "encourage students to think about their interests and the world of work around them."
Population: Grades 3-7.
Publication Date: 2000.
Price Data: $36.25 per 25 consumable booklets (12 pages); volume discounts available.
Foreign Language Edition: Spanish translation available.

c) CAREERS FOR ME PLUS.
Purpose: Designed to "transition student to the next step in their career awareness and education."
Population: Grades 6-9.
Publication Date: 2009.
Price Data, 2010: $47.50 per 25 consumable booklets (24 pages); volume discounts available.
Foreign Language Edition: Spanish translation available.

d) CAREERS FOR ME SN.
Purpose: To assist special needs children in thinking about career interests.
Population: Lower functioning special needs students.
Publication Date: 2003.
Price Data, 2010: $33.75 per 25 consumable folders; volume discounts available.

[449]

Caregiver-Teacher Report Form.

Purpose: Designed "to assess behavioral/emotional problems and identify syndromes of problems that tend to occur together."
Population: Ages 1.5–5.
Publication Dates: 1997– 2000.
Acronym: C-TRF.
Scores, 10: Emotionally Reactive, Anxious/Depressed, Somatic Complaints, Withdrawn, Attention Problems, Aggressive Behavior; Internalizing, Externalizing, Total; DMS oriented scales: Affective Problems, Anxiety Problems, Attention Deficit/Hyperactivity Problems, Oppositional Defiant Problems, Pervasive Developmental Problems.
Administration: Group.
Price Data: Available from publisher.
Time: [10] minutes.
Comments: Ratings by daycare providers and preschool teachers.
Author: Thomas M. Achenbach.
Publisher: ASEBA Research Center for Children, Youth, and Families.

Cross References: For reviews by Karen T. Carey and by Michael Furlong and Renee Pavelski, see 14:67.

[450]
Carey Temperament Scales.

Purpose: Designed to assess "temperamental characteristics in infants and children."
Population: Ages 1 month to 12 years-11 months.
Publication Dates: 1996–1998.
Acronym: CTS.
Scores: 9 categories of temperament: Activity, Rhythmicity, Approach, Adaptability, Intensity, Mood, Persistence, Distractibility, Threshold.
Administration: Individual.
Price Data: Price information available from publisher for questionnaires with hand scoring, software (diskette or CD), and online scoring are available or online at www.b-di.com.
Time: [15–20] minutes for administration. 2-3 minutes for software scoring; 10-15 minutes for hand scoring.
Comments: Parent/caregiver ratings of infant and child temperament; also assesses the caregiver's overall general impression of each category of temperament and provides a general manageability score; measures the nine NYLS temperament dimensions; or use in research and in clinical work with parents of preadolescent children; five separate questionnaires are included in the series, based on age levels in early infancy, infancy, toddlerhood, early childhood and middle childhood; computer scoring software on diskette, CDs and internet scoring are available (CDs are available for PC).
and Macintosh).
Authors: William B. Carey, Sean C. McDevitt, Barbara Medoff-Cooper, William Fullard, and Robin L. Hegvik.
Publisher: Behavioral-Developmental Initiatives.
Cross References: For reviews by Aimée Langlois and E. Jean Newman, see 14:68.

[451]
Caring Relationship Inventory.

Purpose: Designed to "measure the ... elements of love or caring in human relationships."
Population: Premarital and marital counselees.
Publication Dates: 1966–1975.
Acronym: CRI.
Scores, 7: Affection, Friendship, Eros, Empathy, Self-Love, Being Loved, Deficiency Love.
Administration: Individual.
Price Data: Available from publisher.
Time: (40) minutes.
Author: Everett L. Shostrom.
Publisher: EdITS/Educational and Industrial Testing Service.
Cross References: See T4:408 (3 references); for reviews by Donald L. Mosher and Robert F. Stahmann, see 8:333 (5 references); for a review by Albert Ellis, see 7:561; see also P:31 (1 reference).

[452]
Carlson Psychological Survey.

Purpose: Developed to assess and classify offenders quickly and accurately.
Population: Adult and adolescent offenders.
Publication Dates: 1982–1997.
Acronym: CPS.
Scores, 5: Chemical Abuse, Thought Disturbance, Anti-Social Tendencies, Self-Depreciation, Validity.
Administration: Group or individual.
Price Data, 2010: $88 per examination kit including manual on CD (1982, 28 pages), 5 question and answer booklets, 5 scoring sheets, 5 profile sheets, and one machine-scorable question-and-answer document for an Extended Report; $24 per test manual on CD; $60 per 25 question-and-answer booklets; $66 per 25 response sheets (including 25 scoring sheets and 25 profile sheets); $75-$85 (depending on volume) per 10 machine-scorable question-and-answer sheets for Extended Reports; $145 per software package including installation package and 10 coupons for computer reports.
Foreign Language Editions: Psicologico Texto (PT) designed specifically for use with Spanish-literate offenders; question and answer booklets available in French and Spanish.
Time: 15 minutes.
Author: Kenneth A. Carlson.
Publisher: SIGMA Assessment Systems, Inc.
Cross References: See T4:409 (2 references); for a review by H. C. Ganguli, see 9:203.

[453]
The Carolina Curriculum.

Purpose: Designed as an assessment and intervention program for use with young children who have mild to severe disabilities.
Population: Birth to age 5.
Publication Date: 2004.
Scores: 5 domains: Cognition, Communication, Social Adaptation, Fine Motor, Gross Motor.
Administration: Individual
Price Data, 2011: $87.95 per 2-book set; $25 per 10 assessment and development progress charts; $139.95 per printable masters on CD-ROM; $48.95 per special bound book (specify level).
Time: Administration time not reported.
Comments: A criterion-referenced system that links assessment with intervention.
Authors: Nancy M. Johnson-Martin, Susan M. Attermeier, and Bonnie J. Hacker.
Publisher: Paul H. Brookes Publishing Co., Inc.
  a) THE CAROLINA CURRICULUM FOR INFANTS & TODDLERS WITH SPECIAL NEEDS, THIRD EDITION.
Population: Birth to 36 months.

Acronym: CCITSN.
Price Data: $48.95 per special-bound book (512 pages).
b) THE CAROLINA CURRICULUM FOR PRE-SCHOOLERS WITH SPECIAL NEEDS, SECOND EDITION.
Population: 24–60 months.
Acronym: CCPSN.
Price Data: $48.95 per special-bound book (448 pages).

[454]

Carolina Developmental Profile.

Purpose: "Designed to assist the teacher in establishing long-range objectives to increase developmental abilities in six areas: fine motor, gross motor, visual perception, reasoning, receptive language, and expressive language."
Population: Ages 2–5.
Publication Date: 1980.
Acronym: CDP.
Scores, 7: Fine Motor, Gross Motor, Visual Perception, Reasoning, Receptive Language, Expressive Language, Social/Emotional.
Administration: Individual.
Manual: No manual.
Price Data, 2003: $199.95 per complete kit including 10 scoring booklets, toy, supplies, and manipulatives; $14.95 per 10 scoring booklets.
Time: Administration time not reported.
Comments: "Criterion referenced" behavior checklist.
Authors: David L. Lillie and Gloria L. Harbin.
Publisher: Kaplan Early Learning Company.

[455]

Carolina Picture Vocabulary Test (for Deaf and Hearing Impaired).

Purpose: "To measure the receptive sign vocabulary in individuals where manual signing [is] the primary mode of communication."
Population: Deaf and hearing-impaired children ages 4–11.5 years.
Publication Date: 1985.
Acronym: CPVT.
Scores: Total score only.
Administration: Individual.
Price Data, 2011: $152 per complete program; $78 per picture book; $38 per 50 record forms; $49 per manual (38 pages).
Time: (10-15) minutes.
Authors: Thomas L. Layton and David W. Holmes.
Publisher: PRO-ED.
Cross References: For additional information, see 11:62 (1 reference).

[456]

Carroll Depression Scales.

Purpose: Designed as a measure of depression; providing diagnostic as well as level of severity information.
Population: Ages 18 and older.
Publication Date: 1998.
Scores, 6: Major Depression, Dysthymic Disorder, Melancholic Features, Atypical Features, HDRS, Total.
Administration: Individual or Group.
Price Data, 2011: $87 Technical Manual; $56 Software preview version including 3 profile reports and 3 Brief profile reports; $5 per profile report; $3 per Brief profile report.
Foreign Language Editions: Arabic, Chinese, Dutch, French, French-Canadian, German, Greek, Italian, Japanese, Russian, Slovakian, and Spanish available upon special request.
Comments: Interpretation by qualified professionals only.
Author: Bernard Carroll.
Publisher: Multi-Health Systems, Inc.
  a) CARROLL DEPRESSION SCALES.
  Acronym: CDS-R.
  Time: (20) minutes.
  Comments: A 52-item self-report measure.
  b) CARROLL DEPRESSION SCALE—REVISED.
  Acronym: CDS-R.
  Time: (10) minutes.
  Comments: A 52-item self-report measure; includes diagnostic index in addition to severity score provided by CDS.
  c) BRIEF CARROLL DEPRESSION INVENTORY.
  Acronym: Brief CDS-R.
  Time: (2) minutes.
  Comments: A 12-item self-report rapid screening measure of depressive symptoms.
Cross References: For a review by Susan M. Swearer, see 14:69.

[457]

CASAS Life and Work Reading Assessments.

Purpose: Designed to "measure learning progress of members of the youth and adult education population in the content domain of reading."
Population: Youth and adult learners.
Publication Dates: 2005-2010.
Scores, 3: Appraisal, Pre-Test, Post-Test.
Administration: Group.
Levels, 4: A, B, C, D.
Forms, 12: 81, 82, 81X, 82X, 83, 84, 185, 186, 85, 86, 187, 188.
Restricted Distribution: Distribution restricted to agencies completing the CASAS Implementation Training.
Price Data, 2010: $70 per 25 Level A, Form 81; $70 per 25 Level A, Form 82; $70 per 25 Level A, Form

81X; $70 per 25 Level A, Form 82X; $70 per 25 Level B, Form 83; $70 per 25 Level B, Form 84; $70 per 25 Level C, Form 85; $70 per 25 Level C, Form 86; $70 per 25 Level C, Form 185; $70 per 25 Level C, Form 186; $70 per 25 Level D, Form 187; $70 per 25 Level D, Form 188; $20 per Test Administration Manual (2005, 22 pages).

Time: (60) minutes.

Comments: An appraisal test is administered first to identify the appropriate level of pretest. The pretest is administered and the score from the pretest guides the choice of posttest. A chart for guiding pretest/post-test choice is provided in the administration manual. Students move up through the levels of testing as their skills develop.

Author: CASAS.

Publisher: CASAS.

[458]

The Category-Specific Names Test.

Purpose: Designed to detect category-specific deficits both in naming and in comprehension of the spoken or written name within four semantic categories: animals, fruits and vegetables, praxic objects, and non-praxic objects.

Population: Children and adults.

Publication Date: Unavailable.

Scores: Available from publisher.

Administration: Individual.

Price Data, 2001: $415 per complete test.

Time: Administration time not reported.

Author: Pat McKenna.

Publisher: Psychology Press.

[459]

Category Test.

Purpose: "Measures an individual's ability to perform in an ambiguous, problem-solving situation" and is intended to be used "in settings that require the assessment of brain damage and/or problem solving ability."

Population: Ages 9-15 (ICat); [Ages 16-69 (HCT, ACat, RCat)].

Publication Dates: 1989-2008.

Acronym: Cat.

Scores: Information available from publisher.

Administration: Individual.

Forms: 4 computer-adapted versions: Halstead Category Test (HCT), Adaptive Category Test (ACat), Russell Revised Short Form (RCat), Intermediate Category Test (ICat).

Price Data, 2011: $220 per complete kit including Category Test software (version 7.0), technical guide, and software manual (2008, 104 pages).

Time: (30-40) minutes; "up to [95] minutes for impaired clients."

Comments: The Cat is composed of four computer-adapted versions administered depending on respondents' ages. The HCT is the full adult version of the Halstead Category Test; the ACat is a shortened version that uses "a subset of responses on items of [each HCT] subtest... to predict the respondent's final score for that subtest"; the RCat is a shortened version that eliminates one of the HCT subtests and reduces "half the number of items from most [other] subtests"; the ICat "is designed for children"; software is Windows compatible; instructions available in visual and auditory form; each score is based on "the ability to discover and apply certain" problem-solving rules.

Authors: James Choca, Linda Laatsch, Dan Garside, Rahul Gupta, and James Fenstermacher.

Publisher: Multi-Health Systems, Inc.

Cross References: For reviews by Karen T. Carey and Catherine P. Cook-Cottone, see 18:24; for a review by Robert A. Leark of an earlier form, The Computer Category Test, see 15:62.

[460]

Cattell Infant Intelligence Scale.

Purpose: Designed to measure the infant's developmental progress.

Population: Ages 3–30 months.

Publication Dates: 1946–1960.

Acronym: CIIS.

Scores: Ratings in 4 areas: Willingness, Self-Confidence, Social-Confidence, Attention.

Administration: Individual.

Price Data, 2002: $795 per basic set including all necessary equipment, 25 record forms, and carrying case (manual not included); $113 per manual entitled The Measurement of Intelligence of Infants and Young Children (1960, 274 pages); $40 per 25 record forms.

Time: (20-30) minutes.

Comments: Downward extension of Stanford-Binet Intelligence Scale, Second Revision.

Author: Psyche Cattell.

Publisher: Pearson.

Cross References: See T5:433 (14 references), T4:423 (13 references) and T3:381 (19 references); for a review by Fred Damarin, see 8:209 (7 references); see also T2:487 (27 references) and 6:515 (22 references); for reviews by Florence M. Teagarden and Beth L. Wellmann and excerpted reviews by Rachel Stutsman Ball, C. M. Louttit, T. L. McCulloch, Norma V. Schneidmann, and Helen Speyer, see 3:281.

[461]

CERAD Behavior Rating Scale for Dementia, Second Edition.

Purpose: Designed to "assess the behavioral problems and psychiatric symptoms of individuals with no history of mental retardation who have or are suspected to have acquired cognitive deficits."

Population: Adults who have, or are suspected to have, acquired cognitive deficits.

Publication Dates: 1991–2001.

Acronym: BRSD.

Scores, 7: Depressive Symptoms, Inertia, Vegetative Symptoms, Irritability/Aggression, Behavioral Dysregulation, Psychotic Symptoms, Total Weighted Score.

Administration: Individual.

Price Data, 2003: $85 per test kit including manual; $75 per training video.

Time: [20–40] minutes.

Comments: Informant report interview; short form available; may be administered via telephone.

Authors: James L. Mack and Marion Patterson.

Publisher: CERAD, Duke University Medical Center.

Cross References: For a review by Pamilla Ramsden, see 16:44.

[462]

CERAD (Consortium to Establish a Registry for Alzheimer's Disease) Assessment Battery.

Purpose: "To develop brief, standardized instruments for the assessment of patients with probable Alzheimer's disease."

Population: Patients with mild to moderate dementia.

Publication Dates: 1987-1995.

Acronym: CERAD.

Scores: Information gathered in 19 areas: Demographic, Drug Inventory, Informant History (Clinical, Blessed Dementia Rating Scale), Subject History, Short Blessed Test, Depression and Calculation and Language, Examinations (Physical, Neurological), Laboratory Studies, Diagnostic Impression, Neuropsychological Battery (Neuropsychology Battery Status, Verbal Fluency Categories, Boston Naming Test, Mini-Mental State Exam, Word List Memory, Constructional Praxis, Word List Recall, Word List Recognition), Constructional Praxis Recall.

Administration: Individual.

Restricted Distribution: Current use only with permission of CERAD.

Price Data: Available from publisher.

Foreign Language Editions: Forms available in French, Spanish, Italian, Chinese, Japanese, and Korean.

Time: 50–70] minutes.

Comments: Available in electronic format.

Authors: Consortium to Establish a Registry for Alzheimer's Disease, Albert Heyman (Principal Investigator).

Publisher: CERAD, Duke University Medical Center.

Cross References: For reviews by Frank M. Bernt and Gabrielle Stutman, see 12:66 (1 reference).

[463]

Certified Picture Framer Examination.

Purpose: "To provide professional recognition to competent individuals who are engaged in the business of picture framing."

Population: Individuals actively involved in the business of picture framing for one year.

Publication Dates: 1986–1993.

Acronym: CPF.

Scores: Total score only.

Administration: Group.

Price Data: Available from publisher.

Time: (210) minutes.

Comments: Test administered on specific dates at centers established by the publisher.

Author: Certification Board of the Professional Picture Framers Association.

Publisher: Professional Picture Framers Association.

[464]

Change Abilitator.

Purpose: Designed to identify six types of concerns people experience when change is introduced into their organization.

Population: Teams.

Publication Date: 1995.

Scores, 6: Information, Personal, Operational, Impact, Collaboration, Transforming.

Administration: Group.

Price Data: Available from publisher.

Time: (15) minutes.

Comments: Revision of the Stages of Concern Questionnaire.

Author: LHE, INC.

Publisher: HRD Press, Inc.

Cross References: For a review by Cynthia A. Larson-Daugherty, see 14:70.

[465]

Change Agent Questionnaire.

Purpose: Assesses "the underlying assumptions and practical strategies employed by agents of change as they seek to influence others."

Population: Adults.

Publication Dates: 1969-1995.

Acronym: CAQ.

Scores, 20: Client-Centered Change (Philosophy, Strategy, Evaluation, Total), Charismatic Change (Philosophy, Strategy, Evaluation, Total), Custodial Change (Philosophy, Strategy, Evaluation, Total), Compliance Change (Philosophy, Strategy, Evaluation, Total), Credibility Change (Philosophy, Strategy, Evaluation, Total).

Administration: Group.

Manual: No manual.

Price Data, 2001: $8.95 per instrument.

Time: Administration time not reported.
Authors: Jay Hall and Martha S. Williams.
Publisher: Teleometrics International, Inc.

[466]

Chapin Social Insight Test.

Purpose: Designed to "assess the perceptiveness and accuracy with which an individual can appraise others and forecast what they might say and do."
Population: Ages 13 and over.
Publication Dates: 1967–1993.
Acronym: SCLT.
Scores: Total score only.
Administration: Group.
Price Data: Available from publisher at www.mind-garden.com/products/sclts.htm.
Time: (20–30) minutes.
Authors: F. Stuart Chapin (test) and Harrison G. Gough (manual).
Publisher: Mind Garden, Inc.
Cross References: For reviews by Frank M. Bernt and by Collie W. Conoley and Linda Castillo, see 16:45; see also T3:384 (5 references); for reviews by Richard I. Lanyon and David B. Orr of an earlier edition, see 7:51; see also P:34 (3 references).

[467]

Characteristics Scale.

Purpose: To determine teachers' views of important pupil characteristics and behaviors.
Population: Grades K-8.
Publication Dates: 1970-1975.
Scores: Total score only.
Administration: Group.
Manual: No manual.
Price Data, 2001: Now free upon request from publisher.
Time: Administration time not reported.
Comments: Ratings by teachers; research instrument; may be used with or separately from Behavior Rating Scale.
Authors: Patricia B. Elmore and Donald L. Beggs.
Publisher: Patricia B. Elmore.

[468]

Checking Individual Progress in Phonics.

Purpose: Designed to "assess pupils' progress in phonics, identify their learning strategies and improve their skills."
Population: Ages 6 to 7.
Publication Date: 2001.
Acronym: ChIPPs.
Scores: Total words read correctly.
Administration: Individual.
Forms: 2 parallel forms: Version 1 and Version 2.
Price Data: Price data for complete set including

teacher's manual (106 pages), test materials, and reproducible Individual, Class, and Pupil record sheets available from publisher.
Time: Administration time not reported.
Authors: Sue Palmer and Rea Reason.
Publisher: GL Assessment [England].
Cross References: For reviews by Jorge E. Gonzalez and Rebekah Haynes and by William K. Wilkinson, see 17:38.

[469]

Checklist for Child Abuse Evaluation.

Purpose: Designed as a "tool for investigating and evaluating children and adolescents who may have been neglected or abused."
Population: Children and adolescents.
Publication Dates: 1988–1990.
Acronym: CCAE.
Scores: 24 sections: Identification and Case Description, The Child's Status, Accuracy of Allegations by the Reporter, Interview with the Child (Physical/Behavioral Observations, Disclosure, Emotional Abuse, Sexual Abuse, Physical Abuse, Neglect), Events Witnessed or Reported by Others (Neglect, Emotional Abuse, Sexual Abuse, Physical Abuse), The Child's Psychological Status, History and Observed/Reported Characteristics of the Accused, Credibility of the Child–Observed/Reported, Competence of the Child–Observed/Reported, Conclusions (Consistency of Other Information, Allegation Motives, Substantiation of Allegations, Competence of the Child as a Witness, Level of Stress Experienced by the Child, Protection of the Child), Treatment Recommendations.
Administration: Individual.
Price Data, 2006: $138 per introductory kit including manual (1990, 19 pages) and 25 checklists.
Time: Untimed.
Author: Joseph Petty.
Publisher: Psychological Assessment Resources, Inc.
Cross References: For reviews by Denise M. DeZolt and Janice G. Williams, see 12:68.

[470]

Checklist of Adaptive Living Skills.

Purpose: "A criterion-referenced measure of adaptive living skills and a tool for program planning."
Population: Infants to adults.
Publication Date: 1991.
Acronym: CALS.
Scores: 4 areas: Personal Living Skills, Home Living Skills, Community Living Skills, Employment Skills; and 24 subscales: Socialization, Eating, Grooming, Toileting, Dressing, Health Care, Sexuality, Clothing Care, Meal Planning and Preparation, Home Cleaning and Organization, Home Maintenance, Home Safety,

Home Leisure, Social Interaction, Mobility and Travel, Time Management, Money Management and Shopping, Community Safety, Community Leisure, Community Participation, Job Search, Job Performance and Attitudes, Employee Relations, Job Safety.
Administration: Individual.
Price Data, 2006: $117.50 per complete kit including manual (62 pages) and 25 checklists; $75.50 per manual; $82 per 25 checklists.
Time: [60] minutes.
Comments: "Designed to be completed by a respondent who has had the opportunity to observe the learner in natural environments for a period of three or more months"; conceptually and statistically linked to two normative measures of adaptive behavior: Scales of Independent Behavior–Revised (SIB-R; 2352) and Inventory for Client and Agency Planning (ICAP; 1342); companion publication is the Adaptive Living Skills Curriculum.
Authors: Lanny E. Morreau and Robert H. Bruininks.
Publisher: Riverside Publishing.
Cross References: See T5:443 (1 reference); for reviews by Patricia A. Bachelor and James P. Van Haneghan, see 12:69.

[471]

ChemTest (Form AR-C).

Purpose: Designed for selecting candidates with basic chemical knowledge.
Population: Applicants and incumbents for jobs requiring knowledge of chemical principles.
Publication Dates: 2001-2008.
Scores, 9: Physical Knowledge, Acids/Bases & Salts, Compounds, Elements, Miscellaneous, Chemical Knowledge, Mechanical Principles, Gases & Fluids, Total.
Administration: Group.
Price Data, 2011: $22 per consumable self-scoring test booklet or online test administration (minimum order of 20); $24.95 per manual (2008, 16 pages).
Time: (60-70) minutes.
Comments: Self-scoring instrument; available for online test administration.
Author: Roland T. Ramsay.
Publisher: Ramsay Corporation.
Cross References: For a review by John Tivendell of an earlier edition, see 17:39.

[472]

Child Abuse/Husband Abuse/Wife Abuse/ Girlfriend Abuse.

Purpose: Designed to compile an individual's history of abuse.
Population: Children, husbands, wives, girlfriends.
Publication Dates: 1991-2010.
Administration: Individual or group.

Forms, 4: Child Abuse, Husband Abuse, Wife Abuse, Girlfriend Abuse.
Manual: Instructions included with the worksheet.
Price Data, 2011: Now available only in the book, "Psychological Worksheets & Assignments," which includes all 68 tests available from publisher; $98 per book version and $48 per CD version.
Time: Administration time not reported.
Author: Allan Roe.
Publisher: Diagnostic Specialists, Inc.

[473]

The Child Abuse Potential Inventory, Form VI.

Purpose: "To assist in the screening of suspected physical child abuse cases."
Population: Male and female parents or primary caregivers who are suspected of physical child abuse.
Publication Dates: 1980–1993.
Acronym: CAP Inventory.
Scores: 12 scale scores: Abuse scale (Distress, Rigidity, Unhappiness, Problems With Child and Self, Problems With Family, Problems With Others, Total Physical Child Abuse), Validity scales (Lie Scale, Random Response Scale, Inconsistency Scale), Loneliness, Ego-Strength, and 3 Response Distortion Indexes (Faking-Good, Faking-Bad, Random Response).
Administration: Individual administration recommended.
Price Data: Available from publisher.
Time: (12–20) minutes.
Author: Joel S. Milner.
Publisher: Psytec Inc.
Cross References: See T5:448 (30 references) and T4:429 (10 references); for reviews by Stuart N. Hart and Gary B. Melton, see 10:50 (5 references).

[474]

Child Care Inventory.

Purpose: Developed to evaluate child care programs in order to improve program effectiveness or to determine the level of program implementation.
Population: Child care programs.
Publication Date: 1986.
Scores: 11 performance areas: Classroom Arrangement, Safety, Curriculum, Interacting, Scheduling, Child Assessment, Health, Special Needs, Parent Involvement, Outdoor Play, Infant Programs.
Administration: Individual.
Price Data, 2002: $22.95 per complete kit including test booklet and manual (32 pages); 11.95 per test booklet; $12.95 per manual.
Time: Administration time not reported.
Authors: Martha S. Abbott-Shim and Annette M. Sibley.

Publisher: Humanics Test Corporation.

Cross References: For reviews by Lisa G. Bischoff and Annette M. Iverson, see 12:71.

[475]

Child Development Inventory.

Purpose: "Designed to provide systematic ways of obtaining in depth developmental information from parents."

Population: Ages 1–3 to 6–3.

Publication Dates: 1968–1992.

Acronym: CDI.

Scores, 9: Social, Self Help, Gross Motor, Fine Motor, Expressive Language, Language Comprehension, Letters, Numbers, General Development.

Administration: Individual.

Price Data, 2005: $72 per complete set including 10 test booklets, 25 answer sheets, 25 CDI profiles, and manual (2005, 44 pages) with scoring template; $18 per 10 test booklets; $12.50 per 25 answer sheets; $12.50 per 25 CDI profiles; $33 per manual with scoring template.

Time: [30–50] minutes.

Comments: Parent-completed questionnaire; formerly called the Minnesota Child Development Inventory.

Author: Harold Ireton.

Publisher: Child Development Review - Behavior Science Systems, Inc.

Cross References: For reviews by Jean Powell Kirnan and Diana Crespo and by Stephanie Stein, see 13:56; see also T4:436 (14 references); for a review of an earlier edition by Jane A. Rysberg, see 9:712; see also T3:1492 (6 references); for a review by William L. Goodwin, see 8:220 (3 references).

[476]

Child Development Review Parent Questionnaire.

Purpose: A brief screening inventory "designed to help identify children with developmental, behavioral, or health problems."

Population: 18 months to age 5.

Publication Date: 1994.

Acronym: CDR.

Scores, 5: Development (Social, Self-Help, Gross Motor, Fine Motor, Language), Possible Problems, Child Description, Parents' Questions/Concerns, Parents' Functioning.

Administration: Individual.

Price Data, 2005: $12.50 per 25 parent questionnaire/child development charts; $33 per manual (22 pages).

Time: [5–10] minutes.

Comments: Parent-completed questionnaire; scores reflect parents' report of child's present functioning-development; Child Development Chart on back, can be used for observation or for parent report.

Author: Harold Ireton.

Publisher: Child Development Review - Behavior Science Systems, Inc.

Cross References: For reviews by Terry Overton and Gary J. Stainback, see 14:71.

[477]

Child Language Ability Measures.

Purpose: "Designed to measure language development."

Population: Ages 2–8.

Publication Date: 1979.

Acronym: CLAM.

Scores: 6 tests: Vocabulary Comprehension, Grammar Comprehension, Inflection Production, Grammar Imitation, Grammar Formedness Judgment, Grammar Equivalence Judgment.

Administration: Individual.

Price Data: Available from publisher.

Time: (15) minutes per test.

Comments: Tests may be administered separately or in any of 11 combinations.

Authors: Christy Moynihan and Albert Mehrabian.

Publisher: Albert Mehrabian.

Cross References: For a review by Allen Jack Edwards, see 10:51.

[478]

Child Sexual Behavior Inventory.

Purpose: Designed as a "measure of sexual behavior in children"; used in the identification of sexual abuse.

Population: Ages 2–12.

Publication Dates: 1986–1997.

Acronym: CSBI.

Scores, 3: Developmentally Related Sexual Behaviors, Sexual Abuse Specific Items, Total.

Administration: Individual.

Price Data, 2006: $155 per introductory kit including manual (1997, 61 pages) and 50 test booklets.

Time: [10–15] minutes.

Comments: Completed by a child's primary caregiver.

Author: William N. Friedrich.

Publisher: Psychological Assessment Resources, Inc.

Cross References: For reviews by Frank M. Bernt and Thomas McKnight, see 14:72; see also T5:457 (1 reference).

[479]

Child Symptom Inventory-4 [2002 Update].

Purpose: Designed as a "screening instrument for the behavioral, affective, and cognitive symptoms" of childhood psychiatric disorders.

Population: Ages 5–12.

Publication Dates: 1994–2002.

Acronym: CSI-4.

Scores, 13: AD/HD Inattentive, AD/HD Hyper-Impulsive, AD/HD Combined, Oppositional Defiant Disorder, Conduct Disorder, Generalized Anxiety Dis-

order, Schizophrenia, Major Depressive Disorder, Dysthymic Disorder, Autistic Disorder, Asperger's Disorder, Social Phobia, Separation Anxiety Disorder.
Administration: Individual.
Forms, 2: Parent Checklist, Teacher Checklist.
Price Data, 2006: $98 per deluxe kit including screening and norms manual (2002, 179 pages), 25 parent checklists, 25 teacher checklists, 50 symptom count score sheets, and 50 symptom severity profile score sheets; $358 per deluxe kit also including scoring CD; $44 per screening and norms manual; $32 per 50 parent checklists; $60 per 100 parent checklists; $32 per 50 Spanish parent checklists; $32 per 50 teacher checklists; $13 per 50 profiles for parent or teacher checklists; $290 per computer scoring software.
Foreign Language Edition: Spanish edition available
Time: [10–15] minutes.
Comments: Instrument is designed to correspond to the DSM-IV classification system.
Authors: Kenneth D. Gadow and Joyce Sprafkin.
Publisher: Checkmate Plus Ltd.
Cross References: For a review by Kathryn E. Hoff and W. Joel Schneider, see 16:46; for reviews by James C. DiPerna and Robert J. Volpe and by Rosemary Flanagan based on an earlier edition of the manual for this test, see 15:47.

[480]

Child Well-Being Scales and Rating Form.

Purpose: Designed for the assessment of children's welfare.
Population: Child welfare practitioners
Publication Date: 1987.
Scores: No scores.
Administration: Group.
Manual: No manual.
Price Data: Price information available from publisher for test booklet at www.cwla.org/pubs.
Time: Administration time not reported.
Comments: Ratings by child welfare practitioners.
Authors: Stephen Magura and Beth Silverman Moses.
Publisher: Child Welfare League of America.
Cross References: See T5:458 (2 references).

[481]

Childhood Autism Rating Scale, Second Edition.

Purpose: "For identifying the presence of behavioral symptoms of autism to support the diagnostic process and also for research and classification purposes."
Publication Dates: 1986-2010.
Administration: Group.
Price Data, 2010: $150 per complete test kit including 25 Standard Version rating booklets, 25 High-Func-

tioning rating booklets, 25 Questionnaires for Parents or Caregivers, and manual (2010, 109 pages); $35 per 25 Standard Version rating booklets; $35 per 25 High-Functioning rating booklets; $25 per 25 Questionnaires for Parents or Caregivers; $70 per manual.
Time: (5-10) minutes.
Comments: Questionnaires for Parents or Caregivers are included to aid in diagnostic decision-making and supplement data-gathering but are not scored.
Authors: Eric Schopler, Mary. E. Van Bourgondien, G. Janette Wellman, and Steven R. Love.
Publisher: Western Psychological Services.
a) CHILDHOOD AUTISM RATING SCALE, SECOND EDITION-STANDARD VERSION.
Acronym: CARS2-ST.
Population: Ages 2 to 6 (or estimated IQ below 79).
Scores, 16: Relating to People, Imitation, Emotional Response, Body Use, Object Use, Adaptation to Change, Visual Response, Listening Response, Taste, Smell, and Touch Response and Use, Fear or Nervousness, Verbal Communication, Nonverbal Communication, Activity Level, Level and Consistency of Intellectual Response, General Impressions, Total.
b) CHILDHOOD AUTISM RATING SCALE, SECOND EDITION-HIGH-FUNCTIONING VERSION.
Acronym: CARS2-HF.
Population: Ages 6 and over (or estimated IQ above 80).
Scores, 16: Social-Emotional Understanding, Emotional Expression and Regulation of Emotions, Relating to People, Body Use, Object Use in Play, Adaptation to Change/Restricted Interests, Visual Response, Listening Response, Taste, Smell, and Touch Response and Use, Fear or Anxiety, Verbal Communication, Nonverbal Communication, Thinking/Cognitive Integration Skills, Level and Consistency of Intellectual Response, General Impressions, Total.
Cross References: See T5:459 (40 references) and T4:439 (6 references); for reviews by Barry M. Prizant and J. Steven Welsh, see 11:65 (4 references).

[482]

Childhood Trauma Questionnaire.

Purpose: Designed as a self-report inventory for "screening for histories of abuse and neglect."
Population: Ages 12 and up.
Publication Dates: 1997–1998.
Acronym: CTQ.
Scores, 5: Emotional Abuse, Physical Abuse, Sexual Abuse, Emotional and Physical Neglect and Minimization/Denial of Abuse.
Administration: Individual.
Price Data, 2002: $99 per complete kit including 25 READYSCORE answer documents and manual

(1998, 76 pages); $40 per 25 READYSCORE answer documents; $73 per manual.

Time: (5) minutes.

Comments: A 28-item, self-report inventory.

Authors: David P. Bernstein and Laura Fink.

Publisher: Pearson.

Cross References: For reviews by Michael Furlong and Renee Pavelski and by Jonathan Sandoval, see 14:73; see also T5:460 (2 references).

[483]

Children of Alcoholics Screening Test.

Purpose: Measures children's and adults' attitudes, feelings, perceptions, and experiences related to their parents' drinking behavior; also identifies probable children of alcoholics (CoAs) and adult children of alcoholics (ACoAs).

Population: School-age children through adults.

Publication Dates: 1981–1993.

Acronym: CAST.

Scores: Total score only.

Administration: Group or individual.

Price Data: Available from publisher.

Time: (5–10) minutes.

Comments: Reduced rate is available for additional forms used in research or mass testing.

Author: John W. Jones.

Publisher: Camelot Unlimited.

Cross References: See T5:462 (33 references) and T4:440 (8 references); for reviews by Stuart N. Hart and Steven P. Schinke, see 10:52; for reviews by Susanna Maxwell and Barrie G. Stacey, see 9:217.

[484]

Children's Academic Intrinsic Motivation Inventory.

Purpose: "To measure academic intrinsic motivation … defined as enjoyment of school learning characterized by an orientation toward mastery, curiosity, persistence, and the learning of challenging, difficult, and novel tasks."

Population: Grades 4–8.

Publication Date: 1986.

Acronym: CAIMI.

Scores: 5 scales: Reading, Math, Social Studies, Science, General.

Administration: Individual or group.

Price Data, 2006: $162 per introductory kit including 50 test booklets, 50 profile forms, and manual (24 pages).

Time: (20–30) minutes for individual administration; (60) minutes for group administration.

Comments: Self-report inventory.

Author: Adele Gottfried.

Publisher: Psychological Assessment Resources, Inc.

Cross References: See T5:464 (5 references); for a review by C. Dale Posey, see 10:54.

[485]

Childrens Adaptive Behavior Scale, Revised.

Purpose: Provides a means to gather information on the relevant knowledge and concepts requisite to adaptive functioning.

Population: Ages 5–11.

Publication Dates: 1980–2002.

Acronym: CABS.

Scores, 6: Language Development, Independent Functioning, Family Role Performance, Economic-Vocational Activity, Socialization, Total.

Administration: Individual.

Price Data, 2002: $1 per student booklet; $14.95 per manual (1983, 42 pages); $35.95 per specimen set including 5 student booklets, picture book, and manual.

Time: (45–50) minutes.

Comments: Other test materials (e.g., coins, blocks, scissors, paper) must be supplied by examiner.

Authors: Richard H. Kicklighter and Bert O. Richmond.

Publisher: Humanics Test Corporation.

Cross References: See T4:442 (1 reference); for reviews by Kenneth A. Kavale and Esther Sinclair, see 10:55 (1 reference); for reviews by Thomas R. Kratochwill and Corinne R. Smith of the original edition, see 9:218; see also T3:395 (1 reference).

[486]

Children's Aggression Scale.

Purpose: Designed to "evaluate the nature, severity, and frequency of aggressive behaviors in children, distinct from those behaviors better characterized as oppositional/defiant or hostile."

Population: Ages 5-18.

Publication Dates: 2002-2008.

Acronym: CAS.

Scores, 11: Scale scores (Verbal Aggression, Aggression Against Objects and Animals, Physical Aggression, Use of Weapons, Total Aggression Index), Cluster scores (Provoked Physical Aggression, Initiated Physical Aggression, Aggression Toward Peers, Aggression Toward Adults, Aggression Against Family Members [Parent form only], Aggression Against Non-Family Members [Parent form only]).

Administration: Group.

Forms, 2: Parent (CAS-P), Teacher (CAS-T).

Price Data, 2010: $240 per introductory kit including professional manual (2008, 473 pages), 25 Parent rating forms, 25 Teacher rating forms, 25 Parent score summary forms/profiles, and 25 Teacher score summary forms/profiles; $52 per 25 Parent rating forms; $52 per 25 Teacher rating forms; $37 per 25 Parent score summary forms/profiles; $37 per 25 Teacher score summary forms/profiles; $77 per professional manual.

Time: (10-15) minutes.

Comments: Ratings by parents and teachers (multiple forms may be completed by multiple parents and teachers);

Children's Aggression Scale Scoring Program (CAS-SP) offered separately.
Authors: Jeffrey M. Halperin and Kathleen E. McKay.
Publisher: Psychological Assessment Resources, Inc.
Cross References: For reviews by Jeffrey A. Atlas and David F. Ciampi, see 18:25.

[487]

Children's Apperception Test [1991 Revision].

Purpose: A projective "method of investigating personality by studying the dynamic meaningfulness of the individual differences in perception of standard stimuli."
Population: Ages 3–10.
Publication Dates: 1949–1992.
Acronym: C.A.T.
Scores: No scores.
Administration: Individual.
Editions, 3: Animal, Human, Supplement, plus Short Form.
Price Data, 2010: $150 per C.A.T.–A, C.A.T.–S, C.A.T.–H, manual (1991, 24 pages), 25 recording and analysis blanks (short form), and 10 copies of Haworth's Schedule of Adaptive Mechanisms in C.A.T. Responses; $35 per C.A.T.–A , C.A.T.–H, or C.A.T.–S; $14.50 per 25 recording and analysis blanks (short form); $12.50 per 30 Haworth's Schedules; $9 per 10 psychodiagnostic test reports.
Time: (15–20) minutes.
Authors: Leopold Bellak and Sonya Sorel Bellak.
Publisher: C.P.S., Inc.
Cross References: See T5:466 (1 reference); for reviews by Howard M. Knoff and Robert C. Reinehr, see 13:58 (4 references); see also T4:444 (4 references); for reviews by Clifford V. Hatt and Marcia B. Shaffer of an earlier edition, see 9:219 (1 reference); see also T3:396 (1 reference), T2:1451 (23 references), and P:419 (18 references); for reviews by Bernard L. Murstein and Robert D. Wirt, see 6:206 (19 references); for reviews by Douglas T. Keeny and Albert I. Rabin, see 5:126 (15 references); for reviews by John E. Bell and L. Joseph Stone and excerpted reviews by M. M. Genn, Herbert Herman, Robert R. Holt, Laurance F. Shaffer, and Adolf G. Woltmann, see 4:103 (2 references).

[488]

Children's Articulation Test.

Purpose: Designed to "assess child's ability to produce consonants, vowels and diphthongs in an in-depth relationship to other consonants and vowels."
Population: Ages 3–11.
Publication Date: 1989.
Acronym: CAT.
Scores, 7: Medial Vowels/Diphthongs, Final Consonants, Initiating Consonants, Abutting Consonants, Abutting Consonants and Vowels/Diphthongs, Connected Speech, Language Concepts.

Administration: Individual.
Price Data: Available from publisher.
Time: [15] minutes.
Author: George S. Haspiel.
Publisher: Dragon Press [No reply from publisher; status unknown].
Cross References: For reviews by Kathryn W. Kenney and Lawrence J. Turton, see 12:74.

[489]

Children's Attention and Adjustment Survey.

Purpose: "Designed to measure the diagnostic criteria of inattention, impulsivity, hyperactivity, and aggressiveness or conduct problems."
Population: Ages 5–13.
Publication Date: 1990.
Acronym: CAAS.
Scores, 7: Inattention, Impulsivity, ADD, Hyperactivity, ADHD, Conduct Problems, DSM III-R ADHD.
Administration: Individual.
Editions, 2: School, Home.
Price Data, 2006: $49.99 per 25 self-scorable booklets (select School or Home form); $19.99 per 25 scoring profiles; $45.99 per manual (75 pages); $154.99 per starter set including manual and 25 each of Home Form, School Form, and Scoring Profile.
Time: (5–10) minutes per form.
Comments: Ratings by teacher or parent.
Authors: Nadine Lambert, Carolyn Hartsough, and Jonathan Sandoval.
Publisher: Pearson.
Cross References: See T5:469 (3 references); for reviews by Claire B. Ernhart and Stephen L. Koffler, see 12:75 (1 reference).

[490]

Children's Auditory Verbal Learning Test-2.

Purpose: Constructed to "measure auditory verbal learning and memory abilities" in children.
Population: Ages 6-6 to 17-11.
Publication Dates: 1988–1993.
Acronym: CAVLT-2.
Scores, 6: Immediate Memory Span, Level of Learning, Immediate Recall, Delayed Recall, Recognition Accuracy, Total Intrusions.
Administration: Individual.
Price Data, 2005: $106 per introductory kit including 25 test booklets and professional manual (1993, 68 pages).
Time: (25–30) minutes.
Comments: Orally administered.
Author: Jack L. Talley.
Publisher: Psychological Assessment Resources, Inc.
Cross References: For reviews by John O. Anderson and Sherwyn Morreale, see 12:76.

[491]

Children's Category Test.

Purpose: "Designed to assess non-verbal concept formation, ability to benefit from verbal feedback to alter problem solving behavior and abstract reasoning."
Population: Ages 5-0 to 16-11.
Publication Date: 1993.
Acronym: CCT.
Scores, 6: Subtest I, Subtest II, Subtest III, Subtest IV, Subtest V, Total.
Administration: Individual.
Levels, 2: Level 1 (Ages 5 to 8), Level 2 (Ages 9 to 16).
Price Data, 2006: $399 per complete kit including manual (72 pages), 25 Level 1 record forms, 25 Level 2 record forms, stimulus booklets, and color response cards (1 for each level); $37 per 25 record forms.
Time: (15–20) minutes.
Author: Thomas Boll.
Publisher: Pearson.
Cross References: For reviews by Mark D. Shriver and Nicholas A. Vacc, see 13:59.

[492]

Children's Color Trails Test.

Purpose: "Designed to provide an easily administered and objectively scored measure of alternating and sustained visual attention, sequencing, psychomotor speed, cognitive flexibility, and inhibition-disinhibition."
Population: Ages 8–16.
Publication Dates: 1989–2003.
Acronym: CCTT.
Scores, 6: Time Scores, Prompt Scores, Near-Miss Scores, Error Scores (Number Sequence Errors, Color Sequence Errors), Interference Index.
Subtest: 2: CCTT-1, CCTT-2.
Administration: Individual.
Forms, 4: K, X, Y, Z.
Price Data, 2006: $145 per Introductory kit including professional manual (2003, 81 pages), 50 record forms, and 50 copies of Form K, Parts 1 & 2.
Time: (5–7) minutes.
Comments: Also called Kid's Color Trails, Kiddie Color Trails, K Color Trails; modeled after Color Trails Test.
Authors: Antolin M. Llorente, Jane Williams, Paul Satz, and Louis F. D'Elia.
Publisher: Psychological Assessment Resources, Inc.
Cross References: For reviews by Andrew S. Davis and W. Holmes Finch and by Shawn Powell and Michelle A. Butler, see 16:47.

[493]

Children's Communication Checklist-2: United States Edition.

Purpose: "Designed to assess children's communication skills in the areas of pragmatics, syntax, morphology, semantics, and speech."
Population: Ages 4-16.
Publication Date: 2006.
Acronym: CCC-2.
Scores, 12: 10 communication domains: Speech, Syntax, Semantics, Coherence, Initiation, Scripted Language, Context, Nonverbal Communication, Social Relations, Interests; plus General Communication Composite, Social Interaction Difference Index.
Administration: Individual.
Price Data, 2008: $165 per complete kit including manual (2006, 112 pages), 25 caregiver response forms, 25 scoring worksheets, and scoring CD; $89 per manual; $39 per 25 caregiver response forms; $22 per 25 scoring worksheets.
Time: (5-10) minutes.
Comments: Scaled scores, general communication composite, social interaction difference index, confidence intervals, and percentile ranks are provided for each scale score.
Author: D. V. M. Bishop.
Publisher: Pearson.
Cross References: For reviews by Rebecca McCauley and Roger L. Towne, see 18:26.

[494]

Children's Depression Inventory 2nd Edition.

Purpose: Designed to provide "comprehensive multi-rater assessment of depressive symptoms in children."
Population: Ages 7-17.
Publication Dates: 1977-2011.
Acronym: CDI 2.
Scores, 14: Self-Report Full-Length-7: Total Score, Emotional Problems Scale Score, Functional Problems Scale Score, Negative Mood/Physical Symptoms Subscale Score, Negative Self-Esteem Subscale Score, Ineffectiveness Subscale Score, Interpersonal Problems Subscale Score; Self-Report Short-1: Total Score; Parent Report-3: Total Score, Emotional Problems Scale Score, Functional Problems Scale Score; Teacher Report-3: Total Score, Emotional Problems Scale Score, Functional Problems Scale Score.
Administration: Group.
Forms, 4: Self-Report Full-Length, Self-Report Short, Parent Report, Teacher Report.
Price Data, 2011: $365 per complete software kit including technical manual (2011, 172 pages), Software Scoring Installation, 25 self-report response forms, 25 self-report short response forms, 25 parent response forms, and 25 teacher response forms; $80 per technical manual; $250 per handscored kit including 2 manuals, 25 self-report QuikScore forms, 25 self-report short QuikScore forms, 25 parent QuikScore forms, and 25 teacher QuikScore forms.
Foreign Language Edition: Available in Spanish online.
Time: (15) minutes for Self-Report Full-Length; (5) minutes for Self-Report Short; (10) minutes for Parent Report; (5) minutes for Teacher Report.

Comments: This is a multi-rater assessment; available in paper-and-pencil and online administration and scoring.
Authors: Maria Kovacs and MHS Staff.
Publisher: Multi-Health Systems, Inc.
Cross References: For reviews by Janet F. Carlson and Stephen J. Freeman of the 2003 Update, see 17:41; see also T5:472 (235 references) and T4:450 (71 references); for reviews by Michael G. Kavan and Howard M. Knoff of an earlier edition, see 11:66 (63 references).

[495]

Children's Depression Rating Scale, Revised.
Purpose: Constructed as a "screening instrument, diagnostic tool, and severity measure of depression in children."
Population: Ages 6–12
Publication Date: 1996.
Acronym: CDRS-R.
Scores: Total score only.
Administration: Group.
Price Data, 2011: $99 per complete kit including manual (91 pages) and 25 administration booklets; $44 per 25 administration booklets; $60 per manual.
Time: (15–20) minutes.
Comments: Ratings by health care professionals.
Authors: Elva O. Poznanski and Hartmut B. Mokros.
Publisher: Western Psychological Services.
Cross References: For reviews by E. Thomas Dowd and Donald Lee Stovall, see 14:74; see also T5:473 (8 references).

[496]

Children's Interview for Psychiatric Syndromes.
Purpose: Designed to identify "symptoms of 20 common Axis I psychiatric disorders in children and adolescents."
Population: Ages 6–18.
Publication Date: 1999.
Acronym: ChIPS.
Scores, 20: Attention-Deficit/Hyperactivity Disorder, Oppositional Defiant Disorder, Conduct Disorder, Substance Abuse, Specific Phobia, Social Phobia, Separation Anxiety Disorder, Generalized Anxiety Disorder, Obsessive-Compulsive Disorder, Acute Stress Disorder, Posttraumatic Stress Disorder, Anorexia, Bulimia, Depressive Episode, Dysthymic Disorder, Manic Episode, Hypomanic Episode, Enuresis, Encopresis, Schizophrenia/Psychosis.
Administration: Individual.
Price Data, 2006: $34.95 per administration manual (60 pages); $59 per reusable interview administration booklet (30 pages); $33.95 per 20 scoring forms; $28.50 per 20 report forms; $236 per starter kit.
Time: Administration time not reported.

Authors: Elizabeth B. Weller, Ronald A. Weller, Mary A. Fristad, and Marijo Teare Rooney.
Publisher: American Psychiatric Publishing, Inc.
Cross References: For reviews by Janet F. Carlson and R. Joel Farrell II, see 15:48.

[497]

Children's Inventory of Anger.
Purpose: Designed "to measure aspects of a youngster's experience of anger."
Population: Ages 6–16.
Publication Date: 2000.
Acronym: CIA.
Scores, 5: Frustration, Physical Aggression, Peer Relationship, Authority Relations, Total.
Administration: Group or individual.
Price Data, 2006: $93.50 per complete kit including 25 autoscore answer forms, and manual; $42.50 per 25 autoscore answer forms; $54.50 per manual; $105 per disk that offers scoring for 25 uses; $16.50 per PC answer sheet pads of 100.
Time: 10 minutes.
Comments: Self-report inventory.
Authors: W. Michael Nelson III and A. J. Finch, Jr.
Publisher: Western Psychological Services.
Cross References: For reviews by Theresa Volpe-Johnstone and Delores D. Walcott, see 15:49.

[498]

Children's Inventory of Self-Esteem, Second Edition.
Purpose: "Provides … a quick way to assess the relative strength of a child's self-worth."
Population: Ages 5–12.
Publication Dates: 1987–2001.
Acronym: CISE.
Scores, 7: 4 components of self-esteem: Belonging (B), Purpose (P), Control (C), Self (S); Total (T); 2 favored coping styles: Defensive (TD), Aggressive (TA).
Administration: Individual.
Price Data, 2006: $99 per an individual lifetime license for individuals, including examiner's manual (2001, 24 pages), CISE for girls, CISE for boys, answer form, Exploring Your Child's Self-Esteem form, Your Child's Sense of Self form, Your Child's Sense of Purpose form, Your Child's Sense of Control form, Your Child's Sense of Belonging form (all forms personalized with unlimited copying privileges); $125 per school or agency lifetime license; $110 per lifetime license for each school when purchased by school district (minimum 2 schools); $4.95 shipping/handling fee.
Time: (10) minutes.
Comments: 64-item behavior rating scale completed by parents and teachers of child; provides strategies for helping improve self-esteem.

Author: Richard A. Campbell.
Publisher: Brougham Press.
Cross References: For reviews by R. Joel Farrell II and Jacqueline Johnson, see 15:50; for reviews by Kathy E. Green and Nicholas A. Vacc of a previous edition, see 12:78.

[499]

Children's Measure of Obsessive-Compulsive Symptoms.

Purpose: Designed to provide an "objective assessment and quantification of the subjective experience of children and adolescents with both overt and covert behavior problems related to obsessions or compulsions at either a subclinical or clinical level."
Population: Ages 8-19.
Publication Date: 2010.
Acronym: CMOCS.
Scores, 10: Defensiveness, Inconsistent Responding, Fear of Contamination, Rituals, Intrusive Thoughts, Checking, Fear of Mistakes and Harm, Picking/Slowing, Impact, Total.
Administration: Group.
Price Data, 2010: $99 per complete kit including 25 AutoScore forms and manual (62 pages); $45 per 25 AutoScore forms; $65 per manual.
Time: (10-15) minutes.
Authors: Cecil R. Reynolds and Ronald B. Livingston.
Publisher: Western Psychological Services.

[500]

Children's Memory Scale.

Purpose: "Comprehensive assessment of visual/verbal learning and memory skills" in children and adolescents.
Population: Ages 5–16.
Publication Dates: 1997–1998.
Acronym: CMS.
Scores, 34: 14 Core Battery Subtest Scores: Dot Locations (Learning, Total Score, Long Delay); Stories (Immediate, Delayed, Delayed Recognition); Faces (Immediate, Delayed); Word Pairs (Learning, Total Score, Long Delay, Delayed Recognition); Numbers (Total Score); Sequences (Total Score); 6 supplemental scores: Dot Locations (Short Delay), Stories (Immediate Thematic, Delayed Thematic), Word Pairs (Immediate), Numbers (Forward, Backward); 6 Supplemental scores from 3 Supplemental Subtests: Word Lists (Learning, Delayed, Delayed Recognition), Picture Locations (Total Score), Family Pictures (Immediate, Delayed); 8 Indexes: Visual Immediate, Visual Delayed, Verbal Immediate, Verbal Delayed, General Memory, Attention/Concentration, Learning, Delayed Recognition.
Administration: Individual.
Levels, 2: 5–8, 9–16.

Price Data, 2006: $499 per complete kit including manual (1997, 288 pages), 25 record forms for both age levels, 2 stimulus booklets, 5 family picture cards, and response grid in a box along with 8 chips in a pouch; $549 per complete kit available in soft-sided carrying case; $62 per record forms (specify level); $210 per computer Scoring Assistant (available for Windows or Macintosh).
Time: (20–50) minutes.
Author: Morris J. Cohen.
Publisher: Pearson.
Cross References: For reviews by Scott A. Napolitano and Margot B. Stein, see 14:75.

[501]

Children's Organizational Skills Scales.

Purpose: Measures "how children organize their time, materials, and actions to accomplish important tasks at home and school."
Population: Ages 8-13.
Publication Date: 2009.
Acronym: COSS.
Scores, 15: 5 scores per form: Task Planning, Organized Actions, Memory and Materials Management, Total, Inconsistency Index (COSS-Parent & COSS-Teacher only), Positive Impression (COSS-Child only).
Administration: Individual or group.
Forms, 3: COSS-Parent, COSS-Teacher, and COSS-Child.
Price Data, 2011: $220 per complete handscored kit including 25 Parent/Teacher/Child QuikScore forms and technical manual (2009, 153 pages); $276 per complete scoring software kit including 25 Parent/Teacher/Child response forms, technical manual, and unlimited use scoring software; $98 per online kit including 10 Parent, 10 Teacher, and 10 Child online forms, and technical manual; $50 per 25 COSS-Parent QuikScore forms; $50 per 25 COSS-Teacher forms; $50 per 25 COSS-Child forms; $50 per 25 COSS-Parent response forms; $50 per 25 COSS-Teacher response forms; $50 per 25 COSS-Child response forms; $1.80 per COSS-Parent online form; $1.80 per COSS-Teacher online form; $1.80 per COSS-Child online form; $61 per technical manual; $110 per COSS unlimited scoring software.
Time: (20) minutes.
Comments: Global assessment of overall organizational difficulty (COSS-Teacher only) and Impairment Questions (COSS-Teacher & COSS-Parent only) are interpreted qualitatively; ratings by teachers, parents, and child (self-rating); available online and in paper-and-pencil format; forms can be scored by hand, using the COSS scoring software, or using the COSS online program. Online subscription option is available.
Authors: Howard Abikoff and Richard Gallagher.
Publisher: Multi-Health Systems, Inc.
Cross References: For reviews by Michael S. Matthews and Rayne A. Sperling, see 18:27.

[502]

Children's Personality Questionnaire.

Purpose: Designed to measure personality traits to predict and evaluate the course of personal, social, and academic development.
Population: Ages 8–12.
Publication Dates: 1959–1992.
Acronym: CPQ.
Scores, 18: 14 Primary Factors: Warmth, Abstract Thinking, Emotional Stability, Excitability, Dominance, Enthusiasm, Conformity, Boldness, Sensitivity, Withdrawal, Shrewdness, Apprehension, Self-Discipline, Tension; 4 Second Order Factors: Extraversion, Anxiety, Tough Poise, Independence.
Administration: Group or individual.
Forms, 4: A, B, C, D.
Price Data: Available from publisher.
Foreign Language Editions: Information regarding several non-English-language adaptations available from publisher.
Time: (30–60) minutes per form.
Comments: Test booklet is entitled "What You Do and What You Think."
Authors: Rutherford B. Porter and Raymond B. Cattell.
Publisher: Institute for Personality and Ability Testing, Inc. (IPAT)
Cross References: For reviews by Rosa A. Hagin and Terry A. Stinnett, see 13:60 (3 references); see also T4:454 (9 references); for reviews by Steven Klee and Howard M. Knoff of an earlier edition, see 9:222 (11 references); for a review by Harrison G. Gough, see 8:520 (46 references); see also T3:1129 (60 references) and P:38 (14 references); for reviews by Anne Anastasi, by Wilbur L. Layton, and by Robert D. Wirt of the 1963 edition, see 6:122 (2 references).

[503]

Children's Problems Checklist.

Purpose: "To identify relevant problems, establish rapport, and provide written documentation of presenting problems consistent with community standards of care."
Population: Ages 5-12.
Publication Date: 1985.
Acronym: CPC.
Scores: 11 areas: Emotions, Self-Concept, Peers and Play, School, Language and Thinking, Concentration and Organization, Activity Level and Motor Control, Behavior, Values, Habits, Health.
Administration: Individual or group.
Manual: No manual.
Price Data, 2005: $49 per package of 50.
Time: (10-20) minutes.
Comments: Ratings by parent or guardian.
Author: John A. Schinka.
Publisher: Psychological Assessment Resources, Inc.

Cross References: For a review by Wayne C. Piersel, see 10:56.

[504]

Children's PTSD Inventory: A Structured Interview for Diagnosing Posttraumatic Stress Disorder.

Purpose: "Designed for the identification and assessment of posttraumatic stress disorder in children and adolescents."
Population: Ages 6–18.
Publication Date: 2004.
Scores, 7: Exposure, Situational Reactivity, Reexperiencing, Avoidance and Numbing, Increased Arousal, Significant Distress, Total.
Administration: Individual.
Price Data, 2007: $141 per complete kit including manual (52 pages) and 25 inventory forms; $52 per 25 inventory forms; $66 per manual.
Time: (5–20) minutes.
Comments: Inventory forms also available in Spanish and Canadian French; five overall diagnostic categories (PTSD Negative, Acute PTSD, Chronic PTSD, Delayed Onset PTSD, or No Diagnosis) provided.
Author: Philip A. Saigh.
Publisher: Pearson.
Cross References: For reviews by Robert Christopher and by Beth Doll and Allison Osborn, see 17:42.

[505]

Children's Speech Intelligibility Measure.

Purpose: "Designed to provide clinicians with an objective measure of single-word intelligibility of children ages 3.0 to 10.11 whose speech is considered unintelligible."
Population: Ages 3.0–10.11.
Publication Date: 1999.
Acronym: CSIM.
Scores: Total score only.
Administration: Individual.
Price Data, 2004: $94 per complete kit including manual (140 pages), 15 record forms, and microphone switch; $15 per 15 record forms; $50 per manual.
Time: (10-20) minutes.
Authors: Kim Wilcox and Sherrill Morris.
Publisher: Pearson.
Cross References: For a review by Connie T. England and Gabrielle Stutman, see 17:43.

[506]

The Children's Test of Nonword Repetition.

Purpose: To assess short term memory in children.
Population: Ages 4–8.
Publication Date: 1996.

Acronym: CN REP.
Scores: Total score only.
Administration: Individual.
Price Data, 2006: £74 per complete set including record forms, cassette tape, and manual (29 pages).
Time: [15] minutes.
Authors: Susan Gathercole and Alan Baddeley.
Publisher: Pearson Assessment [England].
Cross References: For reviews by Patrick Grehan and Manuel Martinez-Pons, see 16:48.

[507]

Children's Version of the Family Environment Scale.

Purpose: "Provides a measure of young children's subjective appraisal of their family environment."
Population: Ages 5–12.
Publication Date: 1984.
Acronym: CV/FES.
Scores, 10: Cohesion, Expressiveness, Conflict, Independence, Achievement Orientation, Intellectual-Cultural Orientation, Active-Recreational Orientation, Moral-Religious Emphasis, Organization, Control.
Administration: Group.
Price Data, 2002: $64 per complete kit; $14 per manual (15 pages); $34 per 10 (reusable) test answer booklets; $19 per 50 profiles; $19 per 50 examiner's worksheets; $19 per 50 individual student answer sheets.
Time: Administration time not reported.
Comments: Downward extension of the Family Environment Scale (9:408).
Authors: Christopher J. Pino, Nancy Simons, and Mary Jane Slawinowski.
Publisher: Slosson Educational Publications, Inc.
Cross References: For a review by Nancy A. Busch-Rossnagel, see 10:57.

[508]

Chinese Proficiency Test.

Purpose: "Designed to evaluate the proficiency in Chinese listening and reading comprehension attained by Americans and other English-speaking learners of Chinese."
Population: Postsecondary to adults.
Publication Dates: 1986–1992.
Scores, 4: Listening Comprehension, Structure, Reading Comprehension, Total.
Administration: Group.
Price Data, 2002: $25 per test (quantity discounts available); $6 per official score report.
Time: 120(180) minutes.
Comments: Mail-in scoring.
Author: Center for Applied Linguistics.
Publisher: Center for Applied Linguistics.

a) PRELIMINARY CHINESE PROFICIENCY TEST.
Publication Date: 1991.
Acronym: Pre-CPT.
Comments: "Designed to be most appropriate for students who are completing at least one year of language study at the college level or three or four years of instruction at the high school level."
b) CHINESE PROFICIENCY TEST.
Publication Dates: 1986–1992.
Acronym: CPT.
Comments: Available in Cantonese and Mandarin; "designed to be most appropriate for students who have completed two or more years of study at the college level."
Cross References: For reviews by Chi-wen Kao and Antony John Kunnan, see 13:62.

[509]

Choosing A College Major.

Purpose: Designed to "assist students to assess their occupational interests, educational and training goals, and occupational work values to develop an individualized profile that can be matched with occupations related to majors within a field of study."
Population: Students considering college.
Publication Dates: 2004-2005.
Scores, 14: Agriculture, Architecture, The Arts, Biological & Life Sciences, Business & Finance, Communications, Computer Sciences, Education, Engineering, Consumer Sciences, Health Sciences, Humanities, Physical Sciences, Social Sciences.
Administration: Group.
Price Data, 2008: $4.75 per 9 Choosing A College Major test booklets and manuals (2004, 17 pages); $.70 per 7 answer folders.
Time: Administration time not reported.
Comments: Self-assessment.
Author: Francis R. Ferry.
Publisher: CKFR Career Materials, Inc.

[510]

Choosing Outcomes and Accommodations for Children (COACH): A Guide to Educational Planning for Students with Disabilities, Second Edition.

Purpose: To identify meaningful and measurable educational goals for IEPs.
Population: Preschool and school-aged learners with moderate, severe, or profound disabilities
Publication Date: 1998.
Acronym: COACH.
Scores: Item scores only.
Administration: Individual.
Price Data, 2011: $25.00 per 3 student record forms; $42.95 per manual (1998, 400 pages).

Time: (60) minutes (part 1 of 3 parts).
Comments: "Criterion-referenced"; ratings by a team including a parent, student (where appropriate), educators, related service personnel, and family advocate; previous versions available on microfiche from ERIC; previously listed as C.O.A.C.H.: Cayuga-Onondaga Assessment for Children with Handicaps.
Authors: Michael F. Giangreco, Chigee J. Cloninger, and Virginia S. Iverson.
Publisher: Paul H. Brookes Publishing Co., Inc.
Cross References: See T5:553 (1 reference); for a review by Jay Kuder and David E. Kapel, see 11:73.

[511]

Chronic Pain Battery.
Purpose: Constructed to assess chronic pain by collecting "medical, psychological, behavioral, social, demographic and pain data."
Population: Patients ages 18 and over
Publication Dates: 1983–1986.
Acronym: CPB.
Scores, 10: Demographic and Social History, Past and Present Pain History, Past Treatment, Medications, Medical History, Personality-Pain Coping Style, Patient Expectations and Goals, Behavioral-Learning Factors, Psychosocial Factors, Patient Problem Ratings.
Administration: Group or individual.
Manual: No manual.
Price Data, 2011: $31 per online scoring. Volume discounts.
Time: (30–60) minutes.
Comments: Comprises the Pain Assessment Questionnaire–Revised and the Symptom Checklist 90–Revised (2655); self-administered by paper-and-pencil with scoring and report generation online on a secure testing website.
Author: Stephen R. Levitt.
Publisher: Pain Resource Center, Inc.

[512]

Chronic Pain Coping Inventory.
Purpose: Designed to "assess the use of coping strategies that are typically targeted for change in multidisciplinary pain treatment programs."
Population: Ages 20-80.
Publication Dates: 1995-2008.
Acronym: CPCI.
Scores, 9: Guarding, Resting, Asking for Assistance, Exercise/Stretch, Relaxation, Task Persistence, Coping Self-Statements, Pacing, Seeking Social Support.
Administration: Individual or group.
Price Data, 2009: $185 per manual (2008, 60 pages), 25 rating forms, 25 score summary/profile sheets, and 25 pain worksheets; price data for computer scoring software available from publisher.

Time: (15) minutes.
Authors: Mark P. Jensen, Judith A. Turner, Joan M. Romano, and Warren R. Nielson.
Publisher: Psychological Assessment Resources, Inc.
Cross References: For reviews by Tony Cellucci and James P. Donnelly, see 18:28.

[513]

Chronicle Career Quest.
Purpose: Designed to "help individuals identify careers related to personal interests and preferences and move independently from assessment through awareness to career exploration."
Population: Grades 7–10, Grades 9–16 and adult.
Publication Dates: 1989–2005.
Acronym: CCQ.
Scores: 12 G.O.E. clusters: Artistic, Scientific, Plants and Animals, Protective, Mechanical, Industrial, Business Detail, Selling, Accommodating, Humanitarian, Leading Influencing, Physical Performing.
Administration: Group or individual.
Forms, 2: S and L.
Price Data, 2010: $15 per specimen set including 1 each Form S and L (each Form includes Interest Inventory, Interest Profile & Career Paths; 2001, 16 pages each), 1 Reuseable Occupations Booklet (2009, 24 pages), Administrator's Guide (2001, 10 pages), and 1 Technical Manual (2001, 10 pages); $30.75 per 25 Form S Booklets; $31 per 25 Form L Booklets; $32 per 25 Reuseable Occupations Booklets; $7.50 per Administrator's Guide; $18 per Technical Manual; quantity and package pricing available.
Time: (10–15) minutes for Interest Inventory (Form S and Form L); (10–15) minutes for Interpretation Guide (Form S and Form L); (20–45) minutes for Career Paths (Form S); (180–240) minutes for Career Paths (Form L).
Author: Chronicle Guidance Publications, Inc.
Publisher: Chronicle Guidance Publications, Inc.
Cross References: For reviews by Larry G. Daniel and Donald Thompson, see 12:79.

[514]

CID Phonetic Inventory.
Purpose: To evaluate the hearing-impaired "child's speech ability at the phonetic level."
Population: Hearing-impaired children.
Publication Date: 1988.
Scores, 7: Suprasegmental Aspects, Vowels and Diphthongs, Initial Consonants, Consonants with Alternating Vowels, Final Consonants, Alternating Consonants, Average.
Administration: Individual.
Price Data, 2011: $15 per package of 25 CID Picture SPINE rating forms.
Time: (30-35) minutes.

Author: Jean S. Moog.
Publisher: Central Institute for the Deaf (CID).
Cross References: See T5:486 (3 references); for a review by Vincent J. Samar, see 11:67.

[515]

CID Picture SPINE (SPeech INtelligibility Evaluation).

Purpose: To "provide a measure of speech intelligibility for severely and profoundly hearing-impaired children and adolescents."
Population: Hearing-impaired children ages 6–13.
Publication Date: 1988.
Scores: Total score only.
Administration: Individual.
Price Data, 2011: $15 for 25 response forms (4 pages).
Time: (20-30) minutes.
Authors: Randall Monsen, Jean S. Moog, and Ann E. Geers.
Publisher: Central Institute for the Deaf (CID).
Cross References: See T5:487 (2 references) and T4:465 (1 reference); for a review by Vincent J. Samar, see 11:68.

[516]

CID Preschool Performance Scale.

Purpose: Designed to measure the intelligence of hearing-impaired and language-impaired children.
Population: Hearing- and language-impaired and normal children ages 2 to 6.
Publication Date: 1984.
Scores: 7: Manual Planning, Manual Dexterity, Form Perception, Perceptual-Motor Skills, Preschool Skills, Part/Whole Relations, Total.
Administration: Individual.
Price Data, 2005: $850 per complete kit including manipulatives for subtests, manual (29 pages), and 30 recording booklets; $30 per manual; $35 per 30 recording booklets.
Time: (40) minutes.
Comments: Adaptation of the Randall's Island Performance Series.
Authors: Ann E. Geers, Helen S. Lane, and Central Institute for the Deaf.
Publisher: Stoelting Co.
Cross References: For reviews by Bruce A. Bracken and Albert C. Oosterhof, see 12:80.

[517]

Cigarette Use Questionnaire.

Purpose: Designed for "evaluation, referral, and treatment of individuals who smoke cigarettes and wish to quit or must do so for health reasons."
Population: Ages 18-83.
Publication Date: 2006.

Acronym: CUQ.
Scores, 6: Defensiveness, Environmental Cues, Inconsistent Responding, Nicotine Addiction, Negative Emotional Relief, Readiness for Change.
Administration: Group.
Price Data, 2010: $99 per kit including manual (41 pages) and 25 autoscore forms; $45 per 25 autoscore forms; $60 per manual.
Time: (10) minutes.
Comments: Self-report.
Author: Ken Winters.
Publisher: Western Psychological Services.
Cross References: For reviews by Mark A. Albanese and Delores D. Walcott, see 18:29.

[518]

The City University Colour Vision Test, Second Edition 1980.

Purpose: To assess defects of color vision.
Population: Adults and children.
Publication Date: 1980.
Scores, 3: Chroma Four, Chroma Two, Overall.
Administration: Individual.
Manual: No manual (introductory notes and instructions included in binder of test plates).
Price Data, 2001: $268 per complete kit including profile sheets, 10 test pages, and instructions.
Time: Administration time not reported.
Author: Robert Fletcher.
Publisher: Keeler Instruments Inc.
Cross References: For a review by Karen T. Carey, see 13:65.

[519]

Clark-Beck Obsessive-Compulsive Inventory.

Purpose: Developed to "provide an efficient, yet comprehensive and precise self-report screening instrument for obsessive and compulsive symptoms."
Population: Adolescents and adults suspected of having Obsessive Compulsive Disorder.
Publication Date: 2002.
Acronym: CBOCI.
Scores, 3: Obsessions, Compulsions, Total.
Administration: Individual.
Price Data, 2003: $80 per complete kit including manual (68 pages) and 25 record forms; $55 per manual; $35 per 25 record forms; $133 per 100 record forms.
Time: (10–30) minutes.
Comments: Requires eighth grade reading level.
Authors: David A. Clark and Aaron T. Beck.
Publisher: Pearson.
Cross References: For a review by Tony Cellucci, see 16:49.

[520]
The Clark Wilson Group Multi-Level Feedback Instruments and Development Programs.

Purpose: Designed to identify group or individual training needs, assess the effects of training, support interactive and participatory management, and to be used in organizational and management studies.
Population: Organizations, executives, managers, and employees.
Publication Dates: 1973–2002.
Administration: Group.
Price Data: Available from publisher.
Time: (12–18) minutes.
Comments: Paper-and-pencil or web-based administration; publisher suggests allowing 6 weeks to administer surveys and give feedback.
Authors: Clark L. Wilson and others noted below.
Publisher: The Clark Wilson Group.

   a) LEADERSHIP SERIES.

     1) *Executive Leadership.*
     Purpose: Assesses executive competencies such as strategic foresight and oversight.
     Population: Executives.
     Publication Date: 1988.
     Acronym: EXEC.
     Scores, 17: Leadership Vision, Risk-Taking, Financial and Operational Analysis, Marketplace Savvy, Organizational Savvy, Judgement, Decisiveness, Team Growth and Development, Cultural Appreciation, Standards of Performance, Executive Energy, Push/Pressure, Coping with Stress, Sharing Credit, Effectiveness/Outcomes, Temporary Sources of Power, Lasting Sources of Power.
     Authors: Paul M. Connolly and Clark L. Wilson.

     2) *Leadership Practices.*
     Purpose: Designed to provide feedback on an individual's vision, influence, and drive for change.
     Population: Managers and executives.
     Publication Date: 1986.
     Acronym: SLP.
     Scores, 17: Vision/Imagination, Risk-Taking, Organizational Sensitivity, Encouraging Participation, Persuasiveness, Teaming, Standards of Performance, Perseverance, Push/Pressure, Effectiveness/Outcomes, Coping with Stress, Feedback, Energy, Sharing Credit, Trustworthiness, Temporary Sources of Power, Lasting Sources of Power.
     Authors: Clark L. Wilson and Paul M. Connolly.

     3) *Project Leadership Practices.*
     Purpose: Designed to assess leadership skills for project managers.
     Population: Project managers and project leaders.
     Publication Date: 1995.
     Acronym: PLP.
     Scores, 19: Clarification of Goals and Objectives, Organization Courage, Judgement, Planning, Adaptation, Problem Solving, Teaming, Coaching, Manager Relations, Customer Relations, Feedback, Push/Pressure, Delegation/Permissiveness, Recognition/Reinforcement, Approachability, Building Trust, Sources of Power, Effectiveness, Belief in Project.
     Authors: Clark L. Wilson, Paul M. Connolly, and David B. Gillespie.

     4) *Leadership in Health Services.*
     Purpose: Designed to assess leadership and management skills for health administration.
     Population: VPs, directors, senior and middle administrators.
     Acronym: LHS.
     Scores, 21: Vision and Imagination, Strategic and Operational Goals, Understanding the Changing Environment, Managing Financial Drivers, Expertise, Risk-Taking, Empowering Employees, Building a Team Environment, Coaching for Performance, Openness to Feedback, Valuing Diversity, Standards of Performance, Clarity of Communications, Persuasiveness, Managing Conflict, Delegation/Permissiveness, Goal Pressure, Recognizing and Reqarding Others, Building Trust, Tension Level, Overall Effectiveness.
     Authors: Eugene P. Buccini, Richard L. Dowall, and Clark L. Wilson.

   b) MANAGEMENT SERIES.

     1) *Management Practices.*
     Purpose: Assesses basic managerial competencies.
     Population: Managers.
     Publication Date: 1973.
     Acronym: SMP.
     Scores, 23: Clarification of Goals and Objectives, Upward Communication, Orderly Work Planning, Expertise, Work Facilitation, Feedback, Time Emphasis, Control of Details, Goal Pressure, Delegation (Permissiveness), Recognition for Good Performance, Approachability, Teambuilding, Interest in Subordinate Growth, Building Trust, Work Involvement, Coworker Competence, Team Atmosphere, Opportunity for Growth, Tension Level, Organization Climate, General Morale, Commitment.
     Author: Clark L. Wilson.

     2) *Peer Relations.*
     Purpose: Assesses organizational skills for specialists.

Population: Managers and individual contributors.
Publication Date: 1974.
Acronym: SPR.
Scores, 22: Clarity of Your Own Goals, Clarity of Communications, Encouraging Peer Participation, Orderly Work Planning, Problem Solving, Expertise, Teamwork/Cooperation, Feedback to Peers, Time Emphasis, Attention to Details, Pressure on Peers, Acknowledging Peer Contributions, Approachability, Dependability, Work Involvement, Coworker Competence, Team Atmosphere, Opportunity for Growth, Tension Level, Organization Climate, General Morale, Commitment.
Author: Clark L. Wilson.

3) *Working with Others.*
Purpose: Assesses supervisory skills for the first-time or prospective manager.
Publication Date: 1991.
Acronym: WWO.
Scores, 13: Commitment to Work, Assertiveness, Problem Solving/Resourcefulness, Teamwork, Willingness to Listen, Attention to Details, Push/Pressure, Recognizing Co-worker Performance, Effectiveness/Outcomes, Friendliness, Dependability, Working with Diversity, Future Promise.
Author: Clark L. Wilson.

4) *Coaching Practices.*
Purpose: Assesses coaching and appraising skills for performance management.
Population: Managers and executives.
Publication Date: 1993.
Acronym: SCP.
Scores, 14: Commitment to Coaching, Planning for Personal Growth, Coaching Skills, Coaching for Teamwork, Technical/Functional Expertise, Organization Awareness, Assessment Skills, Responding to Defensiveness, Control of Details, Delegation (Permissiveness), Recognizing Good Performance, Approachability, Trust, Overall Effectiveness.
Authors: Richard L. Dowall and Clark L. Wilson.

5) *Leadership Competencies for Managers.*
Population: Managers.
Publication Date: 1998.
Acronym: LCM.
Scores, 21: Vision/Imagination, Clarification of Goals, Risk-Taking, Decision Making/Problem Solving, Managing Costs, Encouraging Participation, Clarity of Communications, Teambuilding, Coaching, Managing Conflict, Feedback, Standards of Performance, Personal Drive, Persuasiveness, Delegation, Goal Pressure, Recognition for Good Performance, Building Trust, Managing Diversity, Tension Level, Overall Effectiveness.
Authors: Clark L. Wilson, Paul Connolly, and Richard L. Dowell.

c) SALES SERIES.
1) *Sales Management Practices.*
Purpose: Assesses managerial competencies for field sales managers.
Population: Sales managers.
Publication Date: 1975.
Acronym: SSMP.
Scores, 23: Clarification of Goals and Objectives, Upward Communication, Orderly Work Planning, Expertise, Work Facilitation, Feedback, Time Emphasis, Control of Details, Goal Pressure, Delegation (Permissiveness), Recognition of Good Performance, Approachability, Teambuilding, Interest in Subordinate Growth, Building Trust, Work Involvement, Coworker Competence, Team Atmosphere, Opportunity for Growth, Tension Level, Organization Climate, General Morale, Commitment.
Author: Clark L. Wilson.

2) *Sales Relations.*
Purpose: Provides feedback on skills of sales representatives from customers and prospects.
Population: Sales representatives.
Publication Date: 1975.
Acronym: SSR.
Scores, 11: Understanding Us, Communicating Effectively, Account Service, Analyzing Needs, Presenting Benefits, Asking for the Order, Answering Objections, Selling Pressure, Professionalism, Approachability, Overall Satisfaction.
Author: Clark L. Wilson.

3) *Client Relations.*
Purpose: Assesses internal and external consulting skills.
Population: Consultants and client service representatives.
Publication Date: 1998.
Acronym: SCR.
Scores, 13: Understanding Us, Communicating Effectively, Account Service, Analyzing Needs, Presenting Benefits, Making Recommendations, Answering Objections, Personal Enthusiasm, Personal Pressure, Acknowledging Client Responses, Professionalism, Approachability, Overall Satisfaction.

d) TEAM SERIES.
1) *Executive Team.*
Purpose: Coordinates efforts of top management groups.
Population: Executive teams.

Publication Date: 1993.

Acronym: XT.

Scores, 16: Clarity of Mission/Strategic Goals, Leadership for Growth/Productivity, Resistance to Change, Marketing Focus, Organization Awareness, Consensus Planning, Team Atmosphere, Information/Data Support, Human Resource Development, Organization Stretch, Monitoring Executive Plans, Satisfying, Internal Problems, Sharing Credit, Coping with Stress, Effectiveness/Outcomes.

Authors: Paul M. Connolly and Clark L. Wilson.

2) *Our Team.*

Purpose: Provides feedback from team members on team negotiating skills and conflict resolution.

Population: Teams (Work Groups, Task Forces, Quality Circles, Project Teams, Design Teams, Teams with or without Leaders).

Publication Date: 1989.

Acronym: OT.

Scores, 14: Clarity of Goals and Priorities, Coworker Competence, Consensus Planning, Team Atmosphere, Newcomer Support, Conflict Resolution, Management Support, Management Feedback, Monitoring the Team's Work, Tension/Stress Level, Domination, Satisfying, Recognition/Satisfaction, Effectiveness/Outcomes.

Author: Clark L. Wilson.

3) *My Team Mates.*

Purpose: Provides feedback from team mates on a member's teaming skills.

Population: Team members.

Publication Date: 1989.

Acronym: MTM.

Scores, 13: Clarity of Personal Goals, Innovativeness, Functional Expertise, Teamwork, Leadership for Consensus, Negotiating Skills, Monitoring Personal Output, Coping with Stress and Ambiguity, Personal Drive, Pressure on Team Mates, Acknowledging Others' Efforts, Personal Values, Personal Effectiveness.

Author: Clark L. Wilson.

Cross References: See T4:469 (1 reference).

[521]

Clarke Sex History Questionnaire for Males–Revised.

Purpose: Designed "to evaluate a sex offender's sexual preference profile as well as evaluating their potential for sexually conventional behavior."

Population: Sex offenders.

Publication Dates: 1999-2002.

Acronym: SHQ-R.

Scores: 23 scales: Childhood and Adolescent Sexual Experiences and Sexual Abuse, Sexual Dysfunction, Female Adult Frequency, Female Pubescent Frequency, Female Child Frequency, Male Adult Frequency, Male Pubescent Frequency, Male Child Frequency, Child Identification, Fantasy Activities with Females, Fantasy Activities with Males, Exposure to Pornography, Transvestism, Fetishism, Feminine Gender Identity, Voyeurism, Exhibitionism Frequency, Exhibiting Behavior, Obscene Phone Calls, Toucheurism and Frotteurism, Sexual Aggression, Lie, Infrequency.

Administration: Individual.

Price Data, 2011: $54 per 3 reusable item booklets; $163 per 10 reusable item booklets; $67 per technical manual; $53 per software preview version (V.5) including technical manual and 2 comprehensive reports; $20 per comprehensive reports.

Time: (60-90) minutes.

Comments: Self-report paper-and-pencil inventory that is scored electronically by publisher or by software by the user.

Authors: Ron Langevin and Dan Paitich.

Publisher: Multi-Health Systems, Inc.

Cross References: For reviews by Roger A. Boothroyd and Delores D. Walcott, see 16:50.

[522]

The Class Activities Questionnaire.

Purpose: Developed to provide "a measure of the instructional climate."

Population: Students and teachers Grades 6–12.

Publication Date: 1982.

Acronym: CAQ.

Scores: 5 dimensions: Lower Thought Processes, Higher Thought Processes, Classroom Focus, Classroom Climate, Student Opinions.

Administration: Group.

Price Data: Available from publisher.

Time: (20–30) minutes.

Author: Joe M. Steele.

Publisher: Creative Learning Press, Inc.

Cross References: See T5:493 (1 reference); for a review by Robert W. Hiltonsmith, see 9:226 (1 reference).

[523]

Classroom Assessment Scoring System.

Purpose: Designed to "assess classroom quality in preschool through third-grade classrooms."

Population: Preschool through third-grade students.

Publication Dates: 2008-2009.

Acronym: CLASS.

Scores, 13: (10 dimension scores) Positive Climate, Negative Climate, Teacher Sensitivity, Regard for Student Perspectives, Behavior Management, Productivity, Instructional Learning Formats, Concept Development, Quality of Feedback, Language Modeling; (3 composite

domain scores) Emotional Support, Classroom Organization, Instructional Support.
Administration: Group.
Price Data, 2011: $49.95 per CLASS Manual Pre-K with Dimensions Overview (2008, 108 pages); $49.95 per CLASS Manual K-3 with Dimensions Overview (2008, 112 pages); $28 per 10 CLASS Pre-K and K-3 forms.
Time: (120-180) minutes.
Comments: The CLASS is a comprehensive observation system; researchers, teachers, principals, school psychologists, educational consultants, or other potential users must receive training to use the test. See the CLASS web site (http://www.classobservation.com) for more information on training.
Authors: Robert C. Pianta, Karen M. La Paro, and Bridget K. Hamre.
Publisher: Paul H. Brookes Publishing Co., Inc.

[524]

The Classroom Communication Skills Inventory: A Listening and Speaking Checklist.

Purpose: Evaluates "oral communication skills that have been determined to be important for listening and speaking in the school setting and are essential for classroom learning."
Population: Students.
Publication Date: 1993.
Acronym: CCSI.
Scores: 10 ratings: Basic Speech and Hearing Processes (Auditory Perception, Speech), Classroom Communication (Attention, Class Participation), Language Content and Structure (Vocabulary, Grammar, Organization of Language), Interpersonal Classroom Communication (Using Language for a Variety of Purposes, Conversing Effectively, Using Appropriate Nonverbal Communication Skills).
Administration: Individual.
Price Data, 2002: $40.30 per teacher's manual (51 pages) and 25 record forms.
Time: (10–15) minutes.
Author: The Psychological Corporation.
Publisher: Pearson.
Cross References: For reviews by Linda Crocker and Dolores Kluppel Vetter, see 13:66.

[525]

Classroom Environment Scale, Second Edition.

Purpose: Designed to "assess the social climate of junior high and high school classrooms. It focuses on teacher-student and student-student relationships and on the organizational structure of a classroom."
Population: Junior high and senior high teachers and students.
Publication Dates: 1974–1987.

Acronym: CES.
Scores, 9: Relationship dimensions (Involvement, Affiliation, Teacher Support), Personal Growth/Goal Orientation dimensions (Task Orientation, Competition), System Maintenance and Change dimensions (Order and Organization, Rule Clarity, Teacher Control, Innovation).
Administration: Group.
Forms, 3: Real Form (Form R), Ideal Form (Form I), Expectations Form (Form E), and a Short Form (Form S) by administering and scoring the first 36 items of Form R.
Price Data: Available from the publisher at www.mindgarden.com/products/cescs.htm.
Foreign Language Edition: Spanish translation of Form R available.
Time: [15–20] minutes.
Comments: One of ten Social Climate Scales (T5:2445).
Authors: Rudolf H. Moos and Edison J. Trickett.
Publisher: Mind Garden, Inc.
Cross References: See T5:495 (16 references) and T4:475 (5 references); for reviews by Richard A. Saudargas and Corinne Roth Smith, see 10:60 (16 references); see also T3:409 (9 references); for reviews by Maurice J. Eash and C. Robert Pace of an earlier edition, see 8:521 (3 references). For a review of the Social Climate Scales, see 8:681.

[526]

Classroom Reading Inventory, Twelfth Edition.

Purpose: Designed to "quickly diagnose a student's present ability to decode words both in isolation and in context, and to answer questions about the meaning."
Population: Elementary grades to adult learners.
Publication Dates: 1965-2012.
Acronym: CRI.
Scores, 5: Word Recognition, Comprehension, Independent Reading Level, Instructional Reading Level, Frustration Reading Level.
Administration: Individual.
Forms: Form A Subskill Format (pretest K-8th), Form A Subskill Format (posttest (K-8th), Form B Reader Response Format (pretest 1st-8th), Form B Reader Response Format (posttest 1st-8th), Form C Subskill Format (pretest high school/adult), Form C Subskill Format (posttest high school/adult).
Price Data: Available from publisher.
Time: (15) minutes.
Authors: Warren H. Wheelock and Connie J. Campbell.
Publisher: McGraw Hill Higher Education.
Cross References: See T5:496 (4 references) and T4:476 (4 references); for reviews by Ira E. Aaron and Sylvia M. Hutchinson and by Janet A. Norris of the Fourth Edition, see 10:61 (4 references); for a review of an earlier edition by Marjorie S. Johnson, see 8:749; see also T2:1618 (1 reference); for an excerpted review by Donald L. Cleland, see 7:715.

[527]

CLEP Examination in American Government.

Purpose: For college accreditation, advanced placement, or assessment of educational attainment.
Population: Persons entering college or already in college.
Publication Dates: 1965–2002.
Scores: Total score only.
Administration: Group.
Price Data: Available from publisher.
Time: (90) minutes.
Comments: Tests administered at centers throughout the United States and internationally; program administered by the College Board and Educational Testing Service.
Author: Educational Testing Service.
Publisher: Educational Testing Service.
Cross References: For additional information and a review by Howard D. Mehlinger, see 8:919. For reviews of the CLEP program, see 8:473 (3 reviews) and 7:664 (3 reviews).

[528]

CLEP Examination in American Literature.

Purpose: For college accreditation, advanced placement, or assessment of educational attainment.
Population: Persons entering college or already in college.
Publication Dates: 1971–2002.
Scores: Total score only; optional essay, locally scored.
Administration: Group.
Price Data: Available from publisher.
Time: (90) minutes.
Comments: Tests administered at centers throughout the United States and internationally; program administered by the College Board and Educational Testing Service.
Author: Educational Testing Service.
Publisher: Educational Testing Service.
Cross References: For additional information and a review by Leo P. Ruth, see 8:64. For reviews of the CLEP program, see 8:473 (3 reviews).

[529]

CLEP Examination in Analyzing and Interpreting Literature.

Purpose: For college accreditation, advanced placement, or assessment of educational attainment.
Population: Persons entering college or already in college.
Publication Dates: 1964–2002.
Scores: Total score only; optional essay, locally scored.
Administration: Group.
Price Data: Available from publisher.
Time: (90) minutes.
Comments: Tests administered at centers throughout the United States and internationally; program administered by the College Board and Educational Testing Service.
Author: Educational Testing Service.
Publisher: Educational Testing Service.
Cross References: For additional information and a review by John C. Sherwood, see 8:65 (1 reference). For reviews of the CLEP program, see 8:473 (3 reviews) and 7:664 (3 reviews).

[530]

CLEP Examination in Calculus with Elementary Functions.

Purpose: For college accreditation, advanced placement, or assessment of educational attainment.
Population: Persons entering college or already in college.
Publication Dates: 1974–2002.
Scores: Total score only.
Administration: Group.
Price Data: Available from publisher.
Time: (90) minutes.
Comments: Tests administered at centers throughout the United Statesand internationally; program administered by the College Board and Educational Testing Service.
Author: Educational Testing Service.
Publisher: Educational Testing Service.
Cross References: For a review by J. Phillip Smith, see 8:255. For reviews of the CLEP program, see 8:473 (3 reviews).

[531]

CLEP Examination in College Algebra.

Purpose: For college accreditation, advanced placement, or assessment of educational attainment.
Population: Persons entering college or already in college.
Publication Dates: 1968-1999.
Scores: Total score only.
Administration: Group.
Price Data: Available from publisher.
Time: (90) minutes.
Comments: Tests administered at centers throughout the United States and internationally; program administered by the College Board and Educational Testing Service.
Author: Educational Testing Service.
Publisher: Educational Testing Service.
Cross References: For additional information and a review by J. Philip Smith, see 8:297. For reviews of the CLEP program, see 8:473 (3 reviews) and 7:664 (3 reviews).

[532]

CLEP Examination in College Algebra–Trigonometry.

Purpose: For college accreditation, advanced placement, or assessment of educational attainment.
Population: Persons entering college or already in college.
Publication Dates: 1968-1999.
Scores: Total score only.
Administration: Group.
Price Data: Available from publisher.
Time: (90) minutes.
Comments: Tests administered at centers throughout the United States and internationally; program administered by the College Board and Educational Testing Service.
Author: Educational Testing Service.
Publisher: Educational Testing Service.
Cross References: For a review by Peter A. Lappan, Jr., see 8:256 (1 reference); for a review by Carl G. Willis, see 7:454. For reviews of the CLEP program, see 8:473 (3 reviews) and 7:664 (3 reviews).

[533]

CLEP Examination in College-Level French Language, Levels 1 and 2.

Purpose: For college accreditation, advanced placement, or assessment of educational attainment.
Population: Persons entering college or already in college.
Publication Dates: 1975–2002.
Scores, 3: Reading Comprehension, Listening Comprehension, Total.
Administration: Group.
Price Data: Available from publisher.
Time: (90) minutes.
Comments: Tests administered at centers throughout the United States and internationally; program administered by the College Board and Educational Testing Service.
Author: Educational Testing Service.
Publisher: Educational Testing Service.
Cross References: For a review by Michio Peter Hagiwara, see 8:115. For reviews of the CLEP program, see 8:473 (3 reviews).

[534]

CLEP Examination in College-Level German Language, Levels 1 and 2.

Purpose: For college accreditation, advanced placement, or assessment of educational attainment.
Population: Persons entering college or already in college.
Publication Dates: 1975–2002.
Scores, 3: Reading Comprehension, Listening Comprehension, Total.
Administration: Group.
Price Data: Available from publisher.
Time: (90) minutes.
Comments: Tests administered at centers throughout the United States and internationally; program administered by the College Board and Educational Testing Service.
Author: Educational Testing Service.
Publisher: Educational Testing Service.
Cross References: For reviews by Stefan R. Fink and Herbert Lederer, see 8:127. For reviews of the CLEP program, see 8:473 (3 reviews).

[535]

CLEP Examination in College-Level Spanish Language, Levels 1 and 2.

Purpose: For college accreditation, advanced placement, or assessment of educational attainment.
Population: Persons entering college or already in college.
Publication Dates: 1975–2002.
Scores, 3: Reading Comprehension, Listening Comprehension, Total.
Administration: Group.
Price Data: Available from publisher.
Time: (90) minutes.
Comments: Tests administered at centers throughout the United States and internationally; program administered by the College Board and Educational Testing Service.
Author: Educational Testing Service.
Publisher: Educational Testing Service.
Cross References: For reviews of the CLEP program, see 8:473 (3 reviews).

[536]

CLEP Examination in Educational Psychology.

Purpose: For college accreditation, advanced placement, or assessment of educational attainment.
Population: Persons entering college or already in college.
Publication Dates: 1967–2002.
Scores: Total score only.
Administration: Group.
Price Data: Available from publisher.
Time: (90) minutes.
Comments: Tests administered at centers throughout the United States and internationally; program administered by the College Board and Educational Testing Service.
Author: Educational Testing Service.
Publisher: Educational Testing Service.
Cross References: For reviews of the CLEP program, see 8:473 (3 reviews) and 7:664 (3 reviews).

[537]

CLEP Examination in English Literature.

Purpose: For college accreditation, advanced placement, or assessment of educational attainment.
Population: Persons entering college or already in college.
Publication Dates: 1970–2002.
Scores: Total score only; optional essay, locally scored.
Administration: Group.
Price Data: Available from publisher.
Time: (90) minutes.
Comments: Tests administered at centers throughout the United States and internationally; program administered by the College Board and Educational Testing Service.
Author: Educational Testing Service.
Publisher: Educational Testing Service.
Cross References: For additional information and a review by Edward M. White, see 8:66. For reviews of the CLEP program, see 8:473 (3 reviews).

[538]

CLEP Examination in General Biology.

Purpose: For college accreditation, advanced placement, or assessment of educational attainment.
Population: Persons entering college or already in college.
Publication Dates: 1970–2002.
Scores: Total score only.
Administration: Group.
Price Data: Available from publisher.
Time: (90) minutes.
Comments: Tests administered at centers throughout the United States and internationally; program administered by the College Board and Educational Testing Service.
Author: Educational Testing Service.
Publisher: Educational Testing Service.
Cross References: For additional information and a review by Clarence H. Nelson, see 8:832. For reviews of the CLEP program, see 8:473 (3 reviews) and 7:664 (3 reviews).

[539]

CLEP Examination in General Chemistry.

Purpose: For college accreditation, advanced placement, or assessment of educational attainment.
Population: Persons entering college or already in college.
Publication Dates: 1964–2002.
Scores: Total score only.
Administration: Group.
Price Data: Available from publisher.
Time: (90) minutes.
Comments: Tests administered at centers throughout the United States and internationally; program administered by the College Board and Educational Testing Service.
Author: Educational Testing Service.
Publisher: Educational Testing Service.
Cross References: For additional information and a review by J. Arthur Campbell, see 8:847. For reviews

of the CLEP program, see 8:473 (3 reviews) and 7:664 (3 reviews).

[540]

CLEP Examination in History of the United States: Early Colonizations to 1877.

Purpose: For college accreditation, advanced placement, or assessment of educational attainment.
Population: Persons entering college or already in college.
Publication Dates: 1980–2002.
Scores: Total score only.
Administration: Group.
Price Data: Available from publisher.
Time: (90) minutes.
Comments: Tests administered at centers throughout the United States and internationally; program administered by the College Board and Educational Testing Service.
Author: Educational Testing Service.
Publisher: Educational Testing Service.

[541]

CLEP Examination in History of the United States II: 1865 to the Present.

Purpose: For college accreditation, advanced placement, or assessment of educational attainment.
Population: Persons entering college or already in college.
Publication Dates: 1980–2002.
Scores: Total score only.
Administration: Group.
Price Data: Available from publisher.
Time: (90) minutes.
Comments: Tests administered at centers throughout the United States and internationally; program administered by the College Board and Educational Testing Service.
Author: Educational Testing Service.
Publisher: Educational Testing Service.

[542]

CLEP Examination in Human Growth and Development.

Purpose: For college accreditation, advanced placement, or assessment of educational attainment.
Population: Persons entering college or already in college.
Publication Dates: 1969–2002.
Scores: Total score only.
Administration: Group.
Price Data: Available from publisher.
Time: (90) minutes.
Comments: Tests administered at centers throughout the United States and internationally; program administered by the College Board and Educational Testing Service.
Author: Educational Testing Service.
Publisher: Educational Testing Service.

Cross References: For reviews of the CLEP program, see 8:473 (3 reviews) and 7:664 (3 reviews).

[543]

CLEP Examination in Information Systems and Computer Applications.

Purpose: For college accreditation, advanced placement, or assessment of educational attainment.
Population: Persons entering college or already in college.
Publication Dates: 1968–2002.
Scores: Total score only.
Administration: Group.
Price Data: Available from publisher.
Time: (90) minutes.
Comments: Tests administered at centers throughout the United States and internationally; program administered by the College Board and Educational Testing Service; previously entitled CLEP Subject Examination in Computers and Data Processing.
Author: Educational Testing Service.
Publisher: Educational Testing Service.
Cross References: For reviews of the CLEP program, see 8:473 (3 reviews) and 7:664 (3 reviews).

[544]

CLEP Examination in Introductory Business Law.

Purpose: For college accreditation, advanced placement, or assessment of educational attainment.
Population: Persons entering college or already in college.
Publication Dates: 1970–2002.
Scores: Total score only.
Administration: Group.
Price Data: Available from publisher.
Time: (90) minutes.
Comments: Tests administered at centers throughout the United States and internationally; program administered by the College Board and Educational Testing Service.
Author: Educational Testing Service.
Publisher: Educational Testing Service.
Cross References: For reviews of the CLEP program, see 8:473 (3 reviews) and 7:664 (3 reviews).

[545]

CLEP Examination in Introductory Psychology.

Purpose: For college accreditation, advanced placement, or assessment of educational attainment.
Population: Persons entering college or already in college.
Publication Dates: 1967–2002.
Scores: Total score only.
Administration: Group.
Price Data: Available from publisher.
Time: (90) minutes.

Comments: Tests administered at centers throughout the United States and internationally; program administered by the College Board and Educational Testing Service; previously entitled CLEP Subject Examination in General Psychology.
Author: Educational Testing Service.
Publisher: Educational Testing Service.
Cross References: See T3:442 (2 references); for additional information and a review by Alfred E. Hall of an earlier edition, see 8:460. For reviews of the CLEP program, see 8:473 (3 reviews) and 7:664 (3 reviews).

[546]

CLEP Examination in Introductory Sociology.

Purpose: For college accreditation, advanced placement, or assessment of educational attainment.
Population: Persons entering college or already in college.
Publication Dates: 1965–2002.
Scores: Total score only.
Administration: Group.
Price Data: Available from publisher.
Time: (90) minutes.
Comments: Tests administered at centers throughout the United States and internationally; program administered by the College Board and Educational Testing Service.
Author: Educational Testing Service.
Publisher: Educational Testing Service.
Cross References: For reviews of the CLEP program, see 8:473 (3 reviews) and 7:664 (3 reviews).

[547]

CLEP Examination in Principles of Accounting.

Purpose: For college accreditation, advanced placement, or assessment of educational attainment.
Population: Persons entering college or already in college.
Publication Dates: 1970–2002.
Scores: Total score only.
Administration: Group.
Price Data: Available from publisher.
Time: (90) minutes.
Comments: Tests administered at centers throughout the United States and internationally; program administered by the College Board and Educational Testing Service.
Author: Educational Testing Service.
Publisher: Educational Testing Service.
Cross References: For reviews of the CLEP program, see 8:473 (3 reviews).

[548]

CLEP Examination in Principles of Macroeconomics.

Purpose: For college accreditation, advanced placement, or assessment of educational attainment.

Population: Persons entering college or already in college.
Publication Dates: 1974–2002.
Scores: Total score only.
Administration: Group.
Price Data: Available from publisher.
Time: (90) minutes.
Comments: Tests administered at centers throughout the United States and internationally; program administered by the College Board and Educational Testing Service.
Author: Educational Testing Service.
Publisher: Educational Testing Service.
Cross References: For reviews of the CLEP program, see 8:473 (3 reviews).

[549]

CLEP Examination in Principles of Management.

Purpose: For college accreditation, advanced placement, or assessment of educational attainment.
Population: Persons entering college or already in college.
Publication Dates: 1969–2002.
Scores: Total score only.
Administration: Group.
Price Data: Available from publisher.
Time: (90) minutes.
Comments: Tests administered at centers throughout the United States and internationally; program administered by the College Board and Educational Testing Service.
Author: Educational Testing Service.
Publisher: Educational Testing Service.
Cross References: For reviews of the CLEP program, see 8:473 (3 reviews) and 7:664 (3 reviews).

[550]

CLEP Examination in Principles of Marketing.

Purpose: For college accreditation, advanced placement, or assessment of educational attainment.
Population: Persons entering college or already in college.
Publication Dates: 1968–2002.
Scores: Total score only.
Administration: Group.
Price Data: Available from publisher.
Time: (90) minutes.
Comments: Tests administered at centers throughout the United States and internationally; program administered by the College Board and Educational Testing Service.
Author: Educational Testing Service.
Publisher: Educational Testing Service.
Cross References: For reviews of the CLEP program, see 8:473 (3 reviews) and 7:664 (3 reviews).

[551]

CLEP Examination in Principles of Microeconomics.

Purpose: For college accreditation, advanced placement, or assessment of educational attainment.
Population: Persons entering college or already in college.
Publication Dates: 1974–2002.
Scores: Total score only.
Administration: Group.
Price Data: Available from publisher.
Time: (90) minutes.
Comments: Tests administered at centers throughout the United States and internationally; program administered by the College Board and Educational Testing Service.
Author: Educational Testing Service.
Publisher: Educational Testing Service.
Cross References: For reviews of the CLEP program, see 8:473 (3 reviews).

[552]

CLEP Examination in Trigonometry.

Purpose: For college accreditation, advanced placement, or assessment of educational attainment.
Population: Persons entering college or already in college.
Publication Dates: 1968–2002.
Scores: Total score only.
Administration: Group.
Price Data: Available from publisher.
Time: (90) minutes.
Comments: Tests administered at centers throughout the United States and internationally; program administered by the College Board and Educational Testing Service.
Author: Educational Testing Service.
Publisher: Educational Testing Service.
Cross References: For reviews of the CLEP program, see 8:473 (3 reviews) and 7:664 (3 reviews).

[553]

CLEP Examination in Western Civilization I: Ancient Near East to 1648.

Purpose: For college accreditation, advanced placement, or assessment of educational attainment.
Population: Persons entering college or already in college.
Publication Dates: 1964–2002.
Scores: Total score only.
Administration: Group.
Price Data: Available from publisher.
Time: (90) minutes.
Comments: Tests administered at centers throughout the United States and internationally; program administered by the College Board and Educational Testing Service.
Author: Educational Testing Service.
Publisher: Educational Testing Service.

Cross References: For reviews of the CLEP program, see 8:473 (3 reviews) and 7:664 (3 reviews).

[554]

CLEP Examination in Western Civilization II: 1648 to Present.

Purpose: For college accreditation, advanced placement, or assessment of educational attainment.
Population: Persons entering college or already in college.
Publication Dates: 1964–2002.
Scores: Total score only.
Administration: Group.
Price Data: Available from publisher.
Time: (90) minutes.
Comments: Tests administered at centers throughout the United States and internationally; program administered by the College Board and Educational Testing Service.
Author: Educational Testing Service.
Publisher: Educational Testing Service.
Cross References: For reviews of the CLEP program, see 8:473 (3 reviews) and 7:664 (3 reviews).

[555]

CLEP Examinations in English Composition and English Composition Test with Essay.

Purpose: For college accreditation, advanced placement, or assessment of educational attainment.
Population: Persons entering college or already in college.
Publication Dates: 1964–2002.
Scores: Total score only.
Administration: Group.
Price Data: Available from publisher.
Time: (45) minutes per composition test; (45) minutes per essay.
Comments: English Composition Test with Essay administered via computer at any time per a test site's schedule; English Composition test administered at centers throughout the United States and internationally; program administered by the College Board and Educational Testing Service.
Author: Educational Testing Service.
Publisher: Educational Testing Service.
Cross References: See T3:412 (1 reference); for additional information, see 8:42 (4 references) and T2:58 (1 reference); for reviews of the CLEP program, see 8:473 (3 reviews) and 7:664 (3 reviews).

[556]

CLEP Examinations in Humanities.

Purpose: For college accreditation, advanced placement, or assessment of educational attainment.
Population: Persons entering college or already in college.
Publication Dates: 1964–2002.
Scores: Total score only.

Administration: Group.
Price Data: Available from publisher.
Time: (90) minutes.
Comments: Tests administered at centers throughout the United States and internationally; program administered by the College Board and Educational Testing Service.
Author: Educational Testing Service.
Publisher: Educational Testing Service.
Cross References: For additional information and a review by William E. Kline, see 8:254 (1 reference); for reviews of the CLEP program, see 8:473 (3 reviews) and 7:664 (3 reviews).

[557]

CLEP Examinations in Mathematics.

Purpose: For college accreditation, advanced placement, or assessment of educational attainment.
Population: Persons entering college or already in college.
Publication Dates: 1964–2002.
Scores: Total score only.
Administration: Group.
Price Data: Available from publisher.
Time: (90) minutes.
Comments: Tests administered at centers throughout the United States and internationally; program administered by the College Board and Educational Testing Service.
Author: Educational Testing Service.
Publisher: Educational Testing Service.
Cross References: For a review by William E. Kline, see 8:254 (1 reference).

[558]

CLEP Examinations in Natural Sciences.

Purpose: For college accreditation, advanced placement, or assessment of educational attainment.
Population: Persons entering college or already in college.
Publication Dates: 1964–2002.
Scores: Total score only.
Administration: Group.
Price Data: Available from publisher.
Time: (90) minutes.
Comments: Tests administered at centers throughout the United States and internationally; program administered by the College Board and Educational Testing Service.
Author: Educational Testing Service.
Publisher: Educational Testing Service.
Cross References: For additional information by George G. Mallinson, see 8:824 (2 references); for reviews of the CLEP program, see 8:473 (3 reviews) and 7:664 (3 reviews).

[559]

CLEP Examinations in Social Sciences and History.

Purpose: For college accreditation, advanced placement, or assessment of educational attainment.
Population: Persons entering college or already in college.
Publication Dates: 1964–2002.
Scores: Total score only.
Administration: Group.
Price Data: Available from publisher.
Time: (90) minutes.
Comments: Tests administered at centers throughout the United States and internationally; program administered by the College Board and Educational Testing Service.
Author: Educational Testing Service.
Publisher: Educational Testing Service.
Cross References: For additional information and a review by Richard E. Gross, see 8:886 (1 reference); for reviews of the CLEP program, see 8:473 (3 reviews) and 7:664 (3 reviews).

[560]

CLEP Examination in Freshman College Composition.

Purpose: For college accreditation, advanced placement, or assessment of educational attainment.
Population: Persons entering college or already in college.
Publication Dates: 1994–2002.
Scores: Total score only; optional essay, scored locally.
Administration: Group.
Price Data: Available from publisher.
Time: (90) minutes.
Comments: Tests administered at centers throughout the United States and internationally; program administered by the College Board and Educational Testing Service; replaces College Composition (T4:491) and Freshman English (T4:498) examinations.
Author: Educational Testing Service.
Publisher: Educational Testing Service.
Cross References: For a review by Leonard S. Feldt of the CLEP Freshman English Examination, see 8:44 (1 reference). For a review by Charlotte Croon Davis of the CLEP College Composition Examination, see 8:43 (2 references).

[561]

Clerical Abilities Battery.

Purpose: Assesses clerical abilities "for use in hiring and promoting clerical personnel."
Population: Clerical applicants and employees and business school students.
Publication Dates: 1985–1987.
Acronym: CAB.
Scores: 7 tests: Filing, Comparing Information, Copying Information, Using Tables, Proofreading, Addition and Subtraction, Reasoning with Numbers.
Administration: Group or individual.
Forms, 2: A, B.
Restricted Distribution: Distribution of Form A restricted to personnel departments in business and industry.
Price Data, 2006: $180 per starter kit including 5 test booklets of each of 7 tests, 7 keys, and manual; $55 per 25 test booklets (specify form: Filing, Copying Information, Comparing Information, Using Tables, Proofreading, Addition and Subtraction, Reasoning with Numbers); $207 per 100 test booklets (specify form); $84 per set of scoring stencils; $36 per manual.
Time: 70(105) minutes for the battery; 5(10) minutes each for first four tests, 15(20) minutes each for next two tests, 20(25) minutes for last test.
Comments: Tests available as separates.
Author: The Psychological Corporation.
Publisher: Pearson.
Cross References: For reviews by Joseph C. Ciechalski and Bikkar S. Randhawa, see 11:71.

[562]

Clerical Aptitude Test: Acorn National Aptitude Tests.

Purpose: Designed to measure qualities associated with good clerical performance.
Population: Grades 7–12 and adult clerks.
Publication Dates: 1943–1950.
Scores, 4: Business Practice, Number Checking, Date and Name and Address Checking, Total.
Administration: Group.
Price Data: Available from publisher.
Time: 40(50) minutes.
Authors: Andrew Kobal, J. Wayne Wrightstone, and Karl R. Kunze.
Publisher: Psychometric Affiliates.
Cross References: See T3:464 (2 references); see also 5:847 (1 reference); for reviews by Marion A. Bills, Donald G. Paterson, Henry Weitz, and E. F. Wonderlic, see 3:623.

[563]

Clerical Aptitudes.

Purpose: "Designed to indicate ability to learn the tasks usually performed in various clerical jobs."
Population: Applicants for office personnel positions.
Publication Dates: 1947–1982.
Scores, 4: Office Vocabulary, Office Arithmetic, Office Checking, Total.
Administration: Individual or group.
Price Data: Available from publisher.
Time: 25 minutes.
Comments: Previously listed as SRA Clerical Aptitudes.
Author: Richardson, Bellows, Henry & Co., Inc.
Publisher: Pearson Performance Solutions [No reply from publisher; status unknown].
Cross References: See T2:791 (2 references); for reviews by Edward N. Hay and G. A. Satter, see 4:732.

[564]

Clerical Skills Series.

Purpose: "Designed to measure proficiency in paper work tasks typical of . . . clerical occupations."
Population: Clerical worker.
Publication Dates: 1966-1986.
Administration: Group.
Price Data, 2006: $65 per complete kit; $33 per profile sheet package; $49.50 per manual (1966, 20 pages) and manuals supplement (1984, 17 pages).
Author: Martin M. Bruce.
Publisher: Martin M. Bruce, Ph.D.
a) ALPHABETIZING-FILING.
Time: 8(13) minutes.
Price Data: $39 per specimen set; $44 per test package; $3.25 per scoring key.
b) ARITHMETIC.
Time: 8(13) minutes.
Price Data: Same as *a* above.
c) CLERICAL SPEED AND ACCURACY.
Time: 3(5) minutes.
Price Data: Same as *a* above.
d) CODING.
Time: 2(7) minutes.
Price Data: Same as *a* above.
e) EYE-HAND ACCURACY.
Time: 5(10) minutes.
Price Data: $39 per specimen set; $44 per test package; no key required.
f) GRAMMAR AND PUNCTUATION.
Time: (5-10) minutes.
Price Data: Same as *a* above.
g) SPELLING.
Time: (15-20) minutes.
Price Data: Same as *a* above.
h) SPELLING-VOCABULARY.
Time: (15-20) minutes.
Price Data: Same as *a* above.
i) VOCABULARY.
Time: (10-15) minutes.
Price Data: Same as *a* above.
j) WORD FLUENCY.
Time: 5(10) minutes.
Price Data: Same as *e* above.
Cross References: For a review by Robert Fitzpatrick, see 7:988.

[565]

Clerical Skills Test.

Purpose: "Designed to assist companies in identifying individuals who have strong reading, mathematical and analytical skills."
Population: Current and prospective employees.
Publication Dates: 1999–2001.
Acronym: CST.

Scores, 7: Writing, Analyzing, Proofreading, Filing, Math, Checking, Total.
Administration: Group.
Price Data, 2005: $79.99 per starter kit including administrator's manual (2001, 28 pages), 5 tests, and 1 test log; $29.99 per administrator's manual; $9.25 per test (online or paper-and-pencil version; paper-and-pencil version sold in quantities of 10).
Time: 21(26) minutes.
Comments: Paper-and-pencil and online versions available.
Author: J. M. Llobet.
Publisher: G. Neil.
Cross References: For a review by Eleanor E. Sanford-Moore, see 17:44.

[566]

Clerical Skills Test Series [Scored By Client].

Purpose: Measures 16 different clerical-administrative skills.
Population: Adults.
Publication Date: 1990.
Scores: 16 skills: Alphabetizing–Filing, Attention to Detail With Words & Numbers, Bookkeeping Skills, Coding, Grammar & Punctuation, Manual Dexterity, Mechanical Comprehension, Numerical Skills, Problem Solving, Proofreading Skills, Reading Comprehension, Receptionist Skills, Spatial Perception, Spelling, Verbal Fluency, English Vocabulary, plus Total Score.
Administration: Group.
Price Data, 2001: $300 per 20 of the same test; quantity discounts available.
Time: (5) minutes per subtest.
Comments: Scored by the client; includes scoring keys; must be proctored.
Author: Stephen Berke.
Publisher: Walden Personnel Performance, Inc. [Canada].
Cross References: For reviews by Phillip L. Ackerman and Eleanor E. Sanford, see 16:51.

[567]

Client/Server Skills Test.

Purpose: To evaluate the candidate's general client/server knowledge.
Population: Information technology professionals who possess some basic knowledge or experience in a client/server environment.
Publication Date: 1994.
Scores: Total Score, Narrative Evaluation, Ranking, Recommendation.
Administration: Group.
Price Data, 2001: $240 per candidate.
Time: (80) minutes.
Comments: Scored by publisher; must be proctored.

Author: Bruce A. Winrow.
Publisher: Walden Personnel Performance, Inc.

[568]

Clifton Assessment Procedures for the Elderly.

Purpose: Designed to assess cognitive and behavioral competence of the elderly.
Population: Ages 60 and over.
Publication Dates: 1979–1981.
Acronym: CAPE.
Administration: Group.
Price Data, 2002: £8.99 per 20 report forms; £9.50 per manual (1979, 34 pages); £11.99 per specimen set.
Time: Administration time not reported.
Comments: Distributed in the U.S.A. by The Psychological Corporation; 2 tests plus combination short version; authors recommend administering both tests concurrently, however, they can be used separately.
Authors: A. H. Pattie and C. J. Gilleard.
Publisher: Hodder & Stoughton Educational [England].
  a) COGNITIVE ASSESSMENT SCALE.
  Acronym: CAS.
  Scores, 4: Information/Orientation, Mental Ability, Psychomotor (adaptation of Gibson Spiral Maze), Total.
  Price Data: £8.99 per 20 tests (CAS); £13.99 per 20 mazes.
  b) BEHAVIOUR RATING SCALE.
  Acronym: BRS.
  Scores, 5: Physical Disability, Apathy, Communication Difficulties, Social Disturbance, Total.
  Price Data: £8.99 per 20 tests.
  Comments: Shortened version of Stockton Geriatric Rating Scale.
Cross References: See T5:537 (4 references) and T4:518 (19 references); for reviews by Alicia Skinner Cook and K. Warner Schaie, see 9:231 (2 references); see also T3:471 (1 reference).

[569]

Clinical Assessment of Articulation and Phonology.

Purpose: Designed to "assess English articulation and phonology in preschool and school aged children."
Population: Ages 3 to 9 years.
Publication Date: 2002.
Acronym: CAAP.
Administration: Individual.
Price Data, 2006: $219 per complete kit including examiner's manual (2002, 136 pages), 50 Articulation Inventory forms, 30 Phonological Checklists forms, stimulus easel, 5 Clinical Assessment of Articulation and Phonology Pals, and Clinical Assessment of Articulation and Phonology Stickers; $29.99 per 50 Articulation Inventory forms; $29.95 per 30 Phonological Checklists forms; $45 for examiner's manual.

Comments: This is a norm-referenced instrument.
Authors: Wayne A. Secord and JoAnn S. Donohue.
Publisher: Super Duper Publications.
  a) ARTICULATION INVENTORY.
  Scores, 2: Consonant Inventory Score, School Age Sentence Score.
  Time: (15-20) minutes.
  b) PHONOLOGICAL PROCESS CHECKLISTS I AND II.
  Scores, 10: Final Consonant Deletion, Cluster Reduction, Syllable Reduction, Gliding, Vocalization, Fronting, Deaffrication, Stopping, Prevocalic Voicing, Postvocalic Devoicing.
  Time: (20) minutes.
Cross References: For reviews by Steven Long and Roger L. Towne, see 17:45.

[570]

Clinical Assessment of Attention Deficit–Adult.

Purpose: Designed to provide a "comprehensive assessment of attention deficit with and without hyperactivity (ADD/ADHD)" in adults.
Population: Ages 19-79.
Publication Dates: 1994-2005.
Acronym: CAT-A.
Scores, 17: Clinical Index, Childhood Memories Clinical Index (Inattention, Impulsivity, Hyperactivity), Childhood Memories Context Clusters (Personal, Academic/Occupational, Social), Childhood Memories Locus Clusters (Internal, External), Current Symptoms Clinical Index (Inattention, Impulsivity, Hyperactivity), Current Symptoms Context Clusters (Personal, Academic/Occupational, Social), Current Symptoms Locus Clusters (Internal, External).
Administration: Group or individual.
Price Data, 2006: $152 per introductory kit including professional manual (2005, 139 pages), 25 rating forms, and 25 score summary/profile forms; $65 per professional manual; $68 per 25 rating forms; $26 per 25 score summary/profile forms; $185 per unlimited use scoring software CD (CAT-SP).
Time: (20-25) minutes.
Comments: Can be computer scored; a child and adolescent form (CAT-C; 571) is also available and shares the same professional manual.
Authors: Bruce A. Bracken and Barbara S. Boatwright.
Publisher: Psychological Assessment Resources, Inc.
Cross References: For reviews by Rama K. Mishra and Sean Reilley, see 17:46.

[571]

Clinical Assessment of Attention Deficit–Child.

Purpose: Designed to provide a "comprehensive assessment of attention deficit with and without hyperactivity (ADD/ADHD)" in children and adolescents.

Population: 8-18 years.
Publication Dates: 1994-2005.
Acronym: CAT-C.
Scores, 12: Clinical (Inattention, Impulsivity, Hyperactivity), Clinical Index, Context (Personal, Academic/Occupational, Social), Locus (Internal, External), Validity (Negative Impression, Infrequency, Positive Impression).
Administration: Individual.
Parts, 3: Self-Report, Parent Report, Teacher Report.
Price Data, 2007: $265 per introductory kit including professional manual, 25 Self-Rating Forms, 25 Parent Rating Forms, 25 Teacher Rating Forms, 25 Self-Rating Score Summary/Profile Forms, 25 Parent Score Summary/Profile Forms, and 25 Teacher Score Summary/Profile Forms; $65 per professional manual; $52 per 25 Self-Rating forms; $52 per 25 Parent Rating Forms; $52 per 25 Teacher Rating Forms; $22 per 25 Parent Score Summary/Profile Forms; $22 per 25 Self-Rating Score Summary/Profile Forms; $22 per 25 Teacher Score Summary/Profile Forms; $185 per unlimited use CAT-C SP scoring software CD.
Time: (10-20) minutes.
Comments: An adult form (CAT-A; 570) is also available and shares the same professional manual.
Authors: Bruce A. Bracken and Barbara S. Boatwright.
Publisher: Psychological Assessment Resources, Inc.
Cross References: For reviews by George J. Demakis and Rosemary Flanagan, see 17:47.

[572]

Clinical Assessment of Behavior.

Purpose: "Assists in the identification of children and adolescents across a wide age range who are in need of behavioral, educational, or psychiatric treatment or intervention."
Population: Ages 2–18.
Publication Dates: 1996–2004.
Acronym: CAB.
Scores, 21: Internalizing Behaviors, Externalizing Behaviors, Critical Behaviors, Social Skills, Competence, Adaptive Behaviors, CAB Behavioral Index, Anxiety, Depression, Anger, Aggression, Bullying, Conduct Problems, Attention-Deficit/Hyperactivity, Autistic Spectrum Behaviors, Learning Disability, Mental Retardation, Executive Function, Gifted and Talented, Emotional Disturbance, Social Maladjustment.
Administration: Individual.
Forms, 3: Parent Extended Rating Form, Parent Rating Form, Teacher Rating Form.
Price Data, 2006: $229 per introductory kit including CD ROM-based scoring program with on-screen professional manual, installation guide, and professional manual (2004, 309 pages), 25 Parent Rating Forms, 25 Parent Extended Forms, and 25 Teacher Rating Forms.
Time: (10–30) minutes.
Comments: Informant-completed behavior rating scale.
Authors: Bruce A. Bracken and Lori K. Keith.

Publisher: Psychological Assessment Resources, Inc.
Cross References: For reviews by Mike Bonner and Metta K. Volker-Fry and by John Hattie, see 16:52.

[573]

Clinical Assessment of Depression.

Purpose: "Developed to aid in the clinical assessment and diagnosis of depression."
Population: Ages 8 to 79.
Publication Dates: 1994–2004.
Acronym: CAD.
Scores: 14: Symptom Scale Scores (Depressed Mood, Anxiety/Worry, Diminished Interest, Cognitive and Physical Fatigue, Total), Validity Scale Scores (Inconsistency, Negative Impression, Infrequency), Critical Item Cluster Scores (Hopelessness, Self-Devaluation, Sleep/Fatigue, Failure, Worry, Nervous).
Administration: Group.
Price Data, 2007: $130 per introductory kit including professional manual (2004, 96 pages), 25 rating forms, and 25 score summary/profile forms; $185 per scoring program (CD-ROM) including unlimited scoring and reports.
Time: 10 minutes.
Authors: Bruce A. Bracken and Karen Howell.
Publisher: Psychological Assessment Resources, Inc.
Cross References: For reviews by Michael G. Kavan and Jody L. Kulstad, see 17:48.

[574]

Clinical Assessment Scales for the Elderly and Clinical Assessment Scales for the Elderly–Short Form.

Purpose: "A comprehensive measure of acute psychopathology in the elderly" and to "screen for acute psychopathology in the elderly."
Population: Ages 55–90.
Publication Dates: 1999–2001.
Scores: 10: Anxiety, Cognitive Competence, Depression, Fear of Aging, Mania, Obsessive-Compulsive, Paranoia, Psychoticism, Somatization, Substance Abuse.
Administration: Individual or group.
Forms, 2: R (caregiver rating), S (self-rating).
Comments: Addresses selected DSM-IV Axis I disorders.
Authors: Cecil R. Reynolds (test and manual) and Erin D. Bigler (test).
Publisher: Psychological Assessment Resources, Inc.
a) CLINICAL ASSESSMENT SCALES FOR THE ELDERLY.
Purpose: "A comprehensive measure of acute psychopathology in the elderly."
Acronym: CASE.
Price Data, 2006: $210 per introductory kit including CASE/CASE-SF professional manual

(2001, 140 pages), 25 CASE Form S item booklets, 25 CASE Form R item booklets, 25 CASE Form S hand-scorable answer sheets, 25 CASE Form R hand-scorable answer sheets, and 50 CASE profile forms.

Time: 20–40(30–50) minutes.

b) CLINICAL ASSESSMENT SCALES FOR THE ELDERLY—SHORT FORM.

Purpose: To "screen for acute psychopathology in the elderly."

Acronym: CASE-SF.

Price Data: $160 per Short Form introductory kit including CASE/CASE-SF professional manual, 25 CASE-SF Form S test booklets, 25 CASE-SF Form R test booklets, and 50 CASE profile forms.

Time: 10–20(20–30) minutes.

Cross References: For reviews by Stephen J. DePaola and Iris Phillips, see 15:51.

[575]

Clinical Evaluation of Language Fundamentals–4 Screening Test.

Purpose: "Designed to screen school age children, adolescents, and young adults for language disorders."

Population: Ages 5-0 to 21-11.

Publication Dates: 1995–2004.

Acronym: CELF-4 Screening Test.

Scores: Total score only.

Administration: Individual.

Price Data, 2006: $225 per kit including examiner's manual (2004, 45 pages), stimulus manual, and 25 record forms; $59 per 25 record forms; $220 per 100 record forms.

Time: 15 minutes (untimed).

Comments: A test in the CELF series of language testing instruments; administered orally with visual stimuli; not for diagnostic use; "criterion-referenced."

Authors: Eleanor Semel, Elisabeth H. Wiig, and Wayne A. Secord.

Publisher: Pearson.

Cross References: For reviews by Aimee Langlois and Gregory Snyder, see 18:30; see T5:542 (2 references); for reviews by Billy T. Ogletree and Marcel O. Ponton of an earlier edition, see 13:69 (1 reference); for reviews by Linda M. Crocker and Jon F. Miller of an earlier edition, see 9:234.

[576]

Clinical Evaluation of Language Fundamentals, Fourth Edition.

Purpose: Constructed as "a clinical tool for the identification, diagnosis and follow-up evaluation of language and communication disorders."

Population: Ages 5–21.

Publication Dates: 1980–2003.

Acronym: CELF-4.

Administration: Individual.

Price Data, 2005: $425 per complete kit including examiner's manual, 2 stimulus manuals, 10 record form1, 10 record form 2, 50 ORS record forms, and 1 luggage tag; $150 per examiner's manual; $215 per 2 stimulus manuals; $110 per stimulus manual 1; $110 per stimulus manual 2; $40 per 50 ORS record forms; $59 per 25 record form 1; $59 per 25 record form 2; $199 per Scoring Assistant; $550 per complete kit/Scoring Assistant Combo.

Time: (30-45) minutes.

Authors: Eleanor Semel, Elisabeth Wiig, and Wayne A. Secord.

Publisher: Pearson.

a) CELF-4, AGES 5–8.

Population: Ages 5–8.

Scores, 22: Core Language (Concepts and Following Directions, Word Structure, Recalling Sentences, Formulated Sentences), Receptive Language (Concepts and Following Directions, Word Classes 1 and 2-Receptive, Sentence Structure), Expressive Language (Word Structure, Recalling Sentences, Formulated Sentences, Language Content (Concepts and Following Directions, Word Classes 1 and 2-Total, Expressive Vocabulary), Language Structure (Word Structure, Recalling Sentences, Formulated Sentences, Sentence Structure), Phonological Awareness, Word Associations, Rapid Automatic Naming, Number Repetition 1, Familiar Sequences 1.

b) CELF-4, AGES 9–12.

Population: Ages 9–12.

Scores, 21: Core Language (Concepts and Following Directions, Recalling Sentences, Formulated Sentences, Word Classes 2-Total) Receptive Language (Concepts and Following Directions, Word Classes 2-Receptive), Expressive Language (Recalling Sentences, Formulated Sentences, Word Classes 2-Expressive), Language Content (Word Classes 2-Total, Expressive Vocabulary [Age 9], Word Definitions [Ages 10–12], Understanding Spoken Paragraphs), Language Memory (Recalling Sentences, Concepts and Following Directions, Formulated Sentences), Phonological Awareness, Word Associations, Rapid Automatic Naming, Number Repetition 1, Familiar Sequences 1.

c) CELF-4, AGES 13-21.

Population: Ages 13-21.

Scores, 20: Core Language (Recalling Sentences, Formulated Sentences, Word Classes 2-Total, Word Definitions), Receptive Language (Word Classes 2-Receptive, Semantic Relationships, Understanding Spoken Paragraphs), Expressive Language (Recalling Sentences, Formulated Sentences, Word Classes 2-Expressive), Language Content (Word Definitions, Sentence Assembly, Understanding Spoken Paragraphs),

Language Memory (Recalling Sentences, Formulated Sentences, Semantic Relationships), Word Associations, Rapid Automatic Naming, Number Repetition 1 and 2, Familiar Sequences 1 and 2.

Cross References: For reviews by Aimee Langlois and Vincent J. Samar, see 16:53; for reviews by Robert R. Haccoun and David P. Hurford of an earlier edition, see 14:76; see also T5:540 (26 references); for reviews by Ronald B. Gillam and John MacDonald of an earlier edition, see 13:68 (38 references); see also T4:521 (5 references); for reviews by Linda Crocker and David A. Shapiro of an earlier edition, see 11:72; for a review by Dixie D. Sanger of an earlier edition, see 9:233 (2 references); see also T3:474.

[577]

Clinical Evaluation of Language Fundamentals Preschool–Second Edition.

Purpose: Designed as a "clinical tool for identifying, diagnosing, and performing follow-up evaluations of language deficits."
Population: Ages 3–6.
Publication Dates: 1992–2004.
Acronym: CELF Preschool-2.
Scores, 16: 11 subtests (Sentence Structure, Word Structure, Expressive Vocabulary, Concepts and Following Directions, Recalling Sentences, Basic Concepts, Word Classes, Recalling Sentences in Context, Phonological Awareness, Pre-Literacy Rating Scale, Descriptive Pragmatics Profile); 5 Composites (Core Language, Receptive Language, Expressive Language, Language Content, Language Structure).
Administration: Individual.
Price Data, 2007: $329 per complete kit; $89 per examiner's manual (2004, 220 pages); $219 per Stimulus Book #1; $52 per Stimulus Book #2; $62 per 25 record forms.
Time: (15–20) minutes.
Comments: A downward extension of the Clinical Evaluation of Language Fundamentals, Fourth Edition (576).
Authors: Elisabeth H. Wiig, Wayne A. Secord, and Eleanor Semel.
Publisher: Pearson.
Cross References: For reviews by Rick Eigenbrood and Gene Schwarting, see 17:49; see also T5:539 (2 references); for reviews by Janet A. Norris and Nora M. Thompson of an earlier edition, see 13:67 (2 references).

[578]

Clinical Evaluation of Language Fundamentals Preschool–Second Edition-Spanish Edition.

Purpose: Designed to provide "comprehensive language evaluation for Spanish-speaking preschool children."

Population: Ages 3-0 to 6-11.
Publication Dates: 2004-2009.
Acronym: CELF Preschool-2 Spanish.
Scores, 15: Basic Concepts, Word Structure, Recalling Sentences, Concepts and Following Directions, Expressive Vocabulary, Sentence Structure, Word Classes, Phonological Awareness, Early Literacy Rating Scale, Descriptive Pragmatics Profile, Core Language Score, Receptive and Expressive Language Index Score, Expressive Language, Language Content, Language Structure Index Score.
Subtests, 10: Basic Concepts, Word Structure, Recalling Sentences, Concepts and Following Directions, Expressive Vocabulary, Sentence Structure, Word Classes, Phonological Awareness, Early Literacy Rating Scale, Descriptive Pragmatics Profile.
Administration: Individual.
Levels, 4: Level 1: Identify whether or not there is a language disorder; Level 2: Describe the nature of the disorder; Level 3: Evaluate early classroom and literacy fundamentals; Level 4: Evaluate language and communication in context.
Price Data, 2010: $379 per CELF Preschool-2 Spanish Kit including manual (2009, 310 pages), 25 record forms, Spanish stimulus manual, and 25 rating scale forms; $105 per manual; $325 per Spanish stimulus manual.
Foreign Language Editions: English-language edition is Clinical Evaluation of Language Fundamentals Preschool-Second Edition (577).
Time: (15-20) minutes for Level 1; remaining subtest time varies.
Comments: This is a parallel edition to the CELF Preschool 2 (577), not a translation; subtests can be used individually.
Authors: Elisabeth H. Wigg, Wayne A. Secord, and Eleanor Semel.
Publisher: Pearson.

[579]

Clinical Evaluation of Language Fundamentals, Third Edition–Observational Rating Scales.

Purpose: Designed to measure "a student's classroom communication and language learning difficulties."
Population: Ages 6–21.
Publication Date: 1996.
Acronym: CELF-3ORS.
Scores: 4 sections: Listening, Speaking, Reading, Writing.
Administration: Individual or group.
Forms, 4: Parent, Teacher, Student, Summary.
Price Data, 2002: $59 per complete kit including rating scales, summary forms, and guide (86 pages); $15 per Teacher rating forms; $15 per Parent rating forms; $20 per summary forms; $27 per guide.
Time: Administration time not reported.

Comments: Ratings by parents, teachers, and students.
Authors: Eleanor Semel, Elisabeth H. Wiig, and Wayne A. Secord.
Publisher: Pearson.
Cross References: For reviews by Robert R. Haccoun and David P. Hurford, see 14:76; see also T5:541 (1 reference).

[580]

Clinical Experience Record for Nursing Students.

Purpose: Evaluates the "performance and progress of nursing students."
Population: Nursing students and nurses.
Publication Dates: 1960–1975.
Acronym: CERNS.
Scores: No scores.
Administration: Individual.
Price Data: Available from publisher.
Time: Administration time not reported.
Comments: Two assessment areas: Clinical Performance Record, Performance/Progress Record.
Authors: John C. Flanagan, Angeline C. Marchese, Grace Fivars, and Shirley A. Tuska (manual).
Publisher: Grace Fivars.
Cross References: For additional information, see 8:1120 (1 reference).

[581]

Clinical Rating Scale for Circumplex Model.

Purpose: Designed to type marital and family systems and identify intervention targets related to Circumplex Model.
Population: Couples and families.
Publication Dates: 1980–2004.
Acronym: CRS.
Scores: 3 rating scales (Cohesion, Flexibility, Communication) yielding Family System Type related to Circumplex Model.
Administration: Group (couple or family).
Price, 2006: $30 for CRS and manual (includes unlimited copying privileges).
Time: (5-10) minutes.
Comments: Rating of couple or family system based on interview and/or observation.
Author: David H. Olson.
Publisher: Life Innovations, Inc.
Cross References: For reviews by Stuart N. Hart and Steven W. Lee of an earlier edition, see 12:81 (4 references).

[582]

The Clock Test.

Purpose: "Intended to assess visual-spatial construction, visual perception, and abstract conceptualization in individuals 65 and older using three subtests, clock drawing, clock reading, and clock setting, to determine an individual's level of cognitive impairment."
Population: Ages 65 and older.
Publication Date: 1995.
Scores, 3: Clock Reading, Clock Drawing, Clock Setting.
Administration: Individual.
Price Data, 2011: $262 per test kit including 25 QuikScore™ forms, 25 profile sheets, stimulus cards tent, and manual (75 pages); $113 per 25 QuikScore™ forms; $25 per 25 profile sheets; $109 per administration tent; $83 per manual.
Time: (5-10) minutes.
Authors: H. Tuokko, T. Hadjistavropoulos, J. A. Miller, A. Horton, and B. L. Beattie.
Publisher: Multi-Health Systems, Inc.
Cross References: For reviews by Howard A. Lloyd and Antony M. Paolo, see 14:78.

[583]

Closed Head Injury Screener.

Purpose: "Designed to help medical doctors and psychologists assess whether patient symptoms are suggestive of closed-head injuries."
Population: English-speaking adults.
Publication Date: 1994.
Acronym: CHIS.
Scores, 3: Medical Facts, Presenting Complaints, Response Validity.
Administration: Individual.
Price Data: Available from publisher (www.mindgarden.com).
Time: Approximately 30 minutes.
Comments: To be used as a supplement to a full face-to-face patient interview; partial paper and pencil/partial oral interview; results interpreted by administrator; not to be used with patients with cognitive deficits that are explainable by a previous diagnosis.
Author: Michael Ivan Friedman.
Publisher: Mind Garden, Inc.
Cross References: For reviews by Thomas J. Cullen, Jr. and Scott A. Napolitano, see 14:79.

[584]

Closed High School Placement Test.

Purpose: Designed as a measure of cognitive and basic skills to assist in placement decisions for entering freshmen.
Population: Eighth grade students.
Publication Dates: 1958–2011.
Acronym: HSPT.
Scores, 8: Cognitive Skills (Verbal, Quantitative, Total), Basic Skills (Reading, Mathematics, Language, Total), Composite.
Administration: Group.

Price Data: Contact STS at (800) 642-6787 for up-to-date pricing.

Time: 150 minutes plus (15–25) minutes per optional test.

Comments: Optional tests include science, mechanical aptitude, and Catholic religion; new form is developed each year.

Author: Scholastic Testing Service, Inc.

Publisher: Scholastic Testing Service, Inc.

Cross References: For reviews by George Engelhard, Jr. and Ernest Kimmel, see 14:80; see also T5:547 (1 reference) and T3:2324 (1 reference); for reviews by Leonard S. Cahen and Irvin J. Lehmann of an earlier edition, see 8:26 (1 reference); see also 7:21 (2 references); for reviews by Marion F. Shaycoft and James R. Hayden of an earlier series, see 6:6; for reviews by William C. Cottle and Robert A. Jones of the 1955 "open" test, see 5:15.

[585]

Closure Flexibility (Concealed Figures).

Purpose: "To measure the ability to hold a configuration in mind despite distracting irrelevancies."

Population: Wide range of higher level occupations personnel.

Publication Dates: 1956–1965.

Scores: Total score only.

Administration: Individual or group.

Price Data, 2002: $91 per start-up kit including 25 test booklets, score key, and interpretation and research manual (1965, 20 pages); $54 per 25 tests (quantity discounts available); $20 per score key; $28 per interpretation and research manual.

Time: (10) minutes.

Authors: L. L. Thurstone and T. E. Jeffrey.

Publisher: Pearson Performance Solutions [No reply from publisher; status unknown].

Cross References: See T5:548 (1 reference), T3:477 (5 references), T2:547 (9 references), and 7:435 (9 references); for a review by Leona E. Tyler, see 6:545 (4 references).

[586]

Closure Speed (Gestalt Completion).

Purpose: "To measure the ability to see apparently disorganized or unrelated parts as a meaningful whole."

Population: Employees in wide range of occupations.

Publication Date: 1959.

Scores: Total score only.

Administration: Individual or group.

Price Data, 2002: $91 per start-up kit including 25 test booklets, score key, and interpretation and research manual (1966, 18 pages); $54 per 25 test booklets (quantity discounts available); $20 per score key; $28 per interpretation and research manual.

Time: 3 minutes.

Authors: L. L. Thurstone and T. E. Jeffrey.

Publisher: Pearson Performance Solutions [No reply from publisher; status unknown].

Cross References: See T4:530 (2 references), T3:478 (2 references), T2:548 (1 reference), and 7:436 (2 references); for a review by Leona E. Tyler, see 6:546 (3 references).

[587]

Cloze Reading Tests 1-3, Second Edition.

Purpose: Designed to provide a method of testing reading skills.

Population: Ages 8-0 to 10-6, 8-5 to 11-10, 9-5 to 12-6.

Publication Dates: 1982–1992.

Scores: Overall performance score.

Administration: Individual or group.

Levels, 3: Level 1 (Ages 8-0 to 10-6), Level 2 (Ages 8-5 to 11-10), Level 3 (Ages 9-5 to 12-6).

Price Data, 2002: £5.99 per 10 tests (specify Test 1, 2, or 3); £11.99 per manual (16 pages); £12.99 per specimen set.

Time: 35(45) minutes.

Author: D. Young.

Publisher: Hodder & Stoughton Educational [England].

Cross References: See T5:550 (5 references) and T4:531 (3 references); for a review by Esther Geva, see 9:237.

[588]

CNS Vital Signs Screening Battery.

Purpose: Designed to "assess neurocognitive state."

Population: Children, adults.

Publication Date: 2003.

Scores, 5: Memory, Mental Speed, Reaction Time, Attention, Cognitive Flexibility.

Subtests, 7: Verbal Memory, Visual Memory, Finger Tapping, Symbol Digit Coding, Stroop, Shifting Attention, Continuous Performance.

Administration: Individual.

Price Data: Available from publisher.

Time: (30) minutes.

Comments: Computer administered and scored; requires Windows 2000 or XP.

Author: CNS Vital Signs.

Publisher: CNS Vital Signs.

Cross References: For reviews by D. Ashley Cohen and Karl R. Hanes, see 16:54.

[589]

Coaching Effectiveness Survey.

Purpose: Designed as a 360° (self and coachees) measure of coaching skills and coaching style preferences. It is an assessment of executives' coaching skills and developmental needs and it contrasts how executives prefer to coach with how the people they coach prefer to be coached.

Population: Executives in leadership positions.
Publication Date: 1997.
Scores, 5: Coaching Behavior, Coaching Attitude, Coaching Process, Coaching Style, Coaching Effectiveness.
Administration: Group.
Forms, 2: Online Coach Questionnaire, Online Coachee Questionnaire.
Price Data, 2005: $49 per complete kit including questionnaires and answer sheets for 1 self-assessment, 12 coachees, and 1 feedback report.
Foreign Language Edition: Available in English and German.
Time: (30) minutes.
Comments: Assessment is administered online via Lore's Assessment Center. Assessment results are emailed to participant. A paper report may be requested for an additional $50 fee per report.
Author: Lore International Institute.
Publisher: Lore International Institute.

[590]

Coaching Process Questionnaire.

Purpose: "Provides managers with an assessment of their coaching ability."
Population: Managers and employees.
Publication Date: 1992.
Acronym: CPQ.
Administration: Group or individual.
Foreign Language Editions: Available in French and Spanish.
Time: [30–40] minutes.
Comments: Self-scored instrument.
Author: Hay Group.
Publisher: Hay Group.
  a) PARTICIPANT VERSION.
  Population: Managers.
  Scores, 5: Diagnostic Skills, Coaching Techniques, Coaching Qualities, Coaching Model, Overall CPQ score.
  Price Data, 2006: $79 per complete kit including 10 questionnaires, and 10 profiles and interpretive notes.
  b) EMPLOYEE VERSION.
  Population: Employees.
  Scores, 5: Diagnostic Skills, Coaching Techniques, Coaching Qualities, Coaching Model, Overall Employee score.
  Price Data: $29 per 10 questionnaires.
Cross References: For reviews by Patricia A. Bachelor and Geneva D. Haertel, see 13:70.

[591]

Coaching Skills Inventory.

Purpose: Identifies and evaluates "success in performing coaching functions" for organizational leaders.

Population: Adults.
Publication Date: 1991.
Acronym: CSI.
Scores, 5: Contact and Core Skills, Counseling, Mentoring, Tutoring, Confronting and Challenging.
Administration: Group.
Forms, 2: Self, Other.
Price Data: Available from publisher.
Time: Administration time not reported.
Comments: Self-administered; self-scored.
Author: Dennis C. Kinlaw.
Publisher: Jossey-Bass, A Wiley Company.

[592]

Coddington Life Events Scales.

Purpose: "Designed to assess the influence of life events and change in a young person's life, and help determine how these events affect their personal growth and ability to adjust."
Population: Ages 5 and under, ages 6–10, ages 11–19.
Publication Dates: 1981–1999.
Acronym: CLES.
Scores: Total Life Change Unit score only.
Administration: Individual or Group.
Forms, 3: Preschool (CLES-P), Child (CLES-C), Adolescent (CLES-A).
Price Data, 2011: $193 per complete kit including technical manual (1999, 58 pages) and 25 QuikScore forms for the CLES-P, CLES-C, and CLES-A; $76 per technical manual; $50 per 25 QuikScore forms (specify CLES-P, CLES-C, or CLES-A); $83 per preview set including technical manual and 3 of each QuikScore forms for the CLES-P, CLES-C, CLES-A.
Time: (15) minutes.
Comments: Self-report, assisted self-report.
Author: R. Dean Coddington.
Publisher: Multi-Health Systems, Inc.
Cross References: For reviews by James A. Athanasou and Howard M. Knoff, see 15:52; see T5:557 (7 references) and T4:1453 (3 references).

[593]

Cognistat (The Neurobehavioral Cognitive Status Examination).

Purpose: Designed to assess intellectual functioning.
Population: Adults.
Publication Dates: 1983–1995.
Acronym: Cognistat.
Scores, 11: Level of Consciousness, Orientation, Attention, Language (Comprehension, Repetition, Naming), Constructional Ability, Memory, Calculations, Reasoning (Similarities, Judgment).
Administration: Individual.
Price Data, 2010: $575 per starter kit including stimulus book, tokens, 25 test booklets, and manual;

$35 per stimulus book; $475 per 25 test booklets; $35 per set of 8 tokens; $75 per manual.
Time: Administration time not reported.
Authors: R. J. Kiernan, J. Mueller, and J. W. Langston.
Publisher: Cognistat, Inc.
Cross References: For reviews by Charles J. Long and Faith Gunning-Dixon and by Steven R. Shaw, see 14:81.

[594]

Cognitive Abilities Scale–Second Edition.

Purpose: Developed to assess the cognitive abilities of infants and young children and to identify children who have delays in cognitive development.
Population: Ages 3-23 months; 24-47 months.
Publication Dates: 1987–2001.
Acronym: CAS-2.
Administration: Individual.
Price Data, 2011: $82 per examiner's manual (2001, 83 pages); $45 per 25 Profile/Examiner Record Booklets (Infant Form); $45 per 25 Profile/Examiner Record Booklets (Preschool Form); $18 per 25 Symbol Reproduction Forms; $46 per 25 Mikey's Favorite Things Book; $34 per Picture Cards; $12 per Ramp; $229 per Manipulatives Kit; $490 per complete kit including examiner's manual, 25 Profile/ Examiner Record Booklets (Infant Form), 25 Profile/ Examiner Record Booklets (Preschool Form), 25 Symbol Reproduction Forms, 25 copies of "Mikey's Favorite Things," Picture Cards, Ramp, and Manipulatives Kit.
Time: (20–30) minutes.
Authors: Sharon Bradley-Johnson and C. Merle Johnson.
Publisher: PRO-ED.
   a) INFANT FORM.
   Population: Ages 3–23 months.
   Scores, 3: Exploration of Objects, Communication with Others, Initiation and Imitation.
   b) PRESCHOOL FORM.
   Population: Ages 24–47 months.
   Scores, 5: Oral Language, Reading, Math, Writing, Enabling Behaviors.
Cross References: For reviews by Bert A. Goldman and Joyce Meikamp, see 15:53; see T5:559 (1 reference); for reviews by A. Dirk Hightower and Gary J. Robertson of the original edition, see 10:65.

[595]

Cognitive Abilities Test, Form 6.

Purpose: Designed to "assess students' abilities in reasoning and problem solving using verbal, quantitative, and spatial (nonverbal) symbols."
Population: Grades K–12.
Publication Dates: 1954–2002.
Acronym: CogAT.
Scores, 4: Verbal Battery, Quantitative Battery, Nonverbal Battery, Composite.
Administration: Group.

Price Data, 2006: $21.80 per Interpretive Guide for Teachers and Counselors (2001, 174 pages); $21.80 per Interpretive Guide for School Administrators (2001, 140 pages); $63 per Research Handbook (2002, 112 pages); $55.75 per norms booklet; $26.80 per 25 practice tests (specify level); $113.10 per 25 machine-scorable test booklets and 1 Directions for Administration (specify Level K, 1, or 2); $88.60 per 25 reusable test booklets and 1 Directions for Administration (specify Level A through H); $16.50 per Directions for Administration (specify level); $45 per 50 answer sheets (Levels A–H); $85 per 100 answer sheets (Levels A–H); $11.85 per scoring key (specify Level K, 1, or 2); $21.80 per scoring key (Levels A–H).
Comments: Scoring service available from publisher.
Authors: David F. Lohman and Elizabeth P. Hagen.
Publisher: Riverside Publishing.
   a) PRIMARY BATTERY.
   Population: Grades K–2.
   Subtests, 6: Oral Vocabulary, Verbal Reasoning, Relational Concepts, Quantitative Concepts, Figure Classification, Matrices.
   Levels: 3 overlapping levels, K, 1, and 2.
   Time: Untimed, approximately 140 minutes, including administration time (Levels 1 and 2) to 170 minutes (Level K).
   b) MULTILEVEL BATTERY.
   Population: Grades 3–12.
   Subtests, 9: Verbal Classification, Sentence Completion, Verbal Analogies, Quantitative Relations, Number Series, Equation Building, Figure Classification, Figure Analogies, Figure Analysis.
   Levels: 8 overlapping Levels, A through H.
   Time: Approximately 145 minutes, including administration time.
Cross References: For reviews by James C. DiPerna and Bruce G. Rogers, see 16:55; see also T5:560 (4 references); for reviews by Bert A. Goldman and Stephen H. Ivens of an earlier edition, see 13:71 (23 references); see also T4:537 (19 references); for reviews by Anne Anastasi and Douglas Fuchs of an earlier edition, see 10:66 (13 references); for a review by Charles J. Ansorge of an earlier edition, see 9:240 (5 references); see also T3:483 (32 references); for reviews by Kenneth D. Hopkins and Robert C. Nichols, see 8:181 (12 references); for reviews by Marcel L. Goldschmid and Carol K. Tittle and an excerpted review by Richard C. Cox of the primary batteries, see 7:343.

[596]

Cognitive Behavior Rating Scales.

Purpose: Intended to "evaluate the presence and severity of cognitive impairment" using observations of family and/or significant others.
Population: Patients with possible neurological impairment.
Publication Date: 1987.

Acronym: CBRS.
Scores: 9 scales: Language Deficit, Apraxia, Disorientation, Agitation, Need for Routine, Depression, Higher Cognitive Deficits, Memory Disorder, Dementia.
Administration: Individual.
Price Data, 2005: $123 per introductory kit including manual, 50 reusable item booklets, and 50 rating booklets.
Time: (15-20) minutes.
Comments: Completed by family and/or significant others.
Author: J. Michael Williams.
Publisher: Psychological Assessment Resources, Inc.
Cross References: For reviews by Ron Edwards and David J. Mealor, see 11:74.

[597]

Cognitive Distortion Scales.

Purpose: Designed to measure cognitive/distortions (dysfunctional thinking patterns) that interfere with optimal functioning.
Population: Ages 18 and over.
Publication Date: 2000.
Acronym: CDS.
Scores, 5: Self-Criticism, Self-Blame, Helplessness, Hopelessness, Preoccupation with Danger.
Administration: Individual or group.
Price Data, 2006: $132 per introductory kit including manual (2000, 40 pages), 25 test booklets, and 25 profile forms.
Time: (10–15) minutes.
Author: John Briere.
Publisher: Psychological Assessment Resources, Inc.
Cross References: For reviews by Sandra D. Haynes and Timothy J. Makatura, see 15:54.

[598]

Cognitive Linguistic Quick Test.

Purpose: "To assess the relative status of five cognitive domains in adults with known or suspected neurological dysfunction."
Population: Adults ages 18–89 with known or suspected acquired neurological dysfunction.
Publication Date: 2001.
Acronym: CLQT.
Scores, 7: 5 Cognitive Domain Scores (Attention, Memory, Language, Executive Functions, Visuospatial Skills), Total Composite Severity Rating, Clock Drawing Severity Rating.
Administration: Individual.
Price Data, 2002: $150 per complete kit including examiner's manual (146 pages), stimulus manual, 15 English record forms, and 15 response forms; $71 per examiner's manual; $61 per stimulus manual; $53 per 25 English record response forms; $32 per 15 Spanish record/response forms.
Foreign Language Editions: Available in English and Spanish versions.

Time: (15–30) minutes.
Comments: Test is composed of 10 tasks (Personal Facts, Symbol Cancellation, Confrontation Naming, Clock Drawing, Story Retelling, Symbol Trails, Generative Naming, Design Memory, Mazes, Design Generation); includes 5 tasks with minimal language demands; hand-scored.
Author: Nancy Helm-Estabrooks.
Publisher: Pearson.
Cross References: For reviews by Tony Cellucci and Thomas McKnight, see 15:55.

[599]

Cognitive Skills Assessment Battery, Second Edition.

Purpose: "To provide teachers with information regarding children's progress relative to teaching goals in the cognitive and physical-motor areas."
Population: PreK–K.
Publication Dates: 1974–1981.
Acronym: CSAB.
Scores: 98 item scores (49 consist of plus or minus) in 18 areas: Basic Information (4 scores), Identification of Body Parts (4 scores), Color Identification (4 scores), Shape Identification (4 scores), Symbol Discrimination (10 scores), Visual-Auditory Discrimination (5 scores), Auditory Discrimination (6 scores), Number Knowledge (10 scores), Letter Naming (2 scores), Vocabulary (6 scores), Information from Pictures (4 scores), Picture Comprehension (4 scores), Story Comprehension (4 scores), Multiple Directions (4 scores), Large Muscle Coordination (4 scores), Visual-Motor Coordination (6 scores), Memory (8 scores), Response During Assessment (8 scores).
Administration: Individual.
Price Data, 2006: $51.95 per testing materials including 30 response sheets (1981, 4 pages); $8.95 per refill (1 class record, 30 pupil response sheets); $3.50 per assessors manual (1981, 61 pages); $3.95 per specimen set (including 1 sample easel page).
Time: (20-25) minutes.
Comments: "Criterion-referenced."
Authors: Ann E. Boehm and Barbara R. Slater.
Publisher: Teachers College Press.
Cross References: See T5:565 (1 reference) and T4:542 (3 references); for reviews by Esther E. Diamond and Susan Embretson (Whitely), see 9:242; see also T3:484 (2 references); for reviews by Kathryn Hoover Calfee and Barbara K. Keogh, see 8:797.

[600]

Cognitive Symptom Checklists.

Purpose: "Developed to assist in the identification and treatment of problems in five basic cognitive areas."
Population: Ages 16 and older.

Publication Date: 1993.
Acronym: CSC.
Scores: 5 checklists: Attention/Concentration, Memory, Visual Processes, Language, Executive Functions.
Administration: Individual or group.
Price Data, 2006: $86 per introductory kit including Clinician's Guide (26 pages), and 25 each of Attention/ Concentration, Memory, Visual Processes, Language, and Executive Functions checklists.
Time: (10–20) minutes per checklist.
Comments: Checklists can be used separately or in any combination.
Authors: Christina O'Hara, Minnie Harrell, Eileen Bellingrath, and Katherine Lisicia.
Publisher: Psychological Assessment Resources, Inc.
Cross References: For reviews by Thomas J. Cullen, Jr. and Michael Lee Russell, see 14:82.

[601]

CogScreen Aeromedical Edition.

Purpose: "Designed to rapidly assess deficits or changes in" various cognitive abilities associated with flying.
Population: Aviators ages 25–73 with 12 or more years of education.
Publication Date: 1995.
Acronym: CogScreen-AE.
Scores, 65: 19 Speed Measures (Math Speed, Visual Sequence Comparison Speed, Matching-to-Sample Speed, Manikin Speed, Divided Attention Sequence Comparison Speed, Divided Attention Indicator Alone Speed, Divided Attention Indicator Dual Speed, Auditory Sequence Comparison Speed, Pathfinder Number Speed, Pathfinder Letter Speed, Pathfinder Combined Speed, Shifting Attention Arrow Direction Speed, Shifting Attention Arrow Color Speed, Shifting Attention Instruction Speed, Shifting Attention Discovery Speed, Dual Task Previous Number Alone Speed, Dual Task Previous Number Dual Speed, Dual Task Tracking Alone Error, Dual Task Tracking Dual Error), 19 Accuracy Measures (Backward Digit Span Accuracy, Math Accuracy, Visual Sequence Comparison Accuracy, Symbol Digit Coding Accuracy, Symbol Digit Coding Immediate Recall Accuracy, Symbol Digit Coding Delayed Recall Accuracy, Matching-to-Sample Accuracy, Manikin Accuracy, Divided Attention Sequence Comparison Accuracy, Auditory Sequence Comparison Accuracy, Pathfinder Number Accuracy, Pathfinder Letter Accuracy, Pathfinder Combined Accuracy, Shifting Attention Arrow Direction Accuracy, Shifting Attention Arrow Color Accuracy, Shifting Attention Instruction Accuracy, Shifting Attention Discovery Accuracy, Dual Task Previous Number Alone Accuracy, Dual Task Previous Number Dual Accuracy), 16 Thruput Measures (Math Thruput, Visual Sequence Comparison Thruput, Symbol Digit Coding Thruput, Matching-to-Sample Thruput, Manikin Thruput, Divided Attention Sequence Compari-

son Thruput, Auditory Sequence Comparison Thruput, Pathfinder Number Thruput, Pathfinder Letter Thruput, Pathfinder Combined Thruput, Shifting Attention Arrow Direction Thruput, Shifting Attention Arrow Color Thruput, Shifting Attention Instruction Thruput, Shifting Attention Discovery Thruput, Dual Task Previous Number Alone Thruput, Dual Task Previous Number Dual Thruput), 11 Process Measures (Divided Attention Indicator Alone Premature Responses, Divided Attention Indicator Dual Premature Responses, Pathfinder Number Coordination, Pathfinder Letter Coordination, Pathfinder Combined Coordination, Shifting Attention Discovery Rule Shifts Completed, Shifting Attention Discovery Failures to Maintain Set, Shifting Attention Discovery Nonconceptual Responses, Shifting Attention Discovery Perseverative Errors, Dual Task Tracking Alone Boundary Hits, Dual Task Tracking Dual Boundary Hits).
Administration: Individual.
Price Data, 1996: $849 per software kit including manual (148 pages), quick start guide, internal light pen package, and Testkey with 10 administrations (specify 3.5-inch or 5.25-inch disk); $69 per manual; $29.50 per administration with Testkey unlock; $75 per extra Testkey (with no administration); $375 per internal light pen package.
Time: (45–60) minutes.
Comments: Requires IBM or compatible 640K, EGA or VGA graphics card, color monitor, and light pen.
Author: Gary G. Kay.
Publisher: CogScreen LLC [No reply from publisher; status unknown].
Cross References: For reviews by Robert W. Elliott and Hilda Wing, see 14:83.

[602]

Coitometer.

Purpose: Designed to "measure knowledge of the physical aspects of human coitus."
Population: Adults.
Publication Dates: 1974–1988.
Scores: Total score only.
Administration: Group.
Manual: No manual.
Price Data, 2005: $2 per test.
Time: [10] minutes.
Comments: Supplementary article available.
Author: Panos D. Bardis.
Publisher: Donna Bardis.

[603]

College ADHD Response Evaluation.

Purpose: Designed to assess ADHD in postsecondary students.
Population: College students, Parents of college students.
Publication Date: 2002.
Acronym: CARE.

Scores, 6: Inattention, Hyperactivity, Impulsivity, Total Score, DSM-IV Inattentive, DSM-IV Hyperactive/Impulsive.
Administration: Individual.
Forms, 2: Student Response Inventory, Parent Response Inventory.
Price Data, 2006: $135 per complete kit including manual (144 pages), 25 each of student inventory, parent inventory, student profile, and parent profile; $50 per manual; $55 per 25 inventories and 25 profiles (specify student or parent).
Time: 10–15 minutes.
Comments: Oral administration permitted.
Authors: Joseph Glutting, David Sheslow, and Wayne Adams.
Publisher: Psychological Assessment Resources, Inc.
  a) STUDENT RESPONSE INVENTORY.
  Population: College students.
  Scores, 6: Inattention, Hyperactivity, Impulsivity, Total Score, DSM-IV Inattentive, DSM-IV Hyperactive/Impulsive.
  b) PARENT RESPONSE INVENTORY.
  Population: Parents of college students.
  Scores, 5: Inattention, Hyperactivity, Total Score, DSM-IV Inattentive, DSM-IV Hyperactive/Impulsive.
Cross References: For reviews by Mary "Rina" M. Chittooran and William K. Wilkinson, see 16:57.

[604]

College Adjustment Scales.

Purpose: Identifies psychological and adjustment problems experienced by college students.
Population: College and university students.
Publication Date: 1991.
Acronym: CAS.
Scores, 9: Anxiety, Depression, Suicidal Ideation, Substance Abuse, Self-Esteem Problems, Interpersonal Problems, Family Problems, Academic Problems, Career Problems.
Administration: Individual or group.
Price Data, 2006: $130 per introductory kit including professional manual (25 pages), 25 reusable item booklets, and 25 answer sheets.
Time: (15–20) minutes.
Authors: William D. Anton and James R. Reed.
Publisher: Psychological Assessment Resources, Inc.
Cross References: For reviews by William E. Martin, Jr. and Edward R. Starr, see 13:72 (3 references); see also T4:544 (1 reference).

[605]

College Basic Academic Subjects Examination.

Purpose: Designed to assess skills and competencies achieved through the general education component of a college curriculum.

Population: College students having completed the general education component of a college curriculum.
Publication Dates: 1989–2010.
Acronym: College BASE, CBASE.
Scores: 40: Competency (Interpretive Reasoning, Strategic Reasoning, Adaptive Reasoning), Skill (Social Science Procedures, Political/Economic Structures, Geography, Significance of U.S. Events, Significance of World Events, Physical Sciences, Life Sciences, Interpreting Results, Laboratory/Field Techniques, Observation/Experimental Design, Geometrical Calculations, 2- & 3-Dimensional Figures, Equations & Inequalities, Evaluating Expressions, Using Statistics, Properties and Notations, Practical Applications, Expository Writing Sample, Conventions of Written English, Writing as a Process, Understanding Literature, Reading Analytically, Reading Critically), Cluster (Social Sciences, History, Fundamental Concepts, Laboratory & Field Work, Geometry, Algebra, General Mathematics, Writing, Reading & Literature), Subject (Social Studies, Science, Mathematics, English), Composite.
Administration: Group.
Price Data, 2010: $80 per 50 test booklets; $50 per 50 answer booklets (includes examiner's manual); Scoring: $25.40 per student for four subjects with essay, and $13.90 per student for four subjects without essay. Includes institutional summary and student score reports.
Time: 45 minutes per subject; 40 minutes for optional essay; plus 20 minutes for administration time.
Comments: "Criterion-referenced"; 180 multiple-choice items, optional essay assignment; All four subjects may be administered or any combination of 1-3 subjects; accommodations packages are available for students with special needs; additional technical reports and data files may be ordered by special request.
Author: Steven J. Osterlind.
Publisher: Assessment Resource Center, University of Missouri-Columbia.
Cross References: See T5:570 (1 reference); for reviews by William E. Coffman and Delwyn L. Harnisch, see 11:76.

[606]

College Board Institutional SAT Subject Test in English Language Proficiency.

Purpose: To measure spoken and written standard American English, and the ability to use English in the classroom and in daily life.
Population: Entering college freshmen.
Publication Dates: 1997–2005.
Acronym: ELPT.
Scores, 3: Listening, Reading (1–50), and Total (901–999).
Administration: Group or individual.
Price Data: Rental fee per student available from publisher.

Time: 60 minutes.
Comments: Available for local administration and scoring by higher educational institutions.
Author: Educational Testing Service.
Publisher: The College Board.
Cross References: For a review of an earlier form of the program, see 7:665.

[607]

College Board On-Campus SAT Subject Test in Biology E/M.

Purpose: To measure content knowledge in biology.
Population: Entering college freshmen.
Publication Dates: 1962–2005.
Scores: Total (200–800).
Administration: Group or individual.
Price Data: Rental fee per student available from publisher.
Time: 60 minutes.
Comments: Available for local administration and scoring by higher educational institutions; student chooses an Ecological (E) or Molecular (M) emphasis; previously known as College Board One-Hour Achievement Test in Biology.
Author: Educational Testing Service.
Publisher: The College Board.
Cross References: See T5:573 (1 reference) and 8:834 (1 reference); for a review by Elizabeth Hagen of an earlier form, see 5:723; for a review by Clark W. Horton of an earlier form, see 4:600; for a review of an earlier form of the program, see 7:665.

[608]

College Board On-Campus SAT Subject Test in Chemistry.

Purpose: To measure content knowledge in chemistry.
Population: Entering college freshmen.
Publication Dates: 1962–2005.
Scores: Total (200–800).
Administration: Group or individual.
Price Data: Rental fee per student available from publisher.
Time: 60 minutes.
Comments: Available for local administration and scoring by higher educational institutions; previously known as College Board One-Hour Achievement Test in Chemistry.
Author: Educational Testing Service.
Publisher: The College Board.
Cross References: See T5:574 (1 reference); for a review by William Hered of earlier forms, see 6:914; for a review by Max D. Engelhart of an earlier form, see 5:742; for a review by Evelyn Raskin of an earlier form, see 4:617; for a review of an earlier form of the program, see 7:665.

[609]

College Board On-Campus SAT Subject Test in Chinese with Listening Subject.

Purpose: To measure content knowledge in Chinese.
Population: Entering college freshmen.
Publication Dates: 1997–2005.
Scores, 4: Subscores in Listening, Usage, Reading (20–80), and Total (200–800).
Administration: Group or individual.
Price Data: Rental fee per student available from publisher.
Time: 60 minutes.
Comments: Available for local administration and scoring by higher educational institutions; CD player and earphones required; program previously known as College Board One-Hour Achievement Test.
Author: Educational Testing Service.
Publisher: The College Board.
Cross References: For a review of an earlier form of the program, see 7:665.

[610]

College Board On-Campus SAT Subject Test in French.

Purpose: To measure content knowledge in French.
Population: Entering college freshmen.
Publication Dates: 1962–2005.
Scores: Total (200–800).
Administration: Group or individual.
Price Data: Rental fee per student available from publisher.
Time: 60 minutes.
Comments: Available for local administration and scoring by higher educational institutions; previously known as College Board One-Hour Achievement Test in French Reading.
Author: Educational Testing Service.
Publisher: The College Board.
Cross References: For a review of an earlier form of the program, see 7:665.

[611]

College Board On-Campus SAT Subject Test in French with Listening.

Purpose: To measure content knowledge in French.
Population: Entering college freshmen.
Publication Dates: 1971–2005.
Scores, 3: Subscores in Listening, Reading (20–80), Total (200–800).
Administration: Group or individual.
Price Data: Rental fee per student available from publisher.
Time: 60 minutes.
Comments: Available for local administration and scoring by higher educational institutions; CD player and earphones required; previously known as College Board

One-Hour Achievement Test in French with Listening and College Placement Test.
Author: Educational Testing Service.
Publisher: The College Board.
Cross References: For a review of an earlier form of the program, see 7:665.

[612]

College Board On-Campus SAT Subject Test in German.

Purpose: To measure content knowledge in German.
Population: Entering college freshmen.
Publication Dates: 1962–2005.
Scores: Total (200–800).
Administration: Group or individual.
Price Data: Rental fee per student available from publisher.
Time: 60 minutes.
Comments: Available for local administration and scoring by higher educational institutions; previously known as College Board One-Hour Achievement Test in German Reading and College Placement Test.
Author: Educational Testing Service.
Publisher: The College Board.
Cross References: See 7:285 (2 references); for a review by Gilbert C. Kettelkamp of earlier forms, see 6:383; for a review by Harold B. Dunkel, see 5:272; for a review by Herbert Schueler, see 4:244. For a review of an earlier form of the program, see 7:665.

[613]

College Board On-Campus SAT Subject Test in German with Listening.

Purpose: To measure content knowledge in German.
Population: Entering college freshmen.
Publication Dates: 1971–2005.
Scores, 3: Subscores in Listening, Reading (20–80), Total (200–800).
Administration: Group or individual.
Price Data: Rental fee per student available from publisher.
Time: 60 minutes.
Comments: Available for local administration and scoring by higher educational institutions; CD player and headphones required; previously known as College Board One-Hour Achievement Test in German with Listening and College Placement Test.
Author: Educational Testing Service.
Publisher: The College Board.
Cross References: See 8:130 (1 reference). For a review of an earlier form of the program, see 7:665.

[614]

College Board On-Campus SAT Subject Test in Italian.

Purpose: To measure content knowledge in Italian.

Population: Entering college freshmen.
Publication Dates: 1962–2005.
Scores: Total (200–800) score only.
Administration: Group or individual.
Price Data: Rental fee per student available from publisher.
Time: 60 minutes.
Comments: Available for local administration and scoring by higher educational institutions; previously known as College Board One-Hour Achievement Test in Italian and College Placement Test.
Author: Educational Testing Service.
Publisher: The College Board.
Cross References: For a review by Paolo Valesio of earlier forms, see 7:300. For a review of an earlier form of the program, see 7:665.

[615]

College Board On-Campus SAT Subject Test in Japanese with Listening.

Purpose: To measure content knowledge in Japanese.
Population: Entering college freshmen
Publication Dates: 1997–2005.
Scores: 4: Subscores in Listening, Usage, Reading (20–80), and Total (200–800).
Administration: Group or individual.
Price Data: Rental fee per student available from publisher.
Time: 60 minutes.
Comments: Active forms of College Board SAT Subject Test in Japanese with Listening available for local administration and scoring by colleges, universities, and other appropriate organizations; CD player and earphones required; program previously known as College Board One-Hour Achievement Test.
Author: Educational Testing Service.
Publisher: The College Board.
Cross References: For a review of an earlier form of the program, see 7:665.

[616]

College Board On-Campus SAT Subject Test in Latin.

Purpose: To measure content knowledge in Latin.
Population: Entering college freshmen.
Publication Dates: 1962–2005.
Scores: Total (200–800).
Administration: Group or individual.
Price Data: Rental fee per student available from publisher.
Time: 60 minutes.
Comments: Available for local administration and scoring by higher educational institutions; previously known as College Board One-Hour Achievement Test in Latin Reading and College Placement Test.

Author: Educational Testing Service.
Publisher: The College Board.
Cross References: For a review by Konrad Gries of an earlier form, see 5:280; for a review by Harold B. Dunkel, see 4:250. For a review of an earlier form of the program, see 7:665.

[617]

College Board On-Campus SAT Subject Test in Literature.

Purpose: To measure content knowledge in literature.
Population: Entering college freshmen.
Publication Dates: 1968–2005.
Score: Total (200–800).
Administration: Group or individual.
Price Data: Rental fee per student available from publisher.
Time: 60 minutes.
Comments: Available for local administration and scoring by higher educational institutions; previously known as College Board One-Hour Achievement Test in Literature.
Author: Educational Testing Service.
Publisher: The College Board.
Cross References: For a review of an earlier form of the program, see 7:665.

[618]

College Board On-Campus SAT Subject Test in Modern Hebrew.

Purpose: To measure content knowledge in Hebrew.
Population: Entering college freshmen
Publication Dates: 1962–2005.
Scores: Total (200–800) score only.
Administration: Group or individual.
Price Data: Rental fee per student available from publisher.
Time: 60 minutes.
Comments: Available for local administration and scoring by higher educational institutions; previously known as College Board One-Hour Achievement Test in Modern Hebrew and College Placement Test.
Author: Educational Testing Service.
Publisher: The College Board.
Cross References: For a review of an earlier form of the program, see 7:665.

[619]

College Board On-Campus SAT Subject Test in Physics.

Purpose: To measure content knowledge in physics.
Population: Entering college freshmen.
Publication Dates: 1962–2005.
Score: Total (200–800).

Administration: Group or individual.
Price Data: Rental fee per student available from publisher.
Time: 60 minutes.
Comments: Available for local administration and scoring by higher educational institutions; previously known as College Board One-Hour Achievement Test in Physics.
Author: Educational Testing Service.
Publisher: The College Board.
Cross References: See T5:587 (1 reference); for a review of an earlier form of the program, see 7:665.

[620]

College Board On-Campus SAT Subject Test in Spanish.

Purpose: To measure content knowledge in Spanish.
Population: Entering college freshmen.
Publication Dates: 1962–2005.
Score: Total (200–800).
Administration: Group or individual.
Price Data: Rental fee per student available from publisher.
Time: (60) minutes.
Comments: Available for local administration and scoring by higher educational institutions; previously known as College Board One-Hour Achievement Test in Spanish Reading.
Author: Educational Testing Service.
Publisher: The College Board.
Cross References: See 8:161 (1 reference) and 7:316 (1 reference); for a review of an earlier form of the program, see 7:665.

[621]

College Board On-Campus SAT Subject Test in Spanish with Listening.

Purpose: To measure content knowledge in Spanish.
Population: Entering college freshmen.
Publication Dates: 1971–2005.
Scores, 3: Subscores in Listening, Reading (20–80), Total (200–800).
Administration: Group or individual.
Price Data: Rental fee per student available from publisher.
Time: (60) minutes.
Comments: Available for local administration and scoring by higher educational institutions; CD player and earphones required; previously known as College Board One-Hour Achievement Test in Spanish with Listening and College Placement Test.
Author: Educational Testing Service.
Publisher: The College Board.
Cross References: For a review of an earlier form of the program, see 7:665.

[622]

College Board On-Campus SAT Subject Test in U.S. History.

Purpose: To measure content knowledge in United States History.
Population: Entering college freshmen.
Publication Dates: 1965–2005.
Scores: Total (200–800).
Administration: Group or individual.
Price Data: Rental fee per student available from publisher.
Time: (60) minutes.
Comments: Available for local administration and scoring by higher educational institutions; previously known as College Board One-Hour Achievement Test in American History and Social Studies.
Author: Educational Testing Service.
Publisher: The College Board.
Cross References: For a review by Howard R. Anderson of an earlier form, see 6:966; for a review by Ralph W. Tyler, see 5:786; for a review by Robert L. Thorndike, see 4:662; for a review of an earlier form of the program, see 7:665.

[623]

College Board On-Campus SAT Subject Test in World History.

Purpose: To measure content knowledge in World History.
Population: Entering college freshmen.
Publication Dates: 1963–2005.
Scores: Total (200–800).
Administration: Group or individual.
Price Data: Rental fee per student available from publisher.
Time: 60 minutes.
Comments: Available for local administration and scoring by higher educational institutions; previously known as College Board One-Hour Achievement Test in World History.
Author: Educational Testing Service.
Publisher: The College Board.
Cross References: For a review by David K. Heenan of an earlier form, see 6:967; for a review of an earlier form of the program, see 7:665.

[624]

College Board On-Campus SAT Subject Test in Writing.

Purpose: To measure students' writing skills.
Population: Entering college freshmen.
Publication Dates: 1962–2005.
Scores: Subscores in Multiple Choice, Writing Sample (20–80), Total (200–800).

Administration: Group or individual.
Price Data: Rental fee per student available from publisher.
Time: 60 minutes (20-minute essay and 40-minute multiple-choice).
Comments: Administration and scoring by higher educational institutions; previously known as College Board One-Hour Achievement Test in Writing and College Placement Test; includes a writing sample and multiple-choice questions.
Author: Educational Testing Service.
Publisher: The College Board.
Cross References: See 8:48 (20 references); for a review by John C. Sherwood of an earlier form, see 7:190 (3 references); for reviews by Charlotte Croon Davis, Robert C. Pooley, and Holland Roberts of earlier forms, see 6:287; for a review by Charlotte Croon Davis with Frederick B. Davis, see 4:178. For a review of an earlier form of the program, see 7:665.

[625]

College Board On-Campus SAT Subject Tests in Mathematics Level 1 and Level 2.

Purpose: To measure content knowledge in mathematics.
Population: Entering college freshmen.
Publication Dates: 1964–2005.
Score: Total (200–800).
Administration: Group or individual.
Price Data: Rental fee per student available from publisher.
Time: 60 minutes for each level.
Comments: Available for local administration and scoring by higher educational institutions; a calculator at least at the level of a scientific calculator is required to solve some, but not all, of the questions; previously known as College Board One-Hour Achievement Test in Mathematics.
Author: Educational Testing Service.
Publisher: The College Board.
Cross References: See T5:585 (1 reference); for a review of an earlier form of the program, see 7:665.

[626]

College Board On-Campus Tests.

Purpose: A portfolio of assessments, programs, and services designed to help higher education personnel determine the placement levels and remediation requirements of incoming, as well as continuing, students.
Population: Entering and continuing college students.
Publication Dates: 1989-2001.
Scores: Provides data in the following assessment areas: Course Placement, Remediation, Selection, Instruction, Guidance, and Counseling. Also used for Exemption by some institutions of higher education.

Administration: Group or individual.

Price Data: Available from publisher.

Comments: Through its On-Campus Testing Program, the College Board offers institutions of higher education the following: Descriptive Tests System (DTS), Institutional SAT Program, Test of Standard Written English (two forms), Essay Reading Service, and special contracts for state departments of education and consortia of higher education institutions; previously entitled Multiple Assessments, Programs, and Services (MAPS) of the College Board.

Author: Educational Testing Service.

Publisher: Educational Testing Service and the College Board.

Cross References: See T5:1746 (1 reference).

[627]

College Board SAT Program.

Purpose: To provide "tests and related educational services for students who plan to continue their education beyond high school."

Population: Candidates for college entrance.

Publication Dates: 1901–2005.

Acronym: SAT Program.

Scores: Price data is available from the publisher for priced and free materials including technical report (1984, 225 pages), supervisor's manual (1998, 69 pages), student bulletins, test familiarization material for students, score use and interpretation booklets for counselors and admissions officers, summary report guides for high schools and for colleges, state and national reports on college-bound seniors, guide to the College Board Admitted Student Evaluation Service (formerly Validity Study Service), and test and technical data; examination fees include reporting of scores to the candidate's secondary school and 1–4 colleges and/or scholarship services.

Administration: Group.

Price Data: Price data is available from the publisher for priced and free materials including technical report (1984, 225 pages), supervisor's manual (1998, 69 pages), student bulletins, test familiarization material for students, score use and interpretation booklets for counselors and admissions officers, summary report guides for high schools and for colleges, state and national reports on college-bound seniors, guide to the College Board Admitted Student Evaluation Service (formerly Validity Study Service), and test and technical data; examination fees include reporting of scores to the candidate's secondary school and 1–4 colleges and/or scholarship services.

Comments: Formerly called the College Board Admissions Testing Program; the SAT I: Reasoning Test is administered 7 times annually (January, March or April, May, June, October, November, December) at centers established by the publisher; The SAT II: Subject Tests are administered 6 times annually (January, May, June, October, November, December) at centers established

by the publisher, though not all tests are available at each administration; English Language Proficiency Test (ELPT) is also offered in April in participating secondary schools; Student Descriptive Questionnaire provides background information to colleges and scholarship services; special administration arrangements available for students with disabilities, including Braille, cassette tape, regular type, and large-type formats, individualized testing, and additional testing time. The SAT I and SAT II score scales were rescaled in 1995; equivalence tables are available for converting scores from the original scale to the new recentered scale. SAT I and SAT II forms are available for local administration and scoring by higher educational institutions through the College Entry-Level Assessment (CELA) Program.

Author: Educational Testing Service.

Publisher: The College Board.

a) COLLEGE BOARD SAT REASONING TEST.

Publication Dates: 1926–1999.

Price Data: Examination fee per candidate available from publisher. Price data for guidelines on the uses of College Board test scores and related data, guide to the College Board Admitted Student Evaluation Service (formerly the Validity Study Service), Technical Handbook, SAT Program Handbooks, Student Bulletins, Taking the SAT I, test preparation materials and software, SAT I Question and Answer Service, SAT I Student Answer Service, SAT Score Verification Service, and clerical scoring service are all available from the publisher.

Time: (180) minutes.

Comments: The SAT I: Reasoning Test replaced the College Board Scholastic Aptitude Test and the Test of Standard Written English in 1994. Scores are reported for Verbal and Mathematical sections of the SAT I. No subscores are provided. Performance data by item type/content available for Verbal and Mathematics beginning in 1994.

b) COLLEGE BOARD SAT SUBJECT TESTS.

Publication Dates: 1901–1999.

Scores: 21 tests in 18 subjects: Writing (including an essay at every national administration), Literature, American History & Social Studies, World History, Mathematics [Math Level IC, Math Level IIC], Biology E/M [Ecological/Molecular], Chemistry, Physics, French (reading only), French (reading and listening), German (reading only), German (reading and listening), Spanish (reading only), Spanish (reading and listening), Modern Hebrew, Italian, Latin, Japanese (reading and listening), Chinese (reading and listening), Korean (reading and listening), and English Language Proficiency.

Price Data: Examination fees per candidate available from publisher. Price data for guidelines on the uses of College Board test scores and related data, guide to the College Board Admitted Student Evaluation Service (formerly the Validity Study

Service), Writing Sample Copy Service, technical handbook, SAT Program Handbooks, student bulletins, Taking the SAT II, test and preparation materials, and clerical scoring service are all available from the publisher.

Time: (60) minutes.

Comments: Formerly called the College Board Achievement Tests; candidate elects 1 to 3 tests as specified by individual college or scholarship program requirments; candidates have the option of reviewing their SAT II scores prior to deciding whether or not to have these scores reported to colleges or scholarship services. The administration schedule of each Subject Test is available from the publisher.

Cross References: See T5:615 (55 references), T3:500 (3 references), 8:472 (6 references), T2:1048 (9 references), and 7:663 (16 references); for reviews by Benno G. Fricke and Dean K. Whitla of an earlier program, see 6:760 (12 references); see also 5:599 (3 references) and 4:526 (9 references). For reviews of individual tests, see 8:46 (2 reviews), 8:128 (1 review), 8:147 (1 review), 8:258 (2 reviews), 7:344 (2 reviews), 6:287 (3 reviews, 6:289 (1 review), 6:383 (1 review), 6:384 (2 reviews), 6:449 (2 reviews), 6:568 (1 review), 6:569 (1 review), 6:914 (1 review), 6:966 (1 review), 6:967 (1 review), 5:272 (1 review), 5:277 (1 review), 5:280 (1 review), 5:318 (1 review), 5:723 (1 review), 5:742 (1 review), 5:749 (1 review), 5:786 (1 review), 4:178 (1 review), 4:237 (1 review), 4:244 (1 review), 4:250 (1 review), 4:285 (1 review), 4:367 (1 review), 4:368 (1 review), 4:600 (1 review), 4:617 (1 review), 4:633 (1 review), and 4:662 (1 review).

[628]

College Board SAT Subject Test in Biology.

Purpose: To measure content knowledge in biology.
Population: Candidates for college entrance with one-year courses in biology and algebra.
Publication Dates: 1915–2005.
Scores: Total (200–800).
Administration: Group.
Price Data: Available from publisher.
Time: Administration time not reported.
Comments: Test administered for the last time in May 1999 at centers established by publisher; available for local administration and scoring by higher educational institutions through the College Entry-Level Assessment (CELA) Program; replaces College Board Achievement Test in Biology.
Authors: Program administered by the College Board and Educational Testing Service.
Publisher: The College Board.
Cross References: See 8:833 (1 reference), 7:813 (2 references), and 6:892 (3 references); for a review by Elizabeth Hagen of an earlier form, see 5:723; for a review by Clark W. Horton, see 4:600. For reviews of an earlier form of the testing program, see 6:760 (2 reviews).

[629]

College Board SAT Subject Test in Biology E/M.

Purpose: To measure content knowledge in biology.
Population: Candidates for college entrance with one-year courses in biology and algebra.
Publication Dates: 1998–2005.
Scores: Total score only.
Administration: Group.
Price Data: Available from publisher.
Time: 60 minutes
Comments: Administered 6 times annually beginning in 1999 (October, November, December, January, May, and June) at centers established by publisher; candidates take a core set of questions and then select a specialized section of questions in either ecological or molecular biology; available for local administration and scoring by higher educational institutions through the College Entry-Level Assessment (CELA) Program; replaces College Board SAT II: Subject Test in Biology.
Authors: Program administered by the College Board and Educational Testing Service.
Publisher: The College Board.

[630]

College Board SAT Subject Test in Chemistry.

Purpose: To measure content knowledge in chemistry.
Population: Candidates for college entrance with one-year course in introductory chemistry at the college-preparatory level.
Publication Dates: 1937–2005.
Scores: Total (200–800) score only.
Administration: Group.
Price Data: Available from publisher.
Time: 60 minutes.
Comments: Test administered 6 times annually (January, May, June, October, November, December) at centers established by publisher; available for local administration and scoring by higher educational institutions through the College Entry-Level Assessment (CELA) Program.
Authors: Program administered by the College Board and Educational Testing Service.
Publisher: The College Board.
Cross References: See T4:567 (1 reference) and 7:844 (3 references); for a review by William Hered of earlier forms, see 6:914 (4 references); for a review by Max D. Engelhart, see 5:742 (2 references); for a review by Evelyn Raskin, see 4:617 (4 references). For reviews of an earlier form of the testing program, see 6:760 (2 reviews).

[631]

College Board SAT Subject Test in Chinese with Listening.

Purpose: To measure content knowledge in Chinese.

Population: Candidates for college entrance with 2–4 years high school Chinese (Mandarin).
Publication Dates: 1994–2005.
Scores: 4: Usage, Listening, Reading, Total.
Administration: Group.
Price Data: Available from publisher.
Comments: Test administered once annually (November) at centers established by publisher; test takers are required to bring a CD player with earphones for use on the Listening section of the test; available for local administration and scoring by higher educational institutions through the College Entry-Level Assessment (CELA) Program.
Authors: Program administered by the College Board and Educational Testing Service.
Publisher: The College Board.

[632]

College Board SAT Subject Test in French.

Purpose: To measure content knowledge in French.
Population: Candidates for college entrance with 2-4 years of high school French.
Publication Dates: 1937–2005.
Scores: Total (200–800) score only.
Administration: Group.
Price Data: Available from publisher.
Time: 60 minutes.
Comments: Test administered 6 times annually (January, May, June, October, November, December) at centers established by publisher; available for local administration and scoring by higher educational institutions through the College Entry-Level Assessment (CELA) Program; replaces College Board Achievement Test in French.
Authors: Program administered by the College Board and Educational Testing Service.
Publisher: The College Board.
Cross References: For a review by Helen L. Jorstad of an earlier form, see 8:116; see also 6:366 (4 references) and 5:263 (2 references); for a review by Walter V. Kaulfers of earlier forms, see 4:237 (7 references). For reviews of an earlier form of the testing program, see 6:760 (2 reviews).

[633]

College Board SAT Subject Test in French with Listening.

Purpose: To measure content knowledge in French.
Population: Candidates for college entrance with 3–4 years high school French.
Publication Dates: 1994–2005.
Scores, 3: subscores in Listening, Reading (20–80), and Total (200–800).
Administration: Group.
Price Data: Available from publisher.
Time: Administration time not reported.

Comments: Test administered once annually (November) at centers established by publisher; test takers are required to bring a CD player with earphones for use on the Listening section of the test; available for local administration and scoring by higher educational institutions through the College Entry-Level Assessment (CELA) Program.
Authors: Program administered by the College Board and Educational Testing Service.
Publisher: The College Board.

[634]

College Board SAT Subject Test in German.

Purpose: To measure content knowledge in German.
Population: Candidates for college entrance with 2–4 years high school German.
Publication Dates: 1937–2005.
Scores: Total (200–800) score only.
Administration: Group.
Price Data: Available from publisher.
Time: 60 minutes.
Comments: Test administered once annually (June) at centers established by publisher; available for local administration and scoring by higher educational institutions through the College Entry-Level Assessment (CELA) Program; replaces College Board Achievement Test in German.
Authors: Program administered by the College Board and Educational Testing Service.
Publisher: The College Board.
Cross References: For a review by Randall L. Jones of an earlier form, see 8:128; for a review by Gilbert C. Kettelkamp of earlier forms, see 6:383; for a review by Harold B. Dunkel, see 5:272 (3 references); for a review by Herbert Shueler, see 4:244 (3 references). For reviews of an earlier form of the testing program, see 6:760 (2 reviews).

[635]

College Board SAT Subject Test in German with Listening.

Purpose: To measure content knowledge in German.
Population: Candidates for college entrance with 2–4 years in high school German.
Publication Dates: 1994–2005.
Scores, 3: subscores in Listening, Reading (20–80), and Total (200–800).
Administration: Group.
Price Data: Available from publisher.
Time: 60 minutes.
Comments: Test administered once annually (November) at centers established by publisher; test takers are required to bring a CD player with earphones for use on the Listening section of the test; available for local administration and scoring by higher educational

institutions through the College Entry-Level Assessment (CELA) Program.
Authors: Program administered by the College Board and Educational Testing Service.
Publisher: The College Board.

[636]

College Board SAT Subject Test in Italian.

Purpose: To measure content knowledge in Italian.
Population: Candidates for college entrance with 2–4 years high school Italian.
Publication Dates: 1990–2005.
Scores: Total score only (200–800).
Administration: Group.
Price Data: Available from publisher.
Comments: Test administered 6 times annually (January, May, June, October, November, December) at centers established by publisher; available for local administration and scoring by higher educational institutions through the College Entry-Level Assessment (CELA) Program; replaces College Board Achievement Test in Italian.
Authors: Program administered by the College Board and Educational Testing Service.
Publisher: The College Board.

[637]

College Board SAT Subject Test in Japanese with Listening.

Purpose: To measure content knowledge in Japanese.
Population: Candidates for college entrance with 2–4 years high school Japanese.
Publication Dates: 1993–2005.
Scores, 4: Usage, Listening, Reading, Total.
Administration: Group.
Price Data: Available from publisher.
Comments: Test administered once annually (November) at centers established by the publisher; test takers required to bring a CD player with earphones for use on the Listening section of the test; available for local administration and scoring by higher educational institutions through the College Entry-Level Assessment (CELA) Program.
Authors: Program administered by the College Board and Educational Testing Service.
Publisher: The College Board.

[638]

College Board SAT Subject Test in Korean with Listening.

Purpose: To measure content knowledge in Korean.
Population: Candidates for college entrance with 2–4 years high school Korean.
Publication Dates: 1994–2005.
Scores, 4: Usage, Listening, Reading (20–80), Total (200–800).

Administration: Group.
Price Data: Available from publisher.
Time: 60 minutes.
Comments: Test administered once annually (November) at centers established by publisher; test takers are required to bring a CD player with earphones for use on the Listening section of the test; available for local administration and scoring by higher educational institutions through the College Entry-Level Assessment (CELA) Program.
Authors: Program administered by the College Board and Educational Testing Service.
Publisher: The College Board.

[639]

College Board SAT Subject Test in Latin.

Purpose: To measure content knowledge in Latin.
Population: Candidates for college entrance with 2–4 years high school Latin.
Publication Dates: 1937–2005.
Scores: Total score only.
Administration: Group.
Price Data: Available from publisher.
Time: 60 minutes
Comments: Test administered 6 times annually (January, May, June, October, November, December) at centers established by publisher; available for local administration and scoring by higher educational institutions through the College Entry-Level Assessment (CELA) Program; replaces College Board Achievement Test in Latin.
Authors: Program administered by the College Board and Educational Testing Service.
Publisher: The College Board.
Cross References: For a review by Konrad Gries of an earlier form, see 5:280 (1 reference); for a review by Harold B. Dunkel, see 4:250 (2 references). For reviews of an earlier form of the testing program, see 6:760 (2 reviews).

[640]

College Board SAT Subject Test in Literature.

Purpose: To measure content knowledge in Literature.
Population: Candidates for college entrance.
Publication Dates: 1968–2005.
Scores: Total (200–800) score only.
Administration: Group.
Price Data: Available from publisher.
Time: 60 minutes.
Comments: Test administered 6 times annually (January, May, June, October, November, December) at centers established by publisher; available for local administration and scoring by higher educational institutions through the College Entry-Level Assessment (CELA) Program; replaces College Board Achievement Test in Literature.

Authors: Program administered by the College Board and Educational Testing Service.
Publisher: The College Board.
Cross References: See T5:604 (1 reference) and 7:217 (2 references). For reviews of an earlier form of the testing program, see 6:760 (2 reviews).

[641]

College Board SAT Subject Test in Modern Hebrew.

Purpose: To measure content knowledge in Modern Hebrew.
Population: Candidates for college entrance with 2–4 years high school Hebrew.
Publication Dates: 1989–2005.
Scores: Total (200–800) score only.
Administration: Group.
Price Data: Available from publisher.
Time: 60 minutes.
Comments: Test administered 6 times annually (January, May, June, October, November, December) at centers established by publisher; available for local administration and scoring by higher educational institutions through the College Entry-Level Assessment (CELA) Program; replaces College Board Achievement Test in Hebrew.
Authors: Program administered by the College Board and Educational Testing Service.
Publisher: The College Board.
Cross References: For reviews of an earlier form of the testing program, see 6:760 (2 reviews).

[642]

College Board SAT Subject Test in Physics.

Purpose: To measure content knowledge in physics.
Population: Candidates for college entrance with one-year course in introductory physics at the college-preparatory level.
Publication Dates: 1937–2005.
Scores: Total (200–800) score only.
Administration: Group.
Price Data: Available from publisher.
Time: 60 minutes.
Comments: Test administered 6 times annually (January, May, June, October, November, December) at centers established by publisher; available for local administration and scoring by higher educational institutions through the College Entry-Level Assessment (CELA) Program; replaces College Board Achievement Test in Physics.
Authors: Program administered by the College Board and Educational Testing Service.
Publisher: The College Board.
Cross References: See T4:574 (2 reference, 8:863 (1 reference), 7:855 (2 references), and 6:926 (4 references); for a review by Theodore G. Phillips of an earlier form, see 5:749 (2 references); for a review by Palmer

O. Johnson, see 4:633 (3 references). For reviews of an earlier form of the testing program, see 6:760 (2 reviews).

[643]

College Board SAT Subject Test in Spanish.

Purpose: To measure content knowledge in Spanish.
Population: Candidates for college entrance with 2–4 years high school Spanish.
Publication Dates: 1937–2005.
Scores: Total (200–800) score only.
Administration: Group.
Price Data: Available from publisher.
Time: 60 minutes.
Comments: Test administered 6 times annually (January, May, June, October, November, December) at centers established by publisher; available for local administration and scoring by higher educational institutions through the College Entry-Level Assessment (CELA) Program; replaces College Board Achievement Test in Spanish.
Authors: Program administered by the College Board and Educational Testing Service.
Publisher: The College Board.
Cross References: See 6:419 (1 reference), 5:287 (1 reference), and 4:259 (3 references) for information on earlier forms. For reviews of an earlier form of the testing program, see 6:760 (2 reviews).

[644]

College Board SAT Subject Test in Spanish with Listening.

Purpose: To measure content knowledge in Spanish.
Population: Candidates for college entrance with 3–4 years high school Spanish.
Publication Dates: 1994–2005.
Scores, 3: Subscores in Listening, Reading (20–80), Total (200–800).
Administration: Group.
Price Data: Available from publisher.
Time: 60 minutes.
Comments: Test administered once annually (November) at centers established by publisher; test takers required to bring a CD player with earphones for use on the Listening section of the test; available for local administration and scoring by higher educational institutions through the College Entry-Level Assessment (CELA) Program.
Authors: Program administered by the College Board and Educational Testing Service.
Publisher: The College Board.

[645]

College Board SAT Subject Test in U.S. History.

Purpose: To measure content knowledge in American history and social studies.

Population: Candidates for college entrance with one-year American history course at the college-preparatory level.
Publication Dates: 1937–2005.
Scores: Total scores reported on the College Board 200–800 scale, subscores reported on a 20–80 scale; ELPT total score reported on a 901–999 scale; ELPT subscores reported on a 1–50 scale.
Administration: Group.
Price Data: Available from publisher.
Time: Administration time not reported.
Comments: Test administered 6 times annually (January, May, June, October, November, December) at centers established by publisher; available for local administration and scoring by higher educational institutions through the College Entry-Level Assessment (CELA) programs; replaces College Board Achievement Test in American History and Social Studies.
Author: Program administered by The College Board and Educational Testing Service.
Publisher: The College Board.
Cross References: See T4:565 (1 reference) and T2:1939 (1 reference); for a review by Howard R. Anderson of earlier forms, see 6:966; for a review by Ralph W. Tyler, see 5:786 (3 references); for a review by Robert L. Thorndike, see 4:662 (6 references). For reviews of an earlier form of the testing program, see 6:760 (2 reviews).

[646]

College Board SAT Subject Test in World History.

Purpose: To measure content knowledge in world history.
Population: Candidates for college entrance.
Publication Dates: 1937–2005.
Scores: Total (200–800) only.
Administration: Group.
Price Data: Available from publisher.
Time: 60 minutes.
Comments: Test administered 2 times annually (June, December) at centers established by publisher; available for local administration and scoring by higher educational institutions through the College Entry-Level Assessment (CELA) Program; replaces College Board Achievement Test in European History and World Cultures.
Authors: Program administered by the College Board and Educational Testing Service.
Publisher: The College Board.
Cross References: For a review by David K. Heenan of an earlier form, see 6:967. For reviews of an earlier form of the testing program, see 6:760 (2 reviews).

[647]

College Board SAT Test.

Purpose: A curriculum-based, college readiness test, which tests the academic skills and knowledge that students acquire in high school and their ability to apply their knowledge.

Population: Candidates for college entrance.
Publication Dates: 1926–2005.
Acronym: SAT.
Scores, 2: Critical Reading, Mathematics, and Writing reported on the College Board 200–800 scale.
Administration: Group.
Forms: Forms issued annually.
Price Data: Examination fees per candidate available from publisher; price data for guidelines on the uses of College Board test scores and related data, guide to the College Board Admitted Student Evaluation Service (formerly the Validity Study Service), technical handbook, SAT Program handbooks, student bulletins, Taking the SAT, test and technical data, SAT Question and Answer Service, SAT Student Answer Service, SAT Score Verification Service, and clerical scoring service are all available from the publisher.
Time: 225 minutes.
Comments: The SAT I is administered 7 times annually (January, March or April, May, June, October, November, and December) at centers established by the publisher. The SAT Reasoning Test replaced the College Board Scholastic Aptitude Test and Test of Standard Written English in 1994. Scores are reported for Verbal, Mathematical, and Writing sections of the SAT. Performance data by item type/content are available for Verbal and Math beginning in 1994. The SAT I scale was rescaled in 1995; equivalence tables are available for converting scores from one scale to another. SAT forms are available for local administration and scoring through the College Entry-Level Assessment (CELA) Program. Special administration arrangements available for students with disabilities, including Braille, cassette tape, regular type and large-type formats, individualized testing, and additional testing time.
Authors: The College Board and Educational Testing Service.
Publisher: The College Board.
Cross References: See T5:592 (107 references) and T4:564 (167 references); for reviews by Sanford J. Cohn and Lee J. Cronbach of an earlier edition, see 9:244 (31 references); see T3:501 (152 references), 8:182 (217 references), and T2:357 (148 references); for reviews by Philip H. Dubois and Wimburn L. Wallace of an earlier form, see 7:344 (298 references); for reviews by John E. Bowers and Wayne S. Zimmerman, see 6:449 (79 references); for a review by John T. Dailey, see 5:318 (20 references); for a review by Frederick B. Davis, see 4:285 (22 references). For reviews of the testing program, see 6:760 (2 reviews).

[648]

College Board SAT II: English Language Proficiency Test.

Purpose: To measure understanding of spoken and written standard American English and ability to use English in the classroom and in daily life.

Population: Candidates for college entrance.
Publication Dates: 1997–2005.
Acronym: ELPT.
Scores: 3 subscores in Listening, Reading (1–50), and Total (901–999); in addition proficiency ratings (below intermediate to advanced high or higher) are provided for Listening and Reading.
Administration: Group.
Price Data: Available from publisher.
Time: Administration time not reported.
Comments: Test administered once annually (November) at centers established by the publisher; also administered once annually (April) in participating high schools; test takers are required to bring a cassette player with earphones for use on the Listening section of the test; available for local administration and scoring by higher-educational institutions through the College Entry-Level Assessment (CELA) Program; the final administration of this test was in January 2005.
Authors: Program administered by the College Board and Educational Testing Service.
Publisher: The College Board.

[649]

College Board Subject Test in Mathematics Level 1 and Mathematics Level 2.

Purpose: To measure content knowledge in mathematics.
Population: Candidates for college entrance.
Publication Dates: 1937–2005.
Scores: Total (200–800) score only.
Administration: Group.
Price Data: Available from publisher.
Time: 60 minutes.
Comments: For Math Level I, administered to candidates with 3 years of college-preparatory math (2 years algebra, 1 year of geometry); for Math Level II, administered to candidates with more than 3 years of college-preparatory Math (2 years algebra, 1 year geometry, and precalculus and/or trigonometry); test administered 6 times annually (January, May, June, October, November, December) at centers established by publisher; available for local administration and scoring by higher educational institutions through the College Entry-Level Assessment (CELA) Program; a calculator at least at the level of a scientific calculator is required to solve some, but not all, of the questions; replaces College Board Achievement Tests in Mathematics, the final administration of the Math Level 2 test was January 1994; it was replaced by the Math Level IIC Subject Test at all administrations beginning in May 1994; the final administration of Math Level 1 test was January 1998; it was replaced by the Math Level IC Subject Test at all administrations beginning May 1998.
Author: Program administered by the College Board and Educational Testing Service.

Publisher: The College Board.
Cross References: See T4:578 (2 references); for reviews by Jeremy Kilpatrick and Peter A. Lappan, Jr. of Level 1, see 8:258 (4 references); see also 7:456 (4 references). For additional information concerning Level 2, see 8:259 (1 reference); see also 7:457 (1 reference). For reviews of an earlier form of the testing program, see 6:760 (2 reviews).

[650]

College English Test: National Achievement Tests.

Purpose: Designed to measure the student's mastery of elements of the English language.
Population: High school and college freshmen.
Publication Dates: 1937–1943.
Scores, 7: Punctuation, Capitalization, Language Usage, Sentence Structure, Modifiers, Miscellaneous Principles, Total.
Administration: Group.
Forms, 2: A, B.
Price Data: Available from publisher.
Time: 45(50) minutes.
Author: A. C. Jordan.
Publisher: Psychometric Affiliates.
Cross References: For a review by Osmond E. Palmer, see 5:178; for reviews by Constance M. McCullough and Robert W. Howard, see 2:1269.1.

[651]

College Level Examination Program.

Purpose: Designed as a way for college accreditation, advanced placement, or assessment of educational attainment.
Population: 1–2 years of college or equivalent.
Publication Dates: 1964–2002.
Acronym: CLEP.
Price Data: Available from publisher.
Time: (90) minutes per test.
Comments: Tests administered at 1,100 centers throughout the United States as well as internationally; as of July, 2001 administered as a computer-based program; program administered by the College Board and Educational Testing Service.
Author: Educational Testing Service.
Publisher: Educational Testing Service.

   a) BUSINESS.
      1) *Information Systems and Computer Applications.*
      2) *Principles of Management.*
      3) *Principles of Accounting.*
      4) *Introductory Business Law.*
      5) *Principles of Marketing.*
   b) COMPOSITION AND LITERATURE.
Comments: Composition and Literature tests have optional essay supplement that is scored by the college.

1) *American Literature.*
2) *Analyzing and Interpreting Literature.*
3) *Freshman College Composition.*
4) *English Literature.*
5) *English Composition (with and without essay).*
Comments: English Composition with Essay scored by faculty for CLEP.
6) *Humanities.*
c) FOREIGN LANGUAGES.
  1) *College French, Levels 1 and 2.*
  2) *College German, Levels 1 and 2.*
  3) *College Spanish, Levels 1 and 2.*
d) HISTORY AND SOCIAL SCIENCES.
  1) *American Government.*
  2) *History of the United States I: Early Coloniza-tion to 1877.*
  3) *History of the United States II: 1865 to the Present.*
  4) *Educational Psychology.*
  5) *Introductory Psychology.*
  6) *Human Growth and Development.*
  7) *Principles of Macroeconomics.*
  8) *Principles of Microeconomics.*
  9) *Introductory Sociology.*
  10) *Western Civilization I: Ancient Near East to 1648.*
  11) *Western Civilization II: 1648 to the Present.*
  12) *Social Sciences and History.*
e) SCIENCE AND MATHEMATICS.
  1) *Calculus with Elementary Functions.*
  2) *College Algebra.*
  3) *College Algebra–Trigonometry.*
  4) *General Biology.*
  5) *General Chemistry.*
  6) *Trigonometry.*
  7) *Mathematics.*
  8) *Natural Sciences.*

Cross References: See 9:245 (1 reference) and T3:506 (7 references); for reviews by Paul L. Dressel, David A. Frisbie, and Wimburn L. Wallace of an earlier program, see 8:473 (15 references); for reviews of the General Examinations, see 8:8 (2 reviews); for reviews of the separate Subject Examinations, see 8:43 (1 review), 8:44 (1 review), 8:64 (1 review), 8:65 (1 review), 8:66 (1 review), 8:255 (1 review), 8:256 (1 review), 8:297 (1 review), 8:365 (1 review), 8:460 (1 review), 8:832 (1 review), 8:847 (1 review), 8:911 (1 review), , 8:919 (1 review), 8:1119 (1 review), and 8:1120 (1 review); see also T2:1050 (4 references); for reviews by Alexander W. Astin, Benjamin S. Bloom, and Warren G. Findley, see 7:664 (7 references).

[652]

College Student Expectations Questionnaire, Second Edition.

Purpose: Designed to evaluate new students' expectations for college including their goals, motivations, and future plans for various college experiences.

Population: Precollege students and first-year students at the beginning of the first semester.
Publication Dates: 1997–2011.
Acronym: CSXQ.
Scores, 16: Background Information, College Activities Scales (Library and Information Technology, Experiences with Faculty, Course Learning, Writing, Campus Facilities, Clubs, Organizations, Service Projects, Student Acquaintances, Scientific and Quantitative Experiences, Conversations), Reading/Writing, Satisfaction, The College Environment, Additional Questions.
Administration: Group.
Price Data, 2011: $200–$500 administration fee depending on mode of administration, includes all survey processing/setup, one customized institutional report containing means, frequency and descriptive information of survey results arrayed by gender, and an electronic data file containing all student responses; $2 per paper survey; $2.75 per student in a self-service online administration where the institution sends all invitations and communications to students; $3 per student in a full-service online administration where CSEQ sends all invitations and communications to students; $150 per hour for special additional analysis.
Time: (10–15) minutes.
Comments: Adapted from the College Student Experiences Questionnaire (CSEQ; 653); longitudinal assessments are possible by comparing results from the CSXQ with data from the CSEQ completed by the same students near the end of the first year or later in the college experience.
Authors: George D. Kuh and C. Robert Pace.
Publisher: Indiana University Center for Postsecondary Research.

[653]

College Student Experiences Questionnaire, Fourth Edition.

Purpose: Designed to measure (a) the quality of effort undergraduate students invest in using educational resources and opportunities provided for their learning and development, (b) the students' perceptions of how much the campus environment emphasizes a diverse set of educational priorities, and (c) how the students' efforts and perceptions relate to personal estimates of progress made toward a holistic set of learning outcomes.
Population: Undergraduate college students.
Publication Dates: 1979-2011.
Acronym: CSEQ.
Scores, 19: Background Information, College Activities Scales (Library, Computer and Information Technology, Course Learning, Writing Experiences, Experiences with Faculty, Art, Music and Theater, Campus Facilities, Clubs and Organizations, Personal Experiences, Student Acquaintances, Scientific and Quantitative Experiences, Conversations), Reading/Writing, Satisfaction, The College Environment, Estimate of Gains, Additional Questions.

Administration: Group.

Price Data, 2011: $200–$500 administration fee depending on mode of administration, includes all survey processing/setup, one customized institutional report containing means, frequency and descriptive information of survey results arrayed by gender, and an electronic data file containing all student responses; $2 per paper survey; $2.75 per student in a self-service online administration where the institution sends all invitations and communications to students; $3 per student in a full-service online administration where CSEQ sends all invitations and communications to students; $150 per hour for special additional analysis.

Time: (30) minutes.

Authors: C. Robert Pace and George D. Kuh.

Publisher: Indiana University Center for Postsecondary Research.

Cross References: For reviews by Kurt F. Geisinger and by M. David Miller and J. Monroe Miller, see 16:58; see also T5:620 (6 references) and T4:588 (4 references); for reviews by David A. Decoster and Susan McCammon of an earlier edition, see 10:67; for reviews by Robert D. Brown and John K. Miller, see 9:246 (1 reference).

[654]

College Student Inventory [part of the Retention Management System].

Purpose: Designed to assess "a variety of motives and background information related to college success," improved student retention, and enhancing student advising effectiveness.

Population: First-year undergraduate college students.

Publication Date: 1988.

Acronym: CSI.

Scores, 4: Academic Motivation (Study Habits, Intellectual Interests, Academic Confidence, Desire to Finish College, Attitude Toward Educators), Social Motivation (Self-Reliance, Sociability, Leadership), General Coping Ability (Ease of Transition, Family Emotional Support, Openness, Career Planning, Sense of Financial Security), Receptivity to Support Services (Academic Assistance, Personal Counseling, Social Enhancement, Career Counseling).

Administration: Group.

Price Data: Available from publisher.

Time: (60) minutes.

Author: Michael L. Stratil.

Publisher: Noel-Levitz.

Cross References: For reviews by Michael H. Campbell and Thomas P. Hogan, see 16:59.

[655]

College Survival and Success Scale.

Purpose: Designed to "identify the concerns college students are experiencing or the concerns that prospective college students can anticipate."

Population: Individuals interested in attending college, or agencies that work with individuals interested in attending college.

Publication Date: 2006.

Acronym: CSSS.

Scores, 5: Commitment to Education, Self-/Resource-Management Skills, Interpersonal/Social Skills, Academic Success Skills, Career Planning Skills.

Administration: Individual or group.

Price Data, 2006: $37.95 per complete kit including 25 test booklets and 1 administrator's guide (8 pages).

Time: (15-25) minutes.

Author: John Liptak.

Publisher: JIST Publishing, Inc.

Cross References: For a review by Heidi M. Carty, see 17:50.

[656]

College-to-Career Transition Inventory.

Purpose: Designed to "help students pinpoint the false beliefs and potential gaps in knowledge and skills that might prevent them from finding a job, further advancing their education, and succeeding in their career."

Population: Individuals transitioning to the workplace from high school, college, vocational, technical, and training programs.

Publication Date: 2010.

Acronym: CCTI; C2C.

Scores, 5: Life Management, Emotional Intelligence, Job Search, Transition to Work, Career Management.

Administration: Group.

Price Data, 2011: $41.95 per 25 assessment booklets.

Time: (20-25) minutes.

Comments: The administrator's guide (14 pages) is available for download on the publisher's web site.

Author: John J. Liptak.

Publisher: JIST Publishing, Inc.

[657]

Collegiate Assessment of Academic Proficiency.

Purpose: Designed to assess selected academic skills typically obtained in a core general education curriculum.

Population: Freshmen–Seniors in college.

Publication Dates: 1989–1991.

Acronym: CAAP.

Administration: Group.

Restricted Distribution: Available to institutions signing a participation agreement and paying a participation fee.

Price Data, 2005: $350 per year institutional participation fee; test module prices (including scoring and reporting) available from publisher.

Time: 40 minutes per test.

Author: ACT, Inc.

Publisher: ACT, Inc.

a) WRITING SKILLS.
Publication Date: 1998.
Scores, 3: Usage/Mechanics, Rhetorical Skills, Total.
b) MATHEMATICS.
Publication Date: 1989.
Scores, 3: Basic Algebra, College Algebra, Total.
c) READING.
Publication Date: 1989.
Scores, 3: Arts/Literature, Social Studies/Sciences, Total.
d) CRITICAL THINKING.
Publication Date: 1989.
Scores: Total score only.
e) SCIENCE REASONING.
Publication Date: 1989.
Scores: Total score only.
f) WRITING (ESSAY).
Publication Date: 1990.
Scores: Total score only.
Comments: Total of 3 individual essays.
Cross References: See T5:621 (2 references); for reviews by Steven V. Owen and Jeffrey K. Smith, see 13:74 (3 references); see also T4:589 (1 reference).

[658]

Color Trails Test.

Purpose: Designed as a test of sustained visual attention and simple sequencing.
Population: Ages 18 and over.
Publication Dates: 1994–1996.
Acronym: CTT.
Scores, 10: Color Trails 1, Color Trails 1 Errors, Color Trails 1 Near-Misses, Color Trails 1 Prompts, Color Trails 2, Color Trails 2 Color Errors, Color Trails 2 Number Errors, Color Trails 2 Near-Misses, Color Trails 2 Prompts, Interference Index.
Administration: Individual.
Forms, 8: Color Trails 1: A, B, C, D; Color Trails 2: A, B, C, D.
Price Data, 2006: $110 per introductory kit including professional manual (1996, 88 pages), 25 record forms, and 25 administrations of the CCT Form A, Parts 1 and 2.
Time: (10) minutes
Comments: The CTT was developed to be free from the influence of language, and is an analogue of the Trail Making Test (TMT). Administration instructions in Spanish and English are provided in the manual. Respondents must be able to recognize Arabic numerals 1–25.
Authors: Louis F. D'Elia, Paul Satz, Craig Lyons Uchiyama, and Travis White.
Publisher: Psychological Assessment Resources, Inc.
Cross References: For reviews by James C. Reed and Surendra P. Singh, see 15:56.

[659]

Colored Overlay Assessment Kits.

Purpose: Designed to help determine the effectiveness of each colored overlay in improving the ease and accuracy of seeing the printed word while reading.
Population: Individuals experiencing reading and writing problems due to suspected visual perception problems.
Publication Date: 1993.
Scores: Not scored.
Administration: Individual.
Price Data, 2005: $29.95 per each 8-color pack (there are 24 assorted colors in all); packets of 4 individual colored overlays are available; An assessment video is also available at www.nrsi.com; additional price information available at www.dyslexiacure.com.
Time: Administration time varies from student to student.
Author: Marie Carbo.
Publisher: National Reading Styles Institute, Inc.

[660]

Columbia Mental Maturity Scale, Third Edition.

Purpose: Designed to provide "an estimate of the general reasoning ability of children."
Population: 3.5–10 years.
Publication Dates: 1954–1972.
Acronym: CMMS.
Scores: Total score only.
Administration: Individual.
Price Data, 2002: $678 per complete kit including 95 item cards, Guide for Administering and Interpreting (1972, 61 pages); $72 per 35 individual record forms; $25 per English-Spanish Reference Handbook for Educators; $75 per Guide for Administering and Interpreting including Spanish Directions.
Time: (15-20) minutes.
Comments: Requires no verbal response and a minimal motor response.
Authors: Bessie B. Burgemeister, Lucille Hollander Blum, and Irving Lorge.
Publisher: Pearson.
Cross References: See T5:624 (31 references), T4:591 (20 references), and T3:534 (15 references); for reviews by Byron R. Egeland and Alan S. Kaufman, and an excerpted review by Joseph M. Petrosko, see 8:210 (18 references); see also T2:489 (43 references); for reviews by Marshall S. Hiskey and T. Earnest Newland of the 1959 edition, see 6:517 (22 references); see also 5:402 (13 references).

[661]

Combined Basic Skills (Form LCS-C & Form B-C).

Purpose: To evaluate literacy and cognitive skills.
Population: Applicants and incumbents for jobs requiring literacy and cognitive skills.

Publication Dates: 1998–2010.
Scores, 4: Reading, Arithmetic, Inspection and Measurement, Process Monitoring & Problem Solving.
Administration: Group.
Price Data, 2011: $15 per consumable self-scoring test booklet or online test administration (minimum order of 20); $24.95 per manual (2010, 34 pages).
Foreign Language Editions: Available in Spanish.
Time: (48) minutes.
Comments: Self-scoring instrument; two alternate equivalent forms; available for online test administration.
Author: Roland T. Ramsay.
Publisher: Ramsay Corporation.
Cross References: For a review by Cher N. Edwards and Scott F. Beers, see 17:51.

[662]

Combined Cognitive Preference Inventory.
Purpose: Designed to measure how a student processes information intellectually.
Population: Students.
Publication Date: [no date on materials].
Acronym: CCPI.
Scores: 4 cognitive preference areas: Recall, Principles, Questioning, Application.
Administration: Group.
Manual: No manual.
Price Data: Available from publisher.
Time: (20) minutes.
Author: Pinchas Tamir.
Publisher: Israel Science Teaching Center [Israel] [No reply from publisher; status unknown].
Cross References: See T5:626 (1 reference).

[663]

The Common-Metric Questionnaire.
Purpose: "Designed to describe, analyze, and evaluate jobs of all types from both public and private sector organizations."
Population: Job incumbents, supervisors, job analysts.
Publication Dates: 1990–1992.
Acronym: CMQ.
Scores: 6 sections: General Background, Contacts With People, Making Decisions, Physical and Mechanical Activities, Work Setting, Selection Test Scores.
Administration: Group.
Price Data: Available from publisher.
Time: (180–240) minutes.
Comments: When individually administered, the CMQ is mailed to the rater who completes it on his/her own time and returns it; the CMQ should only be individually administered to executive, managerial, and professional level employees; small group administration is recommended.
Authors: Robert J. Harvey (questionnaire) and The Psychological Corporation (manuals).

Publisher: Robert J. Harvey (the author) [No reply from publisher; status unknown].
Cross References: For a review by Gerald A. Rosen, see 13:75.

[664]

Communication Activities of Daily Living, Second Edition.
Purpose: "To assess the functional communication skills of adults with neurogenic communication disorders."
Population: Aphasic adults.
Publication Dates: 1980–1999.
Acronym: CADL-2.
Scores: Total score only.
Administration: Individual.
Price Data, 2006: $195 per complete kit; $25 per patient response forms; $40 per examiner record booklets; $78 per picture book; $56 per examiner's manual.
Time: (25–35) minutes.
Comments: Previous edition entitled Communicative Abilities in Daily Living.
Authors: Audrey Holland, Carol Frattali, and David Fromm.
Publisher: PRO-ED.
Cross References: For reviews by Carolyn Mitchell Person and Katharine Snyder, see 14:84; for a review by Rita Sloan Berndt of an earlier edition, see 10:69 (2 references).

[665]

Communication and Symbolic Behavior Scales Developmental Profile: First Normed Edition.
Purpose: Designed to "evaluate communication and symbolic abilities of children whose functional communication is between 6 months and 2 years."
Population: Ages 6–24 months
Publication Dates: 1995–2002.
Acronym: CSBS DP.
Scores, 11: Social Composite (Emotion and Eye Gaze, Communication, Gestures, Total); Speech Composite (Sounds, Words, Total); Symbolic Composite (Understanding, Object Use, Total); Total.
Administration: Individual.
Forms, 3: Infant-Toddler Checklist, Caregiver Questionnaire, Behavior Sample.
Price Data, 2011: $399 per complete kit including manual (2002, 188 pages), 20 infant-toddler checklists, 20 caregiver questionnaires, 20 caregiver questionnaire scoring worksheets, 20 behavior sample scoring worksheets, 20 caregiver perception rating forms, 1 of each (Part 1 and Part 2) sampling and scoring DVDs, and toy kit; $199.95 per test kit including manual, 20 infant-toddler checklists, 20 caregiver questionnaires, 20 caregiver ques-

tionnaire scoring worksheets, 20 of each (Part 1 and Part 2) sampling and scoring DVDs; $259.95 per toy kit; $65 per manual; $40 per 20 of each infant-toddler checklists, caregiver questionnaires, caregiver questionnaire scoring worksheets, behavior sample scoring worksheets, and caregiver perception rating forms; $25 per 50 caregiver questionnaires; $50 per sampling and scoring DVD (specify Part 1 or Part 2), or $99 for DVD set of Part 1 and Part 2; $99.95 for Infant-Toddler Checklist and Easy-Score CD-ROM with instructional user's guide.

Comments: May be used with children "up to 5–6 years if their developmental level of functioning is younger than 24 months."

Authors: Amy M. Wetherby and Barry M. Prizant.

Publisher: Paul H. Brookes Publishing Co., Inc.

a) INFANT-TODDLER CHECKLIST.

Time: (5–10) minutes.

Comments: A screening tool completed by a caregiver; computer scoring available; may be administered independent of other components.

b) CAREGIVER QUESTIONNAIRE.

Time: (15–20) minutes.

Comments: Companion to the behavior sample completed by caregiver.

c) BEHAVIOR SAMPLE.

Time: (30) minutes.

Comments: A "face to face evaluation tool" conducted by professional evaluator with the caregiver present. The caregiver questionnaire is designed to "determine whether a child has a developmental delay or disability in the areas measured."

Cross References: For a review by Karen T. Carey, see 16:60; see also T5:630 (1 reference); for reviews by Steven H. Long and Dolores Kluppel Vetter of the original edition, see 13:76 (3 references).

[666]

Communication Response Style: Assessment.

Purpose: To assess an individual's communication response style.

Population: Adults.

Publication Dates: 1981–1987.

Scores, 4: Empathic Response Score, Critical Response Score, Searching Response Score, Advising Response Score.

Administration: Group or individual.

Manual: No manual.

Price Data: Price information available from publisher for set including test, answer sheets, and interpretation sheets.

Time: (20) minutes.

Comments: Self-administered, self-scored.

Author: Madelyn Burley-Allen.

Publisher: Training House, Inc.

Cross References: For reviews by Janet Norris and Gargi Roysircar Sodowsky, see 11:78.

[667]

Communication Skills Profile.

Purpose: "Designed to help people who want to gain a thorough knowledge of the processes of communication and to improve their effectiveness as communicators."

Population: Individuals or teams within organizations.

Publication Date: 1997.

Scores: 6 scales: Slowing My Thought Processes, Making Myself Understood, Testing My Conclusions, Listening Constructively, Getting to the Essence, Exploring Disagreement.

Administration: Group.

Price Data: Available from publisher.

Time: Administration time not reported.

Author: Elena Tosca.

Publisher: Jossey-Bass, A Wiley Company.

Cross References: For reviews by Robert Brown and Thomas P. Hogan, see 14:86.

[668]

Community-Based Social Skill Performance Assessment Tool.

Purpose: Designed to assess students' social skill performance in the home and in the community.

Population: Ages 14–21 years, with emotional or behavioral disorders.

Publication Date: Not dated.

Acronym: CBSP.

Scores, 5: Positive Social Behavior, Social Skills Mechanics, Anti-Social Behavior, Self-Control, Total.

Administration: Group.

Forms, 2: Male, Female.

Price Data: Price data available from publisher for set including teaching guide and script (no date, 34 pages), male and female testing materials, response form, and response interpretation/scoring guide.

Time: (45) minutes.

Author: Michael Bullis.

Publisher: James Stanfield Co., Inc.

[669]

Community College Student Experiences Questionnaire, Second Edition.

Purpose: Designed to assess community college students' "quality of effort" toward maximizing college opportunities and achieving their goals.

Population: Community college students.

Publication Dates: 1990–2001.

Acronym: CCSEQ-2.

Scores: 9 scales: Quality of Effort (Course Activities, Library Activities, Faculty-Student Acquaintances, Art, Music and Theater, Writing Activities, Science Activities, Vocational Skills), Satisfaction.

Administration: Group.

Price Data, 2006: $1 per copy of questionnaire; $1.50 per copy for scoring and processing; $12 per test manual (2001, 111 pages); $150 per diskette containing results and summary computer report.
Time: (20–30) minutes.
Comments: For use with students fluent in English.
Authors: C. Robert Pace, Patricia H. Murrell, Jack Friedlander, Penny W. Lehman; Corinna A. Ethington, Anne Marie Guthrie, and Penny W. Lehman (test manual, 3rd edition).
Publisher: Center for the Study of Higher Education, The University of Memphis.
Cross References: For reviews by Candice Haas Hollingsead and James P. Van Haneghan, see 14:87; for reviews by Charles Houston and by Rosemary E. Sutton and Hinsdale Bernard of the original edition, see 12:87.

[670]

Community Improvement Scale.

Purpose: Designed as "a device for measuring neighborhood morale" and "obtaining a diagnostic analysis of principal areas of neighborhood morale maintenance."
Population: Citizens in a neighborhood.
Publication Date: No date.
Scores: Total score only.
Administration: Individual or group.
Price Data, 2001: $3 per specimen set.
Time: (10) minutes.
Author: Inez Fay Smith.
Publisher: Psychometric Affiliates.
Cross Reference: For a review by Jody L. Kulstad, see 15:57.

[671]

Community Opinion Inventory, Revised Edition.

Purpose: "To identify areas the public sees as being done well, and areas seen as not done well" in the local school.
Population: Adults who do not have children enrolled in school.
Publication Dates: 1990–2003.
Scores: 6 subscales: Quality of the Instructional Program, Program Awareness, Responsiveness to the Community, Support for Student Learning, Environment for Learning, Resource Management.
Administration: Group.
Parts, 2: A (Likert-scale items), B (customize up to 20 local questions).
Price Data, 2006: $25 per 25 inventories; administrator's manual (26 pages) may be downloaded free from publisher website.
Time: Untimed.
Author: National Study of School Evaluation.
Publisher: National Study of School Evaluation.

[672]

Community Oriented Programs Environment Scale.

Purpose: Designed to "assess the social environments of community-based psychiatric treatment programs, day programs, sheltered workshops, rehabilitation centers and community care homes."
Population: Patients and staff of community oriented psychiatric facilities.
Publication Dates: 1974–1996.
Acronym: COPES.
Scores, 10: Involvement, Support, Spontaneity, Autonomy, Practical Orientation, Personal Problem Orientation, Anger and Aggression, Order and Organization, Program Clarity, Staff Control.
Administration: Group.
Price Data: Available from publisher at www.mindgarden.com/products/cpess.htm.
Foreign Language Edition: Spanish edition available.
Time: Administration time not reported.
Comments: A part of the Social Climate Scales (T5:2445).
Author: Rudolf H. Moos.
Publisher: Mind Garden, Inc.
Cross References: See T5:637 (3 references), T4:605 (11 references) and T3:542 (6 references); for a review by Richard I. Lanyon, see 8:525 (17 references). For a review of the Social Climate Scales, see 8:681.

[673]

Competency-Based Performance Improvement: Organizational Assessment Package.

Purpose: Used to assess an organization's performance improvement program/s and to improve planning for future programs.
Population: Business managers.
Publication Date: 1995.
Scores, 7: 6 categories (Strategic Goals and Business Objectives, Needs Analysis/Assessment/Planning, Competency Modeling, Curriculum Planning, Learning Intervention Design and Development, Evaluation), Total.
Administration: Group.
Price Data: Available from publisher.
Time: Administration time not reported.
Author: David D. Dubois.
Publisher: HRD Press, Inc.
Cross References: For reviews by Stephen F. Davis and Jerry M. Lowe, see 14:88.

[674]

The Competent Speaker Speech Evaluation Form.

Purpose: Designed to measure public speaking competency.

Population: Post-secondary students.
Publication Date: 1993.
Scores, 9: Chooses and Narrows a Topic Appropriately for the Audience and Occasion, Communicates the Thesis/Specific Purpose in a Manner Appropriate for Audience and Occasion, Uses an Organizational Pattern Appropriate to Topic/Audience/Occasion and Purpose, Provides Appropriate Supporting Material Based on the Audience and Occasion, Uses Language That is Appropriate to the Audience/Occasion and Purpose, Uses Vocal Variety in Rate/Pitch and Intensity to Heighten and Maintain Interest, Uses Pronunciation/Grammar and Articulation Appropriate to the Designated Audience, Uses Physical Behaviors that Support the Verbal Message, Total.
Administration: Individual.
Price Data: Available from publisher.
Time: Administration time not reported.
Author: Speech Communication Association.
Publisher: National Communication Association.
Cross References: For reviews by Sandra M. Ketrow and Julia Y. Porter, see 14:89.

[675]

Complex Figure Test.

Purpose: To serve as an index of brain damage.
Population: Ages 16 and over.
Publication Dates: 1970–1973.
Acronym: CFT.
Scores, 4: Interruption, Omission, Sequence, Total.
Administration: Individual.
Price Data: Available from publisher.
Time: Administration time not reported.
Comments: Originally published in Dutch in 1970 as a revision of Test de Copie d'une Figure Complexe (1959) by André Rey.
Author: R. S. H. Visser.
Publisher: Pearson Assessment [England].
Cross References: See T5:641 (8 references) and T4:606 (8 references); for an excerpted review by C. H. Ammons and R. B. Ammons, see 8:528 (1 reference).

[676]

Compliance with Supervisor's Wishes.

Purpose: Measures employees' attitudinal and behavioral compliance with supervisors' wishes.
Population: Employees.
Publication Date: No date.
Acronym: CSW.
Scores, 2: Attitudinal Compliance, Behavioral Compliance.
Administration: Group.
Manual: No manual.
Price Data, 2008: $75 per permission to make 300 copies for institutional or funded projects; $35 per permission to make 300 copies for individual or unfunded projects; quantity discounts available.
Time: Administration time not reported.
Author: M. Afzal Rahim.
Publisher: Center for Advanced Studies in Management.

[677]

Comprehensive Addictions and Psychological Evaluation.

Purpose: Designed to "provide the clinician with a standard set of questions covering specified content of the DSM-IV diagnostic criteria."
Population: Adults.
Publication Dates: 2000-2004.
Acronym: CAAPE.
Scores, 16: Substance Dependence, Substance Abuse, Depression, Mania, Panic, Anxiety and Phobias, Posttraumatic Stress, Obsessions/Compulsions, Psychosis, Conduct Disorder, Antisocial Personality, Paranoid Personality, Schizoid Personality, Borderline Personality, Dependent Personality, Obsessive-Compulsive Personality.
Administration: Individual.
Price Data, 2008: $67.50 per 25 booklets, $20 per manual (2000, 59 pages).
Time: (20) minutes.
Author: Norman G. Hoffmann.
Publisher: The Change Companies.
Cross References: For reviews by Tony Cellucci and William E. Martin, Jr., see 18:31.

[678]

Comprehensive Adult Student Assessment System–Third Edition.

Purpose: Designed to provide a measure to "place students in the appropriate program, level or test, diagnose student learning needs, monitor student progress and certify student proficiency levels."
Population: Adults.
Publication Dates: 1980-2004.
Acronym: CASAS.
Administration: Group.
Restricted Distribution: Agency training is required before test can be provided.
Price Data: Available from publisher.
Time: Administration times vary.
Comments: Third edition includes new technical manual; computer scoring and individual and class score profiles available.
Author: CASAS.
Publisher: CASAS.
   a) APPRAISAL TESTS.
      1) *ESL Appraisal (English as a Second Language).*
      Scores: 4 tests: Listening, Reading, Speaking, Writing.
      Comments: Appraisal determines level of pretests of CASAS Life Skills Series to be administered.

2) *Life Skills Appraisal.*
Scores: 2 tests: Reading, Math.
Comments: Appraisal determines level of CASAS Life Skills Series Pre-Test to be administered.

3) *ECS Appraisal (Employability Competency System).*
Scores: 2 tests: Reading, Math.
Forms, 2: 120, 130.
Comments: Appraisal determines level of CASAS Basic Skills for Employability Pre-Test to be administered.

b) CASAS TESTS FOR MONITORING PROGRESS.
Comments: All tests serve as pre/post tests.

1) *Employability Competency Series.*
  (a) Reading.
  Levels, 4: A, B, C, and D each with 2 forms.
  (b) Math.
  Levels, 4: A, B, C, and D each with 2 forms.
  (c) Listening.
  Levels, 3: A, B, and C each with 2 forms.

2) *Life Skills Series.*
  (a) Reading.
  Levels, 5: (Beginning Literacy, A, B, C, D), Beginning Literacy, Levels C and D each have 2 forms; Levels A and B have 3 forms.
  (b) Math.
  Levels, 4: A, B, C, and D each with 2 forms.
  (c) Listening.
  Levels, 3: A, B, and C each with 2 forms.

Cross References: For reviews by Terri Flowerday and Carol S. Parke, see 16:61; see also T5:645 (1 reference); for reviews by Ralph O. Mueller and Patricia K. Freitag and by William D. Schafer of a previous edition, see 13:78 (2 references).

[679]

Comprehensive Affair Worksheets.

Purpose: Designed to "analyze the reasons for the affair, the affair behaviors and relationship, the impact on the marriage and all the individuals involved, decisions that need to be made and what needs to be done to solve the problems caused by the affair."
Population: Individuals who have had an affair.
Publication Date: 1995.
Scores: 19 sections: Therapy, Marriage Before the Affair, Pre-Affair Involvement, Activities, Relationship, Religion, Communication, Feelings, Sex, Cheating Opinions, Keeping It Secret, Spouse's Reaction, Effects on the Person, Effects on the Spouse, Others Finding Out, Decisions and Planning, Repairing the Marriage, Marital Sex, Other Problems.
Administration: Individual.
Manual: Instructions included with the worksheet.
Price Data, 2011: Now available only in the book "Psychological Worksheets & Assignments," which

includes all 68 tests available from publisher; $98 per book version and $48 per CD version.
Time: [20-60] minutes.
Author: Allan Roe.
Publisher: Diagnostic Specialists, Inc.

[680]

Comprehensive Assessment of Mathematics Strategies.

Purpose: Designed to "identify and assess a student's level of mastery in each of 12 mathematics strategies."
Population: Grades 1–8.
Publication Dates: 2000-2006.
Acronym: CAMS.
Scores, 12: Building Number Sense, Using Estimation, Applying Addition, Applying Subtraction, Applying Multiplication, Applying Division, Converting Time and Money, Converting Customary and Metric Measures, Using Algebra, Using Geometry, Determining Probability and Averages, Interpreting Graphs and Charts.
Administration: Group.
Levels, 8: Grade 1, Grade 2, Grade 3, Grade 4, Grade 5, Grade 6, Grade 7, Grade 8.
Price Data, 2006: $24.90 per 10 student books; $4.95 per teacher guide (for each level); $25.95 per CD Management Software.
Time: (60) minutes.
Comments: Testing materials include practice lessons, self-assessments, and teacher assessments; self-assessments (both of which are completed after the student is exposed to and practices lessons 1–5, and again after the student is exposed to each practices lessons 6–10); class performance chart available; Teacher Assessment 1 "assesses a student's performance for each of the 12 mathematics' strategies"; Teacher Assessment 2 compares a student's level of mastery in the criteria for the 12 mathematics' strategies.
Author: Robert G. Forest.
Publisher: Curriculum Associates, Inc.

[681]

Comprehensive Assessment of Mathematics Strategies II.

Purpose: Designed to measure "improvement in mathematics comprehension after instruction," identify "level of mastery" of mathematics strategies, and provide "practice with self-assessment."
Population: Grades 1–8.
Publication Dates: 2001–2006.
Administration: Group.
Levels, 8: Books 1–8.
Manual: No comprehensive manual. A Teacher's guide is provided for each level (2001–2003, 13 pages each).
Price Data, 2006: $17.90 per 10 student booklets (specify level); $4.95 per Teacher Guide (specify level).

Time: 45 minutes per lesson (5 lessons per book); 20 minutes per self-assessment.

Comments: Intended for use "after students have been diagnosed with Comprehensive Assessment of Mathematics Strategies and have been instructed with Strategies to Achieve Mathematics Success"; Teacher and Self-Assessments also included.

Author: Robert G. Forest.

Publisher: Curriculum Associates, Inc.

  a) BOOK 1.
  Scores, 8: Building Number Sense, Applying Addition, Applying Subtraction, Applying Multiplication, Converting Time and Money, Converting Measures, Using Geometry, Reading Math Pictures.
  b) BOOK 2.
  Scores, 12: Building Number Sense, Using Estimation, Applying Addition, Applying Subtraction, Applying Multiplication, Applying Division, Converting Time and Money, Converting Customary and Metric Measures, Using Algebra, Using Geometry, Determining Probability and Averages, Interpreting Graphs and Charts.
  c) BOOK 3.
  Scores, 12: Same as Book 2.
  d) BOOK 4.
  Scores, 12: Same as Book 2.
  e) BOOK 5.
  Scores, 12: Same as Book 2.
  f) BOOK 6.
  Scores, 12: Same as Book 2.
  g) BOOK 7.
  Scores, 12: Same as Book 2.
  h) BOOK 8.
  Scores, 12: Same as Book 2.

[682]

Comprehensive Assessment of Reading Strategies.

Purpose: Designed to "identify and assess a student's level of mastery with each of 12 reading strategies."

Population: Grades 1-8.

Publication Dates: 1998–2006.

Acronym: CARS.

Scores, 13: Finding Main Idea, Recalling Facts and Details, Understanding Sequence, Recognizing Cause and Effect, Comparing and Contrasting, Making Predictions, Finding Word Meaning in Context, Drawing Conclusions and Making Inferences, Distinguishing Between Fact and Opinion, Identifying Author's Purpose, Interpreting Figurative Language, Distinguishing Between Real and Make-Believe [Books 1-4], Summarizing [Books 5-8].

Administration: Group.

Levels, 8: Grade 1, Grade 2, Grade 3, Grade 4, Grade 5, Grade 6, Grade 7, Grade 8.

Price Data, 2006: $24.90 per 10 student books; $4.95 per teacher's guide; $25.95 per CD Management Software.

Time: (45) minutes.

Comments: Testing materials include practice lessons, self-assessments, and teacher assessments; self-assessment and teacher assessment are completed after student is exposed to and practices the lessons presented in the test materials; class performance charts available; computer software available for generating interpretive reports; assessment consists of 2 assessments to be given at separate times.

Authors: Deborah Adcock and Courtney Bolser (contributing author to test booklet).

Publisher: Curriculum Associates, Inc.

[683]

Comprehensive Assessment of Reading Strategies II.

Purpose: Designed to "measure improvement in reading comprehension after instruction," identify "level of mastery" for specified reading strategies, and provide "practice with self-assessment."

Population: Grades 1–8.

Publication Dates: 2000–2006.

Administration: Group.

Levels, 8: Grades 1–8.

Price Data, 2006: $17.90 per 10 student books (specify level); $4.95 per teacher's guide (specify level).

Time: (45) minutes per lesson, (20) minutes per self-assessment.

Comments: Designed as a follow-up measure for use with the Comprehensive Assessment of Reading Strategies (T6:634; a diagnostic measure) and Strategies to Achieve Reading Success (focused instructional system).

Authors: Deborah Adcock (Teacher Guides 1–8, and Student Books 1–8), Christopher Forest (contributing author on Student Books 1, 3, 4, 6, and 7).

Publisher: Curriculum Associates, Inc.

  a) BOOK 1.
  Population: Grade 1.
  Scores, 8: Finding Main Idea, Recalling Facts and Details, Understanding Sequence, Recognizing Cause and Effect, Making Predictions, Finding Word Meaning in Context, Drawing Conclusions and Making Inferences, Reading Pictures.
  b) BOOK 2.
  Population: Grade 2.
  Scores, 12: Same as Book 1, with the deletion of Reading Pictures and the addition of Comparing and Contrasting, Distinguishing Between Fact and Opinion, Identifying Author's Purpose, Interpreting Figurative Language, and Distinguishing Between Real and Make-believe.
  c) BOOK 3.
  Population: Grade 3.
  Scores, 12: Same as Book 2.
  d) BOOK 4.
  Population: Grade 4.
  Scores, 12: Same as Book 2.

e) BOOK 5.
Population: Grade 5.
Scores, 12: Same as Book 2, with the deletion of Distinguishing Between Real and Make-believe, and the addition of Summarizing.
f) BOOK 6.
Population: Grade 6.
Scores, 12: Same as Book 5.
g) BOOK 7.
Population: Grade 7.
Scores, 12: Same as Book 5.
h) BOOK 8.
Population: Grade 8.
Scores, 12: Same as Book 5.

[684]

Comprehensive Assessment of School Environments.

Purpose: Developed to assess perceptions of the school climate and student, teacher, and parent satisfaction with each individual's personal environment in order "to foster data-based decision making for school improvement."
Population: Junior and senior high schools.
Publication Dates: 1986–1989.
Acronym: CASE.
Administration: Group.
Price Data: Available from publisher.
Time: Administration time not reported.
Comments: Test booklet titles are School Climate Survey, Parent Satisfaction Survey, Teacher Satisfaction Survey, and Student Satisfaction Survey.
Authors: Cynthia Halderson (manuals and climate survey), Edgar A. Kelley (manuals and climate survey), James W. Keefe (manuals and climate survey), Paul S. Berge (technical manual), John A. Glover (climate survey), Carrie Sorenson (climate survey), Carol Speth (climate survey), Neal Schmitt (satisfaction surveys), and Brian Loher (satisfaction surveys).
Publisher: National Association of Secondary School Principals.
a) SCHOOL CLIMATE SURVEY.
Scores: Student, Teacher, and Parent scores for the following 10 subscales: Teacher-Student Relationships, Security and Maintenance, Administration, Student Academic Orientation, Student Behavioral Values, Guidance, Student-Peer Relationships, Parent & Community-School Relationships, Instructional Management, Student Activities.
b) PARENT SATISFACTION SURVEY.
Scores, 9: Parent Involvement, Curriculum, Student Activities, Teachers, Support Services, School Building/Supplies/Maintenance, Student Discipline, School Administrators, School Information Services.
c) TEACHER SATISFACTION SURVEY.
Scores, 9: Administration, Compensation, Opportunities for Advancement, Student Responsibility & Discipline, Curriculum and Job Tasks, Co-workers, Parents and Community, School Building/Supplies/Maintenance, Communication.
d) STUDENT SATISFACTION SURVEY.
Scores, 8: Teachers, Fellow Students, Schoolwork, Student Activities, Student Discipline, Decision-Making Opportunities, School Building/Supplies/Upkeep, Communication.
Cross References: For reviews by Nancy L. Allen and Frederick T. L. Leong, see 11:80.

[685]

Comprehensive Assessment of School Environments Information Management System.

Purpose: Designed to facilitate and encourage the use of data-based planning for school improvement projects.
Population: Secondary schools.
Publication Dates: 1991–1995.
Acronym: CASE-IMS.
Scores, 9: Principal Questionnaire, Teacher Report Form, Student Report Form, Teacher Satisfaction Survey, Student Satisfaction Survey, Parent Satisfaction Survey (optional), School Climate Survey for Teachers, School Climate Survey for Students, School Climate Survey for Parents (optional).
Administration: Group.
Price Data: Available from publisher.
Time: Administration time not reported.
Comments: Computer administered; available in MS/DOS (3.5-inch or 5.25-inch disks) or Macintosh (3.5-inch disk) format.
Author: National Association of Secondary School Principals Task Force on Effective School Environments.
Publisher: National Association of Secondary School Principals.
Cross References: For reviews by Joseph R. Manduchi and Daniel L. Yazak, see 14:90.

[686]

Comprehensive Assessment of Spoken Language.

Purpose: Designed to measure the processes of comprehension, expression, and retrieval in oral language.
Population: Ages 3–21.
Publication Date: 1999.
Acronym: CASL.
Scores: 15 tests: Basic Concepts, Antonyms, Synonyms, Sentence Completion, Idiomatic Language, Syntax Construction, Paragraph Comprehension, Grammatical Morphemes, Sentence Comprehension, Grammaticality Judgment, Nonliteral Language, Meaning from Context, Inference, Ambiguous Sentences, and Pragmatic Judgment; plus Core Composite scores, Category Index scores (Lexical/Semantic, Syntactic, Supralinguistic); Processing Index scores (Expressive, Receptive).
Administration: Individual.
Forms, 2: 1, 2.

Price Data, 2011: $399 per complete kit, including 3 test books, 24 record forms (12 each of forms 1 and 2, for ages 3 to 6 and 7 to 21, respectively), manual, and norms book; $499 for complete kit plus ASSIST SCORING SOFTWARE; $275 ASSIST SCORING SOFTWARE CD-ROM for Macintosh & Windows; $30 record form for ages 3-6 (set of 12); $99 record form for ages 3-6 (set of 48); $35 record form for ages 7-21 (set of 12); $115 record form for ages 7-21 (set of 48); $42.50 manual; $42.50 norms book; $105 test book 1: Lexical/Semantics Tests; $105 Test Book 2: Syntactic Tests; $105 test book 3: Supralinguistic & Pragmatic Tests.
Author: Elizabeth Carrow-Woolfolk.
Publisher: Western Psychological Services.
Cross References: For reviews by Katharine A. Snyder and Gabrielle Stutman, see 15:58.

[687]
Comprehensive Assessment of Symptoms and History.

Purpose: "Designed as a structured interview and recording instrument for documenting the signs, symptoms, and history of subjects evaluated in research studies of the major psychoses and affective disorders."
Population: Psychiatric patients.
Publication Date: 1987.
Acronym: CASH.
Scores: Interview divided into 3 major sections: Present State (Sociodemographic Data, Evaluation of Current Condition, Psychotic Syndrome, Manic Syndrome, Major Depressive Syndrome, Treatment, Cognitive Assessment, Global Assessment Scale, Diagnosis for Current Episode), Past History (History of Onset and Hospitalization, Past Symptoms of Psychosis, Characterization of Course, Past Symptoms of Affective Disorder), Lifetime History (History of Somatic Therapy, Alcoholism, Drug Use and Abuse and Dependence, Modified Premorbid Adjustment Scale, Premorbid or Intermorbid Personality, Functioning During Past Five Years, Global Assessment Scale, Diagnosis for Lifetime).
Administration: Individual.
Price Data: Available from publisher.
Time: [60–180] minutes.
Comments: The CASH is one component of a modular assessment battery available from the publisher.
Author: Nancy C. Andreasen.
Publisher: Nancy C. Andreasen.
Cross References: See T5:650 (16 references); for reviews by Patricia A. Bachelor and Barbara J. Kaplan, see 12:88 (12 references); see also T4:612 (4 references).

[688]
Comprehensive Identification Process [Revised].

Purpose: "Designed to identify children who may have medical, psychological or learning problems that could interfere with their success in school."

Population: Ages 2–6.5.
Publication Date: 1975–1997.
Acronym: CIP.
Administration: Individual.
Price Data: See www.ststesting.com for up-to-date pricing information.
Foreign Language Edition: Earlier edition available in Spanish.
Time: Varies.
Comments: CIP screening team should include at least one member who has a background in early childhood education of the disabled and is skilled in screening and evaluation; alternatives to the standard screening, such as in-home screening or bilingual screening available.
Authors: R. Reid Zehrbach (test), and Joan Good Erickson (Speech and Expressive Language Record Form).
Publisher: Scholastic Testing Service, Inc.
  a) CHILD: RECORD FOLDER.
  Scores, 5: Hearing, Vision, Perceptual Motor, Cognitive-Verbal, Gross Motor.
  Comment: Materials for hearing and vision screening must be obtained locally.
  b) SPEECH AND EXPRESSIVE LANGUAGE RECORD FORM.
  Scores, 6: Articulation/Phonology, Voice, Fluency, Expressive Language, Associated Factors, Total.
  Author: Joan Good Erickson.
  c) OBSERVATION OF BEHAVIOR FORM.
  Scores, 7: Hearing, Vision, Physical/Motor Speech and Expressive Language, Social Behavior (Responses, Interaction), Affective Behavior.
  d) PARENT INTERVIEW FORM.
  Scores, 7: Pregnancy/Birth/Hospitalization, Walking/Toilet Training, Hearing, Vision, Speech and Expressive Language, Medical, Social Affect.
  Comment: History and ratings by parent.
Cross References: For a review by J. Jeffrey Grill, see 14:91; see also T4:616 (1 reference); for reviews by Robert P. Anderson and Phyllis L. Newcomer of an earlier version, see 8:425 (1 reference).

[689]
Comprehensive Mathematical Abilities Test.

Purpose: Developed to "assess a broad spectrum of mathematical abilities in the areas of comprehension (reasoning), calculation and application."
Population: Ages 7:0 to 18:11.
Publication Date: 2003.
Acronym: CMAT.
Scores: (10–18): General Mathematics (Basic Calculations, composed of Addition, Subtraction, Multiplication, Division, and Mathematical Reasoning, composed of Problem Solving, Charts/Tables/and Graphs); Advanced Calculations (Algebra, Geometry, Rational Numbers) [supplemental]; Practical Applications (Time, Money, Measurement) [supplemental]; Global Mathematics Ability.

Administration: Individual.

Price Data, 2010: $320 per complete kit including examiner's manual (199 pages), picture book, 25 profile/examiner record booklets, 25 student response booklet I, and 25 student response booklet II; $101 per examiner's manual; $85 per picture book; $45 per pack of 25 profile/examiner record booklets; $52 per pack of 25 student response booklet I; $52 per pack of 25 student response booklet II; $122 per CMAT scoring & reporting software; $409 for CMAT Print/Software Combo kit (including examiner's manual, picture book, 25 profile/examiner record booklets, 25 student response booklet I, and 25 student response booklet II; scoring and reporting software).

Time: 45–60 minutes.

Comments: Computer scoring available.

Authors: Wayne P. Hresko, Paul L. Schlieve, Shelley R. Herron, Colleen Swain, and Rita J. Sherbenou.

Publisher: PRO-ED.

Cross References: For reviews by George Engelhard, Jr. and Suzanne Lane, see 16:62.

[690]

Comprehensive Personality Profile.

Purpose: Designed to provide a comprehensive assessment of job-relevant personality characteristics that impact the successful fulfillment of job requirements; used within organizations to identify individuals whose personality characteristics are compatible with job demands.

Population: Ages 15 and up.

Publication Dates: 1985–2002.

Acronym: CPP.

Scores, 48: Primary Scales (Emotional Intensity, Intuition, Recognition Motivation, Sensitivity, Assertiveness, Trust, Exaggeration), Secondary Traits (Ego Drive, Interpersonal Warmth, Stability, Empathy, Objectivity, Independence, Aggressiveness, Decisiveness, Tolerance, Efficiency), Interaction Traits (Temperament, Ego Style, Social Style), Management Performance Traits (Ability To Make Unpopular Decisions, Decisiveness To Act Without Precedent, Ingenuity To Create New Ideas, Ability To Motivate Others To Act, Vision To Plan Ahead On A Large Scale, Self-Discipline To Efficiently Manage Time, Communicates With Frankness And Humility, Tolerance For Corporate Red Tape Or Politics, Delegates Responsibility Or Authority, Caution In Making Policy Commitments), Sales Performance Traits (Goal Oriented Drive Toward Immediate Results, Insight To Perceive The Buyer's Need, Ability To Close Sales Without Hesitation, Ability To Make New Contacts (Call Courage), Overcomes Objections With Tact And Diplomacy, Desire To Provide After-The-Sale Service, Desire To Compete And Win At All Costs, Ability To Keep Positive Attitude (Optimism), Ability To Control Emotional Ups And Downs, Ability To Handle Sales Rejection), Administrative Performance Traits (Tolerance To Stay At One Work Station, Desire To Conform To Management Objectives, Ability To Cope With Change And Disruption, Satisfaction To Stay At Job Level Attained, Ability To Be Diplomatic And Cooperative, Patience To Follow Detailed Instructions, Capacity To Follow Systems), Summary Profile.

Administration: Group or individual.

Price Data: Available from publisher.

Foreign Language Editions: Available in French and Spanish.

Time: (15–25) minutes.

Comments: Title on questionnaire is CPP Compatibility Questionnaire; online administration available.

Authors: Wonderlic, Inc. and Larry L. Craft (questionnaire).

Publisher: Wonderlic, Inc.

Cross References: For reviews by Sanford J. Cohn and Ira Stuart Katz, see 14:92; see also T4:617 (1 reference). For reviews by Sanford J. Cohn and Ira Stuart Katz, see 14:92; see also T4:617 (1 reference).

[691]

Comprehensive Receptive and Expressive Vocabulary Test—Second Edition.

Purpose: "To identify ... deficiencies in oral vocabulary ... discrepancies between receptive and expressive vocabulary, [and] ... progress in instructional programs."

Population: Ages 4-0 through 89-11, ages 5-0 through 89-11.

Publication Dates: 1994–2002.

Acronym: CREVT-2.

Scores, 3: Receptive Vocabulary, Expressive Vocabulary, General Vocabulary.

Administration: Individual.

Forms, 2: A, B.

Price Data, 2010: $273 per complete kit; $51 per forms (A or B); $90 per photo album picture book; $90 per examiner's manual (2002, 141 pages).

Time: 20-30 minutes.

Comments: Combines the CREVT and CREVT-A

Authors: Gerald Wallace and Donald D. Hammill.

Publisher: PRO-ED.

Cross References: For reviews by Luanne Andersson and Gretchen Owens, see 15:59; see T5:655 (CREVT, 1 reference) and T5:656 (CREVT); for reviews by Alan S. Kaufman and Mary J. McLellan of the CREVT, see 13:80 (1 reference); for reviews by Margaret E. Malone and Wayne H. Slater of the CREVT-A, see 14:93 (1 reference).

[692]

Comprehensive Sex History.

Purpose: Designed to compile an individual's complete sexual history.

Population: Adults.

Publication Date: 1995.

Administration: Individual.

Forms, 2: Male, Female.

Manual: No manual.

Price Data, 2010: $15 for one set of reusable question sheets for all 5 parts (specify Male or Female).

Time: [60-120] minutes.

Author: Allan Roe.

Publisher: Diagnostic Specialists, Inc.

a) SEXUAL EXPERIENCES.

Population: General adult.

b) DATING EXPERIENCES.

Population: Those who have dated.

c) NON-MARITAL INTERCOURSE.

Population: Those who have had intercourse outside of marriage.

d) MARITAL OR LIVING TOGETHER SEXUAL EXPERIENCES.

Population: Those who have been married or lived together.

e) INAPPROPRIATE SEXUAL BEHAVIORS.

Population: Those who have done inappropriate criminal sexual activities.

[693]

Comprehensive Test of Nonverbal Intelligence.

Purpose: Constructed to measure "nonverbal intellectual abilities."

Population: Ages 6-0 to 90-11.

Publication Date: 1996.

Acronym: CTONI.

Scores, 9: 6 subtest scores (Pictorial Analogies, Geometric Analogies, Pictorial Categories, Geometric Categories, Pictorial Sequences, Geometric Sequences), 3 composite scores (Nonverbal Intelligence Quotient, Pictorial Nonverbal Intelligence Quotient, Geometric Nonverbal Intelligence Quotient).

Administration: Individual.

Price Data: Available from publisher.

Time: (40–60) minutes.

Comments: The publisher advises that a Second Edition is now available.

Authors: Donald D. Hammill, Nils A. Pearson, and J. Lee Wiederholt.

Publisher: PRO-ED.

Cross References: See T5:662 (1 reference); for reviews by Glen P. Aylward and Gabriele van Lingen, see 13:82.

[694]

Comprehensive Test of Phonological Processing.

Purpose: Designed to measure "phonological awareness, phonological memory, and rapid naming."

Population: Ages 5–6, ages 7–24.

Publication Date: 1999.

Administration: Individual.

Price Data, 2010: $285 per complete kit including examiner's manual (159 pages), 25 each profile/examiner record booklets for ages 5 to 6 and ages 7 to 24, picture book, and audio CD; $62 per 25 profile/examiner record booklets for ages 5 to 6; $73 per 25 profile/examiner record booklets for ages 7 to 24; $45 per picture book; $91 per manual; $23 per audio CD.

Time: (30) minutes.

Authors: Richard K. Wagner, Joseph K. Torgesen, and Carol A. Rashotte.

Publisher: PRO-ED.

a) 5- AND 6-YEAR-OLD VERSION.

Population: Ages 5–6.

Scores, 11: Phonological Awareness (Elision, Blending Words, Sound Matching), Phonological Memory (Memory for Digits, Nonword Repetition), Rapid Naming (Rapid Color Naming, Rapid Object Naming), Blending Nonwords (Supplemental Subtest).

b) 7- THROUGH 24-YEAR-OLD VERSION.

Population: Ages 7–24.

Scores, 17: Phonological Awareness (Elision, Blending Words), Phonological Memory (Memory for Digits, Nonword Repetition), Rapid Naming (Rapid Digit Naming, Rapid Letter Naming), Alternate Phonological Awareness (Blending Nonwords, Segmenting Nonwords), Alternate Rapid Naming (Rapid Color Naming, Rapid Object Naming), Phoneme Reversal (Supplemental Subtest), Segmenting Words (Supplemental Subtest).

Cross References: For reviews by David P. Hurford and Claudia R. Wright, see 15:60.

[695]

Comprehensive Test of Visual Functioning.

Purpose: Designed to identify and differentiate type of visual perceptual dysfunction.

Population: Ages 8 and over.

Publication Date: 1990.

Acronym: CTVF.

Scores, 9: Visual/Letter Integration, Visual/Writing Integration, Nonverbal Visual Closure, Nonverbal Visual Reasoning/Memory, Spatial Orientation/Memory/Motor, Spatial Orientation/Motor, Visual Design/Motor, Visual Design/Memory/Motor, Total.

Administration: Individual.

Price Data, 2002: $108 per complete kit including manual (64 pages), stimulus cards/easel, and stimulus items; $28 per manual; $42 per examiner's directions and scoring protocol (18 pages); $29 per 25 examinee test booklets; $29 per stimulus cards/easel.

Time: (25) minutes.

Comments: "Norm-referenced"; includes 4 additional subtests (Visual Acuity, Visual Processing/Figure-Ground

Visual Tracking, Reading Word Analysis) which do not contribute to the overall visual performance quotient.
Authors: Sue L. Larson, Evelyn Buethe, and Gary J. Vitali.
Publisher: Slosson Educational Publications, Inc.
Cross References: For reviews by Stephen R. Hooper and Douglas J. McRae, see 12:89.

[696]
Comprehensive Testing Program 4.
Purpose: "Designed to provide instructionally useful information about student performance in key areas of the school curriculum: listening, reading, vocabulary, writing, and mathematics"; beginning with the spring of Grade 3, includes verbal and quantitative reasoning tests to measure higher order thinking skills.
Population: Grades 1–2, 2–3, 3–4, 4–5, 5–6, 6–7, 7–8, 8–9, 9–10, 10–11.
Publication Dates: 1974–2004.
Acronym: CTP 4.
Administration: Group.
Levels, 10: 1–10.
Price Data: Available from publisher.
Time: (300) minutes for total battery.
Comments: Machine scoring by the publisher; provides "Independent," "Suburban/Public," "International," "Association," and "National" norms; hand-scoring keys and norms booklets are also available from the publisher; partial battery is an option; allows for nonstandard administration. The test can be administered online with immediate scoring and includes science in grades 3-10.
Author: Educational Records Bureau.
Publisher: Educational Records Bureau.
 a) LEVEL 1.
 Population: Grade 1 spring or Grade 2 fall.
 Scores, 4: Auditory Comprehension, Reading Comprehension, Word Analysis, Mathematics Achievement.
 b) LEVEL 2.
 Population: Grade 2 spring or Grade 3 fall.
 Scores, 5: Same as for Level 1 plus Writing Mechanics.
 c) LEVEL 3.
 Population: Grade 3 spring or Grade 4 fall.
 Scores, 7: Verbal Reasoning, Auditory Comprehension, Reading Comprehension, Writing Mechanics, Writing Concepts and Skills, Mathematics Achievement, Quantitative Reasoning.
 d) LEVEL 4.
 Population: Grade 4 spring or Grade 5 fall.
 Scores, 7: Verbal Reasoning, Vocabulary, Reading Comprehension, Writing Mechanics, Writing Concepts and Skills, Mathematics Achievement, Quantitative Reasoning.
 e) LEVEL 5.
 Population: Grade 5 spring or Grade 6 fall.
 Scores, 7: Same as for Level 4.
 f) LEVEL 6.
 Population: Grade 6 spring or Grade 7 fall.
 Scores, 7: Same as for Levels 4 and 5.
 g) LEVEL 7.
 Population: Grade 7 spring or Grade 8 fall.
 Scores, 7: Same as for Levels 4, 5, and 6.
 h) LEVEL 8.
 Population: Grade 8 spring or Grade 9 fall.
 Scores, 8: Same as for Levels 4, 5, 6, and 7 plus Algebra 1.
 i) LEVEL 9.
 Population: Grade 9 spring or Grade 10 fall.
 Scores, 8: Same as for Level 8.
 j) LEVEL 10.
 Population: Grade 10 spring or Grade 11 fall.
 Scores, 7: Same as for Levels 8 and 9 except for omission of Algebra 1.
Cross References: For reviews by Koressa Kutsick Malcolm and William D. Schafer, see 17:52.

[697]
Comprehensive Trail-Making Test.
Purpose: Developed for the evaluation and diagnosis of brain injury and other forms of central nervous system compromise.
Population: Ages 8 to 74-11.
Publication Date: 2002.
Acronym: CTMT.
Scores, 6: Trail 1, Trail 2, Trail 3, Trail 4, Trail 5, Composite Index.
Administration: Individual.
Price Data, 2010: $129 per complete kit; $62 per 10 record booklets; $73 per examiner's manual (79 pages).
Time: (5–12) minutes.
Author: Cecil R. Reynolds.
Publisher: PRO-ED.
Cross References: For a review by Nora M. Thompson, see 15:61.

[698]
Computer Career Assessment Test.
Purpose: Measures aptitude for work in the computer field.
Population: Any adult without prior computer experience.
Publication Date: 2000.
Acronym: CCAT.
Scores: Total Score, Narrative Evaluation, Ranking.
Administration: Group.
Price Data, 2001: $99 for industry; $65 for educational institutions; quantity discounts available.
Time: (60) minutes.
Comments: Available in booklet and internet versions; scored by publisher; must be proctored.
Author: Bruce A. Winrow.

Publisher: Walden Personnel Performance, Inc. [Canada].
Cross References: For reviews by Michael B. Bunch and Thomas R. O'Neill, see 16:63.

[699]

Computer Literacy Skills Profile.

Purpose: To evaluate computer literacy potential.
Population: Candidates whose job responsibilities will include utilizing common software packages.
Publication Date: 1996.
Acronym: COMPLIT.
Scores: Total Score, Narrative Evaluation, Ranking, Recommendation.
Administration: Group.
Price Data, 2001: $235 per candidate; quantity discounts available.
Time: (110) minutes.
Comments: Scored by publisher; must be proctored.
Author: Bruce A. Winrow.
Publisher: Walden Personnel Performance, Inc.

[700]

Computer Operator Aptitude Battery.

Purpose: Predict "ability to perform computer operator job and potential for learning computer programming."
Population: Experienced computer operators and trainees.
Publication Dates: 1973–1974.
Acronym: COAB.
Scores, 4: Sequence Recognition, Formal Checking, Logical Thnking, Total.
Administration: Individual or group.
Price Data, 2002: $193 per Start-up kit including 5 test booklets, 25 answer sheets, and examiner's manual (1974, 19 pages); $112 per 5 test booklets; $76 per 25 answer sheets (quantity discounts available); $28 per examiner's manual.
Time: 45 minutes.
Author: Pearson Performance Solutions [No reply from publisher; status unknown].
Publisher: Pearson Reid London House.

[701]

Computer Programmer Aptitude Battery.

Purpose: To "measure abilities related to success in computer programmer and systems analysis fields."
Population: Students, programmer trainees, entry-level and experienced.
Publication Dates: 1964–1993.
Acronym: CPAB.
Scores, 6: Verbal Meaning, Reasoning, Letter Series, Number Ability, Diagramming, Total.
Administration: Individual or group.
Forms, 2: A, B.

Price Data, 2002: $193 per start-up kit including 5 test reusable booklets (specify Form A or Form B), 25 answer sheets (specify Form A or Form B) and examiner's manual; $166 per Short Form start-up kit; $158 per 25 Short Form A tests (with carbon answer sheets); $112 per 5 test booklets (quantity discount available; specify Form A or Form B); $76 per 25 answer sheets (quantity discount available; specify Form A or Form B); $28 per examiner's manual.
Time: 79 minutes; 55 minutes for short form.
Comments: Short form contains the Reasoning and Diagramming sections and can be used for all levels of programmers but norms for short form available only for entry level.
Author: Science Research Associates.
Publisher: Pearson Performance Solutions [No reply from publisher; status unknown].
Cross References: For reviews by Roderick K. Mahurin and William D. Schafer, see 11:85; see also T3:557 (1 reference); for additional information and a review by Nick L. Smith, see 8:1079 (3 references); see also T2:2334 (2 references); for reviews by Richard T. Johnson and Donald J. Veldman, see 7:1089 (2 references).

[702]

Computerized Assessment of Response Bias: Revised Edition.

Purpose: "To quantitatively assess a given patient's attitude (response bias) in taking neuropsychological or neurocognitive tests."
Population: Severely impaired neurologic patients, mild traumatic brain injury patients, non-neurologic simulators.
Publication Dates: 1992–2000.
Acronym: CARB.
Scores, 24: 4 actions (Block 1, 2, 3, Total) each with 6 scores: Total Correct, Number of Correct Responses Obtained with Left Hand, Number of Correct Responses Obtained with Right Hand, Reaction Time Average, Reaction Time Average for Correct Responses, Reaction Time Average for Incorrect Responses.
Administration: Individual
Forms, 4: Standard or Quick form, each with or without item-specific feedback.
Price Data, 2002: $300 for disk and comprehensive manual (63 pages).
Foreign Language Edition: Spanish language version available.
Time: (22–40) minutes.
Comments: Typically, this is a test of motivation, not ability or impairment; instructions for installing and operating CARB (DOS based) software are included in the manual.
Authors: Robert L. Conder, Jr., Lyle M. Allen, III, David R. Cox, and Carol M. King.
Publisher: CogniSyst, Inc.
Cross References: For reviews by M. Allan Cooperstein and Edward E. Gotts, see 14:95.

[703]

Computerized Oral Proficiency Instrument.

Purpose: Designed to assess "students' oral language proficiency in Arabic or Spanish."

Population: Native English speaking upper high school students, college students, and professionals who are learning the target language.

Publication Date: 2008.

Acronym: COPI.

Scores: 10 ratings: Novice Low, Novice Mid, Novice High, Intermediate Low, Intermediate Mid, Intermediate High, Advanced Low, Advanced Mid, Advanced High, Superior.

Administration: Group.

Editions, 2: Spanish, Arabic.

Levels: 4 proficiency levels: Novice, Intermediate, Advanced, Superior.

Price Data, 2011: $125 per test kit including Test Administration Program on CD-ROM, Training and Rating CD-ROM, and manual (51 pages).

Time: (45-60) minutes.

Comments: Computer-based, semi-adaptive test; technology requirements include a personal computer (not a Macintosh) with a sound card, CD-ROM drive, headset or speakers, microphone, monitor, keyboard, and mouse; publisher recommends using with the Spanish Multimedia Rater Training Program or the Arabic Rater Training Kit, both available separately.

Author: Center for Applied Linguistics.

Publisher: Center for Applied Linguistics.

[704]

Computerized Test of Information Processing.

Purpose: Designed to "measure the degree to which various neurological injuries impact the speed at which information is processed" and to detect "whether a traumatic brain injury patient is putting forth maximum effort."

Population: Ages 15-74.

Publication Date: 2008.

Acronym: CTiP.

Scores, 3: Simple Reaction Time, Choice Reaction Time, Semantic Search Reaction Time.

Administration: Individual.

Price Data, 2011: $262 per software kit includes manual and unlimited use software; $53 per manual.

Time: (15) minutes.

Comments: Version 5 software package requires Microsoft Windows 98 SE through Windows XP; provides the ability to administer assessments and score and generate reports; scoring is automatic and the test can be administered multiple times to the same individual without high practice effects.

Authors: Tom N. Tombaugh and Laura M. Rees.

Publisher: Multi-Health Systems, Inc.

Cross References: For reviews by Brad M. Merker and Jeremy R. Sullivan, see 18:32.

[705]

Comrey Personality Scales.

Purpose: Developed to measure major personality characteristics.

Population: Ages 16 and over.

Publication Date: 1970.

Acronym: CPS.

Scores, 10: Trust vs. Defensiveness (T), Orderliness vs. Lack of Compulsion (O), Social Conformity vs. Rebelliousness (C), Activity vs. Lack of Energy (A), Emotional Stability vs. Neuroticism (S), Extraversion vs. Introversion (E), Mental Toughness vs. Sensitivity (M), Empathy vs. Egocentrism (P), Validity Check (V), Response Bias (R).

Administration: Group.

Price Data: Available from publisher.

Time: (35-50) minutes.

Comments: Comrey Personality Scales, Short Form is also available with same scales and prices.

Author: Andrew L. Comrey.

Publisher: EdITS/Educational and Industrial Testing Service.

Cross References: See T5:672 (6 references), T4:628 (21 references), 9:261 (8 references), and T3:558 (22 references); for a review by Edgar Howarth, see 8:527 (27 references); for reviews by R. G. Demaree and M. Y. Quereshi, see 7:59 (20 references).

[706]

Comrey Personality Scales–Short Form.

Purpose: To provide a comprehensive, multidimensional assessment instrument for measuring eight personality dimensions.

Population: High school, college, and adults.

Publication Dates: 1993–1995.

Acronym: CPS Short Form.

Scores, 10: Trust vs. Defensiveness, Orderliness vs. Lack of Compulsion, Social Conformity vs. Rebelliousness, Activity vs. Lack of Energy, Emotional Stability vs. Neuroticism, Extraversion vs. Introversion, Mental Toughness vs. Sensitivity, Empathy vs. Egocentrism, Validity Check, Response Bias.

Administration: Group.

Price Data: Available from publisher.

Time: Administration time not reported.

Comments: Includes same scales as the Comrey Personality Scales (705) but has fewer items per scale.

Author: Andrew L. Comrey.

Publisher: EdITS/Educational and Industrial Testing Service.

[707]

Concept Assessment Kit–Conservation.

Purpose: To "determine child's level of conservation by his conservation behavior and his comprehension of the principle involved."

Population: Ages 4–7.

Publication Date: 1968.
Acronym: CAK.
Administration: Individual.
Price Data: Available from publisher.
Authors: Marcel L. Goldschmid and Peter M. Bentler.
Publisher: EdITS/Educational and Industrial Testing Service.

a) FORMS A AND B.

Scores, 13: 2 scores (Behavior, Explanation) in each of 6 areas (2-Dimensional Space, Number, Substance, Continuous Quantity, Weight, Discontinuous Quantity), Total.

Time: (15) minutes per form.

b) FORM C.

Scores, 13: 2 scores (Behavior, Explanation) in each of 3 areas and 3 lengths, Total.

Cross References: See T5:674 (5 references), T4:630 (11 references), T3:559 (17 references), 8:238 (32 references), and T2:549 (5 references); for a review by J. Douglas Ayers, and excerpted reviews by Rheta DeVries and Lawrence Kohlberg, by Vernon C. Hall and Michael Mery, and by Charles D. Smock, see 7:437 (5 references).

[708]

Conditional Reasoning Test of Aggression.

Purpose: "To identify people who have a high-probability of engaging in aggressive, harmful behavior."
Population: Employees ages 18 and over.
Publication Date: 2000.
Acronym: CRTA.
Scores: Total score only.
Administration: Group or individual.
Price Data, 2006: $175 per complete kit including manual (63 pages), 25 test booklets, answer sheet, scoring key, and score interpretation; $45 per manual; $135 per 25 test booklets, answer sheet, and score interpretation.
Time: (25) minutes.
Comments: Provides an indirect measure of "potential for aggressive tendencies"; paper-and-pencil format only; hand-scored.
Authors: Lawrence R. James and Michael D. McIntyre.
Publisher: Pearson.
Cross References: For a review by Jayne E. Stake, see 15:64.

[709]

Conduct Disorder Scale.

Purpose: "To identify persons with Conduct Disorder by evaluating the characteristic behaviors that define this condition."
Population: Ages 5–22 years.
Publication Date: 2002.
Acronym: CDS.
Scores, 5: 4 subscales (Aggressive Conduct, Hostility, Deceitfulness/Theft, Rule Violations), Conduct Disorder Quotient.

Administration: Individual
Price Data, 2010: $100 per complete kit including examiner's manual (41 pages), 50 summary/response forms, and storage box; $58 per examiner's manual; $45 per 50 summary/response forms.
Time: (5–10) minutes.
Comments: Based on the diagnostic criteria for conduct disorder specified by the Diagnostic and Statistical Manual of Mental Disorders–Fourth Edition–Text Revision (DSM-IV-TR); provides interpretation guide for classifying degree of severity of conduct disorder (severe, moderate, mild, not applicable).
Author: James E. Gilliam.
Publisher: PRO-ED.
Cross References: For reviews by Michael J. Furlong and Jenne Simental and by Steven I. Pfeiffer, see 16:64.

[710]

Conference Meeting Rating Scale.

Purpose: Designed as "an overall rating procedure for observers in evaluating both the effectiveness of the conference leader and the conference group, conferees in evaluating leader portion of the meeting, and for the conference leader in measuring the reactions of the conference group."
Population: Employees.
Publication Date: No date.
Scores: Total score only.
Administration: Group.
Price Data: Available from publisher.
Time: Administration time not reported.
Author: B. J. Speroff.
Publisher: Psychometric Affiliates.

[711]

Conflict Analysis Battery.

Purpose: Designed to "assess a person's conflict resolution process, qualitatively, quantitatively and graphically along a range of four relational modalities and a symbolic system consisting of a six step dialectic of formal and energetic intertransformations."
Population: School age and adults.
Publication Date: 1988.
Acronym: CAB.
Scores, 11: The personality inventory (Relational Modality Evaluation Scale), projective tests (Balloon Portraits and Story, Conflictual Memories Test, Dream Analysis), Transparent Mask Test, Animal Metaphor Test, Fairy Tale Metaphor Test, Short Story Metaphor, Intensified Animal Metaphor Test, House-Tree-Person Metaphor Test, Scribble Metaphor.
Administration: Individuals and group.
Price Data, 2006: $40 per volume (packages of 12); $60 per textbook entitled "Conflict Analysis, the Formal Theory of Behavior."
Time: Administration time not reported.

Comments: Self-administered inventory and projective test battery; developed for use with Conflict Analysis Training: A Concise Program of Emotional Education.
Author: Albert J. Levis.
Publisher: The Institute of Conflict Analysis.
Cross References: For reviews by Susan M. Brookhart and Carl Isenhart, see 16:65.

[712]
Conflict Management Appraisal.

Purpose: "Designed to provide information about the various ways people react to and try to manage the differences between themselves and others."
Population: Adults.
Publication Dates: 1986–1995.
Acronym: CMA.
Scores, 20: 5 conflict management styles (9/1 Win-Lose, 1/9 Yield-Lose, 1/1 Lose-Leave, 5/5 Compromise, 9/9 Synergistic) for each of 4 contexts (Personal Orientation, Interpersonal Relationships, Small Group Relationships, Intergroup Relationships).
Administration: Individual.
Price Data, 2001: $7.95 per instrument.
Time: (30) minutes.
Comments: Adaptation of the Conflict Management Survey (713); to be used in conjunction with the Conflict Management Survey; ratings by person well acquainted with subject.
Author: Jay Hall.
Publisher: Teleometrics International, Inc.
Cross References: For reviews by William L. Curlette and David N. Dixon, see 12:90.

[713]
Conflict Management Survey.

Purpose: "Designed to provide information about the various ways people react to and try to manage the differences between themselves and others."
Population: Adults.
Publication Dates: 1969–1996.
Acronym: CMS.
Scores, 20: 5 conflict management styles (9/1 Win-Lose, 1/9 Yield-Lose, 1/1 Lose-Leave, 5/5 Compromise, 9/9 Synergistic) for each of 4 contexts (Personal Orientation, Interpersonal Relationships, Small Group Relationships, Intergroup Relationships).
Administration: Group.
Price Data, 2001: $8.95 per instrument.
Time: Administration time not reported.
Comments: Self-ratings.
Author: Jay Hall.
Publisher: Teleometrics International, Inc.
Cross References: For reviews by Frederick Bessai and Douglas J. McRae, see 12:91; for a review by Frank J. Landy of an earlier edition, see 8:1173 (2 references).

[714]
Conflict Style Inventory.

Purpose: Designed to assess an individual's approach to conflict resolution.
Population: Adults.
Publication Dates: 1990–1995.
Acronym: CSI.
Scores, 15: Total Score, Individual [one-on-one] Conflict Situations, Group/Team Conflict Situations on 5 styles: (Avoiding, Smoothing, Bargaining, Forcing, Problem Solving).
Administration: Group.
Price Data: Available from publisher.
Time: (20) minutes.
Comments: Self-scored.
Author: Marshall Sashkin.
Publisher: HRD Press, Inc.
Cross References: For reviews by Trenton R. Ferro and Scott T. Meier, see 14:96.

[715]
Conflict Tactics Scales.

Purpose: Designed to obtain reports of domestic violence among abusive adult partners and "physical maltreatment and neglect of children by parents, as well as nonviolent modes of discipline."
Population: Adults.
Publication Date: 2003.
Administration: Individual.
Price Data, 2010: $87.50 per complete test kit including Handbook (146 pages), 10 CTS2 AutoScore forms, and 10 CTSPC AutoScore forms; $45 per 25 CTS2 AutoScore forms; $45 per 25 CTSPC AutoScore forms; $60 per Handbook; $55 per continuing education questionnaire and evaluation form.
Authors: Murray A. Straus, Sherry L. Hamby, and W. Louise Warren.
Publisher: Western Psychological Services.
  a) REVISED CONFLICT TACTICS SCALES.
  Acronym: CTS2.
  Scores, 5: Negotiation, Psychological Aggression, Physical Assault, Injury, Sexual Coercion.
  Time: (10-15) minutes.
  b) CONFLICT TACTICS SCALES: PARENT-CHILD VERSION.
  Acronym: CTSPC.
  Scores, 6: Nonviolent Discipline, Psychological Aggression, Physical Assault, Weekly Discipline, Neglect, Sexual Abuse.
  Time: (10) minutes.

[716]
Conners' Adult ADHD Diagnostic Interview for DSM-IV.

Purpose: Empirically based structured interview that assists the process of diagnosing ADHD.

Population: Age 18 and older.
Publication Date: 2001.
Acronym: CAADID.
Scores: Childhood and Adult ADHD Diagnosis (specifies Inattentive vs. Hyperactive Impulsive).
Administration: Individual.
Price Data, 2011: $145 per complete kit including technical manual (2001, 52 pages), 10 patient history forms, and 10 diagnostic criteria interview forms; $65 per preview set including technical manual, 1 patient history form, and 1 diagnostic criteria interview form; $58 per technical manual; $57 per 10 patient history forms; $57 per 10 diagnostic criteria interview forms.
Time: (60–90) minutes for Interview; (30–60) minutes for Self-Report.
Comments: Interview format.
Authors: Jeff Epstein, Diane Johnson, and C. Keith Conners.
Publisher: Multi-Health Systems, Inc.
Cross References: For reviews by George J. Demakis and Timothy J. Makatura, see 16:66.

[717]

Conners' Adult ADHD Rating Scales.

Purpose: Designed to assess "psychopathology and problem behaviors associated with adult ADHD."
Population: Ages 18 and over.
Publication Date: 1999.
Administration: Individual or group.
Forms, 6: Self-Report: Long (CAARS-S:L); Self-Report: Short (CAARS-S:S); Self-Report: Screening (CAARS-S:SV); Observer: Long (CAARS-O:L); Observer: Short (CAARS-O:S); Observer: Screening (CAARS-O: SV).
Price Data, 2011: $339 per complete kit including manual (144 pages) and 25 QuikScore™ forms for each of the 6 forms; $77 per manual; $50 per 25 of any one of the Long QuikScore™ forms; $50 per 25 of any of the Short QuikScore™ forms; $50 per 25 of any one of the Screening QuikScore™ forms; $92 per preview set including manual, and 1 QuikScore™ form for each of the 6 forms; $81 per online profile report kit including manual and 3 online profile reports; $87 per online interpretive report kit including manual and 3 online interpretive reports; $5 per each online profile report; $7 per each online interpretive report; Software also available.
Comments: Observer rating and/or self-report. Correctional Setting norms supplement is available.
Authors: C. Keith Conners, Drew Erhardt, and Elizabeth Sparrow.
Publisher: Multi-Health Systems, Inc.

a) CAARS–SELF-REPORT: LONG; CAARS–OBSERVER: LONG.
Scores, 9: Inattention/Memory Problems, Hyperactivity/Restlessness, Impulsivity/Emotional Lability, Problems with Self-Concept, DSM-IV Inattentive Symptoms, DSM-IV Hyperactive-Impulsive Symptoms, DSM-IV Total ADHD Symptoms, ADHD Index, Inconsistency Index.
Time: (20) minutes.

b) CAARS–SELF-REPORT: SHORT; CAARS–OBSERVER: SHORT.
Scores, 6: Inattentive/Memory Problems, Hyperactivity/Restlessness, Impulsivity/Emotional Lability, Problems with Self-Concept, ADHD Index, Inconsistency Index.
Time: (10) minutes.

c) CAARS–SELF-REPORT: SCREENING; CAARS–OBSERVER: SCREENING.
Scores, 4: DSM-IV Inattentive Symptoms, DSM-IV Hyperactive/Impulsivity Symptoms, DSM-IV Total ADHD Symptoms, ADHD Index.
Time: (10) minutes.
Cross References: For reviews by Andrew S. Davis and Rik Carl D'Amato and by Ronald J. Ganellen, see 15:65.

[718]

Conners Comprehensive Behavior Rating Scales.

Purpose: Designed to "assess a wide range of behavioral, emotional, social, and academic concerns" in order to diagnose, develop, and monitor treatment plans for children and adolescents.
Population: Ages 6-18.
Publication Date: 2008.
Acronym: Conners CBRS; Conners CI.
Administration: Individual or group.
Price Data, 2011: $94 per manual (372 pages); $580 per Conners CBRS Software kit including manual, Software Program (USB Key), and 25 Parent/Teacher/Self-Report Response Booklets; $400 per Scoring Software Program (USB Key only); $50 per package of Response Booklets; $128 per Conners CBRS Online Kit including manual, 10 Parent/Teacher online forms, and 5 Self-report online forms; $1.80 per Online form; $220 per Conners Clinical Index Package including manual and 25 Parent/Teacher/Self-Report QuikScore forms; $50 per package of QuikScore forms.
Levels, 6: Conners CBRS-Teacher, Conners CBRS-Parent, Conners CBRS-Self-Report, Conners Clinical Index-Teacher, Conners Clinical Index-Parent, Conners Clinical Index-Self-Report.
Foreign Language Edition: Spanish edition available.
Comments: "The Conners Clinical Index (Conners CI) is extracted from the Conners CBRS form; the same 24 items used to calculate the Conners Clinical Index score on the Conners CBRS form are used on the Conners CI"; The Conners CBRS and Conners CI forms can be administered and scored online; paper-and-pencil forms

can also be scored online; can be scored using the Conners CBRS scoring software program by entering responses from a completed paper-and-pencil administration but cannot be administered through the software.

Author: C. Keith Conners.

Publisher: Multi-Health Systems Inc.

a) CONNERS COMPREHENSIVE BEHAVIOR RATING SCALE-TEACHER.

Population: Ages 6-18.

Acronym: Conners CBRS-T.

Scores, 44: Emotional Distress, Upsetting Thoughts/Physical Symptoms, Social Anxiety, Defiant/Aggressive Behaviors, Academic Difficulties, Academic Difficulties: Language, Academic Difficulties: Math, Hyperactivity, Social Problems, Separation Fears, Perfectionistic and Compulsive Behaviors, Violence Potential Indicator, Physical Symptoms, ADHD Hyperactive/Impulsive, ADHD Inattentive, ADHD Combined, Conduct Disorder, Oppositional Defiant Disorder, Major Depressive Episode, Manic Episode, Mixed Episode, Generalized Anxiety Disorder, Separation Anxiety Disorder, Social Phobia, Obsessive-Compulsive Disorder, Autistic Disorder, Asperger's Disorder, Positive Impression, Negative Impression, Inconsistency Index, Conners Clinical Index, Bullying Perpetration, Bullying Victimization, Enuresis/Encopresis, Panic Attack, Post Traumatic Stress Disorder, Specific Phobia, Substance Use, Tics, Trichotillomania, Impairment in Schoolwork/Grades, Impairment in Friendships/Relationships, Severe Conduct, Self-Harm.

Time: (20) minutes.

b) CONNERS COMPREHENSIVE BEHAVIOR RATING SCALE-PARENT.

Population: Ages 6-18.

Acronym: Conners CBRS-P.

Scores, 46: Emotional Distress, Upsetting Thoughts, Worrying, Defiant/Aggressive Behaviors, Academic Difficulties, Academic Difficulties: Language, Academic Difficulties: Math, Hyperactivity/Impulsivity, Social Problems, Separation Fears, Perfectionistic and Compulsive Behaviors, Violence Potential Indicator, Physical Symptoms, ADHD Hyperactive/Impulsive, ADHD Inattentive, ADHD Combined, Conduct Disorder, Oppositional Defiant Disorder, Major Depressive Episode, Manic Episode, Mixed Episode, Generalized Anxiety Disorder, Separation Anxiety Disorder, Social Phobia, Obsessive-Compulsive Disorder, Autistic Disorder, Asperger's Disorder, Positive Impression, Negative Impression, Inconsistency Index, Conners Clinical Index, Bullying Perpetration, Bullying Victimization, Enuresis/Encopresis, Panic Attack, Pica, Post Traumatic Stress Disorder, Specific Phobia, Substance Use, Tics, Trichotillomania, Impairment in Schoolwork/Grades, Impairment in Friendships/

Relationships, Impairment in Home Life, Severe Conduct, Self-Harm.

Time: Same as *a* above.

c) CONNERS COMPREHENSIVE BEHAVIOR RATING SCALE-SELF-REPORT.

Population: Ages 8-18.

Acronym: Conners CBRS-SR.

Scores, 38: Emotional Distress, Defiant/Aggressive Behaviors, Academic Difficulties, Hyperactivity/Impulsivity, Separation Fears, Violence Potential Indicator, Physical Symptoms, ADHD Hyperactive/Impulsive, ADHD Inattentive, ADHD Combined, Conduct Disorder, Oppositional Defiant Disorder, Major Depressive Episode, Manic Episode, Mixed Episode, Generalized Anxiety Disorder, Separation Anxiety Disorder, Social Phobia, Obsessive-Compulsive Disorder, Positive Impression, Negative Impression, Inconsistency Index, Conners Clinical Index, Bullying Perpetration, Bullying Victimization, Panic Attack, Pervasive Developmental Disorder, Pica, Post Traumatic Stress Disorder, Specific Phobia, Substance Use, Tics, Trichotillomania, Impairment in Schoolwork/Grades, Impairment in Friendships/Relationships, Impairment in Home Life, Severe Conduct, Self-Harm.

Time: Same as *a* above.

d) CONNERS CLINICAL INDEX-TEACHER.

Population: Ages 6-18.

Acronym: Conners CI-T.

Scores, 6: Overall Conners Clinical Index Score, Disruptive Behavior Indicator, Learning and Language Disorder Indicator, Mood Disorder Indicator, Anxiety Disorder Indicator, ADHD Indicator.

Time: (10) minutes.

e) CONNERS CLINICAL INDEX-PARENT.

Population: Ages 6-18.

Acronym: Conners CI-P.

Scores: Same as *d* above.

Time: Same as *d* above.

f) CONNERS CLINICAL INDEX-SELF-REPORT.

Population: Ages 8-18.

Scores: Same as *d* above.

Time: Same as *d* above.

Cross References: For reviews by Jeremy R. Sullivan and John J. Vacca, see 18:33.

[719]

Conners' Continuous Performance Test II.

Purpose: A computerized assessment tool used to assess attention problems and to measure treatment effectiveness.

Population: Ages 6 to adult.

Publication Dates: 1992–1996.

Acronym: CPT II.

Scores, 12: Omissions, Commissions, Hit Reaction Time, Hit Reaction Time Standard Error, Variability of Standard Error, Attentiveness (d prime), Perseverations,

Hit Reaction Time Block Change (Vigilance Measure), Hit Standard Error Block Change (Vigilance Measure), Hit Reaction Time Inter-Stimulus Interval Change (Adjusting to Presentation Speed), Hit Standard Error Inter-Stimulus Change (Adjusting to Presentation Speed), Confidence Index.
Administration: Individual.
Price Data, 2011: $711 per CPT II V.5 installation (includes manual and unlimited use program); $53 per preview kit (includes manual and 3 report uses).
Time: (14) minutes.
Comments: Self-report performance measure; includes Flash Drive; requires Windows 95 or higher.
Authors: C. Keith Conners and the MHS staff.
Publisher: Multi-Health Systems Inc.
Cross References: For reviews by Beverly M. Klecker and Wesley E. Sime, see 15:66; for a review by James Ysseldyke of an earlier version, see 14:97; see also T5:679 (2 references).

[720]

Conners Early Childhood.

Purpose: Designed to "assess a wide range of behavioral, emotional, and social concerns and developmental milestones in preschool-aged children."
Population: Ages 2-6.
Publication Date: 2009.
Acronym: Conners EC.
Administration: Individual or group.
Forms: 5 form options per rater (Parent, Teacher/Childcare Provider).
Price Data, 2010: $355 per Complete Scoring Software kit including 25 each of the Parent and Teacher response booklets, manual (242 pages), and unlimited use scoring software; $140 per Online Kit including 20 of each of the Parent and Teacher Online Forms, and Manual; $165 per Global Index Handscored Kit including 25 each of the Parent and Teacher QuikScore forms and manual; $108 per Global Index Online kit including 10 each of the Parent and Teacher Online forms and manual; $50 per each package of 25 response booklets for any rater or form (Parent or Teacher Full-Length, Behavior, Developmental Milestones, Behavior Short, or Global Index form); $1.80 per each Online form (Parent or Teacher Full-Length, Behavior, Developmental Milestones, Behavior Short, or Global Index form); $84 per manual; $210 per unlimited scoring software (USB); prices are identical for the equivalent Spanish forms.
Foreign Language Edition: Spanish version available for all forms.
Comments: Administration available in paper-and-pencil or online format; scoring available online or using the scoring software (Global Index QuikScore form can also be hand-scored).
Author: C. Keith Conners.
Publisher: Multi-Health Systems, Inc.

a) CONNERS EARLY CHILDHOOD FULL-LENGTH FORMS.
Acronyms: Conners EC-P; Conners EC-T.
Scores: 22 scores per parent; 21 scores per Teacher, including 11 Behavior scores (Inattention/Hyperactivity, Defiance/Temper, Aggression, Defiant/Aggressive Behaviors Total, Social Functioning, Atypical Behaviors, Social Functioning/Atypical Behaviors Total, Anxiety, Mood and Affect, Physical Symptoms, Sleep Problems, parent only), 5 Developmental Milestone scores (Adaptive Skills, Communication, Motor Skills, Play, Pre-Academic/Cognitive), 3 Validity scores (Positive Impression, Negative Impression, Inconsistency Index), and 3 Global Index scores (Restless-Impulsive, Emotional Lability, Total).
Time: (25) minutes.
Comments: Scoring report also includes item ratings for Other Clinical Indicators and Impairment Items, and rater's responses to two additional open-ended questions.

b) CONNERS EARLY CHILDHOOD BEHAVIOR FORMS.
Acronyms: Conners EC BEH-P; Conners EC BEH-T.
Scores: 17 scores per parent; 16 scores per teacher, including 11 Behavior scores (Inattention/Hyperactivity, Defiance/Temper, Aggression, Defiant/Aggressive Behaviors Total, Social Functioning, Atypical Behaviors, Social Functioning/Atypical Behaviors Total, Anxiety, Mood and Affect, Physical Symptoms, Sleep Problems, parent only), 3 Validity scores (Positive Impression, Negative Impression, Inconsistency Index), and 3 Global Index scores (Restless-Impulsive, Emotional Lability, Total).
Time: (15) minutes.
Comments: Scoring report also includes item ratings for Other Clinical Indicators and Impairment Items, and rater's responses to two additional open-ended questions.

c) CONNERS EARLY CHILDHOOD DEVELOPMENTAL MILESTONES FORMS.
Acronyms: Conners EC DM-P; Conners EC DM-T.
Scores: 5 Developmental Milestones scores per rater: Adaptive Skills, Communication, Motor Skills, Play, Pre-Academic/Cognitive.
Time: (10) minutes.
Comments: Scoring report also includes item ratings for Impairment Items, and rater's responses to two additional open-ended questions.

d) CONNERS EARLY CHILDHOOD BEHAVIOR SHORT FORMS.
Acronyms: Conners EC BEH-P[S]; Conners EC BEH-T[S].
Scores: 8 scores per rater, including 6 Behavior scores (Inattention/Hyperactivity, Defiant/Aggres-

sive Behaviors Total, Social Functioning/Atypical Behaviors Total, Anxiety, Mood and Affect, Physical Symptoms), and 2 Validity scores (Positive Impression, Negative Impression).
Time: (10) minutes.
Comments: Scoring report also includes rater's responses to two additional open-ended questions.
e) CONNERS EARLY CHILDHOOD GLOBAL INDEX FORMS.
Acronyms: Conners ECGI-P; Conners ECGI-T.
Scores: 3 Global Index scores per rater: Restless-Impulsive, Emotional Lability, Total.
Time: (5) minutes.
Cross References: For reviews by Sherry K. Bain and Kathleen B. Aspiranti and by Jean N. Clark, see 18:34.

[721]

Conners' Kiddie Continuous Performance Test.

Purpose: Software programs designed to identify attention problems and measure treatment effectiveness in very young children.
Population: Age 4–5.
Publication Date: 2001.
Acronym: K-CPT.
Scores, 14: Omissions, Comissions, Hit RT, Hit RT Standard Error, Variability, Detectability (d), Response Style, Perseverations, Hit RT Block Change, Hit SE Block Change, Hit RT ISI Change, Hit SE ISI Change, and Confidence Index.
Administration: Individual.
Price Data, 2006: $215 per unlimited-use software kit, including manual (2001, 156 pages); $50 per preview version (3 uses).
Time: 7.5 minutes.
Comments: Self-completed; administered and scored on computer running Windows 95 or higher.
Authors: C. Keith Conners and Multi-Health Systems, Inc. staff.
Publisher: Multi-Health Systems, Inc.
Cross References: For reviews by Brian F. French and by Scott A. Napolitano and Courtney Miller, see 16:67.

[722]

Conners-March Developmental Questionnaire.

Purpose: To gather personal history information about a child from the parents prior to meeting with a physician or psychologist.
Population: Children.
Publication Date: 1994.
Scores: Not scored.
Administration: Individual.
Manual: No manual.
Price Data, 2011: $50 per 25 questionnaires.

Time: Administration time not reported.
Comments: Completed by parent. Development questionnaire, key areas covered: description of problems, treatment history, motor development, history of family and child, temperament, home environment, birth history, medical history, school behavior and performance.
Authors: C. Keith Conners and John S. March.
Publisher: Multi-Health Systems, Inc.

[723]

Conners 3rd Edition.

Purpose: Designed to be an assessment of "Attention-Deficit/Hyperactivity Disorder (ADHD) and its most common comorbid problems and disorders in children and adolescents."
Population: Ages 6-18.
Publication Dates: 1989-2008.
Acronym: Conners 3.
Administration: Individual or group.
Forms, 11: Conners 3-Parent Full, Conners 3-Parent Short, Conners 3-Teacher Full, Conners 3-Teacher Short, Conners 3-Self-Report Full, Conners 3-Self-Report Short, Conners 3 ADHD Index-Teacher, Conners 3 ADHD Index-Parent, Conners 3 ADHD Index-Self-Report, Conners 3 Global Index-Teacher, Conners 3 Global Index-Parent.
Price Data, 2011: $355 per Handscore kit including manual (2008, 470 pages), 25 parent/teacher/self-report QuikScore™ forms, and 25 parent/teacher/self-report short QuikScore™ forms; $270 per Reorder Kit, 25 parent/teacher/self-report QuikScore™ forms, and 25 parent/teacher/self-report short QuikScore™ forms; $94 per manual; $50 per package of 25 QuikScore™ forms; $125 per Conners 3 Online Kit including manual, 10 Parent/Teacher online forms, and 5 Self-report forms; $1.80 per Online form; $600 per Conners 3 Software Kit including manual, software program (USB Key), 25 Parent/Teacher/Self-Report response booklets, and 25 Parent/Teacher/Self-Report Short QuikScore™ forms; $50 per package of 25 Response Booklets.
Foreign Language Edition: Spanish versions available for Parent and Self-Report forms.
Time: (20) minutes for full length form; (10) minutes for short forms.
Comments: All forms are available in QuikScore™ format; can also be completed and scored online; paper-and-pencil forms can also be scored online; can also be scored using the scoring software program by entering responses from a completed pencil-and-paper administration but cannot be administered through the software.
Author: C. Keith Conners.
Publisher: Multi-Health Systems, Inc.
a) CONNERS 3-PARENT.
Population: Ages 6-18.
Full-Length Scores, 22: Inattention, Hyperactivity/Impulsivity, Learning Problems, Executive

Functioning, Defiance/Aggression, Peer Relations, DSM-IV-TR ADHD Hyperactive-Impulsive, DSM-IV-TR ADHD Inattentive, DSM-IV-TR ADHD Combined, DSM-IV-TR Conduct Disorder, DSM-IV-TR Oppositional Defiant Disorder, Positive Impression, Negative Impression, Inconsistency Index, Conners 3 ADHD Index, Conners 3 Global Index, Anxiety, Depression, Impairment in Schoolwork/Grades, Impairment in Friendships/Relationships, Impairment in Home Life, Severe Conduct.

Forms, 4: Full, Short, ADHD Index, Global Index.
b) CONNERS 3-TEACHER.
Population: Ages 6-18.
Full-Length Scores, 22: Inattention, Hyperactivity/Impulsivity, Learning Problems, Executive Functioning, Learning Problems/Executive Functioning, Defiance/Aggression, Peer Relations, DSM-IV-TR ADHD Hyperactive-Impulsive, DSM-IV-TR ADHD Inattentive, DSM-IV-TR ADHD Combined, DSM-IV-TR Conduct Disorder, DSM-IV-TR Oppositional Defiant Disorder, Positive Impression, Negative Impression, Inconsistency Index, Conners 3 ADHD Index, Conners 3 Global Index, Anxiety, Depression, Impairment in Schoolwork/Grades, Impairment in Friendships/Relationships, Severe Conduct.

Forms, 4: Full, Short, ADHD Index, Global Index.
c) CONNERS 3-SELF-REPORT.
Population: Ages 8-18.
Full-Length Scores, 20: Inattention, Hyperactivity/Impulsivity, Learning Problems, Defiance/Aggression, Family Relations, DSM-IV-TR ADHD Hyperactive/Impulsive, DSM-IV-TR ADHD Inattentive, DSM-IV-TR ADHD Combined, DSM-IV-TR Conduct Disorder, DSM-IV-TR Oppositional Defiant Disorder, Positive Impression, Negative Impression, Inconsistency Index, Conners 3 ADHD Index, Anxiety, Depression, Impairment in Schoolwork/Grades, Impairment in Friendships/Relationships, Impairment in Home Life, Severe Conduct.

Forms, 3: Full, Short, ADHD Index.
Cross References: For reviews by Sharon Arffa and Thomas M. Dunn, see 18:35; for reviews by Allen K. Hess and Howard M. Knoff of an earlier edition, see 14:98; see also T5:681 (99 references) and T4:636 (50 references); for reviews by Brian K. Martens and Judy Oehler-Stinnett of the original edition, see 11:87 (83 references).

[724]

Consequences.
Purpose: Measure ideational fluency and originality.
Population: Grades 9–16.
Publication Date: 1958.
Scores, 2: Originality, Ideational Fluency.

Administration: Group.
Forms, 2: A1, A2.
Price Data: Available from publisher.
Time: 10(13) minutes.
Comments: Mimeographed manual, third edition (8 pages); Form A1 consists of first 5 items and Form A2 consists of last 5 items of the original 1958 (single-form) 10-item test.
Authors: Paul R. Christensen, P. R. Merrifield, and J. P. Guilford.
Publisher: Charlotte Mackley [No reply from publisher; status unknown].
Cross References: See T5:682 (5 references), T4:637 (2 references) and T2:551 (71 references); for a review by Goldine C. Gleser of the 10-item test, see 6:547 (13 references).

[725]

Constructive Thinking Inventory.
Purpose: "Evaluates an individual's experiential intelligence and coping skills."
Population: Ages 18–81 years.
Publication Date: 2001.
Acronym: CTI.
Scores, 9: Emotional Coping (Self-Acceptance, Absence of Negative Overgeneralization, Nonsensitivity, Absence of Dwelling), Behavioral Coping (Positive Thinking, Action Orientation, Conscientiousness), Personal Superstitious Thinking, Categorical Thinking (Polarized Thinking, Distrust of Others, Intolerance), Esoteric Thinking (Belief in the Unusual, Formal Superstitious Thinking), Naive Optimism (Over-Optimism, Stereotypical Thinking, Polyanna-ish Thinking), Defensiveness, Validity, Global Constructive Thinking.
Administration: Individual or group.
Price Data, 2006: $145 per introductory kit including CD ROM-based scoring program with on-screen user's manual, professional manual (59 pages), 25 test booklets, and 25-report uses.
Time: (15–30) minutes.
Comments: Administered in paper-and-pencil format only; responses are manually entered into scoring program; software generates raw scores, T-scores, and profile; system requirements: Windows 95/98/NT/2000/ME/XP; 8 MB hard disk, 16 MB RAM (Windows 95/98/ME) or 24 MB RAM (Windows NT/2000/XP), CD ROM with internet and telephone.
Author: Seymour Epstein.
Publisher: Psychological Assessment Resources, Inc.

[726]

Contextual Memory Test.
Purpose: Designed to assess awareness of memory capacity, strategy use, and recall in adults with memory dysfunction.
Population: Adults.
Publication Date: 1993.

Acronym: CMT.
Scores, 12: Recall Score (Immediate Recall, Delayed Recall, Total Recall), Cued Recall, Recognition, Awareness Score (Prediction, Estimation of Performance Following Recall, Response to General Questioning [Prior to Recall, Following Recall]), Strategy Use (Effect of Context, Order of Recall, Total Strategy Score).
Administration: Individual.
Price Data, 2002: $105 per complete kit including manual (138 pages), 2 test cards, 14 cut-apart sheets of 80 picture cards, 25 score sheets (12 pages), and carrying case; $37 per 25 score sheets.
Time: (10–20) minutes.
Author: Joan P. Toglia.
Publisher: Pearson.
Cross References: For reviews by Karen Mackler and Alan J. Raphael, see 14:99.

[727]

Contextual Test of Articulation.

Purpose: "Designed to ... identify phonetic contexts that facilitate correct production of phonemes incorrectly produced by children ... who display speech sound production disorders."
Population: Ages 4-9.
Publication Date: 2000.
Acronym: CTA.
Scores: 6 subtests: Consonant Singleton /s/, Consonant Singleton /l/, Consonant Singleton /k/, Consonant Singleton /r/, Semivowel, Consonant Clusters.
Administration: Individual.
Price Data, 2006: $129 per complete kit including manual (46 pages), easel-style spiral, and 195 full-color picture plates.
Time: (15-25) minutes per subtest.
Comments: This test should be administered "after a child's phonemes production errors have been identified."
Authors: Dawn Aase, Charity Hovre, Karleen Krause, Sarah Schelfhout, Jennifer Smith, and Linda J. Carpenter.
Publisher: Thinking Publications.
Cross References: For reviews by Jeffery P. Braden and Sandye M. Ouzts and by Rebecca J. McCauley, see 17:53.

[728]

Continuous Visual Memory Test [Revised].

Purpose: Constructed to assess visual memory.
Population: Ages 7–80+.
Publication Dates: 1983–1997.
Acronym: CVMT.
Scores, 6: Acquisition (Hits, False Alarms, d-Prime, Total), Delayed Recognition, Visual Discrimination.
Administration: Individual.
Price Data, 2006: $170 per kit including manual (1988, 22 pages), norms manual (1997, 51 pages), stimulus cards, and 50 scoring forms.

Time: (45–50) minutes.
Authors: Donald E. Trahan and Glenn J. Larrabee.
Publisher: Psychological Assessment Resources, Inc.
Cross References: For reviews by Michael B. Brown and Alice J. Corkill, see 14:100; see also T5:687 (4 references); for reviews by Nancy B. Bologna and Stephen F. Davis of an earlier edition, see 12:93; see also T4:642 (4 references).

[729]

Controller Staff Selector.

Purpose: To evaluate the bookkeeping and analytical reasoning skills necessary for the position of controller.
Population: Candidates for the position of controller.
Publication Date: 1988.
Acronym: COCON.
Scores: Total Score, Narrative Evaluation, Ranking, Recommendation.
Administration: Group.
Price Data, 2001: $500 per candidate; quantity discounts available.
Time: (319) minutes.
Comments: Scored by publisher; must be proctored; previously listed as Controller/Accountant Staff Selector.
Author: Walden Personnel Performance, Inc.
Publisher: Walden Personnel Performance, Inc. [Canada].

[730]

The Conversational Skills Rating Scale: An Instructional Assessment of Interpersonal Competence.

Purpose: "To assess the skills domain of conversational competence."
Population: Secondary and post-secondary students.
Publication Date: 1995.
Acronym: CSRS.
Scores, 5: Altercentricism, Composure, Expressiveness, Interaction Management, Total.
Administration: Group.
Forms, 7: Rating of Partner Form, Rating of Self Form, Instructor Rating of Student Form, Self Frequency Version, Partner Frequency Version, Self Trait Rating Form, Other Trait Rating Form.
Price Data: Available from publisher.
Time: (5–15) minutes.
Author: Brian H. Spitzberg.
Publisher: National Communication Association.
Cross References: For reviews by Sandra M. Ketrow and Julia Y. Porter, see 14:101.

[731]

Coolidge Assessment Battery.

Purpose: Designed to assess personality disorders and neuropsychological functioning.

Population: Ages 15 and older.
Publication Date: 1999.
Acronym: CAB.
Scores, 46: 7 Axis I scales (Anxiety, Depression, Post-Traumatic Stress, Psychotic Thinking, Schizophrenia, Social Phobia, Withdrawal); 14 Axis II scales (Antisocial, Avoidant, Borderline, Dependent, Depressive, Histrionic, Narcissistic, Obsessive-Compulsive, Paranoid, Passive-Aggressive, Sadistic, Schizoid, Schizotypal, Self-Defeating); 4 Neuropsychological Dysfunction scales (Overall Neuropsychological, Language Functions, Memory and Concentration, Neurosomatic Functions); 4 Executive Functions of the Frontal Lobe scales (Overall Executive Functions, Decision Difficulty, Planning Problems, Task Completion Difficulty); 5 Personality Change due to Medical Condition scales (Aggression, Apathy, Disinhibition, Emotional Lability, Paranoid); 3 Hostility scales (Anger, Dangerousness, Impulsiveness); 5 Normative scales (Apathy, Emotional Lability, Indecisiveness, Maladjustment, Introversion-Extroversion); 4 Validity scales (Answer Choice Frequency, Random Responding, Tendency to Look Good or Bad, Tendency to Deny Blatant Pathology).
Administration: Group or individual.
Price Data, 2010: $48 per manual (1999, 54 pages); $145 per Windows software installation package, includes 10 scoring coupons.
Time: 40 minutes.
Comments: Originally published as the Coolidge Axis II Inventory (14:102); software scoring.
Author: Frederick L. Coolidge.
Publisher: SIGMA Assessment Systems, Inc.
Cross References: For reviews by Mark A. Staal and Peter Zachar, see 15:68; for reviews by Kevin L. Moreland and Paul Retzlaff of an earlier edition, see 14:102; see also T5:690 (3 references).

[732]
The Cooperative Institutional Research Program.
Purpose: "A national longitudinal study of the American higher educational system" based on freshman survey data.
Population: First-time, full-time entering college freshmen.
Publication Dates: 1966–1994.
Acronym: CIRP.
Scores: No scores.
Administration: Group.
Price Data: Available from publisher.
Time: (40) minutes.
Comments: Test entitled Student Information Form (T3:2333); national norms reported annually.
Authors: Alexander W. Astin, William S. Korn, and Ellyne R. Riggs.
Publisher: Higher Education Research Institute, University of California-Los Angeles [No reply from publisher; status unknown].

Cross References: See T5:692 (1 reference) and T4:645 (8 references); for a review by Harvey Resnick, see 9:266. For a review by Albert B. Hood of the Student Information Form, see 8:397 (15 references).

[733]
Coopersmith Self-Esteem Inventories for Children and Adults.
Purpose: "Designed to measure evaluative attitudes toward the self in social, academic, family, and personal areas of experience."
Population: Ages 8-15, 16 and above
Publication Date: 1981.
Acronym: CSEI.
Administration: Group.
Price Data: Available from the publisher at www.mindgarden.com/products/cseisad.htm.
Foreign Language Edition: Spanish edition available.
Time: (10) minutes.
Author: Stanley Coopersmith.
Publisher: Mind Garden, Inc.
  a) SCHOOL FORM.
  Population: Ages 8–15.
  Scores, 6: General Self, Social Self-Peers, Home-Parents, School-Academic, Total Self Score, Lie.
  Comments: Separate answer sheets may be used; school short form also available.
  b) ADULT FORM.
  Population: Ages 16 and above.
Cross References: See T5:694 (134 references) and T4:647 (106 references); for reviews by Christopher Peterson and James T. Austin and by Trevor E. Sewell, see 9:267 (32 references).

[734]
Coping Inventory: A Measure of Adaptive Behavior.
Purpose: "Assess the behavior patterns and skills used to meet personal needs and to adapt to the demands of the environment."
Population: Ages 3-16; Ages 15-Adult.
Publication Date: 1985.
Scores, 9: 3 scores (Productive, Active, Flexible) for Coping with Self, Coping with Environment, plus Adaptive Behavior Index.
Administration: Individual.
Price Data: See www.ststesting.com for up-to-date pricing information.
Levels, 2: Observation Form (ages 3-16) and Self-Rated Form (ages 15-adult).
Time: Administration time not reported.
Author: Shirley Zeitlin.
Publisher: Scholastic Testing Service, Inc.

a) SELF-RATED FORM.
Population: Ages 15-Adult.
Comments: Self-report ratings of adaptive behavior.
b) OBSERVATION FORM.
Population: Ages 3–16.
Comments: Ratings of adaptive behavior by adult informant.
Cross References: See T5:695 (3 references) and T4:648 (1 reference).

[735]
Coping Inventory for Stressful Situations, Second Edition.

Purpose: Designed as a "scale for measuring coping styles."
Population: Adolescents ages 13–18, adults age 18 and over.
Publication Dates: 1990-1999.
Acronym: CISS.
Scores, 5: Task-Oriented Coping, Emotion-Oriented Coping, Avoidance-Oriented Coping, Distraction, Social Diversion.
Administration: Individual or group.
Forms, 3: Adult, Adolescent, Situation-Specific Coping (CISS:SSC).
Price Data, 2011: $117 per CISS Adult Version Complete Kit including 25 Adult QuikScore™ forms, 25 SSC QuikScore™ forms, and manual (1999, 75 pages); $80 per CISS Adolescent Version Complete Kit including 25 Adolescent QuikScore™ forms and manual (1999, 75 pages); $50 per 25 QuikScore™ forms (specify Adult, Adolescent, or SSC); $51 per manual.
Foreign Language Editions: French (European), French (Quebec), Arabic, Armenian, Danish, German, Greek, Hebrew, Icelandic, Italian, Japanese, Korean, Malaysian, Norwegian, Polish, Russion, Spanish (U.S.), and Spanish (European) translations available.
Time: (10) minutes.
Comments: Self-report.
Authors: Norman S. Endler and James D. A. Parker.
Publisher: Multi-Health Systems, Inc.
Cross References: For a review by William C. Tirre, see 15:69; for reviews by E. Thomas Dowd and Stephanie Stein of an earlier edition, see 14:104, see also T5:696 (2 references).

[736]
Coping Resources Inventory.

Purpose: Developed to assess a person's resources for coping with stress.
Population: Middle school-age to adult
Publication Dates: 1987–1988.
Acronym: CRI.
Scores, 6: Cognitive, Social, Emotional, Spiritual/Philosophical, Physical, Total.

Administration: Group.
Price Data, 2010: Available from the publisher at www.mindgarden.com/products/criss.htm.
Time: (10) minutes.
Authors: Allen L. Hammer and M. Susan Marting.
Publisher: Mind Garden, Inc.
Cross References: See T5:697 (6 references); for reviews by Roger A. Boothroyd and Larry Cochran, see 12:95 (1 reference); see also T4:649 (2 references).

[737]
Coping Resources Inventory for Stress.

Purpose: "Designed to measure coping resources which are believed to help lessen the negative effects of stress."
Population: Adults.
Publication Dates: 1988–1993.
Acronym: CRIS.
Scores, 16: Self-Disclosure, Self-Directedness, Confidence, Acceptance, Social Support, Financial Freedom, Physical Health, Physical Fitness, Stress Monitoring, Tension Control, Structuring, Problem Solving, Cognitive Restructuring, Functional Beliefs, Social Ease, Coping Resource Effectiveness.
Administration: Group or individual.
Price Data: Available from publisher.
Foreign Language Editions: Spanish, French, Russian, Chinese, Portugese, and Korean editions available.
Time: (45–90) minutes.
Comments: Computer (PC-CRIS) administration and software package available.
Authors: Kenneth B. Matheny, William L. Curlette, David W. Aycock, James L. Pugh, and Harry F. Taylor.
Publisher: Health Prisms, Inc. [No reply from publisher; status unknown].
Cross References: See T5:698 (1 reference); for reviews by Sharon L. Weinberg and Paul D. Werner, see 13:84; see also T4:650 (3 references).

[738]
Coping Responses Inventory–Adult and Youth.

Purpose: Constructed to "identify and monitor coping strategies in adults and adolescents."
Population: Ages 12–18, 18 and older.
Publication Date: 1993.
Acronym: CRI.
Scores, 8: Logical Analysis, Positive Reappraisal, Seeking Guidance and Support, Problem Solving, Cognitive Avoidance, Acceptance or Resignation, Seeking Alternative Rewards, Emotional Discharge.
Administration: Group.
Levels, 2: Adult and Youth.
Forms, 2: Ideal, Actual.
Price Data, 2006: $158 per CRI-Adult introductory kit including CRI-Adult professional manual (44 pages),

10 reusable item booklets, 50 answer sheets, and "Coping Responses Inventory"; $158 per CRI-Youth introductory kit including CRI-Adult professional manual, 10 reusable item booklets, 50 answer sheets, and "Coping Responses Inventory."
Time: (10–15) minutes.
Author: Rudolf H. Moos.
Publisher: Psychological Assessment Resources, Inc.
Cross References: For reviews by Ashraf Kagee and Everett V. Smith, Jr., see 14:105; see also T5:699 (5 references).

[739]

Coping Scale for Adults.
Purpose: Designed as a self-report inventory that examines coping behavior and facilitates development of coping strategies.
Population: Ages 18 and over.
Publication Date: 1997.
Acronym: CSA.
Scores, 19: Seek Social Support, Focus on Solving the Problem, Work Hard, Worry, Improve Relationships, Wishful Thinking, Tension Reduction, Social Action, Ignore the Problem, Self-Blame, Keep to Self, Seek Spiritual Support, Focus on the Positive, Seek Professional Help, Seek Relaxing Diversions, Physical Recreation, Protect Self, Humor, Not Cope.
Administration: Group.
Forms, 2: Short Form, Long Form.
Price Data, 2006: A$129.95 per complete kit; A$24.95 per 10 short forms; A$29.95 per 10 long forms; A$12.95 per 10 scoring sheets; A$12.95 per 10 profile charts; A$54.95 per manual (60 pages).
Time: Administration time not reported.
Authors: Erica Frydenberg and Ramon Lewis.
Publisher: Australian Council for Educational Research Ltd. [Australia].
Cross References: For reviews by Peter Miles Berger and M. Allan Cooperstein, see 15:70.

[740]

Coping With Health Injuries and Problems.
Purpose: "Helps you quickly identify an individual's typical coping styles and suggests strategies that will best help the individual cope with and overcome his/her health problems."
Population: Adults.
Publication Dates: 1992–2000.
Acronym: CHIP.
Scores, 4: Distraction, Palliative, Instrumental, Emotional Preoccupation.
Administration: Individual or Group.
Price Data, 2011: $86 per complete kit including technical manual (2000, 66 pages) and 25 QuikScore forms; $50 per 25 QuikScore forms; $58 per technical manual.
Time: (15) minutes.

Comments: Self-report.
Authors: Norman S. Endler and James D. A. Parker.
Publisher: Multi-Health Systems, Inc.
Cross References: For reviews by Linda K. Bunker and by Leonard Handler and Amanda Jill Clements, see 15:71.

[741]

Coping With Stress.
Purpose: Constructed as a self-assessment tool to identify sources of stress and responses to stress.
Population: Adults.
Publication Date: 1989.
Scores, 9: Reaction to Stress (Obsessive, Hysteria, Anxiety, Phobia, Total, Normal), Adjustment to Stress (Healthy, Unhealthy), Sources of Stress.
Administration: Group.
Price Data: Price information available from publisher for complete kit including 20 test folders, 20 response sheets, and 20 interpretation sheets.
Time: [20] minutes administration; [10] minutes scoring; [30] minutes interpretation.
Comments: Self-administered, self-scored.
Author: Training House, Inc.
Publisher: Training House, Inc.
Cross References: For a review by Bert W. Westbrook and Suzanne Markel-Fox, see 12:96.

[742]

COPSystem Picture Inventory of Careers.
Purpose: To measure career interest for persons with reading or language difficulties.
Population: Elementary through adult-non-verbal.
Publication Date: 1993.
Acronym: COPS-PIC.
Scores: Interest scores in 14 COPSystem Career Clusters: Science–Professional, Science–Skilled, Technology–Professional, Technology–Skilled, Consumer Economics, Outdoor, Business–Professional, Business–Skilled, Clerical, Communication, Arts–Professional, Arts–Skilled, Service–Professional, Service–Skilled.
Administration: Group.
Price Data: Available from publisher.
Time: (30) minutes.
Author: Lisa Knapp-Lee.
Publisher: EdITS/Educational and Industrial Testing Service.

[743]

The Cornell Class-Reasoning Test, Form X.
Purpose: "A multiple-choice deductive logic class-reasoning test."
Population: Grades 4–12.
Publication Date: 1964.
Scores: Deductive Logic.

Administration: Group.
Manual: No manual.
Price Data: Available from publisher.
Time: Untimed.
Comments: Subtitle on test booklet is Cornell Critical Thinking Test Series.
Authors: Robert H. Ennis, William L. Gardiner, Richard Morrow, Dieter Paulus, and Lucille Ringel.
Publisher: Illinois Critical Thinking Project.
Cross References: See T2:1753 (1 reference).

[744]

The Cornell Conditional-Reasoning Test.

Purpose: Designed as "a multiple-choice deductive logic conditional-reasoning test."
Population: Grades 4–12.
Publication Date: 1964.
Scores: Deductive Logic.
Administration: Group.
Manual: No manual.
Price Data: Available from publisher.
Time: Untimed.
Comments: Subtitle on test booklet is Cornell Critical Thinking Test Series.
Authors: Robert H. Ennis, William L. Gardiner, John Gazzetta, Richard Morrow, Dieter Paulus, and Lucille Ringel.
Publisher: Illinois Critical Thinking Project.
Cross References: See T2:1754 (1 reference).

[745]

Cornell Critical Thinking Tests.

Purpose: Assesses general critical thinking ability including "induction, deduction, evaluation, observation, credibility (of statements made by others), assumption identification, and meaning."
Publication Dates: 1961-1985.
Acronym: CCTT.
Scores: Total score only for each level.
Administration: Group.
Levels, 2: X, Z.
Price Data, 2001: $21.99 per 10 test booklets (specify level); $8.99 per 10 machine-gradable answer sheets; $8.99 per manual (1985, 32 pages); $17.99 per specimen set including both tests, answer sheet, and manual; $39.99 per software (specify Level X or Level Z and Macintosh or Windows; quantity licenses available); includes 10 free tests (any combination of X and Z levels); $.99 per additional per student license.
Time: (50) minutes.
Comments: Identical to 1971 edition except for minor format and wording changes and 1999 publication of software; 1 form.
Authors: Robert H. Ennis, Jason Millman, and Thomas N. Tomko (manual).
Publisher: The Critical Thinking Co.

a) LEVEL X.
Population: Grade 5–college.
Comments: Software version for Grade 7–college population.
b) LEVEL Z.
Population: Advanced and gifted high school students and college students and adults.
Cross References: See T5:705 (10 references) and T4:655 (1 reference); for reviews by Jan N. Hughes and Koressa Kutsick Malcolm, see 11:88 (3 references); see also 9:269 (1 reference), T3:606 (7 references), T2:1755 (2 references), and 7:779 (10 references).

[746]

Cornell Index–Form N2.

Purpose: For collecting pertinent medical and psychiatric data from patients.
Population: Ages 14 and over.
Publication Dates: 1949–1956.
Acronym: C.I.
Scores: Total score only.
Administration: Group or individual.
Price Data, 2006: $60 per 100 copies; $30 per specimen set.
Foreign Language Editions: French Canadian and Spanish editions available.
Time: (5–15) minutes.
Comments: Title on test is C.I. Form N2.
Authors: Arthur Weider.
Publisher: Arthur Weider and James Weider.
Cross References: See T5:708 (9 references), T4:658 (16 references), 9:270 (15 references), T3:609 (33 references), 8:530 (46 references), and T2:1145 (42 references); for reviews by Eugene E. Levitt and David T. Lykken, see 7:61 (32 references); see also P:49 (77 references).

[747]

The Cornell Inventory for Student Appraisal of Teaching and Courses.

Purpose: "Provides teachers with feedback of student opinion."
Population: College teachers.
Publication Dates: 1972–1973.
Scores: Item norms only.
Administration: Group.
Price Data: Not available.
Time: (15–20) minutes.
Authors: James B. Maas and Thomas R. Owen (manual).
Publisher: James B. Maas [No reply from publisher; status unknown].
Cross References: For a review by Wilbert J. McKeachie, see 8:367.

[748]

Cornell Word Form 2.

Purpose: "To assess mental health adjustment using a forced choice word association technique."
Population: Adults.
Publication Dates: 1946–1955.
Acronym: C.W.F.-2.
Scores: Total score only.
Administration: Group or individual.
Price Data, 2006: $60 per 100 copies; $30 per specimen set.
Time: [5–15] minutes.
Comments: Title on test is C.W.F.
Author: Arthur Weider.
Publisher: Arthur Weider and James Weider.
Cross References: See T2:1146 (1 reference), P:50 (2 references), and 5:44 (11 references); for a review by S. B. Sells, see 6:80 (1 reference).

[749]

Correctional Institutions Environment Scale, Second Edition.

Purpose: Designed to measure the "social climate of juvenile and adult correctional programs."
Population: Residents and staff of correctional facilities.
Publication Dates: 1974–1987.
Acronym: CIES.
Scores, 9: Involvement, Support, Expressiveness, Autonomy, Practical Orientation, Personal Problem Orientation, Order and Organization, Clarity, Staff Control.
Administration: Group.
Forms, 4: Real (R), Ideal (I), Expectations (E), Short (S).
Price Data: Available from publisher at www.mind-garden.com/products/cpess.htm.
Foreign Language Editions: Versions adapted for use in French Quebec, Slovenia, Sweden, Spain, and the United Kingdom.
Time: Administration time not reported.
Comments: Part of the Social Climate Scales (T5:2445).
Author: Rudolf H. Moos.
Publisher: Mind Garden, Inc.
Cross References: For reviews by Kevin J. McCarthy and M. David Miller, see 14:106; see also T4:660 (3 references) and T3:612 (1 reference); for a review by Kenneth A. Carlson of an earlier version, see 8:531 (16 references). For a review of the Social Climate Scales, see 8:681.

[750]

Correctional Officers' Interest Blank.

Purpose: Designed for research in the development of selection techniques for correctional officers.
Population: Correctional officer applicants.
Publication Dates: 1953-2001.
Acronym: COIB.
Scores, Total score only or 19 scales: Dominance, Capacity for Status, Sociability, Social Presence, Self-Acceptance, Well-Being, Responsibility, Socialization, Self-Control, Tolerance, Good Impression, Communality, Achievement via Conformance, Achievement via Independence, Intellectual Efficiency, Psychological-Mindedness, Flexibility, Femininity, Empathy.
Administration: Group or individual.
Price Data: Available from publisher at www.mind-garden.com/products/coibs.htm.
Time: (10) minutes.
Author: Harrison G. Gough.
Publisher: Mind Garden, Inc.
Cross References: For reviews by Robert J. Howell and R. Lynn Richards and by Samuel Roll, see 10:75.

[751]

Correctional Policy Inventory: A Survey of Correctional Philosophy and Characteristic Methods of Dealing with Offenders.

Purpose: Developed to identify the correctional philosophies utilized in particular situations.
Population: Correctional managers.
Publication Date: 1970.
Scores, 4: Reintegration, Rehabilitation, Reform, Restraint.
Administration: Group.
Price Data: Available from publisher.
Time: [20] minutes.
Author: Vincent O'Leary.
Publisher: National Council on Crime and Delinquency.
Cross References: See 8:1092 (2 references).

[752]

Cortical Vision Screening Test.

Purpose: "Designed to detect visual impairments in individuals with normal (corrected) or near-normal vision."
Population: Ages 18–80.
Publication Date: 2001.
Acronym: CORVIST.
Scores, 10: Symbol Acuity, Shape Discrimination, Size Discrimination, Shape Detection, Hue Discrimination, Scattered Dot Counting, Fragmented Numbers, Word Reading, Face Perception, Crowding.
Administration: Individual.
Price Data, 2006: £119.50 per complete kit including manual/stimulus book (40 pages) and 25 scoring sheets; £26.50 per 50 scoring sheets.
Time: Untimed.
Authors: Merle James, Gordon T. Plant, and Elizabeth K. Warrington.
Publisher: Pearson Assessment [England].

[753]

The Couples BrainMap™.

Purpose: "To help partners gain new perspective of, and value for, their relationship."
Population: Couples.
Publication Dates: 1981-1986.
Scores, 4: I-Organize, I-Explore, I-Pursue, I-Preserve.
Administration: Group.
Price Data: Available from publisher.
Time: 40(50) minutes.
Comments: Self-administered, self-scored.
Authors: Sherry Lynch, Dudley Lynch, Phyllis Miller, and Sherod Miller.
Publisher: Brain Technologies Corporation.
Cross References: For a review by Alicia Skinner Cook and Richard E. Guest, see 11:91.

[754]

Course Finder.

Purpose: Assesses "students' interests and preferences, and identifies suitable higher education courses at appropriate universities/colleges in Great Britain."
Population: Students entering higher education.
Publication Dates: 1992–1993.
Acronym: CF.
Administration: Group.
Price Data: Available from publisher.
Time: (45–60) minutes.
Comments: For use in Great Britain; was listed in a previous MMY as Course Finder 2000, however, is updated each year. Now also available online at www.ukcoursefinder.com
Authors: Malcolm Morrisby, Glen Fox, and Mark Parkinson.
Publisher: The Morrisby Organisation [England].
Cross References: For a review by Colin Cooper, see 13:85.

[755]

CPF [Second Edition].

Purpose: "To assess extroversion and preference for social contact."
Population: Ages 16–adult.
Publication Dates: 1954–1992.
Acronym: CPF.
Scores, 3: Validity Scores (Uncertainty, Good Impression), Total Extroversion.
Administration: Group or individual.
Price Data, 2010: $35 per introductory kit including manual (1992, 10 pages), 20 test booklets, and scoring key; $30 per 20 test booklets; $10 per manual.
Time: (5–10) minutes.
Comments: Previously listed as a subtest of the Employee Attitude Series of the Job Tests Program (T3:1219).
Author: Samuel E. Krug.
Publisher: Industrial Psychology International Ltd.
Cross References: For reviews by Michael R. Harwell and Allen K. Hess, see 12:97.

[756]

CPI 260®.

Purpose: "The goal of the inventory is to give a true-to-life description of the respondent, in clear, everyday language, in formats that can help the client to achieve a better understanding of self."
Population: Ages 13 and up.
Publication Date: 2002.
Acronym: CPI 260.
Scores, 29: Dominance, Capacity for Status, Sociability, Social Presence, Self-Acceptance, Independence, Empathy, Responsibility, Social Conformity, Self-Control, Good Impression, Communality, Well-Being, Tolerance, Achievement via Conformance, Achievement via Independence, Conceptual Fluency, Insightfulness, Flexibility, Sensitivity, Managerial Potential, Work Orientation, Creative Temperament, Leadership, Amicability, Law Enforcement Orientation, Orientation Toward Others, Orientation Toward Societal Values, Orientation Toward Self.
Administration: Individual or group.
Price Data, 2011: $24.95 each for CPI 260® Client Feedback Report online administration; $39.95 each for CPI 260® Coaching Report for Leaders online administration; $59.95 each for CPI 260® Client Feedback Report and Coaching Report for Leaders online administration; $92.50 each for CPI 260® Manual; $40.50 each for CPI 260® Coaching Report for Leaders User's Guide; $40.50 each for CPI 260® Client Feedback Report Guide for Interpretation.
Time: (25-30) minutes.
Comments: Abbreviated version derived from the California Psychological Inventory (401).
Authors: Harrison G. Gough and Pamela Bradley; Sam Manoogian (Coaching Report for Leaders); Robert J. Devine (Client Feedback Report).
Publisher: CPP, Inc.
Cross References: For reviews by Gary J. Dean and Stephen J. Freeman, see 18:36.

[757]

Crane Oral Dominance Test: Spanish/English.

Purpose: "To determine if the student has a dominant language, if the student is bilingual ..., or if the student needs concentrated language, concept, and memory development to function adequately in either language."
Population: Ages 4-8.
Publication Date: 1976.
Acronym: CODT.

Scores, 4: Spanish Dominant, English Dominant, Bilingual, Indeterminable.
Administration: Individual.
Price Data, 2001: $34.64 per 30 test booklets and manual (11 pages).
Time: (20) minutes.
Comments: Both English and Spanish used in administration and in pupil responses.
Author: Barbara J. Crane.
Publisher: Bilingual Educational Services, Inc.
Cross References: For excerpted reviews by Protase E. Woodford and Porfirio Sanchez, see 8:162 (1 reference).

[758]

Crawford Small Parts Dexterity Test.
Purpose: "A performance test designed to measure fine eye-hand coordination."
Population: High school and adults.
Publication Dates: 1946–1981.
Acronym: CSPDT.
Scores, 2: Pins and Collars, Screws.
Administration: Individual.
Price Data, 2002: $446 per complete set including manual (1981, 22 pages) and spare parts; $18 per manual; replacement parts are available by calling the publisher.
Time: (8–15) minutes.
Authors: John E. Crawford and Dorothea M. Crawford.
Publisher: Pearson.
Cross References: See T4:679 (2 references), T3:627 (4 references), and T2:2223 (12 references); for a review by Neil D. Warren, see 5:871 (8 references); for a review by Raymond A. Katzell, see 4:752; for a review by Joseph E. Moore, see 3:667.

[759]

Creative Behavior Inventory.
Purpose: Designed to measure "behavioral characteristics associated with creativity."
Population: Grades 1–6, 7–12.
Publication Date: 1989.
Acronyms: CBI1, CBI2.
Scores, 5: Contact, Consciousness, Interest, Fantasy, Total.
Administration: Individual.
Levels, 2: I (elementary), II (secondary).
Price Data: Price data for materials including manual (70 pages) available from publisher.
Time: Administration time not reported.
Comments: Ratings by teachers; manual title is Understanding the Creative Activity of Students.
Author: Robert J. Kirschenbaum.
Publisher: Creative Learning Press, Inc.
Cross References: For a review by Richard M. Clark, see 11:93.

[760]

Creativity Assessment Packet.
Purpose: To assess creative potential.
Population: Ages 6 through 18.
Publication Date: 1980.
Acronym: CAP.
Administration: Group.
Price Data, 2010: $137 per complete kit including 25 of each test (Form A and B), 25 test of divergent feeling forms, 25 Williams scale forms and manual (1980, 24 pages); $35 per manual; $29 per test form.
Author: Frank Williams.
Publisher: PRO-ED.
a) TEST OF DIVERGENT THINKING.
Scores, 6: Fluency, Flexibility, Originality, Elaboration, Vocabulary, Comprehension.
Forms, 2: A, B.
Price Data: $29 per 25 tests (specify Form A or Form B).
Time: 20 (25) minutes for grades 6-12; 25 (30) minutes for grades 3-5.
b) TEST OF DIVERGENT FEELING.
Scores, 5: Curiosity, Imagination, Complexity, Risk-Taking, Total.
Price Data: $29 per 25 tests.
Time: 10 (20) minutes.
c) THE WILLIAMS SCALE.
Scores, 9: Fluency, Flexibility, Originality, Elaboration, Curiosity, Imagination, Complexity, Risk-Taking, Total.
Price Data: $29 per 25 tests.
Time: Administration time not reported.
Comments: Ratings by parents and teachers.
Cross References: See T5:724 (6 references) and T4:682 (3 references); for reviews by Fred Damarin and Carl L. Rosen, see 9:280.

[761]

The Creatrix Inventory [Revised].
Purpose: Determines a person's "creative risk-taking propensity."
Population: Members of organizations.
Publication Dates: 1971–2006.
Scores, 2: Creativity, Risk Taking; plotted on matrix to determine 1 of 8 orientations: Sustainer, Modifier, Challenger, Practicalizer, Innovator, Synthesizer, Dreamer, Planner.
Administration: Group.
Price Data: Available from publisher.
Time: Administration time not reported.
Comments: Online administration and scoring; designed for self-assessment and educational purposes.
Authors: Richard E. Byrd and Jacqueline L. Byrd.
Publisher: Creatrix.
Cross References: For reviews by Harrison G. Gough and John F. Wakefield of an earlier version, see 11:95.

[762]

Cree Questionnaire.

Purpose: "To measure an individual's overall creative potential."
Population: Individuals in a variety of occupations; clients in vocational and career counseling.
Publication Dates: 1957–1995.
Acronym: CQ.
Scores, 11: Overall Creative Potential, plus 10 factorially determined dimension scores grouped under 4 broad headings: Social Orientation, Work Orientation, Internal Functioning, and Interests.
Administration: Individual or group.
Price Data, 2002: $114 per start-up kit including 25 test booklets, 25 score sheets, and interpretation and research manual; $54 per 25 test booklets (quantity discounts available); $45 per 25 score sheets; $28 per interpretation and research manual.
Time: No limit (approximately 20 minutes).
Authors: T. G. Thurstone and J. Melinger.
Publisher: Pearson Performance Solutions [No reply from publisher; status unknown].
Cross References: See T5:728 (1 reference); for a review by Janet M. Stoppard, see 9:282; see also T2:1149 (1 reference) and P:53 (3 references); for reviews of an earlier edition by Allyn Miles Munger and Theodor F. Naumann, see 6:84.

[763]

Crichton Vocabulary Scale.

Purpose: Designed to provide an index of a child's "acquired fund of verbal information."
Population: Ages 4.5–11.
Publication Dates: 1950–1988.
Acronym: CVS.
Scores, 3: Definitions of Set One, Definitions of Set Two, Total.
Administration: Individual.
Price Data: Available from publisher.
Time: Administration time not reported.
Comments: Designed for use with Raven's Progressive Matrices (2233).
Author: J. C. Raven.
Publisher: Oxford Psychologists Press, Ltd. [England].
Cross References: See T4:687 (3 references), T3:632 (2 references), and T2:491 (3 references); for a review by Morton Bortner, see 6:518 (1 reference); for reviews by Charlotte Banks and W. D. Wall, see 4:337.

[764]

Criterion Test of Basic Skills [2002 Edition].

Purpose: Developed to assess "the basic reading and arithmetic skills of individual students."
Population: Ages 6 through 11-11.
Publication Dates: 1976–2002.
Acronym: CTOBS-2.
Administration: Individual.
Price Data, 2006: $112 per test kit including manual (2002, 136 pages), 25 Arithmetic recording forms, 25 Reading recording forms, 25 Math problem sheets, and test plates in vinyl folder; $25 per manual; $25 per 25 Arithmetic recording forms; $25 per 25 Reading recording forms; $12 per 25 Math problem sheets; 25 per set of test plates.
Time: (15–20) minutes.
Comments: "Criterion referenced."
Authors: James Evans, Kerth Lundell, and William Brown.
Publisher: Academic Therapy Publications.
 a) READING.
  Scores, 7: Letter Recognition, Letter Sounding, Blending and Sequencing, Phonics Patterns, Multisyllable Words, Sight Words, Letter Writing.
 b) ARITHMETIC.
  Scores, 14: Correspondence, Numbers and Numerals, Addition, Subtraction, Multiplication, Division, Measurement, Telling Time, Symbols, Fractions, Decimals and Percents, Geometric Concepts, Pre-Algebra, Rounding and Estimations.
Cross References: See T3:635 (1 reference).

[765]

Criterion Validated Written Test for Emergency Medical Practitioner.

Purpose: Intended for the selection of paramedic personnel.
Population: Prospective paramedics.
Publication Date: 1995-1999.
Scores: 7 subtests and total: Interest, Teamwork, Problem Solving–Common Sense, Problem Solving–Map Reading, Problem Solving–Logical Thinking, Problem Solving–Relevancy, Attentiveness, Total.
Administration: Group.
Form, 1: EMP 90.
Restricted Distribution: Distribution restricted to civil service commissions and qualified municipal officials.
Price Data: Available from publisher.
Time: 110 minutes.
Comments: Practice test, candidate study guide, and technical manual are available.
Author: McCann Associates, Inc.
Publisher: McCann Associates.

[766]

Critical Reasoning Test Battery.

Purpose: To assist students in subject and career choices and employers with the selection of job candidates.
Population: Students and employees ages 15 and over.
Publication Dates: 1981–1983.
Acronym: CRTB.

Administration: Group.

Restricted Distribution: Distribution restricted to persons who have completed the publisher's training course or members of the Division of Occupational Psychology of the British Psychological Society.

Price Data: Available from publisher.

Comments: 3 subtests available as separates.

Authors: Peter Saville, Roger Holdsworth, Gill Nyfield, David Hawkey, Susan Bawtree, and Ruth Holdsworth.

Publisher: SHL Group plc [United Kingdom].

a) VERBAL EVALUATION.
Publication Dates: 1982–1983.
Acronym: VC1.
Time: 30(35) minutes.
b) INTERPRETING DATA.
Publication Dates: 1982–1983.
Acronym: NC2.
Time: 30(35) minutes.
c) DIAGRAMMATIC SERIES.
Publication Dates: 1982–1983.
Acronym: DC3.
Time: 20(25) minutes.

[767]

Cross-Cultural Adaptability Inventory.

Purpose: "Designed to provide information to an individual about his or her potential for cross-cultural effectiveness."

Population: Trainers and professionals who work with culturally diverse and cross-culturally oriented populations.

Publication Dates: 1987–1995.

Acronym: CCAI.

Scores: 4 scales: Emotional Resilience, Flexibility/Openness, Perceptual Acuity, Personal Autonomy.

Administration: Group.

Price Data: Available from publisher.

Time: (15–30) minutes.

Comments: Observer-rating survey is optional.

Authors: Colleen Kelley and Judith Meyers.

Publisher: Pearson Performance Solutions [No reply from publisher; status unknown].

Cross References: For reviews by Lynn L. Brown and Wendy Naumann, see 14:107.

[768]

Cross Reference Test.

Purpose: Constructed to assess "skill in routine checking tasks."

Population: Clerical job applicants.

Publication Date: 1959.

Scores: Total score only.

Administration: Group.

Price Data: Available from publisher.

Time: 5(10) minutes.

Author: James W. Curtis.

Publisher: Psychometric Affiliates.

Cross References: For a review by Philip H. Kriedt, see 6:1039.

[769]

CRS Placement/Diagnostic Test.

Purpose: Designed to diagnose and locate the student's CRS (Crane Reading System) level.

Population: Grades Preprimer-2.

Publication Dates: 1977-1978.

Scores: Total score only.

Administration: Group.

Price Data: Price information for test materials including general directions (1977, 7 pages) available from publisher.

Foreign Language Edition: Spanish version available.

Time: Administration time not reported.

Author: Barbara J. Crane.

Publisher: Bilingual Educational Services, Inc.

a) ENGLISH VERSION.
1) *Level A.*
Population: Grade Preprimer.
Subtests, 4: Rhyming, Words That Begin Alike, Long Vowel Recognition, Consonant Sounds.
2) *Levels B, C, and D (Beginning Consonant Sounds).*
Population: Preprimer-primer.
Comments: Levels determined by number of errors.
3) *Level E (Blends).*
Population: Grade 1.
4) *Level F (Vowel Recognition).*
Population: Grade 1.
5) *Level G (Digraphs).*
Population: Grade 1.
6) *Levels H, I, and J (Special Vowel Patterns).*
Population: Grades 1-2.
Comments: Levels determined by number of errors.
b) SPANISH VERSION.
1) *Level A.*
Subtests, 2: Rhyming, Words That Begin Alike.
2) *Level B (Beginning Consonant Sounds–S, M, F, R, N, L, Z).*
3) *Level C (Beginning Consonant Sounds–B, P, T, D, V, CH).*
4) *Level D (Beginning Consonant Sounds–C, G, LL, Q, J, Y).*
5) *Level E (Special Patterns).*

[770]

CTB Writing Assessment System.

Purpose: "Includes direct and indirect writing measures to aid educators in evaluating writing programs and students' writing abilities."

Population: Grades 2.0–12.9.

Publication Date: 1993.

Scores, 6: Holistic, Analytic (Content, Organization, Sentence Construction, Vocabulary/Grammar, Spelling/Capitalization).
Administration: Group.
Levels, 4: 12–13 (grades 2.0–4.2), 14–16 (grades 3.6–7.2), 17–19 (grades 6.6–10.2), and 20–22 (grades 9.6–12.9 and adults).
Price Data, 2002: $53.35 per 30 consumable Writing books including administration and scoring manual (specify Narrative, Descriptive, Informative, or Persuasive and specify level); $41.80 per 30 Writing books with independent prompts only (Specify Narrative, Descriptive, Informative, or Persuasive and specify level); $23.10 per 50 Student Information and Score Sheets; additional price information and information regarding scoring services available from publisher.
Comments: Includes books 1–32 with a writing assignment called a "prompt"; each book comes with its own manual; books are available as separates; overall guide is entitled Writing Assessment Guide.
Author: CTB Macmillan/McGraw-Hill.
Publisher: CTB/McGraw-Hill.
  a) LEVEL 12–13.
  Population: Grades 2.0–4.2
  Time: 30–35 (35–40) minutes.
  Comments: 4 books (Personal Expression–Descriptive [Books 1 & 4], Personal Expression–Narrative [Books 2 & 3]) available as separates.
  b) LEVEL 14–16.
  Population: Grades 3.6–7.2.
  Time: 30–35 (35–40) minutes.
  Comments: 8 books (Personal Expression–Descriptive [Books 5 & 8], Personal Expression–Narrative [Books 6 & 7], and Informative [Books 9–12]) available as separates.
  c) LEVEL 17–19.
  Population: Grades 6.6–10.2.
  Time: 40–45 (45–50) minutes.
  Comments: 10 books (Personal Expression–Narrative [Books 13 & 14], Informative [Books 15–18], Persuasive [Books 19–22]) available as separates.
  d) LEVEL 20–22.
  Population: Grades 9.6–12.9.
  Time: 40–45 (45–50) minutes.
  Comments: 10 books (Personal Expression–Narrative [Books 23 & 24], Informative [Books 25–28], Persuasive [Books 29–32]) available as separates.
Cross References: For reviews by George Engelhard, Jr. and Joe B. Hansen, see 13:88.

[771]

Cultural Competence Self-Assessment Instrument.
Purpose: Designed "to help agencies measure their cultural competency in agency policymaking, administrative procedures, and practices."

Population: Business staff and clients of child welfare agencies.
Publication Date: 1993.
Scores: Not scored.
Administration: Group.
Price Data: Price information available from publisher for instrument including manual (48 pages). Visit www.cwla.org/pubs.
Time: Administration time not reported.
Author: Child Welfare League of America, Inc.
Publisher: Child Welfare League of America.

[772]

Culture Fair Intelligence Test.
Purpose: Designed to measure individual intelligence with minimal influence from verbal fluency, educational level, and ethnic/racial group membership.
Population: Ages 4–8 and educable mentally retarded adults, Ages 8–14 and average IQ adults, senior high, college, and high IQ adults.
Publication Dates: 1950-1973.
Acronym: CFIT.
Scores: Total scores only.
Administration: Group or individual.
Foreign Language Editions: Information regarding many non-English-language adaptations available from publisher.
Comments: Formerly called Culture Free Intelligence Test; test booklet title is Test of "g": Culture Fair.
Authors: Raymond B. Cattell and A. Karen S. Cattell (Scales 2 and 3).
Publisher: Institute for Personality and Ability Testing, Inc. (IPAT).
  a) SCALE 1.
  Population: Ages 4–8 and developmentally delayed persons.
  Administration: Individual.
  Price Data, 2005: $64 per introductory kit including 25 test booklets, scoring key, reusable classification cards, and handbook (1950, 15 pages); $27 per 25 test booklets; $8 per scoring key: $22 per reusable classification test cards; $7 per handbook; $16 per specimen set including test booklet, scoring key, and handbook.
  Time: (22) minutes (untimed).
  Comments: Identical to Cattell Intelligence Tests, Scale O: Dartington Scale; materials for Test 5 (Following Directions) must be assembled locally.
  b) SCALE 2.
  Population: Ages 8–14 and adults.
  Forms, 2: A, B.
  Price Data: $51 per introductory kit including test booklet, scoring keys, answer sheets, manual (1973, 27 pages), and technical supplement (1973, 30 pages); $27 per 25 test booklets (specify Form A or B); $8 per scoring keys for answer sheets;

$8 per scoring keys for test booklets; $18 per 50 answer sheets; $15 per manual; $15 per technical supplement.
Time: 12.5 minutes.
c) SCALE 3.
Population: Adults.
Forms, 2: A, B.
Price Data: Same as *b* above.
Time: 12.5 minutes.
Cross References: See T5:745 (25 references), T4:699 (34 references), 9:290 (13 references), T3:643 (51 references), 8:184 (38 references), and T2:364 (61 references); for reviews by John E. Milholland and Abraham J. Tannenbaum, see 6:453 (15 references); for a review by I. MacFarlane Smith of a, see 5:343 (11 references); for reviews by Raleigh M. Drake and Gladys C. Schwesinger, see 4:300 (2 references).

[773]

Culture-Free Self-Esteem Inventories, Third Edition.

Purpose: "A set of self-report inventories used to determine the level of self-esteem in students ages 6-0 through 18-11."
Population: Ages 0-6 through 11-18.
Publication Dates: 1981–2002.
Acronym: CFSEI-3.
Administration: Individual or group.
Levels, 3: Primary, Intermediate, Adolescent.
Price Data, 2010: $211 per complete kit including manual (2002, 60 pages); $32 per 50 primary examiner/record forms; $32 per 50 intermediate profile/scoring forms; $32 per 50 intermediate student response forms; $32 per 50 adolescent profile/scoring forms; $32 per 50 adolescent student response forms; $60 per manual.
Time: (15–20) minutes.
Comments: Newly normed revision of Culture-Free Self-Esteem Inventories, Second Edition; all levels include Defensiveness Score (a lie scale); previous editions entitled Culture-Free Self-Esteem Inventories for Children and Adults; derivative entitled North American Depression Inventories for Children and Adults (T5:1803).
Author: James Battle.
Publisher: PRO-ED.
a) PRIMARY.
Population: Ages 6–8.
Score: Global Self-Esteem Quotient.
Price Data: $32 per 50 primary examiner/record forms.
b) INTERMEDIATE.
Population: Ages 9–12.
Scores, 5: Academic, General, Parental/Home, Social, Global Self-Esteem Quotient.
Price Data: $32 per 50 intermediate profile/scoring forms; $32 per 50 intermediate student response forms.

c) ADOLESCENT.
Population: Ages 13–18.
Scores, 6: Academic, General, Parental/Home, Social, Personal, Global Self-Esteem Quotient.
Price Data: $32 per 50 adolescent profile/scoring forms, $28 per 50 adolescent student response forms.
Cross References: For reviews by Bethany A. Brunsman and Y. Evie Garcia, see 15:72; see T5:746 (4 references); for reviews by Michael G. Kavan and Michael J. Subkoviak of a previous edition, see 12:100 (7 references); see also T4:700 (9 references); for reviews by Gerald R. Adams and Janet Morgan Riggs of the original edition, see 9:291 (1 reference); see also T3:644 (1 reference). For reviews by Patricia A. Bachelor and Michael G. Kavan of the North American Depression Inventories for Children and Adults, see 11:265 (1 reference).

[774]

Curtis Interest Scale.

Purpose: Developed to identify vocational interest patterns.
Population: Grades 9–16 and adults.
Publication Date: 1959.
Scores, 10: Business, Mechanics, Applied Arts, Direct Sales, Production, Science, Entertainment, Interpersonal, Computation, Farming; 1 rating: Desire for Responsibility.
Administration: Group.
Price Data: Available from publisher.
Time: (6–12) minutes.
Comments: Self-administered.
Author: James W. Curtis.
Publisher: Psychometric Affiliates.
Cross References: See T2:2177 (1 reference); for reviews by Warren T. Norman and Leona E. Tyler, see 6:1052.

[775]

[Curtis Object Completion and Space Form Tests].

Purpose: "Devised to provide estimates of individual competence in two basic areas of mechanical aptitude and pattern visualization."
Population: Applicants for mechanical and technical jobs.
Publication Dates: 1960–1961.
Scores: Total scores only.
Administration: Group.
Price Data: Available from publisher.
Time: 1(6) minutes per test.
Author: James W. Curtis.
Publisher: Psychometric Affiliates.
a) OBJECT-COMPLETION TEST.
b) SPACE FORM TEST.
Cross References: For reviews by Richard S. Melton and I. Macfarlane Smith, see 6:1085.

[776]
Curtis Verbal-Clerical Skills Tests.

Purpose: "Devised to provide estimates of individual competence in … verbal skill usually identified with office and clerical work."
Population: Applicants for clerical positions.
Publication Dates: 1963–1965.
Acronym: CVCST.
Scores: 4 tests: Computation, Checking, Comprehension, Capacity.
Administration: Group.
Price Data: Available from publisher.
Time: 8(10) minutes.
Author: James W. Curtis.
Publisher: Psychometric Affiliates.

[777]
Customer Reaction Survey.

Purpose: Assesses customers' perceptions of salespeople's interpersonal skills.
Population: Salespeople.
Publication Dates: 1972-1995.
Acronym: CRS.
Scores: 4: Observed Exposure, Observed Feedback, Preferred Exposure, Preferred Feedback.
Administration: Group.
Price Data, 2006: $9.95 per instrument.
Time: Administration time not reported.
Comments: Ratings by customers; also called Customer Reaction Index; based on the Johari Window Model of interpersonal relations.
Authors: Jay Hall and C. Leo Griffith.
Publisher: Teleometrics International, Inc.

[778]
Customer Service Applicant Inventory.

Purpose: "Evaluates skills and attitudes to help hire customer service oriented, honest, safe, and productive employees."
Population: Job applicants.
Publication Date: 1996.
Acronym: CSAI.
Scores, 12: Validity Scales (Candidness, Accuracy), Interpersonal Scales (Customer Service, Teamwork, Communication, Stress Tolerance), Core Values (Honesty, Drug Avoidance, Safety), Supplemental Scales (Applied Math, Training Readiness), Composite (Employability Index).
Administration: Group or individual.
Price Data: Available from publisher.
Time: (45) minutes.
Comments: Paper-and-pencil or computer administration available.
Author: Pearson Performance Solutions [No reply from publisher; status unknown].
Publisher: Pearson Reid London House.

[779]
Customer Service Aptitude Profile.

Purpose: Designed to "assist in the selection, placement, and development of people to work in customer service roles."
Population: Ages 14 and over.
Publication Date: 2002.
Acronym: Customer Service AP.
Scores, 21: Self-Enhancement, Self-Criticism, Inconsistent Responding Index, Sales Disposition, Initiative-Cold Calling, Sales Closing, Achievement, Motivation, Competitiveness, Goal Orientation, Planning, Initiative-General, Team Player, Managerial, Assertiveness, Personal Diplomacy, Extroversion, Cooperativeness, Relaxed Style, Patience, Self-Confidence.
Administration: Group.
Price Data, 2010: $137 per CD good for 10 uses; $21.50 per Employers Guide (24 pages); $16.50 per 100 PC answer sheets.
Time: (20) minutes.
Comments: Able to be taken online or with paper-and-pencil.
Authors: Sander I. Marcus, Jotham G. Friedland, and Harvey P. Mandel.
Publisher: Western Psychological Services.

[780]
Customer Service Profile.

Purpose: Designed to "identify qualified people for service positions by measuring important attitudes and aptitudes."
Population: Ages 18 and over.
Publication Date: 1994.
Acronym: CSP.
Scores, 6: Validity-Candidness, Validity-Accuracy, Customer Service Attitude, Customer Service Aptitude, Sales Aptitude, Customer Service Index.
Administration: Individual or group.
Price Data, 2005: $16 including 1–999 reports for Internet scoring with booklets; $16 including 1–999 reports for Internet scoring without booklets; $16 including 1–999 reports for QuantaTouch Test; $16 including 1–999 reports for QUANTA Software for Windows with booklets; $16 including 1–999 reports for QUANTA Software for Windows without booklets.
Time: (20–25) minutes.
Comments: Test can be scored using operator-assisted telephone scoring, touch-test telephone scoring, Quanta-based scoring, or mail-in scoring.
Authors: Reid London House.
Publisher: Pearson Performance Solutions [No reply from publisher; status unknown].

[781]
Customer Service Simulator.

Purpose: "Designed to identify individuals who can solve problems while projecting responsiveness and

sensitivity, and who avoid making common interpersonal errors in dealing with customers."
Population: Any position requiring public contact.
Publication Date: 1993.
Acronym: CSS.
Scores, 3: Customer Service Orientation, Interpersonal Sensitivity, Total.
Administration: Group.
Forms, 3: customer Service Representative Version, Team Leader Version, Supervisor Version.
Restricted Distribution: Clients may be required to pay a nominal one-time overhead/sign-up fee.
Price Data, 2011: $295 per candidate for rental/scoring and feedback report.
Time: 90 minutes.
Comments: All versions are available for online administration.
Author: Richard C. Joines.
Publisher: Management & Personnel Systems, Inc.

[782]

Customer Service Skills Inventory.

Purpose: Designed to "assess customer service skills across a variety of customer-contact jobs."
Population: Ages 18 and over.
Publication Dates: 1993–1995.
Acronym: CSSI.
Scores, 8: Pressure Tolerance, Realistic Orientation, Time Appraisal, Independent Judgment, Responsiveness, Sensitivity, Balanced Judgment, Precision Orientation.
Administration: Group or individual.
Price Data, 2005: $139 per start-up kit including examiner's manual (1995, 34 pages) and 10 test booklets; $139 per QUANTA start-up kit including examiner's manual and 10 administrations and scoring (does not include QUANTA software); $28 per examiner's manual; $127 per 10 tests (quantity discounts available).
Time: (25–30) minutes.
Comments: Test can be administered over the Internet or via paper and pencil; can be scored via Internet, QUANTA software, or self-scoring.
Authors: Juan I. Sanchez and Simon L. Fraser.
Publisher: Pearson Performance Solutions [No reply from publisher; status unknown].

[783]

Customer Service Skills Test.

Purpose: To evaluate technical and interpersonal skills of persons for the customer service position; available also to measure computer use skills.
Population: Candidates for customer service positions.
Publication Date: 1992.
Acronym: BASLCUS.
Scores: Total Score, Narrative Evaluation, Ranking, Recommendation.

Administration: Group.
Price Data, 2001: $150 per candidate; quantity discounts available.
Foreign Language Edition: Available in French.
Time: (70) minutes.
Comments: Scored by publisher; available in booklet and internet versions; must be proctored.
Author: Walden Personnel Performance, Inc.
Publisher: Walden Personnel Performance, Inc. [Canada].
Cross References: For reviews by Wayne J. Camara and Jean Powell Kirnan, see 16:68.

[784]

D-1, D-2, and D-3 Police Officer Tests.

Purpose: "Designed to assess the basic abilities identified as being important for successful performance as a police officer."
Population: Candidates for entry-level police officer positions.
Publication Dates: 1999-2006.
Scores: 5 job dimensions: Observation and Memory [Wanted Posters], Ability to Learn Police Material, Police Interest Questionnaire [Non-Cognitive], Verbal and Reading Comprehension (all but D-1), Situational Judgment and Problem Solving.
Administration: Individual or group.
Forms, 3: D-1, D-2, D-3.
Price Data: Available from publisher.
Time: 130 minutes per test.
Comments: D-1, D-2, D-3 are comparable forms; no prior training or experience as a police officer is assumed of candidates taking any of the three forms.
Authors: International Public Management Association for Human Resources & Bruce Davey Associates.
Publisher: International Public Management Association for Human Resources (IPMA-HR).
Cross References: For reviews by Janet Houser and Chockalingam Viswesvaran, see 18:37.

[785]

d2 Test of Attention.

Purpose: Designed to measure processing speed, rule compliance, and quality of performance, allowing for a neuropsychological estimation of individual attention and concentration performance.
Population: Children, adolescents, and adults.
Publication Date: 1998.
Acronym: d2 Test.
Scores: Score information available from publisher.
Administration: Individual.and group.
Price Data, 2011: $98 per complete test including 20 recording blanks, set of 2 scoring keys, and manual (1998, 80 pages); $16 per 50 recording blanks; $28 per set of 2 scoring keys; $65 per manual.

Time: (8) minutes.
Comments: Originally conceived to assess individuals' suitability for driving, the test has also been used as a part of personnel selection in other workplace environments where high levels of visual attention and concentration are demanded.
Authors: Rolf Brickenkamp and Eric Zillmer.
Publisher: Hogrefe Publishing.
Cross References: For reviews by Phillip L. Ackerman and Elaine Clark, see 15:87.

[786]

DABERON-2: Screening for School Readiness, Second Edition.

Purpose: Developed to provide a standardized assessment of school readiness.
Population: Ages 4 through 6.
Publication Dates: 1972–1991.
Scores: Total score only.
Administration: Individual.
Price Data, 2010: $195 per complete kit including 24 presentation cards, 25 screen forms, 25 readiness reports, 5 classroom summary forms, object kit of manipulatives, and administration manual (1991, 38 pages); $19 per set of presentation cards; $41 per 25 screen forms; $41 per 25 readiness reports; $19 per 5 classroom summary forms; $41 per object kit of manipulatives; $59 per administration manual.
Time: (20-40) minutes.
Authors: Virginia A. Danzer, Mary Frances Gerber, Theresa M. Lyons, and Judith K. Voress.
Publisher: PRO-ED.
Cross References: For reviews by Stephen N. Axford and Selma Hughes, see 11:100 (1 reference).

[787]

Das•Naglieri Cognitive Assessment System.

Purpose: "To provide a cognitive processing measure of ability that is fair to minority children, effective for differential diagnosis, and related to intervention."
Population: Ages 0-5 to 11-17.
Publication Date: 1997.
Levels, 2: Ages 5–7, ages 8–17.
Price Data, 2010: $921 per complete kit including stimulus book, administration and scoring manual (305 pages), interpretive handbook, 5 record forms, 5 response booklets ages 5-7, 5 response booklets ages 8-17, 5 figure memory response booklets, scoring templates, and red pencil all in a canvas bag; $76 per administration and scoring manual; $76 per interpretive handbook; $46 per 25 record forms; $29 per 25 response booklets; $29 per figure memory response booklets; $44 per University training CD-ROM; $18 per scoring templates; $41 per multi-pack of forms; $802 CAS complete kit without case.
Comments: PASS theory reconceptualizes intelligence as cognitive processes.

Authors: Jack A. Naglieri and J. P. Das.
Publisher: PRO-ED.
  a) STANDARD BATTERY.
  Scores: 4 scales with 13 subtests: Planning (Matching Numbers, Planned Codes, Planned Connections), Simultaneous (Nonverbal Matrices, Verbal-Spatial Relations, Figure Memory), Attention (Expressive Attention, Number Detection, Receptive Attention), Successive (Word Series, Sentence Repetition, Speech Rate, Sentence Questions).
  Time: [60] minutes.
  b) BASIC BATTERY.
  Scores: 4 scales with 8 subtests: Planning (Matching Numbers, Planned Codes), Simultaneous (Nonverbal Matrices, Verbal-Spatial Relations), Attention (Expressive Attention, Number Detection), Successive (Word Series, Sentence Repetition).
  Time: [45] minutes.
Cross References: For reviews by Joyce Meikamp and Donald Thompson, see 14:109; see also T5:763 (5 references).

[788]

Database Analyst Staff Selector.

Purpose: To evaluate the analytical reasoning and detail skills necessary for successful performance as a database analyst.
Population: Candidates for database positions.
Publication Date: 1992.
Acronym: DBPRDF.
Scores: Total Score, Narrative Evaluation, Ranking, Recommendation.
Administration: Group.
Price Data, 2001: $340 per candidate.
Time: (85) minutes.
Comments: Scored by publisher; must be proctored.
Author: Walden Personnel Performance, Inc.
Publisher: Walden Personnel Performance, Inc. [Canada].

[789]

A Dating Scale.

Purpose: To measure "liberalism of attitudes toward dating."
Population: Adolescents and adults.
Publication Dates: 1962–1988.
Scores: Total score only.
Administration: Group.
Manual: No manual.
Price Data, 2005: $2 per scale.
Time: [10] minutes.
Comments: Supplementary article available.
Author: Panos D. Bardis.
Publisher: Donna Bardis.
Cross References: For additional information and a review by Charles F. Warnath, see 8:335 (3 references).

[790]

Davidson Trauma Scale.

Purpose: "Developed to assess post traumatic stress disorder (PTSD) symptoms and aid in treatment."
Population: Adults who have been exposed to a serious trauma
Publication Date: 1996.
Acronym: DTS.
Scores, 4: Intrusion, Avoidance/Numbing, Hyperarousal, Total.
Administration: Individual or group.
Price Data, 2011: $96 per complete kit including manual (32 pages), and 25 QuikScore™ forms; $50 per 25 QuikScore™ forms; $67 per manual.
Foreign Language Edition: French-Canadian QuikScore™ forms available.
Time: (10) minutes.
Comments: Self-report.
Author: Jonathan Davidson.
Publisher: Multi-Health Systems, Inc.
Cross References: For reviews by Janet F. Carlson and William E. Martin, Jr., see 14:110.

[791]

DCS–A Visual Learning and Memory Test for Neuropsychological Assessment.

Purpose: Designed as "a learning and memory test for detecting memory deficits resulting from neurological disorders."
Population: Ages 6–70.
Publication Date: 1998.
Scores: Score information available from publisher.
Administration: Individual.
Price Data, 2011: $118 per complete kit including folder, 50 record and evaluation sheets, 18 test cards, 5 wooden sticks, and manual (1998, 48 pages).
Time: (20–60) minutes.
Authors: Georg Lamberti and Sigrid Weidlich.
Publisher: Hogrefe Publishing.
Cross References: For a review by Andrew S. Davis and Rik Carl D'Amato, see 15:73.

[792]

Dean-Woodcock Neuropsychological Battery.

Purpose: Designed to provide a "comprehensive assessment of sensory-motor functioning."
Population: Ages 4-0 and over.
Publication Date: 2003.
Acronym: DWNB.
Administration: Individual.
Price Data, 2007: $309.50 per complete kit including manual (269 pages), stimulus book, 25 test records, 25 interview forms, 25 emotional status forms, and a plastic storage box containing a comb, scissors, key, candle, nail, paper clip, pen, ball, plastic fork, plastic spoon, stylus, eye occluder, and three blindfolds; $49.25 per 25 test records; $40.50 per 25 interview forms; $58.75 per 25 emotional status forms.
Comments: Examiner's manual provides verbal instructions in Spanish and English.
Authors: Raymond S. Dean and Richard W. Woodcock.
Publisher: Riverside Publishing.
　a) DEAN-WOODCOCK SENSORY-MOTOR BATTERY.
　Acronym: DWSMB.
　Scores, 21: Sensory (Near Point Visual Acuity, Visual Confrontation, Naming Pictures of Objects, Auditory Acuity), Tactile (Palm Writing, Object Identification, Finger Identification, Simultaneous Localization, Total), Motor (Lateral Preference, Gait and Station, Romberg, Construction, Coordination, Mime Movements, Left-Right Movements, Finger Tapping, Expressive Speech, Grip Strength, Total), Impairment Index.
　Time: (30–45) minutes.
　b) DEAN-WOODCOCK STRUCTURED NEUROPSYCHOLOGICAL INTERVIEW.
　Scores: Not scored.
　Time: (30) minutes.
　Comments: Structured interview can be administered to the subject, a parent, or "other informant who knows the subject well."
　c) DEAN-WOODCOCK EMOTIONAL STATUS EXAMINATION.
　Scores: Not scored.
　Time: (30) minutes.
　Comments: May be administered to subject or to an informant.
Cross References: For reviews by Rik Carl D'Amato and Justin M. Walker and by W. Joel Schneider, see 17:54.

[793]

Decision Making Inventory.

Purpose: "Designed to assess an individual's preferred style of decision making."
Population: High school and college, working adults.
Publication Dates: 1983–1986.
Acronym: DMI.
Scores, 4: Information Gathering Style (Spontaneous, Systematic), Information Processing Style (Internal, External).
Administration: Group.
Forms, 2: H, I.
Price Data: Available from publisher.
Time: (10) minutes.
Authors: William C. Coscarelli, Richard Johnson (test), and JaDean Johnson (test).
Publisher: Jossey-Bass, A Wiley Company.
Cross References: See T5:768 (2 references); for reviews by George Domino and Barbara A. Kerr, see 10:77 (3 references).

[794]

Decision-Making Strategies: A Leadership Inventory.

Purpose: Designed to help "discover your current decision-making pattern."
Population: Adults.
Publication Date: 1983.
Scores, 5: Bargaining, Collaboration, Decide-By-Rule, Unilateral, Total Score.
Administration: Group.
Price Data: Available from publisher.
Time: (15) minutes.
Author: Herbert S. Kindler.
Publisher: The Center for Management Effectiveness, Inc.

[795]

Decoding-Encoding Screener for Dyslexia.

Purpose: Designed to "quickly assess a student's specific reading difficulties."
Population: Grades 1-8.
Publication Date: 2006.
Acronym: DESD.
Scores, 5: DESD Grade Level, Reading Raw Score, Reading Standard Score, Sight-Word Spelling Raw Score, Phonetic Spelling Raw Score.
Administration: Individual.
Price Data, 2011: $115 per kit including stimulus booklet, 100 spelling response forms, 100 record sheets, and manual (63 pages); $27 per stimulus booklet; $10 per 100 spelling response forms; $45 per 100 record sheets; $55 per manual.
Time: (5-10) minutes.
Authors: John R. Griffin, Howard N. Walton, and Garth N. Christenson.
Publisher: Western Psychological Services.

[796]

Decoding Skills Test.

Purpose: Measures the reading levels and decoding skills of elementary school readers and identifies reading disabled children and provides a diagnostic profile of their decoding skill development.
Population: Grades 1.0-5.8+.
Publication Date: 1985.
Acronym: DST.
Scores: 3 subtests yielding 12 Scores: Basal Vocabulary (Instructional Level, Frustration Level), Phonic Patterns (Monosyllabic, Polysyllabic), Contextual Decoding (Instructional Level [Reading Rate, Error Rate, Phonic Words, Comprehension], Frustration Level [Reading Rate, Error Rate, Phonic Words, Comprehension]).
Administration: Individual.
Price Data, 2006: $154 per complete kit including reusable Presentation Book, 10 scoring booklets, and

manual; $71.50 per 1 reusable Presentation Book; $68.50 per 2+ books; $37.95 per scoring booklet; $50 per manual.
Time: 15-30 minutes.
Comments: "Criterion-referenced."
Authors: Ellis Richardson and Barbara DiBenedetto.
Publisher: Western Psychological Services.
Cross References: See T5:769 (8 references); for reviews by Stephen N. Elliott and Timothy S. Hartshorne, see 10:78.

[797]

Decoding Spelling Proficiency Test-Revised.

Purpose: Designed to provide "a detailed profile of crucial literacy skills that underlie reading and spelling."
Population: Ages 6-25.
Publication Dates: 1982-2010.
Acronym: DSPT-R.
Scores, 4: Decoding, Visual Recognition, Auditory-Visual Recognition, Spelling.
Administration: Group.
Forms, 2: Parallel Forms A and B.
Price Data, 2010: $139 per test kit including manual (2010, 219 pages), 25 record Forms A, 25 record Forms B, 25 test booklets Form A, and 25 test booklets Form B; $49 per manual.
Time: (25-40) minutes.
Comments: "The current version…is a revision of the Diagnostic Spelling Potential test"; The four parts can be administered separately or in conjunction with one another.
Authors: Michael Milone and John Arena.
Publisher: Academic Therapy Publications.
Cross References: For information regarding the Diagnostic Spelling Potential Test, see T4:790 (1 reference); for reviews by Marcee J. Meyers and Ruth Noyce of the Diagnostic Spelling Potential Test, see 9:345 (1 reference).

[798]

Defendant Questionnaire.

Purpose: "Designed for defendant (misdemeanor or felony) assessment in court settings."
Population: Defendants (misdemeanor or felony).
Publication Date: 1997.
Acronym: DQ.
Scores: 7 scales: Truthfulness, Alcohol, Drugs, Substance Abuse/Dependency, Violence (Lethality), Antisocial, Stress Coping Abilities.
Administration: Group.
Price Data: Available from publisher.
Foreign Language Editions: Available in English and Spanish.
Time: Administration time not reported.
Comments: Can be administered via paper and pencil test booklet, directly on computer screen, optically scanned answer sheet, human voice audio via headset and computer.

Author: Risk & Needs Assessment, Inc.
Publisher: Behavior Data Systems, Ltd.

[799]

Defining Issues Test.

Purpose: "Gives information about the process by which people judge what ought to be done in moral dilemmas."
Population: Grades 9-12 and college and adults.
Publication Dates: 1979-1987.
Acronym: DIT.
Scores, 12: Consistency Check, M (meaningless items) score, P (principled moral thinking) score, U (utilizer) score, D (composite) score, A (antiestablishment) score, and stage scores (2, 3, 4, 5A, 5B, and 6).
Administration: Group.
Forms, 2: Short form, long form.
Price Data, 2001: $25 per manual including both forms and scoring information (1986, 96 pages); scoring service available from publisher; $1.90 or less per prepaid scoring sheet including all reports, handling costs, etc.
Time: (30-40) minutes for short form; (40-50) minutes for long form.
Comments: 2 optional companion booklets available: Development in Judging Moral Issues from the Center for the Study of Ethical Development, and Moral Development: Advances in Theory and Research from Praeger Press.
Authors: James R. Rest, with model computer scoring programs by Steve Thoma, Mark Davison, Stephen Robbins, and David Swanson.
Publisher: Center for the Study of Ethical Development.
Cross References: See T5:771 (28 references) and T4:724 (10 references); for reviews by Rosemary E. Sutton and by Bert W. Westbrook and K. Denise Bane, see 11:104 (34 references); for reviews by Robert R. McCrae and Kevin L. Moreland, see 9:304 (22 references); see also T3:666 (8 references).

[800]

DeGangi-Berk Test of Sensory Integration.

Purpose: "Designed to overcome problems in detecting sensory integrative dysfunction in the early years."
Population: Ages 3–5.
Publication Date: 1983.
Acronym: TSI.
Scores, 4: Postural Control, Bilateral Motor Integration, Reflex Integration, Total.
Administration: Individual.
Price Data, 2006: $192.50 per complete kit including set of test materials, 25 star design sheets, 25 protocol booklets, and manual (48 pages) in a carrying case; $29 per 100 star designs; $29 per 25 protocol booklets; $42.50 per manual.
Time: (30) minutes.

Comments: Other test materials (e.g., stopwatch, carpeted scooter board, hula hoop) must be supplied by examiner.
Authors: Georgia A. DeGangi and Ronald A. Berk.
Publisher: Western Psychological Services.
Cross References: See T5:772 (2 references); for a review by R. A. Bornstein, see 10:80.

[801]

Degrees of Reading Power [Primary and Standard Test Forms J & K and Advanced Test Forms T & U].

Purpose: Designed to provide direct criterion-referenced, performance measures of reading comprehension.
Population: Grades 1–12 and over.
Publication Dates: 1979–2002.
Acronym: DRP.
Scores: Total DRP score.
Administration: Group.
Levels, 3: Primary, Standard, Advanced.
Price Data, 2006: $53 per Primary/Standard examination set including 1 copy of each J series test form, 5 answer sheets, 1 J & K tests handbook (2000, 124 pages), and 1 norms booklet; $20 per 25 answer sheets (Standard and Advanced tests); $9.50 per 3-year license to use answer sheets per package of test booklets ordered; $36 per J & K tests handbook; $33 per Primary/Standard norms booklet; $20 per 5 test administration procedures (specify Primary, Standard, or Advanced); $32 per Degrees of Reading Power Program technical manual; $19 per scoring key or scoring overlay per test form.
Time: (45) minutes.
Comments: Practice exercises provided; provides readability analysis of instructional material in print; computer or hand scored; group profiles, optional reports, services, and software also available.
Authors: Touchstone Applied Science Associates (TASA), Inc.
Publisher: Questar Assessment, Inc.

a) PRIMARY.
Purpose: To provide a measure of how well students understand the meaning of text.
Population: Grades 1–3.
Forms, 2: J, K.
Levels, 2: 0, 9.
Price Data: $166 per Primary classroom set including 25 practice exercises, 25 test booklets, 25 answer sheets, test administration procedures, J & K tests handbook, norms booklet, and teacher class profile; $16 per 25 Primary practice exercises; $99 per 25 consumable Primary test booklets including 1 test administration procedures.
b) STANDARD.
Purpose: To provide a measure of how well students understand the meaning of text.

Population: Grades 3–12 and over.
Forms, 2: J, K.
Levels, 5: 8, 7, 6, 4, 2.
Price Data: $166 per Standard classroom set including 25 practice exercises, 25 test booklets, 25 answer sheets, test administration procedures, J & K tests handbook, norms booklet, and teacher class profile; $16 per 25 Standard practice exercises; $79 per reusable Standard test booklets including 1 test administration procedures.
c) ADVANCED.
Purpose: To assess how well students are able to reason with textual materials.
Population: Grades 6–12 and over.
Forms, 2: T, U.
Levels, 2: 4, 2.
Price Data: $45 per Advanced examination set including 1 T4 test booklet, 1 T2 test booklet, 5 answer sheets, and Advanced handbook (2002, 98 pages); $149 per Advanced classroom set including 25 practice exercises, 25 test booklets, 25 answer sheets, test administration procedures, and Advanced handbook; $18 per 25 Advanced practice exercises; $89 per 25 Advanced test booklets; $38 per Advanced handbook (T & U test forms).
Cross References: For reviews by Jeffrey K. Smith and Keith F. Widaman, see 16:69; for reviews by Felice J. Green and Howard Margolis of a previous edition, see 14:111; see also T5:773 (5 references); for reviews by Darrell N. Caulley, Elaine Furniss, and Michael Mc-Namara and by Lawrence Cross of an earlier edition, see 12:101 (9 references); see also T4:726 (14 references); for reviews by Roger Bruning and Gerald S. Hanna of an earlier edition, see 9:305 (1 reference).

[802]

Degrees of Word Meaning.

Purpose: Developed to "assess the size of students' reading vocabularies by measuring their understanding of the meaning of words in naturally occurring contexts."
Population: Grades 3–8+.
Publication Date: 1993.
Acronym: DWM.
Scores: Total score only.
Administration: Group.
Levels: 6 overlapping levels.
Price Data, 2005: $32 per user's manual (96 pages); $17 per 5 test administration procedures; $50 per 30 test booklets (select level); $12.50 per 30 practice booklets; $16 per 30 NCS answer sheets; $14 per scoring key (select level).
Time: Untimed.
Author: Touchstone Applied Science Associates (TASA), Inc.
Publisher: Questar Assessment, Inc.
Cross References: For reviews by David P. Hurford and Judith A. Monsaas, see 13:90.

[803]

Delaware County Silent Reading Test, Second Edition.

Purpose: "Designed to measure pupil achievement in typical . . . reading materials."
Population: Grades 1.5, 2, 2.5, 3, 3.5, 4, 5, 6, 7, 8.
Publication Date: 1965.
Scores, 5: Interpretation, Organization, Vocabulary, Structural Analysis, Total.
Administration: Group.
Levels, 10: Grades 1.5, 2, 2.5, 3, 3.5, 4, 5, 6, 7, 8.
Manual: No manual.
Price Data: Available from publisher.
Time: Administration time not reported.
Comments: Teacher's guide for each level.
Authors: Judson E. Newburg and Nicholas A. Spennato.
Publisher: Delaware County Intermediate Unit.
Cross References: For a review by Allen Berger, see 7:686.

[804]

Delis-Kaplan Executive Function System.

Purpose: To "comprehensive assess ... the key components of executive functions believed to be mediated primarily by the frontal lobe."
Population: 8–89 years.
Publication Date: 2001.
Acronym: D-KEFS.
Scores: 9 tests: Trail Making Test, Verbal Fluency Test, Design Fluency Test, Color-Word Interference Test, Sorting Test, 20 Questions Test, Word Context Test, Tower Test, Proverb Test.
Administration: Individual.
Price Data, 2001: $415 per complete kit in box including manual (388 pages), stimulus booklet, sorting cards (3 sets of 6 cards each), 1 tower stand with 5 color disks, 25 record forms, 25 Design Fluency Response booklets, 25 Trail Making response booklet sets (each set contains 25 response booklets for the 5 Trail Making conditions; $470 per complete kit with soft-side case; $520 per complete kit in box with Scoring Assistant (CD-ROM or diskette, Windows only); $575 per complete kit in a soft-side case with Scoring Assistant; $155 per D-KEFS Scoring Assistant (CD-ROM or diskette); $68 per examiner's and technical manual; $53 per examiner's manual; $42 per technical manual (144 pages); $37 per 25 record forms; $21 per 25 Sorting or Color-Word Interference test record forms; $55 per 25 sets of Trail Making Test response booklets (each set contains 25 different response booklets for the 5 Trail Making conditions); $15 per 25 Trail Making or Design Fluency Test record forms; $22 per 25 Verbal Fluency, 20 Questions, or Word Context test record forms; $18 per 25 Tower or Proverb test record forms; $21 per 25 alternate record forms for Sorting, Verbal Fluency, 20 Questions

Tests; $42 per Sorting Test set of cards including 2 sets of standard sorting cards, and 2 practice set; $42 per Sorting Test alternate set of cards including 3 sets of 6 cards each.
Time: (90) minutes for all 9 tests.
Comments: Each test assesses a different executive-function domain; tests may be administered alone or in combination; hand-scorable; D-KEFS Scoring Assistant software available; scoring software generates reports in table or graphical format; for system requirements contact publisher.
Authors: Dean C. Delis, Edith Kaplan, and Joel H. Kramer.
Publisher: Pearson.

   a) D-KEFS TRAIL MAKING TEST.
   Purpose: Assesses "flexibility of thinking on a visual-motor task."
   Form, 1: Standard Record Form.
   Scores, 6: Visual Scanning, Number Sequencing, Letter Sequencing, Number-Letter Switching, Motor Speed, Composite Score.
   b) D-KEFS VERBAL FLUENCY TEST.
   Purpose: Assesses "fluent productivity in the verbal domain."
   Forms, 2: Standard Record Form, Alternate Record Form.
   Scores, 3: Letter Fluency, Category Fluency, Category Switching.
   c) D-KEFS DESIGN FLUENCY TEST.
   Purpose: Assesses "fluent productivity in the spatial domain."
   Form, 1: Standard Record Form.
   Scores, 3: Filled Dots, Empty Dots Only, Switching.
   d) D-KEFS COLOR-WORD INTERFERENCE TEST.
   Purpose: Assesses "verbal inhibition."
   Form, 1: Standard Record Form.
   Scores, 4: Color Naming, Word Reading, Inhibition, Inhibition/Switching.
   e) D-KEFS SORTING TEST.
   Purpose: Assesses "problem-solving, verbal and spatial concept formation, flexibility of thinking on a conceptual task."
   Forms, 2: Standard Record Form, Alternate Record Form.
   Scores, 2: Free Sorting, Sort Recognition.
   Comments: Alternate set of scoring cards available.
   f) D-KEFS TOWER TEST.
   Purpose: Assesses "planning and reasoning in the spatial modality [and] impulsivity."
   Form, 1: Standard Record Form.
   Score: Total Achievement Score.
   g) D-KEFS 20 QUESTIONS TEST.
   Purpose: Assesses "hypothesis testing, verbal and spatial abstract thinking, [and] impulsivity."
   Forms, 2: Standard Record Form, Alternate Record Form.
   Score: Initial Abstraction Score.

   h) D-KEFS WORD CONTEXT TEST.
   Purpose: Assesses "deductive reasoning [and] verbal abstract thinking."
   Form, 1: Standard Record Form.
   Score: Total Consecutively Correct.
   i) D-KEFS PROVERB TEST.
   Purpose: Assesses "metaphorical thinking, generating versus comprehending abstract thought."
   Form, 1: Standard Record Form.
   Scores, 2: Total Achievement scores: Free Inquiry, Multiple Choice.
Cross References: For reviews by Anthony T. Dugbartey and Pamilla Ramsden, see 15:74.

[805]
Dementia Rating Scale–2.

Purpose: To measure and track "mental status in adults with cognitive impairment."
Population: Adults ages 56–89 and older.
Publication Dates: 1973–2001.
Acronym: DRS-2.
Scores, 6: Attention, Initiation/Perseveration, Construction, Conceptualization, Memory, Total.
Administration: Individual.
Price Data, 2006: $240 per introductory kit including professional manual (2001, 47 pages), 50 scoring booklets, 50 profile forms and set of 32 stimulus cards; $210 per Alternate Form introductory kit; $350 per CD ROM based software with unlimited use Scoring and Interpretive Reports.
Time: (15–30) minutes.
Comments: Revised version of the DRS; DRS-2 stimulus cards same as for original DRS; can be administered bedside by appropriately trained personnel; alternate form is also available.
Authors: Steven Mattis (professional manual, stimulus cards, scoring booklet), Paul J. Jurica, and Christopher L. Leitten (professional manual).
Publisher: Psychological Assessment Resources, Inc.
Cross References: For reviews by Iris Phillips and Pamilla Ramsden, see 15:75; see T5:776 (63 references); for a review by R. A. Bornstein of an earlier edition, see 11:107 (2 references).

[806]
Dementia Rating Scale-2 Alternate Form.

Purpose: Designed as an alternate form of the Dementia Rating Scale-2, a measure of cognitive status, to reduce "the practice effects that occur with serial administrations of the DRS-2."
Population: Ages 56-105.
Publication Dates: 1973-2004.
Acronym: DRS-2: AF.
Scores, 6: Attention, Initiation/Perseveration, Construction, Conceptualization, Memory, Total.
Administration: Individual.

Price Data, 2011: $255 per introductory kit, including 50 scoring booklets, 50 profile forms, 1 set of stimulus cards, and professional manual supplement (2004, 29 pages); $132 per 50 scoring booklets; $45 per 50 profile forms; $42 per set of stimulus cards; $57 per professional manual supplement.

Time: [15-30] minutes.

Comments: As noted in the professional manual for the Dementia Rating Scale-2 (15:75), "The Professional Manual Supplement contains information on the development, reliability, and validity of the DRS-2: AF, as well as instructions for administration and scoring. However, this Professional Manual Supplement should be considered an adjunct to the DRS-2 Professional Manual," which must be purchased separately.

Authors: Kara S. Schmidt and Steven Mattis.

Publisher: Psychological Assessment Resources, Inc.

Cross References: For reviews by Iris Phillips and Pamilla Ramsden of the Dementia Rating Scale-2, see 15:75; see also T5:776 (63 references); for a review by R. A. Bornstein of the original Dementia Rating Scale, see 11:107 (2 references).

[807]

Dental Admission Test.

Purpose: "Designed to measure general academic achievement, comprehension of scientific information, and perceptual ability."

Population: United States dental school applicants.

Publication Dates: 1950–2006.

Acronym: DAT.

Scores, 8: Natural Sciences (Biology, General Chemistry, Organic Chemistry, Total), Reading Comprehension, Quantitative Reasoning, Perceptual Ability, Academic Average.

Administration: Group.

Price Data: Available from publisher.

Time: 255(270) minutes.

Comments: Formerly called Dental Aptitude Testing Program; computer-based test administered throughout the year at centers approved by publisher.

Author: Department of Testing Services.

Publisher: American Dental Association.

Cross References: For reviews by Janet Baldwin and Jerry S. Gilmer, see 12:102; for reviews by Henry M. Cherrick and Linda M. DuBois of an earlier edition, see 9:308; see also T3:673 (2 references); for reviews by Robert L. Linn and Christine H. McGuire of an earlier edition, see 8:1085 (7 references); see also T2:2337 (8 references), 7:1091 (28 references), 5:916 (6 references), and 4:788 (2 references).

[808]

Dental Assistant Test.

Purpose: Developed to help screen for dental assistant positions.

Population: Dental assistant applicants.

Publication Date: 1975.

Scores: 8 tests: Attention to Details, Organization Skills, Perception of Objects in Space, Perception of Spatial Perspective, Following Directions, Detail Judgments, Dexterity, Logic and Reasoning.

Administration: Group.

Price Data: Available from publisher.

Time: (40-45) minutes.

Comments: Self-administered.

Authors: Mary Meeker and Robert Meeker.

Publisher: SOI Systems.

[809]

Dental Receptionist Test.

Purpose: Developed to help screen for dental receptionist positions.

Population: Dental receptionist applicants.

Publication Date: 1975.

Scores: 8 tests: Attention to Details, Vocabulary, Verbal Reasoning, Following Directions, Management of Details, Management of Numerical Information, Dexterity, Logic and Reasoning.

Administration: Group.

Price Data: Available from publisher.

Time: (45-50) minutes.

Comments: Self-administered.

Authors: Mary Meeker and Robert Meeker.

Publisher: SOI Systems.

[810]

Denver Articulation Screening Exam.

Purpose: Designed to identify significant developmental delay in the acquisition of speech sounds.

Population: Ages 2.5 to 7.0.

Publication Dates: 1971–1973.

Acronym: DASE.

Scores, 2: DASE Word Score, Intelligibility Rating.

Administration: Individual.

Price Data, 2005: $8 per 25 test forms; $8 per set of picture cards for use with "shy or immature" children; $230 per training videotape; $19 per manual/workbook (1973, 42 pages).

Time: (10–15) minutes.

Comments: Orally administered.

Authors: Amelia F. Drumwright and William K. Frankenburg (manual).

Publisher: Denver Developmental Materials, Inc.

Cross References: See T3:675 (1 reference); for a review by Harold A. Peterson, see 8:958.

[811]

Denver Audiometric Screening Test.

Purpose: Constructed to identify children who have a serious hearing loss.

Population: Ages 3–6.
Publication Date: 1973.
Acronym: DAST.
Scores: 3 ratings for each ear: Pass, Fail, Uncertain.
Administration: Individual.
Price Data, 2005: $6 per 25 test forms; $230 per training videotape; $28 per manual/workbook (30 pages); $23.50 per reference manual.
Time: [5–10] minutes.
Authors: William K. Frankenburg, Marion Downs, and Elynor Kazuk.
Publisher: Denver Developmental Materials, Inc.
Cross References: See T5:784 (1 reference); for a review by Lear Ashmore, see 9:309.

[812]

Denver Eye Screening Test.

Purpose: Developed to detect problems in visual acuity and screen for eye diseases.
Population: Ages 6 months and over.
Publication Date: 1973.
Acronym: DEST.
Scores, 3: Normal, Abnormal, Untestable.
Administration: Individual.
Price Data, 2005: $6 per 25 test forms; $24 per set of test materials including picture cards, cord, and spinning toy; $11 per set of picture cards; $3.00 per cord; $6 per spinning toy; $180 per training videotape; $24 per manual/workbook (37 pages); $19 per reference manual.
Time: (5–10) minutes.
Comments: "Criterion-referenced."
Authors: William K. Frankenburg, Arnold D. Goldstein, and John Barker.
Publisher: Denver Developmental Materials, Inc.
  a) VISION TESTS.
    1) *Fixation.*
    Population: Ages 6 months to 2.5 years.
    2) *Picture Card.*
    Population: Ages 2.5 to 3.
    3) *"E."*
    Population: Ages 3 and over.
  b) TESTS FOR NON-STRAIGHT EYES.
  Population: Ages 6 months and over.

[813]

Denver Prescreening Developmental Questionnaire II.

Purpose: "To facilitate earlier identification of children whose development may be delayed."
Population: Ages 0-9 months, 9-24 months, 2-4 years, 4-6 years.
Publication Dates: 1975–1998.
Acronym: PDQII.
Scores: Item scores only.
Administration: Individual.

Levels, 4: Ages 0-9 months, 9-24 months, 2-4 years, 4-6 years.
Manual: No manual.
Price Data, 2005: $22–$25 (English) per 100 questionnaires (specify level); $24-$28 (Spanish) per 100 questionnaires (specify level).
Time: [12.5] minutes.
Comments: Ratings by parents; previous edition entitled Revised Denver Prescreening Developmental Questionnaire.
Author: William K. Frankenburg.
Publisher: Denver Developmental Materials, Inc.
Cross References: See T5:787 (4 references); for reviews by Stephen N. Axford and William B. Michael of the Revised Denver Prescreening Developmental Questionnaire, see 12:327 (1 reference).

[814]

Denver II (Denver Developmental Screening Test).

Purpose: Designed to screen for developmental delays.
Population: Birth to age 6.
Publication Dates: 1967–1992.
Scores: Item scores in 4 areas (Personal-Social, Fine Motor-Adaptive, Language, Gross Motor) and 5 test behavior ratings (Typical, Compliance, Interest in Surroundings, Fearfulness, Attention Span).
Administration: Individual.
Price Data, 2005: $90 per complete package; $55 per test kit; $25 per 100 test forms; $215 per training videotape (rental price $90); $26 per training manual (1990, 50 pages); $30 per technical manual (1990, 91 pages).
Time: (10–15) minutes for abbreviated version; (20–25) minutes for entire test.
Comments: Revision is intended to be used as a developmental chart designed to give a broad overview of general development in a minimum amount of time.
Authors: W. K. Frankenburg, Josiah Dodds, Phillip Archer, Beverly Bresnick, Patrick Maschka, Norma Edelman, and Howard Shapiro.
Publisher: Denver Developmental Materials, Inc.
Cross References: See T5:788 (3 references); for reviews by Selma Hughes and Pat Mirenda, see 12:103 (3 references); see also T4:740 (18 references).

[815]

Depression and Anxiety in Youth Scale.

Purpose: Designed to help professionals identify depression and anxiety in children and youth.
Population: Ages 0-6 to 0-18.
Publication Date: 1994.
Acronym: DAYS.
Administration: Individual.
Price Data, 2010: $172 per complete kit including 50 student rating scales, 50 teacher rating scales, 50 parent

rating scales, 50 profile/record forms, scoring keys, and manual (39 pages); $29 per 50 record forms; $29 per 50 profile/record forms; $69 per manual.
Authors: Phyllis L. Newcomer, Edna M. Barenbaum, and Brian R. Bryant.
Publisher: PRO-ED.
 a) STUDENT SELF-REPORT SCALE (SCALE S).
 Scores, 2: Depression, Anxiety.
 Time: (15–20) minutes.
 b) TEACHER RATING SCALE (SCALE T).
 Scores, 2: Depression, Anxiety.
 Time: (5–10) minutes.
 c) PARENT RATING SCALE (SCALE P).
 Scores, 3: Depression, Anxiety, Social Maladjustment.
 Time: (6–10) minutes.
Cross References: For reviews by Gloria Maccow and Janet V. Smith, see 13:91.

[816]
Depressive Experiences Questionnaire.
Purpose: Designed to assess an individual's depressive experience.
Population: Adolescents and adults (patients and normals).
Publication Dates: 1976–1989.
Acronym: DEQ.
Scores, 3: Dependency, Self-Criticism, Efficacy.
Administration: Group.
Forms, 2: DEQ, DEQ-A.
Manual: No manual.
Price Data: Available from publisher.
Time: Administration time not reported.
Authors: Sidney J. Blatt, Carrie E. Schaffer, Susan A. Bers, and Donald M. Quinlan.
Publisher: Sidney J. Blatt.
Cross References: See T5:790 (29 references), T4:744 (30 references), 9:316 (2 references), and T3:682 (1 reference).

[817]
Derogatis Affects Balance Scale [Revised].
Purpose: Designed as a multidimensional mood and affects inventory to "measure the affects profile of community, medical, and psychiatric respondents."
Population: Adults.
Publication Dates: 1975–1996.
Acronym: DABS.
Scores, 13: Joy, Contentment, Vigor, Affection, Anxiety, Depression, Guilt, Hostility, Positive Score Total, Negative Score Total, Affects Balance Index, Affects Expressiveness Index, Positive Affects Ratio.
Administration: Individual.
Forms, 2: DABS, DABS-SF (Short Form).
Price Data, 2002: $50 per 50 tests; $25 per 50 profiles; $29.50 per manual (1996, 58 pages).

Time: (5) minutes (DABS); (2–3) minutes (Short Form).
Comments: Self-report inventory, for clinical or research uses; formerly published as the Affects Balance Scale (ABS); scoring is available online ($1 per scoring) at www.derogatis-tests.com.
Author: Leonard R. Derogatis.
Publisher: Clinical Psychometric Research, Inc.
Cross References: For reviews by Mark J. Atkinson and Carlen Hennington, see 14:112; see also T5:791 (16 references), T4:132 (6 references), and 9:61 (6 references).

[818]
Derogatis Interview for Sexual Functioning.
Purpose: "A brief semistructured interview designed to provide an estimate of the quality of an individual's current sexual functioning in quantitative terms."
Population: Adults.
Publication Dates: 1987–1989.
Scores, 6: Sexual Cognition/Fantasy, Sexual Arousal, Sexual Behavior/Experience, Orgasm, Sexual Drive/Relationship, Total Score.
Administration: Individual.
Price Data, 2006: $62.50 per 50 DISF or DISF-SR (specify gender); $25 per 50 DISF or DISF-SR score sheets (specify gender); additional shipping charges apply.
Foreign Language Editions: Polish, French, Finnish, and German editions available.
Time: (15–20) minutes for DISF; (10–15) minutes for DISF-SR.
Author: Leonard R. Derogatis.
Publisher: Clinical Psychometric Research, Inc.
 a) DEROGATIS INTERVIEW FOR SEXUAL FUNCTIONING.
 Acronym: DISF.
 Time: (15–20) minutes.
 Comments: Semistructured interview format using a 4-point Likert scale.
 b) DEROGATIS INTERVIEW FOR SEXUAL FUNCTIONING–SELF REPORT.
 Acronym: DISF-SR.
 Time: (10–15) minutes.
 Comments: Paper-and-pencil format using Likert scales; may be used to gain evaluations of patient's sexual functioning by the patient or the patient's spouse.
Cross References: For a review by Sheri Bauman, see 15:76.

[819]
Derogatis Psychiatric Rating Scale.
Purpose: Multidimensional psychiatric rating scale for use by clinician to assist in validating patient-reported results.
Population: Adults and adolescents.
Publication Dates: 1974–1992.
Acronym: DPRS.

Administration: Individual.
Comments: Formerly called Hopkins Psychiatric Rating Scale (9:483).
Author: Leonard R. Derogatis.
Publisher: Pearson.

a) BRIEF DEROGATIS PSYCHIATRIC RATING SCALE.
Acronym: B-DPRS.
Scores, 10: Primary Dimensions (Somatization, Obsessive-Compulsive, Interpersonal Sensitivity, Depression, Anxiety, Hostility, Phobic Anxiety, Paranoid Ideation, Psychoticism) and Global Pathology Index.
Price Data, 2006: $50 per 100 forms.
Time: (1–2) minutes.

b) DEROGATIS PSYCHIATRIC RATING SCALE.
Acronym: DPRS.
Scores, 18: Same as brief edition plus Sleep Disturbance, Psychomotor Retardation, Hysterical Behavior, Abjection-Disinterest, Conceptual Dysfunction, Disorientation, Excitement, Euphoria.
Price Data: $32 per 100 forms.
Time: (2–5) minutes.
Cross References: For reviews by Samuel Juni and Paul Retzlaff, see 13:92 (1 reference); see also T4:745 (6 references) and 9:483 (1 reference).

[820]

Derogatis Sexual Functioning Inventory.
Purpose: Multidimensional assessment of sexual functioning.
Population: Adults.
Publication Dates: 1975–1979.
Acronym: DSFI.
Scores, 12: Information, Experience, Drive, Attitudes, Psychological Symptoms, Affects, Gender Role, Definition, Fantasy, Body Image, Sexual Satisfaction, Total, Patient's Evaluation of Current Functioning.
Administration: Individual.
Price Data, 2006: $3.50 per nonreusable test (1978, 8 pages); $12.50 per manual (1979, 36 pages); $.50 per profile form (specify male or female).
Time: (45–60) minutes.
Comments: Scoring is available online ($5 per scoring) at www.derogatis-tests.com.
Author: Leonard R. Derogatis.
Publisher: Clinical Psychometric Research, Inc.
Cross References: See T5:793 (24 references) and T4:746 (10 references); for reviews by Edward S. Herold and David L. Weis, see 9:317 (3 references); see also T3:683 (6 references).

[821]

Derogatis Stress Profile.
Purpose: "Designed to assess and represent stress at three distinct but related levels of measurement."
Population: Adults.

Publication Dates: 1984–1986.
Acronym: DSP.
Scores: 3 domains: Environmental Events, Emotional Response, Personality Mediators; 11 dimensions: Time Pressure, Driven Behavior, Attitude Posture, Relaxation Potential, Role Definition, Vocational Satisfaction, Domestic Satisfaction, Health Posture, Hostility, Anxiety, Depression; 2 global scores: Subjective Stress, Total Stress.
Administration: Individual.
Price Data, 2006: $55 per 50 tests; $25 per 50 score profile forms; $12.50 per summary report and scoring instructions (1986, 14 pages).
Time: 10(15) minutes.
Comments: Scoring available online ($2 per scoring) at www.derogatis-tests.com.
Author: Leonard R. Derogatis.
Publisher: Clinical Psychometric Research, Inc.
Cross References: See T5:794 (2 references); for reviews by Mariela C. Shirley and Paul D. Werner, see 13:93 (4 references); see also T4:747 (1 reference).

[822]

Detailed Assessment of Posttraumatic Stress.
Purpose: Designed as a comprehensive diagnostic measure of trauma exposure and posttraumatic stress and associated functions, including dissociative symptoms, substance abuse, and suicidality.
Population: Adults 18 and over who have undergone a significant psychological stressor.
Publication Date: 2001.
Acronym: DAPS.
Scores: 2 validity scales (Positive Bias and Negative Bias) and 11 scales in 3 clusters: Trauma Specification (Relative Trauma Exposure, Peritraumatic Distress, Peritraumatic Dissociation), Posttraumatic Stress (Reexperiencing, Avoidance, Hyperarousal, Posttraumatic Stress–Total, Posttraumatic Impairment), Associated Features (Trauma-Specific Dissociation, Substance Abuse, Suicidality).
Administration: Individual or group.
Price Data, 2006: $189 per introductory kit including professional manual (56 pages), 10 item booklets, 50 hand-scorable answer sheets, and 50 male/female profile forms; $360 per DAPS-IR CD ROM based software kit.
Time: (20–30) minutes.
Comments: Self-administered; CD-ROM based software with Interpretive Report also available (DAPS-IR).
Author: John Briere.
Publisher: Psychological Assessment Resources, Inc.
Cross References: For reviews by Roger A. Boothroyd and Larissa Smith, see 15:77.

[823]

Detention Promotion Tests–Complete Service.
Purpose: Designed as a custom-made test to fit duties and responsibilities for promotion of detention personnel

Population: Detention workers under consideration for promotion.
Publication Dates: 1990–1998.
Scores: 6 subtests: Detention-Related Technical Knowledges, Knowledge of the Behavioral Sciences and Human Relations, Supervisory and Managerial Knowledges, Administrative Knowledges, Knowledge of Inmate Legal Rights, Comprehension Ability, Total.
Administration: Group.
Price Data: Available from publisher.
Time: [210] minutes.
Comments: Candidate study guide available.
Author: McCann Associates, Inc.
Publisher: McCann Associates.

[824]

Detroit Tests of Learning Aptitude–Adult.
Purpose: Designed to measure both general intelligence and discrete mental ability areas.
Population: Ages 16-0 and over.
Publication Date: 1991.
Acronym: DTLA-A.
Scores, 20: 12 subtest scores: Word Opposites, Story Sequences, Sentence Imitation, Reversed Letters, Mathematical Problems, Design Sequences, Basic Information, Quantitative Relations, Word Sequences, Design Reproduction, Symbolic Relations, Form Assembly and 8 composite scores (Linguistic Verbal, Linguistic Nonverbal, Attention-Enhanced, Attention-Reduced, Motor-Enhanced, Motor-Reduced, General Mental Ability, Optimal).
Administration: Individual.
Price Data, 2006: $295 per complete kit including picture book 1, picture book 2, 25 response forms, 25 examiner record booklets, 25 profile/summary forms, and manual (120 pages); $59 per picture book 1; $27 per picture book 2; $35 per 25 response forms; $50 per 25 examiner record forms; $35 per 25 profile/summary forms; $50 per manual; $51 per manipulatives.
Time: (90–150) minutes.
Comments: Upward extension of the Detroit Tests of Learning Aptitude (Second Edition) (10:85) and (Third Edition) (12:107).
Authors: Donald D. Hammill and Bryan R. Bryant.
Publisher: PRO-ED.
Cross References: For reviews by Thomas E. Dinero and Cynthia Ann Druva-Roush, see 12:105.

[825]

Detroit Tests of Learning Aptitude, Fourth Edition.
Purpose: Designed to measure both general intelligence and discrete ability areas.
Population: Ages 0-6 to 0-17.
Publication Dates: 1935–1998.

Acronym: DTLA-4.
Scores: 10 subtest scores: Word Opposites, Design Sequences, Sentence Imitation, Reversed Letters, Story Construction, Design Reproduction, Basic Information, Symbolic Relations, Word Sequences, Story Sequences; and 16 composite scores: General Mental Ability Composite, Optimal Composite, Domain Composites (Verbal, Nonverbal, Attention-Enhanced, Attention-Reduced, Motor-Enhanced, Motor-Reduced, Total), Theoretical Composites (Fluid Intelligence, Crystallized Intelligence, Associative Level, Cognitive Level, Simultaneous Processing, Successive Processing, Verbal Scale, Performance Scale, Total).
Administration: Individual.
Price Data, 2010: $420 per complete kit including examiner's manual (1998, 247 pages), Picture Books 1 and 2, 25 Profile/Summary forms, 25 Examiner Record Booklets, 25 response forms, Story Sequence Chips, and Design Sequence Cubes; $93 per examiner's manual; $112 per Picture Book 1 (for Design Sequences, Design Reproduction and Symbolic Relations); $59 per Picture Book 2 (for Story Sequences and Story Construction); $35 per 25 Profile/Summary forms; $59 per 25 Examiner Record Booklets; $35 per 25 response forms; $24 per Story Sequence Chips; $46 per Design Sequence Cubes; $129 per software scoring and report system (Windows).
Time: (40–120) minutes.
Author: Donald D. Hammill.
Publisher: PRO-ED.
Cross References: For reviews by Jeffrey K. Smith and Ross E. Traub, see 14:113; see also T5:798 (27 references); for reviews by William A. Mehrens and Michael Poteat of an earlier edition, see 12:107 (4 references); see also T4:752 (7 references); for reviews by Arthur B. Silverstein and Joan Silverstein of an earlier edition, see 10:85 (15 references); see also 9:320 (11 references), and T3:691 (20 references); for a review by Arthur B. Silverstein of an earlier edition, see 8:213 (14 references); see also T2:493 (3 references), and 7:406 (10 references); for a review by F. L. Wells, see 3:275 (1 reference); for reviews by Anne Anastasi and Henry Feinburg and an excerpted review by D. A. Worcester and S. M. Corey, see 1:1058.

[826]

Detroit Tests of Learning Aptitude–Primary, Third Edition.
Purpose: "Measures general aptitude."
Population: Ages 0-3 through 9-11.
Publication Dates: 1986–2005.
Acronym: DTLA-P:3.
Scores, 7: Verbal-Enhanced, Verbal-Reduced, Attention-Enhanced, Attention-Reduced, Motor-Enhanced, Motor-Reduced, General Ability.
Administration: Individual.
Price Data, 2010: $229 per complete kit including examiner's manual (2005, 128 pages), picture book, 25 examiner record booklets, and 25 response forms; $72

per picture book; $43 per 25 response forms; $59 per 25
examiner record booklets; $69 per manual.
Time: (15–45) minutes.
Comments: Adaptation of the Detroit Tests of Learn-
ing Aptitude–Second Edition (T5:779).
Authors: Donald D. Hammill and Brian R. Bryant.
Publisher: PRO-ED.
Cross References: For reviews by Bethany A.
Brunsman and Shawn Powell, see 17:55; see also T5:799
(2 references); for reviews by Terry A. Ackerman and
Robert T. Williams of an earlier edition, see 12:106 (1
reference); for reviews by Cathy F. Telzrow and Stanley
F. Vasa of an earlier edition, see 10:84 (1 reference).

[827]

Developing Skills Checklist.

Purpose: Designed to measure skills and behaviors that
children typically develop between prekindergarten and
the end of kindergarten.
Population: Ages 4–6.
Publication Date: 1990.
Acronym: DSC.
Scores: 9 scales: Mathematical Concepts and Operations,
Language, Memory, Auditory, Print Concepts, Motor, Visual,
Writing and Drawing Concepts, Social-Emotional.
Administration: Individual.
Price Data, 2006: $424.50 per complete kit; $17.30
per 50 Writing and Drawing books; $49 per 50 Social-
Emotional Observational Records; $50 per 50 score
sheets (specify hand-recording or machine-scoring);
$49 per 50 Parent Conference Forms; $4.77 per Class
record book; $91 per set of 3 DSC item books; $11.50
per A Day at School; $25 per administration and score
interpretation manual; $16.60 per Concepts of Print
and Writing administration manual; $16.60 per Social-
Emotional Administration manual; $19.40 per norms
book and technical manual (90 pages); $51 per training
video (entitled How to Administer and Score DSC); $36
per 5 replacement bunnies; $225 per La Lista test kit.
Foreign Language Editions: Spanish adaptation
entitled Lista de Destrezas en Desarrollo (La Lista) available as an all-in-Spanish supplement to the DSC. English
DSC kit is also required in order to administer La Lista.
Time: (10–15) minutes per session (untimed).
Author: CTB Macmillan/McGraw-Hill.
Publisher: CTB/McGraw-Hill.
Cross References: For reviews by Elaine Clark and
Claire B. Ernhart, see 12:108 (2 references).

[828]

Developing the High-Performance Workplace.

Purpose: "Created to give organizational members a
tool for assessing employee opinions about the status
of high-performance workplace characteristics in their
work environments."

Population: Organizational employees.
Publication Date: 1996.
Scores, 18: Importance Ratings (Training and Con-
tinuous Learning, Information Sharing, Employee Par-
ticipation, Organization Structure, Worker-Management
Partnerships, Compensation Linked to Performance
and Skills, Employment Security, Supportive Work
Environment, Overall HPW Rating), Quality Ratings
(Training and Continuous Learning, Information Shar-
ing, Employee Participation, Organization Structure,
Worker-Management Partnerships, Compensation
Linked to Performance and Skills, Employment Security,
Supportive Work Environment, Overall HPW Rating).
Administration: Group.
Price Data: Available from publisher.
Time: Administration time not reported.
Authors: David D. Dubois and William J. Rothwell.
Publisher: HRD Press, Inc.
Cross References: For reviews by M. David Miller
and Deniz S. Ones, see 14:114.

[829]

Developing the Leader Within.

Purpose: Assessment of leadership skills by self and others.
Population: Management personnel.
Publication Date: 1995.
Scores: 4 dimensions: Developing Within, Helping
Others Excel, Improving Critical Processes, Showing
Commitment to the Team.
Administration: Group.
Forms, 4: Leader Form, Direct Manager Form, Higher
Manager Form, Colleague Form.
Manual: No manual.
Price Data: Available from publisher at www.mind-
garden.com/products/dlwmr.htm.
Time: Administration time not reported.
Comments: Basic assessment includes leader self-rating
and up to six ratings by colleagues; Direct Manager and
Higher Manager Forms are optional.
Author: L. Phillips-Jones.
Publisher: Mind Garden, Inc.

[830]

Developmental Activities Screening Inventory, Second Edition.

Purpose: To provide early detection of developmental
disabilities in children functioning between the ages of
birth and 60 months.
Population: Ages birth to 60 months.
Publication Dates: 1977–1984.
Acronym: DASI-II.
Scores: Total score only.
Administration: Individual.
Price Data, 2006: $92 per complete kit including
50 record forms, 37 Picture Cards, 5 Set-Configuration
Cards, 2 pairs of Numeral Cards, 3 pairs of Word Cards

4 Shape Cards, and examiner's manual (1984, 103 pages); $25 per 50 record forms; $35 per 56 Picture Cards; $35 per examiner's manual.

Time: (25-30) minutes.

Comments: Behavior checklist; some test materials (form board, bell) must be supplied by examiner.

Authors: Rebecca R. Fewell and Mary Beth Langley.

Publisher: PRO-ED.

Cross References: See T5:803 (3 references); for reviews by Dennis C. Harper and William B. Michael, see 10:87; see also 9:323 (1 reference); for a reviews by Carl J. Dunst of the original edition, see 9:322 (1 reference).

[831]

A Developmental Assessment for Individuals with Severe Disabilities, Second Edition.

Purpose: Designed to aid "in identifying discrete changes in behavior … in five areas of development."

Population: Individuals of all ages who are functioning within the birth to 7-year developmental range.

Publication Dates: 1980–1999.

Acronym: DASH-2.

Scores, 6: Social-Emotional, Language, Sensory-Motor, Activities of Daily Living, Basic Academics, Overall Developmental Age.

Administration: Individual.

Forms: 5 pinpoint scales: Social-Emotional (17 pages), Language (30 pages), Sensory-Motor (35 pages), Activities of Daily Living (21 pages), Basic Academics (25 pages).

Price Data, 2006: $210 per complete kit including manual (23 pages), 5 each of 5 pinpoint scales, 50 priority intervention worksheets, 50 comprehensive program record forms, and 50 cumulative summary sheets; $45 per 10 pinpoint scales (specify area); $20 per 50 priority intervention worksheets; $20 per 50 comprehensive program record forms; $20 per 50 cumulative summary sheets; $45 per manual.

Time: (120–180) minutes.

Comments: Previously titled Developmental Assessment for the Severely Handicapped; also listed as A Developmental Assessment for Students with Severe Disabilities, Second Edition in *Tests in Print V*; may administer all or any combination of the pinpoint scales; "criterion-referenced"; criterion performance levels 1–5; ratings by developmental professionals.

Authors: Mary K. Dykes and Jane N. Erin.

Publisher: PRO-ED.

Cross References: See T5:804 (1 reference); for reviews by Harvey N. Switzky and David P. Wacker of the original edition, see 9:324.

[832]

Developmental Assessment of Life Experiences (2000 Edition).

Purpose: Developed to assess daily living, intellectual, and adaptive skills of persons with disabilities.

Population: Individuals with developmental disabilities.

Publication Dates: 1974–2000.

Acronym: D.A.L.E. System.

Scores: 8 categories: Personal Hygiene, Daily Living Skills, Community Skills/Safety Skills, Language and Educational Skills, Personal Management, Gender Specific–Female, Gender Specific–Male, Leisure Skills.

Administration: Individual.

Price Data, 2000: $10.50 per complete set including manual (2000, 64 pages).

Time: Administration time not reported.

Authors: Gertrude A. Barber, Vincent Olewnik, Joanne Haughey, Traci Gardner, Michelle Sosnowski, Jennifer Lawrence, Nia Bell, Daneen Engel, Pam Johns, and Nadine Hornyak.

Publisher: The Barber Center Press, Inc.

Cross References: For reviews by Martin E. Block and Linda K. Bunker and by Elizabeth L. Jones of an earlier edition, see 12:109; for a review by Frank M. Gresham of an earlier edition, see 9:295.

[833]

Developmental Assessment of Young Children.

Purpose: Designed to identify children birth through 5-11 with possible delays in the domains of cognition, communication, social-emotional development, physical development, and adaptive behavior.

Population: Birth to age 5-11.

Publication Date: 1998.

Scores: General Development Quotient.

Administration: Individual.

Price Data, 2010: $269 per complete kit including examiner's manual (67 pages), 25 each of Adaptive, Cognitive, Communication, Physical, and Social-Emotional scoring forms, 25 profile/summary forms and 25 Early Childhood Development Chart, Second Edition Mini Poster pack; $35 per 25 scoring forms (specify domain); $24 per 25 profile/summary forms; $64 per manual; $38 per 25 Early childhood development chart, 2E-mini poster pack.

Time: (10–20) minutes per subtest.

Comments: Rating by examiner; subtests may be used alone or in any combination.

Authors: Judith K. Voress and Taddy Maddox.

Publisher: PRO-ED.

a) COGNITIVE SUBTEST.

Purpose: Designed to measure "skills and abilitiess that are conceptual in nature."

Scores: Total score only.

b) COMMUNICATION SUBTEST.

Purpose: Constructed to assess "the exchange of ideas, information, and feelings."

Scores: Total score only.

c) SOCIAL-EMOTIONAL SUBTEST.

Purpose: Designed to measure "social awareness, social relationships, and social competence."

Scores: Total score only.

d) PHYSICAL DEVELOPMENT SUBTEST.
Purpose: Designed to measure "motor development."
Scores: Total score only.
e) ADAPTIVE BEHAVIOR SUBTEST.
Purpose: Designed to assess "independent functioning."
Scores: Total score only.
Cross References: For reviews by Billy T. Ogletree and T. Steuart Watson, see 14:115.

[834]

Developmental Assessment Resource for Teachers (DART) English.

Purpose: Designed to "assist teachers of upper primary and middle primary in their assessment of students' viewing, reading, listening, speaking and writing skills."
Population: Australian students in years 3–4, 5–6.
Publication Dates: 1994–1997.
Scores, 5: Viewing, Reading, Listening, Speaking, Writing.
Administration: Group.
Forms, 2: Form A, Form B.
Publisher: Australian Council for Educational Research Ltd. [Australia].
a) DART MIDDLE PRIMARY ENGLISH.
Population: Students in years 3–4 in Australian classrooms.
Publication Date: 1997.
Price Data, 2006: A$169.00 per specimen set including 1 of each test component; A$75.90 per manual (1997, 152 pages); A$14.25 per 10 Viewing answer booklets; A$53.90 per Viewing video; A$21.95 per 10 reusable Reading stimulus booklets (specify Form A or Form B); A$16.45 per 10 Reading answer booklets A; A$14.25 per 10 Reading answer booklets B; A$10.95 per 10 Listening answer booklets; A$14.25 per audio cassette; A$8.75 per 10 reusable Character Review Speaking Guides; A$10.95 per 10 Writing answer booklets.
Time: (40–190) minutes per section.
Authors: Wendy Bodey, Lynne Darkin, Margaret Forster, and Geoff Masters.
b) DART UPPER PRIMARY ENGLISH.
Population: Students in years 5–6 in Australian classrooms.
Publication Date: 1994.
Price Data: A$120 per specimen set including 1 of each test component; A$45 per manual (1994, 159 pages); A$16.95 per 10 Viewing answer booklets; A$49 per Viewing video; A$5 per Viewing poster; A$19.95 per 10 reusable Reading stimulus booklets (specify Form A or Form B); A$9.95 per 10 Reading answer booklets A; A$12.95 per 10 Reading answer booklets B; A$6.95 per 10 Listening answer booklets; A$12.95 per audio cassette; A$9.95 per 10 reusable Speaking poetry booklets; A$9.95 per 10 Writing answer booklets; A$295

per complete package including testing materials for 30 students.
Time: (40–190) minutes per section.
Authors: Margaret Forster, Juliette Mendelovits, and Geoff Masters.
Cross References: For reviews by Valentina McInerney and by Gretchen Owens and Jan Harting-McChesney, see 15:78.

[835]

Developmental Assessment Resource for Teachers (DART) Mathematics.

Purpose: "Provides an estimate of a student's level of achievement on each of four strands of the [Australian] national mathematics profile … and on each of three strands of the national benchmark framework."
Population: Australian students in years 5–6.
Publication Date: 1998.
Acronym: DART MATHEMATICS.
Scores, 5: Number, Space, Measurement, Chance and Data, Data Sense.
Administration: Group.
Forms, 2: Form A, Form B.
Price Data, 2006: A$75 per kit including video, manual (160 pages), 30 grid sheets, 30 measurement sheets, and photocopy master answer booklet and stimulus for all tests; A$54.95 per manual; A$54.95 per video; A$21.95 per each photocopy master answer booklet and stimulus (specify Number, Space, Measurement, Chance and Data or Data Sense; also specify Form A or Form B); A$14.25 per 30 grid sheets; A$14.25 per 30 measurement sheets.
Time: (60) minutes per section.
Authors: Eve Recht, Margaret Forster, and Geoff Masters.
Publisher: Australian Council for Educational Research Ltd. [Australia].
Cross References: For reviews by Carlen Henington and Judith A. Monsaas, see 15:79.

[836]

Developmental History Checklist for Children.

Purpose: To document the developmental history of children.
Population: Ages 5–12.
Publication Date: 1989.
Scores: 7 Content Areas: Presenting Information, Personal Information/Family Background, Early Developmental History, Educational History, Medical History/Health Status, Family History, Current Behavior/Relationships.
Administration: Individual.
Manual: No manual.
Price Data, 2006: $50 per package of 25.
Time: Administration time not reported.

Comments: Designed to be completed by a parent, guardian, or clinician.
Authors: Edward H. Dougherty and John A. Schinka.
Publisher: Psychological Assessment Resources, Inc.

[837]

Developmental Indicators for the Assessment of Learning–Fourth Edition.

Purpose: Designed to "identify children ages 2:6 through 5:11 who are in need of intervention or diagnostic assessment in the following areas: motor, concepts, language, self-help, and social-emotional skills."
Population: Ages 2:6-5:11.
Publication Dates: 1983–2011.
Acronym: DIAL-4.
Scores: 9 regular form: Motor, Concepts, Language, DIAL-4 Total, Behavioral Observations, Parent Self-Help, Parent Social-Emotional, Teacher Self-Help, Teacher Social-Emotional; 5 Speed DIAL-4: Motor, Concepts, Language, Self-Help Development, Social Development.
Administration: Individual.
Forms, 2: Regular Form, Short Form.
Price Data, 2011: $625 per complete kit including manual (2011, 131 pages), 50 record forms (English), 1 record form (Spanish), 50 cutting cards, 25 Teacher Questionnaires (English), manipulatives, dials, Operator's Handbooks in English and Spanish for Motor, Concepts, and Language Areas plus the Speed DIAL and Training Packet; $45 per 50 Speed DIAL record forms; $275 per Speed DIAL kit in English/Spanish.
Foreign Language Edition: Available in Spanish.
Time: (30-45) minutes, regular form; (20) minutes, short form.
Authors: Carol Mardell and Dorothea S. Goldenberg.
Publisher: Pearson.
Cross References: For reviews by Gregory J. Cizek and Doreen Ward Fairbank of the Third Edition, see 14:116; see also T5:809 (2 references); for reviews by Darrell L. Sabers and Scott Spreat of an earlier edition, see 12:110 (1 reference); see also T4:762 (6 references); for reviews by David W. Barnett and G. Michael Poteat of an earlier version, see 10:89 (6 references); see also 9:326 (1 reference) and T3:696 (2 references); for reviews by J. Jeffrey Grill and James J. McCarthy of an earlier edition, see 8:428 (3 references).

[838]

Developmental Observation Checklist System.

Purpose: "For the assessment of very young children with respect to general development (DC), adjustment behavior (ABC), and parent stress and support (PSSC)."
Population: Birth through age 6.
Publication Date: 1994.
Acronym: DOCS.
Scores, 12: Developmental Checklist (Cognition, Language, Social, Motor, Total); Adjustment Behavior Checklist (Mother, Father, Both Parents, Teacher); Parental Stress and Support Checklist (Mother, Father, Both Parents).
Administration: Individual.
Parts, 3: Developmental Checklist, Adjustment Behavior Checklist, Parental Stress and Support Checklist.
Price Data, 2010: $190 per complete kit including examiner's manual (91 pages), 25 profile/record forms, 25 DC profile/record forms, 25 ABC profile/record forms, and 25 PSSC profile/record forms; $70 per manual; $24 per 25 profile/record forms; $59 per 25 DC profile/record forms; $24 per ABC or PSSC profile/record forms.
Time: (30) minutes.
Authors: Wayne P. Hresko, Shirley A. Miguel, Rita J. Sherbenou, and Steve D. Burton.
Publisher: PRO-ED.
Cross References: For reviews by Frank M. Bernt and Gene Schwarting, see 13:95.

[839]

Developmental Profile 3.

Purpose: "Designed to assess the development and functioning of children from birth through age 12."
Population: Ages 0-0 to 12-11.
Publication Dates: 1972-2007.
Acronym: DP-3.
Scores: 5 scales: Physical, Adaptive Behavior, Social-Emotional, Cognitive, Communication, plus General Development Score.
Administration: Individual.
Forms, 2: Interview Form, Parent/Caregiver Checklist.
Price Data, 2011: $210 per complete kit including 25 Interview Forms; 25 Parent/Caregiver Checklists, and manual (2007, 195 pages); $75 per 25 Interview Forms; $75 per 25 Parent/Caregiver Checklists; $80 per manual; $375 per kit with unlimited-use scoring and interpretation CD; $265 per DP-3 CD with unlimited-use scoring and interpretation.
Foreign Lanuage Edition: Spanish Interview form and Parent/Caregiver checklist available.
Time: (20-40) minutes.
Comments: The Interview form is the preferred method of administration; the Parent/Caregiver Checklist, which contains the same content as the Interview may be used when administering the Interview is not possible because of time constraints or clinical/research needs.
Author: Gerald D. Alpern.
Publisher: Western Psychological Services.
Cross References: For reviews by Rosemary Flanagan and Carlen Henington, see 18:38; see T5:811 (14 references) and T4:764 (1 reference); for reviews by A. Dirk Hightower and E. Scott Huebner of an earlier edition, see 10:90 (3 references); for reviews by Dennis C. Harper and Sue White of an earlier edition, see 9:327; see also T3:698 (5 references); for a review by Jane V. Hunt of the original edition, see 8:215 (1 reference).

[840]

Developmental Readiness Scale–Revised II.
Purpose: Designed as a screening instrument for school readiness.
Population: Ages 3–6.
Publication Dates: 1982–2003.
Acronym: DRS-R2.
Scores, 9: Fine Motor, Visual Motor, Numbers, Concepts, Body Image, Language, Personal-Social, Gross Motor, Reading.
Administration: Individual.
Price Data: Available from publisher.
Time: (30–40) minutes.
Author: Barbara Ball.
Publisher: Academic Consulting & Testing Service.
Cross References: For reviews by Hoi K. Suen and by Kathryn E. Hoff and Mark E. Swerdlik, see 15:80.

[841]

Developmental Scoring System for the Rey-Osterrieth Complex Figure.
Purpose: Designed "to provide developmental guidelines for interpretation of the ROCF," which is a "measure [of] visuospatial ability and visuospatial memory."
Population: Ages 5-14.
Publication Dates: 1986-1996.
Acronym: DSS-ROCF.
Scores: 12 scores, 3 ratings: 4 scores (Organization, Structural Elements Accuracy, Incidental Elements Accuracy, Errors) and 1 rating (Style) per ROCF production (Copy, Immediate Recall, Delayed Recall).
Administration: Individual.
Price Data, 2010: $182 per introductory kit including professional manual (1996, 87 pages), ROCF stimulus card, 25 scoring booklets, and 50 response sheets; $70 per 25 scoring booklets; $50 per 50 response sheets; $15 per ROCF stimulus card; $63 per professional manual.
Time: [35] minutes, including 1 15-20 minute delay.
Authors: Jane Holmes Bernstein and Deborah P. Waber.
Publisher: Psychological Assessment Resources, Inc.
Cross References: For reviews by Stefan C. Dombrowski and Gabrielle Stutman, see 18:39.

[842]

Developmental Tasks for Kindergarten Readiness–II.
Purpose: Designed to provide "objective data about the school-readiness of pre-kindergarten children so that effective educational programming can be planned for them."
Population: Pre-kindergarten children.
Publication Dates: 1978–1994.
Acronym: DTKR-II.
Scores, 19: Composite Score (Social Interaction, Name Printing, Body Concepts–Awareness, Body Concepts–Use, Auditory Sequencing, Auditory Association,

Visual Discrimination, Visual Memory, Visual Motor, Color Naming, Relational Concepts, Number Counting, Number Use, Number Naming, Alphabet Knowledge), Acquired Knowledge, Verbal-Conceptual, Visual Skills.
Administration: Individual.
Price Data, 2010: $155 per kit including manual (1994, 97 pages), materials book (cards), and 25 test booklets; $53 per 25 test booklets; $41 per materials book; $67 per test manual.
Time: (20–30) minutes.
Comments: Administered by school personnel for diagnostic-remedial purposes.
Authors: Walter J. Lesiak and Judi Lucas Lesiak.
Publisher: PRO-ED.
Cross References: For reviews by Joseph O. Prewitt and Theresa Graham, see 14:117; see also T4:766 (1 reference); for reviews by Carol A. Gray and Sue White of an earlier edition, see 9:328.

[843]

Developmental Teaching Objectives and Rating Form-Revised, 5th Edition.
Purpose: Designed "for assessing social and emotional development of children and youth."
Population: Ages 0-16.
Publication Dates: 1992-2007.
Acronym: DTORF-R.
Scores, 4: Behavior (Doing), Communication (Saying), Socialization (Relating), Cognition (Thinking).
Administration: Individual.
Levels, 5: Stage I, Stage II, Stage III, Stage IV, Stage V.
Forms, 3: Early Childhood, Elementary, Secondary.
Price Data, 2011: $75 per annual membership for data entry, management, and analysis for online DTORF (www.dtorf.com); $87 per manual including CD of PDFs of instrument.
Time: [30] minutes per individual student.
Comments: Workbook and CD distributed by PRO-ED, Inc.; rating form filled out by people familiar with the child, following observations; older children (and their parents) participate in their own team ratings.
Authors: Mary M. Wood, Constance A. Quirk, and Faye L. Swindle.
Publisher: Developmental Therapy Institute, Inc.
Cross References: For a review by Sharon H. deFur of an earlier edition, see 14:118.

[844]

Developmental Test of Visual Perception-Adolescent and Adult.
Purpose: "To document the presence and degree of visual perceptual or visual-motor difficulties in individual adolescents and adults."
Population: Ages 11-0 to 74-11 years.
Publication Date: 2002.

Acronym: DTVP-A.
Scores, 9: Motor-Reduced Visual Perception (Figure-Ground, Visual Closure, Form Constancy, Motor-Reduced Visual Perception Index), Visual-Motor Integration (Copying, Visual-Motor Search, Visual-Motor Speed, Visual-Motor Integration Index), General Visual Perception Index.
Administration: Individual.
Price Data, 2010: $229 per complete kit including examiner's manual (135 pages), picture book, 25 profile/examiner record forms, 25 response booklets, and storage box; $81 per examiner's manual; $64 per picture book; $35 per 25 profiler/examiner record forms; $62 per 25 response booklets.
Time: (25) minutes.
Comments: Upward extension and redevelopment of the Developmental Test of Visual Perception, Second Edition (DTVP-2; 845); designed to identify candidates for referral to special education, cognitive rehabilitation, or occupational therapy; may be used to distinguish true visual-perception deficits from problems solely with complex eye-hand or perceptual-motor actions; may assist in differential diagnosis of various dementias.
Authors: Cecil R. Reynolds, Nils A. Pearson, and Judith K. Voress.
Publisher: PRO-ED.
Cross References: For reviews by James M. Hodgson and Ralph G. Leverett, see 16:70.

[845]

Developmental Test of Visual Perception, Second Edition.

Purpose: Measures visual-perceptual and visual-motor integration skills.
Population: Ages 4-0 to 10-11.
Publication Dates: 1961–1993.
Acronym: DTVP-2.
Scores, 8: Motor-Reduced Visual Perception (Position in Space, Figure Ground, Visual Closure, Form Constancy), Visual-Motor Integration (Eye-Hand Coordination, Copying, Spatial Relations, Visual-Motor Speed), General Visual Perception.
Administration: Individual.
Price Data, 2010: $229 per complete kit including examiner's manual (1993, 73 pages), picture book, 25 profile/examiner record forms, and 25 response booklets; $69 per examiner's manual; $64 per picture book; $35 per 25 profile/examiner record forms; $75 per 25 response booklets.
Time: (45) minutes.
Comments: 1993 revision of the Marianne Frostig Developmental Test of Visual Perception (DTVP).
Authors: Donald D. Hammill, Nils A. Pearson, and Judith K. Voress.
Publisher: PRO-ED.
Cross References: See T5:816 (1 reference); for reviews by Nancy B. Bologna and Gerald Tindal, see

12:112 (1 reference); see also T4:767 (2 references); for reviews by Richard E. Darnell and David A. Sabatino of the earlier edition, see 9:650 (4 references); see also T3:1371 (25 references), 8:882 (72 references), and T2:1921 (43 references); for reviews by Brad S. Chissom, Newell C. Kephart, and Lester Mann, see 7:871 (117 references); for reviews by James M. Anderson and Mary C. Austin, see 6:553 (7 references).

[846]

Devereux Behavior Rating Scale–School Form.

Purpose: To evaluate "behaviors typical of children and adolescents with moderate to severe emotional disturbance."
Population: Ages 5–18.
Publication Dates: 1990–1993.
Acronym: BRSS.
Scores, 4: Interpersonal Problems, Inappropriate Behaviors/Feelings, Depression, Physical Symptoms/Fears.
Administration: Individual or group.
Forms, 2: Children, Adolescents.
Price Data, 2002: $149 per complete kit including manual (1993, 142 pages), 25 answer documents 5–12, and 25 ready score answer documents 13–18; $80 per manual; $36 per 25 ready score answer documents 5–12; $36 per 25 ready score answer documents 13–18.
Time: (5–10) minutes.
Comments: Ratings by parents and teachers.
Authors: Jack A. Naglieri, Paul A. LeBuffe, and Steven I. Pfeiffer.
Publisher: Pearson.
Cross References: For reviews by Lisa Bloom and Richard F. Farmer, see 13:96 (8 references); see also T5:817 (1 reference); for additional information on the Devereux Adolescent Behavior Rating Scale, see T3:702 (1 reference); for a review by Carl F. Jesness, see 7:66; see also P:60 (1 reference). For reviews by Lisa Bloom and Richard F. Farmer, see 13:96 (8 references). For additional information on the Devereux Child Behavior Rating Scale, see T3:203 (6 references); see also T2:1158 (1 reference); for a review by Allan G. Barclay, see 7:67; see also P:61 (3 references).

[847]

Devereux Early Childhood Assessment.

Purpose: "To assess preschool children's protective factors and behavioral concerns."
Population: Ages 2–5.
Publication Date: 1999.
Acronym: DECA.
Scores, 5: Initiative, Self-Control, Attachment, Total Protective Factors, Behavioral Concerns.
Administration: Individual.
Price Data, 2002: $199.95 per kit including 40 record forms, user's guide (65 pages), technical manual

(42 pages), classroom strategies guide, 20 parent guides, and classroom observation journal in a carrying case.
Foreign Language Edition: Parent guides and record forms also available in Spanish.
Time: (10) minutes.
Comments: Ratings by teachers and parents.
Authors: Paul A. LeBuffe and Jack A. Naglieri.
Publisher: Kaplan Early Learning Company.
Cross References: For reviews by Eric S. Buhs and Mary M. Chittooran, see 15:81.

[848]

Devereux Early Childhood Assessment– Clinical Form.

Purpose: Designed to evaluate "behaviors related to both social and emotional resilience as well as social and emotional concerns in preschool children."
Population: Ages 2:0–5:11.
Publication Dates: 2002–2003.
Acronym: DECA-C.
Scores, 9: Protective Factors (Initiative, Self-Control, Attachment, Total), Behavioral Concerns (Withdrawal/ Depression, Emotional Control Problems, Attention Problems, Aggression, Total).
Administration: Individual.
Price Data: Prices for the manual, record forms, and norms reference card available from publisher.
Time: Administration time not reported.
Comments: Behavior rating scale may be completed by parent or family member or teacher.
Authors: Paul A. LeBuffe and Jack A. Naglieri.
Publisher: Kaplan Early Learning Company.
Cross References: For reviews by Joan C. Ballard and Sandra A. Loew, see 16:71.

[849]

Devereux Early Childhood Assessment for Infants and Toddlers.

Purpose: "Assesses protective factors and screens for social and emotional risks in very young children."
Population: Ages 1 month to 36 months.
Publication Dates: 2007-2009.
Acronym: DECA-I/T.
Scores, 7: 3 Infant scores: Initiative, Attachment/ Relationships, Total Protective Factors (composite of previous 2 scale scores), and 4 Toddler scores: Initiative, Attachment/Relationships, Self-Regulation, Total Protective Factors (composite of previous 3 scale scores).
Administration: Group.
Forms, 2: Infant (1 month to 18 months), Toddler (18 months to 36 months).
Price Data, 2009: $199.95 per complete kit including 20 Infant Record Forms, 30 Toddler Record Forms, 5 reproducible Parent/Teacher Profile Masters for 5 different age ranges (1 mo. to 3 mos., 3 mos. to 6 mos., 6 mos. to 9

mos., 9 mos. to 18 mos., 18 mos. to 36 mos.), User's Guide (2007, 111 pages), Strategies Guide (2009, 158 pages), 20 Parent Strategy Guides ("For Now and Forever"), 3 Adult Resilience Journals ("Building Your Bounce: Simple Strategies For a Resilient You"), and Forms CD (including Technical Manual [2007, 51 pages], Reproducible Planning Forms, and Scoring Profiles), all in a poly box carrying case; $19.95 per 20 Infant Record Forms; $29.95 per 30 Toddler Record Forms; $12.95 per 5 reproducible Parent/Teacher Profile Masters; $39.95 per User's Guide; $49.95 per Strategies Guide; $24.95 per 20 Parent Strategy Guides; $9.95 per Adult Resilience Journal; $99.95 per CD Scoring Assistant; technical manual is free to print from publisher's website.
Time: Administration time not reported.
Comments: Ratings by parents, other family members, or childcare providers; scoring completed by hand or with separately sold CD Scoring Assistant; DECA-I/T is "part of an integrated, comprehensive five-step system" that involves implementing strategies and evaluating progress; other tests in the Devereux series include: the Devereux Early Childhood Assessment (DECA; T7:811), the Devereux Early Childhood Assessment-Clinical Form (DECA-C; T7:812), and the Devereux Student Strengths Assessment (DESSA; 851).
Authors: Mary Mackrain, Paul A. LeBuffe, and Gregg Powell; Kristin Tenney-Blackwell (Strategies Guide only).
Publisher: Kaplan Early Learning Co.
Cross References: For reviews by Jean N. Clark and Mary J. McLellan, see 18:40.

[850]

Devereux Scales of Mental Disorders.

Purpose: Constructed for "evaluating behaviors associated with psychopathology."
Population: Ages 5–12, 13–18.
Publication Dates: 1993–1996.
Acronym: DSMD.
Scores, 10: Conduct, Attention/Delinquency, Anxiety, Depression, Autism, Acute Problems, Internalizing Composite, Externalizing Composite, Critical Pathology Composite, Total.
Administration: Group or individual.
Forms, 2: Child Form, Adolescent Form.
Price Data, 2002: $195 per complete kit including manual (1994, 300 pages), and 25 ReadyScore™ answer documents for each Child Form and Adolescent Form; $64 per ReadyScore™ answer documents (specify form); $80 per manual; $242 per DSMD Scoring Assistant including user's guide (1996, 77 pages), 2 disks, 5 child's record forms, and 5 adolescent record forms.
Time: (15) minutes.
Comments: Revision of Devereux Child Behavior Rating Scale (T3:703) and Devereux Adolescent Behavior Rating Scale (T3:702); ratings by parents, teachers, or other professionals; Scoring Assistant available to provide narrative interpretive reports and other information.

Authors: Jack A. Naglieri, Paul A. LeBuffe, and Steven I. Pfeiffer.
Publisher: Pearson.
Cross References: For reviews by Colin Cooper and Charles A. Peterson, see 14:120; see also T5:818 (1 reference).

[851]

Devereux Student Strengths Assessment.

Purpose: "Developed to provide a measure of social-emotional competencies."
Population: Grades K-8.
Publication Dates: 2008-2009.
Acronym: DESSA.
Scores, 9: Personal Responsibility, Optimistic Thinking, Goal-Directed Behavior, Social-Awareness, Decision Making, Relationship Skills, Self-Awareness, Self-Management, Total (Social-Emotional Composite).
Administration: Group.
Price Data, 2009: $115.95 per complete kit including 25 record forms, manual (2009, 161 pages), and norms reference card, all in a vinyl portfolio; $39.95 per 25 record forms; $32.95 per 25 online administration record forms and scoring report; $74.95 per manual; $6.95 per norms reference card; $9.95 per vinyl portfolio; price information for online administration, scoring, and individual student reports available from publisher.
Time: [10] minutes or less.
Comments: Test is part of a series that includes: the Devereux Early Childhood Assessment-Infant/Toddler Version (DECA-I/T; 849), the Devereux Early Childhood Assessment (DECA; T7:811), and the Devereux Early Childhood Assessment-Clinical Form (DECA-C; T7:812); ratings "by parents, teachers, or staff at schools and child-serving agencies"; individual and classroom profiles available.
Authors: Paul A. LeBuffe, Valerie B. Shapiro, and Jack A. Naglieri.
Publisher: Kaplan Early Learning Company.
Cross References: For reviews by Jeffrey A. Atlas and Koressa Kutsick Malcolm, see 18:41.

[852]

The Devine Inventory [Revised].

Purpose: Designed as a comprehensive measure of work-related behaviors to assist in employee selection and development.
Population: Employees and prospective employees.
Publication Dates: 1989–2005.
Scores, 29: Self-Responsibility, Role Clarity, Approaches Problems Realistically, Openness to Change And Experience, Growth And Development/Learning, Response to Crisis, Trust in Self, Trust in Others, Dominance/Leadership, Negotiating, Decisiveness, Thinking, Detail Mindedness, Structure, Follow-Through, Diligence/Work Ethic, Goal Orientation, Response to Change, Mobility, Energy, Quiescence, Assertiveness, Authority Relationships/Loyalty, Following Rules and Procedures, Recognition, Sociability/Gregariousness, Belonging, Intimacy, Dependability.
Administration: Individual.
Price Data: Available from publisher.
Foreign Language Editions: Spanish, French, German.
Time: (25–30) minutes.
Comments: Administered and scored via the internet.
Author: Donald W. Devine.
Publisher: The Devine Group, Inc.
Cross References: For reviews by Theodore L. Hayes and Paul M. Muchinsky, see 17:56; for reviews by Phillip Benson and William L. Deaton of an earlier edition, see 12:113.

[853]

Diagnosing Organizational Culture.

Purpose: "Designed to help consultants and organizational members identify the shared values and beliefs that constitute an organization's culture."
Population: Adults.
Publication Dates: 1992–1993.
Scores: 5 scores (Power, Role, Achievement, Support, Total) in each of two areas: Existing Culture, Preferred Culture.
Administration: Group.
Price Data: Price information available from publisher for complete kit including trainer's manual (1993, 58 pages) and instrument (1992, 30 pages).
Time: (45–60) minutes.
Authors: Roger Harrison and Herb Stokes (instrument only).
Publisher: Jossey-Bass, A Wiley Company.
Cross References: For a review by John W. Fleenor, see 13:97.

[854]

Diagnostic Achievement Battery, Third Edition.

Purpose: Designed "to assess children's abilities in listening, speaking, reading, writing, and mathematics."
Population: Ages 6-0 to 14-0.
Publication Dates: 1984–2001.
Acronym: DAB-3.
Scores, 22: 14 subtest scores (Story Comprehension, Characteristics, Synonyms, Grammatic Completion, Alphabet/Word Knowledge, Reading Comprehension, Capitalization, Punctuation, Spelling, Writing: Contextual Language, Writing: Story Construction, Mathematics Reasoning, Mathematics Calculation, Phonemic Analysis) and 8 composite scores (Listening, Speaking, Reading, Writing, Mathematics, Spoken Language, Written Language, Total Achievement).
Administration: Individual.

Price Data, 2010: $327 per complete kit including examiner's manual (2001, 152 pages), student booklet, 25 profile/examiner's record booklets, 25 student response booklets, assessment probes, and audiotape; $126 per software kit including manual and CD-ROM; $92 per manual; $53 per 25 student response booklets; $75 per 25 profile/examiner's record booklets; $53 per student booklet; $24 per audiotape; $46 per assessment probes; $432 print/software combo kit.
Time: (90–120) minutes.
Author: Phyllis Newcomer.
Publisher: PRO-ED.
Cross References: For reviews by Michael B. Bunch and Cleborne D. Maddux, see 15:82, see T5:821 (2 references); for reviews by Jean-Jacques Bernier and Martine Hébert and by Ric Brown of an earlier edition, see 12:114 (2 references); see also T4:774 (1 reference); for a review by William J. Webster of the original edition, see 9:333.

[855]

Diagnostic Achievement Test for Adolescents, Second Edition.

Purpose: To measure the spoken language ability and academic achievement levels of students.
Population: Ages 12–0 to 18–11.
Publication Dates: 1986–1993.
Acronym: DATA-2.
Scores, 22: 13 subtest scores (Receptive Vocabulary, Receptive Grammar, Expressive Grammar, Expressive Vocabulary, Word Identification, Reading Comprehension, Spelling, Writing Composition, Math Calculation, Math Problem Solving, Science, Social Studies, Reference Skills) and 9 composite scores (Listening, Speaking, Reading, Writing, Math, Spoken Language, Written Language, Achievement Screener, Total Achievement).
Administration: Individual.
Price Data, 2010: $200 per complete kit including examiner's manual (1993, 73 pages), 25 student response forms, 25 profile/examiner record forms, and a student booklet; $69 per examiner's manual; $35 per 25 student response forms; $69 per 25 profile/examiner record forms; $38 per student booklet.
Time: (60–120) minutes.
Authors: Phyllis L. Newcomer and Brian R. Bryant.
Publisher: PRO-ED.
Cross References: For reviews by Jerrilyn V. Andrews and Gerald E. DeMauro, see 13:98 (1 reference); for reviews by Randy W. Kamphaus and James E. Ysseldyke of an earlier edition, see 10:92.

[856]

Diagnostic Assessments of Reading™, Second Edition.

Purpose: Designed to function as an assessment of individual reading ability for the DARTTS testing and teaching program.

Population: Grades K-12.
Publication Dates: 1992-2006.
Acronym: DAR™-2.
Scores, 10: Word Recognition, Oral Reading Accuracy, Oral Reading Fluency (optional), Silent Reading Comprehension, Spelling, Word Meaning, Print Awareness, Phonological Awareness, Letters and Sounds, Word Analysis.
Administration: Individual.
Forms, 2: Form A, Form B (equivalent forms).
Price Data, 2010: $261 per classroom kit (specify Form A or B) including student book (57 pages), 30 response records with directions for administration booklets, teacher's manual (27 pages), 5-user license for Trial Teaching Strategy program; $78 per student booklet (specify form); $78 per 15 response records with directions for administration booklets (specify form); $30 per teacher's manual (specify form); $40 per technical manual (2006, 159 pages; CD version also available); $127 per DAR ScoringPro software system; $494 forms A and B classroom combo with TTS.
Time: (40) minutes.
Comments: A component of the DARTTS testing and teaching program.
Authors: Florence G. Roswell, Jeanne S. Chall, Mary E. Curtis, and Gail Kearns.
Publisher: PRO-ED.
Cross References: For reviews by Timothy R. Konold and Camille Lawrence and by Natalie Rathvon, see 18:42; for reviews by Kevin D. Crehan and Gene Schwarting of an earlier edition, see 12:115.

[857]

Diagnostic English Language Tests.

Purpose: Designed to measure "ability to cope with the English language demands of upper secondary school in Australia."
Population: Non-English-speaking students entering Australian secondary schools at years 10 and 11.
Publication Date: 1994.
Acronym: DELTA.
Scores, 3: Reading, Writing, Listening.
Administration: Group.
Price Data, 2006: A$139.95 per complete set; A$21.95 per 10 copies Reading Test; A$21.95 per 10 copies Listening Test.
Time: (180) minutes.
Authors: Joy McQueen and Cecily Aldous.
Publisher: Australian Council for Educational Research Ltd. [Australia].
Cross References: For a review by Alfred Longo, see 15:83.

[858]

Diagnostic Evaluation of Language Variation-Norm Referenced.

Purpose: Designed "to be used by clinicians to identify speech and language disorders (or delays) in children."

Population: Ages 4-0 to 9-11.
Publication Date: 2005.
Acronym: DELV-Norm Referenced.
Scores, 5: Total Language Composite, Syntax, Pragmatics, Semantics, Phonology.
Administration: Individual.
Price Data, 2006: $145 per complete test kit including examiner's manual (209 pages), picture manual, and 25 record forms; $85 per examiner's manual; $85 per stimulus book; $59 per 25 record forms.
Time: (45) minutes.
Comments: Appropriate for use with children for whom English is their first and primary language.
Authors: Harry N. Seymour, Thomas W. Roeper, and Jill de Villiers.
Publisher: Pearson.
Cross References: For reviews by Donna Kelly and Thomas Guyette and by Aimee Langlois, see 17:57.

[859]

Diagnostic Evaluation of Language Variation™–Screening Test.

Purpose: Designed to "distinguish variations due to normal developmental language changes or to regional and cultural patterns of language difference from true markers of language disorder or delay."
Population: Ages 4-0 to 12-11.
Publication Date: 2003.
Acronym: DELV—Screening Test.
Administration: Individual.
Parts, 2: Part I, Part II.
Price Data, 2005: $135 per complete test; $80 per examiner's manual (122 pages), $80 per stimulus manual; $59 per 25 record forms; $195 per 100 record forms.
Time: (15–20) minutes.
Comments: "Criterion-referenced."
Authors: Harry N. Seymour, Thomas W. Roeper, and Jill de Villiers with contributions by Peter A. de Villiers.
Publisher: Pearson.
 a) PART I.
 Population: Ages 4-0 to 12-11.
 Scores: Language Variation Status.
 b) PART II.
 Population: Ages 4-0 to 9-11.
 Scores: Diagnostic Risk Status.
Cross References: For reviews by Aimee Langlois and Sheila Pratt, see 16:72.

[860]

Diagnostic Interview for Borderline Patients.

Purpose: Designed to discriminate borderline patients from patients with schizophrenia, neurotic depression, and mixed diagnoses.
Population: Patients.
Publication Dates: [1982–1983].

Scores, 6: Social Adaptation, Impulse Action Patterns, Affects, Psychosis, Interpersonal Relations, Total.
Administration: Individual.
Price Data: Available from publisher.
Time: (50–90) minutes.
Authors: John G. Gunderson (interview), Pamela S. Ludolph (manual), Kenneth R. Silk (manual), Naomi E. Lohr (manual), and Dewey G. Cornell (manual).
Publisher: Pamela S. Ludolph [No reply from publisher; status unknown].
Cross References: See T5:824 (6 references) and T4:779 (19 references); for reviews by Robert E. Deysach and Charles A. Peterson, see 10:95 (12 references).

[861]

Diagnostic Interview for Children and Adolescents–IV.

Purpose: "Designed to assess psychiatric problems in children and adolescents."
Population: Ages 6–17
Publication Dates: 1997–1999.
Acronym: DICA-IV.
Scores: 28 diagnostic categories: Attention Deficit/Hyperactivity Disorder, Oppositional/Defiant Disorder, Conduct Disorder, Alcohol, Tobacco, Inhalant Use, Marijuana, Street Drugs, Major Depressive Disorder, Mania or Hypomania, Dysthymic Disorder, Separation Anxiety Disorder, Panic Disorder, Generalized Anxiety Disorder, Phobias (Social and Specific), Obsessions, Compulsions, Posttraumatic Stress Disorder, Eating Disorders, Elimination Disorders, Menstruation, Gender Identity, Psychotic Symptoms, Somatization, Psychosocial Stressors, Observation (Clinician Use), Pregnancy/Birth (Parent Version), Early Development (Parent Version).
Administration: Individual.
Price Data, 2011: $591 per Child/Adolescent Version (unlimited use); $591 per Parent Version (unlimited use); $1,034 per both versions (unlimited use); $56 per preview version including 3 Child/Adolescent Version uses and 3 Parent Version uses.
Time: (5–20) minutes per category.
Comments: 2 versions: Child/Adolescent, Parent; must be used in conjunction with MHS's PsycManager; Windows compatible computer-administered interview format.
Authors: Wendy Reich, Zila Welner, Barbara Herjanic, and MHS Staff.
Publisher: Multi-Health Systems, Inc.

[862]

Diagnostic Mathematics Assessment.

Purpose: Designed to "evaluate areas of strengths and weaknesses in mathematics."
Population: Grades 1-3.
Publication Date: 2008.
Acronym: DMA.

Scores, 16: Number Sense, Algebra and Functions, Measurement and Geometry, Statistics/ Data Analysis/ and Probability, Mathematical Reasoning, Overall Readiness Score Number Sense, Overall Readiness Score Algebra and Functions, Overall Readiness Score Measurement and Geometry, Overall Readiness Score Statistics, Overall Readiness Score Data Analysis and Probability, Overall Readiness Score Mathematical Reasoning, Standards-Based Readiness Rating Number Sense, Standards-Based Readiness Rating Algebra and Functions, Standards-Based Readiness Rating Measurement and Geometry, Standards-Based Readiness Rating Statistics/ Data Analysis/ and Probability, Standards-Based Readiness Rating Mathematical Reasoning, Overall Readiness Rating.
Administration: Group.
Levels, 2: Grade 1, Grade 2.
Parts, 5: Number Sense, Algebra and Functions, Measurement and Geometry, Statistics/ Data Analysis/ and Probability, Mathematical Reasoning.
Price Data, 2010: $48.25 per starter set Grade 1 including 1 user's manual (20 pages), 1 answer key, 20 test booklets, 1 class record sheet, and 1 class summary report; $48.25 per starter set Grade 2 including 1 user's manual (20 pages), 1 answer key, 20 test booklets, 1 class record sheet, and 1 class summary report; $13.90 per user's manual.
Time: (60) minutes.
Authors: Fredricka K. Reisman.
Publisher: Scholastic Testing Service, Inc.

[863]

Diagnostic Mathematics Profiles.

Purpose: Constructed to diagnose problems in addition, subtraction, multiplication, and division.
Population: Australian school years 3–6.
Publication Date: 1990.
Scores: Item scores only.
Administration: Group or individual.
Parts, 4: Addition, Subtraction, Multiplication, Division.
Price Data, 2006: A$40.70 per test package including 30 copies of each part; A$15.30 per manual (23 pages).
Time: Administration time not reported.
Author: Brian Doig.
Publisher: Australian Council for Educational Research Ltd. [Australia].
Cross References: For reviews by John M. Enger and Arlen R. Gullickson, see 12:116.

[864]

Diagnostic Reading Assessment.

Purpose: Designed to "evaluate areas of strengths and weaknesses in reading."
Population: Grade 1.
Publication Date: 2010.
Acronym: DRA.

Scores, 16: Word Analysis/Decoding, Vocabulary, Comprehension, Language Arts, Reference Skills, Overall Readiness Score Word Analysis/Decoding, Overall Readiness Score Vocabulary, Overall Readiness Score Comprehension, Overall Readiness Score Language Arts, Overall Readiness Score Reference Skills, Standards-Based Readiness Rating Word Analysis/Decoding, Standards-Based Readiness Rating Vocabulary, Standards-Based Readiness Rating Comprehension, Standards-Based Readiness Rating Language Arts, Standards-Based Readiness Rating Reference Skills, Overall Readiness Rating.
Administration: Group.
Parts, 5: Word Analysis/Decoding, Comprehension, Language Arts, Reference Skills.
Price Data, 2010: $48.25 per starter set including 1 manual (15 pages), 1 answer key, 20 test booklets, 1 class record sheet, and 1 class summary report; $13.90 per user's manual; $27 per sample set including 1 user's manual, 1 test booklet, 1 class record sheet, and 1 class summary; $25 per Instructional Strategies manual (21 pages).
Time: (60) minutes.
Author: Ann Bates.
Publisher: Scholastic Testing Service, Inc.

[865]

Diagnostic Screening Test: Achievement.

Purpose: Designed "for estimating practical data about student's overall school achievement level in general, and achievement in Science, Social Studies, and Literature and the Arts more specifically."
Population: Grades K–12.
Publication Date: 1977.
Acronym: DSTA.
Scores, 5: Science, Social Studies, Literature and the Arts, Practical Knowledge, Total Achievement.
Administration: Group.
Price Data, 2002: $58 per complete kit including manual (12 pages) and 50 test forms; $33 per 50 test forms.
Time: (5–10) minutes.
Authors: Thomas D. Gnagey and Patricia A. Gnagey.
Publisher: Slosson Educational Publications, Inc.
Cross References: For a review by Edward F. Iwanicki, see 9:339.

[866]

Diagnostic Screening Test: Language, Second Edition.

Purpose: Designed "for estimating over-all achievement level in written language."
Population: Grades 1–12.
Publication Date: 1977.
Acronym: DSTL.
Scores, 8: Punctuation, Grammar, Spelling Rules, Sentence Structure, Capitalization, Formal Knowledge of Language, Applied Knowledge of Language, Total Language.

Administration: Group.
Price Data, 2005: $65.25 per complete kit including manual (12 pages) and 50 test forms; $33 per 50 test forms.
Time: (5–10) minutes.
Authors: Thomas D. Gnagey and Patricia A. Gnagey.
Publisher: Slosson Educational Publications, Inc.
Cross References: For reviews by Janice Arnold Dole and Edward F. Iwanicki, see 9:340.

[867]

Diagnostic Screening Test: Math, Third Edition.

Purpose: Designed for estimating practical data about students' mathematical skills.
Population: Grades 1–11.
Publication Date: 1980.
Acronym: DSTM.
Scores, 31: Basic Process Scores (Addition, Subtraction, Multiplication, Division, Total), Specialized Process Scores (Money, Time, Percent, U.S. Measurement, Metric Measurement, Total), Concept Scores (Process, Sequencing, Simple Computation, Complex Computation, Special Manipulations, Use of Zero, Decimals, Simple Fractions, Manipulation in Fractions), 11 consolidation index scores.
Administration: Group.
Price Data, 2002: $58 per complete kit including manual (17 pages), 25 test Form A, and 25 test Form B; $29 per 50 test Form A; $29 per 50 test Form B.
Time: (5–20) minutes.
Author: Thomas D. Gnagey.
Publisher: Slosson Educational Publications, Inc.
Cross References: For reviews by Edward F. Iwanicki and Stanley F. Vasa, see 9:341.

[868]

Diagnostic Screening Test: Reading, Third Edition.

Purpose: Designed "for estimating practical data about students' reading skills."
Population: Grades 1–12.
Publication Date: 1979.
Acronym: DSTR.
Scores, 16: Comfort Reading Level, Instructional Reading Level, Frustration Reading Level, Comprehension Reading Level, Listening Level, Phonics/Sight Ratio, Word Attack Skill Analysis (c-v/c, v-r, v-l, v-v, c-v-c, Silent e, Mix, Sight, Total), Consolidation Index.
Administration: Individual.
Price Data, 2005: $65.25 per complete kit including manual (13 pages), 25 test Form A, and 25 test Form B; $36.75 per 50 test Form A; $36.75 per 50 test Form B.
Time: (5–10) minutes.
Authors: Thomas D. Gnagey and Patricia A. Gnagey.
Publisher: Slosson Educational Publications, Inc.

Cross References: For a review by Edward F. Iwanicki, see 9:342; for a review by P. David Pearson of an earlier edition, see 8:755.

[869]

Diagnostic Screening Test: Spelling, Third Edition.

Purpose: Designed to gather diagnostic information regarding spelling skills.
Population: Grades 1–12.
Publication Date: 1979.
Acronym: DSTS.
Scores, 12: 3 scores (Verbal, Written, Total) for each of 3 categories (Phonics, Sight, Total); 3 Consolidation Index scores (Phonics Written, Sight Written, Total Spelling Written).
Administration: Group.
Price Data, 2005: $65.25 per complete kit including manual (13 pages), 25 test Form A, and 25 test Form B; $36.75 per 50 test Form A; $36.75 per 50 test Form B.
Time: (5–10) minutes.
Author: Thomas D. Gnagey.
Publisher: Slosson Educational Publications, Inc.
Cross References: For reviews by Edward F. Iwanicki and Robert E. Schafer, see 9:343 (4 references).

[870]

Diagnostic Supplement to the WJ III® Tests of Cognitive Abilities.

Purpose: Designed to expand "the diagnostic capabilities of the [Woodcock-Johnson III Tests of Cognitive Abilities] for educational, clinical, or research purposes."
Population: Ages 2–90+.
Publication Date: 2003.
Acronym: WJ III® Diagnostic Supplement to the Tests of Cognitive Abilities.
Scores, 11: Memory for Names, Visual Closure, Sound Patterns–Voice, Number Series, Number Matrices, Cross Out, Memory for Sentences, Block Rotation, Sound Patterns–Music, Memory for Names–Delayed, Bilingual Verbal Comprehension–English/Spanish.
Administration: Individual.
Price Data, 2006: $295.50 per complete kit including test book, examiner's manual (119 pages) 25 test records, audio cassette, WJIII Compuscore and Profiles Program, Version 2.1 (Windows and Mac), and scoring guides; $85 per examiner's manual; $57 per 25 test records; $130.50 per WJIII Compuscore and Profiles Program, Version 2.1 (Windows and Mac).
Time: (5–10) minutes per subtest.
Comments: Tests from the Diagnostic Supplement can be combined with other tests from the Woodcock-Johnson III® (15:281) Tests of Cognitive Abilities Standard and Extended Batteries and the WJIII® Tests of Achievement to provide 14 additional interpretive clusters.

Authors: Richard W. Woodcock, Kevin S. McGrew, Nancy Mather, and Fredrick A. Schrank.
Publisher: Riverside Publishing.
Cross References: For reviews by Timothy Sares and Donald L. Thompson, see 16:275.

[871]

Diagnostic Test for High School Mathematics.

Purpose: Designed to "provide diagnostic information on the competencies of individual students in various areas of basic, high school math."
Population: High school students.
Publication Dates: 2001-2003.
Acronym: DT-HSM.
Scores, 20: Whole Numbers, Common Fractions, Decimal Fractions, Percentages, Signed Numbers, Powers and Roots, Substitution, Setting up Equations, Solving Algebraic Equations, Geometry, Graphs, Tables, Estimation, Probability, Statistics, Order of Operations, Ratios, Math Vocabulary, Word Problems, Miscellaneous.
Administration: Group.
Price Data, 2007: $55 per technical manual (2003, 23 pages); $85 per specimen set including one test, one answer sheet, and sample reports.
Time: (90) minutes.
Author: Joel P. Wiesen.
Publisher: APR Testing Services.
Cross References: For reviews by Thomas P. Hogan and Michael S. Trevisan, see 18:43.

[872]

Diagnostic Test for Pre-Algebra Mathematics.

Purpose: Designed to "provide diagnostic information on the competencies of individual students in various areas of basic math."
Population: 8th grade students.
Publication Dates: 2001-2003.
Acronym: DT-PAM.
Scores, 21: Whole Numbers, Common Fractions, Decimal Fractions, Percentages, Units of Measurement, Signed Numbers, Simple Powers, Substitution, Setting up Equations, Solving Equations, Geometry, Comparisons, Graphs, Tables, Estimation, Probability, Statistics, Order of Operations, Ratios, Math Vocabulary, Word Problems.
Administration: Group.
Price Data: Price data available from publisher.
Time: Administration time not reported.
Comments: Available in both print and online administration formats.
Author: APR Testing Services.
Publisher: APR Testing Services.
Cross References: For reviews by George Engelhard, Jr., and Mary L. Garner, see 18:44.

[873]

Diagnostic Test of the New Testament.

Purpose: "Measures and assesses New Testament knowledge."
Population: Ages 17 and older.
Publication Date: 1986.
Scores: Total score only.
Subtests, 5: Introduction to New Testament World and Records, Gospels, Acts, Epistles, Revelation.
Administration: Group or individual.
Manual: No manual.
Restricted Distribution: This test is "for the exclusive use of institutions of higher learning, such as Bible colleges, liberal arts colleges, and seminaries."
Price Data, 2005: $1 per test; $.10 per answer sheet; $2 per scoring key; bulk discount pricing is available.
Time: (40-50) minutes.
Author: Fred R. Johnson.
Publisher: The Association for Biblical Higher Education.

[874]

DIBELS: Dynamic Indicators of Basic Early Literacy Skills, Sixth Edition.

Purpose: Designed to assess "growth and development of early literacy skills."
Population: Grades K–6.
Publication Dates: 2002–2003.
Acronym: DIBELS.
Scores, 7: Initial Sound Fluency, Letter Naming Fluency, Phoneme Segmentation Fluency, Nonsense Word Fluency, Oral Reading Fluency, Oral Retelling Fluency, Word Use Fluency.
Administration: Individual.
Levels, 7: K, 1, 2, 3, 4, 5, 6.
Parts, 2: Benchmark Assessment, Progress Monitoring.
Price Data, 2006: $69 per classroom set (Grades K-3); $55 per classroom set (Grades 4-6); $88.95 per implementation video, "Catch Them Early, Watch them Grow! Using DIBELS in Your School"; $88.95 per implementation CD-ROM.
Time: (10–15) minutes.
Comments: Benchmark Assessments administered to whole class three times per year; progress monitoring components used with at-risk students on a week-to-week basis to determine progress.
Authors: Roland H. Good III, Ruth A. Kaminski, and Louisa C. Moats (overview only).
Publisher: Sopris West.
  a) LETTER NAMING FLUENCY.
  Population: Grades K–1.
  Authors: Ruth A. Kaminski and Roland H. Good III.
  b) INITIAL SOUND FLUENCY.
  Population: Grade K.
  Forms: 20 alternate forms.

Authors: Roland H. Good III, Deborah Laimon, Ruth A. Kaminski, and Sylvia Smith.
c) PHONEME SEGMENTATION FLUENCY.
Population: Grades K–1.
Forms: 20 alternate forms.
Authors: Roland H. Good III, Ruth A. Kaminski, and Sylvia Smith.
d) NONSENSE WORD FLUENCY.
Population: Grades K–2.
Forms: 20 alternate forms.
Authors: Roland H. Good III and Ruth A. Kaminski.
e) ORAL READING FLUENCY.
Population: Grades 1–6.
Forms: 20 alternate forms.
Authors: Roland H. Good III, Ruth A. Kaminski, and Sheila Dill.
f) ORAL RETELLING FLUENCY.
Population: Grades 1–6.
Authors: Roland H. Good III, Ruth A. Kaminski, and Sheila Dill.
g) WORD USE FLUENCY.
Population: Grades K–3.
Authors: Roland H. Good III, Ruth A. Kaminski, and Sylvia Smith.
Cross References: For reviews by Bethany A. Brunsman and Timothy Shanahan, see 16:73.

[875]

Differential Ability Scales-Second Edition.

Purpose: "To profile a child's strengths and weaknesses in a wide range of cognitive abilities."
Population: Ages 2-6 to 17-11.
Publication Dates: 1979-2007.
Acronym: DAS-II.
Subtests: Core, Diagnostic.
Administration: Individual.
Levels, 2: Early Years Battery, School-Age Battery.
Price Data, 2008: $1,120 per complete test kit including administration and scoring manual (2007, 309 pages), normative data tables manual (2007, 165 pages), technical manual (2007, 309 pages), 15 Early Years Battery record forms, 15 School-Age Battery record forms, 10 each of speed of information processing booklets (versions A, B, and C), 4 stimulus books, object recall card, picture similarities cards, phonological process and signed sentences CD, manipulatives, and scoring assistant.
Author: Colin D. Elliott.
Publisher: Pearson.
a) EARLY YEARS BATTERY.
  1) *Lower Level Early Years Battery.*
  Population: Ages 2-6 to 3-5.
  Time: (20) minutes.
  Scores, 8: Verbal Ability (Verbal Comprehension, Naming Vocabulary), Nonverbal Ability (Picture Similarities, Pattern Construction),

Diagnostic Subtests (Recall of Digits Forward, Recognition of Pictures, Early Number Concepts), General Conceptual Ability.
  2) *Upper Level Early Years Battery.*
  Population: Ages 3-6 to 6-11.
  Time: (31) minutes.
  Scores, 19: Verbal Ability (Verbal Comprehension, Naming Vocabulary), Nonverbal Reasoning Ability (Picture Similarities, Matrices), Spatial Ability (Pattern Construction, Copying), Special Nonverbal Composite, School Readiness (Early Number Concepts, Matching Letter-like Forms, Phonological Processing), Working Memory (Recall of Sequential Order, Recall of Digits Backward), Processing Speed (Speed of Information Processing, Rapid Naming), Recall of Objects-Immediate, Recall of Objects-Delayed, Recall of Digits Forward, Recognition of Pictures, General Conceptual Ability.
b) SCHOOL-AGE BATTERY.
Population: Ages 7-0 to 17-11 (and optionally down to age 5-0).
Time: (39) minutes.
Scores, 17: Verbal Ability (Word Definitions, Verbal Similarities), Nonverbal Reasoning Ability (Matrices, Sequential and Quantitative Reasoning), Spatial Ability (Recall of Designs, Pattern Construction), Special Nonverbal Composite, Working Memory (Recall of Sequential Order, Recall of Digits Backward), Processing Speed (Speed of Information Processing, Rapid Naming), Phonological Processing, Recall of Objects-Immediate, Recall of Objects-Delayed, Recall of Digits Forward, Recognition of Pictures, General Conceptual Ability.
Cross References: For reveiws by Andrew S. Davis and W. Holmes Finch and by Gerald Tindal, see 18:45; see T5:837 (14 references) and T4:800 (3 references); for reviews by Glen P. Aylward and Robert C. Reinehr of an earlier edition, see 11:111 (1 reference).

[876]

Differential Aptitude Tests–Australian and New Zealand Editions [Forms V and W].

Purpose: Provides a battery of tests for personnel selection and rehabilitation counseling with relation to successful job performance.
Population: Grades 8–12.
Publication Dates: 1973–1989.
Scores, 9: Verbal Reasoning, Numerical Ability, Abstract Reasoning, Clerical Speed and Accuracy, Mechanical Reasoning, Space Relations, Spelling, Language Use, Verbal Reasoning + Numerical Ability.
Subtests: Available as separates.
Administration: Individual or group.
Price Data, 2006: A$76.30 per exam kit; A$122.95 per manual (1989, 160 pages; A$272.10 per 25 test

booklets (Verbal, Numerical and Abstract Reasoning); A$110.45 per 25 test booklets (Clerical Speed and Accuracy); A$237.95 per 25 test booklets (Mechanical Reasoning); A$184.45 per 25 test booklets (Space Relations); A$153.70 per 25 test booklets (Spelling and Language Usage); A$76.30 per 25 answer sheets; A$55.80 per SP1; A$67.15 per SP2; A$76.30 per scoring keys.
Time: (60-90) minutes for entire battery.
Comments: New Zealand manual information included; Australian manual same as that for the American version of the Differential Aptitude Tests with norms and revisions for the Australian and New Zealand population.
Authors: Marion M. de Lemos (Australian manual), George K. Bennett, Harold G. Seashore, and Alexander G. Wesman.
Publisher: Pearson Assessment and Information [Australia and New Zealand]; Australian Council for Educational Research Ltd. [Australia].
Cross References: For reviews by Lynn Lakota Brown and Jack E. Gebart-Eaglemont, see 15:85.

[877]

Differential Aptitude Tests, Fifth Edition.

Purpose: "Designed to measure students' ability to learn or to succeed in a number of different areas."
Population: Grades 7–9, grades 10–12 and adults.
Publication Dates: 1947–1992.
Acronym: DAT.
Scores: 9 tests (Verbal Reasoning, Numerical Reasoning, Abstract Reasoning, Perceptual Speed and Accuracy [Part 1, Part 2], Mechanical Reasoning, Space Relations, Spelling, Language Usage) and Total Scholastic Aptitude.
Administration: Group.
Levels, 2: 1, 2.
Price Data, 2002: $59 per 25 Form C partial battery test booklets (Levels 1 or 2) including Directions for Administering (1990, 47 pages); $128 per 25 Form C complete battery test booklets (Levels 1 or 2) including Directions for Administering; $128 per 100 Type 1 machine-scorable answer documents with DAT (Levels 1 or 2, Form C), $152 per 100 Type 1 machine-scorable answer documents with DAT (Levels 1 or 2, Form C) and Level 1 or Level 2 Career Interest Inventory; $67 per Ready-Score answer documents with 25 Perceptual Speed and Accuracy–Part 1 answer sheets, Profile Your DAT scores pamphlet, and Levels 1 or 2 of Form C; $34.50 per norms booklet (Fall or Spring); $34.50 per Using the DAT with Adults; $28 per 25 Practice Tests including a practice test for the Career Interest Inventory and Directions; $108.70 per Guide to Careers Student Workbook; $19 per 25 Exploring Aptitudes: An Introduction to the Differential Aptitude Tests; $19 per 25 Using Test Results for Decision-Making; $34.50 per Technical Manual (1992, 192 pages); $5.30 per Directions for Practice Test; $7 per Directions for Administering; price information for scoring and reporting services available from publisher.

Time: 90(150) minutes.
Comments: 2 forms (C, D) per level; partial battery includes only 2 subtests (Verbal Reasoning and Numerical Reasoning); used in conjunction with Career Interest Inventory (T7:419).
Authors: G. K. Bennett, H. G. Seashore, and A. G. Wesman.
Publisher: Pearson.
Cross References: See T5:838 (23 references); for reviews by Keith Hattrup and Neal Schmitt, see 12:118 (16 references); see also T4:802 (31 references); for reviews of Forms V and W by Ronald K. Hambleton and Daryl Sander, see 9:352 (19 references); see also T3:732 (26 references); for reviews by Thomas J. Bouchard, Jr., and Robert L. Linn and an excerpted review by Gerald S. Hanna of earlier forms, see 8:485 (56 references); see also T2:1069 (64 references); for a review by M. Y. Qureshi and an excerpted review by Jack C. Merwin of earlier forms, see 7:673 (139 references); for reviews by J. A. Keats and Richard E. Schutz, see 6:767 (52 references); for reviews by John B. Carroll and Norman Frederiksen, see 5:605 (49 references); for reviews by Harold Bechtoldt, Ralph F. Berdie, and Lloyd G. Humphreys, see 4:711 (27 references); for an excerpted review, see 3:620.

[878]

Differential Aptitude Tests for Personnel and Career Assessment.

Purpose: Designed to measure ability to learn in eight aptitude areas.
Population: Adult.
Publication Dates: 1972–1991.
Acronym: DAT for PCA.
Scores, 8: General Cognitive Abilities Tests (Verbal Reasoning, Numerical Ability, Total), Perceptual Abilities Tests (Abstract Reasoning, Mechanical Reasoning, Space Relations), Clerical and Language Tests (Spelling, Language Usage, Clerical Speed and Accuracy).
Administration: Group or individual.
Price Data, 2002: $146 per 25 General Cognitive Abilities Battery tests; $146 per 25 Perceptual Abilities Battery tests; $146 per 25 Clerical/Language Battery tests; $74 per 25 tests (select Verbal Reasoning, Numerical Reasoning, Abstract Reasoning, Spelling, Language Usage, or Clerical Speed and Accuracy); $74 per 25 tests (select Mechanical Reasoning or Space Relations); $57 per 25 ready-score answer sheets (select battery); $38 per 50 General Cognitive Abilities Battery hand-scorable answer sheets; $38 per 50 Perceptual Abilities Battery or Clerical/Language Battery hand-scorable answer sheets; $38 per 50 specific test hand-scorable answer sheets (select test); $32 per set of General Cognitive Abilities Battery scoring keys; $32 per set of Perceptual Abilities Battery or Clerical/Language Battery scoring keys; $19 per set of scoring keys for specific tests (select test); $45 per

directions for administering (includes norms); $45 per technical manual; $62 per examination kit.

Time: 114(144) minutes.

Comments: Abbreviated form of the Differential Aptitude Tests, Form V/W.

Authors: George K. Bennett, Harold G. Seashore, and Alexander G. Wesman.

Publisher: Pearson.

Cross References: For reviews by Victor L. Willson and Hilda Wing, see 12:119.

[879]

Differential Scales of Social Maladjustment and Emotional Disturbance.

Purpose: Designed to "differentiate between individuals with social maladjustment and those with emotional disturbances."

Population: Ages 6-0 to 17-11.

Publication Date: 2009.

Acronym: DSSMED.

Scores, 2: Social Maladjustment, Emotional Disturbance.

Administration: Individual.

Price Data, 2010: $136 per examiner's manual (53 pages), 25 summary/rating forms, and 25 scoring overlays. $65 examiner's manual; $44 per 25 scoring overlays; $33 per 25 summary/rating forms.

Time: (5-10) minutes.

Comments: To be completed by a teacher or professional who knows the student well and has observed their behavior in a classroom setting for at least 4 weeks.

Authors: David J. Ehrler, Ronnie L. McGhee, Carol G. Phillips, and Elizabeth A. Allen.

Publisher: PRO-ED.

Cross References: For reviews by Sherry K. Bain and Kathleen B. Aspiranti and by Richard F. Farmer, see 18:46.

[880]

Differential Test of Conduct and Emotional Problems.

Purpose: "Designed to effect differentiations between conduct problem, emotionally disturbed and noninvolved populations."

Population: Grades K–12.

Publication Dates: 1990–1991.

Acronym: DT/CEP.

Scores, 2: Emotional Disturbance Scale, Conduct Problem Scale.

Administration: Group.

Price Data, 2002: $78 per complete set including manual (1990, 58 pages), score forms, and scoring template; $29 per 50 score forms; $9 per set of 2 scoring templates.

Time: (15–20) minutes.

Comments: Ratings by teachers.

Author: Edward J. Kelly.

Publisher: Slosson Educational Publications, Inc.

Cross References: For reviews by Richard Brozovich and Alida S. Westman, see 12:120; see also T4:804 (1 reference).

[881]

Digit Vigilance Test.

Purpose: Designed to measure vigilance during rapid visual tracking and accurate selection of target stimuli.

Population: Ages 20–80.

Publication Date: 1995.

Acronym: DVT.

Scores, 2: Total Time, Total Errors.

Administration: Individual.

Forms, 2: 6s, 9s.

Price Data, 2006: $130 per introductory kit including professional user's guide (12 pages), 25 test booklets, and set of 4 scoring keys.

Time: (10) minutes.

Author: Ronald F. Lewis.

Publisher: Psychological Assessment Resources, Inc.

Cross References: For reviews by Raymond S. Dean and Scott Kristian Hill and by Daniel C. Miller, see 14:122.

[882]

Dimensional Assessment for Patient Placement Engagement and Recovery.

Purpose: Designed to "focus the clinician's attention on those areas most likely to influence placement and planning decisions and to document the foundation for those decisions" when treating individuals with substance abuse problems.

Population: Adults and adolescents.

Publication Dates: 2000-2004.

Acronym: DAPPER.

Scores, 6: Intoxication/Withdrawal, Biomedical Conditions/Complications, Emotional/Behavioral/Cognitive Conditions, Readiness to Change, Relapse/Continued Use/Problem Potential, Recovery Environment.

Administration: Individual.

Price Data, 2008: $78.75 per 25 copies; $25 per manual (2004, 31 pages).

Time: Administration time not reported.

Comments: The test may be used up to six times on the same individual; flow charts contained in the manual are intended to "show the levels of care for which a given rating is compatible, not as a firm indication that that level is required." The DAPPER is compatible with the ASAM PPC-2R criteria for patient placement.

Authors: Norman G. Hoffmann, David Mee-Lee, and Gerald D. Shulman.

Publisher: The Change Companies.

[883]

Dimensional Assessment of Personality Pathology-Basic Questionnaire.

Purpose: Designed to "provide a comprehensive assessment of the basic dimensions of personality disorder and clinically relevant personality traits."
Population: Ages 18 and over.
Publication Date: 2009.
Acronym: DAPP-BQ.
Scores, 18: Affective Lability, Anxiousness, Callousness, Compulsivity, Conduct Problems, Cognitive Dysregulation, Identity Problems, Insecure Attachment, Intimacy Problems, Low Affiliation, Narcissism, Oppositionality, Rejection, Restricted Expression, Self-Harm, Stimulus Seeking, Submissiveness, Suspiciousness.
Administration: Group.
Price Data, 2010: $275 per hand scoring examination lit including manual, 10 test booklets, 25 answer sheets, 25 scoring sheets, 25 profile sheets, and 5 online administrations; $180 per Fax-In examination kit including manual, 5 test booklets, and 10 fax-in answer sheets; $35 per test manual.
Time: (35-50) minutes.
Authors: W. John Livesley and Douglas N. Jackson.
Publisher: SIGMA Assessment Systems, Inc.

[884]

Dimensions of Excellence Scales [1991 Edition].

Purpose: Designed to identify, describe and validate successful programs and practices of a school district, as well as to forecast future needs.
Population: Schools or districts.
Publication Dates: 1988–1990.
Acronym: DOES.
Administration: Group.
Price Data, 2001: $2 per school staff survey; $1.25 per parent survey; $1.25 per student survey; $23.95 per manual (1990, 71 pages).
Comments: Ratings by students, parents, and school staff.
Authors: Russel A. Dusewicz and Francine S. Beyer.
Publisher: Research for Better Schools, Inc.
  a) STUDENT SCALE.
  Scores: 4 dimensions: School Climate, Teacher Behavior, Monitoring and Assessment, Student Discipline and Behavior.
  Time: (30) minutes.
  b) PARENT SCALE.
  Scores, 8: Same as *a* above plus Leadership, Curriculum, Staff Development, Parent Involvement.
  Time: (20–30) minutes.
  c) SCHOOL STAFF SCALE.
  Scores, 8: Same as *b* above.
  Time: (45) minutes.

Cross References: For a review by Andrew A. McConney, see 14:123; for reviews by Janet F. Carlson and William P. Erchul of an earlier edition, see 11:112.

[885]

Dimensions of Self-Concept.

Purpose: Designed to "measure non-cognitive factors associated with self-esteem or self-concept in a school setting."
Publication Dates: 1976–1989.
Acronym: DOSC.
Administration: Group.
Price Data: Available from publisher.
Comments: Self-report instrument.
Authors: William B. Michael, Robert A. Smith, and Joan J. Michael.
Publisher: EdITS/Educational and Industrial Testing Service.
  a) FORM E.
  Population: Grades 4–6.
  Scores, 5: Level of Aspiration, Anxiety, Academic Interest and Satisfaction, Leadership and Initiative, Identification vs. Alienation.
  Time: (20–40) minutes.
  b) FORM S.
  Population: Grades 7–12.
  Scores: Same as for *a* above.
  Time: (15–35) minutes.
  c) FORM H.
  Population: College.
  Scores: Same as for *a* above.
  Time: (15–35) minutes.
  d) FORM W.
  Population: Adult workers.
  Scores, 5: Aspiration, Anxiety, Job Interest and Satisfaction, Identification vs. Alienation, Level of Job Stress.
  Time: Administration time not reported.
Cross References: See T5:844 (6 references) and T4:806 (1 reference); for a review by Sharon Johnson-Lewis, see 11:113 (10 references); for reviews by Herbert G. W. Bischoff and Alfred B. Heilbrun, Jr., see 9:353 (4 references); see also T3:734 (5 references).

[886]

The Diplomacy Test of Empathy.

Purpose: Constructed to measure empathic ability.
Population: Business and industrial personnel.
Publication Dates: 1960–1962.
Scores: Total score only.
Administration: Group.
Price Data: Available from publisher.
Time: (20–25) minutes.
Comments: Revision of Primary Empathic Abilities; title on test is Diplomacy Test of Empathic Ability.
Author: Willard A. Kerr.

Publisher: Psychometric Affiliates.
Cross References: See T2:1160 (1 reference) and P:64 (2 references); for reviews by Arthur H. Brayfield and Richard S. Hatch, see 6:85 (1 reference); for a review by Robert L. Thorndike of the earlier test, see 5:99.

[887]

DiSC Classic.
Purpose: Designed to "help adults better understand themselves and others."
Population: Adults
Publication Dates: 1996–2003.
Scores, 4: Dominance, Influence, Steadiness, Conscientiousness.
Administration: Individual or Group.
Price Data: Available from publisher.
Time: (7–10) minutes.
Comments: Update of the Personal Profile System; self-report, self-scored instrument; related scripted seminar available from publisher.
Author: Inscape Publishing.
Publisher: Inscape Publishing.
Cross References: For a review by Collie W. Conoley and Linda Castillo, see 16:74.

[888]

DiSC Indra.
Purpose: Provides "an in-depth understanding of relationship dynamics."
Population: Adults.
Publication Date: 2003.
Scores, 10: Convincing, Sociable, Receptive, Patient, Careful, Serious, Resolute, Competitive, DiSC Vector Angle and Length, Goodness of Fit.
Administration: Individual, dyad, or group.
Price Data: Available from publisher.
Time: (15-20) minutes.
Comments: Self-report rating scale; computerized, on-line assessment.
Authors: Inscape Publishing (test), Pamela Cole and Kathleen Tuzinski (research report).
Publisher: Inscape Publishing.
Cross References: For reviews by Gypsy M. Denzine and Frederick T. L. Leong, see 16:75.

[889]

The Discipline Index.
Purpose: "Systematically obtains information from a child about the child's overall perceptions of each parent's disciplinary practices."
Population: Ages 6–17.
Publication Dates: 1999–2002.
Acronym: DI.
Scores, 6: Mother and Father scores for: Clear Expectations, Effectively Monitors, Consistently Enforces, Fairness, Attunement, Moderates Anger, plus Mother Total, Father Total.
Administration: Individual.
Price Data, 2002: $199 per complete kit including handbook (2000, 140 pages), 8 sets response cards, 8 scoring summaries, stylus-pen, placement dots, updates, and 3-year update service; $99 per 8 response cards with summaries; $159 per 16 response cards with summaries; $199 per 24 response cards with summaries; $198 per computer scoring program (half price when purchased with kit); $129 per handbook.
Time: (35 minutes).
Authors: Anita K. Lampel, Barry Bricklin, and Gail Elliot.
Publisher: Village Publishing.
Cross References: For reviews by Patti L. Harrison and Darrell L. Sabers, see 15:86.

[890]

Dissemination Self-Inventory.
Purpose: "To help people involved in NIDRR-funded disability research and development projects bridge the gap between the creation of disability research outcomes and their use."
Population: Organizations.
Publication Date: 2002.
Scores, 4: Organizational Structure and Policies, Research Design, Dissemination Plan, Evaluation.
Administration: Individual.
Price Data, 2002: $10 per Dissemination Self-Inventory (2002, 24 pages).
Time: [20–35] minutes.
Author: Southwest Educational Development Laboratory.
Publisher: Southwest Educational Development Laboratory.

[891]

Dissociative Experiences Scale.
Purpose: "Developed to serve as a clinical tool to help identify patients with dissociative psychopathology and as a research tool to provide a means of quantifying dissociative experiences."
Population: Late adolescent–adult.
Publication Date: 1986.
Acronym: DES.
Scores: Total score only.
Administration: Group or individual.
Price Data: Available from publisher.
Foreign Language Editions: Available in French, Spanish, Italian, Dutch, Hindi, Cambodian, Czech, Swedish, Norwegian, Japanese, Hebrew, Chinese (Mandarin, Traditional Character, and Simplified Character), Finnish, Korean, Polish, and Turkish.
Time: [10] minutes.

Comments: Self-report inventory; translation also in progress for version of the DES in German; test is in the public domain and is available from publisher for cost of copying, handling, and mailing.
Authors: Eve Bernstein Carlson and Frank W. Putnam.
Publisher: The Sidran Institute.
Cross References: See T5:846 (26 references); for reviews by Samuel Juni and Niels G. Waller, see 12:122 (16 references); see also T4:809 (1 reference).

[892]

Dissociative Features Profile.
Purpose: Developed to "help uncover dissociative pathology in children and adolescents."
Population: Children and adolescents.
Publication Date: 1996.
Acronym: DFP.
Scores, 22: Part I: Evidence of Amnesia, Staring Episodes, Odd Movements, Fluctuations/Relatedness, Fluctuations/Language, Fearfulness, Anger, Physical Complaints, Dividedness (1), Dividedness (2), Total; Part II: Multiplicity, Malevolent Religiosity, Dissociative Coping, Depersonalized Humans, Explicit Emotional Confusion, Categories of Good and Bad, Mutilation, Torture, Magical Transformations, Total; Combined Part I and Part II Total.
Administration: Individual.
Parts, 2: Behaviors, Markers.
Price Data: Price data available from publisher for set of 5 preliminary DFP forms and scoring manual/reference guide (1996, 4 pages).
Time: Untimed.
Comments: "Developed to be used with a typical psychological testing battery" (at least 2 other psychological tests given in conjunction with this test); profile completed by psychological professionals about juvenile clients.
Author: Joyanna L. Silberg.
Publisher: The Sidran Institute.

[893]

Diversity Awareness Profile.
Purpose: "Designed to assist people in becoming aware of ways in which they discriminate against, judge, or isolate others."
Population: Employees or managers.
Publication Date: 1991.
Acronym: DAP.
Scores: Total score only.
Administration: Group.
Forms, 2: Employee, Manager.
Price Data: Price information available from publisher.
Time: (90) minutes.
Author: Karen Grote.
Publisher: Jossey-Bass, A Wiley Company.

Cross References: For reviews by Donald B. Pope-Davis and Jonathan G. Dings and by Gargi Roysircar Sodowsky, see 12:123.

[894]

Domestic Situation Inventory.
Purpose: "Designed to provide an objective, research-based, and statistically sound survey of the elements and risk factors that influence and contribute to domestic violence, specifically a male perpetrating violence against a female partner."
Population: Adults.
Publication Date: 2004.
Acronym: DSI.
Scores: DSI Total Score, The Hopelessness/Depression Scale [optional], The Powerlessness/Helplessness Scale [optional], The Threatening Behaviors Scale [optional], The Violent Behaviors Scale [optional].
Administration: Individual or group.
Price Data, 2006: $37.95 per complete kit including 25 test booklets and 1 administrator's guide (8 pages).
Time: (10-15) minutes.
Author: Robert P. Brady.
Publisher: JIST Publishing, Inc.

[895]

Domestic Violence Inventory.
Purpose: "Designed specifically for risk and needs assessment of people who have committed physical, emotional and verbal abuse."
Population: Ages 12–18, adults.
Publication Dates: 1991–1995.
Acronym: DVI.
Scores: 6 scales: Truthfulness, Violence, Alcohol, Drugs, Control, Stress Coping Ability.
Administration: Group.
Forms, 2: Adult, Juvenile.
Price Data: Available from publisher.
Time: (30) minutes.
Comments: Available in English and Spanish; both computer version and paper-pencil format are scored on IBM-PC compatibles.
Author: Risk & Needs Assessment, Inc.
Publisher: Behavior Data Systems, Ltd.
Cross References: For reviews by Carol Collins and by David M. Kaplan and Molly L. Vanduser, see 14:125.

[896]

Doors and People.
Purpose: Designed to "provide comparable measures of visual and verbal memory" and "test both recall and recognition."
Population: Ages 16–80.
Publication Date: 1994.
Scores, 14: Verbal Recall (People), Visual Recognition (Doors), Visual Recall (Shapes), Verbal Recognition

(Names), Overall, Combined Visual Memory, Combined Verbal Memory, Combined Recall, Combined Recognition, Forgetting (Verbal), Forgetting (Visual), Overall Forgetting, Visual-Verbal Discrepancies, Recall-Recognition Discrepancies.
Administration: Individual.
Price Data, 2006: £251 per complete kit including manual (20 pages), 25 scoring sheets, and 3 stimulus books; £39.50 per 50 scoring sheets.
Time: [35-40] minutes.
Authors: Alan Baddeley, Hazel Emslie, and Ian Nimmo-Smith.
Publisher: Pearson Assessment [England].
Cross References: For a review by William K. Wilkinson, see 17:58.

[897]

Drafter (CAD Operator) (Form DDC).

Purpose: For selecting CAD operator candidates.
Population: Applicants for drafter positions.
Publication Date: 2005.
Scores, 3: Print Reading, Computer Aided Design, Total.
Administration: Group.
Price Data, 2011: $22 per consumable self-scoring test booklet or online test administration (minimum order of 20).
Time: 30(45) minutes.
Comments: Packet of supplemental sheets included and required for test administration; available for online test administration.
Author: Roland T. Ramsay.
Publisher: Ramsay Corporation.

[898]

Draw A Person: A Quantitative Scoring System.

Purpose: "To meet the need for a modernized, recently normed, and objective scoring system to be applied to human figure drawings produced by children and adolescents."
Population: Ages 5-17.
Publication Date: 1988.
Acronym: Draw A Person: QSS.
Scores, 4: Man, Woman, Self, Total.
Administration: Group.
Price Data, 2002: $146 per complete kit including 25 student record/response forms, scoring chart, and manual (1988, 100 pages); $101 per scoring chart and manual; $47 per 25 student record/response forms.
Time: 15(25) minutes.
Author: Jack A. Naglieri.
Publisher: Pearson.
Cross References: See T5:854 (2 references) and T4:814 (3 references); for reviews by Merith Cosden and W. Grant Willis, see 11:114 (1 reference).

[899]

Draw-A-Person Intellectual Ability Test for Children, Adolescents, and Adults.

Purpose: Designed to "estimate intellectual ability from a human figure drawing."
Population: Ages 4-0 to 89-11.
Publication Date: 2004.
Acronym: DAP: IQ.
Scores: DAP IQ.
Administration: Individual or group.
Price Data, 2010: $114 per complete kit including examiner's manual (75 pages), 50 administration/scoring forms, and 50 drawing forms; $53 per examiner's manual; $46 per 50 administration/scoring forms; $29 per 50 drawing forms.
Time: (10-12) minutes.
Authors: Cecil R. Reynolds and Julia A. Hickman.
Publisher: PRO-ED.
Cross References: For reviews by Robert W. Hiltonsmith and Jonathan Sandoval, see 17:59.

[900]

Draw A Person: Screening Procedure for Emotional Disturbance.

Purpose: Designed to screen for children who may have emotional disorders and require further evaluation.
Population: Ages 6–17.
Publication Date: 1991.
Acronym: DAP:SPED.
Scores: Total score only.
Administration: Group and individual.
Price Data, 2010: $161 per complete kit including 25 record forms, manual (77 pages), and 10 scoring templates; $53 per 25 record forms; $75 per manual; $46 per 10 scoring templates.
Time: 20 minutes.
Authors: Jack A. Naglieri, Timothy J. McNeish, and Achilles N. Bardos.
Publisher: PRO-ED.
Cross References: See T5:852 (1 reference); for reviews by Merith Cosden and Gale M. Morrison, see 12:124 (2 references); see also T4:816 (1 reference).

[901]

Driver Risk Inventory–II.

Purpose: "Designed for DUI/DWI offender screening."
Population: Convicted DUI and DWI offenders.
Publication Dates: 1986–1997.
Acronym: DRI-II.
Scores, 6: Truthfulness, Alcohol, Driver Risk, Drug, Stress Coping, Dependency.
Price Data: Available from publisher.
Time: (30–35) minutes.
Comments: Self-administered, computer-scored test.

Author: Behavior Data Systems Ltd.
Publisher: Behavior Data Systems Ltd.
Cross References: For reviews by Tony Cellucci and Kevin J. McCarthy, see 14:127; for a review by Frank Gresham of an earlier version, see 12:125.

[902]

Drug Abuse Screening Test.

Purpose: To assess "potential involvement with drugs."
Population: Clients of addiction treatment.
Publication Date: 1982.
Acronym: DAST-20.
Scores: Total score only.
Administration: Group.
Price Data, 2002: C$9.05 in Ontario (C$12.95 outside Ontario) per test.
Foreign Language Edition: Available in French.
Time: (5–10) minutes.
Comments: Self-report inventory; manual is entitled "Directory of Client Outcome Measures for Addiction Treatment Programs"; has also been listed as Drug Use Questionnaire.
Author: Harvey A. Skinner.
Publisher: Centre for Addiction and Mental Health [Canada].
Cross References: For reviews by Philip Ash and Jeffrey S. Rain, see 13:104.

[903]

Drug-Taking Confidence Questionnaire.

Purpose: "As an assessment tool, the DTCQ identifies a client's coping self-efficacy in relation to 50 drinking or drug-taking situations."
Population: Clients of addiction treatment.
Publication Date: 1997.
Acronym: DTCQ.
Scores: Situation profiles in two areas: Personal States, Situations Involving Other People; 8 subscales: Unpleasant Emotions, Physical Discomfort, Pleasant Emotions, Testing Personal Control, Urges and Temptations to Use, Conflict with Others, Social Pressure to Use, Pleasant Times with Others.
Administration: Group.
Price Data, 2002: C$34.95 per user's guide; C$14.95 per 30 questionnaires (specify alcohol or drug); C$39.95 per sample pack including user's guide and 40 questionnaires (10 alcohol and 30 drug); C$75 per 50 uses of computer-administration software (DOS format); C$100 per 50 uses of software with user's guide; C$250 per 200 uses of software; C$275 per 200 uses of software with user's guide.
Time: (15) minutes.
Comments: User's guide written in both English (160 pages) and French (69 pages); "French versions of DTCQ have not been scientifically validated."

Authors: Helen M. Annis, Sherrilyn M. Sklar, and Nigel E. Turner.
Publisher: Centre for Addiction and Mental Health [Canada].
Cross References: For reviews by Michael H. Campbell and Glenn B. Gelman, see 14:128.

[904]

Drug Use Screening Inventory–Revised.

Purpose: Designed to quantify "severity of mental health and substance use problems in multiple domains of health, behavior, and psychosocial development" and to predict likelihood of mental health disorder, adverse outcomes, and violence proneness.
Population: Youth (ages 10 to 17); Adult (age 18 and over).
Publication Dates: 1990–2011.
Acronym: DUSI-R.
Scores: 10 Domains: Drug and Alcohol Use, Substance Use, Behavior Patterns, Health Status, Psychiatric Disorder, Social Competence, Family System, School Performance, Work Adjustment, Peer Relationships, Leisure/Recreation; also Overall Problem Severity Index and validity/lie scale scores, plus prediction of 6 mental health disorders (ADHD, SUD, Anxiety, Depression, Conduct/Anti-sociality) and prediction of adverse outcomes (DUI, Car Accident, Sell/Deal Drugs, Head Injury, STD), and Violence Proneness.
Administration: Individual or group.
Levels, 2: Youth, Adult.
Parts, 3: Full Assessment (20min), Short Screen (7min), Brief Screen (2min).
Forms, 3: Past Year, Past Month, Past Week.
Price Data, 2011: $5 per DUSI-R Initial Intake Assessment; $2.50 per DUSI-R Follow-up Assessment during treatment; optional online assessment and advance reports system annual license starts at $125; volume discounts available.
Foreign Language and Other Special Editions: Available in Chinese, Danish, Dutch, Flemish, Belgian French, Finnish, French, German, Norwegian, Portuguese, Russian, Spanish, Swedish, Turkish, and English. Audio version available for clients whose reading level is below grade 5.
Time: Full Assessment, 20 minutes; Short Screen, 7 minutes; Brief Screen, 2 minutes.
Comments: Client self-report inventory; covers both mental health and substance use; subscales within each domain and related subscale questions mapped to DSM; online system provides automated scoring and ability to monitor client progress during treatment, monitor client during aftercare. Recommended and current uses include: detection of high risk youths, intake evaluation (youth/adult), intervention/treatment progress monitoring, outcome assessment, program evaluation, and clinical trials.
Author: Ralph E. Tarter.

Publisher: eCenter Research, Inc.

Cross References: For a review by Tony Cellucci, see 16:76.

[905]

DSST/DANTES Subject Standardized Tests.

Purpose: Gives colleges and universities the opportunity to offer non-traditional learners college credit for knowledge acquired outside the traditional classroom. **Population**: Non-traditional students wishing to earn college credit by examination. **Publication Dates**: 1983–2002. **Acronym**: DSST. **Administration**: Group. **Price Data, 2002**: $40 per exam; test centers may also require an administration fee for each examination; scoring by publisher included in price. **Time**: Untimed, requiring approximately (90) minutes per test. **Comments**: Paper-and-pencil administration; additional information available at www.getcollegecredit.com. **Author**: The Chauncey Group International. **Publisher**: The Chauncey Group International.

a) MATHEMATICS.

Scores: Total score for each of 2 tests:

1) *Fundamentals of College Algebra.*
2) *Principles of Statistics.*

b) SOCIAL SCIENCE.

Scores: Total score for each of 14 tests:

1) *Western Europe Since 1945.*
2) *Introduction to the Modern Middle East.*
3) *A History of the Vietnam War.*
4) *Human/Cultural Geography.*
5) *Lifespan Developmental Psychology.*
6) *General Anthropology.*
7) *Introduction to Law Enforcement.*
8) *Criminal Justice.*
9) *Fundamentals of Counseling.*
10) *Art of the Western World.*
11) *Drug and Alcohol Abuse.*
12) *The Civil War and Reconstruction.*
13) *Foundations of Education.*
14) *Rise and Fall of the Soviet Union.*

c) PHYSICAL SCIENCE.

Scores: Total score for each of 5 tests:

1) *Astronomy.*
2) *Here's to Your Health.*
3) *Environment and Humanity: The Race to Save the Planet.*
4) *Principles of Physical Science I.*
5) *Physical Geology.*

d) BUSINESS.

Scores: Total score for each of 12 tests:

1) *Principles of Finance.*
2) *Principles of Financial Accounting.*
3) *Human Resource Management.*
4) *Organizational Behavior.*
5) *Introduction to Computing.*
6) *Introduction to Business.*
7) *Money and Banking.*
8) *Business Mathematics.*
9) *Business Law II.*
10) *Principles of Supervision.*
11) *Personal Finance.*
12) *Management Information Systems.*

e) FOREIGN LANGUAGE.

f) APPLIED TECHNOLOGY.

1) *Technical Writing.*

g) HUMANITIES.

Scores: Total score for each of 3 tests:

1) *Ethics in America.*
2) *Principles of Public Speaking.*
3) *Introduction to World Religions.*

Cross References: For reviews by Laura L. B. Barnes and William A. Mehrens, see 11:103.

[906]

Durrell Analysis of Reading Difficulty, Third Edition.

Purpose: Designed to screen for reading problems. **Population**: Grades 1–6. **Publication Dates**: 1937–1980. **Acronym**: DARD. **Scores, 16 to 21**: Oral Reading, Silent Reading, Listening Comprehension, Word Recognition, Word Analysis, Listening Vocabulary, Sounds in Isolation (Letters, Blends and Digraphs, Phonograms, Initial Affixes, Final Affixes), Spelling, Phonic Spelling of Words, Visual Memory of Words (Primary, Secondary), Identifying Sounds in Words, Prereading Phonics Abilities Inventories (Optional, Including Syntax Matching, Letter Names in Spoken Words, Phonemes in Spoken Words, Naming Lower Case Letters, Writing Letters from Dictation). **Administration**: Individual. **Price Data, 2002**: $137 per examiner's kit including tachistoscope, reading booklet, 5 record booklets, and manual (1980, 63 pages); $45.60 per reading booklet; $43 per tachistoscope; $81.60 per 35 record booklets; $23 per manual. **Time**: (35–50) minutes. **Authors**: Donald D. Durrell and Jane H. Catterson. **Publisher**: Pearson.

Cross References: See T5:861 (5 references) and T4:822 (14 references); for reviews by Nancy L. Roser and Byron H. Van Roekel, see 9:360 (3 references); see also T3:766 (14 references) and T2:1628 (18 references); for reviews by James Maxwell and George D. Spache of an earlier edition, see 5:660; for a review by Helen M. Robinson of the original edition, see 4:561 (2 references); for reviews by Guy L. Bond and Miles A. Tinker, see 2:1533; for a review by Marion Monroe, see 1:1098.

[907]

Dutch Eating Behaviour Questionnaire.

Purpose: Assesses "the structure of an individual's eating behaviour."
Population: Ages 9–adult.
Publication Date: 2002.
Acronym: DEBQ.
Scores, 3: Emotional Eating, External Eating, Restrained Eating.
Administration: Individual.
Price Data, 2006: £87 per complete kit including manual (24 pages), questionnaire, and 25 scoring sheets; £47 per 50 questionnaires and scoring sheets.
Foreign Language Editions: German, French, Swedish, Portugese, Chinese, Greek, and Korean editions available.
Time: (10) minutes.
Author: Tatjana van Strien.
Publisher: Pearson Assessment [England].
Cross References: For a review by Robert Christopher, see 17:60.

[908]

Dyadic Adjustment Scale.

Purpose: Designed to measure the quality of adjustment in marriage and similar dyadic relationships.
Population: People who have any committed couple relationship including unmarried cohabitation.
Publication Dates: 1989-2001.
Acronym: DAS.
Scores: 5: Dyadic Consensus, Dyadic Satisfaction, Affectional Expression, Dyadic Cohesion, Dyadic Adjustment.
Administration: Group or individual.
Price Data, 2011: $78 per complete kit including test manual (54 pages) and 20 QuikScore™ forms (for 10 couples); $51 per 20 QuikScore™ forms (for 10 couples); $39 per manual; $56 per DAS software preview version (includes 3 reports); $5 each (minimum purchase of 50) for Windows software profile reports (with Psychmanager platform).
Time: (5-10) minutes.
Comments: Self-report.
Author: Graham B. Spanier.
Publisher: Multi-Health Systems, Inc.
Cross References: See T5:863 (94 references) and T4:824 (37 references); for reviews by Karen S. Budd and Nancy Heilman and by Richard B. Stuart, see 11:117 (17 references).

[909]

Dyadic Parent-Child Interaction Coding System.

Purpose: For use in assessing the quality of parent-child social interaction, discriminating between parent-child interactions of children with and without disruptive behavior disorders and their parents, and evaluating change after parent training interventions for young children with behavior problems.

Population: Children ages 2-10 and their parents.
Publication Dates: 1981-2005.
Acronym: DPICS.
Scores: 24 behavioral categories that provide frequency scores: parent and child positive and negative verbalization and physical touch categories, child negative vocalization categories (whine, yell), and child responses to parent commands and questions.
Administration: Individual dyads.
Price Data: Now available free of charge; can be downloaded from www.pcit.org.
Time: 15(20) minutes.
Comments: Behavioral coding by clinician in three standard 5-minute situations that vary in amount of parent control required: child-led play; parent-led play; clean-up; abridged version available for clinical use; workbook to assist coder training available.
Authors: Sheila M. Eyberg, Melanie M. Nelson, Maura Duke, and Stephen R. Boggs.
Publisher: Sheila M. Eyberg.
Cross References: See T5:864 (3 references) and T4:825 (11 references); for reviews by Robert J. McMahon and Phillip S. Strain, see 9:361 (1 reference); see also T3:768 (1 reference).

[910]

Dynamic Assessment of Test Accommodations.

Purpose: "Designed to assist the teacher in determining the appropriate accommodations that will allow students with learning disabilities to demonstrate academic ability independent of their handicapping conditions."
Population: Students with special needs in Grades 2 to 7.
Publication Date: 2003.
Acronym: DATA.
Administration: Individual or group.
Levels, 3: Grades 2–3, Grades 4–5, Grades 6–7.
Price Data, 2003: $150 per complete kit including manual, and 3 test booklets (specify level); $5.50 per Reading Screener card; $14 per 25 Reading Screener score sheets; $5.50 per Workbook Symbols card; $65 per manual, $25 per 25 Math booklets (specify level); $45 per 25 Reading booklets (specify level).
Comments: Student must be capable of reading basic text at a rate of at least 10 words per minute before Reading Comprehension is assessed.
Authors: Lynn Fuchs, Douglas Fuchs, Susan Eaton, and Carol Hamlett.
Publisher: Pearson.

a) READING COMPREHENSION.
Scores, 4: Large Print Gain, Extended Time Gain, Read Aloud Gain, No Accommodation.
Time: 40(45) minutes.
b) MATH COMPUTATION.
Scores, 2: Extended Time Gain, No Accommodation.
Time: 24(29) minutes.

c) MATH APPLICATION.
Scores, 4: Extended Time Gain, Calculator Condition Gain, Reader Condition Gain, No Accommodation.
Time: (42) minutes.
Cross References: For reviews by Michelle Athanasiou and Bethany A. Brunsman, see 16:77.

[911]

Dynamic Factors Survey.

Purpose: Measurement of motivational factors related to personality and interest research, personnel selection, and vocational assessment.
Population: Grades 12-16 and adults.
Publication Dates: 1954–1956.
Acronym: DFSV.
Scores: 10: Need for Attention, Liking for Thinking, Adventure vs. Security, Self-Reliance vs. Dependence, Aesthetic Appreciation, Cultural Conformity, Need for Freedom, Realistic Thinking, Need for Precision, Need for Diversion.
Administration: Group.
Price Data: Available from publisher at www.mindgarden.com/products/dfsvs.htm.
Time: (45) minutes.
Authors: J. P. Guilford, Paul R. Christensen, and Nicholas A. Bond, Jr.
Publisher: Mind Garden, Inc.
Cross References: See T2:1151 (7 references) and P:54 (12 references); for reviews by Andrew R. Baggaley, John W. French, and Arthur W. Meadows, see 5:45.

[912]

Dysarthria Examination Battery.

Purpose: Designed to "assess motor speech disorders."
Population: Children and adults.
Publication Date: 1993.
Scores, 5: Respiration, Phonation, Resonation, Articulation, Prosody.
Administration: Individual.
Price Data: Price data available from publisher for complete kit including test booklet, 3 stimulus cards, 20 scoring forms, and manual (48 pages).
Time: (60) minutes.
Author: Sakina S. Drummond.
Publisher: Pearson.
Cross References: For reviews by Steven B. Leder and Malcolm R. McNeil, see 14:129.

[913]

Dyscalculia Screener.

Purpose: To screen pupil(s) to establish whether a pupil has low attainment because of a dyscalculic deficit.
Population: Ages 6–14.
Publication Date: 2003.

Scores: 4 tests: Dot Enumeration, Number Comparison (Numerical Stroop), Arithmetic Achievement, Simple Reaction Time.
Administration: Group.
Price Data, 2003: £150 for Annual License; £50 for License Renewal.
Time: (15–30) minutes.
Comments: Test administered via microcomputer conforming to the following specification: Pentium class system with at least 32 MB of RAM, 100 MB of free hard drive space, running Windows 98, 98SE, NT4, or 2000, with sound card.
Author: Brian Butterworth.
Publisher: GL Assessment [England].
Cross References: For reviews by Cleborne D. Maddux and Gretchen Owens, see 16:78.

[914]

Dyslexia Adult Screening Test.

Purpose: To assess strengths and weaknesses often associated with dyslexia.
Population: 16 years 5 months to adult.
Publication Date: 1998.
Acronym: DAST.
Scores, 12: Rapid Naming, One Minute Reading, Postural Stability, Nonverbal Reasoning, Phonemic Segmentation, Two Minute Spelling, Backwards Span, Verbal Fluency, Semantic Fluency, Nonsense Passage Reading, One Minute Writing, Total.
Administration: Individual.
Price Data, 2006: £140 per complete kit.
Time: 30 minutes.
Authors: Angela J. Fawcett and Rod I. Nicolson.
Publisher: Pearson Assessment [England].
Cross References: For reviews by Manuela H. Habicht and William K. Wilkinson, see 16:79.

[915]

Dyslexia Determination Test, Second Edition.

Purpose: To identify individuals who exhibit dyslexic patterns of responding in the areas of reading, writing, and spelling.
Population: Grades 2–12.
Publication Dates: 1980-1987.
Acronym: DDT.
Scores: 6 subtests: Dysnemkinesia (Writing of Numbers, Writing of Letters), Dysphonesia (Decoding, Encoding), Dyseidesia (Decoding, Encoding).
Administration: Individual.
Price Data: Available from publisher.
Time: (15–20) minutes.
Authors: John R. Griffin and Howard N. Walton.
Publisher: I-MED, Instructional Materials & Equipment Distributors.

Cross References: For a review by Fred M. Grossman, see 9:362.

[916]
Dyslexia Early Screening Test [Second Edition].

Purpose: "Designed to pick out children who are 'at risk' of reading failure early enough to allow them to be given extra support at school."
Population: Ages 4 years, 6 months to 6 years, 5 months.
Publication Dates: 1996-2004.
Acronym: DEST-2.
Scores, 13: Tests of Attainment (Digit Naming, Letter Naming), Diagnostic Tests (Rapid Naming, Bead Threading, Phonological Discrimination, Postural Stability, Rhyme/First Letter, Forwards Digit Span, Sound Order, Shape Copying, Corsi Frog, Vocabulary), At Risk Quotient.
Administration: Individual.
Price Data, 2006: £125 per complete kit including examiner's manual (2004, 106 pages), envelope 1 (containing 7 subtest cards and sample permission letter), envelope 2 (containing score keys), Forward Digit Span tape, Sound Order tape, Corsi Frog, beads, cord, blindfold, balance tester, scoring software with manual, and 50 score sheets in a carrying case; £83 per upgrade kit including examiner's manual, envelope 1 (containing 7 subtest cards and sample permission letter), envelope 2 (containing score keys), Corsi Frog, scoring software with manual, and 50 score sheets in carrying case; £24.50 per manual; £38.50 per 50 score sheets.
Time: (30) minutes.
Authors: Rod I. Nicolson and Angela J. Fawcett.
Publisher: Pearson Assessment [England].
Cross References: For reviews by Lorraine Cleeton and Katharine Snyder, see 17:61; for reviews by Kathleen M. Johnson and William K. Wilkinson of the earlier edition, see 15:88.

[917]
Dyslexia Screening Instrument.

Purpose: Designed to identify students with dyslexia.
Population: Grades 1–12, ages 6–21.
Publication Date: 1994.
Scores, 4: Passed, Failed, Inconclusive, Cannot Be Scored.
Administration: Individual.
Price Data, 2002: $85 per complete kit including teacher rating scale, manual (40 pages), and scoring program software; $16 per 50 rating forms.
Time: (15–20) minutes.
Comments: Rating form is completed by student's teacher; computer scored, DOS 3.0 or higher.
Authors: Kathryn B. Coon, Mary Jo Polk, and Melissa McCoy Waguespack.

Publisher: Pearson.
Cross References: For reviews by Janet E. Spector and Betsy Waterman, see 14:130.

[918]
Dyslexia Screening Test.

Purpose: "A screening instrument … for profil[ing] the strengths and weaknesses often associated with dyslexia."
Population: Ages 6-6 to 16-5.
Publication Date: 2004.
Acronym: DST.
Scores, 11: 3 Tests of Attainment (One Minute Reading, Two Minute Spelling, One Minute Writing), 8 Diagnostic Tests (Rapid Naming, Bead Threading, Postural Stability, Phonemic Segmentation, Backwards Digit Span, Nonsense Passage Reading, Semantic Fluency, Verbal Fluency), At Risk Quotient.
Administration: Individual.
Price Data, 2004: $119 per complete kit including manual (1996, 63 pages), score keys, Backwards Digit Span audiocassette, and carrying case; $55 per 50 record forms.
Time: (30) minutes for entire battery.
Comments: Normed in the United Kingdom.
Authors: Angela J. Fawcett and Rod I. Nicolson.
Publisher: Pearson Assessment [England].
Cross References: For reviews by Karen T. Carey and James E. Ysseldyke, see 16:80.

[919]
Dysphagia Evaluation Protocol.

Purpose: Developed to "assist in evaluating swallowing functioning in adult patients."
Population: Adult patients.
Publication Date: 1997.
Acronym: DEP.
Scores: 14 ratings: History and Observations (Feeding History, Nutritional Status, Respiratory Status), Clinical Evaluation of Swallowing (Observations, Oral Control, Primitive and Abnormal Reflexes, Pharyngeal Control), Feeding Trial (Appetite/Willingness to Participate, Ability to Swallow Without Food Bolus, Oral State, Pharyngeal Stage), Impressions (Summary, Functional Level, Recommendations/Plan).
Administration: Individual.
Price Data, 2002: $72 per complete kit including 15 record forms, pocket manual (40 pages), and manual (64 pages), $13 per 15 record forms; $36 per pocket manual; $36 per manual.
Time: (30) minutes.
Authors: Wendy Avery-Smith, Abbey Brod Rosen, and Donna M. Dellarosa.
Publisher: Pearson.
Cross References: For a review by Maynard D. Filter, see 14:131.

[920]
Early Child Development Inventory.
Purpose: "A brief screening inventory ... designed to help identify children with developmental, behavioral, or health problems."
Population: Ages 1-3 to 3-0.
Publication Date: 1988.
Acronym: ECDI.
Scores: General Development Score, Possible Problems List (24), Child Description, Parent's Questions/Concerns, Parent's Functioning.
Administration: Individual or group.
Price Data, 2005: $12.50 per 25 Parent Questionnaires; $12.50 per manual (15 pages).
Time: (15) minutes.
Comments: Parent-completed questionnaire; scores reflect parent's report of child's present functioning; publisher now recommends using Child Development Review Parent Questionnaire (476) instead of this.
Author: Harold Ireton.
Publisher: Child Development Review - Behavior Science Systems, Inc.
Cross References: For a review by Robert W. Hiltonsmith, see 11:119.

[921]
Early Childhood Attention Deficit Disorders Evaluation Scale.
Purpose: Designed to document behaviors and measure the characteristics of ADHD in school and home environments.
Population: Males, ages 24–84 months; Females ages 24–83 months.
Publication Date: 1995.
Acronym: ECADDES.
Scores, 3: Inattentive, Hyperactive-Impulsive, Total Percentile Rank.
Administration: Individual.
Forms, 3: Home, School, ECADDES/DSM-IV.
Price Data, 2006: $162 per complete kit including 50 School Version rating forms, 50 Home Version rating forms, 50 ECADDES/DSM-IV forms, School Version technical manual (42 pages), Home Version technical manual (42 pages), ECADDES Intervention manual (147 pages), and Parent's Guide (134 pages); $35 per 50 rating forms (specify School Version or Home Version); $35 per 50 Home Version Spanish rating forms; $22 per 50 ECADDES/DSM-IV forms; $15 per technical manual (specify School Version or Home Version); $25 per ECADDES Intervention manual; $15 per Parent's Guide; $35 per computerized Quick Score program (WIN).
Time: (15–20) minutes.
Comments: Ratings by persons familiar with the child's behavior patterns in home or school settings.
Authors: Stephen B. McCarney and Nancy W. Johnson (Intervention Manual and Parent's Guide).

Publisher: Hawthorne Educational Services, Inc.
Cross References: For reviews by Libby G. Cohen and Harold R. Keller, see 14:132.

[922]
The Early Childhood Behavior Scale.
Purpose: Designed to assess behaviors related to early childhood emotional disturbance and behavior disorder.
Population: 36–72 months.
Publication Dates: 1991–1994.
Acronym: ECBS.
Scores, 4: Academic Progress, Social Relationships, Personal Adjustment, Total Percentile Rank.
Administration: Individual.
Price Data, 2006: $105 per complete kit including technical manual (1994, 36 pages), intervention manual (1991, 130 pages), and 50 ratings forms; $15 per technical manual; $25 per intervention manual; $35 per 50 rating forms.
Time: (15–20) minutes.
Comments: Ratings by teachers.
Author: Stephen B. McCarney.
Publisher: Hawthorne Educational Services, Inc.
Cross References: For reviews by Kathleen D. Paget and Jonathan Sandoval, see 13:105.

[923]
Early Childhood Environment Rating Scale–Revised Edition.
Purpose: Designed to measure the quality of the environments in early childhood programs.
Population: Early childhood programs or classrooms (excluding infant and toddler programs).
Publication Dates: 1980–1998.
Acronym: ECERS-R.
Scores, 8: Space and Furnishings, Personal Care Routines, Language-Reasoning, Activities, Interaction, Program Structure, Parents and Staff, Total.
Administration: Group.
Price Data, 2006: $12.95 per complete test.
Foreign Language Editions: Translations of the original ECERS in Italian, Swedish, German, Portugese, Spanish, and Icelandic.
Time: (140) minutes.
Comments: Can be completed by an outside observer or as a self-assessment by program staff.
Authors: Thelma Harms, Richard M. Clifford, and Debbie Cryer.
Publisher: Teachers College Press.
Cross References: For reviews by Kathleen D. Paget and Gene Schwarting, see 14:133; see also T5:875 (11 references) and T4:833 (7 references); for reviews by Richard Elardo and Cathy Fultz Telzrow of the original version, see 9:365.

[924]

Early Childhood Inventory–4.

Purpose: Constructed to assess the "behavioral, affective, and cognitive symptoms of childhood psychiatric disorders."
Population: Ages 3–6.
Publication Dates: 1996–1997.
Acronym: ECI-4.
Scores, 25: AD/HD Inattentive, AD/HD Hyperactive-Impulsive, AD/HD Combined, Oppositional Defiant Disorder, Conduct Disorder, Peer Conflict Scale, Separation Anxiety Disorder, Specific Phobia, Obsessions, Compulsions, Motor Tics, Vocal Tics, Generalized Anxiety Disorder, Selective Mutism, Major Depressive Disorder, Dysthymic Disorder, Adjustment Disorder, Social Phobia, Sleep Problems, Elimination Problems, Posttraumatic Stress Disorder, Feeding Problems, Reactive Attachment Disorder, Autistic Disorder, Asperger's Disorder.
Administration: Individual.
Forms, 2: Parent Checklist, Teacher Checklist.
Price Data, 2006: $102 per deluxe kit including screening manual (2000, 117 pages), norms manual (1997, 184 pages), 25 parent checklists, 25 teacher checklists, 50 parent score sheets, and 50 teacher score sheets; $52 per 50 parent checklists and score sheets; 38 per 50 teacher checklists and score sheets; $22 per screening manual; $22 per norms manual.
Foreign Language Edition: Spanish edition available.
Time: (10–15) minutes.
Comments: Instrument is designed to correspond to the DSM-IV classification system.
Authors: Kenneth D. Gadow and Joyce Sprafkin.
Publisher: Checkmate Plus, Ltd.
Cross References: For a review by Robert C. Reinehr, see 14:134.

[925]

Early Childhood Physical Environment Observation Schedules and Rating Scales.

Purpose: "Intended for the systematic assessment of the quality of the physical environment of child care centers and related early childhood environments."
Population: Directors and staff of child care centers, early childhood teachers.
Publication Dates: 1982–1994.
Scores: 9 scales: Early Childhood Teacher Style and Dimensions of Education Rating Scales (Early Childhood Teacher Style Rating Scale, Early Childhood Dimensions of Education Rating Scale, Teacher Style and Dimensions of Education Validity Check), Early Childhood Physical Environment Scales (Pattern 905: Spatial Organization, Pattern 908: Behavior Settings), Playground and Neighborhood Observation Behavior Maps (Playground Observation Behavior Map, Neighborhood Observation Behavior Map, Neighborhood Observation Supplementary Coding Sheet), Environment/Behavior Observation Schedule for Early Childhood Environments.
Administration: Group.
Time: [10–30] minutes per scale.
Comments: For research purposes only; the publisher advised in March 2006 that this test is no longer commercially available; it can be downloaded free of charge from the UW-Milwaukee Golda Meir Library e-reserve and is available in hard copy at that library and the Library of Congress.
Author: Gary T. Moore.
Publisher: Center for Architecture and Urban Planning Research, University of Wisconsin-Milwaukee.
Cross References: For reviews by Lisa G. Bischoff and Patricia B. Keith, see 13:106.

[926]

Early Coping Inventory.

Purpose: Measures coping related behaviors.
Population: Mental age 4–36 months.
Publication Date: 1988.
Scores, 4: Sensorimotor Organization, Reactive Behavior, Self-Initiated Behavior, Total.
Administration: Individual.
Price Data: See www.ststesting.com for up-to-date prices.
Time: Administration time varies.
Comments: Downward extension of the Coping Inventory (734); ratings of adaptive behavior by an adult.
Authors: Shirley Zeitlin and G. Gordon Williamson with Margery Szczepanski.
Publisher: Scholastic Testing Service, Inc.
Cross References: See T5:878 (1 reference); for reviews by Harlan J. Stientjes and by Logan Wright and Wade L. Hamil, see 11:120.

[927]

Early Intervention Developmental Profile.

Purpose: Designed to yield information for planning comprehensive developmental programs for children with all types of disabilities.
Population: Children who are at developmental ages of 0–36 months.
Publication Dates: 1977–2006.
Scores, 8: Perceptual/Fine Motor, Cognition, Language, Social/Emotional, Self-Care (Feeding, Toileting, Dressing), Gross Motor.
Administration: Individual.
Price Data: Available from publisher and on the web at www.press.umich.edu.
Time: (50–60) minutes.
Comments: Stimulation activities manual included; see Preschool Developmental Profile (2112) for developmental ages from 36 months to 5 years.
Authors: D. Sue Schafer, Martha S. Moersch, Sally J. Rogers, Diane B. D'Eugenio, Sara L. Brown, Carol M. Donovan, and Eleanor Whiteside Lynch.

Publisher: University of Michigan Press.

Cross References: For reviews by Barbara A. Rothlisberg and Gary J. Stainback, see 13:107 (1 reference); see also T4:835 (1 reference).

[928]

Early Language & Literacy Classroom Observation Tool, K-3, Research Edition.

Purpose: Designed to assess "the quality of both the classroom environment and teachers' practices" for language and literacy instruction.

Population: Kindergarten through third-grade classrooms.

Publication Date: 2008.

Acronym: ELLCO K-3.

Scores, 7: General Classroom Environment (Classroom Structure, Curriculum, Total), Language and Literacy (The Language Environment, Books and Reading, Print and Writing, Total).

Administration: Individual.

Price Data, 2010: $30 per user's guide (100 pages); $30 per 5 observation tools.

Time: (210) minutes.

Authors: Miriam W. Smith, Joanne P. Brady, and Nancy Clark-Chiarelli.

Publisher: Paul H. Brookes Publishing Co., Inc.

[929]

Early Language & Literacy Classroom Observation Tool, Pre-K.

Purpose: Designed as a way for educators and researchers "to examine the literacy-related features of classrooms."

Population: Center-based classrooms for 3- to 5-year-old children.

Publication Date: 2008.

Acronym: ELLCO Pre-K.

Scores, 7: General Classroom Environment (Classroom Structure, Curriculum, Total), Language and Literacy (The Language Environment, Books and Book Reading, Print and Early Writing, Total).

Administration: Individual.

Price Data, 2011: $50 per user's guide (101 pages) and 5 observation tools; $30 per 5 observation tools; $30 per user's guide.

Time: (210) minutes.

Authors: Miriam W. Smith, Joanne P. Brady, and Louisa Anastasopoulos.

Publisher: Paul H. Brookes Publishing Co., Inc.

[930]

Early Language Milestone Scale, Second Edition.

Purpose: To assess speech and language development during infancy and early childhood.

Population: Birth to 36 months.

Publication Dates: 1983–1993.

Acronym: ELM Scale-2.

Scores, 4: Auditory Expressive, Auditory Receptive, Visual, Global Language.

Administration: Individual.

Price Data, 2010: $184 per complete kit including manual (1993, 95 pages), object kit, and 100 records; $69 per manual; $64 per 100 record forms; $60 per object kit.

Time: (1–10) minutes.

Author: James Coplan.

Publisher: PRO-ED.

Cross References: See T5:880 (1 reference) for reviews by Philip Backlund and Sherwyn Morreale and by Betsy Waterman, see 13:108; for a review by Ruth M. Noyce of an earlier edition, see 10:99 (2 references).

[931]

Early Language Skills Checklist.

Purpose: Designed as an observation-based checklist for children "whose language development is causing concern."

Population: Ages 3–5.

Publication Date: 1998.

Acronym: ELS.

Scores: No scores; 4 areas: Attention and Listening Skills, Receptive Language, Expressive Language, Social and Intellectual Use of Language.

Administration: Individual.

Price Data, 2002: £9.99 per 10 checklists; £16.99 per specimen set; £15.99 per handbook.

Time: (5–20) minutes.

Authors: James Boyle and Elizabeth McLellan.

Publisher: Hodder & Stoughton Educational [England].

[932]

Early Literacy Skills Assessment.

Purpose: "Designed to provide preschool programs and teachers with an authentic and meaningful way to assess young children's early literacy skills."

Population: Ages 3-5 years.

Publication Dates: 2005–2007.

Acronym: ELSA.

Scores: 12 scores in 4 areas: Comprehension (Prediction, Retelling, Connection to Real Life), Phonological Awareness (Rhyming, Segmentation, Phonemic Awareness), Alphabetic Principle (Sense of Word, Alphabet Letter Recognition, Letter-Sound Correspondence), Concepts About Print (Orientation, Story Beginning, Direction of Text).

Administration: Individual.

Price Data, 2011: $149.95 per complete kit including 2 copies of Violet's Adventure or Dante Grows Up, user guide (48 pages), 60 score sheets, 60 Child Summary forms, 12 Class Summary forms, and 60 Family Report forms; $149.95 per Spanish version complete

kit including 2 copies of La Aventura de Violeta or El Combio en Dante, user guide, 60 score sheets, 60 Child Summary forms, 12 Class Summary forms, and 60 Family Report forms; $39.95 per Violet's Adventure or La Aventura de Violeta; $39.95 per Dante Grows Up or El Cambio en Dante; $49.95 per DVD Scoring the ELSA: Establishing Reliability; $49.95 per ELSA Reports on CD-ROM, which allows user to enter score sheet results to automatically create child, class and family reports.
Foreign Language Edition: Spanish edition (2006) available.
Time: (15-20) minutes; (20–25) minutes for Spanish edition.
Author: Andrea DeBruin-Parecki.
Publisher: High/Scope Educational Research Foundation.
Cross References: For a review by Rick Eigenbrood, see 17:62.

[933]
Early Math Diagnostic Assessment.
Purpose: Designed to "screen and identify children at risk for math difficulties."
Population: Prekindergarten to Grade 3.
Publication Date: 2002.
Acronym: EMDA.
Scores: 2 subtests: Math Reasoning, Numerical Operations.
Administration: Individual.
Price Data, 2003: $110 per complete kit including examiner's manual (84 pages), stimulus book, 25 record forms, 25 response booklets, and 30 "Thumbs Up" worm stickers; $25 per examiner's manual; $75 per stimulus book; $50 per 25 record forms and response booklets.
Time: (20–30) minutes.
Comments: Items selected to "address mathematical domains identified by" the Principles and Standards for School Mathematics (2002) set forth by the National Council of Teachers of Mathematics.
Author: The Psychological Corporation.
Publisher: Pearson.
Cross References: For reviews by Mark J. Gierl and Xuan Tan and by Arturo Olivarez, Jr., see 16:81.

[934]
Early Memories Procedure.
Purpose: "Method of exploring personality organization, especially current life concerns, based on an individual's memory of the past."
Population: Ages 10 and over with at least a fourth-grade reading level.
Publication Dates: 1989–1992.
Scores: No scores.
Administration: Group.
Price Data: Available from publisher.

Time: (90–240) minutes.
Comments: Instrument may be interpreted according to a Freudian, Adlerian, Ego-Psychological, or Cognitive-Perceptual model.
Author: Arnold R. Bruhn.
Publisher: Arnold R. Bruhn and Associates.
Cross References: For reviews by Karl R. Hanes and LeAdelle Phelps, see 13:109; see also T4:840 (1 reference).

[935]
Early Reading Diagnostic Assessment–Second Edition.
Purpose: Designed to evaluate "the essential components of reading defined by Reading First–phonemic awareness, phonics, fluency, vocabulary and comprehension."
Population: Grades K–3.
Publication Dates: 2002–2003.
Acronym: ERDA Second Edition.
Administration: Individual.
Levels, 4: Grades K, 1, 2, and 3.
Price Data: Available from publisher.
Author: The Psychological Corporation.
Publisher: Pearson.
a) GRADE K.
Population: Kindergarten.
Scores, 11: Letter Recognition, Story Retell, Phonological Awareness (Rhyming, Phonemes, Syllables, Composite), Vocabulary (Receptive, Expressive, Composite), Reading Comprehension, Passage Fluency.
Time: (65–75) minutes.
b) GRADE 1.
Population: Grade 1.
Scores, 14: Word Reading, Pseudoword Decoding, Letter Recognition, Listening Comprehension, Phonological Awareness (Phonemes, Rimes, Syllables, Composite), Reading Comprehension, Vocabulary (Receptive, Expressive, Word Opposites, Composite), Passage Fluency.
Time: (90–95) minutes.
c) GRADE 2.
Population: Grade 2.
Scores, 23: Brief Vocabulary (Receptive, Expressive, Composite), Reading Comprehension, Listening Comprehension, Phonological Awareness (Phonemes, Rimes, Syllables, Comprehension), Word Reading, Pseudoword Decoding, Rapid Automatic Naming (Letters, Words, Digits, Words and Digits, Composite), Full Vocabulary (Brief Vocabulary Composite, Synonyms, Word Definitions, Multiple Meanings, Composite), Passage Fluency (Narrative, Informational).
Time: (110) minutes.
d) GRADE 3.
Population: Grade 3.
Scores, 23: Same as Grade 2.
Time: (110) minutes.

Cross References: For reviews by Marie Miller-Whitehead and Steven R. Shaw, see 16:82.

[936]

Early Reading Success Indicator.

Purpose: "To identify children at risk for developing reading difficulties."
Population: Ages 5–10.
Publication Date: 2004.
Acronym: ERSI.
Scores: RAN-Letters, Phonological Processing, Speeded Naming, Word Reading, Pseudoword Decoding.
Administration: Individual.
Price Data, 2007: $69 per complete kit including manual (89 pages), stimulus book, 25 record forms, Pseudoword Decoding Card, and Word Reading Card; $30 for 25 record forms.
Time: (20–25) minutes.
Comments: A brief battery of cognitive tests composed of subtests selected from various products from this publisher: Process Assessment of the Learner: Test Battery for Reading and Writing (16:199), NEPSY: A Developmental Neuropsychological Assessment (T6:1696), and Wechsler Individual Achievement Test—Second Edition (15:275).
Author: PsychCorp.
Publisher: Pearson.
Cross References: For reviews by Jennifer N. Mahdavi and Diane J. Sawyer, see 17:63.

[937]

Early School Inventory.

Population: Ages 5–7.
Publication Dates: 1986–1987.
Acronym: ESI.
Price Data: Available from publisher.
Time: Administration time not reported.
Authors: Joanne R. Nurss and Mary E. McGauvran.
Publisher: Pearson.

a) EARLY SCHOOL INVENTORY–DEVELOP-MENTAL.
Purpose: "Provides a systematic method for gathering information about a child's development for use in planning effective instruction."
Acronym: ESI-D.
Scores, 4: Physical Development, Language Development, Cognitive Development, Social-Emotional Development.
Administration: Group.
b) EARLY SCHOOL INVENTORY–PRELIT-ERACY.
Purpose: Provides information about "a child's progress in acquiring the preliteracy skills needed when learning to read and write."
Acronym: ESI-P.

Scores, 3: Print Concepts, Writing Concepts, Story Structure.
Administration: Individual.
Cross References: For reviews by Damon Krug and Brandon Davis and by Carol Westby, see 13:110.

[938]

Early School Personality Questionnaire.

Purpose: Measures personality dimensions of young children; useful in the treatment of emotional and conduct problems in schools and clinical settings.
Population: Ages 6–8
Publication Date: 1966.
Acronym: ESPQ.
Scores, 17: 13 Primary Factors (Warmth, Abstract Thinking, Emotional Stability, Excitability, Dominance, Enthusiasm, Conformity, Boldness, Sensitivity, Withdrawal, Shrewdness, Apprehension, Tension), 4 Second-Order Factors (Extraversion, Anxiety, Tough Poise, Independence).
Administration: Group or individual.
Price Data: Available from publisher.
Time: (30–50) minutes for each of two parts (untimed).
Authors: Richard W. Coan and Raymond B. Cattell.
Publisher: Institute for Personality and Ability Testing, Inc. (IPAT)
Cross References: See T4:843 (3 references and T3:772 (4 references); for reviews by Jacob O. Sines and Robert L. Thorndike, see 8:540 (8 references); see also T2:1163 (3 references); for a review by Lovick C. Miller, see 7:71 (8 references); see also P:66 (7 references).

[939]

Early Screening Inventory–Revised [2008 Edition].

Purpose: Designed to identify children at risk for possible school failure.
Population: Ages 3-0 to 5-11.
Publication Dates: 1976–2008.
Acronym: ESI-R.
Scores, 3: Visual-Motor/Adaptive, Language and Cognition, Gross Motor.
Administration: Individual.
Levels, 2: Preschool (3 to 4 1/2 years old), Kindergarten (4 1/2 to 6 years old).
Price Data: Available from publisher.
Foreign Language Edition: Spanish versions available for score sheets, Parent Questionnaire, and the administration and scoring chapter of the manual.
Time: (15–20) minutes.
Comments: Originally introduced as the Eliot-Pearson Screening Inventory.
Authors: Samuel J. Meisels, Dorothea B. Marsden, Martha Stone Wiske, and Laura W. Henderson.
Publisher: Pearson.

Cross References: For reviews by Ernest Kimmel and Kathleen D. Paget of the 1997 edition, see 14:135; see also T5:889 (1 reference); for reviews by Denise M. Dezolt and Kevin Menefee of an earlier edition, see 11:122 (1 reference).

[940]

Early Screening Profiles.

Purpose: A comprehensive, brief, multidimensional screening instrument for children.
Population: Ages 2-0 to 6-11.
Publication Date: 1990.
Acronym: ESP.
Scores: 3 Profile Scores: Cognitive/Language, Motor, Self-Help/Social (Parent or Teacher), and 4 Survey Scores: Articulation, Home, Behavior, Health History.
Administration: Individual.
Price Data, 2006: $313.99 per complete kit including manual (297 pages), Motor administration manual (16 pages), test easel, 25 test records, 25 Self-Help/Social Profile Questionnaires, 25 Score Summaries, Sample Home/Health History Survey, tape measure, beads; $33.99 per 25 test records; $18.99 per 25 Self-Help/ Social Profile questionnaires; $18.99 per 25 Home/Health History surveys; $12.99 per 25 score summaries; $67.99 per manual; $99.99 per ESP Training Video.
Time: (15–40) minutes.
Comments: Two levels of scoring: Level I scores are 6 "screening indexes" and 3 descriptive categories; Level II scores are standard scores, percentile ranks, normal curve equivalents (NCEs), stanines, and age equivalents; ecological assessment with ratings by parents and teachers as well as direct assessment of the child; previously listed as AGS Early Screening Profiles.
Authors: Patti L. Harrison (coordinating author and manual author), Alan S. Kaufman (Cognitive/Language Profile), Nadeen L. Kaufman (Cognitive/Language Profile), Robert H. Bruininks (Motor Profile), John Rynders (Motor Profile), Steven Ilmer (Motor Profile), Sara S. Sparrow (Self-Help/Social Profile), and Domenic V. Cicchetti (Self-Help/Social Profile).
Publisher: Pearson.
Cross References: See T5:124 (1 reference); for reviews by David W. Barnett and Cathy Telzrow, see 12:24 (1 reference); see also T4:134 (2 references).

[941]

Early Screening Project.

Purpose: "Allows for the cost-effective screening of problem behaviors to aid in the early remediation of behavior disorders."
Population: Ages 3–6.
Publication Date: 1995.
Acronym: ESP.
Scores, 4: Critical Events Index, Aggressive Behavior Scale [Externalizers], Social Interaction Scale [Internal-

izers], Combined Frequency Index Adaptive Behavior, Combined Frequency Index Maladaptive Behavior.
Administration: Individual and group.
Price Data, 2002: $95 per complete kit including manual (103 pages), instrument packet, social observation training video, and a stopwatch.
Time: (60) minutes total/group.
Authors: Hill M. Walker, Herbert H. Severson, and Edward G. Feil.
Publisher: Sopris West.
Cross References: For a review by J. Jeffrey Grill, see 14:136.

[942]

Early Speech Perception Test.

Purpose: "Developed to obtain increasingly more accurate information about speech discrimination skills as the profoundly hearing-impaired child's verbal abilities develop."
Population: Ages 3–6, ages 6–12.
Publication Date: 1990.
Acronym: ESP.
Administration: Individual.
Price Data, 2011: $220 per ESP kit including manual (32 pages), standard and low verbal scoring forms, box of toys, full-color picture cards, and CD; $15 per audio CD.
Time: (15–20) minutes.
Comments: Information regarding specialized hardware and software equipment necessary for administering the computerized version of the ESP test battery can be found in the test manual.
Authors: Jean S. Moog and Ann E. Geers.
Publisher: Central Institute for the Deaf (CID).
   a) ESP STANDARD VERSION.
   Population: Ages 6–15.
   Scores, 4: Pattern Perception, Spondee Identification, Monosyllable Identification, Total.
   Price Data: $12 per 25 standard version scoring forms.
   b) ESP LOW-VERBAL VERSION.
   Population: Ages 3–6.
   Scores, 4: Pattern Perception Test, Word Identification Test (Spondee Identification, Monosyllable Identification), Total.
   Price Data: $12 per 25 low-verbal version scoring forms.
Cross References: See T5:891 (1 reference); for a review by Arlene E. Carney, see 12:128.

[943]

Early Years Easy Screen.

Purpose: Constructed to screen for strengths and weaknesses in the areas of physical and cognitive development.
Population: Ages 4–5.
Publication Date: 1991.
Acronym: EYES.

Scores, 6: Level of Performance in 6 areas: Pencil Coordination, Active Body, Number, Oral Language, Visual Reading, Auditory Reading.
Administration: Group.
Price Data: Available from publisher.
Time: (160–194) minutes over several sessions.
Comments: Other test materials (e.g., bean bag, beads) must be supplied by examiner.
Authors: Joan Clerehugh, Kim Hart, Rosalind Pither, Kay Rider, and Kate Turner.
Publisher: GL Assessment [England].
Cross References: For a review by Martin J. Wiese, see 12:129.

[944]

Earning Capacity Assessment Form-Second Edition.
Purpose: Designed to "facilitate the systematic analysis and appraisal of loss of earning capacity."
Population: Ages 0 to 99.
Publication Date: 2010.
Acronym: ECAF-2.
Scores: 1 rating: Impairment to Earning Capacity.
Administration: Individual.
Price Data, 2010: $90 per complete kit, including manual (46 pages) and 25 rating forms; $35 per 25 rating forms; $60 per manual.
Time: [5-10] minutes.
Author: Michael Shahnasarian.
Publisher: Psychological Assessment Resources.

[945]

Eating Disorder Inventory-3.
Purpose: Designed to "provide a standardized clinical evaluation of symptomatology associated with eating disorders."
Population: Females ages 13 to 53 years.
Publication Dates: 1984–2004.
Acronym: EDI-3.
Administration: Group.
Price Data, 2007: $246 per introductory kit including professional manual (2004, 223 pages), referral form manual (2004, 36 pages), 25 item booklets, 25 answer sheets, 25 percentile/T-score profile forms, 25 symptom checklists, and 25 referral forms; $260 per CD-ROM based scoring program.
Author: David M. Garner.
Publisher: Psychological Assessment Resources, Inc.
  a) EATING DISORDER INVENTORY-3.
  Population: Females ages 13 to 53 years.
  Scores, 21: 6 composite scores (Eating Disorder Risk Composite, Ineffectiveness Composite, Interpersonal Problems Composite, Affective Problems Composite, Overcontrol Composite, General Psychological Maladjustment Composite), 12 primary scores (Drive for Thinness, Bulimia, Body Dissat-

isfaction, Low Self-Esteem, Personal Alienation, Interpersonal Insecurity, Interpersonal Alienation, Interoceptive Deficits, Emotional Dysregulation, Perfectionism, Asceticism, Maturity Fears), 3 response style indicators (Inconsistency, Infrequency, Negative Impression).
  Time: (20) minutes.
  Comments: Full battery.
  b) EATING DISORDER INVENTORY-3 REFERRAL FORM.
  Population: Adolescents and adults ages 13 and older.
  Acronym: EDI-3 RF.
  Scores, 4: Drive for Thinness, Bulimia, Body Dissatisfaction, BMI.
  Time: (10) minutes.
  Comments: Abbreviated referral form of Eating Disorder Inventory-3 "used to identify individuals who are at risk for eating disorders."
  c) EATING DISORDER INVENTORY-3 SYMPTOM CHECKLIST.
  Population: Adolescents and adults.
  Acronym: EDI-3 SC.
  Scores: Frequency ratings.
  Time: (10) minutes.
  Comments: Symptom checklist used as an aid in the diagnosis of eating disorders.
Cross References: For reviews by Jeffrey A. Atlas and Ashraf Kagee, see 17:64; see also T5:893 (54 references); for reviews by Phillip Ash and Steven Schinke of an earlier edition, see 12:130 (38 references); see also T4:847 (38 references); for a review by Cabrini S. Swassing of an earlier edition, see 10:100 (16 references).

[946]

Eating Inventory.
Purpose: To assess "three dimensions of eating behavior found to be important in recognizing and treating eating-related disorders: cognitive control of eating, disinhibition, and hunger."
Population: Ages 17 and older.
Publication Dates: 1983–1988.
Scores, 3: Cognitive Restraint of Eating, Disinhibition, Hunger.
Administration: Group or individual.
Price Data, 2002: $160 per complete kit including 25 questionnaires, 25 answer sheets, and manual (1988, 37 pages); $46 per 25 questionnaires; $67 per 25 answer sheets; $67 per manual.
Time: (15–20) minutes.
Authors: Albert J. Stunkard and Samuel Messick.
Publisher: Pearson.
Cross References: For reviews by Lisa Bloom and Sandra D. Haynes, see 13:111 (3 references); see also T4:848 (1 reference).

[947]

Eckstein Audiometers.

Purpose: For the measurement and evaluation of hearing losses.
Population: All ages.
Publication Dates: 1961–1973.
Subtests: 7 models (solid state).
Administration: Individual.
Price Data: Available from publisher.
Time: Administration time not reported.
Author: Eckstein Bros., Inc.
Publisher: Eckstein Bros., Inc.

a) EB-47 MICROPROCESSOR SCREENING AUDIOMETER.
Publication Date: 1998.
Comments: For screening in schools and medical offices; 4 frequencies; 4 hearing classifications.
b) MINIATURE AUDIOMETER MODEL 60.
Publication Date: 1961.
Comments: For air conduction screening and threshold testing in schools and medical offices; 7 frequencies.
c) AUDIOMETER MODEL 350-I.
Publication Dates: 1964–1972.
Comments: Air conduction threshold testing in industry.
d) FULL RANGE PORTABLE AUDIOMETERS.
Publication Dates: 1970–1972.
Comments: 2 models (may be AC operated).
  1) *Model 390.*
  Comments: For pure tone air conducting testing.
  2) *Model 390 MB.*
  Comments: Diagnostic Model for pure tone air and bone conducting testing.
e) DIAGNOSTIC AUDIOMETER, MODEL 400.
Publication Date: 1969.
Comments: Air and bone conduction; calibrated speech and pure tone.
f) EB-23-NOISESTIK II - PEDIATRIC HEARING SCREENER.
  Publication Date: 1998.
  Comments: A hearing screener for testing of infants, toddlers, and older persons not able to respond manually to auditory stimulus.

[948]

Edinburgh Picture Test.

Purpose: To assess reasoning ability in young children.
Population: Ages 6-6 to 8-3.
Publication Dates: 1985–1991.
Scores, 6: Doesn't Belong, Classification, Reversed Similarities, Analogies, Sequences, Total.
Administration: Group.
Price Data, 2002: £8.99 per specimen set; £12.99 per 20 test booklets; £6.99 per manual (1988, 15 pages).
Time: (30–60) minutes.
Author: Godfrey Thomson Unit, University of Edinburgh.

Publisher: Hodder & Stoughton Educational [England].
Cross References: For reviews by Carole M. Krauthamer and Bruce G. Rogers, see 12:133.

[949]

Edinburgh Reading Tests.

Purpose: To assess pupil progress in reading.
Population: Ages 7-0 to 9-0, 8-6 to 10-6, 10-0 to 12-6, 12-0 to 16-6.
Publication Dates: 1972–2002.
Administration: Group.
Levels, 4: Stages 1, 2, 3, 4.
Publisher: Hodder & Stoughton Educational [England].

a) STAGE 1 [THIRD EDITION].
Population: Ages 7-0 to 9-0.
Publication Dates: 1977–2002.
Scores, 5: Vocabulary, Syntax, Sequences, Comprehension, Total.
Forms, 2: A, B.
Price Data, 2002: £9.99 per 10 copies of test (specify Form A or Form B); £14.99 per manual; £16.99 per specimen set.
Time: (30–55) minutes.
Author: Educational Assessment Unit, University of Edinburgh.
b) STAGE 2 [FOURTH EDITION].
Population: Ages 8-6 to 10-6.
Publication Dates: 1972–2002.
Scores, 5: Vocabulary, Comprehension of Sequences, Use of Context, Comprehension of Essential Ideas, Total.
Price Data: £9.99 per 10 copies of test booklet; £14.99 per manual; £15.99 per specimen set; £39.99 per scorer/profiler CD-ROM.
Time: (40) minutes for part I; (35) minutes for part II.
Author: Educational Assessment Unit, University of Edinburgh
c) STAGE 3 [FOURTH EDITION].
Population: Ages 10-0 to 12-6.
Publication Dates: 1973–2002.
Scores, 5: Reading for facts and Comprehension of Sequences, Main Ideas, Comprehension of Points of View, Vocabulary, Total.
Price Data: £9.99 per 10 test booklets; £14.99 per manual; £15.99 per specimen set; £39.99 per scorer/profiler CD-ROM.
Time: (40) minutes for part I; (35) minutes for part II.
Author: Educational Assessment Unit, University of Edinburgh.
d) STAGE 4 [THIRD EDITION].
Population: Ages 11-7 to 16+.
Publication Dates: 1977–2002.

Scores, 6: Skimming, Vocabulary, Reading for Facts, Points of View, Comprehension, Total.

Price Data: £10.99 per 10 test booklets; £15.99 per manual; £16.99 per specimen set; £39.99 per scorer/profiler CD-ROM.

Time: 60(70) minutes.

Author: Educational Assessment Unit, University of Edinburgh.

e) SHORTENED EDINBURGH READING TEST.

Purpose: Designed as a survey and screening instrument of written language attainment.

Population: Ages 10-0 to 11-6.

Scores, 3: Vocabulary, Syntax and Sequence, Comprehension.

Time: (40) minutes.

Price Data: £15.99 per 20 copies of test; £14.99 per manual; £15.99 per specimen set.

Comments: Questions selected from items in the full Edinburgh Reading Tests.

Authors: Godfrey Thomson Unit for Educational Research, Moray House Institute of Education, and the Child Health and Education Study, University of Bristol.

Cross References: See T5:901 (2 references) and T4:855 (1 reference); for reviews by Nancy L. Roser and Byron H. Van Roekel of previous editions, see 9:374 (1 reference); see T3:775 (2 references); for reviews by Douglas A. Pidgeon and Earl F. Rankin of the first editions of Stages 2 and 3, see 8:724.

[950]

Educational Development Series (2000 Edition).

Purpose: A battery of ability and achievement tests and questions on interests and plans.

Population: Grades K-12.

Publication Dates: 1963-2000.

Acronym: EDS.

Administration: Group.

Price Data: See www.ststesting.com for up-to-date prices.

Authors: O. F. Anderhalter, R. H. Bauernfeind, V. M. Cashew, Mary E. Greig, Walter M. Lifton, George Mallinson, Jacqueline Mallinson, Joseph F. Papenfuss, and Neil Vail.

Publisher: Scholastic Testing Service, Inc.

a) LEVEL 10G.

Population: Grade K.

Publication Date: 1999.

Scores, 8: Cognitive Skills (Verbal, Nonverbal, Total), Basic Skills (Reading, Language, Mathematics, Total), Battery Average.

Time: (190) minutes in 5 sessions.

b) LEVEL 11G.

Population: Grade 1.

Publication Date: 1999.

Scores, 11: Cognitive Skills (Verbal, Quantitative, Total), Basic Skills (Reading, Language, Mathematics, Total), Reference Skills, Science, Social Studies, Battery Average.

Time: (280-300) minutes in 5 sessions.

c) LEVEL 12G.

Population: Grade 2.

Publication Date: 1999.

Scores, 11: Cognitive Skills (Verbal, Quantitative, Total), Basic Skills (Reading, Language Arts, Mathematics, Total), Reference Skills, Science, Social Studies, Battery Average.

Time: (310 minutes in 5 sessions.

d) LEVEL 13G.

Population: Grade 3.

Publication Date: 1999.

Scores, 11: Same as for *c* above.

Time: (360) minutes in 5 sessions.

e) LEVEL 14G.

Population: Grade 4.

Publication Date: 1999.

Scores, 14: Cognitive Skills (Verbal, Quantitative, Total), Basic Skills (Reading, Language Arts, Mathematics, Total), Reference Skills, Science, Social Studies, Battery Average, Career Interests, School Plans, School Interests.

Time: (400) minutes in 3 sessions.

f) LEVEL 15G.

Population: Grade 5.

Publication Date: 1999.

Scores, 14: Same as for *e* above.

Time: (400) minutes in 3 sessions.

g) LEVEL 15H.

Population: Grade 6.

Publication Date: 1999.

Scores, 14: Same as for *e* above.

Time: (400) minutes in 3 sessions.

h) LEVEL 16H.

Population: Grade 7.

Publication Date: 1999.

Scores, 14: Same as for *e* above.

Time: (400) minutes in 3 sessions.

i) LEVEL 16H.

Population: Grade 8.

Publication Date: 1999.

Scores, 14: Same as for *e* above.

Time: (400) minutes in 3 sessions.

j) LEVEL 17J.

Population: Grade 9.

Publication Date: 2010.

Scores, 14: Same as for *e* above.

Time: (335) minutes in 3 sessions.

k) LEVEL 17K.

Population: Grade 9.

Publication Date: 2010.

Details: Same as for *j* above.

l) LEVEL 18J.

Population: Grade 10.

Publication Date: 2010.
Details: Same as for *j* above.
m) LEVEL 18H.
Population: Grade 11/12.
Publication Date: 1999.
Details: Same as for *j* above.
Time: (390) minutes in 3 sessions.
Cross References: See T4:858 (2 references); for a review by Esther E. Diamond of an earlier edition, see 9:376; see also T3:2325 (1 reference); for reviews by Samuel T. Mayo and William A. Mehrens of forms copyrighted 1976 and earlier see 8:27; see also T2:33 (1 reference); for a review by Robert D. North of forms copyrighted 1968 and earlier see 7:22.

[951]

Educational Interest Inventory.

Purpose: Designed to identify personal preference for different college educational programs.
Population: Prospective college students.
Publication Date: 1989.
Acronym: EII.
Scores: 47 scales: Agriculture (Agribusiness/Agricultural Production, Agricultural Sciences, Renewable Natural Resources), Architecture and Environmental Design, Area/Ethnic Studies, Business/Management (Accounting and Finance, Administration and Management, Human Resources Management, Marketing/Distribution), Communications, Computer and Information Sciences, Education (Pre-Elementary and Elementary, Secondary and Post-Secondary, Special Education, Physical Education, Industrial Arts), Engineering (Chemical, Civil, Electrical/Electronic, Mechanical), Foreign Languages, Health Sciences (General Medicine, Dentistry, Nursing, Pharmacy, Medical Laboratory), Home Economics, Law, Letters, Library and Archival Sciences, Life Sciences/General Biology, Mathematics, Philosophy and Religion, Theology, Physical Sciences (Chemistry, Geological Sciences, Physics), Psychology, Protective Services, Public Affairs/Social Work, Social Sciences (Economics, History, Political Sciences/Government, Sociology), Visual and Performing Arts (Fine Arts, Drama, Music).
Administration: Group.
Price Data: Price information available from publisher for reusable test booklet, answer sheets and profile guides, manual (43 pages), and for specimen set of all Educational Interest Inventory and Career Guidance Inventory components.
Time: [45–60] minutes.
Comments: Self-administered; self-scored; manual is for the EII and the Career Guidance Inventory (437).
Author: James E. Oliver.
Publisher: Wintergreen/Orchard House, Inc.
Cross References: For reviews by Lois T. Strauss and David E. Kapel and by Jim Fortune and Javaid Kaiser, see 11:123.

[952]

Educational Process Questionnaire.

Purpose: "To aid teachers in their own self-development by providing objective information about the processes used in the teacher's own actual classroom."
Population: Grades 4–12.
Publication Dates: 1973–1987.
Acronym: EPQ.
Scores: 5 scale scores: Reinforcement of Self-Concept, Academic Learning Time, Feedback, Expectations, Development of Multiple Talents.
Administration: Group.
Price Data: Available from publisher.
Time: 35(45) minutes.
Comments: Ratings by students.
Author: Institute for Behavioral Research in Creativity.
Publisher: Institute for Behavioral Research in Creativity.
Cross References: For a review by William L. Curlette, see 11:125.

[953]

Edwards Personal Preference Schedule.

Purpose: Developed to measure "a number of relatively independent normal personality variables."
Population: College and adults.
Publication Dates: 1953–1959.
Acronym: EPPS.
Scores, 16: Achievement, Deference, Order, Exhibition, Autonomy, Affiliation, Intraception, Succorance, Dominance, Abasement, Nurturance, Change, Endurance, Heterosexuality, Aggression, Consistency.
Administration: Group or individual.
Price Data, 2002: $91 per 25 schedule booklets; $50 per 50 hand-scorable answer documents; $65 per 50 NCS machine-scorable answer documents; $65 per 50 IBM answer documents; $47 per scoring template for hand-scorable answer documents including manual (1959, 27 pages); $86.50 per keys for IBM answer documents including manual; $42 per manual; $50 per examination kit.
Time: (40–50) minutes.
Author: Allen L. Edwards.
Publisher: Pearson.
Cross References: See T5:908 (12 references), T4:862 (44 references), 9:378 (16 references), T3:780 (70 references), 8:542 (334 references), and T2:1164 (226 references); for reviews by Alfred B. Heilbrun, Jr., and Michael G. McKee, see 7:72 (391 references); see also P:67 (363 references); for reviews by John A. Radcliffe and Lawrence J. Stricker and an excerpted review by Edward S. Bordin, see 6:87 (284 references); for reviews by Frank Barron, Ake Bjerstedt, and Donald W. Fiske and excerpted reviews by John W. Gustad and Laurance F. Shaffer, see 5:47 (50 references).

[954]

The Egan Bus Puzzle Test.

Purpose: "Designed to assess language development and some performance skills of young children."
Population: 20 months to 4 years.
Publication Date: No date on test materials.
Scores, 6: Expressive Verbal Labels, Comprehension (Verbal Labels, Recognition of Shape, Orientation of Piece to Recess), Comprehension of Sentences, Expressive Language.
Administration: Individual.
Price Data, 2001: £89.50 per complete set including manual (no date, 36 pages), board, and 25 forms; £73.50 per board and manual; £22.50 per 25 forms.
Time: (7-8) minutes.
Authors: Dorothy F. Egan and Rosemary Brown.
Publisher: The Test Agency Limited [England] [No reply from publisher; status unknown].
Cross References: For a review by Sheldon L. Stick, see 10:105.

[955]

Ego Function Assessment.

Purpose: Designed as a "mental status examination" to assess ego function.
Population: Adults.
Publication Date: 1989.
Acronym: EFA.
Scores, 12: Reality Testing, Judgment, Sense of Reality, Regulation and Control of Drives, Object Relations, Thought Processes, Adaptive Regression in the Service of the Ego, Defensive Functions, Stimulus Barrier, Autonomous Functions, Synthetic Functions, Mastery-Competence.
Administration: Individual.
Price Data, 2010: $13 per manual (64 pages); $13.50 per 10 blanks.
Time: Administration time not reported.
Author: Leopold Bellak.
Publisher: C.P.S., Inc.
Cross References: For reviews by Beth Doll and Samuel Juni, see 13:112.

[956]

The Ego Strength Q-Sort Test.

Purpose: Designed to "assess the general strength of one's ego."
Population: Grades 9–16 and adults.
Publication Dates: 1956–1958.
Acronym: ESQST.
Scores, 6: Ego-Status, Social Status, Goal Setting and Striving, Good Mental Health, Physical Status, Total.
Administration: Individual or group.
Price Data: Available from publisher.
Time: (50–90) minutes.
Author: Russell N. Cassel.
Publisher: Psychometric Affiliates.

Cross References: See T5:913 (1 reference) and T2:1167 (1 reference); for reviews by Allen L. Edwards and Harrison G. Gough, see 6:88 (3 references).

[957]

Eidetic Parents Test.

Purpose: To provide stimuli meant to arouse eidetic images of parents to aid in exploring emotional attachments that affect current functioning.
Population: Clinical patients and marriage and family counselees.
Publication Date: 1972.
Acronym: EPT.
Scores: No scores; verbal reporting by individuals of subjective visual images (called eidetics) of increasingly surrealistic situations.
Administration: Individual.
Price Data: Available from publisher.
Time: (60) minutes for brief report; "many hours" for comprehensive report.
Author: Akhter Ahsen.
Publisher: Brandon House, Inc. [No reply from publisher; status unknown].
Cross References: For additional information and a review by Charles Warnath and excerpted reviews by Gregory Sarmousakis, Barry Bricklin, and Manas Raychaudhuri, see 8:546 (8 references).

[958]

801 Public Safety Telecommunicator First-Line Supervisor Test.

Purpose: Designed "to assist Emergency Communications Centers … in promoting qualified candidates to the supervisory level."
Population: Candidates for promotion to the public safety telecommunicator first-line supervisor position.
Publication Dates: 2002-2006.
Scores: 6 knowledge areas: Communication Center Operation, Concepts of Supervision, Concepts of Evaluating Subordinate Performance, Concepts of Training, Concepts of Writing and Reviewing Reports and Paperwork, Concepts of Administration.
Administration: Individual or group.
Price Data: Available from publisher.
Time: 150 minutes.
Comments: A reading list is provided to help candidates prepare for the test.
Author: International Public Management Association for Human Resources.
Publisher: International Public Management Association for Human Resources (IPMA-HR).

[959]

Einstein Assessment of School-Related Skills.

Purpose: "To identify children who are at risk for, or are experiencing, learning difficulties; and who therefore should be referred for a comprehensive evaluation."

Population: Grades K–5.
Publication Date: 1988.
Administration: Individual.
Levels, 6: Kindergarten, First Grade, Second Grade, Third Grade, Fourth Grade, Fifth Grade.
Price Data: Available from publisher.
Time: (10) minutes.
Authors: Ruth L. Gottesman and Frances M. Cerullo.
Publisher: Slosson Educational Publications, Inc.
  a) KINDERGARTEN LEVEL.
  Scores, 5: Language/Cognition, Letter Recognition, Auditory Memory, Arithmetic, Visual-Motor Integration.
  b) FIRST GRADE LEVEL.
  Scores, 7: Language/Cognition, Word Recognition, Oral Reading, Reading Comprehension, Auditory Memory, Arithmetic, Visual-Motor Integration.
  c) SECOND GRADE LEVEL.
  Scores: Same as *b* above.
  d) THIRD GRADE LEVEL.
  Scores: Same as *b* above.
  e) FOURTH GRADE LEVEL.
  Scores: Same as *b* above.
  f) FIFTH GRADE LEVEL.
  Scores: Same as *b* above.
Cross References: See T5:916 (1 reference) and T4:871 (1 reference); for a review by Gloria A. Galvin, see 11:126 (1 reference).

[960]

Ekwall/Shanker Reading Inventory–Third Edition.

Purpose: "Designed to assess the full range of students' reading abilities."
Population: Grades 1–9.
Publication Dates: 1979–1993.
Acronym: ESRI.
Administration: Individual.
Price Data: Available from publisher.
Authors: Eldon E. Ekwall and James L. Shanker.
Publisher: Pearson Education.
  a) GRADED WORD LIST.
  Purpose: "To obtain a quick estimate of the student's independent, instructional, and frustration reading levels."
  Acronym: GWL.
  Scores, 3: Independent Reading Level, Instructional Reading Level, Frustration Level.
  Time: (5–10) minutes.
  b) ORAL AND SILENT READING.
  Purpose: To obtain an assessment of the student's independent, instructional, and frustration reading levels in oral and silent reading.
  Scores, 3: 3 scores (Independent Reading Level, Instructional Reading Level, Frustration Level) in each of two areas (Oral, Silent Reading).
  Time: (10–30) minutes.

  c) LISTENING COMPREHENSION.
  Purpose: "To obtain the level at which a student can understand material when it is read to him or her."
  Score: Listening Comprehension Level.
  Time: (5–10) minutes.
  d) THE BASIC SIGHT WORDS AND PHRASES TEST.
  Purpose: To determine basic sight words and basic sight word phrases that can be recognized and pronounced instantly by the student.
  Scores, 2: Basic Sight Words, Basic Sight Phrases.
  Time: (5–12) minutes.
  e) LETTER KNOWLEDGE.
  Purpose: "To determine if the student can associate the letter symbols with the letter names."
  Scores, 2: Letters (Auditory), Letters (Visual).
  Time: Administration time not reported.
  f) PHONICS.
  Purpose: "To determine if the student has mastered letter-sound (phonics)."
  Scores, 9: Initial Consonants, Initial Blends and Digraphs, Ending Sounds, Vowels, Phonograms, Blending, Substitution, Vowel Pronunciation, Application in Context.
  Time: Administration time not reported.
  g) STRUCTURAL ANALYSIS.
  Purpose: "To determine if the student can use structural analysis skills to aid in decoding unknown words."
  Scores, 10: Hearing Word Parts, Inflectional Endings, Prefixes, Suffixes, Compound Words, Affixes, Syllabication, Application in Context (Part I, Part II, Total).
  Time: Administration time not reported.
  h) KNOWLEDGE OF CONTRACTIONS TEST.
  Purpose: "To determine if the student has knowledge of contractions."
  Scores, 3: Number of Words Pronounced, Number of Words Known, Total.
  Time: Administration time not reported.
  i) EL PASO PHONICS SURVEY.
  Purpose: "To determine if the student has the ability to pronounce and blend 90 phonic elements."
  Scores, 4: Initial Consonant Sounds, Ending Consonant, Initial Consonant Clusters, Vowels, Vowel Teams, and Special Letter Combinations.
  Time: Administration time not reported.
  j) QUICK SURVEY WORD LIST.
  Purpose: "To determine quickly if the student has mastered phonics and structural analysis."
  Score: Comments.
  Time: Administration time not reported.
  k) READING INTEREST SURVEY.
  Purpose: "To assess the student's attitude toward reading and school, areas of reading interest, reading experiences, and conditions affecting reading in the home."
  Score: Comments.
  Time: Administration time not reported.

Cross References: For reviews by Koressa Kutsick Malcolm and by Blaine R. Worthen and Richard R. Sudweeks, see 13:113 (2 references); see also T4:872 (3 references); for reviews by Lynn S. Fuchs and Mary Beth Marr of an earlier edition, see 9:380.

[961]

ElecTest (Form AR-C & Form B).

Purpose: For selecting electrical repair and maintenance candidates.

Population: Applicants and incumbents for jobs requiring practical electrical knowledge and skills.

Publication Dates: 1997-2010.

Scores, 10: Motors, Digital & Analog, Electronics, Schematics & Print Reading and Control Circuits, Basic AC/DC Theory and Electrical Maintenance, Computers & PLC and Test Instruments, Power Supplies, Power Distribution and Construction & Installation, Mechanical and Hand & Power Tools, Total.

Administration: Group.

Forms, 2: AR-C, B.

Price Data, 2011: $22 per consumable self-scoring test booklet or online test administration (minimum order of 20); $24.95 per manual (2008, 27 pages).

Foreign Language Edition: Available in Spanish.

Time: (60-70) minutes.

Comments: Self-scoring instrument; online version available; Form B is an alternate equivalent of Form A.

Author: Roland T. Ramsay.

Publisher: Ramsay Corporation.

Cross References: For a review by Eugene P. Sheehan of an earlier edition, see 18:47.

[962]

Electrical and Electronics Test.

Purpose: "Examines knowledge of fundamental laws, symbols and definitions and requires the application of them to familiar equipment."

Population: Students in electrical or electronics programs ages 15 and over.

Publication Date: No date on test materials.

Scores: Total score only.

Administration: Group.

Price Data, 2001: £6.50 per test booklet; £8.50 per answer key; £12.50 per manual; £27 per specimen set.

Time: (15-30) minutes.

Author: The Test Agency Ltd.

Publisher: The Test Agency Limited [England] [No reply from publisher; status unknown].

[963]

Electrical Aptitude Test (Form EA2-C).

Purpose: For evaluating electrical aptitude skills.

Population: Applicants for jobs that require the ability to learn electrical skills.

Publication Dates: 2003–2010.

Scores: Total score only for 6 areas: Mathematics, Electrical Concepts, Electrical Schematics, Process Flow, Signal Flow, Electrical Sequences.

Administration: Group.

Price Data, 2011: $22 per consumable self-scoring test booklet or online test administration (minimum order of 20); $24.95 per manual (2008, 22 pages).

Foreign Language Edition: Available in Spanish.

Time: (18) minutes.

Comments: Self-scoring instrument; available for online test administration.

Author: Roland T. Ramsay.

Publisher: Ramsay Corporation.

Cross References: For a review by Martin W. Anderson, see 17:65.

[964]

Electrical Maintenance Trainee–Form UKE-1RC.

Purpose: Designed for selecting or evaluating electrical trainees with one year of training or experience.

Population: Applicants for jobs requiring electrical knowledge and skills.

Publication Dates: 1991-2010.

Scores, 12: Motors, Digital and Analog Electronics, Schematics and Electrical Print Reading, Control, Power Supplies, Basic AC/DC Theory, Construction Installation and Distribution, Test Instruments, Mechanical/Equipment Operation/Hand and Power Tools, Computers and PLC, Electrical Maintenance, Total.

Administration: Group.

Price Data, 2011: $22 per consumable self-scoring test booklet or online test administration (20 minimum order); $24.95 per manual (2008, 24 pages).

Time: (60-70) minutes.

Comments: Self-scoring instrument; available for online test administration.

Author: Roland T. Ramsay.

Publisher: Ramsay Corporation.

Cross References: For a review by David C. Roberts of an earlier edition, see 13:114.

[965]

Electrical Sophistication Test.

Purpose: "Intended to discriminate between persons with substantial knowledges of electricity and those with no, little, and merely chance knowledge."

Population: Job applicants.

Publication Dates: 1963–1965.

Scores: Total score only.

Administration: Group.

Price Data: Available from publisher.

Time: (5–10) minutes.

Author: Stanley G. Ciesla.

Publisher: Psychometric Affiliates.

Cross References: For a review by Charles F. Ward, see 7:1125.

[966]
Electromechanical Vocational Assessment Manuals.

Purpose: Designed to evaluate a variety of work abilities (tasks) of blind or visually impaired persons.
Population: Blind or visually impaired adults.
Publication Date: 1983.
Scores, 6: Fine Finger Dexterity Work Task Unit, Foot Operated Hinged Box Work Task Unit, Hinged Box Work Task Unit, Index Card Work Task Unit, Multifunctional Work Task Unit, Revolving Assembly Table Work Task Unit.
Administration: Individual.
Price Data: Available from publisher.
Time: 50(60) minutes for any one task unit.
Comments: Special administration equipment required.
Author: Rehabilitation Research and Training Center on Blindness and Low Vision.
Publisher: Rehabilitation Research and Training Center on Blindness and Low Vision.
Cross References: For reviews by John Geisler and Robert Johnson, see 13:115.

[967]
Electron Test (Form HR-C).

Purpose: Designed for selecting or evaluating candidates for industrial electronics jobs.
Population: Electronic technicians and applicants for electronics jobs.
Publication Dates: 1987-2010.
Scores, 7: Digital & Analog Electronics, AC/DC Theory & Schematics, Motors/Regulators/Electronic Equipment/Power Distribution, Power Supplies, Test Instruments, Computers and PLC, Total.
Administration: Group.
Price Data, 2011: $22 per consumable self-scoring test booklet or online test administration (20 minimum order); $24.95 per manual (2010, 17 pages).
Time: (60-70) minutes.
Comments: Self-scoring instrument; available for online test administration.
Author: Roland T. Ramsay.
Publisher: Ramsay Corporation.
Cross References: For reviews by Keith Hattrup and Eugene (Geno) Pichette of an earlier edition, see 13:116.

[968]
Elementary Program Implementation Profile.

Purpose: Designed as an instrument for "evaluating the appropriateness of elementary school programs and for rating the level of implementation of the High/Scope educational approach in a variety of program settings."
Population: Elementary schools.
Publication Date: 1997.
Acronym: PIP.
Scores, 6: Physical Environment, Daily Schedule, Adult-Child Interaction, Instructional Methods/Content and Assessment, Staff Development and Non-School Collaboration, Total.
Administration: Individual.
Price Data, 2001: $6.95 per manual (7 pages); $14.95 per 25 assessment forms.
Time: Administration time not reported.
Comments: Can also be used with non-High/Scope programs.
Author: High/Scope Educational Research Foundation.
Publisher: High/Scope Educational Research Foundation.

[969]
Elementary Student Opinion Inventory.

Purpose: Designed to measure how elementary students feel about their school.
Population: Elementary students.
Publication Date: 2003.
Scores: 4 subscales: Quality of the Instructional Program, Support for Student Learning, School Climate/Environment for Learning, Student/School Relationships.
Administration: Group.
Parts, 2: A (Likert-scale items), B (customize up to 20 local questions).
Price Data, 2006: $25 per 25 inventories; administrative manual may be downloaded free from publisher webpage.
Time: (15) minutes.
Author: National Study of School Evaluation.
Publisher: National Study of School Evaluation.

[970]
Eliot-Price Perspective Test.

Purpose: "Designed to measure the ability to perceive and to imagine object arrangments from different viewpoints."
Population: Grades 2 and over.
Publication Dates: 1974–1975.
Scores: Total score only.
Administration: Group.
Price Data: Available from publisher.
Time: (20) minutes.
Comments: For research use only.
Authors: John Eliot and Lewis Price.
Publisher: John Eliot (the author) [No reply from publisher; status unknown].
Cross References: See T3:792 (1 reference).

[971]
Emo Questionnaire.

Purpose: "Designed to assess an individual's personal-emotional adjustment."

Population: Clinical and research applications.
Publication Dates: 1958–1998.
Scores: 10 diagnostic dimensions: Rationalization, Inferiority Feelings, Hostility, Depression, Fear and Anxiety, Organic Reaction, Projection, Unreality, Sex Problems, Withdrawal, 3 key adjustment factors: Internal, External, Somatic, and 4 normative level adjustment factors: Internal, External, Somatic, General.
Administration: Individual or group.
Forms, 2: A, B.
Price Data, 2002: $97 per start-up kit including 25 test booklets (specify Form A or Form B), 25 score sheets, and interpretation and research manual; $52 per 25 test booklets (quantity discounts available; specify Form A or Form B); $29 per 25 score sheets; $28 per interpretation and research manual.
Time: No limit (approximately 20 minutes).
Authors: George O. Baehr and Melany E. Baehr.
Publisher: Pearson Performance Solutions [No reply from publisher; status unknown].
Cross References: See T5:927 (1 reference) and T4:883 (1 reference); for reviews by Allan L. LaVoie and Paul McReynolds, see 9:383; see also T2:1170 (1 reference); for reviews by Bertram D. Cohen and W. Grant Dahlstrom, see 6:90 (1 reference).

[972]

Emotional and Behavior Problem Scale–Second Edition.
Purpose: "Developed to contribute to the early identification and service delivery for students with behavior disorders/emotional disturbance."
Population: Ages 5–18.
Publication Dates: 1989–2001.
Acronym: EBPS-2.
Scores, 10: Theoretical (Learning Problems, Interpersonal Relations, Inappropriate Behavior, Unhappiness/Depression, Physical Symptoms/Fears), Empirical (Social Aggression/Conduct Disorder, Social-Emotional Withdrawal/Depression, Learning/Comprehension Disorder, Avoidance/Unresponsiveness, Aggressive/Self-Destructive).
Administration: Individual.
Price Data, 2006: $125 per complete kit including technical manual (2001, 47 pages), 50 School Version rating forms, 50 Home Version rating forms, and IEP and intervention manual (2001, 205 pages); $15 per technical manual (specify Home or School); $35 per 50 rating forms; $25 per IEP and intervention manual; $35 per computerized quick score (Windows®); $225 per computerized IEP and intervention manual (Windows®).
Time: (15) minutes.
Comments: Ratings by teachers and/or parents/guardians.
Authors: Stephen B. McCarney and Tamara J. Arthaud.
Publisher: Hawthorne Educational Services, Inc.
Cross References: For reviews by Adrienne Garro and Judy Oehler-Stinnett, see 16:83; for reviews by J.

Jeffrey Grill and Robert C. Reinehr of the original edition, see 12:134.

[973]

Emotional Behavioral Checklist.
Purpose: To assess an individual's overt emotional behavior.
Population: Ages 16 and over.
Publication Date: 1986.
Acronym: EBC.
Scores, 8: Impulsivity-Frustration, Anxiety, Depression-Withdrawal, Socialization, Self-Concept, Aggression, Reality Disorientation, Total EBC.
Administration: Individual.
Manual: No manual.
Price Data, 2011: $42.50 per 25 checklists.
Time: Administration time not reported.
Comments: Included in the Auxiliary Component of the McCarron-Dial System (1637).
Authors: Jack G. Dial, Carolyn Mezger, Theresa Massey, and Lawrence T. McCarron.
Publisher: McCarron-Dial Systems, Inc.
Cross References: For reviews by William A. Stock and Hoi K. Suen, see 11:130.

[974]

Emotional Competence Inventory.
Purpose: "Designed to assess emotional intelligence (the ability to recognize and manage emotions [yours and others])."
Population: Coaches, executive coaches, mid to senior level managers.
Publication Dates: 1999–2002.
Acronym: ECI.
Scores: 4 clusters, 18 competencies: Self-Awareness (Emotional Self-Awareness, Accurate Self-Assessment, Self-Confidence); Self-Management (Emotional Self-Control, Transparency, Adaptability, Achievement Orientation, Initiative, Optimism); Social Awareness (Empathy, Organizational Awareness, Service Orientation); Relationship Management (Developing Others, Inspirational Leadership, Influence, Change Catalyst, Conflict Management, Teamwork & Collaboration).
Administration: Group or individual.
Price Data, 2005: $3,000 Accreditation (2-day program); $1,800 Accreditation (one-day master class); once accredited internet assessments are $150 per participant (this includes unlimited raters); online development tool available for $75 annual subscription.
Time: (50–60) minutes.
Comments: Accreditation required; multirater assessment to be administered by accredited consultants only; accreditation programs run approximately every second month.
Authors: Daniel Goleman, Richard Boyatzis, and the Hay Group.

Publisher: Hay Group.
Cross References: For reviews by T. Steuart Watson and Tonya S. Watson, see 17:66.

[975]

Emotional Disturbance Decision Tree.

Purpose: To "assist in the identification of children who qualify for the Special Education category of Emotional Disturbance based on federal criteria."
Population: Ages 5-18.
Publication Date: 2007.
Acronym: EDDT.
Scores, 10: Inability to Build or Maintain Relationships Scale, Inappropriate Behaviors or Feelings Scale, Pervasive Mood/Depression Scale, Physical Symptoms or Fears Scale, Emotional Disturbance Decision Tree Total Score, Attention-Deficit Hyperactivity Disorder Cluster, Possible Psychosis/Schizophrenia Cluster, Social Maladjustment Cluster, Level of Severity Cluster, Educational Impact Cluster.
Administration: Group.
Price Data, 2008: $140 per professional manual (139 pages), 25 reusable item booklets, 25 response booklets, and 25 score summary booklets.
Time: (20) minutes.
Author: Bryan L. Euler.
Publisher: Psychological Assessment Resources, Inc.
Cross References: For reviews by Jonathan Sandoval and by Christopher A. Sink and Nyaradzo H. Mvududu, see 18:48.

[976]

Emotional Disturbance Decision Tree-Parent Form.

Purpose: Designed to help identify "children who qualify for the federal Special Education category of Emotional Disturbance."
Population: Ages 5-18.
Publication Date: 2010.
Acronym: EDDT-PF.
Scores, 11: Inability to Build or Maintain Relationships Scale, Inappropriate Behaviors or Feelings Scale, Pervasive Mood/Depression Scale, Physical Symptoms or Fears Scale, Emotional Disturbance Characteristic Scale Total Score, Resilience Scale, Attention-Deficit Hyperactivity Disorder Cluster, Possible Psychosis Cluster, Social Maladjustment Cluster, Severity Cluster, Motivation Cluster.
Administration: Group.
Price Data, 2010: $155 per complete kit including 25 response booklets, 25 reusable item booklets, 25 score summary booklets, case, and manual (151 pages); $57 per 25 response booklets; $31 per 25 reusable item booklets; $21 per 25 score summary booklets; $57 per manual.
Foreign Language Edition: Spanish version available.

Time: (15-20) minutes.
Comments: Ratings by parents/guardians; modeled after the EDDT-TF (18:48; called EDDT in its own listing).
Author: Bryan L. Euler.
Publisher: Psychological Assessment Resources, Inc.

[977]

Emotional Judgment Inventory.

Purpose: "Developed to assess emotional intelligence for use in employee selection and development in organizational contexts."
Population: Ages 16 and over.
Publication Dates: 2000–2003.
Acronym: EJI.
Scores, 8: Being Aware of Emotions, Identifying Own Emotions, Identifying Others' Emotions, Managing Own Emotions, Managing Others' Emotions, Using Emotions in Problem Solving, Expressing Emotions Adaptively, Impression Management.
Administration: Group or individual; online or paper-and-pencil.
Price Data: Available from publisher.
Time: (15) minutes.
Author: Scott Bedwell.
Publisher: Institute for Personality and Ability Testing, Inc. (IPAT)
Cross References: For reviews by Phillip L. Ackerman and by Deniz S. Ones and Stephan Dilchert, see 16:84.

[978]

Emotional or Behavior Disorder Scale–Revised.

Purpose: "Designed to document those behaviors most indicative of emotional or behavioral disorders and the behavior problems which exceed the norms of any student in the environment."
Population: Ages 5–18.
Publication Dates: 1991–2003.
Acronym: EBDS-R.
Scores, 6: Behavioral Component (Academic Progress, Social Relationships, Personal Adjustment), Vocational Component (Work Related, Interpersonal Relations, Social/Community Expectations).
Administration: Individual.
Price Data, 2006: $80 per complete kit including technical manual (2003, 66 pages), 50 rating forms, and intervention manual (2003, 407 pages); $15 per technical manual; $35 per 50 rating forms; $30 per intervention manual; $35 per Quick Score; $225 per intervention manual (Windows®).
Time: Administration time not reported.
Comments: Behavior rating scale completed by observers familiar with the student; derived from the Emotional or Behavior Disorder Scale School Version and the Work

Adjustment Scale (T6:2743); accompanied by Intervention manual; computer scoring software available.
Authors: Stephen B. McCarney (scale and manuals) and Tamara J. Arthaud (technical manual).
Publisher: Hawthorne Educational Services, Inc.
Cross References: For reviews by Amy M. Rees and T. Steuart Watson, see 16:85; for reviews by Patti L. Harrison and Steven W. Lee of the original edition, see 13:117.

[979]

Emotional Problems Scales.

Purpose: "To assess emotional and behavioral problems in individuals with mild mental retardation or borderline intelligence."
Population: Ages 14 and over.
Publication Dates: 1984–1991.
Acronym: EPS.
Price Data, 2006: $154 per introductory kit including manual (1991, 31 pages), 25 BRS test booklets, 25 SRI test booklets, SRI scoring keys, and 25 profile forms.
Comments: Previous editions titled Prout-Strohmer Personality Inventory and Strohmer-Prout Behavior Rating Scale.
Authors: H. Thompson Prout and Douglas C. Strohmer.
Publisher: Psychological Assessment Resources, Inc.
  a) BEHAVIOR RATING SCALES.
  Acronym: BRS.
  Scores, 12: Thought/Behavior Disorder, Verbal Aggression, Physical Aggression, Sexual Maladjustment, Distractibility, Hyperactivity, Somatic Concerns, Depression, Withdrawal, Low Self-Esteem, Externalizing Behavior Problems, Internalizing Behavior Problems.
  Administration: Individual.
  Time: [20–50] minutes.
  b) SELF-REPORT INVENTORY.
  Acronym: SRI.
  Scores, 7: Positive Impression, Thought/Behavior Disorder, Impulse Control, Anxiety, Depression, Low Self-Esteem, Total Pathology.
  Administration: Individual.
  Time: (30–35) minutes.
Cross References: For reviews by S. Alvin Leung and John A. Mills, see 13:118. For reviews by Richard Brozovich and Ernest A. Bauer and by Peter F. Merenda of the Prout-Strohmer Personality Inventory, see 11:311.

[980]

Emotional Quotient Inventory.

Purpose: Designed to measure emotional intelligence.
Population: Ages 16 and older.
Publication Date: 1997.
Acronym: EQ-i.

Scores: 21 content scores: Composite Scale Scores (Total EQ, Intrapersonal EQ, Interpersonal EQ, Adaptability EQ, Stress Management EQ, General Mood EQ), Intrapersonal Subscale Scores (Self-Regard, Emotional Self-Awareness, Assertiveness, Independence, Self-Actualization), Interpersonal Subscale Scores (Empathy, Social Responsibility, Interpersonal Relationship), Adaptability Subscale Scores (Reality Testing, Flexibility, Problem Solving), Stress Management Subscale Scores (Stress Tolerance, Impulse Control), General Mood Subscale Scores (Optimism, Happiness), plus 4 validity indicators (Omission Rate, Inconsistency, Positive Impression, Negative Impression).
Administration: Individual or group.
Price Data, 2011: $189 User's Set including technical manual (234 pages), user's manual, and administrators guide; $104 Technical manual; $81 User's manual; $30 administrator's guide; $48 per 10 item booklets; $26 per Leadership user's guide; $142 per Online Business Report Kit (includes Technical manual and 1 Business Report); $137 per Online Development Report Kit (includes Technical manual and 1 Development Report); $137 per Online Resource Report Kit (includes Technical manual and 1 Resource Report); $118 Leadership and Business Report Bundle; $54 per online Business Report; $47 per online Development Report; $47 per online Resource Report; $33 per online Individual Summary Report; $111 per Online Leadership and Resource Report Bundle; $76 Online Group Summary Report. $221 Software Development Report Preview version includes Technical manual and 3 Development Reports; $221 Software Resource Report Preview version includes Technical manual and 3 Resource Reports; $49 per Development Report; $49 per Resource Report; $45 per Individual Summary Report; $79 per Group Summary Report.
Foreign Language Editions: Translations available in Afrikaans, Chinese, Czech, Dutch, French-Canadian, Korean, German, Hebrew, Norwegian, Russian, Spanish (South American), Swedish, Danish, Finnish, French (Euro), Hindi, Indonesian, Italian, Japanese, Portuguese, Slovakian, and Slovene upon special request.
Time: (30–40) minutes.
Comments: Paper-and-pencil and computer administrations available; previously listed as BarOn Emotional Quotient Inventory.
Author: Reuven Bar-On.
Publisher: Multi-Health Systems, Inc.
Cross References: For reviews by Andrew A. Cox and Robert M. Guion, see 14:32.

[981]

Emotional Quotient Inventory: Short.

Purpose: Designed to measure emotionally intelligent behavior in situations where a more detailed assessment is not possible or required. Often used for screening purposes or to monitor change over time.

Population: Age 16 and older.
Publication Date: 2002.
Acronym: EQ-i:S.
Scores, 8: Intrapersonal, Interpersonal, Adaptability, Stress Management, General Mood, Positive Impression, Inconsistency Index, Total EQ.
Administration: Group or individual.
Price Data, 2011: $231 per complete kit including technical manual and 10 complete assessment sets; $82 per technical manual; $178 per 10 complete assessment sets; $357 per software kit including technical manual, getting started guide, and 10 feedback reports; $32 for each software feedback report; $156 per online feedback report kits including technical manual and 3 feedback reports; 34 for each online feedback report.
Time: 10–15 minutes.
Comments: Self-report; previously listed as BarOn Emotional Quotient Inventory: Short Development Edition.
Author: Reuven Bar-On.
Publisher: Multi-Health Systems, Inc.
Cross References: For reviews by R. Anthony Doggett and Carl J. Sheperis and by John T. Willse, see 16:20.

[982]

Emotional Quotient Inventory: Youth Version.

Purpose: "Designed to measure emotional intelligence in young people aged 7 to 18 years."
Population: Ages 7–18.
Publication Date: 2000.
Acronym: EQ-i: YV.
Scores, 8: Intrapersonal Scale, Interpersonal Scale, Adaptability Scale, Stress Management Scale, Total EQ, General Mood Scale, Positive Impression Scale, Inconsistency Index.
Administration: Individual or group.
Forms, 2: EQ-i:YV Long Form; EQ-i:YV(S) Short Form.
Price Data, 2011: $169 per complete kit including manual (86 pages) and 25 QuikScore forms for each of EQ-i:YV and EQ-i:YV(S); $80 per manual; $55 per 25 EQ-i:YV Quikscore forms; $53 per 25 EQ-i:YV(S) Quikscore forms. $150 per online kit including manual, 25 online forms for each of EQ-i:YV and EQ-i:YV(S).
Foreign Language Edition: Spanish edition available upon special request.
Time: (20–25) minutes.
Comments: Self-report; previously listed as BarOn Emotional Quotient Inventory: Youth Version.
Authors: Reuven Bar-On and James D. A. Parker.
Publisher: Multi-Health Systems, Inc.
Cross References: For reviews by Joan C. Ballard and Frederick T. L. Leong, see 15:26.

[983]

Emotional Quotient-360.

Purpose: Designed to provide a "multiperspective view of [an] individual's emotional functioning."
Population: Ages 16 and over.
Publication Date: 2003.
Acronym: EQ-360.
Scores, 21: Intrapersonal (Self-Regard, Emotional Self-Awareness, Assertiveness, Independence, Self-Actualization, Total), Interpersonal (Empathy, Social Responsibility, Interpersonal Relationship, Total), Stress Management (Stress Tolerance, Impulse Control, Total), Adaptability (Reality Testing, Flexibility, Problem Solving, Total), General Mood (Optimism, Happiness, Total), Total EQ.
Administration: Individual.
Price Data, 2011: $79 per technical manual; $49 per 10 reusable item booklets; $43 per 10 additional rater response sheets; $242 per online multirater Feedback Report kit including technical manual and 1 multirater feedback report with Resource or Development Report; $250 per online multirater Feedback Report kit with Business Report Kit including technical manual and 1 multirater feedback report with Business Report; $192 per online multirater Feedback Report with Resource or Development Report; $201 per online multirater Feedback Report with Business Report.
Time: (30) minutes.
Comments: Designed for use in conjunction with the EQ-i (1015); multi-informant rating scale available for paper-and-pencil or on-line administration.
Authors: Reuven Bar-On and Rich Handley.
Publisher: Multi-Health Systems, Inc.
Cross References: For reviews by Deborah L. Bandalos and Ric Brown, see 16:21.

[984]

The Empathy Test.

Purpose: Constructed to assess empathy.
Population: Junior high school and over.
Publication Dates: 1947–1962.
Scores: Total score only.
Administration: Group.
Forms, 3: A, B, C.
Price Data: Available from publisher.
Time: (6-15) minutes.
Authors: W. A. Kerr and B. J. Speroff.
Publisher: Psychometric Affiliates.
Cross References: See T4:890 (2 references), T2:1171 (10 references), and P:73 (1 reference); for a review by Wallace B. Hall, see 6:91 (9 references); for a review by Robert L. Thorndike, see 5:50 (20 references).

[985]

Empirically-Statistically Validated (ESV) Written Tests for Fire Medic.

Purpose: Intended for the selection of cross-trained firefighter/fire medic candidates.

Population: Prospective firefighter/fire medic candidates.
Publication Dates: 1995-2010.
Scores: 7 subtests and total: Interest, Teamwork, Problem Solving–Common Sense, Problem Solving–Mechanical, Problem Solving–Logical Thinking, Problem Solving–Relevancy, Attentiveness, Total.
Administration: Group.
Form, 1: ESV-100.
Restricted Distribution: Distribution restricted to civil service commissions and qualified municipal officials.
Price Data: Available from publisher.
Time: 121 minutes.
Comments: Complimentary Candidate Study Guide is available at the publisher's website; a full-length practice examination for firefighters or fire medics is available for purchase, administered online through the company assessment platform: www.measuredsuccessonline.com.
Author: McCann Associates, Inc.
Publisher: McCann Associates.

[986]
Empirically-Statistically Validated (ESV) Written Tests for Firefighter.
Purpose: For the selection of firefighter candidates.
Population: Prospective firefighters.
Publication Dates: 1976–2010.
Scores: 7 subtests: Interest in Firefighting, Teamwork/Compatibility, Map Reading, Spatial Visualization, Attentiveness (Visual Pursuit), Understanding and Interpreting Table and Text Material About Firefighting, Mechanical Aptitude.
Administration: Group.
Forms, 2: Form ESV-100, M-100.
Restricted Distribution: Distribution restricted to civil service commissions and qualified municipal officials.
Price Data: Available from publisher.
Time: 121 minutes.
Comments: Complimentary Candidate Study Guide is available at the publisher's website; a full-length practice examination is available for purchase, administered online through the company assessment platform: www.measuredsuccessonline.com.
Author: McCann Associates.
Publisher: McCann Associates.

[987]
Empirically-Statistically Validated (ESV) Written Tests for Police Officer.
Purpose: Designed for the selection of police officer candidates.
Population: Prospective police officers.
Publication Dates: 1980–2010.
Scores: 7 subtests and total: Observational Ability, Ability to Exercise Judgment and Common Sense, Interest in Police Work, Ability to Exercise Judgment–Map Reading, Ability to Exercise Judgment–Dealing With People, Ability to Read and Comprehend Police Test Material, Reasoning Ability, Total.
Administration: Group.
Forms, 2: Form ESV 100, Form N-100.
Restricted Distribution: Distribution restricted to civil service commissions and qualified municipal officials.
Price Data: Available from publisher.
Time: 170 minutes.
Comments: Complimentary Candidate Study Guide is available at the publisher's website; a full-length practice examination is available for purchase, administered online through the company assessment platform: www.measuredsuccessonline.com.
Author: McCann Associates.
Publisher: McCann Associates.

[988]
Employability Maturity Interview.
Purpose: "Developed to assess readiness for the vocational rehabilitation planning process."
Population: Rehabilitation clients.
Publication Date: 1987.
Acronym: EMI.
Scores: Total score only.
Administration: Individual.
Price Data: Available from publisher.
Time: (15–20) minutes.
Comments: Based upon the Adult Vocational Maturity Assessment Interview.
Authors: Richard Roessler and Brian Bolton.
Publisher: The National Center on Employment & Disability.
Cross References: See T5:936 (1 reference); for a review by William R. Koch, see 11:132.

[989]
Employee Aptitude Survey, Second Edition.
Purpose: Designed to predict future job performance.
Population: Ages 16 to adult
Publication Dates: 1952–2000.
Acronym: EAS.
Administration: Group or individual.
Price Data: Price data available from publisher for test materials including User's Manual (2005, 64 pages), Technical Manual (1994, 91 pages), Technical Addendum: Fairness of the EAS (2000, 11 pages), and Supplemental Norms Report (1995, 92 pages).
Time: 5-10(10-15) minutes.
Comments: Tests available separately; computerized versions available; transportability procedure available.
Authors: G. Grimsley (*a–h*), F. L. Ruch (*a–g, i, j*), N. D. Warren (*a–g*), and J. S. Ford (*a, c, e–g*).
Publisher: Psychological Services, Inc.

a) TEST 1, VERBAL COMPREHENSION.
Publication Dates: 1956–1984.
Scores: Total score only.
b) TEST 2, NUMERICAL ABILITY.
Publication Dates: 1952–1963.
Scores: Total score only.
c) TEST 3, VISUAL PURSUIT.
Publication Date: 1956.
Scores: Total score only.
d) TEST 4, VISUAL SPEED AND ACCURACY.
Publication Dates: 1952–1980.
Scores: Total score only.
e) TEST 5, SPACE VISUALIZATION.
Publication Dates: 1952–1980.
Scores: Total score only.
f) TEST 6, NUMERICAL REASONING.
Publication Dates: 1957–1985.
Scores: Total score only.
g) TEST 7, VERBAL REASONING.
Publication Dates: 1952–1963.
Scores: Total score only.
h) TEST 8, WORD FLUENCY.
Publication Dates: 1953–1963.
Scores: Total score only.
i) TEST 9, MANUAL SPEED AND ACCURACY.
Publication Dates: 1953–1963.
Scores: Total score only.
j) TEST 10, SYMBOLIC REASONING.
Publication Dates: 1957–1985.
Scores: Total score only.
Cross References: For reviews by Brian Engdahl and Paul M. Muchinsky, see 14:137; see also T5:937 (4 references), T4:894 (1 reference), T3:799 (4 references), and T2:1071 (14 references); for reviews by Paul F. Ross and Erwin K. Taylor, and an excerpted review by John O. Crites of an earlier edition, see 6:769 (4 references); for reviews by Dorothy C. Adkins and S. Rains Wallace of an earlier edition, see 5:607.

[990]

Employee Assistance Program Inventory.

Purpose: "Designed as an intake or screening tool for professionals who provide counseling and other services in working adults."
Population: Adults seeking vocational counseling.
Publication Date: 1994.
Acronym: EAPI.
Scores: 10 scales: Anxiety, Depression, Self-Esteem Problems, Marital Problems, Family Problems, External Stressors, Interpersonal Conflict, Work Adjustment, Problem Minimization, Effects of Substance Abuse.
Administration: Group.
Price Data, 2006: $120 per introductory kit including manual (44 pages), 25 reusable item booklets, and 25 answer sheet/profiles.
Time: (20) minutes.

Authors: William D. Anton and James R. Reed.
Publisher: Psychological Assessment Resources, Inc.
Cross References: For reviews by Michael G. Kavan and David J. Pittenger, see 14:138.

[991]

Employee Effectiveness Profile.

Purpose: "Designed to assist managers in identifying the overall effectiveness of individual employees."
Population: Managers.
Publication Date: 1986.
Scores: Total score only.
Administration: Individual.
Price Data: Price information available from publisher for profiles (24 pages) or short forms.
Time: No time limit.
Author: J. William Pfeiffer.
Publisher: Jossey-Bass, A Wiley Company.
Cross References: For reviews by Lawrence M. Aleamoni and Daniel E. Vogler, see 12:136.

[992]

Employee Involvement Survey.

Purpose: Assesses employees' actual and desired opportunities for personal involvement and influence in the workplace.
Population: Business and industry employees.
Publication Date: 1988.
Acronym: EIS.
Scores, 5: Basic Creature Comfort, Safety and Order, Belonging and Affiliation, Ego-Status, Actualization and Self-Expression.
Administration: Group.
Price Data, 2001: $7.95 per instrument (14 pages).
Time: Administration time not reported.
Comments: Self-administered, self-scored.
Author: Jay Hall.
Publisher: Teleometrics International, Inc.

[993]

Employee Performance Appraisal.

Purpose: "Designed as a tool to aid in performance appraisal and merit review."
Population: Business and industry.
Publication Dates: 1962-1984.
Acronym: EPA.
Scores: 7 merit ratings: Quantity of Work, Quality of Work, Job Knowledge, Initiative, Interpersonal Relationships, Dependability, Potential.
Administration: Group.
Manual: No manual; included in Manuals Supplement (1984) along with 13 tests from this publisher.
Price Data, 2006: $35.20 per package of forms; $19.25 per specimen set.
Time: [10-20] minutes.

Comments: Ratings by supervisors.
Author: Martin M. Bruce.
Publisher: Martin M. Bruce, Ph.D.
Cross References: For a review by Jean Maier Palormo, see 6:1116.

[994]

Employee Productivity Index.

Purpose: "Designed to aid in hiring productive and responsible employees."
Population: Job applicants.
Publication Date: 1989.
Acronym: EPI.
Scores, 7: Dependability Scale, Interpersonal Co-operation Scale, Drug Avoidance Scale, Safety Scale, Validity/Accuracy Scale, Productivity Index, Significant Behavioral Indicators.
Administration: Individual or group.
Forms, 6: Quanta Touch Test, Quanta Software for Windows, Online, Scan, Quanta-Fax, Optical Scoring.
Price Data, 2005: $18 per 1–999 each Quanta Touch Test, Quanta Software for Windows–administration and scoring (no booklets), Quanta Software for Windows–scoring only (one booklet for every coupon ordered), Internet with booklets, internet without booklets, Scan, Quanta-Fax; volume discounts available.
Foreign Language Editions: Available in Spanish.
Time: [20–40] minutes.
Author: London House.
Publisher: Pearson Performance Solutions [No reply from publisher; status unknown].

[995]

Employee Reliability Inventory.

Purpose: Designed to be used as a preemployment instrument for assessing a number of different dimensions of work behavior skills, each of which are associated with reliable and productive work behavior.
Population: Job applicants.
Publication Dates: 1986–1998.
Acronym: ERI.
Scores, 7: Freedom from Disruptive Alcohol and Illegal Drug Use, Courtesy, Emotional Maturity, Conscientiousness, Trustworthiness, Long Term Job Commitment, Safe Job Performance.
Administration: Group.
Price Data, 2010: $17 or less (depending on the administration and scoring methods used) per complete kit including questionnaire, user's manual (1998, 52 pages), all documentation, training, toll-free technical support, and consultation; $55 per Americans With Disabilities Act Kit including user's manual addendum (1992, 19 pages), audio version, Braille version, and large print version.
Foreign Language or Other Special Editions: Braille, Large Print, and Audio versions available.

Time: (12–15) minutes.
Comments: Individual applicant scores are compared to a position specific profile; can be administered online, at a stand alone computer terminal, or by paper and pencil; results for online administration are stored in a database, which is user accessible, and can be used to generate a range of reports.
Author: Gerald L. Borofsky.
Publisher: Bay State Psychological Associates, Inc.
Cross References: See T5:944 (1 reference); for reviews by Robert M. Guion and Lawrence M. Rudner, see 12:137 (3 references); see also T4:899 (2 references).

[996]

Employee Safety Inventory.

Purpose: Designed to "assess the safety attitudes of job applicants and current employees."
Population: Job applicants and employees.
Publication Dates: 1989–1994.
Acronym: ESI.
Scores, 7: Survey Scales (Safety Control, Risk Avoidance, Stress Tolerance), Validity Scales (Validity/Distortion, Accuracy), Composite Score (Safety Index), Supplemental Scale (Driver Attitude).
Administration: Group or individual.
Price Data: Price information for Quanta Touch Test administration and scoring and for Windows administration and scoring available from publisher.
Time: (45) minutes.
Comments: Paper-and-pencil or computer administration available.
Author: London House.
Publisher: Pearson Performance Solutions [No reply from publisher; status unknown].

[997]

Employee Screening Questionnaire.

Purpose: "A personality-based selection measure designed to provide employers with a technique for identifying superior job candidates and to screen out dishonest and unproductive ones."
Population: Ages 16 and over.
Publication Dates: 2001–2002.
Acronym: ESQ.
Scores, 15: Customer Service, Productivity, Accuracy, Commitment/Job Satisfaction, Promotability, Risk of Counter-Productive Behavior, Alcohol and Substance Abuse, Bogus Sick Days, Driving Delinquency, Lateness, Loafing, Sabotage of Employer's Production or Property, Safety Infractions, Theft, Overall Hiring Recommendation.
Administration: Individual or group.
Price Data, 2010: $24 per test manual; $1 per test booklet; $15-$20 (depending on volume) per administration (online or fax-in).

Time: 15 minutes.
Comments: Internet administration or fax-in scoring service available through publisher; recommended by publisher for use in conjunction with the Personnel Assessment Form (PAF).
Author: Douglas N. Jackson.
Publisher: SIGMA Assessment Systems, Inc.
Cross References: For reviews by Paul M. Muchinsky and Frank Schmidt, see 16:86.

[998]

Employee Wellness Evaluation.

Purpose: Designed to "identify potential problems in several areas of significance for employees" as a clinical aid for referral for counseling or "to provide indications of problem prevalence in a workforce."
Population: Employees seeking counseling.
Publication Dates: 1994-1999.
Acronym: EWE.
Scores, 7: Alcohol, Depression, Stress, Anger, Morale, Management, Family Stress.
Administration: Individual and group.
Price Data, 2008: $52.50 per 25 assessments; $15 per EWE guide (1999, 5 pages).
Time: (10-15) minutes.
Author: Norman G. Hoffmann.
Publisher: The Change Companies.
Cross References: For reviews by Elizabeth Bigham and Thomas M. Dunn, see 18:49.

[999]

Employment Inventory.

Purpose: Designed to identify job applicants who will be likely to be productive, exhibit helpful and positive behaviors in interacting with customers, and to stay on the job at least three months.
Population: Job applicants.
Publication Dates: 1985–1993.
Acronym: EI.
Scores, 4: Performance, Tenure, Customer Service, Sales.
Administration: Group.
Price Data: Available from publisher.
Foreign Language Editions: Foreign and bilingual editions available include American Spanish/English, French-Canadian English, Mexican Spanish, British English, and Vietnamese/English.
Time: (30) minutes.
Comments: Online inventory of attitudes and self-descriptions; computer-scored.
Authors: George E. Paajanen, Timothy L. Hansen, and Richard A. McLellan.
Publisher: SHL [United Kingdom].
Cross References: For reviews by Gordon C. Bruner II and Annie W. Ward, see 14:278.

[1000]

Endeavor Instructional Rating System.

Purpose: Student ratings of courses and instructors.
Population: College.
Publication Dates: 1973–1979.
Acronym: EIRS.
Scores, 9: 7 item scores (Hard Work, Advanced Planning, Class Discussion, Personal Help, Presentation Clarity, Grade Accuracy, Increased Knowledge), and 2 composite scores (Student Perception of Achievement, Student-Instructor Rapport).
Administration: Group.
Price Data: Available from publisher.
Time: (5–10) minutes.
Author: Peter W. Frey.
Publisher: Endeavor Information Systems, Inc. [No reply from publisher; status unknown].
Cross References: See 9:386 (1 reference), and T3:818 (2 references); for a review by Kenneth O. Doyle, Jr., see 8:370 (5 references).

[1001]

Endicott Work Productivity Scale.

Purpose: "Designed to describe types of behavior and subjective feelings that are highly likely to reduce productivity and efficiency in work activities."
Population: Adults.
Publication Dates: 1994–1997.
Acronym: EWPS.
Scores: Total score only.
Administration: Individual.
Manual: No manual.
Price Data, 2001: $1 per questionnaire.
Time: [3–5] minutes.
Author: Jean Endicott.
Publisher: Department of Research Assessment and Training.
Cross References: For reviews by Andrew A. Cox and William C. Tirre, see 14:140.

[1002]

Endler Multidimensional Anxiety Scales and EMAS Social Anxiety Scales.

Purpose: Designed to provide "a multidimensional measure of anxiety, with four related scales assessing transitory anxiety response, situational anxiety, perception of immediate threat, and social anxiety."
Population: Adolescents and adults.
Administration: Group.
Time: (25) minutes.
Publisher: Western Psychological Services.
a) ENDLER MULTIDIMENSIONAL ANXIETY SCALES.
Publication Date: 1991.
Scores, 12: Cognitive-Worry, Autonomic-Emotional, Total, Trait Social Evaluation, Trait Physical

Danger, Trait Ambiguous, Trait Daily Routines, Perception Social Evaluation, Perception Physical Danger, Perception Ambiguous, Perception Daily Routines, Perception Threat.

Price Data, 2011: $115 per EMAS kit including 25 AutoScore test forms for EMAS-S, 25 AutoScore test forms for EMAS-T/EMAS-P, and manual (1991, 121 pages); $55 per manual.
Acronym: EMAS.
Authors: Norman S. Endler, Jean M. Edwards, and Romeo Vitelli.
b) EMAS SOCIAL ANXIETY SCALES.
Acronym: EMAS-SAS.
Publication Date: 2002.
Scores, 8: Trait Separation, Trait Self-Disclosure to Family Members, Trait Self-Disclosure to Close Friends, Trait Social Evaluation, Perception Separation, Perception Self-Disclosure, Perception Social Evaluation, Perception Threat.
Price Data: $60 per EMAS-SAS kit including 25 answer sheets, 25 profile forms, scoring template, and manual extension (2002, 50 pages); $27.50 per manual extension.
Authors: Norman S. Endler and Gordon L. Flett.
Cross References: See T5:950 (6 references); for reviews by Deborah L. Bandalos and Steven D. Spaner of the Endler Multidimensional Anxiety Scales, see 12:138 (2 references); see also T4:905 (7 references).

[1003]
English as a Second Language Oral Assessment, Second Edition.
Purpose: Measures the "learner's ability to speak and understand English."
Population: Adult nonnative speakers of English.
Publication Dates: 1978–1996.
Acronym: ESLOA.
Scores, 4: Auditory Comprehension, Basic Vocabulary and Grammatical Structures, Complex Grammatical Structures and Communicating Meaning and Comprehension, Comprehension and Fluency and Pronunciation.
Administration: Individual.
Levels, 4: 1, 2, 3, 4.
Price Data, 2005: $6.50 per 50 answer sheets; $15 per manual (1996, 80 pages).
Time: Administration time not reported.
Authors: Joye Coy Shaffer and Teri McLean.
Publisher: ProLiteracy Worldwide.
Cross References: For reviews by James D. Brown and Charlene Rivera of an earlier edition, see 11:136.

[1004]
English Placement Test [Revised].
Purpose: Designed to "quickly place English language students into homogenous ability levels."

Population: English language learners.
Publication Dates: 1972–2004.
Acronym: EPT.
Scores: Total score only.
Administration: Individual or group.
Forms, 3: A, B, C.
Price Data: Price data for test package including examiner's manual, test booklets for Forms A-C, CDs for the Listening Comprehension section (Forms A-C), and answer sheets available from publisher.
Time: (75) minutes.
Author: University of Michigan.
Publisher: Cambridge-Michigan Language Assessments.
Cross References: For a review by James Dean Brown, see 17:67; see also T4:908 (3 references); for a review by John L. D. Clark of an earlier form, see 8:102.

[1005]
English Skills Assessment.
Purpose: ACER adaptation of STEP Series and DTLS by Educational Testing Service and The College Board.
Population: Grades 11-12 and first year of post-secondary education.
Publication Dates: 1969-1982.
Acronym: ESA.
Scores, 11: Part I (Spelling, Punctuation and Capitalization, Comprehension I, Total), Part II (Comprehension II, Usage, Vocabulary, Sentence Structure, Logical Relationships [optional], Total), Total.
Administration: Group.
Price Data, 2006: A$4.95 per Part I test booklet; A$4.95 per Part II test booklet; A$24.20 per 10 answer sheets; A$4.95 per score key; A$22 per manual; A$42.95per specimen set.
Time: 50(70) minutes for Part I; 60(70) minutes for Part II.
Author: Australian Council for Educational Research (adaptation).
Publisher: Australian Council for Educational Research Ltd. [Australia].
Cross References: See T4:910 (1 reference); for a review by John C. Sherwood, see 9:389.

[1006]
English Test: Municipal Tests: National Achievement Tests.
Purpose: "To test … mastery in language usage (words and sentences), punctuation and capitalization, and expression of ideas."
Population: Grades 3–8.
Publication Dates: 1938–1956.
Scores, 5: Language Usage-Words, Language Usage-Sentences, Punctuation and Capitalization, Expressing Ideas, Total.

Administration: Group.
Forms, 2: A, B.
Levels, 2: Grades 3–6, Grades 6–8.
Price Data: Available from publisher.
Time: 30(35) minutes.
Comments: Subtest of the formerly published Municipal Battery (see 4:20).
Authors: Robert K. Speer and Samuel Smith.
Publisher: Psychometric Affiliates.
Cross References: See T2:77 (1 reference) and 5:190. For reviews of the complete battery, see 5:18 (1 review), 4:20 (1 review), and 2:1191 (2 reviews).

[1007]

English Test: National Achievement Tests.
Purpose: To test skills in English language usage.
Population: Grades 3–12.
Publication Dates: 1936–1957.
Administration: Group.
Levels, 2: Grades 3–8, Grades 7–12; Forms, 2: A, B.
Price Data: Available from publisher.
Time: (40) minutes.
Authors: Robert K. Speer and Samuel Smith.
Publisher: Psychometric Affiliates.
  a) GRADES 3–8.
  Publication Dates: 1936–1938.
  Scores, 7: Capitalization, Punctuation, Language Usage (Sentences), Language Usage (Words), Expressing Ideas, Letter Writing, Total.
  b) GRADES 7–12.
  Publication Dates: 1936–1957.
  Scores, 7: Word Usage, Punctuation, Vocabulary, Language Usage (Sentences), Expressing Ideas, Expressing Feeling, Total.
Cross References: See T2:78 (1 reference) and 5:191; for a review by Winifred L. Post, see 4:162; for a review by Harry A. Greene, see 3:126.

[1008]

Enneagram Personality Portraits Inventory and Profile.
Purpose: Designed to identify an individual's personality type, work style, and leadership style.
Population: Work team members.
Publication Date: 1997.
Scores, 9: Ones–Perfecters/Quality Performers/Stabilizers, Twos–Carers/Helpers/Supporters, Threes–Achievers/Producers/Motivators, Fours–Creators/Expressionists/Individualists, Fives–Observers/Thinkers/Systematizers, Sixes–Groupists/Relaters/Teamsters, Sevens–Cheerers/Animators/Cheerleaders, Eights–Challengers/Asserters/Directors, Nines–Accepters/Receptionists/Reconcilers.
Administration: Group.
Price Data: Available from publisher.

Time: Administration time not reported.
Comments: Classifies respondents into one of nine "types."
Authors: Patrick J. Aspell and Dee Dee Aspell.
Publisher: Jossey-Bass, A Wiley Company.

[1009]

Ennis-Weir Critical Thinking Essay Test.
Purpose: "To help evaluate a person's ability to appraise an argument and to formulate in writing an argument in response, thus recognizing a creative dimension in critical thinking ability."
Population: High school and college.
Publication Dates: 1983-1985.
Scores: Critical Thinking Ability.
Administration: Group.
Price Data: Available free of charge from author's website: http://faculty.ed.uiuc.edu/rhennis.
Time: (40) minutes.
Comments: Supplementary information also available from author's website.
Authors: Robert H. Ennis and Eric Weir.
Publisher: Robert H. Ennis (the author).
Cross References: See T5:959 (2 references); for reviews by James A. Poteet and Gail E. Tompkins, see 10:107.

[1010]

The Enright Forgiveness Inventory.
Purpose: "To measure the degree to which one person forgives another who has hurt him or her deeply and unfairly."
Population: High school and college and adults.
Publication Dates: 2000-2004.
Acronym: EFI.
Scores, 10: 3 Affect scores (Positive Affect, Negative Affect, Total Affect), 3 Behavior scores (Positive Behavior, Negative Behavior, Total Behavior), 3 Cognition scores (Positive Cognition, Negative Cognition, Total Cognition), Total.
Administration: Group or individual.
Price Data, 2005: $40 per manual/sample set (63 pages); additional pricing available at at www.mindgarden.com/products/efins.htm.
Time: (40) minutes.
Authors: Robert D. Enright and Julio Rique.
Publisher: Mind Garden, Inc.
Cross References: For reviews by Laura L. B. Barnes and by James Fauth and Scott T. Meier, see 15:89.

[1011]

Entrepreneurial Quotient.
Purpose: Designed to profile managerial preferences and personality traits to determine whether an individual has a creative, entrepreneurial management style or a more traditional, operational management style; compares an individual's managerial style and personality traits to

those of successful entrepreneurs; designed for use in pre-employment testing and worker development.
Population: Adult.
Publication Dates: 1993–1998.
Acronym: EQ.
Scores, 16: Adaptability, Managerial Traits (Risk Tolerance, Time Management, Creativity, Strategic Thinking, Planning, Goal-Orientation, Total), Personality Traits (Extroversion, Intuition, Thinking, Perceiving, Total), EQ Index, Managerial Type, Personality Type.
Administration: Individual or group.
Price Data: Available from publisher.
Time: 25–35 minutes.
Comments: Online administration available; previously listed as EQ Questionnaire.
Authors: Wonderlic, Inc. and Edward J. Fasiska.
Publisher: Wonderlic, Inc.
Cross References: For reviews by James T. Austin and Paul M. Muchinsky, see 14:141.

[1012]

Entrepreneurial Readiness Inventory.
Purpose: Designed to "help individuals assess whether they have the personality characteristics, behaviors, and resources to successfully start and maintain their own businesses."
Population: Participants in career and employment counseling programs or educational programs that explore career and/or entrepreneurial options.
Publication Date: 2009.
Acronym: ERI.
Scores, 6: Vision, Risk Tolerance, Perseverance, Motivation, Independence, Resources.
Administration: Group.
Price Data, 2011: $21.95 per 10 assessment booklets.
Time: (20-25) minutes.
Author: John J. Liptak.
Publisher: JIST Publishing, Inc.

[1013]

Entrepreneurial Style and Success Indicator [Revised].
Purpose: Designed to help individuals identify their preferred entrepreneurial style and its related strengths and weaknesses, as well as comparing their background to the background of other successful entrepreneurs.
Population: Adults.
Publication Dates: 1988-2006.
Acronym: ESSI.
Scores, 4: Behavioral/Action, Cognitive/Analysis, Interpersonal/Harmony, Affective/Expression, plus 28 Entrepreneurial Success Factors.
Administration: Individual or group.
Price Data, 2006: $19.95 per test booklet (2006, 32 pages); $14.95 per Indicator In-Depth Interpretations

booklet (2006, 48 pages); $34.95 per code for online version; $69.95 per Professional's Guide (2006, 62 pages); $38 per Trainer's Guidelines (1996, 18 pages); $159.95 per Power Point CD & Binder 126 slides; $23.95 per participant workbook entitled Discovering Your Pathway to Entrepreneurial Success (2006, 64 pages).
Time: [120-180] minutes for Basic; [360-720] minutes for Advanced.
Comments: Test can be self-administered and self-scored.
Authors: Ken Keis, Terry D. Anderson, and Howard Shenson.
Publisher: Consulting Resource Group International, Inc.
Cross References: For reviews by Frederick T. L. Leong and Myra N. Womble, see 17:68; for a review by Stephen F. Davis of an earlier edition, see 13:120.

[1014]

Eosys Word Processing Aptitude Battery.
Purpose: For use in selection, allocation, and development of word processor operators.
Population: Job candidates for work processor operator positions.
Publication Date: 1983.
Acronym: WPAB.
Scores, 5: Verbal Skills (WP1), Checking Skills (WP2), Written Instructions (WP3), Coded Information (WP4), Numerical Computation (WP5).
Administration: Group.
Price Data: Available from publisher.
Time: (10) minutes per WP1, WP2, WP5; (12) minutes per WP3; (15) minutes per WP4.
Authors: Gill Nyfield, Susan Bawtree, Michael Pearn (test), David Hawkey (test), and Emma Bird (manual).
Publisher: SHL Group plc [United Kingdom].

[1015]

EQ Index.
Purpose: Measures organizational leaders' emotional intelligence (EQ) at work, specifically their EQ ability as opposed to their personality.
Population: Organizational leaders, managers, and supervisors.
Publication Date: 2002.
Acronym: EQI.
Scores, 5: Self-Awareness, Self-Regulation, Motivation, Empathy, Social Skills.
Administration: Group.
Manual: No manual.
Price Data, 2008: $170 per permission to make 300 copies for institutional or funded projects; $100 per permission to make 300 copies for individual or unfunded projects; quantity discounts available.
Time: Administration time not reported.

Comments: Observer or self-rating.
Authors: M. Afzal Rahim, Clement Psenicka, Panagiotis Polychroniou, Jing-Hua Zhao, C. S. Yu, K. A. Chan, K. W. Yee, M. G. Alves, C. W. Lee, M. S. Rahman, S. Ferdausy, and R. V. Wyk.
Publisher: Center for Advanced Studies in Management.

[1016]

ERB Writing Assessment Program [Revised].
Purpose: Designed to assess six domains of writing proficiency.
Population: Grades 3–4, 5–6, 7–8, 9–10, 11–12.
Publication Dates: 1989–2007.
Acronym: ERB WrAP.
Scores: 6 writing traits: Overall Development, Organization, Support, Sentence Structure, Word Choice, Mechanics.
Administration: Group.
Price Data: Available from publisher. Discount for combination WrAP and online Writing Practice Program (WPP) when ordered together.
Comments: Writing samples scored by Measurement Incorporated. Online WPP provides immediate computer scoring. WPP computer specifications: IE 6.0 or higher, Firefox 1.5 or higher, Safari 2.0 or higher. A 6-point scoring rubric provides analytic scores of 1-6 on each of six writing traits offering detailed information on students' writing skills. Raw scores show growth across grades within a test level; scale scores based on a student's raw score may be compared across grades and test levels; percentile ranks and stanines allow comparison of students' scores on same grade to suburban/public, independent, and international school norms.
Author: Educational Records Bureau.
Publisher: Educational Records Bureau.
a) ELEMENTARY LEVEL.
Purpose: To assess a student's narrative writing.
Population: Grades 3 and 4.
Time: Two [40–60] minute sessions.
b) INTERMEDIATE LEVEL.
Purpose: To assess a student's descriptive writing.
Population: Grades 5 and 6.
Time: Two [40–50] minute sessions.
c) MIDDLE SCHOOL LEVEL.
Purpose: To assess a student's expository writing.
Population: Grades 7 and 8.
Time: Two [40–50] minute sessions.
d) SECONDARY LEVEL.
Purpose: To assess a student's persuasive writing.
Population: Grades 9 and 10.
Time: Two [40–50] minute sessions.
e) COLLEGE PREP LEVEL.
Purpose: To assess a student's critical thinking.
Population: Grades 11 and 12.
Time: Two [40–50] minute sessions.

Cross References: For reviews by Thomas P. Hogan and Bruce G. Rogers, see 17:69; for reviews by G. Michael Poteat and Wayne H. Slater of an earlier edition, see 13:122.

[1017]

Erotometer: A Technique for the Measurement of Heterosexual Love.
Purpose: Designed to measure attitudes toward heterosexual love.
Population: Adults.
Publication Dates: 1971–1988.
Scores: Total score only.
Administration: Group.
Manual: No manual.
Price Data, 2005: $2 per test.
Time: [10] minutes.
Comments: Supplementary article available.
Author: Panos D. Bardis.
Publisher: Donna Bardis.
Cross References: For additional information, see 8:337 (1 reference).

[1018]

ESL/Adult Literacy Scale.
Purpose: Developed to identify "the appropriate starting level for ESL and literacy instruction."
Population: Age 16 through adult.
Publication Date: 1989.
Scores, 6: Listening, Grammar, Life Skills, Reading, Composition, Total.
Administration: Individual.
Manual: No manual.
Price Data, 2006: $25 per 25 test booklets; $5 per scoring template; $5 per instruction card.
Time: [15–20] minutes.
Author: Michael Roddy.
Publisher: Academic Therapy Publications.
Cross References: See T5:971 (2 references); for reviews by Anne L. Harvey and by Dianna L. Newman and Kathleen T. Toms, see 11:138.

[1019]

Essential Skills Assessments: Information Skills.
Purpose: "Broad measures of achievement set within the Essential skills of the New Zealand Curriculum Framework … [for the purpose of] formative assessment."
Population: Ages 9–14.
Publication Date: 2001.
Administration: Group.
Levels, 3: Primary, Intermediate, Secondary.
Price Data, 2002: NZ$36 per full specimen set including 1 each of primary, intermediate, and secondary

tests, and teacher's manual (71 pages); NZ$22.50 per specimen set including all tests and teacher's manual (primary level); NZ$27 per specimen set including all tests and teacher's manual (intermediate level); NZ$22.95 per specimen set including all tests and teacher's manual (secondary level); NZ$450 per CD-ROM pack including CD-ROM with all tests (PDF format), teacher's manual, 1 set of printed tests, and help sheet; NZ$18 per teacher's manual; NZ$9.90 per 10 Finding Information in Books (all levels, specify level); NZ$9.90 per 10 Finding Information in Graphs and Tables (primary level); NZ$12.60 per 10 Finding Information in Graphs and Tables (intermediate level); NZ$11.70 per 10 Finding Information in Graphs and Tables (secondary level); NZ$9.90 per 10 Finding Information in a Library (primary and intermediate levels, specify level); NZ$12.60 per 10 finding Information in a Library (secondary level); NZ$9.90 per 10 Finding Information in Reference Sources (primary and intermediate levels, specify level); NZ$9.90 per 10 Evaluating Information in Text (intermediate level); NZ12.60 per 10 Evaluating Information in Text (secondary level); NZ$12.60 per 10 finding Information in Prose Text (intermediate and secondary levels, specify level).
Time: (30) minutes per test.
Comments: Replaces the Progressive Achievement Tests of Study Skills (T5:2095); tests include both constructed-response and selected-response format items; normed on children living in New Zealand; available in print or CD-ROM format; CD-ROM system requirements: 600 dpi laser or inkjet printer, Adobe Acrobat reader version 3 or 4.
Authors: Cedric Croft, Karyn Dunn, and Gavin Brown.
Publisher: New Zealand Council for Educational Research [New Zealand].
a) FINDING INFORMATION IN BOOKS.
Levels, 2: Primary, Intermediate.
Scores: Total score only.
b) FINDING INFORMATION IN GRAPHS AND TABLES.
Levels, 3: Primary, Intermediate, Secondary.
Scores: Total score only.
c) FINDING INFORMATION IN A LIBRARY.
Levels, 3: Primary, Intermediate, Secondary.
Scores: Total score only.
d) FINDING INFORMATION IN PROSE TEXT.
Levels, 2: Intermediate, Secondary.
Scores: Total score only.
e) FINDING INFORMATION IN REFERENCE SOURCES.
Levels, 2: Primary, Intermediate.
Scores: Total score only.
f) FINDING INFORMATION IN TEXT.
Levels, 2: Intermediate, Secondary.
Scores: Total score only.
Cross References: For a review by Robert L. Johnson, see 15:90; see T5:2095 (1 reference); for reviews by

Michael D. Hiscox and Ronald C. Rodgers of an earlier edition, see 9:1006; see also T3:1913 (1 reference).

[1020]
ETS Tests of Applied Literacy Skills.
Purpose: To measure adult literacy.
Population: Adults.
Publication Date: 1991.
Scores, 3: Total score for each of 3 subtests: Quantitative Literacy, Document Literacy, Prose Literacy.
Administration: Group.
Forms, 2: Forms A and B for each test.
Price Data: Available from publisher.
Time: 6(20) minutes for the battery; 2(20) minutes of any one subtest.
Authors: Educational Testing Service, Irwin J. Kirsch (manual), Anne Jungeblut (manual), and Anne Campbell (manual), with contributions from Norman E. Freeberg, Robert J. Mislevy, Donald A. Rock, and Kentaro Yamamoto.
Publisher: Prentice Hall [No reply from publisher; status unknown].
Cross References: For reviews by Roger A. Richards and Herbert C. Rudman, see 13:123.

[1021]
Evaluating Courses for Inclusion of New Scholarship on Women.
Purpose: A student evaluation questionnaire designed to evaluate course content in terms of information presented about women.
Population: Post-secondary students.
Publication Date: 1988.
Scores: 4 ratings: Evaluation of Course Readings, Evaluation of the Syllabus, Evaluation of the Class, Overall Course Evaluation.
Administration: Group.
Manual: No manual.
Price Data: Available from publisher.
Time: Administration time not reported.
Author: Women's Studies Program, Duke University.
Publisher: Association of American Colleges and Universities.

[1022]
Evaluating Diversity Training.
Purpose: "Designed to help diversity-training managers evaluate the effectiveness of training, instructors, and vendors."
Population: Diversity-training managers.
Publication Date: 1996.
Scores: 17 checklists: Participant Reactions (rating scale, open ended), Self-Assessment of Learning, Learning Self-Assessment, Knowledge of Diversity Issues, Learning Outcomes Role-Play, Participant Post-Training

(open ended, short version, rating scale), Manager's Post training (open ended, satisfaction measure, application estimate), Diversity Behavior, Organizational Results, Vendor Evaluation, Instructor/Facilitator Effectiveness, Experiential Training Evaluation.
Administration: Group.
Price Data: Available from publisher.
Time: Untimed.
Authors: John M. Keller, Andrea Young, and Mary Riley.
Publisher: Jossey-Bass, A Wiley Company.

[1023]
Evaluation Aptitude Test.
Purpose: Constructed to assess deductive reasoning.
Population: Candidates for college and graduate school entrance.
Publication Dates: 1951–1952.
Acronym: EAT.
Scores, 5: Neutral Syllogisms, Emotionally Toned Syllogisms, Total, Emotional Bias, Indecision.
Administration: Group.
Price Data: Available from publisher.
Time: 50(55) minutes.
Author: DeWitt E. Sell.
Publisher: Psychometric Affiliates.
Cross References: For reviews by J. Thomas Hastings and Walker H. Hill, see 5:691.

[1024]
Evaluation Disposition Toward the Environment.
Purpose: Evaluates "value orientation used to approach environmental experiences and responsibilities."
Population: High school and college.
Publication Date: 1976.
Acronym: EDEN.
Scores, 7: Aesthetic, Experiential, Knowledge Seeking, Prudent, Active, Responsible, Practical.
Administration: Group.
Price Data: Available from publisher.
Time: (45) minutes.
Comments: Scoring must be done by publisher.
Author: Norman J. Milchus.
Publisher: Norman Milchus (the author).

[1025]
Evaluation Modality Test.
Purpose: Developed to analyze the characteristics of "the mode in which an individual valuates."
Population: Adults.
Publication Date: 1956.
Acronym: EMT.
Scores, 4: Realism, Moralism, Individualism, Total.
Administration: Individual or group.

Price Data: Available from publisher.
Time: (25–35) minutes.
Author: Hugo O. Engelmann.
Publisher: Psychometric Affiliates.
Cross References: For a review by Wilson H. Guertin, see 5:51.

[1026]
Evaluation of Basic Skills.
Purpose: Designed to provide a concept-based measurement of reading, writing, and mathematics.
Population: Ages 3 to 18.
Publication Dates: 1995–1996.
Scores, 3: Reading, Writing, Mathematics.
Administration: Individual.
Price Data, 2005: $89.95 per complete start-up kit including administration manual (1995, 27 pages), 50 test forms, and 25 pre-test/post-test word tests; $15.95 per administration manual; $12 per 2-tape audio cassette set "Administering the Test"; $195 per application fee as test administrator; $50 per 50 test forms; $40 per 50 pre-test/post-test word tests.
Time: (10) minutes for Mathematics section; untimed for Reading and Writing sections.
Author: Lee Havis.
Publisher: Trust Tutoring.
Cross References: For reviews by Eleanor E. Sanford and Loraine J. Spenciner, see 14:142.

[1027]
Evaluation of Competency to Stand Trial–Revised.
Purpose: "Designed for specialized forensic evaluations related to competency to stand trial."
Population: Ages 18 and over.
Publication Date: 2004.
Acronym: ECST-R.
Scores, 8: Competency Scales (Factual Understanding of Courtroom Proceedings, Rational Understanding of Courtroom Proceedings, Consult with Counsel), Atypical Presentation Scales (Realistic, Psychotic, Nonpsychotic Impairment, Both [Psychotic and Nonpsychotic combined]).
Administration: Individual.
Price Data, 2006: $220 per introductory kit including professional manual (2004, 176 pages), binder with interview booklet, 25 record forms, and 25 profile/summary forms in a soft-sided attaché case.
Time: Untimed.
Comments: Semistructured interview format.
Authors: Richard Rogers, Chad E. Tillbrook, and Kenneth W. Sewell.
Publisher: Psychological Assessment Resources, Inc.
Cross References: For reviews by D. Ashley Cohen and Robert A. Leark, see 16:87.

[1028]

Everyday Life Activities: Photo Series.

Purpose: Designed as a photo series for "language training, teaching, testing and remediation of word-, sentence-, and text/discourse-level abilities."
Population: Children with delay in language development, autistic children, and adults with a language or speech impairment sequel to brain damage.
Publication Date: 1994.
Acronym: ELA.
Scores: Available from publisher.
Administration: Individual.
Price Data, 2001: $743 per book.
Time: Administration time not reported.
Author: Jacqueline Stark.
Publisher: Psychology Press.

[1029]

Examination for the Certificate of Competency in English.

Purpose: Designed as a test of general language proficiency in a variety of contexts; it assesses linguistic, discoursal, sociolinguistic, and pragmatic elements of the English language.
Population: Nonnative speakers of English.
Publication Dates: 1995-2011.
Acronym: ECCE.
Scores, 5: Writing, Listening Comprehension, GVR (Grammar/Vocabulary/Reading), Speaking, Overall Score.
Administration: Group.
Forms, 4: A, B, C, D.
Price Data: Available from publisher.
Time: (30) minutes for Listening; (80) minutes for Grammar/Vocabulary/Reading; (30) minutes for Writing; (10-15) minutes for Speaking.
Comments: Designed for nonnative speakers of English who would like official documentary evidence of intermediate proficiency in the English language, particularly for academic and professional purposes.
Author: The University of Michigan.
Publisher: Cambridge-Michigan Language Assessments.

[1030]

Examination for the Certificate of Proficiency in English.

Purpose: Designed "as a test of general language proficiency in a variety of contexts; it assesses linguistic, discoursal, sociolinguistic, and pragmatic elements of the English language."
Population: English language learners.
Publication Dates: 1953-2011.
Acronym: ECPE.
Scores, 5: Writing, Listening Comprehension, Grammar/Cloze/Vocabulary/Reading, Speaking, Overall Score.
Administration: Group.

Forms: 2 forms per year.
Price Data: Available from publisher.
Time: (150) minutes.
Comments: Administered twice a year at approved test centers around the world; aimed at the C2 level of the Common European Framework of Reference; designed for English language learners who would like official documentary evidence of advanced proficiency in the English language, particularly for academic and professional purposes.
Author: The University of Michigan.
Publisher: Cambridge-Michigan Language Assessments.

[1031]

Examining for Aphasia, Third Edition.

Purpose: "For evaluating possible aphasic language impairments and other acquired impairments that are often closely related to language functions."
Population: Adolescents and adults.
Publication Dates: 1946–1994.
Acronym: EFA-3.
Scores, 41: Agnosias (Common Objects, Pictures, Colors, Geometric Forms, Numerals, Letters, Printed Words, Almost Alike Pictures, Printed Sentences, Nonverbal Noises, Object Identification, Total); Aphasias (Word Identification, Comprehension of Sentences, Comprehension of Multiple Choice, Oral Paragraphs, Silent Reading Sentences, Silent Reading Paragraphs, Total); Apraxias (Body Parts, Simple Skills, Pretend Action, Numerals, Words, Sentences, Total), Aphasios (Automatic Speech, Writing Numerals, Writing Letters, Spelling, Writing from Dictation, Naming Body Parts, Word Finding, Arithmetic Computations, Arithmetic Problems, Total); Composites (Receptive, Expressive, Subaphasic, Aphasia, Total).
Administration: Individual.
Price Data: Available from publisher.
Time: (30–120) minutes.
Comments: Shortened version of test may be administered for screening purposes; the publisher advises that a Fourth Edition is now available.
Author: Jon Eisenson.
Publisher: PRO-ED.
Cross References: For a review by Helen Kitchens, see 13:124: see also T4:940 (2 references), T2:2071 (3 references), and P:76 (2 references); for excerpted reviews by Louis M. DiCarlo and Laurance F. Shaffer, see 5:52 (3 references); for a review by D. Russell Davis and excerpted reviews by Nolan D. C. Lewis and one other, see 4:42; for a review by C. R. Strother and an excerpted review, see 3:39.

[1032]

Executive Administrative Assistant Skills Test.

Purpose: To evaluate the suitability of candidates for the position of executive administrative assistant.

Population: Candidates with all levels of experience for the position of executive administrative assistant.
Publication Date: 1977.
Acronym: PRSECTY.
Scores: Total Score, Narrative Evaluation, Ranking, Recommendation.
Administration: Group.
Price Data, 2001: $355 per candidate.
Time: (45) minutes.
Comments: Scored by publisher; must be proctored.
Author: Walden Personnel Performance, Inc.
Publisher: Walden Personnel Performance, Inc.

[1033]

The Executive Control Battery.

Purpose: "To document the presence and extent of the 'executive dyscontrol' or 'frontal lobe' syndrome."
Population: Adults.
Publication Date: 1999.
Acronym: ECB.
Administration: Individual.
Price Data: Available from publisher.
Comments: Neuropsychological battery; subtests can be administered independently.
Authors: Elkhonon Goldberg, Kenneth Podell, Robert Bilder, and Judith Jaeger.
Publisher: Psych Press [Australia].
  a) THE GRAPHICAL SEQUENCES TEST.
  Purpose: "Designed to elicit perseverations ... and various behavioural stereotypies."
  Scores, 7: Hyperkinetic Motor Perseverations (Occurrences), Perseveration of Elements (Occurrences, Repetitions), Perseveration of Features (Occurrences, Repetitions), Perseverations of Activities (Occurrences, Repetitions).
  Time: (15–20) minutes.
  b) COMPETING PROGRAMS TEST.
  Purpose: "Designed to elicit various types of echopraxia, behavioural stereotypies, and disinhibition."
  Scores, 8: Simple Go/No-Go (Random, Simple Stereotype, Alternating Stereotype, Total Errors), Simple Conflict–Visual (Random, Simple Stereotype, Alternating Stereotype, Total Errors).
  Time: (12–15) minutes.
  c) MANUAL POSTURES TEST.
  Purpose: "Designed to elicit various types of echopraxia."
  Scores: 3 ratings: Correct, Full Mirroring, Other.
  Time: (10–15) minutes.
  d) MOTOR SEQUENCES TEST.
  Purpose: "Designed to elicit various types of motor perseverations, stereotypies, and other deficits of sequential motor organisation."
  Parts, 2: Dynamic Praxis, Bimanual Coordination.
  Time: (10–15) minutes.

  1) *Dynamic Praxis.*
  Scores, 6: Two Stage Movement (Imitation, Continuation, Without Model), Reversal of Two State Movement (Imitation, Continuation Without Model), Three Stage Movement (Imitation, Continuation Without Model.
  2) *Bimanual Coordination.*
  Scores, 6: Distal (Imitation, Continuation Without Model), Proximal (Imitation, Continuation Without Model), Mixed (Imitation, Continuation Without Model).
Cross References: For reviews by Anthony T. Dugbartey and by Shawn Powell and David McCone, see 15:92.

[1034]

Executive Dimensions.

Purpose: Designed to assess leadership effectiveness among top-level senior executives.
Population: Senior executives.
Publication Dates: 2004-2006.
Scores, 16: Sound Judgement, Strategic Planning, Leading Change, Results Orientation, Global Awareness, Business Perspective, Inspiring Commitment, Forging Synergy, Developing and Empowering, Leveraging Differences, Communicating Effectively, Interpersonal Savvy, Courage, Executive Image, Learning from Experience, Credibility.
Administration: Group.
Restricted Distribution: Distribution restricted to persons who have completed the publisher's training course.
Price Data, 2007: $395 per survey set including Development Planning Guide (2005, 20 pages), Facilitator's Guide, internet-based surveys, assessment scoring, and 2 printed feedback reports.
Foreign Language Editions: Spanish, French, German, and Dutch versions available.
Time: Administration time not reported.
Comments: Test administered via secure web page.
Author: Center for Creative Leadership.
Publisher: Center for Creative Leadership.
Cross References: For reviews by Ayres D'Costa and Matt Vassar, see 18:50.

[1035]

Executive Profile Survey.

Purpose: Constructed to assess whether an individual has the attributes for success by measuring behavioral characteristics in comparison with over 2,000 top-level executives.
Population: Prospective executives.
Publication Dates: 1967–1983.
Acronym: EPS.
Scores: 11 dimensions: Ambitious, Assertive, Enthusiastic, Creative, Spontaneous, Self-Focused, Considerate, Open-Minded, Relaxed, Practical, Systematic.

Administration: Group or individual.
Price Data, 2005: $22 per 10 reusable test booklets; $22 per 25 answer sheets; $30 per manual (1983, 79 pages); $34 per introductory kit; $16.50 to $30 per reports.
Time: (60) minutes.
Comments: Self-administered; manual title is Perspectives on the Executive Personality.
Authors: Virgil R. Lang and Samuel E. Krug (manual).
Publisher: Institute for Personality and Ability Testing, Inc. (IPAT).
Cross References: For reviews by S. David Kriska and Gregory J. Marchant, see 12:146; for a review of an earlier edition by William I. Sauser, Jr., see 9:401.

[1036]

Expectations Edition of the Personal Values Inventory.

Purpose: To identify role expectations and compare them with the motivational values of the person in the role.
Population: Adolescents and adults reading at or above sixth grade (U.S.) reading level.
Publication Date: 2001.
Acronym: EE/PVI.
Scores: Blue Motivation, Red-Blue Motivation, Red Motivation, Red-Green Motivation, Green Motivation, Blue-Green Motivation.
Administration: Group or individual.
Manual: No manual.
Price Data, 2002: $4.50 per inventory.
Time: (15–30) minutes.
Comments: For use with the Personal Values Inventory (2018); scores reflect expectations of the person in the role when things are going well and the expected responses when there is conflict or opposition.
Author: Elias H. Porter.
Publisher: Personal Strengths Publishing.

[1037]

Expectations Edition of the Strength Development Inventory.

Purpose: To identify role expectations and compare them with the motivational values of the person in the role.
Population: Adults.
Publication Date: 2001.
Acronym: EE/SDI.
Scores: Altruistic-Nurturing Motivation, Assertive-Nurturing Motivation, Assertive-Directing Motivation, Judicious-Competing Motivation, Analytic-Autonomizing Motivation, Cautious-Supporting Motivation.
Administration: Group or individual.
Manual: No manual.
Price Data, 2002: $4.50 per inventory.
Foreign Language Edition: French edition available entitled Édition sur les attentes de l'inventaire du déploiement des forces de la personnalité.

Time: (15–30) minutes.
Comments: For use with the Strength Deployment Inventory (2565); supersedes the Job Interactions Inventory (14:474); scores reflect expectations of the person in the role when things are going well and the expected responses when there is conflict or opposition.
Author: Elias H. Porter.
Publisher: Personal Strengths Publishing.

[1038]

Experience and Background Inventory (Form S).

Purpose: "Provides quantitative measures of past performance and experience."
Population: Adults [industry].
Publication Dates: 1980–1996.
Acronym: EBI.
Scores: 9 factors: School Achievement, Choice of a College Major, Aspiration Level, Drive/Career Progress, Leadership and Group Participation, Vocational Satisfaction, Financial Responsibility, General Responsibility, Relaxation Pursuits.
Administration: Group.
Price Data, 2002: $102 per start-up kit including 25 test booklets, 25 score sheets, and interprettion and research manual (1996, 15 pages); $54 per 25 test booklets; $32 per 25 score sheets; $28 per interpretation and research manual.
Time: Administration time not reported.
Authors: Melany E. Baehr and Ernest C. Froemel.
Publisher: Pearson Performance Solutions [No reply from publisher; status unknown].
Cross References: For reviews by F. Felicia Ferrara and Chantale Jeanrie, see 15:93.

[1039]

The Experiencing Scale.

Purpose: Assess the degree to which a patient communicates and employs a personal, phenomenological perspective in a therapy session.
Population: Counselors and counselor trainees.
Publication Date: 1969.
Acronym: EXP.
Scores, 2: Mode, Peak; based on a 7-point rating scale.
Administration: Individual.
Price Data, 2001: $26 per Volumes I and II; $42 per Volume III.
Time: Administration time not reported.
Comments: "Evaluating the quality of patient self-involvement in psychotherapy directly from tape recordings or typescripts of the therapy session"; tape or transcript of session required; rated by trained raters from tapes (audio or video).
Authors: M. H. Klein, P. L. Mathieu, E. T. Gendlin, and D. J. Kiesler.
Publisher: Marjorie H. Klein, Ph.D. (the author).

Cross References: See T5:991 (3 references) and T4:943 (1 reference).

[1040]

EXPLORE.

Purpose: Measures the academic progress of eighth and ninth graders in four areas: English, mathematics, reading, and science; helps students explore the range of career options; and assists them in developing a high school coursework plan.
Population: Grades 8–9.
Publication Dates: 1995–2000.
Administration: Group.
Price Data: Available from publisher.
Time: (120) minutes for four academics tests; (45–60) minutes for interest inventory, plans and background information, and needs assessment.
Comments: EXPLORE is the initial component of ACT's Educational Planning and Assessment System (EPAS), which also includes PLAN (2064) in Grade 10, and the ACT in Grades 11 or 12. Special testing with extended time and alternate test formats are available for students who receive special accommodations in school due to professionally diagnosed and documented disabilities.
Author: ACT, Inc.
Publisher: ACT, Inc.
a) EXPLORE ENGLISH TEST.
Purpose: Measures understanding of the conventions of standard written English.
Scores, 3: Usage/Mechanics (Punctuation, Grammar and Usage, Sentence Structure), Rhetorical Skills (Strategy, Organization, Style), Total.
Time: 30 minutes.
b) EXPLORE MATHEMATICS TEST.
Purpose: Measures student's mathematical reasoning skills.
Scores: Total score only.
Time: 30 minutes.
c) EXPLORE READING TEST.
Purpose: Measures reading comprehension as a product of referring and reasoning skills.
Scores: Total score only.
Time: 30 minutes.
d) EXPLORE SCIENCE TEST.
Purpose: Measures scientific reasoning skills.
Scores: Total score only.
Time: 30 minutes.
Cross References: For a review by Sandra A. Loew, see 15:94.

[1041]

Explore the World of Work.

Purpose: Designed to stimulate job awareness and exploration for jobs requiring up to 2 years of training.
Population: Elementary and special education.

Publication Dates: 1989–1991.
Acronym: E-WOW.
Scores, 6: Business/Office/Sales, Industry/Mechanics/Transportation/Construction, Art/Communications/Design, Health/Education/Social Service, Forestry/Agriculture/Natural Resources, Scientific/Technical/Health.
Administration: Group.
Price Data: Available from publisher.
Time: (40–70) minutes.
Comments: Children's Occupational Outlook Handbook suggested to complete follow-up activities on the questionnaire; self-scored.
Authors: Lori Constantino, Bob Kauk, and CFKR Career Materials, Inc. (manuals).
Publisher: CFKR Career Materials.

[1042]

Expressive One-Word Picture Vocabulary Test [2000 Edition].

Purpose: Designed to measure an individual's English-speaking vocabulary.
Population: Ages 2–0 through 18-11.
Publication Dates: 1979–2000.
Acronym: EOWPVT.
Scores: Total score only.
Administration: Individual.
Price Data, 2006: $145 per kit including manual (2000, 128 pages), 25 record forms, and test plates in a vinyl portfolio; $75 per test plates; $30 per 25 record forms; $40 per manual.
Time: (10–15) minutes.
Comments: The editor combines the lower and upper levels in previous editions and extends the use of the test through age 18-11.
Authors: 1990 and earlier edition by Morrison F. Gardner; 2000 edition by Rick Brownell.
Publisher: Academic Therapy Publications.
Cross References: For a review by Alfred Longo, see 15:95; see T5:994 (53 references) and T4:946 (23 references); for reviews by Gregory J. Cizek and Larry B. Grantham of an earlier edition, see 12:147 (6 references); for reviews by Jack A. Cummings and Gilbert M. Spivak of the Lower Level, see 9:403 (2 references).

[1043]

Expressive One-Word Picture Vocabulary Test: Spanish-Bilingual Edition.

Purpose: Designed to "provide an assessment of an individual's combined Spanish and English vocabulary."
Population: Ages 4-0 through 12-11.
Publication Date: 2001.
Acronym: EOWPVT-SBE.
Scores: Total score only.
Administration: Individual.

Price Data, 2006: $140 per test kit including manual (108 pages), test plates, and 25 record forms in portfolio; $38 per Spanish-Bilingual Edition manual; $27 per Spanish-Bilingual record forms.
Time: (10–15) minutes.
Comments: Adaptation of the English edition of the Expressive One-Word Picture Vocabulary Test (1042); co-normed with the Receptive One-Word Picture Vocabulary Test: Spanish-Bilingual Edition (2249).
Author: Rick Brownell.
Publisher: Academic Therapy Publications.
Cross References: For a review by Jill Ann Jenkins, see 16:88.

[1044]

Expressive Vocabulary Test, Second Edition.
Purpose: Designed to assess "expressive vocabulary and word retrieval for Standard American English."
Population: Ages 2:6 to 90+ years.
Publication Dates: 1997-2007.
Acronym: EVT-2™.
Scores: Total score only.
Administration: Individual.
Forms, 2: A, B.
Price Data, 2008: $390 per complete kit (Forms A & B) including 25 record forms for Form A & 25 record forms for Form B, easel for each form, and manual (2007, 238 pages); $45.50 per 25 record forms (specify A or B); $259 per EVT-2 ASSIST™ scoring and reporting software; single form kits also available.
Time: (10-20) minutes.
Comments: Also includes a growth scale value (GSV) to specifically measure progress over time; conormed with the Peabody Picture Vocabulary Test-4 (1966); EVT-2 and PPVT-4 standard scores allow direct comparisons between expressive and receptive vocabulary; items are categorized for multiple levels and types of descriptive analysis; scoring and reporting software (ASSIST) allows for multiple types of individual and group reporting, including aggregation and disaggregation options; evidence-based interventions are embedded within the ASSIST.
Author: Kathleen T. Williams.
Publisher: Pearson.
Cross References: For reviews by Theresa Graham and Natalie Rathvon, see 18:51; for reviews by Frederick Bessai and Orest Eugene Wasyliw of a previous edition, see 14:143.

[1045]

Extended Complex Figure Test
Purpose: Designed to measure both perceptual organization and visual memory in persons with brain injury.
Population: Ages 19–85.
Publication Date: 2003.
Acronym: ECFT.

Scores, 14: Copy Total Correct, Copy Time, Immediate Recall Total Correct, Immediate Recall Time, Delayed Recall Total Correct, Delayed Recall Time, Recognition Total Correct, Recognition Global, Recognition Detail, Recognition Left Detail, Recognition Right Detail, Matching Total Correct, Matching Left Detail, Matching Right Detail.
Administration: Individual.
Price Data, 2006: $159.50 per kit including manual (94 pages), stimulus booklet, and administration scoring booklet; $68.50 per stimulus booklet; $47 per 25 administration and scoring booklets; $58 per manual.
Time: (15–20) minutes.
Author: Philip S. Fastenau.
Publisher: Western Psychological Services.
Cross References: For reviews by Mary "Rina" M. Chittooran and Daniel C. Miller, see 16:89.

[1046]

Eyberg Child Behavior Inventory and Sutter-Eyberg Student Behavior Inventory–Revised.
Purpose: Designed "to measure conduct problems in children ages 2 through 16 years."
Population: Ages 2–16.
Publication Dates: 1978–1999.
Acronym: ECBI; SESBI-R.
Scores, 2: Intensity, Problem.
Administration: Group or individual.
Forms, 2: Eyberg Child Behavior Inventory; Sutter-Eyberg Student Behavior Inventory–Revised.
Price Data, 2006: $162 per introductory kit including professional manual (1999, 64 pages), 50 ECBI test sheets, and 50 SESBI-R test sheets.
Time: (10) minutes.
Comments: ECBI is a rating form completed by parents; SESBI-R is a rating form completed by teachers.
Authors: Sheila Eyberg (SESBI-R, ECBI, and professional manual), Joseph Sutter (SESBI-R), and Donna Pincus (professional manual).
Publisher: Psychological Assessment Resources, Inc.
Cross References: For reviews by Joyce Meikamp and by Susan C. Whiston and Jennifer C. Bouwkamp, see 15:96; for information on the Eyberg Child Behavior Inventory, see T5:997 (30 references) and T4:948 (26 references); for a review by Michael L. Reed of an earlier edition, see 9:404 (6 references); see also T3:858 (2 references). For information on the Sutter-Eyberg Student Behavior Inventory, see T5:2595 (2 references) and T4:2668 (1 reference); for a review by T. Steuart Watson of an earlier edition, see 11:410 (2 references).

[1047]

Eysenck Personality Inventory.
Purpose: Measures two independent dimensions of personality: Extraversion-Introversion and Neuroticism-Stability.
Population: Adults.

Publication Dates: 1963–1969.
Acronym: EPI.
Scores, 3: Extraversion, Neuroticism, Lie.
Administration: Group.
Time: (10–15) minutes.
Comments: Revision of Maudsley Personality Inventory; for revised edition of EPI, see Eysenck Personality Questionnaire–Revised (1048); no reliability data for Lie scores; authors recommend use of both forms to obtain adequate reliability for individual measurements; U.S. and British Editions are identical except for three words and directions.
Authors: H. J. Eysenck and Sybil B. G. Eysenck.
  a) UNITED STATES EDITION.
  Population: Grades 9–16 and adults.
  Publication Dates: 1963–1969.
  Forms, 2: A, B.
  Price Data: Available from publisher.
  Foreign Language Edition: Spanish edition (1972) available.
  Comments: A printing with the title Eysenck Personality Inventory is available for industrial use.
  Publisher: EdITS/Educational and Industrial Testing Service.
  b) BRITISH EDITION.
  Population: Adults.
  Publication Dates: 1963–1964.
  Forms, 2: A, B.
  Price Data: Available from publisher.
  Comments: This test is now superseded by Eysenck Personality Questionnaire [Revised] (1048) except where parallel forms are required.
  Publisher: Hodder & Stoughton Educational [England].
Cross References: See T5:998 (135 references), T4:949 (226 references), 9:405 (91 references), and T3:859 (245 references); for a review by Auke Tellegen, see 8:553 (405 references); see also T2:1174 (140 references); for reviews by Richard I. Lanyon and excerpted reviews by A. W. Heim and James Linder, see 7:776 (121 references); see also P:77 (52 references); for a review by James C. Lingoes, see 6:93 (1 reference).

[1048]

Eysenck Personality Questionnaire [Revised].
Publication Dates: 1975–1994.
Acronym: EPQ-R.
Scores, 5: Psychotocism or Tough-Mindedness, Extraversion, Neuroticism or Emotionality, Lie, Addiction.
Administration: Group.
Time: (10–15) minutes.
Comments: Revision of the still-in-print Eysenck Personality Inventory (1047).
Authors: H. J. Eysenck and Sybil B. G. Eysenck.
  a) UNITED STATES EDITION.
  Purpose: Designed to measure four dimensions of personality in adults.

Population: College and general adults including those with lower education levels.
Publication Dates: 1975–1994.
Price Data: Available from publisher.
Publisher: EdITS/Educational and Industrial Testing Service.
  b) BRITISH EDITION.
  Purpose: Measures three main personality factors: Psychotocism, Extraversion, and Neuroticism.
  Population: Ages 7–15, 16 and over.
  Publication Dates: 1975–1991.
  Price Data: Available from publisher.
  Publisher: Hodder & Stoughton Educational [England].
Cross References: See T5:999 (195 references), T4:950 (190 references), 9:406 (32 references), and T3:860 (72 references); for reviews by Jack Block, Paul Kline, Lawrence J. Stricker, and Auke Tellegen, see 8:554 (84 references).

[1049]

FACES IV (Family Adaptability and Cohesion Evaluation Scale).
Purpose: To determine the structure of the family, in terms of the Circumplex Model.
Population: Families.
Publication Dates: 1985-2009.
Acronym: FACES IV.
Scores: 2 major dimensions: Family Cohesion, Family Flexibility; 6 scales with 2 balanced scales (Balanced Cohesion and Balanced Flexibility) and 4 unbalanced scales (Disengaged and Enmeshed, Rigid and Chaotic).
Administration: Individual or group.
Price Data, 2006: $95 for FACES IV Package, which includes unlimited use (package includes manual, scales, and scoring procedures).
Time: (15-20) minutes.
Comments: FACES II and FACES III are no longer available but are integrated into FACES IV; also known as Family Adaptability & Cohesion Evaluation Scales; self-report instrument; additional information available at www.facesiv.com.
Authors: David H. Olson, Dean Gorall, and Judy Tiesel.
Publisher: Life Innovations, Inc.
Cross References: See T5:1000 (110 references), T4:951 (31 references), and 11:140 (26 references).

[1050]

Facial Action Coding System.
Purpose: Constructed to assess facial movements or expressions.
Population: Adults.
Publication Date: 1978.
Acronym: FACS.
Scores: 66 Action Units.

Administration: Individual.
Price Data: Available from publisher.
Time: Administration time not reported.
Authors: Paul Ekman and Wallace V. Friesen.
Publisher: Paul Ekman (the author) [No reply from publisher; status unknown].
Cross References: See T5:1001 (17 references); for reviews by Kathryn M. Benes and Thomas F. Donlon, see 12:149 (7 references); see also T4:952 (11 references).

[1051]

Facial Expressions of Emotion–Stimuli and Tests.

Purpose: Designed to "assess recognition of facial expressions of emotion."
Population: Adults.
Publication Date: 2002.
Acronym: FEEST.
Administration: Individual.
Price Data, 2006: £384 per CD-ROM including tests and manual.
Time: Untimed.
Comments: Computer administered; requires Pentium PC running Windows 98, 64 Mb RAM and CD-ROM drive; also runs on Apple Macintosh System 7.5 through 9; 2 tests: Ekman 60 Faces, Emotion Hexagon.
Authors: Andrew Young, David Perrett, Andrew Calder, Reiner Sprengelmeyer, and Paul Ekman.
Publisher: Pearson Assessment [England].
  a) EKMAN 60 FACES.
  Scores, 7: Anger, Disgust, Fear, Happiness, Sadness, Surprise, Total.
  b) EMOTION HEXAGON.
  Scores, 7: Same as *a* above.
  Comments: Uses computer-morphed expressions to manipulate test difficulty.
Cross References: For reviews by Albert M. Bugaj and Denice Ward Hood, see 17:70.

[1052]

Faculty Morale Scale for Institutional Improvement.

Purpose: Designed "as a diagnostic instrument—an attitudinal fact-finding device."
Population: Faculty members.
Publication Date: No date.
Scores: Total score only.
Administration: Group.
Price Data, 2001: $3 per specimen set.
Time: Administration time not reported.
Author: A Local Chapter Committee, American Association of University Professors.
Publisher: Psychometric Affiliates.
Cross References: For a review by Keith Hattrup, see 15:97.

[1053]

A Familism Scale.

Purpose: Measures attitudes related to family.
Population: Adolescents and adults.
Publication Dates: 1959–1988.
Scores, 3: Nuclear, Extended, Total.
Administration: Group.
Manual: No manual.
Price Data, 2005: $2 per scale.
Time: (8) minutes.
Comments: Supplementary article available.
Author: Panos D. Bardis.
Publisher: Donna Bardis.
Cross References: See T4:957 (1 reference).

[1054]

Family Adjustment Test.

Purpose: "Designed to measure feelings of intrafamily homeyness-homelessness."
Population: Ages 12 and over.
Publication Dates: 1952–1954.
Acronym: FAT.
Scores, 11: Attitudes Toward Mother, Attitudes Toward Father, Father-Mother Attitude Quotient, Oedipal, Struggle for Independence, Parent-Child Friction-Harmony, Interparental Friction-Harmony, Family Inferiority-Superiority, Rejection of Child, Parental Qualities, Total.
Administration: Group.
Price Data: Available from publisher.
Time: (35–40) minutes.
Comments: Title on test is Elias Family Opinion Survey.
Author: Gabriel Elias.
Publisher: Psychometric Affiliates.
Cross References: See T4:958 (1 reference), T2:1181 (12 references), and P:80 (1 reference); for a review by John Elderkin Bell, see 6:95; for a review by Albert Ellis, see 5:53 (6 references).

[1055]

Family Assessment Form: A Practice-Based Approach to Assessing Family Functioning.

Purpose: Constructed to "standardize the assessment of family functioning and service planning for families receiving home-based services."
Population: Families receiving home-based services
Publication Date: 1997.
Acronym: FAF.
Scores, 6: Parent-Child Interactions, Living Conditions, Caregiver Interactions, Supports for Parents, Financial Conditions, Developmental Stimulation.
Administration: Group.
Price Data: Price information available from publisher for test booklet/manual (79 pages), at www.cwla.org/pubs.
Time: (60–90) minutes.

Comments: Ratings by child welfare practitioners.
Author: Children's Bureau of Southern California.
Publisher: Child Welfare League of America.
Cross References: For reviews by Cindy Carlson and Mary Lou Kelley, see 14:144; see also T5:1007 (1 reference).

[1056]
Family Assessment Measure Version III.
Purpose: "Provides quantitative indices of family strengths and weaknesses."
Population: Families.
Publication Dates: 1993–1995.
Acronym: FAM-III.
Scores, 26: General scale (Task Accomplishment, Role Performance, Communication, Affective Expression, Involvement, Control, Values and Norms, Social Desirability, Defensiveness, Total), Dyadic Relationships (Task Accomplishment, Role Performance, Communication, Affective Expression, Involvement, Control, Values and Norms, Total), Self-Rating (Task Accomplishment, Role Performance, Communication, Affective Expression, Involvement, Control, Values and Norms, Total).
Administration: Individual.
Price Data, 2011: $242 per complete kit including manual (1995, 90 pages), 25 General Scale QuikScore™ forms, 25 Dyadic Relationship Scale QuikScore™ forms, 25 Self-Rating Scale QuikScore™ forms, and 15 ColorPlot Profile of Family Perceptions; $218 per Brief FAM complete kit including manual, 25 Brief FAM General Scale QuikScore™ forms, 25 Brief FAM Dyadic Relationship Scale QuikScore™ forms, 25 Brief FAM Self-Rating Scale QuikScore™ forms, and 15 Progress ColorPlot Profiles; $50 per 25 General Scale QuikScore™ forms (English, Spanish, or French-Canadian); $50 per 25 Dyadic Relationship Scale QuikScore™ forms (English, Spanish, or French-Canadian); $50 per 25 Self-Rating Scale QuikScore™ forms (English, Spanish, or French-Canadian); $50 per 25 Brief General Scale QuikScore™ forms (English, Spanish, or French-Canadian); $50 per 25 Brief FAM Dyadic Relationship Scale QuikScore™ forms (English, Spanish, or French-Canadian); $50 per 25 Brief FAM Self-Rating Scale QuikScore™ forms (English, Spanish, or French-Canadian); $42 per 15 Progress Color Plot Profiles; $42 per 15 Color Plot Profile of Family Perceptions; $82 per manual; software also available; $10 per long profile report; $7 per brief profile report; $56 per preview version including 3 profile reports and manual.
Foreign Language Editions: Spanish and French-Canadian QuikScore™ forms available.
Time: (30–40) minutes.
Authors: Harvey A. Skinner, Paul D. Steinhauer, and Jack Santa-Barbara.
Publisher: Multi-Health Systems, Inc.

Cross References: For reviews by Kenneth J. Manges and Stephen A. Spilland, see 14:145; see also T5:1008 (3 references).

[1057]
Family Day Care Rating Scale.
Purpose: Assesses the quality of family day care.
Population: Consumers of day care services, day care providers, agency supervisors, and researchers.
Publication Date: 1989.
Acronym: FDCRS.
Scores, 6: Space and Furnishings for Care and Learning, Basic Care, Language and Reasoning, Learning Activities, Social Development, Adult Needs.
Administration: Group.
Price Data, 2006: $15.95 per manual (48 pages); $8.95 per 30 scoring sheets.
Time: (2) hours.
Authors: Thelma Harms and Richard M. Clifford.
Publisher: Teachers College Press.
Cross References: For a review by Annette M. Iverson, see 11:141.

[1058]
Family Environment Scale [Third Edition Manual].
Purpose: Designed to assess family members' perceptions of their social environment.
Population: Ages 11–adult
Publication Dates: 1974–1994.
Acronym: FES.
Scores, 11: Cohesion, Expressiveness, Conflict, Independence, Achievement, Intellectual-Cultural, Active-Recreational, Moral-Religious, Organization, Control, Incongruence.
Administration: Group.
Forms, 4: Real (Form R), Ideal (Form I), Expectations (Form E), Children's Version.
Price Data: Available from the publisher at www.mindgarden.com/products/fescs.htm.
Foreign Language Edition: Spanish edition available.
Time: (15–20) minutes.
Comments: One component of the Social Climate Scales (T5:2445).
Authors: Rudolf H. Moos and Bernice S. Moos.
Publisher: Mind Garden, Inc.
Cross References: For reviews by Jay A. Mancini and Michael J. Sporakowski, see 14:146; see also T5:1010 (138 references); for reviews by Julie A. Allison and Brenda H. Loyd of an earlier edition, see 12:151 (76 references); see also T4:961 (136 references); for reviews by Nancy A. Busch-Rossnagel and Nadine M. Lambert of an earlier edition, see 9:408 (18 references); see also T3:872 (14 references); for a review by Philip H. Dreyer, see 8:557 (4 references). For a review of the Social Climate Series, see 8:681.

[1059]
Family Relations Test.

Purpose: "Designed to give concrete representation of the subject's childhood family."
Population: Ages 7–12, ages 13–17, adults, married couples.
Publication Dates: 1965–1978.
Acronym: FRT.
Scores: Nobody, Self, Father, Mother, Siblings, and Others scores for 2 areas: Outgoing Feelings, Incoming Feelings.
Administration: Individual.
Time: (20–25) minutes.
Publisher: GL Assessment [England].
  a) CHILDREN'S VERSION.
  Price Data, 1999: £180 per complete set; £98 per set of figures; £36 per manual (1978, 56 pages).
  Authors: Eva Bene and James Anthony.
    1) Younger Children.
    Population: Ages 7–12.
    Price Data: £18 per 25 record/score sheets.
    2) Older Children.
    Population: Ages 13–17.
    Price Data: £31 per 25 record/score sheets.
  b) ADULT VERSION.
  Population: Adults.
  Price Data: £216 per complete set; £51.50 per 25 record/score sheets.
  Author: Eva Bene.
  c) MARRIED COUPLES VERSION.
  Population: Married couples.
  Price Data: Same as for *b* above.
  Authors: Eva Bene and James Anthony (test).
Cross References: See T5:1011 (4 references), T4:962 (1 reference), 9:409 (3 references), T3:874 (33 references), 8:558 (18 references), and T2:1182 (4 references); for an excerpted review by B. Semeonoff of *a* and *b*, see 7:79 (7 references); see also P:81 (2 references); for reviews by John E. Bell, Dale B. Harris, and Arthur R. Jensen of *a*, see 5:132 (1 reference).

[1060]
Family Relations Test: Children's Version.

Purpose: "To assess the relative importance that different family members have for children" and to explore the child's emotional relations with his family.
Population: Ages 3–15.
Publication Date: 1976.
Administration: Individual.
Levels, 2: Form for Young Children, Form for Older Children.
Price Data, 1999: £180 for complete set including manual (1985, 59 pages), test figures and item cards, scoring and record sheets for older children, and record/score sheets for young children.

Time: 25(40) minutes.
Authors: Eva Bene (test and revised manual) and James Anthony (test).
Publisher: GL Assessment [England].
  a) FORM FOR YOUNG CHILDREN.
  Population: Ages 3–7.
  Scores, 8: Outgoing Feelings (Positive Total, Negative Total), Incoming Feelings (Positive Total, Negative Total), Dependency Feelings, Sum of Positive, Sum of Negative, Total Involvement.
  b) FORM FOR OLDER CHILDREN.
  Population: Ages 7–15.
  Scores, 12: Sum of Outgoing Positive, Sum of Outgoing Negative, Sum of Incoming Positive, Sum of Incoming Negative, Total Involvement, Sum of Positive Mild, Sum of Positive Strong, Sum of Negative Mild, Sum of Negative Strong, Maternal Overprotection, Paternal Overindulgence, Maternal Overindulgence.
Cross References: See T5:1012 (2 references); for reviews by Cindy I. Carlson and Steven I. Pfeiffer, see 11:142; for information on the complete test, see 9:409 (3 references), T3:874 (33 references), 8:558 (18 references), and T2:1182 (4 references); for an excerpted review by B. Semeonoff of the Children's Version and the Adult Version, see 7:79 (7 references); see also P:81 (2 references); for reviews by John E. Bell, Dale B. Harris, and Arthur R. Jensen of the Children's Version, see 5:132 (1 reference).

[1061]
Family Relationship Inventory.

Purpose: "Method of examining family relationships, designed to clarify individual feelings and interpersonal behavior"; within the family, the FRI identifies who feels closest to whom and who feels most distant and provides a Self-Esteem score for each family member.
Population: Young children age 5 and above, adolescents, and adults.
Publication Dates: 1972–1984.
Acronym: FRI.
Scores: 2: Positive, Negative, for each family member.
Administration: Individual or family groups.
Price Data, 2011: $209 per complete kit including item cards, 25 scoring forms, 50 tabulating forms, 50 individual relationship wheel forms, 25 familygram forms, and test manual (1982, 36 pages); $55 per set of item cards; $43.50 per 100 scoring forms; $43.50 per 100 tabulating forms; $43.50 per 100 individual relationship wheels; $43.50 per 100 familygrams.
Time: Administration time not reported.
Comments: Based upon Family Relationship Scale.
Authors: Ruth B. Michaelson, Harry L. Bascom, Louise Nash, W. Lee Morrison, and Robert M. Taylor.
Publisher: Psychological Publications, Inc.
Cross References: See T5:1013 (2 references) and T4:964 (2 references); for a review by Mary Henning-Stout, see 10:112.

[1062]

Family Satisfaction Scale [Revised].

Purpose: Designed to measure satisfaction on the dimensions of family cohesion and family adaptability.
Population: Families.
Publication Dates: 1982-2005.
Scores: Total Family Satisfaction.
Administration: Individual or group.
Price Data, 2006: $30 per manual (7 pages) and scale (unlimited rights for duplication).
Time: (10-15) minutes.
Authors: David H. Olson and Marc Wilson.
Publisher: Life Innovations, Inc.
Cross References: See T5:1014 (7 references).

[1063]

Family System Test.

Purpose: Designed "for representing emotional bonds (cohesion) and hierarchical structures in the family or similar social systems."
Population: Individuals and families.
Publication Dates: 1993–1998.
Acronym: FAST.
Scores: Score information available from publisher.
Administration: Individuals or group.
Price Data, 2011: $437 per complete test including 20 recording blanks, board and schematic figures, and manual (1998, 80 pages); $36 per 20 recording blanks; $55 per manual.
Time: (5–10) minutes for individuals; (10–30) minutes for groups.
Comments: A "figural technique"; "language independent"; authorized English translation of the 1993 German edition "Familiensystemtest" (FAST).
Authors: Thomas Gehring; translated from the German edition by Anita Arnone-Reitezle.
Publisher: Hogrefe Publishing.
Cross References: For reviews by Lisa Bischoff and Richard B. Stuart, see 15:98.

[1064]

A Family Violence Scale.

Purpose: To indicate the occurrence of family violence in one's childhood.
Population: Adolescents and adults.
Publication Dates: 1973–1988.
Scores: Total Family Violence Score.
Administration: Group.
Manual: No manual.
Price Data, 2005: $2 per scale.
Time: Administration time not reported.
Comments: Supplementary article available.
Author: Panos D. Bardis.
Publisher: Donna Bardis.
Cross References: See 8:340 (1 reference).

[1065]

The Farnum String Scale: A Performance Scale for All String Instruments.

Purpose: Measurement of ability to play a stringed instrument.
Population: Grades 7–12.
Publication Date: 1969.
Scores, 4: Total score only for each test (Violin, Viola, Cello, String Bass).
Administration: Individual.
Price Data: Available from publisher.
Time: Administration time not reported.
Author: Stephen E. Farnum.
Publisher: Hal Leonard Publishing Corporation [No reply from publisher; status unknown].
Cross References: For additional information and a review by Walter L. Wehner, see 8:94.

[1066]

Fast Health Knowledge Test, 1986 Revision.

Purpose: "To measure discrimination and judgment in matters of health."
Population: High school and college.
Publication Date: 1986.
Scores, 11: Personal Health, Exercise-Relaxation-Sleep, Nutrition, Consumer Health, Contemporary Health Problems, Substance of Abuse, Safety and First Aid, Disease Control, Mental Health, Family Life and Sex Education, Total.
Administration: Group.
Price Data: Available from publisher.
Time: 40(50) minutes.
Author: Charles G. Fast.
Publisher: Charles G. Fast.
Cross References: For a review by Linda K. Bunker, see 10:113.

[1067]

Fast Track.

Purpose: Designed as a "simple screening tool to identify those who have literacy needs below Level 1 and/or numeracy needs below Entry Level of the Basic Skills Standards."
Population: Adults.
Publication Date: 2000.
Scores: Total score only.
Administration: Individual.
Forms, 3: Fast Track 20 Questions, Fast Track Assessment-Written, Fast Track Assessment-Oral.
Price Data, 2000: £15 per complete kit including manual (24 pages), 50 Fast Track 20 Question, 50 Fast Track Assessment-Written, and 50 Fast Track Assessment-Oral; £9 per manual; £3 per 50 Fast Track 20 Questions; £3 per 50 Fast Track Assessment-Written; £3 per 50 Fast Track Assessment-Oral.

Time: (5-15) minutes.
Comments: This test can be completed as part of a 1:1 interview.
Authors: The Basic Skills Agency.
Publisher: The Basic Skills Agency [England].
Cross References: For a review by Pam Ramsden, see 17:71.

[1068]

Fear of Appearing Incompetent Scale.

Purpose: Designed "to identify if individuals are concerned about maintaining or saving face around others to the extent of sacrificing tangible rewards in order to do so."
Population: Adults and college-age.
Publication Date: No date.
Scores: Total score only.
Administration: Group.
Price Data, 2001: $3 per specimen set.
Time: Administration time not reported.
Authors: L. R. Good and K. C. Good.
Publisher: Psychometric Affiliates.
Cross References: For a review by William C. Tierre, see 15:99.

[1069]

Fear of Powerlessness Scale.

Purpose: Developed as "a self-report measure of the motive to avoid powerlessness."
Population: College-age and adults.
Publication Date: No date.
Scores: Total score only.
Administration: Group.
Price Data, 2001: $3 per specimen set.
Time: Administration time not reported.
Authors: L. R. Good, K. C. Good, and S. B. Golden, Jr.
Publisher: Psychometric Affiliates.
Cross References: For a review by Nathaniel J. Pallone and James J. Hennessy, see 15:100.

[1070]

Fear of Success Scale.

Purpose: Designed as a self-report measure of fear of success.
Population: College students.
Publication Date: No date.
Scores: Total score only.
Administration: Group.
Price Data, 2001: $3 per specimen set.
Time: Administration time not reported.
Authors: L. R. Good and K. C. Good.
Publisher: Psychometric Affiliates.
Cross References: For a review by Laura L. B. Barnes, see 15:101.

[1071]

Fear Survey Schedule.

Purpose: "Designed to identify and quantify patients' reactions to a variety of sources of maladaptive emotional reactions."
Population: College and adults.
Publication Dates: 1964–1977.
Acronym: FSS.
Scores: Total score only.
Administration: Group.
Price Data: Available from publisher.
Time: (15) minutes.
Comments: Self-rating.
Authors: Joseph Wolpe and Peter J. Lang.
Publisher: EdITS/Educational and Industrial Testing Service.
Cross References: See T5:1021 (48 references), T4:974 (30 references), 9:411 (23 references), and T3:883 (53 references); for a review by Charles D. Spielberger, see 8:559 (32 references); see also T2:1185 (14 references); for a review by R. G. Demaree, see 7:80 (17 references).

[1072]

Feedback Edition of the Strength Deployment Inventory.

Purpose: Designed to elicit feedback to describe how a person uses his/her personal strengths in relationships.
Population: Adults.
Publication Dates: 1973–1996.
Acronym: SDI/PVI.
Scores, 20: 7 Motivational Values (Altruistic-Nurturing, Assertive-Directing, Analytic-Autonomizing, Flexible-Cohering, Assertive-Nurturing, Judicious-Competing, Cautious-Supporting), plus 13 scores reflecting Progression through Conflict.
Administration: Individual or group.
Price Data, 2001: $4.50 per test booklet; $30 per manual (1996, 146 pages).
Time: (20–40) minutes.
Comments: Uses self-ratings and ratings of a significant other person; manual is entitled Relationship Awareness Theory Manual of Administration and Interpretation (9th Ed.).
Author: Elias H. Porter.
Publisher: Personal Strengths Publishing.
Cross References: For a review by Richard E. Harding, see 17:72.

[1073]

Feedback Portrait of Overdone Strengths.

Purpose: Designed to elicit feedback to describe how a person uses his/her personal strengths.
Population: Adults.
Publication Date: 1997.

Scores, 3: Profile, Top Overdone Strengths, Least Overdone Strengths.
Administration: Individual or group.
Price Data, 2001: $5.50 per test booklet; $100 per manual.
Time: (20–40) minutes.
Author: Personal Strengths Publishing.
Publisher: Personal Strengths Publishing.

[1074]

Feedback Portrait of Personal Strengths.

Purpose: Designed to elicit feedback to describe how a person uses his/her personal strengths in relationships.
Population: Adults.
Publication Date: 1997.
Scores, 3: Profile, Top Strengths, Least Deployed Strengths.
Administration: Individual or group.
Price Data, 2001: $5.50 per test booklet; $100 per manual.
Time: (20–40) minutes.
Author: Personal Strengths Publishing.
Publisher: Personal Strengths Publishing.
Cross References: For reviews by Frederick Medway and James A. Penny, see 17:73.

[1075]

Feelings, Attitudes, and Behaviors Scale for Children.

Purpose: "Designed to assess a range of emotional and behavioral problems."
Population: Ages 6–13.
Publication Date: 1996.
Acronym: FAB-C.
Scores, 7: Conduct Problems, Self Image, Worry, Negative Peer Relationships, Antisocial, Lie (validity), Problem Index.
Administration: Individual or Group.
Price Data, 2011: $105 per complete kit including manual (47 pages), and 25 QuikScore™ forms; $50 per 25 QuikScore™ forms; $73 per manual; $77 per online profile report kit including manual and 3 profile reports; $5 per profile report.
Time: (10) minutes.
Comments: Self-report.
Author: Joseph H. Beitchman.
Publisher: Multi-Health Systems, Inc.
Cross References: For reviews by Patti L. Harrison and Mary Lou Kelley, see 14:147.

[1076]

50 Grammar Quizzes for Practice and Review.

Purpose: Designed to "guide students to learn correct grammar, improve their writing skills, and write clearly and effectively."

Population: Students.
Publication Date: 1985.
Scores: No scores.
Administration: Group.
Parts, 6: Part I: Writing Clear, Complete Sentences (15 quizzes); Part II: Correcting Errors in Agreement: Pronouns and Antecedents, Subjects and Verbs (3 study guides and 9 quizzes); Part III: Correcting Pronoun and Verb Shifts (2 sets of instructions and 5 quizzes); Part IV: Correcting Errors in the Use of Modifiers (4 quizzes); Part V: Correcting Errors in the Use of Parallel Structure (study guide and 3 quizzes); Part VI: Writing Precise, Effective Sentences (3 study guides and 14 quizzes).
Price Data: Price information available form publisher for complete set of display copy.
Time: Administration time not reported.
Comments: Reproduction rights limited to purchaser of masters and a single classroom teacher.
Author: Joan R. Markos.
Publisher: Walch Education.

[1077]

Figure Classification Test.

Purpose: Designed to "measure abstract reasoning ability."
Population: Applicants for industrial work with 7 to 9 years of schooling.
Publication Date: 1976.
Scores: Total score only.
Administration: Group.
Price Data: Price information available from publisher for test materials including manual (21 pages).
Foreign Language Edition: Manual written in both English and Afrikaans.
Time: 60(70) minutes.
Comments: Separate answer sheets must be used.
Author: T. R. Taylor.
Publisher: Human Sciences Research Council [South Africa].
Cross References: See T4:978 (1 reference).

[1078]

The Filipino Work Values Scale.

Purpose: "Constructed to measure work values."
Population: Filipino employees and students.
Publication Dates: 1987–1988.
Acronym: FWVS.
Scores, 10: Environmental, Familial, Intellectual-Achievement Oriented, Interpersonal, Managerial, Material, Occupational, Organizational, Religious, Variety.
Administration: Group or individual.
Forms, 2: Employee, Student.
Price Data, 2006: $205 per employee edition complete kit including manual (1987, 39 pages), 25 scale

booklets, 25 answer sheets, and manual scoring keys; $205 per student edition complete kit including manual, 25 scale booklets, 25 answer sheets, and manual scoring keys.
Foreign Language Editions: English, Thai; Philippine languages editions: Cebuano, Filipino, Pangasinense.
Time: (15–20) minutes.
Author: Vicentita M. Cervera.
Publisher: MAVEC Specialists Foundation, Inc. [Philippines].
Cross References: For reviews by Gary J. Dean and William I. Sauser, Jr., see 14:148.

[1079]

Fine Dexterity Test.

Purpose: To provide "a measure of manual dexterity using a fine test task."
Population: Applicants for jobs involving fine motor dexterity.
Publication Date: 1983.
Acronym: FDT.
Scores, 2: Finger Dexterity, Fine Tool Dexterity.
Administration: Group.
Price Data: Available from publisher.
Time: 6(8) minutes.
Author: Educational & Industrial Test Services Ltd.
Publisher: Educational & Industrial Test Services Ltd. [England].

[1080]

Fire Promotional Tests (Custom).

Purpose: "Fully-customized content-valid written promotional assessments to test the duties and responsibilities of firefighters."
Population: Firefighters.
Publication Dates: 1979–2010.
Scores: 11 subtests: Knowledge of Fire Protection/Prevention Practices, Fire Investigation Practices, Size-Up and Command Practices, Emergency Scene Practices–All Companies, Emergency Scene Practices–Truck Companies, Emergency Scene Practices–Engine Companies, Emergency Scene Practices–EMS Companies, Supervisory and Managerial Practices, Administrative Practices, Ability to Comprehend Hypothetical Fire Codes, Ability to Read and Comprehend Fire-Service Related Tables and Texts.
Administration: Group.
Price Data: Available from publisher.
Time: (210) minutes.
Comments: Complimentary Candidate Study Guide is available at the publisher's website; two full-length practice examinations are available for purchase, administered online through the company assessment platform: www.measuredsuccessonline.com.
Author: McCann Associates.
Publisher: McCann Associates.

[1081]

Firefighter Learning Simulation.

Purpose: Designed to "simulate the learning process required of entry-level firefighters in Fire Academies."
Population: Applicants for firefighter trainee positions.
Publication Dates: 1983-1998.
Acronym: FLS.
Scores: Total score only.
Administration: Group or individual.
Price Data: Price information available from publisher for test material including Administration Guide and Technical Manual (11 pages), and Training Manual (26 pages).
Time: 90(95) minutes.
Comments: Simulated training manual is provided to examinees in advance of the test.
Author: Psychological Services, Inc.
Publisher: Psychological Services, Inc.
Cross References: For reviews by JoEllen V. Carlson and James W. Pinkney, see 15:102.

[1082]

Firefighter Selection Test [Revised].

Purpose: "To rank-order applicants according to their probability of success in training and success on the job" as a firefighter.
Population: Applicants for firefighter trainee positions.
Publication Dates: 1983–1998.
Acronym: FST.
Scores: Total score only.
Administration: Group or individual.
Price Data: Price data available from publisher for test material including Technical Manual (1998, 22 pages), Administrator's Guide (1998, 6 pages), and Study Guide (1998, 16 pages).
Time: 150 (165) minutes.
Comments: Measures mechanical comprehension, reading comprehension, and report interpretation.
Author: Psychological Services, Inc.
Publisher: Psychological Services, Inc.
Cross References: For reviews by Chantale Jeanrie and Deniz S. Ones, see 15:103; for reviews by David O. Anderson and Cynthia Ann Druva-Roush of an earlier edition, see 11:143.

[1083]

Firestone Assessment of Self-Destructive Thoughts.

Purpose: Constructed "for the clinical assessment of a patient's suicidal potential."
Population: Ages 16–80.
Publication Date: 1996.
Acronym: FAST.
Scores: No scores.
Administration: Group.

Price Data, 2002: $142 per complete kit including manual (176 pages) and 25 ReadyScore® response booklets; $61 per 25 response booklets, $86 per manual.
Time: (20) minutes.
Comments: Includes 11 levels of progressively self-destructive thoughts on a continuum ranging from Social Isolation, Eating Disorders, Substance Abuse, Self-Mutilation, and Suicide.
Authors: Robert W. Firestone and Lisa A. Firestone.
Publisher: Psychological Assessment Resources, Inc.
Cross References: For reviews by William E. Martin and Robert C. Reinehr, see 14:149.

[1084]

Firestone Assessment of Violent Thoughts.

Purpose: "Designed to assess the underlying thoughts that predispose violent behavior."
Population: Ages 18+.
Publication Dates: 1999-2008.
Acronym: FAVT.
Scores, 10: Paranoid/Suspicious, Persecuted Misfit, Self-Depreciating/Pseudo-Independent, Overtly Aggressive, Self-Aggrandizing, Total, Theoretical Subscale scores (Instrumental/Proactive Violence, Hostile/Reactive Violence), Validity scores (Negativity, Inconsistency).
Administration: Group.
Price Data, 2010: $125 per introductory kit including professional manual (2008, 148 pages), 25 rating forms, and 25 score summary/profile forms; $60 per 25 rating forms; $20 per 25 score summary/profile forms; $55 per professional manual.
Time: (15-20) minutes.
Comments: Scores normed for Younger Men (ages 18-39), Older Men (ages 40-75), Younger Women (ages 18-39), and Older Women (ages 40-75).
Authors: Robert W. Firestone and Lisa A. Firestone.
Publisher: Psychological Assessment Resources, Inc.
Cross References: For reviews by Stephen Axford and M. Meghan Davidson, see 18:52.

[1085]

Firestone Assessment of Violent Thoughts-Adolescent.

Purpose: To "assess the underlying thoughts that predispose violent behavior in adolescents."
Population: Ages 11-18.
Publication Dates: 1999-2008.
Acronym: FAVT-A.
Scores, 9: Paranoid/Suspicious, Persecuted Misfit, Self-Depreciating/Pseudo-Independent, Overtly Aggressive, Total, Instrumental/Proactive Violence, Hostile/Reactive Violence, Inconsistency, Negativity.
Administration: Individual.
Price Data, 2011: $120 per introductory kit including professional manual (2008, 167 pages), 25 rating

forms, and 25 score summary/ profile forms; $55 per professional manual; $55 per 25 rating forms; $20 per 25 score summary/profile forms.
Time: 15 minutes.
Authors: Robert W. Firestone and Lisa A. Firestone.
Publisher: Psychological Assessment Resources, Inc.

[1086]

FIRO-B® [Fundamental Interpersonal Relations Orientation–Behavior™].

Purpose: Designed "to measure behavior that derives from interpersonal needs."
Population: Age 13 and over.
Publication Dates: 1958–2000.
Acronym: FIRO-B™.
Scores, 7: 2 Overall Behavior scores (Expressed, Wanted) for each of 3 dimensions (Inclusion, Control, Affection) plus Overall Need score.
Administration: Individual or group.
Price Data, 2011: $12.25 each for FIRO-B® Profile online administration; $89.95 per 10 FIRO-B® self-scorable forms; $14.95 each for FIRO-B® Interpretive Report for Organizations online administration; $20.95 each for Leadership Report Using the FIRO-B® and MBTI® Instruments online administration; $51.50 per FIRO-B® technical guide (2000, 77 pages); $112.50 per 10 Introduction to the FIRO-B® Instrument; $112.50 per 10 Introduction to the FIRO-B® Instrument in Organizations; $112.50 per 10 Participating in Teams (Using Your FIRO-B® Results to Improve Interpersonal Effectiveness); $102.50 per 10 Understanding Your FIRO-B® Results.
Time: (10–15) minutes.
Comments: May be administered via paper-pencil or online at skillsone.com; earlier versions entitled FIRO Awareness Scales.
Authors: William Schutz (original test), Allen L. Hammer (technical guide), and Eugene R. Schnell (technical guide).
Publisher: CPP, Inc.
Cross References: For reviews by Michelle Athanasiou and Donald Oswald, see 15:104; see T5:1036 (13 references) and T4:982 (18 references); for a review by Peter D. Lifton of an earlier edition, see 9:416 (12 references); see also T3:890 (45 references), 8:555 (147 references), and T2:1176 (58 references); for a review by Bruce Bloxom, see 7:78 (70 references); see also P:79 (30 references) and 6:94 (15 references).

[1087]

First Year Algebra Test: National Achievement Tests.

Purpose: Designed to measure the student's knowledge of first year algebra.
Population: One year high school.
Publication Dates: 1958–1962.

Scores: Total score only.
Administration: Group.
Forms, 2: A, B.
Price Data: Available from publisher.
Time: (40–45) minutes.
Authors: Ray Webb and Julius H. Hlavaty.
Publisher: Psychometric Affiliates.
Cross References: For a review by Donald L. Meyer, see 6:600.

[1088]

FirstSTEP: Screening Test for Evaluating Preschoolers.

Purpose: "Designed to identify preschool children who are at risk for developmental delays in the five areas mandated by IDEA (PL 99-457)."
Population: Preschool children.
Publication Dates: 1990–1993.
Scores, 7: Cognitive, Language, Motor, Composite, Social-Emotional, Adaptive Behavior, Parent/Teacher.
Administration: Individual.
Levels, 3: Ages 1–2, Ages 3–4, Ages 5–7.
Price Data, 2002: $195 per complete kit including 5 record forms each for levels 1, 2, and 3, 25 Social-Emotional/Adaptive Behavior booklets, 25 Parent booklets, manipulatives in a plastic case, and manual (1993, 166 pages); $34 per 25 record forms (specify level); $34 per 25 Social-Emotional Scale/Adaptive Behavior checklists; $17 per 25 Parent/Teacher Scales.
Foreign Language Edition: Spanish version entitled PrimerPASO was published in 2003.
Time: (15–20) minutes.
Author: Lucy J. Miller.
Publisher: Pearson.
Cross References: For a review by Terry Overton, see 13:126.

[1089]

The Fisher-Logemann Test of Articulation Competence.

Purpose: "Designed to ... facilitate ... analysis and categorization of articulation errors."
Population: Preschool to adult.
Publication Date: 1971.
Acronym: F-LTOAC.
Scores: No scores.
Administration: Individual.
Price Data, 2010: $224 per complete kit includes examiner's manual, test portfolio, 50 picture test record forms, and 50 sentence test record forms; $35 per manual; $116 per test portfolio; $41 per Picture Test or Sentence Articulation Test record forms.
Time: (45) minutes.
Authors: Hilda B. Fisher and Jerilyn A. Logemann.
Publisher: PRO-ED.

a) PICTURE TEST.
Population: Preschool to adult.
Comments: 3 areas are covered: Singleton Consonants, Consonant Blends, Vowel Phonemes and Diphthongs; a shortened screening form consisting of 11 of the Singleton Consonants may be administered.
b) SENTENCE ARTICULATION TEST.
Population: Grade 3 to adult.
Comments: 5 areas are covered: Consonant Pairs, Singleton Consonants, Nasals, Vowel Phonemes, Diphthongs.
Cross References: See T5:1040 (11 references), T4:986 (6 references), and T3:896 (9 references); for reviews by Marie C. Fontana and Lawrence J. Turton, see 8:961.

[1090]

Fitness Interview Test-Revised.

Purpose: A screening instrument that provides "a structured interview for assessing competency to stand trial."
Population: Juveniles and adults.
Publication Date: 2006.
Acronym: FIT-R.
Scores: Individual item scores only.
Subtests, 3: Understand the Nature or Object of Proceedings, Understand the Possible Consequences, Communicate with Counsel.
Administration: Individual.
Price Data, 2007: $45 per manual (64 pages) and CD-ROM.
Time: Administration time not reported.
Comments: Designed to correspond with case law in the U.S., U.K., and Canada.
Authors: Ronald Roesch, Patricia A. Zapf, and Derek Eaves.
Publisher: Professional Resource Press.
Cross References: For reviews by Rita Budrionis and Joe W. Dixon, see 18:53.

[1091]

Five-Factor Personality Inventory–Children.

Purpose: Developed to "measure personality dispositions in children and adolescents" in order to "identify children who are at risk for adjustment problems at school and in their community."
Population: Ages 9-0 to 18-11.
Publication Date: 2007.
Acronym: FFPI-C.
Scores, 5: Agreeableness, Extraversion, Openness to Experience, Conscientiousness, Emotional Regulation.
Administration: Individual or group.
Price Data, 2010: $159 per complete kit; includes examiner's manual (69 pages) and 25 administration and scoring forms. $81 per examiner's manual; $81 per 25 administration and scoring forms.

Time: (15-40) minutes.

Comments: Descriptive ratings for each of the five scores are provided to aid in the interpretation of personality characteristics as they relate to a child's risk for experiencing adjustment problems.

Authors: Ronnie L. McGhee, David J. Ehrler, and Joseph A. Buckhalt.

Publisher: PRO-ED.

Cross References: For reviews by Merith Cosden and H. Dennis Kade, see 18:54.

[1092]

Five Factor Wellness Inventory.

Purpose: Designed to "assess characters of wellness as a basis for helping individuals make choices for healthier living."

Population: Elementary, high school, and adults.

Publication Date: 2005.

Acronym: 5F-WEL.

Scores, 28: Wellness (Creative Self [Thinking, Emotions, Control, Positive Humor, Work], Coping Self [Realistic Beliefs, Stress Management, Self-Worth, Leisure], Social Self [Friendship, Love], Essential Self [Spirituality, Self-Care, Gender Identity, Cultural Identity], Physical Self [Exercise, Nutrition]), Local Context, Institutional Context, Global Context, Chronometrical Context, Life Satisfaction Index.

Administration: Group or individual.

Levels, 3: Elementary, Teen, Adults.

Price Data, 2005: $40 per manual (71 pages); additional pricing information available at www.mindgarden.com/products/ffwels.htm.

Foreign Language Editions: Hebrew, Korean, Turkish.

Time: (10-20) minutes.

Comments: Users can administer the factor scales only or all scales; can be self-administered; web-based administration and reporting including a development guide.

Authors: Jane E. Myers and Thomas J. Sweeney.

Publisher: Mind Garden, Inc.

Cross References: For reviews by Gerald E. De-Mauro and Susan Lonborg, see 17:74.

[1093]

The Five P's (Parent/Professional Preschool Performance Profile) [2002 Update].

Purpose: Constructed to collect teacher and parent ratings of child's observed performance across all domains of development to create a comprehensive profile of child's current level of functioning, to link assessment to goal setting and remediation, to monitor change over time, and to promote home/school collaboration.

Population: Children with disabilities between the ages of 6 and 59 months.

Publication Dates: 1982–2004.

Scores: Standard Index and Percentile scores may be prepared separately in five domains of development:

Self Help (Toileting and Hygiene, Mealtime Behaviors, Dressing), Language Development (Communicative Competence, Receptive Language, Expressive Language), Social Development (Emerging Self, Relationships to Adults, Relationships to Children, Classroom Adjustment), Motor Development (Gross Motor/Balance/Coordination Skills, Perceptual/Fine Motor Skills), Cognitive Development; Interfering Behaviors for each of the five domains are scored separately.

Administration: Individual.

Price Data, 2004: $150 per materials for class of 10 children including 10 sets of scales, 1 user manual (2002, 40 pages), 10 Information and Directions, 10 graphic profiles, 1 copy of The Five P's Preschool Annual Goals and Short-Term Instructional Objectives; $45 per training video (25 minutes); $10 per user manual; $25 per copy of The Five P's Preschool Annual Goals and Short-Term Instructional Objectives (bound copy); $45 per technical manual, which includes Index and Percentile Score Tables (2004, 132 pages); $85 per sample packet including assessment packet, training video, research papers, and The Five P's Preschool Annual Goals and Short-Term Instructional Objectives.

Foreign Language Edition: Spanish edition available.

Time: (60) minutes.

Comments: Teacher and Parent Observer training protocol and training video available.

Authors: Judith Simon Bloch, John S. Hicks, and Janice L. Friedman.

Publisher: Variety Child Learning Center.

Cross References: For reviews by Kimberly A. Blair and Lisa F. Smith, see 16:91; for reviews by Annie W. Ward and Steven Zucker of an earlier edition, see 13:127; for a review by Barbara Perry-Sheldon, see 10:116.

[1094]

Flanagan Aptitude Classification Tests.

Purpose: Measurement of aptitudes for sixteen on-the-job skills.

Population: Individuals in a variety of lower-level industrial or mechanical positions.

Publication Dates: 1951–1994.

Acronym: FACT.

Scores: Total score only for each test.

Administration: Individual or group.

Price Data, 2002: $85 per start-up kit including 25 test booklets (specify test) and examiner's manual; $67 per 25 test booklets (quantity discounts available; specify test); $28 per examiner's manual.

Author: John C. Flanagan.

Publisher: Pearson Performance Solutions [No reply from publisher; status unknown].

a) FACT 1A, INSPECTION.

Publication Dates: 1953–1956.

Time: 6 minutes.

b) FACT 2A AND 2B, CODING.
Publication Dates: 1953–1956.
Forms, 2: A, B.
Time: 10 minutes.
c) FACT 3A AND 3B, MEMORY.
Publication Dates: 1953–1956.
Forms, 2: A, B.
Time: 4 minutes.
d) FACT 4A, PRECISION.
Publication Dates: 1953–1956.
Time: 8 minutes.
e) FACT 5A, ASSEMBLY.
Publication Dates: 1953–1956.
Time: 12 minutes.
f) FACT 6A, SCALES.
Publication Dates: 1953–1956.
Time: 16 minutes.
g) FACT 7A, COORDINATION.
Publication Dates: 1953–1956.
Time: 2 minutes, 40 seconds.
h) FACT 8A, JUDGEMENT AND COMPREHEN-SION.
Publication Dates: 1953–1956.
Time: No limit (approximately 35 minutes).
i) FACT 9A, ARITHMETIC.
Publication Dates: 1953–1956.
Time: 10 minutes.
j) FACT 10A, PATTERNS.
Publication Dates: 1953–1956.
Time: 20 minutes.
k) FACT 11A, COMPONENTS.
Publication Dates: 1953–1956.
Time: 20 minutes.
l) FACT 12A, TABLES.
Publication Dates: 1953–1956.
Time: 10 minutes.
m) FACT 13A AND 13B, MECHANICS.
Publication Dates: 1953–1956.
Forms, 2: A, B.
Time: 20 minutes.
n) FACT 14A, EXPRESSION.
Publication Dates: 1953–1956.
Time: No limit (approximately 30 minutes).
o) FACT 15A, REASONING.
Publication Dates: 1957–1960.
Time: 24 minutes.
p) FACT 16A, INGENUITY.
Publication Dates: 1957–1960.
Time: 24 minutes.
Cross References: See T3:899 (2 references), and T2:1072 (1 reference); for an excerpted review by Harold D. Murphy (with John P. McQuary), see 7:675 (10 references); for reviews by Norman Frederiksen and William B. Michael, see 6:770 (7 references); for reviews by Harold P. Bechtoldt, Ralph F. Berdie, and John B. Carroll, see 5:608.

[1095]
Flanagan Industrial Tests.
Purpose: Measurement of aptitudes for eighteen on-the-job skills.
Population: Supervisory, technical, office, skilled labor, and other industrial positions.
Publication Dates: 1960–1975.
Acronym: FIT.
Scores: Total score only for each test.
Administration: Individual or group.
Price Data, 2002: $99 per start-up kit including 25 test booklets, scoring stencil, and examinee's manual (1975, 36 pages); $63 per 25 test booklets (quantity discounts available); $20 per scoring stencil; $28 per examiner's manual.
Author: John C. Flanagan.
Publisher: Pearson Performance Solutions [No reply from publisher; status unknown].
a) ARITHMETIC.
Time: 5(7) minutes.
b) ASSEMBLY.
Time: 10(13) minutes.
c) COMPONENTS.
Time: 10(12) minutes.
d) COORDINATION.
Price Data: $82 per start-up kit.
Time: 5(7) minutes.
e) ELECTRONICS.
Time: 15(17) minutes.
f) EXPRESSION.
Time: 5(8) minutes.
g) INGENUITY.
Time: 15(18) minutes.
h) INSPECTION.
Price Data: $117 per start-up kit; $39 per scoring stencil.
Time: 5(9) minutes.
i) JUDGMENT AND COMPREHENSION.
Time: 15(17) minutes.
j) MATHEMATICS AND REASONING.
Time: 15(18) minutes.
k) MECHANICS.
Time: 15(18) minutes.
l) MEMORY.
Time: 10(19) minutes.
m) PATTERNS.
Time: 5(7) minutes.
n) PLANNING.
Time: 15(18) minutes.
o) PRECISION.
Price Data: $82 per start-up kit.
Time: 5(8) minutes.
p) SCALES.
Time: 5(7) minutes.
q) TABLES.
Time: 5(8) minutes.

r) VOCABULARY.
Time: 15(17) minutes.
Cross References: See T5:1043 (1 reference) and T4:989 (1 reference); for reviews by David O. Herman and Arthur C. MacKinney, see 8:981 (3 references); for reviews by C. J. Adcock and Robert C. Droege and an excerpted review by John L. Horn, see 7:977 (1 reference).

[1096]

Fleishman Job Analysis Survey [Revised].

Purpose: "A means for analyzing the knowledge, skills and abilities needed to perform jobs."
Population: Adults.
Publication Dates: 1992–1996.
Acronym: F-JAS.
Scores: 52 Abilities Scales: Cognitive (Oral Comprehension, Written Comprehension, Oral Expression, Written Expression, Fluency of Ideas, Originality, Memorization, Problem Sensitivity, Mathematical Reasoning, Number Facility, Deductive Reasoning, Inductive Reasoning, Information Ordering, Category Flexibility, Speed of Closure, Flexibility of Closure, Spatial Orientation, Visualization, Perceptual Speed, Selective Attention, Time Sharing), Psychomotor (Control Precision, Multilimb Coordination, Response Orientation, Rate Control, Reaction Time, Arm-Hand Steadiness, Manual Dexterity, Finger Dexterity, Wrist-Finger Speed, Speed of Limb Movement), Physical (Static Strength, Explosive Strength, Dynamic Strength, Trunk Strength, Extent Flexibility, Dynamic Flexibility, Gross Body Coordination, Gross Body Equilibrium, Stamina), Sensory/Perceptual (Near Vision, Far Vision, Visual Color Discrimination, Night Vision, Peripheral Vision, Depth Perception, Glare Sensitivity, Hearing Sensitivity, Auditory Attention, Sound Localization, Speech Recognition, Speech Clarity).
Administration: Group.
Levels, 3: Job-Level Analysis, Job Dimension-Level Analysis, Task-Level Analysis.
Price Data: Available from publisher.
Time: (40) minutes.
Comments: Previously referred to as the Task Assessment Scales, Ability Requirement Scale, Manual for the Ability Requirement Scales (MARS); Handbook of Human Abilities brings together ability definitions, tasks, and jobs requiring each ability, and test descriptions and tests available to measure each ability.
Authors: Edwin A. Fleishman, Maureen E. Reilly, and David P. Costanza.
Publisher: Management Research Institute, Inc.
a) SOCIAL/INTERPERSONAL ABILITIES.
Publication Date: 1996.
Acronym: F-JAS-2.
Scores: 21 Social/Interpersonal Skill Scales: Agreeableness, Behavior Flexibility, Coordination, Dependability, Assertiveness, Negotiation, Persuasion, Sociability, Social Conformity, Social Sensitivity, Self Control, Social Confidence, Coaching, Oral Fact Finding, Achievement Striving, Openness to Experience, Self Sufficiency, Perseverance, Resistance to Premature Judgment, Oral Defense, Resilience.
Time: (20) minutes.
b) KNOWLEDGES/SKILLS.
Publication Date: 1992.
Acronym: F-JAS-3.
Scores: 33 Knowledge Scales: Administration and Management, Clerical, Economics and Accounting, Sales and Marketing, Customer and Personal Service, Personnel and Human Resources, Production and Processing, Food Production, Computers and Electronics, Engineering and Technology, Design, Building and Construction, Mechanical, Mathematics, Physics, Chemistry, Biology, Psychology, Sociology and Anthropology, Geography, Medicine and Dentistry, Therapy and Counseling, Education and Training, English Language, Foreign Language, Fine Arts, History and Archeology, Philosophy and Theology, Public Safety and Security, Law/Government and Jurisprudence, Telecommunications, Communications and Media, Transportation.
Time: (25) minutes.
Cross References: For reviews by Jeffrey S. Rain and Ross E. Traub, see 12:153.

[1097]

Flex Style Negotiating.

Purpose: Designed to profile participants' preferred negotiation styles and to define legitimate versus illegitimate behaviors.
Population: Employees and managers.
Publication Date: 1997.
Scores, 3: Social Dimension, Emotional Dimension, Cognitive Dimension.
Administration: Group.
Price Data: Available from publisher.
Time: (25) minutes.
Author: Alexander Watson Hiam.
Publisher: HRD Press, Inc.

[1098]

Fluharty Preschool Speech and Language Screening Test–Second Edition.

Purpose: Designed to identify preschool children whose speech and language skills warrant a comprehensive communication evaluation.
Population: Ages 3-0 to 6-11.
Publication Dates: 1978–2000.
Acronym: FLUHARTY-2.
Scores, 8: Articulation, Repeating Sentences, Following Directives and Answering Questions, Describing Actions, Sequencing Events, Receptive Language, Expressive Language, General Language.
Administration: Individual.

Price Data, 2010: $193 per complete kit including examiner's manual (2000, 65 pages), picture book, 25 profile/examiner record forms, and a set of 12 colored blocks; $41 per 25 profile/examiner record forms; $35 per set of blocks; $64 per picture book; $64 per examiner's manual.
Time: (10) minutes.
Author: Nancy Buono Fluharty.
Publisher: PRO-ED.
Cross References: For reviews by David P. Hurford and Rebecca McCauley, see 15:105; see T5:1047 (7 references) and T4:993 (2 references); for reviews by Nicholas W. Bankson and Harold A. Peterson of an earlier edition, see 9:422 (1 reference).

[1099]

Food Protection Certification Test.

Purpose: "To test persons who have ongoing on-site responsibility for protecting the consumer from food-borne illness in food preparation, serving, or dispensing establishments."
Population: Food industry personnel.
Publication Dates: 1985–1993.
Scores, 3: Purchasing/Receiving/Storing Food, Processing/Serving/Dispensing Food, Employees/Facilities/Equipment.
Administration: Group.
Price Data: Price information available from publisher for registration fee providing for administration and scoring of the test and mailing of results to examinee and for practice test.
Time: (120) minutes.
Comments: Tests administered per request of certified site examiner.
Author: Center for Occupational and Professional Assessment.
Publisher: Educational Testing Service.

[1100]

The Forer Structured Sentence Completion Test.

Purpose: Designed to measure personality variables and attitudes that may be of some value in treatment planning.
Population: Ages 10–18 and adults.
Publication Dates: 1957–1967.
Acronym: FSSCT.
Scores: No scores; 100 items in 18 areas: Interpersonal Figures (Mother, Males, Females, Groups, Father, Authority), Wishes, Causes of Own (Aggression, Anxiety/Fear, Giving Up [Adolescents] or Depression [Adults], Failure, Guilt, Inferiority Feelings [Adolescents]), Reactions To (Aggression, Rejection, Failure, Responsibility, School [Adolescents], Sexual Stimuli [Adults], Love and Marriage [Adults]).
Administration: Group.
Editions, 4: Separate editions for boys, girls, men, and women.

Price Data, 2006: $93.50 per kit including 10 tests, 20 checklists, and manual (1957, 34 pages) for any of each level; $24.75 per 25 tests (specify edition); $24.75 per 25 checklists (specify edition); $32.50 per manual.
Time: [30–45] minutes.
Author: Bertram R. Forer.
Publisher: Western Psychological Services.
Cross References: See T5:1049 (2 references), T2:1461 (3 references), and P:429 (4 references); for reviews by Charles N. Cofer and Percival M. Symonds, see 5:134 (5 references).

[1101]

Forms for Behavior Analysis with Children.

Purpose: A collection of assessment measures "designed to provide a comprehensive portrait of problems with an eye to how the information can be used to design behavioral treatments."
Population: Children and adolescents.
Publication Date: 1983.
Scores: 21 measures: Behavior Analysis History Questionnaire, Behavior Status Checklist, Reinforcement Survey Schedules, Assertive Behavior Survey Schedule, Bodily Cues for Tension and Anxiety, Fear Inventory, Medical History Inventory, Parental Reaction Survey Schedule, Physical Complaint Survey Schedule, School Behavior Status Checklist, Self-Evaluation Scale, Parents' and Children's Reinforcement Survey Schedule, Reinforcement Menu, Response Cost Survey Schedule, School Reinforcement Survey Schedule, Behavior Record Form, Home Visit Observation Form, Behavior Rating Card, Motivation Assessment of Parents and Children, Progress Chart, Session Report.
Administration: Group.
Forms, 5: C (child), A (adolescent), P (parent), S (school personnel), T (therapist).
Price Data, 2001: $39.95 per manual (208 pages) including reproducible forms.
Time: Administration time not reported.
Comments: Forms (C, A, P, S, T) refer to the person who is to complete the form; "Different assessment formats are encompassed, ranging from direct observations and interviews to informant ratings and self-report."
Authors: Joseph R. Cautela, Julie Cautela, and Sharon Esonis.
Publisher: Research Press.
Cross References: For reviews by Sarah J. Allen and Karen T. Carey, see 11:144.

[1102]

Four Picture Test, Third Revised Edition.

Purpose: A projective technique "of the Thematic Apperception type" requiring written, rather than verbal, responses.
Population: Ages 10 and over.

309

Publication Dates: 1948–1983.
Acronym: FPT.
Scores: No scores.
Administration: Group.
Price Data: Price information available from publisher for materials including manual (1983, 26 pages).
Time: (30–45) minutes.
Comments: Projective analysis guidelines provided in manual.
Author: D. J. van Lennep.
Publisher: Pearson Assessment [England].
Cross References: See P:431 (3 references); for a review by S. G. Lee and Johann M. Schepers of an earlier edition, see 6:213 (3 references); for reviews by John E. Bell, E. G. Bradford, and Ephraim Rosen of the original edition, see 4:105 (3 references, 1 excerpt).

[1103]

Fox Adds Up.

Purpose: Designed to assess mathematics skills.
Population: Grades K-3.
Publication Date: 2005.
Subtests: 5 per level: Number/Operations, Algebra, Geometry, Measurement, Data Analysis/Probability.
Administration: Individual.
Levels, 4: Kindergarten, Grade 1, Grade 2, Grade 3.
Price Data, 2006: $245 per complete kit including teacher's guide, observation and scoring records, Activity Cards, Math Manipulatives, and DVD; $55 per 25 observation and scoring records.
Foreign Language Edition: Parent letter available in Spanish.
Time: Administration time not reported.
Comments: Designed to be administered twice during the school year, including once in the fall and once in the spring; directly connects to benchmarks in Fox Letters and Numbers (1044) and Fox in a Box-Second Edition (1104).
Author: CTB/McGraw-Hill.
Publisher: CTB/McGraw-Hill.
  a) KINDERGARTEN.
  Scores, 21: Number/Operations (Counting Cubes, Counting Forward/Backward, Representing Numbers, Coins, Modeling Additions, Modeling Subtraction, Adding, Subtracting), Algebra (Sorting, Patterns, Missing Addends), Geometry (Geometric Shapes, Position Words, Finding Shapes), Measurement (Measurement Totals, Time to the Hour, Nonstandard Units), Data Analysis/Probability (Organizing Data, Choosing a Graph, Likely/Unlikely), Kindergarten Total.
  b) GRADE 1.
  Scores, 20: Number/Operations (Two-Digit Numbers, Counting Backward, Composing/Decomposing Numbers, Comparing Two-Digit Numbers, Addition, Subtraction), Algebra (Sorting, Patterns, Commutative Property), Geometry (Comparing/Contrasting Shapes, Arranging Objects, Re-creating a Design), Measurement (Appropriate Measurement Units, Time to the Half-Hour, Nonstandard Units), Data Analysis/Probability (Organizing Data, Choosing Graph, Reading a Graph, Most Likely Outcome), Grade 1 Total.
  c) GRADE 2.
  Scores, 20: Number/Operations (Place Value, Representing Two-Digit Numbers, Modeling Two-Digit Addition, Modeling Two-Digit Subtraction, Adding Two-Digit Numbers, Subtracting Two-Digit Numbers), Algebra (Sorting, Patterns, Using a Pattern in a Table), Geometry (Compares Geometric Shapes, Using a Grid, Redrawing a Design from Memory), Measurement (Appropriate Measurement Tool, Time to 5 Minutes, Standard and Nonstandard Units), Data Analysis/Probability (Organizing Data, Choosing a Graph, Analyzing a Graph, Most and Least Likely Outcomes), Grade 2 Total.
  d) GRADE 3.
  Scores, 18: Number/Operations (Place Value, Fractions, Multiplication, Division), Algebra (Sorting, Patterns in a Table, Equations), Geometry (Combining Shapes, Using a Map, Flips/Sides/Turns, Three-Dimensional Figures), Measurement (Appropriate Measurement Unit, Elapsed Time, Area/Perimeter), Data Analysis/Probability (Organizing Data, Choosing and Analyzing a Graph, Most Likely Outcome on a Spinner), Grade 3 Total.

[1104]

Fox in a Box-Second Edition.

Purpose: Designed to measure "children's literacy skills."
Population: Grades K-3.
Publication Dates: 1998-2005.
Subtests: 4-6 per level: Phonemic Awareness [Levels 1-2 only], Phonics, Vocabulary [Levels 2-8 only], Reading Comprehension, Fluency [Levels 4-8 only], Listening and Comprehension.
Levels, 8: Level 1 (Fall Kindergarten), Level 2 (Spring Kindergarten), Level 3 (Fall Grade 1), Level 4 (Spring Grade 1), Level 5 (Fall Grade 2), Level 6 (Spring Grade 2), Level 7 (Fall Grade 3), Level 8 (Spring Grade 3).
Price Data, 2006: $245 per complete kit including teacher's guide, observation and scoring records, activity cards, window card, reader, fox puppet, "Monday" book, and Staff Development DVD; $55 per 25 observation scoring records.
Foreign Language Edition: Parent letter available in Spanish.
Comments: Designed to be given twice a year, including once in early fall (October/November) and once in early spring (March/April); spelling section of this test is designed to be administered over 2 to 3 days; directly connects to benchmarks in Fox Letters and Numbers (1105) and Fox Adds Up (1103).

Author: CTB/McGraw-Hill.
Publisher: CTB/McGraw-Hill.
 a) LEVEL 1-FALL KINDERGARTEN.
  1) *Phonemic Awareness.*
  Scores, 4: Rhyme Recognition, Rhyme Generation, Syllable Clapping, Initial Consonants.
  Administration: Individual.
  Time: (10-20) minutes.
  2) *Phonics.*
   (a) Alphabet Recognition.
   Administration: Individual.
   Time: (2-7) minutes.
   (b) Alphabet Writing.
   Administration: Individual or group.
   Time: (2-7) minutes.
   (c) Spelling.
   Administration: Individual or group.
   Time: (5-10) minutes for battery; (2-7) minutes for any one test.
  3) *Reading Comprehension.*
  Scores, 2: Listening Comprehension, Writing Development.
  Administration: Individual or group.
  Time: (40-60) minutes.
  4) *Listening and Writing.*
   (a) Timmy Turtle.
   Administration: Individual.
   Time: (2-7) minutes.
 b) LEVEL 2-SPRING KINDERGARTEN.
  1) *Phonemic Awareness.*
  Scores, 3: Final Consonants, Blending, Segmenting.
  Administration: Individual.
  Time: (5-15) minutes.
  2) *Phonics.*
   (a) Alphabet Recognition.
   Administration: Individual.
   Time: (2-7) minutes.
   (b) Alphabet Writing.
   Administration: Individual or group.
   Time: (2-7) minutes.
   (c) Spelling.
   Administration: Individual or group.
   Time: (10-20) minutes for battery; (2-7) minutes for any one test.
   (d) Decoding.
   Administration: Individual.
   Time: (2-7) minutes.
  3) *Vocabulary.*
   (a) Sight Words.
   Administration: Individual or group.
   Time: (2-7) minutes.
  4) *Reading Comprehension.*
  Scores, 2: Emergent Reading, Oral Expression.
  Administration: Individual.
  Time: (10-20) minutes.

  5) *Listening and Writing.*
   (a) The Squirrel, the Eagle, and the Egg.
   Scores, 2: Listening Comprehension, Writing Development.
   Administration: Individual or group.
   Time: (35-55) minutes.
 c) LEVEL 3-FALL GRADE 1.
  1) *Phonics.*
   (a) Spelling.
   Administration: Individual or group.
   Time: (20-40) minutes for battery; (5-15) minutes for any one test.
   (b) Decoding.
   Administration: Individual.
   Time: (2-7) minutes.
  2) *Vocabulary.*
   (a) Work Knowledge.
   Administration: Individual or group.
   Time: (10-20) minutes.
   (b) Sight Words.
   Administration: Individual.
   Time: (2-7) minutes.
  3) *Reading Comprehension.*
  Scores, 3: Reading Accuracy, Reading Comprehension, Oral Expression.
  Administration: Individual.
  Time: (10-20) minutes.
  4) *Listening and Writing.*
   (a) Danger Dog.
   Scores, 2: Listening Comprehension, Writing Development.
   Administration: Individual or group.
   Time: (35-55) minutes.
 d) LEVEL 4-SPRING GRADE 1.
  1) *Phonics.*
   (a) Spelling.
   Administration: Individual or group.
   Time: (20-40) minutes for battery; (5-15) minutes for any one test.
   (b) Decoding.
   Administration: Individual.
   Time: (2-7) minutes.
  2) *Vocabulary.*
   (a) Work Knowledge.
   Administration: Individual or group.
   Time: (10-20) minutes.
   (b) Sight Words.
   Administration: Individual.
   Time: (2-7) minutes.
  3) *Reading Comprehension.*
  Scores, 3: Reading Accuracy, Reading Comprehension, Oral Expression.
  Administration: Individual.
  Time: (10-20) minutes.
  4) *Fluency.*
  Scores, 2: Reading Rate, Reading Expression.

Administration: Individual.
Time: (1-3) minutes.
5) *Listening and Writing.*
  (a) Magpie Robbery.
  Scores, 3: Listening Comprehension, Writing Expression, Writing Development.
  Administration: Individual or group.
  Time: (35-55) minutes.
e) LEVEL 5-FALL GRADE 2.
  1) *Phonics.*
    (a) Spelling.
    Administration: Individual or group.
    Time: (35-55) minutes for battery; (10-20) minutes for any one test.
    (b) Decoding.
    Administration: Individual.
    Time: (2-7) minutes.
  2) *Vocabulary.*
    (a) Work Knowledge.
    Administration: Individual or group.
    Time: (10-20) minutes.
    (b) Sight Words.
    Administration: Individual.
    Time: (2-7) minutes.
  3) *Reading Comprehension.*
  Scores, 3: Reading Accuracy, Reading Comprehension, Oral Expression.
  Administration: Individual.
  Time: (15-25) minutes.
  4) *Fluency.*
  Scores, 2: Reading Rate, Reading Expression.
  Administration: Individual.
  Time: (1-3) minutes.
  5) *Listening and Writing.*
    (a) Puffin Patrol.
    Scores, 3: Listening Comprehension, Writing Expression, Writing Development.
    Administration: Individual or group.
    Time: (35-55) minutes.
f) LEVEL 6-SPRING GRADE 2.
  1) *Phonics.*
    (a) Spelling.
    Administration: Individual or group.
    Time: (35-55) minutes for battery; (10-20) minutes for any one test.
    (b) Decoding.
    Administration: Individual.
    Time: (2-7) minutes.
  2) *Vocabulary.*
    (a) Work Knowledge.
    Administration: Individual or group.
    Time: (10-20) minutes.
    (b) Sight Words.
    Administration: Individual.
    Time: (2-7) minutes.

3) *Reading Comprehension.*
Scores, 3: Reading Accuracy, Reading Comprehension, Oral Expression.
Administration: Individual.
Time: (15-25) minutes.
4) *Fluency.*
Scores, 2: Reading Rate, Reading Expression.
Administration: Individual.
Time: (1-3) minutes.
5) *Listening and Writing.*
  (a) Dodger's Den Mother.
  Scores, 3: Listening Comprehension, Writing Expression, Writing Development.
  Administration: Individual or group.
  Time: (35-55) minutes.
g) LEVEL 7-FALL GRADE 3.
  1) *Phonics.*
    (a) Spelling.
    Administration: Individual or group.
    Time: (35-55) minutes for battery; (10-20) minutes for any one test.
  2) *Vocabulary.*
    (a) Work Knowledge.
    Administration: Individual or group.
    Time: (10-20) minutes.
    (b) Sight Words.
    Administration: Individual.
    Time: (2-7) minutes.
  3) *Reading Comprehension.*
  Scores, 3: Reading Accuracy, Reading Comprehension, Oral Expression.
  Administration: Individual.
  Time: (15-25) minutes.
  4) *Fluency.*
  Scores, 2: Reading Rate, Reading Expression.
  Administration: Individual.
  Time: (1-3) minutes.
  5) *Listening and Writing.*
    (a) Some Jungles are Noisier Than Others.
    Scores, 3: Listening Comprehension, Writing Expression, Writing Development.
    Administration: Individual or group.
    Time: (45-65) minutes.
h) LEVEL 8-SPRING GRADE 3.
  1) *Phonics.*
    (a) Spelling.
    Administration: Individual or group.
    Time: (35-55) minutes for battery; (10-20) minutes for any one test.
  2) *Vocabulary.*
    (a) Work Knowledge.
    Administration: Individual or group.
    Time: (10-20) minutes.
    (b) Sight Words.
    Administration: Individual.
    Time: (2-7) minutes.

3) *Reading Comprehension.*
Scores, 3: Reading Accuracy, Reading Comprehension, Oral Expression.
Administration: Individual.
Time: (15-25) minutes.
4) *Fluency.*
Scores, 2: Reading Rate, Reading Expression.
Administration: Individual.
Time: (1-3) minutes.
5) *Listening and Writing.*
  (a) Rainforest Surprise.
  Scores, 3: Listening Comprehension, Writing Expression, Writing Development.
  Administration: Individual or group.
  Time: (45-65) minutes.

[1105]
Fox Letters and Numbers.
Purpose: Designed as "an observational assessment of literacy and mathematics for the years proceeding kindergarten."
Population: Prekindergarten students.
Publication Date: 2005.
Subtests, 2: Literacy, Mathematics.
Administration: Individual.
Price Data, 2006: $245 per complete kit including teacher's guide, observation and scoring records, activity cards, storybook, math manipulatives, and Product DVD; $55 per 25 observation and scoring records.
Foreign Language Edition: Parent letter available in Spanish.
Time: Administration time not reported.
Comments: Designed to be administered twice during the school year, including one time early in the fall; directly connects to benchmarks in Fox in a Box-Second Edition (1104) and Fox Adds Up (1103).
Author: CTB/McGraw-Hill.
Publisher: CTB/McGraw-Hill.
  a) LITERACY.
  Scores, 15: Oral Language (Identifying Same/Different Sounds, Following Directions, Story Retell, Labeling Objects, Position Words, Opposites), Phonological Awareness (Rhyme Recognition, Syllable Clapping, Identifying Same/Different Words, Blending Phonemes), Alphabet Knowledge (Naming Letters, Naming Letter Sounds), Print Awareness (Differentiates Numbers/Letters/Print, Handling a Book), Literacy Total.
  b) MATHEMATICS.
  Scores, 14: Number and Operations (Finding How many, Numbers to 10, Conservation of Number, More or Fewer), Geometry (Identifies Shape, Matches Shapes), Measurement (Comparing, Time of Day, Conservation of Length, Nonstandard Units), Algebra (Patterns, Sorting), Data Analysis and Probability (Comparing Groups of Objects, Classifying Groups), Mathematics Total.

[1106]
Frenchay Dysarthria Assessment–Second Edition.
Purpose: Designed to provide a "measurement, differential description, and diagnosis of dysarthria."
Population: Ages 12 to adult.
Publication Dates: 1983-2008.
Acronym: FDA-2.
Scores, 7: Reflexes, Respiration, Lips, Palate, Laryngeal, Tongue, Intelligibility.
Administration: Individual.
Price Data, 2010: $150 per complete kit including 25 rating forms, Intelligibility cards, and examiner's manual (2008, 45 pages); $45 per 25 rating forms; $46 per Intelligibility cards; $73 per examiner's manual.
Foreign Language Editions: Translations available in French, German, Dutch, Norwegian, Swedish, Finnish, Castilian, and Catalan.
Time: (30) minutes.
Comments: Additional items required for administration include: tongue depressor, stopwatch, tape recorder, glass of water, cookie, sterile gloves, and calipers.
Authors: Pamela Enderby and Rebecca Palmer.
Publisher: PRO-ED.
Cross References: For reviews by Jeff Berry and Steven Long and by Patricia Brazier-Carter, see 18:55; see T5:1056 (2 references); for reviews by Steven B. Leder and Malcolm R. McNeil of a previous edition, see 12:154; see also T4:1007 (2 references).

[1107]
Friedman Well-Being Scale.
Purpose: "Designed to assess the level of well-being of an individual."
Population: Adults.
Publication Dates: 1992–1994.
Acronym: FWBS.
Scores, 6: Composite/Total, Sociability, Self-Esteem, Joviality, Emotional Stability, Happiness.
Administration: Group.
Price Data: Available from publisher at www.mindgarden.com/products/fwbss.htm.
Time: (2–3) minutes.
Comments: Scale for rating perception of others or for self-rating; self-administered, administrator scored.
Author: Philip H. Friedman.
Publisher: Mind Garden, Inc.
Cross References: For a review by John W. Fleenor, see 14:152.

[1108]
Frontal Systems Behavior Scale.
Purpose: "Identifies and quantifies behavioral problems associated with frontal lobe lesions."
Population: Ages 18–95.

Publication Date: 2001.

Acronym: FrSBe.

Scores, 4: Apathy (subscale A), Disinhibition (subscale D), Executive Dysfunction (subscale E), Total Score.

Administration: Individual or group.

Forms, 2: Family Rating Form, Self-Rating Form.

Price Data, 2006: $195 per introductory kit including professional manual (109 pages), 25 hand-scorable Self-Rating test booklets, 25 hand-scorable Family Rating test booklets, 25 Self-Rating profile forms, and 25 Family Rating profile forms;

Time: 10 minutes to administer; 10–15 minutes to score.

Comments: Revision of the Frontal Lobe Personality Scale; available in paper-and-pencil form only; obtains ratings of patient's behavior before and after an injury or illness.

Authors: Janet Grace and Paul F. Malloy.

Publisher: Psychological Assessment Resources, Inc.

Cross References: For reviews by Harrison D. Kane and Shawn K. Acheson and by Nora M. Thompson, see 15:106.

[1109]

Fuld Object-Memory Evaluation.

Purpose: Designed to "evaluate memory and learning under conditions that virtually guarantee attention and minimize anxiety."

Population: Ages 70–90 regardless of language and sensory handicaps.

Publication Date: 1977.

Acronym: FOME.

Scores, 5: Total Recall, Storage, Consistency of Retrieval, Ability to Benefit from Reminding, Ability to Say Words in Categories.

Administration: Individual.

Forms, 2: Record Form I, II.

Price Data, 2005: $75 per complete kit; $25 per 30 record forms; $25 per manual (24 pages).

Time: Administration time not reported.

Author: Paula Altman Fuld.

Publisher: Stoelting Co.

Cross References: See T5:1058 (9 references) and T4:1009 (6 references); for a review by Eric F. Gardner, see 9:427.

[1110]

Full Range Test of Visual Motor Integration.

Purpose: Designed to assess the ability of individuals to "accurately relate visual stimuli to motor responses" and "to assist in differentiating normal from pathological aging."

Population: Ages 5-0 through 74-0.

Publication Dates: 1996-2006.

Acronym: FRTVMI.

Scores: Total score only.

Administration: Group or individual.

Price Data, 2010: $194 per complete kit including examiner's manual (2006, 102 pages), 25 profile/examiner record forms for ages 5-10, 25 profile/examiner record forms for ages 11-74, and scoring transparency; $60 per examiner's manual; $68 per 25 profile/examiner record forms for ages 5-10; $68 per 25 profile/examiner record forms for ages 11-74; $8 per scoring transparency.

Time: (5-15) minutes.

Comments: Extensive revision and redevelopment of the Test of Visual-Motor Integration.

Authors: Donald D. Hammill, Nils A. Pearson, Judith K. Voress, and Cecil R. Reynolds.

Publisher: PRO-ED.

Cross References: For reviews by Rik Carl D'Amato and Jamie E. Vannice and by Katharine Snyder, see 17:75; for a review by Deborah Erickson of the Test of Visual-Motor Integration, see 14:395; see also T5:2722 (1 reference).

[1111]

The Fullerton Language Test for Adolescents, Second Edition.

Purpose: Constructed to "distinguish normal from language-impaired adolescents."

Population: Ages 11-18.

Publication Dates: 1980–1986.

Scores, 8: Auditory Synthesis, Morphology Competency, Oral Commands, Convergent Production, Divergent Production, Syllabication, Grammatic Competency, Idioms.

Administration: Individual.

Price Data, 2006: $110 per complete kit including stimulus items, 25 scoring forms and profiles, and manual (1986, 55 pages); $35 per set of stimulus items; $30 per 25 scoring forms and profiles; $45 per manual.

Time: (45) minutes.

Author: Arden R. Thorum.

Publisher: PRO-ED.

Cross References: See T5:1060 (7 references) and T4:1011 (3 references); for a review by Diane J. Sawyer of the experimental edition, see 10:122; for a review by Margaret C. Byrne, see 9:428.

[1112]

Functional Assessment and Intervention System: Improving School Behavior.

Purpose: "Designed to enable interdisciplinary staff (school psychologists, teachers, counselors, and support staff) to systematically identify the intent or function of a student's challenging behaviors and gain a clear understanding of his or her needs."

Population: Early childhood through high school.

Publication Date: 2004.

Acronym: FAIS.

Scores: No scores.

Administration: Individual.

Forms, 2: Social Competence Performance Checklist, Classroom Competence Observation Form.

Price Data, 2004: $85 per complete kit including manual (177 pages) and 25 record forms.

Time: (10) minutes for Social Competence Performance Checklist; (15–30) minutes for observation and support plan development.

Comments: Components of the FAIS can be used with Outcomes: Planning, Monitoring, Evaluating (1920) for planning interventions.

Author: Karen Callan Stoiber.

Publisher: Pearson.

Cross References: For reviews by Robert W. Hiltonsmith and Daniel C. Miller, see 16:93.

[1113]

Functional Assessment of Academic Behavior.

Purpose: Designed as an ecological approach to "evaluate learners in context and address needed instructional, home, and home-school supports for learning."

Population: Grades PreK-12.

Publication Dates: 1987-2002.

Acronym: FAAB.

Scores, 23: 12 classroom components: Instructional Math, Instructional Expectations, Classroom Environment, Instructional Presentation, Cognitive Emphasis, Motivational Strategies, Relevant Practice, Informed Feedback, Academic Engaged Time, Adaptive Instruction, Progress Evaluation, Student Understanding; 5 home components: Home Expectations and Attributions, Discipline Orientation, Home-affective Environment, Parent Participation, Structure for Learning; 6 home-school relationship components: Shared Standards and Expectations, Consistent Structure, Cross-setting Opportunity to Learn, Mutual Support, Positive/Trusting Relationships, Modeling.

Administration: Individual.

Forms, 11: 5 required forms: Instructional Environment Checklist, Instructional Environment Checklist: Annotated Version, Instructional Needs Checklist, Parental Experience With Their Children's Learning and Schoolwork, Intervention Documentation Record; 6 supplemental forms: Observation Record, Student Interview Record, Teacher Interview Record, Parent Interview Record, Supplemental Teacher Interview Questions, Supplemental Student Interview Questions.

Price Data, 2006: $61.95 per Functional Assessment of Academic Behavior book (2002, 105 pages).

Time: Administration time not reported.

Comments: Replaces The Instructional Environment System-III (T6:1223).

Authors: James Ysseldyke and Sandra L. Christenson.

Publisher: Sopris West.

Cross References: For reviews by Jonathan Sandoval and Sandra Ward, see 17:76; see also T5:1275 (1 reference); for reviews by Michael J. Furlong and Jennifer A. Rosenblatt and by Jerry Tindal of The Instructional Environment System-II, see 13:150; for reviews by Kenneth W. Howell and by William T. McKee and Joseph C. Witt of an earlier form, see 10:149.

[1114]

Functional Communication Profile.

Purpose: Designed to measure functional language performance in aphasic patients.

Population: Aphasic adults.

Publication Dates: 1956–1969.

Acronym: FCP.

Scores, 6: Movement, Speaking, Understanding, Reading, Other, Total.

Administration: Individual.

Price Data: Available from publisher.

Time: (15–30) minutes for interview.

Comments: Ratings by experienced clinician following nonstructured interview.

Author: Martha Taylor Sarno.

Publisher: Institute of Rehabilitation Medicine, New York University Medical Center [No reply from publisher; status unknown].

Cross References: See T5:1061 (1 reference), T4:1012 (3 references), and T3:925 (3 references); for reviews by Raphael M. Haller and Harvey Halpern, see 8:962 (11 references).

[1115]

Functional Evaluation for Assistive Technology.

Purpose: To identify "the most appropriate and effective assistive technology (AT) devices to help individuals with learning problems compensate for their difficulties and meet the demands of specific tasks and contexts."

Population: "Individuals with learning problems (of all ages)."

Publication Date: 2002.

Acronym: FEAT.

Scores: Not scored; "examiner interprets the FEAT on a 'per item' basis."

Administration: Individual and group.

Price Data, 2009: $149 per complete kit including 25 of each of the following forms: Contextual Matching Inventory, Checklist of Strengths and Limitations, Checklist of Technology Experiences, Technology Characteristics Inventory, Individual-Technology Evaluation Scale, and Summary and Recommendations Booklet, and 1 examiner's manual (78 pages); $55 per specimen kit including 1 of each of the following: Contextual Matching Inventory, Checklist of Strengths and Limitations, Checklist of Technology Experiences, Technology Characteristics Inventory, Individual-Technology Evaluation Scale, Summary and Recommendations Booklet,

and examiner's manual; $17 per 25 Contextual Matching Inventories; $17 per 25 Checklists of Strengths and Limitations; $17 per 25 Checklists of Technology Experiences; $12 per 25 Technology Characteristics Inventory; $17 per 25 Individual-Technology Evaluation Scales; $25 per 25 Summary and Recommendations Booklets; $55 per examiner's manual.
Time: Administration time not reported.
Comments: The FEAT should be used by an AT evaluation team rather than a single evaluator; "examiner" is the head of the evaluation team; total number of parts administered depends on "individual's AT needs."
Authors: Marshall H. Raskind and Brian R. Bryant.
Publisher: Psycho-Educational Services.

a) CONTEXTUAL MATCHING INVENTORY.
Purpose: To identify "the tasks in which the individual is typically engaged across settings ... and [to determine] whether the [assistive] technology will be successful across those settings."
Comments: Ratings "based on interviews with... teachers, employers, family members, and/or [the] student or employee" being evaluated.
b) CHECKLIST OF STRENGTHS AND LIMITATIONS.
Purpose: To "provide information concerning academic behaviors associated with listening, speaking, reading, writing, mathematics, memory, organization, physical/motor, and behavior."
Administration: Group.
Comments: Ratings by "teachers, employers, family members, and/or [the] student or employee" being evaluated.
c) CHECKLIST OF TECHNOLOGY EXPERIENCES.
Purpose: "To identify the individual's familiarity with [AT] devices that may be evaluated."
Comments: Ratings based on an interview with the student or employee being evaluated.
d) TECHNOLOGY CHARACTERISTICS INVENTORY.
Purpose: "To evaluate [AT] device-specific characteristics such as its reliability/dependability, operational ease, and so forth."
Comments: Ratings by examiner.
e) INDIVIDUAL-TECHNOLOGY EVALUATION SCALE AND RELATED WORKSHEETS.
Purpose: "To obtain "information about the person's interaction with the AT device that is being evaluated."
Forms: 5 additional worksheets "to be used in conjunction with the Individual-Technology Evaluation Scale:" Optical Character Recognition/Speech Synthesis, Speech Synthesis/Screen Reading Systems, Speech Recognition Systems, Word Prediction Software, Spell Checkers.
Comments: Individual-Technology Evaluation Worksheets are reproducible and found in Appendix B of Examiner's Manual; ratings by examiner.

f) SUMMARY AND RECOMMENDATIONS BOOKLET.
Purpose: "To summarize the assessment information, make recommendations, and arrange for follow-ups to assess for effective implementation."
Comments: Completed by examiner.
Cross References: For reviews by Marta Coleman and Suzanne Young, see 18:56.

[1116]

Functional Fitness Assessment for Adults Over 60 Years, Second Edition.

Purpose: Developed as a field test to determine the functional capacity of older adults.
Population: Adults over age 60.
Publication Dates: 1990–1996.
Scores, 7: Body Composition (Body Weight, Standing Height Measurement), Flexibility, Agility/Dynamic Balance, Coordination, Strength/Endurance, Endurance.
Administration: Group.
Price Data, 2001: $12 per manual (1996, 60 pages).
Time: Administration time not reported.
Authors: Wayne H. Osness, Marlene Adrian, Bruce Clark, Werner Hoeger, Dianne Raab, and Robert Wiswell.
Publisher: American Association for Active Lifestyles and Fitness.
Cross References: For reviews by Anita M. Hubley and Anthony M. Paolo, see 15:107; for reviews by Matthew E. Lambert and Cecil R. Reynolds of an earlier edition, see 13:128.

[1117]

Functional Grammar Test.

Purpose: To assess student mastery of English grammar.
Population: High school and college.
Publication Date: 1970.
Acronym: FGT.
Scores: Total score only.
Administration: Group.
Forms, 2: A, B.
Price Data: Available from publisher.
Time: (15–20) minutes.
Author: Joyce E. Lackey.
Publisher: Psychometric Affiliates.

[1118]

Functional Linguistic Communication Inventory.

Purpose: "Designed to quantify the functional linguistic communication skills of moderately and severely demented individuals."
Population: Adults diagnosed with Alzheimer's disease.
Publication Date: 1994.
Acronym: FLCI.

Scores, 10: Greeting and Naming, Question Answering, Writing, Comprehension of Signs and Object-to-Picture Matching, Word Reading and Comprehension, Following Commands, Pantomime, Gesture, Conversation, Total.
Administration: Individual.
Price Data, 2010: $229 per complete kit including manual (31 pages), 25 response record forms, 25 score forms, stimulus book (50 pages), and 3 objects (comb, pencil, mask); $29 per 25 response record forms; $24 per 25 score sheets; $69 per manual; $116 per stimulus book; $19 per kit including comb, pencil, and mask.
Time: (30) minutes.
Authors: Kathryn A. Bayles and Cheryl K. Tomoeda.
Publisher: PRO-ED.
Cross References: For reviews by Cameron J. Camp and Jennifer A. Brush and by Wilfred G. Van Gorp, see 13:129.

[1119]

Functional Skills Screening Inventory, Individual Edition.

Purpose: "To be used in natural settings to assess critical living and working skills in persons with moderate to severe handicapping conditions."
Population: Age 6 through adult.
Publication Dates: 1984-1986.
Acronym: FSSI.
Scores, 9: Categorized into 3 priority levels: Basic Skills and Concepts, Communication, Personal Care, Homemaking, Work Skills and Concepts, Community Living, Social Awareness, Functional Skills Subtotal, Problem Behaviors.
Administration: Individual.
Price Data, 2006: $190 per master print copy including assessment booklet for unlimited assessments, hand-scoring sheets, and user guide (1986, 117 pages); $450 per Windows interactive computer program; web site provides demo with documentation.
Time: [60-120] minutes per assessment.
Comments: A domain-referenced behavioral checklist; Employment Edition and Environmental Edition are also available in Windows format.
Authors: Heather Becker, Sally Schur, Michele Paoletti-Schelp, and Ed Hammer.
Publisher: Functional Resources.
Cross References: See T5:1067 (1 reference); for reviews by Diane Browder and G. Michael Poteat, see 10:123 (3 references).

[1120]

GAINS: A Pre-test and Post-test for Measuring Career Development Competency Progress.

Purpose: A diagnostic tool for assessing level of competency accrued from career development studies.

Population: Grades 4–7, 8–11.
Publication Date: 1995.
Acronym: GAINS I, GAINS II.
Scores, 2: Pre-Test Total, Post-Test Total, Modified Percent Gain.
Administration: Group.
Price Data: Price information available from publisher for classroom set including 30 tests and teacher's guide (specify GAINS I or GAINS II; volume discounts available).
Time: Testing time specified by teacher based on reading ability; pre-test and post-test must use the same time limit.
Author: Norene Lindsay.
Publisher: Wintergreen/Orchard House, Inc.

[1121]

Gambler Addiction Index.

Purpose: Designed for "gambler assessment in clinics, employee assistance programs, counseling settings, courts, probation departments, mental health professionals, and service provider offices."
Population: Ages 17-74.
Publication Dates: 1982-2004.
Acronym: GAI.
Scores, 7: Truthfulness, Gambler Severity, DSM-IV Gambling, Alcohol, Drugs, Suicide, Stress Coping Abilities.
Administration: Group.
Price Data, 2010: $8 per test; volume discounts available.
Foreign Language Edition: Spanish version available.
Time: (35) minutes.
Comments: May be administered via paper and pencil, computer, or human voice audio.
Author: Behavior Data Systems, Ltd.
Publisher: Behavior Data Systems, Ltd.

[1122]

Garos Sexual Behavior Inventory.

Purpose: "Designed to assist forensic specialists and mental health professionals in making assessments and treatment decisions about individuals with problems related to sexuality and sexual behavior."
Population: Ages 18 and over.
Publication Date: 2008.
Acronym: GSBI.
Scores, 8: Discordance, Sexual Obsession, Permissiveness, Sexual Stimulation, Sexual Control Difficulties, Sexual Excitability, Sexual Insecurity, Inconsistent Responding.
Administration: Group.
Price Data, 2010: $99.50 per complete kit including 25 AutoScore forms, 5 reusable administration cards, and manual (63 pages); $42.50 per 25 AutoScore forms; $27.50 per 5 reusable administration cards; $55 per manual.

Time: (20-30) minutes.
Comments: Administration card is entitled Sexual Attitudes Inventory.
Author: Sheila Garos.
Publisher: Western Psychological Services.

[1123]

Gates-MacGinitie Reading Tests®, Fourth Edition, Forms S and T.

Purpose: Designed to assess students' "general level of reading achievement."
Population: Grades K.7–12 and adults.
Publication Dates: 1926–2000.
Acronym: GMRT®.
Scores, 11: Literacy Concepts, Oral Language Concepts, Letters and Letter/Sound Correspondences, Listening Comprehension, Initial Consonants and Consonant Clusters, Final Consonants and Consonant Clusters, Vowels, Basic Story Words, Word Decoding, Vocabulary/Word Knowledge, Comprehension.
Administration: Group.
Levels, 11: PR (Pre-Reading), BR (Beginning Reading), 1, 2, 3, 4, 5, 6, 7/9, 10/12, AR (Adult Reading).
Forms, 2: S, T.
Price Data, 2006: $78.75 per hand-scorable test booklet package (Levels PR–3, specify level and form) including 25 test booklets, one Directions for Administration, one Booklet Scoring Key, one Class Summary Record, and one Decoding Skills Analysis form (for Levels 1 and 2 only); $119.25 per machine-scorable test booklet package (Levels BR–3, specify level and form); $141.50 per Level PR machine-scorable test booklet package (scored by publisher for an additional fee) including 25 test booklets, one Directions for Administration, and materials needed for machine scoring; $78.75 per reusable test booklet package (Levels 4–10/12 and AR) including 25 test booklets, one Directions for Administration, one Booklet Scoring Key, and one Class Summary Record; $113.50 per machine-scorable answer sheet package (Levels 4–10/12 and AR; scored by publisher for an additional fee) including 100 answer sheets and materials for machine scoring (specify level); $42.75 per self-scorable answer sheet package (Levels 4–10/12 and AR) including 25 answer sheets and one Class Summary Record (specify level); $380.75 per self-scorable answer sheet package (Levels 4–10/12 and AR) including 250 answer sheets (specify level); $10.75 per extra copy of Directions for Administration (specify level); $21 per Manual for Scoring and Interpretation (specify level); $14.50 per Linking Testing to Teaching: A Classroom Resource for Reading Assessment and Instruction (specify level); $25.75 per Technical Report; $475 per Score Converting and Reporting Software (for PC only).
Time: (55–100) minutes.
Comments: Norms tables available on CD-ROM.
Authors: Walter H. MacGinitie, Ruth K. MacGinitie, Katherine Maria, and Lois G. Dreyer.

Publisher: Riverside Publishing.
Cross References: For reviews by Kathleen M. Johnson and Patrick P. McCabe, see 16:94; see also T5:1072 (55 references) and T4:1022 (13 references); for a review by Mark E. Swerdlik of the third edition, see 11:146 (78 references); for reviews by Robert Calfee and William H. Rupley of an earlier edition, see 9:430 (15 references); see also T3:932 (77 references) and 8:726A (34 references); for reviews by Carolyn L. Burke and Byron H. Van Roekel and an excerpted review by William R. Powell of an earlier edition, see 7:689.

[1124]

Gates-MacGinitie Reading Tests, 2nd Canadian Edition.

Purpose: Constructed to assess reading achievement.
Population: Grades K.7–12.
Publication Dates: 1978-1992.
Administration: Group.
Forms, 2: 3, 4.
Price Data, 2005: $60.75 to $63.25 per 35 test booklets (select level); $9.40 per scoring key (select level); $14.20 per 10 class record sheets; $45.60 per Teacher's Guide (select level; includes directions for administration, interpretation, and norms tables); $37.90 per Out-of-Level Norms Booklet; $47.70 per preview kit; $29.95 per technical manual; scoring service available from publisher.
Comments: Levels PRE, R, and A are each available as Form 3; Levels B through F have two parallel forms (3, 4).
Authors: Walter H. MacGinitie and Ruth K. MacGinitie.
Publisher: Nelson Education Ltd. [Canada].
  a) LEVEL PRE.
  Population: Grades K.7-1.2.
  Scores: Total score only.
  Price Data: $60.75 per 35 test booklets.
  Time: (90) minutes.
  b) LEVEL R.
  Population: Grades 1.0-1.9.
  Scores: Total score only.
  Time: (70) minutes.
  c) LEVEL A.
  Population: Grades 1.3-1.9.
  Scores, 3: Vocabulary, Comprehension, Total.
  Price Data: $12 per decoding skills analysis forms.
  Time: 55 minutes.
  d) LEVEL B.
  Population: Grade 2.
  Scores, 3: Same as for *c* above.
  Price Data: Same as for *c* above.
  Time: Same as for *c* above.
  e) LEVEL C.
  Population: Grade 3.
  Scores, 3: Same as for *c* above.
  Time: Same as for *c* above.

f) LEVEL D 4.
Population: Grade 4.
Scores, 3: Same as for *c* above.
Price Data: $37.80 per 35 hand-scorable answer sheets; $90.25 per 100 hand-scorable answer sheets; $83.75 per 50 machine-scorable answer sheets; $379.00 per 250 machine-scorable answer sheets; $21.70 per set of scoring stencils.
Time: Same as for *c* above.
g) LEVEL D 5/6.
Population: Grades 5-6.
Scores, 3: same as for *c* above.
Price Data: same as for *f* above.
h) LEVEL E.
Population: Grades 7-9.
Scores, 3: Same as for *c* above.
Price Data: Same as for *f* above.
Time: Same as for *c* above.
i) LEVEL F.
Population: Grades 10-12.
Scores, 3: Same as for *c* above.
Price Data: Same as for *f* above.
Time: Same as for *c* above.
Cross References: See T5:1071 (5 references) and T4:1021 (6 references); for reviews by Mariam Jean Dreher and Susanna W. Pflaum of an earlier edition, see 9:431.

[1125]

Gates-McKillop-Horowitz Reading Diagnostic Test, Second Edition.

Purpose: "Assess the strengths and weaknesses in reading and related areas of a particular child."
Population: Grades 1-6.
Publication Dates: 1962-1981.
Scores, 23: Omissions, Additions, Repetitions, Mispronunciations (Directional Errors, Wrong Beginning, Wrong Middle, Wrong Ending, Wrong in Several Parts, Accent Errors, Total), Reading Sentences, Words-Flash, Words-Untimed, Word-Attack (Syllabication, Recognizing and Blending Common Word Parts, Reading Words, Giving Letter Sounds, Naming Capital Letters, Naming Lower-Case Letters), Vowels, Auditory (Blending, Discrimination), Spelling.
Administration: Individual.
Price Data, 2006: $2.50 per test materials; $7.50 per 30 pupil record booklets; $1 per manual of directions (1981, 16 pages); $3.95 per manual of directions kit (includes test materials, 1 pupil record booklet, manual of directions).
Time: Administration time not reported.
Comments: Revision of Gates-McKillop Reading Diagnostic Tests.
Authors: Arthur I. Gates, Anne S. McKillop, and Elizabeth Cliff Horowitz.
Publisher: Teachers College Press.

Cross References: See T5:1072 (3 references) and T4:1023 (3 references); for reviews by Priscilla A. Drum and by P. David Pearson and Patricia Herman, see 9:432 (2 references); for a review by Harry Singer of an earlier edition, see 8:759 (8 references); see also T2:1629 (11 references); for reviews by N. Dale Bryant and Gabriel M. Della-Piana, see 6:824 (2 references); for a review by George D. Spache of the earlier edition, see 5:662; for a review by T. L. Torgerson, see 3:510 (3 references).

[1126]

The Geist Picture Interest Inventory.

Purpose: Designed to "assess quantitatively eleven male and twelve female general interest areas and identify motivating forces behind occupational choice."
Population: Grade 8–adulthood.
Publication Dates: 1959–1971.
Acronym: GPII.
Scores: 18 (males) or 19 (females) scores: 11 or 12 Interest scores (Persuasive, Clerical, Mechanical, Musical, Scientific, Outdoor, Literary, Computational, Artistic, Social Service, Dramatic, Personal Service–females only), and 7 Motivation scores (Family, Prestige, Financial, Intrinsic and Personality, Environmental, Past Experience, Could Not Say).
Administration: Group or individual.
Forms, 2: M (male), F (female).
Price Data, 2006: $87.95 per kit including 10 tests of each form (male or female), and manual (1971, 42 pages plus tests and motivation questionnaires); $37.95 per 20 tests of male form; $36 per 20 tests of female form; $57 per manual; $14.95 per 20 motivation questionnaires of male form; $11 per 20 motivation questionnaires of female form.
Time: 10–20 minutes.
Author: Harold Geist.
Publisher: Western Psychological Services.
Cross References: See T2:2180 (18 references); for reviews by Milton E. Hahn and Benjamin Shimberg, and an excerpted review by David V. Tiedeman, see 6:1054 (12 references)

[1127]

General Ability Measure for Adults.

Purpose: "Designed to evaluate intellectual ability using abstract designs."
Population: Ages 18–96.
Publication Date: 1997.
Acronym: GAMA.
Scores, 5: Matching, Analogies, Sequences, Construction, GAMA IQ Score.
Administration: Individual and/or group.
Price Data, 2006: $58 per manual (1997, 97 pages); $153 per 10 softcover test booklets; $73.75 per 25 hand-scored answer sheets (test items included); $21 per 25 Q Local answer sheets (test items included); $5.80 per Q Local report; quantity discounts availabe for the reports; price information for Spanish materials available from publisher.

Time: (25) minutes.
Comments: May be self-administered.
Authors: Jack A. Naglieri and Achilles N. Bardos.
Publisher: Pearson.
Cross References: For reviews by Robert Fitzpatrick and Bert A. Goldman, see 14:153.

[1128]

General Chemistry Test: National Achievement Tests.

Purpose: Designed to measure students' knowledge in three areas of general chemistry.
Population: Grades 10–16.
Publication Dates: 1958–1959.
Scores, 4: Uses-Processes-Results, Formulae and Valence, Miscellaneous Facts, Total.
Administration: Group.
Manual: No manual.
Price Data: Available from publisher.
Time: 40(45) minutes.
Authors: Lester D. Crow and Roy S. Cook.
Publisher: Psychometric Affiliates.
Cross References: See T4:1025 (1 reference); for a review by J. A. Campbell, see 6:918.

[1129]

General Clerical Test.

Purpose: Developed to assess clerical speed and accuracy, numerical skills, and language-related skills.
Population: Clerical applicants and workers.
Publication Dates: 1972–1988.
Acronym: GCT.
Scores, 4: Clerical, Numerical, Verbal, Total.
Administration: Group or individual.
Price Data, 2006: $151 per 25 Clerical/Numerical/Verbal test booklets; $99 per 25 Clerical/Numerical test booklets; $72 per 25 Verbal test booklets; $555 per 100 Clerical/Numerical/Verbal test booklets; $358 per 100 Clerical/Numerical test booklets; $215 per 100 Verbal only test booklets; $51 per handscoring key; $52 per manual; 57 per examination kit, including 1 complete test booklet and manual (no key).
Time: 60 minutes.
Author: The Psychological Corporation.
Publisher: Pearson.
Cross References: See T5:1078 (1 reference); for reviews by Dianna L. Newman and Alfred L. Smith, Jr., see 12:158.

[1130]

General Management In-Basket.

Purpose: "Designed to assess supervisory/managerial skills independent of any particular management position, from entry management up through top management positions; may be used for selection and/or career development."

Population: Managers.
Publication Dates: 1985–2011.
Acronym: GMIB.
Scores, 5: Leadership Style and Practices, Handling Priorities and Sensitive Situations, Managing Conflict, Organizational Practices/Management Control, Total.
Administration: Group.
Forms, 4: Private and public sector forms include Executive Version, Engineer Version, Police Versions for each managerial level from Police Sergeant to Police Chief, and Fire Versions for each managerial level from Fire Captain to Fire Chief.
Restricted Distribution: Clients may be required to pay a one-time overhead/sign-up fee.
Price Data, 2011: $575-$625 per candidate (depending on particular version) for rental/scoring and detailed Career Development Report identifying strengths, weaknesses, and developmental needs with specific learning objectives for each of the four factors measured by the test.
Time: 165 minutes.
Comments: All versions are available for online administration.
Author: Richard C. Joines.
Publisher: Management & Personnel Systems, Inc.
Cross References: For reviews by S. David Kriska and William J. Waldron, see 12:160.

[1131]

General Physics Test: National Achievement Tests.

Purpose: "Constructed to test the student's basic knowledge of Physics and his ability to apply that knowledge."
Population: Grades 10–16.
Publication Dates: 1958–1962.
Scores, 3: Uses and Application of Principles, Miscellaneous Facts and Scientists, Total.
Administration: Group.
Manual: No manual.
Price Data: Available from publisher.
Time: 40(45) minutes.
Authors: Lester D. Crow and Roy S. Cook.
Publisher: Psychometric Affiliates.
Cross References: For a review by Theodore G. Phillips, see 6:930.

[1132]

General Processing Inventory.

Purpose: Designed to identify learning disabilities.
Population: Ages 5–75 years.
Publication Dates: 1986–2004.
Acronym: GPI.
Scores, 7: Graphomotor, Short Term Memory Retrieval, Long Term Memory Retrieval, Visual (Dyslexia), Auditory, Speech (Dysphasia), Total.

Subtests, 2: General Elementary Inventory of Language Skills (GEILS), General Elementary Inventory of Mathematics and Numeration (GEIMAN).
Administration: Individual.
Levels, 4: One (5 years old), Two (Above 6 years), Three (Above 8 years), Four (Above 10 years).
Price Data, 2005: $350 per test kit; $400 for training required to administer test.
Time: (60–180) minutes.
Comments: Training required; psychologists and other licensed test administrators will learn to tabulate errors and may send their results to publisher for report writing. There is a fee for report writing dependent on volume.
Author: Ruth M. Geiman.
Publisher: Ruth M. Geiman, Ph.D.
Cross References: For reviews by Sherry K. Bain and Stephen A. Spillane, see 14:154.

[1133]
General Science Test: National Achievement Tests.
Purpose: Designed to measure students' knowledge of general science.
Population: Grades 7–9.
Publication Dates: 1936–1950.
Scores, 7: General Concepts, Identifications, Men of Science, Definitions, Uses of Objects, Miscellaneous Facts, Total.
Administration: Group.
Manual: No manual.
Price Data: Available from publisher.
Time: (30–45) minutes.
Authors: Robert K. Speer, Lester D. Crow, and Samuel Smith.
Publisher: Psychometric Affiliates.
Cross References: For a review by Robert M. W. Travers, see 5:712; for reviews by Francis D. Curtis and G. W. Hunter, see 2:1602.

[1134]
The Gesell Developmental Observation.
Purpose: A comprehensive developmental screening that measures physical/neurological growth, language skills, and adaptive behaviors such as thinking, memory, perception, attention to task, ability to follow directions, short term visual and aduitory memory, cognitive-perceptual thinking, organizational skills, logical mathematical thinking skills, and application of what is learned.
Population: Ages 2.5 through 9 years.
Publication Dates: 1964-2005.
Administration: Individual.
Price Data, 2006: $129 per reusable kit; $55.95 per 30 precollated sheets to test 30 children; $4.95 per pad of 75 Assessment Profile Forms (Summary Sheets).

Comments: Earlier version of the test was called The Gesell School Readiness Test.
Author: The Gesell Institute.
Publisher: The Gesell Institute.
Cross References: See T5:1085 (4 references) and T4:1035 (13 references); for reviews by Robert H. Bradley and Everett Waters of an earlier version, see 9:438; see also T3:953 (6 references) and T2:1703 (4 references); for excerpted reviews by L. J. Borstelmann and Edith Meyer Taylor, see 7:750 (5 references).

[1135]
Gesell Preschool Test.
Purpose: "Designed to measure . . . relative maturity ratings in four basic fields of behavior."
Population: Ages 2.5–6.
Publication Date: 1980.
Scores: Ratings in 4 areas: Motor, Adaptive, Language, Personal-Social.
Administration: Group.
Price Data, 2001: $127.30 per kit (reusable materials only); $29 per formboard; $28 per picture vocabulary cards; $10 per color forms; $9 per letters and numbers; $5.50 per pellets and bottles; $12.50 per copy forms; $14.95 per manual (72 pages); $5 per 25 developmental schedules; $9.50 per 10 one-inch cubes; $13.75 per typical response cards for incomplete man test.
Time: (30-45) minutes.
Comments: Abbreviated adaptation of the Gesell Developmental Schedules (see 6:522) and the Gesell Developmental Tests (see 7:750).
Authors: Jacqueline Haines, Louise Bates Ames, and Clyde Gillespie.
Publisher: The Gesell Institute.
Cross References: See T5:1086 (4 references); for reviews by Nadeen L. Kaufman and Jack A. Naglieri, see 9:437 (8 references).

[1136]
Get Ready to Read!–Revised.
Purpose: Designed as a screening tool to measure preschool students' "understanding of books, printed letters, and words," as well as "the relationship between letters and speech sounds and how sounds can combine to form words" to "determine if they have the necessary early literacy skills to become successful readers."
Population: Ages 3-0 to 5-11.
Publication Dates: 2000-2009.
Acronym: GRTR!.
Scores: Total score only.
Administration: Individual.
Price Data, 2009: $82.95 per complete test kit; $16.55 per 25 child record forms; $1 per summary form; $49.95 per stimulus easel; $25.95 per Early Literacy Manual (2009, 23 pages).

Foreign Language Edition: A Spanish version of the complete test kit is available.
Time: (10-15) minutes.
Comments: Should not be used to screen the same student more than three times in 1 year and at least 3 months should separate screening dates; a summary form is included for administrators to record screening scores at different time points for each student in a particular class or group; the Total score is interpreted using Step Scores or Performance Levels provided in the manual and on the back of the answer sheet; there are four (1-4) Step Scores (providing information about the student's pre-literacy skill level) that correspond to a range of Total scores.
Author: National Center for Learning Disabilities.
Publisher: Pearson.
Cross References: For reviews by Zandra S. Gratz and Timothy Shanahan, see 18:57.

[1137]

Gibson Spiral Maze, Second Edition.

Purpose: Measures "the speed, accuracy, and general style of people's muscular reactions in response to carefully controlled stimuli."
Population: Children and adults.
Publication Dates: 1961–1965.
Scores, 2: Time score, Error score.
Administration: Individual.
Price Data, 2002: £13.99 per test 20 copies; manual and specimen set are now out of print.
Time: (2) minutes.
Comments: Forms part of the Clifton Assessment Procedures for the Elderly (568).
Author: H. B. Gibson.
Publisher: Hodder & Stoughton Educational [England].
Cross References: For reviews by William K. Wilkinson and James Ysseldyke, see 14:155; see also T4:1037 (3 references), T3:955 (1 reference), T2:1191 (3 references), 7:82 (3 references), and P:90 (2 references).

[1138]

Gifted and Talented Evaluation Scales.

Purpose: Designed to help "identify persons who are gifted and talented."
Population: Ages 5-18.
Publication Date: 1996.
Acronym: GATES.
Scores, 5: Intellectual Ability, Academic Skills, Creativity, Leadership, Artistic Talent.
Administration: Individual.
Price Data, 2010: $127 per complete kit including examiner's manual (50 pages) and 50 summary/response forms; $75 per examiner's manual; $59 per 50 summary/response forms.
Time: (5-10) minutes.

Comments: This test is to be completed by a teacher, parent, or guardian of the individual being assessed.
Authors: James E. Gilliam, Betsy O. Carpenter, and Janis R. Christensen.
Publisher: PRO-ED.
Cross References: For reviews by Linda E. Brody and Carolyn M. Callahan, see 17:77.

[1139]

Gifted Evaluation Scale, Second Edition.

Purpose: Designed to help identify gifted students.
Population: Ages 5–18.
Publication Dates: 1987–2000.
Acronym: GES-2.
Scores, 8: 6 subscales (Intellectual, Creativity, Specific Academic Aptitude, Leadership Ability, Performing and Visual Arts, Motivation [optional]), Quotient Score, Percentile Score.
Administration: Individual.
Price Data, 2006: $75 per complete kit including technical manual (1998, 60 pages), 50 rating forms, and Gifted Intervention Manual (1990, 107 pages); $10 per 50 motivation scoring forms; $15 per technical manual; $35 per 50 rating forms; $25 per Gifted Intervention Manual; $5 per subscale percentile tables; $35 per Quick Score (WIN).
Time: (15–20) minutes.
Comments: Ratings by "anyone familiar with the student's behavior patterns and specific skills ... (e.g., teacher, counselor, etc.)."
Authors: Diana Henage (The Gifted Intervention Manual), Stephen B. McCarney and Paul D. Anderson (technical manual and subscale percentile tables).
Publisher: Hawthorne Educational Services, Inc.
Cross References: For reviews by Douglas K. Smith and John W. Young, see 14:156; see also T5:1089 (2 references); for reviews by Carolyn M. Callahan and Ross E. Traub of an earlier edition, see 12:162 (1 reference).

[1140]

Gifted Rating Scales.

Purpose: Designed to "assess observable student behaviors indicating giftedness."
Publication Date: 2003.
Acronym: GRS.
Administration: Individual.
Price Data, 2003: $125 per complete kit including manual (86 pages), 25 Early Child record forms, and 25 School Age record forms; $75 per manual; $40 per 25 Early Child record forms; $40 per 25 School Age record forms.
Comments: Norm-referenced, teacher-completed rating scale.
Authors: Steven I. Pfeiffer and Tania Jarosewich.
Publisher: Pearson.

a) GIFTED RATING SCALE—PRESCHOOL AND KINDERGARTEN.
Population: Ages 4:0 to 6:11.
Acronym: GRS-P.
Scores, 5: Intellectual Ability, Academic Ability, Creativity, Artistic Talent, Motivation.
Time: (10) minutes.
b) GIFTED RATING SCALE–SCHOOL.
Population: Ages: 6:0 to 13:11.
Acronym: GRS-S.
Scores, 6: Same as *a* above with the addition of Leadership Ability.
Time: (15) minutes.
Cross References: For a review by Sandra A. Ward, see 16:95.

[1141]

Gilliam Asperger's Disorder Scale [2003 Update].

Purpose: Designed to evaluate children with unique behavioral problems who may have Asperger's Disorder.
Population: Ages 3–0 through 22–0 years.
Publication Date: 2001.
Acronym: GADS.
Scores, 4: Social Interaction, Restricted Patterns of Behavior, Cognitive Patterns, Pragmatic Skills.
Administration: Individual.
Price Data, 2010: $116 per complete kit including examiner's manual (52 pages) and 25 summary/response forms; $69 per examiner's manual; $53 per 25 summary/response booklets.
Time: (5–10) minutes.
Authors: James E. Gilliam.
Publisher: PRO-ED.
Cross References: For reviews by Connie T. England and Carol M. McGregor, see 16:96; for reviews by Donald Oswald and Theresa Volpe-Johnstone of an earlier edition, see 15:108.

[1142]

Gilliam Autism Rating Scale–Second Edition.

Purpose: Designed to help professionals "identify children with autism from children with other severe behavioral problems."
Population: Ages 3-22.
Publication Dates: 1995-2006.
Acronym: GARS-2.
Scores: 3 subscales: Stereotyped Behaviors, Communication, Social Interaction, plus Autism Index.
Administration: Individual.
Price Data, 2011: $151 per complete kit including examiner's manual (2006, 85 pages), 50 summary/response booklets, and instructional objectives manual (2006, 26 pages); $69 per examiner's manual; $53 per 50

summary/response booklets; $32 per instructional objectives manual. GARS-2 Scoring System and Reporting Software available separately ($94).
Time: (5-10) minutes.
Comments: Appropriate raters include parents, teachers, or other caregivers who have had regular, sustained contact with the individual for at least 2 weeks.
Author: James E. Gilliam.
Publisher: PRO-ED.
Cross References: For reviews by Doreen Ward Fairbank and Adrienne Garro, see 17:78; for reviews by Donald P. Oswald and Steven Welsh of an earlier form, see 13:130.

[1143]

Gilmore Oral Reading Test.

Purpose: "Developed to provide ... a means of analyzing the oral reading performance of pupils."
Population: Grades 1–8.
Publication Dates: 1951–1968.
Acronym: GORT.
Scores, 3: Accuracy, Comprehension, Rate.
Administration: Individual.
Forms, 2: C, D.
Price Data, 2002: $24.50 per examination kit including manual (1968, 31 pages) and record blank; $41.25 per reading paragraphs (both forms); $70 per 35 record blanks (specify Form C or D); $22 per manual.
Time: (15-20) minutes.
Authors: John V. Gilmore and Eunice C. Gilmore.
Publisher: Pearson.
Cross References: See T5:1092 (18 references), T4:1042 (21 references), and T3:958 (13 references); for an excerpted review by Jerry Stafford, see 8:785 (17 references); see also T2:1679 (5 references); for reviews by Albert J. Harris and Kenneth J. Smith, see 7:737 (17 references); for reviews by Lydia A. Duggins and Maynard C. Reynolds of the original edition, see 5:671.

[1144]

Giotto.

Purpose: To provide a wide-ranging measure of personal integrity for use in staff selection.
Population: Unspecified.
Publication Dates: 1996–1997.
Scores: 7 scales: Prudence, Fortitude, Temperance, Justice, Faith, Charity, Hope.
Administration: Group or individual.
Price Data, 2006: $297 per starter kit including 20 question and answer booklets, scoring software, and manual (1997, 79 pages).
Time: (15) minutes.
Comments: Must be scored by computer on Giotto software using Windows 3.1 or Windows 95.
Author: John Rust.

Publisher: Pearson Assessment [England].
Cross References: For reviews by Eugene V. Aidman and by Deniz S. Ones and Stephan Dilchert, see 16:97.

[1145]

Global Assessment Scale.

Purpose: "For evaluating the overall functioning of a subject during a specified time period on a continuum from psychological or psychiatric sickness to health."
Population: Psychiatric patients and possible psychiatric patients.
Publication Dates: 1976-1985.
Acronym: GAS.
Scores: Mental Health-Illness rating of individual on a continuum of 1 to 100.
Administration: Individual.
Price Data, 2001: $.50 per scale; $2.50 per case vignettes and keys (1985, 17 pages); $1 per instructions (1978, 8 pages).
Authors: Robert L. Spitzer, Miriam Gibbon, and Jean Endicott.
Publisher: Department of Research Assessment and Training.
Cross References: See T5:1093 (116 references) and T4:1043 (62 references); for a review by Michael J. Subkoviak, see 11:147 (22 references).

[1146]

GOALS®: A Performance-Based Measure of Achievement.

Purpose: A measure of student achievement using open-ended questions requiring reasoning skills.
Population: Grades 1–12.
Publication Dates: 1992–1994.
Administration: Group.
Forms, 3: A, B, C (Form C is secure and not available through the catalog).
Levels, 11: 1–11.
Price Data, 2002: $23.90 per 25 test booklets including directions for administering; $11.70 per scoring guide; $8 per directions for administering; $26.50 per 1991 norms booklet (separate by content area); $80 per 1992 norms booklet (all content areas); $53 per technical manual (1994, 114 pages); $26.50 per interpretive manual; $4.50 per Option 1 computer scoring by publisher of one domain including scoring and two copies of the Student Performance Roster; $3.40 per each additional domain; $.22 per additional copy of Student Performance Roster); $760 set-up charge for Option 2 computer scoring by publisher including scoring and recording of scores in test booklets; $3.41 per domain scored; $.62 per class profile ($43.25 per order each additional copy); $.51 per school profile ($34.25 per order each additional copy); $.44 per district profile ($25.50 per order each additional copy); $.79 per administrator's data summary-school ($34.50 per order each additional copy);

$.79 per administrator's data summary-district ($25.50 per order each additional copy); $1.03 per administrator's data summary-school and district ($43.25 per each additional copy); $.87 per student profile ($.25 per additional copy); $.68 per student record label; $.68 per master list of test results ($.22 per additional copy); $.68 per student performance roster ($.22 per additional copy); $.44 per student data diskette; $760 per set-up charge for customer data input (plus cost of additional optional reports ordered).
Time: Approximately one class period.
Comments: Produces norm-referenced and holistic-analytic scores.
Author: Harcourt Brace Educational Measurement.
Publisher: Pearson.
a) MATHEMATICS.
  Scores, 5: Content (Problem Solving [All Levels], Procedures [All Levels]), Process (Applying Mathematical Skills and Concepts to Solve Problems [Levels 1–2], Drawing Conclusions Using Mathematical Skills and Concepts [Levels 1–4], Integrating Mathematical Concepts and Skills to Solve Problems [Levels 1–8], Analyzing Problems Using Mathematical Skills and Concepts [Levels 3–11], Creating Solutions Through Synthesis of Mathematical Concepts and Skills [Levels 5–11], Evaluating Problems Using Mathematical Skills and Concepts [Levels 9–11]).
b) LANGUAGE.
  Scores, 5: Content (Narrative Writing, Expository Writing), Process (Skill in Composing, Understanding of Usage, Application in Mechanics).
c) READING.
  Scores, 5: Content (Narrative Text, Informational Text), Process (Global Understanding, Identification and Application of Strategies, Critical Analysis).
d) SCIENCE.
  Scores, 6: Content (Life Science, Physical Science, Earth/Space Science), Process (Collecting and Recording Scientific Data, Applying Science Concepts, Drawing Conclusions).
e) SOCIAL SCIENCE.
  Scores, 5: Content (Geographic/Economic/and Cultural Foundations of Society, Historical and Political Bases of Society), Process (Understanding of Basic Conceptual Social Science Frameworks, Creative Thinking and Problem-Solving Skills, Inquiry and Decision Making Using Social Science Tools).
Cross References: For reviews by C. Dale Carpenter and Darrell L. Sabers, see 13:131.

[1147]

Goldman-Fristoe Test of Articulation–Second Edition.

Purpose: Designed as "a systematic means of assessing an individual's articulation of the consonant sounds of Standard American English."

Population: Ages 2-0 through 21-11.
Publication Dates: 1969–2000.
Acronym: GFTA-2.
Scores: 3 sections: Sounds-in-Words (norm-referenced), Sounds-in-Sentences, Stimulability.
Administration: Individual.
Price Data, 2008: $255 per complete kit, including test manual (2000, 146 pages), test easel, 25 response forms, supplemental developmental norms booklet, and canvas carrying bag; $33 per 25 response forms; $259 for ASSIST CD (Win only)–combined with KLPA-2 ASSIST.
Time: 5–15 minutes.
Comments: Normative scores are available for the Sounds-in-Words section only.
Authors: Ronald Goldman and Macalyne Fristoe.
Publisher: Pearson.
Cross References: For reviews by Steven Long and Katharine A. Snyder, see 15:109; see T5:1095 (48 references) and T4:1045 (15 references); for a review by Donald E. Mowrer of an earlier edition, see 10:126 (7 references); see also T3:960 (21 references); for reviews by Margaret C. Byrne and Ralph L. Shelton, and an excerpted review by Dorothy Sherman, see 7:952 (4 references).

[1148]

Goldman-Fristoe-Woodcock Test of Auditory Discrimination.

Purpose: Tests the ability to discriminate speech sounds against two different backgrounds: quiet and noise.
Population: Ages 3-8 through 70+.
Publication Date: 1970.
Acronym: G-F-W.
Scores: 2 subtests: Quiet, Background Noise.
Administration: Individual.
Price Data, 2008: $154 per kit, including test easel, 50 response forms, audio CD, and manual (31 pages); $33 per 50 response forms; $27.50 per manual.
Time: 10-15 minutes.
Authors: Ronald Goldman, Macalyne Fristoe, and Richard W. Woodcock.
Publisher: Pearson.
Cross References: See T5:1096 (13 references), T4:1046 (8 references), and T3:962 (14 references); for an excerpted review by Alex Bannatyne, see 8:938 (18 references); see also T2:2037 (4 references); for reviews by Eugene C. Sheeley and Ralph L. Shelton and an excerpted review by Barton B. Proger, see 7:938.

[1149]

Goodenough-Harris Drawing Test.

Purpose: Developed for use "as a measure of intellectual maturity."
Population: Ages 3-15.

Publication Dates: 1926-1963.
Scores: Total score only.
Administration: Group or individual.
Price Data, 2002: $70 per 35 test booklets; $67 per set of quality scale cards; $62 per manual (1963, 80 pages); $131 per examiner's kit.
Time: (10-15) minutes.
Comments: Revision and extension of the Goodenough Draw-a-Man Test.
Authors: Florence L. Goodenough and Dale B. Harris (test).
Publisher: Pearson.
Cross References: See T5:1097 (14 references), T4:1049 (20 references), 9:441 (6 references), T3:964 (52 references), 8:187 (87 references), and T2:381 (93 references); for reviews by Anne Anastasi and James A. Dunn, and excerpted reviews by M. L. Kellmer Pringle, Marjorie P. Honzik, Carol Hunter, Adolph G. Woltmann, Marvin S. Kaplan, and Mary J. Rouse, see 7:352 (158 references); see also 6:460 (43 references) and 5:335 (34 references); for a review by Naomi Stewart of the original edition, see 4:292 (60 references).

[1150]

The Gordon Diagnostic System.

Purpose: Aids in the evaluation of Attention Deficit Hyperactivity Disorder as well as useful in titrating stimulant medication; is also used in the neuropsychological assessment of disorders such as subclinical hepatic encephalopathy, AIDS dementia complex, post concussion syndrome, closed head injury, and neurotoxicity.
Population: Children, adolescents, and adults.
Publication Dates: [1982–1996].
Acronym: GDS.
Scores: 11 tests: Standard Vigilance Task, Standard Distractibility Test, Delay Task, Preschool Delay Task, Preschool Vigilance "0" Task, Preschool Vigilance "1" Task, Vigilance "3/5" Task, Adult Vigilance Task, Adult Distractibility Task, Auditory Vigilance Task, Auditory Interference Task.
Administration: Individual.
Price Data, 2005: $1,595 per GDS III microprocessor-based portable unit including all tasks, capacity for automatic output to a printer, instruction manual (1996, 102 pages), interpretive guide, 50 record forms, 4 issues of the ADHD REPORT, and 1-year warranty; $200 plus shipping per 2-month trial rental; $299 plus shipping per optional GDS compatible printer; $30 per 50 GDS record forms; $225 plus shipping per optional auditory module.
Time: (9) minutes per task.
Comments: A micro-processor-based unit that administers tests of attention and impulse control; FDA approved as a medical device.
Author: Michael Gordon.
Publisher: Gordon Systems, Inc.

Cross References: See T5:1099 (5 references); for reviews by Robert G. Harrington and Judy J. Oehler-Stinnett, see 13:132 (6 references); see also T4:1051 (6 references).

[1151]

Gordon Occupational Check List II.

Purpose: "Designed for persons seeking education and job training below the college level."
Population: Grades 8–12 and adults.
Publication Dates: 1961–1981.
Acronym: GOCL II.
Scores, 6 or 12: Business, Outdoor, Arts, Technology (Mechanical, Industrial), Service, and 6 optional summarization scores (preceding 6 areas).
Administration: Group or individual.
Price Data, 2002: $105 per 35 check lists including manual (1982, 19 pages) and 35 job title supplements; $29 per manual; $36.50 per examination kit including check list, manual, and job title supplement.
Time: (20-25) minutes.
Author: Leonard V. Gordon.
Publisher: Pearson.
Cross References: For a review by Donald G. Zytowski, see 9:443; for reviews by John N. McCall and Bert W. Westbrook of an earlier edition, see 7:1019; for reviews by John O. Crites and Kenneth B. Hoyt of an earlier edition, see 6:1056.

[1152]

Gordon Personal Profile–Inventory™ [Revised].

Purpose: Pre-employment assessment for all roles; nine "normal" personality traits are measured.
Population: Grades 9–12 and college and adults.
Publication Dates: 1951–1993.
Acronym: GPP-I.
Administration: Group.
Price Data, 2006: $300 per starter kit including 25 handscorable booklets, 25 machine-scorable booklets, manual, scoring key, and interpretative guide; $85 per package of 25 hand-scorable test booklets; $65 per manual; $45 per score key; $35 per interpretive guide; available online.
Time: (20–25) minutes.
Comments: Combination of Gordon Personal Profile and Gordon Personal Inventory; separate booklet editions still available.
Author: Leonard V. Gordon.
Publisher: Pearson.
   a) GORDON PERSONAL PROFILE.
   Scores, 5: Ascendancy, Responsibility, Emotional Stability, Sociability, Self-Esteem (Total).
   b) GORDON PERSONAL INVENTORY.
   Scores, 4: Cautiousness, Original Thinking, Personal Relations, Vigor.
Cross References: See T5:1101 (2 references); for reviews by Robert M. Guion and Allen K. Hess, see 13:133

(4 references); see also T4:1053 (2 references); for reviews by Douglas Fuchs and Alfred B. Heilbrun, Jr. of an earlier edition, see 10:128 (4 references); see also 9:444 (1 reference), T3:966 (6 references), 8:568 (34 references), 8:569 (52 references), T2:1194 (56 references), and P:93 (23 references); for reviews by Charles F. Dicken and Alfred B. Heilbrun, Jr., see 6:102 (13 references) and 6:103 (25 references); for reviews by Benno G. Fricke and John A. Radcliffe and excerpted reviews by Laurance F. Shaffer and Laurence Siegel, see 5:58 and 5:59 (16 references).

[1153]

Goyer Organization of Ideas Test, Form S (Revised).

Purpose: Intended to assess the ability to organize ideas.
Population: College and adults.
Publication Dates: 1966–1993.
Acronym: GOIT, Form S (Rev.).
Scores: Total score only.
Administration: Individual or group.
Manual: No manual.
Price Data: Available from publisher.
Time: [20–40] minutes.
Author: Robert S. Goyer.
Publisher: Robert S. Goyer.
Cross References: For reviews of an earlier edition by Ric Brown and Robert B. Frary, see 9:445; see also 8:817 (1 reference).

[1154]

Graded Arithmetic-Mathematics Test.

Purpose: Designed to assess overall mathematical attainment.
Population: Ages 5–12.
Publication Dates: 1949–1998.
Scores: Total score only.
Administration: Group.
Price Data, 2002: £9.99 per 20 tests; £9.99 per manual; £10.99 per specimen set.
Time: (30) minutes.
Comments: Oral administration instructions provided.
Authors: P. E. Vernon and K. M. Miller.
Publisher: Hodder & Stoughton Educational [England].
Cross References: For reviews by Kevin D. Crehan and Delwyn L. Harnisch, see 15:110; see T3:972 (3 references) and T2:618 (8 references); for a review by Stanley Nisbet of the original edition, see 5:476.

[1155]

Graded Nonword Reading Test.

Purpose: Designed to "identify reading difficulties associated with impaired phonological skills."
Population: Ages 5-11.
Publication Date: 1996.

Scores: Total score only.
Administration: Individual.
Price Data, 2006: £84 per complete kit including manual (32 pages), 100 scoring sheets, and stimulus book; £26.50 per 100 scoring sheets.
Time: (5) minutes.
Authors: Margaret J. Snowling, Susan E. Stothard, and Janet McLean.
Publisher: Pearson Assessment [England].
Cross References: For reviews by Karen Mackler and Jeffrey Smith, see 17:79.

[1156]

Graded Word Spelling Test, Second Edition.

Purpose: Designed to measure spelling achievement.
Population: Ages 6-0 to adults.
Publication Dates: 1977–1998.
Scores: Total Words Correct.
Administration: Group.
Price Data, 2002: £8.99 per test booklet/manual.
Time: (20–30) minutes.
Author: P. E. Vernon.
Publisher: Hodder & Stoughton Educational [England].
Cross References: For a review by Deborah L. Bandalos, see 14:157; see also T5:1105 (1 reference); for a review by Carol E. Westby of an earlier edition, see 12:165 (3 references); see also T4:1056 (2 references).

[1157]

Graduate and Managerial Assessment.

Purpose: Constructed to assess numerical skills needed in finance-related occupations.
Population: Undergraduate and graduate students.
Publication Date: 1985.
Acronym: GMA.
Scores: 3 tests: Numerical, Abstract, Verbal.
Administration: Group.
Forms, 2: A, B.
Price Data: Available from publisher.
Time: 30(35) minutes per test.
Comments: Test may also be administered online at http://www.gma-online.com.
Author: Psychometric Research Unit, The Hatfield Polytechnic.
Publisher: Psychometric Research & Development Ltd. [England].
Cross References: See T5:1106 (1 reference); for reviews by Philip G. Benson and Rhonda L. Gutenberg, see 10:129.

[1158]

Graduate Management Admission Test.

Purpose: Designed to measure "general verbal and mathematical skills important in the study of management at the graduate level."

Population: Applicants to study in graduate management education.
Publication Dates: 1954-1994.
Acronym: GMAT.
Scores, 3: Verbal, Quantitative, Total.
Administration: Group.
Price Data: Available from publisher.
Time: 180(210) minutes; 210(235) minutes including Writing Assessment.
Comments: Test administered 4 times annually (January, March, June, October) at centers established by publisher; Analytical Writing Assessment added October 1994.
Author: Graduate Management Admission Council.
Publisher: Pearson VUE.
Cross References: See T5:1107 (10 references) and T4:1058 (6 references); for reviews by Lawrence A. Crosby and James Ledvinka, see 9:447 (1 reference); see also T3:973 (6 references), 8:1074 (11 references), and T2:2325 (5 references); for reviews by Jerome E. Doppelt and Gary R. Hanson of earlier forms, see 7:1080 (10 references).

[1159]

Graduate Program Self-Assessment Service.

Purpose: "To assist colleges and universities that are carrying out departmental or program reviews at the graduate level."
Population: Faculty members, students majoring in the department, and recent graduates.
Publication Date: 1986.
Acronym: GPSA.
Scores, 16: Environment for Learning, Scholarly Excellence, Quality of Teaching, Faculty Concern for Students, Curriculum, Departmental Procedures, Available Resources, Student Satisfaction with Program, Internship/Fieldwork/Clinical Experiences, Resource Accessibility, Employment Assistance, Faculty Work Environment, Faculty Program Involvement, Faculty Research Activities, Faculty Professional Activities, Student Accomplishments.
Administration: Group.
Forms, 6: Faculty, Student, Alumni for both Masters and Doctoral Programs.
Price Data: Available from publisher.
Time: (30–45) minutes.
Author: Educational Testing Service.
Publisher: Educational Testing Service.

[1160]

The Graduate Record Examinations Biochemistry, Cell and Molecular Biology Test.

Purpose: Designed to assess the qualifications of graduate school applicants for advanced study and for fellowships in biochemistry, cell biology, molecular biol-

ogy, and genetics, along with related programs such as microbiology and genetics.
Population: Graduate school candidates.
Publication Dates: 1990–2006.
Acronym: GRE.
Scores, 4: Biochemistry, Cell Biology, Molecular Biology and Genetics, Total.
Administration: Group.
Price Data: Available from publisher.
Time: (170) minutes.
Comments: Test administered 3 times annually (April, November, December) at centers established by publisher.
Author: Educational Testing Service.
Publisher: Educational Testing Service.
Cross References: For reviews of the GRE program, see 7:667 (1 review) and 5:601 (1 review).

[1161]

The Graduate Record Examinations Biology Test.

Purpose: Designed to assess the qualifications of graduate school applicants for advanced study and for fellowships in Biology.
Population: Graduate school candidates.
Publication Dates: 1939–2006.
Acronym: GRE.
Scores, 4: Cellular and Molecular Biology, Organismal Biology, Ecology and Evolution, Total.
Administration: Group.
Price Data: Available from publisher.
Time: (170) minutes.
Comments: Test administered 3 times annually (April, November, December) at centers established by publisher.
Author: Educational Testing Service.
Publisher: Educational Testing Service.
Cross References: See T5:1110 (1 reference); for a review by Clark W. Horton of an earlier form, see 5:727. For reviews of the GRE program, see 7:667 (1 review) and 5:601 (1 review).

[1162]

The Graduate Record Examinations Chemistry Test.

Purpose: Designed to assess the qualifications of graduate school applicants for advanced study and for fellowships in chemistry.
Population: Graduate school candidates.
Publication Dates: 1939–2006.
Acronym: GRE.
Scores: Total score only.
Administration: Group.
Price Data: Available from publisher.
Time: (170) minutes.
Comments: Test administered 3 times annually (April, November, December) at centers established by publisher.

Author: Educational Testing Service.
Publisher: Educational Testing Service.
Cross References: See T4:1060 (1 reference), 8:852 (1 reference), and 7:848 (1 reference); for a review by Max D. Engelhart of an earlier form, see 6:919. For reviews of the GRE program, see 7:667 (1 review) and 5:601 (1 review).

[1163]

The Graduate Record Examinations Computer Science Test.

Purpose: Designed to assess the qualifications of graduate school applicants for advanced study and for fellowships in computer science.
Population: Graduate school candidates.
Publication Dates: 1976–2006.
Acronym: GRE.
Scores: Total score only.
Administration: Group.
Price Data: Available from publisher.
Time: (170) minutes.
Comments: Test administered 3 times annually (April, November, December) at centers established by publisher.
Author: Educational Testing Service.
Publisher: Educational Testing Service.

[1164]

The Graduate Record Examinations–General Test.

Purpose: "Designed to assess the verbal reasoning, quantitative reasoning, critical thinking, and analytical writing abilities of graduate school applicants."
Population: Graduate school candidates.
Publication Dates: 1949–2006.
Acronym: GRE.
Scores, 3: Verbal Reasoning, Quantitative Reasoning, Analytical Writing.
Administration: Individual
Price Data: Available from publisher.
Time: (240) minutes for computer-based test.
Comments: Beginning in September 2007, the General Test will be composed of revised Verbal Reasoning, Quantitative Reasoning, and Analytical Writing sections; the same three sections are in the current test; however, each of the sections will be revised to better focus on skills that are necessary for success in graduate school. In addition, the test is changing from an adaptive test, where the questions presented to each examinee vary in part, according to his or her performance, to a linear test, where all examinees testing at the same time receive the same questions.
Author: Educational Testing Service.
Publisher: Educational Testing Service.
Cross References: See T5:1115 (29 references) and T4:1076 (31 references); for reviews by Sanford J. Cohn

and Richard M. Jaeger, see 9:448 (9 references); see also T3:995 (26 references), 8:188 (45 references), T2:382 (15 references), and 7:353 (43 references); for reviews by Robert L. French and Warren W. Willingham of an earlier edition, see 6:461 (17 references); for a review by John T. Dailey, see 5:336 (7 references); for reviews by J. P. Guilford and Carl I. Hovland, see 4:293 (2 references). For reviews of the GRE program, see 7:667 (1 review) and 5:601 (1 review).

[1165]

The Graduate Record Examinations Literature in English Test.

Purpose: Designed to assess the qualifications of graduate school applicants for advanced study and for fellowships in literature in English.
Population: Graduate school candidates.
Publication Dates: 1939–2006.
Acronym: GRE.
Scores: Total score only.
Administration: Group.
Price Data: Available from publisher.
Time: (170) minutes.
Comments: Test administered 3 times annually (April, November, December) at centers established by publisher.
Author: Educational Testing Service.
Publisher: Educational Testing Service.
Cross References: See T5:1118 (1 reference); for a review by Edward M. White, see 8:69; see also 7:219 (1 reference); for a review by Robert C. Pooley of an earlier form, see 5:215. For reviews of the GRE program, see 7:667 (1 review) and 5:601 (1 review).

[1166]

The Graduate Record Examinations Mathematics Test.

Purpose: Designed to assess the qualifications of graduate school applicants for advanced study and for fellowships in mathematics.
Population: Graduate school candidates.
Publication Dates: 1939–2006.
Acronym: GRE.
Scores: Total score only.
Administration: Group.
Price Data: Available from publisher.
Time: (170) minutes.
Comments: Test administered 3 times annually (April, November, December) at centers established by publisher.
Author: Educational Testing Service.
Publisher: Educational Testing Service.
Cross References: See T4:1069 (1 reference) and 8:272 (1 reference); for a review by Paul C. Rosenbloom of an earlier form, see 6:578; for a review by Eric F. Gardner, see 5:427 (1 reference). For reviews of the GRE program, see 7:667 (1 review) and 5:601 (1 review).

[1167]

The Graduate Record Examinations Physics Test.

Purpose: Designed to assess the qualifications of graduate school applicants for advanced study and for fellowships in physics.
Population: Graduate school candidates.
Publication Dates: 1939–2006.
Acronym: GRE.
Scores: Total score only.
Administration: Group.
Price Data: Available from publisher.
Time: (170) minutes.
Comments: Test administered 3 times annually (April, November, December) at centers established by publisher.
Author: Educational Testing Service.
Publisher: Educational Testing Service.
Cross References: See 8:866 (1 reference); for a review by Theodore G. Phillips, see 6:931; for a review by Leo Nedelsky, see 5:754. For reviews of the GRE program, see 7:667 (1 review) and 5:601 (1 review).

[1168]

The Graduate Record Examinations Psychology Test.

Purpose: Designed to assess the qualifications of graduate school applicants for advanced study and for fellowships in psychology.
Population: Graduate school candidates.
Publication Dates: 1939–2006.
Acronym: GRE.
Scores, 3: Experimental Psychology, Social Psychology, Total.
Administration: Group.
Price Data: Available from publisher.
Time: (170) minutes.
Comments: Test administered 3 times annually (April, November, December) at centers established by publisher.
Author: Educational Testing Service.
Publisher: Educational Testing Service.
Cross References: See T5:1122 (2 references), T4:1073 (3 references), 8:461 (3 references), T2:1005 (2 references), and 7:644 (9 references); for a review by Harold Seashore of an earlier form, see 5:583. For reviews of the GRE program, see 7:667 (1 review) and 5:601 (1 review).

[1169]

Graduate Record Examinations: Subject Tests.

Purpose: Designed to assess the qualifications of graduate school applicants in specific fields of study.
Population: Graduate school candidates.
Publication Dates: 1939–2006.
Acronym: GRE.

Scores: 8 tests: Biochemistry/Cell and Molecular Biology, Biology, Chemistry, Computer Science, Literature in English, Mathematics, Physics, Psychology.
Administration: Group.
Price Data: Available from publisher.
Time: (170) minutes.
Comments: Test administered 3 times annually (April, November, December) at centers established by publisher.
Author: Educational Testing Service.
Publisher: Educational Testing Service.
Cross References: See T4:1075 (2 references), T3:994 (5 references), and 8:476 (6 references); for a review by Leona E. Tyler of an earlier program, see 7:667 (10 references); see also 6:762 (1 reference); for a review by Harold Seashore, see 5:601 (12 references); see also 4:527 (24 references).

[1170]

Grandparent Strengths and Needs Inventory.
Purpose: "To help grandparents recognize their favorable qualities and identify aspects of their family relationships in which further growth is needed."
Population: Grandparents of children 6 and over.
Publication Date: 1993.
Acronym: GSNI.
Scores, 6: Satisfaction, Success, Teaching, Difficulty, Frustration, Information Needs.
Administration: Group.
Price Data: See www.ststesting.com for up-to-date prices.
Time: Administration time not reported.
Comments: Parent and grandchild inventories included for comparison purposes.
Authors: Robert D. Strom and Shirley K. Strom.
Publisher: Scholastic Testing Service, Inc.
Cross References: See T5:1128 (4 references); for reviews by Roger A. Boothroyd and Dianna L. Newman, see 13:134 (2 references).

[1171]

Gravidometer.
Purpose: Measures knowledge about human pregnancy.
Population: Adolescents and adults.
Publication Dates: 1974–1988.
Scores: Total score only.
Administration: Group.
Manual: No manual.
Price Data, 2005: $2 per test.
Time: [10] minutes.
Comments: Supplementary article available.
Author: Panos D. Bardis.
Publisher: Donna Bardis.

[1172]

Gray Diagnostic Reading Tests–Second Edition.
Purpose: Designed as "a comprehensive measure of reading skills ... to determine strengths and weaknesses,

document progress in reading programs, [and] help diagnose specific reading problems."
Population: Ages 6-0 to 13-11.
Publication Dates: 1991-2004.
Acronym: GDRT-2.
Scores: 7 subtests: Letter/Word Recognition, Phonetic Analysis, Reading Vocabulary, Meaningful Reading, Listening Vocabulary, Rapid Naming, Phonological Awareness; and 3 composites: Decoding, Comprehension, General Reading.
Administration: Individual.
Forms: 2 equivalent forms: A, B.
Price Data, 2011: $287 per complete kit including examiner's manual (2004, 113 pages), Adventures in Fancyland Storybook, Student Book Form A, Student Book Form B, 25 record Forms A, 25 record Forms B, and storage box; $85 per examiner's manual; $59 per Student Book Form A; $59 per Student Book Form B; $7 per Adventures in Fancyland Storybook; $55 per 25 record Forms A; $55 per 25 record Forms B.
Time: (45-60) minutes.
Comments: Norm-referenced; revision of the Gray Oral Reading Tests-Diagnostic.
Authors: Brian R. Bryant, J. Lee Wiederholt, and Diane Pedrotty Bryant.
Publisher: PRO-ED.
Cross References: For reviews by Howard Margolis and Antonia D'Onofrio and by Lisa F. Smith, see 17:80; see also T5:1130 (2 references); for reviews by William R. Merz, Sr. and Steven A. Stahl of the original edition, see 11:149 (1 reference).

[1173]

Gray Oral Reading Tests, Fourth Edition.
Purpose: Designed "to provide a measure of growth in oral reading and an aid in the diagnosis of oral reading difficulties."
Population: Ages 6-0 to 18-11.
Publication Dates: 1967–2001.
Acronym: GORT-4.
Scores, 4: Rate, Accuracy, Fluency, Comprehension.
AdminisLevels: Forms, 2: A, B.
Price Data, 2011: $259 per kit including 25 each of profile/examiner record forms (Form A and Form B), student book, and examiner's manual (2001, 146 pages); $59 per 25 record forms (specify Form A or B); $59 per student book; $92 per examiner's manual.
Time: (20–30) minutes.
Authors: J. Lee Wiederholt and Brian R. Bryant.
Publisher: PRO-ED.
Cross References: For reviews by Nancy L. Crumpton and Marie Miller-Whitehead, see 15:111; see T5:1131 (18 references); for reviews by John D. King and Deborah King Kundert of an earlier edition, see 12:166 (5 references); see also T4:1084 (9 references); for reviews by Julia A. Hickman and Robert J. Tierney of an earlier edition, see 10:131 (15 references).

[1174]
Gray Silent Reading Tests.

Purpose: "Designed to assess silent reading comprehension."
Population: Ages 7–25.
Publication Date: 2000.
Acronym: GSRT.
Scores: Silent Reading Quotient.
Administration: Group.
Forms, 2: A, B.
Price Data, 2011: $184 per complete kit including 25 profile/response forms, 10 each of reading book Forms A and B, and manual (101 pages); $29 per 25 profile/response forms; $41 per 10 reading books (specify Form A or Form B); $82 per manual.
Time: (15–30) minutes.
Comments: Developed to be used as an adjunct to the Gray Oral Reading Tests (1173) or independently.
Authors: J. Lee Wiederholt and Ginger Blalock.
Publisher: PRO-ED.
Cross References: For reviews by Harold R. Keller and Darrell L. Sabers, see 15:112.

[1175]
Green's Emotional Perception Test.

Purpose: Designed to measure "the ability to judge emotion expressed in another person's tone of voice."
Population: Ages 6 to 90.
Publication Dates: 1986-2008.
Acronym: EPT.
Scores: Total score only.
Administration: Individual.
Price Data, 2010: $200 per 20 test uses and manual (2008, 44 pages); $4 per individual use.
Foreign Language & Other Special Editions: Nonsense version available for non-English speakers.
Time: (6) minutes.
Comments: Test is administered using Microsoft Windows.
Authors: Paul Green, Lloyd Flaro, and Roger Gervais.
Publisher: Green's Publishing Inc. [Canada].

[1176]
Green's Medical Symptom Validity Test.

Purpose: Designed as a computerized "verbal memory screening test with built-in effort testing."
Population: Ages 6 to 68.
Publication Dates: 2003-2004.
Acronym: MSVT.
Scores, 5: Primary Effort (Immediate Recognition, Delayed Recognition, Consistency), Memory (Paired Associates, Free Recall).
Administration: Individual.
Price Data, 2010: $300 per manual (2004, 102 pages), program on CD for use with Microsoft Windows, and 30 test uses; $6 per individual use.

Foreign Language Editions: Available in Danish, Dutch, French, German, Norwegian, Portuguese, Spanish, and Swedish.
Time: [5-15] minutes.
Author: Paul Green.
Publisher: Green's Publishing Inc. [Canada].

[1177]
Green's Non-Verbal Medical Symptom Validity Test.

Purpose: Designed as a "computerized nonverbal memory-screening test, which allows the person's effort on testing to be measured."
Population: Children and adults.
Publication Dates: 2006-2008.
Acronym: NV-MSVT.
Scores, 7: Primary Effort (Immediate Recognition, Delayed Recognition, Consistency, Delayed Recognition-Variations, Delayed Recognition-Archetypes), Memory (Paired Associates, Free Recall).
Administration: Individual.
Price Data, 2010: $300 per manual (2008, 116 pages), program on CD for use with Microsoft Windows, and 30 test uses; $6 per individual use.
Time: [5-15] minutes.
Author: Paul Green.
Publisher: Green's Publishing, Inc. [Canada].

[1178]
Green's Word Memory Test.

Purpose: Designed to "measure verbal and nonverbal memory."
Population: Ages 7 and over.
Publication Dates: 1995-2005.
Acronym: WMT.
Scores, 6: Immediate Recognition, Delayed Recognition, Multiple Choice, Paired Associates, Free Recall, Long Delayed Free Recall.
Administration: Individual.
Price Data, 2010: $300 per Green's WMT for Windows first year (unlimited use).
Foreign Language Editions: Oral, Spanish, French, German, Dutch, Portuguese, Turkish, Russian, Danish, and Hebrew translations available.
Time: Administration time not reported.
Comments: For use with Microsoft Windows; two scores are designed to be sensitive to "poor effort or exaggeration of cognitive difficulties, yet they are insensitive to … cognitive impairment."
Author: Paul Green.
Publisher: Green's Publishing Inc. [Canada].
Cross References: For reviews by M. Alan Cooperstein and Michael P. Gamache of an earlier version, see 14:424.

[1179]

Greenspan Social-Emotional Growth Chart.

Purpose: Designed to help determine a child's social-emotional development and growth.
Population: Birth to 3.5 years.
Publication Date: 2004.
Scores, 3: Total Growth Chart Score, Sensory Processing Score, Highest Stage Mastered.
Administration: Individual.
Price Data, 2006: $99 per complete kit including manual, 25 caregiver reports, and 25 questionnaires; $80 per manual; $25 per 25 caregiver reports; $35 per 25 questionnaires.
Time: (5-15) minutes.
Comments: It is recommended that the questionnaire be administered at each developmental stage.
Author: Stanley I. Greenspan.
Publisher: Pearson.
Cross References: For reviews by Carol M. McGregor and Gretchen Owens, see 17:81.

[1180]

Gregorc Style Delineator.

Purpose: "Designed to aid an individual to recognize and identify the channels through which he/she receives and expresses information."
Population: Adults.
Publication Dates: 1982–2002.
Scores, 4: Concrete Sequential score, Abstract Sequential score, Abstract Random score, Concrete Random score.
Administration: Group.
Price Data, 2002: $69.95 per sample set including An Adult's Guide to Style (2002, 110 pages), Mind Styles Model: Theory Principles and Practice (1998, 28 pages), Mind Styles FAQs Book (2001, 152 pages), Relating with Style (1997, 170 pages), test, Extends Charts, Phoenix bookmark, and Careful Us audio tape; $15.95 per technical manual (1982, 46 pages); $59.50 per 25 instrument packets or $29.95 per 10 instrument packets including guidelines for group administration; $9.95 per audiocassette on careful use; $17.95 per An Adult's Guide to Style; $19.95 per Mind Styles FAQs Book; $19.95 per Relating with Style; $7.50 per Mind Styles Model: Theory, Principles, and Practice.
Time: 3 minutes.
Comments: Self-assessment instrument.
Author: Anthony F. Gregorc.
Publisher: Gregorc Associates, Inc.
Cross References: See T5:1132 (1 reference); for reviews by Stephen L. Benton and Trenton R. Ferro, see 12:167 (3 references); see also T4:1086 (2 references).

[1181]

Grid Test of Schizophrenic Thought Disorder.

Purpose: "Developed to detect the presence of schizophrenic thought disorder."

Population: Adults.
Publication Date: 1967.
Acronym: GTSTD.
Scores, 2: Intensity, Consistency.
Administration: Individual.
Price Data: Available from publisher.
Time: (15–25) minutes.
Comments: 1 form (set of 8 photographs).
Authors: D. Bannister and Fay Fransella.
Publisher: Psychological Test Publications [England] [No reply from publisher; status unknown].
Cross References: See T4:1087 (4 references) and T3:1009 (3 references); for a review by Robert W. Payne, see 8:571 (30 references); see also T2:1198 (8 references); for a review by David Jones, see 7:84 (7 references); see also P:96 (8 references).

[1182]

Griffiths Mental Development Scales [Revised].

Purpose: Designed to measure trends of development that are indicative of intelligence/mental growth.
Publication Dates: 1951–1996.
Administration: Individual.
Forms, 2: Scale 1 (0–2 years), Scale 2 (2–8 years).
Restricted Distribution: Restricted to persons who qualify by attending an approved course; details available from distributor.
Price Data, 2001: £260 per Scale 1; £315 per Scale 2; £2.20 per Scale 2 record book; £1.65 per Scale 1 record form; £24.50 per The Abilities of Babies (1976, 239 pages); £24.50 per The Abilities of Young Children (1996, 114 pages); £39.50 per Scale 1 manual; £29.50 for 8 additional test items for 1996 Revised Scale 1.
Authors: Ruth Griffiths and Michael Huntley (Birth–2 years Scale [Scale 1] and manual, 1996 Revision).
Publisher: The Test Agency Limited [England] [No reply from publisher; status unknown].

a) SCALE 1: BIRTH TO 2 YEARS.
Population: Ages 0–2 years.
Publication Dates: 1951–1996.
Scores, 6: Locomotor, Personal-Social, Hearing and Speech, Eye and Hand, Performance, Total.
Time: (20–40) minutes.
b) SCALE 2: (2 TO 8 YEARS).
Population: Ages 2–8 years.
Publication Dates: 1951–1978.
Scores, 7: Same as Scale 1 above plus Practical Reasoning.
Time: Administration time not reported.
Cross References: See T5:1134 (8 references), T4:1088 (10 references), and 9:450 (1 reference); for a review by C. B. Hindley of an earlier version of Scale 2, see 6:523 (4 references); for a review by Nancy Bayley of Scale 1, see 5:404 (3 references).

[1183]
Grooved Pegboard Test.

Purpose: To assess manipulative dexterity.
Population: Ages 5 to 8-12, 9 to 14-12, 15 to adult.
Publication Date: 1989.
Scores, 3: Total Time, Number of "Drops," Total Pegs Correctly Placed.
Administration: Individual.
Price Data: Available from publisher.
Time: Trial discontinued after 5 minutes.
Comments: Ages 5 to 8-12 only complete first two rows of the Pegboard; "this test requires more complex visual-motor coordination than most pegboards."
Author: Ronald Trites (manual).
Publisher: Lafayette Instrument.
Cross References: See T5:1135 (27 references); for reviews by Roderick K. Mahurin and Erin McClure and Richard K. Stratton, see 12:169 (14 references); see also T4:1089 (2 references).

[1184]
Group Achievement Identification Measure.

Purpose: "To determine the degree to which children exhibit the characteristics of underachievers so that preventative or curative efforts may be administered."
Population: Grades 5-12.
Publication Date: 1986.
Acronym: GAIM.
Scores, 6: Competition, Responsibility, Achievement Communication, Independence/Dependence, Respect/Dominance, Total.
Administration: Group.
Price Data, 2005: $15 per specimen set; $120 per class set of 30 inventories including prepaid computer scoring by publisher; manual for administration and interpretation (12 pages) included with test orders.
Time: (30) minutes.
Comments: Student self-report inventory.
Author: Sylvia B. Rimm.
Publisher: Educational Assessment Service Inc.
Cross References: See T5:1136 (1 reference); for reviews by Robert K. Gable and Jeffrey Jenkins, see 11:150.

[1185]
Group Cohesiveness: A Study of Group Morale.

Purpose: Designed to assess group cohesiveness.
Population: Adults.
Publication Dates: 1957–1958.
Acronym: GC.
Scores, 5: Satisfaction of Individual Motives, Satisfaction of Interpersonal Relations, Homogeneity of Attitude, Satisfaction With Leadership, Total.
Administration: Group.

Price Data: Available from publisher.
Time: (10–15) minutes.
Comments: Self-administered.
Author: Bernard Goldman.
Publisher: Psychometric Affiliates.
Cross References: See T2:1199 (1 reference) and P:97; for reviews by Eric F. Gardner and Cecil A. Gibb, see 6:104 (1 reference).

[1186]
Group Diagnostic Reading Aptitude and Achievement Tests, Intermediate Form.

Purpose: Designed to assess reading achievement and to diagnose reading problems.
Population: Grades 3–9.
Publication Date: [Orig. 1937].
Scores, 13: Achievement [Reading (Paragraph Understanding, Speed, Word Discrimination), Arithmetic, Spelling], Diagnostic [Word Discrimination Errors, Visual (Letter Memory, Form Memory), Auditory (Letter Memory, Discrimination and Orientation), Motor (Copying Text, Cross Out Letters), Language-Vocabulary].
Administration: Group.
Price Data: Available from publisher.
Time: (40) minutes (includes both timed and untimed tests).
Authors: Marion Monroe and Eva Edith Sherman.
Publisher: C. H. Nevins Printing Co.
Cross References: For reviews by Deborah King Kundert and Margaret R. Rogers, see 12:170.

[1187]
Group Embedded Figures Test.

Purpose: Developed to evaluate field-dependence.
Population: Older children, adolescents, adults
Publication Date: 1971.
Acronym: GEFT.
Scores: Total score only.
Administration: Group.
Price Data, 2010: Available from the publisher at www.mindgarden.com/products/gefts.htm.
Time: (20) minutes.
Comments: Adaptation of the individually administered Embedded Figures Test (T6:900); manual is a combined manual for this test and the Embedded Figures Test.
Authors: Philip K. Oltman, Evelyn Raskin, Herman A. Witkin, and Stephen A. Karp (manual).
Publisher: Mind Garden, Inc.
Cross References: See T5:1140 (60 references), T4:1094 (95 references), 9:452 (41 references), and T3:1013 (88 references); for reviews by Leonard D. Goodstein and Alfred E. Hall, see 8:572 (47 references); see also T2:1201 (3 references); for references to reviews of the individual test, see 8:548.

[1188]

Group Environment Scale, Third Edition.

Purpose: Designed to "measure the actual, preferred, and expected, social environments of task-oriented, social, psychotherapy, and self-help groups."

Population: Group members and leaders; clinicians, consultants, and program evaluators

Publication Dates: 1974–2002.

Acronym: GES.

Scores, 10: Cohesion, Leader Support, Expressiveness, Independence, Task Orientation, Self-Discovery, Anger and Aggression, Order and Organization, Leader Control, Innovation.

Administration: Group.

Forms, 3: Real (R), Ideal (I), Expectations (E).

Price Data: Available from the publisher at www. mindgarden.com/products/gescs.htm.

Foreign Language Edition: Spanish translation of Form R available.

Time: Administration time not reported.

Comments: A component of the Social Climate Scales.

Author: Rudolf H. Moos.

Publisher: Mind Garden, Inc.

Cross References: For reviews by Laura L. B. Barnes and Malinda Hendricks Green, see 17:82; see also T5:1141 (5 references) and T4:1095 (5 references); for a review by Arthur M. Nezu of an earlier edition, see 10:132 (6 references); for reviews by Michael J. Curtis and Robert J. Illback, see 9:435 (4 references); for reviews by David P. Campbell and Robyn M. Dawes, see 8:573; see also T3:1015 (1 reference); for a review of the Social Climate Scales, see 8:681.

[1189]

Group Inventory for Finding Creative Talent.

Purpose: "Identify students with attitudes and values usually associated with creativity."

Population: Grades K-2, 3-4, 5-6

Publication Dates: 1976-2010.

Acronym: GIFT.

Scores, 4: Imagination, Independence, Many Interests, Total.

Administration: Group or individual.

Levels, 3: Primary (Grades K-2), Elementary (Grades 3-4), Upper Elementary (Grades 5-6).

Price Data, 2005: $100 per 30 test booklets and scoring service (scoring must be done by publisher); $15 per specimen set.

Foreign Language Edition: Spanish edition available.

Time: (20-45) minutes.

Author: Sylvia B. Rimm.

Publisher: Educational Assessment Service, Inc.

Cross References: See T5:1142 (5 references); for reviews by Patricia L. Dwinell and Dan Wright, see 9:454 (1 reference); see also T3:1016 (1 reference).

[1190]

Group Inventory For Finding Interests.

Purpose: "Identify students with attitudes and interests usually associated with creativity."

Population: Grades 6-1.

Publication Dates: 1979-2010.

Acronym: GIFFI.

Scores: 5 dimensional scores: Creative Arts and Writing, Challenge-Inventiveness, Confidence, Imagination, Many Interests. Administration: Group or individual.

Levels, 2: Level 1: Grades 6-9; Level 2: Grades 9-12.

Price Data, 2005: $120 per 30 test booklets and scoring service (scoring must be done by publisher); $15 per specimen set.

Foreign Language Edition: Spanish edition available.

Time: (20-40) minutes.

Authors: Sylvia B. Rimm and Gary A. Davis.

Publisher: Educational Assessment Service Inc.

Cross References: See T5:1143 (2 references); for a review by M. O'Neal Weeks, see 9:455 (1 reference).

[1191]

Group Literacy Assessment.

Purpose: To sample children's overall skills level with written material.

Population: End of junior school and beginning of secondary school.

Publication Dates: 1981–1999.

Acronym: GLA.

Scores, 3: Proof-Reading, Fill the Gaps, Total.

Administration: Group.

Price Data, 2002: £8.50 per 20 tests; £8.99 per manual (16 pages); £9.99 per specimen set.

Time: 16(30) minutes.

Author: Frank A. Spooncer.

Publisher: Hodder & Stoughton Educational [England].

Cross References: For a review by Gail E. Tompkins of an earlier edition, see 9:456.

[1192]

Group Mathematics Assessment and Diagnostic Evaluation.

Purpose: A group-administered diagnostic mathematics test that measures individual skills in key areas, including concepts, operations, computation, and applications.

Population: Grades K–12.

Publication Date: 2004.

Acronym: G·MADE.

Administration: Group.

Forms: 2 parallel forms, A or B, for each of 9 levels.

Price Data, 2007: $110.99–$184.99 per Form A classroom sets (specify Level) including teacher's manual (102 pages), hand-scoring templates, answer sheets, and

30 student booklets; $201.99–$303.99 per Forms A & B classroom sets (specify Level); $31.99 per norms supplement (specify age-based or grade-based out-of-level); $34.99 per technical manual (122 pages); $349.99 per Scoring and Reporting Software v. 2.1 PC and Mac Version; $2,295.99 per Scoring and Reporting Software Single PC Scanning Version 2.1; $114.99 per Resource Library (specify Level).
Time: (50–90) minutes per level.
Author: Kathleen T. Williams.
Publisher: Pearson.

  a) LEVEL R.
  Population: Ages 5-0 to 7-11.
  Scores, 3: Concepts and Communication, Process and Applications, Total.
  b) LEVEL 1.
  Population: Ages 6-0 to 8-11.
  Scores, 4: Same as a above plus Operations and Computation.
  c) LEVEL 2.
  Population: Ages 6-0 to 9-11.
  Scores, 4: Same as b above.
  d) LEVEL 3.
  Population: Ages 7-0 to 10-11.
  Scores, 4: Same as b.
  e) LEVEL 4.
  Population: Ages 8-0 to 12-11.
  Scores, 4: Same as b.
  f) LEVEL 5.
  Population: Ages 9-0 to 18-0 and above.
  Scores, 4: Same as b.
  g) LEVEL 6.
  Population: Ages 10-0 to 18-0 and above.
  Scores, 4: Same as b.
  h) LEVEL M.
  Population: Ages 11-0 to 18-0 and above.
  Scores, 4: Same as b.
  i) LEVEL H.
  Population: Ages 12-0 to 18-0 and above.
  Scores, 4: Same as b.
Cross References: For reviews by Joseph C. Ciechalski and Kevin D. Crehan, see 17:83.

[1193]
Group Mathematics Test, Third Edition.
Purpose: General assessment of mathematical understanding.
Population: Ages 6.5-8.10 and older underachieving students.
Publication Dates: 1970–1996.
Acronym: GMT.
Scores, 3: Oral, Computation, Total.
Administration: Group.
Forms, 2: A, B.
Price Data, 2002: £7.99 per 20 tests (Form A or B); £8.99 per manual; £9.99 per specimen set.

Time: (40–50) minutes.
Author: D. Young.
Publisher: Hodder & Stoughton Educational [England].
Cross References: See T5:1145 (2 references) and T4:1049 (1 reference); for reviews by Mary Kay Corbitt and Douglas H. Crawford, see 9:457; for a review by John Cook of an earlier edition, see 8:273.

[1194]
Group Process Questionnaire.
Purpose: "Designed to help groups assess how effective they are."
Population: Adults.
Publication Date: 1988.
Scores, 29 to 145: My Rating, Group Rating, and How I Did scores for Behavior Scale (Task Behavior, Maintenance Behavior), for Total Scale, and for 12 optional categories (Initiating, Seeking Information or Opinions, Giving Information or Opinions, Clarifying and Elaborating, Summarizing, Consensus-Testing, Listening, Harmonizing, Gatekeeping, Encouraging, Compromising, Standard Setting/Testing), and My Rating and Group Rating scores for 5 additional optional categories (Leadership, Time Utilization, Results, Acceptance, Inclusion).
Administration: Group.
Price Data: Available from publisher.
Time: (60) minutes.
Comments: Scale for ratings by group members and for self-ratings.
Authors: Richard Hill, D. Joseph Fisher, Tom Webber, and Kathleen A. Fisher.
Publisher: Aviat.

[1195]
Group Reading Assessment and Diagnostic Evaluation.
Purpose: Designed to pinpoint students' individual reading levels.
Population: Pre-K through adult.
Publication Dates: 2001-2002.
Administration: Individual or group.
Levels, 11: P (pre-kindergarten and kindergarten), K (kindergarten and first grade), 1 (kindergarten through second grade), 2, 3, 4, 5, 6, M (middle school, grades 5–9), H (high school, grades 9–12), A (grades 11 to postsecondary).
Forms, 2: Form A, Form B.
Price Data, 2006: $210.99 per Levels 1, 2, or 3 Classroom Set with Forms A and B including 30 each of Form A and Form B student booklets, 1 teacher's administration manual, and 2 scoring and interpretative manual; $222.99 per Levels P and K Classroom Set with Forms A and B; $312.99 per Levels 4, 5, 6, M, H, or

A Classroom Set with Forms A and B; $30.99 per 10 student booklets (each of Levels P–A); $9.99 per 10 answer sheets (Levels 4–A); $43.99 per Forms a and B hand-scoring templates (each of Levels 4–A); $11.99 per teacher's administration manual (each of Levels P–A); $19.99 per scoring and interpretative manual (each of Levels P–A); $32.99 per technical manual (for all levels); $32.99 per Out of Level Norms Supplement (205 page book of norm tables); $109.99 per GRADE Resource Library (each of Levels P–A); $299.99 per GRADE Scoring and Reporting Software (single PC version); $1,995.99 per GRADE Scoring and Reporting Software (single PC scanning version).

Time: (45–90) minutes.

Comments: May be hand scored or computer scored.

Author: Kathleen T. Williams.

Publisher: Pearson.

a) LEVEL P.

Scores, 8: Picture Matching, Picture Differences, Verbal Concepts, Picture Categories, Sound Matching, Rhyming, Listening Comprehension, Total Score.

b) LEVEL K.

Scores, 9: Sound Matching, Rhyming, Print Awareness, Letter Recognition, Same and Different Words, Phoneme-Grapheme Correspondence, Word Reading, Listening Comprehension, Total Score.

c) LEVEL 1, 2.

Scores, 6: Word Reading, Word Meaning, Sentence Comprehension, Passage Comprehension, Listening Comprehension, Total Score.

d) LEVEL 3.

Scores, 6: Word Reading, Vocabulary, Sentence Comprehension, Passage Comprehension, Listening Comprehension, Total Score.

e) LEVEL 4–A.

Scores, 5: Vocabulary, Sentence Comprehension, Passage Comprehension, Listening Comprehension, Total Score.

Cross References: For reviews by Mark H. Fugate and Betsy B. Waterman, see 15:113.

[1196]

Group Reading Test, Fourth Edition.

Purpose: Designed to measure "the reading of single words and of simple sentences."

Population: Ages 6:4 to 8:11 and less able children 8:0 to 11:11.

Publication Dates: 1968–1999.

Acronym: GRT.

Scores: Total score only.

Administration: Group.

Forms, 2: A, B.

Price Data, 2002: £7.99 per 20 Form A or Form B; £9.99 per manual (1999, 27 pages); £4.99 per template A or B; £10.99 per specimen set.

Time: (20) minutes.

Author: Dennis Young.

Publisher: Hodder & Stoughton Educational [England].

Cross References: For reviews by Gretchen Owens and John W. Young, see 14:158; for reviews by William R. Merz, Sr., and Diane J. Sawyer of an earlier edition, see 12:171 (1 reference); see also T4:1102 (4 references); for reviews by Patrick Groff and Douglas A. Pidgeon of the Second Edition, see 9:458 (1 reference); for a review by Ralph D. Dutch of the original edition, see 8:729.

[1197]

Group Reading Test II (6–14).

Purpose: Designed to monitor progress in reading and to screen and identify pupils who require further diagnostic assessment.

Population: Ages 6 years to 15 years 9 months.

Publication Dates: 1985–2000.

Acronym: GRT II(6–14).

Scores, 2: Sentence Completion, Context Comprehension.

Administration: Group.

Forms, 6: Forms A and B, Forms C and D, and Forms X and Y.

Price Data, 2004: Price data for teacher's guide (2000, 75 pages), At-a-Glance Guide, group record sheet, and record forms available from publisher.

Time: (30) minutes.

Comments: Computer and publisher scoring service available; originally published as Macmillan Group Reading Test.

Author: NFER-Nelson Publishing Co., Ltd.

Publisher: GL Assessment [England].

Cross References: For reviews by C. Dale Carpenter and Alice J. Corkill, see 16:98; for reviews by Koressa Kutsick and Gail E. Tompkins of the Macmillan Reading Test, see 10:179.

[1198]

Group Shorr Imagery Test.

Purpose: Designed as a projective measure of personality conflict.

Population: Adults.

Publication Date: 1977.

Acronym: GSIT.

Scores, 6: Item scores in 5 areas (Human, Animal, Inanimate, Botanical, Others) plus Total score for Conflict.

Administration: Group.

Price Data: Available from publisher.

Time: Administration time not reported.

Comments: Tape cassette used for administration; group form of the Shorr Imagery Test (2454).

Author: Joseph E. Shorr.

Publisher: Institute for Psychoimagination Therapy.

[1199]

Group Styles Inventory.

Purpose: Designed to "assess the particular style or styles of your work group following a simulated or real problem-solving session or meeting."
Population: Group members.
Publication Dates: 1990–1993.
Acronym: GSI.
Scores: 12 styles in 3 general clusters: Constructive (Achievement, Self-Actualizing, Humanistic-Encouraging, Affiliative), Passive/Defensive (Approval, Conventional, Dependent, Avoidance), Aggressive/Defensive (Oppositional, Power, Competitive, Perfectionistic).
Administration: Group.
Price Data: Price information for test materials including Participant Guide (50 pages) and Leader's Guide (53 pages) available from publisher.
Time: [10–15] minutes.
Authors: Robert A. Cooke and J. Clayton Lafferty.
Publisher: Human Synergistics International.
Cross References: For reviews by Lawrence M. Aleamoni and Bert A. Goldman, see 12:172.

[1200]

Group Tests of Musical Abilities.

Purpose: Developed to measure an individual's musical ability level.
Population: Ages 7–14.
Publication Date: 1988.
Scores, 2: Pitch, Pulse.
Administration: Group.
Price Data: Price information available from publisher for starter pack including cassette tape, 25 answer sheets, and manual (25 pages).
Time: [15–20] minutes.
Comments: A good quality audiocassette player is needed to administer test.
Author: Janet Mills.
Publisher: GL Assessment [England].
Cross References: For reviews by J. David Boyle and Annabel J. Cohen, see 12:173.

[1201]

Gudjonsson Suggestibility Scales.

Purpose: "Developed in order to measure objectively the vulnerability or proneness of people [to suggestive influence and/or] to give erroneous accounts when interviewed," particularly in forensic contexts.
Population: Ages 6 and over.
Publication Date: 1997.
Scores, 7: Immediate Recall, Delayed Recall, Yield 1, Yield 2, Shift, Total Suggestibility, Confabulation.
Administration: Individual.
Forms: 2 parallel forms: GSS1, GSS2.
Price Data: Available from publisher.
Time: Administration time not reported.

Author: Gisli H. Gudjonsson.
Publisher: Psychology Press (Taylor and Francis Group) [England].
Cross References: For reviews by Marc Janoson and Bruce Frumkin and by Romeo Vitelli, see 17:84.

[1202]

Guide for Occupational Exploration Interest Inventory, Second Edition.

Purpose: Designed to help people identify their interests, then use this information to explore career, learning, and lifestyle alternatives.
Population: High school through adult.
Publication Date: 2002.
Acronym: GOEII.
Scores: Arts/Entertainment/Media, Science/Math/Engineering, Plants and Animals, Law/Law Enforcement/Public Safety, Mechanics/Installers/Repairers, Construction/ Mining/Drilling, Transportation, Industrial Production, Business Detail, Sales and Marketing, Recreation/Travel/Other Personal Services, Education and Social Service, General Management and Support, Medical and Health Services.
Administration: Group or individual.
Price Data, 2006: $29.95 per 25 inventories including copy of administrator's guide (12 pages).
Time: (20-40) minutes.
Comments: Self-administered and self-scored.
Author: J. Michael Farr.
Publisher: JIST Publishing, Inc.
Cross References: For reviews by M. David Miller and Jennifer M. Bergeron and by William I. Sauser, Jr., see 16:99.

[1203]

Guide to the Assessment of Test Session Behavior for the WISC-III and the WIAT.

Purpose: Assesses "whether a child's behavior during WISC-III and/or WIAT testing differs substantially from the behavior of other children of the same age."
Population: Ages 6–16.
Publication Date: 1992.
Acronym: GATSB.
Scores: 4 scales: Avoidance, Inattentiveness, Uncooperative Mood, Total Score.
Administration: Individual.
Price Data, 2002: $80 per complete kit including 25 ready-score answer forms and manual (88 pages); $36 per 25 ready-score answer documents; $140 per 100 ready-score answer documents; $44 per manual.
Time: (5–10) minutes.
Authors: Joseph J. Glutting and Tom Oakland.
Publisher: Pearson.
Cross References: See T5:1155 (1 reference); for reviews by Alice J. Corkill and Eleanor E. Sanford, see 13:135.

[1204]

Hall Occupational Orientation Inventory, Form II and Young Adult/College/Adult Form (Fourth Edition).

Purpose: Designed to help individuals understand their values, needs, interests, and preferred life-styles, and how these relate to career goals and future educational plans.
Population: Junior high students–adults, high school students–adults.
Publication Dates: 1968–2002.
Administration: Group or individual.
Price Data: See www.ststesting.com.
Time: (45–60) minutes.
Author: Lacy G. Hall.
Publisher: Scholastic Testing Service, Inc.
   a) YOUNG ADULT/COLLEGE/ADULT FORM.
   Population: High school–adults.
   Publication Dates: 1968–2002.
   Scores, 29: Creativity-Independence, Information-Knowledge, Belongingness, Security, Aspiration, Esteem, Self-Actualization, Personal Satisfaction, Routine-Dependence, People-Social-Accommodating, Data-Information, Things-Physical, People-Business-Influencing, Ideas-Scientific, Aesthetics-Arts, Geographic Location, Abilities, Monetary-Compensation, Workplace, Coworkers, Time, Qualifications, Risk, Subjective External Authority, Objective External Authority, Subjective Internal Authority, Shaping/Autonomy/and Self-Empowerment, Interdependent, Procrastination.
   b) FORM II.
   Population: Junior high students–adults.
   Publication Dates: 1968–1989.
   Scores, 15: Creativity-Independence, Information-Knowledge, Belongingness, Security, Aspiration, Esteem, Self-Actualization, Personal Satisfaction, Routine-Dependence, People-Social-Accommodating, Data-Information, Things-Physical, People-Business-Influencing, Ideas-Scientific, Aesthetics-Arts.
Cross References: For reviews by John S. Geisler and Joseph G. Law, Jr., see 16:100; for reviews by Gregory Schraw and Hilda Wing of an earlier edition, see 12:175 (1 reference); see also T3:1051 (4 references); for reviews by Robert H. Dolliver and Austin C. Frank of an earlier edition, see 8:1003 (5 references); see also T2:2187 (3 references); for a review by Donald G. Zytowski of the original edition, see 7:104 (4 references).

[1205]

Halpern Critical Thinking Assessment.

Purpose: Designed to assess "critical thinking skills."
Population: Ages 15 and over.
Publication Date: 2010.
Acronym: HCTA.

Scores: 3 scores for each dimension of critical thinking (Verbal Reasoning, Argument Analysis, Thinking as Hypothesis Testing, Likelihood and Uncertainty, Decision Making and Problem Solving): Total Critical Thinking Score, Critical Thinking Score-Constructed Responses, Critical Thinking Score-Forced Choice Responses.
Administration: Group or individual.
Forms, 2: Form S1 (Standard version), Form S2 (Multiple-choice short version).
Price Data: Available from publisher.
Foreign Language Editions: The management software is available in 13 languages; translations of the HCTA are available in 10 languages including Chinese, Spanish, Dutch, and Turkish.
Time: (20) minutes for short-form recognition items; (60-80) minutes constructed response and recognition items.
Comments: Computer administered and scored using the Vienna Test System; single user, server license, or internet testing.
Author: Diane F. Halpern.
Publisher: Schuhfried GmbH [Austria].

[1206]

Halstead-Reitan Neuropsychological Test Battery.

Purpose: "Developed to evaluate the brain-behavior functioning of individuals."
Population: Ages 5-8, 9-14, 15 and over.
Publication Dates: 1979-1993.
Scores: 1 combined score for each battery and for areas of function, plus scores for individual tests.
Price Data: Available from publisher.
Comments: Consists of three neuropsychological test batteries, one for each age level; each battery includes a Neuropsychological Deficit Scale, which provides normative ranges for each test, for areas of function, and for the entire battery in addition to cut-off scores (brain impairment versus normal brain status) for each variable, area, and summary score.
Author: Ralph M. Reitan.
Publisher: Reitan Neuropsychology Laboratory/Press.
   a) REITAN-INDIANA NEUROLOGICAL TEST BATTERY FOR YOUNG CHILDREN.
   Population: Ages 5-8.
      1) Category.
      Comments: Projection box with slide projector and slides necessary for administration.
      2) Tactual Performance.
      Scores, 3: Total Time, Memory, Localization.
      Comments: 6-figure board.
      3) Finger Tapping.
      Comments: Electronic finger tapper necessary for administration.
      4) Matching Pictures.
      5) Individual Performance.
      Subtests, 4: Matching Figures, Star, Matching V's, Concentric Squares.
      6) Marching.

7) *Progressive Figures.*
8) *Color Form.*
Scores, 2: Total Time, Errors.
9) *Lateral Dominance Examination.*
10) *Target.*
11) *Aphasia Screening.*
12) *Sensory Perceptual.*
Subtests, 6: Imperception (Tactile, Auditory, Visual), Tactile Finger Recognition, Finger-Tip Symbol Writing and Recognition, Tactile Form Recognition.
13) *Grip Strength.*
Scores, 2: Preferred Grip, Nonpreferred Grip.
Comments: Hand dynamometer necessary for administration.
14) *Name Writing.*
b) HALSTEAD-REITAN NEUROPSYCHOLOGI-CAL TEST BATTERY FOR OLDER CHILDREN.
Population: Ages 9-14.
1) *Category.*
Comments: Similar to *a* above.
2) *Tactual Performance.*
Comments: Same as *a* above.
3) *Seashore Rhythm Test.*
4) *Speech-Sounds Perception.*
5) *Trail Making.*
6) *Finger Tapping.*
Comments: Manual finger tapping apparatus necessary for administration.
7) *Aphasia Screening.*
8) *Sensory-Perceptual.*
Subtests, 5: Sensory Imperception (Tactile, Auditory, Visual), Finger Agnosia, Finger-Tip Number Writing.
9) *Tactile Form Recognition.*
10) *Grip Strength.*
Scores, 2: Preferred Grip, Nonpreferred Grip.
Comments: Hand dynamometer necessary for administration.
11) *Lateral Dominance.*
12) *Name Writing.*
c) HALSTEAD-REITAN NEUROPSYCHOLOGI-CAL TEST BATTERY FOR ADULTS.
Population: Ages 15 and over.
Comments: Battery has 11 tests same as *b* above with a number of changes in equipment, administration, and scoring forms for this level.
Cross References: See T5:1164 (187 references) and T4:1119 (159 references); for reviews by Raymond S. Dean and Manfred J. Meier, see 9:463 (79 references); see also T3:1052 (4 references).

[1207]

Halstead Russell Neuropsychological Evaluation System.
Purpose: Provides "comprehensive measures of the functions relevant to neuropsychological assessment."
Population: Neuropsychological patients.
Publication Date: 1993.
Acronym: HRNES.
Scores, 3: Percent Impaired Score, Average Index Score, Lateralization Key.
Administration: Individual.
Price Data, 2006: $495 per complete kit including manual (99 pages), 10 recording booklets, and unlimited-use HRNES-R disk; $495 per complete kit with CD including manual, 10 recording booklets, and unlimited-use HRNES-R CD; $54.50 per 10 recording booklets; $57 per manual.
Time: Administration time not reported.
Comments: HRNES computer program compiles raw scores from up to 22 tests, corrects them for age and education, and converts them to scaled scores; includes unlimited use disk.
Authors: Elbert W. Russell and Regina I. Starkey.
Publisher: Western Psychological Services.
Cross References: For reviews by Roderick K. Mahurin and Paul Retzlaff, see 12:176 (1 reference).

[1208]

Hamilton Depression Inventory.
Purpose: Designed to "comprehensively screen for symptoms of depression."
Population: Adults.
Publication Date: 1995.
Acronym: HDI.
Scores: Total score only.
Administration: Group or individual.
Forms, 2: HS and Short Form.
Price Data, 2006: $249 per kit including manual (140 pages), 10 reusable item booklets, 25 summary sheets, 25 answer sheets, 25 short form test booklets, and HDI Scoring Program software (3.5" diskette).
Time: (10) minutes.
Comments: Self-report version of the Hamilton Depression Rating Scale; computer scoring software included; software for administration and interpretation available from publisher.
Authors: William M. Reynolds and Kenneth A. Kobak.
Publisher: Psychological Assessment Resources, Inc.
Cross References: See T5:1166 (230 references); for reviews by Ephrem Fernandez and Carl Isenhart, see 13:136 (43 references).

[1209]

Hammill Multiability Achievement Test.
Purpose: Designed as a "measure of school achievement."
Population: Ages 7-0 to 17-11.
Publication Date: 1998.
Acronym: HAMAT.
Scores, 5: Reading, Writing, Arithmetic, Facts, General Achievement Quotient.

Administration: Individual.
Forms, 2: A, B.
Price Data, 2011: $240 per complete kit including examiner's manual (116 pages), 25 each Form A and Form B response booklets, and 25 each Form A and Form B record forms; $53 per student response booklets (Form A or B); $35 per profile/examiner record forms; $82 per examiner's manual.
Time: (30–60) minutes.
Authors: Donald D. Hammill, Wayne P. Hresko, Jerome J. Ammer, Mary E. Cronin, and Sally S. Quinby.
Publisher: PRO-ED.
Cross References: For reviews by Jeffrey A. Jenkins and Eleanor E. Sanford, see 14:159.

[1210]

The Hand Test [Revised].

Purpose: Designed as "a diagnostic technique that uses pictures of hands as the projective medium."
Population: Ages 5 and older.
Publication Dates: 1959–1991.
Scores, 41: 24 quantitative scores: Interpersonal (Affection, Dependence, Communication, Exhibition, Direction, Aggression, Total), Environmental (Acquisition, Active, Passive, Total), Maladjustive (Tension, Crippled, Fear, Total), Withdrawal (Description, Bizarre, Failure, Total), Experience Ratio, Acting Out Ratio, Pathological, Average Initial Response Time, High Minus Low Score, plus 17 qualitative scores: Ambivalent, Automatic Phrase, Cylindrical, Denial, Emotion, Gross, Hiding, Immature, Inanimate, Movement, Oral, Perplexity, Sensual, Sexual, Original, Repetition.
Administration: Individual.
Price Data, 2006: $164.50 per complete kit including manual (1983, 94 pages), manual supplement: Interpreting Child and Adolescent Responses (1991, 41 pages), 25 scoring booklets, and 1 set of picture cards; $27.50 per 25 scoring booklets; $43.50 per set of picture cards; $53 per manual; $48.95 per manual supplement: Interpreting Child and Adolescent Responses.
Time: (10) minutes.
Author: Edwin E. Wagner.
Publisher: Western Psychological Services.
Cross References: For reviews by Colin Cooper and Susana Urbina, see 14:161; see also T5:1169 (6 references) and T4:1121 (17 references); for a review by Marcia B. Shaffer of an earlier edition, see 10:134 (5 references); see also 9:464 (16 references), T3:1053 (21 references), 8:575 (29 references), T2:1470 (15 references), and P:438 (12 references); for a review by Goldine C. Gleser and an excerpted review by Irving R. Stone of an earlier edition, see 6:216 (6 references).

[1211]

Hand-Tool Dexterity Test.

Purpose: Intended to "provide a measure of proficiency in using ordinary mechanic's tools."

Population: Adolescents and adults.
Publication Dates: 1946–1981.
Acronym: HTDT.
Scores: Total score only.
Administration: Individual.
Price Data, 2006: $390 per complete set including all necessary equipment and manual (1981, 19 pages); $45 per manual.
Time: (5–10) minutes.
Comments: Examinee's score based on time it takes to finish test.
Author: George K. Bennett.
Publisher: Pearson.
Cross References: See T3:1054 (1 reference) and 7:1044 (4 references); for reviews by C. H. Lawshe, Jr. and Neil D. Warren, see 3:649 (2 references).

[1212]

Hanes Sales Selection Inventory.

Purpose: Designed "to help select potentially successful insurance, printing and closely allied salesmen."
Population: Applicants for sales positions.
Publication Date: No date.
Scores: Part II, Part III, Drive Score.
Administration: Group.
Price Data: Available from publisher.
Time: (30) minutes.
Author: Bernard Hanes.
Publisher: Psychometric Affiliates.
Cross References: For a review by Theodore L. Hayes, see 15:114.

[1213]

Haptic Intelligence Scale for Adult Blind.

Purpose: Designed to "measure the intelligence of blind persons on the basis of non-verbal factors."
Population: Blind and partially sighted individuals ages 16 years and older.
Publication Dates: 1964-2004.
Acronym: HIS.
Scores: Digital Symbol, Block Design, Object Assembly, Object Completion, Pattern Board, Bead Arithmetic, Total.
Administration: Individual.
Price Data, 2006: $850 per complete kit including manual (2004, 50 pages), 25 record booklets, and all other necessary materials; $30 per manual; $27 per 25 record booklets.
Time: 91.75(121.75) minutes for the battery.
Comments: It is recommended that this test be used with a verbal test of intelligence for more comprehensive results.
Authors: Harriet C. Shurrager and Phil S. Shurrager.
Publisher: Stoelting Co.
  a) DIGITAL SYMBOL.
    Time: 2(7) minutes.

b) BLOCK DESIGN.
Time: 21(26) minutes.
c) OBJECT ASSEMBLY.
Time: 20(25) minutes.
d) OBJECT COMPLETION.
Time: 15(20) minutes.
e) PATTERN BOARD.
Time: 19(24) minutes.
f) BEAD ARITHMETIC.
Time: 14.75(19.75) minutes.

[1214]

Hare P-Scan.

Purpose: Designed as a "tool for assessing psychopathy and managing risk for antisocial, criminal, and violent behavior."
Population: Ages 13 and older
Publication Date: 1999.
Scores, 4: Interpersonal Facet, Affective Facet, Lifestyle Facet, Total.
Administration: Individual or group.
Price Data, 2011: $81 per complete kit including 25 QuikScore™ forms, 1 manual, and 1 book "Without Conscience"; $33 per 25 QuikScore™ forms; $37 per manual; $61 per kit including manual and 25 QuikScore™ forms.
Time: (10–15) minutes.
Comments: Ratings by evaluator.
Authors: Robert D. Hare and Hugues F. Herve.
Publisher: Multi-Health Systems, Inc.

[1215]

Hare Psychopathy Checklist–Revised: 2nd Edition.

Purpose: Designed for "the assessment of psychopathy in research, clinical and forensic settings."
Population: Ages 18 and over
Publication Dates: 1990–2003.
Acronym: PCL-R.
Scores: 7: Factor 1 (Interpersonal, Affective, Total), Factor 2 (Lifestyle, Antisocial, Total), Total.
Administration: Individual.
Forms, 2: Rating Booklet, Interview Guide.
Price Data, 2011: $357 per complete kit including technical manual (2003, 231 pages), 1 rating booklet, 25 QuikScore™ forms, and 25 interview guides; $130 per technical manual; $72 per rating booklet (reusable, hardcover); $83 per 25 QuikScore™ forms; $135 per 25 interview guides; $181 per preview set including manual, 1 rating booklet, 2 QuikScore forms, and 2 interview guides; $344 for software kit (V.5) includes technical manual and 25 profile reports; $11 per Profile report.
Time: (90–120) minutes for interview; (60) minutes for collateral review, (15-20) minutes for assessment.
Comments: Rating scale based on responses to semi-structured interview and collateral information review.

Expands previous edition for use with female and African American offenders, substance abusers, and offenders in countries other than the U.S.
Author: Robert D. Hare.
Publisher: Multi-Health Systems, Inc.
Cross References: For reviews by Shawn K. Acheson and Joshua W. Payne and by D. Joe Olmi, see 16:101; see also T5:1174 (1 reference); for reviews by Solomon M. Fulero and Gerald L. Stone of a previous edition, see 12:177 (5 references); see also T4:1127 (3 references).

[1216]

Hare Psychopathy Checklist: Screening Version.

Purpose: To screen for psychopathy in forensic and nonforensic settings.
Population: Adults age 18 and over.
Publication Date: 1995.
Acronym: PCL:SV.
Scores, 3: Part 1, Part 2, Total.
Administration: Individual.
Price Data, 2011: $186 per complete kit including 25 interview guides, 25 QuikScore™ forms, and manual (82 pages); $119 per 25 interview guides/QuikScore™ forms; $72 per 25 interview guides; $72 per 25 QuikScore™ forms; $70 per manual.
Time: (30–60) minutes; case history review and scoring require further (20–30) minutes.
Comments: Interview format; shortened version of Hare Psychopathy Checklist–Revised (1215).
Authors: Stephen D. Hart, David N. Cox, and Robert D. Hare.
Publisher: Multi-Health Systems, Inc.
Cross References: For reviews by Ronald J. Ganellen and by Nathaniel J. Pallone and James J. Hennessy, see 14:162.

[1217]

Hare Psychopathy Checklist: Youth Version.

Purpose: Designed for "the assessment of psychopathic traits in adolescents."
Population: Ages 12–18
Publication Date: 2003.
Acronym: PCL:YV.
Scores, 5: Interpersonal, Affective, Behavioral, Antisocial, Total.
Administration: Individual.
Forms, 2: Interview Guide, QuikScore™ Rating Form.
Price Data, 2011: $321 per kit including technical manual, rating booklet, 25 QuikScore forms, and 25 interview guides; $100 per technical manual; $76 per rating booklet (reusable, hardcover); $79 per 25 QuikScore forms; $129 per 25 interview guides.
Time: (90-120) minutes for interview, (60) minutes for collateral interview, (10-20) minutes for completing assessment and scoring.

Comments: Adapted from the Hare Psychopathy Checklist–Revised (1215); expert-completed rating scale based on responses to semistructured interview and collateral information review.
Authors: Adelle E. Forth, David S. Kosson, and Robert D. Hare.
Publisher: Multi-Health Systems, Inc.
Cross References: For a review by John W. Fleenor, see 16:102.

[1218]

Harmonic Improvisation Readiness Record and Rhythm Improvisation Readiness Record.

Purpose: Designed to "help determine objectively whether individual students have the necessary harmonic and rhythmic readiness to learn to improvise" music.
Population: Grades 3 through music graduate school.
Publication Date: 1998.
Scores, 2: Harmonic Readiness, Rhythmic Readiness.
Administration: Group.
Price Data, 2006: $110 per complete kit including 100 harmonic answer sheets, 100 rhythm answer sheets, scoring masks, compact disc, and manual (1998); $20 per 100 answer sheets (specify harmonic or rhythm); $20 per scoring masks; $25 per compact disc.
Time: (20) minutes per test.
Comments: Can be machine scored.
Author: Edwin E. Gordon.
Publisher: GIA Publications, Inc.

[1219]

The Harrington-O'Shea Career Decision-Making System–Revised, 2005 Update.

Purpose: An interest inventory that provides an assessment of career interests, job choices, school subjects, future plans, values, and abilities.
Population: Grade 7 and over.
Publication Dates: 1976-2005.
Acronym: CDM-R.
Administration: Individual or group.
Price Data, 2006: $399.99 per Career Exploration Classroom Set Level 1 or 2, including 25 workbooks, teacher's guide, and video set; $57.99 per CDM Hand-scored Level 1 or 2, including 25 booklets, directions; $29.99 per manual (156 pages); $199.99 per set of career videos; $199.99 per software for Windows or Macintosh: includes CD-ROM, manual, and 50 administrations; $52.99 per 25 scannable forms and 25 Level 2 Interpretive Folders.
Foreign Language Edition: Available in Spanish.
Comments: Hand scored or computer scored; updated every 2 years to reflect changes in occupational forecasts and titles.

Authors: Thomas F. Harrington and Arthur J. O'Shea.
Publisher: Pearson.
a) LEVEL 1.
Population: Middle school students, and other students and adults with reading difficulty.
Publication Dates: 1992–2000.
Scores: 6 Career Interest Areas: Crafts, Scientific, The Arts, Social, Business, Office Operations; 18 Career Clusters: Manual, Skilled Crafts, Technical, Math-Science, Medical-Dental, Literary, Art, Music, Entertainment, Customer Service, Personal Service, Social Service, Education, Sales, Management, Legal, Clerical, Data Analysis.
Time: (20–25) minutes.
b) LEVEL 2.
Population: High school and college students and adults with average or better reading level.
Publication Dates: 1976–2000.
Scores: Same as *a* above and questions in 5 areas: Career Choices, School Subjects, Future Plans, Values, Abilities.
Time: (30–45) minutes.
Cross References: For reviews by Kevin R. Kelly and Mark L. Pope, see 16:103; see also T5:1177 (2 references); for reviews by Debra Neubert and Marcia B. Shaffer of an earlier edition, see 12:179; see also T4:1128 (1 reference); for a review by Caroline Manuele-Adkins of an earlier edition, see 10:136 (1 reference); see also T3:1054 (3 references); for a review by Carl G. Willis of an earlier edition, see 8:1004.

[1220]

Harris Infant Neuromotor Test.

Purpose: Developed as a "family-focused screening tool" for use "in clinical and research settings for the early identification of developmental disorders in infants."
Population: 2.5 months to 12.5 months.
Publication Dates: 2009-2010.
Acronym: HINT.
Score: Total score only.
Administration: Individual.
Price Data, 2010: $36 per manual (2010, 39 pages); $60 per 50 test forms.
Time: (15-25) minutes.
Comments: Additional materials required for administration, but not included: brightly colored ring with string attached, black and white contrasting pictures or designs, disposable paper tape measures for measuring head circumference; after getting a total raw score, it is possible to obtain standard scores based on age norms.
Authors: Susan R. Harris, Antoinette M. Megens, and Linda E. Daniels.
Publisher: Infant Motor Performance Scales, LLC.

[1221]

The Hartman Value Profile.

Purpose: Assesses the development of the capacity to make certain evaluative judgments.
Population: Age 5 and older.
Publication Dates: 1965-1972.
Acronym: HVP.
Scores: 4 parts: The Development of the Capacities to Make Valuations in the Outside World, The Development of the Capacities to Make Valuations of One's Own Self, The Development of the Balance Between the Capacities to Value the Outside World and to Value One's Own Self, The Development of Certain Selected Value Capacities.
Administration: Group or individual.
Price Data, 2004: $35 per 35 copies Regular Form (individual or group administration); $35 per 35 copies of Research Form; $28 per set of Card Form or Pictorial Form (reuseable for individual administration only); $25 per 35 handscoring forms; $42 per manual (269 pages).
Time: (20-30 minutes).
Authors: Robert S. Hartman and Mario Cardenas Trigos.
Publisher: Research Concepts.
Cross References: See T4:1130 (1 reference), T2:1211 (2 references), and P:106 (2 references).

[1222]

Hassles and Uplifts Scales.

Purpose: To identify sources of stress and positive aspects of daily living that help counteract the damaging effects of stress.
Population: Adults.
Publication Date: 1989.
Acronym: HSUP.
Administration: Group.
Price Data: Available from publisher at www.mindgarden.com/products/hsups.htm
Time: (10-15) minutes per test.
Comments: Self-administered; tests available as separates.
Authors: Richard S. Lazarus and Susan Folkman.
Publisher: Mind Garden, Inc.
  a) THE DAILY HASSLES SCALE.
  Scores, 2: Frequency, Severity.
  b) THE UPLIFTS SCALE.
  Scores, 2: Frequency, Intensity.
  c) THE COMBINED HASSLES AND UPLIFTS SCALES.
  Scores, 2: Hassles, Uplifts.
Cross References: See T5:1178 (17 references) and T4:1132 (2 references); for reviews by Karen S. Budd and Nancy Heilman and by Barbara A. Reilly, see 11:155 (6 references).

[1223]

Hay Aptitude Test Battery [Revised].

Purpose: Designed to assess perceptual speed and accuracy.
Population: Applicants for positions that place a heavy emphasis on information processing speed and accuracy.
Publication Dates: 1947-2004.
Scores, 2: Number of Correct Responses, Number of Incorrect Responses.
Administration: Group or individual.
Price Data: Available from publisher.
Foreign Language Editions: French and Spanish versions available.
Author: Edward N. Hay.
Publisher: Wonderlic, Inc.
  a) WARM-UP TEST.
  Purpose: Designed to reduce test-taker anxiety and help acclimate the test taker to the testing setting.
  Time: (1) minute.
  b) NUMBER PERCEPTION TEST.
  Purpose: Designed to assess short-term memory and accuracy with numerical detail.
  Time: (4) minutes.
  c) NAME FINDING TEST.
  Purpose: Assesses short-term memory and accuracy with alphabetical detail.
  Time: (4) minutes.
  d) NUMBER SERIES COMPLETION TEST.
  Purpose: Assesses numerical comprehension, logical thinking, and the ability to perceive patterns and relationships.
  Time: (4) minutes.
Cross References: For reviews by Mark A. Albanese and Michael Kane, see 14:164; for reviews by Sue M. Legg and M. David Miller of an earlier edition, see 12:179; for a review by Robert P. Vecchio of an earlier edition, see 9:470; see also T2:2132 (2 references) and 5:849 (2 references); for reviews by Reign H. Bittner and Edward E. Cureton, see 4:725 (8 references).

[1224]

The Hayling and Brixton Tests.

Purpose: Designed to assess executive functions.
Population: Ages 18-80.
Publication Date: 1997.
Administration: Individual.
Price Data, 2006: £136 per complete kit including manual (20 pages), stimulus book, and 25 scoring sheets; £39.50 per 50 scoring sheets.
Authors: Paul W. Burgess and Tim Shallice.
Publisher: Pearson Assessment [England].
  a) HAYLING TEST.
  Scores, 4: Response Latency, Error Score, Time Taken to Respond, Total.
  Time: [5] minutes.

Comments: Administered verbally; requires no reading or writing.
b) BRIXTON TEST.
Score: Total score only.
Time: [5-10] minutes.
Cross References: For reviews by Kathleen D. Allen and Eugene P. Sheehan, see 17:85.

[1225]

HCR-20: Assessing Risk for Violence.
Purpose: Designed as "a broad-band violence risk assessment instrument with potential applicability to a variety of settings."
Population: Adults (Psychiatric and Correctional Settings).
Publication Date: 1997.
Scores, 4: Final Risk Judgment, Historical Items, Clinical Items, Risk Management Items.
Administration: Individual.
Price Data: Available from publisher.
Time: Administration time not reported.
Comments: "Research instrument."
Authors: Christopher D. Webster, Kevin S. Douglas, Derek Eaves, and Stephen D. Hart.
Publisher: Mental Health, Law, and Policy Institute, Simon Fraser University [Canada].
Cross References: For reviews by Paul A. Arbisi and Colin Cooper, see 15:115.

[1226]

Health and Daily Living Form, Second Edition.
Purpose: To examine the influence of extra treatment factors on treatment outcome as well as to explore the social resources and coping processes people use to prevent and adapt to stressful life circumstances.
Population: Students ages 12-18, Adults.
Publication Dates: 1984-1990.
Acronym: HDLF.
Administration: Group.
Forms, 2: Youth Form, Adult Form B.
Price Data: Available from publisher at www.mind-garden.com/products/hdlfs.htm.
Time: (30-45) minutes.
Comments: May be administered as an interview or as a questionnaire.
Authors: Rudolf H. Moos, Ruth C. Cronkite, and John W. Finney.
Publisher: Mind Garden, Inc.
a) YOUTH FORM.
Population: Students ages 12-18.
Scores: 9 indices: Health-Related (Self-Confidence, Positive Mood, Distressed Mood, Physical Symptoms, Medical Conditions, Health–Risk Behaviors), Social Functioning (Family Activities, Activities with Friends, Social Integration in School).

b) ADULT FORM B.
Population: Adults.
Scores: 41 indices: Health-Related Functioning (Self-Confidence, Physical Symptoms, Medical Conditions, Global Depression, Depressive Mood and Ideation, Endogenous Depression, Depressive Features, Depressed Mood/Past 12 Months, Alcohol Consumption–Quantity, Alcohol Consumption–Quantity/Frequency, Drinking Problems, Smoking Symptoms, Medication Use), Social Functioning and Resources (Social Activities with Friends, Network Contacts, Number of Close Relationships, Quality of Significant Relationship), Family Functioning and Home Environment (Family Social Activities, Family Task Sharing, Tasks Performed by Self, Tasks Performed by Partner, Family Arguments, Negative Home Environment), Children's Health and Functioning (Children's Physical Health Problems, Children's Psychological Health Problems, Children's Total Health Problems, Children's Behavioral Problems, Children's Health–Risk Behaviors), Life Change Events (Negative Life Change Events, Exit Events, Positive Life Change Events), Help-Seeking (Mental Health Professional [past 12 months], Mental Health Professional [ever gone], Non-Mental Health Professional [past 12 months], Non-Mental Health Professional [ever gone]), Family Level Composite (Quality of Conjugal Relationship, Family Social Activities, Family Agreement on Task Sharing, Family Agreement on Household Tasks, Family Arguments, Negative Home Environment).
Cross References: For reviews by Sandra D. Haynes and Ashraf Kagee, see 15:116; see T5:1181 (28 references) and T4:1135 (19 references); for reviews by Arthur M. Nezu and Steven P. Schinke, see 10:137 (8 references).

[1227]

Health and Safety Education Test: National Achievement Tests.
Purpose: Designed to measure students' knowledge of health and safety.
Population: Grades 3–6.
Publication Dates: 1947–1960.
Scores, 5: Good Habits, Cause and Effect, Facts, Application of Rules, Total.
Administration: Group.
Manual: No manual.
Price Data: Available from publisher.
Time: 40(45) minutes.
Authors: Lester D. Crow and Loretta C. Ryan.
Publisher: Psychometric Affiliates.
Cross References: For a review by Clarence H. Nelson, see 5:555.

[1228]

Health Dynamics Inventory.
Purpose: Developed to assess mental health status.

Population: Ages 3-18 (Parent Form), Ages 16-84 (Self Form).
Publication Date: 2003.
Acronym: HDI.
Scores, 13: Morale, Global Symptoms, Global Impairment, Depression, Anxiety, Attention Problems, Psychotic Thinking, Eating Disorders, Substance Abuse, Behavioral Problems, Occupational/Task Impairment, Relationship Impairment, Self-Care Impairment.
Administration: Group or individual.
Forms, 2: Parent, Self.
Price Data, 2011: $340 per complete kit including technical manual (152 pages), 10 each Parent and Self item booklets, 25 each Parent and Self background information questionnaires, and 25 each Parent and Self response forms; $84 per technical manual; $29 per 10 Parent or Self item booklets; $67 per 25 Parent or Self background information questionnaires; $50 per 25 Parent or Self response forms; $94 per preview set including technical manual, 1 Parent and 1 Self item booklets, 3 Parent and 3 Self background information questionnaires, and 3 Parent and 3 Self response forms. $210 per software kit including technical manual and 25 interpretive reports; $190 per summary report kit including technical manual and 25 Health summary report.
Time: (15) minutes.
Comments: Parent form is completed for children ages 3–18 by parent.
Authors: Stephen M. Saunders and James V. Wojcik.
Publisher: Multi-Health Systems, Inc.
Cross References: For reviews by Rik Carl D'Amato and Gregory C. Wochos and by Jeffrey A. Jenkins, see 16:104.

[1229]

Health Education Test: Knowledge and Application: Acorn National Achievement Tests, Revised Edition.

Purpose: Constructed to measure the student's knowledge and application of health information.
Population: Grades 7–13.
Publication Dates: 1946–1956.
Scores, 3: Knowledge, Application, Total.
Administration: Group.
Manual: No manual.
Price Data: Available from publisher.
Time: 40(45) minutes.
Authors: John H. Shaw and Maurice E. Troyer.
Publisher: Psychometric Affiliates.
Cross References: See T2:928 (1 reference) and 5:557 (1 reference); for reviews by H. H. Remmers and Mabel E. Rugen, see 3:421.

[1230]

Health Knowledge Test for College Freshmen: National Achievement Tests.

Purpose: Designed to measure the health knowledge of college freshmen.

Population: College freshmen.
Publication Date: 1956.
Scores: Total score only.
Administration: Group.
Price Data: Available from publisher.
Time: 40(45) minutes.
Author: A. Frank Bridges.
Publisher: Psychometric Affiliates.
Cross References: For a review by James E. Bryan, see 5:558 (3 references).

[1231]

Health Occupations Basic Entrance Test.

Purpose: "A diagnostic instrument [designed] to assist Health Occupation schools evaluate the academic and counseling skills of new applicants to their programs."
Population: Adult applicants to health occupation schools or programs.
Publication Dates: 2000–2001.
Acronym: HOBET.
Scores, 28: 7 Essential Math Skills scores (Whole Numbers, Number System Conversions, Algebra Equations, Percent Operations, Decimal Operations, Fractions Operations, Composite), 3 Reading Comprehension scores (Reading Rate, Reading Rate Placement, Composite), 3 Critical Thinking Appraisal scores (Main Idea of Passage, Inferential Reading, Predicting of Outcomes), Testtaking Skills score, 2 Social Interaction Profile scores (Passive, Aggressive), 5 Stress Level Profile scores (Family, Social, Money/Time, Academic, Work Place), 6 Learning Styles (Auditory Learner, Solitary Learner, Visual Learner, Social Learner, Oral Dependent Learner, Writing Dependent Learner), Composite Percentage.
Administration: Group.
Forms, 2: A, B.
Price Data, 2002: $17 per test by computer; $10.50 per test booklet (36 pages); $8 per answer sheet; $27.50 per Study Guide (150 pages); quantity discounts available.
Time: 150 minutes.
Comments: Generates a Diagnostic Report including Group Report and individual Student Reports; Group Report provides group-level mean percentages and normative comparisons for the 28 scores; optional Study Guide offers test-taking strategy tips and practice tests.
Author: Michael D. Frost.
Publisher: Educational Resources, Inc.
Cross References: For reviews by James T. Austin and Erich C. Fein and by Nambury S. Raju, see 16:105.

[1232]

Health Problems Checklist.

Purpose: To facilitate "the rapid assessment of the health status and potential health problems of clients typically seen in psychotherapy settings."
Population: Adults.

Publication Dates: 1984-1989.
Scores: Items in 13 areas: General Health, Cardiovascular/Pulmonary, Endocrine/Hematology, Gastrointestinal, Dermatological, Visual, Auditory/Olfactory, Mouth/Throat/Nose, Orthopedic, Neurological, Genitourinary, Habits, History; no formal scoring procedure.
Administration: Individual or group.
Manual: No manual.
Price Data, 2006: $50 per package of 50.
Time: (10–20) minutes.
Author: John A. Schinka.
Publisher: Psychological Assessment Resources, Inc.
Cross References: See T5:1186 (1 reference); for a review by Robert M. Kaplan and Michelle T. Toshima of an earlier version, see 10:138.

[1233]

The Health Sciences Reasoning Test.
Purpose: "Was developed for use by educators and researchers to assess the critical thinking skills of health science professionals and health science students."
Population: Health science professionals and students.
Publication Dates: 2006-2007.
Acronym: HSRT.
Scores, 6: Analysis, Evaluation, Inference, Deductive Reasoning, Inductive Reasoning, Total.
Administration: Group.
Price Data: Available from publisher.
Time: (45) minutes.
Comments: This test can be administered online or via paper and pencil.
Authors: Noreen C. Facione and Peter A. Facione.
Publisher: Insight Assessment-The California Academic Press LLC.
Cross References: For reviews by Brian F. French and Sandra D. Haynes, see 18:58.

[1234]

Health Status Questionnaire 2.0.
Purpose: Designed "to measure physical and social functioning and emotional well-being."
Population: Ages 14 and older.
Publication Date: 1994.
Acronym: HSQ® 2.0.
Scores, 8: Health Perception, Physical Functioning, Role Limitations-Physical, Role Limitations-Emotional, Social Functioning, Mental Health, Bodily Pain, Energy/Fatigue.
Administration: Group.
Price Data, 2006: $21 per Q Local answer sheets; $30 per user's guide; $10.25 per 5 test booklets; $1.40 per Q Local single administration report; no charge for progress reports; quantity discounts available for single administration reports.
Time: (5–10) minutes.

Comments: Self-administered; may be administered in paper-and-pencil format or online; contains all items found on the SF-36 Questionnaire (MOS 36-Item Short Form Health Survey) and SF-36 scores are included in the HSQ 2.0 report; scoring via MICROTEST Q Assessment System Software.
Authors: Health Outcomes Institute and the RAND Health Services Program.
Publisher: Pearson.
Cross References: For reviews by John C. Caruso and Theodore L. Hayes, see 15:117.

[1235]

Health Test: National Achievement Tests.
Purpose: To assess students' information, judgment, and evaluation of health knowledge and habits.
Population: Grades 3–8.
Publication Dates: 1937–1957.
Scores, 5: Recognizing Best Habits, Health Comparisons, Causes and Effects, Health Facts, Total.
Administration: Group.
Forms, 2: A, B.
Manual: No manual.
Price Data: Available from publisher.
Time: (40) minutes.
Authors: Robert K. Speer and Samuel Smith.
Publisher: Psychometric Affiliates.
Cross References: For a review by Benno G. Fricke, see 5:560; for a review by Jacob S. Orleans, see 4:485.

[1236]

Healthcare Customer Service Test.
Purpose: Selects customer service oriented workers for hospitals and healthcare settings.
Population: Hospital employees (service, skilled, professional, nursing, administrative, physician, technicians, environmental services).
Publication Dates: 1996–1997.
Acronym: HCST.
Scores, 5: Collaborate, Accommodate, Respect, Engage, Total.
Administration: Group.
Price Data: Available from publisher.
Time: (25–35) minutes, untimed.
Comments: Used for selection; subtests can be used for interview probes.
Author: Healthcare Testing, Inc.
Publisher: Silverwood Enterprises, LLC.
Cross References: For a review by Ronald A. Berk, see 16:106.

[1237]

Help Desk Support Staff Selector.
Purpose: To evaluate essential skills for the Help Desk position.

Population: Candidates for Help Desk positions.
Publication Date: 1993.
Acronym: HEDCO.
Scores: Total Score; Narrative Evaluation, Ranking, Recommendation.
Administration: Group.
Price Data, 2001: $300 per candidate; quantity discounts available.
Time: (180) minutes.
Comments: Scored by publisher; must be proctored.
Authors: Walden Personnel Testing & Training, Inc. and R. Label.
Publisher: Walden Personnel Performance, Inc. [Canada].

[1238]

Help for Preschoolers Assessment Strands: Ages 3-6.

Purpose: Assesses developmental skills/behaviors.
Population: Ages 3-6 years.
Publication Dates: 1987-1995.
Scores: Item scores only; 6 developmental areas: Cognitive, Language, Gross Motor, Fine Motor, Social, Self-Help.
Administration: Individual.
Price Data, 2006: $3.25 per child; price information regarding quantity discounts available from publisher (www.vort.com).
Time: Administration time not reported.
Comments: Adaptation of Behavioral Characteristics Progression (BCP; 312); upward extension of Hawaii Early Learning Profile (Ages 0-3; 1239); "criterion-referenced"; previous version entitled Help for Special Preschoolers Assessment Checklist: Ages 3-6.
Author: VORT Corporation.
Publisher: VORT Corporation.
Cross References: For reviews by Harlan J. Stientjes and Gerald Tindal of an earlier edition, see 11:158.

[1239]

HELP Strands (Hawaii Early Learning Profile): Ages birth-3.

Purpose: Assesses developmental skills/behaviors.
Population: Ages birth-3 years.
Publication Dates: 1984-2004.
Acronym: HELP Strands.
Scores: Item scores only; 6 developmental areas: Cognitive, Language, Gross Motor, Fine Motor, Social, Self-Help.
Administration: Individual.
Price Data, 2006: $3.25 per child; price information for quantity discounts available from publisher (www.vort.com).
Time: Administration time not reported.
Comments: Ratings by professionals; previous version entitled HELP Checklist (Hawaii Early Learning Profile).

Authors: Stephanie Parks (based on original work by Setsu Furuno, Katherine A. O'Reilly, Carol M. Hosaka, Takayo T. Inatsuka, Barbara Zeisloft-Falbey, and Toney Allman).
Publisher: VORT Corporation.
Cross References: For reviews by William Steven Lang and Koressa Kutsick Malcolm of an earlier edition, see 11:157.

[1240]

Herrmann Brain Dominance Instrument [Revised].

Purpose: Designed to measure "a person's preference both for right-brained or left-brained thinking and for conceptual or experiential thinking."
Population: Adults
Publication Dates: 1981–1995.
Acronym: HBDI®.
Scores: 12: Left Mode Preference, Right Mode Preference, Quadrant (Upper Left, Lower Left, Upper Right, Lower Right), Adjective Pairs (subset of 4 Quadrant Scores), Upper (Cerebral) Mode Preference, Lower (Limbic Mode) Preference.
Administration: Group.
Manual: No manual.
Price Data: Available from publisher.
Time: (15–20) minutes.
Comments: Administered via computer; scored by publisher and interpreted by a certified practitioner; hard copy version is available for special needs.
Author: Ned Herrmann.
Publisher: Herrmann International
Cross References: For reviews by F. Felicia Ferrara and Gabriele van Lingen, see 14:165; see also T5:1197 (1 reference); for a review by Rik Carl D'Amato of an earlier edition, see 11:159 (7 references).

[1241]

High Level Battery: Test A/75.

Purpose: To provide "measures of general intelligence, arithmetical ability and certain language abilities."
Population: Adults with at least 12 years of education.
Publication Dates: 1960–1972.
Scores: Total scores only for 4 tests in a single booklet: Mental Alertness, Arithmetical Problems, Reading Comprehension (English, Afrikaans), Vocabulary (English, Afrikaans).
Administration: Group.
Price Data: Available from publisher.
Time: 197 (215) minutes.
Comments: Formerly listed as National Institute for Personnel Research High Level Battery.
Author: D. P. M. Beukes (manual).

Publisher: Human Sciences Research Council [South Africa].
Cross References: See 6:778 (1 reference).

[1242]

High Level Figure Classification Test.

Purpose: Designed to assess intellectual ability.
Population: Grades 10–12.
Publication Date: 1983.
Acronym: HL FCT.
Scores: Total score only.
Administration: Group.
Price Data: Available from publisher.
Foreign Language Edition: Test printed in both English and Afrikaans.
Time: 30(40) minutes.
Authors: M. Werbeloff and T. R. Taylor.
Publisher: Human Sciences Research Council [South Africa].

[1243]

High School Career-Course Planner.

Purpose: Designed "to develop a high school course plan that is consistent with self-assessed career goals."
Population: Grades 8 and 9.
Publication Dates: 1983–1990.
Acronym: HSCCP.
Scores: Total score only.
Administration: Group.
Price Data: Available from publisher.
Time: (50) minutes; (5–8) minutes for computer version.
Comments: Computer version also available.
Author: CFKR Career Materials, Inc.
Publisher: CFKR Career Materials.
Cross References: For reviews by Mary Henning-Stout and James W. Pinkney, see 12:181.

[1244]

High School Personality Questionnaire.

Purpose: Measures primary personality characteristics in adolescents.
Population: Ages 12–18.
Publication Dates: 1958–1984.
Acronym: HSPQ.
Scores, 18: 14 primary factor scores (Warmth, Abstract Thinking, Emotional Stability, Excitability, Dominance, Enthusiasm, Conformity, Boldness, Sensitivity, Withdrawal, Apprehension, Self-Sufficiency, Self-Discipline, Tension), 4 second-order factor scores (Extraversion, Anxiety, Tough Poise, Independence).
Administration: Group or individual.
Price Data, 2005: $35 per 25 reusable test booklets; $18 per scoring keys; $18 per 25 machine-scorable answer sheets; $18 per 50 hand-scoring answer sheets; $20 per 50 hand-scoring answer-profile sheets; $18 per 50 profile sheets; $18 per 50 second-order worksheets; $20 per manual (1984, 98 pages); $23 per computer interpretation introductory kit including manual, reusable test booklet, answer sheet, and prepaid processing form for computer interpretive report; $41 per hand-scoring introductory kit including test booklet, scoring keys, answer sheet, and profile sheet; computer scoring and interpretive services available from publisher for $7 to $30 per individual report depending upon quantity requested.
Foreign Language Editions: Information regarding several non-English-language adaptations available from publisher.
Time: (45-60) minutes.
Comments: Previously listed as Jr.-Sr. High School Personality Questionaire.
Authors: Raymond B. Cattell, Mary D. Cattell, and Edgar Johns (manual and norms).
Publisher: Institute for Personality and Ability Testing, Inc. (IPAT).
Cross References: See T5:1201 (6 references) and T4:1159 (4 references); for reviews by Richard I. Lanyon and Steven V. Owen, see 11:188 (17 references); see also 9:559 (8 references), T3:1233 (22 references), 8:597 (68 references), and T2:1253 (37 references); for reviews by Robert Hogan and Douglas N. Jackson, see 7:97 (53 references); see also P:136 (29 references); for reviews by C. J. Adcock and Philip E. Vernon of an earlier edition, see 6:131 (17 references); see also 5:72 (4 references).

[1245]

High School Placement Test-Open Edition.

Purpose: Designed as a measure of cognitive and basic skills to assist in placement decisions for entering freshmen.
Population: Eighth grade students.
Publication Dates: 1982–2004.
Acronym: HSPT.
Scores, 5: Verbal Skills, Quantitative Skills, Reading, Mathematics, Language.
Administration: Group.
Restricted Distribution: Available for school purchase only.
Price Data: Contact STS at (800) 642-6787 for up-to-date prices.
Time: 150 minutes plus (15–25) minutes per optional test.
Comments: Optional tests available including Science, Mechanical Aptitude, and Catholic Religion.
Author: Scholastic Testing Service, Inc.
Publisher: Scholastic Testing Service, Inc.
Cross References: For reviews by John O. Anderson and Geneva D. Haertel, see 14:166.

[1246]

High School Reading Test: National Achievement Tests.

Purpose: Designed to measure the student's mastery and application of factual material in English, reading, literature, and vocabulary.

Population: Grades 7–12.
Publication Dates: 1939–1952.
Scores, 6: Vocabulary, Word Discrimination, Sentence Meaning, Noting Details, Interpreting Paragraphs, Total.
Administration: Group.
Forms, 2: A, B.
Price Data: Available from publisher.
Time: (40) minutes.
Authors: Robert K. Speer and Samuel Smith.
Publisher: Psychometric Affiliates.
Cross References: For a review by Victor H. Noll, see 5:634; for a review by Holland Roberts, see 4:536; for a review by Robert L. McCaul, see 3:488.

[1247]

Higher Education Learning Profile.

Purpose: "Designed primarily as a diagnostic instrument to assist educational programs evaluate the academic processing skills of new applicants."
Population: Adult applicants to college automotive, business, computer, electronics, legal, technology, and telecommunication programs.
Publication Date: 2001.
Acronym: HELP.
Scores, 28: Essential Math Skills (Whole Numbers, Number System Conversions, Algebra Equations, Percent Operations, Decimal Operations, Fractions Operations, Composite), Reading Comprehension (Reading Rate, Reading Rate Placement, Composite), Critical Thinking Appraisal (Main Idea of Passage, Inferential Reading, Predicting of Outcomes), Testtaking Skills, Social Interaction Profile (Passive, Aggressive), Stress Level Profile (Family, Social, Money/Time, Academic, Work Place), Learning Styles (Auditory Learner, Solitary Learner, Visual Learner, Social Learner, Oral Dependent Learner, Writing Dependent Learner), Composite Percentage.
Administration: Group.
Forms, 3: A, B, C.
Price Data, 2002: $17 per test by computer; $10.50 per test booklet; $8 per answer sheet; $27.50 per Student Study Guide; quantity discounts available.
Time: (150) minutes.
Comments: Generates a Diagnostic Report including the test Group Report, and Individual Student Reports; Group Report provides group-level mean percentages and normative comparisons for the 28 scores; optional Study Guide offers test-taking strategy tips and practice tests.
Author: Educational Resources, Inc.
Publisher: Educational Resources, Inc.

[1248]

Hill Interaction Matrix.

Purpose: "To study group development, group composition, and therapist style."
Population: Prospective members, members, and leaders of psychotherapy groups.

Publication Dates: 1954–1994.
Acronym: HIM.
Scores: Matrix of 4 columns (Topics, Groups, Personal, Relationship) and 4 rows (Conventional, Assertive, Speculative, Confrontive) produces 16 scores, 8 marginal Total scores, Grand Total, and other derivative scores.
Administration: Group or individual.
Price Data: Available from publisher.
Time: (20) minutes.
Author: Wm. Fawcett Hill.
Publisher: Howdah Press [No reply from publisher; status unknown].
  a) HIM A AND B.
  Population: Prospective members and members of psychotherapy groups.
  Publication Dates: 1954–1968.
  Editions, 2: HIM-A, HIM-B.
  b) HIM-G.
  Population: Observers and leaders of psychotherapy groups.
  Publication Dates: 1967–1968.
  Manual: No manual.
Cross References: See T5:1205 (1 reference), T4:1162 (25 references), T3:1099 (9 references), 8:577 (35 references), and T2:1214 (29 references).

[1249]

Hilson Adolescent Profile.

Purpose: "Designed as a screening tool to assess the presence and extent of adolescent behavior patterns and problems."
Population: Age 13 years and above or as determined by a psychologist.
Publication Dates: 1984–1987.
Acronym: HAP.
Scores, 16: Guarded Responses, Alcohol Use, Drug Use, Educational Adjustment Difficulties, Law Violations, Frustration Tolerance, Antisocial/Risk-Taking, Rigidity/Obsessiveness, Interpersonal/Assertiveness Difficulties, Homelife Conflicts, Social/Sexual Adjustment, Health Concerns, Anxiety/Phobic Avoidance, Depression/Suicide Potential, Suspicious Temperament, Unusual Responses.
Administration: Individual or group.
Price Data: Available from publisher.
Time: (45–55) minutes.
Comments: Self-administered; computer-scored.
Author: Robin E. Inwald.
Publisher: Institute for Personality and Ability Testing, Inc. (IPAT) - Public Safety & Security Division.
Cross References: See T5:1207 (1 referfence); for a review by Allen K. Hess, see 11:161.

[1250]

Hilson Adolescent Profile–Version S.

Purpose: "Designed as a screening tool to identify adolescent emotional difficulties, depression and/or

suicidal tendencies, homelife conflicts, and other behavior patterns."
Population: Age 13 years and above or as determined by a psychologist.
Publication Date: 1993.
Acronym: HAP-S.
Scores, 7: Guarded Responses, Educational Adjustment Difficulties, Frustration Tolerance, Homelife Conflicts, Social/Sexual Adjustment, Depression/Suicide Potential, Unusual Responses.
Administration: Individual or group.
Price Data: Available from publisher.
Time: (15–25) minutes.
Comments: Short version of the Hilson Adolescent Profile (1249).
Author: Robin Inwald.
Publisher: Institute for Personality and Ability Testing, Inc. (IPAT) - Public Safety & Security Division.

[1251]

Hilson Career Satisfaction Index.

Purpose: To aid in employee "fitness-for-duty" evaluations, promotion, and special assignment decisions.
Population: Public safety/security officers
Publication Date: 1989.
Acronym: HCSI.
Scores, 13: Stress Patterns, Stress Symptoms, Drug/Alcohol Abuse, Lack of Interpersonal Support, Anger/Hostility Patterns, Disciplinary History, Excusing Attitudes, Aggression/Hostility, Dissatisfaction with Career, Dissatisfaction with Supervisor, Relationship with Co-Workers, Dissatisfaction with Job, Defensiveness.
Administration: Individual or group.
Price Data: Available from publisher.
Time: (25–35) minutes.
Author: Robin Inwald.
Publisher: Institute for Personality and Ability Testing, Inc. (IPAT) - Public Safety & Security Division.
Cross References: See T4:1166 (1 reference).

[1252]

Hilson Personnel Profile/Success Quotient.

Purpose: Designed to aid in the assessment of the qualifications needed for long term career success (e.g., emotional IQ, drive, work ethic, social skills and communication skills).
Population: Age 16 and above or as determined by a psychologist.
Publication Date: 1988.
Acronym: HPP/SQ.
Scores, 16: Candor, Achievement History, Social Ability, "Winner's" Image, Initiative, Success Quotient, Extraversion, Popularity/"Charisma," Sensitivity, Competitive Spirit, Self-Worth, Family Achievement Expectations, Drive, Preparation Style, Goal Orientation, Anxiety about Organization.

Administration: Individual or group.
Price Data: Available from publisher.
Time: (20–30) minutes.
Author: Robin E. Inwald.
Publisher: Institute for Personality and Ability Testing, Inc. (IPAT) - Public Safety & Security Division.
Cross References: For a review by Joseph G. Law, Jr., see 11:162.

[1253]

Hodson Assessment of Phonological Patterns–Third Edition.

Purpose: Designed to "assess and analyze phonological deviations of children with highly unintelligible speech."
Population: Ages 3 to 8.
Publication Dates: 1986-2004.
Acronym: HAPP-3.
Scores, 14: Word/Syllable Structures Omissions (Syllables, Consonant Sequences/Clusters, Prevocalic Singletons, Intervocalic Singletons, Postvocalic Singletons, Total), Consonant Category Deficiencies (Liquids, Nasals, Glides, Stridents, Velars, Anterior Nonstridents, Total), Total Occurrences of Major Phonological Deviations.
Administration: Individual.
Levels, 3: Comprehensive Phonological Evaluation, Preschool Phonological Screening, Multisyllabic Word Screening.
Price Data, 2011: $218 per complete kit including examiner's manual (2004, 64 pages); $41 per 25 Comprehensive Phonological Evaluation Record Forms; $35 per 25 Major Phonological Deviations Analysis Forms; $35 per 25 Substitutions and Other Strategies Analysis Forms; $24 per 50 Preschool Phonological Screening Record Forms; $24 per 50 Multisyllabic Word Screening Record Forms; $11 per 1 Multisyllabic Word Screening Picture Sheet; $59 per 30-piece object kit and 13 picture cards; $70 per examiner's manual.
Time: (15–20) minutes.
Comments: Norm referenced and "criterion referenced"; formerly called The Assessment of Phonological Processes.
Author: Barbara Williams Hodson.
Publisher: PRO-ED.
Cross References: For reviews by David P. Hurford and Vincent J. Samar, see 17:87; see also T5:214 (19 references); for reviews of an earlier version by Allen O. Diefendorf, Michael K. Wynne, and Kathy Kessler and by Kathryn W. Kenney, see 12:36; see also T4:220 (4 references); for a review by Sheldon L. Stick, see 9:91 (1 reference).

[1254]

Hogan Development Survey [Revised].

Purpose: Designed to "assess eleven common dysfunctional dispositions."
Population: Ages 16 and over.

Publication Dates: 1995-2009.
Acronym: HDS.
Scores, 11: Excitable, Skeptical, Cautious, Reserved, Leisurely, Bold, Mischievous, Colorful, Imaginative, Diligent, Dutiful.
Administration: Group.
Price Data, 2011: Available from publisher.
Foreign Language Editions: Available in 35 languages: Czech, French Canadian, French Parisian, German, Slovak, Spanish, Castilian Spanish, Brazilian Portuguese, Danish, Turkish, UK English, US English, Italian, Swedish, Dutch, Norwegian, Indian, Greek, South African, Kenya, Bahasa, Japanese, Korean, Icelandic, New Zealand English, Simplified Chinese, Traditional Chinese, Polish, Russian, Finnish, Romanian, Bulgarian, Thai, Australian, Greek English.
Time: (15-20) minutes.
Comments: Available for online administration.
Authors: Robert Hogan and Joyce Hogan.
Publisher: Hogan Assessment Systems, Inc.
Cross References: For reviews by Glen Fox and E. Scott Huebner of an earlier edition, see 14:168.

[1255]

Hogan Personality Inventory [Revised].

Purpose: Measure of normal personality designed for use in personnel selection, individualized assessment, and career-related decision making.
Population: College students and adults.
Publication Dates: 1985–1995.
Acronym: HPI.
Scores: 7 primary scale scores (Inquisitive, Adjustment, Ambition, Sociability, Interpersonal Sensitivity, Prudence, Learning Approach), 6 occupational scale scores (Service Orientation, Stress Tolerance, Reliability, Clerical Potential, Sales Potential, Managerial Potential), and Validity scale score.
Administration: Group.
Price Data, 2006: Selection Reports starting at $20; Development Reports starting at $40.
Time: (15–20) minutes.
Comments: Web-based administration.
Authors: Robert Hogan and Joyce Hogan (manual).
Publisher: Hogan Assessment Systems, Inc.
Cross References: See T5:1212 (1 reference); for reviews by Stephen N. Axford and Steven G. LoBello, see 13:138 (2 references); see also T4:1169 (7 references); for reviews by James J. Hennessy and Rolf A. Peterson of an earlier edition, see 10:140.

[1256]

Holden Psychological Screening Inventory.

Purpose: "To provide a very brief measure of psychiatric symptomatology, social symptomatology, and depression."
Population: Ages 14 and older.

Publication Date: 1996.
Acronym: HPSI.
Scores, 4: Psychiatric Symptomatology, Social Symptomatology, Depression, Total.
Administration: Individual or group.
Price Data, 2011: $94 per complete kit including manual (50 pages) and 25 QuikScore™ forms; $50 per 25 QuikScore™ forms (English or French-Canadian); $62 per manual; $67 per online profile report kit including manual and 3 profile reports; $5 per online profile report.
Foreign Language Edition: French-Canadian QuikScore™ forms available.
Time: (5–7) minutes.
Comments: Self-report; Windows™ version computer administration and scoring available on CD or 3.5-inch disk.
Author: Ronald R. Holden.
Publisher: Multi-Health Systems, Inc.
Cross References: For reviews by Stephen N. Axford and Janet F. Carlson, see 14:169; see also T5:1213 (1 reference).

[1257]

Holtzman Inkblot Technique.

Purpose: Designed as a projective personality test.
Population: Ages 5 and over.
Publication Dates: 1958–1972.
Acronym: HIT.
Scores, 20–22: Reaction Time (*a* only), Rejection, Location, Space, Form Definiteness, Form Appropriateness, Color, Shading, Movement, Pathognomic Verbalization, Integration, Content (Human, Animal, Anatomy, Sex, Abstract), Anxiety, Hostility, Barrier, Penetration, Balance (*a* only), Popular.
Administration: Group or individual.
Price Data, 2002: $11 per 25 or $40 per 100 Hill clinical summary forms; $31.50 per Workbook for the Holtzman Inkblot Technique.
Author: Wayne H. Holtzman.
Publisher: Pearson.
a) INDIVIDUAL TEST.
Publication Dates: 1958–1972.
Forms, 2: A, B.
Price Data: $687 per complete set for Forms A and B combined including 47 inkblots, 25 record forms with summary sheets, and scoring guide; $369 per complete set (specify Form A or B).
b) GROUP TEST.
Publication Dates: 1958–1972.
Manual: No manual.
Price Data: $21 per 50 Gorham-Holtzman group record forms; $11 per normative item statistics.
Comments: Administration slides for either form must be constructed locally.
Author: Donald R. Gorham (record form).
Cross References: See T4:1170 (12 references); for reviews by Bert P. Cundick and David M. Dush, see 9:480

351

(17 references); see also T3:1106 (25 references); for a review by Rolf A. Peterson, see 8:578 (96 references); see also T2:1471 (42 references); for excerpted reviews by Raymond J. McCall and David G. Martin, see 7:169 (106 references); see also P:439 (90 references); for reviews by Richard N. Coan, H. J. Eysenck, Bertram R. Forer, and William N. Thetford, see 6:217 (22 references).

[1258]

Home & Community Social Behavior Scales.

Purpose: Designed to evaluate social competence and antisocial behavior.
Population: Ages 5–18 (Grades K-12).
Publication Date: 2008.
Acronym: HCSBS.
Scores, 6: Peer Relations, Self-Management/Compliance, Social Competence Total, Defiant/Disruptive, Antisocial/Aggressive, Antisocial Behavior Total.
Administration: Individual.
Price Data, 2008: $49.95 per user's guide (120 pages); $34.95 per 25 test forms.
Time: (5–10) minutes.
Comments: Companion to the School Social Behavior Scales (2377); rated by parent or other home- or community-based rater.
Authors: Kenneth W. Merrell and Paul Caldarella.
Publisher: Paul H. Brookes Publishing Co., Inc.
Cross References: For reviews by Theodore Coladarci and by Stephanie Stein and Phil Diaz, see 16:107.

[1259]

Home Environment Questionnaire, HEQ-2R and HEQ-1R.

Purpose: Measures "dimensions of the child's psychological environment that exert specific types of pressure on the child."
Population: Grades 4–6.
Publication Date: 1983.
Acronym: HEQ.
Scores, 10: P(ress) Achievement, P Aggression-External, P Aggression-Home, P Aggression-Total, P Supervision, P Change, P Affiliation, P Separation, P Sociability, P Socioeconomic Status.
Administration: Individual or Group.
Forms, 2: HEQ-2R for use with two-parent families and HEQ-1R for use with single-parent families.
Price Data: Available from publisher.
Time: Administration time not reported.
Comments: Ratings by child's mother.
Author: Jacob O. Sines.
Publisher: Jacob O. Sines (the author).
Cross References: See T5:1215 (4 references) and T4:1171 (1 reference); for a review by Steven I. Pfeiffer and Julia Pettiette-Doolin, see 10:141 (1 reference).

[1260]

Home Observation for Measurement of the Environment.

Purpose: Designed to measure the quality and quantity of stimulation and support available to a child in the home environment.
Population: Birth to age 3, early childhood, middle childhood, early adolescent.
Publication Dates: 1978–2003.
Acronym: HOME Inventory.
Administration: Individual.
Price Data, 2003: $50 per comprehensive manual; $40 per standard manual (without Disability Adapted or Child Care HOME); $30 per Child Care HOME Manual; $15.00 per pad of Infant Toddler forms; $25 per 50 Early Childhood forms; $12.50 per 25 Middle and Early Adolescent forms.
Time: (60) minutes.
Comment: Focus is on the child in the home environment as a recipient of inputs from objects, events, and transactions occurring in connection with the family surroundings.
Authors: Bettye M. Caldwell and Robert H. Bradley.
Publisher: Home Inventory LLC.
  a) INFANT/TODDLER HOME INVENTORY.
  Population: Birth-3 years.
  Scores, 7: Responsivity, Acceptance, Organization, Learning Materials, Involvement, Variety, Total.
  b) EARLY CHILDHOOD HOME INVENTORY.
  Population: 3-6 years.
  Scores, 9: Learning Materials, Language Stimulation, Physical Environment, Responsivity, Academic Stimulation, Modeling, Variety, Acceptance, Total.
  c) MIDDLE CHILDHOOD HOME INVENTORY.
  Population: 6-10 years.
  Scores, 8: Responsivity, Encouragement of Maturity, Acceptance, Learning Materials, Enrichment, Family Companionship, Paternal Involvement, Total.
  d) EARLY ADOLESCENT HOME INVENTORY.
  Population: Early adolescents.
  Scores 7: Physical Environment, Learning Materials, Modeling, Instructional Activities, Regular Activities, Variety of Experience and Acceptance, Responsivity.
Cross References: See T5:1216 (113 references) and T4:1172 (42 references); for a review by Ann E. Boehm, see 9:481 (13 references); see also T3:1108 (14 references).

[1261]

Home Screening Questionnaire.

Purpose: Constructed to screen the home environment for factors related to the child's growth and development.
Population: Birth to age 3, ages 3–6.
Publication Date: 1981.
Acronym: HSQ.

Scores, 3: Questions, Toy Checklist, Total.
Administration: Individual.
Price Data, 2005: $17 per 25 questionnaires; $18 per reference manual (29 pages).
Time: (15–20) minutes.
Comments: Ratings by parents; abbreviated adaptation of the Home Observation for Measurement of the Environment (1260).
Authors: Cecilia E. Coons, Elizabeth C. Gay, Alma W. Fandal, Cynthia Ker, and William K. Frankenburg.
Publisher: Denver Developmental Materials, Inc.
Cross References: See T5:1217 (1 reference); for a review by S. Ruben Lozano, see 9:482.

[1262]

Home-Visit Kit.

Purpose: Yields information regarding home safety and life-style issues necessary in child custody evaluations.
Population: Families involved in child custody situations.
Publication Dates: 1997–2002.
Scores: Unscored.
Administration: Group.
Price Data, 2002: $189 per kit including 8 Home-Visit booklets, instruction booklet (42 pages), and update service; $99 per 8 Home-Visit booklets; $159 per 16 Home-Visit booklets; $199 per 24 Home-Visit booklets; $119 per Home-Visit instruction booklet.
Time: Administration time not reported.
Comments: Previously listed as The Bricklin/Elliot Child Custody Evaluation.
Authors: Barry Bricklin and Gail Elliot.
Publisher: Village Publishing.

[1263]

The Hooper Visual Organization Test.

Purpose: Measures an individual's ability to organize visual stimuli.
Population: Ages 5 years and over.
Publication Dates: 1957–1983.
Acronym: VOT.
Scores: Total score only.
Administration: Group or individual.
Price Data, 2006: $207 per complete kit including 4 reusable test pictures booklets, manual (1983, 39 pages), 25 test booklets, 100 answer sheets, and scoring key; $27.50 per 25 test booklets; $40 per reusable test pictures booklet; $16.50 per scoring key; $27.50 per 100 answer sheets; $47 per manual.
Time: (15) minutes.
Author: H. Elston Hooper.
Publisher: Western Psychological Services.
Cross References: See T5:1218 (19 references); for reviews by Kathy E. Green and Wilfred G. Van Gorp, see 12:182 (7 references); see also T4:1174 (28 references),

T3:1109 (6 references), T2:1216 (5 references), and P:111 (7 references); for reviews by Ralph M. Reitan and Otfried Spreen of an earlier edition, see 6:116 (4 references).

[1264]

Hopkins Verbal Learning Test–Revised.

Purpose: A "brief assessment of verbal learning and memory (immediate recall, delayed recall, delayed recognition)."
Population: Ages 16 years and older.
Publication Dates: 1991–2001.
Acronym: HVLT-R.
Scores, 4: Total Recall, Delayed Recall, Retention, Recognition Discrimination Index.
Administration: Individual.
Forms, 6: 1–6.
Price Data, 2006: $255 per introductory kit including professional manual (2001, 55 pages) and 25 each of 6 test booklets (Forms 1–6).
Time: (5–10) minutes with a 25-minute delay.
Comments: Forms 1–6 are very similar psychometrically and can be used to eliminate practice effects on repeated administration.
Authors: Jason Brandt and Ralph H. B. Benedict.
Publisher: Psychological Assessment Resources, Inc.
Cross References: For reviews by Timothy Z. Keith and Wendy J. Steinberg, see 16:108.

[1265]

The Hospital Anxiety and Depression Scale with the Irritability-Depression-Anxiety Scale and the Leeds Situational Anxiety Scale.

Purpose: Designed to detect and distinguish "between anxiety and depression and measures the severity of emotional disorder."
Population: Adults.
Publication Date: 1994.
Acronym: HADS.
Scores, 3: Irritability, Anxiety, Depression.
Administration: Group.
Price Data: Available from publisher.
Time: (5) minutes.
Authors: R. P. Snaith and A. S. Zigmond.
Publisher: GL Assessment [England].
Cross References: For reviews by Michael H. Campbell and William E. Martin, Jr., see 15:118.

[1266]

House-Tree-Person and Draw-A-Person as Measures of Abuse in Children: A Quantitative Scoring System.

Purpose: Developed to "evaluate possible child sexual abuse."
Population: Ages 7–11.

Publication Date: 1994.
Acronym: H-T-P/D-A-P.
Scores, 4: Preoccupation with Sexually Relevant Concepts, Aggression and Hostility, Withdrawal and Guarded Accessibility, Alertness for Danger/Suspiciousness and Lack of Trust.
Administration: Individual.
Price Data, 2005: $102 per H-T-P/D-A-P Quantitative Scoring System Kit including "H-T-P/D-A-P as Measures of Abuse in Children," and 25 scoring booklets.
Time: Administration time not reported.
Comments: A projective drawing instrument; for related instruments see The Draw-A-Person, Draw A Person: A Quantitative Scoring System, Draw-A-Person Quality Scale, and Draw A Person: Screening Procedure for Emotional Disturbance.
Author: Valerie Van Hutton.
Publisher: Psychological Assessment Resources, Inc.
Cross References: See T5:1219 (1 reference); for reviews by E. Thomas Dowd and Howard M. Knoff, see 13:139 (2 references).

[1267]

How Am I Doing? A Self-Assessment for Child Caregivers.

Purpose: Designed to identify areas of strength and skill development needs of caregivers of children with disabilities.
Population: Caregivers of children with disabilities.
Publication Date: 1993.
Scores: 8 sections: Arrival and Departure, Free Choice Play, Structured Group Activities, Outside Play, Meal Time, Toileting, Nap Time, Throughout the Day.
Administration: Group.
Price Data: Price data available from publisher.
Time: Administration time not reported.
Author: Irene Carney.
Publisher: Child Development Resources.
Cross References: For reviews by Lisa G. Bischoff and by Frederic J. Medway and Karen Fay, see 13:140.

[1268]

How I Think About Drugs and Alcohol Questionnaire.

Purpose: Designed to "measure adolescents' behaviors and attitudes related to drug use."
Population: Grades 9-12.
Publication Date: 2008.
Acronym: HIT-D&A.
Scores, 9: Soft Drug Use, Hard Drug Use, Drug Abuse, Drug Dependence, Behavior Scale Score, Self- Centered, Blaming Others and Assuming the Worst, Minimizing and Mislabeling, Attitude Scale Score.
Administration: Group.
Price Data, 2011: $25.95 per manual (65 pages) and 20 questionnaires, $23.95 per 20 questionnaires.

Time: (5-10) minutes.
Authors: Alvaro Q. Barriga (test and manual), John C. Gibbs, Granville Bud Potter, M. Konopisos, and K. T. Barriga.
Publisher: Research Press.

[1269]

How I Think Questionnaire.

Purpose: Designed to "measure self-serving cognitive distortion."
Population: Ages 12–21.
Publication Date: 2001.
Acronym: HIT.
Scores, 11: Hit Questionnaire, Overt, Covert, Self-Centered, Blaming Others, Minimizing/Mislabeling, Assuming the Worst, Opposition-Defiance, Physical Aggression, Lying, Stealing, Anomalous Responding.
Administration: Individual.
Price Data, 2006: $25.95 per 20 questionnaires and manual (44 pages); $23.95 per 20 additional questionnaires.
Time: (5–15) minutes.
Authors: John C. Gibbs, Alvaro Q. Barriga, Granville Bud Potter, and Albert K. Kiau.
Publisher: Research Press.
Cross References: For reviews by Jack E. Gebart-Eaglemont and Joseph C. Kush, see 15:119.

[1270]

How Supervise?

Purpose: Designed to assess the knowledge of practices affecting worker efficiency.
Population: Supervisors.
Publication Dates: 1943–1971.
Scores: Total score only.
Administration: Group or individual.
Forms, 3: A, B, M.
Price Data, 2006: $77 per 25 test booklets (specify form); $26 per manual (1971, 17 pages); $30 per examination kit including test booklets for all three forms and manual.
Time: [40] minutes.
Authors: Quentin W. File and H. H. Remmers.
Publisher: Pearson.
Cross References: See T4:1177 (2 references) and T2:2448 (11 references); for a review by Joel T. Campbell, see 6:1189 (9 references); see also 5:926 (18 references); for a review by Milton M. Mandell, see 4:774 (8 references); for reviews by D. Welty Lefever, Charles I. Moiser, and C. H. Ruedisili, see 3:687 (5 references).

[1271]

HRR Pseudoisochromatic Plates for Detecting and Classifying Color Vision Deficiency.

Purpose: Designed to test for color vision; distinguishes those with normal color vision from those with defective color vision. For those with defective color vision, indicates the type (Protan, Deutan, or Tritan) and the degree of defect (mild, medium, or strong).

Population: People who may have color vision deficiency and occupational settings where the work requires a known level of color vision.
Publication Dates: 1991-2002.
Scores, 3: Normal Color Vision, Defective Color Vision (Red-Green Deficiency, Blue-Yellow Deficiency).
Administration: Individual.
Price Data, 2010: $219 per H.R.R. 4th Edition book including 4 demonstration plates, 20 test pages, Directions (in English) and laminated score sheet; other versions available with laminated plates for longer wear. Also available in combo version with Amsler Grids used to detect scotomata. Check www.richmondproducts.com for free 16-page Color Vision Tutorial.
Time: (1–3) minutes.
Authors: Richmond Products, Inc.; LeGrand H. Hardy (manual), Gertrude Rand (manual), and M. Catherine Rittler (manual); J. Neitz (Fourth Edition), and J. Bailey (Fourth Edition).
Publisher: Richmond Products, Inc.
Cross References: For a review by Ayres G. D'Costa, see 15:120.

[1272]

H-T-P: House-Tree-Person Projective Technique.

Purpose: "To provide psychologists and psychiatrists … with an examining procedure with which to acquire diagnostically and prognostically significant data concerning a subject's total personality."
Population: Ages 3 and over
Publication Dates: 1946–1993.
Acronym: H-T-P.
Scores: Total score only.
Administration: Individual.
Price Data, 2011: $199 per complete kit, including 1 copy of The House-Tree-Person Projective Drawing Technique: Manual and Interpretive Guide, 1 copy of House-Tree-Person Drawings: An Illustrated Diagnostic Handbook, 1 copy of Catalog for the Qualitative Interpretation of the House-Tree-Person (H-T-P), 25 H-T-P Interpretation Booklets, and 25 H-T-P Drawing Forms; $75 for The House-Tree-Person Projective Drawing Technique: Manual and Interpretive Guide (165 pages); $45 for a Catalog for the Qualitative Interpretation of the House-Tree-Person (191 pages); $45 for the House-Tree-Person Drawings: An Illustrated Diagnostic Handbook (108 pages); $23 for H-T-P Interpretation Booklet (set of 25, quantity price break available); $23 H-T-P Person Drawing/Interpretation Booklet (set of 25, quantity price break available); $18 H-T-P Drawing Form (set of 25, quantity price break available).
Time: (60–90) minutes.
Authors: John N. Buck, W. L. Warren (revision), Isaac Jolles (interpretive catalog), L. Stanley Wenck (diagnostic handbook), and Emmanuel F. Hammer (clinical research manual).

Publisher: Western Psychological Services.
Cross References: See T5:1160 (4 references), T4:1183 (6 references), T2:1469 (61 references), and P:437 (24 references); for a review by Mary R. Haworth of an earlier edition, see 6:215 (32 references); for a review by Philip L. Harriman, see 5:139 (61 references); for reviews by Albert Ellis and Ephraim Rosen and an excerpted review, see 4:107 (14 references); for reviews by Morris Krugman and Katherine N. Wilcox, see 3:47 (5 references).

[1273]

Hughes Basic Gross Motor Assessment.

Purpose: Designed to detect disorders in motor performance.
Population: Ages 6–12 believed to have minor motor dysfunctions.
Publication Date: 1979.
Acronym: BGMA.
Scores: 8 subtests: Static Balance, Stride Jump, Tandem Walking, Hopping, Skipping, Target, Yo-Yo, Ball Handling Skills.
Administration: Individual.
Price Data: Available from publisher.
Time: Administration time not reported.
Author: Jeanne E. Hughes.
Publisher: Nancy Hughes [No reply from publisher; status unknown].
Cross References: See 9:487 (1 reference).

[1274]

Human Figure Drawing Test.

Purpose: "Designed to provide an objective approach" to human figure drawings.
Population: Clients in psychotherapy.
Publication Date: 1993.
Acronym: HFDT.
Scores, 4: Impairment, Distortion, Simplification, Organic Factors Index.
Administration: Individual.
Price Data, 2006: $86.50 per complete kit including handbook (189 pages), 25 drawing forms, and 25 AUTOSCORE™ forms; $19.25 per 25 drawing forms; $35.75 per 25 AUTOSCORE™ forms; $54.50 per handbook.
Time: (5–20) minutes.
Authors: Jerry Mitchell, Richard Trent, and Roland McArthur.
Publisher: Western Psychological Services.
Cross References: For reviews by Charles A. Peterson and William K. Wilkinson, see 14:170; see also T5:1226 (4 references).

[1275]

Human Information Processing Survey.

Purpose: "Assesses processing preference–left, right, integrated, or mixed [brain functioning]."

Population: Adults.
Publication Date: 1984.
Acronym: HIP Survey.
Scores, 3: Right, Left, Integrated.
Administration: Group.
Editions, 2: Research Edition, Professional Edition.
Price Data, 2005: $56.90 per professional edition starter set including administrator's manual (44 pages), 10 survey forms, and 10 strategy and tactics profiles booklets; $43.85 per 10 survey forms and strategy and tactics profiles; $22 per manual (professional and research editions); $75.50 per research edition starter set including administrator's manual, 20 reusable survey forms, 20 profile forms, and 20 response sheets; $22.65 per 20 profile forms and response sheets (research edition); $23.10 per sample set for each edition.
Time: [40] minutes.
Authors: E. Paul Torrance, William Taggart (manual), and Barbara Taggart.
Publisher: Scholastic Testing Service, Inc.
Cross References: See T5:1227 (2 references) and T4:1186 (1 reference); for a review by J. P. Das, see 10:144 (1 reference).

[1276]

Human Relations Inventory.
Purpose: Designed to measure social conformity.
Population: Grades 9–16 and adults.
Publication Dates: 1954–1959.
Acronym: HRI.
Scores: Total score only.
Administration: Group.
Price Data: Available from publisher.
Time: (20) minutes.
Author: Raymond E. Bernberg.
Publisher: Psychometric Affiliates.
Cross References: See T2:1221 (4 references), P:114 (1 reference), and 6:119 (6 references); for reviews by Raymond C. Norris and John A. Radcliffe, see 5:68.

[1277]

Humanics National After-School Assessment Form.
Purpose: "Designed to help the teacher observe the child in different areas of development and to follow changes over the year."
Population: Ages 6-9.
Publication Dates: 1995-2009.
Scores, 5: Social-Emotional, Language, Cognitive, Motor Skills, Hygiene/Self-Help.
Administration: Individual.
Manual: No manual.
Price Data, 2010: $34.95 per 25 test booklets.
Time: Administration time not reported.
Authors: Jackson Rabbit, Sylvia B. Booth, and Marilyn L. Perling.
Publisher: Humanics Test Corporation.

[1278]

Humanics National Child Assessment Form [Revised].
Purpose: To serve as developmental checklists of skills and behavior that occur during the first 9 years of life.
Population: Ages 0–3, 3–6, 6–9.
Dates: 1981–2002.
Administration: Group.
Levels, 3: Birth to age 3, ages 3 to 6, ages 6 to 9.
Price Data, 2002: $34.95 per 25 assessment forms (specify level).
Time: Administration time varies.
Comments: Behavior checklists to be completed by parents or teachers.
Publisher: Humanics Test Corporation.
  a) BIRTH TO THREE.
  Scores, 5: Social-Emotional, Language, Cognitive, Gross Motor, Fine Motor.
  Price Data: $23.95 per handbook and 5 assessment forms; $18.95 per handbook.
  Authors: Marsha Kaufman (checklist), T. Thomas McMurrain (checklist), Jane A. Caballero (handbook), and Derek Whordley (handbook).
  b) AGES THREE TO SIX.
  Scores, 5: Same as *a* above.
  Price Data: $39.95 per handbook and 5 assessment forms; $18.95 per handbook.
  Authors: Derek Whordley (handbook) and Rebecca J. Doster (handbook).
  c) AGES SIX TO NINE.
  Scores, 5: Same as *a* above.
  Authors: Jackson Rabbit (checklist), Sylvia B. Booth (checklist), and Marilyn L. Perling (checklist).
  Comments: Age level 6 to 9 is not accompanied by a handbook; behavior checklists to be completed by parents or teachers.
Cross References: For reviews by Arthur S. Ellen and David MacPhee of an earlier edition, see 11:170.

[1279]

The Hundred Pictures Naming Test.
Purpose: "A confrontation naming test designed to evaluate rapid naming ability."
Population: Ages 4-6 to 11-11.
Publication Date: 1992.
Acronym: HPNT.
Scores, 3: Error, Accuracy, Time.
Administration: Individual.
Price Data, 2006: A$104.50 per complete kit including manual (84 pages), test book, and 25 response forms; A$13.20 per 25 response forms.
Time: (6) minutes.
Authors: John P. Fisher and Jennifer M. Glenister.
Publisher: Australian Council for Educational Research Ltd. [Australia].

Cross References: For reviews by Jeffrey A. Atlas and Stephen Jurs, see 12:183.

[1280]
Hunter-Grundin Literacy Profiles.

Purpose: Designed to monitor the written and spoken language skills of children.
Population: Ages 6.5–8, 7.10–9.3, 9–10, 9.10–11.5, 10.10–12.7.
Publication Dates: 1979–1989.
Scores: 6 tests: Attitude to Reading (Levels 1 and 2 only), Reading for Meaning, Spelling, Free Writing, Spoken Language, Profile of Personal Interests (Levels 4 and 5 only).
Administration: Individual and group.
Levels: 5 overlapping levels.
Manual: Separate manual for each level.
Price Data: Available from publisher.
Time: (3-10) minutes per test at any one level.
Comments: Ratings by teacher in part.
Authors: Elizabeth Hunter-Grundin and Hans U. Grundin.
Publisher: The Test Agency Limited [England] [No reply from publisher; status unknown].
   a) LEVEL 1.
   Population: Ages 6.5–8.
   b) LEVEL 2.
   Population: Ages 7.10–9.3.
   c) LEVEL 3.
   Population: Ages 9–10.
   d) LEVEL 4.
   Population: Ages 9.10–11.5.
   e) LEVEL 5.
   Population: Ages 10.10–12.7.
Cross References: For reviews by Martha C. Beech and Patricia H. Kennedy of a previous edition, see 9:491.

[1281]
I Can Do Maths.

Purpose: Designed "to inform teachers and parents about children's development in numeracy in the early years of schooling."
Population: Children in the first 3 years of Australian and New Zealand school systems.
Publication Dates: 2000–2001.
Scores, 4: Number, Measurement, Space, Total.
Administration: Group.
Price Data, 2006: A\$58.30 per specimen set including one Level A test booklet, one Level B test booklet, one Level A Ezi-guide, one Level B Ezi-guide, and teacher's guide (36 pages).
Time: (30–40) minutes.
Authors: Brian Doig and Marion de Lemos.
Publisher: Australian Council for Educational Research Ltd. [Australia].

   a) LEVEL A.
   Population: Children in the first 2 years of school.
   Price Data: \$27.50 per 10 Level A test booklets.
   b) LEVEL B.
   Population: Children in the second and third years of school.
   Price Data: Same as Level A above.
Cross References: For a review by Theresa Graham, see 16:109.

[1282]
I-SPEAK Your Language™: A Survey of Personal Styles.

Purpose: Designed to teach employees how to identify and modify their communication style to work best with others in a variety of situations.
Population: Employees.
Publication Dates: 1972–1999.
Scores, 8: Favorable Conditions (Intuitor, Thinker, Feeler, Senser), Stress Conditions (Intuitor, Thinker, Feeler, Senser).
Administration: Group or individual.
Price Data, 2002: \$50 per 10 questionnaires; \$12.95 per Self-Development Exercises manual (1992, 59 pages); \$12.95 per manual (1993, 46 pages); \$25 per specimen set including questionnaire, manual, and Self-Development Exercises manual.
Time: (20) minutes.
Comments: Also available (except Self-Development Exercises manual) in Spanish, French, German, Portugese, Arabic, Norwegian, Bhasa Indonesian.
Author: Drake Beam Morin, Inc.
Publisher: Drake Beam Morin, Inc.
Cross References: For reviews by Mary Anne Bunda and Kimberly A. Lawless, see 13:141.

[1283]
IDEA Feedback for Administrators.

Purpose: Designed "to assist in appraising professional functioning and to suggest how that functioning could be improved."
Population: College and university administrators.
Publication Date: 2001.
Scores: Summary Ratings (Quality of Job, Confidence in Administrator), Strengths in Performing Administrative Roles (Planner, Consultant, Communicator, Expert, Community Builder), Administrative Style (Democratic Practice, Structuring, Vigor), Personal Characteristics (Interpersonal Sensitivity, Integrity, Character).
Administration: Group.
Price Data, 2003: \$150 per administrator including initial and reminder e-mails to administrator, 3 copies of the report that includes responses to open-ended questions, and shipping plus \$1 for each individual notified of survey via e-mail; \$25 cancellation fee after e-mail

addresses loaded into system; $50 fee assessed to correct undeliverable e-mails.

Time: Administration time not reported.

Comments: Online administration; ratings by faculty members and chairperson; publisher scores and generates interpretive reports.

Author: The IDEA Center.

Publisher: The IDEA Center.

[1284]

IDEA Feedback for Department Chairs.

Purpose: Designed to diagnose administrative performance and discover ways to effectively improve it.

Population: College and university department chairpersons.

Publication Dates: 1977–1998.

Scores: 17 scores in 3 areas: Overall Ratings (Summary Judgement, Effectiveness in Performance, Five Types of Administrative Responsibilities); Effectiveness in Performing Twenty Specific Administrative Responsibilities (Administrative Support, Personnel Management, Program Leadership/Support, Building Image/Reputation, Developing Positive Climate); Description of Administrative Methods and Personal Characteristics (Democratic/Humanistic, Goal-Oriented/Structured, Supports Faculty, Promotes Positive Climate, Promotes Department Advancement, Ability to Resolve Issues, Communication Skills, Steadiness, Trustworthiness, Openness).

Administration: Group.

Price Data: Available from publisher.

Time: (15–30) minutes.

Comments: Available for online administration; previous version entitled Departmental Evaluation of Chairperson Activities for Development; publisher scores and generates interpretive reports; online inventory completed by faculty about their department chairs.

Authors: IDEA Center and Donald D. Hoyt (Technical Report, 1998).

Publisher: The IDEA Center.

Cross References: For reviews by John W. Fleenor and M. David Miller, see 15:121; see T4:741 (1 reference).

[1285]

IDEA Oral Language Proficiency Test.

Purpose: To "assist in the initial identification designation and redesignation of a student as being NES, LES, or FES (Non-Limited-Fluent English Speaking)."

Population: Preschool–grade 12.

Publication Dates: 1983–2006.

Acronym: IPT 2004.

Scores: 3 Modality scores: Oral, Listening, Speaking; 4 Diagnostic scores: Vocabulary, Comprehension, Syntax, Verbal Expression.

Administration: Individual.

Price Data: Available from publisher.

Foreign Language Editions: English and Spanish versions available for each level.

Publisher: Ballard & Tighe, Publishers.

   a) PRE-IPT.

   Population: Ages 3–5.

   Publication Date: 2006.

   Time: (8–13) minutes.

   Authors: Constance O. Williams, Enrique F. Dalton, and Phyllis L. Tighe.

   b) IPT-I.

   Population: Grades K–6.

   Publication Date: 2006.

   Time: (14–19) minutes.

   Authors: Wanda S. Ballard, Phyllis L. Tighe, and Enrique F. Dalton.

   c) IPT-II.

   Population: Grades 7–12.

   Publication Date: 2006.

   Time: (15–20) minutes.

   Authors: Enrique F. Dalton and Beverly A. Amori.

Cross References: For reviews by Emilia C. Lopez and Salvador Hector Ochoa, see 14:171; see also T5:1234 (5 references).

[1286]

IDEA Reading and Writing Proficiency Test.

Purpose: To provide "comprehensive assessment for the initial identification and redesignation of Limited English Proficient (LEP) students."

Population: Grades K–12.

Publication Dates: 1992–2006.

Acronym: IPT R & W 2004.

Scores: 2 skill scores: Reading, Writing; 5 Diagnostic Scores for Reading: Vocabulary, Vocabulary in Context, Reading for Understanding, Reading for Life Skills, Language Usage; 3 Diagnostic Scores for Writing: Conventions, Write a Story, Write Your Own Story; 12 Diagnostic Scores for Early Literacy: Visual Recognition, Letter Recognition, Phonemic Awareness, Phonics, Reading Vocabulary, Reading for Life Skills, Reading for Understanding, Sentences and Stories, Copy Letters, Write Name and Copy Sentence, Descriptive/Narrative Writing, Spelling.

Administration: Group.

Levels, 4: Grades K–1, Grades 2–3, Grades 4–6, Grades 7–12.

Price Data: Available from publisher.

Foreign Language Editions: English and Spanish versions available for each level.

Time: (70–115) minutes.

Comments: Used in conjunction with the IPT Oral Language Proficiency Test (1285) with scoring rules available for deriving both a comprehension and an overall score.

Authors: Beverly A. Amori, Enrique F. Dalton, and Phyllis L. Tighe.

Publisher: Ballard & Tighe, Publishers.
Cross References: For reviews by James Dean Brown and Alan Garfinkel, see 13:142.

[1287]
IDEA Student Ratings of Instruction.

Purpose: Designed to provide student ratings of college instructors.
Population: College faculty.
Publication Dates: 1975–1998.
Scores: 5-part report compiled from ratings data: Overall Measures of Teaching Effectiveness, Student Ratings of Progress in Specific Objectives, Teaching Methods/Style, Course Description/Context, Statistical Detail.
Administration: Group.
Price Data: Available from publisher.
Time: (10–20) minutes.
Comments: Available for use in the classroom and in online classes.
Authors: Donald P. Hoyt, William H. Pallett, Amy B. Gross, Richard E. Owens, William E. Cashin (technical reports), Glenn R. Sixbury (technical reports, numbers 7–10), Yih-Fen Chen (technical report number 11).
Publisher: The IDEA Center.
Cross References: For reviews by Raoul A. Arreola and Jennifer J. Fager, see 14:172; see also T4:1195 (1 reference); for a review by John C. Ory of an earlier edition, see 9:493 (2 references).

[1288]
IDEAS: Interest Determination, Exploration and Assessment System™.

Purpose: "To be used as an introduction to career exploration for students and adults."
Population: Grades 7–12 and adults.
Publication Dates: 1977–1994.
Acronym: IDEAS™.
Scores, 16: Mechanical/Fixing, Protective Services, Nature/Outdoors, Mathematics, Science, Medical, Creative Arts, Writing, Community Service, Educating, Child Care, Public Speaking, Business, Sales, Office Practices, Food Service.
Administration: Group or individual.
Price Data, 2006: $70 per 50 test booklets (Youth or Adult version); $21 per manual (1990, 80 pages); $25 per starter kit with self-scored reports; quantity discounts available for the reports; price information for Spanish materials available from publisher.
Time: (40–45) minutes.
Comments: Self-administered, self-scored.
Author: Charles B. Johansson.
Publisher: Pearson.
Cross References: For a review by Robert J. Miller, see 11:172; for a review by M. O'Neal Weeks of an earlier edition, see 9:516.

[1289]
Illinois Test of Psycholinguistic Abilities, Third Edition.

Purpose: Designed "to help children who have weakness in various linguistic processes including spoke or written language."
Population: Ages 5-0 to 12-11.
Publication Dates: 1961–2001.
Acronym: ITPA-3.
Scores, 12: Spoken Analogies, Spoken Vocabulary, Morphological Closure, Syntactic Sentences, Sound Deletion, Rhyming Sequences, Sentence Sequencing, Written Vocabulary, Sight Decoding, Sound Decoding, Sight Spelling, Sound Spelling.
Administration: Individual.
Price Data, 2011: $204 per kit including 25 profile/examiner record booklets, 25 student response booklets, manual (2001, 165 pages), and an audio cassette; $59 per 25 profile/examiner record booklets; $53 per 25 student response booklets; $82 per examiner's manual; $24 per audio cassette; $316 print/software combo kit; $129 per software scoring and report system.
Time: (45–60) minutes.
Authors: Donald D. Hammill, Nancy Mather, and Rhia Roberts.
Publisher: PRO-ED.
Cross References: For a review by Roger L. Towne, see 15:122; see T5:1240 (51 references), T4:1201 (53 references), 9:496 (37 references), and T3:1126 (145 references); for reviews by James Lumsden and J. Lee Wiederholt of an earlier edition, and an excerpted review by R. P. Waugh, see 8:431 (269 references); see also T2:981 (113 references); for reviews by John B. Carroll and Clinton I. Chase, see 7:442 (239 references); see also 6:549 (22 references).

[1290]
Illness Behaviour Questionnaire, Third Edition.

Purpose: In the clinical context, to screen for the presence, and "record aspects of illness behaviour, particularly those attitudes that suggest or are associated with inappropriate or maladaptive modes of responding to one's state of health."
Population: Pain clinic, psychiatric, and general practice patients.
Publication Dates: 1983–1994.
Acronym: IBQ.
Scores, 9: 7 factors (General Hypochondriasis, Disease Conviction, Psychological vs. Somatic Perception of Illness, Affective Inhibition, Affective Disturbance, Denial, Irritability) and Discriminant Function Score and Whitely Index of Hypochondriasis.
Administration: Individual or group.
Price Data, 1999: $40 per manual (1994, 95 pages) including test.
Time: (10) minutes.

Comments: Self-report instrument; the Discriminant Function Score indicates likelihood of conversion disorder.
Authors: Issy Pilowsky and Neil Spence.
Publisher: I. Pilowsky [Australia].
Cross References: For reviews by Colin Cooper and M. Allan Cooperstein, see 15:123; see also T5:1241 (6 references) and T4:1203 (6 references).

[1291]

Illness Effects Questionnaire–Multi-Perspective.

Purpose: Designed to assess "the impact of a patient's illness from multiple perspectives."
Population: Ages 18 and over.
Publication Date: 2002.
Acronym: IEQ–MP.
Administration: Individual.
Forms, 4: Self-Report, Professional, Observer, Treatment.
Price Data, 2011: $317 per complete kit including user's manual (84 pages), 25 of each form, and 25 comparative and integrated profile forms; $73 per user's manual; $61 per 25 of any one form; $101 per preview kit including user's manual, 3 of each form, and 3 comparative and integrated profile forms.
Time: (10) minutes.
Authors: Glen D. Greenberg and Rolf A. Peterson.
Publisher: Multi-Health Systems Inc.
Cross References: For reviews by Alan C. Bugbee, Jr. and Beth Doll, see 16:110.

[1292]

Incentives Management Index.

Purpose: Designed to make explicit sales managers' "assumptions, theories, and practices in the realm of sales motivation."
Population: Sales managers.
Publication Dates: 1972–1995.
Acronym: IMI.
Scores, 5: Basic Creative Comfort, Safety and Order, Belonging and Affiliation, Ego-Status, Actualization and Self-Expression.
Administration: Group.
Price Data, 2001: $8.95 per instrument (1995, 24 pages).
Time: Administration time not reported.
Comments: Self-administered; self-scored.
Authors: Jay Hall and Norman J. Seim.
Publisher: Teleometrics International, Inc.
Cross References: For reviews by Leslie H. Krieger and Patricia H. Wheeler, see 14:173.

[1293]

Independent Living Scales.

Purpose: Designed to assess adults' competence in instrumental activities of daily living.

Population: Adults with cognitive impairments.
Publication Date: 1996.
Acronym: ILS.
Scores, 6: Memory/Orientation, Managing Money, Managing Home and Transportation, Health and Safety, Social Adjustment, Total.
Administration: Individual.
Price Data, 2002: $248 per complete kit including manual (119 pages), 25 record forms, stimulus booklet, and a pouch containing a facsimile of a driver's license, credit card, and key; $37 per 25 record forms.
Time: (45) minutes.
Comments: Four screening items are used to determine whether the examinee has a vision, speech, or hearing impairment; the stimulus booklet is designed for adults who can hear and those with a hearing impairment.
Author: Patricia Anderten Loeb.
Publisher: Pearson.
Cross References: For reviews by Libby G. Cohen and Jack A. Cummings, see 14:174.

[1294]

Independent Mastery Testing System for Math Skills.

Purpose: "To monitor the student's mastery of basic mathematics skills, to diagnose specific student weaknesses, to recommend a program of further study, and to provide the teacher with a comprehensive record of student progress."
Population: Adult students.
Publication Date: 1984.
Acronym: IMTS.
Scores: 13 tests: Adding and Subtracting Whole Numbers, Multiplying and Dividing Whole Numbers, Adding and Subtracting Fractions, Multiplying and Dividing Fractions, Adding and Subtracting Decimals, Multiplying and Dividing Decimals, Percents Skills, Charts and Graphs Skills, Measurement Skills, The Language of Algebra, The Uses of Algebra, Geometry-Angles, Geometry-Plane and Solid Figures.
Administration: Individual.
Forms: 3 parallel forms of each test.
Price Data: Not available.
Time: Administration time not reported.
Comments: Computer-administered instructional management system; Apple II, Apple II+, Apple IIe, or Apple IIc computer necessary for administration.
Authors: Cambridge, The Adult Education Company in association with Moravian College, Bethlehem, PA.
Publisher: Prentice Hall [No reply from publisher; status unknown].
Cross References: For a review by Richard M. Jaeger, see 10:147.

[1295]

Independent Mastery Testing System for Writing Skills.

Purpose: "To monitor the student's mastery of basic grammar and writing skills, to diagnose specific student

weaknesses, to recommend a program of further study, and to provide the teacher with a comprehensive record of student progress."
Population: Adult students.
Publication Date: 1984.
Acronym: IMTS.
Scores: 15 tests: Recognizing Sentences, Verb Tenses, Subject-Verb Agreement-Part A, Subject-Verb Agreement-Part B, Pronouns-Part A, Pronouns-Part B, Plurals and Possessives, Adjectives and Adverbs-Part A, Adjectives and Adverbs-Part B, Sentence Structure, Prepositions and Conjunctions, Logic and Organization, Capitalization, Punctuation, Spelling.
Administration: Individual.
Forms: 3 parallel forms (1, 2, 3) of each test.
Price Data: Available from publisher.
Time: Administration time not reported.
Comments: Computer-administered instructional management system; Apple II, Apple II+, Apple IIe, or Apple IIc computer necessary for administration.
Authors: Cambridge, The Adult Education Company, in association with Moravian College, Bethlehem, PA.
Publisher: Prentice Hall [No reply from publisher; status unknown].
Cross References: For a review by Pamela A. Moss, see 11:173.

[1296]

Independent School Entrance Exam, 3rd Edition.

Purpose: Designed to "assess verbal reasoning, quantitative reasoning, reading comprehension, and mathematics achievement for use in admissions into independent schools."
Population: Grades 4-11, or candidates for Grades 5–12.
Publication Dates: 1989-2010.
Acronym: ISEE.
Scores, 4: Verbal Reasoning, Quantitative Reasoning, Reading Comprehension, Mathematics Achievement.
Administration: Group.
Levels, 3: Lower, Middle, Upper.
Price Data: Available from publisher.
Time: (140) minutes.
Comments: Test booklet title is ISEE.
Author: Educational Records Bureau.
Publisher: Educational Records Bureau.
Cross References: For reviews by Mary Anne Bunda and Joyce R. McLarty of an earlier edition, see 11:174.

[1297]

Index of Teaching Stress.

Purpose: Designed to "assess the effects of a specific student's behavior on a teacher's stress level and self-perception."
Population: Teachers from preschool to 12th grade.
Publication Dates: 2003–2004.

Acronym: ITS.
Scores, 12: Total Stress Score, Attention-Deficit/Hyperactivity Disorder, Student Characteristics (Emotional Lability/Low Adaptability, Anxiety/Withdrawal, Low Ability/Learning Disability, Aggressive/Conduct Disorder, Total); Teacher Characteristics (Sense of Competence/Need for Support, Loss of Satisfaction From Teaching, Disruption of the Teaching Process, Frustration Working With Parents, Total).
Administration: Group.
Price Data, 2007: $134 per introductory kit including manual (2004, 89 pages), 25 reusable item booklets, 25 answer sheets, and 25 profile forms.
Time: (20–25) minutes.
Authors: Richard R. Abidin, Ross W. Greene, and Timothy R. Konold.
Publisher: Psychological Assessment Resources, Inc.
Cross References: For a review by Mildred Murray-Ward, see 17:88.

[1298]

Individual Directions Inventory™.

Purpose: Designed to provide insight into a wide range of personal motivations; useful in individual and organizational development.
Population: Adults.
Publication Dates: 1988–2001.
Acronym: IDI.
Scores: 17 dimensions: Types of Emotional Satisfaction (Giving, Receiving, Belonging, Expressing, Gaining Stature, Entertaining, Creating, Interpreting, Excelling, Enduring, Structuring, Maneuvering, Winning, Controlling, Stability, Independence, Irreproachability).
Administration: Group.
Price Data: Available from publisher.
Time: (30) minutes.
Comments: Purchase and use requires training by publisher or credential review.
Authors: James T. Mahoney (test) and Robert I. Kabacoff (manual).
Publisher: Management Research Group.

[1299]

Individual Employment Plan with 84-Item Employability Assessment.

Purpose: To help service organizations gather information about clients' employability status and assist clients in creating and completing a training and services plan.
Population: Participants in employment programs.
Publication Date: 2002.
Acronym: IEP.
Scores: Personal Issues and Considerations, Health and Physical Considerations, Work Orientation, Career and Life Planning Skills, Job Seeking Skills, Job Adaptation Skills, Education and Training.

Administration: Individual.
Price Data, 2006: $34.95 per 25 inventories including free administrator's guide (8 pages).
Time: (30) minutes.
Comments: Eight-panel foldout.
Authors: LaVerne L. Ludden and Bonnie R. Maitlen.
Publisher: JIST Publishing, Inc.

[1300]
Individual Outlook Test.
Purpose: Designed to assess codependent orientation.
Population: Adults.
Publication Date: 1993.
Acronym: IOT.
Scores, 6: Codependent Orientation, Externally Derived Sense of Self Worth, Anxiety, Dysfunctional Family of Origin, Dependency within Relationships, Dysfunctional Relationships.
Administration: Group or individual.
Price Data: Available from publisher.
Time: (15–20) minutes.
Authors: Laurie A. Sim and Eugene E. Fox (test and manual); Michelle J. Worth and Donald Macnab (manual).
Publisher: Psychometrics Canada Ltd. [Canada].
Cross References: For reviews by Jeffrey A. Atlas and by Susan C. Whiston and Wendi L. Tai, see 16:111.

[1301]
Individual Style Survey.
Purpose: "Intended to be an educational tool for self and interpersonal development."
Publication Dates: 1989–1990.
Administration: Group.
Price Data: Available from publisher.
Time: (60–90) minutes.
Comments: Self-administered, self-scored survey.
Author: Norman Amundson.
Publisher: Psychometrics Canada Ltd. [Canada] [No reply from publisher; status unknown].
a) INDIVIDUAL STYLE SURVEY.
  Population: Adults.
  Publication Date: 1989.
  Acronym: ISS.
  Scores, 14: 8 categories of behavior (Forceful, Assertive, Outgoing, Spontaneous, Empathetic, Patient, Reserved, Analytical) yielding 4 styles (Dominant, Influencing, Harmonious, Cautious) that combine to form 2 summary scores (People/ Task Orientation, Introspective/Interactive Stance).
b) MY PERSONAL STYLE.
  Population: Ages 10–18.
  Publication Date: 1990.
  Acronym: MPS.
  Scores, 14: 8 categories (Carefree, Outgoing, Straight Forward, Forceful, Precise, Reserved,

Patient, Sensitive) yielding 4 styles (Influencing, Strong Willed, Cautious, Peaceful) that combine to form 2 summary scores (People/Task Orientation, Expressive/Thoughtful Stance).
  Comments: Simplified version of the Individual Style Survey for use with young people.
Cross References: For reviews by Jeffrey A. Atlas and William I. Sauser, see 13:144.

[1302]
Industrial Reading Test.
Purpose: "Measures an individual's ability to comprehend written technical materials."
Population: Grade 9 and above vocational students and applicants or trainees in technical or vocational training programs.
Publication Dates: 1976-1989.
Acronym: IRT.
Scores: Total score only.
Administration: Group or individual.
Forms, 2: A, B.
Restricted Distribution: Distribution of Form A restricted to business and industry.
Price Data, 2006: $34 per examination kit; $30 per manual; $28 per Form A Test Booklets; $155 per Form B Test Booklets; $49 per Form A Keys; $49 per Form B Keys; $105 per IBM 805/OpScan Answer Sheets.
Time: (40) minutes.
Comments: Test can be scored by hand or with an IBM 805 or OpScan machine.
Author: The Psychological Corporation.
Publisher: Pearson.
Cross References: For a review by Darrell L. Sabers, see 9:504.

[1303]
Industrial Test Battery.
Purpose: Intended to assess an individual's conceptual reasoning and spatial abilities.
Population: Individuals with less than 7 years of formal schooling.
Publication Date: 1986.
Acronym: ITB.
Scores: Total score only for each test.
Subtests, 3: Anomalous Concept Test (ACT), Anomalous Figure Test (AFT), Series Induction Test (SIT).
Administration: Group.
Price Data: Available from publisher.
Foreign Language Edition: Tests printed in both English and Afrikaans.
Time: 20(30) minutes for ACT; 25(35) minutes for AFT; 30(40) minutes for SIT.
Author: T. R. Taylor.
Publisher: Human Sciences Research Council [South Africa].

[1304]

The Infanib.

Purpose: Designed to provide a systematic scorable method to assess the neurological status of infants, especially infants who are premature or have special conditions.
Population: Infants from 4 to 18 months corrected gestational age.
Publication Date: 1994.
Scores, 20: Hands Open, Hands Closed, Scarf Sign, Heel-To-Ear, Popliteal Angle, Leg Abduction, Dorsiflexion of the Foot, The Foot Grasp, Tonic Labyrinthine Supine, Asymmetric Tonic Neck Reflex, Pull-To-Sitting, Body Denotative, Body Rotative, All-Fours, Tonic Labyrinthine Prone, Sitting, Sideways Parachute, Backwards Parachute, Standing-Positive Support Reaction, Forward Parachute.
Administration: Individual.
Price Data, 2002: $94 per complete kit including 50 screening forms and manual (131 pages); $28 per 50 screening forms.
Time: Untimed.
Comments: "Criterion-referenced" test with ratings determined by therapist.
Author: Patricia H. Ellison.
Publisher: Pearson.
Cross References: For reviews by Jill Ann Jenkins and John J. Vacca, see 14:175.

[1305]

Infant Development Inventory.

Purpose: Designed "for screening or assessing the development of infants in the first eighteen months."
Population: Birth to 18 months.
Publication Dates: 1980–1995.
Acronym: IDI.
Scores, 5: Social, Self-Help, Gross Motor, Fine Motor, Language.
Administration: Individual.
Manual: Brief Instructions only.
Price Data, 2005: $12.50 per 25 parent questionnaires.
Time: [5–10] minutes.
Comments: New version of the Minnesota Infant Development Inventory (T4:1642); observations by mother.
Author: Harold Ireton.
Publisher: Child Development Review - Behavior Science Systems, Inc.
Cross References: For reviews by Alan S. Kaufman and John J. Vacca, see 14:176; see also T5:1259 (2 references); for information on the earlier edition, see T4:1642 (1 reference); for a review by Bonnie W. Camp of the earlier edition, see 9:714.

[1306]

The Infant-Toddler and Family Instrument.

Purpose: Designed as "a relatively short survey of family and child functioning" to "help in making a judgment about whether a child and family need further services and referrals."
Population: Families with infants and toddlers 6–36 months
Publication Date: 2001.
Acronym: ITFI.
Scores, 4: Caregiver Interview, Developmental Map, Checklist for Evaluating Concern, Plan for the Child and Family.
Administration: Individual.
Price Data: Infant-Toddler and Family Instrument (The) Manual: $25.00; Infant-Toddler and Family Instrument (The) Instrument: $25 for package of 5.
Time: (150–165) minutes.
Authors: Nancy H. Apfel and Sally Provence.
Publisher: Paul H. Brookes Publishing Co., Inc.

[1307]

Infant-Toddler Developmental Assessment.

Purpose: Constructed as "an integrated family-centered assessment process that addresses the health and development of children." It is designed to improve the early identification of children (birth to 3 years) who are developmentally at risk.
Population: Birth to 36 months.
Publication Date: 1995.
Acronym: IDA.
Scores: 8 developmental domains: Gross Motor, Fine Motor, Relationship to Inanimate Objects (Cognitive), Language Communication, Self-Help, Relationship to Persons, Emotions and Feeling States (Affects), Coping.
Administration: Individual.
Price Data, 2011: $711 per complete kit including administration manual (223 pages), foundations and study guide, readings, 25 parent report forms (English), 25 health record guides, and 25 record forms all in a canvas carrying case along with manipulatives in a separate carrying case; $96 per administration manual; $96 per foundations and study guide; $40 per 25 parent report forms (English or Spanish); $31 per 25 health record guides; $70 per 25 record forms.
Time: Varies.
Comments: Ratings by multidisciplinary team.
Authors: Sally Provence, Joanna Erikson, Susan Vater, and Saro Palmeri.
Publisher: PRO-ED.
Cross References: For reviews by Melissa M. Groves and E. Jean Newman, see 13:146.

[1308]

Infant/Toddler Environment Rating Scale-Revised Edition.

Purpose: Designed to assess programs for children from birth to 30 months of age in group care settings.

low

Population: Infant/toddler day care centers.
Publication Dates: 1990-2006.
Acronym: ITERS-R.
Scores, 8: Space and Furnishings, Personal Care Routines, Listening and Talking, Activities, Interaction, Program Structure, Parents and Staff, Total.
Administration: Individual.
Price Data, 2006: $14.95 per rating scale (2006, 79 pages) including administration and scoring instructions and score sheet and profile that may be photocopied.
Time: (180) minutes to observe and rate.
Authors: Thelma Harms, Debby Cryer, and Richard M. Clifford.
Publisher: Teachers College Press.
Cross References: For reviews by Karen Carey and Joseph C. Kush, see 17:89; see also T5:1264 (6 references); for reviews by Norman A. Constantine and Annette M. Iverson of an earlier edition, see 12:188.

[1309]
Infant/Toddler Symptom Checklist.

Purpose: Designed as a screening instrument for infants and toddlers with regulatory and sensory-integrative disorders.
Population: 7–30 months.
Publication Date: 1995.
Scores, 9: Self-Regulation, Attention, Sleep, Eating or Feeding, Dressing/Bathing or Touch, Movement, Listening and Language, Looking and Sight, Attachment/Emotional Functioning.
Administration: Individual.
Levels, 6: 7–9 months, 10–12 months, 13–18 months, 19–24 months, 25–30 months, General Screening Version (when age specific administration is inconvenient).
Price Data, 2002: $63 per Infant/Toddler Symptom Checklist including manual (58 pages) and 6 sets of 5 score sheets in 25-page pads in a vinyl storage portfolio; $37 per additional score sheets available in 6 sets of five sheets in 25-page pads.
Time: (10) minutes.
Comments: "Criterion-referenced"; checklist completed by parents or caregiver.
Authors: Georgia A. DeGangi, Susan Poisson, Ruth Z. Sickel, and Andrea Santman Wiener.
Publisher: Pearson.
Cross References: For reviews by Deborah Erickson and Ruth E. Tomes, see 14:178.

[1310]
Influence Strategies Exercise.

Purpose: Designed to identify and develop influence techniques.
Population: Managers and employees.
Publication Date: 1993.
Acronym: ISE.
Scores, 9: Empowerment, Interpersonal Awareness, Bargaining, Relationship Building, Organizational Awareness, Common Vision, Impact Management, Logical Persuasion, Coercion.
Administration: Individual or group.
Parts, 3: Participant Version, Profile and Interpretative Notes, and Feedback Version (optional).
Price Data, 2006: $79 per complete kit including 10 exercises and 10 profiles and interpretive notes (19 pages); $29 per 10 feedback version exercises.
Time: (20–25) minutes.
Comments: Self-administered questionnaire.
Author: Hay Group.
Publisher: Hay Group.
Cross References: For reviews by Collie W. Conoley and Paul M. Muchinsky, see 13:147.

[1311]
The Influence Styles Inventory.

Purpose: Designed to identify and examine the styles and strategies used in "day-to-day problems managers face."
Population: Managers.
Publication Dates: 1997–1998.
Scores, 3: Aggressive, Assertive, Passive.
Administration: Group.
Price Data: Available from publisher.
Time: (20) minutes.
Author: Marshall Sashkin.
Publisher: HRD Press, Inc.

[1312]
Informal Reading Comprehension Placement Test [Revised].

Purpose: "Assesses the instructional and independent comprehension levels of students from pre-readiness (grade 1) through level twelve plus (grade 12)."
Population: Grades 1–8 for typical learners and grades 8–12 remedially; adult education students.
Publication Dates: 1983–1999.
Scores, 3: Word Comprehension, Passage Comprehension, Total Comprehension.
Administration: Individual.
Price Data, 2006: $59.95 per test including Mac/Win CD-ROM, management, and guide; $299.75 per site license version.
Time: (35–50) minutes for the battery; (15–20) minutes for Part 1; (20–30) minutes for Part 2.
Comments: Automatically administered, scored, and managed; for use with adults, the placements are correlated with Tests of Adult Basic Education (2788); test administered in two parts; microcomputer (IBM Windows or MAC) necessary for administration.
Authors: Ann Edson and Eunice Insel.
Publisher: Educational Activities Software.
Cross References: For reviews by Diane J. Sawyer and Gabrielle Stutman, see 13:148; for reviews by Gloria A. Galvin and Claudia R. Wright of an earlier edition, see 11:178.

[1313]

Information System Skills.

Purpose: Constructed to predict "a person's success in operating terminal based information systems."
Population: Information processing job applicants.
Publication Date: 1983.
Acronym: ISS.
Scores, 4: Reasoning, Form Recognition, Document Checking, Speed.
Administration: Group.
Price Data: Available from publisher.
Time: 36 minutes and 30 seconds (45 minutes).
Author: Malcolm Morrisby.
Publisher: Educational & Industrial Test Services Ltd. [England].

[1314]

Informeter: An International Technique for the Measurement of Political Information.

Purpose: Designed to measure political information.
Population: Adults.
Publication Date: 1972.
Scores, 5: Local, National, International, Miscellaneous, Total.
Administration: Group.
Manual: No manual.
Price Data, 2005: $2 per scale.
Time: [15] minutes.
Comments: Supplementary article available.
Author: Panos D. Bardis.
Publisher: Donna Bardis.

[1315]

InQ: Assessing Your Thinking Profile.

Purpose: Designed to "measure individual preferences in the way people think...it is a wide-ranging tool for both individual and group development, and for planning for more effective contacts with others."
Population: Business and industry.
Publication Dates: 1997-2001.
Acronym: InQ.
Scores, 5: Synthesist, Idealist, Pragmatist, Analyst, Realist.
Administration: Group.
Price Data, 2007: $16.95 per Manual of Administration and Interpretation (2001, 73 pages); $69.95 per set of 10 questionnaires.
Foreign Language Edition: Spanish edition available.
Time: (20) minutes.
Comments: Self-administered version of the Inquiry Mode Questionnaire (12:189), which is the trainer-administered version.
Author: InQ Educational Materials, Inc.
Publisher: InQ Educational Materials, Inc.
Cross References: For reviews by Patricia A. Bachelor and Ayres D'Costa, see 18:59.

[1316]

Inquiry Mode Questionnaire: A Measure of How You Think and Make Decisions.

Purpose: Developed to measure "individual preferences in the way people think."
Population: Business and industry.
Publication Dates: 1977–1989.
Acronym: INQ.
Scores, 5: Synthesist, Idealist, Pragmatist, Analyst, Realist.
Administration: Group or individual.
Price Data: Available from publisher.
Time: (20) minutes.
Comments: Manual title is INQ Styles of Thinking.
Authors: Allen F. Harrison and Robert M. Bramson.
Publisher: INQ Educational Materials Inc.
Cross References: For reviews by Philip Benson and Tamela Yelland, see 12:189.

[1317]

Insight: Assessing and Developing Self-Esteem.

Purpose: Designed as a tool to "assess and, where required, improve a (child's) self-esteem."
Population: Ages 3 to 16.
Publication Date: 2002.
Scores, 4: Sense of Self, Sense of Belonging, Sense of Personal Power, Overall.
Administration: Individual or group.
Price Data: Available from publisher.
Time: (10) minutes.
Comments: Reproducible rating scale forms are titled "Self-Esteem Indicator."
Author: Elizabeth Morris.
Publisher: GL Assessment [England].
   a) INSIGHT: PRE-SCHOOL.
   Population: Ages 3 to 5.
   Comments: Rating scale completed by adult observer.
   b) INSIGHT: PRIMARY.
   Population: Ages 5 to 11.
   Comments: Rating scale can be completed by adult observer or by adult and student working together.
   c) INSIGHT: SECONDARY.
   Population: Ages 11 to 16.
   Comments: Rating scale completed by adult observer or by adult and student working together.
Cross References: For reviews by Gerald E. DeMauro and Gypsy M. Denzine, see 16:112.

[1318]

INSIGHT Inventory [Revised].

Purpose: Designed to determine how an individual differs from other individuals in his or her style of influencing others, relating to others, responding to people, making decisions and taking action, and structuring time and handling details.

Population: Adults age 21 and over, students age 16–21.

Publication Dates: 1988–2006.

Scores: 4 traits: Getting Your Way (Direct, Indirect), Responding to People (Reserved, Outgoing), Pacing Activity (Urgent, Steady), Dealing with Details (Unstructured, Precise).

Administration: Group or individual.

Forms, 3: INSIGHT Inventory, Teaming Up with INSIGHT, INSIGHT 360 Degree Style Feedback Set.

Price Data, 2006: $12 per INSIGHT Inventory; $16 per Teaming Up with INSIGHT; $16 per Form F, INSIGHT 360 Degree Style Feedback Set; $295 per Training Kit for adult version including video, training guide, technical manual, and CD with digital slides.

Time: (15–20) minutes.

Comments: Users get two profiles, one reflecting how they see themselves in their work (school) environment and the other reflecting how they see themselves in their personal (at home) environment; "has field theory base which takes into account that participants may change their behavior from one environment (field) to another"; utilizes self-perception; supporting feedback sets provide perceptions of how five others see the user; 1993 revision based on a second collection of norms and a factor analysis of the items; online version available at www.insightinstitute.com.

Author: Patrick Handley.

Publisher: Insight Institute, Inc.

Cross References: For reviews by Sanford J. Cohen and Elizabeth L. Jones, see 14:179; for a review by Susana Urbina of an earlier edition, see 13:149.

[1319]

Instructional Style Indicator [Revised].

Purpose: Designed to identify "instructional preferences and learning effectiveness with others."

Population: Adults.

Publication Dates: 1996-2006.

Acronym: ISI.

Scores, 4: Behavioral/Action/Independent, Cognitive/Analysis/Visual, Interpersonal/Harmony/Auditory, Affective/Expression/Experiential.

Administration: Individual or group.

Price Data, 2006: $13.95 per test booklet (2006, 16 pages); $13.95 per In-Depth Interpretation booklet (2006, 28 pages); $26.95 per access code online version; $37.95 per Trainer's Guidelines (1996, 28 pages).

Time: (30) minutes (90-180 minutes program options).

Comments: Self-administered and self-scored; can be used in conjunction with the Learning Style Indicator (1506).

Authors: Ken Keis, Everett T. Robinson, and Terry D. Anderson.

Publisher: Consulting Resource Group International, Inc.

[1320]

Instrument for Disability Screening [Developmental Edition].

Purpose: To screen for learning disabilities.

Population: Primary grade children.

Publication Date: 1980.

Acronym: IDS.

Scores, 9: Hyperactive/Aggression, Visual, Speech/Auditory, Reading, Drawing/Writing, Inactivity, Concepts, Psychomotor Development, Total.

Administration: Individual.

Manual: No manual.

Price Data: Not available.

Time: (5-15) minutes.

Author: James R. Beatty.

Publisher: James R. Beatty [No reply from publisher; status unknown].

Cross References: See T3:1161 (3 references); for reviews by Norman A. Buktenica and Stephen I. Pfeiffer, see 9:515.

[1321]

Instrument Timbre Preference Test.

Purpose: "To act as an objective aid to the teacher and the parent in helping a student choose an appropriate woodwind or brass instrument to learn to play in beginning instrumental music and band."

Population: Grades 4-12.

Publication Dates: 1984-1985.

Acronym: ITPT.

Scores, 7: Flute, Clarinet, Saxophone and French Horn, Oboe/English Horn/Bassoon, Trumpet and Cornet, Trombone/Baritone/French Horn, Tuba and Sousaphone.

Administration: Group.

Price Data, 2006: $59 per complete kit including 100 test sheets, scoring masks, compact disc, and manual (1984, 53 pages); $14.50 per 100 test sheets; scoring service available from publisher.

Time: (30) minutes.

Author: Edwin E. Gordon.

Publisher: GIA Publications, Inc.

Cross References: For reviews by Richard Colwell and Paul R. Lehman, see 10:150.

[1322]

Instrumen Test (Form AIT-C).

Purpose: For selecting instrument technicians.

Population: Applicants and incumbents for jobs requiring technical knowledge and skills of instrumentation.

Publication Dates: 2001–2005.

Scores, 8: Mathematics & Basic AC/DC Theory, Analog & Digital Electronics and Power Supplies, Schematics & Electrical Print Reading, Process Control, Test Instruments, Mechanical and Hand & Power Tools, Computers & PLC, Total.

Administration: Group.
Price Data, 2011: $22 per consumable self-scoring test booklet or online test administration (minimum order of 20); $24.95 per manual (2005, 15 pages).
Time: (60-70) minutes.
Comments: Self-scoring instrument; available for online administration.
Author: Roland T. Ramsay.
Publisher: Ramsay Corporation.
Cross References: For a review by Suzanne Young, see 17:90.

[1323]

Instruments for Assessing Understanding & Appreciation of Miranda Rights.

Purpose: Designed for use in forensic settings to assess an individual's ability to waive their Miranda Rights in a "voluntary, knowing, and intelligent" manner.
Population: Juveniles and adults.
Publication Date: 1998.
Scores, 4: Comprehension of Miranda Rights, Comprehension of Miranda Rights-Recognition, Comprehension of Miranda Vocabulary, Function of Rights in Interrogation.
Administration: Individual.
Price Data, 2007: $99.95 per complete kit including testing easel, 20 test forms, and manual (104 pages); $64.95 per testing easel; $20 per 20 test forms; $26.95 per manual.
Time: 50(60) minutes.
Author: Thomas Grisso.
Publisher: Professional Resource Press.
Cross References: For reviews by Joe W. Dixon and by Marc Janoson and Thomas Lazzaro, see 18:60.

[1324]

Insurance Selection Inventory.

Purpose: Designed to "evaluate skills and attitudes that are generally appropriate for insurance claims examiner/adjuster, correspondence representative or customer service representative positions."
Population: Ages 18 and over.
Publication Date: 2002.
Acronym: ISI.
Scores, 11: Number Comparison, Verbal Reasoning, Arithmetic Computation, Error Recognition, Applied Arithmetic, Drive, Interpersonal Skills, Cognitive Skills, Self-Discipline, Writing Skills, Work Preference.
Administration: Group.
Forms, 2: Timed, Untimed.
Price Data, 2005: $16 including 1–999 reports for Internet scoring with booklets; $16 including 1–999 reports for Internet scoring without booklets; $16 including 1–999 reports for QuantaTouch Test; $16 including 1–999 reports for QUANTA Software for Windows with booklets; $16 including 1–999 reports for QUANTA Software for Windows without booklets.
Time: (45) minutes.
Comments: Test can be scored via Touch Test, Internet, or Optical Scanning Software.
Author: Pearson Reid London House.
Publisher: Pearson Performance Solutions [No reply from publisher; status unknown].

[1325]

Integrated Assessment System®.

Purpose: "A series of performance tasks that can be used independently or in combination with a norm-referenced achievement test to offer a comprehensive view of student achievement."
Population: Grades 1–9.
Publication Dates: 1990–1992.
Acronym: IAS®.
Subtests: 3.
Administration: Group.
Authors: Roger Farr and Beverly Farr (Language Arts and Spanish only).
Publisher: Pearson.
   a) IAS-LANGUAGE ARTS.
   Population: Grades 1–8.
   Scores, 3: Response to Reading, Management of Content, Command of Language.
   Price Data, 2002: $160.60 per complete grade 1 package including 25 each of three student booklets and one directions for administering; $280.40 per complete grades 2–8 package including 25 each of three reading passages, three sets of guided-writing-activity blackline masters, directions for administering, three packages of 25 response forms, and response form directions; $28.10 per grade 1 examination kit including student booklet, directions for administering, and one passage-specific scoring rubric; $35.50 per grades 2–8 examination kit including one each of reading passage, guided-writing-activity blackline master, response form, response form directions, directions for administering, and one passage-specific scoring rubric; $40.30 per grade 1 activity package including 25 of one student booklet and directions for administering; $100.20 per grades 2–8 activity package including 25 of one reading passage, one directions for administering, and one guided-writing activity blackline master; $9 per grades 2–8 response form package; $10.60 per grades 1–8 directions for administering; $23.30 per grades 1–8 scoring guides; $37.10 per 25 grade 1 reading passage only; $91.20 per 25 grades 2–8 reading passage only; $20.10 per grades 2–8 guided-writing-activity blackline masters; $55 per technical report (1991, 53 pages); $324.90 per scoring workshop kit including videotape, trainer's manual, 25 overhead transparencies, and blackline

masters of model papers and training papers; $200.30 per portfolio starter kit including classroom storage box, 25 student portfolios, and teacher's manual; $64.10 per 25 student portfolio folders; $64.10 per teacher's manual; $98.60 per introductory videotape and viewer's guide; $6.60 per basic scoring service including list report and summary.
Time: (120–240) minutes.

1) *IAS–Language Arts, Spanish Edition.*
Scores: Same as *a* above.
Price Data: $28 per grade 1 examination kit including student booklet, directions for administering, and a passage-specific scoring rubric; $33 per grades 2–8 examination kit including one each of reading passage, guided-writing-activity blackline master, response form, response form directions, directions for administering, and passage-specific scoring rubric; $38.70 per grade 1 activity package including 25 copies of one student booklet and one directions for administering; $97 per grades 2–8 activity package including 25 copies of one reading passage, one directions for administering, and one guided-writing-activity blackline master; $9 per grades 2–8 response form package including 25 response forms and one response form directions; $10.60 per grades 1–8 directions for administering; $22.80 per grades 1–8 scoring guides; $36 per 25 grade 1 reading passage; $88 per 25 grades 2–8 reading passage; $18.60 per grades 2–8 guided-writing-activity blackline masters; $6.60 per basic scoring service including list report and summary.

b) IAS-MATHEMATICS.
Population: Grades 1–9.
Scores, 4: Reasoning, Conceptual Knowledge, Communication, Procedures.
Price Data: $28.10 per examination kit including one of each student booklet, directions for administering, and scoring rubric; $40.90 per activity package including 25 student booklets and one directions for administering; $11.70 per directions for administering; $24.40 per scoring guides; $180.70 per scoring training kit including binder and overhead transparencies; $8 per basic scoring service (holistic only).
Time: (80–90) minutes.

c) IAS-SCIENCE.
Population: Grades 1–8.
Scores, 4: Experimenting, Collecting Data, Drawing Conclusions, Communicating.
Price Data: $27 per examination kit including one each of student booklet, directions for administering, and scoring rubric; $40.90 per activity package including 25 student booklets and one directions for administering; $11.70 per directions for ad-

ministering; $24.40 per scoring guides; $45.60 per manipulative materials; $179 per scoring workshop kit including trainer's manual; $8 per basic scoring service (holistic only).
Time: (80–90) minutes.
Cross References: For reviews by Gabriel M. Della-Piana and Bikkar S. Randhawa, see 13:152.

[1326]

Integrated Writing Test.

Purpose: "Designed to evaluate major components of good writing in students' writing samples."
Population: Grades 2–12.
Publication Date: 1993.
Acronym: IWT.
Scores, 7: Productivity, Clarity, Vocabulary, Spelling, Punctuation, Legibility, Total Test Language Quotient.
Administration: Group.
Levels, 5: Grades 2/3, Grade 4, Grades 5/6, Grades 7 to 9, Grades 10 to 12.
Price Data, 2001: $131.95 per kit including manual (66 pages) and 35 booklets for each grade level; $22.95 per package of 35 booklets; $22.95 per manual.
Time: 15(20) minutes.
Comments: Academic extension of the Developmental Test of Visual-Motor Integration (119); also based upon the National Assessment of Educational Progress Writing Test.
Authors: Keith E. Beery with assistance from the Integrated Teaching Team.
Publisher: Golden Educational Center.
Cross References: For reviews by C. Dale Carpenter and Richard M. Wolf, see 14:181.

[1327]

Interest-A-Lyzer Family of Instruments.

Purpose: Series of instruments "designed to assess various aspects of student interests."
Publication Dates: 1982–1997.
Administration: Group.
Price Data, 2004: $15.95 per manual (1997, 80 pages); $29.95 per 30 Interest-A-Lyzer Forms (specify level); $22.95 per 30 Art Interest-A-Lyzer Forms (specify level); $14.95 per My Book of Things and Stuff (1982, 60 pages).
Time: Untimed.
Author: Joseph S. Renzulli.
Publisher: Creative Learning Press, Inc.

a) INTEREST-A-LYZER.
Population: Grades 4–8.
Scores, 10: Performing Arts, Creative Writing and Journalism, Mathematics, Business Management, Athletics, History, Social Action, Fine Arts and Crafts, Science, Technology.
b) PRIMARY INTEREST-A-LYZER.
Population: Grades Kindergarten–3.

Scores, 10: Same as *a* above.
Authors: Joseph S. Renzulli and Mary G. Rizza.
c) SECONDARY INTEREST-A-LYZER.
Population: Grades 7–12.
Scores, 10: Same as *a* above.
Authors: Thomas P. Hebert, Michelle F. Sorensen, and Joseph S. Renzulli.
d) PRIMARY ART INTEREST-A-LYZER.
Purpose: "Invites students to examine their present and potential interest in art."
Population: Grades Kindergarten–3.
Scores, 7: Painting, Drawing, Photography, Sculpture, Printmaking, Commercial Art, Art History.
e) ART INTEREST-A-LYZER.
Purpose: "Invites students to examine their present and potential interest in art."
Population: Grades 4–12.
Scores, 7: Same as *d* above.
f) MY BOOK OF THINGS AND STUFF.
Purpose: Designed to assess students' "special interests and learning styles."
Population: Grades Kindergarten–6.
Publication Date: 1982.
Scores: No scores.
Author: Ann McGreevy.

[1328]

Interest Explorer.

Purpose: Designed "to explore interests combined with academic skills for the purpose of career and educational planning."
Population: Grades 8–12.
Publication Date: 1999.
Scores: Interest Levels in 14 career areas: Animals and Plants, Arts, Business Services, Computer Technology, Customer Services, Educational and Social Services, Engineering Technology, Legal Services, Management and Administration, Mechanical and Craft Technology, Medical Sciences, Physical and Life Sciences and Mathematics, Protective Services, Sales.
Administration: Group.
Levels, 2: 1, 2.
Price Data: Available from publisher.
Time: Less than one class period for Interest Explorer, plus (260) minutes for ITED for complete battery; (160) minutes for ITED Core battery.
Comments: The Interest Explorer is designed to be used in conjunction with The Iowa Tests of Educational Development (1364).
Author: Riverside Publishing.
Publisher: Riverside Publishing.

[1329]

Interference Learning Test.

Purpose: Designed "for detecting and characterizing mild and moderate as well as severe levels of" neuropsychological impairment.

Population: Ages 16 and over.
Publication Date: 1999.
Scores: Learning Performance (List 1 Total Recall, Best Recall, List 2 Total Recall, Added Words, Lost Words, Middle Recall, Recency Minus Primary, Subjective Organization, Category Clustering, Seriation, Intertrial Consistency, New Word Priority, Repeats, Source Errors, Confabulations), Delayed Recall Performance (Short Delay Recall, Long Delay Recall, Cued Recall, Retroactive Inhibition, Cueing Facilitation, Encoding, Rebound), Recognition Performance (Recognition Correct, Overlap Correct, Novel Foil Correct, Indirect Correct), Total.
Administration: Individual.
Price Data, 2006: $165 per kit including manual (186 pages), 5 Response Record Forms, a stimulus booklet, and 5-use disk for computer scoring and interpretation; $55 per stimulus booklet; $55 per manual; $36 per 20 Response Record Forms; $270 per 20-use disk.
Time: (20–30) minutes.
Comments: Computer administration option available.
Authors: Michael M. Schmidt and Frederick L. Coolidge.
Publisher: Western Psychological Services.
Cross References: For reviews by Joan C. Ballard and Shawn Powell, see 15:125.

[1330]

Intermediate Measures of Music Audiation.

Purpose: "To identify children with exceptionally high music aptitude … who can profit from the opportunity to participate in additional group study and special private instruction … to evaluate the comparative tonal and rhythm aptitudes of each child with exceptionally high music aptitude."
Population: Grades 1-4.
Publication Dates: 1978-1982.
Acronym: IMMA.
Scores, 3: Tonal, Rhythm, Composite.
Administration: Group.
Price Data, 2006: $100 per complete kit containing 1 tonal and rhythm compact disc, 100 tonal answer sheets, 100 rhythm answer sheets, 2 sets of scoring masks, 100 profile cards, 4 class record sheets, research monographs, and test manual (1982, 44 pages); $25 per CD; $41.50 per 500 tonal answer sheets; $41.50 per 500 rhythm answer sheets; $5 per set of tonal or rhythm scoring masks; $15.50 per 100 profile cards; $2 per 10 class record sheets; $20 per manual.
Time: (20) minutes per Tonal test; (20) minutes per Rhythm test.
Comments: Advanced version of the Primary Measures of Music Audiation (2125); tests administered by CD.
Author: Edwin E. Gordon.
Publisher: GIA Publications, Inc.

[1331]

Internalized Shame Scale.

Purpose: Developed to measure an individual's feelings of shame and the negative response patterns that result from internalized chance.
Population: Age 13 and older.
Publication Date: 2001.
Acronym: ISS.
Scores, 2: Shame, Self-Esteem.
Administration: Individual or group.
Price Data, 2011: $131 per complete kit including technical manual (114 pages), 25 QuikScore forms, and 25 patient handouts; $62 per technical manual; $50 per 25 QuikScore forms; $34 per 25 patient handouts.
Time: 15 minutes.
Comments: Self-completed.
Author: David R. Cook.
Publisher: Multi-Health Systems, Inc.
Cross References: For reviews by Sean P. Reilley and by Susan M. Swearer and Kelly Brey Love, see 16:113.

[1332]

International Personality Disorder Examination.

Purpose: To "diagnose personality disorders using DSM-IV or ICD-10 criteria."
Population: Adults.
Publication Dates: 1988–1999.
Acronym: IPDE.
Scores: 11 scores for DSM-IV version: Paranoid, Schizoid, Schizotypal, Antisocial, Borderline, Histrionic, Narcissistic, Avoidant, Dependent, Obsessive-Compulsive, Not Otherwise Specified; 10 scores for ICD-10 version: Paranoid, Schizoid, Dissocial, Emotionally Unstable/Impulsive Type, Emotionally Unstable/Borderline Type, Histrionic, Anankastic, Anxious (Avoidant), Dependent, Unspecified.
Administration: Individual.
Parts, 2: DSM-IV Module, ICD-10 Module.
Price Data, 2006: $185 per introductory kit including professional manual, 25 screening questionnaires (specify for DSM-IV or ICD-10), 15 scoring booklets (specify DSM-IV or ICD-10), and 50 answer sheets (specify DSM-IV or ICD-10).
Time: [60–120] minutes.
Comments: Complete administration includes a self-administered questionnaire as well as a clinical interview with client/subject.
Author: Armand W. Loranger.
Publisher: Psychological Assessment Resources, Inc.
Cross References: For reviews by Felito Aldarondo and Kwong-Liem Karl Kwan and by Gregory J. Boyle, see 15:126.

[1333]

Interpersonal Adjective Scales.

Purpose: "A self-report instrument designed to measure two important dimensions of interpersonal transactions: Dominance and Nurturance."

Population: Ages 18 and up.
Publication Date: 1995.
Acronym: IAS.
Scores, 10: Assured-Dominant, Arrogant-Calculating, Cold-hearted, Aloof-Introverted, Unassured-Submissive, Unassuming-Ingenious, Warm-Agreeable, Gregarious-Extraverted, Dominance, Nurturance.
Administration: Individual or group.
Price Data, 2005: $109 per introductory kit including manual (143 pages), 25 test booklets, 25 scoring booklets, and 25 glossaries.
Time: (15–20) minutes.
Comments: Separate norms are available for college students and adults; glossary is included to be used by subjects during testing.
Author: Jerry S. Wiggins.
Publisher: Psychological Assessment Resources, Inc.
Cross References: For reviews by Steven J. Lindner and Gerald R. Schneck, see 14:184; see also T5:1288 (2 references).

[1334]

Interpersonal Behavior Survey.

Purpose: "Developed to distinguish assertive behaviors from aggressive behaviors."
Population: Grades 9–16 and adults.
Publication Date: 1980.
Acronym: IBS.
Scores, 21: Denial, Infrequency, Impression Management, General Aggressiveness–Rational, Hostile Stance, Expression of Anger, Disregard for Rights, Verbal Aggressiveness, Physical Aggressiveness, Passive Aggressiveness, General Assertiveness–Rational, Self-Confidence, Initiating Assertiveness, Defending Assertiveness, Frankness, Praise, Requesting Help, Refusing Demands, Conflict Avoidance, Dependency, Shyness, plus additional scores (General Aggressiveness–Empirical, General Assertiveness–Empirical) and 10 short-form scores.
Administration: Group.
Price Data, 2006: $143 per complete kit including 5 reusable administration booklets, 50 profile forms, 50 answer sheets, set of scoring keys, manual (78 pages), and 25 autoscore forms for the short form IBS; $27.50 per 10 administration booklets; $32.50 per set of scoring keys; $27.50 per 100 answer sheets; $27.50 per 100 profiles; $52.25 per manual.
Time: 45 minutes.
Comments: Self-report inventory.
Authors: Paul A. Mauger, David R. Adkinson, Suzanne K. Zoss (test), Gregory Firestone (test), and J. David Hook (test).
Publisher: Western Psychological Services.
Cross References: See T5:1290 (4 references) and T4:1251 (5 references); for reviews by Stephen L. Franzoi and Robert R. Hutzell, see 9:518.

[1335]
Interpersonal Communication Inventory.

Purpose: To assess "a client's interpersonal communication as it provides clues to communication difficulties outside of the family relationship."
Population: Grade 9 to adult.
Publication Dates: 1969-1976.
Acronym: ICI.
Scores, 12: Self-Disclosure, Awareness, Evaluation and Acceptance of Feedback, Self-Expression, Attention, Coping with Feelings, Clarity, Avoidance, Dominance, Handling Differences, Perceived Acceptance, Total.
Administration: Group.
Price Data, 1993: $.75 per inventory; $3.50 per guide (1976, 15 pages).
Time: (20) minutes.
Author: Millard J. Bienvenu.
Publisher: Millard J. Bienvenu, Northwest Publications.
Cross References: See T5:1292 (1 reference), T4:1253 (3 references), and T3:1171 (2 references); see also 8:589 (3 references) and T2:1241 (1 reference).

[1336]
Interpersonal Intelligence Inventory.

Purpose: Intended "to identify the teamwork skills individuals demonstrate" in cooperative learning situations.
Population: Grade 6-adult.
Publication Date: 2002.
Acronym: III.
Scores, 5: Attends to Teamwork, Seeks and Shares Information, Communicates with Teammates, Thinks Critically and Creatively, Gets Along with Team.
Administration: Group.
Price Data: See www.ststesting.com for up-to-date pricing information.
Time: Varies.
Comments: Test can be administered in middle schools, high schools, colleges, and universities.
Authors: Paris S. Strom and Robert D. Strom.
Publisher: Scholastic Testing Service, Inc.
Cross References: For reviews by Bruce Biskin and Arthur S. Ellen, see 17:91.

[1337]
Interpersonal Relations Questionnaire.

Purpose: "To identify specific problems in connection with interpersonal relations and identity formation."
Population: "White pupils" in Standards 5-7 in South African schools.
Publication Dates: 1981-1988.
Acronym: IRQ.
Scores, 13: Self-Confidence, Self-Esteem, Self-Control, Nervousness, Health, Family Influences, Personal Freedom, Sociability A, Sociability T, Sociability D, Moral Sense, Formal Relations, Lie Scale.

Administration: Group.
Price Data: Available from publisher.
Time: (105-120) minutes.
Comments: Supplementary manual in English and Afrikaans.
Authors: Marianne Joubert and Dawn Schlebusch (supplementary manual).
Publisher: Human Sciences Research Council [South Africa].

[1338]
Interpersonal Style Inventory.

Purpose: To measure "an individual's characteristic ways of relating to other people ... also evaluates style of impulse control and characteristic modes of dealing with work and play."
Population: Ages 14 and over.
Publication Dates: 1977-1986.
Acronym: ISI.
Scores: 15 in 5 areas: Interpersonal Involvement (Sociable, Help Seeking, Nurturant, Sensitive), Socialization (Conscientious, Trusting, Tolerant), Autonomy (Directive, Independent, Rule Free), Self-Control (Deliberate, Orderly, Persistent), Stability (Stable, Approval Seeking).
Administration: Group.
Price Data, 2006: $99 per complete kit including 2 reusable administration booklets, 20 AutoScore™ answer forms, and manual (1986, 69 pages); $32.50 per 10 administration booklets; $54.50 per manual; $42.50 per 20 AutoScore™ answer forms; $21.90 per 20 profile sheets for adolescents; $13.75 per mail-in answer sheet; $8.80 per FAX service scoring charge.
Time: 30 minutes.
Authors: Maurice Lorr and Richard P. Youniss.
Publisher: Western Psychological Services.
Cross References: See T5:1294 (4 references) and T4:1256 (6 references); for reviews by Randy W. Kamphaus and Gerald L. Stone, see 10:151 (4 references); for reviews by John Duckitt and Stuart A. Karabenick of an earlier edition, see 9:521; see also T3:1173 (1 reference).

[1339]
Interpersonal Style Questionnaire.

Purpose: Designed "to help educators determine their primary interpersonal style."
Population: Educators at grades K-12.
Publication Dates: 1987-1998.
Scores, 4: Achiever, Persuader, Supporter, Analyst.
Administration: Group.
Manual: No manual.
Price Data, 2002: $25 per 20 test booklets.
Time: Administration time not reported.
Comments: Can be used alone or with Working Together, a tool for collaborative teaching, available from publisher.

Author: Anita DeBoer.
Publisher: Sopris West.

[1340]

Interpersonal Trust Surveys.

Purpose: Designed to measure an individual's "propensity to trust and to build trust with other people."
Population: Adults.
Publication Dates: 1996–1997.
Acronym: ITS; ITS-O; OTS.
Administration: Group.
Scores, 6: Shares Information, Reduces Control, Allows for Mutual Influences, Clarifies Expectations, Meets Others' Expectations, Total.
Forms, 3: Interpersonal Trust Survey, Interpersonal Trust Survey–Observer, Organizational Trust Survey.
Price Data: Available from publisher.
Time: Administration time not reported.
Comments: Scored for "My Behavior" and "Others' Behavior"; can be used as part of an educational workshop in interpersonal trust or as a tool for counseling; based on the "behavioral model of interpersonal trust"; scoring software available (must be run with Microsoft Excel).
Author: Guy L. DeFuria.
Publisher: Jossey-Bass, A Wiley Company.
Cross References: For a review by Mark E. Sibicky, see 14:185.

[1341]

Intuitive Mechanics (Weights & Pulleys).

Purpose: "To measure the ability to understand mechanical relationships, to visualize internal movement in a mechanical system."
Population: Industrial positions.
Publication Dates: 1956–1984.
Scores: Total score only.
Administration: Individual or group.
Price Data, 2002: $91 per start-up kit including 25 test booklets, score key, and interpretation and research manual; $54 per 25 test booklets (quantity discounts available); $20 per score key; $28 per interpretation and research manual.
Time: (3) minutes.
Authors: L. L. Thurstone and T. E. Jeffrey.
Publisher: Pearson Performance Solutions [No reply from publisher; status unknown].
Cross References: For a review by William A. Owens, see 9:523.

[1342]

Inventory for Client and Agency Planning.

Purpose: Developed "to assess the status, adaptive functioning, and service needs of clients."
Population: Infant to adult.
Publication Date: 1986.

Acronym: ICAP.
Scores, 10: Maladaptive Behavior Indexes (Internalized, Asocial, Externalized, General), Adaptive Behavior (Motor Skills, Social and Communication Skills, Personal Living Skills, Community Living Skills, Total), Broad Independence Service Level Index.
Administration: Individual.
Price Data, 2006: $167.50 per complete kit in English or Spanish including examiner's manual (165 pages) and 25 test records; $106 per examiner's manual; $65 per 25 test records.
Foreign Language Edition: Also available in Spanish.
Time: (20–30) minutes.
Comments: Statistically related to the Scales of Independent Behavior (2352) and the Woodcock-Johnson Psycho-Educational Battery (2952); to be completed by "a respondent who has known a client for at least 3 months and who sees him or her on a day-to-day basis."
Authors: Robert H. Bruininks, Bradley K. Hill, Richard F. Weatherman, and Richard W. Woodcock.
Publisher: Riverside Publishing.
Cross References: See T5:1300 (11 references) and T4:1260 (3 references); for reviews by Ronn Johnson and Richard L. Wikoff, see 10:152.

[1343]

Inventory of Altered Self-Capacities.

Purpose: Designed to assess difficulties in relatedness, identity, and affect control.
Population: Age 18 and above.
Publication Dates: 1998–2000.
Acronym: IASC.
Scores, 11: Interpersonal Conflicts, Idealization–Disillusionment, Abandonment Concerns, Identity Impairment, Self-Awareness, Identity Diffusion, Susceptibility to Influence, Affect Dysregulation, Affect Skill Deficits, Affect Instability, Tension Reduction Activities.
Administration: Group or individual.
Price Data, 2006: $175 per introductory kit including 25 reusable item booklets, 50 hand-scorable answer sheets, 50 profile forms, and professional manual (2000, 49 pages).
Time: [15–20] minutes.
Author: John Briere.
Publisher: Psychological Assessment Resources, Inc.
Cross References: For a review by Rosemary Flanagan, see 15:127.

[1344]

Inventory of Anger Communication.

Purpose: "To identify the subjective and interactional aspects of anger in assessing how one communicates around anger."
Population: High school and adults.
Publication Dates: 1974-1976.

Acronym: IAC.
Scores: Total score only.
Administration: Group.
Price Data, 1993: $.75 per inventory; $2 per manual (1976, 10 pages).
Time: [15-20] minutes.
Author: Millard J. Bienvenu.
Publisher: Millard J. Bienvenu, Northwest Publications.
Cross References: For additional information, see 8:591 (1 reference).

[1345]

Inventory of Drinking Situations.

Purpose: "Designed to assess situations in which a client drank heavily over the past year."
Population: Ages 18 to 75.
Publication Date: 1987.
Acronym: IDS.
Scores, 8: Personal Status (Unpleasant Emotions, Physical Discomfort, Pleasant Emotions, Testing Personal Control, Urges and Temptations), Situations Involving Other People (Conflict with Others, Social Pressure to Drink, Pleasant Times with Others).
Administration: Group.
Forms, 2: IDS-100, IDS-42 (Brief Version).
Price Data, 2002: C$25 per specimen set including user's guide (53 pages), 25 questionnaires, 25 answer sheets, 25 profiles; C$13.50 per user's guide; C$12.75 per 25 IDS-42 (Brief Version) questionnaires, 25 answer sheets, and 25 profile sheets; C$14.75 per 25 IDS-100 questionnaires, 25 answer sheets, and 25 profile sheets.
Foreign Language Edition: Both forms available in French.
Time: (20–25) minutes.
Comments: IDS-42 (Brief Version) is for research use only.
Authors: Helen M. Annis, J. Martin Graham, and Christine S. Davis.
Publisher: Centre for Addiction and Mental Health [Canada].
Cross References: See T5:1304 (1 reference); for reviews by Merith Cosden and Kevin L. Moreland, see 13:155 (3 references); see also T4:1265 (2 references).

[1346]

Inventory of Drug Taking Situations.

Purpose: "Designed primarily as an assessment instrument, the IDTS generates an individualized profile detailing situations in which a client has used alcohol and/or other drugs over the past year."
Population: Drug or alcohol users.
Publication Date: 1997.
Acronym: IDTS.
Scores: Situation profiles in three areas: Negative Situations, Positive Situations, Temptation Situations;

8 subscales: Unpleasant Emotions, Physical Discomfort, Pleasant Emotions, Testing Personal Control, Urges/Temptations to Use, Conflict with Others, Social Pressure to Use, Pleasant Times with Others.
Administration: Group.
Price Data, 2002: C$34.95 per user's guide; C$14.95 per 30 questionnaires (specify alcohol or drug); C$39.95 per sample pack including user's guide, and 40 questionnaires (10 alcohol and 30 drug);C$75 per 50 uses of computer-administration software (DOS format); C$100 per 50 uses of software with user's guide; C$250 per 200 uses of software; C$275 per 200 uses of software with user's guide.
Time: (15) minutes per each drug class.
Comments: User's guide written in both English (150 pages) and French (72 pages); French version of IDTS have not been scientifically validated; "The IDTS is administered separately for each of the client's major substances of abuse, not once for the client's overall use of drugs."
Authors: Helen M. Annis, Nigel E. Turner, and Sherrilyn M. Sklar.
Publisher: Centre for Addiction and Mental Health [Canada].
Cross References: For reviews by Tony Cellucci and Glenn B. Gelman, see 14:186.

[1347]

Inventory of Learning Processes–R.

Purpose: To measure learning styles of college and university students.
Population: College and university students.
Publication Dates: 1977–1992.
Acronym: ILP-R.
Scores, 14: Academic Self-Concept (Intrinsic Motivation, Self-Efficacy, Non-reiterative Processing, Self-Esteem, Total), Reflective Processing (Deep Processing, Elaborative Processing, Self-Expression, Total), Agentic Processing (Conventional, Serial Processing, Fact Retention, Total), Methodical Study.
Administration: Group.
Price Data: Price information available from publisher for test booklet (includes answer sheets).
Time: Administration time not reported.
Authors: Ronald R. Schmeck and Elke Geisler-Bernstein.
Publisher: Ronald R. Schmeck (the author).
Cross References: For reviews by Kusum Singh and Gerald L. Stone, see 13:156 (5 references).

[1348]

Inventory of Legal Knowledge.

Purpose: "Designed to assist the forensic examiner in assessing response styles of defendants undergoing evaluations of adjudicative competence" and to measure

"a defendant's approach to inquiries about his or her legal knowledge."
Population: Ages 12 and over.
Publication Date: 2010.
Acronym: ILK.
Scores: Total score only.
Administration: Individual.
Price Data, 2010: $129 per complete kit including 10 reusable item booklets, 25 response sheets, and manual (56 pages); $40 per 10 reusable item booklets; $55 per 25 response sheets; $45 per manual.
Time: (15) minutes.
Comments: "The ILK is not a test of adjudicative competence....The ILK is solely a measure of response style; more specifically, it is a measure of a defendant's approach to inquiries about his or her legal knowledge."
Authors: Randy K. Otto, Jeffrey E. Musick, and Christina B. Sherrod.
Publisher: Psychological Assessment Resources, Inc.

[1349]

Inventory of Offender Risk, Needs, and Strengths.

Purpose: Designed "to identify static, dynamic, and protective factors related to offender risk, treatment need, and management."
Population: Ages 18 and older.
Publication Date: 2006.
Acronym: IORNS.
Scores, 28: Overall Risk Index, Static Risk Index, Criminal Orientation, Psychopathy, Intra/Interpersonal Problems, Alcohol Drug Problems, Aggression, Negative Social Influence, Dynamic Need Index, Personal Resources, Environmental Resources, Protective Strength Index, Favorable Impression, Procriminal Attitudes, Irresponsibility, Manipulativeness, Impulsivity, Angry Detachment, Esteem Problems, Relational Problems, Hostility, Aggressive Behaviors, Negative Friends, Negative Family, Cognitive/Behavioral Regulation, Anger Regulation, Education/Training, Inconsistent Response Style.
Administration: Individual or group.
Price Data, 2008: $142 per professional manual (129 pages), 25 response forms, and 25 scoring summary/profile forms.
Time: (20) minutes.
Author: Holly A. Miller.
Publisher: Psychological Assessment Resources, Inc.
Cross References: For reviews by Sheri Bauman and by Geoffrey L. Thorpe and Lindsay R. Owings, see 18:61.

[1350]

Inventory of Perceptual Skills.

Purpose: "Assesses visual and auditory perceptual skills."
Population: Ages 5–10.
Publication Date: 1983.

Acronym: IPS.
Scores, 11: Visual Perception Skills (Visual Discrimination, Visual Memory, Object Recognition, Visual-Motor Coordination, Total), Auditory Perception Skills (Auditory Discrimination, Auditory Memory, Auditory Sequencing, Auditory Blending, Total), Total.
Administration: Individual.
Price Data, 2005: $45 per complete kit including manual (16 pages), stimulus cards, student workbook, and record books; $20 per 10 student record books; $15 per manual; $15 per stimulus cards; $6 per student workbook.
Time: (15) minutes.
Author: Donald R. O'Dell.
Publisher: Stoelting Co.
Cross References: For reviews by Donna Spiker and by Logan Wright, Tim Eck, and Natasha Gwartney, see 12:193.

[1351]

Inventory of Positive Thinking Traits.

Purpose: "Designed to assess the attitudes of individuals in terms of their positivity and negativity."
Population: Adults and adolescents.
Publication Date: 1992.
Scores: Total score only.
Administration: Individual and group.
Price Data, 1998: $.50 per inventory; $1 per guide.
Time: (10) minutes.
Author: Millard J. Bienvenu.
Publisher: Millard J. Bienvenu, Northwest Publications.
Cross References: For a review by Peggy E. Gallaher, see 13:157.

[1352]

An Inventory of Religious Activities and Interests.

Purpose: "Measures interest in activities performed by persons employed in a variety of church-related occupations."
Population: High school and college.
Publication Dates: 1967–1970.
Acronym: IRAI.
Scores: 11 scales: Counselor, Administrator, Teacher, Scholar, Evangelist, Spiritual Guide, Preacher, Reformer, Priest, Musician, Check Scale.
Administration: Group.
Price Data: Available from publisher.
Time: (40–45) minutes for both forms.
Comments: For research use only.
Authors: Sam C. Webb and Richard A. Hunt.
Publisher: Ministry Inventories.
Cross References: See T2:1025A (2 references); for a review by Donald G. Zytowski, see 7:1023.

[1353]

Inventory of School Effectiveness.

Purpose: Designed as a rating by staff of practices and conditions that contribute to improved student performance.

Population: Administrators, teachers, and support staff.
Publication Date: 2005.
Scores: 11 topics: Research-Based Practices (Expect Results, Monitor Performance, Support Student Learning, Maximize Teacher's Effectiveness, Develop a Professional Learning Community, Lead for Improvement), Organizational Conditions for Improving Schools (Quality Teachers, Effective Leadership, Quality Information, Policies and Procedures, Resources and Support Systems).
Administration: Group.
Price Data, 2006: $25 per 25 inventories; administrative manual may be downloaded free from publisher webpage.
Time: (20) minutes.
Comments: Web-based and paper-based; unlimited items can be added to the web-based version; schools can use the "A and B" line to add additional demographic items to the paper version.
Author: National Study of School Evaluation.
Publisher: National Study of School Evaluation.

[1354]

Inventory of Suicide Orientation-30.
Purpose: "To assess and help identify adolescents who are at risk for suicide orientation by measuring the strength of their suicide orientation."
Population: Adolescents.
Publication Dates: 1988–1994.
Acronym: ISO-30.
Scores, 2: Final Raw Score, Final Critical Item Score.
Administration: Group.
Price Data, 2006: $55 per 25 hand-scored answer sheets with test; $25.50 per 25 Q Local answer sheets with test items; $3.95 per Q Local report; quantity discounts available for the reports; price information for Spanish materials available from publisher.
Foreign Language Edition: Hispanic edition available.
Time: [10] minutes.
Authors: John D. King and Brian Kowalchuk.
Publisher: Pearson.
Cross References: For a review by George Domino, see 13:158.

[1355]

Inventory of Vocational Interests: Acorn National Aptitude Tests.
Purpose: Designed to provide evidence of vocationally significant interests.
Population: Grades 7–16 and adults.
Publication Dates: 1943–1960.
Scores, 5: Mechanical, Academic, Artistic, Business and Economic, Farm-Agricultural.
Administration: Group.
Price Data, 2001: $4 per specimen set.
Time: (35) minutes.
Authors: Andrew Kobal, J. Wayne Wrightstone, and Karl R. Kunze.

Publisher: Psychometric Affiliates.
Cross References: For a review by John W. French, see 6:1060; for reviews by Marion A. Bills, Edward S. Bordin, Harold D. Carter, and Patrick Slater, see 3:638.

[1356]

InView.
Purpose: "A cognitive abilities test ... measur[ing] selected verbal, nonverbal, and quantitative reasoning abilities ... important for success in an educational program."
Population: Grades 2–12.
Publication Date: 2001.
Scores, 8: 5 subtest scores (Sequences, Analogies, Quantitative Reasoning, Verbal Reasoning–Words, Verbal Reasoning–Context); 3 composite scores (Verbal Composite, Nonverbal Composite, Total Test Scale Score).
Administration: Group.
Levels, 6: 1 (Grades 2–3), 2 (Grades 4–5), 3 (Grades 6–7), 4 (Grades 8–9), 5 (Grades 10–11), 6 (Grades 11–12).
Price Data, 2006: $109 per 25 InView-1 consumable test books; $85 per 25 InView 2–6 reusable test books (specify level); $37 per 50 InView 2–6 answer sheets; $1,408 per 2,500 InView continuous form answer sheets; $26 per InView 2–6 stencil set (specify level); $23 per examiner's manual, specify level); $41 per Teacher's Guide to InView, Technical Bulletin 1, Technical Report (CD-ROM version), or Norms Book (all levels); $3.12 per Class Record Sheet for Handscoring.
Time: 95 minutes.
Comments: Replaces the Test of Cognitive Skills, Second Edition (TCS/2); conormed with the Primary Test of Cognitive Skills (PTCS) (see 2126) and with TerraNova, The Second Edition (see T7:2563); Level 1 students record answers in test books; Levels 2–6 students use separate answer sheets; variety of score report formats available; on-line feedback on test performance available, contact publisher for details.
Author: CTB/McGraw-Hill.
Publisher: CTB/McGraw-Hill.
Cross References: For reviews by Russell N. Carney and Bruce Thompson, see 16:114; see T5:2677 for information on the Test of Cognitive Skills, Second Edition; for a review by Randy W. Kamphaus of an earlier edition, see 13:325 (8 references); see also T4:2745 (4 references); for reviews by Timothy Z. Keith and Robert J. Sternberg of an earlier edition, see 9:1248; for a review by Lynn H. Fox and an excerpted review by David M. Shoemaker of the Short Form Test of Academic Aptitude, see 8:202 (9 references).

[1357]

Inwald Personality Inventory [Revised].
Purpose: "To aid public safety/law enforcement and security agencies in selecting new officers."
Population: Public safety, security, and law enforcement applicants (post-conditional job offer only).

Publication Dates: 1980-1992.
Acronym: IPI.
Scores, 26: Guardedness, Externalized Behavior Measures (Actions [Alcohol, Drugs, Driving Violations, Job Difficulties, Trouble with the Law and Society, Absence Abuse], Attitudes [Substance Abuse, Antisocial Attitudes, Hyperactivity, Rigid Type, Type A]), Internalized Conflict Measures (Illness Concerns, Treatment Programs, Anxiety, Phobic Personality, Obsessive Personality, Depression, Loner, Unusual Experiences/Thoughts), Interpersonal Conflict Measures (Lack of Assertiveness, Interpersonal Difficulties, Undue Suspiciousness, Family Conflicts, Sexual Concerns, Spouse/Mate Conflicts).
Administration: Individual or group.
Price Data: Available from publisher.
Time: (30–45) minutes.
Author: Robin Inwald.
Publisher: Institute for Personality and Ability Testing, Inc. (IPAT) - Public Safety & Security Division.
Cross References: See T5:1313 (2 references) and T4:1275 (1 reference); for reviews by Brian Bolton and Richard I. Lanyon, see 12:194; for reviews by Samuel Juni and Niels G. Waller of an earlier edition, see 11:183 (2 references); for reviews by Brian Bolton and Jon D. Swartz of an earlier edition, see 9:530.

[1358]
Inwald Survey 5–Revised.

Purpose: To aid in employee selection by identifying a job candidate's lack of integrity, anger patterns, job performance problems, and domestic difficulties.
Population: All occupations including public safety/security, clerical, managerial, sales, and entry-level.
Publication Dates: 1992-2001.
Acronym: IS5-R.
Scores, 12: Lack of Insight/Candor, Frustration/Anger Patterns, Distrust of Others, Work Adjustment Difficulties, Attitudes (Antisocial Behaviors), Behavior Patterns (Integrity Concerns), Lack of Competitive Motivation, Work Effort Concerns, Lack of Sensitivity, Leadership Avoidance, Introverted Personality Style, Domestic Difficulties.
Administration: Individual or group.
Price Data: Available from publisher.
Time: 15-20 minutes.
Comments: "Appropriate under ADA and can be administered pre-employment."
Authors: Robin Inwald.
Publisher: Institute for Personality and Ability Testing, Inc. (IPAT)- Public Safety & Security Division.

[1359]
Iowa Algebra Aptitude Test™, Fifth Edition.

Purpose: Designed to "help teachers and counselors make the most informed decisions possible regarding the initial placement of students in the secondary mathematics curriculum."
Population: Grades 7-8.
Publication Dates: 1931-2006.
Acronym: IAAT.
Scores, 5: Pre-Algebraic Number Skills and Concepts, Interpreting Mathematical Information, Representing Relationships, Using Symbols, Total.
Administration: Group or individual.
Forms, 2: A, B.
Price Data, 2006: $31 per manual Forms A and B; $78 per 25 test booklets (Form A or B); $8 per Directions for Administration booklet (Forms A and B); $35 per 25 self-scoring answer sheets (Forms A and B); $98 per 100 Mark Reflex answer sheets (Forms A and B); $33 per 25 Report to Families booklets (Forms A and B); $1,250 per Licensed Norms (Forms A and B).
Time: 40 minutes for the battery (i.e., 10 minutes for each of four subtests) plus approximately 10 minutes for distribution and collection of materials.
Comments: "Designed to be used in conjunction with other indicators of student progress, such as grades and teacher evaluations."
Authors: Harold L. Schoen and Timothy N. Ansley.
Publisher: Riverside Publishing.
Cross References: For reviews by David Morse and Bruce G. Rogers, see 17:92; for reviews by John W. Fleenor and Judith A. Monsaas of an earlier edition, see 12:195; see also T2:681 (7 references); for reviews by W. L. Bashaw and Cyril J. Hoyt, and an excerpted review by Russell A. Chadbourn of an earlier edition, see 7:505 (8 references); for reviews by Harold Gulliksen and Emma Spaney of an earlier edition, see 4:393; for a review by David Segel, see 3:327 (2 references); for reviews by Richard M. Drake and M. W. Richardson, see 2:144 (1 reference).

[1360]
Iowa Gambling Task.

Purpose: Designed to detect impaired decision making that is mediated by the prefrontal cortex.
Population: Ages 18 and over.
Publication Dates: 1992-2007.
Acronym: IGT.
Scores, 4: Block Net, Total Money, Deck Selection Frequency, Net Total.
Administration: Individual.
Price Data, 2008: $499 per complete testing kit including professional manual (2007, 71 pages), administration card, quick start guide, and administration software program; $50 per professional manual.
Time: [15-20] minutes to administer and score.
Comments: Test administered and scored via personal computer.
Author: Antoine Bechara.
Publisher: Psychological Assessment Resources, Inc.

Cross References: For reviews by Anita M. Hubley and Matthew E. Lambert, see 18:62.

[1361]

Iowa Parent Behavior Inventory.

Purpose: Designed "to measure parental behavior in relation to a child."
Population: Parents.
Publication Dates: 1976–1979.
Acronym: ITBI.
Administration: Group.
Price Data: Price information available from publisher for test and manual (1979, 41 pages including both forms and score sheet).
Time: Administration time not reported.
Authors: Sedahlia Jasper Crase, Samuel G. Clark, and Damaris Pease.
Publisher: Iowa State University Research Foundation, Inc. [No reply from publisher; status unknown].
  a) MOTHER FORM.
  Publication Date: 1977.
  Scores, 6: Parental Involvement, Limit Setting, Responsiveness, Reasoning Guidance, Free Expression, Intimacy.
  b) FATHER FORM.
  Publication Date: 1977.
  Scores, 5: Parental Involvement, Limit Setting, Responsiveness, Reasoning Guidance, Intimacy.
Cross References: See T5:1316 (2 references) and T4:1278 (3 references); for reviews by Verna Hart and Richard L. Wikoff, see 9:531 (1 reference).

[1362]

Iowa Social Competency Scales.

Purpose: To provide an "easily administered and objectively scored individual rating instrument for parents relative to the social behavior (competencies) of normal children."
Population: Ages 3–12.
Publication Dates: 1976–1982.
Acronym: ISCS.
Administration: Group.
Price Data: Available from publisher.
Time: Administration time not reported.
Comments: Ratings by parents.
Authors: Damaris Pease, Samuel G. Clark, and Sedahlia Jasper Crase.
Publisher: Iowa State University Research Foundation, Inc. [No reply from publisher; status unknown].
  a) PRESCHOOL.
  Population: Ages 3–6.
    1) *Mother.*
    Scores, 5: Social Activator, Hypersensitivity, Reassurance, Uncooperativeness, Cooperativeness.
    2) *Father.*
    Scores, 5: Social Activator, Hypersensitivity, Reassurance, Social Ineptness, Attentiveness.
    3) *Combined.*
    Scores, 3: Social Activator, Hypersensitivity, Reassurance.
  b) SCHOOL-AGE.
  Population: Ages 6–12.
  Comments: Adaptation of Devereux Elementary School Behavior Rating Scale.
    1) *Mother.*
    Scores, 6: Task Oriented, Disruptive, Leader, Physically Active, Affectionate Toward Parent, Apprehensive.
    2) *Father.*
    Scores, 5: Capable, Defiant, Leader, Active with Peers, Affectionate Toward Parent.
Cross References: For a review by Gloria E. Miller, see 10:154; see also 9:532 (2 references).

[1363]

Iowa Tests of Basic Skills®, Forms A and B.

Purpose: Designed to measure skills and achievement in fundamental content areas of school curricula: vocabulary, word analysis, reading comprehension, language arts, mathematics, social studies, science, and sources of information.
Population: Grades K–9.
Publication Dates: 1955–2003.
Acronym: ITBS®.
Administration: Group.
Levels, 10: 5–14.
Forms, 2: A and B; 3 batteries: Complete (Levels 5-14), Core (Levels 7–14 only), and Survey (Levels 7–14 only).
Price Data: Available from publisher.
Comments: Provides scores for both norm-referenced and criterion-referenced interpretations.
Authors: H. D. Hoover, S. B. Dunbar, D. A. Frisbie, K. R. Oberley, V. L. Ordman, R. J. Naylor, G. B. Bray, J. C. Lewis, and A. L. Qualls.
Publisher: Riverside Publishing.
  a) LEVEL 5.
  Population: Grades K.1–1.5.
  Scores, 8: Vocabulary, Word Analysis, Reading Words, Listening, Language, Mathematics, Reading Profile Total, Core Total.
  Time: Untimed, approximately 120-145 minutes.
  b) LEVEL 6.
  Population: Grades K.7–1.9.
  Scores, 10: Same as *a* above, with the addition of Reading Comprehension and Reading Total.
  Time: Untimed, approximately 163 minutes.
  c) LEVELS 7 AND 8.
  Population: Grades 1.7–3.2.
  Scores, 18: Vocabulary, Word Analysis, Reading Comprehension, Reading Total, Listening, Spelling, Language, Math Concepts, Math Problems, Math Computation, Math Total, Core Total, Social Studies, Science, Sources of Information, Composite, Reading Profile Total, Survey Battery Total.

Time: Untimed, approximately 260-284 minutes for Core Battery; approximately 344-374 minutes for Complete Battery; approximately 114-136 minutes for Survey Battery.
d) LEVELS 9–14.
Population: Grades 3.0–9.9.
Scores, 21–23: Vocabulary, Reading Comprehension, Reading Total, Spelling, Capitalization, Punctuation, Usage and Expression, Language Total, Math Concepts and Estimation, Math Problem Solving and Data Interpretation, Math Computation, Math Total, Core Total, Social Studies, Science, Maps and Diagrams, Reference Materials, Sources of Information Total, Word Analysis (Level 9 only), Listening (Level 9 only), Composite, Reading Profile Total (Level 9 only), Survey Battery Total.
Time: 250–360 minutes for Core Battery; 362–515 minutes for Complete Battery; 101–142 minutes for Survey Battery.
Cross References: For reviews by George Engelhard, Jr. and Suzanne Lane, see 17:93; see also T5:1318 (24 references); for reviews by Susan M. Brookhart and Lawrence H. Cross of Forms K, L and M, see 13:159 (110 references); see also T4:1280 (33) references; for reviews by Suzanne Lane and Nambury S. Raju of Form J, see 11:184 (24 references); for reviews by Robert L. Linn and Victor L. Willson of Forms G and H, see 10:155 (45 references); for reviews by Peter W. Airasian and Anthony J. Nitko of Forms 7 and 8, see 9:533 (29 references); see also T3:1192 (97 references); for reviews by Larry A. Harris and Fred Pyrczak of Forms 5-6, see 8:19 (58 references); see T2:19 (87 references) and 6:13 (17 references); for reviews by Virgil E. Herrick, G.A.V. Morgan, and H. H. Remmers, and an excerpted review by Laurence Siegel of Forms 1-2, see 5:16. For reviews of the modern mathematics supplement, see 7:481 (2 reviews).

[1364]

Iowa Tests of Educational Development®, Forms A and B.

Purpose: Designed to "provide objective, norm-referenced information about high school students' development in the skills that are the long-term goals of secondary education."
Population: Grades 9–12.
Publication Dates: 1942–2006.
Acronym: ITED®.
Administration: Group.
Levels, 3: 15, 16, 17/18.
Forms, 2: A, B (parallel forms).
Price Data: Available from publisher.
Special Editions: Braille and large-print editions available.
Authors: R. A. Forsyth, T. N. Ansley, L. S. Feldt, and S. D. Alnot.
Publisher: Riverside Publishing.

a) CORE BATTERY.
Scores, 7: Vocabulary, Reading Comprehension, Language: Revising Written Materials, Spelling, Mathematics: Concepts and Problem Solving, Computation, Total.
Time: (160) minutes.
b) COMPLETE BATTERY.
Scores, 10: Vocabulary, Reading Comprehension, Language: Revising Written Materials, Spelling, Mathematics: Concepts and Problem Solving, Computation, Analysis of Social Studies Materials, Analysis of Science Materials, Sources of Information, Total.
Time: (260) minutes.
Cross References: For reviews by Alan C. Bugbee, Jr. and William D. Schafer, see 16:116; for reviews by William A. Mehrens and Michael J. Subkoviak of an earlier edition, see 13:160 (7 references); see also T4:1281 (4 references); for a review by S. E. Phillips of an earlier edition, see 10:156 (3 references); for reviews by Edward Kifer and James L. Wardrop of an earlier form, see 9:534 (5 references); see also T3:1193 (14 references) for reviews by C. Mauritz Lindvall and John E. Milholland of an earlier form, see 8:20 (15 references); see T2:20 (85 references); for reviews by Ellis Batton Page and Alexander G. Wesman of earlier forms, see 6:14 (23 references); for reviews by J. Murray Lee and Stephen Wiseman, see 5:17 (9 references); for a review by Eric Gardner, see 4:17 (3 references); for reviews by Henry Chauncey, Gustav J. Froehlich, and Lavone A. Hanna, see 3:12.

[1365]

Iowa Tests of Music Literacy, Revised.

Purpose: Assesses "a student's comparative strengths and weaknesses in six dimensions of tonal and rhythm audiation and notational audiation" and compares these scores to the student's "music aptitude."
Population: Grades 4–12.
Publication Dates: 1970–1991.
Scores, 9: Tonal Concepts (Audiation/Listening, Audiation/Reading, Audiation/Writing, Total), Rhythm Concepts (Audiation/Listening, Audiation/Reading, Audiation/Writing, Total), Total.
Administration: Group.
Price Data, 2006: $350 per complete kit for all six levels including manual, six cassette tapes, 50 answer sheets, six record folders, and scoring masks; $90 per complete kit for Level One Only including manual, one cassette tape, scoring masks, 50 answer sheets, and 6 record folders; $8 per 50 tonal answer sheets; $8 per 50 rhythm answer sheets; $15 per 50 cumulative record folders; $3 per 6 class record sheets; $15 per manual; $15 per cassette tape (specify level).
Time: 36(45) minutes for Tonal Concepts; 36(45) minutes for Rhythm Concepts.
Author: Edwin E. Gordon.

Publisher: GIA Publications, Inc.

Cross References: For a review by Rudolf E. Radocy, see 13:161; for a review by Paul R. Lehman of an earlier edition, see 8:97 (16 references); see also T2:199 (5 references) and 7:245 (2 references).

[1366]

IPI Job-Tests Program.

Purpose: "Screening, selection, and promotion of job applicants and employees."

Population: Job applicants and employees in industry.

Publication Dates: 1948–1997.

Administration: Group or individual.

Foreign Language Editions: French and Spanish editions available.

Comments: Program is composed of 19 tests "used in different combinations to form specific batteries for each of the job-test fields"; job fields include Sales Personnel, Medical Office Assistant, Clerical Staff, Dental Technician, and Production/Mechanical.

Author: Industrial Psychology International Ltd.

Publisher: Industrial Psychology International Ltd.

a) OFFICE TERMS.
Price Data, 2010: $30 per 20 test booklets; $35 per introductory kit including 20 test booklets, technical manual, and scoring key.
Time: (6) minutes.

b) NUMBERS.
Price Data: Same as *a* above.
Time: (6) minutes.

c) PERCEPTION.
Price Data: Same as *a* above.
Time: Same as *a* above.

d) JUDGMENT.
Price Data: Same as *a* above.
Time: Same as *a* above.

e) FLUENCY.
Price Data: Same as *a* above.
Time: Same as *a* above.

f) PARTS.
Price Data: Same as *a* above.
Time: Same as *a* above.

g) MEMORY.
Price Data: $44 per 20 test booklets; $49 per introductory kit including 20 test booklets, technical manual, and scoring key.
Time: Same as *a* above.

h) BLOCKS.
Price Data: Same as *a* above.
Time: Same as *a* above.

i) DEXTERITY.
Price Data: Same as *a* above.
Time: (3) minutes.

j) DIMENSION.
Price Data: Same as *a* above.
Time: Same as *a* above.

k) PRECISION.
Price Data: Same as *a* above.
Time: Same as *a* above.

l) TOOLS.
Price Data: Same as a above.
Time: Same as *a* above.

m) MOTOR.
Price Data: $30 per 20 record booklets; $35 per introductory kit including 20 record booklets and technical manual; $160 per motor board.
Time: Same as *a* above.

n) SALES TERMS.
Price Data: Same as *a* above.
Time: (5) minutes.

o) APPLIED MATH.
Price Data: Same as *a* above.
Time: (12) minutes.

p) READING COMPREHENSION.
Price Data: $20 per 10 reusable test booklets; $32 per 20 answer/score sheets; $40 per introductory kit including 5 reusable test booklets, 20 answer/score sheets, and technical manual.
Time: Same as *o* above.

q) CPF SECOND EDITION.
Acronym: CPF.
Price Data: Same as *a* above.
Time: (5-10) minutes.
Author: Samuel E. Krug.

r) NPF SECOND EDITION.
Acronym: NPF.
Price Data: Same as *a* above.
Time: Same as *q* above.
Author: Same as *q* above.

Cross References: For reviews by Laura L. B. Barnes and Mary A. Lewis, see 11:185; see also T2:1078 (12 references); for reviews by William H. Helme and Stanley I. Rubin, see 6:774; for a review by Harold P. Bechtoldt of the Factored Aptitude Series, see 5:602; for a review by D. Welty Lefever and an excerpted review by Laurance F. Shaffer of an earlier edition of this series, see 4:712 (1 reference).

[1367]

IPT Early Literacy Test.

Purpose: Designed to "assess the skill development of English learners in kindergarten and first grade relative to their becoming proficient English language readers and writers."

Population: Grades K-1.

Publication Dates: 2000-2004.

Administration: Group.

Price Data: Available from publisher.

Comments: Measures students' developmental stages of reading and writing and helps educators develop instructional programs tailored to meet students' specific needs.

Authors: Beverly Amori and Enrique F. Dalton.

Publisher: Ballard & Tighe, Publishers.

a) READING.

Scores, 9: Visual Recognition, Letter Recognition, Phonemic-Initial Sounds, Phonics-Initial Blends and Digraphs, Reading Vocabulary, Reading for Life Skills, Reading for Understanding Sentences, Reading for Understanding Stories, Total Reading.

Time: (10-30) minutes.

b) WRITING.

Scores, 5: Copy Letters, Write Name and Copy the Sentence, Descriptive or Narrative Writing, Spelling, Total Writing.

Time: (30-45) minutes.

Cross References: For reviews by Merith Cosden and Patti L. Harrison, see 17:94.

[1368]

IRAOS: Interview for the Retrospective Assessment of the Onset and Course of Schizophrenia and Other Psychoses.

Purpose: Designed to provide "a retrospective assessment of symptoms, disability and social development in schizophrenic and affective illness."

Population: Adults who have schizophrenia.

Publication Dates: 1987–2003.

Acronym: IRAOS.

Scores: Item scores only.

Subtest, 5: General Information, Socio-Demographic and Case History Information, Episodes and Intervals of Mental Disorder, Indicators of Psychiatric Illness, Evaluation of Success of Information.

Administration: Individual.

Price Data, 2011: $298 per kit including manual (2003, 60 pages), 5 interview booklets, 50 score sheets, 50 IND forms, 50 TREAT forms, 50 EPIS forms, 50 time schedules, and 50 calendars of episodes.

Time: (90–120) minutes.

Authors: Heinz Häfner, Walter Löffler, Kurt Maurer, Anita Riecher-Rössler, and Astrid Stein.

Publisher: Hogrefe Publishing.

Cross References: For reviews by Allen K. Hess and Janet V. Smith, see 16:117.

[1369]

Irenometer.

Purpose: Measures attitudes toward peace.

Population: Adults.

Publication Dates: 1984–1985.

Scores: Total score only.

Administration: Group.

Manual: No manual.

Price Data, 2005: $2 per scale

Time: [12] minutes.

Comments: Supplementary article available.

Author: Panos D. Bardis.

Publisher: Donna Bardis.

[1370]

IS Manager/Consultant Skills Evaluation.

Purpose: To assess essential skills needed for the position of IS Manager or IS Consultant.

Population: Candidates for IS Manager or IS Consultant positions.

Publication Date: 1992.

Acronym: BAEDPMC.

Scores: Total Score, Narrative Evaluation, Ranking, Recommendation.

Administration: Group.

Price Data, 2001: $500 per candidate; quantity discounts available.

Time: Administration time not reported.

Comments: Scored by publisher; must be proctored.

Author: Bruce A. Winrow.

Publisher: Walden Personnel Performance, Inc. [Canada].

[1371]

IT Consultant Skills Evaluation.

Purpose: Designed "to evaluate technical, intellectual and supervisory skills required for a senior level IT Consultant, Data Processing Consultant, or IT Trainer."

Population: Candidates for the position of senior level IT Consultant, Data Processing Consultant, or IT Trainer.

Publication Dates: 1988–2002.

Scores, 7: Technical-Analytical Skills (Procedural Ability, Error Recognition, Problem Solving, Business Analysis, Project Management, Planning), Management-Related Skills (Business Judgment).

Administration: Group.

Price Data: Available from publisher.

Foreign Language Editions: Available in French and English.

Time: (180) minutes.

Author: Walden Personnel Performance, Inc.

Publisher: Walden Personnel Performance, Inc. [Canada].

[1372]

ITSEA/BITSEA: Infant-Toddler and Brief Infant-Toddler Social and Emotional Assessment.

Purpose: Designed to identify children "who may have social-emotional and behavioral problems and/or delays, or deficits in social-emotional competence."

Population: Ages 12-0 to 35-1 months.

Publication Date: 2006.

Administration: Individual.

Parts: 2 assessments: Brief Infant Toddler Social Emotional Assessment, Infant Toddler Social Emotional Assessment.

Forms, 2: Parent, Childcare Provider.

Price Data, 2006: $275 per ITSEA/BITSEA comprehensive kit including ITSEA/BITSEA Scoring

Assistant software, ITSEA manual, BITSEA manual, 10 ITSEA Parent Forms, 10 ITSEA Childcare Provider Forms 25 BITSEA Parent Forms, and 25 BITSEA Childcare Provider Forms.

Foreign Language Editions: Parent and Childcare Provider Forms available in Spanish.

Comments: These tests are to be completed by a parent/guardian and a childcare provider; the parent form may be completed as an interview.

Publisher: Pearson.

a) BRIEF INFANT TODDLER SOCIAL EMOTIONAL ASSESSMENT.

Acronym: BITSEA.

Scores, 2: Problem Total, Competence Total.

Price Data: $99 per complete kit including BITSEA manual (2006, 62 pages), 25 BITSEA Parent Forms, and 25 BITSEA Childcare Provider Forms; $50 per BITSEA manual; $35 per 25 BITSEA Parent Forms; $35 per 25 BITSEA Childcare Provider Forms.

Time: (5-10) minutes.

Authors: Margaret J. Briggs-Gowan and Alice S. Carter.

b) INFANT TODDLER SOCIAL EMOTIONAL ASSESSMENT.

Acronym: ITSEA.

Scores, 20: Externalizing (Activity/Impulsivity, Aggression/Defiance, Peer Aggression), Internalizing (Depression/Withdrawal, General Anxiety, Separation Distress, Inhibition to Novelty), Dysregulation (Sleep, Negative Emotionality, Eating, Sensory Sensitivity), Competence (Compliance, Attention, Imitation/Play, Mastery Motivation, Empathy, Prosocial Peer Relations), Maladaptive Item Cluster, Social Relatedness Cluster, Atypical Item Cluster.

Price Data: $150 per complete kit including ITSEA manual (2006, 180 pages), 10 BITSEA Parent Forms, and 10 ITSEA Childcare Provider Forms; $25 per ITSEA manual; $25 per 10 ITSEA Parent Forms; $25 per 10 ITSEA Childcare Provider Forms; $75 per ITSEA Scoring Assistant.

Time: (20-30) minutes.

Authors: Alice S. Carter and Margaret J. Briggs-Gowan.

Cross References: For reviews by Abigail Baxter and Timothy R. Konold, see 17:95.

[1373]

IVA+Plus [Integrated Visual and Auditory Continuous Performance Test].

Purpose: "Designed primarily to help in the diagnosis and quantification of the symptoms of Attention-Deficit/Hyperactivity Disorders (ADHD)."

Population: Ages 6 to adult.

Publication Dates: 1993–2010.

Acronym: IVA+Plus CPT.

Scores, 30: Auditory Response Control Quotient, Prudence Auditory, Consistency Auditory, Stamina Auditory, Visual Response Control Quotient, Prudence Visual, Consistency Visual, Stamina Visual, Full Scale Response Control Quotient, Auditory Attention Quotient, Vigilance Auditory, Focus Auditory, Speed Auditory, Visual Attention Quotient, Vigilance Visual, Focus Visual, Speed Visual, Full Scale Attention Quotient, Fine Motor Regulation Quotient (Hyperactivity), Balance, Readiness Auditory, Readiness Visual, Comprehension Auditory, Comprehension Visual, Persistence Auditory, Persistence Visual, Sensory/Motor Auditory, Sensory/Motor Visual, Sustained Visual Attention, Sustained Auditory Attention.

Administration: Individual.

Price Data, 2010: Option 1: $499 per starter kit with Investigator including CD-ROM, interpretation, administration and technical support manuals (included on CD), and 10 testing administrations (licensed for use at one computer); $249 per 10 additional test administrations for starter kit preferred customer ($399 per 25); Option 2: $1,895 per unlimited use kit with Investigator including CD-ROM, interpretation, administration, and technical support manuals (included on CD), and unlimited testing administrations at one computer station; $99 per preferred customer plan; $25 for a two test trial version; $349 per Interpretive Report Writer Kit; $249 per 10 additional reports; $349 per 25 additional reports $649 per 100 additional reports; discounts apply for customers who choose to participate in the preferred customer plan.

Foreign Language Editions: Option available to allow the test stimuli to be spoken in a foreign language (Arabic, Danish, Dutch, French, German, Greek, Hebrew, Hindi, Indonesian, Italian, Japanese, Mandarin, Pashto, Polish, Portuguese, Russian, Spanish, Swahili, Swedish, Taiwanese Dialect, Turkish, Vietnamese, and Welsh) for an additional charge of $369.

Time: 13[20] minutes.

Comments: Computer administered; requires IBM computer with a Pentium III or higher processor, USB mouse, Windows XP, Vista or 7, Internet Explorer 6.0 or higher, and speakers or headphones; optional analyses (Investigator and Special Analyses) and report writers (Standard Report, ADHD Report) may be added to software; the Preferred Customer Plan provides software and normative updates, free technical support for one year, and discounts on the cost of additional testing administrations and Add-Ons.

Authors: Joseph A. Sandford and Ann Turner.

Publisher: BrainTrain.

Cross References: For reviews by Cleborne D. Maddux and Wes Sime, see 17:96; for reviews by Harrison Kane and Susan C. Whiston and by Martin J. Wiese of an earlier edition, see 14:180.

[1374]

Jackson Personality Inventory–Revised.

Purpose: Designed as a "modern measure of normal personality, useful in counseling and business settings."

Population: Adolescents and adults.
Publication Dates: 1976–1997.
Acronym: JPI-R.
Scores: 15 scales in 5 clusters: Analytical (Complexity, Breadth of Interest, Innovation, Tolerance), Emotional (Empathy, Anxiety, Cooperativeness), Extroverted (Sociability, Social Confidence, Energy Level), Opportunistic (Social Astuteness, Risk Taking), Dependable (Organization, Traditional Values, Responsibility).
Administration: Group or individual.
Price Data, 2010: $92 per examination kit including manual on CD (1994, 138 pages), 5 test booklets, 5 Quick Score answer sheets, 5 profile sheets, and coupon and machine-scorable answer sheet for one Basic Report; $24 per manual on CD; $60 per 25 reusable test booklets; $75 per 25 Quick Score answer sheets; $50 per 25 profile sheets; $65–$75 (depending on volume) per 10 machine-scorable answer sheets and coupons for Basic Reports; $145 per software package including installation package and 10 coupons for computer reports; $12-$20 (depending on volume) per online password.
Foreign Language Edition: Available in French (booklets only).
Time: 45 minutes.
Author: Douglas N. Jackson.
Publisher: SIGMA Assessment Systems, Inc.
Cross References: See T5:1333 (8 references); for reviews by David J. Pittenger and Peter Zachar, see 13:162 (21 references); see also T4:1296 (28 references) and T3:1203 (6 references); for reviews by Lewis R. Goldberg and David T. Lykken of an earlier edition, see 8:593 (6 references).

[1375]

Jackson Vocational Interest Survey [1999 Revision].

Purpose: "Designed to yield … a set of scores representing interests and preferences relevant to work …, conceptualized as work roles and work styles."
Population: High school and above.
Publication Dates: 1977–2000.
Acronym: JVIS.
Scores, 50: 34 Basic Interest Scales (Creative Arts, Performing Arts, Mathematics, Physical Science, Engineering, Life Science, Social Science, Adventure, Nature–Agriculture, Skilled Trades, Personal Service, Family Activity, Medical Service, Dominant Leadership, Job Security, Stamina, Accountability, Teaching, Social Service, Elementary Education, Finance, Business, Office Work, Sales, Supervision, Human Relations Management, Law, Professional Advising, Author—Journalism, Academic Achievement, Technical Writing, Independence, Planfulness, Interpersonal Confidence); 10 General Occupational Themes (Expressive, Logical, Inquiring, Practical, Assertive, Socialized, Helping, Conventional, Enterprising, Communicative); 3 Administrative Indices (Unscorable Responses, Response Consistency Index, Infrequency Index); Academic Satisfaction; Similarity to College Students; Similarity to Occupational Classifications.
Administration: Group or individual.
Price Data, 2010: $110 per examination kit including manual on CD (2000, 149 pages), JVIS Applications Handbook, JVIS Occupations Guide, machine-scorable answer sheet for Extended Report, reusable test booklet, hand-scorable answer and profile sheets, and jvis.com password; $24 per test manual on CD; $50 per JVIS Applications Handbook; $40 per JVIS Occupations Guide (2008); $60 per 25 reusable test booklets; $50 per 25 hand-scorable answer sheets; $50 per 25 profile sheets; $95-$105 per Mail-in Extended Report including machine-scorable answer sheet and laser-printed report; $65-$75 per Mail-in Basic Report including machine-scorable answer sheet; $145 per SigmaSoft JVIS for Windows installation package and 10 coupons; $8-$10 (depending on volume) per online password.
Foreign Language Editions: Available in Spanish (booklets only) and in French (booklets and extended reports; also, online administration using SigmaSoft JVIS for Windows and reports).
Time: 45 minutes.
Comments: Former edition no longer available; available in paper-and-pencil format (hand scoring or mail-in scoring), software administration and scoring available using SigmaSoft JVIS for Windows software; system requirements: SigmaSoft JVIS for Windows also can be used for scoring data scanned by an optical mark reader using SigmaSoft Scanning Utility; SigmaSoft JVIS for Windows produces Basic Report, Extended Report, and Data Report. Online scoring available at www.SigmaTesting.com and www.JVIS.com.
Authors: Douglas N. Jackson and Marc Verhoeve (applications handbook).
Publisher: SIGMA Assessment Systems, Inc.
Cross References: For reviews by Eleanor E. Sanford and Wendy J. Steinberg, see 15:129; see T5:1334 (5 references and T4:1297 (1 reference); for reviews by Douglas T. Brown and John W. Shepard of a previous edition, see 10:158 (1 reference); for reviews by Charles Davidshofer and Ruth G. Thomas, see 9:542; see also T3:1204 (1 reference).

[1376]

Jail Inmate Inventory.

Purpose: "Designed for inmate risk assessment and needs identification"; provides information to "help determine inmate risk, establish supervisory levels and identify readiness for classification or status changes."
Population: Jail inmates with a sixth grade or above reading level.
Publication Dates: 1991–1995.
Acronym: JII.
Scores, 6: Truthfulness, Violence, Antisocial, Adjustment, Alcohol, Drugs.

Administration: Group.
Price Data: Available from publisher.
Foreign Language Edition: Spanish Edition available.
Time: (15–20) minutes.
Comments: Can be administered by paper and pencil or by computer; all scoring is done by computer.
Author: Risk & Needs Assessment, Inc.
Publisher: Behavior Data Systems, Ltd.

[1377]

James Madison Test of Critical Thinking.
Purpose: "Designed to evaluate the in-depth critical thinking ability of middle school students through adults."
Population: Grades 7-12+.
Publication Date: 2004.
Acronym: JMTCT.
Scores: Total score only.
Administration: Individual or group.
Forms, 2: A, B.
Price Data, 2006: $64.99 per 50-use CD (specify form); $103.99 per 50-use CD including both forms; quantity discounts available; $9.99 per test online administration.
Time: 50 minutes.
Comments: Can be administered online, over a network, or on a stand-alone computer (Windows or Macintosh); both forms can be used as a pretest or posttest; formerly known as the Comprehensive Test of Critical Thinking.
Authors: Don Fawkes, Bill O'Meara, and Dan Flage.
Publisher: The Critical Thinking Co.
Cross References: For reviews by Jerrell C. Cassady and Suzanne Young, see 17:97.

[1378]

Jesness Behavior Checklist.
Purpose: "Designed as a multiple rating scale to be used by self and others that measures individuals at risk for antisocial behavior."
Population: Delinquents ages 13-20.
Publication Dates: 1970-1971.
Scores, 14: Unobtrusiveness/Obtrusiveness, Friendliness/Hostility, Responsibility/Irresponsibility, Considerateness/Inconsiderateness, Independence/Dependence, Rapport/Alienation, Enthusiasm/Depression, Sociability/Poor Peer Relations, Conformity/Non-Conformity, Calmness/Anxiousness, Effective Communications/Inarticulateness, Insight/Unawareness and Indecisiveness, Social Control/Attention-Seeking, Anger Control/Hypersensitivity.
Administration: Individual.
Editions, 2: Observer, Self-Appraisal.
Price Data, 2011: $182 per complete kit including 10 Observer item booklets, 25 Observer QuikScore™ forms, 10 Self-Appraisal item booklets, 25 Self-Appraisal QuikScore™ forms, and manual (1971, 32 pages); $37 per 10 Observer item booklets; $37 per 25 Observer QuikScore™ forms; $37 per 10 Self-Appraisal item booklets; $44 per 25 Self-Appraisal QuikScore™ forms; $59 per manual.
Time: (10-20) minutes.
Comments: Software also available (observer and self-appraisal entry sheets).
Author: Carl F. Jesness.
Publisher: Multi-Health Systems, Inc.
Cross References: See T5:1340 (5 references); for reviews by Dorcas Susan Butt and Edwin I. Megargee, see 8:594 (3 references).

[1379]

Jesness Inventory–Revised.
Purpose: Designed to be used as a personality inventory for delinquent and conduct-disordered youths and adults.
Population: Ages 8 and over
Publication Dates: 1962–2003.
Acronym: JI-R.
Scores, 24: Randomness Scale, Lie Scale, Asocial Index, Social Maladjustment, Value Orientation, Immaturity, Autism, Alienation, Manifest Aggression, Withdrawal-Depression, Social Anxiety, Repression, Denial, Conduct Disorder, Oppositional Defiant Disorder, Undersocialized/Active [Unsocialized/Aggressive], Undersocialized/Passive [Unsocialized/Passive], Conformist [Immature Conformist], Group Oriented [Cultural Conformist], Pragmatist [Manipulator], Autonomy-Oriented [Neurotic/Acting-Out], Introspective [Neurotic/Anxious], Inhibited [Situational], Adaptive [Cultural Identifier].
Administration: Individual or Group.
Price Data, 2011: $220 per complete kit including technical manual, 10 item booklets, 25 QuikScore forms, and scoring templates; $87 per technical manual; $29 per 10 reusable item booklets; $61 per 25 QuikScore forms; $87 for scoring templates; $117 per online kit including technical manual and 25 online forms; $1.80 per online form; $205 per software kit (V.5) including technical manual and 25 interpretive reports; $7 per profile report; $12 per interpretive report.
Time: (20-30) minutes.
Comments: Software version available; Web administration available.
Author: Carl F. Jesness.
Publisher: Multi-Health Systems, Inc.
Cross References: For reviews by Elizabeth Kelley Rhoades and Georgette Yetter, see 16:118; for reviews by Robert M. Guion and Susana Urbina of a previous edition, see 14:188; see also T5:1341 (3 references) and T3:1209 (9 references); for a review by Dorcas Susan Butt of an earlier edition, see 8:595 (14 references); see also T2:1249 (5 references); for a review by Sheldon A. Weintraub of the Youth Edition of the earlier edition, see 7:94 (10 references); see also P:133 (3 references).

[1380]

Job Activity Preference Questionnaire.

Purpose: To obtain a measure of job interests or preferences.
Population: Adults.
Publication Dates: 1972–1981.
Acronym: JAPQ.
Scores, 16: Making Decisions/Communicating and Having Responsibility, Operating Vehicles, Using Machines-Tools-Instruments, Performing Physical Activities, Operating Keyboard and Office Equipment, Monitoring and/or Controlling Equipment and/or Processes, Working Under Uncomfortable Conditions, Working with Art-Decor/Entertainment, Performing Supervisory Duties, Performing Estimating Activities, Processing Written Information, Working With Buyers-Customers-Salespersons, Working Under Hazardous Conditions, Performing Paced and/or Repetitive Activities, Working with Aerial and Aquatic Equipment, Catering/Serving/Smelling/Tasting.
Administration: Group.
Price Data: Available from publisher.
Time: Administration time not reported.
Comments: Restructured and simplified version of Position Analysis Questionnaire (2079).
Authors: Robert C. Mecham, Alma F. Harris (test), Ernest J. McCormick (test), and P. R. Jeanneret (test).
Publisher: PAQ Services, Inc.
Cross References: For reviews by Norman G. Peterson and Paul R. Sackett, see 9:547.

[1381]

Job and Vocational Attitudes Assessment Questionnaire and Interview.

Purpose: Designed to assess an employee's readiness to return to work following a positive drug screening or addiction treatment.
Population: Employees.
Publication Dates: 1994-2003.
Acronym: JAVAA.
Scores, 9: Recognition/Status, Job Attitudes, Work Relationships, Desire to Work, Recovery Strategy, Emotional Well-being, Anger Resolution, Insight, Support.
Administration: Individual.
Forms, 2: Questionnaire, Interview Guide.
Price Data, 2008: $62.50 per 25 questionnaire forms; $62.50 per 25 interview forms; $37.50 per 25 summary forms; $15 per manual (2003, 29 pages).
Time: Administration time not reported.
Comments: Materials for questionnaire and interview form are purchased separately.
Author: Norman G. Hoffmann.
Publisher: The Change Companies.

[1382]

Job Attitude Analysis.

Purpose: Devised to "reveal a person's underlying attitudes pertinent for success and satisfaction in his work."
Population: Production and clerical workers.
Publication Dates: 1961–1970.
Acronym: JAA.
Scores: Total score only.
Administration: Group.
Price Data: Available from publisher.
Time: Administration time not reported.
Comments: An inventory for employment interviewing and vocational counseling.
Author: P. L. Mellenbruch.
Publisher: Psychometric Affiliates.
Cross References: For additional information, see 7:980 (1 reference).

[1383]

Job Attitude Scale.

Purpose: Designed to assess intrinsic and extrinsic job orientations.
Population: Adults.
Publication Dates: 1971–1988.
Acronym: JAS.
Scores, 17: Praise and Recognition, Growth in Skill, Creative Work, Responsibility, Advancement, Achievement, Salary, Security, Personnel Policies, Competent Supervision, Relations-Peers, Relations-Subordinates, Relations-Supervisor, Working Conditions, Status, Family Needs-Salary, Total Intrinsic.
Administration: Group.
Forms, 2: Full, Abbreviated.
Price Data: Available from publisher.
Time: (15–20) minutes.
Author: Shoukry D. Saleh.
Publisher: Shoukry D. Saleh [Canada] [No reply from publisher; status unknown].
Cross References: For a review by Gregory J. Boyle, see 11:186; see also 8:1049 (9 references).

[1384]

Job Challenge Profile.

Purpose: "Designed to help managers better understand and see their job assignments as opportunities for learning and growth."
Population: Managers, leaders, and executives.
Publication Date: 1999.
Acronym: JCP.
Scores, 10: Unfamiliar Responsibilities, New Directions, Inherited Problems, Problems with Employees, High Stakes, Scope and Scale, External Pressure, Influence Without Authority, Work Across Cultures, Work Group Diversity.
Administration: Individual.
Price Data, 2006: $30 per Facilitator's Guide (76 pages); $15 per Participant's Workbook/Survey (49 pages); quantity discounts are available.
Time: 15-20 minutes.

Comments: Revision of the Developmental Challenge Profile (DCP; no longer available); self-scored; Facilitator's Guide includes details of workshop procedures, reproducible overheads, and handout masters; Participant's Workbook contains test items and action guide.
Authors: Cynthia D. McCauley (Facilitator's Guide, Participant Workbook/Survey), Patricia J. Ohlott (Facilitator's Guide, Survey), and Marian N. Ruderman (Facilitator's Guide, Survey).
Publisher: Jossey-Bass, A Wiley Company.
Cross References: For reviews by Laura L. B. Barnes and Jean Powell Kirnan, see 16:119; for reviews by Jean Powell Kirnan and Kristen Wojcik and by Eugene P. Sheehan of The Developmental Challenge Profile, see 13:94 (2 references).

[1385]

A Job Choice Decision-Making Exercise.

Purpose: Serves as a behavioral decision theory measurement approach to need for affiliation, need for power, and need for achievement.
Population: High school and college and adults.
Publication Dates: 1981–1986.
Acronym: JCE.
Scores, 3: Affiliation, Power, Achievement.
Administration: Group.
Price Data, 2006: $4 per exercise booklet; $35 per Managerial and Technical Motivation book (1986, 178 pages, available from Praeger Publishers, in lieu of manual).
Time: [15–20] minutes.
Authors: Michael J. Stahl and Anil Gulati (scoring software and scoring manual).
Publisher: Assessment Enterprises.
Cross References: For a review by Nicholas A. Vacc and J. Scott Hinkle, see 11:187.

[1386]

Job Descriptive Index (2009 Revision) and The Job in General Scales (2009 Revision).

Purpose: To measure job satisfaction (facet and/or overall).
Population: Employees.
Publication Dates: 1969–2009.
Acronym: JDI; JIG.
Scores: Five facets (Work on Present Job, Pay, Opportunities for Promotion, Supervision, and People on Your Present Job) and the Job in General.
Administration: Group or individual.
Price Data, 2010: There is no charge to use the copyrighted scales, which can be downloaded at https://webapp.bgsu.edu/jdi/. User manuals, scoring services, and national norms may be purchased by contacting http://www.bgsu.edu/departments/psych/io/jdi.
Time: 5-15 minutes.

Authors: Patricia C. Smith, Lorne M. Kendall, and Charles L. Hulin (1969 edition); William K. Balzer, Jenifer A. Kihm, Patricia C. Smith, Jennifer L. Irwin, Peter D. Bachiochi, Chet Robie, Evan F. Sinar, and Luis F. Parra (1997 edition). Gillespie, J., Balzer, W., Gillespie, M., & Brodke, M. et al. (2009 edition).
Publisher: Bowling Green State University.
Cross References: For a review by Michael R. Harwell, see 15:130; see T5:1348 (16 references); for reviews by Charles K. Parsons and Norman D. Sundberg for an earlier edition of the Job Descriptive Index and Retirement Descriptive Index, see 12:199 (33 references); see also T4:1312 (63 references); for reviews by John O. Crites and Barbara A. Kerr of an earlier edition of the Job Descriptive Index, see 9:550 (49 references).

[1387]

JOB-O E Career Awareness and Planning, 3rd Edition.

Purpose: Designed to "increase students' awareness of their interests and how they may relate to future careers."
Population: Upper elementary and lower middle school students.
Publication Dates: 2003-2008.
Acronym: JOB-OE.
Scores, 6: Doers, Thinkers, Creators, Helpers, Persuaders, Organizers.
Administration: Group.
Price Data, 2008: $4.20 per 9 test booklets (2003, 16 pages); $.57 per 9 answer folders.
Time: Administration time not reported.
Comments: The answer booklet contains open-ended questions to prompt students to learn more about the jobs in which they are interested.
Author: Francis Ferry.
Publisher: CFKR Career Materials, Inc.

[1388]

JOB-O 2000+.

Purpose: Designed to "help students to explore work interests, specific job characteristics, and employment information in order to make a career plan."
Population: Middle school students.
Publication Dates: 2006-2007.
Acronym: JOB-O 2000+.
Scores: No scores.
Administration: Group.
Price Data, 2008: $6.36 per 9 JOB-O 2000+ booklets (2006, 16 pages); $1.31 per 9 answer booklets.
Time: Administration time not reported.
Comments: Students are asked questions about their educational goals and occupational interests that provide them with a numerical profile; they then compare this profile to 120 different career profiles to find a match.
Authors: Arthur Cutler, Francis Ferry, Robert Kauk, and Robert Robinett.
Publisher: CFKR Career Materials, Inc.

[1389]

JOB-O.

Purpose: "To facilitate self-awareness, career-awareness, and career exploration."
Publication Dates: 1981–1992.
Administration: Group.
Price Data: Price information available from publisher.
Comments: Also known as Judgement of Occupational Behavior-Orientation.
Authors: Arthur Cutler, Francis Ferry, Robert Kauk, and Robert Robinett.
Publisher: CFKR Career Materials.
a) JOB-O (ELEMENTARY).
Population: Grades 4–7.
Scores: 6 ratings: Mechanical/Construction/Agriculture, Scientific/Technical, Creative/Artistic, Social/Legal/Educational, Managers/Sales, Administrative Support.
Time: Administration time not reported.
b) JOB-O.
Population: Junior high school through adult.
Scores, 8: Education, Interest, Inclusion, Control, Affection, Physical Activity, Hands/Tools/Machinery, Problem-Solving, Creative-Ideas.
Foreign Language Editions: Spanish and Vietnamese test booklets and answer sheets available.
Time: (60–65) minutes.
c) JOB-O A (ADVANCED).
Population: Grades 10–12 and adult.
Scores, 16: Occupational Interest, Training Time, Reasoning Skills, Mathematical Skills, Language Skills, Working with Data, Working with People, Working with Things, Working Conditions, Physical Demands, Leadership, Helping People, Problem-Solving, Initiative, Team Work, Public Contact.
Time: [50–55] minutes.
Comments: May be self-administered.
Cross References: For reviews by F. Marion Asche and Lawrence H. Cross, see 12:200; for a review by James W. Pinkney of an earlier edition, see 10:160; for a review by Bruce J. Eberhardt of an earlier edition, see 9:560.

[1390]

Job Observation and Behavior Scale.

Purpose: Designed as "a work performance evaluation for supported and entry level employees."
Population: Ages 15 and above.
Publication Dates: 1998–2000.
Acronym: JOBS.
Scores, 4: Work-Required Daily Living Activities, Work-Required Behavior, Work-Required Job Duties, Quality of Performance Composite/Total.
Administration: Individual.
Price Data, 2005: $75 per complete kit including 25 record forms and manual (1998, 28 pages); $30 per 25 record forms; $50 per job manual.

Time: (30) minutes.
Authors: Howard Rosenberg and Michael Brady.
Publisher: Stoelting Co.
Cross References: For reviews by Ayres G. D'Costa and Sheldon Zedeck, see 15:131.

[1391]

Job Readiness Skills Pre- and Post-Assessment.

Purpose: Designed to assess examinees on skills related to employability and work maturity/job retention.
Population: Individuals seeking employment.
Publication Dates: 1984–2000.
Administration: Group or individual.
Manual: No manual.
Price Data, 2002: $18 per specimen set including 5 copies each of Pre- and Post-Assessment forms; $52 per set of 25 assessments (specify Pre- or Post-Assessment).
Time: (45–55) minutes.
Comments: Earlier version entitled Assessing Specific Competencies.
Author: Education Associates, Inc.
Publisher: Education Associates.
a) PRE-ASSESSMENT.
Scores: 9 areas: Career Goals, Finding a Job, Resumes, Job Applications, Interviews, Positive Attitudes, Good Appearance, Communication, Written Communication.
b) POST-ASSESSMENT.
Scores: Same as *a* above.
Cross References: For reviews by Robert Fitzpatrick and Robert C. Reinehr of an earlier edition, see 12:33.

[1392]

Job Search Attitude Inventory, Second Edition.

Purpose: Helps identify personal attitudes about looking for a job.
Population: Adult and teen job seekers and career planners.
Publication Date: 2002.
Acronym: JSAI.
Scores, 4: Luck vs. Planning, Uninvolved vs. Involved, Help from Others vs. Self-Help, Passive vs. Active.
Administration: Group or individual.
Price Data, 2006: $39.95 per 25 inventories including copy of administrator's guide (8 pages).
Time: (10–15) minutes.
Comments: Self-administered and self-scored; revised edition features simplified language and directions, plus added practical advice for becoming more self-directed in a job search.
Author: John J. Liptak.
Publisher: JIST Publishing, Inc.
Cross References: For reviews by John W. Fleenor and Thomas R. O'Neill, see 16:120.

[1393]

Job Search Knowledge Scale.
Purpose: Designed to "measure a person's knowledge about finding a job."
Population: Job seekers.
Publication Date: 2005.
Acronyms: JSKS.
Scores, 5: Identifying Job Leads, Direct Application to Employers, Resumes/Cover Letters, Employment Interviews, Following Up.
Administration: Individual or group.
Price Data, 2006: $34.95 per complete kit including 25 test booklets and administrator's guide (8 pages).
Time: (15-25) minutes.
Comments: This test can be self-administered and self-scored.
Author: John Liptak.
Publisher: JIST Publishing, Inc.
Cross References: For reviews by Gary J. Dean and Keith Hattrup, see 17:98.

[1394]

Job Seeking Skills Assessment.
Purpose: "For assessing clients' ability to complete a job application form and participate in the employment interview, and to serve as a guide for integrating the results into program planning."
Population: Vocational rehabilitation clients.
Publication Date: 1988.
Acronym: JSSA.
Scores, 2: Job Application, Employment Interview.
Administration: Group.
Price Data: Available from publisher.
Time: Administration time not reported.
Comments: Designed as a component of the Diagnostic Employability Profile (DEP).
Authors: Suki Hinman, Bob Means, Sandra Parkerson, and Betty Odendahl.
Publisher: The National Center on Employment & Disability.
Cross References: For reviews by Paul M. Muchinsky and William I. Sauser, Jr., see 12:201.

[1395]

Job Stress Survey.
Purpose: "Designed to assess generic sources of occupational stress encountered by men and women employed in a variety of work settings."
Population: Adults ages 18 and older.
Publication Dates: 1991-1999.
Acronym: JSS.
Scores, 9: Job Stress Index, Job Stress Severity, Job Stress Frequency, Job Pressure Index, Job Pressure Severity, Job Pressure Frequency, Lack of Organizational Support Index, Lack of Organizational Support Severity, Lack of Organizational Support Frequency.
Administration: Group.
Forms, 2: Form HS (Hand-Scorable), Form SP (Scoring Program).
Price Data, 2006: $136 per introductory kit including professional manual (1999, 72 pages), 25 test booklets, 25 profile forms, and scoring software on 3.5-inch disk with 5 free uses of the scoring program.
Time: (10-15) minutes.
Comments: Computer scoring program available; Forms HS and SP are identical in content.
Authors: Charles D. Spielberger and Peter R. Vagg.
Publisher: Psychological Assessment Resources, Inc.
Cross References: For reviews by Peter M. Berger and James W. Pinkney, see 15:132.

[1396]

Job Style Indicator [Revised].
Purpose: Designed to help understand "the work behavioral style and task requirements" of a job and to provide "a job compatibility rating when used with the following CRG Style assessments: Personal, Sales, Instructional, Entrepreneurial, and Quick."
Population: Adults.
Publication Dates: 1988-2006.
Acronym: JSI.
Scores, 4: Behavioral/Action, Cognitive/Analysis, Interpersonal/Harmony, Affective/Expression.
Administration: Individual or group.
Price Data, 2006: $7.95 per test booklet (2006, 12 pages); $7.95 per access code online version; $69.95 per professional's guide (2006, 64 pages).
Time: [30-60] minutes.
Comments: Self-administered and self-scored; may be used in conjunction with Personal Style Indicator (2016), Sales Style Indicator (2331), Quick Style Indicator (2223), Entrepreneurial Style and Success Indicator (1013), and the Instructional Style Indicator (1319).
Authors: Ken Keis, Terry D. Anderson, and Everett T. Robinson.
Publisher: Consulting Resource Group International, Inc.
Cross References: For a review by M. David Miller, see 17:99; for reviews by Neal Schmitt and David M. Williamson of an earlier edition, see 13:164.

[1397]

Job Survival and Success Scale.
Purpose: Designed to "identify a person's attitudes and knowledge about keeping a job and getting ahead in the workplace."
Population: Job seekers.
Publication Date: 2005.
Acronym: JSSS.
Scores, 5: Dependability, Responsibility, Human Relations, Ethical Behavior, Getting Ahead.
Administration: Individual or group.

Price Data, 2006: $37.95 per complete kit including 25 test booklets and administrator's guide (8 pages).
Time: (15-25) minutes.
Comments: This test can be self-administered and self-scored.
Author: John Liptak.
Publisher: JIST Publishing, Inc.
Cross References: For reviews by James T. Austin and Stephanie D. Tischendorf and by Stephen B. Johnson, see 17:100.

[1398]

Johnston Informal Reading Inventory.

Purpose: "To assess the reading comprehension of junior and senior high school students."
Population: Grades 7–12.
Publication Date: 1982.
Acronym: JIRI.
Scores, 2: Vocabulary Screening, Reading Comprehension.
Administration: Group or individual.
Price Data: Available from publisher.
Time: (20) minutes.
Comments: Forms B and C are approximately parallel and Form L is longer; "high-interest materials utilized."
Author: Michael C. Johnston.
Publisher: Educational Publications [No reply from publisher; status unknown].
Cross References: For reviews by Margaret R. Rogers and Claudia R. Wright, see 12:202.

[1399]

Joliet 3-Minute Preschool Speech and Language Screen.

Purpose: "Differentiates individuals with intact skills from those with suspected problems in phonology, semantics, and grammar."
Population: 2.5–4.5 years.
Publication Date: 1992.
Scores: 3 areas: Grammar, Semantics, Phonology.
Administration: Individual.
Price Data: Price data available from publisher for complete kit including 12 vocabulary plates on card stock, 2 reproducible scoring sheets, recordkeeping manual, and manual (57 pages).
Time: (3) minutes.
Author: Mary C. Kinzler.
Publisher: Pearson.
Cross References: For a review by Carlos Inchaurralde, see 14:189.

[1400]

Joliet 3-Minute Speech and Language Screen (Revised).

Purpose: To "identify children with age-appropriate phonological, grammatical, and semantic structures."

Population: Grades K, 2, 5.
Publication Dates: 1983–1992.
Scores, 5: Receptive Vocabulary, Grammar (Evoked Sentences), Phonology, Voice, Fluency.
Administration: Individual.
Levels, 3: Grades K, 2, 5.
Price Data: Price information available from publisher for complete kit including manual (1992, 39 pages), vocabulary plates on card stock, recordkeeping manual (15 pages), and 2 reproducible scoring sheets.
Time: (2–5) minutes.
Authors: Mary C. Kinzler and Constance Cowing Johnson.
Publisher: Pearson.
Cross References: For reviews by Martin A. Fischer and by Malcolm R. McNeil and Thomas F. Campbell, see 13:165; for a review by Robert E. Owens, Jr. of the original edition, see 9:555 (1 reference).

[1401]

The Jones-Mohr Listening Test.

Purpose: "To provide feedback on listening efficiency and to measure the effect of skill building in this area."
Population: Persons in educational and training programs.
Publication Date: 1976.
Scores: Total score only.
Administration: Group.
Forms, 2: A, B.
Price Data: Price information available from publisher for kit including 50 test forms, audiocassette, and facilitator's guide (26 pages); 25 test forms (specify form).
Time: (25–30) minutes.
Authors: John E. Jones and Lawrence Mohr.
Publisher: Jossey-Bass, A Wiley Company.
Cross References: For reviews by Lear Ashmore and John F. Schmitt, see 9:556 (1 reference).

[1402]

Jordan Left-Right Reversal Test–Revised.

Purpose: Constructed "to measure letter and number reversals in the area of visual receptive functioning."
Population: Ages 5-0 through 12-11.
Publication Dates: 1973–1990.
Scores: Total score only.
Administration: Individual or group.
Levels: 2 overlapping levels (ages 5-12, 9-12) in a single booklet.
Price Data, 2006: $90 per complete kit including 50 test forms, 50 laterality checklists, 50 remedial checklists, and manual (1990, 64 pages); $30 per 50 test forms; $15 per 50 laterality checklists; $15 per 50 remedial checklists; $30 per manual; $30 per specimen set including manual and sample forms.
Time: (20) minutes.
Comments: Norm-referenced.
Author: Brian T. Jordan.

Publisher: Academic Therapy Publications.
Cross References: For reviews by Christine W. Burns and Jeffrey H. Snow, see 12:203 (1 reference); see also T4:1326 (4 references); for reviews by Mary S. Poplin and Joseph Torgesen, see 9:557; see also T3:1224 (2 references); for reviews by Barbara K. Keogh and Richard J. Reisboard, and excerpted reviews by Alex Bannatyne and Alan Krichev, see 8:434 (5 references).

[1403]

Joseph Picture Self-Concept Scale.

Purpose: Designed to measure "self-concept in children" and "identify children whose negative self-appraisals signal that they are at risk for academic and behavioral difficulties."
Publication Date: 2004.
Scores: Total Self-Concept Score.
Administration: Individual.
Parts, 4: Light-Skin Boys, Dark-Skin Boys, Light-Skin Girls, Dark-Skin Girls.
Price Data, 2006: $198 for complete kit for younger children including 2 stimulus booklets, 20 AutoScore forms, and manual (86 pages); $121 for complete kit for older children including 2 stimulus booklets, 20 AutoScore forms, and manual; $44 per manual; $40 per 20 AutoScore forms (specify Form Y [younger] or Form O [older]); $64 for choice of stimulus booklets; $28.50 for either Form O light-skin or Form O dark-skin version stimulus booklet.
Time: (5-10) minutes.
Comments: Both forms of this test allow participants to "respond using pictures rather than words."
Author: Jack Joseph.
Publisher: Western Psychological Services.
a) FORM Y-YOUNG CHILD INTERVIEW.
Population: Ages 3-0 to 7-11 years.
b) FORM O-OLDER CHILD INTERVIEW.
Population: Ages 7-0 to 13-11 years.
Cross References: For reviews by Eugene V. Aidman and Carlen Henington, see 17:101.

[1404]

Joseph Pre-School and Primary Self-Concept Screening Test.

Purpose: Constructed as an early screen for learning problems.
Population: Ages 3-5 to 9-11.
Publication Date: 1979.
Scores: Global Self Concept.
Administration: Individual.
Price Data, 2005: $150 per complete kit including manual (66 pages), 56 stimulus cards, 100 identity reference drawings, and 100 record forms; $30 per 50 record forms; $80 per set of stimulus cards; $35 per set of identity drawings; $25 per manual.

Time: (5–7) minutes.
Comments: May be used with non-verbal children.
Author: Jack Joseph.
Publisher: Stoelting Co.
Cross References: See T5:1363 (2 references); for reviews by Kathryn Clark Gerken and Cathy Fultz Telzrow, see 9:558.

[1405]

Jung Personality Questionnaire.

Purpose: "To assist pupils in choosing a career."
Population: Standards 7 and 8 and 10 in South African school system.
Publication Date: 1983.
Acronym: JPQ.
Scores, 4: Extraversion vs. Introversion, Thinking vs. Feeling, Sensation vs. Intuition, Judgement vs. Perception.
Administration: Group.
Price Data: Available from publisher.
Foreign Language Edition: Afrikaans edition available.
Time: (25–35) minutes.
Comments: "Criterion-referenced."
Author: L. B. H. duToit.
Publisher: Human Sciences Research Council [South Africa].

[1406]

Jungian Type Survey: The Gray-Wheelwrights Test (16th Revision).

Purpose: "Designed to delineate types of personality structure."
Population: Adults.
Publication Date: 1964.
Scores, 6: Introversion, Extraversion, Intuition, Sensation, Thinking, Feeling.
Administration: Group.
Price Data: Price information available from publisher for reusable question sheet, answer sheet, and manual (8 pages).
Time: (20) minutes.
Authors: Horace Gray (test only), Joseph B. Wheelwright (test and manual), Jane H. Wheelwright (test and manual), and John A. Bueler (manual only).
Publisher: C. G. Jung Institute of San Francisco, Inc.

[1407]

Junior Eysenck Personality Inventory.

Purpose: "Designed to measure … neuroticism or emotionality, and extraversion-introversion in children."
Population: Ages 7–16.
Publication Dates: 1963–1970.
Acronym: JEPI.
Scores, 3: Extraversion, Neuroticism, Lie.
Administration: Group.
Price Data: Available from publisher.

Foreign Language Edition: Spanish edition available.
Time: [15–20] minutes.
Author: Sybil B. G. Eysenck.
Publisher: EdITS/Educational and Industrial Testing Service.
Cross References: See T5:1367 (7 references), T4:1331 (13 references), 9:561 (10 references), T3:1229 (24 references), 8:596 (36 references), and T2:1252 (14 references); for reviews by Maurice Chazan and Robert D. Wirt and excerpted reviews by Gertrude H. Keir and B. Semeonoff, see 7:96 (19 references); see also P:135 (7 references).

[1408]

Junior High School Mathematics Test: Acorn Achievement Tests.

Purpose: Designed to test the pupil's knowledge of junior high level mathematics concepts, skills, and insights.
Population: Grades 7–9.
Publication Dates: 1942–1952.
Scores, 4: Concepts, Problem Analysis, Problems, Total.
Administration: Group.
Price Data: Available from publisher.
Time: 52(57) minutes.
Author: Harry Eisner.
Publisher: Psychometric Affiliates.
Cross References: For a review by Myron F. Rosskopf, see 5:429; for a review by William Betz, see 3:310.

[1409]

Junior Rating Scale.

Purpose: Designed to provide teachers with a framework to record and display visually ratings of pupils' strengths and needs.
Population: Ages 8–11.
Publication Date: 1990.
Acronym: JRS.
Scores: 5 subscale scores: Language/Education, Motor Skills, Behaviour, Social Integration, General Development.
Administration: Individual.
Price Data: Available from publisher.
Time: Untimed.
Comments: Developed from Infant Rating Scale (9:505).
Authors: J. A. Abraham and G. A. Lindsay.
Publisher: GL Assessment [England].

[1410]

Junior South African Individual Scales.

Purpose: Measures general intellectual level.
Population: South African children ages 3.0–7.11.
Publication Dates: 1981–1988.
Acronym: JSAIS.
Scores, 27: Verbal (Vocabulary, Reading Knowledge, Story Memory, Picture Riddles, Word Association, Social Reasoning, Picture Analogies, Word Fluency), Numeri-cal (Number and Quantity A, Number and Quantity B, Number and Quantity A & B, Memory for Digits A, Memory for Digits B, Memory for Digits A & B), Visual-Spatial (Form Board, Block Designs, Absurdities A, Absurdities B, Form Discrimination A & B, Grouping, Gestalt Completion, Picture Series, Picture Puzzles, Visual Memory A, Visual Memory B, Visual Memory A & B, Copying).
Administration: Individual.
Price Data: Available from publisher.
Foreign Language Edition: Afrikaans edition available.
Time: (60–90) minutes.
Authors: Elizabeth M. Madge (manuals, Parts 1-3), A. R. vandenBerg (manual, Part 3), Maryna Robinson (manual, Part 3), and J. Landman (appendix to manuals).
Publisher: Human Sciences Research Council [South Africa].
Cross References: See T5:1370 (1 reference) and T4:1335 (1 reference).

[1411]

Just-in-Time Training Assessment Instrument.

Purpose: "Intended to measure ... perceptions of how frequently and how effectively [an] organization has created a work environment that supports JITT."
Population: Adults.
Publication Date: 1996.
Acronym: JITT.
Scores, 2: Frequency, Effectiveness.
Administration: Group.
Price Data: Available from publisher.
Time: (15–20) minutes.
Author: William J. Rothwell.
Publisher: HRD Press, Inc.

[1412]

Juvenile Automated Substance Abuse Evaluation.

Purpose: Intended to "measure adolescent alcohol and drug use/abuse ... attitudes and life-stress issues."
Population: Adolescents.
Publication Dates: 1989–1997.
Acronym: JASAE.
Scores, 6: Test Taking Attitude, Life Circumstance Evaluation, Drinking Evaluation Category, Alcohol Addiction Evaluation, Drug Use Evaluation, Summary.
Administration: Individual or group.
Price Data: Available from publisher.
Time: (20) minutes.
Comments: Self-administered; computer scored, IBM compatible with either DOS or Windows required; provides DSM–IV classification for alcohol and drug use and ASAM patient placement criteria for treatment recommendations; available in English and Spanish.

Author: ADE Incorporated.
Publisher: ADE Incorporated.
Cross References: For reviews by Mark Pope and Jody L. Swartz-Kulstad, see 14:190.

[1413]

Juvenile Justice Policy Inventory.

Purpose: "Designed to assess both individual attitudes toward juvenile justice policies and characteristic methods of dealing with juvenile offenders."
Population: Juvenile justice professionals.
Publication Date: 1973.
Scores, 4: Reintegration, Rehabilitation, Reform, Restraint.
Administration: Group.
Price Data: Available from publisher.
Time: Administration time not reported.
Author: Vincent O'Leary.
Publisher: National Council on Crime and Delinquency.

[1414]

Juvenile Presentence Evaluation.

Purpose: Designed for juvenile presentence evaluation and "assesses attitudes and behaviors important to juvenile adjustment profiles."
Population: Presentenced juveniles.
Publication Dates: 1998-2003.
Acronym: JPE.
Scores, 9: Truthfulness, Suicide, Resistance, Self-Esteem, Violence (Lethality), Alcohol, Drugs, Distress, Stress Coping Abilities.
Administration: Group.
Price Data, 2010: $8 per test; volume discounts available.
Foreign Language Edition: Spanish version available.
Time: (35) minutes.
Comments: May be administered via paper and pencil, computer, or human voice audio.
Author: Risk & Needs Assessment, Inc.
Publisher: Behavior Data Systems, Ltd.

[1415]

Juvenile Pretrial Test.

Purpose: Designed to assist in making decisions about "counseling, treatment, probation, levels of supervision, and incarceration alternatives."
Population: Juvenile offenders.
Publication Date: 1998.
Acronym: JPT.
Scores, 7: Validity (Truthfulness), Alcohol Severity, Drugs Severity, Lethality (Violence), Distress, Adjustment, Stress Quotient.
Administration: Group.
Price Data, 2010: $8 per test; volume discounts available.
Foreign Language Edition: Spanish version available.
Time: (25-30) minutes.

Comments: May be administered via paper and pencil, computer, or human voice audio.
Author: Risk & Needs Assessment, Inc.
Publisher: Behavior Data Systems, Ltd.

[1416]

Juvenile Substance Abuse Profile.

Purpose: "Designed for troubled youth ... assessment in juvenile courts, screening programs, schools systems, and treatment agencies."
Population: Troubled youth.
Publication Date: 2002.
Acronym: JSAP.
Scores, 5: Truthfulness, Aggressiveness, Alcohol, Drugs, Stress Coping Abilities.
Administration: Group.
Price Data, 2010: $8 per test; volume discounts available.
Foreign Language Edition: Spanish version available.
Time: (20) minutes.
Comments: May be administered via paper and pencil, computer, or human voice audio.
Author: Behavior Data Systems, Ltd.
Publisher: Behavior Data Systems, Ltd.

[1417]

Kaplan Baycrest Neurocognitive Assessment.

Purpose: "Test of neurocognitive functioning."
Population: Ages 20–89.
Publication Date: 2000.
Acronym: KBNA.
Scores: 8 index scores: Attention/Concentration, Immediate Memory Recall, Delayed Memory Recall, Delayed Memory Recognition, Spatial Processing, Verbal Fluency, Reasoning/Conceptual Shifting, Total Index.
Administration: Individual.
Price Data, 2002: $239 per complete kit including manual (188 pages), stimulus book (94 pages), 8 response chips, cassette, 25 response booklets, 25 record forms, and response grid (packaged in a box); $70 per manual; $70 per stimulus book; $43 per 25 response booklets; $43 per 25 record forms; $11 per response grid.
Time: (60–90) minutes.
Comments: Test contains 25 subtests (Orientation, Sequences, Numbers, Word Lists 1, Complex Figure 1, Motor Programming, Auditory Signal Detection, Symbol Cancellation, Clocks, Word Lists 2, Complex Figure 2, Picture Naming, Sentence Reading–Arithmetic, Reading Single Words, Spatial Location, Verbal Fluency, Praxis, Picture Recognition, Expression of Emotion, Practical Problem Solving, Conceptual Shifting, Picture Description–Oral, Auditory Comprehension, Repetition, Picture Description–Written); detailed analysis of neurocognitive functioning can be obtained through examination of 94

component Process Scores; Process Scores are categorized as below average, equivocal, or average.
Authors: Larry Leach, Edith Kaplan, Dmytro Rewilak, Brian Richards, and Guy-B. Proulx.
Publisher: Pearson.
Cross References: For reviews by Raymond S. Dean and John J. Brinkman, Jr., and by Harrison D. Kane and Shawn K. Acheson, see 16:121.

[1418]

Katz Adjustment Scales–Relative Report Form.

Purpose: Designed to assess aspects of community adjustment of psychiatric patients "to identify whether follow-up rehabilitation services are required."
Population: Adults with psychiatric, medical, or neurological disorders.
Publication Dates: 1961–1999.
Acronym: KAS-R.
Administration: Individual.
Parts, 3: General Behavior, Socially Expected Activities, Use of Leisure Time.
Price Data, 2006: $114.50 per complete kit including manual (1998, 94 pages), response card, and 25 AutoScore answer forms; $60.50 per manual; $40 per 25 AutoScore answer forms; $21.50 per 10 Spanish language test forms; $17 per 5 response cards; $18 per mail-in answer booklet; $265 per 25-use PC disk; $16.50 per 50 PC answer booklets; volume discounts available.
Time: (35–45) minutes; (10–15) minutes for Short Form.
Comments: Informant (relative or close friend) completes behavior rating scale; computer scoring available; formerly a subscale of the Katz Adjustment Scale; Spanish language form available for research purposes; Short Form includes General Psychopathology, Stability, Social Aggression Index, Emotionality Index, Disorientation, Withdrawal Index, and Psychopathology Index.
Authors: Martin M. Katz and W. Louise Warren.
Publisher: Western Psychological Services.

a) GENERAL BEHAVIOR.
Scores, 16: Inconsistent Responding, General Psychopathology, Stability, Social Aggression Index (Belligerence, Negativism, Verbal Expressiveness), Emotionality Index (Anxiety Index [Anxiousness, Nervousness], Depression Index [Depression, Helplessness]), Disorientation/Withdrawal Index (Confusion, Expressive Deficit, Withdrawal/Retardation), Severe Psychopathology Index (Bizarreness, Hyperactivity, Suspiciousness).
b) SOCIALLY EXPECTED ACTIVITIES.
Scores, 3: Level of Performance of Socially Expected Activities, Level of Expectations for Performance of Socially Expected Activities, Expectation/Performance Discrepancy.
c) USE OF LEISURE TIME.
Scores, 2: Level of Performance of Leisure Activities, Level of Satisfaction with Leisure Activities.

Cross References: For a review by Roger A. Boothroyd, see 16:122; for information on an earlier edition of the Katz Adjustment Scales, see T4:1340 (30 references), T3:1240 (18 references), 8:599 (3 references), T2: 1255 (12 references), and P:138 (10 references).

[1419]

Kaufman Adolescent and Adult Intelligence Test.

Purpose: "An individually administered measure of general intelligence developed from fluid and crystallized theory."
Population: Ages 11 to 85+.
Publication Date: 1993.
Acronym: KAIT.
Scores, 9 to 14: Crystallized Scale (Definitions, Auditory Comprehension, Double Meanings, Famous Faces [alternate subtest], Total), Fluid Scale (Rebus Learning, Logical Steps, Mystery Codes, Memory for Block Designs [alternate subtest], Total), Measures of Delayed Recall [optional] (Rebus Delayed Recall, Auditory Delayed Recall), Mental Status [supplementary subtest], Total.
Administration: Individual.
Price Data, 2008: $783 per complete kit including 2 test easels, manual (161 pages), 25 individual test records, 25 Mystery Codes item booklets, Auditory Comprehension audiocassette, set of 6 Memory for Design Blocks with holder, and carrying Case; $72 per record set including 25 each, record booklets and mystery code booklets; $78 per manual; $129 per KAIT training video.
Time: 60 minutes for Core Battery; 90 minutes for Expanded Battery.
Authors: Alan S. Kaufman and Nadeen L. Kaufman.
Publisher: Pearson.
Cross References: See T5:1378 (14 references); for reviews by Dawn P. Flanagan and Timothy Z. Keith, see 12:204 (6 references); see also T4:1342 (1 reference).

[1420]

Kaufman Assessment Battery for Children, Second Edition.

Purpose: Designed to measure the "processing and cognitive abilities of children and adolescents."
Population: Ages 3-18.
Publication Dates: 1983-2004.
Acronym: KABC-II.
Scores, 7–23: Sequential (Number Recall, Word Order, Hand Movements, Total), Simultaneous (Block Counting, Conceptual Thinking, Face Recognition, Pattern Reasoning [Ages 5 and 6], Rover, Story Completion [Ages 5 and 6], Triangles, Gestalt Closure, Total), Planning [Ages 7–18 only] (Pattern Reasoning, Story Completion, Total), Learning (Atlantis, Rebus, Atlantis Delayed, Rebus Delayed, Total), Knowledge (Expressive Vocabulary, Riddles, Verbal Knowledge,

Total), Nonverbal Index, Mental Processing Index, Fluid-Crystallized Index.
Administration: Individual.
Price Data, 2008: $826 per complete kit, including 4 easels, manual (2004, 236 pages), all necessary stimulus and manipulative materials, 25 record forms, and soft-sided briefcase; $55.75 per manual; $58 per 25 record forms; $259 per computer ASSIST scoring software; $129 per training video.
Time: (25–70) minutes.
Comments: Nonverbal scale available for hearing impaired, speech-and-language disordered, and non-English-speaking children (an adaptation that examiners can make when verbal concerns are present).
Authors: Alan S. Kaufman and Nadeen L. Kaufman.
Publisher: Pearson.
Cross References: For reviews by Jeffery P. Braden and Sandye M. Ouzts and by Robert M. Thorndike, see 16:123; see also T5:1379 (103 references) and T4:1343 (114 references); for reviews by Anne Anastasi, William E. Coffman, and Ellis Batten Page of an earlier edition, see 9:562 (3 references).

[1421]

Kaufman Brief Intelligence Test, Second Edition.
Purpose: Intended as a brief measure of verbal and nonverbal intelligence.
Population: Ages 4–90.
Publication Dates: 1990–2004.
Acronym: KBIT-2.
Scores: 3: Verbal, Nonverbal, IQ Composite.
Subtests: 3: Verbal Knowledge, Riddles, Matrices.
Administration: Individual.
Price Data, 2008: $226 per complete kit including easel, manual (2004, 147 pages), 25 individual test record forms, and carry bag; $46.50 per 25 individual test records; $66 per scoring and administration manual.
Time: (15–30) minutes.
Comments: Examiners are encouraged to teach individuals, using teaching items, how to solve the kinds of items included in subtests.
Authors: Alan S. Kaufman and Nadeen L. Kaufman.
Publisher: Pearson.
Cross References: For reviews by Ronald A. Madle and Steven R. Shaw, see 17:102; see also T5:1380 (21 references); for reviews by M. David Miller and John W. Young of an earlier version, see 12:205 (9 references); see also T4:1344 (4 references).

[1422]

Kaufman Developmental Scale.
Purpose: Designed to assess the "level of development … and an overall level of functioning."
Population: Birth to age 9 and mentally retarded of all ages.

Publication Dates: 1972–1975.
Acronym: KDS.
Scores, 7: Gross Motor, Fine Motor, Receptive, Expressive, Personal Behavior, Inter-Personal Behavior, Total.
Administration: Individual.
Price Data, 2005: $425 per complete kit including test materials, manual (1974, 83 pages), 25 record forms, and carrying case; $55 per 25 evaluation booklets; $30 per 25 record forms; $55 per manual.
Time: (30) minutes.
Author: H. Kaufman.
Publisher: Stoelting Co.
Cross References: For a review by Dorothy H. Eichorn, see 8:218.

[1423]

Kaufman Functional Academic Skills Test.
Purpose: A quick measure of reading and math functional skills designed as a brief, individually administered test to determine performance in reading and mathematics as applied to daily life.
Population: Ages 15–85+.
Publication Date: 1994.
Acronym: K-FAST.
Scores, 3: Arithmetic Subtest, Reading Subtest, Functional Academic Skills Composite.
Administration: Individual.
Price Data, 2008: $160 per complete kit including manual (110 pages), test easel, and 25 record forms; $132 per test easel; $38.50 per 25 record forms.
Time: (15–25) minutes.
Comments: Examinees may respond in any language.
Authors: Alan S. Kaufman and Nadeen L. Kaufman.
Publisher: Pearson.
Cross References: See T5:1382 (1 reference); for reviews by Steven R. Shaw and Robert T. Williams, see 13:166 (2 references).

[1424]

Kaufman Infant and Preschool Scale.
Purpose: Designed to measure "early, high-level cognitive thinking, and indicates possible need for intervention."
Population: Ages 1 month–48 months and mentally retarded individuals whose preacademic functioning age does not exceed 48 months.
Publication Date: 1979.
Acronym: KIPS.
Scores: Tasks in 3 areas: General Reasoning, Storage, Verbal Communication.
Administration: Individual.
Price Data, 2005: $300 per complete kit including all manipulatives, stimulus cards, and 10 evaluation booklets; $33 per 10 evaluation booklets; $20 per set of stimulus cards; $28 per manual (40 pages).

Time: (20-30) minutes.
Author: H. Kaufman.
Publisher: Stoelting Co.
Cross References: For reviews by Roy A. Kress and Phyllis Anne Teeter, see 9:563.

[1425]

Kaufman Short Neuropsychological Assessment Procedure.

Purpose: A brief, individually administered measure of the cognitive functioning of adolescents and adults.
Population: Ages 11 through 85+.
Publication Date: 1994.
Acronym: K-SNAP.
Scores, 5: Gestalt Closure, Number Recall, Four-Letter Words, Recall/Closure Composite, K-SNAP Composite.
Administration: Individual.
Price Data, 2008: $243 per complete kit including manual (128 pages), easel, and 25 record forms; $38.50 per 25 record forms; $165.50 per easel.
Time: 30 minutes.
Authors: Alan S. Kaufman and Nadeen L. Kaufman.
Publisher: Pearson.
Cross References: See T5:1384 (2 references); for reviews by Karen Geller and Martine Hebert, see 13:167 (2 references).

[1426]

Kaufman Survey of Early Academic and Language Skills.

Purpose: Designed as an easy-to-administer measure of children's language skills (expressive and receptive vocabulary), numerical skills, and articulation.
Population: 3-0 to 6-11.
Publication Date: 1993.
Acronym: K-SEALS.
Scores, 3: Vocabulary; Numbers, Letters, and Words; Articulation Survey.
Administration: Individual.
Price Data, 2006: $244.99 per complete kit including manual (109 pages), easel, 25 test records, and carrying bag; $34.99 per 25 record booklets; $45.99 per manual.
Time: (15–25) minutes.
Comments: The Early Academic Scales can be interpreted only for ages 5-0 to 6-11.
Authors: Alan S. Kaufman and Nadeen L. Kaufman.
Publisher: Pearson.
Cross References: For reviews by Phillip L. Ackerman and by Laurie Ford and Kerri Turk, see 12:206.

[1427]

Kaufman Test of Educational Achievement–Second Edition, Comprehensive Form.

Purpose: Designed to measure "achievement in reading, mathematics, written language, and oral language."

Population: Ages 4.6–25.
Publication Dates: 1985–2004.
Acronym: KTEA-II.
Scores, 23: Reading (Letter and Word Recognition, Reading Comprehension, Composite), Mathematics (Math Concepts & Applications, Math Computation, Composite), Written Language (Written Expression, Spelling, Composite), Oral Language (Listening Comprehension, Oral Expression, Composite), Comprehensive Achievement Composite, Phonological Awareness, Nonsense Word Decoding, Sound-Symbol Composite, Decoding Composite, Word Recognition Fluency, Decoding Fluency, Reading Fluency Composite, Associational Fluency, Naming Facility [RAN], Oral Fluency Composite.
Administration: Individual.
Forms, 2: Parallel forms A and B.
Price Data, 2008: $613 per complete Form A and B kit including Comprehensive Form A and Form B kits with 2 manuals (2004, 442 pages) and 2 norms books; $341.50 per comprehensive kit (Form A or B) including 2 easels, manual, norms book, 25 record forms, 25 student response booklets, 25 error analysis booklets, 2 each of 3 Written Expression booklets, all necessary stimulus materials, administration CD, puppet, and tote bag; $38.50 per manual; $38.50 per norms book; $86 per 25 record forms, 25 student response booklets, and 24 Error Analysis Booklets; $29 per 25 error analysis booklets; $11.25 per 10 Written Expression booklets; $259 per Computer ASSIST computer scoring program.
Time: (30–85) minutes.
Comments: Computer and hand scoring available.
Authors: Alan S. Kaufman and Nadeen L. Kaufman.
Publisher: Pearson.
Cross References: For reviews by Mike Bonner and C. Dale Carpenter, see 16:124; for reviews by John Poggio and William D. Schafer of an earlier edition, see 14:191; see also T5:1386 (26 references) and T4:1348 (5 references); for reviews by Elizabeth J. Doll and Jerome M. Sattler of an earlier edition, see 10:161.

[1428]

Keegan Type Indicator.

Purpose: Measures perception, judgment, and attitude (extraversion/introversion) based on C. G. Jung's theory of psychological types.
Population: Adults.
Publication Dates: 1980–2006.
Acronym: KTI.
Scores, 3: Extraversion vs. Introversion, Sensation vs. Intuition, Thinking vs. Feeling.
Administration: Group.
Price Data: Price data, including user's manual (1980, 12 pages) and instructor's manual (1980, 21 pages), available from publisher.
Time: [20] minutes.
Author: Warren J. Keegan.

Publisher: Keegan (Warren) Associates Press.
Cross References: For a review by Arlene C. Rosenthal, see 10:162.

[1429]

Keirsey Temperament Sorter II.

Purpose: Designed to be used "for assessing temperament, character, and personality."
Population: College and adult.
Publication Dates: 1978–2003.
Acronym: KTS-II.
Scores, 16: Artisan-Promoter (ESTP), Artisan-Crafter (ISTP), Artisan-Performer (ESFP), Artisan-Composer (ISFP), Guardian-Supervisor (ESTJ), Guardian-Inspector (ISTJ), Guardian-Provider (ESFJ), Guardian-Protector (ISFJ), Rational-Fieldmarshal (ENTJ), Rational-Architect (ENFP), Rational-Mastermind(INTJ), Rational-Inventor (INTP), Idealist-Champion (ENFP), Idealist-Header (INFP), Idealist-Counselor (INFJ), Idealist-Teacher (ENFJ).
Administration: Group.
Price Data, 2004: KTS-II may be taken free online; $14.95 per Classic Temperament Report; $19.95 per Career Temperament Report; $27.95 per Career Personality Package; price information available from publisher for Statistical Study (2003, 89 pages) and for Academic Platform or Corporate Platform delivery; $15.95 per "Please Understand Me II" (1998, 352 pages).
Foreign Language Editions: Available in American English, Spanish, French, German, Italian, Polish, Portuguese, and Japanese.
Time: (10–15) minutes.
Authors: David Keirsey (instrument and "Please Understand Me II") and Alpine Media Corporation (Statistical Study).
Publisher: Keirsey.com.
Cross References: For a review by Peter Zachar, see 16:125.

[1430]

Kendrick Assessment Scales of Cognitive Ageing.

Purpose: Designed "to provide an accurate and flexible means of screening for and predicting possible dementia."
Population: Ages 40–92.
Publication Dates: 1979–1999.
Acronym: KOLT.
Administration: Individual.
Price Data, 1999: £125 per complete set including 10 record forms, manual (1999), and material for the four subtests; £15 per 10 record forms.
Time: Untimed.
Comments: Revision of Kendrick Cognitive Tests for the Elderly (T4:1352).
Authors: Don Kendrick and Geoff Watts.
Publisher: GL Assessment [England].

a) OBJECT LEARNING TEST.
Acronym: KOLT.
Scores: Total score only.
Forms, 2: A, B (4 cards).
Comments: Test of recall of everyday objects.
b) DIGIT COPYING TEST.
Acronym: KDCT.
Scores: Total score only.
Comments: Test of speed performance.
c) WATTS VISUO-SPATIAL TEST.
Acronym: WVST.
Scores: Total score only.
Comments: Test of visuo-spatial ability.
d) KENDRICK ATTENTION AND REASONING TEST.
Acronym: KART.
Scores: Total score only.
Comments: Test of reasoning and attention.
Cross References: See T5:1390 (7 references), T4:1352 (1 reference), and 11:189 (2 references); for reviews by Joseph D. Matarazzo and K. Warner Schaie of an earlier edition, see 9:566 (2 references).

[1431]

Kent Inventory of Developmental Skills [1996 Standardization].

Purpose: Designed to assess the developmental status and progress of healthy infants, infants at risk, and young children with developmental disabilities.
Population: Infants up to 15 months of age and young children whose developmental age is less than 15 months.
Publication Dates: 1978–1999.
Acronym: KIDS.
Scores, 12: Developmental Ages and Standard Scores for: Cognitive, Motor, Language, Self-Help, Social Domains, Full Scale.
Administration: Individual.
Price Data: Price information available from publisher for complete kit including 25 profile sheets, 25 answer sheets, reusable administration and scoring booklet, 5 scoring templates, set of developmental timetables, manual, and 2-use disk for on-site computer scoring and interpretation.
Time: (45) minutes.
Comments: Relies on caregiver report; also yields individualized developmental timetables; includes hand-scoring materials and an expanded computer report, including a list of developmentally appropriate activities selected to match each child's specific competencies; earlier editions entitled The Kent Infant Development Scale.
Authors: Jeanette Reuter with Lewis Katoff and Jeffrey Wozniak (3rd edition of the test manual and user's guide) and James Whiteman (computer-scoring disk).
Publisher: Western Psychological Services.
Cross References: For reviews by Diane J. Sawyer and Gary J. Stainback, see 14:192; see also T5:1391 (2

references); for reviews by Candice Feiring and Edward S. Shapiro of an earlier edition, see 10:163 (2 references); for a review by Candice Feiring of an earlier version, see 9:567; see also T3:1246 (1 reference).

[1432]

Kent Visual Perceptual Test.

Purpose: Designed to "identify and characterize visual processing deficits in school or neuropsychological settings."
Population: Ages 5–11.
Publication Dates: 1995–2000.
Acronym: KVPT.
Administration: Individual.
Price Data, 2005: $207 per complete kit including 10 copy tests, memory test stimuli, discrimination test stimuli, 10 scoring and error analysis booklets, and professional manual (2000, 128 pages).
Time: (25–30) minutes.
Author: Lawrence E. Melamed.
Publisher: Psychological Assessment Resources, Inc.
    a) KENT VISUAL PERCEPTION TEST–DISCRIMI-
    NATION.
    Purpose: Designed to assess visual discrimina-
    tion skills.
    Acronym: KVPT-D.
    Scores, 2: Error Analysis, Total.
    b) KENT VISUAL PERCEPTION TEST–COPY.
    Purpose: Designed to assess visual reproduction
    skills.
    Acronym: KVPT-C.
    Scores, 4: KVPT-C1, KVPT-C2, KVPT-C3,
    Total.
    c) VISUAL PERCEPTION TESTS–IMMEDIATE
    MEMORY.
    Purpose: Designed to assess immediate memory.
    Acronym: KVPT-M.
    Scores, 2: Error Analysis, Total.
Cross References: For reviews by Ralph G. Leverett and Katharine A. Snyder, see 16:126; for a review by Annie W. Ward of an earlier edition, see 14:193.

[1433]

KeyMath-3 Diagnostic Assessment.

Purpose: Designed to assess understanding and ap-
plications of mathematics concepts and skills.
Population: Ages 4-6 to 21-11.
Publication Dates: 1971-2007.
Acronym: KeyMath-3 DA.
Scores, 14: Basic Concepts (Numeration, Algebra, Geometry, Measurement, Data Analysis and Probability, Total), Operations (Mental Computation and Estimation, Addition and Subtraction, Multiplication and Division, Total), Applications (Foundations of Problem Solving, Applied Problem Solving, Total), Total.
Administration: Individual.

Forms, 2: A, B.
Price Data, 2008: $699 per complete kit including manual (2007, 371 pages), Form A and Form B test easels, 25 Form A & Form B record forms, and carrying bag; $399 per single form (specify form) kit including manual, test easels, 25 record forms, and carrying bag; $76 per 25 record forms (specify form); $259 per KeyMath-3 ASSIST scoring software.
Time: (30-40) minutes Grades PK-2; (75-90) minutes Grades 3 and up.
Author: Austin J. Connolly.
Publisher: Pearson.
Cross References: For reviews by Theresa Graham and by Suzanne Lane and Debra Moore, see 18:63; for reviews by G. Gage Kingsbury and James A. Wollack of a previous edition, see 14:194; see also T5:139 (15 references) and T4:1355 (5 references); for reviews by Michael D. Beck and Carmen J. Finley of an earlier edition, see 11:191 (26 references); see also T3:1250 (12 references); for an excerpted review by Alex Bannatyne of an earlier edition, see 8:305 (10 references).

[1434]

KEYS® to Creativity.

Purpose: Designed to measure how "employees perceive stimulants and barriers to creativity."
Population: Employees.
Publication Date: 1995.
Scores, 10: 8 environment scales (6 environmental stimulants to creativity: Organizational Encouragement of Creativity, Supervisory Encouragement of Creativity, Work Group Supports, Freedom, Sufficient Resources, Challenging Work; 2 obstacles to creativity: Organizational Impediments, Workload Pressure); 2 outcome scales (Creativity, Productivity).
Administration: Group.
Price Data, 2006: $20 per survey booklet (5–50 book-lets); quantity discounts available; $75 per group comparisons.
Time: (15–20) minutes.
Comments: Costs of survey booklets includes scoring, standard feedback results, one KEYS User's Guide (205 pages), and one KEYS: Interpreting the Results.
Authors: Teresa M. Amabile and Center for Creative Leadership.
Publisher: Center for Creative Leadership.
Cross References: For a review by Carolyn M. Callahan, see 14:195; see also T5:1393 (1 reference).

[1435]

Khan-Lewis Phonological Analysis–Second Edition.

Purpose: Measures phonological process usage in speech and allows tracking of intervention planning and progress.
Population: Ages 2-0 to 21-11.
Publication Dates: 1986-2002.

Acronym: KLPA-2.

Scores, 11: 5 Reduction Processes (Deletion of Final Consonants, Syllable Reduction, Stopping of Fricatives and Affricates, Cluster Simplification, Liquid Simplification), 3 Place and Manner Processes (Velar Fronting, Palatal Fronting, Deaffrication), 2 Voicing Processes (Initial Voicing, Final Devoicing), Total Score.

Administration: Individual.

Price Data, 2008: $149 per kit including manual (2002, 206 pages), 25 analysis forms, Sound Change booklet, and 25 Phonological Summary and Progress Report worksheets; $44 per 25 analysis forms, $259 per ASSIST CD (Win only)—combined with GFTA-2 ASSIST.

Time: 10–30 minutes.

Comments: Supplements the Goldman-Fristoe Test of Articulation–Second Edition (GFTA-2; 1147); scores based on completely transcribed responses to the Sounds-in-Words subtest of the GFTA-2; to complete the KLPA-2, examiner needs both complete KLPA-2 kit and GFTA-2 (the easel); is conormed with the Goldman-Fristoe Test of Articulation, Second Edition.

Authors: Linda M. L. Khan and Nancy P. Lewis.

Publisher: Pearson.

Cross References: For reviews by Carlos Inchaurralde and Steven Long, see 16:127; see also T5:1394 (13 references) and T4:1356 (1 reference); for a review by Donald E. Mowrer of an earlier edition, see 10:164.

[1436]

Khatena-Morse Multitalent Perception Inventory.

Purpose: Identifies giftedness in music, art, and leadership.

Population: Age 6–adult.

Publication Dates: 1985–1994.

Acronym: KMMPI.

Scores, 6: Artistic, Musical, Creative Imagination, Initiative, Leadership, Versatility.

Administration: Group.

Forms, 2: A, B.

Price Data: See www.ststesting.com for up-to-date prices.

Time: (30–45) minutes.

Authors: Joe Khatena and David T. Morse.

Publisher: Scholastic Testing Service, Inc.

Cross References: For reviews by Carolyn M. Callahan and William Steve Lang, see 13:169.

[1437]

Khatena-Torrance Creative Perception Inventory.

Purpose: Developed as measures of creative personality.

Population: Age 12–adult.

Publication Dates: 1976–1998.

Acronym: KTCPI.

Administration: Group.

Price Data: See www.ststesting.com for up-to-date prices.

Time: (10–20) minutes per checklist.

Comments: Includes 2 self-report checklists designed to identify candidates for creativity programs.

Publisher: Scholastic Testing Service, Inc.

a) WHAT KIND OF PERSON ARE YOU?

Purpose: Designed to "yield an index of the individual's disposition or motivation to function in creative ways."

Acronym: WKOPAY?

Scores: 5 factors: Acceptance of Authority, Self-Confidence, Inquisitiveness, Awareness of Others, Disciplined Imagination.

Author: E. Paul Torrance.

b) SOMETHING ABOUT MYSELF.

Purpose: Designed as an autobiographical "screening device for the identification of creative people."

Acronym: SAM.

Scores: 6 factors: Environmental Sensitivity, Initiative, Self-Strength, Intellectuality, Individuality, Artistry.

Author: Joe Khatena.

Cross References: For reviews by Carolyn M. Callahan and Gregory Schraw, see 16:128; see also T5:1396 (5 references); for reviews by David L. Bolton and William Steve Lang of a previous edition, see 13:168 (2 references); for a review by Philip E. Vernon of an earlier edition, see 9:569 (3 references).

[1438]

Kilmann-Saxton Culture-Gap Survey [Revised].

Purpose: Assesses "actual versus desired cultural norms."

Population: Work team members, employees.

Publication Dates: 1983–1991.

Acronym: CGS.

Scores, 4: Task Support, Social Relationships, Task Innovation, Personal Freedom.

Administration: Group.

Price Data, 2001: $8.50 per survey.

Time: (30) minutes.

Authors: Ralph H. Kilmann and Mary J. Saxton.

Publisher: Kilmann Diagnostics.

Cross References: For reviews by Russell N. Carney and Norman D. Sundberg, see 13:170; for reviews by Andres Barona and Gargi Roysircar Sodowsky of an earlier edition, see 11:192.

[1439]

Kilmanns Organizational Belief Survey.

Purpose: Assesses beliefs about one's level of control in their organizational surroundings.

Population: Employees.

Publication Date: 1991.

Scores, 8: Control Score, My Work Group, My Department, My Organization, Individual Profile, Work Group Profile, Department Profile, Organizational Profile.

Administration: Group.

Price Data, 2001: $8.50 each questionnaire/booklet.

Time: Administration time not reported.

Comments: A component of the Workshop for Implementing the Five Tracks, part of a completely integrated set of materials for creating and maintaining long-term organizational success; self-scored.

Authors: Ralph H. Kilmann and Ines Kilmann.

Publisher: Kilmann Diagnostics.

[1440]

Kindergarten Diagnostic Instrument–Second Edition.

Purpose: "Designed to assess developmental readiness skills in children."

Population: Children ages 4–6 years or older children with known or suspected developmental delays.

Publication Date: 2000.

Acronym: KDI-2.

Scores, 22: 13 subtest scores (Body Awareness, Concept Mastery, Form/Letter Identification, General Information, Gross Motor, Memory for Sentences, Number Skills, Phonemic Awareness, Verbal Associations, Visual Discrimination, Visual Memory, Visual-Motor Integration, Vocabulary), 6 subskills (Form Identification, Letter Identification, Verbal Associations–Similarities, Verbal Associations–Opposites, Visual Discrimination–Similarities, Visual Discrimination–Differences), Nonverbal Factor Score, Verbal Factor Score, Total Test Score.

Administration: Individual.

Price Data, 2004: $175 per complete test kit including administration manual (146 pages), 3 stimulus booklets, 13 1-inch wooden blocks, and 25 student response booklets in a carrying case; $495 per assessment bundle including complete test kit, 50 student response booklets, 50 My Kindergarten Fun Books-II (40 pages), and scoring program for Windows; $32 per 25 student response booklets; $50 per 25 My Kindergarten Fun Books-II; $275 per KDI-2 Scoring Program for Windows (one-time license fee, additional cost applies for sites screening more than 300 children annually); $30 per training video; quantity discounts available on all items.

Time: (35–45) minutes.

Comments: KDI-2 Scoring Program for Windows stores students' pre-kindergarten and kindergarten data, generates local schoolwide norms, assesses performance compared to local norms, generates individual reports, test-retest reports; contact publisher for KDI-2 Scoring Program system requirements.

Authors: Daniel C. Miller (KDI-2, Training Video, My Kindergarten Fun Book-II) and Michie A. Miller (Training Video, My Kindergarten Fun Book-II).

Publisher: Kindergarten Interventions and Diagnostic Services, Inc.

Cross References: For reviews by Glen P. Aylward and Lisa F. Smith, see 16:129.

[1441]

Kindergarten Inventory of Social-Emotional Tendencies.

Purpose: "Designed to screen for social skill deficits and signs of emotional immaturity in preschool and kindergarten aged children."

Population: Ages 4–6.

Publication Date: 1997.

Acronym: KIST.

Scores: 7 domains: Communication Skills, Daily Living Skills, Hyperactive/Inattentive Behaviors, Maladaptive Behaviors, Separation Anxiety Behaviors, Socialization or Peer Relation Skills, Sleeping & Eating Behaviors.

Administration: Individual.

Price Data: Available from publisher.

Time: (10) minutes.

Comments: Ratings by child's primary caregiver, or by a teacher who knows the child well.

Authors: Daniel C. Miller and Michie A. Miller.

Publisher: Kindergarten Interventions and Diagnostic Services, Inc.

Cross References: For reviews by Amy M. Rees and Cynthia A. Rohrbeck, see 16:130.

[1442]

Kindergarten Language Screening Test, Second Edition.

Purpose: Designed to help identify children "who need further diagnostic testing to determine whether or not they have language deficits that will accelerate academic failure."

Population: Ages 4-0 through 6-11.

Publication Dates: 1978–1998.

Acronym: KLST-2.

Scores: Total score only.

Administration: Individual.

Price Data, 2011: $150 per complete kit including examiner's manual (1998, 30 pages), 50 profile/examiner record forms, picture book, and 3 picture cards; $46 per examiner's manual; $53 per 50 profile/examiner record forms; $46 per picture book; $15 per 3 picture cards.

Time: (5) minutes.

Authors: Sharon V. Gauthier and Charles L. Madison.

Publisher: PRO-ED.

Cross References: For reviews by Timothy R. Konold and Leslie Eastman Lukin, see 14:196; see also T4:1359 (2 references).

[1443]

Kindergarten Readiness Test [Scholastic Testing Service, Inc.].

Purpose: Designed "to assist in determining a student's readiness for beginning kindergarten."

Population: Preschool-kindergarten students.

Publication Date: 2006.
Acronym: KRT.
Scores, 8: Vocabulary, Identifying Letters, Visual Discrimination, Phonemic Awareness, Comprehension and Interpretation, Mathematical Knowledge, Full Battery Total, Readiness Classification.
Administration: Group.
Price Data: See www.ststesting.com for up-to-date prices.
Foreign Language Edition: Spanish edition available.
Time: (30) minutes.
Authors: O. F. Anderhalter and Jan Perney.
Publisher: Scholastic Testing Service, Inc.
Cross References: For reviews by Kathleen M. Johnson and by Mark E. Swerdlik and Kathryn E. Hoff, see 18:64.

[1444]

Kindergarten Readiness Test [Slosson Educational Publications, Inc.].
Purpose: Determines the readiness of children to begin kindergarten.
Population: Ages 4–6.
Publication Date: 1988.
Acronym: KRT.
Scores: Total score only.
Administration: Individual.
Price Data, 2002: $118 per complete kit; $38 per manual (39 pages); $55 per 25 test booklets; $14 per 25 performance grid sheets; $14 per 25 letter to parent; $14 per 25 scoring interpretation; $21 per stimulus items.
Time: (15) minutes.
Authors: Sue L. Larson and Gary J. Vitali.
Publisher: Slosson Educational Publications, Inc.
Cross References: For reviews by Michael D. Beck and by Rosemary E. Sutton and Catharine C. Knight, see 12:207.

[1445]

Kinetic Drawing System for Family and School: A Handbook.
Purpose: Designed "as a projective technique which assesses a child's perceptions of relationships among the child, peers, family, school, and significant others."
Population: Ages 5-20.
Publication Date: 1985.
Scores: 5 diagnostic categories: Actions of and Between Figures, Figure Characteristics, Position/Distance/Barriers, Style, Symbols.
Administration: Individual.
Price Data, 2006: $81.50 per complete kit including 25 scoring booklets and handbook (65 pages); $37.95 per 25 scoring booklets; $48.50 per handbook (including scoring booklet).
Time: (20-40) minutes.
Comments: A combination of the Kinetic Family Drawing and Kinetic School Drawing.

Authors: Howard M. Knoff and H. Thompson Prout (handbook).
Publisher: Western Psychological Services.
Cross References: See T5:1401 (4 references) and T4:1362 (2 references); for reviews by Bert P. Cundick and Richard A. Weinberg, see 10:166 (4 references).

[1446]

Kipnis-Schmidt Profiles of Organizational Influence Strategies.
Purpose: To "measure how people use influence in their organizations."
Population: Organizational members.
Publication Date: 1982.
Acronym: POIS.
Scores, 12 or 14: Friendliness, Bargaining, Reason, Assertiveness, Sanctions (Form S only), Higher Authority, Coalition scores for each of 2 areas (First Attempt to Influence, Attempts to Overcome Resistance to Influence).
Administration: Group.
Forms, 3: M (Influencing Your Manager), C (Influencing Your Co-Workers), S (Influencing Your Subordinates).
Price Data: Price information available from publisher for set of 10 forms (specify Form M, C, S, or respondent's guides); trainer's package including 1 copy of each instrument, respondent's guide, and manual (16 pages).
Time: (20–30) minutes.
Authors: David Kipnis and Stuart M. Schmidt.
Publisher: Jossey-Bass, A Wiley Company.
Cross References: See T5:1402 (3 references) and T4:1363 (2 references).

[1447]

The Kirkpatrick Management and Supervisory Skills Series.
Purpose: Designed to assess "Key management skills and practices."
Publication Date: 1995.
Scores: Total score only.
Administration: Group.
Price Data: Available from publisher.
Time: (20) minutes per inventory.
Author: Donald L. Kirkpatrick.
Publisher: Donald L. Kirkpatrick (the author).
a) COMMUNICATION INVENTORY.
Purpose: Constructed to "improve knowledge, attitudes, and skills" related to communication.
Population: Supervisors and all levels of managers.
Acronym: CI.
b) HUMAN RELATIONS INVENTORY.
Purpose: Constructed to assess "the relationships that exist between supervisor and subbordinate."
Population: Same as *a* above.
Acronym: HRI.
c) MANAGING CHANGE INVENTORY.
Purpose: Designed to "cover principles, facts, and attitudes that are basic to managing change effectively."

Population: All levels of managers.
Acronym: MCI.
d) MODERN MANAGEMENT INVENTORY.
Purpose: Designed to measure "philosophy, principles, and approaches related to the effective performance of managers."
Population: Same as *c* above.
Acronym: MMI.
e) COACHING AND PERFORMANCE APPRAISAL INVENTORY.
Purpose: Constructed to assess "concepts, principles, and techniques that are important ingredients" of on-the-job coaching.
Population: Same as *c* above.
Acronym: CPAI.
f) TIME MANAGEMENT INVENTORY.
Purpose: Constructed to measure "Key factors in better time utilization and delegation."
Population: Same as *c* above.
Acronym: TMI.
g) LEADERSHIP, MOTIVATION, AND DECISION-MAKING INVENTORY.
Purpose: Constructed to "make managers more conscious of their need to be leaders."
Population: Same as *c* above.
Acronym: LMDMI.
Cross References: For a review by L. Carolyn Pearson and Lee Droegemueller, see 14:197.

[1448]

Kirton Adaption-Innovation Inventory [1998 Edition].

Purpose: Designed as a measure of one's preferred cognitive style of problem solving (creativity and decision making) so that one can distinguish between cognitive style and capacity.
Population: British and U.S. adults and teenagers over age 14.
Publication Dates: 1976–1998.
Acronym: KAI.
Scores, 4: Sufficiency v. Proliferation of Originality, Efficiency, Rule/Group Conformity, Total.
Administration: Individual or group.
Price Data: Available from publisher; volume discounts available.
Foreign Language Editions: Translations available for Italian, Slovak, French, and Dutch adults and teenagers.
Time: (5–10) minutes.
Comments: See publisher website (www.kaicentre.com) for expanded information on theory and research and for access to extensive reference/publication list.
Author: M. J. Kirton.
Publisher: Occupational Research Centre [England].
Cross References: For reviews by Lynn L. Brown and Ric Brown, see 14:198; see also T5:1404 (15 references) and T4:1364 (9 references); for reviews by Gregory

J. Boyle and Gerald E. DeMauro of an earlier edition, see 11:193 (8 references).

[1449]

Kit of Factor Referenced Cognitive Tests.

Purpose: "To provide research workers with a means of identifying certain aptitude factors in factor-analytic studies."
Population: Various grades 6-college level.
Publication Dates: 1954–1978.
Administration: Group.
Price Data, 2002: $30 per complete set including 72 tests and manual (1976, 230 pages); $10 per manual; a license agreement is required for the use of the tests ($.10 a copy with a minimum of $35 for graduate students, $.20 a copy with a minimum of $50 for other researchers).
Time: Administration time given separately for each test.
Comments: Formerly called the Kit of Reference Tests for Cognitive Factors.
Authors: Tests and manual written by Ruth B. Ekstrom, John W. French, Harry H. Harman, and Diran Dermen.
Publisher: Educational Testing Service.
a) FACTOR CF: FLEXIBILITY OF CLOSURE.
   1) *Hidden Figures Test.*
   2) *Hidden Patterns Test.*
   3) *Copying Test.*
b) FACTOR CS: SPEED OF CLOSURE.
   1) *Gestalt Completion Test.*
   2) *Concealed Words Test.*
   3) *Snowy Pictures.*
c) FACTOR CV: VERBAL CLOSURE.
   1) *Scrambled Words.*
   2) *Hidden Words.*
   3) *Incomplete Words.*
d) FACTOR FA: ASSOCIATIONAL FLUENCY.
   1) *Controlled Associations Test.*
   2) *Opposites Test.*
   3) *Figures of Speech.*
e) FACTOR FE: EXPRESSIONAL FLUENCY.
   1) *Making Sentences.*
   2) *Arranging Words.*
   3) *Rewriting.*
f) FACTOR FF: FIGURAL FLUENCY.
   1) *Ornamentation Test.*
   2) *Elaboration Test.*
   3) *Symbols Test.*
g) FACTOR FI: IDEATIONAL FLUENCY.
   1) *Topics Test.*
   2) *Theme Test.*
   3) *Thing Categories Test.*
h) FACTOR FW: WORD FLUENCY.
   1) *Word Endings Test.*
   2) *Word Beginnings Test.*
   3) *Word Beginnings and Endings Test.*
i) FACTOR I: INDUCTION.
   1) *Letter Sets Test.*
   2) *Locations Test.*
   3) *Figure Classifications.*

j) FACTOR IP: INTEGRATIVE PROCESSES.
  1) *Calendar Test.*
  2) *Following Directions.*
k) FACTOR MA: ASSOCIATIVE MEMORY.
  1) *Picture–Number Test.*
  2) *Object–Number Test.*
  3) *First and Last Names Test.*
l) FACTOR MS: MEMORY SPAN.
  1) *Auditory Number Span Test.*
  2) *Visual Number Span Test.*
  3) *Auditory Letter Span Test.*
m) FACTOR MV: VISUAL MEMORY.
  1) *Shape Memory Test.*
  2) *Building Memory.*
  3) *Map Memory.*
n) FACTOR N: NUMBER.
  1) *Addition Test.*
  2) *Division Test.*
  3) *Subtraction and Multiplication Test.*
  4) *Addition and Subtraction Correction.*
o) FACTOR P: PERCEPTUAL SPEED.
  1) *Finding A's Test.*
  2) *Number Comparison Test.*
  3) *Identical Pictures Test.*
p) FACTOR RG: GENERAL REASONING.
  1) *Arithmetic Aptitude Test.*
  2) *Mathematics Aptitude Test.*
  3) *Necessary Arithmetic Operations Test.*
q) FACTOR RL: LOGICAL REASONING.
  1) *Nonsense Syllogisms Test.*
  2) *Diagramming Relationships.*
  3) *Inference Test.*
  4) *Deciphering Languages.*
r) FACTOR S: SPATIAL ORIENTATION.
  1) *Card Rotations Test.*
  2) *Cube Comparisons Test.*
s) FACTOR SS: SPATIAL SCANNING.
  1) *Maze Tracing Speed Test.*
  2) *Choosing a Path.*
  3) *Map Planning Test.*
t) FACTOR V: VERBAL COMPREHENSION.
  1) *Vocabulary Test I.*
  2) *Vocabulary Test II.*
  3) *Extended Range Vocabulary Test.*
  4) *Advanced Vocabulary Test I.*
  5) *Advanced Vocabulary Test II.*
u) FACTOR VZ: VISUALIZATION.
  1) *Form Board Test.*
  2) *Paper Folding Test.*
  3) *Surface Development Test.*
v) FACTOR XF: FIGURAL FLEXIBILITY.
  1) *Toothpicks Test.*
  2) *Planning Patterns.*
  3) *Storage Test.*
w) FACTOR XU: FLEXIBILITY OF USE.
  1) *Combining Objects.*

  2) *Substitute Uses.*
  3) *Making Groups.*
  4) *Different Uses.*

Cross References: See T5:1405 (40 references), T4:1365 (92 references), 9:572 (27 references), T3:1257 (78 references), and T2:561 (103 references).

[1450]

Klein Group Instrument® for Effective Leadership and Participation in Teams.

Purpose: Designed "to assess a range of behaviors that are essential for effective leadership and teamwork."
Population: Team and group participants of ages 14+.
Publication Date: 2008.
Acronym: KGI®.
Scores, 13: Leadership (Assertiveness, Group Facilitation, Initiative, Total), Negotiation Orientation (Perspective Taking, Constructive Negotiation Approach, Total), Task Focus (Task Analysis, Task Implementation, Total), Interpersonal Focus (Positive Group Affiliation, Feeling Orientation, Total).
Administration: Group or Individual.
Price Data, 2008: $30 per individual online administration including a downloadable User's Guide and Individual Profile of results; $50 per group online administration (plus $25 per group member) including a downloadable User's Guide, Individual Profile, and Group Profile per group member, and 1 downloadable administration manual per group; $50 per administration manual (138 pages).
Time: (25-30) minutes.
Comments: Available online.
Author: Robert R. Klein.
Publisher: Center for Applications of Psychological Type, Inc.
Cross References: For reviews by Philip G. Benson and Myra N. Womble, see 18:65.

[1451]

Knox's Cube Test–Revised.

Purpose: A nonverbal mental test designed to measure attention span and memory of children and adults.
Population: Ages 3 and over.
Publication Dates: 1980–2002.
Acronym: KCT-R.
Scores: Total score only.
Administration: Individual.
Price Data, 2005: $105 per complete kit including manual, tapping cubes, and 15 test/record booklets; $25 per 15 report booklets.
Time: (10-15) minutes.
Comments: Items unchanged from previous edition; Junior and Senior forms have been eliminated.
Author: Mark H. Stone.
Publisher: Stoelting Co.

Cross References: For reviews by Carolyn M. Callahan and Anita M. Hubley, see 16:131; see also T5:1407 (5 references) and T4:1367 (7 references); for reviews by Raymond S. Dean and Jerome M. Sattler of the previous edition, see 9:574 (2 references).

[1452]

Kohlberg's Moral Judgment Interview.
Purpose: To identify stages of moral development.
Population: Ages 10 and over.
Publication Date: 1983.
Scores: Moral Development Stages.
Price Data: Available from publisher.
Time: Administration time not reported.
Authors: Anne Colby and Lawrence Kohlberg.
Publisher: Cambridge University Press.
Cross References: See T5:1408 (9 references), T4:1368 (9 references), and T3:1262 (2 references).

[1453]

The Kohlman Evaluation of Living Skills.
Purpose: "An occupational therapy evaluation that is designed to determine a person's ability to function in basic living skills."
Population: Occupational therapy clients with living skill deficits.
Publication Dates: 1981–1992.
Acronym: KELS.
Scores: 5 areas: Self-care, Safety and Health, Money Management, Transportation and Telephone, Work and Leisure.
Administration: Individual.
Price Data: Available from publisher.
Time: (30–45) minutes.
Comments: Evaluation combines interview questions and tasks; can be used with the elderly, with persons who have cognitively disabling conditions, in court for the determination of commitment, and in discharge planning at acute-care hospitals.
Author: Linda Kohlman Thomson.
Publisher: The American Occupational Therapy Association, Inc.
Cross References: For a review by Gabriele van Lingen, see 14:199.

[1454]

The Kohs Block-Design Test.
Purpose: Designed as "performance tests that have been standardized to measure intelligence."
Population: Mental ages 5–20.
Publication Date: [1919].
Scores: Total score only.
Administration: Individual.
Price Data, 2005: $140 per complete kit including cubes, cards, manual (20 pages), and 50 record blanks; $25 per 50 record blanks; $20 per set of design cards; $100 per set of blocks; $25 per manual.

Time: (30-40) minutes.
Comments: Formerly called The Block-Design Test; modifications appear in Arthur Point Scale of Performance Tests, New Guinea Performance Scales, Ohwaki-Kohs Tactile Block Design Intelligence Test for the Blind, and Pacific Design Construction Test.
Author: S. C. Kohs.
Publisher: Stoelting Co.
Cross References: See T5:1410 (4 references), T4:1370 (5 references), T3:1265 (4 references), and T2:545 (74 references).

[1455]

Kolbe Index.
Purpose: Designed to focus on the "predisposition of a subject to respond to specific behavioral settings with certain patterns of behavior."
Publication Dates: 1987–1997.
Administration: Group or individual.
Price Data: Available from publisher.
Comments: A series of instruments designed to enhance personnel selection and increase self-awareness about instructive talent and potential.
Author: Kathy Kolbe.
Publisher: Kolbe Corp.
  a) KOLBE A™ INDEX.
    Purpose: Designed to measure conative style.
    Population: Adults.
    Acronym: KCI-A.
    Scores, 4: Fact Finder, Follow Thru, Quick Start, Implementor.
    Time: (25) minutes.
  b) KOLBE B™ INDEX.
    Purpose: Designed to "identify the characteristics perceived as necessary to succeed in a given job."
    Population: Job applicants.
    Acronym: KCI-B.
    Time: (15–20) minutes.
  c) KOLBE C™ INDEX.
    Purpose: Designed to "identify the characteristics necessary to function successfully in a specific job."
    Population: Supervisors.
    Acronym: KCI-C.
  d) KOLBE Y™ INDEX.
    Purpose: Designed to assist the respondent in identifying his/her "talent for certain types of activities."
    Population: Youth (5th grade reading level).
    Acronym: KCI-Y.
Cross References: For reviews by Raoul A. Arreola and Chockalingam Viswesvaran, see 14:200; for reviews by Collie Wyatt Conoley and Frank Gresham of an earlier edition, see 12:208.

[1456]

Koppitz Developmental Scoring System for the Bender Gestalt Test, Second Edition.
Purpose: Designed "to document the presence and degree of visual-motor difficulties in individual examinees."

Population: Ages 5-7, 8-85+.
Publication Dates: 1963-2007.
Acronym: KOPPITZ-2.
Scores: Total score only.
Administration: Individual.
Levels, 2: Ages 5-7, 8-85+.
Price Data, 2011: $239 per complete kit including 25 examiner record forms ages 5-7, 25 examiner record forms ages 8-85+, 25 emotional indicators record forms, Bender Gestalt II stimulus cards, examiner's manual (2007, 192 pages), scoring template; $45 per 25 examiner record forms (specify ages 5-7 or 8-85+); $28 per 25 emotional indicators record forms; $59 per Bender Gestalt II stimulus cards set; $91 per examiner's manual (2007, 200 pages); $11 per scoring template.
Time: (6-20) minutes.
Comments: An update of the Bender Gestalt Test for Young Children; current edition utilizes drawings from the Bender Visual-Motor Gestalt Test, Second Edition (16:30).
Author: Cecil R. Reynolds.
Publisher: PRO-ED.
Cross References: For reviews by Joseph C. Kush and Katharine A. Snyder, see 18:66.

[1457]

Krantz Health Opinion Survey.

Purpose: "To measure attitudes toward different treatment approches."
Population: College, healthy adults, and chronic disease populations.
Publication Date: 1980.
Acronym: KHOS.
Scores, 3: Information, Behavioral Involvement, Total.
Administration: Group.
Manual: No manual.
Price Data: Test materials now available free of charge from author.
Time: (10-15) minutes.
Authors: David S. Krantz, Andrew Baum, and Margaret V. Wideman.
Publisher: David S. Krantz.
Cross References: See T5:1412 (4 references) and T4:1373 (1 reference); for a review by James A. Blumenthal, see 9:578 (1 reference); see also T3:1267 (1 reference).

[1458]

Krug Asperger's Disorder Index.

Purpose: To identify individuals who have Asperger's Disorder, to target goals for intervention on the IEP, and for use in research.
Population: Ages 6-0 to 21-11.
Publication Date: 2003.
Acronym: KADI.

Scores: Total score only.
Administration: Individual.
Price Data, 2006: $90 per complete kit; $54 per examiner's manual (39 pages); $20 per 50 profile/examiner record forms (specify ages 6-11 or ages 12-22).
Time: Untimed.
Comments: Ratings by parents, close relatives, teachers, educational assistants, or counselors.
Authors: David A. Krug and Joel R. Arick.
Publisher: PRO-ED.
Cross References: For reviews by Leah M. Nellis and Stephen E. Trotter, see 16:132.

[1459]

Kuder Career Search.

Purpose: Assesses activity preferences to suggest possible satisfying occupations.
Population: Middle school through adult.
Publication Date: 1999.
Acronym: KCS.
Scores, 6: Outdoor/Mechanical, Science/Technical, Arts/Communication, Social/Personal Services, Sales/Management, Business Operations.
Administration: Individual or group.
Price Data: Available from publisher.
Time: (20–25) minutes including scoring.
Comments: Uses preference profile to find best matches from a database of approximately 2,000 employed adults and yields first-person accounts of their occupations/jobs; with Kuder Skills Assessment (1462) and Super's Work Values Inventory–Revised (2620), plus the Kuder Electronic Career Portfolio constitutes the Kuder Career Planning System.
Authors: Frederic Kuder and Donald G. Zytowski.
Publisher: Kuder, Inc.

[1460]

Kuder General Interest Survey, Form E.

Purpose: Constructed to assess "broad interest areas" related to occupational choices.
Population: Grades 6–12.
Publication Dates: 1963–1991.
Scores, 11: Outdoor, Mechanical, Computational, Scientific, Persuasive, Artistic, Literary, Musical, Social Service, Clerical, Verification.
Administration: Group.
Price Data: Available from publisher.
Time: [45–60] minutes.
Comments: Extension of the Kuder vocational interest inventories series.
Author: G. Frederic Kuder.
Publisher: Kuder, Inc.
Cross References: See T5:1413 (1 reference); for reviews by Mark Pope and Donald Thompson, see 12:209; see also T4:1374 (4 references), T3:1269 (4 references),

and 8:1009 (16 references); for reviews by Barbara A. Kirk, Paul R. Lohnes, and John N. McCall of an earlier edition, and excerpted reviews by T. R. Husek and Robert F. Stahmann, see 7:1024 (8 references).

[1461]

Kuder Occupational Interest Survey, Revised (Form DD).

Purpose: Measures individual interests in order to "suggest promising occupations and college majors in rank order, based on examinee's interest pattern."
Population: Grade 10 through adult.
Publication Dates: 1956–1985.
Acronym: KOIS.
Scores, 4: Dependability, Vocational Interest Estimates (10 areas), Occupational Scales (approximately 100), College Major Scales (approximately 40).
Administration: Group.
Price Data: Available from publisher.
Time: (30–45) minutes.
Comments: Includes Vocational Interest Estimate scales identical in content to those of the Kuder Preference Record, Form C and the Kuder General Interest Survey, Form E.
Authors: Frederic Kuder, Esther E. Diamond, and Donald G. Zytowski (manual supplement).
Publisher: Kuder, Inc.
Cross References: See T4:1375 (1 reference); for reviews by Edwin L. Herr and Mary L. Tenopyr, see 10:167 (3 references); see also T3:1270 (12 references), 8:1010 (41 references), and T2: 2194 (13 references); for reviews by Robert H. Dolliver and W. Bruce Walsh, and excerpted reviews by Frederick G. Brown and Robert F. Stahmann, see 7:1025 (19 references).

[1462]

Kuder Skills Assessment.

Purpose: Assesses self-efficacy in six skill areas.
Population: Middle school through adult.
Publication Date: 2001.
Acronym: KSA.
Scores, 6: Outdoor/Mechanical, Science/Technical, Arts/Communication, Social/Personal Services, Sales Management, Business Operations.
Administration: Individual or group.
Price Data: Available from publisher.
Time: (15–20) minutes.
Comments: Online administration; instant scoring; combined report with Kuder Career Search (1459) available; with Kuder Career Search and Super's Work Values Inventory–Revised (2620), plus the Kuder Electronic Career Portfolio, constitutes the Kuder Career Planning System.
Authors: Donald G. Zytowski and Darrell Luzzo.
Publisher: Kuder, Inc.

[1463]

Kuhlmann-Anderson Tests, Eighth Edition.

Purpose: "Designed to provide a measure of an individual's academic potential through assessing cognitive skills related to the learning process."
Population: Grades K, 1, 2–3, 3–4, 5–6, 7–9, 9–12.
Publication Dates: 1927–1982.
Acronym: KA.
Scores, 6: 3 raw scores (Verbal, Nonverbal, Full) and 3 derived scores.
Administration: Group.
Price Data: See www.ststesting.com for prices.
Levels, 7: K, A, BC, CD, EF, G, and H.
Manual: Separate manual of directions for each level.
Authors: F. Kuhlmann (fourth and earlier editions) and Rose G. Anderson.
Publisher: Scholastic Testing Service, Inc.
  a) LEVEL K.
    Population: Kindergarten.
    Time: 28(50–75) minutes in 2 days.
  b) LEVEL A.
    Population: Grade 1.
    Time: 28(50–75) minutes in 2 days.
  c) LEVEL BC.
    Population: Grades 2, 3.
    Time: 28(50–75) minutes in 2 days.
  d) LEVEL CD.
    Population: Grades 3, 4.
    Time: 35(50–75) minutes.
  e) LEVEL EF.
    Population: Grades 5, 6.
    Time: 40(50–75) minutes.
  f) LEVEL G.
    Population: Grades 7–9.
    Time: 40(50–75) minutes.
  g) LEVEL H.
    Population: Grades 9–12.
    Time: 40(50–75) minutes.
Cross References: See T4:1377 (2 references); for reviews by Michael D. Hiscox and Ronald C. Rodgers, see 9:579 (2 references); see T3:1272 (13 references) and T2:398 (53 references); for reviews by William B. Michael and Douglas A. Pidgeon, and an excerpted review by Frederick B. Davis of the seventh edition, see 6:466 (11 references); see also 5:348 (15 references); for reviews by Henry E. Garrett and David Segel of an earlier edition, see 5:302 (10 references); for reviews by W. G. Emmett and Stanley S. Maryolf, see 3:236 (25 references); for a review by Henry E. Garrett, see 2:1404 (15 references); for reviews by Psyche Cattell, S. A. Courtis, and Austin H. Turney, see 1:1049.

[1464]

Kundu Introversion Extraversion Inventory.

Purpose: Designed to obtain a measure of the introversion-extraversion dimension of adult behavior to be used for diagnosis, selection, or career guidance.

Population: Adults.
Publication Date: 1976.
Scores: Total score only.
Administration: Group.
Price Data: Available from publisher.
Time: (20–40) minutes.
Author: Ramanath Kundu.
Publisher: Ramanath Kundu [India] [No reply from publisher; status unknown].

[1465]

Kundu Neurotic Personality Inventory.
Purpose: Designed to measure neurotic tendencies.
Population: Adults.
Publication Dates: 1965–1987.
Acronym: KNPI.
Scores: Item scores only.
Administration: Individual or group.
Price Data: Available from publisher.
Foreign Language Edition: Bengali edition available.
Time: (20–30) minutes.
Author: Ramanath Kundu.
Publisher: Ramanath Kundu [India] [No reply from publisher; status unknown].
Cross References: See T2:1257 (2 references) and P:140 (5 references).

[1466]

The Lake St. Clair Incident.
Purpose: To examine group and individual decision-making processes, help individuals and groups perceive and evaluate their interactions and styles of communicating, and utilize the instrument to simply have fun or create an environment.
Population: Adults.
Publication Dates: 1977-1978.
Acronym: LSC.
Scores, 3: Autocratic, Consultative, Consensual.
Administration: Individual in part.
Price Data, 2006: $46.95 per 10 test booklets and 1 manual (1977, 22 pages); $27.50 per manual; $46.95 per 25 test booklets.
Time: (65-80) minutes.
Author: Albert A. Canfield.
Publisher: Western Psychological Services.
Cross References: For a review by Jack L. Bodden, see 9:582.

[1467]

Language Arts Objective Sequence.
Purpose: "Helps evaluate students' current [language arts] performance levels and identify specific goals and objectives."
Population: Grades 1–12.
Publication Date: 2001.

Scores: 9 ratings/objectives: Readiness (Level 3), Listening (Levels 3, 2), Speaking (Levels 3, 2, 1), Reading–Word Recognition (Level 3), Reading–Comprehension (Levels 3, 2, 1), Writing–Handwriting (Level 3), Writing–Spelling (Levels 3, 2), Writing Process (Levels 3, 2, 1), Writing–Grammar (Levels 3, 2, 1).
Administration: Individual.
Levels, 3: 1, 2, 3.
Price Data, 2006: $39.95 per assessment manual (120 pages) including 24 reproducible forms and checklists; $150 per report generating software (for Windows) Language Arts Objective Sequence Reports (LOSR) including LOS manual.
Time: Administration time not reported.
Comments: Intended to be used by teachers as an informal "curriculum guide, bank of objectives, rubric guide, or structured observation system"; some objectives do not include all 3 levels.
Authors: Jacqueline Robertson and Sheldon Braaten.
Publisher: Research Press.

[1468]

Language Assessment Scales, 2nd Edition–Oral.
Purpose: Designed to "measure those English and language skills necessary for functioning in a mainstream academic environment."
Population: Grades 1–6, 7--2.
Publication Dates: 1987–1991.
Acronym: LAS-O.
Scores, 6: Vocabulary, Listening Comprehension, Story Retelling, Minimal Sound Pairs, Phonemes, Total.
Administration: Individual.
Levels, 2: 1, 2.
Parts, 2: Oral Language (for Level 1 & 2), Pronunciation (for Grades 2–12).
Forms, 2: C, D.
Price Data, 2006: $80 per test review kit including administration manual, scoring and interpretation manual, student test booklet or multicopy scoresheet, and cue picture booklet along with test reviewer's guide (specify level and form); $51 per 50 answer documents; $54 per reusable cue picture booklet; $26 per audiocassette (specify level and form); $40 per administration manual (specify level); $42 per scoring and interpretation manual (specify level); $40 per technical report (1991, 144 pages); $193 per examiner's kit (specify level).
Foreign Language Edition: Spanish edition (1990) available.
Time: [15] minutes.
Comments: Language Proficiency Score also incorporates Language Assessment Scales, Reading and Writing (1469).
Authors: Edward A. DeAvila and Sharon E. Duncan.
Publisher: CTB/McGraw-Hill.
Cross References: See T5:1420 (1 references); for reviews by Natalie L. Hedberg and Pamela S. Tidwell, see 12:210 (1 reference); for a review of the Language Assessment Scales by Lyn Haber, see 9:584 (1 reference).

[1469]

Language Assessment Scales, 2nd Edition, Reading and Writing.

Purpose: Designed to measure "English language skills in reading and writing necessary for functioning in a mainstream academic environment."
Population: Language-minority students in Grades 2–3, 4–6, 7–11.
Publication Dates: 1988–2000.
Acronym: LAW R/W.
Scores, 3: Reading, Writing, Total.
Administration: Group.
Levels, 3: 1, 2, 3.
Forms, 2: A, B.
Price Data, 2006: $125 per 35 Level 1 Reading test booklets and examiner's manual (67 pages); $80 per 35 Level 2 or Level 3 Reading test booklets and Reading/Writing examiner's manual (Level 2, 79 pages; Level 3, 73 pages); $61 per 35 Writing test booklets (specify level); $53 per 50 student answer documents (sepecify Level 2 or Level 3); $188 per 9 Level 1 scoring stencils (Reading only); $22 per Level 2 or Level 3 scoring stencil (Reading only); $19 per administration manual (specify level); materials also available in Spanish; $29 per technical manual (98 pages); $336 for LASSCORE site license.
Time: (50–75) minutes for Level 1; (49–87) minutes for Level 2; (53–86) minutes for Level 3.
Comments: May be used in conjunction with LAS Oral, 2nd Edition (1468).
Authors: Sharon E. Duncan and Edward A. DeAvila.
Publisher: CTB/McGraw-Hill.
Cross References: See T5:1421 (4 references); for reviews by C. Dale Carpenter and Thomas W. Guyette, see 12:211; see also T4:1386 (5 references).

[1470]

Language Assessment Skills Links Benchmark Assessment.

Purpose: Designed to "measure students' skills in speaking, listening, reading and writing."
Population: Grades K-12.
Publication Date: 2005.
Acronym: LAS Links Benchmark Assessment.
Scores, 6: Speaking, Listening, Reading, Writing, Comprehension, Oral.
Administration: Individual or group.
Levels, 5: Grades K-1; Grades 2-3; Grades 4-5; Grades 6-8; Grades 9-12.
Price Data, 2006: $$25 per 10 student books; $15 per student answer documents (specify book number and grades); $14.95 per examiner's guide (99-111 pages, specify level); $17.50 per 10 student profile sheets (specify grades).
Comments: Test is designed for English language learners.
Author: CTB/McGraw-Hill.
Publisher: CTB/McGraw-Hill.

a) SPEAKING.
Time: (2-8) minutes.
Subtests, 4: Speak in Words, Speak in Sentences, Make Conversation, Tell a Story.
b) LISTENING.
Time: (5-15) minutes.
Subtests, 3: Listen for Information, Listen in the Classroom, Listen/Comprehend.
c) READING.
Time: (10-20) minutes.
Subtests, 3: Analyze Words, Read Words, Read for Understanding.
d) WRITING.
Time: (5-15) minutes.
Subtests, 3-4: Use Conventions, Write About, Write Why, Write in Detail (not included in Grades K-1).

[1471]

Language Assessment Skills Links K-12 Assessments.

Purpose: Designed to "measure students' skills in speaking, listening, reading, writing, and comprehension."
Population: Grades K-12.
Publication Date: 2005.
Acronym: LAS Links K-12.
Scores, 7: Speaking, Listening, Reading, Writing, Overall, Comprehension, Oral.
Levels, 5: Grades K-1; Grades 2-3; Grades 4-5; Grades 6-8; Grades 9-12.
Price Data, 2006: $92.45 per classroom kit including consumable student book, cue picture book, examiner's guide (66-69 pages), and audio CD (specify Grades K-1 or 2-3); $43.55 per classroom kit including reusable student book, student answer book, examiner's guide and audio CD (specify Grades 4-5, 6-8, or 9-12); $35 per 10 consumable student books (specify Grades K-1 or 2-3); $42 per 10 reusable student books (specify Grades 4-5, 6-8, or 9-12); $50.40 per cue picture book (specify Grades K-1 or 2-3); $15 pr 10 student answer books (specify Grades 4-5, 6-8, 9-12); $19.95 per examiner's guide (specify grades); $24.95 per audio cassette (specify grades); $24.95 per audio CD (specify grades); $17.50 per student profile sheets; $39.50 per interpretation guide.
Comments: Test is designed for English-language learners.
Author: CTB/McGraw-Hill.
Publisher: CTB/McGraw-Hill.
a) SPEAKING.
Administration: Individual.
Time: (5-15) minutes.
Subtests, 4: Speak in Words, Speak in Sentences, Make Conversation, Tell a Story.
b) LISTENING.
Administration: Individual or group.
Time: (10-20) minutes.
Subtests, 3: Listen for Information, Listen in the Classroom, Listen/Comprehend.

c) READING.
Administration: Individual or group.
Time: (35-45) minutes.
Subtests, 3: Analyze Words, Read Words, Read for Understanding.
d) WRITING.
Administration: Individual or group.
Time: (35-45) minutes.
Subtests, 3: Use Conventions, Write About, Write Why, Write in Detail [not included in Grades K-1].

[1472]

Language Processing Test 3: Elementary.

Purpose: Designed to identify "students' language processing strengths and weaknesses in a hierarchical framework."
Population: Ages 5-0 to 11-11.
Publication Dates: 1985-2005.
Acronym: LPT 3.
Scores, 8: Labeling, Stating Functions, Associations, Categorization, Similarities, Differences, Multiple Meanings, Attributes.
Administration: Individual.
Price Data: Available from publisher.
Time: (30) minutes.
Authors: Gail J. Richard and Mary Anne Hanner.
Publisher: LinguiSystems, Inc.
Cross References: For a review by Natalie Rathvon, see 17:103; see also T5:1424 (5 references); for reviews by Thomas W. Guyette and Lyn Haber of an earlier edition, see 10:169.

[1473]

Language Proficiency Test Series.

Purpose: Designed to aid in student placement and the evaluation of student language proficiency in reading, writing, listening, and speaking.
Population: Grades K–12, specifically ELL students.
Publication Dates: 1998-2001.
Acronym: LPTS.
Scores, 3: Reading, Writing, Listening/Speaking.
Administration: Individual or group.
Forms, 24: Listening/Speaking: L/S 1–Grades K–2, L/S 2–Grades 3–5, L/S 3–Grades 6–8, L/S 4–Grades 9–12, Reading: R1–Grades K–2, R2–Grades 3–5, R3–Grades 6–8, R4–Grades 9–12, Writing: W1–Grades K–2, W2–Grades 3–5, W3–Grades 6–8, W4–Grades 9–12; alternate forms available for all subjects and grade clusters.
Price Data, 2010: $32 per administrator's sample set including Administration and Scoring Guide plus one test booklet each for Reading, Writing, and Listening/Speaking at grade level of choice (K-2, 3–5, 6–8, or 9–12); $59.50 per 25 Grades K–2 or for Grades 3–5 (Form A or B) Reading Test booklets; $51.50 per 25 Grades 6–8 or Grades 9–12 (Form A or B) Reading Test booklets;

$12.50 per 25 scannable answer sheets for Reading Test (Grades 6–12 only); $1.25 each for scoring Reading Test booklet; $26.50 per 25 Writing Test booklets (Grades K-2, 3–5, 6–8, or 9–12, Form A or B); $1.25–$2.30 each for scoring Writing Test booklet; $26.50 per 25 Listening/Speaking Test booklets (Grades K-2, 3–5, 6–8, or 9–12, Form A or B); $1.25–$2.85 each for scoring Listening/Speaking Test booklet; $59.50 per technical manual (2004, 36 pages).
Time: (25) minutes average per test.
Author: MetriTech, Inc.
Publisher: MetriTech, Inc.
Cross References: For reviews by Marie Miller-Whitehead and Judith A. Monsaas, see 15:134.

[1474]

Language Sampling, Analysis, and Training–Third Edition.

Purpose: "Designed to analyze the syntax and morphology of children who are producing a significant number of utterances containing at least three morphemes."
Population: Children with language delay.
Publication Dates: 1974–1999.
Acronym: LSAT-3.
Scores, 39: Word Morpheme (Sentences Total, Words Total, Morphemes Total, Words/Sentences Means, Morphemes/Sentence Means, Word-Morpheme Index), Noun Phrase Constituents (Pronouns, Prepositions, Possessive Marker, Demonstratives, Articles, Plurals, Locatives, Conjunctions), Verb Phrase Constituents (Modals, Particles, Copula, Present Progressive Tense, Present Tense-3rd Singular, Past Tense, Irregular), Simple Sentence Constructions (Noun Phrase, Verb Phrase, Verb Phrase + Noun Phrase, Noun Phrase + Verb Phrase + [Noun Phrase], Noun Phrase + Copula + N/Adj, Unclassifiable Constructions), Complex Sentences (Coordination, Subordination-Infinitives, Adverbials, Indirect Questions, Verb + [that] + Sentence, Relatives, Direct Quotations, Complex in More Than One Way, Unclassifiable, Percentage Complex), Questions, Negatives.
Administration: Individual.
Price Data, 2006: $100 per complete kit including manual (1999, 163 pages), analysis forms, and transcription sheets; $40 per manual; $40 per analysis forms; $30 per transcription sheets.
Time: Administration time varies.
Comments: Visual and verbal stimuli for eliciting language sample determined by examiner; tape recording recommended for recording responses; a detailed tutorial with self-checking exercises covering all steps in the procedure, multicultural issues, setting targets, training, measuring and reporting change are new inclusions in the third edition handbook.
Authors: Dorothy Tyack and Gail Portnuff Venable.
Publisher: PRO-ED.

Cross References: For a review by Sheila Pratt, see 14:201; for a review by Margaret C. Byrne of an earlier edition, see 9:590.

[1475]

LARR Test of Emergent Literacy.

Purpose: Designed to provide "a simple measure of young children's level of literacy on entry to compulsory schooling."
Population: Students entering school.
Publication Date: 1993.
Acronym: LARRTEL.
Scores: Total score only.
Administration: Group.
Price Data: Available from publisher.
Time: (25) minutes.
Comments: Based on the Linguistic Awareness Reading Readiness (LARR) Test (T6:1434).
Author: National Foundation for Educational Research.
Publisher: GL Assessment [England].
Cross References: For a review by Jill Ann Jenkins, see 16:133.

[1476]

Law Enforcement Applicant Inventory.

Purpose: Designed to "identify individuals who have the integrity and attitudes important to become model law enforcement officers and security personnel."
Population: Ages 18 and over.
Publication Dates: 1991–1996.
Acronym: LEAI.
Scores, 12: Honesty, Nonviolence, Drug Avoidance, Risk Avoidance, Safety, Stress Tolerance, Validity/Distortion, Validity/Accuracy, Candidate Potential Index, Criminal Justice Orientation, Background and Work Experience, Narrative Information.
Administration: Individual or group.
Price Data, 2005: $16 including 1–999 reports for Internet scoring with booklets; $16 including 1–999 reports for Internet scoring without booklets; $16 including 1–999 reports for QuantaTouch Test; $16 including 1–999 reports for QUANTA Software for Windows with booklets; $16 including 1–999 reports for QUANTA Software for Windows without booklets.
Time: (30–45) minutes.
Comments: Test can be scored via Touch Test, Internet, or Optical Scanning Software.
Author: Pearson Reid London House.
Publisher: Pearson Performance Solutions [No reply from publisher; status unknown].

[1477]

Law Enforcement Assessment and Development Report.

Purpose: Intended to evaluate personality implications for performance in law enforcement jobs.

Population: Applicants and incumbents for law enforcement and other public safety positions.
Publication Dates: 1967–1987.
Acronym: LEADR.
Scores, 37: 4 personality dimensions (Emotional Adjustment, Integrity/Control, Intellectual Efficiency, Interpersonal Relations); 16 normal personality primary factor scores; 17 pathological characteristics; Performance Index; Tough Poise; Independence; Leadership, Accident Proneness.
Administration: Group or individual.
Price Data, 2005: $40 per 25 reusable test booklets; $18 per 25 answer sheets; $30 per manual (1987, 43 pages); $33 per introductory kit including manual, test booklet, answer sheet, and prepaid processing form; $19.50 to $30 per individual score report.
Time: (120) minutes.
Comments: Represents a computer-based analysis from the Clinical Analysis Questionnaire (T7:540); on-site software scoring and report options available.
Author: IPAT staff.
Publisher: Institute for Personality and Ability Testing, Inc. (IPAT).
Cross References: For a review by David S. Hargrove, see 10:170; for a review by Lawrence Allen of the earlier edition, see 9:593.

[1478]

Law School Admission Test.

Purpose: "To measure skills that are considered essential for success in law school."
Population: Law school entrants.
Publication Dates: 1948–2011.
Acronym: LSAT.
Scores: Total score plus unscored writing sample.
Administration: Group.
Price Data, 2011: $139 per LSAT; $68 per late registration; $35 per test center change; $68 per test date change; $252 per nonpublished test center (U.S.A., Canada, Puerto Rico); $335 per nonpublished test center (all other countries); $42 per hand scoring; $42 per former registrants score report; $124 per Credential Assembly Service (CAS) subscription (5 years no report); $16 per law school report.
Time: 175 minutes; 35 minutes per writing sample.
Comments: Test administered 4 times annually (June, September/October, December, February) at centers established by the publisher.
Author: Law School Admission Council, Inc.
Publisher: Law School Admission Council, Inc.
Cross References: See T5:1434 (2 references); for reviews by James B. Erdmann and by Robert F. McMorris, Elizabeth L. Bringsjord, and Wei-Ping Liu, see 13:174 (8 references); see also T4:1400 (4 references); for a review by Gary B. Melton of an earlier edition, see 9:594 (2 references); see also T3:1292 (6 references), 8:1093 (7 references), and T2:2349 (7 references); for a review by Leo A. Munday of earlier forms, see 7:1098

(23 references); see also 5:928 (7 references); for a review by Alexander G. Wesman, see 4:815 (6 references).

[1479]

Leader Behavior Analysis II.

Purpose: Developed to assess leadership style.
Population: Middle and upper level managers.
Publication Date: 1991.
Acronym: LBAII.
Scores, 6: Style Flexibility, Style Effectiveness, Directing Style, Coaching Style, Supporting Style, Delegating Style.
Administration: Group.
Editions, 2: Self, Other.
Price Data: Price information available from publisher for complete kit including 1 LBAII-Self instrument, 8 LBAII-Other instruments, data summary sheet, and scoring instructions.
Time: [15-20] minutes.
Comments: Ratings by employees and self-ratings.
Authors: Drea Zigarmi, Douglas Forsyth, Kenneth Blanchard, and Ronald Hambleton (tests).
Publisher: The Ken Blanchard Companies.
Cross References: See T5:1436 (1 reference); for reviews by H. John Bernardin and Donna K. Cooke and by Sharon McNeely, see 12:212; see also T4:1402 (1 reference).

[1480]

Leader Behavior Questionnaire, Revised.

Purpose: Constructed as a measure of "organizational leadership."
Population: Managers and employees.
Publication Dates: 1988–1996.
Acronym: LBQ.
Scores: Visionary Leadership Behavior Scales (Clear Leadership, Communicative Leadership, Consistent Leadership, Caring Leadership, Creative Leadership) Visionary Leadership Characteristics Scales (Confident Leadership, Empowered Leadership, Visionary Leadership), Visionary Culture Building Scales (Organizational Leadership, Cultural Leadership).
Administration: Group.
Forms, 2: Self, Other.
Price Data, 1996: $7.95 per self questionnaire; $2.95 per other questionnaire; $24.95 per trainer's guide (1996, 63 pages).
Time: (10–20) minutes.
Author: Marshall Sashkin.
Publisher: HRD Press, Inc.
Cross References: For reviews by Janet Barnes-Farrell and Hilda Wing, see 14:202.

[1481]

Leadership and Self-Development Scale.

Purpose: Measurement of the effectiveness of a leadership workshop for college women.

Population: College.
Publication Dates: 1976-1979.
Scores, 9: Assertiveness, Risk Taking, Self-Concept, Setting Goals, Decision Making, Obtaining a Followership, Conflict Resolution, Group Roles, Evaluation.
Administration: Group.
Manual: No manual; mimeographed research report (1976, 20 pages).
Price Data, 2001: Now free upon request from publisher.
Time: Administration time not reported.
Authors: Virginia Hoffman and Patricia B. Elmore.
Publisher: Patricia B. Elmore.
Cross References: For a review by Robert R. Mc-Crae, see 9:597; see also T3:1298 (2 references).

[1482]

Leadership Appraisal Survey.

Purpose: "An assessment of leadership practices and attitudes as viewed through the eyes of others."
Population: Adults.
Publication Dates: 1971-1997.
Scores, 5: Philosophy, Planning, Implementation, Evaluation, Total.
Administration: Group.
Manual: No manual.
Price Data, 2001: $7.95 per instrument.
Time: Administration time not reported.
Comments: Self-administered survey.
Author: Jay Hall.
Publisher: Teleometrics International, Inc.
Cross References: See T3:2351 (1 reference); for a review by Abraham K. Korman of the Styles of Leadership and Management, see 8:1185 (8 references).

[1483]

Leadership Competency Inventory.

Purpose: Measures an individual's use of four competencies related to leadership.
Population: Managers and employees.
Publication Dates: 1993–1996.
Acronym: LCI.
Scores, 4: Information Seeking, Conceptual Thinking, Strategic Orientation, Service Orientation.
Administration: Group or individual.
Price Data, 2006: $69 per complete kit including 10 profiles and interpretive notes (20 pages), and 10 questionnaires; $29 per 10 (employee version) questionnaires; $55 per 10 Development Assistant booklets.
Time: [30–40] minutes.
Comments: Self-scored questionnaire.
Author: Hay Group.
Publisher: Hay Group.
Cross References: For a review by L. Carolyn Pearson, see 13:175.

[1484]

Leadership Development Report.

Purpose: "An expert system providing insight into how a manager's personality affects his or her performance and how to modify a manager's behavior within his or her natural limits."
Population: Adults.
Publication Dates: 1996–2000.
Acronym: LDR.
Scores, 34: Impulsivity, Understanding, Complexity, Risk Taking, Breadth of Interests, Innovation, Endurance, Cognitive Structure, Order, Organization, Play, Self-Esteem, Anxiety, Tolerance, Change, Achievement, Aggression, Responsibility, Abasement, Value Orthodoxy, Energy Level, Harm Avoidance, Affiliation, Dominance, Exhibition, Interpersonal Affect, Succorance, Social Participation, Social Adroitness, Conformity, Defendence, Social Recognition, Nurturance, Autonomy.
Administration: Group or individual.
Price Data, 2010: $24 per test manual; $5 per test booklet; $70-$98 (depending on volume) per report available through fax-in scoring system or online at www.sigmatesting.com.
Time: 40 minutes.
Comments: Includes items from the Jackson Personality Inventory–Revised (1374), The Personality Research Form (2028), and The Survey of Work Styles (2646) (all still available for sale). The LDR can be administered in two ways: answer sheets can be faxed to publisher, bound reports are returned via courier or sent by email; or test can be administered and scored directly through a www.sigmatesting.com account.
Authors: Douglas N. Jackson and Julie Carswell.
Publisher: SIGMA Assessment Systems, Inc.
Cross References: For a review by Mark A. Staal, see 15:135.

[1485]

Leadership Effectiveness Analysis™.

Purpose: Developed to identify leadership skills and behaviors in a 360 degree context.
Population: Managers, supervisors, individual contributors at all levels.
Publication Dates: 1981–2001.
Acronym: LEA.
Scores, 23: Conservative, Innovative, Technical, Self, Strategic, Persuasive, Outgoing, Excitement, Restraint, Structuring, Tactical, Communication, Delegation, Control, Feedback, Management Focus, Dominant, Production, Cooperation, Consensual, Authority, Empathy, Exaggeration.
Administration: Group.
Price Data: Available from publisher.
Foreign Language Editions: English (American), English (British), Chinese (Simplified characters), Chinese (Traditional characters), Danish, Dutch, Finnish, French, German, Italian, Japanese, Portuguese (Brazil), Spanish, and Swedish.
Time: (45) minutes.
Comments: Requires training by publisher before purchase and use.
Authors: James T. Mahoney (test) and Robert I. Kabacoff (manual).
Publisher: Management Research Group.

[1486]

Leadership/Impact.

Purpose: Provides people in leadership with information about their current performance as well as insights into ways they can enhance their effectiveness through the leadership strategies they employ and the impact they have on others.
Population: Leaders at the executive level.
Publication Date: 1996.
Acronym: L/I.
Scores: 3 Dimensions of Effectiveness: Organizational Effectiveness, Personal Effectiveness, Balance; 12 Types of Impact on Others: Impact (Achievement, Self-Actualizing, Humanistic-Encouraging, Affiliative), Passive/Defensive (Approval, Conventional, Dependent, Avoidance), Aggressive/Defensive (Oppositional, Power, Competitive, Perfectionistic); 10 Domains of Leadership: Personal Focus (Envisioning, Role Modeling), Interpersonal Focus (Mentoring, Stimulating Thinking, Referring, Monitoring, Providing Feedback), Organizational Focus (Reinforcing, Influencing, Creating a Setting).
Administration: Individual or group.
Price Data: Price data for test materials including Facilitator's Guide available from publisher.
Time: Administration time not reported.
Comments: Ratings by self and at least three coworkers.
Author: Robert A. Cooke.
Publisher: Human Synergistics International.

[1487]

Leadership Opinion Questionnaire.

Purpose: To measure supervisory leadership dimensions.
Population: Supervisors and prospective supervisors.
Publication Dates: 1960–1989.
Acronym: LOQ.
Scores, 2: Structure, Consideration.
Administration: Individual or group.
Price Data, 2002: $72 per start-up kit including 25 test booklets and examiner's manual; $53 per 25 test booklets (quantity discounts available); $28 per examiner's manual; price data available from publisher for Quanta Computer Administration and Scoring software (Windows); $72 per Quanta start-up kit including examiner's manual and 25 administrations and scoring (does not include Quanta software).

Time: No limit (approximately 10–15 minutes).
Author: Edwin A. Reishman.
Publisher: Pearson Performance Solutions [No reply from publisher; status unknown].
Cross References: See T5:1444 (4 references), T4:1409 (7 references), T3:1300 (10 references), 8:1177 (52 references), and T2:2454 (15 references); for a review by Cecil A. Gibb, see 7:1149 (41 references); for reviews by Jerome E. Doppelt and Wayne K. Kirchner, see 6:1190 (6 references).

[1488]

Leadership Practices Inventory [Pfeiffer & Company International Publishers].
Purpose: Designed to provide ratings of five leadership behaviors.
Population: Managers.
Publication Dates: 1990–1992.
Acronym: LPI.
Scores, 5: Challenging the Process, Inspiring a Shared Vision, Enabling Others to Act, Modeling the Way, Encouraging the Heart.
Administration: Group.
Editions, 2: Self, Other.
Price Data: Price information available from publisher for trainer's package including LPI: Self-Assessment booklet and inventory, LPI: Other inventory, technical manual (1992, 31 pages) and trainer's manual (1990, 39 pages); LPI: Self-Assessment booklet and inventory; LPI: Other inventory; IBM-PC (or compatible) scoring software.
Time: Administration time not reported.
Comments: Scale for ratings by employees and for self-ratings.
Authors: James M. Kouzes and Barry Z. Posner.
Publisher: Jossey-Bass, A Wiley Company.
Cross References: See T5:1448 (1 reference); for reviews by Frederick T. L. Leong and Mary A. Lewis, see 12:213; see also T4:1411 (2 references).

[1489]

Leadership Practices Inventory–Individual Contributor [Second Edition].
Purpose: "Designed to assist a nonmanagerial leader in assessing the extent to which he or she engages in certain leadership behaviors."
Population: Nonmanagerial leaders.
Publication Dates: 1990–1997.
Acronym: LPI-IC.
Scores, 5: Challenging, Inspiring, Enabling, Modeling, Encouraging.
Administration: Group.
Forms, 2: Self, Observer.
Price Data: Available from publisher.
Time: Administration time not reported.

Comments: Nonmanagerial version of the Leadership Practices Inventory (1488); a 30-item Self or Observer rating; hand or computer scored (computer scoring recommended); computer scoring software available.
Authors: James M. Kouzes and Barry Z. Posner.
Publisher: Jossey-Bass, A Wiley Company.
Cross References: For reviews by John M. Enger and L. Carolyn Pearson, see 14:204; for reviews by Frederick T. L. Leong and Mary A. Lewis of an earlier edition of the Leadership Practices Inventory, see 12:213; see also T4:1411 (2 references).

[1490]

The Leadership Q-Sort Test (A Test of Leadership Values).
Purpose: Designed to "assess an individual's values with respect to the leadership role."
Population: Adults.
Publication Date: 1958.
Acronym: LQST.
Scores, 7: Personal Integrity, Consideration of Others, Mental Health, Technical Information, Decision Making, Teaching and Communication, Total.
Administration: Individual or group.
Price Data: Available from publisher.
Time: (40–45) minutes.
Author: Russell N. Cassel.
Publisher: Psychometric Affiliates.
Cross References: For reviews by Joel T. Campbell, Cecil A. Gibb, and William Stephenson, see 6:134 (6 references).

[1491]

Leadership Skills Inventory [Revised] [Consulting Resource Group International, Inc.].
Purpose: Designed to benchmark 60 leadership competencies and skills required for effective leadership; also offers 360° feedback with the LSI-Others version.
Population: Adults.
Publication Dates: 1992-2006.
Acronym: LSI.
Scores, 6: Self-Management Skills, Interpersonal Communication Skills, Coaching/Counseling and Problem Management Skills, Skills for Developing Teams and Organizations, Versatility and Organizational Development Skills, Total Score.
Administration: Individual or group.
Price Data, 2006: $16.95 per Leadership Skills Inventory-Self (2006, 20 pages); $9.95 per Leadership Skills Inventory-Others (2006, 8 pages); $38 per Trainer's Guidelines (1996, 18 pages); $50 per Transforming Leadership Book–Second Edition (1998, 340 pages).
Editions, 3: Self (print), Others (print), Self (online).
Time: (30) minutes.
Comments: Self-administered and self-scored.

Authors: Ken Keis and Terry D. Anderson.
Publisher: Consulting Resource Group International, Inc.

> *a)* LEADERSHIP SKILLS INVENTORY-OTHERS.
> **Acronym**: LSI-O.
> **Price Data**: $9.95 per test booklet.
> *b)* LEADERSHIP SKILLS INVENTORY-SELF.
> **Acronym**: LSI-S.
> **Price Data**: $16.95 per test booklet.
> *c)* ONLINE LEADERSHIP SKILLS INVENTORY-SELF.
> **Acronym**: Online LSI-S.
> **Price Data**: $16.95 per online assessment code.

Cross References: For reviews by Alan D. Moore and Nambury S. Raju of an earlier edition, see 16:134; for reviews by Mary Henning-Stout and George C. Thornton, III of an earlier edition, see 13:176.

[1492]
Leadership Skills Profile.

Purpose: Designed to analyze "the strengths and weaknesses of managerial and executive candidates."
Population: Ages 18 and over.
Publication Date: 2003.
Acronym: LSP.
Scores, 42: Leadership Dimensions: Technical Orientation, Analytical Orientation, Decisiveness, Creativity, Thoroughness, Objectivity, Risk Taking, Open-Mindedness, First Impression, Interpersonal Relations, Sensitivity, Social Astuteness, Conflict Management, Communication, Formal Presentation, Persuasiveness, Negotiation, Listening, Achievement/Motivation, Self Discipline, Flexibility, Independence, Self Esteem, Emotional Control, Dependability, Ambition, General Leadership Effectiveness, Assuming Responsibility, Vision, Emphasizing Excellence, Organizational Spokesperson, Subordinate Involvement, Facilitating Teamwork, Inspirational Role Model, Short-Term Planning, Strategic Planning, Organizing the Work of Others, Delegation, Monitoring and Controlling, Motivating Others, Attracting Staff, Productivity.
Administration: Individual or group.
Price Data, 2010: $24 per test manual; $5 per test booklet; $160-$235 (depending on volume) per administration through fax-in scoring or online scoring at www.SigmaTesting.com.
Time: 40 minutes.
Comments: Publisher scoring services provided via internet or fax. Two reports available: Selection and Development.
Author: Douglas N. Jackson.
Publisher: SIGMA Assessment Systems, Inc.
Cross References: For reviews by Philip G. Benson and John S. Geisler, see 16:135.

[1493]
Leadership Spectrum Profile.

Purpose: To identify leadership business priorities in a given situation, develop business acumen, improve team effectiveness, enhance strategic thinking, and to reflect that leadership requirements change by context or circumstance.
Population: Senior leaders, teams, and individuals in leadership positions.
Publication Dates: 1998–2000.
Acronym: LSP.
Scores: 6 choices: Inventor (new products/services), Catalyst (market growth), Developer (reduce risk and improve accountabilities), Performer (increase efficiency, quality, and resource utilization), Protector (build culture and develop talent), and Challenger (position for the future, check assumptions and trends) .
Administration: Group.
Price Data, 2005: $24.95 per manual/test booklet (2000, 31 pages), volume discounts available; $45 per Priority Balancing Handbook (110 pages); price information for online version is available from publisher.
Foreign Language Edition: Japanese language version is available.
Time: (12–18) minutes.
Comments: Results reflect the business priorities that are currently driving the leader; online version is available at www.leadershipspectrum.com.
Author: Mary Lippitt.
Publisher: Enterprise Management Ltd.
Cross References: For reviews by Janet F. Carlson and by L. Carolyn Pearson and Sharon Ann Richardson, see 17:104.

[1494]
Leadership Versatility Index.

Purpose: Designed to measure "versatility on two complementary pairs of leadership dimensions: forceful and enabling, and strategic and operational."
Population: Managers, executives.
Publication Dates: 2001-2007.
Acronym: LVI.
Scores, 7: Overall Versatility, Forceful-Enabling Versatility, Strategic-Operational Versatility, Specific Leadership Behavior Items, Team Productivity, Team Vitality, Overall Effectiveness.
Administration: Group.
Forms, 2: Standard LVI 360, LVI 360-plus.
Restricted Distribution: Special authorization from publisher is required to use the LVI.
Price Data, 2008: $275 per complete Standard LVI 360 test kit; $350 per LVI 360-plus kit including open-ended questions.
Time: (20) minutes.
Comments: The Standard LVI 360 includes only numerical feedback and the LVI 360-plus includes open-ended questions.
Authors: Robert E. Kaplan and Robert B. Kaiser.
Publisher: Kaplan DeVries Inc.
Cross References: For reviews by Mark A. Staal and Matt Vassar, see 18:67.

[1495]

Leadex: Leadership Assessment System.
Purpose: Designed to help "managers at all levels become more effective by increasing their self-awareness and self-understanding."
Population: Managers.
Publication Date: 1990.
Scores, 6: Vision and Values, Direction, Persuasion, Support, Development, Appreciation.
Administration: Individual or group.
Forms, 2: A (Self Rating), B (Feedback Questionnaire).
Price Data: Available from publisher.
Time: Administration time not reported.
Author: Karl Albrecht.
Publisher: Karl Albrecht International.

[1496]

Learned Behaviors Profile–Self/Other.
Purpose: "Designed to help people explore their patterns of behavior."
Population: Adults.
Publication Date: 1990.
Acronym: LBP.
Scores, 6: Caretaker, People-Pleaser, Workaholic, Martyr, Perfectionist, Tap Dancer.
Administration: Group.
Editions, 2: Self, Other.
Price Data: Price information available from publisher for LBP: Self inventory (31 pages); LBP: Other inventory (6 pages); each includes administrator's guide (no date, 2 pages).
Time: Administration time not reported.
Comments: Self-administered, self-scored.
Authors: J. William Pfeiffer and Judith A. Pfeiffer.
Publisher: Jossey-Bass, A Wiley Company.
Cross References: For reviews by Diane Billings Findley and John R. Graham, see 11:197.

[1497]

Learning Ability Profile.
Purpose: Designed to provide "a quantifiable index of the subject's inductive and deductive reasoning, cognitive and problem solving skills."
Population: Grades 5-16 and adults.
Publication Dates: 1975-1978.
Acronym: LAP.
Scores, 5: Total and 4 derived scores (Certainty, Problem Solving, Flexibility, Frustration).
Administration: Group.
Price Data, 1999: $130 per person.
Time: Untimed.
Author: Margherita M. Henning.
Publisher: Walden Personnel Performance, Inc. [Canada].
Cross References: For reviews by Philip M. Clark and Robert J. Illback, see 9:599 (1 reference).

[1498]

Learning Accomplishment Profile Diagnostic Edition.
Purpose: "Designed to provide the teacher of the young child with a simple criterion-referenced tool for systematic assessment of the child's existing skills."
Publication Dates: 1992–1997.
Administration: Individual or group.
Parts, 4: LAP-D Normed Assessment, LAP-D Screen, LAP (Revised Edition), Early LAP.
Comments: May be administered in station or individual format.
Publisher: Kaplan Early Learning Company.
   a) LEARNING ACCOMPLISHMENT PROFILE DIAGNOSTIC EDITION NORMED ASSESSMENT.
Purpose: "Facilitates standardized, norm referenced assessment … of developmental skills."
Population: Ages 30–60 months.
Publication Date: 1992.
Acronym: LAP-D.
Scores, 8: 4 development areas: Fine Motor (Writing, Manipulation), Language (Comprehension, Naming), Gross Motor (Body Movement, Object Movement), Cognitive (Counting, Matching).
Price Data, 2001: $624.95 per Normed Assessment including examiner's manual (62 pages), technical report, scoring booklets, and training manual (55 pages); $25.95 per 20 scoring protocols; $19.95 per technical report; $9.95 per examiner's manual; $12.95 per 10 Partial Person pads; $9.95 per 10 Plain Paper pads or 10 Diamond Design Cutting pads; $199.95 per single-user software (diskette or CD-ROM); $899.95 per 5-user site license (diskette); $1,799.95 per 10-user site license (diskette).
Time: (45–90) minutes.
Comments: "Designed to assist in making relevant educational decisions with regard to young children and to enable the teacher to develop developmentally appropriate instructional objectives and strategies"; hand or computer scoring available; LAP-D Windows software Version 3.5 system requirements: Windows 3.1, 3.51, or 98, 80486 or higher microprocessor, VGA or higher resolution screen supported by Windows, 8MB or more RAM, Windows-compatible printer.
Authors: Aubrey D. Nehring, Ema F. Nehring, John R. Bruni, Jr., and Patricia L. Randolph.
   b) LEARNING ACCOMPLISHMENT PROFILE DIAGNOSTIC EDITION NORMED SCREEN.
Purpose: "Quick initial developmental instruments designed as entry level to the diagnostic process."
Population: Ages 3–5 years.
Publication Date: 1997.
Acronym: LAP-D Screen.
Scores, 6: 4 developmental areas: Fine Motor (Writing, Manipulation), Language (Comprehension, Naming), Gross Motor, Cognitive.

Price Data: $124.95 per Screen kit (specify age 3, age 4, or Kindergarten) including examiner's manual, 25 scoring booklets, 3 Kindergarten Progress Charts, and screening items (specify English or Spanish); $349.95 per ages 3/4/5 Screen package (specify English or Spanish); $9.95 per 30 scoring profiles (specify age 3, age 4, or Kindergarten, specify English or Spanish); $52.95 per Screen manuals for ages 3, 4, and 5 (specify English or Spanish).

Time: (12–15) minutes, untimed.

Comments: Designed to be completed by the child's classroom teacher; items selected from LAP-D Standardized Assessment.

Author: Kaplan Press.

c) LEARNING ACCOMPLISHMENT PROFILE–REVISED EDITION.

Purpose: "A systematic, ongoing, criterion-referenced assessment of a child's existing skills in fine and gross motor, cognitive/language, personal/social, and self-help skills."

Population: Ages 3–6 years.

Publication Date: 1995.

Acronym: LAP-R.

Ratings, 7: Gross Motor, Fine Motor, Pre-Writing, Cognitive, Language, Self-Help, Personal/Social.

Price Data: $274.95 per kit including manipulatives, supplies, toys for use during assessment, 380 Learning Activities for Young Children cards, 20 scoring booklets, instruction manual (132 pages), and IEP forms; $89.95 per 10 manuals (specify English or Spanish); $6.50 per Social or Self-Help Observation Checklist.

Time: Administration time not reported.

Authors: Anne R. Sanford and Janet G. Zelman.

d) EARLY LEARNING ACCOMPLISHMENT PROFILE.

Purpose: "An ongoing, criterion-referenced assessment system covering gross motor, fine motor, cognitive, language, self-help, and social/emotional domains."

Population: Birth to 36 months.

Publication Date: 1995.

Acronym: E-LAP.

Ratings, 6: Gross Motor, Fine Motor, Cognitive, Language, Self-Help, Social/Emotional.

Price Data: $334.95 per Early Learning kit including manipulatives, toys, supplies, 20 scoring booklets, Early Learning Activity Cards, and instruction manual (111 pages); $89.95 per 10 manuals (specify English or Spanish); $22.95 per 20 scoring booklets (specify English or Spanish); $9.95 per manual.

Time: Administration time not reported.

Authors: M. Elayne Glover, Jodi L. Preminger, and Anne R. Sanford.

Cross References: For a review by Loraine J. Spenciner, see 16:136.

Learning and Study Strategies Inventory–High School Version.

Purpose: Designed to assist high school students "in determining their study skills strategies, problems and attitudes, and learning practices."

Population: Grades 9–12.

Publication Date: 1990.

Acronym: LASSI-HS.

Scores, 10: Attitude, Motivation, Time Management, Anxiety, Concentration, Information Processing, Selecting Main Ideas, Study Aids, Self Testing, Test Strategies.

Administration: Group.

Price Data, 2006: $2.75 per self-scored form, internet, or computer-scored form; quantity discounts available.

Time: (25–30) minutes.

Authors: Claire E. Weinstein and David R. Palmer.

Publisher: H & H Publishing Co., Inc.

Cross References: For reviews by Kenneth A. Kiewra and Robert T. Williams, see 13:177 (4 references).

Learning and Study Strategies Inventory, Second Edition.

Purpose: Designed to assess "students' awareness about and use of learning and study strategies related to skill, will and self-regulation components of strategic learning."

Population: Grades 9 and over.

Publication Dates: 1987-2002.

Acronym: LASSI.

Scores, 10: Anxiety Scale, Attitude Scale, Concentration Scale, Information Processing Scale, Motivation Scale, Self-Testing Scale, Selecting Main Ideas Scale, Study Aids Scale, Time Management Scale, Test Strategies Scale.

Administration: Individual or group.

Foreign Language Edition: Spanish Version available for college students.

Time: (15-20) minutes.

Comments: This test can be self-administered and self-scored; can be computer administered and scored.

Authors: Claire E. Weinstein, Ann C. Schulte, and David R. Palmer.

Publisher: H&H Publishing Company, Inc.

a) COLLEGE VERSION.

Population: College students.

Price Data: $3.25 per complete kit including test booklet and user's manual (2002, 28 pages).

b) HIGH SCHOOL VERSION.

Population: Grades 9-12.

Price Data: $2.75 per complete kit including test booklet and user's manual (2002, 28 pages).

c) SPANISH VERSION.

Population: College students.

Price Data: $3 per complete kit including test booklet and user's manual (2002, 28 pages).

Cross References: For reviews by Heidi M. Carty and Claudia R. Wright, see 17:105; see also T5:1455 (13 references) and T4:1417 (1 reference); for reviews by Martha W. Blackwell and Steven C. Hayes of an earlier edition, see 11:198 (3 references).

[1501]

Learning/Behavior Problems Checklist.

Purpose: Designed "to identify children at risk of or already experiencing behavior problems or learning disorders."
Population: Students in the primary grades.
Publication Date: 1990.
Scores: Not scored.
Administration: Individual.
Price Data, 2002: $10 per 25 checklists.
Time: [5–10] minutes.
Comments: Ratings by teachers.
Author: Academic Consulting & Testing Service.
Publisher: Academic Consulting & Testing Service.

[1502]

Learning Disabilities Diagnostic Inventory.

Purpose: Designed to identify specific learning disabilities and to help diagnose dysphasia, dyslexia, dysgraphia, dyscalculia, and disorders in executive function.
Population: Ages 8-0 to 17-11.
Publication Date: 1998.
Acronym: LDDI.
Scores, 6: Listening, Speaking, Reading, Writing, Mathematics, Reasoning.
Administration: Individual.
Price Data, 2011: $137 per complete kit including examiner's manual (106 pages) and 50 rating summary booklets; $59 per examiner's manual; $87 per 50 rating summary booklets.
Time: (10–20) minutes.
Authors: Donald D. Hammill and Brian R. Bryant.
Publisher: PRO-ED.
Cross References: For reviews by Terry B. Gutkin and John MacDonald, see 14:206.

[1503]

Learning Disability Evaluation Scale (Renormed).

Purpose: "Developed to aid in diagnosis, placement, and planning for learning disabled children and adolescents."
Population: Grades K–12.
Publication Dates: 1983–1996.
Acronym: LDES.
Scores, 7: Listening, Thinking, Speaking, Reading, Writing, Spelling, Mathematical Calculations.
Administration: Individual.
Price Data, 2005: $152 per complete kit including 50 Pre-Referral Learning Problem Checklist forms, 50 Pre-Referral Intervention Strategies Documentation forms, 50 LDES rating forms, LDES technical manual (1996, 71 pages), Learning Disability Intervention manual (1995, 223 pages), and Parents' Guide to Learning Disabilities (1991, 200 pages); $30 per 50 Pre-Referral Learning Problem Checklist forms; $30 per 50 Pre-Referral Intervention Strategies Documentation forms; $35 per 50 LDES rating forms; $15 per technical manual; $25 per Learning Disability Intervention manual; $17 per Parents' Guide to Learning Disabilities; $25 per computerized Quick Score (Win); $225 per computerized manual (Win).
Time: (15–20) minutes.
Comments: Ratings by teacher; the 1996 edition is renormed but content is not revised.
Authors: Stephen B. McCarney (test and manual) and Angela Marie Bauer (manual).
Publisher: Hawthorne Educational Services, Inc.
Cross References: For reviews by Patricia B. Keith and Loraine J. Spenciner, see 14:207; for reviews by Glen P. Aylward and Scott W. Brown of an earlier edition, see 12:214 (1 reference).

[1504]

Learning Organization Practices Profile.

Purpose: Designed "to facilitate a diagnostic process by which an organization can measure its capacity as a learning organization."
Population: Organizations.
Publication Date: 1994.
Acronym: LOPP.
Scores, 12: Vision and Strategy, Executive Practices, Managerial Practices, Climate, Organizational and Job Structure, Information Flow, Individual and Team Practices, Work Processes, Performance Goals and Feedback, Training and Education, Rewards and Recognition, Individual and Team Development.
Administration: Group.
Price Data: Available from publisher.
Time: Administration time not reported.
Author: Michael J. O'Brien.
Publisher: Jossey-Bass, A Wiley Company.
Cross References: For reviews by Neil P. Lewis and Michael J. Zickar, see 14:208.

[1505]

Learning Skills Profile.

Purpose: To assess the gap between personal aptitudes and critical skills required by a job.
Population: Junior high to adults.
Publication Date: 1993.
Acronym: LSP.
Scores, 36: 3 scores: Personal Learning Skill, Job Skill Demand, and Learning Gap in each of 12 skill areas: Interpersonal Skills (Leadership Skill, Relationship Skill,

Help Skill), Analytical Skills (Theory Skill, Quantitative Skill, Technology Skill), Information Skills (Sense-Making Skill, Information-Gathering Skill, Information Analysis Skill), Behavioral Skills (Goal Setting Skill, Action Skill, Initiative Skill).

Administration: Group or individual.

Price Data, 2006: $50 per complete kit including 10 workbooks and profiles, and 1 set of reusable LSP cards and instructions; $40 per 10 workbooks; $15 per reusable LSP cards, instructions, and profiles; also available online at $10 per person.

Time: [45–60] minutes.

Comments: Self-scored profile.

Authors: Richard E. Boyatzis and David A. Kolb.

Publisher: Hay Group.

Cross References: See T5:1467 (1 reference); for a review by David O. Herman, see 13:179.

[1506]

Learning Style Indicator [Revised].

Purpose: Designed to identify "preferred learning style and preferences."

Population: Ages 15 years and over.

Publication Dates: 1996-2006.

Acronym: LSI.

Scores, 4: Behavioral/Action/Independent, Cognitive/Analysis/Visual, Interpersonal/Harmony/Auditory, Affective/Expression/Experiential.

Administration: Individual or group.

Price Data, 2006: $12.95 per test booklet (2006, 12 pages); $13.95 per In-Depth Interpretations booklet (2006, 28 pages); $24.95 per access code online version; $37.95 per Trainer's Guidelines (1996, 28 pages).

Time: (30) minutes (90-180 minutes program options).

Comments: Self-administered and self-scored; can be used in conjunction with the Instructional Style Indicator (1319).

Authors: Ken Keis and Everett T. Robinson.

Publisher: Consulting Resource Group International, Inc.

[1507]

Learning Style Inventory [Price Systems, Inc.]

Purpose: Identifies "the conditions under which an individual is most likely to learn, remember, and achieve."

Population: Grades 3–12.

Publication Dates: 1975-2009.

Acronym: LSI.

Scores: 22 areas: Noise Level, Light, Temperature, Design, Motivation, Persistent, Responsible, Structure, Learning Alone/Peer Oriented, Authority Figures Present, Learn in Several Ways, Auditory, Visual, Tactile, Kinesthetic, Requires Intake, Evening/Morning, Late Morning, Afternoon, Needs Mobility, Parent Figure Motivated, Teacher Motivated, plus a Consistency score.

Administration: Group or individual.

Price Data, 2010: $22.50 per 10 answer sheets for Grades 3 & 4 or for Grade 5 thru 12 (includes scoring); $7.50 or less per group and subscale summaries available from publisher only in addition to individual profiles; $.60 per individual interpretative booklet; $16 per manual (1997, 100 pages); $3.25 per research report; $395 per computerized self-administered inventory program in English ($495 for multi-language version) with 100 administrations ($60 per 100 additional administrations) (Windows); $495 for Scanwin program permitting schools to scan and profile forms on site (includes multi-language capability); $.60 per answer form to use with Scanwin.

Time: (20–30) minutes.

Comments: PC compatible computer required for (optional) computerized administration; NCS Pearson Optical Mark Reader with dual pencil reader; Scrantron 8000, 8200, 8400, or SCANMARK 2550, 2660, 2800, 4000 or 5500 Scanner with dual pencil read for Scanwin; may be taken online at www.learningstyle.com.

Authors: Rita Dunn, Kenneth Dunn, and Gary E. Price.

Publisher: Price Systems, Inc.

Cross References: See T5:1470 (5 references); for reviews by Thomas R. Knapp and Craig S. Shwery, see 13:180 (9 references); see also T4:1432 (3 references); for reviews by Jan N. Hughes and Alida S. Westman of an earlier edition, see 11:203 (6 references).

[1508]

Learning Style Inventory, Version 3.1.

Purpose: Identifies an individual's learning preference and explores the opportunities that different learning styles present.

Population: Ages 18-60.

Publication Dates: 1976–2005.

Acronym: LSI3.1.

Scores: 4 scores: Concrete Experience, Active Experimentation, Reflective Observation, Abstract Conceptualization; 4 learning styles: Accommodating, Diverging, Converging, Assimilating.

Administration: Group or individual.

Price Data, 2006: $90 per 10 self-scoring booklets; $50 per facilitator's guide to learning (2000, 81 pages); PowerPoint slides free with purchase; also available online at $15 per person. Free technical manual and bibliography of research.

Foreign Language Editions: French and Spanish versions available.

Time: [20–30] minutes.

Author: David A. Kolb.

Publisher: Hay Group.

Cross References: For reviews by Cecil R. Reynolds and David Shum, see 15:136; see T5:1469 (13 references) and T4:1438 (12 references); for a review by Noel Gregg of an earlier edition, see 10:173 (17 references); see also 9:607 (7 references).

[1509]

Learning Style Profile.
Purpose: Designed to evaluate student learning style as the basis for student advisement and placement, instructional strategy, and the evaluation of learning.
Population: Grades 6–12.
Publication Dates: 1986–1990.
Acronym: LSP.
Scores, 23: Cognitive Skills (Analytic, Spatial, Discrimination, Categorizing, Sequential Processing, Memory), Perceptual Responses (Visual, Auditory, Emotive), Persistence Orientation, Verbal Risk Orientation, Study and Instructional Preferences (Verbal-Spatial, Manipulative, Study Time [Early Morning, Late Morning, Afternoon, Evening], Grouping, Posture, Mobility, Sound, Lighting, Temperature).
Administration: Group.
Price Data: Available from publisher.
Foreign Language Edition: Spanish version available.
Time: (50–60) minutes.
Authors: James W. Keefe (test, Handbook II), John S. Monk (test), Charles A. Letteri (test, Handbook I), Marlin Languis (test), Rita Dunn (test), John M. Jenkins (Handbook I), and Patricia Rosenlund (Handbook I).
Publisher: National Association of Secondary School Principals.
Cross References: For reviews by Sonya Blixt and James A. Jones and by Philip Nagy, see 12:217 (1 reference); see also T4:1433 (1 reference).

[1510]

Learning Style Questionnaire.
Purpose: Developed to "help individuals measure their preferences for learning."
Population: Adults.
Publication Date: 1999.
Acronym: LSQ.
Scores, 4: Participation, Reflecting, Structuring, Experiencing.
Administration: Group.
Price Data, 2001: $6.50 per questionnaire; $29.95 per leader's guide (24 pages).
Time: (20–30) minutes.
Author: Chris Hutcheson.
Publisher: HRD Press, Inc.

[1511]

Learning Styles Inventory [Western Psychological Services].
Purpose: Provides a quick measure of learning preferences.
Population: Junior High School, High School, College, Adults in business settings.
Publication Dates: 1976–1988.
Acronym: LSI.
Scores, 21: Conditions for Learning (Peer, Organization, Goal Setting, Competition, Instructor, Detail,

Independence, Authority), Area of Interest (Numeric, Qualitative, Inanimate, People), Mode of Learning (Listening, Reading, Iconic, Direct Experience), Expectation for Course Grade (A-expectation, B-expectation, C-expectation, D-expectation, Total expectation).
Administration: Group.
Forms, 4: A (College), B (High School), C (Junior High School), E (College-Easy).
Price Data, 2006: $109.50 per complete kit including 2 each of Forms A, B, C, and E inventory booklets, 1 Form ABC computer-scorable booklet, 1 Form E computer-scorable booklet, 2 prepaid mail-in booklets for computer scoring and interpretation, and manual (1988, 76 pages); $58 per 10 inventory booklets (specify form); $14 per computer-scorable booklet (price depends on quantity ordered and includes scoring service by publisher); $53.50 per manual.
Time: (15–20) minutes.
Comments: Previously listed as Canfield Learning Styles Inventory.
Author: Albert A. Canfield.
Publisher: Western Psychological Services.
Cross References: See T5:392 (2 references) and T4:378 (5 references); for a review by Stephen L. Benton, see 11:57 (2 references); for reviews by John Biggs and C. Dean Miller of an earlier edition, see 9:609 (1 reference).

[1512]

Learning Styles Inventory [Educational Activities, Inc.].
Purpose: Designed to assess an individual's learning style of receiving and expressing information.
Population: Intermediate and secondary level students.
Publication Dates: 1993-2000.
Acronym: LSI.
Scores, 9: Visual Language, Visual Numeric, Auditory Language, Auditory Numeric, Tactile Concrete, Social Individual, Social Group, Oral Expressiveness, Written Expressiveness.
Administration: Group.
Price Data, 2006: $98 per CD-ROM, management, and documentation; $490 per site license.
Foreign Language Editions: Available in English and Spanish with audio.
Time: Administration time not reported.
Comments: Pencil-and-paper or computer (Windows/Mac) administered.
Authors: Jerry F. Brown and Richard M. Cooper.
Publisher: Educational Activities Software.
Cross References: For reviews by Robert Brown and Robert J. Drummond, see 14:209.

[1513]

Learning Styles Inventory [Piney Mountain Press, Inc.].
Purpose: Designed to identify learning needs of students.

Population: Grades 6–12.

Publication Dates: 1988–2000.

Scores: 9 subtopics in 2 areas: Learning (Auditory Language, Visual Language, Auditory Numerical, Visual Numerical, Auditory-Visual-Kinesthetic), Working (Group Learner, Individual Learner, Oral Expressive, Written Expressive).

Administration: Individual or group.

Price Data, 2002: $195 per single station software; $395 per multistation software including instructor guide, software, multimedia CD, video, and response sheets; $995 for Network version.

Time: [11] minutes.

Author: Al Babich.

Publisher: Piney Mountain Press, Inc.

Cross References: For reviews by Kevin D. Crehan and Mark H. Fugate, see 12:218.

[1514]

Learning Styles Inventory, Version III.

Purpose: Designed to identify "student preferences for particular instructional techniques."

Population: Elementary and middle school students.

Publication Dates: 1978–2002.

Acronym: LSI-III.

Scores, 9: Direct Instruction, Instruction through Technology, Simulations, Projects, Independent Study, Peer Teaching, Drill and Recitation (Elementary school only), Discussion (Middle school only), Teaching Games (Middle school only).

Administration: Group.

Forms, 3: Elementary school, Middle school, Teacher.

Price Data, 2004: $17.95 per technical and administration manual (2002, 95 pages); $29.95 per class set including 30 student instruments, 1 teacher instrument, and 1 classroom summary sheet.

Time: (15) minutes.

Authors: Joseph S. Renzulli, Mary G. Rizza, and Linda R. Smith.

Publisher: Creative Learning Press, Inc.

Cross References: For reviews by Theodore Coladarci and Jennifer N. Mahdavi, see 17:106; see also T5:1474 (2 references) and T4:1435 (1 reference); for a review by Benson P. Low of a previous edition, see 9:608.

[1515]

Learning Tactics Inventory.

Purpose: "Provides ... individuals with information about how they learn and illustrates behaviors that they can adopt to become more versatile learners."

Population: Managers, leaders, executives.

Publication Date: 1999.

Acronym: LTI.

Scores: 4 learning tactics: Action, Thinking, Feeling, Accessing Others.

Administration: Individual.

Price Data, 2006: $32 per Facilitator's Guide (41 pages); $17 per Participant's Workbook/Survey; quantity discounts are available.

Time: 15 minutes.

Comments: An inventory of the behaviors individuals have reported using when engaged in the task of learning from experience; self-scored; Facilitator's Guide includes details of workshop procedures, reproducible overheads, and handout masters.

Authors: Maxine Dalton.

Publisher: Jossey-Bass Pfeiffer.

Cross References: For reviews by Kathleen A. Dolgos and William B. Michael, see 15:137.

[1516]

Learning/Working Styles Inventory.

Purpose: "Developed to assess learning styles and preferred working conditions."

Population: Grades 7–12 and adults.

Publication Dates: 1989–2000.

Scores: 25 subtopics in 5 areas: Physical Domain (Kinesthetic, Visual, Tactile, Auditory), Social Domain (Group, Individual), Environmental Domain (Formal Design, Informal Design, Bright Lights, Dim Lights, Warm Temperature, Cool Temperature, With Sound, Without Sound), Mode of Expression Domain (Oral Expressive, Written Expressive), Work Characteristics Domain (Outdoors, Indoors, Sedentary, Non-Sedentary, Lifting, Non-Lifting, Data, People, Things).

Administration: Group and individual.

Price Data, 2002: $195 per single station software, $395 per multistation software including instructor guide, software, multimedia CD, video, and response sheets; $995 for Network version.

Time: [15] minutes.

Comments: Previously entitled Vocational Learning Styles.

Author: Helena Hendrix-Frye.

Publisher: Piney Mountain Press, Inc.

Cross References: For reviews by Leo M. Harvill and Craig N. Mills of the earlier edition (Vocational Learning Styles), see 12:410.

[1517]

Leatherman Leadership Questionnaire [Revised].

Purpose: "To aid in selecting leaders, providing specific feedback to participants on their leadership knowledge for career counseling, conducting accurate needs analysis, and screening for assessment centers or giving pre/post assessment feedback."

Population: Managers, supervisors, team leaders, and potential leaders.

Publication Dates: 1987–1992.

Acronym: LLQ.

Scores, 28: Assigning Work, Career Counseling, Coaching Employees, Oral Communication, Managing Change, Handling Employee Complaints, Dealing with Employee Conflicts, Counseling Employees, Helping an Employee Make Decisions, Delegating, Taking Disciplinary Action, Handling Emotional Situations, Setting Goals/Planning with Employees, Handling Employee Grievances, Conducting Employee Meetings, Giving Positive Feedback, Negotiating, Conducting Performance Appraisals, Establishing Performance Standards, Persuading/Influencing Employees, Making Presentations to Employees, Problem Solving with Employees, Conducting Selection Interviews, Team Building, Conducting Termination Interviews, Helping an Employee Manage Time, One-on-One Training, Total.

Subtests, 2: May be administered in separate parts.

Administration: Group.

Price Data: Available from publisher.

Time: (300–325) minutes for battery; (150–165) minutes per part.

Comments: Complete test administered in 2 parts; machine scored by publisher.

Author: Richard W. Leatherman.

Publisher: International Training Consultants, Inc. [No response from publisher; status unknown].

Cross References: For reviews by Jeffrey S. Rain and Lawrence M. Rudner, see 12:219; for reviews by Walter Katkovsky and William D. Porterfield of an earlier edition, see 11:205.

[1518]

Leeds Scales for the Self-Assessment of Anxiety and Depression.

Purpose: Self-assessment measure of the severity of symptoms of clinical anxiety and depression.

Population: Psychiatric patients.

Publication Date: 1976.

Scores, 4: Depression (General, Specific), Anxiety (General, Specific).

Administration: Group or individual.

Price Data: Available from publisher.

Time: Administration time not reported.

Comments: Self-rating scale.

Authors: R. P. Smith, G. W. K. Bridge, and Max Hamilton.

Publisher: Psychological Test Publications [England] [No reply from publisher; status unknown].

Cross References: See T5:1481 (4 references) and T4:1440 (11 references); for reviews by John Duckitt and H. J. Eysenck, see 9:611 (4 references).

[1519]

Leisure Interest Inventory.

Purpose: Designed to assess "preferred leisure activities."

Population: College students.

Publication Date: 1969.

Acronym: LII.

Scores, 5: Sociability, Games, Art, Mobility, Immobility.

Administration: Group.

Price Data: Available from publisher.

Time: (20-25) minutes.

Author: Edwina E. Hubert.

Publisher: Edwina E. Hubert, Ph.D.

[1520]

Leisure/Retirement Activities Card Sort.

Purpose: "To introduce a new perspective on adult development and a model of understanding the process of change as it relates to retirement; to stimulate personal thinking on handling retirement; and to assist participants to identify and begin planning for avenues of new growth or expanded satisfaction in retirement living" and "to incorporate leisure activities into your life style."

Population: Adults.

Publication Dates: 1977-2005.

Scores: Item scores only.

Administration: Group or individual.

Price Data, 2011: $9 per one card sort deck and one worksheet.

Time: (75–120) minutes.

Comments: Previously known as Retirement Activities Card Sort Planning Kit; 8 supplementary activities included in manual; distributors are available in Canada, Australia, Egypt, and U.S.A. List of distributor information is available at www.CareerNetwork.Org.

Author: Richard L. Knowdell.

Publisher: Career Research & Testing, Inc.

Cross References: For reviews by M. Allan Cooperstein and Robert B. Frary of the Retirement Activities Card Sort Planning Kit, see 13:262.

[1521]

Leisure to Occupations Connection Search.

Purpose: Designed to allow the user to explore career options based on leisure-time interests.

Population: Seventh-grade students through adults

Publication Date: 1999.

Acronym: LOCS.

Scores: Scores interests in 100 leisure activities.

Administration: Individual.

Price Data, 2006: $29.95 for two packages of 25 inventories and a professional's manual (6 pages).

Time: (45) minutes.

Comments: Lists related occupations for each leisure activity; 12-panel foldout; self-scoring and self-interpreting; consumable; no other components needed.

Authors: Carl McDaniels and Sue Rife Mullins.

Publisher: JIST Publishing, Inc.

[1522]

Leiter International Performance Scale–Revised.

Purpose: Constructed as a "nonverbal cognitive assessment."

Population: Ages 2.0–20.11, adults.

Publication Dates: 1936–1998.

Acronym: Leiter-R.

Scores, 31: Visualization and Reasoning (Figure Ground, Design Analogies, Form Completion, Matching, Sequential Order, Repeated Patterns, Picture Context, Classification, Paper Folding, Figure Rotation), VR Composite (Fluid Reasoning, Brief IQ, Fundamental Visualization, Spatial Visualization, Full IQ), Attention and Memory Associated Pairs, Immediate Recognition, Forward Memory, Attention Sustained, Reverse Memory, Visual Coding, Spatial Memory, Delayed Pairs, Delayed Recognition, Attention Divided), AM Composite (Memory Screen, Associative Memory, Memory Span, Attention, Memory Process, Recognition Memory).

Administration: Individual.

Price Data, 2005: $895 per complete kit (in rolling backpack) including manual (1997, 378 pages), 3 easel books, VR response cards, AM response cards, manipulatives, 20 each VR and AM record forms, Attention Sustained booklets A, B, and C, and the Growth Profile Booklet and the rating scales; $850 per complete kit (in cloth carrying case); $25 per 20 record forms (specify battery); $15 per 20 Attention Sustained booklets (specify form); $10 per 20 rating scale record forms (specify form); $25 per 20 Growth Profile booklets, $75 per manual.

Time: (90) minutes.

Comments: May calculate growth scores (criterion-referenced scores) to assess improvement in cognitive skills; computer scoring software available requiring Windows 3.1, Windows 95 or Windows 98 operating systems.

Authors: Gale H. Roid and Lucy J. Miller.

Publisher: Stoelting Co.

Cross References: For reviews by Gary L. Marco and Terry A. Stinnett, see 14:211; see also T5:1485 (64 references), T4:1446 (33 references), T3:1319 (16 references), and T2:505 (18 references); for a review by Emmy E. Werner of the original version, see 6:526 (10 references); see also 5:408 (17 references); for a review by Gwen F. Arnold and an excerpted review by Laurance F. Shaffer, see 4:349 (25 references).

[1523]

Level of Service/Case Management Inventory: An Offender Assessment System.

Purpose: Designed to help "determine an offender's risk/needs level so that an appropriate level of service can be provided."

Population: Offenders ages 16 and over.

Publication Date: 2004.

Acronym: LS/CMI.

Scores, 9: Total Score plus 8 Risk/Need factors: Criminal History, Education/Employment, Family/Marital, Leisure/Recreation, Companions, Alcohol/Drug Problem, Procriminal Attitude/Orientation, Antisocial Pattern.

Administration: Individual.

Price Data, 2011: $308 per complete kit including user's manual (228 pages), scoring guide, and 25 each of interview guides, offender history forms, QuikScore forms, ColorPlot profiles, and case management protocols; $197 per reorder kit including 25 each of interview guides, offender history forms, QuikScore forms, ColorPlot profile forms, and case management protocols; $91 per user's manual; $98 per 25 interview guides; $20 per 25 offender history forms; $60 per 25 QuikScore forms; $28 per 25 ColorPlot profile forms; $267 per software kit including user's manual and 25 profile reports.

Time: (20–30) minutes plus interview.

Comments: Online version available.

Authors: D. A. Andrews, James L. Bonta, and J. Stephen Wormith.

Publisher: Multi-Health Systems, Inc.

Cross References: For reviews by Sheri Bauman and Geoffrey L. Thorpe, see 17:108.

[1524]

The Level of Service Inventory–Revised [2003 Norms Update].

Purpose: Designed as a "quantitative survey of attributes of offenders and their situations relevant to level of service decisions."

Population: Ages 16 and older.

Publication Dates: 1995–2003.

Acronym: LSI-R.

Scores: Total score only.

Administration: Individual.

Price Data, 2011: $248 per LSI-R U.S. Norms complete kit including manual (2001, 63 pages), LSI-R U.S. Norms Supplement (2003, 16 pages), 25 interview guides, 25 QuikScore forms, and 25 U.S. ColorPlot profile forms; $90 per LSI-R manual, LSI-R Norms Supplement, and 1 U.S. ColorPlot profile form; $149 per 25 each of interview guides, QuikScore forms, and U.S. ColorPlot profiles; $98 per 25 interview guides; $61 per 25 QuikScore forms; $30 per 25 U.S. Norms ColorPlot profile forms; $117 per U.S. norms preview set including LSI-R manual, LSI-R U.S. Norms Supplement, 3 each of interview guides, QuikScore forms, and U.S. ColorPlot profile forms; $220 per software kit, including manual and 25 profile reports.

Foreign Language Editions: LSI-R is available in Spanish but the U.S. ColorPlot profile forms are not.

Time: (30–45) minutes.

Comments: Software version also available.

Authors: Don A. Andrews and James L. Bonta.

Publisher: Multi-Health Systems, Inc.

Cross References: For reviews by David F. Ciampi and Andrew A. Cox, see 17:107; for reviews by Solomon M. Fulero and Romeo Vitelli of an earlier edition, see 14:212.

[1525]

Level of Service Inventory–Revised: Screening Version.

Purpose: Designed to provide "a risk/needs assessment important to offender treatment planning."
Population: Ages 16 and older.
Publication Date: 1998.
Acronym: LSI-R:SV.
Scores: Total score only.
Administration: Individual.
Price Data, 2011: $143 per complete kit including 25 interview guides, 25 QuikScore™ forms, and manual (1998, 26 pages); $83 per 25 interview guides/QuikScore™ forms; $37 per 25 interview guides; $61 per 25 QuikScore™ forms; $70 per manual; $72 per training set including 3 interview guides, 3 QuikScore™ forms, and manual; software and online versions also available.
Time: (10–15) minutes.
Authors: Don Andrews and James Bonta.
Publisher: Multi-Health Systems, Inc.
Cross References: For reviews by Ira S. Katz and Kevin J. McCarthy, see 15:138.

[1526]

Level of Service/Risk, Need, Responsivity.

Purpose: "Designed to assist professionals in management and treatment planning with adult and late adolescent male and female offenders in justice, forensic, correctional, prevention, and related agencies."
Population: "Male and female offenders 16 years of age and older."
Publication Date: 2008.
Acronym: LS/RNR.
Scores, 9: Criminal History, Education/Employment, Family/Marital, Leisure/Recreation, Companions, Procriminal Attitude/Orientation, Alcohol/Drug Problem, Antisocial Pattern, Total (General Risk/Need Factors).
Administration: Individual.
Parts, 2: Interview Guide, QuikScore; Sections, 8: Specific Risk/Need Factors, Prison Experience-Institutional Factors, Other Client Issues, Special Responsivity Considerations, Risk/Need Summary and Override, Risk/Need Profile, and Program/Placement Decision.
Price Data, 2011: $161 per complete kit including 25 interview guides, 25 QuikScore forms, 25 ColorPlot forms, and scoring guide (63 pages); $98 per 25 interview guides; $60 per 25 QuikScore forms; $28 per 25 ColorPlot forms; $36 per scoring guide.
Time: [40–120] minutes.
Comments: Test is part of the LSI family of instruments including the Level of Service Inventory-Revised (LSI-R; 17:107), the Level of Service Inventory-Revised: Screening Version (LSI-R:SV; T7:1449), the Youth Level of Service/Case Management Inventory (YLS/CMI; 17:108), and the Level of Service/Case Management Inventory (LS/CMI; T72842); the Interview Guide is a semi-structured interview used to obtain ratings for the QuikScore form; Sections 2 through 8 provide additional information that is not numerically scored.
Authors: D. A. Andrews, James L. Bonta, and J. Stephen Wormith.
Publisher: Multi-Health Systems, Inc.
Cross References: For reviews by Jeffrey A. Jenkins and Mark H. Stone, see 18:68.

[1527]

Levine-Pilowsky [Depression] Questionnaire.

Purpose: A questionnaire technique for classifying depression.
Population: Adults.
Publication Date: 1979.
Acronym: LPD.
Scores: 9 subscales: Insomnia (Initial), Sleep (General), Paranoia, Appetite, Insomnia (Late), Crying, Diurnal Variation, Hopelessness, Intensity of Depression.
Administration: Individual or group.
Manual: No manual.
Price Data: Available from publisher.
Time: (10) minutes.
Author: I. Pilowsky.
Publisher: I. Pilowsky [Australia].
Cross References: See T4:1448 (3 references).

[1528]

Lexington Developmental Scales.

Purpose: To "provide an individual graph or profile which depicts the child's developmental age level."
Population: Ages birth-6 years.
Publication Dates: 1973-1977.
Acronym: LDS.
Scores: Contains behavioral and experimental items rated by examiner in 4 areas: Motor, Language, Cognitive, Personal and Social.
Administration: Individual administration to ages birth-2 years.
Price Data: Not available.
Time: (60) minutes in children birth-2 years; time varies for older children.
Comments: Long and Short Forms; may be used by parents and volunteers; "particularly helpful in pre- and post-testing"; additional testing materials must be supplied by the examiner.
Authors: United Cerebral Palsy of the Bluegrass, John V. Irwin, Margaret Norris Ward, Ann B. Greis, Carol C. Deen, Valerie C. Cooley, Alice A. Auvenshine, Rhea A. Taylor, C. A. Coleman.

Publisher: Child Development Centers of the Bluegrass, Inc.

Cross References: See T5:1490 (2 references) and T4:1450 (1 reference); for reviews by Michael J. Roznowski and Zona R. Weeks, see 9:615 (1 reference); see also T3:1322 (1 reference).

[1529]

The Life Adjustment Inventory.

Purpose: Developed to survey "the extent to which a secondary school curriculum meets the needs of all its pupils."

Population: Grades 9–12.

Publication Date: 1951.

Scores, 14: General Feeling of Adjustment to the Curriculum, Reading and Study Skills, Communication and Listening Skills, General Social Skills and Etiquette, Boy-Girl Relationships, Religion/Morals/Ethics, Functional Citizenship, Vocational Orientation and Preparation, Education for Physical and Mental Health, Education for Family Living, Orientation to Science, Consumer Education, Development of Appreciation for and Creativity in the Arts, Education for Wise Use of Leisure Time.

Administration: Group.

Price Data: Available from publisher.

Time: (20–25) minutes.

Authors: Ronald C. Doll and J. Wayne Wrightstone.

Publisher: Psychometric Affiliates.

Cross References: See P:145 (1 reference); for reviews by John W. M. Rothney and Helen Schacter, see 4:67.

[1530]

Life Attitudes Schedule: A Risk Assessment for Suicidal and Life-Threatening Behaviors.

Purpose: Designed to "measure the cognitive, affective, and action-oriented components of suicide proneness."

Population: Ages 15–20.

Publication Date: 2004.

Administration: Individual or group.

Forms, 2: Life Attitudes Schedule, Life Attitudes Schedule: Short.

Price Data, 2011: $145 per complete kit including technical manual (70 pages), 10 item booklets, and 25 QuikScore forms each for LAS and LAS:S; $60 per technical manual; $31 per 10 item booklets (reusable); $50 per 25 LAS QuikScore forms; $50 per 25 LAS:S QuikScore forms.

Authors: Peter M. Lewinsohn, Jennifer Langhinrichsen-Rohling, Paul Rohde, and Richard A. Langford.

Publisher: Multi-Health Systems, Inc.

  a) LIFE ATTITUDES SCHEDULE.

  Acronym: LAS.

  Scores, 12: Composite Scores (Physical, Psychological), Content Scales (Health-Related, Death-Related, Injury-Related, Self-Related), Modality Type Scales (Actions, Thoughts, Feelings), Valence Scales (Negative, Positive), Total.

  Time: (30) minutes.

  b) LIFE ATTITUDES SCHEDULE: SHORT.

  Acronym: LAS:S.

  Scores, 3: Physical, Psychological, Total.

  Time: (10) minutes.

Cross References: For reviews by Thomas P. Hogan and Janet Smith, see 17:109.

[1531]

Life Stressors and Social Resources Inventory–Adult Form.

Purpose: "Provides an integrated picture of an individual's current life context" including "stable life stressors and social resources."

Population: Healthy adults, psychiatric patients, and medical patients.

Publication Dates: 1988–1994.

Acronym: LISRES-A.

Scores: 16 scales: 9 Life Stressor Scales (Physical Health, Home/Neighborhood, Financial, Work, Spouse or Partner, Children, Extended Family, Friends, Negative Life Events); 7 Social Resources Scales (Financial, Work, Spouse or Partner, Children, Extended Family, Friends, Positive Life Events).

Administration: Individual or group.

Price Data, 2006: $165 per introductory kit including manual (1994, 40 pages), 10 reusable item booklets, and 50 hand-scorable answer/profile forms.

Time: [10] minutes.

Comments: May be administered using either a self-report or a structured interview format.

Authors: Rudolf H. Moos (instrument and manual) and Bernice S. Moos (manual).

Publisher: Psychological Assessment Resources, Inc.

Cross References: See T5:1495 (1 reference); for reviews by M. Allan Cooperstein and Richard B. Stuart, see 13:184 (1 reference).

[1532]

Life Stressors and Social Resources Inventory–Youth Form.

Purpose: "Provides an integrated picture of a youth's current life context ... assesses stable life stressors and social resources as well as changes in them over time."

Population: Ages 12–18.

Publication Dates: 1990–1994.

Acronym: LISRES-Y.

Scores, 16: 9 Life Stressors Scales (Physical Health, Home and Money, Parents, Siblings, Extended Family, School, Friends, Boyfriend/Girlfriend, Negative Life Events); 7 Social Resources Scales (Parents, Siblings, Extended Family, School, Friends, Boyfriend/Girlfriend, Positive Life Events).

Administration: Individual or Group.

Editions, 2: Youth, Adult.

Price Data, 2006: $165 per introductory kit including manual (1994, 38 pages), 10 item booklets, and 50 hand-scorable answer/profile forms.

Time: (45) minutes for self-report; (45–90) minutes for structured interview.

Comments: Available as self-report or structured interview; structured interview "allows an interviewer to use the inventory with youths whose reading and comprehension skills are below a sixth-grade level."

Authors: Rudolf H. Moos and Bernice S. Moos.

Publisher: Psychological Assessment Resources, Inc.

Cross References: See T5:1496 (1 reference); for reviews by Kevin D. Crehan and Albert Oosterhof, see 13:185 (1 reference).

[1533]

Life Style Questionnaire.

Purpose: To provide information regarding vocational interests and attitudes.

Population: Ages 14 and over.

Publication Date: No date on test materials.

Acronym: LSQ.

Scores: 13 scales: Expressive/Imaginative, Logical/Analytical, Managerial/Enterprising, Precise/Administrative, Active/Concrete, Supportive/Social, Risk Taking/Uncertainty, Perseverance/Determination, Self Evaluation, Sensitivity/Other Awareness, Affiliation, Degree to Which a Vocation is Associated with Self Fulfillment, Degree of Certainty.

Administration: Group or individual.

Price Data, 2001: £35 per specimen set; £4 per answer sheet and graph; £6.50 per questionnaire booklet; £25 per manual (26 pages); £459 per computer software version.

Time: Administration time not reported.

Author: James S. Barrett.

Publisher: The Test Agency Limited [England] [No reply from publisher; status unknown].

Cross Reference: For a review by Robert B. Slaney, see 9:619.

[1534]

Life Styles Inventory.

Purpose: Designed to assess an individual's thinking and behavioral styles.

Population: Adults.

Publication Dates: 1973–1990.

Acronym: LSI.

Administration: Individual.

Price Data: Price data for test materials including Leader's Guide (1989, 211 pages), Self-Development Guide (1989, 75 pages), and Description by Others Self-Development Guide (1990, 123 pages) available from publisher.

Time: (20-25) minutes.

Author: J. Clayton Lafferty.

Publisher: Human Synergistics International.

a) LSI1: LIFE STYLES INVENTORY (SELF DESCRIPTION).

Scores, 12: Constructive Styles (Achievement, Self-Actualizing, Humanistic-Encouraging, Affiliative), Passive/Defensive Styles (Approval, Conventional, Dependent, Avoidance), Aggressive/Defensive Styles (Oppositional, Power, Competitive, Perfectionistic).

b) LSI2: LIFE STYLES INVENTORY (DESCRIPTION BY OTHERS).

Scores, 12: Same as for *a* above.

Comments: Administered to manager and 4 or 5 others.

Cross References: For reviews by Gregory J. Boyle and Patricia Schoenrade, see 12:222; see also T4:1459 (6 references); for reviews by Henry M. Cherrick and Linda M. DuBois, see 9:620 (1 reference).

[1535]

Lifestyle Assessment Questionnaire.

Purpose: Provides individuals with a measurement of their lifestyle status in various wellness categories, offers a health risk appraisal component that lists the individual's top ten risks of death, projects an achievable health age, makes suggestions for lifestyle improvement, and offers a stimulus for positive lifestyle change by providing a guide to successful implementation of that change.

Population: Adults ages 18–60 with a minimum of 12th grade education.

Publication Dates: 1978–1989.

Scores, 16: Physical (Exercise, Nutrition, Self-Care, Vehicle Safety, Drug Usage), Social/Environmental, Emotional (Emotional Awareness and Acceptance, Emotional Management), Intellectual, Occupational, Spiritual, Actual Age, Appraised Health Age, Achievable Health Age, Top 10 Risks of Death, Lifestyle Improvement Suggestions.

Administration: Group.

Price Data: Available from publisher.

Time: (45–60) minutes.

Comments: Scoring by National Wellness Institute; information on up to four wellness areas included in scoring report; individual and group reports available.

Authors: Dennis Elsenrath, Bill Hettler, and Fred Leafgren.

Publisher: National Wellness Institute, Inc.

Cross References: For reviews by Michael B. Brown and William E. Martin, Jr., see 13:186 (3 references); see also T4:1461 (3 references).

[1536]

Light's Retention Scale.

Purpose: Developed to assist in determining if grade retention will have a positive or negative outcome for a particular student.

Population: Grades K-12.
Publication Dates: 1981-2006.
Acronym: LRS.
Scores: Total score only.
Administration: Individual.
Price Data, 2007: $95 per complete kit including 50 recording forms, 50 parent guides, and manual (2006, 96 pages); $35 per 50 recording forms; $25 per 50 parent guides; $25 per 50 Spanish parent guides; $35 per manual.
Time: (10-15) minutes.
Comments: A nonpsychometric instrument used as a counseling tool with a specific retention candidate; Spanish parent guides available.
Author: H. Wayne Light.
Publisher: Academic Therapy Publications.
Cross References: For reviews by Loraine J. Spenciner and Hoi K. Suen, see 18:69; for reviews by Bruce K. Alcorn and Frederic J. Medway of the 1991 Revision, see 11:208 (2 references); for reviews by Michael J. Hannafin and Patti L. Harrison of an earlier edition, see 9:622, see also T3:1328 (1 reference).

[1537]

The Lincoln-Oseretsky Motor Development Scale.

Purpose: "Designed to test the motor ability of children."
Population: Ages 6–14.
Publication Dates: 1948-1956.
Scores: Total score only.
Administration: Individual.
Price Data, 2005: $235 per complete kit including 50 record blanks and manual (1948, 79 pages); $20 per 50 record blanks; $20 per 50 mazes; $20 per 50 concentric circles; $25 per manual.
Time: Administration time not reported.
Comments: Revision of Oseretsky Tests of Motor Proficiency.
Author: William Sloan.
Publisher: Stoelting Co.
Cross References: See T4:1464 (5 references), T3:1331 (5 references), and T2:1895 (27 references); for a review by Anna Espenschade, see 5:767 (10 references).

[1538]

Lindamood Auditory Conceptualization Test–Third Edition.

Purpose: Designed to measure "the ability to (a) discriminate one speech sound or phoneme from another and (b) segment a spoken word into its constituent phonemic units."
Population: Ages 5-0 through 18-11.
Publication Dates: 1971–2004.
Acronym: LAC-3.
Scores, 6: Isolated Phoneme Patterns, Tracking Phonemes, Counting Syllables, Tracking Syllables, Tracking Syllables and Phonemes, Total.

Administration: Individual.
Price Data, 2011: $218 per complete kit including examiner's manual, 25 examiner record booklets, LiPS/KAC blocks, felt kit, and CD; $106 per examiner's manual & CD; $79 per 25 examiner record booklets; $29 per LiPS/KAC blocks; $9 per felt kit.
Time: (20–30) minutes.
Comments: "Criterion referenced"; requires no reading by examinees.
Authors: Patricia C. Lindamood and Phyllis Lindamood.
Publisher: PRO-ED.
Cross References: For reviews by Vincent J. Samar and Dolores Kluppel Vetter, see 17:110; see also T5:1503 (16 references) and T4:1465 (2 references); for reviews by Nicholas G. Bountress and James R. Cox of a previous edition, see 9:623 (1 reference).

[1539]

Listen Up: Skills Assessment.

Purpose: Designed to measure listening comprehension, interpretation, and ability to follow directions.
Population: Grades 7–12 and adults.
Publication Dates: 1985–1995.
Scores, 6: Evaluating Message Content, Understanding Meaning in Conversations, Understanding and Remembering Lectures, Evaluating Emotional Meanings in Messages, Following Instructions and Directions, Total.
Administration: Group.
Price Data: Available from publisher.
Time: [40–80] minutes.
Authors: Kittie W. Watson and Larry L. Barker.
Publisher: Jossey-Bass, A Wiley Company.
Cross References: For reviews by Cleborne D. Maddux and Sandra J. Wanner, see 14:213.

[1540]

Listening Comprehension Test Series.

Purpose: Designed to "assess the communication skills that enable a child to listen, understand and respond appropriately to information."
Population: Ages 4–14.
Publication Date: 1999.
Scores: Total score only.
Administration: Individual or group.
Levels, 5: A, B, C, D, E.
Price Data: Price data for starter set including teacher's guide group record sheet, 20 pupil booklets, At-a-Glance Guide, and audiocassette available from publisher.
Time: Untimed.
Comments: Linked to the National Curriculum for England and Wales, the Scottish 5–14 Guidelines, and the Northern Ireland Curriculum.
Authors: Neil Hagues, Rifat Siddiqui, and Paul Merwood.

Publisher: GL Assessment [England].
Cross References: For a review by Michael D. Beck, see 16:137.

[1541]

The Listening Inventory.

Purpose: Developed as an initial screener for students "who may be at risk for having (Central) Auditory Processing Disorder."
Population: Ages 4-17.
Publication Date: 2006.
Acronym: TLI.
Scores, 7: Linguistic Organization, Decoding & Language Mechanics, Attention & Organization, Sensory-Motor Skills, Social & Behavioral Skills, Auditory Processes, Total Score.
Administration: Individual.
Price Data, 2007: $85 per complete kit including 25 listening inventory forms, 25 profile forms, and manual (64 pages); $50 per 25 listening inventory forms and 25 profile forms; $35 per manual.
Time: 15 minutes.
Authors: Donna Geffner and Deborah Ross-Swain.
Publisher: Academic Therapy Publications.
Cross References: For reviews by Tiffany L. Hutchins and Sandra Ward, see 18:70.

[1542]

The Listening Skills Test.

Purpose: Designed to measure "comprehension monitoring and message appraisal."
Population: 3 years 6 months to 6 years 11 months.
Publication Date: 2001.
Acronym: LIST.
Scores: 4 subtests: Referent Identification, Message Appraisal, Comprehension of Directions, Verbal Message Evaluation.
Administration: Individual.
Price Data, 2006: £81 per complete test kit including 25 record forms, stimulus manual, and manual (101 pages).
Time: (20–30) minutes.
Authors: Peter Lloyd, Ian Peers, and Caroline Foster.
Publisher: Pearsoon Assessment [England].
Cross References: For reviews by Pam Lindsey and Gene Schwarting, see 15:139.

[1543]

Listening Styles Profile.

Purpose: "Designed to identify habitual listening responses and to encourage participants to think about how preference traits might be expressed in actual settings."
Population: Adults.
Publication Date: 1995.
Scores, 4: People Oriented, Action Oriented, Content Oriented, Time Oriented.
Administration: Group.

Price Data: Available from publisher.
Time: (5–10) minutes.
Comments: Can be used to evaluate self or another person.
Authors: Kittee W. Watson and Larry L. Barker.
Publisher: Jossey-Bass, A Wiley Company.
Cross References: For reviews by Mildred Murray-Ward and Sandra Ward, see 14:214.

[1544]

Literature Tests/Objective and Essay.

Purpose: To assess students' literal and interpretive comprehension of over 200 works of contemporary and classical literature.
Population: Middle school and high school.
Publication Dates: 1929–1990.
Scores: Total score only.
Administration: Group.
Manual: No manual.
Price Data, 2005: $4.75 per 50-question test; $5.75 per 100-question test; $5.75 per essay test.
Time: Administration time not reported.
Comments: Over 700 tests on specific literary works; formerly called Book Review Tests and Objective Tests in English.
Author: Perfection Learning Corp.
Publisher: Perfection Learning Corp.

[1545]

Living in the Reader's World: Locator Test.

Purpose: Diagnose nonproficient reader's appropriate starting point in a 4-book adult education reading program.
Population: Adults at reading grade levels 2.0–6.0.
Publication Date: 1983.
Administration: Group.
Price Data: Not available.
Time: Administration time not reported.
Comments: Upward extension of the Maryland/Baltimore County Design for Adult Basic Education (1616).
Author: Cambridge, The Adult Education Co.
Publisher: Prentice Hall [No reply from publisher; status unknown].

[1546]

Location Learning Test.

Purpose: To measure visuo-spatial learning and recall.
Population: Elderly adults.
Publication Date: 2000.
Acronym: LLT.
Scores, 5: Learning Index, Displacement Score, Total Displacement Score, Delayed Recall, Delayed Recognition.
Administration: Individual.
Forms, 2: A, B.
Price Data, 2006: £113.50 per complete kit including manual (15 pages), 25 scoring sheets, test grids, practice grids, and picture cards; £35.50 per 50 scoring sheets.

Time: (25) minutes.
Authors: Romola S. Bucks, Jonathan R. Willison, and Lucie M. T. Byrne.
Publisher: Pearson Assessment [England].
Cross References: For reviews by Anita M. Hubley and Claudia R. Wright, see 17:111.

[1547]

LOCO (Learning Opportunities Coordination): A Scale for the Assessment of Coordinated Learning Opportunities in Living Units for People with a Handicap.

Purpose: Designed "for indicating to what extent a Living Unit for people with handicaps is able to contribute significantly to their social and personal development and to maintain a level of reasonable independence."
Population: Residents of any type of living units where people with a handicap live with the assistance of care givers.
Publication Date: 1987.
Acronym: LOCO.
Scores, 4: Basic Training Conditions, Essential Items, Additional Items, Total.
Administration: Group.
Price Data: Available from publisher.
Time: Administration time not reported.
Comments: Can be used in conjunction with P-A-C (Progress Assessment Chart) (2155).
Authors: H. C. Gunzburg and A. L. Gunzburg.
Publisher: SEFA (Publications) Ltd. [England].

[1548]

Loewenstein Occupational Therapy Cognitive Assessment.

Purpose: "A cognitive battery of tests for both primary assessments and ongoing evaluation in the occupational therapy treatment of brain-injured patients."
Population: Ages 6 to 12 and brain-injured adults.
Publication Date: 1990.
Acronym: LOTCA.
Scores: 21 tests in 4 areas: Orientation (Orientation for Place, Orientation for Time), Visual and Spatial Perception (Object Identification, Shapes Identification, Overlapping Figures, Object Constancy, Spatial Perception, Praxis), Visual Motor Organization (Copying Geometric Forms, Reproduction of a Two-Dimensional Model, Pegboard Construction, Colored Block Design, Plain Block Design, Reproduction of a Puzzle, Drawing a Clock), Thinking Operations (Categorization, ROC Unstructured, ROC Structured, Pictorial Sequence A, Pictorial Sequence B, Geometric Sequence).
Administration: Individual.
Price Data: Price data available from publisher for complete kit including manual (56 pages), test booklet, and other materials packed in a plastic carrying case.

Time: (30–45) minutes.
Authors: Loewenstein Rehabilitation Hospital; Malka Itzkovich (manual), Betty Elazar (manual), Sarah Averbuch (manual), Naomi Katz (principal researcher), and Levy Rahmani (advisor).
Publisher: Maddak Inc.
Cross References: For reviews by Elaine Clark and Stephen R. Hooper, see 13:187.

[1549]

Logical Reasoning.

Purpose: Designed to measure sensitivity to logical necessity, consistency and inconsistency, and relationships.
Population: Grades 9–16 and adults.
Publication Date: 1955.
Scores: Total score only.
Administration: Group.
Parts, 2: 1, 2.
Price Data: Available from publisher.
Time: 20(25) minutes.
Comments: Two parallel parts may be administered separately or together.
Authors: Alfred F. Hertzka and J. P. Guilford.
Publisher: Charlotte Mackley [No reply from publisher; status unknown].
Cross References: See T5:1514 (1 reference), T4:1476 (3 references), and T2:1761 (10 references); for reviews by Duncan Howie and Charles R. Langmuir, see 5:694 (1 reference).

[1550]

The Lollipop Test: A Diagnostic Screening Test of School Readiness–Revised.

Purpose: "A screening test to identify the child's deficits (and strengths) in readiness skills."
Population: First grade entrants.
Publication Dates: 1981–2002.
Scores, 5: Identification of Colors and Shapes and Copying Shapes, Picture Description and Position and Spatial Recognition, Identification of Numbers and Counting, Identification of Letters and Writing, Total.
Administration: Individual.
Price Data, 2002: $59.95 per complete kit including 25 test booklets, stimulus cards, and manual (1989, 35 pages); $34.95 per 25 test booklets; $14.95 per set of stimulus cards; $15.95 per manual.
Foreign Language Edition: Available in Spanish.
Time: (15–20) minutes.
Author: Alex L. Chew.
Publisher: Humanics Test Corporation.
Cross References: See T5:1515 (1 reference) and T4:1477 (2 references); for reviews by Sylvia T. Johnson and Albert C. Oosterhof, see 11:210 (5 references); for reviews by Isabel L. Beck and Janet A. Norris of an earlier edition, see 9:629.

[1551]

Looking at MySELF, Form II.

Purpose: Designed to "help students to acquire the attitudes, knowledge, and interpersonal skills to help them understand and respect self and others."
Population: Grades 7-12.
Publication Dates: 1991-2006.
Acronym: LAM.
Scores, 14: Self-Esteem, Speaking/Listening, Money/Wealth, Leadership, Artistic Things, Adventure, Helping People, Education, Creativity, Prestige, Community Service, Decision Making, Goal Setting, Career Awareness.
Administration: Group.
Price Data, 2008: $4.20 per 9 Looking at MySELF booklets (2006, 16 pages); $.57 per 9 activity folders.
Time: Administration time not reported.
Comments: The activity folder contains questions to probe students to think about their self-esteem, interests, and goals.
Author: CFKR Career Materials, Inc.
Publisher: CFKR Career Materials, Inc.

[1552]

Lore Leadership Assessment.

Purpose: Measures perceived skill and effectiveness in the five dimensions of the Lore Leadership Model: moral, intellectual, courageous, collaborative, and visionary/inspirational; measures executive's leadership skill levels as well as their impact on the people they are leading.
Population: Executives in leadership positions.
Publication Dates: 1998–2001.
Scores, 6: Overall Leadership Effectiveness, Moral Leadership, Intellectual Leadership, Courageous Leadership, Collaborative Leadership, Visionary/Inspirational Leadership.
Administration: Group.
Forms, 2: Self-Assessment, Assessment of Other.
Manual: No manual.
Price Data, 2005: $49 per online assessment with electronic report.
Foreign Language Editions: Available in English and German.
Time: [30] minutes.
Comments: Test forms are administered online via the internet at Lore's Assessment Center.
Author: Lore International Institute.
Publisher: Lore International Institute.
Cross References: For a review by Connie Kubo Della-Piana of the original edition, see 14:215.

[1553]

Lorimer Braille Recognition Test: A Test of Ability in Reading Braille Contractions.

Purpose: Designed to test blind children's performance in reading Braille contractions.
Population: Students (ages 7–13) in Grade 2 Braille.

Publication Date: 1962.
Scores: Total score only.
Administration: Group.
Price Data: Price data, including manual (27 pages) (available in printed form or Braille), available from publisher.
Time: Administration time not reported.
Author: John Lorimer.
Publisher: Association for the Education and Welfare of the Visually Handicapped [England] [No reply from publisher; status unknown].
Cross References: See 6:854 (1 reference).

[1554]

LSI Conflict.

Purpose: Enables individuals to identify and understand how their thinking patterns and coping behaviors influence their ability to deal with conflict situations.
Population: Adults.
Publication Date: 1990.
Scores: 12 patterns of thinking and behavior: Constructive (Pragmatist, Self-Empowered, Conciliator, Relationship Builder), Passive/Defensive (Accommodator, Regulator, Insulator, Avoider), Aggressive/Defensive (Escalator, Dominator, Competitor, Perfectionist).
Administration: Individual or group.
Price Data: Price data for test materials including Self-Development Guide and Leader's Guide available from publisher.
Time: Administration time not reported.
Author: J. Clayton Lafferty.
Publisher: Human Synergistics International.

[1555]

Luria-Nebraska Neuropsychological Battery: Children's Revision.

Purpose: "To diagnose general and specific cognitive deficits, including lateralization and localization of focal brain impairments, and to aid in the planning and evaluation of rehabilitation programs."
Population: Ages 8–12.
Publication Date: 1987.
Acronym: LNNB-C.
Scores, 16: Clinical scales (Motor Functions, Rhythm, Tactile Functions, Visual Functions, Receptive Speech, Expressive Speech, Writing, Reading, Arithmetic, Memory, Intellectual Processes), Optional scales (Spelling, Motor Writing), Summary scales (Pathognomonic, Left Sensorimotor, Right Sensorimotor).
Administration: Individual.
Price Data, 2006: $549.50 per complete kit including manual (266 pages) and all required materials in a carrying case; $26.95 per 10 patient response booklets; $59.95 per 10 administration and scoring booklets; $93.50 per manual; $21.50 per prepaid WPS Test Report answer

sheet; $319.00 per 25-use computer disk (PC with DOS); $12.50 each per FAX scoring service.

Time: (150) minutes.

Comments: Uses the same stimulus materials, with the addition of 3 extra cards and an audiotape, as Form I of the adult version of the Luria-Nebraska Neuropsychological Battery (1556); other test materials (e.g., tape recorder, stopwatch, eraser, door key) must be supplied by examiner.

Author: Charles J. Golden.

Publisher: Western Psychological Services.

Cross References: See T5:1524 (2 references) and T4:1487 (2 references); for a review by Stephen R. Hooper, see 11:211 (3 references).

[1556]

Luria-Nebraska Neuropsychological Battery: Forms I and II.

Purpose: Designed "to diagnose general and specific cognitive deficits, including lateralization and localization of focal brain impairments, and to aid in the planning and evaluation of rehabilitation programs."

Population: Ages 15 and over

Publication Dates: 1980–1985.

Acronym: LNNB.

Scores, 27: Clinical and Summary scales (Motor Functions, Rhythm, Tactile Functions, Visual Functions, Receptive Speech, Expressive Speech, Writing, Reading, Arithmetic, Memory, Intellectual Processes, Intermediate Memory [Form II only], Pathognomonic, Left Hemisphere, Right Hemisphere, Profile Elevation, Impairment), Localization scales (Left Frontal, Left Sensorimotor, Left Parietal-Occipital, Left Temporal, Right Frontal, Right Sensorimotor, Right Parietal-Occipital, Right Temporal), Optional scales (Spelling, Motor Writing), plus 28 Factor scales.

Administration: Individual.

Forms, 2: I, II.

Price Data, 2006: $549.50 per Form I set including manual (1985, 423 pages), test materials, 10 administration and scoring booklets, and 10 patient response booklets; $489.50 per Form II set; $59.95 per 10 administration and scoring booklets (Form I); $54.95 per 10 administration and scoring booklets (Form II); $25 per 10 patient response booklets (Forms I and II); $152 per manual; $319 per 25-use (PC with DOS) disk for LNNB, Forms I, II, and Children's Revision; $12.50 per FAX service scoring charge.

Time: (90-150) minutes.

Comments: Uses cards adapted from Luria's Neuropsychological Investigation by Anne-Lise Christensen (Form II includes improved, spiral-bound stimulus cards); tape provided for rhythm subtest; Form I can be scored by hand or computer; Form II is computer scored only.

Authors: Charles J. Golden, Arnold D. Purisch, and Thomas A. Hammeke.

Publisher: Western Psychological Services.

Cross References: See T5:1525 (25 references) and T4:1488 (16 references); for reviews by Jeffrey H. Snow and Wilfred G. Van Gorp, see 11:212 (105 references); for a review by Russell L. Adams, see 9:637 (41 references); see also T3:1346 (8 references).

[1557]

MAC Checklist for Evaluating, Preparing, and/or Improving Standardized Tests for Limited English Speaking Students.

Purpose: Aids in the review, critique, or preparation of ESL assessment instruments.

Population: ESL test developers, reviewers, and users.

Publication Date: 1981.

Scores: 5 criterion categories: Evidence of Validity, Evidence of Examinee Appropriateness, Evidence of Proper Item Construction, Evidence of Technical Merit, Evidence of Administrative Excellence.

Administration: Group.

Price Data: Available from publisher.

Time: Administration time not reported.

Author: Jean D'Arcy Maculaitis.

Publisher: MAC Testing & Consulting, LLC.

Cross References: For reviews by Eugene E. Garcia and Charles W. Stansfield, see 10:177.

[1558]

MacArthur-Bates Communicative Development Inventories, Second Edition.

Purpose: Designed as parent-completed assessments "of key language milestones" yielding "information on the course of language development."

Publication Dates: 1993-2007.

Acronym: CDI.

Administration: Individual.

Price Data, 2011: $121.95 per complete kit, including 20 Words and Gestures forms, 20 Words and Sentences forms, CDI III, and user's guide (2007, 207 pages); $99.95 per kit including 20 Words and Gestures forms, 20 Words and Sentences forms, and user's guide; $25 per 20 Words and Gestures forms; $25 per 20 Words and Sentences forms; $20 per 25 CDI-III forms; $59.95 per manual.

Foreign Language Edition: Spanish edition available.

Time: (20-40) minutes.

Comments: Previous version known as MacArthur Communicative Development Inventories.

Authors: Larry Fenson, Virginia A. Marchman, Donna J. Thal, Philip S. Dale, J. Steven Reznick, and Elizabeth Bates.

Publisher: Paul H. Brookes Publishing Co., Inc.

a) WORDS AND GESTURES.

Population: Ages 8-18 months.

Scores, 7: Early Words (First Signs of Understanding, Phrases Understood, Starting to Talk, Vocabulary Checklist), Actions and Gestures (Early Gestures, Later Gestures, Total Gestures).
b) WORDS AND SENTENCES.
Population: Ages 16-30 months.
Scores, 7: Words Children Use (Vocabulary Checklist, How Children Use Words), Sentences and Grammar (Word Endings/Part 1, Word Forms, Word Endings/Part 2), Combining Words (Examples of the Child's Three Longest Sentences, Complexity).
c) CDI-III.
Population: Ages 30-37 months.
Scores, 3: Vocabulary Checklist, Sentences, Using Language.
Cross References: See T5:1528 (8 references); for a review by Carol Westby of the MacArthur Communicative Development Inventories, see 13:188 (14 references).

[1559]

Machinist Test–Form AR-C.

Purpose: Designed for selecting or evaluating applicants or incumbents for machine shop jobs.
Population: Machinist job applicants or incumbents.
Publication Dates: 1981-2007.
Scores, 10: Heat Treating, Layout/Cutting and Assembly, Print Reading, Steel/Metals and Materials, Rigging, Mechanical Principles and Repair, Machine Tools, Tools/Material and Equipment, Machine Shop Lubrication, Total.
Administration: Group.
Price Data, 2011: $22 per consumable self-scoring test booklet (20 minimum order); $24.95 per manual (2007, 19 pages).
Time: (60-70) minutes.
Comments: Self-scoring instrument; previously listed as Ramsay Corporation Job Skills-Machinist Test; available for online test administration.
Author: Roland T. Ramsay.
Publisher: Ramsay Corporation.
Cross References: For reviews by John Peter Hudson, Jr. and James W. Pinkney of an earlier edition, see 13:253.

[1560]

Maculaitis Assessment of Competencies II.

Purpose: "A comprehensive assessment of English Language proficiency for students ... whose first language is not English."
Population: Grades K–12.
Publication Dates: 1982–2001.
Acronym: MAC II.
Scores, 5: 4 subtests (Speaking, Listening, Reading, Writing), Total Battery.
Forms, 2: A, B.
Price Data: Available from publisher.

Comments: Updated and revised version of Maculaitis Assessment of Competencies (MAC), subtests can be administered separately; hand- or machine-scorable; machine scoring performed by publisher; variety of score reports available including Roster Reports, Individual Student Labels, Individual Student Record Form Reports, Summary Reports; Green 10-minute screening test for new students also available.
Author: Jean D'Arcy Maculaitis.
Publisher: Questar Assessment, Inc.
  a) RED LEVEL.
  Population: Grades K–1.
  Administration: Individual.
  Time: (25) minutes.
  b) BLUE LEVEL.
  Population: Grades 2–3.
  Administration: Individual or group.
  Time: (75) minutes.
  c) ORANGE LEVEL.
  Population: Grades 4–5.
  Administration: Individual or group.
  Time: (121) minutes.
  d) IVORY LEVEL.
  Population: Grades 6–8.
  Administration: Individual or group.
  Time: (126) minutes.
  e) TAN LEVEL.
  Population: Grades 9–12.
  Administration: Individual or group.
  Time: (131) minutes.

[1561]

Maintenance Electrician A Test (Form BTA-RC).

Purpose: Designed for selecting manufacturing or processing maintenance candidates.
Population: Applicants and incumbents for jobs requiring electrical knowledge and skills at the highest level.
Publication Dates: 2000-2009.
Scores, 8: Motors, Digital Electronics and Analog Electronics, Schematics & Print Reading and Control Circuits, Power Supplies/Power Distribution and Construction & Installation, Basic AC/DC Theory and Electrical Maintenance & Troubleshooting, Test Instruments and Computers & PLC, Mechanical Maintenance, Total.
Administration: Group.
Price Data, 2011: $22 per consumable self-scoring test booklet or online test administration (minimum order of 20); $24.95 per manual (2009, 18 pages).
Time: (60-70) minutes.
Comments: Self-scoring instrument; available for online test administration.
Author: Roland T. Ramsay.
Publisher: Ramsay Corporation.
Cross References: For a review by Kevin R. Kelly of an earlier edition, see 17:112.

[1562]

Maintenance Electrician B Test (Form BTB-C).

Purpose: For selecting manufacturing or processing maintenance candidates.
Population: Applicants and incumbents for jobs requiring electrical knowledge and skills.
Publication Dates: 2000–2005.
Scores, 8: Motors, Digital Electronics and Analog Electronics, Schematics & Print Reading and Control Circuits, Power Supplies/Power Distribution and Construction & Installation, AC/DC Theory and Electrical Maintenance, Test Instruments and Computers & PLC, Mechanical Maintenance and Hand & Power Tools, Total.
Administration: Group.
Price Data, 2011: $22 per consumable self-scoring test booklet or online test administration (minimum order of 20); $24.95 per manual (2000, 16 pages).
Time: (60-70) minutes.
Comments: Self-scoring instrument; available for online test administration.
Author: Roland T. Ramsay.
Publisher: Ramsay Corporation.
Cross References: For a review by Jay R. Stewart, see 17:113.

[1563]

MAINTEST (Form A, Form B, & Form C).

Purpose: Measures practical mechanical and electrical knowledge.
Population: Applicants and incumbents for jobs requiring practical mechanical and electrical knowledge and skills.
Publication Dates: 1991–2010.
Scores, 22: Hydraulics, Pneumatics, Welding, Power Transmission, Lubrication, Pumps, Piping, Rigging, Mechanical Maintenance, Shop Machines and Tools & Equipment, Combustion, Motors, Digital Electronics, Schematics & Print Reading, Control Circuits, Power Supplies, Basic AC & DC Theory, Power Distribution, Test Instruments, Computers & PLC, Electrical Maintenance, Total.
Administration: Group.
Price Data, 2011: $65 per paper-and-pencil test or online test administration (minimum order of 10) no charge for manual (2005, 28 pages); price per test administration is $45 when 20 test administrations are purchased.
Foreign Language Edition: Available in Spanish.
Time: (130-170) minutes.
Comments: Tests scored by publisher; Forms B and C are alternate forms of Form A.
Author: Roland T. Ramsay.
Publisher: Ramsay Corporation.
Cross References: For a review by Michael J. Zickar, see 17:114; for reviews by Nambury S. Raju and William J. Waldron of an earlier edition, see 13:189.

[1564]

Major Field Tests.

Purpose: Designed to measure the basic knowledge and understanding achieved by students in a major field of study.
Population: Undergraduate students completing an academic major program and MBA.
Publication Dates: 1988–2006.
Acronym: MFT.
Scores: Total score only.
Administration: Group.
Price Data: Available from publisher at www.ETS.org/MFT.
Time: (120) minutes; MBA: 180 minutes.
Comments: Objective, end-of-program content tests in 16 disciplines; yields individual scores and subscores, group mean scores, and "assessment indicators" (group reliable subscores); delivered in two formats: online and paper-and-pencil; because there are no preset test administration dates, institutions and departments may schedule testing at their convenience; colleges and academic departments can choose where to administer the exams, as long as it is in a proctored environment, and with Internet connections for the online tests.
Author: Educational Testing Service.
Publisher: Educational Testing Service.

[1565]

Major-Minor Finder [2006 Update].

Purpose: Designed to help individuals "assess their aptitudes and interests and use the information to find college majors they are most likely to not only enjoy but succeed in."
Population: High school and college.
Publication Dates: 1978-2006.
Acronym: MMF.
Scores: No scores; decisions based on number of matches for each major.
Administration: Group.
Price Data, 2008: $4.20 per 9 Major-Minor Finder booklets (2006, 16 pages); $.57 per 9 answer booklets.
Time: Administration time not reported.
Author: CFKR Career Materials, Inc.
Publisher: CFKR Career Materials, Inc.
Cross References: For a review by James W. Pinkney of the 1986-1996 Edition, see 10:181; for reviews by Rodney L. Lowman and Daryl Sander of an earlier edition, see 9:643.

[1566]

Make A Picture Story.

Purpose: "A projective psychological test" intended "as an aid in inferring psychodynamic interpretations and structural aspects of personality."
Population: Age 6 and over.

Publication Dates: 1947–1952.
Acronym: MAPS.
Scores: Not scored.
Administration: Individual.
Price Data, 2006: $104.50 per complete kit including manual (1952, 92 pages), 22 stimulus cards, 67 cut-out figures, and 25 Location sheets; $27.50 per 100 Location sheets.
Time: Untimed.
Comments: A projective test similar to the Thematic Apperception Test (2796); best when used as a component of a battery of psychological tests; guidelines for qualitative interpreting of subjects' responses provided.
Author: Edwin S. Shneidman.
Publisher: Western Psychological Services.
Cross References: See T3:1361 (66 references), T2:1482 (10 references) and P:452 (4 references); for a review by Arthur R. Jensen, see 6:230 (10 references); see also 5:149 (18 references); for reviews by Albert Rabin and Charles R. Strother, see 4:113 (19 references).

[1567]

Making a Terrific Career Happen.

Purpose: For use in guiding examinees in self-evaluation and exploration of careers.
Population: High school graduates, college students, and adults.
Publication Date: 1992.
Acronym: MATCH.
Scores: Science-Professional, Science-Skilled, Technology-Professional, Technology-Skilled, Consumer Economics, Outdoor, Business-Professional, Business-Skilled, Clinical, Communication, Arts-Professional, Arts-Skilled, Service-Professional, Service-Skilled.
Administration: Group.
Price Data: Available from publisher.
Time: Administration time varies.
Comments: Self-administered and interpreted.
Author: Lisa Knapp-Lee.
Publisher: EdITS/Educational and Industrial Testing Service.

[1568]

Malingering Probability Scale.

Purpose: Designed to "assess whether an individual is attempting to produce false evidence of psychological distress."
Population: Ages 17 and over
Publication Date: 1998.
Acronym: MPS.
Scores, 6: Depression and Anxiety, Dissociative Disorders, Post-Traumatic Stress, Schizophrenia, Inconsistency, Malingering.
Administration: Individual.
Price Data, 2006: $160 per kit for mail-in computer scoring including reusable administration card, 5 prepaid mail-in answer sheets, and manual; $450 per kit for on-site computer scoring including reusable administration card, 20-use disk, 100 PC answer sheets, and manual; $7 per reusable administration card; $30 per five pack of reusable administration cards; $60 per manual; $21.95 per mail-in answer sheet; $399 per 20-use disk (PC with Microsoft Windows), free U.S. shipping; $17.50 per 100 PC answer sheets.
Time: (20) minutes.
Comments: May be administered by paper and pencil or personal computer; computer scored (only) and interpreted locally or by publisher FAX or mail-in service.
Authors: Leigh Silverton and Chris Gruber (manual).
Publisher: Western Psychological Services.
Cross References: For reviews by Solomon M. Fulero and Radhika Krishnamurthy, see 14:216.

[1569]

Management and Graduate Item Bank.

Purpose: "For use in the selection, development or guidance of personnel at graduate level or in management positions."
Population: Graduate level and senior management applicants for the following areas: finance, computing, engineering, corporate planning, purchasing, personnel, and marketing.
Publication Dates: 1985–1987.
Acronym: MGIB.
Scores, 2: Verbal Critical Reasoning, Numerical Critical Reasoning.
Administration: Group.
Price Data: Available from publisher.
Time: 60(65) minutes.
Comments: Abbreviated adaptation of the Advanced Test Battery (128); subtests available as separates.
Authors: Saville & Holdsworth Ltd. and Linda Espey (supplementary norms manual).
Publisher: SHL Group plc [United Kingdom].
Cross References: For reviews by James T. Austin and H. John Bernardin and by R. W. Faunce, see 11:213.

[1570]

Management and Leadership Questionnaire.

Purpose: Designed to "provide information about an individual's management and leadership competencies and skills."
Population: Ages 18-64.
Publication Date: 2011.
Acronym: MLQ30.
Scores, 36: Strategic and Creative Thinking, Thinking and Managing Globally, Developing Strategy and Acting Strategically, Managing Knowledge and Information, Creating and Innovating, Managing costs and Financial Performance, Leading and Deciding, Attracting and Managing Talent, Motivating People and Inspiring Them

to Excel, Coaching and Developing People, Managing Culture and Diversity, Making Sound Decisions, Developing and Changing, Displaying Initiative and Drive, Showing courage and Strength, Learning and Developing Continuously, Managing and Implementing Change, Adapting and Coping with Pressure, Implementing and Improving, Executing Strategies and Plans, Improving Processes and Systems, Managing customer Relationships and Services, Analyzing Issues and Problems, Managing Plans and Projects, Communicating and Presenting, Facilitating and Improving Communication, Influencing and Persuading People, Managing Feelings and Emotions, Speaking with Confidence and Presenting to Groups, Writing and Reporting, Relating and Supporting, Relating and Networking, Listening and Showing Understanding, Building Trust and Modeling Integrity, Identifying and Resolving Conflict, Cultivating Teamwork and Collaboration.
Administration: Group.
Forms, 2: Normative and Ipsative.
Price Data, 2011: $14.95 per test.
Time: (30) minutes.
Comments: Assessment, scoring, and feedback conducted online.
Author: MySkillsProfile.com.
Publisher: MySkillsProfile.com Limited [England].

[1571]

Management & Leadership Systems.

Purpose: Designed to assess management and leadership skills and team effectiveness.
Population: Management personnel.
Publication Dates: 1992–2001.
Acronym: MLS.
Administration: Group.
Price Data, 2001: $495 per Facilitator's kit including User's Manual (2001, 230 pages), Guide to Management & Leadership, High-Performing Teams Action Planning Workbook, 6 Management & Leadership Profiles, 6 Team Effectiveness Profiles, 6 Management Candidate Profiles, and transparency masters; $35 per Guide to Management & Leadership; $35 per High-Performing Teams Action Planning workbook; $195 annual licensing fee for scoring software.
Foreign Language Editions: Available in English, Spanish, French, and Portuguese.
Time: (20) minutes per test.
Comments: Inventories may be completed via paper-and-pencil, or on-line via the internet; microcomputer software requirements are Windows 98 or newer, 32 MB RAM, and 10 MB free on hard drive; the option to have the publisher generate the MLP, TEKP, MCP, and SIP is available, thus eliminating licensing of the scoring software; reports can be printed in different languages.
Author: Curtiss S. Peck.
Publisher: Assessment Systems International, Inc.

a) MANAGEMENT & LEADERSHIP PROFILE.
Purpose: Designed to measure "both present behavior and desired behavior based on the needs and expectations of the people who are evaluating the manager."
Acronym: MLP.
Scores, 15: Clarity of Purpose (Goals, Communication), Planning and Problem Avoidance (Planning, Involvement, Decision Making), Task Accomplishment (Competence, Motivation, Work Facilitation), Providing Feedback (Feedback), Exercising Control (Managing Performance, Accountability, Delegation), Individual & Team Relationships (Relationships, Linking, Teamwork).
b) TEAM EFFECTIVENESS PROFILE.
Purpose: "Provides a way of measuring and giving feedback to teams on how they manage their processes and projects."
Acronym: TEP.
Scores, 15: Clarity of Purpose (Goals, Communication), Planning and Problem Avoidance (Planning, Involvement, Innovation/Risk, Decision Making), Task Accomplishment (Values, Competence, Motivation, Quality/Continuous Improvement), Providing Feedback (Feedback), Exercising Control (Control, Delegation), Individual & Team Relationships (Linking, Teamwork).
c) MANAGEMENT CANDIDATE PROFILE.
Purpose: "Measures day-to-day behavior that is correlated with effective management and leadership behavior. The MCP helps people understand the skills required to become effective managers and provides a clear picture of the candidate's strengths and softspots in ten important areas."
Acronym: MCP.
Scores, 10: Goals, Communication, Planning, Innovation/Risk, Decision Making, Motivation, Quality/Continuous Improvement, Feedback, Control, Relationships.
d) SELLING WITH INTEGRITY PROFILE.
Purpose: "Measure the perceptions of current behavior and desired behavior of internal and external sales people. The SIP is completed by customers, sales manager, and sales person."
Acronym: SIP.
Scores, 7: Professionalism, Identification of Needs, Partnering, Competence, Negotiation, Close, Service.
Cross References: For reviews by Stephen F. Davis and William J. Waldron, see 14:217.

[1572]

Management and Organizational Skills Test.

Purpose: Measures "an individual's knowledge and understanding of how relatively complex organizations function as well as knowledge of the competencies and skills required for success in management and executive positions."

Population: Job applicants.
Publication Date: 2004.
Acronym: MOST.
Scores: Total score only.
Administration: Group.
Price Data, 2005: $29.95 per manual (10 pages); $50 per 10 test booklets.
Time: (45–60) minutes.
Comments: Web-based test version is self-administering.
Authors: E. P. Prien and Leonard D. Goodstein.
Publisher: HRD Press, Inc.
Cross References: For reviews by Paul M. Muchinsky and by Carolyn L. Pearson and Ibrahim Duyar, see 17:115.

[1573]

Management Appraisal Survey.

Purpose: "An assessment of managerial practices and attitudes as viewed through the eyes of employees."
Population: Employees.
Publication Dates: 1967-1996.
Scores, 5: Overall Leadership Style, Philosophy, Planning, Implementation, Evaluation.
Administration: No manual.
Price Data, 2001: $7.95 per instrument.
Time: Administration time not reported.
Comments: Self-administered survey.
Authors: Jay Hall, Jerry B. Harvey, and Martha S. Williams.
Publisher: Teleometrics International, Inc.
Cross References: For reviews by H. John Bernardin and George C. Thornton, III, see 10:182; see also T3:2351 (1 reference); for a review by Abraham K. Korman of the Styles of Leadership and Management, see 8:1185 (8 references).

[1574]

Management Aptitude Test.

Purpose: Designed to "evaluate critical thinking skills typically relevant to management positions."
Population: Age 18 and over.
Publication Date: 1993.
Acronym: MAT.
Scores, 7: Administrative Skills, Business Control, Communication, Planning/Organizing, Problem Solving, Supervisory Skills, Manager Potential Index.
Administration: Group or individual.
Price Data, 2005: $43 per 1–999 profiles using Inernet without booklets; $43 per 1–999 profiles using Quanta-TouchTest™, $43 per 1–999 profiles using Quanta® software for Windows without booklets.
Time: (90–100) minutes.
Comments: Test can be scored using operator-assisted telephone scoring, touch-test telephone scoring, and Quanta-based scoring.
Author: Reid London House.

Publisher: Pearson Performance Solutions [No reply from publisher; status unknown].

[1575]

Management Development Questionnaire.

Purpose: A personal competence assessment instrument "designed to help managers identify their weakness and strengths and decide what they need to do to develop themselves."
Population: Managers.
Publication Date: 1997.
Acronym: MDQ.
Scores, 20: Initiative, Risk Taking, Innovation, Flexibility/Adaptability, Analytical Thinking, Decision Making, Planning, Quality Focus, Oral Communication, Sensitivity, Relationships, Teamwork, Achievement, Customer Focus, Business Awareness, Learning Orientation, Authority/Presence, Motivating Others, Developing People, Resilience.
Administration: Individual.
Price Data: Available from publisher.
Time: (35) minutes.
Author: Alan Cameron.
Publisher: HRD Press, Inc.
Cross References: For reviews by Samuel Hinton and Eugene P. Sheehan, see 15:140.

[1576]

Management Effectiveness Profile System.

Purpose: "Identifies managers' current strengths and weaknesses and provides direction for individual development."
Population: Managers and coworkers.
Publication Dates: 1983–1993.
Acronym: MEPS.
Scores: 2 scores (Self, Other) in 14 management skill areas: Problem Solving, Time Management, Planning, Goal Setting, Performance Leadership, Organizing, Team Development, Delegation, Participation, Integrating Differences, Providing Feedback, Stress Processing, Maintaining Integrity, Commitment.
Administration: Individual or group.
Forms, 2: Self Description, Description by Others.
Price Data: Available from publisher.
Comments: Originally called Management Practices Audit; administered to manager and 4 or 5 coworkers.
Author: Human Synergistics International.
Publisher: Human Synergistics International.

[1577]

Management Interest Inventory.

Purpose: "To assist both organizations and individuals in making decisions relating to selection, placement, and career development at management level."
Population: Managers.
Publication Dates: 1983–1986.

Scores, 54: Management Functions Preference Scores and Experience Scores (Production Operations, Technical Services, Research and Development, Distribution, Purchasing, Sales, Marketing Support, Personnel and Training, Data Processing, Finance, Legal and Secretarial, Administration, Total, Spread Across Functions); Management Skills Preference Scores and Experience Scores (Information Collecting, Information Processing, Problem-Solving, Decision-Making, Modelling, Communicating Orally, Communicating in Writing, Organising Things, Organising People, Persuading, Developing, Representing, Total).
Administration: Group.
Price Data: Available from publisher.
Time: (20–40) minutes.
Authors: Roger Holdsworth (test), Ruth Holdsworth (test), Lisa Cramp (test), and Miranda Blum (manual).
Publisher: SHL Group plc [United Kingdom].
Cross References: For a review by David M. Saunders, see 11:216.

[1578]

Management Inventory on Leadership, Motivation and Decision-Making.

Purpose: Designed for use in the training and selection of managers.
Population: Managers and manager trainees.
Publication Date: 1991.
Acronym: MILMD.
Scores: Total score only.
Administration: Group.
Price Data, 2001: $40 per 20 test and answer booklets; $5 per Instructor Manual (1991, 8 pages); $10 per Review Set including one test, one answer booklet, and Instructor Manual.
Time: (15-20) minutes.
Author: Donald L. Kirkpatrick.
Publisher: Donald L. Kirkpatrick (the author).
Cross References: For reviews by Kevin R. Murphy and Eugene P. Sheehan, see 12:226.

[1579]

Management Inventory on Managing Change.

Purpose: To assess managers' attitudes, knowledge, and opinions regarding principles and approaches for facilitating change.
Population: Managers.
Publication Dates: 1978-1983.
Acronym: MIMC.
Scores: Total score only.
Administration: Group or individual.
Price Data, 2001: $40 per 20 tests and answer booklets; $5 per instructor's manual (1983, 8 pages); $10 per review set (includes test, answer booklet, and manual).

Time: (15-25) minutes.
Author: Donald L. Kirkpatrick.
Publisher: Donald L. Kirkpatrick (the author).

[1580]

Management Inventory on Modern Management.

Purpose: "Developed to cover eight different topics of importance to managers."
Population: Managers.
Publication Date: 1984.
Acronym: MIMM.
Scores: 8 areas: Leadership Styles, Selecting and Training, Communicating, Motivating, Managing Change, Delegating, Decision Making, Managing Time; Total score is sum of the 8 areas.
Administration: Group or individual.
Price Data, 2001: $40 per 20 tests and answer booklets; $5 per manual (12 pages); $10 per specimen set.
Time: (20) minutes.
Comments: Self-scored training tool.
Author: Donald L. Kirkpatrick.
Publisher: Donald L. Kirkpatrick (the Author).
Cross References: For a review by Lenore W. Harmon, see 10:183.

[1581]

Management Inventory on Performance Appraisal and Coaching.

Purpose: "To determine the need for training in "performance appraisal and coaching.'"
Population: Managers.
Publication Date: 1990.
Acronym: MIPAC.
Scores: Total score only.
Administration: Group.
Price Data, 2001: $40 per 20 tests and answer booklets; $10 per optional audiocassette; $5 per manual (7 pages); $10 per specimen set.
Time: (20-25) minutes.
Comments: Self-administered, self-scored.
Author: Donald L. Kirkpatrick.
Publisher: Donald L. Kirkpatrick (the author).

[1582]

Management Inventory on Time Management.

Purpose: Tests time management ability of managerial personnel.
Population: Managers.
Publication Date: 1980.
Acronym: MITM.
Scores: Total score only.
Administration: Group or individual.

Price Data, 2001: $40 per 20 tests and answer booklets; $5 per instructor's manual (8 pages); $10 per review set (includes test, answer booklet, and manual).
Time: (15-25) minutes.
Author: Donald L. Kirkpatrick.
Publisher: Donald L. Kirkpatrick (the author).

[1583]
Management of Differences Inventory.

Purpose: To provide feedback to an individual concerning his/her manner of handling differences in managerial situations.
Population: Business managers.
Publication Dates: 1981–1994.
Acronyn: MODI.
Scores, 9: Maintain, Smooth, Dominate, Decide by Rule, Coexist, Bargain, Yield, Release, Collaborate.
Administration: Group.
Forms, 2: Self, Feedback.
Price Data, 2002: $8.95 per Self form; $8.95 per Feedback form; minimum of 20 (volume discounts available).
Time: (20) minutes.
Comments: Self-administered; self-scored.
Author: Herbert S. Kindler.
Publisher: The Center for Management Effectiveness, Inc.

[1584]
Management Practices Update.

Purpose: To provide individuals with information about managerial behavior in areas of interpersonal relationships, the management of motivation, and personal "style" of management.
Population: Individuals involved in the management of others.
Publication Date: 1987.
Acronym: MPU.
Scores, 12: Section I (Exposure, Feedback), Section II (Basic, Safety, Belonging, Ego Status, Actualization), Section III (Team Management, Middle-of-the-Road Management, Task Management, Country Club Management, Impoverished Management).
Administration: Group.
Parts, 3: I (Interpersonal Relationships), II (Management of Motivation), III (Analysis of Management Style).
Price Data, 2001: $8.95 per instrument (25 pages).
Time: Administration time not reported.
Comments: Represents a shortened version of Personnel Relations Survey (2035), Management of Motives Index, and Styles of Management Inventory (2608).
Author: Jay Hall.
Publisher: Teleometrics International, Inc.

[1585]
Management Readiness Profile.

Purpose: Designed to "measure the attitudes and aptitudes that are commonly critical to management success."

Population: Ages 18 and over.
Publication Dates: 1989–2000.
Acronym: MRP.
Scores, 9: Managerial Interest, Leadership, Energy Level, Practical Thinking, Interpersonal Skills, Business Ethics, Management Readiness Index, Candidness, Accuracy.
Administration: Group or individual.
Price Data, 2005: $20 including 1–999 reports for Internet scoring with booklets; $20 including 1–999 reports for Internet scoring without booklets; $20 including 1–999 reports for QuantaTouch Test; $20 including 1–999 reports for QUANTA Software for Windows with booklets; $20 including 1–999 reports for QUANTA Software for Windows without booklets.
Foreign Language Editions: Available in Spanish and French Canadian.
Time: (20–25) minutes.
Comments: Test can be scored over Touch Test, Internet, and Optical Scanning Software.
Author: Reid London House.
Publisher: Pearson Performance Solutions [No reply from publisher; status unknown].

[1586]
Management Relations Survey.

Purpose: To assess employees' perceptions of their practices toward their managers.
Population: Subordinates to managers.
Publication Dates: 1970-1995.
Acronym: MRS.
Scores, 2: Exposure, Feedback.
Administration: Group.
Price Data, 2001: $7.95 per instrument.
Time: Administration time not reported.
Comments: Companion instrument to Personnel Relations Survey (2035); based on the Johari Window Model of interpersonal relations.
Author: Jay Hall.
Publisher: Teleometrics International, Inc.
Cross Reference: For a review by Walter C. Borman, see 8:1178 (1 reference).

[1587]
Management Situation Checklist.

Purpose: Designed to help determine how management style matches management demands, to define vulnerabilities from management style and develop strategies for improving vulnerabilities.
Population: Managers.
Publication Date: 1986.
Acronym: MSC.
Scores, 6: Coercive, Authoritative, Affiliative, Democratic, Pacesetting, Coaching.
Administration: Group or individual.

Price Data, 2006: $33 per 10 booklets.
Time: [20–30] minutes.
Comments: Self-rating checklist; self-scored; is a companion to the Managerial Style Questionnaire (1602).
Author: Hay Group.
Publisher: Hay Group.

[1588]

Management Style Inventory [Training House, Inc.].

Purpose: "This exercise is designed to give you some insights into your management style and how it affects others."
Population: Industry.
Publication Dates: 1986–1987.
Scores, 5: Team Builder, Soft, Hard, Middle of Road, Ineffective.
Administration: Group or individual.
Price Data: Price information available from publisher for complete sets including test, answer sheet, and interpretation sheet.
Time: (20) minutes.
Comments: Self-administered, self-scored.
Author: Training House, Inc.
Publisher: Training House, Inc.
Cross References: For reviews by Ernest J. Kozma and Charles K. Parsons, see 11:220.

[1589]

Management Styles Inventory.

Purpose: Assesses individual management style under a variety of conditions.
Population: Adults.
Publication Dates: 1964-1995.
Scores, 5: Philosophy, Planning and Goal Setting, Implementation, Performance Evaluation, Total.
Administration: Group.
Price Data, 2001: $8.95 per instrument.
Time: Untimed.
Comments: Self-administered survey.
Authors: Jay Hall, Jerry B. Harvey, and Martha S. Williams.
Publisher: Teleometrics International Inc.
Cross References: For reviews by Ralph F. Darr, Jr. and Charles K. Parsons, see 12:227.

[1590]

Management Success Profile.

Purpose: "Provides a standardized measure of potential for success in management and is an ideal instrument for selecting supervisors, unit managers, and team leaders. The MSP assesses the individual's interest in, motivation toward, and knowledge about management positions."
Population: Adults (management position candidates).
Publication Date: 1996.
Acronym: MSP.

Scores: Validity (Candidness, Accuracy), Management Focus (Work Background, Leadership), Motivation and Attitudes (Management Responsibility, Productivity, Customer Service Orientation), Management Style (Practical Thinking, Adaptability, Coaching), Stability and Risk (Business Ethics, Job Commitment), Overall Management Profile Index.
Administration: Group.
Price Data: Available from publisher.
Time: (45) minutes.
Comments: Toll free customer service hotline for immediate assistance with Profile (1-800-221-8378).
Author: London House.
Publisher: Pearson Performance Solutions [No reply from publisher; status unknown].

[1591]

Management Team Roles–Indicator.

Purpose: "A team roles model and questionnaire [that] identifies the contribution ... made by each individual to the success of [his or her work] team" and "indicates which [of 8 distinct] Jungian function-attitudes are primarily being used at present."
Population: Adults.
Publication Date: 2000.
Acronym: MTR-i.
Scores: 8 team roles: Coach, Crusader, Explorer, Innovator, Sculptor, Curator, Conductor, Scientist.
Administration: Group.
Price Data, 2001: £49.50 per specimen set including technical manual (2000, 95 pages), question card, answer sheet, report, and 360 Degree feedback form; £35 per 10 self-score answer sheets; £35 per 10 report and 360 Degree feedback forms; £42.50 per technical manual.
Time: (10–15) minutes.
Comments: Can be completed online.
Author: Stephen P. Myers.
Publisher: The Test Agency Limited [England] [No reply from publisher; status unknown].
Cross References: For reviews by Gary J. Dean and John Tivendell, see 15:141.

[1592]

Management Transactions Audit.

Purpose: Assesses "one's interpersonal transactions and their implications for managerial effectiveness."
Population: Managers.
Publication Dates: 1973–1997.
Acronym: MTA.
Scores, 9: Transaction Scores (Parent Subsystem, Adult Subsystem, Child Subsystem); Tension Index Scores (Subordinates [Disruptive, Constructive], Colleagues [Disruptive, Constructive], Superiors [Disruptive, Constructive]).
Administration: Group.
Manual: No manual.
Price Data, 2001: $8.95 per instrument.

Time: [15-30] minutes.
Comments: Self-administered survey.
Authors: Jay Hall and C. Leo Griffith.
Publisher: Teleometrics International, Inc.
Cross References: For reviews by Stephan J. Motowidlo and Ronald N. Taylor, see 8:1180.

[1593]

Manager Style Appraisal.
Purpose: A measure of managerial style.
Population: Adults.
Publication Dates: 1967-1995.
Scores, 5: Philosophy, Planning and Goal Setting, Implementation, Performance Evaluation, Total.
Administration: Group.
Price Data, 2001: $7.95 per instrument.
Time: Untimed.
Comments: Self-administered survey.
Authors: Jay Hall, Jerry B. Harvey, and Martha S. Williams.
Publisher: Teleometrics International, Inc.
Cross References: For reviews by Kenneth N. Anchor and Claudia J. Morner, see 12:228.

[1594]

Manager/Supervisor Staff Selector.
Purpose: "Measures important intellectual and personality characteristics needed for the successful manager/supervisor."
Population: Candidates for managerial and supervisory positions.
Publication Dates: 1976–1984.
Scores: 10 tests: Problem Solving Ability, Numerical Skills, Fluency, Business, Judgment, Supervisory Practices, CPF (interest in working with people), NPF (emotional stability), Adult Personality Inventory, Work Motivation Inventory.
Administration: Group.
Price Data, 2001: $500 per person; quantity discounts available.
Foreign Language Edition: French edition available.
Time: (240) minutes.
Comments: Graded by publisher; comprehensive report prepared for each candidate; must be proctored.
Authors: Tests from various publishers compiled, distributed, and scored by Walden Personnel Testing.
Publisher: Walden Personnel Performance, Inc. [Canada].
Cross References: For a review by Eric F. Gardner, see 10:186.

[1595]

Managerial and Professional Job Functions Inventory.
Purpose: "For defining the basic dimensions of jobs and assessing their relative importance for the job" and "assessing one's ability to perform them."

Population: Middle and upper level managers and higher-level professionals.
Publication Dates: 1978–1997.
Acronym: MPJFI.
Scores, 16: Setting Organizational Objectives, Financial Planning and Review, Improving Work Procedures and Practices, Interdepartmental Coordination, Developing and Implementing Technical Ideas, Judgment and Decision-Making, Developing Teamwork, Coping with Difficulties and Emergencies, Promoting Safety Attitudes and Practices, Communications, Developing Employee Potential, Supervisory Practices, Self-Development and Improvement, Personnel Practices, Promoting Community-Organization Relations, Handling Outside Contacts.
Administration: Individual or group.
Price Data, 2002: $101 per start-up kit including 25 test booklets (specify Importance or Ability), 25 score sheets, and interpretation and research manual; $54 per 25 test booklets (specify Importance or Ability); $31 per 25 score sheets; $28 per interpretation and research manual.
Time: No limit (approximately 40–60 minutes).
Authors: Melany E. Baehr, Wallace G. Lonergan, and Bruce A. Hunt.
Publisher: Pearson Performance Solutions [No reply from publisher; status unknown].
Cross References: For reviews by L. Alan Witt and Sheldon Zedeck, see 11:222.

[1596]

Managerial Assessment of Proficiency MAP™.
Purpose: "Shows a participant's strengths and weaknesses in twelve areas of managerial competency and two dimensions of management style."
Population: Managers.
Publication Dates: 1985–1988.
Acronym: MAP.
Scores, 19: Administrative Competencies (Time Management and Prioritizing, Setting Goals and Standards, Planning and Scheduling Work, Administrative Composite), Communication Competencies (Listening and Organizing, Giving Clear Information, Getting Unbiased Information, Communication Composite), Supervisory Competencies (Training/Coaching/Delegating, Appraising People and Performance, Disciplining and Counseling, Supervisory Composite), Cognitive Competencies (Identifying and Solving Problems, Making Decisions/Weighing Risk, Thinking Clearly and Analytically, Cognitive Composite), Proficiency Composite, Theory X Style (Parent-Child), and Theory Y Style (Adult-Adult).
Administration: Group.
Price Data: Available from publisher.
Time: (360–420) minutes.
Comments: May be purchased with licensing agreement, contracted for in-house administration, or used

by attending a public workshop provided by publisher; administered in part by videocassette.

Author: Scott B. Parry.

Publisher: Training House, Inc.

Cross References: For a review by Jerard F. Kehoe, see 11:223.

[1597]

Managerial Competence Index.

Purpose: "To assess the probable competence of one's approach to management."

Population: Individuals who manage or are being assessed for their potential to manage others.

Publication Dates: 1980-1989.

Acronym: MCI.

Scores, 5: Team Management, Middle-of-the-Road Management, Task Management, Country Club Management, Impoverished Management.

Administration: Group.

Price Data, 2001: $8.95 per instrument (1989, 21 pages).

Time: Administration time not reported.

Author: Jay Hall.

Publisher: Teleometrics International, Inc.

Cross References: For a review by Kurt F. Geisinger, see 11:224.

[1598]

Managerial Competence Review.

Purpose: To identify a manager's preferred managerial style and assess the relative competence of his/her approach to management.

Population: Subordinates to managers.

Publication Dates: 1980–1989.

Acronym: MCR.

Scores, 5: Relative measures of concern for people and concern for production ("9/9," "1/9," "5/5," "9/1," "1/1").

Administration: Group.

Price Data, 2001: $7.95 per instrument (1989, 17 pages).

Time: Administration time not reported.

Comments: Companion instrument for Managerial Competence Index (1597).

Author: Jay Hall.

Publisher: Teleometrics International, Inc.

[1599]

Managerial Competency Questionnaire.

Purpose: "Developed to measure the use of seven competencies that have been found to be critical for effective managers."

Population: Managers.

Publication Date: 1997.

Acronym: MCQ.

Scores, 7: Achievement Orientation, Developing Others, Directiveness, Impact and Influence, Inter-personal Understanding, Organizational Awareness, Team Leadership.

Administration: Individual or group.

Price Data, 2006: $69 per 10 questionnaire, and interpretive notes (24 pages); $29 per 10 questionnaires only; $55 per 10 Development Assistant booklets. Refer to the Manager Competency Portfolio for a more comprehensive on-line alternative.

Time: [30–40] minutes.

Comments: Self-report questionnaire.

Author: Hay Group.

Publisher: Hay Group.

[1600]

Managerial Philosophies Scale.

Purpose: Surveys the "manager's assumptions and working theories about the nature of those whose activities he or she coordinates."

Population: Managers.

Publication Dates: 1975–1995.

Acronym: MPS.

Scores, 2: Theory X (Reductive Management Beliefs), Theory Y (Developmental Management Beliefs).

Administration: Group.

Manual: No manual.

Price Data, 2001: $8.95 per instrument.

Time: [15-30] minutes.

Comments: Self-administered survey.

Authors: Jacob Jacoby and James R. Terborg.

Publisher: Teleometrics International, Inc.

Cross References: See T3:1366 (1 reference).

[1601]

Managerial Scale for Enterprise Improvement.

Purpose: Designed "to measure management morale."

Population: Managers.

Publication Date: No date.

Scores: Total score only.

Administration: Group.

Price Data, 2001: $2 per specimen set.

Time: (12) minutes.

Author: Herbert A. Kaufman.

Publisher: Psychometric Affiliates.

Cross References: For a review by Nambury S. Raju, see 15:142.

[1602]

Managerial Style Questionnaire.

Purpose: Measures individuals' perception of how they manage based on the assessment of six managerial styles.

Population: Persons in managerial situations.

Publication Dates: 1980–1996.

Acronym: MSQ.

Scores, 6: Coercive, Authoritative, Affiliative, Democratic, Pacesetting, Coaching.

Administration: Group or individual.
Forms, 2: Participant, Employee.
Price Data, 2006: $79 per 10 Participant version questionnaires, profiles, and interpretive notes; $29 per 10 Employee version questionnaires; $25 per trainer's guide (1994, 28 pages) hardcopy of free electronic copy with purchase.
Foreign Language Editions: Available in Spanish and French.
Time: [30–40] minutes.
Comments: Self-scored instrument.
Author: Hay Group.
Publisher: Hay Group.
Cross References: For a review by H. John Bernardin and Joan E. Pynes, see 10:185; for a review by Frank L. Schmidt of an earlier edition, see 8:1182 (1 reference).

[1603]

Manchester Personality Questionnaire.

Purpose: Designed to provide an occupational personality test with a focus on traits relevant to creative and innovative behavior.
Population: Adults.
Publication Dates: 1993–1996.
Acronym: MPQ.
Administration: Group.
Author: CIM Test Publishers.
Publisher: The Test Agency Limited [England]; North American Distributor: Human Resource Development Press [No reply from publisher; status unknown].

a) MPQ FACTOR 14.
Purpose: An assessment of 14 personality traits covering the Big Five personality factors.
Scores, 19: Big Five Factors (Creativity, Agreeableness, Achievement, Extroversion, Resilience), Originality, Rule Consciousness, Openness to Change, Assertiveness, Social Confidence, Empathy, Communicativeness, Independence, Rationality, Competitiveness, Conscientiousness, Perfectionism, Decisiveness, Apprehension.
Price Data, 2001: £65 per administration set including user's manual (1996, 72 pages), reusable questionnaire, answer sheet, and profile chart; £55 per user's manual; £6.50 per reusable question booklet; £62.50 per 25 answer sheets; £25 per 25 profile charts; £450 per MPQ Expert System.
Time: (20) minutes.
b) MANCHESTER CREATIVITY QUESTIONNAIRE FACTOR 7.
Purpose: An assessment of the personality attributes of creativity.
Scores, 9: Global Factor (Creativity), Originality, Rule Consciousness, Openness to Change, Assertiveness, Independence, Achievement, Radicalness, Response Style.
Price Data: £65 per 10 combined question/answer booklets.
Time: Administration time not reported.

Cross References: For reviews by Jack E. Gebart-Eaglemont and Carl Isenhart, see 13:191.

[1604]

Manifest Needs Questionnaire.

Purpose: "Measures the relative power of four work-related motivation factors: the need for achievement, for affiliation, for autonomy, and for dominance."
Population: Adult employees of a company or organization.
Publication Date: [No date].
Acronym: MNQ.
Scores, 4: Need for Achievement, Need for Affiliation, Need for Autonomy, Need for Dominance.
Administration: Group.
Price Data, 2008: $49.95 per 10 questionnaires.
Time: Administration time not reported.
Author: InQ Educational Materials, Inc.
Publisher: InQ Educational Materials, Inc.

[1605]

Manifestation of Symptomatology Scale.

Purpose: Designed "to identify problems of children and adolescents."
Population: Ages 11–18.
Publication Date: 1999.
Acronym: MOSS.
Scores, 20: Validity Scores (Inconsistent Responding, Random Responding, Faking Good, Faking Bad), Summary Index (Affective State, Home, Acting Out), Content Scales (Sexual Abuse, Alcohol and Drugs, Suspiciousness, Thought Process, Self-Esteem, Depression, Anxiety, Mother, Father, Home Environment, Impulsivity, School, Compliance).
Administration: Group or individual.
Price Data, 2006: $99 per kit including 25 AutoScore forms and manual (69 pages); $49.50 per 25 AutoScore forms; $55 per manual.
Time: (15–20) minutes.
Comments: Self-report inventory.
Author: Neil L. Mogge.
Publisher: Western Psychological Services
Cross References: For reviews by Ronald A. Berk and Richard B. Stuart, see 15:143.

[1606]

The Manson Evaluation, Revised Edition.

Purpose: Identifies alcoholics and potential alcoholics.
Population: Adults.
Publication Dates: 1948–1987.
Scores, 8: Anxiety, Depressive Fluctuations, Emotional Sensitivity, Resentfulness, Incompleteness, Aloneness, Interpersonal Relations, Total.
Administration: Individual or group.
Editions, 2: Paper-and-pencil, microcomputer.

Price Data, 2006: $82.50 per complete kit including 25 AutoScore™ test profile forms and manual (1987, 28 pages); $37.95 per 25 AutoScore™ test booklets/profiles (1987); $49.50 per manual.
Time: 5–10 minutes.
Comments: Self-administered; computer program and mail-in answer sheets can be used for both the Manson Evaluation and the Alcadd Test (137).
Authors: Morse P. Manson and George J. Huba.
Publisher: Western Psychological Services.
Cross References: For reviews by Tony Toneatto and Jalie A. Tucker, see 11:226; see also T2:1271 (2 references) and P:152 (1 reference); for a review by Dugal Campbell, see 6:137 (5 references); for reviews by Charles H. Honzik and Albert L. Hunsicker, see 4:68 (4 references).

[1607]

Manual Dexterity Test.

Purpose: Designed to provide "a measure of manual speed and skill."
Population: Ages 16 and over.
Publication Date: No date.
Acronym: MDT.
Scores, 4: Speed, Speed and Skill, Manual Speed (average scale score of Speed, Speed and Skill), Manual Skill (difference between Speed, Speed and Skill scale scores).
Administration: Group.
Price Data: Available from publisher.
Time: 2 minutes and 15 seconds (8 minutes).
Author: Educational & Industrial Test Services Ltd.
Publisher: Educational & Industrial Test Services Ltd. [England].

[1608]

MAPP: Motivational Appraisal of Personal Potential.

Purpose: Intended to measure "an individual's potential and motivation for given areas of work."
Population: Employees at all levels.
Publication Date: 1995.
Acronym: MAPP.
Scores, 13: Interest in Job Content, Temperament for the Job, Aptitude for the Job, Orientation to People, Affinity for Objects and Things, Approach to Data and Information, Reasoning and Thinking Style, Mathematical Capability, Language Levels, Personal Style, Personal Traits, Interpersonal and Social Tendencies, Learning Style.
Administration: Group.
Price Data: Available form publisher.
Time: (20–25) minutes.
Comments: Available as paper-and-pencil or computerized version.
Author: International Assessment Network.

Publisher: International Assessment Network.
Cross References: For reviews by Martha E. Hennen and Abbot Packard, see 14:218.

[1609]

A Marital Communication Inventory.

Purpose: Designed to assess the communications dimension of a marital relationship for purposes of counseling and marriage enrichment.
Population: Married couples.
Publication Dates: 1968-1979.
Acronym: MCI.
Scores: Total score only.
Administration: Group.
Price Data, 1993: $1.50 per inventory; $2 per manual (1978, 8 pages).
Time: (20) minutes.
Author: Millard J. Bienvenu.
Publisher: Millard J. Bienvenu, Northwest Publications.
Cross References: See T5:1580 (5 references) and T4:1536 (4 references); for a review by Joseph P. Stokes, see 9:651 (1 reference).

[1610]

Marital Evaluation Checklist.

Purpose: "Provides a brief yet comprehensive survey of the most common characteristics and problem areas in a marital relationship."
Population: Married couples in counseling.
Publication Date: 1984.
Acronym: MEC.
Scores: 3 areas: Reasons for Marrying, Problems of the Current Relationship, Motivation for Counseling.
Administration: Group.
Price Data, 2006: $50 per package of 50.
Time: (30-40) minutes.
Comments: Self-administered checklist.
Author: Leslie Navran.
Publisher: Psychological Assessment Resources, Inc.
Cross References: See T5:1581 (1 reference); for a review by Richard B. Stuart, see 10:187.

[1611]

Marital Satisfaction Inventory–Revised.

Purpose: Designed to "identify, separately for each partner in a relationship, the nature and extent of distress along several key dimensions of their relationship."
Population: Couples who are married or living together.
Publication Dates: 1979–1998.
Acronym: MSI-R.
Scores, 13: Conventionalization, Global Distress, Affective Communication, Problem-Solving Communication, Aggression, Time Together, Disagreement About Finances, Sexual Dissatisfaction, Role Orientation, Family History of Distress, Dissatisfaction with Children, Conflict over Child Rearing, Inconsistency.

Administration: Group.
Price Data, 2006: $121 per complete kit including 40 AutoScore™ answer forms and manual (1997, 126 pages); $42.50 per 20 AutoScore™ answer forms; $54.50 per manual; $18.50 per 6 Spanish research administration booklets; $18.50 per mail-in answer booklet; $265 per 20-use disk (PC with Microsoft Windows); $16.50 per 100 PC answer sheets; $12.50 per FAX Service Scoring charge.
Foreign Language Edition: Spanish research edition administration booklet available but without separate norms.
Time: 20 to 25 minutes.
Comments: 150-item self-report inventory; hand or computer scoring available; computer-generated interpretation available.
Author: Douglas K. Snyder.
Publisher: Western Psychological Services.
Cross References: For reviews by Frank Bernt and Mary Lou Bryant Frank, see 14:219; see also T5:1582 (15 references) and T4:1538 (7 references); for reviews by David N. Dixon and E. M. Waring of an earlier edition, see 9:652 (2 references).

[1612]

The Maroondah Assessment Profile for Problem Gambling.

Purpose: Designed as "an instrument that assists counselors in developing treatment intervention for their clients with gambling problems."
Population: People with gambling problems.
Publication Date: 1999.
Acronym: G-MAP.
Scores, 17: Beliefs About Winning (Control, Prophecy, Uninformed), Feelings (Good Feelings, Relaxation, Boredom, Numbness), Situations (Oasis, Transition, Desperation, Mischief), Attitudes to Self (Low Self-Image, "Winner," Entrenchment, Harm to Self), Social (Shyness, Friendship).
Administration: Group or individual.
Price Data, 2006: A$240.90 per kit including 10 questionnaires, manual (2000, 234 pages), 10 answer sheets, 18 photocopiable action sheet masters, 10 profile sheets, 10 response reports, and computer scoring program disk; $108.90 per manual (incl disk); $60.50 per 10 questionnaires; $42.90 per 10 answer sheet; $22 per 10 profile sheets; $5.50 per response form; $29.70 per 18 action sheets.
Time: (20) minutes.
Comments: Self-report inventory; Scoring program calculates scores for all factors and provides unlimited scoring.
Authors: Tim Loughnan, Mark Pierce, and Anastasia Sagris-Desmond.
Publisher: Australian Council for Educational Research Ltd. [Australia].
Cross References: For reviews by George Engelhard, Jr. and Michael G. Kavan, see 15:144.

[1613]

The Marriage Checkup Questionnaire.

Purpose: "Designed to be used by couples to assess their marriage relationship."
Population: Married couples.
Publication Date: 2002.
Scores, 2: Current Level of Satisfaction, Current Level of Communication.
Administration: Group.
Price Data, 2009: $3.99 per questionnaire; $12.99 per optional counseling book, "How to Counsel a Couple in 6 Sessions or Less" (167 pages).
Time: (60-120) minutes.
Comments: Current Level of Communication score has two parts.
Author: Norman H. Wright.
Publisher: Regal Books.

[1614]

Martin and Pratt Nonword Reading Test.

Purpose: Designed to "investigate the [phonological] recoding skills of students."
Population: Ages 6–16.
Publication Date: 2001.
Scores: Total score only.
Administration: Individual.
Forms, 2: A, B.
Price Data, 2006: A$120 per starter set including record booklet, stimulus book, and manual (60 pages); A$16.50 per 10 record booklets (A or B); A$35 per stimulus book; A$60 per manual.
Time: (5–10) minutes.
Authors: Frances Martin and Chris Pratt.
Publisher: Australian Council for Educational Research Ltd. [Australia].
Cross References: For reviews by Kris L. Baack and Annabel J. Cohen, see 16:139.

[1615]

Maryland Addictions Questionnaire.

Purpose: Intended to survey "issues relevant to the severity of patients' alcohol and drug abuse history."
Population: Ages 17 and older.
Publication Date: 1997.
Acronym: MAQ.
Scores, 15: Validity (Response Inconsistency, Defensiveness), Summary (Emotional Distress, Resistance to Treatment, Admission of Problems), Substance Abuse (Alcoholism Severity, Drug Abuse Severity, Craving, Substance Abuse Control, Resentment), Treatment (Motivation for Treatment, Social Anxiety, Antisocial Behaviors, Cognitive Symptoms, Affective Disturbance).
Administration: Group.
Price Data, 2006: $99 per complete kit including manual (102 pages) and 25 AutoScore™ answer sheets;

$47 per 25 AutoScore™ answer sheets; $15.95 per mail-in answer sheet; $16.50 per 100-pad PC answer sheets; $54.95 per manual; $299 per PC disk good for 25 uses (3.5-inch, Microsoft Windows required); $11.50 per FAX Scoring Service.
Time: (15–20) minutes.
Comments: Author suggests should be administered as an intake measure for individuals entering addiction treatment programs.
Authors: William E. O'Donnell, Clinton B. DeSoto, and Janet L. DeSoto.
Publisher: Western Psychological Services.
Cross References: For reviews by Carl Isenhart and John A. Mills, see 14:220.

[1616]

Maryland/Baltimore County Design for Adult Basic Education.

Purpose: "Diagnoses a student's strengths, weaknesses, and deficiencies in skill areas that are prerequisite to literacy."
Population: Adult nonreaders.
Publication Date: 1982.
Scores: 21 subtest scores in 5 areas: Background Knowledge, Alphabet Recognition and Reproduction, Auditory Perception and Discrimination, Visual Perception and Discrimination, Sight Vocabulary.
Administration: Group and individual.
Price Data: Not available.
Time: (120–180) minutes.
Comments: Commonly called the "BCD Test."
Author: Baltimore County Public Schools Office of Adult Education.
Publisher: Prentice Hall [No reply from publisher; status unknown].
Cross References: For reviews by Mary M. Dupuis and Sharon L. Smith, see 9:658.

[1617]

Maryland Parent Attitude Survey.

Purpose: Designed to measure child-rearing attitudes.
Population: Parents.
Publication Dates: [1957-1966].
Acronym: MPAS.
Scores, 4: Disciplinarian, Indulgent, Protective, Rejecting.
Administration: Group.
Price Data, 2001: $5 per complete package including test, scoring instructions and tables, T scores, and copy of article.
Time: [20–60] minutes.
Comments: For research use only; tests may be reproduced locally.
Author: Donald K. Pumroy.
Publisher: Donald K. Pumroy.
Cross References: See T4:1551 (1 reference).

[1618]

Maslach Burnout Inventory, Third Edition.

Purpose: Constructed to measure three aspects of burnout.
Population: Members of the helping professions including educators and human service professionals.
Publication Dates: 1981–1996.
Scores, 3: Emotional Exhaustion, Depersonalization, Personal Accomplishment.
Administration: Group.
Price Data, 2001: $65 per review kit including Human Services Survey booklet, Educators Survey booklet, General Survey booklet, set of scoring keys, and manual (1996, 56 pages); $28 per 25 nonreusable survey booklets (specify Human Services, Educators, or General); $17.50 per 25 Human Services Survey or Educators Survey demographic data sheets; $14 per 25 scoring keys; $42 per manual.
Authors: Wilmar B. Schaufeli, Michael P. Leiter, Christina Maslach, and Susan E. Jackson.
Publisher: Mind Garden, Inc.
  a) HUMAN SERVICES SURVEY.
  Acronym: MBI-HSS.
  Population: Staff members in the Human Services profession.
  Time: (10–15) minutes.
  b) EDUCATORS SURVEY.
  Acronym: MBI-ES.
  Population: Educators.
  Time: (5–10) minutes.
  c) GENERAL SURVEY.
  Acronym: MBI-GS.
  Population: Other workers in the service professions.
  Foreign Language Edition: Spanish translation of HSS and ES forms available.
  Time: (10-15) minutes.
Cross References: For reviews by Robert Fitzpatrick and Claudia R. Wright, see 16:140; see also T5:1590 (69 references) and T4:1552 (30 references); for reviews by David S. Hargrove and Jonathan Sandoval of an earlier edition, see 10:189 (34 references).

[1619]

Massachusetts Youth Screening Instrument–Version 2.

Purpose: "To identify youths with potential mental, emotional, or behavioral problems at entry points in the juvenile justice system."
Population: Ages 12-17.
Publication Dates: 1998-2006.
Acronym: MAYSI-2.
Administration: Individual.
Forms, 2: Male, Female.
Restricted Distribution: To use the MAYSI-2 one must be registered with the National Youth Screening Assistance Project.

Price Data, 2009: $194.95 per manual and MAY-SIWARE software; $20 per set of 7 screening forms.
Foreign Language Edition: Spanish language paper-and-pencil version is available, plus the software (MAYSIWARE) version also presents the MAYSI items in Spanish, on screen and audio.
Time: (15) minutes.
Authors: Thomas Grisso and Richard Barnum.
Publisher: Professional Resource Press.
a) MALE.
Scores, 7: Alcohol/Drug Use, Angry-Irritable, Depressed-Anxious, Somatic Complaints, Suicide Ideation, Thought Disturbance, Traumatic Experiences.
b) FEMALE.
Scores, 6: Alcohol/Drug Use, Angry-Irritable, Depressed-Anxious, Somatic Complaints, Suicide Ideation, Traumatic Experiences.
Cross References: For reviews by Randy G. Floyd and by Renee M. Tobin and Corinne Zimmerman, see 18:71.

[1620]
Matching Assistive Technology & Child.
Purpose: A series of instruments designed to assess "infants' and childrens' need for assistive technology" to determine the most appropriate child-technology match.
Population: Children with disabilities, ages 0–5.
Publication Date: 1997.
Administration: Individual.
Price Data: Available from publisher.
Time: (90) minutes for entire battery.
Comments: To be used by Early Intervention and Special Education professionals with parents.
Author: Marcia J. Scherer.
Publisher: The Institute for Matching Person & Technology, Inc.
a) TECHNOLOGY UTILIZATION WORKSHEET FOR MATCHING ASSISTIVE TECHNOLOGY & CHILD.
Purpose: Designed to "review technologies the child is currently using, has used in the past, and needs."
Scores: No formal scores; examines perceptions in 10 areas: Communication, Mobility/Gross Motor, Vision, Hearing, Fine Motor Skills, Daily Living, Health Maintenance, Play, Self-Care, Learning/Cognition.
Comments: Completed by parent and/or educator.
b) WORKSHEET FOR MATCHING ASSISTIVE TECHNOLOGY & CHILD.
Purpose: Designed to "obtain parent perspectives of a child's particular limitations, goals, and interventions as well as strengths which can be built upon in planning interventions."
Scores: No scores; examines perceptions of 10 areas: Communication, Mobility/Gross Motor, Vision, Hearing, Fine Motor Skills, Daily Living, Health Maintenance, Play, Self-Care, Learning/Cognition.
Comments: Completed by the child's parent.

c) SURVEY OF TECHNOLOGY USE.
Purpose: Designed to "help identify technologies and technology functions/features a child is likely to feel comfortable or successful in using."
Acronym: SOTU.
Scores: No formal scores.
Comments: Completed by educator and/or parent.
d) MATCHING ASSISTIVE TECHNOLOGY & CHILD.
Purpose: Designed to help "select the most appropriate assistive technology for a child's use while pinpointing areas for training and further assessment."
Acronym: MATCH.
Scores: No formal scores.
Comments: Completed by caregiver or educator.
Cross References: For reviews by Libby G. Cohen and by T. Steuart Watson and R. Anthony Doggett, see 15:145.

[1621]
Matching Familiar Figures Test.
Purpose: Measurement of constructs of reflection and impulsivity.
Population: Ages 5–12, 13 and over.
Publication Date: 1965.
Acronym: MFF.
Scores: Total score only.
Administration: Individual.
Levels, 2: Elementary, Adolescent/Adult.
Manual: No manual.
Price Data: Available from publisher.
Time: Administration time not reported.
Authors: Jerome Kagan (test) and Neil J. Salkind (norms booklet).
Publisher: Jerome Kagan [No reply from publisher; status unknown].
Cross References: See T5:1592 (28 references), T4:1553 (106 references), and 9:662 (71 references).

[1622]
Matching Person and Technology.
Purpose: Designed for "selecting and evaluating technologies used in rehabilitation, education, the workplace and other settings."
Population: Clients, patients, students, or employees, and those professionals working with them.
Publication Dates: 1991–2005.
Acronym: MPT.
Administration: Individual or group.
Forms, 2: Consumer, Professional.
Price Data: Available from publisher.
Time: (15) minutes per test.
Comments: CD version (2005) is available with additional administration tools and supplemental resources.
Author: Marcia J. Scherer.
Publisher: The Institute for Matching Person & Technology, Inc.

a) SURVEY OF TECHNOLOGY USE.
Purpose: Constructed to measure "the consumer's present use of, experiences with, and feelings toward technological devices."
Acronym: SOTU.
Scores, 4: Experience with Current Technologies, Perspectives on Technologies, Typical Activities, Personal/Social Characteristics.
b) ASSISTIVE TECHNOLOGY DEVICE PREDIS-POSITION ASSESSMENT.
Purpose: Designed to "help individuals select appropriate assistive technologies."
Acronym: ATD PA.
Scores, 4: Subjective View of Capabilities, Subjective Well-Being/Quality of Life, Temperament and Psychosocial Characteristics, Device and Person Degree of Match.
c) EDUCATIONAL TECHNOLOGY PREDISPOSI-TION ASSESSMENT.
Purpose: Designed "for teachers who are helping students use technology to reach educational goals."
Acronym: ET PA.
Scores, 4: Educational Goal, The Student, Educational Technology, Educational Environment.
d) WORKPLACE TECHNOLOGY PREDISPOSI-TION ASSESSMENT.
Purpose: "Designed to assist employers in identifying factors that might inhibit the acceptance or use of a new technology in the workplace."
Acronym: WT PA.
Scores, 4: The Technology, The Employee Being Trained to Use the Technology, The Workplace Environment, Match Between Person and Technology.
e) HEALTH CARE TECHNOLOGY PREDISPOSI-TION ASSESSMENT.
Purpose: "Developed to assist health care professionals in identifying factors that might inhibit the acceptance or appropriate use of health care technologies."
Acronym: HCT PA.
Scores, 5: Health Problem, Consequences of HCT Use, Characteristics of the Health Care Technology, Personal Issues, Attitudes of Others.
Cross References: For reviews by Patricia A. Bachelor and by Laura L. B. Barnes and Carrie L. Winterowd, see 14:221.

[1623]

MATE [Marital ATtitude Evaluation].
Purpose: "Designed to explore the relation between two people who have close contact with each other."
Population: Couples.
Publication Date: 1989.
Acronym: MATE.
Scores: 5 scales: Inclusion Behavior, Inclusion Feelings, Control Behavior, Control Feelings, Affection.

Administration: Group.
Manual: Information included in manual of FIRO Awareness Scales (1086).
Price Data: Available from publisher at www.mind-garden.com/products/mates.htm.
Time: Administration time not reported.
Comments: Based on FIRO Awareness Scales (1086).
Author: Will Schutz.
Publisher: Mind Garden, Inc.

[1624]

Math-Level Indicator.
Purpose: Designed to survey the basic mathematical skills of students.
Population: Grades 4–12.
Publication Date: 2003.
Acronym: MLI.
Scores: Total score only.
Administration: Group.
Price Data, 2006: $144.99 per starter set including manual, 1 package (25) Red forms, 1 package (25) Blue forms, 2 hand-scoring templates, and 2 scannable answer sheets packages (25 each); $25.99 per manual; $36.99 per 25 forms (specify Red or Blue); $41.99 per 2 hand-scoring templates; $19.99 per 25 scannable answer sheets.
Time: (30) minutes.
Comments: Designed to work with the Group Mathematics Assessment and Diagnostic Evaluation (G•MADE; 1192).
Author: Kathleen T. Williams.
Publisher: Pearson.
Cross References: For reviews by Zandra S. Gratz and Dixie McGinty, see 16:141.

[1625]

Mathematical Olympiads.
Purpose: Constructed "to discover and challenge secondary school students with outstanding mathematical talent."
Population: Secondary school.
Publication Dates: 1972-2001.
Scores: Total score only.
Administration: Group.
Manual: No manual.
Price Data: Available from publisher.
Author: Committee on the American Mathematics Competitions.
Publisher: Mathematical Association of America; American Mathematics Competitions.
a) USA MATHEMATICAL OLYMPIAD.
Acronym: USAMO.
Time: 10–20) minutes over 2 sessions.
Comments: Test administered annually in April; selection to participate is based on both the AMC12 and AIME scores.

b) INTERNATIONAL MATHEMATICAL OLYMPIAD.
Acronym: IMO.
Time: (10–20) minutes over 2 sessions.
Comments: Test administered annually in July; selection to participate is based on USAMO scores and other scores obtained during the training session.
Cross References: For reviews by Phillip L. Ackerman and William R. Koch, see 11:228.

[1626]

Mathematics 7.

Purpose: "Assess the mathematics attainment of children near the end of the school year in which they reach their seventh birthday."
Population: Ages 6-10 to 7-9.
Publication Date: 1987.
Scores: 1 individual total score, 4 item analysis categories: Understanding, Computational Skill, Application, Factual Recall.
Administration: Group.
Price Data: Price information available from publisher for specimen set including Teacher's Guide (24 pages), test booklet, and group record sheet.
Time: (30–50) minutes.
Comments: Downward extension of Mathematics 8–12 Series; no norms for categories; orally administered.
Author: Test Development Unit of the Foundation for Educational Research in England and Wales.
Publisher: GL Assessment [England].
Cross References: For reviews by Camilla Persson Benbow and Kevin Menefee, see 11:230.

[1627]

Mathematics Attitude Inventory.

Purpose: "To measure the attitudes toward mathematics of secondary school and college students."
Population: Grades 7-12 and undergraduate students.
Publication Date: 1979.
Acronym: MAI.
Scores, 6: Perception of the Mathematics Teacher, Anxiety Toward Mathematics, Value of Mathematics in Society, Self-Concept in Mathematics, Enjoyment of Mathematics, Motivation in Mathematics.
Administration: Group.
Price Data: Free, upon request. Information available from publisher for tests, scoring key, and manual (26 pages).
Time: 15 minutes.
Comments: Tests may be reproduced locally.
Author: Richard S. Sandman.
Publisher: Quantitative Methods in Education, University of Minnesota.
Cross References: See T5:1599 (6 references); for reviews by Harvey Resnick and Richard F. Schmid, see 9:664 (3 references); see also T3:1410 (1 reference).

[1628]

Mathematics Competency Test.

Purpose: Constructed to assess "mathematics achievement."
Population: Ages 11 to adult.
Publication Date: 1996.
Scores: Total score only.
Administration: Group.
Price Data, 2006: A$18.15 per 10 test booklets; $36.30 per manua; $38 per specimen set.
Time: (40) minutes.
Authors: P. E. Vernon, K. M. Miller, and J. F. Izard.
Publisher: Australian Council for Educational Research Ltd. [Australia]; Hodder & Stoughton Educational [England].
Cross References: For reviews by Joseph C. Ciechalski and G. Michael Poteat, see 14:222.

[1629]

Mathematics Self-Efficacy Scale.

Purpose: Intended to measure beliefs regarding ability to perform various math-related tasks and behaviors.
Population: College freshmen.
Publication Date: 1993.
Acronym: MATH.
Scores, 3: Mathematics Task Self-Efficacy, Math-Related School Subjects Self-Efficacy, Total Mathematics Self-Efficacy Score.
Administration: Group.
Forms, 2: A, B.
Price Data: Available from publisher at www.mindgarden.com/products/maths.htm.
Time: (15) minutes.
Authors: Nancy E. Betz and Gail Hackett.
Publisher: Mind Garden, Inc.
Cross References: For reviews by Joseph C. Ciechalski and Everett V. Smith, Jr., see 14:223; see also T5:1602 (1 reference).

[1630]

A Mathematics Test for Grades Four, Five and Six.

Purpose: Designed to measure "achievement in modern mathematics."
Population: Grades 4–6.
Publication Date: 1969.
Scores, 13: Understanding Numeration Systems, Set Terminology, Mathematical Structure, Addition and Subtraction of Whole Numbers, Multiplication of Whole Numbers, Division of Whole Numbers, Common Fractions, Decimal Fractions and Per Cent, Measurements, Geometry, Solving Problems with the Use of Number Sentences, Graphs and Scale Drawings, Total.
Administration: Group.
Price Data: Available from publisher.

Time: (120–180) minutes in 2 sessions.
Author: Stanley J. LeJeune.
Publisher: Psychometric Affiliates.
Cross References: For a review by William H. Nibbelink, see 8:280; for a review by Arthur Mittman, see 7:476.

[1631]

Mather-Woodcock Group Writing Tests.

Purpose: "Designed for early identification of problems/weaknesses, measurement of growth in writing skills, instructional planning, and curriculum evaluation."
Population: Grades 2.0–16.9.
Publication Date: 1997.
Acronym: GWT.
Scores: 3 clusters (Total Writing, Basic Writing Skills, Expressive Writing Ability), and 4 subtests (Dictation Spelling, Writing Samples, Editing, Writing Fluency).
Administration: Group.
Price Data, 2006: $229.50 per complete package including 25 writing booklets at selected level, administration instructions (96 pages), scoring key, 25 writing evaluation scales, manual, and scoring software (3.5 disk-Windows/Mac and user's manual); $90 per additional packages of booklets includes 25 writing booklets, 25 writing evaluation scales, and scoring key.
Time: (60) minutes or less.
Authors: Nancy Mather and Richard W. Woodcock.
Publisher: Riverside Publishing.
Cross References: For a review by Bruce Thompson, see 14:224.

[1632]

Matrix Analogies Test.

Purpose: Developed to "measure nonverbal reasoning ability."
Population: Ages 5-0 to 17-11.
Publication Date: 1985.
Author: Jack A. Naglieri.
Publisher: Pearson.
a) SHORT FORM.
Acronym: MAT-SF.
Administration: Group.
Scores: Total score only.
Price Data, 2002: $105 per 15 test booklets; $58 per 25 answer sheets; $43 per manual (1985, 45 pages); $51 per examination kit.
Time: 25(30) minutes.
b) EXPANDED FORM.
Acronym: MAT-EF.
Administration: Individual.
Scores, 5: Pattern Completion, Reasoning by Analogy, Serial Reasoning, Spatial Visualization, Total.
Price Data: $218 per complete kit including stimulus book, 50 answer sheets, manual (1985,

82 pages) and case; $98 per stimulus manual; $58 per 50 answer sheets; $73 per examiner's manual.
Time: (20–25) minutes.
Cross References: See T5:1607 (15 references) and T4:1566 (8 references); for a review by Robert F. McMorris, David L. Rule, and Wendy J. Steinberg, see 10:191 (1 reference).

[1633]

Matrix-Predictive Uniform Law Enforcement Selection Evaluation Inventory.

Purpose: Designed to "assess the future job-performance liabilities of law enforcement officer candidates."
Population: Law enforcement officer candidates.
Publication Date: 2008.
Acronym: M-PULSE.
Scores, 47: Interpersonal Difficulties, Off-Duty Misconduct, Property Damage, Motor Vehicle Accidents, Inappropriate Use of Weapon, Excessive Force, Sexually Offensive Conduct, Potential for Reprimands/Suspensions, Potential for Resignation, Potential for Termination, Chemical Abuse/Dependency, Procedural and Conduct Mistakes, Misuse of Vehicle, Discharge of Weapon, Unprofessional Conduct, Racially Offensive Conduct, Lawsuit Potential, Criminal Conduct, Impression Management, Negative Self-Issues, Negative Emotions, Egocentrism, Inadequate Views of Police Work, Poor Emotional Controls, Negative Perceptions of Law Enforcement, Inappropriate Attitudes About the Use of Force, Overly Traditional Officer Traits, Suspiciousness, Unethical Behavior, Lack of Personal Integrity, Negative Views of Department/Leadership, Amorality, Unpredictability, Risk Taking, Novelty Seeking, Social Incompetence, Lack of Teamwork, Unreliability, Reckless-Impulsivity, Rigidity, Lack of Integrity/Ethics, Emotional Instability-Stress Intolerance, Poor Decision-Making and Judgment, Passivity-Submissiveness, Poor Service Orientation, Substance Abuse.
Administration: Individual or group.
Price Data, 2011: $60 per technical manual (58 pages); $45 per 10 item booklets; $33 per 50 data entry sheets; $25 per online profile report.
Time: (60-80) minutes.
Comments: Can be administered online or via paper and pencil.
Authors: Robert D. Davis and Cary D. Rostow.
Publisher: Multi-Health Systems, Inc.
Cross References: For reviews by J. M. Blackbourn, Conn Thomas, and Jennifer G. Fillingim and by Gary J. Dean, see 18:72.

[1634]

Mayer-Salovey-Caruso Emotional Intelligence Test.

Purpose: Designed to assess emotional intelligence, measuring a person's capacity for reasoning with emotional information.

Population: Age 17 and older.
Publication Date: 2002.
Acronym: MSCEIT.
Scores, 4: Managing Emotions, Understanding Emotions, Using Emotions, Perceiving Emotions.
Administration: Individual or group.
Price Data, 2011: $65 per user's manual; $59 per package of 3 reusable item booklets; $95 per online personal summary report kit including user's manual and 1 personal summary report; $41 per online personal summary report; $45 per online resource report; $94 per software preview version including getting started guide and 3 personal summary reports.
Time: (30-45) minutes.
Comments: Self-completed.
Authors: John D. Mayer, Peter Salovey, and David R. Caruso.
Publisher: Multi-Health Systems, Inc.
Cross References: For reviews by S. Alvin Leung and by Catherine Cook-Cottone and Scott T. Meier, see 16:143.

[1635]

The MbM Questionnaire: Managing by Motivation, Third Edition.

Purpose: Designed for "helping managers understand their own needs" ... and "to identify the needs of their employees."
Population: Managers and supervisors.
Publication Dates: 1986–1996.
Acronym: The MbM Questionnaire.
Scores: 4 scales: Safety/Security, Social/Belonging, Self-Esteem, Self-Actualization.
Administration: Group.
Price Data: Available from publisher.
Time: (10) minutes.
Author: Marshall Sashkin.
Publisher: HRD Press, Inc.
Cross References: For reviews by John W. Fleenor and Robert K. Gable, see 14:225.

[1636]

McCall-Crabbs Standard Test Lessons in Reading.

Purpose: Measurement of reading progress.
Population: Reading level grades 3-8.
Publication Dates: 1926–1979.
Scores: Item and grade equivalent scores.
Administration: Group.
Levels, 6: Overlapping levels labeled A, B, C, D, E, F.
Price Data, 2006: $3.95 per test booklet (any level); $6.95 per 30 answer sheets; $1.50 per manual/answer key (1979, 16 pages).
Time: 3 minutes for any one test; 180 minutes for each booklet (60 tests per booklet).
Comments: Fourth edition.

Authors: William A. McCall and Lelah Crabbs Schroeder; revision by Robert P. Starr.
Publisher: Teachers College Press.
Cross References: See T4:1568 (1 reference); for a review by Brendan John Bartlett, see 9:669.

[1637]

McCarron-Dial System.

Purpose: A battery of neurometric and behavioral measures to be used for vocational, educational, and neuropsychological assessment particularly in meeting the programming needs of handicapped persons.
Population: Normal and handicapped individuals ages 3 to adult.
Publication Dates: 1973-2005.
Acronym: MDS.
Scores: 5 factors: Verbal-Spatial-Cognitive, Sensory, Motor, Emotional, Integration-Coping.
Administration: Individual.
Parts: 3 components (Auxiliary Component, Haptic Visual Discrimination Test [HVDT], McCarron Assessment of Neuromuscular Development [MAND]).
Price Data, 2011: $3,660 per complete System including Auxiliary, HVDT, and MAND Components; price data for software for computer-assisted programs supporting the MDS available from publisher; price information for workshops and training available from publisher.
Comments: "A commitment to receive training is required for all purchasers of the McCarron-Dial System"; components available as separates.
Authors: Lawrence McCarron and Jack G. Dial.
Publisher: McCarron-Dial Systems, Inc.

a) AUXILIARY COMPONENT.
Publication Dates: 1973-2005.
Price Data: $650 per set of materials in carrying case; $42.50 per 50 IEP forms; $42.50 per 25 IPP forms; $170 per manual (2005, 259 pages).
Comments: Manual title is Revised McCarron-Dial Evaluation System Manual; kit includes Bender Visual Motor Gestalt Test, and Koppitz Scoring Manual for The Bender Gestalt Test for Young Children, the McCarron-Dial System Individual Evaluation Profile (IEP), the McCarron-Dial Individual Program Plan (IPP), the Observational Emotional Inventory, the Emotional Behavioral Checklist, and the Dial Behavior Rating Scale.

1) *Dial Behavior Rating Scale.*
Purpose: To provide an abbreviated assessment of essential personal, social, and work adjustment behaviors that relate to vocational placement, adjustment to work, and personal-social adjustment.
Publication Dates: 1973-1986.
Acronym: BRS.
Price Data: $42.50 per 25 forms.
Author: Jack G. Dial.

2) *Observational Emotional Inventory.*
Publication Date: 1986.
Acronym: OEI.
Price Data: $42.50 per 25 forms.
Time: 120 minutes on each of 5 days.
Comments: Behavior checklist.
3) *Emotional Behavioral Checklist.*
Purpose: To assess an individual's overt emotional behavior.
Publication Date: 1986.
Acronym: EBC.
Price Data: $42.50 per 25 forms.
Comments: Behavior Checklist (alternate to OEI).
b) HAPTIC VISUAL DISCRIMINATION TEST.
Purpose: To measure an individual's haptic-visual integration skills.
Publication Dates: 1976-1988.
Acronym: HVDT.
Scores, 4: Shape, Size, Texture, Configuration.
Price Data: $1365 per complete kit including score forms, photographic plates, folding screen, sets of shapes, sizes, textures, and configurations, manual (1988, 261 pages) in a carrying case; $45.25 per 50 score forms; $81.75 per manual.
Time: (10-15) minutes per hand.
Comments: Manual title is Sensory Integration: The Haptic Visual Processes.
c) McCARRON ASSESSMENT OF NEUROMUS-CULAR DEVELOPMENT.
Purpose: "A standardized and quantitative procedure for assessing fine and gross motor abilities."
Population: Ages 3.5 to adult.
Publication Dates: 1976–1997.
Acronym: MAND.
Scores, 3: Fine Motor, Gross Motor, Total.
Price Data: $1,645 per complete kit including score forms, a dynamometer, stopwatch-timer, components for fine and gross motor testing, and manual (1997, 221 pages) in carrying case; $58.50 per 25 score forms; $88 per manual.
Time: (15) minutes.
Comments: Manual title is Revised McCarron Assessment of Neuromuscular Development Manual.
Author: Lawrence T. McCarron.
Cross References: For reviews by Calvin P. Garbin and David C. Solly, see 11:231 (1 reference).

[1638]

McCarthy Scales of Children's Abilities.
Purpose: Developed to "determine . . . general intellectual level as well as . . . strengths and weaknesses in important abilities."
Population: Ages 2.6–8.6.
Publication Dates: 1970–1972.
Acronym: MSCA.

Scores, 6: Verbal, Perceptual-Performance, Quantitative, Composite (General Cognitive), Memory, Motor.
Administration: Individual.
Price Data, 2002: $583 per complete set including all necessary equipment, 25 drawing booklets, 25 record forms, and manual (1972, 217 pages); $57 per 25 drawing booklets; $220 per 100 drawing booklets; $43 per 25 record forms; $157 per 100 record forms; $66 per manual.
Time: (45–60) minutes.
Author: Dorothea McCarthy.
Publisher: Pearson.
Cross References: See T5:1612 (101 references) and T4:1571 (97 references); for reviews by Kathleen D. Paget and David L. Wodrich, see 9:671 (29 references); see also T3:1424 (60 references); for reviews by Jane V. Hunt, Jerome M. Sattler, and Arthur B. Silverstein, and excerpted reviews by Everett E. Davis, by Linda Hufano and Ralph Hoepfner, by R. B. Ammons and C. H. Ammons, and by Alan Krichev, see 8:219 (29 references).

[1639]

McCarthy Screening Test.
Purpose: Designed to "identify children who are likely to encounter difficulty in coping with schoolwork."
Population: Ages 4–6.5.
Publication Dates: 1970–1978.
Acronym: MST.
Scores, 6: Right-Left Orientation, Verbal Memory, Draw-A-Design, Numerical Memory, Conceptual Grouping, Leg Coordination.
Administration: Individual.
Price Data, 2002: $225 per complete set including all necessary equipment, manual (1978, 71 pages), 25 record forms, 25 drawing booklets, and carrying case: $58 per 25 drawing booklets; $230 per 100 drawing booklets; $37 per 25 record forms; $152 per 100 record forms; $52 per manual.
Time: (20) minutes.
Comments: Adaptation of the McCarthy Scales of Children's Abilities; criterion-referenced; percentile cutoff scores provided for classification as "at risk" for learning problems.
Author: Dorothea McCarthy.
Publisher: Pearson.
Cross References: See T5:1613 (2 references) and T4:1572 (9 references); for reviews by Nadeen L. Kaufman and Jack A. Naglieri, see 9:672 (3 references); see also T3:1425 (2 references).

[1640]

McDowell Vision Screening Kit.
Purpose: "Designed for screening children's vision problems."
Population: 2 1/2 to 5 1/2 years.
Publication Date: 1994.

Scores, 15: Distance Vision, Near Point Vision, Ocular Alignment/Motility (Cover/Uncover, Light Reflex), Color Perception, Ocular Function (Pupils, Scanning, Shifts Attention, Blink, Tracking, Convergence, Conjugate Gaze, Visual Fields, Distant/Near Accommodation, Nystagmus).
Administration: Individual.
Price Data, 2006: $154 per kit including all test materials, 100 recording forms, and manual (40 pages); $32.50 per 100 recording forms; $49.50 per manual.
Time: (10–20) minutes.
Comments: Recording form for use in screening young children or disabled students; administrator scored.
Authors: P. Marlene McDowell and Richard L. McDowell.
Publisher: Western Psychological Services.
Cross References: For a review by Cynthia A. Rohrbeck, see 14:226.

[1641]

The mCircle™ Instrument.

Purpose: "Tests for and explores appropriate uses for five strategies routinely used by individuals to solve problems and reach resolution in human interaction."
Population: Business and industry.
Publication Date: 1986.
Scores, 5: Get Out, Give In, Take Over, Trade Off, Breakthrough.
Administration: Group.
Price Data: Available from publisher.
Time: (30-40) minutes.
Comments: Self-administered, self-scored.
Authors: Paul Kordis and Dudley Lynch.
Publisher: Brain Technologies Corporation.
Cross References: For reviews by Stephen Jurs and Rick Lindskog, see 11:232.

[1642]

MD5 Mental Ability Test.

Purpose: "To assess mental ability quickly, easily and over a wide range of educational and ability levels, in staff selection, placement and counselling."
Population: Supervisors to managers.
Publication Date: No date on test materials.
Scores: Total score only.
Administration: Group.
Price Data, 2001: £3.25 per question/answer book; £5 per scoring key; £19.50 per technical manual; £300 per computer system version.
Time: (15) minutes.
Author: The Test Agency.
Publisher: The Test Agency Limited [England] [No reply from publisher; status unknown].
Cross References: For reviews by M. Harry Daniels and David J. Mealor, see 10:193.

[1643]

MDS Vocational Interest Exploration System.

Purpose: "A computer-assisted interest exploration process that facilitates the discovery of personal preferences and job opportunities."
Population: High school–adults.
Publication Date: 1991.
Acronym: VIE.
Scores: 3 steps: Selection of Jobs Based on Work Preferences, Occupational Exploration, Job Review Comparison.
Administration: Individual.
Price Data, 2011: $470 per set including computer program (Windows or Macintosh), 4 VIE job manuals, instructor's manual (135 pages), 25 VIE system guides with work preference questionnaires and job review forms.
Time: Administration time not reported.
Comments: Three supplementary forms are also provided with materials: Pre-Post Job Knowledge Form, Understanding of Self and Job Questionnaire, and Vocational Goal Planning Exercise.
Authors: Lawrence T. McCarron and Harriette P. Spires.
Publisher: McCarron-Dial Systems, Inc.
Cross References: For reviews by Douglas J. McRae and Myra N. Womble, see 13:194.

[1644]

Meadow-Kendall Social-Emotional Assessment Inventory for Deaf and Hearing Impaired Students.

Purpose: "Can be used to flag students who need extra attention in particular areas .... useful in communicating with parents who are reluctant to admit that their child needs special attention ... helpful in implementing an individualized program so that social and emotional areas are emphasized in the curriculum for the child who needs them."
Population: Ages 3–6, 7–21.
Publication Date: 1983.
Acronym: SEAI.
Administration: Group.
Levels: 2 levels.
Price Data, 2001: $8 per 10 forms; $15 per manual (37 pages).
Time: Administration time not reported.
Comments: Behavior checklist to be completed by adult informant.
Authors: Kathryn P. Meadow and others listed below.
Publisher: Laurent Clerc National Deaf Education Center.

a) PRE-SCHOOL.
   Population: Ages 3-6.
   Scores, 5: Sociable/Communicative Behaviors, Impulsive Dominating Behaviors, Developmental-Lags, Anxious/Compulsive Behaviors, Special Items.

Authors: Kathryn P. Meadow, Pamela Getson, Chi K. Lee, Linda Stamper, and the Center for Studies in Education and Human Development.
b) SCHOOL-AGE.
Population: Ages 7-21.
Scores, 3: Social Adjustment, Self Image, Emotional Adjustment.
Authors: Kathryn P. Meadow, Michael A. Karchmer, Linda M. Petersen, and Lawrence Rudner.
Cross References: See T5:1618 (3 references) and T4:1579 (2 references); for reviews by Marilyn E. Demorest and Kenneth L. Sheldon, see 10:194 (1 reference).

[1645]
Measure of Achieving Tendency.

Purpose: Developed to assess achievement motivation.
Population: Ages 15 and older.
Publication Dates: 1969–1993.
Acronym: MACH.
Scores: Total score only.
Administration: Group or individual.
Price Data: Available from publisher for complete kit including scales, scoring directions, norms, manual (1994, 8 pages), and literature review.
Time: (10–15) minutes.
Comments: Current revision also based on previous edition entitled A Questionnaire Measure of Individual Differences in Achieving Tendency.
Author: Albert Mehrabian.
Publisher: Albert Mehrabian.
Cross References: For reviews by James T. Austin and E. Scott Huebner, see 13:195 (1 reference); for a review by Timothy S. Hartshorne of an earlier edition, see 10:301; for a review by Jayne E. Stake of an earlier edition, see 9:682; see also T3:1442 (1 reference).

[1646]
Measure of Child Stimulus Screening and Arousability.

Purpose: Designed to assess child individual differences in positive and/or negative emotionality, emotional sensitivity, or emotional reactivity.
Population: Ages 3 months to 7 years.
Publication Date: 1978.
Scores: Total score only.
Administration: Group or individual.
Manual: No manual.
Price Data: Available from publisher for test kit including scale, scoring directions, norms, and descriptive material.
Time: [15] minutes.
Comments: Ratings by parents.
Authors: Albert Mehrabian and Carol A. Falender.
Publisher: Albert Mehrabian.
Cross References: See T5:1621 (1 reference); for a review by Steven Klee, see 9:678; see also T3:1439 (2 references).

[1647]
Measure of Existential Anxiety.

Purpose: Designed as a measure of existential anxiety.
Population: Adults and college-age.
Publication Date: No date.
Scores: Total score only.
Administration: Group.
Price Data, 2001: $3 per specimen set.
Time: Administration time not reported.
Authors: L. R. Good and K. C. Good.
Publisher: Psychometric Affiliates.
Cross References: For a review by Matthew E. Lambert, see 15:146.

[1648]
Measure of Individual Differences in Dominance-Submissiveness.

Purpose: Constructed as a "general measure of trait dominance-submissivenessthe general feeling of control and influence versus lack of control over one's surroundings and life situations."
Population: Ages 15 and older.
Publication Dates: 1978–1994.
Scores: Total score only.
Administration: Group or individual.
Price Data: Available from publisher for test kit including scale, scoring directions, norms, and manual (1994, 7 pages).
Time: (10–15) minutes.
Authors: Albert Mehrabian and Melissa Hines (original edition).
Publisher: Albert Mehrabian.
Cross References: For reviews by Robert H. Deluty and Douglas N. Jackson of an earlier edition, see 9:679.

[1649]
Measure of Questioning Skills.

Purpose: Designed "to measure the quantity and quality of questions."
Population: Grades 3–10.
Publication Dates: 1986–1993.
Scores, 4: Gathering Information, Organizing Information, Extending Information, Composite.
Administration: Group.
Forms, 2: A, B.
Price Data: See www.ststesting.com for up-to-date prices.
Time: (20) minutes.
Authors: Ralph Himsl and Garnet W. Millar.
Publisher: Scholastic Testing Service, Inc.
Cross References: For a review by Darrell R. Sabers, see 14:228.

[1650]
A Measure of Self-Esteem.

Purpose: Designed as a "measure of self-esteem ... that was constructed on the assumption that low self-esteem

is indicated when someone feels inferior, inadequate, unworthy, disliked, helpless, etc."
Population: College-age and adults.
Publication Date: No date.
Scores: Total score only.
Administration: Group.
Price Data, 2001: $3 per specimen set.
Time: Administration time not reported.
Authors: L. R. Good and K. C. Good.
Publisher: Psychometric Affiliates.
Cross References: For a review by Jeffrey A. Atlas, see 15:147.

[1651]

Measure of Self-Evaluation.

Purpose: Developed to measure an individual's need for self-evaluation.
Population: Adults.
Publication Date: No date.
Scores: Total score only.
Administration: Group.
Price Data, 2001: $3 per specimen set.
Time: Administration time not reported.
Comments: Manual is entitled An Objective Measure of the Self-Evaluation Motive.
Authors: L. R. Good and K. C. Good.
Publisher: Psychometric Affiliates.
Cross References: For a review by Jody L. Kulstad, see 15:148.

[1652]

Measure of Vindication.

Purpose: Designed to measure the vindication motive.
Population: College-age and adults.
Publication Date: No date.
Scores: Total score only.
Administration: Group.
Price Data, 2001: $3 per specimen set.
Time: Administration time not reported.
Authors: L. R. Good and K. C. Good.
Publisher: Psychometric Affiliates.
Cross References: For a review by Dennis Doverspike, see 15:149.

[1653]

The Measurement of Moral Judgment.

Purpose: Measures moral judgment through dilemma interviews.
Population: Ages 10 and over.
Publication Date: 1984.
Scores: 1 score dichotomized as moral stage (I to V) and moral type (A: Heteronomous or B: Autonomous).
Administration: Individual.
Forms, 3: Parallel Forms A, B, and C consist of 3 standard dilemmas each.

Price Data: Available from publisher.
Time: (10-15) minutes.
Authors: Anne Colby, Lawrence Kohlberg, John Gibbs, and Marcus Lieberman.
Publisher: Cambridge University Press.
Cross References: See T5:1625 (1 reference), 9:681 (9 references), and T3:1262 (2 references).

[1654]

Measures in Post Traumatic Stress Disorder: A Practitioner's Guide.

Purpose: A set of tests that may be used to assist in identifying post traumatic stress disorder.
Population: Adults.
Publication Date: 1998.
Administration: Individual and group.
Price Data, 1998: £95 per practitioner's guide (77 pages); sample sheets are free.
Time: Administration time not reported.
Comments: Some of these tests may also have other uses and may be available separately from other sources.
Authors: Stuart Turner and Deborah Lee.
Publisher: GL Assessment [England].
   a) GENERAL HEALTH QUESTIONNAIRE–28.
   Publication Date: 1981.
   Acronym: GHQ-28.
   Scores: 4 subscales; Somatic Symptoms, Anxiety and Insomnia, Social Dysfunction, Severe Depression.
   Comments: Self-report measure; see T6:1038.
   b) HOSPITAL ANXIETY AND DEPRESSION SCALE.
   Purpose: Designed to detect anxiety and depressive states.
   Publication Dates: 1983–1994.
   Acronym: HADS.
   Scores: 2 subscales; Anxiety, Depression.
   Comments: Self-report.
   c) THE IMPACT OF EVENT SCALE.
   Purpose: Designed as a measure of specific responses to trauma.
   Acronym: IES.
   Scores: 2 subscales; Intrusion, Avoidance.
   Comments: Self-report.
   d) DISSOCIATIVE EXPERIENCES SCALE II.
   Purpose: A measure of dissociation.
   Publication Date: 1993.
   Acronym: DES-II.
   Comments: Self-report; see 891.
   e) INTERNALISED SHAME SCALE.
   Purpose: Developed to measure the extent to which respondents have internalised shame feelings.
   Publication Date: 1990.
   Acronym: ISS.
   Scores, 2: Shame, Positive Self-Esteem.
   Comments: Self-administered.

f) TRAUMA, ATTITUDES AND BELIEFS SCALE.
Purpose: A descriptive measure intended to identify feelings of personal change and alienation.
Acronym: TABS.
Comments: Self-administered.
g) TRAUMA INTERVIEW SCHEDULE.
Acronym: TIS.
Comments: A structured interview.
h) CLINICIAN-ADMINISTERED PTSD SCALE FOR DSM-IV.
Acronym: CAPS.
Comments: A structured interview designed to assess the 17 symptoms of PTSD outlined in the DSM-IV.

[1655]

Measures of Academic Progress.

Purpose: Designed to provide "educators the information they need to improve teaching and learning" in the areas of reading, language usage, mathematics, and science as well as develop instructional strategies and promote school improvement.
Population: Grades 3-10.
Publication Dates: 2003-2011.
Acronym: MAP.
Administration: Group.
Restricted Distribution: To administer the MAP, professionals must have completed the MAP training requirements.
Price Data, 2010: Prices are available for administration training and MAP licensing on a sliding scale depending on district size and proportion of students tested. Pricing for the tests and training will be provided upon request.
Time: Untimed (typically 60 to 75 minutes).
Comments: MAP tests are computer administered and adaptive; sublistings vary by state, typical example below.
Author: Northwest Evaluation Association.
Publisher: Northwest Evaluation Association.
  a) LANGUAGE.
  Scores, 6: Writing Process, Composition Structure, Grammar/Usage, Punctuation, Capitalization, Total.
  b) MATHEMATICS.
  Scores, 9: Number/Numeration Systems, Operations/Computation, Equations/Numerals, Geometry, Measurement, Problem Solving, Statistics/Probability, Applications, Total.
  c) READING.
  Scores, 5: Word Meaning, Literal Comprehension, Interpretive Comprehension, Evaluative Comprehension, Total.
  d) SCIENCE CONCEPTS.
  Scores, 3: Concepts, Processes, Total.
  e) GENERAL SCIENCE.
  Scores, 4: Life Sciences, Earth/ Space Sciences, Physical Sciences, Total.

Cross References: For reviews by Gregory J. Cizek and by Mark J. Gierl and Cecilia B. Alves, see 18:73.

[1656]

Measures of Affiliative Tendency and Sensitivity to Rejection.

Population: Ages 15 and older.
Publication Dates: 1976–1994.
Administration: Group or individual.
Price Data: Available from publisher for complete kit including scales, scoring directions, norms, manual (1994, 13 pages), and literature review.
Time: (10–15) minutes.
Author: Albert Mehrabian.
Publisher: Albert Mehrabian.
  a) AFFILIATIVE TENDENCY.
  Purpose: "Designed to measure friendliness, sociability, and social skills conducive to positive and comfortable social exchanges."
  Scores: Total score only.
  b) SENSITIVITY TO REJECTION.
  Purpose: "Designed to assess social submissiveness."
  Scores: Total score only.
Cross References: For reviews by Sheila Mehta and Scott T. Meier, see 13:196; for a review by Peter D. Lifton of an earlier edition, see 9:683; see also T3:1443 (1 reference).

[1657]

Measures of Individual Differences in Temperament.

Purpose: Provides three basic temperament scores (Trait Pleasure-Displeasure, Trait Arousability, Trait Dominance-Submissiveness) for a comprehensive description of temperament; includes formulas that can employ these basic temperament scores to compute a variety of personality-scale scores (e.g., Trait Anxiety, Neuroticism, Depression, Exuberance, Dependency, Achievement, Affiliation, Shyness, Dependency).
Population: Ages 15 and older.
Publication Dates: 1978–1994.
Scores: Total scores only.
Administration: Group or individual.
Price Data: Available from publisher for complete kit including scales, scoring directions, norms, computational formulas, four manuals (1994, 10 pages, 8 pages, 7 pages, 5 pages), and literature review.
Time: (30–45) minutes.
Author: Albert Mehrabian.
Publisher: Albert Mehrabian.
Cross References: For a review by John B. Gormly of an earlier edition, see 9:684; see also T3:1444 (1 reference).

[1658]

Measures of Pleasure-, Arousal-, and Dominance-Inducing Qualities of Parental Attitudes.

Purpose: Constructed for "a comprehensive measurement of the emotional climate parents create for their children."
Population: Parents of children ages 3 months to 7 years.
Publication Date: 1980.
Scores, 3: Pleasure-Inducing Parental Attitude, Arousal-Inducing Parental Attitude, Dominance-Inducing Parental Attitude.
Administration: Individual.
Manual: No manual.
Price Data: Available from publisher for complete kit including scale, scoring directions, norms, and descriptive material.
Time: [20] minutes.
Authors: Carol Ann Falender and Albert Mehrabian.
Publisher: Albert Mehrabian.
Cross References: For reviews by Douglas N. Jackson and Charles Wenar, see 9:686; see also T3:1448 (1 reference).

[1659]

Measures of Psychosocial Development.

Purpose: "Assesses personality development through eight stages of life."
Population: Ages 13–86 years.
Publication Dates: 1980-1988.
Acronym: MPD.
Scores, 27: 8 Positive scores (Trust [P1], Autonomy [P2], Initiative [P3], Industry [P4], Identity [P5], Intimacy [P6], Generativity [P7], Ego Integrity [P8]), 8 Negative scores (Mistrust [N1], Shame and Doubt [N2], Guilt [N3], Inferiority [N4], Identity Confusion [N5], Isolation [N6], Stagnation [N7], Despair [N8]), 8 Resolution scale scores (R1, R2, R3, R4, R5, R6, R7, R8), 3 Total scores (Total Positive [TP], Total Negative [TN], Total Resolution [TR]).
Administration: Individual or group.
Price Data, 2006: $153 per introductory kit including 25 reusable item booklets, 50 answer sheets, 25 male profile forms, 25 female profile forms, and manual (1988, 31 pages).
Time: (15-20) minutes.
Comments: Based upon Erikson's theory of human development.
Author: Gwen A. Hawley.
Publisher: Psychological Assessment Resources, Inc.
Cross References: See T5:1631 (4 references); for reviews by James C. Carmer and Robert K. Gable, see 11:233.

[1660]

Mechanic Evaluation Test–Forms A1R-C, B1-C, C1-C.

Purpose: Designed for selecting or evaluating industrial mechanics.

Population: Mechanic job applicants or incumbents.
Publication Dates: 1992-2009.
Administration: Group.
Levels, 3: C Mechanic, B Mechanic, A Mechanic.
Price Data, 2011: $22 per consumable self-scoring booklet or online test administration (20 minimum order); $24.95 per manual (18 pages).
Foreign Language Edition: Available in Spanish.
Time: (60-70) minutes.
Comments: Self-scoring instrument; available for online test administration.
Author: Roland T. Ramsay.
Publisher: Ramsay Corporation.
  a) A MECHANIC.
    Scores: 6 areas: Welding & HVAC, Pneumatics and Lubrication, Print Reading and Shop, Electrical, Mechanical & Miscellaneous, Total.
  b) B MECHANIC.
    Scores: 5 areas: Welding/ Plumbing & HVAC, Pneumatics and Lubrication, Print Reading/ Mechanical & Shop, Electrical, Total.
  c) C MECHANIC.
    Scores: 6 areas: Welding/ Plumbing & HVAC, Pneumatics and Lubrication, Mechanical & Print Reading, Electrical, Shop/ Tools & Machines, Rigging & Miscellaneous, Total.
Cross References: For reviews by David O. Anderson and Alan C. Bugbee of an earlier edition, see 13:254.

[1661]

Mechanical Aptitude Test: Acorn National Aptitude Tests.

Purpose: Designed to measure interests and abilities associated with aptitudes for skilled trades.
Population: Grades 7–16 and adults.
Publication Dates: 1943–1952.
Scores, 5: Verbal (Comprehension of Mechanical Tasks, Use of Tools and Materials, Matching Tools and Operations), Nonverbal (Use of Tools and Materials), Total.
Administration: Group.
Price Data: Available from publisher.
Time: 45(50) minutes.
Authors: Andrew Kobal, J. Wayne Wrightstone, and Karl R. Kunze.
Publisher: Psychometric Affiliates.
Cross References: For reviews by Reign H. Bittner, James M. Porter, Jr., and Alec Rodger, see 3:669.

[1662]

Mechanical Aptitude Test (Form MAT-3-C).

Purpose: Designed for evaluating mechanical aptitude.
Population: Applicants for jobs that require the ability to learn mechanical skills.
Publication Dates: 2002-2010.

Scores: Total score only covering 4 areas: Household Objects, Work-Production and Maintenance, School-Science and Physics, Hand and Power Tools.
Administration: Group.
Price Data, 2011: $22 per consumable self-scoring test booklet or online test administration (minimum order of 20); $24.95 per manual (2010, 21 pages).
Foreign Language Edition: Available in Spanish.
Time: 20(30) minutes.
Comments: Self-scoring instrument; available for online test administration.
Author: Roland T. Ramsay.
Publisher: Ramsay Corporation.
Cross References: For a review by M. David Miller of an earlier edition, see 17:116.

[1663]

Mechanical Aptitudes.

Purpose: Measures ability to learn and succeed in an industrial, mechanical or maintenance position.
Population: Applicants for industrial positions, training programs, and vocational counseling.
Publication Dates: 1947–1995.
Scores, 4: Mechanical Knowledge, Space Relations, Shop Arithmetic, Total.
Administration: Individual or group.
Price Data, 2002: $177 per start-up kit including 5 test booklets, 25 answer sheets, 100 profile sheets, and examiner's manual; $91 per 5 test booklets (quantity discounts available); $41 per 25 answer sheets (quantity discounts available); $37 per 100 profile sheets (quantity discounts available); $28 per examiner's manual.
Time: 35 minutes.
Comments: Previously listed as SRA Mechanical Aptitudes.
Author: Richardson, Bellows, Henry & Co., Inc.
Publisher: Pearson Performance Solutions [No reply from publisher; status unknown].
Cross References: See T2:2267 (8 references); for reviews by Alec Rodger and Douglas G. Schultz, see 4:764.

[1664]

Mechanical Maintenance Trainee (Form UKM-1C).

Purpose: Designed for selecting mechanical maintenance trainees.
Population: Applicants with mechanical training and experience necessary for entry into a training program.
Publication Dates: 1998-2010.
Scores, 13: Hydraulics, Pneumatics, Print Reading, Welding, Power Transmission, Lubrication, Pumps, Piping, Rigging, Maintenance, Shop Machines, Tools/Material & Equipment, Total.
Administration: Group.
Price Data, 2011: $22 per consumable self-scoring test booklet or online test administration (minimum order of 20); $24.95 per manual (2008, 22 pages).

Time: (60-70) minutes.
Comments: Self-scoring instrument; available for online test administration.
Author: Roland T. Ramsay.
Publisher: Ramsay Corporation.
Cross References: For a review by Kevin J. McCarthy of an earlier edition, see 17:117.

[1665]

Mechanical Movements.

Purpose: Assesses the ability to visualize a mechanical system where there is internal movement or displacement of parts.
Population: Assesses the ability to visualize a mechanical system where there is internal movement or displacement of parts.
Publication Dates: 1959–1963.
Scores: Total score only.
Administration: Individual or group.
Price Data, 2002: $91 per start-up kit including 25 test booklets, score key, and interpretation and research manual (1963, 14 pages); $54 per 25 test booklets (quantity discounts available); $20 per score key; $28 per interpretation and research manual.
Time: 14 minutes.
Authors: L. L. Thurstone and T. E. Jeffrey.
Publisher: Pearson Performance Solutions [No reply from publisher; status unknown].
Cross References: For a review by William A. Owens, see 6:1089.

[1666]

Mechanical Technician A (Forms AR-XC and MTA-YC).

Purpose: Designed for selecting or evaluating above journey level maintenance technicians for jobs in the metals or manufacturing industry.
Population: Applicants and incumbents for jobs requiring mechanical maintenance knowledge and skills at the highest level.
Publication Dates: 2003-2009.
Scores, 6: Hydraulics & Pneumatics, Print Reading, Power Transmission & Lubrication, Pumps & Piping, Mechanical Maintenance Principles, Total.
Administration: Group.
Forms, 2: AR-XC, MTA-YC.
Price Data, 2011: $22 per consumable self-scoring test booklet or online test administration (minimum order of 20); $24.95 per manual (2009, 24 pages).
Time: (60-70) minutes.
Comments: Self-scoring instrument; available for online test administration; Form MTA-YC is an alternate equivalent of Form AR-XC.
Author: Roland T. Ramsay.
Publisher: Ramsay Corporation.

Cross References: For reviews by Michael D. Biderman and Bart L. Weathington and by Mary L. Garner of an earlier edition, see 17:118.

[1667]

Mechanical Technician B (Forms MTB-XC and MTB-YC).

Purpose: For selecting or evaluating mid-journey level maintenance technicians for jobs in the metals or manufacturing industry.
Population: Applicants and incumbents for jobs requiring mechanical maintenance knowledge and skills.
Publication Dates: 2003–2005.
Scores, 8: Hydraulics & Pneumatics, Print Reading, Burning/Fabricating/Welding & Rigging, Power Transmission & Lubrication, Pumps & Piping, Mechanical Maintenance Principles, Shop Equipment & Tools, Total.
Administration: Group.
Forms, 2: MTB-XC, MTB-YC.
Price Data, 2011: $22 per consumable self-scoring test booklet or online test administration (minimum order of 20); $24.95 per manual (2005, 18 pages).
Foreign Language Edition: Available in Spanish.
Time: (60-70) minutes (untimed).
Comments: Self-scoring instrument; Form MTB-YC is an alternate equivalent of Form MTB-XC; available for online test administration.
Author: Roland T. Ramsay.
Publisher: Ramsay Corporation.
Cross References: For a review by Gregory J. Cizek, see 17:119.

[1668]

Mechanical Technician C (Forms CR-XC and MTC-YC).

Purpose: For selecting or evaluating entry-journey level maintenance technicians for jobs in the metals or manufacturing industry.
Population: Applicants and incumbents for jobs requiring mechanical knowledge and skills.
Publication Dates: 2003-2008.
Scores, 8: Hydraulics & Pneumatics, Print Reading, Burning/Fabricating/Welding & Rigging, Power Transmission & Lubrication, Pumps & Piping, Mechanical Maintenance Principles, Shop Equipment & Tools, Total.
Administration: Group.
Forms, 2: MTC-YC, MTC-XC.
Price Data, 2011: $22 per consumable self-scoring test booklet or online test administration (minimum order of 20); $24.95 per manual (2008, 25 pages).
Time: (60-70) minutes.
Comments: Self-scoring instrument; available for online test administration; Form MTC-YC is an alternate equivalent of Form CR-XC.
Author: Roland T. Ramsay.

Publisher: Ramsay Corporation.
Cross References: For a review by Russell W. Smith of an earlier edition, see 17:120.

[1669]

Mechanical Understanding Test.

Purpose: Designed to assess how well people understand "the basic principles of physics and mechanics that determine success in handling and manipulating objects and machines."
Population: Adults.
Publication Date: 2004.
Acronym: MUT.
Scores: Total score only.
Administration: Group.
Price Data: Available from publisher.
Time: (30–40) minutes.
Authors: Erich P. Prien, Leonard D. Goodstein, and Kristin O. Prien.
Publisher: HRD Press, Inc.
Cross References: For reviews by Phillip L. Ackerman and Michael B. Bunch, see 17:121.

[1670]

MecTest (Form AU-C).

Purpose: Designed for selecting or evaluating journey-level maintenance mechanics.
Population: Applicants and incumbents for maintenance jobs.
Publication Dates: 1991–2008.
Scores, 9: Hydraulics and Pneumatics, Print Reading, Welding and Rigging, Power Transmission, Lubrication, Pumps and Piping, Mechanical Maintenance, Shop Machines/Tools/Equipment, Total.
Administration: Group.
Price Data, 2011: $22 per consumable self-scoring test booklet (20 minimum order); $24.95 per manual (2008, 24 pages).
Foreign Language Edition: Available in Spanish.
Time: (60-70) minutes.
Comments: Self-scoring instrument; available for online test administration.
Author: Roland T. Ramsay.
Publisher: Ramsay Corporation.
Cross References: For a review by Robert J. Drummond of an earlier edition, see 13:197.

[1671]

Medical College Admission Test.

Purpose: "Designed primarily to aid members of admissions committees in the . . . selection of applicants" for medical colleges.
Population: Applicants for admission to member colleges of the Association of American Medical Colleges and to other participating institutions.

Publication Dates: 1946-1994.
Acronym: MCAT.
Scores, 4: Verbal Reasoning, Physical Sciences, Biological Sciences, Writing Sample.
Administration: Group.
Price Data: Available from publisher.
Time: (345) minutes.
Comments: Administered 2 times annually (April, August) at centers established by publisher.
Author: Constructed under the direction of the Association of American Medical Colleges.
Publisher: Administered at the direction of the Association of American Medical Colleges.
Cross References: See T5:1638 (3 references), T4:1600 (11 references), 9:691 (9 references), T3:1576 (40 references), 8:1101 (40 references), and T2:2355 (30 references); for reviews by Nancy S. Cole and James M. Richards, Jr. of earlier forms, see 7:1100 (57 references); for reviews by Robert L. Ebel and Philip H. DuBois, see 6:1137 (43 references); for a review by Alexander G. Wesman, see 5:932 (4 references); for a review by Morey J. Wantman, see 4:817 (11 references).

[1672]

Medical Ethics Inventory.
Purpose: Designed to provide "profiles of the value preferences of medical students regarding medical ethical dilemmas."
Population: First year medical students.
Publication Date: 1982.
Acronym: MEI.
Scores, 6: Social, Economic, Theoretical, Political, Religious, Aesthetic.
Administration: Group.
Price Data: Available from publisher.
Time: [30-40] minutes.
Authors: Cynthia J. Stolman and Rodney L. Doran.
Publisher: Rodney L. Doran [No reply from publisher; status unknown].
Cross References: For reviews by Joseph D. Matarazzo and Gary B. Melton, see 10:197.

[1673]

Meeker Behavioral Correlates.
Purpose: Assesses "major dimensions of intellectual abilities and personality characteristics" for management matching of teams.
Population: Industry.
Publication Date: 1981.
Scores: Ratings by self in 6 areas: Comprehension, Memory, Leadership, Convergent Production Skills, Creativity, Team Contributions.
Administration: Group.
Price Data: Available from publisher.
Time: [20] minutes.

Comments: Self-ratings.
Author: Mary Meeker.
Publisher: SOI Systems.
Cross Reference: For a review by William I. Sauser, Jr., see 10:198.

[1674]

Memory and Behavior Problems Checklist and The Burden Interview.
Publication Dates: 1983–1990.
Administration: Individual.
Price Data, 2001: $5.25 per manual including the instruments.
Authors: Steven H. Zarit and Judy M. Zarit.
Publisher: Gerontology Center, The Pennsylvania State University.
 a) MEMORY AND BEHAVIOR PROBLEMS CHECKLIST.
Purpose: Designed to "determine how frequently a dementia patient engages in problematic behaviors and which problems are especially upsetting for family members."
Population: Dementia patients and their families.
Acronym: MBPC.
Scores, 3: Frequency of Problems, Severity of Functional Behavior Problems, Mean Distress.
Comments: Administered by an interviewer to family members of a dementia patient.
 b) THE BURDEN INTERVIEW.
Purpose: "Designed to assess the stresses experienced by family caregivers of elderly and disabled persons."
Population: Caregivers of elderly and disabled persons.
Scores, 2: Personal Strain, Role Strain.
Comments: Administered by an interviewer or self-administered.
Cross References: For reviews by Sally Kuhlenschmidt and Richard A. Wantz, see 14:229; see also T5:1643 (2 references).

[1675]

Memory Assessment Scales.
Purpose: Developed to provide a comprehensive battery that assesses short- and long-term verbal and visual (nonverbal) memory.
Population: Ages 18 and over.
Publication Date: 1991.
Acronym: MAS.
Scores, 16: Short-Term Memory (Verbal Span, Visual Span, Total), List Acquisition, Delayed List Recall, Delayed Prose Recall, Global Memory Scale (Verbal Memory [List Recall, Immediate Prose Recall, Total], Visual Memory [Visual Reproduction, Immediate Visual Recognition, Total], Total), Delayed Visual Recognition, Names-Faces (Immediate, Delayed) and 7 Verbal Process

scores: Total Intrusions, List Clustering (Acquisition, Recall, Delayed Recall), Cued List Recall (Recall, Delayed Recall), List Recognition.
Administration: Individual.
Price Data, 2006: $289 per introductory kit including stimulus card set, 25 record forms, manual (131 pages), and attache case.
Time: [40-45] minutes.
Author: J. Michael Williams.
Publisher: Psychological Assessment Resources, Inc.
Cross References: See T5:1644 (1 reference); for reviews by Ronald A. Berk and John W. Young, see 12:229.

[1676]
Memory for Intentions Test.
Purpose: Designed to measure "everyday aspects" of prospective memory performance.
Population: Ages 18 to 95.
Publication Date: 2010.
Acronym: MIST.
Scores, 8: 2-Minute Time Delay, 15-Minute Time Delay, Time Cue, Event Cue, Verbal Response, Action Response, Prospective Memory Total, Retrospective Recognition Total; 1 optional score: Delayed Prospective Memory Task.
Administration: Individual.
Forms, 2: A, B.
Price Data, 2010: $240 per complete kit including 25 Form A record forms, 25 Form B record forms, 25 Form A word search sheets, 25 Form B word search sheets, 25 score summary sheets, 25 request for records forms, digital clock, carrying case, and manual (62 pages); $180 per introductory kit including 25 Form A record forms, 25 Form A word search sheets, 25 score summary sheets, 25 request for records forms, digital clock, carrying case, and manual; $40 per 25 record forms (Form A or Form B); $25 per 25 word search sheets (Form A or Form B); $30 per 25 score summary sheets; $25 per 25 request for records forms; $15 per digital clock; $65 per manual.
Time: (30) minutes.
Comments: Additional materials required for administration, but not included in test materials: red pen, postcard, envelope, tape recorder.
Authors: Sarah Raskin, Carol Buckheit, and Christina Sherrod (manual).
Publisher: Psychological Assessment Resources, Inc.

[1677]
Memory Test for Older Adults.
Purpose: Designed as a brief instrument to assess verbal and visuospatial learning and memory in older adults.
Population: Ages 55–84.
Publication Date: 2002.
Acronym: MTOA, MTOA:S, MTOA:L.
Scores, 8: Free Recall Word List Total Score, Free Recall Word List Retention, Free Recall + Cued Recall Word List Total Score, Free Recall + Cued Recall Word List Retention Score, Recognition Score, Geometric Figure Total Score, Geometric Figure Retention Score, Geometric Figure Copy Score.
Administration: Individual.
Forms, 2: Long, Short.
Price Data, 2011: $202 per complete kit including 1 long form (MTOA:L), 1 short form (MTOA:S), geometric cards, 25 short form record forms, 25 long form record forms, and technical manual; $57 per 25 long or short record forms; $73 per technical manual; $60 per package of 25 MTOA:L Record forms; $60 per package of 25 MTOA:S Record forms.
Time: Administration time not reported.
Authors: Anita M. Hubley and Tom M. Tombaugh.
Publisher: Multi-Health Systems, Inc.
Cross References: For reviews by Stephen J. Freeman and by W. Joel Schneider and Mark E. Swerdlik, see 16:144.

[1678]
Menometer.
Purpose: Designed to measure "knowledge of the physical aspects of human menstruation."
Population: Adolescents and adults.
Publication Dates: 1974–1988.
Scores: Total score only.
Administration: Group.
Manual: No manual.
Price Data, 2005: $2 per scale.
Time: [10] minutes.
Comments: For a supplementary source, see Panos D. Bardis, "Research Instruments for Population Studies," Society and Culture, July 1974, 5(2), 177-191.
Author: Panos D. Bardis.
Publisher: Donna Bardis.

[1679]
Menstrual Distress Questionnaire.
Purpose: Designed as "a self-report inventory for use in the diagnosis and treatment of premenstrual and menstrual distress."
Population: Women who experience strong to severe premenstrual or menstrual distress.
Publication Dates: 1968–1991.
Acronym: MDQ.
Scores, 8: Pain, Water Retention, Autonomic Reactions, Negative Affect, Impaired Concentration, Behavior Change, Arousal, Control.
Administration: Group or individual.
Forms, 2: Form C, Form T.
Price Data: Available from publisher.
Foreign Language Edition: Spanish edition available.
Time: (15) minutes for Form C; (5) minutes for Form T.
Author: Rudolph H. Moos.

Publisher: Western Psychological Services.
Cross References: See T5:1647 (4 references); for reviews by Jennifer J. Fager and Donna L. Sundre, see 12:230 (12 references); see T4:1608 (7 references), 9:695 (6 references), and T3:1466 (4 references).

[1680]

Mental Status Checklist for Adolescents.

Purpose: To assist professionals in the assessment of adolescents' mental status.
Population: Ages 13–17.
Publication Date: 1988.
Scores: Item scores only.
Administration: Individual.
Price Data, 2006: $50 per package of 25.
Time: Administration time not reported.
Comments: Reliability and validity data not reported; problems checklist.
Authors: Edward H. Dougherty and John A. Schinka.
Publisher: Psychological Assessment Resources, Inc.
Cross References: For a review by Julian Fabry, see 11:234.

[1681]

Mental Status Checklist for Adults, 1988 Revision.

Purpose: "Surveys items that are commonly included in a comprehensive mental status examination."
Population: Adults.
Publication Dates: 1986–1988.
Scores: 10 Content Areas: Presenting Problems, Behavioral/Physical Descriptions, Emotional State, Mental Status, Health and Habits, Legal Issues, Current Living Situation, Diagnoses, Treatment Recommendations, Disposition.
Administration: Individual.
Manual: No manual.
Price Data, 2006: $50 per package of 25.
Time: Administration time not reported.
Author: John A. Schinka.
Publisher: Psychological Assessment Resources, Inc.

[1682]

Mental Status Checklist for Children.

Purpose: Assess childhood problems and plan for treatment approaches.
Population: Ages 5–12.
Publication Date: 1989.
Scores: Item scores only.
Administration: Individual.
Manual: No manual.
Price Data, 2006: $50 per package of 25.
Time: (10–20) minutes.
Comments: Downward extension of the Mental Status Checklist–Adult (1681); scale for ratings by parents, caregivers, or self-ratings.

Authors: Edward H. Dougherty and John A. Schinka.
Publisher: Psychological Assessment Resources, Inc.
Cross References: For reviews by David Lachar and Marcia B. Shaffer, see 11:235.

[1683]

Mentoring Skills Assessment.

Purpose: Provides awareness about successful mentoring or being a successful mentee; feedback report is designed to improve mentoring and mentee skills; the mentor form is designed to rate skills in the areas of quality and frequency of mentoring skills.
Population: Mentors, coaches, and mentees.
Publication Dates: 1995–1998.
Acronym: MSA.
Scores, 27: Importance, Quality, Frequency on each of the following scales: Listening, Encouraging, Inspiring/Instilling Vision, Coaching, Instructing, Managing Risks, Opening Doors, Demonstrating Personal Mastery, Giving Constructive Feedback.
Administration: Group.
Forms, 2: Mentor/Colleague or Mentee/Colleague.
Manual: No manual.
Price Data: Available from publisher (www.mindgarden.com).
Time: Administration time not reported.
Comments: Web-based and paper-based; multirater.
Author: Linda Phillips-Jones.
Publisher: Mind Garden, Inc.

[1684]

Mentoring Style Indicator™.

Purpose: Assesses 4 mentoring styles (Informational, Guiding, Collaborative, Confirming) and associated mentoring behaviors; identifies the style of mentoring that mentors prefer to provide and proteges prefer to receive.
Population: Mentors and proteges.
Publication Dates: 1987–2005.
Acronym: MSI.
Scores, 6: Informational Mentoring, Guiding Mentoring, Collaborative Mentoring, Confirming Mentoring, Preferred Mentoring Style.
Administration: Individual and group.
Price Data: Available from publisher; discounts on bulk orders.
Time: (20-25) minutes.
Comments: Versions available for new hires, career development, leadership development, generic, sales, healthcare, youth, new teachers, college students, college faculty, and educational administrators; can be answered online as part of the web-based Colaboro® Mentoring Management System™; scoring is automatically done online; Preferred Mentoring Style and an interpretation is printed out.
Author: William A. Gray.
Publisher: Corporate Mentoring Solutions® Inc.

a) MSI FOR MENTORING NEW HIRES.
Population: Mentors and proteges wanting orientation.
b) MSI FOR CAREER DEVELOPMENT.
Population: Mentors and proteges wanting to explore career options.
c) MSI FOR LEADERSHIP DEVELOPMENT.
Population: Mentors and proteges wanting to become leaders.
d) MSI–GENERIC.
Population: Mentors and proteges wanting to handle generic work challenges.
e) MSI FOR SALES.
Population: Mentors and proteges wanting to handle common sales challenges.
f) MSI FOR HEALTHCARE PROFESSIONALS.
Population: Mentors and proteges wanting to handle healthcare challenges.
g) MSI FOR MENTORING NEW TEACHERS.
Population: Mentors and new teachers wanting induction into the profession.
h) MSI FOR EDUCATIONAL ADMINISTRATORS.
Population: Educational administrators and proteges wanting to become administrators.
i) MSI FOR MENTORING COLLEGE/UNIVERSITY STUDENTS.
Population: Mentors and college students wanting to handle freshman and transfer challenges.
j) MSI FOR MENTORING COLLEGE/UNIVERSITY FACULTY.
Population: Mentors and proteges wanting to get tenured and promoted.
k) MSI FOR MENTORING YOUTH.
Population: Mentors and youthful proteges wanting adult assistance.
Cross References: For reviews by Raoul A. Arreola and Russell N. Carney, see 13:198.

[1685]

Merrill-Palmer-Revised Scales of Development.

Purpose: Designed to assess cognitive, social-emotional, self-help, and fine and gross motor development in infants and children.
Population: Ages 0-1 to 6-6 years.
Publication Dates: 1926-2004.
Acronym: M-P-R.
Administration: Individual.
Price Data, 2006: $925 per complete kit including manual (2004, 267 pages), infant stimuli book, easel book, Fido book, choke-safe toys and manipulatives, 20 Cognitive Battery record forms, 20 Social Emotional Development Parent Scales, 20 Social Emotional Temperament Style Parent Forms, 20 Gross Motor record forms, 20 Self-Help/Adaptive Development Scale Parent Forms, 20 Expressive Language Evaluator Forms, 20 Expressive

Language Parent Forms, 20 Summary Reports/Growth Score Profiles, 20 Copying Response Sheets A, and 20 Copying Response Sheets B; $55 per manual; $30 per 20 Cognitive Battery record forms; $10 per 20 Social Emotional Development Parent Scales; $20 per 20 Spanish Social Emotional Development Parent Scales; $10 per 20 Social Emotional Temperament Style Parent Forms; $20 per 20 Spanish Social Emotional Temperament Style Parent Forms; $20 per 20 Gross Motor Record Forms; $10 per 20 Self-Help/Adaptive Development Scale Parent Forms; $20 per 20 Spanish Self-Help Parent Report Forms; $10 per 20 Expressive Language Evaluator Forms; $10 per 20 Expressive Language Parent Forms; $20 per 20 Summary Reports/Growth Score Profiles; $2.50 per 20 Copying Response Sheets A; $2.50 per 20 Copying Response Sheets B.
Foreign Language Editions: Spanish editions of parent reports available.
Time: (40-50) minutes.
Comments: Portions of this test are to be completed by a parent/guardian; previous edition entitled Merrill-Palmer Scale of Mental Tests.
Authors: Gale H. Roid and Jackie L. Sampers.
Publisher: Stoelting Co.
a) EXPRESSIVE LANGUAGE-EXAMINER FORM.
1) Element of Attire, Body Parts, Verbs.
Population: Ages 1-1 years and older.
2) Adverbs, Adjectives, Prepositions, Pronouns.
Population: Ages 1-6 years and older.
b) EXPRESSIVE LANGUAGE-PARENT REPORT.
Scores: 2 scales, 4 subscales: 0-12 months, 13 months and older (Word Combination, Word Meanings/Semantics, Gestural, Expressive Verbal).
c) SELF-HELP/ADAPTIVE-PARENT.
Forms, 5: 0-11 months, 12-23 months, 24-35 months, 36-37 months, 48-78 months.
d) GROSS MOTOR-EXAMINER.
Scores: 7 scales, 23 subscales: 0-12 months (Lifts Head, Supported Sitting, Reaching, Rolls, Balance Responses, Independent Sitting, Stomach Creep, Hand/Knee Creep), 13-24 months (Pull to Standing, Cruises Furniture, Independent Walking), 25-36 months (Child Squats to Pick Up Toy, Climbing Into Chair, Stairs, Special Walking), 37-48 months (Running, Jumping #1), 49-78 months (Throwing/Catching, Kicking, Dynamic Walking, Static Balance, Jumping #2, Hopping Movements), Quality of Movement, Tone.
e) SOCIAL-EMOTIONAL DEVELOPMENTAL-PARENT.
Forms, 5: Same as *c* above.
f) SOCIAL-EMOTIONAL TEMPERAMENT-PARENT.
Forms, 2: 0-17 months, 18-78 months.
g) COGNITIVE BATTERY-EXAMINER.
Scores, 6: Cognitive, Memory, Fine Motor, Speed, Receptive Language, Visual Motor; 8 scales, 49

subscales: 1-5 months (Warm-up, Visual Regard, Small Rattle Play, Visual Preference), 6-12 months (Spin Toy, Large Rattle Play, Dangle Toy, Push-Spin Toy, Object Permanence), 13-23 months (Novel Problem, Blocks, Chips in the Box, Round Peg Board (A), Body Parts, Pop Out, Simple Puzzle, Square Peg Board (B), Fido Book), 24-35 months (Ring Stack, Color Matching, Identifies Emotions, Picture Details, Goodnight Baby, Bead Stringing, Two Puzzles, Find It, Goes Together, Square Pegs, Same), 36-47 months (Fingers, Questions, Where Do They Go?, Word Pictures, See It?, Shapes Puzzle), 48-59 months (Puzzle Fun, Big/Small, Touch Picture, Draw It, Hidden Picture, Different Pictures), 60-78 months (Find 'em, High/Low, Count 'em, Fun with Cards, Touch 'em, What's Next?, Different Pictures, Let's Draw It).

  1) *Testing Behaviors-Examiner.*
  Scores: 4 scales, 6 subscales: 1-5 months (Emotionality), 6-11 months (Attention), 12-17 months (Fearful/Cautious), 18-78 months (Organized/Cooperative, Active/Eager, Angry/Oppositional).
h) SUMMARY REPORT-EXAMINER.
  1) *Developmental Index.*
  Scores, 7: Developmental Index, Cognitive, Fine Motor, Receptive Language, Memory (ages 1-4 years and older), Speed (ages 1-4 years and older), Visual Motor.
  2) *Gross Motor.*
  Score: Gross Motor.
  3) *Language.*
  Scores, 2: Overall Expressive Language, Overall Language.
  4) *Social-Emotional.*
  Score: Social-Emotional.
  5) *Self-Help.*
  Score: Self-Help/Adaptive.
Cross References: For reviews by Sandra Loew and by Loraine J. Spenciner and Dolores J. Appl, see 17:122; see also T5:1653 (29 references) and T4:1614 (19 references); for a review by Jack A. Naglieri of an earlier edition, see 9:697 (4 references).

[1686]

Meta-Motivation Inventory.

Purpose: Designed to measure personal and managerial style.
Population: Managers and persons in leadership positions.
Publication Date: 1979.
Acronym: MMI.
Scores, 32: Motivation for Achievement, Perfection, Assertiveness, Independence, Achievement, Meta-Achievement, Deterministic, Approval, Conventional, Dependent, Avoidance, Helplessness, Need for Control,

Persuasiveness, Manipulation, Reactive, Authoritarian, Exploitive, Concern for People, Cooperation, Affiliation, Humanistic, Synergy, Meta-Humanistic, Self-Actualization, Stress, Repression, Anger, Judgemental, Creativity, Growth Potential, Fun Scale.
Administration: Group.
Price Data: Available from publisher.
Time: Administration time not reported.
Comments: Self-administered.
Author: John A. Walker.
Publisher: Meta-Visions.
Cross References: For reviews by John K. Butler, Jr. and Denise M. Rousseau, see 9:698.

[1687]

Metaphon.

Purpose: Designed to be "a complete assessment and therapy programme for children with phonological disorders."
Population: Ages 3.5–7.
Publication Date: 1990.
Scores: Total score only.
Administration: Individual.
Parts, 4: Screening, Probing, Intervention, Monitoring.
Price Data: Available from publisher.
Time: (15) minutes.
Authors: Elizabeth Dean, Janet Howell, Ann Hill, and Daphne Waters.
Publisher: GL Assessment [England].
Cross References: For a review by Allan O. Diefendorf, Kathy Kessler, and Michael K. Wynne, see 12:231.

[1688]

Metropolitan Achievement Tests, Eighth Edition.

Purpose: Designed to provide assessment of students' achievement in reading, mathematics, language arts, science, and social studies at appropriate levels.
Publication Dates: 1931–2001.
Acronym: METROPOLITAN8.
Administration: Group.
Forms, 2: Complete Battery, Short Form.
Price Data, 2002: $31.50 per multiple-choice Complete Battery examination kit (for preview only) including Complete Battery test booklet, directions for administering, practice test with directions (Preprimer through Intermediate 4 only), separate answer document (Elementary 1 through Secondary 3 only), and open-ended assessment preview brochure (specify level); $16 per multiple-choice Complete Battery 25 practice tests (specify Level Preprimer through Intermediate 2/3/4); $7 per directions for administering practice tests; $122.50 per 25 machine-scorable multiple-choice Complete Battery test booklets (specify preprimer–Elementary 1); $93 per 25 reusable multiple-choice Complete Battery test booklets (specify Elementary 1–Secondary 3); $76 per

100 Complete Battery machine-scorable answer documents (specify Elementary 1–Secondary 3); $11.50 per directions for administering (specify level); $7 per 25 test booklet place markers; $31.50 per multiple-choice Complete Battery response key-list of correct responses (specify level); $16 per 25 multiple-choice Short Form practice tests (specify Primary 1–Intermediate 2/3/4); $7 per directions for administering Short Form practice tests; $104 per 25 multiple-choice Short Form machine-scorable test booklets (specify Primary 1–Elementary 1); $83 per 25 multiple-choice Short Form reusable test booklets (specify Elementary 2–Secondary 3); $11.50 per directions for administering (specify Primary 1–Secondary); $69 per 100 multiple-choice Short Form machine-scorable answer documents (specify Elementary 1–Secondary 3); $31.50 per multiple-choice Short Form response key-list of correct responses (specify level); $14 per 25 Parent Guide to METROPOLITAN8 (specify English or Spanish); $66 per norms book (specify Fall or Spring); $60 per technical manual; $40 per Compendium of Instructional Objectives (also available in CD-ROM version); $25 per Guide for Classroom Planning (specify Primary 1/2, Elementary 1/2, Intermediate 1/2/3/4, or Secondary 1/2/3); $21 per Understanding Test Results (specify Primary 1/2–Secondary 1/2/3); price information for scoring and reporting services available from publisher.

Author: Harcourt Educational Measurement.

Publisher: Pearson.

a) PREPRIMER.

Population: Grades K.0–K.5.

Scores, 4: Sounds and Print, Mathematics, Language, Complete Battery.

Time: (90–100) minutes.

b) PRIMER.

Population: Grades K.5–1.5.

Scores, 4: Same as for Preprimer.

Time: (90–100) minutes.

c) PRIMARY 1.

Population: Grades 1.5–2.5.

Scores, 12: Sounds and Print, Reading Vocabulary, Reading Comprehension, Total Reading, Mathematics Concepts and Problem Solving, Mathematics Computation, Total Mathematics, Language, Spelling, Science, Social Studies, Complete Battery.

Time: (265–292) minutes.

d) PRIMARY 2.

Population: Grades 2.5–3.5.

Scores, 12: Same as for Primary 1.

Time: (270–296) minutes.

e) ELEMENTARY 1.

Population: Grades 3.5–4.5.

Scores, 12: Same as for Primary 1.

Time: (275–328) minutes.

f) ELEMENTARY 2.

Population: Grades 4.5–5.5.

Scores, 11: Same as for Primary 1 minus Sounds and Print.

Time: (255–298) minutes.

g) INTERMEDIATE 1.

Population: Grades 5.5–6.5.

Scores, 11: Same as Elementary 2.

Time: (275–316) minutes.

h) INTERMEDIATE 2.

Population: Grades 6.5–7.5.

Scores, 11: Same as for Elementary 2.

Time: (275–316) minutes.

i) INTERMEDIATE 3.

Population: Grades 7.5–8.5.

Scores, 11: Same as for Elementary 2.

Time: (275–316) minutes.

j) INTERMEDIATE 4.

Population: Grades 8.5–9.5.

Scores, 11: Same as for Elementary 2.

Time: (275–316) minutes.

k) SECONDARY 1.

Population: Grade 9.

Scores, 9: Reading Vocabulary, Reading Comprehension, Sounds and Print/Total Reading, Mathematics, Language, Spelling, Science, Social Studies, Complete Battery.

Time: (240–288) minutes.

l) SECONDARY 2.

Population: Grade 10.

Scores, 9: Same as for Secondary 1.

Time: (240–288) minutes.

m) SECONDARY 3.

Population: Grades 11–12.

Scores, 9: Same as for Secondary 1.

Time: (240–288) minutes.

Cross References: For reviews by Michael R. Harwell and Leslie Eastman Lukin, see 16:146; see also T5:1657 (25 references); for reviews by Carmen J. Finley and Ronald K. Hambleton, see 12:232 (37 references); see also T4:1618 (31 references); for reviews by Anthony J. Nitko and Bruce G. Rogers of an earlier edition, see 10:200 (44 references); for reviews by Edward H. Haertel and Robert L. Linn, see 9:699 (30 references); see also T3:1473 (89 references); for reviews by Norman E. Gronlund and Richard M. Wolf and an excerpted review by Joseph A. Wingard and Peter M. Bentler of an earlier edition, see 8:22 (41 references); see also T2:22 (20 references) and 7:14 (25 references); for reviews by Henry S. Dyer and Warren G. Findley of an earlier edition, see 6:16 (16 references); for a review by Warren G. Findley, see 4:18 (10 references); see also 3:13 (7 references); for reviews by E. V. Pullias and Hugh B. Wood, see 2:1189 (3 references); for reviews by Jack W. Dunlap, Charles W. Odell, and Richard Ledgerwood, see 1:874. For reviews of subtests, see 8:283 (1 review), 8:732 (2 reviews), 6:627 (2 reviews), 6:797 (1 review), 6:877 (2 reviews), 6:970 (2 reviews), 4:416 (1 review), 4:543 (2 reviews), 2:1458.1 (2 reviews), 2:1551 (1 review), 1:892 (2 reviews), and 1:1105 (2 reviews).

[1689]

METROPOLITAN8 Writing Test.

Purpose: Designed to provide a "norm-referenced measure of student achievement in written expression."
Population: Grades 1–12.
Publication Dates: 1931–2001.
Acronym: METROPOLITAN8 Writing.
Scores: Analytical Scoring option yields Content Development, Organizational Strategies, Word Choice, Sentence Formation, Usage, and Writing Mechanics scores; Holistic Scoring option yields total score only.
Administration: Group.
Levels, 11: Primary 1 and 2; Elementary 1 and 2; Intermediate 1, 2, 3, and 4; Secondary 1, 2, and 3.
Forms, 22: 2 forms for each level.
Price Data: Available from publisher.
Time: Untimed (40–50 minutes).
Comments: Scoring and reporting services available from publisher; may be used alone, or in combination with the Metropolitan Achievement Tests (1688) Language Test.
Author: Harcourt Educational Measurement.
Publisher: Pearson.
Cross References: For reviews by Stephen L. Benton and Natalie Rathvon, see 16:147.

[1690]

Metropolitan Performance Assessment: Integrated Performance Tasks.

Purpose: Designed to show progression in the "acquisition of concepts, strategies, and skills needed to perform language/literacy and quantitative/mathematics tasks" usually taught through kindergarten.
Population: Ages 4-4 to 6-3; ages 5-5 to 7-0.
Publication Date: 1995.
Acronym: MPA.
Scores, 3: Holistic, Analytic (Language/Literacy, Quantitative/Mathematics).
Administration: Group.
Levels, 2: 1, 2.
Price Data, 2002: $40 per examination kit including task booklet, set of manipulative sheets, directions for administering, scoring guide, and teacher observation form (Level 1 or Level 2); $49 per task package including 25 booklets, 25 sets of manipulative sheets, directions for administering, and teacher observation form (Level 1 or Level 2); $26.50 per scoring guide (Level 1 or Level 2); $6.40 per directions for administering (Level 1 or Level 2); $57 per preliteracy inventory including 25 record forms, Homer the Goose Storybook, and directions for administering; $23.85 per developmental inventory; $13.25 per portfolio assessment guidelines with information for interpreting preliteracy and devlopmental inventories; $17 per literacy environment inventory; $65.75 per Handbook of Early Childhood Activities.

Time: Untimed.
Comments: Handbook of Early Childhood Activities covers many areas assessed in the MPA, but may also be used independently of the program.
Author: Joanne R. Nurss.
Publisher: Pearson.
Cross References: For reviews by Theodore Coladarci and Delwyn L. Harnisch, see 14:230.

[1691]

Metropolitan Readiness Tests®, Sixth Edition.

Purpose: Designed to assess basic and advanced skills important in beginning reading and mathematics.
Population: PreKindergarten through grade 1.
Publication Dates: 1933–1995.
Acronym: MRT®6.
Administration: Individual (Level 1) or Group (Level 2).
Price Data, 2002: $19 per 25 parent-teacher conference reports (specify level); $19 per story comprehension big book.
Time: (85) minutes per level; (10) minutes for the practice items for each level.
Authors: Joanne R. Nurss and Mary E. McGauvran.
Publisher: Pearson.
a) LEVEL 1.
Population: PreKindergarten and beginning Kindergarten.
Administration: Individual.
Scores: 5 tests: Beginning Reading Skill Area (Visual Discrimination, Beginning Consonants, Sound-Letter Correspondence), Story Comprehension, Quantitative Concepts and Reasoning, plus Prereading Composite.
Price Data: $121 per complete kit including stimulus manual, story comprehension big book, manual (1995, 43 pages), 25 parent-teacher conference reports, and 25 student record forms; $32 per 25 student record forms; $31 per manual; $57.25 per stimulus manual; $29 per exam kit including Level I flyer, story comprehension big book flyer, manual, student record form, and parent-teacher conference report.
b) LEVEL 2.
Population: Middle and end of kindergarten and beginning of grade 1.
Administration: Group.
Scores: 5 tests: Beginning Reading Skill Area (Beginning Consonants, Sound-Letter Correspondence, Aural Cloze with Letter), Story Comprehension, Quantitative Concepts and Reasoning, plus Prereading Composite.
Price Data: $164 per starter kit including 25 test booklets, directions for administering, story comprehension big book, 25 practice booklets, class record and analysis chart, norms book, answer

keys, parent-teacher conference reports, 25 Birthday Surprise Task booklets, 25 Birthday Surprise manipulative sheets, Birthday Surprise directions for administering, scoring guide, and teacher observation form; $82 per 25 handscorable test booklets also including directions for administration, 25 practice booklets, and class record and analysis chart; $29.50 per answer keys; $41 per manual; $31 per norms book (1995, 72 pages); $17 per exam kit including test booklet, directions for administering, practice booklet, class record and analysis chart, and parent-teacher conference report.

Cross References: For reviews by Randy W. Kamphaus and Christine Novak, see 14:231; see also T5:1659 (14 references) and T4:1619 (35 references); for a review by Michael M. Ravitch of an earlier edition, see 9:700 (11 references); see also T3:1479 (73 references), 8:802 (111 references), and T2:1716 (55 references); for reviews by Robert Dykstra and Harry Singer of an earlier edition, see 7:757 (124 references); for a review by Eric F. Gardner and an excerpted review by Fay Griffith, see 4:570 (3 references); for a review by Irving H. Anderson, see 3:518 (5 references); for a review by W. J. Osburn, see 2:1552 (10 references).

[1692]
Meyer-Kendall Assessment Survey.
Purpose: Constructed to assess work-related personality style.
Population: Business employees and job applicants.
Publication Dates: 1986–1991.
Acronym: MKAS.
Scores, 12: Objectivity, Social Desirability Bias, Dominance, Extraversion, People Concerns, Attention to Detail, Anxiety, Stability, Psychosomatic Tendencies, Determination, Achievement Motivation, Independence.
Administration: Group or individual.
Price Data, 2002: $92.50 per complete kit including 2 prepaid assessment sheets, 2 prepaid pre-assessment sheets, and manual (1991, 72 pages); $29.50 per mail-in assessment sheet (price includes scoring and report by publisher); $8.50 per pre-assessment sheet; $45 per manual.
Time: (15–20) minutes.
Authors: Henry D. Meyer and Edward L. Kendall.
Publisher: Western Psychological Services.
Cross References: For reviews by Mark H. Daniel and Gregory H. Dobbins, see 12:234.

[1693]
Michigan Alcoholism Screening Test.
Purpose: Designed as a screening test for assessing alcohol abuse.
Population: Adults.
Publication Dates: 1971–1980.
Acronym: MAST.
Scores: Total score only.
Administration: Group or individual.
Manual: No manual available.
Price Data, 2006: $40 per copy, which includes scoring key and permission to duplicate the test.
Foreign Language Editions: French, Japanese, Spanish, and Vietnamese versions available.
Time: (10) minutes.
Comments: Can be self-administered.
Author: Melvin L. Selzer.
Publisher: Melvin L. Selzer.
Cross References: For reviews by Jane Close Conoley and Jeff Reese and by Janice W. Murdoch, see 14:232; see also T5:1661 (85 references).

[1694]
Michigan English Language Assessment Battery.
Purpose: Designed "to evaluate the advanced level English language proficiency of adult non-native speakers of English."
Population: Adult non-native speakers of English.
Publication Dates: 1985–2010.
Acronym: MELAB.
Scores, 5: Writing, Listening, GCVR [includes Grammar, Cloze Reading, Vocabulary, Reading], Final Score, Speaking Test (optional).
Administration: Group or individual.
Forms: Multiple equivalent forms.
Price Data: Available from publisher.
Time: (145–160) minutes for complete battery; (30) minutes for Writing; (35) minutes for Listening; (80) minutes for Grammar/Cloze/Vocabulary/Reading; (15) minutes for optional oral interview.
Comments: "Used primarily to draw inferences about a test-taker's ability to study in an institution where English is the medium of instruction" or for test takers who require evidence of English language ability for professional purposes; candidates register to take exam through authorized test centers; publisher scores all examinations and issues official score report directly to institutions selected by examinee.
Author: University of Michigan.
Publisher: Cambridge-Michigan Language Assessments.
Cross References: For reviews by Ayres D'Costa and Alan Garfinkel, see 14:233.

[1695]
Michigan English Language Institute College English Test–Grammar, Cloze, Vocabulary, Reading.
Purpose: "To provide educational institutions and researchers with information about the English language

competencies of their own students, employees, or research participants."
Population: Adult nonnative speakers of English.
Publication Date: 2001.
Acronym: MELICET-GCVR.
Scores: Total score only.
Administration: Group.
Forms, 2: AA, BB.
Price Data: The complete testing package includes 20 test booklets, 100 answer sheets, stencil, and a user's manual. Purchasers need to specify Form AA or BB. Prices for each package are available from the publisher.
Time: 75 minutes.
Comments: All items are in a multiple-choice format. Items are scored by punched stencil. Purchasers may use their own scannable answer sheets. The test is nonsecure; it is administered and scored by educational institutions or researchers who have purchased the test for use within their institution.
Author: The University of Michigan.
Publisher: Cambridge-Michigan Language Assessments.
Cross References: For a review by Thomas P. Hogan, see 15:151.

[1696]

Michigan English Language Institute College English Test–Listening.

Purpose: "To provide educational institutions and researchers with information about the English language competencies of their own students, employees, or research participants."
Population: Adult nonnative speakers of English.
Publication Date: 2003.
Acronym: MELICET-L.
Scores: Total score only.
Administration: Group.
Forms, 2: A1, B1.
Restricted Distribution: Distribution restricted to authorized educational institutions and researchers.
Price Data: The complete testing package includes 20 test booklets, 100 answer sheets, stencil, and a user's manual (16 pages); specify Form A1 or B1; prices for each package are available from the publisher.
Time: 45 minutes.
Comments: All items are in a multiple-choice format. Items are scored by punched stencil. Purchasers may use their own scannable answer sheets. The test is nonsecure; it is administered and scored by educational institutions or researchers who have purchased the test for use within their institution.
Author: The University of Michigan.
Publisher: Cambridge-Michigan Language Assessments.
Cross References: For reviews by Marsha Bensoussan and by Catherine P. Cook-Cottone and Jennifer Piccolo and by Alan Garfinkel, see 16:148.

[1697]

Michigan English Test.

Purpose: Designed to assess "general English language proficiency" by measuring "listening, reading, grammar, and vocabulary skills in personal, public, occupational, and educational contexts."
Population: Adolescents and adults at or above a secondary level of education.
Publication Dates: 2009-2011.
Acronym: MET.
Scores, 3: Section I: Listening, Section II: Reading and Grammar, Final Score.
Administration: Group.
Forms: 11 forms per year, one per month excluding December.
Price Data: Available from publisher.
Time: (135) minutes.
Comments: A paper-and-pencil test that is administered monthly, except December, only at authorized test centers.
Author: The University of Michigan.
Publisher: Cambridge-Michigan Language Assessments.

[1698]

MicroCog: Assessment of Cognitive Functioning.

Purpose: "Assesses important neurocognitive functions in adults."
Population: Ages 18–89.
Publication Dates: 1993–2004.
Scores: 9 areas: Attention/Mental Control, Memory, Reasoning/Calculation, Spatial Processing, Reaction Time, Information Processing Accuracy, Information Processing Speed, General Cognitive Functioning, General Cognitive Proficiency.
Administration: Individual.
Price Data, 2006: $235 per complete kit including manual (1993, 106 pages, user's guide (2004, 94 pages), CD-ROM Windows software with booklet insert, and 10 report credits; $155 per 10 report credits; bulk discounts available for report credits.
Time: (50–60) minutes for Standard form; (30) minutes for Brief form.
Comments: Computer administered and scored.
Authors: Douglas Powell, Edith Kaplan, Dean Whitla, Sandra Weintraub, Randolph Catlin, and Harris Funkenstein.
Publisher: Pearson.
Cross References: For reviews by Charles J. Long and Stephanie L. Cutlan and by Cynthia A. Rohrbeck, see 13:199.

[1699]

The MIDAS: Multiple Intelligences Developmental Assessment Scales [Revised].

Purpose: "A self-report designed to provide an objective measure of the multiple intelligences using a process approach."

Publication Dates: 1994-2007.
Acronym: MIDAS.
Administration: Group or individual.
Price Data, 2011: $250 per Professional kit including MIDAS Questionnaire (select 2 age groups-reproducible), 50 MIDAS Profiles (pre-paid bulk scoring), The MIDAS: A Professional Manual (rev ed., 2007, 136 pages), and 1 interpretative workbook (reproducible); $350 per Classroom kit including MIDAS Questionnaire (select 1 age group-reproducible), 100 MIDAS Profiles (bulk pre-paid mail-in scoring included), The MIDAS Teacher's Handbook, Common Miracles in Your School, Select 1 of the two (2) reproducible workbooks above, 1 hour technical support, and discount bulk scoring rate; $900 per Guidance kit including MIDAS Questionnaires for Teens and Adults (reproducible), 200 MIDAS Profiles (pre-paid bulk scoring), The MIDAS: Professional Manual, The Challenge! Guide to Career Development, Student High Impact Project (SHIP) reproducible, and 1 hour technical support; $2,500 per School kit including MIDAS Questionnaires for 2 age groups-reproducible, bulk scoring for 1,000 profiles, on-site DOS scoring program (upon request during checkout), The MIDAS: A Professional Manual, Common Miracles in Your School (bulk pricing available), Student High Impact Project (SHIP) (reproducible), Teacher's Handbook for MI in the Classroom (bulk pricing available), Stepping Stones: A Teacher's Workbook (reproducible), Stepping Stones: Student Workbook for MI (reproducible), The Challenge! Guide to Career Success (reproducible), 2 hours on-site training (plus travel expenses), and 3 hours of telephone (free), Discounted Bulk Scoring Rate; $500 per Staff Development kit including MIDAS Questionnaire for adults (reproducible), 100 MIDAS Profiles (pre-paid bulk scoring), Teacher's Handbook: Multiple Intelligences in the Classroom, Common Miracles in Your School, Stepping Stones Workbook for Teachers (reproducible), 1 hour of technical support, Staff Development Packet (reproducible)-forthcoming, inquire; $40 per MIDAS preview package including 3 profiles, 1 book, interpretative packet, and Teacher's Handbook for MI in the Classroom; $45 per Teacher's Profile Package including Teacher's Handbook for MI in the Classroom, Common Miracles in Your School, and 1 MIDAS Adult Profile; $150 per The Basic Research kit, 100 MIDAS profiles, Professional Manual or Teacher's Handbook, Brief Interpretative Packet, data imported into database (either SPSS or Excel database-upon request), and 1 workbook (upon request); $300 per 100 MIDAS Profiles (with kit purchase); $400 per 100 MIDAS Profiles (without kit purchase); $100 per MIDAS Database; $7 per MIDAS Personal Profile (with purchase of book or package); $15 per MIDAS profile (bulk discounts available); $20 per Teacher's Handbook: Multiple Intelligences in the Classroom; $40 per The MIDAS: A Professional Manual (rev ed.).
Foreign Language Editions: Korean (MIDAS-K) and Chinese (C-MIDAS) and Danish (MIDAS-DK);

research editions available: Greek, Dutch, Singaporean, Spanish, Malaysian, Romanian, Farsi, Arabic, Turkish, Icelandic, and Bahasa.
Time: (25-35) minutes via self-completion using Online MIDAS System (OMS) or paper questionnaire; (60-90) minutes via structured interview.
Comments: This assessment can be administered via self-completion or as a structured interview; can be completed by an individual who is close to the subject; parents complete the MIDAS-KIDS: My Young Child version; the web-based administrative system automatically scores the responses and returns the profile via email within minutes.
Author: C. Branton Shearer.
Publisher: Multiple Intelligences Research and Consulting, Inc.

a) MIDAS.
Population: Ages 20 and up.
Scores: 11 scales and 26 subscales: Basic Scales: Musical (Appreciation, Vocal Ability, Instrumental Skill, Composing), Kinesthetic (Athletics, Dexterity), Logical-Mathematical (Strategy Games, Everyday Skills with Math, Everyday Problem Solving, School Math), Spatial (Spatial Awareness, Artistic Design, Working with Objects), Linguistic (Rhetorical Skill, Expressive Sensitivity, Written/Academic Ability), Interpersonal (Social Sensitivity, Social Persuasion, Interpersonal Work), Intrapersonal (Personal Knowledge/Efficacy, Self/Other Efficacy, Calculations, Spatial Problem-Solving), Naturalist (Animal Care, Plant Care, Science), Intellectual Style Scales: Leadership (Social Adeptness, Communication Skill, Managerial Skill), Innovation (Musical, Kinesthetic, Logical-Mathematical, Spatial, Linguistic, Interpersonal, Intrapersonal), General Logic (Logical-Mathematical, Spatial, Interpersonal, Intrapersonal).
b) TEEN-MIDAS.
Population: Ages 15-19.
Scores: Same as *a* above.
c) MIDAS-KIDS: ALL ABOUT ME.
Population: Ages 9-14.
Scores: 10 scales and 24 subscales: Basic Scales: Musical (Musicality, Vocal, Appreciation, Instrument), Kinesthetic (Physical Ability, Dance, Working with Hands), Logical-Mathematical (Problem Solving, Calculations), Spatial (Artistic, Constructions, Imagery), Linguistic (Linguistic Sensitivity, Writing, Reading), Interpersonal (Leadership, Understanding People, Getting Along with Others), Intrapersonal (Self Knowledge, Managing Feelings, Effective Relationships, Goal Achievement), Naturalist (Animal Care, Earth Science), Intellectual Style Scales: Technical, Innovative.
d) MIDAS-KIDS: MY YOUNG CHILD.
Population: Ages 5-9.
Scores: Same as *c* above, except without Intellectual Style Scales.

Cross References: For reviews by Robert W. Hiltonsmith and W. Joel Schneider, see 17:123; for reviews by Abbot Packard and Michael S. Trevisan of an earlier version, see 14:234.

[1700]

The Middle Infant Screening Test.

Purpose: Designed to screen for reading and writing difficulties in first year school children.
Population: Ages 5-8 and over.
Publication Date: 1993.
Acronym: MIST.
Scores, 5: Listening Skills, Letter Sounds, Written Vocabulary, Three-Phoneme Words, Sentence Dictation.
Administration: Group.
Price Data: Available from publisher.
Time: (50–60) minutes.
Comments: "Criterion referenced"; designed for use with the Forward Together skills recovery program.
Author: Sybil Hannavy.
Publisher: GL Assessment [England].

[1701]

The Middlesex Elderly Assessment of Mental State.

Purpose: "Developed as a screening test to detect gross impairment of specific cognitive skills in the elderly."
Population: Adults.
Publication Date: 1989.
Acronym: MEAMS.
Scores, 12: Orientation, Name Learning, Naming, Comprehension, Remembering Pictures, Arithmetic, Spatial Construction, Fragmented Letter Perception, Unusual Views, Usual Views, Verbal Fluency, Motor Perseveration.
Administration: Individual.
Forms, 2: Version A, Version B.
Price Data, 2006: £175 per complete kit including manual (14 pages), 25 scoring sheets, and 2 stimulus books; £33.50 per 50 scoring sheets.
Time: [10] minutes.
Author: Evelyn Golding.
Publisher: Pearson Assessment [England].
Cross References: For reviews by Stephen J. Freeman and Matthew E. Lambert, see 17:124.

[1702]

Milani-Comparetti Motor Development Screening Test.

Purpose: "The test provides the clinician with a synopsis of the child's motor development by systematically examining the integration of primitive reflexes and the emergence of volitional movement against gravity."
Population: Ages 1–16 months.

Publication Dates: 1977–1992.
Scores, 27: Body Lying Supine, Hand Grasp, Foot Grasp, Supine Equilibrium, Body Pulled Up From Supine, Sitting Posture, Sitting Equilibrium, Sideways Parachute, Backward Parachute, Body Held Vertical, Head Righting, Downward Parachute, Standing, Standing Equilibrium, Locomotion, Landau Response, Forward Parachute, Body Lying Prone, Prone Equilibrium, All Fours, All Fours Equilibrium, Symmetric Tonic Neck Reflex, Body Derotative, Standing Up From Supine, Body Rotative, Asymmetrical Tonic Neck Reflex, Moro Reflex.
Administration: Individual.
Price Data: Price data for test including manual (1992, 48 pages) available from publisher.
Time: (10–15) minutes.
Comments: Behavior checklist.
Authors: Wayne Stuberg (Project Director), Pam Dehne, Jim Miedaner, and Penni White (Content Consultants).
Publisher: Munroe-Meyer Institute for Genetics & Rehabilitation.
Cross References: See T5:1668 (1 reference); for reviews by Linda K. Bunker and Ruth E. Tomes, see 11:236.

[1703]

MILCOM Patient Data Base System.

Purpose: Designed to record a patient's medical history.
Population: Medical patients.
Publication Dates: 1971–1985.
Scores: Item scores only.
Administration: Individual.
Manual: No manual.
Price Data: Available from publisher.
Foreign Language Edition: Spanish version available.
Time: Administration time not reported.
Comments: Questionnaire includes health questionnaire and 18-part physical exam.
Author: MILCOM Systems, A Division of Hollister, Inc.
Publisher: MILCOM Systems, A Division of Hollister, Inc.

[1704]

Military Environment Inventory.

Purpose: "Asesses the social environment of varied types of military contexts."
Population: Military personnel.
Publication Date: 1986.
Acronym: MEIN.
Scores, 7: Involvement, Peer Cohesion, Officer Support, Personal Status, Order and Organization, Clarity, Officer Control.
Administration: Group.
Forms, 4: Real Form (Form R), Short Form (Form S), Ideal Form (Form I), Expectations Form (Form E).

Price Data: Available from publisher at www.mind-garden.com/products/meins.htm.
Time: Administration time not reported.
Comments: One of 10 Social Climate Scales.
Author: Rudolf H. Moos.
Publisher: Mind Garden, Inc.
Cross References: For reviews by David O. Herman and Alfred L. Smith, Jr., see 11:237 (1 reference).

[1705]

Mill Hill Vocabulary Scale.

Purpose: Provides a measure of acquired verbal knowledge.
Population: Ages 6.5-16.5, Ages 18–adult.
Publication Dates: 1943–1998.
Acronym: MHV.
Scores: Total score only.
Administration: Group or individual.
Forms, 2: A, B.
Price Data: Price information available from publisher for test booklets and for specimen set including one of each test booklet, scoring key, and appropriate sections of the Raven's manuals (Section 1–1998, 119 pages; Section 5–1998, 124 pages).
Time: (15–40) minutes.
Comments: To be used in conjunction with the Raven's Progressive Matrices (2233); short-form also available.
Authors: J. C. Raven, J. H. Court, and J. Raven.
Publisher: Oxford Psychologists Press, Ltd. [England]
   a) JUNIOR.
      Population: Ages 6.5–16.5.
   b) SENIOR.
      Population: Ages 18–adult.
Cross References: See T5:1671 (8 references); for reviews by Theodore L. Hayes and William K. Wilkinson, see 13:200 (30 references); see also T4:1629 (51 reference), 9:705 (8 references), T3:1485 (29 references), and T2:402 (32 references); for a review by Morton Bortner of an earlier edition, see 6:471 (16 references); see also 4:303 (7 references); for a review by David Wechsler, see 3:239 (3 references).

[1706]

Miller Analogies Test.

Purpose: Measures background knowledge and analytical abilities critical to the commencement of study in graduate school.
Population: Graduate school applicants.
Publication Dates: 1926–2006.
Acronym: MAT.
Scores: Total score only.
Administration: Group or individual.
Price Data: Available from publisher.
Time: 60 minutes.
Comments: Paper-and-pencil or computer-based, on-demand.
Author: Harcourt Assessment, Inc.

Publisher: Pearson.
Cross References: See T5:1672 (5 references); for reviews by Robert B. Frary and Stephen H. Ivens, see 12:235 (2 references); see also T4:1630 (1 reference), T3:1486 (16 references), 8:192 (31 references), T2:404 (15 references), and 7:363 (57 references); for reviews by Lloyd G. Humphreys, William B. Schrader, and Warren W. Willingham, see 6:472 (26 references); for a review by John T. Dailey, see 5:352 (28 references); for reviews by J. P. Guilford and Cart I. Hovland, see 4:304 (16 references).

[1707]

Miller Assessment for Preschoolers.

Purpose: Designed "to identify children who exhibit moderate 'preacademic' problems."
Population: Ages 2-9 to 5-8.
Publication Date: 1982.
Acronym: MAP.
Scores, 6: Foundations, Coordination, Verbal, Non-Verbal, Complex Tasks, Total.
Administration: Individual.
Levels: 6 developmental levels (ages 2-9 to 3-2, 3-3 to 3-8, 3-9 to 4-2, 4-3 to 4-8, 4-9 to 5-2, 5-3 to 5-8).
Price Data, 2002: $695 per complete kit including manual (220 pages), score sheets, and all items needed for administration and scoring; $100 per examiner's manual; $299 per training tape; $99 per training tape rental; $72 per workshop set; $36 per 6 cue sheets; $34 per 25 score sheets; $34 per 25 drawing booklets; $34 per 25 record booklets.
Time: (20–30) minutes.
Author: Lucy Jane Miller.
Publisher: Pearson.
Cross References: See T5:1673 (11 references) and T4:1631 (6 references); for reviews by Dennis J. Deloria and William B. Michael, see 9:706.

[1708]

Miller Common Sense Scale.

Purpose: "Designed to permit the individual to compare his/her level of common sense with other individuals … and to determine changes that should be made as a result of this information."
Population: Ages 15 to adult.
Publication Date: 1997.
Scores: Total score only.
Administration: Group.
Price Data, 2001: $35 per administration via webpage (Visa or MasterCard are required to use this test).
Time: (15) minutes.
Comments: Administered and scored on the internet; printout of results is provided. [Editor's note: Since November 2002, the webpage for administration of this test has been unavailable.]
Author: Harold J. Miller.

Publisher: Meta Development LLC [Canada] [No reply from publisher; status unknown].
Cross References: For a review by Carl Isenhart, see 15:152.

[1709]
Miller Depression Scale.
Purpose: Designed to "measure an individual's depression level."
Population: Ages 15 years and over.
Publication Date: 1997.
Scores: Total score only.
Administration: Individual or group.
Manual: No manual.
Price Data, 2001: $35 per administration via webpage (Visa or MasterCard are required to use this test).
Time: (15) minutes.
Comments: "Designed to be given and scored over the internet"; printout of results provided; can be used to monitor treatment effectiveness. [Editor's note: Since November 2002, the webpage for administration of this test has been unavailable.]
Author: Harold J. Miller.
Publisher: Meta Development LLC [Canada] [No reply from publisher; status unknown].
Cross References: For a review by Cederick O. Lindskog, see 15:153.

[1710]
Miller Emotional Maturity Scale.
Purpose: Designed to "measure the individual's emotional maturity."
Population: Adults with reading levels at 7th grade or above.
Publication Date: 1991.
Scores, 8: Secure, Stable, Independent, Optimistic, Responsible, Assertive, Social, Honest.
Administration: Individual or group.
Manual: No manual.
Price Data, 2001: $35 per administration via webpage (Visa or MasterCard are required to use this test).
Time: (30–45) minutes.
Comments: "Designed to be administered and scored on the internet"; printout of results is provided. [Editor's note: Since November 2002, the webpage for administration of this test has been unavailable.]
Author: Harold J. Miller.
Publisher: Meta Development LLC [Canada] [No reply from publisher; status unknown].
Cross References: For reviews by Robert J. Drummond and Jeffrey A. Jenkins, see 15:154.

[1711]
Miller Forensic Assessment of Symptoms Test.
Purpose: Designed to "provide information regarding the probability that an individual is malingering psychiatric illness."
Population: Ages 18 and over.
Publication Dates: 1995–2001.
Acronym: M-FAST.
Scores, 8: Reported vs. Observed, Extreme Symptomatology, Rare Combinations, Unusual Hallucinations, Unusual Symptom Course, Negative Image, Suggestibility, Total.
Administration: Individual.
Price Data, 2006: $135 per introductory kit including professional manual and 25 interview booklets.
Time: (5–10) minutes.
Author: Holly A. Miller.
Publisher: Psychological Assessment Resources, Inc.
Cross References: For reviews by Marc Janoson and by Nathaniel J. Pallone and James J. Hennessy, see 15:155.

[1712]
Miller Function and Participation Scales.
Purpose: Designed "to determine if a child has a developmental delay in the functional motor abilities needed to participate in early school years."
Population: Ages 2.6-7.11.
Publication Date: 2006.
Acronym: M-FUN.
Administration: Individual.
Parts, 2: Performance Assessment, Participation Assessment.
Price Data, 2008: $369 per complete kit with manipulatives.
Time: (40-60) minutes.
Author: Lucy J. Miller.
Publisher: Pearson.
a) PERFORMANCE ASSESSMENT.
Levels, 3: Ages 2.6-3.11, Ages 4.0-5.11, Ages 6.0-7.11.
Forms, 2: Ages 2.6-3.11, Ages 4.0-7.11.
1) Ages 2.6-3.11.
Scores, 21: Follow the Path, Flying Birds, Clouds, Hidden Forks, Find the Rabbits, Copying Shapes, Writing, Visual Motor Behavior Rating, Clay Play, Penny Bank, Origami, Snack Time, Fine Motor Behavior Rating, Statue, Throw and Catch, Soccer, Jumping, Gross Motor Behavior Rating, Visual Motor, Fine Motor, Gross Motor.
2) Ages 4.0-5.11.
Scores, 22: Amazing Mazes, Race Car, Hidden Forks, Find the Puppies, Draw a Kid, Writing, Go Fishing (1-4), Visual Motor Behavior Rating, Go Fishing (5-7), Clay Play, Penny Bank, Origami, Snack Time, Fine Motor Behavior Rating, Statue, Ball Balance, Soccer, Jumping, Gross Motor Behavior Rating, Visual Motor, Fine Motor, Gross Motor.
3) Ages 6.0-7.11.
Scores, 23: Amazing Mazes, Race Car, Hidden Forks, Find the Puppies, Draw a

Kid, Writing, Go Fishing (1-4), Visual Motor Behavior Rating, Go Fishing (5-7), Clay Play, Penny Bank, Origami, Snack Time, Fine Motor Behavior Rating, Statue, Ball Balance, Bouncing Ball, Soccer, Jumping, Gross Motor Behavior Rating, Visual Motor, Fine Motor, Gross Motor.
b) PARTICIPATION ASSESSMENT.
Scores, 3: Home Observations, Classroom Observations, Test Observations.
Population: Ages 2.6-7.11.
Cross References: For reviews by Abigail Baxter and C. Dale Carpenter, see 18:74.

[1713]

Miller Getting Along With People Scale.

Purpose: "Designed to help individuals determine how well they get along with other people."
Population: Ages 15 to adult.
Publication Date: 1996.
Scores: Total score only.
Administration: Group.
Price Data, 2001: $35 per administration via webpage (Visa or MasterCard are required to use this test).
Time: (15) minutes.
Comments: Administered and scored on the internet; printout of results provided. [Editor's note: Since November 2002, the webpage for administration of this test has been unavailable.]
Author: Harold J. Miller.
Publisher: Meta Development LLC [Canada] [No reply from publisher; status unknown].
Cross References: For reviews by Albert M. Bugaj and Jean Powell Kirnan, see 15:156.

[1714]

Miller Happiness Scale.

Purpose: "Designed to measure eight areas of an individual's happiness."
Population: Grade 7 reading level or higher.
Publication Date: 1998.
Scores, 8: Personal Happiness, Health Happiness, Spiritual Happiness, Intimate Relationship Happiness, Family Happiness, Friendship Happiness, Work Happiness, Leisure Happiness.
Administration: Group.
Price Data, 2001: $35 per administration via webpage (Visa or MasterCard are required to use this test).
Time: (30–45) minutes.
Comments: Administered and scored on the internet; printout of results is provided. [Editor's note: Since November 2002, the webpage for administration of this test has been unavailable.]
Author: Harold J. Miller.
Publisher: Meta Development LLC [Canada] [No reply from publisher; status unknown].

Cross References: For reviews by Julie A. Allison and Raoul A. Arreola, see 15:157.

[1715]

Miller Love Scale.

Purpose: "Designed to measure eight areas of love."
Population: Ages 16 to adult.
Publication Date: 1998.
Scores, 8: Self-Love, Love Motivation, Value, Perception of Partner, Love Thoughts, Love Feelings, Love Behavior, Spiritual Love.
Administration: Group.
Price Data, 2001: $35 per administration via webpage (Visa or MasterCard are required to use this test).
Time: (30–45) minutes.
Comments: Administered and scored on the internet; printout of results is provided. [Editor's note: Since November 2002, the webpage for administration of this test has been unavailable.]
Author: Harold J. Miller.
Publisher: Meta Development LLC [Canada] [No reply from publisher; status unknown].
Cross References: For reviews by Jill Ann Jenkins and S. Alvin Leung, see 15:158.

[1716]

Miller Marriage Satisfaction Rating Scale.

Purpose: "Designed to compare one's level of marriage satisfaction to the marriage satisfaction of other married people."
Population: Individuals who are dating, living together or who are married.
Publication Date: 1997.
Scores: Total score only.
Administration: Group.
Price Data, 2001: $35 per administration via web page (Visa or MasterCard are required to use this test).
Time: (15) minutes.
Comments: Administered and scored on the internet; online documentation lists as Miller Marriage Satisfaction Scale but test itself is entitled Miller Marriage Satisfaction Rating Scale; printout of results is provided. [Editor's Note: Since November 2002, the webpage for administration of this test has been unavailable.]
Author: Harold J. Miller.
Publisher: Meta Development LCC [Canada] [No reply from publisher; status unknown].
Cross References: For reviews by Frank M. Bernt and Cindy I. Carlson, see 15:159.

[1717]

Miller Motivation Scale.

Purpose: "Designed to measure positive and negative aspects of the individual's motivation."
Population: Individuals who have a grade seven reading level or greater.

Publication Dates: 1986–1988.

Scores, 8: Creative, Innovative, Productive, Cooperative, Attention, Power, Revenge, Give-Up.

Administration: Group.

Price Data, 2001: $35 per administration via webpage (Visa or MasterCard are required to use this test).

Time: (30–45) minutes.

Comments: Administered and scored on the internet; printout of results is provided. [Editor's note: Since November 2002, the webpage for administration of this test has been unavailable.]

Author: Harold J. Miller.

Publisher: Meta Development LLC [Canada] [No reply from publisher; status unknown].

Cross References: For a review by Michael J. Roszkowski, see 15:160.

[1718]

Miller Psychological Independence Scale.

Purpose: Designed to "measure the individual's psychological independence in a dependent-independent continuum."

Population: High school students and athletes.

Publication Date: 1996.

Scores, 8: Independent Behavior, Independence in Relationships, Perfection, Effectiveness, Egocentric, Independent Thoughts, Independent Feelings, Control.

Administration: Group.

Price Data, 2001: $35 per administration via webpage (Visa or MasterCard are required to use this test).

Time: (30–45) minutes.

Comments: "Designed to be given on the internet"; results immediately available in a six-page printout. [Editor's note: Since November 2002, the webpage for administration of this test has been unavailable.]

Author: Harold J. Miller.

Publisher: Meta Development LLC [Canada] [No reply from publisher; status unknown].

Cross References: For a review by Brian F. Bolton, see 15:161.

[1719]

Miller Self-Concept Scale.

Purpose: Designed to "measure components of the individual's self-concept."

Population: Individuals with a seventh-grade or higher reading level.

Publication Date: 1989.

Scores, 8: Intrapsychic, Family, Friendship Self-Concept, Work/School Self-Concept, Locus of Control, Attribution, Courage, Flexibility.

Administration: Group.

Price Data, 2001: $35 per administration via webpage (Visa or MasterCard are required to use this test).

Time: (30–45) minutes.

Comments: "Designed to be given and scored on the internet"; results are immediately available in a six-page printout. [Editor's note: Since November 2002, the webpage for administration of this test has been unavailable.]

Author: Harold J. Miller.

Publisher: Meta Development LLC [Canada] [No reply from publisher; status unknown].

Cross References: For reviews by Trenton R. Ferro and Judith A. Rein, see 15:162.

[1720]

Miller Stress Scale.

Purpose: "Designed to measure the individual's stress in several areas of the individual's life."

Population: Individuals with reading level at or above the 7th grade.

Publication Date: 1992.

Scores, 8: Stressful Behavior, Relationship Stress, Family Stress, Work Stress, Physical Stress, Stressful Thoughts, Stressful Feelings, Coping.

Administration: Group.

Price Data, 2001: $35 per administration via webpage (Visa or MasterCard are required to use this test).

Time: (30–45) minutes.

Comments: "Designed to be given and scored on the internet"; results are available immediately in a six-page printout. [Editor's note: Since November 2002, the webpage for administration of this test has been unavailable.]

Author: Harold J. Miller.

Publisher: Meta Development LLC [Canada] [No reply from publisher; status unknown].

Cross References: For a review by Michael J. Scheel and Brad M. Merker, see 15:163.

[1721]

Millon Adolescent Clinical Inventory.

Purpose: Designed to assess "an adolescent's personality, along with self-reported concerns and clinical syndromes."

Population: Ages 13–19.

Publication Date: 1993.

Acronym: MACI.

Scores, 27: Personality Patterns (Introversive, Inhibited, Doleful, Submissive, Dramatizing, Egotistic, Unruly, Forceful, Conforming, Oppositional, Self-Demeaning, Borderline Tendency), Expressed Concerns (Identify Diffusion, Self-Devaluation, Body Disapproval, Sexual Discomfort, Peer Insecurity, Social Insensitivity, Family Discord, Childhood Abuse), Clinical Syndromes (Eating Dysfunctions, Substance Abuse Proneness, Delinquent Predisposition, Impulsive Propensity, Anxious Feelings, Depressive Affect, Suicidal Tendency), and 3 Modifying Indices (Disclosure, Desirability, Debasement).

Administration: Individual or group.

Price Data, 2008: $103 per computer (Q Local) starter kit including manual (123 pages), 3 answer sheets with test items, and three interpretive report administrations; $25 per individual computer interpretive report administrations (quantity discounts available); $350 per hand-scoring starter kit including manual, hand-scoring user's guide, 10 test booklets, 50 answer sheets, 50 profile forms, and answer keys; $53.50 per audio CD; $43 per manual; price data for Spanish materials available from publisher.

Foreign Language Edition: Spanish materials available.

Time: (25-30) minutes.

Comments: Self-report personality inventory; paper-and-pencil and on-line administration available; computer (Q Local), mail-in scoring, and hand-scoring options; available in profile and interpretive report formats; Facet scales also available, contact publisher for details.

Authors: Theodore Millon, Carrie Millon, Roger Davis, and Seth Grossman.

Publisher: Pearson.

Cross References: See T5:1685 (2 references); for reviews by Paul Retzlaff and Richard B. Stuart, see 12:236 (6 references); see also T4:1633 (14 references); for reviews by Douglas T. Brown and Thomas A. Widiger of the Millon Adolescent Personality Inventory, see 9:707.

[1722]

Millon Adolescent Personality Inventory.

Purpose: Designed to assess an adolescent's personality.

Population: Ages 13-18.

Publication Dates: 1976-1982.

Acronym: MAPI.

Scores: 20 scales: Personality Styles (Introversive, Inhibited, Cooperative, Sociable, Confident, Forceful, Respectful, Sensitive) Expressed Concerns (Self-Concept, Personal Esteem, Body Comfort, Sexual Acceptance, Peer Security, Social Tolerance, Family Rapport, Academic Confidence) Behavioral Correlates (Impulse Control, Social Conformity, Scholastic Achievement, Attendance Consistency).

Administration: Group or individual.

Price Data, 2008: $112 per Computer (Q Local) starter kit, including manual, 3 answer sheets, 1 test booklet, and three report administrations; $27.50 per individual computer interpretive report administrations (quantity discounts available; hand-scoring not available); $53.50 per audio CD; $44 per manual; price data for Spanish materials available from publisher.

Time: (20-30) minutes.

Authors: Theodore Millon, Catherine J. Green, and Robert B. Meagher, Jr.

Comments: Self-report personality inventory; paper-and-pencil and online administration available; computer (Q Local), mail-in scoring, and hand-scoring options.

Publisher: Pearson.

Cross References: For reviews by Douglas T. Brown and Thomas A. Widiger, see 9:707.

[1723]

Millon Behavioral Medicine Diagnostic.

Purpose: Designed to "assess psychological factors that can influence the course of treatment of medically ill patients ... especially for patients in which psychosocial factors may play a role in the course of the disease and treatment outcome."

Population: Clinical and rehabilitation patients ages 18–85.

Publication Date: 2001.

Acronym: MBMD.

Scores, 39: Validity Indicator, Response Patterns (Disclosure, Desirability, Debasement), Negative Health Habits (Alcohol, Drug, Eating, Caffeine, Inactivity, Smoking), Psychiatric Indications (Anxiety-Tension, Depression, Cognitive Dysfunction, Emotional Lability, Guardedness), Coping Styles (Introversion, Inhibited, Dejected, Cooperative, Sociable, Confident, Nonconforming, Forceful, Respectful, Oppositional, Denigrated), Stress Moderators (Illness Apprehension, Functional Deficits, Pain Sensitivity, Social Isolation, Future Pessimism, Spiritual Absence), Treatment Prognostics (Interventional Fragility, Medication Abuse, Information Discomfort, Utilization Excess, Problematic Compliance), Management Guides (Adjustment Difficulties, Psych Referral).

Administration: Individual or group.

Price Data, 2006: $110 per Q Local starter kit with interpretive reports including manual, softcover test booklet, 3 answer sheets with test items to conduct and receive 3 interpretive Q Local administrations; $21 per 25 Q Local answer sheets with test items; $51 per manual (183 pages); $51 per compact disc; $24.50 per Q Local interpretive report; $16.75 per Q Local profile report; $117 per mail-in scoring service starter kit with interpretive reports including manual, softcover test booklet, 3 answer sheets with test items to conduct 3 assessments and receive 3 interpretive reports using mail-in socring service; $27.50 per mail-in interpretive report (test items and answer sheets included); $19.75 per mail-in profile reports (test items and answer sheets included); $337 per hand-scoring starter kit including manual, hand-scoring user's guide, 10 test booklets, 50 answer sheets, 50 worksheets, and 50 profile forms and answer keys; $28 per 10 hand-scoring test booklets; $19 per 25 large print answer sheets; quantity discounts available; price information for Spanish materials available from publisher.

Foreign Language Edition: Available in Spanish.

Time: (20–25) minutes.

Comments: Upgrading of the Millon Behavioral Health Inventory (T5:1686); self-administered; may be administered in paper-and pencil format, via computer, or via audiocassette; interpretive reports with healthcare provider summary and profile available; scoring options include handscoring, mail-in, Q Local Assessment System software.

Authors: Theodore Millon, Michael Antoni, Carrie Millon, Sarah Minor, and Seth Grossman.

Publisher: Pearson.

Cross References: For reviews by Mark J. Atkinson and John C. Caruso, see 15:164; for information regarding the original Millon Behavioral Health Inventory, see T5:1686 (7 references) and T4:1634 (6 references); for reviews of the Millon Behavioral Health Inventory by Mary J. Allen and Richard I. Lanyon, see 9:708 (1 reference).

[1724]

Millon Clinical Multiaxial Inventory–III [Manual Third Edition].

Purpose: Designed to provide diagnostic and treatment information to clinicians in the areas of personality disorders and clinical syndromes.

Population: Individuals 18 years and older.

Publication Dates: 1976–2006.

Acronym: MCMI-III.

Scores, 28: Modifying Indices (Disclosure, Desirability, Debasement, Validity), Clinical Personality Patterns (Schizoid, Avoidant, Depressive, Dependent, Histrionic, Narcissistic, Antisocial, Sadistic [Aggressive], Compulsive, Negativistic [Passive-Aggressive], Masochistic [Self-Defeating]), Severe Personality Pathology (Schizotypal, Borderline, Paranoid), Clinical Syndromes (Anxiety, Somatoform, Bipolar: Manic, Dysthymia, Alcohol Dependence, Drug Dependence, Post-Traumatic Stress Disorder), Severe Clinical Syndromes (Thought Disorder, Major Depression, Delusional Disorder).

Administration: Individual or group.

Price Data, 2008: Clinical Report pricing: $141 per Computer (Q_Local) Starter Kit including manual, 3 answer sheets, 1 test booklet, and three report administrations; $36 per Individual computer interpretive report administrations (quantity discounts available); $351 per hand-scoring starter kit including manual, hand-scoring user's guide, 10 test booklets, 50 answer sheets, 50 worksheets, 50 profile forms and answer keys; Corrections Report pricing: $150 per Computer (Q_Local) Starter Kit including manual, 3 answer sheets, 1 test booklet, and three report administrations; $33.50 per Individual computer interpretive report administrations (quantity discounts available, hand-scoring not available); $53.50 per Audio CD; $52 per manual; price data for Spanish materials available from publisher.

Foreign Language Edition: Spanish materials available.

Time: 25-30 minutes.

Comments: Designed to coordinate with DSM-IV categories of clinical syndromes and personality disorders; revision of the Millon Clinical Multiaxial Inventory—III (13:201); includes optional Corrections Report for use with correctional inmates; self-report personality inventory; paper-and-pencil and on-line administration available; Computer (Q_Local), mail-in scoring, and hand-scoring options; available in profile and interpretive report formats; Facet scales also available (contact publisher for details).

Authors: Theodore Millon, Roger Davis, Carrie Millon, and Seth Grossman.

Publisher: Pearson.

Cross References: For reviews by James P. Choca and Thomas A. Widiger, see 14:236; see also T5:1687 (47 references); for reviews by Allen K. Hess and Paul Retzlaff of the third edition, see 13:201 (81 references); see also T4:1635 (104 references); for reviews by Thomas M. Haladyna and Cecil R. Reynolds of the second edition, see 11:239 (74 references); for reviews by Allen K. Hess and Thomas A. Widiger of the original edition, see 9:709 (1 reference); see also T3:1488 (3 references).

[1725]

Millon College Counseling Inventory.

Purpose: Designed to "help counselors identify, predict, and understand a broad range of psychological issues that are common among college students seen primarily in college counseling settings."

Population: College students ages 16-40.

Publication Date: 2006.

Acronym: MCCI.

Scores, 36: Personality Style Scales (Introverted, Inhibited, Dejected, Needy, Sociable, Confident, Unruly, Conscientious, Oppositional, Denigrated), Severe Personality Tendencies Scale (Borderline), Expressed Concerns Scales (Mental Health Upset, Identity Quandaries, Family Disquiet, Peer Alienation, Romantic Distress, Academic Concerns, Career Confusion, Abusive Experiences, Living Arrangement Problems, Financial Burdens, Spiritual Doubts), Clinical Signs Scales (Suicidal Tendencies, Depressive Outlook, Anxiety/Tension, Post-Traumatic Stress, Eating Disorders, Anger Dyscontrol, Attention [Cognitive] Deficits, Obsessions/Compulsions, Alcohol Abuse, Drug Abuse), Response Tendency Scales (Validity, Disclosure, Desirability, Debasement), plus 7 Noteworthy Responses (Risky Behaviors, Homesickness, Expectation Pressures, Escapist Distractions, Minority Prejudice, Somatic Concerns, Reality Distortions).

Administration: Group or individual.

Price Data, 2009: $206 per hand-scoring starter kit, including 50 answer sheets with test items, answer keys, and manual (2006, 115 pages); $46.50 per 50 answer sheets for hand-scoring; $53.50 per audio CD; $33.50 per manual; $66.50 per computer (Q-Local) starter kit, including manual, 3 answer sheets with test items, and 3 Q_Local administrations (does not include Q_Local software); $27.50 per 25 Q_Local answer sheets; $8 per administration for Q_Local interpretive report; $76.05 per mail-in starter kit with interpretive report including 3 answer sheets, manual, and all materials necessary to conduct 3 assessments and receive interpretive reports using the mail-in scoring service; $21 per mail-in interpretive report (price includes answer sheet and scoring).

Time: (20-25) minutes.

Comments: Self-report personality inventory; paper-and-pencil and on-line administration available; computer (Q_Local), mail-in scoring, and hand-scoring options.

Authors: Theodore Millon, Stephen N. Strack, Carrie Millon, and Seth Grossman.
Publisher: Pearson.
Cross References: For reviews by Mark A. Albanese and Georgia Hinman and by Andrew A. Cox, see 18:75.

[1726]

Millon Index of Personality Styles Revised.

Purpose: "Designed to measure personality styles of normally functioning adults."
Population: 18 years and older.
Publication Dates: 1994-2004.
Acronym: MIPS Revised.
Scores, 28: 6 Motivating Styles (Pleasure-Enhancing, Pain-Avoiding, Actively Modifying, Passively Accommodating, Self-Indulging, Other-Nurturing), 8 Thinking Styles (Externally Focused, Internally Focused, Realistic/Sensing, Imaginative/Intuiting, Thought-Guided, Feeling-Guided, Conservation-Seeking, Innovation-Seeking), 10 Behavior Styles (Asocial/Withdrawing, Gregarious/Outgoing, Anxious/Hesitating, Confident/Asserting, Unconventional/Dissenting, Dutiful/Conforming, Submissive/Yielding, Dominant/Controlling, Dissatisfied/Complaining, Cooperative/Agreeing), 3 Validity Indices (Positive Impression, Negative Impression, Consistency), Clinical Index.
Administration: Group or individual.
Form: 1 form with 2 reporting options: Interpretive, Profile.
Price Data, 2008: $43 per manual (2004, 176 pages); $183 per hand-scoring starter kit, including manual, 10 test booklets, 50 answer sheets, and answer keys; $90 per computer (Q Local) starter kit, including manual, 3 answer sheets, 1 test booklet, and three interpretive report administrations; $17.75 per individual computer interpretive report administrations (quantity discounts available).
Time: (25-30) minutes.
Comments: Self-report personality inventory; paper-and-pencil and on-line administration available; computer (Q Local), mail-in scoring, and hand-scoring options; available in profile and interpretive report formats.
Authors: Theodore Millon.
Publisher: Pearson.
Cross References: For reviews by S. Alvin Leung and David J. Pittenger, see 17:125; see also T5:1688 (1 reference); for reviews by James P. Choca and Peter Zachar of an earlier version, see 13:202.

[1727]

Millon Pre-Adolescent Clinical Inventory.

Purpose: To "identify, predict, and understand a broad range of psychological disorders that are common in 9-12 year olds seen in clinical settings."
Population: Ages 9-12.
Publication Date: 2005.
Acronym: M-PACI.

Scores: 16 scales: Emerging Personality Patterns (Confident, Outgoing, Conforming, Submissive, Inhibited, Unruly, Unstable), Current Clinical Signs (Anxiety/Fears, Attention Deficits, Obsessions/Compulsions, Conduct Disorder, Disruptive Behaviors, Depressive Moods, Reality Distortions), Response Validity Indicators (Invalidity, Response Negativity).
Administration: Individual or group.
Price Data, 2008: $220 per hand-scoring starter kit, including manual (115 pages), 50 answer sheets, 50 profile forms, and answer keys; $53.50 per audio CD; $40.50 per manual; $86.25 per computer (Q Local) starter kit, including manual, 3 answer sheets with test items, and three report administrations; $19.25 per individual computer report administrations (quantity discounts available).
Time: (15–20) minutes.
Comments: Self-report personality inventory; paper-and-pencil and on-line administration available; computer (Q Local), mail-in scoring, and hand-scoring options; available in profile and interpretive report formats.
Authors: Theodore Millon, Robert Tringone, Carrie Millon, and Seth Grossman.
Publisher: Pearson.
Cross References: For a review by Jeffrey A. Atlas and Steven I. Pfeiffer, see 17:126.

[1728]

The Milwaukee Evaluation of Daily Living Skills.

Purpose: "To assess basic daily living skills for use with the chronically mentally ill."
Population: Ages 18 and over.
Publication Date: 1989.
Acronym: MEDLS.
Scores, 20: Basic Communication Skills, Bathing, Brushing Teeth, Denture Care, Dressing, Eating, Eyeglass Care, Hair Care, Maintenance of Clothing, Make-up Use, Medication Management, Nail Care, Personal Health Care, Safety in Community, Safety in Home, Shaving, Time Awareness, Use of Money, Use of Telephone, Use of Transportation.
Administration: Individual.
Price Data: Available from publisher.
Time: (80) minutes.
Author: Carol A. Leonardelli.
Publisher: SLACK Incorporated.

[1729]

Mind Body Wellness Geriatric Rehabilitation and Restorative Assessment System.

Purpose: Designed to "assess pathology and general quality of life for residents who need assisted living or nursing home care based on their levels of behavioral, emotional, and illness symptoms."

Population: Ages 55 and up.
Publication Date: 2008.
Acronym: GRRAS.
Administration: Individual.
Scores: 3 subtests: Psychological Resistance to Activities of Daily Living Index, Geriatric Multidimensional Pain and Illness Inventory, Geriatric Level of Dysfunction Scale.
Price Data, 2009: $205 per introductory kit including professional manual (117 pages), 25 PRADLI rating forms, 25 GMPI rating forms, 25 GLDS rating Forms, and 25 GRRAS profile forms in a soft-sided attaché case; $70 per professional manual; $25 per 25 profile forms; $299 per unlimited-use CD-ROM scoring system.
Comments: The Mind Body Wellness Rehabilitation and Restorative Assessment System Software Portfolio (GRRAS-SP) is available to score and generate reports for all three forms of the GRRAS; the GRRAS-SP requires Windows 2000/XP/Vista, NTFS file system, CD-ROM drive for installation, and internet connection or telephone for software activation.
Authors: P. Andrew Clifford, Kristi D. Roper, and Daisha J. Cipher.
Publisher: Psychological Assessment Resources, Inc.
    a) PSYCHOLOGICAL RESISTANCE TO ACTIVITIES OF DAILY LIVING INDEX.
    Acronym: PRADLI.
    Price Data: $40 per 25 PRADLI rating forms; $125 per PRADLI kit including professional manual, 25 PRADLI rating forms, and 25 profile forms.
    Time: (15) minutes.
    b) GERIATRIC MULTIDIMENSIONAL PAIN AND ILLNESS INVENTORY.
    Acronym: GMPI.
    Price Data: $40 per 25 GMPI rating forms; $125 per GMPI kit including professional manual, 25 GMPI rating forms, and 25 profile forms.
    Time: (15) minutes.
    c) GERIATRIC LEVEL OF DYSFUNCTION SCALE.
    Acronym: GLDS.
    Price Data: $45 per 25 GLDS rating forms; $130 per GLDS kit including professional manual, 25 GLDS rating forms, and 25 profile forms.
    Time: (15) minutes.
Cross References: For reviews by John J. Brinkman and Amber Carter and by Timothy J. Makatura, see 18:76.

[1730]
Mindex: Your Thinking Style Profile.

Purpose: Designed to measure "thinking style," an individual's "unique way of processing ideas and deriving meaning" from experience.
Population: Adults.
Publication Date: 1983.
Scores, 20: Thinking Style Preference (Red Earth, Blue Earth, Red Sky, Blue Sky), Sensory Mode Preference (Kinesthetic, Visual, Auditory), Structure Preference

(Time Orientation, Detail Orientation, Technical Orientation, Goal Orientation), Mental Flexibility (Tolerance for Ambiguity, Opinion Flexibility, Semantic Flexibility, Positive Orientation, Sense of Humor, Investigative Orientation, Resistance to Enculturation), Thinking Fluency (Idea Fluency, Logical Fluency).
Administration: Individual.
Price Data: Available from publisher.
Time: Administration time not reported.
Author: Karl Albrecht.
Publisher: Karl Albrecht International.

[1731]
MindMaker6™.

Purpose: To determine personality or personal style using hemispheric dominance theories for use in training, consulting, and counseling clients.
Population: Adults.
Publication Dates: 1985-1987.
Scores, 6: Kins-Person, Loner, Loyalist, Achiever, Involver, Choice-Seeker.
Administration: Group.
Price Data: Available from publisher.
Time: (30-40) minutes.
Authors: Kenneth L. Adams and Dudley Lynch.
Publisher: Brain Technologies Corporation.
Cross References: For a review by Thomas A. Wrobel, see 11:240.

[1732]
Miner Sentence Completion Scale.

Purpose: Intended for use in "selection, vocational and career guidance, identifying talent supplies, and evaluating training primarily."
Population: Workers and prospective workers in management, professional, and entrepreneurial or task-oriented occupations.
Publication Dates: 1961–1986.
Acronym: MSCS.
Administration: Group.
Forms, 3: Form H (Management domain), Form P (Professional domain), Form T (Task domain).
Price Data, 2002: $30 per 50 tests with scoring sheets; $10 per scoring guide (Form H, 1964, 64 pages, with 1977 supplement, 15 pages, and 1989 supplement, 4 pages; Form P, 1981, 49 pages; Form T, 1986, 56 pages).
Time: (20–30) minutes.
Comments: Form H available as free-response or multiple-choice version; directions included for scoring rare response patterns.
Author: John B. Miner.
Publisher: Organizational Measurement Systems Press.
    a) FORM H.
    Scores, 9: Authority Figures, Competitive Games, Competitive Situations, Assertive Role,

Imposing Wishes, Standing Out from Group, Routine Administrative Functions, Supervisory Job, Total.

b) FORM P.

Scores, 6: Acquiring Knowledge, Independent Action, Accepting Status, Providing Help, Professional Commitment, Total.

c) FORM T.

Scores, 6: Self Achievement, Avoiding Risks, Feedback of Results, Personal Innovation, Planning for the Future, Total.

Cross References: See T5:1689 (4 references) and T4:1637 (1 reference); for reviews by Frederick T. L. Leong and Linda F. Wightman, see 11:241 (2 references); see also T2:1484 (4 references); for a review by C. J. Adcock, see 7:172 (2 references); see also P:450 (3 references) and 6:230a (2 references).

[1733]
Mini-Battery of Achievement.
Purpose: Constructed as a brief, wide-range test of basic skills and knowledge.
Population: Ages 4–adult.
Publication Date: 1994.
Acronym: MBA.
Scores, 5: Basic Skills (Reading, Writing, Mathematics, Total), Factual Knowledge.
Administration: Individual.
Price Data, 2006: $231.50 per complete kit including test book with manual, 25 test records with subject worksheets, and scoring and reporting program (Windows and Mac); $176.50 per test book, $35 per 25 test records with subject worksheets; $28.50 per scoring and reporting program.
Time: (20–30) minutes.
Comments: Previously listed as Woodcock-McGrew-Werder Mini-Battery of Achievement.
Authors: Richard W. Woodcock, Kevin S. McGrew, and Judy K. Werder.
Publisher: Riverside Publishing.
Cross References: See T5:2903 (2 references); for reviews by William B. Michael and Eleanor E. Sanford, see 13:363.

[1734]
Mini Inventory of Right Brain Injury, Second Edition.
Purpose: Designed for "screening neurocognitive deficits associated with right hemisphere lesions."
Population: Ages 20-80.
Publication Dates: 1989–2000.
Acronym: MIRBI-2.
Scores, 10: Visual Scanning, Integrity of Gnosis, Integrity of Body Image, Visuoverbal Processing, Visuosymbolic Processing, Integrity of Visuomotor Praxis, Higher-Level Language Skills, Expressing Emotion, General Affect, General Behavior.

Administration: Individual.
Price Data, 2011: $187 per complete kit; $69 per examiner record booklets; $41 per response forms; $24 per response sheets; $24 per caliper; $69 per manual (2000, 58 pages).
Time: (15–30) minutes.
Authors: Patricia A. Pimental and Jeffrey A. Knight.
Publisher: PRO-ED.
Cross References: For reviews by Daniel C. Miller and David Shum, see 15:165; for reviews of an earlier edition by R. A. Bornstein and by John E. Obrzut and Carol A. Boliek, see 11:242.

[1735]
Mini-Mental State Examination.
Purpose: Designed to "measure cognitive status in adults."
Population: Adults.
Publication Dates: 1975–2001.
Acronym: MMSE.
Scores: Total score only with items in 11 sections: Orientation to Time, Orientation to Place, Registration, Attention and Calculation, Recall, Naming, Repetition, Comprehension, Reading, Writing, Drawing.
Administration: Individual.
Price Data, 2006: $112 per introductory kit including MMSE clinical guide, pocket norms card, user's guide (2001, 11 pages), and 50 test forms; $285 per Mental Status Reporting Software (which incorporates the MMSE and an additional checklist) on CD-ROM providing unlimited scoring, interpretation, and reports.
Time: (5–10) minutes.
Authors: Marshal F. Folstein, Susan E. Folstein, and Paul R. McHugh, and Gary Fanjiang (manual only).
Publisher: Psychological Assessment Resources, Inc.
Cross References: For reviews by Mark A. Albanese and Sandra B. Ward, see 15:166.

[1736]
Minnesota Clerical Test.
Purpose: Designed to measure speed and accuracy in clerical work.
Population: Grades 8–12 and adults.
Publication Dates: 1933–1979.
Acronym: MCT.
Scores, 2: Number Comparison, Name Comparison.
Administration: Group or individual.
Price Data, 2006: $89 per per starter kit, including 25 test booklets key and manual; $30 per key for hand scoring test booklets; $36 per manual;
Time: 15(20) minutes.
Authors: Dorothy M. Andrew, Donald G. Paterson, and Howard P. Longstaff.
Publisher: Pearson.
Cross References: See T5:1693 (3 references) and T4:1640 (3 references); for reviews by Michael Ryan

and Ruth G. Thomas, see 9:713 (2 references); see also T3:1493 (5 references), T2:2135 (23 references), and 6:1040 (10 references); for a review by Donald E. Super, see 5:850 (46 references); for reviews by Thelma Hunt, R. B. Selover, Erwin K. Taylor, and E. F. Wonderlic, see 3:627 (22 references); for a review by W. D. Commins, see 2:1664 (18 references).

[1737]

Minnesota Handwriting Assessment.
Purpose: "Used to assess manuscript and D'Nealian handwriting of students."
Population: Grades 1–2.
Publication Date: 1999.
Acronym: MHA.
Scores, 6: Rate, Legibility, Form, Alignment, Size, Spacing.
Administration: Group or individual.
Price Data, 2002: $56 per kit including 25 manuscript sheets, 25 D'Nealian sheets, and manual (99 pages).
Time: (2.5–10) minutes.
Author: Judith Reisman.
Publisher: Pearson.
Cross References: For reviews by Kathy J. Bohan and Andrew A. Cox, see 16:149.

[1738]

Minnesota Importance Questionnaire.
Purpose: "To measure twenty psychological needs and six underlying values that have been found to be relevant to work adjustment, specifically to satisfaction with work."
Population: Ages 16 and over.
Publication Dates: 1967-1981.
Acronym: MIQ.
Scores, 21: Ability Utilization, Achievement, Activity, Independence, Variety, Compensation, Security, Working Conditions, Advancement, Recognition, Authority, Social Status, Co-workers, Social Services, Moral Values, Company Policies, Supervision-Human Relations, Supervision-Technical, Creativity, Responsibility, Autonomy (ranked form only).
Administration: Group.
Forms, 2: Ranked form (1975, 9 pages), paired form (1975, 18 pages).
Price Data, 2001: $39.50 per complete kit including 50 answer sheets, 10 reusable booklets, manual (1981, 73 pages), and Occupational Reinforcer Patterns (1986); $.70 or less per reusable booklet ($7 minimum); $.12 or less per answer sheet ($6 minimum); $8.50 per manual; scoring service offered by publisher.
Foreign Language Edition: Spanish edition available.
Time: (15-25) minutes for ranked form; (30-40) minutes for paired form.
Authors: James B. Rounds, Jr., George A. Henly, René V. Dawis, Lloyd H. Lofquist, and David J. Weiss.

Publisher: Vocational Psychology Research.
Cross References: See T5:1694 (10 references) and T4:1641 (3 references); for reviews by Barbara Lachar and Wilbur L. Layton, see 11:243 (4 references); for reviews by Lewis E. Albright and Sheldon Zedeck, see 8:1050 (40 references); see also T3:1495 (14 references), T2:2283 (8 references), and 7:1063 (29 references).

[1739]

Minnesota Job Description Questionnaire.
Purpose: "Designed to measure the reinforcer characteristics of jobs."
Population: Employees and supervisors.
Publication Dates: 1967-1968.
Acronym: MJDQ.
Scores: 21 reinforcer dimensions: Ability Utilization, Achievement, Activity, Advancement, Authority, Company Policies and Practices, Compensation, Co-Workers, Creativity, Independence, Moral Values, Recognition, Responsibility, Security, Social Service, Social Status, Supervision-Human Relations, Supervision-Technical, Variety, Working Conditions, Autonomy.
Administration: Group.
Forms, 2: E (for employees), S (for supervisors).
Price Data, 2001: $.73-$.75 per copy (Form S); $.78-$.80 per copy (Form E); $6 per manual (1968, 96 pages); $1.75 per person for scoring service.
Time: [20] minutes.
Comments: For research use only; 20 scores parallel scores of the Minnesota Importance Questionnaire (1738) and Minnesota Satisfaction Questionnaire (1743).
Authors: Fred H. Borgen, David J. Weiss, Howard E. A. Tinsley, René V. Dawis, and Lloyd H. Lofquist.
Publisher: Vocational Psychology Research.
Cross References: See T5:1695 (2 references), T4:1643 (3 references), and T3:1497 (4 references); for a review by Sheldon Zedeck, see 8:1051 (15 references); see also T2:2284 (8 references).

[1740]

Minnesota Manual Dexterity Test.
Purpose: "Measures the capacity for simple but rapid eyehand coordination as well as arm-hand dexterity."
Population: Ages 13–adult.
Publication Date: [Undated].
Scores: Total time for each of two tests.
Administration: Group.
Tests, 2: Placing Test, Turning Test.
Price Data: Available from publisher.
Time: Administration time not reported.
Author: Lafayette Instrument.
Publisher: Lafayette Instrument.
Cross References: For reviews by Deborah Erickson and Alida S. Westman, see 12:237.

[1741]

Minnesota Multiphasic Personality Inventory-Adolescent.

Purpose: Designed for use with adolescents to assess a number of the major patterns of personality and emotional disorders.
Population: Ages 14-18
Publication Date: 1992.
Acronym: MMPI-A.
Scores, 68: 8 Validity Scales (Cannot Say (?), Lie (L), Infrequency 1 (F1), Infrequency 2 (F2), Infrequency (F), Defensiveness (K), Variable Response Inconsistency (VRIN), True Response Inconsistency (TRIN); 10 Clinical Scales (Hypochondriasis, Depression, Hysteria, Psychopathic Deviate, Masculinity-Femininity, Paranoia, Psychasthenia, Schizophrenia, Hypomania, Social Introversion); 28 Harris-Lingoes Subscales (Subjective Depression, Psychomotor Retardation, Physical Malfunctioning, Mental Dullness, Brooding, Denial of Social Anxiety, Need for Affection, Lassitude-Malaise, Somatic Complaints, Inhibition of Aggression, Familial Discord, Authority Problems, Social Imperturbability, Social Alienation, Self-Alienation, Persecutory Ideas, Poignancy, Naivete, Social Alienation, Emotional Alienation, Lack of Ego Mastery-Cognitive, Lack of Ego Mastery-Conative, Lack of Ego Mastery-Defective Inhibition, Bizarre Sensory Experiences, Amorality, Psychomotor Acceleration, Imperturbability, Ego Inflation); 3 Si Subscales (Shyness/Self-Consciousness, Social Avoidance, Alienation); 15 Adolescent Content Scales (Anxiety, Obsessiveness, Depression, Health Concerns, Alienation, Bizarre Mentation, Anger, Cynicism, Conduct Problems, Low Self-Esteem, Low Aspirations, Social Discomfort, Family Problems, School Problems, Negative Treatment Indicators); 6 Supplementary Scales (Anxiety, Repression, MacAndrew Alcoholism Scale–Revised, Alcohol/Drug Problem Acknowledgment, Alcohol/Drug Problem Proneness, Immaturity).
Administration: Group or individual.
Price Data, 2006: $50 per manual; $35 per Adolescent Interpretive System User's Guide; $35 per 10 softcover test booklets; $50 per 1 hardcover test booklet; $80 per audiocassette; $86 hand-scoring materials package (50 answer sheets, 50 Validity/Clinical scales profile forms); $46 profile and record forms, 50 per each package for Validity/Clinical scales, clinical subscales, Content scales, Content Component scales, Supplementary scales; price information for scoring and interpretive reports available from Pearson Assessments.
Time: 45–60 minutes.
Comments: May be administered by audiocassette or microcomputer.
Authors: James N. Butcher, Carolyn L. Williams, John R. Graham, Robert P. Archer, Auke Tellegen, Yossef S. Ben-Porath, and Beverly Kaemmer (manual).
Publisher: University of Minnesota Press; distributed by Pearson.

Cross References: See T5:1698 (28 references); for reviews by Charles D. Claiborn and Richard I. Lanyon, see 12:238 (4 references); see also T4:1646 (4 references).

[1742]

Minnesota Multiphasic Personality Inventory-2.

Purpose: "Designed to assess a number of the major patterns of personality and emotional disorders."
Population: Ages 18 and over.
Publication Dates: 1942–1990.
Acronym: MMPI-2.
Scores, 75: 7 Validity Indicators: Cannot Say (?), Lie (L), Infrequency (F), Correction (K), Back F (FB), Variable Response Inconsistency (VRIN), True Response Inconsistency (TRIN); 10 Clinical Scales: Hypochondriasis (Hs), Depression (D), Conversion Hysteria (Hy), Psychopathic Deviate (Pd), Masculinity-Femininity (Mf), Paranoia (Pa), Psychasthenia (Pt), Schizophrenia (Sc), Hypomania (Ma), Social Introversion (Si); 15 Supplementary Scales: Anxiety (A), Repression (R), Ego Strength (Es), MacAndrew Alcoholism Scale-Revised (MAC-R), Overcontrolled Hostility (O-H), Dominance (Do), Social Responsibility (Re), College Maladjustment (Mt), Gender Role-Masculine (GM), Gender Role-Feminine (GF), 2 Post-Traumatic Stress Disorder Scales (PK & PS); Marital Distress Scale (MDS), Addiction Potential Scale (APS), Addiction Admission Scale (AAS); 15 Content Scales: Anxiety (ANX), Fears (FRS), Obsessiveness (OBS), Depression (DEP), Health Concerns (HEA), Bizarre Mentation (BIZ), Anger (ANG), Cynicism (CYN), Antisocial Practices (ASP), Type A (TPA), Low Self-Esteem (LSE), Social Discomfort (SOD), Family Problems (FAM), Work Interference (WRK), Negative Treatment Indicators (TRT); 3 Si subscales: Shyness/Self-Consciousness (Si1), Social Avoidance (Si2), Alienation-Self and Others (Si3); 28 Harris-Lingoes Subscales: Subjective Depression (D1), Psychomotor Retardation (D2), Physical Malfunctioning (D3), Mental Dullness (D4), Brooding (D5), Denial of Social Anxiety (Hy1), Need for Affection (Hy2), Lassitude-Malaise (Hy3), Somatic Complaints (Hy4), Inhibition of Aggression (Hy5), Familial Discord (Pd1), Authority Problems (Pd2), Social Imperturbability (Pd3), Social Alienation (Pd4), Self-Alienation (Pd5), Persecutory Ideas (Pa1), Poignancy (Pa2), Naivete (Pa3), Social Alienation (Sc1), Emotional Alienation (Sc2), Lack of Ego Mastery, Cognitive (Sc3), Conative (Sc4), Defective Inhibition (Sc5), Bizarre Sensory Experiences (Sc6), Amorality (Ma1), Psychomotor Acceleration (Ma2), Imperturbability (Ma3), Ego Inflation (Ma4).
Administration: Group or individual.
Price Data, 1999: $27 per 10 reusable softcover test booklets (English or Hispanic); $36 per reusable hardcover test booklet (English); $77 per 100 hand-scorable answer sheets and profile forms; $78 per audiocassette

(English or Hispanic); $38.50 per 50 profile forms (specify Supplementary Scales, Content Scales, Content Component Scales, or Harris-Lingoes Subscales); $67 per answer keys (specify scale and for softcover or hardcover test booklets); $43 per manual for administration and scoring (1989, 166 pages); $18 per Adult Clinical System User's Guide (1989, 71 pages); $18 per Revised Personnel System User's Guide (1989, 76 pages); price data available from publisher for IBM compatible microcomputer edition based on type of score or interpretive report desired; price data available from publisher for scoring service by publisher based on type of score or interpretive report desired.

Time: (90) minutes.

Comments: Revision of the Minnesota Multiphasic Personality Inventory; may be administered by audiocassette or microcomputer.

Authors: James N. Butcher, W. Grant Dahlstrom, John Graham, Auke Tellegen, and Beverly Kaemmer.

Publisher: Published by University of Minnesota Press; distributed by Pearson.

Cross References: See T5:1697 (600 references) and T4:1645 (504 references); for reviews by Robert P. Archer and David S. Nichols, see 11:244 (637 references); see also 9:715 (339 references) and T3:1498 (749 references); for reviews by Henry A. Alker and Glen D. King of the original version, see 8:616 (1,188 references); see also T2:1281 (549 references); for reviews by Malcolm D. Gynther and David A. Rodgers, see 7:104 (831 references); see also P:166 (1,066 references); for a review by Arthur L. Benton, see 4:71 (211 references); for reviews by Arthur L. Benton, H. J. Eysenck, L. S. Penrose, and Julian B. Rotter, and an excerpted review, see 3:60 (76 references).

[1743]

Minnesota Satisfaction Questionnaire.

Purpose: "Designed to measure an employee's satisfaction with his/her job."

Population: Business and industry.

Publication Dates: 1963-1977.

Acronym: MSQ.

Administration: Group.

Price Data, 2001: $.38 to $.39 per questionnaire for Short Form; $.64 to $.66 per questionnaire for Long Form; $4.95 per manual (1967, 130 pages); $6.60 per specimen set including MSQ Long Form, MSQ Long Form (1967 revision), MSQ Short Form, and manual; $1.10 per booklet for scoring service (Short Form); $1.65 per booklet for scoring service (Long Form).

Authors: David J. Weiss, René V. Dawis, George W. England, and Lloyd H. Lofquist.

Publisher: Vocational Psychology Research.

a) LONG FORM.

Scores, 21: Ability Utilization, Achievement, Activity, Advancement, Authority, Company Policies

and Practices, Compensation, Coworkers, Creativity, Independence, Moral Values, Recognition, Responsibility, Security, Social Service, Social Status, Supervision-Human Relations, Supervision-Technical, Variety, Working Conditions, General Satisfaction.

Editions, 2: 1967 revision, 1977 edition.

Time: (15-20) minutes.

b) SHORT FORM.

Scores, 3: Intrinsic, Extrinsic, General.

Time: (5-10) minutes.

Cross References: See T5:1701 (56 references), T4:1649 (49 references), 9:721 (21 references), and T3:1508 (27 references); for a review by Robert M. Guion, see 8:1052 (82 references); see also T2:2285 (11 references); for reviews by Lewis E. Albright and John P. Foley, Jr., see 7:1064 (18 references).

[1744]

Minnesota Satisfactoriness Scales.

Purpose: "Designed to measure an employee's satisfactoriness on a job."

Population: Employees.

Publication Dates: 1965-1970.

Acronym: MSS.

Scores, 5: Performance, Conformance, Dependability, Personal Adjustment, General Satisfactoriness.

Administration: Group.

Price Data, 2001: $.33-.35 per test; manual (1970, 53 pages plus test) no longer in print, photocopies available for $3.50; $1.25 per person for scoring service.

Time: (5) minutes.

Comments: Ratings by supervisors.

Authors: Dennis L. Gibson, David J. Weiss, René V. Dawis, and Lloyd H. Lofquist.

Publisher: Vocational Psychology Research.

Cross References: See T5:1702 (4 references), T4:1650 (6 references), and T3:1509 (2 references); for a review by Jerome E. Doppelt, see 8:1061 (9 references).

[1745]

Mirror-Couple Relationship Inventory.

Purpose: To reflect to a couple how each partner sees self and other partner.

Population: Engaged and married couples.

Publication Date: 1980.

Scores: 24 scales: 11 content scales (Parents, Lifestyle, Career, Money, Sex, Leisure, Friends, Religion, Children, Future, Rank Importance), 12 process scales (Personality, Awareness, OK Alone, Freedom, Problem Solving, Fight/Flight, Values Self, Values Partner, Positive Communication, Negative Communication, Stress, Satisfaction), and 1 Attitude scale.

Administration: Group or individual.

Price Data: Available from publisher.

Time: Administration time not reported.

Authors: Joan A. Hunt and Richard A. Hunt.
Publisher: Ministry Inventories.
Cross References: See T5:1705 (4 references).

[1746]

Mirror Edition of the Personal Values Inventory.

Purpose: Designed to describe how a person uses his/her personal strengths in relationships.
Population: Adolescents and adults reading at sixth grade level or above.
Publication Dates: 1973–1997.
Scores, 20: 7 Motivational Values.
Administration: Individual or group.
Price Data, 2001: $4.50 per test booklet; $30 per manual (1996, 146 pages).
Time: (20–40) minutes.
Comments: Manual is entitled Relationship Awareness Theory Manual of Administration and Interpretation (9th Ed.).
Author: Elias H. Porter.
Publisher: Personal Strengths Publishing.
Cross References: For a review by Ric Brown, see 16:150.

[1747]

The Missouri Children's Picture Series.

Purpose: Assessment of personality.
Population: Ages 5–16.
Publication Dates: 1971, c1963–1964.
Acronym: MCPS.
Scores, 8: Conformity, Masculinity-Femininity, Maturity, Aggression, Inhibition, Activity Level, Sleep Disturbance, Somatization.
Administration: Group.
Price Data: Available from publisher.
Time: (25-35) minutes.
Authors: Jacob O. Sines, Jerome D. Pauker, and Lloyd K. Sines.
Publisher: Jacob O. Sines (the author).
Cross References: See T5:1706 (3 references), T4:1655 (6 references), and T3:1515 (3 references); for reviews by Dale B. Harris and Lovick C. Miller, and an excerpted review by George Gilmore, see 8:625 (11 references); see also T2:1287 (4 references).

[1748]

Missouri Kindergarten Inventory of Developmental Skills, Alternate Form.

Purpose: A screening battery providing a comprehensive assessment measure to use at or before kindergarten entrance.
Population: Ages 48-72 months.
Publication Date: 1982.

Acronym: KIDS.
Scores: 6 areas: Number Concepts, Auditory Skills, Language Concepts, Paper and Pencil Skills, Visual Skills, Gross Motor Skills.
Administration: Individual.
Price Data, 2010: $1.38 per Student Packet (including Pupil Record Sheet, Answer Sheets, and Parent/Guardian Questionnaire); $13.94 for Manual Packet (includes Administration and Scoring Manual, Color Cards, and one Student Packet); $4.72 for the Instructional Guidebook; $17.30 per specimen set (includes Manual Packet and Instructional Guidebook).
Time: 35 minutes.
Comments: Can be given anytime within the year preceding kindergarten as well as at kindergarten entrance.
Author: Missouri Department of Elementary and Secondary Education.
Publisher: Assessment Resource Center, University of Missouri-Columbia.
Cross References: For reviews by Mary Henning-Stout and James E. Ysseldyke, see 11:246.

[1749]

MKM Binocular Preschool Test.

Purpose: To evaluate "the near point performance of preschool and other nonreading children."
Population: Preschool.
Publication Dates: 1963–1965.
Scores: Item scores only.
Administration: Individual.
Price Data: Available from publisher.
Time: [1–2] minutes.
Comments: Stereoscope necessary for administration.
Authors: Leland D. Michael, James W. King, and Arlene Moorhead (instructions).
Publisher: MKM.

[1750]

MKM Monocular and Binocular Reading Test.

Purpose: "To detect children who are likely to have reading problems associated with poor binocular coordination and macular suppression."
Population: Grades 1–2, 3 and over.
Publication Dates: 1963–1964.
Scores: Item scores only.
Administration: Individual.
Levels, 2: 1, 2.
Price Data: Available from publisher.
Time: [3–10] minutes.
Comments: Stereoscope necessary for administration.
Authors: Leland D. Michael, James W. King, and Arlene Moorhead (instructions).
Publisher: MKM.
Cross References: See T2:1920 (1 reference).

[1751]

MKM Picture Arrangement Test.

Purpose: Tests directionality.
Population: Grades K–6.
Publication Dates: 1963–1965.
Scores: No scores.
Administration: Individual.
Price Data: Available from publisher.
Time: [1–2] minutes.
Authors: Leland D. Michael and James W. King.
Publisher: MKM.

[1752]

The MLR Visual Diagnostic Skills Test.

Purpose: Designed to "provide an objective measure of one's ability to identify common technical-physical performance problems and to prescribe appropriate remedies."
Population: Undergraduate through graduate school.
Publication Dates: 1983-2008.
Scores: Total score only.
Subtests, 2: Woodwind, Brass.
Administration: Group.
Price Data, 2010: $50 per Visual Diagnostic Skills Test CD-ROM, including composite test, brass subtest, woodwind subtest, test manual, and answer sheets.
Time: (45) minutes.
Comments: This test can be used as a pre-test/post-test companion to the Visual Diagnostic Skills Program; the two additional subtests (Woodwind, Brass) are provided to accommodate pretest/posttest visual diagnostic skills assessment but no studies have been undertaken to determine the subtests' reliability, content validity, and construct validity.
Authors: James O. Froseth and John R. Woods.
Publisher: GIA Publications, Inc.

[1753]

Mobile Vocational Evaluation.

Purpose: "Computer assisted testing system that measures vocationally related abilities and interests."
Population: Adults.
Publication Date: 1983.
Acronym: MVE.
Scores, 29: 17 ability factors (Finger Dexterity, Wrist-Finger Speed, Arm-Hand Steadiness, Manual Dexterity, Two-Arm Coordination, Two-Hand Coordination, Perceptual Accuracy, Spatial Perception, Aiming, Reaction Time, Abstract Reasoning, Numerical Reasoning, Verbal Reasoning, Reading and Arithmetic Grade Levels, Leadership Structure and Consideration, Following Directions, Sales Attitude); 12 interest categories (Artistic, Scientific, Plants and Animals, Protective, Mechanical, Industrial, Business Detail, Selling, Accommodating, Humanitarian, Leading-Influencing, Physical Performing).
Administration: Group and individual.

Price Data, 2006: $5,300 for the entire system including 10 each of nine standardized paper-and-pencil tests with manuals, scoring keys, and oral directions, cassette tape with cassette tape player, 10 interest inventory test booklets with scoring forms, system manual, software (IBM or MAC), data processing user's guide, and professional consultation.
Time: (180) minutes.
Author: Edward J. Hester.
Publisher: Hester Evaluation Systems, Inc.

[1754]

Modern Occupational Skills Tests, Second Edition.

Purpose: Developed to assess skills in checking, numeracy, verbal skills, and office administration skills for use in "recruitment, selection and development of clerical and related staff."
Population: Potential and current office employee.
Publication Dates: 1989-2001.
Acronym: MOST.
Scores: Total score only for each test.
Administration: Group.
Editions, 2: British, Australian.
Price Data: Available from publisher.
Foreign Adaptation: Australian Edition available from Australian Council for Educational Research Ltd. [Australia].
Comments: Some parts of this series are available for online administration at www.gma-online.com.
Authors: Charles Johnson, Steve Blinkhorn, Robert Wood, and Jonathan Hall.
Publisher: Psychometric Research & Development Ltd. [England].
  a) NUMERICAL ESTIMATION.
  Time: 12 minutes.
  b) NUMERICAL AWARENESS.
  Time: 8 minutes.
  c) NUMERICAL CHECKING.
  Time: 8 minutes.
  d) TECHNICAL CHECKING.
  Time: 12 minutes.
  e) WORD MEANINGS.
  Time: 12 minutes.
  f) VERBAL CHECKING.
  Time: 8 minutes.
  g) DECISION MAKING.
  Time: 15 minutes.
  h) SPELLING AND GRAMMAR.
  Time: 8 minutes.
  i) FILING.
  Time: 12 minutes.
Cross References: For reviews by Joseph C. Ciechalski and Bikkar S. Randhawa of the original edition, see 12:239.

[1755]

Modern Photography Comprehension Test.

Purpose: Developed to assess knowledge of photography.
Population: Photography students.
Publication Dates: 1953-1969.
Scores: Total score only.
Administration: Group.
Price Data, 2006: $49.50 per test package; $2.35 per key; $2 per direction sheet; $10.50 per specimen set.
Time: (15-20) minutes.
Comments: Revision of What Do You Know About Photography?
Author: Martin M. Bruce.
Publisher: Martin M. Bruce, Ph.D.
Cross References: For a review by David P. Campbell, see 7:547.

[1756]

Modified Vygotsky Concept Formation Test.

Purpose: "Measures an individual's ability to think in abstract concepts."
Population: Older children and adolescents and adults.
Publication Dates: 1940–1984.
Scores, 2: Convergent Thinking, Divergent Thinking.
Administration: Individual.
Price Data, 2005: $195 per Kasanin-Hanfmann test kit; $35 per modified manual (1984, 75 pages); $28 per 30 record forms.
Time: (30) minutes.
Comments: Modified manual used in conjunction with Kasanin-Hanfmann Concept Formation Test (Vigotsky Test) (T3:1239).
Author: Paul L. Wang (modified manual).
Publisher: Stoelting Co.
Cross References: For reviews by Kathryn A. Hess and Gregory Schraw, see 12:240; for information on the Kasanin-Hanfmann Concept Formation Test, see also T3:1239 (1 reference), T2:1140 (9 references), P:47 (7 references), and 6:78 (11 references); for a review of an earlier edition by Kate Levine Kogan (with William S. Kogan), see 4:35 (8 references); for a review of an earlier edition by O. L. Zangwill, see 3:27 (21 references).

[1757]

Monitoring Basic Skills Progress–Second Edition.

Purpose: "Designed to monitor students' progress in mathematics over the course of a school year" using curriculum-based measurements.
Population: Grades 1–6.
Publication Dates: 1998–1999.
Administration: Group.
Price Data, 2011: $81 per complete program including Basic Math Manual, Basic Math Computation Blackline Masters, and Basic Math Concepts and Applications Blackline Masters; $27 per Basic Math Manual (available for individual purchase, the blackline masters are not available individually).
Comments: "Derived from the curriculum-based measurement (CBM) model of student monitoring"; for use in general or special education classrooms. No data collection system (software or print) is currently available.
Authors: Lynn S. Fuchs, Carol L. Hamlett, and Douglas Fuchs.
Publisher: PRO-ED.
   a) BASIC MATH COMPUTATION.
   Purpose: Designed to "monitor student progress, identify students who require intervention, and improve instructional programs" in mathematics.
   Population: Grades 1–6.
   Scores: Total score only.
   Time: (2–6) minutes.
   b) MATH CONCEPTS AND APPLICATIONS.
   Population: Grades 2–6.
   Comments: Includes a set of 18-25 reproducible tests for each grade level; level of difficulty gradually increases with each grade level.
Cross References: For reviews by Mary J. McLellan and Jeffrey K. Smith, see 14:238; for a review by Joseph C. Witt and Kevin M. Jones of an earlier edition, see 12:241.

[1758]

The Mooney Problem Check Lists, 1950 Revision.

Purpose: "Intended to help individuals express their personal problems."
Population: Junior high–adults.
Publication Dates: 1941–1950.
Acronym: MPCL.
Administration: Group.
Price Data, 2002: $36 per combined levels examination kit (for use without separate answer documents) including Check Lists and manual (1950, 15 pages); $12 per combined examination kit (for use with separate answer documents) including Check List, answer document, and manual; $4 per 25 checklists (for use without separate answer documents) and manual (specify level); $151 per 100 checklists (for use without separate answer documents) and manual (specify level).
Time: (35) minutes.
Authors: Ross L. Mooney and Leonard V. Gordon (manuals, *c*, and *d*).
Publisher: Pearson.
   a) JUNIOR HIGH SCHOOL FORM.
   Population: Grades 7–9.
   Publication Dates: 1942–1950.
   Scores, 7: Health and Physical Development, School, Home and Family, Money-Work-The Future, Boy and Girl Relations, Relations to People in General, Self-Centered Concerns.

b) HIGH SCHOOL FORM.
Population: Grades 9–12.
Publication Dates: 1941–1950.
Scores, 11: Health and Physical Development, Finances-Living Conditions-Employment, Social and Recreational Activities, Social-Psychological Relations, Personal-Psychological Relations, Courtship-Sex-Marriage, Home and Family, Morals and Religion, Adjustment to School Work, The Future-Vocational and Educational, Curriculum and Teaching Procedure.
c) COLLEGE FORM.
Population: Grades 13–16.
Publication Dates: 1941–1950.
Scores, 11: Same as for High School Form.
d) ADULT FORM.
Population: Adults.
Publication Date: 1950.
Scores, 9: Health, Economic Security, Self-Improvement, Personality, Home and Family, Courtship, Sex, Religion, Occupation.
Cross References: See T5:1716 (5 references), T4:1667 (14 references), T3:1531 (19 references), 8:626 (48 references), T2:1289 (92 references), and P:173 (55 references); for a review by Thomas C. Burgess, see 6:145 (25 references); see also 5:89 (26 references); for reviews by Harold E. Jones and Morris Krugman, see 4:73 (13 references); for reviews by Ralph C. Bedell and Theodore F. Lentz of an earlier form of *a–c*, see 3:67 (17 references).

[1759]

Morrisby Profile.

Purpose: "Designed to give a complete statement, in objective terms, about the basic mental structure of a person."
Population: Age 14–adults.
Publication Dates: 1955–1992.
Acronym: MP.
Scores: 12 tests: Compound Series, General Abilities-Verbal, General Abilities-Numerical, General Abilities-Perceptual, Shapes, Mechanical Ability, Speed Tests 1–4 (Modal Profile), Speed Tests 5–6 (Dexterity).
Administration: Group.
Price Data: Available from publisher.
Time: (165–180) minutes.
Comments: Although more commonly used as a battery of tests to provide a profile of an individual's attributes, often for vocational guidance, component tests can be used in isolation for selection purposes (e.g., the Compound Series test is used to measure Abstract Reasoning, and the three General Ability tests are used together to identify relative strengths in verbal, numerical, and perceptual abilities).
Author: The Morrisby Organisation.
Publisher: The Morrisby Organisation [England].

Cross References: For a review by Patricia A. Bachelor, see 16:151; for information on the Differential Test Battery, see T3:733 (2 references) and T2:1070 (6 references); for reviews by E. A. Peel, Donald E. Super, and Philip E. Vernon, see 5:606.

[1760]

Motivated Skills Card Sort.

Purpose: To identify skills that are central to personal and career satisfaction and success by rank ordering skills on two dimensions: Competency and Motivation.
Population: Adults
Publication Dates: 1977-2005.
Scores: Skills Ratings Matrix.
Administration: Group or individual.
Price Data, 2011: $9 per one deck of cards and one worksheet.
Time: (45–60) minutes.
Comments: Distributors are available in Canada, Australia, Egypt, and U.S.A. List of istributor informaiton is available at www.CareerNetwok.Org.
Author: Richard L. Knowdell.
Publisher: Career Research & Testing, Inc.
Cross References: For reviews by Albert M. Bugaj and Gary J. Robertson, see 13:204.

[1761]

Motivated Strategies for Learning Questionnaire.

Purpose: "To assess college students' motivational orientations and their use of different learning strategies for a college course."
Population: College students
Publication Date: 1991.
Acronym: MSLQ.
Scores, 15: 3 Motivation Scales [Value Component (Intrinsic Goal Orientation, Extrinsic Goal Orientation, Task Value), Expectancy Component (Control of Learning Beliefs, Self-Efficacy for Learning and Performance), Affective Component (Test Anxiety)]; 2 Learning Strategies Scales [Cognitive and Metacognitive Strategies (Rehearsal, Elaboration, Organization, Critical Thinking, Metacognitive Self-Regulation), Resource Management Strategies (Time and Study Environment, Effort Regulation, Peer Learning, Help Seeking)].
Administration: Group.
Price Data: Available from publisher.
Time: (20–30) minutes.
Authors: Paul R. Pintrich, David A. F. Smith, Teresa Garcia, and Wilbert J. McKeachie.
Publisher: Combined Program in Education and Psychology, University of Michigan
Cross References: See T5:1720 (5 references); for reviews by Jeri Benson and Robert K. Gable, see 13:205 (5 references).

[1762]
Motivation Assessment Scale.
Purpose: Designed to assess the motivation underlying problem behaviors so as to curb those behaviors.
Population: People with mental disabilities.
Publication Date: 1992.
Scores, 4: Sensory, Escape, Attention, Tangible.
Administration: Individual.
Price Data: Available from publisher.
Time: 10 minutes.
Comments: A rating tool designed and validated to provide results equivalent to a functional assessment of behavior; may be administered to or completed by someone in close contact with the target individual; can be completed by paper and pencil or as an interview; results identify the maintaining consequence for the target behavior given the particular setting and rater; also available in electronic and Internet subscription versions, which score and summarize results.
Authors: V. Mark Durand and Daniel B. Crimmins.
Publisher: Monaco & Associates Incorporated.
Cross References: For reviews by Roger A. Boothroyd and James P. Van Haneghan, see 14:239; see also T5:1722 (2 references).

[1763]
Motivational Patterns Inventory.
Purpose: "Designed to help members of an organization explore dominant motivations that can affect the way they contribute to the success of that organization."
Population: Organizational members.
Publication Date: 1990.
Scores, 3: Farmer, Hunter, Shepherd.
Administration: Group.
Price Data: Price information available from publisher for inventory (33 pages) including administrator's guide (2 pages).
Time: Administration time not reported.
Comments: Self-scored.
Authors: Richard E. Byrd and William R. Neher.
Publisher: Jossey-Bass, A Wiley Company.
Cross References: For reviews by Larry G. Daniel and Barbara A. Reilly, see 12:245.

[1764]
Motive to Attain Social Power.
Purpose: Designed to evaluate one's "probable enjoyment or dislike (motivational preference) for a variety of socialized power activities."
Population: Undergraduates.
Publication Date: No date.
Scores: Total score only.
Administration: Group.
Price Data, 2001: $3 per specimen set.
Time: Administration time not reported.
Authors: L. R. Good and K. C. Good.
Publisher: Psychometric Affiliates.

Cross References: For a review by Gary J. Dean, see 15:168.

[1765]
Motives, Values, Preferences Inventory.
Purpose: Designed to assess "the fit between an individual and the organizational culture" and "a person's motives."
Population: Adults.
Publication Dates: 1987–1996.
Acronym: MVPI.
Scores: 10 scales: Aesthetics, Affiliation, Altruistic, Commerce, Hedonism, Power, Recognition, Science, Security, Tradition.
Administration: Group.
Price Data, 2006: Selection Reports starting at $20; Development Reports starting at $40.
Time: (20) minutes.
Comments: Web-based administration.
Authors: Joyce Hogan and Robert Hogan (manual).
Publisher: Hogan Assessment Systems, Inc.
Cross References: For reviews by Brent W. Roberts and Sheldon Zedeck, see 14:240.

[1766]
Motor-Free Visual Perception Test, 3rd Edition.
Purpose: Designed to assess an individual's "visual perceptual ability without any motor involvement needed to make a response."
Population: Ages 4–0 through 94+.
Publication Dates: 1972-2003.
Acronym: MVPT-3.
Scores: Total score only.
Administration: Individual.
Price Data, 2006: $120 per test kit including manual (2003, 95 pages), test plates, and 25 recording forms in portfolio; $30 per manual; $65 per set of test plates; $25 per 25 recording forms.
Time: (20-30) minutes.
Comments: Revision includes updated norms and new test items.
Authors: Ronald P. Colarusso and Donald D. Hammill.
Publisher: Academic Therapy Publications.
Cross References: For reviews by Gary L. Canivez and John D. King, see 16:152; for reviews by Nancy B. Bologna and Theresa Volpe-Johnstone of an earlier edition, see 14:241; see also T5:1725 (8 references) and T4:1677 (6 references); for a review by Carl L. Rosen of an earlier edition and an excerpted review by Alan Krichev, see 8:883 (9 references).

[1767]
Motor-Free Visual Perception Test–Vertical.
Purpose: Designed to assess problems in visual perception in individuals with hemispatial visual neglect.

Population: People with brain injuries.
Publication Date: 1997.
Acronym: MVPT-V.
Scores: Total score only.
Administration: Individual.
Price Data, 2006: $80 per complete test kit including manual (35 pages), test plates, and 50 recording forms; $16 per 50 recording forms; $38 per test plates; $23 per manual.
Time: (10) minutes.
Comments: Contents of test based on the Motor-Free Visual Perception Test (1766).
Authors: Louisette Mercier, Rejean Hebert, Ronald Colarusso, and Donald Hammill.
Publisher: Academic Therapy Publications.
Cross References: For a review by Matthew E. Lambert, see 14:242.

[1768]

Movement Assessment Battery for Children.

Purpose: Designed to assess motor skills and motor development difficulties.
Population: Ages 4–12 years.
Publication Dates: 1972–1992.
Acronym: Movement ABC.
Administration: Individual.
Price Data, 2006: £575.50 per complete kit including manual (1992, 260 pages), 50 checklists, 10 of each record form, bibliography, and all manipulatives in briefcase; £17 per 50 checklists; £50.50 per 25 record forms (specify level); £83 per manual.
Authors: Sheila E. Henderson and David A. Sugden.
Publisher: Pearson Assessment [England].
  a) MOVEMENT ABC.
  Scores, 3: Manual Dexterity, Ball Skills, Static and Dynamic Balance.
  Administration: Individual.
  Levels, 4: Age Band 1 (Ages 4–6); Age Band 2 (Ages 7–8); Age Band 3 (Ages 9–10); Age Band 4 (Ages 11–12).
  Time: (20–30) minutes.
  Comments: Developed from the Test of Motor Impairment (9:1265).
  b) MOVEMENT ABC CHECKLIST.
  Scores, 5: Child Stationary/Environment Stable, Child Moving/Environment Stable, Child Stationary/Environment Changing, Child Moving/Environment Changing, Behavioral Problems Related to Motor Difficulties.
  Administration: Group or individual.
  Time: Administration time not reported.
  Comments: Behavior Checklist used by teachers, parents, and other professionals.
Cross References: For reviews by Larry M. Bolen and Carol E. Kessler, see 14:243; see also T5:1725 (8 references); for a review by Jerome D. Pauker of an earlier edition, see 8:881 (2 references); see also T2:1904 (4 references).

[1769]

Mullen Scales of Early Learning: AGS Edition.

Purpose: A comprehensive measure of cognitive functioning for infants and preschool children.
Population: Birth to 68 months.
Publication Dates: 1984–1995.
Scores, 6: Gross Motor Scale, Cognitive Scales (Visual Reception, Fine Motor, Receptive Language, Expressive Language), Early Learning Composite.
Administration: Individual.
Price Data, 2002: $635.95 per complete kit; $28.95 per 25 record forms; $199.95 per Mullen ASSIST (Macintosh/Windows CD-ROM).
Time: (15–60) minutes.
Comments: Previous editions entitled Infant Mullen Scales of Early Learning and Preschool Mullen Scales of Early Learning.
Author: Eileen M. Mullen.
Publisher: Pearson.
Cross References: For reviews by Mary Mathai Chittooran and Carol E. Kessler, see 14:244; see also T5:1728 (2 references); for a review by Verna Hart of the earlier edition, see 11:177.

[1770]

Multi-Craft Aptitude Test (Form A-3).

Purpose: To evaluate mechanical and electrical aptitude.
Population: Applicants for jobs that require the ability to learn mechanical and electrical skills.
Publication Dates: 2004–2008.
Scores: Total score only covering 9 areas: General Science, Power Tools, Hand Tools, Household Items, Electrical Concepts, Electrical Schematic Maze, Process Flow, Signal Flow, Electrical Sequences.
Administration: Group.
Price Data, 2011: $22 per consumable self-scoring test booklet or online test administration (minimum order of 20); $24.95 per manual (2008, 20 pages).
Foreign Language Edition: Available in Spanish.
Time: 24(30) minutes.
Author: Roland T. Ramsay.
Publisher: Ramsay Corporation.
Cross References: For a review by Kevin J. McCarthy, see 17:127.

[1771]

Multi-Craf Test (Forms MC-C and B).

Purpose: Designed for selecting or evaluating maintenance employees.
Population: Applicants and incumbents for jobs requiring mechanical and electrical knowledge and skills.
Publication Dates: 2000–2009.
Scores, 8: Hydraulics & Pneumatics, Welding & Rigging, Power Transmission/Lubrication/Mechanical Maintenance

& Shop Machines/Tools and Equipment, Pumps/Piping & Combustion, Motors/Control Circuits & Schematics and Print Reading, Digital Electronics/Power Supplies/Computers & PLC and Test Instruments, Basic AC & DC Theory/Power Distribution and Electrical Maintenance, Total.
Administration: Group.
Forms, 2: MC-C, B.
Price Data, 2011: $22 per consumable self-scoring test booklet or online test administration (minimum order of 20); $24.95 per manual (2009, 23 pages).
Foreign Language Edition: Available in Spanish.
Time: (60-70) minutes.
Comments: Self-scoring instrument; Form B is an alternate equivalent of Form MC-C; available for online test administration.
Author: Roland T. Ramsay.
Publisher: Ramsay Corporation.
Cross References: For a review by Vicki S. Packman of an earlier edition, see 17:128.

[1772]
Multiaxial Diagnostic Inventory-Revised Edition.
Purpose: "Developed to serve as a criterion-referenced diagnostic screening instrument designed to assess personality disorders and clinical syndromes."
Population: Children, adolescents, adults.
Publication Dates: 1989-1994.
Acronym: MDI-R.
Administration: Individual or group.
Levels, 4: Personality Scales, Adult Clinical Scales, Adolescent Clinical Scales, Child Clinical Scales.
Price Data, 2008: $74.95 per manual and 10 copies of each scale.
Time: Administration time not reported.
Comments: "Criterion-referenced."
Author: William F. Doverspike.
Publisher: Professional Resource Press.
  a) PERSONALITY SCALES.
  Population: Adults.
  Scores, 12: Paranoid, Schizoid, Schizotypal, Borderline, Histrionic, Narcissistic, Antisocial, Avoidant, Dependent, Obsessive-Compulsive, Passive-Aggressive, Depressive.
  b) ADULT CLINICAL SCALES.
  Population: Adults.
  Scores, 13: Dysthymic Disorder, Major Depressive Disorder, Bipolar Disorder, Psychotic Disorder, Dissociative Disorder, Posttramautic Stress, Anxiety Disorder, Panic Disorder, Somatoform Disorder, Anorexia Nervosa, Bulimia Nervosa, Alcohol Abuse, Substance Abuse.
  c) ADOLESCENT CLINICAL SCALES.
  Population: Ages 10-12.
  Scores, 12: Attention-Deficit/Hyperactivity Disorder, Oppositional Defiant Disorder, Conduct Disorder, Alcohol Abuse, Substance Abuse, Dysthymic Disorder, Major Depressive Disorder, Anxiety, Separation Anxiety, Psychotic Disorder, Anorexia Nervosa, Bulimia Nervosa.
  d) CHILD CLINICAL SCALES.
  Population: Children.
  Scores, 12: Attention-Deficit/Hyperactivity Disorder, Oppositional Defiant Disorder, Conduct Disorder, Alcohol Abuse, Substance Abuse, Dysthymic Disorder, Major Depressive Disorder, Anxiety, Separation Anxiety, Psychotic Disorder, Anorexia Nervosa, Bulimia Nervosa.
Cross References: For reviews by Ashraf Kagee and Robert Wright, see 18:77.

[1773]
MultiCraft Trainee Test.
Purpose: For selecting MultiCraft (mechanical and electrical) trainees.
Population: Applicants for jobs where some knowledge and skill in mechanical and electrical areas is needed.
Publication Dates: 2004-2009.
Scores, 8: Hydraulics & Pneumatics, Welding/Cutting & Rigging, Power Transmission/Lubrication/Mechanical Maintenance & Shop Machines and Tools & Equipment, Pumps/Piping & Combustion, Motors/Control Circuits and Schematics & Print Reading, Digital & Analog Electronics/Power Supplies/Computers & PLC and Test Instruments, Basic AC/DC Theory/Power Distribution and Electrical Maintenance, Total.
Administration: Group.
Price Data, 2011: $22 per consumable self-scoring test booklet or online administration (minimum order of 20); $24.95 per manual (2009, 19 pages).
Foreign Language Edition: Available in Spanish.
Time: 60-70 minutes.
Comments: Reusable test with separate answer sheets and key; available for online administration.
Author: Roland T. Ramsay.
Publisher: Ramsay Corporation.

[1774]
The Multidimensional Addictions and Personality Profile.
Purpose: Designed as "an objective measure of substance abuse and personal adjustment problems."
Population: Adolescents and adults experiencing substance abuse and mental health disorders.
Publication Dates: 1988–2006.
Acronym: MAPP.
Scores, 15: Substance Abuse Subscales (Psychological Dependence, Abusive/Secretive/Irresponsible Use, Interference, Signs of Withdrawal, Total), Personal Adjustment Subscales (Frustration Problems, Interpersonal Problems, Self-Image Problems, Total), Defensiveness

and Inconsistency Scores (Defensiveness, Inconsistency, Total); Minimizing Response Pattern Scales (Substance Abuse, Personal Adjustment, Total).
Administration: Group and individual.
Price Data: Available from publisher.
Foreign Language Editions: French and Spanish translation package available (including printed questions with audio tape).
Time: (20–25) minutes.
Comments: Previous edition entitled The COMPASS; IBM or compatible with 2 disk drives and at least 640K RAM, monitor, and printer required for computer scoring option.
Authors: John R. Craig and Phyllis Craig.
Publisher: Diagnostic Counseling Services, Inc.
Cross References: For reviews by Carl Isenhart and Keith F. Widaman, see 14:245.

[1775]

Multidimensional Anxiety Questionnaire.

Purpose: Designed "for the evaluation of anxiety symptoms in adults."
Population: Ages 18–89.
Publication Date: 1999.
Acronym: MAQ.
Scores, 5: Physiological-Panic, Social Phobia, Worry-Fears, Negative Affectivity, Total.
Administration: Group or individual.
Price Data, 2006: $118 per introductory kit including 25 hand-scorable booklets, professional manual (94 pages), and 50 profile forms.
Time: (10) minutes.
Author: William M. Reynolds.
Publisher: Psychological Assessment Resources, Inc.
Cross References: For reviews by Stephanie Stein and Robert E. Wall, see 15:169.

[1776]

Multidimensional Anxiety Scale for Children.

Purpose: "Designed to assess a variety of anxiety dimensions in children and adolescents."
Population: Ages 8–19.
Publication Date: 1997.
Administration: Individual or Group.
Price Data, 2011: $167 per MASC/MASC-10 complete kit including MASC manual (62 pages) and 25 MASC and MASC-10 QuikScore™ forms; $118 per MASC kit including manual and 25 MASC QuikScore™ forms; $73 per manual; $50 per 25 MASC QuikScore™ forms; $50 per 25 MASC-10 QuikScore™ forms.
Comments: Self-report.
Author: John March.
Publisher: Multi-Health Systems, Inc.
    a) MULTIDIMENSIONAL ANXIETY SCALE FOR CHILDREN.
    Acronym: MASC.

Scores, 13: Physical Symptoms (Tense Symptom Subscale, Somatic Symptoms Subscale, Total), Harm Avoidance (Perfectionism Subscale, Anxious Coping Subscale, Total), Social Anxiety (Humiliation Fears Subscale, Performance Fears Subscale, Total), Separation/Panic, Total Anxiety, Anxiety Disorders Index, Inconsistency Index.
Time: (15) minutes.
Comments: Self-report measure; can be orally administered to young children or poor readers; for use only by psychology professionals with training in assessment.
    b) MASC-10: MULTIDIMENSIONAL ANXIETY SCALE FOR CHILDREN–10 ITEM.
    Acronym: MASC-10.
    Scores, 4: Physical Symptoms, Harm Avoidance, Social Anxiety, Separation/Panic.
    Time: (2–5) minutes.
    Comments: A shortened, 10-item version of the MASC tapping the four basic anxiety scales.
Cross References: For reviews by John C. Caruso and Robert Christopher, see 14:246.

[1777]

Multidimensional Aptitude Battery-II.

Purpose: Designed "to provide a measure of general cognitive ability or intelligence."
Population: Ages 16 and over.
Publication Dates: 1984–1998.
Acronym: MAB-II.
Scores, 13: Verbal (Information, Comprehension, Arithmetic, Similarities, Vocabulary, Total); Performance (Digit Symbol, Picture Completion, Spatial, Picture Arrangement, Object Assembly, Total), Total.
Administration: Group or individual.
Price Data, 2010: $80 per machine-scoring examination kit including Verbal and Performance booklets, manual on CD (1998, 107 pages), Verbal and Performance answer sheets, and one coupon for computerized scoring; $110 per hand-scoring examination scoring kit including Verbal and Performance booklets, manual on CD (1998, 107 pages), Verbal and Performance answer sheets, record form, and set of scoring templates; $24 per test manual on CD; $65 per 10 Verbal or Performance test booklets; $130 per 25 Verbal or Performance test booklets; $65 per 25 Verbal or Performance answer sheets; $53 per 25 record forms; $45 per scoring templates; $85–$95 (depending on volume) per 10 machine-scorable answer sheets and coupons for Mail-in Extended Reports; $105–$115 (depending on volume) per 10 machine-scorable answer sheets and coupons for Mail-in Clinical Reports; $145 per software installation package, includes 10 coupons for computer reports.
Time: 100 minutes.
Comments: Paper-and-pencil or computer administration available.
Author: Douglas N. Jackson.

Publisher: SIGMA Assessment Systems, Inc.
Cross References: For reviews by Donald L. Thompson and Keith F. Widaman, see 15:170; see T5:1731 (3 references), and T4:1678 (13 references); for reviews by Sharon B. Reynolds and Arthur B. Silverstein of an earlier edition, see 10:202 (5 references).

[1778]

Multidimensional Health Profile.

Purpose: Developed to provide a brief but comprehensive assessment of psychosocial and health functioning for general use in health-related settings.
Population: Ages 18–90.
Publication Dates: 1992–1998.
Administration: Group or Individual.
Forms, 2: Psychosocial Functioning (MHP-P), Health Functioning (MHP-H).
Price Data, 2006: $149 per introductory kit including professional manual, 25 MHP-P booklets, and 25 MHP-H booklets.
Time: (15) minutes for either form.
Authors: Linda S. Ruehlman, Richard I. Lanyon, and Paul Karoly.
Publisher: Psychological Assessment Resources, Inc.
  a) MULTIDIMENSIONAL HEALTH PROFILE-PSYCHOSOCIAL FUNCTIONING.
  Acronym: MHP-P.
  Scores, 17: Number of Stressful Events, Perceived Stress, Coping Skills, Total Social Support, Emotional Support, Informational Support, Tangible Support, Negative Social Exchange, Total Psychological Distress, Depressed Affect, Guilt, Motor Retardation, Anxious Affect, Somatic Complaints, Cognitive Disturbance, Life Satisfaction, Global Stress.
  Comments: 58-item self-report questionnaire to assess psychosocial functioning.
  b) MULTIDIMENSIONAL HEALTH PROFILE-HEALTH FUNCTIONING.
  Acronym: MHP-H.
  Scores, 20: Self-Help, Professional Help, Help from Friends, Spiritual Help, Positive Health Habits, Negative Health Habits, Self-Efficacy, Health Vigilance, Health Values, Trust in Health Care Personnel, Trust in Health Care System, Hypochondriasis, Overall Health, Recent Health, Presence of a Chronic Illness, Impairment Due to a Chronic Illness, Office Visits, Overnight Hospital Treatment, Emergency Room Treatment, Over the Counter Medication.
  Comments: 69-item self-report questionnaire to assess health functioning.
Cross References: For reviews by Wendy Naumann and Terri L. Weaver, see 14:247.

[1779]

Multidimensional Perfectionism Scale.

Purpose: Designed to assess "different aspects of perfectionism."

Population: Ages 18 and over.
Publication Date: 2004.
Acronym: MPS.
Scores: 3 subscales: Self-Oriented Perfectionism, Other-Oriented Perfectionism, Socially Prescribed Perfectionism.
Administration: Individual or group.
Price Data, 2011: $140 per complete kit including technical manual (88 pages) and 25 QuikScore forms; $75 per technical manual; $50 per 25 QuikScore forms; $79 per Online Profile Report Kit including technical manual and 3 profile reports; $5 per each online Profile report; $81 per Online Interpretive Report Kit including technical manual and 3 interpretive reports; $7 per each online Interpretive report; $140 per software kit including technical manual, and 25 interpretive reports; $5 per each software Profile report; $7 per each software Interpretive report.
Time: (15) minutes.
Comments: Self-report inventory.
Authors: Paul L. Hewitt and Gordon L. Flett.
Publisher: Multi-Health Systems, Inc.
Cross References: For a review by Collie Conoley, see 17:129.

[1780]

Multidimensional Self Concept Scale.

Purpose: Designed to provide a multidimensional assessment of self concept in clinical and research settings.
Population: Grades 5–12.
Publication Date: 1992.
Acronym: MSCS.
Scores, 7: Social, Competence, Affect, Academic, Family, Physical, Total.
Administration: Group or individual.
Price Data, 2011: $127 per complete set; $69 per 50 record booklets; $64 per examiner's manual (82 pages).
Time: (20) minutes.
Author: Bruce A. Bracken.
Publisher: PRO-ED.
Cross References: See T5:1734 (6 references); for reviews by Francis X. Archambault, Jr. and W. Grant Willis, see 12:246 (1 reference); see also T4:1682 (1 reference).

[1781]

The Multidimensional Self-Esteem Inventory.

Purpose: "Measures global self-esteem and its eight components."
Population: Adults.
Publication Dates: 1983–1988.
Acronym: MSEI.
Scores, 11: Competence, Lovability, Likability, Self-control, Personal Power, Moral Self-approval, Body Appearance, Body Functioning, Identity Integration, Defensive Self-enhancement, Global Self-esteem.

Administration: Individual or group.
Price Data, 2006: $165 per introductory kit including manual (1988, 22 pages), 25 reusable test booklets, 50 rating forms, and 50 profile forms.
Time: (15-30) minutes.
Comments: Originally called Self-Report Inventory.
Authors: Edward J. O'Brien and Seymour Epstein.
Publisher: Psychological Assessment Resources, Inc.
Cross References: See T5:1735 (12 references) and T4:1683 (2 references); for reviews by Barbara J. Kaplan and Joseph G. Ponterotto, see 11:250 (1 reference).

[1782]
Multifactor Leadership Questionnaire for Teams.

Purpose: To assess and develop a plan for enhancing team leadership.
Population: Management personnel.
Publication Date: 1996.
Acronym: MLQT.
Scores, 6: Transformational Leadership, Transactional Leadership, Non-Transactional Leadership, Outcomes of Leadership Styles (Extra Effort, Effectiveness, Satisfaction).
Administration: Group.
Price Data: Available from publisher at www.mindgarden.com/products/tmlq.htm.
Time: Administration time not reported.
Comments: Same instrument as MLQTR (1783) but packaged for researchers only.
Authors: Bernard M. Bass and Bruce J. Avolio.
Publisher: Mind Garden, Inc.

[1783]
Multifactor Leadership Questionnaire for Teams Report.

Purpose: To assess and develop a plan for enhancing team leadership.
Population: Management personnel.
Publication Date: 1996.
Acronym: MLQTR.
Scores, 12: Transformational Leadership: Idealized Attributes, Idealized Behaviors, Inspirational Motivation, Intellectual Stimulation, Individualized Consideration, Transactional Leadership: Contingent Reward, Management-by-Exception (Active), Passive/Avoidant: Management-by-Exception (Passive), Laissez-faire, Outcomes of Leadership: Extra Effort, Effectiveness, Satisfaction.
Administration: Group.
Price Data: Available from publisher at www.mindgarden.com/products/tmlq.htm.
Time: (20) minutes.
Comments: Web-based administration and reporting available.

Authors: Bernard M. Bass and Bruce J. Avolio.
Publisher: Mind Garden, Inc.

[1784]
Multifactor Leadership Questionnaire, Third Edition.

Purpose: Measures a broad range of leadership types; identifies the characteristics of a transformational leader and helps individuals discover how they measure up in their own eyes and in the eyes of those with whom they work.
Population: Researchers, consultants, leaders, supervisors, colleagues, peers, direct reports.
Publication Dates: 1985–2004.
Acronym: MLQ.
Scores, 12: Transformational Leadership (Idealized Attributes, Idealized Behaviors, Inspirational Motivational, Intellectual Stimulation, Individualized Consideration), Transactional Leadership (Contingent Reward, Management-by-Exception: Active), Passive-Avoidant Behaviors (Management-by-Exception: Passive, Laissez-Faire), Extra Effort, Effectiveness, and Satisfaction with the Leadership.
Administration: Group.
Forms, 3: Leader 5X-Short, Rater 5X-Short, Actual-Ought.
Price Data: Available from publisher www.mindgarden.com/translead.htm.
Foreign Language Editions: Translations and reports available in English, German, Italian, Swedish, Spanish, Turkish, and Portuguese; MLQ translations only: French, Norwegian, Hebrew, Arabic, Chinese, Thai, Korean, and others.
Time: (15) minutes.
Comments: Both paper form-based and Web-based forms are available; scoring and reporting provided by publisher (including both multirater and an Actual vs Ought Feedback Report); previous edition listed as Multifactor Leadership Questionnaire for Research, Second Edition.
Authors: Bruce J. Avolio and Bernard M. Bass.
Publisher: Mind Garden, Inc.
Cross References: For reviews by John W. Fleenor and Eugene P. Sheehan, see 17:130; for a review by David J. Pittenger of an earlier edition, see 14:248; see also T5:1736 (5 references); for reviews by Frederick Bessai and Jean Powell Kirnan and Brooke Snyder of an earlier edition, see 12:247 (5 references); see also T4:1684 (5 references).

[1785]
Multilevel Academic Survey Test.

Purpose: Developed "for use by school personnel who make decisions about student performance in reading and mathematics."

Population: K–8 and high school students with reading or mathematics skills deficits.
Publication Date: 1985.
Acronym: MAST.
Scores: Total score only for each test.
Price Data, 2002: $79 per examination kit including Grade Level test booklet, answer sheet, Curriculum Level record form, and manual (189 pages); $52 per 25 grade 1 evel test booklets; $33 per 25 grade level self-scoring answer sheets; $51 per 25 curriculum level record forms.
Authors: Kenneth W. Howell, Stanley H. Zucker, and Mada Kay Morehead.
Publisher: Pearson.

a) GRADE LEVEL TEST.
1) *Primary.*
Population: Grades K–2.
Administration: Individual.
Time: (10–15) minutes.
2) *Short.*
Population: Grades 3–12.
Administration: Group.
Time: 22(27) minutes.
3) *Extended.*
Population: Grades 3-12.
Administration: Group.
Time: 30(35) minutes.
Comments: Administered to students who have taken the short form when a larger sample of performance is required.
b) CURRICULUM LEVEL TEST.
Population: Grades K–8.
Administration: Group.
Time: 1–5 minutes per test.
Comments: "Criterion-referenced."
1) *Reading.*
Tests, 4: Graded Oral Reading, Graded Comprehension, Diagnostic Oral Reading, Comprehension Problem Profile.
2) *Mathematics.*
Tests, 8: Basic Facts Screening, Addition, Multiplication, Division, Fractions, Decimals/Ratios/Percents, Problem Solving, Applications Content.
Cross References: See T5:1738 (1 reference) and T4:1685 (1 reference); for reviews by Ellen H. Bacon and Thomas G. Haring, see 10:203.

[1786]

Multilingual Aphasia Examination, Third Edition.

Purpose: Designed to evaluate the presence, severity, and qualitative aspects of aphasic disorder.
Population: Ages 6–69.
Publication Dates: 1978–1994.
Acronym: MAE.
Scores, 11: Visual Naming, Sentence Repetition, Controlled Word Association, Oral Spelling, Written Spelling, Block Spelling, MAE Token Test, Aural Comprehension of Words and Phrases, Reading Comprehension of Words and Phrases, Rating of Articulation, Rating of Praxic Features of Writing.
Administration: Individual.
Price Data: Not available.
Foreign Language Edition: Spanish edition available.
Time: Administration time not reported.
Authors: A. L. Benton, deS. Hamsher, and A. B. Sivan.
Publisher: AJA Associates [No reply from publisher; status unknown].
Cross References: For reviews by Nancy B. Bologna and by Malcolm R. McNeil and Wiltrud Fassbinder, see 14:249; see also T5:1740 (36 references).

[1787]

Multimodal Life History Inventory.

Purpose: To provide "therapists with an in-depth assessment tool for adult counseling."
Population: Adult counseling clients.
Publication Dates: 1980-1991.
Scores: No scores.
Administration: Group.
Manual: No manual.
Price Data, 2006: $25.95 per set of 20 inventories; price information for Spanish version available from publisher.
Foreign Language Edition: Spanish version available.
Time: Administration time not reported.
Comments: Self-report to be completed in the client's "own time"; previously listed as Multimodal Life History Questionnaire.
Authors: Arnold A. Lazarus and Clifford N. Lazarus.
Publisher: Research Press.

[1788]

Multiphasic Environmental Assessment Procedure.

Purpose: Characterizes the "physical and social environments of residential care settings for older adults."
Population: Nursing home residents, residential care facilities, congregate apartments.
Publication Dates: 1979–1998.
Acronym: MEAP.
Administration: Individual.
Price Data: Available from publisher.
Time: [4–8] hours.
Comments: Administration time dependent on size and complexity of facility.
Authors: Rudolf H. Moos and Sonne Lemke.
Publisher: SAGE Publications [No reply from publisher; status unknown].
a) PHYSICAL AND ARCHITECTURAL FEATURES CHECKLIST.
Acronym: PAF.

Scores, 8: Community Accessibility, Physical Amenities, Social-Recreational Aids, Prosthetic Aids, Orientational Aids, Safety Features, Staff Facilities, Space Availability.
b) POLICY AND PROGRAM INFORMATION FORM.
Acronym: POLIF.
Scores, 9: Expectations for Functioning, Acceptance of Problem Behavior, Policy Choice, Resident Control, Policy Clarity, Provision for Privacy, Availability of Health Services, Availability of Daily Living Assistance, Availability of Social-Recreational Activities.
c) RESIDENT AND STAFF INFORMATION FORM.
Acronym: RESIF.
Scores, 6: Resident Social Resources, Resident Heterogeneity, Resident Functional Abilities, Resident Activity Level, Resident Activities in the Community, Staff Resources.
d) SHELTERED CARE ENVIRONMENT SCALE.
Acronym: SCES.
Scores, 7: Cohesion, Conflict, Independence, Self-Disclosure, Organization, Resident Influence, Physical Comfort.
e) RATING SCALE.
Acronym: RS.
Scores, 4: Physical Attractiveness, Environmental Diversity, Resident Functioning, Staff Functioning.
Cross References: See T5:1743 (2 references); for reviews by Julian Fabry and Kenneth Sakauye, see 12:248; see also T4:1688 (4 references), 9:733 (1 reference), and T3:1546 (4 references).

[1789]

Multiphasic Sex Inventory II.

Purpose: "To assess a wide range of psychosexual characteristics of the sexual offender."
Population: Adult males, ages 18–84.
Publication Dates: 1984–2003.
Acronym: MSI II.
Scores: 42 scales and indices: Suicide, Sexual Ethics, Sex Knowledge and Beliefs, Repeated Items, Infrequency, Social Sexual Desirability, Sexual Obsessions, Dissimulation, Lie, Molester Comparison, Rapist Comparison, Child Molest, Rape, Exhibitionism, Voyeurism, Sex Harassment, Net Sex, Obscene Call, Pornography, Transvestism, Fetishism & NOS Paraphilias, Bondage Discipline, Sexual Sadism, Masochism, Physiologic Dysfunction, Desire, Premature Ejaculation, Body Image, Social Sexual Inadequacies, Emotional Neediness, Cognitive Distortion and Immaturity, Antisocial Behavior, Conduct Disorder, Sociopathy, Domestic Violence, Substance Abuse, Denial, Justification, Scheming, Superoplimism, Gender Identity, Treatment Attitudes.
Administration: Group.
Price Data: Available from publisher.

Foreign Language Edition: Spanish language version available.
Time: (45–120) minutes.
Comments: May be administered via audio cassette or paper-pencil; computer scoring done by publisher.
Authors: H. R. Nichols and Ilene Molinder.
Publisher: Nichols & Molinder Assessments.
Cross References: For reviews by Paul A. Arbisi and Albert Bugaj, see 16:153; see also T5:1744 (8 references) and T4:1689 (2 references).

[1790]

Multiple Affect Adjective Check List–Revised.

Purpose: "To measure both state and affect traits."
Population: Ages 20–79.
Publication Dates: 1960–1999.
Acronym: MAACL-R.
Scores, 7: Anxiety, Depression, Hostility, Positive Affect, Sensation Seeking, Dysphoria, Positive Affect and Sensation Seeking.
Administration: Group.
Price Data, 2005: $11 per 25 hand-scoring or machine-scoring lists (specify State or Trait) [$41.75 per 100, $166.50 per 500]; $16.50 per scoring key; $28.75 per manual (1999, 71 pages); $26.75 per bibliography (1991, 1,000 references); $31 per specimen set including manual and 1 copy of all forms.
Time: 5(10) minutes.
Comments: Previous edition still available.
Authors: Marvin Zuckerman and Bernard Lubin.
Publisher: EdITS/Educational and Industrial Testing Service.
Cross References: For reviews by Gerald E. DeMauro and Paul Retzlaff, see 16:154; see also T5:1745 (89 references) and T4:1690 (96 references); for a review by John A. Zarske of an earlier edition, see 10:205 (84 references); see also 9:734 (47 references), T3:1547 (108 references), 8:628 (102 references), and T2:1293 (56 references); for reviews by E. Lowell Kelly and Edwin I. Megargee of an earlier edition, see 7:112 (60 references); see also P:176 (28 references).

[1791]

Multiscale Dissociation Inventory.

Purpose: To assess the clinical severity of dissociative disturbance.
Population: Ages 18 and older.
Publication Dates: 1998–2002.
Acronym: MDI.
Scores, 6: Disengagement, Depersonalization, Derealization, Emotional Constriction, Memory Disturbance, Identity Dissociation.
Administration: Individual or group.
Price Data, 2006: $122 per introductory kit including professional manual (2002, 40 pages), 25 test booklets, and 25 profile forms.

Time: (5–10) minutes.
Comments: Self-report; requires 6th grade reading level; normed on 440 adults with a histories of at least one DSM-IV-TR "Criterion A" traumatic event.
Author: John Briere.
Publisher: Psychological Assessment Resources, Inc.
Cross References: For reviews by Frederick T. L. Leong and Paul Retzlaff, see 16:156.

[1792]

Multiscore Depression Inventory for Adolescents and Adults.

Purpose: "To provide an objective measure of the severity of self-reported depression."
Population: Ages 13 through adult.
Publication Date: 1986.
Acronym: MDI.
Scores, 10: Low Energy Level, Cognitive Difficulty, Guilt, Low Self-Esteem, Social Introversion, Pessimism, Irritability, Sad Mood, Instrumental Helplessness, Learned Helplessness.
Administration: Group.
Forms, 2: Short Form version available by administering first 47 items of questionnaire.
Price Data, 2006: $132 per kit including scoring keys, 25 hand-scored test/answer sheets, 25 profile forms, and manual (111 pages); $21.95 per set of scoring keys; $31 per 100 hand-scored test/answer sheets; $20.50 or less per prepaid mail-in WPS Test Report answer sheet; $31 per 100 profile forms; $54.50 per manual; $335.50 per 25-use disk (PC with DOS) for administration, scoring, and interpretation; $16.50 per 100 PC answer sheets; $13.25 per FAX service scoring charge.
Time: (20) minutes; (10) minutes for Short Form.
Comments: Self-report format; IBM PC, XT, or AT or compatible computer required for optional computer administration or scoring.
Author: David J. Berndt.
Publisher: Western Psychological Services.
Cross References: See T5:1748 (1 reference) and T4:1693 (2 references); for reviews by David N. Dixon and Stephen G. Flanagan, see 11:251.

[1793]

Multiscore Depression Inventory for Children.

Purpose: Designed to assess depression and "features related to depression."
Population: Ages 8–17
Publication Date: 1996.
Acronym: MDI-C.
Scores, 9: Anxiety, Self-Esteem, Sad Mood, Instrumental Helplessness, Social Introversion, Low Energy, Pessimism, Defiance, Total.
Administration: Group.

Price Data, 2011: $120 per complete kit, including 25 AutoScore™ test forms, 25 profile forms, and 1 manual; $45 per 25 AutoScore™ test forms; $55 per manual; $27.50 per 50 profile forms; $19.25 per mail-in answer sheet, which includes test items; $375 per CD including 25 uses (PC with Windows 98, 2000, ME, XP, Vista, or Windows 7); Free U.S. shipping on this product; $17.50 per 100 PC answer sheets, for use with the MDI-C CD.
Time: (15–20) minutes.
Authors: David J. Berndt and Charles F. Kaiser.
Publisher: Western Psychological Services.
Cross References: For reviews by Jill Ann Jenkins and Michael G. Kavan, see 14:250.

[1794]

Murphy-Meisgeier Type Indicator for Children® [Revised].

Purpose: "Intended to help students develop greater awareness of their preferred ways for processing information, making decisions, and forming relationships."
Population: Grades 2-12.
Publication Dates: 1987-2008.
Acronym: MMTIC™.
Scores, 4: Extraversion or Introversion, Sensing or Intuition, Thinking or Feeling, Judging or Perceiving.
Administration: Individual or group.
Price Data, 2011: $7 per online assessment including scoring and a personalized student report; $3 per additional Professional report (designed for counselors); $3 per additional Career Report; $3.50 for additional Verified Type Report; $25 per year for access to the MMTIC Facilitator Interface, which allows quantity purchases, set up and management of different groups and individuals, report generation, data management, and free downloadable support materials (including MMTIC manual, 2008, 96 pages).
Time: (15-20) minutes.
Comments: Each report provides the indicated preference for the respondent on the four dichotomies that are scored.
Authors: Elizabeth Murphy and Charles Meisgeier.
Publisher: Center for Applications of Psychological Type, Inc.
Cross References: For reviews by Joyce Meikamp and Jeanette Lee-Farmer and by David Morse, see 18:78; see T5:1750 (1 reference); for reviews by Joanne Jensen and Norman Constantine and by Hoi K. Suen of an earlier edition, see 12:249.

[1795]

Music Achievement Tests 1, 2, 3, and 4.

Purpose: Constructed to measure musical achievement.
Publication Dates: 1968–1986.
Acronym: MAT.

Administration: Group.
Price Data: Available from publisher.
Comments: Record player necessary for administration.
Author: Richard Colwell.
Publisher: MAT [No reply from publisher; status unknown].

   a) TEST 1.
   Population: Grades 3–12.
   Scores, 4: Pitch Discrimination, Interval Discrimination, Meter Discrimination, Total.
   Time: (18) minutes.
   b) TEST 2.
   Population: Grades 4–12.
   Scores, 6: Major-Minor Mode Discrimination, Feeling for Tonal Center, Auditory-Visual Discrimination (Pitch, Rhythm, Total), Total.
   Time: (28) minutes.
   c) TEST 3.
   Population: Grades 4–12.
   Scores, 5: Tonal Memory, Melody Recognition, Pitch Recognition, Instrument Recognition, Total.
   Time: (32) minutes.
   d) TEST 4.
   Population: Grades 5–12.
   Scores, 7: Musical Style (Composers, Texture, Total), Auditory-Visual Discrimination, Chord Recognition, Cadence Recognition, Total.
   Time: (38) minutes.
Cross References: For reviews by J. David Boyle and Rudolf E. Radocy, see 12:250; see also T2:207 (5 references); for a review by Paul R. Lehman, see 7:248 (5 references).

[1796]

Music Apperception Test.

Purpose: Designed for application in "clinical, educational, organizational and neuropsychology, art and creativity, and language and cognition."
Population: Ages 8 to 45.
Publication Date: 2007.
Acronym: MAT.
Scores, 39: Response Latency, Fluency (Compositional Fluency, Post-Compositional Fluency, Run-on Fluency, Total), Content Categories (Human, Human Mythic, Human Group, Participant Observer, Total Human, Animal, Animal Mythic, Total Animal, Natural, Man Made, Abstract, Morbid, Total Other), Interaction (Solitary, Mutual, Conflict, Detach), Tangential Response (Self, Music Centered, Other, Total Non-Story Reference), Affective Fit (Hedonic Tone, Affect Expressed, Common Theme, Common Interaction, Common Setting, Total), Narrative Style (Logical, Balanced, Kinetic/Imagistic, Disorganized/Other), Morbid Content, Adaptive Response to Change, Time to Termination.
Administration: Individual.
Forms, 4: Standard, Extended, Short Form (A, B).

Price Data, 2007: $189 per starter kit including manual (2007, 125 pages), manual supplement (2007, 115 pages), 20 record forms, administration CD, and carrier bag; $32 per 20 record forms; $40 per manual; $30 per manual supplement; $89 per administration CD; $18 per carrier bag; $30 per administration email coding and interpretation.
Time: (8-25) minutes.
Comments: Test administered via CD; requires the use of a tape or digital recorder to record examinee response.
Author: Leland van den Daele.
Publisher: Psychodiagnostics, Inc.
Cross References: For reviews by Mary L. Garner and Jeffrey K. Smith, see 18:79.

[1797]

Music Teacher Self-Assessment.

Purpose: Designed to provide means for music teachers to view and analyze their teaching.
Population: Music teachers.
Publication Date: 1996.
Administration: Individual.
Scores: No scores.
Price Data, 2008: $34.95 per workbook (36 pages), self-assessment, and VHS tape.
Time: Administration time not available.
Authors: James O. Froseth and Molly A. Weaver.
Publisher: GIA Publications.

[1798]

Musical Aptitude Profile [1995 Revision].

Purpose: Designed to evaluate music aptitude.
Population: Grades 4–12.
Publication Dates: 1965–1995.
Scores, 11: Tonal Imagery (Melody, Harmony, Total), Rhythm Imagery (Tempo, Meter, Total), Musical Sensitivity (Phrasing, Balance, Style, Total), Total.
Administration: Group.
Price Data, 2006: $140 per complete kit; $25 per 100 answer sheets; $30 per 100 profile cards; $2 per class record sheet; $25 per sensitivity compact disc; $25 per tonal and rhythm compact disc; $20 per scoring masks (with school purchase order only; $20 per manual (1995, 162 pages).
Time: (110) minutes.
Comments: Test must be scored manually.
Author: Edwin E. Gordon.
Publisher: GIA Publications, Inc.
Cross References: For reviews by Christopher M. Johnson and James W. Sherbon, see 16:157; see also T5:1752 (1 reference); for reviews by Annabel J. Cohen and James W. Sherbon of an earlier edition, see 12:251; see also T4:1697 (2 references); T3:1552 (4 references); 8:98 (25 references), and T2:209 (11 references); for reviews by Robert W. Lundin and John McLeish, see 7:249 (33 references).

[1799]

My Vocational Situation.

Purpose: Designed to diagnose difficulties in vocational decision-making.
Population: High school and college and adult.
Publication Date: 1980.
Acronym: MVS.
Scores, 3: Vocational Identity, Occupational Information, Barriers.
Administration: Group.
Price Data, 2001: $14.50 per 25 item booklets (for hand scoring); $5.50 per manual (8 pages).
Time: (5-10) minutes.
Authors: John L. Holland, Denise Daiger, and Paul G. Power.
Publisher: CPP, Inc.
Cross References: See T5:1754 (27 references) and T4:1701 (24 references); for a review by Bert W. Westbrook, see 9:738 (1 reference).

[1800]

My Worst Experience Scale.

Purpose: Designed to "assess youngsters' reports of their most stressful experiences and their thoughts, behaviors, and feelings associated with those experiences."
Population: Ages 9–18.
Publication Date: 2002.
Acronym: MWES.
Scores, 12: DSM IV PTSD Criterion Subscales (Impact of the Event, Re-experience of the Trauma, Avoidance and Numbing, Increased Arousal), Symptoms Subscales (Depression, Hopelessness, Somatic Symptoms, Oppositional Conduct, Hypervigilance, Dissociation and Dreams, General Maladjustment), Total.
Administration: Group or individual.
Price Data, 2006: $126.50 per test kit including 25 AutoScore™ answer forms, manual (78 pages), and 100 school alienation and trauma survey forms; $49.50 per manual; $54.95 per 25 AutoScore™ answer forms; $26.95 per 100 school alienation and trauma survey forms; $280 per 25-use disk; $16.50 per PC answer booklet; $13.75 per mail-in answer booklet; volume discounts available.
Time: (20–30) minutes.
Comments: Self-report questionnaire; computer administration and scoring available.
Authors: Irwin A. Hyman, and Pamela A. Snook (scale and manual), J. M. Berna, M. A. Kohr, J. DuCette, and G. Britton (scale).
Publisher: Western Psychological Services.
Cross References: For reviews by Frederic J. Medway and Heidi K. Moore, see 16:158.

[1801]

Myers-Briggs Type Indicator®, Form M.

Purpose: Designed for "the identification of basic preferences on each of the four dichotomies specified or implicit in Jung's theory" and "the identification and description of the 16 personality types that result from interactions among the preferences."
Population: Ages 14 and older.
Publication Dates: 1943–1998.
Acronym: MBTI®.
Scores, 4: Extraversion vs. Introversion, Sensing vs. Intuition, Thinking vs. Feeling, Judging vs. Perceiving.
Administration: Individual or group.
Price Data, 2011: $46.95 per complete online administration with interpretation; $109.50 per 10 self-scorable forms; $12.95 per Profile online administration; $19.95 per Interpretative Report online administration; $23.5 per Interpretive Report for Organizations online administration; $13.95 per MBTI Career Report online administration; $23.95 per Team Report online administration; $23.95 per Work Styles Report online administration; $23.95 per Decision-Making Styles Report online administration; $23.95 per Stress Management Report online administration; $23.95 per Communication Style Report online administration; $119.50 per manual (1998, 440 pages).
Foreign Language Editions: U.S. English, U.K. English, Latin American Spanish, Japanese, Chinese-Traditional, Chinese-Simplified, Danish, Dutch, French, German, Swedish, European Spanish, Brazilian Portuguese, Argentine Spanish, Canadian French, Norwegian, Italian, Greek, Portuguese, Finnish.
Time: (15–25) minutes.
Comments: Scoring options: Online, self-scorable, template scoring, software on-site scoring, mail-in scoring; Extensive support materials are available, visit www.cpp.com to review all MBTI®-related products.
Authors: Katharine C. Briggs, Isabel Briggs Myers, Mary H. McCaulley (revised manual), Naomi L. Quenk (revised manual), and Allen L. Hammer (revised manual).
Publisher: CPP, Inc.
Cross References: For reviews by John W. Fleenor and Paul M. Mastrangelo, see 14:251; see also T5:1755 (78 references) and T4:1702 (45 references); for a review by Jerry S. Wiggins of an earlier edition, see 10:206 (42 references); for a review by Anthony J. DeVito of an earlier edition, see 9:739 (19 references); see also T3:1555 (42 references); for a review by Richard W. Coan, of an earlier edition, see 8:630 (115 references); see also T2:1294 (120 references) and P:177 (56 references); for reviews by Gerald A. Mendelsohn and Norman D. Sundberg and an excerpted review by Laurence Siegel, see 6:147 (10 references).

[1802]

Myers-Briggs Type Indicator® Step II (Form Q).

Purpose: "Provides an in-depth personalized account of personality preferences."
Population: Age 12 and over.
Publication Date: 2001.
Acronym: MBTI Step II–Form Q.

Scores, 24: Four dichotomies (Extraversion vs. Introversion, Sensing vs. Intuition, Thinking vs. Feeling, Judging vs. Perceiving), 20 facets: 5 Extraversion–Introversion facets (Initiating–Receiving, Expressive–Contained, Gregarious–Intimate, Active–Reflective, Enthusiastic–Quiet), 5 Sensing–Intuition facets (Concrete–Abstract, Realistic–Imaginative, Practical–Conceptual, Experiential–Theoretical, Traditional–Original), 5 Thinking–Feeling facets (Logical–Empathetic, Reasonable–Compassionate, Questioning–Accommodating, Critical–Accepting, Tough–Tender), 5 Judging–Perceiving facets (Systematic–Casual, Planful–Open-Ended, Early Starting–Pressure-Prompted, Scheduled–Spontaneous, Methodical–Emergent).
Administration: Individual or group.
Price Data, 2011: $24.95 each for MBTI® Step II™ Profile online administration; $36.95 each for MBTI® Step II™ Interpretive Report online administration; $107.50 each for MBTI® Step II™ manual; $49.95 each for MBTI® Step II™ User's Guide; $299 each for Working With MBTI® Step II™ Results; $18.50 each for Understanding Your MBTI® Step II™ Results.
Foreign Language Editions: Available in U.S. English, U.K. English, Latin American Spanish, Japanese, Chinese Traditional, Chinese Simplified, Danish, Dutch, French, German, Swedish, European Spanish, Canadian French.
Time: (25–35) minutes.
Comments: Includes all items comprising Step I, Form M of MBTI® (1801); can be used to generate all reports produced by Step I, Form M of MBTI®; provides advice for enhancing communication, conflict and change management, and decision making skills; computer or web-administered scoring available.
Authors: Katharine C. Briggs, Isabel Briggs Myers, Naomi L. Quenk (Profile Form, Interpretive Form, MBTI Step II Manual), Jean Kummerow (Profile Form, Interpretive Form), Allen L. Hammer (MBTI Step II Manual), and Mark S. Major (MBTI Step II Manual).
Publisher: CPP, Inc.
Cross References: For reviews by Allen K. Hess and Kevin Lanning, see 15:172; for information about other components of this program, see T5:1755 (78 references) and T4:1702 (45 references); for reviews by John W. Fleenor and Paul M. Mastrangelo of Form M, see 14:251 (1 reference); for a review by Jerry S. Wiggins, see 10:206 (42 references); for a review by Anthony J. DeVito, see 9:739 (19 references); see also T3:1555 (42 references); for a review by Richard Coan, see 8:630 (115 references); see also T2:1294 (120 references) and P:177 (56 references); for reviews by Gerald A. Mendelsohn and Norman D. Sundberg and an excerpted review by Laurence Siegel, see 6:147 (10 references).

[1803]
Naglieri Nonverbal Ability Test.
Purpose: A "measure of nonverbal reasoning and problem solving independent of educational curricula and cultural or language background."

Population: Grades K–12.
Publication Dates: 1996–1997.
Acronym: NNAT.
Scores, 5: Pattern Completion (PC), Reasoning by Analogy (RA), Serial Reasoning (SR), Spatial Visualization (SV), Total (Nonverbal Ability Index–NAI).
Administration: Group.
Levels, 7: A (Kindergarten), B (Grade 1), C (Grade 2), D (Grades 3–4), E (Grades 5–6), F (Grades 7–9), G (Grades 10–12).
Price Data, 2002: $24.90 per examination kit (specify Level A–G) including one copy each machine-scorable or reusable test booklets, multilevel directions for administration, and machine-scorable answer documents (for Levels E–G); $92.80 per 25 machine-scorable test booklets including directions for administering and order for scoring services (specify Level A–D); $67.30 per 25 reusable test booklets for use with machine-scorable and hand-scorable answer documents (specify Level E–G); $67.30 per 25 hand-scorable test booklets including directions and 1 multilevel class record (specify Level A–D); $26 per 25 combined D/E/F/G machine-scorable answer documents; $26 per 25 combined D/E/F/G hand-scorable answer documents; $44.50 per side by side keys for hand-scorable test booklets (specify Level A–D); $22 per stencil keys for hand-scorable answer documents (specify Level D–G); $30 per response keys for all levels (list of correct responses); $60 per fall or spring norms book; $78.50 per technical manual; $9 per additional copy of directions for administering (all levels); price information for scoring and reporting services available from publisher.
Time: 30 (45) minutes.
Comments: An extension and revision of the Matrix Analogies Test (1632); appropriate for non-English-speaking students, students with hearing, language, or motor impairment, and impaired color vision; a general measure of ability or identification of students with learning problems.
Author: Jack A. Naglieri.
Publisher: Pearson.
Cross References: For reviews by Terry A. Stinnett and Michael S. Trevisan, see 14:252.

[1804]
Naglieri Nonverbal Ability Test–Individual Administration.
Purpose: Designed to provide a brief nonverbal measure of general ability.
Population: Ages 5-0 to 17-11.
Publication Date: 2003.
Acronym: NNAT-I.
Scores: Total score only.
Administration: Individual.
Price Data, 2004: $233 per complete kit including manual (139 pages), stimulus book, 25 parent reports,

and 25 each of record forms A and B; $110 per stimulus book; $5 per manual; $55 per 25 record forms (specify Form A or B); $55 per 25 parent reports.

Time: (25–30) minutes.

Comments: This test and the Naglieri Nonverbal Ability Test (Multilevel Form) (T6:1680) are the second editions of the still in-print Matrix Analogies Test (Expanded Form and Short Form) (T6:1531).

Author: Jack A. Naglieri.

Publisher: Pearson.

Cross References: For reviews by Connie T. England and Brian F. French, see 16:159; see also T5:1607 (15 references) and T4:1566 (8 references); for a review by Robert F. McMorris, David L. Rule, and Wendy J. Steinberg of the Matrix Analogies Test, see 10:191 (1 reference).

[1805]

NASA Moon Survival Task.

Purpose: To explore the performance characteristics of a decision-making group and the significance of member contributions to the quality of group production.

Population: Individuals who work, or anticipate working, in a group setting.

Publication Dates: 1963-1989.

Scores, 4: Commitment, Conflict, Creativity, Consensus.

Administration: Individual in part.

Price Data, 2001: $8.95 per instrument (1989, 21 pages).

Time: Administration time not reported.

Author: Jay Hall.

Publisher: Teleometrics International Inc.

Cross References: See T5:1757 (2 references).

[1806]

National Assessment of Educational Progress–Released Exercises.

Purpose: "A continuing, congressionally mandated national survey of knowledge, skills, and understanding, of young Americans" in the fields of mathematics, science, reading, writing, U.S. history, geography, and other subject areas.

Population: Grades 4, 8, and 12 (main NAEP); Ages 9, 13, and 17 (Long-Term Trend NAEP).

Publication Dates: 1983–2002.

Acronym: NAEP.

Scores: No individual scores, scaled results (average proficiency) are provided for designated reporting subgroups.

Administration: Group.

Price Data: Released items available on the NAEP website.

Comments: Released-exercise set, which is approximately one-third to one-half of the complete assessment package; administered to national samples of specified age groups biennially since 1969 (1969–1998 now out of print); released exercises are in the public domain and may be copied without restriction following receipt of permission from the author (NCES); student, teacher, and school questionnaires are also available; details of the assessments, procedures, analyses, and results can be found in a series of reports available from the author and publisher; ETS has served as the primary NAEP contractor since 1983. Available on the web at NCES. ed.gov/nationsreportand/itmrls.

Authors: National Assessment of Educational Progress; National Center for Education Statistics; Office of Educational Research and Improvement; U.S. Dept. of Education.

Publisher: Educational Testing Service.

a) MATHEMATICS.

Scores: 5 content areas (Numbers and Operations, Measurement, Geometry, Data Analysis/Statistics and Probability, Algebra and Functions), Estimation Skills; 3 process areas (Conceptual Understanding, Procedural Knowledge, Problem Solving).

Comments: Assessment dates: 1986, 1990, 1992, 1996.

b) SCIENCE.

Scores: 3 content areas (Life Sciences, Physical Sciences, Earth & Space Sciences); 3 thinking skills/areas (Conducting Inquiries, Solving Problems, Knowing Science).

Comments: Assessment dates: 1986, 1990.

c) READING.

Scores: 3 purposes (Reading for Literary Experience, Reading to Gain Information, Reading to Perform a Task); 4 stances (Initial Understanding, Developing Interpretation, Personal Reflection and Response, Demonstrating a Critical Stance).

Comments: Assessment dates: 1984, 1986, 1988, 1990, 1992, 1994, 1998, 2000, 2002.

d) WRITING.

Scores: 3 purposes (Informative, Narrative, Persuasive).

Comments: Assessment dates: 1984, 1988, 1992, 1998, 2002.

e) U.S. HISTORY.

Scores: 4 themes (Change and Continuity in American Democracy, The Gathering and Interaction of Peoples/Cultures/and Ideas, Economic and Technological Changes and Their Relation to Society/Ideas/and the Environment, The Changing Role of America in the World).

Comments: Assessment dates: 1988, 1994, 2001.

f) GEOGRAPHY.

Scores: 3 content areas (Space and Place, Environment and Society, Spatial Dynamics and Dimensions).

Comments: Assessment dates: 1988, 1994, 2001.

g) FINE ARTS.

Scores: 4 content areas (Music, Dance, Theatre, Visual Arts).

Comments: Assessment date: 1997.

Cross References: See T5:1759 (18 references).

[1807]

National Educational Development Tests.

Purpose: To provide students with information in their development of skills that are necessary to do well on college admissions tests and in college work itself.
Population: Grades 9–10.
Publication Dates: 1983–1984.
Acronym: NEDT.
Scores, 6: English Usage, Mathematics Usage, National Sciences Reading, Social Studies Reading, Composite Score, Educational Ability.
Administration: Group.
Price Data: Available from publisher for combined test materials and standard scoring services, student materials consist of test booklets and answer sheets, Student Handbook, Certificates of Educational Development, and Student Information Bulletin; administrative materials consist of identification sheets, Supervisor's and Examiner's Manuals (1984, 14 pages), and Interpretive Manuals.
Time: 150(180) minutes.
Comments: Tests administered 2 times annually (October and February).
Author: Science Research Associates, Inc.
Publisher: CTB/McGraw-Hill.
Cross References: See T4:1707 (1 reference); for reviews by Patti L. Harrison and Howard M. Knoff, see 11:255.

[1808]

National German Examination for High School Students.

Purpose: To evaluate students' achievement in German study, may be used as a diagnostic tool.
Population: 2, 3, or 4 years high school.
Publication Dates: 1960-2006.
Scores: Total score only.
Administration: Group.
Levels, 3: 2nd year, 3rd year, 4th year.
Price Data, 2006: $5 per test, includes scoring service; Interpretive data (17 pages) available; test booklets, tapes, and answer sheets are to be returned to Software, Inc.
Time: 60(65) minutes.
Comments: Also called AATG National Standardized Testing Program; formerly called AATG German Test and National German Contest for High School Students; tests administered annually in December and January under auspices of high school guidance departments and administration; test is new each year.
Author: American Association of Teachers of German.
Publisher: American Association of Teachers of German, Inc.
Cross References: For reviews by Gilbert C. Kettelkamp and Theodor F. Naumann of an earlier edition, see 6:382.

[1809]

National Institute for Personnel Research Normal Battery.

Purpose: "Designed as a selection device for use mainly with Bantu clerks in various industrial and government organizations."
Population: South African Standards 6–10 and job applicants with 8–11 years of education.
Publication Dates: 1960–1973.
Subtests, 5: Mental Alertness, Reading Comprehension, Vocabulary, Spelling, Computation.
Administration: Group.
Price Data: Price information available from publisher for test materials including manual (1969, 129 pages).
Author: S. M. A. Waterhouse (manual).
Publisher: Human Sciences Research Council [South Africa].
Cross References: See T2:1085 (2 references) and 6:779.

[1810]

National Police Officer Selection Test.

Purpose: Measures skills critical to the successful performance of entry-level officers.
Population: Police officer candidates.
Publication Dates: 1991–1992.
Acronym: POST.
Partial Batteries: POST III or POST IV.
Administration: Group.
Restricted Distribution: Available to authorized police personnel only.
Price Data: Price information available from publisher for administration guide (1991, 12 pages), examiner's manual (1992, 13 pages; required with first purchase), and study guide.
Comments: Test may be self-scored or scored by Stanard & Associates, Inc.
Author: Stanard & Associates, Inc.
Publisher: Stanard & Associates, Inc.
  a) POST III.
  Scores, 4: Mathematics, Reading Comprehension, Grammar, Total.
  Price Data: Price information available from publisher for 1-250 POST III (scored by publisher) and 1–250 POST III (self-scored).
  Time: 66 (71) minutes.
  b) POST IV.
  Scores, 5: Mathematics, Reading Comprehension, Grammar, Incident Report Writing, Total.
  Price Data: Price information available from publisher for 1-250 POST IV (scored by publisher) and 1–250 POST IV (self-scored).
  Time: 83 (88) minutes.
Cross References: See T5:1763 (1 reference); for reviews by Jim C. Fortune and Abbot Packard and by Kurt F. Geisinger, see 12:253.

[1811]

National Spanish Examinations.

Purpose: Designed as a motivational extracurricular contest for students of members of the American Association of Teachers of Spanish and Portuguese (AATSP) and chapters.
Population: Second semester of 1, 2, 3, 4–6 year Spanish students.
Publication Dates: 1957–2002.
Acronym: NSE.
Scores: Total score only.
Administration: Group.
Levels, 6: 01, 1, 2, 3, 4, 5 (3, 4, and 5 include a Bilingual/Native Supplement).
Manual: Directions for Administering, 2002, 10 pages (revised annually).
Restricted Distribution: Available only to current members of AATSP.
Price Data: Available from publisher.
Time: 60 minutes.
Comments: New form constructed annually for administration in February and March at local secondary schools or centers established by local chapters of the AATSP; summary of results of top three scorers in each level published in Hispania in September following the completion of the testing program; now available as online test only (no paper copies).
Author: Test Development Committees, American Association of Teachers of Spanish and Portuguese.
Publisher: National Spanish Exam.
Cross References: See 8:168 (2 references); for a review by Walter V. Kalfers of earlier forms, see 7:323 (1 reference); see also 6:428 (8 references).

[1812]

National Survey of Student Engagement.

Purpose: Designed to provide colleges and universities information about the student experience and institutional performance to use to improve undergraduate education, inform accountability and accreditation efforts, and facilitate national and sector benchmarking efforts.
Population: Bachelor's degree-seeking undergraduate students at 4-year colleges and universities.
Publication Dates: 2000–2011.
Acronym: NSSE.
Scores, 8: Level of Academic Challenge, Active and Collaborative Learning, Student Interactions with Faculty Members, Enriching Educational Experiences, Supportive Campus Environment, Deep Learning, Background Information, Consortium Questions.
Administration: Group.
Price Data, 2011: The base cost includes a $300 nonrefundable registration fee plus an administration fee determined by undergraduate enrollment. This fee ranges from $1,500 to $7,500. Participating institutions receive: (a) an institutional report with respondent characteristics, mean and frequency distributions, benchmark comparisons, multi-year benchmark report, major field reports, student experience in brief, and an executive snapshot; (b) a data file and codebook; and (c) resources that include psychometric portfolio, accreditation toolkits, examples of how institutions are using their data, and much more. There are also optional fees for institutions that wish to oversample and/or participate in a consortium.
Time: (10–15) minutes.
Authors: George D. Kuh (test and technical report); J. C. Hayek, R. M. Carini, J. A. Oimet, R. M. Gonyea, and J. Kennedy (technical report).
Publisher: Indiana University Center for Postsecondary Research.
Cross References: For reviews by William I. Sauser, Jr. and Eugene P. Sheehan, see 16:160.

[1813]

Neale Analysis of Reading Ability: Second Revised British Edition.

Purpose: Designed to measure reading accuracy, comprehension and rate and to provide diagnostic information about children's reading difficulties.
Population: Ages 6-0 to 12-11.
Publication Dates: 1958–1997.
Acronym: NARA II.
Scores, 3: Comprehension, Accuracy, Rate; plus 4 supplementary diagnostic scores (Discrimination of Initial and Final Sounds, Names and Sounds of the Alphabet, Graded Spelling, Auditory Discrimination and Blending).
Administration: Individual.
Forms, 3: 1, 2, Diagnostic Tutor Form (not norm referenced).
Price Data: Available from publisher.
Time: (20) minutes.
Comments: Revision includes new norms and larger standardization sample.
Authors: Marie D. Neale (test and manual); Second Revised British Edition and standardization by Chris Whetton, Louise Caspall, and Kay McCulloch.
Publisher: GL Assessment [England].
Cross References: For reviews by Marie Miller-Whitehead and Elizabeth Kelley Rhoades, see 16:161; see also T5:1765 (36 references) and T4:1714 (7 references); for reviews by Cleborne D. Maddux and G. Michael Poteat of an earlier edition, see 11:257 (41 references); see also T3:1567 (13 references) and T2:1683 (7 references); for reviews by M. Alan Brimer and Magdalen D. Vernon, and an excerpted review, see 6:843.

[1814]

Neale Analysis of Reading Ability, 3rd Edition [Australian Standardisation].

Purpose: Designed to "assess reading progress objectivity [and] to obtain structured diagnostic observations of an individual's reading behaviour."
Population: Ages 6 to 12.

Publication Dates: 1958–1999.
Scores, 3: Accuracy, Comprehension, Rate.
Administration: Individual.
Forms, 2: 1, 2.
Price Data, 2006: A$38.50 per test booklet; A$1.95 per individual record standardised test (specify form); A$1.95 per individual record diagnostic tutor (specify form); A$54.95 per manual (1999, 141 pages); A$99.95 per specimen set including test booklet, 1 each individual record standarised test Form 1 and 2, 1 each individual record diagnostic tutor Form A and B, and manual; A$149.95 per specimen set plus video; A$49.95 per video; A$21.95 per audio cassette.
Time: Administration time not reported.
Comments: Includes six supplementary diagnostic tests (Discrimination of Initial and Final Sounds, Names and Sounds of the Alphabet, Graded Spelling, Auditory Discrimination and Blending, Word Lists, and Silent Reading/Writing).
Authors: Marie D. Neale, Michael McKay, and John Barnard.
Publisher: Australian Council for Educational Research Ltd. [Australia].
Cross References: For reviews by Valentina McInerney and Bruce G. Rogers, see 15:173.

[1815]

NEEDS Survey.

Purpose: Designed "to provide a concise but comprehensive profile of an individual's functioning" relative to the treatment of substance abuse.
Population: Adults.
Publication Date: 1994.
Acronym: NEEDS.
Scores, 10: Test Taking Attitude, Basic Problem Solving and Reading, Emotional Stability, Substance Abuse, Employment, Personal Relationship and Support System, Physical Health, Education, Criminal History, Overall "Needs."
Administration: Individual or group.
Price Data: Available from publisher.
Time: (26) minutes.
Comments: Self-administered; computer-scored, IBM compatible with either DOS or Windows required; provides DSM-IV classification for alcohol and drug abuse and ASAM patient placement criteria for treatment recommendations; available in English or Spanish.
Author: ADE Incorporated.
Publisher: ADE Incorporated.
Cross References: For reviews by Anita M. Hubley and Paul M. Mastrangelo, see 14:253.

[1816]

Nelson-Denny Reading Test CD-ROM Version 1.2.

Purpose: "To provide a trustworthy assessment of student ability in three areas of academic achievement: vocabulary, reading comprehension, and reading rate."

Population: Grades 9–16 and adults.
Publication Dates: 1929–2000.
Scores, 4: Vocabulary, Comprehension, Total, Reading Rate.
Administration: Group.
Forms, 2: G and H.
Price Data, 2011: $26 per Manual for Scoring and Interpretation; $9 per administration for 25 to 499 test administrations; $8 per administration for 500-999 test administrations; $7 per administration for 1000+ administrations.
Time: 35(56) minutes.
Comments: Requires Windows 95, 98, NT, or 2000; creates reports including the Individual Narrative, Individual Longitudinal, Group Longitudinal, Group Longitudinal Summary, List of Student Scores, and the Group Summary; a computerized alternative identical in content to paper-pencil Forms G and H and considered by the publisher to be parallel forms.
Authors: James I. Brown, Vivian Vick Fishco, and Gerald S. Hanna.
Publisher: PRO-ED.
Cross References: For reviews by Alice Corkill and by Darrell L. Sabers and Amy M. Olson, see 17:132; see also T5:1767 (9 references); for reviews by Mildred Murray-Ward and Douglas K. Smith of Forms G and H, see 13:206 (52 references); see also T4:1715 (30 references); for reviews by Robert J. Tierney and James E. Ysseldyke of Forms E and F, see 9:745 (12 references); see also T3:1568 (38 references); for reviews by Robert A. Forsyth and Alton L. Raynor of Forms C and D, see 8:735 (31 references); see also T2:1572 (46 references); for reviews by David B. Orr and Agatha Townsend an excerpted review by John O. Crites of Forms A and B, see 6:800 (13 references); for a review by Ivan A. Booker, see 4:544 (17 references); for a review by Hans C. Gordon, see 2:1557.

[1817]

Nelson-Denny Reading Test, Forms G and H.

Purpose: "To assess student achievement and progress in vocabulary, comprehension, and reading rate."
Population: Grades 9–16 and adult.
Publication Dates: 1929–1993.
Scores, 4: Vocabulary, Comprehension, Total, Reading Rate.
Administration: Group.
Price Data, 2011: $204 per complete kit, which includes 25 Form G Test Booklets, 25 Form H Test Booklets, 50 Self-Scorable Answer Sheets, Directions for Administration, and a Manual for Scoring and Interpretation.
Time: 35 minutes; 56 minutes for extended time administration.
Comments: Computer-administered version is available on CD-ROM in Windows format.

Authors: James I. Brown, Vivian Vick Fishco, and Gerald S. Hanna.
Publisher: PRO-ED.
Cross References: See T5:1767 (9 references); for reviews by Mildred Murray-Ward and Douglas K. Smith, see 13:206 (52 references); see also T4:1715 (30 references); for reviews by Robert J. Tierney and James E. Ysseldyke of Forms E and F, see 9:745 (12 references); see also T3:1568 (38 references); for reviews by Robert A. Forsyth and Alton L. Raynor of Forms C and D, see 8:735 (31 references); see also T2:1572 (46 references); for reviews by David B. Orr and Agatha Townsend and an excerpted review by John O. Crites of Forms A and B, see 6:800 (13 references); for a review by Ivan A. Booker, see 4:544 (17 references); for a review by Hans C. Gordon, see 2:1557.

[1818]

NEO-4.

Purpose: Designed as a four-factor version of the Revised NEO Personality Inventory.
Population: Ages 17 and older.
Publication Date: 1998.
Scores, 28: Extraversion (Warmth, Gregariousness, Assertiveness, Activity, Excitement-Seeking, Positive Emotions, Total); Openness to Experience (Fantasy, Aesthetics, Feelings, Actions, Ideas, Values, Total); Agreeableness (Trust, Straightforwardness, Altruism, Compliance, Modesty, Tender-Mindedness, Total); Conscientiousness (Competence, Order, Dutifulness, Achievement Striving, Self-Discipline, Deliberation, Total).
Administration: Group or individual.
Forms, 2: Form S (self-reports), Form R (observer ratings).
Price Data, 2006: $202 per introductory kit including NEO-4 manual supplement (19 pages), 10 each Form S and Form R reusable item booklets, 25 hand-scorable answer sheets, 25 profile forms, 25 style graph booklets, and 25 Your NEO-4 summary forms.
Time: [25–35] minutes.
Comments: Questionnaire items, scoring keys, and scale norms are identical to those found in the Revised NEO Personality Inventory (NEO PI-R; T7:1729) for the four factors of Extraversion, Openness to Experience, Agreeableness, and Conscientiousness and users are encouraged to consult the professional manual for the NEO PI-R.
Authors: Paul T. Costa and Robert R. McCrae.
Publisher: Psychological Assessment Resources, Inc.
Cross References: For reviews by Theresa M. Bahns and Carlen Hennington, see 14:254.

[1819]

NEO Personality Inventory-3.

Purpose: Designed to measure "the five major dimensions, or domains, of personality and the most important traits or facets that define each domain."

Population: Ages 12 and older.
Publication Dates: 1978-2010.
Administration: Group.
Price Data, 2010: $165 per complete NEO-FFI-3 Adult Form S Kit including NEO Inventories professional manual (2010, 145 pages), 25 NEO-FFI-3 Form S Adult item booklets, and 25 Your NEO Summary feedback sheets; $165 per complete NEO-FFI-3 Adolescent Form S Kit including NEO Inventories Professional Manual, 25 NEO-FFI-3 Form S Adolescent item booklets, and 25 Your NEO Summary feedback sheets; $65 per NEO Inventories professional manual: NEO-PI-3, NEO-FFI-3, NEO PI-R.
Comments: A major innovation of this edition is the modification of the NEO PI-R in which 37 items were replaced; the NEO-PI-3 is now "suitable for assessing personality in middle school-aged children and adolescents, as well as adults"; clinicians may continue using the NEO PI-R; "The NEO-FFI-3 is a revision of the NEO-FFI in which 15 … items have been replaced to improve readability and psychometric properties."
Authors: Robert R. McCrae and Paul T. Costa, Jr.
Publisher: Psychological Assessment Resources, Inc.
a) NEO PERSONALITY INVENTORY-3.
Acronym: NEO-PI-3.
Scores, 35: 30 facets in 5 domains: Neuroticism (Anxiety, Angry Hostility, Depression, Self-Consciousness, Impulsiveness, Vulnerability), Extraversion (Warmth, Gregariousness, Assertiveness, Activity, Excitement-Seeking, Positive Emotions), Openness (Fantasy, Aesthetics, Feelings, Actions, Ideas, Values), Agreeableness (Trust, Straightforwardness, Altruism, Compliance, Modesty, Tender-Mindedness), Conscientiousness (Competence, Order, Dutifulness, Achievement Striving, Self-Discipline, Deliberation).
Forms, 2: Form S (self-report), Form R (observer ratings).
Time: (30-40) minutes.
b) REVISED NEO PERSONALITY INVENTORY.
Acronym: NEO PI-R.
Scores, 35: 30 facets in 5 domains: Neuroticism (Anxiety, Angry Hostility, Depression, Self-Consciousness, Impulsiveness, Vulnerability), Extraversion (Warmth, Gregariousness, Assertiveness, Activity, Excitement-Seeking, Positive Emotions), Openness (Fantasy, Aesthetics, Feelings, Actions, Ideas, Values), Agreeableness (Trust, Straightforwardness, Altruism, Compliance, Modesty, Tender-Mindedness), Conscientiousness (Competence, Order, Dutifulness, Achievement Striving, Self-Discipline, Deliberation).
Forms, 2: Form S (self-report), Form R (observer ratings).
Time: (30-40) minutes.
c) NEO FIVE-FACTOR INVENTORY-3.
Acronym: NEO-FFI-3.

Scores, 5: Neuroticism, Extraversion, Openness, Agreeableness, Conscientiousness.

Forms, 4: Form S (self-report), Form R (observer ratings), Adolescent, Adult.

Time: (5-10) minutes.

Cross References: See T5:2218 (135 references); for reviews by Michael D. Botwin and Samuel Juni of the Revised Edition, see 12:330 (50 references); see also T4:2263 (49 references); for reviews by Allen K. Hess and Thomas A. Widiger of an earlier edition, see 11:258 (5 references); for a review by Robert Hogan of an earlier edition of a, see 10:214 (6 references).

[1820]

Neonatal Behavioral Assessment Scale, 3rd Edition.

Purpose: Designed to evaluate an infant's behavioral and neurological status.

Population: Ages 3 days through 2 months.

Publication Dates: 1973–1995.

Acronym: NBAS.

Scores, 53: (Each item represents a score) in 3 domains: Behavioral (28 items), Supplementary (7 items), Reflex (18 items).

Administration: Individual.

Price Data: Available from publisher.

Time: (20–30) minutes.

Comments: Previous version entitled Brazelton Neonatal Behavioral Assessment Scale-380; a 53-item rating scale of infant behavior and reflexes; not for use with infants recovering from illness or premature birth; to be administered by clinicians trained in neonatal behavior.

Authors: T. Berry Brazelton and J. Kevin Nugent.

Publisher: Cambridge University Press.

Cross References: For reviews by Carol M. McGregor and Hoi K. Suen, see 14:255; see also T5:1770 (17 references), T4:321 (9 references), 9:157 (9 references), and T3:311 (31 references); for a review by Anita Miller Sostek of an earlier edition, and an excerpted review by Stephen Wolkind of an earlier edition, see 8:208 (15 references).

[1821]

NEPSY-II-Second Edition.

Purpose: "Designed to assess neuropsychological development."

Population: Ages 3-0 to 16-11.

Publication Dates: 1998-2007.

Acronym: NEPSY-II.

Scores, 32: Attention/Executive Functioning (Animal Sorting, Auditory Attention and Response Set, Clocks, Design Fluency, Inhibition, Statue), Language (Body Part Naming and Identification, Comprehension of Instructions, Oromotor Sequences, Phonological Processing, Repetition of Nonsense Words, Speeded Naming, Word Generation), Memory and Learning (List Memory, Memory for Designs, Memory for Faces, Memory for Names, Narrative Memory,

Sentence Repetition, Word List Interference), Sensorimotor (Fingertip Tapping, Imitating Hand Positions, Manual Motor Sequences, Visuomotor Precision), Social Perception (Affect Recognition, Theory of Mind), Visuospatial Processing (Arrows, Block Construction, Design Copying, Geometric Puzzles, Picture Puzzles, Route Finding).

Administration: Individual.

Forms, 2: Ages 3-4, Ages 5-16.

Price Data, 2007: $845 per complete kit including administration manual (2007, 183 pages), clinical and interpretive manual (2007, 290 pages), 2 stimulus books, 25 record forms (ages 3-4), 25 record forms (ages 5-16), 25 response booklets (ages 3-4), 25 response booklets (ages 5-16), administration cards, scoring templates, manipulatives, and training CD; $49 per 25 record forms (ages 3-4); $59 per 25 record forms (ages 5-16); $49 per 25 response booklets (ages 3-4); $59 per 25 record forms (ages 5-16); $20 per scoring template; $50 per set of administration cards; $30 per memory grid; $105 per set of 12 blocks; $85 per administration manual; $120 per clinical and interpretive manual; $130 per stimulus book; $100 per training CD.

Time: (45-90) minutes for ages 3-4; (60-180) minutes for ages 5-16.

Comments: Also contains optional qualitative behavioral observations and supplemental scores; earlier edition entitled: NEPSY: A Developmental Neuropsychological Assessment.

Authors: Marit Korkman, Ursula Kirk, and Sally Kemp.

Publisher: Pearson.

Cross References: For reviews by Rik Carl D'Amato and Jonathan E. Titley and by Scott A. Napolitano, see 18:80; for reviews by Sandra D. Haynes and Daniel C. Miller of an earlier edition, see 14:256.

[1822]

Network Analyst Staff Selector.

Purpose: To evaluate essential skills needed for the network analyst.

Population: Candidates for technical network positions.

Publication Date: 1992.

Acronym: NETAL.

Scores: Total Score, Narrative Evaluation, Ranking, Recommendation.

Administration: Group.

Price Data, 2001: $340 per candidate; quantity discounts available.

Time: (150) minutes.

Comments: Scored by publisher; must be proctored.

Author: Bruce A. Winrow.

Publisher: Walden Personnel Performance, Inc. [Canada].

[1823]

Network Technician Staff Selector.

Purpose: To measure network knowledge and analytical skills.

Population: Candidates for the position of network technician.
Publication Date: 1992.
Acronym: NETECH.
Scores: Total Score, Narrative Evaluation, Ranking, Recommendation.
Administration: Group.
Price Data, 2001: $340 per candidate.
Time: (107) minutes.
Comments: Scored by publisher; must be proctored.
Author: Bruce A. Winrow.
Publisher: Walden Personnel Performance, Inc. [Canada].

[1824]

Neurobehavioral Functioning Inventory.

Purpose: "Designed to measure the frequency of neurobehavioral problems associated with traumatic brain injury and other neurological disorders."
Population: Patients ages 17 and older.
Publication Date: 1999.
Acronym: NFI.
Scores, 6: Depression, Somatic, Memory/Attention, Communication, Aggression, Motor.
Administration: Individual or group.
Price Data, 2002: $137 per complete kit including manual (120 pages), 25 Family record forms, and 25 Patient record forms; $79 per manual; $39 per 25 record forms (Family or Patient).
Time: (30) minutes.
Comments: Self-scoring self-report forms.
Authors: Jeffrey S. Kreutzer, Ronald T. Seel, and Jennifer H. Marwitz.
Publisher: Pearson.
Cross References: For reviews by Raymond S. Dean and John J. Brinkman, Jr., and by Thomas McKnight, see 16:162.

[1825]

Neuropsychiatry Unit Cognitive Assessment Tool.

Purpose: Designed to "assist in the diagnosis and management of cognitive disorders and serve as a guide to more in-depth formal neuropsychological testing."
Population: Ages 18+.
Publication Date: 2008.
Acronym: NUCOG.
Scores, 6: Attention, Memory, Executive Function, Language, Visuoconstructional Function, Total.
Administration: Individual.
Price Data, 2008: A$136.95 per kit including manual (64 pages), 10 Interview Schedule/Cognitive Profiles, and 10 Subject Completion Sheets; A$119.96 per manual.
Time: (20) minutes.
Authors: Mark Walterfang and Dennis Velakoulis.

Publisher: Australian Council for Educational Research Ltd. [Australia].
Cross References: For a review by Anthony T. Dugbartey, see 18:81.

[1826]

Neuropsychological Assessment Battery.

Purpose: "Developed for the assessment of a wide array of cognitive skills and functions in adults with known or suspected disorders of the central nervous system."
Population: Ages 18–97.
Publication Dates: 2001–2003.
Forms, 2: Form 1, Form 2 (equivalent forms).
Price Data: Available from publisher.
Time: Administration time not reported.
Comments: Modules may be purchased and administered individually; NAB Training Program on DVD is included with each module; software portfolio available for use on CD-ROM.
Authors: Robert A. Stern and Travis White.
Publisher: Psychological Assessment Resources, Inc.
  a) SCREENING MODULE.
  Scores, 6: Attention, Language, Memory, Spatial, Executive Function, Total.
  Comments: May be used to determine whether more in-depth, followup examinations are necessary.
  b) ATTENTION MODULE.
  Scores, 12: Digits (2), Dots, Numbers & Letters (7), Driving Scenes, Total.
  c) LANGUAGE MODULE.
  Scores, 6: Oral Production, Auditory Comprehension, Naming, Writing, Bill Payment, Total.
  d) MEMORY MODULE.
  Scores, 5: List Learning, Shape Learning, Story Learning, Daily Living Memory, Total.
  Comments: Also available as a stand-alone test with a separate manual.
  e) SPATIAL MODULE.
  Scores, 5: Visual Discrimination, Design Construction, Figure Drawing, Map Reading, Total.
  f) EXECUTIVE FUNCTIONS.
  Scores, 5: Mazes, Judgment, Categories, Word Generation, Total.
Cross References: For reviews by Timothy J. Makatura and by Wilfred G. Van Gorp and Jason Hassenstab, see 16:163.

[1827]

The Neuropsychological Impairment Scale.

Purpose: Designed to screen for "neuropsychological symptoms."
Population: Ages 18–88 years.
Publication Date: 1994.
Acronym: NIS.
Scores, 14: Defensiveness, Affective Disturbance, Response Inconsistency, Subjective Distortion Index,

Global Measure of Impairment, Total Items Circled, Symptom Intensity Measure, Critical Items, Cognitive Efficiency, Attention, Memory, Frustration Tolerance, Learning-Verbal, Academic Skills.
Administration: Group.
Forms, 3: Self-Report, Observer Report, Senior Interview.
Price Data, 2006: $148.50 per complete kit including 25 self-report AutoScore™ answer forms, 25 observer-report AutoScore™ answer forms, and manual (71 pages) with Senior Interview Supplement and Response Card; $46.50 per 25 self-report AutoScore™ answer forms; $46.50 per 25 observer-report AutoScore™ answer forms; $61.50 per manual; $98 per Senior Interview kit including 25 Senior Interview AutoScore™ answer forms, 1 manual with Senior Interview Supplement and Response Card; $46.50 per 25 Senior Interview AutoScore™ answer forms; $155 10 use disk for use with self report, observer report, and senior interview; $16.50 per PC Answer Sheet in packages of 100.
Time: (15–20) minutes.
Comments: Self-Report form and Observer-Report form both utilize the 14 scores listed above, Senior Interview provides Global Measure of Impairment and scores for Defensiveness, Affective Disturbance, and Inconsistency.
Authors: William E. O'Donnell, Clinton B. DeSoto, Janet L. DeSoto, and Don McQ. Reynolds.
Publisher: Western Psychological Services.
Cross References: For a review by Robert A. Leark, see 14:257; see also T5:1775 (3 references).

[1828]

Neuropsychological Status Exam.

Purpose: Designed to organize data useful in neuropsychological assessment.
Population: Neuropsychological patients.
Publication Date: 1983.
Acronym: NSE.
Scores: Checklists in 13 areas: Patient Data, Referral Data, Tentative Findings, Neuropsychological Symptom Checklist, Premorbid Status, Physical Status, Emotional Status, Cognitive Status, Test Administration, Results of Neuropsychological Testing, Diagnostic Comments, Effects on Patient Functioning, Treatment Recommendations.
Administration: Individual.
Price Data, 2005: $59 per complete kit including 25 NSE and 25 NSC (Checklist) forms and manual (13 pages).
Time: Administration time not reported.
Author: John A. Schinka.
Publisher: Psychological Assessment Resources, Inc.

[1829]

Neuropsychology Behavior and Affect Profile.

Purpose: Designed to assess psychological changes in personality that accompany selective neurological disorders.

Population: Brain-impaired individuals ages 15 and over.
Publication Dates: 1989–1994.
Acronym: NBAP.
Scores, 5: Indifference, Inappropriateness, Pragnosia, Depression, Mania.
Administration: Individual.
Forms, 2: Form S, Form O.
Price Data: Available from publisher at www.mind-garden.com/products/nbaps.htm.
Time: Administration time not reported.
Comments: Form S is self-administered by patients judged capable of accurate self-report; Form O is filled out by significant other when Form S is deemed inappropriate.
Authors: Linda Nelson, Paul Satz, and Louis F. D'Elia.
Publisher: Mind Garden, Inc.
Cross References: For a review by Surendra P. Singh, see 14:258.

[1830]

New Jersey Test of Reasoning Skills—Form B.

Purpose: Assesses elementary reasoning and inquiry skills.
Population: Reading level grade 5 and over.
Publication Dates: 1983-1985.
Scores: 22 skill areas: Converting Statements, Translating into Logical Form, Inclusion/Exclusion, Recognizing Improper Questions, Avoiding Jumping to Conclusions, Analogical Reasoning, Detecting Underlying Assumptions, Eliminating Alternatives, Inductive Reasoning, Reasoning with Relationships, Detecting Ambiguities, Discerning Causal Relationships, Identifying Good Reasons, Recognizing Symmetrical Relationships, Syllogistic Reasoning (Categorical), Distinguishing Differences of Kind and Degree, Recognizing Transitive Relationships, Recognizing Dubious Authority, Reasoning with 4-Possibilities Matrix, Contradicting Statements, Whole-Part and Part-Whole Reasoning, Syllogistic Reasoning (Conditional).
Administration: Group.
Manual: No manual.
Price Data, 2001: $2.40 per test booklet.
Time: (30-45) minutes.
Author: Virginia Shipman.
Publisher: Institute for the Advancement of Philosophy for Children.
Cross References: See T4:1723 (1 reference); for reviews by Arthur S. Ellen and Rosemary E. Sutton, see 11:259 (1 reference).

[1831]

New Standards Reference Examinations: English Language Arts.

Purpose: Designed to assess student performance "in the areas of reading and writing."
Population: Elementary, middle, and high school students.
Publication Dates: 1996–2003.
Acronym: NSRE: English Language Arts.

Scores, 4: Reading: Basic Understanding, Reading: Analysis and Interpretation, Writing: Effectiveness, Writing: Conventions.
Administration: Group.
Levels, 3: Elementary, Middle, High School.
Forms, 2: E, F.
Price Data: Available from publisher.
Time: Three 55-minute sessions.
Comments: Scoring service provided by publisher.
Author: National Center on Education and the Economy; Learning Research and Development Center, University of Pittsburgh.
Publisher: Pearson.
Cross References: For a review by Dorothy M. Singleton, see 16:164.

[1832]

New Standards Reference Examinations: Mathematics.

Purpose: Designed to assess student performance in mathematics.
Population: Elementary, middle, and high school students.
Publication Dates: 1996–2003.
Acronym: NSRE: Mathematics.
Scores, 3: Skills, Concepts, Problem Solving.
Administration: Group.
Levels, 3: Elementary, Middle, High School.
Forms, 2: C, D.
Price Data: Available from publisher.
Foreign Language Edition: Spanish edition available.
Time: Three (55–65) minute sessions.
Comments: Scoring service provided by publisher.
Author: National Center on Education and the Economy; Learning Research and Development Center, University of Pittsburgh.
Publisher: Pearson.
Cross References: For reviews by Maria del R. Medina-Diaz and Carol S. Parke, see 16:165.

[1833]

New Technology Tests: Computer Commands.

Purpose: To "provide a measure of aptitude for those entering employment or training in occupations where computers are used as basic operational tools ... it focuses on skills relating to the rapid identification of differences between two pieces of information, and the use of commands to bring about change."
Population: Applicants for computer-related jobs.
Publication Date: 1987.
Scores: Total score only.
Administration: Group.
Price Data: Available from publisher.
Time: 20 [25] minutes.
Comments: New Technology Tests: Computer Rules (1834) also available.

Author: Psychometric Research & Development Ltd.
Publisher: Psychometric Research & Development Ltd. [England].
Cross References: For a review by Bruce W. Hall, see 11:260.

[1834]

New Technology Tests: Computer Rules.

Purpose: To "provide a measure of aptitude for those entering employment or training in occupations where computers are used as a basic operational tool ... the emphasis in this test is primarily on following rules."
Population: Applicants for computer-related jobs.
Publication Date: 1987.
Scores: Total score only.
Administration: Group.
Price Data: Available from publisher.
Time: 30[35] minutes.
Comments: New Technology Tests: Computer Commands (1833) also available.
Author: Psychometric Research & Development Ltd
Publisher: Psychometric Research & Development Ltd. [England].
Cross References: For a review by Bruce W. Hall, see 11:261.

[1835]

New York Longitudinal Scales Adult Temperament Questionnaire, Second Edition.

Purpose: Designed to measure the nine NYLS dimensions of temperament in adulthood.
Population: Ages 13-89.
Publication Dates: 1995-2008.
Acronym: ATQ2.
Scores, 9: Activity Level, Rhythmicity, Adaptability, Approach, Intensity, Mood, Persistence, Distractibility, Threshold.
Administration: Group.
Price Data, 2011: $69.95 per complete kit including test manual (2008, 34 pages), user's guide, and 25 questionnaires with scoring and profile sheets; $49.95 per 25 questionnaires with scoring and profile sheets; volume discounts available.
Time: (10-15) minutes.
Comments: Self-report ratings; internet scoring available using ATQ2 iReport Writer software.
Authors: Stella Chess and Alexander Thomas.
Publisher: Behavioral-Developmental Initiatives.
Cross References: For reviews by James A. Athanasou and Stephen N. Axford of the original edition, see 16:166.

[1836]

NewGAP.

Purpose: Constructed to assess reading comprehension using Cloze technique.

Population: Grades 2-5; ages 7 through 12.
Publication Date: 1990.
Scores: Total score only.
Administration: Group or individual.
Forms, 2: I, II.
Price Data, 2006: $55 per complete kit including 25 each of Forms I and II, scoring template, and manual (39 pages); $22 per 50 test forms (25 each Form I and II); $6 per scoring template; $24 per manual; $24 per specimen set.
Time: 15(20) minutes.
Comments: Norm-referenced.
Authors: John McLeod and Rita McLeod.
Publisher: Academic Therapy Publications.
Cross References: For reviews by Terry A. Ackerman and Ruth Johnson, see 12:254.

[1837]
NICU Network Neurobehavioral Scale.

Purpose: Designed to examine "the neurobehavioral organization, neurologic reflexes, motor development, and active and passive tone as well as signs of stress and withdrawal of the at-risk or drug-exposed infant."
Population: Infants between 30 to 48 weeks corrected or conceptional age.
Publication Date: 2005.
Acronym: NNNS.
Scores, 13: Habituation, Attention, Handling, Quality of Movement, Regulation, Nonoptimal Reflexes, Asymmetry, Stress/Abstinence, Arousal, Hypertonicity, Hypotonicity, Excitability, Lethargy.
Administration: Individual.
Restricted Distribution: Examiners must obtain training and certification from the publisher to administer the test.
Price Data, 2010: $349 per complete test kit including manual, scoring sheets, and tool kit (includes ball, bell rattle, flashlight, foot probe, and head supports); $50 per manual (242 pages); $30 per 20 scoring sheets; $325 per tool kit.
Time: (20) minutes.
Comments: Examiners are instructed to gather observations and then complete the scoring sheet; scores should not be completed while conducting the examination. The standardized administration procedures are designed to accommodate the current state of arousal and age of the infant being assessed. The authors state that the scale is "not appropriate for infants who are younger than 30 weeks gestational age."
Authors: Barry M. Lester and Edward Z. Tronick.
Publisher: Paul H. Brookes Publishing Co., Inc.

[1838]
901 Correctional Facility First-Line Supervisor Test.

Purpose: Designed "to assist correctional facilities … in promoting qualified candidates to the supervisory level."

Population: Candidates for promotion to the correctional facility first-line supervisory position.
Publication Dates: 2002-2006.
Scores: 6 knowledge areas: Concepts of Supervision, Correctional Facility Operation, Concepts for Writing and Reviewing Reports and Paperwork, Concepts of Evaluating Subordinate Performance, Concepts of Training, Concepts of Administration.
Administration: Individual or group.
Price Data: Available from publisher.
Time: 150 minutes.
Comments: A reading list is available to help candidates prepare for the test.
Author: International Public Management Association for Human Resources.
Publisher: International Public Management Association for Human Resources (IPMA-HR).

[1839]
19 Field Interest Inventory.

Purpose: Measures vocational interests in 19 broad vocational areas.
Population: Standards 8–10 in South African school system and college and adults.
Publication Dates: 1970–1971.
Acronym: 19FII.
Scores, 21: Fine Arts, Performing Arts, Language, Historical, Service, Social Work, Sociability, Public Speaking, Law, Creative Thought, Science, Practical-Male, Practical-Female, Numerical, Business, Clerical, Travel, Nature, Sport, Work-Hobby, Active-Passive.
Administration: Group.
Price Data: Available from publisher.
Time: (45) minutes.
Authors: F. A. Fouche and N. F. Alberts.
Publisher: Human Sciences Research Council [South Africa].
Cross References: For additional information, see 7:1027.

[1840]
NOCTI Experienced Worker Assessments.

Purpose: "Designed to measure an individual's knowledge of higher-level concepts, theories, and applications in the related occupation."
Population: Career and technical education teachers, potential teachers, and journey workers.
Publication Dates: 1993–2002.
Scores: Duty category scores and total scores are reported for 52 Written and Performance tests: Advertising and Design, Air Cooled Gas Engine Repair, Appliance Repair, Architectural Drafting, Audio Visual Communications Technology, Automotive Technician, Building and Home Maintenance Services, Building Construction Occupations, Building Trades Maintenance, Cabinetmaking and Millwork, Carpentry, Collision Repair,

Collision Repair/Refinishing Technology, Computer Programming, Computer Technology, Cosmetology, Diesel Engine Repair, Diesel Mechanics, Drafting Occupations, Early Child Care and Education, Electrical Construction, Electrical Installation, Electromechanical Technology, Electronic Product Servicing, Electronics Communications, Electronics Technology, Graphic Imaging Technology, Heating/Ventilation & Air Conditioning (HVAC), Heating/Ventilation/Air Conditioning & Refrigeration (HVAC/R), Heavy Equipment Mechanics, Hospitality Management–Food & Beverage, Hospitality Management–Lodging, Industrial Electrician, Industrial Electronics, Industrial Technology, Marine Mechanics, Masonry, Materials Handling, Metalworking Occupations, Motorcycle Mechanics, Painting and Decorating, Plumbing, Precision Machining, Quantity Food Preparation, Quantity Foods, Refinishing Technology, Retail Commercial Baking, Retail Trades, Sheet Metal, Technical Drafting, Tool and Die Making, Welding.

Administration: Group.

Parts, 2: Written, Performance.

Price Data, 2005: $180 per complete test including written and performance parts, instructions for administration, scoring and reporting services and certificates of competence, if applicable.

Time: (180) minutes for all written tests; (1.5–6) hours for performance tests.

Comments: The National Occupational Competency Testing Institute (NOCTI) is a not-for-profit organization with a primary mission to serve all levels of the career-technical education field and to assist in developing a world-class workforce. NOCTI's assessment services include customization of assessments to better meet client needs. Assessments are designed to meet psychometric standards that utilize the psychomotor, cognitive, and affective domains of learning to assess competence. Most standardized assessments have both written (cognitive) and performance (psychomotor) components.

Author: National Occupational Competency Testing Institute.

Publisher: National Occupational Competency Testing Institute/The Whitener Group.

Cross References: For a review of an earlier version of the NOCTI program, see 8:1153 (6 references). Reviews and references for previous separate NOCTI TOCT tests: Appliance Repair: For reviews by Geneva D. Haertel and Cyril J. Sadowski, see 13:208; for a review by Richard C. Erickson, see 10:227; Architectural Drafting: See 9:776 (1 reference); for a review by Gary E. Lintereur, see 8:1131; Audio-Visual Communications Technology: For reviews by JoEllen V. Carlson and Anne L. Harvey, see 11:262; for reviews by Patricia A. Bachelor and Connie Kubo Della-Piana, see 13:209; Auto Body Repair: For reviews by Robert J. Drummond and Dale P. Scannell, see 13:210; see also 9:777 (1 reference); Automotive Technician: For reviews by Dale P. Scannell and George C. Thornton III, see 13:211; see also 9:778 and T3:1595

(1 reference); for a review by Charles W. Pendleton, see 8:1133; Brick Masonry: For a review by Thomas S. Baldwin, see 10:229; Building and Home Maintenance Services: For a review by Gary E. Lintereur, see 10:230; Cabinet Making and Millwork: See 9:782 (1 reference); for a review by Gary E. Lintereur, see 8:1134; Carpentry: See 9:783 (1 reference); for a review by Daniel L. Householder, see 8:1535; Child Care and Guidance: For reviews by Patricia B. Keith and by Jean Powell Kirnan and Jennifer DeNicolis, see 12:255; Commercial Art: For a review by Gary E. Lintereur, see 10:231; Diesel Engine Repair: See 9:786 (1 reference); for a review by Charles W. Pendleton, see 8:1138; Electrical Installation: See 9:788 (1 reference) and T3:1601 (1 reference); for a review by Alan R. Suess, see 8:1139 (1 reference); Electronics Communications: See 9:789 (1 reference); for a review by Emil H. Hoch, see 8:1140; Industrial Electrician: See 9:792 (1 reference); for a review by Alan R. Suess, see 8:1141; Industrial Electronics: See 9:793 (1 reference); for a review by Emil H. Hoch, see 8:1142; Machine Drafting: See 9:794 (1 reference); for a review by Tim L. Wentling, see 8:1143; Machine Trades: For a review by Thomas S. Baldwin, see 10:239; see also 9:795 (1 reference) and 8:1144 (1 reference); Masonry: See 9:797 (1 reference); Mechanical Technology: For reviews by Bruce K. Alcorn and David O. Anderson, see 12:256; Microcomputer Repair: For reviews by Kurt F. Geisinger and David O. Herman, see 12:257; Plumbing: See 9:801 (1 reference); for a review by Richard C. Erickson, see 8:1147; Quantity Food Preparation: See 9:804 (1 reference); Scientific Data Processing: For reviews by Jim C. Fortune and Myra N. Womble, see 13:212; for a review by William M. Bart, see 11:263; Sheet Metal: See 9:807 (1 reference) and T3:1612 (1 reference); for a review by Daniel L. Householder, see 8:1150; Small Engine Repair: See 9:808 (1 reference); for a review by Kenneth E. Poucher, see 8:1151; Welding: See 9:809 (1 reference); for a review by Richard C. Erickson, see 8:1152.

[1841]

NOCTI Job Ready Assessments.

Purpose: "Designed to measure an individual's knowledge of basic processes including the identification and use of terminology and tools."

Population: Students in career and technical education programs.

Publication Dates: 1983–2005.

Scores: Duty category and total scores are reported for 85 Written and Performance tests: Accounting, Administrative Assisting, Advertising and Design, Agriculture Mechanics, Air Cooled Gas Engine Repair, Appliance Repair, Architectural Drafting, Audio-Visual Communications, Auto Diesel Mechanics, Automotive Technician, Building Construction Occupations, Building Trades Maintenance, Business and Information Processing,

CAD/CAM, Cabinetmaking, Carpentry, Clothing and Textiles Management and Production, Collision Repair, Collision Repair/Refinishing Technology, Commercial Foods, Computer Networking Fundamentals, Computer Programming, Computer Repair Technology, Computer Technology, Construction Electricity, Construction Masonry–Blocklaying, Construction Masonry–Bricklaying, Construction Masonry–Stone, Cosmetology, Criminal Justice, Dental Assisting, Dental Lab Technology, Diesel Engine Mechanics, Early Childhood Care & Education, Electrical Construction, Electrical Occupations, Electronic Product Servicing, Electronic Technology, Electronics, Floriculture, Food Production Management and Services, Forestry Products and Processing, General Drafting and Design, Graphic Communications Tech, Health Assisting, Heating/Ventilation & Air Conditioning, Heating/Ventilation/Air Conditioning & Refrigeration, Heavy Equipment Maintenance and Repair, Home Health Aide, Horticulture-Landscaping, Horticulture–Olericulture, Hospitality Management–Food & Beverage, Hospitality Management–Lodging, Industrial Electricity, Industrial Electronics, Industrial Maintenance Mechanic, Manufacturing Technology, Marine Mechanics, Medical Assisting, Metalworking and Fabrication, Motorcycle Mechanics, Nursing Assisting, Painting and Decorating, Plumbing, Practical Nursing, Pre-Engineering/Engineering Technology, Precision Machining, Production Agriculture, Refinishing Technology, Retail Commercial Baking, Retail Trades, Robotics Technology, Technical Drafting, Television Broadcasting, Truck and Bus Mechanics, Visual Communications, Warehousing Services, Welding, Workplace Readiness.
Administration: Group.
Parts, 2: Written, Performance.
Price Data, 2005: $20 per complete online test (Written and Performance) including instructions for administration, scoring and reporting services, and certificates of completion, if applicable; $17.50 if purchased separately (Written only or Performance only); $25 per complete paper/pencil test combination; $23 if purchased separately.
Time: (180) minutes for most Written tests; (1–5) hours for Performance tests.
Comments: The National Occupational Competency Testing Institute (NOCTI) is a not-for-profit organization with a primary mission to serve all levels of the career-technical education field and to assist in developing a world-class workforce. NOCTI's assessment services include customization of assessments to better meet client needs. Assessments meet psychometric standards that utilize the psychomotor, cognitive, and affective domains of learning to assess competence. Most standardized assessments have both written (cognitive) and performance (psychomotor) components. Assessments are reviewed for revision every 2 years.
Author: National Occupational Competency Testing Institute.

Publisher: National Occupational Competency Testing Institute/The Whitener Group.

[1842]

Noncognitive Variables and Questionnaire.
Purpose: To aid in admission decisions and advising regarding minority college student applicants.
Population: Minority college student applicants.
Publication Dates: 1978–1998.
Acronym: NCQ.
Scores, 8: Positive Self-Concept or Confidence, Realistic Self-Appraisal, Understands and Deals with Racism, Prefers Long-Range Goals to Short-Term or Immediate Needs, Availability of Strong Support Person, Successful Leadership Experience, Demonstrated Community Service, Knowledge Acquired in a Field.
Administration: Group.
Manual: No manual.
Price Data: Available from publisher.
Time: [20] minutes.
Author: William E. Sedlacek.
Publisher: University of Maryland, University Counseling Center [No reply from publisher; status unknown].
Cross References: For reviews by Gregory J. Marchant and Lisa F. Smith, see 14:259.

[1843]

Non-Reading Intelligence Tests, Levels 1–3.
Purpose: Measures "aspects of language and thinking that are not fully represented in the earlier stages of learning in reading and mathematics."
Population: Ages 6-4 to 8-3, 7-4 to 9-3, 8-4 to 10-11.
Publication Dates: 1989–1992.
Acronym: NRIT.
Scores, 5: Total score for each of four subtests (A, B, C, D), Grand Total.
Administration: Group.
Levels: 3 overlapping levels.
Price Data, 2002: £16.99 per specimen set including manual (1989, 48 pages) and one copy each of the three test forms; £11.99 per manual; £7.99 per 20 Level 1, Level 2 or Level 3 test sheets; £5.99 per marking template.
Time: (60) minutes for Levels 1 and 2; (45–60) minutes for Level 3.
Comments: Incorporates the Non-Readers Intelligence Test (9:811) as Level 1 and the Oral Verbal Intelligence Test (8:197) as Level 3, along with a newer intermediate test as Level 2.
Author: Dennis Young.
Publisher: Hodder & Stoughton Educational [England].
Cross References: For reviews by Carole M. Krauthamer and Esther E. Diamond, see 12:258; see also T4:1816 (1 reference). For a review by A. E. G. Pilliner of the Oral Verbal Intelligence Test, see 8:197; for reviews by Calvin O. Dyer and Steven I. Pfeiffer of the Non-Readers Intelligence Test, Third Edition, see 9:811.

[1844]

Nonverbal Form.

Purpose: Measures general learning ability independent of language and reading skills.
Population: Measures general learning ability independent of language and reading skills.
Publication Dates: 1946–1986.
Scores: Total score only.
Administration: Individual or group.
Price Data: Available from publisher.
Time: 10 minutes.
Comments: Previously listed as SRA Nonverbal Form.
Authors: Robert N. McMurray and Joseph E. King.
Publisher: Pearson Performance Solutions [No reply from publisher; status unknown].
Cross References: See T2:449 (12 references); for a review by W. D. Commins, see 4:318; for an excerpted review, see 3:261 (incorrectly listed under 3:260 in the first printing of *The Third Mental Measurements Yearbook*).

[1845]

Non-Verbal Intelligence Test–Revised (SON-R).

Purpose: Developed as an untimed, nonverbal test of intelligence.
Population: Dutch, German, French, Czech, Slovak children ages 2-6 to 7-0; Dutch children ages 5-6 to 17-0.
Publication Dates: 1939–2009.
Administration: Individual.
Price Data: Available from publisher.
Foreign Language Editions: Dutch, German, French, Danish, Czech, and Slovak editions available.
Comments: Administered in pantomime (for hearing impaired) or orally.
Publisher: Hogrefe Publishing.
  a) SNIJDERS-OOMEN NON-VERBAL INTELLIGENCE SCALE FOR YOUNG CHILDREN.
  Population: Dutch, German, French, Czech, Slovak children ages 2-6 to 7-0.
  Acronym: SON-R 2 1/2–7.
  Scores, 6: Sorting, Mosaic, Combination, Memory, Copying, Total.
  Time: (45–50) minutes.
  Comments: Also called Non-Verbal Intelligence Scale SON-R 2 1/2–7.
  Authors: J. T. Snijders and N. Snijders-Oomen.
  b) SON-R 5 1/2-17.
  Population: Dutch children ages 5-6 to 17-0.
  Acronym: SON-R 5 1/2–17.
  Scores, 8: Categories, Mosaics, Hidden Pictures, Patterns, Situations, Analogies, Stories, Total.
  Time: (60–120) minutes.
  Comments: Revised version of the SON-'58 and SSON; older versions out-of-print.
  Authors: J. T. Snijders, P. J. Tellegen, J. A. Laros, N. Snijders-Oomen (test), and M. A. H. Huijnen (test).

Cross References: See T5:2441 (2 references) and T4:2491 (2 references); for reviews by Douglas K. Detterman and Timothy Z. Keith of an earlier edition, see 9:1146; see also T3:2221 (1 reference) and T2:512 (5 references); for a review by J. S. Lawes of the 1958 edition, see 6:529 (2 references).

[1846]

Nonverbal Personality Questionnaire and Five-Factor Nonverbal Personality Questionnaire.

Purpose: Designed to "measure normal personality characteristics" with the use of pictures instead of words.
Population: Ages 18 and over.
Publication Date: 2004.
Administration: Group or individual.
Price Data, 2010: $24 per test manual (72 pages)
Comments: Tests can be administered together and use the same manual; can be used in research, counseling, and business settings.
Authors: Sampo V. Paunonen, Douglas N. Jackson, and Michael C. Ashton (manual).
Publisher: SIGMA Assessment Systems, Inc.
  a) NONVERBAL PERSONALITY QUESTIONNAIRE.
  Acronym: NPQ.
  Scores, 17: Achievement, Affiliation, Aggression, Autonomy, Dominance, Endurance, Exhibition, Thrill-Seeking, Impulsivity, Nurturance, Order, Play, Sentience, Social Recognition, Succorance, Understanding, Deviation.
  Price Data: $50 per handscorable examination kit including test manual, picture booklet, 5 answer sheets, and 5 profile sheets; $60 per 10 picture booklets; $75 per 25 answer sheets; $50 per 25 profile sheets; $8-$14 (depending on volume) per online administration at www.SigmaTesting.com.
  Time: (20–35) minutes.
  Authors: Sampo V. Paunonen and Douglas N. Jackson.
  b) FIVE-FACTOR NONVERBAL PERSONALITY QUESTIONNAIRE.
  Acronym: FF-NPQ.
  Scores, 5: Extraversion, Agreeableness, Conscientiousness, Neuroticism, Openness to Experience.
  Price Data: $50 per examination kit including test manual, picture booklet, 5 answer sheets, and 5 profile sheets; $60 per 10 picture booklets; $65 per 25 answer sheets; $50 per 25 profile sheets; $6-$12 (depending on volume) per online administration at www.SigmaTesting.com.
  Time: (10–15) minutes.
  Authors: Sampo Paunonen, Douglas N. Jackson, and Michael C. Ashton.
Cross References: For reviews by Ashraf Kagee and Sean Reilley, see 17:133.

[1847]

Nonverbal Reasoning.

Purpose: "To measure the capacity to reason logically as indicated by solutions to pictoral problems."
Population: Individuals in a variety of occupations.
Publication Dates: 1957–1986.
Scores: Total score only.
Administration: Individual or group.
Price Data, 2002: $94 per start-up kit including 25 test booklets, score key, and interpretation and research manual; $58 per 25 test booklets (quantity discounts available); $20 per score key; $28 per interpretation and research manual.
Time: No limit (approximately 20 minutes).
Author: Raymond J. Corsini.
Publisher: Pearson Performance Solutions [No reply from publisher; status unknown].
Cross References: See T4:1817 (1 reference) and T2:414 (2 references); for reviews by James E. Kennedy and David G. Ryans, see 6:478.

[1848]

Non-Verbal Reasoning Test Series.

Purpose: Designed to assess "a pupil's ability to recognise similarities, analogies and patterns in unfamiliar designs."
Population: Ages 7.3-15.3.
Publication Date: 1993.
Scores: Total score only.
Administration: Group.
Levels, 3: Age 8 and 9; Age 10 and 11; Ages 12–14.
Price Data: Available from publisher.
Time: (40–45) minutes.
Authors: Pauline Smith and Neil Hagues.
Publisher: GL Assessment [England].
Cross References: For reviews by Sally Kuhlenschmidt and Julia Y. Porter, see 16:167.

[1849]

Norris Educational Achievement Test.

Purpose: Designed to assess educational ability.
Publication Dates: 1991–1992.
Acronym: NEAT.
Administration: Individual.
Forms, 2: A, B.
Price Data, 2002: $128.50 per complete kit including 10 test booklets (5 Form A, 5 Form B), administration and scoring manual (1992, 234 pages), and technical manual (1992, 86 pages); $38.50 per 25 test booklets (select Form A or B); $65 per administration and scoring manual; $49.95 per technical manual.
Authors: Janet Switzer and Christian P. Gruber (manuals).
Publisher: Western Psychological Services.
 a) READINESS.
 Population: Ages 4-0 to 6-11.

Scores, 4: Fine Motor Coordination, Math Concepts, Letters, Total.
Time: (10–15) minutes.
 b) ACHIEVEMENT.
 Population: Ages 6-0 to 17-11.
 Scores, 4-6: Word Recognition, Spelling, Arithmetic, Total plus 2 supplemental scores (Oral Reading and Comprehension, Written Language).
 Time: (20–30) minutes for basic battery; (30–40) minutes for entire battery.
Cross References: See T5:1802 (1 reference); for reviews by A. Harry Passow and Michael S. Trevisan, see 12:260.

[1850]

Novaco Anger Scale and Provocation Inventory.

Purpose: "Designed to assess anger as a problem of psychological functioning and physical health and to assess therapeutic change."
Population: Ages 9–84 years.
Publication Date: 2003.
Acronym: NAS-PI.
Administration: Individual or group.
Price Data, 2007: $92 per complete kit including 25 AutoScore test forms and manual (64 pages); $53 per manual; $43.50 per 25 AutoScore test forms (bulk discounts available); Computerized Components: $152.50 per 25-use Computer Scoring CD for Windows; $16.50 per 100 PC answer sheets.
Comments: Can be administered as a whole or as two separate parts.
Author: Raymond W. Novaco.
Publisher: Western Psychological Services.
 a) THE NOVACO ANGER SCALE.
 Purpose: Designed to assess "how an individual experiences anger."
 Scores: Cognitive, Arousal, Behavior, NAS Total, Anger Regulation.
 Time: (10-20) minutes.
 b) THE PROVOCATION INVENTORY.
 Purpose: Designed to identify "the kinds of situations that lead to anger."
 Scores: PI Total.
 Time: (5-15) minutes.
Cross References: For reviews by Albert Bugaj and Geoffrey L. Thorpe, see 17:134.

[1851]

NPF [Second Edition].

Purpose: "To assess stress tolerance and overall adjustment."
Population: Ages 16-adult.
Publication Dates: 1955-1992.
Acronym: NPF.

Scores, 3: Validity Scores (Uncertainty, Good Impression), Total Adjustment.
Administration: Group or individual.
Price Data, 2010: $35 per introductory kit including manual (1992, 10 pages), 20 test booklets, and scoring key; $30 per 20 test booklets; $10 per manual.
Time: (5-10) minutes.
Comments: Previously listed as a subtest of the Employee Attitude Series of the Job-Tests Program (T3:1219).
Author: Samuel E. Krug.
Publisher: Industrial Psychology International Ltd.
Cross References: For reviews by Charles D. Claiborn and Howard M. Knoff, see 12:261.

[1852]

NSight Aptitude/Personality Questionnaire.

Purpose: A "method for measuring a person's work-related characteristics … [that can be used] for hiring and promoting people who are similar to those already successful in the job."
Population: Adults.
Publication Dates: 1990–2002.
Acronym: NAPQ.
Scores, 26: 3 Cognitive Characteristics (Verbal Reasoning/Comprehension, Numerical Reasoning, Word Knowledge); 1 Achievement Characteristic (Visual Perception); 19 Personality Characteristics measured along 6 subtopics: Thinking Style (Emotional Decision Maker, Analytical Thinker, Logical Thinker, Practical), Drives (Security Oriented, Cooperative, Rule Bound), Stress (Anxious, Tolerant, Apprehensive), Communication (Serious, Reserved, Assuming), Leadership (Passive, Submissive, Suspicious), Reliability (Indifferent, Changeable, Expedient); 3 Validity Scales (Lie, Faking Bad, Faking Good).
Administration: Group.
Price Data, 2002: $168 per assessment including 11-page report and telephone consultation; quantity discounts available.
Time: (120) minutes for Cognitive Characteristics Inventory; Personality Inventory untimed.
Author: Stephen Overcash.
Publisher: Directional Insight International, Inc.
Cross References: For a review by John S. Geisler, see 15:174.

[1853]

Number Test DE.

Purpose: "To provide a measure of the child's understanding of the four number processes (addition, subtraction, multiplication and division)."
Population: Ages 10-6 to 12-6.
Publication Date: 1965.
Scores: Total score only.
Administration: Group.

Price Data: Available from publisher.
Time: (50–60) minutes.
Comments: Formerly called Number Test 1.
Author: E. L. Barnard.
Publisher: GL Assessment [England].
Cross References: See T3:1652 (1 reference).

[1854]

Numeracy Impact Tests.

Purpose: "Designed to assess the impact of intervention strategies which are intended to raise the level of achievement of pupils who are working on the borderline between levels 3 and 4 in mathematics."
Population: Ages 10–11.
Publication Date: 2000.
Scores: Total score only.
Administration: Group.
Forms: 2 tests: A, B.
Price Data, 2003: £18.90 per 10 test booklets; £16.80 per evaluation pack.
Time: (30) minutes.
Authors: Tandi Clausen-May, Helen Claydon, and Graham Ruddock.
Publisher: GL Assessment [England].
Cross References: For reviews by Dixie McGinty and Georgette Yetter, see 16:168.

[1855]

Nurse Entrance Test.

Purpose: "Designed … as a diagnostic instrument to assist nursing programs evaluate the academic and social skills of new applicants to their programs."
Population: Adult applicants to nursing schools.
Publication Dates: 1998–2001.
Acronym: NET.
Scores, 28: 7 Essential Math Skills scores (Whole Numbers, Number System Conversions, Algebra Equations, Percentage Operations, Decimal Operations, Fraction Operations, Essential Math Skills), 3 Reading Comprehension scores (Reading Rate, Reading Rate Placement, Reading Comprehension), 3 Critical Thinking Appraisal scores (Main Idea of Passage, Inferential Reading, Predicting of Outcomes), Testtaking Skills score, 2 Social Interaction Profile scores (Passive, Aggressive), 5 Stress Level Profile scores (Family, Social, Money/Time, Academic, Work Place), 6 Learning Styles (Auditory Learner, Solitary Learner, Visual Learner, Social Learner, Oral Dependent Learner, Writing Dependent Learner), Composite Percentage.
Administration: Group.
Price Data, 2002: $17 per test by computer; $10.50 per test; $8 per answer sheet; $27.50 per Study Guide.
Time: (150) minutes.
Comments: Generates a Diagnostic Report including NET Group Report, individual Student Reports; Group

Report provides group-level mean percentages and normative comparisons for the 28 scores; optional Study Guide offers test-taking strategy tips and practice tests.
Author: Michael D. Frost.
Publisher: Educational Resources, Inc.
Cross References: For reviews by Mark A. Albanese and Patricia A. Bachelor, see 16:169.

[1856]

O*NET Career Interests Inventory: Based on the "O*NET Interest Profiler" developed by the U.S. Department of Labor.
Purpose: To allow users to rank six career interest areas and relate them to specific careers.
Population: Youth and adults.
Publication Date: 2002.
Scores: 6 interest categories: Realistic, Investigative, Artistic, Social, Enterprising, Conventional.
Administration: Group or individual.
Price Data, 2006: $29.95 per 25 inventories including copy of administrator's guide (8 pages).
Time: (20–60) minutes.
Comments: Twelve-panel foldout; a compact, shorter, and less expensive version of the Department of Labor's "O*NET Interest Profiler"; based on the "O*NET Interest Profiler" developed by the U.S. Department of Labor.
Author: JIST Publishing, Inc.
Publisher: JIST Publishing, Inc.
Cross References: For reviews by Mark Pope and Eleanor E. Sanford, see 16:172.

[1857]

O*NET Career Values Inventory: Based on the "O*NET Work Importance Locator" developed by the U.S. Department of Labor.
Purpose: To allow users to rank six work values and relate them to specific careers.
Population: Youth and adults
Publication Date: 2002.
Scores: Achievement, Independence, Recognition, Relationships, Support, Working Conditions.
Administration: Group or individual.
Price Data, 2006: $29.95 per 25 inventories including administrator's guide (8 pages).
Time: (20–60) minutes.
Comments: Twelve-panel foldout; a compact, shorter, and less expensive version of the Department of Labor's "O*NET Work Importance Locator"; based on the "O*NET Work Importance Locator" developed by the U.S. Department of Labor.
Author: JIST Publishing, Inc.
Publisher: JIST Publishing, Inc.
Cross References: For reviews by Kathy Green and Richard E. Harding, see 16:173.

[1858]

O*NET Interest Profiler.
Purpose: "Provides … self-knowledge about [one's] … vocational personality type … [and] fosters career awareness."
Population: Age 14 and older.
Publication Dates: 1985–2000.
Acronym: IP.
Scores, 11: Interest Areas (Realistic, Investigative, Artistic, Social, Enterprising, Conventional), Job Zones (Little or No Preparation Needed, Some Preparation Needed, Medium Preparation Needed, Considerable Preparation Needed, Extensive Preparation Needed).
Administration: Group.
Price Data: Available from publisher.
Time: (20–60) minutes.
Comments: Replaces the Job Search Inventory (T5:1351); self-administered and self-scored; pencil-and-paper format; Computerized Interest Profile is administered and scored on computer; part of the O*NET Career Exploration Tools; intended for career exploration, planning, and counseling purposes only; results should not be used for employment or hiring decisions.
Author: U.S. Department of Labor, Employment and Training Administration.
Publisher: U.S. Department of Labor, Employment and Training Administration.
Cross References: For reviews by Michael B. Brown and William B. Michael, see 16:174; for reviews by Ralph O. Mueller and Sheldon Zedeck of the Job Search Inventory, see 13:163.

[1859]

O*NET Work Importance Locator.
Purpose: "Helps users identify what is important to them in a job."
Population: Ages 16 and older.
Publication Date: 2000.
Acronym: WIL.
Scores, 6: Achievement, Independence, Recognition, Relationships, Support, Working Conditions.
Administration: Group.
Price Data: Available from publisher.
Time: (15–45) minutes.
Comments: Available in paper-and-pencil format only; related Work Importance Profiler is administered and scored on computer; part of O*NET Career Exploration Tools; intended for career exploration, planning, and counseling purposes only; results should not be used for employment or hiring decisions.
Author: U.S. Department of Labor, Employment and Training Administration.
Publisher: U.S. Department of Labor, Employment and Training Administration.
Cross References: For reviews by Karl N. Kelley and William B. Michael, see 16:175.

[1860]
The OAD Survey.
Purpose: "Measures seven work-related personality traits and seven perceptions of how an individual believes he/she must behave in his/her job."
Population: Employees.
Publication Dates: 1990-2002.
Acronym: OAD.
Scores, 7: Autonomy, Extroversion, Patience, Detail, Versatility Level, Emotional Control, Creativity.
Administration: Individual and group.
Restricted Distribution: Completion of a 3-day seminar is required for participants to administer and use the survey within their organization.
Price Data: Available from publisher.
Foreign Language Editions: Available in 10 languages.
Time: Not timed.
Comments: Web-based scoring process is available.
Author: Michael J. Gray.
Publisher: Organization Analysis and Design LLC.
Cross References: For reviews by Arthur S. Ellen and Jeffrey A. Jenkins, see 17:135.

[1861]
OARS Multidimensional Functional Assessment Questionnaire.
Purpose: Designed to assess individual functioning in the elderly.
Population: Ages 65 and over.
Publication Dates: 1975–1988.
Acronym: OARS MFAQ.
Scores: One of 6 ratings (Excellent, Good, Mildly Impaired, Moderately Impaired, Severely Impaired, Totally Impaired) for 5 scales: Social Resources, Economic Resources, Mental Health, Physical Health, Activities of Daily Living.
Administration: Individual.
Price Data: Price data for test materials including manual (1988, 191 pages) available from publisher.
Time: (45) minutes.
Comments: Orally administered to the subject or to someone who knows the subject well.
Author: Center for the Study of Aging and Human Development.
Publisher: Center for the Study of Aging and Human Development, Duke University Medical Center.
Cross References: See T5:1808 (3 references) and T4:1855 (9 references); for reviews by Keith S. Dobson and Bruce R. Fretz, see 9:847 (4 references); see also T3:1659 (1 reference).

[1862]
Oaster Stressors Scales.
Purpose: Designed to index an individual's level of stressors by using derived trait scales.
Population: Adults.
Publication Date: 1983.
Scores: 4 profiles: Classic/Overload Stressor Pattern of Type A Behavior, Overload Stressor Pattern, Underload Stressor Pattern/Goal-Blocked Type A, Type B Behavior Pattern.
Administration: Group.
Price Data: Available from publisher.
Time: Administration time not reported.
Author: Thomas R. Oaster.
Publisher: Thomas R. Oaster.

[1863]
Object-Oriented Programmer Analyst Staff Selector.
Purpose: To measure knowledge of object-oriented terminology and C++.
Population: Candidates for the position of object-oriented programmer analyst.
Publication Date: 1994.
Acronym: OOPS.
Scores: Total Score, Narrative Evaluation, Ranking, Recommendation.
Administration: Group.
Price Data, 2001: $350 per candidate; quantity discounts available.
Time: (120) minutes.
Comments: Scored by publisher.
Author: Bruce A. Winrow.
Publisher: Walden Personnel Performance, Inc. [Canada].
Cross References: For reviews by Dennis Doverspike and Matthew E. Lambert, see 16:170.

[1864]
Observation Ability Test for the Police Service.
Purpose: Designed as a testing instrument for police jobs or any other jobs with high observational requirements.
Population: Candidates for police entry-level positions.
Publication Dates: 1980-2010.
Scores, 1: Observation Ability.
Administration: Group.
Restricted Distribution: Distribution restricted to civil service commissions and qualified municipal officials.
Price Data: Available from publisher.
Time: (35) minutes.
Comments: Typically utilized as a portion of the Empirically-Statistically Validated (ESV) Written Tests for Police Officer.
Author: McCann Associates.
Publisher: McCann Associates.

[1865]
Observation of Type Preference.
Purpose: Designed to provide a view of MBTI® type from others who work with an executive.

Population: Executives in leadership positions.
Publication Date: 1995.
Acronym: OTP.
Scores, 8: Introversion, Extraversion, Intuitive, Sensate, Thinking, Feeling, Judging, Perceiving.
Administration: Group.
Manual: Manual not available.
Price Data, 2005: $49 per complete set including questionnaires and answer sheets; $50 per report for an additional paper report.
Time: [30] minutes.
Comments: Assessment is administered online via Lore's Assessment Center; results are emailed to participant and additional paper report may be requested for additional charge; complements the Myers-Briggs Type Indicator (MBTI; 1801) and helps executives understand how others view their operating style, which is useful in coaching when executives' own operating style preferences differ significantly from how they are perceived.
Author: Lore International Institute.
Publisher: Lore International Institute.

[1866]

Observational Assessment of Temperament.
Purpose: Assesses temperamental characteristics, primarily in industrial/organizational settings.
Population: Higher level specialized and managerial personnel.
Publication Dates: 1979–1996.
Acronym: CAT.
Scores: 3 behavior factors: Extroversive/Impulsive vs. Introversive/Reserved, Emotional/Responsive vs. Non-emotional/Controlled, Self-Reliant/Individually Oriented vs. Dependent/Group Oriented.
Administration: Group.
Price Data, 2002: $54 per 25 tests (including background research, scoring iinstructions, and norms).
Time: (10) minutes.
Comments: Can be used as a self-assessment or for the assessment of the observed behavior of others; assesses the three behavior factors measured by the Temperament Comparator (2699).
Author: Melany E. Baehr.
Publisher: Pearson Performance Solutions [No reply from publisher; status unknown].
Cross References: For reviews by Stephen J. DePaola and David J. Pittenger, see 15:175.

[1867]

Observational Emotional Inventory–Revised.
Purpose: "Provides a stucture for observing and rating overt emotional behaviors which interfere with educational or vocational potential."
Population: Students and adults.
Publication Date: 1986.

Acronym: OEI-R.
Scores: 8: Impulsivity-Frustration, Anxiety, Depression-Withdrawal, Socialization, Self-Concept, Aggression, Reality Disorientation, Total Score.
Administration: Group.
Price Data, 2011: $59.50 per package of 25 inventories.
Time: 120 minutes each day for 5 days.
Comments: Problems checklist.
Authors: Lawrence T. McCarron and Jack G. Dial.
Publisher: McCarron-Dial Systems, Inc.
Cross References: For a review by Joseph G. Ponterotto, see 11:266.

[1868]

Occupational Aptitude Survey and Interest Schedule–Third Edition.
Purpose: To assist in career development.
Population: Grades 8–12 and adults.
Publication Dates: 1983–2002.
Acronym: OASIS-3:AS.
Administration: Group or individual.
Price Data, 2006: $51 per machine score kit.
Time: (30–45) minutes per survey.
Comments: Machine scoring is available.
Author: Randall M. Parker.
Publisher: PRO-ED.
  a) APTITUDE SURVEY.
  Acronym: OASIS-3:AS.
  Scores, 6: General Ability, Verbal Aptitude, Numerical Aptitude, Spatial Aptitude, Perceptual Aptitude, Manual Dexterity.
  Price Data: $170 per complete kit including 10 student test booklets, 50 handscorable answer sheets, 50 profile sheets, and examiner's manual (2002, 45 pages); $45 per 10 student test booklets; $45 per 50 handscorable answer sheets; $28 per 50 profile sheets; $60 per examiner's manual.
  b) INTEREST SCHEDULE.
  Acronym: OASIS-3:IS.
  Scores, 12: Artistic, Scientific, Nature, Protective, Mechanical, Industrial, Business Detail, Selling, Accommodating, Humanitarian, Leading-Influencing, Physical Performing.
  Price Data: $174 per complete kit including 25 student test booklets, 50 handscorable answer sheets, 50 profile sheets, 50 scoring forms, and examiner's manual (2002, 53 pages); $40 per 25 student test booklets; $28 per 50 handscorable answer sheets; $28 per 50 profile sheets; $28 per scoring forms; $56 per examiner's manual; $56 per Interpretation Workbook.
Cross References: For reviews by Michael B. Bunch and William B. Michael, see 16:171; for reviews by Laura L. B. Barnes and Thomas E. Dinero of an earlier version of the Aptitude Survey, see 12:263 (2 references); see also T4:1862 (2 references). For reviews by Robert

J. Miller and Donald G. Zytowski of an earlier version of the Interest Schedule, see 12:264; see also T4:1863 (2 references); for reviews by Christopher Borman and Ruth G. Thomas of an earlier edition, see 20:244 (1 reference).

[1869]

Occupational Interest Inventories.
Purpose: Interest assessment to be used in career guidance, placement, selection, and counseling.
Population: Adults.
Publication Date: 1982.
Administration: Group.
Price Data: Available from publisher.
Time: (25–45) minutes per inventory.
Authors: Ruth Holdsworth and Lisa Camp (manual and user's guide).
Publisher: SHL Group plc [United Kingdom].
  a) GENERAL OCCUPATIONAL INTEREST INVENTORY.
  Population: Adults of average educational level.
  Acronym: GOII.
  Scores, 18: Medical, Welfare, Personal Services, Selling Goods, Selling Services, Supervision, Clerical, Office Equipment, Control, Leisure, Art and Design, Crafts, Plants, Animals, Transport, Construction, Electrical, Mechanical.
  b) ADVANCED OCCUPATIONAL INTEREST INVENTORY.
  Population: Adults of above average educational level.
  Acronym: AOII.
  Scores, 19: Medical, Welfare, Education, Control, Commercial, Managerial, Administration, Legal, Financial, Data Processing, Information, Media, Art and Design, Biological Sciences, Physical Sciences, Process, Mechanical, Electrical/Electronic, Construction.

[1870]

Occupational Interests Card Sort.
Purpose: To identify and rank occupational interests.
Population: Adults.
Publication Dates: 1977-2009.
Scores: Interests Work Sheet.
Administration: Group or individual.
Price Data, 2011: $14 per deck of cards and worksheet; additional price information available online from www.CareerTrainer.Com.
Time: (20–30) minutes.
Comments: Distributors are available in Canada, Australia, Egypt, and U.S.A. List of distributor information is available at www.CareerNetwork.Org.
Author: Richard L. Knowdell.
Publisher: Career Research & Testing, Inc.
Cross References: For reviews by Michael B. Bunch and Donald Thompson, see 13:213.

[1871]

Occupational Personality Assessment.
Purpose: Designed as a "computer simulation of a vocational assessment."
Population: Individuals seeking vocational counseling.
Publication Date: 1993.
Acronym: OPA.
Administration: Individual.
Price Data: Available from publisher.
Time: Administration time not reported.
Comments: Self-administered computerized test requires IBM or compatible Windows for administration.
Authors: Don Schaeffer and Joyce Schaeffer.
Publisher: Measurement for Human Resources.
  a) INTEREST TEST.
  Purpose: "Designed to assess what kinds of things a person would enjoy doing."
  Scores, 3: Interest Profile, Experience Profile, How Much Interest and Experience Match.
  Comments: Scores are based on Holland's RIASEC occupational codes.
  b) COMMERCIAL ORIENTATION.
  Purpose: Designed to measure "skills and attitudes related to commercial business."
  Scores, 4: Focus on Making Money, Tactical Orientation, Reading Business Tables, Total.
  c) MOTIVATION.
  Purpose: Constructed to assess "motivational preferences."
  Scores, 8: Personal Motives (Peaceful, Sensory, Acquisitive, Work Driven), Work Motives (Intellect, Beauty, Independent Authority, Pleasing Others).
  d) MANAGEMENT.
  Purpose: Designed to assess "management style."
  Scores, 7: Aggressiveness, Field Independence, Toughness, Determination, Fluctuating Salary, Fluctuating Income Tolerance, Management Style Preference.
Cross References: For a review by Peter F. Merenda, see 13:214.

[1872]

Occupational Stress Inventory–Revised Edition.
Purpose: Designed as a "measure of three dimensions of occupational adjustment: occupational stress, psychological strain, and coping resources."
Population: Age 18 years and over.
Publication Dates: 1981–1998.
Acronym: OSI-R.
Scores, 14: Occupational Roles Questionnaire (Role Overload, Role Insufficiency, Role Ambiguity, Role Boundary, Responsibility, Physical Environment); Personal Strain Questionnaire (Vocational Strain, Psychological Strain, Interpersonal Strain, Physical Strain); Personal Resources Questionnaire (Recreation, Self-Care, Social Support, Rational Cognitive Coping).

Administration: Individual or group.

Price Data, 2006: $172 per introductory kit including professional manual, 25 reusable item booklets, 50 rating sheets, 50 gender-specific profile forms, and 50 generic profile forms.

Time: (30) minutes.

Comments: Self-administered.

Author: Samuel H. Osipow.

Publisher: Psychological Assessment Resources, Inc.

Cross References: For reviews by Patricia K. Freitag and Robert Wall, see 14:260; see also T5:1825 (7 references) and T4:1870 (4 references); for reviews by Mary Ann Bunda and Larry Cochran of an earlier edition, see 11:269 (1 reference).

[1873]

Occupational Test Series-Basic Skills Tests.

Purpose: Designed for the "assessment of current levels of skill in comprehension, writing and dealing with numbers."

Population: New trainees and employees.

Publication Date: 1988.

Scores, 7: Literacy (Reading Comprehension and Information-Seeking, Writing [optional], Total), Numeracy (Calculating, Approximating, Problem-Solving, Total).

Administration: Group.

Price Data: Price information available from publisher for Reference Set, reusable Literacy Newspapers, Literacy Administration pack, Numeracy Administration pack, and reusable Numeracy Question Booklets.

Time: 35(45) minutes for Literacy Test (both sections); 20(30) minutes for Reading section of Literacy Test; (35) minutes for Numeracy Test.

Authors: Pauline Smith and Chris Whetton.

Publisher: GL Assessment [England].

Cross References: For reviews by Phyllis Kuehn and Mark Pope, see 12:267.

[1874]

Occupational Test Series: General Ability Tests.

Purpose: "Assessing persons without previous work experience; selection for supervisory and similar management posts."

Population: Employees and candidates for employment.

Publication Date: 1988.

Scores: 4 tests: Verbal, Non-Verbal, Numerical, Spatial.

Administration: Group.

Price Data: Price information available from publisher for Reference Set, test booklet (specify Verbal, Non-Verbal, Numerical, or Spatial), Administration Pack (specify Non-Verbal, Numerical, or Spatial), and Test Taker's Guide.

Time: 25(30) minutes for Verbal; 30(35) minutes for each (Non-Verbal, Numerical, Spatial).

Comments: Tests may be administered separately.

Authors: Pauline Smith and Chris Whetton.

Publisher: GL Assessment [England].

Cross References: For reviews by Philip G. Benson and Michael S. Trevisan, see 11:270.

[1875]

Oetting Michaels Anchored Ratings for Therapists.

Purpose: Designed for use by supervisors to rate therapists in training.

Population: Graduate students and interns in counseling and clinical training.

Publication Date: 1989.

Acronym: OMART.

Scores: Developmental ratings on 34 dimensions of therapist effectiveness: Interviewing (Relationship with the Client, Dealing with Therapist Identification Issues, Personal Style, Exploration of Client Goals, Exploration of Issues, Exploration of Feelings, Time During the Interview, Responsiveness to Nonverbal Cues, Use of Language), Conceptualization of Therapy (Knowledge of Personality Theory, Applying Psychotherapy Theory, Knowledge of DSM III, Ability to Analyze Course of Therapy, Treatment Plans), Reaction to Supervision (Interaction During Supervision, Openness to Feedback, Confidence, Self Evaluation), Sensitivity to Client Issues (Dealing with Dependency, Dealing with Client/Therapist Sexual Feelings, Awareness of Environmental Influences, Sensitivity to Cultural Differences, Sensitivity to Sex-Role Stereotypes, Handling of Conflicts of Client/Therapist Values), Trainee Issues (Management of Personal Stress, Interference Because of Therapist's Adjustment Problems, Self-Direction of Professional Development), Other (Dealing with Ambiguity, Therapist's Attitudes to Authority, Writing Reports, General Test Interpretation, Intellective Assessment, Appropriate Handling of Sexual Material).

Administration: Individual.

Price Data: Available from publisher (license to reproduce provided for Ph.D.s or Ed.D.s).

Time: [20–30] minutes.

Comments: Completed by supervisor.

Authors: E. R. Oetting and Laurie Michaels.

Publisher: E. R. Oetting, Colorado State University.

Cross References: For a review by John S. Geisler, see 14:262.

[1876]

Oetting's Computer Anxiety Scale.

Purpose: Developed "to provide a general measure of computer anxiety."

Population: Entering college freshmen.

Publication Date: 1983.

Acronym: COMPAS.

Scores, 8: Hand Calculator, Trust, General Attitude, Data Entry, Word Processing, Business Operations, Computer Science, Total; Total score only for short form.

Administration: Group.
Price Data: License to reproduce for Ph.D.s or Ed.D.s available from publisher.
Time: [15] minutes.
Author: E. R. Oetting.
Publisher: E. R. Oetting, Colorado State University.
Cross References: For reviews by Benjamin Kleinmuntz and Steven L. Wise, see 10:245.

[1877]
Offender Assessment Index.

Purpose: Designed "for evaluating misdemeanor and felony defendants" in adult courts.
Population: Adult defendants.
Publication Dates: 1985-1997.
Acronym: OAI.
Scores, 7: Truthfulness, Resistance, Violence, Alcohol, Drugs, Substance Abuse/Dependency, Stress Coping Abilities.
Administration: Group.
Price Data, 2010: $8 per test; volume discounts available.
Foreign Language Edition: Spanish version available.
Time: (30-35) minutes.
Comments: May be administered via paper and pencil, computer, or human voice audio.
Author: Risk & Needs Assessment, Inc.
Publisher: Behavior Data Systems, Ltd.

[1878]
Offer Self-Image Questionnaire for Adolescents, Revised.

Purpose: Designed to measure the self-image of adolescents.
Population: Ages 13–19.
Publication Dates: 1971–1992.
Acronym: OSIQ-R.
Scores, 13: Emotional Tone, Impulse Control, Mental Health, Social Functioning, Family Functioning, Vocational Attitudes, Self-Confidence, Self-Reliance, Body Image, Sexuality, Ethical Values, Idealism, Total Self-Image.
Administration: Group or individual.
Price Data, 2006: $109.50 per complete kit including manual (1992, 75 pages), 2 reusable administration booklets, and 5 WPS Test Report prepaid mail-in answer sheets; $35.75 per 10 reusable administration booklets; $49.50 per manual; $17.50 per mail-in answer sheet; $260 per 25-use WPS Test Report IBM Microcomputer scoring disk; $16.50 per 100 answer sheets for use with Microcomputer disk; $10.50 per FAX scoring.
Time: 30 minutes.
Comments: Computer scored via disk or prepaid mail-in answer sheet.

Authors: Daniel Offer (test/manual), E. Ostrov (manual), K. I. Howard (manual), and S. Dolan (manual).
Publisher: Western Psychological Services.
Cross References: See T5:1832 (17 references); for reviews by Sarah J. Allen and by Michael Furlong and Mitchell Karno, see 12:268 (9 references); see also T4:1877 (6 references); for reviews of an earlier edition by Robert Hogan and Roy P. Martin, see 9:855 (5 references); see also T3:1673 (1 reference) and 8:633 (10 references).

[1879]
Office Arithmetic Test (Form CA).

Purpose: For evaluating the ability to perform arithmetic computations at various levels of difficulty.
Population: Applicants and incumbents for jobs requiring the ability to calculate computations generally found in an office environment.
Publication Dates: 1990-2005.
Scores: Total score only.
Administration: Group.
Price Data, 2011: $12 per paper-and-pencil (answer key provided) or online test administration.
Time: 30(45) minutes.
Author: Roland T. Ramsay.
Publisher: Ramsay Corporation.
Cross References: For reviews by Frederick Bessai and Anita Tesh, see 13:255.

[1880]
Office Proficiency Assessment and Certification [OPAC System].

Purpose: "Assess[es] the knowledge, skills, and abilities of … job candidates [and students]" "for both the corporate and educational environments."
Population: Ages 18 and over.
Publication Dates: 1994–2002.
Acronym: OPAC System.
Scores, 41: 28 office skills scores [Computer Applications (Windows, Editing/Formatting from a Rough Draft, Spreadsheet, Intermediate Excel, Database, PowerPoint), Keyboarding Skills (Keyboarding, 10-Key, Data Entry–Vendor, Data Entry–Inventory, Data Entry–Invoice), Clerical Skills (Formatting a Letter, Transcription, Alphabetic Filing, Minutes Composition, Numeric Filing, Proofreading 1, Proofreading 2, Content Proofreading Practice), Financial Skills (Bank Deposit, Bank Reconciliation, Petty Cash, Basic Math), Professional Skills (Legal and Medical Keyboarding, Legal and Medical Proofreading, Legal and Medical Terminology, Legal and Medical Transcription)]; 13 Hogan Personality Inventory scores [7 primary scale scores (Intellectance, Adjustment, Ambition, Sociability, Likeability, Prudence, School Success), 6 occupational scale scores (Service Orientation, Stress Tolerance, Reliability, Clerical Potential, Sales Potential, Managerial Potential)].

Administration: Individual or group.
Price Data, 2002: $2,295 per Single-User OPAC including CD-ROM, administrator manual (2001, 200 pages), candidate manual (2001, 92 pages), one test station packet per station, and 3 dictation cassette tapes; $4,295 per Multi-User OPAC (up to 5 test stations); $6,295 per Multi-User OPAC (up to 10 test stations, plus $200 for each test station over 10); all packages include one year OPAC Plus Customer Support offering unlimited technical support, free updates, and free upgrades; $50 per administrator manual; $30 per Test Station Pack; price information available from publisher for additional site licenses and OPAC Plus subscriptions available.
Time: Time limits for OPAC tests set by user; (15–20) minutes for Hogan Personality Inventory.
Comments: Computer administered; System requirements: Windows 95, 98, or ME (16 MB additional RAM, 32 MB recommended), Windows 2000, XKP, NT 4.0 (128 MB RAM, 256 MB recommended), 16-bit color SVGA monitor, Pentium 133 or higher; self-administered, self-scored; user selects tests to be administered; test writer provides custom test development inhouse enabling user to create additional tests in other content areas; assists user in determining cutoff scores and examining content validity; includes Hogan Personality Inventory (HPI).
Author: International Association of Administrative Professionals.
Publisher: Biddle Consulting Group Inc.

[1881]

Office Reading Test (Form G).

Purpose: "Measures the ability to read, comprehend, and answer questions based on a printed passage."
Population: Applicants or incumbents in an office environment where the ability to read and comprehend is a job requirement.
Publication Dates: 1990–1999.
Scores: Total score only.
Administration: Group.
Price Data, 2011: $12 per pencil-and-paper test administration (with scoring key provided) or online test administration; $24.95 per manual (2005, 11 pages).
Time: 30(45) minutes.
Author: Roland T. Ramsay.
Publisher: Ramsay Corporation.
Cross References: For reviews by Laura L. B. Barnes and Steven J. Osterlind, see 13:256 (1 reference).

[1882]

Office Skills Achievement Test.

Purpose: Constructed to assess office skills.
Population: Office employees.
Publication Dates: 1962–1963.
Scores, 7: Business Letter, Grammar, Checking, Filing, Arithmetic, Written Directions, Total.

Administration: Group.
Price Data: Available from publisher.
Time: 20(25) minutes.
Author: P. L. Mellenbruch.
Publisher: Psychometric Affiliates.
Cross References: For reviews by Douglas G. Schultz and Paul W. Thayer, see 6:1043.

[1883]

Office Skills Assessment Battery.

Purpose: Designed to "provide objective information to aid in your hiring and placement decisions."
Population: Administrative support and clerical position applicants.
Publication Date: 1991.
Acronym: OSAB.
Administration: Individual or group.
Forms, 5: Quanta Touch Test, Quanta Software for Windows–administration and scoring, Quanta Software for Windows–scoring only, RLH Online, Mail-in Scoring.
Price Data, 2002: $18 per 25–99 each Quanta Touch Test, Quanta Software for Windows–administration and scoring (no booklets), Quanta Software for Windows–scoring only (one booklet for every coupon ordered), RLH Online, OSAB-S, OSAB-A, OSAB-S&A; volume discounts available.
Author: London House.
Publisher: Pearson Performance Solutions [No reply from publisher; status unknown].
a) OFFICE SKILLS ASSESSMENT BATTERY–SKILLS.
Acronym: OSAB-S.
Scores, 9: Number Comparison, Checking, Filing, Grammar, Office Vocabulary, Spelling, Punctuation/Capitalization, Career Development, Office Skills Index.
Time: (50–70) minutes for battery; 3(8) minutes for Sessions 1, 2, and 4; 5(10) minutes for Session 3.
b) OFFICE SKILLS ASSESSMENT BATTERY–ATTITUDES.
Acronym: OSAB-A.
Scores, 12: Work Conduct, Work Accountability, Work Performance, Office Practices, Tenure, Energy Level, Stress Tolerance, Career Interests, Background/Education/Work Experience, Office Attitudes Index, Candidness, Accuracy.
Time: [10–20] minutes.

[1884]

Office Skills Tests.

Purpose: Designed for measurement of aptitudes for twelve on-the-job skills.
Population: Applicants for clerical positions.
Publication Dates: 1977–1984.
Acronym: OST.
Scores: Total score only for each of 12 tests: Checking, Coding, Filing, Forms Completion, Grammar, Numerical

Skills, Oral Directions, Punctuation, Reading Comprehension, Spelling, Typing, Vocabulary.
Administration: Individual or group.
Forms, 2: A, B for each test.
Price Data, 2002: $93 per start-up kit including 25 test booklets, scoring stencil, and examiner's manual (specify test; $126 per start-up kit including Oral Directions audiocassette; $56 per 25 test booklets (specify test; quantity discounts available); $20 per scoring stencil (specify test); $28 per examiner's manual; $37 per Oral Directions audiocassette.
Time: (3–10) minutes.
Author: Science Research Associates.
Publisher: Pearson Performance Solutions [No reply from publisher; status unknown].
Cross References: See T5:1836 (1 references); for reviews by Benjamin Shimberg and Paul W. Thayer, see 9:857.

[1885]

Official GED Practice Test.

Purpose: To help candidates determine their readiness to take the full-length GED tests.
Population: Candidates preparing for the full-length GED.
Publication Dates: 1979–1983.
Scores, 5: Writing Skills, Social Studies, Science, Reading Skills, Mathematics.
Administration: Group.
Forms, 2: A, B.
Price Data: Not available.
Foreign Language Edition: Spanish edition available.
Time: 202.5(227.5) minutes for complete test.
Comments: Suggested standards of mastery for full length GED given for each state.
Author: American Council on Education.
Publisher: Prentice Hall [No reply from publisher; status unknown].

[1886]

The Ohio Penal Classification Test.

Purpose: Developed to assess mental abilities of penal populations.
Population: Penal institutions.
Publication Dates: 1952–1954.
Acronym: OPCT.
Scores, 5: Block Counting, Digit-Symbol, Number Series, Memory Span, Total.
Administration: Group.
Price Data: Available from publisher.
Time: (25–30) minutes.
Comments: Also available for industrial use under the title Ohio Classification Test (1957).
Authors: DeWitt E. Sell, Robert W. Scollay, and Leroy N. Vernon (manual for industrial edition).
Publisher: Psychometric Affiliates.

Cross References: See T2:418 (2 references); for a review by Norman Eagle, see 5:358.

[1887]

Older Persons Counseling Needs Survey.

Purpose: To assess the needs of older persons and their desires for counseling.
Population: Ages 60 and over.
Publication Date: 1993.
Scores, 3: Needs, Desires, Total.
Administration: Group or individual.
Price Data: Available from publisher at www.mindgarden.com/products/opcns.htm.
Time: (10–15) minutes.
Author: Jane E. Myers.
Publisher: Mind Garden, Inc.
Cross References: For reviews by Dennis C. Harper and Lawrence J. Ryan, see 14:264.

[1888]

Oliver Organization Description Questionnaire.

Purpose: Describes occupational organizations along four dimensions.
Population: Adults.
Publication Date: 1981.
Acronym: OODQ.
Scores, 4: H (Hierarchy), P (Professional), T (Task), G (Group).
Administration: Group.
Price Data, 2002: $30 per 50 tests with scoring sheets; $5 per scoring guide (1981, 13 pages).
Time: (15–20) minutes.
Author: John E. Oliver, Jr.
Publisher: Organizational Measurement Systems Press.
Cross References: For a review by Peter Villanova and H. John Bernardin, see 11:271.

[1889]

OMNI Personality Inventory and OMNI-IV Personality Disorder Inventory.

Purpose: "Comprehensive self-report instruments for measuring normal and abnormal personality traits."
Population: Ages 18–74 years.
Publication Date: 2001.
Administration: Individual or group.
Price Data, 2006: $172 per OMNI introductory kit including OMNI professional manual (75 pages), 25 OMNI test booklets, OMNI CD-ROM software system with on-screen manual, and 5 free on-screen administrations of the OMNI; $150 per OMNI-IV Introductory kit including OMNI professional manual (75 pages), 25 OMNI-IV test booklets, OMNI-IV CD-ROM software system with on-screen manual, and 5 free on-screen administrations of the OMNI-IV.

Comments: Paper-and-pencil and computer administration available; computer-scored only (cannot be hand-scored); CD-ROM based scoring software generates interpretive report.

Author: Armand W. Loranger.

Publisher: Psychological Assessment Resources, Inc.

a) OMNI PERSONALITY INVENTORY.

Acronym: OMNI.

Scores, 44: 2 Validity Scales: Variable Response Inconsistency (VRIN), Current Distress (CD); 25 Normal Scales: Aestheticism (AE), Ambition (AM), Anxiety (AN), Assertiveness (AS), Conventionality (CO), Depression (DE), Dutifulness (DU), Excitement (EC), Exhibitionism (EH), Energy (EN), Flexibility (FL), Hostility (HS), Impulsiveness (IM), Intellect (IT), Irritability (IR), Modesty (MD), Moodiness (MO), Orderliness (OR), Self-Indulgence (SI), Sincerity (SN), Sociability (SO), Self-Reliance (SR), Tolerance (TO), Trustfulness (TR), Warmth (WR); 10 Personality Disorder Scales: Paranoid (PAR), Schizoid (SCH), Schizotypal (SCT), Antisocial (ANT), Borderline (BOR), Histrionic (HIS) Narcissistic (NAR), Avoidant (AVD), Dependent (DEP), Obsessive-Compulsive (OBC); 7 Personality Factor Scales: Agreeableness (AGRE), Conscientiousness (CONC), Extraversion (EXTR), Narcissism (NARC), Neuroticism (NEUR), Openness (OPEN), Sensation-Seeking (SENS).

Time: (60–90) minutes.

Comments: 375-item self-report inventory; measure both normal and abnormal personality traits as specified in DSM-IV.

b) OMNI-IV PERSONALITY DISORDER INVENTORY.

Acronym: OMNI-IV.

Scores, 12: 2 Validity Scales: Variable Response Inconsistency (VRIN), Current Distress (CD); 10 Personality Disorder Scales: Paranoid (PAR), Schizoid (SCH), Schizotypal (SCT), Antisocial (ANT), Borderline (BOR), Histrionic (HIS), Narcissistic (NAR), Avoidant (AVD), Dependent (DEP), Obsessive-Compulsive (OBC).

Time: (35–45) minutes.

Comments: 210 items taken from the OMNI; assesses personality disorders as specified in DSM-IV.

Cross References: For a review by Kevin Lanning, see 15:177.

[1890]

An Online Computerized Adaptive Placement Exam in Spanish, French, German, Russian, and ESL.

Purpose: Designed to assist appropriate placement into college-level beginning Spanish, French, German, Russian, and ESL courses.

Population: College students.

Publication Dates: 1986–1996.

Acronym: WebCAPE (S, F, G, R, or E).

Scores: Total score only.

Administration: Individual.

Price Data: Available from publisher.

Time: (20–25) minutes.

Comments: Tests taken online (creativeworks.byu.edu/hrc).

Authors: Jerry W. Larson, Kim L. Smith, Don Jensen, Randall L. Jones, Marshall Murray, and Diane Strong-Krause.

Publisher: Brigham Young University, Humanities Technology and Research Support Center.

Cross References: For reviews by G. Gage Kingsbury and Steven L. Wise, see 12:364.

[1891]

Opinions About Deaf People Scale.

Purpose: To measure hearing adults' beliefs about the capabilities of deaf adults.

Population: Adults.

Publication Date: Undated.

Scores: Total score only.

Administration: Group.

Price Data: Now available to the public at no charge.

Time: Administration time not reported.

Authors: Paul James Berkay, J. Emmett Gardener, and Patricia L. Smith.

Publisher: National Clearinghouse of Rehabilitation Training Materials.

Cross References: For reviews by Jeffery P. Braden and by Vincent J. Samar and Ila Parasnis, see 14:265.

[1892]

Opposite Strengths Inventory of Strengths.

Purpose: "To identify eight patterns of human strengths."

Population: Managers and adults in organizational settings.

Publication Dates: 1977– 2011.

Acronym: OSIS

Scores: Core Strengths.

Administration: Individual.

Forms, 2: Self-report (1977, 2 pages, for self-ratings), Other-report (1977, 2 pages, for ratings by unlimited numbers of others).

Restricted Distribution: Inventory and all reports available only to Opposite Strengths Certified Executive Coaches and Certified Facilitators..

Price Data, 2011: Scoring service, part of executive coaching or culture transformation service; otherwise $375; online printing only.

Time: (10) minutes.

Comments: Forms available only at www.opposite-strengths.com.

Authors: J. W. Thomas, Clyde C. Mayo (manual), and T. J. Thomas (interpretive reports).
Publisher: Opposite Strengths, Inc.

[1893]

OPQ32.

Purpose: "Designed to give information on individual styles or preferences at work."
Population: Employees and employee candidates.
Publication Dates: 1984–1999.
Acronym: OPQ32.
Scores: 32 scales: Relationships with People (Persuasive, Controlling, Outspoken, Independent Minded, Outgoing, Affiliative, Socially Confident, Modest, Democratic, Caring), Thinking Style (Data Rational, Evaluative, Behavioural, Conventional, Conceptual, Innovative, Variety Seeking, Adaptable, Forward Thinking, Detail Conscious, Conscientious, Rule Following), Feelings and Emotions (Relaxed, Worrying, Tough Minded, Optimistic, Trusting, Emotionally Controlled, Vigorous, Competitive, Achieving, Decisive).
Administration: Group.
Forms, 2: OPQ32n, OPQ32i.
Price Data: Available from publisher.
Time: Untimed; administration time not reported.
Comments: May be administered via Palm-top (PSION) Personal Questionnaire Administrator, personal computer, booklet and answer sheet, or on the internet; previous version was listed as Occupational Personality Questionnaire.
Author: SHL Group plc.
Publisher: SHL Group plc [United Kingdom].
Cross References: See T5:1822 (7 references); for a review by Thomas M. Haladyna of the earlier edition, see 11:267.

[1894]

Optometry Admission Testing Program.

Purpose: "Designed to measure general academic ability and comprehension of scientific information."
Population: Optometry school applicants.
Publication Dates: 1987-2006.
Acronym: OAT.
Scores, 8: Academic Average, Quantitative Reasoning, Reading Comprehension, Physics, Biology, General Chemistry, Organic Chemistry, Total Science.
Administration: Group.
Price Data: Available from publisher.
Time: 245(285) minutes.
Comments: Administered via computer.
Author: Optometry Admission Testing Program.
Publisher: Optometry Admission Testing Program.
Cross References: For reviews by Alan C. Bugbee, Jr. and James E. Carlson, see 12:269; for a review by Penelope Kegel-Flom of the Optometry College Admission Test, see 8:1104 (3 references).

[1895]

OQ-45.2 (Outcome Questionnaire).

Purpose: Designed to measure "patient progress in therapy."
Population: Adult therapy patients.
Publication Dates: 1996–2004.
Scores, 4: Symptom Distress, Interpersonal Relations, Social Role, Total.
Administration: Individual.
Price Data: Price data for manual (2004, 54 pages), questionnaire, and scoring services available from publisher.
Foreign Language Editions: Spanish, German, French, Dutch, Swedish, Norwegian, Hebrew, and Japanese editions available.
Time: (5–15) minutes.
Comments: Designed for repeated administration over the course of therapy; computer scoring available; may be administered orally.
Authors: Michael J. Lambert, Jared S. Morton, Derick Hatfield, Cory Harmon, Stacy Hamilton, Rory C. Reid, Kenichi Shumokawa, Cody Christopherson, and Gary Burlingame.
Publisher: OQ Measures LLC.
Cross References: For reviews by William E. Hanson and Brad M. Merker and by Steven I. Pfeiffer, see 16:176.

[1896]

OQ-10.2 [A Brief Screening & Outcome Questionnaire].

Purpose: "Designed as a brief screening instrument … intended to alert the physician to the possibility that the patient was experiencing enough psychological distress to consider follow-up with other specific diagnostic tests or interviews."
Population: Ages 17-80 years.
Publication Dates: 1998-2000.
Acronym: OQ-10.2.
Scores: Total score only.
Administration: Individual or group.
Restricted Distribution: Requires licensure from American Professional Credentialing Services LLC.
Price Data, 2006: Licensing cost available from publisher; $25 per administration and scoring manual (1998, 10 pages); $25 per test.
Foreign Language Editions: English, Spanish, and French editions available.
Time: (1-5) minutes.
Authors: Michael J. Lambert, Arthur M. Finch, John Okishi, Gary M. Burlingame (manual only), Celeste McKelvey (manual only), and Curtis W. Reisinger.
Publisher: OQ Measures LLC.
Cross References: For reviews by Jody L. Kulstad and Michael J. Scheel, see 17:136.

[1897]

OQ-30.1 [Outcome Questionnaire for Adults].

Purpose: Designed to "measure patient progress following psychological and medical interventions."
Population: Ages 17-80 years.
Publication Dates: 2001-2003.
Acronym: OQ 30.1.
Scores: Total score only.
Administration: Individual or group.
Restricted Distribution: Requires licensure from American Professional Credentialing Services LLC.
Price Data, 2006: Licensing cost available from publisher; $25 per administration and scoring manual (2003, 18 pages); $25 per test.
Foreign Language Editions: English, Spanish, and French editions available.
Time: (2-15) minutes.
Comments: Test can be administered orally.
Authors: Michael J. Lambert, Derek R. Hatfield, David A. Vermeersch (manual only), Gary M. Burlingame, Curtis W. Resinger, and G. S. (Jeb) Brown (manual only).
Publisher: OQ Measures LLC.
Cross References: For reviews by Collie Conoley and Pam Ramsden, see 17:137.

[1898]

Oral and Written Language Scales: Listening Comprehension (LC) and Oral Expression (OE) Scales.

Purpose: Assesses receptive and expressive oral language.
Population: Ages 3–21.
Publication Date: 1995.
Acronym: OWLS LC/OE.
Scores, 3: Listening Comprehension, Oral Expression, Oral Composite.
Administration: Individual.
Price Data, 2008: $260 per complete kit, including manual (212 pages), Listening Comprehension Easel, Oral Expression Easel, and 25 record forms; $40.25 per 25 record forms; $221 per ASSIST™ for OWLS LC/OE (Windows or Macintosh).
Time: (5–15) minutes for LC; (10–25) minutes for OE.
Authors: Elizabeth Carrow-Woolfolk.
Publisher: Western Psychological Services.
Cross References: For reviews by Steve Graham and Koressa Kutsick Malcolm, see 14:266.

[1899]

Oral and Written Language Scales: Written Expression (WE) Scale.

Purpose: Constructed as an "assessment of written language."
Population: Ages 5–21.
Publication Date: 1996.
Acronym: OWLS WE.
Scores, 2: Written Expression, Language Composite (when used with OWL Listening Comprehension and Oral Expression Scales).
Administration: Individual or group.
Price Data, 2011: $160 per complete kit, including manual (255 pages), 25 response booklets, 25 record forms, and 1 Administration Card; $95 for just the manual; $41 per 25 response booklets; $37 per 25 record forms; $340 for WE Kit with ASSIST SCORING SOFTWARE; $230 per ASSIST™ for OWLS WE (Windows or Macintosh).
Time: (15-25) minutes.
Comments: May be used alone or in combination with OWLS Listening Comprehension and Oral Expression (1898).
Author: Elizabeth Carrow-Woolfolk.
Publisher: Western Psychological Services
Cross References: For reviews by C. Dale Carpenter and Koressa Kutsick Malcolm, see 14:267.

[1900]

Oral English/Spanish Placement Test.

Purpose: A measure of bilingualism to aid in placing children properly for efficient instruction.
Population: Ages 4–20.
Publication Dates: 1974–1976.
Acronym: OE/SPPT.
Scores: Total score and grade level equivalents.
Administration: Individual.
Tests, 2: English, Spanish.
Price Data, 2006: $20 per packet (includes manual and 1 English and 1 Spanish rating/answer sheets); permission to copy answer sheets is included.
Time: (1–2) minutes for children with little or no proficiency; (2–5) minutes for children with slightly better proficiency.
Comments: Performance rated by examiner; no reading by examinees.
Author: Steve Moreno.
Publisher: Moreno Educational Co.
Cross References: For a review by Stephen Powers, see 9:902.

[1901]

Oral-Motor/Feeding Rating Scale.

Purpose: Constructed to assess "oral-motor movement/feeding dysfunction."
Population: Ages 1 and over.
Publication Date: 1990.
Scores: Item scores only.
Administration: Individual.
Price Data, 2002: $40 per complete kit including 25 progress charts and manual (26 pages); $23 per 25 progress charts.
Time: (60) minutes or less.

Comments: Ratings by professional.
Author: Judy Michels Jelm.
Publisher: Pearson.
Cross References: For reviews by Glen E. Ray and Donna Spiker, see 12:271.

[1902]

Oral Speech Mechanism Screening Examination, Third Edition.

Purpose: "To provide the speech-language pathologist and other professionals with a method for assessing the adequacy of the oral mechanism for speech and related functions."
Population: Age 5 through adults.
Publication Dates: 1981–2000.
Acronym: OSMSE-3.
Scores: 9 areas: Lips, Tongue, Jaw, Teeth, Hard Palate, Soft Palate, Pharynx, Breathing, Diadochokinesis.
Administration: Individual.
Price Data, 2011: $117 per complete kit; $35 per 50 scoring forms; $24 per audio CD; $65 per examiner's manual.
Time: (10–15) minutes.
Authors: Kenneth O. St. Louis and Dennis M. Ruscello.
Publisher: PRO-ED.
Cross References: For a review by Roger L. Towne, see 14:268; see also T5:1852 (6 references) and T4:1900 (4 references); for reviews by Charles Wm. Martin and Malcolm R. McNeil of an earlier edition, see 11:272.

[1903]

Organic Dysfunction Survey Schedules.

Purpose: To assist in discovering psychological and medical factors that may contribute to treatment.
Population: Adult clients.
Publication Date: 1981.
Acronym: ODSS.
Scores: 22 survey schedules: Arthritis, Asthma, Cancer, Cardiac, Covert Thermal, Cues for Tension and Anxiety, Dysmenorrhea, Gastrointestinal, Guidelines for Cardiac Rehabilitation, Headache, Hypertension, Nutrition, Organic Dysfunction-Medical, Organic Dysfunction-Psychological, Pain, Physical Complaint, Reactions Toward Illness, Renal Failure, Seizure, Stress, Stroke, Vomiting.
Administration: Group or individual.
Manual: No manual.
Price Data, 2001: $79.95 per set of schedules.
Time: Administration time not reported.
Author: Joseph R. Cautela.
Publisher: Cambridge Center for Behavioral Studies.
Cross References: See T5:1853 (1 reference); for reviews by Julian Fabry and George N. Prigitano, see 9:909.

[1904]

Organizational and Team Culture Indicator.

Purpose: Measures unconscious archetypal stories based on an aggregate assessment and relates these to an organization's or team's values and strengths; interpretative results also gauge the relative balance of attention to building stable systems, achieving results, creating and sustaining community, and fostering learning and growth; is intended to help an organization optimize customer service, support employee satisfaction and communication, and generate strong brand identity.
Population: Adults.
Publication Dates: 2003–2004.
Acronym: OTCI.
Scores: 12 Archetypes: Creator, Everyperson, Hero, Caregiver, Innocent, Magician, Jester, Lover, Sage, Ruler, Explorer, Revolutionary.
Administration: Individual or group.
Restricted Distribution: Distribution of Professional Report is restricted to persons who have completed the publisher's or author's training course.
Price Data, 2004: $45 per manual (2004, 141 pages); $18 per Basic Report (print version) including 1 instrument, 1 self-scorable report form, and 1 Understanding Archetypes in Your Organization (2003, 49 pages); $15 per Basic Report (online version); prices for administering the OTCI in the aggregate format using the OTCI Professional Report for interpretation available from publisher.
Time: Administration time not reported.
Comments: Results are available in either Basic or more comprehensive Professional Report Format; Basic Report is available for online or self-scored administration and Professional Report format is available only through qualified professionals.
Authors: Carol S. Pearson (test and manual) and Allen L. Hammer (manual).
Publisher: Center for Applications of Psychological Type.
Cross References: For a review by Stephen B. Johnson, see 16:178.

[1905]

Organizational Assessment Survey.

Purpose: Designed to help businesses identify problems leading to low productivity and employee dissatisfaction.
Population: Adult.
Publication Date: 1985.
Acronym: OAS.
Scores, 4: Accomplishment, Recognition, Power, Affiliation.
Administration: Group or individual.
Price Data, 2005: $49.50 per OAS Report Kit including manual, reusable test booklets, and processing of 2 reports; $15.75–$21 each per individual report; $8.50–$12 each per group report.
Time: Untimed.
Authors: Larry A. Breskamp and Martin L. Maehr.
Publisher: MetriTech, Inc.

[1906]

Organizational Behavior Profile.

Purpose: Designed to detect signs of codependency in organizations.
Population: Organizations.
Publication Date: 1993.
Acronym: OBP.
Scores, 4: Closed/Open, Denial/Collusion, Excessive Changes/Crisis Management/Confusion, Excessive Promises.
Administration: Group.
Price Data: Available from publisher.
Time: Administration time not reported.
Comments: Self-scored inventory; completed by members to measure the organization.
Authors: Jeanette Goodstein and Earnie Larsen.
Publisher: Jossey-Bass, A Wiley Company.

[1907]

Organizational Beliefs Questionnaire.

Purpose: "Intended to give concerned managers a deeper understanding of their own organization's culture."
Population: Organizations.
Publication Date: 1997.
Acronym: OBQ.
Scores, 10: Work Can Be As Much Fun As Play, Seek Constant Improvement, Accept Specific And Difficult Goals, Accept Responsibility For Your Actions, Care About One Another, Quality Is Crucially Important, Work Together To Get The Job Done, Have Concern For Measures Of Our Success, There Must Be Hands-On Management, A Strong Set Of Shared Values And Beliefs Guide Our Actions.
Administration: Group.
Price Data: Available from publisher.
Time: Administration time not reported.
Comments: Computerized interpretive information provided by publisher, including scale summaries and individual item analyses.
Author: Marshall Sashkin.
Publisher: HRD Press, Inc.
Cross References: For reviews by Cynthia A. Larson-Daugherty and Mary Roznowski, see 14:269.

[1908]

Organizational Change-Readiness Scale.

Purpose: Constructed "to analyze the ability of an organization to manage change effectively and to plan improvement actions."
Population: Employees.
Publication Date: 1996.
Acronym: OCRS.
Scores: 5 scales: Structural Readiness, Technological Readiness, Climatic Readiness, Systemic Readiness, People Readiness.

Administration: Group.
Price Data, 1996: $6.50 per assessment inventory; $24.95 per facilitator's guide (24 pages).
Time: (20) minutes.
Comments: Redevelopment of Organizational Change-Readiness Survey.
Authors: John E. Jones and William L. Bearley.
Publisher: HRD Press, Inc.
Cross References: For reviews by Gary J. Dean and Eugene P. Sheehan, see 14:270.

[1909]

Organizational Character Index.

Purpose: Designed to determine the character of a department, team, or organization.
Population: Adults working for an organization.
Publication Date: 2000.
Acronym: OCI.
Scores, 4: Extroversion or Introversion, Sensing or Intuition, Thinking or Feeling, Judging or Perceiving.
Administration: Individual or group.
Price Data, 2011: $7 per Organizational Character Index self-scorable booklet.
Time: (15) minutes.
Comments: Can be self-administered and scored; book entitled The Character of Organizations serves as manual.
Author: William Bridges.
Publisher: CPP, Inc.

[1910]

Organizational Climate Exercise II.

Purpose: Assesses the current climate within an organization/department versus how one thinks it should be.
Population: Work groups.
Publication Dates: 1991–1993.
Acronym: OCE.
Scores, 12: Actual Organizational Climate and Ideal Organizational Climate on 6 dimensions: Flexibility, Responsibility, Standards, Rewards, Clarity, Team Commitment.
Administration: Group or individual.
Price Data, 2006: $79 per complete kit including 10 questionnaires and 10 profiles and interpretive notes (11 pages); $29 per 10 Feedback Version questionnaires; $25 per Trainer's Guide (1993, 31 pages) hardcopy or free electronic version.
Foreign Language Editions: French and Spanish editions available.
Time: [30] minutes.
Comments: Self-scored instrument; publisher recommends Pulse Surveys as an alternative on-line version.
Author: Hay Group.
Publisher: Hay Group.
Cross References: For reviews by Mary Anne Bunda and Erich P. Prien, see 13:217.

[1911]

Organizational Culture Inventory.

Purpose: Designed to measure an organization's current and ideal norms and expectations.
Population: Organizational members.
Publication Dates: 1987–1989.
Acronym: OCI.
Scores: 12 culture styles: Constructive Cultures (Achievement, Self-Actualizing, Humanistic-Encouraging, Affiliative), Passive/Defensive Cultures (Approval, Conventional, Dependent, Avoidance Style), Aggressive/Defensive Cultures (Oppositional, Power, Competitive, Perfectionistic).
Administration: Group or individual.
Forms, 2: OCI Ideal, OCI Current.
Price Data: Price information available from publisher for test materials including Leader's Guide (1989, 74 pages).
Time: [15-20] minutes.
Authors: Robert A. Cooke and J. Clayton Lafferty.
Publisher: Human Synergistics International.
Cross References: See T5:1862 (2 references); for reviews by Charlene M. Alexander and Gargi Roysircar Sodowsky, see 12:272 (1 reference).

[1912]

Organizational Description Questionnaire.

Purpose: Designed to "measure how often each member of the organization perceives the culture of their unit/department/organization to be using a full range of specific leadership factors."
Population: Organizations.
Publication Date: 1992.
Acronym: ODQ.
Scores, 2: Transactional, Transformational.
Administration: Group.
Price Data: Available from publisher at www.mindgarden.com/products/odq.htm.
Time: (20–25) minutes.
Comments: Web-based administration and reporting available.
Authors: Bernard M. Bass and Bruce J. Avolio.
Publisher: Mind Garden, Inc.

[1913]

Organizational Effectiveness Inventory.

Purpose: Determines the impact of organizational, group, and job level factors on organizational effectiveness.
Population: Organization members.
Publication Date: 1997.
Acronym: OEI.
Scores: 41 Outcomes and Causal Factors: Mission and Philosophy (Articulation of Mission, Customer-Service Focus), Structures (Empowerment, Employee Involvement), Systems (Selection /Placement, Training and De-velopment, Respect for Members, Fairness of Appraisals, Use of Rewards, Use of Punishment, Goal Clarity, Goal Challenge, Participative Goal Setting, Goal Acceptance), Technology (Autonomy, Skill Variety, Feedback, Task identity, Significance, Interdependence), Skills/Qualities (Upward Communication, Downward Communication, Communication for Learning, Interaction Facilitation, Task Facilitation, Goal Emphasis, Consideration, Personal Bases of Power, Organizational Bases of Power), Individual Outcomes–Positive Indices (Role Clarity, Motivation, Satisfaction, Intention to Stay), Individual Outcomes–Negative Indices (Role Conflict, Job Insecurity, Stress), Group Outcomes (Intra-Unit Cooperation, Inter-Unit Coordination, Departmental–Level Quality), Organizational Outcomes (Organizational–Level Quality, External Adaptability).
Administration: Individual or group.
Price Data: Available from publisher.
Time: Administration time not reported.
Author: Robert A. Cooke.
Publisher: Human Synergistics International.

[1914]

Organizational Justice Inventory.

Purpose: Measures employees' perception of their organization's commitment to justice.
Population: Employees.
Publication Date: 2000.
Acronym: OJI.
Scores, 4: Procedural Justice, Distributive Justice, Interpersonal Justice, Informational Justice.
Administration: Group.
Manual: No manual.
Price Data, 2008: $150 per permission to make 300 copies for institutional or funded projects; $75 per permission to make 300 copies for individual or unfunded projects; quantity discounts available.
Time: Administration time not reported.
Authors: M. Afzal Rahim, Nace R. Magner, and Debra L. Shapiro.
Publisher: Center for Advanced Studies in Management.

[1915]

Orleans-Hanna Algebra Prognosis Test, Third Edition.

Purpose: Designed to "determine algebra readiness" and as a predictor of student success in first-year algebra.
Population: Grades 7–11.
Publication Dates: 1928–1998.
Scores: Total score only.
Administration: Group.
Price Data, 2005: $85 per 25 test booklets and manual (1998, 55 pages); $35 per 25 hand-scorable answer documents including class record; $21 per key

to use with hand-scorable answer documents; $30 per 25 student report forms; $35 per 25 machine-scorable answer documents.

Time: 35(40) minutes.

Author: Gerald S. Hanna.

Publisher: Pearson.

Cross References: For reviews by Joseph C. Ciechalski and Kevin D. Crehan, see 17:138; see also T4:1910 (3 references); for reviews by Dietmar Küchemann and Charles Secolsky of an earlier edition, see 9:912 (1 reference); see also T2:688 (11 references); for reviews by W. L. Bashaw and Cyril J. Hoyt of an earlier edition, see 7:510 (3 references); for reviews by Harold Gulliksen and Emma Spany, see 4:396 (1 reference); for a review by S. S. Wilks, see 2:1444 (4 references).

[1916]
OSOT Perceptual Evaluation.

Purpose: Designed to identify perceptual impairment in adults.

Population: Adults.

Publication Date: 1991.

Scores, 19: Scanning, Spatial Neglect, Motor Planning, Copying 2 Dimensional Designs, Copying 3 Dimensional Designs, Body Puzzle, Draw-a-Person, Right/Left Discrimination, Clock, Peg Board, Draw-a-House, Shape Recognition, Colour Recognition, Size Recognition, Figure Ground Discrimination, Proprioception, Stereognosis R, Stereognosis L, Total.

Administration: Individual.

Price Data, 2005: $859 per test kit; $37.70 per English manual (included in kit, 60 pages), $36.70 per French manual.

Time: Administration time not reported.

Authors: Pat Fisher, Marian Boys, and Claire Holzberg.

Publisher: Nelson Education Ltd. [Canada].

Cross References: For a review by Raoul A. Arreola, see 12:274.

[1917]

Otis-Lennon School Ability Test, Eighth Edition.

Purpose: "Designed to measure those verbal, quantitative, and figural reasoning skills that are most closely related to scholastic achievement."

Population: Ages 4-6 to 18-2.

Publication Dates: 1977-2003.

Acronym: OLSAT 8.

Scores, 3: Verbal, Nonverbal, Total.

Administration: Group.

Levels, 7: A, B, C, D, E, F, G.

Forms, 1: 5.

Restricted Distribution: OLSAT 8 is sold only to accredited schools and school districts.

Price Data, 2009: $7.90 per directions for administering for the practice test (Form 5, Levels A-F); $9.70 per 10 practice test packs (Form 5, Levels A-F); $19.70 per directions for administering (Form 5, Levels A, B, C, and D and E/F/G combined); $54.60 per 10 machine-scorable test packs (Form 5, Levels A-D); $43.35 per 10 reusable test packs (Form 5, Levels E-G); $43.85 per 30 machine-scorable answer documents (Form 5, Levels E/F/G combined); $8.10 per class records (Form 5, Levels A-G); $26.25 per response keys for hand scoring (Form 5, Levels A-G); $68.25 per norms book (specify spring [2003, 94 pages] or fall [2003, 94 pages]); $50.40 per technical manual (2003, 65 pages).

Time: (77) minutes over 2 sessions for Levels A-B; (72) minutes over 2 sessions for Level C; 50 (60) minutes over 1 session for Level D; 40 (60) minutes over 1 session for Levels E-G.

Comments: Administered orally at Levels A-B; Level C is partially self-administered; Levels D-G are self-administered; originally titled Otis-Lennon Mental Ability Test.

Author: Pearson.

Publisher: Pearson.

Cross References: For reviews by Cleborne D. Maddux and David Morse, see 18:82; for reviews by Lizanne DeStefano and Bert A. Goldman of the Seventh Edition, see 14:271; see also T5:1866 (45 references) and T4:1913 (8 references); for reviews by Anne Anastasi and Mark E. Swerdlik of an earlier edition, see 11:274 (48 references); for reviews by Calvin O. Dyer and Thomas Oakland of an earlier edition, see 9:913 (7 references); see also T3:1754 (64 references), 8:198 (35 references), and T2:424 (10 references); for a review by John E. Milholland and excerpted reviews by Arden Grotelueschen and Arthur E. Smith of an earlier edition, see 7:370 (6 references).

[1918]
Our Class and Its Work.

Purpose: "To measure those teaching behaviors believed to contribute to student achievement in the classroom."

Population: Grades 3–12.

Publication Date: 1983.

Acronym: OCIW.

Scores, 9: Didactic Instruction, Enthusiasm, Feedback, Instructional Time, Opportunity to Learn, Pacing, Structuring Comments, Task Orientation, Total.

Administration: Group.

Price Data: Available from publisher.

Time: Administration time not reported.

Comments: Self-report instrument.

Authors: Maurice J. Eash and Hersholt C. Waxman.

Publisher: Maurice J. Eash [No reply from publisher; status unknown].

Cross References: See T4:1914 (1 reference); for reviews by James R. Barclay and F. Charles Mace, see 10:269 (1 reference).

[1919]

Outcome Assessment and Reporting System.

Purpose: Designed to provide "relevant longitudinal data," throughout the treatment period, documenting "observations that are related to positive outcomes for the treatment of substance dependence."
Population: Adolescents and adults.
Publication Date: 2005.
Acronym: OAARS.
Scores, 13: Emotional Volatility, Ability to Focus on Treatment, Affective and Anxiety Problems/Disorders, Awareness and Understanding of the Condition, Openness and Personal Commitment to Change, Willingness to Involve Others in Treatment, Indication of Ability to Follow-Through on the Treatment Plan, Level of Engagement in Treatment, Social/Interpersonal Supports, The Recovery Environment, Discharge/Program Completion Status, Engagement, Recovery Status.
Administration: Individual.
Price Data, 2008: $99 per kit; $5 per manual (7 pages).
Time: Administration time not reported.
Comments: The scale is to be completed three times throughout the course of treatment; items to assess treatment effectiveness are to be completed 3 to 6 months after treatment.
Authors: Norman G. Hoffmann, Gerald D. Shulman, and David Mee-Lee.
Publisher: The Change Companies.

[1920]

Outcomes: Planning, Monitoring, Evaluating.

Purpose: "A tool for monitoring student progress toward selected goals."
Population: Grades K–12.
Publication Date: 2002.
Acronym: PME.
Scores: 11 categories: Concern Description, Goals and Benchmarks, Benchmark Sealing, Social-Validation Criteria, Intervention Planning, Progress-Monitoring Procedures, Progress Chart, Progress Analysis, Evaluation of Outcomes, Next-Step Strategies, Special Education Considerations.
Administration: Individual.
Price Data, 2002: $85 per complete kit including manual (2002, 139 pages), binder, and 25 record forms; $50 per manual; $40 per 25 record forms.
Time: Untimed.
Comments: Provides a framework for documenting education professionals' problem-solving efforts; helps identify concerns, describe context of problem, rate baseline performance, operationalize goals, plan intervention, monitor and graph student progress, evaluate intervention outcomes, plan next steps.
Authors: Karen Callan Stoiber and Thomas R. Kratochwill.

Publisher: Pearson.
Cross References: For a review by Gypsy M. Denzine, see 15:178.

[1921]

Overall Assessment of the Speaker's Experience of Stuttering.

Purpose: Designed to "provide clinicians with a measure of the overall impact of stuttering on a person's life."
Population: Individuals 18 and over who stutter.
Publication Date: 2008.
Acronym: OASES.
Scores, 4: General Information, Your Reaction to Stuttering, Communication in Daily Situations, Quality of Life.
Administration: Individual or group.
Price Data, 2008: $70 per starting kit including technical manual (41 pages) and 25 record forms; $25 per 25 record forms; $65 per Q local scoring and reporting software starter kit including technical manual, 3 record forms, and 3 Q local administrations; $25 per local scoring record forms; $8 per profile report; $72.50 per mail-in scoring service starter kit including technical manual, 3 record forms, and 3 interpretive reports; $12 per mail-in scoring interpretive report; $9.50 per mail-in scoring profile report.
Foreign Language Edition: Record forms are available in Spanish.
Time: (15-20) minutes.
Authors: J. Scott Yaruss and Robert W. Quesal.
Publisher: Pearson.
Cross References: For reviews by Sandra D. Haynes and by Jeanette Lee-Farmer and Joyce Meikamp, see 18:83.

[1922]

Overeating Questionnaire.

Purpose: Designed to measure "key habits, thoughts, and attitudes related to obesity."
Population: Ages 9–98 years.
Publication Date: 2004.
Acronym: OQ.
Scores, 12: 2 Validity scores (Inconsistent Responding, Defensiveness), 6 Eating-Related Habits and Attitudes scores (Overeating, Undereating, Craving, Expectations About Eating, Rationalizations, Motivation to Lose Weight), 4 general Health Habits and Psychosocial Functioning scores (Health Habits, Body Image, Social Isolation, Affective Disturbance).
Administration: Group or individual.
Price Data, 2007: $93.50 per complete kit including 25 AutoScore answer sheets and manual (51 pages); $42.50 per 25 AutoScore answer sheets (bulk discounts available); $55 per manual; Computerized components: $307.50 per 25-use computer disk for Windows; $16.50 per 100 PC answer sheets.

Time: 20 minutes.

Comments: Written for individuals with a fourth-grade reading level and higher.

Authors: William E. O'Donnell and W. L. Warren.

Publisher: Western Psychological Services.

Cross References: For reviews by James P. Donnelly and Sandra D. Haynes, see 17:139.

[1923]

P-BDQ Police Officer Background Data Questionnaire.

Purpose: Assesses backgrounds and personal characteristics of entry-level police officer candidates.

Population: Candidates for entry-level police officer positions.

Publication Dates: 1999-2000.

Acronym: P-BDQ.

Scores: 5 biodata subtypes: Background, Lifestyle, Interest, Personality, Ability.

Administration: Individual or group.

Price Data: Available from publisher.

Time: 30 minutes.

Comments: "It is recommended that this test be used in conjunction with one of IPMA-HR's other entry-level police officer tests."

Authors: International Public Management Association for Human Resources & Bruce Davey Associates.

Publisher: International Public Management Association for Human Resources (IPMA-HR).

Cross References: For a review by Thomas R. O'Neill, see 18:84.

[1924]

P.C. User Aptitude Test.

Purpose: To evaluate the practical and analytical skills required for the effective use of microcomputers.

Population: Applicants for positions involving the use of microcomputers.

Publication Date: 1986.

Acronym: WMICRO.

Scores: Total Score, Narrative Evaluation, Ranking, Recommendation.

Administration: Group.

Price Data, 2001: $235 per candidate; quantity discounts available.

Foreign Language Edition: French edition available.

Time: 75 minutes.

Comments: Graded by publisher; must be proctored; previously listed as Microcomputer User Aptitude Test.

Author: Richard Label.

Publisher: Walden Personnel Performance, Inc. [Canada].

Cross References: For a review by Robert Fitzpatrick, see 11:473.

[1925]

P-Det 1.0 and 2.0 Police Detective Tests.

Purpose: Developed "to assist law enforcement departments … in promoting qualified candidates to the detective position."

Population: Candidates for promotion to the police detective position.

Publication Dates: 2004-2006.

Acronym: P-Det 1.0, P-Det 2.0.

Scores: 3 knowledge areas: Police Investigation Procedures, Laws Related to Police Work, Concepts for Writing and Completing Reports/Records and Paperwork.

Administration: Individual or group.

Forms, 2: P-Det 1.0, P-Det 2.0.

Price Data: Available from publisher.

Time: 120 minutes per test.

Comments: P-Det 1.0 and P-Det 2.0 are comparable forms; reading lists are available to help candidates prepare for the tests.

Author: International Public Management Association for Human Resources.

Publisher: International Public Management Association for Human Resources (IPMA-HR).

Cross References: For a review by Karl N. Kelley, see 18:85.

[1926]

P-1SV and P-2SV Police Officer Tests.

Purpose: Developed to "assess the competencies that new police officers need to perform successfully on the job."

Population: Candidates for entry-level police officer positions.

Publication Dates: 2003-2006.

Acronym: P-1SV, P-2SV.

Scores: 5 job dimensions: Ability to Learn and Apply Police Information, Ability to Observe and Remember Details, Verbal Ability, Ability to Follow Directions, Ability to Use Judgment and Logic.

Administration: Individual or group.

Forms, 2: P-1SV, P-2SV.

Price Data: Available from publisher.

Time: 130 minutes per test.

Comments: P-1SV and P-2SV are parallel forms; no prior training or experience as a police officer is assumed of candidates taking the tests.

Author: International Public Management Association for Human Resources.

Publisher: International Public Management Association for Human Resources (IPMA-HR).

Cross References: For a review by Deniz S. Ones and Stephan Dilchert, see 18:86.

[1927]

Pain Assessment Battery, Research Edition.

Purpose: Constructed as "a comprehensive assessment tool for evaluating and documenting the physical,

experiential, behavioral, and psychological dimensions of chronic pain."
Population: Patients with chronic pain.
Publication Dates: 1993–1999.
Acronym: PAB-RE.
Scores: 7 tests: Pain History and Status Interview, Pain Imagery Interview, Pain Experience Scale, Pain Coping Interview–Research Edition, Stress Symptoms Checklist, Coping Style Profile, Interview Behavior Checklist.
Administration: Individual.
Price Data, 2002: $400 per test.
Time: (10–120) minutes.
Comments: Research instrument; computer-administered (DOS version only).
Authors: Bruce N. Eimer and Lyle M. Allen, III.
Publisher: CogniSyst, Inc.
Cross References: For reviews by M. Allan Cooperstein and F. Felicia Ferrara, see 14:272.

[1928]
Pain Patient Profile.
Purpose: "Designed to identify patients who are experiencing emotional distress associated with primary complaints of pain and assess the severity of distress in comparison to community and pain patient population national sample."
Population: Pain patients aged 17–76.
Publication Dates: 1992–1995.
Acronym: P-3®.
Scores, 4: Depression, Anxiety, Somatization, Validity Index.
Administration: Group.
Price Data, 2006: $55 per Q Local interpretive starter kit including manual (1995, 89 pages) and 3 answer sheets with test items to conduct and receive 3 Q Local administrations (starter kits with 10 or 30 Q Local administrations available); $63 per mail-in scoring starter kit including manual and 3 answer sheets with test items to conduct and receive 3 interpretive reports; $92.50 per 50 hand-scorable answer sheets; $10.25 per Q Local interpretive report; $13.25 per mail-in interpretive report including answer sheet with test items; $33 per manual; quantity discounts available for the reports; price information for Spanish materials available from publisher.
Foreign Language Edition: Spanish materials available.
Time: (10–15) minutes.
Authors: C. David Tollison and Jerry C. Langley.
Publisher: Pearson.
Cross References: For reviews by Gregory J. Boyle and Ronald J. Ganellen, see 14:273.

[1929]
Pair Attraction Inventory.
Purpose: "Designed to measure both complementarity and symmetry in pair relationships."
Population: College and adults.

Publication Dates: 1970–1971.
Acronym: PAI.
Scores, 7: Mother-Son, Daddy-Doll, Bitch-Nice Guy, Master-Servant, Hawks, Doves, Person-Person.
Administration: Individual.
Price Data: Available from publisher.
Time: (20-30) minutes.
Author: Everett L. Shostrom.
Publisher: EdITS/Educational and Industrial Testing Service.
Cross References: For a review by James R. Clopton, see 8:349 (10 references).

[1930]
Panic and Agoraphobia Scale.
Purpose: "Determine[s] the severity of panic disorder with or without agoraphobia and ... monitor[s] treatment efficacy."
Population: Age 16 and older.
Publication Date: 1999.
Acronym: PAS.
Scores, 5: Panic Attacks, Agoraphobic Avoidance, Anticipatory Anxiety, Disability, Worries About Health.
Administration: Individual and group.
Forms, 2: Observer-rated, self-rated.
Price Data, 2011: $98 per kit including manual (88 pages), 50 observer-rated scales, and 50 patient questionnaires.
Time: (5–10) minutes for observer-rated scale.
Comments: Self-administered; computerized version of self-rated scale in preparation; compatible with DSM-IV and ICD-10 classifications.
Author: Borwin Bandelow.
Publisher: Hogrefe Publishing.
Cross References: For reviews by C. G. Bellah and by James Donnelly and Scott T. Meier, see 15:179.

[1931]
Paper and Pencil Games.
Purpose: Constructed to measure "figural, quantitative and verbal skills closely related to scholastic achievement."
Population: Pupils in their second, third and fourth years in South African school system.
Publication Date: 1996.
Acronym: PPG.
Administration: Group.
Levels, 2: 2, 3.
Price Data, 2002: R5.13 per test booklet (specify level); R3.99 per Level 2 short version test booklet; R1.14 per practice test; R39.90 per manual (90 pages) (English only); R28.50 per directions for administration (specify language).
Foreign Language Editions: Available in Afrikaans, Ndebele, Northern Sotho, Swati, Southern Sotho, Tsonga, Tswana, Venda, Xhosa, and Zulu.

Time: (150–180) minutes including 20-minute break.
Author: N. C. W. Claassen.
Publisher: Human Sciences Research Council [South Africa].

    a) LEVEL 2.
    Population: School years 2–3.
    Scores, 5: Classification, Verbal and Quantitative Reasoning, Figure Series, Comprehension, Pattern Completion.
    b) LEVEL 3.
    Population: School years 3–4.
    Scores, 5: Figure Series, Verbal and Quantitative Reasoning, Pattern Completion, Comprehension, Number Series.
Cross References: For a review by Gary L. Marco, see 14:274.

[1932]

PAR: Proficiency Assessment Report.

Purpose: Developed to identify proficiency in 22 abilities associated with effective management.
Population: Supervisors and managers.
Publication Date: 1989.
Scores, 24: 22 Ability Scores, 2 Style Scores.
Administration: Group or individual.
Manual: No manual.
Price Data: Available from publisher.
Time: (30) minutes.
Comments: Ratings by manager and self; administered prior to training program and then discussed in pairs.
Author: Training House, Inc.
Publisher: Training House, Inc.
Cross References: For reviews by Stephen F. Davis and S. Alvin Leung, see 12:276.

[1933]

Parallel Spelling Tests, Second Edition.

Purpose: Designed to help "chart children's progress in spelling."
Population: Ages 6 to 13 years.
Publication Dates: 1983–1998.
Scores: Total score only.
Administration: Group.
Price Data, 2002: £16.99 per test booklet/manual (1998, 40 pages).
Time: (20) minutes per test.
Comments: Teachers create tests from two banks of items: A (for ages 6 to 10) and B (for ages 9 to 13).
Author: Dennis Young.
Publisher: Hodder & Stoughton Educational [England].
Cross References: For reviews by Theresa G. Siskind and Lisa F. Smith, see 14:275; for reviews by Steven R. Shaw and Mark E. Swerdlik and by Claudia R. Wright of an earlier edition, see 12:277.

[1934]

A Parent-Adolescent Communication Inventory.

Purpose: "Designed to measure the parent's perceived communication with the adolescent."
Population: Parents and adolescents.
Publication Dates: 1968–1979.
Acronym: PACI.
Scores: Total score only.
Administration: Group.
Price Data: Price information available from publisher for parent or adolescent form and user's guide (1969, 4 pages).
Time: (20) minutes.
Author: Millard J. Bienvenu.
Publisher: Millard J. Bienvenu, Northwest Publications.
Cross References: See T5:1876 (1 reference) and T4:1929 (1 reference); for a review by Mark W. Roberts, see 9:916 (12 references); see also T3:1761 (2 references) and T2:1310 (1 reference); for a review by David B. Orr of an earlier edition, see 7:119 (3 references).

[1935]

Parent Adolescent Relationship Questionnaire.

Purpose: Designed to "examine and understand the parent-adolescent relationship."
Population: Parents of adolescents ages 11-18 and adolescents ages 11-18.
Publication Date: 2009.
Acronym: PARQ.
Scores, 31: Conventionalization, Global Distress, Communication, Problem Solving, School Conflict, Sibling Conflict, Eating Conflict, Malicious Intent, Perfectionism, Ruination, Cohesion, Coalitions, Mother-Father Coalition, Spouse-Adolescent Coalition, Parent-Adolescent Coalition, Triangulation, Adolescent in Middle, Parent in Middle, Spouse in Middle (Parent Form), Mother Communication, Father Communication, Mother Problem Solving, Father Problem Solving, Mother School Conflict, Father School Conflict, Autonomy, Unfairness, Father-Adolescent Coalition, Mother-Adolescent Coalition, Father in the Middle, Mother in the Middle (Adolescent Form).
Administration: Group.
Forms, 2: Parent Profile Form, Adolescent Profile Form.
Price Data, 2010: $240 per introductory kit including professional manual (171 pages), 10 parent reusable item booklets, 25 parent response booklets, 25 parent profile forms, 10 adolescent reusable item booklets, 25 adolescent response booklets, 25 adolescent profile forms; $60 per professional manual.
Time: (15-20) minutes, Parent Form; (15-20) minutes, Adolescent Form.
Authors: Arthur L. Robin, Thomas Koepke, Ann W. Moye, and Rebecca Gerhardstein.
Publisher: Psychological Assessment Resources, Inc.

[1936]

Parent As A Teacher Inventory [Revised].

Purpose: "Intended to help mothers and fathers of preschool and primary grade children … recognize their favorable qualities and identify realms in which further personal growth is needed."
Population: Mothers and fathers of children ages 3–9.
Publication Dates: 1984-1995.
Acronym: PAAT.
Scores, 6: Creativity, Frustration, Control, Play, Teaching/Learning, Total.
Administration: Group or individual.
Price Data: See www.ststesting.com for up-to-date pricing.
Foreign Language Edition: Spanish edition available.
Time: (30–45) minutes.
Author: Robert D. Strom.
Publisher: Scholastic Testing Service, Inc.
Cross References: See T5:1878 (1 reference); for reviews by Alice J. Corkill and Ralph F. Darr, Jr., see 13:218 (4 references); see also T4:1922 (6 references); for a review by Elizabeth A. Robinson of an earlier edition, see 9:917 (1 reference).

[1937]

Parent Awareness Skills Survey.

Purpose: Constructed to identify strengths and weaknesses in a parent's sensitivity to typical child care situations.
Population: Parents involved in custody decisions.
Publication Dates: 1990–2002.
Acronym: PASS.
Scores, 18: 6 categories (Awareness of Critical Issues, Awareness of Adequate Solutions, Awareness of Communicating in Understandable Terms, Awareness of Acknowledging Feelings, Awareness of the Importance of Relevant Aspects of a Child's Past History, Awareness of Feedback Data) for each of the following conditions (Spontaneous Level, Probe Level One, Probe Level Two).
Administration: Individual.
Price Data, 2002: $189 per complete kit including 8 booklets, 8 scoring summaries, answer pen, updates, and manual and scoring guide; $99 per 8 booklets; $159 per 16 booklets; $199 per 24 booklets; $129 per manual and scoring guide.
Time: [30–60] minutes.
Comments: Orally administered.
Author: Barry Bricklin.
Publisher: Village Publishing.
Cross References: For reviews by Lisa G. Bischoff and Debra E. Cole, see 12:279.

[1938]

Parent Behavior Form.

Purpose: "Designed to assess … dimensions of perceived parent behavior."

Population: Parents; ratings by ages 8–12, 12–18 and adults.
Publication Date: No date.
Acronym: PBF.
Scores, 15: Acceptance, Active Involvement, Egalitarianism, Cognitive Independence, Cognitive-Understanding, Cognitive Competence, Lax Control, Conformity, Achievement, Strict Control, Punitive Control, Hostile Control, Rejection, Inconsistent Responding, Social Desirability.
Administration: Group or individual.
Forms, 5: PBF, PBF-S, PBF Elementary, Form A, Form C-B.
Price Data: Available from publisher.
Time: Administration time not reported.
Comments: Ratings of parent behavior by their children; form for parent self-rating available.
Authors: Leonard Worell and Judith Worell.
Publisher: Judith Worell, Ph.D.
Cross References: See T5:1881 (3 references) and T4:1925 (1 reference); for reviews by JoEllen V. Carlson and Stephen Olejnik, see 11:277 (1 reference).

[1939]

Parent-Child Communication Inventory.

Purpose: "To better understand how parents and their children communicate."
Population: Children and parents.
Publication Date: 1974.
Acronym: PCCI.
Scores, 2: Total Child, Total Parent.
Administration: Group.
Manual: No manual.
Price Data: Price information available from publisher for child form, parent form, and guide.
Time: Administration time not reported.
Author: Millard J. Bienvenu.
Publisher: Millard J. Bienvenu, Northwest Publications.

[1940]

Parent-Child Relationship Inventory.

Purpose: "Assesses parents' attitudes toward parenting and toward their children."
Population: Parents of 3–15-year-old children.
Publication Date: 1994.
Acronym: PCRI.
Scores, 9: 7 content scales (Parental Support, Satisfaction With Parenting, Involvement, Communication, Limit Setting, Autonomy, Role Orientation), 2 validity indicators (Social Desirability, Inconsistency).
Administration: Group.
Price Data, 2006: $99 per complete kit including manual (57 pages) and 25 AutoScore™ answer sheets; $47 per 25 AutoScore™ answer sheets; $58 per manual; $17.50 per each mail-in computer scored and interpreted answer sheet; $329 per 25-use disk (PC with Microsoft

Windows); $16.50 per 100 microcomputer answer sheets; $13 each for FAX service scoring.

Time: (15) minutes.

Comments: Self-report; microcomputer edition available.

Author: Anthony B. Gerard.

Publisher: Western Psychological Services.

Cross References: See T5:1883 (1 reference); for reviews by Roger A. Boothroyd and Gregory J. Marchant, see 13:220.

[1941]
Parent/Family Involvement Index.

Purpose: "Measure of the extent to which parents are involved in their child's special education program."

Population: Parents with children in special education programs.

Publication Dates: 1984–1985.

Acronym: P/FII.

Scores, 13: Contact with Teacher, Participation in the Special Education Process, Transportation, Observations at School, Educational Activities at Home, Attending Parent Education/Consultation Meetings, Classroom Volunteering, Involvement with Administration, Involvement in Fund Raising Activities, Involvement in Advocacy Groups, Disseminating Information, Involvement Total, Total.

Administration: Group.

Price Data: Price information available from publisher for index and mimeographed paper (1985, 21 pages).

Time: (12–15) minutes.

Comments: Ratings by teachers.

Authors: John D. Cone, David D. DeLawyer, and Vicky V. Wolfe.

Publisher: John D. Cone.

Cross References: For reviews by Marilyn Friend and Koressa Kutsick, see 10:270.

[1942]
Parent Opinion Inventory, Revised Edition.

Purpose: Designed "to provide the school personnel or administrator(s) with the opinions of parents in regard to how they believe the school is meeting the needs of students."

Population: Parents of school children.

Publication Dates: 1976–2003.

Scores: 4 subscales: Parent/School/Community Relations, Quality of the Instructional Program, Support for Student Learning, School Climate/Environment for Learning.

Administration: Group.

Parts, 2: A (Likert-scale items), B (customize up to 20 local questions).

Price Data, 2006: $25 per 25 inventories; administrator's manual may be downloaded free from publisher webpage.

Foreign Language Edition: Available in Spanish.

Time: Untimed.

Author: National Study of School Evaluation.

Publisher: National Study of School Evaluation.

[1943]
Parent Perception of Child Profile.

Purpose: Designed to elicit a parent's knowledge and understanding of a child.

Population: Parents.

Publication Dates: 1991–2002.

Acronym: PPCP.

Scores, 13: Interpersonal Relations, Daily Routine, Health History, Developmental History, School History, Fears, Communication Style, Depth of Knowledge, Scope of Knowledge, Emotional Tone, Value/Philosophy, Areas Needing Attention, Recall.

Administration: Individual.

Price Data, 2002: $189 per comprehensive starting kit including directions (1991, 11 pages), 8 Q-books, 8 recall worksheets, 8 summary forms, "answer" pen (black), "other source" pen (red), and updates; $99 per 8 Q-books with recall worksheets and summary sheets; $159 per 16 Q-books with recall worksheets and summary sheets; $199 per 24 Q-books with recall worksheets and summary sheets; $109 per directions.

Time: (60) minutes.

Comments: Self- or evaluator-administered.

Authors: Barry Bricklin and Gail Elliot.

Publisher: Village Publishing.

Cross References: For reviews by Robert W. Hiltonsmith and Mary Lou Kelley, see 12:280.

[1944]
Parent Success Indicator [Revised Edition].

Purpose: Designed to "identify favorable qualities of parents and aspects of their behavior where education seems warranted."

Population: Ages 10-14 and parents of ages 10-14.

Publication Dates: 1984-2009.

Acronym: PSI.

Scores, 6: Communication, Use of Time, Teaching, Frustration, Satisfaction, Information.

Administration: Group.

Forms, 2: Parent, Adolescent.

Price Data, 2010: $73.90 per starter set including manual (2009, 31 pages), 20 Parent Inventory booklets, 20 Child Inventory booklets, and 20 profiles; $15.80 per manual.

Foreign Language Editions: Spanish, Japanese, and Mandarin versions available.

Time: (15-20) minutes.

Comments: Parents provide self-assessments, adolescents provide observations of their parents.

Authors: Robert D. Strom and Paris S. Strom.

Publisher: Scholastic Testing Service, Inc.

Cross References: For reviews by C. Ruth Solomon Scherzer and Suzanne Young of an earlier edition, see 16:179.

[1945]
Parent/Teacher Conference Checklist.
Purpose: Designed "to provide a self-evaluation of the teacher's role in the parent/teacher conference."
Population: Teachers.
Publication Date: 1988.
Scores: Not scored.
Administration: Individual.
Manual: No manual.
Price Data, 2002: $10 per 25 forms.
Time: [5–10] minutes.
Comments: Self-report inventory; title on checklist is Parent Conference Evaluation Form.
Author: Academic Consulting & Testing Service.
Publisher: Academic Consulting & Testing Service.

[1946]
The Parenthood Questionnaire.
Purpose: Designed to obtain information from youth concerning their opinions and knowledge of parenting and child development.
Population: Youth who are prospective parents or who may work with children in the future.
Publication Dates: 1977–1978.
Scores: 9 subsections: Opinions About Marriage and Having Children, Feelings About Parenthood, Feelings About Myself, Opinions About Children, Understanding of Children, Child Care Skills, Before Birth, Family Life Situations, Knowledge and Opinions About Sex.
Administration: Group.
Price Data: Available from publisher.
Foreign Language Edition: Spanish version available.
Time: Administration time not reported.
Comments: Intended for use in parent-training or child care training programs; manual title is Education for Parenthood: A Program, Curriculum, and Evaluation Guide.
Authors: James C. Petersen, Jean M. Baker, Larry A. Morris, and Rachel Burkholder.
Publisher: The Assessment and Development Centre.
Cross References: For reviews by Sarah J. Allen and Cynthia A. Rohrbeck, see 15:180.

[1947]
Parenting Alliance Measure.
Purpose: "Measures the strength of the perceived alliance between parents of children ages 1 to 19 years"; and "reflects the parents' ability to cooperate with each other in meeting the needs of the child."
Population: Parents of children ages 1–19 years.
Publication Dates: 1988–1999.
Acronym: PAM.
Scores: Total score only.
Administration: Group.
Price Data, 2006: $119 per introductory kit including professional manual and 50 hand-scorable test forms.
Time: (5–15) minutes.
Authors: Richard R. Abidin (test) and Timothy R. Konold (manual and test).
Publisher: Psychological Assessment Resources, Inc.
Cross References: For reviews by Cindy I. Carlson and Mary M. Clare, see 15:181.

[1948]
Parenting Relationship Questionnaire.
Purpose: Designed to "capture a parent's perspective of the parent-child relationship."
Population: Parents of children ages 2-5, 6-18.
Publication Date: 2006.
Acronym: PRQ.
Scores, 7: Attachment, Communication (child and adolescent only), Discipline Practices, Involvement, Parenting Confidence, Satisfaction with School (child and adolescent only), Relational Frustration.
Administration: Individual.
Levels, 2: Preschool, Child and Adolescent.
Forms, 3: Parent Feedback Report, Preschool, Child and Adolescent.
Price Data, 2009: $133 per hand-scored starter set including 25 of each hand-scored form (preschool, child/adolescent, and parent feedback), and manual (104 pages); $356 per PRQ Assist starter set including 25 of each form (preschool, child/adolescent, and parent feedback), manual, and Assist computer scoring software; $32 per 25 hand-scored forms (specify preschool or child/adolescent); $27 per 25 computer-entry forms (specify preschool or child/adolescent); $44 per 25 scannable forms (specify preschool or child/adolescent); $27 per 25 parent feedback report forms; $64 per manual; $36 per test item audio CD; $267 per Assist scanning software.
Foreign Language Edition: Also available in Spanish.
Time: (10-15) minutes.
Comments: For use in conjunction with the Behavior Assessment System for Children, Second Edition (BASC-2; 297) or as a stand-alone instrument; alternative starter sets and upgrades available for current BASC-2 users, contact publisher for details.
Authors: Randy W. Kamphaus and Cecil R. Reynolds.
Publisher: Pearson.
Cross References: For reviews by Mary M. Clare and Sandra Ward, see 18:87.

[1949]
Parenting Satisfaction Scale™.
Purpose: Designed to assess "parents' attitudes toward parenting."

Population: Adults with dependent children.
Publication Date: 1994.
Acronym: PSS.
Scores, 3: Satisfaction with Spouse/Ex-Spouse Parenting Performance, Satisfaction with the Parent-Child Relationship, Satisfaction with Parenting Performance.
Administration: Group.
Price Data, 2002: $119 per comprehensive kit including manual (47 pages) and 25 ReadyScore® answer documents; $37 per 25 ReadyScore® answer documents; $87 per manual.
Time: (30) minutes.
Authors: John Guidubaldi and Helen K. Cleminshaw.
Publisher: Pearson.
Cross References: For reviews by Ira Stuart Katz and Janet V. Smith, see 14:276; see also T5:1888 (1 reference).

[1950]

Parenting Stress Index, Third Edition.

Purpose: To identify stressors experienced by parents that are related to dysfunctional parenting.
Population: Parents of children ages 1 month to 12 years.
Publication Dates: 1983–1995.
Acronym: PSI.
Scores, 15: Child Domain (Adaptability, Acceptability, Demandingness, Mood, Hyperactivity and Distractibility, Reinforces Parent), Parent Domain (Depression, Attachment, Restrictions of Role, Sense of Competence, Social Isolation, Relationship with Spouse, Parental Health), Life Stress, Total Score.
Administration: Group.
Forms, 2: Full Length, Short Form.
Price Data, 2006: $158 per introductory kit including manual, 10 reusable item booklets, and 25 hand-scorable answer sheet/profile forms; $595 per PSI Software Portfolio including unlimited scoring/reporting software for hand-administered forms, 10 PSI software test booklets, 10 PSI software short form test booklets, and 5 free on-screen administrations.
Time: (20–30) minutes.
Comments: PSI Software Portfolio (CD-ROM) allows for on-screen administration and scoring, or scoring of hand-entered item responses from either PSI form.
Authors: Richard R. Abidin, and PAR Staff (Software Portfolio).
Publisher: Psychological Assessment Resources, Inc.
Cross References: See T5:1889 (20 references); for reviews by Julie A. Allison and by Laura L. B. Barnes and Judy J. Oehler-Stinnett, see 13:221 (51 references); see also T4:1933 (22 references); for reviews by Frank M. Gresham and Richard A. Wantz of an earlier edition, see 10:271 (2 references).

[1951]

Parents' Evaluation of Developmental Status.

Purpose: Designed to help "identify children at risk for school problems and those with undetected developmental and behavioral disabilities"; "helps providers decide when to refer, reassure, advise, wait and see versus screen."
Population: Birth–8 years.
Publication Dates: 1997–1998.
Acronym: PEDS.
Scores, 3: Low Risk, Medium Risk, High Risk.
Administration: Individual.
Price Data: Available from publisher.
Foreign Language Edition: Spanish version available.
Time: (2–5) minutes.
Comments: Questionnaire for parents about children; can be administered as an interview or in paper and pencil form.
Author: Frances Page Glascoe.
Publisher: Ellsworth & Vandermeer Press, LLC.
Cross References: For reviews by Lisa Bischoff and Mark W. Roberts, see 14:277.

[1952]

Parents' Observation of Study Behaviors Survey.

Purpose: To measure students' improvement in study habits and behaviors.
Population: Grades 6–13.
Publication Date: 1991.
Scores, 4: Positive Attitudes, Useful Work Habits, Efficient Learning Tools, Effective Test Taking.
Administration: Individual.
Price Data, 2001: $3 per survey.
Time: Administration time not reported.
Comments: Ratings by parents.
Author: The Cambridge Stratford Study Skills Institute.
Publisher: The Cambridge Stratford Study Skills Institute.

[1953]

Parents' Observations of Infants and Toddlers (POINT).

Purpose: "Designed to identify young children with potential problems who may be in need of further diagnostic assessment."
Population: Ages 2-36 months.
Publication Date: 2006.
Acronym: POINT.
Scores, 4: Being Healthy & Early Moving Skills, Thinking/Talking & Early Learning Skills, Feelings/Learning About Others & Everyday Skills, Total.
Administration: Individual.
Levels, 6: Level 1 (2-6 months), Level 2 (6-9 months), Level 3 (9-12 months), Level 4 (12-18 months), Level 5 (18-24 months), Level 6 (24-36 months).
Price Data, 2007: $200 per complete basic kit including manual (2006, 112 pages), 12 record forms for each level in choice of Spanish or English, 1 set of record forms in the other language, 1 set of transparent scoring masks for each level, 1 set duplication masters of

POINT Parent Conference Plan form, and the POINT Report Card in English and Spanish; $230 per complete bilingual kit including manual, 12 record forms for each level in both English and Spanish, 1 set of transparent scoring masks for each level, 1 set of duplication masters of the POINT Parent Conference Plan form and POINT Report Card in English and Spanish; $30 per POINT Portfolio; $35 per 12 record forms for each level in English or Spanish; $15 per 24 record forms for one level; $30 per 6 sets of transparent scoring masks; $10 per set of 3 Conference Plan and Report Card duplication masters. **Foreign Language Editions**: Spanish version available; standardized in Spanish and English. **Time**: (15-20) minutes. **Comments**: Test to be completed by one or two parents/guardians and/or one or two caregivers. **Authors**: Carol D. Mardell and Dorothea S. Goldenberg. **Publisher**: Pearson. **Cross References**: For reviews by Jean N. Clark and Loraine J. Spenciner, see 17:141.

[1954]

Parker Team Development Survey.

Purpose: Identifies teams' strengths and weaknesses across 12 characteristics of effective teams, as perceived by teams' participants. **Population**: Team and group participants. **Publication Dates**: 1992–2003. **Acronym**: PTDS. **Scores, 24**: 2 scores (Description, Importance) per team characteristic: Clear Purpose, Informality, Participation, Listening, Civilized Disagreement, Consensus Decisions, Open Communication, Clear Roles and Work Assignments, Shared Leadership, External Relations, Style Diversity, Self-Assessment. **Administration**: Group. **Manual**: No manual. **Price Data, 2011**: $56.50 per 10 Parker Team Development Surveys; $75 per Parker Team Development Survey Program. **Time**: Administration time not reported. **Comments**: For measurement of groups, not individuals. **Authors**: Glenn M. Parker. **Publisher**: CPP, Inc.

[1955]

Parker Team Player Survey.

Purpose: "Helps individuals identify their primary team player styles." **Population**: Employees. **Publication Date**: 1991. **Acronym**: PTPS. **Scores, 4**: Contributor, Collaborator, Communicator, Challenger. **Administration**: Group or individual.

Foreign Language Editions: Available in English, Spanish, and French. **Time**: (15) minutes. **Comments**: Self-scored. **Author**: Glenn M. Parker. **Publisher**: CPP, Inc.
   a) PARKER TEAM PLAYER SURVEY.
   Price Data, 2011: $14.95 per test booklet/manual (23 pages).
   b) PTPS: STYLES OF ANOTHER PERSON.
   Price Data: $13.50 per test booklet/manual.
Cross References: For reviews by Gary J. Dean and Richard B. Stuart, see 13:222 (1 reference).

[1956]

A Partial Index of Modernization: Measurement of Attitudes Toward Morality.

Purpose: Designed to measure attitudes toward morality issues. **Population**: Children and adults. **Publication Date**: 1972. **Scores**: Total score only. **Administration**: Group. **Manual**: No manual. **Price Data, 2005**: $2 per scale. **Time**: [8] minutes. **Comments**: Supplementary article available. **Author**: Panos D. Bardis. **Publisher**: Donna Bardis. **Cross References**: See 8:464 (1 reference).

[1957]

Participative Management Survey.

Purpose: To assess the extent to which a leader provides opportunities and support for employee involvement. **Population**: Individuals involved in a leadership capacity with others. **Publication Date**: 1988. **Acronym**: PMS. **Scores, 5**: Basic Creature Comfort, Safety, Belonging, Ego-Status, Actualization. **Administration**: Group or individual. **Price Data, 2001**: $8.95 per instrument (17 pages). **Time**: Administration time not reported. **Author**: Jay Hall. **Publisher**: Teleometrics International, Inc.

[1958]

Partners in Play: Assessing Infants and Toddlers in Natural Contexts.

Purpose: Designed "for the identification and follow-up of infants and toddlers … who might be eligible for early intervention services." **Population**: Ages 1-36 months.

Publication Date: 2007.

Acronym: PIP.

Scores, 5: Neuromotor Domain, Sensory-Perceptual Domain, Cognitive Domain, Language Domain, Social-Emotional Behavior.

Administration: Individual.

Parts, 5: Initial Caregiver Interview, Caregiver Report of Child Development, Unstructured Caregiver-Child Play, Unstructured Examiner-Child Play, Structured Examiner-Child Play.

Price Data, 2006: $19.95 per book including assessment (219 pages).

Authors: Gail L. Ensher, Tasia P. Bobish, Eric F. Gardner, Carol L. Reinson, Deborah A. Bryden, and Daniel J. Foertsch.

Publisher: Thomson Delmar Learning.

a) CAREGIVER FORMS/INTERVIEWS.

Time: (30-45) minutes.

1) *Initial Caregiver Interview.*

Scores: Not scored.

2) *Caregiver Report of Child Development.*

Scores, 5: Neuromotor Skills, Sensory-Perceptual Skills, Cognitive Domain, Language Skills, Social-Emotional Skills.

b) PLAY INTERACTIONS.

Comments: It is preferable to conduct all play interactions in one session; if they need to be broken up into two sessions, complete both unstructured interactions in one session, and schedule another session within 5 days to conduct the structured interaction.

1) *Unstructured Caregiver-Child Play.*

Scores: 5 scales, 13 subscales: Language Domain (Strategies for Communication, Communication of Needs/Intent, Understanding of Language Communication [3-36 months], Vocalized Turn-Taking [1-18 months], Joint Referencing with Caregiver), Social-Emotional Behavior (Quality of Social Interaction with Caregiver [1-36 months only], Emotional Stability), Cognitive Domain (Play Strategies Observed [5-36 months]), Sensory-Perceptual Domain (Moving/Maneuvering in the Environment [3-36 months], Skill in Eating [1-18 months], Skill in Drinking), Neuromotor Domain (Picking Up Finger Food/Self-Feeding [9-24 months], Self-Feeding with Eating Utensils [11-36 months]).

Time: (20-30) minutes.

2) *Unstructured Examiner-Child Play.*

Scores: 5 scales, 15 subscales: Language Domain (Response to Common Sounds in the Environment, Intelligibility of Speech and Language [1-36 months]), Imitation Skills [5-36 months]), Social-Emotional Behavior (Quality of Interaction with Unfamiliar People, Attentiveness to Play Activities, Attention-Gaining Behaviors Observed [5-36 months]), Neuromotor

Domain (Quality of Movement [3-36 months], Large Motor Milestones [5-36 months], Hand Skills Observation [3-36 months], Body Symmetry, Transition Into/Out of Various Positions [9-36 months], Protective Responses [5-12 months]), Sensory-Perceptual Domain (Response to Touch), Cognitive Domain (Purposeful Behavior in Play [7-36 months], Problem-Solving Skills [11-36 months]).

Time: (20-30) minutes.

3) *Structured Examiner-Child Play.*

Scores: 5 scales, 15 subscales: Neuromotor Domain (Play with Rattles [3-12 months], Play with Balls [7-36 months]), Sensory-Perceptual Domain (Tracking, Play with Bubble Tumbler [13-36 months], Undressing/Dressing [9-36 months]), Cognitive Domain (Attention to Faces/Designs [1-18 months], Response to Hidden Objects [5-12 months], Early Understanding of Cause/Effect [5-24 months], Play with Blocks/Shape Sorter [9-36 months], Play with Pictures and Point [5-36 months], Advanced Doll Play [13-36 months], Problem-Solving [13-36 months]), Language Domain (Response to Bell, Early Social Games [3-18 months]), Social Emotional Behavior (Adaptability [11-36 months]).

Time: (30-40) minutes.

[1959]

PASAT 2000 [Poppleton Allen Sales Aptitude Test].

Purpose: "Designed to measure those personality attributes which have a direct relevance to success in sales roles."

Population: Adults.

Publication Date: 1999.

Acronym: PASAT 2000.

Scores: 11 scales: Motivational, Emotional, Social, Adaptability, Conscientious, Emotional Stability, Social Control, Self-Assurance, Attentive Distortion, Adaptive Distortion, Social Distortion.

Administration: Group.

Price Data: Available from publisher.

Time: (20) minutes.

Authors: Steve Poppleton and Peter Jones.

Publisher: The Test Agency Limited [England] [No reply from publisher; status unknown].

Cross References: For reviews by Richard E. Harding and John Tivendell, see 15:182; for reviews by Larry Cochran and David O. Herman of an earlier edition of the Poppleton Allen Sales Aptitude Test, see 10:285.

[1960]

Pathways to Independence, Second Edition.

Purpose: Assess skills that contribute to personal and social independence.

Population: Disadvantaged school-aged children and mentally and otherwise handicapped teenagers and adults and rehabilitating brain-damaged and geriatric patients.

Publication Dates: 1982–1998.

Scores: Checklists for recording behavior in 11 areas: Eating and Drinking, Domestic Tasks, Cleanliness and Health, Clothing, Giving Information, Use of Information, Time, Money, Freedom of Movement, Use of Amenities, Leisure.

Administration: Individual.

Manual: No manual.

Price Data, 2002: £22.99 per 10 checklists, including instructions and profile sheet; £4.99 per specimen copy.

Time: Administration time not reported.

Authors: Dorothy M. Jeffree and Sally Cheseldine.

Publisher: Hodder & Stoughton Educational [England].

Cross References: See T5:1897 (1 reference) and T4:1940 (2 references).

[1961]

The Patterned Elicitation Syntax Test with Morphonemic Analysis.

Purpose: Designed to determine "whether a child's expressive grammatical skills are age appropriate."

Population: Ages 3–0 to 7–6.

Publication Dates: 1981–1993.

Acronym: PEST.

Scores, 13: Articles, Adjectives, Auxilaries/Modals/Copulas, Conjunctions, Negatives, Plurals, Possessives, Pronouns, Questions, Verbs, Subject/Verb Agreement, Embedded Elements, Total.

Administration: Individual.

Price Data: Price information available from publisher for complete kit including manual (1993, 18 pages), stimulus picture book, and 10 data form booklets.

Time: (15–20) minutes.

Comments: Previously titled The Patterned Elicitation Syntax Test.

Authors: Edna Carter Young and Joseph J. Perachio.

Publisher: Pearson.

Cross References: For reviews by Clinton W. Bennett and Sheila R. Pratt, see 13:223 (2 references); for a review by Carolyn Peluso Atkins of an earlier edition, see 9:921.

[1962]

Paulhus Deception Scales: Balanced Inventory of Desirable Responding Version 7.

Purpose: Designed to measure the tendency to give socially desirable responses to tests.

Population: Ages 16 and older.

Publication Dates: 1998–1999.

Acronym: PDS.

Scores, 2: Impression Management, Self-Deceptive Enhancement.

Administration: Individual or group.

Price Data, 2011: $80 per complete kit including 25 QuikScore™ forms and manual; $50 per 25 QuikScore™ forms; $55 per manual.

Time: (5–7) minutes.

Comments: Self-report; software also available; multiple translations available.

Authors: Delroy L. Paulhus.

Publisher: Multi-Health Systems, Inc.

Cross References: For reviews by Kwong-Liem Karl Kwan and Romeo Vitelli, see 15:183; see T5:1898 (1 reference).

[1963]

PDD Behavior Inventory.

Purpose: Designed to assist in the assessment of children who have been diagnosed with a pervasive developmental disorder.

Population: Ages 1-6 to 12-5.

Publication Dates: 1999-2005.

Acronym: PDDBI.

Scores, 51: 29 Approach/Withdrawal Problems scores: Approach/Withdrawal Problems Composite, Receptive/Ritualistic/Pragmatic Problems Composite, Sensory/Perceptual Repetitive Approach Behaviors (Visual Behaviors, Non-Food Taste Behaviors, Touch Behaviors, Proprioceptive/Kinesthetic Behaviors, Receptive Manipulative Behaviors), Ritualism/Resistance to Change (Resistance to Change in the Environment, Resistance to Change in Schedules/Routines, Rituals), Social Pragmatic Problems (Problems with Social Approach, Social Awareness Problems, Inappropriate Reactions to the Approaches of Others), Semantic/Pragmatic Problems (Aberrant Vocal Quality When Speaking, Problems with Understanding Words, Verbal Pragmatic Deficits), Arousal Regulation Problems (Kinesthetic Behaviors, Reduced Responsiveness, Sleep Regulation Problem [extended form only]), Specific Fears (Sadness When Away From Caregiver/Other Significant Figure/or in New Situation, Anxious When Away From Caregiver/Other Significant Figure/or in New Situation, Auditory Withdrawal Behaviors, Fears and Anxieties, Social Withdrawal Behaviors [extended form only]), Aggressiveness (Self-Directed Aggressive Behaviors, Incongruous Negative Affect, Problems When Caregiver or Other Significant Figure Returns From Work/an Outing/or Vacation, Aggressiveness Toward Others, Overall Temperament Problems [extended form only]); 22 Receptive/Expressive Social Communication Abilities scores: Receptive/Expressive Social Communication Abilities Composite, Expressive Social Communication Abilities Composite, Social Approach Behaviors (Visual Social Approach Behaviors, Positive Affect Behaviors, Gestural Approach Behaviors, Responsiveness to Social Inhibition Cues, Social Play Behaviors, Imaginative Play Behaviors, Empathy Behaviors, Social Interaction Behaviors [parent/caregiver form

only], Social Imitative Behaviors), Expressive Language (Vowel Production, Consonant Production at the Beginning/Middle/and End of Words, Diphthong Production, Expressive Language Competence, Verbal Affective Tone, Pragmatic Conversational Skills), Learning/Memory/Receptive Language (General Memory Skills, Receptive Language Competence [extended form only]), Autism Composite, SOCPP-SOCAPP Discrepancy Score, SEMPP-EXPRESS Discrepancy Score.
Administration: Individual or group.
Forms, 4: Parent/Guardian or Teacher, Standard or Extended.
Price Data, 2007: $230 per complete kit including professional manual (2005, 545 pages), 25 Parent Rating forms, 25 Teacher Rating forms, 25 Parent Score Summary sheets, 25 Teacher Score Summary sheets, and 50 Profile forms; $75 per professional manual; $60 per 25 Parent Rating forms; $60 per 25 Teacher Rating forms; $15 per 25 Parent Score Summary sheets; $15 per 25 Teacher Score Summary sheets; $25 per 50 Profile forms; $225 per unlimited use PDDBI Scoring Program software CD.
Time: (30-45) minutes for Extended forms; (20-30) minutes to Standard forms.
Comments: Ratings from both parents and multiple teachers/school personnel is desirable.
Authors: Ira L. Cohen and Vicki Sudhalter.
Publisher: Psychological Assessment Resources, Inc.
Cross References: For reviews by Karen Carey and by Kathryn E. Hoff and Renee M. Tobin, see 17:142.

[1964]

Peabody Developmental Motor Scales–Second Edition.

Purpose: Designed "to assess gross motor skills and fine motor skills."
Population: Birth to 72 months.
Publication Dates: 1983–2000.
Acronym: PDMS-2.
Scores, 9: Reflexes, Stationary, Locomotion, Object Manipulation, Grasping, Visual-Motor Integration, Gross Motor, Fine Motor, Total Motor.
Administration: Individual.
Price Data, 2011: $509 per complete kit including examiner's manual (2000, 234 pages), 25 profile/summary forms, 25 examiner record booklets, administration guide, motor activities program manual, black-and-white motor development chart, 25 black-and-white motor development parent charts, and manipulatives; $418 per complete test including everything in complete kit except the motor activities program; $81 per 25 examiner record booklets; $35 per 25 profile/summary forms; $93 per motor activities program; $81 per object kit; $18 per shape cards/BLM kit; $106 per administration guide; $93 per examiner's manual; $24 per 25 black-and-white motor development parent charts; $30 per full-color parent

chart; $129 per software CD (PC; Windows 95/98).
Time: (45–60) minutes.
Authors: M. Rhonda Folio and Rebecca R. Fewell.
Publisher: PRO-ED.
Cross References: For reviews by Linda K. Bunker and Peggy Kellers and by Donald Lee Stovall, see 15:184; see T5:1901 (19 references) and T4:1943 (3 references); for a review by Homer B. C. Read, Jr. of an earlier edition, see 9:922.

[1965]

Peabody Individual Achievement Test–Revised [1997 Normative Update].

Purpose: Designed to measure academic achievement.
Population: Grades K–12; ages 5-0 through 21-11.
Publication Dates: 1970–1998.
Acronym: PIAT-R/NU.
Scores, 9: General Information, Reading Recognition, Reading Comprehension, Total Reading, Mathematics, Spelling, Total Test, Written Expression, Written Language.
Administration: Individual.
Levels: 2 for Written Expression subtest (Level I: Grades K–1; Level II: Grades 2–12).
Price Data, 2006: $385.99 per complete kit including 4 easels, 50 combined test record and written expression response booklets, and NU manual (1998, 271 pages); $87.99 per 50 combined test record/written expression response booklets; $112.99 per manual; $199.99 per software package (Windows or Macintosh).
Time: (60) minutes.
Comments: This test (PIAT-R/NU [1998 Normative Update]) is the same as the PIAT-R (1989) but with new norms.
Author: Frederick C. Markwardt Jr.
Publisher: Pearson.
Cross References: For reviews by Lawrence H. Cross and Jennifer J. Fager, see 14:279; see also T5:1902 (103 references) and T4:1944 (33 references); for reviews by Kathryn M. Benes and Bruce G. Rogers of an earlier version, see 11:280 (125 references); see also 9:923 (39 references), T4:1944 (33 references), and T3:1769 (67 references); for excerpted reviews by Alex Bannatyne and Barton B. Proger of the original edition, see 8:24 (36 references); see also T2:26 (2 references); for a review by Howard B. Lyman of the original edition, see 7:17.

[1966]

Peabody Picture Vocabulary Test, Fourth Edition.

Purpose: Designed for use as a measure of receptive vocabulary for Standard American English.
Population: Ages 2:6–90+.
Publication Dates: 1959-2007.
Acronym: PPVT-4.

Scores: Total score only.
Administration: Individual.
Forms, 2: A, B.
Price Data, 2008: $390 per complete kit (Forms A & B) including administration easels, 25 record booklets Form A & 25 record booklets Form B, and examiner's manual (2007, 219 pages); $40.50 per 25 record booklets (specify A or B); $259 per PPVT-4 ASSIST™ scoring and reporting software; single form kits also available.
Time: (10-15) minutes.
Comments: Also includes a growth scale value (GSV) to specifically measure progress over time; conormed with the Expressive Vocabulary Test-2 (1044); PPVT-4 and EVT-2 standard scores allow direct comparisons between receptive and expressive vocabulary; items are categorized for multiple levels of descriptive analysis; evidence-based interventions are embedded in the scoring and reporting software (AS-SIST) and allow for multiple individual and group reports with aggregation and disaggregation options.
Authors: Lloyd M. Dunn and Douglas M. Dunn.
Publisher: Pearson.
Cross References: For reviews by Joseph C. Kush and Steven R. Shaw, see 18:88; for reviews by Frederick Bessai and Orest Eugene Wasyliw of the third edition, see 14:280; see also T5:1903 (585 references) and T4:1945 (426 references); for reviews by R. Steve McCallum and Elisabeth H. Wiig of an earlier edition, see 9:926 (117 references); see also T3:1771 (301 references), 8:222 (213 references), T2:516 (77 references), and 7:417 (201 references); for reviews by Howard B. Lyman and Ellen V. Piers, see 6:530 (21 references).

[1967]

Pearson-Marr Archetype Indicator®.

Purpose: Designed to help people discover the stories that define the personal archetypal journey in professional and personal lives; provides a unique perspective that facilitates the understanding of life patterns and how they affect a person's choices, behaviors, and future vision.
Population: Adolescent–adult.
Publication Dates: 1989–2003.
Acronym: PMAI®
Scores, 12: Innocent, Orphan, Warrior, Caregiver, Seeker, Lover, Destroyer, Creator, Ruler, Magician, Saga, Jester.
Administration: Group.
Price Data, 2011: $22 per Introduction to Archetypes (2003, 64 pages), questionnaire, and individualized scoring sheet; $18 per online administration; $35 per manual (2003, 103 pages).
Time: 15 minutes
Comments: Self-administered and self-scored; can also be administered and scored online.
Authors: Carol S. Pearson and Hugh K. Marr.
Publisher: Center for Applications of Psychological Type, Inc.

Cross References: For reviews by Carl Isenhart and William E. Martin, Jr., see 16:180.

[1968]

Pediatric Attention Disorders Diagnostic Screener.

Purpose: Designed to assist clinicians in diagnosing children with ADHD by using multiple sources and multiple types of assessments.
Population: Parent- or school-referred children ages 6-12.
Publication Date: 2000-2008.
Acronym: PADDS.
Scores, 22: 4 scores per SNAP-IV form (Parent/Guardian, Teacher): ADHD-Inattention, Hyperactivity/Impulsivity, ADHD-Combined Type, Total (calculated as likelihood ratio); Total count of behavioral responses (Redirection/Re-instruction, Fidgeting, Emotional Reaction) per Target Test; Raw score and likelihood ratio per Target Test (Target Recognition, Target Sequence, Target Tracking); 5 cumulative, Post-test probabilities of being diagnosed with ADHD (calculated each time additional assessment is entered into PADDS system).
Administration: Individual.
Parts, 4: SNAP-IV Rating Scale, Computer Administered Diagnostic Interview, Structured Assessment of Testing Behaviors, Target Tests of Executive Functioning.
Price Data, 2008: $695 per PADDS full version including Clinical Manual (66 pages), Software Installation and Use Manual (30 pages), and CD-ROM (Version 1.0.45) with unlimited uses; $395 per PADDS standard version including Clinical Manual, Software Installation and Use Manual, and CD-ROM (Version 1.0.45) with 5 pre-loaded uses; $100 per 10 additional uses; quantity discounts available.
Time: (35-45) minutes; (25-30) minutes to administer all three Target Tests of Executive Functions; (10-15) minutes to input data from previously completed CADI and SNAP-IV forms.
Comments: Also called Pediatric ADHD Screener, Target Tests of Executive Functioning; testing software is Windows compatible and requires Adobe Reader (included) for viewing of summary reports.
Authors: Thomas K. Pedigo, Kenneth L. Pedigo, and Vann B. Scott, Jr. (Clinical Manual).
Publisher: Targeted Testing Inc.
  a) SNAP-IV RATING SCALE.
    Purpose: Identifies "Parent and teacher ratings [of the child] of the behavior criteria for ADHD based on criteria set by the [DSM-IV-R]."
    Publication Date: 1992.
    Acronym: SNAP-IV.
    Scores, 8: 4 scores per form: ADHD-Inattention, Hyperactivity/Impulsivity, ADHD-Combined Type, Total (calculated as likelihood ratio).
    Administration: Group.
    Forms, 2: Parent/Guardian, Teacher.

Foreign Language Editions: Available in Spanish; contact publisher for availability of other languages.

Time: Administration time not reported.

Comments: Separate ratings by parent/guardian and teacher.

Authors: James M. Swanson, W. Nolan, and W. E. Pelham.

b) COMPUTER ADMINISTERED DIAGNOSTIC INTERVIEW.

Purpose: Screens for "possible co-morbid conditions that can mimic or exacerbate ADHD symptoms."

Acronym: CADI.

Scores: Not scored; Clinical feedback may be provided for 6 possible domains: Medical History/Systems Review, Developmental History, Social/Emotional Functioning, Depression/Anxiety, Attention/Hyperactivity, Behavior/School History.

Administration: Group.

Foreign Language Editions: Available in Spanish; contact publisher for availability of other languages.

Time: Administration time not reported.

Comments: Interview can be computer administered and completed during child's session, or interview and protocol can be printed out and completed prior to child's session. Ratings by Parent/Guardian.

c) STRUCTURED ASSESSMENT OF TESTING BEHAVIORS.

Purpose: Designed to "help assess and quantify behavior changes in subjects across administration as in pre-medication and post-medication challenges."

Scores, 3: Total count of behavioral responses (Redirection/Re-instruction, Fidgeting, Emotional Reaction) per Target Test.

Administration: Individual.

Time: (25-30) minutes.

Comments: Ratings by administrator of Target Tests.

d) TARGET TESTS OF EXECUTIVE FUNCTIONING.

Purpose: Computer presented tasks "aimed at providing objective assessment of a subject's ability to employ various but not all executive processes: (planning, attending, organizing input, storing and retrieving information, modulating emotions and sustaining effort)."

Acronym: TTEF.

Scores, 6: 2 scores (Raw score and likelihood ratio) per Target Test (Target Recognition, Target Sequence, Target Tracking).

Administration: Individual.

Time: (25-30) minutes to administer all three Target Tests.

Cross References: For reviews by Rama K. Mishra and Janet Reed, see 18:89.

[1969]

Pediatric Behavior Rating Scale.

Purpose: "To assist in the identification of serious emotional dysregulation and related disorders-most notably early onset bipolar disorder."

Population: Ages 3-18.

Publication Date: 2008.

Acronym: PBRS.

Scores, 10: Atypical, Irritability, Grandiosity, Hyperactivity/Impulsivity, Aggression, Inattention, Affect, Social Interactions, Total Bipolar Index, Inconsistency Score.

Administration: Group.

Forms, 2: Parent (PBRS-P), Teacher (PBRS-T).

Price Data, 2010: $235 per introductory kit including professional manual (128 pages), 25 reusable Parent item booklets, 25 reusable Teacher item booklets, 25 Parent response booklets, 25 Teacher response booklets, 25 Parent score summary/profile forms, and 25 Teacher score summary/profile forms; $31 per 25 reusable Parent item booklets; $31 per 25 reusable Teacher item booklets; $47 per 25 Parent response booklets; $47 per 25 Teacher response booklets; $21 per 25 Parent score summary/profile forms; $21 per 25 Teacher score summary/profile forms; $52 per professional manual.

Time: [15-20] minutes.

Comments: Pediatric Behavior Rating Scale Scoring Program (PBRS-SP) offered separately.

Authors: Richard M. Marshall and Berney J. Wilkinson.

Publisher: Psychological Assessment Resources, Inc.

Cross References: For reviews by Janet Reed and Tony C. Wu, see 18:90.

[1970]

Pediatric Early Elementary Examination (PEEX2).

Purpose: Designed to "enable health care and other professionals to derive an empirical description of a child's development and functional neurologic status."

Population: Ages 6–9.

Publication Dates: 1983–1996.

Acronym: PEEX-2.

Scores, 6: Fine Motor/Graphomotor Functions, Attention Checkpoints, Language Functions, Gross Motor Functions, Memory Functions, Visual Processing Functions.

Administration: Individual.

Price Data, 2006: $111.30 per complete set including all materials except observer's guide and video; $18.60 per manual (1998, 65 pages); $74.05 per record form and response book; $21.75 per stimulus book; $38.10 per observer's guide; $23.55 per specimen set including observer's guide, record form, and examiner's manual; $54.30 per clinician's training video tape; quantity discounts available.

Time: (60) minutes.

Comments: Recommended for use as part of a multifaceted assessment process.
Authors: Developed under the direction of Melvin D. Levine and Adrian D. Sandler.
Publisher: Educators Publishing Service, Inc.
Cross References: For reviews by Denise M. DeZolt and Carl J. Dunst of an earlier edition, see 13:224 (1 reference); for reviews by J. Jeffrey Grill and Neil H. Schwartz of another earlier edition, see 10:272.

[1971]

Pediatric Evaluation of Disability Inventory.

Purpose: Designed as a "comprehensive clinical assessment instrument that samples key functional capabilities and performance."
Population: Ages 6 months to 7.5 years.
Publication Date: 1992.
Acronym: PEDI.
Scores, 9: Self-Care (Functional Skills, Caregiver Assistance, Modification Frequencies), Mobility (Functional Skills, Caregiver Assistance, Modification Frequencies), Social Function (Functional Skills, Caregiver Assistance, Modification Frequencies).
Administration: Individual.
Price Data: Available from publisher.
Time: (45–60) minutes.
Comments: Should be completed by the person or group of persons familiar with the child's typical performance in the domains surveyed; software program (IBM-compatible) available for data entry, scoring, and generation of individual summary score profiles.
Authors: Stephen M. Haley, Wendy J. Coster, Larry H. Ludlow, Jane T. Haltiwanger, and Peter J. Andrellos.
Publisher: Health and Disability Research Institute, Boston University.
Cross References: For a review by Billy T. Ogletree, see 14:281.

[1972]

Pediatric Examination of Educational Readiness (PEER).

Purpose: "A combined neurodevelopmental, behavioral, and health assessment "that generates descriptive observations to be used in planning health, education, and developmentally oriented services."
Population: Ages 4-6.
Publication Dates: 1982–1988.
Acronym: PEER.
Scores: 27 or 28 rating scores: Developmental Attainment (Orientation, Gross Motor, Visual-Fine Motor, Associated Observations, Sequential, Linguistic, Preacademic Learning), Associated Observations (Selective Attention/Activity, Processing Efficiency, Adaptation), Neuromaturation (Associated Move-

ments, Other Minor Neurological Signs), Other Physical Findings (General Physical Examination, Neurological Examination, Auditory and Vision Testing, Dressing and Undressing [optional]), Task Analysis (Visual, Verbal, Sequential, Somesthetic, Total, Short-Term Memory, Experiential Acquisition, Total, Fine Motor, Motor Sequential, Verbal Sequential, Verbal Expressive, Total).
Administration: Individual.
Price Data, 2006: $104.15 per complete set including examiner's manual, stimulus booklet, PEER kit, and 24 record forms; $40.15 per 24 record forms; $15.55 per stimulus booklet; $19.40 per PEER kit including ball, plastic sticks, wooden blocks, key, and rubber band; $29.50 per examiner's manual (80 pages); $30.25 per specimen set including record form and examiner's manual; quantity discounts available.
Time: (40-50) minutes excluding physical examination.
Authors: Developed under the direction of Melvin D. Levine and Elizabeth A. Schneider (manual).
Publisher: Educators Publishing Service, Inc.
Cross References: See T4:1947 (1 reference).

[1973]

Pediatric Examination of Educational Readiness at Middle Childhood.

Purpose: Constructed to "survey neurodevelopmental areas that may be associated with academic difficulties."
Population: Ages 9 to 15.
Publication Dates: 1984–1996.
Acronym: PEERAMID-2.
Scores: 6 major sections: Fine Motor/Graphomotor Function, Attention Checkpoints, Language Functions, Gross Motor Functions, Memory Functions, Visual Processing Functions.
Administration: Individual.
Price Data, 2006: $131.80 per complete kit including manual (1996, 80 pages), stimulus booklet, PEERAMID 2 kit, 12 record forms, and 12 response booklets; $86.40 per 12 record forms and 12 response booklets; $21.75 per stimulus booklet; $5.50 per PEERAMID 2 kit including cup and ball; $18.60 per examiner's manual (1996, 80 pages); $23.55 per specimen set including observer's guide, record form, and examiner's manual; $42.85 observer's guide; $54.30 per clinician's training video; quantity discounts available.
Time: (60) minutes.
Comments: Publisher suggests should only be used as a part of a multifaceted evaluation.
Author: Melvin D. Levine.
Publisher: Educators Publishing Service, Inc.
Cross References: For reviews by Joseph C. Kush and Robert G. Morwood, see 14:282; see also T5:1908 (1 reference); for reviews by Cathy W. Hall and Jan N. Hughes of the original edition, see 10:273.

[1974]

Pediatric Extended Examination at Three (PEET).

Purpose: "To aid in the early detection and clarification of problems with learning, attention, and behavior in three- to four-year-old children."

Population: Ages 3-4

Publication Date: 1986.

Acronym: PEET.

Scores, 20: Developmental Attainment (Gross Motor, Language, Visual-Fine Motor, Memory, Intersensory Integration), Assessment of Behavior Rating Scale (Initial Adaptation, Reactions during Assessment), Global Language Rating Scale, Physical Findings (General Physical Examination, Neurological Examination, Auditory and Vision Testing), Task Analysis (Reception, Discrimination, Sequencing, Memory, Fine Motor Output, Gross Motor Output, Expressive Language, Instructional Output, Experiential Application).

Administration: Individual.

Price Data, 2006: $151.80 per complete kit including 24 record booklets, PEET kit (ball, target, key, wooden blocks, plastic sticks, car, crayon, doll, buttoning strip, checkers, and objects for stereognosis task), stimulus booklet (40 pages), and examiner's manual (64 pages); $32.95 per 24 record forms; $21.75 per stimulus booklet; $16.65 per examiner's manual; $81.45 per PEET kit; $17.60 per specimen set including examiner' s manual and record form; quantity discounts available.

Time: Administration time not reported.

Authors: James A. Blackman, Melvin D. Levine, and Martha Markowitz.

Publisher: Educators Publishing Service, Inc.

Cross References: For reviews by William B. Michael and Hoi K. Suen, see 11:281.

[1975]

Pediatric Test of Brain Injury.

Purpose: Designed to "estimate a child's ability in applying neurocognitive-linguistic skills that are vulnerable to pediatric brain injury and relevant to functioning well in school" and track "recovery starting in the acute phase and continuing until…performance indicates functioning in the normal range."

Population: Ages 6-16 who have sustained traumatic brain injury or acquired brain injury.

Publication Date: 2010.

Acronym: PTBI.

Scores, 11: Orientation, Following Commands, Word Fluency, What Goes Together, Digit Span, Naming, Story Retelling-Immediate, Yes/No/Maybe, Picture Recall, Story Retelling-Delayed, Overall Performance Rating.

Administration: Individual.

Price Data, 2010: $349.95 per complete test kit including examiner's manual (127 pages), stimulus book, and test forms; $49.95 per 10 test forms.

Time: (30-35) minutes.

Comments: Specialists trained to assess children and adolescents with cognitive-communication impairments, including brain injury, are qualified to administer the PTBI. Results from each score are reported in a performance profile pattern and are combined to provide a level of overall performance.

Authors: Gillian Hotz, Nancy Helm-Estabrooks, Nickola W. Nelson, and Elena Plante.

Publisher: Paul H. Brookes Publishing Co., Inc.

[1976]

PEEK–Perceptions, Expectations, Emotions, and Knowledge About College.

Purpose: "Designed to assess prospective student's expectations about what college will be like."

Population: Prospective college students.

Publication Date: 1995.

Acronym: PEEK.

Scores, 3: Academic Expectations, Personal Expectations, Social Expectations.

Administration: Group or individual.

Price Data, 2006: $2 per publisher-scored form; $1.50 per internet form (volume discounts available).

Time: (15–25) minutes.

Comments: Self-report questionnaire; can be machine scored by publisher or locally via the internet.

Authors: Claire E. Weinstein, David R. Palmer, and Gary R. Hanson.

Publisher: H & H Publishing Co., Inc.

Cross References: For reviews by David Gillespie and Daniel L. Yazak, see 14:283.

[1977]

Peg Board.

Purpose: Developed to measure manual dexterity.

Population: Applicants for electrical and light engineering assembly jobs.

Publication Date: 1983.

Scores, 4: Preferred Hand, Non-Preferred Hand, Both Hands, Assemblies.

Administration: Group.

Price Data: Available from publisher.

Time: 3 minutes and 50 seconds (7 minutes).

Author: Educational & Industrial Test Services Ltd.

Publisher: Educational & Industrial Test Services Ltd. [England].

[1978]

Penna Assessor Adaptive Ability Tests.

Purpose: "For use in the selection, training, and career development of personnel in the UK."

Population: Junior school–adult.

Publication Dates: 1988–1990.

Administration: Individual.
Price Data: Available from publisher.
Time: [15] minutes per subtest.
Comments: All subtests are computer administered; previously listed as Selby MillSmith Adaptive Ability Tests.
Author: Selby MillSmith Ltd.
Publisher: Penna Assessment PLC [England] [No reply from publisher: status unknown].

a) NUMERIC ABILITY TEST.
Purpose: "To assess basic numeracy and numerical skills at all levels of the organisation."
Scores: Total score only.
b) LANGUAGE ABILITY TEST.
Purpose: "Assesses the individual's range and clarity in the use of vocabulary."
Scores: Total score only.
c) ADMINISTRATIVE ABILITY TEST.
Purpose: "To assess the speed and accuracy of an individual's administrative capabilities."
Scores, 3: Numbers, Addresses, Codes.
Cross References: For reviews by Colin Cooper and Glen Fox, see 13:279.

[1979]

Penna Assessor Values Indices.

Purpose: "A measure of personal values associated with work and the working environment."
Population: Adults.
Publication Dates: 1985–1991.
Administration: Individual or group.
Editions, 2: Management Values Index, Supervisory Values Index.
Price Data: Available from publisher.
Comments: Test may be paper-and-pencil or computer administered; previously listed as Selby MillSmith Values Indices.
Author: Adrian W. Savage.
Publisher: Penna Assessment PLC [England] [No reply from publisher: status unknown].

a) MANAGEMENT VALUES INDEX.
Purpose: "For selection, assessment and training and development at managerial and senior levels within an organisation."
Population: Managers.
Acronym: MVI.
Scores, 27: Core Scales [Achievement Values (Work Ethic, Responsibility, Risk Taking, Task Orientation, Leadership, Activity, Need for Status, Self Esteem), Expertise Values (Need for Mental Challenge, Innovation, Analysis, Attention to Detail), Consolidation Values (Need for Stability, Need for Structure, Career Development), Interpersonal Values (Sociability, Inclusion, Personal Warmth, Tactfulness, Tolerance)], [Second Order Indices (Executive Index, Stability Index, Conscientiousness Index, Expert Orientation Index, Team Orientation Index, Empathy Index, Motivational Distortion Index)].
Time: (30–45) minutes.

b) SUPERVISORY VALUES INDEX.
Purpose: "For selection, assessment and training and development at supervisory and 'A' level standard."
Scores, 26: Core Scales [Achievement Values (Work Ethic, Responsibility, Risk Taking, Task Orientation, Leadership, Activity, Need for Status, Self Esteem), Expertise Values (Need for Mental Challenge, Innovation, Analysis, Attention to Detail), Consolidation Values (Need for Stability, Need for Structure, Career Development), Interpersonal Values (Sociability, Inclusion, Personal Warmth, Tactfulness, Tolerance)], Second Order Indices (Initiative Index, Team Orientation Index, Stability Index, Enquiry Index, Conscientiousness Index, Motivational Distortion Index).
Time: (30–45) minutes.
Cross References: For reviews by Peter Miles Berger and Gerald R. Schneck, see 14:343.

[1980]

People Performance Profile.

Purpose: Designed to determine how employees perceive their organization, their work team, and themselves.
Population: Organization members.
Publication Date: 1985.
Acronym: PPP.
Scores, 20: Organizational Performance (Planning, Management Procedures, Motivational Climate, Physical Environment, Organizational Stress Factors), Work-Team Performance (Supervision, Role Clarity, Communications, Conflict Management, Problem Solving, Meeting Effectiveness, Job Satisfaction, Group Productivity), Personal Fitness (Health, Exercise, Nutrition, Alcohol and Drug Use, Interpersonal Support, Time Management, Personal Stress Management).
Administration: Group.
Price Data: Available from publisher.
Time: Administration time not reported.
Authors: Bob Crosby, John Scherer (survey, leader's guide), and Gil Crosby (work-team guide).
Publisher: Jossey-Bass, A Wiley Company.
Cross References: For reviews by Seymour Adler and Larry Cochran, see 10:274.

[1981]

The People Process.

Purpose: Designed to help determine personalities and assist in relating to people "of the same or different personality traits."
Population: Adults.
Publication Date: 1992.
Scores: 4 processes: Energy, Information, Decisions, Actions.
Administration: Group.
Price Data: Available from publisher.

Time: (120–240) minutes.
Author: Pam Hollister.
Publisher: Jossey-Bass, A Wiley Company.

[1982]

People Smarts: Behavioral Profiles.

Purpose: Designed to reveal perceptions of behavioral styles in the workplace.
Population: Adults.
Publication Date: 1994.
Scores: 4 profiles: Relater, Socializer, Thinker, Director.
Administration: Group.
Price Data: Price information available from publisher for trainer's package including trainer's guide (100 pages), 1 self-assessment, 1 observer assessment, 1 scoring matrix, 1 reminder card, 1 45-minute videocassette, and 1 People Smarts book (224 pages); participant's package including 1 workbook, 1 self-assessment, 1 scoring matrix, and 5 observer assessments; 1 self-assessment or 1 observer assessment; scoring matrix; reminder card; participant workbook; People Smarts book.
Time: Administration time not reported.
Author: Tony Alessandra.
Publisher: Jossey-Bass, A Wiley Company.

[1983]

Per-Flu-Dex Tests.

Purpose: Developed to test "a variety of abilities to cope with the needs for effective performance."
Population: High school and college and industry.
Publication Date: 1955.
Administration: Group.
Price Data: Available from publisher.
Time: 7(25) minutes; 1(5) minutes for any one test.
Author: Frank J. Holmes.
Publisher: Psychometric Affiliates.

a) PER-SYMB TEST.
Purpose: Symbol number substitution.
b) PER-VERB TEST.
Purpose: Letter perception and counting.
c) PER-NUMB TEST.
Purpose: Number counting and perception.
d) FLU-VERB TEST.
Purpose: Word completion and verbal fluency.
e) FLU-NUMB TEST.
Purpose: Arithmetic computation.
f) THE DEX-MAN SCALE.
Purpose: Manual speed of movement.
g) DEX-AIM TEST.
Purpose: Aiming accuracy and speed.
Cross References: See T2:2286 (2 references); for reviews by Andrew L. Comrey and John W. French, see 5:901.

[1984]

Perception-Of-Relationships-Test.

Purpose: Constructed to measure the degree to which a child seeks psychological "closeness" with each parent;

and the types of behaviors the child has had to develop to permit or accommodate interaction with each parent.
Population: Children age 3 and over.
Publication Dates: 1964–2002.
Acronym: PORT.
Scores: No scores.
Administration: Individual.
Price Data, 2002: $199 per complete kit including 8 test/scoring booklets, handbook (1990, 179 pages); pen, eraser, and updates; $99 per 8 test/scoring booklets; $159 per 16 test/scoring booklets; $199 per 24 test/scoring booklets; $149 per handbook; $198 per IBM computer scoring profile (3.5-inch disk).
Time: [30] minutes.
Comments: Projective test for use in custody decisions.
Author: Barry Bricklin.
Publisher: Village Publishing.
Cross References: For reviews by Janet F. Carlson and Judith Conger, see 12:283.

[1985]

Perceptions of Parental Role Scales.

Purpose: "To measure perceived parental role responsibilities."
Population: Parents.
Publication Date: 1982.
Acronym: PPRS.
Scores: 13 areas in 3 domains: Teaching the Child (Cognitive Development, Social Skills, Handling of Emotions, Physical Health, Norms and Social Values, Personal Hygiene, Survival Skills), Meeting the Child's Basic Needs (Health Care, Food/Clothing/Shelter, Child's Emotional Needs, Child Care), Family as an Interface With Society (Social Institutions, the Family Unit Itself).
Administration: Group.
Price Data: Available from publisher.
Time: (15) minutes.
Comments: Self-administered.
Authors: Lucia A. Gilbert and Gary R. Hanson.
Publisher: Lucia A. Gilbert, Ph.D.
Cross References: For reviews by Cindy I. Carlson and Mark W. Roberts, see 11:282.

[1986]

Perceptual-Motor Assessment for Children & Emotional/Behavioral Screening Program.

Purpose: "Designed for screening visual, auditory and haptic perception; fine and gross motor abilities; and perceptual memory in children."
Population: Ages 4-0-15-11.
Publication Date: 1988.
Acronym: P-MAC/ESP.
Scores: 12: 3 scores for the Perceptual Memory Task-Abbreviated (PMT-A): Spatial Relations, Auditory-Visual Colors Recognition, Auditory-Visual Colors Sequence; 3 scores for Haptic Visual Discrimination Test-Abbreviated

(HVDT-A): Shape, Size, Texture; 6 scores for McCarron Assessment of Neuromuscular Development-Abbreviated (MAND-A): Beads in Box, Finger Tapping, Nut and Bolt, Hand Strength, Standing on One Foot, Finger-Nose-Finger.
Subtests, 3: PMT-A, HVDT-A, MAND-A.
Administration: Individual.
Price Data, 2011: $2,090 per P-MAC including P-MAC battery, computer program, manual (219 pages), 25 Protocol/Data Entry Forms, and 5 GEM volumes; $250 per ESP including 25 Behavioral Checklists for Students, computer program, and manual; $2,340 per combined P-MAC & ESP; $56.50 per each of 5 GEM volumes; $58.50 per 25 P-MAC Protocol/Data Entry Forms; $42.50 per 25 Behavioral Checklists for Students; $78.75 per P-MAC manual; $33.75 per separate ESP manual.
Time: (45) minutes.
Comments: P-MAC battery consists of selected subtests from the MAND, HVDT, and PMT; 5 age-specific volumes of Guides for Educational Management (GEM) that provide expanded recommendations and functional implications; computer software included; Behavioral Checklist for Students for ESP program.
Authors: Jack G. Dial (P-MAC and ESP), Lawrence McCarron (P-MAC), and Garry Amann (P-MAC and ESP).
Publisher: McCarron-Dial Systems, Inc.
Cross References: See T5:1919 (1 reference); for reviews by Barbara A. Rothlisberg and E. W. Testut, see 12:284.

[1987]

Perceptual Speed (Identical Forms).

Purpose: Designed to assess "the ability to rapidly compare visual configurations and identify two figures as similar or identical or to identify some particular detail that is buried in distracting material."
Population: Visual inspectors, proofreaders, clerical personnel.
Publication Dates: 1984–1996.
Scores: Total score only.
Administration: Group or individual.
Price Data, 2002: $51 per 25 tests; $28 per interpretation and research manual (1959, 10 pages); $20 per score key.
Time: 5 minutes.
Comments: Primarily used in industry and governmental organizations (norms provided to these personnel).
Authors: L. L. Thurstone and T. E. Jeffrey.
Publisher: Pearson Performance Solutions [No reply from publisher; status unknown].
Cross References: For reviews by John W. Fleenor and Paul M. Mastrangelo, see 15:185.

[1988]

[Performance Review Forms].

Purpose: To provide a format to accomplish an appraisal of managerial performance in relation to accountability and personal characteristics.

Population: Employees, managers.
Publication Dates: 1960-1961.
Scores: Ratings in 3 areas: Accountability, Performance, Developmental Program.
Administration: Individual.
Author: Seymour Levy.
Publisher: Martin M. Bruce, Ph.D.
 a) COUNSELING INTERVIEW SUMMARY.
 Purpose: For summarizing a performance review interview.
 Population: Employees, managers.
 Publication Date: 1960.
 Forms, 2: Employee, Management.
 Price Data, 2006: $6.25 per employee forms; $3.50 per employee specimen set; $8.25 per management forms; $4.95 per management specimen set; $9.75 per guide to counseling.
 Time: (10) minutes.
 b) MANAGERIAL PERFORMANCE REVIEW.
 Purpose: Ratings by supervisors preparatory to performance review interview.
 Population: Managers.
 Publication Date: 1961.
 Price Data: $52 per forms; $27 per specimen set.
 Time: (40-50) minutes.

[1989]

Performance Series.

Purpose: A computer-adaptive assessment of student performance and progress, modified to measure the different academic objectives of individual state standards.
Population: Grades 2-10.
Publication Dates: 2002-2006.
Scores, 21: Reading (Vocabulary, Fiction, Nonfiction, Long Passages, Total), Mathematics (Number & Operations, Algebra, Geometry, Measurement, Data Analysis & Probability, Total), Language Arts (Capitalization, Parts of Speech, Punctuation, Sentence Structure, Total), Science (Ecology, Science Processes, Living Things, Total), Total.
Administration: Group.
Price Data, 2006: $12-$15 per student annual subscription cost.
Time: (60) minutes per subject area.
Comments: Web-administered, computer-adaptive instrument for Windows or Macintosh platforms; bookmarking allows students to take assessments over more than one test period.
Author: Scantron Corporation.
Publisher: Scantron Corporation.
Cross References: For reviews by Carlen Henington and David Morse, see 17:143.

[1990]

Performance Skills Leader.

Purpose: Designed to identify "leadership strengths and developmental needs."

Population: Employees in leadership positions.
Publication Date: 1996.
Acronym: PS Leader.
Scores, 24: Strategic Focus (Vision, Business Knowledge, Change Management), Business Focus (Quality Centered, Planning and Executing, Budgeting, Technology Management and Application), Work Force Focus (Coaching, Team Leadership, Creativity and Innovation, Commitment to Work Force Diversity, Human Resource Management), Interpersonal Focus (Interpersonal Skills, Oral Communication, Influencing, Writing, Conflict Resolution and Negotiation), Personal Focus (Self-Development, Action Orientation, Results Focus, Flexibility, Problem Solving and Decision Making, Role Modeling, Time Management).
Administration: Group.
Price Data: Available from publisher.
Time: Administration time not reported.
Author: Human Technology, Inc.
Publisher: HRD Press, Inc.
Cross References: For reviews by Trenton R. Ferro and George C. Thornton III, see 14:284.

[1991]

Personal Achievement Formula.

Purpose: Constructed to identify an individual's managerial strategy and his/her view of the organizational culture.
Population: Managers.
Publication Dates: 1976–1997.
Scores: 4 scores (Personal Achievement Formula, Organizational Culture, Group Achievement Formula, Group Assessment of Organization) each falling in one of 4 domains (Human Relations Specialist, Low Achiever, Average Achiever, High Achiever).
Administration: Group.
Price Data, 2001: $8.95 per instrument.
Time: Administration time not reported.
Author: Jay Hall.
Publisher: Teleometrics International, Inc.

[1992]

Personal Audit.

Purpose: Assess individual personality characteristics.
Population: Individuals in a variety of professional occupations.
Publication Dates: 1941–1992.
Administration: Individual or group.
Price Data: Available from publisher.
Authors: Clifford R. Adams and William M. Lepley.
Publisher: Pearson Performance Solutions [No reply from publisher; status unknown].
   a) FORM SS (SHORT FORM).
   Scores, 6: Seriousness, Firmness, Frankness, Tranquility, Stability, Tolerance.
   Time: No limit (approximately 40 minutes).

   b) FORM LL (LONG FORM).
   Scores, 9: 6 scores listed in *a* above plus Steadiness, Persistence, Contentment.
   Time: No limit (approximately 50 minutes).
Cross References: See T2:1314 (4 references) and P:192 (6 references); for a review by William Seeman, see 4:75 (3 references); for a review by Percival M. Symonds, see 3:64 (10 references).

[1993]

Personal Characteristics Inventory™.

Purpose: Used for selection and developmental purposes; designed to gauge individual standing on the "Big Five" primary dimensions of personality to predict important work, education, and life outcomes and to help organizations identify promising candidates more effectively and provide feedback to individuals regarding strengths and areas where improvement is necessary.
Population: Ages 15 and over.
Publication Dates: 1995–2005.
Acronym: PCI.
Scores, 26: Conscientiousness (Dependability, Achievement Striving, Efficiency, Total), Stability (Even Temperament, Self-Confidence, Total), Extraversion (Sociability, Need for Recognition, Leadership Orientation, Total), Agreeableness (Cooperation, Consideration, Total), Openness (Abstract Thinking, Creative Thinking, Total), Occupational Score (Manager, Sales, Clerical, Production, Driver), Teamwork, Integrity, Learning Orientation, Commitment to Work.
Administration: Group or individual.
Price Data: Available from publisher.
Foreign Language Editions: French and Spanish editions available.
Time: 25–30 minutes.
Comments: Online administration available.
Authors: Michael K. Mount, Murray R. Barrick, and Wonderlic Consulting.
Publisher: Wonderlic, Inc.
Cross References: For reviews by Susan M. Brookhart and Mark L. Pope, see 16:181.

[1994]

Personal Creativity Assessment.

Purpose: Designed "to allow individuals to determine how they measure up in the realm of creativity."
Population: Age 18 and above.
Publication Date: 1999.
Acronym: PCA.
Scores, 2: Enabler, Barrier.
Administration: Group or individual.
Price Data, 2001: $29.95 per Creativity by Design leader's guide (73 pages).
Time: (20–25) minutes.
Author: Alexander Watson Hiam.
Publisher: HRD Press, Inc.

[1995]

Personal Directions®.

Purpose: An executive coaching tool designed to aid in the structured exploration of an individual's personal choices regarding life balance issues, career planning, feelings of satisfaction and security, and opportunities for growth and development.

Population: Adults.

Publication Dates: 1997–2001.

Scores: 46 dimensions: Types of Emotional Satisfaction (Giving, Receiving, Belonging, Expressing, Gaining Stature, Entertaining, Creating, Interpreting, Excelling, Enduring, Structuring, Maneuvering, Winning, Controlling, Stability, Independence, Irreproachability), Areas of Emphasis (Career, Economic, Community, Interpersonal, Recreation, Travel, Nature, Palate, Arts, Practical Arts, Home, Romance, Family, Intellectual, Ideological, Physical, Emotional, Spiritual), World Outcomes (Level of Satisfaction, Level of Dissatisfaction, Level of Security, Level of Insecurity, Level of Growth, Balance of World, Level of Present Support, Internal Focus of World, External Focus of World, Flexibility of Boundaries, Level of Public Success).

Administration: Group.

Price Data: Available from publisher.

Foreign Language Editions: Available in English (American), English (British), Danish, Dutch, French, German, Italian, and Swedish.

Time: (45) minutes.

Comments: Purchase and use requires training by publisher.

Authors: James T. Mahoney, Joan W. Chadbourne (test), and Robert I. Kabacoff (manual).

Publisher: Management Research Group.

[1996]

Personal Effectiveness Inventory.

Purpose: Provides insights into attitudes, beliefs, and behavior, and increases skills for effectiveness.

Population: Adults.

Publication Date: 1996.

Acronym: PEI.

Scores, 15: Self-Development (Self-Image, Control, Approval, Amicability), Relationship Building (Trust, Cooperation, Interpersonal, Inclusion), Goal Achievement (Satisfaction, Directedness, Expectations, Effectiveness), Time Orientation (Past, Present, Future).

Administration: Individual.

Price Data: Price data for test materials including Self-Development Guide (70 pages) available from publisher.

Time: Administration time not reported.

Author: Human Synergistics International.

Publisher: Human Synergistics International.

[1997]

Personal Experience Inventory.

Purpose: "Assesses all forms of substance abuse plus related psychosocial problems and personal risk factors."

Population: Ages 12–18.

Publication Dates: 1988–1989.

Acronym: PEI.

Scores: 45 scores/screens: Chemical Involvement Problem Severity Section: Basic Scales (Personal Involvement with Chemicals, Effects from Drug Use, Social Benefits of Drug Use, Personal Consequences of Drug Use, Polydrug Use), Clinical Scales (Social-Recreational Drug Use, Psychological Benefits of Drug Use, Transsituational Drug Use, Preoccupation with Drugs, Loss of Control), Validity Indicators (Infrequent Responses, Defensiveness, Pattern Misfit), Drug Use Frequency/Duration/Age of Onset (Alcohol, Marijuana, LSD, Psychedelics, Cocaine, Amphetamines, Quaaludes, Barbiturates, Tranquilizers, Heroin, Opiates, Inhalants); Psychosocial Section: Personal Risk Factor Scales (Negative Self-Image, Psychological Disturbance, Social Isolation, Uncontrolled, Rejecting Convention, Deviant Behavior, Absence of Goals, Spiritual Isolation), Environmental Risk Factor Scales (Peer Chemical Environment, Sibling Chemical Use, Family Pathology, Family Estrangement), Problem Screens (Psychiatric Referral, Eating Disorder, Sexual Abuse, Physical Abuse, Family Chemical Dependency, Suicide Potential), Validity Indicators (Infrequent Responses, Defensiveness).

Administration: Group.

Parts, 2: Chemical Involvement Problem Severity Section, Psychosocial Section.

Price Data, 2006: $165 per kit for mail-in computer scoring including 5 prepaid mail-in answer booklets for computer scoring and interpretation and manual (1989, 103 pages); $132 per kit for on-site computer scoring including 5-use disk (PC with Windows), 5 PC answer booklets, and manual; $55 per manual; $26.95 per mail-in answer booklet; $329 per 25-use disk (PC with Windows); $24.75 per 10 PC answer booklets; $13 per FAX service scoring.

Time: 45 minutes.

Authors: Ken C. Winters and George A. Henly.

Publisher: Western Psychological Services.

Cross References: See T5:1931 (1 reference) and T4:1971 (2 references); for reviews by Tony Toneatto and Jalie A. Tucker, see 11:284.

[1998]

Personal Experience Inventory for Adults.

Purpose: Designed to yield "comprehensive information about an individual's substance abuse patterns and problems."

Population: Age 19 and older.

Publication Dates: 1995–1996.

Acronym: PEI-A.

Scores, 37: Problem Severity Scales (Personal Involvement with Drugs, Physiological Dependence, Effects of Use, Social Benefits of Use, Personal Consequences

of Use, Recreational Use, Transsituational Use, Psychological Benefits of Use, Preoccupation, Loss of Control, Infrequency–1, Self-Deception, Social Desirability–1, Treatment Receptiveness), Psychosocial Scales (Negative Self-Image, Psychological Disturbance, Social Isolation, Uncontrolled, Rejecting Convention, Deviant Behavior, Absence of Goals, Spiritual Isolation, Peer Drug Use, Interpersonal Pathology, Estrangement in the Home, Infrequency–2, Social Desirability–2), Problem Screens (Suicide Risk, Work Environment Risk, Past Family Pathology, Other Impulse-Related Problems, Significant Other Drug Problem, Sexual Abuse Perpetrator, Physical Abuse Perpetrator, Physical/Sexual Abuse Victim, Need for Psychiatric Referral, Miscellaneous).
Administration: Group.
Parts, 2: Problem Severity Scales, Psychosocial Scales.
Price Data, 2006: $165 per kit for mail-in computer scoring including 5 prepaid mail-in answer booklets and manual (1996, 100 pages); $132 per kit with disc for on-site computer scoring including 5-use disk, 5 PC answer booklets, and manual; $132 per kit with CD for on-site computer scoring including 5-use CD, 5 PC answer booklets, and manual; $26.95 or less per mail-in answer booklet; $329 or less per 25-use (PC with Windows) scoring disk; $329 or less per 25-use (PC with Windows) scoring CD; $25 or less per 10 PC answer booklets for use with computer disk; $55 per manual.
Time: (45–60) minutes.
Comments: Untimed self-report inventory; computer scored only.
Author: Ken C. Winters.
Publisher: Western Psychological Services.
Cross References: For reviews by Mark D. Shriver and Claudia R. Wright, see 13:225.

[1999]

Personal Experience Screening Questionnaire.
Purpose: "Designed as a brief screening tool to aid ... in the identification of teenagers likely to need a drug abuse assessment referral."
Population: Adolescents.
Publication Date: 1991.
Acronym: PESQ.
Scores, 3: Infrequency, Defensiveness, Problem Severity.
Administration: Group.
Price Data, 2006: $91 per complete kit including 25 AutoScore™ test forms and manual (30 pages); $41 per 25 AutoScore™ test forms; $53 per manual.
Time: (10) minutes.
Author: Ken C. Winters.
Publisher: Western Psychological Services.
Cross References: For reviews by Stuart N. Hart and Richard W. Johnson, see 12:286 (1 reference).

[2000]

Personal Experience Screening Question-naire for Adults.
Purpose: Designed to "screen for the abuse of alcohol and other drugs by adults."

Population: Ages 19 and over.
Publication Date: 2003.
Acronym: PESQ-A.
Scores, 2: Problem Severity, Defensiveness.
Administration: Individual or group.
Price Data, 2006: $91 per kit including Autoscore™ test forms and manual; $41 per 25 Autoscore™ test forms; $53 per manual; volume discount available.
Time: (10) minutes.
Comments: Self-report behavior inventory.
Author: Ken C. Winters.
Publisher: Western Psychological Services.
Cross References: For reviews by Jody L. Kulstad and William E. Martin, Jr., see 16:182.

[2001]

Personal History Checklist for Adolescents.
Purpose: To obtain historical information during routine intake procedures.
Population: Adolescent clients of mental health services.
Publication Date: 1989.
Scores: Item scores only.
Administration: Individual.
Manual: No manual.
Price Data, 2006: $50 per package of 25.
Time: Administration time not reported.
Comments: Can be completed by client or clinician.
Authors: Edward H. Dougherty and John A. Schinka.
Publisher: Psychological Assessment Resources, Inc.

[2002]

Personal History Checklist for Adults.
Purpose: To obtain historical information during routine intake procedures.
Population: Adult clients of mental health services.
Publication Date: 1989.
Scores: Item scores only.
Administration: Individual.
Manual: No manual.
Price Data, 2006: $50 per package of 25.
Time: Administration time not reported.
Comments: Checklist can be completed by client or clinician.
Author: John A. Schinka.
Publisher: Psychological Assessment Resources, Inc.
Cross References: For a review by Thomas A. Widiger, see 11:285.

[2003]

Personal Inventory of Needs.
Purpose: Designed as a self-assessment tool to identify the strengths of basic needs.
Population: Employees.
Publication Date: 1990.

Scores, 3: Achievement, Affiliation, Power.
Administration: Group or individual.
Price Data: Price information available from publisher for complete kit including 20 inventories, 20 response sheets, and 20 interpretation sheets.
Time: [30] minutes administration; [30] minutes interpretation.
Comments: Self-administered, self-scored; based on David McClelland's research at MIT.
Author: Training House, Inc.
Publisher: Training House, Inc.
Cross References: For reviews by Gary J. Dean and Trenton R. Ferro, see 12:287.

[2004]

Personal Opinion Matrix.

Purpose: Surveys the impressions and reactions of those who are managed.
Population: Employees.
Publication Dates: 1977-1983.
Scores, 2: Managerial Review, Climate.
Administration: Group.
Manual: No manual.
Price Data, 2001: $7.95 per instrument.
Time: Administration time not reported.
Comments: Self-administered survey.
Author: Jay Hall.
Publisher: Teleometrics International, Inc.
Cross References: For a review by Gregory H. Dobbins, see 10:276 (7 references).

[2005]

Personal Orientation Dimensions.

Purpose: Designed to "measure attitudes and values in terms of concepts of the actualizing person."
Population: High school, college, and adults.
Publication Dates: 1975–1977.
Acronym: POD.
Scores, 13: Orientation (Time Orientation, Core Centeredness), Polarities (Strength, Weakness, Anger, Love), Integration (Synergistic Integration, Potentiation), Awareness (Being, Trust in Humanity, Creative Living, Mission, Manipulation Awareness).
Administration: Group.
Price Data: Available from publisher.
Time: Administration time not reported.
Comments: A refinement and extension of concepts first measured by the Personal Orientation Inventory (2006); self-administering.
Author: Everett L. Shostrom.
Publisher: EdITS/Educational and Industrial Testing Service.
Cross References: For reviews by Gloria Maccow and Claudia R. Wright, see 14:285; see also T5:1938 (1 reference) and T4:1977 (1 reference).

[2006]

Personal Orientation Inventory.

Purpose: Designed as a "measure of values and behavior seen to be of importance in the development of the self-actualizing person."
Population: High school, college, and adults.
Publication Dates: 1962–1996.
Acronym: POI.
Scores, 12: Time Ratio, Support Ratio, Self-Actualizing Value, Existentiality, Feeling Reactivity, Spontaneity, Self-Regard, Self-Acceptance, Nature of Man, Synergy, Acceptance of Aggression, Capacity for Intimate Contact.
Administration: Group.
Price Data: Available from publisher.
Time: (30–40) minutes.
Comments: Self-administered.
Author: Everett L. Shostrum.
Publisher: EdITS/Educational and Industrial Testing Service.
Cross References: See T5:1939 (15 references), T4:1978 (42 references), 9:943 (24 references), and T3:1789 (98 references); for an excerpted review by Donald J. Tosi and Cathy A. Lindamood, see 8:641 (433 references); see also T2:1315 (80 references); for reviews by Bruce Bloxom and Richard W. Coan, see 7:121 (97 references); see also P:193 (26 references).

[2007]

Personal Problems Checklist–Adult.

Purpose: "To facilitate the rapid assessment of an individual's problems as seen from that person's point of view."
Population: Adults.
Publication Date: 1985.
Scores: 13 areas: Social, Appearance, Vocational, Family and Home, School, Finances, Religion, Emotions, Sex, Legal, Health and Habits, Attitude, Crises.
Administration: Individual or group.
Manual: No manual.
Price Data, 2006: $50 per package of 25.
Time: (10) minutes.
Author: John A. Schinka.
Publisher: Psychological Assessment Resources, Inc.
Cross References: See T5:1941 (1 reference); for a review by Harold R. Keller, see 10:278.

[2008]

Personal Problems Checklist for Adolescents.

Purpose: "To identify relevant problems, establish rapport, and provide written documentation of presenting problems consistent with community standards of care."
Population: Adolescents.
Publication Dates: 1985–1989.
Acronym: PPC.
Scores: 13 problem areas: Social and Friends, Appearance, Job, Parents, Family and Home, School, Money,

Religion, Emotions, Dating and Sex, Health and Habits, Attitudes and Opinions, Crises.
Administration: Individual or group.
Manual: No manual.
Price Data, 2006: $50 per package of 25.
Time: (10–20) minutes.
Comments: Adolescent version of the Personal Problems Checklist (2007).
Author: John A. Schinka.
Publisher: Psychological Assessment Resources, Inc.
Cross References: See T5:1942 (1 reference); for reviews by Brian K. Martens and Toni E. Santmire, see 10:279.

[2009]

Personal Profile System.
Purpose: "Helps people identify their behavioral style and pinpoints what they might do to become more effective and successful people."
Population: Employees.
Publication Dates: 1977-1983.
Scores: Behavioral Patterns (Work).
Administration: Group.
Price Data: Available from publisher.
Time: (60-360) minutes depending on preferred program format.
Comments: Self-report instrument.
Author: Performax Systems International, Inc.
Publisher: Inscape Publishing.
Cross References: For a review by Ellen McGinnis, see 10:280.

[2010]

Personal Reaction Index.
Purpose: Assesses how people feel regarding the aspects of their work environment.
Population: Employees.
Publication Dates: 1974-1995.
Scores, 6: Degree of Participation, Feelings of Satisfaction, Feelings of Responsibility, Feelings of Commitment, Feelings of Frustration, Perceived Decision Quality.
Administration: Group.
Manual: No manual.
Price Data, 2001: $2.95 per instrument.
Time: Administration time not reported.
Comments: Self-administered survey.
Author: Jay Hall.
Publisher: Teleometrics International, Inc.
Cross References: For reviews by Ralph M. Alexander and Daniel G. Spencer, see 9:946.

[2011]

Personal Resource Questionnaire.
Purpose: Provides information about adults' social networks and perceived levels of social support.
Population: Ages 18–80.

Publication Dates: 1981–1987.
Acronym: PRQ-85.
Scores: Part I, 3 scores: Size of Network, Number of Problems Experienced, Degree of Satisfaction with Help Received; Part II, total score only.
Administration: Group.
Parts, 2: I, II.
Manual: No manual.
Price Data: Price information available from publisher for instructions and Questionnaire; additional copies may be photocopied locally.
Time: (10–15) minutes.
Comments: May be self-administered; Parts I and II can be administered independently of each other.
Authors: Patricia Brandt and Clarann Weinert.
Publisher: Patricia Brandt and Clarann Weinert.
Cross References: See T5:1947 (8 references); for a review by Esther E. Diamond, see 11:286.

[2012]

Personal Stress Assessment Inventory.
Purpose: A self-assessment instrument designed to identify those who would most likely benefit from participation in stress-management training.
Population: Adults.
Publication Dates: 1981–1993.
Acronym: PSAI.
Scores, 6: Predisposition, Resilience, Sources of Stress, Overall Stress Factor, Health Symptoms, Personal Reactions.
Administration: Group or individual.
Price Data, 2002: $8.95 per inventory; minimum of 20 (volume discounts available).
Time: (20–30) minutes.
Comments: Self-administered; self-scored.
Author: Herbert S. Kindler.
Publisher: The Center for Management Effectiveness, Inc.
Cross References: For reviews by E. Scott Huebner and Norman D. Sundberg, see 14:286.

[2013]

Personal Stress Navigator.
Purpose: "Samples the magnitude and types of stress [and stress symptoms] experienced by the respondent and assesses relative vulnerability to stress."
Population: Adults.
Publication Dates: 1983-1987.
Scores, 16: Situational (Family, Individual Roles, Social Being, Environment, Financial, Work/School), Symptom (Muscular System, Parasympathetic Nervous System, Sympathetic Nervous System, Emotional, Cognitive System, Endocrine, Immune System), Vulnerability, Total Situational Stress, Total Symptoms.
Administration: Group.
Price Data: Available from publisher.

Time: [20-30] minutes.

Comments: Self-administered; v5.0 is available in paper-and-pencil format (optically scannable for computer scoring and interpretation), PC format (computer administration, scoring, and interpretation), and on the World Wide Web (http://www.bbinst.org/); entitled Stress Audit on previous listing.

Authors: Lyle H. Miller, Alma Dell Smith, and Bruce L. Mehler (manual only).

Publisher: Stress Directions, Inc.

Cross References: For a review by Rolf A. Peterson, see 10:347.

[2014]

Personal Style Assessment.

Purpose: To assess an individual's personal style of communication.

Population: Adults.

Publication Dates: 1980–1987.

Scores, 4: Thinker, Intuitor, Sensor, Feeler.

Administration: Group.

Manual: No manual.

Price Data: Price information available from publisher for tests and interpretation sheets.

Time: (15–25) minutes.

Comments: Self-administered, self-scored.

Author: Training House, Inc.

Publisher: Training House, Inc.

Cross References: For reviews by Cathy W. Hall and Gerald L. Stone, see 11:287.

[2015]

Personal Style Assessment, Jung-Parry Form.

Purpose: To assess an individual's relative strength on Jung's four personal styles, or "psychological types."

Population: Adults.

Publication Date: 1992.

Scores, 4: Thinker, Intuitor, Sensor, Feeler.

Administration: Group or individual.

Manual: No manual.

Price Data: Price information available from publisher for set including tests, answer sheets, and interpretation folder.

Time: (20–30) minutes.

Comments: Self-administered; self-scored.

Author: Scott B. Parry.

Publisher: Training House, Inc.

Cross References: For a review by Vicki S. Packman, see 13:227.

[2016]

Personal Style Indicator [Revised].

Purpose: Designed to increase mutual understanding, acceptance, and communication among people and to increase self-awareness.

Population: Ages 15 years–adults.

Publication Dates: 1988-2006.

Acronym: PSI.

Scores, 4: Behavioral/Action, Cognitive/Analysis, Interpersonal/Harmony, Affective/Expression.

Administration: Individual or group.

Price Data, 2006: $13.95 per test booklet (2006, 20 pages); $14.95 per In-Depth Interpretations booklet (2006, 28 pages); $26.95 per access code for online version; $69.95 per Professional's Guide (2006, 64 pages); $35 per Trainer's Guidelines (1996, 70 pages); $159.95 per PSI Power Point CD and binder (2006, 116 slides); $23.95 per participant workbook Building Relationships With Style (2006, 68 pages); $22.95 per Why Aren't You More Like Me? book second edition (1994, 226 pages); $109.95 per CRG Models Master Handouts binder and CD for PSI-color PDFs (2005, 26 pages).

Foreign Language Editions: Available online in English, French, and German, and in print in English, French, Japanese, Dutch, and Spanish; the In-Depth interpretations booklet is available in English, Japanese, Dutch, Spanish, and French.

Time: [90] minutes; [180-720] minutes advanced.

Comments: Self-administered and self-scored.

Authors: Ken Keis, Terry D. Anderson, and Everett T. Robinson.

Publisher: Consulting Resource Group International, Inc.

Cross References: For a review by Gypsy M. Denzine, see 17:144; for reviews by James T. Austin and Kusum Singh of an earlier edition, see 13:228.

[2017]

Personal Styles Inventory [PSI-120] [1999 Revision].

Purpose: Provides a comprehensive assessment of nonpathological personality characteristics.

Population: Adults.

Publication Dates: 1990–2005.

Acronym: PSI-120.

Scores, 24: Styles of Expressing Emotions (Sympathetic, Enthusiastic, Expansive, Confronting, Self-Willed, Reserved, Modest, Patient), Styles of Doing Things (Agreeing, Sociable, Excitement-Seeking, Venturing, Restless, Self-Directed, Self-Motivated, Organizing), Styles of Thinking (Traditional, Dedicated, Imaginative, Inquiring, Individualistic, Analytical, Practical, Focused).

Administration: Group or individual.

Price Data: Available from publisher.

Time: (20–30) minutes.

Comments: Interactive administration is available online; computerized interpretation reports are available.

Authors: Joseph T. Kunce, Corrine S. Cope, and Russel M. Newton.

Publisher: Educational & Psychological Consultants, Inc.

Cross References: For reviews by Frederick Medway and Janet Smith, see 17:145; see also T5:1954 (1 reference); for reviews by Paul A. Arbisi and Mary Henning-Stout of an earlier edition, see 13:229 (2 references); see also T4:1993 (4 references).

[2018]

Personal Values Inventory [Personal Strengths Publishing].

Purpose: Designed to facilitate self-discovery of personal style of approaching tasks, conflicts, decision-making, and relationships.
Population: Adolescents and adults with sixth grade or above reading levels.
Publication Dates: 1973–1997.
Acronym: PVI.
Scores: 7 Motivational Values (a set of values that helps a person decide how to act when things are going well); 13 scores reflecting predictable progressive responses to conflict and opposition.
Administration: Group or individual.
Editions, 2: Personal Values Inventory; Mirror Edition of the Personal Values Inventory.
Price Data, 2001: $10 per self-scorable inventory; $30 per manual (1996, 146 pages).
Time: (20–40) minutes.
Comments: Highest scores represent motivational values and valued relating style for an individual; self-scorable; for corporate (e.g., training workshops), and clinical (e.g., individual and group counseling) uses; can be self-administered, but trained administrators and interpreters recommended; Mirror Edition uses self-ratings and ratings from a significant other person.
Authors: Elias H. Porter and Sara E. Maloney.
Publisher: Personal Strengths Publishing.

[2019]

Personal Values Questionnaire.

Purpose: Measures individuals' "values related to achievement, affiliation, and power."
Population: Adults.
Publication Date: 1993.
Acronym: PVQ.
Scores, 3: Achievement, Affiliation, Power.
Administration: Individual.
Price Data, 2006: $69 per complete kit including 10 questionnaires and 10 profiles and interpretive notes (11 pages).
Time: [30] minutes.
Comments: Self-scored profile; also available online.
Author: Hay Group.
Publisher: Hay Group.
Cross References: For reviews by Brian F. Bolton and Gary J. Dean, see 13:230.

[2020]

Personality Adjective Check List.

Purpose: "Developed primarily as a self-report instrument for measuring personality in counseling clients and normal adults."

Population: Ages 16-adult.
Publication Dates: 1987-1991.
Acronym: PACL.
Scores, 9: Introversive, Inhibited, Cooperative, Sociable, Confident, Forceful, Respectful, Sensitive, PI (indicator of potential personality problems).
Administration: Group.
Price Data, 2001: $79 per start-up kit including manual (92 pages), scoring keys, 50 test sheets, and 50 profile sheets; $30 per manual; $30 per 50 test sheets; $25 per 50 profile sheets; $15 per scoring key set; $425 per WinPACL and AutoPACL software with narrative interpretations.
Time: (10-15) minutes.
Comments: Conceived as a tool for measuring the personality styles outlined by Theodore Millon among counseling clients and normal adults.
Author: Stephen Strack.
Publisher: 21st Century Assessment.
Cross References: See T5:1958 (1 reference); for reviews by Allen K. Hess and Howard M. Knoff, see 12:289 (1 reference); see also T4:1996 (3 references).

[2021]

Personality Advantage Questionnaire.

Purpose: Designed to "identify personality strengths, and set those strengths in a work context."
Population: Employees.
Publication Date: 1998.
Acronym: PAQ.
Scores, 5: Communication Style, Emotions, Drive and Determination, Relationships with People, Thinking Style.
Administration: Individual.
Manual: No manual.
Price Data, 2001: $14.95 per diskette.
Time: Administration time not reported.
Author: Human Resource Development Press.
Publisher: HRD Press, Inc.

[2022]

Personality Assessment Inventory-Adolescent.

Purpose: An "objective test of personality designed to provide information on critical client variables in professional settings."
Population: Ages 12-18.
Publication Dates: 1990-2007.
Acronym: PAI-A.
Scores, 53: Somatic Complaints (Conversion, Somatization, Health Concerns, Total), Anxiety (Cognitive, Affective, Physiological, Total), Anxiety-Related Disorders (Obsessive-Compulsive, Phobias, Traumatic Stress, Total), Depression (Cognitive, Affective, Physiological, Total), Mania (Activity Level, Grandiosity, Irritability, Total), Paranoia (Hypervigilance, Persecution, Resentment, Total), Schizophrenia (Psychotic Experiences, Social Detachment, Thought Disorder, Total), Borderline

Features (Affective Instability, Identity Problems, Negative Relationships, Self-Harm, Total), Antisocial Features (Antisocial behaviors, Egocentricity, Stimulus-Seeking, Total), Alcohol Problems, Drug Problems, Aggression (Aggressive Attitude, Verbal Aggression, Physical Aggression, Total), Suicidal Ideation, Stress, Nonsupport, Treatment Rejection, Dominance, Warmth, Inconsistency, Infrequency, Negative Impression, Positive Impression.
Administration: Group.
Price Data, 2008: $295 per complete kit including professional manual (2007, 190 pages), 2 reusable item booklets, 2 administration folios, 25 hand-scored answer sheets, 25 profile forms-adolescent, 25 critical items forms-adolescent, and 1 professional report service answer sheet in a soft-sided attaché case; $32 per reusable item booklet; $34 per 10 soft cover item booklets; $48 per 25 hand-scored answer sheets; $30 per 25 profile forms-adolescent; $35 per 25 critical items forms-adolescent; $70 per professional manual.
Time: 45(55) minutes.
Comments: Designed to complement its parent instrument, the Personality Assessment Inventory (2023).
Author: Leslie C. Morey.
Publisher: Psychological Assessment Resources, Inc.
Cross References: For reviews by H. Dennis Kade and Jonathan Sandoval, see 18:92.

[2023]

Personality Assessment Inventory [2007 Professional Manual].

Purpose: Designed to provide information relevant to clinical diagnosis, treatment planning, and screening for psychopathology.
Population: Ages 18 and over.
Publication Dates: 1991-2007.
Acronym: PAI.
Scores, 54: Somatic Complaints (Conversion, Somatization, Health Concerns, Total), Anxiety (Cognitive, Affective, Physiological, Total), Anxiety-Related Disorders (Obsessive-Compulsive, Phobias, Traumatic Stress, Total), Depression (Cognitive, Affective, Physiological, Total), Mania (Activity Level, Grandiosity, Irritability, Total), Paranoia (Hypervigilance, Persecution, Resentment, Total), Schizophrenia (Psychotic Experiences, Social Detachment, Thought Disorder, Total), Borderline Features (Affective Instability, Identity Problems, Negative Relationships, Self-Harm, Total), Antisocial Features (Antisocial Behaviors, Egocentricity, Stimulus-Seeking, Total), Alcohol Problems, Drug Problems, Aggression (Aggressive Attitude, Verbal Aggression, Physical Aggression, Total), Suicidal Ideation, Stress, Nonsupport, Treatment Rejection, Dominance, Warmth, Inconsistency, Infrequency, Negative Impression, Positive Impression.
Administration: Group.
Price Data, 2009: $295 per complete kit including professional manual (2007, 385 pages), 2 reusable item

booklets, 2 administration folios, 25 hand-scored answer sheets, 25 adult profile forms-revised, 25 critical item forms-revised, and 1 professional report service answer sheet; $36 per 10 item booklets; $33 per reusable item booklet; $50 per 25 hand-scored answer sheets; $36 per 25 adult profile forms-revised; $33 per 25 college profile forms; $30 per 25 critical item forms-revised; $70 per professional manual; $33 per administration folio.
Time: 55(75) minutes.
Author: Leslie C. Morey.
Publisher: Psychological Assessment Resources, Inc.
Cross References: For reviews by Andrew A. Cox and by Geoffrey L. Thorpe and Rachel D. Burrows, see 18:93; see T5:1959 (8 references); for reviews of a previous edition by Gregory J. Boyle and Michael G. Kavan, see 12:290 (8 references); see also T4:1997 (3 references).

[2024]

Personality Assessment Screener.

Purpose: "Designed to identify individuals in need of further assessment for emotional problems, behavioral problems, or both."
Population: Ages 18 and older.
Publication Dates: 1991–1997.
Acronym: PAS.
Scores, 11: Negative Affect, Acting Out, Health Problems, Psychotic Features, Social Withdrawal, Hostile Control, Suicidal Thinking, Alienation, Alcohol Problem, Anger Control, Total.
Administration: Individual or group.
Price Data, 2006: $85 per complete kit including manual (1997, 69 pages) and 25 hand-scorable response forms.
Time: (5) minutes.
Comments: Screening version of the Personality Assessment Inventory (2023).
Author: Leslie C. Morey.
Publisher: Psychological Assessment Resources, Inc.
Cross References: For a review by Matthew Burns, see 14:288.

[2025]

Personality Disorder Interview-IV: A Semistructured Interview for the Assessment of Personality Disorders.

Purpose: Constructed to "facilitate reliable and valid interview assessments of DSM-IV personality disorders."
Population: Ages 18 and older.
Publication Date: 1995.
Acronym: PDI–IV.
Scores, 21: 12 Personality Disorder Scores (Antisocial, Avoidant, Borderline, Dependent, Histrionic, Narcissistic, Obsessive-Compulsive, Paranoid, Schizoid, Schizotypal, Depressive, Passive-Aggressive); 9 Thematic Content Area Scores (Attitudes Toward Self, Attitudes Toward Others, Security/Comfort with

Others, Friendships and Relationships, Conflicts and Disagreements, Work and Leisure, Social Norms, Mood, Appearance and Perception).
Administration: Individual.
Price Data, 2006: $145 per introductory kit including hardcover manual (1995, 277 pages), 2 of each Interview Booklet, 10 score summary booklets, and 10 profile booklets.
Time: [120] minutes.
Comments: Corresponds with DSM—IV Personality Disorder diagnosis criteria.
Authors: Thomas A. Widiger, Steve Mangine, Elizabeth M. Corbitt, Cynthia G. Ellis, and Glenn V. Thomas.
Publisher: Psychological Assessment Resources, Inc.
Cross References: For reviews by Samuel Juni and Paul Retzlaff, see 14:289.

[2026]

Personality Inventory for Children, Second Edition.

Purpose: "Assesses both broad and narrow dimensions of behavioral, emotional, cognitive, and interpersonal adjustment."
Population: Ages 5–19 years (Kindergarten–Grade 12).
Publication Dates: 1977–2001.
Acronym: PIC-2.
Administration: Group.
Forms, 2: Standard Form, Behavioral Summary.
Price Data, 2002: $175 per kit including 2 reusable administration booklets, 50 answer sheets, 1 set of scoring templates, 25 Behavioral Summary AutoScore forms, 50 Standard Form profile sheets, manual (2001, 212 pages), 25 Behavioral Summary profile sheets, and 50 Critical Items summary sheets; $50 per manual; $25 per reusable administration booklet, quantity discount available; $19.50 per 5 Spanish translation administration booklets, quantity discount available; $19.50 per 100 answer sheets; $32.50 per set of scoring templates.
Foreign Language Editions: Spanish editions available for both forms.
Comments: Complete revision and restandardization of Personality Inventory for Children, Revised (PIC-R); old edition no longer available; coordinates with Personality Inventory for Youth (PIY, 2027) and Student Behavior Survey (SBS, 2594).
Authors: David Lachar and Christian P. Gruber.
Publisher: Western Psychological Services.
  a) STANDARD FORM.
  Scores, 33: 9 Adjustment Scales and 21 Adjustment Subscales: Cognitive Impairment (Inadequate Abilities, Poor Achievement, Developmental Delay), Impulsivity and Distractibility (Disruptive Behavior, Fearlessness), Delinquency (Antisocial Behavior, Dyscontrol, Noncompliance), Family Dysfunction (Conflict Among Members, Parent Maladjustment), Reality Distortion (Developmental Deviation,

Hallucinations and Delusions), Somatic Concern (Psychosomatic Preoccupation, Muscular Tension and Anxiety), Psychological Discomfort (Fear and Worry, Depression, Sleep Disturbance/Preoccupation with Death), Social Withdrawal (Social Introversion, Isolation), Social Skill Deficits (Limited Peer Status, Conflict With Peers), 3 Response Validity Scales (Defensiveness, Dissimulation, Inconsistency).
  Price Data: $19.50 per 100 Standard Form profiles or 100 Critical Items summary sheets.
  Time: (40) minutes.
  Comments: Hand-scored; computer scoring option will be available 2003 and will include mail, fax, or computer disks; system requirements DOS 3.0 or above, 512K memory, 286 processor, 1 MB free disk space, 3.5-inch high-density floppy drive.
  b) BEHAVIORAL SUMMARY.
  Scores, 12: 8 Short Adjustment Scales (Impulsivity and Distractibility–Short, Delinquency–Short, Family Dysfunction–Short, Reality Distortion–Short, Somatic Concern–Short, Psychological Discomfort–Short, Social Withdrawal–Short, Social Skill Deficits–Short), 3 Composite Scales (Externalization–Composite, Internalization–Composite, Adjustment–Composite), Total Score.
  Price Data: $29.95 per 25 Behavioral Summary AutoScore answer forms, quantity discount available; $19.50 per 100 Behavioral Summary profiles.
  Time: (15) minutes.
  Comments: "A quick screening version of the Standard Form; focuses on current behavior that can support the development of a treatment plan; can be administered using standard PIC-2 test materials"; hand-score only.
Cross References: For reviews by Radhika Krishnamurthy and Susana Urbina, see 16:183; see T5:1962 (23 references) and T4:1998 (21 references); for a review by Howard M. Knoff of an earlier edition, see 10:281 (20 references); for reviews by Cecil R. Reynolds and June M. Tuma of an earlier edition, see 9:949 (5 references); see also T3:1796 (5 references).

[2027]

Personality Inventory for Youth.
Purpose: "Assesses emotional and behavioral adjustment, family character and interaction, and school adjustment and academic ability."
Population: Ages 9–19.
Publication Date: 1995.
Acronym: PIY.
Scores, 37: Validity, Inconsistency, Dissimulation, Defensiveness, Cognitive Impairment (Poor Achievement and Memory, Inadequate Abilities, Learning Problems, Total), Impulsivity and Distractibility (Brashness, Distractibility and Overactivity, Impulsivity, Total), Delinquency (Antisocial Behavior, Dyscontrol, Noncompliance,

Total), Family Dysfunction (Parent-Child Conflict, Parent Maladjustment, Marital Discord, Total), Reality Distortion (Feelings of Alienation, Hallucinations and Delusions, Total), Somatic Concern (Psychosomatic Syndrome, Muscular Tension and Anxiety, Preoccupation with Disease, Total), Psychological Discomfort (Fear and Worry, Depression, Sleep Disturbance, Total), Social Withdrawal (Social Introversion, Isolation, Total), Social Skill Deficits (Limited Peer Status, Conflict with Peers, Total).

Administration: Group.

Price Data, 2006: $247.50 per complete kit including administration and interpretation guide, technical guide, 100 answer sheets, 1 set of scoring templates, 100 profile forms (male and female), 100 critical items summary sheets (male and female), 2 reusable administration booklets, and audiotape; $27.50 per reusable administration booklet; $24.75 per Spanish Research Edition reusable administration booklet; $26.50 per 100 answer sheets; $26.50 per 100 profile forms; $26.50 per 100 critical items summary sheets; $20.50 per mail-in answer sheet; $329.50 per 25-use disk (PC with Microsoft Windows); $12 per FAX service scoring charge; $35.75 per set of scoring templates; $16.50 per audiotape; $52.25 per administration and interpretation guide; $54.50 per technical guide.

Time: (45) minutes.

Authors: David Lachar and Christian P. Gruber.

Publisher: Western Psychological Services.

Cross References: For reviews by Lizanne DeStefano and by Gregory J. Marchant and T. Andrew Ridenour, see 13:231.

[2028]

Personality Research Form, 3rd Edition.

Purpose: Designed as an "extensively validated comprehensive measure of normal personality."

Population: Grade 6-college, adults.

Publication Dates: 1964-1997.

Acronym: PRF.

Administration: Group or individual.

Forms, 5: A, B, AA, BB, and E (Form E sent out unless specified; contact publisher for availability and prices of other forms).

Price Data, 2010: $92 per examination kit including manual on CD (1984, 72 pages), 5 reusable test booklets, 5 hand-scorable answer sheets, 5 profile sheets, scoring template, and one machine-scorable answer sheet and coupon for an Extended Report; $24 per test manual on CD; $60 per 25 reusable test booklets; $50 per 25 hand-scorable answer sheets; $50 per 25 profile sheets; $22 per scoring template; $95–$105 (depending on volume) per 10 machine-scorable answer sheets and coupons for Mail-in Extended Report; $65–$75 (depending on volume) per 10 machine-scorable answer sheets and coupons for Mail-in Basic Report; $145 per software installation package,

includes 10 coupons for computer reports; $12-$20 (depending on volume) per online password.

Foreign Language Editions: Available in Spanish and French (Form E test booklets only).

Comments: The PRF is available for online scoring at www.sigmatesting.com.

Author: Douglas N. Jackson.

Publisher: SIGMA Assessment Systems, Inc.

  a) FORM A.

  Population: Ages 16-adult.

  Publication Dates: 1965-1985.

  Scores, 15: Achievement, Affiliation, Aggression, Autonomy, Dominance, Endurance, Exhibition, Harmavoidance, Impulsivity, Nurturance, Order, Play, Social Recognition, Understanding, Infrequency.

  Time: (30-45) minutes.

  b) FORM B.

  Comments: Parallel form to Form A.

  c) FORM AA.

  Population: College students.

  Publication Dates: 1965-1985.

  Scores, 22: Same as Form A and Form B plus Abasement, Change, Cognitive Structure, Defendence, Sentience, Succorance, Desirability.

  Time: (40-70) minutes.

  d) FORM BB.

  Comments: Parallel form to Form AA.

  e) FORM E.

  Population: Grade 6-adult.

  Publication Dates: 1974-1987.

  Scores, 22: Same as Form AA.

  Time: 45 minutes.

Cross References: See T5:1965 (86 references) and T4:2000 (45 references); for reviews by Robert Hogan and Jerry S. Wiggins, see 10:282 (68 references); see also 9:950 (42 references) and T3:1798 (116 references); for a review by Robert Hogan of an earlier edition, see 8:643 (132 references); see also T3:1322 (23 references); for reviews by Anne Anastasi, E. Lowell Kelly, and Jerry Wiggins, and excerpted reviews by John O. Crites, Lonnie D. Valentine, Jr., and Ruth Wessler with Jane Loevinger of an earlier edition, see 7:123 (27 references); see also P:201 (13 references).

[2029]

Personality Self-Portrait [Revised].

Purpose: Designed to illustrate "the wide range of normal personality styles that combine to create each individual's unique personality profile and demonstrates how each personality style influences relationships, work and home life."

Population: Ages 18 and over.

Publication Dates: 1995–1996.

Acronym: PSP.

Scores, 14: Vigilant, Solitary, Idiosyncratic, Adventurous, Mercurial, Dramatic, Self-Confident, Sensitive,

Devoted, Conscientious, Leisurely, Aggressive, Self-Sacrificing, Serious.
Administration: Individual.
Price Data, 2011: $189 per complete kit including 5 reusable item booklets, 20 Quikscore forms, and 20 interpretation guides; $55 per 5 reusable item booklets; $33 per 20 Quikscore forms; $115 per 20 interpretive guides, $8 per Online profile report (minimum purchase of 20).
Time: [30] minutes.
Comments: Self-report questionnaire; online administration available.
Authors: John M. Oldham and Lois B. Morris.
Publisher: Multi-Health Systems, Inc.
Cross References: For reviews by Gregory J. Boyle and Sandra D. Haynes, see 16:184.

[2030]

Personalized Achievement Summary System.
Purpose: Designed to provide information useful for monitoring academic progress, selecting curriculum and evaluating and planning instructional programming in home school settings.
Population: Grades 3–8.
Publication Dates: 1987–2006.
Acronym: P.A.S.S.
Scores, 20: Reading (Word Meaning, Literal Comprehension, Interpretive Comprehension, Evaluative Comprehension, Total); Mathematics (Numeration and Number Systems, Fractions, Decimals/Percent/and Currency, Geometry and Measurement, Graphs/Charts/and Statistics, Word Problems and Problem Solving, Computation, Total); Language Usage (Grammar, Capitalization, Punctuation, Composition, Study Skills, Spelling, Total).
Administration: Individual.
Price Data, 2010: $36, includes shipping and handling. Quantity discounts apply.
Time: Untimed.
Comments: Items licensed from the Portland (Oregon) Public Schools.
Author: Hewitt Research Foundation.
Publisher: Hewitt Research Foundation.
Cross References: For reviews by Douglas F. Kauffman and Michael S. Trevisan, see 16:185.

[2031]

Personalysis®.
Purpose: Constructed "to inventory personality characteristics of individuals at five different levels" yielding information on "how to maximize personal, interpersonal, and group effectiveness in the work place."
Population: Leaders, employees, families, individuals.
Publication Dates: 1975–2001.
Scores, 32: Preferred Style–Rational Self (Authoritative, Democratic, Structured, Self Directed), Communication Expectations–Socialized Self (Direction, Involvement,

Methodology, Input), Motivational Needs–Instinctive Self (Authority, Influence, Control, Understanding), Defensive Self (Coerce, Provoke, Resist, Reject), Irrational Self (Hostile, Rebellious, Stubborn, Withdrawn); Act, Adapt, Analyze, and Assess scores for Preferred Style–Rational Self, Back-Up Style–Socialized Self, and Functional Stress–Instinctive.
Administration: Individual or group.
Price Data: Available from publisher.
Time: Untimed.
Comments: Self-administered.
Author: James R. Noland.
Publisher: Personalysis Corporation.
Cross References: For reviews by Jack Gebart-Eaglemont and S. Alvin Leung, see 16:186; for reviews by George Engelhard, Jr. and L. Alan Witt of an earlier edition, see 12:291.

[2032]

Personnel Assessment Form.
Purpose: To measure mental ability and intelligence for employee selection and placement planning.
Population: Ages 16 and older.
Publication Dates: 2004–2006.
Acronym: PAF.
Scores: Verbal Subtest Score, Quantitative Subtest Score, Total Score.
Subtest: Verbal Subtest, Quantitative Subtest.
Administration: Group and individual.
Forms, 2: A, C.
Price Data, 2010: $24 per manual; $5 per Form A test booklet or Form C test booklet; $15-$20 (depending on volume) per report via fax-in scoring or online administration.
Time: 14 minutes.
Comments: The PAF is available through fax-in scoring and online administration at www.sigmatesting.com.
Author: Douglas N. Jackson.
Publisher: SIGMA Assessment Systems, Inc.
Cross References: For reviews by Jean P. Kirnan and James W. Pinkney, see 17:146.

[2033]

[Personnel Interviewing Form].
Purpose: Designed to help business and industry to obtain various information from interviewees.
Population: Business and industry.
Publication Dates: 1956-1984.
Administration: Individual.
Manual: No manual.
Time: (20-30) minutes.
Author: Judd-Safian Associates.
Publisher: Martin M. Bruce, Ph.D.
a) INITIAL INTERVIEW TABULATION.
Scores: For recording ratings in 10 areas: Appearance, Voice and Speech, Poise, Health, Education,

Manner, Responsiveness, Experience, Job Stability, Motivation.
Price Data, 2006: $5.40 per specimen set; $9.35 per package of forms.
b) DEPTH INTERVIEW PATTERN.
Scores: For interviewing in 5 areas: Work Evaluation, Educational and Social Evaluation, Economic Evaluation, Personality Evaluation, Ambitions Evaluation.
Price Data: $14.50 per specimen set; $27.00 per package of forms.
c) EMPLOYMENT REFERENCE INQUIRY.
Purpose: For securing employee evaluation from previous employers.
Price Data: $4.75 per specimen set; $9.35 per package of forms.

[2034]

Personnel Reaction Blank.

Purpose: A personality-based integrity test to help in hiring trustworthy, dependable employees.
Population: Ages 15 to adult.
Publication Dates: 1972–2003.
Acronym: PRB.
Scores, 5: Personality Reliability Index, which is a composite of 4 subscales: Sense of Well-Being, Positive Background Indicators, Compliance with Rules and Routines, Conventional Occupational Preferences.
Administration: Group or individual; online and paper-and-pencil.
Price Data: Available from publisher.
Time: (15) minutes.
Comments: In addition to the scores, the report produces a narrative statement for each score that describes typical behavior of low scorers and high scorers; the summary page of the report provides item responses and number of missing responses for each scale.
Authors: Harrison G. Gough, Richard Arvey, and Pamela Bradley.
Publisher: Institute for Personality and Ability Testing, Inc. (IPAT).
Cross References: For a review by Donna L. Sundre of an earlier version, see 13:232.

[2035]

Personnel Relations Survey [Revised].

Purpose: "Designed to assess the understanding and behavior of managers in their interpersonal relationships."
Population: Managers.
Publication Dates: 1967–2000.
Acronym: PRS.
Scores, 6: Relationships with Employees (Exposure, Feedback); Relationships with Colleagues (Exposure, Feedback); Relationships with Superiors (Exposure, Feedback).
Administration: Group.

Manual: Leader's Guide available.
Price Data, 2006: $9.95 per instrument.
Time: Administration time not reported.
Comments: Self-administered, self-scored; based on the Johari Window Model of interpersonal relationships.
Authors: Jay Hall and Martha S. Williams.
Publisher: Teleometrics International, Inc.
Cross References: For a review by Matthew E. Lambert, see 14:29.

[2036]

Personnel Selection Inventory.

Purpose: Helps identify job applicants who are likely to be honest and have positive attitudes toward work, safety and customer service and provides a valid, fair, and cost effective means of identifying applicants who are likely to be productive and responsible.
Population: Job applicants.
Publication Dates: 1975–1980.
Acronym: PSI.
Scores: 21 scales: Honesty, Supervision Attitudes, Tenure, Drug Avoidance Scale, Nonviolence Scale, Employee/Customer Relations Scale, Risk Avoidance Scale, Stress Tolerance Scale, Safety Scale, Work Values Scale, Math Scale, Responsibility, Productivity, Customer Service Aptitude Scale, Customer Service Attitude Scale, Sales Aptitude Scale, Customer Service Index, Candidness Validity Scale, Employability Index, Detailed Personal and Behavioral History.
Administration: Individual or group.
Forms: 20 versions available including non-integrity test versions.
Price Data: Available from publisher.
Time: Varies based on version.
Comments: Previously listed as London House Personnel Selection Inventory.
Author: London House.
Publisher: Pearson Performance Solutions [No reply from publisher; status unknown].
Cross References: See T5:1972 (1 reference) and T4:1478 (1 reference); for a review by William I. Sauser, see 9:631; see also T3:1339 (2 references).

[2037]

Personnel Test Battery.

Purpose: Designed to assess numerical skills, language proficiency, and perceptual accuracy.
Population: Office and sales groups.
Publication Dates: 1979–1981.
Acronym: PTB.
Subtests: Available as separates.
Administration: Group.
Levels, 2: 1, 2.
Restricted Distribution: Restricted to persons who have completed the publisher's training course or

members of the Division of Occupational Psychology of the British Psychological Society.
Price Data: Available from publisher.
Authors: Peter Saville, Gill Nyfield, Roger Holdsworth (test), and Ruth Holdsworth (manual).
Publisher: SHL Group plc [United Kingdom].
  a) LEVEL 1.
  Comments: "Basic skills and comprehension"; 3 tests plus 2 optional tests for Levels 1 and 2.
    1) *Verbal Usage.*
    Acronym: VPI.
    Time: 10(15) minutes.
    2) *Numerical Comprehension.*
    Acronym: NP2.
    Time: 7(12) minutes.
    3) *Checking.*
    Acronym: CP3.
    Time: 7(12) minutes.
    4) *Basic Checking.*
    Acronym: CP7.
    Time: 5(10) minutes.
    Comments: Optional test for Levels 1 and 2.
    5) *Audio Checking.*
    Acronym: CP8.
    Time: (15) minutes.
    Comments: Optional test for Levels 1 and 2; test administered by cassette tape.
  b) LEVEL 2.
  Comments: "Higher-order reasoning skills"; 3 tests plus 2 optional tests for Levels 1 and 2.
    1) *Classification.*
    Acronym: CP4.
    Time: 7(12) minutes.
    2) *Verbal Meaning.*
    Acronym: VP5.
    Time: 10(15) minutes.
    3) *Numerical Reasoning.*
    Acronym: NP6.
    Time: 10(15) minutes.

[2038]

Personnel Tests for Industry.

Purpose: To assist in the selection, placement, training, and promotion of individuals in industrial settings.
Population: Trade school and adults.
Publication Dates: 1945–1995.
Acronym: PTI.
Scores: Total score only.
Administration: Group or individual.
Publisher: Pearson.
  a) PTI-VERBAL TEST.
  Publication Dates: 1952–1969.
  Acronym: PTI-V.
  Forms, 2: A, B.
  Price Data, 2006: $50 per examination kit including all forms of Verbal and Numerical booklets

and manual; $100 per 25 test booklets (manual, booklets, key) (specify Form A or B); $285 per 100 test booklets (includes manual, booklet, key).
  Time: 5(15) minutes.
  Author: Alexander G. Wesman.
  b) PTI-NUMERICAL TEST.
  Publication Dates: 1952–1969.
  Acronym: PTI-N.
  Forms, 2: A, B.
  Price Data: Same as for *a* above.
  Time: 20(25) minutes.
  Author: Jerome E. Doppelt.
  c) PTI-ORAL DIRECTIONS TEST.
  Publication Dates: 1945–1995.
  Acronym: PTI-ODT.
  Comments: For information on revision of this subtest, see 2039.
Author: Charles R. Langmuir.
Cross References: See T5:1974 (1 reference), T4:2008 (5 references), T3:1808 (3 references), T2:433 (5 references), and 7:373 (3 references); for a review by Erwin K. Taylor, see 5:366; see also 4:309 (1 reference); for reviews by Charles D. Flory, Irving Lorge, and William W. Turnbull on the Oral Directions Test, see 3:245.

[2039]

Personnel Tests for Industry–Oral Directions Test [Second Edition].

Purpose: A test of general ability designed to "assess an individual's ability to follow directions presented orally" and as a selection tool "to predict performance in a variety of vocational and technical training settings."
Population: Adolescents and adults.
Publication Dates: 1974-1995.
Acronym: PTI-ODT.
Scores: Total score only.
Administration: Individual or group.
Forms, 2: S, T.
Price Data, 2007: $200 per complete set including recording, manual (1995, 67 pages), script, key, 100 answer documents, directions for administering, and cassette tape Form S or T; $50 per examination kit including scripts and answer documents for both forms and manual.
Time: (15) minutes.
Comments: Tape-recorded administration; one of three subtests of Personnel Tests for Industry (2038).
Author: Charles R. Langmuir.
Publisher: Pearson.
Cross References: For reviews by Caroline M. Adkins and Bruce Biskin, see 17:147; for information for Personnel Tests for Industry, see T5:1974 (1 reference), T4:2008 (5 references), T3:1808 (3 references), T2:433 (5 references), and 7:373 (3 references); for a review by Erwin K. Taylor, see 5:366; see also 4:309 (1 reference); for reviews by Charles D. Flory, Irving Lorge, and William W. Turnbull of the Oral Directions Test, see 3:245.

[2040]

Pervasive Developmental Disorder in Mental Retardation Scale [Second Revised Edition].

Purpose: "A simple classification and screening instrument designed for the identification of Pervasive Developmental Disorders in persons with mental retardation/intellectual disability."
Population: Ages 2-80.
Publication Dates: 1990-2006.
Acronym: PDD-MRS.
Scores: Total score only.
Administration: Individual.
Price Data, 2006: €123,40 (U.S. $148.08) per starter set including manual (2006, 53 pages) and 75 record forms; €49,50 (U.S. $59.40) per manual; €73,90 (U.S. $88.68) per 75 record forms.
Foreign Language Editions: First published in Dutch; English, German, and Italian versions are available.
Time: (10-20) minutes.
Comments: Norms of the scale are based on data of 1,230 children, adolescents, and adults in the profound, severe, moderate, and mild ranges of mental retardation.
Author: D. W. Kraijer.
Publisher: PITS: Psychologische Instrumenten Tests en Services [The Netherlands].
Cross References: For a review by Tawnya Meadows, see 17:148.

[2041]

Pervasive Developmental Disorders Screening Test, Second Edition.

Purpose: Designed as "a clinical screening tool for autism (autistic disorder)/AD and other pervasive developmental disorders, such as pervasive developmental disorder, not otherwise specified (PDD-NOS) and Asperger's Disorder."
Population: Ages 12 to 48 months.
Publication Date: 2004.
Acronym: PDDST-II.
Scores: Total score only.
Administration: Individual.
Forms, 3: Stage 1–Primary Care Screener, Stage 2–Developmental Clinic Screener, Stage 3–Autism Clinic Severity Screener.
Price Data, 2007: $125 per complete kit including manual (42 pages) and record forms; $30 per 25 Stage 1 record forms; $30 per 25 Stage 2 record forms; $30 per 25 Stage 3 record forms.
Time: (10–20) minutes.
Comments: Parent-report screening measure.
Author: Bryna Siegel.
Publisher: Pearson.
Cross References: For reviews by Mary (Rina) M. Chittooran and Theresa Volpe-Johnstone, see 17:149.

[2042]

Pharmacy College Admission Test.

Purpose: Developed to measure the abilities, aptitudes, and skills that pharmacy schools have deemed essential for success in basic pharmacy curricula.
Population: Pharmacy school applicants.
Publication Dates: 1974– 2006.
Acronym: PCAT.
Scores, 7: Verbal Ability, Biology, Reading Comprehension, Quantitative Ability, Chemistry, Composite, Writing.
Administration: Group.
Restricted Distribution: Distribution restricted and test administered at testing centers; details may be obtained from publisher.
Price Data: Available from publisher.
Time: 235 minutes.
Comments: Paper-and-pencil; national test dates.
Author: Harcourt Assessment, Inc.
Publisher: Pearson.
Cross References: For reviews by Mark Albanese and Leo M. Harvill, see 13:233.

[2043]

Phelps Kindergarten Readiness Scale.

Purpose: Constructed to assess the academic strengths and weaknesses of children prior to enrolling in kindergarten or shortly after starting school.
Population: Pre-kindergarten and early kindergarten.
Publication Dates: 1991–2010.
Acronym: PKRS.
Scores, 4: Verbal Processing, Perceptual Processing, Auditory Processing, Total Readiness.
Administration: Individual.
Price Data: Available from publisher.
Time: (15) minutes.
Author: LeAdelle Phelps.
Publisher: Psychology Press Inc.
Cross References: For a review by Theresa H. Elofson, see 12:292.

[2044]

Phonemic-Awareness Skills Screening.

Purpose: "The PASS is a quick screening that pinpoints" three "specific areas of phonological weakness": to identify students with problems, to determine strengths and weaknesses, to document progress.
Population: Grades 1–2.
Publication Date: 2000.
Acronym: PASS.
Scores: 8 subtests: Rhyming, Sentence Segmentation, Blending, Syllable Segmentation, Deletion, Phoneme Isolation, Phoneme Segmentation, Substitution, Total.
Administration: Individual.
Price Data, 2006: $30 per complete kit including examiner's manual (16 pages) and 25 record forms; $20 per 25 record forms; $13 per examiner's manual.

Time: (15) minutes.
Comments: Can be administered by a teacher or assistant, requires "no specialized training in testing"; subtests may be administered separately.
Authors: Linda Crumrine and Helen Lonegan.
Publisher: PRO-ED.
Cross References: For reviews by Steven Long and by Vincent J. Samar and Ricki Korey Birnbaum, see 15:187.

[2045]

Phonics-Based Reading Test.

Purpose: "Designed to assess reading skills" and "To measure an individual's ability to apply phonics concepts when reading single words and connected text."
Population: Ages 6-0 through 12-11.
Publication Date: 2002.
Acronym: PRT.
Scores, 4: Decoding, Fluency, Comprehension, Total Reading Standard Score.
Administration: Individual.
Price Data, 2006: $82 per test kit including manual (109 pages), stimulus book, and 25 student test booklets; $25 per stimulus book; $27 per 25 student test booklets; $30 per manual.
Time: (20–30) minutes.
Comments: Norm- and criterion-referenced.
Author: Rick Brownell.
Publisher: Academic Therapy Publications.
Cross References: For reviews by Karen Mackler and Annita Marie Ward, see 16:187.

[2046]

Phonological Abilities Test.

Purpose: "A screening test for the identification of children at risk of reading difficulties and as a diagnostic test to assess the nature and extent of phonological difficulties in older children with recognized reading problems."
Population: Ages 5–7.
Publication Date: 1997.
Acronym: PAT.
Scores, 8: Rhyme Detection, Rhyme Production, Word Completion—Syllables, Word Completion—Phonemes, Phoneme Deletion—Beginning Sounds, Phoneme Deletion—End Sounds, Speech Rate, Letter Knowledge.
Administration: Individual.
Price Data, 2006: £90 per complete kit including examiner's manual (45 pages), stimulus manual, alphabet cards, and record forms in carrying case; £29.50 per 25 record forms; £36.50 per examiner's manual; £44.50 per stimulus manual; £21.50 per alphabet cards.
Time: 30 minutes.
Comments: Normed in the U.K.; tests can be given individually or in combination; normative data are also available for 4-year-olds.

Authors: Valerie Muter, Charles Hulme, and Margaret Snowling.
Publisher: Pearson Assessment [England].
Cross References: For a review by Annita Marie Ward, see 15:188.

[2047]

Phonological Assessment Battery [Standardised Edition].

Purpose: Designed to identify "those children who need special help by providing an individual assessment of the child's phonological skills."
Population: Ages 6–15.
Publication Date: 1997.
Acronym: PLAB.
Scores: 6 tests: Alliteration, Naming Speed, Rhyme, Spoonerisms, Fluency, Non-Word Reading.
Administration: Individual.
Price Data, 1998: £75 per complete set including 10 record booklets and manual (130 pages); £10 per 10 record booklets; sample sheets are free.
Time: (30–40) minutes.
Comments: Is also appropriate for children whose first language is not English.
Authors: Norah Frederickson, Uta Frith, and Rea Reason.
Publisher: GL Assessment [England].
Cross References: For a review by Claudia R. Wright, see 15:189.

[2048]

Phonological Awareness Skills Program.

Purpose: "Designed to provide a means for placing students at the appropriate entry points in the Phonological Awareness Skills Program Curriculum."
Population: Ages 4 to 10.
Publication Date: 1999.
Acronym: PASP.
Scores: Total score only.
Administration: Individual.
Price Data, 2010: $100 per complete kit including 25 record forms, curriculum manual, and instrument manual (24 pages); $21 per 25 record forms.
Time: (2–4) minutes.
Authors: Jerome Rosner.
Publisher: PRO-ED.
Cross References: For a review by Janet Norris, see 15:190.

[2049]

Phonovisual Diagnostic Tests [1975 Revision].

Purpose: "Designed to test phonetic skills as taught by the Phonovisual Method."
Population: Grades 3-12.

Publication Date: 1975.
Scores: Total score only.
Administration: Group.
Tests: 6 tests consisting of 24 words each.
Price Data, 2001: $9.50 per set of tests and instructions.
Time: Administration time not reported.
Authors: Edna B. Smith and Mazie C. Lloyd.
Publisher: Phonovisual Products, Inc.
Cross References: For reviews by Charles M. Brown and George D. Spache of an earlier edition, see 6:829.

[2050]

Photo Articulation Test, Third Edition.

Purpose: Constructed as a "systematic method for eliciting speech sounds from children and identifying errors in articulation."
Population: Ages 3–8.
Publication Dates: 1969–1997.
Acronym: PAT-3.
Scores: Total score only.
Administration: Individual.
Price Data, 2011: $206 per complete kit; $53 per summary/response forms; $53 per examiner's manual; $75 per photo album picture book; $41 per picture card deck.
Time: (20) minutes.
Authors: Barbara A. Lippke, Stanley E. Dickey, John W. Selmar, and Anton L. Sodor.
Publisher: PRO-ED.
Cross References: For a review by David P. Hurford, see 14:291; see also T5:1982 (15 references), T4:2017 (12 references), 9:957 (2 references), and T3:1814 (5 references); for a review by Lawrence D. Shriberg of an earlier edition, see 8:969 (1 reference); see also 7:962 (2 references).

[2051]

PHSF Relations Questionnaire.

Purpose: Constructed "to measure … the personal, home, social and formal relations of high school pupils, students and adults, in order to determine the level of adjustment."
Population: Standards 6–10 in South African school system, college, and adults.
Publication Dates: 1969–1971.
Acronym: PHSF.
Scores, 12: Personal (Self-Confidence, Self-Esteem, Self-Control, Nervousness, Health), Home (Family Influences, Personal Freedom), Social (Sociability-Group, Sociability-Specific Person, Moral Sense), Formal Relations, Validity Scale.
Administration: Group.
Price Data: Available from publisher.
Time: (30) minutes.

Comments: Test materials in both English and Afrikaans.
Authors: F. A. Fouche and P. E. Grobbelaar.
Publisher: Human Sciences Research Council [South Africa].

[2052]

Picha-Seron Career Analysis.

Purpose: "Provides a description and analysis of an individual's workstyle and relates this workstyle to 178 selected technical, managerial and professional occupations (career profile and occupational profile) or to an in-depth workstyle analysis (personnel profile)."
Population: Middle school-adult.
Publication Dates: 1991-1993.
Acronym: PSCA.
Administration: Individual or group.
Price Data: Available from publisher.
Time: [10-15] minutes.
Author: Merron S. Seron.
Publisher: International Career Planning Services, Inc.
  a) PSCA-CAREER PROFILE.
  Population: Middle school-secondary school.
  Acronym: PSCA-CP.
  Scores, 16: Workstyle Graph Interpretations (Dominance, Influence, Adaptance, Compliance), Occupational Strengths (Practical, Analytical, Creative, Service, Managerial, Supportive), Learning Styles (Cognitive Organization, Internality, Time Orientation), Occupational Scales (178).
  b) PSCA-OCCUPATIONAL PROFILE.
  Population: College-adult.
  Acronym: PSCA-OP.
  Scores, 18: Workstyle Graphs (Ideal Self, Pressure Self, Usual Self), other scores same as *a* above.
  c) PSCA-PERSONNEL PROFILE.
  Population: Adults.
  Acronym: PSCA-PP.
  Scores, 18: Verification Score, Workstyle Graphs (Ideal Self, Pressure Self, Usual Self), Workstyle Graph Interpretations (Dominance, Influence, Adaptance, Compliance), Strength of Occupational Area (Practical, Analytical, Creative, Service, Managerial, Supportive), Learning Styles (Internality, Cognitive Organization, Time Orientation), Major Workstyles.
Cross References: For reviews by Michael B. Bunch and Bertram C. Sippola, see 12:295.

[2053]

Pictographic Self Rating Scale.

Purpose: Designed to assess pupils' attitudes toward their academic subjects and classroom activities.
Population: High school and college.
Publication Dates: 1955–1957.
Scores: Total score only.
Administration: Group.

Price Data: Available from publisher.
Time: (35) minutes.
Author: Einar R. Ryden.
Publisher: Psychometric Affiliates.
Cross References: For reviews by Stanley E. Davis and John D. Krumboltz, see 6:701 (2 references).

[2054]

Pictorial Reasoning Test.

Purpose: Assesses general learning ability independent of language and reading skills.
Population: Entry-level positions in a variety of occupations.
Publication Dates: 1966–1994.
Acronym: PRT.
Scores: Total score only.
Administration: Individual or group.
Price Data: Available from publisher.
Time: 15 minutes.
Comments: Previously listed as SRA Pictorial Reasoning Test.
Authors: Robert N. McMurry and Phyllis D. Arnold (test), and Bruce A. Campbell (manual).
Publisher: Pearson Performance Solutions [No reply from publisher; status unknown].
Cross References: For reviews by Raymond A. Katzell and John E. Milholland, and an excerpted review by John L. Horn, see 7:381.

[2055]

The Pictorial Scale of Perceived Competence and Social Acceptance for Young Children.

Purpose: Measures "perceived competence and perceived social acceptance" in young children.
Population: Preschool through second grade.
Publication Dates: 1980–1983.
Scores, 4: Cognitive Competence, Peer Acceptance, Physical Competence, Maternal Acceptance.
Administration: Individual.
Forms, 2: Preschool/Kindergarten, First/Second Grade.
Price Data: Available from publisher.
Time: Administration time not reported.
Comments: Downward extension of the Perceived Competence Scale for Children.
Authors: Susan Harter and Robin Pike in collaboration with Carole Efron, Christine Chao, and Beth Ann Bierer.
Publisher: Susan Harter, University of Denver.
Cross References: See T5:1987 (23 references) and T4:2022 (6 references); for reviews by William B. Michael and Susan M. Sheridan, see 11:292 (9 references).

[2056]

Pictorial Test of Intelligence, Second Edition.

Purpose: Designed to "identify children who are significantly below their peers in important abilities and to identify children among these who are physically disabled who are more able to think and reason than their traditional communication skills support."
Population: Ages 3–8.
Publication Dates: 1964–2001.
Acronym: PTI-2.
Scores, 4: Verbal Abstractions, Form Discrimination, Quantitative Concepts, Pictorial Intelligence Quotient.
Administration: Individual.
Price Data, 2011: $164 per kit including examiner's manual (2001, 87 pages), picture book, and 25 profile/examiner record booklets; $46 per 25 record booklets; $53 per manual; $70 per picture book.
Time: (15–30) minutes.
Author: Joseph L. French.
Publisher: PRO-ED.
Cross References: For reviews by Michelle Athanasiou and by Dawn P. Flanagan and Leonard F. Caltabiano, see 15:191; see T3:1823 (3 references); for an excerpted review by Thomas A. Smith, see 8:223 (11 references); see also T2:517 (1 reference); for reviews by Philip Himelstein and T. Ernest Newland, see 7:418 (17 references); see also 6:531 (2 references).

[2057]

Picture Identification Test.

Purpose: "Designed to measure judgments, attitudes, sex-of picture differences, organizing principle strength, and need ego relationships associations pertaining to 22 needs based on the Murray need system."
Population: 12 years and older.
Publication Dates: 1959–1979.
Acronym: PIT.
Scores: 4 scores (Judgment Problem, Ego Problem, Organizing Principle, Sex-of-Picture) for each of 22 needs (Abasement, Achievement, Affiliation, Aggression, Autonomy, Blame Avoidance, Counteraction, Deference, Dependence, Dominance, Exhibition, Gratitude, Harm Avoidance, Inferiority Avoidance, Nurturance, Order, Play, Rejection, Sentience, Sex, Succorance, Understanding), plus scores for 3 need dimensions (Combative, Personal-Social, Competitive), 6 Dimension Confusion scores, 3 Dimension Weight scores, 9 Sex-of-Picture Dimension Attitude score, scores for 10 need clusters (Friendliness, Intimacy, Inhibition, Competition, Dominance, Sociability, Independence, Aggression, Performance, Failure Avoidance), 10 Cluster Problem scores, 10 Combative Dimension Cluster Problem scores, 10 Persona-Social Dimension Cluster Problem scores, 10 Competitive Dimension Cluster Problem scores, 20 Combative Dimension Cluster Conflict score, 9 Personal-Social Dimension Cluster Conflict scores, 10 Competitive Dimension Cluster Conflict scores, 13 Averaged Set Problem scores, 1 General Motivation System Function score.
Administration: Group or individual.
Price Data: Available from publisher.

Time: [40] minutes.
Author: Jay L. Chambers.
Publisher: Jay L. Chambers.
Cross References: See T4:2026 (2 references), T3:1825 (3 references), T2:1490 (2 references), and P:463 (17 references).

[2058]

Picture Interest Career Survey.

Purpose: "Provides an easy way for people with limited reading ability or special needs to explore their career interests and find a job that fits."
Population: Ages 10-65.
Publication Date: 2007.
Acronym: PICS.
Scores, 6: Realistic, Investigative, Artistic, Social, Enterprising, Conventional.
Administration: Group.
Price Data, 2008: $42.95 per 25 tests.
Time: (15) minutes.
Author: Robert P. Brady.
Publisher: JIST Publishing, Inc.
Cross References: For reviews by Sheri Bauman and Julia Y. Porter, see 18:94.

[2059]

Piers-Harris Children's Self-Concept Scale, Second Edition.

Purpose: Designed to aid in the "assessment of self-concept in children and adolescents."
Population: Ages 7–18.
Publication Dates: 1969–2002.
Acronym: Piers-Harris 2.
Scores, 7: Behavioral Adjustment, Intellectual and School Status, Physical Appearance and Attributes, Freedom From Anxiety, Popularity, Happiness and Satisfaction, Total.
Administration: Group or individual.
Price Data, 2006: $119 per complete kit including 20 AutoScore™ answer forms, manual (2002, 135 pages); $43.50 per 20 AutoScore™ answer forms; $60.50 per manual; $19.25 per 20 Spanish answer forms; $20.50 per mail-in answer sheet; $291.50 per 25-Use Disk (PC with Windows); $16.50 per 100 PC answer sheets; $11 per fax scoring.
Foreign Language Edition: Spanish answer forms available.
Time: (10–15) minutes.
Authors: Ellen V. Piers (test and manual), David S. Herzberg (test and manual), and Dale B. Harris (test).
Publisher: Western Psychological Services.
Cross References: For reviews by Mary Lou Kelley and Donald P. Oswald, see 16:188; see also T5:1991 (108 references) and T4:2030 (123 references); for reviews by Jayne H. Epstein and Patrick J. Jeske of an earlier edition, see 9:960 (38 references); see also T3:1831 (107

references), 8:646 (95 references); and T2:1326 (10 references); for a review by Peter M. Bentler of an earlier edition, see 7:124 (8 references).

[2060]

A Pill Scale.

Purpose: Designed to measure attitudes toward oral contraception.
Population: Adults.
Publication Dates: 1969–1988.
Scores: Total score only.
Administration: Group.
Manual: No manual.
Price Data, 2005: $2 per scale.
Time: [10] minutes.
Comments: Supplementary article available.
Author: Panos D. Bardis.
Publisher: Donna Bardis.
Cross References: See 8:350 (3 references).

[2061]

PIM 8–12.

Purpose: Designed "to assess the extent to which children have acquired the mathematical skills and concepts covered by each year's curriculum."
Population: Ages 8–12.
Publication Dates: 1983–1985.
Scores, 5: Understanding, Computation, Application, Factual Recall, Total.
Administration: Group.
Levels, 5: Mathematics 8, Mathematics 9, Mathematics 10, Mathematics 11, Mathematics 12.
Price Data: Price information available from publisher for test booklets (specify Mathematics 8, 9, 10, 11, or 12), Teacher's Guide, and specimen set including 1 each of 8–12 test booklets, teacher's guide, and group record sheet.
Time: (60–80) minutes for each level.
Authors: Alan Brighouse, David Godber, and Peter Patilla.
Publisher: GL Assessment [England].

[2062]

PIP Developmental Charts, Second Edition.

Purpose: Assess behaviors to establish several developmental levels.
Population: Mentally handicapped children birth to age 5.
Publication Dates: 1976–1998.
Scores: Profile of 5 areas of development: Physical, Social, Eye-Hand, Development of Play, Language.
Administration: Individual.
Manual: No manual (instructions for administration and scoring included on test).
Price Data, 2002: £12.99 per 10 charts; £3.99 per specimen copy.

Time: Administration time not reported.
Authors: Dorothy M. Jeffree and Ray McConkey.
Publisher: Hodder & Stoughton Educational [England].
Cross References: For reviews by Joan F. Goodman and Robert L. Slonaker, see 9:961.

[2063]

PL-1 and PL-2 Police Administrator Tests (Lieutenant).
Purpose: Developed as knowledge-based tests suitable for the command level and to assist police departments in promoting qualified candidates to a higher rank.
Population: Candidates for promotion to the police administrator position.
Publication Dates: 1998-2006.
Acronym: PL-1, PL-2.
Scores: 4 knowledge areas: Police Procedures: Patrol and Investigation, Laws Related to Police Work, Concepts of Supervision, Concepts of Administration.
Administration: Individual or group.
Forms, 2: PL-1, PL-2.
Price Data: Available from publisher.
Time: 150 minutes per test.
Comments: PL-1 and PL-2 are comparable forms; reading lists are available to help candidates prepare for the tests.
Author: International Public Management Association for Human Resources.
Publisher: International Public Management Association for Human Resources (IPMA-HR).
Cross References: For a review by Russell W. Smith, see 18:95.

[2064]

PLAN.
Purpose: Measures knowledge and skills attained early in secondary education in four curriculum areas: English, mathematics, reading, and science. Serves as a predictor of success on the ACT, an early indicator of college readiness, and a tool to help students explore careers that match their interests.
Population: Grade 10.
Publication Dates: 1989-2005.
Administration: Group.
Price Data: Available from publisher.
Time: 115 minutes for 4 academic tests; (60-70) minutes for student information, Interest Inventory, Study Power Assessment, and High School Course information.
Comments: Formerly called P-ACT+; special testing with extended time and alternate test formats are available for students who receive special accommodations in school due to professionally diagnosed and documented disabilities.
Author: ACT, Inc.
Publisher: ACT, Inc.

a) PLAN ENGLISH TEST.
Purpose: Measures understanding of the conventions of standard written English.
Scores, 7: Usage/Mechanics (Punctuation, Basic Grammar, Sentence Structure), Rhetorical Skills (Strategy, Organization, Style), Total.
Time: 30 minutes.
b) PLAN MATHEMATICS TEST.
Purpose: Measures student's mathematical reasoning skills.
Scores, 5: Algebra (Pre-Algebra, Elementary Algebra), Geometry (Coordinate Geometry, Plane Geometry), Total.
Time: 40 minutes.
c) PLAN READING TEST.
Purpose: Measures reading comprehension as a product of referring and reasoning skills.
Scores: Total score only.
Time: 20 minutes.
d) PLAN SCIENCE TEST.
Purpose: Measures scientific reasoning skills.
Scores: Total score only.
Time: 25 minutes.
Cross References: See T5:1997 (1 reference); for reviews by Martha Blackwell and Mary Henning-Stout, see 12:296.

[2065]

Plane Geometry: National Achievement Tests.
Purpose: To measure students' knowledge of plane geometry.
Population: High school.
Publication Dates: 1958–1960.
Scores: Total score only.
Administration: Group.
Forms, 2: A, B.
Price Data: Available from publisher.
Time: 40(45) minutes.
Authors: Ray Webb and Julius H. Hlavaty.
Publisher: Psychometric Affiliates.
Cross References: For a review by Dorothy L. Jones, see 7:540.

[2066]

Plane Trigonometry: National Achievement Tests.
Purpose: To measure students' knowledge of plane trigonometry.
Population: Grades 10–16.
Publication Dates: 1958–1960.
Scores: Total score only.
Administration: Group.
Forms, 2: A, B.
Price Data: Available from publisher.

Time: 40(45) minutes.
Authors: Ray Webb and Julius H. Hlavaty.
Publisher: Psychometric Affiliates.

[2067]

Planning, Organizing, & Scheduling Test, Revised Edition.

Purpose: Designed to measure an individual's "ability to plan, organize the actions and resources of, and schedule events around an activity."
Population: Adults.
Publication Date: 2004.
Acronym: POST.
Scores: Total score only.
Administration: Individual or group.
Manual: No manual.
Price Data: Available from publisher.
Time: 20(25) minutes.
Authors: Erich P. Prien and Leonard D. Goodstein.
Publisher: HRD Press, Inc.

[2068]

The Play Observation Scale [Revised].

Purpose: To assess the social and cognitive levels of children's play behaviors in natural settings.
Population: Preschool to elementary school children.
Publication Dates: 1989-2001.
Acronym: POS.
Scores: 28 possible ratings: 7 Non-Play (Transition, Unoccupied, Onlooker, Aggression, Rough-and-Tumble, Teacher Conversation, Peer Conversation); 15 Play, 5 cognitive ratings (Functional, Exploratory, Constructive, Dramatic, Games) in each of 3 social areas (Solitary, Parallel, Group); 3 Affective (Positive, Negative, Neutral).
Administration: Individual.
Price Data: Price available from publisher for complete kit including manual (20 pages).
Time: (3) minutes per observation.
Author: Kenneth H. Rubin.
Publisher: Kenneth H. Rubin, Ph.D. (the author).
Cross References: For reviews by Denise M. DeZolt and Mark H. Fugate of an earlier edition, see 13:234.

[2069]

Police Promotional Tests (Custom).

Purpose: "Fully-customized content-valid written promotional assessments to test the duties and responsibilities of police officers."
Population: Police officers.
Publication Dates: 1979–2010.
Scores: 7 subtests: Technical Police Knowledge, Investigative Knowledge, Legal Knowledge, Supervisory and Managerial Knowledge, Administrative Knowledge, Deductive Reasoning in Police Situations, Ability to Read and Comprehend Police Related Tables and Texts.

Administration: Group.
Restricted Distribution: Distribution restricted to civil service commissions and qualified municipal officials.
Price Data: Available from publisher.
Time: (210) minutes.
Comments: Complimentary Candidate Study Guide is available at the publisher's website; two full-length practice examinations are available for purchase, administered online through the company assessment platform: www.measuredsuccessonline.com.
Author: McCann Associates.
Publisher: McCann Associates.

[2070]

Police Selection Test.

Purpose: "Designed to measure abilities important for successful performance in training and on-the-job" as a police officer.
Population: Police officer applicants.
Publication Dates: 1989–2005.
Acronym: PST.
Scores: Total score only.
Administration: Group or individual.
Forms, 3: A, A-1, B-1.
Price Data: Price information available from publisher for test material including Technical manual (1990, 17 pages), Technical Report Addendum: The Development of PST Short Forms A-1 & B-1 (2005, 9 pages), User's Manual (2005, 10 pages), Study Guide and sample questions (1990, 21 pages).
Time: 120(125) minutes for long form; 60(65) minutes for short forms.
Comments: Measures reading comprehension, quantitative problem solving, data interpretation, writing skills, and verbal problem solving.
Author: Psychological Services, Inc.
Publisher: Psychological Services, Inc.
Cross References: For reviews by Jim C. Fortune and Deniz S. Ones, see 14:292.

[2071]

Polish Proficiency Test.

Purpose: "Designed to assess the general proficiency in listening and reading comprehension attained by English-speaking learners of Polish."
Population: Postsecondary to adult.
Publication Date: 1992.
Acronym: PPT.
Scores, 3: Listening Comprehension, Reading Comprehension, Structure.
Administration: Group.
Price Data, 2005: $25 per test; quantity discounts available; $6 per official score report.
Time: 120 (150) minutes.
Comments: Machine-scorable.
Author: Center for Applied Linguistics.

Publisher: Center for Applied Linguistics.
Cross References: For a review by Jack Gebart-Eaglemont, see 16:189.

[2072]
Polyfactorial Study of Personality.
Purpose: Developed "to offer diagnostic profiles approximating those which would be obtained with projective instruments."
Population: Adults.
Publication Dates: 1959-1984.
Acronym: PSP.
Scores, 11: Hypochondriasis, Sexual Identification, Anxiety, Social Distance, Sociopathy, Depression, Compulsivity, Repression, Paranoia, Schizophrenia, Hyperaffectivity.
Administration: Group.
Price Data, 2006: $54.50 per test package; $59 per IBM answer sheet/profile sheet package; $39 per set of IBM scoring stencils; $41.50 per manual (1959, 11 pages) and manuals supplement (1984, 17 pages); $53.50 per specimen set.
Time: (45-50) minutes.
Authors: Ronald H. Stark and Martin M. Bruce.
Publisher: Martin M. Bruce, Ph.D.
Cross References: For reviews by Bertram D. Cohen and Donald R. Peterson and an excerpted review by Edward S. Bordin, see 6:160.

[2073]
Portable Tactual Performance Test.
Purpose: Designed to assess the speed of movement, tactile perception, and problem-solving ability.
Population: Ages 5 to adult.
Publication Date: 1984.
Acronym: P-TPT.
Scores, 3: Dominant Hand, Non-dominant Hand, Both Hands.
Administration: Individual.
Price Data, 2006: $415 per introductory kit including 50 recording forms, 6-hole and 10-hole form boards in case, and manual (8 pages).
Time: (10-15) minutes per trial (three trial limit).
Comments: A portable alternative to the original Tactual Performance Test for use with the Halstead-Reitan Neuropsychological Test Battery (1206).
Author: Psychological Assessment Resources, Inc.
Publisher: Psychological Assessment Resources, Inc.
Cross References: For a review by Calvin P. Garbin, see 11:295.

[2074]
Porteus Mazes.
Purpose: "Designed to examine the individual's ability or ... tendency to use planning capacity, prudence and mental alertness in a new situation of a concrete nature."
Publication Dates: 1914–1965.

Scores, 2: Quantitative, Qualitative.
Administration: Group.
Price Data, 2002: $19 per 100 score sheets; $56 per manual (1965, 324 pages).
Comments: Formerly called The Porteus Maze Test.
Author: S. D. Porteus.
Publisher: Pearson.
  a) VINELAND REVISION.
  Population: Ages 3–12, 14, adult.
  Price Data: $225 per basic set including mazes and 100 score sheets.
  Time: Administration time not recorded.
  b) PORTEUS MAZE EXTENSION.
  Population: Ages 7–12, 14, adult.
  Price Data: $165 per basic set including mazes and 100 score sheets.
  Time: [25] minutes.
  Comments: For use only as a practice-free retest of *a*.
  c) PORTEUS MAZE SUPPLEMENT.
  Population: Ages 7–12, 14, adult.
  Price Data: $155 per basic set including 100 each of 8 mazes.
  Time: [25] minutes.
  Comments: For use only as a third retest after *a* and *b*.
Cross References: See T5:2010 (24 references), T4:2051 (25 references), 9:965 (19 references), T3:1853 (34 references), 8:224 (25 references), and T2:518 (52 references); for reviews by Richard F. Docter and John L. Horn, and excerpted reviews by William D. Altus, H. B. Gibson, D. C. Kendrick, and Laurance F. Shaffer, see 7:419 (67 references); see also 6:532 (38 references) and 5:412 (28 references); for reviews by C. M. Louttit and Gladys C. Schwesinger, see 4:356 (56 references).

[2075]
Portland Digit Recognition Test [Revised].
Purpose: "Designed for neuropsychological assessment of exaggeration and malingering."
Population: Adults.
Publication Dates: 1989-2001.
Acronym: PDRT.
Scores, 3: Easy Items, Hard Items, Total.
Administration: Individual.
Price Data, 2006: $149 per complete kit.
Time: (40) minutes.
Author: Laurence M. Binder.
Publisher: Laurence M. Binder, Ph.D. (the author).
Cross References: For reviews by Charles J. Long and Stephanie Western and by Orest E. Wasyliw of an earlier version, see 12:297 (1 reference); see also T4:2052 (1 reference).

[2076]
Portland Problem Behavior Checklist–Revised.
Purpose: "Developed to aid school and mental health personnel to identify problem behaviors, make classification

or diagnostic decisions, and evaluate counseling, intervention, or behavior consultation procedures."
Population: Grades K–12.
Publication Dates: 1980–1992.
Acronym: PPBC-R.
Administration: Individual.
Price Data, 2001: $45 per complete kit; $20 per 25 male or female forms.
Time: Untimed.
Comments: Respondents are professionals working with children; scoring form also includes opportunity to report on "other" problems (those not specifically included as a subscale).
Author: Steven A. Waksman.
Publisher: Enrichment Press.

a) FORM FOR FEMALES, GRADES K–6.
Scores, 4: Conduct Problems, Peer Problems, Personal Problems, Total.
b) FORM FOR FEMALES, GRADES 7–12.
Scores, 5: Academic Problems, Personal Problems, Conduct Problems, Anxiety Problems, Total.
c) FORM FOR MALES, GRADES K–6.
Scores, 5: Conduct Problems, Academic Problems, Anxiety Problems, Peer Problems, Total.
d) FORM FOR MALES, GRADES 7–12.
Scores, 6: Academic Problems, Anxiety Problems, Peer Problems, Conduct Problems, Personal Problems, Total.
Cross References: For reviews by Thomas McKnight and Robert Spies, see 14:293; for reviews by Terry A. Stinnett and John G. Svinicki of an earlier edition, see 10:287 (1 reference).

[2077]

Portrait of Overdone Strengths.

Purpose: Designed to demonstrate how one may "overdo or misapply" personal strengths, thereby contributing to unwarranted conflict in relationships.
Population: Adults.
Publication Dates: 1973–1996.
Scores, 3: Profile, Most Overdone Strengths, Least Overdone Strengths.
Administration: Group or individual.
Price Data, 2001: $5.50 per test booklet; $100 per facilitation guide.
Time: (20–40) minutes.
Comments: To be used with the Strength Deployment Inventory (2565); self-report using Q Sort; Feedback Edition of the Portrait of Overdone Strengths uses self-ratings and ratings from a significant other person.
Author: Personal Strengths Publishing.
Publisher: Personal Strengths Publishing.

[2078]

Portrait of Personal Strengths.

Purpose: "Designed to help you see how you use your strengths when things are going well in your relationships."

Population: Adults.
Publication Dates: 1973–1996.
Scores, 3: Profile, Top Strengths (6), Least Deployed Strengths (6).
Administration: Group or individual.
Price Data, 2001: $5.50 per test booklet; $100 per facilitation guide.
Time: (20–40) minutes.
Comments: To be used with the Strength Deployment Inventory (2565); self-report by Q Sort; Feedback Edition of the Portrait of Personal Strengths uses self-rating and ratings from a significant other person.
Author: Personal Strengths Publishing.
Publisher: Personal Strengths Publishing.

[2079]

Position Analysis Questionnaire.

Purpose: Constructed to analyze "jobs in terms of work activities and work-situation variables."
Population: Business and industrial jobs.
Publication Dates: 1969–1989.
Acronym: PAQ.
Scores: 45 dimensions in 7 divisions: Information Input, Mental Processes, Work Output, Relationships with Other Persons, Job Context, Other Job Characteristics, Overall Dimensions.
Administration: Individual.
Price Data: Available from publisher.
Time: Administration time not reported.
Comments: Ratings by 2 or more analysts; also provides estimates of selected employment tests useful for personnel selection and job evaluation points.
Authors: Ernest J. McCormick, Robert C. Mecham, and P. R. Jeanneret.
Publisher: PAQ Services, Inc.
Cross References: See T5:2016 (2 references); for reviews by Ronald A. Ash and George C. Thornton III, see 12:299 (2 references); see also T4:2054 (17 references) and T3:1855 (12 references); for a review by Alan R. Bass, see 8:983 (17 references).

[2080]

Position Classification Inventory.

Purpose: Designed "as an inventory for classifying positions and occupations" to assess the demands, rewards, and opportunities of work environments.
Population: Adults.
Publication Date: 1991.
Acronym: PCI.
Scores, 6: Realistic, Investigative, Artistic, Social, Enterprising, Conventional.
Administration: Individual or group.
Price Data, 2007: $90 per introductory kit including manual, 25 reusable item booklets, and 25 answer sheets/profile forms; $27 per manual; $35 per 25 reusable item booklets; $34 per 25 answer sheets/profile forms.

Time: (10) minutes.
Authors: Gary D. Gottfredson and John L. Holland.
Publisher: Psychological Assessment Resources, Inc.
Cross References: For a review by Keith Hattrup, see 17:150.

[2081]

Positive and Negative Syndrome Scale.

Purpose: "Designed to assist in the assessment of schizophrenia."
Population: Psychiatric patients.
Publication Dates: 1986–2006.
Acronym: PANSS.
Scores: Standard Model: Positive, Negative, Composite Index, General Psychopathology, Anergia, Thought Disturbances, Activation, Paranoid/Belligerence, Depression, Supplemental; Pentagonal Model: Positive, Negative, Activation, Dysphoric Mood, Autistic Preoccupation.
Administration: Individual.
Price Data, 2011: $252 per complete kit including manual (2006, 76 pages), 25 QuikScore™ forms, 25 Structured Clinical Interview forms, and 25 Informant Questionnaire forms; $58 per manual; $50 per 25 QuikScore™ forms; $96 per 25 SCI-PANSS Structured Clinical Interview forms; $87 per 25 IQ-PANSS Informant Questionnaire forms.
Time: (30-40) minutes.
Comments: Completed by clinician.
Authors: Stanley R. Kay, Lewis A. Opler, and Abraham Fiszbein.
Publisher: Multi-Health Systems, Inc.
Cross References: See T5:2017 (17 references); for reviews by Barbara J. Kaplan and Cecil R. Reynolds, see 12:300 (15 references); see also T4:2055 (1 reference).

[2082]

Post-Assault Traumatic Brain Injury Interview and Checklist.

Purpose: "Designed to assist in treatment planning for neuropsychological and neurological evaluation, treatment, and rehabilitation."
Population: Assault victims.
Publication Date: 1997.
Acronym: P-TBI-IC.
Scores: 13 symptom areas: Hallmarks of Brain Injury Alertness, Prosody, Memory, Sensorimotor Functions, Speech, Academic Abilities, Cognitive Problem Solving, Organic Depression, Organic Anxiety, Organic Impulsivity, Laterality, Treatment Problems.
Administration: Group or individual.
Price Data, 2002: $75 per complete kit including manual (11 pages), and 10 test booklets; $50 per 10 test booklets; $30 per manual; student, volume, and research discounts available.
Time: Administration time not reported.

Comments: Ratings by health care professionals, shelter personnel, sexual assault center personnel, and from data obtained from client, significant others, and other health care professionals.
Authors: Martha E. Banks and Rosalie J. Ackerman.
Publisher: ABackans DCP, Inc.
Cross References: For reviews by James C. Reed and by Wilfred G. Van Gorp and Colleen A. Ewing, see 15:192.

[2083]

Postpartum Depression Screening Scale.

Purpose: Designed to assess the presence, severity, and type of postpartum depression symptoms.
Population: New mothers ages 14–49.
Publication Date: 2002.
Acronym: PDSS.
Scores, 10: Inconsistent Responding Index, Sleeping/Eating Disturbances, Anxiety/Insecurity, Emotional Lability, Mental Confusion, Loss of Self, Guilt/Shame, Suicidal Thoughts, Short Total Score, Total Score.
Administration: Group.
Price Data, 2005: $72.50 per kit including manual (59 pages) and 25 AutoScore™ test forms; $32.50 per 25 AutoScore™ test forms; $45 per manual; $17.50 per 10 test forms in Spanish.
Time: (5–10) minutes; (1–2) minutes for short form.
Comments: May be orally administered; allows for detection of women in need of psychiatric evaluation; short form consists of just 7 items and yields a short total score.
Authors: Cheryl Tatano Beck and Robert K. Gable.
Publisher: Western Psychological Services.
Cross References: For reviews by Paul A. Arbisi and Delores D. Walcott, see 16:190.

[2084]

Posttraumatic Stress Diagnostic Scale.

Purpose: Designed to identify the presence and symptom severity of posttraumatic stress disorder.
Population: Ages 18-65.
Publication Date: 1995.
Acronym: PDS.
Scores, 5: Symptom Severity Score, Number of Symptoms Endorsed, Symptom Severity Rating, Level of Impairment in Functioning, PTSD Diagnosis.
Administration: Group.
Price Data, 2008: $52 per Q Local starter kit; $62 per hand-scoring starter kit; $37 per manual/user's guide (54 pages); $17 per 5 reusable test booklets; $22 per 25 Q Local answer sheets; $146 per 50 hand-scoring answer sheets with 50 scoring worksheets; $6.25 per Q Local profile report.
Time: (10–15) minutes.
Author: Edna B. Foa.
Publisher: Pearson.

Cross References: For reviews by Stephen N. Axford and Beth Doll, see 14:294; see also T5:2018 (1 reference).

[2085]

Posture and Fine Motor Assessment of Infants.

Purpose: Designed to identify motor delays in infants and to monitor progress in the first year of life.
Population: Ages 2–12 months.
Publication Date: 2000.
Acronym: PFMAI.
Scores, 2: Posture, Fine Motor.
Administration: Individual.
Levels, 2: PFMAI-I (2–6 months), PFMAI-II (6–12) months.
Price Data, 2001: $55 per manual (99 pages).
Time: (25–30) minutes.
Authors: Jane Case-Smith and Rosemarie Bigsby.
Publisher: Pearson.
Cross References: For reviews by Linda K. Bunker, B. Ann Boyce, and Gregory Hanson, and by John J. Venn, see 16:191.

[2086]

Power and Performance Measures.

Purpose: Battery of nine aptitude and ability tests designed to measure both potential and achievement in a wide range of occupational settings.
Population: Ages 16 and over.
Publication Dates: 1990–1996.
Acronym: PPM.
Scores: Verbal Reasoning, Verbal Comprehension, Perceptual Reasoning, Spatial Ability, Numerical Reasoning, Numerical Computation, Mechanical Understanding, Clerical Speed and Accuracy, Applied Logic.
Administration: Group or individual.
Price Data, 2001: £55 per technical handbook (1996, 54 pages); £6.50 per question booklet; £2.75 per answer sheet; £133 per specimen set.
Time: (3–12) minutes.
Author: James S. Barrett.
Publisher: The Test Agency Ltd. [England] [No reply from publisher; status unknown].
Cross References: For a review by Kurt F. Geisinger, see 16:192.

[2087]

Power Base Inventory.

Purpose: Assesses the techniques individuals use to influence others.
Population: Work team members, leaders, managers, supervisors.
Publication Dates: 1985–1999.
Acronym: PBI.
Scores, 6: Information, Expertise, Goodwill, Authority, Reward, Discipline.
Administration: Group or individual.
Price Data, 2011: $14.95 per inventory.
Time: (15) minutes.
Comments: Self-scored.
Authors: Kenneth W. Thomas and Gail Fann Thomas.
Publisher: CPP, Inc.
Cross References: For a review by Judy L. Elliott, see 13:235.

[2088]

Power Management Inventory.

Purpose: "Designed to assess a manager's characteristic management of influence dynamics; that is, how a given manager prefers to handle situations calling for the exercise of power and authority."
Population: Managers.
Publication Dates: 1981–2000.
Acronym: PMI.
Scores, 4: Power Motive (Personalized, Socialized, Affiliative), Power Style.
Administration: Group.
Manual: No manual.
Price Data, 2001: $8.95 per instrument.
Time: Administration time not reported.
Comments: Self-administered survey; companion to Power Management Profile (2089).
Authors: Jay Hall and James Hawker.
Publisher: Teleometrics International, Inc.
Cross References: For reviews by Philip G. Benson and William A. Owens, see 9:967.

[2089]

Power Management Profile.

Purpose: Assesses "the methods and reasons which most characterize your manager's handling of power situations."
Population: Managers.
Publication Dates: 1981–1995.
Acronym: PMP.
Scores, 5: Power Motive (Personalized, Socialized, Affiliative), Power Style, Moral.
Administration: Group.
Manual: No manual.
Price Data, 2001: $8.95 per instrument.
Time: Administration time not reported.
Comments: Self-administered survey; companion to Power Management Inventory (2088).
Authors: Jay Hall and James Hawker.
Publisher: Teleometrics International, Inc.
Cross References: For a review by Rhonda L. Gutenberg, see 9:968.

[2090]

The Power of Influence Test.

Purpose: Designed as an instrument that "records the attitudes of pupils toward each other and tells which pupils have friendship capacity."

Population: Grade 5 and over.
Publication Date: No date.
Scores: Total score only.
Administration: Group.
Price Data: Available from publisher.
Time: (5) minutes.
Comments: Also referred to as The Sociometric Test.
Authors: Roy Cochrane and Wesley Roeder.
Publisher: Psychometric Affiliates.
Cross References: For reviews by Salvador Hector Ochoa and Jeffrey K. Smith, see 15:193.

[2091]

Power Reading Assessment Kit.

Purpose: Created to "determine a student's reading level and best entry level into the Power Reading Program."
Population: Students.
Publication Date: 2005.
Scores, 3: Reading Accuracy, Comprehension, Fluency.
Administration: Individual.
Levels, 24: Reading levels from Primer (.3) to 10th grade (10.8).
Price Data, 2006: $129.95 per Reading Assessment Kit including teacher's guide (191 pages), 24 leveled, recorded Power Reading stories on 24 audiotapes or CDs with line-by-line word counts for fluency assessment, story cards for comprehension assessment, examiner worksheets, record-keeping charts, graphs, and timer.
Time: (5-10) minutes.
Author: Marie Carbo.
Publisher: National Reading Styles Institute, Inc.

[2092]

Practical Adolescent Dual Diagnostic Interview.

Purpose: "To elicit information relevant to the identification and diagnosis of mental health and substance use disorders in adolescents."
Population: Ages 12–18.
Publication Dates: 2000-2001.
Acronym: PADDI.
Scores, 17: Major Depressive Episode, Manic Episode, Mixed Episode, Psychotic Symptoms, Panic Attacks, Anxiety and Phobias, Posttraumatic Stress Disorder, Obsessions/Compulsions, Conduct Disorder, Oppositional Defiant Disorder, Personality Disorders, Paranoid Personality Traits, Dependent Personality Traits, Sexual Orientation, Substance Abused Disorders, Dangerousness to Self or Others, Child Abuse—Victimization.
Administration: Individual.
Price Data: Available from publisher.
Time: (20–40) minutes.
Comments: A structured diagnostic interview compatible with the DSM-IV diagnostic criteria; can be administered by paraprofessionals as a screening device.

Authors: Todd W. Estroff and Norman G. Hoffmann.
Publisher: Change Companies.
Cross References: For reviews by C. G. Bellah and Michael G. Kavan, see 16:193.

[2093]

Pragmatic Language Skills Inventory.

Purpose: Designed to help identify children "who have pragmatic language disabilities."
Population: Ages 5-12.
Publication Date: 2006.
Acronym: PLSI.
Scores: 3 subscales: Classroom Interaction, Social Interaction, Personal Interaction; Pragmatic Language Index.
Administration: Individual
Price Data, 2011: $110 per complete kit including examiner's manual (59 pages) and 25 summary/response forms; $64 per manual; $53 per 25 summary/response forms.
Time: (5-10) minutes.
Comments: Appropriate raters include teachers, parents, teacher assistants, or other qualified persons who work closely with the child and are well acquainted with the child's language characteristics.
Authors: James E. Gilliam and Lynda Miller.
Publisher: PRO-ED.
Cross References: For reviews by Thomas W. Guyette and Donna J. Kelly and by Aimee Langlois, see 17:151.

[2094]

The Praxis Series: Professional Assessments for Beginning Teachers.

Purpose: Includes tests that correspond to two key milestones in the development as a teacher entering a teacher training program and obtaining a license to teach.
Population: Beginning teachers.
Publication Dates: 1993–1998.
Administration: Group.
Restricted Distribution: Secure instruments administered at centers established by the publisher.
Comments: Tests administered 7 times annually; earlier versions previously available as NTE Programs (1940–1992).
Author: Educational Testing Service.
Publisher: Educational Testing Service.
  a) PRAXIS I: ACADEMIC SKILLS ASSESSMENTS.
  Purpose: Designed to be taken early in a student's college career to measure reading, writing and mathematical skills.
  Price Data, 2006: PPST tests: $35 per test; CPPST tests: $75 for one test, $110 for two tests, $145 for three tests; $125 for CPPST combined test.
  Time: PPST tests: 60 minutes per test; PI-CBT tests: 120 minutes per test.

Comments: Includes the paper-based Pre-Professional Skills Test (PPST®) and the Praxis I Computer-Based Tests (PI-CPPST) in Reading, Writing, and Mathematics.
b) PRAXIS II: SUBJECT ASSESSMENTS.
Purpose: Measures a student's content knowledge of subjects he or she will teach.
Price Data: $60 each per 1-hour Multiple-Choice tests; $75 each per 1-hour Constructed-Response tests; $75 each per 2-hour Multiple-Choice tests; $190 each per 2-hour Constructed-Response tests; $85 each per 2-hour Multiple-Choice and Constructed-Response tests; $115 each per Principals of Learning and Teaching test.
Comments: Includes: Subject Assessments/Specialty Area test, 1-hour Multiple-Choice tests, 1-hour Constructed-Response tests, 2-hour Multiple-Choice tests, 2-hour Constructed-Response tests, and Principals of Learning and Teaching (PLT) test.
c) PRAXIS III: CLASSROOM PERFORMANCE ASSESSMENT.
Comments: Developed to assess teachers' classroom performance for licensure needs of some states. To determine whether required in a particular state, contact that state's department of education.
Cross References: For information on earlier editions of the NTE Core Battery, see T4:1824 (5 references), T3:1624 (1 reference), and 8:382 (2 references). For information on earlier editions of the Pre-Professional Skills Test, see T4:2071 (6 references); for reviews by Don B. Oppenheim and Edys S. Quellmalz of an earlier edition, see 9:975.

[2095]

Predictive Ability Test, Adult Edition.

Purpose: Measures "the ability to predict" as the basis for determining intelligence.
Population: Ages 17 and over.
Publication Date: 1974.
Acronym: PAT.
Scores: Overall performance score.
Administration: Group.
Price Data: Available from publisher.
Time: [30-40] minutes.
Author: Myles I. Friedman.
Publisher: Myles I. Friedman.
Cross References: For a review by Arthur R. Jensen, see 9:971.

[2096]

Pre-Kindergarten Screen.

Purpose: Designed "to be a quick screening instrument for children between the ages of 4 years 0 months and 5 years 11 months who may be at risk for early academic difficulty."
Population: Ages 4 through 6.

Publication Date: 2000.
Acronym: PKS.
Scores, 10: Gross Motor Skills, Fine Motor Skills, Following Directions, Block Tapping, Visual Matching, Visual Memory, Imitation, Basic Academic Skills, Delayed Gratification, Total.
Administration: Individual.
Price Data, 2006: $65 per test kit including manual (56 pages), 50 record forms, and test plates; $25 per 50 record forms; $18 per test plates; $22 per manual.
Time: [15] minutes.
Authors: Raymond E. Webster and Angela Matthews.
Publisher: Academic Therapy Publications.
Cross References: For reviews by Mary M. Chittooran and Mary Lou Kelley, see 15:194.

[2097]

PreLAS® 2000.

Purpose: Designed to "assess oral language proficiency and preliteracy skills in young children"; the PreLAS2000 "assesses receptive language and expressive language, which requires all the processing capacities of comprehension plus cognitive organization and the performance of appropriate motor behavior to make the requisite speech sounds"; helps measure the language development of first- and second-language students in both English and Spanish.
Population: Ages 4-6.
Publication Date: 1998.
Scores, 12: Oral Language Component (Simon Says, Art Show, Say What You Hear, Human Body, Story #1, Story #2); Pre-Literacy Component (Letters, Numbers, Colors, Shapes, Reading, Writing).
Administration: Individual.
Parts, 2: Oral Language Component, Pre-Literacy Component.
Price Data, 2006: $216 per examiner's kit including manual (79 pages); $34 per technical report.
Time: (15-25) minutes.
Authors: Sharon E. Duncan and Edward A. De Avila.
Publisher: CTB/McGraw-Hill.
Cross References: For reviews by Sheila Pratt and Annita Marie Ward, see 15:195.

[2098]

Preliminary SAT/National Merit Scholarship Qualifying Test.

Purpose: "Measures reasoning, math problem-solving, and writing skills generally associated with academic achievement in college—for guidance in grades 10-11 and entry to scholarship programs in grade 11."
Population: Grades 10-11.
Publication Dates: 1959-1998.
Acronym: PSAT/NMSQT.
Scores, 4: Verbal, Mathematical, Writing Skills, Section Index (for scholarship consideration by NMSC).

Administration: Group.

Price Data: Available from publisher.

Special Editions: Braille, cassette, script, and large-type editions available.

Time: [140] minutes.

Comments: A shortened version of SAT I; administered in October at participating secondary schools; testing accommodations available for students with disabilities.

Authors: Administered for the College Board and National Merit Scholarship Corporation by Educational Testing Service.

Publisher: Educational Testing Service.

Cross References: See T5:2031 (11 references), T4:2067 (6 references), and T3:1866 (7 references); for reviews by Jerome E. Doppelt and J. Thomas Hastings, see 8:199 (15 references); see also T2:436 (4 references) and 7:375 (10 references); for a review by Wayne S. Zimmerman of earlier forms, see 6:487 (2 references).

[2099]

Preliminary Test of English as a Foreign Language.

Purpose: Designed to evaluate the English language skills of nonnative speakers of English at the beginning levels of study.

Population: College and other institutional applicants, grade 11 and over, from non-English-language countries.

Publication Dates: 1983–1989.

Acronym: Pre-TOEFL®.

Scores, 4: 3 section scores for Listening Comprehension, Structure and Written Expression, Reading Comprehension and Vocabulary, and a Total score.

Administration: Group.

Price Data: Price information available from publisher for examination fee per institution per administration; fee includes machine scoring by publisher, test results, and use of booklets and administrative materials which must be returned to publisher.

Time: 70 minutes.

Comments: A shorter test measuring the same components of language proficiency as the regular TOEFL; 2 forms per year; Pre-TOEFL is offered only through the TOEFL Institutional Testing Program.

Authors: Jointly sponsored by College Entrance Examination Board, Graduate Record Examination Board, and Educational Testing Service.

Publisher: Educational Testing Service.

Cross References: For reviews by Roger A. Richards and Charlene Rivera, see 11:298. For reviews by Brenda H. Loyd and Kikumi K. Tatsuoka of the Test of English as a Foreign Language, see 9:1257 (1 reference); see also T3:2441 (9 references), 8:110 (15 references), and T2:238 (4 references); for reviews by Clinton I. Chase and George Domino of the TOEFL, see 7:266 (10 references).

[2100]

Pre-Literacy Skills Screening.

Purpose: Provides a quick look at the reading readiness skills of children beginning school.

Population: Kindergarten.

Publication Date: 1999.

Acronym: PLSS.

Scores, 11: Rhyme, Sentence Repetition, Naming Accuracy, Naming Time, Blending, Sentence Segmentation, Letter Naming, Syllable Segmentation, Deletion, Multisyllabic Word Repetition, Overall Score.

Administration: Individual.

Price Data, 2011: $60 per complete kit including 25 record forms, and examiner's manual (30 pages); $24 per 25 record forms; $39 per examiner's manual.

Time: (15) minutes.

Authors: Linda Crumrine and Helen Lonegan.

Publisher: PRO-ED

Cross References: For reviews by Carol E. Kessler and Koressa Kutsick Malcolm, see 15:196.

[2101]

A Premarital Communication Inventory.

Purpose: "To help counselors assess the marriageability of a couple."

Population: Premarital couples.

Publication Dates: 1968-1982.

Acronym: PCI.

Scores: Total score only.

Administration: Group.

Price Data, 1993: $.75 per inventory; $2.50 per manual (1982, 6 pages).

Time: (20) minutes.

Author: Millard J. Bienvenu.

Publisher: Millard J. Bienvenu, Northwest Publications.

Cross References: For a review by James R. Clopton, see 8:351.

[2102]

PREPARE/ENRICH.

Purpose: Designed as a series of tests for use in assessing couples' relationships.

Population: Premarital and married couples.

Scores: 17 scores common to all four tests: Idealistic Distortion, Personality Issues, Communication, Conflict Resolution, Financial Management, Leisure Activities, Sexual Expectations, Role Relationship, Spiritual Beliefs, Couple Closeness, Couple Flexibility, Family Closeness, Family Flexibility, Self-Confidence, Assertiveness, Avoidance, Partner Dominance.

Administration: Individual or group.

Price Data, 2006: $150 per training in day workshop, which includes Counselor's Manual and 5 couple inventories including PREPARE, PREPARE-MC (Marriage with Children), PREPARE-CC (Cohabiting

Couples), ENRICH, and MATE; $195 per self-training option for professional counselors including the above materials and the day workshop on a 3 DVD set.; online version available.

Time: (30–45) minutes.

Comments: Counselor Computer Report (15 pages) and Building Strong Marriage Booklet for Couple (25 pages) with six couple exercises are available; additional information is available at www.prepare-enrich.com.

Publisher: Life Innovations, Inc.

a) PREMARITAL PERSONAL AND RELATION-SHIP EVALUATION.

Purpose: Designed to help couples getting ready for marriage (who do not have children) assess their relationship.

Population: Couples planning to marry who do not have children.

Publication Dates: 1978–1998.

Acronym: PREPARE.

Scores, 20: 17 scores common to all 5 tests plus Marital Expectations, Children and Parenting, Family and Friends.

Authors: David H. Olson, David G. Fournier, and Joan M. Druckman.

b) PREMARITAL PERSONAL AND RELATION-SHIP EVALUATION–MARRIED WITH CHILDREN.

Purpose: Designed to help couples who are planning to marry (and who already have children) assess their relationship and identify important issues.

Population: Couples planning to marry who have children.

Publication Dates: 1981–1998.

Acronym: PREPARE-MC.

Scores, 20: Same as *a* above.

Authors: David H. Olson, David G. Fournier, and Joan M. Druckman.

c) ENRICHING RELATIONSHIP ISSUES, COMMUNICATION AND HAPPINESS.

Purpose: Designed to assess relationship strengths and areas for growth.

Population: Married couples or couples who have cohabitated for 2 or more years.

Publication Dates: 1981–1998.

Acronym: ENRICH.

Scores, 19: 17 scores common to all 5 tests plus: Marital Satisfaction, Children and Parenting.

Authors: David H. Olson, David G. Fournier, and Joan M. Druckman.

d) MATURE AGE TRANSITION EVALUATION.

Purpose: Designed to help mature couples who are preparing for marriage assess their relationships.

Population: Couples over 50 planning marriage.

Publication Dates: 1995–1998.

Acronym: MATE.

Scores, 20: 17 scores common to all 5 tests plus: Life Transitions, Intergenerational Issues, Health Issues.

Authors: David H. Olson and Elinor Adams.

e) PREPARE FOR COHABITING COUPLES.

Purpose: Designed to help couples who are living together and are planning to marry.

Acronym: PREPARE CC.

Cross References: For reviews by Corine Fitzpatrick and Jay A. Mancini, see 14:295; see also T5:2034 (7 references).

[2103]

Pre-Reading Inventory of Phonological Awareness.

Purpose: "Designed to assess phonological awareness in young students."

Population: Ages 4.0–6.11.

Publication Dates: 2000–2003.

Acronym: PIPA.

Scores, 6: Rhyme Awareness, Syllable Segmentation, Alliteration Awareness, Sound Isolation, Sound Segmentation, Letter–Sound Knowledge.

Administration: Individual.

Price Data, 2007: $160 per complete kit including manual (2003, 82 pages), stimulus book, and 25 record forms; $49 per 25 record forms; $120 per stimulus book; $89 per manual.

Time: (25–30) minutes.

Authors: Barbara Dodd, Sharon Crosbie, Beth McIntosh, Tania Teitzel, and Anne Ozanne.

Publisher: Pearson.

Cross References: For reviews by David P. Hurford and Maura Jones Moyle, see 17:152.

[2104]

Pre-Referral Intervention Manual-Third Edition.

Purpose: To provide appropriate intervention strategies for learning and behavior problems.

Population: Grades K-12.

Publication Dates: 1988-2006.

Acronym: PRIM-3.

Scores: Not scored.

Administration: Individual.

Price Data, 2006: $105 per complete kit including manual (2006, 570 pages), 50 checklist forms, and 50 intervention strategies documentation forms; $40 per manual; $35 per 50 learning and behavior problem checklists; $30 per 50 intervention strategies documentation forms; $225 per Pre-Referral Intervention Manual (WIN).

Time: Administration time not reported.

Comments: Intervention strategies in 13 areas: Memory/Abstractions/Generalizations/Organizations, Listening, Speaking, Reading, Writing, Spelling, Mathematical Calculations, Academic Performance, Interpersonal Relationships, Depression and Motivation, Inappropriate Behavior Under Normal Circumstances, Rules and Regulations, Group Behavior.

Authors: Stephen B. McCarney and Kathy Cummins Wunderlich.
Publisher: Hawthorne Educational Services, Inc.
Cross References: For a review by Rosemary Flanagan, see 17:153; for reviews by Anthony W. Paolitto and Gabriele van Lingen of an earlier form, see 13:236.

[2105]

Preschool and Kindergarten Behavior Scales, Second Edition.

Purpose: "Designed for use in evaluating social skills and problem behaviors of preschool and kindergarten-age children."
Population: Ages 3–6.
Publication Dates: 1994–2002.
Acronym: PKBS-2.
Scores, 12: Social Skills (Social Cooperation, Social Interaction, Social Independence, Total), Problem Behavior (Externalizing Problems, Internalizing Problems, Total), Supplemental Problem Behavior Subscales (Self-Control/Explosive, Attention Problems/Overactive, Antisocial/Aggressive, Social Withdrawal, Anxiety/Somatic Problems).
Administration: Individual.
Price Data, 2011: $127 per complete kit including examiner's manual (2002, 103 pages) and 50 profile/record forms (specify English or Spanish); $82 per examiner's manual; $47 per 50 record forms (specify English or Spanish).
Foreign Language Edition: Spanish version available.
Time: (8–12) minutes.
Comments: Ratings by home-based raters or school-based raters; Supplemental Problem Behavior Subscales can be used to identify more specific symptoms of emotional and behavioral problems.
Author: Kenneth W. Merrell.
Publisher: PRO-ED.
Cross References: For reviews by Doreen Ward Fairbank and Ronald A. Madle, see 16:194; see also T5:2036 (1 reference); for reviews by David MacPhee and T. Steuart Watson of an earlier edition, see 13:237.

[2106]

Preschool and Kindergarten Interest Descriptor.

Purpose: "Identify children with attitudes and interests usually associated with preschool and kindergarten creativity."
Population: Ages 3-6.
Publication Date: 1983.
Acronym: PRIDE.
Scores: 4 dimension scores: Originality, Imagination-Playfulness, Independence-Perseverance, Many Interests.
Administration: Group.
Price Data, 2005: $120 per complete set including manual (10 pages) and 30 scales; $15 per specimen set.
Time: (20-35) minutes.
Comments: Downward extension of the Group Inventory for Finding Creative Talent (1189); scale for rating by parents.
Author: Sylvia B. Rimm.
Publisher: Educational Assessment Service, Inc.
Cross References: For reviews by Gloria A. Galvin and Sue White, see 10:289.

[2107]

Preschool and Primary Inventory of Phonological Awareness.

Purpose: "Designed to identify children who have poor phonological awareness" and are at risk for literacy problems.
Population: Ages 3 years to 6 years, 11 months.
Publication Date: 2000.
Acronym: PIPA.
Scores: 6 subtests: Syllable Segmentation, Rhyme Awareness, Alliteration Awareness, Phoneme Isolation, Phoneme Segmentation, Letter Knowledge.
Administration: Individual.
Price Data, 2006: £92 per complete kit including record forms, stimulus manual, and manual (54 pages).
Time: (25–30) minutes; (5) minutes per subtest.
Authors: Barbara Dodd, Sharon Crosbie, Beth McIntosh, Tania Teitzel, and Anne Ozanne.
Publisher: Pearson Assessment [England].
Cross References: For reviews by Carlos Inchaurralde and Gene Schwarting, see 16:195.

[2108]

Pre-School Behavior Checklist.

Purpose: "To help identify children with emotional and behavioral problems by providing a tool for the systematic and objective description of behavior."
Population: Ages 2 through 5.
Publication Date: 1988.
Acronym: PBCL.
Scores: Total score only.
Administration: Group.
Price Data, 2006: ATP prices: $67 per test kit including 25 recording forms, scoring acetate, 50 Developmental Activities Checklist forms, and manual; $20 per 25 recording forms; $10 per scoring acetate; $15 per 50 Developmental Activities Checklist forms; $22 per manual; $22 per specimen set including manual and sample forms; NFER-Nelson prices: Available from publisher.
Time: (8–10) minutes.
Comments: Behavior checklist.
Authors: Jacqueline McGuire and Naomi Richman.
Publisher: GL Assessment [England]; licensed to Academic Therapy Publications.
Cross References: See T5:2038 (5 references); for reviews by Roger D. Carlson and Gary Stoner, see 11:299.

[2109]
The Preschool Behavior Questionnaire.
Purpose: Designed as a screening tool to identify emotional/behavioral problems in children.
Population: Ages 3-6.
Publication Date: 1974.
Acronym: PBQ.
Scores, 4: Hostile-Aggressive, Anxious-Fearful, Hyperactive-Distractible, Total.
Administration: Group.
Price Data, 2011: $30 per 50 questionnaires, 50 scores sheets, and manual (16 pages).
Time: [5-10] minutes.
Comments: Modification of Michael A. Rutter's 1967 unpublished Children's Behavior Questionnaire; available in English and Spanish.
Authors: Lenore Behar and Samuel Stringfield.
Publisher: Lenore Behar.
Cross References: See T5:2039 (24 references) and T4:2077 (15 references); for a review by Robert A. Fox, see 9:978 (6 references).

[2110]
Preschool Child Observation Record, Second Edition.
Purpose: Designed to create a "picture of children's development and abilities."
Population: Ages 2-6 to 6-0 years.
Publication Dates: 1992-2003.
Acronym: COR.
Scores: 7 areas: Initiative, Social Relations, Creative Representation, Movement/Music, Language and Literacy, Mathematics/Science, Total.
Administration: Indivdual or group.
Price Data, 2006: $174.95 per complete kit including 2 Observation Items manuals (2003, 45 pages), user's guide, What's Next? Planning Children's Activities Around Preschool Child Observations Guide, 25 Child Anecdotes booklets, 25 Parent Guide booklets (includes Spanish version), 1 Class Summary form, 25 Child Information and Developmental Summary forms, 50 Parent Report forms (includes Spanish version), Preschool COR poster, High/Scope Preschool Key Experiences poster, 2 complete desk posters, and 2 sets of COR category tabs; $14.95 per 2 Observation Items manuals; $15.95 per user's guide; $16.95 per What's Next? Planning Children's Activities Around Preschool Child Observations Guide; $39.95 per 25 Child Anecdotes booklets; $39.95 per 25 Parent Guide booklets (includes Spanish version); $11.95 per 1 Class Summary form and 25 Child Information and Developmental Summary forms; $16.95 per 50 Parent Report forms (includes Spanish version); $5.95 per Preschool COR poster; $5.95 per High/Scope Preschool Key Experiences poster; $8.95 per 2 complete desk posters.

Foreign Editions: Parent Guide booklets (2003) and Parent Report forms available in Spanish.
Time: Untimed.
Comments: This test is to be completed by teachers and parents/guardians; previous version was entitled High/Scope Child Observation Record for Ages 2 1/2-6.
Authors: High/Scope Educational Research Foundation.
Publisher: High/Scope Educational Research Foundation.
Cross References: For reviews by Jean N. Clark and Leah M. Nellis, see 17:154; for reviews by Glen P. Aylward and Mary Mathai Chittooran of an earlier version, see 14:167.

[2111]
Preschool Development Inventory.
Purpose: A brief screening inventory "designed to help identify children with developmental, behavioral, or health problems."
Population: Ages 3-6.
Publication Dates: 1984-1998.
Acronym: PDI.
Scores: General Development Score, Possible Problems List (24); 4 ratings: Child Description, Special Problems or Handicaps, Parent's Questions/Concerns, Parent's Functioning.
Administration: Individual.
Price Data, 2005: $12.50 per manual (1998, 25 pages); $12.50 per 25 parent questionnaires.
Time: (15) minutes.
Comments: Parent-completed questionnaire; replaces the Minnesota Preschool Inventory (aka Minnesota PreKindergarten Inventory) (9:720) and the Preschool Developmental Inventory (10:291) and publisher now recommends using Child Development Review Parent Questionnaire (476) over this.
Author: Harold Ireton.
Publisher: Child Development Review - Behavior Science Systems, Inc.
Cross References: For reviews by Lena R. Gaddis and Diane J. Sawyer, see 13:238; see also T4:2079 (1 reference); for a review by R. A. Bornstein of an earlier edition, see 10:291.

[2112]
Preschool Developmental Profile.
Purpose: "Designed to write an individualized education program and to serve as a way of measuring a child's developmental progress."
Population: Children who function at the 3-6-year developmental age.
Publication Dates: 1977-2006.
Scores, 10: Perceptual/Fine Motor, Cognition (Classification, Number, Space, Seriation, Time), Speech and Language, Social Emotional, Self-Care, Gross Motor.
Administration: Individual.

Price Data: Available from publisher and at www.press.umich.edu.
Time: (50–60) minutes.
Comments: See Early Intervention Developmental Profile (927) for developmental ages of 0 to 36 months.
Authors: Diane B. D'Eugenio, Martha S. Moersch, Sara L. Brown, Judith E. Drews, B. Suzanne Haskin, Eleanor Whiteside Lynch, and Sally J. Rogers.
Publisher: University of Michigan Press.
Cross References: For reviews by Doreen Ward Fairbank and David MacPhee, see 13:239.

[2113]

Preschool Evaluation Scale.

Purpose: Designed to assess behavior related to developmental delays.
Population: Birth–72 months.
Publication Dates: 1991–1992.
Acronym: PES.
Scores, 6: Large Muscle Skills, Small Muscle Skills, Cognitive Thinking, Expressive Language Skills, Social/Emotional, Self-Help Skills.
Administration: Individual.
Levels, 2: Birth–35 months, 36–72 months.
Price Data, 2006: $180 per complete kit including school and home technical manuals ($15 each), 50 School Version birth–35 months rating forms, 50 Home Version birth–35 months rating forms, 50 School Version 36–72 months rating forms, 50 Home Version 36–72 months rating forms (each pkg. [50] $35; forms also available in Spanish); $35 per computerized quick score (WIN).
Time: (20–25) minutes.
Comments: Ratings by parents or child care providers.
Author: Stephen B. McCarney.
Publisher: Hawthorne Educational Services, Inc.
Cross References: For reviews by Mary Mathai Chittooran and Lena R. Gaddis, see 13:240.

[2114]

Preschool Language Assessment Instrument–Second Edition.

Purpose: Designed to test "children's discourse abilities" in "aspects of early educational exchanges."
Population: Ages 3-0 to 5-11.
Publication Dates: 1978–2003.
Acronym: PLAI-2.
Administration: Individual.
Forms, 2: Age 3 years, Ages 4–5 years.
Price Data, 2011: $226 per complete kit including examiner's manual (2003, 71 pages), picture book, 25 profile/examiner record booklets–3-year-olds, and 25 profile/examiner record booklets–4/5-year-olds; $61 per examiner's manual; $89 per picture book; $46 per 25 profile/examiner's record booklets for 3-year-olds; $46 per 25 profile/examiner's record booklets for 4/5-year-olds.

Time: (30) minutes.
Comments: Includes nonstandardized procedures for analyzing adequacy of response and interfering behaviors.
Authors: Marion Blank, Susan A. Rose, and Laura J. Berlin.
Publisher: PRO-ED.
a) AGES 3 YEARS.
Scores, 6: Discourse Ability (Matching, Selective Analysis, Reordering and Reasoning, Receptive, Expressive, Total).
b) AGES 4–5 YEARS.
Scores, 7: Discourse Ability (Matching, Selective Analysis, Reordering, Reasoning, Receptive, Expressive, Total).
Cross References: For reviews by Koressa Kutsick Malcolm and Rebecca McCauley, see 16:197; see also T5:2044 (6 references) and T4:2083 (2 references); for reviews by William O. Haynes and Kenneth G. Shipley of a previous edition, see 9:979.

[2115]

Preschool Language Scales, Fifth Edition.

Purpose: Designed to "identify children who have a language delay or disorder."
Population: Ages birth to 7-11.
Publication Dates: 1969-2011.
Acronym: PLS-5.
Scores, 5: Auditory Comprehension, Expressive Communication, Total Language; 2 optional scores: Articulation, Mean Length of Utterance.
Administration: Individual.
Price Data, 2011: $335 per complete kit with manipulatives including examiner's manual (2011, 119 pages), administration and scoring nanual (2011, 191 pages), picture manual, 15 record forms, and 25 Home Communication Questionnaires; $275 per basic kit without manipulatives including examiner's manual, administration and scoring manual, picture manual, 15 record forms, and 25 Home Communication Questionnaires; $125 per set of manipulatives; $60 per 15 record forms; $10 per 25 Home Communication Questionnaires; $55 per examiner's manual; $160 per picture manual; $105 per administration and scoring manual.
Foreign Language Edition: Spanish edition available.
Time: (25-50) minutes.
Comments: Fifth edition includes some new items, scoring changes, and norms based on 2008 U.S. Census data.
Authors: Irla Lee Zimmerman, Violette G. Steiner, and Roberta Evatt Pond.
Publisher: Pearson.
a) ARTICULATION SCREENER.
Purpose: Designed to evaluate articulation in single words.
Population: Ages 2-6 to 7-11.
Scores: Total score only.
Comments: "Criterion-referenced" optional subtest.

b) LANGUAGE SAMPLE CHECKLIST.
Purpose: Designed to evaluate spontaneous speech.
Population: Ages 1 to 7-11.
Scores: Mean Length of Utterance.
Comments: Supplemental measure to help validate information obtained from the Expressive Communication scale.
c) HOME COMMUNICATION QUESTIONNAIRE.
Purpose: Designed to give "the caregiver's perspective of a child's communication behaviors" at home, preschool, or daycare.
Population: Ages birth to 2-11.
Scores: Not scored.
Time: (10-15) minutes.
Comments: Supplemental questionnaire.
Cross References: For reviews by Terri Flowerday and Hoi K. Suen of a previous edition, see 16:198; see also T5:2045 (6 references); for reviews by J. Jeffrey Grill and Janet A. Norris of a previous edition, see 13:241 (26 references); see also T4:2084 (24 references); for an excerpted review by Barton B. Proger of a previous edition, see 8:929 (3 references); see also T2:2024 (1 reference); for a review by Joel Stark and an excerpted review by C. H. Ammons, see 7:965.

[2116]

Preschool Motor Speech Evaluation & Intervention.

Purpose: To assess oral motor and motor speech abilities of children from 18 to 60 months who are exhibiting significant speech delays.
Population: Ages 18–60 months.
Publication Date: 2000.
Scores: No scores.
Administration: Individual.
Price Data, 2006: $59 per complete kit including spiral-bound soft cover manual with an assessment form and several reproducible pages.
Time: (75–160) minutes.
Comments: Parent interview/observation.
Author: Margaret M. Earnest.
Publisher: PRO-ED.

[2117]

Preschool Program Quality Assessment, Second Edition.

Purpose: "Designed to evaluate the quality of early childhood programs and identify staff training needs."
Population: Center-based early childhood education settings.
Publication Dates: 1998-2003.
Acronym: PQA.
Administration: Individual or group.
Forms, 2: A, B.
Price Data, 2011: $27.95 per Starter Pak, which includes administration manual (2003, 32 pages), 1 Form

A-Classroom Items, 1 Form B-Agency Items, and set of Index Tabs; $13.95 per administration manual; $7.95 per Form B-Agency items; $7.95 per Form A-Classroom Items; $1.95 per index tab set.
Time: Administration time not reported.
Comments: "Based on classroom observations and interviews with teaching and administrative staff."
Author: High/Scope Educational Research Foundation.
Publisher: High/Scope Educational Research Foundation.
a) FORM A-CLASSROOM ITEMS.
Scores, 5: Learning Environment, Daily Routine, Adult-Child Interaction, Curriculum Planning/Assessment, Classroom Score.
b) FORM B-AGENCY ITEMS.
Scores, 4: Parent Involvement/Family Services, Staff Qualifications/Development, Program Management, Agency Score.
Cross References: For reviews by Abigail Baxter and Stephen B. Johnson, see 17:155; for reviews by Michael B. Bunch and William J. Sauser, Jr. of an earlier version, see 15:198.

[2118]

Preschool Screening Instrument.

Purpose: Designed to identify potential learning problems in prekindergarten children.
Population: Ages 3-0 to 5-3.
Publication Date: 1979.
Acronym: PSSI.
Scores, 6: Human Figure Drawing, Visual Motor Perception/Fine Motor, Gross Motor, Language Development, Speech, Behavior.
Administration: Individual.
Price Data, 2005: $90 per complete kit including 25 student record forms, 25 parental questionnaires, story card, manipulatives, and manual (40 pages); $30 per 25 student record forms; $20 per 25 parental questionnaires; $23 per manual.
Time: (5–8) minutes.
Author: Stephen Paul Cohen.
Publisher: Stoelting Co.
Cross References: For a review by Gene Schwarting, see 9:981.

[2119]

The Pre-School Screening Test.

Purpose: To screen children for special educational needs.
Population: 3 years 6 months to 4 years 5 months.
Publication Date: 2001.
Acronym: PREST.
Scores, 14: PREST 1 (Rapid Naming, Bead Threading & Paper Cutting, Digits & Letters, Repetition, Shape Copying, Corsi Frog, At-Risk Total), PREST 2 (Balance, Phonological Discrimination, Digit Span, Rhyme, Sound Order, Teddy and Form Matching, At-Risk Total).

Administration: Individual.
Price Data, 2006: £97 per complete kit including manual (98 pages), score keys, sample permission letter, test cards, beads, cord, sound order tape, frog pond card and frog, 50 double-sided record forms, and training video in a bag; £29 per manual; £38.50 per 50 record forms.
Time: (10–30) minutes.
Authors: Angela Fawcett, Rod Nicolson, and Ray Lee.
Publisher: Pearson Assessment [England].
Cross References: For reviews by Sherry K. Bain and Young Ju Lee and by Gene Schwarting, see 16:196.

[2120]
Preschool Skills Test.

Purpose: "Designed to assess the [developmental] skills of preschool-aged, early elementary or mentally handicapped children."
Population: Age 2 through Grade 2 level children.
Publication Dates: 1983–1993.
Scores: 7 developmental areas: Fine Motor, Personal/Social, Visual, Visual Identification, Number Concepts, Discrimination/Matching, Readiness/Academic.
Administration: Individual.
Price Data: Available from publisher.
Time: [20–30] minutes.
Comments: Previous edition entitled Preschool Screening Test.
Author: Carol Lepera.
Publisher: Preschool Skills Test.
Cross References: For reviews by Doreen Ward Fairbank and Mark E. Swerdlik, see 14:296; for a review by Ruth Tomes of an earlier edition, see 12:303.

[2121]
Present State Examination.

Purpose: Clinical interview questionnaire for ratings of psychiatric symptoms reported by patient during preceding month.
Population: Adult psychiatric patients.
Publication Dates: 1967–1974.
Acronym: PSE.
Scores: 38 syndrome scores and various derived scores.
Administration: Individual.
Price Data: Available from publisher.
Time: (45–60) minutes.
Comments: No scoring instructions except description of computer scoring program.
Authors: J. K. Wing, J. E. Cooper, and N. Sartorius.
Publisher: Cambridge University Press.
Cross References: See T5:2050 (142 references), T4:2091 (237 references), 9:985 (71 references), and T3:1883 (70 references); for a review by Jack Zusman, Isabel C. A. Moyes, Clive A. Sims, and David Goldberg, see 8:649.

[2122]
The Press Test.

Purpose: Measures how well an individual performs tasks when experiencing stress.
Population: Managers and high-level professionals.
Publication Dates: 1959–1987.
Scores, 5: Reading Speed, Color-Naming Speed, Color-Naming Speed With Distraction, Difference Between Color-Naming Speed With and Without Distraction, Difference Between Reading Speed and Color-Naming Speed.
Administration: Individual or group.
Price Data: Available from publisher.
Time: (6–10) minutes.
Authors: Melany E. Baehr and Raymond J. Corsini.
Publisher: Pearson Performance Solutions [No reply from publisher; status unknown].
Cross References: For a review by Robert P. Vecchio, see 9:986; see also T3:1884 (2 references), T2:1333 (1 reference), and P:213 (1 reference); for reviews by William H. Helme and Allyn Miles Munger, see 6:163.

[2123]
The Prevocational Assessment and Curriculum Guide.

Purpose: Designed to "assess and identify the prevocational training needs of handicapped persons."
Population: Mentally retarded individuals.
Publication Dates: 1978–1993.
Acronym: PACG.
Scores: 9 categories: Attendance/Endurance, Independence, Production, Learning, Behavior, Communication, Social Skills, Grooming/Eating, Toileting.
Administration: Individual.
Price Data, 2011: $12 per complete kit including 10 inventories, summary profile sheets, curriculum guides, and one manual (6 pages); $8 per set of 10 additional forms.
Time: [15–20] minutes.
Comments: Ratings by professional acquainted with individual; title on test is PACG Inventory.
Authors: Dennis E. Mithaug, Deanna K. Mar, and Jeffrey E. Stewart.
Publisher: Exceptional Education.
Cross References: For reviews by Richard A. Wantz and Jean M. Williams, see 12:304.

[2124]
Prevocational Assessment Screen.

Purpose: "Designed to assess a student's motor and perceptual abilities in relation to performance requirements within a local vocational training program."
Population: Grades 8-12.
Publication Dates: 1985–2000.
Acronym: PAS.

Scores, 16: Time and Error scores for 8 modules: Alphabetizing, Etch A Sketch Maze, Calculating, Small Parts, Pipe Assembly, O Rings, Block Design, Color Sort.
Administration: Individual.
Price Data, 2002: $1,195 per complete kit including manual (50 pages) and computer software for use in scoring and reporting.
Time: (50) minutes.
Author: Michele Rosinek.
Publisher: Piney Mountain Press, Inc.
Cross References: For reviews by Stephen L. Koffler and James B. Rounds, see 12:305.

[2125]
Primary Measures of Music Audiation.
Purpose: To assess basic music aptitudes.
Population: K-3.
Publication Date: 1979.
Acronym: PMMA.
Scores, 3: Tonal, Rhythm, Composite.
Administration: Group.
Price Data, 2006: $100 per complete kit including 1 tonal and rhythm compact disc, 100 total answer sheets and 100 rhythm answer sheets, 1 set of scoring masks, 100 profile cards, 4 class record sheets, and test manual (107 pages); $25 per CD ; $41.50 per 100 tonal or rhythm answer sheets; $5 per set of scoring masks; $15.50 per 100 profile cards; $2 per 10 class record sheets; $20 per manual.
Time: (20) minutes per tonal tape and (20) minutes per rhythm tape.
Comments: For upward extension, see Intermediate Measures of Music Audiation (1330); test administered by CD.
Author: Edwin E. Gordon.
Publisher: GIA Publications, Inc.
Cross References: See T4:2099 (2 references); for reviews by Paul R. Lehman and Walter L. Wehner, see 9:988; see also T3:1891 (1 reference).

[2126]
Primary Test of Cognitive Skills.
Purpose: Designed to "measure verbal, spatial, memory, and conceptual abilities."
Population: Grades K–1.
Publication Date: 1990.
Acronym: PTCS.
Scores, 5: Spatial, Memory, Concepts, Verbal, Total.
Administration: Group.
Price Data: Price information available from publisher for test materials including manual (70 pages), norms book (82 pages), and technical bulletin (23 pages); scoring service available from publisher.
Time: Untimed, (30) minutes per subtest; (120) minutes total test.

Authors: Janellen Huttenlocher and Susan Cohen Levine.
Publisher: CTB/McGraw-Hill.
Cross References: For reviews by Sherry K. Bain and Laura L. B. Barnes and David E. McIntosh, see 12:307.

[2127]
Primary Test of Nonverbal Intelligence.
Purpose: Intended for "assessing [nonverbal] reasoning abilities in young children."
Population: Ages 3-0 to 9-11.
Publication Date: 2008.
Acronym: PTONI.
Scores: Total score only.
Administration: Individual.
Price Data, 2011: $220 per complete kit including picture book, 25 record forms, and examiner's manual (84 pages); $100 per picture book; $50 per 25 record forms; $79 per examiner's manual.
Foreign Language & Other Special Editions: Test directions are available in eight foreign languages: Spanish, French, traditional Chinese (Mandarin), simplified Chinese, German, Tagalog, Vietnamese, Italian, Japanese; alternate directions for children with hearing impairments can be administered using American Sign Language, Manually Coded English, Aural/Oral English, and Sign-Supported Speech/English.
Time: (5-15) minutes.
Comments: Children respond to items by pointing to the correct picture in the picture book.
Authors: David J. Ehrler and Ronnie L. McGhee.
Publisher: PRO-ED.
Cross References: For reviews by Connie Theriot England and Koressa Kutsick Malcolm, see 18:96.

[2128]
Principles of Adult Mentoring Inventory.
Purpose: Designed "to provide a self-assessment instrument for those who have assumed the role of mentor in their contact with adult learners."
Population: Adults.
Publication Date: 1998.
Acronym: PAMI.
Scores, 7: Relationship Emphasis/Trust, information Emphasis/Advice, Facilitative Focus/Alternatives, Conforntive Focus/Challenge, Mentor Model/Motivation, Employee Vision/Initiative, Total.
Administration: Individual.
Price Data, 2001: $39.95 per leader's guide (51 pages); $4.95 per critique form.
Time: Administration time not reported.
Author: Norman H. Cohen.
Publisher: HRD Press, Inc.
Cross References: For reviews by L. Carolyn Pearson and Trey Martindale and by Cecil R. Reynolds, see 15:197.

[2129]

PrinTest (Forms A-C and BR-C).

Purpose: Designed for selecting or evaluating entry-level production or maintenance employees where the reading of prints and drawings is required.
Population: Applicants or incumbents for jobs requiring print reading abilities.
Publication Dates: 1990-2010.
Acronym: RCJS-PrinTest.
Scores: Total score only.
Administration: Group.
Price Data, 2011: $22 per consumable self-scoring test booklet or online test administration; $24.95 per manual (2010, 23 pages).
Time: 35(45) minutes.
Comments: Self-scoring instrument; available for online test administration.
Author: Roland T. Ramsay.
Publisher: Ramsay Corporation.
Cross References: For reviews by James W. Pinkney and Nambury S. Raju of an earlier edition, see 13:258.

[2130]

Prison Inmate Inventory.

Purpose: "Designed for inmate risk assessment and needs identification."
Population: Prison inmates.
Publication Date: 1996.
Acronym: PII.
Scores: 10 scales: Truthfulness, Violence, Antisocial, Adjustment, Self-Esteem, Alcohol, Drugs, Judgment, Distress, Stress Coping Abilities.
Administration: Group.
Price Data: Available from publisher.
Time: (35) minutes.
Comments: Available in English and Spanish; both computer version and paper-pencil format are scored on IBM-PC compatibles.
Author: Risk & Needs Assessment, Inc.
Publisher: Behavior Data Systems, Inc.
Cross References: For reviews by R. J. DeAyala and John A. Mills, see 14:297.

[2131]

Problem Behavior Inventory [Adult & Adolescent Screening Forms].

Purpose: Designed to help "clinicians structure and focus the diagnostic interview."
Population: Adults and adolescents.
Publication Date: 1991.
Scores: No scores.
Administration: Group.
Forms, 2: Adult, Adolescent.
Price Data, 2011: $45 Adult Problem Behavior Inventory (set of 25); $45 Adolescent Problem Behavior Inventory (set of 25).

Time: (10-20) minutes.
Author: Leigh Silverton.
Publisher: Western Psychological Services.

[2132]

Problem Experiences Checklist.

Purpose: Developed for use prior to the initial intake interview to identify potential problems for further discussion.
Population: Adolescents, adults.
Publication Date: 1991.
Scores: No scores.
Administration: Individual.
Editions, 2: Adolescent, Adult.
Manual: No manual.
Price Data, 2006: $27.50 per 25 checklists (specify Adult or Adolescent).
Time: [10-15] minutes.
Author: Leigh Silverton.
Publisher: Western Psychological Services.
Cross References: For reviews by Mark H. Daniel and Michael J. Sporakowski, see 12:309.

[2133]

Problem-Solving Decision-Making Style Inventory.

Purpose: Provides feedback on one's perception of problem-solving and decision-making styles of self or others.
Population: High school and college and adults in organizational settings.
Publication Date: 1982.
Scores, 4: Delegative, Facilitative, Consultative, Authoritative.
Administration: Group.
Forms, 2: Self, Other.
Manual: No manual (administrative and scoring directions included in instrument).
Price Data: Price information available from publisher.
Time: Administration time not reported.
Comments: Self-administered ratings questionnaire.
Authors: Paul Hersey and Walter E. Natemeyer.
Publisher: Jossey-Bass, A Wiley Company.
Cross References: For reviews by David N. Dixon and Paul McReynolds, see 10:295.

[2134]

The Problem Solving Inventory.

Purpose: "To assess an individual's perceptions of his or her own problem-solving behaviors and attitudes."
Population: Age 16 and above.
Publication Date: 1988.
Acronym: PSI.
Scores, 4: Problem-Solving Confidence, Approach-Avoidance Style, Personal Control, Total.
Administration: Group and individual.

Price Data, 2001: $31.25 per 25 test booklets; $13.50 per scoring key; $32 per manual (23 pages); $47 per preview kit including manual, test booklet, and scoring key.
Time: (10-15) minutes.
Comment: Self-ratings scale.
Author: P. Paul Heppner.
Publisher: P. Paul Heppner (the author) [No reply from publisher; status unknown].
Cross References: See T5:2065 (35 references) and T4:2108 (26 references); for reviews by Cameron J. Camp and Steven G. LoBello, see 11:303 (11 references).

[2135]

Process Assessment of the Learner–Second Edition: Diagnostic Assessment for Math.

Purpose: "Designed for measuring the development of math processes in children."
Population: Grades K-6.
Publication Date: 2007.
Acronym: PAL-II M.
Scores: 48 scores across 17 subtests: Numeral Writing (Automatic Legible Numeral Writing at 15 Seconds [NWAL], Legible Numeral Writing [NWL], Total Time [NWTT], Reversals [NWR], Omissions [NOW], Transpositions [NWTR]), Oral Counting (Oral Counting [OC]), Numeric Coding (Numeric Coding [NC]), Fact Retrieval: Look and Write (Addition [FRLW-A], Subtraction [FRLW-S], Mixed Addition and Subtraction [FRLW-AS], Multiplication [FRLW-M], Division [FRLW-D], Mixed Multiplication and Division [FRLW-MD]), Fact Retrieval: Listen and Say, (Addition [FRLS-A], Subtraction [FRLS-S], Mixed Addition and Subtraction [FRLS-AS], Multiplication [FRLS-M], Division [FRLS-D], Mixed Multiplication and Division [FRLS-MD]), Computation Operations (Task A-Spatial Alignment [CO-SA], Task B-Verbal Explanation [CO-VE], Task C-Problem Solution [CO-PS], Computation Operations Composite [COC]), Place Value (Oral [PVO], Written [PVW], Problem Response Written [PVPW], Place Value Composite [PVC]), Part-Whole Relationships (Part-Whole Concepts [PWC], Part-Whole Fractions and Mixed Numbers [PWF], Part-Whole Time [PWT], Part-Whole Relationships Composite [PWRC]), Finding the Bug (Finding the Bug [FB]), Multi-Step Problem Solving (Multi-Step Problem Solving [MSPS]), Quantitative Working Memory (Quantitative Working Memory [QWM]), Spatial Working Memory (Oral [SWMO], Drawing [SWMD]), RAN: Digits (Single Digits Total Time [RAN-DTT], Single Digits Rate Change [RAN-DRC]), RAN: Double Digits (Double Digits Total Time [RAN-DDTT], Double Digits Rate Change [RAN-DDRC]), RAN: Digits and Double Digits Total Scores (Digits + Double Digits Rate Change [RAN-D-DDRC], Digits + Double Digits Total Errors [RAN-D-DDTE], Digits + Double Digits Total Time Composite [RAN-D-DDC]), RAS: Words and Digits (Words and Digits Total

Time [RAS-WDTT], Words and Digits Rate Change [RAS-WDRC], Words and Digits Total Errors [RAS-WDTE]), Fingertip Writing (Fingertip Writing [FW]).
Administration: Individual.
Levels, 5: Kindergarten, Grade 1, Grade 2, Grade 3, Grades 4-6.
Price Data, 2009: $338 per Math Kit including 10 Response Booklets, 10 Record Forms, Stimulus Book, Stimulus Booklet, Administration and Scoring Manual (141 pages), and Comprehensive User's Guide CD; $74 per 25 Response Booklets; $54 per 25 Record Forms; $109.20 per Stimulus Book; $78 per Stimulus Booklet; $104 per Comprehensive User's Guide CD.
Time: (60-120) minutes to administer all subtests; time limit varies across individual subtests.
Comments: The PAL-II M has three applications: (a) "Tier 1: universal screening for early intervention and prevention," (b) "Tier 2: problem-solving consultation and progress monitoring," (c) "Tier 3: differential diagnosis and treatment planning;" number and type of subtests administered depends on grade level and application.
Author: Virginia Wise Berninger.
Publisher: Pearson.
Cross References: For reviews by Laura Hamilton and by Katherine Ryan and Michael J. Culbertson, see 18:97.

[2136]

Process Assessment of the Learner–Second Edition: Diagnostic Assessment for Reading and Writing.

Purpose: "Designed for measuring reading and writing skills and related processes in children."
Population: Grades K-6.
Publication Dates: 1998-2007.
Acronym: PAL-II RW.
Scores, 83: Alphabet Writing Automatic Legible Letter Writing (AWAL), Alphabet Writing Legible Letter Writing (AWL), Alphabet Writing Total Time (AWTT), Copying Task A Automatic Legible Letter Writing (CPAAL), Copying Task A Legible Letter Writing (CPAL), Copying Task A Total Time (CPATT), Copying Task B Legibility (0-30 seconds) (CPBL-30), Copying Task B Legibility (0-60 seconds) (CPBL-60), Copying Task B Legibility (0-90 seconds) (CPBL-90), Copying Task B Copy Accuracy (CPBCA), Handwriting Total Automatic Letter Legibility Composite (HWGTALC), Handwriting Total Legibility Composite (HWGTLC), Handwriting Total Time Composite (HWGTTC), Handwriting Total Reversals (HWGTRC), Handwriting Total Inversions (HWGTI), Handwriting Total Omissions (HWGTO), Handwriting Total Repetitions (HWGTRP), Handwriting Total Transpositions (HWGTTR), Handwriting Total Case Confusions (HWGTCC), Handwriting Total Format Confusions (HWGTFC), Receptive Coding (RC), Expressive Coding (EC), Orthographic Coding Composite

(ORC), Rhyming (RY), Syllables (SY), Phonemes (PN), Rimes (RI), Phonological Coding Composite (PLC), Are They Related? (RR), Does It Fit? (DF), Sentence Structure (ST), Morphological/Syntactic Coding Composite (MSCC), Pseudoword Decoding Fluency at 60 seconds (PDF-60), Pseudoword Decoding Accuracy (PDA), Find the True Fixes (FF), Morphological Decoding Fluency Accuracy (MDFA), Morphological Decoding Fluency (MDF), Morphological Decoding Composite (MDC), Word Choice Accuracy (WCA), Word Choice Fluency (WCF), Sentence Sense Accuracy (SSA), Sentence Sense Fluency (SSF), Compositional Fluency Total Number of Words (CFTW), Compositional Fluency Total Correctly Spelled Words (CFCSW), Compositional Fluency Total Complete Sentences (CFCST), Expository Note Taking Accuracy (NTA), Expository Note Taking Fact Errors (NTFE), Expository Report Writing Quality (RWQ), Expository Report Writing Organizational Quality of Report Writing (RWO), Expository Report Writing Irrelevant Thoughts Added (RWITA), Cross-Genre Compositional and Expository Writing Total Number of Words (CGWTW), Cross-Genre Compositional and Expository Writing Total Correctly Spelled Words (CG-WCSW), Cross-Genre Compositional and Expository Writing Total Complete Sentences (CGWCS), Letters (WML), Words (WMW), Letters and Words Composite (WML-WC), Sentences: Listening (WMSL), Sentences: Writing (WMSW), Sentences: Listening and Sentences: Writing Composite (WMSL-SWC), Verbal Working Memory Composite (WMVC), RAN-Letters Rate Change Raw Score (RAN-LRC), RAN-Letters Total Time (RAN-LTT), RAN-Letter Groups Rate Change Raw Score (RAN-LGRC), RAN-Letter Groups Total Time (RAN-LGTT), RAN-Words Rate Change Raw Score (RAN-WRC), RAN-Words Total Time (RAN-WTT), RAN-Letters -Letter Groups and -Words Total Rate Change Score (RAN-L-LG-WRC), RAN-Letters -Letter Groups and -Words Total Errors (RAN-L-LG-WTE), RAN-Letters -Letter Groups and -Words Total Time Composite (RAN-L-LG-WC), RAS-Words and Digits Total Time (RAS-WDTT), RAS-Words and Digits Rate Change Raw Score (RAS-WDRC), RAS-Words and Digits Total Errors (RAS-WDTE), Oral Motor Planning Total Time (OMT), Oral Motor Planning Total Errors (OME), Finger Repetition-Dominant Hand Total Time (FSRP-DTT), Finger Repetition-Non-Dominant Hand Total Time (FSRP-NTT), Finger Succession-Dominant Hand Total Time (FSS-DTT), Finger Succession-Non-Dominant Hand Total Time (FSS-NTT), Finger Succession Total Errors (FSSTE), Finger Sense Frequent Motoric Overflow (FSFMO), Finger Sense Occasional Motoric Overflow (FSOMO), Finger Localization (FSL), Finger Recognition (FSRC).
Administration: Individual.
Levels, 5: Kindergarten, Grade 1, Grade 2, Grade 3, Grades 4-6.

Price Data, 2009: $468 per complete kit including 10 Response Booklets, 10 Record Forms, Stimulus Book, Stimulus Booklets (A and B), administration and scoring manual for Reading and Writing (2007, 225 pages), and Comprehensive User's Guide CD; $74 per 25 Response Booklets; $79 per 25 Record Forms; $109.20 per Stimulus Book; $78 per Stimulus Booklet-A; $78 per Stimulus Booklet-B; $104 per Comprehensive User's Guide CD.
Time: (60-120) minutes to administer all subtests; time limit varies across individual subtests.
Comments: The PAL-II RW has three applications: (a) "Tier 1: universal screening for early intervention and prevention," (b) "Tier 2: problem-solving consultation and progress monitoring," (c) "Tier 3: differential diagnosis and treatment planning"; number of subtests administered depends on grade level and application; "designed to complement the Wechsler Intelligence Scale for Children-Fourth Edition (WISC-IV) and the Wechsler Individual Achievement Test-Second Edition (WIAT-II Update)"; previous edition entitled Process Assessment of the Learner: Test Battery of Reading and Writing.
Author: Virginia Wise Berninger.
Publisher: Pearson.
Cross References: For reviews by S. Kathleen Krach and Jennifer N. Mahdavi, see 18:98; for a review by Karen E. Jennings of an earlier edition, see 16:199.

[2137]

Productive Practices Survey.

Purpose: "To assess, describe, and pinpoint specific practices of the manager which support–or fail to support–organizational productivity."
Population: Managers.
Publication Dates: 1987–1996.
Acronym: PPS.
Scores, 12: Dimension I (Management Values, Support Structure, Managerial Credibility, Total), Dimension II (Impact, Relevance, Community, Total), Dimension III (Task Environment, Social Context, Problem Solving, Total).
Administration: Group.
Price Data, 2001: $8.95 per instrument.
Time: (30-35) minutes.
Comments: Based on model of organizational functioning called Competence Theory; self ratings; self scored.
Author: Jay Hall.
Publisher: Teleometrics International, Inc.

[2138]

Productivity Assessment Questionnaire.

Purpose: Assesses an employee's opinions about productivity in the organization in which they work.
Population: Employees.
Publication Date: 1984.

Scores: 11 areas: Policy, Leadership, Objectives, Inputs, Performance, Technology, Work Procedures, HRD, Work Quality, Managerial Skills, Quality of Work Life.
Administration: Group.
Price Data, 2006: $40 per 10 questionnaires; quantity discounts available.
Time: (10-12) minutes.
Comments: Self-administered and self-scored; can be made available for electronic administration.
Author: Robert C. Preziosi.
Publisher: Preziosi Partners, Inc.
Cross References: For a review by Robert M. Guion, see 10:297.

[2139]
Productivity Environmental Preference Survey.

Purpose: Identifies "how adults prefer to function, learn, concentrate and perform in their occupational or educational environment."
Population: Adults age 18 and older.
Publication Dates: 1975-2010.
Acronym: PEPS.
Scores, 20: Sound, Light, Temperature, Design, Motivated/Unmotivated, Persistent, Responsible, Structure, Learning Alone/Peer-Oriented Learner, Authority-Oriented Learner, Several Ways, Auditory Preferences, Visual Preferences, Tactile Preferences, Kinesthetic Preferences, Requires Intake, Evening/Morning, Late Morning, Afternoon, Needs Mobility.
Administration: Group or individual.
Price Data, 2011: $22.50 per 10 answer sheets for adults (includes scoring); $7.50 or less per group and subscale summary available from publisher only in addition to individual profiles; $.60 per individual interpretative booklet; $14 per manual (1996, 66 pages); $395 per computerized self-administered inventory program with 100 administrations (multi-language version $495) ($60 per 100 additional administrations) (Windows); $495 for Scanwin program permitting schools and businesses to scan and profile forms on site, includes multi-language capability; $.60 per answer form to use with Scanwin.
Time: (20–30) minutes.
Comments: PC compatible computer required for (optional) computerized administration; NCS Pearson Optical Mark Reader with dual pencil reader; Scrantron 8000, 8200, 8400, or SCANMARK 2550, 2660, 2800, 4000, or 5500 Scanner with dual pencil read for Scanwin; online administration available at www.learningstyle.com.
Authors: Gary E. Price, Rita Dunn, and Kenneth Dunn.
Publisher: Price Systems, Inc.
Cross References: See T5:2069 (3 references); for reviews by Javaid Kaiser and Thaddeus Rozecki, see 13:242 (6 references); see also T4:2114 (2 references); for reviews by Craig N. Mills and Bertram C. Sippola of an earlier edition, see 11:306 (9 references).

[2140]
Professional and Managerial Position Questionnaire.

Purpose: Constructed for use in analyzing professional and managerial jobs.
Population: Professional and managerial jobs.
Publication Dates: 1980–1992.
Acronym: PMPQ.
Scores: 3 categories: Job Functions, Personal Requirements, Other Information.
Administration: Group.
Price Data: Available from publisher.
Time: Administration time not reported.
Authors: J. L. Mitchell, E. J. McCormick, S. Morton McPhail (manual), P. Richard Jeanneret (manual), and Robert C. Mecham (manual).
Publisher: PAQ Services, Inc.
Cross References: For reviews by Mary Anne Bunda and William I. Sauser, Jr., see 12:311; for reviews of an earlier edition by Gregory H. Dobbins and George Thornton, see 9:993.

[2141]
Professional Employment Test.

Purpose: Designed to measure reading comprehension, reasoning, quantitative problem solving, and data interpretation for use in selecting personnel for professional, administrative, and managerial occupations.
Population: Potential managerial, administrative, and professional employees.
Publication Dates: 1986–2004.
Acronym: PET.
Scores: Total score only.
Administration: Group or individual.
Forms, 8: A, B, C, D, A-1, B-1, C-1, D-1.
Price Data: Price information available from publisher for test material including Technical Manual (2004, 40 pages), Supplemental Technical Manual for Form A-1 (1988, 9 pages), Supplemental Technical Manual for Forms C, D, C-1, and D-1 (2004, 11 pages), and User's Manual (2004, 19 pages).
Time: 80(85) minutes for long form; 40(45) minutes for short form.
Comments: Computerized versions available.
Authors: William W. Ruch, Richard H. McKillip, and Ricki Buckly.
Publisher: Psychological Services, Inc.
Cross References: For reviews by Gregory J. Cizek and Jayne E. Stake, see 12:312.

[2142]
The Professional Judgment Rating Form.

Purpose: Designed to judge "the extent to which novices approach problems with critical thinking".
Population: "Novice professionals."

Publication Dates: 1998-2006.
Acronym: PJRF.
Scores: Overall Rating.
Administration: Individual.
Price Data: Available from publisher.
Time: Administration time not reported.
Authors: Peter A. Facione, Stephen W. Blohm, Noreen C. Facione, and Carol Ann F. Giancarlo.
Publisher: Insight Assessment-The California Academic Press LLC.

[2143]

Profile of Aptitude for Leadership.

Purpose: To measure an individual's relative strength in each of four leadership styles (or types of leader).
Population: Adults.
Publication Date: 1991.
Acronym: PAL.
Scores, 4: Manager (Administrator), Supervisor (Coach), Entrepreneur (Leader), Technician (Specialist).
Administration: Group or individual.
Manual: No manual.
Price Data: Price information available from publisher for test, answer sheet, and interpretation folder.
Time: (20) minutes.
Comments: Self-administered; self-scored.
Author: Training House, Inc.
Publisher: Training House, Inc.
Cross References: For reviews by Jack E. Gebart-Eaglemont and Neal Schmitt, see 13:243.

[2144]

Profile of Creative Abilities.

Purpose: "Designed to measure the creative abilities of students."
Population: Ages 5-0 to 14-11.
Publication Date: 2007.
Acronym: PCA.
Scores: Creativity Index, Drawing (New Elements, Originality, Orientation, Perspectives, Total), Categories (Fluency, Flexibility, Total), Home Rating Scale Total, School Rating Scale Total.
Price Data, 2011: $167 per complete kit including 25 Home Rating Scales, 25 School Rating Scales, 25 Student Forms, 25 Summary and Scoring Booklets, Picture Booklet, and examiner's manual (2007, 97 pages); $29 per 25 Home Rating Scales; $29 per 25 School Rating Scales; $29 per 25 Student Forms; $29 per 25 Summary and Scoring Booklets; $11 per Picture Booklet; $53 per examiner's manual.
Authors: Gail R. Ryser.
Publisher: PRO-ED.
　　a) PCA SUBTESTS.
　　Purpose: Designed to "measure two aspects of divergent production."

Scores: Creativity Index, Drawing (New Elements, Originality, Orientation, Perspective, Total), Categories (Fluency, Flexibility, Total).
Subtests, 2: Drawing, Categories.
Administration: Group (Drawing) and individual (Categories).
Time: (30-40) minutes.
　　b) PCA RATING SCALES.
　　Purpose: Designed to "measure creative abilities, domain-relevant skills, creativity-relevant skills, and intrinsic task motivation."
Scores: Total score only for each scale.
Administration: Group.
Forms, 2: Home Rating Scale, School Rating Scale.
Time: Administration time not reported.
Comments: Home ratings by parents/guardians; school ratings by teachers/educators.
Cross References: For reviews by Steven I. Pfeiffer and John F. Wakefield, see 18:99.

[2145]

Profile of Mood States.

Purpose: "Developed to measure mood or affective states."
Population: Age 18 and older.
Publication Dates: 1971–2003.
Acronym: POMS.
Scores, 7: Tension-Anxiety, Depression-Dejection, Anger-Hostility, Vigor-Activity, Fatigue-Inertia, Confusion-Bewilderment, Total Mood Disturbance.
Administration: Individual or group.
Price Data, 2010: $66 per POMS Standard Kit (technical manual and 25 POMS standard QuikScore forms); $31 per technical manual; $50 per 25 Standard QuikScore forms; $50 per 25 Brief QuikScore forms.
Time: (5-10) minutes.
Comments: Earlier experimental forms called Lorr Outpatient Mood Scale and Psychiatric Outpatient Mood Scale; self-administering. Different Norm groups are available: Adult norms; Geriatric norms; College norms; and psychiatric outpatients norms.
Authors: Douglas M. McNair, Maurice Lorr, and Leo F. Droppleman.
Publisher: Multi-Health Systems, Inc.
Cross References: See T5:2076 (187 references) and T4:2122 (191 references), 9:998 (46 references), and T3:1904 (84 references); for reviews by William J. Eichman and Thaddeus E. Weckowicz, see 8:651 (33 references); see also T2:1337 (17 references).

[2146]

Profile of Mood States, Bi-Polar Form.

Purpose: Developed to measure mood dimensions in terms of six bipolar affective states.
Population: Age 18 and older.
Publication Dates: 1984–2003.

Acronym: POMS-BI.
Scores, 6: Composed–Anxious, Elated–Depressed, Agreeable–Hostile, Energetic–Tired, Clearheaded–Confused, Confident–Unsure.
Administration: Individual or Group.
Price Data, 2011: $74 per POMS Bipolar Kit (POMS technical manual, POMS Bipolar supplement, & 25 POMS Bipolar QuikScore forms); $49 per POMS technical manual and POMS Bipolar supplement; $21 per POMS Bipolar supplement; $50 per 25 POMS Bipolar QuikScore forms.
Time: (5-10) minutes.
Authors: Maurice Lorr, Douglas M. McNair, and W. P. Heuchert.
Publisher: Multi-Health Systems, Inc.
Cross References: See T5:2077 (9 references).

[2147]

Profile of Nonverbal Sensitivity.

Purpose: "Designed to measure ability to decode nonverbal cues conveyed by the face, body, and tone of voice."
Population: Grades 3-16 and adults.
Publication Date: 1979.
Acronym: PONS.
Scores: Total score only.
Administration: Group.
Price Data: Price information available from publisher for manual (1979, 90 pages), 50 question sheets, and 50 child's version question sheets.
Authors: Robert Rosenthal, Judith Hall, Dane Archer, Robin DiMatteo, and Peter Rogers.
Publisher: Irvington Publishers, Inc.
  a) THE FULL PONS TEST.
  Purpose: Matching facial expressions, body movements, and tone of voice to situations.
  Price Data: Price information available from publisher for VHS video cassette.
  Time: 45(50) minutes.
  b) AUDIO CASSETTE VERSION.
  Purpose: To test sensitivity to tone of voice.
  Price Data: Price information available from publisher for audio cassette.
  Time: 60(65) minutes.
  Comments: Cassette tape includes the audio sections of the Full PONS, male, female, and child speakers.
  c) FACE AND BODY PONS.
  Price Data: Price information available from publisher for VHS video cassette.
  Time: 8(13) minutes.
  Comments: Visual-only-no-sound test; contains 20 face-only and 20 body-only items from the Full PONS test.
  d) BRIEF EXPOSURE PONS.
  Price Data: Price information available from publisher for VHS video cassette.
  Time: 8(13) minutes.

Comments: Contains same 40 items as *c* but the exposure times are shortened to from 2 seconds to 1/24, 3/24, 9/24, and 27/24 seconds.
  e) NON-VERBAL DISCREPANCY TEST.
  Purpose: Measures how well the viewer detects discrepant audio versus visual signals.
  Price Data: Price information available from publisher for VHS video cassette.
  Time: 30(35) minutes.
Cross References: See T5:2078 (7 references) and T4:2124 (7 references).

[2148]

ProfileXT Assessment.

Purpose: "Multi-purpose assessment that is used for selection, coaching, training, promotion, managing, and succession planning."
Population: Present and potential employees.
Publication Dates: 1999-2007.
Acronym: PXT.
Scores: 21 scores in 4 subgroups: Thinking Style Scale (Learning Index, Verbal Skill, Verbal Reasoning, Numerical Ability, Numeric Reasoning), Behavioral Trait Scales (Energy Level, Assertiveness, Sociability, Manageability, Attitude, Decisiveness, Accommodating, Independence, Objective Judgment), Occupational Interests Scales (Enterprising, Financial/Administrative, People Service, Technical, Mechanical, Creative), Distortion Scale.
Administration: Group or individual.
Forms, 2: Online, Paper and Pencil.
Price Data: Available from publisher.
Time: (50-70) minutes.
Comments: Web-based administration available; 8 result reports: Placement Report, Coaching Report, Individual Report, Succession Planning Report, Candidate Matching Report, Job Profile Summary Report, Job Summary Graph, and Job Analysis Report.
Author: Profiles International, Inc.
Publisher: Profiles International, Inc.
Cross References: For reviews by Caroline Manuele Adkins and by Richard T. Kinnier and Nicole L. Nieset, see 18:100.

[2149]

Program for Assessing Youth Employment Skills.

Purpose: Measures attitudes concerning job-holding skills and supervision, self-confidence, cognitive measures, and vocational interest for persons with low verbal skills.
Population: Adolescents and young adults with low verbal skills.
Publication Dates: 1967–1979.
Acronym: PAYES.
Scores: 7 subtests: Job-Holding Skills, Attitudes Toward Supervision, Self-Confidence, Job Knowledge,

Job-Seeking Skills, Practical Reasoning, Vocational Interest Inventory.
Administration: Group.
Forms: 1 form in 3 booklets: Booklet 1 (1979, 18 pages), Booklet 2 (1979, 31 pages), Booklet 3 (1979, 11 pages).
Price Data: Not available.
Time: (75) minutes.
Comments: May be orally administered.
Author: Simon & Schuster Higher Education Group.
Publisher: Prentice Hall [No reply from publisher; status unknown].
Cross References: For reviews by Shirley A. White and Dan Zakay, see 9:1001.

[2150]

Program Self-Assessment Service.

Purpose: "To assist colleges and universities that are carrying out departmental or program reviews at the undergraduate level."
Population: Faculty members, students majoring in the department, and recent graduates.
Publication Date: 1986.
Acronym: PSAS.
Scores, 16: Environment for Learning, Scholarly Excellence, Quality of Teaching, Faculty Concern for Students, Curriculum, Departmental Procedures, Available Resources, Student Satisfaction With Program, Internship/Fieldwork/Clinical Experiences, Resource Accessibility, Employment Assistance, Faculty Work Environment, Faculty Program Involvement, Faculty Research Activities, Faculty Professional Activities, Student Accomplishments.
Administration: Group.
Forms, 3: Faculty, Student, Alumni.
Price Data: Available from publisher.
Time: (30-45) minutes.
Author: Educational Testing Service.
Publisher: Educational Testing Service.
Cross References: For a review by Darrell L. Sabers, see 10:298.

[2151]

Programmer Analyst Aptitude Test [One-Hour Version].

Purpose: To evaluate the candidate's aptitude and potential for programming and analyzing business problems.
Population: Entry-level and experienced applicants for programmer analyst positions.
Publication Date: 1997.
Acronym: PROGANI.
Scores: Total Score, Narrative Evaluation, Ranking, Recommendation.
Administration: Group.
Price Data, 2001: $235 per person; quantity discounts available.
Foreign Language Edition: Available in French.

Time: (60) minutes.
Comments: Available in booklet and Internet versions; scored by publisher; must be proctored.
Author: Bruce A. Winrow.
Publisher: Walden Personnel Performance, Inc. [Canada].
Cross References: For a review by Suzanne Young, see 16:200.

[2152]

Programmer Analyst Aptitude Test [Two-Hour Version].

Purpose: "To evaluate the candidate's aptitude and potential for programming and analyzing business problems."
Population: Applicants for programmer analyst positions.
Publication Date: 1984.
Acronym: PAAT.
Scores: Programming, Analytical, Total, Narrative Evaluation, Ranking, Recommendation.
Administration: Group.
Price Data, 2001: $350 per candidate; quantity discounts available.
Time: (120) minutes.
Comments: Tests scored by publisher only; must be proctored.
Author: Bruce Winrow.
Publisher: Walden Personnel Performance, Inc. [Canada].
Cross References: For reviews by Frederick Bessai and Ralph F. Darr, Jr., see 11:308.

[2153]

Programmer Aptitude Battery.

Purpose: Designed to assess aptitude for programming.
Population: Adults naive to programming task.
Publication Date: 1988.
Acronym: PAB.
Scores, 4: Procedures, Matrices I, Matrices II, Grand Total.
Administration: Group.
Price Data: Available from publisher.
Foreign Language Edition: Test printed in both English and Afrikaans.
Time: 100(135) minutes.
Author: T. R. Taylor.
Publisher: Human Sciences Research Council [South Africa].

[2154]

Programmer Aptitude Series.

Purpose: Assess skills needed in the data processing environment.
Population: Computer programming personnel.
Publication Dates: 1979–1983.
Acronym: PAS.

Administration: Group or individual.

Restricted Distribution: Distribution restricted to persons who have completed the publisher's training course or members of the Division of Occupational Psychology of the British Psychological Society.

Price Data: Available from publisher.

Comments: Consists of tests from within the Advanced, Personnel, and Technical Test Batteries; subtests available as separates.

Authors: Peter Saville (VA1, NA2, manual), Gill Nyfield (CP7, manual), Roger Holdsworth (VA3, NA4), David Hawkey (DA5, ST7, DT8, ST9), Sue Bawtree (CP7), Steve Blinkhorn (VA3), and Alan Iliffe (NA4).

Publisher: SHL Group plc [United Kingdom].

a) LEVEL 1.
Publication Dates: 1979–1981.
Purpose: Basic programming.

1) *Number Series.*
Publication Date: 1980.
Acronym: NA2.
Time: 15(20) minutes.

2) *Diagramming.*
Publication Date: 1980.
Acronym: DA5.
Time: 20(25) minutes.

3) *Verbal Concepts.*
Publication Date: 1980.
Acronym: VA1.
Time: 15(20) minutes.

4) *Basic Checking.*
Publication Dates: 1980–1981.
Acronym: CP7.
Time: 10(15) minutes.

5) *Spatial Recognition.*
Publication Dates: 1980–1981.
Acronym: ST9.
Time: 15(20) minutes.

b) LEVEL 2.
Publication Dates: 1979–1983.
Purpose: Complex programming skills.

1) *Number Series.*
Details same as for Level 1.

2) *Diagramming.*
Details same as for Level 1.

3) *Verbal Critical Reasoning.*
Publication Date: 1983.
Acronym: VA3.
Time: 30(35) minutes.

4) *Basic Checking.*
Details same as for Level 1.

5) *Special Reasoning.*
Publication Dates: 1979–1981.
Acronym: ST7.
Time: 20(25) minutes.

c) LEVEL 3.
Publication Dates: 1979–1983.
Population: Systems analysts and management.

1) *Verbal Concepts.*
Details same as for Level 1.

2) *Number Series.*
Details same as for Level 1.

3) *Verbal Reasoning.*
Details same as for Level 2.

4) *Numerical Critical Reasoning.*
Publication Dates: 1979–1983.
Acronym: NA4.
Time: 35(40) minutes.

5) *Diagrammatic Reasoning.*
Publication Dates: 1979–1981.
Acronym: DT8.
Time: 15(20) minutes.

[2155]

Progress Assessment Chart of Social and Personal Development.

Purpose: Constructed to assess progress in social development.

Publication Dates: 1966–1982.

Administration: Individual.

Price Data: Available from publisher.

Foreign Language Editions: Dutch, French, German, Portuguese, and Spanish editions available.

Time: Administration time not reported.

Comments: Behavior checklist.

Author: H. C. Gunzburg.

Publisher: SEFA (Publications) Ltd. [England].

a) PRIMARY PROGRESS ASSESSMENT CHART OF SOCIAL DEVELOPMENT, FORM P.
Population: Young mentally handicapped children, severely handicappted young children, and profoundly handicapped adults, very young normal children.
Acronym: P-PAC.
Scores: 4 areas: Self-Help, Communication, Occupation, Socialisation.

b) PROGRESS ASSESSMENT CHART OF SOCIAL AND PERSONAL DEVELOPMENT, FORM 1.
Population: Handicapped children and adolescents.
Acronym: PAC-1.
Scores: 5 areas: Same as a above plus Personal Assessment.

c) PROGRESS ASSESSMENT CHART OF SOCIAL AND PERSONAL DEVELOPMENT, FORM A1.
Population: Same as b above.
Acronym: A-PAC1.
Scores: Same as b above.
Comments: Extension of PAC-1.

d) PROGRESS ASSESSMENT CHART OF SOCIAL AND PERSONAL DEVELOPMENT, FORM 2.
Population: Mentally handicapped adolescents and adults.
Acronym: PAC-2.
Scores: Same as b above.

e) PROGRESS ASSESSMENT CHART OF THE SOCIAL DEVELOPMENT OF CHILDREN WITH DOWN'S SYNDROME, FORM 1.

Population: Mentally handicapped children with Down's Syndrome.

Acronym: M-PAC1.

Scores: Same as *a* above.

Authors: H. C. Gunzberg and Janice Sinson.

f) ELEMENTARY PROGRESS ASSESSMENT CHART, FORM S/E.

Population: Profoundly and severely handicapped persons.

Acronym: S/E PAC.

Scores: Same as *a* above.

g) PROGRESS ASSESSMENT CHART S1 OF SOCIAL AND PERSONAL DEVELOPMENT, FORM S1.

Population: Same as *f* above.

Acronym: S-PAC1.

Scores: Same as *b* above.

h) PROGRESS ASSESSMENT CHART OF SOCIAL AND PERSONAL DEVELOPMENT, FORM S2.

Population: Same as *f* above.

Acronym: S-PAC2.

Scores: Same as *b* above.

Cross References: See T5:2088 (1 reference); for reviews by Betty N. Gordon and Joel Hundert, see 9:1003; see also T3:1908 (1 reference), T2:1338 (3 references), 7:125 (1 reference), and P:216 (5 references).

[2156]

Progress in English 5–14.

Purpose: Designed as "a comprehensive standardized English test series that assesses reading and writing skills."

Population: Ages 4.0–15.05.

Publication Dates: 1994–2001.

Acronym: PiE 5–14.

Administration: Group.

Price Data: Available from publisher.

Comments: Assessments linked to curriculum guidelines for England and Wales, Scotland and Northern Ireland.

Publisher: GL Assessment [England].

a) PROGRESS IN ENGLISH 5.

Population: Ages 4.0–6.03.

Scores, 3: Initial Literacy, Understanding of Whole Text, Total.

Time: (40) minutes.

Authors: Lynn Howard, Anne Kispal, and Neil Hagues, National Foundation for Educational Research.

b) PROGRESS IN ENGLISH 6.

Population: Ages 5.0-7.05.

Scores, 5: Early Reading, Early Reading-Spelling, Understanding of Whole Text, Understanding Language in Context.

Time: (40-45) minutes.

Authors: Anne Kispal, and Neil Hagues, National Foundation for Educational Research.

c) PROGRESS IN ENGLISH 7.

Population: Ages 6.0–8.05.

Scores, 5: Understanding of Whole Text, Understanding Language in Context, Grammar, Spelling, Total.

Time: (60) minutes.

Authors: Anne Kispal, and Neil Hagues, National Foundation for Educational Research.

d) PROGRESS IN ENGLISH 8.

Population: Ages 7.0–9.5.

Scores, 5: Spelling, Grammar, Understanding of Whole Text, Understanding Language in Context, Total.

Time: (60) minutes.

Authors: Anne Kispal, Neil Hagues, and Graham Ruddock, National Foundation for Educational Research.

e) PROGRESS IN ENGLISH 9.

Population: Ages 8.0–10.05.

Scores, 6: Same as *d* above.

Time: (60) minutes.

Authors: Anne Kispal, Neil Hagues, and Graham Ruddock, National Foundation for Educational Research.

f) PROGRESS IN ENGLISH 10.

Population: Ages 9.0–11.05.

Scores, 6: Spelling, Grammar, Understanding of Whole Text, Vocabulary(Frequency and Spelling), Style, Total.

Time: (60) minutes.

Authors: Anne Kispal, Neil Hagues, and Graham Ruddock, National Foundation for Educational Research.

g) PROGRESS IN ENGLISH 11.

Population: Ages 10.0–12.05.

Scores, 6: Same as *f* above.

Time: (60) minutes.

Authors: Anne Kispal, Neil Hagues, and Graham Ruddock, National Foundation for Educational Research.

h) PROGRESS IN ENGLISH 12.

Population: Ages 11.0–13.05.

Scores, 6: Same as *f* above.

Time: (60) minutes.

Authors: Anne Kispal, Neil Hagues, and Graham Ruddock, National Foundation for Educational Research.

i) PROGRESS IN ENGLISH 13.

Population: Ages 12.0–14.05.

Scores, 6: Same as *f* above.

Time: (60) minutes.

Authors: Anne Kispal, Neil Hagues, and Graham Ruddock, National Foundation for Educational Research.

j) PROGRESS IN ENGLISH 14.

Population: Ages 13.0–15.05.

Scores, 6: Same as *f* above.
Time: (60) minutes.
Authors: Anne Kispal, and Neil Hagues, National Foundation for Educational Research.
Cross References: For reviews by Andrew A. Cox and Natalie Rathvon, see 16:201.

[2157]

Progressive Achievement Test of Mathematics, 2nd Edition.

Purpose: To assist classroom teachers in determining the mathematics skills of their students.
Population: Ages 8-14.
Publication Dates: 1974-2007.
Acronym: PAT Mathematics.
Scores: Total score only.
Administration: Group.
Levels, 7: Individual tests for 7 year levels.
Price Data, 2011: NZ$4 per test booklet; NZ$1.78 per 10 answer sheets; NZ$20 per teacher's manual (2007, 64 pages); NZ$2.40 per marking key; price data for specimen sets for split year levels available from publisher.
Time: (35-45) minutes.
Comments: Electronic marking service available to generate specific reports for each child/classroom/year level.
Authors: Charles Darr, Alex Neill, and Andrew Stephanou.
Publisher: New Zealand Council for Educational Research [New Zealand].
Cross References: For reviews by Linda E. Brady and Suzanne Lane of an earlier edition, see 12:313; see also T3:1911 (1 reference); for a review by Harold C. Trimble of an earlier edition, see 8:288; for reviews by James C. Impara and A. Harry Passow of an earlier Australian edition, see 11:309.

[2158]

Progressive Achievement Tests in Mathematics–3rd Edition.

Purpose: Designed "to provide information to teachers about the level of achievement attained by their students in the skills and understanding of mathematics."
Population: Australian students in years 3-10.
Publication Dates: 1983–2005.
Acronym: PATMaths 3rd edition.
Scores: Total score only.
Administration: Group.
Price Data, 2005: A$6.50 per test booklet; A$149.95 per specimen set including one of each test booklet, teacher's manual, answer sheet, and CD-ROM; A$50 per 10 answer sheets–OMR or non-OMR available.
Time: (45) minutes.
Author: Australian Council for Educational Research Press.

Publisher: Australian Council for Educational Research Ltd. [Australia].
   a) LEVEL 1.
   Population: Years 4–6.
   b) LEVEL 2.
   Population: Years 6–9.
   c) LEVEL 3.
   Population: Years 7–9.
Cross References: For reviews by Kevin D. Crehan and Cindy M. Walker of an earlier edition, see 15:199; see T5:2091 (5 references); for reviews by James C. Impara and A. Harry Passow of an earlier edition, see 11:309 (2 references). For information on the New Zealand edition, see T3:1911 (1 reference); for additional information and a review by Harold C. Trimble, see 8:288.

[2159]

Progressive Achievement Tests in Reading: Comprehension and Vocabulary–Third Edition.

Purpose: "Tests designed to assist teachers in their assessment of students' reading comprehension skills and vocabulary knowledge."
Population: Years 3-9 in Australian school system.
Publication Dates: 1973–2001.
Acronym: PAT-R.
Scores, 2: Reading Comprehension, Reading Vocabulary .
Administration: Individual or group.
Parts, 2: PAT-R: Comprehension, PAT-R: Vocabulary.
Levels, 4: 4 levels for Comprehension and for Vocabulary: Test Form 1 (Years 3–5), Test Form 2 (Years 4–6), Test Form 3 (Years 6–8), Test Form 4 (Years 7–9).
Price Data, 2006: A$130 per specimen set including revised teacher's manual with score keys (2001, 79 pages), Comprehension test forms 1–4 (reusable), Comprehension answer sheets (10 each for Forms 1–4), Vocabulary test forms 1–4 (reusable), Vocabulary answer sheets (10 each for Forms 1–4); $85 per revised manual with score keys; $6.30 per Comprehension test form (any of Levels 1–4); $3.85 per Vocabulary test for (any of Levels 1–4); $11 per 10 Comprehension answer sheets or 10 Vocabulary answer sheets (any of Levels 1–4).
Time: 40(55) minutes (Comprehension); 25 minutes (Vocabulary).
Comments: Developed especially, but not exclusively, for use in Australian schools; hand- or machine-scorable; machine scoring performed by publisher; two types of reports available (PAT-R Report, PAT-R Diagnostic Report).
Author: Australian Council for Educational Research, Ltd.
Publisher: Australian Council for Educational Research Ltd. [Australia].
Cross References: For a review by Mark H. Fugate, see 15:200; for information on an earlier edition, see T5:2092 (4 references); for reviews by Paul C. Burnett and Richard Lehrer of an earlier edition, see 11:310 (4 references); see also T3:1912 (4 references); for a review

by Douglas A. Pidgeon of an earlier edition, see 8:738 (1 reference); see also T2:1579 (1 reference); for excerpted reviews by Milton L. Clark and J. Elkins, see 7:699.

[2160]

Progressive Achievement Test of Listening Comprehension [Revised].

Purpose: "Intended ... to assist teachers in determining levels of development attained by their students in the basic skills of listening comprehension."

Population: Ages 7–14.

Publication Dates: 1971–1994.

Acronym: PAT: Listening Comprehension.

Scores: Total score only.

Administration: Group.

Levels: 8 overlapping levels labeled Parts 1–8: Primary: Parts 1–4 (Standards 1–4); Intermediate: Parts 5–6 (Forms 1–2); Secondary: Parts 7–8 (Forms 3–4).

Price Data, 2001: NZ$1.80 per Primary, Intermediate, or Secondary test booklet; $4.50 per Primary, Intermediate, or Secondary teacher's script; $.99 per scoring key; $1.44 per 10 answer sheets; $9 per Intermediate audiotape; $9.90 per Secondary audiotape; $9 per teacher's manual (1994, 32 pages).

Time: (55) minutes.

Comments: 2 forms (A & B) available (Form A is used in odd-numbered years and Form B is used in even-numbered years); this test was specifically developed for use in New Zealand schools.

Authors: Neil A. Reid, Ian C. Johnston, and Warwick B. Elley.

Publisher: New Zealand Council for Educational Research [New Zealand].

Cross References: For a review by Sherwyn Morreale and Philip Backlund, see 13:245 (1 reference); see also T4:2140 (2 references) and T3:1910 (1 reference); for a review by Roger A. Richards of an earlier edition, see 8:453 (2 references).

[2161]

Progressive Achievement Tests of Reading [2008 Revision].

Purpose: Designed to "assist classroom teachers to determine the level of achievement attained by their students in reading comprehension and reading vocabulary."

Population: Years 4-10.

Publication Dates: 1969-2008.

Scores, 2: Reading Comprehension, Reading Vocabulary.

Administration: Group.

Levels, 7: 1, 2, 3, 4, 5, 6, 7.

Price Data: Available from publisher.

Comments: Scores on the tests are converted to scores on the Reading Comprehension and Reading Vocabulary measurement scales. This allows progress to be measured across tests.

Authors: Charles Darr, Sue McDowall, Hilary Ferral, Juliet Twist, and Verena Watson.

Publisher: New Zealand Council for Educational Research [New Zealand].

  a) READING COMPREHENSION.

  Acronym: PATC.

  Time: (55) minutes.

  b) READING VOCABULARY.

  Acronym: PATV.

  Time: (35) minutes.

Cross References: See T5:2094 (3 references); for a review by Herbert C. Rudman of an earlier edition, see 12:314 (3 references); see also T4:2141 (7 references) and T3:1912 (2 references); for a review by Douglas A. Pidgeon, see 8:738 (1 reference); see also T2:1579 (1 reference); for excerpted reviews by Milton L. Clark and J. Elkins, see 7:699.

[2162]

Project Implementation Profile.

Purpose: To identify and measure behavioral variables that may be related to project success.

Population: Project managers and team members.

Publication Date: 1992.

Acronym: PIP.

Scores, 11: Project Mission, Top Management Support, Project Schedule, Client Consultation, Personnel, Technical Tasks, Client Acceptance, Monitoring and Feedback, Communication, Trouble-Shooting, Overall Performance.

Administration: Group.

Price Data: Available from publisher.

Time: (20) minutes.

Authors: Jeffrey K. Pinto and Dennis P. Slevin.

Publisher: Innodyne, Inc.

Cross References: For reviews by Sally Kuhlenschmidt and Kimberly A. Lawless, see 13:246.

[2163]

Project Leader Skills Evaluation.

Purpose: To assess essential skills needed for the position of Project Leader.

Population: Candidates for Project Leader position.

Publication Date: 1993.

Scores: Total Score, Narrative Evaluation, Ranking, Recommendation.

Administration: Group.

Price Data, 2001: $235 per candidate; quantity discounts available.

Foreign Language Edition: Available in French.

Time: [60] minutes.

Comments: Scored by publisher; available in booklet and Internet versions; must be proctored.

Author: Bruce A. Winrow.

Publisher: Walden Personnel Performance, Inc. [Canada].

Cross References: For reviews by Laura L. B. Barnes and Alan D. Moore, see 16:202.

[2164]

Project Management Competency Assessment.

Purpose: Designed to assess project manager competencies.
Population: Project managers.
Publication Date: 1996.
Scores, 18: Project Definition, Organization Awareness, Team Leadership, Time Management, Resource Management, Lost Management, Quality Management, Risk Management, Team Facilitation, Managing Conflict, Negotiating Changes, Communication Management, Project Integration, Receiving Feedback, Results Focus, Goal Pressure, Delegation, Recognition.
Administration: Group.
Manual: No manual.
Price Data: Available from publisher.
Time: Administration time not reported.
Comments: Ratings by self and/or coworkers; can be used alone or in conjunction with Project Management Knowledge & Skills Assessment (14:298).
Author: Clark L. Wilson.
Publisher: The Clark Wilson Group for the exclusive use of Educational Services Institute.

[2165]

Projective Storytelling Cards.

Purpose: "This is neither a test nor a technique, but a carefully designed system of card pictures, characters, and potential themes that serve as the basis for endless interactive assessment and treatment uses."
Population: Children and adolescents.
Publication Dates: 1993–2000.
Scores: No scores.
Administration: Individual.
Price Data, 2000: $35 per 35-card set including user's manual (2000, 67 pages); $40 per 12-card Child Exploitation Series; $165 per 35-card set and 12-card set; $17.50 per Court Preparation Set including 5 cards plus booklet of "Chris Tells the Truth."
Time: Administration time not reported.
Comments: Projective nontest; up to 47 different cards; cards are available in minority sets, nonminority sets, and racially mixed sets.
Authors: Kent R. Caruso and Richard J. Pulcini.
Publisher: Northwest Psychological Publishers, Inc.

[2166]

Proof-Reading Tests of Spelling.

Purpose: Constructed to measure a child's ability to discriminate between words spelled correctly and incor-

rectly in the context of meaningful paragraphs.
Population: Ages 8–13.
Publication Date: 1981.
Acronym: PRETOS.
Scores, 2: Production, Recognition.
Administration: Group.
Levels, 5: Test 2, Test 3, Test 4, Test 5, Test 6.
Price Data: Available from publisher.
Time: 30 minutes.
Authors: Cedric Croft, Alison Gilmore, Neil Reid, and Peter Jackson.
Publisher: New Zealand Council for Educational Research [New Zealand].
Cross References: See T4:2146 (2 references); for a review by Sally Anita Whiting, see 9:1009.

[2167]

Prospector: Discovering the Ability to Learn and to Lead.

Purpose: "Designed to assess openness to learning from experience."
Population: Managers and executives.
Publication Date: 1996.
Scores, 11: Seeks Opportunities to Learn, Has the Courage to Take Risks, Seeks Broad Business Knowledge, Adapts to Cultural Differences, Acts with Integrity, Is Committed to Making a Difference, Brings Out the Best in People, Is Insightful: Sees Things from New Angles, Seeks and Uses Feedback, Learns from Mistakes, Is Open to Criticism.
Administration: Group.
Price Data, 2006: $225 per set including an unlimited number of questionnaires (Prospector is only available on-line), feedback reports, one learning guide, and one facilitators guide (96 pages); quantity discounts are available.
Time: [10–15] minutes.
Authors: Morgan W. McCall, Gretchen M. Spreitzer, and Joan Jay Mahoney.
Publisher: Center for Creative Leadership.
Cross References: For reviews by Theodore L. Hayes and Neil P. Lewis, see 14:299.

[2168]

PSACS Public Safety Assessment Center System for Police Sergeant.

Purpose: Designed "to help assess the promotional potential of police officers for the position of police sergeant."
Population: Candidates for promotion to the police sergeant position.
Publication Date: 2006.
Acronym: PSACS.
Scores: 7 competencies: Problem Identification and Analysis, Decision Making/Decisiveness, Oral

Communication, Written Communication, Interpersonal and Community Relations, Planning and Supervising, Applied Technical Knowledge.
Administration: Individual or group.
Price Data: Available from publisher.
Time: 2 days.
Comments: Part of Public Safety Assessment Center System; modifications for rank structure or job title for sheriff's departments can be made; system includes subordinate role play exercise, video-based technical exercise, and an in-basket exercise; the system contains multiple simulation exercises, some of which are automated; also includes educational and training materials for jurisdictions to administer the assessment center without incurring the added cost of hiring a consultant; exercises vary by rank and are updated every other year.
Author: International Public Management Association for Human Resources.
Publisher: International Public Management Association for Human Resources (IPMA-HR).

[2169]

PSB Aptitude for Practical Nursing Examination.

Purpose: Designed as a "method of selection, placement, guidance and counseling of incoming practical/vocational nursing students."
Population: Applicants for admission to practical/vocational nursing schools.
Publication Dates: 1961-2006.
Scores, 8: Academic Aptitude (Verbal, Arithmetic, Nonverbal, Total), Spelling, Information in the Natural Sciences, Judgment and Comprehension in Practical Nursing Situations, Vocational Adjustment Index.
Administration: Individual or group.
Price Data, 2006: $15 per electronic test.
Time: (135) minutes.
Comments: Electronic tests available at www.psbtests.com.
Authors: Anna S. Evans, Phyllis G. Roumm, and George A. W. Stouffer, Jr., with technical assistance from Psychological Services Bureau, Inc.
Publisher: Psychological Services Bureau, Inc.
Cross References: For reviews by Mark Albanese and Anita Tesh of the Revised PSB Aptitude for Practical Nursing Examination, see 13:264.

[2170]

PSB Health Occupations Aptitude Examination.

Purpose: Measures "abilities, skills, knowledge, and attitudes important for successful performance of students in the allied health education programs."
Population: Candidates for admission to programs of

study for the allied health occupations.
Publication Dates: 1978–1999.
Scores, 8: Academic Aptitude (Verbal, Arithmetic, Nonverbal, Total), Spelling, Reading Comprehension, Information in the Natural Sciences, Vocational Adjustment Index.
Administration: Group or individual.
Price Data, 2006: $15 per electronic test.
Time: (135) minutes.
Comments: Electronic tests available at www.psbtests.com.
Authors: Psychological Services Bureau, Inc. with consultant contributions.
Publisher: Psychological Services Bureau, Inc.
Cross References: For reviews by Betty Bergstrom and Hilda Wing of the Revised PSB Health Occupations Aptitude Examination, see 13:265; for reviews by Stephen B. Dunbar and Lawrence M. Rudner of an earlier edition, see 11:312.

[2171]

PSB Reading Comprehension Examination.

Purpose: To reveal the examinee's comprehension or understanding of what is read.
Population: Secondary and postsecondary students applying or enrolled in terminal vocational or occupational programs, general population.
Publication Dates: 2000-2006.
Scores: Total score only.
Administration: Group or individual.
Price Data, 2006: $15 per electronic test.
Time: (60) minutes.
Comments: Electronic tests available at www.psbtests.com.
Authors: Psychological Services Bureau, Inc., with consultant contributions.
Publisher: Psychological Services Bureau, Inc.
Cross References: For reviews by Ray Fenton and Felice J. Green of the Revised PSB–Reading Comprehension Examination, see 13:267; for reviews by Joseph C. Ciechalski and by Brandon Davis and John A. Glover of an earlier edition, see 11:314.

[2172]

PSB Registered Nursing School Aptitude Examination.

Purpose: Predicts "readiness or suitability for specialized instruction in a school/program of professional nursing."
Population: Prospective nursing students.
Publication Dates: 1978-2006.
Scores, 8: Academic Aptitude (Verbal, Arithmetic, Nonverbal, Total), Spelling, Reading Comprehension, Information in the Natural Sciences, Vocational Adjustment Index.
Administration: Individual or group.

Price Data, 2006: $15 per electronic test.
Time: (105) minutes.
Comments: Electronic tests available at www.psbtests.com; previously listed as PSB Nursing School Aptitude Examination (RN).
Authors: Anna S. Evans, Phyllis G. Roumm, and George A. W. Stouffer, Jr.
Publisher: Psychological Services Bureau, Inc.
Cross References: For reviews by Mark H. Daniel and William B. Michael of the Revised PSB–Nursing School Aptitude Examination (R.N.), see 13:266; for reviews by Kurt F. Geisinger and James C. Impara of an earlier edition, see 11:313.

[2173]

PSC-Survey ADT.

Purpose: "Evaluates a job applicant's attitudes toward companies, business, work and trust attitudes."
Population: Job applicants.
Publication Date: 1987.
Scores, 4: Alienation, Trustworthiness, Total, False Positives.
Administration: Group or individual.
Price Data: Available from publisher.
Time: (15–20) minutes.
Comments: On-site scoring available.
Authors: Alan L. Strand and Mark L. Strand.
Publisher: Predictive Surveys Corporation.
Cross References: For a review by Chantale Jeanrie, see 13:247.

[2174]

PSC Survey-SA.

Purpose: "Measures attitudes toward the position of supervisor for selection or promotion."
Population: Job applicants or current employees.
Publication Date: 1987.
Scores, 6: Attitudes Toward Companies and Business, Attitudes Toward Managers and Executives, Attitudes Toward Peers and Associates, Attitudes Toward Being a Supervisor, Attitudes Toward Subordinates, Total.
Administration: Group or individual.
Price Data: Available from publisher.
Time: (10–15) minutes.
Authors: Alan L. Strand and Mark L. Strand.
Publisher: Predictive Surveys Corporation.
Cross References: For reviews by L. Carolyn Pearson and E. Lea Witta, see 13:248.

[2175]

PSI Basic Skills Tests for Business, Industry, and Government.

Purpose: "Designed to assess abilities and skills that are important for clerical, Administrative, and customer service positions."

Population: Prospective administrative, customer service, and clerical employees.
Publication Dates: 1981–1984.
Acronym: BST.
Scores: 15 subtest scores: Language Skills, Reading Comprehension, Vocabulary, Computation, Problem Solving, Decision Making, Following Oral Directions, Following Written Directions, Forms Checking, Reasoning, Classifying, Coding, Filing Names, Filing Numbers, Visual Speed and Accuracy.
Administration: Group or individual.
Price Data: Price information available from publisher for test material including User's Manual (2005, 59 pages), Technical Manual (2001, 61 pages), Technical Report Addendum: Meta-Analysis of the Validity of the Basic Skills Tests (2002, 14 pages), Validation Report (1982, 93 pages).
Time: 1.5-10(5-15) minutes for each test.
Comments: Tests available separately; computerized versions available; transportability procedure available.
Authors: William W. Ruch, Allen N. Shub, Sheryl M. Moinat, and David A. Dye.
Publisher: Psychological Services, Inc.
Cross References: See T5:2105 (1 reference); for reviews by Michael J. Stahl and Sheldon Zedeck, see 9:1010.

[2176]

PST-100SV and PST-80SV Public Safety Telecommunicator Tests.

Purpose: Designed to assess critical abilities required for entry-level public safety telecommunicator positions.
Population: Candidates for entry-level public safety communicator positions.
Publication Date: 1995.
Acronym: PST-80SV, PST-100SV.
Scores: 5 knowledge areas: Listening Skills, Reading Comprehension, Ability to Learn and Apply Information, Reasoning Ability, Ability to Use Situational Judgment.
Administration: Individual or group.
Forms, 2: PST-80SV, PST-100SV.
Price Data: Available from publisher.
Time: 144 minutes for PST-100SV; 120 minutes for PST-80SV.
Comments: The two versions contain exactly the same questions with the exception of the Listening Skills subtest, which has an audio component and so the PST-80SV version of the exam is available for those jurisdictions that do not have the audio equipment needed to administer the Listening Skills subtest.
Author: International Public Management Association for Human Resources.
Publisher: International Public Management Association for Human Resources (IPMA-HR).
Cross References: For a review by Myra N. Womble, see 18:101.

[2177]

PSUP 1.1, 2.1, and 3.1 Police Supervisor Tests (Corporal/Sergeant).

Purpose: Designed as "a promotional test for first-line police supervisor."

Population: Candidates for promotion to the police supervisor or corporal/sergeant position.

Publication Dates: 2003-2006.

Acronym: PSUP 1.1, PSUP 2.1, PSUP 3.1.

Scores: 5 knowledge areas: Laws Related to Police Work, Police Field Operations, Investigative Procedures, Supervisory Principles and Concepts & Reports, Records and Paperwork.

Administration: Individual or group.

Forms, 3: PSUP 1.1, PSUP 2.1, PSUP 3.1.

Price Data: Available from publisher.

Time: 150 minutes per test.

Comments: PSUP 1.1, PSUP 2.1, PSUP 3.1 are comparable forms; reading lists are available to help candidates prepare for the tests.

Authors: International Public Management Association for Human Resources & Bruce Davey Associates.

Publisher: International Public Management Association for Human Resources (IPMA-HR).

Cross References: For a review by Jay R. Stewart, see 18:102.

[2178]

PsychEval Personality Questionnaire.

Purpose: "Measures both normal personality and pathology-oriented traits to provide a multidimensional profile of the individual."

Population: Ages 16 and over; adults.

Publication Dates: 2002-2007.

Acronym: PEPQ.

Administration: Individual or group.

Price Data, 2010: $84 per interpretation introductory kit including manual (2006, 133 pages), test booklet, answer sheet, and pre-paid mail-in processing certificate; $59.75 per manual; $24.75 per 10 reusable test booklets; $22.25 per 25 answer sheets; publisher scoring rate varies by quantity ($24.25 to $36 per report); $83 per Protective Services Report Plus introductory kit including manual (2007, 116 pages), questionnaire, answer sheet, and pre-paid mail-in report processing certificate; $59.75 per Protective Services Report manual; $23.50 to $35 per Protective Services Report Plus (volume discounts available).

Time: (75-90) minutes.

Comments: Computer administration and scoring available; Reports: Protective Services Report Plus available for post-offer selection and fitness for duty evaluations for personnel in high-risk, public safety professions; PEPQ Interpretation available for use in both personal and vocational counseling.

Authors: Raymond B. Cattell, A. Karen S. Cattell, Heather E. P. Cattell, Mary T. Russell, and Scott Bedwell.

Publisher: Institute for Personality and Ability Testing, Inc. (IPAT).

a) RESPONSE STYLE INDICES.

Scores, 3: Impression Management, Infrequency, Acquiescence.

b) NORMAL PERSONALITY SCALES.

Scores: 16 Primary Factors: Warmth, Reasoning, Emotional Stability, Dominance, Liveliness, Rule-Consciousness, Social Boldness, Sensitivity, Vigilance, Abstractedness, Privateness, Apprehension, Openness to Change, Self-Reliance, Perfectionism, Tension; 5 Global Factors: Extraversion, Anxiety, Tough-Mindedness, Independence, Self-Control.

Comments: Items and norms from the 16PF Fifth Edition (2471).

c) PATHOLOGY ORIENTED SCALES.

Scores, 12: Psychological Inadequacy, Health Concerns, Suicidal Thinking, Anxious Depression, Low Energy State, Self-Reproach, Apathetic Withdrawal, Paranoid Ideation, Obsessional Thinking, Alienation and Perceptual Distortion, Thrill-Seeking, Threat-Immunity.

d) INDICES.

Scores, 4: Quick-Eval, Depressive Characteristics, Distorted Thought Patterns, Risk-Taking.

e) OCCUPATIONAL INTEREST SECTION.

Scores, 6: Realistic Theme, Investigative Theme, Artistic Theme, Social Theme, Enterprising Theme, Conventional Theme.

Cross References: For reviews by Eugene V. Aidman and Frederick T. L. Leong, see 18:103.

[2179]

Psychiatric Content Analysis and Diagnosis.

Purpose: "For measuring the magnitude of various psychological states and traits from the content analysis of verbal behavior."

Population: Children and adults.

Publication Dates: 1993-2000.

Acronym: PCAD.

Scores, 13: Anxiety Scale, Hostility Scales (Hostility Directed Outward, Hostility Directed Inward, Ambivalent Hostility), Social Alienation–Personal Disorganization Scale, Cognitive and Intellectual Impairment Scale, Depression Scale, Hope Scale, Health-Sickness Scale, Achievement Striving Scale, Human Relations Scale, Dependency Strivings Scale, Quality of Life Scale.

Administration: Individual or group.

Price Data, 2005: $299.95 per software license including media and manual (2000, 83 pages).

Time: (5) minutes; more if multiple speakers.

Comments: Earlier version listed in previous Buros publications as Psychologic and Neuropsychiatric Assessment Manual.

Authors: Louis A. Gottschalk and Robert Bechtel.
Publisher: GB Software LLC.
Cross References: For a review by William M. Reynolds, see 14:300.

[2180]

Psychiatric Diagnostic Screening Questionnaire.

Purpose: "Designed to screen for the DSM-IV (Diagnostic and Statistical Manual of Mental Disorders, Fourth Edition) Axis I disorders most commonly encountered in medical and outpatient mental health settings."
Population: Adult psychiatric patients.
Publication Date: 2002.
Acronym: PDSQ.
Scores, 14: Major Depressive Disorder, Posttraumatic Stress Disorder, Bulimia/Binge-Eating Disorder, Obsessive-Compulsive Disorder, Panic Disorder, Psychosis, Agoraphobia, Social Phobia, Alcohol Abuse/Dependence, Drug Abuse/Dependence, Generalized Anxiety Disorder, Somatization Disorder, Hypochondriasis, Total.
Administration: Individual.
Price Data, 2006: $114.50 per test kit including manual, 25 test booklets, 25 summary sheets, and CD containing 13 follow-up interview guides (one for each disorder); $49.50 per manual; $43.50 per 25 test booklets; $29 per 100 summary sheets; volume discounts available.
Time: (15–20) minutes.
Comments: Self-report questionnaire.
Author: Mark Zimmerman.
Publisher: Western Psychological Services.
Cross References: For reviews by Michael G. Kavan and Sean P. Reilley, see 16:203.

[2181]

Psychiatric Evaluation Form.

Purpose: Designed "to record scaled judgments of a subject's functioning during a one week period" on dimensions of psychopathology.
Population: Psychiatric patients and nonpatients.
Publication Dates: 1967-1968.
Acronym: PEF.
Scores, 28: 20 psychopathological scores in Part I (Narcotics-Drugs, Agitation-Excitement, Suicide-Self Mutilation, Grandiosity, Somatic Concerns, Anti-Social Attitudes-Acts, Speech Disorganization, Hallucinations, Social Isolation, Belligerence-Negativism, Disorientation-Memory, Alcohol Abuse, Anxiety, Inappropriate, Suspicion-Persecution, Daily Routine-Leisure Time, Denial of Illness, Depression, Retardation-Lack of Emotion, Overall Severity of Illness), 3 occupational roles and 2 social roles; 3 admission scores (Duration, Stress, Reason for Admission).
Administration: Individual.
Price Data, 2001: $3.50 per booklet including score sheet; $1 per instruction manual; $4 per teaching tape/key; additional price data available from publisher.

Time: (20-40) minutes.
Authors: Robert L. Spitzer, Jean Endicott, Alvin Mesnikoff, and George Cohen.
Publisher: Department of Research Assessment and Training.
Cross References: See T5:2108 (5 references) and T4:2153 (9 references); for reviews by Goldine C. Gleser and Jerome D. Pauker, see 7:126 (1 reference); see also T3:1922 (15 references) and T2:1339 (4 references).

[2182]

Psychiatric Self-Assessment & Review.

Purpose: "To assist psychiatrists in keeping abreast of new knowledge and scientific developments in the field of psychology."
Population: Physicians.
Publication Date: 1999.
Acronym: PSA-R.
Scores: Total score only.
Administration: Individual.
Price Data: Available from publisher.
Time: Administration time not reported.
Comments: Self-administered and self-scored; information regarding obtaining Continuing Medical Education credit for this examination available from publisher.
Authors: American Psychiatric Association.
Publisher: American Psychiatric Association.

[2183]

The Psychiatric Status Schedule: Subject Form, Second Edition.

Purpose: Designed to evaluate social and role functioning as well as mental status.
Population: Psychiatric patients and nonpatients.
Publication Dates: 1966-1968.
Acronym: PSS-2.
Scores, 43: 18 symptom scores (Inappropriate Affect–Appearance–Behavior, Interview Belligerence–Negativism, Agitation–Excitement, Retardation–Lack of Emotion, Speech Disorganization, Grandiosity, Suspicion–Persecution–Hallucinations, Reported Overt Anger, Depression–Anxiety, Suicide–Self-Mutilation, Somatic Concerns, Social Isolation, Daily Routine–Leisure Time Impairment, Antisocial Impulses or Acts, Alcoholic Abuse, Drug Abuse, Disorientation Memory, Denial or Illness), 5 role functioning scores (Wage Earner, Housekeeper, Student or Trainee, Mate, Parent), 5 summary symptom and role scales (Subjective Distress, Behavioral Disturbance, Impulse Control Disturbance, Reality Testing Disturbance, Summary Role), 20 supplemental scores (Anxiety, Auditory Hallucinations, Catatonic Behavior, Conversion Reaction, Delusions–Hallucinations, Depression–Suicide, Disassociation, Elated Mood, Guilt, Lack of Emotion, Obsessions–Compulsions, Persecutory Delusions, Pho-

bia, Psychomotor Retardation, Sex Deviation, Silliness, Somatic Delusions or Hallucinations, Visual Hallucinations, Miscellaneous, Validity Check).
Administration: Individual.
Price Data: Available from publisher.
Time: (30-50) minutes.
Comments: Most sections dealing with signs and symptoms of psychiatric disorder are from Mental Status Schedule.
Authors: Robert L. Spitzer, Jean Endicott, and George M. Cohen.
Publisher: Department of Research Assessment and Training.
Cross References: See T5:2109 (1 reference), T4:2154 (14 references), T3:1923 (18 references), and T2:1340 (6 references); for a review by Hans H. Strupp, see 7:127 (5 references).

[2184]

Psycho-Epistemological Profile.
Purpose: "Designed to provide a profile of an individual's epistemological hierarchy."
Population: College and adults.
Publication Dates: 1968–1980.
Acronym: PEP.
Scores, 3: Metaphoric, Rational, Empirical.
Administration: Group.
Price Data: Available from publisher.
Foreign Language Edition: French edition available.
Time: (20–30) minutes.
Comments: Experimental form.
Authors: J. R. Royce and L. P. Mos.
Publisher: Psychometric Affiliates.
Cross References: See T5:2112 (1 reference) and T4:2157 (2 references); for reviews by Bruce A. Bracken and Thomas J. Kehle, see 9:1013; see also 8:653 (2 references).

[2185]

Psychoeducational Profile–Third Edition.
Purpose: Designed as a measure of autism and related developmental disabilities.
Population: Ages 6 months to 7 years 5 months.
Publication Dates: 1979-2005.
Acronym: PEP-3.
Administration: Individual.
Price Data, 2011: $536 per complete kit including examiner's manual, guide to item administration, picture book, 10 examiner scoring/summary booklets, 10 response booklets, 10 caregiver report forms, and object kit; $70 per examiner's manual; $47 per guide to item administration; $47 per picture book; $32 per 10 examiner scoring/summary booklets; $23 per 10 response booklets; $23 per 10 caregiver report forms; $333 per object kit.
Time: (45-90) minutes.

Comments: Includes a norm-referenced scale and parent/caregiver scale; caregiver "must be an adult who is familiar with the behavior of the child being evaluated."
Authors: Eric Schopler, Margaret D. Lansing, Robert J. Reichler, and Lee M. Marcus.
Publisher: PRO-ED.
a) PERFORMANCE PART.
1) *Developmental Abilities.*
Scores: 6 subscales: Cognitive Verbal/Preverbal, Expressive Language, Receptive Language, Fine Motor, Gross Motor, Visual-Motor Imitation.
2) *Maladaptive Behaviors.*
Scores: 4 subscales: Affective Expression, Social Reciprocity, Characteristic Motor Behaviors, Characteristic Verbal Behaviors.
3) *Composites.*
Scores: 3 subscales: Communication, Motor, Maladaptive Behaviors.
b) CAREGIVER REPORT.
1) *Clinical Sections.*
Scores: 3 subtests: Problem Behaviors, Personal Self-Care, Adaptive Behavior.
Cross References: For reviews by Pat Mirenda and Leah M. Nellis, see 17:156; see also T5:2111 (2 references); for reviews by Pat Mirenda and Gerald Tindal of an earlier edition, see 12:316 (2 references); for reviews by Gerald S. Hanna and Martin J. Wiese of the original edition, see 11:317.

[2186]

Psycholinguistic Assessments of Language Processing in Aphasia.
Purpose: Designed as "an assessment of language processing in adult acquired aphasia."
Population: Adults with aphasia.
Publication Date: 1992.
Acronym: PALPA.
Scores: Available from publisher.
Administration: Individual.
Price Data, 2001: $397 per box file including 60 tests.
Time: Administration time not reported.
Authors: Janice Kay, Ruth Lesser, and Max Coltheart.
Publisher: Psychology Press.

[2187]

Psychological Indicator for Assessing Quantities of Love with Regard to Various Types of Love.
Purpose: Designed to assess a person's love for various activities, lifestyles, and people.
Population: Contact publisher for details.
Publication Dates: 2004-2005.
Administration: Group or individual.

Manual: No manual.
Price Data, 2010: $20-50 per survey, based on ability to pay.
Time: Administration time not reported.
Comments: Survey price range is based upon the consumer's ability to pay.
Authors: James T. Struck, with contributions from Marina Garavaglia and Darren Rubin.
Publisher: Dinosaurs, Trees, Religion and Galaxies.

[2188]

Psychological Processing Checklist–Revised.

Purpose: Designed to assess processing deficits by differentiating "between learning disabilities, under-achievement and other disabling conditions" to inform intervention development.
Population: Ages 5-10.
Publication Dates: 2003-2008.
Acronym: PPC-R.
Scores, 7: Auditory Processing, Social Perception, Visual Processing, Organization, Visual-Motor Process-ing, Attention, Total Score.
Administration: Individual or group.
Price Data, 2011: $105 per complete test kit; $71 per technical manual (2008, 84 pages): $50 per 25 QuikScore forms.
Time: (15) minutes.
Comments: To be completed by the student's regular or special education teacher.
Authors: Mark E. Swerdlik, Peggy Swerdlik, Jeffrey H. Kahn, and Tim Thomas.
Publisher: Multi-Health Systems, Inc.
Cross References: For reviews by Joyce Meikamp and Jeanette Lee-Farmer and by Tawnya J. Meadows and Natasha Segool, see 18:104; for reviews by Bruce A. Bracken and Keith F. Widaman of the earlier edi-tion, see 16:204.

[2189]

Psychological Screening Inventory.

Purpose: Developed to screen for mental health problems.
Population: Ages 16 and over.
Publication Date: 1973-1978.
Acronym: PSI.
Scores, 5: Alienation, Social Nonconformity, Discom-fort, Expression, Defensiveness.
Administration: Group or individual.
Price Data, 2010: $84 per examination kit including manual (1978, 44 pages), 5 question-and-answer sheets, 5 profile sheets, and set of scoring templates; $32 per test manual; $50 per set of scoring templates; $60 per testing kit (including 25 question-and-answer sheets and 25 profile sheets).
Foreign Language Edition: Available in Spanish (question and answer sheets only).

Time: 15 minutes.
Author: Richard I. Lanyon.
Publisher: SIGMA Assessment Systems, Inc.
Cross References: See T5:2115 (6 references), T4:2159 (20 references), 9:1015 (2 references), and T3:1931 (18 references); for a review by Stephen L. Golding, see 8:654 (32 references); see also T2:1342 (7 references).

[2190]

Psychometric Behavior Checklist.

Purpose: For recording unusual test taking behavior.
Population: Adults.
Publication Date: 1960.
Acronym: PBC.
Score: Total score only.
Administration: Group.
Price Data: Available from publisher.
Time: Administration time not reported.
Comments: Also called Maryland Test Behavior Checklist.
Authors: Bernard G. Berenson, Kathryn C. Biersdorf, Thomas M. Magoon, Martha J. Maxwell, Donald K. Pumroy, and Marjorie H. Richey.
Publisher: University of Maryland, University Counsel-ing Center [No reply from publisher; status unknown].
Cross References: See 6:166 (1 reference).

[2191]

Psychopathic Personality Inventory–Revised.

Purpose: Designed to help "assess psychopathic per-sonality traits."
Population: Ages 18-86.
Publication Date: 2005.
Acronym: PPI-R.
Scores, 15: 8 Content scores (Machiavellian Egocen-tricity, Rebellious Nonconformity, Blame Externalization, Carefree Nonplanfulness, Social Influence, Fearlessness, Stress Immunity, Coldheartedness), Total, 4 Valid-ity scores (Virtuous Responding, Deviant Responding, Inconsistent Responding 15, Inconsistent Responding 40), 3 Factor scores (Self-Centered Impulsivity, Fearless Dominance, Coldheartedness).
Administration: Individual or group.
Price Data, 2007: $210 per introductory kit includ-ing professional manual (166 pages), 25 item booklets, 25 response forms, and 25 scoring summary forms; $72 per professional manual; $46 per 25 response forms; $55 per 25 reusable item booklets; $46 per 25 scoring summary forms.
Time: (20-30) minutes.
Comments: "PPI-R scores and profiles should not be used as the sole basis for diagnostic and treatment decisions that require the integration of information from varying sources."

Authors: Scott O. Lilienfeld and Michelle R. Widows.
Publisher: Psychological Assessment Resources, Inc.
Cross References: For reviews by Gerald E. De-Mauro and S. Alvin Leung, see 17:157.

[2192]
Psychosocial Adjustment to Illness Scale.

Purpose: "Designed to assess the quality of a patient's psychosocial adjustment to a current medical illness or its residual effects."
Population: Medical patients or their immediate relatives.
Publication Date: 1983.
Acronym: PAIS and PAIS-SR.
Scores, 8: Health Care Orientation, Vocational Environment, Domestic Environment, Sexual Relationship, Extended Family, Social Environment, Psychological Distress, Total.
Administration: Individual.
Editions, 3: Interview, Self-Report, Caretaker version.
Price Data, 2006: $3 per reusable booklet (interview); $1.30 per self-report booklet; $.50 per score/profile sheet (select edition); $.25 per score sheet; $29 per manual (56 pages).
Time: (20–30) minutes.
Comments: Scoring is available online, $1.50 per scoring, at www.derogatis-tests.com.
Author: Leonard R. Derogatis.
Publisher: Clinical Psychometric Research, Inc.
Cross References: See T5:2117 (5 references) and T4:2161 (3 references); for a review by Cabrini S. Swassing, see 10:299.

[2193]
Psychosocial Evaluation & Threat Risk Assessment.

Purpose: Designed to "assist school personnel in ... determining the nature and degree of violence risk among students."
Population: Ages 11-18.
Publication Date: 2005.
Acronym: PETRA.
Scores, 15: 4 Domain scores (Psychological Domain, Ecological Domain, Resiliency Problems Domain, Total Domain), 8 Cluster scores (Depressed Mood, Alienation, Egocentricism, Aggression, Family/Home, School, Stress, Coping Problems), 2 Response Style Indicator scores (Social Desirability, Inconsistency), PETRA Threat Assessment Matrix score.
Administration: Individual or group.
Price Data, 2007: $115 per introductory kit including professional manual (2005, 85 pages), 25 rating forms, and 25 score summary/profile forms; $50 per professional manual; $50 per 25 rating forms; $25 per 25 score summary/profile forms.
Time: (10-15) minutes.

Author: Jay Schneller.
Publisher: Psychological Assessment Resources, Inc.
Cross References: For reviews by Michael Furlong and Diane Tanigawa and by Georgette Yetter, see 17:158.

[2194]
Psychosocial Pain Inventory [Revised].

Purpose: "Provides a standardized method of evaluating psychosocial factors important in maintaining and exacerbating chronic pain problems."
Population: Adults with chronic pain.
Publication Dates: 1980–1985.
Acronym: PSPI.
Scores: Item scores only.
Administration: Individual.
Price Data, 2006: $115 per introductory kit including manual (1985, 38 pages) and 50 forms.
Time: [60-120] minutes.
Authors: R. K. Heaton, R. A. W. Lehman, and C. J. Getto.
Publisher: Psychological Assessment Resources, Inc.
Cross References: For reviews by Julie A. Allison and Dennis C. Harper, see 14:301; see also T4:2162 (1 reference).

[2195]
Psychotherapy Outcome Kit (Including Quality of Emotional Life Self-Report).

Purpose: Designed to assist mental health care providers in collecting treatment outcome data.
Population: Age 15 and under, Age 16 and older.
Publication Date: 1994.
Scores: Total score only.
Administration: Individual.
Price Data: Available from publisher at www.mindgarden.com
Time: Administration time not reported.
Author: David P. Isenberg.
Publisher: Mind Garden, Inc.
> *a)* CHILD VERSION.
> **Population**: Age 15 and under.
> **Comments**: Child Version QELSR completed by parent/guardian.
> *b)* ADULT VERSION.
> **Population**: Age 16 and older.
> **Comments**: Adult Version QELSR completed by patient.
Cross References: For reviews by Matthew Burns and George Domino, see 14:302.

[2196]
PsychProfiler.

Purpose: Assists in the "identification and treatment of disorders in children, adolescents and adults."
Scores, 54: 22 "Positive Screen Cutoff" conclusions (YES/NO) per population level: Generalised Anxiety

Disorder, Obsessive-Compulsive Disorder, Post-Traumatic Stress Disorder, Attention-Deficit/Hyperactivity Disorder (Hyperactive-Impulsive Type, Inattentive Type, Combined Type), Conduct Disorder, Oppositional Defiant Disorder, Expressive Language Disorder, Mixed Receptive-Expressive Language Disorder, Phonological Disorder, Dysthymic Disorder, Anorexia Nervosa, Bulimia Nervosa, Disorder of Written Expression, Mathematics Disorder, Reading Disorder, Asperger's Disorder, Autistic Disorder, Tic Disorder-Motor, Tic Disorder-Vocal, Tourette's Disorder; 1 additional conclusion unique to Child and Adolescent level: Separation Anxiety Disorder; 4 additional conclusions unique to Adult level: Panic Disorder, Specific Phobia, Major Depressive Disorder, Antisocial Personality Disorder; 1 "Reliability Measure" per form per population level (Parent-Report, Self-Report, Teacher-Report [Child and Adolescent]; Self-Report, Observer-Report [Adult]).
Administration: Group.
Price Data, 2008: A$775.01 per Adult PsychProfiler (APP) Kit including manual (2007, 174 pages), APP software, 10 APP Self-Report Forms, and 10 APP Observer-Report Forms; A$795 per Child and Adolescent PsychProfiler (CAPP) kit including manual, CAPP software, 10 CAPP Parent-Report Forms, 10 CAPP Self-Report Forms, and 10 CAPP Teacher-Report Forms; A$1,385 per complete kit including APP kit and CAPP kit; A$59.50 per 10 APP Self-Report Forms; A$59.50 per 10 APP Observer-Report Forms; A49.50 per 10 CAPP Parent-Report Forms; A$49.50 per 10 CAPP Self-Report Forms; A$49.50 per CAPP Teacher-Report Forms; A$495 per APP software; A$495 per CAPP software; A$199.95 per manual.
Comments: Available for computer or paper-and-pencil administration; software is Windows compatible.
Authors: Shane Langsford, Stephen Houghton, and Graham Douglas.
Publisher: Australian Council for Educational Research Ltd. [Australia].
  a) CHILD AND ADOLESCENT PSYCHPROFILER.
  Population: Ages 2-17.
  Publication Dates: 1999-2007.
  Acronym: CAPP.
  Forms, 3: Parent Report, Self-Report (only administered to children ages 10+), Teacher-Report.
  Time: (15) minutes per form.
  Comments: Formerly called Child and Adolescent Disorder Screening Instrument (CADSI).
  b) ADULT PSYCHPROFILER.
  Population: Ages 18+.
  Publication Date: 2007.
  Acronym: APP.
  Forms, 2: Self-Report, Observer Report.
  Time: (25) minutes per form.
Cross References: For a review by Mark E. Swerdlik and W. Joel Schneider, see 18:105.

[2197]

Psypercept-170.

Purpose: "Designed to measure work-related personality and interest variables among managers."
Population: Managers.
Publication Date: 1996.
Acronym: Psypercept-170.
Scores, 17: Directive, Inclusive, Expressive, Persuasive, Persistent, Accommodating, Calming, Inventive, Discerning, Aspiring, Urgent, Materialistic, Numerical, Altruistic, Technological, Artistic, Procedural.
Administration: Individual or group.
Price Data, 2001: $300 per assessment set including 5 reusable test booklets, 50 answer sheets, 50 data summary sheets, 1 set of hand-scoring keys, and manual (66 pages); $75 per 5 reusable test booklets; $75 per 50 answer sheets; $50 per 50 data summary sheets; $60 per set of hand-scoring keys; $75 per manual.
Time: (35–45) minutes.
Comments: A 170-item self-administered questionnaire; "For use in assessing and developing the talents of executives, managers, and supervisors."
Author: Joseph Hartman.
Publisher: Joseph Hartman, Ph.D.
Cross References: For reviews by Patricia A. Bachelor and William I. Sauser, Jr., see 15:201.

[2198]

The Pupil Rating Scale Revised: Screening for Learning Disabilities.

Purpose: To identify students with deficits in learning.
Population: Grades K–6.
Publication Dates: 1971–1981.
Scores, 8: Verbal (Auditory Comprehension, Spoken Language, Total), Nonverbal (Orientation, Motor Coordination, Personal-Social Behavior, Total), Total.
Administration: Individual.
Price Data, 2002: $53 per 50 record forms; $49 per manual (1981, 84 pages).
Time: (10–15) minutes.
Comments: Ratings by teachers.
Author: Helmer R. Myklebust.
Publisher: Pearson.
Cross References: See T5:2123 (1 reference) and T4:2165 (2 references); for a review by Shavaun M. Wall, see 9:1019 (3 references); see also T3:1934 (8 references); for a review by Nicholas J. Anastasiow of an earlier edition and an excerpted review by Barton B. Proger, see 8:439 (5 references).

[2199]

Purdue Interest Questionnaire.

Purpose: To help students identify an appropriate specialization within or outside of engineering.
Population: Freshmen engineering students.

Publication Dates: 1976–1980.
Acronym: PIQ.
Scores: 18 scale scores: 11 engineering, 5 transfer, 2 general.
Administration: Group.
Price Data: Available from publisher.
Time: Administration time not reported.
Comments: Separate answer sheets (machine scored) must be used.
Authors: William K. LeBold and Kevin D. Shell (manual).
Publisher: Purdue Research Foundation [No reply from publisher; status unknown].
Cross References: See T4:2167 (1 reference) and 9:1020 (1 reference).

[2200]

Purdue Pegboard.

Purpose: Measures an individual's ability to move hands, fingers, and arms (gross movement) and to control movements of small objects (finger tip dexterity).
Population: Assembly, general factory and various industrial positions and vocational rehabilitation.
Publication Dates: 1941–1992.
Scores, 5: Right Hand, Left Hand, Both Hands, Right plus Left plus Both Hands, Assembly.
Administration: Individual or group.
Price Data, 2002: $346 per start-up kit including 100 profile sheets, pegboard with complete set of washers, collars, and pegs, and examiner's manual; $70 per 100 profile sheets (quantity discounts available); $47 per replacement set of pegs, washers, and collars; $28 per examiner's manual.
Time: (3–9) minutes.
Author: Purdue Research Foundation.
Publisher: Pearson Performance Solutions [No reply from publisher; status unknown].
Cross References: See T5:2125 (30 references), T4:2168 (34 references), T3:948 (13 references), T2:2234 (51 references), and 6:1081 (15 references); for a review by Neil D. Warren, see 5:873 (11 references); see also 4:751 (12 references); for reviews by Edwin F. Ghiselli, Thomas W. Harrell, and Albert Gibson Packard, see 3:666 (3 references).

[2201]

The Purpose in Life Test.

Purpose: To detect "existential vacuum."
Population: Adults.
Publication Dates: 1962–1981.
Acronym: PIL.
Scores: Total score only.
Administration: Individual or group.
Price Data: Available from publisher.
Time: (10–15) minutes.
Comments: 1976 form identical to 1969 version except for minor format changes; 1981 manual identical to 1969 version.

Authors: James C. Crumbaugh and Leonard T. Maholick.
Publisher: Psychometric Affiliates.
Cross References: See T5:2126 (16 references), T4:2169 (17 references), 9:1021 (9 references), T3:1960 (21 references), 8:656 (54 references), and T2:1350 (4 references); for reviews by John R. Braun and George Domino, see 7:130 (7 references).

[2202]

Putney Auditory Comprehension Screening Test.

Purpose: Designed to "assess auditory comprehension in severely physically disabled patients."
Population: Adults.
Publication Date: 2002.
Acronym: PACST.
Score: Total score only.
Administration: Individual.
Price Data, 2006: £62 per complete kit including manual (23 pages) and 25 questionnaire/scoring sheets; £33 per 50 questionnaire/scoring sheets.
Time: Untimed.
Comments: Requires only the ability to provide verbal or nonverbal "yes" or "no" responses.
Authors: J. G. Beaumont, Julia Marjoribanks, Sarah Flury, and Tracey Lintern.
Publisher: Pearson Assessment [England].
Cross References: For reviews by Jeffery P. Braden and Hailey E. Krouse and by Daniel C. Miller, see 17:159.

[2203]

The Pyramid Scales.

Purpose: "Assesses adaptive behavior in handicapped persons of all ages."
Population: Handicapped persons ages birth to 78.
Publication Date: 1984.
Scores, 20: Sensory (Tactile Responsiveness, Auditory Responsiveness, Visual Responsiveness), Primary (Gross Motor, Eating, Fine Motor, Toileting, Dressing, Social Interaction, Washing/Grooming, Receptive Language, Expressive Language), Secondary (Recreation/Leisure, Writing, Domestic Behavior, Reading, Vocational, Time, Numbers, Money).
Administration: Individual.
Price Data: Available from publisher.
Time: (30–45) minutes.
Comments: "Criterion-referenced"; behavior checklist for measuring adaptive behavior by directly observing client or by interviewing adult informant.
Author: John D. Cone.
Publisher: John D. Cone.
Cross References: See T5:2127 (2 references) and T4:2170 (1 reference); for a review by John G. Svinicki, see 10:300.

[2204]

The Pyramids and Palm Trees Test.

Purpose: Designed "to assess a person's ability to access detailed semantic representations from words and from pictures."
Population: Ages 18-80.
Publication Date: 1992.
Scores: Total score only.
Administration: Individual.
Price Data, 2007: £105.44 per complete kit including manual, 25 scoring sheets, word card, and stimulus book; £15.28 per 25 scoring sheets.
Time: Administration time not reported.
Authors: David Howard and Karalyn Patterson.
Publisher: Pearson Assessment [England].
Cross References: For reviews by Arturo Olivarez, Jr. and Allison Boroda, see 17:160.

[2205]

The Q-Tags Test of Personality.

Purpose: "Designed to enquire into the self-development influences."
Population: Ages 6 and over.
Publication Dates: 1967–1969.
Acronym: Q-TTP.
Administration: Group or individual.
Price Data, 2005: $22 per 25 answer sheets; $44 per specimen set (including 4 series of 54 tags, 4 paper boards, manual [1969, 27 pages], list of directions, and 25 answer sheets).
Time: (60–80) minutes in 2 sessions.
Comments: Self-administering.
Authors: Arthur G. Storey and Louise I. Masson.
Publisher: Institute of Psychological Research, Inc. [Canada].
  a) [BIOGRAPHICAL FORM].
  Population: Ages 6 and over.
  Scores, 13: 6 factor scores (Affective, Assertive, Effective, Hostility, Reverie, Social) in each of 2 areas (He or She Is, He or She Should Be), Correlation of Self and Ideal Self.
  b) [AUTOBIOGRAPHICAL FORM].
  Population: Ages 12 and over.
  Scores, 13: 6 factor scores (same as *a* above) in each of 2 areas (I Am, I Wish I Were), Correlation of Self and Ideal Self.
Cross References: See T4:2171 (1 reference) and T2:1351 (2 references); for a review by Joan Preston, see 7:131 (2 references); see also P:225 (5 references).

[2206]

Quality Culture Assessment.

Purpose: Designed to assess and evaluate organizational practices, policies, and procedures.
Population: Managers and personnel.

Acronym: QCA.
Administration: Group.
Manual: No manual.
Price Data: Available from publisher.
Time: Administration time not reported.
Authors: Juran Institute and Teleometrics International.
Publisher: Teleometrics International, Inc.
  a) QUALITY POTENTIAL ANALYSIS.
  Publication Dates: 1982–1995.
  Acronym: QPA.
  Scores, 2: As It Is Now, As I Would Like It To Be.
  b) QUALITY CULTURE ANALYSIS.
  Publication Date: 1995.
  Acronym: QCA.
  Scores, 9: Quality Values (Senior Leadership, Goals and Objectives, Rewards and Recognition), Empowered Employees (Self-Control, Recovery, Participation), Customer Focus (Individual Customer Focus, Managerial Customer Focus, Organizational Customer Focus).

[2207]

Quality of Life Enjoyment and Satisfaction Questionnaire.

Purpose: Designed to measure the "degree of enjoyment and satisfaction experienced by subjects in various areas of daily functioning."
Population: Adults with mental or medical disorders.
Publication Date: 1990.
Acronym: Q-LES-Q.
Scores, 9: 6 scores (Physical Health, Subjective Feelings, Leisure Time Activities, Social Relationships, General Activities, Overall Life Enjoyment and Satisfaction); 3 optional scores (Work, Household Duties, School/Coursework).
Administration: Group.
Forms, 2: Regular Form, Short Form.
Price Data, 2001: $1.50 per regular form; $.50 per short form; $1.50 per summary scale scores.
Time: Regular Form: [5–15] minutes; Short Form: [3–5] minutes.
Comments: Self-report measure.
Author: Jean Endicott.
Publisher: Department of Research Assessment and Training.
Cross References: For reviews by John C. Caruso and Mary Lou Bryant Frank, see 14:303.

[2208]

Quality of Life Inventory.

Purpose: Developed to provide a measure of a person's quality of life and their satisfaction with life.
Population: Ages 18 and over.
Publication Date: 1994.
Acronym: QOLI®.

Scores: 17 scales: Health, Self-Esteem, Goals-and-Values, Money, Work, Play, Learning, Creativity, Helping, Love, Friends, Children, Relatives, Home, Neighborhood, Community, Overall Quality of Life.
Administration: Group or individual.
Price Data, 2006: $98 per hand-scoring starter kit including manual (84 pages), 50 answer sheets, and 50 worksheets; $95 per Q Local starter kit including 25 answer sheets to conduct and receive 25 Q Local profile reports; $75 per hand-scoring reorder kit including 50 answer sheets and 50 worksheets; $21 per Q Local answer sheets; $2.25 per Q Local profile report; $40 per manual; quantity discounts available for the reports.
Time: (5) minutes.
Comments: Useful for outcomes measurement as well as individual counseling.
Author: Michael B. Frisch.
Publisher: Pearson.
Cross References: For reviews by Laura L. B. Barnes and Richard W. Johnson, see 14:304.

[2209]
Quality of Life Questionnaire.
Purpose: "Designed to assess the relationship between the quality of an individual's life and other behaviors and afflictions, such as physical health, psychological health, and alcohol or substance use."
Population: Ages 18 and over.
Publication Date: 1989-2003.
Acronym: QLQ.
Scores: 17: Material Well-Being, Physical Well-Being, Personal Growth, Marital Relations, Parent-Child Relations, Extended Family Relations, Extramarital Relations, Altruistic Behavior, Political Behavior, Job Characteristics, Occupational Relations, Job Satisfiers, Creative/ Aesthetic Behavior, Sports Activity, Vacation Behavior, Social Desirability, Total Quality of Life.
Administration: Individual or Group.
Price Data, 2011: $86 per complete kit including 25 QuikScore™ answer forms, 10 question booklets, and manual (38 pages); $31 per 10 reusable question booklets; $34 per 25 QuikScore™ answer forms; $40 per manual; $45 per QLQ Online Report Kit including manual and 3 QLQ reports; $5 per Online Report.
Time: (30) minutes.
Comments: Self-report; Online version available.
Authors: David R. Evans and Wendy E. Cope.
Publisher: Multi-Health Systems, Inc.
Cross References: See T5:2132 (4 references) and T4:2172 (1 reference); for reviews by Gary B. Seltzer and Richard B. Stuart, see 11:318.

[2210]
Quality Potential Assessment.
Purpose: "Designed to provide information about an organization, such as data on its policies, practices, and logistics, and the degree to which the data contribute to encouraging staff to give their best to the organization."
Population: Adults.
Publication Dates: 1992–1995.
Acronym: QPA.
Scores: Actual and Desired ratings in 10 areas: Collaboration (Management Values, Support Structure, Managerial Credibility, Climate), Commitment (Impact, Relevance, Community), Creativity (Task Environment, Social Context, Problem Solving).
Administration: Group.
Price Data: Available from publisher.
Time: Administration time not reported.
Author: Jay Hall.
Publisher: Teleometrics International, Inc.
Cross References: For reviews by Theodore L. Hayes and Michael J. Zickar, see 14:305.

[2211]
Qualls Early Learning Inventory.
Purpose: Designed to provide a diagnostic review of six key developmental aras of learning that are important for success in school.
Population: Grades K–1.
Publication Date: 2003.
Acronym: QELI.
Scores, 6: General Knowledge, Oral Communication, Written Language, Math Concepts, Work Habits, Attentive Behavior.
Administration: Individual or group.
Price Data, 2006: $30 per 25 Inventories and 1 Teacher's Directions and Interpretive Guide; Score Reports: $.60 per student and $.36 for extra copy per student for Profile Narrative, $.75 per student and $.36 for extra copy per student for Class Diagnostic Report, and $.47 per student and $.24 for extra copy per student for Class, Building, and System Summary.
Time: (10) minutes per student.
Comments: Teacher-completed rating scale; observation of individual students; computer scoring and individual and group score reports available through Riverside Scoring Service; test was previously listed as Iowa Early Learning Inventory.
Authors: A. L. Qualls, H. D. Hoover, S. B. Dunbar, and D. A. Frisbie.
Publisher: Riverside Publishing.
Cross References: For reviews by Leslie Eastman Lukin and Carol M. McGregor, see 16:115.

[2212]
Quant Q.
Purpose: Designed to "target reasoning skills in relation to quantitative problems. The problems are designed to measure one's ability to think 'outside of the box' when solving quantitative problems."

Population: Undergraduates, students seeking advanced degrees, professionals, college prep students, adults of all ages.
Publication Date: 2005.
Scores: Total score only.
Administration: Group.
Manual: No manual.
Price Data: Available from publisher.
Time: (50) minutes.
Comments: This test can be administered online or via paper and pencil.
Author: Stephen W. Blohm.
Publisher: Insight Assessment-The California Academic Press LLC.

[2213]

Questionnaire Measure of Trait Arousability (Or Its Converse, Stimulus Screening).

Purpose: Designed to measure individual differences in positive and/or negative emotionality, emotional sensitivity, or emotional reactivity.
Population: Ages 15 and older.
Publication Dates: 1976–1994.
Scores: Total score only.
Administration: Group or individual.
Price Data: Available from publisher for specimen set including manual (1994, 8 pages) and literature review.
Time: (10–15) minutes.
Comments: Previously known as Questionnaire Measure of Stimulus Screening and Arousability.
Author: Albert Mehrabian.
Publisher: Albert Mehrabian.
Cross References: For a review by Robert A. Leark, see 13:249; for a review by James J. Jupp of the earlier edition, see 9:1025.

[2214]

QUESTS: A Life-Choice Inventory.

Purpose: To assess outcomes of substance abuse prevention education.
Population: Grades 9–12.
Publication Dates: 1974–1976.
Acronym: QUESTS.
Scores, 6: Needs Recognition, Values Classification, Adaptive Autonomy, Perception of Reality, Self-Worth, Total.
Administration: Group.
Price Data: Available from publisher.
Time: (23–30) minutes.
Comments: Scoring must be done by publisher.
Authors: Norman J. Milchus, Omar D. Numey, and David N. Rodwell.
Publisher: Norman Milchus (the author).

[2215]

QUIC Tests.

Purpose: Designed "to establish or verify the functional level of proficiency in the areas of either mathematics or the communicative arts."

Population: Grades 2–12.
Publication Dates: 1989–2006.
Scores, 8: Mathematics (Computation, Concepts, Problem Solving, Total), Communicative Arts (Reading, Reference Skills, Language Arts, Total).
Administration: Individual or group.
Forms, 2: G, H.
Price Data: See www.ststesting.com for up-to-date prices.
Time: (35) minutes or less.
Comments: Self-administered; competency-based interpretation.
Author: Scholastic Testing Service, Inc.
Publisher: Scholastic Testing Service, Inc.
Cross References: For a review by Delwyn L. Harnisch, see 11:320.

[2216]

Quick Informal Assessment [Third Edition].

Purpose: Designed to quickly and informally "assess a student's proficiency level in English."
Population: Grades K-12.
Publication Dates: 1997-2006.
Acronym: QIA.
Scores: Total score only.
Administration: Individual.
Forms: 6 alternate forms: A-F.
Price Data, 2006: $130 per complete set including English and Spanish examiner's manuals, test picture book, and 50 class profile forms.
Foreign Language Editions: Available in Spanish and English.
Time: (5) minutes.
Comments: Students classified into one of five levels of language proficiency: beginning, early intermediate, intermediate, early advanced, advanced; leveled score system.
Author: Constance O. Williams.
Publisher: Ballard & Tighe, Publishers.
Cross References: For reviews by Alan Garfinkel and Alfred P. Longo of an earlier edition, see 13:250.

[2217]

Quick Language Assessment Inventory.

Purpose: Designed to provide information about student's English and Spanish language background.
Population: Grades K–6.
Publication Date: 1974.
Scores: Total score and grade level equivalents.
Administration: Individual.
Price Data: Available from publisher.
Time: (1–2) minutes.
Comments: Designed for children suspected of needing English as a second language; parents or guardians provide information about child's English and Spanish background.
Author: Steve Moreno.

Publisher: Moreno Educational Co.
Cross References: For reviews by Giuseppe Costantino and Beth L. Evard, see 9:1026.

[2218]

Quick Neurological Screening Test II.

Purpose: "Designed to assess areas of neurological integration as they relate to learning."
Population: Ages 5 through 18.
Publication Dates: 1974-1998.
Acronym: QNST-II.
Scores, 15: Hand Skill, Figure Recognition and Production, Palm Form Recognition, Eye Tracking, Sound Patterns, Finger to Nose, Thumb and Finger Circle, Double Simultaneous Stimulation of Hand and Cheek, Rapidly Reversing Repetitive Hand Movements, Arm and Leg Extensions, Tandem Walk, Standing on One Leg, Skipping, Left-Right Discrimination, Behavioral Irregularities.
Administration: Individual.
Price Data, 2006: $95 per test kit including manual (93 pages), 25 scoring forms, 25 geometric form reproduction sheets, 25 remedial guideline forms, and cue cards; $35 per manual; $20 per 25 scoring forms; $10 per 25 geometric form reproduction sheets; $12 per 25 remedial guideline forms; $18 per directions for administration and scoring printed on 20 cue cards; $35 per specimen set including manual and sample forms.
Time: (20-30) minutes.
Comments: Screening for early identification of learning disabilities; 1998 edition provides extensive literature reviews, clarified directions for administration, and reformatted test protocol sheets.
Authors: Margaret C. Mutti, Harold M. Sterling, Nancy A. Martin, and Norma V. Spalding.
Publisher: Academic Therapy Publications.
Cross References: For a review by Edward E. Gotts, see 14:306; see also T5:2141 (1 reference) and T4:2183 (3 references); for a review by Russell L. Adams of an earlier edition, see 9:1027.

[2219]

Quick Phonics Survey.

Purpose: Designed to "assess a child's understanding of sound/symbol relationships, transfers, and associations."
Population: Grades 1- 7.
Publication Date: 1976.
Acronym: QPS.
Scores: Total score only.
Administration: Individual.
Manual: No manual.
Price Data, 2006: $15 per plasticized stimulus card and 50 recording forms with directions.
Time: Administration time not reported.
Comments: Criterion-referenced.

Author: John Arena.
Publisher: Academic Therapy Publications.
Cross References: For reviews by Beth D. Bader and Dawn P. Flanagan, see 12:318.

[2220]

Quick Picture Reading Test.

Purpose: Designed "to quickly characterize an individual's general reading ability" through a picture-matching task.
Publication Date: 2010.
Acronym: QPRT.
Scores: Total score only.
Administration: Group.
Price Data, 2009: $65 per complete kit including 10 Adult AutoScore forms, 10 Child AutoScore forms, and manual (56 pages); $32 per 25 AutoScore forms (specify Adult or Child); $50 per manual.
Time: (10) minutes.
Authors: Amber M. Klein and David S. Herzberg.
Publisher: Western Psychological Services.
  a) CHILD FORM.
  Population: Ages 8-19.
  b) ADULT FORM.
  Population: Ages 17-89.

[2221]

Quick Quizzes for U.S. History Classes.

Purpose: To be used as pre- or post-tests, self-tests, or study guides for 52 U.S. History topics.
Population: Grades 6–12.
Publication Date: 1989.
Scores: Total score only.
Administration: Group.
Manual: No manual.
Price Data: Price information available from publisher for 52 blackline master quiz forms and answer booklet.
Time: Administration time not reported.
Authors: E. Richard Churchill and Linda R. Churchill.
Publisher: Walch Education.

[2222]

Quick Spelling Inventory.

Purpose: To "identify the grade level at which a student can function in spelling."
Population: Grades 2-8.
Publication Date: 1988.
Acronym: QSI.
Scores: Total score only.
Administration: Group or individual.
Manual: No manual.
Price Data, 2006: $15 per 50 recording forms and plasticized word list with directions.
Time: Administration time not reported.
Author: John Arena.

Publisher: Academic Therapy Publications (High Noon Division).

Cross References: For reviews by Kevin D. Crehan and Dale P. Scannell, see 11:322.

[2223]

Quick Style Indicator.

Purpose: Designed to help identify "personal style as it relates to people, tasks, time and situations."

Population: Adults and teenagers.

Publication Dates: 1996-2006.

Acronym: QSI.

Scores, 4: Behavioral/Action, Cognitive/Analysis, Interpersonal/Harmony, Affective/Expression.

Administration: Individual or group.

Price Data, 2006: $11.95 per test booklet (2006, 12 pages); $14.94 per In-Depth Interpretations booklet (2006, 48 pages).

Time: (30) minutes; (90-180 minutes program options).

Comments: Shorter version of Personal Style Indicator (2016); self-administered and self-scored.

Authors: Ken Keis, Terry D. Anderson, Marilyn Hamilton, and Everett T. Robinson.

Publisher: Consulting Resource Group International, Inc.

[2224]

The Quick Test.

Purpose: Designed to assess intelligence based on verbal-perceptual performance.

Population: Ages 2 and over

Publication Dates: 1958-1962.

Acronym: QT.

Scores: Total score only.

Administration: Individual.

Forms, 3: 1, 2, 3.

Price Data, 2010: $65 per tester's set including 3 plates, 100 record sheets, instruction cardboard, item cardboard, and manual (1962, 54 pages); $30 per manual; $35 per 100 record sheets; $15 per set of 3 plates; $5 per Instruction cardboard; $5 per Item cardboard.

Time: (3-10) minutes.

Authors: R. B. Ammons and C. H. Ammons.

Publisher: Psychological Test Specialists.

Cross References: See T5:2146 (20 references), T4:2191 (44 references), 9:1028 (19 references), T3:1969 (44 references), 8:225 (33 references), and T2:522 (15 references); for excerpted reviews by Peter F. Merenda and B. Semeonoff, see 7:422 (30 references); for reviews by Boyd R. McCandless and Ellen V. Piers, see 6:534 (3 references).

[2225]

A Quick Test of Cognitive Speed.

Purpose: Designed to "screen adolescents and adults for parietal lobe dysfunctions indicative of mild cognitive impairments, acquired neurogenic disorders of language and communication … or degenerative neurological disorders such as Alzheimer's or Parkinson's disease."

Population: Adolescents and adults.

Publication Date: 2002.

Acronym: AQT.

Scores, 5: Color-Form, Color-Number, Color-Letter, Color-Animal, Color-Object.

Administration: Individual.

Price Data, 2004: $249 per complete kit including examiner's manual (88 pages), stimulus manual, and 25 record forms; $75 per examiner's manual; $150 per stimulus manual; $50 per 25 record forms.

Foreign Language Edition: Spanish and French-Canadian directions included in examiner's manual.

Time: [3–5] minutes.

Comments: "Criterion-referenced"; previously entitled Alzheimer's Quick Test: Assessment of Parietal Function.

Authors: Elisabeth H. Wiig, Niels Peter Nielsen, Lennart Minthon, and Siegbert Warkentin.

Publisher: Pearson.

Cross References: For reviews by Shawn K. Acheson and Joan C. Ballard of this test when it was entitled Alzheimer's Quick Test: Assessment of Parietal Function, see 16:11.

[2226]

Quickview Social History.

Purpose: Psychosocial inventory designed to help standardize the collection of client information.

Population: Individuals 16 years and older.

Publication Dates: 1983–1992.

Administration: Group.

Price Data, 2008: $92 per Q Local starter kit; $97 per mail-in scoring starter kit; $5 per user's guide (1992, 33 pages); $48.50 per 10 reusable softcover test booklets; $62 per 1 reusable hardcover test booklet; $22 per 25 Q Local answer sheets; $13 per Q Local report; $16 per mail-in scoring report.

Time: (30–45) minutes.

Author: Ronald A. Giannetti.

Publisher: Pearson.

a) BASIC REPORT.

Scores: 9 areas of inquiry: Demographic Data, Developmental History, Family of Origin, Educational History, Marital History, Occupational History/Financial Status, Legal History, Military History, Symptom Screen.

Comments: The report also has a follow-up summary that includes contradictory responses, indeterminate responses, and client-requested follow-up sections.

b) CLINICAL SUPPLEMENT.

Scores: Includes 8 areas of inquiry listed in Basic Report, plus Physical and Psychological Symptom Screens including: Adult Problems (Substance

Use, Psychotic Symptoms, Mood Symptoms, Anxiety Disorders, Somatoform Symptoms, Psychosexual Disorders, Sleep and Arousal, Antisocial Personality, Other Current or Past Potential Adult Problems/Stressors), Developmental Problems (Activity Level/Lability, Conduct Problems, Anxious/Avoidant, Eating/Weight, Tic/Elimination/Sleep, Other Disorders/Delays, Other Potential Developmental Problems/Stressors).

Cross References: For reviews by David N. Dixon and Edward R. Starr, see 13:251.

[2227]
Racial Attitude Survey.

Purpose: Measures attitudes toward an examiner-selected group of people using a generic semantic differential method.
Population: Teenagers through adults.
Publication Dates: 1989–2008.
Scores, 9: Physical, Ego Strength (Dominance, Control, Anxiety, Ethics, General Social, On-the-Job), Social Distance, Casual Contact.
Administration: Individual or group.
Manual: No manual.
Price Data: Price information for online testing for theses and other research is available from publisher at www.racialattitudesurvey.com & www.culturaldiversitytest.com. Individuals may take test online at those sites free of charge to learn about the test.
Time: [20] minutes.
Comments: Previously entitled Racial Attitude Test; technical information provided is from thesis by Cynthia Lewis.
Author: Thomas J. Rundquist.
Publisher: Nova Media, Inc.
Cross References: For a review by Deborah L. Bandalos, see 16:206.

[2228]
Rahim Leader Power Inventory.

Purpose: Measures employees' perception of, and relationship with, immediate supervisors, in order to assess supervisors' power bases.
Population: Employees.
Publication Date: 1988.
Acronym: RLPI.
Scores, 5: Coercive, Reward, Legitimate, Expert, Referent.
Administration: Group.
Manual: No manual.
Price Data, 2008: $150 per permission to make 300 copies for institutional or funded projects; $75 per permission to make 300 copies for individual or unfunded projects; quantity discounts available.
Time: Administration time not reported.
Author: M. Afzal Rahim.
Publisher: Center for Advanced Studies in Management.

[2229]
Rahim Organizational Conflict Inventories.

Purpose: "Designed to measure three independent dimensions of organizational conflict: Intrapersonal, Intragroup, Intergroup" (ROCI-I) and "designed to measure five independent dimensions that represent styles of handling interpersonal conflict: Integrating, Obliging, Dominating, Avoiding, and Compromising" (ROCI-II).
Population: Managers, employees, supervisors.
Publication Date: 1983.
Acronym: ROCI.
Administration: Group.
Price Data, 2006: $25 per manual (70 pages).
Comments: Self-administering; separate answer sheets must be used.
Author: M. Afzalur Rahim.
Publisher: Center for Advanced Studies in Management.

a) RAHIM ORGANIZATIONAL CONFLICT INVENTORY I.
Acronym: ROCI-I.
Scores: 3 subscales: Intrapersonal, Intragroup, Intergroup.
Price Data: $150 per permission to make 300 copies for institutional or funded projects; $75 per permission to make 300 copies for individual or unfunded projects; quantity discounts available.
Time: (10–12) minutes.
b) RAHIM ORGANIZATIONAL CONFLICT INVENTORY II.
Acronym: ROCI-II.
Scores, 5: Integrating, Obliging, Dominating, Avoiding, Compromising.
Price Data: $170 per permission to make 300 copies for institutional or funded projects; $100 per permission to make 300 copies for individual or unfunded projects; quantity discounts available.
Time: (10–12) minutes.
Cross References: See T5:2149 (5 references) and T4:2195 (1 reference); for a review by George C. Thornton III, see 10:303 (3 references).

[2230]
RAND-36 Health Status Inventory.

Purpose: Designed to assess "general health status."
Population: Adults.
Publication Date: 1998.
Acronym: R-36 HSI.
Scores, 10: Physical Functioning, Role Limitations Due to Physical Health Problems, Pain, General Health Perceptions, Emotional Well-Being, Role Limitations Due to Emotional Problems, Social Functioning, Energy/Fatigue/Physical Health Composite, Mental Health Composite, Global Health Composite.
Administration: Group or individual.
Forms, 2: RAND-36, RAND-12 (a short form).

Price Data, 2002: $60 per complete kit including manual (126 pages), 25 question/answer sheets, and 25 hand-scoring worksheets; $8 per 25 question/answer sheets; $8 per 25 hand-scoring worksheets; $8 per 25 RAND-12 HSI question/answer sheets; $50 per manual.
Time: Administration time not reported.
Comments: Paper-and-pencil or computer administered; hand-scoring forms also available.
Author: Ron D. Hays.
Publisher: Pearson.
Cross References: For reviews by Corine Fitzpatrick and Richard I. Frederick, see 14:307.

[2231]

Randt Memory Test.

Purpose: Designed "as a global survey and evaluation of patients' complaints concerning their memory."
Population: Ages 20-90.
Publication Dates: 1983-1989.
Acronym: RMT.
Scores, 10: Acquisition Recall (Five Items Acquisition, Paired Words Acquisition, Short Story Verbatim, Digit Span, Incidental Learning), Delayed Recall (Five Items Recall, Paired Words Recall, Picture Recall, General Information), Memory Index.
Administration: Individual.
Forms, 5: Alternative forms for repeated measures.
Price Data, 2001: $95 per complete test including 10 administration booklets, 5 sets of picture cards, and manual (1989, 36 pages); $45 per 50 administration booklets.
Time: (20-25) minutes.
Authors: C. T. Randt and E. R. Brown.
Publisher: Life Science Associates.
Cross References: See T5:2159 (4 references) and T4:2204 (2 references); for a review by Joseph D. Matarazzo, see 10:304 (1 reference).

[2232]

Rapid Automatized Naming and Rapid Alternating Stimulus Tests.

Purpose: "Designed to estimate an individual's ability to see a visual symbol … and name it accurately and rapidly."
Population: Ages 5-0 to 18-11.
Publication Date: 2005.
Acronym: RAN/RAS.
Scores, 6: Rapid Automatized Naming (Objects, Colors, Numbers, Letters), Rapid Alternating Stimulus (2-Set Letters and Numbers, 3-Set Letters/Numbers and Colors).
Administration: Individual.
Price Data, 2011: $150 per complete kit including examiner's manual (112 pages), 50 record forms, and set of 6 cards; $69 per examiner's manual; $59 per 50 record forms; $29 per set of 6 cards.
Time: (5–10) minutes.
Authors: Maryanne Wolf and Martha Bridge Denckla.
Publisher: PRO-ED.

Cross References: For reviews by Russell N. Carney and by Rayne A. Sperling and Nicholas D. Warcholak, see 17:161.

[2233]

Raven's Progressive Matrices.

Purpose: Constructed as a nonverbal assessment of perception and thinking skills.
Population: Ages 6–65
Publication Dates: 1938–2000.
Acronym: RPM.
Scores: Total score only.
Price Data: Available from publisher.
Comments: Formerly called Progressive Matrices; may be used with Crichton Vocabulary Scale (763) or Mill Hill Vocabulary Scale (1705).
Authors: J. C. Raven, J. H. Court (manual), and J. Raven (manual).
Publisher: Oxford Psychologists Press, Ltd. [England]
a) STANDARD.
  Population: Ages 6–65.
  Acronym: SPM.
  Administration: Group.
  Time: (45) minutes.
  Comments: Includes Classic, Parallel, and Plus Versions.
b) COLOURED.
  Population: Ages 5–11 and people with mental defects and elderly people.
  Acronym: CPM.
  Administration: Individual.
  Forms, 2: Board, Book.
  Time: (15–30) minutes.
c) ADVANCED.
  Population: Ages 11 and over with average or high intellectual ability.
  Acronym: APM.
  Administration: Group.
    1) *Set I.*
    Time: (10) minutes.
    2) *Set II.*
    Time: 40(45) or 60(65) minutes.
Cross References: See T5:2163 (356 references), T4:2208 (260 references), 9:1007 (67 references), T3:1914 (200 references), 8:200 (190 references), T2:439 (122 references), and 7:376 (194 references); for a review by Morton Bortner, see 6:490 (78 references); see also 5:370 (62 references); for reviews by Charlotte Banks, W. D. Wall, and George Westby, see 4:314 (32 references); for reviews by Walter C. Shipley and David Wechsler of the 1938 edition, see 3:258 (13 references); for a review by T. J. Keating, see 2:1417 (8 references).

[2234]

Reading and Arithmetic Indexes.

Purpose: "Measures level of development in reading and math." "Assesses proficiency levels in reading and math."

Population: Age 14–adult applicants for entry level jobs and special training programs.
Publication Dates: 1968–1996.
Administration: Group.
Forms, 2: Reading Index, Arithmetic Index.
Price Data, 1998: $53 per 25 tests (specify Arithmetic Index or Reading Index); $19.75 per examiner's manual.
Author: Science Research Associates..
Publisher: Pearson Performance Solutions [No reply from publisher; status unknown].
    a) READING–ARITHMETIC INDEX.
    Purpose: "Measures level of development in reading and math."
    Acronym: RAI.
    Scores, 11: Reading Index (Picture-Word Association, Word Decoding, Comprehension of Phrases, Comprehension of Sentences, Comprehension of Paragraphs, Total), Arithmetic Index (Addition and Subtraction of Whole Numbers, Multiplication and Division of Whole Numbers, Basic Operations Involving Fractions, Basic Operations Involving Decimals and Percentages, Total).
    Time: (25) minutes per Index.
    b) READING AND ARITHMETIC INDEXES (12).
    Purpose: "Assesses proficiency levels in reading and math."
    Acronym: RAI-12.
    Scores, 14: Reading Index (Picture-Word Association, Word Decoding, Comprehension of Phrases, Comprehension of Sentences, Comprehension of Paragraphs I, Comprehension of Paragraphs II, Total), Arithmetic Index (Addition and Subtraction of Whole Numbers, Multiplication and Division of Whole Numbers, Basic Operations Involving Fractions, Basic Operations Involving Decimals and Percentages, Basic Operations Involving Square Roots and Powers, Basic Operations Involving Geometry and Word Problems, Total).
    Time: (35) minutes per Index.
Cross References: For reviews by D. Joe Olmi and Jay R. Stewart, see 15:202; for a review by Dorothy C. Adkins of an earlier edition, see 7:20. See T4:2538 (1 reference) and 8:813 (3 references) for information regarding the Reading Index. See T5:171 (2 references) and 8:307 (3 references) for information regarding the Arithmetic Index.

[2235]

Reading Comprehension Battery for Aphasia, Second Edition.

Purpose: "Designed to provide systematic evaluation of the nature and degree of reading impairment in adolescents and adults with aphasia."
Population: Pre-adolescent to geriatric aphasic people.
Publication Dates: 1979–1998.
Acronym: RCBA-2.
Scores, 19: Word–Visual, Word–Auditory, Word–Semantic, Functional Reading, Synonyms, Sentence–Pic-

ture, Paragraph–Picture, Paragraph–Factual, Paragraph–Inferential, Morpho–Syntax, Overall Score of Core Subtests, Letter Discrimination, Letter Naming, Letter Recognition, Lexical Decision, Semantic Categorization, Oral Reading: Words, Oral Reading: Sentences, Overall Score of Supplemental Subtests.
Administration: Individual.
Price Data, 2011: $206 per complete kit including examiner's manual (1998, 38 pages), picture book, supplementary picture book, and 25 profile/summary record forms; $35 per examiner's manual, $64 per picture book or supplementary picture book; $53 per 25 profile/summary record forms.
Time: (30) minutes.
Comments: Instrument is criterion-referenced.
Authors: Leonard L. LaPointe and Jennifer Horner.
Publisher: PRO-ED.
Cross References: For reviews by Candice Haas Hollingsead and Robert Wall, see 14:308; see also T5:2172 (1 reference), T4:2220 (5 references), and 9:1033 (1 reference).

[2236]

Reading Evaluation Adult Diagnosis, Fifth Edition.

Purpose: Designed for assessing existing reading competencies.
Population: Illiterate adult students.
Publication Dates: 1972–1999.
Acronym: READ.
Scores: 3 parts, 21 scores: Sight Words (List 1, List 2, List 3, List 4), Word Analysis Skills (Letter Sound Relationships, Letter Names [Upper-Case], Letter Names [Lower-Case], Reversals, CVC, CV[CC], Final Digraphs, Initial Digraphs, Final Blends, Initial Blends, Multi-Syllabic Words, Silent Letters, Soft C & G, Suffixes), Reading/Listening Inventory (Word Recognition, Reading Comprehension, Listening Comprehension).
Administration: Individual.
Price Data, 2005: $15 per test booklet/manual (1999, 51 pages); $6.50 per answer pad.
Time: Administration time not reported.
Authors: Original test by Ruth J. Colvin and Jane H. Root; 1999 revision by Kathleen A. Hinchman and Rebecca Schoultz.
Publisher: ProLiteracy Worldwide.
Cross References: For reviews by Howard Margolis and Timothy Shanahan, see 14:309; for reviews by Mary E. Huba and Diane J. Sawyer of an earlier edition, see 11:326 (1 reference).

[2237]

Reading Fluency Indicator.

Purpose: A brief, individually administered test of oral reading fluency that measures rate, accuracy, comprehension, and prosody.

Population: Grades 1–12.
Publication Date: 2004.
Acronym: RFI.
Scores: Total Reading Time, Total Miscues, Total Comprehension Passage Level, Words Read per Minute, Miscue Descriptive Analysis (Addition, Omission, Provided Word, Repetition, Reversal, Substitution), Prosody Rating System, Comprehension Descriptive Analysis (Literal Comprehension Questions, Inferential Comprehension Questions).
Administration: Individual.
Levels, 10: P, K, 1–6, M, H.
Price Data, 2006: $154.99 per starter set including manual (42 pages), passage book, and 30 progress record forms; $82.99 per passage book; $30.99 per 20 progress record forms; $82.99 per manual.
Time: (5–10) minutes.
Comments: May be used as supplement to the Group Reading Assessment and Diagnostic Evaluation (1195); "criterion-referenced."
Author: Kathleen T. Williams.
Publisher: Pearson.
Cross References: For reviews by Alice Corkill and George Engelhard, Jr., see 17:162.

[2238]

Reading-Free Vocational Interest Inventory: 2.

Purpose: "To measure the vocational interest of the special needs student/adult and regular classroom students."
Population: Ages 12 to 69.
Publication Dates: 1975–2000.
Acronym: RFVII:2.
Scores: 11 scales: Automotive, Building Trades, Clerical, Animal Care, Food Service, Patient Care, Horticulture, Housekeeping, Personal Service, Laundry Service, Materials Handling, plus 5 cluster scores: Mechanical, Outdoor, Mechanical–Outdoor, Food Service–Handling Operations, Clerical–Social Service.
Administration: Individual.
Price Data, 2011: $121 per complete kit including 20 test booklets, manual (2000, 123 pages), and Occupational Title Lists 2 (2001, 42 pages); $61 per sample set including 10 test booklets and manual; $45.50 per examination set including 1 test booklet and manual; $45 per 20 test booklets (discounts available for orders of 40 or more); $44 per manual; $35 Occupational Title Lists: 2.
Time: 20 (30) minutes.
Comments: Revision of Reading-Free Vocational Interest Inventory; earlier edition listed as AAMD-Becker Reading-Free Vocational Interest Inventory; self-administered; hand-scorable only.
Author: Ralph L. Becker.
Publisher: Elbern Publications.
Cross References: For reviews by Zandra S. Gratz and Mark Pope, see 15:203; for information on an earlier edition, see T4:2177; for a review by Robert J. Miller of an earlier edition, see 11:327; see also T3:1996 (2 references); for reviews by Esther E. Diamond and George Domino of an earlier edition, see 8:988 (6 references).

[2239]

Reading-Level Indicator.

Purpose: Designed "to identify individual reading at a second-to-sixth-grade level and functional nonreaders."
Population: Upper elementary to college students.
Publication Dates: 2000-2002.
Scores, 5: Sentence Comprehension Score, Vocabulary Score, Total Raw Score, Instructional Reading Level, Independent Reading Level.
Administration: Group or individual.
Forms, 2: Blue Form, Purple Form.
Price Data, 2006: $73.99 per starter Set including Manual, 1 package (25) Purple forms, 1 package (25) Blue forms; $26.99 per 25 forms (specify Purple or Blue); $26.99 per manual; $73.99 per Spanish Companion.
Foreign Language Edition: Spanish translation available.
Time: (4–20) minutes.
Comments: Designed to work with Group Reading Assessment and Diagnostic Evaluation (GRADE; 1195), a diagnostic reading test.
Author: Kathleen T. Williams.
Publisher: Pearson.
Cross References: For reviews by Elizabeth Kelley Boyles and Robert E. Wall, see 15:204.

[2240]

Reading Progress Tests.

Purpose: Designed to "provide a continuous measure of individual and group progress in reading comprehension."
Population: Ages 5-0 to 12-2.
Publication Dates: 1996–1997.
Acronym: RPT.
Scores: Total score only.
Administration: Group.
Price Data, 2002: £12.99 per Stage One manual (1996, 48 pages); £13.50 per Stage Two manual (1997, 47 pages); £14.99 per Stage One specimen set; £16.99 per Stage Two specimen set.
Time: (20) minutes per test.
Authors: Denis Vincent, Mary Crumpler, and Mike de la Mare.
Publisher: Hodder & Stoughton Educational [England].

a) STAGE ONE.
  1) *Literacy Baseline*.
  Purpose: "To provide a 'baseline' from which to measure subsequent progress."
  Population: Children in first term of their first year of compulsory schooling (ages 5-0 to 6-4).
  Price Data: £6.99 per 10 copies.

2) *RPT Test 1.*
Purpose: Constructed to "assess developing reading skills."
Population: Year 1 (ages 5-8 to 7-2).
Price Data: £6.99 per 10 copies.
Time: (45–50) minutes.
3) *RPT Test 2.*
Population: Year 2 (ages 6-8 to 8-1).
Price Data: £6.99 per 10 copies.
b) STAGE TWO.
1) *RPT Test 3.*
Population: Year 3 (ages 7-8 to 9-2).
Price Data: £6.99 per 10 copies; £11.50 per 10 Test 3 broadsheets.
2) *RPT Test 4.*
Population: Year 4 (ages 8-8 to 10-2).
Price Data: £6.99 per 10 copies; £11.50 per 10 Test 4 broadsheets.
3) *RPT Test 5.*
Population: Year 5 (ages 9-8 to 11-2).
Price Data: £6.99 per 10 copies; £11.50 per 10 Test 5 broadsheets.
4) *RPT Test 6.*
Population: Year 6 (ages 10-8 to 12-2).
Price Data: £6.99 per 10 copies; £11.50 per 10 Test 6 broadsheets.
Cross References: For a review by Sharon deFur, see 17:163.

[2241]

Reading Skills Diagnostic Test III, Level 4.

Purpose: Assesses "three areas in encoding/decoding" of reading including content, processes, and basic capacity.
Population: Grades 2.5–12.
Publication Dates: 1967–1983.
Acronym: RSDT-III.
Scores, 12: Letter Writing, Short Term Memory–Letters, Simple Phonics, Open Syllable Writing, Syllable Writing, Word Writing, Short Term Memory–Words, Long Vowels, Consonant Diphthongs, Vowel Diphthongs, Sight Word Writing (2 parts), Context Clues.
Administration: Group.
Price Data: Available from publisher.
Time: (40–60) minutes.
Author: Richard H. Bloomer.
Publisher: Brador Publications, Inc. [No reply from publisher; status unknown].
Cross References: For reviews by Ira E. Aaron and Edward R. Sipay, see 8:772; see also T2:1644 (1 reference).

[2242]

Reading Style Inventory 2000.

Purpose: Designed to identify "the way each student learns best then (match) those strengths to the most effective reading methods, materials and strategies."

Population: Grade 1 to adults.
Publication Dates: 1980–2000.
Acronym: RSI.
Scores: 52 elements: Global Tendencies, Analytical Tendencies, Perceptual Strengths (Auditory Strengths, Visual Strengths, Tactile Strengths, Kinesthetic Strengths), Reading Methods (Carbo Recorded-Book Method, Fernald Method, Individualized Method, Modeling Methods, Language-Experience Method, Orton-Gillingham Method, Phonics Method, Whole-Word Method, Recorded Books, Computers), Preferred Reading Environment (Quiet–No Talking, Quiet–No Music, Dim Light, Warm Temperatures, Informal Design, Highly Organized), Emotional Profile (Peer Motivated, Adult Motivated, Self-Motivated, Persistent, Responsible), These Students Prefer (Choices, Direction, Work Checked), Sociological Preferences (Read to a Teacher, Read with Peers, Read Alone, Read with Peers/Teacher, Read with One Peer), Physical Preferences (Intake While Reading, Read in the Morning, Read in Early Afternoon, Read in Late Afternoon, Read in Evening, Mobility), Reading Materials (Audio-Visuals, Basal Reader Phonics, Basal Reader Whole-Word, Computers, Fernald Materials, Reading Activities, Orton-Gillingham Materials, Reading Kits, Recorded-Books, Tradebooks, Newspapers, etc.; Workbooks and Worksheets).
Administration: Individual and group.
Forms, 3: Primary, Intermediate, Adult.
Price Data, 2006: Price per administration varies by volume.
Time: Administration time not reported.
Comments: Available online only at www.nrsi.com.
Author: National Reading Styles Institute.
Publisher: National Reading Styles Institute, Inc.
Cross References: For reviews by Alice Corkill and by Thomas Emerson Hancock and Kathleen Allen, see 16:207; see also T5:218 (2 references); for reviews by Jeri Benson and Alice J. Corkill of a previous edition, see 11:328 (1 reference).

[2243]

Reading Test (Comprehension and Speed): Municipal Tests: National Achievement Tests.

Purpose: Measures reading comprehension and speed.
Population: Grades 3–6, 6–8.
Publication Dates: 1938–1957.
Scores, 5: Following Directions, Sentence Meaning, Paragraph Meaning, Reading Speed, Total.
Administration: Group.
Price Data: Available from publisher.
Time: (32) minutes.
Comments: Subtest of Municipal Battery; 2 forms: A, B.
Authors: Robert K. Speer and Samuel Smith.
Publisher: Psychometric Affiliates.

Cross References: For a review by Larry A. Harris, see 8:741. For reviews of the complete battery, see 5:18 (1 review), 4:20 (1 review), and 2:1191 (2 reviews).

[2244]

Reading Test SR-A & SR-B.

Purpose: "Designed to provide a means of estimating the reading attainment of primary school children."
Population: Ages 7-6 to 11-11.
Publication Dates: 1970–1982.
Scores: Total score only.
Administration: Group.
Editions, 2: SR-A, SR-B.
Price Data: Price information available from publisher for test booklets and manual (1971, 17 pages).
Time: 20(25) minutes.
Authors: Brian Pritchard and the National Foundation for Educational Research in England and Wales.
Publisher: GL Assessment [England].
Cross References: For reviews by Robert C. Calfee and Marian Jean Dreher, see 10:311.

[2245]

Reading Tests EH 1-2.

Purpose: Provides a measure of reading ability.
Population: Ages 11-0 to 15-1.
Publication Dates: 1961–1966.
Scores: 2 tests: Vocabulary, Comprehension.
Administration: Group.
Price Data: Price information available from publisher for test booklets (specify EH1 [Vocabulary] or EH2 [Comprehension]) and for manual.
Time: (15–20) minutes for EH1; (40–45) minutes for EH2.
Author: S. M. Bate.
Publisher: GL Assessment [England].
Cross References: See T3:2004 (1 reference).

[2246]

Ready to Learn: A Dyslexia Screener.

Purpose: Designed as a screening instrument for underlying early learning and prereading skills "so that children at risk for developing reading problems can be identified early."
Population: Ages 3-6 to 6-5.
Publication Dates: 1996-2004.
Scores: 16 subscale scores: (Rapid Naming, Bead Threading and Paper Cutting, Corsi Frog, Balance, Phonological Discrimination, Digit Span, Rhyming, Sound Order, Teddy & Form Matching, Vocabulary, Shape & Letter Copying [optional for ages 3-6 to 4-5], Repetition [optional for ages 3-6 to 4-5], Digit Naming [optional for ages 3-6 to 4-5], Letter Naming [optional for ages 3-6 to 4-5], First Letter Sound [ages 4-6 to 6-5], Postural Sound [ages 4-6 to 6-5]), Risk Index [one score for each of the above scale scores].

Administration: Individual.
Price Data, 2006: $250 per complete kit including manual (2004, 109 pages), 25 record forms, audio CD, stimulus book, set of manipulatives, and soft case; $110 per manual; $43 per 25 record forms; $12 per audio CD; $80 per stimulus book; $43 per set of manipulatives; $18 per Balance Test manipulative; $6.50 per CORSI Frog manipulative; $18 per 13 beads and a cord manipulative.
Time: (30-45) minutes.
Comments: This test can be completed in two sessions if necessary.
Authors: Angela J. Fawcett, Rod I. Nicolson, and Ray Lee.
Publisher: Pearson.
Cross References: For reviews by R. Anthony Doggett and Kristin N. Johnson-Gros and by Kathleen M. Johnson, see 17:164.

[2247]

Reality Check Survey.

Purpose: Assesses "how managerial actions serve employee needs."
Population: Adults.
Publication Dates: 1989–1995.
Acronym: RCS.
Scores: Total score only.
Administration: Group.
Price Data, 2001: $7.95 per instrument.
Time: Untimed.
Comments: Self-administered survey.
Author: Jay Hall.
Publisher: Teleometrics International, Inc.
Cross References: For reviews by S. Alvin Leung and Sheldon Zedeck, see 12:322.

[2248]

Receptive-Expressive Emergent Language Test, Third Edition.

Purpose: Designed to identify babies or young children with delayed language acquisition, to determine discrepancy between receptive and expressive processes of emergent language and to document intervention effects.
Population: Ages 0–36 months.
Publication Dates: 1971–2003.
Acronym: REEL-3.
Scores, 3: Receptive Language Ability, Expressive Language Ability, Language Ability.
Administration: Individual.
Price Data, 2011: $116 per complete kit including examiner's manual (2003, 98 pages) and 25 profile/examiner record booklets; $69 per examiner's manual; $53 per 25 profile/examiner record booklets.
Time: (20–30) minutes.
Comments: Informants knowledgeable about child's language behavior are interviewed; first edition titled The

Bzoch-League Receptive Expressive Emergent Language Scale: For the Measurement of Language Skills in Infancy.
Authors: Kenneth R. Bzoch, Richard League, and Virginia L. Brown.
Publisher: PRO-ED.
Cross References: For reviews by David P. Hurford and Gabrielle Stutman, see 16:208; see also T5:2189 (7 references); for reviews by Lyle F. Bachman and Lynn S. Bliss of a previous edition, see 12:323 (2 references); see also T4:2238 (3 references) and T3:338 (5 references); for excerpted reviews by Alex Bannatyne, Dale L. Johnson, and Barton B. Proger of the first edition, see 8:956 (5 references); see also T2:2067 (2 references).

[2249]

Receptive One-Word Picture Vocabulary Test–Spanish-Bilingual Edition.

Purpose: Designed to provide "an assessment of an individual's combined Spanish and English hearing vocabulary."
Population: Ages 4.0–12.11
Publication Date: 2001.
Acronym: ROWPVT-SBE.
Scores: Total score only.
Administration: Individual.
Price Data, 2006: $140 per test kit including manual (92 pages), test plates, and 25 Spanish-Bilingual record forms in portfolio; $38 per manual; $27 per 25 Spanish-Bilingual record forms; $75 per book of test plates (uses same plate booklet as English edition).
Time: (15–20) minutes.
Comments: Co-normed with the Expressive One-Word Picture Vocabulary Test–Spanish-Bilingual Edition (1043) to allow for comparisons of an individual's expressive and receptive vocabulary.
Author: Rick Brownell.
Publisher: Academic Therapy Publications.
Cross References: For reviews by S. Kathleen Krach and Maria del R. Medina-Diaz, see 16:209.

[2250]

Receptive One-Word Picture Vocabulary Test [2000 Edition].

Purpose: Designed to assess an individual's English hearing vocabulary.
Population: Ages 2–0 through 18-11.
Publication Dates: 1985–2000.
Acronym: ROWPVT.
Scores: Total score only.
Administration: Individual.
Price Data, 2006: $145 per kit including manual (2000, 110 pages), 25 record forms, and test plates; $30 per 25 record forms; $75 per test plates; $40 per manual.
Time: (10–15) minutes.
Comments: Lower and upper levels have been combined into this edition.

Authors: 1985 edition by Morrison F. Gardner; 2000 edition prepared by Rick Brownell.
Publisher: Academic Therapy Publications.
Cross References: For reviews by Doreen W. Fairbank and Sheila Pratt, see 15:205; see T5:2190 (9 references); T4:2239 (1 reference); for reviews by Janice A. Dole and Janice Santogrossi of an earlier edition, see 10:312; for reviews by Laurie Ford and William D. Schafer of an earlier edition of the upper level, see 11:329.

[2251]

Recognition Memory Test.

Purpose: Allows clinicians to quickly distinguish between right- and left-hemisphere brain damage.
Population: Adult patients referred for neuropsychological assessment.
Publication Date: 1984.
Acronym: RMT.
Scores, 2: Words, Faces.
Administration: Individual.
Price Data, 2006: $185 per kit including 1 reusable test booklet and word card, 25 record forms. and manual (16 pages); $32.50 per 100 record forms; $38.50 per manual.
Time: (15) minutes.
Author: Elizabeth K. Warrington.
Publisher: Western Psychological Services.
Cross References: See T5:2193 (59 references) and T4:2241 (12 references); for a review by Russell L. Adams, see 10:313 (1 reference).

[2252]

Recovery Attitude and Treatment Evaluator.

Purpose: Intended for use after diagnosis of alcohol or other drug dependency to determine the "patient's level of resistance to treatment and other important information" to be considered in treatment planning.
Population: Adults.
Publication Dates: 1987–1996.
Acronym: RAATE–CE; RAATE–QI.
Scores: 5 dimensions: Resistance to Treatment, Resistance to Continuing Care, Acuity of Biomedical Problems, Acuity of Psychiatric/Psychological Problems, Social/Family Environmental Status.
Administration: Individual.
Forms, 2: Clinical Evaluation, Initial Questionnaire.
Price Data: Available from publisher.
Time: (30–45) minutes for Clinical Evaluation; [20–30] minutes for Initial Questionnaire.
Authors: David Mee-Lee, Norman G. Hoffmann, and Maurice B. Smith (manual).
Publisher: Change Companies.
Cross References: For reviews by Philip Ash and Tony Toneatto, see 14:311.

[2253]

REHAB: Rehabiliation Evaluation Hall and Baker.

Purpose: "Designed to assess people with a major psychiatric handicap."

Population: Psychiatric patients who live in residential care.
Publication Dates: 1984–1994.
Acronym: REHAB.
Scores, 8: Deviant Behaviour, General Behaviour (Social Activity, Speech Disturbance, Self Care, Community Skills, Overall Rating), Speech Skills.
Administration: Individual.
Price Data, 2005: $405 (£215) per complete set including 50 assessment forms, 5 rater guides, 1 scoring key, 25 score sheets, 25 individual presentation sheets, 25 group presentation sheets, manual (1994, 136 pages), and carrying case; $33 (£17.50) per 25 assessment forms; $44 (£23) per 5 raters guides; $34 (£17.50) per scoring key; $19.50 (£10.50) per 25 score sheets; $27.50 (£14.50) per 25 individual presentation sheets; $46 (£26) per 25 group presentation sheets; $88 (£45.50) per manual; $105 (£60) per carrying case.
Time: (1) week.
Comments: A multipurpose behavior rating scale requiring observation of the target client over a period of one week; raters can include any direct care staff.
Authors: Roger Baker and John N. Hall.
Publisher: Dr. Baker Partnership [England].
Cross References: For reviews by James P. Choca and Pamilla Morales, see 14:312; see also T5:2195 (2 references).

[2254]
Rehabilitation Checklist.

Purpose: Designed to help determine the needs of clients recovering from serious and soft-tissue physical injuries, cognitive impairment (mild to moderate brain injury), and related psychological adjustment and/or trauma.
Population: Adults.
Publication Dates: 1998–1999.
Acronym: RCL.
Scores, 7: (Physical, Cognitive, Emotional, Psychosocial, Employability, Job), plus Total and Total Rehabilitation subscale.
Administration: Group.
Price Data, 2011: $133 per complete kit including 25 QuikScore™ forms and manual (1998, 54 pages); $79 per 25 QuikScore™ forms; $77 per manual.
Time: (15) minutes.
Comments: Self-report.
Author: J. Douglas Salmon, Jr.
Publisher: Multi-Health Systems, Inc.
Cross References: For reviews by Michael G. Kavan and Carolyn Mitchell Person, see 15:206.

[2255]
Rehabilitation Survey of Problems and Coping.

Purpose: Intended for use as a symptom rating and disability management tool.

Population: Age 14 and over
Publication Date: 2002.
Acronym: R-SOPAC.
Scores, 12: Overall Total, Problem Total, Coping Total, Emotional Overall, Emotional Problem, Emotional Coping, Physical Overall, Physical Problem, Physical Coping, Cognitive Overall, Cognitive Problem, Cognitive Coping.
Administration: Group or individual.
Parts, 2: Survey of Problems, Survey of Coping.
Price Data, 2011: $122 per complete kit including technical manual (112 pages) and 25 QuikScore forms™; $88 per technical manual; $50 per 25 QuikScore™ forms.
Time: (10–15) minutes.
Comments: One of several measures comprising a broad battery of rehabilitation-oriented instruments together entitled the Rehabilitation Assessment Series (RAS).
Authors: J. Douglas Salmon, Jr. and Marek Celinski.
Publisher: Multi-Health Systems, Inc.
Cross References: For reviews by Theodore L. Hayes and Nambury S. Raju, see 16:210.

[2256]
Reiss-Epstein-Gursky Anxiety Sensitivity Index.

Purpose: To measure the fear of anxiety in order to "identify patients with high anxiety sensitivity" and "to obtain information relevant to the diagnosis of panic disorder or posttraumatic stress disorder; to evaluate treatment outcomes; to assess soldiers at risk to panic under stress."
Population: Adults and adolescents.
Publication Date: 1987.
Acronym: ASI.
Scores: Total Anxiety Sensitivity.
Administration: Individual or group.
Price Data: Available from publisher.
Time: [5] minutes.
Comments: Translated into 18 languages: Catalan, Chinese, Dutch, Farsi, French, German, Greek, Icelandic, Italian, Japanese, Polish, Portuguese, Russian, Spanish, Swedish, Turkish.
Authors: Steven Reiss and Rolf A. Peterson.
Publisher: IDS Publishing Inc.
Cross References: See T5:2199 (14 references) and T4:2244 (2 references); for a review by Harrison G. Gough, see 11:330.

[2257]
A Religion Scale.

Purpose: Measures attitudes toward religion.
Population: Adolescents and adults.
Publication Date: 1961.
Scores: Total score only.
Administration: Group.

Manual: No manual.
Price Data, 2005: $2 per scale.
Time: [10] minutes.
Comments: Supplementary article available.
Author: Panos D. Bardis.
Publisher: Donna Bardis.
Cross References: See 8:465 (2 references).

[2258]
The Renfrew Bus Story, North American Edition.
Purpose: Designed as a "test of narrative recall."
Population: Ages 3.6–7.0
Publication Date: 1994.
Scores, 4: Information, Sentence Length, Complexity, Independence.
Administration: Individual.
Price Data, 2011: $75 per complete kit including manual (56 pages), 15 record forms, and story booklet; $15 per 15 record forms.
Time: Administration time approximately 5-10 minutes.
Comments: American adaptation of original British version.
Authors: Judy Cowley and Cheryl Glasgow.
Publisher: Learning Tools LLC.
Cross References: For reviews by Sherry K. Bain and Robert R. Haccoun, see 14:314.

[2259]
Repeatable Battery for the Assessment of Neuropsychological Status.
Purpose: Designed to measure "attention, language, visuospatial/constructional abilities, and immediate and delayed memory."
Population: Ages 20–89.
Publication Date: 1998.
Acronym: RBANS.
Scores, 18: Immediate Memory (List Learning, Short Memory, Total), Visuospatial/Constructional (Figure Copy, Line Orientation, Total), Language (Picture Naming, Semantic Fluency, Total), Attention (Digit Span, Coding, Total), Delayed Memory (List Recall, List Recognition, Story Memory, Figure Recall, Total), Total.
Administration: Individual.
Forms, 2: A, B.
Price Data, 2002: $149 per primary form kit including manual, record form A, stimulus book A, and coding scoring template A; $125 per alternative form kit including 25 record form B, stimulus book B, and coding scoring template B; $44 per 25 record forms (specify form); $81 per stimulus book (specify form); $13 per coding scoring template (specify form); $37 per manual.
Time: (20–30) minutes.
Author: Christopher Randolph.
Publisher: Pearson.

Cross References: For reviews by Stephen J. Freeman and Timothy J. Makatura, see 14:315.

[2260]
Report Completion Exercise for Firefighter, Police Officer, and Correctional Officer.
Purpose: "Video-based test designed to assess observation and listening skills as well as written communication skills."
Population: Candidates for entry-level firefighter, police officer, and correctional officer positions.
Publication Date: 2005.
Scores: Total score only.
Administration: Individual or group.
Price Data: Price data available from publisher (administration fee is waived if ordered with another testing product).
Time: 30 minutes.
Comments: Departments choosing to administer one of the tests must develop their own scoring criteria; administered via videos; joint technical report available for all three tests.
Author: International Public Management Association for Human Resources.
Publisher: International Public Management Association for Human Resources (IPMA-HR).
  a) FIREFIGHTER REPORT COMPLETION EXERCISE.
  Population: Entry-level firefighter candidates.
  Publication Date: 2005.
  Acronym: F-RCE.
  b) POLICE OFFICER REPORT COMPLETION EXERCISE.
  Population: Entry-level police officer candidates.
  Publication Date: 2005.
  Acronym: P-RCE.
  c) CORRECTIONAL OFFICER REPORT COMPLETION EXERCISE.
  Population: Entry-level correctional officer candidates.
  Publication Date: 2005.
  Acronym: C-RCE.
Cross References: For a review by Chockalingam Viswesvaran, see 18:106.

[2261]
Research Personnel Review Form.
Purpose: Designed "to provide a means for the periodic review of scientific, engineering, and technical personnel, and the environment in which they work."
Population: Research and engineering and scientific firms.
Publication Dates: 1959–1960.
Acronym: RPRF.
Scores: No scores.
Administration: Group.

Price Data: Available from publisher.
Time: Administration time not reported.
Author: Morris I. Stein.
Publisher: The Mews Press.

[2262]

Resiliency Scales for Children & Adolescents.

Purpose: Designed to assess "core characteristics of personal resiliency in children and adolescents."
Population: Ages 9-18.
Publication Dates: 2006-2007.
Scores, 13: Sense of Mastery (Optimism, Self-Efficacy, Adaptability, Total), Sense of Relatedness (Trust, Support, Comfort, Tolerance, Total), Emotional Reactivity (Sensitivity, Recovery, Impairment, Total).
Administration: Individual or group.
Price Data, 2008: $99 per complete kit including manual (2007, 183 pages) and 25 combination scales booklets; $64 per 25 combination scales booklets; $47 per manual.
Time: (10-25) minutes.
Comments: A downward extension of the Resiliency Scales for Adolescents.
Author: Sandra Prince-Embury.
Publisher: Pearson.
Cross References: For reviews by Christopher A. Sink and Nyaradzo H. Mvududu and by John J. Venn, see 18:107.

[2263]

Responsibility and Independence Scale for Adolescents.

Purpose: Measures adolescents' adaptive behaviors.
Population: Ages 12.0–19.11.
Publication Date: 1990.
Acronym: RISA.
Scores, 3: Responsibility, Independence, Adaptive Behavior Total.
Subtest: Subscales, 9: Self-Management, Social Maturity, Social Communication, Domestic Skills, Money Management, Citizenship, Personal Planning, Transportation Skills, Career Development.
Administration: Individual.
Price Data, 2006: $210.50 per complete kit including test book, examiner's manual (176 pages), 25 response forms; $76.50 per examiner's manual, $46 per 25 response forms.
Time: (30–45) minutes.
Comments: Administered in a standardized interview format to a respondent who is familiar with the adolescent.
Authors: John Salvia, John T. Neisworth, and Mary W. Schmidt.
Publisher: Riverside Publishing.
Cross References: For reviews by D. Joe Olmi and James P. Van Haneghan, see 13:325 (2 references).

[2264]

Retail Management Applicant Inventory.

Purpose: Designed for "personnel selection and placement and the identification of strengths and areas to improve" in the field of retail management.
Population: Retail management applicants.
Publication Dates: 1994–1998.
Acronym: RMAI.
Scores, 13: Validity (Candidness, Accuracy), Management Focus (Background and Work Experience, Management and Leadership Interest), Motivation and Attitudes (Management Responsibility, Customer Service, Energy Level, Management Orientation), Job Knowledge (Managerial Arithmetic, Understanding Management Procedures and Practices), Stability and Risk (Business Ethics, Job Stability), Management Potential Index.
Administration: Individual or group.
Forms, 5: Quanta Touch Test, Quanta Software for Windows–administration and scoring, Quanta Software for Windows–scoring only, RLH Online, Mail-in Scoring.
Price Data, 2005: $32 per 25–99 each Quanta Touch Test, Quanta Software for Windows—administration and scoring (no booklets), Quanta Software for Windows—scoring only (one booklet for every coupon ordered), RLH Online; volume discounts available.
Time: [40–60] minutes.
Author: London House.
Publisher: Pearson Performance Solutions [No reply from publisher; status unknown].

[2265]

Retail Sales Skills Test.

Purpose: To evaluate the knowledge necessary for successful performance as a retail salesperson.
Population: Candidates for the position of retail salesperson.
Publication Date: 1994.
Acronym: RETSALES.
Scores: Total Score, Narrative Evaluation, Ranking, Recommendation.
Administration: Group.
Price Data, 2001: $150 per candidate; quantity discounts available.
Time: (70) minutes.
Comments: Scored by publisher; must be proctored.
Author: Walden Personnel Performance, Inc.
Publisher: Walden Personnel Performance, Inc.

[2266]

Retail Store Manager Staff Selector.

Purpose: To evaluate the knowledge necessary for successful performance in retail store management.
Population: Candidates for the position of store manager or assistant manager.
Publication Date: 1996.
Acronym: RSALES.

Scores: Total Score, Narrative Evaluation, Ranking, Recommendation.
Administration: Group.
Price Data, 2001: $500 per candidate; quantity discounts available.
Time: (255) minutes.
Comments: Scored by publisher; must be proctored.
Author: Walden Personnel Performance, Inc.
Publisher: Walden Personnel Performance, Inc. (Canada).

[2267]

The Retention/Promotion Checklist.

Purpose: Assists parents, teachers, and administrators in their decision of whether to retain or promote a student to the next grade level.
Population: Grades K-8.
Publication Date: 1998.
Scores: Not scored.
Administration: Individual.
Price Data, 2011: $29.95 per checklist (124 pages) including a selection of freely reproducible pages containing The Retention/Promotion Checklist, Checklist Summary Form, Individual Retention Plan, Individual Promotion Plan, and appendices used for aiding the decision process.
Time: Administration time not reported.
Comments: Checklist should be completed by all members of the child study team including parents, teachers, and administrators.
Authors: Jim Grant and Irv Richardson.
Publisher: Crystal Springs Books.

[2268]

Retirement Descriptive Index.

Purpose: Designed to measure satisfaction with facets of retirement.
Population: Retirees
Publication Dates: 1969–1993.
Acronym: RDI.
Scores, 4: Present Work and Activities, Financial Situation, Present Health, People You Associate With.
Administration: Group or individual.
Price Data, 2010: There is no charge to use the copyrighted scales. For permission, e-mail jdi_ra@bgnet.bgsu.edu or phone (419) 372-8247 at the Department of Psychology, Bowling Green State University, Bowling Green, OH 43403.
Time: 5 minutes.
Comments: Previously listed with the Job Descriptive Index (1386).
Authors: Patricia C. Smith, Lorne M. Kendall, and Charles L. Hulin.
Publisher: Bowling Green State University.
Cross References: For reviews by Charles K. Parsons and Norman D. Sundberg of the Job Descriptive Index

and Retirement Descriptive Index, see 12:199 (33 references); see also T4:1312 (63 references).

[2269]

Revised Behavior Problem Checklist [PAR Edition].

Purpose: Developed to "rate problem behaviors observed in adolescents and young children."
Population: Ages 5–18.
Publication Dates: 1979–1987.
Acronym: RBPC.
Scores, 6: Conduct Disorder, Socialized Aggression, Attention Problems-Immaturity, Anxiety-Withdrawal, Psychotic Behavior, Motor Tension-Excess.
Administration: Individual.
Price Data, 2006: $182 per introductory kit including professional manual, 50 test booklets, and 50 profiles.
Time: 20(30) minutes.
Comments: Ratings by teachers, parents, and child care staff.
Authors: Herbert C. Quay and Donald R. Peterson.
Publisher: Psychological Assessment Resources, Inc.
Cross References: See T5:2211 (52 references) and T4:2254 (45 references); for reviews by Denise M. Dezolt and by Edward S. Shapiro and Stewart M. Shear, see 11:332 (80 references); for a review by Anthony A. Cancelli, see 9:1043 (31 references); see also T3:2012 (6 references).

[2270]

Revised Children's Manifest Anxiety Scale: Second Edition.

Purpose: "Designed to assess the level and nature of anxiety in children and adolescents."
Population: Ages 6-19.
Publication Dates: 1985-2008.
Acronym: RCMAS-2.
Administration: Group.
Scores, 6: Inconsistent Responding Index, Defensiveness, Total Anxiety, Physiological Anxiety, Worry, Social Anxiety.
Price Data, 2008: $99.50 per kit including 25 autoscore forms, one audio CD, and one technical manual (2008, 83 pages); $44.50 per 25 autoscore forms; $59.50 per technical manual; $15.50 per audio CD; $49.50 per Spanish version including 25 English autoscore forms and 25 Spanish item sheets.
Foreign Language Edition: Spanish version available.
Time: (10-15) minutes.
Comments: The revised edition includes the addition of an inconsistent responding index.
Authors: Cecil R. Reynolds and Bert O. Richmond.
Publisher: Western Psychological Services.
Cross References: For reviews by Gypsy M. Denzine and Margot B. Stein, see 18:108; see T5:2214 (140

references) and T4:2257 (47 references); for a review by Frank M. Gresham of an earlier edition, see 10:314.

[2271]

Revised Evaluating Acquired Skills in Communication.

Purpose: Constructed to assess communication skills in the areas of semantics, syntax, morphology, and pragmatics.
Population: Children 3 months to 8 years with severe language impairments.
Publication Dates: 1984-1991.
Acronym: EASIC.
Scores: Ratings in 10 areas: Labels/Nouns and Pronouns, Verbs and Action Commands, Comprehension of Three-Word Phrases, Affirmation and Negation, Prepositional Location Commands, Comprehension of Singular and Plural, Adjectives and Attributes, Money Concepts, Categorization and Association, Interrogatives.
Administration: Individual.
Price Data: Price data available from publisher for complete kit including manual (1991, 54 pages).
Time: Administration time not reported.
Author: Anita Marcott Riley.
Publisher: Pearson.
Cross References: For reviews by William O. Haynes and John H. Kranzler, see 12:329; for reviews by Barry W. Jones and Robert E. Owens, Jr. of an earlier edition, see 10:109.

[2272]

Revised Hamilton Rating Scale for Depression.

Purpose: Designed as a clinician-rated scale for evaluating individuals already diagnosed with depressive illness.
Population: Depressed individuals
Publication Date: 1994.
Acronym: RHRSD.
Scores, 22: General Screening, Depressed Mood, Feelings of Guilt, Suicide, Insomnia, Nocturnal Waking, Early Morning Waking, Work and Activities, Sexual Symptoms, Loss of Insight, Retardation, Agitation, Worry, Somatic Anxiety, Gastrointestinal Somatic Symptoms, General Somatic Symptoms, Hypochondriasis, Loss of Weight, Diurnal Variation, Obsessive-Compulsive Symptoms, Paranoid Symptoms, Depersonalization/Derealization.
Administration: Individual.
Price Data, 2011: $120 per kit, including 20 AutoScore RHRSD Clinician Forms, 20 AutoScore RHRSD Self-Report Problem Inventories, and 1 Manual; $45 per 25 AutoScore RHRSD Clinician Forms; $45 per 25 AutoScore RHRSD Self-Report Problem Inventories; $60 manual; $250 RHRSD CD; $17.50 per 100 Clinician Form RHRSD PC Answer Sheets, for use with the RHRSD CD; $17.50 per 100 Self-Report Problem Inventory RHRSD PC answer sheets, for use with the RHRSD CD.
Time: (5–10) minutes.

Comments: A self-report scale is also provided; The RHRSD CD will administer, score, and interpret both the RHRSD Clinician Form and the Self-Report Problem Inventory; requires PC with Windows 98, ME, XP, 2000, Vista, or Windows 7; Each CD is good for 20 uses.
Author: W. L. Warren.
Publisher: Western Psychological Services.
Cross References: For reviews by Paul C. Burnett and Barbara J. Kaplan, see 13:263 (382 references); see also T4:2261 (10 references).

[2273]

Revised Minnesota Paper Form Board Test, Second Edition.

Purpose: "Designed to measure aspects of mechanical ability requiring the capacity to visualize and manipulate objects in space."
Population: Grade 9 and over.
Publication Dates: 1934–1995.
Acronym: RMPFBT.
Scores: Total score only.
Administration: Group.
Forms, 4: Series AA, BB, MA, MB.
Price Data, 2006: $60 per examination kit including test booklets for 4 forms and manual; $95 per 25 Form AA or BB test booklets for booklet scoring; $120 per 25 test booklets for Forms MA and MB for use with scannable or hand-scorable answer document; $10 per key for Forms AA and BB; $50 per key for hand scoring scannable answer document for Forms MA and MB; $75 per 50 scannable answer documents for use with Form MA or MB; $45 per manual.
Foreign Adaptations: Australian edition: 1981; revised edition prepared by J. Jenkinson; Australian Council for Education Research [Australia]; British norms supplement: 1978; Gil Nyfield, NFER-Nelson Publishing Co. [England].
Time: 20(40) minutes.
Authors: Rensis Likert and W. H. Quasha.
Publisher: Pearson.
Cross References: For reviews by L. Carolyn Pearson and Michael J. Roszkowski, see 14:316; see also T5:2217 (3 references) and T4:2262 (2 references); for a review by Paul W. Thayer of an earlier edition, see 9:1045 (2 references); see also T3:2015 (19 references), T2:2266 (37 references), 7:1056 (19 references), and 6:1092 (16 references); for a review by D. W. McElwain, see 5:885 (29 references); for reviews by Clifford E. Jurgensen and Raymond A. Katzell, see 4:763 (38 references); for a review by Dewey B. Stuit, see 3:677 (48 references); for a review by Alec Rodger, see 2:1673 (9 references).

[2274]

Revised Pre-Reading Screening Procedures [1997 Edition].

Purpose: Designed to "find among children of average to superior intelligence the ones who show difficulties

in Auditory, Visual, and/or Kinesthetic modalities that often indicate Specific Language Disability (SLD)."
Population: First grade entrants.
Publication Dates: 1968–1997.
Scores: 7 areas: Visual, Visual-Kinesthetic-Motor, Auditory, Auditory-Visual, Auditory-Visual-Kinesthetic-Motor, Language, Letter Knowledge.
Administration: Group.
Price Data, 2006: $65.65 per test booklet (32 pages) including 12 Teacher Observation/Summary sheets, 12 Practice Pages, and 12 cardboard markers; $21.75 per Teacher's Manual (1997, 94 pages) including instructions plus detachable key; $24.45 per Teacher's Cards and Chart (2 sets of 5 x 10 cards and 2 copies of a wall chart used in giving the tests); $23.55 per specimen set including Teacher's Manual and 1 test booklet; quantity discounts available.
Time: Administration time not reported.
Authors: Beth H. Slingerland and Marty Aho.
Publisher: Educators Publishing Service, Inc.
Cross References: For a review by Maurine A. Fry of an earlier edition, see 9:1046; see also T2:1721 (1 reference); for reviews by Colleen B. Jamison and Roy A. Kress of an earlier edition, see 7:732 (1 reference).

[2275]

The Revised Sheridan Gardiner Test of Visual Acuity.
Purpose: To measure visual acuity.
Population: Age 5 and over.
Publication Dates: 1970–c1993.
Scores, 2: Distance Vision, Near Vision.
Administration: Individual.
Manual: No manual.
Price Data, 2001: $36 per test.
Time: Administration time not reported.
Authors: Mary D. Sheridan and Peter A. Gardiner.
Publisher: Keeler Instruments Inc. (U.S. Distributor).
Cross References: See T2:1926 (1 reference).

[2276]

Revised Token Test.
Purpose: Designed as a quantitative and descriptive test for "auditory disorders associated with aphasia and brain damage."
Population: Ages 20-80; Preliminary normative data based on the following standardization samples: non-brain-damaged, left hemisphere brain-damaged, right hemisphere brain-damaged.
Publication Date: 1978.
Acronym: RTT.
Scores, 22: 10 Subtest mean scores, Overall mean score, 11 Linguistic Element mean scores.
Administration: Individual.
Price Data, 2011: $175 per complete kit including 25 scoring forms, 25 profile forms, administration manual,

24 tokens, and manual (118 pages); $41 per profile forms; $35 per administration manual and scoring forms; $43 per tokens; $59 per examiner's manual.
Time: Administration time varies with condition.
Comments: Reconstruction of the Token Test.
Authors: Malcolm Ray McNeil and Thomas E. Prescott.
Publisher: PRO-ED.
Cross References: See T5:2225 (21 references) and T4:2270 (5 references); for reviews by Michael D. Franzen and Charles J. Golden and by Thomas Hammeke, see 9:1048; see also T3:2017 (5 references).

[2277]

Rey Auditory Verbal Learning Test: A Handbook.
Purpose: Designed to measure "verbal learning and memory."
Population: Ages 7–89.
Publication Date: 1996.
Acronym: RAVLT.
Scores, 3: Learning, Recall, Recognition.
Administration: Individual.
Price Data, 2006: $87.95 per complete kit including handbook (148 pages) and 25 record sheets and score summaries; $27.50 per 25 record sheets and score summaries; $64 per handbook.
Time: (15) minutes.
Author: Michael Schmidt.
Publisher: Western Psychological Services.
Cross References: For reviews by Karen Mackler and Steven R. Shaw, see 14:317; see also T5:2226 (42 references).

[2278]

Rey Complex Figure Test and Recognition Trial.
Purpose: Designed to assess "visuospatial constructional ability and visuospatial memory."
Population: Ages 6–89.
Publication Dates: 1995–1996.
Acronym: RCFT.
Scores, 9: Immediate Recall, Delayed Recall, Recognition Total Correct, Copy, Time to Copy, Recognition True Positives, Recognition False Positives, Recognition True Negatives, Recognition False Negatives.
Administration: Individual.
Price Data, 2006: $252 per introductory kit including manual (1995, 126 pages), 25 test booklets, stimulus card, and supplemental norms for children and adolescents (1996, 21 pages).
Time: (45) minutes, including a 30-minute delay interval.
Authors: John E. Meyers and Kelly R. Meyers.
Publisher: Psychological Assessment Resources, Inc.
Cross References: For reviews by D. Ashley Cohen and Deborah D. Roman, see 14:318; see also T5:2227 (62 references).

[2279]

Reynell Developmental Language Scales [U.S. Edition].

Purpose: Developed to measure verbal comprehension and expressive language skills.
Population: Ages 1 to 6.
Publication Dates: 1977–1990.
Acronym: RDLS.
Scores, 2: Verbal Comprehension, Expressive Language.
Administration: Individual.
Price Data, 2006: $549 per complete kit including a set of stimulus materials, 10 record forms, and manual (1990, 91 pages) in carrying case; $54.50 per 25 record forms; $66 per manual.
Time: (30) minutes.
Comments: Two Verbal Comprehension scales available to accommodate simple oral responses or pointing responses; British version available.
Authors: Joan K. Reynell and Christian P. Gruber.
Publisher: Western Psychological Services.
Cross References: See T5:2229 (16 references); for reviews by Dawn P. Flanagan and Rebecca J. McCauley, see 12:331 (3 references); see also T4:2272 (2 references); for reviews by Doris V. Allen and Diane Nelson Bryen of the British version, see 9:1049 (5 references); see also T3:2018 (16 references); for reviews by Katharine G. Butler and Joel Stark of the British version, see 8:974 (3 references); see also T2:2025 (3 references).

[2280]

Reynolds Adolescent Adjustment Screening Inventory.

Purpose: Designed as "a screening measure of adolescent adjustment."
Population: Ages 12–19.
Publication Dates: 1998–2001.
Acronym: RAASI.
Scores, 5: Antisocial Behavior, Anger Control Problems, Emotional Distress, Positive Self, Adjustment Total Score.
Administration: Individual or group.
Price Data, 2006: $140 per introductory kit including 50 test booklets and professional manual (2001, 134 pages).
Time: (5) minutes.
Author: William M. Reynolds.
Publisher: Psychological Assessment Resources, Inc.
Cross References: For reviews by Lynn Lakota Brown and Kevin M. Jones, see 15:207.

[2281]

Reynolds Adolescent Depression Scale–2nd Edition.

Purpose: Designed "to assess the severity of depressive symptomatology in adolescents in school and clinical settings."
Population: Ages 11–20.

Publication Dates: 1986–2002.
Acronym: RADS-2.
Scores, 5: Dysphoric Mood, Anhedonia/Negative Affect, Negative Self-Evaluation, Somatic Complaints, Depression Total.
Administration: Individual or group.
Price Data, 2006: $134 per introductory kit including professional manual (2002, 172 pages), 25 hand-scorable test booklets, and 25 summary/profile forms.
Time: (5–10) minutes.
Comments: Self-report measure; hand scored; may be administered aloud; test booklet is titled "About Myself."
Author: William M. Reynolds.
Publisher: Psychological Assessment Resources, Inc.
Cross References: For reviews by Kimberly A. Blair and Janet F. Carlson, see 16:211; see also T5:2230 (21 references) and T4:2274 (11 references); for reviews by Barbara J. Kaplan and Deborah King Kundert of an earlier edition, see 11:333 (6 references).

[2282]

Reynolds Adolescent Depression Scale-2nd Edition: Short Form.

Purpose: "Designed as a brief screening measure for the assessment of depression in adolescents."
Population: Ages 11-20.
Publication Dates: 1987-2008.
Acronym: RADS-2:SF.
Scores: Total score only.
Administration: Group.
Price Data, 2010: $79 per introductory kit including professional manual (2008, 91 pages) and 25 test booklets; $40 per 25 test booklets; $45 per professional.
Time: (2-3) minutes.
Comments: Abbreviated version of Reynolds Adolescent Depression Scale-2nd Edition (2281); self-report measure; may be administered aloud.
Author: William M. Reynolds.
Publisher: Psychological Assessment Resources, Inc.
Cross References: For reviews by Michael G. Kavan and Rama K. Mishra, see 18:109.

[2283]

Reynolds Bully-Victimization Scales for Schools.

Purpose: Designed to evaluate "school-related violence and its impact on students."
Publication Date: 2003.
Acronym: RBVSS.
Administration: Individual or group.
Levels, 3: Bully-Victimization Scale, Bully-Victimization Distress Scale, School Violence Anxiety Scale.
Price Data, 2003: $160 per complete kit including manual (181 pages), 30 Bully-Victimization Scale forms, 30 School Violence Anxiety Scale forms, 30 Bully-Victim-

ization Distress forms, Bully-Victimization Scale scoring key–English/Spanish, and Bully-Victimization Distress Scale scoring key–English/Spanish; $65 per manual; $30 per 30 Bully-Victimization Scale (specify English or Spanish); $30 per 30 School Violence Anxiety Scale (specify English or Spanish); $30 per 30 Bully-Victimization Distress Scale (specify English or Spanish); $10 per Bully-Victimization Scale scoring key–English/Spanish; $10 per Bully-Victimization Distress Scale scoring key–English/Spanish.
Foreign Edition: Spanish edition available.
Time: (5–10) minutes per scale.
Comments: Scales may be used individually or as a battery; automated group testing available.
Author: William Reynolds.
Publisher: Pearson.
　　a) BULLY-VICTIMIZATION SCALE.
　　Purpose: "Designed to measure bullying behavior and victimization among peers in or near school settings."
　　Population: Grades 3–12.
　　Acronym: BVS.
　　Scores, 2: Bullying, Victimization.
　　b) BULLY-VICTIMIZATION DISTRESS SCALE.
　　Purpose: Designed to "evaluate the dimensions of students' psychological distress specific to being bullied."
　　Population: Grades 3–12.
　　Acronym: BVDS.
　　Scores, 3: Total Distress (Externalizing, Internalizing, Total).
　　c) SCHOOL VIOLENCE ANXIETY SCALE.
　　Purpose: Designed to "measure student anxiety about schools as unsafe or threatening environments."
　　Population: Grades 5–12.
　　Acronym: SVAS.
　　Scores: Total score only.
Cross References: For reviews by Christopher A. Sink and Cher I. Edwards and by Susan M. Swearer and Kelly Brey Love, see 16:212.

[2284]

Reynolds Child Depression Scale-2nd Edition and Short Form.

Purpose: "Designed to screen for depression in children."
Population: Ages 7-13 years.
Publication Dates: 1981-2010.
Acronyms: RCDS-2; RCDS-2:SF.
Scores: Total score only.
Administration: Individual or group.
Forms, 2: Reynolds Child Depression Scale-2nd Edition; Reynolds Child Depression Scale-2nd Edition: Short Form.
Price Data, 2011: $145 per complete kit including 25 full length test booklets, 25 short test forms, and manual (2010, 133 pages); $58 per 25 full length test booklets; $40 per 25 short forms; $60 per manual.
Time: (10-15) minutes for full length form; (2-3) minutes for short form.

Comments: Both forms should be administered orally to children in Grades 2 through 4.
Author: William M. Reynolds.
Publisher: Psychological Assessment Resources, Inc.
Cross References: See T5:2231 (7 references) and T4:2275 (3 references); for reviews by Janet F. Carlson and Cynthia A. Rohrbeck of an earlier edition, see 11:334 (1 reference).

[2285]

Reynolds Depression Screening Inventory.

Purpose: Constructed as a "self-report measure of the severity of depressive symptoms."
Population: Ages 18–89.
Publication Date: 1998.
Acronym: RDSI.
Scores: Total score only.
Administration: Individual or group.
Price Data, 2006: $71 per introductory kit including manual (64 pages) and 25 booklets.
Time: (5–10) minutes.
Authors: William M. Reynolds and Kenneth A. Kobak.
Publisher: Psychological Assessment Resources, Inc.
Cross References: For reviews by Michael H. Campbell and Rosemary Flanagan, see 14:320.

[2286]

Reynolds Intellectual Assessment Scales and the Reynolds Intellectual Screening Test.

Purpose: Designed to assess verbal and nonverbal intelligence and memory.
Population: Ages 3–94.
Publication Dates: 1998–2003.
Administration: Individual.
Price Data, 2006: $385 per RIAS/RIST combination kit including 3-volume set of stimulus books, 25 RIAS record forms and 25 RIST record forms, and professional manual (2003, 267 pages) in a softsided attache case; $165 per RIAS scoring program software on CD-ROM including unlimited use software for scoring and report generation of RIAS and RIST.
Authors: Cecil R. Reynolds and Randy W. Kamphaus.
Publisher: Psychological Assessment Resources, Inc.
　　a) REYNOLDS INTELLECTUAL SCREENING TEST.
　　Purpose: Designed to identify quickly those who need a more comprehensive intellectual assessment.
　　Acronym: RIST.
　　Scores, 3: Guess What, Odd-Item Out, Total RIST Index.
　　Time: (10–15) minutes.
　　Comments: Brief screening test comprising two RIAS subtests.
　　b) REYNOLDS INTELLECTUAL ASSESSMENT SCALES.
　　Purpose: Designed to measure intellectual level.
　　Acronym: RIAS.

Scores, 10: Verbal Intelligence Index (Guess What, Verbal Reasoning), Nonverbal Intelligence Index (Odd-Item Out, What's Missing), Composite Intelligence Index, Composite Memory Index (Verbal Memory, Nonverbal Memory).
Time: (30–35) minutes.
Cross References: For reviews by Bruce A. Bracken and Gregory Schraw, see 16:213.

[2287]

Rhode Island Test of Language Structure.
Purpose: "Provides a measure of English language development–a profile of the child's understanding of language structure–and assessment data."
Population: Hearing-impaired children ages 3-20, hearing children ages 3-6.
Publication Date: 1983.
Acronym: RITLS.
Scores: Measures syntax response errors for 20 sentence types, both simple and complex, including Relative and Adverbial Clauses, Subject and Other Complements, Reversible and Nonreversible Passives, Datives, Deletions, Negations, Conjunctives, Embedded Imperatives.
Administration: Individual.
Price Data, 2011: $164 per complete kit including scoring forms, test booklet, and manual (114 pages); $35 per scoring forms; $77 per test booklet; $60 per manual.
Time: (25-35) minutes.
Authors: Elizabeth Engen and Trygg Engen.
Publisher: PRO-ED.
Cross References: See T5:2233 (4 references) and T4:2276 (1 reference); for reviews by Lynn S. Bliss and Joan I. Lynch, see 10:315.

[2288]

The Riley Articulation and Language Test, Revised.
Purpose: To identify children in need of speech therapy.
Population: Grades K–2.
Publication Dates: 1966–1971.
Acronym: RALT.
Scores, 3: Language Proficiency and Intelligibility, Articulation Function, Language Function.
Administration: Individual.
Price Data, 2006: $58 per complete kit including 25 tests and manual (1971, 7 pages); $29 per 25 tests; $33 per manual.
Time: (3–5) minutes.
Author: Glyndon D. Riley.
Publisher: Western Psychological Services.
Cross References: For reviews by Ralph L. Shelton and Lawrence D. Shriberg, see 8:975 (1 reference); for a review by Raphael M. Haller of the original edition, see 7:967 (1 reference).

[2289]

Risk-Sophistication-Treatment Inventory.
Purpose: Designed to assess juvenile offenders' risk for dangerousness, sophistication-maturity, and amenability to treatment.
Population: Juvenile offenders ages 9–18.
Publication Dates: 1998–2004.
Acronym: RSTI.
Scores, 12: Risk for Dangerousness (Violent and Aggressive Tendencies, Planned and Extensive Criminality, Psychopathic Features, Total), Sophistication-Maturity (Autonomy, Cognitive Capacities, Emotional Maturity, Total), Treatment Amenability (Psychopathology-Degree and Type, Responsibility and Motivation to Change, Consideration and Tolerance of Others, Total).
Administration: Individual.
Price Data, 2007: $174 per introductory kit including professional manual (2004, 109 pages), 25 interview booklets, and 25 rating forms.
Time: (50–65) minutes for semistructured interview; [15–20] minutes for rating form.
Comments: Semistructured interview and rating scale.
Author: Randall T. Salekin.
Publisher: Psychological Assessment Resources, Inc.
Cross References: For reviews by John S. Geisler and Steven I. Pfeiffer, see 17:165.

[2290]

Risk Taking Inventory & Guide.
Purpose: Designed to "help respondents see the filters through which they assess risk" and "also guides them in improving the likelihood of gains while reducing uncertainty and the likelihood of losses."
Population: Managers.
Publication Date: 1997.
Scores, 3: Risk-Preference Pattern, Risk-Avoidance Pattern, Risk-Neutral Pattern.
Administration: Group.
Manual: No manual.
Price Data, 2002: $8.95 per inventory and guide; minimum of 20 (volume discounts available).
Time: [15] minutes including self-scoring.
Author: Herbert S. Kindler.
Publisher: The Center for Management Effectiveness, Inc.

[2291]

Rivermead Assessment of Somatosensory Performance.
Purpose: "Designed to provide therapists and doctors with a brief, quantifiable and reliable assessment of somatosensory functioning after neurological disorders such as stroke, MS, peripheral neuropathies, head injury and spinal cord injury."

Population: Age 18 and over.
Publication Date: 2000.
Acronym: RASP.
Scores: Total score only.
Subtests, 7: Sharp/Dull Discrimination, Surface Pressure Touch, Surface Localization, Temperature Discrimination, Movement, Direction Proprioception Discrimination, Sensory Extinction, Two-Point Discrimination.
Administration: Individual.
Price Data, 2006: £184 per complete kit including manual (19 pages), 25 scoring sheets, reference card, 2 aesthesiometers/neurometers, 2 neurotemps, two-point discriminator/neurodisk, and 30 neurotips; £35 per 50 scoring sheets.
Time: (25–35) minutes.
Authors: Charlotte E. Winward, Peter W. Halligan, and Derick T. Wade.
Publisher: Pearson Assessment [England].
Cross References: For reviews by Thomas M. Dunn and Timothy Makatura, see 17:166.

[2292]

The Rivermead Behavioural Memory Test-Extended Version.

Purpose: Designed "to predict everyday memory problems in people with acquired, non-progressive brain injury and monitor change over time."
Population: Ages 16-65.
Publication Dates: 1985-1999.
Acronym: RBMT-E.
Scores, 12: First Names, Second Names, Belongings and Appointments, Picture Recognition, Story (Immediate), Story (Delayed), Face Recognition, Route (Immediate), Route (Delayed), Messages (Immediate), Messages (Delayed), Orientation and Date.
Administration: Individual.
Forms: 2 versions: A, B.
Price Data, 2006: £295.50 per complete kit including manual (1999, 20 pages), 25 scoring sheets, 2 stimulus books, picture cards, and timer.
Time: (25-30) minutes.
Authors: Barbara A. Wilson, Linda Clare, Janet M. Cockburn, Alan D. Baddeley, Robyn Tate, and Peter Watson.
Publisher: Pearson Assessment [England].
Cross References: For reviews by Andrew S. Davis and W. Holmes Finch and by Harrison Kane and Daniel Krenzer, see 17:167.

[2293]

The Rivermead Behavioural Memory Test [Second Edition].

Purpose: "Developed to detect impairment of everyday memory functioning and to monitor change following treatment for memory difficulties."
Publication Dates: 1985-2003.
Acronym: RBMT-II.
Administration: Individual.
Price Data: Available from publisher.
Time: (25-30) minutes.
Publisher: Pearson Assessment [England].
  a) THE RIVERMEAD BEHAVIOURAL MEMORY TEST.
  Population: Brain-damaged persons, ages 16-96 years.
  Publication Dates: 1985-2003.
  Scores, 2: Screening Score, Standardized Profile Score.
  Comments: For multiple administrations with the same subject, four parallel versions available.
  Authors: Barbara Wilson (test, manual, supplementary manual 2), Janet Cockburn (test, manual, supplementary manuals 2 and 3), and Alan Baddely (test, manual, supplementary manual 2).
  b) THE RIVERMEAD BEHAVIOURAL MEMORY TEST FOR CHILDREN.
  Population: Brain-damaged children, ages 5–11 years.
  Publication Date: 1991.
  Score: Standardized Profile Score.
  Comments: Separate test; materials from adult version used for most subtests, but some additional materials needed.
  Authors: Barbara A. Wilson (test and manual), Rebecca Ivani-Chalian (test and manual), and Frances Aldrich (manual).
Cross References: For reviews by Anthony M. Paolo and by Goran Westergren and Ingela Westergren, see 14:321; see also T5:2239 (35 references).

[2294]

Roberts-2.

Purpose: Designed to provide an "assessment of a child's or adolescent's level of social cognitive understanding."
Population: Ages 6-18 years.
Publication Dates: 1982-2005.
Scores, 28: 2 Theme Overview scales (Popular Pull, Complete Meaning), 6 Available Resources scales (Support from Self-Feeling, Support from Self-Advocacy, Support from Other-Feeling, Support from Other-Help, Reliance on Other, Limit Setting), 5 Problem Identification scales (Recognition, Description, Clarification, Definition, Explanation), 5 Resolution scales (Simple Closure or Easy Outcome, Easy and Realistically Positive Outcome, Constructive Resolution, Constructive Resolution of Feeling and Situation, Elaborated Process with Possible Insight), 4 Emotion scales (Anxiety, Aggression, Depression, Rejection), 4 Outcome scales (Unresolved Outcome, Nonadaptive Outcome, Maladaptive Outcome, Unrealistic Outcome), 2 Unusual or Atypical Responses scales (Unusual-Refusal/No Score/Antisocial, Atypical Categories).

Administration: Individual.

Editions, 3: Set of Test Pictures Featuring White Children and Adolescents, Set of Test Pictures Featuring Black Children and Adolescents, Set of Test Pictures Featuring Hispanic Children and Adolescents.

Price Data, 2008: $180 per complete kit including manual (2005, 171 pages), Casebook, Quick Scoring Guide, Set of Test Pictures Featuring White Children and Adolescents, and 25 record forms; $49.95 per manual; $59.95 per Set of Test Pictures Featuring White, Black, or Hispanic Children and Adolescents; $34.50 per 25 record forms; $55 per Continuing Education Questionnaire and Evaluation Form; $55 per Casebook (including 1 Quick Scoring Guide).

Time: (30-40) minutes.

Comments: Previous version entitled Roberts Apperception Test for Children.

Authors: Glen E. Roberts (test and manual) and Chris Gruber (manual only).

Publisher: Western Psychological Services.

Cross References: For reviews by Frederic J. Medway and by Rachel J. Valleley and Brandy L. Clarke, see 18:110; for reviews by Merith Cosden and Niels G. Waller of an earlier version, see 14:322; see also T5:2242 (8 references) and T4:2285 (5 references); for a review by Jacob O. Sines of an earlier edition, see 9:1054.

[2295]

Rockford Infant Developmental Evaluation Scales.

Purpose: Developed as a developmental checklist offering an informal assessment of developmental function.

Population: Birth-4 years.

Publication Date: 1979.

Acronym: RIDES.

Scores, 5: Personal-Social/Self-Help, Fine Motor/Adaptive, Receptive Language, Expressive Language, Gross Motor.

Administration: Individual.

Price Data: See www.ststesting.com for up-to-date prices.

Time: Administration time varies; author recommends administration in several sessions in one week.

Comments: 3 ways of administering items: ask parents for information, observe spontaneous actions and informal play, present specific tasks or set up situation that will elicit a particular kind of response.

Author: Developed by PROJECT RHISE, Children's Development Center, Rockford, IL.

Publisher: Scholastic Testing Service, Inc.

Cross References: See T5:2243 (1 reference); for a review by Dennis C. Harper, see 9:1055.

[2296]

Roeder Manipulative Aptitude Test.

Purpose: Measures manual and finger dexterity and hand-eye coordination.

Population: Elementary school to adult.

Publication Date: 1967.

Scores, 1 to 3: Left Hand Dexterity (optional), Right Hand Dexterity (optional), Total.

Administration: Group.

Price Data: Available from publisher.

Time: 5(10) minutes.

Author: Wesley S. Roeder.

Publisher: Lafayette Instrument.

Cross References: For reviews by Jean Powell Kirnan and Shauna Faltin and by Suzanne Lane, see 12:333.

[2297]

Rogers Criminal Responsibility Assessment Scales.

Purpose: "To quantify essential psychological and situational variables at the time of the crime and to implement criterion-based decision models for criminal responsibility."

Population: Adults.

Publication Date: 1984.

Acronym: R-CRAS.

Scores: 5 scales: Patient Reliability, Organicity, Psychopathology, Cognitive Control, Behavioral Control.

Administration: Individual.

Price Data, 2006: $104 per introductory kit including professional manual and 50 examination booklets.

Time: Administration time not reported.

Comments: "Criterion-referenced."

Author: Richard Rogers.

Publisher: Psychological Assessment Resources, Inc.

Cross References: See T4:2288 (1 reference); for a review by Robert J. Howell and R. Lynn Richards, see 10:316.

[2298]

Rokeach Value Survey.

Purpose: Constructed to identify values of importance to the respondent.

Population: Ages 11 and over.

Publication Dates: 1967-1983.

Scores: No scores.

Administration: Group.

Price Data, 2001: $67 per 25 test booklets; $32.95 per manual (322 pages).

Time: (10-20) minutes.

Comments: Rankings of 18 terminal values ("end-states of existence") and 18 instrumental values ("modes of behavior"); manual title is Understanding Human Values.

Author: Milton Rokeach.

Publisher: Sandra Ball-Rokeach [No reply from publisher; address unknown].

Cross References: See T5:2246 (14 references); for reviews by Susan M. Brookhart and Eleanor E. Sanford, see 12:334 (14 references); see also T4:2290 (28 references), 9:1058 (17 references), and T3:2029 (49 references); for reviews by Jacob Cohen and Tom Kitwood, see 8:660 (155 references); see also T2:1355 (39 references).

[2299]

Rorschach.

Purpose: A projective technique for clinical assessment and diagnosis.
Population: Ages 5 and over.
Publication Dates: 1921–1998.
Scores: Many variations of scoring and interpretation are in use with no single method generally accepted.
Administration: Individual.
Price Data, 2011: $98 per set of 10 plates; $25.30 per 100 recording sheets; $38 per set of 5 lotion charts; $63 per manual (1998, 228 pages).
Time: (20–30) minutes.
Comments: Variously referred to by such titles as Rorschach Method, Rorschach Test, Rorschach Psychodiagnostics.
Author: Hermann Rorschach.
Publisher: Hogrefe Publishing.
Cross References: For a review by Allen K. Hess, Peter Zachar, and Jeffrey Kramer, see 14:323; see also T5:2247 (136 references), T4:2292 (273 references), 9:1059 (79 references), and T3:2030 (155 references); for reviews by Richard H. Dana and Rolf A. Peterson, see 8:661 (360 references); see also T2:1499 (376 references); for reviews by Alvin G. Burstein, John F. Knutson, Charles C. McArthur, Albert I. Rabin, and Marvin Resnikoff, see 7:175 (455 references); see also P:470 (719 references); for reviews by Richard H. Dana, Leonard D. Eron, and Arthur R. Jensen, see 6:237 (734 references); for reviews by Samuel J. Beck, H. J. Eysenck, Raymond J. McCall, and Laurance F. Shaffer, see 5:154 (1078 references); for a review by Helen Sargent, see 4:117 (621 references); for reviews by Morris Krugman and J. R. Wittenborn, see 3:73 (452 references); see also 2:1246 (147 references).

[2300]

Ross Information Processing Assessment–Geriatric.

Purpose: A clinical instrument designed to identify, describe, and quantify cognitive-linguistic deficits in the geriatric population following traumatic brain injury.
Population: Geriatric patients.
Publication Date: 1996.
Acronym: RIPA-G.
Scores, 12: Immediate Memory, Recent Memory, Temporal Orientation, Spatial Orientation, Orientation to Environment, Recall of General Information, Problem Solving and Abstract Reasoning, Organization of Information, Auditory Processing and Comprehension, Problem Solving and Concrete Reasoning, Naming Common Objects, Functional Oral Reading.
Administration: Individual.
Price Data: Available from publisher.
Time: (45–60) minutes.
Comments: 10 core subtests, 2 supplemental subtests; publisher advises that a revised edition is now available.

Authors: Deborah Ross-Swain and Paul T. Fogle.
Publisher: PRO-ED.
Cross References: For reviews by Surendra P. Singh and Wilfred G. Van Gorp, see 14:324.

[2301]

Ross Information Processing Assessment–Primary.

Purpose: Designed to "assess information processing skills in children ages 5-0 through 12-11 who have acquired or developmental problems involving the brain."
Population: 5-0 to 12-11
Publication Date: 1999.
Acronym: RIPA-P.
Scores, 12: 8 subtests (Immediate Memory, Recent Memory, Recall of General Information, Spatial Orientation, Temporal Orientation, Organization, Problem Solving, Abstract Reasoning); 4 composite scores (Memory, Orientation, Thinking and Reasoning, Information Processing).
Administration: Individual.
Price Data, 2011: $150 per complete kit including manual (61 pages), 25 profile/summary forms, and 25 record forms; $68 per manual; $35 per 25 profile/summary forms; $53 per 25 record forms.
Time: (45) minutes for complete battery.
Comments: Certain subtests not administered to younger children.
Author: Deborah Ross-Swain.
Publisher: PRO-ED.
Cross References: For reviews by Dawn P. Flanagan and Leonard F. Caltabiano and by Matthew E. Lambert, see 15:208.

[2302]

Ross Information Processing Assessment, Second Edition.

Purpose: Designed to assess "cognitive-linguistic deficits following traumatic brain injury."
Population: Ages 15–90.
Publication Dates: 1986–1996.
Acronym: RIPA-2.
Scores, 20: 10 Subtest scores (Immediate Memory, Recent Memory, Temporal Orientation [Recent Memory, Remote Memory], Spatial Orientation, Orientation to Environment, Recall of General Information, Problem Solving and Abstract Reasoning, Organization, Auditory Processing and Retention); 10 Diacritical scores (Errors, Perseveration, Repeat Instructions/Stimulus, Denial/Refusal, Delayed Response, Confabulation, Partially Correct, Irrelevant, Tangential, Self-Corrected).
Administration: Individual.
Price Data, 2011: $172 per complete kit including examiner's manual (1996, 68 pages), 25 record forms, and 25 profile/summary forms in storage box; $64 per 25 record forms; $41 per 25 profile/summary forms; $75 per examiner's manual.

Time: (60) minutes.
Author: Deborah Ross-Swain.
Publisher: PRO-ED.
Cross References: For a review by Stephen R. Hooper, see 14:325; see also T4:2294; for a review by Jonathan Ehrlich of an earlier edition, see 11:337.

[2303]

Rothwell Miller Interest Blank (Revised).

Purpose: "Designed primarily to give an assessment of vocational interests as an aid to a career interview . Other applications include company selection and promotion, and clinical and rehabilitation counselling."
Population: Ages 13 and over.
Publication Dates: 1958–1994.
Acronym: RMIB.
Scores, 12: Outdoor, Mechanical, Computational, Scientific, Persuasive, Aesthetic, Literary, Musical, Social Service, Clerical, Practical, Medical.
Forms, 3: A, B, and C.
Administration: Individual or group.
Price Data: Available from publisher.
Foreign Language and Special Editions: Culturally adapted editions (English language): Australian, New Zealand, Philippine, Singapore, South African editions; Foreign language editions: French and Greek language editions available (Afrikaans, German, Hungarian, Icelandic, and Romanian editions in progress).
Time: (15–30) minutes.
Comments: In addition to main task of ranking occupations in order of preference, there is an opportunity for free choice responses; can be used in conjunction with the complementary measure Rothwell Miller Values Blank (2305).
Authors: J. W. Rothwell (original test), K. M. Miller (original test and revision), and B. Tyler (1994 revision).
Publisher: Miller & Tyler, Limited [England].
Cross References: For reviews by Richard E. Harding and William K. Wilkinson, see 13:269; for reviews by A. W. Heim and Clive Jones of an earlier edition, see 7:1034 (2 references).

[2304]

Rothwell-Miller Interest Blank.

Purpose: Designed to assess vocational interests.
Population: Ages 12 and over.
Publication Date: 1986.
Acronym: RMIB.
Scores, 12: Outdoor, Mechanical, Computational, Scientific, Persuasive, Artistic, Literary, Musical, Social Service, Clerical, Practical, Medical.
Administration: Group.
Price Data: Available from publisher.
Foreign Language Edition: Test printed in English and Afrikaans.

Time: 30(40) minutes.
Authors: B. A. Hall, M. E. Halstead, and T. R. Taylor.
Publisher: Human Sciences Research Council [South Africa].

[2305]

Rothwell Miller Values Blank.

Purpose: "Designed as a measure of work related values to be used primarily in career guidance, in conjunction with an occupational interests measure. Other applications include company selection (with school leavers or older basic level staff) and clinical and rehabilitation counselling."
Population: Ages 15 and older.
Publication Dates: 1968–1994.
Acronym: RMVB.
Scores, 5: Rewards, Interest, Security, Pride in Work, Autonomy.
Administration: Individual or group.
Price Data: Available from publisher.
Foreign Language Editions: French and Greek language editions available; Afrikaans, German, Hungarian, Icelandic, and Romanian editions in progress.
Time: [10–20] minutes.
Comments: Previously entitled Choosing a Career; developed as a complementary measure to be used with the Rothwell Miller Interest Blank (2304).
Authors: J. W. Rothwell, K. M. Miller, and B. Tyler.
Publisher: Miller & Tyler, Limited [England].
Cross References: For reviews by John S. Geisler and William I. Sauser, Jr., see 14:328.

[2306]

Rotter Incomplete Sentences Blank, Second Edition.

Purpose: Primarily used "as a screening instrument of overall adjustment."
Population: College students, adults, high-school students.
Publication Dates: 1950–1992.
Acronym: RISB.
Score: Index of Overall Adjustment.
Administration: Individual or group.
Forms, 3: College, Adult, High School.
Price Data, 2002: $34 per 25 response sheets or $127 per 100 response sheets(specify High School, College, or Adult; $82 per manual (1992, 256 pages).
Time: (20–40) minutes.
Authors: Julian B. Rotter, Michael I. Lah, and Janet E. Rafferty.
Publisher: Pearson.
Cross References: See T5:2258 (6 references); for reviews by Gregory J. Boyle and Mary J. McLellan, see 12:335 (3 references); see also T4:2300 (11 references), T3:2037 (11 references), 8:663 (21 references), T2:1501 (48 references), P:472 (35 references), 6:239 (17 references), and 5:156 (18 references); for reviews by Charles

N. Cofer and William Schofield of an earlier edition and an excerpted review by Adolf G. Woltmann, see 4:130 (6 references).

[2307]

Ruff Figural Fluency Test.
Purpose: Developed with the "aim of providing clinical information regarding nonverbal capacity for fluid and divergent thinking, ability to flexibly shift cognitive set, planning strategies, and executive ability to coordinate this process."
Population: Ages 16–70.
Publication Dates: 1988–1996.
Acronym: RFFT.
Scores, 3: Unique Designs, Perseverative Errors, Index of Planning Efficiency (Error Ratio).
Administration: Individual.
Price Data, 2006: $118 per introductory kit including 25 test booklets and professional manual (1996, 43 pages).
Time: 5 minutes.
Comments: Especially useful in neuropsychological applications.
Author: Ronald M. Ruff.
Publisher: Psychological Assessment Resources, Inc.
Cross References: For reviews by Raymond S. Dean and John J. Brinkman, Jr. and by Vincent J. Samar, see 15:209.

[2308]

Ruff-Light Trail Learning Test.
Purpose: "To assess visuospatial learning and memory."
Population: Ages 16–70.
Publication Date: 1999.
Acronym: RULIT.
Scores, 7: Learning (Total Correct, Total Step Errors, Trials to Completion), Immediate Memory (Trial 2 Correct, Trial 2 Errors), Delayed Memory (Delayed Correct, Delayed Errors).
Administration: Individual.
Price Data, 2006: $130 per introductory kit including professional manual, 50 test booklets, and stimulus cards.
Time: (5–15) minutes with a 60-minute delay.
Comments: Two alternate versions of a 15-step trail; long-term memory is evaluated by having the respondent retrace the trail after a 60-minute delay.
Authors: Ronald M. Ruff and C. Christopher Allen.
Publisher: Psychological Assessment Resources, Inc.
Cross References: For reviews by D. Ashley Cohen and Joseph G. Law, Jr., see 15:210.

[2309]

Ruff Neurobehavioral Inventory.
Purpose: Designed to measure cognitive, emotional, physical, and psychosocial problems both before and after a specified event–usually an injury or neuropsychiatric–illness.
Population: Ages 18 and older.
Publication Date: 2003.

Acronym: RNBI.
Scores, 26: Inconsistency, Infrequency, Negative Impression, Positive Impression, Cognitive Composite, Emotional Composite, Physical Composite, Quality of Life Composite, Attention & Concentration, Executive Functions, Learning & Memory, Speech & Language, Anger & Aggression, Anxiety, Depression, Paranoia & Suspicion, Posttraumatic Stress Disorder, Substance Abuse, Neurological Status, Pain, Somatic Complaints, Abuse, Activities of Daily Living, Psychosocial Integration & Recreation, Vocation & Finance, Spirituality.
Administration: Individual or group.
Price Data, 2006: $158 per introductory kit including 25 reusable item booklets, 25 answer booklets, 25 profile booklets, and professional manual (123 pages).
Time: [30–45] minutes.
Authors: Ronald M. Ruff and Kristin M. Hibbard.
Publisher: Psychological Assessment Resources, Inc.
Cross References: For reviews by Andrew S. Davis and W. Holmes Finch and by Wilfred G. Van Gorp and Jason Hassenstab, see 16:214.

[2310]

Ruff 2 & 7 Selective Attention Test.
Purpose: Developed to "measure two overlapping aspects of visual attention: sustained attention, and selective attention."
Population: Ages 16–70 years.
Publication Dates: 1995–1996.
Acronym: 2 & 7 Test.
Scores, 11: Automatic Detection Speed, Automatic Detection Errors, Automatic Detection Accuracy, Controlled Search Speed, Controlled Search Errors, Controlled Search Accuracy, Total Speed, Total Accuracy, Speed Difference, Accuracy Difference, Total Difference.
Administration: Individual.
Price Data, 2006: $155 per introductory kit including manual and 50 test booklets.
Time: (5) minutes.
Authors: Ronald M. Ruff and C. Christopher Allen.
Publisher: Psychological Assessment Resources, Inc.
Cross References: For a review by Daniel C. Miller, see 15:211.

[2311]

Rust Advanced Numerical Reasoning Appraisal.
Purpose: Measures the ability to recognize, understand, and apply mathematical and statistical reasoning abilities.
Population: Adults.
Publication Dates: 2001–2002.
Acronym: RANRA.
Scores: Total score only.
Administration: Group or individual.
Price Data, 2006: £195 per complete kit.

Time: 20 minutes.
Author: John Rust.
Publisher: Pearson Assessment [England].
Cross References: For reviews by Cederick O. Lindskog and Eleanor E. Sanford, see 16:215.

[2312]

Rust Inventory of Schizotypal Cognitions.
Purpose: For assessment of risk of schizotypal symptoms.
Population: Age 16 and over.
Publication Date: 1989.
Acronym: RISC.
Scores: Total score only.
Administration: Individual.
Price Data, 2006: £67.50 per complete kit including record forms and manual (57 pages).
Time: (10) minutes.
Author: John Rust.
Publisher: Pearson Assessment [England].
Cross References: For reviews by Gregory J. Boyle and George Domino, see 13:270 (3 references); see also T4:2303 (3 references).

[2313]

The Rutgers Drawing Test.
Purpose: A nonverbal "test of perception through motor response."
Population: Ages 4–6, 6–9.
Publication Dates: 1961–1973.
Scores: Total score only.
Administration: Group.
Price Data, 2005: $24 per specimen set; $44 per 25 test forms (specify Form A or Form B).
Time: Administration time not reported.
Author: Anna Spiesman Starr.
Publisher: Institute of Psychological Research, Inc. [Canada].
  a) FORM A.
  Population: Ages 4–6.
  b) FORM B.
  Population: Ages 6–9.
Cross References: For a review by Melvyn I. Semmel, see 7:446 (6 references); see also 6:559 (2 references).

[2314]

Safran Student's Interest Inventory, Third Edition.
Purpose: Developed to identify occupational interests.
Population: Grades 5-9, 8-12.
Publication Dates: 1960-1985.
Scores, 7: Economic, Technical, Outdoor, Service, Humane, Artistic, Scientific.
Administration: Group.
Levels, 2: 1 (grades 5-9), 2 (grades 8-12).

Price Data, 2005: $74.50 per 35 test booklets (select level); $44.10 per 35 students' manuals (1985, 8 pages); $41.30 per counsellor's manual (1985, 39 pages); $42.40 per preview kit.
Time: (40) minutes.
Comments: Self-administered.
Authors: Carl Safran, Douglas W. Feltham, and Edgar N. Wright.
Publisher: Nelson Education Ltd. [Canada].
Cross References: For reviews by Albert M. Bugaj and Caroline Manuele-Adkins, see 12:336; for a review by Thomas T. Frantz of an earlier edition, see 7:1035; see also 6:1069 (1 reference).

[2315]

Sales Achievement Predictor.
Purpose: Constructed to assess "characteristics that are critical for success in sales."
Population: Adults.
Publication Date: 1995.
Acronym: Sales AP.
Scores, 21: Validity Scores (Inconsistent Responding, Self-Enhancing, Self-Critical), Special Scores (Sales Disposition, Initiative-Cold Calling, Sales Closing), Basic Domain Scores (Achievement, Motivation, Competitiveness, Goal Orientation, Planning, Initiative-General, Team Player, Managerial, Assertiveness, Personal Diplomacy, Extroversion, Cooperativeness, Relaxed Style, Patience, Self-Confidence).
Administration: Group.
Price Data, 2006: $165 per kit including manual (73 pages), 2 mail-in answer sheets; $54.50 per mail-in answer sheet; $60.50 per manual; $430 per 10-use computer CD (PC with Windows); $16.50 per 100 PC answer sheets; $38.50 per FAX service scoring.
Time: 20 minutes.
Comments: Microsoft Windows 3.1 or above required for computer scoring.
Authors: Jotham G. Friedland, Sander I. Marcus, and Harvey P. Mandel.
Publisher: Western Psychological Services.
Cross References: For reviews by Gordon C. Bruner II and Brent W. Roberts, see 14:329.

[2316]

Sales Aptitude Test.
Purpose: "To measure an individual's sales aptitude."
Population: Sales people and sales managers.
Publication Dates: 1993–1996.
Scores: Total score only.
Administration: Group.
Price Data, 2002: $106 per start-up kit including 25 test booklets and examiner's manual (1996, 11 pages); $91 per 25 tests; $28 per examiner's manual; price information for Quanta scoring software available from publisher.

Time: (30) minutes.
Comments: Paper-and-pencil or computer administration available.
Author: Science Research Associates.
Publisher: Pearson Performance Solutions [No reply from publisher; status unknown].
Cross References: For reviews by Deniz S. Ones and Sheldon Zedeck, see 15:212.

[2317]
Sales Attitude Check List.
Purpose: To measure attitudes toward selling and habits in the sales situation.
Population: Applicants for sales positions.
Publication Dates: 1960–1992.
Acronym: SACL.
Scores: Total score only.
Administration: Individual or group.
Price Data, 2002: $97 per start-up kit including 25 test booklets and examiner's manual; $81 per 25 test booklets (quantity discounts available); $28 per examiner's manual.
Time: No limit (approximately 10–15 minutes).
Author: Erwin K. Taylor.
Publisher: Pearson Performance Solutions [No reply from publisher; status unknown].
Cross References: For reviews by Walter C. Borman and Stephan J. Motowidlo, see 9:1066 (1 reference); for a review by John P. Foley, Jr., see 6:1177.

[2318]
Sales Competency Inventory.
Purpose: Designed to measure the frequency with which respondents display certain competencies associated with effective sales performance.
Population: Salespeople.
Publication Date: 1996.
Scores, 5: Achievement Orientation, Customer Service Orientation, Impact and Influence, Initiative, Interpersonal Understanding.
Administration: Individual or group.
Price Data, 2006: $69 per 10 Profile and Interpretive Notes (22 pages) and 10 questionnaires; $29 per 10 Employee Version questionnaires; $55 per 10 Development Assistant booklets.
Time: [30–40] minutes.
Comments: Self-scoring and interpretive information provided.
Author: Hay Group.
Publisher: Hay Group.

[2319]
Sales Comprehension Test.
Purpose: "Designed to aid in the appraisal of sales ability and potential."
Population: Sales applicants and employees.

Publication Dates: 1947-1994.
Acronym: SCT.
Scores: Total score only.
Administration: Group.
Price Data, 2006: $119.50 per test; $3.75 per key; $36.50 per profiles; $53 per manual (1976, 20 pages), manual supplement (1984, 17 pages), manual supplement (1985, 4 pages), and norms supplement (1994, 4 pages); $4.50 per norms supplement (1988, 1 page); $56.95 per specimen set.
Foreign Language Editions: Spanish, Dutch, French, German, and Italian editions available.
Time: (15-20) minutes.
Comments: Revision of the Aptitudes Associates Test of Sales Aptitude.
Author: Martin M. Bruce.
Publisher: Martin M. Bruce, Ph.D.
Cross References: See T2:2406 (3 references) and 6:1178 (7 references); for a review by Raymond A. Katzell, see 5:947 (10 references).

[2320]
Sales Effectiveness Survey.
Purpose: Designed as a 360° measure of more than 70 competencies and personality traits that are common among the most successful salespeople.
Population: Sales and business development professionals.
Publication Date: 1996.
Scores, 7: Overall Sales Effectiveness, Comparative Sales Effectiveness, Personal Sales Characteristics, Basic Sales Skills, Selling Skills, Account Management Skills, Opportunity Management Skills.
Administration: Group.
Manual: No manual.
Price Data, 2005: $49 per set including questionnaires and answer sheets for 1 self-assessment, 6 others, 6 customers, and 1 feedback report; $50 fee for additional paper report.
Time: [30] minutes.
Comments: Assessment is administered online via Lore's Assessment Center; assessment results are emailed to participant; a paper report may be requested for an additional fee; the group report, available separately, summarizes the results for an entire sales group without identifying the individuals and enables the sales manager to look at the strengths and developmental needs of the group as a whole.
Author: Lore International Institute.
Publisher: Lore International Institute.

[2321]
Sales Motivation Inventory, Revised.
Purpose: Designed for "assessment of interest in, and motivation for, sales work."

Population: Prospective and employed salespeople.
Publication Dates: 1953-1988.
Acronym: SMI.
Scores: Total score only.
Administration: Group.
Price Data, 2006: $119.50 per test package; $52.65 per manual/manuals supplement; $4.50 per norms supplement; $36.50 per profile sheet package; $3.75 per scoring key; $55.95 per specimen set.
Foreign Language Edition: French edition also available.
Time: (20-30) minutes.
Author: Martin M. Bruce.
Publisher: Martin M. Bruce, Ph.D.
Cross References: For a review by Leo M. Harvill, see 11:338; for reviews by Robert M. Guion and Stephan J. Motowidlo of an earlier edition, see 9:1067; see also T2:2408 (5 references); for a review by S. Rains Wallace, see 5:948 (2 references).

[2322]

Sales Motivation Survey.

Purpose: Designed to assess the kinds of needs and values salespeople see as important considerations in making decisions about their work.
Population: Salespeople.
Publication Dates: 1972–1995.
Scores, 5: Basic Creative Comfort, Safety and Order, Belonging and Affiliation, Ego-Status, Actualization and Self-Expression.
Administration: Group.
Price Data, 2001: $7.95 per instrument.
Time: Administration time is not reported.
Comments: Self-administered; self-scored.
Authors: Jay Hall and Norman J. Seim.
Publisher: Teleometrics International, Inc.
Cross References: For reviews by Leslie H. Krieger and Sheldon Zedeck, see 14:330.

[2323]

Sales Performance Assessment™.

Purpose: Designed to identify an individual's strengths and weaknesses in the area of sales.
Population: Salespeople.
Publication Dates: 1985-2005.
Acronym: SPA.
Scores, 25: Market Awareness, Technical, Strategic, Structure, Sales Focus, Prospecting, Entrepreneurship, Communication, Outgoing, Optimistic, Excitement, Persuasive Negotiation, Insight, Aggressiveness, Tactical, Empathy, Customer Identification, Team Player, Persistence, Production, Management Focus, Idealism, Ego Drive, Materialism, Exaggeration.
Administration: Group.
Price Data: Available from publisher.

Foreign Language Editions: Available in English (American), English (British), Dutch, French, and German.
Time: (45) minutes.
Comments: Purchase and use requires training by publisher; test previously listed as Sales Effectiveness Analysis.
Authors: James T. Mahoney (test) and Management Research Group Staff (manual).
Publisher: Management Research Group.

[2324]

Sales Personality Questionnaire.

Purpose: Developed to assess personality characteristics necessary for sales success.
Population: Sales applicants.
Publication Dates: 1987–1990.
Acronym: SPQ.
Scores, 12: Interpersonal (Confidence, Empathy, Persuasive), Administration (Systematic, Conscientious, Forward Planning), Opportunities (Creative, Observant), Energies (Relaxed, Resilient, Results Oriented), Social Desirability.
Administration: Group.
Price Data: Available from publisher.
Time: (20-30) minutes.
Author: Saville & Holdsworth Ltd.
Publisher: SHL Group plc [United Kingdom].
Cross References: For reviews by Wayne J. Camara and Michael J. Roszkowski, see 12:337.

[2325]

Sales Potential Inventory.

Purpose: "Designed to help select top sales performers and determine the sales ability levels of current employees in any external or internal sales position."
Population: Job applicants and employees in sales positions.
Publication Dates: 2000–2001.
Acronym: S.P.I.
Scores, 2: S.P.I. score, Deception Scale score.
Administration: Group.
Price Data, 2005: $79.99 per starter kit including administrator's manual (2001, 28 pages), 5 tests, and 1 test log; $9.29 per 10 tests (volume discount available); $9.29 per 10 test logs for the online test version (volume discount available); $29.99 per administrator's manual.
Time: (15-20) minutes.
Comments: Online and paper-and-pencil versions of test are available; online version includes interpretive reports and follow-up interview questions.
Author: J. M. Llobet.
Publisher: G. Neil.
Cross References: For a review by Kathy E. Green, see 17:168.

[2326]

Sales Professional Assessment Inventory.

Purpose: Designed "to assess the individual's interest, motivation and skills needed for success in the sales profession."

Population: Salespeople.
Publication Dates: 1989–1992.
Acronym: SPAI.
Scores, 15: Validity (Candidness, Accuracy), Sales Motivation (Sales/Work Experience, Sales Interest, Sales Responsibility, Sales Orientation, Energy Level, Self Development), Sales Readiness (Sales Skills, Sales Understanding, Sales Arithmetic, Customer Service), Dependability (Business Ethics, Job Stability), Overall Index (Sales Potential).
Administration: Group or individual.
Price Data: Price information for Quanta Touch Test administration and scoring and for Windows administration and scoring available from publisher.
Time: (45) minutes.
Author: London House.
Publisher: Pearson Performance Solutions [No reply from publisher; status unknown].

[2327]

Sales Relations Survey.
Purpose: Designed to assess the interpersonal practices and customer orientation of salespeople.
Population: Salespeople.
Publication Dates: 1972–1995.
Scores, 2: Exposure, Feedback.
Administration: Group.
Price Data, 2001: $8.95 per instrument.
Time: Administration time not reported.
Comments: Self-administered; self-scored.
Author: Jay Hall.
Publisher: Teleometrics International, Inc.

[2328]

The Sales Sentence Completion Blank.
Purpose: "Designed to aid in the selection of competent sales personnel."
Population: Applicants for sales positions.
Publication Dates: 1961-1982.
Acronym: SSCB.
Scores: Total score only.
Administration: Group.
Price Data, 2006: $65.95 per test package; $19.50 per manual (1961, 25 pages); $28.05 per specimen set.
Time: (20-35) minutes.
Author: Norman Gekoski.
Publisher: Martin M. Bruce, Ph.D.
Cross References: For a review by William E. Kendall, and an excerpted review by John O. Crites, see 6:1181.

[2329]

Sales Skills Test.
Purpose: Designed "to evaluate the knowledge, skills, and abilities for a sales position."
Population: Adult sales position applicants.
Publication Dates: 2001–2002.

Scores, 6: Sales Principles, Sales Terms, Vocabulary, Sales Comprehension, Sales Situations, Math/Logic & Attention to Detail.
Administration: Individual.
Price Data: Available from publisher.
Time: (65) minutes.
Comments: Scoring available by mail, courier service, fax service, telephone, or "super-fast" fax service.
Author: Bruce Winrow.
Publisher: Walden Personnel Testing and Consulting, Inc. [Canada].
Cross References: For reviews by JoEllen V. Carlson and Paul M. Muchinsky, see 16:216.

[2330]

Sales Staff Selector.
Purpose: "Evaluates the suitability of candidates of all levels of experience for the position of Sales Representative."
Population: Candidates for sales representative positions.
Publication Date: 1984.
Scores, 4: Total score, Narrative Evaluation, Ranking, Recommendation.
Administration: Group.
Price Data, 2001: $150 per candidate; quantity discounts available.
Foreign Language Edition: French edition available.
Time: (65) minutes.
Comments: Scored by publisher; available in booklet and internet versions.
Author: Walden Personnel Performance, Inc.
Publisher: Walden Personnel Performance, Inc. [Canada].
Cross References: For reviews by Philip G. Benson and Richard W. Johnson, see 10:319.

[2331]

Sales Style Indicator [Revised].
Purpose: Designed to help an individual identify their preferred selling style and "assist individuals and teams to increase their sales and customer service performance."
Population: Sales personnel, sales managers, and customer service representatives.
Publication Dates: 1991-2006.
Acronym: SSI.
Scores, 4: Behavioral/Action, Cognitive/Analysis, Interpersonal/Harmony, Affective/Expression.
Administration: Individual or group.
Price Data, 2006: $13.95 per test booklet (2006, 20 pages); $14.95 per In-Depth Interpretations Booklet (2006, 48 pages); $26.95 per code for online version, which includes assessment and in-depth interpretations; $159.95 per SSI Power Point CD and binder (2006, 143 Slides); $23.95 per Why Don't You Sell The Way That I Buy? participant workbook (2006, 80 pages); $38 per Trainer's Guidelines (1996, 24 pages).

Foreign Language Editions: Available online in English, French, and German, and in print in English and French; the In-Depth interpretations booklet is available in English and French.
Time: 15 minutes to administer; 90-180 minutes for short program; up to 2 days for the full program.
Comments: Test can be self-administered, self-scored, and self-interpreted; full 1-2-day training program available using "Why Don't You Sell The Way That I Buy?" workbook and SSI Power Point as support.
Authors: Ken Keis, Terry D. Anderson, and Bruce Wares.
Publisher: Consulting Resource Group International, Inc.
Cross References: For reviews by Wayne J. Camara and Gerald A. Rosen of an earlier edition, see 13:271.

[2332]

Sales Transaction Audit.

Purpose: Intended as an assessment of sales style and its impact on salesperson-customer transactions.
Population: Salespeople.
Publication Dates: 1972-1980.
Acronym: STA.
Scores, 3: Parent, Adult, Child.
Administration: Group.
Manual: No manual.
Price Data, 2001: $8.95 per instrument.
Time: Administration time not reported.
Authors: Jay Hall and C. Leo Griffith.
Publisher: Teleometrics International, Inc.
Cross References: For a review by Chantale Jeanrie, see 14:331; for a review by Stephen L. Cohen of an earlier edition, see 8:1127.

[2333]

SalesMax.

Purpose: A computerized testing system designed "to measure personality traits and sales knowledge that contribute to effectiveness in the sales role."
Population: Potential employees for consultative sales positions (selection) or current employees (development reports available).
Publication Dates: 1998-2010.
Scores, 25: Sales Personality (Energetic, Follows Through, Optimistic, Resilient, Assertive, Social, Expressive, Serious-Minded, Self-Reliant, Accommodating, Positive About People), Sales Knowledge (Prospecting/ Pre-qualifying, First Meetings/First Impressions, Probing/Presenting, Overcoming Objections, Influencing/ Convincing, Closing), Sales Motivations (Recognition/ Attention, Control, Money, Freedom, Developing Expertise, Affiliation, Security/Stability, Achievement).
Administration: Group or individual.
Price Data, 2011: $150 one-time fee for account set-up and user training; reports are $128 to $170 each.

Foreign Language Editions: Portuguese, Hungarian, and Dutch versions available.
Time: [90] minutes for all modules; [20] minutes for 1 or 2 modules.
Comments: Earlier version entitled SalesMax System Internet Version.
Author: Assess Systems.
Publisher: Bigby, Havis & Associates, Inc., d/b/a Assess Systems.
Cross References: For reviews by Gerald R. Schneck and Michael Spangler of an earlier version called SalesMax System Internet Version, see 15:213.

[2334]

Salford Sentence Reading Test (Revised).

Purpose: To assess level of oral reading achievement.
Population: Ages 6-0 to 10-6.
Publication Dates: 1976-2000.
Acronym: SSRT (R).
Scores: Reading Age.
Administration: Individual.
Forms, 2: X and Y.
Price Data, 2002: £8.99 per set of 2 test cards (X and Y); £8.99 per manual (2000, 16 pages); £6.99 per 20 record sheets; £17.99 per specimen set including one each of test cards X and Y, record sheet, and manual.
Time: [2-3] minutes.
Authors: G. E. Bookbinder; revision by Denis Vincent and Mary Crumpler.
Publisher: Hodder & Stoughton Educational [England].
Cross References: See T4:2320 (1 reference); for a review by J. Douglas Ayers of an earlier edition, see 8:791.

[2335]

SAQ-Adult Probation III.

Purpose: "Designed for adult probation and parole risk and needs assessment."
Population: Adult probationers and parolees.
Publication Dates: 1985-1997.
Acronym: SAQ.
Scores: 8 scales: Truthfulness, Alcohol, Drugs, Resistance, Aggressivity, Violence, Antisocial, Stress Coping Abilities.
Administration: Group.
Price Data: Available from publisher.
Time: (30) minutes.
Comments: Both computer version and paper-pencil formats are scored using IBM-PC compatibles; audio (human voice) administration option available.
Author: Risk & Needs Assessment, Inc.
Publisher: Behavior Data Systems, Ltd.
Cross References: For reviews by John R. Hays and by Robert Spies and Mark Cooper, see 14:332; for a review by Tony Toneatto of an earlier edition, see 12:338.

[2336]

SAQS Chicago Q Sort.

Purpose: Developed to "describe people to be sorted out in terms of continuum of applicability about self or others" to obtain a measure of similarity.
Population: College and adults.
Publication Dates: 1956–1957.
Acronym: SAQS.
Scores: Total score only.
Administration: Group.
Price Data: Available from publisher.
Time: (10–15) minutes.
Author: Raymond Corsini.
Publisher: Psychometric Affiliates.
Cross References: See T2:1358 (5 references) and P:232 (2 references); for reviews by William Stephenson and Clifford H. Swenson, Jr., see 5:103 (2 references).

[2337]

SASB [Structural Analysis of Social Behavior] Intrex Questionnaires.

Purpose: Designed to measure the patient's perceptions of self and others, based on trait x state x situational philosophy and Structural Analysis of Social Behavior.
Population: Psychiatric patients and normals.
Publication Dates: 1980–2000.
Acronym: SASB Intrex.
Scores: Pattern Coefficient Scores, cluster profiles, and weighted affiliation and autonomy scores for each of 3 areas: Interpersonal Transitive-Focus on Other, Interpersonal Intransitive-Focus on Self, Intrapsychic Introjection; 3 forms (short, medium, long), 6 subtests: Self (Best, Worst), He/I Present Tense (Best, Worst), She/I Present Tense (Best, Worst), Mother/I Past Tense, Father/I Past Tense, Mother with Father/Father with Mother Past Tense.
Administration: Individual or group.
Price Data, 2000: $120 (research use) or $160 (clinical use) per questionnaire and coding software package including all 3 forms of Intrex questionnaire (short, medium, long), electronic forms, questionnaire user's manual (2000, 56 pages), SASBWorks coding programs (Process, Content, Complex, Markov), and coding reference manual (2000, 59 pages); $80 (research use) or $120 (clinical use) per all 3 forms of Intrex questionnaire with electronic forms and questionnaire user's manual; $80 per all 4 SASBWorks coding programs with coding reference manual; $.20 (research use, $10 minimum) or $2 (clinical use, $20 minimum) royalty fee per administration; $25 per questionnaire user's manual; $15 per coding reference manual; miscellaneous specialized SASB coding programs also available (contact intrex@psych.utah.edu for details).
Time: (60) minutes for complete battery, short form.
Comments: PC systems with DOS or Windows 95/98/2000 and Microsoft Access2000, Excel (1997 version or later), and Word necessary to process SASBWorks coding programs. Information and updates available online at: http://www.psych.utah.edu/benjamin/sasb/
Author: Lorna Smith Benjamin.
Publisher: University of Utah, Department of Psychology.
Cross References: For reviews by Dennis Doverspike and Thomas P. Hogan, see 15:214; see T5:1298 (1 reference); for a review by Scott T. Meier of an earlier edition, see 12:192; see also T4:1258 (2 references).

[2338]

SAT On-Campus Program SAT Test and SAT Subject Tests.

Purpose: To place students at the appropriate level of study in college, and/or to help determine admission status.
Population: Entering college freshmen.
Publication Dates: 1962–2005.
Scores: SAT Reasoning Test provides a Verbal, Mathematics, and Writing score on the College Board 200 to 800 scale. SAT Subject Tests provide total test scores on the College Board's 200 to 800 score scale, except for the English Language Proficiency Test that is on a score scale from 901 to 999. Some SAT Subject Tests also provide subscores.
Subtests: Tests: SAT Reasoning Test and SAT Subject Tests. Subject Tests include: English Language Proficiency; Literature; Writing; Mathematics Levels I and Mathematics 2; Biology E/M (Ecological/Molecular); Chemistry, Physics; Reading Language Tests in French, German, Modern Hebrew, Italian, Latin, and Spanish; and Reading and Listening Language Tests in Chinese, French, German, Japanese, Korean, and Spanish.
Administration: Group or individual.
Price Data: Available from publisher.
Comments: Available for local administration and scoring by higher educational institutions. The Institutional SAT tests are offered through the College Board's SAT On-Campus Testing Program. Institutional SAT Reasoning test answer sheets are scored locally with MicroScore software; Institutional SAT Subject test answer sheets are scored using clear scoring templates. The Institutional SAT Subject Tests were previously known as the College Placement Tests and the One-Hour Achievement Tests. The Institutional SAT Reasoning Test was previously known as the Scholastic Aptitude Test and SAT.
Author: Educational Testing Service.
Publisher: The College Board.
Cross References: See T5:1274 (2 references) and T3:507 (2 references); for a review by John R. Hills of the College Placement Tests, see 7:665.

[2339]

Scale for the Assessment of Negative Symptoms.

Purpose: To assess negative symptoms of schizophrenia.
Population: Psychiatric inpatients and outpatients of all ages.

Publication Dates: 1981-1984.
Acronym: SANS.
Scores: 25 behavioral rating scores within 5 areas: Affective Flattening or Blunting, Alogia, Avolition-Apathy, Anhedonia-Asociality, Attention.
Administration: Individual.
Price Data: Available from publisher.
Foreign Language Editions: Available in Spanish, French, Italian, German, Portuguese, Japanese, Chinese, and Greek.
Time: [15-30] minutes.
Comments: May be used in conjunction with the Scale for the Assessment of Positive Symptoms (SAPS; 2340).
Author: Nancy C. Andreasen.
Publisher: Nancy C. Andreasen.
Cross References: See T5:2288 (85 references); for reviews by Suzanne King and Niels G. Waller, see 12:339 (75 references); see also T4:2325 (37 references); for information on an earlier edition, see 9:1069 (2 references).

[2340]

Scale for the Assessment of Positive Symptoms.

Purpose: "Designed to assess positive symptoms, principally those that occur in schizophrenia."
Population: Psychiatric inpatients and outpatients of all ages.
Publication Date: 1984.
Acronym: SAPS.
Scores: 35 behavior ratings within 5 areas: Hallucinations, Delusions, Bizarre Behavior, Positive Formal Thought Disorder, Inappropriate Affect.
Administration: Individual.
Price Data: Available from publisher.
Time: [15-30] minutes.
Comments: Intended to serve as a complementary instrument to the Scale for the Assessment of Negative Symptoms (SANS; 2339).
Author: Nancy C. Andreasen.
Publisher: Nancy C. Andreasen.
Cross References: See T5:2289 (69 references); for reviews by John D. King and Suzanne King, see 12:340 (44 references); see also T4:2326 (24 references).

[2341]

Scale for the Assessment of Thought, Language, and Communication.

Purpose: Designed to assess clinical and pathological characteristics of language behavior.
Population: Manics, depressives, and schizophrenics.
Publication Date: 1980.
Acronym: TLC.
Scores: 19 ratings: Poverty of Speech, Poverty of Content of Speech, Pressure of Speech, Distractible Speech, Tangentiality, Derailment, Incoherence, Illogicality, Clanging, Neologisms, Word Approximations,

Circumstantiality, Loss of Goal, Perseveration, Echolalia, Blocking, Stilted Speech, Self-Reference, Global Rating.
Administration: Individual.
Price Data: Price data for materials including manual (19 pages) available from publisher.
Time: [45-60] minutes.
Author: Nancy C. Andreasen.
Publisher: Nancy C. Andreasen.
Cross References: See T5:2290 (2 references) and T4:2327 (4 references).

[2342]

Scale of Feelings and Behavior of Love: Revised.

Purpose: Designed to "identify the patterns of behavior and feelings people exhibit and experience in their love relationships."
Population: College and adults.
Publication Dates: 1973-1992.
Scores, 8: Verbal Expression of Affection, Self-Disclosure, Toleration of Loved Ones' Bothersome Aspects, Moral Support/Encouragement and Interest, Feelings Not Expressed, Material Evidence of Affection, Total Love Scale, Love Scale Index.
Administration: Group.
Price Data: Available from publisher.
Time: (30) minutes.
Comments: Separate answer sheets may be used; current edition now included in Innovations in Clinical Practice: A Source Book (Vol. II).
Authors: Clifford H. Swensen, Michele Killough Nelson, Jan Warner, and David Dunlap.
Publisher: Clifford H. Swensen.
Cross References: See T4:2328 (1 reference); for a review by H. Thompson Prout of an earlier edition, see 9:1072.

[2343]

Scale of Job-Related Social Skill Performance.

Purpose: Designed to assess the strengths and weaknesses of a student's social skill performance in various work settings.
Publication Date: [Undated].
Administration: Individual.
Price Data: Price data available from publisher for complete kit including teaching guide and script, response form, and interpretation/scoring guide.
Authors: Michael Bullis, Vicki Nishioka-Evans, H. D. Bud Fredericks, and Cheryl D. Davis.
Publisher: James Stanfield Co., Inc.
   a) SCALE OF JOB-RELATED SOCIAL SKILLS KNOWLEDGE.
   Population: Ages 15–25.
   Acronym: SSSK.
   Scores: Total score only.

Time: (45) minutes.
Comments: Administered using a verbal role playing method.
b) SCALE OF JOB-RELATED SOCIAL SKILL PERFORMANCE.
Population: Ages 14–21.
Acronym: SSSP.
Scores: 6 scales: Positive Social Behaviors, Self Control, Personal Issues, Body Movements, Personal Appearance, Negative Social Behaviors.
Time: Administration time not reported.

[2344]

Scale of Marriage Problems: Revised.

Purpose: Designed to measure marital conflicts.
Population: Couples.
Publication Dates: 1975–1992.
Scores, 7: Problem-Solving, Childrearing, Relatives, Personal Care, Money, Outside Relationships, Total.
Administration: Group.
Price Data: Available from publisher.
Time: Administration time not reported.
Comments: Current edition now included in Innovations in Clinical Practice: A Source Book (Vol. II).
Authors: Clifford H. Swensen, Michele Killough Nelson, Jan Warner, and David Dunlap.
Publisher: Clifford H. Swensen.
Cross References: For reviews by Cindy Carlson and Delores D. Walcott, see 14:334.

[2345]

Scaled Curriculum Achievement Levels Test.

Purpose: Assesses individual and group achievement in mathematics computation, reading, and language usage.
Population: Grades 3–8.
Publication Date: 1992.
Acronym: SCALE.
Administration: Group.
Levels: 9 levels in each of 3 subtests: Mathematics Computation (M1-M9), Reading (R1-R9), Language Usage (L1-L9).
Price Data, 2006: $109.50 per complete kit including 6 reusable administration booklets (2 each for Mathematics Computation, Reading, and Language Usage), 10 class placement/record sheets, 30 answer forms (10 each for Mathematics Computation, Reading, and Language Usage), and manual (135 pages); $16.50 per 100 class placement/record sheets; $52 per manual.
Authors: Victor W. Doherty and Gale H. Roid.
Publisher: Western Psychological Services.
a) MATHEMATICS COMPUTATION.
Scores: Total score only.
Price Data: $28.50 per 10 reusable administration booklets; $17.50 per 10 AutoScore™ answer forms.
Time: (20–25) minutes.

b) READING.
Scores: Same as *a* above.
Price Data: $41 per 10 reusable administration booklets; $17.50 per 10 AutoScore™ answer forms.
Time: Same as *a* above.
c) LANGUAGE USAGE.
Scores: Sames as *a* above.
Price Data: $36 per 10 reusable administration booklets; $17.50 per 10 AutoScore™ answer forms.
Time: (15–20) minutes.
Cross References: For reviews by Russell N. Carney and Robert K. Gable, see 12:341.

[2346]

Scales for Assessing Emotional Disturbance.

Purpose: Designed to assist in "the identification of children who qualify for the federal special education category of emotional disturbance."
Population: Students ages 5-0 to 18-11.
Publication Date: 1998.
Acronym: SAED.
Scores, 7: Inability to Learn, Relationship Problems, Inappropriate Behavior, Unhappiness or Depression, Physical Symptoms or Fears, Socially Maladjusted, Overall Competence.
Administration: Individual.
Price Data: Available from publisher.
Time: (10) minutes.
Comments: Should be "completed … by teachers or other school personnel who have had substantial contact with the student"; the publisher advises that a Second Edition is now available.
Authors: Michael H. Epstein and Douglas Cullinan.
Publisher: PRO-ED.
Cross References: For reviews by Sandra J. Carr and Gretchen Owens, see 14:333.

[2347]

Scales for Diagnosing Attention-Deficit/ Hyperactivity Disorder.

Purpose: "To help identify children and adolescents who have attention-deficit/hyperactivity disorder (ADHD)."
Population: Ages 5-0 through 18-11.
Publication Date: 2002.
Acronym: SCALES.
Scores, 4: Inattention, Hyperactivity, Impulsivity, Total.
Administration: Individual.
Forms, 2: Summary/School Rating Scale Form (SRS), Home Rating Scale Form (HRS).
Price Data, 2011: $110 per complete kit including examiner's manual (78 pages), 25 summary/school rating forms, and 25 home rating forms; $60 per examiner's manual; $35 per 25 summary/school rating forms; $24 per 25 home rating forms.
Time: 15–20 minutes.

Comments: Completed by parents and teachers of target child; designed as part of a comprehensive ADHD assessment; identifies specific behavioral targets for intervention; allows for ratings on DSM-IV-TR criterion for ADHD.
Authors: Gail Ryser. and Kathleen McConnell.
Publisher: PRO-ED.
Cross References: For a review by Joseph G. Law, Jr., see 15:215.

[2348]

Scales for Identifying Gifted Students.

Purpose: "Designed to assist school districts in the identification of students as gifted."
Population: Ages 5-18 years.
Publication Date: 2004.
Acronym: SIGS.
Scores: 7 areas: General Intellectual Ability, Language Arts, Mathematics, Science, Social Studies, Creativity, Leadership.
Administration: Individual.
Forms, 2: Home Rating Scale, School Rating Scale.
Price Data, 2006: $150 per complete kit including manual (57 pages), 25 Home Rating Scale forms, 25 School Rating forms, and 25 Summary forms; $65 per manual; $35 per 25 Home Rating Scale forms; $35 per 25 School Rating Scale forms; $20 per 25 Summary forms.
Foreign Language: Available in a Spanish-speaking version.
Time: (10-15) minutes.
Comments: This test "is designed to be completed by a teacher, counselor, or other professional who has an opportunity to observe the student for an extended period of time."
Authors: Gail R. Ryser and Kathleen McConnell.
Publisher: Prufrock Press Inc.
Cross References: For reviews by Michael S. Matthews and Sandra Ward, see 17:169.

[2349]

Scales for Rating the Behavioral Characteristics of Superior Students.

Purpose: Designed to aid teachers in the identification of gifted children.
Population: Population unspecified, developed from research with students in Grades 4–6.
Publication Date: 1976.
Acronym: SRBCSS.
Scores, 10: Learning, Motivational, Creativity, Leadership, Artistic, Musical, Dramatics, Communication (Precision, Expressiveness), Planning.
Administration: Group.
Price Data: Available from publisher.
Time: Administration time not reported.
Comments: Scales for rating by teachers.
Authors: Joseph S. Renzulli, Linda H. Smith, Alan J. White, Carolyn M. Callahan, and Robert K. Hartman.

Publisher: Creative Learning Press, Inc.
Cross References: See T5:2295 (9 references); for reviews by Edward N. Argulewicz and James O. Rust, see 9:1073 (1 reference).

[2350]

Scales of Cognitive Ability for Traumatic Brain Injury.

Purpose: To "provide a systematic method of assessing cognitive deficits associated with traumatic brain injury."
Population: Patients with acquired brain damage; adolescents and adults.
Publication Date: 1992.
Acronym: SCATBI.
Scores, 46: Perception and Discrimination (Sound Recognition, Shape Recognition, Word Recognition [no distraction], Word Recognition [with distraction], Color Discrimination, Shape Discrimination, Size Discrimination, Discrimination of Color/Shape/Size, Discrimination of Pictured Objects, Auditory Discrimination [real words], Auditory Discrimination [nonsense], Total); Orientation (Premorbid Questions, Postmorbid Questions, Total); Organization (Identifying Pictured Categories, Identifying Pictured Category Members, Word Associations, Sequencing Objects [size], Sequencing Words [alphabetical], Sequencing Events [time of year], Sequencing Events [pictured task steps], Sequencing Events [recall task steps], Total); Recall (Memory for Graphic Elements, Naming Pictures, Immediate Recall of Word Strings, Delayed Recall of Word Strings, Cued Recall of Words, Cued Recall of Words in Discourse, Word Generation, Immediate Recall of Oral Directions, Recall of Oral Paragraphs, Total); Reasoning (Figural Reasoning: Matrix Analogies, Convergent Thinking: Central Theme, Deductive Reasoning: Elimination, Inductive Reasoning: Opposites, Inductive Reasoning: Analogies, Divergent Thinking: Homographs, Divergent Thinking: Idioms, Divergent Thinking: Proverbs, Divergent Thinking: Verbal Absurdities, Multiprocess Reasoning: Task Insight, Multiprocess Reasoning: Analysis, Total).
Administration: Individual.
Price Data, 2011: $318 per complete kit; $65 per 25 record forms; $66 per stimulus card set; $82 per stimulus manual; $82 per examiner's manual; $35 per audio CD.
Time: 30 to 120 minutes.
Authors: Brenda Adamovich and Jennifer Henderson.
Publisher: PRO-ED.
Cross References: For reviews by Charles J. Long and Faith Gunning and by Deborah D. Roman, see 13:273.

[2351]

Scales of Early Communication Skills for Hearing-Impaired Children.

Purpose: "Designed to evaluate speech and language development of hearing-impaired children between the ages of two and eight years."

Population: Ages 2-0 to 8-11.
Publication Date: 1975.
Acronym: SECS.
Scores, 4: Receptive Language Skills, Expressive Language Skills, Nonverbal Receptive Skills, Nonverbal Expressive Skills.
Administration: Individual.
Price Data, 2011: $12 per package of 25 rating forms.
Time: [60] minutes (through observation).
Comments: Ratings by teachers.
Authors: Jean S. Moog and Ann E. Geers.
Publisher: Central Institute for the Deaf (CID).
Cross References: See T5:2298 (3 references); for reviews by Vincent J. Samar and Marc Marschark and by E. W. Testut, see 12:342.

[2352]

Scales of Independent Behavior–Revised.

Purpose: "Designed to measure functional independence and adaptive functioning in school, home, employment, and community settings."
Population: Infants to adults, with or without developmental disabilities.
Publication Dates: 1984–1996.
Acronym: SIB-R.
Scores, 24: Full Scale (Gross-Motor Skills, Fine Motor Skills, Social Interaction, Language Comprehension, Language Expression, Eating and Meal Preparation, Toileting, Dressing, Personal Self-Care, Domestic Skills, Time and Punctuality, Money and Value, Work Skills, Home/Community Orientation), Maladaptive Behavior Scale [optional] (Hurtful to Self, Unusual or Repetitive Habits, Withdrawal or Inattentive Behavior, Socially Offensive Behavior, Uncooperative Behavior, Hurtful to Others, Destructive to Property, Disruptive Behavior).
Administration: Individual.
Forms, 3: Full Scale, Short Form, Early Development.
Price Data, 2006: $240.50 per complete kit including interview book, comprehensive manual (1996, 306 pages), 15 full scale response booklets with IPRs, 5 short form response booklets with IPRs, and 5 early development form response booklets with IPRs; $86 per comprehensive manual; $61 per 25 full scale response booklets with IPRs; $38.50 per 25 short form response booklets with IPRs; $38.50 per 25 early development form response booklets with IPRs; $52.50 per 25 short form for the visually impaired response booklets.
Time: (45–60) minutes for Full Scale; (15–20) minutes for Short Form; (15–20) minutes for Early Development.
Comments: SIB-R in conjunction with the Woodcock-Johnson® Psychoeducational Battery–Revised can be used as a comprehensive diagnostic system for measuring adaptive behavior, problem behavior, cognitive ability, language proficiency, and achievement; can be administered either via interview or checklist; short and early development forms available as part of test kit; computerized scoring system available in Windows or Macintosh; visually impaired short form also available.
Authors: Robert H. Bruininks, Richard W. Woodcock, Richard F. Weatherman, and Bradley K. Hill.
Publisher: Riverside Publishing.
Cross References: For reviews by Gloria Maccow and Leland C. Zlomke, see 14:337; see also T5:2299 (7 references) and T4:2335 (6 references); for reviews by Bonnie W. Camp and Louis J. Heifetz of the earlier version, see 10:321.

[2353]

SCAN-3 for Adolescents and Adults: Tests for Auditory Processing Disorders.

Purpose: "Designed to identify auditory processing disorders in adolescents and adults."
Population: Ages 13-50.
Publication Dates: 1986-2009.
Acronym: SCAN-3:A.
Scores, 21: 4 screening test scores: Gap Detection, Auditory Figure-Ground 0 dB, Competing Words-Free Recall, Total (P/F); 5 diagnostic test scores: Auditory Processing Composite (Filtered Words, Auditory Figure-Ground 0 dB, Competing Words-Directed Ear, Competing Sentences, Total); 3 supplementary test scores: Auditory Figure-Ground +8 dB, Auditory Figure-Ground +12 dB, Time Compressed Sentences; ear advantage summary score for each of the following: Auditory Figure-Ground 0 dB, Competing Words-Free Recall, Filtered Words, Competing Words-Directed Ear-Directed Right Ear, Competing Words-Directed Ear-Directed Left Ear, Competing Sentences, Auditory Figure-Ground +8 dB, Auditory Figure-Ground +12 dB, Time Compressed Sentences.
Administration: Individual.
Price Data, 2010: $255 per complete kit including 25 record forms, manual (2009, 120 pages), and Audio CD; $57 per 25 record forms; $97 per manual; $107 per Audio CD.
Time: (10-15) minutes for the screening tests; (20-30) minutes for the diagnostic and supplementary tests.
Comments: Screening test scores are "criterion-referenced"; Auditory Figure-Ground 0 dB test is identical across the screening and diagnostic levels; all scores (except for Gap Detection) are calculated as a composite of the participant's right ear score and left ear score, and the ear-advantage score is the difference between the right and left ear scores; additional materials required: "CD player with a track display or a two-channel audiometer" or access to a computer, two sets of stereo headphones, and a stereo Y-adapter if necessary; revision of SCAN-A: A Test for Auditory Processing Disorders in Adolescents and Adults.
Author: Robert W. Keith.
Publisher: Pearson.
Cross References: For reviews by Jerrell Cassady and Catherine Wagner and by Rick Eigenbrood, see

18:111; for reviews by William R. Merz, Sr. and Jaclyn B. Spitzer of the earlier edition entitled SCAN-A: A Test for Auditory Processing Disorders in Adolescents and Adults, see 13:275.

[2354]

SCAN-3 for Children: Tests for Auditory Processing Disorders.

Purpose: "Designed to identify auditory processing disorders in children."
Population: Ages 5-12.
Publication Dates: 1986-2009.
Acronym: SCAN-3:C.
Scores, 21: 4 screening test scores: Gap Detection (ages 8-12 only), Auditory Figure-Ground +8 dB, Competing Words-Free Recall, Total (P/F); 5 diagnostic test scores: Auditory Processing Composite (Filtered Words, Auditory Figure-Ground +8 dB, Competing Words-Directed Ear, Competing Sentences, Total); 3 supplementary test scores: Auditory Figure-Ground +12 dB, Auditory Figure-Ground 0 dB, Time Compressed Sentences; ear advantage summary score for each of the following: Auditory Figure-Ground +8 dB, Competing Words-Free Recall, Filtered Words, Competing Words-Directed Ear-Directed Right Ear, Competing Words-Directed Ear-Directed Left Ear, Competing Sentences, Auditory Figure-Ground +12 dB, Auditory Figure-Ground +0 dB, Time Compressed Sentences.
Administration: Individual.
Price Data, 2010: $255 per complete kit including 25 record forms, manual (2009, 124 pages), and Audio CD; $57 per 25 record forms; $97 per manual; $107 per Audio CD.
Time: (10-15) minutes for the screening tests; (20-30) minutes for the diagnostic and supplementary tests.
Comments: Screening test scores are "criterion-referenced"; Auditory Figure-Ground +8 dB test is identical across the screening and diagnostic levels; all scores (except for Gap Detection) are calculated as a composite of the participant's right ear score and left ear score, and the ear-advantage score is the difference between the right and left ear scores; additional materials required: "CD player with a track display or a two-channel audiometer" or access to a computer, two sets of stereo headphones, and a stereo Y-adapter if necessary; revision of SCAN-C Test for Auditory Processing Disorders in Children-Revised.
Author: Robert W. Keith.
Publisher: Pearson.
Cross References: For reviews by Gary L. Canivez and Connie Theriot England, see 18:112; for reviews by Annabel J. Cohen and Jaclyn B. Spitzer and Abbey L. Berg of an earlier edition entitled SCAN-C Test for Auditory Processing Disorders in Children-Revised, see 16:217; for an earlier edition see also T5:2300 (1 reference); for a review by Sami Gulgoz of the original edition, see 11:341 (2 references).

[2355]

The Scenotest: A Practical Technique for Understanding Unconscious Problems and Personality Structure.

Purpose: A projective instrument intended "to help very quickly assess emotional problems in children."
Population: Children and adolescents.
Publication Dates: 1971-1998.
Scores: Score information available from publisher.
Administration: Individual.
Price Data, 2011: $1,804 per complete test kit excluding manual (von Staabs, 1998, 110 pages, $52).
Time: Administration time not reported.
Comments: Material in the test kit consists of flexible human figures and accessories including animals, trees, symbolic figures, and items from everyday life.
Authors: G. von Staabs (original edition) and Joseph A. Smith (manual translated from the German edition).
Publisher: Hogrefe Publishing.
Cross References: For reviews by Joseph C. Kush and Paul Retzlaff, see 15:216.

[2356]

The SCERTS Model: A Comprehensive Educational Approach for Children with Autism Spectrum Disorders.

Purpose: "Criterion-referenced" assessment designed as a "multidisciplinary approach to enhancing communication and social-emotional abilities" of people with Autism Spectrum Disorders and related disabilities.
Population: People of all ages with Autism Spectrum Disorders and related disabilities.
Publication Date: 2006.
Acronym: SCERTS.
Scores: 3 Communication Stages: Social Partner, Language Partner, Conversational Partner; 3 domains: Social Communication (Joint Attention, Symbol Use), Emotional Regulation (Mutual Regulation, Self-Regulation), Transactional Support (Interpersonal Support, Learning Support).
Administration: Individual.
Price Data, 2010: $109.95 per two-volume manual (344 pages, 400 pages) set.
Time: (120-240) minutes.
Comments: An ongoing curriculum-based assessment, planning, and implementation model.
Authors: Barry M. Prizant, Amy M. Wetherby, Emily Rubin, Amy C. Laurent, and Patrick J. Rydell.
Publisher: Paul H. Brookes Publishing Co., Inc.

[2357]

Schaie-Thurstone Adult Mental Abilities Test.

Purpose: Designed to "measure the mental abilities of adults."

Population: Ages 22-84.
Publication Dates: 1985-1998.
Acronym: STAMAT.
Scores: 7 scale scores: Recognition Vocabulary (V), Figure Rotation (FR), Object Rotation (OR, Form OA only), Letter Series (LS), Word Series (WS, Form OA only), Number Addition (N), Word Fluency (W).
Administration: Group.
Forms, 2: Form A (for "Adult," essentially the Thurstone Primary Mental Abilities Test Form II-17 (PMA) with new adult norms), Form OA (for "Older Adult," large-type version of the original plus two additional scales for adults over age 55).
Price Data: Price information available from publisher for Form OA expendable test booklets, Form A booklets, Form A answer sheets, Form A scoring key, profiles for both OA and A, manual (86 pages), and specimen set.
Time: (50–60) minutes.
Comments: Norms updated in 1998.
Author: K. Warner Schaie.
Publisher: K. Warner Schaie (the author).
Cross References: See T5:2304 (4 references) and T4:2339 (3 references); for a review by Eric F. Gardner, see 10:322.

[2358]

Schedule for Affective Disorders and Schizophrenia, Third Edition.

Purpose: "To record information regarding a subject's functioning and psychopathology."
Population: Adults.
Publication Dates: 1977-1988.
Acronym: SADS.
Administration: Individual.
Price Data, 2001: $.50 per SADS/SADS-L suggested procedures; $2.50 per SADS/SADS-L instructions and clarifications (1985, 24 pages).
Time: [30–120] minutes.
Authors: Robert L. Spitzer, Jean Endicott, Jo Ellen Loth (SADS-LB, SADS-LI), Patricia McDonald-Scott (SADS-LI), and Patricia Wasek (SADS-LI).
Publisher: Department of Research Assessment and Training.
    a) SCHEDULE FOR AFFECTIVE DISORDERS AND SCHIZOPHRENIA.
    Scores, 24: Current Syndromes (Depressive Mood/Ideation, Endogenous Features, Depressive-Associated Features, Suicidal Ideation/Behavior, Anxiety, Manic Syndrome, Delusions-Hallucinations, Formal Thought Disorder, Impaired Functioning, Alcohol or Drug Abuse, Behavioral Disorganization, Miscellaneous Psychopathology, GAS [worst period], Extracted Hamilton); Past Week Functioning (Depressive Syndrome, Endogenous Features, Manic Syndrome, Anxiety, Delusions-Hall-Disorganization, GAS rating, Ex-

tracted Hamilton, Miscellaneous Psychopathology); Past Other than Diagnosis (Social Functioning, Suicidal Behavior).
    Price Data: $3 per SADS booklet; $.50 per SADS score sheet; $1.50 per SADS summary scales scores; $.50 per editing and coding instructions; $2.50 per instructions/clarifications.
    b) SCHEDULE FOR AFFECTIVE DISORDERS AND SCHIZOPHRENIA LIFETIME (VARIOUS VERSIONS).
    1) *SADS-L.*
    Purpose: To record information regarding a subject's functioning and psychopathology; includes current disturbance.
    Price Data: $2 per SADS-L booklet; $.50 per SADS-L score sheet.
    2) *SADS-LB.*
    Purpose: To record information regarding a subject's functioning and psychopathology; includes current disturbance and additional items related to bipolar affective disorder.
    Price Data: $2 per SADS-LB booklet; $.50 per SADS-LB score sheet.
    3) *SADS-LI.*
    Purpose: To record information regarding a subject's functioning and psychopathology; specifies follow-up interval.
    Price Data: $2 per SADS-LI booklet; $.50 per SADS-LI score sheet.
Cross References: See T5:2305 (248 references); for reviews by Paul A. Arbisi and James C. Carmer, see 12:343 (414 references); see also T4:2340 (152 references).

[2359]

Schedule for Nonadaptive and Adaptive Personality.

Purpose: "Designed to assess trait dimensions in the domain of personality disorders."
Population: Ages 18 and older.
Publication Date: 1993.
Acronym: SNAP.
Scores: 34 scales: Trait (Mistrust, Manipulativeness, Aggression, Self-harm, Eccentric Perceptions, Dependency, Exhibitionism, Entitlement, Detachment, Impulsivity, Propriety, Workaholism), Temperament (Negative Temperament, Positive Temperament, Disinhibition), Diagnostic (Paranoid, Schizoid, Schizotypal, Antisocial, Borderline, Histrionic, Narcissistic, Avoidant, Dependent, Obsessive-Compulsive, Passive-Aggressive, Sadistic, Self-Defeating), Validity (Variable Response Inconsistency, True Response Inconsistency, Desirable Response Inconsistency, Deviance, Rare Virtues, Invalidity Index).
Administration: Individual or group.
Price Data, 2006: $55 per starter kit including 10 test booklets, 100 answer sheets, set of scoring keys, 25 profile forms, and manual for administration, scoring,

and interpretation (92 pages); $10 per 10 test booklets; $15 per 100 answer sheets; $35 per set of 34 scoring keys; $5 per 25 profile forms (specify diagnostic scales or validity trait, and temperament scales); $15 per manual for administration, scoring, and interpretation; price data for scoring disks available from publisher.
Time: 45 minutes.
Author: Lee Anna Clark.
Publisher: University of Minnesota Press.
Cross References: For reviews by Lizanne DeStefano and Niels G. Waller, see 14:338; see also T5:2306 (1 reference) and T4:2341 (1 reference).

[2360]

A Schedule of Adaptive Mechanisms in CAT Response.

Purpose: "Designed to aid in qualitative evaluation of C.A.T. stories."
Population: Children.
Publication Date: [ca. 1963].
Scores: 12 categories: Defense Mechanisms (Reaction-Formation, Undoing and Ambivalence, Isolation, Repression and Denial, Deception, Symbolization, Projection and Introjection, Fear and Anxiety, Regression, Controls Weak or Absent), Identification (Adequate/Same-Sex, Confused/or Opposite Sex).
Administration: Individual.
Manual: No manual.
Price Data, 2010: $12.50 per 30 forms.
Time: Administration time not reported.
Comments: See Children's Apperception Test (487).
Author: Mary Haworth.
Publisher: C.P.S., Inc.

[2361]

The Schedule of Growing Skills: Second Edition.

Purpose: Designed as an assessment of child development.
Population: Ages 0–5 years.
Publication Dates: 1987–1996.
Acronym: SGS II.
Scores, 9: Passive Postural, Active Postural, Locomotor, Manipulative, Visual, Hearing and Language, Speech and Language, Interactive Social, Self-Care Social.
Administration: Individual.
Price Data, 1998: £120 per starter set including 10 child records, 50 profiles, user's guide (1996, 109 pages), and all stimulus materials; £40 per conversion kit including user's guide, picture book, shape formboard, fish formboard, pegboard and pegs, STYCAR distant vision card B and key card, pom pom, and baby rattle; £65 per 10 record forms; £40 per 50 profiles; £30 per reference manual.
Time: (20) minutes.

Authors: Martin Bellman, Sundara Lingam, and Anne Aukett.
Publisher: GL Assessment [England].
Cross References: For reviews by Carol M. McGregor and Leah M. Nellis, see 15:217; see T5:2308 (1 reference); for reviews by Michelle M. Creighton and Scott R. McConnell and by Donna Spiker of an earlier edition, see 11:342.

[2362]

Schedules for Clinical Assessment in Neuropsychiatry, Version 2.0.

Purpose: "Aimed at assessing, measuring and classifying the psychopathology and behavior associated with the major psychiatric syndromes of adult life."
Population: Adults.
Publication Dates: 1982-1995.
Acronym: SCAN.
Scores: Item scores only.
Administration: Individual.
Parts, 3: Present State Examination, Item Group Checklist, Clinical History Schedule.
Price Data, 2006: $34.95 per manual; $32.50 per Glossary; $28.50 per recording booklets.
Foreign Language Editions: Contact publisher for information regarding availability of foreign language editions.
Time: Administration time not reported.
Comments: Computer administration and scoring available for DOS and Windows.
Author: World Health Organization.
Publisher: American Psychiatric Publishing, Inc.
  a) PRESENT STATE EXAMINATION.
  Acronym: PSE10.
  Subtests, 2: Part One, Part Two.
  Comments: Part One covers somatoform, dissociative, anxiety, depressive, and bipolar disorders and problems associated with basic bodily functions and use of alcohol and other substance use. Part Two covers psychotic and cognitive disorders and observed abnormalities of speech, affect, and behavior.
  b) ITEM GROUP CHECKLIST.
  Acronym: IGC.
  Comments: 40 Item Groups cover disorders in subchapters F2 (psychotic disorders), F3 (affective disorders), and F40-42 (neurotic disorders) of ICD10.
  c) CLINICAL HISTORY SCHEDULE.
  Acronym: CHS.
  Comments: Includes broader clinical and social history data.

[2363]

Scholastic Abilities Test for Adults.

Purpose: "Designed to be a general measure of scholastic accomplishment."

Population: Ages 16 through 70.
Publication Date: 1991.
Acronym: SATA.
Scores: 9 subtest scores: Verbal Reasoning, Nonverbal Reasoning, Quantitative Reasoning, Reading Vocabulary, Reading Comprehension, Math Calculation, Math Application, Writing Mechanics, Writing Composition, and 9 composite scores: Scholastic Abilities, General Aptitude, Total Achievement, Verbal, Quantitative, Reading, Mathematics, Writing, Achievement Screener.
Administration: Group.
Price Data, 2011: $206 per complete kit including 10 test books, 25 response booklets, 25 profile/examiner record forms, and examiner's manual (102 pages); $64 per 10 test books; $53 per 25 response booklets; $35 per 25 profile/examiner record forms; $64 per examiner's manual.
Time: (60-120) minutes.
Authors: Brian R. Bryant, James R. Patton, and Caroline Dunn.
Publisher: PRO-ED.
Cross References: See T5:2309 (2 references); for reviews by Nambury S. Raju and Douglas K. Smith, see 12:344.

[2364]

School-Age Care Environment Rating Scale.

Purpose: Designed to assess the quality of center-based child care for school-aged children.
Population: Child care programs.
Publication Dates: 1980–1996.
Acronym: SACERS.
Scores, 7: Space and Furnishings, Health and Safety, Activities, Interactions, Program Structure, Staff Development, Total.
Administration: Group.
Price Data, 2006: $15.95 per rating scale (1996, 44 pages); $8.95 per 30 scoring sheets.
Time: (120) minutes.
Comments: An adaptation of the Early Childhood Environment Rating Scale (923); for use with center-based care (not family child care homes); respondents cue evaluators of the child-care environment; "Also includes a set of 6 supplementary items for centers that include children with special needs."
Authors: Thelma Harms, Ellen Vineberg Jacobs, and Donna Romano White.
Publisher: Teachers College Press.
Cross References: For reviews by Patricia B. Keith and Hillary Michaels, see 14:339.

[2365]

School Archival Records Search.

Purpose: "Designed to overlay existing school records so that they can be coded and quantified systematically."
Population: Grades 1–12.

Publication Date: 1991.
Acronym: SARS.
Scores: 11 archival variables: Demographics, Attendance, Achievement Test Information, School Failure, Disciplinary Contacts, Within-School Referrals, Certification for Special Education, Placement Out of Regular Classroom, Receiving Chapter I Services, Out-of-School Referrals, Negative Narrative Comments.
Administration: Group.
Price Data, 2002: $35 per complete kit including user's guide, technical manual (86 pages), and 50 instrument packets.
Time: Administration time varies.
Authors: Hill M. Walker, Alice Block-Pedego, Bonnie Todis, and Herbert H. Severson.
Publisher: Sopris West.
Cross References: For reviews by John Crawford and Robert Fitzpatrick, see 13:275 (1 reference).

[2366]

School Assessment Survey.

Purpose: "Designed to measure schoolwide characteristics."
Population: Elementary through senior high school teachers and administrators.
Publication Date: 1985.
Acronym: SAS.
Scores, 9: Goal Consensus, Facilitative Leadership, Centralization of Influence: Classroom Instruction, Centralization of Influence: Curriculum and Resources, Vertical Communication, Horizontal Communication, Staff Conflict, Student Discipline, Teaching Behavior.
Administration: Group.
Price Data, 2001: $9.99 per kit including manual (69 pages).
Time: [30-40] minutes.
Authors: Bruce L. Wilson and William A. Firestone.
Publisher: Research for Better Schools, Inc.
Cross References: See T5:2312 (1 reference); for reviews by LeAnn M. Gamache and by Dean Nafziger and Joanne L. Jensen, see 12:345 (1 reference); see also T4:2355 (1 reference).

[2367]

School Effectiveness Questionnaire.

Purpose: Assesses variables that have an impact on school effectiveness.
Population: Students, teachers, parents.
Publication Date: 1993.
Acronym: SEQ.
Scores, 11: Effective Instructional Leadership, Clear and Focused Mission, Safe and Orderly Environment, Positive School Climate, High Expectations, Frequent Assessment/Monitoring of Student Achievement, Emphasis on Basic Skills, Maximum Opportunities

for Learning, Parent/Community Involvement, Strong Professional Development, Teacher Involvement in Decision Making.
Administration: Group.
Forms, 4: Level 1 Students (Elementary), Level 2 Students (High School), Teachers, Parents.
Price Data, 2002: $13 per 10 reusable questionnaires (Teacher Form); $33 per 10 reusable questionnaires (Level 1, Level 2, Parent Forms); $18 per manual (45 pages); $85 per 100 Type 2 machine-scorable answer documents; $22 per examination kit including manual, one each of all four questionnaires, and one answer document.
Time: (15–20) minutes.
Comments: Optional data analysis software available from publisher.
Authors: Lee Baldwin, Freeman Coney III, Diane Färdig, and Roberta Thomas.
Publisher: Pearson.
Cross References: For reviews by Robert Fitzpatrick and Michael Harwell, see 13:276.

[2368]

School Environment Preference Survey.

Purpose: "Designed to measure the student's commitment to the set of attitudes, values and behaviors that have been characteristically fostered and rewarded in traditional school environments."
Population: Grades 4–12.
Publication Date: 1978.
Acronym: SEPS.
Scores, 5: Self-Subordination, Traditionalism, Rule Conformity, Uncriticalness, Structured Role Orientation.
Administration: Group.
Price Data: Available from publisher.
Time: (10–15) minutes.
Author: Leonard V. Gordon.
Publisher: EdITS/Educational and Industrial Testing Service.
Cross References: See T5:2315 (1 reference) and T4:2360 (1 reference); for a review by Joan Silverstein, see 10:324.

[2369]

School Function Assessment.

Purpose: Designed to "measure a student's performance of functional tasks that support his or her participation in the academic and social aspects of an elementary school program."
Population: Grades K–6.
Publication Date: 1998.
Acronym: SFA.
Scores, 26: Participation, Task Supports (Physical Tasks Assistance, Physical Tasks Adaptations, Cognitive/Behavioral Tasks Assistance, Cognitive/Behavioral Tasks Adaptations), Activity Performance (Travel, Maintaining

and Changing Positions, Recreational Movement, Manipulation with Movement, Using Materials, Setup and Cleanup, Eating and Drinking, Hygiene, Clothing Management, Up/Down Stairs, Written Work, Computer and Equipment Use, Functional Communication, Memory and Understanding, Following Social Conventions, Compliance with Adult Directives and School Rules, Task Behavior/Completion, Positive Interaction, Behavior Regulation, Personal Care Awareness, Safety).
Administration: Individual.
Price Data, 2002: $149 per complete kit including 25 record forms with 3 rating scale guides and user's manual (136 pages); $59 per 25 record forms with 3 rating scale guides.
Time: Untimed; (5–10) minutes per scale.
Comments: Ratings to be completed by an educational and therapeutic professional who is familiar with the child's typical performance.
Authors: Wendy Coster, Theresa Deeney, Jane Haltiwanger, and Stephen Haley.
Publisher: Pearson.
Cross References: For reviews by Wayne C. Piersel and William D. Schafer, see 14:340.

[2370]

The School Leadership Series.

Purpose: Consists of two assessments developed to provide states with assessments to use as part of the licensure process for principals, superintendents, and school leaders.
Population: Prospective school principals, superintendents, and school leaders.
Publication Date: 1998.
Scores: Total score only.
Administration: Group.
Restricted Distribution: Secure instruments administered three time annually at centers established by the publisher.
Price Data, 2006: $425 per School Leaders Assessment; $250 per School Superintendent Assessment.
Time: 360 minutes in three 120-minute modules.
Comments: State department of education for a particular state should be consulted to determine whether the School Leaders Licensure Assessment or the Superintendent Assessment is required.
Author: Educational Testing Service.
Publisher: Educational Testing Service.

[2371]

School Life Questionnaire.

Purpose: Designed to provide "data on students' ratings of their school connectedness, engagement and motivation to learn."
Population: Upper Primary and Secondary students.
Publication Dates: 1984-2009.

Acronym: SLQ.

Scores: 8 scales: General Satisfaction, Interaction with Teachers, Relevance/Opportunity, Success/Achievement, Social Integration, Negative Feelings, Status [Secondary version], Adventure [Primary version].

Administration: Group.

Forms, 2: Primary School, Secondary School.

Price Data, 2009: A$5.45 per Survey Form; contact publisher for cost of scoring and report service; manual (2009, 11 pages) is free to print from publisher's website: www.acer.edu.au/slq.

Time: (40) minutes.

Comments: Available "online or in paper-and-pencil format"; publisher provides scoring and summary report; summary report does not provide data for individual students.

Author: Australian Council for Educational Research Ltd.

Publisher: Australian Council for Educational Research Ltd. [Australia].

[2372]

School Motivation and Learning Strategies Inventory.

Purpose: Designed to measure "strategies students actively employ in learning and test taking."

Population: Ages 8-12, 13-18.

Publication Date: 2006.

Acronym: SMALSI.

Scores, 11: Study Strategies, Note-Taking and Listening Skills, Reading and Comprehension Strategies, Writing and Research Skills, Test-Taking Strategies, Time Management (teen only), Organizational Techniques (teen only), Time Management/Organizational Techniques (child only), Academic Motivation, Test Anxiety, Attention and Concentration.

Administration: Group.

Levels, 2: Child, Teen.

Forms, 2: Child Form, Teen Form.

Price Data, 2008: $199 per complete kit including manual (108 pages), 25 child test forms, 25 child profile sheets, child scoring template, 25 teen test forms, 25 teen profile sheets, teen scoring template, and audio CD; $135 per child or teen kit including manual, 25 test forms and 25 profile sheets (specify form), scoring template (specify form), and audio CD; $45 per 25 test forms, $32.50 per scoring template, $28 per 100 profile sheets (specify forms); $16.50 per audio CD; $52.50 per manual; $399 per scoring CD.

Time: (20-30) minutes.

Comments: The same manual is used for both Child and Teen forms.

Authors: Kathy Chatham Stroud and Cecil R. Reynolds.

Publisher: Western Psychological Services.

Cross References: For reviews by Christine Novak and Claudia R. Wright, see 18:113.

[2373]

School Readiness Checklist.

Purpose: Designed "to involve the parent in planning the child's educational program."

Population: Kindergarten entrants.

Publication Date: 1989.

Scores: Not scored.

Administration: Individual.

Manual: No manual.

Price Data, 2002: $10 per 25 checklists.

Time: [5–10] minutes.

Comments: Ratings by parents.

Author: Academic Consulting & Testing Service.

Publisher: Academic Consulting & Testing Service.

[2374]

School-Readiness Evaluation by Trained Teachers.

Purpose: To screen all school entrants to identify different levels of school-readiness.

Population: South African school beginners.

Publication Date: 1984.

Acronym: SETT.

Scores, 9: Language and General Development (Basic Level, Potential Level, Total), Physical Motor Development (Motor Ability, Integration, Total), Emotional Social Development (Sociability, Emotionality, Total).

Administration: Individual.

Price Data: Available from publisher.

Time: (30) minutes.

Comments: Parent Questionnaire for the Evaluation of School-Readiness and Nursery-School Questionnaire for the Evaluation of School-Readiness may be used in conjunction with this test.

Author: Marianne Joubert.

Publisher: Human Sciences Research Council [South Africa].

[2375]

School Readiness Test.

Purpose: Designed to test the student's readiness for first grade academics.

Population: End of kindergarten through first 3 weeks of Grade 1.

Publication Dates: 1974–2004.

Acronym: SRT.

Scores, 9: Vocabulary, Identifying Letters, Visual Discrimination, Phonemic Awareness, Comprehension and Interpretation, Mathematical Knowledge, Developmental Spelling Ability, Optional Handwriting Assessment, Total.

Administration: Group.

Price Data: See www.ststesting.com for up-to-date pricing.

Foreign Language Edition: Spanish edition available.

Time: (80) minutes.

Comments: Subtest scores convert to Individual Readiness Ratings of adequate, marginal, and low; Total score converts to Overall Readiness Ratings of high, above average, average, marginal, not ready without special attention, and not ready without much special attention.
Authors: O. F. Anderhalter and Jan Perney.
Publisher: Scholastic Testing Service, Inc.
Cross References: For reviews by Esther Stavrou Toubanos and Larry Weber, see 12:346; for a review by Thorsten R. Carlson of an earlier edition, see 8:808.

[2376]
School Situation Survey.

Purpose: Designed to measure "school-related student stress."
Population: Grades 4-12.
Publication Date: 1989.
Acronym: SSSR.
Scores, 7: Sources of Stress (Teacher Interactions, Academic Stress, Peer Interactions, Academic Self-Concept), Manifestations of Stress (Emotional, Behavioral, Physiological).
Administration: Group.
Price Data: Available from publisher at www.mind-garden.com/products/sssrs.htm.
Time: (10-15) minutes.
Authors: Barbara J. Helms and Robert K. Gable.
Publisher: Mind Garden, Inc.
Cross References: For reviews by Theodore Coladarci and LeAdelle Phelps, see 12:347; see also T4:2368 (1 reference).

[2377]
School Social Behavior Scales, Second Edition.

Purpose: Designed to evaluate social competence and antisocial behavior of children and youth in Grades K-12 (ages 5-18).
Population: Grades K–12.
Publication Dates: 1993–2002.
Acronym: SBSS-2.
Scores, 8: Social Competence Scale (Peer Relations, Self-Management/Compliance, Academic Behavior, Social Competence Total), Antisocial Behavior Scale (Hostile/Irritable, Antisocial/Aggressive, Defiant/Disruptive, Antisocial Behavior Total).
Administration: Individual.
Price Data, 2006: $36 per 25 rating forms; $49 per user's guide (2002, 114 pages).
Time: (8–10) minutes.
Comments: Companion to Home & Community Social Behavior Scales (1258); rated by teachers or other school personnel.
Author: Kenneth W. Merrell.
Publisher: Paul H. Brookes Publishing Co., Inc.

Cross References: For reviews by Rosemary Flanagan and by Michael J. Furlong and Alicia Soliz, see 16:218; for reviews by Stephen R. Hooper and Lesley A. Welsh of a previous edition, see 13:277 (2 references); see also T4:2369 (1 reference).

[2378]
School Social Skills.

Purpose: Developed to assess social skills exhibited in a school setting.
Population: Elementary school and junior high school and high school.
Publication Date: 1984.
Acronym: S3.
Scores: Ratings in 4 categories: Adult Relations, Peer Relations, School Rules, Classroom Behaviors.
Administration: Individual.
Price Data, 2002: $58 per complete kit including manual (25 pages); $38 per 50 rating scales; $25 per manual.
Time: (10) minutes.
Comments: Ratings by teachers.
Authors: Laura J. Brown, Donald D. Black, and John C. Downs.
Publisher: Slosson Educational Publications, Inc.
Cross References: For reviews by Beth D. Bader and William K. Wilkinson, see 12:348; see also T4:2370 (1 reference).

[2379]
Schubert General Ability Battery.

Purpose: Developed as a test of an individual's ability to understand and think in terms of words, numbers, and ideas.
Population: Grades 12–16 and adults.
Publication Dates: 1946–1965.
Acronym: SGAB.
Scores, 5: Vocabulary, Analogies, Arithmetic Problems, Syllogisms, Total.
Administration: Group.
Price Data, 2005: $72.75 per complete kit including 25 tests and manual (1965, 24 pages); $41 per 25 tests.
Time: 16(25) or 32(40) minutes.
Authors: Herman J. P. Schubert and Daniel S. P. Schubert (test).
Publisher: Slosson Educational Publications, Inc.
Cross References: See 7:386 (1 reference); for a review by William B. Schrader, see 5:382.

[2380]
SCID Screen Patient Questionnaire and SCID Screen Patient Questionnaire Extended.

Purpose: "An Axis I symptoms and disorders screening tool."

Population: Psychiatric or general medical patients ages 18 or older.
Publication Dates: 1991–1999.
Acronym: SSPQ, SSPQ-X.
Scores, 6: Mood Disorders, Anxiety Disorders, Substance Use Disorders, Somatoform Disorders, Eating Disorders, Schizophrenia and Other Psychotic Disorders.
Administration: Individual.
Price Data, 2011: $515 per SSPQ unlimited-use software program; $645 per SSPQ-X unlimited-use software program; $56 per SSPQ software preview version (3 uses); $56 per SSPQ-X software preview version.
Time: (20) minutes SSPQ; (30–45) minutes for SSPQ-X.
Comments: SSPQ is an abbreviated computer-administered screening version of the Structured Clinical Interview for DSM-IV (SCID-I) and an adaptation of the MiniSCID for DSM-IIIR; SSPQ-X is an extended adaptation of the SSPQ; System requirements: Pentium, 120 MB hard drive, VGA or SVGA color monitor, 16 MB RAM, 3.5-inch floppy disk drive, CD-ROM drive, Windows 95 or higher.
Authors: Michael B. First, Miriam Gibbon, Janet B. W. Williams, and Robert L. Spitzer.
Publishers: Multi-Health Systems, Inc.; American Psychiatric Association.
Cross References: For reviews by Mark H. Stone and Peter Zachar, see 15:218; for reviews by Paul D. Werner and Thomas A. Widiger of the clinician version, see 14:373 (9 references); see also T5:2519 (56 references).

[2381]
Science Assessment Series 1 and 2.

Purpose: Designed to assist teachers in "checking children's understanding of the science taught" during primary and secondary education.
Population: Ages 5–9, Ages 8–13.
Publication Date: 2001.
Administration: Group.
Levels, 2: Series 1, Series 2.
Price Data: Available from publisher.
Comments: Designed to correspond to the national curricula of England and Wales, Northern Ireland, and Scotland.
Authors: Terry Russell and Linda McGuigan.
Publisher: GL Assessment [England].
  a) SCIENCE ASSESSMENT SERIES 1.
  Population: Ages 5–9.
  Scores: 5 subtest units: Humans and Other Animals, Planets, Materials, Light and Sound, Electricity and Forces.
  Time: (45) minutes per unit.
  b) SCIENCE ASSESSMENT SERIES 2.
  Population: Ages 8–13.
  Scores: 8 subtest units: Humans and Other Animals, Planets, Living Things in the Environment,

Materials, Changing Materials, Electricity, Light and Sound, Forces and the Earth and Beyond.
  Time: (45) minutes per unit.
Cross References: For reviews by Bruce G. Rogers and William D. Schafer, see 16:219.

[2382]
Scientific Orientation Test.

Purpose: "Designed to measure a range of affective outcomes for students of science or science-related subjects."
Population: Students in school years 5 to 12.
Publication Date: 1995.
Acronym: S.OR.T.
Scores, 4: Interest in Science, Scientific Attitude, Attitude to School Science, Total.
Administration: Group or individual.
Price Data: Available from publisher.
Time: (40) minutes.
Comments: Includes 5 subtests yielding 13 subscores; formerly titled A Test of Interests.
Author: G. Rex Meyer.
Publisher: GRM Educational Consultancy [Australia].
Cross References: For reviews by Bruce G. Rogers and Herbert C. Rudman, see 14:341.

[2383]
SCL-90 Analogue™.

Purpose: A brief rating scale "for collecting observer data on a patient's psychological symptomatic distress."
Population: Adults and adolescents.
Publication Date: 1976.
Scores, 10: Primary Dimensional Scales (Somatization, Obsessive Compulsive, Interpersonal Sensitivity, Depression, Anxiety, Hostility, Phobic Anxiety, Paranoid Ideation, Psychoticism), Global Psychopathology Scale.
Administration: Group.
Price Data, 2006: $45.25 per 100 forms.
Time: (1–3) minutes.
Comments: Designed for use by health professionals without in-depth training or knowledge of psychopathology.
Author: Leonard R. Derogatis.
Publisher: Pearson.
Cross References: See T5:2326 (3 references).

[2384]
Screening Assessment for Gifted Elementary and Middle School Students, Second Edition.

Purpose: "Used to identify students who are gifted in academics and reasoning."
Population: Ages 5–14.
Publication Dates: 1987–2001.
Acronym: SAGES-2.
Scores, 3: Mathematics/Science, Language Arts/Social Studies, Reasoning.
Administration: Group.

Price Data, 2011: $247 per kit including 10 K–3 mathematics/science student response booklets, 10 K–3 language arts/social studies student response booklets, 10 K–3 reasoning student response booklets, 10 4–8 mathematics/science student response booklets, 10 4–8 language arts/social studies student response booklets, 10 4–8 reasoning response booklets, manual (2001, 128 pages), 50 K–3 profile/scoring sheets, 50 4–8 profile/response sheets, and a 4–8 scoring transparency; $24 per 10 K–3 mathematics/science student response booklets; $24 per 10 K–3 language arts/social studies student response booklets; $24 per 10 K–3 reasoning student response booklets; $19 per 10 4–8 mathematics/science student response booklets; $19 per 10 4–8 language arts/social studies student response booklets; $19 per 10 4–8 reasoning student response booklets; $60 per manual; $35 per 50 K–3 profile/scoring sheets; $35 per 50 4–8 profile/response sheets; $13 per 4–8 scoring transparency.
Time: (30–45) minutes.
Comments: This edition replaces both the earlier Screening Assessment for Gifted Elementary Students (T5:2328) and the Screening Assessment for Gifted Elementary Students–Primary (T5:2329).
Authors: Susan K. Johnsen and Anne L. Corn.
Publisher: PRO-ED.
Cross References: For reviews by Carolyn M. Callahan and Howard M. Knoff, see 15:219; see T5:2328 (1 reference); for reviews by Lewis R. Aiken and Susana Urbina of an earlier edition, see 12:349; for a review by E. Scott Huebner of an earlier edition, see 10:327.

[2385]
Screening Kit of Language Development.
Purpose: Assesses preschool language development in order to identify language disorders/delays.
Population: Ages 2–5.
Publication Dates: 1983–2002.
Acronym: SKOLD.
Scores, 6: Vocabulary, Comprehension, Story Completion, Individual and Paired Sentence Repetition with Pictures, Individual Sentence Repetition without Pictures, Comprehension of Commands.
Administration: Individual.
Editions, 2: Standard English, Black English.
Price Data, 2002: $93 per complete kit including manual (37 pages), stimulus book, and 1 set of standard English scoring forms or 1 set of Black English scoring forms; $42 per 25 standard English scoring forms; $42 per 25 Black English scoring forms; $30 per stimulus materials and scoring guidelines; $26 per examiner's manual.
Time: (15) minutes.
Authors: Lynn S. Bliss and Doris V. Allen.
Publisher: Slosson Educational Publications, Inc.
Cross References: See T4:2381 (1 reference).

[2386]
Screening Test for Developmental Apraxia of Speech–Second Edition.
Purpose: Developed "to screen for the potential presence of developmental apraxia of speech in children."
Population: Ages 4-0 to 12-11.
Publication Dates: 1980–2001.
Acronym: STDAS-2.
Scores: 3: Prosody, Verbal Sequencing, Articulation.
Administration: Individual.
Price Data, 2011: $110 per complete kit including examiner's manual (2001, 37 pages) and 50 profile/examiner record forms; $53 per 50 profile/examiner record forms; $64 per examiner's manual.
Time: (10–15) minutes.
Author: Robert W. Blakeley.
Publisher: PRO-ED.
Cross References: For reviews by Rebecca McCauley and Janet Norris, see 15:220; see T5:2332 (2 references) and T4:2383 (3 references); for a review by Ronald K. Sommers of an earlier edition, see 11:347.

[2387]
Screening Test for Educational Prerequisite Skills.
Purpose: Developed to screen for skills needed for beginning kindergarten.
Population: Ages 4–5 years.
Publication Dates: 1976–1990.
Acronym: STEPS.
Scores: 5 areas: Motor Skills, Intellectual Skills, Verbal Information Skills, Cognitive Strategies, Attitudes.
Administration: Individual.
Price Data, 2006: $165 per complete kit including test materials (pictures, bears, pencil), 25 AutoScore™ forms, 25 AutoScore™ home questionnaires, and manual (1990, 68 pages); $42 per set of test materials; $54.95 per 25 AutoScore™ forms; $36 per 25 AutoScore™ home questionnaires; $48.50 per manual.
Time: (8–10) minutes.
Author: Frances Smith.
Publisher: Western Psychological Services.
Cross References: For reviews by John Christian Busch, M. Elizabeth Graue, and Jeffrey K. Smith, see 12:351.

[2388]
Screening Test for the Luria-Nebraska Neuropsychological Battery: Adult and Children's Forms.
Purpose: Screening tests for "predicting which individuals would probably show 'normal' or 'clinical' patterns if they were administered the appropriate form of the full Luria-Nebraska Neuropsychological Battery."
Population: Ages 8–12, 13 and older.

Publication Date: 1987.
Acronym: ST-LNNB.
Scores: Cutoff score only.
Administration: Individual.
Forms, 2: Children's Form, Adult Form.
Price Data, 2006: $157 per complete set including 25 administration and scoring booklets for children, 25 administration and scoring booklets for adults, set of stimulus cards adult and children, and manual for adult and children; $32.50 per 25 administration and scoring booklets (specify adult or children's form); $58 per set of stimulus cards; $53 per manual.
Time: (20) minutes.
Comments: For screening purposes only.
Author: Charles J. Golden.
Publisher: Western Psychological Services.
Cross References: For reviews by Arlene Coopersmith Rosenthal and W. Grant Willis, see 11:348.

[2389]
Screening Test of Adolescent Language.

Purpose: Designed to identify adolescents at risk of having language disorders.
Population: Junior and senior high school.
Publication Date: 1980.
Acronym: STAL.
Scores, 5: 4 subtests (Vocabulary, Auditory Memory Span, Language Processing, Proverb Explanation), Total.
Administration: Individual.
Price Data, 2006: $69 per kit, including manual (24 pages), mini-screen, 50 tests, and administration and scoring card and scoring instructions; $27.50 per 50 test forms; $42.50 per manual.
Time: (7) minutes.
Authors: Elizabeth M. Prather, Sheila Van Ausdal Breecher, Marimyn Lee Stafford, and Elizabeth Matthews Wallace.
Publisher: Western Psychological Services.
Cross References: See T4:2387 (1 reference); for a review by Ronald K. Sommers, see 9:1086 (1 reference).

[2390]
Search Institute Profiles of Student Life: Attitudes and Behaviors.

Purpose: Designed to "assist … communities in measuring 40 developmental assets related to youth well-being."
Population: Grades 6–12.
Publication Dates: 1989–1996.
Scores: Total score only.
Administration: Group.
Price Data, 2001: $55 per 25 copies of survey; $700 per 80-page report.
Time: (50) minutes.
Author: Search Institute.
Publisher: Search Institute.

Cross References: For reviews by George Engelhard, Jr. and Carol M. McGregor, see 15:221; for reviews by Ernest A. Bauer and Sharon Johnson-Lewis of an earlier edition, see 11:350.

[2391]
Secondary Level English Proficiency Test.

Purpose: "A measure of ability in two primary areas: understanding spoken English and understanding written English."
Population: Grades 7-12.
Publication Date: 1980-2003.
Acronym: SLEP.
Scores, 3: 2 section scores for Listening Comprehension and Reading Comprehension, and a Total score.
Administration: Individuals or group.
Forms, 3: 1, 2, 3.
Price Data: Available from publisher.
Time: 85(90) minutes.
Comments: Can be administered in a single session or in two separate sessions.
Author: Educational Testing Service.
Publisher: Educational Testing Service.
Cross References: See T4:2393 (2 references); for reviews by Brenda H. Loyd and Michael J. Subkoviak, see 9:1090.

[2392]
Secondary-School Record.

Purpose: "Designed to present a summary of the student's academic record and summarize ratings by several teachers."
Population: Grades 9–12.
Publication Dates: 1941–1964.
Acronym: SSR.
Price Data: Available from publisher.
Time: Administration time not reported.
Comments: Transcript form only still available.
Author: National Association of Secondary School Principals.
Publisher: National Association of Secondary School Principals.
Cross References: See 4:516 (1 reference).

[2393]
Secondary Screening Profiles.

Purpose: Designed to help "identify pupils' individual strengths and weaknesses upon entry to secondary school (junior high)," and also as a "standardised basis for screening special education needs."
Population: Junior high students, ages 10–13 years.
Publication Dates: 1995–1999.
Acronym: SSP.
Scores, 3: Reasoning, Reading, Mathematical.
Administration: Group.

Forms, 6: Reading, Forms A and B; Mathematics, Forms A and B; Reasoning, Forms A and B.
Price Data, 2002: £12.99 per 20 test forms; £16.99 per manual; £16.99 per specimen set.
Time: (20–40) minutes for each form.
Author: Centre for Research on Learning and Instruction, University of Edinburgh.
Publisher: Hodder & Stoughton Educational [England].
Cross References: For reviews by John O. Anderson and Susan J. Maller, see 15:222.

[2394]

The Seeking of Noetic Goals Test.

Purpose: Constructed "to measure the strength of motivation to find life meaning."
Population: Adolescents and adults.
Publication Date: 1977.
Acronym: SONG.
Scores: Total score only.
Administration: Group.
Price Data: Available from publisher.
Time: (10) minutes.
Comments: Complementary scale to the Purpose in Life Test.
Author: James C. Crumbaugh.
Publisher: Psychometric Affiliates.
Cross References: For reviews by Brenda Bailey-Richardson and Kevin L. Moreland, see 9:1092, see also T3:2124 (1 reference).

[2395]

Seguin-Goddard Formboards.

Purpose: Designed for testing spatial perception and motor coordination.
Population: Age 4 to adult.
Publication Date: [1911].
Scores: No scores.
Price Data, 2005: $185 per "flush" formboard; $340 per "raised" formboard.
Time: [5-10] minutes.
Comments: Used in the Halstead-Reitan Neuropsychological Test Battery (1206), Merrill-Palmer Scale of Mental Tests (1685), and Arthur Point Scale of Performance Tests (T5:182).
Authors: E. Seguin, H. H. Goddard, and N. Norsworthy.
Publisher: Stoelting Co.
Cross References: See T4:2397 (1 reference), T3:2125 (1 reference), and T2:578 (25 references).

[2396]

Select Associate Screening System.

Purpose: Designed to assist organizations in making employee selection decisions for associate and entry-level positions.
Publication Dates: 1995-2010.
Acronym: SELECT.

Administration: Group.
Price Data, 2011: $150 one-time fee for account set-up and user training. Report costs are $15 to $40 each (depending on quantity of order and complexity of report). Annual licenses for larger volume usage are also available.
Time: (15-40) minutes depending on survey.
Authors: Bigby, Havis & Associates, Inc., d/b/a Assess Systems.
Publisher: Bigby, Havis & Associates, Inc., d/b/a Assess Systems.
a) SELECT FOR ADMINISTRATIVE SUPPORT.
Purpose: "A personality-based survey designed to measure characteristics that have been found to predict job effectiveness in administrative or clerical positions."
Population: Applicants for administrative support positions.
Scores, 2: Provides Overall Performance and Integrity indices with recommended ranges; subscale results for Energy, Multi-Tasking, Attention to Detail, Self-Reliance, Task Focus, Interpersonal Insight, Criticism Tolerance, Acceptance of Diversity, Self-Control, Productive Attitude; optional modules available for willingness to perform job tasks and Counterproductive Behaviors.
b) SELECT FOR ENTRY LEVEL RETAIL MANAGERS.
Purpose: Designed to measure "personality characteristics related to effective job performance in managerial jobs that require individuals to produce sales, lead associates, and build customer loyalty."
Population: Applicants for entry level retail management positions.
Scores, 2: Provides Overall Performance and Integrity indices with recommended ranges; subscale results for Energy, Frustration Tolerance, Persuasiveness, Positive Sales Attitude, Leadership, Good Judgment, Organization and Attention to Detail; optional modules available for Retail Manager Math and Counterproductive Behaviors.
c) SELECT FOR RETAIL SALES ASSOCIATES.
Purpose: Designed to measure "personality characteristics related to effective job performance in sales-oriented jobs that require associates to sell and build customer loyalty."
Population: Applicants for retail sales associate positions.
Scores, 2: Provides Overall Performance and Integrity indices with recommended ranges; subscale results for Energy, Frustration Tolerance, Initiative, Positive Sales Attitude, Leadership, Persuasiveness, Good Judgment; optional modules available for Retail Math, willingness to perform job tasks, and Counterproductive Behaviors.
d) SELECT FOR RETAIL CLERK/CASHIER.
Purpose: Designed to measure "personality characteristics related to effective job performance in

retail jobs that require employees to enjoy serving the customer."

Population: Applicants for clerk or cashier positions in a retail store.

Scores, 2: Provides Overall Performance and Integrity indices with recommended ranges; subscale results for Positive Service Attitude, Energy, Accommodation to Others, Frustration Tolerance, Acceptance of Diversity; optional modules available for Retail Math, willingness to perform job tasks, and Counterproductive Behaviors.

e) SELECT FOR PRODUCTION AND DISTRIBUTION.

Purpose: "A personality-based survey designed to measure characteristics important to team-oriented manufacturing and distribution jobs."

Population: Applicants for production, manufacturing, and distribution positions.

Scores, 2: Provides Overall Performance and Integrity indices with recommended ranges; subscale results for Energy, Frustration Tolerance, Acceptance of Diversity, Self-Control, Productive Attitude, Acceptance of Structure; optional modules available for willingness to perform job tasks and Counterproductive Behaviors.

f) SELECT FOR LEASING AGENTS.

Purpose: Designed to measure "personality characteristics related to effective job performance in rental property sales positions."

Population: Applicants for leasing agent positions.

Scores, 2: Provides Overall Performance and Integrity indices with recommended ranges; subscale results for Energy, Assertiveness, Positive Sales Attitude, Social Comfort, Accommodation to Others, Frustration Tolerance, Criticism Tolerance, Self-Reliance, Acceptance of Diversity; optional modules available for Leasing Agent Math, willingness to perform job tasks, and Counterproductive Behaviors.

g) SELECT FOR HEALTH CARE.

Purpose: "A work-personality survey designed to measure characteristics important in most health care jobs."

Population: Applicants for jobs in hospitals or care-giving environments that have high patient (or patient family) contact.

Scores, 2: Provides Overall Performance and Integrity indices with recommended ranges; subscale results for Positive Service Attitude, Energy, Accommodation to Others, Frustration Tolerance, Accountability, Rapport, Empathy, Acceptance of Diversity, Multi-Tasking; optional modules available for willingness to perform job tasks and Counterproductive Behaviors.

h) SELECT FOR CUSTOMER SERVICE.

Purpose: Designed to measure personality characteristics that contribute to success in customer service jobs.

Population: Applicants for general customer service representative positions.

Scores, 2: Provides Overall Performance and Integrity indices with recommended ranges; subscale results for Energy, Frustration Tolerance, Accommodation to Others, Acceptance of Diversity, Positive Service Attitude; optional modules available for Retail Math, willingness to perform job tasks, and Counterproductive Behaviors.

i) SELECT FOR PERSONAL SERVICE.

Purpose: Designed to measure personality characteristics that contribute to success in customer service jobs.

Population: Applicants for positions that require providing high quality customer service as well as developing and maintaining a client base.

Scores, 2: Provides Overall Performance and Integrity indices with recommended ranges; subscale results for Energy, Frustration Tolerance, Accommodation to Others, Acceptance of Diversity, Positive Service Attitude, Social Comfort; optional modules available for willingness to perform job tasks and Counterproductive Behaviors.

j) SELECT FOR RECEPTIONISTS.

Purpose: Designed to measure personality characteristics that contribute to success in customer service jobs.

Population: Applicants for receptionist or information clerk positions.

Scores, 2: Provides Overall Performance and Integrity indices with recommended ranges; subscale results for Energy, Frustration Tolerance, Accommodation to Others, Acceptance of Diversity, Positive Service Attitude, Social Comfort; optional modules available for willingness to perform job tasks and Counterproductive Behaviors.

k) SELECT FOR CALL CENTERS-INBOUND SERVICE.

Purpose: Designed to "measure personality characteristics related to effective job performance in call center positions."

Population: Applicants for service-oriented jobs in call centers.

Scores, 2: Provides Overall Performance and Integrity indices with recommended ranges; subscale results for Energy, Frustration Tolerance, Accommodation to Others, Acceptance of Diversity, Positive Service Attitude; optional modules available for willingness to perform job tasks and Counterproductive Behaviors.

l) SELECT FOR CALL CENTERS-INBOUND SALES.

Purpose: Designed to "measure personality characteristics related to effective job performance in call center positions."

Population: Applicants for jobs that require representatives to answer customer calls and use effective selling and persuasion techniques.

Scores, 2: Provides Overall Performance and Integrity indices with recommended ranges; subscale results for Energy, Accountability, Positive Sales Attitude, Preference for Structure, Influence, Social

Comfort, Frustration Tolerance; optional modules available for willingness to perform job tasks and Counterproductive Behaviors.

m) SELECT FOR CALL CENTERS-OUTBOUND SALES.

Purpose: Designed to "measure personality characteristics related to effective job performance in call center positions."

Population: Applicants for jobs that require representatives to actively solicit and sell to potential customers.

Scores, 2: Provides Overall Performance and Integrity indices with recommended ranges; subscale results for Energy, Multi-Tasking Ability, Accountability, Positive Sales Attitude, Assertiveness, Social Comfort, Diplomacy, Acceptance of Diversity, Frustration Tolerance, Criticism Tolerance; optional modules available for willingness to perform job tasks and Counterproductive Behaviors.

n) SELECT FOR CALL CENTERS-HELP DESK.

Purpose: Designed to "measure personality characteristics related to effective job performance in call center positions."

Population: Applicants for help desk and technical phone support positions.

Scores, 2: Provides Overall Performance and Integrity indices with recommended ranges; subscale results for Energy, Frustration Tolerance, Accountability, Criticism Tolerance, Assertiveness, Collaboration, Problem Solving, Multi-Tasking, Acceptance of Diversity; optional modules available for willingness to perform job tasks and Counterproductive Behaviors.

o) SELECT FOR CONVENIENCE STORE MANAGERS.

Purpose: "Work-personality survey designed to measure characteristics important in convenience store jobs."

Population: Applicants for convenience store manager positions.

Scores, 2: Provides Overall Performance and Integrity indices with recommended ranges; subscale results for Energy, Frustration Tolerance, Persuasiveness, Positive Sales Attitude, Leadership, Good Judgment, Organization and Attention to Detail; optional modules available for math and Counterproductive Behaviors.

p) SELECT FOR CONVENIENCE STORE ASSOCIATES.

Purpose: "Work-personality survey designed to measure characteristics important in convenience store jobs."

Population: Applicants for convenience store associate positions.

Scores, 3: Provides Overall Performance, Integrity, and Math Ability indices with recommended ranges; subscale results for Positive Service Attitude, Accommodation to Others, Frustration Tolerance, Acceptance of Diversity, Self-Control, Energy; optional modules available for willingness to perform job tasks and Counterproductive Behaviors.

q) SELECT FOR BANKING SALES ASSOCIATES.

Purpose: "Personality-based survey designed to measure characteristics that have been found to predict job effectiveness for positions in retail banking work environments."

Population: Applicants for positions that are responsible for handling daily customer transactions as well as selling retail banking services.

Scores, 2: Provides Overall Performance and Integrity indices with recommended ranges; subscale results for Positive Service Attitude, Acceptance of Diversity, Accommodation to Others, Energy, Resilience/Frustration Tolerance, Interpersonal Influence, Social Comfort, Preference for Objective Measures, Dependability, Process Focused, Multi-Tasking, Self-Reliance, Leadership, Responsibility, Flexible Thinking; optional modules available for Retail Banking Associate Math, willingness to perform job tasks, and Counterproductive Behaviors.

r) SELECT FOR IN-STORE SALES ASSOCIATES.

Purpose: "Personality-based survey designed to measure characteristics that have been found to predict job effectiveness for positions in retail banking work environments."

Population: Applicants for sales associate positions within an in-store banking environment.

Scores, 2: Provides Overall Performance and Integrity indices with recommended ranges; subscale results for Positive Service Attitude, Acceptance of Diversity, Accommodation to Others, Energy, Resilience/Frustration Tolerance, Interpersonal Influence, Social Comfort, Preference for Objective Measures, Dependability, Process Focused, Multi-Tasking, Self-Reliance, Leadership, Responsibility, Flexible Thinking; optional modules available for Retail Banking Associate Math, willingness to perform job tasks, and Counterproductive Behaviors.

s) SELECT FOR BRANCH MANAGERS.

Purpose: "Personality-based survey designed to measure characteristics that have been found to predict job effectiveness for positions in retail banking work environments."

Population: Applicants for positions that require managing daily operations of a bank branch and promoting customer service.

Scores, 2: Provides Overall Performance and Integrity indices with recommended ranges; subscale results for Positive Service Attitude, Acceptance of Diversity, Accommodation to Others, Energy, Resilience/Frustration Tolerance, Interpersonal Influence, Social Comfort, Preference for Objective Measures, Dependability, Process Focused, Multi-Tasking, Self-Reliance, Leadership, Responsibility, Flexible Thinking; optional modules available for Retail Banking Manager Math, Job Experience Checklist, and Counterproductive Behaviors.

t) SELECT FOR BANKING SERVICE ASSOCIATES.
Purpose: "Personality-based survey designed to measure characteristics that have been found to predict job effectiveness for positions in retail banking work environments."
Population: Applicants for service-only positions, including bank tellers.
Scores, 2: Provides Overall Performance and Integrity indices with recommended ranges; subscale results for Positive Service Attitude, Acceptance of Diversity, Accommodation to Others, Energy, Resilience/Frustration Tolerance, Interpersonal Influence, Social Comfort, Preference for Objective Measures, Dependability, Process Focused, Multi-Tasking, Self-Reliance, Leadership, Responsibility, Flexible Thinking; optional modules available for Retail Banking Associate Math, willingness to perform job tasks, and Counterproductive Behaviors.
Cross References: For reviews by James T. Austin and Vicki S. Packman of an earlier version called SELECT Associate Screening System-Internet Version, see 14:344.

[2397]

[Selection Interview Forms].
Purpose: Designed to help interviewers obtain appropriate and valid information from job applicants.
Population: Business and industry.
Publication Date: 1962.
Scores: Ratings in 8 areas (Motivation for the Job, Adequacy of Work Experience, Supervisory Experience and Ability, Achievements at School, Vocational Adjustment, Family Background and Personal Adjustments, Wife's and Family's Role, Health) plus Total.
Administration: Individual.
Author: Benjamin Balinsky.
Publisher: Martin M. Bruce, Ph.D.
a) SELECTION INTERVIEW FORM.
Price Data, 2006: $13.75 per specimen set; $26.40 per package of forms.
Time: [60-90] minutes.
b) INTERVIEW RATING FORM.
Price Data: $10.45 per specimen set; $19.80 per package of forms.
Time: [15] minutes.

[2398]

Self-Appraisal Questionnaire.
Purpose: "Multi-dimensional self-administered questionnaire designed to predict violent and non-violent offender recidivism among correctional/forensic populations and to assist with the assignment of these populations to appropriate treatment/correctional programs and different institutional security levels."
Population: Offenders,. age 18 and older.
Publication Date: 2005.
Acronym: SAQ.

Scores, 8: Criminal Tendencies, Antisocial Personality Problems, Conduct Problems, Criminal History, Alcohol/Drug Abuse, Antisocial Associates, Anger, Total.
Administration: Individual or group.
Price Data, 2011: $93 per complete kit including technical manual (80 pages) and 25 QuikScore forms; $63 per technical manual; $47 per 25 QuikScore forms.
Time: (10–15) minutes.
Comments: Can be administered verbally.
Author: Wagdy Loza.
Publisher: Multi-Health Systems Inc.
Cross References: For reviews by Phillip L. Ackerman and and Rita Budrionis, see 17:170.

[2399]

Self-Assessment in Writing Skills.
Purpose: Developed as a self-assessment tool to assess writing skills.
Population: Clerical, managerial, and sales employees.
Publication Date: 1990.
Scores, 3: Content and Style, Organization and Format, Total.
Administration: Group or individual.
Price Data: Price information available from publisher for complete kit including 20 inventories, 20 scoring sheets for part 1, and 20 scoring sheets for part 2.
Time: [90–120] minutes.
Comments: Self-administered, self-scored.
Author: Training House, Inc.
Publisher: Training House, Inc.
Cross References: For reviews by Gabriel M. Della-Piana and Stephen Jurs, see 12:352.

[2400]

Self-Audit.
Purpose: Designed as an "assessment instrument ... for use at intake (pre-treatment) and post-treatment intervals."
Population: Ages 16 to 76.
Publication Date: 2001.
Acronym: SA.
Scores, 9: Truthfulness, Distress, Resistance, Morale, Violence, Alcohol, Drugs, Self-Esteem, Stress Coping Abilities.
Administration: Group.
Price Data, 2011: $8 per test; volume discounts available.
Foreign Language Edition: Spanish version available.
Time: (30-35) minutes.
Comments: May be administered via paper and pencil, computer, or human voice audio.
Author: Behavior Data Systems, Ltd.
Publisher: Behavior Data Systems, Ltd.

[2401]

Self-Awareness Profile.
Purpose: "This self-assessment provides insight into the basic personality attributes that influence the way we behave."

Population: Industry.
Publication Dates: 1980–1987.
Scores, 4: Dominance, Influence, Conformity, Evenness.
Administration: Individual or group.
Price Data: Price information available from publisher for complete sets including 16-item inventory, interpretation sheet, planning sheet, and 20 sets of cards containing profiles on 10 different personalities, to be sorted by participants ("most like me, next most," etc.).
Time: (80–100) minutes.
Author: Scott B. Parry.
Publisher: Training House, Inc.
Cross References: For a review by Timothy M. Osberg, see 11:353.

[2402]

The Self-Concept and Motivation Inventory: What Face Would You Wear?

Purpose: To assess motivation and academic self-concept.
Population: Age 4–kindergarten, grades 1–3, 3–6, 7–12.
Publication Dates: 1967–1977.
Acronym: SCAMIN.
Administration: Group.
Price Data: Available from publisher.
Authors: Norman J. Milchus, George A. Farrah, and William Reitz.
Publisher: Norman Milchus (the author).
  a) PRE-SCHOOL/KINDERGARTEN FORM.
  Population: Age 4–kindergarten.
  Scores, 14: Motivation (Goal and Achievement Needs, Achievement Investment, Self-Concept), Total (optional).
  Time: (25–30) minutes.
  b) EARLY ELEMENTARY FORM.
  Population: Grades 1-3.
  Scores, 5: Motivation (Goal and Achievement Needs, Achievement Investment), Self-Concept (Role Expectations, Self-Adequacy), Total (optional).
  Time: (25–30) minutes.
  c) LATER ELEMENTARY FORM.
  Population: Grades 3–6.
  Scores, 10: Same as *b* above plus 6 optional Sources of Support Climate scores (Parents, Teachers, Peers and Siblings, Academic Self, Academic Activity Climate, School Climate), Total (optional).
  Time: (30–35) minutes.
  d) SECONDARY FORM.
  Population: Grades 7–12.
  Scores, 20: Same as *b* above plus 16 optional scores: Sources of Support Climate (Parents, Teachers, Peers, Academic Self, Physical and Social Self, Adults and Counselors, Academic Activity Climate, School Climate), Immediate-Intrinsic Orientation (Evaluated Competition, Tasks and Projects, Discovery and Creativity, Skills), Fulfillment Orientation (Aspiration, Cooperation and Conformity, Responsibility, Acceptance and Praise).
  Time: (40) minutes.
Cross References: See T5:2355 (3 references) and T4:2408 (3 references); for a review by Lorrie Shepard, see 8:670 (4 references).

[2403]

Self-Description Questionnaire–I, II, III.

Purpose: To measure aspects of self-concept.
Population: Ages 5–12, 13–17, 16–Adult.
Publication Dates: 1987–1992.
Acronym: SDQ.
Administration: Group.
Price Data: Available from publisher.
Comments: Self-report measures.
Author: Herbert W. Marsh.
Publisher: SELF Research Centre [Australia].
  a) SELF-DESCRIPTION QUESTIONNAIRE–I.
  Population: Ages 8–12.
  Scores, 11: Academic (Mathematics, Reading, General–School, Total), Non-Academic (Physical Abilities, Physical Appearance, Peer Relations, Parent Relations, Total), Global (General–Self, Total–Self).
  Time: (15–20) minutes.
  b) SELF-DESCRIPTION QUESTIONNAIRE–II.
  Population: Ages 13–17.
  Scores, 12: Academic (Mathematics, Verbal, General–School), Non-Academic (Physical Abilities, Physical Appearance, Same Sex Peer Relations, Opposite Sex Peer Relations, Parent Relations, Emotional Stability, Honesty/Trustworthiness), Global (General–Self, Total–Self).
  Time: (20–25) minutes.
  c) SELF-DESCRIPTION QUESTIONNAIRE–III.
  Population: Ages 16–Adult.
  Scores, 14: Academic (Mathematics, Verbal, Problem-Solving, General–Academic), Non-Academic (Physical Abilities, Physical Appearance, Same Sex Peer Relations, Opposite Sex Peer Relations, Parent Relations, Spiritual Values/Religion, Honesty/Trustworthiness, Emotional Stability), Global (General–Self, Total–Self).
  Time: (20–25) minutes.
Cross References: See T5:2358 (17 references); for reviews by Jeffrey A. Atlas, Robert K. Gable, and Steven Isonio, see 13:280 (42 references); see also T4:2412 (10 references).

[2404]

Self-Directed Learning Readiness Scale/ Learning Preference Assessment.

Purpose: The SDLRS/LPA is designed to measure attitudes, abilities, and characteristics that comprise readiness to engage in self-directed learning.

Population: Ages 7-14, age 14 and over.
Publication Dates: 1977-2005.
Acronym: SDLRS.
Scores: Total score only.
Administration: Individual or group.
Price Data, 2006: $4.95 each scale; quantity discounts available.
Foreign Language Editions: The adult form has been translated into Spanish, French, German, Italian, Korean, Chinese, Japanese, Finnish, Greek, Portuguese, Afrikaans, and Lithuanian.
Time: [25] minutes.
Comments: A self-scoring form, entitled the Learning Preference Assessment, is available for use in workshops; an elementary form is available for Grades 3–7.
Authors: Lucy M. Guglielmino (all forms) and Paul J. Guglielmino (self-scoring form).
Publisher: Guglielmino & Associates.
Cross References: See T5:2359 (2 references).

[2405]

Self-Directed Search, 4th Edition [Forms R, E, CE, and CP].

Purpose: A vocational inventory designed to identify "a person's particular activities, competencies, and self-estimates compared with various occupational groups."
Population: Ages 12 and above.
Publication Dates: 1970–1997.
Acronym: SDS.
Scores, 6: Realistic, Investigative, Artistic, Social, Enterprising, Conventional.
Administration: Group.
Editions, 4: Form R (Regular), Form E (Easy), Form CP (Career Planning), Form CE (Career Explorer).
Price Data, 2006: $186 per SDS Form R Comprehensive Kit including manuals, 25 booklets and occupational finders, 25 "You and Your Career" booklets, 10 leisure activity finders, and 10 educational opportunities finders; $99 per SDS software portfolio (CD-ROM) including unlimited scoring and report generation for Form R and 5 free on-screen administrations.
Foreign Language Editions: "Adaptations available in the following countries/continents: Australia, Canada, China, Finland, France, Greece, Guyana, Hungary, Indonesia, Israel, Italy, Japan, Netherlands, New Zealand, Nigeria, Norway, Poland, Portugal, Russia, Saudi Arabia, Slovenia, South Africa, South America, Spain, Switzerland"; English-Canadian, Spanish, Vietnamese, and Braille editions also available.
Time: (30–50) minutes.
Comments: Self-administered, -scored, and -interpreted; computer software available; based on the Holland typology of vocational preferences.
Authors: John L. Holland (test and manuals), Amy B. Powell (manuals), and Barbara A. Fritzsche (manuals).
Publisher: Psychological Assessment Resources, Inc.

Cross References: For a review by Michael B. Brown, see 14:345; see also T5:2360 (13 references); for reviews by Joseph C. Ciechalski and Esther E. Diamond of an earlier edition, see 13:281 (48 references); see also T4:2414 (23 references); for reviews by M. Harry Daniels and Caroline Manuele-Adkins, see 10:330 (19 references); for a review by Robert H. Dolliver, see 9:1098 (12 references); see also T3:2134 (55 references); for a review by John O. Crites and excerpted reviews by Fred Brown, Richard Seligman, Catherine C. Cutts, Robert H. Dolliver, and Robert N. Hanson, see 8:1022 (88 references); see also T2:2211 (1 reference).

[2406]

Self-Directed Search–Revised 2001 Australian Edition.

Purpose: Designed as an instrument "for students and adults wishing to explore their career options."
Population: Ages 15 and over.
Publication Dates: 1970–2006.
Acronym: SDS.
Scores: 4 scales: Activities, Competencies, Occupations, Summary.
Administration: Group or individual.
Price Data, 2006: A$30.80 per 10 assessment booklets; $39.95 per 10 Occupations finder; $16.50 per 10 "You and Your Career"; $5.95 per Alphabetical Occupations Finder; $60.50 per manual; $70.40 per specimen set.
Foreign Language and Special Editions: Spanish, Vietnamese, French, and Braille editions available.
Time: (50) minutes.
Authors: John L. Holland, Meredith Shears (Australian Manual), and Adrian Harvey-Beavis (Australian Manual).
Publisher: Australian Council for Educational Research Ltd. [Australia].
Cross References: For a review by Nancy L. Crumpton, see 15:223.

[2407]

Self-Esteem Index.

Purpose: "Designed to measure the way individuals perceive themselves."
Population: Ages 7-0 to 18-11.
Publication Date: 1991.
Acronym: SEI.
Scores, 5: Familial Acceptance, Academic Competence, Peer Popularity, Personal Security, Self-Esteem Quotient.
Administration: Group.
Price Data, 2011: $147 per complete kit including 50 student response booklets, 50 profile/record forms, and manual (1991, 51 pages); $46 per 50 student response booklets; $46 per 50 profile/record forms; $55 per examiner's manual.
Time: (30-35) minutes.
Authors: Linda Brown and Jacquelyn Alexander.

Publisher: PRO-ED.
Cross References: See T5:2361 (4 references); for reviews by E. Scott Huebner and by Ralph O. Mueller and Paula J. Dupuy, see 11:354.

[2408]

The Self-Esteem Inventory.

Purpose: Developed to examine an individual's self-esteem.
Population: Adolescents and adults.
Publication Date: 1995.
Scores: Total score only.
Administration: Group.
Manual: No manual.
Price Data: Available from publisher.
Time: Administration time not reported.
Author: Millard J. Bienvenu.
Publisher: Millard J. Bienvenu, Northwest Publications.

[2409]

Self-Esteem Questionnaire.

Purpose: Measures self-esteem and satisfaction with self-esteem.
Population: Ages 9 and over.
Publication Dates: 1971–1976.
Acronym: SEQ.
Scores, 2: Self-Esteem, Self-Other Satisfaction.
Administration: Group.
Price Data: Not available.
Time: (15–20) minutes.
Author: James K. Hoffmeister.
Publisher: Test Analysis & Development Corporation.
Cross References: See T4:2416 (3 references).

[2410]

The Self Image Profiles.

Purpose: To quickly assess self image and self esteem in children and adolescents.
Publication Date: 2001.
Acronym: SIP.
Administration: Group or individual.
Price Data, 2006: £73.50 per complete kit including Adolescent Profiles, Child Profiles, 25 SIP-C record forms, 25 SIP-A record forms, and manual (43) pages.
Author: Richard J. Butler.
Publisher: Pearson Assessment [England].
a) THE SELF IMAGE PROFILE FOR CHILDREN.
Population: Ages 7–11.
Acronym: SIP-C.
Scores, 11: Positive Self Image, Negative Self Image, Sense of Difference, Self Esteem, Aspects of Self (Behaviour, Social, Emotional, Outgoing, Academic, Resourceful, Appearance).
Time: (12–25) minutes.
b) THE SELF IMAGE PROFILE FOR ADOLESCENTS.
Population: Ages 12–16.

Acronym: SIP-A.
Scores, 14: Positive Self Image, Negative Self Image, Sense of Difference, Self Esteem, Aspects of Self (Expressive, Caring, Outgoing, Academic, Emotional, Hesitant, Feel Different, Inactive, Unease, Resourceful).
Time: (9–17) minutes.
Cross References: For a review by Jayne E. Stake, see 15:224.

[2411]

Self-Motivated Career Planning Guide.

Purpose: To help the individual develop vocational objectives through self-administered exercises.
Population: High school and college and adults.
Publication Dates: 1978–1984.
Acronym: SMCP.
Scores: 7 pencil/paper exercises (Personal Orientation Survey, Education Summary, Career Experience Summary, Personal Career Life Summary, Career Strengths and Interests, Next Career Steps, Personal Development Summary) plus a 16PF personality assessment and interpretive report (Personal/Career Development Profile).
Administration: Group or individual.
Price Data, 2005: $25 per self-motivated Career Planning Guide (1984, 88 pages); testing materials and report purchased separately.
Foreign Language Edition: Spanish edition available.
Time: (50–120) minutes per exercise.
Authors: Verne Walter and Melvin Wallace.
Publisher: Institute for Personality and Ability Testing, Inc. (IPAT).
Cross References: For reviews by Larry Cochran and Samuel Juni, see 11:355; for reviews by Robert H. Dolliver and Kevin W. Mossholder of an earlier edition, see 9:1099.

[2412]

Self Observation Scales.

Purpose: Designed as a measure of self-concept.
Population: Grades K–3, 4–6, 7–9, 10–12.
Publication Dates: 1974–1979.
Acronym: SOS.
Administration: Group.
Forms: 1 or 2 for each of 4 levels.
Price Data: Available from publisher.
Time: (20–30) minutes.
Comments: Publisher recommends use of local norms; self-report; interactive computer version of the SOS available.
Authors: A. Jackson Stenner and William G. Katzenmeyer.
Publisher: NTS Research Corporation [No reply from publisher; status unknown].

a) PRIMARY LEVEL.
Population: Grades K–3.
Scores: 4 scales: Self Acceptance, Self Security, Social Maturity, School Affiliation.
Forms, 2: A, C.
Comments: Orally administered.
b) INTERMEDIATE LEVEL.
Population: Grades 4–6.
Scores: 7 scales: Same as *a* above plus Social Confidence, Teacher Affiliation, Peer Affiliation.
Forms, 2: A, C.
c) JUNIOR HIGH LEVEL.
Population: Grades 7–9.
Scores: 7 scales: Same as *a* above except include Self Assertion in place of Social Maturity.
d) SENIOR HIGH LEVEL.
Population: Grades 10–12.
Scores: 7 scales: Same as *c* above.
Cross References: See T4:2418 (2 references); see 9:1100 (3 references).

[2413]

Self-Perception Profile for College Students.
Purpose: To measure college students' self-concept.
Population: College students.
Publication Date: 1986.
Scores: 13 domains: Creativity, Intellectual Ability, Scholastic Competence, Job Competence, Athletic Competence, Appearance, Romantic Relationships, Social Acceptance, Close Friendships, Parent Relationships, Finding Humor in One's Life, Morality, Global Self-Worth.
Administration: Group.
Price Data: Available from publisher.
Time: 30(40) minutes.
Authors: Jennifer Neemann and Susan Harter.
Publisher: Susan Harter, University of Denver.
Cross References: See T5:2369 (12 references); for reviews by Robert D. Brown and Stephen F. Davis, see 11:357 (1 reference).

[2414]

Self-Perceptions Inventory [2006 Revision].
Purpose: To describe "the present affective dimensions of children and adults primarily in regard to themselves and in their relationships with others."
Population: Grades 1–12, adults, student teachers, instructors, nurses, nursing students, administrators and coordinators.
Publication Dates: 1965–2006.
Acronym: SPI.
Administration: Group.
Price Data, 2006: $30 per 25 forms; $30 per separate test manual (specify for Student Forms, Adult Forms, Teacher Forms, Nursing Forms, or Educational Leadership Forms [2006]); $60 per composite manual (2006).

Time: (5–20) minutes per test.
Authors: Louise M. Soares and Anthony T. Soares.
Publisher: Castle Consultants.
a) STUDENT FORMS.
Population: Grades 1–12.
Scores: 11 scales: Self Concept, Ideal Concept, Reflected Self/Classmates, Reflected Self/Friends, Reflected Self/Teachers, Reflected Self/Parents or Guardians, Reflected Self/Others, Perceptions of Others/Males, Perceptions of Others/Females, Student Self, Perceptions of Others/Students, Reflected Self of Mothers Alone or Fathers Alone.
b) ADULT FORMS.
Population: Grades 9–12 and adults.
Scores: 11 scales: Self Concept, Ideal Concept, Reflected Self/Friends, Reflected Self/Teachers/Professors, Reflected Self/Parents, Reflected Self/Partners, Reflected Self/Others, Perceptions of Others, Student Self, Perceptions of Others/Students, Reflected Self of Mothers Alone or Fathers Alone.
c) TEACHER FORMS.
Population: Student teachers and other instructors.
Scores: 8 scales: Self as a Teacher, Ideal as a Teacher, Self as a College Professor, Self as a Student Teacher, Self as an Intern, Reflected Self of Administrators/Classroom Aides/Colleagues/Community/Department Heads/Parents/Students/Supervisors, Perceptions of Others/Teachers.
d) NURSING FORMS.
Population: Nurses and nursing students.
Scores: 6 scales: Self Concept, Self as a Nurse, Ideal as a Nurse, Reflected Self by Administrators/Colleagues/Instructors/Nurses' Aides/Patients/Physicians' Assistants/Students/Supervisors, Perceptions of Others/Nurses.
e) EDUCATIONAL LEADERSHIP.
Population: Administrators and Coordinators.
Scores: 9 scales: Self Concept, Self as an Educational Leader, Ideal Educational Leader, Self as an Educational Manager, Reflected Self/Leader, Reflected Self/Manager, Perceptions of Others/Leaders, Perceptions of Others/Managers [Community/Parents/Peers/School Board/Students/Supervisors/Teachers], Ideal Educational Manager.
Cross References: For reviews by Mary M. Clare and Aimin Wang of the 1999 Revision, see 15:226; see T4:2421 (1 reference); for a review by Janet Morgan Riggs of an earlier edition, see 9:1101; for a review by Lorrie Shepard of an earlier edition, see 8:673 (2 references). For reviews by Gerald E. DeMauro and Michael R. Harwell of an earlier edition of the Nursing forms, see 11:356.

[2415]

Self-Perceptions of Adolescents.
Purpose: Designed to measure an adolescent's concept of self.

Population: Adolescents.
Publication Dates: 1965-2007.
Scores: 8 scales: Self as a Person (Self Concept, Ideal Concept, Reflected Self, Perceptions of Others), Self as a Student (Self Concept, Ideal Concept, Reflected Self, Perceptions of Others).
Administration: Group.
Forms, 8: Self as a Person Scales (Self Concept, Ideal Concept, Reflected Self/Other, Perceptions of Others), Self as a Student (Student Self, Ideal Concept as a Student, Reflected Self as a Student/Other, Perceptions of Others/Student Self).
Price Data, 2007: $40 per 25 scales (specify form); $40 per test manual (2007, 39 pages); $.40 per scale for scoring; $40 per analysis of profile charts and reports.
Time: (5-20) minutes.
Comments: Developed from the original Self-Perceptions Inventory (15:226) and is part of the SPI series that includes: Self-Perceptions of Adults (2416), Self-Perceptions of Children (2417), Self-Perceptions of College Students, Self-Perceptions of School Administrators (2418), Self-Perceptions of University Instructors (2419), Self-Perceptions of Teachers, and Self-Perceptions of Nurses.
Author: Louise M. Soares.
Publisher: Castle Consultants.
Cross References: For reviews by Stephen Axford and Eric S. Buhs, see 18:114; for reviews by Mary M. Clare and Aimin Wang of the 1999 Revision of the Self-Perceptions Inventory, see 15:226; see also T4:2421 (1 reference); for a review by Janet Morgan Riggs of an earlier edition, see 9:1101; for a review by Lorrie Shepard of an earlier edition, see 8:673 (2 references).

[2416]

Self-Perceptions of Adults.

Purpose: Designed to measure an adult's concept of self.
Population: Adults.
Publication Dates: 1965-2006.
Scores: 8 scales: Self as a Person (Self Concept, Ideal Concept, Reflected Self, Perceptions of Others), Self as a Working Adult (Self Concept, Ideal Concept, Reflected Self, Perceptions of Others).
Administration: Group.
Forms, 16: Self as Person Scales (Self Concept/Adjectives, Self Concept/Sentences, Ideal Concept/Adjectives, Ideal Concept/Sentences, Reflected Self/Adjectives, Reflected Self/Sentences, Perceptions of Others/Adjectives, Perceptions of Others/Sentences), Self as a Working Adult (Self Concept/Adjectives, Self Concept/Sentences, Ideal Concept/Adjectives, Ideal Concept/Sentences, Reflected Self/Adjectives, Reflected Self/Sentences, Perceptions of Others/Adjectives, Perceptions of Others/Sentences).
Price Data, 2008: $40 per 25 scales (specify form); $40 per 50 answer sheets; $.25 per customized booklet; $.40 per profile chart; $40 per test manual (2006, 44 pages); $.40 per scale for scoring.

Time: (5-20) minutes.
Comments: Developed from the original Self-Perceptions Inventory (15:226) and is part of the SPI series that includes: Self-Perceptions of Adolescents (2415), Self-Perceptions of Children (2417), Self-Perceptions of College Students, Self-Perceptions of School Administrators (2418), Self-Perceptions of University Instructors (2419), Self-Perceptions of Teachers, and Self-Perceptions of Nurses.
Author: Louise M. Soares.
Publisher: Castle Consultants.
Cross References: For reviews by Nancy L. Crumpton and Richard F. Farmer, see 18:115; for reviews by Mary M. Clare and Aimin Wang of the 1999 Revision of the Self-Perceptions Inventory, see 15:226; see also T4:2421 (1 reference); for a review by Janet Morgan Riggs of an earlier edition, see 9:1101; for a review by Lorrie Shepard of an earlier edition, see 8:673 (2 references).

[2417]

Self-Perceptions of Children.

Purpose: Designed to assess children's self-concepts and "determine developmental differences in the self during the typical growth periods of childhood."
Publication Dates: 1965-2008.
Acronym: SPI/Children.
Administration: Group.
Price Data, 2009: $40 per 25 scales (specify form); $40 per test manual (2008, 38 pages); $.40 per scoring per scale; $40 per analysis report.
Time: (10) minutes per scale.
Authors: Louise M. Soares and Anthony T. Soares (test).
Publisher: Castle Consultants.
Comments: Revision of the Student Forms of the Self-Perceptions Inventory (2414).
   a) SELF AS PERSON.
   Population: Ages 6-8.
   Scores, 4: Self Concept, Student Self, Perceptions of Others (Self), Perceptions of Others (Student).
   b) SELF AS STUDENT.
   Population: Ages 9-11.
   Scores, 4: Self Concept, Student Self, Perceptions of Others (Self), Perceptions of Others (Student).
Cross References: For reviews by Kathleen D. Allen and Cher Edwards, see 18:116; for reviews by Mary M. Clare and Aimin Wang of the entire Self-Perceptions Inventory [1999 Revision], see 15:226; see also T4:2421 (1 reference); for a review by Janet Morgan Riggs of an earlier edition, see 9:1101; for a review by Lorrie Shepard of an earlier edition, see 8:673 (2 references). For reviews by Gerald E. DeMauro and Michael R. Harwell of an earlier edition of the Nursing forms, see 11:356.

[2418]

Self-Perceptions of School Administrators.

Purpose: Designed to measure a school administrator's concept of self.

Population: Adults.
Publication Dates: 1965-2005.
Scores: 8 scales: Self as a Person (Self Concept, Ideal Concept, Reflected Self, Perceptions of Others), Self as a School Administrator (Self Concept, Ideal Concept, Reflected Self, Perceptions of Others).
Administration: Group.
Forms, 8: Self as Person Scales (Self Concept, Ideal Concept, Reflected Self, Perceptions of Others), Self as a School Administrator (Self Concept, Ideal Concept, Reflected Self, Perceptions of Others).
Price Data, 2008: $40 per 25 scales (specify form); $40 per 50 answer sheets; $.25 per customized booklet; $.40 per profile chart; $40 per test manual (2005, 40 pages); $.40 per scale for scoring.
Time: (5-20) minutes.
Comments: Developed from the original Self-Perceptions Inventory (15:226) and is part of the SPI series that includes: Self-Perceptions of Adolescents (2415), Self-Perceptions of Children (2417), Self-Perceptions of College Students, Self-Perceptions of Adults (2416), Self-Perceptions of University Instructors (2419), Self-Perceptions of Teachers, and Self-Perceptions of Nurses.
Author: Louise M. Soares.
Publisher: Castle Consultants.
Cross References: For reviews by Marta Coleman and Suzanne Young, see 18:117; for reviews by Mary M. Clare and Aimin Wang of the 1999 Revision of the Self-Perceptions Inventory, see 15:226; see also T4:2421 (1 reference); for a review by Janet Morgan Riggs of an earlier edition, see 9:1101; for a review by Lorrie Shepard of an earlier edition, see 8:673 (2 references).

[2419]

Self-Perceptions of University Instructors.
Purpose: Designed to measure an adult's concept of self.
Population: University instructors.
Publication Dates: 1965-2008.
Scores: 16 scales: Self as a Person [College Professors] (Self Concept, Ideal Concept, Reflected Self, Perceptions of Others), Self as a Person [Adjunct Faculty] (Self Concept, Ideal Concept, Reflected Self, Perceptions of Others), Self as a College Professor (Self Concept, Ideal Concept, Reflected Self, Perceptions of Others), Self as an Adjunct Faculty Member (Self Concept, Ideal Concept, Reflected Self, Perceptions of Others).
Administration: Group.
Forms, 16: Self as a Person [College Professors] (Self Concept, Ideal Concept, Reflected Self, Perceptions of Others), Self as a Person [Adjunct Faculty] (Self Concept, Ideal Concept, Reflected Self, Perceptions of Others), Self as a College Professor (Self Concept, Ideal Concept, Reflected Self, Perceptions of Others), Self as an Adjunct Faculty Member (Self Concept, Ideal Concept, Reflected Self, Perceptions of Others).
Price Data, 2008: $40 per 25 scales (specify form); $40 per 50 answer sheets; $40 per test manual (2008,

41 pages); $.40 per scale for scoring and profiles; $40 per report for analysis.
Time: (5-20) minutes.
Comments: Developed from the original Self-Perceptions Inventory (15:226) and is part of the SPI series that includes: Self-Perceptions of Adolescents (2415), Self-Perceptions of Children (2417), Self-Perceptions of College Students, Self-Perceptions of Adults (2416), Self-Perceptions of University Instructors (2419), Self-Perceptions of Teachers, and Self-Perceptions of Nurses.
Author: Louise M. Soares.
Publisher: Castle Consultants.
Cross References: For reviews by Theodore Coladarci and Sandra M. Harris, see 18:118; for reviews by Mary M. Clare and Aimin Wang of the 1999 Revision of the Self-Perceptions Inventory, see 15:226; see also T4:2421 (1 reference); for a review by Janet Morgan Riggs of an earlier edition, see 9:1101; for a review by Lorrie Shepard of an earlier edition, see 8:673 (2 references).

[2420]

Self Worth Inventory.
Purpose: "Helps respondents increase their understanding of self-worth and how it is developed."
Population: Adults and teenagers.
Publication Dates: 1990-2006.
Acronym: SWI.
Scores, 8: Self, Family, Peers, Work, Projected Self, Self-Concept, Self-Esteem, Self-Worth.
Administration: Individual and group.
Price Data, 2006: $13.95 per inventory (1990, 8 pages); $13.95 per access code online version; $38 per SWI Trainer's Guidelines (1996, 24 pages).
Time: 60 minutes (short program); 120-180 minutes (longer program).
Comments: May be self-administered.
Author: Everett Robinson.
Publisher: Consulting Resource Group International, Inc.
Cross References: For reviews by Jayne E. Stake and Norman D. Sundberg, see 13:282.

[2421]

The Senior Apperception Technique [1985 Revision].
Purpose: A projective instrument to gather information on forms of depression, loneliness, or rage in the elderly.
Population: Ages 65 and over.
Publication Dates: 1973–1985.
Acronym: S.A.T.
Scores: No scores.
Administration: Individual.
Price Data, 2010: $33 per manual (1985, 12 pages) and set of picture cards.
Time: Administration time not reported.
Author: Leopold Bellak.
Publisher: C.P.S., Inc.

Cross References: For reviews by Paul A. Arbisi and Michael G. Kavan, see 13:283; see also T3:2148 (2 references); for a review by K. Warner Schaie of an earlier edition, see 8:676 (1 reference).

[2422]

Senior Aptitude Tests.

Purpose: Constructed "to measure a number of aptitudes of pupils . . . for the purpose of guidance and selection."
Population: Standards 8–10 in South African schools, college, and adults.
Publication Dates: 1969–1970.
Acronym: SAT.
Scores, 12: Verbal Comprehension, Numerical Fluency, Word Fluency, Visual Perception Speed, Reasoning (Deductive, Inductive), Spatial Visualization (2 Dimensional, 3 Dimensional), Memory (Paragraphs, Symbols), Psychomotor Coordination, Writing Speed.
Administration: Group.
Price Data: Available from publisher.
Time: 88(120) minutes.
Comments: Test materials in English and Afrikaans.
Authors: F. A. Fouche and N. F. Alberts.
Publisher: Human Sciences Research Council [South Africa].
Cross References: See T5:2373 (1 reference) and T4:2430 (1 reference).

[2423]

Senior South African Individual Scale–Revised.

Purpose: Measures general intelligence.
Population: Ages 7-0 to 16-11.
Publication Dates: 1964–1991.
Acronym: SSAIS-R.
Scores: 11 tests: Verbal (Vocabulary, Comprehension, Similarities, Number Problems, Story Memory, Memory for Digits), Nonverbal (Pattern Completion, Block Designs, Missing Parts, Form Board, Coding).
Administration: Individual.
Price Data: Available from publisher.
Time: Tests 1–9: (75) minutes; Tests 10–11: (10) minutes; Tests 3, 4, 7, and 8 (Abbreviated Scale): (45) minutes.
Comments: Developed for Afrikaans-speaking and English-speaking South African students.
Author: Human Sciences Research Council.
Publisher: Human Sciences Research Council [South Africa].
Cross References: For information regarding an earlier edition, see T3:2153 (1 reference) and 7:413 (1 reference).

[2424]

Sensory Evaluation Kit.

Purpose: "Designed to increase functional performance through the primary use of smell."

Population: Ages 2 to adult.
Publication Date: 1991.
Scores, 20: Motor, Tactile, Visual, Auditory, Olfactory, Gustatory, Problem Solving, Attention Span, Directions (2-Step, No Cuing), Interpretation of Signs/Symbols, Memory, Body Scheme (Body Parts, R/L Discrimination), Motor Planning, Stereognosis, Figure/Ground, Color Perception, Form Constancy, Position in Space.
Administration: Individual.
Price Data: Available from publisher.
Time: Administration time not reported.
Author: Bonnye S. Klein.
Publisher: Maddak Inc.
Cross References: For reviews by J. Jeffrey Grill and Ellen Weissinger, see 13:284.

[2425]

Sensory Integration and Praxis Tests.

Purpose: Designed to assess several practic abilities, various aspects of sensory processing status, and behavioral manifestations of deficits in integration of sensory inputs from these systems.
Population: Ages 4–8.11.
Publication Date: 1989.
Acronym: SIPT.
Scores: 17 tests: Space Visualization, Figure-Ground Perception, Standing and Walking Balance, Design Copying, Postural Praxis, Bilateral Motor Coordination, Praxis Verbal Command, Constructional Praxis, Postrotary Nystagmus, Motor Accuracy, Sequencing Praxis, Oral Praxis, Manual Form Perception, Kinesthesia, Finger Identification, Graphesthesia, Localization of Tactile Stimuli.
Administration: Individual.
Price Data, 2002: $1,15 per set for mail-in scoring including all test materials, 25 copies of each consumable test form, 10 complete sets of all 17 computer-scored answer sheets with 10 transmittal sheets, manual (307 pages), and carrying case; $1,150 per set for PC scoring including all test materials, 25 copies of each consumable test form, 1 disk, 10 PC answer booklets, manual, and carrying case; $29.50 per one each of 17 test answer sheets and 1 transmittal sheet; $14.50 per transmittal sheet; $3.90 per individual test answer sheet; $255 per 10-use disk (PC with Microsoft Windows) with 10 PC answer booklets; $18.50 per 25 test booklets (specify Design Copying, Motor Accuracy, or Kinesthesia); $70 per manual; $132.50 per training administration video (VHS); $179.50 per training administration 2 CD-ROM set.
Time: (10) minutes or less per individual test.
Comments: Extension and revision of the Southern California Sensory Integration Tests (SCSIT) and the Southern California Postrotary Nystagmus Test (SCPNT); computer-scoring only; stopwatch capable of recording 1/10 seconds needed (available from publisher).
Author: A. Jean Ayres.

Publisher: Western Psychological Services.
Cross References: See T5:2377 (4 references); for a review by James E. Ysseldyke, see 12:353 (18 references); see also T4:2433 (9 references). For a review by Byron P. Rourke of the SCPNT, see 9:1157 (20 references); for information on the SCSIT, see 9:1158 (5 references) and T3:2244 (21 references); for reviews by Homer B. C. Reed, Jr. and Alida S. Westman of the SCSIT, see 8:875 (5 references); see also T2:1887 (18 references).

[2426]

Sensory Integration Inventory–Revised for Individuals with Developmental Disabilities.

Purpose: "Designed to screen for [occupational therapy] clients who might benefit from a sensory integration treatment approach."
Population: Developmentally disabled occupational therapy clients school aged to adults, including autism spectrum and PDD.
Publication Dates: 1990–1992.
Acronym: SI Inventory.
Scores: Item scores in each of 4 sections interpreted individually: Tactile, Vestibular, Proprioception, General Reactions.
Administration: Individual.
Price Data: Available from publisher.
Time: Administration time not reported.
Comments: A semistructured interview of a person who works/lives closely with the client (e.g., parent or therapeutic staff member); space also provided for qualitative comments.
Authors: Judith E. Reisman and Bonnie Hanschu.
Publisher: P.D.P. Press, Inc.
Cross References: For a review by William Verdi, see 14:346.

[2427]

Sensory Processing Measure.

Purpose: "Enables assessment of sensory processing issues, praxis, and social participation in elementary school-aged children."
Population: Ages 5-12.
Publication Date: 2007.
Acronym: SPM.
Scores, 15: Social Participation, Vision, Hearing, Touch, Body Awareness, Balance and Motion, Planning and Ideas, Total Sensory Systems, Environment Difference, Art Class Total, Music Class Total, Physical Education Class Total, Recess/Playground Total, Cafeteria Total, School Bus Total.
Administration: Group.
Price Data, 2010: $155 per comprehensive kit including 25 Home AutoScore Forms, 25 Main Classroom AutoScore Forms, School Environments Form CD, and manual (102 pages); $125 per School kit including 25 Main Classroom AutoScore Forms, School Environments

Form CD, and manual; $99 per Home kit including 25 Home AutoScore Forms and manual; $42 per 25 AutoScore Forms; $32 per 25 School Environments Form CD (unlimited use); $66 per manual; $22 per Continuing Education (CE) Questionnaire and Evaluation Form.
Time: (15-20) minutes each for the Home and Main Classroom Forms; (5) minutes for each School Environment Form.
Comments: The Home and Main Classroom Forms may be used individually or together, but the School Environments Forms may only be used in conjunction with the Main Classroom Form.
Authors: L. Diane Parham and Cheryl Ecker (Home Form); Heather Miller Kuhaneck, Diana A. Henry, and Tara J. Glennon (Main Classroom and School Environments Forms).
Publisher: Western Psychological Services.
Cross References: For reviews by Michael K. Cruce and by T. Steuart Watson and Michael F. Woodin, see 18:119.

[2428]

Sensory Processing Measure-Preschool.

Purpose: "Enables assessment of sensory processing issues, praxis, and social participation in children of preschool age."
Population: Children ages 2-5 who have not started kindergarten.
Publication Date: 2010.
Acronym: SPM-P.
Scores: 8 for each form: Social Participation, Vision, Hearing, Touch, Body Awareness, Balance and Motion, Planning and Ideas, Total Sensory Systems.
Administration: Individual.
Forms, 2: Home, School.
Price Data, 2011: $125 per complete kit including 25 Home AutoScore forms, 25 School AutoScore forms, and manual (94 pages); $42 per 25 AutoScore forms (Home or School); $66 per manual.
Time: (15-20) minutes.
Comments: The Home and School Forms are intended for use together, but each form may also be used separately; the SPM-P is "the companion instrument to the Sensory Processing Measure (2427), which facilitates assessment of sensory processing issues for elementary school-aged children."
Authors: Cheryl Ecker and L. Diane Parham (Home Form); Heather Miller Kuhaneck, Diana A. Henry, and Tara J. Glennon (School Form).
Publisher: Western Psychological Services.

[2429]

Sensory Profile.

Purpose: "To measure a child's sensory processing abilities."
Publication Dates: 1999–2002.

Administration: Individual or group.
Levels, 2: Infant/Toddler Sensory Profile–Clinical Edition, Sensory Profile.
Price Data, 2002: $150 per software kit including user's manual (1999, 146 pages), e-record forms, and 1-year subscription; $105 per software stand-alone including 1-year subscription for e-record forms; $65 per manual; $45 per e-record forms including subscription renewal for 1-year.
Foreign Language Edition: Available in Spanish.
Comments: Profiles completed by child's caregiver; can be administered and scored electronically using personal computer or PDA (Windows and Palm OS), contact publisher for details.
Publisher: Pearson.

a) INFANT/TODDLER SENSORY PROFILE–CLINICAL EDITION.
Population: Birth to 36 months.
Publication Date: 2002.
Scores, 6: General Processing, Auditory Processing, Visual Processing, Tactile Processing, Vestibular Processing, Oral Sensory Processing.
Price Data: $119 per Infant/Toddler Sensory Profile complete kit including user's manual (2002, 21 pages), 25 English caregiver questionnaires, and 25 summary score sheets; $75 per user's manual; $31.50 per 25 caregiver questionnaires (English or Spanish); $16.50 per 25 summary score sheets.
Time: 15(25) minutes.
Comments: Ages birth to 6 months: 5 scores (General Processing, Auditory Processing, Visual Processing, Tactile Processing, Vestibular Processing).
Author: Winnie Dunn.

b) SENSORY PROFILE.
Population: Ages 3–10.
Forms, 2: Sensory Profile, Short Sensory Profile.
Scores, 23: 6 Sensory Processing categories (Auditory Processing, Visual Processing, Vestibular Processing, Touch Processing, Multisensory Processing, Oral Sensory Processing); 5 Modulation categories (Sensory Processing Related to Endurance/Tone, Modulation Related to Body Position and Movement, Modulation of Movement Affecting Activity Level, Modulation of Sensory Input Affecting Emotional Responses, Modulation of Visual Input Affecting Emotional Responses and Activity Level); 3 Behavioral and Emotional Responses categories (Emotional/Social Responses, Behavioral Outcomes of Sensory Processing, Items Indicating Thresholds for Response); 9 Factor Scores (Sensory Seeking, Emotionally Reactive, Low Endurance/Tone, Oral Sensitivity, Inattention/Distractibility, Poor Registration, Sensory Sensitivity, Sedentary, Fine Motor/Perceptual).
Price Data: $119 per Sensory Profile complete kit including user's manual, and 25 each of each of caregiver questionnaires, short sensory profiles, and

summary score sheets; $65 per user's manual; $32 per 25 caregiver questionnaires (English or Spanish); $15 per 25 short sensory profiles (English or Spanish); $19 per 25 summary score sheets (English or Spanish).
Time: (15–30) minutes.
Comments: 125-question profile.
Author: Winnie Dunn.

c) SHORT SENSORY PROFILE.
Purpose: "To help service providers in screening settings quickly identify children with sensory processing difficulties."
Population: Ages 5–10.
Acronym: SSP.
Scores, 8: Tactile Sensitivity, Taste/Smell Sensitivity, Movement Sensitivity, Underresponsive/Seeks Sensation, Auditory Filtering, Low Energy/Weak, Visual/Auditory Sensitivity, Total.
Time: (10) minutes.
Authors: Daniel N. McIntosh, Lucy Jane Miller, Vivian Shyu, and Winnie Dunn.
Cross References: For reviews by Doreen W. Fairbank and John J. Vacca, see 16:220.

[2430]

Sensory Profile School Companion.

Purpose: Assesses a student's sensory processing abilities and their effect on the student's functional performance in the classroom and school environment.
Population: Ages 3-0 to 11-11.
Publication Date: 2006.
Scores, 13: 4 Quadrant scores (Registration, Seeking, Sensitivity, Avoiding), 4 School Factor scores (School Factors 1, 2, 3, 4), 5 Section scores (Auditory, Visual, Movement, Touch, Behavior).
Administration: Individual.
Price Data, 2007: $140 per complete kit including user's manual (2006, 106 pages), 25 teacher questionnaires, and 25 summary score sheets; $45 per 25 teacher questionnaires; $29 per 25 summary score sheets; $95 per user's manual.
Time: 15(30) minutes.
Author: Winnie Dunn.
Publisher: Pearson.
Cross References: For reviews by Elizabeth Bigham and Shawn Powell, see 18:120.

[2431]

Sentence Completion Series.

Purpose: Designed to "identify underlying concerns and specific areas of distress."
Population: Adolescents and adults.
Publication Dates: 1991–1992.
Acronym: SCS.
Scores: No scores.

Administration: Individual or group.

Forms, 8: Adult, Adolescent, Family, Marriage, Parenting, Work, Illness, Aging.

Price Data, 2006: $108 per introductory kit including manual and 15 of each of 8 forms.

Time: [10–45] minutes.

Comments: Forms may be administered alone or in any combination; clinicians evaluates responses.

Authors: Larry H. Brown and Michael A. Unger.

Publisher: Psychological Assessment Resources, Inc.

Cross References: For reviews by Kevin L. Moreland and Paul D. Werner, see 14:347.

[2432]

Sentence Completion Tests.

Purpose: "These tests provide a projective technique for individuals to express in their own way their own unique feelings, behaviors, attitudes, assets, needs, problems, thoughts, opinions of self, relationships, likes, dislikes, moods, frustrations, inhibitions, fantasies, backgrounds, responses from others, desires, mistakes, habits, secrets, idiosyncrasies, dreams, attitudes toward the test, etc."

Publication Dates: 1989-1995.

Administration: Group.

Price Data, 2001: $10 per 20 tests; $95 for 2 copies of all tests and Lifetime License to copy for personal or institutional use.

Time: Administration time not reported.

Comments: Master List includes sentence completion stems and alternatives used in the development of all the tests.

Author: Allan Roe.

Publisher: Diagnostic Specialists, Inc.

a) GENERAL INCOMPLETE SENTENCES TEST.

Population: General including college, clinical, hospitalized, and private practice adults.

Acronym: GIST.

Foreign Language Edition: Spanish GIST is available.

b) SHORT INCOMPLETE SENTENCES.

Population: Adult and adolescent clients.

Acronym: SIS.

c) FULL INCOMPLETE SENTENCES TEST.

Purpose: To be used for courts, custody, and diagnostic decisions.

Acronym: FIST.

d) FULL I AM TEST.

Purpose: "Helpful for eliciting identity problems."

Acronym: FIAT.

e) KIDS INCOMPLETE SENTENCES TEST.

Population: Ages 5-12.

Acronym: KIST.

f) TEENAGE SENTENCE COMPLETION.

Population: Ages 13-19.

Acronym: TASC.

g) MARRIAGE INCOMPLETE SENTENCES TEST.

Population: Married couples.

Acronym: MIST.

h) RELATIONSHIP INCOMPLETE SENTENCES TEST.

Population: Any relationship.

Acronym: RIST.

i) FULL LENGTH ALCOHOL SENTENCE COMPLETION.

Population: Alcohol users.

Acronym: FLASC.

j) DRUG INQUIRY SENTENCE COMPLETION.

Population: Drug users.

Acronym: DISC.

k) TALKING HONESTLY AND OPENLY ABOUT OUR RELATIONSHIP.

Population: Sex offenders.

Acronym: THOR.

l) SEXUAL ABUSE SURVIVOR'S TEST.

Population: Sex abuse victim.

Acronym: SAST.

[2433]

Sequenced Inventory of Communication Development, Revised Edition.

Purpose: Designed as a diagnostic assessment to evaluate the communication abilities of normal and retarded children.

Population: Ages 4 months through 4 years.

Publication Dates: 1975–1984.

Acronym: SICD-R.

Administration: Individual.

Price Data, 2006: $435 per complete kit (includes all test materials in a sturdy carrying case, 50 record/booklet/profiles, 1 instruction manual, and 1 test manual); $54.95 per 25 record booklet/profile forms; $36 per instruction manual; $36 per test manual.

Foreign Language Editions: Cuban-Spanish edition available; Spanish translation included in test manual and separate Spanish-language forms with pictures are available.

Time: (30–75) minutes.

Comments: Some test accessories (e.g., paper, coins, and picture book) must be assembled locally.

Authors: Dona Lea Hedrick, Elizabeth M. Prather, and Annette R. Tobin, with contributions by Doris V. Allen, Lynn S. Bliss, and Lillian R. Rosenberg.

Publisher: Western Psychological Services.

a) RECEPTIVE SCALE.

Scores, 3: Awareness, Discrimination, Understanding.

b) EXPRESSIVE SCALE.

Scores, 4: Imitating, Initiating, Responding, Verbal Output.

Cross References: See T5:2382 (40 references) and T4:2438 (21 references); for reviews by Carol Mardell-Czudnowski and Mary Ellen Pearson, see 10:331 (6 references); for reviews by Barbara W. Hodson and Joan I. Lynch of the earlier edition, see 9:1109 (4 references); see also T3:2159 (4 references).

[2434]

Service Ability Inventory.

Purpose: Designed "to select job applicants who have a service orientation ... to determine the service skill levels of current employees."
Population: Current and prospective employees.
Publication Dates: 1999–2004.
Acronym: S.A.I.
Scores, 7: Service Orientation, Interpersonal Skills, Tolerance for Stress, Team Skills, Patience, Coping Skills, Deception Scale.
Administration: Individual or group.
Price Data: $79.99 per starter kit including 5 tests, administrator's manual (2004, 32 pages), and 1 test log.
Time: (20–25) minutes.
Comments: Online and paper-and-pencil versions of test are available; online version includes interpretive reports and follow-up interview questions.
Author: J. M. Llobet.
Publisher: G. Neil.
Cross References: For reviews by Michael B. Bunch and Denice Ward Hood, see 17:171.

[2435]

Service Animal Adaptive Intervention Assessment.

Purpose: Constructed for "evaluating predispositions to and outcomes of service animal use."
Population: Occupational, physical, and recreational therapists, assistive technology professionals, and animal assisted therapy specialists.
Publication Date: 1998.
Acronym: SAAIA.
Scores, 5: Knowledge and Experience of Animals, Typical Activities/Skills, Personal/Social Characteristics, Requirements of Service Animal Compared to Resources of Person, Total Predisposition Score.
Administration: Group or individual.
Price Data, 2001: $29.95 per complete kit including all assessments as masters for photocopying and manual (10 pages).
Time: (90–120) minutes.
Comments: Ratings by professionals; also includes qualitative information.
Author: Susan A. Zapf.
Publisher: The Institute for Matching Person & Technology, Inc.
Cross References: For reviews by Ronald A. Berk and Judith A. Rein, see 15:227.

[2436]

ServiceFirst.

Purpose: Constructed to measure "customer service orientation or potential."
Population: Employees in service-oriented positions.

Publication Dates: 1990–2001.
Scores, 5: Active Customer Relations, Polite Customer Relations, Helpful Customer Relations, Personalized Customer Relations, Total.
Administration: Group.
Price Data, 2006: $30 per test kit including sample test booklet, sample answer sheet, test manual (2001, 47 pages), administration and scoring manual, and demonstration administration and scoring manual; $10 per administrator's manual; $10 per reusable test booklet; scoring service $11.50 to $15 per applicant.
Time: (20) minutes.
Comments: Internet-based administration and scoring is available at www.peoplefocus.com; paper-and-pencil and PC administration also available with scoring via telephone or fax by publisher, or onsite with a computer disk.
Author: Larry Fogli.
Publisher: People Focus.
Cross References: For reviews by Michael B. Bunch and Mary A. Lewis, see 14:348.

[2437]

701 and 702 Fire Supervisor Tests (Lieutenant).

Purpose: Designed to measure knowledge in the firefighting field as promotional tests for fire department first-line supervisors.
Population: Candidates for promotion to the fire supervisor or lieutenant position.
Publication Dates: 2001-2006.
Scores: 9 knowledge areas: Fire Behavior and Fire Service, Firefighting Tactics and Procedures, Rescue and Safety, Firefighting Equipment and Apparatus, Building Construction, Supervisory Practices, Fire Prevention and Fire Safety, Hazardous Materials, Emergency Medical Care (Test 701 only).
Administration: Individual or group.
Forms, 2: 701, 702.
Price Data: Available from publisher.
Time: 120 minutes per test.
Comments: Reading lists are available to help candidates prepare for the tests.
Authors: International Public Management Association for Human Resources & Bruce Davey Associates.
Publisher: International Public Management Association for Human Resources (IPMA-HR).

[2438]

Severe Cognitive Impairment Profile.

Purpose: Designed to "measure and track impairment of cognitive abilities in adults with primary progressive dementia."
Population: Ages 42–90 and older.
Publication Dates: 1995–1998.
Acronym: SCIP.
Scores, 9: Comportment, Attention, Language, Memory, Motor, Conceptualization, Arithmetic, Visuospatial, Total.

Administration: Individual.

Price Data, 2005: $399 per introductory kit including professional manual (1998, 67 pages), 25 record forms, and manipulative materials to administer subtests, all packaged in sturdy briefcase.

Time: (30–45) minutes.

Author: Guerry M. Peavy.

Publisher: Psychological Assessment Resources, Inc.

Cross References: For reviews by Joan C. Ballard and Lawrence J. Ryan, see 14:349.

[2439]

The Severe Impairment Battery.

Purpose: Designed "to assess severe dementia in the elderly."

Population: Ages 51-91.

Publication Date: 1993.

Acronym: SIB.

Scores, 7: Attention, Orientation, Language, Memory, Visual-Spatial Ability, Construction, Total.

Administration: Individual.

Price Data, 2007: £238.48 per complete kit including manual (16 pages), 25 scoring sheets, stimulus cards, plastic shapes, spoon, cup, and full distractor pack in bag; £60.51 per 25 score sheets.

Time: 20 minutes.

Comments: Test takes into account specific behavioral and cognitive deficits associated with severe dementia; provides an assessment of social interaction skills abstracted from the Communication Activities of Daily Living (664).

Authors: J. Saxton, K. L. McGonigle, A. A. Swihart, and F. Boller.

Publisher: Pearson Assessment [England].

Cross References: For a review by Brad M. Merker and John Linck, see 17:172.

[2440]

The Severity and Acuity of Psychiatric Illness Scales–Adult Version.

Purpose: Designed to assess the severity and acuity of psychiatric illness in adult mental health service recipients.

Population: Adults.

Publication Date: 1998.

Scores, 6: Severity (Complexity Indicator, Probability of Admission, Total), Acuity (Clinical Status, Nursing Status, Total).

Administration: Individual.

Price Data, 2002: $75 per starter kit including training manual (52 pages), 10 reusable Severity item booklets, 25 Severity scale rating sheets, 10 reusable Acuity item booklets, and 25 Acuity scale rating sheets; $18 per 10 Severity scale item booklets; $15 per 25 Severity scale rating sheets; $18 per 10 Acuity scale item booklets; $15 per 25 Acuity scale rating sheets; $120 per training manual.

Time: (5) minutes.

Comments: Computer versions available; two scales (Severity and Acuity) can be used separately or together; results to be used as an "integrated outcomes-management and decision-support system for assisting treatment decision-making"; ratings are done by caregivers about clients/patients.

Author: John S. Lyons.

Publisher: Pearson.

Cross References: For reviews by Mark J. Atkinson and Roger A. Boothroyd, see 14:350.

[2441]

Sex-Role Egalitarianism Scale.

Purpose: "Developed to measure attitudes toward the equality of men and women."

Population: High school to adult.

Publication Date: 1993.

Acronym: SRES.

Scores, 6: Marital Roles, Parental Roles, Employment Roles, Social-Interpersonal-Heterosexual Roles, Educational Roles, Total.

Administration: Group or individual.

Price Data, 2010: $65 per examination kit including manual on CD (1993, 58 pages), 5 Form B question-and-answer documents, and 5 profile sheets; $24 per test manual on CD; $60 per 25 Form B question-and-answer documents; $45 per 25 Form K Research Forms; $50 per 25 profile sheets; $50 per 25 Short Form BB or KK question-and-answer sheets; $60 per researcher's kit including manual on CD, one Form K question-and-answer document, and one each of Form BB and KK Short Forms.

Time: 25 minutes.

Comments: Two full forms, B and K; two abbreviated forms, BB and KK.

Authors: Lynda A. King and Daniel W. King.

Publisher: SIGMA Assessment Systems, Inc.

Cross References: See T5:2389 (1 reference); for a review by Carol Collins, see 13:285.

[2442]

Sexometer.

Purpose: Designed to measure one's sex information.

Population: Adolescents and adults.

Publication Dates: 1974–1988.

Scores: Total score only.

Administration: Group.

Manual: No manual.

Price Data, 2005: $2 per scale.

Time: [20] minutes.

Comments: Supplementary article available.

Author: Panos D. Bardis.

Publisher: Donna Bardis.

Cross References: See 8:353 (1 reference).

[2443]

Sexual Adaptation and Functioning Test.

Purpose: Designed "as an aid in the planning of psychotherapeutic intervention techniques and to gain insight into an individual's sexual adaptation and sexual functioning."
Population: White adults ages 16 and over.
Publication Dates: 1985–1986.
Acronym: SAFT.
Scores: Total score only.
Administration: Individual.
Restricted Distribution: Distribution restricted to psychologists registered with the South African Medical and Dental Council.
Price Data: Available from publisher.
Foreign Language Edition: Afrikaans edition available.
Time: (90–100) minutes.
Comments: Projective test; self-administered using audiotaped instructions.
Author: Louise Olivier.
Publisher: Human Sciences Research Council [South Africa].

[2444]

Sexual Adjustment Inventory.

Purpose: "Designed to identify sexually deviate and paraphiliac behavior."
Population: People accused or convicted of sexual offenses.
Publication Date: 1991.
Acronym: SAI.
Scores: 13 scales: Test Item Truthfulness, Sex Item Truthfulness, Sexual Adjustment, Child Molest, Sexual Assault, Exhibitionism, Incest, Alcohol, Drugs, Violence, Antisocial, Distress, Judgment.
Administration: Group.
Forms, 2: Adult, Juvenile.
Price Data: Available from publisher.
Time: (35–40) minutes.
Comments: Both computer version and paper-pencil format are scored using IBM-PC compatibles.
Author: Risk & Needs Assessment, Inc.
Publisher: Behavior Data Systems, Ltd.
Cross References: For reviews by Richard F. Farmer and Sheila Mehta, see 14:351.

[2445]

Sexual Communication Inventory.

Purpose: Designed to help couples develop their skills for communicating about sexual matters in their relationship.
Population: Premarital and marital counselees.
Publication Date: 1980.
Acronym: SCI.
Scores: Overall score.
Administration: Group.

Price Data, 1993: $.75 per inventory; $2 per manual (6 pages).
Time: (20) minutes.
Author: Millard J. Bienvenu.
Publisher: Millard J. Bienvenu, Northwest Publications.
Cross References: For a review by Richard B. Stuart, see 9:1118.

[2446]

Sexual Violence Risk-20.

Purpose: Designed as a "method" (not a test or scale) of assessing an individual's risk for committing sexual violence.
Population: Individuals suspected to be at-risk for committing sexual violence.
Publication Dates: 1997–1998.
Acronym: SVR-20.
Scores: Not scored; ratings in five areas: Psychosocial Adjustment, Sexual Offenses, Future Plans, Other Considerations, Summary Risk Rating.
Administration: Individual.
Price Data: Available from publisher.
Time: Administration time not reported.
Comments: "Designed to assist evaluations of risk for sexual violence"; administration and coding by trained professionals only; rating done by the professional about a client/offender.
Authors: Douglas P. Boer, Stephen D. Hart, P. Randall Kropp, and Christopher D. Webster.
Publisher: British Columbia Institute Against Family Violence [Canada].
Cross References: For reviews by Rita M. Budrionis and Paul Retzlaff, see 15:228.

[2447]

Sexuality Experience Scales.

Purpose: To be used in sex counseling as an aid in interviewing, diagnosis of sexual dysfunction, and evaluation of therapy, as well as in research.
Population: Adults.
Publication Date: 1981.
Acronym: SES.
Scores, 4: Sexual Morality, Psychosexual Stimulation, Sexual Motivation, Attraction to Marriage.
Administration: Group.
Editions, 2: Female, Male.
Price Data: Available from publisher.
Time: Administration time not reported.
Authors: J. Frenken and P. Vennix.
Publisher: Pearson Assessment [England].
Cross References: See T5:2396 (1 reference) and T4:2449 (2 references).

[2448]

SF-36 Health Survey.

Purpose: Designed as a "survey of general health concepts."

Population: Ages 14 and older.
Publication Dates: 1989–2005.
Acronym: SF-36.
Scores: 8 scales: Physical Functioning, Role-Physical, Bodily Pain, General Health, Vitality, Social Functioning, Role-Emotional, Mental Health, plus 2 summary component scores.
Administration: Group.
Price Data: Available from publisher; administration and scoring software available from various vendors authorized by the publisher.
Foreign Language Editions: Translated into 60+ languages.
Time: Administration time not reported.
Comments: Permissions to use the SF-36 are granted through a combined licensing program of Medical Outcomes Trust, QualityMetric Incorporated, and Health Assessment Lab. The program itself is administered by QualityMetric, on behalf of the three organizations. Additional information is available at www.qualitymetric.com and www.sf-36.org.
Author: John E. Ware, Jr.
Publisher: Medical Outcomes Trust.
Cross References: For reviews by Ashraf Kagee and Nathaniel J. Pallone, see 14:352; see also T5:2397 (1 reference).

[2449]

Shapes Analysis Test.

Purpose: Designed as a test of spatial perception.
Population: Ages 14 and over.
Publication Date: 1972.
Acronym: SAT.
Scores, 3: 2-Dimensional, 3-Dimensional, Total.
Administration: Group.
Price Data, 2001: £21 per 19 booklets; £35 per 50 answer sheets; £10 per manual (20 pages); £15 per specimen set.
Time: 25(35) minutes.
Authors: A. W. Heim, K. P. Watts, and V. Simmonds.
Publisher: The Test Agency Limited [England] [No reply from publisher; status unknown].
Cross References: For a review by Charles T. Myers, see 8:1046 (2 references).

[2450]

Shapiro Control Inventory.

Purpose: Designed to "categorize, refine, and articulate a person's state of consciousness regarding control."
Population: Ages 14–88.
Publication Date: 1994.
Acronym: SCI.
Scores, 9: General Domain (Overall Sense of Control, Positive Sense of Control, Negative Sense of Control), Modes of Control (Positive Assertive, Positive Yielding,

Negative Assertive, Negative Yielding), Domain-Specific Sense of Control, Overall Desire for Control.
Administration: Group or individual.
Price Data: Available from publisher.
Foreign Language Editions: Spanish, Japanese, and Polish editions under development.
Time: (20–30) minutes.
Author: Deane H. Shapiro, Jr.
Publisher: Behaviordata, Inc.
Cross References: See T5:2399 (1 reference); for reviews by Wesley E. Sime and Claudia R. Wright, see 13:286.

[2451]

Ship Destination Test.

Purpose: Constructed to measure "general reasoning."
Population: Grades 9 and over.
Publication Dates: 1955–1956.
Scores: Total score only.
Administration: Group.
Price Data: Available from publisher.
Time: 15(20) minutes.
Authors: Paul R. Christensen and J. P. Guilford.
Publisher: Charlotte Mackley [No reply from publisher; status unknown].
Cross References: See T5:2401 (1 reference) and T2:457 (13 references); for a review by William B. Schrader, see 6:500 (8 references); for a review by C. J. Adcock, see 5:383.

[2452]

Shipley-2.

Purpose: Measures cognitive functioning and impairment in children and adults, including crystallized knowledge and fluid reasoning.
Population: Ages 7-89.
Publication Dates: 1939-2009.
Scores: 7 scores possible, 4 scores per profile form: Vocabulary, Abstraction, Composite A, and Impairment Index (AQ) for Composite A Form, or Vocabulary, Block Patterns, Composite B, and Impairment Index (BQ) for Composite B Form.
Administration: Group.
Price Data, 2010: $120 per kit including 20 Vocabulary AutoScore forms, 10 Abstraction AutoScore forms, 10 Block Patterns forms, and manual (1009, 148 pages); $35 per 25 AutoScore forms; $80 per manual; $199 per unlimited-use CD; $33 per Continuing Education (CE) Questionnaire and Evaluation Form.
Time: (20-25) minutes.
Comments: Previous edition called Shipley Institute of Living Scale; earlier versions entitled Shipley-Institute of Living Scale for Measuring Intellectual Impairment and Shipley-Hartford Retreat Scale for Measuring Intellectual Impairment.

Authors: Walter C. Shipley (all forms and manual), Christian P. Gruber (manual, Abstraction form, Vocabulary form, Composite A profile sheet, Composite B profile sheet), Thomas A. Martin (manual, Block Patterns form, Composite B profile sheet), and Amber M. Klein (manual).

Publisher: Western Psychological Services.

Cross References: For reviews by Theodore L. Hayes and Tracy Thorndike-Christ, see 18:121; for information for previous edition see T5:2402 (71 references) and T4:2453 (63 references); for a review by William L. Deaton of the Shipley Institute of Living Scale, see 11:360 (56 references); see also 9:1122 (13 references), T3:2179 (64 references), 8:677 (39 references), and T2:1380 (34 references); for a review by Aubrey J. Yates, see 7:138 (21 references); see also P:244 (38 references), 6:173 (13 references), and 5:111 (23 references); for reviews by E. J. G. Bradford, William A. Hunt, and Margaret Ives, see 3:39 (25 references).

[2453]

Shoplifting Inventory.

Purpose: "Designed to evaluate people charged or convicted of shoplifting."

Population: Shoplifting offenders.

Publication Date: 1995.

Acronym: SI.

Scores: 9 scales: Truthfulness, Entitlement, Shoplifting, Antisocial, Peer Pressure, Self-Esteem, Impulsiveness, Alcohol, Drugs.

Administration: Group.

Price Data: Available from publisher.

Time: (35) minutes.

Comments: Both computer version and paper-pencil format are scored on IBM-PC compatibles.

Author: Risk & Needs Assessment, Inc.

Publisher: Behavior Data Systems, Ltd.

Cross References: For reviews by G. Gage Kingsbury and Kwong-Liem Karl Kwan, see 14:353.

[2454]

Shorr Imagery Test.

Purpose: "Designed to elicit and score the degree of conflict in the visual images projected by the subject."

Population: College students and adults.

Publication Dates: 1974–1977.

Acronym: SIT.

Scores, 6: Item scores in 5 areas (Human, Animal, Inanimate, Botanical, Others) plus Total score for Conflict.

Administration: Individual.

Price Data: Available from publisher.

Time: (15–40) minutes.

Comments: For information for Group Shorr Imagery Test, see 1198.

Author: Joseph E. Shorr.

Publisher: Institute for Psychoimagination Therapy.

[2455]

Short Category Test, Booklet Format.

Purpose: A sensitive indicator of brain damage measuring an individual's ability to solve problems requiring careful observation, development of organizing principles, and responsiveness to feedback.

Population: Ages 20 and over.

Publication Dates: 1986–1987.

Scores: Total score only.

Subtests, 5: 1, 2, 3, 4, 5.

Administration: Individual.

Price Data, 2006: $192.50 per complete kit including 100 answer sheets, set of stimulus cards, and manual (1987, 40 pages); $126.50 per set of stimulus cards, 5 booklets (1986, 20 cards per booklet); $27.50 per 100 answer sheets; $49.50 per manual.

Time: (15–30) minutes.

Comments: Revision of the Halstead-Reitan Category Test.

Authors: Linda Wetzel and Thomas J. Boll.

Publisher: Western Psychological Services.

Cross References: See T5:2405 (1 reference); for reviews by Scott W. Brown and Hope J. Hartman, see 11:361.

[2456]

Short Employment Tests, Second Edition.

Purpose: "Measures verbal, numerical, and clerical skills."

Population: Adults.

Publication Dates: 1951–1993.

Acronym: SET.

Scores, 4: Verbal, Numerical, Clerical, Total.

Administration: Group or individual.

Forms: 2 forms of each subtest (Verbal, Numerical, Clerical Aptitude).

Price Data, 2006: $249 per starter kit, including 25 each of the Verbal, Numerical, and Clerical Aptitude test booklets, scoring key, and manual; $95 per package of 25 test bookets (specify version and Form 1 or 2); $320 per package of 100 test booklets (specify version and Form 1 or 2); $30 per combination scoring key; $45 per manual.

Time: 5(10) minutes.

Comments: Distribution of Form 1 restricted to banks that are members of the American Banking Association.

Authors: George K. Bennett and Marjorie Gelink.

Publisher: Pearson.

Cross References: For reviews by Caroline Manuele-Adkins and by Bert W. Westbrook and Michael C. Hansen, see 13:287; see also T4:2456 (3 references); for reviews by Samuel Juni and Ronald Baumanis and by Leonard J. West of an earlier edition, see 9:1124 (1 reference); see also T3:2180 (1 reference); for reviews by Ronald N. Taylor and Paul W. Thayer, see 8:1037 (4 references); see also T2:2151 (6 references); for a review by Leonard W. Ferguson, see 6:1045 (9 references); for a review by P. L. Mellenbruch, see 5:854 (16 references).

[2457]

Short Tests of Clerical Ability.

Purpose: Designed to measure aptitudes and abilities in tasks common to various office jobs.
Population: Applicants for office positions.
Publication Dates: 1959–1997.
Acronym: STCA.
Administration: Individual or group.
Price Data, 2002: $73 per start-up kit including 25 test booklets and examiner's manual (specify Arithmetic, Business Vocabulary, Checking, Coding, Directions–Oral and Written, Filing, or Language); $54 per 25 test booklets (specify test; quantity discounts available); price information available from publisher for Quanta Computer Administration and Scoring software (Windows); $73 per Quanta start-up kit including examiner's manual, 25 administrations and scoring, and oral directions sheet (does not include Quanta software).
Author: Science Research Associates.
Publisher: Pearson Performance Solutions [No reply from publisher; status unknown].
   a) ARITHMETIC.
   Scores, 3: Computation, Business Arithmetic, Total.
   Time: 6 minutes.
   b) BUSINESS VOCABULARY.
   Time: 5 minutes.
   c) CHECKING.
   Time: 5 minutes.
   d) CODING.
   Time: 5 minutes.
   e) DIRECTIONS–ORAL AND WRITTEN.
   Time: 5 minutes.
   f) FILING.
   Time: 5 minutes.
   g) LANGUAGE.
   Time: 5 minutes.
Cross References: For reviews by Lorraine D. Eyde and Dean R. Malsbary, see 8:1039 (1 reference); for reviews by Philip H. Kriedt and Paul W. Thayer, see 6:1046.

[2458]

Shortened Edinburgh Reading Test.

Purpose: Designed as a survey measure of children's reading skills in the upper primary school, and as a screening instrument to detect children who might need remedial help in reading.
Population: Ages 10-0 to 11-6.
Publication Date: 1985.
Scores, 5: Vocabulary, Syntax, Comprehension, Retention, General Reading Quotient.
Administration: Group.
Price Data, 2002: £15.99 per 20 test booklets; £16.99 per manual; £15.99 per specimen set.
Time: (40–45) minutes.

Author: The Godfrey Thomson Unit, University of Edinburgh.
Publisher: Hodder & Stoughton [England].
Cross References: For reviews by Douglas K. Smith and Betsy Waterman, see 14:354.

[2459]

SIGMA Survey for Police Officers.

Purpose: "Designed to identify job applicants possessing the cognitive skills necessary to use sound practical judgement in police situations, and to write meaningful and credible police incident reports."
Population: Ages 18 and over.
Publication Dates: 2001–2002.
Acronym: SSPO.
Scores, 6: Incident Report Writing (Spelling, Grammar, Vocabulary, Total), Police Problem Solving, Total.
Administration: Individual or group.
Forms, 4: A, B, C, and D.
Price Data, 2010: $24 per test manual; $5 per booklet; $15-$20 (depending on volume) per report.
Time: 35 minutes.
Comments: Fax-in scoring service available through publisher; available in Canadian format and American format; publisher recommends use of the SSPO in conjunction with the Employee Screening Questionnaire (997).
Author: Douglas N. Jackson.
Publisher: SIGMA Assessment Systems, Inc.
Cross References: For reviews by Thomas M. Dunn and Chockalingam Viswesvaran, see 16:221.

[2460]

SIGMA Survey for Sales Professionals.

Purpose: Designed to analyze "the strengths and weaknesses of sales and sales manager job candidates on 28 dimensions of expected job performance."
Population: 18 and over.
Publication Dates: 2002–2003.
Acronym: 3SP.
Scores, 28: Technical Orientation, Creativity, Thoroughness, Risk Taking, Open Mindedness, First Impression, Interpersonal Relations, Sensitivity, Social Astuteness, Communication, Formal Presentation, Persuasiveness, Negotiation, Listening Skill, Achievement and Motivation, Self-Discipline, Flexibility, Independence, Self Esteem, Emotional Control, Dependability, Ambition, Organizational Spokesperson, Assuming Responsibility, Vision, Short-Term Planning, Strategic Planning, Productivity.
Administration: Group and individual.
Price Data, 2010: $24 per test manual; $5 per test booklet; $40-$58 (depending on volume) per report via fax-in scoring or online administration.
Time: 40 minutes.

Comments: Publisher scoring services available via fax-in scoring or online administration at www.sigma-testing.com.
Author: Douglas N. Jackson.
Publisher: SIGMA Assessment Systems, Inc.
Cross References: For reviews by Martha E. Hennen and Stephen B. Johnson, see 16:222.

[2461]

SIGMA Survey for Security Officers.

Purpose: Designed as a "test for screening job applicants for the position of security officer."
Population: Ages 18 and over.
Publication Dates: 1996–2003.
Acronym: SSSO.
Scores, 5: Security Officer Problem Solving, Incident Report Writing Aptitude (Spelling, Grammar and Punctuation, Total), Overall Score.
Administration: Individual or group.
Parts, 2: Security Problem Solving, Incident Report Writing.
Price Data, 2010: $24 per test manual; $5 per test booklet; $15-$17 (depending on volume) per report.
Time: 30 minutes.
Comments: Fax-in scoring services available through publisher; recommended by publisher for use in conjunction with the Employee Screening Questionnaire (997). Canadian and American version available.
Author: Douglas N. Jackson.
Publisher: SIGMA Assessment Systems, Inc.
Cross References: For reviews by James T. Austin and Erich C. Fein and by David J. Pittenger, see 16:223.

[2462]

Signposts Early Assessment System.

Purpose: Designed to provide an integrated set of measures with an emphasis on literacy development focusing on prereading and reading skills.
Population: Grades K–3.5.
Publication Dates: 2000–2001.
Scores: Total score only.
Subtests: 4 components: Early Literacy Battery, Pre-DRP Tests, Performance Tasks, Informal Assessments.
Administration: Group (individual for some components).
Levels, 5: SA-1 (Grades K–K.5), SA-2 (Grades K.5–1.4), SA-3 (Grades 1.0–1.9), SA-4 (Grades 1.7–2.7), SA-5 (Grades 2.5–3.5).
Price Data, 2006: $50 per examination set including 1 test booklet of each level, administration procedures, handbook (2001, 68 pages), and norms book (2001, 31 pages); $99 per classroom set including 25 test booklets (specify level) including administration procedures, a class record, handbook, and norms book; $72 per 25 test booklets (specify level) including administration

procedures and a class record sheet; $10 per scoring key (specify level); $24 per handbook; $20 per norms book.
Time: (110–165) minutes.
Comments: Scoring keys must be purchased separately.
Author: Touchstone Applied Science Associates, Inc.
Publisher: Questar Assessment, Inc.
Cross References: For reviews by Thomas P. Hogan and Judith A. Monsaas, see 16:224.

[2463]

Singer-Loomis Type Deployment Inventory.

Purpose: Designed to assess "personality factors that may help an individual in self-understanding and in utilizing skills, talents, and abilities, so as to better deal with interactions between oneself and the environment."
Population: High school and college and adults.
Publication Dates: 1984–1997.
Acronym: SL-TDI.
Scores: Profile of 8 scores: Introverted, Extroverted for each of 4 functions (Thinking, Feeling, Sensing, Intuition), plus Extraversion, Introversion, Judging, Perceiving.
Administration: Group.
Price Data: Available from publisher.
Time: (30–40) minutes.
Comments: Self-report type profile based on Jung's typology.
Authors: June Singer, Mary Loomis, Elizabeth Kirkhart (revision), and Larry Kirkhart (revision).
Publisher: Moving Boundaries, Inc.
Cross References: For reviews by Joni R. Hays and Kevin Lanning, see 14:356; for a review by Richard B. Stuart of the earlier edition, see 10:334 (1 reference).

[2464]

SIPOAS: Styles in Perception of Affect Scale.

Purpose: "A personality scale measuring the ability to respond to the subtle, changing physical cues arising from the body's response to perceptions, memories and associations, and to integrate them into optimal emotional and behavioral response."
Population: Age 18 to adult.
Publication Date: 1995.
Acronym: SIPOAS.
Scores: 3 styles: BB (Based on Body), EE (Emphasis on Evaluation), LL (Looking to Logic).
Administration: Individual or group.
Price Data, 2002: $20 per 25 copies of questionnaire including scoring template with scoring criteria (can be mechanically reproduced); $22.50 per complete research report (203 pages); $14.25 per administration/interpretation manual.
Time: [20–30] minutes.
Comments: Paper-and-pencil test; may be completed by the individual or administered by an assistant to an individual or group. Can be used to determine

predominant styles, which is helpful for selecting the optimal psychotherapeutic modality and for predicting therapy outcome. Also has application in marital therapy and in personnel and organizational decision making, and may have application in legal justice settings such as jury selection, witness coaching, child custody and probation/parole issues.
Author: Michael Bernet.
Publisher: Institute for Somat Awareness.
Cross References: For reviews by Brian F. Bolton and S. Alvin Leung, see 14:357.

[2465]
Situational Attitude Scale.
Purpose: "Measures the attitudes of whites toward blacks."
Population: College and adults.
Publication Dates: c1969–1972.
Acronym: SAS.
Scores, 11: 10 situation scores, Total.
Administration: Group.
Forms, 2: A, B.
Price Data: Available from publisher.
Time: Untimed.
Authors: William E. Sedlacek and Glenwood C. Brooks, Jr.
Publisher: University of Maryland, University Counseling Center [No reply from publisher; status unknown].
Cross References: See T5:2413 (1 reference) and T4:2466 (2 references); for reviews by Ralph Mason Dreger and Marvin E. Shaw, see 8:678 (1 reference); see also T2:1381 (3 references).

[2466]
Situational Confidence Questionnaire.
Purpose: Designed to help clients identify high-risk drinking relapse situations.
Population: Adult alcoholics.
Publication Dates: 1987–1988.
Administration: Group.
Editions, 2: Computerized, print.
Authors: Helen M. Annis and J. Martin Graham.
Publisher: Centre for Addiction and Mental Health [Canada].
a) SITUATIONAL CONFIDENCE QUESTION-NAIRE.
Acronym: SCQ-39.
Scores, 9: Unpleasant Emotions/Frustrations, Physical Discomfort, Social Problems at Work, Social Tension, Pleasant Emotions, Positive Social Situations, Urges and Temptations, Testing Personal Control, Average.
Price Data, 2002: C$14.75 per 25 questionnaires; C$13.50 per user's guide (1988, 49 pages); C$25 per specimen set including user's guide and 25 questionnaires.

Time: (10–15) minutes.
b) ALCOHOL CONFIDENCE QUESTIONNAIRE.
Acronym: ACQ-16.
Scores: Total score only.
Time: Administration time not reported.
Comments: Brief version of the Situational Confidence Questionnaire; test items listed in SCQ user's guide.
Cross References: See T5:2414 (7 references); for reviews by Merith Cosden and Cecil R. Reynolds, see 13:288 (4 references); see also T4:2467 (1 reference).

[2467]
Situational Leadership®.
Purpose: Designed to identify successful leaders as "those who can adapt their behavior to meet the demands of their own unique situation."
Population: Managers, leaders, administrators, supervisors, and staff.
Publication Dates: 1973–1998.
Acronym: SL.
Administration: Group.
Manual: No manual.
Price Data: Available from publisher.
Time: Administration time not reported.
Comments: Related programs, Situational Leadership Simulator and Situational Leadership: Leveraging Human Performance, and Situational Leadership One-Day, also available.
Authors: Paul Hersey and Ron Campbell.
Publisher: Leadership Studies, Inc.
a) LEADER EFFECTIVENESS AND ADAPTABILITY.
Publication Dates: 1973–1998.
Acronym: LEAD.
Comments: Ratings of self and others.
Forms, 2: LEAD Self, LEAD Other.
b) READINESS STYLE MATCH.
Publication Date: 1979.
Acronym: RSM.
Scores: Ratings in 4 areas: Major Objectives, Readiness, Integration of Style and Readiness, Readiness Style Match Matrix.
Forms, 2: Staff Member Rating Form, Manager Rating Form.
c) READINESS SCALE.
Publication Date: 1977.
Acronym: MS.
Scores: 2 scores (Task Readiness, Psychological Readiness) for each of 5 major objectives or responsibilities.
Forms, 2: Self Rating Form, Manager Rating Form.
d) POWER PERCEPTION PROFILE.
Publication Date: 1979–1998.
Acronym: PPP.
Scores, 7: Coercive, Connection, Expert, Information, Legitimate, Referent, Reward.
Forms, 2: Perception of Self, Perception of Other.

e) LEADERSHIP SCALE.
Publication Date: 1980–1997.
Acronym: LS.
Scores: 2 scores (Total Task-Behavior, Total Relationship-Behavior) for each of 5 major objectives or responsibilities.
Forms, 2: Staff Member Form, Manager Form.
Cross References: For reviews by Bruce J. Eberhardt and Sheldon Zedeck, see 9:1133.

[2468]

Situational Outlook Questionnaire®.

Purpose: "Measures the climate for creativity, innovation, and change in an organization, within teams, and can be used for leadership development."
Population: Adult employees or members of a company, organization, or team.
Publication Dates: 1995-2007.
Acronym: SOQ.
Scores, 9: Challenge/Involvement, Freedom, Trust/Openness, Idea-Time, Playfulness/Humor, Conflict, Idea-Support, Debate, Risk-Taking.
Administration: Group.
Restricted Distribution: "The SOQ is only to be administered by those who have completed a qualification program."
Price Data, 2008: $75 per manual (2007, 390 pages).
Time: (25) minutes.
Comments: Includes analysis of narrative comments from open-ended questions; Web-based assessment; manual title is "Assessing the Context for Change, Second Edition"; in addition to computing scores for individual participants, averages for the organization are also computed for comparison purposes; "The SOQ is only to be administered by those who have completed a qualification program."
Authors: Scott G. Isaksen and Göran Ekvall, with contributions from Hans Akkermans, Glenn V. Wilson, and John P. Gaulin.
Publisher: The Creative Problem Solving Group, Inc.
Cross References: For reviews by Julia Y. Porter and John Sample, see 18:122.

[2469]

Situational Preference Inventory.

Purpose: "Designed to assess individual styles of social interaction."
Population: Grades 9-16 and adults.
Publication Dates: 1968-1973.
Acronym: SPI.
Scores, 3: Cooperational, Instrumental, Analytic.
Administration: Group.
Price Data: Available from publisher.
Time: (10-15) minutes.
Comments: Self-administered.

Author: Carl N. Edwards.
Publisher: Carl N. Edwards.
Cross References: See T2:1382 (2 references).

[2470]

Six Factor Personality Questionnaire.

Purpose: Designed as a measure of six personality dimensions or broad factors.
Population: Adults.
Publication Date: 2000.
Acronym: SFPQ.
Scores, 6: Extraversion, Agreeableness, Independence, Openness to Experience, Methodicalness, Industriousness.
Administration: Individual or group.
Price Data, 2010: $82 per examination kit including manual on CD (2000, 68 pages), 5 quick score answer sheets, 5 profile sheets, and one machine-scorable answer sheet for a Mail-in Basic Report; $24 per test manual on CD; $60 per 25 test booklets; $65 per Quick Answer Score sheets; $50 per 25 profile forms; $65–$75 (depending on volume) per 10 machine-scorable answer sheets and coupons for Mail-in Basic Report; $145 per SigmaSoft SFPQ for Windows Software installation package, includes 10 scoring coupons; $12-$20 (depending on volume) per online password.
Time: 20 minutes.
Comments: Available for online administration at www.sigmatesting.com.
Authors: Douglas N. Jackson, Sampo V. Paunonen, and Paul F. Tremblay.
Publisher: SIGMA Assessment Systems, Inc.
Cross References: For a review by Jeffrey A. Jenkins, see 15:229.

[2471]

Sixteen Personality Factor Questionnaire, Fifth Edition.

Purpose: Designed to measure personality traits.
Population: Ages 16 and over.
Publication Dates: 1949–2002.
Acronym: 16PF.
Scores, 24: 16 Primary Factor Scores (Warmth, Reasoning, Emotional Stability, Dominance, Liveliness, Rule-Consciousness, Social Boldness, Sensitivity, Vigilance, Abstractedness, Privateness, Apprehension, Openness to Change, Self-Reliance, Perfectionism, Tension); 5 Global Factors (Extraversion, Anxiety, Tough-Mindedness, Independence, Self-Control); 3 Response Style Indices (Impression Management, Infrequency, Acquiescence).
Administration: Group or individual.
Price Data: Available from publisher.
Time: (35–50) minutes.
Comments: Computer administration, interpretive reports, and scoring available; online or paper-and-pencil

administration; the following interpretive reports are available: 16PF Interpretive Report, 16PF Profile Report, 16PF Competency Report, 16PF Practitioner Report, 16PF Profile and Manager Feedback Report, 16PF Career Development Report, 16PF Leadership Coaching Report, 16 PF Management Potential Report, 16PF Teamwork Development Report.

Authors: Raymond B. Cattell, A. Karen S. Cattell, and Heather E. P. Cattell.

Publisher: Institute for Personality and Ability Testing, Inc. (IPAT).

Cross References: See T5:2417 (43 references); for reviews by Mary J. McLellan and Pamela Carrington Rotto, see 12:354 (38 references); see also T4:2470 (140 references); for reviews of an earlier edition by James N. Butcher and Marvin Zuckerman, see 9:1136 (67 references); see also T3:2208 (182 references); for reviews by Bruce M. Bloxom, Brian F. Bolton, and James A. Walsh, see 8:679 (619 references); see also T2:1383 (244 references); for reviews by Thomas J. Bouchard, Jr. and Leonard G. Rorer, see 7:139 (295 references); see also P:245 (249 references); for a review by Maurice Lorr, see 6:174 (81 references); for a review by C. J. Adcock, see 5:112 (21 references); for reviews by Charles M. Harsh, Ardie Lubin, and J. Richard Wittenborn, see 4:87 (8 references).

[2472]

16PF Adolescent Personality Questionnaire.

Purpose: Designed to "measure normal personality of adolescents, problem-solving abilities, and preferred work activities," and to identify problems in areas known to be problematic to adolescents.

Population: Ages 11–22.

Publication Date: 2001.

Acronym: APQ.

Scores, 21: 21 normal personality scales: Primary Personality Factor Scales (Warmth, Reasoning, Emotional Stability, Dominance, Liveliness, Rule-Consciousness, Social Boldness, Sensitivity, Vigilance, Abstractedness, Privateness, Apprehension, Openness to Change, Self-Reliance, Perfectionism, Tension), Global Factor Scales (Extraversion, Anxiety, Tough-Mindedness, Independence, Self-Control); plus a ranking of Work Activity Preferences (Manual, Scientific, Artistic, Helping, Sales/Management, and Procedural), Personal Discomfort (Discouragement, Worry, Poor Body Image, Overall Discomfort), "Getting in Trouble" (Anger or Aggression, Problems with Authority, Alcohol or Drugs, Overall Trouble), Context (Home or School), Coping/Managing Difficulty, Impression Management, Missing Responses, Central Responses, Predicted Grade Point Average.

Administration: Group or individual.

Price Data: Available from publisher.

Time: (54–65) minutes (untimed).

Comments: Computerized scoring and interpretive reports available (APQ Guidance Report and APQ Psychological Report); optional Life's Difficulties section provides an opportunity for the youth to indicate particular problems in areas known to be problematic for adolescents, making the APQ appropriate for screening and for introducing sensitive topics in a counseling setting.

Author: J. M. Schuerger.

Publisher: Institute for Personality and Ability Testing, Inc. (IPAT).

Cross References: For reviews by William M. Reynolds and by Susan C. Whiston and Jennifer C. Bouwkamp, see 15:230.

[2473]

16PF® Human Resource Development Report.

Purpose: Assesses an individual's management potential and style, provides insights into the individual's personality, and focuses on five management dimensions frequently identified in research on successful managers.

Population: Managerial candidates.

Publication Dates: 1982–1997.

Acronym: HRDR.

Scores, 26: 5 management dimensions: Leadership, Interaction with Others, Decision-Making Abilities, Initiative, Personal Adjustment; 16 primary factor scores; 5 global factor scores.

Administration: Group or individual.

Price Data, 2006: $33 per introductory kit including test booklet, answer sheet, prepaid processing form to receive Human Resource Development Report, and user's guide (1997, 55 pages); $20 per 10 reusable test booklets; $18 per 25 machine-scorable answer sheets; $30 per user's guide; $16.50 to $30 per Human Resource Development Report available from publisher scoring service.

Time: 35–50 minutes.

Comments: Based on the Sixteen Personality Factor Questionnaire (2471); mail-in, fax, on-site software, and Net Assess internet delivery options available; can be generated from 4th or 5th edition of 16PF questionnaire.

Author: IPAT staff.

Publisher: Institute for Personality and Ability Testing, Inc. (IPAT).

Cross References: For reviews by S. Alvin Leung and Mary A. Lewis, see 11:169.

[2474]

16PF Select.

Purpose: A shorter version of the 16PF Fifth Edition personality measure, which was designed for personnel selection.

Population: Ages 16 and over.

Publication Date: 1999.

Acronym: 16PF Select.

Scores, 12: Warmth, Calmness, Dominance, Liveliness, Rule-Consciousness, Social Boldness, Trust,

Imagination, Self-Assuredness, Openness, Self-Reliance, Organization.

Administration: Individual or group.

Price Data, 2006: $58 per introductory kit including manual (1999, 75 pages), dimension specification form, questionnaire/answer sheet booklet and prepaid mail-in report processing certificate; $30 per manual; $30 per 10 questionnaire/answer sheet booklets; $15.50 to $30 per report.

Time: (20) minutes (untimed).

Comments: A shorter version of the 16PF Fifth Edition (2471).

Authors: Raymond B. Cattell, A. Karen S. Cattell, Heather E. P. Cattell, and Mary L. Kelly.

Publisher: Institute for Personality and Ability Testing, Inc. (IPAT).

Cross References: For reviews by Paul A. Arbisi and Stephen E. Trotter, see 15:231; for information about the complete 16PF see T5:2417 (43 references); for reviews of an earlier edition of the 16PF by Mary J. McLellan and Pamela Carrington Rotto, see 12:354 (38 references); see also T4:2470 (140 references); for reviews by James N. Butcher and Marvin Zuckerman, see 9:1136 (67 references); see also T3:2208 (182 references); for reviews by Bruce M. Bloxom, Brian F. Bolton, and James A. Walsh, see 8:679 (619 references); see also T2:1383 (244 references); for reviews of an earlier edition by Thomas J. Bouchard, Jr. and Leonard G. Rorer, see 7:139 (295 references); see also P:245 (249 references); for a review by Maurice Lorr, see 6:174 (81 references); for a review by C. J. Adcock, see 5:112 (21 references); for reviews by Charles M. Harsh, Ardie Lubin, and J. Richard Wittenborn, see 4:87 (8 references).

[2475]

Skills and Attributes Inventory.

Purpose: Assesses the relative importance of job-related skills and attributes for a position as well as the degree to which an individual possesses thos skills and attributes.

Population: Non-management positions.

Publication Dates: 1976–1979.

Acronym: SAI.

Scores, 13: General Functioning Intelligence, Visual Acuity, Visual and Coordination Skills, Physical Coordination, Mechanical Skills, Graphic and Clerical Skills, General Clerical Skills, Leadership Ability, Tolerance in Interpersonal Relations, Organization Identification, Conscientiousness and Reliability, Efficiency Under Stress, Solitary Work.

Administration: Individual or group.

Price Data, 2002: $101 per start-up kit (specify Importance or Ability) including 25 test booklets, 25 score sheets, and interpretation and research manual; $54 per 25 test booklets (specify Importance or Ability); $31 per 25 score sheets; $28 per interpretation and research manual.

Time: No limit (approximately 30–45 minutes).

Author: Melany E. Baehr.

Publisher: Pearson Performance Solutions [No reply from publisher; status unknown].

Cross References: For a review by Lenore W. Harmon, see 9:1137.

[2476]

Skills Assessment Module.

Purpose: To assess a student's affective, cognitive, and manipulative strengths and weaknesses in relation to vocational skills required in various training programs within a school system.

Population: Average, handicapped, and disadvantaged vocational training school students ages 14-18.

Publication Dates: 1985–2000.

Acronym: SAM.

Scores, 13: Digital Discrimination, Clerical Verbal, Motor Coordination, Clerical Numerical, Following Written Directions, Finger Dexterity, Aiming, Reading a Ruler (Measurement), Manual Dexterity, Form Perception, Spatial Perception, Color Discrimination, Following Diagrammed Instructions.

Administration: Individual in part.

Price Data, 2002: $2,995 for complete test including all subtests.

Time: (90-150) minutes.

Comments: Module includes Career Development ITEP software, Basic Skills Locater Test (275), Learning Styles Inventory (1513), Auditory Directions Screen, Voc-Ties Interest Survey, and 13 hands on performance work samples.

Author: Michele Rosinek.

Publisher: Piney Mountain Press, Inc.

Cross References: For reviews by Jean Powell Kirnan and Wilbur L. Layton, see 11:364.

[2477]

Skills Confidence Inventory, Revised Edition.

Purpose: Designed as part of the process of educational or career exploration to measure the confidence of career professionals in their abilities to successfully perform various work-related tasks and activities.

Population: Ages 15 and up.

Publication Dates: 1996-2004.

Scores, 6: Realistic, Investigative, Artistic, Social, Enterprising, Conventional.

Administration: Individual or group.

Price Data, 2011: $12.25 each for Strong Interest Inventory® and Skills Confidence Inventory online administration; $39.50 per Skills Confidence Inventory manual.

Time: (45-55) minutes.

Comments: This instrument can only be taken with the Strong Interest Inventory (25760) and is available online at www.skillsone.com.

Authors: Nancy E. Betz, Fred H. Borgen, and Lenore W. Harmon.
Publisher: CPP, Inc.
Cross References: For reviews by Joseph C. Ciechalski and Gypsy M. Denzine, see 18:123.

[2478]
Skills Inventory for Teams.

Purpose: To aid early intervention practitioners to "evaluate their ability to work as part of a team."
Population: Early intervention practitioners.
Publication Dates: 1978–1992.
Acronym: SIFT.
Scores, 12: Clarity of Purpose, Cohesion, Clarity of Roles, Communication, Use of Resources, Decision Making/Problem Solving, Responsibility Implementation, Conflict Resolution, View of Family Role, Evaluation, External Support, Internal Support.
Administration: Group.
Price Data: Price information for administration guide and inventory (1992, 66 pages) available from publisher.
Time: Administration time not reported.
Comments: Previously called Skills Inventory for Teachers; self-administered inventory.
Authors: Corinne Garland, Adrienne Frank, Deana Buck, and Patti Seklemian.
Publisher: Child Development Resources.
Cross References: For reviews by Robert Johnson and E. Lea Witta, see 13:289.

[2479]
SKILLSCOPE®.

Purpose: Assesses managerial strengths and developmental needs from managers' and coworkers' perspectives.
Population: Managers.
Publication Dates: 1988-1997.
Scores: 15 Skill Areas: Getting Information, Communication, Taking Action, Risk Taking, Administration, Conflict Management, Relationships, Selecting/Developing, Influencing, Flexibility, Knowledge of Job, Energy/Drive, Time Management, Coping With Pressure, Self-Management.
Administration: Group.
Price Data, 2006: $155 per set including 9 survey instruments, a feedback report, a development planning guide, and a facilitators's guide (2006, 63 pages); $195 per group profile; quantity discounts available.
Time: [20–30] minutes.
Comments: SKILLSCOPE questionnaires can be returned to the Center for Creative Leadership for confidential scoring or the questionnaires can be completed on-line; managers are rated by self and by coworkers.
Author: Robert E. Kaplan.
Publisher: Center for Creative Leadership.
Cross References: For a review by Linda F. Wightman, see 12:355.

[2480]
Slingerland Screening Tests for Identifying Children with Specific Language Disability.

Purpose: "To screen from among a group of children those with potential language difficulties and those with already present specific language disabilities who are in need of special attention."
Population: Grades 1–2.5, 2.5–3.5, 3.5–4, 5–6
Publication Dates: 1962–2005.
Subtests, 8 or 9: Copying-Chart, Copying-Page, Visual Perception-Memory, Visual Discrimination, Visual Perception-Memory with Kinesthetic Memory, Auditory Recall, Auditory Sounds, Auditory Association, Orientation (Form D only); plus individual Echolalia test.
Administration: Group (Echolalia test individually administered).
Author: Beth H. Slingerland.
Publisher: Educators Publishing Service, Inc.

    a) FORMS A, B, C, REVISED EDITION.
    Population: Grades 1–2.5, 2.5–3.5, 3.5–4.
    Publication Dates: 1962-2005.
    Scores, 13 (8 tests): Visual Copying Far Point, Visual Copying Near Point, Total, Visual Perception-Memory, Visual Discrimination, Visual Perception-Memory with Kinesthetic Memory, Auditory Recall (Letters, Numbers, Spelling), Auditory Discrimination of Sounds, Auditory-Visual Association, Total Errors (excluding Visual Copying), Total Errors plus Self-Corrections and Poor Formations.
    Price Data, 2006: $33 per 12 tests (A, B, or C); $20 per cards and charts (A, B, or C); $17.80 per teacher's manual (2005, 172 pages); $20.80 per specimen set including manual and one each of above tests; quantity discounts available.
    Time: 56(66) minutes in 2 or 3 sessions.
    Authors: Revisions by Beth H. Slingerland and Alice S. Ansara.
      1) *Form A.*
      Population: Grades 1–2.5.
      2) *Form B.*
      Population: Grades 2.5–3.5.
      3) *Form C.*
      Population: Grades 3.5–4.
    b) FORM D.
    Population: Grades 5–6.
    Publication Date: 1974.
    Scores, 14 (9 tests): Visual Copying Far Point, Visual Copying Near Point, Total, Visual Perception-Memory, Visual Discrimination, Visual Perception-Memory with Kinesthetic Memory, Auditory Recall (Letters, Numbers, Spelling), Auditory Discrimination of Sounds, Auditory-Visual Association, Auditory Perception and Individual Orientation, Total Errors (excluding Visual Copying), Total Errors and Confusions.
    Price Data: $24.80 per 12 tests and 12 summary sheets; $22.75 per cards and charts including directions

for administration and scoring; $14.20 per teacher's manual; $15.20 per specimen set including teacher's manual, Form D test, summary sheet, and list of material needed; quantity discounts available.
Time: (110-125) minutes in 2 sessions.
Cross References: See T4:2478 (2 references); for reviews by Martin Fujiki and Elisabeth H. Wiig, see 9:1141 (4 references); see also T3:2214 (2 references); for an excerpted review by Barton B. Proger, see 8:446 (3 references); see also T2:989 (4 references); for reviews by Evelyn Deno and Joseph M. Wepman of a, see 7:969 (3 references).

[2481]
Slosson Articulation, Language Test with Phonology.

Purpose: Measures the communicative competence of a child by combining into a single score the assessment of articulation, phonology and language.
Population: Ages 3-0 to 5-11.
Publication Date: 1986.
Acronym: SALT-P.
Scores, 4: Consonants + Vowels/Diphthongs, Phonological Processes, Language Errors, Composite Score.
Administration: Individual.
Price Data, 1992: $50 per complete kit; $14 per examiner's manual (12 pages); $20 per 50 scoring forms; $18 per test book/picture plates; $70 per video tape.
Time: (7-10) minutes.
Comments: Instructional video tape with taped administration of test available.
Author: Wilma Jean Tade.
Publisher: Slosson Educational Publications, Inc.
Cross References: For reviews by Clinton W. Bennett and Robert A. Reineke, see 12:357.

[2482]
Slosson Full-Range Intelligence Test.

Purpose: Constructed as a "quick estimate of general cognitive ability."
Population: Ages 5–21.
Publication Dates: 1988–2002.
Acronym: S-FRIT.
Scores, 8: General Cognition (Full-Range Intelligence Quotient, Rapid Cognitive Index, Best g Index), Cognitive Subdomains (Verbal Index, Abstract Index, Quantitative Index, Memory Index, Performance Index).
Administration: Individual.
Forms, 2: Item Profiles/Score Summaries Form, Brief Score Form.
Price Data, 2002: $110 per complete kit including examiner's manual (1994, 80 pages), normative/technical manual (1994, 93 pages), picture book, 50 motor response forms, 50 brief score forms, and 50 item profiles/score summaries: $38 per 50 forms (specify Motor response,

brief score, or item profiles/score summaries); $70 per examiner's manual; $40 per normative/technical manual; $26.50 per picture book.
Time: (20–35) minutes.
Authors: Bob Algozzine, Ronald C. Eaves, Lester Mann, H. Robert Vance, and Steven W. Slosson (Brief Score Form).
Publisher: Slosson Educational Publications, Inc.
Cross References: For reviews by Gerald S. Hanna and Gerald Tindal, see 14:359.

[2483]
Slosson Intelligence Test 3rd [2002 Edition].

Purpose: Designed for use as a "quick estimate of general verbal cognitive ability."
Population: Ages 4-65 and over.
Publication Dates: 1961–2002.
Acronym: SIT-R3.
Scores: Total score only.
Administration: Individual.
Price Data, 2005: $110.25 per complete kit including 50 test forms, manual (1991, 45 pages), and norms tables/technical manual (1991, 39 pages); $27 per 50 test forms; $47 per norms tables/technical manual; $47 per manual.
Time: (10-20) minutes.
Authors: Richard L. Slosson, Charles L. Nicholson (revision), and Terry H. Hibpshman (revision).
Publisher: Slosson Educational Publications, Inc.
Cross References: See T5:2432 (33 references); for reviews by Randy W. Kamphaus and T. Steuart Watson, see 12:358 (16 references); see also T4:2482 (43 references); for reviews by Thomas Oakland and William M. Reynolds of an earlier edition , see 9:1142 (11 references); see also T3:2217 (82 references), 8:227 (62 references), and T2:524 (12 references); for reviews by Philip Himelstein and Jane V. Hunt, see 7:424 (31 references).

[2484]
Slosson Oral Reading Test–Revised.

Purpose: Designed as a "quick estimate to target word recognition levels for children and adults."
Population: Preschool–adult.
Publication Dates: 1963–2002.
Acronym: SORT-R.
Scores: Total score only.
Administration: Individual.
Price Data, 2002: $60 per complete kit; $40 per manual (1990, 38 pages); $26 per 50 score sheets; $14 per spiral-bound word lists; $7 per large print word lists.
Special Editions: Large print edition available for individuals with visual handicaps.
Time: (3-5) minutes.
Comments: Grade equivalent (GE) and age equivalent (AE) scores are also available.
Authors: Richard L. Slosson and Charles L. Nicholson.

Publisher: Slosson Educational Publications, Inc.
Cross References: See T5:2433 (4 references); for reviews by Steven R. Shaw and Carol E. Westby, see 12:359 (4 references); see T4:2483 (16 references), T3:2218 (15 references), T2:1688 (5 references), and 6:844.

[2485]
Slosson Test of Reading Readiness.
Purpose: "Designed to identify children who are at risk of failure in programs of formal reading instruction."
Population: Latter kindergarten-grade 1.
Publication Date: 1991.
Acronym: STRR.
Scores, 12: Visual Skills (Recognition of Capital Letters, Recognition of Lower Case Letters, Matching Capital and Lower Case Letters, Visual Discrimination-Matching Word Forms, Total), Auditory Skills (Auditory Discrimination-Rhyming Words, Auditory Discrimination and Memory–Recognition of Beginning Sounds, Total), Cognitive Skills (Sequencing, Opposites, Total), Total Inventory.
Administration: Individual.
Price Data, 1992: $48 per complete kit; $18 per manual (24 pages); $12 per test stimulus booklet; $16 per 50 scoring booklets; $6 per 50 letter to parent.
Time: (15) minutes.
Authors: Leslie Anne Perry and Gary J. Vitali.
Publisher: Slosson Educational Publications, Inc.
Cross References: For reviews by Gerald S. Hanna and Diane J. Sawyer, see 12:360.

[2486]
Smedley Hand Dynamometer.
Purpose: Developed to "measure the muscular torque (grip) of the hand and forearm."
Population: Ages 6–18.
Publication Dates: [1920–1953].
Scores: Total score only.
Administration: Individual.
Price Data, 2005: $215 per hand dynamometer.
Time: Administration time not reported.
Author: F. Smedley.
Publisher: Stoelting Co.
Cross References: See T2:1901 (10 references).

[2487]
Smell Identification Test™ [Revised].
Purpose: Designed to measure an individual's ability to "identify a number of odorants at the suprathreshold level."
Population: People 5 years and up with suspected olfactory dysfunction.
Publication Dates: 1981–1995.
Acronym: SIT; UPSIT.
Scores: Total score only.

Administration: Individual.
Price Data: Available from publisher.
Time: [10–15] minutes.
Comments: A 40-item forced-choice questionnaire; also known as University of Pennsylvania Smell Identification Test; for use only by individuals "professionally engaged in the scientific or medical evaluation of smell function"; related versions include the Pocket Smell Test, the Cross-Cultural Smell Identification Test, and the Picture Identification Test (equivalent to the SIT except stimuli are pictures rather than odors).
Author: Richard L. Doty.
Publisher: Sensonics, Inc.
Cross References: For a review by Ralph G. Leverett, see 14:360; see also T5:2437 (4 references).

[2488]
Smoker Complaint Scale.
Purpose: Designed to measure changes in physiological/emotional/craving states as a function of smoking cessation.
Population: Persons quitting smoking.
Publication Date: 1984.
Acronym: SCS.
Scores: Total score and item scores only.
Administration: Individual or group.
Manual: No manual.
Price Data: Instrument now available without charge from publisher.
Foreign Language Editions: Translations available in Danish, Dutch, English for Australia, German, Italian, and Norwegian.
Time: (1-5) minutes.
Comments: Self-administered; also available online at www.proqolid.org.
Author: Nina G. Schneider.
Publisher: Nina G. Schneider, Ph.D.
Cross References: See T5:2440 (1 reference).

[2489]
Social Adjustment Scale–Self Report.
Purpose: Designed to assess "the ability of an individual to adapt to, and derive satisfaction from, their social roles."
Population: Age 17 and older
Publication Date: 1999.
Acronym: SAS-SR.
Scores, 7: Work, Social and Leisure Activities, Relations with Extended Family, Primary Relationship, Parenthood, Family Life, Overall Mean.
Administration: Individual or group.
Price Data, 2011: $174 per complete kit including 10 question booklets, 25 QuikScore™ forms, and manual; $49 per 10 question booklets; $50 per 25 QuikScore™ forms; $94 per manual.
Foreign Language Editions: Available in Afrikaans, Cantonese, Czech, Danish, Dutch, Finnish,

Flemish, French (European), French-Canadian, German, Greek, Hebrew, Hungarian, Italian, Japanese, Korean, Mandarin, Norwegian, Portuguese, Russian, Spanish (European), Spanish (South American), and Swedish.
Time: (15–20) minutes.
Author: Myrna Weissmann.
Publisher: Multi-Health Systems, Inc.
Cross References: For reviews by Julie A. Allison and Romeo Vitelli, see 15:232.

[2490]

Social Behavior Assessment Inventory.
Purpose: Assesses social skill levels in students.
Population: Grades K–9.
Publication Dates: 1978–1992.
Acronym: SBAI.
Scores, 30: Environmental Behaviors (Care for the Environment, Dealing with Emergencies, Lunchroom Behavior, Movement Around Environment), Interpersonal Behaviors (Accepting Authority, Coping with Conflict, Gaining Attention, Greeting Others, Helping Others, Making Conversation, Organized Play, Positive Attitude Toward Others, Playing Informally, Property: Own and Others), Self-Related Behaviors (Accepting Consequences, Ethical Behavior, Expressing Feelings, Positive Attitude Toward Self, Responsible Behavior, Self-Care), Task-Related Behaviors (Asking and Answering Questions, Attending Behavior, Classroom Discussion, Completing Tasks, Following Directions, Group Activities, Independent Work, On-Task Behavior, Performing Before Others, Quality of Work).
Administration: Individual or group.
Price Data, 2006: $140 per introductory kit including Social Skills in the Classroom–2nd ed., manual (1992, 34 pages), and 25 rating booklets.
Time: (30–45) minutes.
Comments: Observations made by teacher or trained paraprofessional.
Authors: Thomas M. Stephens and Kevin D. Arnold.
Publisher: Psychological Assessment Resources, Inc.
Cross References: See T5:2444 (1 reference); for reviews by Kathryn A. Hess and David MacPhee, see 12:361; see also T4:2493 (1 reference); for a review by Ronald S. Drabman of an earlier edition, see 9:1148; see also T3:2226 (1 reference).

[2491]

Social Competence and Behavior Evaluation, Preschool Edition.
Purpose: "Designed to assess patterns of social competence, affective expression, and adjustment difficulties."
Population: Children aged 30 months to 76 months (2 1/2 to 6 years).
Publication Date: 1995.
Acronym: SCBE.

Scores: 8 Basic scales (Depressive-Joyful, Anxious-Secure, Angry-Tolerant, Isolated-Integrated, Aggressive-Calm, Egotistical-Prosocial, Oppositional-Cooperative, Dependent-Autonomous); 4 Summary scales (Social Competence, Internalizing Problems, Externalizing Problems, General Adaptation).
Administration: Group.
Price Data, 2006: $92.50 per complete kit including 25 AutoScore™ forms and manual (67 pages); $44 per 25 AutoScore™ forms; $53 per manual.
Time: (15) minutes.
Comments: Ratings by teachers or other child care professionals.
Authors: Peter J. LaFreniere and Jean E. Dumas.
Publisher: Western Psychological Services.
Cross References: For reviews by Ronald A. Madle and G. Michael Poteat, see 14:362.

[2492]

Social-Emotional Dimension Scale–Second Edition.
Purpose: "Designed to provide school personnel … with a means for rating student behavior problems that may interfere with academic functioning."
Population: Ages 6.0-18.11.
Publication Dates: 1986–2004.
Acronym: SEDS-2.
Administration: Individual.
Price Data, 2011: $171 per complete kit: $53 per examiner's manual; $46 per 25 comprehensive forms; $47 per 50 screener forms; $47 per 50 screener summary forms.
Comments: Norm-referenced behavior rating scale.
Authors: Jerry B. Hutton and Timothy G. Roberts.
Publisher: PRO-ED.
a) SCREENER FORM.
Scores: Total score only.
Time: (5–8) minutes.
b) COMPREHENSIVE FORM.
Scores, 8: Externalizing Behavior (Interpersonal Relationships, Conduct Problems, Total), Internalizing Behavior (Inappropriate Behavior, Depression, Anxiety/Inattention, Total), Overall Social-Emotional Disturbance.
Time: (15–20) minutes.
c) FUNCTIONAL ASSESSMENT INTERVIEW.
Scores: Not scored.
Time: (30) minutes.
Cross References: For a review by Mark D. Shriver, see 16:226; for a review by Jean Powell Kirnan of the earlier edition, see 11:368.

[2493]

Social-Emotional Wellbeing Survey.
Purpose: Allows "schools…to survey their students and receive a report on a wide variety of social, emotional and, behavioural outcomes of their student population."

Population: Ages 3-18.
Publication Dates: 2003-2009.
Acronym: SEWB.
Scores: Item summaries only.
Administration: Group.
Forms, 4: Teacher-Early Years (Kinder-Grade 2), 'Student-Primary (Grades 2-6), Student-Secondary (Grades 5-12), Teacher Perceptions (Grades 2-12).
Price Data, 2009: A$7.50 per Survey Form; A$440 per ACER report service; A$270 per ACER report service for schools using only the Teacher Form-Early Years; cost of additional reports "determined by the nature of the request and negotiated between ACER and the client"; manual (2009, 18 pages) is free to print from publisher's website: www.acer.edu.au/sewb.
Time: (30) minutes.
Comments: Based on surveys developed by Michael E. Bernard and published by ACER in 2003: Social and Emotional Wellbeing Survey (Student Form, Grades 2-4; Student Form, Grades 5-12; Teacher Form, Grades 2-12) and Survey of Young Children's Social and Emotional Wellbeing (Teacher Form, pre-Grade 2); publisher provides scoring and summary report; Teacher Form-Early Years completed by teacher "on behalf of student"; Student Form-Primary may be read aloud to student; Student Form-Secondary also includes "perceptions of home, school and community"; Teacher Perceptions Form (optional) completed by teacher and reflects teacher perceptions of particular student; item summaries only; data are aggregated across like subjects; 50 items per Teacher Form-Early Years, 53 items per Student Form-Primary, 94 items per Student Form-Secondary, 60 items per Teacher Perceptions Form; the client school's scores are separated by gender and year level, and are compared "against 'All Schools' results"; summary report does not provide data for individual students; "to protect student anonymity, at least five students of each gender, at each year level [per form used], must complete a survey."
Author: Australian Council for Educational Research Ltd.
Publisher: Australian Council for Educational Research Ltd. [Australia].

[2494]

Social Phobia and Anxiety Inventory.

Purpose: Constructed for assessment of the "somatic, cognitive and behavioral aspects of social phobia."
Population: Ages 14 and older.
Publication Date: 1996.
Acronym: SPAI.
Scores, 3: Social Phobia, Agoraphobia, Difference.
Administration: Individual or group.
Price Data, 2011: $105 per complete kit including manual (42 pages) and 25 QuikScore™ forms; $50 per 25 QuikScore™ forms; $73 per manual.
Time: (15) minutes.

Comments: Self-report.
Authors: Samuel M. Turner, Deborah C. Beidel, and Constance V. Dancu.
Publisher: Multi-Health Systems, Inc.
Cross References: For reviews by George Engelhard, Jr. and Delores D. Walcott, see 14:363.

[2495]

Social Phobia & Anxiety Inventory for Children.

Purpose: "Assesses the frequency and range of social fears and anxiety in children and adolescents."
Population: Ages 8–14.
Publication Date: 1998.
Acronym: SPAI-C.
Scores: Total score only.
Administration: Group or individual.
Price Data, 2011: $105 per complete kit including manual and 25 QuikScore™ forms; $50 per 25 QuikScore™ forms; $73 per manual (1998, 40 pages); $50 per 25 Spanish QuikScore™ forms.
Time: (20–30) minutes.
Comments: Self-report; "has been translated into several languages."
Authors: Deborah C. Beidel, Samuel M. Turner, and Tracy L. Morris.
Publisher: Multi-Health Systems, Inc.
Cross References: For reviews by Sarah J. Allen and Loraine J. Spenciner, see 15:233.

[2496]

The Social Problem-Solving Inventory for Adolescents.

Purpose: Designed to "measure self-reported covert and overt social problem solving behaviors in personal as well as social contexts."
Population: Grades 6-7, 9-10, college.
Publication Date: 2003.
Acronym: SPSI-A.
Scores, 13: Automatic Process, Problem Orientation (Cognition, Emotion, Behavior), Problem-Solving Skills (Problem Identification, Alternative Generation, Consequence Prediction, Implementation, Evaluation, Reorganization), Total Score.
Administration: Group.
Forms, 2: Long, Short.
Price Data, 2006: $6 per reproducible Electronic Long & Short versions; $19 per manual (2003, 114 pages); contact publisher for electronic scoring and interpretation pricing.
Foreign Language Editions: Long and Short versions available in English, Spanish, Romanian, and Persian.
Time: Administration time not reported.
Authors: Marianne Frauenknecht and David R. Black.
Publisher: SPSI-A, LLC.

a) LONG VERSION.
Population: Grades 9-10.
b) SHORT VERSION.
Population: Grades 6-7, 9-10, college.
Cross References: For reviews by Stephanie Stein and Claudia R. Wright, see 18:124.

[2497]

Social Problem-Solving Inventory–Revised.

Purpose: Designed to measure people's "ability to resolve problems of everyday living."
Population: Ages 13 and over.
Publication Dates: 1990–2002.
Acronym: SPSI-R.
Administration: Individual or group.
Price Data, 2011: $139 per complete kit including technical manual (2002, 100 pages), 25 long forms, and 25 short forms; $73 per technical manual; $50 per 25 long QuikScore™ forms; $50 per 25 short QuikScore™ forms.
Foreign Language Editions: Also available in French-Canadian, German, Russian, Spanish, and Turkish upon special request.
Authors: Thomas J. D'Zurilla, Arthur M. Nezu, and Albert Maydeu-Olivares.
Publisher: Multi-Health Systems, Inc.
a) LONG VERSION.
Acronym: SPSI-R: L.
Scores, 10: Positive Problem Orientation, Negative Problem Orientation, Rational Problem Solving (Problem Definition and Formulation, Generation of Alternative Solutions, Decision Making, Solution Implementation and Verification), Impulsivity/Carelessness Style, Avoidance Style and Total.
Time: (15–20) minutes.
b) SHORT VERSION.
Acronym: SPSI-R: S.
Scores, 5: Positive Problem Orientation, Negative Problem Orientation, Rational Problem Solving, Impulsivity/Carelessness Style, Avoidance Style.
Time: (10) minutes.
Cross References: For reviews by Pam Lindsey and Gretchen Owens, see 16:227.

[2498]

Social Responsiveness Scale.

Purpose: Designed to help "establish the diagnosis of autism spectrum conditions."
Population: Ages 4-18 years.
Publication Date: 2005.
Acronym: SRS.
Scores, 6: Social Awareness, Social Cognition, Social Communication, Social Motivation, Autistic Mannerisms, Total.
Administration: Group or individual.
Price Data, 2007: $91 per complete kit including 15 Parent AutoScore forms, 15 Teacher AutoScore

forms, and manual (69 pages); $50 per manual; $38.50 per 25 Parent AutoScore forms; $38.50 per 25 Teacher AutoScore forms, bulk discounts available; Computerized components: $115.50 per 25-use Windows SRS scoring CD, bulk discounts available; $16.50 per 100 PC answer sheets; $22 per Continuing Education Questionnaire and Evaluation Form.
Time: (15-20) minutes.
Comments: This test is to be completed by a parent, teacher, or other custodial caretaker.
Authors: John N. Constantino and Christian P. Gruber.
Publisher: Western Psychological Services.
Cross References: For reviews by Francine Conway and John J. Venn, see 17:173.

[2499]

Social Reticence Scale.

Purpose: To assess an individual's shyness.
Population: High school and college and adults.
Publication Date: 1986.
Acronym: SRTS.
Scores: Total score only.
Administration: Individual or group.
Price Data: Available from publisher at www.mind-garden.com/products/srtss.htm.
Time: (5-10) minutes.
Authors: Warren H. Jones and Stephen Briggs.
Publisher: Mind Garden, Inc.
Cross References: See T4:2499 (1 reference); for reviews by Owen Scott, III and William K. Wilkinson, see 11:370 (1 reference).

[2500]

Social Skills Improvement System Rating Scales.

Purpose: "Assists professionals in screening and classifying students suspected of having significant social skills deficits."
Population: Ages 3-18 years.
Publication Dates: 1990-2008.
Acronym: SSIS Rating Scales.
Scores, 51: 2 scale scores with 7 and 5 subscales, respectively, per teacher, parent, and student rater: Social Skills (Communication, Cooperation, Assertion, Responsibility, Empathy, Engagement, Self-Control) and Problem Behaviors (Externalizing, Bullying, Hyperactivity/Inattention, Internalizing, Autism Spectrum [not included on Student forms]), 1 Academic Competence Scale score [Teacher form only], and 3 Validity Indexes per rater (F Index, Response Pattern Index, Response Consistency Index).
Administration: Group.
Forms, 4: Teacher, Parent, Student (ages 8-12), Student (ages 13-18).
Price Data, 2010: $245.80 per Hand-Scored Starter Set (English) including Rating Scales manual (2008,

227 pages), 25 of each rating form; $322.60 per Hand-Scored Starter Set (English/Spanish) including Rating Scales manual and 25 of each rating form; $53.05 per 25 Computer-Entry (English) Teacher, Parent, Student (ages 8-12), or Student (ages 13-18) forms; $42.60 per 25 Hand-Scored (English) Teacher, Parent, Student (ages 8-12), or Student (ages 13-18) forms; $103 per Rating Scales manual; $254 per ASSIST Software CD-ROM (Win/Mac); $600.75 per Rating Scales ASSIST Software for Scanning CD-ROM (Win); additional Starter Sets available with ASSIST Software.

Foreign Language Edition: Spanish edition available for Parent and Student forms.

Time: (15-20) minutes.

Comments: Student form not administered for children age 7 and younger; revision of Social Skills Rating System (T7:2375); SSIS Rating Scales are part of larger Social Skills Improvement System, which includes SSIS Performance Screening Guide, SSIS Classwide Intervention Program, and SSIS Intervention Guide; hand-scored or computer-entry forms available for all Rating Scales; Parent and Student forms available as audio recordings; optional ASSIST Scoring and Reporting System Software available (computer-entry or scanning version).

Authors: Frank M. Gresham and Stephen N. Elliott.

Publisher: Pearson.

Cross References: For reviews by Beth Doll and Kristin Jones and by Jeanette Lee-Farmer and Joyce Meikamp, see 18:125; for information regarding the Social Skills Rating System, see T5:2452 (24 references); for reviews by Kathryn M. Benes and Michael Furlong and by Mitchell Karno of the Social Skills Rating System, see 12:362 (10 references); see also T4:2502 (4 references).

[2501]

Social Skills Inventory, Research Edition.

Purpose: "To assess basic social communication skills."

Population: Ages 14 and over reading at or above the eighth grade level.

Publication Date: 1989.

Acronym: SSI.

Scores, 7: Emotional Expressivity, Emotional Sensitivity, Emotional Control, Social Expressivity, Social Sensitivity, Social Control, Total.

Administration: Group and individual.

Price Data: Available from the publisher at www.mindgarden.com/products/ssins.htm.

Time: (30–45) minutes.

Comments: Test booklet title is Self-Description Inventory; self-administered; web version is available.

Author: Ronald E. Riggio.

Publisher: Mind Garden, Inc.

Cross References: See T5:2451 (4 references) and T4:2501 (4 references); for reviews by Judith C. Conger and Susan M. Sheridan, see 11:371 (3 references).

[2502]

Social Skills Training: Enhancing Social Competence with Children and Adolescents.

Purpose: Designed to measure social skills problems and help design appropriate intervention programs to develop social competence.

Population: Ages 5–18.

Publication Date: 1995.

Administration: Individual.

Forms, 3: Parent, Teacher, Pupil.

Price Data, 2004: Price data for user's guide (267 pages) photocopiable resource book, 8 photo cards, and research and technical supplement (37 pages) available from publisher.

Time: Administration time not reported.

Comments: Assessments are incorporated in Social Skills Training: Enhancing Social Competence with Children and Adolescents program.

Author: Susan H. Spence.

Publisher: GL Assessment [England].

a) SOCIAL COMPETENCE WITH PEERS QUESTIONNAIRE.

Forms, 3: Parent, Teacher, Pupil.

Scores, 3: Total score for each form.

b) SOCIAL WORRIES QUESTIONNAIRE.

Forms, 3: Parent, Teacher, Pupil.

Scores, 3: Total score for each form.

c) SOCIAL SITUATION CHECKLIST.

Scores, 1: Total score only.

d) SOCIAL SKILLS QUESTIONNAIRE.

Forms, 3: Parent, Teacher, Pupil.

Scores, 3: Total score for each form.

e) ASSESSMENT OF PERCEPTION OF EMOTION FROM FACIAL EXPRESSION.

Scores: Total score only.

f) ASSESSMENT OF PERCEPTION OF EMOTION FROM POSTURE CUES.

Scores: Total score only.

Cross References: For reviews by Kathleen M. Johnson and Caroline Manuele-Adkins, see 16:228.

[2503]

Social Styles Analysis.

Purpose: Constructed to identify a person's social style of presentation and interaction.

Population: Adults.

Publication Date: 1989.

Scores: 4 categories: Analytical, Driver, Amiable, Expressive.

Administration: Group.

Editions, 2: Self, Other.

Manual: No manual.

Price Data: Price information available from publisher for package for self analysis (5.25-inch or 3.5-inch diskette); package for other analyses (5.25-inch or 3.5-inch diskette).

Time: Administration time not reported.
Comments: IBM microcomputer necessary for scoring.
Author: Wilson Learning Corporation.
Publisher: Jossey-Bass, A Wiley Company.
Cross References: For a review by C. Dale Carpenter, see 11:372.

[2504]

Socio-Sexual Knowledge and Attitudes Assessment Tool–Revised.

Purpose: Designed to assess sexual knowledge and attitudes of individuals with developmental disabilities.
Population: Developmentally disabled adults (ages 16-71), can be used with other adults.
Publication Dates: 1976–2003.
Acronym: SSKAAT-R.
Scores, 8: Anatomy, Women's Bodies and Women's Knowledge of Men, Men's Bodies and Men's Knowledge of Women, Intimacy, Pregnancy/Childbirth and Child Rearing, Birth Control and STDs, Sexual Boundaries, Total.
Administration: Individual.
Price Data, 2005: $295 per complete kit including easel, stimulus cards, 20 record forms, and manual (2003, 47 pages); $55 per 20 record forms; $75 per training video (DVD format).
Time: Untimed.
Authors: Dorothy Griffiths and Yona Lunsky.
Publisher: Stoelting Co.
Cross References: For a review by Mary M. Clare, see 16:229; for a review by Edward S. Herold of an earlier edition, see 9:1152; see also T3:2237 (1 reference).

[2505]

Softball Skills Test.

Purpose: "To improve teaching and evaluation of softball skills."
Population: Grades 5-12 and college.
Publication Date: 1991.
Scores, 4: Batting, Fielding Ground Balls, Overhand Throwing, Baserunning.
Administration: Individual.
Price Data, 2001: $14 per manual (64 pages).
Time: Administration time not reported.
Author: Roberta E. Rikli, Editor.
Publisher: American Association for Active Lifestyles and Fitness.
Cross References: For a review by Don Sebolt, see 12:363.

[2506]

Solid Geometry: National Achievement Tests.

Purpose: To measure achievement in solid geometry.
Population: High school students.
Publication Dates: 1958–1960.
Scores: Total score only.

Administration: Group.
Forms, 2: A, B.
Price Data: Available from publisher.
Time: 40 minutes.
Comments: No specific manual; combined manual (1958, 12 pages) for this test and following tests: Plane Trigonometry (T6:1918), Plane Geometry (T6:1917), and First Year Algebra Test (T6:1003).
Authors: Ray Webb and Julius H. Hlavaty (manual).
Publisher: Psychometric Affiliates.
Cross References: For a review by Sheldon S. Myers, see 6:653.

[2507]

Sources of Stress Scale [2006 Revision].

Purpose: Designed as "an instrument to identify origins of perceived and current anxiety, to quantify the intensity of such stresses, and to determine the pattern of such perceptions for predictions and subsequent interventions."
Population: High school and adults.
Publication Dates: 1986-2006.
Acronym: S.O.S.S.
Administration: Group.
Price Data, 2006: $30 per 25 scales; $.40 per answer sheet; $30 per test manual (2006, 37 pages); $.30 per scoring scale; $.50 per answer sheet; $.25 for profile charts.
Time: [5-15] minutes per scale.
Comments: Self-rating scale.
Authors: Louise M. Soares and Anthony T. Soares.
Publisher: Castle Consultants.
  a) CORPORATE EXECUTIVE FORM.
  Scores: 12 categories: Daily Issues, Professional Issues, Internal Personnel, Outside Influence, Changes, Finances/Money, The Future, Health, My Personal Life, Myself, Personal Relationships, Time Management.
  b) GRADUATE STUDENT FORM.
  Scores: 12 categories: Campus Life, Academic Activities, Field Experiences, College Personnel, plus last 8 categories from *a* above.
  c) CORPORATE EXECUTIVE FORM.
  Scores: 12 categories: Daily Issues, Professional Issues, Internal Personnel, Outside Influence, Changes, Finances/Money, The Future, Health, My Personal Life, Myself, Personal Relationships, Time Management.
  d) HIGH SCHOOL FORM.
  Scores: 12 categories: Extracurricular Activities, Academic Activities, Life at School, High School, plus last 8 categories from *a* above.
  e) NURSING FORM.
  Scores: 12 categories: Same as *a* above.
  f) PARENT FORM.
  Scores: 12 categories: Children, Family Issues, Spouse/Partner, Work/Job/Occupation, plus last 8 categories from *a* above.

g) POLITICIAN FORM.
Scores: 12 categories: Same as *a* above.
h) SCHOOL ADMINISTRATOR FORM.
Scores: 12 categories: Instructional Leadership, Organizational Issues, Legal & Political Issues, Resource Allocation, plus last 8 categories from *a* above.
i) SENIOR CITIZEN FORM.
Scores: 12 categories: Same as *f* above but including Quality of Life Issues and excluding Work/Job/Occupation.
j) TEACHER FORM.
Scores: 12 categories: Classroom Issues, Professional Issues, School Issues, plus last 9 categories from *a* above.
k) YOUNG ADULTS FORM.
Scores: 12 categories: Same as *f* above.
Cross References: For reviews by Deborah Bandalos and by Jerrell C. Cassady and Molly M. Jameson, see 17:174; for reviews by JoAnn Murphey and Wesley E. Sime of an earlier edition, see 15:235.

[2508]
The Southern California Ordinal Scales of Development.
Purpose: To provide "differential assessment of educational needs and abilities."
Population: Multihandicapped, developmentally delayed, and learning disabled children.
Publication Dates: 1977–1985.
Acronym: SCOSD.
Scores: 6 scales: Cognition, Communication, Social-Affective Behavior, Practical Abilities, Fine Motor Abilities, Gross Motor Abilities.
Administration: Individual.
Price Data, 2002: $130 per complete instrument.
Time: (60–120) minutes per scale.
Comments: A Piagetian-based assessment system.
Authors: Donald I. Ashurst, Elaine Bamberg, Julika Barrett, Ann Bisno, Artice Burke, David C. Chambers, Jean Fentiman, Ronald Kadish, Mary Lou Mitchell, Lambert Neeley, Todd Thorne, and Doris Wents.
Publisher: Foreworks.
Cross References: See T5:2459 (1 reference); for reviews by Cameron J. Camp and Arlene C. Rosenthal, see 10:338.

[2509]
Space Relations (Paper Puzzles).
Purpose: Developed as an assessment of mechanical aptitude.
Population: Ages 17 and over.
Publication Dates: 1984–1996.
Scores: Total score only.
Administration: Group.
Price Data, 2002: $91 per start-up kit including 25 test booklets, score key, and interpretation and research

manual; $54 per 25 tests; $28 per interpretation and research manual; $20 per score key.
Time: (9) minutes.
Authors: L. L. Thurstone and T. E. Jeffrey.
Publisher: Pearson Performance Solutions [No reply from publisher; status unknown].
Cross References: For reviews by Phillip L. Ackerman and Mark A. Albanese, see 15:236.

[2510]
Space Thinking (Flags).
Purpose: To measure the ability to visualize a stable figure, drawing or diagram when it is moved into different positions.
Population: Industrial employees.
Publication Dates: 1959–1984.
Scores: Total score only.
Administration: Individual or group.
Price Data, 2002: $91 per start-up kit including 25 test booklets, score key, and interpretation and research manual; $54 per 25 test booklets (quantity discounts available); $20 per score key; $28 per interpretation and research manual.
Time: 5 minutes.
Authors: L. L. Thurstone and T. E. Jeffrey.
Publisher: Pearson Performance Solutions [No reply from publisher; status unknown].
Cross References: See T4:2515 (1 reference), T3:898 (1 reference), and T2:2245 (1 reference); for a review by I. MacFarlane Smith, see 6:1086.

[2511]
Spadafore ADHD Rating Scale.
Purpose: Designed "to examine the wide range of behaviors that are frequently associated with ADHD symptoms."
Population: Ages 5 through 19.
Publication Date: 1997.
Acronym: S-ADHD-RS.
Scores, 4: Impulsivity/Hyperactivity, Attention, Social Adjustment, ADHD Index.
Administration: Individual.
Price Data, 2006: $80 per test kit including manual (80 pages) 25 scoring protocols, 25 observation forms, and 25 medication tracking forms; $25 per 25 scoring protocols; $15 per 25 observation forms; $15 per 25 medication tracking forms; $25 per manual.
Time: Untimed.
Comments: Rating scale to be completed by classroom teachers about a child; also included in kit: behavioral observation form and medication monitoring form; previously listed as Spadafore Attention Deficit Hyperactivity Disorder Rating Scale.
Authors: Gerald J. Spadafore and Sharon J. Spadafore.
Publisher: Academic Therapy Publications.
Cross References: For reviews by Scott T. Meier and Judy Oehler-Stinnett, see 14:364.

[2512]

Spadafore Diagnostic Reading Test.

Purpose: Constructed to assess decoding and comprehension skills in reading.
Population: Grades 1–12; ages 6 through adults.
Publication Date: 1983.
Acronym: SDRT.
Scores, 15: 3 performance levels (Independent, Instructional, Frustration) for each of 5 subtests (Decoding [Word Recognition, Oral Reading], Comprehension [Oral Reading, Silent Reading, Listening]).
Administration: Individual.
Price Data, 2006: $65 per complete kit including manual (60 pages), test plates, and 10 test booklets; $28 per set of test plates; $15 per 10 test booklets; $22 per manual; $22 per specimen set.
Time: (30–60) minutes.
Comments: Criterion-referenced.
Author: Gerald J. Spadafore.
Publisher: Academic Therapy Publications.
Cross References: See T4:2516 (1 reference); for a review by James R. Sanders and Blaine R. Worthen, see 9:1159.

[2513]

Spanish Assessment of Basic Education, Second Edition.

Purpose: "Designed to measure achievement in the basic skills … with students for whom Spanish is the language of instruction."
Population: Grades 1.0–1.9, 1.6–2.9, 2.6–3.9, 3.6–4.9, 4.6–6.9, 7.0–8.9.
Publication Dates: 1991–1994.
Acronym: SABE/2.
Administration: Group.
Price Data, 2006: $24 per 35 practice tests (select level); $63 per 100 student diagnostic profiles (select level); $24 per 35 parent reports (select level); $3.15 per class record sheet; $23 per examiner's manual (1991, 41–57 pages) (select level); $27 per user's guide (1991, 64 pages); $31 per technical report (1994, 43 pages); $23 per norms book (1994, 159 pages); scoring service available from publisher.
Author: CTB Macmillan/McGraw-Hill.
Publisher: CTB/McGraw-Hill.
a) LEVEL 1.
Population: Grades 1.0–1.9.
Scores, 11: Word Attack, Vocabulary, Reading Comprehension, Mechanics, Expression, Mathematics Computation, Mathematics Concepts and Applications, Total Reading, Total Mathematics, Total Language, Total Battery.
Price Data: $228 per 35 scannable test books.
Time: (205) minutes.
b) LEVEL 2.
Population: Grades 1.6–2.9.

Scores: Same as *a* above.
Price Data: Same as *a* above.
Time: (219) minutes.
c) LEVEL 3.
Population: Grades 2.6–3.9.
Scores: Same as *a* above.
Price Data: Same as *a* above.
Time: (255) minutes.
d) LEVEL 4.
Population: Grades 3.6–4.9.
Scores, 12: Vocabulary, Reading Comprehension, Spelling, Mechanics, Expression, Mathematics Computation, Mathematics Concepts and Applications, Study Skills, Total Reading, Total Mathematics, Total Language, Total Battery.
Price Data: $179 per 35 reusable test books; $68 per 50 answer sheets (for CompuScan® or handscoring); $72 per set of 3 handscoring stencils.
Time: (249) minutes.
e) LEVEL 5.
Population: Grades 4.6–6.9.
Scores: Same as *d* above.
Price Data: Same as *d* above.
Time: (260) minutes.
f) LEVEL 6.
Population: Grades 7.0–8.9.
Scores: Same as *d* above.
Price Data: Same as *d* above.
Time: (259) minutes.
Cross References: For reviews by Maria Prendes Lintel and Emelia C. Lopez, see 13:291.

[2514]

Spanish/English Reading Comprehension Test [Revised].

Purpose: Designed to "determine the degrees of bilingualism."
Population: Grades 1–6.
Publication Dates: 1974–1993.
Scores: Total score and grade level equivalents.
Administration: Group or individual.
Forms, 2: English, Spanish.
Price Data, 2006: $20 per packet including manual (1993, 42 pages) and 1 English and 1 Spanish rating/answer sheet (permission to copy answer sheets is included).
Time: (30) minutes.
Comments: Spanish Reading based on Mexican curriculum materials; English Reading based on U.S.A. curriculum materials; English Reading Comprehension Test is translated from the Spanish version; pretesting and posttesting used.
Author: Steve Moreno.
Publisher: Moreno Educational Co.
Cross References: For reviews by Jorge E. Gonzalez and Craig S. Shwery and by Salvador Hector Ochoa, see 15:237; for reviews by Esteban L. Olmedo and David T. Sanchez, see 9:1161.

[2515]

Spanish Reading Inventory.

Purpose: To help teachers and other professionals determine a student's reading proficiency in Spanish.
Population: Grades 1–4+.
Publication Date: 1997.
Scores, 7: Independent, Instructional, Frustration, Word Recognition in Isolation, Word Recognition in Context, Comprehension-Oral, Comprehension-Silent.
Administration: Individual.
Forms, 2: A, B.
Price Data, 2003: $52.95 per complete kit (specify Form A or Form B); $32.95 per performance booklets (specify Form A or Form B).
Time: Administration time not reported.
Author: Jerry L. Johns.
Publisher: Kendall/Hunt Publishing Company.
Cross References: For a review by Salvador Hector Ochoa, see 16:230.

[2516]

SPAR Spelling and Reading Tests, Third Edition.

Purpose: Designed as a "group test of literacy."
Population: Ages 7-0 to 12-11 years.
Publication Dates: 1976–1998.
Acronym: SPAR.
Scores, 2: Reading Total Score, Spelling Total Score.
Administration: Group.
Parts, 2: Reading Test, Spelling Test.
Price Data, 2002: £7.99 per 20 For A or Form B; £9.99 per manual (1976, 32 pages) including photocopiable version of spelling test; £4.99 per scoring template (A or B); £11.99 per specimen set including 1 copy each of Test Forms A and B, and manual.
Time: 13 minutes for Spelling Test; (20–25) minutes for Reading Test.
Comments: Reading Test is available in parallel Forms (A and B); Spelling Test is created from three parallel banks of items found in the manual.
Author: Dennis Young.
Publisher: Hodder & Stoughton Educational [England].
Cross References: For reviews by Timothy Z. Keith and Brenda A. Stevens, see 14:365; see also T5:2467 (1 reference); for reviews by Cleborne D. Maddux and William R. Merz, Sr. of the second edition, see 12:365 (2 references); see also T4:2520 (3 references); for reviews by J. Douglas Ayers of earlier editions of the Spelling Test and the Reading Test, see 8:76 and 8:742.

[2517]

Spatial Awareness Skills Program.

Purpose: Constructed to identify "children whose spatial awareness skills are developing more slowly than expected" and provide "information about how to remedy a deficit."

Population: Ages 4 to 10.
Publication Date: 1999.
Acronym: SASP.
Scores: Total score only.
Administration: Individual.
Price Data, 2010: $126 per complete kit including curriculum manual, instrument manual, 25 student response booklets, and scoring transparency; $50 per 25 student response booklets.
Time: (5) minutes.
Comments: Previously titled Test of Visual Analysis Skills (T5:2721); designed to be used with the Spatial Awareness Skills Program (SASP) Curriculum; criterion-referenced.
Author: Jerome Rosner.
Publisher: PRO-ED.
Cross References: For reviews by Connie T. England and Robert M. Thorndike, see 15:238.

[2518]

Spatial Reasoning.

Purpose: Designed to assess "a pupil's ability to manipulate shapes and patterns."
Population: Ages 5.4–15.5.
Publication Date: 2002.
Scores: Total score only.
Administration: Group.
Levels, 4: Age 6 and 7; Age 8 and 9; Age 10 and 11; Ages 12–14.
Price Data: Available from publisher.
Time: 20(35–40) minutes for Age 6 and 7; 27(40–45) minutes for Age 8 and 9; 28(45) minutes for Age 10 and 11; 33(45–50) minutes for Ages 12–14.
Comments: Designed to complement the publisher's Verbal (2853) and Non-Verbal Reasoning (1848) series of tests.
Authors: Pauline Smith and Thomas R. Lord.
Publisher: GL Assessment [England].
Cross References: For reviews by Kathy Bohan and Beth Doll, see 16:231.

[2519]

Speaking Proficiency English Assessment Kit.

Purpose: "To assess the English speaking proficiency of people who are not native speakers of English."
Population: Nonnative speakers of English.
Publication Date: 1996.
Acronym: SPEAK.
Scores: Total score only.
Administration: Individual or group.
Price Data: Available from publisher.
Time: (20) minutes.
Comments: Produced by the Test of English as a Foreign Language Program; provides a measure of an individual's speaking ability at the intermediate to advanced levels for

English language programs, international teaching assistant training programs, and businesses.
Author: Educational Testing Service.
Publisher: Educational Testing Service.

[2520]

Speech and Language Evaluation Scale.

Purpose: "Designed for in-school screening and referral of students with speech and language problems."
Population: Ages 4.5-18.
Publication Dates: 1989-1990.
Acronym: SLES.
Scores, 6: Speech (Articulation, Voice, Fluency), Language (Form, Content, Pragmatics).
Administration: Individual.
Price Data, 2006: $135 per complete kit including 50 pre-referral checklist forms, 50 pre-referral intervention strategies documentation forms, technical manual (1989, 47 pages), 50 rating forms, and Speech and Language Classroom Intervention Manual (1990, 206 pages); $30 per 50 pre-referral checklist forms; $30 per 50 intervention strategies documentation forms; $15 per technical manual; $35 per 50 rating forms; $25 per Speech and Language Intervention Manual; $25 per computerized quick score (WIN).
Time: (15-20) minutes.
Comments: Ratings by teachers.
Authors: Diane R. Fressola, Sandra Cipponeri-Hoerchler, Jacquelyn S. Hagan, Steven B. McDannold, Jacqueline Meyer (manual), and Stephen B. McCarney (technical manual).
Publisher: Hawthorne Educational Services, Inc.
Cross References: For reviews by Katharine G. Butler and Penelope K. Hall, see 12:367.

[2521]

Speech-Ease Screening Inventory (K–1).

Purpose: "Designed to screen the articulation, language development," and auditory comprehension of kindergartners and first-graders.
Population: Grades K–1.
Publication Date: 1985.
Scores: Item scores only in 5 areas (Articulation, Language Association, Auditory Recall, Vocabulary, Basic Concepts) and in 4 optional areas (Auditory, Similarities and Differences, Language Sample, Linguistic Relationships) plus 5 observational ratings (Voice Quality, Fluency, Syntax, Oral-Peripheral, Hearing).
Administration: Individual.
Price Data, 2011: $115 per complete kit; $38 per 100 screening forms; $31 per 50 summary sheets (specify kindergarten or first grade); $47 per manual (32 pages).
Time: (7-10) minutes.
Authors: Teryl Pigott, Jane Barry, Barbara Hughes, Debra Eastin, Patricia Titus, Harriett Stensel, Kathleen Metcalf, and Belinda Porter.

Publisher: PRO-ED.
Cross References: For reviews by Kris L. Baack and Eleanor E. Sanford, see 12:368.

[2522]

Speech Evaluation of the Patient with a Tracheostomy Tube.

Purpose: Designed to help speech-language pathologists "assess the potential of an adult patient with an artificial airway to use a device that promotes phonation."
Population: Adults with artificial airways.
Publication Dates: 1994–1997.
Scores: 6 evaluative areas: Current Airway Assessment Information, Ventilation Status, Nutritional and Swallowing Status, Clinical Observations/Assessment, Patient Goals, Recommendations.
Administration: Individual.
Price Data, 2006: $61 per kit including manual (1997, 124 pages) and reproducible diagrams and laminated evaluation report form.
Time: Administration time not reported.
Comments: Not a standardized test but author provides clinical recommendations based on the information provided on a patient's report form.
Author: Nancy Conway.
Publisher: PRO-ED.

[2523]

Speech Perception Instructional Curriculum and Evaluation.

Purpose: "Designed to provide a guide for developing listening skills in severely and profoundly deaf children."
Population: Hearing-impaired individuals ages 3–12.
Publication Date: 1995.
Acronym: SPICE.
Scores: Rates total of 16 goals within 4 categories: Detection (Detects Speech, Indicates Onset and Termination of Speech), Suprasegmental Perception (Discriminates between 2 Stimuli Differing in Duration/Stress/and/or Intonation, Identifies Among 3 Stimuli Differing in Duration/Stress/and/or Intonation, Identifies Among 4 Stimuli Differing in Duration/Stress/and/or Intonation, Differentiates Stimuli With Similar Duration but Differing in Stress and/or Intonation; Identifies Among Sentences Differing Only in Duration of Key Words, Vowels and Consonants (Identifies Among Six Sounds, Identifies Words of Similar Duration and Differing in Vowels and/or Consonants, Identifies Monosyllables With the Same Consonants and Differing Vowels; Engages in Discussion About a Familiar Topic, Engages in Connected Discourse Tracking), Connected Speech (Identifies Key Words in the Context of Sentences, Practiced Sentences, Converses Using Picture Context, Engaged in Discussion About a Familiar Topic, Engages in Connected Discourse Tracking.

Administration: Individual.
Price Data, 2011: $375 per complete kit including manual (221 pages), rating forms, box of 16 toys for listening activities, 374 illustrated word and sentence cards, auditory training screen; $20 additional auditory training screen.
Time: Administration time not reported.
Comments: Informally documents present auditory skill level, helps identify instructional objectives; instructional videotape contains 18 teaching segments; can be adapted for individuals over age 12 through adult.
Authors: Jean S. Moog, Julia J. Biedenstein, and Lisa S. Davidson.
Publisher: Central Institute for the Deaf (CID).

[2524]

The Speed and Capacity of Language Processing Test.

Purpose: "Designed to provide a wholistic measure of the efficacy of language comprehension."
Population: Ages 16–65.
Publication Date: 1992.
Acronym: SCOLP.
Scores, 2: The Speed of Comprehension Test, The Spot-the-Word Test.
Administration: Individual.
Price Data, 2006: £92 per complete kit including manual (16 pages), 3 acetates, and 6 packs of 25 scoring sheets; £18 per 25 scoring sheets (specify Speed of Comprehension Test A, Speed of Comprehension Test B, Speed of Comprehension Test C, Speed of Comprehension Test D, Spot-the-Word Vocabulary Test A, or Spot-the-Word Vocabulary Test B).
Time: Untimed.
Comments: Each subtest comes with different versions for the purpose of retesting: The Speed of Comprehension Test has 4 versions (A, B, C, D) and The Spot-the-Word Test has 2 versions (A, B).
Authors: Alan Baddeley, Hazel Emslie, and Ian Nimmo-Smith.
Publisher: Pearson Assessment [England].
Cross References: For a review by Kay B. Stevens and J. Randall Price, see 17:175.

[2525]

Spelling Performance Evaluation for Language and Literacy, Second Edition.

Purpose: Designed to identify language knowledge deficits based on analysis of "a student's patterns of misspelling."
Population: Grades 2-12 and adults.
Publication Dates: 2002-2006.
Acronym: SPELL-2.
Scores, 5: Phonological Awareness, Orthographic Knowledge, Morphological Knowledge, Semantic Relationships, Mental Orthographic Images.

Administration: Individual.
Price Data, 2007: $445 per complete kit including examiner's manual (2006, 138 pages), CD-ROM for single computer use, unlimited administrations; $150 for pay-per-student kit including examiner's manual, CD-ROM for single computer use, single administration credit ($75 per additional test session); volume discounts available.
Time: (30-90) minutes.
Comments: Test is computer adaptive; student performance will determine which of 11 test modules are to be administered.
Authors: Julie J. Masterson, Kenn Apel, and Jan Wasowicz.
Publisher: Learning by Design
Cross References: For reviews by Sharon deFur and Kay Stevens, see 18:126.

[2526]

Spelling Test: National Achievement Tests.

Purpose: Assesses achievement in the spelling of common words.
Population: Grades 3–4, 5–8, 7–9, 10–12.
Publication Dates: 1936–1957.
Scores: Total score only.
Administration: Group.
Manual: No manual.
Price Data: Available from publisher.
Time: (25) minutes.
Comments: 1956–1957 tests identical to tests copyrighted 1939.
Authors: Robert K. Speer and Samuel Smith.
Publisher: Psychometric Affiliates.
Cross References: For a review by James A. Fitzgerald, see 5:230; for a review by W. J. Osburn, see 1:1161.

[2527]

Spiritual Well-Being Scale.

Purpose: "Developed as a general indicator of the subjective state of religious and existential well-being."
Population: Adults.
Publication Dates: 1982-1991.
Acronym: SWBS.
Scores, 3: Religious Well-Being, Existential Well-Being, Total Spiritual Well-Being.
Administration: Individual or group.
Price Data, 2001: $20 per specimen set including scale, manual (1991, 6 pages), bibliography, and scoring and research information; $2.25 or less per scale; volume discounts and student discounts available.
Time: (10-15) minutes.
Comments: Even-numbered items produce Existential Well-Being Scale (EWB); odd-numbered items produce Religious Well-Being Scale (RWB).
Authors: Craig W. Ellison and Raymond F. Paloutzian.
Publisher: Life Advance, Inc.

Cross References: See T5:2474 (1 reference); for reviews by Ayres D'Costa and Patricia Schoenrade, see 12:369 (1 reference); see also T4:2529 (1 reference).

[2528]
Sport Personality Questionnaire.

Purpose: "Designed to provide information about the personality and mental factors that contribute to elite performance in sport. It is intended to be used by sport psychologists and coaches to help athletes understand and develop the mental skills needed to perform successfully in competition."
Population: Athletes ages 16 to 65.
Publication Date: 2011.
Acronym: SPQ20.
Scores, 27: 20 Scale scores (Competitiveness, Aggressiveness, Self-Efficacy, Flow, Achievement, Power, Conscientiousness, Ethics, Adaptability, Self-Awareness, Intuition, Relationships, Empathy, Emotions, Managing Pressure, Fear of Failure, Burnout, Self-Talk, Visualization, Goal Setting); 7 Summary scores (Overall Mental Skills, Leadership Potential, Achievement and Competitiveness, Confidence and Resilience, Interaction and Sportsmanship, Power and Agressiveness, Response Style).
Administration: Group.
Price Data, 2011: $14.95 per test.
Time: [15-20] minutes.
Comments: Assessment, scoring, and feedback conducted online.
Author: MySkillsProfile.com, Ltd.
Publisher: MySkillsProfile.com, Limited [England].

[2529]
Sports Emotion Test.

Purpose: "Designed to show how an athlete responds affectively to a competition."
Population: High school through adult athletes.
Publication Dates: 1980-1983.
Acronym: SET.
Scores, 24: 4 scores (Intensity, Concentration, Anxiety, Physical Readiness) for 6 different points in time (24 Hours Before, At Breakfast, Just Before, After Start, At Peak, Something Wrong).
Administration: Group.
Price Data: License to reproduce for PhDs and EdDs available from publisher.
Time: (10-20) minutes.
Authors: E. R. Oetting and C. W. Cole (profile).
Publisher: E. R. Oetting, Colorado State University.
Cross References: For reviews by Robert D. Brown and Robert P. Markley, see 10:339.

[2530]
Spousal Assault Risk Assessment Guide.

Purpose: "Helps criminal justice professionals predict the likelihood of domestic violence."
Population: Individuals suspected of or being treated for spousal or family-related assault.
Publication Date: 1999.
Acronym: SARA.
Scores: Total score only.
Administration: Individual.
Price Data, 2010: $95 per complete kit including 25 checklist forms, 25 assessment forms, and manual; $35 per 25 QuikScore forms; $24 per 25 checklist forms; $44 per manual.
Time: Administration time not reported.
Comments: Completed by clinician/rater (criminal justice professional) after all available sources of information from suspect/offender, victim, etc. are gathered.
Authors: P. Randall Kropp, Stephen D. Hart, Christopher D. Webster, and Derek Eaves.
Publisher: Multi-Health Systems, Inc.
Cross References: For reviews by Ira S. Katz and Michael J. Scheel, see 15:239.

[2531]
Standard Progressive Matrices, New Zealand Standardization.

Purpose: Designed as a measure of nonverbal reasoning skills.
Population: New Zealand children ages 8–15 and adults.
Publication Date: 1985.
Acronym: SPM.
Scores: Total score only.
Administration: Group.
Price Data: Available from publisher.
Time: 30 minutes.
Authors: J. Raven (manual), J. C. Raven (manual), J. H. Court (manual), and New Zealand Council for Educational Research.
Publisher: New Zealand Council for Educational Research [New Zealand].
Cross References: See T5:2478 (2 references); for information on all editions of the Progressive Matrices, see 9:1007 (67 references), T3:1914 (200 references), 8:200 (190 references), T2:439 (122 references), and 7:376 (194 references); for a review by Morton Bortner, see 6:490 (78 references); see also 5:370 (62 references); for reviews by Charlotte Banks, W. D. Wall, and George Westby, see 4:314 (32 references); for reviews by Walter C. Shipley and David Wechsler of the 1938 edition, see 3:258 (13 references); for a review by T. J. Keating, see 2:1417 (8 references).

[2532]
The Standard Timing Model.

Purpose: "Designed to simulate the motions, functions and operations of automatic production machines" for use in selection, evaluation, and training of employees.
Population: Mechanics, electricians, and operators.
Publication Date: 1971.

Scores: 4 tasks.
Administration: Individual.
Price Data: Available from publisher.
Time: [60] minutes.
Author: Scientific Management Techniques, Inc.
Publisher: Scientific Management Techniques, Inc.
Cross References: For reviews by Sami Gulgoz and Gary L. Marco, see 12:370.

[2533]

Standardized Bible Content Tests, Forms I and J.

Purpose: Intended for "assessment of biblical knowledge (Bible/Theology/World View)."
Population: College freshman and seniors.
Publication Dates: 1956-1996.
Acronym: SBCT.
Scores: Total score only.
Administration: Group or individual.
Restricted Distribution: Open to any Bible college.
Price Data, 2009: ABHE Member institutions 1.50 per exam; non-members $3.50 per exam.
Time: (45) minutes.
Author: Commission on Professional Development of the Accrediting Association of Bible Colleges.
Publisher: Association for Biblical Higher Education.
Cross References: See 7:651 (1 reference).

[2534]

Standardized Reading Inventory, Second Edition.

Purpose: "Designed primarily to assess children's independent, instructional, and frustration reading levels in word recognition and comprehension skills."
Population: Ages 6-0 to 14-6.
Publication Dates: 1986–1999.
Acronym: SRI-2.
Scores, 4: Passage, Comprehension, Word Accuracy, Vocabulary in Context, Reading Quotient.
Administration: Individual.
Forms, 2: A, B.
Price Data, 2011: $306 per complete kit including manual (1999, 134 pages), story book, 25 each Forms A and B vocabulary sheets, 25 each Forms A and B record booklets, and 50 profile scoring forms; $24 per 25 vocabulary sheets (specify form); $64 per 25 record booklets (specify form); $29 per 50 profile scoring forms; $50 per story book; $59 per examiner's manual.
Time: (30–90) minutes.
Comments: Second Edition is norm-referenced.
Author: Phyllis L. Newcomer.
Publisher: PRO-ED.
Cross References: For reviews by Alan Solomon and Brenda A. Stevens, see 14:366; for reviews by Kenneth W. Howell and Cleborne D. Maddux of the original edition, see 10:340.

[2535]

Standardized Test of Computer Literacy and Computer Anxiety Index (Version AZ), Revised.

Purpose: To measure general computer literacy and identify students who have computer-related anxieties.
Population: Students in introductory computer literacy courses.
Publication Date: 1984.
Acronym: STCL and CAIN.
Administration: Group.
Price Data: Available from publisher.
Authors: Michael Simonson, Mary Montag (manual and achievement test), and Matt Maurer (manual and anxiety survey).
Publisher: Iowa State University Research Foundation, Inc. [No reply from publisher; status unknown].
a) STANDARDIZED TEST OF COMPUTER LITERACY (VERSION AZ), REVISED.
Purpose: Measures achievement in computer literacy.
Scores, 3: Computer Systems, Computer Applications, Computer Programming.
Time: 90(105) minutes.
Comments: May be administered in one session or in separate sessions for each of 3 sections.
b) COMPUTER ANXIETY INDEX.
Time: Administration time not reported.
Comments: Test booklet title is Computer Opinion Survey.
Cross References: For reviews by Ron Edwards and Kevin L. Moreland, see 10:341.

[2536]

Stanford Achievement Test–Abbreviated Version–8th Edition.

Purpose: "Measures student achievement in reading, mathematics, language, spelling, study skills, science, social science, and listening."
Population: Primary (1.5–4.5), Intermediate (4.5–7.5), Advanced (7.5–9.9), TASK (9.0–12.9).
Publication Dates: 1989–1992.
Administration: Group.
Price Data, 2002: $52 per examination kit (for preview only) including complete battery test booklet, directions for administering, practice test with directions (Primary 1 through Advanced 2 only), and hand-scorable answer document (Primary 3 through TASK 3 only); $29 per 25 complete/partial battery hand-scorable test booklets; $21 per copy of directions for administration (specify level); $7.50 per copy of class records; $64 per fall or spring national norms booklet (1988), and $103 per SAT abbreviated national norms booklet (1991).
Comments: For fall testing, the publisher recommends the use of the previous grade level test.
Author: The Psychological Corporation.
Publisher: Pearson.

a) PRIMARY 1.
Population: Grades 1.5–2.5.
Scores, 12: Word Study Skills, Word Reading, Reading Comprehension, Total Reading, Language/English, Spelling, Listening, Concepts of Number, Mathematics Computation, Mathematics Applications, Total Mathematics, Environment.
Price Data: $156 per 25 complete battery Type 2 machine-scorable test booklets; $129 per 25 hand-scorable test booklets; $39.80 for keys for hand scoring (hand scoring requires Norms Booklets) complete/partial battery hand-scorable test booklets (Primary 1–Primary 3).
Time: 167 minutes for Partial battery; 187 minutes for Basic battery; 210 minutes for Complete battery.
b) PRIMARY 2.
Population: Grades 2.5–3.5.
Scores, 12: Word Study Skills, Reading Vocabulary, Reading Comprehension, Total Reading, Language/English, Spelling, Listening, Concepts of Numbers, Mathematics Computation, Mathematics Applications, Total Mathematics, Environment.
Price Data: Same as *a* above.
Time: 160 minutes for Partial battery; 180 minutes for Basic battery; 203 minutes for Complete battery.
c) PRIMARY 3.
Population: Grades 3.5–4.5.
Scores, 16: Word Study Skills, Reading Vocabulary, Reading Comprehension, Total Reading, Language Mechanics, Language Expression, Total Language, Study Skills, Spelling, Listening, Concepts of Number, Mathematics Computation, Mathematics Applications, Total Mathematics, Science, Social Science.
Price Data: $156 per 25 complete battery machine-scorable test booklets; $129 per 25 complete battery hand-scorable test booklets; $156 per 25 Type 2 partial battery machine-scorable test booklets; $129 per 25 partial battery hand-scorable test booklets; $129 per 25 complete battery reusable test booklets; $129 per 25 partial battery reusable test booklets; $117 per 100 complete/partial battery Type 2 machine-scorable answer folders; $29 per 25 Form J complete/partial battery hand-scorable answer folders; $46 per keys for hand scoring complete battery hand-scorable answer folders (Primary 3–TASK 3).
Time: 152 minutes for Partial battery; 197 minutes for Basic battery; 233 minutes for Complete battery.
d) INTERMEDIATE 1–3.
Population: Grades 4.5–7.5.
Scores, 15: Reading Vocabulary, Reading Comprehension, Total Reading, Language Mechanics, Language Expression, Total Language, Study Skills, Spelling, Listening, Concepts of Numbers, Mathematics Computation, Mathematics Applications, Total Mathematics, Science, Social Science.
Price Data: $129 per 25 complete battery reusable test booklets; $128 per 25 partial battery reusable

test booklets; $117 per 100 complete/partial battery Type 2 machine-scorable answer folders; $29 per 25 Form J complete/partial battery hand-scorable answer folders; $46 per keys for hand scoring complete battery hand-scorable answer folders (Primary 3–TASK 3); see *c* above for additional price information.
Time: 142 minutes for Partial battery; 187 minutes for Basic battery; 223 minutes for Complete battery.
e) ADVANCED 1–2.
Population: Grades 7–8.
Scores, 15: Reading Vocabulary, Reading Comprehension, Total Reading, Language Mechanics, Language Expression, Total Language, Study Skills, Spelling, Listening, Concepts of Numbers, Mathematics Computation, Mathematics Applications, Total Mathematics, Science, Social Science.
Price Data: Same as *d* above.
Time: 142 minutes for Partial battery; 186 minutes for Basic battery; 222 minutes for Complete battery.
f) TASK 1–3.
Population: Grades 9–12.
Scores, 9: Reading Vocabulary, Reading Comprehension, Total Reading, Language/English, Study Skills, Spelling, Mathematics, Science, Social Science.
Price Data: $118 per 25 complete battery reusable test booklets; $117 per 100 complete/partial battery Type 2 machine-scorable answer folders; $29 per 25 Form J complete/partial battery hand-scorable answer folders.
Time: 95 minutes for Partial battery; 119 minutes for Basic battery; 155 minutes for Complete battery.
Cross References: See T5:2483 (1 reference); for reviews by Stephen N. Elliott, James A. Wollack, and Kevin L. Moreland, see 12:371.

[2537]

Stanford Achievement Test, Tenth Edition.

Purpose: Measures student achievement in reading, language, spelling, study skills, listening, mathematics, science and social science.
Population: Grades K.0–12.9.
Publication Dates: 1923–2003.
Acronym: Stanford 10.
Administration: Group.
Forms, 4: A, B, D, E.
Levels, 13: Stanford Early School Achievement Test 1, Stanford Early School Achievement Test 2, Primary 1, Primary 2, Primary 3, Intermediate 1, Intermediate 2, Intermediate 3, Advanced 1, Advanced 2, Stanford Test of Academic Skills 1, Stanford Test of Academic Skills 2, Stanford Test of Academic Skills 3.
Price Data: Available from publisher.
Comments: A variety of assessment options are available including full-length and abbreviated multiple-choice batteries; large-print and Braille editions are available.

Author: Harcourt Assessment, Inc.
Publisher: Pearson.

a) STANFORD EARLY SCHOOL ACHIEVEMENT TEST 1.
Population: Grades K.0–K.5.
Acronym: SESAT 1.
Forms, 2: Basic Battery, Complete Battery.
Scores, 6: Reading (Sounds and Letters, Word Reading, Total), Mathematics, Listening to Words and Stories, Environment.
Time: (105) minutes for Basic Battery; (135) minutes for Complete Battery.

b) STANFORD EARLY SCHOOL ACHIEVEMENT TEST 2.
Population: Grades K.5–1.5.
Acronym: SESAT 2.
Forms, 2: Basic Battery, Complete Battery.
Scores, 7: Reading (Sounds and Letters, Word Reading, Sentence Reading, Total), Mathematics, Listening to Words and Stories, Environment.
Time: (140) minutes for Basic Battery; (170) minutes for Complete Battery.

c) PRIMARY 1.
Population: Grades 1.5–2.5.
Forms, 4: Basic Battery, Complete Battery, Abbreviated Battery, Language.
Scores, 11-12: Reading (Word Study Skills, Word Reading, Sentence Reading, Reading Comprehension, Total), Mathematics (Mathematics Problem Solving, Mathematics Procedures, Total), Language, Spelling, Listening (not available in Abbreviated Battery), Environment.
Time: (295) minutes for Basic Battery; (325) minutes for Complete Battery; (212) minutes for Abbreviated Battery.

d) PRIMARY 2.
Population: Grades 2.5–3.5.
Forms, 4: Same as *c* above.
Scores, 10-11: Reading (Word Study Skills, Reading Vocabulary, Reading Comprehension, Total), Mathematics (Mathematics Problem Solving, Mathematics Procedures, Total), Language, Spelling, Listening (not available in Abbreviated Battery), Environment.
Time: (265) minutes for Basic Battery; (295) minutes for Complete Battery; (189) minutes for Abbreviated Battery.

e) PRIMARY 3.
Population: Grades 3.5–4.5.
Forms, 4: Same as *c* above.
Scores, 11-12: Reading (Word Study Skills, Reading Vocabulary, Reading Comprehension, Total), Mathematics (Mathematics Problem Solving, Mathematics Procedures, Total), Language, Spelling, Listening (not available in Abbreviated Battery), Science, Social Science.
Time: (280) minutes for Basic Battery; (330) minutes for Complete Battery; (203) minutes for Abbreviated Battery.

f) INTERMEDIATE 1.
Population: Grades 4.5–5.5.
Forms, 4: Same as *c* above.
Scores, 11-12: Same as *c* above.
Time: (280) minutes for Basic Battery; (330) minutes for Complete Battery; (201) minutes for Abbreviated Battery.

g) INTERMEDIATE 2.
Population: Grades 5.5–6.5.
Forms, 4: Same as *c* above.
Scores, 10-11: Reading (Reading Vocabulary, Reading Comprehension, Total), Mathematics (Mathematics Problem Solving, Mathematics Procedures, Total), Language, Spelling, Listening (not available in Abbreviated Battery), Science, Social Science.
Time: (260) minutes for Basic Battery; (310) minutes for Complete Battery; (187) minutes for Abbreviated Battery.

h) INTERMEDIATE 3.
Population: Grades 6.5–7.5.
Forms, 4: Same as *c* above.
Scores, 10-11: Same as *g* above.
Time: (260) minutes for Basic Battery; (310) minutes for Complete Battery; (187) minutes for Abbreviated Battery.

i) ADVANCED 1.
Population: Grades 7.5–8.5.
Forms, 4: Same as *c* above.
Scores, 10-11: Same as *g* above.
Time: (260) minutes for Basic Battery; (310) minutes for Complete Battery; (186) minutes for Abbreviated Battery.

j) ADVANCED 2.
Population: Grades 8.5–9.9.
Forms, 4: Same as *c* above.
Scores, 10-11: Same as *g* above.
Time: (260) minutes for Basic Battery; (310) minutes for Complete Battery; (185) minutes for Abbreviated Battery.

k) STANFORD TEST OF ACADEMIC SKILLS 1.
Population: Grades 9.0–9.9.
Acronym: TASK 1.
Forms, 4: Same as *c* above.
Scores, 8: Reading (Reading Vocabulary, Reading Comprehension, Total), Mathematics, Language, Spelling, Science, Social Science.
Time: (180) minutes for Basic Battery; (230) minutes for Complete Battery; (160) minutes for Abbreviated Battery.

l) STANFORD TEST OF ACADEMIC SKILLS 2.
Population: Grades 10.0–10.9.
Acronym: TASK 2.
Forms, 4: Same as *c* above.
Scores, 8: Same as *k* above.
Time: Same as *k* above.

m) STANFORD TEST OF ACADEMIC SKILLS 3.
Population: Grades 11.0–12.9.

Acronym: TASK 3.
Forms, 4: Same as *c* above.
Scores, 8: Same as *k* above.
Time: Same as *k* above.
Cross References: For reviews by Russell N. Carney and David T. Morse, see 16:232; see T5:2484 (15 references); for reviews by Ronald A. Berk and Thomas M. Haladyna of an earlier edition, see 13:292 (80 references); for reviews of the Stanford Achievement Test-Abbreviated-8th Edition by Stephen N. Elliott and James A. Wollack and by Kevin L. Moreland, see 12:371; for information on an earlier edition of the Stanford Achievement Test, see T4:2551 (44 references); for reviews by Frederick G. Brown and Howard Stoker, see 11:377 (78 references); for reviews by Mark L. Davison and by Michael J. Subkoviak and Frank H. Farley of the 1982 Edition, see 9:1172 (19 references); see also T3:2286 (80 references); for reviews by Robert L. Ebel and A. Harry Passow and an excerpted review by Irvin J. Lehmann of the 1973 edition, see 8:29 (51 references); see also T2:36 (87 references); for an excerpted review by Peter F. Merenda of the 1964 edition, see 7:25 (44 references); for a review by Miriam M. Bryan and an excerpted review by Robert E. Stake (with J. Thomas Hastings), see 6:26 (13 references); for a review by N. L. Gage of an earlier edition, see 5:25 (19 references); for reviews by Paul R. Hanna (with Claude E. Norcross) and by Virgil E. Herrick, see 4:25 (20 references); for reviews by Walter W. Cook and Ralph C. Preston, see 3:18 (33 references). For reviews of subtests, see 9:1173 (1 review), 9:1174 (1 review), 9:1175 (1 review), 8:291 (2 reviews), 8:745 (2 reviews), 7:209 (2 reviews), 7:537 (1 review), 7:708 (1 review), 7:802 (1 review), 7:895 (1 review), 6:637 (1 review), 5:656 (2 reviews), 5:698 (2 reviews), 5:799 (1 review), 4:419 (1 review), 4:555 (1 review), 4:593 (2 reviews), 3:503 (1 review), and 3:595 (1 review); for a review of the Stanford Test of Academic Skills [1982 Edition] by John C. Ory, see 9:1182; see also T3:2298 (3 references); for reviews by Clinton I. Chase and Robert L. Thorndike of an earlier edition, see 8:31.

[2538]

Stanford-Binet Intelligence Scales, Fifth Edition.

Purpose: Designed to assess "intelligence and cognitive abilities."
Population: Ages 2-0 to 89-9.
Publication Dates: 1916–2003.
Acronym: SB5.
Scores, 13: Nonverbal Fluid Reasoning, Verbal Fluid Reasoning, Nonverbal Knowledge, Verbal Knowledge, Nonverbal Quantitative Reasoning, Verbal Quantitative Reasoning, Nonverbal Visual-Spatial Processing, Verbal Visual-Spatial Processing, Nonverbal Working Memory, Verbal Working Memory, Nonverbal IQ, Verbal IQ, Full Scale IQ.

Subtests: Subtests and Partial Batteries: Abbreviated Battery (Nonverbal Fluid Reasoning and Verbal Knowledge).
Administration: Individual.
Price Data, 2006: $937 per complete kit including examiner's manual (336 pages), 3 item books, technical manual, 25 test records, child card, layout card, and manipulatives in a storage case all in a canvas bag; $113.50 per examiner's manual; $113.50 per technical manual; $56.50 per 25 test records.
Time: (45–75) minutes; (15–20) minutes for Abbreviated Battery.
Author: Gale H. Roid.
Publisher: PRO-ED.
Cross References: For reviews by Judy A. Johnson and Rik Carl D'Amato and by Joseph C. Kush, see 16:233; for information on an earlier edition, see T5:2485 (245 references) and T4:2553 (120 references); for reviews by Anne Anastasi and Lee J. Cronbach, see 10:342 (89 references); see also 9:1176 (41 references), T3:2289 (203 references), 8:229 (176 references), and T2:525 (428 references); for a review by David Freides, see 7:425 (258 references); for a review by Elizabeth D. Fraser and excerpted reviews by Benjamin Balinski, L. B. Birch, James Maxwell, Marie D. Neale, and Julian C. Stanley, see 6:536 (110 references); for reviews by Mary R. Haworth and Norman D. Sundberg of the second revision, see 5:413 (121 references); for a review by Boyd R. McCandless, see 4:358 (142 references); see also 3:292 (217 references); for excerpted reviews by Cyril Burt, Grace H. Kent, and M. Krugman, see 2:1420 (132 references); for reviews by Francis W. Maxfield, J. W. M. Rothney, and F. L. Wells, see 1:1062.

[2539]

Stanford-Binet Intelligence Scales for Early Childhood, Fifth Edition.

Purpose: Designed to assess intelligence and cognitive abilities.
Population: Ages 2 years to 7 years, 3 months.
Publication Date: 2005.
Acronym: Early SB5.
Scores, 14: Full Scale IQ (Nonverbal IQ, Verbal IQ), Nonverbal IQ (Nonverbal Fluid Reasoning, Nonverbal Knowledge, Nonverbal Quantitative Reasoning, Nonverbal Visual-Spatial Processing, Nonverbal Working Memory); Verbal IQ (Verbal Fluid Reasoning, Verbal Knowledge, Verbal Quantitative Reasoning, Verbal Visual-Spatial Processing, Verbal Working Memory); Abbreviated Battery IQ (Nonverbal Fluid Reasoning, Verbal Knowledge).
Administration: Individual.
Price Data, 2006: $355 per complete package including examiner's manual (282 pages), Item Book 1, Item Book 2, 25 record forms, manipulatives kit, child card, layout card, and carrying case; $49.50 per 25 record forms; $54.50 per examiner's manual.

Time: (15–50) minutes.

Comments: Adaptation of Stanford-Binet Intelligence Scales, Fifth Edition (2538).

Author: Gale H. Roid.

Publisher: PRO-ED.

Cross References: For reviews by Christopher A. Sink and Christie Eppler and by John J. Vacca, see 17:176.

[2540]

Stanford Diagnostic Mathematics Test, Fourth Edition.

Purpose: Designed to measure "competence in the basic concepts and skills that are prerequisite to problem solving in mathematics."

Publication Dates: 1976–1996.

Acronym: SDMT.

Administration: Group.

Parts, 2: Multiple Choice, Free Response.

Forms: 1 for Red, Orange, and Green levels; 2 (J, K) for Purple, Brown, and Blue levels.

Price Data, 2002: $37.50 per examination kit including multiple-choice test booklet and free-response test booklet (specify level) and directions for administering for each, answer document, practice test and practice test directions for administering, and ruler/marker; $17 per 25 practice tests and directions (specify level); $112 per 25 machine-scorable multiple-choice test booklets (specify Red, Orange, or Green level); $76 per 25 hand-scorable multiple-choice test booklets (specify Red, Orange, or Green level), directions for administering, and class record; $76 per 25 free-response test booklets (specify Red, Orange, or Green level) and directions for administering; $112 per hand-scorable multiple-choice/free-response combination kit including 25 hand-scorable multiple-choice test booklets and directions for administering, 25 free-response test booklets and directions for administering, and class record (specify Red, Orange, or Green level); $139 per machine-scorable multiple-choice/free response combination kit including 25 machine-scorable multiple-choice test booklets and directions for administering and 25 free-response test booklets and directions for administering (specify Red, Orange, or Green level); $76 per 25 reusable multiple-choice test booklets and directions for administering (specify Purple, Brown, or Blue level and Form J or K); $76 per 25 free response test booklets and directions for administering (specify Purple, Brown, or Blue level and Form J or K); $112 per reusable multiple-choice/free-response combination kit including 25 reusable multiple-choice test booklets and directions for administering and 25 free-response test booklets and directions for administering (specify Purple, Brown, or Blue level and Form J or K); $15 per set of response keys for multiple-choice tests (specify level and form); $16 per side-by-side keys for hand-scorable test booklets including blackline master of student record form (specify Red, Orange, or Green level); $15.50 per scoring guide for free-response tests including blackline master of student record form (specify level and form); $22 per stencil keys for hand-scorable answer documents (specify Purple, Brown, or Blue level and Form J or K); $30 per 25 hand-scorable answer documents with blackline master of student record form and class record (specify Purple, Brown, or Blue level); $38 per 25 Purple/Brown/Blue level machine-scorable answer documents type I; $6.50 per 25 ruler/markers; $52 per Fall (1996, 166 pages) or Spring (1996, 166 pages) multilevel norms booklet; $22 per teacher's manual for interpreting (specify Level Red/Orange [1996, 61 pages], Green/Purple [1996, 64 pages], or Brown/Blue [1996, 63 pages]); $10 per directions for administering (specify multiple-choice or free-response, and Level Red, Orange, Green, or Purple/Brown/Blue); $6.50 per practice test directions for administering (specify Red, Orange, Green, Purple, or Brown Level); $6.50 per class record (specify Red, Orange, Green, or Purple/Brown/Blue level); price information for various scoring services available from publisher.

Author: Harcourt Brace Educational Measurement.

Publisher: Pearson.

a) RED LEVEL.

Population: Grades 1.5–2.5.

Scores, 9: Concepts and Applications (Number Systems and Numeration, Patterns and Functions, Graphs and Tables, Problem Solving, Geometry and Measurement, Total), Computation (Addition of Whole Numbers, Subtraction of Whole Numbers, Total).

Time: 65 minutes for multiple choice; 90 minutes for free response.

b) ORANGE LEVEL.

Population: Grades 2.5–3.5.

Scores, 9: Same as for Red level.

Time: Same as for Red level.

c) GREEN LEVEL.

Population: Grades 3.5–4.5.

Scores, 11: Concepts and Applications (Number Systems and Numeration, Patterns and Functions, Graphs and Tables, Problem Solving, Geometry and Measurement, Total), Computation (Addition of Whole Numbers, Subtraction of Whole Numbers, Multiplication of Whole Numbers, Division of Whole Numbers, Total).

Time: Same as for Red level.

d) PURPLE LEVEL.

Population: Grades 4.5–6.5.

Scores, 12: Concepts and Applications (Number Systems and Numeration, Statistics and Probability, Graphs and Tables, Problem Solving, Geometry and Measurement, Patterns and Functions [free response only], Total), Computation (Addition of Whole Numbers, Subtraction of Whole Numbers, Multiplication of Whole Numbers, Division of Whole Numbers, Total).

Time: 65 minutes for multiple choice; 80 minutes for free response.

e) BROWN LEVEL.
Population: Grades 6.5–8.9.
Scores, 15: Concepts and Applications (Number Systems and Numeration, Patterns and Functions [free response only], Statistics and Probability, Graphs and Tables, Problem Solving, Geometry and Measurement, Total), Computation (Addition and Subtraction of Whole Numbers, Multiplication of Whole Numbers [multiple choice only], Division of Whole Numbers [multiple choice only], Multiplication and Division of Whole Numbers [free response only], Operations with Fractions and Mixed Numbers, Operations with Decimals and Percents, Equations, Total).
Time: Same as Purple level.
f) BLUE LEVEL.
Population: Grades 9.0–13.0.
Scores, 12: Concepts and Applications (Number Systems and Numeration, Patterns and Functions [free response only], Statistics and Probability, Graphs and Tables, Problem Solving, Geometry and Measurement, Total), Computation (Operations with Whole Numbers, Operations with Fractions and Mixed Numbers, Operations with Decimals and Percents, Equations, Total).
Time: Same as Purple level.
Cross References: See T5:2486 (3 references); for reviews by Irvin J. Lehmann, Philip Nagy, and G. Michael Poteat, see 13:293; see also T4:2554 (5 references); for reviews by Bruce G. Rogers and Lorrie A. Shepard of an earlier edition, see 9:1177 (2 references); see also T3:2291 (1 reference); for reviews by Glenda Lappan and Larry Souder, see 8:292.

[2541]

Stanford Diagnostic Reading Test, Fourth Edition.

Purpose: "Intended to diagnose students' strengths and weaknesses in the major components of the reading process."
Publication Dates: 1978–1996.
Acronym: SDRT4.
Administration: Group.
Forms, 2: J, K (for Purple, Brown, and Blue levels).
Price Data, 2002: $37.50 per examination kit including multiple-choice test booklet and directions for administering, practice test and directions for administering, answer document, class record form, Reading Questionnaire, Reading Strategies Survey, Story Retelling (Story and Response Form), and directions for each (specify level); $17 per 25 practice tests and directions for administering (specify Red, Orange, Green, Purple, or Brown level); $111 per 25 machine-scorable test booklets type 1 and directions for administering (specify Red, Orange, or Green level); $76 per 25 hand-scorable test booklets, directions for administering, and class record

(specify Red, Orange, or Green level); $76 per 25 reusable test booklets and directions for administering (specify level and form); $37.50 per 25 Reading Questionnaires and directions for administering (specify level and form); $37.50 per 25 Reading Strategies Surveys and directions for administering (specify Level Red/Orange, Green/Purple, or Brown/Blue); $44.50 per Story Retelling manual (1995, 15 pages) and 25 Story and Response forms (specify Level Red/Orange, Green/Purple, or Brown/Blue); $37.50 per 25 machine-scorable answer documents type 1 (for Purple/Brown/Blue levels); $30 per 25 hand-scorable answer documents with blackline master of student record form and class record (for Purple/Brown/Blue levels); $15 per side-by-side keys for hand-scorable test booklets including blackline master of student record form (specify Red, Orange, or Green level); $15 per response keys (specify Purple, Brown, or Blue level and Form J or K); $22 per stencil keys for hand-scorable answer documents (specify Purple, Brown, or Blue level and Form J or K); $6.50 per class record (specify Level Red, Orange, Green, or Purple/Brown/Blue); $6.90 per 25 row markers; $52 per Fall or Spring Multilevel norms booklet (1996, 103 pages); $22 per teacher's manual for interpreting (specify Level Red/Orange [1996, 67 pages], Green/Purple [1996, 68 pages], or Brown/Blue [1996, 62 pages]); $10 per test directions for administering (specify Level Red, Orange, Green, or Purple/Brown/Blue); $6.50 per practice test directions for administering (specify Level Red, Orange, Green, Purple, or Brown); $6.50 per Reading Questionnaire directions for administering; $6.50 per Reading Strategies Survey directions for administering; $9 per Story Retelling manual; price information for scoring services available from publisher.
Authors: Bjorn Karlsen and Eric F. Gardner.
Publisher: Pearson.
a) RED LEVEL.
Population: Grades 1.5–2.5.
Scores, 19: Phonetic Analysis (Consonants-Single, Consonants-Blends, Consonants-Digraphs, Consonants Total, Vowels-Short, Vowels-Long, Vowels Total, Total), Vocabulary (Word Reading, Listening Vocabulary, Nouns, Verbs, Others, Total), Comprehension (Sentences, Riddles, Cloze, Total), Paragraphs with Questions.
Time: 105(110) minutes.
b) ORANGE LEVEL.
Population: Grades 2.5–3.5.
Scores, 19: Phonetic Analysis (Consonants-Single, Consonants-Blends, Consonants-Digraphs, Consonants Total, Vowels-Short, Vowels-Long, Vowels Total, Total), Vocabulary (Listening Vocabulary, Reading Vocabulary, Synonyms, Classification, Total), Comprehension (Cloze, Total), Paragraphs with Questions, Recreational Reading, Textual Reading, Functional Reading.
Time: 100(105) minutes.

c) GREEN LEVEL.
Population: Grades 3.5–4.5.
Scores, 25: Phonetic Analysis (Consonants-Single, Consonants-Blends, Consonants-Digraphs, Consonants Total, Vowels-Short, Vowels-Long, Vowels-Other, Vowels Total, Total), Vocabulary (Listening Vocabulary, Reading Vocabulary, Synonyms, Classification, Word Parts, Content Area Words, Total), Comprehension, Paragraphs with Questions, Recreational Reading, Textual Reading, Functional Reading, Initial Understanding, Interpretation, Critical Analysis and Reading Strategies.
Time: 100(105) minutes.
d) PURPLE LEVEL.
Population: Grades 4.5–6.5.
Scores, 16: Vocabulary (Reading Vocabulary, Synonyms, Classification, Word Parts, Content Area Words, Total), Comprehension, Paragraphs with Questions, Recreational Reading, Textual Reading, Functional Reading, Initial Understanding, Interpretation, Critical Analysis, Reading Strategies, Scanning.
Time: 85(90) minutes.
e) BROWN LEVEL.
Population: Grades 6.5–8.9.
Scores, 16: Same as Purple Level.
Time: 85(90) minutes.
f) BLUE LEVEL.
Population: Grades 9.0–12.9.
Scores, 16: Same as Purple Level.
Time: 85(90) minutes.
Cross References: See T5:2487 (19 references); for reviews by George Engelhard, Jr. and by Mark E. Swerdlik and Jayne E. Bucy, see 13:294 (9 references); see also T4:2555 (24 references); for reviews by Robert J. Tierney and James E. Ysseldyke of an earlier edition, see 9:1178 (7 references); see also T3:2292 (15 references); for a review by Bryon H. Van Roekel, see 8:777 (13 references); see T2:1651 (2 references); for a review by Lawrence M. Kasdon of Levels 1–2 of an earlier edition, see 7:725 (3 references).

[2542]

Stanford Early School Achievement Test, Third Edition.

Purpose: Measures school achievement.
Population: Grades K.0–K.5, K.5–1.5.
Publication Dates: 1969–1991.
Acronym: SESAT.
Administration: Group.
Forms, 2: J, L.
Price Data, 2002: $185 per 25 machine-scorable tests (Type 1, Form J; Type 2, Form L) (scored by publisher) (select level); $23.90 per 25 practice tests and one directions for administering (select level); $7.50 per class record form; $35.50 per 25 previews for parents (select level); $21 per administration directions (select

level and form); $7.50 per administration directions for practice test (select level); $67.50 per norms booklet (1988, Form J Only; 1991, Forms J and L) (select level); $47 per coordinator's handbook; $51.50 per examination kit including test booklet, administration directions, and practice test with directions (select level and form).
Comments: Downward extension of the Stanford Achievement Test Series.
Author: The Psychological Corporation.
Publisher: Pearson.
a) LEVEL 1.
Population: Grades K.0–K.5.
Scores, 8: Sounds and Letters, Word Reading, Total, Mathematics, Listening to Words and Stories, Total for Basic Battery, Environment, Total for Complete Battery.
Price Data: $185 per 25 machine-scorable test booklets (Type 1, Form J; Type 2, Form L); $119 per 25 hand-scorable test booklets (select form); $175 per set of scoring keys (select form).
Time: (190) minutes over 9 sessions.
b) LEVEL 2.
Population: Grades K.5–1.5.
Scores, 9: Sounds and Letters, Word Reading, Sentence Reading, Total, Mathematics, Listening to Words and Stories, Basic Battery Total, Environment, Complete Battery Total.
Price Data: $185 per 25 machine-scorable test booklets (Type 1, Form J; Type 2, Form L); $126 per 25 hand-scorable test booklets (select form); $175 per set of scoring keys (select form).
Time: (225) minutes over 9 sessions.
Cross References: See T5:2488 (10 references) and T4:2556 (2 references); for reviews by Phillip L. Ackerman and C. Dale Carpenter, see 11:378 (8 references); for a review by Mary J. Allen of an earlier edition, see 9:1179 (1 reference); see also T3:2293 (9 references); for a review by Courtney B. Cazden of an earlier edition, see 8:30 (6 references); see also T2:38 (1 reference); for reviews by Elizabeth Hagen and William A. Mehrens of Level 1, see 7:28.

[2543]

Stanford English Language Proficiency Test.

Purpose: Designed to evaluate "the listening, reading, writing, speaking, and comprehension skills" of English language learners.
Population: Grades preK-12.
Publication Dates: 2005-2006.
Acronym: Stanford ELP.
Administration: Individual or group.
Forms, 3: A, B, C.
Levels, 6: Readiness, Preliteracy, Primary, Elementary, Middle Grades, High School.
Restricted Distribution: Distribution is restricted to accredited schools and school districts.

Price Data, 2007: $45 per Exam kit including Test Booklet, Directions for Administering, Screening Test, Screening Test Directions, Response Booklet (Readiness-High School), Practice Test, and Practice Test Directions for Administering; $7 per Practice Test Directions for Administering; $12.30 per 10 Practice Test packs; $14.40 per 5 Screening tests; $7 per Screening Test Directions for Administering; $42.80 per cassettes (standardized recording of all directions and stimuli for Listening, Speaking, and Writing [Forms A, B, C-Primary, Elementary, Middle Grades, High School]); $12.80 per Directions for Administering; $39 per 10 machine-scorable test packs (Form A-Preliteracy, Primary); $39 per 10 machine-scorable test packs (Form B-Primary); $39 per 10 machine-scorable test packs (Form C-Primary); $27.80 per 10 machine-scorable response booklet packs (Form A-Readiness, Elementary, Middle Grades, High School); $27.80 per 10 machine-scorable response booklet packs (Form B or C-Elementary, Middle Grades, High School); $11.20 per Speaking booklet (Form A, B, or C-Primary); $46.90 per 10 reusable test packs (Form A, B, or C-Elementary, Middle Grades, High School); $7.50 per class record; $23.50 per response keys (Form A, B, or C); $33.50 per Speaking/Writing Training Manual with DVD for Readiness-Preliteracy and Primary-High School; $50 per teacher Pre-and Post-Test Online Training; $45 per technical report/manual (2005, 191 pages); new technical manuals available Fall 2007 for SELP/SSLP Readiness-Preliteracy and SELP/SSLP Primary-High School.
Foreign Language Edition: Stanford Spanish Language Proficiency Test edition available.
Comments: Test requires the use of a cassette player.
Author: Harcourt Assessment, Inc.
Publisher: Pearson.
a) READINESS.
Population: PreK.
Subtests, 4: Listening, Basic Academic Concepts, Writing, Speaking.
Scores, 6: Listening, Speaking, Comprehension (Listening and Basic Academic Concepts), Social (Listening and Speaking), Early Academic (Basic Academic Concepts and Writing), Productive (Speaking and Writing).
Time: (40) minutes.
b) PRELITERACY.
Population: Grade K-beginning 1.
Subtests, 5: Listening, Speaking, Early Reading, Early Writing, Writing.
Scores, 6: Listening, Speaking, Comprehension (Listening and Basic Academic Concepts), Early Academic (Basic Academic Concepts and Writing), Productive (Speaking and Writing).
Time: (90) minutes.
c) PRIMARY.
Population: Grades K-2.

Subtests, 5: Listening, Speaking, Reading, Writing Conventions, Writing.
Scores: 8 scales: 5 Content scales (Listening, Speaking, Reading, Total Writing [Writing conventions, Writing], Comprehension [Listening and Reading]), 3 Communication scales (Social [Listening, Speaking], Academic [Reading, Writing Conventions, Writing], Productive [Speaking, Writing]).
Time: (85-95) minutes.
d) ELEMENTARY.
Population: Grades 3-5.
Subtests: Same as Primary.
Scores: Same as Primary.
Time: Same as Primary.
e) MIDDLE GRADES.
Population: Grades 6-8.
Subtests: Same as Primary.
Scores: Same as Primary.
Time: (95-105) minutes.
f) HIGH SCHOOL.
Population: Grades 9-12.
Subtests: Same as Primary.
Scores: Same as Primary.
Time: Same as Middle Grades.
Cross References: For reviews by Dixie McGinty and Gerald Tindal, see 17:177.

[2544]

Stanford Reading First.

Purpose: Designed to "identify students in kindergarten through grade three who are at risk of reading below grade level by assessing reading foundation skills and monitoring reading progress."
Population: Grades K.0-K-5, K.5-1.5, 1.5-2.5, 2.5-3.5, 3.5-4.5.
Publication Dates: 2002-2004.
Scores, 10: Sounds and Letters, Word Study Skills, Word Reading, Sentence Reading, Reading Vocabulary, Reading Comprehension, Listening to Words and Stories, Listening Vocabulary, Speaking Vocabulary, Oral Reading Fluency.
Administration: Individual and group.
Levels, 5: Stanford Early School Achievement Test Level 1, Stanford Early School Achievement Test Level 2, Primary 1, Primary 2, Primary 3.
Parts, 2: Multiple-Choice, Oral Fluency.
Price Data, 2009: $53.40 per technical data report (2004, 85 pages); $73.60 per training kit; $35 per 10 machine-scorable test packs (specify level); $13.25 per Oral Reading Fluency reusable booklet (specify level); $14 per directions for administering (specify level); $27.55 per response key (specify level); $9 per class record (specify level).
Time: (75) minutes.

Comments: Multiple-Choice component items are taken from Reading and Listening subtests of the Stanford Achievement Test Series, Tenth Edition (16:232), and the Oral Fluency items are new to Reading First.
Author: Pearson.
Publisher: Pearson.
Cross References: For reviews by C. Dale Carpenter and Jeffrey K. Smith, see 18:127.

[2545]

Stanford Writing Assessment Program, Third Edition.

Purpose: Provides for the direct assessment of written expression in four modes: Descriptive, Narrative, Expository, and Persuasive.
Population: Grades 3–12.
Publication Dates: 1982–1997.
Scores: 4 writing modes: Descriptive, Narrative, Expository, Persuasive.
Administration: Group.
Levels, 9: Primary 3, Intermediate 1, Intermediate 2, Intermediate 3, Advanced 1, Advanced 2, TASK 1, TASK 2, TASK 3.
Forms, 2: S, T (Form T is a secure form).
Price Data, 2002: $25.50 per 25 writing prompts, 25 response forms, and Directions for Administering (specify Descriptive, Narrative, Expository, or Persuasive); $8 per Directions for Administering (specify Descriptive, Narrative, Expository, or Persuasive); $11 per writing exam kit including 1 prompt each of Descriptive, Narrative, Expository and Persuasive, 1 Directions for Administering, 1 response form, and Reviewer's Edition; $75 per norms book; $22 per manual for interpreting (1997, 70 pages) (all forms and levels); scoring prices available from publisher.
Time: (50) minutes.
Comments: Holistic and analytic scoring available; computer scoring available; Form T is a secure form; Third edition provides information about student strengths and weaknesses, which can assist in instructional planning.
Authors: Harcourt Brace Educational Measurement.
Publisher: Pearson.
Cross References: For reviews by Linda Crocker and Sharon H. deFur, see 14:367; for reviews by Philip Nagy and Wayne H. Slater of an earlier editions, see 13:295.

[2546]

The Stanton Profile.

Purpose: Designed to provide "pre-employment personality and attitudinal assessments."
Population: Employment applicants.
Publication Dates: 1987–1995.
Scores, 6: 4 content scores (Work Motivation, Adaptability/Flexibility, Service Orientation, Trustworthiness), 2 validity checks (Social Desirability Bias, Infrequent Response Patterns).
Administration: Group or individual.

Manual: No manual.
Price Data: Available from the publisher.
Time: Untimed, generally requiring approximately 20 minutes.
Author: William G. Harris.
Publisher: ChoicePoint.

[2547]

The Stanton Survey and the Stanton Survey Phase II.

Purpose: Provides indications of previous counterproductive work behavior and attitudes toward honesty.
Population: Applicants for employment.
Publication Dates: 1964–1995.
Scores: Total score only.
Administration: Individual or group.
Price Data: Available from publisher.
Time: Untimed.
Comments: Available in hard copy or via telephonic IVR.
Authors: Carl S. Klump, Homer B. C. Reed, Jr., and Sherwood Perman.
Publisher: ChoicePoint.
  a) THE STANTON SURVEY.
  b) THE STANTON SURVEY PHASE II.
Cross References: For reviews by H. C. Ganguli and Kenneth G. Wheeler, see 9:1185. (An additional review by William G. Harris is available electronically from the Buros Institute national database: available from EBSCO and Ovid and from Tests Reviews Online via the Buros webpage.)

[2548]

STAR Early Literacy®.

Purpose: A computer-adaptive, progress-monitoring assessment designed to assess the early literacy skills of beginning readers.
Population: Prekindergarten–Grade 3.
Publication Dates: 2001-2010.
Scores, 8: Graphophonemic Knowledge, General Readiness, Phonemic Awareness, Phonics, Comprehension, Structural Analysis, Vocabulary, Scaled Score.
Administration: Group.
Price Data: Price information quote is available from publisher for a one-time school fee (based on each school/district's specific needs) plus an annual subscription cost per student.
Time: (10) minutes.
Comments: Reports criterion-referenced scores; software includes report capabilities (e.g., diagnostic reports); capable of sharing databases with other Renaissance Learning software; data may be maintained on-site or hosted by the publisher; may be administered as often as weekly for progress monitoring. Information regarding complete system requirements available at http://www.renlearn.com/support/sysreq.asp.

Author: Renaissance Learning, Inc.
Publisher: Renaissance Learning, Inc.
Cross References: For reviews by Theresa Graham and Sandra B. Ward, see 15:240.

[2549]

STAR Math®.

Purpose: A computer-adaptive, progress-monitoring assessment designed to assess students' mathematical abilities and overall mathematics achievement.
Population: Grades 1–12.
Publication Dates: 1998–2010.
Scores: Total score only.
Administration: Group.
Price Data: Price information quote available from publisher for a one-time school fee (based on each school/district's specific needs) plus an annual subscription cost per student.
Time: (15) minutes.
Comments: Reports norm-referenced (percentile ranks, normal curve equivalents, grade equivalents) and criterion-referenced (math instructional levels) scores; software includes report capabilities (e.g., diagnostic reports); capable of sharing databases with other Renaissance Learning software; may be administered as often as weekly for progress monitoring. Information regarding complete system requirements available at http://www.renlearn.com/support/sysreq.asp.
Author: Renaissance Learning, Inc.
Publisher: Renaissance Learning, Inc.
Cross References: For reviews by Mary L. Garner and G. Michael Poteat, see 16:234; for reviews by Joseph C. Ciechalski and Cindy M. Walker of an earlier version, see 15:241.

[2550]

STAR Reading®.

Purpose: A computer-adaptive, progress-monitoring assessment designed to assess students' reading comprehension and overall reading achievement.
Population: Grades 1–12.
Publication Dates: 1996–2010.
Scores: Total score only.
Administration: Group.
Price Data: Price information quote available from publisher for a one-time school fee (based on each school/district's specific needs) plus an annual subscription cost per student.
Time: (10) minutes.
Comments: Reports norm-referenced (percentile ranks, normal curve equivalents, grade equivalents) and criterion-referenced (instructional reading levels) scores; software includes report capabilities (e.g., diagnostic reports); capable of sharing databases with other Renaissance Learning software; data may be maintained on-site or hosted by the publisher; may be administered as often as

weekly for progress monitoring. Information regarding complete system requirements available at http://www.renlearn.com/support/sysreq.asp.
Author: Renaissance Learning, Inc.
Publisher: Renaissance Learning, Inc.
Cross References: For reviews by Lori Nebelsick-Gullett and by Betsy B. Waterman and David M. Sargent, see 15:242; for reviews by Theresa Volpe-Johnstone and Sandra Ward of the original edition, see 14:368.

[2551]

STAR Supplementary Tests of Achievement in Reading.

Purpose: "Designed to supplement the assessments that teachers make about their pupils' progress and achievement in reading."
Population: Ages 7–13.
Publication Dates: 2000–2003.
Administration: Group.
Levels, 3: STAR Test (Year 3), STAR Test (Years 4–6), STAR Test (Years 7–9).
Forms, 2: A, B.
Price Data, 2006: NZ$38.70 per specimen set (specify level) including teacher's manual (2001, 35 pages), 1 test booklet each of Forms A and B, 1 set answer keys each of Forms A and B; NZ$9.90 per 10 test booklets (specify Form A or B, specify level); NZ$9 per photocopiable masters answer key (Level 3, 4–6, specify Form A or B); NZ$9 per photocopiable masters marking key (Level 7–9, specify Form A or B).
Comments: Normed on children living in New Zealand.
Author: Warwick B. Elley.
Publisher: New Zealand Council for Educational Research [New Zealand].
a) STAR TEST (3)
Scores, 4: Word Recognition, Sentence Comprehension, Paragraph Comprehension, Vocabulary Range.
b) STAR TEST (4–6).
Scores, 4: Word Recognition, Sentence Comprehension, Paragraph Comprehension, Vocabulary Range.
Time: 20(35) minutes.
c) STAR TEST (7–9).
Scores, 6: Word Recognition, Sentence Comprehension, Paragraph Comprehension, Vocabulary Range, The Language of Advertising, Reading Different Genres or Styles of Writing.
Time: 30(45) minutes.
Cross References: For a review by John W. Young, see 15:243.

[2552]

START–Strategic Assessment of Readiness for Training.

Purpose: Designed to diagnose adults' learning strengths and weaknesses for workplace application.

Population: Adults.
Publication Date: 1994.
Acronym: START.
Scores, 8: Anxiety, Attitude, Motivation, Concentration, Identifying Important Information, Knowledge Acquisition Strategies, Monitoring Learning, Time Management.
Administration: Group or individual.
Price Data, 2006: $4.95 per assessment (volume discounts available).
Time: (15) minutes.
Authors: Claire E. Weinstein and David R. Palmer.
Publisher: H & H Publishing Co., Inc.
Cross References: For reviews by Phillip L. Ackerman and Patricia A. Bachelor, see 14:369.

[2553]

State-Trait Anger Expression Inventory-2.

Purpose: "Designed to measure the experience, expression, and control of anger for adolescents and adults."
Population: Ages 16 and over.
Publication Dates: 1988–1999.
Acronym: STAXI-2.
Scores, 12: State Anger Scale (Feeling Angry, Feel like Expressing Anger Verbally, Feel like Expressing Anger Physically, Total), Trait Anger Scale (Angry Temperament, Angry Reaction, Total), Angry Expression and Anger Control Scales (Anger Expression–Out, Anger Expression–In, Anger Control–Out, Anger Control–In), Anger Expression Index.
Administration: Group or individual.
Price Data, 2006: $226 per introductory kit including professional manual, 25 reusable item booklets, 50 rating sheets, and 50 profile forms; $445 per interpretive report software (CD-ROM) with unlimited scoring and interpretive reports.
Time: (12–15) minutes.
Author: Charles D. Spielberger.
Publisher: Psychological Assessment Resources, Inc.
Cross References: For reviews by Stephen J. Freeman and Beverly M. Klecker, see 15:244; see T5:2496 (6 references); for reviews by David J. Pittenger and Alan J. Raphael of the Revised Research Edition, see 13:296 (52 references); see also T4:2562 (12 references); for reviews by Bruce H. Biskin and Paul Retzlaff of the STAXI-Research Edition, see 11:379 (8 references).

[2554]

State-Trait Anger Expression Inventory-2: Child and Adolescent.

Purpose: Designed to "assess state and trait anger with anger expression and control."
Population: Ages 9 to 18 years.
Publication Date: 2009.
Acronym: STAXI-2 C/A.
Scores, 9: State Anger, State Anger-Feelings, State Anger-Expression, Trait Anger, Trait Anger-Temperament, Trait Anger-Reaction, Anger Expression-Out, Anger Expression-IN, Anger Control.
Administration: Group.
Price Data, 2010: $155 per introductory kit including professional manual (87 pages), 25 rating booklets, and 25 profile forms; $52 per professional manual; $80 per 25 rating booklets; $36 per 25 profile forms.
Time: (10-15) minutes.
Authors: Thomas M. Brunner and Charles D. Spielberger.
Publisher: Psychological Assessment Resources, Inc.

[2555]

State-Trait Anxiety Inventory.

Purpose: Designed to assess anxiety as an emotional state (S-Anxiety) and individual differences in anxiety proneness as a personality trait (T-Anxiety).
Population: Grades 9-16 and adults.
Publication Dates: 1968-1984.
Acronym: STAI.
Scores, 2: State Anxiety, Trait Anxiety.
Administration: Group.
Forms, 2: X, Y.
Parts, 2: 2 parts for each form labeled Form 1 (State), Form 2 (Trait).
Price Data: Available from publisher at www.mindgarden.com/products/staisad.htm.
Foreign Language Edition: Spanish edition available; many researcher translations available.
Time: (10-20) minutes.
Comments: Title on test is Self-Evaluation Questionnaire.
Authors: Charles D. Spielberger; Form Y and manual prepared in collaboration with R. L. Gorsuch, R. Lushene, P. R. Vagg, and G. A. Jacobs.
Publisher: Mind Garden, Inc.
Cross References: See T5:2497 (680 references), T4:2563 (646 references), 9:1186 (158 references), and T3:2300 (277 references); for reviews by Ralph Mason Dreger and Edward S. Katkin, see 8:683 (268 references); see also T2:1391 (45 references) and 7:141 (20 references).

[2556]

State-Trait Anxiety Inventory for Children.

Purpose: Designed to measure anxiety in children; distinguishes between a general proneness to anxious behavior rooted in the personality and anxiety as a fleeting emotional state.
Population: Upper elementary through junior high school children.
Publication Dates: 1970-1973.
Acronym: STAIC.
Scores, 2: State Anxiety, Trait Anxiety.
Administration: Group.
Price Data: Available from publisher at www.mindgarden.com/products/staisch.htm.
Foreign Language Edition: Spanish edition available.

Time: (20) minutes.
Comments: Downward extension of State-Trait Anxiety Inventory (2555); title on test is "How-I-Feel Questionnaire"; self-administering; can be administered verbally to younger children.
Authors: Charles D. Spielberger, C. Drew Edwards, Robert E. Lushene, Joseph Montuori, Denna Platzek.
Publisher: Mind Garden, Inc.
Cross References: See T5:2498 (78 references), T4:2564 (58 references), and T3:2301 (15 references); for a review by Norman S. Endler, see 8:684 (19 references); see also T2:1392 (2 references).

[2557]

State Trait-Depression Adjective Check Lists.
Purpose: "To measure both state and trait depression mood and feelings."
Population: Ages 14 and over.
Publication Dates: 1967–2002.
Acronym: ST-DACL.
Scores, 6: State-Positive Mood, State-Negative Mood, State Mood-Total, Trait-Positive Mood, Trait-Negative Mood, Trait Mood-Total.
Administration: Group.
Forms, 4: 1, 2, A-B, C-D.
Price Data: Price information available from publisher for introductory kit including manual (2002, 83 pages), 25 forms 1 & 2, 25 forms C-D, and 25 profile forms.
Time: (4–8) minutes per list.
Comments: Developed from the Depression Adjective Check List.
Author: Bernard Lubin.
Publisher: EdITS/Educational and Industrial Testing Service.
Cross References: See T5:2499 (1 reference); for reviews by Andres Barona and by Janet F. Carlson and Betsy Waterman of an earlier edition, see 13:297 (21 references); see also T4:742 (79 references), 9:315 (21 references), T3:681 (46 references), 8:536 (20 references), and T2:1154 (2 references); for reviews of the earlier edition by Leonard D. Goodstein and Douglas M. McNair, see 7:65 (3 references); see also P:57 (4 references).

[2558]

Station Employee Applicant Inventory.
Purpose: Designed to help "assess a potential employee's willingness to contribute to team efforts, practice safe work habits, handle cash and merchandise with complete trustworthiness, stay on the job once hired" and "follow company policies."
Population: Service station applicants.
Publication Date: 1997.
Acronym: SEAI.
Scores, 9: Validity/Candidness, Honesty, Interpersonal Cooperation, Drug Avoidance, Applied Arithmetic, Skills and Abilities, Safety, Tenure, Employability Index.

Administration: Individual or group.
Forms, 2: Paper and pencil, computer.
Price Data, 2005: $24 per 1–999 each Quanta Touch Test, Quanta Software for Windows–administration and scoring (no booklets), Quanta Software for Windows–scoring only (one booklet for every coupon ordered), RLH Online; volume discounts available.
Foreign Language Edition: Available in Spanish.
Time: (45–60) minutes.
Author: London House.
Publisher: Pearson Performance Solutions [No reply from publisher; status unknown].

[2559]

Stephens Oral Language Screening Test.
Purpose: To screen children "for potential problems in syntax and/or articulation associated with their production of standard American English dialects."
Population: Prekindergarten-grade 1.
Publication Date: 1977.
Acronym: SOLST.
Scores, 2: Syntax, Articulation.
Administration: Individual.
Price Data: Available from publisher.
Time: (9) minutes.
Author: M. Irene Stephens.
Publisher: Interim Publishers [No reply from publisher; status unknown].
Cross References: See 9:1193 (2 references).

[2560]

The Stieglitz Informal Reading Inventory: Assessing Reading Behaviors from Emergent to Advanced Levels.
Purpose: Designed to provide educators with information about students' reading behaviors.
Population: Grades 1–9.
Publication Date: 1992.
Acronym: SIRI.
Scores, 7: Graded Words in Context (Independent, Instructional, Frustration), Graded Reading Passages (Word Recognition, Oral Comprehension, Prior Knowledge, Interest).
Administration: Individual.
Price Data: Available from publisher.
Time: (20–30) minutes.
Author: Ezra L. Stieglitz.
Publisher: Pearson Education.
Cross References: For reviews by Koressa Kutsick Malcolm and Stephanie Stein, see 13:298.

[2561]

Stirling Eating Disorder Scales.
Purpose: Developed as a comprehensive measure of anorexia and bulimia.

Population: Adolescents and adults.
Publication Dates: 1995–1996.
Acronym: SEDS.
Scores: 8 scales: Anorexic Dietary Cognitions, Anorexic Dietary Behavior, Bulimic Dietary Cognitions, Bulimic Dietary Behavior, Perceived External Control, Low Assertiveness, Low Self-Esteem, Self-Directed Hostility.
Administration: Individual.
Price Data, 2006: £74 per complete kit including 25 record forms, 25 profile sheets, and manual (1995, 33 pages).
Time: (30) minutes.
Authors: Gwenllian-Jane Williams and Kevin Power.
Publisher: Pearson Assessment [England].
Cross References: For reviews by Jeffrey A. Atlas and Ronald A. Berk, see 16:235.

[2562]

Stoelting Brief Nonverbal Intelligence Test.
Purpose: Designed as a nonverbal, nonlanguage measure of cognitive functions.
Population: Ages 6-0 to 20-11.
Publication Date: 1999.
Acronym: S-BIT.
Scores, 7: Figure Ground, Form Completion, Sequential Order, Repeated Patterns, S-BIT IQ, Visualization, Fluid Reasoning.
Administration: Individual.
Price Data, 2005: $295 per complete kit including 20 record forms, examiner's manual (1999, 191 pages), easel book, and response cards; $20 per 20 record forms; $50 per examiner's manual; $170 per easel book; $35 per carrying case; $70 per response cards.
Time: (25) minutes.
Authors: Gale H. Roid and Lucy J. Miller.
Publisher: Stoelting Co.
Cross References: For reviews by Russell N. Carney and Susana Urbina, see 15:245.

[2563]

Stokes/Gordon Stress Scale.
Purpose: Developed to measure stressors in healthy individuals over age 65.
Population: Healthy individuals over age 65.
Publication Date: 1987.
Acronym: SGSS.
Scores: Total stress score.
Administration: Group.
Price Data: Available from publisher.
Time: (15–30) minutes.
Comments: Self-administered in person or by mail.
Authors: Shirlee A. Stokes and Susan E. Gordon.
Publisher: Lienhard School of Nursing.
Cross References: For a review by Sharon L. Weinberg, see 13:299; see also T4:2572 (1 reference).

[2564]

Strategic Decision Making Inventory.
Purpose: Designed as a guide to business managers to help them think strategically in their decision making process (deciding how to decide).
Population: Business managers.
Publication Date: 1983.
Scores, 2: Flexibility, Appropriateness.
Administration: Group.
Price Data, 2002: $8.95 per inventory; minimum of 20 (volume discounts available).
Time: [15–20] minutes.
Comments: Self-administered; self-scored.
Author: Herbert S. Kindler.
Publisher: The Center for Management Effectiveness, Inc.

[2565]

Strength Deployment Inventory.
Purpose: Designed to assess "personal strengths in relating to others" under two conditions: when things are going well, and when there is conflict.
Population: Adults.
Publication Dates: 1973–1996.
Acronym: SDI.
Scores: 7 Motivational Values Systems: (Altruistic-Nurturing, Assertive-Directing, Analytic-Autonomizing, Flexible-Cohering, Assertive-Nurturing, Judicious-Competing, Cautious-Supporting); 13 scores reflecting progression through stages of conflict.
Administration: Group or individual.
Price Data, 2001: $22 per Premier Edition including Standard Edition of the Strength Deployment Inventory, interpretive cards, and 2 exercises; Portrait of Personal Strengths and Portrait of Overdone Strengths; $5.50 per either Portrait available separately; $10 per Standard Edition; $14 per Component Edition including interpretive cards; $30 per manual (1996, 146 pages).
Foreign Language Editions: Standard Edition available in French, Swedish, and Spanish; Premier Edition available in Swedish and Dutch.
Time: (20–40) minutes for Standard Edition; (20–40) minutes per exercise in Premier Edition.
Comments: Self-scorable; for corporate (e.g., team building), clinical (e.g., relationship counseling), and career development (e.g., outplacement and welfare-to-work) uses; Feedback Edition uses self-rating and ratings of a significant other person.
Author: Elias H. Porter.
Publisher: Personal Strengths Publishing.
Cross References: For a review by Frederick T. L. Leong, see 14:371.

[2566]

Stress Assessment Questionnaire.
Purpose: Designed to "provide an integrated multifactor stress assessment measure for counseling and self-development."

Population: Ages 16-65.
Publication Date: 2010.
Acronym: SAQ.
Scores, 16: Work, Relationship, Parenting, Emotional Symptoms, Behavioral Symptoms, Physical Symptoms, Social Support, Self-Regulation, Problem Solving, Distraction, Health, Procrastination, Perfectionism, Self-Esteem, Depression, Anxiety.
Administration: Group.
Price Data, 2011: $14.95 per assessment.
Time: (10-15) minutes.
Comments: Assessment, scoring, and feedback conducted online.
Author: MySkillsProfile.com.
Publisher: MySkillsProfile.com Limited [England].

[2567]

Stress in General Scale.

Purpose: To measure job stress.
Population: Employees.
Publication Dates: 1992–2002.
Acronym: SIG.
Scores, 2: Pressure, Threat.
Administration: Individual or group.
Price Data, 2010: There is no charge to use the copyrighted scales. For permission, e-mail jdi_ra@bgnet.bgsu.edu or phone 419.372.8247 at the Department of Psychology, Bowling Green State University, Bowling Green, OH 43403.
Time: 3-5 minutes.
Comments: Previously listed with the Job Descriptive Index (1386).
Authors: Jeffrey M. Stanton, William K. Balzer, Patricia C. Smith, Luis Fernando Parra, and Gail H. Ironson.
Publisher: Bowling Green State University.
Cross References: For reviews by Christopher G. Bellah and by Leonard Handler and Amanda Jill Clemence, see 15:246.

[2568]

Stress Index for Parents of Adolescents.

Purpose: Designed to "identify stressful areas in parent-adolescent interactions."
Population: Parents of adolescents ages 11–19 years.
Publication Date: 1998.
Scores, 11: Adolescent Domain (Moodiness/Emotional Lability, Social Isolation/Withdrawal, Delinquency/Antisocial, Failure to Achieve or Persevere), Parent Domain (Life Restrictions, Relationship with Spouse/Partner, Social Alienation, Incompetence/Guilt), Adolescent-Parent Relationship Domain, Life Stressors, Total Parenting Stress.
Administration: Individual.
Price Data, 2006: $120 per introductory kit including 25 reusable item booklets, 25 hand-scorable answer sheet/profile forms, and professional manual (70 pages).

Time: (20) minutes.
Authors: Peter L. Sheras and Richard R. Abidin.
Publisher: Psychological Assessment Resources, Inc.
Cross References: For reviews by Elizabeth L. Jones and Susan M. Swearer, see 14:372.

[2569]

Stress Indicator & Health Planner [Revised].

Purpose: Designed to help an individual assess their current levels of stress, health, and wellness.
Population: Adults.
Publication Dates: 1990-2006.
Acronym: SIHP.
Scores, 10: Physical Distress, Psychological Distress, Behavioral Distress, Total Distress, Interpersonal Stress Assessment, Nutritional, Health Assessment, Total Wellness Assessment, Time-Stress Assessment, Occupational Stress Assessment.
Administration: Individual or group.
Parts, 5: Personal Distress Assessment, Interpersonal Stress Assessment, Wellness Assessment, Time-Stress Assessment, Occupational Stress Assessment.
Price Data, 2006: $14.95 per test booklet (2006, 24 pages); $38 per Professional/Trainer's Guidelines (1993, 15 pages); $14.95 per online version code.
Time: [30-60] minutes for basic; [180-360] minutes for facilitated/advanced.
Comments: Test can be self-administered and self-scored and includes a health planner.
Authors: Ken Keis, Terry D. Anderson, and Gwen Faulkner.
Publisher: Consulting Resource Group International, Inc.
Cross References: For reviews by Dennis C. Harper and Barbara L. Lachar of an earlier edition, see 13:300.

[2570]

Stress Management Questionnaire [Revised].

Purpose: Identifies how one responds to life stressors and copes with stress.
Population: Adults and adolescents.
Publication Dates: 1980–1999.
Acronym: SMQ.
Scores, 11: Warning Signs (Hostility/Anger, Perfectionism, Time Orientation, Disappointment, Negative Mood, Underachievement, Tension), Stress Effects (Physical, Live Work Satisfaction), Stressors (Life Events, Hassles).
Administration: Group or individual.
Forms, 2: Participant, Companion.
Price Data, 2001: $14 per questionnaire (discounts available).
Time: (20–25) minutes.
Comments: Manual title is "Stressmaster Trainer's Manual"; questionnaire completed by self and by a close companion; self-scored.

Author: James C. Petersen.
Publisher: The Assessment and Development Centre.
Cross References: For a review by Jayne E. Stake of an earlier version, see 10:348.

[2571]

Stress Processing Report.

Purpose: Enables individuals to identify, understand and change their reactions to stress, thereby improving their receptivity to organizational change.
Population: Adults.
Publication Date: 1994.
Acronym: SPR.
Scores: 19 domains: Self (Self-Image, Past View, Control, Approval, Growth, Effectiveness), Others (Inclusion, Interpersonal, Intimacy, Trust), Process (Receptiveness, Synergy, Cooperation, Time Orientation, Time Utilization), Goals (Satisfaction, Directedness, Expectations, Future View).
Administration: Individual or group.
Price Data: Price data for test materials including Self-Development Guide and Leader's Guide available from publisher.
Time: Administration time not reported.
Author: Human Synergistics International.
Publisher: Human Synergistics International.

[2572]

Stress Profile.

Purpose: "Developed to provide a brief yet comprehensive stress and health risk assessment."
Population: Adults.
Publication Date: 1999.
Scores, 16: Stress, Health Habits, Exercise, Rest/Sleep, Eating/Nutrition, Prevention, ARC Item Cluster, Social Support Network, Type A Behavior, Cognitive Hardiness, Coping Style, Positive Appraisal, Negative Appraisal, Threat Minimization, Problem Focus, Psychological Well-Being.
Administration: Group.
Price Data, 2006: $110 per kit including 25 AutoScore™ forms, manual (63 pages), and 1 reusable administration booklet; $46.75 per 25 AutoScore™ forms to be used with administration booklet; $54.50 per manual; $29 per 25 disposable administration booklets; $61 per 5 reusable administration booklets (quantity discounts available); $18 for WPS Test Report mail-in answer sheet; $260 per 25-use disk; $10.50 for FAX service.
Time: (20–30) minutes.
Comments: Can be administered and scored by hand or by computer.
Author: Kenneth M. Nowack.
Publisher: Western Psychological Services.
Cross References: For reviews by Carl Isenhart and Kevin J. McCarthy, see 15:247.

[2573]

Stress Resiliency Profile.

Purpose: Designed to identify some ways individuals unintentionally contribute to their own stress levels.
Population: Employees.
Publication Dates: 1974-1992.
Acronym: SRP.
Scores, 3: Deficiency Focusing, Necessitating, Skill Recognition.
Administration: Group or individual.
Price Data, 2011: $112.50 per 10 test booklet/manual.
Time: (15) minutes.
Comments: Self-administered and self-scored.
Authors: Kenneth W. Thomas and Walter G. Tymon, Jr.
Publisher: CPP, Inc.
Cross References: For reviews by John A. Mills and William R. Merz, Sr., see 13:301.

[2574]

Stromberg Dexterity Test.

Purpose: "Developed as an aid in choosing workers for jobs which require speed and accuracy of arm and hand movement."
Population: Trade school and adults.
Publication Dates: 1945–1981.
Acronym: SDT.
Scores: Total score only.
Administration: Individual.
Price Data, 2006: $700 per complete set including all necessary equipment and manual in case; $45 per manual.
Time: (5–10) minutes.
Author: Eleroy L. Stromberg.
Publisher: Pearson.
Cross References: See T3:2317 (2 references) and T2:2235 (8 references); for a review by Julian C. Stanley, see 4:755 (1 reference).

[2575]

Strong Interest Explorer.

Purpose: Self-scorable assessment intended to help individuals learn more about their interests to help them "define a career direction, select classes or activities," and/or "choose a major or technical program."
Population: High school and community college students, or early career populations.
Publication Dates: 1933-2001.
Acronym: SIE.
Scores, 14: Working with Numbers, Health and Science, Music and Arts, Writing and Mass Communications, Cultural Relations, Helping Others, Teaching and Training, Law and Politics, Office and Project Management, Business/Sales/and Marketing, Working with Computers, Outdoor Environment/Plants & Animals, Construction and Engineering, Protective Services.

Administration: Individual or group.
Price Data, 2011: $9.25 each for Strong Interest Explorer Self-Scorable.
Time: (8-10) minutes.
Comments: It is suggested the SIE be given in a classroom or group setting and led by a teacher or counselor; developed as a simplified alternative to the Strong Interest Inventory (2576).
Author: Judy Chartrand.
Publisher: CPP, Inc.
Cross References: For reviews by Bert A. Goldman and Eugene P. Sheehan, see 18:128.

[2576]

Strong Interest Inventory®.

Purpose: Intended to generate an in-depth assessment of "interests among a broad range of occupations, work and leisure activities, and educational subjects"… "to help individuals match their interests with occupational, educational, and leisure pursuits that are compatible with those interests."
Population: Ages 16 and over.
Publication Dates: 1927-2005.
Acronym: Strong.
Scores, 290: 6 General Occupational Themes: Realistic, Investigative, Artistic, Social, Enterprising, Conventional; 30 Basic Interest Scales: Realistic (Mechanics & Construction, Computer Hardware & Electronics, Military, Protective Services, Nature & Agriculture, Athletics), Investigative (Science, Research, Medical Science, Mathematics), Artistic (Visual Arts & Design, Performing Arts, Writing & Mass Communication, Culinary Arts), Social (Counseling & Helping, Teaching & Education, Human Resources & Training, Social Sciences, Religion & Spirituality, Healthcare Services), Enterprising (Marketing & Advertising, Sales, Entrepreneurship, Politics & Public Speaking, Law), Conventional (Office Management, Taxes & Accounting, Programming & Information Systems, Finance & Investing); 244 Occupational Scales: Accountant (f, m), Actuary (f, m), Administrative Assistant (f, m), Advertising Account Manager (f, m), Architect (f, m), Art Teacher (f, m), Artist (f, m), Athletic Trainer (f, m), Attorney (f, m), Automobile Mechanic (f, m), Banker (f, m), Biologist (f, m), Bookkeeper (f, m), Broadcast Journalist (f, m), Business Education Teacher (f, m), Buyer (f, m), Carpenter (f, m), Chef (f, m), Chemist (f, m), Chiropractor (f, m), College Instructor (f, m), Community Service Director (f, m), Computer & IS Manager (f, m), Computer Scientist (f, m), Computer Systems Analyst (f, m), Corporate Trainer (f, m), Cosmetologist (f, m), Credit Manager (f, m), Dentist (f, m), Dietitian (f, m), Editor (f, m), Elected Public Official (f, m), Electrician (f, m), Elementary School Teacher (f, m), Emergency Medical Technician (f, m), Engineer (f, m), Engineering Technician (f, m), English Teacher (f, m),

ESL Instructor (f, m), Farmer/Rancher (f, m), Financial Analyst (f, m), Financial Manager (f, m), Firefighter (f, m), Flight Attendant (f, m), Florist (f, m), Food Service Manager (f, m), Foreign Language Teacher (f, m), Forester (f, m), Geographer (f, m), Geologist (f, m), Graphic Designer (f, m), Health Information Specialist (f, m), Horticulturist (f, m), Housekeeping/Maintenance Manager (f, m), Human Resources Manager (f, m), Interior Designer (f, m), Investments Manager (f, m), Landscape/Grounds Manager (f, m), Law Enforcement Officer (f, m), Librarian (f, m), Licensed Practical Nurse (f, m), Life Insurance Agent (f, m), Marketing Manager (f, m), Mathematician (f, m), Mathematics Teacher (f, m), Medical Illustrator (f, m), Medical Technician (f, m), Medical Technologist (f, m), Military Enlisted (f, m), Military Officer (f, m), Minister (f, m), Musician (f, m), Network Administrator (f, m), Nursing Home Administrator (f, m), Occupational Therapist (f, m), Operations Manager (f, m), Optician (f, m), Optometrist (f, m), Paralegal (f, m), Parks & Recreation Manager (f, m), Pharmacist (f, m), Photographer (f, m), Physical Education Teacher (f, m), Physical Therapist (f, m), Physician (f, m), Physicist (f, m), Production Worker (f, m), Psychologist (f, m), Public Administrator (f, m), Public Relations Director (f, m), Purchasing Agent (f, m), R&D Manager (f, m), Radiologic Technologist (f, m), Realtor (f, m), Recreation Therapist (f, m), Registered Nurse (f, m), Rehabilitation Counselor (f, m), Reporter (f, m), Respiratory Therapist (f, m), Restaurant Manager (f, m), Retail Sales Manager (f, m), Retail Sales Representative (f, m), Sales Manager (f, m), School Administrator (f, m), School Counselor (f, m), Science Teacher (f, m), Social Science Teacher (f, m), Social Worker (f, m), Sociologist (f, m), Software Developer (f, m), Special Education Teacher (f, m), Speech Pathologist (f, m), Technical Sales Representative (f, m), Technical Support Specialist (f, m), Technical Writer (f, m), Top Executive (f, m), Translator (f, m), Travel Consultant (f, m), University Professor (f, m), Urban & Regional Planner (f, m), Veterinarian (f, m), Vocational Agriculture Teacher (f, m); 5 Personal Style Scales: Work Style, Learning Environment, Leadership Style, Risk Taking, Team Orientation; 9 Administrative Indexes: Total Percentage, Occupations, Subject Areas, Activities, Leisure Activities, People, Your Characteristics, Total Response Index, Typicality Index.
Administration: Individual or group.
Price Data, 2011: $9.25 each for Strong Profile online administration; $9.25 each for Strong Profile, College Edition online administration; $8.50 each for Strong Profile, High School Edition online administration; $15.25 each for Strong Interpretive Report online administration; $12.25 each for Strong Interest Inventory and Skills Confidence Inventory online administration; $12.25 each for Strong and MBTI® Career Report (NOTE: this report requires simultaneous or previous purchase of an MBTI® administration); $69.50 each for Strong Interest Inventory manual (2005, 286 pages); $29.50 each for Strong Interest Inventory User's Guide;

$39.50 each for Strong Interest Inventory College Profile User's Guide; $39.50 each for Skills Confidence Inventory Manual; $10.75 each for Where Do I Go Next (Using Your Strong Results to Manage Your Career); $10.75 each for Career Exploration for College Students (Using the Strong and MBTI® Tools To Chart Your Course); mail-in scoring options are available for most Strong instruments (see www.cpp.com for a complete listing of options).

Time: (35-40) minutes.

Authors: David A. C. Donnay, Michael L. Morris, Nancy A. Schaubhut, and Richard C. Thompson; Judith Grutter and Allen L. Hammer (user's guide).

Publisher: CPP, Inc.

Cross References: For reviews by Kevin R. Kelly and by Neeta Kantamneni and Michael J. Scheel, see 18:129; for reviews by Kevin R. Kelly and Eugene P. Sheehan of the 1994 Edition, see 15:248; see also T5:1790 (19 references); for reviews by John Christian Busch and by Blaine R. Worthen and Perry Sailor of the Fourth Edition, see 12:374 (43 references); see also T4:2581 (64 references); for reviews by Wilbur L. Layton and Bert W. Westbrook, see 9:1195 (17 references); see also T3:2318 (99 references); for reviews by John O. Crites, Robert H. Dolliver, Patricia W. Lunneborg, and excerpted reviews by Richard W. Johnson, David P. Campbell, and Jean C. Steinhauer, see 8:1023 (289 references, these references are for SVIB-M, SBIV-W, and SCII). For references on the Strong Vocational Interest Blank For Men, see T2:2212 (133 references); for reviews by Martin R. Katz and Charles J. Krauskopf and excerpted reviews by David P. Campbell and John W. M. Rothney, see 7:1036 (485 references); for reviews by Alexander W. Astin and Edward J. Furst, see 6:1070 (189 references); see also 5:868 (153 references); for reviews by Edward S. Bordin and Elmer D. Hinckley, see 4:747 (98 references); see also 3:647 (102 references); for reviews by Harold D. Carter, John G. Darley, and N. W. Morton, see 2:1680 (71 references); for a review by John G. Darley, see 1:1178. For references on the Strong Vocational Interest Blank For Women, see T2:2213 (30 references); for reviews by Dorothy M. Clendenen and Barbara A. Kirk, see 7:1037 (92 references); see also 6:1071 (12 references) and 5:869 (19 references); for a review by Gwendolen Schneidler Dickson, see 3:649 (38 references); for a review by Ruth Strang, see 2:1681 (10 references); for a review by John G. Darley, see 1:1179.

[2577]

The Strong Narrative Assessment Procedure.

Purpose: Designed to "evaluate language and narrative skills of students with diverse impairments such as language, learning, and cognitive challenges."

Population: Grades K-8.

Publication Date: 1998.

Acronym: SNAP.

Scores, 56: Awareness of Story Structure (Setting Includes Place and Time, Identification of Central Characters), Major Plot Episodes (Statement of Problem, Statement of Plan to Solve Problem, Statement of Problem Resolution), Use of Stylistic Devices (Formal Beginning of Story, Formal Conclusion), Coherence (Logical Story Consequence, Correct Sequence of Events, Use of Transition Terms), Total Story Retelling, Responses to Comprehension Questions (Factual, Inferential), Length (Number of C-units, Number of Words), Syntax (Average Words per C-unit, Total Number of Clauses, Number of Subordinate Clauses, Number of Clauses per C-unit, Number of Adverbial Clauses, Number of Nominal Clauses, Number of Relative Clauses, Complex Subordination, Cohesion (Number of Incomplete/Erroneous Reference Cohesion Ties, Number of Complete Reference Cohesion Ties, Total Reference Cohesion Ties, Percentage of Incomplete/Erroneous Reference Ties, Successful Revisions of Reference Ties, Total Number of Conjunction Cohesion Ties, Number of Additive Ties, Number of Temporal Ties, Number of Causal Ties, Number of Adversative Ties, Percentage of Additive Ties, Percentage of Temporal Ties, Percentage of Causal Ties, Percentage of Adversative Ties, Examples of Types of Conjunction Cohesion Ties, Examples of Conjunction Cohesion Ties Used Erroneously, Story Grammar (Total Number of Story Grammar Components, Number of Settings, Percentage of Settings, Number of Initiating Events, Percentage of Initiating Events, Number of Internal Responses, Percentage of Internal Responses, Number of Plans, Percentage of Plans, Number of Attempts, Percentage of Attempts, Number of Consequences, Percentage of Consequences, Number of Reactions, Percentage of Reactions, Number of Complete Episodes, Results of Story Retelling Questionnaire).

Administration: Individual or group.

Price Data, 2006: $99 per complete kit including manual (221 pages), 4 Mercer Mayer books, and 2 audiocassettes (1 story per side).

Time: 45(40-60) minutes per battery.

Comments: This test requires the use of a cassette tape player; 4 picture books/stimulus stories include: A Boy, A Dog and A Frog; Where Are You?; One Frog Too Many; Frog Goes to Dinner.

Author: Carol J. Strong.

Publisher: Thinking Publications.

Cross References: For reviews by Natalie Rathvon and Annita Marie Ward, see 17:178.

[2578]

Stroop Color and Word Test [Adult and Children's Versions, Revised].

Purpose: Designed to test "the ability of the individual to separate the word and color naming stimuli."

Publication Dates: 1978-2003.

Scores, 4: Word, Color, Color-Word, Interference.

Administration: Individual or group.

Forms, 2: Children's Version, Adult Version.

Price Data, 2006: $85 per complete kit including manual and 25 test booklets (specify Children's or Adult Version); $35 per manual (specify Children's [2003, 35 pages] or Adult Version [2002, 72 pages]); $55 per 25 test bookets (specify Children's or Adult Version); $25 per computerized scoring; $80 per Spanish test booklet; $40 per Spanish manual.

Foreign Language Edition: Spanish version available.

Time: (5-15) minutes.

Publisher: Stoelting Co.

a) CHILDREN'S VERSION.

Population: Ages 5-14 years.

Authors: Charles J. Golden, Shawna M. Freshwater, and Zarabeth Golden.

b) ADULT VERSION.

Population: Ages 15 years and older.

Authors: Charles J. Golden and Shawna M. Freshwater.

Cross References: For reviews by Mark Roybal and Louise M. Soares, see 17:179; see also T5:2516 (122 references) and T4:2582 (40 references); for reviews by James R. Evans and George W. Hynd of an earlier edition of the adult version, see 9:1196 (15 references); see also T3:2319 (1 reference).

[2579]

Stroop Neuropsychological Screening Test.

Purpose: Provides "an efficient and sensitive neuropsychological screening measure based on the Stroop procedure."

Population: Ages 18 and over.

Publication Date: 1989.

Acronym: SNST.

Scores, 2: Color, Color-Word.

Administration: Individual.

Price Data, 2006: $126 per introductory kit including manual, 25 Form C stimulus sheets, 25 Form C-W stimulus sheets, and 50 record forms.

Time: 4 minutes (timed).

Authors: Max R. Trenerry, Bruce Crosson, James DeBoe, and William R. Leber.

Publisher: Psychological Assessment Resources, Inc.

Cross References: See T5:2517 (8 references) and T4:2583 (3 references); for reviews by Manfred J. Meier and Cecil R. Reynolds, see 11:382 (1 reference).

[2580]

Structure of Intellect Learning Abilities Test.

Purpose: "Designed to assess a wide variety of cognitive abilities or factors of intelligence in children and adults."

Population: Preschool–adult.

Publication Dates: 1975–1985.

Acronym: SOI-LA.

Administration: Group or individual.

Price Data, 2006: $236.50 per complete kit including 10 standard test booklets (5 Form A and 5 Form B), set of scoring keys, set of stimulus cards, 10 worksheets/profiles, and manual (1985, 165 pages); $28.50 per 5 standard test booklets (specify Form A or B); $44 per scoring keys for Forms A, B, and G; $86 per manual (1985, 165 pages).

Authors: Mary Meeker, Robert Meeker, and Gale H. Roid (manual).

Publisher: Western Psychological Services.

a) FORM A.

Population: Grade 2–adult.

Scores: 26 subtests in 5 test areas: Cognition (Cognition of Figural Units, Cognition of Figural Classes, Cognition of Figural Systems, Cognition of Figural Transformations, Cognition of Symbolic Relations, Cognition of Symbolic Systems, Cognition of Semantic Units, Cognition of Semantic Relations, Cognition of Semantic Systems), Memory (Memory of Figural Units, Memory of Symbolic Units–Visual, Memory of Symbolic Systems–Visual, Memory of Symbolic Units–Auditory, Memory of Symbolic Systems–Auditory, Memory of Symbolic Implications), Evaluation (Evaluation of Figural Units, Evaluation of Figural Classes, Evaluation of Symbolic Classes, Evaluation of Symbolic Systems), Convergent Production (Convergent Production of Figural Units, Convergent Production of Symbolic Systems, Convergent Production of Symbolic Transformations, Convergent Production of Symbolic Implications), and Divergent Production (Divergent Production of Figural Units, Divergent Production of Semantic Units, Divergent Production of Symbolic Relations) yielding 14 general ability scores: Cognition, Memory, Evaluation, Convergent Production, Divergent Production, Figural, Symbolic, Semantic, Units, Classes, Relations, Systems, Transformations, Implications.

Time: (150–180) minutes.

b) FORM B.

Purpose: Alternative to Form A.

c) GIFTED SCREENING FORM (FORM G).

Population: Grade 2–adult.

Subtests, 12: From Form A which best predict gifted status.

Price Data: $26 per 5 test booklets.

Time: (60–90) minutes.

d) PRIMARY FORM (FORM P).

Population: Grades K–3.

Subtests, 11: Similar to Form A, 5 measuring figural abilities, 3 measuring symbolic abilities, and 3 measuring semantic abilities.

Price Data: $27.50 per 5 test booklets; $45 per scoring key.

Time: (60–90) minutes.

Comments: Formerly called Process and Diagnostic Screening Test.

Cross References: See T5:2518 (4 references); for reviews by Jack A. Cummings and Dianna L. Newman, see 10:349 (5 references); for reviews by William E. Coffman and Donald A. Leton of an earlier form, see 9:1197 (2 references); see also T3:2320 (2 references).

[2581]

Structure of Temperament Questionnaire.

Purpose: Designed to "measure the traits which appear as consistent patterns and dynamics of behavior, more or less independently of the content of the situation."
Population: Ages 15-75.
Publication Date: 2007.
Administration: Group.
Price Data, 2009: $147 per complete Extended STQ or Compact STQ test kits including professional manual, 50 response forms, and 50 scoring summary/profile forms; $77 per 50 Extended STQ or Compact STQ carbonless response forms; $20 per 50 scoring summary/profile forms.
Foreign Language Editions: Complete test kits available in Chinese, Polish, Russian and Urdu.
Authors: Vladimir Rusalov and Irina Trofimova.
Publisher: Psychological Services Press.
  a) EXTENDED STQ.
  Acronym: STQ-E.
  Scores, 13: Motor Ergonicity, Social Ergonicity, Intellectual Ergonicity, Motor Plasticity, Social Plasticity, Intellectual Plasticity, Motor Tempo, Social Tempo, Intellectual Tempo, Object-Related Emotionality, Social Emotionality, Intellectual Emotionality, Validity Scale.
  Time: (30) minutes.
  b) COMPACT STQ.
  Acronym: STQ-77.
  Scores, 13: Motor Ergonicity, Social Ergonicity, Motor Tempo, Social Tempo, Sensitivity to Physical Sensations, Empathy, Intellectual Ergonicity, Plasticity, Sensitivity to Probabilities, Self-Confidence, Impulsivity, Neuroticism, Validity Scale.
  Time: (15) minutes.
  c) SHORT STQ.
  Acronym: STQ-26.
  Scores, 13: Motor Ergonicity, Social Ergonicity, Intellectual Ergonicity, Motor Plasticity, Social Plasticity, Intellectual Plasticity, Motor Tempo, Social Tempo, Intellectual Tempo, Object-Related Emotionality, Social Emotionality, Intellectual Emotionality, Validity Scale.
  Time: (10) minutes.
Cross References: For reviews by Gerald E. De-Mauro and Steven V. Rouse, see 18:130.

[2582]

Structured Assessment of Violence Risk in Youth.

Purpose: Designed to "assist professional evaluators in assessing and making judgments about a juvenile's risk for violence."

Population: Ages 12-18.
Publication Dates: 2002-2006.
Acronym: SAVRY.
Scores: Total rating only.
Administration: Individual.
Price Data, 2010: $98 per complete kit including professional manual (2006, 97 pages) and 50 rating forms; $62 per 50 rating forms; $46 per professional manual.
Time: [10-15] minutes.
Comments: Completed by a mental health professional utilizing multiple sources to provide accurate estimates of behavior; structured interview questions also included.
Authors: Randy Borum, Patrick Bartel, and Adelle Forth.
Publisher: Psychological Assessment Resources, Inc.
Cross References: For reviews by Cynthia Hazel and Shawn Powell, see 18:131.

[2583]

Structured Clinical Interview for DSM-IV Axis I Disorders: Clinician Version.

Purpose: Constructed as "a semistructured interview for making the major DSM-IV Axis I diagnoses."
Population: Psychiatric or general medical patients ages 18 or older.
Publication Date: 1997.
Acronym: SCID-CV.
Scores, 6: Mood Episodes, Psychotic Symptoms, Psychotic Disorders, Mood Disorders, Substance Use Disorders, Anxiety and Other Disorders.
Administration: Individual.
Price Data, 2006: $116 per complete kit including user's guide (138 pages), administration booklet (84 pages), and 5 score sheets; $45.50 per packet of 5 score sheets; $52 per user's guide; $48.95 per administration booklet.
Time: (45–90) minutes.
Comments: Shortened, clinician version of the Structured Clinical interview for DSM-IV Axis I Disorders: Research Version.
Authors: Michael B. First, Robert L. Spitzer, Miriam Gibbon, and Janet B. W. Williams.
Publisher: American Psychiatric Publishing, Inc.
Cross References: For reviews by Paul D. Werner and Thomas A. Widiger, see 14:373; see also T5:2519 (56 references).

[2584]

Structured Clinical Interview for DSM-IV Axis II Personality Disorders.

Purpose: Designed as "a semistructured diagnostic interview for assessing the 10 DSM-IV Axis II personality disorders as well as Depressive Personality Disorder and Passive-Aggressive Personality Disorder."
Population: Adults receiving psychiatric or general medical care.
Publication Date: 1997.

Acronym: SCID-II.

Scores, 13: Avoidant, Dependent, Obsessive-Compulsive, Passive-Aggressive, Depressive, Paranoid, Schizotypal, Schizoid, Histrionic, Narcissistic, Borderline, Antisocial, Not Otherwise Specified.

Administration: Individual.

Price Data, 2006: $84 per complete kit including user's guide and packet of 5 interviews and questionnaire; $45.50 per 5 interviews and questionnaires; $53 per user's guide.

Time: Administration time not reported.

Comments: Also includes optional, self-report SCID-II Personality Questionnaire.

Authors: Michael B. First, Miriam Gibbon, Robert L. Spitzer, Janet B. W. Williams, and Lorna Smith Benjamin.

Publisher: American Psychiatric Publishing, Inc.

Cross References: For reviews by Paul A. Arbisi and Suzanne G. Martin, see 14:374; see also T5:2520 (25 references).

[2585]

Structured Clinical Interview for DSM-IV Dissociative Disorders–Revised.

Purpose: "Can be used to assess dissociative symptoms and disorders in subjects with a variety of psychiatric illnesses."

Population: Adults with psychiatric illnesses.

Publication Date: 1994.

Acronym: SCID-D-R.

Scores, 5: Amnesia, Depersonalization, Derealization, Identity Confusion, Identity Alteration.

Administration: Individual.

Price Data, 2006: $69 per Interviewer's Guide (168 pages); $45.50 package of 5 interviews; $97 per Interviewer's Guide and package of 5 interviews.

Time: Administration time not reported.

Comments: Composed of both closed- and open-ended questions and does not provide quantitative information regarding a subject; can be used as part of an overall battery of psychiatric diagnostic instruments, or can be administered independently.

Author: Marlene Steinberg.

Publisher: American Psychiatric Publishing, Inc.

[2586]

Structured Interview for the Five-Factor Model of Personality.

Purpose: Designed to "assess both normal and abnormal personality functioning" using the Five-Factor Model.

Population: Ages 18 and above.

Publication Date: 1997.

Acronym: SIFFM.

Scores, 35: Neuroticism (Anxiety, Hostility, Depression, Self-Consciousness, Impulsiveness, Vulnerability, Total), Extraversion (Warmth, Gregariousness, Assertive-ness, Activity, Excitement-Seeking, Positive Emotions, Total), Openness to Experience (Fantasy, Aesthetics, Feelings, Actions, Ideas, Values, Total), Agreeableness (Trust, Straightforwardness, Altruism, Compliance, Modesty, Tender-Mindedness, Total), Conscientiousness (Competence, Order, Dutifulness, Achievement-Striving, Self-Discipline, Deliberation, Total).

Administration: Individual.

Price Data, 2006: $128 per introductory kit including 25 interview booklets and professional manual (85 pages).

Time: (60) minutes.

Authors: Timothy J. Trull and Thomas A. Widiger.

Publisher: Psychological Assessment Resources, Inc.

Cross References: For reviews by Paul M. Mastrangelo and Susana Urbina, see 15:249.

[2587]

Structured Interview of Reported Symptoms, 2nd Edition.

Purpose: Designed to "evaluate feigning of psychiatric symptoms" and "the manner in which it is likely to occur."

Population: Ages 18 and over.

Publication Dates: 1986-2010.

Acronym: SIRS-2.

Scores, 14: Primary Scales (Rare Symptoms, Symptom Combinations, Improbable or Absurd Symptoms, Blatant Symptoms, Subtle Symptoms, Selectivity of Symptoms, Severity of Symptoms, Reported vs. Observed Symptoms), Classification Scale (Rare Symptoms-Total), Supplementary Scales (Direct Appraisal of Honesty, Defensive Symptoms, Improbable Failure, Overly Specified Symptoms, Inconsistency of Symptoms); plus 2 indexes (Modified Total Index, Supplementary Scale Index).

Administration: Individual.

Price Data, 2010: $285 per complete kit including 25 interview booklets, 2 security templates, and manual (2010, 130 pages); $220 per 25 interview booklets; $10 per set of 2 security templates; $80 per manual.

Foreign Language Edition: Interview booklet available in Spanish.

Time: (30-45) minutes.

Authors: Richard Rogers (interview booklet and manual), Kenneth W. Sewell (manual), and Nathan D. Gillard (manual).

Publisher: Psychological Assessment Resources.

Cross References: For reviews by David N. Dixon and Ronald J. Ganellen of an earlier edition, see 12:375.

[2588]

Structured Inventory of Malingered Symptomatology.

Purpose: Designed as a screening measure of malingering to assess symptoms of both feigned psychopathology and cognitive function.

Population: Ages 18 and over.

Publication Date: 2005.
Acronym: SIMS.
Scores, 6: Neurologic Impairment, Affective Disorders, Psychosis, Low Intelligence, Amnestic Disorders, Total.
Administration: Individual.
Price Data, 2007: $120 per complete kit including professional manual (46 pages) and 25 response forms; $68 per professional manual; $60 per 25 response forms.
Time: (10-15) minutes.
Comments: This test can be self-administered.
Authors: Glenn P. Smith and Michelle R. Widows.
Publisher: Psychological Assessment Resources, Inc.
Cross References: For reviews by Thomas M. Dunn and Ronald J. Ganellen, see 17:180.

[2589]

Structured Photographic Articulation Test II Featuring Dudsberry.

Purpose: Designed to assess children's articulation and phonological skills.
Population: Ages 3-0 through 9-11 years.
Publication Dates: 1989–2001.
Acronym: SPAT-D II.
Scores: Total score only.
Administration: Individual.
Price Data: Available from publisher.
Time: Administration time not reported.
Comments: Forty photographs are used to assess 59 singleton consonants and 10 consonant blends; revision of the Structured Photographic Articulation Test Featuring Dudsberry (SPAT-D).
Authors: Janet I. Dawson and Patricia J. Tattersall.
Publisher: Janelle Publications, Inc.
Cross References: For reviews by Mildred Murray-Ward and Roger L. Towne, see 16:236; for reviews by Clinton W. Bennett and Susan Felsenfeld of the earlier edition, see 12:376.

[2590]

Structured Photographic Expressive Language Test-Preschool 2.

Purpose: Designed to "probe a child's ability to generate early developing morphological and syntactic forms."
Population: Ages 3 to 5-11.
Publication Dates: 1983-2004.
Acronym: SPELT-P 2.
Scores: Total score only.
Administration: Individual.
Price Data, 2008: $165 per manual (2005, 79 pages), 37 color photographs, and 50 response forms.
Time: (20) minutes.
Comments: Includes a system of alternative response structures for assessment of the African American population.
Authors: Janet Dawson, Connie Stout, Julia Eyer, Patricia Tattersall, Janice Fonkalsrud, and Karen Croley.
Publisher: Janelle Publications, Inc.

Cross References: For reviews by Tiffany L. Hutchins and Roger L. Towne, see 18:132; see T5:2524 (13 references) and T4:2588 (1 reference); for a review by Joan D. Berryman of an earlier edition, see 9:1198 (2 references).

[2591]

Structured Photographic Expressive Language Test-Third Edition.

Purpose: Designed to "examine expressive use of morphology and syntax."
Population: Ages 4 to 9-11.
Publication Dates: 1983-2003.
Acronym: SPELT-3.
Score: Total score only.
Administration: Individual.
Price Data, 2008: $165 per manual (2003, 97 pages), 54 color photographs, 30 response forms, and storage box.
Time: (20) minutes.
Comments: Includes a system of alternative response structures for assessment of the African American population.
Authors: Janet I. Dawson, Connie E. Stout, and Julia A. Eyer.
Publisher: Janelle Publications.
Cross References: For reviews by Jorge E. Gonzalez and Craig S. Shwery and by Darrell L. Sabers and Huaping Sun, see 18:133; see T5:2524 (13 references) and T4:2588 (1 reference); for a review by Joan D. Berryman of an earlier edition, see 9:1198 (2 references).

[2592]

Student Adaptation to College Questionnaire.

Purpose: "Designed to assess how well a student is adapting to the demands of the college experience."
Population: College freshmen.
Publication Date: 1989.
Acronym: SACQ.
Scores, 5: Academic Adjustment, Social Adjustment, Personal Emotional Adjustment, Attachment, Full Scale.
Administration: Group or individual.
Price Data, 2006: $98.50 per complete kit including 25 hand-scorable questionnaires and manual (76 pages) $47 per 25 hand-scorable questionnaires; $55 per manual; $14.50 per computer-scored mail-in answer sheet (quantity discounts available).
Time: 15 to 20 minutes.
Authors: Robert W. Baker and Bohdan Siryk.
Publisher: Western Psychological Services.
Cross References: See T5:2525 (13 references) and T4:2590 (9 references); for a review by E. Jack Asher, Jr., see 11:383 (4 references).

[2593]

Student Adjustment Inventory.

Purpose: Designed as "an instrument for identifying common affective-social problems."
Population: Upper elementary, junior high, senior high, and beginning college students.

Publication Dates: 1975–1989.
Acronym: SAI.
Scores, 7: Self-Esteem, Group Interaction, Self-Discipline, Communication, Energy/Effort, Learning/Studying, Attitude Towards Learning Environment.
Administration: Group or individual.
Price Data, 2005: $34 per report kit including manual (1989, 23 pages), 2 reusable test booklets, 5 answer sheets, and processing of 5 mail-in reports; $10 per 10 reusable test booklets; $8 per 50 answer sheets; $10 per manual; $5.45-$6.35 per mail-in report; $225 per SAI microcomputer version per 50 administrations (IBM 3.5-inch disk).
Time: (20–30) minutes.
Comments: Available in pencil and paper or micro-computer versions.
Author: James R. Barclay.
Publisher: MetriTech, Inc.
Cross References: For reviews by Philip Ash and Mark J. Benson, see 12:377.

[2594]
Student Behavior Survey.

Purpose: A multidimensional assessment to rate behavior and classroom performance to reflect the presence of problems in emotional and behavioral adjustment.
Population: Ages 5–18.
Publication Date: 2000.
Acronym: SBS.
Scores: 11 scales: Academic Performance, Academic Habits, Social Skills, Parent Participation, Health Concerns, Emotional Distress, Unusual Behavior, Social Problems, Verbal Aggression, Physical Aggression, Behavior Problems.
Administration: Individual.
Price Data, 2006: $95 per introductory kit including 25 AutoScore™ answer/profile forms and manual (72 pages); $40 per 25 AutoScore™ answer/profile forms; $59.50 per manual.
Time: Untimed.
Comments: Ratings by teachers.
Authors: David Lachar, Sabine A. Wingenfeld, Rex B. Kline, and Christian P. Gruber.
Publisher: Western Psychological Services.
Cross References: For reviews by Stephen N. Axford and by Michael J. Furlong and Renee Pavelski, see 15:250.

[2595]
Student Developmental Task and Lifestyle Assessment.

Purpose: "Assisting students in understanding their own development and establishing goals and plans to shape their own futures."
Population: College students ages 17-24.
Publication Date: 1987.
Acronym: SDTLA.

Scores, 12: Establishing and Clarifying Purpose Task (Educational Involvement Subtask, Career Planning Subtask, Life Management Subtask, Lifestyle Planning Subtask, Cultural Participation Subtask), Developing Mature Interpersonal Relationships Task (Peer Relationships Subtask, Tolerance Subtask, Emotional Autonomy Subtask), Academic Autonomy Task, Salubrious Lifestyle Scale, Intimacy Scale, Response Bias Scale.
Administration: Group.
Price Data: $150 for online setup and processing of results plus $2 per completed student inventory.
Time: (30-40) minutes.
Comments: Revision of the Student Developmental Task Inventory, Revised, Second Edition.
Authors: Roger B. Winston, Jr., Theodore K. Miller, and Diane L. Cooper.
Publisher: Appalachian State University.
Cross References: See T5:2527 (17 references) and T4:2592 (9 references); for reviews by Mary Henning-Stout and Willam D. Porterfield, see 11:384 (13 references); for reviews by Fred H. Borgen and Steven D. Brown of the Second Edition, see 9:1199 (5 references).

[2596]
Student Instructional Report II.

Purpose: Designed to objectively capture students' evaluations of faculty performance.
Population: College faculty and administrators.
Publication Dates: 1971–2006.
Acronym: SIR II.
Scores: 45 item scores plus up to 10 optional locally prepared items.
Administration: Group.
Price Data: Available from publisher at www.ets.org/SIRII.
Time: (10–15) minutes.
Comments: Students anonymously answer questions covering multiple dimensions of their college instruction; the informed feedback and timely responses are intended to be helpful to faculty who are experimenting with new classroom practices and teaching methods; a Distance Learning Version is also available (e-SirII).
Author: Educational Testing Service.
Publisher: Educational Testing Service.
Cross References: See T5:2531 (3 references), T4:2597 (1 reference), and T3:2334 (3 references); for reviews by Frank Costin and William C. McGaghie of the earlier edition, see 8:398 (16 references); see also T2:894 (1 reference).

[2597]
Student Opinion Inventory, Revised Edition.

Purpose: To assess students' opinions concerning many facets of the school and to "solicit students' recommendations for improvement."
Population: Grades 5–12.

Publication Dates: 1974–2003.
Scores: 4 subscales: Quality of the Instructional Program, Support for Student Learning, School Climate/Environment for Learning, Student Activities/Intervention in School.
Administration: Group.
Parts, 2: A (Likert-scale items), B (customize up to 20 local questions).
Price Data, 2006: $25 per 25 inventories; administrator's manual may be downloaded free from publisher website.
Time: (35–40) minutes.
Author: National Study of School Evaluation.
Publisher: National Study of School Evaluation.
Cross References: See T3:2335 (1 reference).

[2598]

Student Rights Scales.

Purpose: Designed to determine student and teacher perceptions of student rights in junior and senior high school.
Population: Grades 7–12.
Publication Dates: 1982–1986.
Acronym: SRS.
Scores, 5: General Rights, Due Process, Academic Self Determination, Freedom of Expression, Personal Conduct.
Administration: Group.
Price Data: Available from publisher.
Time: Administration time not reported.
Comments: For research use only.
Author: Thomas R. Oaster.
Publisher: Thomas R. Oaster.
Cross References: For reviews by Steven W. Lee and David Moshman, see 10:351.

[2599]

Student Self-Concept Scale.

Purpose: An individually or group-administered multidimensional measure of self-concept.
Population: Grades 3–12.
Publication Date: 1993.
Acronym: SSCS.
Scores, 13: Self-Confidence (Self-Image, Academic, Social, Lie, Composite), Importance (Self-Image, Academic, Social, Lie), Outcome Confidence (Self-Image, Academic, Social, Composite).
Administration: Group or individual.
Levels, 2: Grades 3–6, grades 7–12.
Price Data, 2006: $46.99 per 25 record booklets (specify Level 1 or Level 2); $64.99 per manual (82 pages).
Time: (20–30) minutes.
Authors: Frank M. Gresham, Stephen N. Elliott, and Sally E. Evans-Fernandez.
Publisher: Pearson.

Cross References: For reviews by Jeri Benson and Frederick T. L. Leong, see 13:303.

[2600]

Student Styles Questionnaire™.

Purpose: "Designed to detect individual differences students display in their preferences, temperaments, and personal styles."
Population: Ages 8–13.
Publication Date: 1996.
Acronym: SSQ.
Scores, 8: Extroverted, Introverted, Practical, Imaginative, Thinking, Feeling, Organized, Flexible.
Administration: Group or individual.
Price Data, 2002: $98 per starter kit including manual (241 pages), classroom applications booklet, 5 Ready Score™ answer documents, and question booklet; $66 per 25 question booklets; $35 per 25 Ready Score™ answer documents; $18 per 25 record forms; $75 per manual; $22 per classroom applications booklet; $107 per microcomputer kit including 3.5-inch diskette, user's guide, and 25 record forms (Windows only).
Time: (30) minutes.
Authors: Thomas Oakland, Joseph Glutting, and Connie Horton.
Publisher: Pearson.
Cross References: For reviews by Gregory Schraw and Jay R. Stewart, see 14:375.

[2601]

Student Talent and Risk Profile.

Purpose: To identify talented students as well as students "at-risk" for counseling, guidance, and special teaching strategies.
Population: Grades 5–12.
Publication Date: 1990.
Acronym: STAR Profile.
Scores, 7: Academic Performance, Creativity, Artistic Potential, Leadership, Emotional Maturity, Educational Orientation, At Risk.
Administration: Group.
Price Data: Available from publisher.
Time: (60–65) minutes.
Comments: Revision of Biographical Inventory Form U.
Author: Institute for Behavioral Research in Creativity.
Publisher: Institute for Behavioral Research in Creativity.
Cross References: For reviews by Barbara Kerr and John W. Shepard, see 12:378; for reviews by Christopher Borman and Courtland C. Lee of Biographical Inventory Form U, see 9:150.

[2602]

Student-Teacher Relationship Scale.

Purpose: "Provides a quantitative self-report assessment of the relationship between a teacher and a specific student."

Population: Teachers of preschool through Grade 3 students.
Publication Date: 2001.
Acronym: STRS.
Scores, 4: Conflict, Closeness, Dependency, Total.
Administration: Group or individual.
Price Data, 2006: $96 per introductory kit including professional manual (58 pages), and 50 response forms.
Time: (5–10) minutes per individual; (10–15) minutes per group.
Comments: Intended to inform consultation and intervention efforts as part of the Student, Teachers, and Relationship Support (STARS) program.
Author: Robert C. Pianta.
Publisher: Psychological Assessment Resources, Inc.
Cross References: For reviews by Gerald Giraud and by Jorge E. Gonzalez and Chris Gonzalez, see 15:251.

[2603]

Study Attitudes and Methods Survey [Revised Short Form].

Purpose: "Developed to measure non-cognitive factors associated with success in school."
Population: Junior high, high school, college.
Publication Dates: 1972–1985.
Acronym: SAMS.
Scores, 6: Academic Interest-Love of Learning, Academic Drive-Conformity, Study Methods, Study Anxiety, Manipulation, Alienation Toward Authority.
Administration: Group.
Price Data: Available from publisher.
Time: (20–25) minutes.
Authors: William B. Michael, Joan J. Michael, and Wayne S. Zimmerman.
Publisher: EdITS/Educational and Industrial Testing Service.
Cross References: For reviews by Robert G. Harrington and Kenneth A. Kiewra, see 14:376; see also T5:2538 (1 reference), T4:2604 (6 references), and T3:2340 (2 references); for reviews by Allen Berger and John W. Lombard of an earlier edition, see 8:818 (6 references); see also T2:1766 (4 references).

[2604]

Stuttering Prediction Instrument for Young Children.

Purpose: Designed to "measure severity and predict chronicity."
Population: Ages 3-8.
Publication Date: 1981.
Acronym: SPI.
Scores, 5: Reactions, Part-Word Repetitions, Prolongations, Frequency, Total.
Administration: Individual.
Price Data, 2011: $121 per complete kit including 50 tests, picture plates, and manual (45 pages); $59 per 50 test forms; $69 per manual with picture plates.

Time: Administration time not reported.
Comments: Information taken from parent interview, observation and tape recording of the child's speech, and analysis of the tape recording.
Author: Glyndon D. Riley.
Publisher: PRO-ED.
Cross References: See T5:2542 (2 references) and T4:2612 (1 reference).

[2605]

Stuttering Severity Instrument for Children and Adults, Third Edition.

Purpose: "Measures stuttering severity for both children and adults."
Population: School-age children and adults.
Publication Dates: 1980–1994.
Acronym: SSI-3.
Scores, 8: Frequency, Duration, Physical Concomitants (Distracting Sounds, Facial Grimaces, Head Movements, Movements of the Extremities, Total), Total.
Administration: Individual.
Forms, 2: Reading, Nonreading.
Price Data: Available from publisher.
Time: Administration time not reported.
Comments: Tape recorder necessary for speech sample; the publisher advises that a Fourth Edition is now available.
Author: Glyndon D. Riley.
Publisher: PRO-ED.
Cross References: See T5:2543 (3 references); for reviews by Ronald B. Gillam and Rebecca McCauley, see 13:304 (21 references); see also T4:2613 (5 references).

[2606]

Style of Learning and Thinking.

Purpose: To indicate a student's learning stategy and brain hemisphere preference in problem solving.
Population: Grades K–5, 6–12.
Publication Date: 1988.
Acronym: SOLAT.
Scores, 3: Whole Brain, Left Brain, Right Brain.
Administration: Group.
Forms, 2: Elementary, Youth.
Price Data: See www.ststesting.com for up-to-date pricing.
Time: [30-40] minutes.
Comments: Self-scored.
Authors: E. Paul Torrance, Bernice McCarthy, Mary Kolesinski, and Jamie Smith.
Publisher: Scholastic Testing Service, Inc.
Cross References: See T5:2545 (6 references); for reviews by Kenneth A. Kiewra and Damian McShane and by Donald U. Robertson and Virginia L. Brown, see 11:390 (2 references).

[2607]

Styles of Leadership Survey.
Purpose: Assesses individual leadership skills under a variety of conditions.
Population: Adults.
Publication Dates: 1968-1995.
Scores, 5: Philosophy, Planning and Goal Setting, Implementation, Performance and Evaluation, Total.
Administration: Group.
Price Data, 2001: $8.95 per instrument.
Time: Untimed.
Comments: Self-administered survey.
Authors: Jay Hall, Jerry B. Harvey, and Martha S. Williams.
Publisher: Teleometrics International, Inc.
Cross References: See T5:2547 (1 reference); for reviews by Kenneth N. Anchor and Norman D. Sundberg, see 12:379 (1 reference); see T3:2351 (1 reference); for a review by Abraham K. Korman of [Styles of Leadership and Management], see 8:1185 (8 references).

[2608]

Styles of Management Inventory.
Purpose: Assesses individual management style under a variety of conditions.
Population: Adults.
Publication Dates: 1964-2000.
Scores, 5: Philosophy, Planning and Goal Setting, Implementation, Performance Evaluation, Total.
Administration: Group.
Price Data, 2001: $8.95 per instrument.
Time: Untimed.
Comments: Self-administered survey.
Authors: Jay Hall, Jerry B. Harvey, and Martha S. Williams.
Publisher: Teleometrics International, Inc.
Cross References: For reviews by Richard W. Faunce and Linda F. Wightman, see 12:380; see T3:2351 (1 reference); for a review by Abraham K. Korman of [Styles of Leadership and Management], see 8:1185 (8 references).

[2609]

Styles of Teamwork Inventory.
Purpose: Assess individual feelings about working in teams and the behaviors one typically employs in work-team situations.
Population: Individuals whose work responsibilities require work-team cooperation.
Publication Dates: 1963-1995.
Acronym: STI.
Scores, 5: Synergistic, Compromise, Win-Lose, Yield-Lose, Lose-Leave.
Administration: Group.
Price Data, 2001: $8.95 per instrument.
Time: Administration time not reported.
Comments: Based on Team Behaviors Model of analysis of individual behaviors in a team setting; self

ratings; self scored; formerly called Group Encounter Survey (T3:1014).
Author: Jay Hall.
Publisher: Teleometrics International, Inc.
Cross References: See 8:1048 (2 references).

[2610]

Substance Abuse Life Circumstance Evaluation.
Purpose: "Designed to assess alcohol and drug use/abuse behavior, as well as the role that attitude and stress may play in this use/abuse."
Population: Adults.
Publication Date: 1988.
Acronym: SALCE.
Scores, 6: Test-Taking Attitude, Life Circumstance Evaluation, Drinking Evaluation Category, Alcohol Addiction Evaluation, Drug Use Evaluation, Summary Score.
Administration: Individual or group.
Price Data: Available from publisher.
Time: (20) minutes.
Comments: Self-administered; computer scored, IBM compatible with Windows required; provides both DSM-IV classification and ASAM patient placement criteria.
Author: ADE Incorporated.
Publisher: ADE Incorporated.
Cross References: For a review by Anita M. Hubley, see 14:377.

[2611]

Substance Abuse Relapse Assessment.
Purpose: Designed to help "develop relapse prevention goals and monitor treatment progress."
Population: Adolescents and adults.
Publication Date: 1993.
Acronym: SARA.
Scores: 4 parts: Substance Abuse Behavior, Antecedents of Substance Abuse, Consequences of Substance Abuse, Responses to Slips and Relapses.
Administration: Individual.
Price Data, 2006: $130 per introductory kit including 25 interview record forms, 25 each of 3 relapse prevention planning forms, and manual (31 pages) with stimulus card.
Time: (60) minutes.
Authors: Lawrence Schonfeld, Roger Peters, and Addis Dolente.
Publisher: Psychological Assessment Resources, Inc.
Cross References: For reviews by Michael G. Kavan and Jeffrey S. Rain, see 13:306.

[2612]

Substance Abuse Screening Test.
Purpose: "Designed to screen-out those students who are unlikely to have a substance abuse problem."
Population: Ages 13–adult.

Publication Date: 1993.
Acronym: SAST.
Scores: Total Level of Risk.
Administration: Group.
Forms, 2: Response Form, Observation Report.
Price Data, 2002: $56 per complete kit including 50 Response Forms, 50 Observation Reports, and manual (34 pages); $21 per 50 Response Forms; $21 per 50 Observation Reports; $29 per manual.
Time: (5) minutes.
Authors: Terry Hibpshman and Sue Larson.
Publisher: Slosson Educational Publications, Inc.
Cross References: For reviews by Mary Lou Kelley and Mariela C. Shirley, see 13:307.

[2613]
The Substance Abuse Subtle Screening Inventory–3.
Purpose: Designed to "identify individuals who have a high probability of having a substance dependence disorder."
Population: Ages 18–73.
Publication Dates: 1983–1997.
Acronym: SASSI-3.
Scores: 10 subscales: Face Valid Alcohol, Face Valid Other Drugs, Symptoms, Obvious Attributes, Subtle Attributes, Defensiveness, Supplemental Addiction Measure, Family vs. Controls, Correctional, Random Answering Pattern.
Administration: Individual or group.
Price Data: Available from publisher.
Time: [15] minutes.
Comments: May be administered as paper-and-pencil instrument with hand scoring or scoring by optical scanning, computer administered, or via audiotape for people with special needs regarding vision or literacy.
Author: Glenn A. Miller.
Publisher: The SASSI Institute.
Cross References: For reviews by Ephrem Fernandez and David J. Pittenger, see 15:252; see T5:2553 (6 references); for reviews by Barbara Kerr and Nicholas A. Vacc of an earlier edition, see 12:381 (1 reference); see also T4:2623 (1 reference).

[2614]
Substance Use Disorders Diagnostic Schedule-IV.
Purpose: "Designed to elicit information related to the diagnosis of substance use disorders."
Population: Adults suspected of abusing alcohol or drugs.
Publication Dates: 1995–2001.
Acronym: SUDDS-IV.
Scores: Number of Current Dependence Symptoms in Past Year, Number of Current Dependence Categories, Number of Current Abuse Symptoms in Past Year, Number of Current Abuse Categories for 10 Substance Categories (Alcohol, Marijuana, Cocaine, Sedatives/

Tranquilizers, Stimulants, Heroin/Other Opioids, Hallucinogens, PCP, Inhalants, Other/Mixed), DSM-IV Psychoactive Substance Use Disorder Diagnosis Codes (Dependence, Abuse), Ratings for Stress, Depression and Anxiety Screens.
Administration: Individual.
Price Data: Available from publisher.
Time: (30–45) minutes.
Comments: Structured diagnostic interview; also available as a computer-administered interview; designed primarily to provide comprehensive diagnostic information for substance use disorders according to DSM-IV criteria; provides information for patient placement according to American Society of Addiction Medicine criteria.
Authors: Norman G. Hoffmann and Patricia Ann Harrison.
Publisher: Change Companies.
Cross References: For reviews by Tony Cellucci and Mark H. Stone, see 15:253; for reviews by Andres Barona and Steven I. Pfeiffer of an earlier edition, see 13:308 (2 references).

[2615]
Subsumed Abilities Test.
Purpose: Designed "to determine an individual's or group's ability to learn or to use a previously learned written language, system of mathematics, coding system, or other visual symbol system."
Population: Ages 9 and over.
Publication Dates: 1957-1984.
Acronym: SAT.
Scores, 5: Recognition, Abstraction, Conceptualization, Total (Demonstrated Abilities), Potential Abilities.
Administration: Individual or group.
Price Data, 2006: $69 per test package; $39.50 per manual (1963, 12 pages) and manual supplement (1984, 17 pages); $29 per key-tabulation sheet package; $46.50 per specimen set.
Time: 30(40) minutes.
Comments: Subtitle on manual is A Measure of Learning Efficiency.
Author: Joseph R. Sanders.
Publisher: Martin M. Bruce, Ph.D.
Cross References: See T2:582 (2 references); for a review by Naomi Stewart, see 6:560.

[2616]
Suffolk Reading Scale 2.
Purpose: Designed to assess "reading ability."
Population: Ages 6.0 to 14.11.
Publication Dates: 1986–2002.
Acronym: SRS2.
Scores: Total score only.
Administration: Individual or group.
Levels, 3: 1 (Ages 6.0 to 8.11), 2 (Ages 8.0 to 11.11), 3 (Ages 10.0 to 14.11).
Forms, 2: A, B.

Price Data: Available from publisher.
Time: (50) minutes.
Author: Fred Hagley.
Publisher: GL Assessment [England].
Cross References: For reviews by Jennifer N. Mahdavi and Howard Margolis, see 16:237; see also T5:2556 (3 references); for reviews by Robert B. Cooter, Jr. and Richard Lehrer of an earlier edition, see 11:392.

[2617]

Suicidal Ideation Questionnaire.

Purpose: Designed to "screen for suicidal ideation in adolescents."
Population: Grades 7–9 (SIQ), 10–12 (SIQ-JR).
Publication Dates: 1987–1988.
Acronym: SIQ.
Scores: Total Suicidal Ideation.
Administration: Individual or small group.
Levels, 2: SIQ (senior high school), SIQ-JR (junior high school).
Price Data: 2006: $148 per introductory kit including manual (1988, 47 pages), 25 each SIQ and SIQ-JR hand-scorable answer sheets, and scoring keys for SIQ and SIQ-JR.
Time: (5–10) minutes.
Author: William M. Reynolds.
Publisher: Psychological Assessment Resources, Inc.
Cross References: See T5:2556 (11 references) and T4:2627 (1 reference); for reviews by James C. Carmer and Collie W. Conoley, see 11:393 (2 references).

[2618]

Suicide Intervention Response Inventory [Revised].

Purpose: Designed to assess "the paraprofessional's ability to select an appropriate response to the self-destructive client."
Population: Mental health paraprofessionals.
Publication Dates: 1980–1997.
Acronym: SIRI.
Scores: Total score only.
Administration: Group.
Price Data: Available from publisher.
Time: (15) minutes.
Author: Robert A. Neimeyer.
Publisher: Robert A. Neimeyer, Ph.D.
Cross References: See T5:2558 (3 references).

[2619]

Suicide Probability Scale.

Purpose: Designed to "measure an individual's self-reported attitudes and behaviors which have a bearing on suicide risk."
Population: Ages 14 and over.
Publication Date: 1982.
Acronym: SPS.

Scores, 5: Hopelessness, Suicide Ideation, Negative Self-Evaluations, Hostility, Total.
Administration: Group or individual.
Price Data, 2006: $121 per kit including 25 tests, 25 profiles, and manual (73 pages plus test and profile); $43.50 per 25 tests; $42 per 100 profiles; $49.50 per manual; $10 per FAX Service scoring charge.
Time: (5–10) minutes.
Authors: John G. Cull and Wayne S. Gill.
Publisher: Western Psychological Services.
Cross References: See T5:2559 (13 references) and T4:2629 (6 references); for a review by Stephen L. Golding, see 9:1210.

[2620]

Super's Work Values Inventory–Revised.

Purpose: Assesses relative importance of selected attributes of occupations and jobs.
Population: Middle school through adult.
Publication Date: 2001.
Acronym: WVI-R.
Scores, 12: Achievement, Co-Workers, Creativity, Income, Independence, Lifestyle, Mental Challenge, Prestige, Security, Supervision, Work Environment, Variety.
Administration: Individual or group.
Price Data: Available from publisher.
Time: (15–20) minutes.
Comments: Online administration; instant scoring; with Kuder Career Search (1459) and Kuder Skills Assessment (1462), plus the Kuder Electronic Career Portfolio, constitutes the Kuder Career Planning System.
Authors: Donald E. Super; revised by Donald G. Zytowski.
Publisher: Kuder, Inc.
Cross References: See T4:2998 (9 references) and T3:2567 (17 references); for an excerpted review by Frederick Brown of an earlier edition, see 8:1030 (52 references); see also T2:2221 (12 references); for reviews by Ralph F. Berdie and David V. Tiedeman, and an excerpted review by John W. French, see 7:1042 (33 references).

[2621]

SuperSelect.

Purpose: Designed to "assess the work related attitudes, opinions, and behaviors of job applicants for the supermarket bagger, cashier, and courtesy clerk positions."
Population: Age 18 and over.
Publication Date: 2001.
Acronym: BCCC.
Scores, 13: Customer Service, Interpersonal Skills, Communication, Productivity, Work Conduct, Integrity, Drug Avoidance, Adaptability, Candidness, Accuracy, Performance Index, Dependability Index, Overall Composite Index.
Administration: Individual or group.
Price Data: Available from publisher.

Time: Administration time not reported.
Author: Reid London House.
Publisher: Pearson Performance Solutions [No reply from publisher; status unknown].

[2622]

Supervisory Behavior Description Questionnaire.

Purpose: "Designed to measure the behavior patterns of supervisory and management personnel on two major dimensions of leadership: 'Consideration' and 'Structure.'"
Population: Supervisors and prospective supervisors.
Publication Dates: 1970–1996.
Acronym: SBD.
Scores, 2: Consideraton, Structure.
Administration: Group.
Price Data: Available from publisher.
Time: (20) minutes.
Comments: Paper-and-pencil or computer administration available.
Author: Edin A. Reishman.
Publisher: Pearson Performance Solutions [No reply from publisher; status unknown].
Cross References: For reviews by Albert M. Bugaj and Michael J. Roszkowski, see 15:254.

[2623]

Supervisory Inventory on Communication.

Purpose: Designed to assess supervisor's knowledge of certain principles, facts, and techniques of communication.
Population: Supervisors and prospective supervisors.
Publication Dates: 1965-1979.
Acronym: SIC.
Scores: Total score only.
Administration: Group.
Price Data, 2001: $40 per 20 SIC tests and answer booklets; $5 per instructor's manual (1979, 11 pages); $10 per specimen set (including test, answer booklet, manual and leader's guide).
Time: (20) minutes.
Author: Donald L. Kirkpatrick.
Publisher: Donald L. Kirkpatrick (the author).
Cross References: For a review by Joyce L. Carbonell, see 9:1211; see also 7:1152 (1 reference).

[2624]

Supervisory Inventory on Human Relations.

Purpose: Designed to assess supervisors' knowledge of human relations principles, facts, and techniques.
Population: Supervisors and prospective supervisors.
Publication Dates: 1960-1982.
Acronym: SIHR.
Scores: Total score only.
Administration: Group.
Price Data, 2001: $40 per 20 tests and answer booklets; $5 per instructor's manual (1982, 12 pages);

$10 per specimen set (including test, answer booklet, and manual).
Time: (15-20) minutes.
Authors: Donald L. Kirkpatrick and Earl Planty (test).
Publisher: Donald L. Kirkpatrick (the author).
Cross References: See T2:2463 (1 reference); for a review by Seymour Levy of the original edition, see 6:1193 (1 reference).

[2625]

Supervisory Practices Test, Revised.

Purpose: "Designed to aid in appraising supervisory ability and potential."
Population: Supervisors.
Publication Dates: 1957-1984.
Acronym: SPT.
Scores: Total score only.
Administration: Group.
Price Data, 2006: $58.95 per specimen set; $119.50 per test package; $53.00 per manual (1974, 14 pages), manual supplement (1984, 17 pages), and norms supplement; $36.50 per profile sheet package; $3.75 per key.
Foreign Language Editions: French, German, and Spanish editions available.
Time: (20-30) minutes.
Author: Martin M. Bruce.
Publisher: Martin M. Bruce, Ph.D.
Cross References: See T3:2363 (1 reference), T2:2466 (2 references), and 6:1194 (4 references); for reviews by Clifford E. Jurgensen and Mary Ellen Oliverio, see 5:955.

[2626]

Supervisory Simulator.

Purpose: "Designed to assess supervisory skills of first-level supervisors, forepersons and/or team leaders independent of any particular job title or organization; may be used for selection and/or career development."
Population: First-level supervisors, forepersons, or team leaders.
Publication Dates: 1991–2011.
Acronym: SupSim.
Scores, 3: Leadership/Decision Making, Team Relations, Total .
Administration: Group or individual.
Forms, 5: Public and private sector forms include Blue-Collar Teams, Office/Clerical Teams, Police, Fire, Transportation.
Restricted Distribution: Clients may be required to pay a nominal one-time overhead/sign-up fee.
Price Data, 2011: $320-$360 per candidate (depending on the version) for rental/scoring and a detailed Career Development Report that identifies strengths, weaknesses, and developmental needs with specific learning objectives for each of the two factors measured by the test.
Time: (75) minutes.

Comments: All versions are available for online administration.
Author: Richard C. Joines.
Publisher: Management & Personnel Systems, Inc.

[2627]

Supervisory Skills Inventory.

Purpose: Developed to assess a supervisor's day-to-day, on-the-job behavior as seen by self and collectively by five other people.
Population: First-line supervisors.
Publication Date: 1982.
Acronym: SSI.
Scores: 2 scores (Self, Other) in 12 supervisory skill areas: Setting Goals, Planning and Organizing, Directing and Delegating, Solving Problems, Enforcing Work Rules, Relating to and Supporting Staff, Maintaining and Controlling Materials and Equipment, Building Teams, Assuring Safety, Evaluating Performance, Training and Coaching, Reacting to Stress, plus 5 summary perception scores.
Administration: Group.
Forms, 2: Self-Description, Description by Others.
Price Data: Available from publisher.
Comments: Administered to supervisor and 4 or 5 workers.
Author: Human Synergistics International.
Publisher: Human Synergistics International.

[2628]

Supplementary Spelling Assessments.

Purpose: Designed to "augment the assessments of spelling teachers make on the basis of how, and how well, children spell in their writing."
Population: Years 4-7.
Publication Date: 2007.
Acronym: SSpA.
Administration: Group.
Price Data, 2010: $38.70 per specimen set including teacher manual (52 pages), administration and scoring guide, 1 test booklet of Part 1: Tests 1, 2, and 3 and Part 2: Diagnostic Assessments 1 and 2.
Author: Cedric Croft.
Publisher: New Zealand Council for Educational Research [New Zealand].
  a) PART 1: ACHIEVEMENT AND PROGRESS.
  Time: (35) minutes.
  Population: Years 4-6.
    1) *Test 1*.
    Scores, 4: Dictated Words, Beginning Sounds, Recognising Errors in Words, Recognising Errors in Sentences.
    2) *Test 2*.
    Scores, 5: Dictated Words, Dictated Paragraph, Recognising Errors in Words, Recognising Errors in Sentences, Recognising Correct Words.

  3) *Test 3*.
    Scores, 5: Dictated Words, Dictated Paragraph, Recognising Errors in Words, Recognising Errors in Sentences, Recognising Correct Words.
  b) PART 2: DIAGNOSTIC ASSESSMENTS.
  Time: Untimed.
  Population: Years 5-6.
  Scores, 6: Beginning Sounds/Initial Consonants, Beginning Sounds/Prefixes, Ending Sounds/Suffixes, Short and Long Vowel Sounds, Silent Letters, Shortened Words/Contractions.

[2629]

Support Staff Opinion Inventory.

Purpose: Designed to measure general perceptions about the school from support staff.
Population: School support staff.
Publication Date: 2005.
Scores: 4 subscales: Quality of the Instructional Program, Support for Student Learning, School Climate/Environment, School Organization and Administration.
Administration: Group.
Parts, 2: A (Likert-scale items), B (customize up to 20 local questions)
Price Data, 2006: $25 per 25 inventories; administrator's manual may be downloaded free from publisher webpage.
Foreign Language Edition: Available in Spanish.
Time: (15) minutes.
Author: National Study of School Evaluation.
Publisher: National Study of School Evaluation.

[2630]

Supports Intensity Scale.

Purpose: Designed to help service providers "understand the support needs of people with intellectual disabilities (i.e., mental retardation) and closely related developmental disabilities."
Population: Individuals ages 16–72 with intellectual or closely related developmental disabilities.
Publication Date: 2004.
Acronym: SIS.
Scores, 9: Home Living, Community Living, Lifelong Learning, Employment, Health and Safety, Social, Support Needs Index, Exceptional Medical Needs, Exceptional Behavioral Needs.
Administration: Individual.
Price Data, 2006: $125 per complete set including user's manual (128 pages) and 25 interview forms; $95 per user's manual; $38.75 per 25 interview forms; $375 per Electronic Scoring Program on CD-ROM; Pricing for SISOnline, web-based scoring application determined on case-by-case basis available from publisher (www.siswebsite.org).
Time: Administration time not reported.

Comments: Semistructured, multiple informant interview format.
Authors: James R. Thompson, Brian R. Bryant, Edward M. Campbell, Ellis M. Craig, Carolyn M. Hughes, David A. Rotholz, Robert L. Schalock, Wayne P. Silverman, Marc J. Tassé, and Michael L. Wehmeyer.
Publisher: American Association on Intellectual and Developmental Disabilities.
Cross References: For reviews by Sandra A. Loew and David J. Pittenger, see 16:238.

[2631]

SUP'R Star Profiles.

Purpose: Designed to identify an individual's dominant personality type.
Population: Adults.
Publication Date: 1994.
Scores: 4 personality types: Self-Reliant, Upbeat, Patient, Reasoning.
Administration: Group.
Price Data: Available from publisher.
Time: (15–20) minutes.
Author: James H. Brewer.
Publisher: BEST Instruments, LLC.
Cross References: For reviews by Jeffrey B. Brookings and Carol Collins, see 13:309.

[2632]

Survey Ballot for Industry.

Purpose: Designed "specifically as the psychological measuring instrument for economical assessment of job satisfaction levels of worker groups."
Population: Employee groups.
Publication Date: No date.
Scores, 11: Job Security, Welfare Interest, Supervision, Working Conditions, Co-Workers, Pay, Freedom of Communication, Management Good Intent, Management Good Judgment, Company Effect on Happiness, Total Satisfaction.
Administration: Group.
Price Data, 2001: $4 per specimen set.
Time: Administration time not reported.
Author: W. A. Kerr.
Publisher: Psychometric Affiliates.

[2633]

Survey of Employee Access.

Purpose: Measures effective managerial behavior.
Population: Adults.
Publication Dates: 1989–2000.
Acronym: SEA.
Scores, 5: Access to the Problem, Access to People, Access to Information and Resources, Access to Emotional/Procedural Supports, Access to Solution.
Administration: Group.
Price Data, 2001: $7.95 per instrument.

Time: Untimed.
Comments: Self-administered survey.
Author: Jay Hall.
Publisher: Teleometrics International, Inc.
Cross References: For reviews by Marcia J. Belcher and Robert Fitzpatrick, see 12:382.

[2634]

Survey of Functional Adaptive Behaviors.

Purpose: To assess an individual's skill level of adaptive behavior.
Population: Ages 16 and over.
Publication Date: 1986.
Acronym: SFAB.
Scores, 5: Residential Living Skills, Daily Living Skills, Academic Skills, Vocational Skills, SFAB Total Score.
Administration: Individual.
Manual: No manual.
Price Data, 2011: $71.25 per 25 surveys.
Authors: Jack G. Dial, Carolyn Mezger, Theresa Massey, Steve Carter, and Lawrence T. McCarron.
Publisher: McCarron-Dial Systems, Inc.
Cross References: For reviews by Steven W. Lee and Steven I. Pfeiffer, see 11:404.

[2635]

Survey of Goals for Student Learning.

Purpose: "Designed to help schools assess the extent of students' achievement of essential goals for their learning and the level of priority that should be assigned to each goal."
Population: Teachers and administrators.
Publication Date: 1997.
Scores: 2 subscales: Level of Student Achievement, Level of Priority for Improvement.
Administration: Group.
Price Data, 2006: $25 per 25 inventories; administrator's manual may be downloaded from publisher webpage.
Time: (30) minutes.
Comments: Ten additional goals for student learning can be added to both parts of the survey.
Author: National Study of School Evaluation.
Publisher: National Study of School Evaluation.

[2636]

Survey of Influence Effectiveness.

Purpose: Designed as a 360° assessment to measure an executive's influence skills and interpersonal effectiveness; a multidimensional survey that identifies how effectively an individual influences others by comparing self-perceptions to the perceptions of others.
Population: Executives in leadership positions.
Publication Date: 1994.
Administration: Group.
Forms, 2: Self, Other.
Manual: No manual.

Price Data, 2005: $49 per set including question-naires and answer sheets for 1 self-assessment, 6 others, 6 customers, and 1 feedback report; $50 per additional paper report.

Time: [30] minutes.

Comments: Assessment is administered online via Lore's Assessment Center; results are emailed to partici-pant; a paper report may be requested for an additional fee; the SIE is based on an influence framework that features 10 positive influence tactics, 4 negative tactics, and 10 sources of power.

Author: Lore International Institute.

Publisher: Lore International Institute.

a) SELF FORM.

Scores, 4: Influence Tactic Frequency, Influence Tactic Appropriateness, Influence Tactic Skills and Effectiveness, Source of Power.

Comments: 10 Influence tactics are measured and reported.

b) OTHER FORM.

Scores, 7: Positive Influence Tactic Frequency, Negative Influence Tactic Frequency, Influence Tactic Appropriateness, Influence Tactic Skills and Effectiveness, Overall Influence Assessment, Sources of Power Recommendations.

Comments: A 128-item rating form.

[2637]

Survey of Instructional and Organizational Effectiveness.

Purpose: Designed "to help schools identify the strengths and limitations of the effectiveness of the instructional practices and organizational conditions of their school."

Population: Teachers and administrators.

Publication Date: 1997.

Scores: 2 subscales: Indicators of Quality Instructional Systems, Indicators of Quality Organizational Systems.

Administration: Group.

Price Data, 2006: $25 per 25 inventories; administra-tor's manual may be downloaded from publisher webpage.

Time: (30) minutes.

Author: National Study of School Evaluation.

Publisher: National Study of School Evaluation.

[2638]

Survey of Interpersonal Values.

Purpose: Designed to measure certain values involving an individual's relationships with others.

Population: Individuals in a variety of occupations and job levels.

Publication Dates: 1960–1993.

Acronym: SIV.

Scores, 6: Support, Conformity, Recognition, Inde-pendence, Benevolence, Leadership.

Administration: Individual or group.

Price Data, 2002: $163 per start-up kit including 25 test booklets, 100 profile sheets, scoring stencil, and

examiner's manual; $64 per 25 test booklets (quantity discounts available); $70 per 100 profile sheets; $20 per scoring stencil; $28 per examiner's manual.

Time: No limit (approximately 15 minutes).

Author: Leonard V. Gordon.

Publisher: Pearson Performance Solutions [No reply from publisher; status unknown].

Cross References: See T5:2581 (3 references), T4:2653 (3 references), and T3:2366 (14 references); for reviews by John D. Black and Allan L. LaVoie, see 8:688 (51 references); see also T2:1407 (78 references) and P:261 (48 references); for reviews by Lee J. Cronbach, Leonard D. Goodstein, and John K. Hemphill and an excerpted review by Laurence Siegel, see 6:184 (12 references).

[2639]

Survey of Management Practices.

Purpose: To assess a manager's organizational practices, and whether they enhance employee productivity.

Population: Subordinates of managers.

Publication Dates: 1987–1995.

Acronym: SMP.

Scores, 12: Dimension I (Management Values, Sup-port Structure, Managerial Credibility, Total), Dimension II (Impact, Relevance, Community, Total), Dimension III (Task Environment, Social Context, Problem Solving, Total).

Administration: Group.

Price Data, 2001: $7.95 per instrument.

Time: Administration time not reported.

Comments: Manager behavior rated by subordinates.

Author: Jay Hall.

Publisher: Teleometrics International, Inc.

[2640]

Survey of Organizational Climate.

Purpose: To assess an individual's opinion of his/her organizational climate.

Population: Employees.

Publication Dates: 1977–1985.

Scores, 12: Clarity of Goals, Job Interest and Chal-lenge, Rewards and Satisfactions, Standards of Excel-lence, Degree of Responsibility, Personal Development, Working Relationships, Advancement/Mobility, Job Security, Management's Credibility, Personnel Policies and Procedures, Self-Confidence.

Administration: Group or individual.

Manual: No manual.

Price Data: Price information available from publisher for kit including 20 copies of survey, 20 answer sheets, and 20 interpretation sheets.

Time: (20) minutes.

Comments: Self-scored.

Author: Training House, Inc.

Publisher: Training House, Inc.

Cross References: For a review by Charles K. Parsons, see 11:406.

[2641]

Survey of Organizational Culture.

Purpose: Identification of organizational purpose and mission, perception of customers, and interrelationships of organization members.
Population: Employees of organizations.
Publication Dates: 1987–1989.
Acronym: SOC.
Scores: 15 scales: Culture (Orientation to Customers, Orientation to Employees, Orientation to Stakeholders, Impact of Mission, Managerial Depth, Decision Level/Autonomy, Communication/Openness, Human Scale, Incentive/Motivation, Cooperation/Competition, Organizational Congruence, Behavior Under Pressure, Theory-S/Theory-T, 13 Scales Aggregated), Job Characteristics (Job Satisfaction, Organizational Commitment).
Administration: Group.
Editions, 2: Select Items, Professional.
Manual: No manual.
Price Data: Available from publisher.
Time: (20–25) minutes.
Authors: Robert W. Tucker and Walt J. McCoy.
Publisher: Human Services Resource Group [No reply from publisher; status unknown].
Cross References: For a review by Bertram C. Sippola, see 11:407.

[2642]

Survey of Pain Attitudes.

Purpose: "Developed to assess a patient's attitudes and beliefs about pain."
Population: Ages 21-80 currently suffering from chronic pain.
Publication Dates: 1987-2007.
Acronym: SOPA.
Administration: Group.
Scores, 7: Adaptive Beliefs (Control Scale, Emotion Scale), Maladaptive Beliefs (Disability Scale, Harm Scale, Medication Scale, Solicitude Scale, Medical Cure Scale).
Price Data, 2008: $175 per introductory kit including technical manual (2007, 52 pages), 25 rating forms, 25 score summary/profile sheets, and 25 pain worksheets; $60 per technical manual; $65 per 25 rating forms; $35 per 25 score summary/profile sheets; $25 per 25 pain worksheets.
Time: (10-15) minutes.
Authors: Mark P. Jensen and Paul Karoly.
Publisher: Psychological Assessment Resources, Inc.
Cross References: For reviews by Jennifer G. Fillingim and Conn Thomas and by Stephen J. Freeman, see 18:134.

[2643]

Survey of Personal Values.

Purpose: To "measure certain critical values that help to determine the manner in which individuals cope with the problems of everyday living."

Population: Individuals in a variety of occupations, high school and college students.
Publication Dates: 1964–1992.
Acronym: SPV.
Scores,6: Practical Mindedness, Achievement, Variety, Decisiveness, Orderliness, Goal Orientation.
Administration: Individual or group.
Price Datam 2002: $163 per start-up kit including 25 test booklets, 100 profile sheets, scoring stencil, and examiner's manual: $64 per 25 test booklets (quantity discount available); $70 per 100 profile sheets; $20 per scoring stencil; $28 per examiner's manual.
Time: No limit (approximately 15 minutes).
Author: Leonard V. Gordon.
Publisher: Pearson Performance Solutions [No reply from publisher; status unknown].
Cross References: For reviews by William P. Erchul and Rodney L. Lowman, see 10:354; see also T3:2370 (5 references) and T2:1409 (5 references); for a review by Gene V Glass, see 7:148 (6 references); see also P:263 (3 references).

[2644]

Survey of Student Assessment of Study Behaviors.

Purpose: Designed to help students understand their current study behaviors.
Population: Grades 6–13.
Publication Date: 1991.
Scores, 6: Positive Attitudes, Useful Work Habits, Efficient Learning Tools, Good Comprehension, High Performance Writing, Effective Test Taking.
Administration: Individual.
Price Data, 2001: $3 per survey.
Time: Administration time not reported.
Comments: Self-report survey.
Author: The Cambridge Stratford Study Skills Institute.
Publisher: The Cambridge Stratford Study Skills Institute.

[2645]

Survey of Teenage Readiness and Neurodevelopmental Status.

Purpose: "Provides an overview of an adolescent's own perceptions of his or her functioning and performance strategies across a variety of neurocognitive and psychosocial domains."
Population: Ages 13–19.
Publication Date: 2001.
Acronym: STRANDS.
Scores, 13: Attention, Memory, Sequencing, Language, Visual Processing, Motor Functions, Organization and Strategies, Higher-Order Cognition, School Skills, School Life, Social Life, School and Work Preferences, Reasons.
Administration: Individual.
Price Data, 2006: $86.95 per complete set including manual for administration, scoring and interpretation

(114 pages), 12 student questionnaires (15 pages), 12 student interview booklets (30 pages), and 12 profile sheets; $23.45 per specimen set including manual for administration, scoring, and interpretation, 1 student questionnaire, and 1 student interview booklet; $21.20 per manual; $73.60 per 12 pair of student questionnaires and student interview booklets; $6.20 per 12 profile sheets (quantity discounts available).

Time: (40) minutes for Student Interview; (20) minutes for Student Questionnaire.

Comments: Examines the relationship between metacognitive knowledge and actual strategic behavior; consists of 2 parts: structured clinical student interview (closed- and open-ended questions), student-completed questionnaire.

Authors: Melvin D. Levine and Stephen R. Hooper.

Publisher: Educators Publishing Service, Inc.

Cross References: For a review by Scott T. Meier, see 16:239.

[2646]

Survey of Work Styles.

Purpose: A "measure of six components of the Type A behavior pattern."

Population: Adults.

Publication Dates: 1987–1998.

Acronym: SWS.

Scores, 8: Impatience, Anger, Time Urgency, Work Involvement, Job Dissatisfaction, Competitiveness, Scale A, Total.

Administration: Group or individual.

Price Data, 2010: $75 per research test kit including manual on CD, 2nd edition (1993, 22 pages), 5 handscorable question-and-answer documents, 5 scoring sheets, and one set of templates; $24 per test manual on CD; $41 per 25 question-and-answer documents; $30 per 25 scoring sheets; $22 per set of scoring templates; $17 per machine-scorable question-and-answer document for a Mail-in Developmental Report; $12 per machine-scorable question-and-answer document for a Mail-in Basic Report; $145 per software installation package, includes 10 coupons for computer reports; $12-$20 (depending on volume) per online password.

Time: 15 minutes.

Comments: Available for online scoring at www.sigmatesting.com.

Authors: Douglas N. Jackson and Anna Mavrogiannis Gray.

Publisher: SIGMA Assessment Systems, Inc.

Cross References: See T5:2592 (1 reference); for a review by Peggy A. Hicks, see 13:311 (1 reference); see also T4:2664 (1 reference).

[2647]

Survey of Work Values, Revised, Form U.

Purpose: To measure work values.

Population: Employees.

Publication Dates: 1975-1976.

Scores, 6: Social Status, Activity Preference, Upward Striving, Attitude Toward Earnings, Pride in Work, Job Involvement.

Administration: Group or individual.

Manual: No manual.

Price, 2010: There is no charge to use the copyrighted scales. For permission, e-mail jdi_ra@bgnet.bgsu.edu or phone (419) 372-8247 at the Department of Psychology, Bowling Green State University, Bowling Green, OH 43403.

Time: 15 minutes.

Authors: Bowling Green State University.

Publisher: Bowling Green State University.

Cross References: For reviews by Julie A. Allison and by H. John Bernardin and Donna K. Cooke, see 12:383 (1 reference); see also T4:2665 (1 reference).

[2648]

Surveys of Research Administration and Environment.

Purpose: Designed "to gather both facts and opinions on a variety of factors related to the jobs of scientists, engineers, and technicians."

Population: Research and engineering and scientific firms.

Publication Dates: 1959–1960.

Scores: No scores.

Administration: Group.

Price Data: Available from publisher.

Author: Morris I. Stein.

Publisher: The Mews Press.

a) STEIN SURVEY FOR ADMINISTRATION.

Population: Supervisors and administrators.

Comments: Also part of Technical Personnel Recruiting Inventory (2688).

Time: (30–40) minutes.

b) STEIN RESEARCH ENVIRONMENTAL SURVEY.

Population: Research and technical personnel.

Time: (90–120) minutes.

[2649]

Swallowing Ability and Function Evaluation.

Purpose: "Designed for evaluating and treating dysphagia."

Population: Adolescents and adults.

Publication Date: 2003.

Acronym: SAFE.

Scores, 3: Physical Examination, Oral Phase, Pharyngeal Phase.

Administration: Individual.

Price Data, 2011: $150 per complete kit including examiner's manual (37 pages), Treatment and Resource Manual (235 pages), and 50 profile/examiner record forms; $60 per examiner's manual; $69 per Treatment Manual; $32 per 50 profile/examiner record forms.

Time: (20–25) minutes.

Authors: Peggy Kipping, Deborah Ross-Swain and Patricia Yee.
Publisher: PRO-ED.
Cross References: For a review by Carolyn Mitchell Person, see 16:240.

[2650]
Swanson-Cognitive Processing Test.

Purpose: Designed to assess "different aspects of mental processing ability and potential."
Population: Ages 5 to adult.
Publication Date: 1996.
Acronym: S-CPT.
Scores: 11 subtest scores: Rhyming Words, Visual Matrix, Auditory Digit Sequence, Mapping and Directions, Story Retelling, Picture Sequence, Phrase Recall, Spatial Organization, Semantic Association, Semantic Categorization, Nonverbal Sequence; 3 composite scores: Semantic, Episodic, Total; 4 component scores: Auditory, Visual, Prospective, Retrospective; 4 supplementary scores: Strategy Efficiency Index, Processing Difference Index, Instructional Efficiency Index, Stability Index.
Administration: Individual.
Price Data, 2011: $247 per complete kit including manual (183 pages), 25 profile/examiner record booklets, picture book, card decks, and strategy cards in storage box; $81 per 25 profile/examiner record booklets; $69 per manual; $35 per picture book; $60 per card deck; $24 per strategy cards.
Time: (120) minutes.
Author: H. Lee Swanson.
Publisher: PRO-ED.
Cross References: See T5:2596 (1 reference); for reviews by Carolyn M. Callahan and Ralph F. Darr, Jr., see 13:312.

[2651]
Symbol Digit Modalities Test.

Purpose: Designed as an early screening of cerebral dysfunction.
Population: Ages 8 and over.
Publication Date: 1973.
Acronym: SDMT.
Scores: Total score only.
Administration: Group or individual.
Forms, 2: Written, Oral.
Price Data, 2006: $91 per complete kit including 25 WPS AutoScore™ test forms and manual (10 pages plus test); $46.50 per 25 AutoScore™ test forms; $48.50 per manual.
Time: 1.5(10) minutes.
Author: Aaron Smith.
Publisher: Western Psychological Services.
Cross References: See T5:2599 (43 references), T4:2671 (20 references), and T3:2380 (2 references); for reviews by Brad S. Chissom and James C. Reed, see 8:878; see also T2:1889 (4 references).

[2652]
Symbol Imagery Test.

Purpose: "Designed to measure a student's symbol imagery for letters in both random and orthographically regular combinations."
Population: Ages 6-0 to 17-11.
Publication Date: 2010.
Acronym: SI Test.
Scores: Total score only.
Administration: Individual.
Price Data, 2011: $149.95 per complete kit, including letters and words cards, 25 examiner's record booklets, and examiner's manual (128 pages); $99.95 per examiner's manual.
Time: (10-20) minutes.
Author: Nanci Bell.
Publisher: Gander Publishing.

[2653]
Symbolic Play Test, Second Edition.

Purpose: Developed to assess early concept formation and symbolization based on a child's spontaneous non-verbal play.
Population: Ages 1–3.
Publication Dates: 1976–1988.
Scores: Total score only.
Administration: Individual.
Price Data, 1999: £145 per complete set including toys, 25 record forms, and manual (1988, 39 pages); £14.50 per 25 record forms; £25 per manual.
Time: (10–15) minutes.
Authors: Marianne Lowe and Anthony J. Costello.
Publisher: GL Assessment [England].
Cross References: See T5:2601 (3 references); for reviews by Anthony W. Paolitto and Harvey N. Switzky, see 12:384; see also T4:2673 (2 references) and T3:2383 (1 reference).

[2654]
Symptom Assessment–45 Questionnaire.

Purpose: "Designed as a brief yet comprehensive general assessment of psychiatric symptomalogy."
Population: Ages 13 and over, reading at the 6th grade level or higher.
Publication Dates: 1996–1998.
Acronym: SA-45.
Scores, 11: 9 subscales (Anxiety, Depression, Hostility, Interpersonal Sensitivity, Obsessive-Compulsive, Paranoid Ideation, Phobic Anxiety, Psychoticism, Somatization), 2 composite scores (Global Severity Index, Positive Symptom Total).
Administration: Individual or group.
Price Data, 2011: $94 per complete kit including technical manual (113 pages) and 25 QuikScore forms; $50 per 25 QuikScore forms; $62 per technical manual.

Time: (10–15) minutes.
Comments: Derived from the original Symptom Checklist–90 (SCL-90; 2655); self-report inventory.
Authors: Strategic Advantage, Inc. and Mark Marush.
Publisher: Multi-Health Systems, Inc.
Cross References: For reviews by William M. Reynolds and Chockalingam Viswesvaran, see 14:378.

[2655]

Symptom Checklist-90-Revised.

Purpose: "Designed primarily to reflect the psychological symptom patterns of psychiatric and medical patients," as well as nonpatients.
Population: Adults and adolescents age 13 and older.
Publication Date: 1975.
Acronym: SCL-90-R®.
Scores: 9 primary symptom dimensions: Somatization, Obsessive-Compulsive, Interpersonal Sensitivity, Depression, Anxiety, Hostility, Phobic Anxiety, Paranoid Ideation, Psychoticism; plus 3 indices of distress: Global Severity Index, Positive Symptom Distress Index, Positive Symptom Total.
Administration: Group or individual.
Price Data, 2006: $57.25 per Q Local starter kit with interpretive reports including manual and 3 answer sheets with test items to conduct and receive 3 Q Local administrations; $26 per 25 Q Local answer sheets; $10 per Q Local interpretive reports; $4.15 per Q Local profile reports; $65 per mail-in scoring service starter kit with interpretive reports including manual, softcover test booklet, and 3 answer sheets to conduct and receive 3 administrations using the mail-in scoring service; $13 per mail-in interpretive reports; $7.15 per mail-in profile reports; $100 per hand-scoring starter kit including manual, 50 answer sheets with test items, 50 profile forms, 2 worksheets, and answer keys (specify Nonpatient Adult, Nonpatient Adolescent, Outpatient Psychiatric, Inpatient Psychiatric); $52.50 per hand-scoring answer sheets with test items; $24.50 per 50 profile forms and 2 worksheets (specify Nonpatient Adult, Nonpatient Adolescent, Outpatient Psychiatric, Inpatient Psychiatric); $24.75 per answer keys; $34 per manual; $10.25 per 5 test booklets; $51.50 per compact disc; quantity discounts available for the reports; price data for Spanish materials available from publisher.
Foreign Language Edition: Spanish materials available.
Time: (12–15) minutes.
Comments: Self-report test; companion clinician and observer rating forms also available.
Author: Leonard R. Derogatis.
Publisher: Pearson.
Cross References: See T5:2603 (593 references) and T4:2674 (318 references); for reviews by Jerome D. Pauker and Robert W. Payne, see 9:1082 (61 references); see also T3:2100 (13 references).

[2656]

System for Testing and Evaluation of Potential.

Purpose: "To evaluate managerial and professional personnel."
Population: Managerial and professional personnel.
Publication Dates: 1986–1995.
Acronym: LH-STEP.
Administration: Group or individual.
Price Data, 2002: $287 per job analysis kit including 10 job analysis questionnaires, computer scoring, individual and composite reports, and a recommendation regarding which LH-STEP battery to use.
Author: Human Resources Center, The University of Chicago.
Publisher: Pearson Performance Solutions [No reply from publisher; status unknown].
a) LH-STEP (STANDARD REPORT).
Scores: 6 ratings: Potential Estimates (Executive, Middle Manager, Supervisors and Nonsupervisory Professionals), Job Skills (Executive, Middle Manager, Supervisors and Nonsupervisory Professionals); 39 scores: Predictor Profile: (School Achievement, Drive, Vocational Satisfaction, Financial Responsibility, General Family Responsibility, Leadership, Relaxation Pursuits, Non-Verbal Reasoning, Word Fluency, Vocabulary, Closure Flexibility, Creative Potential, Sales Aptitude, Personal Insight, Extroversion, Emotional Responsiveness, Self-Reliance, Ability to Work Under Pressure, Level of Stress Response, Internal Adjustment, External Adjustment, Social Adjustment, General Adjustment), Job Skills: Organization (Setting Organizational Objectives, Financial Planning and Review, Improving Work Procedures and Practices, Interdepartmental Coordination), Leadership (Developing and Implementing Technical Ideas, Judgment and Decision Making, Developing Group Cooperation and Teamwork, Coping With Difficulties and Emergencies, Promoting Safety Attitudes and Practices, Communications), Human Resources (Developing Employee Potential, Supervisory Practices, Self-Development and Improvement, Personnel Practices), Community (Promoting Community/Organization Relations, Handling Outside Contacts).
Price Data: $230 or less per battery.
Time: (190–210) minutes.
b) LH-STEP (EXTENDED REPORT).
Scores: 6 ratings: same as LH-STEP Standard Report; 63 scores: same as LH-STEP Standard Report, plus Calm, Cautious, Composed, Decisive, Demonstrative, Even-Tempered, Persevering, Seeks Company, Self-Confident, Serious, Steady Worker, Talkative, Reaction Time to Verbal Stimuli, Reaction Time to Color Stimuli, Dominance, Independence, Autonomous Work Environment,

Pressure Performance, Energy Level, Speed of Reaction, Ideational Spontaneity, Theoretical Interests, Artistic Interests, Mechanical Interests; 12 tests: Managerial and Professional Job Functions Inventory for Ability, Experience and Background Inventory, Word Fluency, Temperament Comparator, Vocabulary Inventory, Non-Verbal Reasoning, Sales Inventory, Cree Questionnaire, The Press Test, Closure Flexibility, EMO Questionnaire, Management Style Questionnaire.
Price Data: $230 or less per battery.
Time: (190–210) minutes.

[2657]

System of Multicultural Pluralistic Assessment.

Purpose: Designed as "a comprehensive system for assessing the level at which children function in cognitive abilities, perceptual motor abilities, and adaptive behavior."
Population: Ages 5–11.
Publication Dates: 1977–1978.
Acronym: SOMPA.
Administration: Individual.
Price Data, 2002: $327 per basic kit including parent interview manual (1977, 150 pages), 25 parent interview record forms, 6 ABIC scoring keys, student assessment manual (1978, 125 pages), 25 student assessment record forms, 25 profile folders, and technical manual (1979, 164 pages).
Foreign Language Edition: Spanish edition available.
Authors: Jane R. Mercer and June F. Lewis.
Publisher: Pearson.
a) STUDENT ASSESSMENT.
Population: Ages 5–11.
Publication Date: 1978.
Scores: 6 instruments: Physical Dexterity Tasks, Bender Visual Motor Gestalt Test, Weight by Height, Visual Acuity (Snellen Test), Auditory Acuity (audiometer), WISC-R (WPPSI for children under 6 years).
Price Data: $209 per SOMPA student assessment kit including 25 record forms, 25 profile folders, and manual.
Time: (60) minutes, several test sessions should be scheduled.
Comments: The following instruments are not available in the SOMPA test kit and must be obtained by the tester: Bender Gestalt, Snellen Test, audiometer, WISC-R, or WPPSI.
b) PARENT INTERVIEW.
Population: Parents.
Publication Date: 1977.
Scores: 3 instruments: Sociocultural Scales, Adaptive Behavior Inventory for Children (ABIC), Health History Inventory.
Price Data: $265 per SOMPA parent interview kit including 25 record forms, 25 profile folders, and manual.

Cross References: See T5:2606 (5 references) and T4:2676 (11 references); for reviews by Lloyd G. Humphreys, Cecil R. Reynolds, and Jonathan Sandoval, see 9:1222 (6 references).

[2658]

Systematic Analysis of Language Transcripts 2010 Bilingual SE Version.

Purpose: Designed to assess the expressive language proficiency of native Spanish-speaking bilingual (Spanish/English) children by providing a series of analyses comparing their English and Spanish language samples to samples from age- or grade-matched bilingual peers.
Population: Preschool-Grade 3 native Spanish-speaking bilingual children.
Publication Dates: 2009-2010.
Acronym: SALT 2010 Bilingual SE version.
Scores, 2: Subordination Index, Narrative Scoring Scheme.
Administration: Individual.
Price Data, 2010: $99 per SALT Bilingual SE Version including software and printed SALT manual (2009, 115 pages).
Foreign Language and Other Special Editions: English, Research, and Instructional editions available.
Time: Unlimited.
Comments: Computer software for Windows® 2000, XP, Vista, 7.
Authors: Jon F. Miller and Aquiles Iglesias.
Publisher: SALT Software, LLC.

[2659]

Systematic Analysis of Language Transcripts 2010 English Version.

Purpose: Aids the transcription process and provides a series of analyses comparing an individual language sample to samples from age or grade-matched peers whose primary language is English.
Population: Preschool through high school.
Publication Dates: 2009-2010.
Acronym: SALT 2010 English version.
Scores: 3 handscoring: Subordination Index, Narrative Scoring Scheme, Expository Scoring Scheme; 5 computer analyses: Syntax, Morphology, Lexicon, Fluency and Rate, Discourse.
Administration: Group.
Price Data, 2010: $99 per SALT English Version including software and printed SALT manual.
Foreign Language and Other Special Editions: Bilingual (Spanish/English), Research, and Instructional editions available.
Time: Unlimited.
Comments: Computer software for Windows® 2000, XP, Vista, 7.
Author: Jon F. Miller.
Publisher: SALT Software, LLC.

[2660]

Systematic Screening for Behavior Disorders.

Purpose: To screen and identify students at risk for developing serious behavior problems.
Population: Grades K–6.
Publication Dates: 1990–1992.
Acronym: SSBD.
Administration: Individual and group.
Price Data, 2002: $195 per complete kit including technical manual (1992, 80 pages), user's guide (1992, 151 pages), observer training manual (1992, 136 pages), videotape, and 25 sets of classroom screening forms.
Authors: Hill M. Walker and Herbert H. Severson.
Publisher: Sopris West.
 a) STAGE I.
 Scores: 2 rankings: Internalizing, Externalizing.
 Time: (30–45) minutes.
 Comments: Rankings by teacher.
 b) STAGE II.
 Scores, 6: 3 scores: Total Critical Events, Total Adaptive Behavior, Total Maladaptive Behavior in two areas: Internalizing, Externalizing.
 Time: (30–45) minutes.
 Comments: Ratings by teachers.
 c) STAGE III.
 Scores, 11: Academic Engaged Time (Total); Peer Social Behavior (Social Engagement, Participation, Parallel Play, Alone, No Code, Social Interaction, Negative Interaction, Positive Interaction, Total Positive Behavior, Total Negative Behavior).
 Administration: Individual and group.
 Time: (60–90) minutes.
 Comments: Observations by trained staff member.
Cross References: See T5:2607 (1 reference); for reviews by Mary Lou Kelley and by Leland C. Zlomke and Robert Spies, see 13:313.

[2661]

Systems Analysis Aptitude Test.

Purpose: "Measures aptitude for business systems design using a real-life problem."
Population: Applicants for computer systems analyst position.
Publication Date: 1973.
Acronym: SAAT.
Administration: Group.
Restricted Distribution: Restricted to employers of systems analysts, not available to school personnel.
Price Data, 2001: $465 per candidate.
Time: (240) minutes.
Comments: Detailed report on system designed by each candidate.
Author: Jack M. Wolfe.
Publisher: Rose Wolfe Family Partnership LLP [Canada].

[2662]

Systems Programming Aptitude Test.

Purpose: "To evaluate the aptitude and potential of systems programming candidates of all experience levels, for work in all types of systems programming tasks."
Population: Systems programmers.
Publication Date: 1979.
Acronym: SPAT.
Administration: Group.
Price Data, 2001: $440 per person.
Time: Untimed.
Comments: Detailed report provided on each candidate.
Author: Jack M. Wolfe.
Publisher: Rose Wolfe Family Partnership LLP [Canada].
Cross References: For reviews by Samuel Juni and David Marshall, see 10:356.

[2663]

T.A. Survey.

Purpose: "Evaluates an individual's trust attitudes which predict trust performance."
Population: Employees.
Publication Dates: 1970–1981.
Scores: Total score only.
Administration: Group or individual.
Price Data: Price information available from publisher for surveys and yearly license fee.
Time: (15) minutes.
Comments: Also called Trustworthiness Attitude Survey.
Authors: Alan L. Strand and others.
Publisher: Predictive Surveys Corporation.
Cross References: For reviews by John K. Butler, Jr. and Denise M. Rousseau, see 9:1223.

[2664]

Tapping Students' Science Beliefs: A Resource for Teaching and Learning.

Purpose: Designed to "assess the belief students have about certain natural phenomena and permits appropriate learning experiences to be planned."
Population: Primary grade level students.
Publication Date: 1993.
Acronym: TSSB.
Scores, 5: Skateboard News, What Happened Last Night, The Day We Cooked Pancakes in School, Children's Week, Our School Garden.
Administration: Group.
Price Data, 2006: A$43.95 per complete kit including manual (77 pages), 5 unit tests with 1 student score sheet and 1 group profile sheet per unit; A10.95 per manual.
Time: (30) minutes per unit.
Authors: Brian Doig and Ray Adams.

Publisher: Australian Council for Educational Research Ltd. [Australia].
Cross References: For reviews by Jerrilyn V. Andrews and James P. Van Haneghan, see 13:314.

[2665]

The Tapping Test: A Predictor of Typing and Other Tapping Operations.

Purpose: Measures the student's ability to learn typing.
Population: High school.
Publication Dates: 1959–1970.
Acronym: TARC.
Scores: Total score only.
Administration: Group.
Price Data: Available from publisher.
Time: [30] minutes.
Authors: John C. Flanagan, Grace Fivars (manual), Shirley A. Tuska (manual), and Carol F. Hershey (manual).
Publisher: Grace Fivars.
Cross References: See T2:796 (3 references); for reviews by Ray G. Price and Henry Weitz, see 6:52 (2 references).

[2666]

Target Mathematics Tests.

Purpose: Designed "to provide achievement tests which reflect the content of the National Curriculum in Mathematics" in Great Britain.
Population: Levels 2–5, 2–6.
Publication Date: 1993.
Scores: Total score only.
Administration: Group.
Forms, 2: Test 4, Test 5.
Price Data, 2002: £9.99 per 20 test booklets (specify test); £9.99 per manual; £10.99 per specimen set.
Time: [30] minutes.
Author: D. Young.
Publisher: Hodder & Stoughton Educational [England].
Cross References: For reviews by Kevin D. Crehan and Gerald E. DeMauro, see 14:380.

[2667]

Tasks of Emotional Development Test.

Purpose: Assesses "the emotional and social adjustment of children" by means of projective techniques.
Population: Ages 6-11, 12-18.
Publication Dates: 1960-1971.
Acronym: T.E.D.
Scores: LATENCY: 5 scores: (Perception, Outcome, Affect, Motivation, Spontaneity) in each of 12 areas (Peer Socialization, Trust, Aggression Toward Peers, Attitudes For Learning, Respect For Property of Others, Separation From Mother Figure, Identification With Same-Sex Parent, Acceptance of Siblings, Acceptance of Need-Frustration, Acceptance of Parents' Affection

to One Another, Orderliness and Responsibility, Self-Image); ADOLESCENCE: 5 scores in each of 13 areas: Same as for Latency plus Heterosexual Socialization.
Administration: Individual.
Levels, 2: Latency (Ages 6-11); Adolescence (Ages 12-18).
Price Data: Available from publisher.
Time: [30-40] minutes.
Authors: Haskel Cohen and Geraldine Rickard Weil.
Publisher: Massachusetts School of Professional Psychology/T.E.D. Test.
Cross References: See T5:2614 (2 references) and T4:2686 (1 reference); for excerpted reviews by Edward Earl Gates and by C. H. Ammons and R. B. Ammons, see 8:691 (7 references); see also T2:1517 (2 references) and P:481 (1 reference).

[2668]

Tasks of Executive Control.

Purpose: Designed to "assess attention, working memory, and inhibitory control."
Population: Ages 5 to 18.
Publication Dates: 2006-2010.
Acronym: TEC.
Administration: Individual.
Forms, 5: Forms 1, 2, and 3 are statistically equivalent; Forms 4 and 5 are to be used in research.
Price Data, 2010: $375 per introductory test kit CD-ROM including TEC software program with onscreen help, professional manual (2010, 188 pages), 1 set of keytops, quick start guide, and 10 bonus onscreen administrations; $80 per professional manual; $70 per 10 onscreen administrations; $165 per 25 onscreen administrations; $300 per 50 onscreen administrations.
Time: (20-30) minutes.
Comments: The TEC is a computer-administered test and requires the following technical supports: CD-ROM drive for installation; keyboard (USB/wireless not recommended); 60Hz noninterlaced (16.76 ms) refresh rate; 12.5-inch diagonal CRT or LCD (14.5-inch diagonal widescreen); AGP or PCI Express video card with 32MB on-board RAM, 128MHz RAMDAC; 16-bit, 1024x768 (XGA) display.
Authors: Peter K. Isquith, Robert M. Roth, and Gerard A. Gioia.
Publisher: Psychological Assessment Resources, Inc.
  a) AGES 5 TO 7 YEARS.
  Scores, 23: 3 Factor Scores: Response Control, Selective Attention, Response Speed; 10 Summary Scores: Accuracy, Target Correct, Standard Correct, Target Omissions, Standard Omissions, Incorrect, Commissions, Target RT, Standard RT, Standard RTSD, Standard ICV; 10 Task Scores: Target Correct, Standard Correct, Target Omissions, Standard Omissions, Incorrect, Commissions, Target RT, Standard RT, Standard RTSD, Standard ICV.

b) AGES 8 TO 18 YEARS.

Scores, 24: 4 Factor Scores: Sustained Accuracy, Selective Attention, Response Speed, Response Variability; 10 Summary Scores: Accuracy, Target Correct, Standard Correct, Target Omissions, Standard Omissions, Incorrect, Commissions, Target RT, Standard RT, Standard RTSD, Standard ICV; 10 Task Scores: Target Correct, Standard Correct, Target Omissions, Standard Omissions, Incorrect, Commissions, Target RT, Standard RT, Standard RTSD, Standard ICV.

[2669]

TAV Selection System.

Purpose: Constructed to measure "interpersonal reactions" for use in vocational selection and counseling.
Population: Adults.
Publication Dates: 1963-1968.
Acronym: TAV.
Administration: Group.
Price Data: Available from publisher.
Time: (180) minutes for the battery, (15-20) minutes for any one test.
Comments: Self-administered.
Author: R. R. Morman.
Publisher: TAV Selection System.
  a) TAV ADJECTIVE CHECKLIST.
  Scores, 3: Toward People (T), Away from People (A), Versus People (V).
  b) TAV JUDGMENTS.
  Scores, 3: Same as *a* above.
  c) TAV PERSONAL DATA.
  Scores, 3: Same as *a* above.
  d) TAV PREFERENCES.
  Scores, 3: Same as *a* above.
  e) TAV PROVERBS AND SAYINGS.
  Scores, 3: Same as *a* above.
  f) TAV SALESMAN REACTIONS.
  Scores, 3: Same as *a* above.
  g) TAV MENTAL AGILITY.
  Scores, 3: Follow Directions and Carefulness, Weights and Balances, Verbal Comprehension.
Cross References: For a review by Robert G. Demaree, see 8:986 (1 reference); see also T2:2113 (3 references); for an excerpted review by John O. Crites, see 7:983 (1 reference); see also P:263A (11 references).

[2670]

The Taylor-Helmstadter Pair Comparison Scale of Aesthetic Judgment.

Purpose: Constructed to assess aesthetic judgment.
Population: Ages 4 and over.
Publication Dates: 1973-1976.
Scores: Total score only.
Administration: Group.
Price Data: Available from publisher.

Time: [20–30] minutes.
Comments: Two carousel slide projectors necessary for administration.
Author: Anne P. Taylor.
Publisher: Anne P. Taylor.
Cross References: See T3:2395 (1 reference).

[2671]

Taylor-Johnson Temperament Analysis® [2007 Edition].

Purpose: Designed to "measure a number of ... personality variables or attitudes and behavioral tendencies which influence personal, social, marital, parental, family, scholastic, and vocational adjustment."
Population: Ages 11 and up.
Publication Dates: 1941–2007.
Acronym: T-JTA®.
Scores, 11: Nervous vs. Composed, Depressive vs. Light-Hearted, Active-Social vs. Quiet, Expressive-Responsive vs. Inhibited, Sympathetic vs. Indifferent, Subjective vs. Objective, Dominant vs. Submissive, Hostile vs. Tolerant, Self-Disciplined vs. Impulsive, Test-Taking Attitude, Total Mids; computer scoring software includes 8 additional scales: Overall Adjustment, Emotional Stability, Alienating, Interpersonal Effectiveness, Self-Esteem, Outgoing/Gregarious, Industrious/Persevering, Consistency (validity scale).
Administration: Individual or group.
Forms, 4: Regular Edition (criss-cross and self-report forms); Form "S" for Adolescents (criss-cross and self-report).
Price Data, 2011: $245 per manual with 2007 norms and handbook; $189 per test manual with 2007 norm tables; $68.50 per handbook; $72 per 2007 norm tables; $699 per computer scoring software Kit (manual, Software, with 15 scoring coupons); $259 per handscoring kit (manual, 2007 norms, scoring stencils, 5 question booklets, 25 answer sheets, 25 profiles, 5 report booklets); $194.50 per online kit (manual, online registration fee); computer scoring software (25 scoring coupons $699). 10 question booklets $34.50; 100 answer sheets $43.50; 100 Shaded Profiles $43.50; Self Profile $15.50; Criss-Cross Profiles (set of 5) $37; Brief and Interpretive Reports also available.
Foreign Language Editions: Available in Spanish, German, French, Portuguese, Japanese, Chinese, Korean, and Danish; norms for Chinese, Spanish, and German editions only.
Time: Untimed.
Comments: Can be used as a self-report questionnaire or as a tool for obtaining perceptions of another person (criss-cross form); Form S can be used with adolescents or with adults with poor reading skills; 2002 Edition (reviewed) based upon 2002 norms; 2006 and 2007 editions based on norms for those years.
Authors: Original edition by Roswell H. Johnson, revision by Robert M. Taylor, Lucile P. Morrison (manual),

W. Lee Morrison (statistical consultant), and Richard C. Romoser (statistical consultant).
Publisher: Psychological Publications, Inc.
Cross References: For reviews by Stephen N. Axford and Gregory J. Boyle of the 2002 Edition, see 16:241; for reviews by Michael J. Sporakowski and Stephen E. Trotter of the 1996 Edition, see 14:381; for reviews by Jeffrey A. Jenkins and Barbara J. Kaplan of an earlier edition, see 13:315; see also T4:2690 (3 references); for reviews by Cathy W. Hall and Paul McReynolds, see 10:357; see also T3:2396 (1 reference) and T2:840 (3 references); for a review by Robert F. Stahmann, see 8:692 (18 references); for a review by Donald L. Mosher of an earlier edition, see 7:572 (1 reference); see also P:264 (3 references) and 6:130 (10 references); for a review by Albert Ellis of the original edition, see 4:62 (6 references); for a review by H. Meltzer of the original edition, see 3:57.

[2672]

TEACCH Transition Assessment Profile, Second Edition.

Purpose: Designed to "assess and develop goals for [adolescents and older children] in the autism spectrum [or who have] related developmental disorders."
Population: Children and adolescents grades 3-12 and adults "with mild to severe mental disabilities."
Publication Dates: 1988-2007.
Acronym: TTAP.
Scores, 18: 6 scores per scale: Vocational Skills, Vocational Behaviors, Independent Functioning, Leisure Skills, Functional Communication, Interpersonal Behavior.
Administration: Individual.
Parts, 3: Direct Observation Scale, Home Scale, School/Work Scale.
Price Data, 2011: $84 per complete kit including 10 profile/scoring forms and manual (2007, 221 pages); $22 per 10 profile/scoring forms; There is an assembled materials kit available for purchase through TEACCH http://www.oeenterprises.org/ttap.html.
Time: (1.5-2) hours to complete the Direct Observation Scale; (1) hour each to complete the Home and School/Work Scales.
Comments: Revision of The Adolescent and Adult Psychoeducational Profile: Volume IV (AAPEP; 11:8); "Direct Observation Scale is administered by a teacher, psychologist, job coach, or other trained professional"; Home and School/Work Scales are behavior checklists completed through interviews with parents and with teachers and supervisors, respectively; other test materials for the Direct Observation Scale (e.g., washers, bolts, pill bottles) may be supplied by examiner or purchased from OE Enterprises, Inc.; set of reproducible forms included in the manual act as supplements to the TTAP by providing an ongoing, informal assessment: Cumulative Record of Skills (CRS), Community Site Assessment Worksheet (CSAW), Community Skills Checklist

(CSC), Community Behaviors Checklist (CBC), and Daily Accomplishment Chart (DAC).
Authors: Gary Mesibov, John B. Thomas, S. Michael Chapman, and Eric Schopler.
Publisher: PRO-ED.
Cross References: For reviews by Lena R. Gaddis and J. Jeffrey Grill of an earlier edition entitled Adolescent and Adult Psychoeducational Profile: Volume IV, see 11:8; see also T5:70 (1 reference).

[2673]

Teacher Assessment of Grammatical Structures.

Purpose: "Developed to evaluate a child's understanding and use of the grammatical structures of English and to suggest a sequence for teaching these structures."
Population: Ages 2–4, 5–9, 9 and over.
Publication Date: 1983.
Acronym: TAGS.
Scores: 3 ratings: Imitated, Prompted, Spontaneous Production.
Administration: Individual.
Price Data, 2011: $25 per manual (203 pages) for all 3 levels; $15 per 25 rating forms (specify TAGS-P, Pre-Sentence Level; TAGS-S, Simple Sentence Level; or TAGS-C, Complex Sentence Level).
Time: Administration time not reported.
Comments: Ratings are based on informal administration in classroom or therapy setting.
Authors: Jean S. Moog and Victoria J. Kozak.
Publisher: Central Institute for the Deaf (CID).
   a) TAGS-P, PRE-SENTENCE LEVEL.
     Population: Ages up to 6 years for hearing-impaired children, ages 2–4 for language-impaired children.
     Comments: Assesses receptive and expressive skills.
   b) TAGS-S, SIMPLE-SENTENCE LEVEL.
     Population: Ages 5–9 years for hearing-impaired children, ages 3 and over for language-impaired children.
     Comments: Assesses expressive skills.
   c) TAGS-C, COMPLEX SENTENCE LEVEL.
     Population: Ages 8 and over for hearing-impaired children, ages 3.5 and over for language-impaired children.
Cross References: See T5:2620 (1 reference) and T4:2691 (1 reference); for reviews by Elizabeth M. Prather and Kenneth G. Shipley, see 10:358 (1 reference).

[2674]

Teacher Observation Scales for Identifying Children with Special Abilities.

Purpose: Designed as an assessment instrument for identifying gifted children, tailored to be culturally appropriate for use in New Zealand.
Population: Junior and middle primary school.
Publication Date: 1996.
Scores, 5: Learning Characteristics, Social Leadership Characteristics, Creative Thinking Characteristics,

Self-Determination Characteristics, Motivational Characteristics.
Administration: Individual.
Price Data, 2001: NZ$12.60 per 20 observation scales; $12.60 per teacher's handbook (9 pages).
Time: Administration time not reported.
Authors: Don McAlpine and Neil Reid.
Publisher: New Zealand Council for Educational Research [New Zealand].
Cross References: For reviews by Ira Stuart Katz and Kenneth A. Kiewra, see 14:382.

[2675]

Teacher Opinion Inventory, Revised Edition.

Purpose: To assess teachers' opinions concerning many facets of the school, to "compile teachers' recommendations for improvement," and to provide "data to guide the school's professional staff in decision making relative to program development."
Population: Elementary and secondary school teachers.
Publication Dates: 1975–2003.
Scores: 4 subscales: Quality of the Instructional Program, Support for Student Learning, School Climate/Environment for Learning, School Organization and Administration.
Administration: Group.
Parts, 2: A (Likert-scale items), B (customize up to 20 local questions).
Price Data, 2006: $25 per 25 inventories; administrator's manual may be downloaded free from publisher website.
Time: Untimed.
Author: National Study of School Evaluation.
Publisher: National Study of School Evaluation.

[2676]

Teacher Performance Assessment [2006 Revision].

Purpose: "Developed to provide both an objective assessment and a self-assessment of classroom instructional activities from individuals who work in different roles and who make different contributions to the schools."
Population: Teachers, student teachers, interns, classroom assistants.
Publication Dates: 1991–2006.
Acronym: TPA.
Scores, 3: Performance Assessment, Self-Assessment, Reflected Self-Assessment.
Administration: Group.
Forms, 8: Classroom Teachers, Substitute Teachers, Field Associates, Internship I, Internship II, Student Teachers, Classroom Aides, Residents; plus supervisor forms for each (each form provides two formats–categories of teaching competencies–and categories with related cluster performances).
Price, 2006: $30 per 25 scales (specify form); $.50 per answer sheet; $.50 per customized booklet; $30 per manual (2006); $.40 per scale for scoring.

Time: (15) minutes.
Authors: Louise M. Soares and Anthony T. Soares.
Publisher: Castle Consultants.
Cross References: For reviews by Raoul A. Arreola and Samuel Hinton of an earlier edition, see 15:256.

[2677]

Teacher Values Inventory.

Purpose: Measures "teacher's preferences and opinions."
Population: Teachers.
Publication Dates: 1980–1981.
Acronym: TVI.
Scores, 6: Theoretical, Economic, Aesthetic, Social, Political, Religious.
Administration: Group.
Price Data: Available from publisher.
Foreign Language Edition: Hindi version available.
Time: Administration time not reported.
Authors: Harbhajan L. Singh and S. P. Ahluwalia.
Publisher: National Psychological Corporation [India] [No reply from publisher; status unknown].

[2678]

Teaching Resource and Assessment of Critical Skills.

Purpose: Designed to assist decision making about an individual's skills and potential to live in an unsupervised setting.
Population: People with special needs.
Publication Date: 1989.
Acronym: TRACS.
Scores: Unscored.
Administration: Individual.
Price Data, 1998: $124 per program including resource, assessment and skill log booklets, user's guide (49 pages), master forms, and audio tape.
Time: Administration time not reported.
Authors: Lauren Meiklejohn and Mark Rice.
Publisher: Program Development Associates (Distributor).

[2679]

Team Competency Assessment.

Purpose: Designed to "evaluate the level at which a team is performing on ten team competencies."
Population: Team members.
Publication Date: Not dated.
Scores, 11: Committing to a Team Approach, Communicating Effectively Within Teams, Utilizing Team Member Abilities, Resolving Team Conflicts, Creating a Shared Team Purpose, Planning for Results, Making Meetings Work, Evaluating Team Process and Performance, Making Team Decisions by Consensus, Solving Team Problems, Climate.
Administration: Group.

Price Data: Available from publisher.
Time: Administration time not reported.
Comments: A 65-item questionnaire; can be computer administered, scored, and interpreted (requiring IBM Windows compatible) or available in pencil-paper format; can be used separately or as one component of a team skills workshop.
Author: Human Technology, Inc.
Publisher: HRD Press, Inc.

[2680]
Team-Development Inventory.

Purpose: "A means by which work-team members can give each other feedback concerning how they are working together."
Population: Work-team members.
Publication Date: 1982.
Acronym: TDI.
Scores, 8: Each team member rank orders all members on 8 dimensions: Participation, Collaboration, Flexibility, Sensitivity, Risk Taking, Commitment, Facilitation, Openness.
Administration: Group.
Price Data: Price information available from publisher for kit including 10 instruments, 10 handouts, and facilitator's guide (16 pages).
Time: (35–50) minutes.
Author: John E. Jones.
Publisher: Jossey-Bass, A Wiley Company.

[2681]
Team Effectiveness Survey.

Purpose: Designed to assess process issues associated with team dynamics.
Population: Team members.
Publication Dates: 1968-1996.
Acronym: TES.
Scores: 4 scores for each team member: Exposure, Feedback, Defensive, Supportive, plus Total Team Effectiveness score.
Administration: Group.
Price Data, 2001: $8.95 per instrument.
Time: Administration time not reported.
Author: Jay Hall.
Publisher: Teleometrics International, Inc.
Cross References: For reviews by Gregory H. Dobbins and Harrison G. Gough, see 12:388; for a review by William G. Mollenkopf of an earlier version, see 8:1055.

[2682]
The Team Leadership Practices Inventory.

Purpose: Focuses on the behaviors and actions of high-performing teams and self-directed work groups.
Population: Managers.
Publication Date: 1992.
Acronym: LPI.

Scores, 15: 3 scores: Self-Average, Team-Average, Total in each of 5 areas: Challenging the Process, Inspiring a Shared Vision, Enabling Others to Act, Modeling the Way, Encouraging the Heart.
Administration: Group.
Price Data: Price information available from publisher for trainer's package including 3 booklets, self-assessment, and observer and trainer's manual (47 pages); deluxe trainer's package including the leadership challenge, self-assessment and analysis, and trainer's manual; IBM scoring program including manual (12 pages); instrument and participant's manual.
Time: (20–140) minutes.
Comments: Self-scored inventory.
Authors: James M. Kouzes and Barry Z. Posner.
Publisher: Jossey-Bass, A Wiley Company.
Cross References: For reviews by Jeffrey B. Brookings and William J. Waldron, see 13:317.

[2683]
Team Process Diagnostic.

Purpose: To analyze and classify group processes according to their implications for member and team effectiveness.
Population: Individuals whose work responsibilities require work-team cooperation.
Publication Dates: 1974–1989.
Scores: 9 clusters in 3 modes: Problem Solving (Integrative, Content-Bound, Process-Bound), Fight (Perceptual Difference, Status-Striving, Frustration), Flight (Fear, Indifference, Powerlessness).
Administration: Group.
Price Data: Price information available from publisher for instrument (1989, 21 pages).
Time: Administration time not reported.
Comment: Team associate ratings, self ratings, self scored.
Author: Jay Hall.
Publisher: Teleometrics International, Inc.
Cross References: For a review by Lawrence A. Aleamoni, see 11:416.

[2684]
Team Skills (Form AR-C).

Purpose: Designed to evaluate a candidate's ability to work as a member or leader of a team.
Population: Applicants and incumbents for jobs requiring knowledge of team principles.
Publication Dates: 1998-2009.
Scores: Total score only covering 7 areas: Conflict Resolution, Group Dynamics, Team Decision Making, Productivity and Motivation, Communication Skills, Leader & Member Skills, Interpersonal Skills.
Administration: Group.
Price Data, 2011: $14 per consumable self-scoring test booklet or online test administration (minimum order of 20); $24.95 per manual (2009, 15 pages).

Foreign Language Edition: Available in Spanish.
Time: (30-50) minutes.
Comments: Self-scoring instrument; available for online test administration.
Author: Roland T. Ramsay.
Publisher: Ramsay Corporation.
Cross References: For a review by Gerald Tindal of an earlier edition, see 17:181.

[2685]
Teamness Index.

Purpose: To "survey ... conditions of work and the array of feelings that might exist among two or more people as they seek to work together."
Population: Individuals whose work responsibilities require work-team cooperation.
Publication Dates: 1988–1995.
Scores: Item scores only.
Administration: Group.
Price Data, 2001: $8.95 per instrument.
Time: Administration time not reported.
Comments: Self-ratings; self-scored.
Author: Jay Hall.
Publisher: Teleometrics International, Inc.
Cross References: For reviews by Barbara Lachar and Frederick T. L. Leong, see 11:417.

[2686]
Teamwork Appraisal Survey.

Purpose: To assess "an associate's feelings about working in teams and the behaviors he or she employs in work-team situations."
Population: Individuals whose work responsibilities require work-team cooperation.
Publication Date: 1987.
Acronym: TAS.
Scores, 5: Synergistic, Compromise, Win-Lose, Yield-Lose, Lose-Leave.
Administration: Group.
Price Data: Price information available from publisher for instrument (24 pages).
Time: Administration time not reported.
Comment: Based on Team Behaviors Model of analysis of individual behaviors in a team setting; work associates rate each other's behavior.
Author: Jay Hall.
Publisher: Teleometrics International, Inc.

[2687]
Teamwork-KSA Test.

Purpose: Designed to "measure the essential knowledge, skills, and abilities that are predictive of working effectively in teams."
Population: Adults (industry),
Publication Date: 1994.
Scores: 7 subscales: Conflict Resolution, Collaborative Problem Solving, Communication, Interpersonal Skills, Goal Setting and Performance Management, Planning and Task Coordination, Self-Management Skills, plus Overall Score.
Administration: Group or individual.
Price Data, 2002: $127 per 10 tests; $28 per examiner's manual (1994, 23 pages); price data for scoring software available from publisher.
Time: [30–40] minutes.
Comments: Paper-and-pencil or computer administered.
Authors: Michael J. Stevens and Michael A. Campion.
Publisher: Pearson Performance Solutions [No reply from publisher; status unknown].
Cross References: For reviews by Patricia A. Bachelor and Patricia H. Wheeler, see 15:257.

[2688]
Technical Personnel Recruiting Inventory.

Purpose: Intended for use in research and development within industrial organizations; also for use in hiring.
Population: Research, engineering, and scientific firms.
Publication Dates: 1959–1960.
Scores: Item scores only.
Administration: Group.
Price Data: Available from publisher.
Author: Morris I. Stein.
Publisher: The Mews Press.
  a) INDIVIDUAL QUALIFICATION FORM.
  Population: Supervisors.
  Comments: For description of available position.
  b) PERSONAL DATA FORM FOR SCIENTIFIC, ENGINEERING, AND TECHNICAL PERSONNEL.
  Population: Job applicants.
  c) STEIN SURVEY FOR ADMINISTRATORS.
  Population: Administrators.
  Time: (30-40) minutes.
  Comments: Description of company's research environment; also part of Surveys of Research Administration and Environment (2648).
Cross References: For additional information, see 6:1167.

[2689]
Technical Support Staff Selector.

Purpose: To measure knowledge and aptitude for technical support positions.
Population: Candidates for the position of technical support.
Publication Date: 1994.
Acronym: TECHSUP.
Scores: Total Score, Narrative Evaluation, Ranking, Recommendation.
Administration: Group.
Price Data, 2001: $400 per candidate; quantity discounts available.
Time: (80) minutes.
Comments: Scored by publisher; must be proctored.
Author: Bruce A. Winrow.
Publisher: Walden Personnel Performance, Inc.

[2690]

Technical Test Battery.
Purpose: "Designed for occupational selection and placement."
Population: Technical job applicants and incumbents entry level to professional.
Publication Date: 1990.
Acronym: TTB.
Scores: Total score only for each of 9 tests.
Administration: Individual or group.
Price Data: Available from publisher.
Comments: Subtests available as separates.
Author: Saville & Holdsworth Ltd.
Publisher: SHL Group plc [United Kingdom].
  a) FOLLOWING INSTRUCTIONS (VTS1).
  Time: 20(25) minutes.
  b) NUMERICAL COMPUTATION (NT2).
  Time: 10(15) minutes.
  c) MECHANICAL COMPREHENSION (MT4).
  Time: 15(20) minutes.
  d) NUMERICAL ESTIMATION (NTS2).
  Time: 10(15) minutes.
  e) MECHANICAL COMPREHENSION (MTS3).
  Time: 15(20) minutes.
  f) FAULT FINDING (FTS4).
  Time: 20(25) minutes.
  g) DIAGRAMMATIC THINKING (DTS6).
  Time: 20(25) minutes.
  h) SPATIAL REASONING (ST7).
  Time: 20(25) minutes.
  i) DIAGRAMMATIC REASONING (DT8).
  Time: 15(20) minutes.
Cross References: For a review by Sami Gulgoz, see 11:419.

[2691]

Technical Test Battery [British Edition].
Purpose: Assess vocational skills and abilities.
Population: Apprentice and technical personnel.
Publication Dates: 1979–1982.
Acronym: TTB.
Administration: Group.
Restricted Distribution: Persons who have completed the publisher's training course or members of the Division of Occupational Psychology of the British Psychological Society.
Price Data: Available from publisher.
Comments: Subtests available as separates.
Authors: David Hawkey, Peter Saville, Robert Page (MT4), and Gill Nyfield (manual).
Publisher: SHL Group plc [United Kingdom].
  a) LEVEL 1.
  Purpose: "Basic skills and comprehension."
  Publication Dates: 1979–1981.
    1) *Verbal Comprehension.*
    Acronym: VT 1.
    Time: 10(15) minutes.
    2) *Numerical Computation.*
    Acronym: NT 2.
    Time: 10(15) minutes.
    3) *Visual Estimation.*
    Acronym: ET 3.
    Time: 10(15) minutes.
    4) *Mechanical Comprehension.*
    Acronym: MT 4.
    Time: 15(20) minutes.
  b) LEVEL 2.
  Purpose: "Higher older reasoning and analytical skills."
  Publication Dates: 1979-1981.
    1) *Verbal Reasoning.*
    Acronym: VT 5.
    Time: 10(15) minutes.
    2) *Numerical Reasoning.*
    Acronym: NT 6.
    Time: 10(15) minutes.
    3) *Spatial Reasoning.*
    Acronym: ST 7.
    Time: 20(25) minutes.
    4) *Diagrammatic Reasoning.*
    Acronym: DT 8.
    Time: 15(20) minutes.
    5) *Spatial Recognition (optional test for Levels 1 and 2).*
    Acronym: ST 9.
    Time: 15(20) minutes.

[2692]

Technology and Internet Assessment.
Purpose: Designed to determine strengths and weaknesses in eight areas related to computer, Internet, and information skills.
Population: Middle school, high school, and college students, potential and existing employees.
Publication Date: 1999.
Acronym: TIA.
Scores, 8: Use of Technology, Specific Computer Skills, Acquisition of Technology Knowledge, Basic Internet Knowledge, Internet Information Skills, Adapting to Technological Change, Impact of Technology, Ethics of Technology.
Administration: Individual or group.
Price Data, 1999: $3 per test (100 copies or less); $2.50 per test (over 100 copies); user's manual free.
Time: (20–30) minutes.
Comments: Administration and results via World Wide Web.
Author: Michael Ealy.
Publisher: H & H Publishing Co., Inc.

[2693]

Teele Inventory for Multiple Intelligences.
Purpose: Designed to examine the dominant intelligences of individuals from the age of 3 to adults to

identify the dominant ways individuals learn and process information.
Population: Age 3 to adult.
Publication Dates: 1992–1997.
Acronym: TIMI.
Scores, 7: Linguistic, Logical-Mathematical, Musical, Spatial, Bodily-Kinesthetic, Intrapersonal, Interpersonal.
Administration: Individual or group.
Price Data, 2006: $250 per complete kit including 35 pictorial inventories, 35 answer sheets, 1 scoring transparency and a teacher's manual (1997) plus postage; $25 per single set, includes one inventory, 35 answer sheets, and 1 scoring transparency; $10 per 35 scoring sheets plus transparency; $325 per test kit, includes 35 pictorial inventories, 35 answer sheets, 1 scoring transparency plus set of 25 rigid polished vinyl overhead transparencies for presentations.
Time: (15-20) minutes.
Comments: A spatial, forced-choice pictorial inventory that does not require the English language to complete.
Author: Sue Teele.
Publisher: Sue Teele & Associates.
Cross References: For reviews by Allen K. Hess and Sally Kuhlenschmidt, see 16:242.

[2694]

Telemarketing Applicant Inventory.

Purpose: "Provides a standardized measure of telemarketing potential and is an ideal instrument for selecting inbound and outbound telemarketing professionals" and is "ideal for personnel selection and placement, as well as identification of basic training needs."
Population: Applicants for telephone sales and service positions.
Publication Dates: 1992–2003.
Acronym: TMAI.
Scores, 13: Candidness, Accuracy, Sales Interest/Skill, Sales Responsibility, Productivity, Confidence/Influence, Interpersonal Orientation, Stress Tolerance, Job Stability, Job Stimulation Rating, Communicator Competence, Applied Verbal Reasoning, Readiness Index.
Administration: Individual.
Price Data: Available from publisher.
Time: (40–50) minutes.
Author: NCS Pearson, Inc.
Publisher: Pearson Performance Solutions [No reply from publisher; status unknown].

[2695]

Telemarketing Staff Selector.

Purpose: To evaluate the necessary knowledge and skills needed for the position of telemarketing representative.
Population: Candidates for the position of telemarketing representative.
Publication Date: 1997.
Scores: Total Score, Narrative Evaluation, Ranking, Recommendation.

Administration: Group.
Price Data, 2001: $150 per candidate; quantity discounts available.
Time: (81) minutes.
Comments: Scored by publisher; must be proctored.
Author: Walden Personnel Performance, Inc.
Publisher: Walden Personnel Performance, Inc.

[2696]

Telephone Interview for Cognitive Status.

Purpose: Designed to serve as a "brief test of global cognitive functioning" for administration over the telephone.
Population: Ages 60–98.
Publication Dates: 1987–2003.
Acronym: TICS.
Scores: Total score only.
Administration: Individual.
Price Data, 2006: $70 per introductory kit including manual (2003, 31 pages) and 50 record forms.
Time: (10) minutes.
Authors: Jason Brandt and Marshal F. Folstein.
Publisher: Psychological Assessment Resources, Inc.
Cross References: For reviews by Ronald J. Ganellen and Robert M. Thorndike, see 16:243.

[2697]

TEMAS (Tell-Me-A-Story).

Purpose: A culturally revelant apperception test for children.
Population: Ages 5–18.
Publication Dates: 1986–1988.
Acronym: TEMAS.
Scores, 34: Quantitative Scales (Cognitive Functions [Reaction Time, Total Time, Fluency, Total Omissions], Personality Functions [Interpersonal Relations, Aggression, Anxiety/Depression, Achievement Motivation, Delay of Gratification, Self-Concept, Sexual Identity, Moral Judgment, Reality Testing], Affective Functions [Happy, Sad, Angry, Fearful]), Qualitative Indicators (Affective Functions [Neutral, Ambivalent, Inappropriate Affect], Cognitive Functions [Conflict, Sequencing, Imagination, Relationships, Total Transformations, Inquiries, Omissions and Transformations scores for each of the following: Main Character, Secondary Character, Event, Setting]).
Administration: Individual.
Forms, 2: Short, Long.
Versions, 2: Minority, Nonminority.
Price Data, 2006: $291.50 per complete kit including nonminority stimulus cards (1986, 36 cards), minority stimulus cards (1986, 36 cards), 25 record booklets, administration instruction card, and manual (1988, 166 pages); $98 per set of stimulus cards; $24.75 per 25 record booklets; $13 per administration instruction card; $68.75 per manual.

Time: (45) minutes (short form); (120) minutes (long form).
Authors: Giuseppe Costantino, Robert G. Malgady (manual and record booklet), and Lloyd H. Rogler (manual).
Publisher: Western Psychological Services.
Cross References: See T5:2647 (2 references) and T4:2716 (1 reference); for a review by William Steve Lang, see 11:422.

[2698]

Temperament and Atypical Behavior Scale.
Purpose: Designed to measure temperament and dysfunctional behavior.
Population: 11–71 months
Publication Date: 1999.
Acronym: TABS.
Scores, 5: Detached, Hyper-Sensitive/Active, Underreactive, Dysregulated, Temperament and Regulatory Index.
Administration: Individual.
Price Data, 2011: $95 per complete set including manual (122 pages), screener with 50 forms, and 30 assessment tools; $25 per 50 screener forms; $30 per 30 assessment tool forms; $50 per manual.
Time: (5) minutes for screener; (15) minutes for assessment tool.
Comments: Ratings by parents, surrogates, or other professionals.
Authors: Stephen J. Bagnato, John T. Neisworth, John Salvia, and Frances M. Hunt.
Publisher: Paul H. Brookes Publishing Co., Inc.
Cross References: For reviews by Harold R. Keller and Loraine J. Spenciner, see 16:244.

[2699]

Temperament Comparator.
Purpose: "Designed to assess the relatively permanent temperament traits which are characteristic of an individual's behavior."
Population: Managers, supervisors, salespeople, and other higher-level professionals.
Publication Dates: 1958–1996.
Acronym: TC.
Scores, 15: Trait Scores (Calm, Cautious, Decisive, Demonstrative, Composed, Even-Tempered, Persevering, Seeks Company, Self-Confident, Serious, Steady Worker, Talkative), Factor Scores (Extroversive/Impulsive vs. Introvertive/Cautious, Emotionally Responsive vs. Non-Emotionally Controlled, Self-Reliant/Self-Oriented vs. Dependent/Group Oriented).
Administration: Individual or group.
Price Data, 2002: $99 per start-up kit including 25 test booklets, 25 score sheets, and interpretation and research manual; $54 per 25 test booklets (quantity discounts available); $29 per 25 score sheets; $28 per interpretation and research manual.
Time: No limit (approximately 15 minutes).

Author: Melany E. Baehr.
Publisher: Pearson Performance Solutions [No reply from publisher; status unknown].
Cross References: See T5:2648 (1 reference); for reviews by Paul M. Muchinsky and Aharon Tziner, see 9:1234; see also T2:1413 (1 reference); for reviews by Lawrence J. Stricker and Robert L. Thorndike, see 6:187 (1 reference).

[2700]

Temperament Inventory.
Purpose: Designed to measure a set of four genetically determined temperaments.
Population: College and adults.
Publication Dates: 1977–1980.
Acronym: TI.
Scores: 4: Phlegmatic, Sanguine, Choleric, Melancholy.
Administration: Group.
Price Data, 2005: $1.75 per test booklet; $7.99 per scoring templates; $3.99 per guide book.
Foreign Language Editions: Test booklets are available in English, French, German, and Spanish.
Time: Administration time not reported.
Comments: Includes 80 yes-or-no questions. The guide book, Understanding Your Temperament, is available for self-administering, self-scoring, and self-interpreting the scores from a Christian viewpoint; scoring templates are available (specify English or international) for efficient scoring.
Authors: Robert J. Cruise and W. Peter Blitchington.
Publisher: Andrews University Press.
   a) [GROUP EDITION].
   Publication Date: 1977.
   b) UNDERSTANDING YOUR TEMPERAMENT.
   Publication Date: 1979.
Cross References: For reviews by Allan L. LaVoie and Paul McReynolds, see 9:1235 (1 reference); see also T3:2411 (1 reference).

[2701]

Tennessee Self-Concept Scale, Second Edition.
Purpose: Designed as a multidimensional self-concept assessment instrument.
Population: Ages 7 to 90.
Publication Dates: 1964–1996.
Acronym: TSCS: 2.
Scores, 15: Validity scores (Inconsistent Responding, Self-Criticism, Faking Good, Response Distribution); Summary scores (Total Self-Concept, Conflict); Self-Concept scales (Physical, Moral, Personal, Family, Social, Academic/Work); Supplementary scores (Identity, Satisfaction, Behavior).
Administration: Group.
Price Data, 2006: $110 per complete kit including 24 AutoScore™ answer forms (12 for adults and 12 for

children) and manual (1996, 141 pages); $46.75 per 25 AutoScore™ forms (specify Adult of Child); $16.50 per 10 Spanish Research edition answer sheets (specify Adult or Child); $14.85 per mail-in answer sheet (specify Adult or Child); $295 per 25-use disk (PC with Windows; specify Adult or Child form); $16.50 per 100 answer sheets for use with disk; $10.20 per FAX Service Scoring; $65.50 per manual.

Time: (10–20) minutes.

Comments: Self-administered; WPS TEST RE-PORT Service available for computerized scoring and test interpretation.

Authors: William H. Fitts and W. L. Warren.

Publisher: Western Psychological Services.

    a) TSCS:2 ADULT FORM.

    Population: Ages 13 and older.

    b) TSCS:2 CHILD FORM.

    Population: Ages 7–14.

    c) TSCS:2 SHORT FORM.

    Population: Adults (13 and older); child (7–14).

    Comments: The Short Form consists of the first 20 items on the adult and child forms.

Cross References: See T5:2652 (12 references); for reviews by Ric Brown and John Hattie, see 13:320 (41 references); see also T4:2723 (32 references); for reviews by Francis X. Archambault, Jr. and E. Thomas Dowd, see 11:424 (89 references); see also 9:1236 (60 references), T3:2413 (120 references), 8:693 (384 references), and T2:1415 (80 references); for reviews by Peter M. Bentler and Richard M. Suinn and an excerpted review by John O. Crites of an earlier edition, see 7:151 (88 references); see also P:266 (30 references).

[2702]

Tennis Skills Test Manual.

Purpose: Designed to assess essential skills needed to play tennis.

Population: High school and college.

Publication Date: 1989.

Scores, 3: Ground Stroke, Serve, Volley.

Administration: Individual.

Price Data, 2001: $14 per manual (50 pages).

Time: Administration time not reported.

Authors: Larry Hensley, Graham Hatcher, Gloria Hook, Paul Hook, Carolyn Lehr, and Jacqueline Shick.

Publisher: American Association for Active Lifestyles and Fitness.

Cross References: For reviews by Claude A. Sandy and William A. Stock, see 12:390; see also T4:2724 (1 reference).

[2703]

TerraNova, Third Edition.

Purpose: "An assessment system designed to measure concepts, processes, and skills taught throughout the (U.S.) nation."

Population: Grades K-12.

Publication Dates: 1997-2009.

Acronym: TerraNova 3.

Administration: Group.

Levels, 12: 10 (Grades K-6 to 1-6), 11 (Grades 1-6 to 2-6), 12 (Grades 2-0 to 3-2), 13 (Grades 2-6 to 4-2), 14 (Grades 3-6 to 5-2), 15 (Grades 4-6 to 6-2), 16 (Grades 5-6 to 7-2), 17 (Grades 6-6 to 8-2), 18 (Grades 7-6 to 9-2), 19 (Grades 8-6 to 10-2), 20 (Grades 9-6 to 11-2), 21/22 (Grades 10-6 to 12-9).

Price Data, 2009: Price data for Teacher's Guide (2009, 353 pages) and Technical Report (on CD only, 2008, 384 pages) available from publisher; $61.05 per norms book (specify Fall norms, Winter norms, or Spring norms).

Time: Administration time varies by test and level.

Comments: Earlier versions were called California Achievement Test and Comprehensive Test of Basic Skills.

Author: CTB/McGraw-Hill.

Publisher: CTB/McGraw-Hill.

    a) TERRANOVA, THIRD EDITION SURVEY EDITION.

    Purpose: Designed to "yield norm-referenced information and some curriculum-referenced information in a minimum of testing time."

    Price Data: $151 per 25 consumable Survey test books (Levels 12-13, specify level); $136 per 25 reusable Survey test books (Levels 14-21/22, specify level); $24.65 per Survey Test Directions for Teachers (Levels 12-21/22, specify level); $17.70 per 25 packages of math manipulatives (Levels 13-21/22, specify level); $6.20 per Survey Directions for Practice Activities (Levels 12-18, specify level).

    Comments: All items are selected-response items.

        1) *Level 12.*

        Population: Grades 2-0 to 3-2.

        Scores: 4 Survey scores (Reading, Mathematics, Science, Social Studies).

        Time: (135) minutes.

        2) *Level 13-21/22.*

        Population: Grades 2-6 to 12-9.

        Scores: 5 Survey scores (Reading, Language, Mathematics, Science, Social Studies).

        Time: (170) minutes.

    b) TERRANOVA, THIRD EDITION COMPLETE BATTERY.

    Purpose: Designed to be "capable of generating precise norm-referenced achievement scores and a full complement of objective mastery scores."

    Price Data: $193.75 per 25 consumable Complete Battery test books (Levels 10-13, specify level); $151 per 25 reusable Complete Battery test books (Levels 14-21/22, specify level); $24.65 per Complete Battery Directions for Teachers (Levels 10-21/22, specify level); $17.70 per 25 packages of math manipulatives (Levels 13-21/22, specify level); $24.65 per 25 Complete Battery Practice Activities

(Levels 10-18, specify level); $6.20 per Complete Battery Teacher Directions for Practice Activities (Levels 10-18, specify level).

Comments: A combination of the Survey items and additional selected-response items.

1) *Level 10.*

Population: Grades K-6 to 1-6.

Scores: 2 Complete Battery scores (Reading, Mathematics).

Time: (95) minutes.

2) *Levels 11-12.*

Population: Grades 1-6 to 3-2.

Scores: 4 Complete Battery scores (Reading, Mathematics, Science, Social Studies).

Time: (160-180) minutes.

3) *Levels 13-21/22.*

Population: Grades 2-6 to 12-9.

Scores: 5 Complete Battery scores (Reading, Language, Mathematics, Science, Social Studies).

Time: (245) minutes.

c) TERRANOVA, THIRD EDITION MULTIPLE ASSESSMENTS.

Purpose: This edition "combines selected-response items of the Survey edition with sections of constructed-response items that allow students to produce their own short and extended responses."

Price Data: $202.50 per 25 consumable Multiple Assessments test books (Levels 11-21/22, specify level); $24.15 per Multiple Assessments Directions for Teachers (Levels 11-21/22, specify level); $17.70 per 25 packages of math manipulatives (Levels 13-21/22, specify level); $24.65 per 25 Multiple Assessments Practice Activities (Levels 11-21/22, specify level); $6.20 per Multiple Assessments Teacher Directions for Practice Activities (Levels 11-21/22, specify level).

1) *Levels 11-12.*

Population: Grades 1-6 to 3-2.

Scores: 4 Multiple Assessments scores (Reading, Mathematics, Science, Social Studies).

Time: (260-270) minutes.

2) *Levels 13-21/22.*

Population: Grades 2-6 to 12-9.

Scores: 5 Multiple Assessments scores (Reading, Language, Mathematics, Science, Social Studies).

Time: (335) minutes.

d) TERRANOVA, THIRD EDITION PLUS TESTS.

Purpose: Designed to "provide additional in-depth information about students' basic skills."

Price Data: $65.80 per 25 Form C Plus test booklets (Levels 11-13, specify level); $56.70 per 25 Form C Plus test booklets (Levels 14-21/22, specify level); $24.65 per Complete Battery/Plus Directions for Teachers (specify Level 16-18, 19-21/22).

Time: Administration time not reported.

Comments: "Used in conjunction with the Survey, Complete Battery, and Multiple Assessments components."

1) *Level 11.*

Population: Grades 1-6 to 2-6.

Scores, 3: Word Analysis, Vocabulary, Mathematics Computation.

2) *Levels 12-13.*

Population: Grades 2-0 to 4-2.

Scores, 5: Word Analysis, Vocabulary, Language Mechanics, Spelling, Mathematics Computation.

3) *Levels 14-21/22.*

Population: Grades 3-6 to 12-9.

Scores, 4: Vocabulary, Language Mechanics, Spelling, Mathematics Computation.

Cross References: For reviews by John O. Anderson and Michael Harwell, see 18:135; for reviews by Gregory J. Cizek and Robert L. Johnson of the Second edition, see 16:245; for reviews by Judith A. Monsaas and Anthony J. Nitko of an earlier edition, see 14:383; for information on the Comprehensive Tests of Basic Skills, see T5:665 (95 references); see also T4:623 (23 references); for reviews by Kenneth D. Hopkins and M. David Miller of the CTBS, see 11:81 (70 references); for reviews by Robert L. Linn and Lorrie A. Shepard of an earlier form, see 9:258 (29 references); see also T3:551 (59 references); for reviews by Warren G. Findley and Anthony J. Nitko of an earlier edition, see 8:12 (13 references); see also T2:11 (1 references); for reviews by J. Stanley Ahmann and Frederick G. Brown and excerpted reviews by Brooke B. Collison and Peter A. Taylor (rejoinder by Verna White) of Forms Q and R, see 7:9. For reviews of subtests of earlier editions, see 8:721 (1 review), 8:825 (1 review), 7:685 (1 review), 7:514 (2 reviews), and 7:778 (1 review).

[2704]

Test Anxiety Profile.

Purpose: Constructed to measure "how much anxiety a person generally experiences in different types of testing situations."

Population: Grades 9–12 and college.

Publication Date: 1980.

Acronym: TAP.

Scores, 12: 2 anxiety scores (Feeling of Anxiety, Thought Interference) for 6 different situations (Multiple Choice Test, Time-Limit Test, "Pop" Quiz, Essay Test, Giving Talk, Math Test).

Administration: Group.

Price Data: License to reproduce for Ph.D.s or Ed.D.s available from publisher.

Time: (20) minutes.

Authors: E. R. Oetting, C. W. Cole (test), and J. L. Deffenbacher (manual).

Publisher: E. R. Oetting, Colorado State University.

Cross References: See T4:2725 (2 references); for reviews by Steven D. Brown and John P. Galassi, see 9:1237.

[2705]
Test Attitude Inventory.
Purpose: "Developed to measure individual differences in test anxiety as a situation-specific personality trait."
Population: High school and college students.
Publication Dates: 1977–1980.
Acronym: TAI; TSAN.
Scores, 3: Worry, Emotionality, Total.
Administration: Group.
Price Data: Available from publisher at www.mind-garden.com/products/tsans.htm.
Time: (5–10) minutes.
Comments: Self-report inventory of test anxiety; title of manual is Test Anxiety Inventory.
Author: Charles D. Spielberger.
Publisher: Mind Garden, Inc.
Cross References: See T5:2656 (25 references) and T4:2726 (16 references); for reviews by John P. Galassi and Thomas R. Knapp, see 9:1238 (3 references); see also T3:2417 (2 references).

[2706]
Test de Vocabulario en Imágenes Peabody: Adaptación Hispanoamericana.
Purpose: Designed to measure "an individual's receptive or hearing vocabulary of single Spanish words spoken by the examiner"; described as an "achievement test, since it shows the extent of Spanish vocabulary acquisition of the subject" as well as a "screening test of scholastic aptitude."
Population: Ages 2-6 to 17-11.
Publication Date: 1986.
Acronym: TVIP.
Scores: Total score only.
Administration: Individual.
Price Data, 2008: $165 per test easel, manual (172 pages), 25 record forms, and shelf box.
Time: (15) minutes.
Comments: A Spanish language adaptation of the 1981 Peabody Picture Vocabulary Test–Revised, with manuals in Spanish and English.
Authors: Lloyd M. Dunn, Eligio R. Padilla, Delia E. Lugo, and Leota M. Dunn.
Publisher: Pearson.

[2707]
Test for Auditory Comprehension of Language–Third Edition.
Purpose: Designed as a measure of receptive spoken vocabulary, grammar, and syntax.
Population: Ages 3-0 to 9-11.
Publication Dates: 1973–1999.
Acronym: TACL-3.
Scores: 4: Vocabulary, Grammatical Morphemes, Elaborated Phrases and Sentences, Total.
Administration: Individual.
Price Data, 2011: $315 per complete kit; $93 per manual (1999, 117 pages); $178 per picture book; $53 per 25 profile/examiner record booklets.
Time: (15–25) minutes.
Author: Elizabeth Carrow-Woolfolk.
Publisher: PRO-ED.
Cross References: For reviews by Ramasamy Manikam and Christine Novak, see 14:384; see also T5:2657 (37 references) and T4:2727 (20 references); for reviews by Nicholas W. Bankson and William O. Haynes of an earlier edition, see 10:363; see also T3:2472 (25 references); for reviews by John T. Hatten and Huberto Molina of an earlier edition, see 8:454 (6 references); see also T2:997A (2 references).

[2708]
Test for Colour-Blindness.
Purpose: To identify congenital color vision deficiency.
Population: Ages 4 and over.
Publication Dates: 1917–1970.
Scores: Total score only.
Administration: Individual.
Price Data: Available from distributor.
Time: Administration time not reported.
Author: Shinobu Ishihara.
Publisher: Graham-Field (U.S. Distributor) [No reply from distributor; status unknown].
Cross References: See T5:2658 (2 references), T4:2729 (3 references), T3:2419 (1 reference), T2:1932 (29 references), 7:882 (13 references), and 6:962 (58 references).

[2709]
Test for Creative Thinking–Drawing Production.
Purpose: "Meant to be a screening instrument which allows for a first rough, simple, and economic assessment of a person's creative potential."
Population: Age 4–adult.
Publication Date: 1996.
Acronym: TCT-DP.
Scores, 15: Continuations, Completions, New Elements, Connections Made with Lines, Connections that Contribute to a Theme, Boundary-Breaking Being Fragment–Dependent, Perspective, Humour/Affectivity/Emotionality/Expressive Power of the Drawing, Unconventionality A–Uncoventional Manipulation, Unconventionality B–Symbolic/Abstract/Fictional, Unconventionality C–Symbol-Figure-Combinations, Unconventionality D–Nonstereotypical Utilization of Given Fragments/Figures, Speed, Total.
Administration: Group.
Forms, 2: A, B.
Price Data: Available from publisher.
Time: (30) minutes.
Authors: Klaus K. Urban and Hans G. Jellen.
Publisher: Pearson Assessment [England].

Cross References: For reviews by Alice J. Corkill and William Steve Lang, see 14:385.

[2710]

Test for Examining Expressive Morphology.

Purpose: "Developed to help clinicians evaluate expressive morpheme development with children whose language skills range from three to eight years of age."
Population: Ages 3-0 to 8-12.
Publication Date: 1983.
Acronym: TEEM.
Scores, 7: (6 morphemes plus 1 age level approximation): Present Progressives, Plurals, Possessives, Past Tenses, Third-Person Singulars, Derived Adjectives, Total.
Administration: Individual.
Price Data: Price information available from publisher for complete kit including manual (43 pages), test booklet, and 25 scoring forms.
Time: (5-7) minutes.
Authors: Kenneth G. Shipley, Terry A. Stone, and Marlene B. Sue.
Publisher: Pearson.
Cross References: See T5:2660 (4 references) and T4:2730 (1 reference); for reviews by Doris V. Allen and Janice A. Dole, see 10:364.

[2711]

Test for the Reception of Grammar.

Purpose: "Designed to assess understanding of grammatical contrasts in English."
Population: Ages 4–12 years and also dysphasic adults.
Publication Dates: 1983–1989.
Acronym: TROG.
Scores, 21: Noun, Verb, Adjective, Two Element Combination, Negative, Three Element Combination, Singular/Plural Personal Pronoun, Reversible Active, Masculine/Feminine Personal Pronoun, Singular/Plural Noun Inflection, Comparative/Absolute, Reversible Passive, In and On, Postmodified Subject, X But Not Y, Above and Below, Not Only X But Also Y, Relative Clause, Neither X nor Y, Embedded Sentence, Total.
Administration: Individual.
Price Data: Available from publisher.
Time: (10–20) minutes.
Comments: An 80-item, orally administered, multiple-choice test; "suitable for American as well as British subjects."
Author: Dorothy Bishop.
Publisher: Dorothy Bishop [England].
Cross References: For a review by Roger L. Towne, see 15:258, see T5:2662 (8 references).

[2712]

Test Lessons in Primary Reading, Second Enlarged and Revised Edition.

Purpose: "Designed to evaluate students' reading progress and thinking skills."
Population: Children.
Publication Date: 1980.
Scores: Item scores only.
Administration: Group.
Price Data, 2006: $5.95 per lesson booklet; $2.95 per teacher's manual/answer key (17 pages).
Time: Administration time not reported.
Authors: William A. McCall and Mary Lourita Harby.
Publisher: Teachers College Press.

[2713]

Test of Academic Achievement Skills–Reading, Arithmetic, Spelling, and Listening Comprehension.

Purpose: Measures a child's reading, arithmetic, spelling, and listening comprehension skills.
Population: Ages 4-0 to 12-0.
Publication Date: 1989.
Scores, 6: Spelling, Total Reading (Letter/Word Identification, Listening Comprehension, Total), Arithmetic, Total.
Administration: Individual.
Price Data: Not available.
Time: (15–25) minutes.
Author: Morrison F. Gardner.
Publisher: Psychological & Educational Publications, Inc.
Cross References: For reviews by C. Dale Carpenter and Steve Graham, see 13:321.

[2714]

Test of Academic Performance.

Purpose: Developed to assess achievement in four curriculum areas: Mathematics, Spelling, Reading, and Writing.
Population: Grades K–12.
Publication Date: 1989.
Acronym: TOAP.
Scores, 6: Basic subtests (Mathematics, Spelling, Reading Recognition, Reading Comprehension), Optional subtests (Written Composition, Copying Rate).
Administration: Individual and group.
Price Data, 2002: $119 per complete set including examiner's manual (182 pages), 25 student response forms, 25 record forms, and package of four reading stimulus cards; $75 per examiner's manual; $43 per 25 student response forms and record forms.
Time: (20–45) minutes.
Authors: Wayne Adams, Lynn Erb, and David Sheslow.
Publisher: Pearson.
Cross References: For reviews by Steve Graham and Cleborne D. Maddux, see 13:322.

[2715]

Test of Adolescent/Adult Word Finding.

Purpose: Developed to assess word finding skills.
Population: Ages 12-80.

Publication Date: 1989.

Acronym: TAWF.

Scores: 5 sections (Picture Naming: Nouns, Sentence Completion Naming, Description Naming, Picture Naming: Verbs, Category Naming) yielding 4 scores: Accuracy, Comprehension, Item Response Time, Word Finding Profile.

Administration: Individual.

Forms, 2: Complete, Brief.

Price Data, 2011: $334 per complete kit including test book, 25 response booklets, examiner's manual (204 pages), and technical manual (121 pages); $53 per 25 response forms; $167 per test book; $69 per examiner's manual; $69 per technical manual.

Time: (20-30) minutes for complete test; [10] minutes for brief test.

Comments: Upward extension of the Test of Word Finding (2777); speed can be measured in actual or estimated Item Response Time; tape recorder and stopwatch required on Section 1 only when using Actual Item Response Time Option.

Author: Diane J. German.

Publisher: PRO-ED.

Cross References: See T5:2667 (1 reference); for reviews by Ronald B. Gillam and Richard E. Harding, see 12:391.

[2716]

Test of Adolescent and Adult Language, Fourth Edition.

Purpose: Designed "(a) to identify adolescents and adults who score significantly below their peers and therefore might need help improving their language proficiency, (b) to determine areas of relative strength and weakness among language abilities, and (c) to serve as a research tool in studies investigating language problems in adolescents and adults."

Population: Ages 12-0 to 24-11.

Publication Dates: 1980-2007.

Acronym: TOAL-4.

Scores, 7: Spoken Language (Word Opposites, Word Derivations, Spoken Analogies), Written Language (Word Similarities, Sentence Combining, Orthographic Usage), General Language.

Administration: Individual or group.

Price Data, 2011: $224 per complete kit including 25 examiner record booklets, 25 written language forms, and manual (2007, 109 pages); $64 per 25 examiner record booklets; $87 per 25 written language forms; $87 per manual.

Time: (60) minutes.

Authors: Donald D. Hammill, Virginia L. Brown, Stephen C. Larsen, and J. Lee Wiederholt.

Publisher: PRO-ED.

Cross References: For reviews by Aimee Langlois and Dolores Kluppel Vetter, see 18:136; see T5:2668 (7

references); for reviews by John MacDonald and Roger A. Richards of an earlier edition, see 13:323 (6 references); see also T4:2738 (9 references); for reviews by Allen Jack Edwards and David A. Shapiro of an earlier edition, see 10:365; for a review by Robert T. Williams of an earlier edition, see 9:1243.

[2717]

Test of Articulation in Context.

Purpose: Designed to "examine a student's phonological abilities in the contest of spontaneous conversation, and can be used to screen, predict change, diagnose and assess a student's phonological progress following treatment."

Population: Preschool through elementary-school-aged children.

Publication Date: 1998.

Acronym: TAC.

Scores, 4: Sound Production, Speech Mechanism, Intelligibility, Adverse Effect on Educational Performance.

Administration: Individual.

Price Data, 2006: $133 per kit including 25 response forms, 4 laminated test boards, manual (45 pages), and canvas carrying bag; $51 per 25 response forms.

Time: Untimed.

Author: Teresa Lanphere.

Publisher: PRO-ED.

Cross References: For a review by Thomas W. Guyette, see 14:386.

[2718]

Test of Attitude Toward School.

Purpose: To assess a student's attitude toward school.

Population: Boys in grades 1, 3, 5.

Publication Dates: 1973-1984.

Acronym: TAS.

Scores, 2: Scholastic Attitude Score, Evaluation by the Teacher

Administration: Individual.

Price Data, 2005: $22 per set of 16 drawings; $54.95 per 25 teacher questionnaires (1984, 3 pages); $19.80 per manual (1984, 116 pages).

Time: Administration time not reported.

Comments: Projective test.

Authors: Guy Thibaudeau, Cathy Ingram-LeBlanc (translation from French), and Michael Dewson (verification of technical terms).

Publisher: Institute of Psychological Research, Inc. [Canada].

Cross References: For a review by Bert A. Goldman, see 11:425.

[2719]

Test of Auditory Analysis Skills.

Purpose: Constructed to assess "a child's auditory perceptual skills."

Population: Ages 5-8.

Publication Dates: 1975–1993.
Acronym: TAAS.
Scores: Total score only.
Administration: Individual.
Manual: No manual (directions on each form).
Price Data, 2006: $16 per 50 test forms.
Time: Administration time not reported.
Comments: Criterion-referenced; may be used in conjunction with the Test of Visual Analysis Skills; test is reproduced from author's book Helping Children Overcome Learning Difficulties (1993, Walker Publishing Company, New York).
Author: Jerome Rosner.
Publisher: Academic Therapy Publications.
Cross References: See T5:2671 (3 references); for reviews by Allan O. Diefendorf and Kathy S. Kessler and by Rick Lindskog of the earlier edition, see 11:426.

[2720]

Test of Auditory Comprehension.

Purpose: Designed to be used for the selection of auditory training objectives and measurement of progress in comprehension.
Population: Hearing impaired ages 4–17.
Publication Dates: 1976–1981.
Acronym: TAC.
Scores, 10: Linguistic vs. Nonlinguistic, Linguistic/Human Nonlinguistic/Environmental, Stereotypic Messages, Single Element Core Noun Vocabulary, Recalls Two Critical Elements, Recalls Four Critical Elements, Sequences Three Events, Recalls Five Details, Sequences Three Events With Competing Message, Recalls Five Details With Competing Message.
Administration: Individual.
Price Data: Publisher advises in April 2006 that test is now out of print although support materials (score sheets, tapes, curriculum, etc.) will remain available for several years.
Time: (30) minutes.
Comments: Test administered by cassette tape.
Authors: Audiologic Services and Southwest School for the Hearing Impaired, Office of the Los Angeles County Superintendent of Schools.
Publisher: Foreworks.
Cross References: See T5:2672 (2 references) and T4:2741 (7 references); for a review by James R. Cox, see 9:1246.

[2721]

Test of Auditory Processing Skills–Third Edition.

Purpose: "To measure a child's functioning in various areas of auditory perception."
Population: Ages 4–0 through 18-11.
Publication Dates: 1985-2005.
Acronym: TAPS-3.

Scores, 9: Word Discrimination, Phonological Segmentation, Phonological Blending, Number Memory Forward, Number Memory Reversed, Word Memory, Sentence Memory, Auditory Comprehension, Auditory Reasoning.
Administration: Individual.
Price Data, 2007: $130 per complete set including 25 test booklets, Auditory Figure-Ground CD, and manual (2005, 102 pages); $65 per 25 test booklets; $20 per Auditory Figure-Ground CD; $45 per manual.
Foreign Language Edition: Spanish version is available.
Time: (60) minutes (untimed).
Authors: Nancy A. Martin and Rick Brownell (TAPS-3); earlier editions by Morrison F. Gardner.
Comments: Represents a complete reshaping of the Test of Auditory-Perceptual Skills, Revised.
Publisher: Academic Therapy Publications.
Cross References: For reviews by Timothy R. Konold and Rebecca Blanchard and by Dolores Kluppel Vetter, see 18:137; for reviews by Annabel J. Cohen and by Anne R. Kessler and Jaclyn B. Spitzer of the Test of Auditory-Perceptual Skills, see 13:324 (2 references).

[2722]

Test of Auditory Processing 3: Spanish-Bilingual Edition.

Purpose: Designed to assess "auditory skills commonly utilized in academic and everyday activities."
Population: Spanish-bilingual children ages 5-0 to 18-11.
Publication Dates: 1985-2009.
Acronym: TAPS-3:SBE.
Scores, 13: Word Discrimination, Phonological Segmentation, Phonological Blending, Number memory Forward, Number Memory Reversed, Word Memory, Sentence Memory, Auditory Comprehension, Auditory Reasoning, Phonologic Index, Memory Index, Cohesion Index, Overall Score.
Subtests, 9: Word Discrimination, Phonological Segmentation, Phonological Blending, Number memory Forward, Number Memory Reversed, Word Memory, Sentence Memory, Auditory Comprehension, Auditory Reasoning.
Administration: Individual.
Price Data, 2010: $140 per complete kit including manual (2009, 104 pages), 25 test booklets, and Auditory Figure-ground CD; $50 per manual.
Foreign Language Edition: English edition available.
Time: 60(10) minutes.
Comments: Spanish edition, based on but not a translation of the English-language Test of Auditory Processing Skills¬Third Edition (18:137).
Author: Nancy A. Martin.
Publisher: Academic Therapy Publications.
Cross References: For reviews by Timothy R. Konold and Rebecca Blanchard and by Dolores Kluppel Vetter of the Test of Auditory Processing Skills-Third

Edition, see 18:137; for reviews by Annabel J. Cohen and by Anne R. Kessler and Jaclyn B. Spitzer of the Test of Auditory-Perceptual Skills, Revised, see 13:324 (2 references).

[2723]
Test of Childhood Stuttering.
Purpose: Assesses "speech fluency skills and stuttering-related behaviors."
Population: Ages 4 through 12.
Publication Date: 2010.
Acronym: TOCS.
Scores, 9: 5 Speech Fluency Scores (Rapid Picture Naming, Modeled Sentences, Structured Conversation, Narration, Speech Fluency Index), 4 Observation Rating Scale Scores (Speech Fluency Rating Scale Score, Speech Fluency Rating Scale Index, Disfluency-Related Consequences Rating Scale Score, Disfluency-Related Consequences Rating Scale Index).
Administration: Individual.
Price Data, 2011: $183 per complete kit including examiner's manual (134 pages), picture book, 25 examiner record booklets, and 25 Observational Rating scales; $44 per 25 examiner record booklets; $67 per examiner's manual; $29 per 25 Observational Rating scales; $46 per picture book.
Time: 20 to 30 minutes.
Authors: Ronald B. Gillam, Kenneth J. Logan, and Nils A. Pearson.
Publisher: PRO-ED.
Cross References: For a review by Kathy Shapley and Thomas Guyette, see 18:138.

[2724]
Test of Creativity.
Purpose: To gain a quick measure of a person's creativity.
Population: Adolescents and adults.
Publication Date: 1994.
Scores: Total score only.
Administration: Group.
Manual: No manual.
Price Data: Price information available from publisher for tests including self-assessment, answer sheet and feedback, and Types of Creativity.
Time: 35(40) minutes.
Comments: Self-administered, self-scored.
Author: Training House, Inc.
Publisher: Training House, Inc.

[2725]
Test of Early Language Development–Third Edition: Spanish Version.
Purpose: Designed to identify children in need of intervention in the area of language development and gather information on their strengths and weaknesses in different skill areas involved in language development;

the test may also be used "as a measure in research studying language development in young children and to accompany other assessment techniques."
Population: Ages 2-0 to 7-11.
Publication Date: 2007.
Acronym: TELD-3:S.
Scores, 3: Receptive Language, Expressive Language, Spoken Language Ability.
Administration: Individual.
Price Data, 2011: $167 per complete kit including 25 student response forms, 25 profile examiner record books, picture book, manipulatives, and examiner's manual (79 pages); $35 per 25 examiner's record booklets; $35 per examiner's manual; $65 per picture book.
Foreign Language Edition: The test is also available in English (14:388).
Time: (15-40) minutes.
Comments: The test must be administered and interpreted by "fluent Spanish speakers with knowledge of and speaking ability in the appropriate Spanish dialect"; authors also advise that although "results may contribute to the selection of long-term educational goals, they should not be used as the basis for planning day-to-day instructional programs for individual children."
Authors: Margarita Ramos and Jorge Ramos with Wayne P. Hresko, D. Kim Reid, and Donald D. Hammill.
Publisher: PRO-ED.
Cross References: For reviews by Sandra T. Acosta and Arturo Olivarez, Jr., see 18:139.

[2726]
Test of Early Language Development, Third Edition.
Purpose: Designed to measure the early development of spoken language in the areas of receptive and expressive language, syntax, and semantics.
Population: Ages 2-0 to 7-11.
Publication Date: 1981–1999.
Acronym: TELD-3.
Scores, 3: Receptive Language, Expressive Language, Spoken Language Quotient.
Administration: Individual.
Forms, 2: A, B.
Price Data, 2011: $327 per complete kit; $88 per manual (1999, 159 pages); $81 per Picture Book; $53 each per profile/Examiner Record booklet; $65 per manipulatives.
Time: (15–40) minutes.
Authors: Wayne P. Hresko, D. Kim Reid, and Donald D. Hammill.
Publisher: PRO-ED.
Cross References: For reviews by Sherwyn P. Morreale and Hoi K. Suen, see 14:388; see also T5:2680 (19 references) and T4:2749 (6 references); for reviews by Javaid Kaiser and David A. Shapiro of an earlier edition, see 12:393 (4 references); for reviews by Janice Arnold Dale and Elizabeth M. Prather of an earlier edition, see 9:1250 (1 reference).

[2727]

Test of Early Mathematics Ability, Third Edition.

Purpose: Designed as a test of early mathematical ability.
Population: Ages 3-0 to 8-11.
Publication Dates: 1983–2003.
Acronym: TEMA-3.
Scores: Math Ability Score.
Administration: Individual.
Forms, 2: A, B.
Price Data, 2011: $308 per complete kit including examiner's manual (2003, 71 pages), picture book Form A, picture book Form B, 25 examiner record booklets Form A, 25 examiner record booklets Form B, 25 worksheets Form A, 25 worksheets Form B, assessment probes, 5-inch x 8-inch cards, 20 blocks, 20 tokens, and mesh bag; $60 per picture book A; $57 per picture book B; $29 per 25 Form A or Form B examiner record booklets; $23 per 25 Form A or Form B worksheets; $41 per Assessment Probes manual (2003, 82 pages); $48 per examiner's manual; $28 per objects kit.
Time: Untimed.
Authors: Herbert P. Ginsburg and Arthur J. Baroody.
Publisher: PRO-ED.
Cross References: For reviews by Kevin D. Crehan and Judith A. Monsaas, see 16:246; see also T5:2681 (2 references); for a review by Jerry Johnson and Joyce R. McLarty of an earlier edition, see 11:428 (1 reference); for a review by David P. Lindeman, see 9:1252.

[2728]

Test of Early Reading Ability–Deaf or Hard of Hearing.

Purpose: Designed to measure "children's ability to attribute meaning to printed symbols, their knowledge of the alphabet and its functions, and their knowledge of the conventions of print."
Population: Deaf and hard of hearing children ages 3-0 to 13-11.
Publication Date: 1991.
Acronym: TERA-D/HH.
Scores: Total score only.
Administration: Individual.
Forms, 2: A, B.
Price Data, 2011: $219 per complete kit including picture book, 25 Form A and 25 Form B profile/examiner record forms, and manual (49 pages); $75 per picture book; $44 per 25 profile/examiner record forms (select Form A or B); $59 per manual.
Time: (20–30) minutes.
Comments: Adaptation of the Test of Early Reading Ability-2 (2729).
Authors: D. Kim Reid, Wayne P. Hresko, Donald D. Hammill, and Susan Wiltshire.
Publisher: PRO-ED.
Cross References: For reviews by Barbara A. Rothlisberg and Esther Stavrou Toubanos, see 12:394.

[2729]

Test of Early Reading Ability, Third Edition.

Purpose: Designed to "assess children's mastery of early developing reading skills."
Population: Ages 3-6 to 8-6.
Publication Dates: 1981–2001.
Acronym: TERA-3.
Scores, 3: Alphabet, Conventions, Meaning.
Administration: Individual.
Forms, 2: A, B.
Price Data, 2011: $303 per complete kit including examiner's manual (2001, 127 pages), 2 picture books (Form A and Form B), 25 Form A profile/examiner record forms, and 25 Form B profile/examiner record forms; $93 per examiner's manual; $75 per picture book (specify Form A or Form B); $35 per 25 profile/examiner record forms (specify Form A or Form B).
Time: (30) minutes.
Authors: D. Kim Reid, Wayne P. Hresko, and Donald D. Hammill.
Publisher: PRO-ED.
Cross References: For reviews by Sharon H. deFur and Lisa F. Smith, see 15:259; see T5:2682 (13 references) and T4:2751 (2 references); for reviews by Michael D. Beck and Robert W. Hiltonsmith of an earlier edition, see 11:429 (1 reference); for reviews by Isabel L. Beck and Janet A. Norris of the original edition, see 9:1253.

[2730]

Test of Early Written Language, Second Edition.

Purpose: "Measures early writing ability in children."
Population: Ages 3–0 to 10–1.
Publication Dates: 1988–1996.
Acronym: TEWL-2.
Scores, 3: Basic Writing, Contextual Writing, Global Writing.
Administration: Individual or group.
Forms, 2: A, B.
Price Data: Available from publisher.
Time: (30–45) minutes.
Comments: The publisher advises that a Third Edition is now available.
Authors: Wayne P. Hresko, Shelley R. Herron, and Pamela K. Peak.
Publisher: PRO-ED.
Cross References: For reviews by David P. Hurford and Michael S. Trevisan, see 13:326; for a review by Patricia Wheeler of an earlier edition, see 11:430.

[2731]

Test of Economic Knowledge, Second Edition.

Purpose: Measures knowledge of economic concepts.
Population: Grades 7–9.

Publication Date: 1987.
Acronym: TEK.
Scores: Total score only.
Administration: Group.
Forms, 2: A, B.
Price Data, 2001: $19.95 per 25 test booklets (specify Form A or B); $14.95 per examiner's manual (61 pages).
Time: (40) minutes.
Comments: "Designed to replace the Junior High School Test of Economics."
Authors: William B. Walstad and John C. Soper.
Publisher: Council for Economic Education.
Cross References: For reviews by William A. Mehrens and Anthony J. Nitko, see 11:431.

[2732]

Test of Economic Literacy, Third Edition.

Purpose: Designed to "evaluate a student's performance and make decisions about economics instruction at the senior high school level."
Population: Grades 11–12.
Publication Dates: 1978–2001.
Acronym: TEL.
Scores: Total score only.
Administration: Group.
Forms, 2: A, B.
Price Data, 2001: $22.95 per 25 test booklets (specify Form A or B); $17.95 per examiner's manual (2001, 75 pages), which includes scoring keys and a model answer sheet (may be duplicated locally).
Time: (40-50) minutes.
Authors: William B. Walstad and Ken Rebeck.
Publisher: Council for Economic Education.
Cross References: For a review by John W. Young, see 15:260; see T5:2686 (2 references); for reviews by Jennifer J. Fager and Dan Wright of an earlier edition, see 12:395; for a review by Anna S. Ochoa, see 9:1256; see also T2:1968 (19 references); for reviews by Edward J. Furst and Christine H. McGuire, and an excerpted review by Robert L. Ebel, see 7:901 (10 references).

[2733]

Test of English for International Communication (TOEIC).

Purpose: To evaluate the English proficiency of those whose native language is not English.
Population: Adult nonnative speakers of English.
Publication Dates: 1980–1999.
Acronym: TOEIC.
Scores, 3: Listening Comprehension, Reading Comprehension, Total.
Administration: Group.
Price Data: Price varies for Secure and Institutional Programs; price data available from publisher for ICS Program, 5 test booklets and answer sheets, audiocassette, and test administration manual (1998, 26 pages); volume discounts available.

Time: (120) minutes.
Comments: Secure Program administered on set dates and scored by TOEIC program office; Institutional and ICS Program administered by the client on-site and/or by TOEIC representative; one-half of test (100 questions) administered by audiocassette tape recording; separate answer sheet.
Author: Educational Testing Service.
Publisher: The Chauncey Group International.
Cross References: For reviews by Dan Douglas and Roger A. Richards, see 11:432.

[2734]

The Test of Everyday Attention.

Purpose: To measure "selective attention, sustained attention and attentional switching."
Population: Ages 18–80.
Publication Date: 1994.
Acronym: TEA.
Scores, 9: Map Search, Elevator Counting, Elevator Counting with Distraction, Visual Elevator, Elevator Counting with Reversal, Telephone Search, Telephone Search While Counting, Lottery, Total.
Administration: Individual.
Forms, 3: A, B, C.
Price Data, 2006: £269.50 per complete kit including manual (32 pages), 25 scoring sheets, cue book, stimulus cards and maps, 3 CDs, and 1 videotape; £41.50 per 50 scoring sheets.
Time: (45–60) minutes.
Authors: Ian H. Robertson, Tony Ward, Valerie Ridgeway, and Ian Nimmo-Smith.
Publisher: Pearson Assessment [England].
Cross References: For reviews by William D. Schafer and Terry A. Stinnett, see 17:183.

[2735]

The Test of Everyday Attention for Children.

Purpose: To measure "selective attention, sustained attention and attentional switching."
Population: Ages 6–16.
Publication Date: 1998.
Acronym: TEA-ch.
Scores: 9 subtests: Sky Search, Score!, Creature Counting, Sky Search DT, Map Mission, Score DT, Walk/Don't Walk, Opposite Worlds, Code Transmission.
Administration: Individual.
Forms, 2: A, B.
Price Data, 2006: £355.50 per complete kit including manual, 25 scoring sheets, cue book, stimulus cards and maps, and 2 audiotapes; £81 per 50 scoring sheets.
Time: (55–60) minutes.
Authors: Tom Manly, Ian H. Robertson, Vicky Anderson, and Ian Nimmo-Smith.
Publisher: Pearson Assessment [England].
Cross References: For reviews by Merilee McCurdy and Amanda Albertson and by Martin J. Wiese, see 17:182.

[2736]

The Test of Everyday Reasoning.

Purpose: Designed to supplement information on applications for employment, educational assessments, and program evaluations by assessing basic reasoning skills.
Population: Middle school students, high school students, and adults.
Publication Dates: 2000-2007.
Acronym: TER.
Scores, 6: Analysis, Evaluation, Inference, Deductive Reasoning, Inductive Reasoning, Total.
Administration: Group.
Price Data: Available from publisher.
Time: (50) minutes.
Authors: Peter A. Facione and Stephen W. Blohm.
Publisher: Insight Assessment-The California Academic Press LLC.
Cross References: For reviews by Timothy J. Makatura and by Renee M. Tobin and Corinne Zimmerman, see 18:140.

[2737]

Test of Gross Motor Development–Second Edition.

Purpose: To "measure gross motor abilities that develop early in life."
Population: Ages 3-10.
Publication Dates: 1985–2000.
Acronym: TGMD-2.
Scores, 2: Locomotor, Object Control.
Administration: Individual.
Price Data, 2011: $121 per kit including 50 profile/examiner record booklets, and examiner's manual (2000, 69 pages) in a sturdy storage box; $64 per 50 profile/examiner record booklets; $64 per manual.
Time: (15–20) minutes.
Author: Dale A. Ulrich.
Publisher: PRO-ED.
Cross References: For reviews by Libby G. Cohen and G. Michael Poteat, see 15:261; see T5:2689 (2 references) and T4:2762 (2 references); for reviews by Linda K. Bunker and Ron Edwards of an earlier edition, see 10:370.

[2738]

Test of Handwriting Skills–Revised.

Purpose: Designed to assess "neurosensory integration ability as evidenced by manuscript or cursive writing."
Population: Ages 6 to 18.
Publication Date: 2007.
Acronym: THS-R.
Scores: Total score only.
Administration: Group.
Forms, 2: Manuscript, Cursive.
Price Data, 2007: $120 per test kit including 15 manuscript test booklets, 15 cursive test booklets, 30 record forms, manual (190 pages), and training video; $35 per 15 test booklets and record forms (specify manuscript or cursive); $35 per manual; $15 per training video.
Time: (15-20) minutes.
Comments: Examiner's manual contains scoring directions for both manuscript and cursive formats.
Author: Michael Milone.
Publisher: Academic Therapy Publications.
Cross References: For reviews by Phillip L. Ackerman and Gene Schwarting, see 18:141.

[2739]

The Test of Infant Motor Performance.

Purpose: Designed to test "postural and selective motor control needed for functional performance in daily life during infancy."
Population: Ages birth to 17 weeks (term-born infants); 34 weeks postconceptual age through 4 months post-term (premature infants).
Publication Dates: 2001-2006.
Acronym: TIMP; TIMPSI.
Scores: Total score only.
Administration: Individual.
Forms, 2: Test of Infant Motor Performance, Version 5.1, TIMP Screening Items Version 1.0.
Price Data, 2010: $36 per manual (2005, 37 pages); $65 per 25 TIMP test forms; $10 per 100 Percentile Rank score sheets; $85 per self-instructional Compact Disc V. 4; $15 per age calculator; $60 per 50 TIMPSI test forms.
Foreign Language Editions: French and Portuguese editions available for the TIMP.
Time: (21-45) minutes.
Comments: Additional materials required for administration but not included: rattle, squeaky object, shiny red ball, age calculation wheel; after getting a total raw score, it is possible to obtain standard scores based on age norms as well as percentile rank scores; electronic version of the TIMP available (the TIMP Online).
Authors: Suzann K. Campbell, Gay L. Girolami, Thubi H. A. Kolobe, Elizabeth T. Osten, and Maureen C. Lenke.
Publisher: Infant Motor Performance Scales, LLC.

[2740]

Test of Inference Ability in Reading Comprehension.

Purpose: "Designed to provide diagnostic information about the inference ability of students."
Population: Grades 6–8.
Publication Dates: 1987–1989.
Scores: Total score only.
Administration: Individual or group.
Forms, 2: Multiple-choice, Constructed-response.
Price Data: Price information available from publisher for tests (specify multiple-choice or constructed-response), manual (1989, 24 pages), and technical report (1989, 58 pages).

Time: (40–45) minutes per form.
Authors: Linda M. Phillips (constructed-response format and multiple-choice format) and Cynthia C. Patterson (multiple-choice format).
Publisher: Linda Phillips (the author).
Cross References: For reviews by Douglas K. Smith and Robert Wall, see 13:327.

[2741]

Test of Information Processing Skills.

Purpose: Designed to assess "how well a person learns and retains new information and the effects of interference on those processes."
Population: Ages 5-0 and over.
Publication Dates: 1981-2009.
Acronym: TIPS.
Scores, 6: Visual Modality, Auditory Modality, Delayed Recall, Word Fluency, Modality, Process.
Administration: Individual.
Parts, 4: Part 1: Visual Modality, Part 2: Auditory Modality, Part 3: Delayed Recall, Part 4: Word Fluency.
Price Data, 2010: $140 per test kit including manual (2009, 224 pages), plates, and 25 protocols; $50 per manual.
Time: 30(15) minutes.
Comments: Based on the Learning Efficiency Test.
Author: Raymond E. Webster.
Publisher: Academic Therapy Publications.
Cross References: For information on the Learing Efficiency Test, see T5:1462 (3 references); for reviews by Alice J. Corkill and Gregory Schraw of the 1992 Revision of the Learning Efficiency Test, see 12:215; see also T4:1423 (1 reference); for a review by Robert G. Harrington of an earlier form of the Learning Efficiency Test, see 9:601.

[2742]

Test of Interpersonal Competence for Employment.

Purpose: Designed to assess social interaction skills necessary for job tenure for mentally retarded adults.
Population: Mildly retarded adolescents and adults.
Publication Date: 1986.
Acronym: TICE.
Scores, 6: Handling Criticism and Correction, Requesting Assistance, Following Instructions, Cooperative Work Behavior, Handling of Teasing and Provocation, Resolving Personal Concerns.
Administration: Group.
Price Data: Price data available from publisher for set including teaching guide and script (56 pages).
Time: (60) minutes.
Authors: Gilbert Foss, Doug Cheney, and Michael Bullis.
Publisher: James Stanfield Co., Inc.

Cross References: For reviews by Sharon H. deFur and Lawrence J. Ryan, see 15:262.

[2743]

Test of Irregular Word Reading Efficiency.

Purpose: Designed to use "the pronunciation of phonetically irregular words to measure reading comprehension."
Population: Ages 3-94.
Publication Date: 2007.
Acronym: TIWRE.
Score: Reading Efficiency Index.
Administration: Individual.
Forms, 3: Form 1, Form 2, Form 3.
Price Data, 2009: $159 per manual (93 pages), 25 record forms, 25 profile forms, and 3 laminated stimulus cards.
Time: (2) minutes.
Comments: Three equivalent forms are to be used to monitor progress over time; a profile form is included with a score log and a table for comparing scores.
Authors: Cecil R. Reynolds and Randy W. Kamphaus.
Publisher: Psychological Assessment Resources, Inc.
Cross References: For reviews by Mildred Murray-Ward and Michael S. Trevisan, see 18:142.

[2744]

Test of Kindergarten/First Grade Readiness Skills.

Purpose: "To assess a child's readiness for kindergarten or for first grade."
Population: Ages 3–6 through 7–0.
Publication Date: 1987.
Acronym: TKFGRS.
Scores, 3: Reading, Spelling, Arithmetic.
Administration: Individual.
Price Data, 2006: $60 per test kit including manual, 25 record booklets, and 8 stimulus cards.
Time: (20–25) minutes.
Author: Karen Gardner Codding.
Publisher: Academic Therapy Publications.
Cross References: For reviews by D. Joe Olmi and J. Steven Welsh, see 13:328.

[2745]

Test of Language Competence–Expanded Edition.

Purpose: "To evaluate delays in the emergence of linguistic competence and in the use of semantic, syntactic, and pragmatic strategies."
Population: Ages 5 through 18.
Publication Date: 1989.
Acronym: TLC-Expanded.
Scores: 5 subtest scores: Ambiguous Sentences, Listening Comprehension: Making Inferences, Oral Expression: Recreating Speech Acts, Figurative Language, Remembering Word Pairs (supplemental subtest for Level 2 only), plus 4

composite scores: Expressing Intents, Interpreting Intents, Screening Composite, TLC-Expanded Composite.

Administration: Individual.

Price Data, 2006: $459 per complete kit with briefcase including 25 Level 1 & 2 record forms, Level 1 & 2 stimulus manuals, administration manual (1989, 311 pages), and technical manual (1989, 98 pages); $399 per complete kit without briefcase; $55 per 25 Level 1 or Level 2 record forms.

Time: (60) minutes.

Authors: Elisabeth H. Wiig and Wayne Secord.

Publisher: Pearson.

a) LEVEL 1.

Population: Ages 5 through 9.

Price Data: $55 per 25 record forms.

b) LEVEL 2.

Population: Ages 10 through 18.

Price Data: $55 per 25 record forms.

Cross References: See T5:2693 (10 references); for reviews by Dolores Kluppel Vetter and Carol E. Westby, see 11:435 (1 reference).

[2746]

Test of Language Development–Intermediate, Third Edition.

Purpose: To determine strengths and weaknesses in language skills.

Population: Ages 8-0 to 12-11.

Publication Dates: 1977–1997.

Acronym: TOLD-I:3.

Scores, 12: General Intelligence/Aptitude Quotient, Spoken Language Quotient (SLQ), Listening Quotient (LiQ), Speaking Quotient (SpA), Semantics Quotient (SeQ), Syntax Quotient (SyQ), Sentence Combining (SC), Picture Vocabulary (PV), Word Ordering (WO), Generals (GL), Grammatic Comprehension (GC), Malapropism (MP).

Administration: Individual.

Price Data: Available from publisher.

Time: (30–60) minutes.

Comments: Primary edition also available; the publisher advises that a Fourth Edition is now available.

Authors: Donald D. Hammill and Phyllis L. Newcomer.

Publisher: PRO-ED.

Cross References: For reviews by David P. Hurford and Pat Mirenda, see 14:389; see also T5:2694 (27 references) and T4:2767 (7 references); for reviews by Rebecca McCauley and Kenneth G. Shipley of the TOLD-I:2, see 11:436 (5 references). For a review by Doris V. Allen of an earlier version of the entire Test of Language Development, see 9:1261 (5 references).

[2747]

Test of Language Development–Primary, Third Edition.

Purpose: To determine children's specific strengths and weaknesses in language skills.

Population: Ages 4-0 to 8-11.

Publication Dates: 1977–1997.

Acronym: TOLD-P:3.

Scores: 15 subtests (Picture Vocabulary, Relational Vocabulary, Oral Vocabulary, Grammatic Understanding, Sentence Imitation, Grammatic Completion, Word Discrimination [Optional], Phoenemic Analysis [Optional], Word Articulation [Optional]); Composites (Listening, Organizing, Speaking, Semantics, Syntax, Spoken Language).

Administration: Individual.

Parts, 2: Subtests, Composites.

Price Data: Available from publisher.

Time: (60) minutes.

Comments: Intermediate edition also available; orally administered; examiners need formal training in assessment; PRO-SCORE Computer Scoring System available for Macintosh, Windows, and DOS (1998); the publisher advises that a Fourth Edition is now available.

Authors: Phyllis L. Newcomer and Donald D. Hammill.

Publisher: PRO-ED.

Cross References: For reviews by Ronald A. Madle and Gabrielle Stutman, see 14:390; see also T5:2695 (72 references) and T4:2768 (21 references); for reviews by Linda Crocker and Carol E. Westby of a previous edition, see 11:437 (20 references).

[2748]

Test of Mathematical Abilities for Gifted Students.

Purpose: "Designed to identify students who have talent or giftedness in mathematics."

Population: Ages 6–12.

Publication Date: 1998.

Acronym: TOMAGS.

Scores: Total score only.

Administration: Group or individual.

Levels, 2: Primary, Intermediate.

Price Data, 2011: $200 per complete kit including manual (53 pages), 25 each Primary Level and Intermediate Level student booklets, and 25 each Primary Level and Intermediate Level profile/scoring sheets; $53 per 25 student booklets (specify level); $24 per 25 profile/scoring sheets (specify level); $65 per manual.

Time: (30–60) minutes.

Authors: Gail R. Ryser and Susan K. Johnsen.

Publisher: PRO-ED.

Cross References: For reviews by Robert B. Frary and Delwyn L. Harnisch, see 14:391.

[2749]

Test of Mathematical Abilities, Second Edition.

Purpose: "A measure of math ability."

Population: Ages 8-0 to 18-11.

Publication Dates: 1984–1994.

Acronym: TOMA-2.

Scores, 6: Vocabulary, Computation, General Information, Story Problems, Attitude Toward Math, Total.
Administration: Group.
Price Data, 2011: $106 per complete kit including 25 profile/record forms and examiner's manual (1994, 51 pages); $53 per 25 profile/record forms; $57 per examiner's manual.
Time: (60-90) minutes.
Authors: Virginia L. Brown, Mary E. Cronin, and Elizabeth McEntire.
Publisher: PRO-ED.
Cross References: For reviews by Delwyn L. Harnisch and Rosemary Sutton, see 13:329 (1 reference); for a review by Mark L. Davison of the earlier edition, see 9:1263.

[2750]

Test of Mechanical Concepts.

Purpose: "Designed to measure an individual's ability to visualize and understand basic mechanical relationships."
Population: Applicants for industrial positions.
Publication Dates: 1976–1995.
Scores,4: Mechanical Interrelationships, Mechanical Tools and Devices, Spatial Relations, Total.
Administration: Individual or group.
Forms, 2: A, B.
Price Data, 2002: $106 per start-up kit including 25 test booklets (specify Form A or Form B) and examiner's manual; $91 per 25 test booklets (quantity discounts available; specify Form A or Form B); $28 per examiner's manual.
Time: No limit (approximately 35–45 minutes).
Author: Science Research Associates.
Publisher: Pearson Performance Solutions [No reply from publisher; status unknown].
Cross References: See T5:2700 (1 reference); for reviews by Lorraine D. Eyde and Lyle F. Schoenfeldt, see 8:1045.

[2751]

Test of Memory and Learning, Second Edition.

Purpose: Designed to assess the "key features of memory" and to "evaluate learning as reflected in changes in recall and recognition over multiple trials of various stimuli."
Population: Ages 5-0 to 59-11.
Publication Dates: 1994-2007.
Acronym: TOMAL-2.
Scores, 25: 10 Verbal subtest scores (Memory for Stories, Word Selective Reminding, Object Recall, Paired Recall, Digits Forward, Letters Forward, Digits Backward, Letters Backward, Memory for Stories Delayed, Word Selective Reminding Delayed); 6 Nonverbal subtest scores (Facial Memory, Abstract Visual Memory, Visual Sequence Memory, Memory for Location, Visual Selective Reminding, Manual Imitation); 3 core composite scores (Verbal Memory Index, Nonverbal Memory Index, Composite Memory Index); 6 supplemental composite scores (Verbal Delayed Recall Index, Attention/Concentration Index, Sequential Recall Index, Free Recall Index, Associative Recall Index, Learning Index).
Administration: Individual.
Price Data, 2011: $416 per complete kit including Picture Book A, Picture Book B, 25 profile forms, 25 examiner record booklets, Delayed Recall Cue Cards, Visual Selective Reminding Test Board, 15 vinyl chips, and examiner's manual (2007, 165 pages); $81 per Picture Book A; $92 per Picture Book B; $47 per 25 profile forms; $69 per 25 examiner record booklets; $35 per set of Delayed Recall Cue Cards; $19 per Visual Selective Reminding Test Board; $10 per 15 vinyl chips; $82 per manual (2007, 159 pages).
Time: Core battery (30-35) minutes; Supplemental subtests (25-35) minutes.
Authors: Cecil R. Reynolds and Judith K. Voress.
Publisher: PRO-ED.
Cross References: For reviews by R. Anthony Doggett and Steven R. Shaw, see 18:143; for reviews by Karen Geller and Susan J. Maller of an earlier edition, see 13:330 (1 reference).

[2752]

Test of Memory Malingering.

Purpose: "To assist neuropsychologists in discriminating between true memory-impaired patients and malingerers."
Population: Ages 16 to 84.
Publication Date: 1996.
Acronym: TOMM.
Scores: Total score only.
Administration: Individual.
Price Data, 2011: $206 per complete kit including manual (45 pages), TOMM Research Monograph, 25 recording forms, and 1 set of stimulus booklets; $53 per 25 recording forms; $102 per set of 3 stimulus booklets; $75 per manual; $26 per Research Monograph; $84 per TOMM Software preview kit including user's manual and 3 reports; $9 per TOMM Software Reports.
Time: (15–20) minutes.
Comments: Self-completed; Windows™ computer software available on CD or 3.5-inch disk to administer, score, and report results of TOMM.
Author: Tom N. Tombaugh.
Publisher: Multi-Health Systems, Inc.
Cross References: For reviews by M. Allan Cooperstein and Romeo Vitelli, see 14:392.

[2753]

Test of Minimal Articulation Competence.

Purpose: Assesses articulation performance in children and adults.
Population: Ages 3 to adult.
Publication Date: 1981.

Acronym: T-MAC.
Scores, 3: Vowel/Diphthong, Consonant, Total.
Administration: Individual.
Parts, 3: Complete Test, Screening Test, Rapid Screening Test.
Price Data, 2002: $119 per complete program including Examiner's Manual and 25 record forms; $46 per 25 record forms; $80 per examiner's manual including administration, scoring, and interpretation information.
Time: Administration time not reported.
Author: Wayne Secord.
Publisher: Pearson.
Cross References: See T5:2703 (2 references); for a review by Barbara W. Hodson, see 9:1264.

[2754]

Test of Narrative Language.
Purpose: Designed to measure "children's ability to understand and tell stories."
Population: Ages 5-0 to 11-11.
Publication Date: 2004.
Acronym: TNL.
Scores, 3: 2 subtests: Narrative Comprehension, Oral Narration, plus Narrative Language Ability Index.
Administration: Individual.
Price Data, 2011: $184 per complete kit including examiner's manual (119 pages), picture book, and 25 examiner record booklets; $69 per examiner's manual; $75 per picture book; $53 per 25 examiner record booklets.
Time: (15–20) minutes.
Authors: Ronald B. Gillam and Nils A. Pearson.
Publisher: PRO-ED.
Cross References: For reviews by Abigail Baxter and Gabriele van Lingen, see 16:247.

[2755]

Test of Nonverbal Intelligence, Fourth Edition.
Purpose: "Developed to assess aptitude, intelligence, abstract reasoning, and problem solving in a completely language-free format."
Population: Ages 6-0 to 89-11.
Publication Dates: 1982-2010.
Acronym: TONI4.
Scores: Total score only.
Administration: Individual.
Forms, 2: Form A, Form B.
Price Data, 2010: $361 per kit including examiner's manual (2010, 107 pages), picture book, Critical Reviews and Research Findings (1982-2009), 50 Form A answer booklets and record forms, and 50 Form B answer booklets and record forms.
Foreign Language Editions: Spanish, French, German, Chinese, Vietnamese, Korean, Tagalog instructions available.

Time: (15-20) minutes.
Author: Linda Brown, Rita J. Sherbenou, and Susan K. Johnsen.
Publisher: PRO-ED.
Cross References: For reviews by Jeffrey A. Atlas and Gerald E. DeMauro of the Third Edition, see 14:393; see also T5:2704 (47 references) and T4:2775 (10 references); for reviews by Kevin K. Murphy and T. Steuart Watson of the Second Edition, see 11:439 (9 references); for reviews by Philip M. Clark and Samuel T. Mayo of the original edition, see 9:1266.

[2756]

Test of Oral Structures and Functions.
Purpose: "Assesses oral structures and motor integrity during verbal and nonverbal oral functioning."
Population: Ages 7–Adults.
Publication Dates: 1986–2002.
Acronym: TOSF.
Scores, 16: Speech Survey (Articulation, Rate/Prosody, Fluency, Voice, Total); Verbal Oral Functioning (Resonance, Balance, Sequenced Syllables, Mixed Syllable Sequence, Sequenced Vowels, Sequenced Syllable Rates, Total); Nonverbal Oral Functions (Isolated Functioning, Sequenced Functioning); Survey of Orofacial Structures; History-Behavioral Survey.
Administration: Individual.
Price Data, 2002: $85 per complete kit including manual (36 pages), 25 test booklets, finger cots, tongue blades, penlight, and balloons; $35 per examiner's manual; $40 per 25 test booklets; $8 per oroscope penlight.
Time: (20) minutes.
Author: Gary J. Vitali.
Publisher: Slosson Educational Publications, Inc.
Cross References: See T5:2706 (2 references); for reviews by Ronald B. Gillam and Roger L. Towne, see 12:397.

[2757]

Test of Phonological Awareness in Spanish.
Purpose: To assess phonological awareness in children whose first language is Spanish.
Population: Ages 4-0 to 10-11.
Publication Date: 2004.
Acronym: TPAS.
Scores, 5: Phonological Awareness Ability, Initial Sounds, Final Sounds, Rhyming Words, Deletion.
Administration: Individual.
Price Data, 2011: $96 per complete kit; $58 per examiner's manual; $45 per examiner record booklets.
Time: (10–15) minutes.
Authors: Cynthia A. Riccio, Brian Imhoff, Jan E. Hasbrouck, and G. Nicole Davis.
Publisher: PRO-ED.
Cross References: For reviews by Carlos Inchaurralde and Vincent J. Samar, see 16:248.

[2758]

Test of Phonological Awareness–Second Edition: PLUS.

Purpose: Designed to measure "young children's ability to isolate individual phonemes in spoken words and their knowledge of relationships between letters and phonemes in English."
Population: Ages 5–8.
Publication Dates: 1994–2004.
Acronym: TOPA-2+.
Scores: 2 subtests: Phonological Awareness, Letter Sounds.
Administration: Individual or group.
Levels, 2: Kindergarten, Early Elementary.
Price Data, 2011: $240 per complete kit including examiner's manual (2004, 78 pages), 50 Kindergarten summary forms, 50 Early Elementary summary forms, 25 student booklets for Kindergarten, and 25 student booklets for Early Elementary; $84 per examiner's manual; $35 per 50 Kindergarten summary forms; $35 per 50 Early Elementary summary forms; $55 per 25 Kindergarten student booklets; $55 per 25 Early Elementary student booklets.
Time: (15–30) minutes for Early Elementary version; (30-45) minutes for Kindergarten version.
Authors: Joseph K. Torgesen and Brian R. Bryant.
Publisher: PRO-ED.
Cross References: For a review by Ray Fenton, see 16:249; for reviews by Steven H. Long and by Rebecca McCauley of a previous edition, see 13:333 (3 references).

[2759]

Test of Phonological Awareness Skills.

Purpose: Designed to measure sound comparison, phoneme blending, and phoneme segmentation.
Population: Ages 5-0 to 10-11.
Publication Date: 2003.
Acronym: TOPAS.
Scores, 5: Rhyming, Incomplete Words, Sound Sequencing, Phoneme Deletion, Phonological Awareness.
Administration: Individual.
Price Data, 2011: $127 per complete kit; $58 per examiner's manual: $45 per 25 examiner record booklets; $17 per Block kit; $20 per audio cassette.
Time: (15–30) minutes.
Authors: Phyllis L. Newcomer and Edna Barenbaum.
Publisher: PRO-ED.
Cross References: For a review by Catherine P. Cook-Cottone and Jennifer Piccolo, see 16:250.

[2760]

Test of Pragmatic Language.

Purpose: Designed "to provide an in-depth screening of the effectiveness and appropriateness of a student's pragmatic, or social, language skills."
Population: Ages 5-0 to 13-11.
Publication Date: 1992.
Acronym: TOPL.

Scores, 3: Listening Skills, Speaking Skills, Total.
Administration: Individual.
Price Data: Available from publisher.
Time: (45) minutes.
Comments: The publisher advises that a Second Edition is now available.
Authors: Diana Phelps-Terasaki and Trisha Phelps-Gunn.
Publisher: PRO-ED.
Cross References: For reviews by Salvador Hector Ochoa and William K. Wilkinson, see 12:398.

[2761]

Test of Preschool Early Literacy.

Purpose: Designed to "identify children at risk of having or developing problems in literacy."
Population: Ages 3-0 to 5-11.
Publication Date: 2007.
Acronym: TOPEL.
Scores, 4: Print Knowledge, Definitional Vocabulary, Phonological Awareness, Early Literacy Index.
Administration: Individual.
Price Data, 2011: $237 per complete kit including examiner's manual (72 pages), picture book, and 25 record booklets; $97 per picture book; $59 per 25 record booklets; $93 per examiner's manual.
Time: (30) minutes.
Authors: Christopher J. Lonigan, Richard K. Wagner, Joseph K. Torgesen, and Carol A. Rashotte.
Publisher: PRO-ED.
Cross References: For reviews by Ronald A. Madle and by Gretchen Owens and Claire Lenz, see 18:144.

[2762]

Test of Pretend Play.

Purpose: To assess symbolic play, conceptual development, and use of symbols.
Population: Ages 1–6.
Publication Dates: 1997–1998.
Acronym: ToPP.
Scores: Scores for 4 sections (Self With Everyday Objects, Toy and Non-representational Material, Representational Toy Alone, Self Alone), and Total Score.
Administration: Individual.
Price Data, 2006: £356.50 per complete kit including 25 record forms, manipulables, and manual (1997, 58 pages).
Time: (45) minutes.
Authors: Vicky Lewis and Jill Boucher.
Publisher: Pearson Assessment [England].
Cross References: For reviews by Pam Lindsey and Louise M. Soares, see 15:263.

[2763]

Test of Problem Solving 3: Elementary.

Purpose: Designed to assess children's critical thinking and problem solving skills.
Population: Ages 6.0-12.11.

Publication Dates: 1984-2005.
Acronym: TOPS 3.
Scores, 7: Making Inferences, Sequencing, Negative Questions, Problem Solving, Predicting, Determining Causes, Total.
Administration: Individual.
Price Data: Available from publisher.
Time: (35-40) minutes.
Authors: Linda Bowers, Rosemary Huisingh, and Carolyn LoGiudice.
Publisher: LinguiSystems, Inc.
Cross References: For a review by Patti L. Harrison, see 17:184; see also T5:2710 (8 references).

[2764]

Test of Reading Comprehension, Third Edition.

Purpose: Designed to "quantify the reading comprehension ability of individuals."
Population: Ages 7-0 to 17-11.
Publication Dates: 1978–1995.
Acronym: TORC-3.
Scores: 9 subtests: General Vocabulary, Syntactic Similarities, Paragraph Reading, Sentence Sequencing, Supplementary (Mathematics Vocabulary, Social Studies Vocabulary, Science Vocabulary, Reading the Directions of Schoolwork), Reading Comprehension Quotient.
Administration: Group or individual.
Price Data: Available from publisher.
Time: (60) minutes.
Comments: The publisher advises that a Fourth Edition is now available.
Authors: Virginia L. Brown, Donald D. Hammill, and J. Lee Wiederholt.
Publisher: PRO-ED.
Cross References: See T5:2712 (1 reference); for reviews by Felice J. Green and Carole Perlman, see 13:334 (3 references); see also T4:2785 (3 references); for reviews by James A. Poteet and Robert J. Tierney of an earlier edition, see 10:372 (4 references); for reviews by Brendon John Bartlett and Joyce Hood of the original edition, see 9:1270; see also T3:2456 (1 reference).

[2765]

Test of Sensory Functions in Infants.

Purpose: Developed to measure "sensory processing and reactivity in infants."
Population: Infants ages 4-18 months.
Publication Date: 1989.
Acronym: TSFI.
Scores, 6: Reactivity to Tactile Deep Pressure, Adaptive Motor Functions, Visual-Tactile Integration, Ocular-Motor Control, Reactivity to Vestibular Stimulation, Total.
Administration: Individual.
Price Data, 2006: $192.50 per complete kit including set of test materials, 100 administration and scoring forms, and manual (45 pages) in carrying case; $29 per 100 administration and scoring forms; $42.50 per manual.
Time: (20) minutes.
Authors: Georgia A. DeGangi and Stanley I. Greenspan.
Publisher: Western Psychological Services.
Cross References: See T5:2715 (1 reference); for a review by Mark Albanese, see 11:441.

[2766]

Test of Silent Contextual Reading Fluency.

Purpose: Designed as a quick and accurate method of assessing silent reading ability.
Population: Ages 7 to 18 years.
Publication Date: 2006.
Acronym: TOSCRF.
Scores: Total score only.
Administration: Group or individual.
Forms: 4 equivalent forms: A, B, C, D.
Price Data, 2011: $272 per complete kit including examiner's manual (98 pages), 25 Student record Forms A, 25 Student record Forms B, 25 Student record Forms C, and 25 Student record Forms D; $64 per examiner's manual; $53 per 25 Student record forms.
Time: (10) minutes.
Authors: Donald D. Hammill, J. Lee Wiederholt, and Elizabeth A. Allen.
Publisher: PRO-ED.
Cross References: For reviews by Lisa F. Smith and Louise M. Soares, see 17:185.

[2767]

Test of Silent Word Reading Fluency.

Purpose: Measures the ability to recognize printed words accurately and efficiently.
Population: Ages 6-6 to 17-11.
Publication Date: 2004.
Acronym: TOSWRF.
Scores: Total score only.
Forms, 2: A, B.
Price Data, 2011: $156 per complete kit including examiner's manual, 50 student record forms A, and 50 student record forms B; $64 per examiner's manual; $53 per 50 student record forms (specify Form A or B); $85 per 100 student record forms (specify A kit or B kit).
Time: 3 minutes per form.
Authors: Nancy Mather, Donald D. Hammill, Elizabeth A. Allen, and Rhia Roberts.
Publisher: PRO-ED.
Cross References: For reviews by Michael D. Beck and John W. Young, see 16:251.

[2768]

Test of Social Insight.

Purpose: Designed to "appraise the characteristic mode of reaction the individual uses in resolving interpersonal (social) problems."

Population: Grades 6-12, 13-16 and adults.
Publication Dates: 1959-1984.
Acronym: TSI.
Scores, 6: Withdrawal, Passivity, Cooperation, Competition, Aggression, Total.
Administration: Group.
Levels, 2: Youth Edition, Adult Edition.
Price Data, 2006: $95 per test package; $57.50 per manual (1963, 19 pages) and manual supplement (1984, 19 pages); $85 per IBM answer sheet/profile sheet package; $45 per set of IBM scoring stencils; $61.50 per specimen set.
Time: [20-25] minutes.
Author: Russell N. Cassel.
Publisher: Martin M. Bruce, Ph.D.
Cross References: See T3:2461 (1 reference) and T2:1419 (3 references). For reviews by John D. Black and John Pierce-Jones, and an excerpted review by Edward S. Bordin, see 6:190 (4 references).

[2769]
Test of Spoken English.
Purpose: Measures the ability of nonnative speakers of English to communicate orally in English.
Population: Nonnative speakers of English.
Publication Dates: 1979–2006.
Acronym: TSE.
Scores: Total score only.
Administration: Group.
Price Data: Examination fee per candidate available from publisher.
Time: (20–25) minutes.
Comments: Because TOEFL iBT will assess all four language skills (listening, reading, writing, and speaking), using integrated tasks to evaluate communicative competency in English for nonnative speakers, ETS will discontinue TSE as a stand-alone testing program in areas where TOEFL iBT is being delivered.
Author: International Language Programs, Educational Testing Service.
Publisher: Educational Testing Service.
Cross References: See T5:2717 (1 reference); for reviews by Michael J. Subkoviak and Kikumi K. Tatsuoka, see 9:1273.

[2770]
Test of Supervisory Skills.
Purpose: Designed to measure an individual's understanding of "the roles and responsibilities of a first-line supervisor."
Population: Business supervisors and potential business supervisors.
Publication Date: 2004.
Acronym: TOSS.
Scores, 8: Management of Performance Quality, Staffing/Personnel Actions, Communications, Interpersonal Relations, Problem Analysis/Resolution, Project Planning, Direct Supervision, Total.

Administration: Individual or group.
Price Data, 2005: $29.95 per technical and administrative manual; $50 per 10 question booklets; $75 per 25 answer sheets.
Time: (30–45) minutes.
Comments: Available in paper-and-pencil and Web-based versions.
Authors: Erich P. Prien and Leonard D. Goodstein.
Publisher: HRD Press, Inc.
Cross References: For reviews by Ayres G. D'Costa and John W. Fleenor, see 17:186.

[2771]
Test of Understanding in College Economics-Fourth Edition.
Purpose: Intended "to provide norming data for a large national sample of students in [economics] principles classes, allowing instructors to compare performance in their classes on both pretests and posttests to the performance of the national sample of students and instructors."
Population: Introductory economics students.
Publication Dates: 1967-2007.
Acronym: TUCE-4.
Scores: 2 tests: Microeconomics, Macroeconomics.
Administration: Group.
Price Data, 2008: $24.95 per 25 booklets (2007, 44 pages).
Time: (45) minutes.
Authors: William B. Walstad, Michael Watts, and Ken Rebeck.
Publisher: Council for Economic Education.
Cross References: For reviews by George Engelhard, Jr. and Jean P. Kirnan, see 18:145; for reviews by Joseph C. Ciechalski and Jennifer J. Fager of the third edition, see 13:335; see also T2:1970 (10 references); for a review by Christine H. McGuire of an earlier edition, see 7:902.

[2772]
Test of Variables of Attention (Version 8.0).
Purpose: Developed to assess attention and impulsivity.
Population: Ages 4–80.
Publication Dates: 1988–2011.
Acronym: TOVA.
Administration: Individual.
Price Data: Available from publisher.
Time: (21.6) minutes.
Comments: Computerized continuous performance test (CPT) compatible with Windows, Mac, and Linux computers.
Authors: Lawrence M. Greenberg.
Publisher: The TOVA Company.
   a) T.O.V.A. VISUAL.
   Scores, 4: Commission, Omission, Response Time, Response Time Variability and Signal Detection.

b) T.O.V.A. AUDITORY.
Scores: Same as *a* above.
Cross References: For reviews by Sandra Loew and by Susan C. Whiston and Harrison Kane of an earlier version, see 14:394; see also T5:2720 (2 references); for reviews by Rosa A. Hagin and Peter Della Bella and by Margot B. Stein of an earlier edition, see 13:336 (1 reference).

[2773]

Test of Visual-Motor Skills.
Purpose: To assess a child's visual-motor functioning.
Population: Ages 2-0 through 13-11.
Publication Dates: 1986–1995.
Acronym: TVMS-R.
Scores: Total score plus 8 error scores.
Administration: Group or individual.
Price Data, 2006: $90 per test kit including manual, 15 test booklets, 15 scoring forms, and protractor; $28 per manual; $34 per 15 test booklets; $25 per scoring-criterion forms; $3 per protractor.
Time: (3–5) minutes.
Authors: Morrison F. Gardner.
Publisher: Academic Therapy Publications.
Cross References: For reviews by Deborah Erickson and Janet E. Spector of an earlier edition, see 13:337 (2 references); see also T4:2791 (1 reference).

[2774]

Test of Visual-Motor Skills–Upper Level.
Purpose: To assess a child's visual-motor functioning.
Population: Ages 2–0 through 13-11.
Publication Dates: 1986–1995.
Acronym: TVMS.
Scores: Total score plus 8 error scores.
Administration: Group or individual.
Price Data, 2006: $70 per test kit including manual, 25 test booklets, 25 scoring forms, and protractor; $17 per manual; $44 per test booklets, $3 per protractor; $6 per 25 scoring sheets.
Time: (3-5) minutes.
Author: Morrison F. Gardner.
Publisher: Academic Therapy Publications.

[2775]

Test of Visual Perceptual Skills, 3rd Edition.
Purpose: Constructed to "determine a child's visual-perceptual strengths and weaknesses."
Population: Ages 4-0 through 18-11.
Publication Dates: 1982-2006.
Acronym: TVPS-3.
Scores: 7 subtests: Visual Discrimination, Visual Memory, Spatial Relationships, Form Constancy, Sequential Memory, Visual Figure-Ground, Visual Closure, Total Score.
Administration: Individual.

Price Data, 2006: $150 per test kit including manual (2006, 88 pages), test plates, and 25 record forms; $40 per manual; $80 per test plates; $30 per 25 record forms.
Time: (30) minutes (untimed).
Authors: Nancy Martin (TVPS-3); earlier editions by Morrison F. Gardner.
Publisher: Academic Therapy Publications.
Cross References: For reviews by Phillip L. Ackerman and Brian F. French, see 18:146; see T5:2724 (13 references); for reviews by Nancy A. Busch-Rossnagel and Joseph W. Denison of an earlier edition entitled Test of Visual-Perceptual Skills (Non-Motor), see 9:1276.

[2776]

Test of Word Finding in Discourse.
Purpose: Designed to assess children's word-finding skills in discourse.
Population: Ages 6-6 to 12-11.
Publication Date: 1991.
Acronym: TWFD.
Scores, 2: Productivity Index, Word-Finding Behaviors Index.
Administration: Individual.
Price Data, 2011: $137 per complete test including manual (173 pages) and 25 test record forms; $46 per 25 test record forms; $93 per manual.
Time: (15-20) minutes.
Author: Diane J. German.
Publisher: PRO-ED.
Cross References: For reviews by James Dean Brown and Rebecca J. Kopriva, see 12:399; see also T4:2800 (1 reference).

[2777]

Test of Word Finding, Second Edition.
Purpose: Designed as a diagnostic tool for the assessment of children's word finding skills.
Population: Ages 4–12.
Publication Dates: 1986–2000.
Acronym: TWF-2.
Scores, 11: 8 scores for Standardized Assessment (Picture Naming: Nouns, Sentence Completion Naming, Picture Naming: Verbs, Picture Naming: Categories, Comprehension Check for Picture Naming: Nouns, Comprehension Check for Sentence Completion Naming, Comprehension Check for Picture Naming: Verbs, Comprehension Check for Picture Naming: Categories); 5 scores for Informal Assessment (Delayed Response Procedure, Secondary Characteristics Tally, Phonemic Cueing Procedure, Imitation Procedure, Response Analysis for Nouns).
Administration: Individual.
Levels, 3: Preprimary, Primary, Intermediate.
Forms, 2: Standardized Assessment, Informal Assessment.
Price Data, 2011: $444 per complete kit including examiner's manual (2000, 194 pages), picture books 1

and 2, 10 preprimary profile/examiner record forms, 10 primary profile/examiner record forms, and 10 intermediate profile/examiner record forms; $19 per 10 preprimary profile/examiner record forms; $24 per 10 profile/examiner record forms (specify primary or intermediate); $93 per examiner's manual; $172 per picture book 1; $127 per picture book 2.
Time: (20–30) minutes.
Author: Diane J. German.
Publisher: PRO-ED.
Cross References: For a review by D. Joe Olmi, see 15:264; see T5:2725 (10 references); for reviews by Sharon L. Weinberg and Susan Ellis Weisman of an earlier edition, see 11:443 (1 reference); for reviews by Mavis Donahue and Priscilla A. Drum of an earlier edition, see 10:373.

[2778]

Test of Word Knowledge.

Purpose: Developed to "assess a student's skill in the reception and expression of ... semantics."
Population: Ages 5–17.
Publication Date: 1992.
Acronym: TOWK.
Scores, 11: Expressive Vocabulary, Receptive Vocabulary, Word Opposites, Word Definitions, Synonyms, Multiple Contexts, Figurative Usage, Conjunctions and Transition Words, Receptive Composite, Expressive Composite, Total.
Administration: Individual.
Levels, 2: Ages 5–8, Ages 8–17.
Price Data, 2006: $195 per complete kit including stimulus manual, examiner's manual (118 pages), and 12 record forms; $40 per 12 record forms.
Time: (25) minutes for Level 1; (65) minutes for Level 2.
Authors: Elisabeth H. Wiig and Wayne Secord.
Publisher: Pearson.
Cross References: See T5:2727 (1 reference); for a review by Rick Lindskog, see 13:338 (3 references).

[2779]

Test of Word Reading Efficiency.

Purpose: Constructed as a "measure of an individual's ability to pronounce printed words accurately and fluently."
Population: Ages 6-0 to 24-11.
Publication Date: 1999.
Acronym: TOWRE.
Scores, 3: Sight Word Efficiency, Phonemic Decoding Efficiency, Total Word Reading Efficiency.
Administration: Individual.
Forms, 2: A, B.
Price Data: Available from publisher.
Time: (5–8) minutes.
Comments: Publisher advises that a Second Edition is now available.

Authors: Joseph K. Torgesen, Richard K. Wagner, and Carol A. Rashotte.
Publisher: PRO-ED.
Cross References: For reviews by Gerald Tindal and John J. Vacca, see 15:265.

[2780]

Test of Written Expression.

Purpose: Constructed as a "norm-referenced test of writing."
Population: Ages 6-6 to 14-11.
Publication Date: 1995.
Acronym: TOWE.
Scores, 2: Items, Essay.
Administration: Individual or group.
Price Data, 2011: $167 per complete kit including manual (58 pages), 25 profile/examiner record forms, and 25 student booklets in storage box; $53 per 25 student booklets; $59 per profile/examiner record forms; $66 per examiner's manual.
Time: (60) minutes.
Authors: Ron McGhee, Brian R. Bryant, Stephen C. Larsen, and Diane M. Rivera.
Publisher: PRO-ED.
Cross References: For reviews by Mildred Murray-Ward and Carole Perlman, see 13:339 (1 reference).

[2781]

Test of Written Language–Third Edition.

Purpose: Designed to "(a) identify students who perform significantly more poorly than their peers in writing and who as a result need special help; (b) determine a student's particular strengths and weaknesses in various writing abilities; (c) document a student's progress in a special writing program; and conduct research in writing."
Population: Ages 7-6 to 17-11.
Publication Dates: 1978–1996.
Acronym: TOWL-3.
Scores: 8 subtest scores (Vocabulary, Spelling, Style, Logical Sentences, Sentence Combining, Contextual Conventions, Contextual Language, Story Construction) plus 3 composite scores (Contrived Writing, Spontaneous Writing, Overall Writing).
Administration: Individual or group.
Forms, 2: A, B.
Price Data: Available from publisher.
Time: (90) minutes.
Comments: The publisher advises that a Fourth Edition is now available.
Authors: Donald D. Hammill and Stephen C. Larsen.
Publisher: PRO-ED.
Cross References: See T5:2731 (8 references); for reviews by Joe B. Hansen and by Jayne E. Bucy and Mark E. Swerdlik, see 13:340 (16 references); see also T4:2804 (2 references); for reviews by Stephen L. Benton and Joseph M. Ryan of an earlier edition, see 11:44 (6 references); for reviews by Edward A. Polloway and Robert T. Williams of the original edition, see 9:1278

[2782]

Test of Written Spelling, Fourth Edition.

Purpose: Designed to assess students' spelling abilities.
Population: Ages 6-0 to 18-11.
Publication Dates: 1976–1999.
Acronym: TWS-4.
Scores: Total score only.
Administration: Group.
Price Data, 2006: $85 per complete kit including manual (1999, 59 pages) and 50 answer sheets; $50 per examiner's manual; $40 per 50 answer sheets.
Time: (15) minutes.
Authors: Stephen C. Larsen, Donald D. Hammill, and Louisa C. Moats.
Publisher: PRO-ED.
Cross References: For a review by Gerald E. De-Mauro, see 15:266; see T5:2732 (2 references); for reviews by Alfred P. Longo and Hoi K. Suen of an earlier edition, see 13:341 (5 references); see also T4:2805 (4 references); for reviews by Deborah B. Erickson and Ruth M. Noyce of an earlier edition, see 10:374; for reviews by John M. Bradley and Deborah B. Erickson of an earlier edition, see 9:1279.

[2783]

Test on Appraising Observations.

Purpose: Designed to test one aspect of critical thinking: judging credibility.
Population: Grade 10 to adult.
Publication Dates: 1983–1990.
Administration: Group.
Price Data: Available from publisher.
Authors: Stephen P. Norris (multiple-choice format and constructed-response format) and Ruth King (multiple-choice format).
Publisher: Faculty of Education, Memorial University of Newfoundland [Canada].
    a) MULTIPLE-CHOICE FORMAT.
    Publication Date: 1983.
    Scores: Total score only.
    Parts, 2: A, B.
    Time: (40–45) minutes.
    b) CONSTRUCTED-RESPONSE VERSION.
    Publication Date: 1986.
    Scores, 2: Answer-Choice, Justification.
    Time: (40–45) minutes.
Cross References: For reviews by Michael Kane and Jeffrey K. Smith, see 13:342; see also T4:2806 (1 reference).

[2784]

Tests of Achievement and Proficiency™, Forms K, L, and M.

Purpose: Designed to "provide a comprehensive and objective measure of students' progress in a high school curriculum."
Population: Grades 9–12.

Publication Dates: 1978–1996.
Acronym: TAP™.
Administration: Group.
Forms, 3: K, L, M; 2 batteries: Complete and Survey.
Levels, 4: 15, 16, 17, 18.
Price Data: Available from publisher.
Special Editions: Braille and large-print editions available.
Authors: Dale P. Scannell, Oscar M. Haugh, Brenda H. Loyd, and C. Frederick Risinger.
Publisher: Riverside Publishing.
    a) COMPLETE BATTERY.
    Scores, 15: Vocabulary, Reading Comprehension, Written Expression, Math Concepts and Problem Solving, Math Computation [optional], Social Studies, Science, Information Processing, Reading Total, Math Total, Core Total, Composite, plus Advance Skills Scores for reading, language, and mathematics.
    Time: (255) minutes; (275) minutes with optional test.
    b) SURVEY BATTERY.
    Scores, 10: Reading (Vocabulary, Comprehension, Total), Written Expression, Math Concepts and Problem Solving, Math Computation [optional], Total, plus Advanced Skills Scores for reading, language, and mathematics.
    Time: (90) minutes; (100) minutes with optional test.
Cross References: For reviews by Susan M. Brookhart and Darrell L. Sabers, see 14:396; see also T5:2735 (1 reference), T4:2810 (1 reference), and 11:445 (4 references); for a review by Elaine Clark of Forms G and H, see 10:375 (2 references); for reviews by John M. Keene, Jr. and James L. Wardrop of an earlier form, see 9:1282.

[2785]

Tests of Achievement in Basic Skills: Mathematics.

Purpose: To assess mathematics achievement.
Population: Preschool-kindergarten, Grades 1, 2, 3–4, 4–6, 7–9, 10–adult.
Publication Dates: 1970–1976.
Acronym: TABS-M.
Administration: Group.
Price Data: Available from publisher.
Time: (45–70) minutes.
Comments: May be used separately or as part of instructional Individualized Mathematics Program (IMP); "criterion-referenced tests"; 18-69 item scores, each item measuring a specific objective, and part and total scores; separate answer sheets (Digitek) must be used with Levels B-D.
Authors: James C. Young and Robert R. Knapp (Level C manuals).
Publisher: EdITS/Educational and Industrial Testing Service.
    a) LEVEL K.
    Population: Preschool-kindergarten.

Publication Date: 1974.
Scores: 18 item scores in 3 areas: Arithmetic Skills, Geometry-Measurement, Modern Concepts.
b) LEVEL 1.
Population: Grade 1.
Publication Date: 1974.
Scores: 36 item scores in 3 areas: same as *a* above.
c) LEVEL 2.
Population: Grade 2.
Publication Date: 1974.
Scores: 41 item scores in 3 areas: same as *a* above.
d) LEVEL A.
Population: Grades 3–4.
Publication Date: 1973.
Scores: 49 item scores in 3 areas: same as *a* above.
e) LEVEL B.
Population: Grades 4–6.
Publication Dates: 1972–1973.
Scores: 73 items and total scores in 3 areas: same as *a* above, plus Total.
f) LEVEL C.
Population: Grades 7–9.
Publication Dates: 1970–1971.
Scores: 68 items and total scores in 3 areas: same as *e* above.
g) LEVEL D.
Population: Grades 10-12.
Publication Dates: 1972–1976.
Scores: 47 items and total scores in 2 areas: Arithmetic Skills, Arithmetic Application, plus Total.
Cross References: For reviews by James Braswell and C. Alan Riedesel, and an excerpted review by Barton B. Proger, see 8:293 (2 references); see also 7:492 (1 reference).

[2786]

Tests of Adult Basic Education Work-Related Foundation Skills.

Purpose: "To provide pre-instructional information about an examinee's level of achievement on basic skills, … to identify areas of weakness … measure growth, … and involve the examinee in appraising his or her learning needs to assist … [in preparing] an instructional program to meet the examinee's individual needs."
Population: Adults in vocational/technical programs, students in adult basic education programs 2-year colleges, and secondary school ROP & JTPA programs.
Publication Dates: 1994–1996.
Acronym: TABE WF.
Scores, 6: Reading, Math Computation, Applied Math, Total Mathematics (Math Computation and Applied Math), Language, Total Battery.
Administration: Group.
Forms, 4: General, Business/Office, Health, Trade/Technical.
Price Data, 2002: $33.65 per review kit including general test book, trade/technical test book, health test book, business/office test book, examiner's manual (1994, 30 pages), and individual diagnostic profile; $54 per manual and 25 locator tests; $83.40 per manual and general trade technical, health, or business/office test book; $24.50 per 25 locator test SCOREZE answer sheets; $29 per general trade/technical, health, or business/office SCOREZE answer sheets; $28.80 per 50 CompuScan answer sheets; $23.95 per 50 Scantron Opt. 2 answer sheets; $12.75 per 25 individual diagnostic profiles; $17.40 per handscoring stencil; $2.85 per group record sheet; $15.80 per examiner's manual; $15.30 per norms book; $14.25 per technical bulletin; $14.25 per technical report (1996, 33 pages) for use with this test and the TABE Work-Related Problem Solving available from publisher.
Time: 120(160) minutes.
Author: CTB Macmillan/McGraw-Hill.
Publisher: CTB/McGraw-Hill.
Cross References: For reviews by Kurt F. Geisinger and Jeffrey A. Jenkins, see 13:344.

[2787]

Tests of Adult Basic Education Work-Related Problem Solving.

Purpose: "Designed to help employers, educators, and training professionals diagnose how an examinee deals with the different aspects of problem solving."
Population: Students in secondary schools, vocational education programs, adult basic education programs, and junior colleges, and employees in industry.
Publication Dates: 1994–1996.
Acronym: TABE-PS.
Scores, 5: Competency scores (Employs Reading and Math Skills to Identify and Define a Problem, Examines Situations Using Problem-Solving Techniques, Makes Decisions About Possible Solutions, Evaluates Outcomes and Effects of Implementing Solutions), Total Number Correct Score.
Administration: Group.
Forms, 2: 7, 8.
Price Data, 2006: $23 per review kit including examiner's manual/scoring guide (1994, 56 pages), and test book; $67 per 25 test books with 1 manual; $40 per 25 practice exercise test book; $32 per 25 scannable answer sheet; $21 per examiner's manual/scoring guide.
Time: 70(75) minutes for Form 7; 60(65) minutes for Form 8.
Comments: May be administered alone or in conjunction with other TABE materials; test includes a Practice Exercise which was included in the norming studies and so should be administered along with the test; includes Individual Diagnostic Profile, and Interview/Interest Questionnaire.
Author: CTB/McGraw-Hill.
Publisher: CTB/McGraw-Hill.
Cross References: For reviews by Gale M. Morrison and Jerry Tindal, see 13:345.

[2788]

Tests of Adult Basic Education, Forms 9 & 10.

Purpose: "Designed and developed to provide achievement scores that are valid for most types of adult education decision-making."

Population: Adults.

Acronym: TABE.

Subtests, 4-11: Pre-Reading (Level L), Reading, Mathematics Computation, Applied Mathematics, Language, Language Mechanics (optional), Vocabulary (optional), Spelling (optional), Science/Social Studies (Level A), Algebra/Geometry (Level A), Writing (Level A).

Administration: Individual or group.

Editions, 2: Complete Battery, Survey.

Forms, 2: 9, 10.

Price Data, 2006: $36 per 25 hand-scored SCOREZE answer sheets; $31 per 50 CompuScan answer sheets; $16 per 25 Individual Diagnostic Profiles; $32 per review materials; $19 per test directions book; $27 per 25 examinee books; $4 per group record sheet; $19 per norms book; $21 per Technical Report CD (116 pages printed); $24.50 per 25 Getting to Know TABE Workbooks; $60 per Guide to Administering TABE 9 & 10 book; $40 per TABE Teacher's Guide for Reading and Language: Linking Assessments to Learning book; $40 per TABE Teacher's Guide for Mathematics: linking Assessments to Learning book; $46 per 10 consumable test books; $46 per 10 reusable test books; $35 per audio tape; $19 per large print test directions; $58 per large print test book; $57 per 25 large print SCOREZE answer sheets; $8 per online test administration (bulk discounts available).

Special Editions: Form 9 is available in Large Print, Braille, and Audio.

Comments: Both forms available online.

Author: CTB/McGraw-Hill.

Publisher: CTB/McGraw-Hill.

a) COMPLETE BATTERY.

Purpose: Designed to "assess skill levels and help determine appropriate career or training programs."

Publication Dates: 1957-2004.

Levels, 4-5: L (Limited Literacy), E (Easy), M (Medium), D (Difficult), A (Advanced).

Scores, 4: Total Mathematics (Mathematics Computation, Applied Mathematics), Total Battery (Pre-Reading/Reading, Total Mathematics, Language).

Price Data: $101 per 25 Complete Battery test books; $42 per Complete Battery scoring stencils; $236 per Braille Complete Battery Test book; $48 per Writing test book; $16 per Writing Assessment and scoring manual; $72 per Science/Social Studies test book; $13 per Science/Social Studies test directions; $32 per 25 Science/Social Studies SCOREZE answer sheets; $23.50 per 50 Science/Social Studies CompuScan answer sheets; $21.25 per Science/Social Studies scoring stencils; $72 per Algebra/Geometry test book; $13 per Algebra/Geometry test directions; $32 per 25 Algebra/Geometry SCOREZE answer sheets; $23.50 per 50 Algebra/Geometry CompuScan answer sheets; $21.25 per Algebra/Geometry scoring stencils; $16 per Science/Social Studies and Algebra/Geometry tables book.

1) *Pre-Reading*.

Scores, 4: Match Letters, Recognize Letters, Recognize Beginning/Ending Sounds, Middle Sounds.

Levels: Level L only.

Time: 13(23) minutes.

2) *Reading*.

3) *Mathematics Computation*.

Scores, 2-6: Add Whole Numbers [Levels L-M], Subtract Whole Numbers [Levels L-M], Multiply Whole Numbers [Levels E-D], Divide Whole Numbers [Levels E-D], Decimals [Levels E-A], Fractions [Levels M-A], Integers [Levels D, A], Percents [Levels D, A], Order of Operations [Level A], Algebraic Operations [Level A].

Time: 15(25) minutes for Level L; 24(34) minutes for Levels E-A.

4) *Applied Mathematics*.

Scores, 6-9: Number & Number Operations, Computation in Context, Estimation [Levels E-A], Measurement, Geometry & Spatial Sense, Data Analysis, Statistics & Probability [Levels E-A], Patterns/Functions/Algebra, Problem Solving & Reasoning [Levels E-A].

Levels: Level L only.

Time: 45(55) minutes for Level L; 50(60) minutes for Levels E-A.

5) *Language*.

Scores, 6: Usage, Sentence Formation, Paragraph Development, Capitalization, Punctuation, Writing Conventions.

Levels: Levels E-A only.

Time: 55(65) minutes.

6) *Vocabulary*.

Scores, 3: Word Meaning, Multi-Meaning Words, Words in Context.

Levels: Levels E-A only.

Time: 14(24) minutes.

Comments: This subtest is optional.

7) *Language Mechanics*.

Scores, 2: Sentences/Phrases/Clauses, Writing Conventions.

Levels: Levels E-A only.

Time: 14(24) minutes.

Comments: This subtest is optional.

8) *Spelling*.

Scores, 3: Vowel, Consonant, Structural Unit.

Levels: Levels E-A only.

Time: 10(20) minutes.

Comments: This subtest is optional.

9) *Science/Social Studies.*
Scores: Scores not presented.
Level: Level A only.
Time: Administration time not reported.
Comments: This subtest is optional.
10) *Algebra/Geometry.*
Scores: Scores not presented.
Level: Level A only.
Time: Administration time not reported.
Comments: This subtest is optional.
11) *Writing.*
Scores: Scores not presented.
Level: Level A only.
Time: 45(55) minutes.
Comments: This subtest is optional.
b) SURVEY.
Purpose: Provides a skill snapshot for placement information.
Publication Dates: 1987-2004.
Levels, 4: Same as Complete Battery except for omission of Level L.
Scores, 2: Same as Complete Battery.
Price Data: $101 per Survey test book; $42 per Survey scoring stencils; $212 per Braille Survey test book.
 1) *Reading.*
 Scores, 5: Same as Complete Battery.
 Time: 25(35) minutes.
 2) *Mathematics Computation.*
 Scores, 5-6: Same as Complete Battery.
 Time: 15(25) minutes.
 3) *Applied Mathematics.*
 Scores, 9: Same as Complete Battery.
 Time: 25(35) minutes.
 4) *Language.*
 Scores, 6: Same as Complete Battery.
 Time: 25(35) minutes.
 5) *Language Mechanics.*
 Scores, 3: Same as Complete Battery.
 Time: 14(24) minutes.
 Comments: This subtest is optional.
 6) *Vocabulary.*
 Scores, 3: Same as Complete Battery.
 Time: 14(24) minutes.
 Comments: This subtest is optional.
 7) *Spelling.*
 Scores, 3: Same as Complete Battery.
 Time: 10(20) minutes.
 Comments: This subtest is optional.
c) LOCATOR TEST.
Purpose: Designed to "help teachers in assigning the level of the TABE test to administer."
Subtests, 4: Reading, Mathematics Computation, Applied Mathematics, Language.
Scores: Total score only.
Price Data: $58 per 2 Practice Exercise and Locator Test books; $21 per Practice and Locator Test

scoring stencils; $130 per Braille Practice Exerci and Locator Test books.
Time: 37(47) minutes for Complete Battery; 35(4 minutes for Survey.
d) WORD LIST.
Scores: Total score only.
Price Data: $26 per Word List Test book; $5 per large print word list.
Time: 15(25) minutes.
e) PRACTICE EXERCISE.
Scores: Not scored.
Price Data: Same as *c* above.
Time: 20(30) minutes.
Cross References: For a review by Judith A. Mor saas, see 17:187; for reviews by Michael D. Beck an Bruce G. Rogers of an earlier edition, see 13:343; f reviews by Robert W. Lissitz and Steven J. Osterlind an earlier edition, see 11:446 (2 references); for reviev by Thomas F. Donlon and Norman E. Gronlund of a earlier edition, see 8:33 (1 reference); for a review A. N. Hieronymus and an excerpted review by S. Al Cohen of an earlier edition, see 7:32.

Tests of General Educational Developmen [GED Tests].

Purpose: To "assess skills representative of the typical ou comes of a traditional high school education" for the purpo of awarding a high school equivalency (GED) credential
Population: Candidates for high school equivalenc diplomas.
Publication Dates: 1944–2002.
Acronym: GED Tests.
Scores: Battery of 5 tests: Language Arts an Writing, Language Arts and Reading, Social Studie Science, Mathematics.
Administration: Group or individual.
Forms: 11 U.S. English Operational (secure) full-leng forms available; 7 U.S. English forms available of Offici GED Practice test (8 half-length, 1 full-length).
Price Data, 2010: Operational (secure) forms n available for purchase and are available only to an administered at Official GED Testing Centers; Offici GED Practice Tests half-length (available from Stec Vaughn Co., (800) 531-5015): $37.50 per 10 test ba teries; $15.98 per set of 50 universal machine-scorab answer sheets; $12.98 per set of 10 self-scoring answ sheets (for use with half-length practice test U.S. Englis Form CC only); full-length U.S. English practice tes $36 per set of 5; $14.91 per set of 25 correspondir answer sheets; $24.20 per administrator's set includir teacher's manual (1989, 203 pages), scoring materials, ar conversion tables, available in U.S. English half-lengt U.S. English full-length, Spanish, or French; $40.5 per 10 Spanish-language edition batteries (or $.88 f one test and one universal answer sheet); $15.98 p

50 Spanish-language universal answer sheets; $40.50 per 10 French-language edition batteries (or $4.88 for one test and one universal answer sheet); $15.98 per 50 French-language universal answer sheets; $13.80 per 1 Large Print practice test (U.S. English only) and universal answer sheet; $47.87 per 1 audiocassette practice test (U.S. English only) with large print reference copy. Canadian English practice test batteries (2 forms) available from Gage Publishing Ltd., (416) 293-8141: C27.50 per 10 batteries (avalable singly at C$4.98 each); C$13.68 per 50 Canadian English universal answer sheets; C$25.99 per Canadian English administrator's set. U.S. English (4 forms) and Canadian English (2 forms) computer-delivered practice tests available on CD-ROM through NTC/Contemporary Publishing, (800) 621-1918; outside the U.S., Canada, and their territories through Sylvan Learning Systems (800) 627-4276.

Foreign Language and Special Editions: Operational (secure) full-length GED batteries: Canadian English-language (6 forms), Spanish-language (3 forms), French-language (2 forms), and U.S. English large print (3 forms), audiocassettte (2 forms), and Braille (2 forms) available. Computer-delivered U.S. English-language tests available only outside U.S., Canada, and their territories. Official GED Practice Tests: Canadian English, Spanish, French, U.S. English large print, and audiocassette.

Time: 120 minutes for Language Arts, Writing; 70 minutes for Social Studies; 80 minutes for Science; 65 minutes for Language Arts, Reading; 90 minutes for Mathematics [all times are for Operational (secure forms) of the tests and do not include time required to give and clarify verbal test-taking instructions].

Comments: Tests administered throughout the year at official GED centers; tests originated in 1942 for granting high school/college credit for veterans, in mid-1950s GED program extended to all non-high school graduates; extensive 1988 revisions include addition of essay component to Writing Skills test and increased emphasis on higher order cognitive skills (e.g., application, analysis/evaluation, and math problem solving) throughout the battery; last test series was released in January 2002.

Author: General Educational Development Testing Service of the American Council on Education.

Publisher: General Educational Development Testing Service of the American Council on Education.

Cross References: See T4:2816 (2 references); for reviews by Bruce G. Rogers and Michael S. Trevisan, see 11:447 (2 references); for reviews by J. Stanley Ahmann and A. Harry Passow, see 9:1284 (1 reference); see also T3:2485 (2 references), 8:35 (20 references), and 7:34 (21 references); for a review by Robert J. Solomon of earlier forms, see 5:29 (39 references); for a review by Gustav J. Froehlich, see 4:26 (27 references); for reviews by Herbert S. Conrad and Warren G. Findley, see 3:20 (11 references). For reviews by Charlotte W. Croon of an earlier form of the expression subtest, see 3:122; for

reviews by W. E. Hall and C. Robert Pace of an earlier form of the social studies reading subtest, see 3:528.

[2790]
Tests of Reading Comprehension, Second Edition.

Purpose: "They aim at assessing the extent to which readers are able to obtain meaning from text."

Population: Grades 3–7, 6–10, and individuals with special needs.

Publication Dates: 1987–2003.

Acronym: TORCH.

Scores, 14: Grasshoppers, The Bear Who Liked Hugging People, Lizards Love Eggs, Getting Better, Feeding Puff, Shocking Things/Earthquakes!, The Swamp-creature, The Cats, A Horse of Her Own, Iceberg Towing, The Accident, The Killer Smog of London, I Want to be Andy, The Red Ace of Spades.

Administration: Individual or group.

Price Data, 2006: A$109.95 per complete kit including reading booklet, one of each answer sheet, and manual; A$89.95 per manual; A$8.95 per test booklet; A$11 per pack of 10 answer sheets for each of 12 levels.

Time: (30) minutes, untimed.

Comments: "Content-referenced" and/or "norm-referenced."

Authors: Leila Mossenson, Peter Hill, and Geoffrey Masters.

Publisher: Australian Council for Educational Research Ltd. [Australia].

Cross References: See T5:2743 (3 references) and T4:2817 (1 reference); for reviews by Robert B. Cooter, Jr. and Diane J. Sawyer of the earlier edition, see 11:448.

[2791]
TestWell: Health Risk Appraisal.

Purpose: "Designed to provide an awareness of how current behaviors and physical health measurements impact health risks."

Population: Adults ages 18–60 with a minimum of 10th grade education.

Publication Date: 1992.

Scores, 5: Appraised Age, Achievable Age, Positive Lifestyle Behaviors, Top 10 Risks of Death, Suggestions for Improvement.

Administration: Group.

Manual: No manual.

Price Data: Available from publisher.

Time: (20) minutes.

Comments: Scoring by National Wellness Institute; individual and group reports available.

Author: National Wellness Institute, Inc.

Publisher: National Wellness Institute, Inc.

Cross References: For reviews by Barbara L. Lachar and Steven G. LoBello, see 13:346.

[2792]

TestWell: Wellness Inventory for Windows.

Purpose: Designed to promote awareness of wellness.
Population: Adults with a minimum of 10th grade education.
Publication Date: 1992.
Scores, 11: Physical Fitness and Nutrition, Social Awareness, Medical Self-Care, Spirituality and Values, Emotional Management, Intellectual Wellness, Environmental Wellness, Safety, Occupational Wellness, Sexuality and Emotional Awareness, Total.
Administration: Group.
Manual: No manual.
Price Data: Available from publisher.
Time: (20) minutes.
Comments: Requires IBM or compatible computer hardware.
Author: National Wellness Institute, Inc.
Publisher: National Wellness Institute, Inc.
Cross References: For reviews by William W. Deardorff and Theodore L. Hayes, see 13:347; see also T4:2821 (1 reference).

[2793]

TestWell: Wellness Inventory for Windows—College Version.

Purpose: "Designed to address lifestyle choices facing today's college students."
Population: College students.
Publication Date: 1993.
Scores, 11: Physical Fitness, Nutrition, Social Awareness, Self-Care and Safety, Emotional and Sexuality, Intellectual Wellness, Environmental Wellness, Emotional Management, Occupational Wellness, Spirituality and Values, Total.
Administration: Group.
Price Data: Available from publisher.
Time: (20) minutes.
Author: National Wellness Institute, Inc.
Publisher: National Wellness Institute, Inc.
Cross References: For reviews by David L. Bolton and Richard E. Harding, see 13:348.

[2794]

Texas Functional Living Scale.

Purpose: Intended to be a "performance-based measure of instrumental activities of daily living."
Population: "Individuals ages 16-90 diagnosed with a variety of clinical disorders or requiring an assessment of functional abilities."
Publication Dates: 2006-2009.
Acronym: TFLS.
Scores, 5: Time, Money and Calculation, Communication, Memory, Total.
Administration: Individual.

Price Data, 2009: $149 per complete kit including 25 record forms, 25 response forms, clear plastic bottle, 2 stimulus cards, 5 simulated phone books, and examiner's manual (2009, 104 pages); $15 per 2 stimulus cards; $15 per 5 simulated phone books; $70 per examiner's manual.
Time: (10-20) minutes.
Comments: Initial version also referred to as the Test of Everyday Functional Abilities (TEFA); paper-and-pencil format; examiner must provide the following materials: stopwatch, timer, calendar for the current year, small edible objects/candies to mimic pills, 2 pencils, zip-top bag(s) for money, telephone, 1 $5 bill, 2 $1 bills, 7 quarters, 5 dimes, 5 nickels, and 5 pennies.
Authors: C. Munro Cullum, Myron F. Weiner, and Kathleen C. Saine.
Publisher: Pearson.
Cross References: For reviews by Pam Lindsey-Glenn and Jennifer M. Strang, see 18:147.

[2795]

Thanatometer.

Purpose: Measures attitudes concerning death.
Population: Adults.
Publication Date: 1986.
Scores: Total score only.
Administration: Group or individual.
Manual: No manual.
Price Data, 2005: $2 per scale.
Time: [5-10] minutes.
Comments: Supplementary article available.
Author: Panos D. Bardis.
Publisher: Donna Bardis.

[2796]

Thematic Apperception Test.

Purpose: "A method of revealing to the trained interpreter some of the dominant drives, emotions, sentiments complexes and conflicts of a personality."
Population: Ages 4 and over.
Publication Dates: 1935–1943.
Acronym: TAT.
Scores: Total score only.
Administration: Individual.
Price Data: Available from publisher.
Time: 100(200) minutes in 2 sessions 1 day apart.
Author: Henry A. Murray.
Publisher: Harvard University Press.
Cross References: See T5:2749 (87 references), T4:2824 (107 references), 9:1287 (51 references), and T3:2491 (105 references); for a review by Jon D. Swartz, see 8:697 (241 references); see also T2:1519 (231 references); for a review by Richard H. Dana and Leonard D. Eron, see 7:181 (297 references); see also P:484 (33 references); for a review by C. J. Adcock, see 6:245 (28 references); for reviews by Leonard D. Eron and Arthur R. Jensen, see 5:164 (311 references); for a review b

Arthur L. Benton, see 4:136 (198 references); for reviews by Arthur L. Benton, Julian Rotter, and J. R. Wittenborn and an excerpted review, see 3:103 (102 references).

[2797]

Theological School Inventory.

Purpose: Assesses motivation for entering the ministry.
Population: Incoming seminary students.
Publication Dates: 1962–1972.
Acronym: TSI.
Scores, 12: Definiteness, Natural Leading, Special Leading, Concept of the Call, Flexibility, Acceptance by Others, Intellectual Concern, Self-Fulfillment, Leadership Success, Evangelistic Witness, Social Reform, Service to Persons.
Administration: Group.
Price Data: Available from publisher.
Time: Administration time not reported.
Authors: James E. Dittes, Frederick Kling, Ellery Pierson, and Harry DeWire.
Publisher: Ministry Inventories.
Cross References: See T2:1028 (7 references) and P:273 (5 references).

[2798]

Therapy Attitude Inventory.

Purpose: Provides ratings of parental satisfaction with parent training interventions for child behavior problems.
Population: Parents.
Publication Date: 1974.
Scores: Total score only.
Administration: Individual.
Price Data, 1994: No charge for first copy; may photocopy for research or clinical use.
Time: (5) minutes.
Author: Sheila M. Eyberg.
Publisher: Sheila M. Eyberg (the author).
Cross References: See T5:2752 (2 references) and T4:2827 (1 reference); for a review by Terry B. Gutkin, see 9:1289 (2 references); see also T3:2494 (1 reference).

[2799]

Thinking Creatively in Action and Movement.

Purpose: Designed to sample creative thinking abilities of preschool children with limited verbal and drawing skills.
Population: Ages 3–6.
Publication Date: 1981.
Acronym: TCAM.
Scores, 3: Fluency, Originality, Imagination.
Administration: Individual.
Price Data: See www.ststesting.com for up-to-date pricing information.
Time: (10–30) minutes.
Author: E. Paul Torrance.

Publisher: Scholastic Testing Service, Inc.
Cross References: See T5:2754 (5 references) and T4:2829 (2 references); for reviews by Joseph S. Renzulli and James O. Rust, see 9:1290.

[2800]

Thinking Creatively With Sounds and Words.

Purpose: Developed to assess creative thinking through response to sound and words.
Population: Grades 3–12, adults.
Publication Dates: 1973-1990.
Acronym: TCSW.
Scores, 2: Sounds and Images, Onomatopoeia and Images.
Administration: Group.
Levels, 2: I (Grades 3-12), II (adult).
Forms, 2: A, B.
Price Data: See www.ststesting.com for up-to-date prices.
Time: (30–35) minutes for each test.
Authors: E. Paul Torrance, Joe Khatena, and Bert F. Cunnington (except technical manual).
Publisher: Scholastic Testing Service, Inc.
Cross References: See T5:2755 (2 references) and T4:2830 (5 references); for a review by Lynn H. Fox, see 9:1291 (3 references); see also T3:2496 (5 references); for reviews by Philip M. Clark and Mary Lee Smith, see 8:248 (6 references); see also T2:587 (17 references).

[2801]

Thomas-Kilmann Conflict Mode Instrument.

Purpose: Designed to assess "an individual's behavior in conflict situations."
Population: Managers.
Publication Date: 1974.
Acronym: TKI.
Scores: 5: Competing, Collaborating, Compromising, Avoiding, Accommodating.
Administration: Group or individual.
Price Data, 2011: $14.95 each for Thomas-Kilmann Conflict Mode Instrument Profile and Interpretive Report online administration; $14.95 per Thomas-Kilmann Conflict Mode Instrument self-scorable; $112.50 per 10 for Introduction to Conflict Management; $112.50 per 10 for Introduction to Conflict and Teams; $175 per Conflict Workshop Facilitator's Guide.
Time: [15] minutes.
Comments: Self-administered, self-scored, online at skillsone.com.
Authors: Kenneth W. Thomas and Ralph H. Kilmann.
Publisher: CPP, Inc.
Cross References: See T5:2756 (2 references); for reviews by Richard E. Harding and Ronn Johnson, see 10:377 (4 references).

[2802]

3-Minute Reading Assessments.
Purpose: Designed to "assess reading performance throughout the year" and "identify students who need help."
Publication Date: 2005.
Scores, 4: Word Recognition Accuracy, Reading Fluency-Automaticity, Reading Fluency-Expression, Comprehension.
Administration: Individual.
Time: (3-5) minutes.
Comments: The authors suggest students be assessed at regular intervals throughout the year in order to track progress over time (the four equivalent forms for each grade are provided for this purpose).
Authors: Timothy V. Rasinski and Nancy Padak.
Publisher: Scholastic Inc.

a) 3-MINUTE READING ASSESSMENTS GRADES 1-4.
Population: Grades 1-4.
Levels, 4: Grade 1, Grade 2, Grade 3, Grade 4.
Forms, 4: Form A, Form B, Form C, Form D.
Parts, 2: Student, Teacher.
Price Data, 2010: $14.99 per complete set Grades 1-4.

b) 3-MINUTE READING ASSESSMENTS GRADES 5-8.
Population: Grades 5-8.
Levels, 4: Grade 5, Grade 6, Grade 7, Grade 8.
Forms, 4: Form A, Form B, Form C, Form D.
Parts, 2: Student, Teacher.
Price Data: $14.99 per complete set Grades 5-8.

[2803]

Thurstone Temperament Schedule.
Purpose: Measures personality traits related to job performance.
Population: Variety of occupations from entry-level to management.
Publication Dates: 1949–1991.
Acronym: TTS.
Scores, 6: Active, Impulsive, Dominant, Stable, Sociable, Reflective.
Administration: Individual or group.
Price Data, 2002: $75 per start-up kit including 25 test booklets and examiner's manual; $56 per 25 test booklets (quantity discount available); $28 per examiner's manual.
Time: No limit (approximately 15–20 minutes).
Comments: Administered via paper and pencil; hand-scored carbon format.
Author: L. L. Thurstone.
Publisher: Pearson Performance Solutions [No reply from publisher; status unknown].
Cross References: See T5:2757 (1 reference), T4:2833 (6 references), T3:2499 (2 references), T2:1423 (32 references), P:277 (20 references), and 6:192 (17 references); for a review by Neil J. Van Steenberg, see 5:118 (12 references); for reviews by Hans J. Eysenck, Charles M. Harsh, and David G. Ryans, and an excerpted review by Laurance F. Shaffer, see 4:93.

[2804]

Thurstone Test of Mental Alertness.
Purpose: Measures general mental ability to learn and comprehend.
Population: Wide variety of occupations.
Publication Dates: 1943–1998.
Acronym: TMA.
Scores, 3: Quantitative, Linguistic, Total.
Administration: Individual or group.
Forms, 2: A, B.
Price Data, 2002: $86 per start-up kit including 25 test booklets and examiner's manual (specify Form A or Form B); $68 per 25 test booklets (quantity discounts available; specify Form A or Form B); $28 per examiner's manual; price data available from publisher for Quanta computer administration and scoring software (Windows); $86 per Quanta start-up kit including examiner's manual, 25 administrations and scoring (does not include Quanta software).
Time: 20 minutes.
Authors: Thelma Gwinn Thurstone and L. L. Thurstone.
Publisher: Pearson Performance Solutions [No reply from publisher; status unknown].
Cross References: See T5:2758 (1 reference) and T2:469 (5 references); for a review by Robert D. North, see 7:392 (4 references); for a review by Joshua A. Fishman, see 5:391; see also 4:326 (3 references); for reviews by Anne Anastasi and Emily T. Burr of an earlier edition, see 3:265.

[2805]

Tiffany Control Scales.
Purpose: Designed to evaluate personality problems related to one's experience of control across different situations.
Population: Ages 12–60+.
Publication Dates: 1985–2007.
Acronym: TCS.
Scores, 16: Control from Self/Internal, Control over Self, Control over the Environment, Control from the Environment, Coping Index, Passive/Assertive/Aggressive Index, Extratensive/Intratensive Index, Repression, Expressive, Self-Directed, Non-Self-Directed, and 5 other measures.
Administration: Individual or group.
Editions, 2: Paper and pencil, computer administered.
Price Data, 2001: $12.50 per 25 paper and pencil tests; $495.95 per computer edition, unlimited use; $50 per limited use edition (5 uses); demo and sample report are free; $25 per test for mail-in scoring; $19.95 per manual (1999, 83 pages).
Foreign Language Edition: Spanish version available.
Time: (10-20) minutes.

Comments: For research or clinical use or in employment screening; may be customized to fit examiner's needs; self-rating instrument; scoring and interpretation by computer.
Authors: Donald W. Tiffany and Phyllis G. Tiffany.
Publisher: Psychological Growth Associates, Inc.
Cross References: For a review by Brian F. Bolton, see 14:397.

[2806]

The Time of Your Life.

Purpose: Constructed as a self-assessment tool to provide "insight" into time management.
Population: Employees.
Publication Date: 1988.
Scores: Total score only.
Administration: Group or individual.
Price Data: Price available from publisher for complete kit including 20 inventories and 20 scoring and interpretation sheets.
Time: [30] minutes.
Comments: Self-administered, self-scored.
Author: Training House, Inc.
Publisher: Training House, Inc.
Cross References: For reviews by Ralph F. Darr, Jr. and Richard W. Faunce, see 12:400.

[2807]

Timed Typings for Holidays.

Purpose: To measure typing skill growth, develop fluency, and help reach for new speed goals.
Population: Students in typing classes.
Publication Date: 1988.
Scores: Total score only.
Administration: Group.
Manual: No manual.
Price Data: Price information available from publisher for blackline masters.
Time: (1–5) minutes per writing.
Authors: Berkley H. Rudd and Carol R. Scott.
Publisher: Walch Education.

[2808]

TMJ Scale.

Purpose: "Designed to measure the [clinical significance of] symptom patterns of dental patients with temporo-mandibular joint disorders and orofacial pain."
Population: Dental and medical patients ages 13 and over.
Publication Dates: 1984–1987.
Scores: 10: Physical Domain (Pain Report, Palpation Pain, Perceived Malocclusion, Joint Dysfunction, Range of Motion Limitation, Non-TM Disorder), Psychosocial Domain (Psychological Factors, Stress, Chronicity), Global Scale.
Administration: Individual or group.

Price Data, 2011: $21 per online test scoring. Volume discounts.
Time: (10–15) minutes.
Comments: Self-administered by paper-and-pencil or online on a secure testing website; Scoring and report generation online on a secure testing website.
Authors: Stephen R. Levitt, Tom F. Lundeen, and Michael W. McKinney.
Publisher: Pain Resource Center, Inc.
Cross References: For a review by William W. Deardorff, see 12:402; see also T4:2842 (3 references).

[2809]

Toddler and Infant Motor Evaluation.

Purpose: Designed to be used for "diagnostic, comprehensive assessment of children who are suspected to have motor delays or deviations, the development of appropriate remediation programs, and treatment efficacy research."
Population: Ages 4 months to 3.5 years.
Publication Date: 1994.
Acronym: TIME.
Scores: 5 Primary Subtests: Mobility, Stability, Motor Organization, Social-Emotional, Functional Performance; 3 Clinical Subtests: Quality Rating, Component Analysis Rating, Atypical Positions.
Administration: Individual.
Price Data, 2002: $451 per complete kit including manual (324 pages), 10 record forms, timer, rattle, 2 balls, squeak toy, toy car, 3 containers, toy telephone, 2 shoelaces, 6 blocks, and nylon tote bag; $37.50 per 10 record forms; $137 per manual.
Time: (15–40) minutes.
Comments: Diagnostic assessment tool designed to be used by licensed/highly trained physical and occupational therapists, or appropriately trained adaptive physical educators, special education teachers, or others with expertise in the motor domain; administered utilizing a partnership between parent(s) or caretaker(s) and a trained examiner.
Authors: Lucy J. Miller and Gale H. Roid.
Publisher: Pearson.
Cross References: For reviews by Larry M. Bolen and William R. Merz, Sr., see 14:399.

[2810]

The Toglia Category Assessment.

Purpose: Designed "to examine the ability of adults with brain injury or psychiatric illness to establish categories and switch conceptual set."
Population: Adults 18 and over who have neurological impairment.
Publication Date: 1994.
Acronym: TCA.
Scores: Total score only.
Administration: Individual.

Price Data: Price data for "Dynamic Assessment of Categorization TCA: The Toglia Category Assessment" (1994, 43 pages), score sheets, and manipulatives available from publisher.
Time: (10–20) minutes.
Authors: Joan Toglia assisted by Naomi Josman.
Publisher: Maddak Inc.
Cross References: For reviews by Thomas McKnight and by Scott A. Napolitano and Courtney Miller, see 16:252.

[2811]

The Token Test for Children, Second Edition.

Purpose: Designed to identify "children who are significantly below their peers in early receptive language development."
Population: Children ages 3-0 to 12-11.
Publication Dates: 1978-2007.
Scores: Total score only.
Administration: Individual.
Parts, 4: I, II, III, IV.
Price Data, 2011: $156 per complete kit including 50 examiner record forms, 20 tokens, and manual (2007, 69 pages); $53 per 50 examiner record forms; $34 per 20 tokens; $75 per manual.
Time: (10-15) minutes.
Authors: Ronnie L. McGhee, David J. Ehrler, and Frank DiSimoni.
Publisher: PRO-ED.
Cross References: For reviews by Christine Novak and Zarabeth Gerling and by Gene Schwarting, see 18:148; see T5:2768 (43 references) and T4:2846 (24 references); for reviews by William M. Reynolds and John Salvia of an earlier edition, see 9:1295 (9 references); see also T3:2509 (1 reference).

[2812]

Tooze Braille Speed Test: A Test of Basic Ability in Reading Braille.

Purpose: "A speed test which seeks to give a quick appraisal of the child's ability to read Braille characters."
Population: Students (Ages 7-13) in Grades 1 or 2 Braille.
Publication Date: 1962.
Scores: Total score only.
Administration: Individual.
Price Data: Available from publisher.
Time: 1(5) minutes.
Author: F. H. G. Tooze.
Publisher: Association for the Education and Welfare of the Visually Handicapped [England] [No reply from publisher; status unknown].

[2813]

Torrance Tests of Creative Thinking.

Purpose: To identify and evaluate creative potential through words (verbal forms) and pictures (figural forms).

Population: Grades K through adult.
Publication Dates: 1966–2006.
Acronym: TTCT.
Administration: Individual and group.
Price Data: See www.ststesting.com for up-to-date pricing information.
Foreign Language Editions: Spanish edition available.
Author: E. Paul Torrance.
Publisher: Scholastic Testing Service, Inc.
  a) VERBAL TEST.
  Scores: 3 for equivalent Forms A and B: Fluency, Flexibility, Originality.
  Administration: Individual for Grades K to 3.
  Time: 45(60) minutes.
  Comments: Test booklet is titled Thinking Creatively With Words.
  b) FIGURAL TEST.
  Scores: 4 for equivalent Forms A and B: Fluency, Flexibility, Originality, Elaboration.
  Time: 30(45) minutes.
  Comments: Test booklet is titled Thinking Creatively with Pictures.
Cross References: See T5:2771 (45 references) and T4:2849 (33 references); for reviews by Clinton I. Chase and Donald J. Treffinger, see 9:1296 (20 references); see also T3:2512 (107 references), 8:249 (229 references), and T2:589 (88 references); for reviews by Leonard L. Baird and Robert L. Thorndike, and excerpted reviews by Ralph Hoepfner, John L. Holland, and Michael A. Wallach, see 7:448 (243 references).

[2814]

Tower of London–Drexel University: 2nd Edition.

Purpose: A neuropsychological instrument "designed to assess higher-order problem solving–specifically, executive planning abilities–in children and adults."
Population: Ages 7 and above.
Publication Dates: 1999–2005.
Acronym: TOLDX 2nd Ed.
Scores, 8: Total Move Score, Total Correct Score, Total Time Violation, Total Rules Violation, Total Initiation Time, Total Execution Time, Total Problem-Solving Time, Total Stimulus-Bound.
Administration: Individual.
Forms, 2: Adult, Child.
Price Data, 2011: $339 per complete kit including technical manual (2005, 94 pages), 2 peg boards with beads, 25 child record forms, and 25 adult record forms; $296 per complete adult kit including technical manual, 2 peg boards with beads, and 25 adult record forms; $296 per complete child kit including technical manual, 2 peg boards with beads, and 25 child record forms; $105 per technical manual; $50 per 25 child or adult record forms.
Time: (10–15) minutes.
Comments: Administered individually by clinicians; special instructions for mentally challenged populations.

Authors: William C. Culbertson and Eric A. Zilmer.
Publisher: Multi-Health Systems, Inc.
  a) CHILD.
  Population: Ages 7–15.
  b) ADULT.
  Population: Ages 16 and older.
Cross References: For reviews by Brad M. Merker and John Linck and by Gregory Schraw, see 17:188; for reviews by Carolyn M. Callahan and James P. Van Haneghan of the previous edition, see 15:267.

[2815]

TPRI.

Purpose: Designed to "measure students' progress in the acquisition of important skills related to early reading."
Population: K-3.
Publication Date: 2010.
Acronym: TPRI.
Scores, 5: Phonemic Awareness, Graphophonemic Knowledge, Word Reading, Listening Comprehension, Reading Accuracy/ Fluency/ and Comprehension.
Administration: Group.
Levels, 2: Progress Monitoring for Beginning Readers, Progress Monitoring for Emergent Readers.
Price Data, 2010: $69.95 per Progress Monitoring for Emergent Readers kit including PMER Teacher's Guide and Task Card Booklet; $69.95 per Progress Monitoring for Beginning Readers kit including PMBR Teacher's Guide and Story Comprehension Booklet; $29.95 per 15 PMER Student Record Sheets; $29.95 per 15 PMER Student Record Sheets.
Time: Administration time not reported.
Comments: The assessment has an administration schedule that can assess progress at the beginning of the year, middle of the year, and end of the year.
Author: Texas Education Agency.
Publisher: Paul H. Brookes Publishing Co., Inc.

[2816]

Trade Aptitude Test Battery.

Purpose: "To select prospective pupils for admission to technical institutes and colleges."
Population: First-year South African students in the technical fields.
Publication Dates: 1981–1983.
Acronym: TRAT.
Scores, 16: Dexterity, Co-ordination, Patterns, Components, Classification, Assembly, Computations, Inspection, Graphs, Mechanical Insight, Mathematics, Spatial Perception/2-D, Vocabulary, Figure Series, Woordeskat, Spatial Perception/3-D.
Administration: Group.
Price Data: Available from publisher.
Time: 288(293) minutes.
Comments: Test materials in both English and Afrikaans.
Authors: J. J. Taljaard and J. W. von Mollendorf (test).
Publisher: Human Sciences Research Council [South Africa].

[2817]

Trainer's Assessment of Proficiency (TAP).

Purpose: Constructed as a "self-assessment exercise that measures relative strengths in twelve instructional skills."
Population: Trainers.
Publication Date: 1991.
Acronym: TAP.
Scores, 12: Assessing Needs and Entering Behavior, Setting Objectives and Terminal Behavior, Analyzing Participants and Situations, Eliciting Relevant Responses and Testing, Applying Classroom Facilitation Skills, Forming Questions and Probes Effectively, Maintaining Adult Relationships, Giving Feedback and Reinforcement, Building Toward Transfer of Training, Getting All Learners to Participate, Managing Classroom Time Effectively, Displaying Good Flow/Logic/Organization.
Administration: Group.
Forms, 2: Long, Short.
Price Data: Available from publisher.
Time: (60) minutes for Short form; (180) minutes for Long form.
Comments: Videocassette recorder necessary for administration of inventory.
Author: Scott B. Parry.
Publisher: Training House, Inc.
Cross References: For reviews by Mark W. Roberts and Daniel E. Vogler, see 12:403.

[2818]

Trait Evaluation Index.

Purpose: "Designed to elicit comprehensive, multi-dimensional appraisals of 'normal' personality dimensions."
Population: College and adults.
Publication Dates: 1967-1984.
Acronym: TEI.
Scores: 29 scores (Social Orientation, Compliance, Benevolence, Elation, Ambition, Motivational Drive, Self-Confidence, Dynamism, Independence, Personal Adequacy, Caution, Self-Organization, Responsibility, Propriety, Courtesy, Verbal Orientation, Intellectual Orientation, Perception, Self-Control, Fairmindedness, Adaptability, Sincerity) plus 4 general supplementary scores (Overall Adjustment, Masculinity, Femininity, Consistency) and 3 supplementary scores for engineers (Employment Stability, Productivity-Creativity, Job Satisfaction).
Administration: Group.
Price Data, 2006: $94.20 per test package; $83.40 per IBM answer/profile sheet package; $46 per set of IBM scoring stencils; $56.40 per manual (1968, 38 pages) and manual supplement (1984, 17 pages); $75.50 per specimen set; $137.45 per German edition test package.
Foreign Language Edition: German edition available.
Time: (30-50) minutes.
Author: Alan R. Nelson.

Publisher: Martin M. Bruce, Ph.D.
Cross References: See T2:1424 (1 reference); for reviews by Harold Borko and Jacob Cohen, see 7:155 (1 reference).

[2819]

The Trait Pleasure-Displeasure Scale.

Purpose: One of three fundamental dimensions of temperament in Mehrabian's Temperament Model; provides a general assessment of psychological adjustment-maladjustment.
Population: Ages 15 and older.
Publication Dates: 1978–1994.
Scores: Total score only.
Administration: Group or individual.
Price Data: Available from publisher for complete kit including scale, scoring directions, norms, manual (1994, 10 pages), and literature review.
Time: (10–15) minutes.
Author: Albert Mehrabian.
Publisher: Albert Mehrabian (the author).
Cross References: For reviews by Thaddeus Rozecki and Chockalingam Viswesvaran, see 13:351 (1 reference).

[2820]

Transdisciplinary Play-Based Assessment, 2nd Edition.

Purpose: Designed as a multidimensional approach to identifying service needs, developing intervention plans, and evaluating progress in children.
Population: Birth to age 6.
Publication Dates: 1993-2008.
Acronym: TPBA2.
Scores: 4 domains: Sensorimotor, Emotional and Social, Communication, Cognitive Development.
Administration: Individual.
Price Data, 2009: $329.95 per 3-volume set with forms CD including Administration Guide for TPBA2 & TPBI2 (2008, 408 pages), Transdisciplinary Play-Based Intervention, 2nd Edition, Transdisciplinary Play-Based Assessment, 2nd Edition, and forms CD; $149.95 per 3-volume set including Administration Guide for TPBA2 & TPBI2, Transdisciplinary Play-Based Intervention, 2nd Edition, and Transdisciplinary Play-Based Assessment, 2nd Edition; $54.95 per Transdisciplinary Play-Based Assessment, 2nd Edition; $59.95 per Transdisciplinary Play-Based Intervention, 2nd Edition; $54.95 per Administration Guide for TPBA2 & TPBI2; $39.95 per 5 tablets of forms; $229.95 per forms CD.
Time: (60-90) minutes.
Comments: Ratings by transdisciplinary team; no domain scores; compares observations to Age Tables that outline appropriate skills for each age.
Author: Toni Linder.
Publisher: Paul H. Brookes Publishing Co., Inc.

Cross References: For reviews by David R. Holliway and Becky L. Spritz, see 18:149; for reviews by Terry Overton and Gary J. Stainback of the previous edition, see 13:352.

[2821]

Transition Behavior Scale–Second Edition.

Purpose: "Developed to be an educational-relevant measure of predicted success in employment and independent living based upon school personnel's observation of a student's behavior or skills."
Population: Ages 12–18.
Publication Dates: 1989–2000.
Acronym: TBS-2.
Scores, 3: Work-Related, Interpersonal Relations, Social/Community Expectations.
Administration: Group or individual.
Price Data, 2006: $125 per complete kit including 50 school version rating forms, 50 self-report rating forms, school version technical manual (2000, 41 pages), self-report technical manual (2000, 36 pages), and IEP and intervention manual (2000, 188 pages); $35 per 50 school version rating forms; $35 per 50 self-report rating forms; $15 per school version technical manual; $15 per self-report technical manual; $25 per IEP and intervention manual.
Time: (15–20) minutes.
Authors: Stephen B. McCarney and Paul D. Anderson.
Publisher: Hawthorne Educational Services, Inc.
Cross References: For reviews by Susan K. Green and Michael S. Trevisan, see 16:253; for reviews by Martha Blackwell and David O. Herman of the original edition, see 12:404.

[2822]

Transition Competence Battery for Deaf and Hard of Hearing Adolescents and Young Adults.

Purpose: To measure work and social skills necessary to successfully work and live in the community for persons who are deaf and hard of hearing to successfully work and live in the community.
Population: Deaf and hard of hearing adolescents and young adults.
Publication Date: 1993.
Acronym: TCB.
Scores, 6: Job-Seeking Skills, Work Adjustment Skills, Job-Related Social and Interpersonal Skills, Money Management Skills, Health and Home Skills, Community Awareness Skills.
Administration: Group.
Price Data: Price data for complete set available from publisher.
Time: (180) minutes.
Comments: In addition to the written form, a video form is also available in which the test is presented in sign language.

Authors: John Reiman, Michael Bullis, and Cheryl Davis.
Publisher: James Stanfield Co., Inc.
Cross References: For a review by Connie T. England, see 15:268.

[2823]

Transition Planning Inventory (Updated Version).

Purpose: Designed to help identify "preferences and interests and areas of transition strength and needs."
Population: Students with disabilities who desire to plan for the future.
Publication Date: 1997-2006.
Acronym: TPI-UV.
Scores: Ratings in 9 areas: Employment, Further Education, Daily Living, Leisure Activities, Community Participation, Health, Self-Determination, Communication, Interpersonal Relationships.
Administration: Group or individual.
Forms, 5: Student, Home, School, Profile and Further Recommendations, Modified Form for Students with Significant Disabilities.
Versions, 2: Paper and pencil, Computer.
Price Data, 2011: $200 per complete kit including Administration and Resource Guide (2006, 184 pages), 25 Profile and Further Assessment Recommendation forms, 25 School forms, 25 Home forms, 25 Student forms, Informal Assessments for Transition Planning resource, and Case Studies in Transition Planning book; $28 per Administration and Resource Guide; $29 per 25 Profile and Further Assessment Recommendation forms; $29 per 25 School forms; $29 per 25 Home forms; $29 per 25 Student forms; $34 per Case Studies in Assessment for Transition Planning; $40 per Informal Assessments in Transition Planning.
Foreign Language Editions: Home forms available in Spanish, Chinese, Japanese, and Korean.
Time: (15-30) minutes per form.
Comments: The Home and Student forms can be administered independently, individually (assisted), in small groups, or orally; Student, Home, School, and Profile and Further Recommendations forms should all be used when working with students without significant disabilities.
Authors: Gary M. Clark and James R. Patton.
Publisher: PRO-ED.
Cross References: For reviews by Pam Lindsey and Julia Y. Porter, see 17:189; for reviews by Robert K. Gable and by Rosemary E. Sutton and Theresa A. Quigney of an earlier form, see 14:400.

[2824]

Transition-to-Work Inventory.

Purpose: Designed to "measure a person's leisure interests in order to help him or her turn these interests into possible employment opportunities in a full- or part-time job, small business enterprise, or home-based business."
Population: Job seekers.
Publication Date: 2004.
Acronym: TWI.
Scores, 14: Arts/Entertainment/Media, Science/Math/Engineering, Plants/Animals, Law/Law Enforcement/Public Safety, Mechanics/Installers/Repairers, Construction/Mining/Drilling, Transportation, Industrial Production, Business Detail, Sales/Marketing, Recreation/Travel/Other Personal Services, Education/Social Sciences, General Management/Support, Medical/Health Services.
Administration: Individual or group.
Price Data, 2006: $34.95 per complete kit including 25 test booklets and administrator's guide (4 pages).
Time: (20-30) minutes.
Comments: This test can be self-administered and self-scored.
Author: John Liptak.
Publisher: JIST Publishing, Inc.

[2825]

Transition-to-Work Inventory: A Job Placement System for Workers with Severe disAbilities.

Purpose: "Designed to assist employers, supported employment counselors, and other transition professionals in identifying the best match between the skills of an individual with disabilities and the requirements of the job."
Population: Individuals with severe disabilities.
Publication Dates: 1995–1996.
Acronym: TWI™.
Scores, 3: Job Analysis Rating, Worker Analysis Rating, Difference Score.
Administration: Individual.
Parts, 2: Job Analysis Scale, Worker Analysis Scale.
Price Data, 2006: $105 per starter kit including user and accommodation manual, 10 job analysis booklets, 25 worker analysis booklets, and 25 profile sheets; $23 per 10 worker analysis booklets; $41 per 25 job analysis booklets; $22 per individual profile sheets; $68 per manual and accommodation guide.
Time: (30–35) minutes per scale.
Comments: Ratings by transition professionals.
Authors: Lee Friedman, Carl Cameron, and Jennifer Fletcher.
Publisher: Pearson.
Cross References: For reviews by Chantale Jeanrie and Erich P. Prien, see 14:401.

[2826]

Trauma and Attachment Belief Scale.

Purpose: Measures beliefs related to five need areas that are sensitive to the effects of traumatic experiences.
Population: Ages 9–18, 17–78.
Publication Date: 2003.
Acronym: TABS.

Scores, 11: Self-Safety, Other-Safety, Self-Trust, Other-Trust, Self-Esteem, Other-Esteem, Self-Intimacy, Other-Intimacy, Self-Control, Other-Control, Total.
Administration: Group.
Forms, 2: Profile Sheet, Profile Sheet for Youth.
Price Data, 2011: $115 per kit including 25 Adult AutoScore™ test/profile forms, 25 Youth AutoScore™ test/profile forms, and manual (52 pages); $45 per 25 AutoScore™ test/profile forms (Adult); $45 per 25 AutoScore™ test/profile forms (Youth); $55 per manual.
Time: (10–15) minutes.
Comments: Previously known as Traumatic Stress Institute (TSI) Belief Scale.
Author: Laurie Anne Pearlman.
Publisher: Western Psychological Services.
Cross References: For reviews by Eugene V. Aidman and Adrienne Garro, see 16:254.

[2827]

Trauma Assessment Inventories.

Purpose: "Designed to screen for Posttraumatic Stress Disorder" and designed to assess "Cognitive and emotional aspects of guilt associated with a specific traumatic event."
Population: Ages 18 years and older.
Publication Date: 2004.
Administration: Individual.
Price Data, 2006: $192.50 per complete kit including Screening Kit and Treatment Kit; Computerized Components: $96 per 20-use CD for Computer Scoring Only; $40 per 25 AutoScore forms (specify screening or treatment); $16.50 per 100 computerized answer sheets (specify screening or treatment).
Author: Edward S. Kubany.
Publisher: Western Psychological Services.
  a) SCREENING KIT.
  Purpose: "Designed to screen for Posttraumatic Stress Disorder."
  Price Data: $109 per complete screening kit including 25 AutoScore forms, 25 test forms, and screening manual (47 pages); $44 per screening manual.
  Time: (10-20) minutes.
  Comments: This test can be abbreviated if time constraints are an issue.
    1) *Traumatic Life Events Questionnaire.*
    Acronym: TLEQ.
    Scores, 3: Count of Events, Count of Events Associated with Fear or Hopelessness, Occurrences.
    Price Data: $29 per 25 test forms.
    2) *PTSD Screening and Diagnostic Scale.*
    Acronym: PSDS.
    Scores, 7: Criterion A, Criterion B, Criterion C, Criterion D, PSDS Symptom Score, Criterion E, Criterion F.

  b) TREATMENT KIT.
  Purpose: Designed to assess "Cognitive and emotional aspects of guilt associated with a specific traumatic event."
  Price Data: $88 per complete treatment kit including 25 AutoScore forms, 25 test forms, and treatment manual (59 pages); $52 per treatment manual.
  Time: Administration time not reported.
    1) *The Trauma-Related Guilt Inventory.*
    Acronym: TRGI.
    Scores, 6: Global Guilt, Distress, Guilt Cognitions (Wrongdoing, Insufficient Justification, Hindsight-Bias/Responsibility).
    Comments: This test is written at a 5th-grade reading level.
Cross References: For reviews by James P. Donnelly and Kerry Donnelly and by Carl J. Sheperis and April K. Heiselt, see 17:190.

[2828]

Trauma Symptom Checklist for Children.

Purpose: Designed "to measure acute and chronic posttraumatic stress and related psychological symptomatology."
Population: Ages 8–16.
Publication Date: 1996.
Acronym: TSCC.
Scores: 8 scales: Underresponse, Hyperresponse, Anxiety, Depression, Anger, Posttraumatic Stress, Dissociation, Sexual Concerns.
Administration: Group or individual.
Price Data, 2006: $146 per introductory kit including professional manual, 25 test booklets, 25 male profile forms, and 25 female profile forms; $275 per software portfolio (CD-ROM) including unlimited scoring, reports, and profiles.
Time: (15–20) minutes.
Author: John Briere.
Publisher: Psychological Assessment Resources, Inc.
Cross References: For reviews by Gregory J. Boyle and Chockalingam Viswesvaran, see 15:269.

[2829]

Trauma Symptom Checklist for Young Children.

Purpose: Designed "to measure acute and chronic posttraumatic stress and related psychological symptomatology."
Population: Ages 3–12 years.
Publication Dates: 1999–2005.
Acronym: TSCYC.
Scores, 11: Validity scales (Response Level, Atypical Response), Clinical scales (Anxiety, Depression, Anger/Aggression, Posttraumatic Stress-Intrusion, Posttraumatic Stress-Avoidance, Posttraumatic Stress-Arousal, Posttraumatic Stress-Total, Dissociation, Sexual Concerns).
Administration: Group.
Price Data, 2007: $185 per introductory kit including professional manual (2005, 61 pages), 25 item booklets, 25 hand-scorable answer sheets, 25 profile forms (Male &

Female Ages 3–4 Years), 25 profile forms (Male & Female Ages 5–9 Years), and 25 profile forms (Male & Female Ages 10–12 Years; $285 per scoring program (CD-ROM) including unlimited scoring, reports, and profiles.
Time: (15–20) minutes.
Comments: Instrument is answered by the child's parents and/or caretakers.
Author: John Briere.
Publisher: Psychological Assessment Resources, Inc.
Cross References: For reviews by Karen Mackler and Terry A. Stinnett, see 17:191.

[2830]

Trauma Symptom Inventory.

Purpose: Designed for the "evaluation of acute and chronic posttraumatic symptomatology."
Population: Ages 18 and older.
Publication Date: 1995.
Acronym: TSI.
Scores, 13: Validity Scales (Response Level, Atypical Response, Inconsistent Response); Clinical Scales (Anxious Arousal, Depression, Anger/Irritability, Intrusive Experiences, Defensive Avoidance, Dissociation, Sexual Concerns, Dysfunctional Sexual Behavior, Impaired Self-Reference, Tension Reduction Behavior).
Administration: Group.
Price Data, 2006: $189 per introductory kit including manual (67 pages), 10 item booklets, 25 hand-scorable answer sheets, and 25 each of male and female profile forms; $275 per Scoring Program including unlimited scoring reports.
Time: (20) minutes.
Comments: Computer scoring system available from publisher.
Author: John Briere.
Publisher: Psychological Assessment Resources, Inc.
Cross References: For reviews by Ephrem Fernandez and Jack E. Gebart-Eaglemont, see 14:402; see also T5:2782 (3 references).

[2831]

Treatment Intervention Inventory.

Purpose: Designed for intake, referral and post-treatment comparisons of adult counseling clients.
Population: Ages 12–18; Adult counseling clients.
Publication Dates: 1991–1997.
Acronym: TII; TII-J.
Scores, 9: Truthfulness, Anxiety, Depression, Self-Esteem, Distress, Family, Alcohol, Drug, Stress Coping Abilities.
Administration: Group.
Levels, 2: Adult, Juvenile.
Price Data: Available from publisher.
Time: (35) minutes Adult; (25–30) minutes Juvenile.
Comments: "A computerized, self-report assessment"; administration by paper and pencil or by computer; computer scored.
Author: Behavior Data Systems Ltd.

Publisher: Behavior Data Systems Ltd.
Cross References: For reviews by Janice G. Murdoch and Linda J. Zimmerman, see 14:403.

[2832]

Triadal Equated Personality Inventory.

Purpose: To measure personality variables.
Population: Adult males.
Publication Dates: 1960–1963.
Acronym: TEPI.
Scores, 22: Dominance, Self-Confidence, Decisiveness, Independence, Toughness, Suspiciousness, Conscientiousness, Introversion, Restlessness, Solemnity, Foresight, Industriousness, Warmth, Enthusiasm, Conformity, Inventiveness, Persistence, Sex Drive, Recognition Drive, Cooperativeness, Humility-Tolerance, Self-Control.
Administration: Group.
Price Data: Available from publisher.
Time: (50–120) minutes.
Author: Research Staff, United Consultants.
Publisher: Psychometric Affiliates.
Cross References: For a review by Jacob Cohen, see 7:156.

[2833]

Triage Assessment for Addictive Disorders.

Purpose: "Designed to cover diagnostic information for current dependence or abuse of alcohol and drugs."
Population: Adults.
Publication Dates: 1995–2000.
Acronym: TAAD.
Scores, 2: Abuse, Dependence.
Administration: Individual.
Price Data: Available from publisher.
Time: (10) minutes.
Comments: Structured interview; screens for DSM-IV diagnostic criteria, providing an estimate of the likelihood that an individual meets the criteria for abuse or dependency; covers current problems only; can be administered by paraprofessionals; scores indicate number of positive symptoms and criteria for alcohol abuse and dependence specifically, and number of positive symptoms and criteria for drug abuse and dependence collectively.
Author: Norman G. Hoffmann.
Publisher: The Change Companies.
Cross References: For reviews by JoAnn Murphey and by Wendy Naumann and Robin Rix, see 15:270.

[2834]

Triage Assessment for Psychiatric Disorders.

Purpose: A semi-structured interview that assists clinicians in screening for frequently diagnosed psychiatric disorders.
Population: Adults.
Publication Dates: 1991-1999.
Acronym: TAPD.
Scores: Item scores only.

Administration: Individual.
Price Data, 2008: $52.50 per 25 interview forms; $15 per administration guide (1999, 5 pages).
Time: 15-20 minutes.
Author: Norman G. Hoffmann.
Publisher: The Change Companies.

[2835]

Tutor Evaluation and Self-Assessment Tool.

Purpose: "A structured profile that evaluates tutors' effectiveness … to improve growth and development."
Population: Tutors of all subjects and grade levels.
Publication Date: 1996.
Acronym: TESAT.
Scores, 12: Greeting, Identification of Task, Breaking the Task into Parts, Identification of Thought Process, Setting Agenda, Addressing the Task, Tutee Summary of Content, Tutee Summary of Underlying Process, Confirmation, What Next?, Arranging and Planning Next Session, Closing.
Administration: Group.
Price Data, 2001: $198 per 100 TESATs, quantity discount available; $64.95 (+$3.50 shipping) per Tutor Trainer's Manual (64 pages); $85 per transparency set, $23.95 per Master Tutor Guidebook (124 pages) (quantities up to 29); $16.95 per Master Tutor Guidebook (quantities of 30 or more); Orders of 100 or more Master Tutor Guidebooks include free Tutor Trainer's Manual, transparency set, and 100 tests.
Time: Untimed.
Comments: Administered in paper-and-pencil format only using carbonated compilation and scoring sheets; ranks tutors into one of four skill categories (outstanding, proficient, adequate, needs improvement) for each of 12 steps of the "Tutor Cycle," based on the author's tutoring model; can be completed by tutor for self-assessment or by other evaluator.
Author: Ross B. MacDonald.
Publisher: The Cambridge Stratford Study Skills Institute.

[2836]

Typing 5.

Purpose: Assesses typing skills.
Population: Administrative assistants, secretaries, and any position requiring typing ability.
Publication Date: 1975.
Scores, 2: Speed, Accuracy.
Administration: Individual or group.
Price Data, 1998: $70.50 per start-up kit (specify Form A, B, or C) including 25 test booklets, 25 practice sheets, and examiner's manual; $44 per 25 test booklets (specify Form A, B, or C; quantity discounts available); $14.75 per 25 practice sheets (quantity discounts available); $19.75 per examiner's manual.

Time: 5 minutes per test.
Comments: Previously listed as SRA Typing 5.
Author: Science Research Associates.
Publisher: Pearson Performance Solutions [No reply from publisher; status unknown].
  a) FORM A–TYPING SPEED.
  b) FORM B–BUSINESS LETTER.
  c) FORM C–NUMERICAL.
Cross References: For reviews by Charles J. Cranny and Lawrence W. Erickson, see 8:1035.

[2837]

The Uncritical Inference Test.

Purpose: "Helps students learn to distinguish between observations (or facts) and inferences, assumptions, beliefs, and judgments."
Population: Adolescents and adults.
Publication Dates: 1955–1982.
Scores: Total score only.
Administration: Group.
Manual: No manual.
Price Data, 2006: $1 per test (minimum order of 10 paper tests); electronic delivery via email attachment or download in PDF format (from www.time-binding. org/store.htm) includes license for multiple usages at $.75 per use.
Time: Administration time not reported.
Author: William V. Haney.
Publisher: Institute of General Semantics.

[2838]

Understanding and Managing Stress.

Purpose: Assesses stress level and health-related behaviors.
Population: Adults.
Publication Date: 1989.
Scores: Continuum of risk scores (low, medium, high) for each of 22 areas: Changes on the Job/Total, Changes on the Job/High-Impact, Changes in Personal Life/Total, Changes in Personal Life/High-Impact, Chronic Stressful Conditions on the Job, Chronic Stressful Conditions in Personal Life, Strain Response, Psychological Outlook, General Lifestyle/Importance to Health, General Lifestyle/Present Effectiveness, Social Support, Nutritional Habits and Awareness/Total, Physical Exercise Habits and Awareness, Drinking Habits, Behavioral Habits, Tobacco, Systolic Blood Pressure Reading, Diastolic Blood Pressure Reading, Total Cholesterol, High-Density Lipoprotein (HDL) Level, Ratio of Total Cholesterol to HDL, Triglyceride Level.
Administration: Group.
Price Data: Price information available from publisher for handbook (64 pages).
Time: Administration time not reported.
Comments: Self-administered, self-scored.
Author: John D. Adams.

Publisher: Jossey-Bass, A Wiley Company.
Cross References: For reviews by William J. Waldron and by William K. Wilkinson and Christopher P. Migotsky, see 12:405.

[2839]

Understanding Communication.

Purpose: Developed "to measure comprehension of verbal material in the form of short sentences and phrases."
Population: Variety of occupations.
Publication Dates: 1959–1992.
Scores: Total score only.
Administration: Individual or group.
Price Data, 2002: $91 per start-up kit including 25 test booklets, score key, and interpretation and research manual; $54 per 25 test booklets (quantity discounts available); $20 per score key; $28 per interpretation and research manual.
Time: 15 minutes.
Author: Thelma Gwinn Thurstone.
Publisher: Pearson Performance Solutions [No reply from publisher; status unknown].
Cross References: See T4:2864 (1 reference) and T2:1747 (1 reference); for reviews by C. E. Jurgensen and Donald E. P. Smith, see 6:840.

[2840]

Uniform Child Custody Evaluation System.

Purpose: Constructed as a "uniform child custody evaluation procedure."
Population: Professionals involved in custody evaluation.
Publication Date: 1994.
Acronym: UCCES.
Scores: No scores.
Administration: Individual.
Forms, 25: General Data and Administrative Forms (UCCES Checklist, Initial Referral Form, Chronological Record of all Case Contacts Form, Case Notes Form, Consent for Psychological Services to Child(ren) Form, Authorization to Release Information Form, Suitability for Joint Custody Checklist, Collateral Interview Form, Consent for Evaluation of Minor(s) Form, UCCES Summary Chart), Parent Forms (Parent's Family/Personal History Questionnaire, Parent Interview Form, Parenting Abilities Checklist, Suitability for Joint Custody Interview, Analysis of Response Validity Checklist, Behavioral Observations of Parent-Child Interaction Form, Home Visit Observation Form, Agreement Between Parent and Evaluator Form, Explanation of Custody Evaluation Procedures for Parents and Attorneys), Child Forms (Child History Questionnaire, Child Interview Form, Child Abuse Interview Form, Abuse/Neglect Checklist, Child's Adjustment to Home and Community Checklist, Parent-Child Goodness of Fit Observation Form and Checklist).
Price Data, 2006: $180 per introductory kit including manual (47 pages), 2 sets of Parent Forms, 2 sets of Child Forms, and 1 set of Administrative and Data Forms.

Time: Administration time varies.
Authors: Harry L. Munsinger and Kevin W. Karlson.
Publisher: Psychological Assessment Resources, Inc.
Cross References: For a review by Steven Zucker, see 13:353.

[2841]

Universal Nonverbal Intelligence Test™.

Purpose: "Designed to provide a ... fair measure of the general intelligence and cognitive abilities of children and adolescents ... who may be disadvantaged by traditional verbal and language-loaded measures."
Population: Ages 5 years through 17 years, 11 months.
Publication Dates: 1998-2005.
Acronym: UNIT™.
Scores, 11: Symbolic Memory, Cube Design, Spatial Memory, Analogic Reasoning, Object Memory, Mazes, Memory Quotient, Reasoning Quotient, Symbolic Quotient, Nonsymbolic Quotient, Full Scale IQ.
Administration: Individual.
Forms: Abbreviated Battery, Standard Battery, Extended Battery.
Price Data, 2011: $748 per complete test kit including examiner's manual, 2 stimulus books, 16 response chips, response grid, 9 cubes, response mat, 10 symbolic memory cards, 25 record forms, 25 mazes response booklets, black pencil, red pencil, and Administration at a Glance all in a canvas carrying case; $106 per examiner's manual; $63 per 25 record forms; $70 per mazes response booklets.
Time: (10–15) minutes, Abbreviated Battery; (30) minutes, Standard Battery; (45) minutes, Extended Battery.
Authors: Bruce A. Bracken and R. Steve McCallum.
Publisher: PRO-ED.
Cross References: For a review by Deborah L. Bandalos, see 14:404.

[2842]

University Residence Environment Scale [Revised].

Purpose: Designed to "assess the social climate of university student living groups."
Population: University students and staff.
Publication Dates: 1974–1988.
Acronym: URES.
Scores: 10: Involvement, Emotional Support, Independence, Traditional Social Orientation, Competition, Academic Achievement, Intellectuality, Order and Organization, Student Influence, Innovation.
Administration: Group.
Forms, 4: Real (R), Ideal (I), Expectations (E), Short (S).
Price Data: Available from publisher at www.mindgarden.com/products/uress.htm.
Time: Administration time not reported.

Comments: Part of the Social Climate Scales (T5:2445); focuses on student-student and student-staff relationships and the organizational structure of a living group; for use in student living groups and in program evaluation and counseling; can also be completed by observers and other nonresidents, such as parents and student visitors; provides information about student living groups and encourages staff to become involved in program planning and design.
Author: Rudolf H. Moos.
Publisher: Mind Garden, Inc.
Cross References: For reviews by Barbara A. Rothlisberg and Theresa G. Siskind, see 14:405; see also T4:2865 (8 references) and T3:2534 (3 references); for reviews by Fred H. Borgen and James V. Mitchell, Jr. of an earlier edition, see 8:700 (12 references).

[2843]

Useful Field of View.

Purpose: Designed as a "computer-administered and computer-scored test of visual attention," which may be used to help predict the degree to which a person may perform some everyday activities, such as driving a motor vehicle, safely.
Population: Adults.
Publication Date: 1998.
Acronym: UFOV.
Scores, 3: Central Vision and Processing Speed, Divided Attention, Selective Attention.
Administration: Individual.
Price Data, 1998: $130 per complete kit including user's manual (106 pages), reference card, CD, and use counter.
Time: (15) minutes.
Comments: Microsoft Windows 95 required with video card and CD ROM drive; not for use with laptops.
Authors: Karlene K. Ball and Daniel L. Roenker.
Publisher: Pearson.
Cross References: For reviews by Gregory Schraw and James P. Van Haneghan, see 15:271.

[2844]

Utah Test of Language Development, Fourth Edition.

Purpose: Designed to "identify children who are significantly below their peers in language proficiency."
Population: Ages 3-0 to 9-11.
Publication Dates: 1958–2003.
Acronym: UTLD-4.
Scores, 8: Picture Identification, Word Functions, Morphological Structures, Sentence Repetition, Word Segmentation, Total Language Composite, Content Composite, Form Composite.
Administration: Individual.
Price Data, 2006: $140 per complete kit including examiner's manual, picture book, and 25 profile/

examiner record booklets, all in a sturdy storage box; $50 per examiner's manual; $60 per picture book; $35 per 25 profile/examiner record booklets.
Time: (15–30) minutes.
Comments: Earliest edition of this test was called the Utah Verbal Language Development.
Author: Merlin J. Mecham.
Publisher: PRO-ED.
Cross References: For reviews by David P. Hurford and Judith R. Johnston, see 16:255; see also T5:2801 (3 references) and T4:2872 (1 reference); for a review by Lynn S. Bliss of the third edition, see 11:454 (2 references); for reviews by Joan I. Lynch and Michelle Quinn of an earlier edition, see 9:1306 (3 references); see also T3:2541 (5 references) and T2:2097 (4 references); for reviews by Katharine G. Butler and William H. Perkins of an earlier edition, see 7:973.

[2845]

Validity Indicator Profile.

Purpose: Designed to assess response styles to help determine whether the results of cognitive, neuropsychological, or other types of testing should be considered representative of an individual's overall capacities.
Population: Individuals 18-69.
Publication Date: 1997.
Acronym: VIP.
Scores, 2: Nonverbal Subtest Response Style, Verbal Subtest Response Style.
Administration: Group.
Price Data, 2008: $123 per Q Local software starter kit; $128 per mail-in scoring starter kit; $44.50 per manual; $41.50 per 1 reusable test booklet; $22 per 25 Q Local answer sheets; $18.50 per Q Local interpretive report; $14 per Q Local profile report; $21.50 per mail-in interpretive report; $17 per mail-in profile report.
Time: (50) minutes for both subtests; (20) minutes for verbal subtest and (30) minutes for nonverbal subtest.
Comments: The scoring options are Q Local software or mail-in scoring; the report options are Interpretive or Profile.
Author: Richard I. Frederick.
Publisher: Pearson.
Cross References: For reviews by Jack E. Gebart-Eaglemont and Stephen H. Ivens, see 14:406.

[2846]

Valpar Test of Essential Skills.

Purpose: Designed to "help examinees demonstrate in a relatively short period of time important basic English and math skills required of workers in most of the occupations or training programs in the United States and Canada."
Population: Ages 15 and over.
Publication Dates: 1998–1999.

Acronym: VTES.
Administration: Individual or group.
Price Data, 2006: $30 per manual (1998, 76 pages), $75 per 25 answer sheets; $50 per 10 math test booklets (specify Form A or Form B); $50 per 10 English booklets (specify Form A or Form B); $50 per Evaluation Kit including 1 manual, 10 answer sheets, 2 math test booklets, 2 English test booklets, and scoring software.
Comments: Time limited; criterion-referenced; computer scoring only; requires IBM PC or compatible, 486 or higher; "percent correct" scores provided for all subtests and totals for English and Math; test booklets are reusable.
Authors: Bryan B. Christopherson and Alex Swartz.
Publisher: Valpar International Corporation.
a) VTES ENGLISH.
Scores, 6: Vocabulary/Grade Level, Spelling/Grade Level, Usage/Grade Level, Reading/Grade Level, Total/Grade Level, Total/General Educational Development-L (GED-L).
Forms, 2: Alternate Forms: Form A and Form B.
Time: (60) minutes.
b) VTES MATH.
Scores, 6: Computation/Grade Level, Usage/Grade Level, Total/Grade Level, Computation/General Educational Development-M (GED-M), Usage/General Educational Development-M (GED-M), Total/General Educational Development-M (GED-M).
Forms, 2: Alternate Forms: Form A and Form B.
Time: (60) minutes.
Cross References: For reviews by Arthur S. Ellen and by Shawn Powell and Michelle A. Butler, see 16:256.

[2847]

Values Preference Indicator [Revised].

Purpose: Provides respondents with the tools to examine their values and priorities for the purpose of self-learning, group discussion, team development, and gaining insight into corporate culture.
Population: Adults.
Publication Dates: 1990-2006.
Acronym: VPI.
Scores, 21: Accomplishment, Acknowledgment, Challenge, Cooperation, Creativity, Expertise, Friendship, Honesty, Independence, Instruction, Intimacy, Organization, Pleasure, Quality, Recognition, Responsibility, Security, Spirituality, Tranquility, Variety, Wealth.
Administration: Individual or group.
Price Data, 2006: $13.95 per test booklet (2006, 12 pages); $13.95 per code for online version; $38 per Trainer's Guidelines (1996, 22 pages).
Time: [30-45] minutes to administer; 90-180 for program.
Comments: Test can be self-administered and self-scored.
Authors: Ken Keis and Everett T. Robinson.
Publisher: Consulting Resource Group International, Inc.

[2848]

Vasectomy Scale: Attitudes.

Purpose: To measure attitudes toward vasectomy.
Population: Adults.
Publication Dates: 1974–1988.
Scores: Total score only.
Administration: Group.
Manual: No manual.
Price Data, 2005: $2 per scale.
Time: [10] minutes.
Comments: Supplementary article available.
Author: Panos D. Bardis.
Publisher: Donna Bardis.

[2849]

Verb and Sentence Test.

Purpose: "Developed to investigate disorders affecting the production and comprehension of verbs and sentences."
Population: People with aphasia, aged 18–80 years.
Publication Date: 2002.
Acronym: VAST.
Scores: 10 subtests: Verb Comprehension, Sentence Comprehension, Grammaticality Judgement, Action Naming, Verb Finite, Verb Infinitive, Sentence Construction, Anagrams Without Picture, Anagrams With Picture, Wh-Anagrams.
Administration: Individual.
Price Data: Available from publisher.
Time: (180) minutes for complete battery.
Comments: Subtests may be administered individually.
Authors: Roelien Bastiaanse, Susan Edwards, and Judith Rispens.
Publisher: Pearson Assessment [England].
Cross References: For reviews by Shawn K. Acheson and Mildred Murray-Ward, see 17:192.

[2850]

Verbal Form.

Purpose: Designed to measure general ability to learn and comprehend.
Population: Employees in a wide variety of occupations.
Publication Dates: 1946–1984.
Scores, 3: Quantitative, Linguistic, Total.
Administration: Individual or group.
Forms, 2: A, B.
Price Data, 2002: $78 per start-up kit including 25 test booklets (specify Form A or Form B) and examiner's manual; $60 per 25 test booklets (quantity discounts available; specify Form A or Form B); $28 per examiner's manual; price data available from publisher for Quanta computer administration and scoring software (Windows); $78 per Quanta start-up kit including examiner's manual, 25 administrations, and scoring (does not include Quanta software).

Time: 15 minutes.
Comments: Previously listed as SRA Verbal Form.
Authors: Thelma Gwinn Thurstone and L. L. Thurstone.
Publisher: Pearson Performance Solutions [No reply from publisher; status unknown].
Cross References: See T4:2542 (3 references), T3:2276 (3 references), T2:452 (1 reference), and 7:383 (2 references); for reviews by W. D. Commins and Willis C. Schaefer, see 4:319.

[2851]

Verbal Motor Production Assessment for Children.

Purpose: "Designed to aid in the systematic assessment of the neuromotor integrity of the motor speech system in children ... [with] speech production disorders."
Population: Speech-disordered children ages 3–12.
Publication Date: 1999.
Acronym: VMPAC.
Scores, 8: Global Motor Control, Focal Oromotor Control, Sequencing, Connected Speech and Language Control, Speech Characteristics, Auditory, Visual, Tactile.
Administration: Individual.
Price Data, 2005: $115 per complete kit including examiner's manual (206 pages), 11 stimulus cards, 15 record forms, and training videotape (45 minutes); $80 per examiner's manual; $32 per 15 record forms; $32 per stimulus cards; $43 per training videotape.
Time: (30) minutes.
Authors: Deborah Hayden and Paula Square.
Publisher: Pearson.
Cross References: For a review by Katharine Snyder, see 16:257.

[2852]

Verbal Reasoning.

Purpose: To measure the capacity to reason logically based on verbal problems.
Population: Wide variety of occupations and vocational counseling.
Publication Dates: 1958–1961.
Scores: Total score only.
Administration: Individual or group.
Price Data, 2002: $92 per start-up kit including 25 test booklets, score key, and interpretation and research manual (1961, 20 pages); $55 per 25 test booklets (quantity discounts available); $20 per score key; $28 per interpretation and research manual (1961, 20 pages).
Time: 15 minutes.
Authors: Raymond J. Corsini and Richard Renck.
Publisher: Pearson Performance Solutions [No reply from publisher; status unknown].
Cross References: See T3:2553 (1 reference); for reviews by James E. Kennedy and David G. Ryans, see 6:509.

[2853]

Verbal Reasoning Tests.

Purpose: Designed to "assess a pupil's verbal skills."
Population: Ages 7.3–10.3; Ages 9.3–12.3; 11.3–14.3.
Publication Date: 1993.
Scores, 5: Vocabulary, Relationships, Sentences, Reasoning, Symbol Manipulation.
Administration: Group.
Levels, 3: 8 and 9, 10 and 11, 12 and 13.
Price Data: Available from publisher.
Authors: Neil Hagues and Denise Courtenay.
Publisher: GL Assessment [England].
  a) VERBAL REASONING 8 and 9.
  Population: Ages 7.3–10.3.
  Time: (40) minutes.
  b) VERBAL REASONING 10 and 11.
  Population: Ages 9.3–12.3.
  Time: (45) minutes.
  c) VERBAL REASONING 12 and 13.
  Population: Ages 11.3–14.3.
  Time: (50) minutes.
Cross References: For reviews by Hoi K. Suen and by Rosemary E. Sutton and Jeremy Genovese, see 16:258.

[2854]

Versant.

Purpose: Measures speaking and listening skills over the telephone and measures facility in spoken English and Spanish, which includes the ease and immediacy in understanding and producing basic conversational English and Spanish.
Population: Ages 8–79.
Publication Dates: 2000–2006.
Scores, 5: Overall Score, Sentence Mastery, Vocabulary, Fluency, Pronunciation.
Administration: Individual.
Forms, 3: 5 minutes, 10 minutes, 15 minutes.
Price Data, 2005: $24 per 5-minute test; $40 per 10-minute or 15-minute test.
Time: (5–15) minutes.
Comments: Test administered via telephone or PC; previously titled Ordinate Spoken English Test.
Authors: Ordinate Corporation and Harcourt Assessment.
Publisher: Pearson.
Cross References: For reviews by Dennis Doverspike and Alan Garfinkel, see 16:177.

[2855]

VESPAR: A Verbal and Spatial Reasoning Test.

Purpose: "Designed to measure fluid intelligence in neurological patients."
Population: People "who have suffered physical or cognitive impairments as a result of neurological illness."
Publication Date: 1995.

Acronym: VESPAR.
Scores: Available from publisher.
Administration: Individual.
Price Data, 2001: $198 per multi-part test.
Time: Administration time not reported.
Authors: Dawn W. Langdon and Elizabeth K. Warrington.
Publisher: Psychology Press.

[2856]

Victoria Symptom Validity Test.

Purpose: Designed to "assess possible exaggeration or feigning of cognitive impairments."
Population: Ages 18 and over.
Publication Date: 1997.
Acronym: VSVT.
Scores, 6: Total Items Correct, Easy Items Correct, Difficult Items Correct, Easy Items Response Latency, Difficult Items Response Latency, Right-Left Preference.
Administration: Individual.
Price Data, 2006: $99 per introductory kit including unlimited use software (CD-ROM) for administering, scoring, and reports, with professional manual (93 pages).
Time: 18-25 minutes.
Authors: Daniel Slick, Grace Hopp, Esther Strauss, and Garrie B. Thompson.
Publisher: Psychological Assessment Resources, Inc.
Cross References: For reviews by Stephen J. Freeman and Linda J. Zimmerman, see 14:407.

[2857]

VIEW: An Assessment of Problem Solving Style.

Purpose: Designed to assess "problem-solving styles."
Population: Ages 12 years and older.
Publication Dates: 2002-2004.
Scores, 3: Orientation to Change, Manner of Processing, Ways of Decoding.
Administration: Individual or group.
Price Data, 2006: $25 per manual (70 pages); $165 per complete kit including facilitator's guide (219 pages) and 10 paper copies of VIEW (required for all first-time orders); $90 per 10 paper copies; $50 per set-up fee for on-line access; $90 per 10 on-line uses; discounts available for nonprofit schools, religious organizations, college and university faculty, and researchers.
Foreign Editions: Information regarding translated tests available from publisher.
Time: (10-15) minutes.
Comments: Available in online and print versions.
Authors: Edwin C. Selby, Donald J. Treffinger, Scott G. Isaksen, and Kenneth J. Lauer (technical manual only).
Publisher: Center for Creative Learning.
Cross References: For reviews by Gregory Schraw and Mark A. Staal, see 17:193.

[2858]

ViewPoint.

Purpose: An assessment of work attitudes designed for use in employee selection.
Population: Applicants for nonexempt or entry-level positions in industries.
Publication Dates: 1998–2003.
Scores: 10 scales: WorkView Total, ServiceView Total, Conscientiousness, Trustworthiness, Managing Work Pressure, Getting Along with Others, Drug/Alcohol Avoidance, Safety Orientation, Carelessness, Faking.
Administration: Group or individual.
Price Data, 2005: Available from publisher for test materials including Technical Manual (1999, 62 pages), Technical Report Addendum: A Meta-Analysis of the Validity of ViewPoint (2001, 13 pages), and User's Manual (2005, 56 pages).
Comments: Published in five different forms, each one covering a different combination of work and service attitudes; computerized versions are available.
Authors: W. M. Gibson, M. L. Holcom, S. W. Stang, and W. W. Ruch.
Publisher: Psychological Services, Inc.
  a) WORKVIEW 6.
  Acronym: W6.
  Time: (15–20) minutes.
  b) WORKVIEW 4.
  Acronym: W4.
  Time: (10–15) minutes.
  c) SERVICEVIEW.
  Acronym: SV.
  Time: (10–15) minutes.
  d) WORKVIEW 6 + SERVICE.
  Acronym: W6SV.
  Time: (20–30) minutes.
  e) WORKVIEW 4 + SERVICE.
  Acronym: W4SV.
  Time: (20–25) minutes.
Cross References: For a review by Robert Fitzpatrick, see 16:259.

[2859]

ViewPoint General Personality Survey.

Purpose: "A general-purpose measure of normal personality [based on the Big Five structure] designed for business settings."
Population: "[Job] candidates across a broad range of positions."
Publication Dates: 2001-2009.
Acronym: ViewPoint GPS.
Scores, 37: 5 Major Scales based on 22 Component Scales: Agreeableness (Caring, Helpful, Complying, Considerate, Trusting), Conscientiousness (Thoroughness, Achievement Focus, Diligence, Initiative, Organization), Stability (Even Tempered, Self-Confidence,

Optimism, Composure), Extraversion (Influential, Likes Attention, Sociable, Lively), Openness (Inventiveness, Flexibility, Curiosity, Quick Thinking); 8 Occupational Scales grouped into 3 categories: Associate (Implementing, Providing Service), Leadership (Establishing, Managing), Specialist (Analyzing, Creating, Selling), no category (Loyalty); 2 Special Scales: Careful Responding, Impression Management.

Administration: Group.

Price Data, 2009: $32 per online test per quantity of 5-99 tests purchased (includes overall PPI scoring report, but not PPI Caregiver Profile); $18 per online PPI Caregiver Profile per quantity of 5-24 Profiles purchased; $24 per online PPI Caregiver Profile with optional Problem Solving Index per quantity of 5-24 Profiles purchased; quantity discounts available; contact publisher for pricing information regarding paper-and-pencil version; Technical Manual (Version 8, 2009, 104 pages), Caregiver Profile: Administrator's Guide (Version 8, 2008, 27 pages), and Caregiver Profile: PPI Manual Supplement (Version 8, 2008, 24 pages) can be downloaded free of charge with authorization from publisher.

Foreign Language Editions: Spanish and Chinese editions available.

Time: Online administration: (20-25) minutes, (15) additional minutes for optional component of the Caregiver Profile; paper-and-pencil administration: (25-30) minutes, (20-25) additional minutes for optional component.

Comments: Distributed exclusively by PSI Services LLC under the title "ViewPoint General Personality Survey" (ViewPoint GPS); available online or in paper-and-pencil format; optional PPI Caregiver Profile is a special method of scoring the ViewPoint GPS and is distributed under the title "CareView."

Authors: Joseph D. Abraham and John D. Morrison, Jr. (PPI Technical Manual [Version 8] and PPI Caregiver Profile: Administrator's Guide [Version 8]).

Publisher: A & M Psychometrics, LLC; sole distributor: PSI Services LLC.

a) PPI CAREGIVER PROFILE.

Purpose: "A special method of scoring the PPI [that provides] a targeted assessment of candidates for Direct Support Professional and other caregiving positions."

Population: "Applicants for the position of Direct Support Professional and closely related jobs."

Scores, 5: Nurturing (i.e., PPI Agreeableness), Dependable (i.e., PPI Conscientiousness), Positive Attitude (i.e., PPI Optimism), Performance/Retention Index (i.e., mean of first three scores), Problem Solving Index (optional score based on the Numerical Ability (EAS2) subtest).

Comments: Numerical Ability (EAS2) is a subtest of the Employee Aptitude Survey (EAS) published by PSI Services LLC; the EAS2 is offered in conjunction with the PPI.

Cross References: For reviews by Michael D. Biderman and Chockalingam Viswesvaran, see 18:91.

[2860]

Vigil Continuous Performance Test.

Purpose: Designed to "measure a person's ability to concentrate on a simple or relatively complex task over time."

Population: Ages 6 to 90.

Publication Dates: 1996–1998.

Scores, 4: Errors of Omission, Errors of Commission, Hit Rate, Reaction Time.

Administration: Individual.

Price Data, 2003: $545 per complete kit including Windows Version Binder and three 3.5-inch disks.

Time: [8] minutes.

Comments: Test is computer administered and scored; requires IBM compatible 386 or 486 20 MB hard drive, 3.5-inch disk drive, Windows 3.1, mouse, color V6A or Super V6A, monitor, and Sound System compatible with Sound Blaster Pro Deluxe Soundboard.

Author: The Psychological Corporation.

Publisher: Pearson.

Cross References: For a review by Joseph C. Kush, see 16:260.

[2861]

Vineland Adaptive Behavior Scales, Second Edition.

Purpose: Designed as an adaptive behavior assessment system that measures self-sufficiency across the life-span.

Population: Birth to age 90-11.

Publication Dates: 1935-2008.

Acronym: Vineland-II.

Scores, 16: 3 Communication scores: Receptive, Expressive, Written; 5 Daily Living Skills scores: Personal, Domestic, Community, Academic (Teacher Rating Form only), School Community (Teacher Rating Form only); 3 Socialization scores: Interpersonal Relationships, Play and Leisure Time, Coping Skills; 2 Motor Skills scores: Gross, Fine; Adaptive Behavior Composite, Maladaptive Behavior Index (optional), Maladaptive Behavior Critical Items (optional).

Administration: Individual.

Foreign Language Edition: Spanish interview and rating forms available for Survey and Expanded Interview forms.

Comments: A revision of the Vineland Social Maturity Scale by Edgar A. Doll.

Authors: Sara S. Sparrow, Domenic V. Cicchetti, and David A. Balla.

Publisher: Pearson.

a) SURVEY INTERVIEW FORM, PARENT/CAREGIVER RATING FORM.

Purpose: Designed to assess adaptive behavior via parent/caregiver report.

Population: Birth to age 90-11.

Price Data, 2009: $154.50 per Survey Forms starter kit including 10 Survey Interview forms, 10 Parent/Caregiver Rating forms, 10 Survey Interview reports to parents, 10 Survey reports to caregivers, and Survey Forms manual (2005, 326 pages); $74 per 25 Survey Interview forms; $74 per 25 Parent/Caregiver Rating forms; $29.75 per 25 Survey Interview forms report to parents; $29.75 per 25 Survey Forms report to caregivers; $103 per Survey Forms manual; $267 per Survey Forms ASSIST™ scoring software for Mac/Windows.
Time: 45(65) minutes.
b) TEACHER RATING FORM.
Purpose: Assessment of adaptive behavior within classroom and school settings.
Population: Ages 3-0 to 18-11.
Price Data: $103 per Teacher Rating Forms starter kit including 10 Teacher Rating Forms, 10 Teacher Rating reports to parents/caregivers, and Teacher Rating Form manual (2006, 238 pages); $68 per 25 Teacher Rating Forms; $29.85 per 25 Teacher Rating Form reports to parents/caregivers; $85.50 per Teacher Rating Form manual; $267 per Teacher Rating Form ASSIST™ scoring software for Mac/Windows.
Time: 20(40) minutes.
c) EXPANDED INTERVIEW FORM.
Purpose: Designed to provide a comprehensive assessment of adaptive behavior via a semistructured interview.
Population: Birth to age 90.
Price Data: $180 per Expanded Interview Form starter kit including 10 Expanded Interview Forms, 10 Expanded Form report to parents, 10 Expanded Form report to caregivers, and Expanded Form manual (2008, 326 pages); $350 per Expanded Form starter kit with ASSIST™ software; $72 per Expanded Interview Forms; $30 per 25 Expanded Form report to parents; $31 per 25 Expanded Form report to caregivers; $85.50 per Expanded Form manual.
Time: 25(90) minutes.
Cross References: For reviews by Stephanie Stein and Keith F. Widaman, see 18:150; see T5:2813 (156 references) and T4:2882 (62 references); for a review by Jerome M. Sattler of an earlier edition, see 10:381 (9 references); for a review by Iris Amos Campbell of an earlier Survey Form and Expanded Form, see 9:1327 (8 references); see also T3:2557 (38 references), 8:703 (23 references), T2:1428 (50 references), P:281 (21 references), 6:194 (20 references), and 5:120 (15 references); for reviews by William M. Cruickshank and Florence M. Teagarden of an earlier edition, see 4:94 (21 references); for reviews by C. M. Louttit and John W. M. Rothney and an excerpted review, see 3:107 (58 references); for reviews by Paul H. Furfey, Elaine F. Kinder, and Anna S. Starr, see 1:1143.

[2862]
Vineland Social-Emotional Early Childhood Scales.
Purpose: Designed to assess the social and emotional functioning of young children.
Population: Birth to age 5-11.
Publication Date: 1998.
Acronym: SEEC.
Scores, 4: Interpersonal Relationships, Play and Leisure Time, Coping Skills, Composite.
Administration: Individual.
Price Data, 2006: $71.99 per complete kit; $32.99 per 25 record forms; $199.99 for reporting software (Early Childhood Assessment ASSIST).
Foreign Language Edition: Spanish edition available.
Time: (15–25) minutes.
Comments: Administered as a structured oral interview; interviewee should be the person with the most knowledge of the child's social and emotional functioning (e.g., parent, grandparent, legal guardian).
Authors: Sara S. Sparrow, David A. Balla, and Dominic V. Cicchetti.
Publisher: Pearson.
Cross References: For reviews by Joseph C. Kush and Donald Lee Stovall, see 14:408.

[2863]
A Violence Scale.
Purpose: Designed to measure attitudes toward violence.
Population: Adolescents and adults
Publication Date: 1973.
Scores: Total score only.
Administration: Group.
Manual: No manual.
Price Data, 2005: $2 per scale.
Time: [10] minutes.
Comments: Supplementary article available.
Author: Panos D. Bardis.
Publisher: Donna Bardis.
Cross References: See 8:704 (1 reference).

[2864]
Visual Analog Mood Scales.
Purpose: Designed to "assess internal mood states in neurologically impaired adults and in patients in medical and psychiatric settings."
Population: Ages 18 and over.
Publication Dates: 1996–1997.
Acronym: VAMS.
Scores: 8 scales: Afraid, Confused, Sad, Angry, Energetic, Tired, Happy, Tense.
Administration: Group or individual.
Price Data, 2006: $122 per introductory kit including 25 response booklets, professional manual (1997, 48 pages), and metric ruler.

Time: 5 minutes.
Comments: Self-administered or administered by examiner.
Author: Robert A. Stern.
Publisher: Psychological Assessment Resources, Inc.
Cross References: For reviews by S. Alvin Leung and William E. Martin, Jr., see 15:272.

[2865]

Visual Association Test.
Purpose: "Designed to detect anterograde amnesia and certain brain disorders it is connected with."
Population: Ages 16–94.
Publication Date: 2003.
Acronym: VAT.
Scores, 12: Form A: Trial 1 & 2, Trial 3 (optional), Delayed Reproduction (optional); Parallel Form B: idem; Long Form (Form A + B): idem.
Administration: Individual.
Forms, 3: Form A, Form B, Long Form (Form A + B).
Price Data: Available from publisher (www.pits-online.nl/en).
Foreign Language Editions: Dutch, English, and German editions available.
Time: 5-15 minutes (depending on the form chosen).
Comments: Based on the Visual Association Method; manual includes section for each language.
Authors: J. Lindeboom and B. Schmand.
Publisher: PITS: Psychologische Instrumenten Tests en Services [The Netherlands].
Cross References: For a review by Stephen J. Freeman, see 16:261.

[2866]

The Visual Aural Digit Span Test.
Purpose: Intended as a "standardized test of intersensory integration and short-term memory for school-age children."
Population: Ages 5-6 to 12.
Publication Date: 1977.
Acronym: VADS Test.
Scores, 11: Aural-Oral, Visual-Oral, Aural-Written, Visual-Written, Aural Input, Visual Input, Oral Expression, Written Expression, Intrasensory Integration, Intersensory Integration, Total.
Subtests, 4: Aural-Oral, Visual-Oral, Aural-Written, Visual-Written.
Administration: Individual.
Price Data, 2002: $61 per examination kit including 1 package of stimulus cards, Directions for Administering, and 100 visual scoring forms); $34 per 100 visual scoring forms; $83 per manual (1977, 216 pages).
Time: [10–15] minutes.
Author: Elizabeth M. Koppitz.
Publisher: Pearson.
Cross References: See T5:2816 (1 reference) and T4:2884 (1 reference); for reviews by H. Lee Swanson

and Robert H. Zabel, see 9:1329 (2 references); see also T3:2560 (2 references).

[2867]

Visual Functioning Assessment Tool.
Purpose: "Assessment of a student's visual functioning in the educational setting."
Population: Visually impaired in grades preschool and over.
Publication Date: 1980.
Acronym: VFAT.
Scores: No scores.
Administration: Individual.
Price Data, 2005: $95 per complete kit; $38 per reproducible recording booklet; $65 per manual (123 pages).
Time: Untimed.
Authors: Kathleen Byrnes Costello, Patricia Pinkney, and Wendy Scheffers.
Publisher: Stoelting Co.

[2868]

Visual Motor Assessment.
Purpose: "Designed to identify visual-motor problems in children and adults."
Population: Ages 6 and older
Publication Dates: 1962-2006.
Acronym: ViMo.
Scores, 5: Total Rotation Score, T-Score, Total SPCD (Separation of the Circle-Diamond Figure), Total DCD (Distortion of the Circle-Diamond Figure), Total DD (Distortion of the Dot Figure).
Administration: Individual.
Price Data, 2011: $123 per complete kit including technical manual (104 pages), 25 record forms, and 2 sets of test cards; $73 per technical manual; $50 per 25 record forms.
Time: (5-15) minutes.
Comments: Formerly known as the Minnesota Percepto-Diagnostic (MPD) Test.
Author: Gerald B. Fuller.
Publisher: Multi-Health Systems, Inc.
Cross References: For reviews by Mark Roybal and by Kay B. Stevens and J. Randall Price, see 17:194; for information on the Minnesota Percepto-Diagnostic Test, see T5:1699 (2 references), T4:1647 (6 references), 9:719 (3 references), 8:872 (22 references), T2:1485 (17 references), and P:475 (19 references); for reviews by Richard W. Coan and Eugene E. Levitt of the original edition of the Minnesota Percepto-Diagnostic Test, see 6:231 (2 references).

[2869]

The Visual Object and Space Perception Battery.
Purpose: Designed to assess visual object and space perception.
Population: Adults.

Publication Date: 1991.
Acronym: VOSP.
Scores: 9 tests: Shape Detection Screening Test, Incomplete Letters, Silhouettes, Object Decision, Progressive Silhouettes, Dot Counting, Position Discrimination, Number Location, Cube Analysis.
Administration: Individual or group.
Price Data, 2007: £174.32 per complete kit including manual (20 pages), 25 scoring sheets, and 3 stimulus books; £19.39 per 25 scoring sheets.
Time: Untimed.
Comments: Tests may be administered separately, in groups, or as a complete battery.
Authors: Elizabeth K. Warrington and Merle James.
Publisher: Pearson Assessment [England].
Cross References: For a review by Ayres G. D'Costa, see 17:195.

[2870]
Visual Patterns Test.
Purpose: Designed to measure "short term visual memory."
Population: Ages 18 and over.
Publication Date: 1997.
Acronym: VPT.
Score: Total score only.
Administration: Individual.
Forms: 2 parallel forms: A, B.
Price Data, 2006: £70 per complete kit including manual (12 pages), stimulus cards, and response sheet; £35 per 50 scoring sheets.
Time: [10] minutes.
Authors: Sergio Della Sala, Colin Gray, Alan Baddeley, and Lindsay Wilson.
Publisher: Pearson Assessment [England].
Cross References: For reviews by Valentina McInerney and Steven R. Shaw, see 17:196.

[2871]
Visual Search and Attention Test.
Purpose: Constructed to "measure attentional processes commonly disrupted in acute and chronic brain damage or disease."
Population: Ages 18 and over.
Publication Dates: 1987–1990.
Acronym: VSAT.
Scores, 3: Left, Right, Total.
Administration: Individual.
Price Data, 2006: $156 per introductory kit including 50 test booklets and manual (1990, 18 pages).
Time: 6 minutes.
Authors: Max R. Trenerry, Bruce Crosson, James DeBoe, and William R. Leber.
Publisher: Psychological Assessment Resources, Inc.
Cross References: See T5:2820 (1 reference); for reviews by Stephen R. Hooper and Wilfred G. Van Gorp, see 12:407.

[2872]
Visual Skills Appraisal.
Purpose: "Developed to assist teachers and other educators, who may not have specialized training in visual skills assessment, to identify visual inefficiencies that affect school performance."
Population: Grades K–4; ages 5 through 9.
Publication Date: 1984.
Acronym: VSA.
Scores: 6 subtests: Pursuits, Scanning, Aligning, Locating, Eye-Hand Coordination, Fixation Unity.
Administration: Individual.
Price Data, 2006: $85 per complete kit including manual (112 pages), stimulus cards, 25 design completion forms, 25 red/green trail forms, 25 score sheets, and red/green glasses; $12 per stimulus cards; $12 per 25 design completion forms, 25 red/green trail forms, or 25 score sheets; $10 per red/green glasses; $27 per manual.
Time: (10–15) minutes.
Comments: Criterion-referenced.
Authors: Regina G. Richards and Gary S. Oppenheim in consultation with G. N. Getman.
Publisher: Academic Therapy Publications.
Cross References: See 11:456 (1 reference).

[2873]
Voc-Tech Quick Screener.
Purpose: Designed to identify job interests.
Population: Non-college bound high school students and adults.
Publication Dates: 1984–1990.
Acronym: VTQS.
Scores, 14: Administrative Support/Clerical, Agriculture/Animals and Forestry, Construction Trades, Design/Graphics and Communication, Food/Beverage Services, Health Services, Health Technicians, Industrial Production Trades, Marketing/Sales, Mechanical/Craftsmanship Trades, Personal Services, Protective Services, Science/Engineering Technicians, Transportation/Equipment Operators.
Administration: Group.
Price Data: Available from publisher.
Time: (20–25) minutes.
Authors: Robert Kauk and Robert Robinett.
Publisher: CFKR Career Materials.
Cross References: For reviews by Albert M. Bugaj and Del Eberhardt, see 12:411.

[2874]
Vocabulary Test: National Achievement Tests.
Purpose: Measures the student's vocabulary and judgment in the choice of effective words.
Population: Grades 3–8, 7–12.
Publication Dates: 1939–1957.
Scores: Total score only.

Administration: Group.
Price Data: Available from publisher.
Time: (15) minutes.
Authors: Robert K. Speer and Samuel Smith.
Publisher: Psychometric Affiliates.
Cross References: For a review by Clifford Woody, see 3:168.

[2875]

Vocational Assessment and Curriculum Guide.

Purpose: "Designed to assess and identify skill deficits in terms of competitive employment expectations; to prescribe training goals designed to reduce identified deficits; to evaluate program effectiveness by reassessing the worker after training."
Population: Mentally handicapped employees.
Publication Dates: 1982–2003.
Acronym: VACG.
Scores, 10: Attendance/Endurance, Independence, Production, Learning, Behavior, Communication Skills, Social Skills, Grooming/Eating, Reading/Writing, Math.
Administration: Group.
Price Data, 2011: $12 per complete kit including manual (5 pages), 10 test booklets, curriculum guides, and summary profile sheets; $8 per set of 10 extra forms.
Time: (15–20) minutes.
Authors: Frank R. Rusch, Richard P. Schutz, Dennis E. Mithaug, Jeffrey E. Stewart, and Deanna K. Mar.
Publisher: Exceptional Education.
Cross References: For reviews by Hinsdale Bernard and Gerald R. Schneck, see 13:356; see also T4:2898 (1 reference).

[2876]

Vocational Decision-Making Interview, Revised Edition.

Purpose: Designed to improve the vocational decision making of people with learning and other disabilities.
Population: People with learning and other disabilities, including vision impairments, limited academic skills, limited English-language proficiency, or with displaced workers and people in substance abuse programs.
Publication Dates: 1993–1999.
Acronym: VDMI.
Scores, 3: Decision-Making Readiness, Employment Readiness, Self-Appraisal.
Administration: Individual.
Price Data, 2006: $26.95 per 10 assessments; a Tips booklet included free with each 10 assessments; price information for administration manual available from publisher.
Time: (20–40) minutes.
Comments: Not self-administered or self-scored; six-panel foldout; consumable; no other components needed.

Authors: Thomas Czerlinsky, and Shirley K. Chandler.
Publisher: JIST Publishing, Inc.
Cross References: For reviews by Karen T. Carey and Donald W. Tiffany of an earlier version, see 14:409.

[2877]

Vocational Interest, Experience and Skill Assessment (VIESA), 2nd Canadian Edition.

Purpose: Designed to stimulate career exploration.
Population: Grades 8-10, 11-adults.
Publication Dates: 1985–1992.
Acronym: VIESA, 2nd Canadian Edition.
Scores: Scores for Interests, Skills, and Experiences in 4 areas: People, Data, Things, Ideas.
Administration: Group or individual.
Levels, 2: 1 (grades 8-10), 2 (grade 11-adult).
Price Data, 2005: $68.50 per 25 guide books and job family charts (specify level); $36.60 per preview kit Level 1 & 2; $35.40 per user's handbook.
Time: (40-45) minutes.
Comments: Self-scored inventory of career-related interests, experiences, skills and values, with supporting materials for counselors; adapted from VIESA, U.S. Edition.
Author: ACT Career Planning Services.
Publisher: Nelson Education Ltd. [Canada].
Cross References: For reviews by David J. Bateson and Brenda H. Loyd; see 12:409; for information for VIESA, 2nd Edition, see 9:1338; for a review by Charles J. Krauskopf of an earlier edition, see 8:1025.

[2878]

Vocational Interest Inventory and Exploration Survey (Voc-Ties).

Purpose: Designed to "assess a student's interest in school based training programs" and provide "information about the training area."
Population: Vocational education students.
Publication Dates: 1991–2000.
Scores: 15 vocational training interest areas: Auto Mechanics, Business and Office, Construction, Cosmetology, Drafting, Electromechanics, Electronics, Family and Consumer Science, Food Service, Graphic Arts, Health Services, Horticulture/Agriculture, Marketing, Metals, Technology Education.
Administration: Individual or group.
Price Data, 2002: $595 per media kit including guide, video cassette, software, and answer sheets; $195 per single station version; $495 per multi-station version; $995 per Network version.
Time: (15-20) minutes.
Authors: Nancy L. Scott and Charles Gilbreath.
Publisher: Piney Mountain Press, Inc.
Cross References: For reviews by Larry Cochran and Kevin R. Murphy of an earlier edition, see 12:408.

[2879]

Vocational Interest Survey for Australia.

Purpose: Designed to "assist Australians facing career decisions by providing an assessment of their vocational interests."
Population: Job applicants.
Publication Dates: 1989–1995.
Acronym: VISA.
Scores, 8: Caring, Culture, Service, Managing, Clerical, Science, Practical, Environmental.
Administration: Group or individual.
Price Data, 2006: A$173.05 per complete test.
Time: 20 minutes.
Author: Robert Pryor.
Publisher: Pearson Assessment and Information [Australia and New Zealand].
Cross References: For reviews by Eugene V. Aidman and Neroli Sawyer and by Robert Fitzpatrick, see 15:273.

[2880]

Vocational Opinion Index.

Purpose: Constructed to measure "an individual's attitudes, perceptions and motivations that impact on his/her ability to get and/or hold a job."
Population: Disadvantaged trainees in vocational skills programs.
Publication Dates: 1973-1976.
Acronym: VOI.
Scores, 13: Attractions to Work (Overall, Benefits to Children, Benefits to Worker, Better Life Style, Independence), Losses Associated with Work (Overall, Personal Freedom, Time for Family), Barriers to Employment (Medical, Child Care and Family, New Situation and People, Ability to Get and Hold a Job, Transportation).
Administration: Group.
Forms, 2: A, B.
Price Data: Available from publisher.
Foreign Language Edition: Spanish edition available.
Time: (20-40) minutes.
Author: Associates for Research in Behavior, Inc.
Publisher: ARBOR, Inc.
Cross Reference: For reviews by Bruce Shertzer and Donald G. Zytowski, see 9:1340.

[2881]

Vocational Preference Inventory, 1985 Edition.

Purpose: Designed to "assess career interests."
Population: High school and college and adults.
Publication Dates: 1953–1985.
Acronym: VPI.
Scores: 11 scales: Realistic, Investigative, Social, Conventional, Enterprising, Artistic, Self-Control, Masculinity-Femininity, Status, Infrequency, Acquiescence.
Administration: Individual or group.

Price Data, 2006: $99 per introductory kit including 50 test booklet/answer sheet/profile combinations and manual (1985, 36 pages).
Time: (15–30) minutes.
Author: John L. Holland.
Publisher: Psychological Assessment Resources, Inc.
Cross References: See T5:2835 (28 references) and T4:2910 (9 references); for reviews by John W. Shepard and Nicholas A. Vacc, see 10:382 (17 references); for reviews by James B. Rounds and by Nicholas A. Vacc and James Pickering of an earlier edition, see 9:1342 (19 references); see also T3:2581 (45 references); for an excerpted review by W. Bruce Walsh of an earlier edition, see 8:1028 (175 references); see also T2:1430 (48 references); for reviews by Joseph A. Johnston and Paul R. Lohnes, see 7:157 (39 references); see also P:283 (31 references); for reviews by Robert L. French and H. Bradley Sagen of an earlier edition, see 6:115 (13 references).

[2882]

A Voice Assessment Protocol For Children and Adults.

Purpose: "Assesses five parameters of the voice: pitch, loudness, quality, breath features, and rate/rhythm."
Population: Children and adults.
Publication Date: 1987.
Scores: 5 assessments: Pitch, Loudness, Quality, Breath Features, Rate/Rhythm.
Administration: Individual.
Price Data, 2011: $87 per complete kit including 25 protocols, audiocassette, and manual (24 pages); $35 per 25 protocols; $19 per audiocassette; $35 per manual.
Time: Administration time not reported.
Author: Rebekah H. Pindzola.
Publisher: PRO-ED.
Cross References: See T5:2837 (1 reference); for a review by Maynard D. Filter, see 11:459.

[2883]

Vulpe Assessment Battery–Revised.

Purpose: Designed as "a comprehensive, process-oriented, criterion-referenced assessment that emphasizes children's functional abilities."
Population: Children functioning between full term birth to six years of age.
Publication Date: 1994.
Acronym: VAB-R.
Scores: 8 scales: Basic Senses and Functions, Gross Motor, Fine Motor, Language, Cognitive Processes and Specific Concepts, Adaptive Behaviors, Activities of Daily Living, Environmental Assessment.
Administration: Individual or group.
Price Data, 2002: $109 per complete kit including manual (1994, 480 pages) and 50 record sheets; $21 per 50 record sheets.

Time: Administration time not reported.
Comments: Ratings by person familiar with the child.
Author: Shirley German Vulpe.
Publisher: Slosson Educational Publications, Inc.
Cross References: For reviews by Theresa Graham and Diane J. Sawyer, see 14:411.

[2884]
W-APT Programming Aptitude Test.
Purpose: To evaluate the aptitude and potential for computer programming work at all levels of experience.
Population: Programmers and general population.
Publication Date: 1984.
Acronym: W-APT.
Scores: Total score only.
Administration: Group.
Price Data, 2001: $190 per candidate.
Time: (60) minutes.
Comments: Detailed report provided on each candidate.
Author: Jack M. Wolfe.
Publisher: Rose Wolfe Family Partnership LLP [Canada].

[2885]
Wagner Enneagram Personality Style Scales.
Purpose: Designed "to measure the nine personality styles described by Enneagram."
Population: Ages 18 years and over.
Publication Date: 1999.
Acronym: WEKPSS.
Scores, 9: The Good Person, The Loving Person, The Effective Person, The Original Person, The Wise Person, The Loyal Person, The Joyful Person, The Powerful Person, The Peaceful Person.
Administration: Group or individual.
Price Data, 2006: $160 per kit including 25 autoscore forms, manual (114 pages), 100 glossary sheets, 100 brief guides to WEPSS results; $57.50 per 25 answer forms; $65 per manual; $21.50 per 100 glossary sheets; $21.50 per brief guide to WEPSS results; $16.50 per mail-in answer form; $325 per 25-use PC scoring disk; $17.50 per 100 PC answer sheets.
Time: (20–40) minutes.
Comments: Paper-and-pencil or computer administration available.
Author: Jerome P. Wagner.
Publisher: Western Psychological Services.
Cross References: For reviews by Frank M. Bernt and Johnnie A. Brown, see 15:274.

[2886]
WAIS-R NI.
Purpose: Constructed as a "process approach to neuropsychological assessment of cognitive functions."
Population: Ages 16–74.
Publication Date: 1991.

Scores, 14: Verbal (Information, Comprehension, Arithmetic, Similarities, Digit Span, Vocabulary, Total), Performance (Digit Symbol, Picture Completion, Block Design, Picture Arrangement, Object Assembly, Total), Total.
Administration: Individual.
Price Data, 2002: $541 per complete kit including manual (153 pages), stimulus booklet, sentence arrangement booklet, 25 response booklets, 25 record forms, 3 puzzles/boxes, spatial span board, object assembly layout shield, and 3 Koh's blocks; $1,155 per combination kit including WAIS-R NI complete kit, WAIS-R complete set and attaché case; $31 per 25 digit symbol response booklets; $110 per 25 record forms.
Time: Administration time varies by number of supplemental subtests administered.
Comments: It is necessary to have the Wechsler Adult Intelligence Scale–Revised (WAIS-R; T4:2937) complete set in order to administer WAIS-R NI.
Authors: Edith Kaplan, Deborah Fein, Robin Morris, and Dean C. Delis.
Publisher: Pearson.
Cross References: For reviews by Keith Hattrup and David C. S. Richard, see 14:412.

[2887]
Waksman Social Skills Rating Scale.
Purpose: "Developed to assist psychologists, educators, and other clinicians to identify specific and clinically important social skill deficits in children and adolescents."
Population: Grades K-12.
Publication Dates: 1983-1992.
Acronym: WSSRS.
Scores, 3: Aggressive, Passive, Total.
Administration: Individual.
Price Data, 2001: $45 per complete kit including 50 each of male and female forms, and manual (1992, 10 pages); 420 per 25 male or female forms.
Time: 10 minutes.
Author: Steven A. Waksman.
Publisher: Enrichment Press.
Cross References: See T5:2841 (1 reference) and T4:2915 (2 references); for reviews by Harold R. Keller and Ellen McGinnis, see 10:383.

[2888]
Walden Structured Analysis and Design Concepts Proficiency Test.
Purpose: "Evaluates candidate's knowledge of structured analysis and design methodology, as well as commonly used tools and techniques."
Population: Candidates for EDP systems analysts/designers.
Publication Date: 1983.
Scores: Total Score, Narrative Evaluation, Ranking, Recommendation.
Administration: Group.
Price Data, 2001: $140 per candidate.

Time: (45) minutes.
Comments: Scored by publisher; must be proctored; test previously listed as Wolfe-Winrow Structured Analysis and Design Concepts Proficiency Test.
Author: Bruce A. Winrow.
Publisher: Walden Personnel Performance, Inc. [Canada].
Cross References: For reviews by David O. Anderson and Cynthia Ann Druva-Roush, see 11:474.

[2889]

Ward Atmosphere Scale [Third Edition].

Purpose: Designed to evaluate treatment program social climates in health care settings.
Population: Patients and staff members.
Publication Dates: 1974–1996.
Acronym: WASC.
Scores, 10: Involvement, Support, Spontaneity, Autonomy, Practical Orientation, Personal Problems Orientation, Anger and Aggression, Order and Organization, Program Clarity, Staff Control.
Administration: Group.
Forms, 3: Real, Ideal, Expectations.
Price Data: Available from publisher at www.mindgarden.com/products/wascs.htm.
Foreign Language Editions: Translations available in Danish, Dutch, Finnish, French, German, Hebrew, Italian, Norwegian, Spanish, and Swedish.
Time: Administration time not reported.
Comments: Used to describe, plan for, and monitor change or improvements in treatment programs by examining patient and staff social climate perceptions.
Author: Rudolph H. Moos.
Publisher: Mind Garden, Inc.
Cross References: For reviews by Ronald A. Berk and Mary Anne Bunda, see 14:413; see also T5:2850 (3 references), T4:2925 (17 references), and T3:2587 (16 references); for a review by Earl S. Taulbee of an earlier edition, see 8:706 (31 references). For a review of the Social Climate Scales, see 8:681.

[2890]

Warehouse/Plant Worker Staff Selector.

Purpose: To assess the intellectual skills needed for the position of plant worker.
Population: Applicants for plant work.
Publication Date: 1991.
Acronym: PLANT.
Scores: Total Score, Narrative Evaluation, Ranking, Recommendation.
Administration: Group.
Price Data, 2001: $95 per candidate; quantity discounts available.
Time: (60) minutes.
Comments: Scored by publisher.

Author: Walden Personnel Performance, Inc.
Publisher: Walden Personnel Performance, Inc. [Canada].

[2891]

Washer Visual Acuity Screening Technique.

Purpose: To assess visual acuity for near and far vision in very young children and mentally challenged or low functioning individuals.
Population: Mental ages 2.5-adult.
Publication Date: 1984.
Acronym: WVAST.
Scores, 6: Farpoint (Both Eyes, Right Eye, Left Eye), Nearpoint (Both Eyes, Right Eye, Left Eye).
Administration: Individual.
Price Data: See www.ststesting.com for up-to-date pricing.
Time: Administration time varies.
Comments: Criterion-referenced scores.
Author: Rhonda Wiczer Washer.
Publisher: Scholastic Testing Service, Inc.

[2892]

The Watkins-Farnum Performance Scale: A Standardized Achievement Test for All Band Instruments.

Purpose: Designed to measure performance and progress on a musical instrument.
Population: Music students.
Publication Dates: 1942–1962.
Scores: Total score only.
Administration: Individual.
Forms, 2: A, B.
Price Data: Available from publisher.
Time: [20-30] minutes.
Authors: John G. Watkins and Stephen E. Farnum.
Publisher: Hal Leonard Publishing Corporation [No reply from publisher; status unknown].
Cross References: See T2:216 (4 references); for a review by Herbert D. Wing, see 5:253 (2 references); for related reviews, see 3:1228 (4 excerpts).

[2893]

Watson-Barker Listening Test.

Purpose: To measure adult interpersonal listening abilities.
Population: Adults in business, professions, and college.
Publication Dates: 1984–1994.
Scores, 6: Evaluating Message Content, Understanding Meaning in Conversations, Understanding and Remembering Information in Lectures, Evaluating Emotional Meanings in Messages, Following Instructions and Directions, Total.
Administration: Group.
Forms, 3: A (pre-test), B (post-test), Short Form (for demonstration and listening awareness).

Price Data: Available from publisher.
Time: (40) minutes.
Comments: Administered by video tape.
Authors: Kittie W. Watson and Larry L. Barker with Charles Roberts and Patrice Johnson.
Publisher: Jossey-Bass, A Wiley Company.
Cross References: For a review by James R. Clopton, see 10:384.

[2894]

Watson-Barker Listening Test–High School Version.

Purpose: "Designed to assess overall listening ability."
Population: Grades 7–12.
Publication Dates: 1985–1991.
Acronym: HS-WBLT.
Scores, 6: Evaluating Message Content, Understanding Meaning in Conversations, Understanding and Remembering Information in Lectures, Evaluating Emotional Meanings in Messages, Following Instructions and Directions, Total.
Administration: Group.
Forms, 2: A (pre-test) and B (post-test).
Price Data: Price information available from publisher for Form A and B package (including video tape, facilitator's guide [1991, 42 pages], and 20 answer sheets per group [A & B]).
Time: 40 minutes.
Comments: May be self-scored for awareness training; VHS video tape player and 17-inch (minimum size) color TV monitor needed; high school version of Watson-Barker Listening Test (2893).
Authors: Kittie W. Watson, Larry L. Barker, and Charles V. Roberts.
Publisher: SPECTRA Incorporated, Publishers.
Cross References: For reviews by Michael R. Harwell and by Carol Kehr Tittle and Deborah Hecht, see 11:461; for reviews by James R. Clopton and Joseph P. Stokes of the adult version, see 10:384.

[2895]

Watson-Glaser Critical Thinking Appraisal.

Purpose: Constructed to assess critical thinking abilities related to reading comprehension.
Population: Grades 9-12 and college and adults.
Publication Dates: 1942-1980.
Acronym: WGCTA.
Scores, 6: Inference, Recognition of Assumptions, Deduction, Interpretation, Evaluation of Arguments, Total.
Administration: Group or individual.
Forms, 2: A, B.
Price Data, 2006: $195 per starter kit including 10 test booklets, 25 answer documents, score key, and manual; $115 per set of 10 test booklets; $175 per set of 25 test booklets; $65 per 25 answer documents; $35 per hand scoring key; $45 per manual.
Time: (40–60) minutes.

Comments: Revision of Form YM and ZM.
Authors: Goodwin Watson and Edward M. Glaser.
Publisher: Pearson.
Cross References: See T5:2856 (13 references) and T4:2933 (5 references); for reviews by Allen Berger and Gerald C. Helmstadter, see 9:1347 (4 references); see also T3:2594 (15 references), 8:822 (49 references), and T2:1775 (35 references); for excerpted reviews by John O. Crites and G. C. Helmstadtler, see 7:783 (74 references); see also 6:867 (24 references); for reviews by Walker H. Hill and Carl I. Hovland of an earlier edition, see 5:700 (8 references); for a review by Robert H. Thouless and an excerpted review by Harold P. Fawcett, see 3:544 (3 references).

[2896]

Watson-Glaser Critical Thinking Appraisal, Short Form.

Purpose: Designed to help "select employees for any job requiring careful, analytical thinking."
Population: Adults with at least a ninth grade education.
Publication Date: 1994.
Acronym: WGCTA-S.
Scores: Composite score derived from following content areas: Inference, Recognition of Assumptions, Deduction, Interpretation, Evaluation of Arguments.
Administration: Group or individual.
Price Data, 2006: $175 per starter kit including 10 test booklets, 25 answer document, scoring key, and manual (87 pages); $95 per 10 test booklets; $145 per 25 test booklets; $60 per 25 answer documents; $35 per key for hand scoring key; $45 per manual; also available for online administration.
Time: (30–45) minutes.
Comments: Developed as a shorter version of the WGCTA Form A; Form S norms are developed from norms of original WGCTA (2895).
Authors: Goodwin B. Watson and Edward M. Glaser.
Publisher: Pearson.
Cross References: See T5:2857 (1 reference); for reviews by Kurt F. Geisinger and Stephen H. Ivens, see 13:358. For information on the original edition of the WGCTA, see T4:2933; for reviews by Allen Berger and Gerald C. Helmstadter, see 9:1347 (4 references); see also T3:2594 (15 references), 8:822 (49 references), and T2:1775 (35 references); for excerpted reviews by John O. Crites and G. C. Helmstadter, see 7:783 (74 references); see also 6:867 (24 references); for reviews by Walker H. Hill and Carl I. Hovland of an earlier edition, see 5:700 (8 references); for a review by Robert H. Thouless and an excerpted review by Harold P. Fawcett, see 3:544 (3 references).

[2897]

Ways of Coping Questionnaire.

Purpose: "To identify the thoughts and actions an individual has used to cope with a specific stressful encounter."
Population: Adults.

Publication Date: 1988.
Scores: 8: Confrontive Coping, Distancing, Self-Controlling, Seeking Social Support, Accepting Responsibility, Escape-Avoidance, Planful Problem-Solving, Positive Reappraisal.
Administration: Group.
Price Data: Available from publisher at www.mindgarden.com/products/wayss.htm.
Time: (10-15) minutes.
Comments: Self-administered.
Authors: Susan Folkman and Richard S. Lazarus.
Publisher: Mind Garden, Inc.
Cross References: See T5:2858 (129 references) and T4:2936 (25 references); for reviews by Judith C. Conger and Kathryn D. Hess, see 11:462 (16 references).

[2898]

Wechsler Abbreviated Scale of Intelligence.
Purpose: Designed as a "short and reliable measure of intelligence"; serves as a quick measure of an individual's verbal, nonverbal, and general cognitive functioning in any setting.
Population: Ages 6–89.
Publication Date: 1999.
Administration: Individual.
Price Data, 2006: $250 per complete kit; $62 per 25 record forms; $235 per 100 record forms; $130 per stimulus book; $130 per manual (238 pages).
Author: The Psychological Corporation.
Publisher: Pearson.
   a) TWO SUBTEST FORM.
   Scores, 3: Verbal (Vocabulary), Performance (Matrix Reasoning), Full Scale IQ.
   Time: (15) minutes.
   b) FOUR SUBTEST FORM.
   Scores, 7: Verbal (Vocabulary, Similarities), Performance (Block Design, Matrix Reasoning), Verbal IQ, Performance IQ, Full Scale IQ.
   Time: (30) minutes.
Cross References: For reviews by Timothy Z. Keith and by Cederick O. Lindskog and Janet V. Smith, see 14:414.

[2899]

Wechsler Adult Intelligence Scale-Fourth Edition.
Purpose: "Designed to assess the cognitive ability of adolescents and adults"; "provides subtest and composite scores that represent intellectual functioning in specific cognitive domains, as well as a composite score that represents general intellectual ability."
Population: Ages 16-0 to 90-11.
Publication Dates: 1939-2008.
Acronym: WAIS-IV.
Scores, 6: Verbal Comprehension Index, Perceptual Reasoning Index, Processing Speed Index, General Ability Index, Full Scale.
Subtests, 15: Block Design, Similarities, Digit Span, Matrix Reasoning, Vocabulary, Arithmetic, Symbol Search, Visual Puzzles, Information, Coding, Letter-Number Sequencing, Figure Weights, Comprehension, Cancellation, Picture Completion.
Administration: Individual.
Price Data, 2008: $1,079 per complete test kit including Symbol Search scoring key, Coding scoring key, Cancellation scoring templates, 25 record forms, 25 response booklet #1, 25 response booklet #2, administration and scoring manual (2008, 258 pages), technical manual (2008, 218 pages), 2 stimulus books, and Block Design block set.
Time: (59-100) minutes.
Comments: If there are significant differences between Index scores, the General Ability Index can be used to further inform interpretation; Letter-Number Sequencing, Figure Weights, and Cancellation are supplemental subtests for individuals 16-0 to 69-11 only.
Author: David Wechsler.
Publisher: Pearson.
Cross References: For reviews by Gary L. Canivez and Gregory Schraw, see 18:151; for reviews by Allen K. Hess and Bruce G. Rogers of the third edition, see 14:415; see also T5:2860 (1422 references) and T4:2937 (1131 references); for reviews by Alan S. Kaufman and Joseph D. Matarazzo of the revised edition, see 9:1348 (291 references); see also T3:2598 (576 references), 8:230 (351 references), and T2:529 (178 references); for reviews by Alvin G. Burstein and Howard B. Lyman of the original edition, see 7:429 (538 references); see also 6:538 (180 references); for reviews by Nancy Bayley and Wilson H. Guertin, see 5:414 (42 references).

[2900]

Wechsler Fundamentals: Academic Skills.
Purpose: Designed as "a brief achievement test that measures broad skills in the areas of reading, spelling, and math computation."
Population: Children Kindergarten-Grade 12, adults age 18-50.
Publication Date: 2008.
Scores, 5: Word Reading, Reading Comprehension, Reading Composite, Spelling, Numerical Operations.
Administration: Group and individual.
Forms, 2: A & B.
Price Data, 2009: $182 per examination kit Form A including 25 Summary of Skills Inventory and Word Reading record forms, 25 Spelling and Numerical Operations response booklets, 25 Reading Comprehension response booklets (5 each of Grade K-3, Grade 4-5, Grade 6-8, Grade 9-12, and Adult), word card, and administration and scoring manual (268 pages); $91 per combination set (specify Form A or Form B) including 25 Summary of Skills Inventory and Word Reading record forms, 25 Spelling and Numerical Operations response booklets, and 25 Reading Comprehension response booklets (5 each of Grade K-3, Grade 4-5, Grade 6-8,

Grade 9-12, and Adult); $44 per 25 Spelling and Numerical Operations response booklets (specify Form A or B); $10.40 per Word Card (specify Form A or Form B); $44 per 25 Summary of Skills Inventory and Word Reading record forms (specify Form A or B); $93.60 per administration and scoring manual; price information available from publisher for CD for technical and interpretive manual (83 pages).
Time: (45) minutes.
Author: Pearson.
Publisher: Pearson.
Cross References: For reviews by Susan M. Brookhart and Georgette Yetter, see 18:152.

[2901]

Wechsler Individual Achievement Test–Second Edition Abbreviated.

Purpose: "Identif[ies] and track[s] basic academic skills and intervention needs in children and adults."
Population: Grades K–16; ages 6–85 years.
Publication Date: 2001.
Acronym: WIAT-II-A.
Scores, 4: 3 subtests (Word Reading, Numerical Operations, Spelling), Composite Score.
Administration: Individual.
Price Data, 2003: $130 per test kit including manual (206 pages), combination record forms/response booklets, 2 word cards, and bag; $55 per manual; $48 per 25 combination record forms/response booklets; $15 per set of 2 word cards.
Time: (15–25) minutes.
Comments: Subtests are taken from the WIAT-II (T7:2747); can be used with Wechsler Abbreviated Scale of Intelligence (2898) for a brief cognitive and achievement battery.
Author: The Psychological Corporation.
Publisher: Pearson.
Cross References: For a review by Kathleen M. Johnson, see 15:276.

[2902]

Wechsler Individual Achievement Test-Third Edition.

Purpose: "Designed to measure the achievement of students" in prekindergarten through Grade 12 in the areas of "listening, speaking, reading, writing and mathematics."
Population: Ages 4-0 to 19-11.
Publication Dates: 1992-2009.
Acronym: WIAT-III.
Scores, 24: 16 subtests (Listening Comprehension, Early Reading Skills, Reading Comprehension, Math Problem Solving, Alphabet Writing Fluency, Sentence Composition, Word Reading, Essay Composition, Pseudoword Decoding, Numerical Operations, Oral Expression, Oral Reading Fluency, Spelling, Math Fluency-Addition, Math Fluency-Subtraction, Math Fluency-Multiplication), 8 composite scores (Oral Language, Total Reading, Basic Reading, Reading Comprehension and Fluency, Written Expression, Mathematics, Math Fluency, Total Achievement).
Administration: Individual.
Price Data, 2010: $625 per complete test kit including Scoring Assistant (Windows only); $117 per 25 record forms and 25 response booklets.
Time: Administration time varies depending on the grade level of the student and the number of subtests administered.
Comments: Examiners may choose to administer one subtest, a subset of subtests, or all 16 subtests; not all subtests contribute to the Total Achievement composite; the Math Fluency subtests do not contribute to the Total Achievement composite; the Early Reading Skills subtest and the Alphabet Writing Fluency subtest are administered to students in prekindergarten through Grade 3 but only contribute to the Total Achievement composite for prekindergarten through Grade 1; the Oral Reading Fluency subtest is administered to students in Grades 1-12 but only contributes to the Total Achievement composite for Grades 2-12; the Spelling subtest is administered to students in kindergarten through Grade 12 but only contributes to the Total Achievement composite for kindergarten through Grade 2; the publisher advises that adult norms for ages 20-50 were published in 2010.
Author: Pearson.
Publisher: Pearson.
Cross References: For reviews by M. David Miller and John T. Willse, see 18:153; for reviews by Beth J. Doll and by Gerald Tindal and Michelle Nutter of the Second Edition, see 15:275; see also T5:2861 (4 references); for reviews by Terry Ackerman and Steven Ferrara of a previous edition, see 13:359 (17 references).

[2903]

Wechsler Intelligence Scale for Children–Fourth Edition.

Purpose: Designed to assess "the cognitive ability of children"; provides four index scores that reflect different abilities, important in the expression of intelligent behavior in the classroom and beyond.
Population: Ages 6-0 to 16-11.
Publication Dates: 1971–2003.
Acronym: WISC-IV.
Scores: 15 to 20: Verbal Comprehension (Similarities, Vocabulary, Comprehension, Information [supplemental], Word Reasoning [supplemental], Total), Perceptual Reasoning (Block Design, Picture Concepts, Matrix Reasoning, Picture Completion [supplemental], Total), Working Memory (Digit Span, Letter-Number Sequencing, Arithmetic [supplemental], Total), Processing Speed (Coding, Symbol Search, Cancellation [supplemental], Total), Full Scale IQ.
Administration: Individual.

Price Data, 2006: $925 per Basic Kit in hard or soft case including administration manual (2003, 282 pages), technical manual, stimulus book #1, 25 record forms, 25 response booklet #1, 25 response booklet #2, block design set, symbol search scoring key, coding scoring key with coding recall [for use with both WISC-IV and WISC-IV Integrated], and cancellation scoring templates; $875 per Basic Kit in box; $1049 per Basic Kit with Scoring Assistant in box; $1099 per Basic Kit with Scoring Assistant in hard or soft case; $1,249 per Basic Kit with Writer in soft case; $99 per 25 record forms; $62 per 25 response booklet #1, $62 per 25 response booklet #2; $365 per 100 record forms; $235 per 100 response booklet #1; $235 per 100 response booklet #2; $210 per scoring assistant; $425 per writer; $250 per scoring assistant upgrade to writer.

Time: Core subtests (65–80) minutes; Supplemental: (10–15) minutes.

Author: David Wechsler.

Publisher: Pearson.

Cross References: For reviews by Susan J. Maller and Bruce Thompson, see 16:262; see also T5:2862 (740 references); for reviews by Jeffrey P. Braden and Jonathan Sandoval of an earlier edition, see 12:412 (409 references); see also T4:2939 (911 references); for reviews by Morton Bortner, Douglas K. Detterman, and by Joseph C. Witt and Frank Gresham of an earlier edition, see 9:1351 (299 references); see also T3:2602 (645 references); for reviews by David Freides and Randolph H. Whitworth, and excerpted reviews by Carol Kehr Tittle and Joseph Petrosko, see 8:232 (548 references); see also T2:533 (230 references); for reviews by David Freides and R. T. Osborne of the original edition, see 7:431 (518 references); for a review by Alvin G. Burstein, see 6:540 (155 references); for reviews by Elizabeth D. Fraser, Gerald R. Patterson, and Albert I. Rabin, see 5:416 (111 references); for reviews by James M. Anderson, Harold A. Delp, and Boyd R. McCandless, and an excerpted review by Laurance F. Shaffer, see 4:363 (22 references).

[2904]

Wechsler Intelligence Scale for Children–Fourth Edition Integrated.

Purpose: "Designed to assess the cognitive ability and problem-solving process of children"; provides a comprehensive measure of learning strengths and difficulties.

Population: Ages 6-0 to 16-11.

Publication Dates: 1971–2004.

Scores, 47: Verbal Comprehension Index (Similarities, Vocabulary, Comprehension, Information [supplemental], Word Reasoning [supplemental], Index), Perceptual Reasoning Index (Block Design, Picture Concepts, Matrix Reasoning, Picture Completion [supplemental], Index), Working Memory Index (Digit Span, Letter-Number Sequencing, Arithmetic [supplemental], Index), Processing Speed Index (Coding, Symbol Search, Cancellation [supplemental], Index), Full Scale IQ, Process Subtests (Similarities Multiple Choice, Vocabulary Multiple Choice, Picture Vocabulary Multiple Choice, Comprehension Multiple Choice, Information Multiple Choice, Block Design No Time Bonus, Block Design Multiple Choice, Block Design Multiple Choice No Time Bonus, Block Design Process Approach, Elithorn Mazes, Elithorn Mazes No Time Bonus, Digit Span Forward, Digit Span Backward, Visual Digit Span, Spatial Span Forward, Spatial Span Backward, Letter Span Nonrhyming, Letter Span Rhyming, Letter-Number Sequencing Process Approach, Arithmetic With Time Bonus, Arithmetic Process Approach-Part A, Arithmetic Process Approach-Part A With Time Bonus, Arithmetic Process Approach-Part B, Written Arithmetic, Cancellation Random, Cancellation Structured, Coding Recall, Coding Copy).

Administration: Individual.

Price Data, 2007: $999 per complete basic kit including administration manual (2004, 487 pages), technical and interpretive manual (2004, 343 pages), WISC-IV stimulus book 1, WISC-IV Integrated stimulus books 2 and 3, block design set, 25 WISC-IV record forms, 10 WISC-IV Integrated record forms, 10 WISC-IV response book 1, 10 WISC-IV response book 2, 10 WISC-IV Integrated response book 3, Block Design Process Approach Grid Overlays, Visual Digit Span Item Card and Sleeve, Spatial Span Board, and scoring templates; $475 per integrated writer; $79 per rolling case; $275 per integrated scoring assistant software.

Time: (65–80) minutes for the 10 core subtests; additional time required for supplemental subtests; time for Process subtests varies by number of subtests administered.

Comments: Combination of the Wechsler Intelligence Scale for Children–Fourth Edition (2903) and the revised and renormed Wechsler Intelligence Scale for Children–Third Edition as a Process Instrument; guidelines are provided for administering test to children who are deaf or hard of hearing.

Authors: David Wechsler, Edith Kaplan, Deborah Fein, Joel Kramer, Robin Morris, Dean Delis, and Arthur Maelender.

Publisher: Pearson.

Cross References: For reviews by Ronald A. Madle and by Joyce Meikamp and Carolyn H. Suppa, see 17:197; for reviews by Susan J. Maller and Bruce Thompson of the WISC-IV, see 16:262; see also T5:2862 (740 references); for reviews by Jeffrey P. Braden and Jonathan Sandoval of an earlier edition, see 12:412 (409 references); see also T4:2939 (911 references); for reviews by Morton Bortner, Douglas K. Detterman, and by Joseph C. Witt and Frank Gresham of an earlier edition, see 9:1351 (299 references); see also T3:2602 (645 references); for reviews by David Freides and Randolph H. Whitworth, and excerpted reviews by Carol Kehr Tittle and Joseph Petrosko, see 8:232 (548 references); see also T2:533 (230 references); for reviews by David Freides and R. T. Osborne of the original edition, see 7:431 (518 references); for a review by Alvin G. Burstein, see 6:540 (155 references); for reviews by Elizabeth D. Fraser, Gerald R. Patterson, and Albert I. Rabin, see 5:416 (111 references); for reviews by James M. Anderson, Harold A. Delp, and Boyd R. McCandless, and an an excerpted review by Laurance F. Shaffer, see 4:363 (22 references).

[2905]
Wechsler Memory Scale–Fourth Edition.

Purpose: Developed to "assess various memory and working memory abilities" among "individuals with suspected memory deficits or diagnosed with a range of neurological, psychiatric, and developmental disorders."
Publication Dates: 1945-2009.
Acronym: WMS-IV.
Subtest: Brief Cognitive Status Exam (optional).
Administration: Individual.
Price Data, 2009: $675 per complete test kit including administration and scoring manual (2009, 167 pages), technical and interpretive manual (2009, 258 pages), Stimulus Book #1, Stimulus Book #2, 25 Adult record forms, 25 Older Adult record forms, 25 response booklets, Design and Spatial Addition card set, scoring template, memory grid.
Comments: Roman numerals I and II indicate a subtest's immediate and delayed conditions, respectively; Standard administration guidelines require that 20-30 minutes should elapse between the completion of a subtest's immediate condition and the beginning of the delayed condition.
Author: David Wechsler.
Publisher: Pearson.
  a) ADULT BATTERY.
  Population: Ages 16-0 to 69-11.
  Time: [80-115] minutes.
  Scores, 12: 7 subtests; 6 primary (Logical Memory I, Logical Memory II, Verbal Paired Associates I, Verbal Paired Associates II, Designs I, Designs II, Visual Reproduction I, Visual Reproduction II, Spatial Addition, Symbol Span; 1 option (Brief Cognitive Status Exam); 5 indices (Auditory Memory, Visual Memory, Visual Working Memory, Immediate Memory, Delayed Memory).
  b) OLDER ADULT BATTERY.
  Population: 65-0 to 90-11.
  Time: [50-70] minutes.
  Scores, 10: 6 subtests; 5 primary (Logical Memory I, Logical Memory II, Verbal Paired Associates I, Verbal Paired Associates II, Visual Reproduction I, Visual Reproduction II, Symbol Span); 1 optional (Brief Cognitive Status Exam); 4 indices (Auditory Memory, Visual Memory, Immediate Memory, Delayed Memory).
Cross References: For reviews by Jerrell Cassady and Athena Dacanay and by Mary (Rina) M. Chittooran, see 18:154; for reviews by Rik Carl D'Amato and Cecil

R. Reynolds of the third edition, see 14:416; see also T5:2863 (431 references) and T4:2940 (117 references); for reviews by E. Scott Huebner and Robert C. Reinehr of an earlier edition, see 11:465 (166 references); see also 9:1355 (49 references), T3:2607 (96 references), 8:250 (36 references), T2:592 (70 references), and 6:561 (9 references); for reviews by Ivan Norma Mensh and Joseph Newman of the original version, see 4:364 (6 references); for a review by Kate Levine Kogan, see 3:302 (3 references).

[2906]
Wechsler Memory Scale–Third Edition Abbreviated.

Purpose: Designed to quickly assess adult memory function; to survey auditory and visual immediate and delayed memory; provides an estimate of general memory functioning when extended memory testing is not indicated or feasible.
Population: Ages 16–89.
Publication Dates: 1997–2003.
Acronym: WMS-III Abbreviated.
Scores, 11: Total Memory Composite, Delayed Memory Composite, Immediate Memory Composite, Logical Memory I, Family Pictures I, Logical Memory II, Family Pictures II, Logical Memory I–Family Pictures I, Logical Memory II–Family Pictures II, Immediate Memory Composite–Delayed Memory Composite, Predicted WMS-III General Memory Index Score.
Administration: Individual.
Price Data, 2006: $178 per complete kit including technical manual (2002, 207 pages), stimulus book, and 25 record forms; $43 per 25 record forms; $87 per stimulus book.
Time: 15–20 minutes.
Comments: Abbreviated adaptation of the Wechsler Memory Scale–Third Edition (T6:2695); provides statistics for comparing Total Memory with WAIS-III (IQ) and Serial Assessment.
Author: David Wechsler.
Publisher: Pearson.
Cross References: For reviews by Ronald K. Hambleton and by Joyce Meikamp and Carolyn H. Suppa, see 16:263.

[2907]
Wechsler Nonverbal Scale of Ability.

Purpose: Designed as a nonverbal measure of general cognitive ability.
Population: Ages 4-0 to 21-11.
Publication Date: 2006.
Acronym: WNV.
Scores, 7: Matrices, Coding, Object Assembly, Recognition, Spatial Span, Picture Arrangement, Full Scale Score.
Administration: Individual.

Levels, 2: Ages 4-0 to 7-11, 8-0 to 21-11.

Price Data, 2007: $675 per complete kit including administration and scoring manual (198 pages), technical and interpretive manual (125 pages), norms booklet (U.S./Canada), stimulus book, 25 record forms, 25 response booklets, spatial span board, object assembly puzzles, picture arrangement cards, pencil, soft cover carrying case, and Wechsler Nonverbal scoring assistant; $42 per 25 record forms; $31 per 25 response booklets; $210 per object assembly puzzle set; $163 per picture arrangement card set; $130 per administration and scoring manual; $76 per technical and interpretive manual; $26 per norms booklet (U.S./Canada); $130 per stimulus book.

Time: 2-subtest battery: (15-20) minutes; 4-subtest battery: (45) minutes.

Comments: Examinee instructions are delivered via pictorial sequences.

Authors: David Wechsler and Jack A. Naglieri.

Publisher: Harcourt Assessment, Inc.

    a) AGES 4-0 to 7-11.

    Scores: Matrices, Coding (4-subtest battery only), Object Assembly (4 subtest battery only), Recognition, Full Scale Score.

    b) AGES 8-0 to 21-11.

    Scores: Matrices, Coding (4 subtest battery only), Spatial Span, Picture Arrangement (4 subtest battery only), Full Scale Score.

Cross References: For reviews by Cleborne D. Maddux and Gerald Tindal, see 18:155.

[2908]

Wechsler Objective Language Dimensions.

Purpose: Designed to assess language skills.

Population: Ages 6 years to 16 years, 11 months.

Publication Date: 1996.

Acronym: WOLD.

Scores, 4: Listening Comprehension, Oral Expression, Written Expression, Total Composite Score.

Administration: Individual.

Price Data, 2006: £150.50 per complete kit including manual (209 pages), stimulus booklet, and 50 record forms; £52 per 50 record forms; £59.50 per manual; £59.50 per stimulus booklet.

Time: 30 minutes.

Author: David Wechsler.

Publisher: Pearson Assessment [England].

Cross References: For reviews by Judith R. Johnston and Dolores Kluppel Vetter, see 16:264.

[2909]

Wechsler Objective Numerical Dimensions.

Purpose: Intended to assess a child's progress in acquiring fundamental numeracy skills.

Population: Ages 6 years to 16 years, 11 months.

Publication Date: 1996.

Acronym: WOND.

Scores, 3: Composite Score, Mathematics Reasoning, Numerical Operations.

Administration: Individual.

Price Data, 2006: £150.50 per complete kit including manual (134 pages), stimulus booklet, and 50 record forms; £52 per 50 record forms.

Time: 30 minutes.

Author: David Wechsler.

Publisher: Pearson Assessment [England].

Cross References: For reviews by Mary L. Garner and Jerry Johnson, see 16:265.

[2910]

Wechsler Objective Reading Dimensions.

Purpose: Designed to assess literacy skills.

Population: Ages 6–16 years.

Publication Dates: 1990–1993.

Acronym: WORD.

Scores, 4: Basic Reading, Spelling, Reading Comprehension, Total Composite Score.

Administration: Individual.

Price Data, 2006: £150.50 per complete kit including manual (1993, 157 pages), stimulus booklet, and 50 record forms; £52 per 50 record forms.

Time: (20) minutes.

Author: David Wechsler.

Publisher: Pearson Assessment [England].

Cross References: For reviews by Thomas Emerson Hancock and Alfred P. Longo, see 16:266.

[2911]

Wechsler Preschool and Primary Scale of Intelligence–Third Edition.

Purpose: Developed "for assessing the intelligence of young children."

Population: Ages 2-6 to 3-11, ages 4-0 to 7-3.

Publication Dates: 1949–2002.

Acronym: WPPSI-III.

Administration: Individual.

Price Data, 2006: $850 per complete box kit including all necessary stimulus and manipulative materials, administration and scoring manual (2002, 267 pages), technical and interpretive manual (2002, 228 pages), 25 record forms for ages 2-6 to 3-11, 25 record forms for ages 4-0 to 7-3, and 25 response booklets; $899 per complete kit including materials listed above (specify attaché or soft-sided case); $999 per complete kit with WPPSI-III Scoring Assistant in box; $1050 per complete kit with WPPSI-III Scoring Assistant in attaché or soft-sided case; $1225 per complete kit in soft-sided case with WPPSI-III Writer; $155 per complete manual including both administration and scoring manual and technical and interpretive manual; $130 per administration and scoring manual; $130 per technical and interpretive manual; $130 per stimulus booklet (specify 1 or

2); $62 per 25 response booklets; $235 per 100 response booklets; $62 per 25 record forms for ages 2-6 to 3-11; $235 per 100 record forms for ages 2-6 to 3-11; $99 per 25 record forms for ages 4-0 to 7-3; $365 per 100 record forms for ages 4-0 to 7-3; $210 per WPPSI-III Scoring Assistant (CD-ROM); $425 per WPPSI-III Writer including a comprehensive user's manual; $299 per WPPSI-III Scoring Assistant to Writer Upgrade including a CD-ROM and comprehensive user's manual.
Author: David Wechsler.
Publisher: Pearson.

> *a*) 2:6–3:11 AGE BAND.
> **Population**: Ages 2-6 to 3-11.
> **Scores, 7 to 9**: Verbal (Receptive Vocabulary, Information, Picture Naming [supplemental], Total), Performance (Block Design, Object Assembly, Total), Global Language Composite [supplemental], Total.
> **Time**: (30–45) minutes.
> *b*) 4:0–7:3 AGE BAND.
> **Population**: Ages 4-0 to 7-3.
> **Scores, 10 to 19**: Verbal (Information, Vocabulary, Word Reasoning, Comprehension [supplemental], Similarities [supplemental], Receptive Vocabulary [optional], Picture Naming [optional], Total), Performance (Block Design, Matrix Reasoning, Picture Concepts, Picture Completion [supplemental], Object Assembly [supplemental], Total), Global Language Composite [optional], Total.

Cross References: For reviews by Ronald A. Madle and by Merilee McCurdy and Lynae A. Johnsen, see 16:267; see also T5:2864 (146 references) and T4:2941 (38 references); for reviews by Bruce A. Bracken and Jeffery P. Braden of an earlier edition, see 11:466 (118 references); for a review by B. J. Freeman, see 9:1356 (33 references); see also T3:2608 (280 references), 8:234 (84 references), and T2:538 (30 references); for reviews by Dorothy H. Eichorn and A. B. Silverstein, and excerpted reviews by C. H. Ammons and by O. A. Oldridge and E. E. Allison, see 7:434 (56 reference).

[2912]

Wechsler Test of Adult Reading.

Purpose: Developed as an assessment tool for estimating premorbid (pre-injury) intellectual functioning and to predict a person's pre-injury IQ and memory abilities.
Population: Ages 16–89.
Publication Date: 2001.
Acronym: WTAR.
Scores: Total score only.
Administration: Individual.
Price Data, 2006: $125 per complete kit including manual, 25 record forms, word card, and audiotape; $45 per 25 record forms.
Time: (5–10) minutes.
Comments: Co-normed with the Wechsler Adult Intelligence Scale–Third Edition (T7:2746) and the Wechsler Memory Scale–Third Edition (T7:2751); U.K. norms available.
Author: The Psychological Corporation.
Publisher: Pearson.
Cross References: For reviews by Nora M. Thompson and Sandra Ward, see 16:268.

[2913]

Weidner-Fensch Speech Screening Test.

Purpose: Designed "to be used in screening out children with speech difficulties from those who have normally developed speech."
Population: Grades 1–3.
Publication Date: No date.
Scores: Item scores only.
Administration: Individual.
Forms, 2: A, B.
Price Data, 2001: $4 per specimen set.
Time: (5–10) minutes.
Authors: William E. Weidner and Edwin A. Fensch.
Publisher: Psychometric Affiliates.
Cross References: For a review by Kris L. Baack, see 16:269.

[2914]

Weiss Comprehensive Articulation Test.

Purpose: "For making a thorough diagnosis of articulation and its associated parameters."
Population: All ages.
Publication Dates: 1978–1980.
Acronym: WCAT.
Scores, 5: Articulation, Articulation Age, Intelligibility, Stimulability, Number of Misarticulations.
Administration: Individual.
Forms, 2: Nonreading Subjects, Reading Subjects.
Price Data, 2011: $143 per complete kit including picture cards, sentence card, 50 picture response forms, 50 sentence response forms, and manual (1980, 32 pages); $46 per 100 picture response forms; $46 per 100 sentence response forms.
Time: [20] minutes.
Author: Curtis E. Weiss.
Publisher: PRO-ED.
Cross References: See T5:2866 (5 references) and T4:2942 (2 references); for a review by Richard J. Schissel, see 9:1357.

[2915]

WeldTest (Form AC).

Purpose: Designed for selecting and evaluating journey-level, industrial welders.
Population: Welding job applicants.
Publication Dates: 1984-2007.
Scores: 7 areas: Print Reading, Welding/Cutting Torch and Arc Air Cutting, Welder Maintenance and Operation,

Tools/Machines/Material and Equipment, Mobile Equipment and Rigging, Production Welding Practices, Total.
Administration: Group.
Price Data, 2011: $22 per consumable self-scoring test booklet or online test administration; $24.95 per manual (2005, 16 pages).
Time: (60-70) minutes.
Comments: Self-scoring instrument; available for online test administration.
Author: Roland T. Ramsay.
Publisher: Ramsay Corporation.
Cross References: For reviews by John Peter Hudson, Jr. and David C. Roberts of an earlier edition, see 13:360.

[2916]

Wellness Evaluation of Lifestyle [2004 Update].

Purpose: Designed to help respondents make healthy lifestyle choices based on their responses to each of the five life tasks and subtasks defined in the Wheel of Wellness; the life tasks of spirituality, self-direction, work & leisure, friendship, and love interact with a variety of life forces and global events.
Population: Ages 18 and over.
Publication Dates: 1994–2004.
Acronym: WEL.
Scores, 21: Spirituality, Self-Direction, Sense of Worth, Sense of Control, Realistic Beliefs, Emotional Awareness and Coping, Intellectual Stimulation, Problem Solving and Creativity, Sense of Humor, Nutrition, Exercise, Self-Care, Stress Management, Gender Identity, Culture Identity, Work, Leisure, Friendship, Love, Total Wellness, Perceived Wellness.
Administration: Group or individual.
Price Data: Available from publisher.
Time: (15–20) minutes.
Comments: Web-based administration and reporting available at www.mindgarden.com/products/wells.htm.
Authors: Jane E. Myers, Thomas J. Sweeney, and J. Melvin Witmer.
Publisher: Mind Garden, Inc.
Cross References: For reviews by Richard F. Farmer and Trenton R. Ferro, see 16:270; for reviews by Andrew A. Cox and Ashraf Kagee of a previous edition, see 15:277.

[2917]

Welsh Figure Preference Test.

Purpose: A nonverbal approach to personality measurement and research incorporating the Barron-Welsh Art Scale.
Population: Ages 6 and over.
Publication Dates: 1959-1980.
Acronym: WFPT.
Scores, 27: Like, Don't Like, Repeat, Conformance, Origence, Intellectence, Female Response, Movement, Figure Ground, Shading, Black, Anxiety, Repression, Conformity, Neuropsychiatric, Consensus Like, Female-Male, Children, Figure Ground Reversal, Sex Symbol (male and female).
Administration: Group or individual.
Price Data: Available from publisher at www.mindgarden.com/products/wfpts.htm.
Time: (50) minutes.
Comments: For research use only; self-administering.
Author: George S. Welsh.
Publisher: Mind Garden, Inc.
Cross References: See T5:2869 (1 reference) and T4:2945 (5 references); for a review by Julien Worland, see 9:1360 (1 reference); see also T3:2613 (4 references), T2:1437 (34 references), and P:287 (24 references); for a review by Harold Borko and an excerpted review by Gordon V. Anderson, see 6:197 (20 references); for information for Barron-Welsh Art Scale, see T3:243 (15 references).

[2918]

Wepman's Auditory Discrimination Test, Second Edition.

Purpose: Measures children's ability to hear spoken English accurately, specifically to "discriminate between commonly used phonemes in the English language."
Population: Ages 4-8 years.
Publication Dates: 1958–1987.
Acronym: ADT.
Scores: Total score yielding Qualitative score, Standard score, Percentile rank.
Administration: Individual.
Forms, 2: 1A, 2A.
Price Data, 2006: $109.50 per complete kit including 200 tests (100 each of Forms 1A and 2A) and manual (1987, 58 pages); $40 per 100 tests (specify form); $44 per manual.
Time: 5 minutes.
Authors: Joseph M. Wepman (test) and William M. Reynolds (manual).
Publisher: Western Psychological Services.
Cross References: See T5:2870 (5 references) and T4:2946 (1 reference); for a review by Mary Pannbacker and Grace Middleton, see 11:467 (5 references); see also T3:226 (31 references), 8:932 (74 references), and T2:2028 (82 references); for a review by Louis M. Di-Carlo of the original edition, see 6:940 (2 references).

[2919]

Wesman Personnel Classification Test.

Purpose: Developed to measure verbal reasoning and numerical ability.
Population: Grades 10-12 and applicants and employees.
Publication Dates: 1946-1965.
Acronym: PCT.
Scores, 3: Verbal, Numerical, Total.
Administration: Group or individual.
Forms, 3: A, B, C.

Price Data, 2006: $90 per starter kit, including 25 test booklets (specify form) and manual (1965, 28 pages).
Time: 28 minutes.
Author: Alexander G. Wesman.
Publisher: Pearson.
Cross References: See T5:2871 (4 references), T4:2947 (5 references), T3:2614 (4 references), and T2:480 (2 references); for a review by Arthur C. Mac-Kinney, and an excerpted review by Jack C. Merwin, see 7:400 (7 references); see also 5:399 (8 references); for reviews by John C. Flanagan and Erwin K. Taylor, see 4:331 (3 references); for an excerpted review, see 3:253.

[2920]
The Wessex Head Injury Matrix.

Purpose: "Designed to assess and monitor recovery in patients after severe head injury."
Population: Ages 16 and over.
Publication Date: 2000.
Acronym: WHIM.
Scores: Not scored.
Administration: Individual.
Price Data, 2006: £69 per complete kit including manual and 25 scorint sheets; £71 per 50 scoring sheets.
Time: Untimed.
Authors: Agnes Shiel, Barbara A. Wilson, Lindsay McLellan, Sandra Horn, and Martin Watson.
Publisher: Pearson Assessment [England].
Cross References: For reviews by Sandra D. Haynes and H. Dennis Kade, see 17:198.

[2921]
Western Aphasia Battery-Revised.

Purpose: "Designed to evaluate a patient's language function following stroke, dementia, or other acquired neurological disorder."
Population: Adults with acquired neurological disorders.
Publication Dates: 1980-2007.
Acronym: WAB-R.
Scores, 16: Spontaneous Speech (Information Content, Fluency/Grammatical Competence and Paraphasias, Total), Auditory Verbal Comprehension (Yes/No Questions, Auditory Word Recognition, Sequential Commands, Total), Repetition, Naming and Word Finding (Object Naming, Word Fluency, Sentence Completion, Responsive Speech, Total), Language Quotient, Cortical Quotient, Aphasia Quotient.
Administration: Individual.
Forms, 3: Part 1, Part 2, Bed-Side Administration.
Price Data, 2010: $318 per complete kit including examiner's manual (2007, 153 pages), stimulus book, 25 record forms, 25 bedside record forms, Raven's Progressive Matrices test booklet, and manipulatives; $43 per 20 record forms (Part 1); $32 per 10 record forms (Part 2); $27 per 25 bedside record forms; $124 per stimulus book; $65 per manipulative set; $81 per examiner's manual.

Time: (30-45) minutes for full battery; (15) minutes for bedside administration; (45-60) minutes for the Reading, Writing, Apraxia Constructional, Viuospatial, Calculation, and Supplemental Writing and Reading sections administration.
Comments: Utilizes criterion-referenced scores.
Author: Andrew Kertesz.
Publisher: Pearson.
Cross References: For reviews by Shawn K. Acheson and by Andrew S. Davis and W. Holmes Finch, see 18:156; see T5:2873 (74 references) and T4:2949 (33 references); for a review by Francis J. Pirozzolo of an earlier edition, see 9:1362 (1 reference).

[2922]
The Western Personality Inventory.

Purpose: Combines the Manson Evaluation and the Alcadd Test to predict the likelihood of alcoholic addiction or abuse.
Population: Adults.
Publication Dates: 1963–1988.
Acronym: WPI.
Scores, 14: Anxiety, Depressive Fluctuations, Emotional Sensitivity, Resentfulness, Incompleteness, Aloneness, Interpersonal Relations, Total, Regularity of Drinking, Preference for Drinking over Other Activities, Lack of Controlled Drinking, Rationalization of Drinking, Excessive Emotionality, Total.
Administration: Individual or group.
Manual: No manual; use manuals for The Manson Evaluation and The Alcadd Test.
Price Data, 2006: $104.50 per complete kit including 5 AutoScore test forms, 2 prepaid mail-in answer sheets for computer scoring and interpretation, Manson Evaluation Manual, and Alcadd Manual; $49.50 per Manson Evaluation Manual or Alcadd Manual; $11.55 per mail-in answer sheet.
Time: 10 to 20 minutes.
Comments: Combination of The Manson Evaluation (1606) and The Alcadd Test (137).
Author: Morse P. Manson.
Publisher: Western Psychological Services.

[2923]
The WH Question Comprehension Test: Exploring the World of WH Question Comprehension for Students With an Autism Spectrum Disorder.

Purpose: Designed to indicate a student's competence in WH question form comprehension through appropriate match of question form and response.
Population: Ages 3 and up with cognitive impairments.
Publication Dates: 2002-2004.
Scores: 6 areas: Who, What, Where, When, Why, How.
Administration: Individual.
Price Data, 2006: $25 per combination test booklet/manual (2004, 175 pages).
Time: (20-30) minutes.

Comments: Test can be administered in multiple sessions if necessary.
Author: Beverly Vicker.
Publisher: Indiana Resource Center for Autism.
Cross References: For reviews by Francine Conway and Doreen W. Fairbank, see 17:199.

[2924]
What Do You Say?

Purpose: Designed as a self-assessment tool to identify communication style and relate it to two basic types of human interactions: parent-child (McGregor's Theory X) and adult-adult (Theory Y).
Population: Employees.
Publication Dates: 1986–1991.
Scores, 4: Empathic, Critical, Searching, Advising.
Administration: Group or individual.
Price Data: Price available from publisher for complete kit including 20 inventories, 20 answer sheets, and 20 interpretation booklets.
Time: [20] minutes administration; [10] minutes scoring; [30-60] minutes interpretation.
Comments: Self-administered, self-scored.
Author: Training House, Inc.
Publisher: Training House, Inc.
Cross References: For reviews by William L. Deaton and Gerald L. Stone, see 12:413.

[2925]
Whisler Strategy Test.

Purpose: "To discover how effective the individual is in drawing on his abilities and knowledges to demonstrate his general competence."
Population: Business and industry.
Publication Dates: 1955–1961.
Scores, 6: 4 direct scores (Number Circled-Boldness, Number Attempted-Speed, Number Right-Accuracy, Net Strategy), and 2 derived scores (Caution, Hypercaution).
Administration: Group.
Price Data: Available from publisher.
Time: (25) minutes.
Comments: Measures "intelligence action" or strategic ability.
Author: Laurence Whisler.
Publisher: Psychometric Affiliates.
Cross References: See T5:2877 (1 reference) and T2:2292 (1 reference); for reviews by Jean Maier Palormo and Paul F. Ross, see 6:1110 (1 reference).

[2926]
The Whitener Group Industrial Assessments.

Purpose: "Designed to measure an individual's knowledge of competencies related specifically to industrial occupations. These assessments consist of only a written portion; intended for evaluating individuals with a combination of education, training, and work experience." Suggested uses include: selecting skilled workers (worry free); giving promotions based on objective, verifiable standards; providing blueprints for employee development; analyzing job requirements; and developing precise job descriptions, training curriculum, performance analysis charts, objective performance appraisals, valid interview protocol, and career paths.
Population: Industrial and potential industrial employees.
Publication Dates: 1996–2002.
Scores: Duty support scores and total scores are reported for 23 tests: Die Making, Electricity/Electronics, Electrical/Electronics Maintenance, General Industrial/Mechanical, General Maintenance, General Technical Skills, Industrial Maintenance Technician, Instrumentation and Control, Industrial Mechanic, Instrumentation and Electrician Technician, Lead Maintenance, Machine Repair, Maintenance, Maintenance Mechanic, Maintenance and Repair Mechanic, Maintenance Technician, Manufacturing Technician, Master Machine Repair, Mechanical Systems, Mechanical and Fluid Power Maintenance, Mechanical Maintenance, Pipefitter, Toolmaker.
Administration: Group.
Price Data, 2005: $75 per standardized industrial test, online or paper/pencil administration, including instructions for administration, scoring, and reporting services; contact publisher for pricing information on customized assessment services.
Time: (180) minutes per test.
Comments: Previously listed as NOCTI Industrial Assessments.
Authors: National Occupational Competency Testing Institute/The Whitener Group.
Publisher: National Occupational Competency Testing Institute/The Whitener Group.

[2927]
Who Am I?

Purpose: Assesses "a child's readiness for particular types of learning experiences and identifies the levels that children have reached in their understanding and use of conventional symbols and relevant early learning skills."
Population: Preschool–Year 2 in Australian school system.
Publication Date: 1999.
Scores, 4: Copying, Symbols, Drawing, Total.
Administration: Group or individual.
Price Data, 2006: A$59.95 per specimen set including task booklet, assessment manual (36 pages), and administration instructions; A$27.50 per 10 task booklets; A$44.95 per assessment manual; A$9.95 per administration instructions.
Time: (10–20) minutes.
Authors: Marion de Lemos and Brian Doig.
Publisher: Australian Council for Educational Research Ltd. [Australia].
Cross References: For reviews by G. Michael Poteat and Donald L. Stovall, see 15:278.

[2928]

Wide Range Achievement Test–Expanded Early Reading Assessment.

Purpose: Designed to measure "pre-reading and beginning reading skills."
Population: Ages 4.6–7.11.
Publication Date: 2003.
Acronym: ERA.
Scores, 7: Pre-Reading Skills (Letter/Word Discrimination, Letter-Sound Discrimination, Total), Reading Skills (Word Reading, Sentence Reading, Total), Total.
Administration: Individual.
Price Data, 2006: $210 per complete kit including manual (112 pages), flipbook, and 25 record forms.
Time: (35) minutes.
Author: Gary J. Robertson.
Publisher: Psychological Assessment Resources, Inc.
Cross References: For reviews by Leslie Eastman Lukin and Patrick P. McCabe, see 16:271.

[2929]

Wide Range Achievement Test–Expanded Edition.

Purpose: An achievement test battery "designed to assess the core curricular domains of reading, mathematics, and oral and written language."
Population: Grades 2–12; Ages 5–24.
Publication Dates: 2001-2002.
Comments: Designed to complement the WRAT-3.
Author: Gary J. Robertson.
Publisher: Psychological Assessment Resources, Inc.
a) WRAT-EXPANDED GROUP ASSESSMENT (FORM G).
Population: Grades 2–12.
Scores, 5: Reading (Basic Reading, Reading Comprehension), Mathematics, Nonverbal Reasoning.
Administration: Group.
Levels, 5: G-1 (Grade 2), G-2 (Grades 3–4), G-3 (Grades 5–6), G-4 (Grades 7–9), G-5 (Grades 10–12).
Price Data, 2006 : $250 per WRAT–Expanded Group Assessment (Form G) comprehensive package including 10 booklets and scoring forms for each level, manuals for each level (2001, 71–75 pages each), and technical supplement (2001, 80 pages).
Time: (125–135) minutes.
b) WRAT-EXPANDED INDIVIDUAL ASSESSMENT (FORM I).
Population: Ages 5–24.
Scores, 5: Reading, Mathemaics, Listening Comprehension, Oral Expression, Written Language.
Administration: Individual.
Time: [30] minutes.
Cross References: For reviews by George Engelhard, Jr., and by Bo Zhang and Cindy M. Walker, see 16:272.

[2930]

Wide Range Achievement Test 4.

Purpose: Designed to "measure the basic academic skills of reading, spelling, and math computation."
Population: Ages 5-94.
Publication Dates: 1940-2006.
Acronym: WRAT4.
Scores, 5: Word Reading, Sentence Comprehension, Spelling, Math Computation, Reading Composite.
Administration: Individual and group.
Levels, 2: Ages 5-7, Ages 8-94.
Forms, 3: Blue, Green, Combined.
Price Data, 2009: $250 per professional manual (2006, 494 pages), 25 blue test/response forms, 25 green test/response forms, 25 blue sentence comprehension response booklets, 25 green sentence comprehension response booklets, set of 2 word reading/spelling cards, set of 3 sentence comprehension cards, and 1 place marker.
Time: (15-45) minutes.
Comments: "The Blue Form and the Green Form can be used interchangeably with comparable results, thus permitting retesting within short periods of time without the potential practice effects that may occur from repeating the same items."
Authors: Gary S. Wilkinson and Gary J. Robertson.
Publisher: Psychological Assessment Resources, Inc.
Cross References: For reviews by Kathryn E. Hoff and Mark E. Swerdlik and by Darrell L. Sabers and Amy M. Olson, see 18:157; see T5:2879(237 references); for reviews by Linda Mabry and Annie W. Ward of the WRAT3, see 12:414 (111 references); see also T4:2956 (121 references); for reviews by Elaine Clark and Patti L. Harrison, see 10:389 (161 references); for reviews by Paula Matuszek and Philip A. Saigh of an earlier edition, see 9:1364 (103 references); see also T3:2621 (249 references), 8:37 (117 references), and T2:50 (35 references); for reviews by Jack C. Merwin and Robert L. Thorndike of an earlier edition, see 7:36 (49 references); see also 6:27 (15 references); for reviews by Paul Douglas Courtney, Verner M. Sims, and Louis P. Thorpe of the 1946 edition, see 3:21.

[2931]

Wide Range Achievement Test Fourth Edition Progress Monitoring Version.

Purpose: Designed "to monitor the progress of students with learning difficulties, students in special education placements, underachieving students in regular education, or students who exhibit other conditions that affect school learning."
Population: Ages 5-94.
Publication Dates: 1940-2006.
Acronym: WRAT4-PMV.
Scores, 4: Word Reading, Sentence Comprehension, Spelling, Math Computation.
Administration: Group.

Levels, 6: Level 1 (Grades K-1), Level 2 (Grades 2-3), Level 3 (Grades 4-5), Level 4 (Grades 6-8), Level 5 (Grades 9-12), Level 6 (Grades 13-16).
Forms, 4: Form 1, Form 2, Form 3, Form 4.
Price Data, 2009: $288 per introductory kit including professional manual, 25 level equivalent profile forms, 25 word reading record sheets, 1 word reading list card, 25 sentence comprehension record booklets, set of 3 sentence comprehension cards, 25 spelling response booklets, 1 spelling card, 25 math computation response booklets, and math computation cards.
Time: (15) minutes.
Comments: Adaptation of the Wide Range Achievement Test 4 (2930).
Authors: Gale H. Roid and Mark F. Ledbetter, with significant contributions by Melissa Messer.
Publisher: Psychological Assessment Resources, Inc.
Cross References: For reviews by William D. Schafer and John J. Venn, see 18:158.

[2932]

Wide Range Assessment of Memory and Learning, Second Edition.

Purpose: Designed for use in "clinical assessments of memory including evaluation of immediate and/or delay recall as well as differentiating between verbal, visual or more global memory deficits."
Population: Ages 5–90.
Publication Dates: 1990–2003.
Acronym: WRAML2.
Scores, 25: Verbal Memory (Story Memory, Verbal Learning, Total), Visual Memory (Design Memory, Picture Memory, Total), Attention/Concentration (Finger Windows, Number Letter, Total), General Memory; Optional scores: Working Memory (Verbal Working Memory, Symbolic Working Memory, Total), Verbal Recognition (Story Recognition, Verbal Learning Recognition, Total), Visual Recognition (Design Recognition, Picture Memory Recognition, Total), General Recognition, Sound Symbol, Sentence Memory, Story Memory Recall, Verbal Learning Recall, Sound Symbol Recall.
Administration: Individual.
Price Data, 2006: $475 per complete kit including administration and technical manual (2003, 245 pages), 25 examiner forms, 25 Picture Memory response forms, 2 Picture Memory Recognition forms, 2 china markers, 25 Design Memory response forms, 25 Design Memory Recognition forms, 4 Picture Memory plates, 5 Design Memory cards, 1 Finger Windows board, 2 Symbolic Working Memory boards, and soft canvas briefcase; $195 per scoring software (CD-ROM) including unlimited scoring and reports.
Time: [60] minutes.
Authors: David Sheslow and Wayne Adams.
Publisher: Psychological Assessment Resources, Inc.
Cross References: For reviews by Thomas M. Dunn and Sandra D. Haynes, see 16:273; see also T5:2880 (7 references); for reviews by Richard M. Clark and Frederic J. Medway of a previous edition, see 11:470.

[2933]

Wide Range Assessment of Visual Motor Abilities.

Purpose: A standardized assessment of visual-motor, visual-spatial, and fine motor skills.
Population: Ages 3–17 years.
Publication Date: 1995.
Acronym: WRAVMA.
Scores, 4: Fine Motor, Visual-Spatial, Visual-Motor, Visual-Motor Integration Composite.
Administration: Individual.
Price Data, 2006: $260 per introductory kit including manual (151 pages), 25 drawing forms, 25 visual matching forms, 25 examiner record forms, pegboard and pegs, pencils, markers, and sharpener, all in a soft-side canvas attache' case.
Time: (15–30) minutes; (5–10) minutes per subtest.
Comments: Best results when "integrated with data from other standardized tests and clinical observations"; test should be interpreted by "those with graduate or equivalent professional training in cognitive assessment."
Authors: Wayne Adams and David Sheslow.
Publisher: Psychological Assessment Resources, Inc.
Cross References: For reviews by Linda K. Bunker and Keith F. Widaman, see 14:418.

[2934]

Wide Range Intelligence Test.

Purpose: "Designed to measure an individual's cognitive abilities."
Population: Ages 4–85.
Publication Date: 2000.
Acronym: WRIT.
Scores, 7: Verbal (Verbal Analogies, Vocabulary, Total), Visual (Matrices, Diamonds, Total), Total.
Administration: Individual.
Price Data, 2006: $275 per regular introductory kit including test manual, Matrices and Diamonds easel stimulus book, 25 examiner forms, and set of 21 Diamond Chips, all packaged in a canvas carrying case.
Time: (20–30) minutes.
Authors: Joseph Glutting, Wayne Adams, and David Sheslow.
Publisher: Psychological Assessment Resources, Inc.
Cross References: For reviews by Terry A. Stinnett and Keith F. Widaman, see 15:279.

[2935]

Wide Range Interest and Occupation Test, Second Edition.

Purpose: Designed to provide participants "with a better understanding of themselves, the types of occupations they prefer, their pattern of likes and dislikes among work-related activities, and the intensity and consistency of their response pattern."
Population: Ages 9–80.
Publication Dates: 1970–2003.
Acronym: WRIOT2.

Scores, 39: Occupational Cluster (Art, Music, Drama, Sales, Management, Clerical–Office, Personal Service, Food Service, Cleaning Service, Protective Service, Social Service, Science, Health Care, Build and Repair, Factory and Assembly Line, Heavy Equipment and/or Machine Operation, Plants and Animals); Interest Cluster (Spoken Words, Numbers, People, Things, Perceived Ability, Income, Leadership, Strenuous, Outdoors, Risk, Creative, Routine, Likes, Dislikes, Occupational Clarity, Inconsistency) Holland Type Cluster (Realistic, Investigative, Artistic, Social, Enterprising, Conventional).
Administration: Individual.
Price Data: Available from publisher.
Time: (30) minutes.
Comments: A nonverbal measure of occupational interest; previous edition called the Wide Range Interest-Opinion Test.
Authors: Joseph J. Glutting and Gary S. Wilkinson.
Publisher: Pearson.
Cross References: For reviews by Albert M. Bugaj and Caroline Manuele-Adkins, see 16:274; see also T4:2959 (1 reference); for reviews by Louis M. Hsu and Caroline A. Manuele of a previous edition, see 9:1366; for a review by Donald G. Zytowski, see 8:1029.

[2936]

The Wiesen Test of Mechanical Aptitude.

Purpose: Designed to measure mechanical aptitude for purpose of personnel selection.
Population: Applicants (18 years and older) for jobs requiring mechanical aptitude.
Publication Dates: 1997–1999.
Acronym: WTMA.
Scores, 12: Total Score and 11 research scores: Basic Machines, Movement of Simple and Complex Objects, Center of Gravity and Gravity, Basic Electricity/Electronics, Transfer of Heat, Basic Physical Properties of Matter and Materials, Miscellaneous, Academic, Kitchen Objects, Non-Kitchen Objects, Other Everyday Objects.
Administration: Individual or group.
Price Data, 2005: $215 per introductory kit including manual, 10 item booklets, 25 answer sheets, and 1 scoring key.
Time: 30 minutes.
Comments: A 60-item multiple-choice objective test.
Author: Joel P. Wiesen.
Publisher: Psychological Assessment Resources, Inc.
Cross References: For reviews by John M. Enger and Nambury S. Raju, see 14:419.

[2937]

Wife's or Husband's Marriage Questions.

Purpose: Designed to diagnose and treat marital problems.
Population: Husbands, wives.
Publication Date: 1994-2010.
Administration: Individual or group.

Forms, 2: Wife's Marriage Questions, Husband's Marriage Questions.
Manual: No manual.
Price Data, 2011: Now available only in the book, "Psychological Worksheets & Assignments," which includes all 68 tests available from publisher; $98 per book version and $48 per CD version.
Time: [15-30] minutes.
Author: Allan Roe.
Publisher: Diagnostic Specialists, Inc.

[2938]

Wiig Assessment of Basic Concepts.

Purpose: "Designed to evaluate a child's understanding and use of basic word opposites and related concepts."
Publication Date: 2004.
Acronym: WABC.
Scores, 10: Scores in 7 areas (Color/Shape, Size/Weight/Volume, Distance/Speed/Time, Quantity/Completeness, Location/Direction, Condition/Quality, Sensation/Emotion/Evaluation), Receptive raw score, Expressive raw score, Total raw score.
Administration: Individual.
Price Data, 2006: $179 per complete kit including Level 1 and Level 2 Storybooks, 50 Level 1 record forms, 50 Level 2 record forms, clipboard with calculator, Puppy Bank reinforcer with 30 Doggy Dog tokens, 75 WABC stickers, and tote bag; $29.96 per 50 Level 1-A Day at the Zoo record forms; $29.96 per 50 Level 2-A Day at the Park record forms; $4.95 per 75 WABC stickers; $14.95 per clipboard.
Time: (10-15) minutes.
Author: Elisabeth H. Wiig.
Publisher: Super Duper Publications.
  a) LEVEL 1: A DAY AT THE ZOO.
  Population: Ages 2-6 to 5-11 years.
  b) LEVEL 2: A DAY AT THE PARK.
  Population: Ages 5-0 to 7-11 years.
Cross References: For reviews by Carol M. McGregor and Thomas McKnight, see 17:200.

[2939]

Wiig Criterion Referenced Inventory of Language.

Purpose: "Designed to assist speech-language pathologists and special and regular educators in the diagnosis of children with language disorders and language delays."
Population: Ages 4 through 13.
Publication Date: 1990.
Acronym: Wiig CRIL.
Scores: 4 modules: Semantics, Morphology, Syntax, Pragmatics.
Administration: Individual.
Price Data, 2006: $299 per complete kit including Professional's Guide (63 pages), all 4 stimulus manuals, and 10 each of all four record forms; price information for the

module package (specify Semantics, Morphology, Syntax, or Pragmatics) including stimulus manual and 10 record forms available from publisher; $49 per 20 record forms (specify Semantics, Morphology, Syntax, or Pragmatics).
Time: Untimed.
Author: Elisabeth H. Wiig.
Publisher: Pearson.
Cross References: For reviews by Clinton W. Bennett and Judith R. Johnston, see 13:361.

[2940]
Wilson Driver Selection Test.

Purpose: Constructed to measure aptitudes related to safe driving.
Population: Prospective motor vehicle operators.
Publication Dates: 1961-1984.
Scores, 7: Visual Attention, Depth Visualization, Recognition of Simple Detail, Recognition of Complex Detail, Eye-Hand Coordination, Steadiness, Total.
Administration: Group.
Price Data, 2006: $149.40 per test package; $3.75 per key; $54.60 per manual (1961, 28 pages) and manual supplement (1984, 17 pages); $59.95 per specimen set.
Time: 26(50) minutes.
Author: Clark L. Wilson.
Publisher: Martin M. Bruce, Ph.D.
Cross References: For reviews by Willard A. Kerr and D. H. Schuster, see 6:1200.

[2941]
Winslow Discovery Profile.

Purpose: Measures 16 personality characteristics to assist in hiring the best available applicants for many hourly positions in organizations.
Population: Applicants for hourly positions, current employees, coaching program participants.
Publication Date: 2009.
Scores: Assessment Validity (Objectivity, Accuracy), Interpersonal Traits (Sociability, Recognition, Conscientiousness, Exhibition, Trust, Nurturance); Organizational Traits (Alertness, Structure, Order, Flexibility, Creativity, Responsibility); Dedication Traits (Ambition, Endurance, Assertiveness, Boldness, Coachability, Leadership); Self-Control Traits (Self-Confidence, Composure, Tough-Mindedness, Autonomy, Contentment, Control).
Administration: Individual or group.
Price Data: Available from publisher.
Time: (45) minutes.
Comments: Internet-based administration and results are immediately available online.
Author: Winslow Research Institute.
Publisher: Winslow Research Institute.

[2942]
Winslow Dynamics Profile.

Purpose: Measures 24 personality characteristics to aid in applicant selection and/or employee development;

can also be used for personal coaching programs and for self-improvement "to assist individuals in achieving career success and personal contentment."
Population: Applicants for positions, current employees, coaching program participants.
Publication Dates: 1995-2009.
Scores: Assessment Validity (Objectivity, Accuracy), Interpersonal Traits (Sociability, Recognition, Conscientiousness, Exhibition, Trust, Nurturance); Organizational Traits (Alertness, Structure, Order, Flexibility, Creativity, Responsibility); Dedication Traits (Ambition, Endurance, Assertiveness, Boldness, Coachability, Leadership); Self-Control Traits (Self-Confidence, Composure, Tough-Mindedness, Autonomy, Contentment, Control).
Administration: Individual or group.
Price Data, 2011: Fees range from $195-$145 per report depending on quantity purchased. Fee includes the Assessment Profile, free re-takes (when the participant's answers to the Profile are invlaid), Participant's Report, Manager's Report, Executive Report, Position Compatibility Summary Report, Group Profiles, and Sub-group Profiles.
Time: (30) minutes or less.
Comments: Previously listed as Personal Dynamics Profile; internet-based administration and delivery or reports on confidential website provided free of charge to clients.
Authors: Denis Waitley, Lem Burnham, Charles C. Kaufman, J. Michael Priddy, Joan L. Francis, Thomas A. Tutko, Bruce C. Ogilvie, and Leland P. Lyon.
Publisher: Winslow Research Institute.

[2943]
Winslow Success Profile.

Purpose: A personality assessment instrument designed to measure 11 personality characteristics of individuals; can be utilized by organizations in hiring the best available applicants for minimum hourly positions and developing current employees in those positions to their potential.
Population: Current personnel and potential employees.
Publication Dates: 1968-2009.
Scores: Assessment Validity (Objectivity, Accuracy), Competitiveness Traits (Drive, Assertiveness, Determination, Leadership), Self-Control Traits (Self-Confidence, Emotional Control, Mental Toughness), Dedication Traits (Coachability, Conscientiousness, Responsibility, Trust), Composite Traits (Competitiveness, Self-Control, Dedication).
Administration: Individual and group.
Price Data, 2010: Fee per participant ranges from $25-49 depending on quantity of Profile Passwords purchased; fee includes assessment profile, free retakes (when participant's answers are invalid) Participant's Report, Manager's Report, Executive Report, PCS Summary Forms, Group Profiles, and Subgroup Profiles.
Foreign Language Editions: Available in English, Spanish, and French.

Time: (30) minutes or less.
Comments: Previously listed as Personal Success Profile; short version of comprehensive Winslow Dynamics Profile (2942); derivation of Athletic Success Profile (aka The Athletic Motivation Inventory, AMI), which measures the mental attitudes of individuals participating in competitive sport; internet-based administration and delivery of reports.
Authors: Denis Waitley, Lem Burnham, Charles C. Kaufman, J. Michael Priddy, Linda G. Griggs, Joan L. Francis, Thomas A. Tutko, Leland P. Lyon, and Bruce C. Ogilvie.
Publisher: Winslow Research Institute.
a) PERSONAL SUCCESS SURVEY.
    Publication Dates: 1990-2009.
    Scores, 3: Ambition, Self-Confidence, Mental Toughness.
    Price Data: Available from publisher.
    Time: (10) minutes.
    Comments: This is a paper-and-pencil, self-scoring assessment, measuring 3 of the 11 personality traits in the Winslow Success Profile; derivation of the Athletic Success Profile.

[2944]

Wisconsin Behavior Rating Scale.

Purpose: "A least biased adaptive behavior scale" to "provide adequate assessment, intervention, and evaluation" of severely and profoundly retarded individuals and of persons functioning below the developmental level of 3 years.
Population: Persons functioning below the developmental level of 3 years.
Publication Dates: 1979-1991.
Acronym: WBRS.
Scores, 12: Gross Motor, Fine Motor, Expressive Language, Receptive Language, Play Skills, Socialization, Domestic Activity, Eating, Toileting, Dressing, Grooming, Total.
Administration: Group.
Price Data, 2005: $20 per 25 scales; $70 per 100 scales (1991, 12 pages); $6 per specimen set including scale and manual (1983, 30 pages).
Time: (10-15) minutes.
Comments: "The assessment is performed by interviewing informants who are most familiar with the behavior of the person being evaluated."
Authors: Agnes Song, Stephen Jones, Janet Lippert, Karin Metzgen, Jacqueline Miller, and Christopher Borreca.
Publisher: Central Wisconsin Center for the Developmentally Disabled.
Cross References: For reviews by Pat Mirenda and Harvey N. Switzky, see 11:472 (1 reference).

[2945]

Wisconsin Card Sorting Test.

Purpose: "Developed...as a measure of abstract reasoning among normal adult populations" and "has increasingly been employed as a clinical neuropsychological instrument."
Population: Ages 6.5–89.
Publication Dates: 1981–1993.
Acronym: WCST.
Scores, 11: Number of Trials Administered, Total Number Correct, Total Number of Errors, Perseverative Responses, Perseverative Errors, Nonperseverative Errors, Conceptual Level Responses, Number of Categories Completed, Trials to Complete First Category, Failure to Maintain Set, Learning to Learn.
Administration: Individual.
Price Data, 2006: $325 per introductory kit including manual (1993, 234 pages), 2 decks of cards, and 50 record booklets; $640 per WCST Computer Version Research Edition software (CD-ROM)including unlimited on screen administration, scoring, and reports with 25 record forms; $450 per WCST Scoring Program Research Edition software (CD-ROM) including unlimited scoring and reports with 25 record forms.
Time: (20–30) minutes.
Comments: Additional materials necessary for testing include a pen or pencil and a clipboard.
Authors: Robert K. Heaton, Gordon J. Chelune, Jack L. Talley, Gary G. Kay, and Glenn Curtiss.
Publisher: Psychological Assessment Resources, Inc.
Cross References: For reviews by Elaine Clark and Deborah D. Roman, see 14:420; see also T5:2892 (309 references) and T4:2967 (96 references); for reviews by Byron Egeland and Robert P. Markley of an earlier edition, see 9:1372 (11 references).

[2946]

Wisconsin Card Sorting Test–64 Card Version.

Purpose: "Developed...as a measure of abstract reasoning among normal adult populations" and "has increasingly been employed as a clinical neuropsychological instrument."
Population: Ages 6.5–89.
Publication Dates: 1981–2000.
Acronym: WCST-64.
Scores, 10: Total Number Correct, Total Number of Errors, Perseverative Responses, Perseverative Errors, Nonperseverative Errors, Conceptual Level Responses, Number of Categories Completed, Trials to Complete First Category, Failure to Maintain Set, Learning to Learn.
Administration: Individual.
Price Data, 2006: $250 per introductory kit including manual (1993, 234 pages), 50 record booklets, and 1 card deck; $540 per Computer Version 2 software (CD-ROM)including unlimited on-screen administration, scoring, and reports, with 25 record forms; $315 per Computer Version 2 Scoring Program software (CD-ROM) including unlimited scoring and reports with 25 record forms.
Time: Untimed.
Comments: Abbreviated form of the standard 128-card version of the Wisconsin Card Sorting Test (2945).
Authors: Susan K. Kongs, Laetitia L. Thompson, Grant L. Iverson, and Robert K. Heaton.

Publisher: Psychological Assessment Resources, Inc.

Cross References: For a review by Michael S. Trevisan, see 15:280; for information on the Wisconsin Card Sorting Test, Revised and Expanded, see T5:2892 (309 references) and T4:2967 (96 references); for reviews by Byron Egeland and Robert P. Markley of an earlier edition, see 9:1372 (11 references).

[2947]

The Wolfe Computer Operator Aptitude Test.

Purpose: Used "to evaluate a candidate's potential for work as a computer operator."

Population: Applicants for computer training or employment.

Publication Dates: 1979–1982.

Acronym: WCOAT.

Scores: Total score only.

Administration: Group.

Price Data, 2001: $165 per candidate.

Foreign Language Edition: French edition available.

Time: (90) minutes.

Comments: Detailed report provided on each candidate.

Author: Jack M. Wolfe.

Publisher: Rose Wolfe Family Partnership LLP [Canada].

[2948]

Wolfe-Spence Programming Aptitude Test.

Purpose: Designed as a screening test to identify persons who should receive further consideration for hiring or training for programming.

Population: Applicants in computer programming.

Publication Date: 1970.

Scores: Total score and percentile.

Administration: Group.

Price Data, 2001: $180 per candidate.

Time: (120) minutes.

Authors: Jack M. Wolfe and Richard J. Spence.

Publisher: Rose Wolfe Family Partnership LLP [Canada].

[2949]

Wonderlic Basic Skills Test.

Purpose: Designed to measure individual language and math skills; intended to serve in the selection and placement of individuals into suitable jobs that match identified skills, and the selection and placement of individuals into appropriate educational programs.

Population: Intended for high school students and adults.

Publication Dates: 1994–2003.

Acronym: WBST.

Scores, 24: Test of Verbal Skills (Word Knowledge, Sentence Construction, Information Retrieval, Verbal GED Level 1, Verbal GED Level 2, Verbal GED Level 3, Verbal GED Level Achieved, Verbal Grade Level Equivalent, Verbal Total), Test of Quantitative Skills (Explicit, Applied, Interpretive, Quantitative GED Level 1, Quantitative GED Level 2, Quantitative GED Level 3, Quantitative GED Level Achieved, Quantitative Grade Level Equivalent, Quantitative Total), Skills Composite (Skills Composite GED Level 1, Skills Composite GED Level 2, Skills Composite GED Level 3, Skills Composite GED Level Achieved, Skills Composite Grade Level Equivalent, Total Skills Composite).

Subtests, 2: Test of Verbal Skills, Test of Quantitative Skills.

Administration: Group or individual.

Forms: 2 equivalent forms for each subtest: VS-1, VS-2 for Test of Verbal Skills; QS-1, QS-2 for Test of Quantitative Skills.

Price Data: Available from publisher.

Time: (20) minutes for each subtest.

Comments: Designed for use in both education and business environments. The Verbal and Quantitative Skills subtests may be administered together or separately, and are available as separate booklets; an online version is available for administration in proctored settings. The WBST has been approved by the U.S. Department of Education for use in qualifying postsecondary students for Title IV Federal financial assistance. Schools using the WBST for this purpose must follow special procedures and guidelines published in the WBST User's Manual for Ability-to-Benefit Testing.

Authors: Eliot R. Long, Victor S. Artese, and Winifred L. Clonts.

Publisher: Wonderlic, Inc.

Cross References: For reviews by Thomas F. Donlon and Gerald S. Hanna, see 13:362.

[2950]

Wonderlic Personnel Test and Scholastic Level Exam.

Purpose: Designed for use by businesses and educational institutions to measure general cognitive ability; designed to determine whether an individual possesses the cognitive ability that is necessary to learn, be trained quickly, and solve problems at the level of complexity that is required.

Population: Ages 15 and up.

Publication Dates: 1937–2005.

Acronym: WPT and SLE.

Scores: Total score only.

Administration: Individual or group.

Forms: 6 alternate forms of the WPT, and 4 alternate forms of the SLE.

Price Data: Available from publisher.

Foreign Language and Special Editions: Chinese, French, Korean, Puerto Rican, Spanish, Swedish, U.K., Metric, large print, braille, and audio editions.

Time: 12 minutes.

Comments: An online version is available for administration in proctored settings.

Author: Wonderlic, Inc.

Publisher: Wonderlic, Inc.

Cross References: For reviews by Kurt F. Geisinger and Gregory Schraw, see 14:421; see also T5:2899 (20 references) and T4:2972 (11 references); for a review by Marcia J. Belcher of an earlier edition, see 11:475 (10 references); for reviews by Frank L. Schmidt and Lyle F. Schoenfeldt, see 9:1385 (8 references); see also T3:2638 (24 references), and T2:482 (10 references); for reviews by Robert C. Droege and John P. Foley, Jr., see 7:401 (28 references); for reviews by N. M. Downie and Marvin D. Dunnette, see 6:513 (17 references); see also 5:400 (59 references); for reviews by H. E. Brogden, Charles D. Flory, and Irving Lorge, see 3:269 (7 references); see also 2:1415 (2 references).

[2951]

Woodcock Diagnostic Reading Battery.

Purpose: "Provides a diagnostic test that assesses reading achievement and important related abilities."

Population: Ages 4 to 90+.

Publication Date: 1997.

Acronym: WDRB.

Scores, 17: Letter-Word Identification, Word Attack, Reading Vocabulary, Passage Comprehension, Incomplete Words, Sound Blending, Oral Vocabulary, Listening Comprehension, Memory for Sentences, Visual Matching, Total Reading, Broad Reading, Basic Reading Skills, Reading Comprehension, Phonological Awareness, Oral Comprehension, Reading Aptitude.

Administration: Individual.

Price Data, 2006: $374.50 per complete test kit including test book, examiner's manual (162 pages), norms tables, and 25 test records; $51 per package of 25 test records; $61 per examiner's manual.

Time: (50–60) minutes.

Comments: Battery comprises selected tests from the Woodcock-Johnson® Psycho-Educational Battery–Revised (2952); for educational, clinical, or research purposes; optional to use any combination of the subtests that are relevant to individual subjects.

Author: Richard W. Woodcock.

Publisher: Riverside Publishing.

Cross References: For reviews by D. Joe Olmi and Herbert C. Rudman, see 14:422.

[2952]

Woodcock-Johnson® III.

Purpose: Designed "to provide a co-normed set of tests for measuring general intellectual ability, specific cognitive abilities, scholastic aptitude, oral language, and academic achievement."

Population: Ages 2-90+.

Publication Dates: 1977–2001.

Acronym: WJ III®.

Administration: Individual.

Parts, 2: Tests of Cognitive Abilities, Tests of Achievement.

Price Data, 2006: $509.50 per Achievement Battery (Form A or B) including Achievement Standard and Extended test books, examiner's manual, audio cassette, 25 test records, 25 response booklets, CompuScore® and Profiles Program version 1.1b (Windows and Macintosh), technical manual, and scoring guides; $599.50 per Achievement Battery with leather carrying case (Form A or B); $70 per 25 Achievement test records and subject response booklets (Form A or B; $690 per Tests of Cognitive Abilities Battery including Cognitive Standard and Extended test books, examiner's manual, audio cassette, 25 test records, 25 response booklets, 5 Brief Intellectual ability Test Records, CompuScore® and Profiles Program version 1.1b (Windows and Macintosh), technical manual, and scoring guides; $779.50 per Tests of Cognitive Abilities Battery with leather carrying case; $70 per 25 Cognitive test records and subject response booklets; $32 per 25 Brief Intellectual Ability Test Records.

Comments: Tests can be administered separately; previous edition was entitled Woodcock-Johnson Psycho-Educational Battery–Revised; can be scored only with the Compuscore® software included or optional Report Writer; minimum system requirements: Microsoft Windows 95/98/NT 4.0/2000/Me/XP, PC with 486 processor, VGA monitor, 16 MB of RAM, 5MB of free hard disk space, Windows-supported printer (Windows System) or Apple system 7.5.5–9.1, Macintosh computer with 68020 processor, Macintosh-compatible printer (Macintosh System), 16 MB RAM, 10MB of free hard disk space; 1989 edition still available.

Authors: Richard W. Woodcock, Kevin S. McGrew, Nancy Mather; and Fredrick A. Schrank (Compuscore® and Profiles Program).

Publisher: Riverside Publishing.

a) TESTS OF ACHIEVEMENT.

Scores: 11 Standard Battery (Form A or B) test scores: Letter-Word Identification, Reading Fluency, Passage Comprehension, Story Recall, Understanding Directions, Calculation, Math Fluency, Applied Problems, Spelling, Writing Fluency, Writing Samples, and 3 Standard Battery Supplemental test scores: Story Recall–Delayed, Handwriting Legibility Scale, Writing Evaluation Scale, plus 6 Standard Battery cluster scores derived from combinations of the above test scores: Broad Reading, Oral Language-Standard, Broad Math, Math Calculation Skills, Broad Written Language, Written Expression, and 4 Supplementary Battery cluster scores: Academic Skills, Academic Fluency, Academic Applications, Total Achievement; 7 Extended Battery (Form A or B) test scores: Word Attack, Reading Vocabulary, Picture Vocabulary, Oral Comprehension, Quantitative Concepts, Editing, Academic Knowledge, and 3

Extended Battery Supplemental test scores: Spelling of Sounds, Sound Awareness, Punctuation & Capitalization, plus 9 Extended Battery cluster scores derived from combinations of standard and extended battery tests: Basic Reading Skills, Reading Comprehension, Oral Language–Extended, Oral Expression, Listening Comprehension, Math Reasoning, Basic Writing Skills, Academic Knowledge, Phoneme/Grapheme Knowledge.

Forms, 2: A, B.

Time: Approximately (5) minutes per test; (55–65) minutes for Standard Battery.

b) TESTS OF COGNITIVE ABILITIES.

Scores: 10 Standard Battery test scores: Verbal Comprehension, Visual-Auditory Learning, Spatial Relations, Sound Blending, Concept Formation, Visual Matching, Numbers Reversed, Incomplete Words, Auditory Working Memory, Visual-Auditory Learning–Delayed, plus 3 Standard Battery cluster scores: Verbal Ability, Thinking Ability, Cognitive Efficiency, and 10 Extended Battery test scores: General Information, Retrieval Fluency, Picture Recognition, Auditory Attention, Analysis–Synthesis, Decision Speed, Memory for Words, Rapid Picture Naming, Planning, Pair Cancellation plus 3 Extended Battery cluster scores: Verbal Ability, Thinking Ability, Cognitive Efficiency; 16 factor cluster scores: Comprehension–Knowledge, Long-Term Retrieval, Visual-Spatial Thinking, Auditory Processing, Fluid Reasoning, Processing Speed, Short-Term Memory, Quantitative Knowledge, Reading-Writing Ability, Phonemic Awareness, Working Memory, Broad Attention, Cognitive Fluency, Executive Processes, Delayed Recall, Knowledge.

Time: Approximately (5) minutes per test; (35–45) minutes per Standard Battery; (90–115) minutes per Extended Battery.

Cross References: For reviews by Gregory J. Cizek and Jonathan Sandoval, see 15:281; see T5:2901 (140 references); for reviews by Jack A. Cummings and by Steven W. Lee and Elaine Flory Stefany of the 1991 edition, see 12:415 (56 references); see also T4:2973 (90 references); for reviews by Jack A. Cummings and Alan S. Kaufman of the 1977 edition, see 9:1387 (6 references); see also T3:2639 (3 references).

[2953]
Woodcock-Johnson III® Diagnostic Reading Battery.

Purpose: "Measures important dimensions of phonological awareness, phonics knowledge, reading achievement, and related oral language abilities."

Population: Ages 2–80+.

Publication Date: 2004.

Acronym: WJ III DRB.

Scores, 8: Basic Reading Skills, Reading Comprehension, Phonics Knowledge, Phonemic Awareness, Oral Language Comprehension, Brief Reading, Broad Reading, Total Reading.

Subtests, 10: Letter-Word Identification, Passage Comprehension, Word Attack, Reading Vocabulary, Reading Fluency, Spelling of Sounds, Sound Awareness, Sound Blending, Oral Vocabulary, Oral Comprehension.

Administration: Individual.

Price Data, 2007: $397.25 per complete kit with carrying case including test book, audio CD package, comprehensive manual (197 pages), software package, and 25 test records and subject response booklets; $61.25 per 25 test records and subject response booklets; $67 per comprehensive manual; $146 per scoring and reporting program (Windows/Mac).

Time: (50-60) minutes.

Comments: Composed of 8 tests from the WJ III Tests of Achievement and 2 tests from the WJ III Tests of Cognitive Abilities (see Woodcock-Johnson III; 2952); includes software for scoring and printing reports.

Authors: Fredrick A. Schrank, Nancy Mather, and Richard W. Woodcock.

Publisher: Riverside Publishing.

Cross References: For reviews by Connie England and by Howard Margolis and Antonia D'Onofrio, see 17:201.

[2954]
Woodcock Language Proficiency Battery–Revised.

Purpose: Intended to measure abilities and achievement in oral language, reading, and written language as well as English language competence.

Population: Ages 2–90+.

Publication Dates: 1980-1991.

Acronym: WLPB-R.

Scores, 25: Oral Language (Memory for Sentences, Picture Vocabulary, Oral Vocabulary, Listening Comprehension, Verbal Analogies), Reading (Letter-Word Identification, Passage Comprehension, Work Attack, Reading Vocabulary), Written Language (Dictation, Writing Samples, Proofing, Writing Fluency), Punctuation and Capitalization, Spelling, Usage, Handwriting, Oral Language, Broad Reading, Basic Reading Skills, Reading Comprehension, Broad Written Language, Basic Writing Skills, Written Expression, Broad English Ability.

Administration: Individual.

Price Data, 2006: $381.50 per complete kit in English or Spanish including test book, audio cassette, 25 test records and 25 subject response booklets, examiner's manual (238 pages), and norms tables; $66 per 25 test records and 25 subject response booklets; $70.50 per examiner's manual; $56 per norms tables.

Foreign Language Edition: Spanish edition available.

Time: (20-60) minutes.

Comments: Battery is a subset of the tests included

in the Woodcock-Johnson® Psycho-Educational Battery–Revised (2952).
Authors: Richard W. Woodcock (English Form); Richard W. Woodcock and Ana F. Muñoz-Sandoval (Spanish Form).
Publisher: Riverside Publishing.
Cross References: See T5:2902 (5 references); for reviews by Irvin J. Lehmann and G. Michael Poteat, see 12:416 (3 references); see also T4:2974 (1 reference); for reviews by Ruth Noyce and Michelle Quinn, see 9:1388.

[2955]

Woodcock-Muñoz™ Language Survey– Revised.

Purpose: Designed "to provide a broad sampling of proficiency in oral language, language comprehension, reading, and writing."
Population: Ages 2–90+.
Publication Dates: 1993-2005.
Acronym: WMLS-R.
Scores, 7: Picture Vocabulary, Verbal Analogies, Letter Word Identification, Dictation, Understanding Directions, Story Recall, Passage Comprehension.
Administration: Individual.
Forms, 3: English A, English B, and Spanish.
Price Data, 2007: $323.50 per English complete kit including test book, 25 test records and 25 dictation worksheets, manual (174 pages), audio CD, and a scoring and reporting program; $323.50 per Spanish complete kit including test book, 25 test records and 25 dictation worksheets, manual (174 pages), audio CD, and a scoring and reporting program; $40.75 per package of 25 test records and 25 dictation worksheets; $90 per manual, $23 per audio CD; $118.50 per scoring and reporting program (Windows).
Foreign Language Edition: Also available in Spanish.
Time: (45-55) minutes for complete; (25) minutes for screening.
Comments: There is a computer program for scoring and generating narrative reports for any combination of tests from the test.
Authors: R. W. Woodcock, A. F. Muñoz-Sandoval, M. L. Ruef, and C. G. Alvarado.
Publisher: Riverside Publishing.
Cross References: For reviews by James Dean Brown and Salvador Hector Ochoa, see 17:202; for reviews by Linda Crocker and Chi-Wen Kao of an earlier edition, see 13:364.

[2956]

Woodcock Reading Mastery Tests–Revised [1998 Normative Update].

Purpose: To measure reading readiness, basic skills, and comprehension.
Population: Grades K through postsecondary; ages 5-0 through 75+.
Publication Dates: 1973–1998.

Scores, 11: Readiness Cluster (Visual-Auditory Learning, Letter Identification, Total), Basic Skills Cluster (Word Identification, Word Attack, Total), Reading Comprehension Cluster (Word Comprehension, Passage Comprehension, Total), Total Reading–Full Scale, Total Reading–Short Scale, plus a Supplementary Letter Checklist.
Administration: Individual.
Forms, 2: G, H (includes Reading Achievement tests only).
Price Data, 2008: $489.25 per Form G/H Kit including G & H test books, 25 each NU Form G & H test records, sample NU Form, G+H Summary record form, Pronunciation Guide Cassette, Sample Report to Parents, NU examiner manual (1998, 214 pages), and carry bag; $606.75 per Form G/H Kit with ASSIST, including ASSIST Kit, G & H test books, 25 each NU Form G & H test records, sample NU Form, G+H Summary Record Form, Pronunciation Guide Cassette, Sample Report to Parents, NU manual, and carry bag; $126.50 per examiner's manual.
Time: (10-30) minutes for each form.
Comments: Test same as 1987 edition but with 1998 norms for Grades K–12 and ages 5–22; information available from publisher for software (ASSIST) scoring and hand-scoring.
Author: Richard W. Woodcock.
Publisher: Pearson.
Cross References: For reviews by Linda Crocker and Mildred Murray-Ward, see 14:423; see also T5:2905 (123 references) and T4:2976 (34 references); for reviews by Robert B. Cooter, Jr. and Richard M. Jaeger of an earlier edition, see 10:391 (38 references); see also T3:2641 (17 references); for reviews by Carol Anne Dwyer and J. Jaap Tuinman, and excerpted reviews by Alex Bannatyne, Richard L. Allington, Cherry Houck (with Larry A. Harris), and by Barton B. Proger of the 1973 edition, see 8:779 (7 references).

[2957]

Word Fluency.

Purpose: Measures ability to produce appropriate words rapidly for fluency in verbal expression.
Population: Positions requiring sharp verbal communication skills.
Publication Dates: 1959–1961.
Scores: Total score only.
Administration: Individual or group.
Price Data, 2002: $73 per start-up kit including 25 test booklets and interpretation and research manual (1959, 30 pages); $54 per 25 test booklets (quantity discounts available); $28 per interpretation and research manual.
Time: 10 minutes.
Author: Human Resources Center, The University of Chicago.
Publisher: Pearson Performance Solutions [No reply from publisher; status unknown].

Cross References: See T5:2907 (9 references), T4:2979 (6 references), T3:2645 (1 reference), and T2:594 (2 references); for a review by James E. Kennedy, see 6:562.

[2958]

Word Identification and Spelling Test.

Purpose: Designed to "assess a student's fundamental literacy skills."
Population: Ages 7.0–18.11.
Publication Date: 2004.
Acronym: WIST.
Scores, 4: Word Identification, Spelling, Sound-Symbol Knowledge, Fundamental Literacy Ability Index.
Administration: Individual.
Levels, 2: Elementary, Secondary.
Price Data, 2011: $269 per complete kit including examiner's manual (142 pages), 25 Elementary examiner record booklets, 25 Secondary examiner record booklets, 50 Spelling response forms, word card-Regular Words, word card-Irregular Words, word card-Letter/Pseudo Words, Elementary Spelling card, Secondary Spelling card, and Irregular Spelling card; $75 per examiner's manual; $46 per 25 examiner's record booklets (specify Elementary or Secondary); $19 per 50 Spelling response forms; $19 per word card (specify Regular, Irregular or Letter/Pseudo Words); $19 per Spelling card (specify Elementary or Secondary).
Time: (40) minutes.
Authors: Barbara A. Wilson and Rebecca H. Felton.
Publisher: PRO-ED.
Cross References: For reviews by W. Joel Schneider and Kathryn E. Hoff and by John T. Willse, see 16:276.

[2959]

Word Identification Scale.

Purpose: Designed as "an informal reading survey that allows a teacher to quickly identify" a student's readability level in terms of "decoding and word recognition skills."
Population: Students in Grades 1–12.
Publication Dates: 1988–1999.
Acronym: WIS.
Scores: Total score only.
Administration: Individual.
Manual: No manual.
Price Data, 2006: $15 per complete set including plasticized word card with instructions and 50 recording forms.
Time: (5–10) minutes.
Author: John Arena.
Publisher: Academic Therapy Publications.

[2960]

Word Recognition and Phonic Skills.

Purpose: "Designed to give the teacher two assessments of a child's word recognition ability."
Population: Ages 5.0 to 8.6.
Publication Date: 1994.

Acronym: WRaPS.
Scores: Word Recognition.
Administration: Group.
Price Data, 2002: £6.99 per 10 test booklets; £10.99 per diagnostic scoring template; £10.99 per manual (31 pages); £10.99 per specimen set including one copy of test form and manual.
Time: (30) minutes.
Authors: Clifford Carver and David Moseley.
Publisher: Hodder & Stoughton Educational [England].
Cross References: For reviews by Robert G. Harrington and Joyce R. McLarty, see 14:425; see also T5:2910 (1 reference).

[2961]

The Word Test 2: Elementary.

Purpose: Designed to assess expressive vocabulary and semantics.
Population: Ages 6.0-11.11.
Publication Dates: 1981-2004.
Scores, 7: Associations, Synonyms, Semantic Absurdities, Antonyms, Definitions, Multiple Definitions, Total.
Administration: Individual.
Price Data: Available from publisher.
Time: (30) minutes.
Authors: Linda Bowers, Rosemary Huisingh, Carolyn LoGiudice, and Jane Orman.
Publisher: LinguiSystems, Inc.
Cross References: For a review by Darrell L. Sabers and Huaping Sun, see 17:203; see also T5:2911 (6 references) and T4:2983 (2 references); for reviews by Mavis Donahue and Nambury S. Raju of the original edition, see 9:1393.

[2962]

Wordchains: A Word Reading Test for All Ages.

Purpose: Designed to "screen for specific learning difficulties" and to help teachers "identify individual pupils with poor reading skills."
Population: Ages 7 and over.
Publication Date: 1999.
Scores, 2: Letterchains, Wordchains.
Administration: Individual or group.
Price Data: Available from publisher.
Time: (15) minutes.
Author: Louise Miller Guron.
Publisher: GL Assessment [England].
Cross References: For reviews by Colin Cooper and Steven R. Shaw, see 16:278.

[2963]

Work Adjustment Inventory.

Purpose: "Designed to evaluate adolescents' and young adults' temperament toward work activities, work environments, other employees, and other aspects of work."

Population: Adolescents and young adults.
Publication Date: 1994.
Acronym: WAI.
Scores, 7: Activity, Empathy, Sociability, Assertiveness, Adaptability, Emotionality, WAI Quotient.
Administration: Group or individual.
Price Data, 2006: $105 per complete kit; $50 per 50 record forms; $59 per manual.
Time: (15–20) minutes.
Author: James E. Gilliam.
Publisher: PRO-ED.
Cross References: For reviews by Mark J. Benson and Wayne J. Camara, see 13:365.

[2964]

Work Aspect Preference Scale.
Purpose: "Constructed to assess the qualities of work that individuals consider important to them."
Population: Grades 10–12 and college and adults.
Publication Dates: 1983-1999.
Acronym: WAPS.
Scores: 13 scales: Independence, Co-Workers, Self-Development, Creativity, Money, Life Style, Prestige, Altruism, Security, Management, Detachment, Physical Activity, Surroundings, plus 3 second order dimensions: On-Work Orientation, Human/Personal Concern, Freedom.
Administration: Group.
Price Data, 2005: : A$2.50 per question/answer booklet; $1.05 per profile; $75.60 per manual (41 pages).
Time: (10-20) minutes.
Author: Robert Pryor.
Publisher: Australian Council for Educational Research Ltd. [Australia].
Cross References: See T5:2915 (8 references) and T4:2987 (1 reference).

[2965]

Work Attitudes Questionnaire (Version for Research).
Purpose: "Designed to differentiate the 'workaholic' or the Type A personality from the highly committed worker."
Population: Managers.
Publication Dates: 1980–1981.
Acronym: WAQ.
Scores, 3: Work Commitment, Psychological Health, Total.
Administration: Group.
Price Data: Available from publisher (now free of charge).
Time: Administration time not reported.
Authors: Maxene S. Doty and Nancy E. Betz.
Publisher: Nancy E. Betz, Ph.D.
Cross References: For a review by Mary L. Tenopyr, see 9:1395.

[2966]

Work Engagement Profile.
Purpose: Designed to measure "intrinsic rewards and… work engagement."
Population: Employees.
Publication Dates: 1993-2009.
Acronym: WEP.
Scores, 4: Sense of Meaningfulness, Sense of Choice, Sense of Competence, Sense of Progress.
Administration: Individual.
Price Data, 2010: $14.25 per Work Engagement Profile including 1 self-scorable assessment and 1 interpretive information booklet; $134.50 per 10 copies of Work Engagement Profile including self-scorable assessments and interpretive information booklets.
Time: (12) minutes.
Comments: Earlier versions were entitled Empowerment Inventory and Profile of Intrinsic Motivation.
Authors: Kenneth W. Thomas and Walter G. Tymon, Jr.
Publisher: CPP, Inc.
Cross References: For reviews by Leslie Eastman Lukin and Patricia Schoenrade of the Empowerment Inventory, see 13:119.

[2967]

Work Environment Scale, Second Edition.
Purpose: Developed to "measure the social environment of different types of work settings."
Population: Employees and supervisors.
Publication Dates: 1974-1989.
Acronym: WES.
Scores, 10: Involvement, Peer Cohesion, Supervisor Support, Autonomy, Task Orientation, Work Pressure, Clarity, Control, Innovation, Physical Comfort.
Administration: Group.
Forms, 3: Real (R), Ideal (I), Expected (E).
Price Data, 2001: $35.50 per 25 test booklets (Form R); $49.75 per 25 test booklets (select Form I or E); $19.25 per 25 answer sheets; $44 per 25 self-scorable answer sheets; $17 per set of scoring stencils; $8.50 per 25 profiles; $37.50 per 25 interpretive report forms; $48.80 per manual (57 pages); $13.20 per preview kit (nonprepaid).
Foreign Language Edition: Spanish edition available.
Time: [15-20] minutes.
Comments: A part of the Social Climate Scales (T5:2445).
Authors: Rudolf H. Moos and Paul N. Insel (tests).
Publisher: Mind Garden, Inc.
Cross References: See T5:2917 (5 references); for reviews by Ralph O. Mueller and Eugene P. Sheehan, see 12:417 (6 references); see also T4:2989 (19 references); for a review by Rabindra N. Kanungo, see 9:1398 (1 reference); see also T3:2652 (2 references) and 8:713 (3 references). For a review of the Social Climate Scales, see 8:681.

[2968]

The Work Experience Survey.

Purpose: Designed as a "structured interview protocol for identifying barriers (and possible solutions) to career maintenance" for a disabled person.
Population: "Individuals with disabilities who are either employed or about to begin employment."
Publication Date: 1995.
Acronym: WES.
Scores: Not scored.
Administration: Individual.
Price Data: Available from publisher.
Time: (30–60) minutes.
Comments: Administered in a face-to-face or telephone interview.
Authors: Richard T. Roessler (survey and manual), Cheryl A. Reed (manual), and Phillip D. Rumrill (manual).
Publisher: The National Center on Employment & Disability.
Cross References: For reviews by Albert M. Bugaj and Lawrence H. Cross, see 14:426.

[2969]

Work Information Inventory.

Purpose: Designed to assess employee morale by utilizing the direction of perception techniques.
Population: Employee groups in industry.
Publication Date: 1958.
Acronym: WII.
Scores: Total score only.
Administration: Group.
Price Data: Available from publisher.
Time: (15) minutes.
Author: Raymond E. Bernberg.
Publisher: Psychometric Affiliates.
Cross References: For additional information and a review by Albert K. Kurtz, see 8:1057.

[2970]

Work Keys Assessments.

Purpose: A job skills assessment system that measures "real world" skills.
Population: Grades 9 to adult.
Publication Dates: 1992–1994.
Administration: Individual or group.
Price Data: Available from publisher.
Author: ACT, Inc.
Publisher: ACT, Inc.
  a) READING FOR INFORMATION ASSESSMENT.
  Purpose: "Measures the learner's skill in reading and understanding work-related instructions and policies."
  Scores: Total score only.
  Levels: 5 reading skill levels.
  Time: (45) minutes.
  b) APPLIED MATHEMATICS ASSESSMENT.
  Purpose: "Measures the learner's skill in applying mathematical reasoning to work-related problems."
  Scores: Total score only.

  Levels: 5 mathematics skill levels.
  Time: (45) minutes.
  c) LISTENING ASSESSMENT.
  Purpose: "Measures the learner's skill at listening to and understanding work-related messages."
  Scores: Total score only.
  Levels: 5 listening skill levels.
  Time: [40] minutes.
  Comments: Constructed-response; administered via audiotape; hand-scored by ACT.
  d) WRITING ASSESSMENT.
  Purpose: "Measures the learner's skill at writing work-related messages."
  Scores: Total score only.
  Levels: 5 writing skill levels.
  Time: [40] minutes.
  Comments: Constructed-response; administered via audiotape; hand-scored by ACT.
  e) LOCATING INFORMATION ASSESSMENT.
  Purpose: "Measures the learner's skill in using information taken from workplace graphics such as diagrams, floor plans, tables, forms, graphs, charts, and instrument gauges."
  Scores: Total score only.
  Levels: 4 information skill levels.
  Time: (45) minutes.
  f) TEAMWORK ASSESSMENT.
  Purpose: "Measures the learner's skill in choosing behaviors and/or actions that simultaneously support team interrelationships and lead toward the accomplishment of work tasks."
  Scores: Total score only.
  Parts: 2.
  Levels: 4 teamwork skill levels.
  Time: (62) minutes.
  Comments: Administered via videotape.
  g) APPLIED TECHNOLOGY ASSESSMENT.
  Purpose: "Measures the learner's skill in solving problems of a technological nature."
  Scores: Total score only.
  Levels: 4 applied technology levels.
  Time: (45) minutes.
  h) OBSERVATION ASSESSMENT.
  Purpose: "Measures the learner's skill in paying attention to instructions and demonstrations, and in noticing details."
  Scores: Total score only.
  Levels: 4 observation levels.
  Time: (60) minutes.
  Comments: Administered via videotape.

[2971]

[Work Motivation].

Purpose: Assesses assumptions and practices characterizing attempts to motivate employees, and evaluate employee motivational needs and values.
Population: Managers, employees.
Publication Dates: 1967–2000.

Scores, 5: Basic-Creature Comfort, Safety and Order, Belonging and Affiliation, Ego-Status, Actualization and Self-Expression.
Administration: Group.
Manual: No manual.
Price Data, 2001: $7.95 per instrument.
Time: [15-30] minutes.
Comments: Self-administered inventory.
Authors: Jay Hall and Martha Williams.
Publisher: Teleometrics International, Inc.
    a) MANAGEMENT OF MOTIVES INDEX.
    Purpose: Assesses assumptions and practices characterizing attempts to motivate employees.
    Acronym: MMI.
    b) WORK MOTIVATION INVENTORY.
    Purpose: Evaluate employee motivational needs and values.
    Acronym: WMI.
Cross References: See T3:2655 (4 references) and 8:1189 (3 references).

[2972]
Work Orientation and Values Survey.

Purpose: Identifies and categorizes 32 work values, reflecting survey taker's approach to world of work.
Population: Adult and teenage job seekers and career planners.
Publication Date: 2002.
Acronym: WOVS.
Scores, 8: Earnings and Benefits, Working Conditions, Time Orientation, Task Orientation, Mission Orientation, Coworker Relations, Supervisor Relations, Managing Others.
Administration: Group or individual.
Price Data, 2006: $24.95 per 25 inventories including copy of administrator's guide (8 pages).
Time: (15–20) minutes.
Comments: Self-administered and self-scored.
Author: Robert P. Brady.
Publisher: JIST Publishing, Inc.
Cross References: For reviews by Alan C. Bugbee, Jr. and Bert A. Goldman, see 17:204.

[2973]
Work Performance Assessment.

Purpose: Designed to assess "work-related social/interpersonal skills."
Population: Job trainees.
Publication Dates: 1987–1988.
Acronym: WPA.
Scores: 19 supervisory demands: Greet Each Trainee, Direct Trainee to Work Station and Explain Nature of Work, Provide Vague Instructions, Explain Supervisory Error, Provide Detailed Instructions, Observe Trainees Working, Stand Next to Trainee, Create a Distraction, Show New Way to Work, Introduce Time Pressure, Criticize Trainee's Work, Compliment Trainee's Work, Ask Trainees to Switch Tasks, Ask Trainees to Socialize, Direct Trainees to Work Together, Ask Trainees to Criticize Each Other, Ask Trainees to Compliment Each Other, Observe Trainees Completing the Task Together, Socialize with Each Trainee, yielding a Total Score.
Administration: Group.
Price Data: Available from publisher.
Time: (60–70) minutes.
Comments: Ratings by supervisor.
Authors: Richard Roessler, Suki Hinman, and Frank Lewis.
Publisher: The National Center on Employment & Disability.
Cross References: For reviews by Caroline Manuele-Adkins and Gerald R. Schneck, see 13:367.

[2974]
Work Personality Index.

Purpose: "Designed to identify personality traits that directly relate to work performance."
Population: High school to adult.
Publication Date: 2001.
Acronym: WPI.
Scores, 17: Teamwork, Concern for Others, Outgoing, Democratic, Attention to Detail, Rule-Following, Dependability, Ambition, Energy, Persistence, Leadership, Innovation, Analytic Thinking, Self-Control, Stress Tolerance, Initiative, Flexibility, and 5 factors: Achievement, Conscientiousness, Social Orientation, Practical Intelligence, Adjustment.
Administration: Group or individual.
Price Data: Available from publisher.
Foreign Language Editions: Available in English and French.
Time: (20–40) minutes.
Comments: May be administered via paper and pencil or on the internet.
Authors: Donald Macnab and Shawn Bakker.
Publisher: Psychometrics Canada Ltd. [Canada].
Cross References: For reviews by Janet F. Carlson and Joseph G. Law, Jr., see 16:279.

[2975]
Work Personality Profile.

Purpose: Designed to "assess fundamental work role requirements that are essential to achievement and maintenance of suitable employment."
Population: Vocational rehabilitation clients.
Publication Date: 1986.
Acronym: WPP.
Scores, 16: Acceptance of Work Role, Ability to Profit from Instruction or Correction, Work Persistence, Work Tolerance, Amount of Supervision Required, Extent Trainee Seeks Assistance from Supervisor, Degree of Comfort or Anxiety with Supervisor, Appropriateness of Personal Relations with Supervisor, Teamwork, Ability to Socialize with Co-Workers, Social Communication Skills, Task Orientation, Social Skills, Work Motivation, Work Conformance, Personal Presentation.
Administration: Individual.

Price Data: Price available from publisher for complete set including manual (40 pages), diskette, and 50 tests.
Time: (5–10) minutes.
Comments: Observational ratings by vocational evaluators; to be administered after one week (20-30 hours) in evaluation setting; available on diskette.
Authors: Brian Bolton and Richard Roessler.
Publisher: The National Center on Employment & Disability.
Cross References: See T5:2924 (4 references) and T4:2994 (1 reference); for a review by Ralph O. Mueller and Paula J. Dupuy, see 11:476.

[2976]

Work Potential Profile.

Purpose: "Developed as a tool for the initial descriptive assessment of long-term unemployed individuals."
Population: Ages 16 and older.
Publication Date: 1997.
Scores, 25: Coping (General Satisfaction, Stress and Anxiety, Self-image, Self-Discipline, Time Sense/Use, Total), Freedom from Major Barriers (Preoccupation with Health, Agitation/Aggression, Depression/Resentment, Pervasive Distrust/Delusions, Total), Social Resources (Attitude Towards Others, Social Skills, Total), Abilities (Communication and Literacy, Technology Use, Numeracy, Problem Solving, Total), Motivation (Work Motivation, Intrinsic Motivation, Extrinsic Motivation, Need for Status, Total), Physical Abilities.
Administration: Group.
Price Data, 2006: A$149.50 per complete set; $59.95 per manual; $19.95 per 10 questionnaire; $19.95 per 10 answer booklets; $19.95 per 10 group record forms;$19.95 per 10 individual record forms; $39.95 per set of 9 score keys.
Time: (10–30) minutes.
Author: Helga A. H. Rowe.
Publisher: Australian Council for Educational Research Ltd. [Australia].
Cross References: For reviews by JoEllen V. Carlson and Robert Fitzpatrick, see 15:282.

[2977]

Work Preference Match: A Career Exploration Tool.

Purpose: Designed to "help career decision makers identify priorities and evaluate career or job choices based on those priorities."
Population: Career decision makers.
Publication Date: 2006.
Acronym: WPM.
Scores: No formal scores.
Administration: Individual or group.
Price Data, 2006: $39.95 per complete kit including 25 booklets and 1 administrator's guide (8 pages); bulk discounts available.
Time: Untimed.
Comments: This is a "structured self-exploration tool."
Author: Lynn R. Dowd.
Publisher: JIST Publishing, Inc.

[2978]

Work Preference Questionnaire.

Purpose: To determine preferred job activities.
Population: Business and industry.
Publication Date: 1982.
Scores: Weighted combinations of 150 items into 16 dimensions of work: Making Decisions/Communicating and Having Responsibility, Operating Vehicles, Using Machines-Tools-Instruments, Performing Physical Activities, Operating Keyboard and Office Equipment, Monitoring and/or Controlling Equipment and/or Processes, Working Under Uncomfortable Conditions, Working With Art-Decor Entertainment, Performing Supervisory Duties, Performing Estimating Activities, Processing Written Information, Working With Buyers-Customers-Salespersons, Working Under Hazardous Conditions, Performing Paced and/or Repetitive Activities, Working With Aerial and Aquatic Equipment, Catering/Serving/Smelling/Tasting.
Administration: Group.
Price Data: Available from publisher.
Time: Administration time not reported.
Comments: Also known as Work Activity Questionnaire.
Authors: Robert C. Mecham, Alma F. Harris (test), Ernest J. McCormick (test), and P. R. Jenneret (test).
Publisher: PAQ Services, Inc.

[2979]

Work Profile Questionnaire.

Purpose: "Designed to look at work preference, and identify situations in which people are most likely to flourish and be effective."
Population: Job applicants.
Publication Date: 2001.
Acronym: WPQ.
Scores, 5: Communication Style, Emotions, Drive and Determination, Relationships with People, Thinking Style.
Administration: Individual.
Price Data, 2001: £22 per completed questionnaire.
Time: (5) minutes.
Author: Allan Cameron.
Publisher: The Test Agency Limited [England] [No reply from publisher; status unknown].

[2980]

Work Profile Questionnaire: Emotional Intelligence.

Purpose: "Designed to measure emotional intelligence … and also identifies respondents' preferred [work] team role."
Population: Adults.
Publication Date: 1999.
Acronym: WPQei.
Scores, 8: Self-Awareness, Empathy, Intuition, Emotions, Motivation, Innovation, Social Skills, Emotional Intelligence.
Administration: Group.
Price Data, 2001: £37.50 per technical manual; £85 per 10 self-scoring questionnaire/answer sheet/profile set; £25 per computer-based WPQei Administrator and Narrative Report Generator.

Time: Untimed.
Comments: Based on the Belbin model of work team functioning; can be administered in paper-and-pencil or personal computer format; requires IBM-compatible PC running Microsoft Windows 95/98/NT, 800x600 resolution display with 256 colors, recommends Pentium processor at 90 Mhz or more, 8 Mb RAM.
Author: Allan Cameron.
Publisher: The Test Agency Limited [England] [No reply from publisher; status unknown].
Cross References: For reviews by Mark Pope and Larissa Smith, see 15:283.

[2981]

Work Readiness Profile.

Purpose: "Developed as a criterion-referenced tool for the initial descriptive assessment of individuals with disabilities."
Population: Older adolescents and adults with disabilities.
Publication Date: 1995.
Scores, 14: Physical Effectiveness (Health, Travel, Movement, Fine Motor Skills, Gross Motor Skills and Strength, Total Average), Personal Effectiveness (Social and Interpersonal, Work Adjustment, Communication Effectiveness, Abilities and Skills, Literacy and Numeracy, Total Average), Hearing, Vision.
Administration: Group.
Price Data, 2006: A$77 per set including manual (64 pages), 10 answer books, 10 group record forms, and 10 individual record forms; A$16.50 per 10 answer books; A$6.60 per 10 group record forms; A$6.60 per 10 individual record forms; A$49.50 per manual.
Time: (10–15) minutes.
Comments: Self-administered or ratings by informant.
Author: Helga A. H. Rowe.
Publisher: Australian Council for Educational Research Ltd. [Australia].
Cross References: For reviews by Jean Powell Kirnan and S. Alvin Leung, see 14:427.

[2982]

Work Skills Series Production.

Purpose: Designed to measure the ability to understand instructions, work with numbers, and accurately check machine settings visually.
Population: Manufacturing and production employees and prospective employees.
Publication Date: 1990.
Acronym: WSS.
Scores: Total score only for each of 3 tests: Understanding Instructions (VWP1), Working with Numbers (NWP2), Visual Checking (CWP3).
Administration: Individual or group.
Price Data: Available from publisher.
Time: 12 minutes for VWP1; 10 minutes for NWP2; 7 minutes for CWP3; 29(40) minutes for complete battery.
Author: Saville & Holdsworth Ltd.
Publisher: SHL Group plc [United Kingdom].

Cross References: For reviews by Brian Bolton and Wayne J. Camara, see 12:418.

[2983]

Work Team Simulator.

Purpose: "Designed to identify individuals who have the attitude and skills needed to be an effective member of a work team; test requires candidates to respond in narrative fashion to a series of job-related situations in order to determine how they will relate to other team members and their supervisor."
Population: Team members.
Publication Date: 1991.
Acronym: WTS.
Scores, 3: Group Decision Making, Team Relations, Total.
Administration: Group.
Forms, 4: Private and public sector forms: Blue Collar, Clerical/Office, Fire Fighter, Transportation Agency Blue Collar.
Restricted Distribution: Clients may be required to pay a nominal one-time overhead/sign-up fee.
Price Data, 2011: $295 per candidate for rental/scoring and feedback report.
Time: 75 minutes.
Comments: All versions are available for online administration.
Author: Richard C. Joines.
Publisher: Management & Personnel Systems, Inc.

[2984]

Work Temperament Inventory.

Purpose: Identifies "personal traits" of the worker that are then matched to suitable occupations.
Population: Workers.
Publication Date: 1993.
Acronym: WTI.
Scores: 12 scales: Directive, Repetitive, Influencing, Variety, Expressing, Judgments, Alone, Stress, Tolerances, Under, People, Measurable.
Administration: Group.
Price Data: Available from publisher.
Time: (15–20) minutes.
Authors: Brian Bolton and Jeffrey Brookings.
Publisher: The National Center on Employment & Disability.
Cross References: For reviews by Peter F. Merenda and Alan J. Raphael, see 13:368.

[2985]

Working–Assessing Skills, Habits, and Style.

Purpose: "Designed to assess personal habits, skills, and styles that are associated with a positive work ethic."
Population: High school and college students and potential employees.
Publication Date: 1996.
Scores: 9 competencies: Taking Responsibility, Working in Teams, Persisting, Having A Sense of Quality,

Life-Long Learning, Adapting to Change, Problem Solving, Information Processing, Systems Thinking.
Administration: Group or individual.
Price Data, 2006: $4 each (quantity discounts available); technical and applications manuals available upon request (price information available from publisher); user's manual free with each order.
Time: (30–35) minutes.
Comments: Inventory for self-rating; can be self-administered and self-scored, or assessed online with automatic scoring.
Authors: Curtis Miles (test and user's manual), Phyllis Grummon (test, user's manual, and technical manual), and Karen M. Maduschke (technical manual).
Publisher: H & H Publishing Co., Inc.
Cross References: For reviews by Wayne Camara and Joyce Meikamp, see 14:429.

[2986]

Working Memory Test Battery for Children.

Purpose: To evaluate working memory in children and young adolescents.
Population: Ages 5–15.
Publication Date: 2001.
Acronym: WMTB-C.
Scores: 9 subtests: Digit Recall, Word List Matching, Word List Recall, Block Recall, Nonword List Recall, Listening Recall, Counting Recall, Mazes Memory, Backward Digit Recall.
Administration: Individual.
Price Data, 2006: £275.50 per complete battery including forms, stimulus books, and manual (183 pages).
Time: (60) minutes.
Authors: Susan Pickering and Sue Gathercole.
Publisher: Pearson Assessment [England].
Cross References: For a review by Rayne A. Sperling and Daniel L. McCollum, see 16:280.

[2987]

Workplace Skills Survey.

Purpose: Designed to provide "information regarding basic work ethics and employment skills."
Population: Job applicants and employees.
Publication Date: 1998.
Acronym: WSS.
Scores, 7: Communication, Adapting to Change, Problem Solving, Work Ethics, Technological Literacy, Teamwork, Composite.
Administration: Individual or group.
Price Data, 2010: $45 per introductory kit including 5 reusable test booklets, 20 answer/score sheets, and technical manual (9 pages); $34 per 20 answer/score sheets; $20 per 10 reusable test booklets.
Time: 20 minutes.
Author: Industrial Psychology International Ltd.
Publisher: Industrial Psychology International Ltd.
Cross References: For reviews by Jean P. Kirnan and William I. Sauser, Jr., see 17:205.

[2988]

Workplace Skills Survey–Form E.

Purpose: Designed to assess students' work place readiness and employment skills.
Population: Students in school-to-work and vocational programs.
Publication Date: 2000.
Acronym: WSS-Form E.
Scores, 9: Career Planning, Job Attainment, Communication, Adapting and Coping with Change, Problem Solving, Work Ethics, Technological Literacy, Teamwork, Overall.
Administration: Individual or group.
Price Data, 2010: $4.50 per assessment per student includes manual, answer documents, shipment of test materials to the school, scoring, analysis reporting (individual student reports and data CD), and shipment of reports to the school; $25 per 25 reusable test booklets.
Time: 50 minutes.
Comments: Scoring and analysis provided by publisher.
Author: Industrial Psychology International Ltd.
Publisher: Industrial Psychology International Ltd.

[2989]

World Government Scale.

Purpose: Measures attitudes toward world government.
Population: Students.
Publication Date: 1985.
Scores: Total score only.
Administration: Group.
Manual: No manual.
Price Data, 2005: $2 per scale.
Time: [12] minutes.
Comments: Supplementary article available.
Author: Panos D. Bardis.
Publisher: Donna Bardis.

[2990]

World of Work Inventory.

Purpose: "Designed to assist clients in thinking about themselves in relation to their total environment" in relation to their personal career development.
Population: Ages 13–65+.
Publication Dates: 1970–2006.
Acronym: WOWI.
Scores, 35: Career Interest Activities (17 scores: Public Service, The Sciences, Engineering & Related, Business Relations, Managerial, The Arts, Clerical, Sales, Service, Primary Outdoor, Processing, Machine Work, Bench Work, Structural Work, Mechanical & Electrical Work, Graphic Arts, Mining); Job Satisfaction Indicators (12 scores: Versatile, Adaptable to Repetitive Work, Adaptable to Performing Under Specific Instructions, Dominant, Gregarious, Isolative, Influencing, Self-Controlled, Valuative, Objective, Subjective, Rigorous); Aptitude/Achievement (6 scores: Verbal, Numerical, Abstractions, Spatial-Form, Mechanical/Electrical, Organizing Skill).
Administration: Individual or group.

Price Data, 2004: Online administration: $13 per single profile report with summary; $19.50 per profile report with interpretative report, and $189 online site license fee; Paper-and-pencil administration: $7 per test booklet and $19.95 per interpretation manual (2001, 70 pages).
Time: (60) minutes for online version; (90) minutes for paper-and-pencil short form.
Authors: Robert E. Ripley, Gregory P. M. Neidert, and Nancy L. Ortman.
Publisher: World of Work, Inc.
Cross References: For reviews by Jeffrey A. Jenkins and Eugene P. Sheehan, see 16:281.

[2991]

Worley's ID Profile.

Purpose: Designed to identify temperament.
Population: Ages 6 and over.
Publication Dates: 1995–2000.
Acronym: WIDP.
Scores, 8: 3 profile scores: Social, Leadership, Relationship; 5 behavior scores: Introverted Sanguine, Sanguine, Phlegmatic, Melancholy, Choleric.
Administration: Individual or group.
Forms, 2: Adult and Youth (Ages 6 to 16).
Price Data: Available from publisher.
Foreign Language Editions: Available in English, Spanish, and Portuguese.
Time: (10) minutes.
Author: John W. Worley.
Publisher: Worley's Identity Discovery Profile, Inc.
Cross References: For reviews by Eugene V. Aidman and Frederick T. L. Leong, see 15:284.

[2992]

Writing Process Test.

Purpose: "Measures the quality of students' written products."
Population: Grades 2–12.
Publication Dates: 1991–1992.
Acronym: WPT.
Scores, 14: Development [First Pass (Purpose/Focus, Audience, Vocabulary, Style/Tone, Total), Second Pass (Support/Development, Organization/Coherence, Total)], Fluency [Third Pass (Sentence Structure/Variety, Grammar/ Usage, Capitalization/Punctuation, Spelling, Total)], Total.
Administration: Group.
Editions, 2: Individual, Classroom.
Price Data, 2011: $204 per complete kit including test manual (1992, 144 pages), technical manual (1992, 40 pages), 25 analytic scales, 25 Form A first draft booklets, and 25 revision booklets; $66 per test manual; $23 per 25 analytic record forms; $25 per 25 Form A first draft booklet; $24 per 25 Form B first draft booklet; $17 per 25 revision booklets; $21 per scorer folder; $42 per technical manual; $23 per 25 Training and Calibration Record Forms; $66 per scoring videotape.
Time: [45] minutes (+30 minutes for revision).
Authors: Robin Warden and Thomas A. Hutchinson.

Publisher: PRO-ED.
Cross References: For reviews by Ernest W. Kimmel and Sandra Ward, see 13:369 (1 reference).

[2993]

The Written Expression Test.

Purpose: To "measure written expression objectively."
Population: Grades 1 to 6.
Publication Dates: 1979-1982.
Acronym: WET.
Scores, 5: Productivity, Mechanics, Handwriting, Maturity, Composite.
Administration: Individual or group.
Price Data: Not available.
Time: (30) minutes.
Authors: Clark Johnson and Sharon Hubly.
Publisher: McClain [No reply from publisher; status unknown].
Cross References: See T5:2934 (1 reference); for reviews by Noel Gregg and Lyn Haber, see 10:396.

[2994]

Written Language Assessment.

Purpose: Assesses writing ability.
Population: Grades 3–12.
Publication Date: 1989.
Acronym: WLA.
Scores, 5: General Writing Ability, Productivity, Word Complexity, Readability, Written Language Quotient.
Administration: Group.
Price Data, 2006: $80 per complete kit including manual (111 pages), 25 each of 3 writing record forms, 25 scoring/profile forms, and hand counter; $25 per 25 each of 3 writing record forms; $15 per 25 scoring/profile forms; $25 per manual; $15 per hand counter; $25 per specimen set.
Time: (45–60) minutes.
Authors: J. Jeffrey Grill and Margaret M. Kirwin.
Publisher: Academic Therapy Publications.
Cross References: See T5:2935 (2 references); for reviews by Stephen Jurs and Mary Ross Moran, see 11:477.

[2995]

Written Language Syntax Test.

Purpose: Designed as a "screening instrument used to provide information on student performance in written language syntax."
Population: Ages 10–17 hearing-impaired.
Publication Date: 1981.
Acronym: WLST.
Scores: Total score only.
Administration: Group or individual.
Levels, 3: 1, 2, 3.
Price Data: Price information available from publisher for tests (specify Level 1, 2, or 3), screening tests, individual data folders, and administrator's package including manual (33 pages) and one copy of each item.
Time: (10–20) minutes for screening test, (40-60) minutes per test.

Comments: Contains "Screening Test" to determine appropriate level for administration.
Author: Sharon R. Berry.
Publisher: Gallaudet University Press.
Cross References: For reviews by Michael W. Casby and Judith R. Johnston, see 9:1404.

[2996]

Y-OQ-SR 2.0 [Youth Outcome Questionnaire-Self Report].

Purpose: Designed to "assess behavior change as the adolescent clients themselves perceive it."
Population: Ages 12-18 years.
Publication Dates: 1999-2005.
Acronym: Y-OQ-SR 2.0.
Scores, 7: Intrapersonal Distress, Somatic, Interpersonal Relations, Social Problems, Behavioral Dysfunction, Critical Items, Total.
Administration: Individual or group.
Restricted Distribution: Requires licensure from American Professional Credentialing Services LLC.
Price Data, 2006: Licensing cost available from publisher; $25 per administration and scoring manual (1999, 15 pages); $25 per test.
Foreign Language Editions: English, Spanish, and French editions available.
Time: (7-15) minutes.
Authors: M. Gawain Wells, Gary M. Burlingame, Paul M. Rose (manual only), and Michael J. Lambert (test only).
Publisher: OQ Measures LLC.
Cross References: For reviews by John S. Geisler and Joseph C. Kush, see 17:207.

[2997]

Y-OQ-30.1 [Youth Outcome Questionnaire-Omni Version].

Purpose: Designed to measure "the treatment process for children and adolescents receiving any form of behavioral health treatment including psychoactive medications."
Population: Ages 12-18 years.
Publication Dates: 1998-2002.
Acronym: Y-OQ-30.1.
Scores: Total score only.
Administration: Individual or group.
Restricted Distribution: Requires licensure from American Professional Credentialing Services LLC.
Price Data, 2006: Licensing cost available from publisher; $25 per administration and scoring manual (2003, 21 pages); $25 per test.
Foreign Language Editions: English, Spanish, and French editions available.
Time: (2-15) minutes.
Comments: Test can be parent-reported and self-reported.
Authors: Gary M. Burlingame, Bruce W. Jasper (manual only), Gary Peterson (manual only), M. Gawain Wells, Curtis W. Reisinger, G. S. (Jeb) Brown (manual only).
Publisher: OQ Measures LLC.

Cross References: For reviews by Sandra Loew and by W. Joel Schneider and Mark E. Swerdlik, see 17:206.

[2998]

Young Children's Achievement Test.

Purpose: Designed to help determine early academic abilities.
Population: Ages 4-0 to 7-11.
Publication Date: 2000.
Acronym: YCAT.
Scores, 6: General Information, Reading, Mathematics, Writing, Spoken Language, and Early Achievement Composite.
Administration: Individual.
Price Data, 2011: $240 per complete kit including examiner's manual (154 pages), picture book (48 pages), 25 student response forms, and 25 profile/examiner record booklets; $75 per examiner's manual; $81 per picture book; $35 per 25 student response forms; $59 per 25 profile/examiner record booklets.
Time: (25–45) minutes.
Authors: Wayne P. Hresko, Pamela K. Peak, Shelley R. Herron, and Deanna L. Bridges.
Publisher: PRO-ED.
Cross References: For reviews by Russell N. Carney and Susan J. Maller, see 15:285.

[2999]

Youth Level of Service/Case Management Inventory 2.0.

Purpose: Designed for use in "assessing risk, need, and responsivity factors in youth and in the formulation of a case plan."
Population: Juvenile offenders, ages 12-18.
Publication Dates: 2002-2011.
Acronym: YLS/CMI 2.0.
Scores: 9 Risk Ratings: Prior and Current Offenses/Dispositions, Family Circumstances/Parenting, Education/Employment, Peer Relations, Substance Abuse, Leisure/Recreation, Personality/Behavior, Attitudes/Orientation, Total.
Administration: Individual.
Parts, 7: Assessment of Risks and Needs, Summary of Risks and Needs, Assessment of Other Needs and Special Considerations, Final Risk/Need Level and Professional Override, Program/Placement Decision, Case Management Plan, Case Management Review.
Price Data, 2011: $195 per complete kit including 25 interview guides, 25 Quikscore forms, 25 case management forms, and user's manual (2011, 92 pages); $79 per 25 interview guides; $47 per 25 Quikscore forms; $28 per 25 case management forms; $63 per user's manual.
Time: [30-40] minutes.
Comments: Reflects the theory and structure of the Level of Service Inventory-Revised (17:107).
Authors: Robert D. Hoge and D. A. Andrews.
Publisher: Multi-Health Systems, Inc.

Cross References: For reviews by Pam Lindsey and Stephen E. Trotter of an earlier edition, see 16:282.

[3000]

Youth Outcome Questionnaire (Y-OQ-2.01).

Purpose: Designed as a "measure of treatment progress for children and adolescents receiving psychological or psychiatric treatment."
Population: Ages 4–17.
Publication Dates: 1996-2005.
Acronym: Y-OQ-2.0.
Scores, 7: Intrapersonal Distress, Somatic, Interpersonal Relations, Critical Items, Social Problems, Behavioral Dysfunction, Total.
Administration: Individual.
Price Data: Price data for manual (1996, 27 pages) and questionnaires available from publisher.
Time: (7–20) minutes.
Comments: Behavior rating scale completed by parent or "significant adult figure."
Authors: Gary M. Burlingame (test and manual), Michael J. Lambert (test and manual), M. Gawain Wells (manual), Matthew J. Hoag (manual), Carolen A. Hope (manual), R. Scott Nebeker (manual), Kimberly Konkel (manual), Pamela McCollam (manual), Gary Peterson (manual), Mark Latkowski (manual), and Curtis W. Reisinger (manual).
Publisher: OQ Measures LLC.
Cross References: For reviews by Susan K. Green and John Hattie, see 16:283.

[3001]

Youth Program Quality Assessment.

Purpose: "Designed to evaluate the quality of youth programs and identify staff training needs."
Population: Youth-serving programs.
Publication Date: 2005.
Acronyms: Youth PQA.
Administration: Individual or group.
Forms, 2: A, B.
Price Data, 2006: $39.95 per complete kit including administration manual (35 pages), Form A-Program Offering Items, and Form B-Organization Items; $19.95 per administration manual; $10.95 per Form A-Program Offering Items; $10.95 per Form B-Organization Items.
Comments: This test is based on observations and interviews by either "independent raters or as a self-assessment."
Author: High/Scope Educational Research Foundation.
Publisher: High/Scope Educational Research Foundation.
a) FORM A-PROGRAM OFFERING ITEMS.
Purpose: "Focuses on youth experiences during a program offering."
Scores, 5: Safe Environment, Supportive Environment, Interaction, Engagement, Total.
Time: (120) minutes.

b) FORM B-ORGANIZATION ITEMS.
Purpose: "Assesses the organization's infrastructure."
Scores, 4: Youth Centered Policies/Practices, High Expectations for All Students/Staff, Access, Total.
Time: (60) minutes.
Cross References: For a review by Georgette Yetter, see 17:208.

[3002]

Youth Risk and Resilience Inventory.

Purpose: Designed "to identify individual assets or resilience factors" and "screen for the presence of risk factors such as teasing, intimidation, bullying, physical abuse, violence, and victimization; to identify signs of emotional stress; and to assess their impact on the individual."
Population: Ages 10 to 17.
Publication Date: 2006.
Acronyms: YRRI.
Scores, 2: Risk Factor, Resilience Factor.
Administration: Individual or group.
Price Data, 2006: $23.95 per complete kit including 25 test booklets and administrator's guide (8 pages); bulk discounts are available.
Time: Administration time not reported.
Comments: There is an optional "My Journal" section at the end of the test; this option does not affect the numeric scores.
Author: Robert P. Brady.
Publisher: JIST Publishing, Inc.
Cross References: For reviews by Merith Cosden and Timothy R. Konold, see 17:209.

[3003]

Youth's Inventory–4.

Purpose: Designed to determine "the extent to which the adolescent patient is aware of his or her symptoms" [of adolescent psychopathology], as determined by self-report.
Population: Ages 12–18.
Publication Date: 1999.
Acronym: YI-4.
Scores, 11: AD/HD Inattentive, Hyperactive–Impulsive, Combined, Oppositional Defiant Disorder, Conduct Disorder, Generalized Anxiety Disorder, Major Depressive Disorder, Dysthymic Disorder, Separation Anxiety Disorder, Eating Problems, Bipolar Disorder.
Administration: Individual.
Price Data, 2006: $75 per deluxe kit including 50 checklists, 50 symptom count score sheets, 50 symptom severity profile score sheets, and manual (1999, 170 pages); $52 per 50 checklists.
Foreign Language Edition: Spanish edition available.
Time: [15] minutes.
Authors: Kenneth D. Gadow and Joyce Sprafkin.
Publisher: Checkmate Plus, Ltd.
Cross References: For reviews by Harold R. Keller and John J. Vacca, see 15:286.

INDEX OF
MMY TEST REVIEWERS

This record of Mental Measurements Yearbook *test reviewers lists all individuals reviewing in the 18 editions of the* MMY *series. The numbers after the names represent the* Mental Measurements Yearbooks *in which their reviews appeared.*

Based on the recommendation of our National Advisory Council, the Buros Institute of Mental Measurements is now making special recognition of the long-term contributions of reviewers to the Mental Measurements Yearbook *series. To receive the "Distinguished Reviewer" designation, an individual must have contributed to six or more editions of this series beginning with* The Ninth Mental Measurements Yearbook. *By virtue of their long-term service, these reviewers exemplify an outstanding dedication in their professional lives to the principles of improving the science and practice of testing. Individuals receiving awards as Distinguished Reviewers as of the publication of* The Eighteenth Mental Measurements Yearbook *(2010) are indicated with an asterisk (*) below.*

Ira E. Aaron, 9-10
Harold H. Abelson, 3
Murray Aborn, 4
Shawn K. Acheson, 15-18
*Phillip L. Ackerman, 11-18
Terry A. Ackerman, 11-13
Sandra T. Acosta, 18
Fred L. Adair, 8
Carol Adams, 9
Clifford R. Adams, 6
Elizabeth C. Adams, 4
Georgia S. Adams, 7-8
Gerald R. Adams, 9
Mary Friend Adams, 8
Russell L. Adams, 9-10
Susan F. Adams, 12
C. J. Adcock, 5-7
*Caroline M. Adkins, 17
Dorothy C. Adkins, 3-7
Dan L. Adler, 5
Seymour Adler, 10

Janet G. Afflerbach, 5
Lois G. Afflerbach, 5
Frederick B. Agard, 3
J. Stanley Ahmann, 6-9
Eugene V. Aidman, 14-18
Lewis R. Aiken, 9, 12
Mary D. Ainsworth, 5
Peter W. Airasian, 8-10
*Mark A. Albanese, 11-18
Amanda Albertson, 17
Lewis E. Albright, 6-8
Norma A. Albright, 2
Bruce K. Alcorn, 11-12
Felito Aldarondo, 15
John Charles Alderson, 8
Lawrence M. Aleamoni, 8-9, 11-12
Charlene M. Alexander, 12
Ralph A. Alexander, 9
Bob Algozzine, 9
Henry A. Alker, 7-8
Doris V. Allen, 9-10

Kathleen Allen, 15
Lawrence Allen, 9
Mary J. Allen, 9
Nancy L. Allen, 11
Robert M. Allen, 8
Sarah J. Allen, 11-12, 15
Richard L. Allington, 9-10
Julie A. Allison, 12-15
John C. Almack, 1-2
William D. Altus, 4
Cecilia B. Alves, 18
Jean D. Amberson, 4
Sueann Robinson Ambron, 8
Vera M. Amerson, 3
Anne Anastasi, 1-11
Nicholas Anastasiow, 7-8
Kenneth N. Anchor, 12
Charles V. Anderson, 8
David O. Anderson, 11-13
Howard R. Anderson, 1-7
Irving H. Anderson, 1, 3
James M. Anderson, 3-4, 6
*John O. Anderson, 11-12, 14-16, 18
Kenneth E. Anderson, 4, 6
Martin W. Anderson, 17
Robert P. Anderson, 8-9
Louanne Andersson, 15
V. Jerrilyn. Andrews, 11-13
Lawrence Andrus, 2
Harvey A. Andruss, 3
Charles J. Ansorge, 9
Edgar Anstey, 6
Dolores J. Appl, 17
Paul A. Arbisi, 12-16
Francis X. Archambault, Jr., 9, 11-12
Robert P. Archer, 11
Joyce A. Arditti, 12
Sharon Arffa, 18
Edward N. Argulewicz, 9
James A. Armentrout, 8
Christian O. Arndt, 2
Dwight L. Arnold, 4-5
Gwen F. Arnold, 4
Edward Aronow, 12
Raoul A. Arreola, 12-15
Judith A. Arter, 9
F. Marion Asche, 12
Philip Ash, 11-14
Ronald A. Ash, 9, 12
E. Jack Asher, Jr., 11
Theodore A. Ashford, 3, 5
Lear Ashmore, 8-9
Kathleen B. Aspiranti, 18
Alexander W. Astin, 6-7
Michelle Athanasiou, 15-17
James Athanasou, 15-16
Carolyn Peluso Atkins, 9

Samuel D. Atkins, 1-2
Mark J. Atkinson, 14-15
Deborah H. Atlas, 12
*Jeffrey A. Atlas, 11-18
Kathryn Hu-Pei Au, 9
Mark W. Aulls, 9
*James T. Austin, 9, 11-14, 16-17
Mary C. Austin, 6
*Stephen N. Axford, 11-17
Frederic L. Ayer, 3-4
George W. Ayer, 8
J. Douglas Ayers, 6-8, 11
Glen P. Aylward, 11-14, 16
Kris L. Baack, 12, 16
James C. Babcock, 2
*Patricia A. Bachelor, 11-16, 18
Lyle F. Bachman, 11-12
Philip A. Backlund, 13-14
Ellen H. Bacon, 10-11
Beth D. Bader, 12
Andrew R. Baggaley, 5-6
Stephen J. Bagnato, 9
Theresa M. Bahns, 14
Brenda Bailey-Richardson, 9
Sherry K. Bain, 12, 14, 16, 18
Leonard L. Baird, 7
Janet Baldwin, 12
Thomas S. Baldwin, 7-8, 10
Benjamin Balinsky, 4-5
Rachel S. Ball, 2
Joan C. Ballard, 14-16
Warren R. Baller, 4-5
Irol W. Balsley, 6
Deborah L. Bandalos, 12, 14, 16-17
K. Denise Bane, 11
Charlotte E. K. Banks, 4-5
Nicholas W. Bankson, 8-11
Allan G. Barclay, 7
James R. Barclay, 9-10
Benjamin D. Barker, 14
*Laura L. B. Barnes, 11-17
Walter Barnes, 1
Janet Barnes-Farrell, 14
David W. Barnett, 10-12
Rita M. Barnett, 12
W. Leslie Barnette, Jr., 8
Andrés Barona, 11, 13
A. S. Barr, 3
Rebecca C. Barr, 7-8
Richard S. Barrett, 6
Thomas C. Barrett, 6
Frank Barron, 5
William M. Bart, 11-12
Brendan John Bartlett, 9
Lauren R. Barton, 17
W. L. Bashaw, 7
Alan R. Bass, 8

David J. Bateson, 12
Donald H. Baucom, 9
Ernest A. Bauer, 11-12
Robert H. Bauernfeind, 5-8
Sheri Bauman, 15
Ronald Baumanis, 9
Deborah N. Bauserman, 9
Abigail Baxter, 16
Brent Baxter, 3-5
Ernest Edward Bayles, 1
Nancy Bayley, 2-3, 5
Kenneth L. Bean, 5-6
Robert M. Bear, 3-4
Harold P. Bechtoldt, 4-7
Isabel L. Beck, 9
Michael D. Beck, 11-13, 16
Roland L. Beck, 2-3
Samuel J. Beck, 2, 5
Wesley C. Becker, 6
Ralph C. Bedell, 3, 5
H. R. Beech, 6
Martha C. Beech, 9
Fred S. Beers, 1
Scott F. Beers, 17
Isaac I. Bejar, 8
Marcia J. Belcher, 11
John E. Bell, 4-6
Peter Della Bella, 13
C.G. Bellah, 15-16
Camilla Persson Benbow, 11
Kathryn M. Benes, 11-12
James K. Benish, 13-15
Albert A. Bennett, 2-3
Clinton W. Bennett, 12-13
George K. Bennett, 3-7
Jeri Benson, 11, 13
Mark J. Benson, 12-13
Nicholas Benson, 13
*Philip G. Benson, 9-12, 16, 18
Marsha Bensoussan, 13, 16
Peter M. Bentler, 6-7
Arthur L. Benton, 3-4, 7
Sheryl Benton, 16
Stephen L. Benton, 11-12, 16
H. E. Benz, 2
Ralph F. Berdie, 3-7
Abbey L. Berg, 16
Harry D. Berg, 3-8
Paul Conrad Berg, 7
Allen Berger, 7-9
Michael Berger, 8
Peter Miles Berger, 14-15
Jennifer M. Bergeron, 16
Betty Bergstrom, 13
*Ronald A. Berk, 9, 12-16
Hinsdale Bernard, 12-13
H. John Bernardin, 9-12

Rita Sloan Berndt, 9-10
Jean-Jacques Bernier, 11-12
Robert G. Bernreuter, 1-4
Frank M. Bernt, 12-16
Jeff Berry, 18
Joan D. Berryman, 9
Frederick Bessai, 11-14
Emmett A. Betts, 6
William Betz, 1, 3
Charles L. Bickel, 2
Michael D. Biderman, 17-18
John Biggs, 9
Elizabeth Bigham, 18
Marion A. Bills, 3
Walter V. Bingham, 1
William C. Bingham, 6, 8
L. B. Birch, 6-7
Ricky Korey Birnbaum, 15
Herbert G. W. Bischoff, 9, 14
Lisa G. Bischoff, 11-15
Bruce H. Biskin, 11-12, 17
Reign H. Bittner, 3-4
Harold H. Bixler, 3-4
Ake Bjerstedt, 5-6
Donald B. Black, 6-7
Hillel Black, 6
John D. Black, 5-6, 8-9
J. M. Blackbourn, 18
J. M. Blackburn, 2
James H. Blackhurst, 1
E. G. Blackstone, 3
Martha Blackwell, 11-12
Kimberly Ann Blair, 15-16
C. B. Blakemore, 6
Rebecca Blanchard, 18
Emery P. Bliesmer, 6
Lynn S. Bliss, 10-12
Sonya Blixt, 12
Jack Block, 8
Martin E. Block, 12
Paul J. Blommers, 3-6
Benjamin S. Bloom, 3-5, 7
Lisa A. Bloom, 12-13
Bruce M. Bloxom, 7-9
Milton L. Blum, 3-4
James A. Blumenthal, 9
Cynthia R. Bochna, 16
Jack L. Bodden, 7-9
Ann E. Boehm, 9
Kathy J. Bohan, 16
Larry M. Bolen, 14
Carol A. Boliek, 11
Joan Bollenbacher, 5
Nancy B. Bologna, 12, 14
*Brian F. Bolton, 8-9, 11-15
David L. Bolton, 12-13
Guy L. Bond, 2

Stephen J. Boney, 12
Mike Bonner, 15-16
Sarah Bonner, 16
Gwyneth M. Boodoo, 9
Ivan A. Booker, 1-4
Daniel R. Boone, 7-8
Roger A. Boothroyd, 12-16
Edward S. Bordin, 3-5
Fred H. Borgen, 7-9
William Borgman, 9
Harold Borko, 6-7
Christopher Borman, 9-10
Walter C. Borman, 8-9
John R. Bormuth, 7
Robert A. Bornstein, 9-12
Allison Boroda, 17
Morton Bortner, 6, 8-9
Michael D. Botwin, 12
Thomas J. Bouchard, Jr., 7-8
William R. Boulton, 9
Nicholas G. Bountress, 9
Jennifer C. Bouwkamp, 15
John E. Bowers, 6
B. Ann Boyce, 16
*Gregory J. Boyle, 11-16
J. David Boyle, 12
Elizabeth Kelley Boyles, 15
Bruce A. Bracken, 9-12, 16
Jeffrey P. Braden, 11-12, 14, 16-17
E. J. G. Bradford, 3-4
John M. Bradley, 9
Robert H. Bradley, 9
Thomas B. Bradley, 9
Francis F. Bradshaw, 1
John C. Brantley, 11
Marla R. Brassard, 9
James Braswell, 7-8
John R. Braun, 7-9
Patricia Brazier-Carter, 18
Arthur H. Brayfield, 4-6
W. C. Brenke, 3
Burke H. Bretzing, 9
Ann Brewington, 3
Ann Brickner, 7
Robert G. Bridgham, 7
M. Alan Brimer, 5-7
Elizabeth L. Bringsjord, 13
John J. Brinkman, Jr., 15-16, 18
Frank W. Broadbent, 9
Stanley L. Brodsky, 8
Linda E. Brody, 10, 12, 17
Hubert E. Brogden, 3-4
*Susan M. Brookhart, 12-14, 16-18
Jeffrey B. Brookings, 13
Nelson Brooks, 1-6
M. Eustace Broom, 2
R. A. Brotemarkle, 3

W. Dale Brotherton, 13
Diane Browder, 10
Alfred S. Brown, 3
Andrew W. Brown, 2
Charles M. Brown, 6
Clara M. Brown, 1-2
Douglas T. Brown, 9-10
Frederick G. Brown, 7-9, 11
James Dean Brown, 11-13, 16
Johnnie A. Brown, 15
Lynn L. Brown, 14-15
Michael B. Brown, 13-14, 16
Ric Brown, 9, 12-14, 16
Robert D. Brown, 9-11, 13-14
Scott W. Brown, 11-12
Steven D. Brown, 9
Virginia L. Brown, 11
William A. Brownell, 1-5
Richard Brozovich, 11-12
Leo J. Brueckner, 1-4
Gordon C. Bruner, II, 14
Roger S. Bruning, 9-10
Bethany A. Brunsman, 15-17
Jennifer A. Brush, 13
James E. Bryan, 5-8
Miriam M. Bryan, 4, 6-8
N. Dale Bryant, 5-8
Diane Nelson Bryen, 9
Aaron D. Buchanan, 8
Jayne E. Bucy, 13
Karen S. Budd, 11
Rita M. Budrionis, 15, 17-18
William D. Buffington, 8
*Albert M. Bugaj, 12-17
Alan C. Bugbee, Jr., 12-13, 16
Eric S. Buhs, 15, 18
Norman A. Buktenica, 9
*Michael B. Bunch, 11-17
Mary Anne Bunda, 11-14
*Linda K. Bunker, 9-12, 14-16
Robert L. Burch, 4
Kenneth E. Burchett, 8
Thomas C. Burgess, 6
Carolyn L. Burke, 7
Paul C. Burnett, 11, 13
R. Will Burnett, 4
Christine W. Burns, 12
Donald G. Burns, 4
Matthew Burns, 14-17
Emily T. Burr, 3
Rachel D. Burrows, 18
Alvin G. Burstein, 6-7
Cyril Burt, 3, 5
Nancy W. Burton, 7
John Christian Busch, 12
Nancy A. Busch-Rossnagel, 9-10
Brenda R. Bush, 10-11

Ray R. Buss, 9
R. T. Busse, 11
Guy T. Buswell, 2
H. J. Butcher, 7
James N. Butcher, 8-9
John K. Butler, Jr., 9
Katharine G. Butler, 7-8, 10-12
Michelle A. Butler, 16
Dorcas Susan Butt, 8-9
Margaret C. Byrne, 7-9
Leonard S. Cahen, 7-8
G. P. Cahoon, 3-4
James R. Caldwell, 7
Kathryn Hoover Calfee, 8
Robert C. Calfee, 8-10
*Carolyn M. Callahan, 12-17
Leroy G. Callahan, 8
Leonard F. Caltabiano, 15
Wayne J. Camara, 12-14, 16
Bonnie W. Camp, 9-10
Cameron J. Camp, 10-11, 13
David P. Campbell, 6-8
Donald T. Campbell, 4-6
Dugal Campbell, 6
Hank Campbell, 10
Iris Amos Campbell, 9
J. Arthur Campbell, 6, 8-9
Joel T. Campbell, 6-7
Michael H. Campbell, 14-16
Thomas F. Campbell, 13
Vincent N. Campbell, 7
Anthony A. Cancelli, 9
Gary L. Canivez, 14, 16, 18
Joyce L. Carbonell, 9
*Karen T. Carey, 11-14, 16-18
Cindy I. Carlson, 11, 14-15
James E. Carlson, 12
*Janet F. Carlson, 11-17
*JoEllen V. Carlson, 11-16
Kenneth A. Carlson, 8
Roger D. Carlson, 11
Thorsten R. Carlson, 7-8
James C. Carmer, 11-12
Arlene E. Carney, 12
Russell N. Carney, 12-13, 15-17
*C. Dale Carpenter, 9-14, 16, 18
Sandra J. Carr, 14
W. L. Carr, 2
David J. Carroll, 8-9
James L. Carroll, 9
John B. Carroll, 4-8
L. Ray Carry, 7
Amber Carter, 18
Harold D. Carter, 1-4
Launor F. Carter, 4
W. H. Cartwright, 3
Heidi M. Carty, 15, 17

John C. Caruso, 14-15
J. Manuel Casas, 9-10
Michael W. Casby, 9
Thomas F. Cash, 9
Jerrell C. Cassady, 17-18
Frank P. Cassaretto, 5
Linda Castillo, 16
Burton M. Castner, 2
Robert S. Cathcart, 5
Psyche Cattell, 1, 3
Raymond B. Cattell, 2
Darrell N. Caulley, 12
Courtney B. Cazden, 7-8
Stella Center, 1
Tony Cellucci, 14-16, 18
Edward J. Cervenka, 8
Robert W. Ceurvorst, 9
Hester Chadderdon, 1-2, 4
Robert C. Challman, 4, 6-7
E. G. Chambers, 3-5
Tiffany Chandler, 17
Carolyn Chaney, 11
Laura H. Chapman, 8
Clinton I. Chase, 7-10
Henry Chauncey, 3, 6
Maurice Chazan, 7
Henry M. Cherrick, 9
Kathleen Barrows Chesterfield, 9
Brad S. Chissom, 7-8
*Mary "Rina" Mathai Chittooran, 13-18
James P. Choca, 13-14
Andrew Christensen, 9
Sandra L. Christenson, 11
Robert Christopher, 14, 17
Edmund P. Churchill, 3
Ruth D. Churchill, 3, 5
David F. Ciampi, 17-18
*Joseph C. Ciechalski, 11-18
*Gregory J. Cizek, 11-18
Charles D. Claiborn, 9, 12
*Mary M. Clare, 15-16, 18
Cherry Ann Clark, 5
D. F. Clark, 7
Elaine Clark, 10, 12-15
Gale W. Clark, 5
J. F. Clark, 5
Jean N. Clark, 17-18
John L. D. Clark, 7-8
John R. Clark, 2
Kenneth E. Clark, 4
Philip M. Clark, 8-9
Richard M. Clark, 9, 11
Willis W. Clark, 6
Brandy L. Clarke, 17-18
H. Harrison Clarke, 4
Glen U. Cleeton, 3
Lorraine Cleeton, 17

W. V. Clemans, 6
Amanda Jill Clemence, 15
Dorothy M. Clendenen, 5-7
Jeanette N. Cleveland, 9
Victor B. Cline, 7
James R. Clopton, 8-10
Richard W. Coan, 6-8
Harriet C. Cobb, 9
Larry R. Cochran, 9-12
Charles N. Cofer, 3-5
William E. Coffman, 3, 5-9, 11
Andrew D. Cohen, 12
Annabel J. Cohen, 12-13, 16
Bertram D. Cohen, 6, 8
D. Ashley Cohen, 14-17
Jacob Cohen, 6-8
John Cohen, 3
Libby G. Cohen, 14-15
S. Alan Cohen, 7
Stephen L. Cohen, 8
Sanford J. Cohn, 9, 14
Theodore Coladarci, 12, 14, 16-18
Nicholas Colangelo, 10
Debra E. Cole, 12
Nancy S. Cole, 7-9
Marta Coleman, 18
Thomas R. Coleman, 9
Roberta R. Collard, 7
Carol J. Collins, 13-14
Deborah Collins, 12
Richard Colwell, 7-10
W. D. Commins, 1-4
Andrew L. Comrey, 5, 7-8
Judith C. Conger, 11-12
Collie W. Conoley, 11-13, 16-17
Jane Close Conoley, 14
Clinton C. Conrad, 2
Herbert S. Conrad, 1-4
Norman A. Constantine, 11-12
Francine Conway, 17
Alicia Skinner Cook, 9, 11
John Cook, 7-9
Walter W. Cook, 2-3, 5
Catherine P. Cook-Cottone, 16, 18
Donna K. Cooke, 12
Norma Cooke, 9
William W. Cooley, 6
Clyde H. Coombs, 3
Colin Cooper, 13-16
Mark Cooper, 14-15
M. Allan Cooperstein, 13-15
Robert B. Cooter, Jr., 10-11
Mary Kay Corbitt, 9
Stephen M. Corey, 1-2
Virginia E. Corgan, 10
*Alice J. Corkill, 11-14, 16-17
Ethel L. Cornell, 1

*Merith Cosden, 11-14, 17-18
Giuseppe Costantino, 9-10
William C. Cottle, 5
Stuart A. Courtis, 1, 4
Douglas Courtney, 3-4
John A. Courtright, 9-10
Andrew A. Cox, 14-18
James R. Cox, 9
Marion Monroe Cox, 1, 3
Richard C. Cox, 8
John A. Cox, Jr., 5
Hazel M. Crain, 9
Rick Crandall, 8
A. Garr Cranney, 8
Charles J. Cranny, 8
Albert B. Crawford, 2
Douglas H. Crawford, 9
John Crawford, 13
William R. Crawford, 6-7
*Kevin D. Crehan, 11-17
Michelle M. Creighton, 11
Diana Crespo, 13
William J. E. Crissy, 4
R. Lenox Criswell, 2
John O. Crites, 6-9
Linda M. Crocker, 9-11, 13-14
Lysle W. Croft, 3-4
Lee J. Cronbach, 3-10
Lawrence A. Crosby, 9
Lawrence H. Cross, 12-14
Susan L. Crowley, 12
Douglas P. Crowne, 6
Michael K. Cruce, 18
William M. Cruickshank, 4
Nancy L. Crumpton, 15, 18
Michael J. Culbertson, 18
Thomas J. Cullen, Jr., 14
Thomas E. Culliton, Jr., 6
Jack A. Cummings, 9-10, 12, 14
Oliver W. Cummings, 9
Rhoda Cummings, 14
Bert P. Cundick, 9-10
Edward E. Cureton, 1-2, 4
Louise W. Cureton, 4
Thomas K. Cureton, 3
William L. Curlette, 11-12
William Curr, 5
Francis D. Curtis, 1-2
Mary E. Curtis, 9
Michael J. Curtis, 9
Stephanie L. Cutlan, 13
Athena Dacanay, 18
Peter A. Dahl, 8
W. Grant Dahlstrom, 4-6, 8
John T. Dailey, 4-5
Edgar Dale, 3
Reginald R. Dale, 5

Edward J. Daly III, 15
Moira Daly, 17
Fred L. Damarin, 8-9
*Rik Carl D'Amato, 11-12, 14-18
Larry G. Daniel, 12
Mark H. Daniel, 12-14
John C. Daniels, 5
M. Harry Daniels, 9-10
John G. Darley, 1-2
Richard E. Darnell, 8-9
Ralph F. Darr, Jr., 11-13
J. P. Das, 9-10
Jane Dass, 8
John H. Daugherty, 3
James M. Daum, 9
Charles Davidshofer, 9
M. Meghan Davidson, 18
Andrew S. Davis, 15-17
Brandon Davis, 11, 13
Charlotte Croon Davis, 3-6, 8
D. Russell Davis, 4-5
Edwin W. Davis, 3
Frederick B. Davis, 1-5, 7
Paul C. Davis, 6
Robert A. Davis, 3
Stanley E. Davis, 6
Steven F. Davis, 11-14
Parker Davis, Jr., 3
Mark L. Davison, 9
Helen C. Dawe, 3
Robyn M. Dawes, 8
Carolyn Dawson, 8
Linda S. Day, 11
*Ayres G. D'Costa, 11-15, 17-18
*Gary J. Dean, 12-15, 17-18
Raymond S. Dean, 9, 14-16
Sandra F. Dean, 17
Lester W. Dearborn, 6
William W. Deardorff, 12-13
William L. Deaton, 11-12
R. J. De Ayala, 14
David A. Decoster, 10
James Deese, 5
Sharon H. deFur, 14-15, 17-18
Frank P. DeLay, 2
Connie Kubo Della-Piana, 13-14
Gabriel M. Della-Piana, 6, 11-13
Vincent J. Dell'Orto, 8
Dennis J. Deloria, 7-9
Harold A. Delp, 4
Robert H. Deluty, 9
George J. Demakis, 16-17
Randy Demaline, 8
Robert G. Demaree, 4, 7-8
*Gerald E. DeMauro, 11-18
Marilyn E. Demorest, 10
George D. Demos, 6

Jennifer Denicolis, 12
Joseph W. Denison, 9
Evelyn Deno, 7
Gypsy M. Denzine, 15-18
Stephen J. DePaola, 15
Susan K. Deri, 3
Mayhew Derryberry, 3
Lawrence G. Derthick, 5
Harry R. DeSilva, 2
Lizanne Destefano, 11-12, 14
Douglas K. Detterman, 9
M. Vere DeVault, 7
Edward F. deVillafranca, 8
Anthony J. DeVito, 9
Joseph C. Dewey, 1-2
Michael L. Dey, 9
Robert E. Deysach, 10
Denise M. DeZolt, 11-13
Esther E. Diamond, 8-9, 11-13
Joseph O. Prewitt Diaz, 14
Phil Diaz, 16
Louis M. DiCarlo, 6
Charles F. Dicken, 6
Gwendolen S. Dickson, 1, 3
Paul B. Diederich, 1-2, 7
Allan O. Diefendorf, 11-12
John S. Diekhoff, 3-5
Stephen Dilchert, 16-18
Thomas E. Dinero, 12
Jonathan G. Dings, 12
Robert L. Dipboye, 8
James Clyde DiPerna, 14-16
Jean Dirks, 9
David N. Dixon, 9-13
Joe W. Dixon, 18
Gregory H. Dobbins, 9-10, 12
Keith S. Dobson, 9
Richard F. Docter, 7
Leland K. Doebler, 9
R. Anthony Doggett, 15-18
Janice A. Dole, 9-10
Kathleen A. Dolgos, 15
*Beth Doll, 10, 12-18
Robert H. Dolliver, 7-9
Stefan C. Dombrowski, 18
George Domino, 7-10, 12-14
Mavis L. Donahue, 9-10
Hei-Ki Dong, 9
Thomas F. Donlon, 8, 12-13
James Donnelly, 15, 17-18
Kerry Donnelly, 17
Antonia D'Onofrio, 17
Jerome E. Doppelt, 4-8
Dan Douglas, 11
Harl R. Douglass, 2-3
Dennis Doverspike, 15-16
E. Thomas Dowd, 9, 11-14

N. M. Downie, 6
John Downing, 8
Kenneth O. Doyle, Jr., 8
Vincent R. D'Oyley, 7
Ronald S. Drabman, 9
Raleigh M. Drake, 2-5
Richard M. Drake, 2-3
Penelope W. Dralle, 12
Ralph Mason Dreger, 8
Mariam Jean Dreher, 9-10
Arnold Dresden, 1
Paul L. Dressel, 3-8
James Drever, 2
Philip H. Dreyer, 8-9
Laura A. Driscoll, 8
Robert C. Droege, 7
Lee Droegemueller, 14
Priscilla A. Drum, 8-10
Robert J. Drummond, 11-15
Cynthia Ann Druva-Roush, 11-12
Judy R. Dubno, 9, 13
Linda M. DuBois, 9
Philip H. DuBois, 3, 6-7
John H. Duckitt, 9
Curtis Dudley-Marling, 9
Gerald G. Duffy, 7
Anthony T. Dugbartey, 15, 17-18
Lydia A. Duggins, 5
Stanley G. Dulsky, 2-3
Stephen B. Dunbar, 11
Harold B. Dunkel, 2-6
Jack W. Dunlap, 1-3
James A. Dunn, 7
S. S. Dunn, 5-6
Thomas M. Dunn, 16-18
Marvin D. Dunnette, 6
Carl J. Dunst, 9-10, 13
Daniel R. Dupecher, 8
Mary M. Dupuis, 9
Paula J. Dupuy, 11
Richard P. Duran, 9
Walter N. Durost, 4-8
David M. Dush, 9
Ralph D. Dutch, 6-8
Ibrahim Duyar, 17
August Dvorak, 2
Beatrice J. Dvorak, 3
Patricia L. Dwinell, 9
Carol Anne Dwyer, 8
Calvin O. Dyer, 9
Henry S. Dyer, 5-6
Robert Dykstra, 7-8
Norman Eagle, 5, 7-8
Douglas B. Eamon, 9
Maurice J. Eash, 8
Howard Easley, 2
Robert L. Ebel, 4-8

Bruce J. Eberhardt, 9-10
Del Eberhardt, 12
Tim Eck, 12
Kelly Eder, 16
Allen Jack Edwards, 10, 12
Bateman Edwards, 2
Cher I. Edwards, 16-18
Reginald Edwards, 5
Ron Edwards, 10-11
Byron R. Egeland, 8-9
Stewart Ehly, 10
Lee H. Ehman, 8
Linnea C. Ehri, 9
Jonathan Ehrlich, 11
William J. Eichman, 6-8
Dorothy H. Eichorn, 5-8
Rick Eigenbrood, 16-18
Philip Eisenberg, 3
Richard Elardo, 9
Bradley Elison, 12
John Elkins, 9
Arthur S. Ellen, 11, 16-17
William Eller, 6
Warwick B. Elley, 8
Judy L. Elliott, 13
M. H. Elliott, 3
Robert W. Elliott, 14
Stephen N. Elliott, 9-12
Steven D. Elliott, 9
Albert Ellis, 3-7
Theresa H. Elofson, 12
Susan Embretson (Whitely), 9
Lon L. Emerick, 8
W. G. Emmett, 3-4
Norman S. Endler, 8-9
Brian Engdahl, 14
*George Engelhard, Jr., 11-18
Max D. Engelhart, 1-2, 4-6
John M. Enger, 11-14
Connie T. England, 15-18
Bertram Epstein, 4
Jayne H. Epstein, 9
William P. Erchul, 10-11
James B. Erdmann, 11-13
Gerald L. Ericksen, 6-7
*Deborah B. Erickson, 9-14
Lawrence W. Erickson, 6-8
Richard C. Erickson, 8, 10
Emanuel E. Ericson, 2
Claire B. Ernhart, 12
Leonard D. Eron, 5-7
Joan Ershler, 11
Anna S. Espenschade, 4-5
Barbara F. Esser, 6-7
Alvin C. Eurich, 1-2
James R. Evans, 9
Beth L. Evard, 9

Alexander Even, 7
Colleen A. Ewing, 15
Lorraine D. Eyde, 8-9
H. J. Eysenck, 9
Julian Fabry, 9, 11-12
Jennifer J. Fager, 12-14
*Doreen Ward Fairbank, 12-17
Shauna Faltin, 12
Xitao Fan, 13
Frank H. Farley, 9
Richard F. Farmer, 13-14, 16, 18
Paul R. Farnsworth, 1-3, 5-6
Roger Farr, 7-8
R. Joel Farrell II, 15
Wiltrud Fassbinder, 14
Ray N. Faulkner, 1-2
Richard W. Faunce, 11-12
James Fauth, 15
Harold P. Fawcett, 2-5
Jay W. Fay, 1
Karen Fay, 13
Ethel M. Feagley, 3
Howard F. Fehr, 4
Elizabeth Fehrer, 3
Erich C. Fein, 16
Henry Feinberg, 1
Candice Feiring, 9-10
Shirley C. Feldmann, 8
Leonard S. Feldt, 5-8
Susan Felsenfeld, 12
Ray Fenton, 12-13, 16
George A. Ferguson, 3-6
Leonard W. Ferguson, 6
Ephrem Fernandez, 13-15
F. Felicia Ferrara, 14-15
Steven Ferrara, 11, 13
Robert H. Ferrell, 5
Trenton R. Ferro, 12-16
C. E. Ficken, 2
James A. Field, Jr., 5
Gordon Fifer, 5
Nikola N. Filby, 8
Jennifer G. Fillingim, 18
Maynard D. Filter, 11, 14
W. Holmes Finch, 16-18
Amy Finch-Williams, 10
Diane Billings Findley, 11
Warren G. Findley, 2-8
Stefan R. Fink, 8
Louis J. Finkle, 9
Carmen J. Finley, 11-12
Martin A. Fischer, 13
Seymour Fisher, 6
Wayne D. Fisher, 6
Joshua A. Fishman, 5
John L. Fisk, 9
Donald W. Fiske, 5

James A. Fitzgerald, 5
Colleen Fitzmaurice, 10
Anne R. Fitzpatrick, 11
Corine Fitzpatrick, 14-16
*Robert Fitzpatrick, 7-16
Dawn P. Flanagan, 12, 15
John C. Flanagan, 1, 3-4, 6
Rosemary Flanagan, 14-18
Stephen G. Flanagan, 11
*John W. Fleenor, 11-17
Lisa Fleisher, 9
C. M. Fleming, 4
W. G. Fleming, 6
Charles D. Flory, 1, 3
Robert E. Floden, 9
Terri Flowerday, 16
Randy G. Floyd, 18
Joseph J. Foley, 8
John P. Foley, Jr., 5-7
Mary O. Folsom, 7
Janet H. Fontaine, 14
Marie C. Fontana, 8
Thomas G. Foran, 1
Donna Ford, 12
Laurie Ford, 11-12
Rex L. Forehand, 9
Bertram R. Forer, 6
Frank J. Fornoff, 6, 8-9
Elaine Forsyth, 3
Robert A. Forsyth, 7-8
Tomlinson Fort, 2
Jim C. Fortune, 11-14
Judson W. Foust, 2
Hanford M. Fowler, 4-5
Raymond D. Fowler, Jr., 7-8
Charles Fox, 2
Glen Fox, 13-14
Hazel M. Fox, 10
Lynn H. Fox, 8-9
Robert A. Fox, 9
Austin C. Frank, 8
Mary Lou Bryant Frank, 14
Thomas T. Frantz, 7-8
Michael D. Franzen, 9
Stephen L. Franzoi, 9
Robert B. Frary, 9, 12-14
Barry J. Fraser, 9
Elizabeth D. Fraser, 5-6
Richard I. Frederick, 14
Wayne A. Frederick, 5
Norman Frederiksen, 3-8
Norman Fredman, 12
B. J. Freeman, 9
Frank S. Freeman, 4-5
Stephen J. Freeman, 14-18
David Freides, 7-8
J. Joseph Freilinger, 8

Patricia K. Freitag, 13-14
Brian F. French, 16, 18
John W. French, 3-8
Joseph L. French, 7
Robert L. French, 6
Sidney J. French, 3
Bruce R. Fretz, 9
Benno G. Fricke, 5-6
Marilyn Friend, 10
David A. Frisbie, 8-9
Clifford P. Froehlich, 4-5
Gustav J. Froehlich, 3-6
Benjamin Fruchter, 5
Bruce Frumkin, 17
Edward B. Fry, 6-8
Maurine A. Fry, 9
Douglas H. Fryer, 3
Verne C. Fryklund, 2
Douglas Fuchs, 10
Lynn S. Fuchs, 9-10
Mark H. Fugate, 12-13, 15
Martin Fujiki, 9-10
Solomon M. Fulero, 12, 14
Paul H. Furfey, 1
*Michael Furlong, 12-18
Elaine Furniss, 12
Edward J. Furst, 6-8
Robert K. Gable, 9, 11-14
Lena R. Gaddis, 11-13
N. L. Gage, 4-5
Eugene L. Gaier, 5
Rosslyn Gaines, 7
John P. Galassi, 9
Peggy E. Gallaher, 13
Gloria A. Galvin, 10-11
Leann M. Gamache, 12
Michael P. Gamache, 14
Bessie Lee Gambrill, 2
*Ronald J. Ganellen, 12-17
H. C. Ganguli, 9
Calvin P. Garbin, 11
Eugene E. Garcia, 9-10
Y. Evie Garcia, 15
Eric F. Gardner, 4-10
Sol L. Garfield, 7
Alan Garfinkel, 8-9, 11, 13-14, 16
Mary E. Garner, 16-18
Ruth Garner, 9
Edgar R. Garrett, 7
Henry E. Garrett, 1-5
Adrienne Garro, 16-17
Jack E. Gebart-Eaglemont, 13-16
Ann L. Gebhardt, 2
Karl W. Gehrkens, 2
Kurt F. Geisinger, 11-14, 16
John Geisler, 13-17
Kenneth E. Gell, 2

Karen Geller, 13
Glenn B. Gelman, 14
Jeremy Genovese, 16
Judy Lynn Genshaft, 9
J. Raymond Gerberich, 2-6
Kathryn Clark Gerken, 9-10
Zarabeth Gerling, 18
Joanne C. Gersten, 8
Maribeth Gettinger, 10
Esther Geva, 9
John J. Geyer, 7-8
Edwin E. Ghiselli, 3
Cecil A. Gibb, 5-7
Mark J. Gierl, 16, 18
H. H. Giles, 1-2
Ronald B. Gillam, 11-13
David Gillespie, 14
Jerry S. Gilmer, 12
Gerald Giraud, 15
John W. Gittinger, 5
Gene V Glass, 7-8
Hugh W. Glenn, 14
James R. Glennon, 6
Goldine C. Gleser, 6-9
Jerry S. Glimer, 12
John A. Glover, 11
Joshua M. Gold, 15
Lewis R. Goldberg, 7-8
Charles J. Golden, 9
Stephen L. Golding, 8-9
*Bert A. Goldman, 6-7, 11-15, 17-18
Leo Goldman, 6
Ronald Goldman, 8
Steven H. Goldman, 9
Marcel L. Goldschmid, 7
Diane Goldsmith, 12
Keith Goltry, 2
Chris Gonzales, 15
Jorge E. Gonzales, 15, 17-18
Ronald H. Good, III, 11
Elizabeth J. Goodacre, 7
Florence L. Goodenough, 2-3
Joan F. Goodman, 9
Clarence J. Goodnight, 7
Leonard D. Goodstein, 6-8
William L. Goodwin, 8
Rodney K. Goodyear, 9
Betty N. Gordon, 9
Edwin Gordon, 7
Hans C. Gordon, 2-3
Leonard V. Gordon, 6-8
John B. Gormly, 9
Elliot L. Gory, 9, 11
Edward Earl Gotts, 9, 14
Harrison G. Gough, 4-9, 11-12
Neil Gourlay, 5
Eric Grady, 18

C. Ray Graham, 8
Grace Graham, 1-2
John R. Graham, 11-12
Steve Graham, 9, 11-14
Theresa Graham, 14-18
Susan L. Graham-Clay, 9
Larry B. Grantham, 12
Vicki, Gratopp, 12
Zandra S. Gratz, 15-16, 18
M. Elizabeth Graue, 12
Carol A. Gray, 9
William S. Gray, 1, 3-4
Felice J. Green, 13-14
Kathy E. Green, 12-13, 16-17
Russel F. Green, 6-7
Susan K. Green, 16
Edward B. Greene, 3-5
Harry A. Greene, 2-3
Jeffrey H. Greenhaus, 9
Noel Gregg, 10
Patrick Grehan, 16
Frank M. Gresham, 9-13
Konrad Gries, 4-5
Amy-Jane Griffith, 18
*J. Jeffrey Grill, 8-14
Arnold B. Grobman, 7
Hulda Grobman, 7-8
Martin G. Groff, 9
Patrick Groff, 9
Norman E. Gronlund, 8
Richard E. Gross, 5-8
Fred M. Grossman, 9-10
Foster E. Grossnickle, 1-4
William R. Grove, 3-4
Melissa M. Groves, 13
Wilson H. Guertin, 5-6
Richard E. Guest, 11
Walter S. Guiler, 4
J. P. Guilford, 1-5
Robert M. Guion, 8-10, 12-14
Sami Gulgoz, 11-12
Arlen R. Gullickson, 7-8, 12
R. Gulliford, 7
Harold Gulliksen, 1-2, 4
John Flagg Gummere, 2
Faith Gunning-Dixon, 13-14
John W. Gustad, 5
Rhonda L. Gutenberg, 9-10
George M. Guthrie, 8-9
John T. Guthrie, 7-8
Barbara Lapp Gutkin, 10
Terry B. Gutkin, 9, 14
*Thomas W. Guyette, 9-10, 12, 14, 17-18
Natasha Gwartney, 12
Malcolm D. Gynther, 7-8
Lyn R. Haber, 9-10
Manuella H. Habicht, 16

Robert R. Haccoun, 14
Laura B. Hadley, 2
Atiqa Hachimi, 16
John H. Haefner, 5-6
Edward H. Haertel, 9, 13
Geneva D. Haertel, 13-14
Elizabeth Hagen, 5-7
Rosa A. Hagin, 9, 11, 13
Michio P. Hagiwara, 7-8
Amos L. Hahn, 9
Milton E. Hahn, 3-4, 6
A. Ralph Hakstian, 7-8
Thomas M. Haladyna, 11-13
Robert Leslie Hale, 9
Alfred E. Hall, 8
Bruce W. Hall, 11
Cathy W. Hall, 9-11
Penelope K. Hall, 11-12
W. E. Hall, 3
Wallace B. Hall, 6
Raphael M. Haller, 7-8
Harvey Halpern, 8
Ronald K. Hambleton, 8-9, 11-12, 16
Wade L. Hamil, 11
Laura Hamilton, 18
Scott B. Hamilton, 9
Thomas A. Hammeke, 9
Nelson G. Hanawalt, 3-5
Thomas E. Hancock, 15-17
Leonard Handler, 15
C. H. Handschin, 2
Karl R. Hanes, 13, 16
Kenneth M. Hanig, 18
Gerald S. Hanna, 8-9, 11-14
Lavone A. Hanna, 2-3
Paul R. Hanna, 4
Michael J. Hannafin, 9
Mary Elizabeth Hannah, 9
Jane Hansen, 9
Joe B. Hansen, 13
Jo-Ida C. Hansen, 8-9
Michael C. Hansen, 13
Gary R. Hanson, 7
Gregory Hanson, 16
William E. Hanson, 14-16
*Richard E. Harding, 10, 12-17
David S. Hargrove, 10
Thomas G. Haring, 10-11
Marilyn J. Haring-Hidore, 9
Lenore W. Harmon, 8-10
Delwyn L. Harnisch, 11-15
Dennis C. Harper, 9-10, 13-14
Robert A. Harper, 6-7
Thomas H. Harrell, 11
Thomas W. Harrell, 3
Philip L. Harriman, 4-6
Robert G. Harrington, 9-10, 13-14

Albert J. Harris, 3, 6-7
Chester W. Harris, 3-4
Dale B. Harris, 4-8
David P. Harris, 7-8
Jerry D. Harris, 9
Jesse G. Harris, Jr., 6
Larry A. Harris, 7-8
Robert C. Harris, 7
Sandra M. Harris, 18
Theodore L. Harris, 6
Mary T. Harrison, 7
*Patti L. Harrison, 9-11, 13-15, 17
Charles M. Harsh, 3-4
Stuart N. Hart, 10, 12
Verna Hart, 9, 11
Jan Harting-McChesney, 15
Ruth N. Hartley, 8
Bruce W. Hartman, 10
Hope J. Hartman, 11
George W. Hartmann, 1, 4
Rodney T. Hartnett, 8-9
Timothy S. Hartshorne, 10
Louis D. Hartson, 1
Maurice L. Hartung, 1, 3
Anne L. Harvey, 11
Leo M. Harvill, 11-13
*Michael R. Harwell, 11-16, 18
Glen Hass, 3
Jason Hassenstab, 16
J. O. Hassler, 1-2
J. Thomas Hastings, 4-6, 8
Richard S. Hatch, 6
Starke R. Hathaway, 3
Clifford V. Hatt, 9
John T. Hatten, 8-9
John Hattie, 12-13, 16
Keith Hattrup, 12-15, 17
G. E. Hawkins, 2
James Hawkins, 16
David G. Hawkridge, 7-8
Mary R. Haworth, 5-6
Linda White Hawthorne, 9
Edward N. Hay, 3-5
James R. Hayden, 5-6
Steven C. Hayes, 11
*Theodore L. Hayes, 13-18
Leslie M. Haynes, 4
Rebekah Haynes, 17
*Sandra D. Haynes, 13-18
William O. Haynes, 9-10, 12
Joni R. Hays, 14
Cynthia Hazel, 18
E. Charles Healey, 10
Kenneth L. Heaton, 4
Martine Hébert, 11-13
Deborah Hecht, 11
Daniel Heck, 14

Natalie L. Hedberg, 11-12
Earle R. Hedrick, 2
David K. Heenan, 5-6
Lloyd H. Heidgerd, 6
Louis J. Heifetz, 10
Edith S. Heil, 10
Louis M. Heil, 2
Alfred B. Heilbrun, Jr., 5-10
Nancy Heilman, 11
Alice W. Heim, 4-7
April K. Heisett, 17
Harry Heller, 2
William H. Helme, 6
G. C. Helmstadter, 7, 9
John K. Hemphill, 6-7
Carlen Henington, 13-15, 17-18
V. A. C. Henmon, 1
Martha E. Hennen, 14, 16
James J. Hennessy, 10, 14-16
Mary Henning-Stout, 10-13
Edwin R. Henry, 4
Stephan A. Henry, 10
William E. Henry, 4-5
William Hered, 6
David O. Herman, 12-13
Patricia Herman, 9
Edward S. Herold, 9
Edwin L. Herr, 9-10
Virgil E. Herrick, 4-5
*Allen K. Hess, 9-16
Brian Hess, 15
Kathryn D. Hess, 11-12
Robert M. Hess, 12
John R. Hester, 11
William L. Heward, 9
Julia A. Hickman, 10
Peggy A. Hicks, 13
Elfrieda H. Hiebert, 9
A. N. Hieronymus, 5-7
A. Dirk Hightower, 10
E. H. C. Hildebrandt, 3
Scott Kristian Hill, 14
Walker H. Hill, 5
John R. Hills, 6-9
*Robert W. Hiltonsmith, 9, 11-13, 16-17
Philip Himelstein, 7
Elmer D. Hinckley, 4
C. B. Hindley, 6
Laura Hines, 9
J. Scott Hinkle, 11
Georgia Hinman,18
Samual Hinton, 15
Michael D. Hiscox, 9
Marshall S. Hiskey, 6-7
Jean Hoard, 2
James R. Hobson, 2-5
Emil H. Hoch, 8

Elton Hocking, 3-4
James O. Hodges, 8
James M. Hodgson, 16
Barbara W. Hodson, 9
Kathryn E. Hoff, 15-18
James V. Hoffman, 9
Robert Hogan, 7-10
Thomas P. Hogan, 8, 14-18
Dorothy E. Holberg, 3
Raymond H. Holden, 7
Candice Haas Hollingsead, 14
Davidd R. Holliway, 18
Warren S. Holmes, 2
Robert R. Holt, 4
Wayne H. Holtzman, 5, 7
Charles Holzwarth, 2
Susan P. Homan, 9
L. Michael Honaker, 11
Charles H. Honzik, 4
Marjorie P. Honzik, 6-7
Albert B. Hood, 8
Darlene Ward Hood, 17
Joyce E. Hood, 8-9
Stephen B. Hood, 8
Stephen R. Hooper, 10-14
Kenneth D. Hopkins, 6-9, 11
John L. Horn, 7
Thomas D. Horn, 7-8
John E. Horrocks, 5-6
William R. Horstman, 17
Clark W. Horton, 2-5
Daniel L. Householder, 8
Janet Houser, 17-18
Charles Houston, 12
Carl I. Hovland, 3-5
Robert W. Howard, 2
Edgar Howarth, 8
George W. Howe, 9
Kenneth W. Howell, 9-10
Robert J. Howell, 10
Duncan Howie, 5
Monica M. Hoye, 3
Cyril J. Hoyt, 4-7
Kenneth B. Hoyt, 6
Louis M. Hsu, 9
Te-Fang Hua, 13
Mary E. Huba, 11
Carl J. Huberty, 7-9
*Anita M. Hubley, 13-18
Edith M. Huddleston, 4
John Peter Hudson, Jr., 13
E. Scott Huebner, 10-11, 13-14
Mildred H. Huebner, 7-8
David P. Huford, 17
Jan N. Hughes, 10-11
Selma Hughes, 11-12
Violet Hughes, 2

Doncaster G. Humm, 2
Lloyd G. Humphreys, 3-6, 9
Joel Hundert, 9
John D. Hundleby, 6
Stephen Hunka, 6
Albert L. Hunsicker, 4
E. Patricia Hunt, 2
Jane V. Hunt, 7-8
Thelma Hunt, 3
William A. Hunt, 3
George W. Hunter, 1-2
Archer W. Hurd, 1
David P. Hurford, 13-16
Tiffany Hutchins, 18
Sylvia M. Hutchinson, 10
Robert R. Hutzell, 9
George W. Hynd, 9
Robert J. Illback, 9
Ludwig Immergluck, 3
James C. Impara, 11
Henry A. Imus, 3
Carlos Inchaurralde, 14, 16
Mario Iona, 8
Carl Isenhart, 13-16
Steven Isonio, 13
Stephen H. Ivens, 12-14
Annette M. Iverson, 11-12
Margaret Ives, 3
Edward F. Iwanicki, 8-9
Douglas N. Jackson, 7-9
Joseph F. Jackson, 2-3
Robert W. B. Jackson, 5
Richard M. Jaeger, 8-10
Alice N. Jameson, 3
Molly M. Jameson, 17
Colleen B. Jamison, 7
Marc Janoson, 15, 17-18
Patsy Arnett Jaynes, 11
Frank C. Jean, 1
Chantale Jeanrie, 13-15
*Jeffrey A. Jenkins, 11-18
Jill Ann Jenkins, 14-16
John R. Jennings, 5
Karen E. Jennings, 15-16
Arthur R. Jensen, 5-7, 9
Joanne L. Jensen, 12
Patrick J. Jeske, 9
Carl F. Jesness, 7
Richard Jessor, 5
Frank B. Jex, 6
James E. Jirsa, 9
Lynae A. Johnsen, 16
A. Pemberton Johnson, 5
Cecil D. Johnson, 5
Christopher Johnson, 15-16
Dale D. Johnson, 8
Jacqueline Johnson, 15

Willard A. Kerr, 3-4, 6-7
Anne R. Kessler, 13
Carol E. Kessler, 14-15
Kathy S. Kessler, 11-12
Sandra M. Ketrow, 14
Gilbert C. Kettelkamp, 6
Thomas E. Kieren, 8
Kenneth A. Kiewra, 11-14
Edward Kifer, 9
Jeremy Kilpatrick, 7-8
Ernest W. Kimmel, 11, 13-14
Elaine F. Kinder, 1
Glen D. King, 8
John D. King, 12, 16
Joseph E. King, 3
Suzanne King, 12
Forrest A. Kingsbury, 2
G. Gage Kingsbury, 12, 14
Albert J. Kingston, 6-8
Lucien B. Kinney, 2, 4
Richard T. Kinnier, 13, 17-18
John R. Kinzer, 3
Wayne K. Kirchner, 6
Barbara A. Kirk, 7
*Jean Powell Kirnan, 11-18
Karyll Kiser, 12
Philip M. Kitay, 6-7
Helen Kitchens, 13-14
Tom Kitwood, 8
Paul M. Kjeldergaard, 6
Seymour G. Klebanoff, 4
Beverly M. Klecker, 14-15
Steven Klee, 9
Benjamin Kleinmuntz, 6-10
Milton V. Kline, 6
Paul Kline, 7-8
William E. Kline, 7-8
Martin Kling, 7-8
Robert R. Knapp, 7
Samuel J. Knapp, 9
Thomas R. Knapp, 9, 13
Catharine C. Knight, 12
*Howard M. Knoff, 9-15
John F. Knutson, 7
William R. Koch, 11-12
Stephen L. Koffler, 12-13
Kate L. Kogan, 3-4
William S. Kogan, 4
Timothy R. Konold, 14, 17-18
David Kopel, 1-2
Rebecca J. Kopriva, 12
Abraham K. Korman, 8
Stephen M. Koziol, Jr., 8
Ernest J. Kozma, 11
S. Kathleen Krach, 16
Jack J. Kramer, 9
Jeffrey Kramer, 14

John H. Kranzler, 12, 14
David R. Krathwohl, 5
Thomas R. Kratochwill, 9
Charles J. Krauskopf, 7-8
Carole M. Krauthamer, 12
Daniel Krenzler, 17
Roy A. Kress, 7-9
A. C. Krey, 1
Philip H. Kriedt, 6
Leslie H. Krieger, 14
Radhika Krishnamurthy, 14, 16
S. David Kriska, 12
Russell P. Kropp, 5
Hailey E. Krouse, 17
Damon Krug, 13
Morris Krugman, 3-5
John D. Krumboltz, 6
David J. Krus, 9
Dietmar Kuchemann, 9
Frederic Kuder, 2-3
Jay Kuder, 11
Phyllis Kuehn, 12
Sally Kuhlenschmidt, 13-14, 16
F. Kuhlmann, 2
Jody L. Kulstad, 15-17
Deborah King Kundert, 10-12
Antony John Kunnan, 13, 16
Dana G. Kurfman, 7-8
Albert K. Kurtz, 4-6, 8
Joseph C. Kush, 14-18
Koressa Kutsick, 10
W. C. Kvaraceus, 3-4
Kwong-Liem Karl Kwan, 13-15
Lou LaBrant, 2
Barbara Lachar, 11, 13
David Lachar, 11
Eleanor M. Ladd, 8
Robert Lado, 7
Linda A. Lagomarsino, 9
*Matthew E. Lambert, 11, 13-18
Nadine M. Lambert, 9
Elaine L. La Monica, 8
W. Elmer Lancaster, 2
Daniel Landis, 7
Herbert A. Landry, 2
Edward Landy, 5
Frank J. Landy, 8
*Suzanne Lane, 11, 15-18
William Steve Lang, 11-14
Theos A. Langlie, 1
Aimée Langlois, 12, 14, 16-18
Charles R. Langmuir, 3-6
Gerald V. Lannholm, 3-5
Kevin Lanning, 14-15
Richard I. Lanyon, 7-9, 11-12
Luis M. Laosa, 8
Glenda Lappan, 8-9

Peter A. Lappan, Jr., 6-8
William S. Larson, 2-6
Cynthia A. Larson-Daugherty, 14
Julian J. Lasky, 7
Robert L. Lathrop, 7
Kelly Laugle, 16
Allan L. LaVoie, 8-9
*Joseph G. Law, Jr., 11-16
J. S. Lawes, 6-7
Kimberly A. Lawless, 13
Camille Lawrence, 18
C. H. Lawshe, Jr., 3
Gary W. Lawson, 9
Martha E. Layman, 4
Wilbur L. Layton, 4-11
Thomas Lazarro, 18
Robert A. Leark, 13-16
Courtney LeClaire, 17
Steven B. Leder, 12, 14
Herbert Lederer, 8
Richard Ledgerwood, 1
James Ledvinka, 9
Courtland C. Lee, 9
J. Murray Lee, 1, 5
S. G. Lee, 6-7
Steven W. Lee, 10-13
Young Ju Lee, 16
Jeanette Lee-Farmer, 18
D. Welty Lefever, 1-6
Sue M. Legg, 12
Paul R. Lehman, 7-10
Irvin J. Lehmann, 6-13
Richard Lehrer, 11
Roger T. Lennon, 4-5
Theodore F. Lentz, 3
Francis E. Lentz, Jr., 9-10
J. Paul Leonard, 2-3
*Frederick T. L. Leong, 11-18
Richard Lesh, 9
Donald A. Leton, 7-9
*S. Alvin Leung, 11-17
Ralph G. Leverett, 13-14, 16
Eugene E. Levitt, 6-8
C. Michael Levy, 9
Philip M. Levy, 6
Seymour Levy, 6
Mary A. Lewis, 11-14
Neil P. Lewis, 14
Roy D. Lewis, 5
Lester M. Libo, 7-8
Peter D. Lifton, 9
John Liggett, 5-6
Glynn D. Ligon, 9
Paul M. Limbert, 1
John Linck, 17
David P. Lindeman, 9
Steven J. Lindner, 14

E. F. Lindquist, 5
Mary Montgomery Lindquist, 8-9
Pam Lindsey-Glenn, 15-18
*Rick Lindskog, 11-16
C. Mauritz Lindvall, 7-8
W. Line, 2
James C. Lingoes, 6
James B. Lingwall, 8
Robert L. Linn, 8-10
Maria Prendes Lintel, 13-14
Gary E. Lintereur, 8, 10
Richard Lippa, 9
Robert W. Lissitz, 11
William M. Littell, 7
Orrel E. Little, 3
Wei-Ping Liu, 13
Alice K. Liveright, 2
Howard A. Lloyd, 14
John Wills Lloyd, 9
Steven G. LoBello, 11-13
Aileene S. Lockhart, 7
Jane Loevinger, 4, 8
Sandra Loew, 14-17
R. Duane Logue, 8
Paul R. Lohnes, 6-8
Walter F. W. Lohnes, 7
Paul S. Lomax, 3
John W. Lombard, 7-8
Susan Lonborg, 17
Charles J. Long, 12-14
John A. Long, 3
Louis Long, 3
*Steven H. Long, 11-13, 15-18
Andrew Longacre, 2
Alfred P. Longo, 13, 15-16
Frank M. Loos, 4
Emilia C. Lopez, 13-14
Peter G. Loret, 6
Irving Lorge, 2-3, 5
Margaret F. Lorimer, 6
Maurice Lorr, 5-8
C. M. Louttit, 1-4
Kelly Brey Love, 16
Kenneth Lovell, 6-7
Benson P. Low, 9
Jerry M. Lowe, 14
Rodney L. Lowman, 9-10
Brenda H. Loyd, 9, 12
S. Ruben Lozano, 9
Ardie Lubin, 4
William H. Lucio, 6
William H. Lucow, 5
Leslie Eastman Lukin, 13-14, 16
James Lumsden, 5, 8
Robert W. Lundin, 5-7
Clifford E. Lunneborg, 7-8
Patricia W. Lunneborg, 8-9

David T. Lykken, 6-8
Howard B. Lyman, 6-7
Joan I. Lynch, 9-10
Hugh Lytton, 8
Henry S. Maas, 3
Linda Mabry, 12
Gloria Maccow, 13-14
John MacDonald, 13-14
F. Charles Mace, 9-10
Gordon N. MacKenzie, 3-4
Arthur C. MacKinney, 6-8
Karen Mackler, 14, 16-17
Saunders MacLane, 6
David MacPhee, 11-13
George F. Madaus, 8-9
Faith Madden, 4
*Cleborne D. Maddux, 10-18
Ronald A. Madle, 14-18
Thomas W. Mahan, Jr., 6
Jennifer N. Mahdavi, 16-18
Roderick K. Mahurin, 11-12
James Mainwaring, 5
Timothy J. Makatura, 14-18
*Koressa Kutsick Malcolm, 11, 13-18
Julius B. Maller, 1-2
Susan J. Maller, 13-16
George G. Mallinson, 6-8
Jacqueline V. Mallinson, 6-8
Berenice Mallory, 2
Margaret E. Malone, 13-14
Dean R. Malsbary, 8
Jay A. Mancini, 14
Milton M. Mandell, 4
Joseph R. Manduchi, 14
Kenneth J. Manges, 14
Ramasamy Manikam, 14
Lester Mann, 7-9
M. Jacinta Mann, 5
John Manning, 5, 7
Winton H. Manning, 6
Herschel T. Manuel, 2-5
*Caroline Manuele-Adkins, 9-10, 12-13, 16-18
Gregory J. Marchant, 12-14
Gary L. Marco, 11-14
Carol Mardell-Czudnowski, 10
Howard Margolis, 14, 17
Suzanne Markel-Fox, 12
Robert P. Markley, 9-10
Howard J. Markman, 9
Melvin R. Marks, 6
Mary Beth Marr, 9
Marc Marschark, 12
Herbert W. Marsh, 9
David Marshall, 10
Brian K. Martens, 10-11
Charles Wm. Martin, 11
Roy P. Martin, 9

Suzanne G. Martin, 14
William E. Martin, Jr., 13-16, 18
Trey Martindale, 15
Manuel Martinez-Pons, 16
Stanley S. Marzolf, 3
Bertram B. Masia, 6
Carolyn E. Massad, 8
M. Mastrangelo, 15
Paul Mastrangelo, 14
Joseph D. Matarazzo, 9-10
Johnny L. Matson, 9
Ross W. Matteson, 4
Michael S. Matthews, 17-18
Paula Matuszek, 9
Francis N. Maxfield, 1-2
James Maxwell, 3-5
Susanna Maxwell, 9
Samuel T. Mayo, 6-9
Arthur B. Mays, 2
James J. Mazza, 10
Dawn Mazzie, 16
Charles C. McArthur, 7
Patrick P. McCabe, 16
John N. McCall, 7
Raymond J. McCall, 5
W. C. McCall, 2
William A. McCall, 2
James M. McCallister, 3
R. Steve McCallum, 9
Susan McCammon, 10
Boyd R. McCandless, 4, 6-7
James J. McCarthy, 7-9
Kevin J. McCarthy, 12, 14-15, 17
James Leslie McCary, 8
Robert L. McCaul, 2-3
Clara J. McCauley, 2
*Rebecca J. McCauley, 11-18
Erin McClure, 12
Daniel L. McCollum, 16
David McCone, 15
Scott R. McConnell, 11
Andrew J. McConney, 14
Richard J. McCowan, 14
Sheila C. McCowan, 14
Robert R. McCrae, 9
R. W. McCulloch, 5
Constance M. McCullough, 2-3, 5, 7
Merilee McCurdy, 14, 16-17
S. P. McCutchen, 1-2
Hiram L. McDade, 9
Arthur S. McDonald, 6
D. W. McElwain, 4-5
William C. McGaghie, 8
Ellen McGinnis, 10
Dixie McGinty, 16-17
Carol M. McGregor, 14-17
Kevin S. McGrew, 10

Christine H. McGuire, 5-8
Valentina McInerney, 15, 17
David E. McIntosh, 12
Robert M. McIntyre, 9
Michael G. McKee, 7
William T. McKee, 10
Margaret G. McKim, 3-4
Thomas McKnight, 14-17
Joyce R. McLarty, 11, 14
Kenneth F. McLaughlin, 6
John McLeish, 4, 7
Mary J. McLellan, 12-14, 18
Jonathon C. McLendon, 6
John McLeod, 8
Robert J. McMahon, 9
Robert F. McMorris, 9-13
Douglas M. McNair, 7-8
Michael McNamara, 12
Sharon McNeely, 12
Malcolm R. McNeil, 10-14
Jeanette McPherrin, 2
John V. McQuitty, 3-4
Louis L. McQuitty, 4
Douglas J. McRae, 11-13
Leija V. McReynolds, 8
Paul McReynolds, 7-10
Damian McShane, 11
Richard A. Meade, 5
Arthur W. Meadows, 5
Tawnya Meadows, 17-18
David J. Mealor, 9-11
I. G. Meddleton, 5
Albert E. Meder, Jr., 5
Maria Del R. Medina-Diaz, 13-14, 16
Frederic J. Medway, 11, 13, 16-18
Paul E. Meehl, 3
Sheila Mehta, 14-14
Edwin I. Megargee, 7-8
Howard D. Mehlinger, 7-8
William A. Mehrens, 7-9, 11-13
Sheila Mehta, 13
Manfred J. Meier, 7-9, 11
Norman C. Meier, 2
Scott T. Meier, 12-16
Joyce Meikamp, 14-18
William B. Meldrum, 1, 3
P. L. Mellenbruch, 5
Gary B. Melton, 9-10, 12
Richard S. Melton, 6, 8
H. Meltzer, 3
David M. Memory, 9
Gerald A. Mendelsohn, 6
Kevin Menefee, 11-12
Robert J. Menges, 8
Ivan N. Mensh, 4
Gerald M. Meredith, 7
Peter F. Merenda, 11-14

Brad M. Merker, 15-16
Philip R. Merrifield, 6
Jack C. Merwin, 6-8
William R. Merz, Sr., 12-14
Bernadine Meyer, 5
Donald L. Meyer, 6
John H. Meyer, 3
C. Edward Meyers, 8
Marcee J. Meyers, 9
Joan J. Michael, 7
*William B. Michael, 4-13, 15-16
Hillary Michaels, 14
William J. Micheels, 4-5
Grace Middleton, 11
Christopher P. Migotsky, 12
T. R. Miles, 5-6, 8
John E. Milholland, 5-8
C. Dean Miller, 9
Courtney Miller, 16
Daniel C. Miller, 14-17
Gloria E. Miller, 10
J. Monroe Miller, 16
John K. Miller, 9
Jon F. Miller, 9
Lovick C. Miller, 7-8
*M. David Miller, 11-12, 14-18
Robert B. Miller, 14
Robert J. Miller, 11-14
Sherri K. Miller, 11
Marie Miller-Whitehead, 15-16
Jason Millman, 6-9
Craig N. Mills, 9, 11-12
John A. Mills, 13-14
J. B. Miner, 2
J. H. Minnick, 2
*Patricia L. Mirenda, 10-12, 14-15, 17
Lorenz Misbach, 3
Rama K. Mishra, 17-18
Ronald W. Mitchell, 7
James V. Mitchell, Jr., 7-8
Carolyn Mitchell-Person, 14-15
Arthur Mittman, 6-8
Glenn Moe, 9
Huberto Molina, 8
William G. Mollenkopf, 3-4, 8
Floyd V. Monaghan, 7
Eason Monroe, 3
Marion Monroe, 1, 3
*Judith A. Monsaas, 12-17
Alan D. Moore, 16
Debra Moore, 18
Heidi K. Moore, 16
Joseph E. Moore, 2-4, 6
Terence Moore, 6
Walter J. Moore, 7
Pamilla Morales, 14
Mary Ross Moran, 11-12

*Kevin L. Moreland, 9-14
G. A. V. Morgan, 5-7
Alice E. Moriarty, 7
Claudia J. Morner, 12, 14
Sherwyn P. Morreale, 12-14
John B. Morris, 5
Coleman Morrison, 6
Frances Crook Morrison, 5-6
Gale M. Morrison, 9, 12-13
Nathan Morrison, 3
Thomas F. Morrison, 2
Irving Morrissett, 8
David T. Morse, 16-18
H. T. Morse, 3
N. W. Morton, 1-2, 4
P. L. Morton, 2
Robert G. Morwood, 14
Harold E. Moser, 5
Donald L. Mosher, 7-8
David Moshman, 10
Charles I. Mosier, 2-3
C. Scott Moss, 6
Pamela A. Moss, 9, 11
Kevin W. Mossholder, 9-10
Stephan J. Motowidlo, 8-9
Donald E. Mowrer, 10
Robert R. Mowrer, 10
*Paul M. Muchinsky, 9, 12-14, 16-17
Daniel J. Mueller, 10
Kate Hevner Mueller, 5
Ralph O. Mueller, 11-13
Ann M. Muench, 11
Ina V. S. Mullis, 8
Leo A. Munday, 7
Allyn M. Munger, 6
Janice W. Murdoch, 14
Joann Murphey, 15
Carolyn Colvin Murphy, 10
Joseph A. Murphy, 7-8
Kevin R. Murphy, 9-12
Wilbur F. Murra, 1-2
Elsie Murray, 4
Mildred Murray-Ward, 13-14, 16-18
James L. Mursell, 1-3
Bernard I. Murstein, 6-8
Nyaradzo H. Mvududa, 18
Charles T. Myers, 5, 8
Roberta S. Myers, 9
Sheldon S. Myers, 6-7
Dean H. Nafziger, 8, 11-12
Jack A. Naglieri, 9, 11
Philip Nagy, 12-13
Louis C. Nanassy, 5
Scott A. Napolitano, 14, 16, 18
Doris E. Nason, 8
Diana S. Natalicio, 8-9
Theodor F. Naumann, 6-7

Wendy Naumann, 14-15
Lori Nebelsick-Gullett, 15
Leo Nedelsky, 5-6
Charles O. Neidt, 5-6
Leah M. Nellis, 14-17
Edward A. Nelsen, 9
Clarence H. Nelson, 3-8
Jack L. Nelson, 8
Rosemery O. Nelson-Gray, 11
Myrna K. Ness, 9
Debra Neubert, 11-12
Charles Neuringer, 8
Andrew F. Newcomb, 9
Theodore Newcomb, 2
Phyllis L. Newcomer, 8-9
Gwendolyn Newkirk, 10
T. Ernest Newland, 6-7
Bernard H. Newman, 7
Dianna L. Newman, 10-13
E. Jean Newman, 13-14
Isadore Newman, 12
Joseph Newman, 4
Kenneth R. Newton, 5
Arthur M. Nezu, 10
William H. Nibbelink, 8
Lois Nichols, 12
David S. Nichols, 9, 11
Robert C. Nichols, 6, 8-9
Nicole L. Nieset, 17-18
John Nisbet, 5-7
Stanley D. Nisbet, 4-7
Michael Nissenbaum, 12
*Anthony J. Nitko, 8-14
Amanda Nolen, 18
Victor H. Noll, 1-7
Patricia Noller, 9
Claude E. Norcross, 4
Warren T. Norman, 5-7
*Janet A. Norris, 9-15
Raymond C. Norris, 5
Robert D. North, 5-7
Paul A. Northrop, 1-2
Christine Novak, 12, 14, 18
Ruth M. Noyce, 9-10
Edward S. Noyes, 2-3
Jum C. Nunnally, 7
Michelle Nutter, 15
Thomas Oakland, 8-9
C. A. Oakley, 2-3
C. O. Oakley, 3
Lindsey O'Brennan, 18
Thomas C. O'Brien, 7-8
John E. Obrzut, 9, 11
Anna S. Ochoa, 8-9
*Salvador Hector Ochoa, 12-17
Charles W. Odell, 1-3
*Judy Oehler-Stinnett, 10-14, 16

Lynn R. Offermann, 13
Billy T. Ogletree, 13-14
Kevin E. O'Grady, 9-10
Stephen Olejnik, 11-12, 14
Arturo Olivarez, Jr., 16-18
Donald W. Oliver, 6
Mary Ellen Oliverio, 5, 7-8
Esteban L. Olmedo, 9
*D. Joe Olmi, 11-16
Amy M. Olson, 17-18
Carl J. Olson, 7
Thomas R. O'Neill, 16-18
Deniz S. Ones, 14-18
Albert C. Oosterhof, 12-13
Don B. Oppenheim, 9
Pedro T. Orata, 2
Michael D. Orlansky, 9
Jacob S. Orleans, 2-6
David B. Orr, 6-7
John C. Ory, 9
Timothy M. Osberg, 11
Allison Osborn, 17
Agnes E. Osborne, 3
Alan Osborne, 7-8
R. T. Osborne, 7
Worth J. Osburn, 1-2, 4
Stuart Oskamp, 7-8
Alton O'Steen, 2
Steven J. Osterlind, 11-13
Nicki N. Ostrom, 9
Donald P. Oswald, 13, 15-16
Jay L. Otis, 3-4
Sandye M. Ouzts, 16-17
Terry Overton, 11-14
Steven V. Owen, 11-14
Gretchen Owens, 14-16
Robert E. Owens, Jr., 9-10
William A. Owens, 6, 8-9
Lindsay R. Owings, 18
Heidi K. Paa, 15
C. Robert Pace, 3-8
Abbot Packard, 12, 14
Albert G. Packard, 3
Vicki S. Packman, 13-14, 17
Ellis Batten Page, 6-9
Kathleen D. Paget, 9-10, 13-14
Nathaniel J. Pallone, 14-16
Ian C. Palmer, 12
Orville Palmer, 5
Osmond E. Palmer, 5-7
Jean M. Palormo, 6
Josephine B. Pane, 7
Mary Pannbacker, 11
Anthony W. Paolitto, 12-14
Anthony M. Paolo, 14-15
Ila Parasnis, 14
Gino Parisi, 7

Carol S. Parke, 16
Jayne A. Parker, 9
Anna Parsek, 2
Charles K. Parsons, 9-12, 16
A. Harry Passow, 4, 8-9, 11-12
Thanos Patelis, 15-16
Donald G. Paterson, 2-4
Gerald R. Patterson, 5
Willard W. Patty, 4
Walter Pauk, 7
Jerome D. Pauker, 6-9
Sharon E. Paulson, 13
Renee Pavelski, 14-15
David A. Payne, 6-7
Douglas S. Payne, 9
Frank D. Payne, 9
Joshua W. Payne, 16
Robert W. Payne, 6-9
William G. Peacher, 4
L. Carolyn Pearson, 13-15
Mary Ellen Pearson, 9-11
P. David Pearson, 9
John Gray Peatman, 2
Elazar J. Pedhazur, 8-9
E. A. Peel, 4-5
Charles W. Pendleton, 8
Douglas A. Penfield, 12
John P. Penna, 8
James A. Penny, 17
L. S. Penrose, 3
William H. Perkins, 7
Carole Perlman, 13
Kathleen N. Perret, 5
Barbara Perry-Sheldon, 10
Carolyn Mitchell Person, 14, 16
Michael Persampieri, 15
Charles C. Peters, 1
Jerry L. Peters, 10
Charles A. Peterson, 9-10, 12-14
Christopher Peterson, 9
Donald R. Peterson, 6
Francisca Esteban Peterson, 14
Gary W. Peterson, 9
Harold A. Peterson, 7-10
Norman G. Peterson, 9
Reece L. Peterson, 9
Rolf A. Peterson, 8, 10
Shailer Peterson, 3
Julia Pettiette-Doolin, 10
*Steven I. Pfeiffer, 9-18
Susanna W. Pflaum, 9
LeAdelle Phelps, 10, 12-13
Roger P. Phelps, 7-8
Gary W. Phillips, 9
Iris Phillips, 15
S. E. Phillips, 9-10
Theodore G. Phillips, 5-7

Nick J. Piazza, 10
Jennifer Piccolo, 16
Eugene (Geno) Pichette, 13
James Pickering, 9
Hale C. Pickett, 3
Douglas A. Pidgeon, 5-9
John Pierce-Jones, 5-6
Ellen V. Piers, 6
Wayne C. Piersel, 9-10, 13-14
Myrtle L. Pignatelli, 2
Len Pikaart, 7-8
A. E. G. Pilliner, 5-8
Paul Pimsleur, 6
*James W. Pinkney, 9-10, 12-13, 15, 17
Rudolf Pintner, 1
Francis J. Pirozzolo, 9
David J. Pittenger, 13-17
Barbara S. Plake, 9
Gus P. Plessas, 6-9
Lynnette B. Plumlee, 3, 5-7
John Poggio, 14
Edward Polloway, 9-10
Joseph G. Ponterotto, 11
Marcel O. Ponton, 13
Robert C. Pooley, 2-7
Mark Pope, 11-12, 14-16
Donald B. Pope-Davis, 12
Mary S. Poplin, 9
Julia Y. Porter, 14, 16-18
Lyman W. Porter, 6
James M. Porter, Jr., 3
William D. Porterfield, 11
Stanley D. Porteus, 2
C. Dale Posey, 10
Winifred L. Post, 4-5
*G. Michael Poteat, 10-16
James A. Poteet, 9-10
Kenneth E. Poucher, 8
Shawn Powell, 15-18
Thomas E. Powell, 11
Stephen Powers, 9
Elizabeth M. Prather, 9-11
Michael W. Pratt, 9
Sheila R. Pratt, 13-16
Norman T. Pratt, Jr., 1-2
Daniel A. Prescott, 1
Joan Preston, 7
Ralph C. Preston, 3-4
H. Vernon Price, 5
J. Randall Price, 17
Jack Price, 7
Ray G. Price, 3, 6-7
Roy A. Price, 2-3
Erich P. Prien, 13-14
Kristin O. Prien, 14
Hugh F. Priest, 7
George P. Prigatano, 9

M. L. Kellmer Pringle, 4-7
Barry M. Prizant, 11
Glen W. Probst, 7
Barton B. Proger, 8-9
H. Thompson Prout, 9
Richard C. Pugh, 12-13
Earl V. Pullias, 2
Alan C. Purves, 7-8
Joan E. Pynes, 10
Fred Pyrczak, 8
Edys S. Quellmalz, 9
M. Y. Quereshi, 7-8
Theresa A. Quigney, 14
Michelle Quinn, 9
Albert I. Rabin, 4-5, 7
S. Rachman, 6
John A. Radcliffe, 5-6
Rudolf E. Radocy, 12-13
Jeffrey S. Rain, 12-13
*Nambury S. Raju, 9, 11-16
Pamilla Ramsden, 15-17
Bikkar S. Randhawa, 11-14
John F. Randolph, 3
Earl F. Rankin, 7-8
Alan J. Raphael, 13-14
Evelyn Raskin, 4
Leslie T. Raskind, 10
Natalie Rathvon, 16
Michael M. Ravitch, 9
Glen E. Ray, 12
Alton L. Raygor, 6, 8
S. A. Rayner, 5
Mark D. Reckase, 9
Homer B. C. Reed, Jr., 8-9
James C. Reed, 7-9, 12-15
Janet Reed, 18
Michael L. Reed, 9
Edwin H. Reeder, 3-4
Amy M. Rees, 16
Jeff Reese, 14
Ronald E. Reeve, 9
William R. Reevy, 6
Sean P. Reilley, 16-17
Barbara A. Reilly, 11-12
David H. Reilly, 9
Judith A. Rein, 15-16
Robert C. Reinehr, 11-14
Robert A. Reineke, 11-12
Richard J. Reisboard, 8
Ralph M. Reitan, 6-7
Willard E. Reitz, 7
H. H. Remmers, 1, 3, 5
K. Ann Renninger, 9
Joseph S. Renzulli, 9
Harvey Resnick, 9
*Paul Retzlaff, 11-16
*Cecil R. Reynolds, 9, 11-15

Maynard C. Reynolds, 5
Sharon B. Reynolds, 10
William M. Reynolds, 9, 14-15
Marvin Reznikoff, 7
Elizabeth Kelley Rhoades, 16-17
James A. Rice, 8
Gilbert J. Rich, 3
David C. Richard, 14
R. Lynn Richards, 10
Roger A. Richards, 5-9, 11, 13-14
T. W. Richards, 4
James M. Richards, Jr., 7-8
J. A. Richardson, 5
M. W. Richardson, 1-2
S. C. Richardson, 5
Sharon Ann Richardson, 17
Bert O. Richmond, 9
James H. Ricks, Jr., 4-6, 8
T. Andrew Ridenour, 13
Paul R. Rider, 2
Stanley E. Ridley, 9
C. Alan Riedesel, 6-8
William Rieman, III, 3-4
Michelle L. Ries, 14
Edward G. Rietz, 5
Henry L. Rietz, 1
Janet Morgan Riggs, 9
Seymour Rigrodsky, 7
Alice R. Rines, 8
Henry D. Rinsland, 1-4
Charlene Rivera, 11
Harry N. Rivlin, 4-5
Robin Rix, 15
James P. Rizzo, 6
Brandy M. Roane, 18
Oscar H. Roberts, 7
Brent W. Roberts, 14
David C. Roberts, 13
Holland Roberts, 2-6
Mark W. Roberts, 9, 11, 14
Donald U. Robertson, 11
Gary J. Robertson, 9-10, 13
Elizabeth A. Robinson, 9
Eric Robinson, 12
G. Edith Robinson, 7
H. Alan Robinson, 6-8
Helen M. Robinson, 4-7
Richard D. Robinson, 8
Alec Rodger, 2-4
David A. Rodgers, 7
Ronald C. Rodgers, 9
*Bruce G. Rogers, 9-17
Carl R. Rogers, 2
Cyril A. Rogers, 5
Frederick R. Rogers, 2
Margaret R. Rogers, 12
Virginia M. Rogers, 7

W. Todd Rogers, 7
Cynthia A. Rohrbeck, 11, 13-16
Samuel Roll, 10
Deborah D. Roman, 12-14
Thomas A. Romberg, 7-8
Leonard G. Rorer, 7
Carl L. Rosen, 7-9
Ephraim Rosen, 4
Gerald A. Rosen, 13
Marvin Rosen, 8
John H. Rosenbach, 7-9
Robert L. Rosenbaum, 8
Jennifer A. Rosenblatt, 13
Sylvia Rosenfield, 9-10
Arlene Coopersmith Rosenthal, 9-11
Nancy L. Roser, 8-9
Benjamin Rosner, 5-7
Jerome Rosner, 7
Alan O. Ross, 6
C. C. Ross, 2-3
Charles S. Ross, 4-5
Paul F. Ross, 6
Myron F. Rosskopf, 5
*Michael J. Roszkowski, 9-10, 12-15
Rodney W. Roth, 11
Harold F. Rothe, 4
Robert D. Rothermel, 9
Barbara A. Rothlisberg, 11-14
John W. M. Rothney, 1, 3-7
Julian B. Rotter, 3
Pamela Carrington Rotto, 12
James B. Rounds, 9-10, 12
Byron P. Rourke, 9
Steven V. Rouse, 18
Denise M. Rousseau, 9-10
Mark C. Roybal, 17
Harold L. Royer, 6
Arthur B. Royse, 5-6
Thaddeus Rozecki, 13
Ronald H. Rozensky, 11
Mary Roznowski, 14
Donald L. Rubin, 11
Stanley I. Rubin, 6
Floyd L. Ruch, 3-4, 6
Giles M. Ruch, 2
Herbert C. Rudman, 9, 12-14
Lawrence M. Rudner, 11-12
Robert Rueda, 10
C. H. Ruedisili, 3
Mabel E. Rugen, 3
David L. Rule, 10
Edward A. Rundqust, 3
William H. Rupley, 9
David H. Russell, 2-4
Harry J. Russell, 2-3
Michael Lee Russell, 13-14
James O. Rust, 9-10

John Rust, 12
Leo P. Ruth, 8
Roger A. Ruth, 7-8
Joseph M. Ryan, 11
Katherine Ryan, 18
Lawrence J. Ryan, 14-15
Michael Ryan, 9-10
David G. Ryans, 3-4, 6
Jane A. Rysberg, 9-10
Richard Rystrom, 7-8
David A. Sabatino, 9
*Darrell L. Sabers, 8-18
Donna S. Sabers, 13
Everett B. Sackett, 1, 6
Paul R. Sackett, 9
Cyril J. Sadowski, 12-13
H. Bradley Sagen, 6-7
Philip A. Saigh, 9
Perry Sailor, 12
Kenneth Sakauye, 12
Rachel Salisbury, 2
John Salvia, 9
*Vincent J. Samar, 11-12, 14-17
John Sample, 18
David T. Sanchez, 9
Daryl Sander, 9
C. Sanders, 5
James R. Sanders, 9
*Jonathan Sandoval, 9-10, 12-15, 17-18
Claude A. Sandy, 12
*Eleanor E. Sanford-Moore, 11-17
Dixie D. Sanger, 9
Toni E. Santmire, 9-10
Janice Santogrossi, 10
H. J. Sants, 6
Bert R. Sappenfield, 5-6
Irwin G. Sarason, 6
Theodore R. Sarbin, 4
Timothy Sares, 16
David M. Sargent, 15
Helen Sargent, 4
I. David Satlow, 5
George A. Satter, 3-4
Jerome M. Sattler, 8-10
Richard A. Saudargas, 10
Aulus W. Saunders, 2
David M. Saunders, 11
David R. Saunders, 5
*William I. Sauser, Jr., 9-17
Jean-Guy Savard, 7
*Diane J. Sawyer, 9-14, 17
Neroli Sawyer, 15
Gilbert Sax, 8
Peter Scales, 9
Dale P. Scannell, 9, 11-13
Douglas E. Scates, 1, 3, 5
William L. Schaaf, 4

Willis C. Schaefer, 4
*William D. Schafer, 11-14, 16-18
Joyce Parr Schaie, 8
K. Warner Schaie, 8-9
Michael J. Scheel, 15, 17-18
Susan J. Schenck, 9-10
Johann H. Schepers, 6
C. Ruth Solomon Scherzer, 16
Alvin W. Schindler, 1-2, 4
Steven P. Schinke, 10, 12
Richard J. Schissel, 9-10
Richard F. Schmid, 9
Frank L. Schmidt, 8-9, 13, 16
Steven W. Schmidt, 18
John F. Schmitt, 9
Neal Schmitt, 9, 12-13
Gerald R. Schneck, 13-15
Arnold E. Schneider, 3
W. Joel Schneider, 16-18
Leroy H. Schnell, 2-3
Lyle F. Schoenfeldt, 7-10
Patricia Schoenrade, 12-13
Wiliiam Schofield, 4-6
Fred J. Schonell, 2, 4-5
Richard V. Schowengerdt, 14
William B. Schrader, 4-6
H. E. Schrammel, 1
Fredrick A. Schrank, 9-10
*Gregory Schraw, 12, 14-18
Robert L. Schreiner, 8
Herbert Schueler, 3-6
Douglas G. Schultz, 4, 6-7
Geoffrey F. Schultz, 11
Harold A. Schultz, 4, 6
Dale H. Schunk, 9
Richard Schupbach, 8
Donald H. Schuster, 6-7
Richard E. Schutz, 6-9
Joseph J. Schwab, 3
*Gene Schwarting, 9, 12-18
Neil H. Schwartz, 9-10
Mariette Schwarz, 6
Dean M. Schweickhard, 2
Gladys C. Schwesinger, 4
Craig S. Scott, 8
Louise B. Scott, 5
Owen Scott, III, 11
May V. Seagoe, 4
Carl E. Seashore, 2
Harold G. Seashore, 3-6
Virginia Seavey, 3
Don Sebolt, 12
Charles Secolsky, 9
William Seeman, 4
Stanley J. Segal, 6
David Segel, 1, 3-4
Esther F. Segner, 2

William U. Snyder, 3
Louise M. Soares, 15-17
Gargi Roysircar Sodowsky, 11-12
Alicia Soliz, 16
David C. Solly, 11
Alan Solomon, 14
Rhonda H. Solomon, 14
Robert J. Solomon, 5-6
Ronald K. Sommers, 8-9, 11
Anita Miller Sostek, 8
Larry Sowder, 8
George D. Spache, 3-7
Steven D. Spaner, 12
Emma Spaney, 4-5
Michael Spangler, 15-16
C. Spearman, 2
Donald Spearritt, 5
Janet E. Spector, 13-14
Robert K. Speer, 2
Daniel G. Spencer, 9
Douglas Spencer, 2-3
Loraine J. Spenciner, 14-18
Peter L. Spencer, 2
Rayne A. Sperling, 16, 18
Charles D. Spielberger, 8
Robert Spies, 13-14
Donna Spiker, 11-12, 17
Stephen A. Spillane, 14
Susan K. Spille, 12
Herbert F. Spitzer, 3-4
Jaclyn B. Spitzer, 9, 11, 13, 16
Gilbert M. Spivack, 9
Bernard Spolsky, 6
Michael J. Sporakowski, 12, 14
Scott Spreat, 12
Otfried Spreen, 6
Becky L. Spritz, 18
Mark A. Staal, 15, 17-18
Barrie G. Stacey, 9
Michael J. Stahl, 9-10
Steven A. Stahl, 11, 14
Robert F. Stahmann, 8
Gary J. Stainback, 11, 13-14
Jayne E. Stake, 9-13, 15
Robert E. Stake, 6
John M. Stalnaker, 1-2, 4-6
Roy W. Stanhope, 5
Julian C. Stanley, 4-6
Charles W. Stansfield, 8-10, 14
Joel Stark, 7-8
C. P. Starke, 4
Stanley Starkman, 9
Anna S. Starr, 1
Edward R. Starr, 13
Russell G. Stauffer, 5-6
John E. Stecklein, 6
Elaine Flory Stefany, 12

Leslie P. Steffe, 7-8
Harry L. Stein, 5-6
Jack M. Stein, 6-7
Margot B. Stein, 13-14, 18
*Stephanie Stein, 11-18
Wendy J. Steinberg, 10, 15-16
Hugh Stephenson, 15
William Stephenson, 4-6
F. E. Sterling, 9
Robert J. Sternberg, 9
Brenda A. Stevens, 14
Kay B. Stevens, 17-18
Jay R. Stewart, 13-15, 17-18
Krista J. Stewart, 9-10
Naomi Stewart, 4-6
Sheldon L. Stick, 9-10
Charles A. Stickland, 4
Harlan J. Stientjes, 11-12
*Terry A. Stinnett, 10-15, 17
William A. Stock, 11-12
Jill M. Stoefen-Fisher, 9
Howard Stoker, 11
Joseph P. Stokes, 9-10
Clarence R. Stone, 2
Gerald L. Stone, 9-13
L. Joseph Stone, 4-5
Mark Stone, 9, 15, 18
Gary Stoner, 11, 12
Janet M. Stoppard, 9
Donald Lee Stovall, 14-15
Phillip S. Strain, 9
David Strand, 10
Jennifer M. Strang, 18
Ruth M. Strang, 1-2, 5
Richard K. Stratton, 12
Christine F. Strauss, 12
Lois T. Strauss, 11
Lawrence J. Stricker, 6, 8
Ruth Strickland, 5
Douglas C. Strohmer, 9
Stanley R. Strong, 8-9
Charles R. Strother, 3-5
J. B. Stroud, 3
Hans H. Strupp, 7
*Richard B. Stuart, 9-13, 15
Dewey B. Stuit, 3-4
George W. Sturrock, 5
*Gabrielle Stutman, 12-18
Frederick H. Stutz, 3, 5
Michael J. Subkoviak, 9, 11-13
Richard R. Sudweeks, 13
*Hoi K. Suen, 11-18
Alan R. Suess, 7-8, 10
Richard M. Suinn, 7
Gail M. Sullivan, 11
Jeremy R. Sullivan, 18
Patricia M. Sullivan, 9

W. L. Sumner, 4
Norman D. Sundberg, 5-9, 11-14
Donna L. Sundre, 12-13
Yong H. Sung, 9
Donald E. Super, 3-6, 8
Carolyn H. Suppa, 16-17
J. P. Sutcliffe, 5
John Sutherland, 5-6
Rosemary E. Sutton, 11-14, 16
Marilyn N. Suydam, 7-9
John G. Svinicki, 10
Edward O. Swanson, 6
H. Lee Swanson, 9
Richard A. Swanson, 7-8
Robert M. Swanson, 8
Robert S. Swanson, 8
Jon D. Swartz, 8-9
Jody L. Swartz-Kulstad, 14
Cabrini S. Swassing, 10
Susan M. Swearer, 14, 16
Clifford H. Swensen, 9
*Mark E. Swerdlik, 9, 11-18
Harvey N. Switzky, 9, 11-12
Percival M. Symonds, 2-5
Hilda Taba, 1-2, 4
Wendi L. Tai, 16
Harold Takooshian, 12
Xuan Tan, 16
Diane Tanigawa, 17
Abraham J. Tannenbaum, 6
Kikumi K. Tatsuoka, 9, 11
Maurice Tatsuoka, 11
Earl S. Taulbee, 8
Calvin W. Taylor, 5
Cie Taylor, 9
Erwin K. Taylor, 3-7
Howard R. Taylor, 3-4
Hugh Taylor, 7
John M. Taylor, 10
Ronald N. Taylor, 8
Wallace W. Taylor, 2-3
Florence M. Teagarden, 2-5
Lorene Teegarden, 2
Phyllis Anne Teeter, 9
Auke Tellegen, 8-9
Cathy Fultz Telzrow, 9-10, 12
Mildred C. Templin, 4
Edward A. Tenney, 2
W. Wesley Tennyson, 5
Mary L. Tenopyr, 9-10
James S. Terwilliger, 11-12
Anita S. Tesh, 12-13
E. W. Testut, 11
James B. Tharp, 2, 4
Paul W. Thayer, 6, 8-10
Herbert A. Thelen, 3
William N. Thetford, 6

C. L. Thiele, 2-3
Charles S. Thomas, 1-2
Cleveland A. Thomas, 5
Conn Thomas, 18
Ruth G. Thomas, 9-10
Albert S. Thompson, 1-2, 4-6
Anton Thompson, 4
Bruce Thompson, 14, 16
Donald Thompson, 12-16
John H. Thompson, 1
Nora M. Thompson, 11-13, 15-16
Richard A. Thompson, 8
Edith I. M. Thomson, 3
Godfrey H. Thomson, 2
Robert L. Thorndike, 2-8
Robert M. Thorndike, 8, 15-17
Tracy Thorndike-Christ, 18
George C. Thornton III, 9-10, 12-14
Geoffrey L. Thorpe, 17-18
Robert H. Thouless, 3
Pamela S. Tidwell, 12
David V. Tiedeman, 4-8
Ernest W. Tiegs, 1-3
Robert J. Tierney, 9-10
Donald W. Tiffany, 14
Joseph Tiffin, 1
James A. Till, 8
Murray H. Tillman, 8
*Gerald Tindal, 11-15, 17-18
Miles A. Tinker, 4
William C. Tirre, 14-15
Stephanie D. Tischendorf, 17
C. Alan Titchenal, 10
Jonathan E. Titley, 18
Carol Kehr Tittle, 7, 9, 11-12
John Tivendell, 15, 17
Renee M. Tobin, 17-18
Hazel M. Toliver, 3
Robert Tolsma, 9
Ruth E. Tomes, 11-12, 14
Gail E. Tompkins, 9-10
Kathleen T. Toms, 11
Tony Toneatto, 11-12, 14
Barry W. Tones, 10
Herbert A. Tonne, 1, 3, 5
Herbert A. Topps, 3
T. L. Torgerson, 3
Joseph Torgesen, 9
Michelle T. Toshima, 10
Esther Stavrou Toubanos, 12
*Roger L. Towne, 11-12, 14-18
Agatha Townsend, 3, 5-6
Marion R. Trabue, 1-2
Ross E. Traub, 12, 14
Kenneth J. Travers, 7
Robert M. W. Travers, 3-5
Arthur E. Traxler, 1-7

Donald J Treffinger, 9
*Michael S. Trevisan, 11-16
Carolyn Triay, 11
Frances O. Triggs, 3
Harold C. Trimble, 6-8
Marie E. Trost, 2
Stephen E. Trotter, 14-16
Maurice E. Troyer, 3
R. M. Tryon, 1-2
Robert C. Tryon, 2
Jalie A. Tucker, 11
Bruce W. Tuckman, 8
J. Jaap Tuinman, 8
Simon H. Tulchin, 2-3
June M. Tuma, 9
Timothy L. Turco, 10
Kerri Turk, 12
Mary E. Turnbull, 4-6
Clarence E. Turner, 2-6
Mervyn L. Turner, 5
Austin H. Turney, 1-2
Lawrence J. Turton, 7-10, 12
F. T. Tyler, 3
Leona E. Tyler, 4-7
Ralph W. Tyler, 2-3, 5
Thomas A. Tyler, 8
Aharon Tziner, 9
Judy A. Ungerer, 9
C. C. Upshall, 3
Susana Urbina, 12-16
Marguerite Uttley, 3
Nicholas A. Vacc, 9-13
John J. Vacca, 14-18
Curtis C. Vail, 1
Rebecca W. Valcarce, 9
Paolo Valesio, 7
Robert E. Valett, 7
Rachel J. Valleley, 17-18
William J. Valmont, 8
Forrest L. Vance, 6-7
Henry Van Engen, 4
*Wilfred G. Van Gorp, 11-16
James P. Van Haneghan, 12-15, 18
Gerald R. Van Hecke, 8
Gabriele van Lingen, 13-14, 16
Byron H. Van Roekel, 5-9
Neil J. Van Steenberg, 4-5
Wendy Van Wyhe, 12
Molly L. Vanduser, 14
Jamie E. Vannice, 17
Stanley F. Vasa, 9-10
Matt Vassar, 18
Robert P. Vecchio, 9
Donald J. Veldman, 6-7
Frank R. Vellutino, 8
John J. Venn, 16-18
William M. Verdi, 13-14

Magdalen D. Vernon, 5-6
Philip E. Vernon, 2, 4-9
Dolores Kluppel Vetter, 11, 13, 16-18
Verna L. Vickery, 5
Donald J. Viglione, Jr., 9
Peter Villanova, 11
Roland Vinette, 3
Jan Visser, 14
Chockalingam Viswesvaran, 13-14
Morris S. Viteles, 2-3
Romeo Vitelli, 14-15, 17
Daniel E. Vogler, 12
Metta Volker-Fry, 16
Robert J. Volpe, 15
Theresa Volpe-Johnstone, 14-15, 17
Alex Voogel, 11
David P. Wacker, 9-10
J. R. Jefferson Wadkins, 7-8
Catherine Wagner, 18
Edwin E. Wagner, 9
Guy W. Wagner, 1
John Wagner, 7
William W. Waite, 3-4
J. V. Waits, 3
John F. Wakefield, 11, 18
Delores D. Walcott, 14-16, 18
William J. Waldron, 12-14
Cindy M. Walker, 15-16
Helen M. Walker, 1
Justin M. Walker, 17
Robert Wall, 13-15
Shavaun M. Wall, 9
W. D. Wall, 4
S. Rains Wallace, 4-5
Wimburn L. Wallace, 5-8
Norman E. Wallen, 6
Niels G. Waller, 11-14
James A. Walsh, 7-8
W. Bruce Walsh, 7
Edwin Wandt, 4, 7
Aimin Wang, 15
Sandra J. Wanner, 14
Morey J. Wantman, 4-6
Richard A. Wantz, 10, 12, 14
F. W. Warburton, 4-5
Annie W. Ward, 11-15
Annita Marie Ward, 15-17
Charles F. Ward, 7
*Sandra Ward, 13-18
William C. Ward, 7-8
George Wardlow, 10
James L. Wardrop, 8-10
E. M. Waring, 9
David M. Wark, 7
Charles F. Warnath, 6, 8
Neil D. Warren, 3, 5
Willard G. Warrington, 5-7

Ruth W. Washburn, 3
Orest E. Wasyliw, 12, 14
Alan T. Waterman, 2
Betsy Waterman, 13-15
Eugene A. Waters, 2
Everett Waters, 9
John G. Watkins, 6
Marley W. Watkins, 9
Ralph K. Watkins, 2
Richard W. Watkins, 7-8
Betty U. Watson, 9
Goodwin Watson, 1-3
Robert I. Watson, 3
*T. Steuart Watson, 11-18
Tonya S. Watson, 17
Bart L. Weathington, 17
J. Fred Weaver, 5
Terri L. Weaver, 14
Larry Weber, 12
Harold Webster, 5-6
William J. Webster, 7, 9
David Wechsler, 2-3
Thaddeus E. Weckowicz, 8
M. O'Neal Weeks, 9
Zona R. Weeks, 9
Walter L. Wehner, 8-9
Charles C. Weidemann, 1-2
David P. Weikart, 7
Richard A. Weinburg, 10
Sharon L. Weinberg, 9, 11-13
Annette B. Weinshank, 9
Sheldon A. Weintraub, 7-8
David L. Weis, 9
Susan Ellis Weismer, 11
David J. Weiss, 7-8
Ellen Weissinger, 12-13
Henry Weitz, 3-8
R. A. Weitzman, 9
Carolyn M. Welch, 3
Wayne W. Welch, 8
A. T. Welford, 4
Beth L. Wellman, 3
F. L. Wells, 1-3
J. Steven Welsh, 11, 13
Lesley A. Welsh, 13
Charles Wenar, 9
Tim L. Wentling, 8
Joseph M. Wepman, 7
Emmy E. Werner, 6-7
Paul D. Werner, 13-14
Edgar B. Wesley, 1-4
Alexander G. Wesman, 4-7
Leonard J. West, 7-9
Bert W. Westbrook, 7-9, 11-13
Carol E. Westby, 11-13
George Westby, 4-6
Goran Westergren, 14

Ingela Westergren, 14
Stephanie Western, 12
Alida S. Westman, 8-9, 11-12
Frederick L. Westover, 4
Harry G. Wheat, 2
D. K. Wheeler, 5
Kenneth G. Wheeler, 9
Patricia H. Wheeler, 11-12, 14-15
Susan C. Whiston, 14-16
Edward M. White, 8
Howard R. White, 4
Karl R. White, 9
Kenneth V. White, 11
Shirley A. White, 9
Sue White, 9-10
Sally Anita Whiting, 9
Dean K. Whitla, 6
Carroll A. Whitmer, 2-3
Richard G. Whitten, 13
Randolph H. Whitworth, 8
Lillian A. Whyte, 9
Katherine Wickstrom, 17
Keith F. Widaman, 14-16, 18
Thomas A. Widiger, 9, 11, 14
J. Lee Wiederholt, 8-9
Margaret Rogers Wiese, 11
Martin J. Wiese, 10-12, 14, 17
James D. Wiggins, 9
Jerry S. Wiggins, 6-7, 10
Linda F. Wightman, 11-12
Elisabeth H. Wiig, 9
Richard L. Wikoff, 9-10
Katherine W. Wilcox, 3
Terry M. Wildman, 12
*William K. Wilkinson, 10-17
S. S. Wilks, 1-2
Haydn S. Williams, 5
J. Robert Williams, 6
Janice G. Williams, 11-13
Jean M. Williams, 12
John M. Williams, 11
Robert T. Williams, 9-13
David M. Williamson, 13
Edmund G. Williamson, 1-2
Warren W. Willingham, 6
Carl G. Willis, 7-8
Margaret Willis, 2
W. Grant Willis, 11-12
John M. Willits, 3, 5
John T. Willse, 16, 18
Victor L. Willson, 8-10, 12
J. Richard Wilmeth, 6
Beverly J. Wilson, 17
David R. Wilson, 9
Guy M. Wilson, 1-3
James W. Wilson, 7
Robert M. Wilson, 9

Marlene Wadsworth Winell, 9
Herbert D. Wing, 4-6
Hilda Wing, 11-14
Harris Winitz, 8
William L. Winnett, 7
George P. Winship, Jr., 6-7
R. Winterbourn, 5
Carrie L. Winterowd, 14
Robert D. Wirt, 6-7
Steven L. Wise, 9-10, 12
Emory E. Wiseman, 7
Stephen Wiseman, 3, 5
Ernest C. Witham, 2
E. Lea Witla, 13
Joseph C. Witt, 9-10, 12-13
L. Alan Witt, 11–12
E. Lea Witta, 13
J. Richard Wittenborn, 3-4
Donna Wittmer, 12
Paul A. Witty, 3
Gregory C. Wochos, 16
David L. Wodrich, 9, 14
Kristen Wojcik, 13
Richard M. Wolf, 8-9, 11-14
Dael L. Wolfle, 1-2, 4
Leroy Wolins, 6
James A. Wollack, 12, 14
Myra N. Womble, 13, 17-18
E. F. Wonderlic, 3
Hugh B. Wood, 2
Jamie G. Wood, 17
Michelle Wood, 13
Ray G. Wood, 3
Michael F. Woodin, 18
Clifford Woody, 1, 3
D. A. Worcester, 2-4
Edward A. Workman, 9
Julien Worland, 9
Blaine R. Worthen, 7-9, 12-13
F. Lynwood Wren, 3
C. Gilbert Wrenn, 1-2, 5
Benjamin D. Wright, 9
*Claudia R. Wright, 11-18

Dan Wright, 9-12
Logan Wright, 11-12
Robert Wright, 18
Robert L. Wright, 7
William J. Wright, 8
J. Wayne Wrightstone, 1-3, 5
Jack Wrigley, 5
Thomas A. Wrobel, 11
Tony C. Wu, 18
Michael K. Wynne, 12
Kaoru Yamamoto, 8
Alfred Yates, 5
Aubrey J. Yates, 7
Daniel L. Yazak, 14
Albert H. Yee, 7
Frank R. Yekovich, 9
Tamela Yelland, 12
Georgette Yetter, 16-18
Dale Yoder, 4
John W. Young, 12, 14-16
Suzanne Young, 16-18
*James E. Ysseldyke, 8-12, 14, 16
William Yule, 8
Robert H. Zabel, 9
Peter Zachar, 13-16
Louis C. Zahner, 2-3, 5
Dan Zakay, 9
O. L. Zangwill, 3
John A. Zarske, 9-10
*Sheldon Zedeck, 8-9, 11-15
Paul F. Zelhart, 10
Bo Zhang, 16
Michael J. Zickar, 14, 17
Edwin Ziegfeld, 2-4
Corinne Zimmerman, 18
Linda J. Zimmerman, 14
Wayne S. Zimmerman, 6-7
Fred Zimring, 9
Joseph E. Zins, 9
Leland C. Zlomke, 10-14
Steven Zucker, 13
Marvin Zuckerman, 9
Donald G. Zytowski, 7-9, 12

INDEX OF TITLES

This title index includes a comprehensive listing of tests currently in print and included in this volume as well as out-of-print (or status unknown) tests that were listed in Tests in Print VII *and* The Seventeenth *and* Eighteenth Mental Measurements Yearbooks. *Numbers without colons refer to in-print tests included in this volume. Numbers with colons refer to out-of-print tests not listed in this volume; readers interested in these tests are referred to the last volume listing the tests. For example, T7:1826 refers to test 1826 in* Tests in Print VII; *16:199 refers to test 199 in* The 16th MMY. *Superseded titles are listed with a cross reference to the present title. All numbers refer to test entries, not to page numbers.*

A-4 Police Officer Video Test, 1

AAMD Adaptive Behavior Scale, see AAMR Adaptive Behavior Scale–School, Second Edition, 3

AAMD-Becker Reading-Free Vocational Interest Inventory, see Reading-Free Vocational Interest Inventory: 2, 2238

AAMR Adaptive Behavior Scale–Residential and Community, Second Edition, 2

AAMR Adaptive Behavior Scale–School, Second Edition, 3

AATG German Test, see National German Examination for High School Students, 1808

AATG National Standardized Testing Program, see National German Examination for High School Students, 1808

Abbreviated Torrance Test for Adults, 4

Aberrant Behavior Checklist, 5

Abortion Scale, 6

Abstract Reasoning Test, 7

Abuse Disability Questionnaire, 8

Abuse Risk Inventory for Women, 9

Abuse Risk Inventory for Women, Experimental Edition, see Abuse Risk Inventory for Women, 9

Academic Advising Inventory, 10

Academic Aptitude Test: Non-Verbal Intelligence: Acorn National Aptitude Tests, 11

Academic Aptitude Test: Verbal Intelligence: Acorn National Aptitude Tests, 12

Academic Competence Evaluation Scales, 13

Academic Freedom Survey, 14

Academic Intervention Monitoring System, 15

Academic Perceptions Inventory [2000 Revision], 16

ACCESS–A Comprehensive Custody Evaluation Standard System, 17

Accountant Staff Selector, 19

Access Management Survey, 18

Accounting Aptitude Test, 20

Accounting Program Admission Test, 21

ACCUPLACER, 22

ACCUPLACER: Computerized Placement Tests, see ACCUPLACER, 22

ACDI-Corrections Version and Corrections Version II, 23

ACER Adult Form B, see ACER Word Knowledge Test, 31

ACER Advanced Test B40, 24

ACER Advanced Test B90: New Zealand Edition, 25

ACER Advanced Tests AL and AQ (Second Edition) and BL-BQ, 26

ACER Applied Reading Test, 27

ACER Mechanical Comprehension Test, T7:27

ACER Mechanical Reasoning Test [Revised 1997], 28

ACER Short Clerical Test, 29

ACER Test of Employment Entry Mathematics, 30

ACER Tests of Basic Skills–Orchid Series, T7:31

ACER Word Knowledge Test, 31

INDEX OF RECENTLY OUT-OF-PRINT TESTS

The Index of Recently Out-of-Print Tests is a cumulative listing of tests that appeared in Tests in Print *III through* The Eighteenth Mental Measurements Yearbook *but that do not appear in* Tests in Print *VIII. The publishers of most of these tests have advised that the tests are now out of print. For some others, status has been unknown for over 10 years and the last known publisher is no longer in business and the tests are not published by a different publisher so out-of-print status has been assumed. Those tests in this index that appeared in* Tests in Print *VII and/or* The Seventeenth *and* Eighteenth Mental Measurements Yearbooks *but are not in* Tests in Print *VIII are also integrated into the Index of Titles. All numbers refer to test entries, not page numbers. For example, T4:233 refers to test 233 in* Tests in Print *IV, 12:121 refers to test 121 in* The 12th MMY, *and 15:301 refers to test 301 in* The 15th MMY.

A. I. Survey, T6:1

A.P.U. Arithmetic Test, T3:193

A.P.U. Vocabulary Test, T3:194

A.S.S.E.T.S.: A Survey of Students' Educational Talents and Skills, T5:217

AAHPER Cooperative Health Education Test, T3:1

AAHPER Cooperative Physical Education Tests, T3:2

AAHPER Sport Skills Tests, T3:4

AAHPER Youth Fitness Test, T3:5

AAHPERD Health Related Physical Fitness Test, 9:2

AAHPERD-Kennedy Foundation Special Fitness Test for the Mentally Retarded, T3:3

The ABC Inventory to Determine Kindergarten and School Readiness, T6:4

Ability Explorer, 14:431

AC Test of Creative Ability, T3:10

Academic Aptitude Test, T3:11

Academic Proficiency Battery, T6:14

Academic Readiness and End of First Grade Progress Scale, T3:16

Academic Readiness Scale, T3:17

Academic-Technical Aptitude Tests, T4:12

Accounting Clerk Staff Selector, T5:16

ACER Advanced Test BL-BQ, New Zealand Revision, T6:23

ACER Advanced Test N, T3:20

ACER and University of Melbourne Music Evaluation Kit, 9:6

ACER Arithmetic Tests: Standardized for Use in New Zealand, T3:23

ACER Checklists for School Beginners, 9:7

ACER Chemistry Test Item Collection: Year 12 (Chemtic), 9:8

ACER Early School Series, 9:10

ACER Higher Test PL-PQ, New Zealand Revision, T6:26

ACER Higher Tests, 9:11

ACER Intermediate Test A, T3:29

ACER Intermediate Test F, T6:27

ACER Intermediate Test G, T6:28

ACER Intermediate Tests C and D, T3:30

ACER Junior Non-Verbal Test, T3:31

ACER Junior Test A, T3:32

ACER Listening Test, 9:14

ACER Lower Grades General Ability Scale, Second Edition, T3:34

ACER Mathematics Profile Series, 9:15

ACER Mathematics Tests: AM Series, 9:16

ACER Mechanical Comprehension Test, T7:27

ACER Number Test, T3:39

ACER Paragraph Reading Test, 9:18

ACER Physics Unit Tests: Diagnostic Aids, 9:19

VCM: Physical Therapist Assistant, 9:1321

VCM: Restaurant Service (Waiter, Waitress, Cashier), 9:1322

VCM: Wastewater Treatment Technician, 9:1323

VCM: Water Treatment Technician, 9:1324

VCM: Word Processing Specialist, 9:1325

Verbal Auditory Screening for Children, T3:2550

Verbal Communication Scales, 9:1326

Verbal Language Developmental Scale, T3:2551

The Verbal Power Test of Concept Equivalence, T3:2552

Veterinary College Admission Test, T6:2648

Vice President and Senior Executive Staff Selector, T4:2880

Vincent Mechanical Diagrams Test, 1979 Revision, T6:2651

Visco Child Development Screening Test, 9:1328

Visual Discrimination Test, T6:2657

Visual Memory Scale, T3:2562

Visual Memory Test, T6:2659

Visual Pattern Recognition Test and Diagnostic Schedule, 9:1331

Visual Perceptual Skills Inventory, T4:2888

Visual-Verbal Test, 1981 Edition, T4:2891

The Visual-Verbal Test: A Measure of Conceptual Thinking, T3:2565

VITAL Checklist and Curriculum Guide, T4:2892

Vocabulary Comprehension Scale, T4:2893

Vocabulary Test for High School Students and College Freshmen, T3:2567

Vocabulary Test: McGraw-Hill Basic Skills System, T4:2894

Vocational Adaptation Rating Scales, T6:2663

The Vocational Apperception Test: Advanced Form, T5:2825

Vocational Behavior Checklist, T5:2827

Vocational Competency Measures, 9:1336

Vocational Exploration and Insight Kit, T4:2900

Vocational Information Profile, T4:2901

Vocational Integration Index, 14:410

Vocational Interest and Sophistication Assessment, T5:2829

Vocational Interest Inventory–Revised, T6:2668

Vocational Interest Profile, T3:2577

Vocational Interest Questionnaire for Pupils in Standards 6-10, T4:2907

Vocational Interest, Experience, and Skill Assessment, T5:2830

Vocational Preference Index, 9:1341

Vocational Research Interest Inventory, T5:2836

Vocational Training Screening Test, 9:1343

Wachs Analysis of Cognitive Structures, 9:1344

Wahler Physical Symptoms Inventory, T5:2839

Wahler Self-Description Inventory, T3:2584

Walden CICS/VS Command Level Proficiency Test, T5:2842

Walden DOS JCL (VS, VSE) Proficiency Test, T5:2843

Walden OS/JCL Proficiency Test, T5:2844

Walden Structured COBOL Proficiency Test, T5:2846

Walden TSO/SPF Proficiency Test, T5:2847

Walker Problem Behavior Identification Checklist, T6:2679

Walker-McConnell Scale of Social Competence and School Adjustment, 11:460

Walton-Sanders English Test, T3:2586

Ward Behavior Inventory, T3:2588

The Washington Pre-College Test, T4:2927

Washington Speech Sound Discrimination Test, T3:2590

Watson Diagnostic Mathematics Test: Computation, Fourth Edition, T4:2931

Watson English Usage and Appreciation Test, Fourth Edition, T4:2932

Watson Number-Readiness Test, Fifth Edition, T4:2934

Watson Reading-Readiness Test, T4:2935

Weber Advanced Spatial Perception Test, T3:2597

Weights and Pulleys: A Test of Intuitive Mechanics, T3:2610

Weinberg Depression Scale for Children and Adolescents, T6:2698

Weiss Intelligibility Test, 9:1358

Weller-Strawser Scales of Adaptive Behavior, 9:1359

Weller-Strawser Scales of Adaptive Behavior for the Learning Disabled, T5:2868

The Wessex Revised Portage Language Checklist, T6:2705

The Western Personnel Tests, T4:2951

Wharton Attitude Survey, T6:2708

What I Like to Do: An Inventory of Students' Interest, T3:2618

Whitaker Index of Schizophrenic Thinking, T6:2711

Wichita Auditory Processing Test, 10:388

Wide Range Employability Sample Test, 9:1365

Wide Range Intelligence-Personality Test [1978 Edition], T4:2958

Wide-Span Reading Test, T6:2718

Williams Awareness Sentence Completion, T5:2887

Williams Intelligence Test for Children with Defective Vision, T6:2722

The Wilson Syntax Screening Test, T7:2785

The Wilson Teacher-Appraisal Scale, T5:2890

Wilson-Patterson Attitude Inventory, 9:1369

Wing Standardised Tests of Musical Intelligence, T3:2631

WISC-R Split-Half Short Form, 9:1370

Wisconsin Tests of Reading Skill Development: Comprehension, T3:2634

Wisconsin Tests of Reading Skill Development: Study Skills, T3:2634

Wisconsin Tests of Reading Skill Development: Word Attack, T3:2635

WLW Personal Survey, Form 3, 9:1374

Wolf Expressive/Receptive Language & Speech Checklist, T5:2893

Wolf Student Behavior Screening, T5:2894

Wolfe Programming Language Test: COBOL, T5:2896

INDEX OF ACRONYMS

This Index of Acronyms refers the reader to the appropriate test in Tests in Print VIII. *In some cases tests are better known by their acronyms than by their full titles, and this index can be of substantial help to the person who knows the former but not the latter. Acronyms are only listed if the author or publisher has made substantial use of the acronym in referring to the test, or if the test is widely known by the acronym. A few acronyms are also registered trademarks (e.g., SAT); where this is known to us, only the test with the registered trademark is referenced. There is some danger in the overuse of acronyms, but this index, like all other indexes in this work, is provided to make the task of identifying a test as easy as possible. All numbers refer to test numbers, not page numbers.*

PDI-IV: Personality Disorder Interview-IV: A Semis-
tructured Interview for the Assessment of Personality
Disorders, 2025
PDI: Preschool Development Inventory, 2111
PDMS-2: Peabody Developmental Motor Scales–Second
Edition, 1964
PDQII: Denver Prescreening Developmental Question-
naire II, 813
PDRT: Portland Digit Recognition Test [Revised], 2075
PDS: Posttraumatic Stress Diagnostic Scale, 2084
PDS:BIDR: Paulhus Deception Scales: Balanced Inven-
tory of Desirable Responding Version 7, 1962
PDSQ: Psychiatric Diagnostic Screening Question-
naire, 2180
PDSS: Postpartum Depression Screening Scale, 2083
PEDI: Pediatric Evaluation of Disability Inventory, 1971
PEDS: Parents' Evaluation of Developmental Status,
1951
PEEK: PEEK–Perceptions, Expectations, Emotions, and
Knowledge About College, 1976
PEER: Pediatric Examination of Educational Readiness
(PEER), 1972
PEERAMID-2: Pediatric Examination of Educational
Readiness at Middle Childhood, 1973
PEET: Pediatric Extended Examination at Three
(PEET), 1974
PEEX-2: Pediatric Early Elementary Examination
(PEEX2), 1970
PEF: Psychiatric Evaluation Form, 2181
PEI-A: Personal Experience Inventory for Adults, 1998
PEI: Personal Effectiveness Inventory, 1996
PEI: Personal Experience Inventory, 1997
PEP-3: Psychoeducational Profile–Third Edition, 2185
PEP: Psycho-Epistemological Profile, 2184
PEPQ: PsychEval Personality Questionnaire, 2178
PEPS: Productivity Environmental Preference Survey,
2139
PES: Preschool Evaluation Scale, 2113
PESQ-A: Personal Experience Screening Questionnaire
for Adults, 2000
PESQ: Personal Experience Screening Questionnaire, 1999
PEST: The Patterned Elicitation Syntax Test with
Morphonemic Analysis, 1961
PET: Professional Employment Test, 2141
PETRA: Psychosocial Evaluation & Threat Risk As-
sessment, 2193
PFMAI: Posture and Fine Motor Assessment of In-
fants, 2085
PHSF: PHSF Relations Questionnaire, 2051
PIAT-R/NU: Peabody Individual Achievement Test–Re-
vised [1997 Normative Update], 1965
PIC-2: Personality Inventory for Children, Second
Edition, 2026
PICS: Picture Interest Career Survey, 2058
PiE 5–14: Progress in English 5–14, 2156
Piers-Harris 2: Piers-Harris Children's Self-Concept
Scale, Second Edition, 2059

PII: Prison Inmate Inventory, 2130
PIL: The Purpose in Life Test, 2201
PIP: Elementary Program Implementation Profile, 968
PIP: Partners in Play: Assessing Infants and Toddlers
in Natural Contexts, 1958
PIP: Project Implementation Profile, 2162
PIPA: Pre-Reading Inventory of Phonological Aware-
ness, 2103
PIPA: Preschool and Primary Inventory of Phonological
Awareness, 2107
PIQ: Purdue Interest Questionnaire, 2199
PIT: Picture Identification Test, 2057
PIY: Personality Inventory for Youth, 2027
PJRF: Professional Judgment Rating Form, 2142
PKBS-2: Preschool and Kindergarten Behavior Scales,
Second Edition, 2105
PKRS: Phelps Kindergarten Readiness Scale, 2043
PKS: Pre-Kindergarten Screen, 2096
PL-1: PL-1 and PL-2 Police Administrator Tests
(Lieutenant), 2063
PL-2: PL-1 and PL-2 Police Administrator Tests
(Lieutenant), 2063
PLAB: Phonological Assessment Battery [Standardised
Edition], 2047
PLAI-2: Preschool Language Assessment Instrument–
Second Edition, 2114
PLANT: Warehouse/Plant Worker Staff Selector, 2890
PLP: The Clark Wilson Group Multi-Level Feedback
Instruments and Development Programs, 520
PLS-5: Preschool Language Scales, Fifth Edition, 2115
PLSI: Pragmatic Language Skills Inventory, 2093
PLSS: Pre-Literacy Skills Screening, 2100
PMAI: Pearson-Marr Archetype Indicator®, 1967
PME: Outcomes: Planning, Monitoring, Evaluating,
1920
PMI: Power Management Inventory, 2088
PMMA: Primary Measures of Music Audiation, 2125
PMP: Power Management Profile, 2089
PMPQ: Professional and Managerial Position Question-
naire, 2140
PMS: Participative Management Survey, 1957
PMT: Assessment of Individual Learning Style: The
Perceptual Memory Task, 209
POD: Personal Orientation Dimensions, 2005
POI: Personal Orientation Inventory, 2006
POINT: Parents' Observations of Infants and Toddlers
(POINT), 1953
POIS: Kipnis-Schmidt Profiles of Organizational Influ-
ence Strategies, 1446
POLIF: Multiphasic Environmental Assessment Pro-
cedure, 1788
POMS-BI: Profile of Mood States, Bi-Polar Form, 2146
POMS: Profile of Mood States, 2145
PONS: Profile of Nonverbal Sensitivity, 2147
PORT: Perception-Of-Relationships-Test, 1984
POS: The Play Observation Scale [Revised], 2068
POST: National Police Officer Selection Test, 1810

SCALE: Scaled Curriculum Achievement Levels Test, 2345

SCALES: Scales for Diagnosing Attention-Deficit/Hyperactivity Disorder, 2347

SCAMIN: The Self-Concept and Motivation Inventory: What Face Would You Wear?, 2402

SCAN-3:A: SCAN-3 for Adolescents and Adults: Tests for Auditory Processing Disorders, 2353

SCAN-3:C: SCAN-3 for Children: Tests for Auditory Processing Disorders, 2354

SCAN: Schedules for Clinical Assessment in Neuropsychiatry, Version 2.0, 2362

SCAP: ACT Survey Services, 54

SCATBI: Scales of Cognitive Ability for Traumatic Brain Injury, 2350

SCBE: Social Competence and Behavior Evaluation, Preschool Edition, 2491

SCERTS: The SCERTS Model: A Comprehensive Educational Approach for Children with Autism Spectrum Disorders, 2356

SCES: Multiphasic Environmental Assessment Procedure, 1788

SCI: Shapiro Control Inventory, 2450

SCI: The Sexual Communication Inventory, 2445

SCICA: Achenbach System of Empirically Based Assessment, 32

SCID-CV: Structured Clinical Interview for DSM-IV Axis I Disorders: Clinician Version, 2583

SCID-D-R: Structured Clinical Interview for DSM-IV Dissociative Disorders–Revised, 2585

SCID-II: Structured Clinical Interview for DSM-IV Axis II Personality Disorders, 2584

SCIP: Severe Cognitive Impairment Profile, 2438

SCL-90-R: Symptom Checklist-90-Revised, 2655

SCLT: Chapin Social Insight Test, 466

SCOLP: The Speed and Capacity of Language Processing Test, 2524

SCOSD: The Southern California Ordinal Scales of Development, 2508

SCP: The Clark Wilson Group Multi-Level Feedback Instruments and Development Programs, 520

SCQ-39: Situational Confidence Questionnaire, 2466

SCR: The Clark Wilson Group Multi-Level Feedback Instruments and Development Programs, 520

SCS: Sentence Completion Series, 2431

SCS: Smoker Complaint Scale, 2488

SCT: Sales Comprehension Test, 2319

SDI: Strength Deployment Inventory, 2565

SDI/PVI: Feedback Edition of the Strength Deployment Inventory, 1072

SDLRS: Self-Directed Learning Readiness Scale/Learning Preference Assessment, 2404

SDMT: Stanford Diagnostic Mathematics Test, Fourth Edition, 2540

SDMT: Symbol Digit Modalities Test, 2651

SDQ: Self-Description Questionnaire–I, II, III, 2403

SDRT: Spadafore Diagnostic Reading Test, 2512

SDRT4: Stanford Diagnostic Reading Test, Fourth Edition, 2541

SDS: Self-Directed Search–Revised 2001 Australian Edition, 2406

SDS: Self-Directed Search, 4th Edition [Forms R, E, CE, and CP], 2405

SDT: Stromberg Dexterity Test, 2574

SDTLA: Student Developmental Task and Lifestyle Assessment, 2595

SEA: Survey of Employee Access, 2633

SEAI: Meadow-Kendall Social-Emotional Assessment Inventory for Deaf and Hearing Students, 1644

SEAI: Station Employee Applicant Inventory, 2558

SECS: Scales of Early Communication Skills for Hearing-Impaired Children, 2351

SEDS-2: Social-Emotional Dimension Scale–Second Edition, 2492

SEDS: Stirling Eating Disorder Scales, 2561

SEEC: Vineland Social-Emotional Early Childhood Scales, 2862

SEI: Self-Esteem Index, 2407

SELECT: Select Associate Screening System, 2396

SEPS: School Environment Preference Survey, 2368

SEQ: School Effectiveness Questionnaire, 2367

SEQ: Self-Esteem Questionnaire, 2409

SES: Sexuality Experience Scales, 2447

SESAT 1: Stanford Achievement Test, Tenth Edition, 2537

SESAT 2: Stanford Achievement Test, Tenth Edition, 2537

SESAT: Stanford Early School Achievement Test, Third Edition, 2542

SET: Short Employment Tests, Second Edition, 2456

SET: Sports Emotion Test, 2529

SETT: School-Readiness Evaluation by Trained Teachers, 2374

SEWB: Social-Emotional Wellbeing Survey, 2493

SF-36: SF-36 Health Survey, 2448

SFA: School Function Assessment, 2369

SFAB: Survey of Functional Adaptive Behaviors, 2634

SFPQ: Six Factor Personality Questionnaire, 2470

SGAB: Schubert General Ability Battery, 2379

SGS II: The Schedule of Growing Skills: Second Edition, 2361

SGSS: Stokes/Gordon Stress Scale, 2563

SHQ-R: Clarke Sex History Questionnaire for Males–Revised, 521

SI Inventory: Sensory Integration Inventory–Revised for Individuals with Developmental Disabilities, 2426

SI Test: Symbol Imagery Test, 2652

SI: Shoplifting Inventory, 2453

SIB-R: Scales of Independent Behavior–Revised, 2352

SIB: Severe Impairment Battery, 2439

SIC: Supervisory Inventory on Communication, 2623

SICD-R: Sequenced Inventory of Communication Development, Revised Edition, 2433

SIE: Strong Interest Explorer, 2575

CLASSIFIED SUBJECT INDEX

The Classified Subject Index classifies all tests included in Tests in Print VIII into 18 major categories: Achievement, Behavior Assessment, Developmental, Education, English and Language, Fine Arts, Foreign Language, Intelligence and General Aptitude, Mathematics, Miscellaneous, Neuropsychological, Personality, Reading, Science, Sensory–Motor, Social Studies, Speech and Hearing, and Vocations. Each category appears in alphabetical order and tests are ordered alphabetically within each category. The Miscellaneous category has 15 subcategories with tests ordered alphabetically within the subcategories. Each test entry includes test title, population for which the test is intended, and the test entry number in Tests in Print VIII. All numbers refer to test entry numbers, not to page numbers. Brief suggestions for the use of this index are presented in the introduction. Revised definitions of the categories were effective with the Fourteenth Mental Measurements Yearbook. Most tests in TIP VIII have been classified using the revised definitions, which are provided below.

Achievement

Tests that measure acquired knowledge across school subject content areas. Included here are test batteries that measure multiple content areas and individual subject areas not having separate classification categories. (Note: Some batteries include both achievement and aptitude subtests. Such batteries may be classified under the categories of either Achievement or Intelligence and Aptitude depending upon the principal content area.)

See also Fine Arts, Intelligence and General Aptitude, Mathematics, Reading, Science, and Social Studies.

Behavior Assessment

Tests that measure general or specific behavior within educational, vocational, community, or home settings. Included here are checklists, rating scales, and surveys that measure observer's interpretations of behavior in relation to adaptive or social skills, functional skills, and appropriateness or dysfunction within settings/situations.

Developmental

Tests that are designed to assess skills or emerging skills (such as number concepts, conservation, memory, fine motor, gross motor, communication, letter recognition, social competence) of young children (0-7 years) or tests which are designed to assess such skills in severely or profoundly disabled school-aged individuals. Included here are early screeners, developmental surveys/profiles, kindergarten or school readiness tests, early learning profiles, infant development scales, tests of play behavior, social acceptance/social skills; and preschool psycho-educational batteries. Content specific screeners, such as those assessing readiness, are classified by content area (e.g., Reading).

See also Neuropsychological and Sensory-Motor.

Education

General education-related tests, including measures of instructional/school environment, effective schools/teaching, study skills and strategies, learning styles and strategies, school attitudes, educational programs/curriculae, interest inventories, and educational leadership.

Specific content area tests (i.e., science, mathematics, social studies, etc.) are listed by their content area.

English and Language

Tests that measure skills in using or understanding the English language in spoken or written form. Included here are tests of language proficiency, applied literacy, language comprehension/development/proficiency, English skills/proficiency, communication skills, listening comprehension, linguistics, and receptive/expressive vocabulary. (Tests designed to measure the mechanics of speaking or communicating are classified under the category Speech and Hearing.)

Fine Arts

Tests that measure knowledge, skills, abilities, attitudes, and interests within the various areas of fine and performing arts. Included here are tests of aptitude, achievement, creativity/talent/giftedness specific to the Fine Arts area, and tests of aesthetic judgment.

Foreign Languages

Tests that measure competencies and readiness in reading, comprehending, and speaking a language other than English.

Intelligence and General Aptitude

Tests that measure general acquired knowledge, aptitudes, or cognitive ability and those that assess specific aspects of these general categories. Included here are tests of critical thinking skills, nonverbal/verbal reasoning, cognitive abilities/processing, learning potential/aptitude/efficiency, logical reasoning, abstract thinking, creative thinking/creativity, entrance exams and academic admissions tests.

Mathematics

Tests that measure competencies and attitudes in any of the various areas of mathematics (e.g., algebra, geometry, calculus) and those related to general mathematics achievement/proficiency. (Note: Included here are tests that assess personality or affective variables related to mathematics.)

Miscellaneous

Tests that cannot be sorted into any of the current MMY categories as listed and defined above. Included here are tests of handwriting, ethics and morality, religion, driving and safety, health and physical education, environment (e.g., classroom environment, family environment), custody decisions, substance abuse, and addictions. (See also Personality.)

Neuropsychological

Tests that measure neurological functioning or brain-behavior relationships either generally or in relation to specific areas of functioning. Included here are neuropsychological test batteries, questionnaires, and

screening tests. Also included are tests that measure memory impairment, various disorders or decline associated with dementia, brain/head injury, visual attention, digit recognition, finger tapping, laterality, aphasia, and behavior (associated with organic brain dysfunction or brain injury).

See also Developmental, Intelligence and General Aptitude, Sensory-Motor, and Speech and Hearing.

Personality

Tests that measure individuals' ways of thinking, behaving, and functioning within family and society. Included here are projective and apperception tests, needs inventories, anxiety/depression scales; tests assessing substance use/abuse (or propensity for abuse), risk taking behavior, general mental health, emotional intelligence, self-image/-concept/-esteem, empathy, suicidal ideation, schizophrenia, depression/hopelessness, abuse, coping skills/stress, eating disorders, grief, decision-making, racial attitudes; general motivation, attributions, perceptions; adjustment, parenting styles, and marital issues/satisfaction.

For content-specific tests, see subject area categories (e.g., math efficacy instruments are located in Mathematics). Some areas, such as substance abuse, are cross-referenced with the Personality category.

Reading

Tests that measure competencies and attitudes within the broadly defined area of reading. Included here are reading inventories, tests of reading achievement and aptitude, reading readiness/early reading ability, reading comprehension, reading decoding, and oral reading. (Note: Included here are tests that assess personality or affective variables related to reading.)

Science

Tests that measure competencies and attitudes within any of the various areas of science (e.g., biology, chemistry, physics), and those related to general science achievement/proficiency. (Note: Included here are tests that assess personality or affective variables related to science.)

Sensory-Motor

Tests that are general or specific measures of any or all of the five senses and those that assess fine or gross motor skills. Included here are tests of manual dexterity, perceptual skills, visual-motor skills, perceptual-motor skills, movement and posture, laterality preference, sensory integration, motor development, color blindness/discrimination, visual perception/organization, and visual acuity. (Note: See also the categories Neuropsychological and Speech and Hearing.)

Social Studies

Tests that measure competencies and attitudes within the broadly defined area of social studies. Included here are tests related to economics, sociology, history, geography, and political science, and those related to general social studies achievement/proficiency. (Note: Also included here are tests that assess personality or affective variables related to social studies.)

Speech and Hearing

Tests that measure the mechanics of speaking or hearing the spoken word. Included here are tests of articulation, voice fluency, stuttering, speech sound perception/discrimination, auditory discrimination/comprehension, audiometry, deafness, and hearing loss/impairment. (Note: See Developmental, English and Language, Neuropsychological, and Sensory-Motor.)

Vocations

Tests that measure employee skills, behaviors, attitudes, values, and perceptions relative to jobs, employment, and the work place or organizational environment. Included here are tests of management skill/style/competence, leader behavior, careers (development, exploration, attitudes); job- or work-related selection/admission/entrance tests; tests of work adjustment, team or group processes/communication/effectiveness, employability, vocational/occupational interests, employee aptitudes/competencies, and organizational climate.

See also Intelligence and General Aptitude, and Personality and also specific content area categories (e.g., Mathematics, Reading).

ACHIEVEMENT

BEHAVIOR ASSESSMENT

DEVELOPMENTAL

EDUCATION

ENGLISH AND LANGUAGE

FINE ARTS

FOREIGN LANGUAGES

INTELLIGENCE AND GENERAL APTITUDE

MATHEMATICS

MISCELLANEOUS

CRIMINAL JUSTICE AND FORENSIC

DRIVING AND SAFETY

FAMILY AND RELATIONSHIPS

HEALTH AND
PHYSICAL EDUCATION

Five Factor Wellness Inventory; Elementary, high school, and adults, see 1092

Functional Fitness Assessment for Adults over 60 Years, Second Edition; Adults over age 60, see 1116

Health and Daily Living Form, Second Edition; Students ages 12-18, Adults, see 1226

Health Problems Checklist; Adults, see 1232

Health Status Questionnaire 2.0; Ages 14 and older, see 1234

Katz Adjustment Scales–Relative Report Form; Adults with psychiatric, medical, or neurological disorders, see 1418

Krantz Health Opinion Survey; College, healthy adults, and chronic disease populations, see 1457

Matching Assistive Technology & Child; Children with disabilities, ages 0–5, see 1620

Medical Ethics Inventory; First year medical students, see 1672

Menometer; Adolescents and adults, see 1678

MILCOM Patient Data Base System; Medical patients, see 1703

Multidimensional Health Profile; Ages 18–90, see 1778

Organic Dysfunction Survey Schedules; Adult clients, see 1903

Overeating Questionnaire; Ages 9–98 years, see 1922

Pain Assessment Battery, Research Edition; Patients with chronic pain, see 1927

Psychosocial Pain Inventory [Revised]; Adults with chronic pain, see 2194

RAND-36 Health Status Inventory; Adults, see 2230

Rehabilitation Checklist; Adults, see 2254

Sexometer; Adolescents and adults, see 2442

Sexual Adaptation and Functioning Test; White adults ages 16 and over, see 2443

SF-36 Health Survey; Ages 14 and older, see 2448

Softball Skills Test; Grades 5-12 and college, see 2505

Stirling Eating Disorder Scales; Adolescents and adults, 2 see 561

Stress Indicator & Health Planner [Revised]; Adults, see 2569

Structured Inventory of Malingered Symptomatology; Ages 18 and over, see 2588

Tennis Skills Test Manual; High school and college, see 2702

Test of Auditory Analysis Skills; Ages 5-8, see 2719

TestWell: Health Risk Appraisal; Adults ages 18–60 with a minimum of 10th grade education, see 2791

TestWell: Wellness Inventory for Windows; Adults with a minimum of 10th grade education, see 2792

TestWell: Wellness Inventory for Windows–College Version; College students, see 2793

Y-OQ-30.1 [Youth-Outcome Questionnaire–Omni Version]; Ages 12-18 years, see 2997

HANDWRITING

Minnesota Handwriting Assessment; Grades 1–2, see 1737

Test of Handwriting Skills–Revised; Ages 6 to 18, see 2738

LEARNING DISABILITIES

Achievement Identification Measure; School age children, see 33

Dyslexia Determination Test, Second Edition; Grades 2–12, see 915

Functional Evaluation for Assistive Technology; "Individuals with learning problems (of all ages)," see 1115

Jordan Left-Right Reversal Test–Revised; Ages 5-0 through 12-11, see 1402

Pathways to Independence, Second Edition; Disadvantaged school-aged children and mentally and otherwise handicapped teenagers and adults and rehabilitating brain-damaged and geriatric patients, see 1960

PHILOSOPHY AND RELIGION

Assessment of Spirituality and Religious Sentiments; Ages 15 and over, see 219

PSYCHOLOGY

The Experiencing Scale; Counselors and counselor trainees, see 1039

RECORD AND REPORT FORMS

Quickview Social History; Individuals 16 years and older, see 2226

SOCIO-ECONOMIC STATUS

The American Home Scale; Grades 8–16, see 149

TEST PROGRAMS

ACT Test; Grades 11–12, see 55

Advanced Placement Examinations; High school students desiring credit for college-level courses and admission to advanced courses, see 127

CLEP Examination in Human Growth and Development; Persons entering college or already in college, see 542

CLEP Examination in Introductory Psychology; Persons entering college or already in college, see 545

College Board On-Campus Tests; Entering and continuing college students, see 626

College Level Examination Program ; 1-2 years of college or equivalent, see 651

DSST/DANTES Subject Standardized Tests; Nontraditional students wishing to earn college credit by examination, see 905

Educational Development Series (2000 Edition); Grades K-12, see 950

The Graduate Record Examinations Psychology Test; Graduate school candidates, see 1168

Graduate Record Examinations: Subject Tests; Graduate school candidates, see 1169

NEUROPSYCHOLOGICAL

PERSONALITY

READING

ACER Applied Reading Test; Apprentices, trainees, technical and trade personnel, see 27

Assessing Reading: Multiple Measures–Second Edition; Grades K-12, see 196

Basic Early Assessment of Reading™; Grades K–3, see 266

Basic Reading Inventory, Eighth Edition; Pre-primer through Grade 12, see 273

Bench Mark Measures; Ungraded, see 324

The Boder Test of Reading-Spelling Patterns; Grades K–12 and adult, see 346

Burns/Roe Informal Reading Inventory: Preprimer to Twelfth Grade, Sixth Edition; Beginning readers–Grade 12, see 383

Burt Word Reading Test, New Zealand Revision; Ages 6-0 to 12-11 years, see 384

California Diagnostic Reading Tests; Grades 1.1-12, see 399

CASAS Life and Work Reading Assessments; Youth and adult learners, see 457

Classroom Reading Inventory, Twelfth Edition; Elementary grades to adult learners, see 526

Cloze Reading Tests 1-3, Second Edition; Ages 8-0 to 10-6, 8-5 to 11-10, 9-5 to 12-6, see 587

Comprehensive Assessment of Reading Strategies; Grades 1-8, see 682

Comprehensive Assessment of Reading Strategies II; Grades 1-8, see 683

Crane Oral Dominance Test: Spanish/English; Ages 4-8, see 757

CRS Placement/Diagnostic Test; Grades Preprimer-2, see 769

Decoding-Encoding Screener for Dyslexia; Grades 1-8, see 795

Decoding Skills Test; Grades 1.0-5.8+, see 796

Decoding Spelling Proficiency Test-Revised; Ages 6-25, see 797

Degrees of Reading Power [Primary and Standard Test Forms J & K and Advanced Test Forms T & U]; Grades 1–12 and over, see 801

Degrees of Word Meaning; Grades 3–8+, see 802

Delaware County Silent Reading Test, Second Edition; Grades 1.5, 2, 2.5, 3, 3.5, 4, 5, 6, 7, 8, see 803

Diagnostic Assessments of Reading™, Second Edition; Grades K-12, see 856

Diagnostic Reading Assessment; Grade 1, see 864

Diagnostic Screening Test: Reading, Third Edition; Grades 1–12, see 868

DIBELS: Dynamic Indicators of Basic Early Literacy Skills, Sixth Edition; Grades K–6, see 874

Durrell Analysis of Reading Difficulty, Third Edition; Grades 1–6, see 906

Dyslexia Adult Screening Test; 16 years 5 months to adult, see 914

Dyslexia Early Screening Test [Second Edition]; Ages 4 years, 6 months to 6 years, 5 months, see 916

Dyslexia Screening Instrument; Grades 1–12, ages 6–21, see 917

Dyslexia Screening Test; Ages 6-6 to 16-5, see 918

Early Reading Diagnostic Assessment–Second Edition; Grades K–3, see 935

Early Reading Success Indicator; Ages 5–10, see 936

Edinburgh Reading Tests; Ages 7-0 to 9-0, 8-6 to 10-6, 10-0 to 12-6, 12-0 to 16-0, see 949

Ekwall/Shanker Reading Inventory–Third Edition; Grades 1–9, see 960

Gates-MacGinitie Reading Tests®, Fourth Edition, Forms S and T; Grades K.6–12 and adults, see 1123

Gates-MacGinitie Reading Tests, 2nd Canadian Edition; Grades K.7–12, see 1124

Gates-McKillop-Horowitz Reading Diagnostic Test, Second Edition; Grades 1-6, see 1125

Get Ready to Read!–Revised; Ages 3-0 to 5-11, see 1136

Gilmore Oral Reading Test; Grades 1–8, see 1143

Graded Nonword Reading Test; Ages 5-11, see 1155

Gray Diagnostic Reading Tests–Second Edition; Ages 6-0 to 13-11, see 1172

Gray Oral Reading Tests, Fourth Edition; Ages 6-0 to 18-11, see 1173

Gray Silent Reading Tests; Ages 7–25, see 1174

Group Diagnostic Reading Aptitude and Achievement Tests, Intermediate Form; Grades 3–9, see 1186

Group Reading Assessment and Diagnostic Evaluation; Pre-K through adult, see 1195

Group Reading Test, Fourth Edition; Ages 6:4 to 8:11 and less able children 8:0 to 11:11, see 1196

Group Reading Test II (6-14); Ages 6 years to 15 years 9 months, see 1197

High School Reading Test: National Achievement Tests; Grades 7-12, see 1246

Industrial Reading Test; Grade 9 and over vocational students and applicants or trainees in technical or vocational training programs, see 1302

Informal Reading Comprehension Placement Test [Revised]; Grades 1–8 for typical learners and grades 8–12 remedially; adult education students, see 1312

Johnston Informal Reading Inventory; Grades 7-12, see 1398

LARR Test of Emergent Literacy; Students entering school, see 1475

Living in the Reader's World: Locator Test; Adults at reading grade levels 2.0-6.0, see 1545

The Lollipop Test: A Diagnostic Screening Test of School Readiness–Revised; First grade entrants, see 1550

Martin and Pratt Nonword Reading Test; Ages 6–16, see 1614

Maryland/Baltimore County Design for Adult Basic Education; Adult nonreaders, see 1616

SCIENCE

SENSORY-MOTOR

Sensory Evaluation Kit; Ages 2 to adult, see 2424

Sensory Integration Inventory–Revised for Individuals with Developmental Disabilities; Developmentally disabled occupational therapy clients school aged to adults, see 2426

Sensory Processing Measure; Ages 5-12, see 2427

Sensory Processing Measure–Preschool; Children ages 2-5 who have not started kindergarten, see 2428

Sensory Profile; Birth to 36 months, Ages 3–10, Ages 5-10, see 2429

Sensory Profile School Companion; Ages 3-0 to 11-11, see 2430

Smedley Hand Dynamometer; Ages 6–18, see 2486

Spatial Reasoning; Ages 5.4–15.5, see 2518

Speech Perception Instructional Curriculum and Evaluation; Hearing-impaired individuals ages 3–12, see 2523

Swallowing Ability and Function Evaluation; Adolescents and adults, see 2649

The Tapping Test: A Predictor of Typing and Other Tapping Operations; High school, see 2665

Test for Colour-Blindness; Ages 4 and over, see 2708

The Test of Everyday Attention; Ages 18–80, see 2734

The Test of Everyday Attention for Children; Ages 6–16, see 2735

Test of Gross Motor Development–Second Edition; Ages 3-10, see 2737

Test of Visual Perceptual Skills, 3rd Edition; Ages 4-0 through 18-11, see 2775

Useful Field of View; Adults, see 2843

The Visual Aural Digit Span Test; Ages 5-6 to 12, see 2866

Visual Functioning Assessment Tool; Visually impaired in grades preschool and over, see 2867

Visual Motor Assessment; Ages 6 and older, see 2868

Visual Skills Appraisal; Grades K–4; ages 5 through 9, see 2872

Washer Visual Acuity Screening Technique; Mental ages 2.5-adult, see 2891

Wide Range Assessment of Visual Motor Abilities; Ages 3–17 years, see 2933

SOCIAL STUDIES

Advanced Placement Examination in Comparative Government and Politics; High school students desiring credit for college-level courses and admission to advanced courses, see 103

Advanced Placement Examination in European History; High school students desiring credit for college-level courses and admission to advanced courses, see 108

Advanced Placement Examination in Human Geography; High school students desiring credit for college-level courses and admission to advanced courses, see 112

Advanced Placement Examination in Macroeconomics; High school students desiring credit for college-level courses and admission to advanced courses, see 115

Advanced Placement Examination in Microeconomics; High school students desiring credit for college-level courses and admission to advanced courses, see 116

Advanced Placement Examination in United States Government and Politics; High school students desiring credit for college-level courses and admission to advanced courses, see 124

Advanced Placement Examination in U.S. History; High school students desiring credit for college-level courses and admission to advanced courses, see 125

Advanced Placement Examination in World History; High school students desiring credit for college-level courses and admission to advanced courses, see 126

Basic Economics Test, Second Edition; Grades 5–6, see 267

CLEP Examination in American Government; Persons entering college or already in college, see 527

CLEP Examination in History of the United States: Early Colonizations to 1877; Persons entering college or already in college, see 540

CLEP Examination in History of the United States II: 1865 to the Present; Persons entering college or already in college, see 541

CLEP Examination in Introductory Sociology; Persons entering college or already in college, see 546

CLEP Examination in Principles of Macroeconomics; Persons entering college or already in college, see 548

CLEP Examination in Principles of Microeconomics; Persons entering college or already in college, see 551

CLEP Examination in Western Civilization I: Ancient Near East to 1648; Persons entering college or already in college, see 553

CLEP Examination in Western Civilization II: 1648 to the Present; Persons entering college or already in college, see 554

CLEP Examinations in Humanities; Persons entering college or already in college, see 556

CLEP Examinations in Social Sciences and History; Persons entering college or already in college, see 559

College Board On-Campus SAT Subject Test in U.S. History; Entering college freshmen, see 622

College Board On-Campus SAT Subject Test in World History; Entering college freshmen, see 623

College Board SAT Subject Test in U.S. History; Candidates for college entrance with one-year American history course at the college-preparatory level, see 645

SPEECH AND HEARING

VOCATIONS

PUBLISHERS DIRECTORY
AND INDEX

This directory and index gives the names and test entry numbers of all publishers represented in Tests *in Print VIII. Current addresses are listed for all publishers for which this is known. Those publishers for which a current address is not available are listed as "Address Unknown." This directory and index also provides telephone and FAX numbers and e-mail and Web page addresses for those publishers who responded to our request for this information. Please note that all test numbers refer to test entry numbers, not page numbers. Publishers are an important source of information about catalogs, specimen sets, price changes, test revisions, and other details.*

A & M Psychometrics, LLC
1209 S Owasso Ave.
Tulsa, OK 74120
Tests: 2859

ABackans DCP, Inc.
1700 West Market Street
Dept. RD301
Akron, OH 44313
Telephone: 330-745-4450
FAX: 330-745-4450
E-mail: ABackans@abackans.com
Web: abackans.com
Tests: 38, 2082

Academic Consulting & Testing Service
P.O. Box 1883
Lake Oswego, OR 97035
Telephone: 503-639-3292
FAX: 503-639-3292
E-mail: HEDSbyACTS@aol.com
Tests: 225, 840, 1501, 1945, 2373

Academic Therapy Publications
20 Commercial Boulevard
Novato, CA 94949-6191
Telephone: 800-422-7249
FAX: 415-883-3720
E-mail: atp@aol.com
Web: www.academictherapy.com/
Tests: 236, 260, 764, 797, 1018, 1042, 1043, 1402, 1536, 1541, 1836, 2045, 2218, 2219, 2222, 2249, 2250, 2511, 2512, 2719, 2721, 2722, 2738, 2741, 2773, 2774, 2775, 2872, 2959, 2994, 1766, 1767, 2096, 2744

Acanthus Publishing
343 Commercial St.
Unit 214, Union Wharf
Boston, MA 02109
Telephone: 617-230-2167
FAX: 215-243-7495
E-mail: info@acanthuspublishing.com
Web: www.AcanthusPublishing.com
Tests: 422

ACS DivCHED Examinations Institute
UW Milwaukee
Chemistry Department
3210 North Cramer Street
Milwaukee, WI 53211
Tests: 40, 41, 42, 43, 44, 45, 46, 47, 48, 49, 50, 51, 52, 53

ACT, Inc.
500 ACT Drive
P.O. Box 168
Iowa City, IA 52243-0168
Telephone: 319-337-1000
FAX: 319-341-2335
Web: www.act.org
Tests: 54, 55, 443, 657, 1040, 2064, 2970

ADE Incorporated
P.O. Box 660
Clarkston, MI 48347
Telephone: 800-334-1918
Tests: 1412, 1815, 2610

Adult Self Expression Scale
c/o John P. Galassi
CB #3500
Peabody Hall
University of North Carolina
Chapel Hill, NC 27599-3500
Tests: 95

Alpha Educational Associates
122 Deerhurst Park Blvd.
Buffalo, NY 14217
Tests: 1391

American Association for Active Lifestyles and Fitness
1900 Association Drive
Reston, VA 22091
Telephone: 800-213-7193
FAX: 703-476-9527
E-mail: aaalf@aahperd.org
Web: www.aahperd.org/aapar/
Tests: 1116, 2505, 2702

American Association of Teachers of German, Inc.
112 Haddontowne Court, #104
Cherry Hill, NJ 08034-3668
Telephone: 856-795-5553
FAX: 856-795-9398
E-mail: headquarters@aatg.org
Web: www.aatg.org
Tests: 1808

American Association on Intellectual and Developmental
    Disabilities
444 North Capitol Street, NW, Suite 846
Washington, DC 20001-1512
Tests: 2630

American Dental Association
211 East Chicago Avenue, 6th Floor
Chicago, IL 60611-2678
Telephone: 312-440-7465
FAX: 312-587-4105
E-mail: kramerg@ada.org
Web: www.ada.org
Tests: 417, 807

American Management Association
Address Unknown
Tests: 147

American Psychiatric Association
1000 Wilson Blvd., Suite #1625
Arlington, VA 22209-3901
Tests: 2182, 496, 2362, 2583, 2584, 2585, 2380

Dr. Nancy C. Andreasen
Department of Psychiatry
MHCRC, 2911 JPP
200 Hawkins Drive
Iowa City, IA 52242-1057
Telephone: 319-356-1553
FAX: 319-353-8300
E-mail: luann-godlove@uiowa.edu
Web: http://iowa-mhcrc.psychiatry.uiowa.edu/
Tests: 687, 2339, 2340, 2341

Andrews University Press
Sutherland House
8360 W Campus Circle Dr
Berrien Springs, MI 49104-1700
Telephone: 269-471-6915
FAX: 269-471-6224
E-mail: aupress@andrews.edu
Web: www.andrews.edu/universitypress/
Tests: 2700

AOTA Press
The American Occupational Therapy Association, Inc.
4720 Montgomery Lane
Bethesda, MD 20814-3425
Tests: 156, 1453

Appalachian State University
Office of Testing Services
287 Rivers St., Room 245
Boone, NC 28608
Tests: 2595

APR Testing Services
62 Candlewood Rd
Scarsdale, NY 10583-6040
Telephone: 617-244-7405
E-mail: jwiesen@aprtestingservices.com
Web: aprtestingservices.com
Tests: 871, 872

ARBOR, Inc.
ARBOR Corporate Center
One West Third Street
Media, PA 19063
Tests: 2880

Arnold R. Bruhn and Associates
7910 Woodmont Avenue, Suite 1300
Bethesda, MD 20814
Tests: 934

ASEBA Research Center for Children, Youth, and
    Families
1 South Prospect Street
Burlington, VT 05401-3456
Telephone: 802-264-6432
FAX: 802-264-6433
E-mail: mail@ASEBA.org
Web: www.ASEBA.org
Tests: 449, 32

Assessio U.S.
909 Marina Village Parkway #291
Alameda, CA 94501-1048
Telephone: 925-676-6265
FAX: 925-676-0519
E-mail: info@assessio.com
Web: www.assessio.us
Tests: 2436

The Assessment and Development Centre
6890 E. Sunrise Drive, #120-382
Tucson, AZ 85750
Telephone: 520-299-5501
FAX: 520-299-5348
E-mail: stressmaster@qwest.net
Web: www.stressmaster.com
Tests: 2570, 1946, 276

Assessment Enterprises
925 Hayslope Drive
Knoxville, TN 37919
Telephone: 865-690-4498
E-mail: mstahl@utk.edu
Tests: 1385

Assessment Resource Center
University of Missouri–Columbia
College of Education
2800 Maguire Blvd.
Columbia, MO 65211
Telephone: 800-366-8232
FAX: 573-822-8937
E-mail: umcarck-12@missouri.edu
Web: www.arc.missouri.edu
Tests: 605, 1748

Assessment Systems International, Inc.
544 East Ogden Avenue, Suite 700–391
Milwaukee, WI 53202
Telephone: 414-224-1400
FAX: 414-224-1401
E-mail: cspeck@execpc.com
Web: www.asi-intl.com
Tests: 1571

Association for Biblical Higher Education
5850 T.G. Lee Blvd, Ste, 130
Orlando, FL 32822-4408
Telephone: 407-207-0808
FAX: 407-207-0840
E-mail:exdir@abhe.org
Web: www.abhe.org
Tests: 873, 2533

Association for the Education and Welfare of the Visu-
    ally Handicapped
ATTN: Mrs. S. A. Clamp, Deputy Head
St. Vincent's School for the Blind
Yew Tree Lane, West Derby
West Derby, Liverpool L12 9HN
England
Tests: 1553, 2812

Association of American Colleges and Universities
1818 "R" Street, NW
Washington, DC 20009
Tests: 1021

Association of American Medical Colleges
2501 "M" Street, NW, Lobby 26
Washington, DC 20037-1300
Tests: 1671

Athletic Success Institute
2308 Crystal Court
Antioch, CA 94509
Tests: 224

Australian Council for Educational Research Ltd.
19 Prospect Hill Road
Camberwell, Melbourne, Victoria 3124
Australia
Telephone: +61 3 9277 5411
FAX: +61 3 9277 5500
E-mail: power@acer.edu.au
Web: www.acer.edu.au
Tests: 7, 24, 26, 27, 28, 29, 30, 31, 78, 176, 194, 232,
    242, 739, 834, 835, 857, 863, 1005, 1279, 1281, 1612,
    1614, 1814, 1825, 2158, 2159, 2196, 2371, 2406,
    2493, 2664, 2790, 2927, 2964, 2976, 2981

Australian Department of Immigration and Multicultural Affairs
Benjamin Offices
Chan St.
Belconnen, ACT 2617
Australia
Tests: 241

AVIAT
c/o Denison Consulting
121 West Washington, Suite 201
Ann Arbor, MI 48104
Tests: 1194

Professor Sandra Ball-Rokeach
Address Unknown
Tests: 2298

Ballard & Tighe Publishers
471 Atlas Street
Brea, CA 92822-0219
Telephone: 800-321-4332
FAX: 714-255-9828
E-mail: info@ballard-tighe.com
Web: www.ballard-tighe.com
Tests: 1285, 1286, 1367, 2216

The Barber Center Press, Inc.
136 East Avenue
Erie, PA 16507
Telephone: 814-453-7661
FAX: 814-455-1132
E-mail: gabcmain@drbarbercenter.org
Web: www.drbarbercenter.org
Tests: 6, 350, 602, 789, 1017, 1053, 1064, 1171, 1314, 1369, 1678, 1956, 2060, 2257, 2442, 2795, 2848, 2863, 2989

Barrett & Associates, Inc.
1772 State Road
Cuyahoga Falls, OH 44223
Telephone: 330-762-2323
FAX: 330-928-2768
E-mail: gbarrett@barrett-associates.com
Web: www.barrett-associates.com
Tests: 237

The Basic Skills Agency
Commonwealth House
1-19 New Oxford Street
London WC1A 1NU
England
Tests: 1067

Bay State Psychological Associates
225 Friend Street
Boston, MA 02114
Telephone: 800-438-2772
FAX: 617-367-5888
E-mail: jerry@eri.com
Web: www.eri.com
Tests: 995

James R. Beatty
College of Business Administration
San Diego State University
San Diego, CA 92182
Tests: 1320

Lenore Behar
1821 Woodburn Road
Durham, NC 27705
Telephone: 919-489-1888
FAX: 919-489-1832
E-mail: lbehar@nc.rr.com
Web: www.lenorebehar.com
Tests: 2109

Behavior Data Systems, Ltd.
P.O. Box 44256
Phoenix, AZ 85064-4256
Tests: 2831, 23, 77, 92, 93, 798, 895, 901, 1121, 1376, 1414, 1415, 1416, 1877, 2130, 2335, 2400, 2444, 2453

Behavioral-Developmental Initiatives
14636 North 55th Street
Scottsdale, AZ 85254
Telephone: 800-405-2313
FAX: 602-494-2688
E-mail: bdi@temperament.com
Web: www.b-di.com
Tests: 450, 1835

Behaviordata, Inc.
20833 Stevens Creek Blvd., Suite 100
Cupertino, CA 95014-2154
Tests: 2450

The Ber-Sil Co.
3412 Seaglen Drive
Rancho Palos Verdes, CA 90275-6140
Tests: 331

BEST Instruments, LLC
P.O. Box 501
Niceville, FL 32588
Tests: 332, 2631

Nancy E. Betz, Ph.D.
240b Lazenby Hall
1827 Neil Avenue Mall
The Ohio State University
Columbus, OH 43210
Telephone: 614-292-4166
FAX: 614-292-4537
E-mail: betz.3@osu.edu
Web: faculty.psy.ohio-state.edu/betz/
Tests: 432, 2965

Biddle Consulting Group Inc.
195 Blue Ravine Rd., Suite 270
Folsom, CA 95630-4760
Telephone: 800-999-0438 x 242
FAX: 916-563-7557
E-mail: blane@opac.com
Web: www.opac.com
Tests: 1880

Millard J. Bienvenu, Ph.D.
Northwest Publications
710 Watson Drive
Natchitoches, LA 71457
Tests: 192, 1335, 1344, 1351, 1609, 1934, 1939, 2101,
    2408, 2445

Bigby, Havis & Associates, Inc., d/b/a Assess Systems
12750 Merit Drive, Suite 300
Dallas, TX 75251
Telephone: 972-233-6055
FAX: 972-233-3154
E-mail: kcapelle@assess-systems.com
Web: www.assess-systems.com
Tests: 2333, 193, 2396

Bilingual Educational Services, Inc.
2514 South Grand Avenue
Los Angeles, CA 90007-9979
Telephone: 213-749-6213
FAX: 213-749-1820
Tests: 757, 769

Laurence M. Binder, Ph.D.
4900 SW Griffith Dr.
Suite 244
Beaverton, OR 97005
Telephone: 503-626-5246
FAX: 503-626-1686
E-mail: pdxlarry@aol.com
Tests: 2075

Biofeedback Certification Institute of America
10200 W. 44th Avenue, Suite 304
Wheat Ridge, CO 80033-2840
Web: www.bcia.org
Tests: 339

Birkman International, Inc.
3040 Post Oak Blvd., Suite 1425
Houston, TX 77056
Telephone: 800-215-2760
FAX: 713-963-9142
E-mail: birkmanresearch@birkman.com
Web: www.birkman.com
Tests: 341

Dr. Dorothy Bishop
c/o TROG Research Fund
Age and Cognitive Performance Research Centre
University of Manchester
Manchester M13 9PL
England
Tests: 2711

Sidney J. Blatt
Yale University School of Medicine
Department of Psychiatry
25 Park Street
New Haven, CT 06519
Telephone: 203-785-2090
FAX: 203-785-7357
E-mail: sidney.blatt@yale.edu
Tests: 217, 816

Bowling Green State University
JDI Office
Department of Psychology
Bowling Green, OH 43403
Telephone: 419-372-8247
FAX: 419-372-6013
E-mail: JDI_RA@bgnet.bgnet.bgsu.edu
Web: www.bgsu.edu/departments/psych/io/jdi/index.
    html
Tests: 1386, 2268, 2567, 2647

Brador Publications, Inc.
38 Main Street
Livonia, NY 14487
Tests: 344, 2241

Brain Injury Rehabilitation Trust
Kerwin Court, Five Oaks Road
Slinfold, Nr Horsham
West Sussex RH13 0TP
England
Telephone: 01403 799163
FAX: 01403 791738
E-mail: michael.oddy@thedtgroup.org
Web: www.birt.co.uk
Tests: 357

Brain Technologies Corporation
P.O. Box 358655
Gainesville, FL 32635
Telephone: 352-792-1036
FAX: 888-639-2814
E-mail: info@braintechnologies.com
Web: www.brainmeup.com
Tests: 358, 753, 1641, 1731

BrainTrain
727 Twin Ridge Lane
Richmond, VA 23235
Telephone: 804-320-0105
FAX: 804-320-0242
E-mail: info@braintrain.com
Web: www.braintrain.com
Tests: 1373

Branden Publishing Co.
P.O. Box 812094
Wellesley, MA 02482
Telephone: 781-235-3634
FAX: 781-790-1056
E-mail: branden@brandenbooks.com
Web: www.brandenbooks.com
Tests: 337

Brandon House, Inc.
P.O. Box 240
Bronx, NY 10471
Tests: 130, 957

Brigham Young University
Humanities Technology and Research Support Center
Foreign Language Testing
Provo, UT 84602
Tests: 1890

British Columbia Institute Against Family Violence
551-409 Granville St.
Vancouver, British Columbia V6C 1T2
Canada
Telephone: 604-669-7055
FAX: 604-669-7054
E-mail: resource@bcifv.org
Tests: 2446

Paul H. Brookes Publishing Co., Inc.
P.O. Box 10624
Baltimore, MD 21285-0624
Telephone: 800-638-3775
FAX: 410-337-8539
E-mail: custserv@brookespublishing.com
Web: www.brookespublishing.com
Tests: 131, 132, 198, 420, 453, 510, 523, 665, 928, 929,
    1258, 1306, 1558, 1837, 1975, 2356, 2377, 2698,
    2815, 2820

Brougham Press
12469 S Greenwood St.
Olathe, KS 66062-6070
Telephone: 800-360-6244
FAX: 913-782-1116
E-mail: CISE@BroughamPress.com
Web: www.broughampress.com.au
Tests: 498

Martin M. Bruce, Ph.D.
26 Laurel Way
Madison, NJ 07940-1002
Telephone: 561-393-2428
Tests: 178, 223, 379, 389, 430, 564, 993, 1755, 1988,
    2033, 2072, 2319, 2321, 2328, 2397, 2615, 2625,
    2768, 2818, 2940

C. G. Jung Institute of San Francisco, Inc.
337 Spruce St.
San Francisco, CA 94118-1883
Telephone: 415-221-2266
FAX: 415-387-5915
E-mail: johnbeebe@msn.com
Tests: 1406

C. H. Nevins Printing Co.
Address Unknown
Tests: 1186

C.P.S., Inc.
P.O. Box 345
Englewood, NJ 07631
Telephone: 201-947-2002
FAX: 201-947-2002
E-mail: CPSPSYCH1@aol.com
Web: www.CPSPublishingInc.com
Tests: 487, 955, 2360, 2421

Caliper Corporation
506 Carnegie Center, Suite 300
P.O. Box 2050
Princeton, NJ 08543-2050
Tests: 405

Callier Center for Communication Disorders
University of Texas at Dallas
1966 Inwood Road
Dallas, TX 75235
Tests: 407

Cambridge Center for Behavioral Studies
P.O. Box 7067
Beverly, MA 01915-0091
Telephone: 978-369-2227
FAX: 978-369-2227
E-mail: center@behavior.org
Web: www.behavior.org
Tests: 296, 1903

Cambridge-Michigan Language Assessments
University of Michigan
500 East Washington Street
Ann Arbor, MI 48104-2028
Telephone: 734-615-9629
FAX: 734-763-0369
E-mail: elicertif@umich.edu
Web: www.lsa.umich.edu/eli/testing
Tests: 1004, 1029, 1030, 1694, 1695, 1696, 1697

The Cambridge Stratford Study Skills Institute
8560 Main Street
Williamsville, NY 14221
Telephone: 800-466-2232
FAX: 716-626-9076
E-mail: cambridges@aol.com
Web: www.cambridgestratford.com
Tests: 1952, 2644, 2835

Cambridge University Press
100 Brook Hill Drive
West Nyack, NY 10994-2133
Web: cambridge.org/us
Tests: 1653, 1820, 2121, 1452

Camelot Unlimited
c/o Michael Lavelli
597 Crosswind Lane
Lindenhurst, IL 60046
E-mail: camelotunlimited@yahoo.com
Tests: 483

Career Cruising
1867 Yonge Street, Suite 1002
Toronto, Ontario M4S 1Y5
Canada
Tests: 438

Career Kids
PO Box 7032
Auburn, CA 95604-7032
Tests: 448

Career Research & Testing, Inc.
PO Box 611930
San Jose, CA 95161-1930
Telephone: 408-272-3085
FAX: 408-259-8438
E-mail: rknowdell@mac.com
Web: www.careernetwork.com
Tests: 447, 1520, 1760, 1870

CASAS
5151 Murphy Canyon Road, Suite 220
San Diego, CA 92123-4339
Telephone: 858-292-2900
FAX: 858-292-2910
E-mail: bwalsh@casas.org
Web: www.casas.org
Tests: 457, 678

Castle Consultants
111 Teeter Rock Road
Trumbull, CT 06611
Telephone: 203-375-5353
FAX: 203-375-2999
E-mail: cassie@castleconsultants.us
Web: www.castleconsultants.us
Tests: 16, 204, 2414, 2415, 2416, 2417, 2418, 2419, 2507, 2676

Center for Advanced Studies in Management
1574 Mallory Court
Bowling Green, KY 42103
Tests: 676, 1015, 1914, 2228, 2229

Center for Applications of Psychological Type, Inc.
2815 Northwest 13th Street, Suite 401
Gainesville, FL 32609
Web: www.capt.org
Tests: 1904, 1450, 1794, 1967

Center for Architecture and Urban Planning Research
P.O. Box 413
University of Wisconsin–Milwaukee
Milwaukee, WI 53201-0413
Tests: 925

Center for Creative Leadership
One Leadership Place
P.O. Box 26300
Greensboro, NC 27438-6300
Telephone: 336-288-7210
FAX: 336-282-3284
E-mail: info@leaders.ccl.org
Web: www.ccl.org
Tests: 326, 1034, 1434, 2167, 2479

Center for Creative Learning
4921 Ringwood Meadow
Sarasota, FL 34235
Telephone: 941-342-9928
FAX: 941-342-0064
E-mail: info@creativelearning.com
Web: www.creativelearning.com
Tests: 2857

The Center for Management Effectiveness, Inc.
P.O. Box 1202
Pacific Palisades, CA 90272
Telephone: 310-459-6052
FAX: 310-459-9307
E-mail: info@cmeinc.org
Web: www.cmeinc.org
Tests: 794, 1583, 2012, 2290, 2564

Center for the Study of Aging and Human Development
Box 3003
Duke University Medical Center
Durham, NC 27710
Telephone: 919-660-7500
FAX: 919-686-8569
E-mail: betty.ray@duke.edu
Web: www.geri.duke.edu
Tests: 1861

Center for the Study of Ethical Development
University of Minnesota
206 Burton Hall
178 Pillsbury Drive, SE
Minneapolis, MN 55455
Telephone: 612-624-0876
FAX: 612-624-8241
E-mail: tich0016@tc.umn.edu
Web: www.centerforthestudyofethicaldevelopment.net
Tests: 799

Center for the Study of Higher Education
The University of Memphis
308 Browning Hall
Memphis, TN 38152
Telephone: 901-678-2775
FAX: 901-678-4291
E-mail: ccseqlib@cc.memphis.edu
Web: www.memphis.edu/cshe
Tests: 669

Central Institute for the Deaf (CID)
825 South Taylor Ave.
St. Louis, MO 63110
Telephone: 314-977-0135
FAX: 314-977-0025
E-mail: kreadmond@cid.edu
Web: www.cid.edu
Tests: 514, 515, 942, 2351, 2523, 2673

Central Wisconsin Center for the Developmentally
    Disabled
ATTN: Psychology Department
317 Knutson Drive
Madison, WI 53704
Telephone: 608-301-9227
FAX: 608-301-9423
E-mail: kesligp@dhfs.state.wi.us
Tests: 2944

Centre for Addiction and Mental Health
Marketing Services
33 Russell Street
Toronto, Ontario M5S 2S1
Canada
Telephone: 416-595-6059
FAX: 416-593-4694
E-mail: marketing@camh.net
Web: www.camh.net
Tests: 138, 190, 902, 903, 1345, 2466

CERAD
Center for the Study of Aging and Human Development
Box 3003
Duke University Medical Center
Durham, NC 27710
Telephone: 919-660-7530
FAX: 919-668-0453
E-mail: ldg@geri.duke.edu
Web: cerad.mc.duke.edu
Tests: 461, 462

CFKR Career Materials
P.O. Box 99
Meadow Vista, CA95722-0099
Tests: 186, 435, 1041, 1243, 1389, 2873, 1387, 1388,
    1565, 509, 1551

Jay L. Chambers, Ph.D.
Deceased
Tests: 2057

The Change Companies
5221 Sigstrom Drive
Carson City, NV 89706
Tests: 90, 315, 677, 882, 998, 1381, 1919, 2092, 2252,
    2614, 2833, 2834

The Chauncey Group International
Educational Testing Service
664 Rosedale Road
Princeton, NJ 08540-2218
Tests: 2733

Checkmate Plus, Ltd.
P.O. Box 696
Stony Brook, NY 11790-0696
Telephone: 800-779-4292
FAX: 631-360-3432
E-mail: info@checkmateplus.com
Web: www.checkmateplus.com
Tests: 67, 86, 96, 479, 924, 3003

Child Development Centers of the Bluegrass, Inc.
465 Springhill Drive
Lexington, KY 40503
Tests: 1528

Child Development Resources
P.O. Box 280
Norge, VA 23127-0280
Tests: 1267, 2478

Child Development Review-Behavior Science Systems,
    Inc.
P.O. Box 19512
5905 Elliot Avenue South
Minneapolis, MN 55419-9998
Telephone: 612-850-8700
FAX: 360-351-1374
E-mail: heidi@childdevrev.com
Web: www.childdevrev.com/
Tests: 475, 476, 920, 1305, 2111

Child Welfare League of America
1726 M St NW
Ste 500
Washington, DC 20036-4522
Telephone: 202-688-4200
FAX: 202-833-1689
E-mail: books@cwla.org
Web: www.cwla.org/pubs
Tests: 480, 771, 1055

ChoicePoint
P.O. Box 49429
Charlotte, NC 28277-2712
Telephone: 888-310-2558
FAX: 888-286-5724
Tests: 2546, 2547

Chronicle Guidance Publications, Inc.
66 Aurora Street
Moravia, NY 13118-3569
Telephone: 800-622-7284
FAX: 315-497-0339
E-mail: CustomerService@ChronicleGuidance.com
Web: www.ChronicleGuidance.com
Tests: 513

The Clark Wilson Group, Inc.
4900 Nautilus Court N., Suite 220
Boulder, CO 80301-3242
Telephone: 800-537-7249
FAX: 303-581-9326
E-mail: info@clarkwilsongroup.com
Web: www.clarkwilsongroup.com
Tests: 520, 2164

Clinical Psychometric Research, Inc.
1228 Wine Spring Lane
Towson, MD 21204
Telephone: 800-245-0277; 410-321-6165
FAX: 410-321-6341
E-mail: mdero@aol.com
Web: www.derogatis-tests.com
Tests: 817, 818, 820, 821, 2192

CNS Vital Signs
598 Airport Blvd, Suite 1400
Morrisville, NC 27550-7203
Telephone: 919-933-2000
FAX: 919-933-2830
Web: www.cnsvs.com
Tests: 588

Cognistat, Inc.
P.O. Box 460
Fairfax, CA 94978
Telephone: 800-922-5840
Web: www.cognistat.com
Tests: 593, 702, 1927

CogScreen, LLC
4910 Massachusetts Ave., NW, Suite 100
Washington, DC 20016
Web: www.cogscreen.com
Tests: 601

The College Board
45 Columbus Avenue
New York, NY 10023-6992
Telephone: 212-713-8000
Web: www.collegeboard.com
Tests: 22, 99, 100, 101, 102, 103, 104, 105, 106, 107,
    108, 109, 110, 111, 112, 113, 114, 115, 116, 117,
    118, 119, 120, 121, 122, 123, 124, 125, 126, 606,
    607, 608, 609, 610, 611, 612, 613, 614, 615, 616,
    617, 618, 619, 620, 621, 622, 623, 624, 625, 627,
    628, 629, 630, 631, 632, 633, 634, 635, 636, 637,
    638, 639, 640, 641, 642, 643, 644, 645, 646, 647,
    648, 649, 2338, 626

Combined Program in Education and Psychology
University of Michigan
1406 School of Education
610 East University Avenue
Ann Arbor, MI 48109-1259
E-mail: mslq@umich.edu
Tests: 1761

John D. Cone
Department of Psychology & Family Studies
United States International University
10455 Pomerado Road
San Diego, CA 92131
Tests: 1941, 2203

Consortium on Reading Excellence, Inc. (CORE)
2560 Ninth Street, Suite 220
Berkeley, CA 94710
Tests: 196

Consulting Resource Group International, Inc.
P.O. Box 8000, PMB 386
Sumas, WA 98295-8000
Telephone: 604-852-0566
FAX: 604-850-3003
E-mail: info@crgleader.com
Web: www.crgleader.com
Tests: 1013, 1319, 1396, 1491, 1506, 2016, 2223, 2331,
  2420, 2569, 2847

Corporate Mentoring Solutions® Inc.
Corporate Head Office
11316 Ravens Croft Place
N Saanichton, British Columbia V8L 5R4
Canada
Telephone: 877-955-0314
FAX: 250-652-6853
E-mail: wgray@mentoring-solutions.com
Web: www.mentoring-solutions.com
Tests: 1684

Council for Economic Education
122 East 42nd St.
Suite 2600
New York, NY 10168
Telephone: 800-338-1192
FAX: 212-730-1793
Web: www.CouncilforEconEd.org
Tests: 267, 2731, 2732, 2771

CPP, Inc.
1055 Joaquin Road, 2nd Floor
Mountain View, CA 94043
Telephone: 800-624-1765
FAX: 650-969-8608
E-mail: custserve@cpp.com
Web: www.cpp.com
Tests: 69, 401, 429, 436, 756, 1086, 1799, 1801, 1802,
  1909, 1954, 1955, 2087, 2477, 2573, 2575, 2576,
  2801, 2966

Creative Learning Press, Inc.
P.O. Box 320
Mansfield Center, CT 06250
Web: WWW.CREATIVELEARNINGPRESS.COM
Tests: 522, 759, 1327, 1514, 2349

The Creative Problem Solving Group, Inc.
P.O. Box 648
6 Grand View Trail
Orchard Park, NY 14127
Telephone: 716-667-1324
FAX: 716-667-6070
E-mail: sgiaway@cpsb.com
Web: www.cpsb.com
Tests: 2468

Creatrix
135 Black Oaks Lane
Wayzata, MN 55391
Telephone: 952-925-1757
E-mail: team@creatrix.com
Web: www.creatrix.com
Tests: 761

The Critical Thinking Co.
P.O. Box 1610
Seaside, CA 93955-1610
Telephone: 800-458-4849
FAX: 831-393-3277
E-mail: info@criticalthinking.com
Web: www.criticalthinking.com
Tests: 745, 1377

Crystal Springs Books
10 Sharon Road
P.O. Box 500
Peterborough, NH 03458-0500
Tests: 2267

CTB/McGraw-Hill
20 Ryan Ranch Road
Monterey, CA 93940-5703
Telephone: 831-393-0700
Web: www.ctb.com
Tests: 89, 250, 393, 398, 399, 770, 827, 1103, 1104,
  1105, 1356, 1468, 1469, 1470, 1471, 1807, 2097,
  2126, 2513, 2703, 2786, 2787, 2788

Curriculum Associates, LLC
153 Rangeway Road
P.O. Box 2001
North Billerica, MA 01862-0901
Telephone: 800-225-0248
FAX: 800-366-1158
E-mail: info@cainc.com
Web: www.curriculumassociates.com
Tests: 368, 369, 370, 371, 372, 373, 680, 681, 682, 683

Delaware County Reading Council
c/o Delaware County Intermediate Unit #25
200 Yale Avenue
Morton, PA 19070
Tests: 803

Denver Developmental Materials, Inc.
P.O. Box 371075
Denver, CO 80237-5075
Telephone: 800-419-4729
FAX: 303-355-5622
E-mail: sales@denverii.com
Web: www.denverii.com
Tests: 810, 811, 812, 813, 814, 1261

Department of Research Assessment and Training
1051 Riverside Drive, Unit 123
New York, NY 10032
Telephone: 212-543-5536
FAX: 212-543-5386
E-mail: je10@columbia.edu
Tests: 1001, 1145, 2181, 2183, 2207, 2358

Development Associates, Inc.
1000 Wilson Blvd., Suite 1000
Arlington, VA 22201-3901
Telephone: 703-276-0677
FAX: 703-276-0432
E-mail: devassoc@devassoc.com
Web: www.devassoc.com
Tests: 94

Developmental Therapy Institute, Inc.
P.O. Box 5153
Athens, GA 30604-5153
Web: www.uga.edu/dttp
Tests: 843

The Devine Group, Inc.
Corporate Headquarters
7755 Montgomery Road, Suite 180
Cincinnati, OH 45236
Web: www.wingnut.com/
Tests: 852

Diagnostic Counseling Services, Inc.
P.O. Box 6178
Kokomo, IN 46904-6178
Tests: 1774

Diagnostic Specialists, Inc.
1170 North 660 West
Orem, UT 84057
Telephone: 801-225-7698
FAX: 801-229-1944
E-mail: allanroe@earthlink.com
Tests: 129, 472, 679, 692, 2432, 2937

Dinosaurs, Trees, Religion and Galaxies
7333 N Ridge Blvd., Apt. 108
Chicago, IL 60645
Telephone: 773-764-0214
E-mail: dinosaurs_galaxies@yahoo.com
Web: jamestimothystruck.page4.me
Tests: 2187

Directional Insight International, Inc.
1111 McKinley Street
Ft. Worth. TX 76126
Telephone: 800-852-2001
FAX: 817-249-6266
E-mail: test@nsightsuccess.com
Web: www.nsightsuccess.com
Tests: 1852

Dr. Baker Partnership
10 Elgin Rd.
Bournemouth BH4 9NL
United Kingdom
Telephone: 011-44-1202-763836
FAX: 011-44-1202-761766
Tests: 2253

Rodney L. Doran, Ph.D., Professor of Science Education
State University of New York at Buffalo
Department of Learning and Instruction
593 Baldy Hall
Buffalo, NY 14260
Tests: 1672

Dragon Press
127 Sycamore Avenue
Mill Valley, CA 94941-2821
Tests: 488

Drake Beam Morin, Inc.
750 3rd Av., 28th FL
New York, NY 10017
E-mail: inquiries@dbm.com
Web: www.dbm.com
Tests: 1282

Dr. Maurice J. Eash, Director
Institute of Learning and Teaching
University of Massachusetts–Boston
Harbor Campus
Boston, MA 02125-3393
Tests: 1918

eCenter Research, Inc.
915 Lake Drive East, Unit 4
Jackson's Point
Ontario L0E 1L0
Canada
Tests: 904

Eckstein Bros., Inc.
5601 West Slauson Avenue, Suite 170
Culver City, CA 90230-6534
Tests: 947

Ed & Psych Associates
Address Unknown
Tests: 70

Edge Training Systems, Inc.
491 Southlake Blvd.
Richmond, VA 23236
Web: www.edgetrainingsystems.com
Tests: 1517

EdITS/Educational and Industrial Testing Service
P.O. Box 7234
San Diego, CA 92167
Web: www.edits.net
Tests: 424, 439, 440, 441, 442, 451, 705, 706, 707, 742,
    885, 1071, 1407, 1567, 1790, 1929, 2005, 2006, 2368,
    2557, 2603, 2785, 1048, 1047

Educational & Psychological Consultants, Inc.
1001 Cherry St. Ste 302
Columbia, MO 65201-7931
Telephone: 573-446-6232
E-mail: kuncej@missouri.edu
Tests: 2017

Educational Activities Software
301 Meadow Brook Estates Lane
Wentzville, MO 63385-4552
Tests: 180, 1312, 1512

Educational Assessment Service, Inc.
W6050 Apple Road
Watertown, WI 53098-3937
Telephone: 920-261-1118
FAX: 920-261-6622
E-mail: order@sylviarimm.com
Web: www.sylviarimm.com
Tests: 33, 34, 1184, 1189, 1190, 2106

Educational Publications
532 E. Blackridge
Tucson, AZ 85705
Tests: 1398

Educational Records Bureau
220 East 42nd Street, Suite 100
New York, NY 10017-5006
Telephone: 212-672-9800
FAX: 212-370-4096
E-mail: info@erbtest.org
Web: www.erbtest.org
Tests: 696, 1016, 1296

Educational Resources, Inc.
7500 W 160th St.
Stilwell, KS 66085
E-mail: testing@eriworld.com
Web: www.eriworld.com
Tests: 1231, 1247, 1855

Educational Testing Service
Publication Order Services
ETS Corporate Headquarters
Rosedale Road
Princeton, NJ 08541
Telephone: 609-921-9000
FAX: 609-734-5410
E-mail: etsinfo@ets.org
Web: www.ets.org
Tests: 127, 527, 528, 529, 530, 531, 532, 533, 534, 535,
    536, 537, 538, 539, 540, 541, 542, 543, 544, 545,
    546, 547, 548, 549, 550, 551, 552, 553, 554, 555,
    556, 557, 558, 559, 560, 626 651, 905, 1099, 1159,
    1160, 1161, 1162, 1163, 1164, 1165, 1166, 1167,
    1168, 1169, 1449, 1564, 1806, 2094, 2098, 2099,
    2150, 2370, 2391, 2519, 2596, 2769

Educators Publishing Service, Inc.
P.O. Box 9031
Cambridge, MA 02139-9031
Telephone: 800-225-5750
FAX: 888-440-2665
E-mail: feedback.eps@schoolspecialty.com
Web: www.eps.schoolspecialty.com
Tests: 165, 324, 1970, 1972, 1973, 1974, 2274, 2480, 2645

Carl N. Edwards, Ph.D.
P.O. Box 279
Dover, MA 02030
Telephone: 774-200-0201
FAX: 508-785-2526
E-mail: cedwards@socialaw.com
Tests: 2469

Dr. Paul Ekman
Paul Ekman Group, LLC
300 Montgomery Street #833
San Francisco, CA 94104-1918
FAX: 415-476-7629
Tests: 1050

Elbern Publications
P.O. Box 9497
Columbus, OH 43209
Telephone: 614-231-1950
FAX: 614-237-2637
E-mail: ebecker@wowway.com
Tests: 292, 2238

Dr. John Eliot
2705 Silverdale Dr.
Silver Spring, MD 20906
Tests: 970

Patricia B. Elmore, Ph.D.
College of Education and Human Services, Dean's Office
Mail Code 4624
Southern Illinois University–Carbondale
Carbondale, IL 62901
Telephone: 618-453-2415
FAX: 618-453-1646
E-mail: pbelmore@siu.edu
Web: www.siu.edu/
Tests: 308, 467, 1481

Ellsworth & Vandermeer Press, LLC
1013 Austin Court
Nolensville, TN 37135
Tests: 1951

Endeavor Information Systems, Inc.
1317 Livingston Street
Evanston, IL 60201
Tests: 1000

Enhanced Performance Systems, Inc.
1010 University Avenue, Suite 265
San Diego, CA 92103
Telephone: 619-497-0156
FAX: 619-497-0820
E-mail: rdaws@epstais.com
Web: www.epstais.com
Tests: 231

Robert H. Ennis, Ph.D.
3904 Trentwood Place
Sarasota, FL 34243
Telephone: 941-358-0906
E-mail: rhennis@illinois.edu
Web: faculty.ed.uiuc.edu/rhennis
Tests: 1009

Enrichment Press
5441 SW Macadam Avenue, #206
Portland, OR 97239
Telephone: 503-222-4046
FAX: 503-222-9989
Tests: 2076, 2887

Enterprise Management Ltd.
4531 Roanoak Way
Palm Harbor, FL 34685
Telephone: 727-934-9810
E-mail: mlippitt@enterprisemgt.com
Web: www.enterprisemgt.com
Tests: 1493

Exceptional Education
P.O. Box 15308
Seattle, WA 98155
Telephone: 206-262-9538
FAX: 206-262-9538
E-mail: jeffs_ttools@hotmail.com
Tests: 2123, 2875

Sheila M. Eyberg, Ph.D.
Department of Clinical & Health Psychology
Box100165
University of Florida
Gainesville, FL 32610
E-mail: seyberg@phhp.ufl.edu
Web: www.pcit.org
Tests: 909, 2798

Faculty of Education
Memorial University of Newfoundland
St. John's, Newfoundland A1B 3X8
Canada
Tests: 2783

Dr. Charles G. Fast, Publisher
2601 Woodwind Ct.
Kirksville, MO 63501-5705
Tests: 1066

Grace Fivars
Psychometric Techniques Associates
5701 Centre Avenue, #511
Pittsburgh, PA 15206-3707
Tests: 580, 2665

Foreworks
Box 33493
Portland, OR 97292
Telephone: 503-653-2614
E-mail: eric@foreworks.com
Web: www.foreworks.com
Tests: 2720, 2508

Myles I. Friedman
College of Education
University of South Carolina
Columbia, SC 29208
Tests: 2095

Functional Resources
3905 Huntington Drive
Amarillo, TX 79019-4047
Telephone: 806-353-1114
FAX: 806-353-1114
E-mail: webmaster@winfssi.com
Web: www.winfssi.com
Tests: 1119

G. Neil
720 International Parkway
P.O. Box 450939
Sunrise, FL 33345-0939
Telephone: 800-999-9111
FAX: 954-846-0777
E-mail: hrassessments@gneil.com
Web: www.gneil.com
Tests: 170, 565, 2325, 2434

Gallaudet University Press
800 Florida Avenue, NE
Washington, DC 20002-3695
Telephone: 800-621-2736
FAX: 800-621-8476
Web: gupress.gallaudet.edu
Tests: 2995

Gander Publishing
P.O. Box 780
Avila Beach, CA 93424
Tests: 2652

GB Software LLC
4607 Perham Road
Corona del Mar, CA 92625
Web: www.gb-software.com
Tests: 2179

Ruth M. Geiman, Ph.D.
8184 Crete Ln.
Blacklick, OH 43004
Telephone: 937-901-1809
E-mail: rgeiman@wideopenwest.com
Tests: 1132

General Educational Development Testing
Service of the American Council on Education
One Dupont Circle, NW, Suite 250
Washington, DC 20036-1163
Telephone: 202-939-9490
E-mail: ged@ace.nche.edu
Web: www.gedtest.org
Tests: 2789

Gerontology Center
217 Washington Avenue
Bellefonte, PA 16801
Web: gerontology.ssri.psu.edu/
Tests: 1674

The Gesell Institute
310 Prospect Street, 2nd Floor
New Haven, CT 06511
Telephone: 203-777-3481
FAX: 203-776-5001
E-mail: gesell.inst@att.net
Web: www.gesellinstitute.org
Tests: 1134, 1135

GIA Publications, Inc.
7404 South Mason Avenue
Chicago, IL 60638
Telephone: 708-496-3800
FAX: 708-496-3828
E-mail: custserv@giamusic.com
Web: www.giamusic.com
Tests: 98, 146, 1218, 1321, 1330, 1365, 1752, 1797, 1798, 2125

Lucia A. Gilbert
Office of the Executive Vice President & Provost
Main 201 (G1000)
University of Texas at Austin
Austin, TX 78712
Telephone: 512-232-3310
FAX: 512-471-0577
E-mail: lucia@mail.utexas.edu
Web: www.utexas.edu/student/connexus/lucia/instruments.html
Tests: 1985

GL Assessment
The Chiswick Centre
414 Chiswick High Road
London W4 5TF
England
Tests: 134, 135, 206, 245, 316, 374, 375, 376, 385, 468, 913, 943, 1059, 1060, 1197, 1200, 1265, 1317, 1409, 1430, 1475, 1540, 1626, 1654, 1687, 1700, 1813, 1848, 1853, 1854, 1873, 1874, 2047, 2061, 2108, 2156, 2244, 2245, 2361, 2381, 2502, 2518, 2616, 2653, 2853, 2962

Golden Educational Center
857 Lake Blvd.
Redding, CA 96003
Telephone: 800-800-1791
FAX: 530-244-5939
E-mail: info@goldened.com
Web: www.goldened.com
Tests: 1326

Gordon Systems, Inc.
P.O. Box 746
DeWitt, NY 13214
Telephone: 315-446-4849 (#2) or 1-800-550-2343
FAX: 315-446-2012
E-mail: info@gsi-add.com
Tests: 1150

Robert S. Goyer
Department of Communication
Arizona State University
Tempe, AZ 85287
Tests: 1153

Graham-Field Health Products, Inc.
2935 Northeast Parkway
Atlanta, GA 30360
Telephone: 800-347-5678
FAX: 800-726-0601
E-mail: cs@grahamfield.com
Web: www.grahamfield.com
Tests: 2708

Green's Publishing Inc.
Suite 201, 17010-103 Ave.
Edmonton, Alberta T5S 1K7
Canada
Telephone: 780-484-5550
FAX: 780-484-5631
E-mail: drpgreen@telus.net
Web: www.wordmemorytest.com
Tests: 1175, 1176, 1177, 1178

Gregorc Associates, Inc.
15 Doubleday Road
P.O. Box 351
Columbia, CT 06237
Telephone: 860-228-0093
FAX: 860-228-0093
Web: www.gregorc.com
Tests: 1180

GRM Educational Consultancy
P.O. Box 154
Beecroft, New South Wales 2119
Australia
Tests: 2382

Guglielmino & Associates
7339 Reserve Creek Drive
Port St. Lucie, FL 34986
Telephone: 772-429-2425
FAX: 772-429-2423
E-mail: guglielmino@rocketmail.com
Web: www.guglielmino734.com
Tests: 2404

Guilford Publications, Inc.
72 Spring Street
New York, NY 10012
Telephone: 212-431-9800
FAX: 212-966-6708
E-mail: estefeni.estremera@guilford.com
Web: www.guilford.com
Tests: 66, 256, 257, 258

H&H Publishing Company, Inc.
1231 Kapp Drive
Clearwater, FL 33765-2116
Web: www.hhpublishing.com
Tests: 1499, 1500, 1976, 2552, 2692, 2985

Hal Leonard Publishing Corporation
7777 West Bluemound Road
P.O. Box 13819
Milwaukee, WI 53213
Tests: 1065, 2892

Susan Harter, Ph.D.
University of Denver
Department of Psychology
2155 South Race Street
Denver, CO 80208-0204
Tests: 2055, 2413

Joseph Hartman, Ph.D.
P.O. Box 37485
Raleigh, NC 27627-7485
Telephone: 904-333-2812
E-mail: jhartman611@nc.rr.com
Tests: 2197

Harvard University Press
79 Garden Street
Cambridge, MA 02138
Web: www.hup.harvard.edu
Tests: 2796

Dr. Robert J. Harvey
1030 S. Jefferson Forest Lane
Blacksburg, VA 24060-8984
Tests: 663

Hawthorne Educational Services, Inc.
800 Gray Oak Drive
Columbia, MO 65201
Telephone: 800-542-1673
FAX: 800-442-9509
E-mail: adina_laird@hes-inc.com
Web: www.hawthorne-ed.com/
Tests: 58, 87, 226, 227, 299, 300, 301, 921, 922, 972, 978, 1139, 1503, 2104, 2113, 2520, 2821

Hay Group
Hay Resources Direct
116 Huntington Avenue
Boston, MA 02116-5712
Telephone: 800-729-8074
FAX: 617-927-5008
Web: www.haygroup.com
Tests: 63, 590, 974, 1310, 1483, 1505, 1508, 1587, 1599, 1602, 1910, 2019, 2318

Health and Disability Research Institute
Boston University
53 Bay State Road
Boston, MA 02215
Telephone: 617-353-1295
FAX: 612-358-1355
E-mail: smhaley@bu.edu
Web: www.sph.bu.edu/HDRI
Tests: 1971

Health Prisms, Inc.
210 Walhalla Ct.
Atlanta, GA 30350-1189
Tests: 737

Mary J. Heppner, Ph.D.
Career Center
305 Noyes Hall
University of Missouri
Columbia, MO 65211
Tests: 446

P. Paul Heppner
Address Unknown
Tests: 2134

Herrmann International
794 Buffalo Creek Road
Lake Lure, NC28746
Telephone: 828-625-9153
FAX: 828-625-1402
E-mail: dorothy@hbdi.com
Web: www.hbdi.com
Tests: 1240

Hester Evaluation Systems, Inc.
2410 SW Granthurst Avenue
Topeka, KS 66611-1274
Telephone: 800-832-3825
FAX: 785-357-4041
E-mail: hester@inlandnet.net
Web: www.hestertesting.com
Tests: 1753

Hewitt Research Foundation
P.O. Box 9
2103 Main Street
Washougal, WA 98671-0009
Telephone: 800-890-4097
FAX: 360-835-8697
E-mail: info@hewitthomeschooling.com
Web: www.hewitthomeschooling.com
Tests: 2030

Higher Education Research Institute
UCLA Graduate School of Education
405 Hilgard Avenue
3005 Moore Hall
Los Angeles, CA 90024-1521
Tests: 732

HighScope Educational Research Foundation
600 North River Street
Ypsilanti, MI 48198-2898
Telephone: 734-485-2000
FAX: 734-485-0704
E-mail: info@highscope.org
Web: www.highscope.org
Tests: 932, 968, 2110, 2117, 3001

Hodder & Stoughton Educational
Hodder Headline PLC
338 Euston Road
London NW1 3BH
England
Telephone: 0207 873 6000
FAX: 0207 873 6299
E-mail: chas.knight@hodder.co.uk
Web: www.hoddertests.co.uk
Tests: 1628, 270, 271, 568, 587, 931, 948, 949, 1137, 1154, 1156, 1191, 1193, 1196, 1843, 1933, 1960, 2062, 2240, 2334, 2393, 2458, 2516, 2666, 2960, 1047, 1048

Hogan Assessment Systems, Inc.
2622 East 21st Street
Tulsa, OK 74114
Web: www.hoganassessments.com
Tests: 1254, 1255, 1765

Hogrefe Psykologisk Forlag A/S [Denmark]
Kongevejen 155
2830 Virum
Copenhagen
Denmark
Telephone: +45 3538 1655
FAX: +45 3538 1665
E-mail: dk-psych@dpf.dk
Web: www.dpf.dk
Tests: 255

Hogrefe Publishing
875 Massachusetts Avenue
7th Floor
Cambridge, MA 02139
Telephone: 866-823-4726
FAX: 617-354-6875
E-mail: customerservice@hogrefe-publishing.com
Web: www.hogrefe.com
Tests: 35, 772, 785, 791, 1063, 1368, 1845, 1930, 2299, 2355

Home Inventory LLC
c/o Lorraine Coulson
2627 Winsor Drive
Eau Claire, WI 54703-1778
Telephone: 715-835-4393
Tests: 1260

Houghton Mifflin Company
College Division, Education
222 Berkeley Street
Boston, MA 02116-3764
Telephone: 617-351-5000
FAX: 617-351-1134
Web: www.hmhco.com
Tests: 383

Howdah Press
c/o Priscilla S. Hill, Ph.D.
3530 Damien #117
LaVerne, CA 91750
Tests: 1248

HRD Press, Inc.
22 Amherst Road
Amherst, MA 01002–9709
Telephone: 800-822-2801
FAX: 413-253-3490
E-mail: info@hrdpress.com
Web: www.hrdpress.com
Tests: 464, 673, 714, 828, 1097, 1311, 1411, 1480, 1510, 1572, 1575, 1635, 1669, 1907, 1908, 1990, 1994, 2021, 2067, 2128, 2679, 2770

Edwina E. Hubert, Ph.D.
313 Wellesley Dr., SE
Albuquerque, NM 87106-1421
Tests: 1519

Nancy Hughes, Ph.D.
University of Kansas
Psychological Clinic
315 Fraser Hall
Lawrence, KS 66045
Tests: 1273

Human Sciences Research Council
Distributed by Mindmuzik Media
P. O. Box 2904 Brooklyn Square
Pretoria, Gauteng 0075
South Africa
Telephone: +27 (0)12-346-6008
FAX: +27 90) 346 4773
E-mail: frikkie@mindmuzik.com
Web: www.mindmuzik.com
Tests: 177, 345, 1077, 1241, 1242, 1303, 1337, 1405, 1410, 1809, 1839, 1931, 2051, 2153, 2304, 2374, 2422, 2423, 2443, 2816

Human Services Resource Group
College of Business Administration
University of Nebraska–Omaha
Omaha, NE 68182-0048
Tests: 2641

Human Synergistics International
39819 Plymouth Road, C-8020
Plymouth, MI 48170-8020
Telephone: 800-622-7584
FAX: 734-459-5557
E-mail: info@humansynergistics.com
Web: www.humansynergistics.com
Tests: 1199, 1486, 1534, 1554, 1576, 1911, 1913, 1996, 2571, 2627

Humanics Test Corporation
P.O. Box 1608
Lake Worth, FL 33460
Telephone: 800-874-8844
FAX: 888-874-8844
Tests: 474, 485, 1277, 1278, 1550

I-MED Instructional Materials & Equipment Distributors
1520 Cotner Avenue
Los Angeles, CA 90025
Tests: 915

The IDEA Center
211 South Seth Child Road
Manhattan, KS 66502-3089
Telephone: 800-255-2757
FAX: 785-320-2400
E-mail: info@theideacenter.org
Web: www.theideacenter.org
Tests: 1283, 1284, 1287

IDS Publishing Corporation
P.O. Box 389
Worthington, OH 43085
Telephone: 614-885-2323
FAX: 614-885-2323
Web: www.idspublishing.com
Tests: 2256

Illinois Critical Thinking Project; Department of Educational Policy Studies
University of Illinois at Urbana-Champaign
360 Education Bldg.
1310 South Sixth Street
Champaign, IL 61820
Tests: 743, 744

Indiana Resource Center for Autism
Indiana Institute on Disability and Community
2853 East Tenth Street
Bloomington, IN 47408-2696
Tests: 2923

Indiana University Center for Postsecondary Research
1900 East Tenth Street
Eigenmann Hall, Suite 419
Bloomington, IN 47406-7512
Telephone: 812-856-5824
FAX: 812-856-5150
E-mail: nsse@indiana.edu
Web: www.iub.edu/~cseq or www.iub.edu/~nsse
Tests: 652, 653, 1812

Industrial Psychology International, Ltd.
4106 Fieldstone Road
P.O. Box 6479
Champaign, IL 61826-6479
Telephone: 800-747-1119
FAX: 217-398-5798
E-mail: ipi@metritech.com
Web: www.metritech.com
Tests: 755, 1366, 1851, 2987, 2988

Infant Motor Performance Scales, LLC
1301 W. Madison St., #526
Chicago, IL 60607
Telephone: 312-733-9604
FAX: 312-733-0565
E-mail: skc@thetimp.com
Web: www.thetimp.com
Tests: 1220, 2739

Innodyne, Inc.
734 Orchard Hill Drive
Pittsburgh, PA 15238
Telephone: 412-963-6701
FAX: 412-963-6751
Web: www.innodyneinc.com
Tests: 2162

INQ Educational Materials, Inc.
6933 Armour Drive
Oakland, CA 94611-1317
Telephone: 888-339-2323
FAX: 510-339-6729
E-mail: Paul@YourThinkingProfile.com
Web: www.YourThinkingProfile.com
Tests: 1315, 1604, 1316

Inscape Publishing
6465 Wayzata Blvd., Suite 800
Minneapolis, MN 55426
Tests: 887, 888, 2009

Insight Assessment–The California Academic Press LLC
217 La Cruz Avenue
Millbrae, CA 94030
Telephone: 650-697-5628
FAX: 650-692-0141
E-mail: info@insightassessment.com
Web: www.insightassessment.com
Tests: 388, 396, 397, 400, 1233, 2142, 2212, 2736

Insight Institute, Inc.
7205 NW Waukomis Drive
Kansas City, MO 64151
Telephone: 800-861-4769
FAX: 816-587-7198
E-mail: phandley@insightinstitute.com
Web: www.insightinstitute.com
Tests: 1318

Institute for Behavioral Research in Creativity
699 E. South Temple, Ste. 330
Salt Lake City, UT 84102-1491
Telephone: 801-487-3209
FAX: 801-262-1739
Web: www.ibric.net
Tests: 952, 2601, 340

The Institute for Matching Person & Technology, Inc.
486 Lake Road
Webster, NY 14580
Telephone: 585-671-3461
FAX: 585-671-3461
E-mail: impt97@aol.com
Web: members.aol.com/IMPT97/MPT.html
Tests: 2435, 1620, 1622

Institute for Personality and Ability Testing, Inc. (IPAT)
P.O. Box 1188
Champaign, IL 61824-1188
Telephone: 217-352-4739
FAX: 217-352-9674
E-mail: custserv@ipat.com
Web: www.ipat.com
Tests: 502, 938, 977, 1035, 1244, 1477, 2034, 2178, 2411, 2471, 2472, 2473, 2474

Institute for Personality and Ability Testing, Inc. (IPAT)
  - Public Safety & Security Division
1801 Woodfield Dr.
Savoy, IL 61874
E-mail: custserv@ipat.com
Tests: 1249, 1250, 1251, 1252, 1357, 1358

International Public Management Association for Human
  Resources (IPMA-HR)
1617 Duke Street
Alexandria, VA 22314
Telephone: 800-381-8378
FAX: 703-684-0948
E-mail: assessment@ipma-hr.org
Web: testing.ipma-hr.org
Tests: 2437

Iowa State University Research Foundation, Inc.
Child Development Department
101 Child Development Building
Research Laboratories
Ames, IA 50011
Tests: 2535, 1361, 1362

Irvington Publishers, Inc.
R. R. 1, Box 85-1
Lower Mill Road
North Stratford, NH 03590
Tests: 2147

Israel Science Teaching Center
Hebrew University
Jerusalem 91904
Israel
Tests: 662

James Stanfield Co., Inc.
P.O. Box 41058
Santa Barbara, CA 93140
Telephone: 800-421-6534
FAX: 805-897-1187
E-mail: orderdesk@stanfield.com
Web: www.stanfield.com
Tests: 668, 2343, 2742, 2822

Janelle Publications, Inc.
P.O. Box 811
1189 Twombly Road
DeKalb, IL 60115
Telephone: 800-888-8834
Web: janellepublications.com
Tests: 2589, 2590, 2591

JIST Publishing, Inc.
7321 Shadeland Sta., Ste. 200
Indianapolis, IN 46256-3936
Telephone: 800-648-5478
FAX: 800-547-8329
E-mail: info@jist.com
Web: www.jist.com
Tests: 259, 423, 434, 655, 656, 894, 1012, 1202, 1299,
  1392, 1393, 1397, 1521, 1856, 1857, 2058, 2824,
  2876, 2972, 2977, 3002

Jossey-Bass, A Wiley Company
989 Market Street
San Francisco, CA 94103
Web: www.wiley.com
Tests: 197, 320, 425, 591, 667, 793, 853, 893, 991, 1008,
  1022, 1340, 1384, 1401, 1446, 1488, 1489, 1496,
  1504, 1515, 1539, 1543, 1763, 1906, 1980, 1981,
  1982, 2133, 2503, 2680, 2682, 2838, 2893

Jerome Kagan
Harvard University
33 Kirkland Street
1510 William James Hall
Cambridge, MA 02138
Tests: 1621

Kaplan DeVries Inc.
1903 G Ashwood Ct.
Greensboro, NC 27455
Telephone: 336-288-8200
FAX: 336-282-6878
E-mail: LVI@kaplandevries.com
Web: www.versatileleader.com
Tests: 1494

Kaplan Early Learning Company
1310 Lewisville-Clemmons Road
P.O. Box 67
Lewisville, NC 27023-0609
Tests: 454, 847, 848, 849, 851, 1498

Karl Albrecht International
3728 Old Cobble Road
San Diego, CA 92111-4050
Web: www.karlalbrecht.com
Tests: 1495, 1730

KBA, LLC
P.O. Box 3673
Carbondale, IL 62902
Tests: 330

Keeler Instruments Inc.
456 Parkway
Broomall, PA 19008
Telephone: 610-353-4350
FAX: 610-353-7814
Web: www.keelerusa.com
Tests: 518, 2275

Keirsey.com
Professional Products Division
P.O. Box 6279
San Mateo, CA 94403
Telephone: 650-276-0770
FAX: 650-312-8342
Web: www.keirsey.com
Tests: 1429

The Ken Blanchard Companies
125 State Place
Escondido, CA 92029
Web: www.kenblanchard.com/estore
Tests: 1479

Kendall/Hunt Publishing Company
4050 Westmark Drive
P.O. Box 1840
Dubuque, IA 52004-1840
Telephone: 800-228-0810
FAX: 800-772-9165
E-mail: orders@kendallhunt.com
Web: www.kendallhunt.com
Tests: 273, 2515

KIDS, Inc.
1156 Point Vista Road
Hickory Creek, TX 76065
Web: www.kidsinc.com
Tests: 1440, 1441

Kilmann Diagnostics
One Suprema Drive
Newport Coast, CA 92657
Tests: 1438, 1439

Dr. Donald L. Kirkpatrick
842 Kirkland Court
Pewaukee, WI 53072
Telephone: 262-695-5851
E-mail: dleekirk1@aol.com
Tests: 1447, 1578, 1579, 1580, 1581, 1582, 2623, 2624

Marjorie H. Klein, Ph.D.
Department of Psychiatry
6001 Research Park Blvd.
Madison, WI 53717
Telephone: 608-263-6066
FAX: 608-265-4008
E-mail: mhklein@falstaff.wisc.edu
Tests: 1039

Kolbe Corp
3421 N. 44th Street
Phoenix, AZ 85018
Telephone: 602-840-9770
FAX: 602-952-2706
E-mail: info@kolbe.com
Web: www.kolbe.com
Tests: 1455

David S. Krantz
Department of Medical and Clinical Psychology
University of the Health Sciences
4301 Jones Bridge Road
Bethesda, MD 20814-4799
E-mail: krantz@bob.usuhs.mil
Tests: 1457

Krieger Publishing Company
1725 Krieger Dr.
Malabar, FL 32950
Web: www.krieger-publishing.com
Tests: 85

Kuder, Inc.
302 Visions Parkway
Adel, IA 50003-1632
Telephone: 800-314-8972
FAX: 515-993-5422
E-mail: info@kuder.com
Web: www.kuder.com
Tests: 1459, 1460, 1461, 1462, 2620

Ramanath Kundu
Department of Psychology
University of Calcutta
92, Acharya Prafulla Chandra Road
Calcutta 700009
India
Tests: 1464, 1465

Lafayette Instrument
P.O. Box 5729
3700 Sagamore Parkway North
Lafayette, IN 47904-5729
Telephone: 765-423-1505
FAX: 765-423-4111
E-mail: info@lafayetteinstrument.com
Web: www.lafayetteinstrument.com
Tests: 1183, 1740, 2296

Laurent Clerc National Deaf Education Center
KDES Suite 3600
Gallaudet University
800 Florida Avenue, NE
Washington, DC 20002-3695
Telephone: 202-651-5340
FAX: 202-651-5708
Web: clerccenter.gallaudet.edu
Tests: 1644

Law School Admission Council, Inc.
Box 40
Newtown, PA 18940-0040
Web: www.lsac.org
Tests: 1478

Leadership Studies, Inc.
230 West Third Avenue
Escondido, CA 92025
Web: www.situational.com
Tests: 2467

Learning by Design
P.O. Box 5448
Evanston, IL 60201-5448
Tests: 2525

Learning Tools LLC
PO Box 1066
Orchard Park, NY 14127-8066
Telephone: 413-588-8199
FAX: 440-425-9511
E-mail: info@busstoryus.com
Web: www.busstoryus.com
Tests: 2258

Lienhard School of Nursing
Pace University
Pleasantville/Briarcliff Campus
Bedford Road
Pleasantville, NY 10570
Tests: 2563

Life Advance, Inc.
81 Front Street
Nyack, NY 10960
Telephone: 845-358-2539
E-mail: craig.ellison@nyack.edu
Tests: 2527

Life Innovations, Inc.
P.O. Box 190
Minneapolis, MN 55440-0190
Telephone: 651-635-0511
FAX: 651-636-1668
E-mail: dolson@prepare-enrich.com
Tests: 581, 1049, 1062, 2102

Life Science Associates
One Fenimore Road
Bayport, NY 11705-2115
Telephone: 631-472-2111
FAX: 631-472-8146
E-mail: lifesciassoc@pipeline.com
Web: lifesciassoc.home.pipeline.com
Tests: 2231

LIMRA International
300 Day Hill Rd
Windsor, CT 06095-1783
Tests: 200, 444

LinguiSystems, Inc.
3100 4th Avenue
East Moline, IL 61244-9700
Telephone: 800-776-4332
E-mail: testing@linguisystems.com
Web: www.linguisystems.com
Tests: 1472, 2763, 2961

Lore International Institute
P.O. Box 1287
1130 Main Avenue
Durango, CO 81301
Telephone: 970-385-4955
FAX: 970-385-7804
E-mail: assessmentcenter@lorenet.com
Web: www.lorenet.com
Tests: 589, 1552, 1865, 2320, 2636

Pamela S. Ludolph, Ph.D.
311 Awixa Road.
Ann Arbor, MI 48104-1811
Tests: 860

James B. Maas
The Center for Improvement of Undergraduate Education
115 Rand Hall
Cornell University
Ithaca, NY 14850
Tests: 747

MAC Testing & Consulting, LLC
788 Shrewsbury Avenue
Building 2, Suite 201
Tinton Falls, NJ 07724
Telephone: 732-741-6112
FAX: 732-936-0162
E-mail: DrMac@mactesting.com
Web: www.mactesting.com
Tests: 1557

Charlotte Mackley
948 South 2350 E
Springville, UT 84663
Tests: 144, 1546, 2451, 724

Maddak Inc.
6 Industrial Road
Pequannock, NJ 07440-1993
Web: www.maddak.com
Tests: 282, 1548, 2424, 2810

Madison Geriatric Research, Education, and Clinical
    Center
VA Medical Center
2500 Overlook Terrace
Madison, WI 53705
Tests: 213

Management & Personnel Systems, Inc.
157 Twin Peaks Dr.
Walnut Creek, CA 94595-1728
Telephone: 800-576-7455
FAX: 925-977-8200
E-mail: mpscorp@value.net
Web: www.mps-corp.com
Tests: 781, 1130, 2626, 2983

Management Research Group
14 York Street, #301
Portland, ME 04101-4556
Telephone: 207-775-2173
FAX: 207-775-6796
E-mail: info@mrg.com
Web: www.mrg.com
Tests: 1298, 1995, 171, 1485, 2323

Management Research Institute, Inc.
11304 Spur Wheel Lane
Potomac, MD 20854
Tests: 1096

Marchman Psychology Associates
PO Box 1268
Iowa City, IA 52244-1268
Tests: 1786

Massachusetts School of Professional Psychology
T.E.D. Test
221 Rivermoor Street
Boston, MA 02132
Telephone: 617-327-6777
FAX: 617-327-4447
E-mail: ce@mspp.edu
Tests: 2667

MAT
Boston University
School of Music
855 Commonwealth Avenue
Boston, MA 02215
Tests: 1795

Mathematial Association of America; American Math-
    ematics Competitions
Steven R. Dunbar, Director
University of Nebraska–Lincoln
1740 Vine Street
Lincoln, NE 68588-0658
Telephone: 800-527-3690; 402-472-2257
FAX: 402-472-6087
E-mail: amcinfo@unl.edu
Web: www.unl.edu/amc
Tests: 150, 152, 153, 154, 1625

MAVEC Specialists Foundation, Inc.
13 Miller St., San Francisco Del Monte
Quezon City 1105
Philippines
Tests: 1078

McCann Associates
North American Business Office
370 Scotch Road, Suite 100
Ewing, NJ 08628-1301
Telephone: 866-933-0508
FAX: 267-746-1440
Web: www.mccanntesting.com
Tests: 765, 823, 985, 986, 987, 1080, 1864, 2069

McCarron-Dial Systems, Inc.
P.O. Box 35285
Dallas, TX 75235-0285
Telephone: 214-634-2863
FAX: 214-634-9970
E-mail: mds@mccarrondial.com
Web: mccarrondial.com
Tests: 37, 61, 209, 973, 1637, 1643, 1867, 1986, 2634

McClain
10 Blue Grouse Ridge Road
Littleton, CO 80127-5704
Tests: 2993

McGraw-Hill Higher Education
2 Penn Plaza, 20th Floor
New York, NY 10121
Tests: 526

Measurement for Human Resources
83 Rouge Au Avenue
Winnipeg, Manitoba R2C 3X5
Canada
Tests: 1871

Albert Mehrabian, Ph.D.
1130 Alta Mesa Road
Monterey, CA 93940
Telephone: 888-363-1732
E-mail: am@kaaj.com
Web: www.kaaj.com/psych/scales
Tests: 188, 251, 477, 1645, 1646, 1648, 1656, 1657, 1658, 2213, 2819

Mental Health, Law, and Policy Institute
Simon Fraser University
8888 University Drive
Burnaby, British Columbia V5A 1S6
Canada
Telephone: 604-291-4554
FAX: 604-268-6695
E-mail: roesch@sfu.ca
Web: www.sfu.ca/~mhlpi/
Tests: 1225

Meta Development LLC
4313 Garnet Street
Regina, Saskatchewan S4S 6J8
Canada
Tests: 1708, 1709, 1710, 1713, 1714, 1715, 1716, 1717, 1718, 1719, 1720

Meta-Visions
5076 Queen Victoria Lane
Kalamazoo, MI 49009-7799
Telephone: 616-353-7111
FAX: 616-353-9577
E-mail: JWalkerMI@aol.com
Tests: 1686

MetriTech, Inc.
4106 Fieldstone Road
Champaign, IL 61822
Telephone: 800-747-4868
FAX: 217-398-5798
E-mail: mtinfo@metritech.com
Web: www.metritech.com
Tests: 65, 1473, 1905, 2593

The Mews Press
Box 2052
Amagansett, NY 11930
FAX: 212-475-2428
Tests: 2261, 2648, 2688

Norman Milchus
468 Essex Drive
Rochester Hills, MI 48307-3504
Tests: 1024, 2214, 2402

MILCOM Systems
A Division of Hollister, Inc.
2000 Hollister Drive
Libertyville, IL 60048
Tests: 1703

Miller & Tyler Limited
Psychological Assessment and Counselling
96 Greenway
London N20 8EJ
England
Telephone: 44-020-8445-7463
FAX: 44-020-8445-0143
Tests: 2305, 2303

Mind Garden, Inc.
855 Oak Grove Ave., Suite 215
Menlo Park, CA 94025
Telephone: 650-322-6300
FAX: 650-322-6398
E-mail: info@mindgarden.com
Web: www.mindgarden.com
Tests: 9, 208, 215, 278, 323, 394, 402, 466, 525, 583, 672, 733, 736, 749, 750, 829, 911, 1010, 1058, 1092, 1107, 1187, 1188, 1222, 1226, 1618, 1623, 1629, 1679, 1683, 1704, 1782, 1783, 1784, 1829, 1887, 1912, 2195, 2376, 2499, 2501, 2555, 2556, 2705, 2842, 2889, 2897, 2916, 2917, 2967

Ministry Inventories
ATTN: Richard A. Hunt, Ph.D.
Fuller Graduate School of Psychology
180 N. Oakland Avenue
Pasadena, CA 91101
Tests: 1352, 1745, 2797

MKM
401 3rd Street, Suite 1
Rapid City, SD 57701
Tests: 1749, 1750, 1751

Monaco & Associates Incorporated
4125 Gage Center Drive, Suite 204
Topeka, KS 66604
Telephone: 785-272-5501
FAX: 785-272-5152
E-mail: greg@monacoassociates.com
Web: www.monacoassociates.com
Tests: 1900, 2217, 2514

The Morrisby Organisation
Focus 31 North
Cleveland Road
Hemel Hempstead, Hertfordshire HP2 7EY
England
Telephone: 01442 215521
FAX: 01442 240531
E-mail: info@morrisby.com
Web: www.morrisby.com
Tests: 754, 1079, 1313, 1607, 1759, 1977

Moving Boundaries, Inc.
1375 SW Blaine Court
Gresham, OR 97080
Tests: 2463

Multi-Health Systems, Inc.
P.O. Box 950
North Tonawanda, NY 14120-0950
Telephone: 800-456-3003
FAX: 888-540-4484
E-mail: customerservice@mhs.com
Web: www.mhs.com
Tests: 718, 719, 1056, 1291, 2398, 163, 164, 166, 244,
    325, 456, 459, 494, 501, 521, 582, 592, 704, 716,
    717, 720, 721, 722, 723, 735, 740, 790, 861, 908,
    980, 981, 982, 983, 1075, 1214, 1215, 1216, 1217,
    1228, 1256, 1331, 1378, 1379, 1523, 1524, 1525,
    1526, 1530, 1633, 1634, 1677, 1776, 1779, 1962,
    2029, 2081, 2145, 2146, 2188, 2209, 2254, 2255,
    2489, 2494, 2495, 2497, 2530, 2654, 2752, 2814,
    2868, 2999, 2380

Multiple Intelligences Research and Consulting, Inc.
1316 South Lincoln Street
Kent, OH 44240
Telephone: 330-677-8534
E-mail: sbranton@kent.edu
Web: www.miresearch.org
Tests: 1699

Munroe-Meyer Institute for Genetics & Rehabilitation
University of Nebraska Medical Center
985450 Nebraska Medical Center
Omaha, NE 68198-5450
Telephone: 402-559-7467
FAX: 402-559-5737
Web: www.unmc.edu/mmi
Tests: 1702

MySkillsProfile.com Limited
23 Dunkeld Road
Ecclesall, Sheffield S11 9HN
England
FAX: 44-114-238-5559
Web: MySkillsProfile.com
Tests: 1570, 2566, 2528

National Association of Secondary School Principals
1904 Association Drive
Reston, VA 20191-1537
Telephone: 703-860-0200
Web: www.principals.org/
Tests: 684, 685, 1509, 2392

The National Center on Employment & Disability
P.O. Box 1358
Hot Springs, AR 71902
Tests: 988, 1394, 2968, 2973, 2975, 2984

National Clearinghouse for Rehabilitation Training
    Materials
6524 Old Main Hill
Utah State University
Logan, UT 84322-6524
Web: www.ncrtm.org
Tests: 1891

National Communication Association
1765 N Street, NW
Washington, DC 20036
Web: www.natcom.org
Tests: 195, 674, 730

National Council on Crime and Delinquency
NCCD Headquarters
1970 Broadway, Suite 500
Oakland, CA 94612
Telephone: 510-208-0500
FAX: 510-208-0511
Web: nccd-crc.org
Tests: 751, 1413

National Occupational Competency Testing Institute/
    The Whitener Group [NOCTI]
500 N. Bronson Avenue
Big Rapids, MI 49307-2737
Telephone: 800-334-6283
FAX: 231-796-4699
E-mail: nocti@nocti.org
Web: www.nocti.org
Tests: 1840, 1841, 2926

National Psychological Corporation
4/230, Kacheri Ghat
AGRA-4
India
Tests: 2677

National Reading Styles Institute, Inc.
P.O. Box 737
Syosset, NY 11791-0737
Telephone: 516-921-5500
FAX: 516-921-5591
E-mail: readingstyle@nrsi.com
Web: www.nrsi.com
Tests: 659, 2091, 2242

National Spanish Exam
2051 Mt. Zion Drive
Golden, CO 80401-1737
Telephone: 303-278-1021
FAX: 303-278-6400
E-mail: martha.quiat@mho.net
Web: viking.valpo.k12.in.us/~cessna/nse/index.htm
Tests: 1811

National Study of School Evaluation
1866 Southern Ln
Decatur, GA 30033-4033
Tests: 671, 969, 1353, 1942, 2597, 2629, 2635, 2675

National Wellness Institute, Inc.
1300 College Court
P.O. Box 827
Stevens Point, WI 54481-2962
Telephone: 800-243-8694
FAX: 715-342-2979
Web: nationalwellness.org
Tests: 1535, 2791, 2792, 2793

Robert A. Neimeyer, Ph.D.
Department of Psychology
Memphis State University
Memphis, TN 38152
Telephone: 901-678-4680
FAX: 901-678-2579
E-mail: neimeyer@memphis.edu
Tests: 2618

Nelson Education Ltd.
1120 Birchmount Road
Toronto, Ontario M1K 5G4
Canada
Telephone: 416-752-9448
FAX: 416-752-9646
E-mail: inquire@nelson.com
Web: www.nelson.com
Tests: 416, 419, 1124, 1916, 2314, 2877

New Zealand Council for Educational Research
Education House West
178-182 Willis Street
Box 3237
Wellington 6000
New Zealand
Telephone: 00 64 4 384 7939
FAX: 00 64 4 384 7933
E-mail: karyn.dunn@nzcer.org.nz
Web: www.nzcer.org.nz
Tests: 25, 384, 1019, 2157, 2160, 2161, 2166, 2531, 2551, 2628, 2674

Nichols & Molinder Assessments
437 Bowes Drive
Fircrest, WA 98466-7047
Tests: 1789

Noel-Levitz
2350 Oakdale Blvd
Coralville, IA 52241-9702
Telephone: 319-337-4700
FAX: 319-337-5274
E-mail: info@noellevitz.com
Web: www.noellevitz.com
Tests: 654

Norland Software
P.O. Box 84499
Los Angeles, CA 90073-0499
Telephone: 310-825-9689
FAX: 310-825-9689
E-mail: emiller@ucla.edu
Web: www.calcaprt.com
Tests: 395

Northwest Evaluation Association
121 NW Everett St
Portland, OR 97209-4049
Tests: 1655

Northwest Psychological Publishers, Inc.
P.O. Box 494958
Redding, CA 96049-4958
Tests: 2165

Nova Media, Inc.
1724 N. State
Big Rapids, MI 49307-9073
Telephone: 231-796-4637
E-mail: trund@netonecom.net
Web: www.racialattitudesurvey.com & www.cultural-diversitytest.com
Tests: 2227

NTS Research Corporation
209 Markham Drive
Chapel Hill, NC 27514
Tests: 2412

Dr. Thomas R. Oaster
Address Unknown
Tests: 2598, 1862

The Occupational Research Centre
"Cornerways"
Cardigan Street
Newmarket, Suffolk CB8 8HZ
United Kingdom
Web: www.kaicentre.com
Tests: 1448

E. R. Oetting, Ph.D.
Psychology Department
Colorado State University
Fort Collins, CO 80523
Telephone: 970-491-1615
FAX: 970-491-0527
E-mail: goetting@lamar.colostate.edu
Tests: 1875, 1876, 2529, 2704

Opposite Strengths, Inc.
100 Congress Avenue, Suite 2000
Austin, TX 78701-3500
Telephone: 512-469-3500
FAX: 512-857-0998
E-mail: contact@oppositestrengths.com
Web: www.oppositestrengths.com
Tests: 1892

Optometry Admission Testing Program
211 East Chicago Avenue, 6th Floor
Chicago, IL 60611-2678
Telephone: 312-440-2684
FAX: 312-587-4105
E-mail: kramerg@ada.org
Tests: 1894

OQ Measures LLC
P.O. Box 521047
Salt Lake City, UT 84152-1047
Telephone: 888-647-2673
Web: www.oqmeasures.com/site/
Tests: 1895, 1896, 1897, 2996, 2997, 3000

Organization Analysis and Design LLC
168 High Street
Norwell, MA 02061
Tests: 1860

Organizational Measurement Systems Press
P.O. Box 70586
Eugene, OR 97401
Telephone: 541-484-2715
FAX: 541-465-1602
E-mail: barb_john_miner@msn.com
Tests: 1732, 1888

Oxford Psychologists Press, Ltd.
Lambourne House
311-321 Banbury Road
Oxford OX2 7JH
United Kingdom
Tests: 763

P.D.P. Press, Inc.
1137 N. McKusick Rd. Lane
Stillwater, MN 55082
Tests: 2426

Pain Assessment Resources
4790 Caughlin Parkway Ste 173
Reno, NV 89519
Telephone: 800-782-1501 or 775-828-2955
FAX: 775-828-4275
E-mail: office@painassessmentresources.com
Web: www.painassessmentresources.com
Tests: 311

Pain Resource Center, Inc.
P.O. Box 763
Hillsborough, NC 27278
Tests: 511, 2808

PAQ Services, Inc.
11 Bellwether Way, Suite 107
Bellingham, WA 98225
Web: www.paq.com
Tests: 1380, 2079, 2140, 2978

Pearson
5601 Green Valley Drive
Minneapolis, MN 55437
Telephone: 800-627-7271 or 952-681-3232
FAX: 800-632-9011 or 952-681-3299
E-mail: pearsonassessments@pearson.com
Web: www.pearsonassessments.com
Tests: 13, 15, 20, 21, 60, 64, 72, 88, 140, 143, 162, 173,
212, 235, 238, 261, 262, 263, 264, 281, 283, 28,4
285, 286, 287, 288, 289, 290, 291, 295, 297, 328,
329, 335, 336, 346, 347, 348, 354, 355, 356, 360,
361, 363, 364, 377, 378, 380, 382, 390, 403, 404,
411, 426, 427, 460, 482, 489, 491, 493, 500, 504,
505, 519, 524, 561, 575, 576, 577, 578, 579, 598,
660, 708, 726, 758, 804, 819, 837, 846, 850, 858,
859, 875, 877, 878, 898, 906, 910, 912, 917, 919,
933, 935, 936, 937, 939, 940, 946, 953, 1044, 1088,

1112, 1127, 1129, 1136, 1140, 1143, 1146, 1147, 1148, 1149, 1151, 1152, 1179, 1192, 1195, 1203, 1211, 1219, 1234, 1257, 1270, 1288, 1293, 1302, 1304, 1309, 1325, 1354, 1372, 1399, 1400, 1417, 1419, 1420, 1421, 1423, 1425, 1426, 1427, 1433, 1435, 1624, 1632, 1638, 1639, 1688, 1689, 1690, 1691, 1698, 1705, 1706, 1707, 1712, 1721, 1722, 1723, 1724, 1725, 1726, 1727, 1736, 1737, 1758, 1769, 1785, 1803, 1804, 1821, 1824, 1831, 1832, 1901, 1915, 1917, 1920, 1921, 1928, 1948, 1949, 1953, 1961, 1965, 1966, 2038, 2039, 2041, 2042, 2074, 2084, 2085, 2103, 2115, 2135, 2136, 2198, 2208, 2225, 2226, 2230, 2233, 2237, 2239, 2246, 2259, 2262, 2271, 2273, 2283, 2306, 2353, 2354, 2367, 2369, 2383, 2429, 2430, 2440, 2456, 2500, 2536, 2537, 2540, 2541, 2542, 2543, 2544, 2545, 2574, 2599, 2600, 2655, 2657, 2706, 2710, 2714, 2745, 2753, 2778, 2794, 2809, 2825, 2843, 2845, 2851, 2854, 2860, 2861, 2862, 2866, 2886, 2895, 2896, 2898, 2899, 2900, 2901, 2902, 2903, 2904, 2905, 2906, 2907, 2911, 2912, 2919, 2921, 2935, 2939, 2956

Pearson Assessment
Halley Court
Jordan Hill, Oxford OX2 8EJ
United Kingdom
Telephone: 0845 630 88 88
FAX: 0845 630 55 55
E-mail: info@psychcorp.co.uk
Web: www.psychcorp.co.uk
Tests: 246, 248, 252, 317, 318, 319, 408, 506, 675, 752, 896, 907, 914, 916, 918, 1051, 1102, 1144, 1155, 1224, 1542, 1546, 1701, 1768, 2046, 2107, 2119, 2202, 2204, 2291, 2292, 2293, 2311, 2312, 2410, 2439, 2447, 2524, 2561, 2709, 2734, 2735, 2762, 2849, 2869, 2870, 2908, 2909, 2910, 2920, 2986

Pearson Assessment and Information
Level 6, 287 Elizabeth Street
Sydney, New South Wales 2000
Australia
FAX: 61 2 9261 4975
E-mail: info@pearsonpsychcorp.com.au
Web: www.pearsonpsychcorp.com.au
Tests: 239, 240, 876, 2879

Pearson Education
501 Boylston St., Ste 900
Boston, MA 02116-3725
Tests: 960, 2560

Pearson Performance Solutions
One North Dearborn, Suite 1600
Chicago, IL 60602
Tests: 2621, 56, 168, 169, 265, 410, 412, 413, 563, 585, 586, 700, 701, 762, 767, 778, 780, 782, 971, 994, 996, 1038, 1094, 1095, 1324, 1341, 1476, 1487, 1574, 1585, 1590, 1595, 1663, 1665, 1844, 1847, 1866, 1883, 1884, 1987, 1992, 2036, 2054, 2122, 2200, 2234, 2264, 2316, 2317, 2326, 2457, 2475, 2509, 2510, 2558, 2622, 2638, 2643, 2656, 2687, 2694, 2699, 2750, 2803, 2804, 2836, 2839, 2850, 2852, 2957

Pearson VUE
5601 Green Valley Dr.
Bloomington, MN 55437-1099
Telephone: 952-681-3000
FAX: 952-681-3899
Web: www.pearsonvue.com
Tests: 1158

Penna PLC
St. Mary's Court
20 St. Mary at Hill
London EC3R 9EE
United Kingdom
Telephone: +44 (0) 207 648 2420
FAX: +44 (0) 207 648 2439
Tests: 220, 221, 222, 1978, 1979

Perfection Learning Corporation
1000 North Second Avenue
P.O. Box 500
Logan, IA 51546-0500
Web: www.perfectionlearning.com
Tests: 1544

Personal Strengths Publishing
P.O. Box 2605
Carlsbad, CA 92018-2605
Telephone: 800-624-7347
FAX: 760-602-0087
E-mail: mail@PersonalStrengths.com
Web: www.PersonalStrengths.com
Tests: 1036, 1037, 1072, 1073, 1074, 1746, 2018, 2077, 2078, 2565

Personalysis Corporation
5847 San Felipe, Suite 650
Houston, TX 77057-3008
Telephone: 713-784-4421
FAX: 713-784-9909
E-mail: info@personalysis.com
Web: www.personalysis.com
Tests: 2031

Dr. Linda Phillips
Director, Centre for Research on Literacy
Faculty of Educacion
University of Alberta
Edmonton, Alberta T6G 2G5
Canada
Telephone: 780-492-4250
FAX: 780-492-0113
Tests: 2740

Phonovisual Products, Inc.
119-A E. Chapline St., First Floor
P.O. Box 90
Sharpsburg, MD 21782
Telephone: 800-283-4888
FAX: 240-358-0228
E-mail: phonovisual@aol.com
Web: www.phonovisual.com
Tests: 2049

Dr. Ralph L. Piedmont
Loyola University Maryland, Pastoral Counseling
    Department
8890 McGaw Road
Columbia, MD 21045
Telephone: 410-617-7625
FAX: 410-617-7644
E-mail: rpiedmont@loyola.edu
Tests: 219

Dr. Issy Pilowsky
University of Sydney
Department of Psychological Medicine
Camperdown
New South Wales 2006
Australia
E-mail: ipilowsk@mail.usyd.edu.au
Tests: 1290, 1527

Piney Mountain Press, Inc.
P.O. Box 986
Dahlonega, GA 30533
Telephone: 800-255-3127
FAX: 800-905-3127
E-mail: cyberguy@alltel.net
Web: www.pineymountain.com
Tests: 275, 1513, 1516, 2124, 2476, 2878

PITS: Psychologische Instrumenten Tests en Services
Postbus 1084
2302 BB Leiden
The Netherlands
Telephone: ++ (0)71-5318786
FAX: ++ (0)71-5728165
E-mail: info@pits-online.nl
Web: www.pits-online.nl
Tests: 157, 2040, 2865

Predictive Surveys Corporation
5802 Howard Avenue
LaGrange, IL 60525
Telephone: 708-246-1271
E-mail: markstrand@prodigy.net
Tests: 2173, 2174, 2663

Prentice-Hall
College Book Division
200 Old Tappan Rd.
Old Tappan, NJ 07675
Tests: 1020, 1294, 1545, 1616, 1295, 1885, 2149

Preschool Skills Test
c/o Carol Lepera
10126 Wood Meadow Ct.
Fort Wayne, IN 46845
E-mail: clepera@frontier.com
Tests: 2120

Preziosi Partners, Inc.
9441 Hollyhock Court
Ft. Lauderdale, FL 33328
Tests: 2138

Price Systems, Inc.
763 N 1750 Rd
Lawrence, KS 66049-9016
Telephone: 785-843-7892
FAX: 785-843-0101
E-mail: learn@learningstyle.com
Web: learn.humanesources.com/
Tests: 1507, 2139

PRO-ED
8700 Shoal Creek Blvd.
Austin, TX 78757-6897
Telephone: 800-897-3202
FAX: 800-397-7633
E-mail: info@proedinc
Web: www.proedinc.com
Tests: 2, 3, 59, 82, 167, 172, 184, 191, 199, 201, 210,
    211, 228, 243, 253, 254, 266, 274, 293, 294, 307,
    309, 343, 351, 352, 366, 455, 594, 664, 689, 691,
    693, 694, 697, 709, 760, 773, 786, 787, 815, 824, 825,
    826, 830, 831, 833, 838, 842, 844, 845, 854, 855, 856,
    879, 899, 900, 930, 1031, 1089, 1091, 1098, 1106,
    1110, 1111, 1118, 1138, 1141, 1142, 1172, 1173,
    1174, 1209, 1253, 1289, 1307, 1442, 1456, 1458,
    1474, 1502, 1538, 1734, 1757, 1780, 1816, 1817,
    1868, 1902, 1964, 2044, 2048, 2050, 2056, 2093,
    2100, 2105, 2114, 2116, 2127, 2144, 2185, 2232,
    2235, 2248, 2276, 2287, 2300, 2301, 2302, 2346,
    2347, 2350, 2363, 2384, 2386, 2407, 2492, 2517,
    2521, 2522, 2534, 2538, 2539, 2604, 2605, 2649,
    2650, 2672, 2707, 2715, 2716, 2717, 2723, 2725,
    2726, 2727, 2728, 2729, 2730, 2737, 2746, 2747,

2748, 2749, 2751, 2754, 2755, 2757, 2758, 2759, 2760, 2761, 2764, 2766, 2767, 2776, 2777, 2779, 2780, 2781, 2782, 2811, 2823, 2841, 2844, 2882, 2914, 2958, 2963, 2992, 2998

Professional Picture Framers Association
3000 Picture Place
Jackson, MI 49201
Telephone: 517-788-8100
FAX: 517-788-8371
E-mail: ppfa@ppfa.com
Tests: 463

Professional Resource Press
P.O. Box 3197
Sarasota, FL 34230-3197
Tests: 1090, 1323, 1619, 1772

Profiles International, Inc.
Profiles Office Park
5205 Lake Shore Drive
Waco, TX 76710-1732
Tests: 2148

Program Development Associates
P.O. Box 2038
Syracuse, NY 13220-2038
Web: www.disabilitytraining.com
Tests: 2678

ProLiteracy Worldwide
1320 Jamesville Avenue
Syracuse, NY 13210
Telephone: 315-422-9121 Ext. 353
FAX: 315-422-6369
E-mail: corpcom@proliteracy.org
Web: www.proliteracy.org
Tests: 1003, 2236

Prufrock Press Inc.
P.O. Box 8813
Waco, TX 76714-8813
Telephone: 800-998-2208
FAX: 800-240-0333
E-mail: info@prufrock.com
Web: www.prufrock.com
Tests: 2348

Psych Press
Level 4 398 Lonsdale Street
Melbourne, VIC 3000
Australia
Telephone: +61 3 9670 0590
FAX: +61 3 9642 3577
E-mail: info@psychpress.com.au
Web: www.psychpress.com
Tests: 1033

Psycho-Educational Services
5114 Balcones Woods Drive
Suite 307-163
Austin, TX 78759
Web: www.psycho-educational.com
Tests: 1115

Psychodiagnostics, Inc.
3155 Patrick Lane, Suite One
Las Vegas, NV 89120
Telephone: 866-530-7742
FAX: 888-214-4393
E-mail: psyinfo@psychodiagnostics.com
Web: www.psychodiagnostics.com
Tests: 1796

Psychological & Educational Publications, Inc.
P.O. Box 520
Hydesville, CA 95547-0520
Tests: 2713

Psychological Assessment Resources, Inc.
16204 N. Florida Avenue
Lutz, FL 33549-8119
Telephone: 800-331-8378
FAX: 800-727-9329
E-mail: custsupp@parinc.com
Web: www.parinc.com
Tests: 68, 74, 75, 81, 83, 84, 97, 145, 303, 304, 305, 306, 310, 349, 353, 365, 367, 428, 431, 445, 469, 478, 484, 486, 490, 492, 503, 512, 570, 571, 572, 573, 574, 596, 597, 600, 603, 604, 658, 725, 728, 738, 805, 806, 822, 836, 841, 881, 944, 945, 975, 976, 979, 990, 1027, 1046, 1083, 1084, 1085, 1108, 1208, 1232, 1264, 1266, 1297, 1332, 1333, 1343, 1348, 1349, 1360, 1395, 1432, 1531, 1532, 1610, 1659, 1675, 1676, 1680, 1681, 1682, 1711, 1729, 1735, 1775, 1778, 1781, 1791, 1818, 1819, 1826, 1828, 1872, 1889, 1935, 1947, 1950, 1963, 1969, 2001, 2002, 2007, 2008, 2022, 2023, 2024, 2025, 2073, 2080, 2191, 2193, 2194, 2269, 2278, 2280, 2281, 2282, 2284, 2285, 2286, 2289, 2297, 2307, 2308, 2309, 2310, 2405, 2431, 2438, 2490, 2553, 2554, 2568, 2579, 2582, 2586, 2587, 2588, 2602, 2611, 2617, 2642, 2668, 2696, 2743, 2828, 2829, 2830, 2840, 2856, 2864, 2871, 2881, 2928, 2929, 2930, 2931, 2932, 2933, 2934, 2936, 2945, 2946

Psychological Growth Associates, Inc.
Products Division
3813 Tiffany Drive
Lawrence, KS 66049
Telephone: 785-841-1141
FAX: 785-749-2190
E-mail: 73204.303@compuserve. com
Tests: 2805

Psychological Publications, Inc.
2205 First St., Suite 110
Simi Valley, CA 93065
Telephone: 800-345-8378
FAX: 805-527-9266
E-mail: tjta@aol.com
Web: www.tjta.com
Tests: 1061, 2671

Psychological Services Bureau, Inc.
977 Seminole Trail
Charlottesville, VA 22901-2894
Telephone: 877-932-8378
FAX: 434-293-5885
E-mail: info@psbtests.com
Web: www.psbtests.com
Tests: 2169, 2170, 2171, 2172

Psychological Services Press
92 Bowman St.
Hamilton, Ontario L8S 2T6
Canada
Telephone: 905-527-0129
FAX: 905-527-5726
E-mail: PS-support@sympatico.ca
Web: www3.sympatico.ca/itrofimova/PS-STQ.htm
Tests: 2581

Psychological Services, Inc.
2950 N. Hollywood Way, Suite 200
Burbank, CA 91505-1072
Web: corporate.psionline.com/contact/
Tests: 989, 1081, 1082, 2070, 2141, 2175, 2858

Psychological Test Publications
Scamp's House
107 Pilton Street
Barnstaple, Devon
England
Tests: 1181, 1518

Psychological Test Specialists
Box 9229
Missoula, MT 59807-9229
Telephone: 406-728-1710
E-mail: Rachel@AmmonsScientific.com
Web: www.ammonsscientific.com
Tests: 2224

Psychology Press
270 Madison Avenue
New York, NY 10016
Telephone: 212-216-7800
FAX: 212-643-1430
Web: www.psypress.com
Tests: 342, 409, 458, 1028, 2186, 2855, 2043

Psychology Press (Taylor and Francis Group)
c/o Julie Norton
27 Church Road
Hove, East Sussex BN3 2FA
England
E-mail: Julie.Norton@tandf.co.uk
Tests: 1201

Psychometric Affiliates
118 Oakcrest Road
Huntsville, AL 35811-9072
Telephone: 256-859-2441
Tests: 11, 12, 14, 141, 149, 151, 155, 181, 182, 562, 650,
670, 710, 768, 774, 775, 776, 886, 956, 965, 984,
1006, 1007, 1023, 1025, 1052, 1054, 1068, 1069,
1070, 1087, 1117, 1128, 1131, 1133, 1185, 1212,
1227, 1229, 1230, 1235, 1246, 1276, 1355, 1382,
1408, 1490, 1529, 1601, 1630, 1647, 1650, 1651,
1652, 1661, 1764, 1882, 1886, 1983, 2053, 2065,
2066, 2090, 2184, 2201, 2243, 2336, 2394, 2506,
2526, 2632, 2832, 2874, 2913, 2925, 2969

Psychometric Research & Development Ltd.
47 Holywell Hill
St. Albans, Herts AL1 1HD
England
Telephone: +44 0 1727 841455
Web: www.prd.co.uk
Tests: 1157, 1754, 1833, 1834

Psychometrics Canada Ltd.
7125 - 77 Avenue
Edmonton, Alberta T6B 0B5
Canada
Telephone: 800-661-5158
FAX: 780-469-2283
E-mail: info@psychometrics.com
Web: www.psychometrics.com
Tests: 1300, 2674, 1301

Psytec Inc.
P.O. Box 564
DeKalb, IL 60115
Telephone: 815-758-1415
FAX: 815-758-1725
Tests: 473

Donald K. Pumroy, Ph.D.
4006 Oliver Street
Hyattsville, MD 20782
Telephone: 301-864-8935
FAX: 301-864-8935
E-mail: dpumroy@earthlink.net
Tests: 1617

Purdue Research Foundation
Engineering and Administration Building
Purdue University
West Lafayette, IN 47907
Tests: 2199

Quality Metric
24 Albion Road
Building 400
Lincoln, RI 02865
Web: www.qualitymetric.com
Tests: 2448

Quantitative Methods in Education
University of Minnesota
178 Pillsbury Drive, SE
206 Burton Hall
Minneapolis, MN 55455
Tests: 1627

Questar Assessment, Inc.
4 Hardscrabble Heights
P.O. Box 382
Brewster, NY 10509-0382
Telephone: 800-800-2598
FAX: 845-277-3548
E-mail: info@QuestarAI.com
Web: www.QuestarAI.com
Tests: 801, 802, 1560, 2462

Ramsay Corporation
Boyce Station Offices
1050 Boyce Road
Pittsburgh, PA 15241-3907
Web: www.ramsaycorp.com
Tests: 136, 471, 661, 897, 961, 963, 964, 967, 1322,
    1559, 1561, 1562, 1563, 1660, 1662, 1664, 1666,
    1667, 1668, 1670, 1770, 1771, 1773, 1879, 1881,
    2129, 2684, 2915

Regal Books
c/o Gospel Light
1957 Eastman Ave.
Ventura, CA 93003
Tests: 1613

Reitan Neuropsychology Laboratory/Press
P.O. Box 66080
Tucson, AZ 85728-6080
Telephone: 520-577-2970
FAX: 520-577-2940
E-mail: reitanlabs@aol.com
Tests: 1206

Renaissance Learning, Inc.
P.O. Box 8036
Wisconsin Rapids, WI 54495-8036
Telephone: 800-656-6740
FAX: 877-279-7642
E-mail: answers@renlearn.com
Web: www.renlearn.com
Tests: 2548, 2549, 2550

Renovex Corporation
1421 Jersey Avenue, N
Minneapolis, MN 55427
Tests: 202

Research Concepts
1368 East Airport Road
Muskegon, MI 49444
Telephone: 231-739-7401
Tests: 1221

Research for Better Schools, Inc.
112 North Broad Street
Philadelphia, PA 19102-1510
Telephone: 215-574-9300
FAX: 215-574-0133
E-mail: maguire@rbs.org
Web: www.rbs.org
Tests: 207, 218, 884, 2366

Research Press
P.O. Box 9177
Champaign, IL 61826
Telephone: 800-519-2707
FAX: 217-352-1221
E-mail: rp@researchpress.com
Web: www.researchpress.com
Tests: 313, 1101, 1268, 1269, 1467, 1787

Richmond Products, Inc.
4400 Silver Avenue, SE
Albuquerque, NM 87108
Telephone: 505-275-2406
FAX: 810-885-8319
E-mail: Lloydpo@aol.com
Web: www.RichmondProducts.com
Tests: 1271

Riverside Publishing
3800 Golf Road, Suite 100
Rolling Meadows, IL 60008
Telephone: 800-323-9540
FAX: 630-467-7192
Web: www.riversidepublishing.com
Tests: 279, 280, 298, 327, 338, 470, 595, 792, 870, 1123,
    1328, 1342, 1342, 1359, 1363, 1364, 1631, 1733,
    2211, 2263, 2352, 2784, 2951, 2952, 2953, 2954, 2955

Rocky Mountain Behavioral Science Institute, Inc.
305 West Magnolia St., #291
Fort Collins, CO 80521
Telephone: 800-447-6354
FAX: 970-221-0595
E-mail: info@rmbsi.com
Web: www.rmbsi.com
Tests: 73, 148

Rose Wolfe Family Partnership LLP
c/o Walden Personnel Performance, Inc.
1445 Lambert-Closse, Suite 301
Montreal, Quebec H3Z 1Z5
Canada
Telephone: 514-989-9555
FAX: 514-989-9934
E-mail: ssilver@waldentesting.com
Web: www.waldentesting.com
Tests: 175, 2662, 2948, 2661, 2884, 2947

Routledge (Taylor and Francis Group)
c/o Julie Norton
Psychology Press
27 Church Road
Hove, East Sussex BN3 2FA
England
E-mail: Julie.Norton@tandf.co.uk
Tests: 229

Kenneth H. Rubin, Ph.D., Director
Center for Children, Relationships & Culture
Department of Human Development, 3304 Benjamin
    Building
University of Maryland
College Park, MD 20742-1131
Tests: 2068

SAGE Publications
2455 Teller Road
Thousand Oaks, CA 09320
Tests: 1788

Dr. Shoukry D. Saleh
Chairman, Department of Management Sciences
University of Waterloo
Waterloo, Ontario N2L 3G1
Canada
Tests: 1383

SALT Software, LLC
23441 Gingers Drive
Muscoda, WI 53573-5591
Telephone: 888-440-7258
FAX: 608-739-3676
E-mail: info@saltsoftware.com
Web: www.saltsoftware.com
Tests: 2658, 2689

The SASSI Institute
201 Camelot Lane
Springville, IN 47462
Telephone: 800-726-0526
FAX: 800-546-7995
E-mail: sassi@sassi.com
Web: www.sassi.com
Tests: 2613

Scantron Corporation
7676 Hazard Center Dr., Suite 1050
San Diego, CA 92108-4515
Telephone: 800-722-6876
FAX: 619-615-0522
E-mail: marjorie–reynolds@scantron.com
Web: www.scantron.com
Tests: 1989

Dr. K. Warner Schaie
Address Unknown
Tests: 2357

Ronald R. Schmeck, Ph.D.
Department of Psychology
Southern Illinois University at Carbondale
Carbondale, IL 62901-6502
Tests: 1347

Nina G. Schneider, Ph.D.
Greater LA VA Healthcare, Nicotine Research Unit
Bldg. 210, 2nd Floor, 11301 Wilshire Blvd.
Mail Code: 691/B151D
Los Angeles, CA 90073
Telephone: 310-268-3059
FAX: 310-268-4125
Tests: 2488

Scholastic Inc.
557 Broadway
New York, NY 10012
Tests: 2802

Scholastic Testing Service, Inc.
480 Meyer Road
Bensenville, IL 60106-1617
Telephone: 800-642-6787
FAX: 630-766-8054
E-mail: sts@mail.ststesting.com
Web: www.ststesting.com
Tests: 4, 584, 688, 734, 862, 864, 926, 950, 1170, 1204,
    1245, 1275, 1336, 1436, 1437, 1443, 1463, 1649,
    1936, 1944, 2215, 2295, 2375, 2606, 2799, 2800,
    2813, 2891

Schuhfried
Hyrtlstrasse 45
2340 Moedling
Austria
Telephone: +43 2236 42315
FAX: +43 2236 46597
E-mail: info@schuhfried.at
Web: www.schuhfried.at
Tests: 1205

Scientific Management Techniques, Inc.
Towne Square Complex
12 Parmenter Road, Unit A-5
Londonderry, NH 03053
Telephone: 603-421-0222
FAX: 603-421-1881
E-mail: scibos@aol.com
Web: www.scientific-management.com
Tests: 2532

Search Institute
The Banks Building
615 First Avenue NE, Suite 125
Minneapolis, MN 55413
Telephone: 800-888-7828
FAX: 612-376-8956
E-mail: si@search-institute.org
Web: www.search-institute.org
Tests: 2390

SEFA (Publications) Ltd.
"The Globe"
4 Great William St.
Stratford-upon-Avon CV37-6RY
England
FAX: +43-2236-29554
E-mail: admin@sefa.org.uk
Web: www.sefa.org.uk
Tests: 1547, 2155

SELF Research Centre
University of Western Sydney
Bankstown Campus
Locked Bag 1797
Penrith South DC
New South Wales 1797
Australia
Tests: 2403

Melvin Selzer, M.D.
6967 Paseo Laredo
La Jolla, CA 92037
Telephone: 619-459-1035
Tests: 1693

Sensonics, Inc.
P.O. Box 112
Haddon Heights, NJ 08035
Web: www.sensonics.com
Tests: 2487

SHL
The Pavilion
1 Atwell Place
Thames Ditton, Surrey KT7 0NE
United Kingdom
Tests: 999 1014, 128, 247, 766, 1569, 1577, 1869, 1893,
2037, 2154, 2324, 2690, 2691, 2982

The Sidran Institute
P.O. Box 436
Brooklandville, MD 21022-0436
Web: www.sidran.org
Tests: 80, 891, 892

SIGMA Assessment Systems, Inc.
P.O. Box 610757
Port Huron, MI 48061-0757
Telephone: 800-265-1285
FAX: 800-361-9411
E-mail: SIGMA@SigmaAssessmentSystems.com
Web: www.SigmaAssessmentSystems.com
Tests: 189, 272, 433, 452, 731, 883, 997, 1374, 1375,
1484, 1492, 1777, 1846, 2028, 2032, 2189, 2441,
2459, 2460, 2461, 2470, 2646

Silverwood Enterprises, LLC
P.O. Box 363
Sharon Center, OH 44273
Telephone: 330-239-1646
FAX: 330-239-0250
E-mail: silverasoc@aol.com
Tests: 142, 1236

Jacob O. Sines
207 Black Springs Circle
Iowa City, IA 52246
Tests: 1259, 1747

SLACK Incorporated
6900 Grove Road
Thorofare, NJ 08086-9447
Web: www.slackinc.com
Tests: 1728

Slosson Educational Publications, Inc.
P.O. Box 544
East Aurora, NY 14052-0544
Telephone: 888-756-7766
FAX: 800-655-3840
E-mail: slosson@slosson.com
Web: www.slosson.com
Tests: 5, 158, 185, 507, 695, 865, 866, 867, 868, 869,
880, 959, 1444, 2378, 2379, 2385, 2481, 2482, 2483,
2484, 2485, 2612, 2756, 2883

SOI Systems
45755 Goodpasture Road
P.O. Box D
Vida, OR 97488
Telephone: 541-896-3936
FAX: 541-896-3983
E-mail: soi@soisystems.com
Web: www.soisystems.com
Tests: 808, 809, 1673

Sopris West
4093 Specialty Place
Longmont, CO 80504-5400
Telephone: 800-547-6747
FAX: 303-776-5934
E-mail: www.sopriswest.com
Web: www.sopriswest.com
Tests: 874, 941, 1113, 1339, 2365, 2660

Southwest Educational Development Laboratory
4700 Mueller Blvd.
Austin, TX 78723-3081
Web: www.sedl.org
Tests: 890

SPECTRA Inc.
1004 Palmyra Drive
Tega Cay, SC 29706-8539
Tests: 2894

SPSI-A, LLC
P.O. Box 147
Oshtemo, MI 49077-1078
Tests: 2496

Stanard & Associates, Inc.
309 West Washington Street, Suite 1000
Chicago, IL 60606
Web: www.stanard.com
Tests: 1810

Stoelting Co.
620 Wheat Lane
Wood Dale, IL 60191-1164
Telephone: 630-860-9700
FAX: 630-860-9775
E-mail: psychtests@stoeltingco.com
Web: www.stoeltingco.com/tests
Tests: 8, 230, 302, 516, 1109, 1213, 1350, 1390, 1404,
1422, 1424, 1451, 1454, 1522, 1537, 1685, 1756,
2118, 2395, 2486, 2504, 2562, 2578, 2867

Stress Directions, Inc.
2464 Massachusetts Avenue, Suite 315C
Cambridge, MA 02140
Telephone: 617-547-3499
FAX: 617-547-3498
E-mail: lmiller@stressdirections.com
Web: www.stressdirections.com
Tests: 2013

Student Development Associates, Inc.
Address Unknown
Tests: 10

Sue Teele & Associates
P.O. Box 7302
Redlands, CA 92375
Telephone: 909-793-1916
FAX: 909-793-1916
E-mail: scandsteele@msn.com
Tests: 2693

Super Duper Publications
P.O. Box 24997
Greenville, SC 29616-2497
Telephone: 800-277-8737
FAX: 800-978-7379
E-mail: custserv@superduperinc.com
Web: www.superduperinc.com
Tests: 569, 2938

Clifford H. Swensen
Department of Psychological Sciences
Purdue University
1364 Psychological Sciences Building
West Lafayette, IN 47907-1364
Telephone: 765-496-6977
FAX: 765-496-2670
E-mail: cswensen@psych.purdue.edu
Tests: 2342, 2344

Targeted Testing Inc.
1109 Trout St. BHR
Okeechobee, FL 34974
Telephone: 863-824-7542
FAX: 863-763-8216
E-mail: info@targettest.com
Web: www.targettest.com
Tests: 1968

TAV Selection System
12807 Arminta Street
North Hollywood, CA 91605
Telephone: 818-765-1884
Tests: 2669

Anne P. Taylor
9 Tumble Weed, NW
Albuquerque, NM 87120-1823
Tests: 2670

Teachers College Press
1234 Amsterdam Avenue
New York, NY 10027
Telephone: 212-678-3929
FAX: 212-678-4149
E-mail: tcpress@tc.columbia.edu
Web: www.teacherscollegepress.com
Tests: 216, 599, 923, 1057, 1125, 1308, 1636, 2364, 2712

Teleometrics International, Inc.
4567 Lake Shore Drive
Waco, TX 76710
Telephone: 800-527-0406
FAX: 254-772-9588
E-mail: teleo.info@teleometrics.com
Web: www.teleometrics.com
Tests: 18, 465, 712, 713, 777, 992, 1292, 1482, 1573,
     1584, 1586, 1589, 1592, 1593, 1597, 1598, 1600,
     1805, 1957, 1991, 2004, 2010, 2035, 2088, 2089,
     2137, 2206, 2210, 2247, 2322, 2327, 2332, 2607,
     2608, 2609, 2633, 2639, 2681, 2683, 2685, 2686, 2971

The Test Agency Ltd.
Burgner House
4630 Kingsgate
Oxford Business Park South
Oxford OX4 2SU
England
Telephone: +44 (0) 1865 402900
FAX: +44 (0) 1865 402888
E-mail: info@testagency.com
Web: www.testagency.com
Tests: 954, 962, 1182, 1280, 1533, 1591, 1642, 1959,
     2086, 2449, 2979, 2980, 1603

Test Analysis & Development Corporation
2400 Park Lake Drive
Boulder, CO 80301
Telephone: 303 666-8651
FAX: 303 665-6045
E-mail: jimh@testanalysis.com
Tests: 2409

Toby J. Tetenbaum
Fordham University
113 West 60th Street, Room 1119
New York, NY 10023
Tests: 233

Thinking Publications
424 Galloway Street
P.O. Box 163
Eau Claire, WI 54702-0163
Tests: 203, 727, 2577

Thomson Delmar Learning
Executive Woods
5 Maxwell Drive
P.O. Box 8007
Clifton Park, NY 12065-2919
Tests: 1958

The TOVA Company
3321 Cerritos Ave.
Los Alamitos, CA 90720-2105
Telephone: 800-729-2886
FAX: 714-229-8782
E-mail: info@tovatest.com
Web: www.tovatest.com
Tests: 2772

Training House, Inc.
22 Amherst Road
Pelham, MA 01002-9745
Tests: 161, 174, 205, 666, 741, 1588, 1596, 1932, 2003,
     2014, 2015, 2143, 2399, 2401, 2640, 2724, 2806,
     2817, 2924

TRT Associates, Inc.
1579 Monroe Drive, Suite F510
Atlanta, GA 30324
Telephone: 404-406-8781
FAX: 404-873-3959
E-mail: trtbasis@hotmail.com
Web: www.mindspring.com/~trtbasis
Tests: 277

Trust Tutoring
9525 Georgia Ave., Ste 200
Silver Spring, MD 20910-1416
Telephone: 800-301-3131
FAX: 301-589-0733 *51
E-mail: havis@erols.com
Web: trusttutoring.com
Tests: 1026

Twenty-First (21st) Century Assessment
P.O. Box 608
South Pasadena, CA 91031–0608
Telephone: 800-374-2100
FAX: 626-441-0614
Web: www.21stcenturyassessment.com
Tests: 2020

U.S. Department of Labor
Division Chief for Evaluation and Skill Assessment
Office of Policy and Research
200 Constitution Avenue, NW
Washington, DC 20210
Tests: 1858, 1859

United States Military Entrance Processing Command
ATTN: Operations Directorate
2500 Green Bay Road
North Chicago, IL 60064-3094
Web: www.asvabprogram.com/
Tests: 187

University of Maryland
Department of Curriculum & Instruction
Reading Center
College Park, MD 20742
Tests: 1842, 2190, 2465

University of Michigan Press
839 Greene Street
Ann Arbor, MI 48104
Telephone: 734-764-4388
FAX: 734-615-1540
E-mail: um.press.bus@umich.edu
Web: www.press.umich.edu
Tests: 927, 2112

University of Minnesota Press
Test Division
Mill Place, Suite 290
111 Third Avenue South
Minneapolis, MN 55401-2520
Web: www.upress.umn.edu/tests
Tests: 2359, 1741, 1742

University of Utah
Department of Psychology–SBS
390 South 1530 East
Salt Lake City, UT 84112-0251
Tests: 2337

Valpar International Corporation
P.O. Box 5767
Tucson, AZ
85703-5767
E-mail: valparbbc@aol.com
Tests: 2846

Variety Child Learning Center
47 Humphrey Drive
Syosset, NY 11791-4098
Telephone: 516-921-7171
FAX: 516-921-8130
E-mail: jfriedman@vclc.org
Web: www.vclc.org
Tests: 1093

Village Publishing
73 Valley Drive
Furlong, PA 18925
Telephone: 800-553-7678
FAX: 215-794-3386
E-mail: VP@custody-vp.com
Web: www.custody-vp.com
Tests: 17, 214, 359, 889, 1262, 1937, 1943, 1984

Vocational and Rehabilitation Research Institute
3304 - 33rd Street, NW
Calgary, Alberta T2L 2A6
Canada
Tests: 62

Vocational Psychology Research
N612 Elliott Hall
University of Minnesota–Twin Cities
75 East River Road
Minneapolis, MN 55455-0344
Telephone: 612-625-1367
FAX: 612-626-0345
E-mail: vpr@tc.umn.edu
Web: www.psych.umn.edu/psylabs/vpr
Tests: 1738, 1739, 1743, 1744

VORT Corporation
P.O. Box 60132-W
Palo Alto, CA 94306
Tests: 312, 1238, 1239

Walch Education
40 Walch Drive
Portland, ME 04103-1286
Web: www.walch.com
Tests: 1076, 2221, 2807

Walden Personnel Performance, Inc.
1445 Lambert-Closse, Suite 301
Montreal, Quebec H3H 1Z5
Canada
Telephone: 514-989-9555
FAX: 514-989-9934
E-mail: ssilver@waldentesting.com
Web: www.waldentesting.com
Tests: 19, 159, 160, 268, 386, 387, 406, 566, 567, 698,
    699, 729, 783, 788, 1032, 1237, 1370, 1371, 1497,
    1594, 1822, 1823, 1863, 1924, 2151, 2152, 2163,
    2265, 2266, 2329, 2330, 2689, 2695, 2888, 2890

Warren Keegan Associates Press
350 Theodore Fremd Ave.
Rye, NY 10580
Telephone: 914-967-9421
FAX: 914-967-8179
E-mail: wkeegan@keeganandco.com
Web: www.keeganandco.com
Tests: 1428

Arthur Weider and James Weider
552 Laguardia Pl.
New York, NY 10012-1459
Telephone: 212-777-7303
FAX: 212-388-0001
E-mail: aweider2000@msm.com
Tests: 746, 748

West Virginia Rehabilitation Research and Training
    Center
Barron Drive
P.O. Box 1004
Institute, WV 25112-1004
Tests: 966

Western Psychological Services
625 Alaska Ave.
Torrance, CA 90503-5124
Telephone: 424-201-8800
FAX: 424-201-6950
E-mail: customerservice@wpspublish.com
Web: www.wpspublish.com
Tests: 36, 39, 57, 76, 79, 91, 133, 137, 183, 234, 314,
    321, 322, 362, 381, 481, 495, 497, 499, 517, 686,
    715, 779, 795, 796, 800, 839, 1002, 1045, 1100,
    1122, 1126, 1207, 1210, 1263, 1272, 1274, 1329,
    1334, 1338, 1403, 1418, 1431, 1445, 1466, 1511,
    1555, 1556, 1566, 1568, 1605, 1606, 1611, 1615,
    1640, 1692, 1792, 1793, 1800, 1827, 1849, 1850,
    1878, 1898, 1899, 1922, 1940, 1997, 1998, 1999,
    2000, 2026, 2027, 2059, 2083, 2131, 2132, 2180,
    2220, 2251, 2270, 2272, 2277, 2279, 2288, 2294,
    2315, 2345, 2372, 2387, 2388, 2389, 2425, 2427,
    2428, 2433, 2452, 2455, 2491, 2498, 2572, 2580,
    2592, 2594, 2619, 2651, 2697, 2701, 2765, 2826,
    2827, 2885, 2918, 2922

Winslow Research Institute
1933 Windward Point
Discovery Bay, CA 94505
Telephone: 925-516-8686
FAX: 925-516-7015
E-mail: winslow@winslowresearch.com
Web: www.winslowresearch.com
Tests: 2941, 2942, 2943

Wintergreen/Orchard House, Inc.
2 LAN Drive, Suite 100
Westford, MA 01886
Tests: 437, 951, 1120

Wonderlic, Inc.
400 Lakeview Parkway, Suite 200
Vernon Hills, IL 60061
Telephone: 800-323-3742
FAX: 847-680-9492
E-mail: sales@wonderlic.com
Web: www.wonderlic.com
Tests: 690, 1011, 1223, 1993, 2949, 2950

Judith Worell, Ph.D.
Address Unknown
Tests: 1938

World Health Organization
Management of Substance Dependence
Dr. Maristela Monteiro
CH-1211
Geneva 27
Switzerland
Telephone: 41-22-791-4791
FAX: 41-22-791-4851
E-mail: monteirom@who.int
Web: www.who.int
Tests: 139

World of Work, Inc.
410 West 1st Street, Suite #103
Tempe, AZ 85281-2574
Web: wowi.com
Tests: 2990

Worley's Identity Discovery Profile, Inc.
190 Bishop Road
Fitchburg, MA 01420-2993
Telephone: 978-448-2047
FAX: 978-448-3910
E-mail: widp@worleyid.com
Web: www.worleyid.com
Tests: 2991

INDEX OF NAMES

This index indicates whether a citation refers to authorship of a test or of a test review for a specific test in a previous Mental Measurements Yearbook. Numbers refer to test entries in Tests in Print VIII, not to pages. The abbreviations and numbers following the names may be interpreted as follows: "test, 73" indicates authorship of test 73; "rev, 86" is based on information listed in the cross references for a test and indicates authorship of a previous review of test 86.

Aaron, I. E.: rev, 526, 2241
Aarons, M.: test, 245
Aase, D.: test, 727
Aasland, O. G.: test, 139
Abbott-Shim, M. S.: test, 474
Abell, E. L.: rev, 393
Abidin, R. R.: test, 1297, 1947, 1950, 2568
Abikoff, H.: test, 501
Abraham, J. A.: test, 1409
Abraham, J. D.: test, 2859
Academic Consulting & Testing Service: test, 225, 1501, 1945, 2373
Academic Freedom Committee, Illinois Division, American Civil Liberties Union: test, 14
Accardo, P. J.: test, 420
Achenbach, T. M.: test, 32, 449
Acheson, S. K.: rev, 310, 352, 1108, 1215, 1417, 2225, 2849, 2921
Ackerman, M. J.: test, 39
Ackerman, P. L.: rev, 231, 566, 785, 977, 1426, 1625, 1669, 2398, 2509, 2542, 2552, 2738, 2775
Ackerman, R. J.: test, 38, 2082
Ackerman, T.: rev, 2902
Ackerman, T. A.: rev, 826, 1836
Acosta, S. T.: rev, 2725
ACS DivCHED Examinations Institute: test, 40, 41, 42, 43, 44, 45, 46, 47, 48, 49, 50, 51, 52, 53
ACT Career Planning Services: test, 2877
ACT, Inc.: test, 54, 55, 443, 657, 1040, 2064
Adamovich, B.: test, 2350

Adams, C.: test, 206
Adams, C. R.: test, 1992
Adams, E.: test, 2102
Adams, G. R.: rev, 773
Adams, J. D.: test, 2838
Adams, K. L.: test, 1731
Adams, M. F.: rev, 267
Adams, R.: test, 2664
Adams, R. L.: rev, 1556, 2218, 2251
Adams, W.: test, 603, 2714, 2932, 2933, 2934
Adcock, C. J.: rev, 1095, 1244, 1732, 2451, 2471, 2474, 2796
Adcock, D.: test, 682, 683
Addiction Research Foundation: test, 190
ADE Incorporated: test, 1412, 1815, 2610
Adkins, C. M.: rev, 2039, 2148
Adkins, D. C.: rev, 989
Adkinson, D. R.: test, 1334
Adler, S.: rev, 1980
Adrian, M.: test, 1116
Ahluwalia, S. P.: test, 2677
Ahmann, J. S.: rev, 2703, 2789
Aho, M.: test, 2274
Ahrens, J. B.: test, 430
Ahsen, A.: test, 130, 957
Aidman, E. V.: rev, 231, 362, 1144, 1403, 2178, 2826, 2879, 2991
Aiken, L. R.: rev, 55, 2384
Airasian, P. W.: rev, 393, 1363
Akkermans, H.: test, 2468

Albanese, M.: rev, 2042, 2169, 2765
Albanese, M. A.: rev, 145, 408, 441, 517, 1223, 1725, 1735, 1855, 2509
Alberts, N. F.: test, 1839, 2422
Albertson, A.: rev, 2735
Albrecht, K.: test, 1495, 1730
Albright, L. E.: rev, 1738, 1743
Alcorn, B. K.: rev, 1536, 1840
Aldarondo, F.: rev, 1332
Alderman, N.: test, 317
Aldous, C.: test, 857
Aldrich, F.: test, 2293
Aleamoni, L. A.: rev, 2683
Aleamoni, L. M.: rev, 991, 1199
Alessandra, T.: test, 1982
Alexander, C. M.: rev, 1911
Alexander, J.: test, 2407
Alexander, R. M.: rev, 2010
Algozzine, B.: test, 2482
Alker, H. A.: rev, 1742
Alleman, E.: test, 142
Allen, C. C.: test, 2308, 2310
Allen, D. V.: rev, 2279, 2710, 2746; test, 2385, 2433
Allen, E. A.: test, 879, 2766, 2767
Allen, K.: rev, 2242
Allen, K. D.: rev, 1224, 2417
Allen, L.: rev, 249, 1477
Allen, L. M., III: test, 702, 1927
Allen, M. J.: rev, 1723, 2542
Allen, N. L.: rev, 684
Allen, S. J.: rev, 307, 1101, 1878, 1946, 2495
Allington, R. L.: rev, 2956
Allison, E. E.: rev, 2911
Allison, J. A.: rev, 220, 1058, 1714, 1950, 2194, 2489, 2647
Allman, T.: test, 1239
Almond, P. J.: test, 243
Alnot, S. D.: test, 1364
Alpern, G.: test, 839
Alpine Media Corporation: test, 1429
Altus, W. D.: rev, 2074
Alvarado, C. G.: test, 279, 338
Alves, C. B.: rev, 1655
Alves, M. G.: test, 1015
Amabile, T. M.: test, 1434
Aman, M. G.: test, 5
Amann, G.: test, 1986
American Association of Teachers of German: test, 1808
American College Testing: test, 2970
American Council on Education: test, 1885
American Institute of Certified Public Accountants: test, 21
American Institutes for Research: test, 1671
American Mathematical Association of Two Year Colleges: test, 150, 152, 153, 154
The American Occupational Therapy Association, Inc.: test, 156
American Psychiatric Association: test, 2182

American Statistical Association: test, 150, 152, 153, 154
Ames, L. B.: test, 1135
Ammer, J. J.: test, 343, 1209
Ammons, C. H.: rev, 3, 675, 1638, 2115, 2667, 2911; test, 2224
Ammons, R. B.: rev, 3, 675, 1638, 2667; test, 2224
Amori, B.: test, 1367
Amori, B. A.: test, 1285, 1286
Amundson, N.: test, 1301
Anastasi, A.: rev, 56, 502, 595, 825, 1149, 1420, 1917, 2028, 2538, 2804
Anastasiow, N. J.: rev, 2198
Anastasopoulos, L.: test, 929
Anastopoulos, A. D.: test, 66
Anchor, K. N.: rev, 1593, 2607
Anderhalter, O. F.: test, 950, 1443, 2375
Anderson, D. O.: rev, 1082, 1660, 1840, 2888
Anderson, G. R.: test, 230
Anderson, G. V.: rev, 2917
Anderson, H. R.: rev, 622, 645
Anderson, I. H.: rev, 1691
Anderson, J. M.: rev, 845, 2903, 2904
Anderson, J. O.: rev, 414, 415, 416, 419, 490, 1245, 2393, 2703
Anderson, K. E.: rev, 42, 53
Anderson, M. W.: rev, 963
Anderson, P. D.: test, 87, 1139, 2821
Anderson, R. G.: test, 1463
Anderson, R. P.: rev, 688
Anderson, T. D.: test, 1013, 1319, 1396, 1491, 2016, 2223, 2331, 2569
Anderson, V.: test, 2735
Andersson, L.: rev, 691
Andreasen, N. C.: test, 687, 2339, 2340, 2341
Andrellos, P. J.: test, 1971
Andrew, D. M.: test, 1736
Andrews, D.: test, 1525
Andrews, D. A.: test, 1523, 1524, 1526, 2999
Andrews, J. V.: rev, 273, 855, 2664
Annis, H. M.: test, 903, 1345, 1346, 2466
Ansley, T. N.: test, 1359, 1364
Ansorge, C. J.: rev, 595
Anthony, J.: test, 1059, 1060
Anton, W. D.: test, 604, 990
Antoni, M.: test, 1723
Apel, K.: test, 2525
Apfel, N. H.: test, 1306
Appl, D. J.: rev, 1685
APR Testing Services: test, 872
Arbisi, P. A.: rev, 288, 1225, 1789, 2017, 2083, 2358, 2421, 2474, 2584
Archambault, F. X., Jr.: rev, 1780, 2701
Archer, D.: test, 743, 2147
Archer, P.: test, 814
Archer, R. P.: rev, 1742; test, 1741
Arditti, J. A.: rev, 39
Arena, J.: test, 797, 2219, 2222, 2959

Bloxom, B. M.: rev, 2471, 2474
Blum, L. H.: test, 660
Blum, M.: test, 1577
Blumenthal, J. A.: rev, 1457
Boatwright, B. S.: test, 570, 571
Bobish, T. P.: test, 1958
Bochna, C. R.: rev, 1104
Bock, S. J.: test, 191
Bodden, J. L.: rev, 426, 427, 1466
Boder, E.: test, 346
Bodey, W.: test, 834
Boehm, A. E.: rev, 370, 371, 1260; test, 347, 348, 599
Boer, D. P.: test, 2446
Boggs, S. R.: test, 909
Bohan, K.: rev, 2518
Bohan, K. J.: rev, 1737
Bolen, L. M.: rev, 1768, 2809
Boliek, C. A.: rev, 327, 1734
Boll, T.: test, 491
Boll, T. J.: test, 2455
Boller, F.: test, 2439
Bologna, N. B.: rev, 728, 845, 1766, 1786
Bolser, C.: test, 682
Bolton, B.: rev, 156, 292, 401, 1357, 2982; test, 988, 2975, 2984
Bolton, B. F.: rev, 1718, 2019, 2464, 2471, 2474, 2805
Bolton, D. L.: rev, 429, 1437, 2793
Bond, G. L.: rev, 906
Bond, N. A., Jr.: test, 911
Bonner, M.: rev, 291, 572, 1427
Bonner, S.: rev, 13, 327
Bonta, J.: test, 1525
Bonta, J. L.: test, 1523, 1524, 1526
Bookbinder, G. E.: test, 2334
Booker, I. A.: rev, 1816, 1817
Boone, D. R.: rev, 352
Booth, S. B.: test, 1277, 1278
Boothroyd, R. A.: rev, 364, 521, 736, 822, 1170, 1418, 1762, 1940, 2440
Bordin, E. S.: rev, 223, 953, 1355, 2576, 2768
Borgen, F. H.: rev, 379, 2595, 2842; test, 1739, 2477
Borko, H.: rev, 2818, 2917
Borman, C.: rev, 340, 1868
Borman, W. C.: rev, 1586, 2317
Bornstein, R. A.: rev, 800, 805, 806, 1734, 2111
Boroda, A.: rev, 279, 2204
Borofsky, G. L.: test, 995
Borreca, C.: test, 2944
Borstelmann, L. J.: rev, 1134
Bortner, M.: rev, 3, 763, 1705, 2233, 2531, 2903, 2904
Borum, R.: test, 2582
Botwin, M. D.: rev, 130, 1819
Bouchard, T. J., Jr.: rev, 278, 877, 2471, 2474
Boucher, J.: test, 2762
Bountress, N. G.: rev, 1538
Bouwkamp, J. C.: rev, 1046, 2472
Bowers, J. E.: rev, 647

Bowers, L.: test, 2763, 2961
Bowling Green State University: test, 2647
Boyatzis, R.: test, 974
Boyatzis, R. E.: test, 63, 1505
Boyce, B. A.: rev, 131, 2085
Boyle, G. J.: rev, 188, 281, 1332, 1383, 1448, 1534, 1928, 2023, 2029, 2306, 2312, 2671, 2828
Boyle, J.: test, 931
Boyle, J. D.: rev, 1200, 1795
Boyles, E. K.: rev, 365, 2239
Boys, M.: test, 1916
Braaten, S.: test, 313, 1467
Bracken, B. A.: rev, 516, 2184, 2188, 2286, 2911; test, 354, 355, 356, 570, 571, 572, 573, 1780, 2841
Braden, J. P.: rev, 236, 727, 1420, 1891, 2202, 2903, 2904, 2911
Bradford, E. G.: rev, 1102
Bradford, E. J. G.: rev, 2452
Bradley, J. M.: rev, 2782
Bradley, P.: test, 401, 756, 2034
Bradley, R. H.: rev, 1134; test, 1260
Bradley-Johnson, S.: test, 199, 594
Brady, J. P.: test, 928, 929
Brady, M.: test, 1390
Brady, R. P.: test, 894, 2058, 2972, 3002
Bramson, R. M.: test, 1316
Brandt, J.: test, 1264, 2696
Brandt, P.: test, 2011
Brannigan, G. G.: test, 327
Braskamp, L. A.: test, 1905
Braswell, J.: rev, 2785
Braun, J. R.: rev, 2201
Bray, G. B.: test, 1363
Brayfield, A. H.: rev, 886
Brazelton, T. B.: test, 1820
Brazier-Carter, P.: rev, 1106
Breecher, S. V. A.: test, 2389
Bresnick, B.: test, 814
Brewer, J. H.: test, 332, 2631
Brickenkamp, R.: test, 785
Bricker, D.: test, 131, 132, 198
Bricklin, B.: rev, 957; test, 17, 359, 889, 1262, 1937, 1943, 1984
Bridges, A. F.: test, 1230
Bridges, D.: test, 2998
Bridges, W.: test, 1909
Briere, J.: test, 597, 822, 1343, 1791, 2828, 2829, 2830
Brigance, A. H.: test, 369
Briggs, K. C.: test, 1801, 1802
Briggs, S.: test, 2499
Briggs-Gowan, M. J.: test, 1372
Brighouse, A.: test, 2061
Brimer, M. A.: rev, 1813
Bringsjord, E. L.: rev, 393, 1478
Brinkman, J. J.: rev, 400, 1729
Brinkman, J. J., Jr.: rev, 172, 1417, 1824, 2307
Britton, G.: test, 1800

Burrows, R. D.: rev, 2023
Burson, S. L., Jr.: rev, 42
Burstein, A. G.: rev, 2299, 2899, 2903, 2904
Burt, C.: rev, 2538
Burt, M. K.: test, 336
Burton, S. D.: test, 838
Busch, J. C.: rev, 2387, 2576
Busch-Rossnagel, N. A.: rev, 507, 1058, 2775
Bush, B. R.: rev, 381
Buss, A. H.: test, 133
Busse, R. T.: rev, 32
Butcher, J. N.: rev, 2471, 2474; test, 390, 1741, 1742
Butler, J. K., Jr.: rev, 1686, 2663
Butler, K. G.: rev, 210, 2279, 2520, 2844
Butler, M. A.: rev, 492, 2846
Butler, R. J.: test, 2410
Butt, D. S.: rev, 1378, 1379
Butterworth, B.: test, 913
Byrd, J. L.: test, 761
Byrd, R. E.: test, 761, 1763
Byrne, L. M. T.: test, 1546
Byrne, M. C.: rev, 1111, 1147, 1474
Bzoch, K. R.: test, 2248

Caballero, J. A.: test, 1278
Cahen, L. S.: rev, 584
Caldarella, P.: test, 1258
Calder, A.: test, 1051
Caldwell, B. M.: test, 1260
Calfee, K. H.: rev, 599
Calfee, R.: rev, 1123
Calfee, R. C.: rev, 2244
Caliper: test, 405
Callahan, C. M.: rev, 246, 349, 396, 1138, 1139, 1434, 1436, 1437, 1451, 2384, 2650, 2814; test, 2349
Caltabiano, L. F.: rev, 2056, 2301
Camara, W.: rev, 2985
Camara, W. J.: rev, 259, 783, 2324, 2331, 2963, 2982
The Cambridge Stratford Study Skills Institute: test, 1952, 2644
Cambridge, The Adult Education Company: test, 1294, 1295, 1545
Cameron, A.: test, 1575, 2979, 2980
Cameron, C.: test, 2825
Camp, B. W.: rev, 343, 1305, 2352
Camp, C. J.: rev, 213, 1118, 2134, 2508
Camp, L.: test, 1869
Campbell, A.: test, 1020
Campbell, B. A.: test, 2054
Campbell, C. J.: test, 526
Campbell, D.: rev, 137, 1606; test, 410, 411, 412, 413
Campbell, D. P.: rev, 1188, 1755, 2576
Campbell, E. M.: test, 2630
Campbell, I. A.: rev, 2861
Campbell, J. A.: rev, 42, 102, 539, 1128
Campbell, J. T.: rev, 1270, 1490
Campbell, M. H.: rev, 654, 903, 1265, 2285

Campbell, R.: test, 2467
Campbell, R. A.: test, 498
Campbell, S. K.: test, 2739
Campbell, T. F.: rev, 1400
Campion, M. A.: test, 2687
Canadian Test Centre: test, 414
Canadian Test Centre, Educational Assessment Services: test, 415, 418
Cancelli, A. A.: rev, 2269
Canfield, A. A.: test, 1466, 1511
Canivez, G. L.: rev, 70, 1766, 2354, 2899
Capt, B.: test, 198
Capute, A. J.: test, 420
Carbo, M.: test, 659, 2091
Carbonell, J. L.: rev, 2623
Cardall, A. J.: test, 421
Career Cruising: test, 438
Career Kids: test, 448
Carey, K.: rev, 1308, 1963
Carey, K. T.: rev, 2, 199, 449, 459, 518, 665, 918, 1101, 2876
Carey, W. B.: test, 450
Carini, R. M.: test, 1812
Carlson, C.: rev, 1055, 2344
Carlson, C. I.: rev, 1060, 1716, 1947, 1985
Carlson, E.: test, 80
Carlson, E. B.: test, 891
Carlson, J.: rev, 20, 21
Carlson, J. E.: rev, 1894
Carlson, J. F.: rev, 84, 884, 288, 494, 496, 790, 1256, 1493, 1984, 2281, 2284, 2557, 2974
Carlson, J. V.: rev, 19, 1081, 1840, 1938, 2329, 2976
Carlson, K. A.: rev, 749; test, 452
Carlson, R. D.: rev, 2108
Carlson, T. R.: rev, 2375
Carmer, J. C.: rev, 1659, 2358, 2617
Carney, A. E.: rev, 942
Carney, C. G.: test, 431
Carney, I.: test, 1267
Carney, R. N.: rev, 1356, 1438, 1684, 2232, 2345, 2537, 2562, 2998
Carpenter, B. A.: test, 1138
Carpenter, C. D.: rev, 210, 372, 1146, 1197, 1326, 1427, 1469, 1712, 2503, 2542, 2544, 2713
Carpenter, D.: rev, 1899
Carpenter, L. J.: test, 727
Carr, S. J.: rev, 2346
Carrington Rotto, P.: rev, 2474
Carroll, B.: test, 456
Carroll, D. J.: rev, 324; test, 949
Carroll, J. B.: rev, 877, 1094, 1289
Carrow-Woolfolk, E.: test, 686, 1898, 1899, 2707
Carswell, J.: test, 1484
Carter, A.: rev, 400, 1729
Carter, A. S.: test, 1372
Carter, H. D.: rev, 1355, 2576
Carter, S.: test, 2634

Clark, E.: rev, 172, 785, 827, 1548, 2784, 2930, 2945
Clark, G. M.: test, 2823
Clark, J. L. D.: rev, 1004
Clark, J. N.: rev, 720, 849, 1953, 2110
Clark, L. A.: test, 2359
Clark, M. L.: rev, 2159, 2161
Clark, P. M.: rev, 1497, 2755, 2800
Clark, R. M.: rev, 759, 2932
Clark, S. G.: test, 1361, 1362
Clark-Chiarelli, N.: test, 928
Clarke, B. L.: rev, 2294
Clausen-May, T.: test, 1854
Claydon, H.: test, 1854
Cleeton, G. U.: rev, 421
Cleeton, L.: rev, 318, 916
Cleland, D. L.: rev, 526
Clemence, A. J.: rev, 740, 2567
Cleminshaw, H. K.: test, 1949
Clendenen, D. M.: rev, 2576
Clerehugh, J.: test, 943
Clifford, P. A.: test, 1729
Clifford, R. M.: test, 923, 1057, 1308
Cloninger, C. J.: test, 510
Clonts, W. L.: test, 2949
Clopton, J. R.: rev, 1929, 2101, 2893, 2894
CNS Vital Signs: test, 588
Coan, R.: rev, 1802
Coan, R. N.: rev, 1257, 1801
Coan, R. W.: rev, 2006, 2868; test, 938
Cobb, H. C.: rev, 24, 25, 26
Cochran, L.: rev, 736, 1872, 1959, 1980, 2411, 2878
Cochrane, R.: test, 2090
Cockburn, J.: test, 319, 2293
Cockburn, J. M.: test, 2292
Codding, K. G.: test, 2744
Coddington, R. D.: test, 592
Coetzee, T. M.: test, 177
Cofer, C. N.: rev, 1100, 2306
Coffman, W. E.: rev, 605, 1420, 2580
Cohen, A. J.: rev, 1200, 1614, 1798, 2354, 2721, 2722
Cohen, B. D.: rev, 971, 2072
Cohen, D. A.: rev, 252, 353, 588, 1027, 2278, 2308
Cohen, G.: test, 2181
Cohen, G. M.: test, 2183
Cohen, H.: test, 2667
Cohen, I. L.: test, 1963
Cohen, J.: rev, 2298, 2818, 2832
Cohen, L. G.: rev, 921, 1293, 1620, 2737
Cohen, M. J.: test, 500
Cohen, N. H.: test, 2128
Cohen, S. A.: rev, 2788
Cohen, S. L.: rev, 2332
Cohen, S. P.: test, 2118
Cohn, S. J.: rev, 647, 690, 1164, 1318
Coladarci, T.: rev, 1258, 1514, 1690, 2376, 2419
Colarusso, R.: test, 1767
Colarusso, R. P.: test, 1766

Colby, A.: test, 1452, 1653
Cole, C. W.: test, 2529, 2704
Cole, D. E.: rev, 97, 1937
Cole, N. S.: rev, 1671
Cole, P.: test, 888
Coleman, C. A.: test, 1528
Coleman, M.: rev, 1115, 2418
Collard, R. R.: rev, 284
The College Board: test, 22, 628, 629, 630, 631, 632, 633, 634, 635, 636, 637, 638, 639, 640, 641, 642, 643, 644, 645, 646, 647, 648, 649
College Board and National Merit Scholarship Corporation: test, 2098
College Entrance Examination Board: test, 2099
Collins, C.: rev, 23, 895, 2441, 2631
Collins, D.: rev, 227
Collison, B. B.: rev, 2703
Coltheart, M.: test, 2186
Colvin, R. J.: test, 2236
Colwell, R.: rev, 1321; test, 1795
Commins, W. D.: rev, 1736, 1844, 2850
Commission on Professional Development of the Accrediting Association of Bible Colleges: test, 2533
Committee on the American Mathematics Competitions: test, 1625
Comrey, A. L.: rev, 224, 1983; test, 705, 706
Conder, R. L., Jr.: test, 702
Cone, J. D.: test, 1941, 2203
Coney, R., III: test, 2367
Conger, J.: rev, 1984
Conger, J. C.: rev, 2501, 2897
Connard, P.: test, 199
Conners, C. K.: test, 716, 717, 718, 719, 720, 721, 722, 723
Connolly, A. J.: test, 1433
Connolly, P. M.: test, 520
Conoley, C.: rev, 1779, 1897
Conoley, C. W.: rev, 288, 466, 887, 1310, 1455, 2617
Conoley, J. C.: rev, 1693
Conrad, H. S.: rev, 2789
Consortium on Reading Excellence: test, 196
Consortium to Establish a Registry for Alzheimer's Disease: test, 462
Constantine, N. A.: rev, 1308, 1794
Constantino, J. N.: test, 2498
Constantino, L.: test, 1041
Conway, F.: rev, 2498, 2923
Conway, N.: test, 2522
Cook, A. S.: rev, 568, 753
Cook, D. R.: test, 1331
Cook, J.: rev, 1193
Cook, R. S.: test, 1128, 1131
Cook, W. W.: rev, 2537
Cook-Cottone, C.: rev, 1634
Cook-Cottone, C. P.: rev, 459, 1696, 2759
Cooke, D. K.: rev, 1479, 2647
Cooke, N.: rev, 172
Cooke, R.: test, 206

Drews, J. E.: test, 2112
Dreyer, L. G.: test, 1123
Dreyer, P. H.: rev, 95, 1058
Dreyfus, D.: test, 269
Drinka, T. J. K.: test, 213
Droege, R. C.: rev, 1095, 2950
Droegemueller, L.: rev, 1447
Droppleman, L. F.: test, 2145
Druckman, J. M.: test, 2102
Drum, P. A.: rev, 1125, 2777
Drummond, R. J.: rev, 140, 446, 1710, 1512, 1670, 1840, 2553
Drummond, S. S.: test, 912
Drumwright, A. F.: test, 810
Druva-Roush, C. A.: rev, 824, 1082, 2888
Dubno, J. R.: rev, 237
Dubois, D. D.: test, 673, 828
DuBois, L. M.: rev, 807, 1534
DuBois, P. H.: rev, 647, 1671
DuCette, J.: test, 1800
Duckitt, J.: rev, 1338, 1518
Dugbartey, A. T.: rev, 352, 804, 1033, 1825
Duggins, L. A.: rev, 1143
Duke, L. M.: test, 353
Duke, M.: test, 909
Dulay, H. C.: test, 336
Dumas, J. E.: test, 2491
Dunbar, S. B.: rev, 2170; test, 1363, 2211
Duncan, S. E.: test, 89, 1468, 1469, 2097
Dunkel, H. B.: rev, 612, 634, 639
Dunlap, D.: test, 2342, 2344
Dunlap, J. W.: rev, 1688
Dunn, C.: test, 2363
Dunn, D. M.: test, 1966
Dunn, J. A.: rev, 1149
Dunn, K.: test, 1019, 1507, 2139
Dunn, L. M.: test, 375, 1966, 2706
Dunn, R.: test, 1507, 1509, 2139, 2429
Dunn, T. M.: rev, 723, 998, 2291, 2459, 2588, 2932
Dunn, W.: test, 72, 2430
Dunnette, M. D.: rev, 2950
Dunst, C. J.: rev, 284, 830, 1970
DuPaul, G. J.: test, 66
Dupuis, M. M.: rev, 1616
Dupuy, P. J.: rev, 2407, 2975
Durand, V. M.: test, 1762
Durrell, D. D.: test, 906
Dusewicz, R. A.: test, 884
Dush, D. M.: rev, 1257
Dutch, R. D.: rev, 1196
duToit, L. B. H.: test, 1405
Duyar, I.: rev, 1572
Dwinell, P. L.: rev, 1189
Dwyer, C. A.: rev, 2956
Dye, D. A.: test, 2175
Dyer, C. O.: rev, 1843, 1917
Dyer, H. S.: rev, 1688

Dykes, M. K.: test, 831
Dykstra, R.: rev, 1691

Eagle, N.: rev, 1886
Ealy, M.: test, 2692
Earnest, M. M.: test, 2116
Eash, M. J.: rev, 525; test, 1918
Eastin, D.: test, 2521
Eaton, S.: test, 910
Eaves, D.: test, 1090, 1225, 2530
Eaves, R. C.: test, 2482
Ebel, R. L.: rev, 1671, 2537, 2732
Eberhardt, B. J.: rev, 1389, 2467
Eberhardt, D.: rev, 2873
Eck, T.: rev, 1350
Ecker, C.: test, 2427, 2428
Eckstein Bros., Inc.: test, 947
Edelman, N.: test, 814
Eder, K.: rev, 286
Edgeworth, J. A.: test, 252
Edson, A.: test, 1312
Education Associates: test, 1391
Educational & Industrial Test Services Ltd.: test, 1079, 1313, 1607, 1977
The Educational Institute of Scotland: test, 949
Educational Records Bureau: test, 696, 1016, 1296
Educational Resources, Inc.: test, 1247
Educational Testing Service: test, 99, 100, 101, 102, 103, 104, 105, 106, 107, 108, 109, 110, 111, 112, 113, 114, 115, 116, 117, 118, 119, 120, 121, 122, 123, 124, 125, 126, 127, 527, 528, 529, 530, 531, 532, 533, 534, 535, 536, 537, 538, 539, 540, 541, 542, 543, 544, 545, 546, 547, 548, 549, 550, 551, 552, 553, 554, 555, 556, 557, 558, 559, 560, 606, 607, 608, 609, 610, 611, 612, 613, 614, 615, 616, 617, 618, 619, 620, 621, 622, 623, 624, 625, 626, 627, 628, 629, 630, 631, 632, 633, 634, 635, 636, 637, 638, 639, 640, 641, 642, 643, 644, 645, 646, 647, 648, 649 , 651, 1020, 1159, 1160, 1161, 1162, 1163, 1164, 1165, 1166, 1167, 1168, 1169, 1564, 2094, 2098, 2099, 2150, 2338, 2370, 2391, 2519, 2596, 2733
Edwards, A. J.: rev, 477, 2716
Edwards, A. L.: rev, 402, 956; test, 953
Edwards, C.: rev, 2417
Edwards, C. D.: test, 2556
Edwards, C. I.: rev, 2283
Edwards, C. N.: rev, 661; test, 2469
Edwards, J. M.: test, 1002
Edwards, R.: rev, 596, 2535, 2737; test, 73, 148
Edwards, S.: test, 2849
Efron, C.: test, 2055
Egan, D. F.: test, 954
Egeland, B.: rev, 2945, 2946
Egeland, B. R.: rev, 274, 660
Ehrler, D. J.: test, 879, 1091, 2127
Ehrlich, J.: rev, 2302
Eichman, W. J.: rev, 2145

Huba, M. E.: rev, 2236
Hubchen, K.: test, 1910
Hubert, E. E.: test, 1519
Hubley, A. M.: rev, 213, 310, 329, 367, 404, 1116, 1360, 1451, 1546, 1815, 2610; test, 1677
Hubly, S.: test, 2993
Hudson, J. P., Jr.: rev, 1559, 2915
Huebner, E. S.: rev, 174, 839, 1254, 1645, 2012, 2384, 2407, 2905
Hufano, L.: rev, 1638
Hughes, B.: test, 2521
Hughes, C. M.: test, 2630
Hughes, J. E.: test, 1273
Hughes, J. N.: rev, 745, 1507, 1973
Hughes, S.: rev, 786, 814
Hughson, E. A.: test, 62
Huijnen, M. A. H.: test, 1845
Huisingh, R.: test, 2763, 2961
Hulin, C. L.: test, 1386, 2268
Hulme, C.: test, 2046
Human Resources Center, The University of Chicago: test, 2656, 2957
Human Resources Development Press, Inc.: test, 2021
Human Sciences Research Council: test, 2423
Human Synergistics: test, 1576, 2627
Human Synergistics International: test, 1996, 2571
Human Technology, Inc.: test, 1990, 2679
Humphreys, G. W.: test, 342
Humphreys, L. G.: rev, 328, 1706, 2657, 877
Hundert, J.: rev, 2155
Hunsicker, A. L.: rev, 137, 1606
Hunt, B. A.: test, 1595
Hunt, F. M.: test, 2698
Hunt, J. A.: test, 1745
Hunt, J. V.: rev, 839, 1638, 2483
Hunt, R. A.: test, 1352, 1745
Hunt, T.: rev, 1736
Hunt, W. A.: rev, 2452
Hunter, C.: rev, 1149
Hunter, G. W.: rev, 1133
Hunter-Grundin, E.: test, 1280
Huntley, M.: test, 1182
Hurford, D. P.: rev, 579, 694, 802, 1098, 1253, 2050, 2103, 2248, 2730, 2746, 2844
Husek, T. R.: rev, 1460
Hutcheson, C.: test, 1510
Hutchings, E. M. J.: test, 949
Hutchings, M. J.: test, 949
Hutchins, T. L.: rev, 1541, 2590
Hutchinson, S. M.: rev, 526
Hutchinson, T. A.: test, 2992
Huttenlocher, J.: test, 2126
Hutton, J. B.: test, 2492
Hutzell, R. R.: rev, 1334
Hyman, I. A.: test, 1800
Hynd, G. W.: rev, 2578

The IDEA Center: test, 1283, 1284
Iglesias, A.: test, 2658
Iliffe, A.: test, 128, 2154
Illback, R. J.: rev, 1188, 1497
Ilmer, S.: test, 940
Imhoff, B.: test, 2757
Impara, J. C.: rev, 2157, 2158, 2172
Inatsuka, T. T.: test, 1239
Inchaurralde, C.: rev, 293, 1399, 1435, 2107, 2757
Industrial Psychology International, Ltd.: test, 1366, 2987, 2988
Ingram, D. E.: test, 241
Ingram-LeBlanc, C.: test, 2718
Innovative Training Systems, Inc.: test, 64
InQ Educational Materials, Inc.: test, 1315, 1604
Inscape Publishing, Inc.: test, 887, 888
Insel, E.: test, 1312
Insel, P. N.: test, 2967
The Institute for Behavioral Research in Creativity: test, 340, 952, 2601
Integrated Teaching Team: test, 1326
International Assessment Network: test, 1608
International Association of Administrative Professionals: test, 1880
International Public Management Association for Human Resources: test, 1, 71, 249, 391, 392, 784, 958, 1838, 1923, 1925, 1926, 2063, 2168, 2176, 2177, 2260, 2437
International Testing and Training Programs, Educational Testing Service: test, 2769
Inwald, R.: test, 1250, 1251, 1357, 1358
Inwald, R. E.: test, 1249, 1252
Iona, M.: rev, 118
IPAT Staff: test, 1477, 2473
Ireton, H.: test, 476, 920, 1305, 2111
Ireton, H. R.: test, 475
Ironson, G. H.: test, 2567
Irwin, J. L.: test, 1386
Irwin, J. V.: test, 1528
Isaksen, S. G.: test, 2468, 2857
Isenberg, D. P.: test, 2195
Isenhart, C.: rev, 711, 1208, 1603, 1615, 1708, 1774, 1967, 2572
Ishihara, S.: test, 2708
Isonio, S.: rev, 2403
Isquith, P. K.: test, 303, 304, 305, 306, 2668
Itskowitz, R.: test, 255
Itzkovich, M.: test, 1548
Ivani-Chalian, R.: test, 2293
Ivens, S. H.: rev, 595, 1706, 2845, 2896
Iverson, A. M.: rev, 474, 1057, 1308
Iverson, G. L.: test, 2946
Iverson, V. S.: test, 510
Ives, M.: rev, 2452
Iwanicki, E. F.: rev, 865, 866, 867, 868, 869
Izard, J.: test, 30
Izard, J. F.: test, 1628

Jackson, D. N.: rev, 1244, 1648, 1658; test, 189, 272, 433, 883, 997, 1374, 1375, 1484, 1492, 1777, 1846, 2028, 2032, 2459, 2460, 2461, 2470, 2646
Jackson, M. T.: test, 87
Jackson, P.: test, 2166
Jackson, S. E.: test, 1618
Jacobs, E. V.: test, 2364
Jacobs, G.A.: test, 2555
Jacoby, J.: test, 1600
Jaeger, J.: test, 1033
Jaeger, R. M.: rev, 1164, 1294, 2956
James, L. R.: test, 708
James, M.: test, 752, 2869
Jameson, M. M.: rev, 2507
Jamison, C. B.: rev, 2274
Janoson, M.: rev, 1201, 1323, 1711
Jansing, C.: rev, 46
Jarosewich, T.: test, 1140
Jarrico, S.: test, 346
Jasper, B. W.: test, 2997
Javorsky, D. J.: test, 353
Jaynes, P. A.: rev, 269
Jeanneret, P. R.: test, 1380, 2079, 2140, 2978
Jeanrie, C.: rev, 1038, 1082, 2173, 2332, 2825
Jeffree, D. M.: test, 1960, 2062
Jeffrey, T. E.: test, 585, 586, 1341, 1665, 1987, 2509, 2510
Jellen, H. G.: test, 2709
Jelm, J. M.: test, 1901
Jenkins, J.: rev, 148, 1184
Jenkins, J. A.: rev, 35, 66, 441, 1043, 1209, 1228, 1304, 1475, 1526, 1710, 1715, 1793, 1860, 2470, 2671, 2786, 2990
Jenkins, J. M.: test, 1509
Jennings, J. R.: rev, 28
Jennings, K. E.: rev, 378, 2136
Jensen, A. R.: rev, 1059, 1060, 1566, 2095, 2299, 2796
Jensen, D.: test, 1890
Jensen, J.: rev, 1794
Jensen, J. L.: rev, 2366
Jensen, M. P.: test, 512, 2642
Jeske, P. J.: rev, 2059
Jesness, C. F.: rev, 846; test, 1378, 1379
Jirsa, J. E.: rev, 60
JIST Publishing, Inc.: test, 1856, 1857
Johansson, C. B.: test, 426, 427, 1288
Johns, E.: test, 1244
Johns, J. L.: test, 273, 2515
Johns, P.: test, 832
Johnsen, L. A.: rev, 2911
Johnsen, S. K.: test, 2384, 2748, 2755
Johnson, C.: test, 1754, 2993
Johnson, C. C.: test, 1400
Johnson, C. M.: rev, 146, 1798; test, 594
Johnson, D.: test, 269, 716
Johnson, D. L.: rev, 2248
Johnson, F. R.: test, 873

Johnson, J.: rev, 398, 498, 2727, 2909; test, 198, 793
Johnson, J. A.: rev, 2538
Johnson, K. M.: rev, 15, 262, 916, 1123, 1443, 2246, 2502, 2901
Johnson, M. S.: rev, 526
Johnson, N. W.: test, 921
Johnson, P.: test, 2893
Johnson, P. O.: rev, 42, 642
Johnson, R.: rev, 966, 1342, 1836, 2478, 2801; test, 793
Johnson, R. H.: test, 2671
Johnson, R. L.: rev, 1019, 2703
Johnson, R. T.: rev, 155, 701
Johnson, R. W.: rev, 251, 432, 1999, 2208, 2330, 2576
Johnson, S. B.: rev, 1397, 1904, 2117, 2460
Johnson, S. T.: rev, 1550
Johnson-Gros, K. N.: rev, 285, 2246
Johnson-Lewis, S.: rev, 885, 2390
Johnson-Martin, N. M.: test, 453
Johnston, I. C.: test, 2160
Johnston, J. A.: rev, 2881
Johnston, J. R.: rev, 2844, 2908, 2939, 2995
Johnston, M. C.: test, 1398
Joines, R. C.: test, 781, 1130, 2626, 2983
Jolles, I.: test, 1272
Jolly, J. B.: test, 291
Jones, B. W.: rev, 254, 2271
Jones, C.: rev, 2303
Jones, C. F.: rev, 297
Jones, D.: rev, 1181
Jones, D. L.: rev, 2065
Jones, E. L.: rev, 832, 1318, 2568
Jones, H. E.: rev, 1758
Jones, J. A.: rev, 1509
Jones, J. E.: test, 1401, 1908, 2680
Jones, J. W.: test, 483
Jones, K.: rev, 2500
Jones, K. M.: rev, 68, 261, 297, 299, 1757, 2280
Jones, P.: test, 1959
Jones, R. A.: rev, 584
Jones, R. L.: rev, 634; test, 1890
Jones, S.: test, 2944
Jones, W. H.: test, 2499
Jordan, A. C.: test, 650
Jordan, B. T.: test, 1402
Jorstad, H. L.: rev, 632
Joseph, J.: test, 1403, 1404
Josman, N.: test, 2810
Joubert, M.: test, 1337, 2374
Judd-Safian Asssociates: test, 2033
Juhnke, G. A.: rev, 190
Jungeblut, A.: test, 1020
Juni, S.: rev, 390, 819, 891, 955, 1357, 1819, 2025, 2411, 2456, 2662
Jupp, J. J.: rev, 2213
Juran Institute: test, 2206
Jurgensen, C. E.: rev, 2273, 2625, 2839
Jurs, S.: rev, 1279, 1641, 2399, 2994

Kabacoff, R. I.: test, 171, 1298, 1485, 1995
Kade, H. D.: rev, 1091, 2022, 2920
Kadish, R.: test, 2508
Kaemmer, B.: test, 1741, 1742
Kagan, J: test, 1621
Kagee, A.: rev, 91, 738, 945, 1226, 1772, 1846, 2448, 2916
Kahn, J. H.: test, 2188
Kaiser, C. F.: test, 1793
Kaiser, J.: rev, 951, 2139, 2726
Kaiser, R. B.: test, 1494
Kalfers, W. V.: rev, 1811
Kaminski, R. A.: test, 874
Kamphaus, R. W.: rev, 153, 154, 274, 855, 1338, 1356, 1691, 2483; test, 261, 262, 297, 1948, 2286, 2743
Kane, H.: rev, 1373, 2292, 2772
Kane, H. D.: rev, 1108, 1417
Kane, M.: rev, 1223, 2783
Kantamneni, N.: rev, 2576
Kanungo, R. N.: rev, 2967
Kao, C.: rev, 508
Kao, C. W.: rev, 2955
Kapel, D. E.: rev, 510, 951
Kaplan, B.: test, 2479
Kaplan, B. J.: rev, 687, 1781, 2081, 2272, 2281, 2671
Kaplan, D. M.: rev, 76, 895
Kaplan, E.: test, 352, 353, 403, 404, 804, 1417, 1698, 2886, 2904
Kaplan, M. S.: rev, 1149
Kaplan, R. E.: test, 1494, 2479
Kaplan, R. M.: rev, 1232
Kaplan Press: test, 1498
Karabenick, S. A.: rev, 1338
Karchmer, M. A.: test, 1644
Karlsen, B.: test, 88, 2541
Karlson, K. W.: test, 2840
Karno, M.: rev, 1878, 2500
Karoly, P.: test, 1778, 2642
Karp, S. A.: test, 1187
Kasdon, L. M.: rev, 274, 2541
Katkin, E. S.: rev, 2555
Katkovsky, W.: rev, 1517
Katoff, L.: test, 1431
Katz, I. S.: rev, 690, 1525, 1949, 2530, 2674
Katz, M. M.: test, 1418
Katz, M. R.: rev, 2576
Katz, N.: test, 1548
Katzell, R. A.: rev, 758, 2054, 2273, 2319
Katzenmeyer, W. G.: test, 2412
Kauffman, D. F.: rev, 2030
Kauffman, G. B.: rev, 47
Kaufman, A. S.: rev, 235, 279, 377, 660, 691, 1305, 2952; test, 940, 1419, 1420, 1421, 1423, 1425, 1426, 1427
Kaufman, C. C.: test, 2942, 2943
Kaufman, H.: test, 1422, 1424
Kaufman, H. A.: test, 1601
Kaufman, M.: test, 1278

Kaufman, N. L.: rev, 235, 377, 691, 1135, 1305, 1639; test, 940, 1419, 1420, 1421, 1423, 1425, 1426, 1427
Kauk, B.: test, 1041
Kauk, R.: test, 186, 435, 1388, 1389, 2873
Kaulfers, W. V.: rev, 632
Kavale, K. A.: rev, 485
Kavan, M. G.: rev, 281, 494, 573, 773, 990, 1612, 1793, 2023, 2092, 2180, 2254, 2282, 2421, 2611
Kay, G. G.: test, 601, 2945
Kay, J.: test, 2186
Kay, S. R.: test, 2081
Keating, T. J.: rev, 2233, 2531
Keats, J. A.: rev, 877
Keefe, J. W.: test, 684, 1509
Keegan, W. J.: test, 1428
Keene, J. M., Jr.: rev, 2784
Keeny, D. T.: rev, 487
Kegel-Flom, P.: rev, 1894
Kehle, T. J.: rev, 2184
Kehoe, J. F.: rev, 427, 1596
Keikamp, J.: rev, 57
Keir, G. H.: rev, 1407
Keirsey, D.: test, 1429
Keis, K.: test, 1013, 1319, 1396, 1491, 1506, 2016, 2223, 2331, 2569, 2847
Keith, L. K.: test, 572
Keith, P. B.: rev, 925, 1503, 1840, 2364
Keith, R. W.: test, 235, 2353, 2354
Keith, T. Z.: rev, 376, 725, 1264, 1356, 1419, 1845, 2516, 2898
Keller, H. R.: rev, 347, 921, 1174, 2007, 2698, 2887, 3003
Keller, J. M.: test, 1022
Kellers, P.: rev, 1964
Kelley, C.: test, 767
Kelley, E. A.: test, 684
Kelley, K. N.: rev, 1859, 1925
Kelley, M. L.: rev, 32, 133, 166, 296, 1055, 1075, 1943, 2059, 2096, 2612, 2660
Kellogg, C. E.: test, 335
Kelly, D.: rev, 858
Kelly, D. J.: rev, 2093
Kelly, E. J.: test, 880
Kelly, E. L.: rev, 401, 1790, 2028
Kelly, K. R.: rev, 1219, 1561, 2576
Kelly, M. L.: test, 2474
Kelner, S. P.: test, 1483, 1599
Kelner, S. P., Jr.: test, 1910
Kemp, S.: test, 1821
Kendall, E. L.: test, 1692
Kendall, L. M.: test, 1386, 2268
Kendall, W. E.: rev, 2328
Kendrick, D. C.: rev, 2074; test, 1430
Kennedy, J.: test, 1812
Kennedy, J. E.: rev, 1847, 2852, 2957
Kennedy, P. H.: rev, 1280
Kenney, K. W.: rev, 488, 1253

Lykken, D. T.: rev, 746, 1374
Lyman, H. B.: rev, 1965, 1966, 2899
Lynch, D.: test, 358, 753, 1641, 1731
Lynch, E. W.: test, 927, 2112
Lynch, J. I.: rev, 2287, 2433, 2844
Lynch, S.: test, 753
Lyon, L. P.: test, 224, 2942, 2943
Lyons, J. S.: test, 2440
Lyons, T. M.: test, 786

Maas, H. S.: rev, 149
Maas, J. B.: test, 747
Mabey, B.: test, 247
Mabry, L.: rev, 2930
Maccow, G.: rev, 815, 2005, 2352
MacDonald, J.: rev, 576, 1502, 2716
MacDonald, R. B.: test, 2835
Mace, F. C.: rev, 1918
MacGinitie, R. K.: test, 1123, 1124
MacGinitie, W. H.: test, 1123, 1124
Mack, J. L.: test, 461
Mackenzie, R.: test, 949
MacKinney, A. C.: rev, 1095, 2919
Mackler, K.: rev, 726, 1155, 2045, 2277, 2829
Mackrain, M.: test, 849
Macnab, D.: test, 1300, 2974
MacPhee, D.: rev, 1278, 2105, 2112, 2490
Maculaitis, J. D.: test, 1557, 1560
Maddox, T.: test, 274, 833
Maddux, C. D.: rev, 206, 270, 433, 854, 913, 1373, 1539,
    1813, 1917, 2516, 2534, 2714, 2907
Madge, E. M.: test, 1410
Madison, C. L.: test, 1442
Madle, R. A.: rev, 68, 381, 1421, 2105, 2491, 2747,
    2761, 2904, 2911
Maduschke, K. M.: test, 2985
Maehr, M. L.: test, 1905
Maelender, A.: test, 2904
Magner, N. R.: test, 1914
Magoon, T. M.: test, 2190
Magura, S.: test, 480
Mahdavi, J. N.: rev, 936, 1514, 2136, 2616
Mahler, J.: test, 196
Maholick, L. T.: test, 2201
Mahoney, J. J.: test, 2167
Mahoney, J. T.: test, 171, 1298, 1485, 1995, 2323
Mahurin, R. K.: rev, 701, 1183, 1207
Maitlen, B. R.: test, 1299
Majors, M. S.: test, 1802
Makatura, T. J.: rev, 227, 597, 716, 1729, 1826, 2259,
    2291, 2736
Malcolm, K. K.: rev, 240, 348, 370, 371, 696, 745, 851,
    960, 1239, 1898, 1899, 2100, 2114, 2127, 2560
Malgady, R. G.: test, 2697
Maller, S. J.: rev, 418, 2393, 2751, 2903, 2904, 2998
Mallinson, G.: test, 950
Mallinson, G. G.: rev, 558

Mallinson, J.: test, 950
Malloy, P. F.: test, 1108
Maloney, S. E.: test, 2018
Malsbary, D. R.: rev, 2457
Management Research Group Staff: test, 2323
Mancini, J. A.: rev, 1058, 2102
Mandel, H. P.: test, 36, 779, 2315
Mandell, M. M.: rev, 1270
Manduchi, J. R.: rev, 685
Manges, K. J.: rev, 1056
Mangine, S.: test, 2025
Manikam, R.: rev, 80, 2707
Manly, T.: test, 2735
Mann, L.: rev, 301, 845; test, 2482
Manoogian, S.: test, 756
Mansfield, R.: test, 2019
Manson, M. P.: test, 137, 1606, 2922
Manuele, C. A.: rev, 2935
Manuele-Adkins, C.: rev, 1219, 2314, 2405, 2456, 2502,
    2935, 2973
Mar, D. K.: test, 2123, 2875
March, J.: test, 1776
March, J. S.: test, 722
Marchant, G. J.: rev, 1035, 1842, 1940, 2027
Marchese, A. C.: test, 580
Marchman, V. A.: test, 1558
Marco, G. J.: rev, 1522
Marco, G. L.: rev, 1931, 2532
Marcus, L. M.: test, 2185
Marcus, S. I.: test, 36, 779, 2315
Mardell, C.: test, 837
Mardell, C. D.: test, 1953
Mardell-Czudnowski, C.: rev, 2433
Margolis, H.: rev, 801, 1172, 2236, 2616, 2953
Maria, K.: test, 1123
Marjoribanks, J.: test, 2202
Markel-Fox, S.: rev, 741
Markley, R. P.: rev, 2529, 2945, 2946
Markos, J. R.: test, 1076
Markowitz, M.: test, 1974
Markwardt, F. C., Jr.: test, 1965
Marlett, N. J.: test, 62
Marr, H. K.: test, 1967
Marr, M. B.: rev, 960
Marscark, M.: rev, 2351
Marsden, D. B.: test, 939
Marsh, H. W.: test, 2403
Marshall, C. W.: test, 189
Marshall, D.: rev, 2662
Marshall, R. M.: test, 1969
Marston, N. C.: test, 70
Martens, B. K.: rev, 723, 2008
Martin, A. W.: test, 211
Martin, C. W.: rev, 183, 1902
Martin, D. G.: rev, 1257
Martin, F.: test, 1614
Martin, N.: test, 2775

Martin, N. A.: test, 2218, 2721, 2722
Martin, R. P.: rev, 1878
Martin, S. G.: rev, 2584
Martin, T. A.: test, 2452
Martin, W. E., Jr.: rev, 397, 604, 677, 790, 1265, 1083, 1535, 1967, 2000, 2864
Martindale, T.: rev, 2128
Martinez-Pons, M.: rev, 306, 506
Marting, M. S.: test, 736
Marush, M.: test, 2654
Marwitz, J. H.: test, 1824
Maryolf, S. S.: rev, 1463
Maschka, P.: test, 814
Maslach, C.: test, 1618
Massey, T.: test, 973, 2634
Masson, L. I.: test, 2205
Masters, G.: test, 834, 835, 2790
Masterson, J. J.: test, 2525
Mastrangelo, P.: rev, 1815
Mastrangelo, P. M.: rev, 1801, 1802, 1987, 2586
Matarazzo, J. D.: rev, 1430, 1672, 2231
Mathematical Association of America: test, 150, 152, 153, 154
Mathematics Assessment Resource Service: test, 250
Matheny, K. B.: test, 737
Mather, N.: test, 279, 870, 1289, 1631, 2767, 2952, 2953
Mathieu, P. L.: test, 1039
Matthews, A.: test, 2096
Matthews, M. S.: rev, 501, 2348
Mattis, S.: test, 805, 806
Matuszek, P.: rev, 2930
Mauger, P. A.: test, 1334
Maurer, K.: test, 1368
Maurer, M.: test, 2535
Maxfield, F. W.: rev, 2538
Maxwell, J.: rev, 906, 2538
Maxwell, K. L.: test, 216
Maxwell, M. J.: test, 2190
Maxwell, S.: rev, 483
Maydeu-Olivares, A.: test, 2497
Mayer, J. D.: test, 1634
Mayo, C. C.: test, 1892
Mayo, S. T.: rev, 950, 2755
McAlpine, D.: test, 2674
McArthur, C. C.: rev, 2299
McArthur, R.: test, 1274
McBer and Company: test, 590, 1310, 1602
McCabe, P. P.: rev, 1123, 2928
McCall, J. N.: rev, 1151, 1460
McCall, M. W.: test, 2167
McCall, R. J.: rev, 1257, 2299
McCall, W. A.: test, 1636, 2712
McCallum, R. S.: rev, 1966; test, 2841
McCammon, S.: rev, 653
McCampbell, E.: test, 349
McCandless, B. R.: rev, 347, 2224, 2538, 2903, 2904

McCann Associates, Inc.: test, 765, 823, 985, 986, 987, 1080, 1864, 2069
McCarney, S. B.: test, 58, 87, 226, 227, 299, 300, 301, 921, 922, 972, 978, 1139, 1503, 2104, 2113, 2821
McCarron, L.: test, 61, 209, 1986
McCarron, L. T.: test, 37, 973, 1637, 1643, 1867, 2634
McCarron, M. B.: test, 37
McCarthy, B.: test, 2606
McCarthy, D.: test, 1638, 1639
McCarthy, J. J.: rev, 837
McCarthy, K. J.: rev, 81, 749, 901, 1525, 1664, 1770, 2572
McCarty, J. J.: test, 151, 155
McCaul, R. L.: rev, 1246
McCauley, C. D.: test, 1384
McCauley, R.: rev, 194, 493, 1098, 2114, 2386, 2605, 2746, 2758
McCauley, R. J.: rev, 727, 2279
McCaulley, M. H.: test, 1801
McClellan, R. A.: test, 999
McClure, E.: rev, 1183
McCollam, P.: test, 3000
McCollum, D. L.: rev, 2986
McConaughey, S. H.: test, 32
McCone, D.: rev, 1033
McConkey, R.: test, 2062
McConnell, K.: test, 2347, 2348
McConnell, S. R.: rev, 2361
McConney, A. A.: rev, 884
McCormick, E. J.: test, 1380, 2079, 2140, 2978
McCowan, R. J.: rev, 189, 464
McCowan, S. C.: rev, 189, 464
McCoy, W. J.: test, 2641
McCrae, R. R.: rev, 799, 1481; test, 1818, 1819
McCulloch, K.: test, 374, 1813
McCulloch, T. L.: rev, 460
McCullough, C. M.: rev, 650
McCurdy, M.: rev, 58, 201, 2735, 2911
McDaniels, C.: test, 1521
Mullins, S. R.: test, 1521
McDannold, S. B.: test, 2520
McDermott, P. A.: test, 70
McDevitt, S. C.: test, 450
McDonald, S.: test, 248
McDonald-Scott, P.: test, 2358
McDowall, S.: test, 2161
McDowell, P. M.: test, 1640
McDowell, R. L.: test, 1640
McElwain, D. W.: rev, 2273
McEntire, E.: test, 2749
McGaghie, W. C.: rev, 2596
McGauvran, M. E.: test, 937, 1691
McGhee, R.: test, 2780
McGhee, R. L.: test, 879, 1091, 2127
McGinnis, E.: rev, 2009, 2887
McGinty, D.: rev, 1624, 1854, 2543
McGonigle, K. L.: test, 2439
McGreevy, A.: test, 1327

Messer, M.: test, 2931

Messick, S.: test, 946

Metcalf, K.: test, 2521

MetriTech, Inc.: test, 1473

Metzgen, K.: test, 2944

Meyer, D. L.: rev, 1087

Meyer, G. R.: test, 2382

Meyer, H. D.: test, 1692

Meyer, J.: test, 2520

Meyers, J.: test, 767

Meyers, J. E.: test, 2278

Meyers, K. R.: test, 2278

Meyers, M. J.: rev, 797

Mezger, C.: test, 973, 2634

MHS Staff: test, 494, 719, 721, 861

Michael, J. J.: test, 885, 2603

Michael, L. D.: test, 1749, 1750, 1751

Michael, W. B.: rev, 397, 813, 830, 1094, 1463, 1515, 1707, 1733, 1858, 1859, 1868, 1974, 2055, 2172; test, 885, 2603

Michaels, H.: rev, 2364

Michaels, L.: test, 1875

Michaelson, R. B.: test, 1061

Middleton, G.: rev, 2918

Miedaner, J.: test, 1702

Migotsky, C. P.: rev, 2838

Miguel, S. A.: test, 838

Milchus, N. J.: test, 1024, 2214, 2402

MILCOM Systems, A Division of Hollister, Inc.: test, 1703

Miles, C.: test, 2985

Milholland, J. E.: rev, 772, 1364, 1917, 2054

Millar, G.: test, 1649

Miller, C. D.: rev, 1511

Miller, C.: rev, 721, 2810

Miller, D. C.: rev, 157, 881, 1045, 1112, 1734, 1821, 2202, 2310; test, 1440, 1441

Miller, E. N.: test, 395

Miller, G. A.: test, 2613

Miller, G. E.: rev, 1362

Miller, H. A.: test, 1349, 1711

Miller, H. J.: test, 1708, 1709, 1710, 1713, 1714, 1715, 1716, 1717, 1718, 1719, 1720

Miller, J.: test, 2944

Miller, J. A.: test, 582

Miller, J. F.: rev, 575; test, 2658, 2659

Miller, J. K.: rev, 653

Miller, J. M.: rev, 653

Miller, K. M.: test, 1154, 1628, 2303, 2305

Miller, L.: test, 2093

Miller, L. C.: rev, 3, 938, 1747

Miller, L. H.: test, 2013

Miller, L. J.: test, 1088, 1522, 1707, 1712, 2429, 2562, 2809

Miller, M. D.: rev, 313, 653, 749, 828, 1202, 1223, 1284, 1396, 1421, 1662, 2703, 2902

Miller, M. A.: test, 1440, 1441

Miller, P.: test, 753

Miller, R. J.: rev, 65, 228, 1288, 1868, 2238

Miller, S.: test, 753

Miller, T. K.: test, 2595

Miller Kuhaneck, H.: test, 2428

Miller-Whitehead, M.: rev, 935, 1173, 1473, 1813

Millis, S. R.: test, 157

Millman, J.: test, 745

Millon, C: test, 1721, 1723, 1724, 1725, 1727

Millon, T: test, 1721, 1722, 1723, 1724, 1725, 1726, 1727

Mills, C. N.: rev, 368, 1516, 2139

Mills, J.: test, 1200

Mills, J. A.: rev, 979, 1615, 2130, 2573

Milner, J. S.: test, 473

Milone, M.: test, 196, 797, 2738

Miner, J. B.: test, 1732

Minor, S.: test, 1723

Minthon, L.: test, 2225

Mirenda, P.: rev, 162, 191, 245, 814, 2185, 2746, 2944

Mishra, R. K.: rev, 318, 570, 1968, 2282

Mislevy, R. J.: test, 1020

Missouri Department of Elementary and Secondary Education: test, 1748

Mitchell, J.: test, 1274

Mitchell, J. L.: test, 2140

Mitchell, J. V., Jr.: rev, 2842

Mitchell, M. L.: test, 2508

Mitchell-Person, C.: rev, 199, 294

Mithaug, D. E.: test, 2123, 2875

Mittman, A.: rev, 1630

Moats, L. C.: test, 874, 2782

Moersch, M. S.: test, 927, 2112

Mogge, N. L.: test, 1605

Mohr, L.: test, 1401

Moinat, S. M.: test, 2175

Moiser, C. I.: rev, 1270

Mokros, H. B.: test, 495

Molina, H.: rev, 2707

Molinder, I.: test, 1789

Mollenkopf, W. G.: rev, 2681

Monk, J. S.: test, 1509

Monroe, M.: rev, 906; test, 1186

Monsaas, J. A.: rev, 802, 835, 1359, 1473, 2462, 2703, 2727, 2788

Monsen, R.: test, 515

Montag, M.: test, 2535

Montuori, J.: test, 2556

Moog, J. S.: test, 514, 515, 942, 2351, 2523, 2673

Mooney, R. L.: test, 1758

Moore, A. D.: rev, 1491, 2163

Moore, D.: rev, 1433

Moore, G. T.: test, 925

Moore, H. K.: rev, 1800

Moore, J. E.: rev, 758

Moore-Hirschl, S.: test, 2567

Moorhead, A.: test, 1749, 1750

Moos, B. S.: test, 1058, 1531, 1532

Moos, R. H.: test, 525, 672, 738, 749, 1058, 1188, 1226, 1531, 1532, 1679, 1704, 1788, 2842, 2889, 2967

Morales, P.: rev, 294, 2253

Moran, M. R.: rev, 58, 2994

Moravian College: test, 1294, 1295

Moray House Institute of Education: test, 949

Morehead, M. K.: test, 196, 1785

Moreland, K. L.: rev, 731, 799, 1345, 2394, 2431, 2535, 2536, 2537

Moreno, S.: test, 1900, 2217, 2514

Morey, L. C.: test, 2022, 2023, 2024

Morgan, A.: test, 351

Morgan, D. L.: test, 82

Morgan, G.: test, 176

Morgan, G. A. V.: rev, 1363

Morman, R. R.: test, 2669

Morner, C. J.: rev, 54, 1593

Morreale, S.: rev, 490, 930, 2160

Morreale, S. P.: rev, 2726

Morreau, L. E.: test, 470

Morrill, W. H.: test, 436

Morris, E.: test, 1317

Morris, L. A.: test, 1946

Morris, L. B.: test, 2029

Morris, M. L.: test, 2576

Morris, R.: test, 2886, 2904

Morris, S.: test, 505

Morris, T. L.: test, 2495

Morrisby, M.: test, 754

The Morrisby Organisation: test, 1759

Morrison, G. M.: rev, 900, 2787

Morrison, J. D., Jr.: test, 2859

Morrison, L. P.: test, 2671

Morrison, W. L.: test, 1061, 2671

Morrow, R.: test, 744

Morse, D.: rev, 1359, 1794, 1917, 1989

Morse, D. T.: rev, 2537; test, 1436

Morton, J. S.: test, 1895

Morton, N. W.: rev, 328, 2576; test, 335

Morton, R. L.: rev, 182

Morwood, R. G.: rev, 1973

Mos, L. P.: test, 2184

Moseley, D.: test, 2960

Moses, B. S.: test, 480

Mosher, D. L.: rev, 451, 2671

Moshman, D.: rev, 2598

Moss, P. A.: rev, 1295

Mossenson, L.: test, 2790

Mossholder, K. W.: rev, 2411

Mostue, P.: test, 1910

Motowidlo, S. J.: rev, 1592, 2317, 2321

Mount, M. K.: test, 1993

Mowrer, D. E.: rev, 1147, 1435

Moxley, R.: test, 2479

Moye, A. W.: test, 1935

Moyes, I. C. A.: rev, 2121

Moyle, M. J.: rev, 2103

Moynihan, C.: test, 477

Mu Alpha Theta: test, 150, 152, 153, 154

Muchinsky, P. M.: rev, 852, 989, 997, 1011, 1310, 1394, 1572, 2329, 2699

Mueller, J.: test, 593

Mueller, R. O.: rev, 413, 678, 1858, 2407, 2967, 2975

Mueller-Hanson, R.: test, 35

Muench, A. M.: rev, 218

Mufer, V.: test, 2046

Mullen, E. M.: test, 1769

Multi-Health Systems Staff: test, 325

Munday, L. A.: rev, 1478

Munger, A. M.: rev, 762, 2122

Muñoz-Sandoval, A. F.: test, 279, 338, 2955

Munro, J.: test, 194

Munsinger, H. L.: test, 2840

Murdoch, J. W.: rev, 1693

Murphey, J.: rev, 2507, 2833

Murphy, C.: test, 145

Murphy, C. C.: rev, 383

Murphy, E.: test, 1794

Murphy, H. D.: rev, 1094

Murphy, J. A.: rev, 110

Murphy, K. K.: rev, 2755

Murphy, K. R.: rev, 413, 1578, 2878; test, 229

Murray, H. A.: test, 2796

Murray, M.: test, 1890

Murray-Ward, M.: rev, 212, 1104, 1297, 1543, 1816, 1817, 2589, 2743, 2780, 2849, 2956

Murrell, P. H.: test, 669

Murstein, B. L.: rev, 487

Musick, J. E.: test, 1348

Mutti, M.: test, 2218

Mvududu, N. H.: rev, 975, 2262

Myers, C. T.: rev, 2449

Myers, I. B.: test, 1801, 1802

Myers, J. E.: test, 1092, 1887, 2916

Myers, S. S.: rev, 2506

Myers, S. P.: test, 1591

Myklebust, H. R.: test, 2198

Myles, B. S.: test, 191

MySkillsProfile.com, Ltd.: test, 1570, 2528, 2566

Nafziger, D.: rev, 2366

Nafziger, D. H.: rev, 218

Naglieri, J.: test, 244

Naglieri, J. A.: rev, 327, 1135, 1639, 1685; test, 787, 846, 847, 848, 850, 851, 898, 900, 1127, 1632, 1803, 2907

Nagy, P.: rev, 1509, 2540, 2545

Napolitano, S. A.: rev, 500, 583, 721, 1821, 2810

Nash, L.: test, 1061

Natemeyer, W. E.: test, 2133

National Assessment of Educational Progress: test, 1806

National Association of Secondary School Principals: test, 2392

National Association of Secondary School Principals Task Force on Effective School Environments: test, 685

National Center for Education Statistics: test, 1806

National Center for Learning Disabilities: test, 1136

National Center on Education and the Economy: test, 1831, 1832

National Computer Systems: test, 1590

National Computer Systems, Inc.: test, 168

National Council of Teachers of Mathematics: test, 150, 152, 153, 154

National Foundation for Educational Research: test, 1475, 2156

National Foundation for Educational Research in England and Wales: test, 2244

National Institute for Personnel Research of Human Sciences Research Council: test, 345

National Occupational Competency Testing Institute: test, 1840, 1841, 2926

National Reading Styles Institute: test, 2242

National Study of School Evaluation: test, 671, 969, 1353, 1942, 2597, 2629, 2635, 2637, 2675

National Wellness Institute, Inc.: test, 2791, 2792, 2793

Naumann, T. F.: rev, 762, 1808

Naumann, W.: rev, 767, 1778, 2833

Navran, L.: test, 1610

Naylor, R. J.: test, 1363

NCS London House: test, 778

NCS Pearson, Inc.: test, 2694

Neale, M.: test, 1813

Neale, M. D.: rev, 2538; test, 1814

Nebeker, R. S.: test, 3000

Nebelsick-Gullett, L.: rev, 2550

Nedelsky, L.: rev, 118, 1167

Neeley, L.: test, 2508

Neemann, J.: test, 2413

Neher, W. R.: test, 1763

Nehring, A. D.: test, 1498

Nehring, E. F.: test, 1498

Neidert, G.P.M.: test, 2990

Neidt, C. O.: rev, 393

Neill, A.: test, 2157

Neimeyer, R. A.: test, 2618

Neisworth, J. T.: test, 2263, 2698

Neitz, J.: test, 1271

Nellis, L. M.: rev, 274, 305, 343, 355, 1458, 2110, 2185, 2361

Nelson, A. R.: test, 2818

Nelson, C. H.: rev, 100, 538, 1227

Nelson, L.: test, 1829

Nelson, M. K.: test, 2342, 2344

Nelson, M. M.: test, 909

Nelson, N. W.: test, 1975

Nelson, W. M., III: test, 497

Nelson-Gray, R. O.: rev, 298, 312

Nennessy, J. J.: rev, 1255

Neubert, D.: rev, 1219

New Zealand Council for Educational Research: test, 2531

Newborg, J.: test, 280

Newburg, J. E.: test, 803

Newcomer, P. L.: rev, 688; test, 815, 854, 855, 2534, 2746, 2747, 2759

Newhouse, Paul A.: test, 32

Newland, T. E.: rev, 660, 2056

Newman, D. L.: rev, 1018, 1129, 1170, 2580

Newman, E. J.: rev, 377, 450, 1307

Newman, I.: rev, 97

Newman, J.: rev, 329, 2905

Newton, R. M.: test, 2017

Nezu, A. M.: rev, 1188, 1226; test, 2497

NFER-Nelson Publishing Co., Ltd.: test, 1197, 1833, 1834

Nibbelink, W. H.: rev, 1630

Nicholas, M.: test, 351

Nichols, C. W.: test, 208, 215

Nichols, D. S.: rev, 1742

Nichols, H. R.: test, 1789

Nichols, R. C.: rev, 595

Nicholson, C. L.: test, 2483, 2484

Nicolson, R.: test, 2119

Nicolson, R. I.: test, 914, 916, 918, 2246

Nideffer, R. M.: test, 231

Nielsen, N. P.: test, 2225

Nielson, W. R.: test, 512

Nieset, N. L.: rev, 2148

Nihira, K.: test, 2, 3

Nimmo-Smith, I.: test, 318, 896, 2524, 2734, 2735

Nisbet, J.: rev, 134

Nisbet, S.: rev, 1154

Nishioka-Evans, V.: test, 2343

Nitko, A. J.: rev, 393, 1363, 1688, 2703, 2731

Nolan, W.: test, 1968

Noland, J. R.: test, 2031

Nolen, A.: rev, 204

Noll, V. H.: rev, 151, 347, 1246

Norcross, C. E.: rev, 2537

Norman, W. T.: rev, 774

Norris, J.: rev, 666, 2048, 2386

Norris, J. A.: rev, 526, 577, 1550, 2115, 2729

Norris, R. C.: rev, 1276

Norris, S. P.: test, 2783

Norsworthy, N.: test, 2395

North, R. D.: rev, 393, 950, 2804

Northwest Evaluation Association: test, 1655

Novaco, R. W.: test, 1850

Novak, C.: rev, 1691, 2372, 2707, 2811

Nowack, K. M.: test, 2572

Noyce, R.: rev, 797, 2954

Noyce, R. M.: rev, 930, 2782

Nugent, J. K.: test, 1820

Numey, O. D.: test, 2214

Nurss, J. R.: test, 937, 1690, 1691

Nutter, M.: rev, 2902

Nyfield, G.: test, 128, 766, 1014, 2037, 2154, 2691

Palormo, J. M.: rev, 993, 2925
Paloutzian, R. E.: test, 2527
Pannbacker, M.: rev, 2918
Paoletti-Schelp, M.: test, 1119
Paolitto, A. W.: rev, 228, 2104, 2653
Paolo, A. M.: rev, 582, 1116, 2293
Papenfuss, J. F.: test, 950
PAR Staff: test, 1950
Parachio, J. J.: test, 1961
Parasnis, I.: rev, 1891
Parham, L. D.: test, 2427, 2428
Parke, C. S.: rev, 678, 1832
Parker, G. M.: test, 1954, 1955
Parker, J. A.: rev, 260, 308
Parker, J. D. A.: test, 735, 740, 982
Parker, R. M.: test, 1868
Parkerson, S.: test, 1394
Parkinson, M.: test, 754
Parks, S.: test, 1239
Parra, L. F.: test, 1386, 2567
Parry, S. B.: test, 1596, 2015, 2401, 2817
Parsons, C. K.: rev, 386, 1386, 1588, 1589, 2268, 2640
Passow, A. H.: rev, 55, 267, 1849, 2157, 2158, 2537, 2789
Patelis, T.: rev, 271
Paterson, D. G.: rev, 178, 562; test, 1736
Patilla, P.: test, 2061
Patterson, C. C.: test, 2740
Patterson, G. R.: rev, 2903, 2904
Patterson, K.: test, 2204
Patterson, M.: test, 461
Pattie, A. H.: test, 568
Patton, J. R.: test, 2363, 2823
Pauker, J. D.: rev, 1768, 2655, 2181; test, 1747
Paul, K. B.: test, 2567
Paulhus, D. L: test, 1962
Paulus, D.: test, 744
Paunonen, S. V.: test, 1846, 2470
Pavelski, R.: rev, 482, 2594
Payne, J. W.: rev, 1215
Payne, R. W.: rev, 1181, 2655
Peak, P. K.: test, 2730, 2998
Pearlman, L. A.: test, 2826
Pearn, M.: test, 1014
Pearson: test, 1917, 2544, 2902
Pearson, C.: rev, 1447
Pearson, C. L.: rev, 1572
Pearson, C. S.: test, 1904
Pearson, L.: test, 385
Pearson, L. C.: rev, 1483, 1489, 1493, 2128, 2174, 2273
Pearson, M. E.: rev, 2433
Pearson, N. A.: test, 274, 693, 844, 845, 1110, 2723, 2754
Pearson, P. D.: rev, 868, 1125
Pearson Reid London House: test, 1324
Pease, D.: test, 1361, 1362
Peavy, G. M.: test, 2438
Peck, C. S.: test, 1571
Pecora, P. J.: test, 32

Pedigo, K. L.: test, 1968
Pedigo, T. K.: test, 1968
Peel, E. A.: rev, 1759
Peers, I.: test, 1542
Pelham, W. E.: test, 1968
Pendleton, C. W.: rev, 1840
Penfield, D. A.: rev, 372
Penna, J. P.: rev, 45
Penny, J. A.: rev, 136, 1074
Penrose, L. S.: rev, 1742
Perfection Learning Corp.: test, 1544
Performax Systems International, Inc.: test, 2009
Perkins, W. H.: rev, 2844
Perling, M. L.: test, 1277, 1278
Perlman, C.: rev, 2764, 2780
Perman, S.: test, 2547
Perney, J.: test, 1443, 2375
Perrett, D.: test, 1051
Perry, L. A.: test, 2485
Perry-Sheldon, B.: rev, 1093
Persampieri, M.: rev, 216
Person, C. M.: rev, 664, 2254, 2649
Personal Strengths Publishing: test, 1073, 1074, 2077, 2078
Peters, R.: test, 2611
Petersen, J. C.: test, 1946, 2570
Peterson, C.: rev, 733
Peterson, C. A.: rev, 363, 364, 850, 860, 1274
Peterson, D. R.: rev, 2072; test, 2269
Peterson, F. E.: rev, 173
Peterson, G.: test, 2997, 3000
Peterson, G. W.: test, 445
Peterson, H. A.: rev, 810, 1098
Peterson, L. M.: test, 1644
Peterson, N. G.: rev, 1380
Peterson, R. A.: rev, 1255, 1257, 2013, 2299; test, 1291, 2256
Peterson, S.: rev, 49
Petrosko, J.: rev, 2903, 2904
Petrosko, J. M.: rev, 660
Pettiette-Doolin, J.: rev, 1259
Petty, J.: test, 469
Pfeiffer, J. A.: test, 1496
Pfeiffer, J. W.: test, 991, 1496
Pfeiffer, S. I.: rev, 84, 321, 322, 709, 1060, 1259, 1320, 1727, 1843, 1895, 2144, 2289, 2614, 2634; test, 846, 850, 1140
Pflaum, S. W.: rev, 1124
Phelps, L.: rev, 403, 934, 2376; test, 2043
Phelps-Gunn, T.: test, 2760
Phelps-Terasaki, D.: test, 2760
Phillips, C. G.: test, 879
Phillips, I.: rev, 574, 805, 806
Phillips, L. M.: test, 2740
Phillips, S. E.: rev, 1364
Phillips, T. G.: rev, 642, 1131, 1167
Phillips-Jones, L.: test, 829, 1683
Pianta, R. C.: test, 523, 2602

Rodgers, D. A.: rev, 1742
Rodgers, R. C.: rev, 1463
Rodwell, D. N.: test, 2214
Roe, A.: test, 129, 472, 679, 692, 2432, 2937
Roe, B. D.: test, 383
Roeder, W.: test, 2090
Roeder, W. S.: test, 2296
Roenker, D. L.: test, 2843
Roeper, T. W.: test, 858, 859
Roesch, R.: test, 1090
Roessler, R.: test, 988, 2973, 2975
Roessler, R. T.: test, 2968
Rogers, B. G.: rev, 393, 595, 948, 1016, 1359, 1688, 1814, 1965, 2381, 2382, 2540, 2788, 2789, 2899
Rogers, M. R.: rev, 1186, 1398
Rogers, P.: test, 743, 2147
Rogers, R.: test, 1027, 2297, 2587
Rogers, S. J.: test, 927, 2112
Rogler, L. H.: test, 2697
Rohde, P.: test, 1530
Rohrbeck, C. A.: rev, 9, 67, 329, 1441, 1640, 1698, 1946, 2284
Roid, G. H.: test, 1522, 1685, 2345, 2538, 2539, 2562, 2580, 2809, 2931
Rokeach, M.: test, 2298
Roll, S.: rev, 750
Rollins, J.: test, 248
Roman, D. D.: rev, 282, 366, 2278, 2350, 2945
Romano, J. M.: test, 512
Romoser, R. C.: test, 2671
Rooney, M. T.: test, 496
Root, J. H.: test, 2236
Roper, K. D.: test, 1729
Rorer, L. G.: rev, 69, 2471, 2474
Rorschach, H.: test, 2299
Rose, P. M.: test, 2996
Rose, S. A.: test, 2114
Rosen, A. B.: test, 919
Rosen, C. L.: rev, 760, 1766
Rosen, E.: rev, 1102, 1272
Rosen, G. A.: rev, 663, 2331
Rosenberg, H.: test, 1390
Rosenberg, L. R.: test, 2433
Rosenblatt, J. A.: rev, 1113
Rosenbloom, P. C.: rev, 1166
Rosenlund, P.: test, 1509
Rosenthal, A. C.: rev, 209, 1428, 2388, 2508
Rosenthal, R.: test, 743, 2147
Roser, N. L.: rev, 906, 949
Rosinek, M.: test, 2124, 2476
Rosner, J.: test, 2048, 2517, 2719
Ross, C. S.: rev, 181
Ross, P. F.: rev, 989, 2925
Ross-Swain, D.: test, 236, 294, 1541, 2300, 2301, 2302, 2649
Rosskopf, M. F.: rev, 1408
Rostow, C. D.: test, 1633
Roswell, F. G.: test, 856

Roszkowski, M. J.: rev, 284, 411, 1375, 1717, 2273, 2324, 2622
Roth, R. M.: test, 304, 2668
Rothlisberg, B. A.: rev, 842, 927, 1986, 2728
Rothney, J. W. M.: rev, 1529, 2538, 2576, 2861
Rotholz, D. A.: test, 2630
Rothwell, J. W.: test, 2303, 2305
Rothwell, W. J.: test, 828, 1411
Rotter, J.: rev, 2796
Rotter, J. B.: rev, 1742; test, 2306
Rotto, P. C.: rev, 2471
Roumm, P. G.: test, 2169, 2172
Rounds, J. B., Jr.: rev, 437; test, 1738
Rounds, J. B.: rev, 426, 2124, 2881
Rourke, B. P.: rev, 2425
Rouse, M. J.: rev, 1149
Rouse, S. V.: rev, 2581
Rousseau, D. M.: rev, 1686, 2663
Rowe, H. A. H.: test, 2976, 2981
Rowland, C.: test, 162
Roybal, M.: rev, 2578, 2868
Royce, J. R.: test, 2184
Rozecki, T.: rev, 2139, 2819
Roznowski, M.: rev, 189, 1907
Roznowski, M. J.: rev, 1528
Rubin, D.: test, 2187
Rubin, E.: test, 2356
Rubin, K. H.: test, 2068
Rubin, S. I.: rev, 1366
Ruch, F. L.: test, 989
Ruch, W. W.: test, 2141, 2175, 2858
Rudd, B. H.: test, 2807
Ruddock, G.: test, 1854, 2156
Ruderman, M. N.: test, 1384
Rudman, H. C.: rev, 435, 1020, 2161, 2382, 2951
Rudner, L.: test, 1644
Rudner, L. M.: rev, 995, 1517, 2170
Ruedisili, C. H.: rev, 1270
Ruef, M. L.: test, 279, 338
Ruehlman, L. S.: test, 1778
Ruff, R. M.: test, 2307, 2308, 2309, 2310
Ruffle, T. M.: test, 32
Rugen, M. E.: rev, 1229
Rule, D. L.: rev, 1632, 1804
Rumrill, P. D.: test, 2968
Rundquist, T. J.: test, 2227
Rupley, W. H.: rev, 1123
Rusalov, V.: test, 2581
Ruscello, D. M.: test, 1902
Rusch, F. R.: test, 2875
Russell, E. W.: test, 1207
Russell, M. L.: rev, 366, 600
Russell, M. T.: test, 2178
Russell, T.: test, 2381
Rust, J.: rev, 25; test, 1144, 2311, 2312
Rust, J. O.: rev, 2349, 2799
Ruth, L. P.: rev, 528

Schinke, S.: rev, 148, 945
Schinke, S. P.: rev, 483, 1226
Schissel, R. J.: rev, 2914
Schlebusch, D.: test, 1337
Schlieve, P. L.: test, 689
Schmand, B.: test, 157, 2865
Schmeck, R. R.: test, 1347
Schmid, R. F.: rev, 1627
Schmidt, F.: rev, 332, 997
Schmidt, F. L.: rev, 1602, 2950
Schmidt, K. S.: test, 310, 806
Schmidt, M.: test, 2277
Schmidt, M. M.: test, 1329, 2263
Schmidt, S. M.: test, 1446
Schmidt, S. W.: rev, 204
Schmitt, J. F.: rev, 1401
Schmitt, N.: rev, 877, 1396, 2143; test, 684
Schmuckler, J.: rev, 46
Schneck, G. R.: rev, 28, 1333, 1979, 2333, 2875, 2973
Schneider, E. A.: test, 1972
Schneider, N. G.: test, 2488
Schneider, W. J.: rev, 301, 309, 479, 792, 1677, 1699, 2196, 2958, 2997
Schneidmann, N. V.: rev, 460
Schnell, L. H.: rev, 182
Schneller, J.: test, 2193
Schoen, H. L.: test, 1359
Schoendorf, K.: test, 39
Schoenfeldt, L. F.: rev, 2750, 2950
Schoenrade, P.: rev, 1534, 2527, 2966
Schofield, W.: rev, 329, 2306
Scholastic Testing Service, Inc.: test, 584, 1245, 2215
Schonfeld, L.: test, 2611
Schopler, E.: test, 481, 2185, 2672
Schowengerdt, R. V.: rev, 70
Schrader, W. B.: rev, 11, 12, 1706, 2379, 2451
Schram, M.: test, 213
Schrank, F. A.: rev, 186, 346, 433; test, 279, 870, 2952, 2953
Schraw, G.: rev, 303, 1204, 1437, 1756, 2286, 2600, 2741, 2814, 2843, 2857, 2899, 2950
Schretlen, D.: test, 365
Schroeder, L. C.: test, 1636
Schubert, D. S. P.: test, 2379
Schubert, H. J. P.: test, 2379
Schueler, H.: rev, 612
Schuerger, J. M.: test, 2472
Schuler, H.: test, 35
Schulte, A. C.: test, 1500
Schultz, D. G.: rev, 1663, 1882
Schultz, G. F.: rev, 34
Schur, S.: test, 1119
Schuster, D. H.: rev, 2940
Schuster, J. W.: test, 216
Schutz, R. E.: rev, 263, 877
Schutz, R. P.: test, 2875
Schutz, W.: test, 1086, 1623

Schwarting, G.: rev, 356, 370, 371, 577, 838, 856, 923, 1542, 1971, 2107, 2118, 2119, 2738, 2811
Schwartz, N. H.: rev, 1970
Schweigert, P.: test, 162
Schwesinger, G. C.: rev, 772, 2074
Science Research Associates: test, 700, 701, 1807, 1884, 2234, 2316, 2457, 2750, 2836
Scientific Management Techniques, Inc.: test, 2532
Scolley, R. W.: test, 1886
Scott, C. R.: test, 2807
Scott, N. L.: test, 2878
Scott, O., III: rev, 2499
Scott, V. B., Jr.: test, 1968
The Scottish Education Department: test, 949
Search Institute: test, 2390
Seashore, H.: rev, 1168, 1169
Seashore, H. G.: test, 876, 877, 878
Sebolt, D.: rev, 2505
Secolsky, C.: rev, 1915
Secord, W.: test, 577, 2745, 2753, 2778
Secord, W. A.: test, 569, 575, 576, 578, 579
Sedlacek, W. E.: test, 1842, 2465
Seel, R. T.: test, 1824
Seeman, W.: rev, 1992
Segel, D.: rev, 1359, 1463
Segool, N.: rev, 2188
Seguin, E.: test, 2395
Seifert, K.: test, 422
Seim, N. J.: test, 1292, 2322
Seklemian, P.: test, 2478
Selby, E. C.: test, 2857
Selby MillSmith Ltd: test, 220, 221, 222, 1978
Seligman, R.: rev, 2405
Sell, D. E.: test, 1023, 1886
Sells, S. B.: rev, 748
Selmar, J. W.: test, 2050
Selover, R. B.: rev, 1736
Seltzer, G. B.: rev, 2209
Selzer, M. L.: test, 1693
Semel, E.: test, 575, 576, 577, 578, 579
Semeonoff, B.: rev, 1059, 1407, 2224
Semmel, M. I.: rev, 3, 2313
Seron, M. S.: test, 2052
Severson, H. H.: test, 941, 2365, 2660
Sewell, K. W.: test, 1027, 2587
Sewell, T. E.: rev, 733
Seymour, H. N.: test, 858, 859
Shaffer, J. C.: test, 1003
Shaffer, L. F.: rev, 401, 487, 953, 1031, 1152, 1366, 1522, 2074, 2299, 2803, 2903, 2904
Shaffer, M. B.: rev, 158, 359, 487, 1210, 1219, 1682
Shahnasarian, M.: test, 944
Shallice, T.: test, 1224
Shanahan, T.: rev, 346, 383, 874, 1136, 2236
Shanker, J. L.: test, 960
Shapiro, D. A.: rev, 576, 2716, 2726
Shapiro, D. H., Jr.: test, 2450

Shapiro, D. L.: test, 1914
Shapiro, E.: test, 15
Shapiro, E. S.: rev, 383, 1431, 2269
Shapiro, H.: test, 814
Shapiro, J. P.: test, 234
Shapiro, V. B.: test, 851
Shapley, K.: rev, 2723
Shaw, J. H.: test, 1229
Shaw, M. E.: rev, 2465
Shaw, S. R.: rev, 211, 365, 593, 935, 1421, 1423, 1933, 1966, 2277, 2484, 2751, 2870, 2962
Shaycoft, M. F.: rev, 584
Shear, S. M.: rev, 2269
Shearer, C. B.: test, 1699
Shears, M.: test, 2406
Sheehan, E. P.: rev, 961, 1224, 1375, 1384, 1575, 1578, 1784, 1812, 1908, 2575, 2576, 2967, 2990
Sheeley, E. C.: rev, 1148
Sheldon, K. L.: rev, 1644
Shell, K. D.: test, 2199
Shellenberger, S.: rev, 336
Shelton, R. L.: rev, 1147, 1148, 2288
Shenson, H.: test, 1013
Shepard, J. W.: rev, 224, 1375, 2601, 2881
Shepard, L.: rev, 2402, 2414, 2416, 2417, 2418, 2419
Shepard, L. A.: rev, 2540, 2703
Sheperis, C. J.: rev, 8, 305, 981, 2827
Sheras, P. L.: test, 2568
Sherbenou, R. J.: test, 689, 838, 2755
Sherbon, J. W.: rev, 98, 146, 1798
Sheridan, M. D.: test, 2275
Sheridan, S. M.: rev, 2055, 2501
Sherman, D.: rev, 1147
Sherman, E. E.: test, 1186
Sherrod, C.: test, 1676
Sherrod, C. B.: test, 1348
Shertzer, B.: rev, 2880
Sherwood, J. C.: rev, 529, 624, 1005
Sheslow, D.: test, 603, 2714, 2932, 2933, 2934
Shick, J.: test, 2702
Shiel, A.: test, 408, 2920
Shimberg, B.: rev, 1126, 1884
Shimokawa, K.: test, 1895
Shipley, K. G.: rev, 2114, 2673, 2746; test, 2710
Shipley, W. C.: rev, 335, 2233, 2531; test, 2452
Shipman, V.: test, 1830
Shirley, M. C.: rev, 821, 2612
SHL Group PLC: test, 1893
Shneidman, E. S.: test, 1566
Shoemaker, D. M.: rev, 1356
Shores, J. H.: rev, 393
Shorr, J. E.: test, 1198, 2454
Shostrom, E. L.: test, 451, 1929, 2005, 2006
Shoultz, R.: test, 2236
Shriberg, L. D.: rev, 2050, 2288
Shriver, M. D.: rev, 58, 201, 491, 1998, 2492
Shub, A. N.: test, 2175

Shueler, H.: rev, 634
Shulman, G. D.: test, 90, 315, 882, 1919
Shum, D.: rev, 1508, 1734
Shurrager, H. C.: test, 1213
Shurrager, P. S.: test, 1213
Shwery, C. S.: rev, 1507, 2514, 2591
Shyu, V.: test, 2429
Sibicky, M. E.: rev, 1340
Sibley, A. M.: test, 474
Sickel, R. Z.: test, 1309
Siddiqui, R.: test, 1540
Siegel, B.: test, 2041
Siegel, L.: rev, 1152, 1363, 1801, 1802, 2638
Silberg, J. L.: test, 892
Silk, K. R.: test, 860
Silver, S.: test, 788
Silverman, W. P.: test, 2630
Silverstein, A. B.: rev, 825, 1638, 1777, 2911
Silverstein, J.: rev, 825, 2368
Silverton, L.: test, 76, 1568, 2131, 2132
Sim, L. A.: test, 1300
Sime, W.: rev, 360, 1373
Sime, W. E.: rev, 190, 719, 2450, 2507
Simental, J.: rev, 709
Simmond, V.: test, 134
Simmonds, V.: test, 2449
Simon, C. S.: test, 203
Simon & Schuster Higher Education Group: test, 2149
Simons, N.: test, 507
Simonson, M.: test, 2535
Simpson, B.: test, 176
Simpson, R. L.: test, 191
Sims, C. A.: rev, 2121
Sims, V. M.: rev, 149, 2930
Sinar, E. F.: test, 1386
Sinclair, E.: rev, 485
Sines, J. O.: rev, 938, 2294; test, 1259, 1747
Sines, L. K.: test, 1747
Singer, E. A.: test, 353
Singer, H.: rev, 1125, 1691
Singer, J.: test, 2463
Singh, H. L.: test, 2677
Singh, K.: rev, 1347, 2016
Singh, N. N.: test, 5
Singh, S. P.: rev, 38, 658, 1829, 2300
Singleton, D. M.: rev, 131, 1831
Singleton, R. M.: test, 316
Sink, C. A.: rev, 236, 422, 975, 2262, 2283, 2539
Sipay, E. R.: rev, 2241
Sipe, J. W.: test, 202
Sippola, B. C.: rev, 2052, 2139, 2641
Siryk, B.: test, 2592
Siskind, T. G.: rev, 1933, 2842
Sivan, A. B.: test, 1786
Sixbury, G. R.: test, 1287
Skinner, H. A.: test, 138, 902, 1056
Sklar, S. M.: test, 903, 1346

Slaney, R. B.: rev, 435, 1533
Slater, B. R.: test, 599
Slater, P.: rev, 1355
Slater, W. H.: rev, 89, 1016, 2545
Slawinowski, M. J.: test, 507
Sleator, E. K.: test, 65
Slentz, K.: test, 198
Slevin, D. P.: test, 2162
Slick, D.: test, 2856
Slingerland, B. H.: test, 2274, 2480
Slivnick, P.: test, 14
Sloan, W.: test, 1537
Slonaker, R. L.: rev, 2062
Slosson, R. L.: test, 2483, 2484
Slosson, S. W.: test, 2482
Smedley, F.: test, 2486
Smith, A.: test, 2651
Smith, A. D.: test, 2013
Smith, A. E.: rev, 1917
Smith, A. L., Jr.: rev, 1129, 1704
Smith, C. R.: rev, 59, 485, 525
Smith, D. A. F.: test, 1761
Smith, D. E. P.: rev, 2839
Smith, D. K.: rev, 1139, 1816, 1817, 2363, 2458, 2740
Smith, E. B.: test, 2049
Smith, E. V., Jr.: rev, 65, 738, 1629
Smith, F.: test, 2387
Smith, G. P.: test, 2588
Smith, G. R.: rev, 16
Smith, I. F.: test, 670
Smith, I. M.: rev, 772, 775, 2510
Smith, J.: rev, 15, 1155, 1530, 2017; test, 727, 2606
Smith, J. K.: rev, 270, 657, 801, 825, 1757, 1796, 2090, 2387, 2544, 2783
Smith, J. P.: rev, 530, 531
Smith, J. V.: rev, 65, 72, 815, 1368, 1949
Smith, K. J.: rev, 1143
Smith, K. L.: test, 1890
Smith, L.: rev, 822, 2980
Smith, L. F.: rev, 1093, 1172, 1440, 1842, 1933, 2729, 2766
Smith, L. H.: test, 1514, 2349
Smith, M. B.: test, 2252
Smith, M. L.: rev, 2800
Smith, M. W.: test, 928, 929
Smith, N. L.: rev, 701
Smith, P.: test, 374, 1848, 1873, 1874, 2518
Smith, P. C.: test, 1386, 2268, 2567
Smith, P. L.: test, 1891
Smith, R. A.: test, 885
Smith, R. P.: test, 1518
Smith, R. W.: rev, 1668, 2063
Smith, S.: test, 181, 182, 874, 1006, 1007, 1133, 1235, 1246, 2243, 2526, 2874
Smith, S. L.: rev, 1616
Smith, T. A.: rev, 2056
Smock, C. D.: rev, 347, 707
Smyth, S.: test, 197

Snaith, R. P.: test, 1265
Snijders, J. T.: test, 1845
Snijders-Oomen, N.: test, 1845
Snook, P. A.: test, 1800
Snow, J. H.: rev, 1402, 1556
Snowling, M.: test, 2046
Snowling, M. J.: test, 1155
Snyder, B.: rev, 1784
Snyder, D. K.: test, 1611
Snyder, G.: rev, 354, 575
Snyder, K.: rev, 664, 916, 1110, 2851
Snyder, K. A.: rev, 380, 686, 1147, 1432, 1456
Soares, A. T.: test, 16, 204, 2414, 2417, 2507, 2676
Soares, L. M.: rev, 335, 415, 2578, 2762, 2766; test, 16, 204, 2414, 2415, 2416, 2417, 2418, 2419, 2507, 2676
Society of Actuaries: test, 150, 152, 153, 154
Sodor, A. L.: test, 2050
Sodowsky, G. R.: rev, 666, 893, 1438, 1911
Soliz, A.: rev, 2377
Solly, D. C.: rev, 1637
Solomon, A.: rev, 2534
Solomon, P. R.: test, 145
Solomon, R. H.: rev, 131, 355
Solomon, R. J.: rev, 2789
Somerville, J. A.: test, 353
Sommers, R. K.: rev, 183, 2386, 2389
Song, A.: test, 2944
Soper, J. C.: test, 2731, 2732
Sorensen, M. F.: test, 1327
Sorenson, C.: test, 684
Sosnowski, M.: test, 832
Sostek, A. M.: rev, 1820
Souder, L.: rev, 2540
Southwest Educational Development Laboratory: test, 890
Spache, G. D.: rev, 906, 1125, 2049
Spadafore, G. J.: test, 2511, 2512
Spadafore, S. J.: test, 2511
Spalding, N. V.: test, 2218
Spaner, S. D.: rev, 1002
Spaney, E.: rev, 1359
Spangler, M.: rev, 326, 328, 386, 2333
Spanier, G. B.: test, 908
Spany, E.: rev, 1915
Sparrow, E.: test, 717
Sparrow, S. S.: test, 940, 2861, 2862
Spector, J. E.: rev, 917, 2773
Speech Communication Association: test, 195, 674
Speer, R. F.: test, 1246
Speer, R. K.: test, 181, 182, 1006, 1007, 1133, 2243, 2526, 2874
Speer, R. V.: test, 1235
Spence, N.: test, 1290
Spence, R. J.: test, 2948
Spence, S. H.: test, 2502
Spencer, D. G.: rev, 2010
Spencer, L. M.: test, 1910

Strand, D.: rev, 331, 1560
Strand, M. L.: test, 2173, 2174
Strang, J. M.: rev, 2794
Strang, R.: rev, 2576
Strategic Advantage, Inc.: test, 2654
Stratil, M. L.: test, 654
Stratton, R. K.: rev, 1183
Straus, L. T.: rev, 951
Straus, M. A.: test, 715
Strauss, E.: test, 2856
Strauss, H.: test, 255
Stricker, L. J.: rev, 953, 1048, 2699
Stringfield, S.: test, 2109
Strohmer, D. C.: test, 979
Strom, P. S.: test, 1336, 1944
Strom, R. D.: test, 1170, 1336, 1936, 1944
Strom, S. K.: test, 1170
Stromberg, E. L.: test, 2574
Strong, C. J.: test, 2577
Strong-Krause, D.: test, 1890
Strother, C. R.: rev, 1031, 1566
Stroud, K. C.: test, 2372
Struck, J. T.: test, 2187
Strupp, H. H.: rev, 2183
Stuart, R. B.: rev, 908, 1063, 1531, 1605, 1610, 1721, 1955, 2209, 2445, 2463
Stuberg, W.: test, 1702
Stuit, D. B.: rev, 2273
Stunkard, A. J.: test, 946
Stutman, G.: rev, 380, 462, 505, 686, 841, 1312, 2248, 2747
Subkoviak, M. J.: rev, 773, 1145, 1364, 2391, 2537, 2769
Sudhalter, V.: test, 1963
Sudweeks, R. R.: rev, 960
Sue, M. B.: test, 2710
Suen, H. K.: rev, 275, 381, 840, 973, 1536, 1794, 1820, 1974, 2115, 2726, 2782, 2853
Suess, A. R.: rev, 1840
Sugden, D. A.: test, 1768
Suinn, R. M.: rev, 2701
Sullivan, J. R.: rev, 704, 718
Sun, H.: rev, 2591, 2961
Sundberg, N. D.: rev, 288, 1386, 1438, 1801, 1802, 2012, 2268, 2420, 2538, 2607
Sundre, D. L.: rev, 1679, 2034
Super, D. E.: rev, 1736, 1759; test, 2620
Suppa, C. H.: rev, 57, 383, 2904, 2906
Sutton, R.: rev, 2749
Sutton, R. E.: rev, 669, 799, 1444, 1830, 2823, 2853
Suydam, M. N.: rev, 271
Svinicki, J.: test, 280
Svinicki, J. G.: rev, 2076, 2203
Swain, C.: test, 689
Swanson, D.: test, 799
Swanson, H. L.: rev, 2866; test, 2650
Swanson, J. M.: test, 1968
Swart, D. J.: test, 177

Swartz, A.: test, 2846
Swartz, J. D.: rev, 188, 1357, 2796
Swartz-Kulstad, J. L.: rev, 76, 1412
Swassing, C. S.: rev, 945, 2192
Swearer, S. M.: rev, 456, 1331, 2283, 2568
Sweeney, T. J.: test, 1092, 2916
Swensen, C. H.: rev, 217; test, 2342, 2344
Swenson, C. H., Jr.: rev, 2336
Swerdlik, M. E.: rev, 301, 309, 368, 840, 1123, 1443, 1677, 1917, 1933, 2120, 2196, 2541, 2781, 2930, 2997; test, 2188
Swerdlik, P.: test, 2188
Swihart, A. A.: test, 2439
Swindle, F. L.: test, 843
Switzer, J.: test, 1849
Switzky, H. N.: rev, 58, 312, 831, 2653, 2944
Sykken, D. T.: rev, 402
Symonds, P. M.: rev, 1100, 1992
Szczepanski, M.: test, 926

Tade, W. J.: test, 2481
Tafrate, R. C.: test, 163, 164
Taggart, B.: test, 1275
Taggart, W.: test, 1275
Tai, W. L.: rev, 1300
Taljaard, J. J.: test, 2816
Talley, J. L.: test, 490, 2945
Tamir, P.: test, 662
Tan, X.: rev, 933
Tanigawa, D.: rev, 246, 2193
Tannenbaum, A. J.: rev, 772
Tarter, R. E.: test, 904
Tasse, M. J.: test, 2630
Tate, R.: test, 2292
Tatsuoka, K. K.: rev, 2099, 2769
Tattersall, P.: test, 2590
Tattersall, P. J.: test, 2589
Taulbee, E. S.: rev, 2889
Taylor, A. P.: test, 2670
Taylor, E. K.: rev, 989, 1736, 2038, 2039, 2919; test, 2317
Taylor, E. M.: rev, 1134
Taylor, H. F.: test, 737
Taylor, H. R.: rev, 421
Taylor, K. M.: test, 432
Taylor, P. A.: rev, 2703; test, 1528
Taylor, R. L.: test, 201
Taylor, R. M.: test, 1061, 2671
Taylor, R. N.: rev, 1592, 2456
Taylor, T. R.: test, 1077, 1242, 1303, 2153, 2304
Teagarden, F. M.: rev, 460, 2861
Tearnan, B. H.: test, 311
Teele, S.: test, 2693
Teeter, P. A.: rev, 69, 1424
Teitzel, T.: test, 2103, 2107
Teleometrics International: test, 2206
Tellegen, A.: rev, 1047, 1048; test, 1741, 1742

Tredoux, M.: test, 177
Treffinger, D. J.: rev, 2813; test, 2857
Tremblay, P. F.: test, 2470
Trenerry, M. R.: test, 2579, 2871
Trent, R.: test, 1274
Trevisan, M. S.: rev, 27, 264, 444, 871, 1699, 1803, 1849, 1874, 2030, 2730, 2743, 2789, 2821, 2946
Trickett, E. J.: test, 525
Trigos, M. C.: test, 1221
Trimble, H. C.: rev, 2157, 2158
Tringone, R.: test, 1727
Triolo, S. J.: test, 229
Trites, R.: test, 1183
Trofimova, I.: test, 2581
Tronick, E. Z.: test, 1837
Trotter, S. E.: rev, 234, 1458, 2474, 2553, 2671, 2999
Troyer, M. E.: test, 1229
Trull, T.: test, 2586
Tucker, J. A.: rev, 1606, 1997
Tucker, R. W.: test, 2641
Tuinman, J. J.: rev, 2956
Tuma, J. M.: rev, 2026
Tuokko, H.: test, 582
Turco, T. L.: rev, 355, 370, 371
Turk, K.: rev, 1426
Turnbull, W. W.: rev, 2038, 2039
Turner, A.: test, 1373
Turner, J. A.: test, 512
Turner, K.: test, 943
Turner, N. E.: test, 903, 1346
Turner, S.: test, 1654
Turner, S. M.: test, 2494, 2495
Turney, A. H.: rev, 1463
Turton, L. J.: rev, 243, 253, 488, 1089
Tuska, S. A.: test, 580, 2665
Tutko, T. A.: test, 224, 2942, 2943
Tuzinski, K.: test, 888
Twist, J.: test, 2161
Twombly, E.: test, 131, 132
Tyack, D.: test, 1474
Tyler, B.: test, 2303, 2305
Tyler, L. E.: rev, 585, 586, 774, 1169
Tyler, R. W.: rev, 622, 645
Tymon, W. G., Jr.: test, 2573, 2966
Tziner, A.: rev, 2699

U.S. Dept. of Education: test, 1806
U.S. Department of Labor, Employment and Training Administration: test, 1858, 1859
U.S. Military Entrance Processing Command: test, 187
Uchiyama, C. L.: test, 658
Ullmann, R. K.: test, 65
Ulrich, D. A.: test, 2737
Unger, M. A.: test, 2431
United Cerebral Palsy of the Bluegrass: test, 1528
University of Michigan: test, 179, 1004, 1029, 1030, 1694, 1695, 1696, 1697

Urban, K. K.: test, 2709
Urbina, S.: rev, 251, 272, 1210, 1318, 1379, 2026, 2384, 2562, 2586

Vacc, N. A.: rev, 190, 427, 491, 498, 1385, 2613, 2881
Vacca, J. J.: rev, 132, 242, 370, 371, 718, 1304, 1305, 2429, 2539, 2779, 3003
Vagg, P. R.: test, 1395, 2555
Vail, N.: test, 950
Valentine, L. D., Jr.: rev, 2028
Valesio, P.: rev, 614
Valleley, R. J.: rev, 131, 2294
Van Bourgondien, M. E.: test, 481
van den Berg, J. M.: test, 27
van den Daele, L.: test, 1796
Van Gorp, W. G.: rev, 38, 167, 1118, 1263, 1556, 1826, 2082, 2300, 2309, 2871
Van Haneghan, J.: rev, 198
Van Haneghan, J. P.: rev, 470, 669, 1762, 2263, 2664, 2814, 2843
Van Hecke, G. R.: rev, 50
Van Hutton, V.: test, 1266
van Lennep, D. J.: test, 1102
van Lingen, G.: rev, 693, 1240, 1453, 2104, 2754
Van Roekel, B. H.: rev, 906, 949, 1123, 2541
Van Steenberg, N. J.: rev, 2803
van Strien, T.: test, 907
Vance, F. L.: rev, 69
Vance, H. R.: test, 2482
vandenBerg, A. R.: test, 1410
VanDuser, M. L.: rev, 76
Vannice, J. E.: rev, 1110
VanVelsor, E.: test, 2479
Vasa, S. F.: rev, 826, 867
Vassar, M.: rev, 1034, 1494
Vater, S.: test, 1307
Vecchio, R. P.: rev, 1223, 2122
Velakoulis, D.: test, 1825
Veldman, D. J.: rev, 701
Venable, G. P.: test, 1474
Venn, J. J.: rev, 284, 2085, 2262, 2498, 2931
Vennix, P.: test, 2447
Verdi, W.: rev, 2426
Verhoeve, M.: test, 1375
Vermeersch, D. A.: test, 1897
Vernon, L. N.: test, 1886
Vernon, M. D.: rev, 1813
Vernon, P. E.: rev, 1244, 1437, 1759; test, 1154, 1156, 1628
Vetter, D. K.: rev, 375, 524, 665, 1538, 2716, 2721, 2722, 2745, 2908
Vicker, B.: test, 2923
Villanova, P.: rev, 1888
Vincent, D.: test, 376, 2240
Visser, J.: rev, 295
Visser, R. S. H.: test, 675
Viswesvaran, C.: rev, 784, 1455, 2260, 2459, 2654, 2819, 2828, 2859

Woody, C.: rev, 2874
Worcester, D. A.: rev, 825
Worell, J.: test, 1938
Worell, L.: test, 1938
Workman, E.: rev, 302
Worland, J.: rev, 2917
World Health Organization: test, 2362
Worley, J. W.: test, 2991
Wormith, J. S.: test, 1523, 1526
Worth, M. J.: test, 1300
Worthen, B. R.: rev, 960, 2512, 2576
Wozniak, J.: test, 1431
Wright, B. D.: rev, 374
Wright, C. R.: rev, 150, 195, 694, 1312, 1398, 1500, 1546, 1618, 1933, 1998, 2005, 2047, 2372, 2450, 2496
Wright, D.: rev, 370, 371, 1189, 2732
Wright, E. N.: test, 416, 2314
Wright, L.: rev, 79, 926, 1350
Wright, N. H.: test, 1613
Wright, R.: rev, 1772
Wrightstone, J. W.: test, 11, 12, 562, 1355, 1529, 1661
Wrobel, T. A.: rev, 1731
Wu, T. C.: rev, 1969
Wunderlich, K. C.: test, 300, 2104
Wyk, R. V.: test, 1015
Wylie, E.: test, 241
Wynne, M. K.: rev, 1253, 1687

Yamamoto, K.: test, 1020
Yanico, B.: test, 431
Yaruss, J. S.: test, 1921
Yates, A. J.: rev, 2452
Yazak, D. L.: rev, 685, 1976
Yee, K. W.: test, 1015
Yegidis, B. L.: test, 9
Yelland, T.: rev, 272, 1316
Yetter, G.: rev, 1379, 1854, 2193, 2900, 3001
Yockelson, S.: test, 132
Yorkston, K. M.: test, 210
Young, A.: test, 1022, 1051
Young, D.: test, 587, 1193, 1196, 1843, 1933, 2516, 2666
Young, E. C.: test, 1961
Young, J. C.: test, 2785
Young, J. W.: rev, 1139, 1196, 1421, 1675, 2551, 2732, 2767

Young, R.: test, 242
Young, S.: rev, 1115, 1322, 1377, 1944, 2151, 2418
Youniss, R. P.: test, 1338
Ysseldyke, J.: rev, 719, 1137; test 1113
Ysseldyke, J. E.: rev, 295, 355, 855, 918, 1748, 1816, 1817, 2425, 2541
Yu, C. S.: test, 1015

Zabel, R. H.: rev, 2866
Zachar, P.: rev, 731, 1374, 1429, 1726, 2299, 2380
Zakay, D.: rev, 2149
Zangwill, O. L.: rev, 1756
Zapf, P. A.: test, 1090
Zapf, S. A.: test, 2435
Zarit, J. M.: test, 1674
Zarit, S. H.: test, 1674
Zarske, J. A.: rev, 69, 1790
Zedeck, S.: rev, 326, 1390, 1595, 1738, 1739, 1765, 1858, 2175, 2247, 2316, 2322, 2467
Zehler, A. M.: test, 94
Zehrbach, R. R.: test, 688
Zeisloft-Falbey, B.: test, 1239
Zeitlin, S.: test, 734, 926
Zelman, J. G.: test, 1498
Zhang, B.: rev, 2929
Zhao, J.: test, 1015
Zickar, M. J.: rev, 325, 1504, 1563, 2210
Zigarmi, D.: test, 1479
Zigmond, A. S.: test, 1265
Zillmer, E.: test, 785
Zillmer, E. A.: test, 2814
Zimmerman, C.: rev, 1619, 2736
Zimmerman, I. L.: test, 2115
Zimmerman, L. J.: rev, 2831, 2856
Zimmerman, M.: test, 2180
Zimmerman, W. S.: rev, 647, 2098; test, 2603
Zlomke, L. C.: rev, 381, 2352, 2660
Zoss, S. K.: test, 1334
Zucker, S.: rev, 1093, 2840
Zucker, S. H.: test, 1785
Zuckerman, M.: rev, 2471, 2474; test, 1790
Zusman, J.: rev, 2121
Zytowski, D. G.: rev, 1151, 1204, 1352, 1868, 2880, 2935; test, 1459, 1461, 1462, 2620

SCORE INDEX

This Score Index lists all the scores, in alphabetical order, for all the tests included in Tests in Print VIII. *Because test scores can be regarded as operational definitions of the variable measured, sometimes the scores provide better leads to what a test actually measures than the test title or other available information. The Score Index is very detailed, and the reader should keep in mind that a given variable (or concept) of interest may be defined in several different ways. Thus the reader should look up these several possible alternative definitions before drawing final conclusions about whether tests measuring a particular variable of interest can be located in* TIP VIII. *If the kind of score sought is located in a particular test or tests, the reader should then read the test descriptive information carefully to determine whether the test(s) in which the score is found is (are) consistent with reader purpose. Used wisely, the Score Index can be another useful resource in locating the right score in the right test. As usual, all numbers in the index are test numbers, not page numbers.*

A (antiestablishment): 799
A Horse of Her Own: 2790
A Strong Set Of Shared Values And Beliefs Guide Our
    Actions: 1907
A Words: 357
A-expectation: 1511
A/2 Trials-B/2 Trials: 2865
A1-A5 Total: 357
A6: 357
Abandonment Concerns: 1343
Abasement: 69, 953, 1484, 2028, 2057
Abbreviated Battery IQ: 2539
Aberrant Vocal Quality When Speaking: 1963
Abilities: 1204, 1219, 2976
Abilities and Skills: 2981
Ability: 391, 1923
Ability Deficits: 381
Ability Scores: 1932
Ability to Abstract: 282
Ability to Analyze Course of Therapy: 1875
Ability To Be Diplomatic And Cooperative: 690
Ability to Benefit from Reminding: 1109
Ability To Close Sales Without Hesitation: 690

Ability to Comprehend Hypothetical Fire Codes: 1080
Ability To Control Emotional Ups And Downs: 690
Ability To Cope With Change And Disruption: 690
Ability to Exercise Judgment and Common Sense: 987
Ability to Exercise Judgment-Dealing With People: 987
Ability to Exercise Judgment-Map Reading: 987
Ability to Focus on Treatment: 1919
Ability to Follow Directions: 1926
Ability to Follow Instructions: 62
Ability to Get and Hold a Job: 2880
Ability To Handle Sales Rejection: 690
Ability To Keep Positive Attitude [Optimism]: 690
Ability to Learn and Apply Information: 2176
Ability to Learn and Apply Police Information: 1, 1926
Ability to Learn Police Material: 784
Ability to Learn/Remember and Apply Information: 249
Ability To Make New Contacts [Call Courage]: 690
Ability To Make Unpopular Decisions: 690
Ability To Motivate Others To Act: 690
Ability to Observe and Remember Details: 1926
Ability to Observe/Listen to/ and Remember Informa-
    tion: 1
Ability to Profit from Instruction or Correction: 2975

Computer Programming: 1840, 1841, 2535
Computer Repair Technology: 1841
Computer Science: 104, 127, 1163, 1169, 1876
Computer Sciences: 509
Computer Scientist: 426
Computer Scientist (f, m): 2576
Computer Systems Analyst (f, m): 2576
Computer Systems: 2535
Computer Technology: 1328, 1840, 1841
Computer Use Skills: 783
Computers: 2242
Computers & PLC: 1322, 1563
Computers & PLC and Test Instruments: 961
Computers and Electronics: 1096
Computers and PLC: 964, 967
Conative (Sc4): 1742
Concealed Words Test: 1449
Concentration: 1499, 2529, 2552
Concentration and Organization: 503
Concentration Impairment and Sublimation: 85
Concentration Scale: 1500
Concentration/Sustained Attention: 230
Concentric Square: 1206
Concept Attainment: 62
Concept Development: 523
Concept Formation: 245, 349, 2952
Concept Mastery: 1440
Concept of the Call: 2797
Concept of Word: 212
Concept Production: 344
Concept Recognition: 344
Concept Scores: 867
Concept Synthesis: 344
Conceptos Cuantitativos: 279
Concepts: 82, 837, 840, 1320, 1408, 1655, 1832, 2126, 2215
Concepts About Print: 932
Concepts and Applications: 393, 2540
Concepts and Communication: 1192
Concepts and Following Directions: 576, 577, 578
Concepts and Problem Solving: 1364
Concepts for Writing and Completing Reports/Records and Paperwork: 1925
Concepts for Writing and Reviewing Reports and Paperwork: 1838
Concepts of Administration: 958, 1838, 2063
Concepts of Evaluating Subordinate Performance: 1838
Concepts of Evaluating Subordinate Performance: 958
Concepts of Number: 2536
Concepts of Supervision: 958, 1838, 2063
Concepts of Training: 958, 1838
Concepts of Writing and Reviewing Reports and Paperwork: 958
Conceptual: 57, 1893
Conceptual/Analytical: 231
Conceptual Composite: 57
Conceptual Dysfunction: 819

Conceptual Fluency: 756
Conceptual Grouping: 1639
Conceptual Incongruity: 4
Conceptual Knowledge: 1325
Conceptual Level: 217
Conceptual Level Responses: 2945, 2946
Conceptual Shifting: 1417
Conceptual Thinking: 1420, 1483
Conceptual Understanding: 1806
Conceptualization: 805, 806, 2438, 2615
Conceptualization of Therapy: 1875
Concern Description: 1920
Concern for Others: 2974
Concern for People: 1686
Concern with Physical Harm: 8
Conciliator: 1554
Conclusions: 469
Concrete—Abstract: 1802
Concrete Experience: 63, 1508
Concrete Random score: 1180
Concrete Sequential score: 1180
Concreteness: 38
Condition/Quality: 2938
Conditions for Learning: 1511
Conduct: 299, 850
Conduct/Anti-Sociality: 904
Conduct Disorder: 79, 83, 84, 86, 479, 496, 677, 718, 861, 924, 1379, 1727, 1772, 1789, 2092, 2196, 2269, 3003
Conduct Disorder as a Child/Adolescent: 315
Conduct Disorder Quotient: 709
Conduct Problem Scale: 880
Conduct Problems: 32, 297, 314, 489, 572, 883, 1075, 1741, 2076, 2226, 2398, 2492
Conducting Employee Meetings: 1517
Conducting Inquiries: 1806
Conducting Performance Appraisals: 1517
Conducting Selection Interviews: 1517
Conducting Termination Interviews: 1517
Conductor: 1591
Confabulation: 38, 353, 1201, 2302
Confabulations: 1329
Confidence: 446, 737, 1190, 1875, 2324
Confidence and Resilience: 2528
Confidence in Administrator: 1283
Confidence in Success: 35
Confidence Index: 719
Confidence/Influence: 2694
Confident: 1722, 1723, 1725, 1727, 2020
Confident/Asserting: 1726
Confident Leadership: 1480
Confident—Unsure: 2146
Configural Accuracy: 353
Configural Presence: 353
Configuration: 1637
Confirmation: 2835
Confirming Mentoring: 1684

Expository Report Writing Irrelevant Thoughts Added (RWITA): 2136
Expository Report Writing Organizational Quality of Report Writing (RWO): 2136
Expository Report Writing Quality (RWQ): 2136
Expository Scoring Scheme: 2659
Expository Writing: 1146
Expository Writing Sample: 605
Exposure: 504, 1584, 1586, 2035, 2327, 2681
Exposure to Pornography: 521
Expressed: 1086
Expressed Concerns: 1721, 1722
Expressed Concerns Scales: 1725
Expressing: 1298, 1995, 2984
Expressing Emotion: 1734
Expressing Emotions Adaptively: 977
Expressing Feeling: 1007, 2490
Expressing Ideas: 1006, 1007
Expressing Intents: 2745
Expression: 385, 393, 1094, 1095, 2189, 2513
Expression of Anger: 1334
Expression of Criticism: 231
Expression of Emotion: 1417
Expression of Ideas: 231
Expression of Support: 231
Expressional Fluency: 1449
Expressions of Feelings and Emotions: 4
Expressive: 332, 407, 1031, 1375, 1422, 2114, 2197, 2333, 2410, 2503, 2805, 2861, 2938
Expressive Attention: 787
Expressive Brief Vocabulary: 935
Expressive Coding (EC): 2136
Expressive Communication: 280, 284, 285, 2115
Expressive Composite: 2778
Expressive—Contained: 1802
Expressive Deficit: 1418
Expressive Gesture and Sign Language: 302
Expressive Grammar: 855
Expressive/Imaginative: 1533
Expressive Index: 686
Expressive Language: 243, 454, 475, 576, 577, 578, 688, 931, 954, 1093, 1098, 1685, 1769, 1963, 1974, 2185, 2203, 2279, 2295, 2591, 2725, 2726, 2944
Expressive Language Ability: 2248
Expressive Language Competence: 1963
Expressive Language Disorder: 2196
Expressive Language Skills: 370, 371, 2113, 2351
Expressive Language/Speech Production: 293
Expressive Prosody: 38
Expressive-Responsive vs. Inhibited: 2671
Expressive School Readiness Composite: 354
Expressive Sensitivity: 1699
Expressive Social Communication Abilities: 1963
Expressive Speech: 792, 1555, 1556
Expressive Subdomain: 372
Expressive Total Composite: 354
Expressive Verbal: 1685

Expressive Verbal Labels: 954
Expressive Vocabulary: 82, 576, 577, 578, 691, 855, 935, 1420, 2778
Expressive Vocabulary [Age 9]: 576
Expressive Writing Ability: 1631
Expressiveness: 507, 730, 749, 1058, 1188, 2349
Extended: 1053
Extended Family: 1531, 1532, 2192
Extended Family Relations: 2209
Extended Range Vocabulary Test: 1449
Extended Time Gain: 910
Extending Information: 1649
Extensive Preparation Needed: 1858
Extent Flexibility: 1096
Extent of Anger: 164
Extent Trainee Seeks Assistance from Supervisor: 2975
External: 350, 570, 571, 793, 971
External Adaptability: 1913
External Adjustment: 2656
External Conflict: 445
External Distractibility: 231
External Eating: 907
External Focus of World: 171, 1995
External Pressure: 1384
External Relations: 1954
External Stressors: 990
External Support: 2478
Externalization: 314, 2026
Externalized: 1342
Externalized Behavior Measures: 1357
Externalizing: 32, 449, 1372, 2500, 2660
Externalizing Anger: 164
Externalizing Behavior: 2492
Externalizing Behavior Problems: 979
Externalizing Behaviors: 572
Externalizing Composite: 850
Externalizing Disorder Factor: 83
Externalizing Distress: 2283
Externalizing Problems: 297, 2105, 2491
Externally Derived Sense of Self Worth: 1300
Externally Focused: 1726
Extra Effort: 1784
Extracted Hamilton: 2358
Extracurricular Activities: 2507
Extramarital Relations: 2209
Extratensive/Intratensive Index: 2805
Extraversion: 411, 502, 938, 1047, 1048, 1091, 1244, 1252, 1406, 1407, 1692, 1818, 1819, 1846, 1865, 1889, 1993, 2178, 2463, 2470, 2472, 2586, 2859
Extraversion/Introversion: 222
Extraversion or Introversion: 1794
Extraversion vs. Introversion: 705, 706, 1405, 1428, 1801, 1802
Extraverted vs. Introverted: 2471
Extreme Symptomatology: 1711
Extrinsic: 1743
Extrinsic Goal Orientation: 1761

Practical-Male: 1839
Practical Mindedness: 2643
Practical Nursing: 1841
Practical Orientation: 672, 749, 2889
Practical Problem Solving: 1417
Practical Reasoning: 1182, 2149
Practical Skills: 386, 406
Practical Thinking: 1585, 1590
Practical v. Carefree: 442
Practicalizer: 761
Practiced Sentences: 2523
Pragmatic Conversational Skills: 1963
Pragmatic Judgment: 686
Pragmatic Knowledge: 254
Pragmatic Language Index: 2093
Pragmatic Skills: 1141
Pragmatics: 82, 858, 2520, 2939
Pragmatist: 1315, 1316, 1379, 1554
Pragnosia: 1829
Praise: 1334
Praise and Recognition: 1383
Praxis: 351, 1417, 1548
Praxis Verbal Command: 2425
Prayer Fulfillment: 219
Pre-Academic/Cognitive: 720
Pre-Affair: 129
Pre-Affair Involvement: 679
Pre-Algebra: 764, 2064
Pre-Algebra/Elementary Algebra: 55
Pre-Algebraic Number Skills and Concepts: 1359
Pre-Elementary and Elementary: 951
Pre-Engineering/Engineering Technology: 1841
Pre-Kindergarten Education: 2094
Pre-Literacy Component: 2097
Pre-Literacy Rating Scale: 577
Pre-Reading: 2788
Pre-Reading Skills: 2928
Pre-Test: 457
Pre-Writing: 1498
Preacademic Learning: 1972
Preacher: 1352
Precipitating Factors Cluster: 74
Precise: 1317
Precise/Administrative: 1533
Precise-Sell: 332
Precise/Systematic: 332
Precision: 1094, 1095, 1366, 2349
Precision Machining: 1840, 1841
Precision Metal Work: 437
Precision Orientation: 782
Precision Production: 437
Predicted Grade Point Average: 2472
Predicted WMS-III General Memory Index Score: 2906
Predicting of Outcomes: 1231, 1247, 1855
Predicting: 2763
Prediction: 726, 932
Predictive Ability: 2095

Predictor Profile: 2656
Predisposing Factors Cluster: 74
Predisposition: 2012
Preference for Difficult Tasks: 35
Preference for Drinking over Other Activities: 137, 2
Preference for Objective Measures: 2396
Preference for Structure: 2396
Preferred Culture: 853
Preferred Exposure: 777
Preferred Feedback: 777
Preferred Grip: 1206
Preferred Hand: 1977
Preferred Mentoring Style: 1684
Preferred Reading Environment: 2242
Preferred Style-Adult: 2031
Preferred Style of Leader Overall: 221
Preferred Style of Leader-Coach: 221
Preferred Style of Leader-Expert: 221
Preferred Style of Leader-Fighter: 221
Prefers Long-Range Goals to Short-Term or Immediate
    Needs: 1842
Prefixes: 960
Pregnancy/Birth/Hospitalization: 688
Pregnancy/Birth—Parent Version: 861
Pregnancy/Childbirth and Child Rearing: 2504
Prehandwriting: 370
Premature Ejaculation: 1789
Premorbid or Intermorbid Personality: 687
Premorbid Questions: 2350
Premorbid Status: 1828
Preoccupation: 1998
Preoccupation with Danger: 597
Preoccupation with Disease: 2027
Preoccupation with Drugs: 1997
Preoccupation with Health: 2976
Preoccupation with Sexually Relevant Concepts: 1266
Preparation Style: 1252
Preparing for Clinical Intervention: 339
Prepositional Location Commands: 2271
Prepositions: 1474, 1685
Prepositions and Conjunctions: 1295
Prepositions and Irregular Plural Nouns: 370, 371
Prepositions: 370
Prereading Composite: 1691
Prereading Phonics Abilities Inventories: 906
Preschool Delay Task: 1150
Preschool Skills: 516
Preschool Vigilance "0" Task: 1150
Preschool Vigilance "1" Task: 1150
Presence of a Chronic Illness: 1778
Present Health: 2268
Present Progressive Tense: 1474
Present Progressives: 2710
Present State: 687
Present Tense-3rd Singular: 1474
Present Work and Activities: 2268
Presentation Clarity: 1000